EDUCATION YEAR BOOK 1

PITMAN PUBLISHING

Editorial Team Michaela Evans
Rachel Vermont
Beverley Crisp
Brenda Carpenter
Maureen Coulson
Johan Gregory

Production Stuart Miller

Advertisement Sales Adrian Clark

Published by Pitman Publishing, 128 Long Acre, London WC2E 9AN
Telephone: 0171-379 7383
Fax: 0171-240 5771

DPA
DIRECTORY PUBLISHERS ASSOCIATION

First published 1939

British Library Cataloguing in Publication Data

A catalogue record for this book is available from the British Library

ISBN 0-273-61650-1

Set in 7pt Univers on a Linotron 202
Printed by Page Bros (Norwich) Limited

Editorial Advisory Panel

Contents

Education Year Book 1996/97

In order to ensure that our coverage is complete for the next edition of the book, your help would be much appreciated. The form below is for users to complete if they feel an organisation should be included. Please photocopy this page and return it to:

The Editor
Education Year Book
Pitman Publishing
128 Long Acre
London
WC2E 9AN

The following organisation should be included in the directory

Name of organisation: ....

Address: ....

Tel No: ....

Fax No: ....

Contact: ....

Type of organisation: ....

Information supplied by:

Name: ....

Address: ....

Tel No: ....

Whilst every effort will be made to include suggestions in the next edition, Pitman Publishing retain the right to decide on all editorial content of the year book

Preface

Once again *Education Year Book* has been updated as a guide to the broad spectrum of the United Kingdom's educational provision in the 1990s.

This 56th Edition contains updated information on Education committees and Governor Training Units in the Local Authority sections, and also up to date coverage of grant maintained schools.

The editorial team is most grateful to all the institutions, organisations, and individuals who have given information and advice which all help to make this new edition as up to date and comprehensive as possible.

Any suggestions for new entries or improvements will be gratefully received.

Editorial Team

Changes to Local Government

England

The Local Government Commission is currently reviewing local government structure in England and is making provisional recommendations to the Department of Environment (see chapter one) who should be contacted for up-to-date information on proposed changes.

Wales

On 5th July 1994, the Local Government (Wales) Bill received Royal Assent and became the Local Government (Wales) Act. The Welsh Office have provided the following list of 22 unitary authorities that will come into being on 1st April 1996. Shadow authorities will come into being after elections on 4th May 1995.

Existing Local Authority Area	Proposed Unitary Authority
Ynys Mon/Anglesey	Anglesey *Sir Fon*
Arfon, Dwyfor and Merionnydd	Caernarfonshire & Merionethshire *Sir Gaernarfon a Merionnydd*
Aberconwy and Colwyn (minus the communities of Trefnant and Cefnmeiriadog)	Aberconwy and Colwyn *Aberconwy a Cholwyn*
Rhuddlan, communities of Trefnant and Cefnmeiriadog (from Colwyn), Glyndwr (minus the communities of Chirk, Glyntraian, Llansantffraid Glyn Ceiriog, Ceiriog Ucha, Llansilin, Llangedwyn and Llanrhaeadr-ym-Mochnant	Denbighshire *Sir Ddinbych*
Delyn and Alyn & Deeside	Flintshire *Sir y Fflint*
Wrexham Maelor and communities of Chirk, Glyntraian, Llansantffraid Glyn Ceiriog, Ceiriog Ucha (from Glyndwr)	Wrexham *Wrecsam*
Brecknock, Radnorshire and Montgomery plus the communities of Llansilin, Llangedwyn and Llanrhaeadr-ym-Mochnant (from Glyndwr) and Llanelly (from Blaenau Gwent)	Powys *Powys*

Ceredigion	Cardiganshire *Sir Aberteifi*
Preseli Pembrokeshire and South Pembrokeshire	Pembrokeshire *Sir Benfro*
Carmarthen, Llanelli and Dinefwr	Carmarthenshire *Sir Gaerfyrddin*
Swansea and the communities of Gowerton, Llwchwr, Gorseinon, Penllergaer, Grovesend, Pont-Lliw, Llangyfelach, Pontardulais Mawr and Clydach (from Lliw Valley)	Swansea *Abertawe*
Neath and Port Talbot, plus the communities of Cilybebyll, Ystalyfera, Cwmllynfell, Pontardawe and Gwaen-cae-Gurwen	Neath & Port Talbot *Castellnedd a Phort Talbot*
Minus the communities of Wick, Ewenny and St Brides Major (from Ogwr)	Bridgend *Pen-y-Bont ar Ogwr*
Cardiff plus the community of Pentyrch (from Taff-Ely)	Cardiff *Caerdydd*
Rhondda, Cynon Valley, Taff-Ely (minus the community of Pentyrch)	Rhondda, Cynon, Taff *Rhondda, Cynon, Taf*
Merthyr Tydfil	Merthyr Tydfil
Blaenau Gwent	Blaenau Gwent
Islwyn and Rhymney Valley, communities of Rhymney, New Tredegar and Darran Valley	Caerphilly *Caerffili*
Torfaen	Torfaen *Tor-faen*
Newport	Newport *Casnewydd*
Monmouth	Monmouthshire *Sir Fynwy*
The Vale of Glamorgan together with the communities of Wick, Ewenny and St Brides Major (from the District of Ogwr)	The Vale of Glamorgan *Bro Morgannwg*

Scotland

On 3rd November 1994, the Local Government etc (Scotland) Bill received Royal Assent and became the Local Government etc (Scotland) Act. The Scottish Office has provided the following list of 32 unitary authorities that will come into being on 1st April 1996. Shadow authorities will come into being after elections in April 1995.

Existing Local Authority Area	Proposed Unitary Authority
Highland	Highland
Moray District Council	Moray

Changes to Local Government

Banff and Buchan, Gordon District Councils, Kincardine and Deeside District Council north of and including Stonehaven	Aberdeenshire
City of Aberdeen District Council plus Westhill	City of Aberdeen
Angus District Council, Tayside electoral divisions 30 (Monifieth) and 31 (Sidlaw) and Grampian electoral divisions 57 and 56 (adjusted to run south of Stonehaven)	Angus and Mearns
City of Dundee District Council, excluding Tayside electoral divisions 30 (Monifieth) and 31 (Sidlaw)	City of Dundee
Perth and Kinross District Council, Invergowrie	Perthshire and Kinross
Stirling	Stirling
Argyll and Bute Strathclyde electoral division 7 (Helensburgh)	Argyll and Bute
Clydebank District Council plus Strathclyde electoral divisions 6 (Dumbarton) and 8 (Vale of Leven)	Dumbarton and Clydebank
Bearsden and Milngavie District Council, plus Strathclyde electoral divisions 43 (Kirkintilloch), 44 (Strathkelvin North), 45 (Bishopsbriggs) and the South Lenzie/Waterside district ward in Strathclyde electoral division 46 (Chryston), excluding the South Lenzie/ Waterside district ward	East Dunbartonshire
Cumbernauld and Kilsyth, Motherwell and Monkslands District Councils, plus Strathclyde electoral division 46 (Chryston), excluding the South Lenzie/Waterside district ward	North Lanarkshire
Clydesdale, Hamilton and East Kilbride District Councils, plus Strathclyde electoral divisions 35 (Toryglen/King's Park), 37 (Rutherglen/Fernhill) and 38 (Cambuslang/Halfway)	South Lanarkshire
Clackmannan District	Clackmannan District
Falkirk District	Falkirk District
Fife, Kincardine Bridge and surrounding area	Fife
Midlothian	Midlothian
Covering the area of the existing District Council	City of Edinburgh
West Lothian	West Lothian
East Lothian	East Lothian
The Borders, including Berwickshire District Council	The Borders
Dumfries and Galloway	Dumfries and Galloway
Kyle and Carrick District	South Ayrshire
Cunninghame District Council	North Ayrshire
Inverclyde	Inverclyde
West Renfrewshire, excluding Inverclyde, Relston	Renfrewshire

Covering the existing Eastwood District Council plus proposed Strathclyde electoral division 79 (Barrhead) and those parts of proposed Strathclyde electoral divisions 76 (Paisley Gleniffer), 77 (Paisley Central) and 78 (Paisley Abercorn) which formed part of the former East Renfrewshire Parliamentary constituency	East Renfrewshire
Kilmarnick and London, Cumnock and Doun Valley	East Ayrshire
Covering the area of the existing District Council excluding Strathclyde electoral divisions 37 (Rutherglen) and 38 (Cambuslang/Halfway)	City of Glasgow
(Existing Islands Council)	Orkney
(Existing Islands Council)	Shetland
(Existing Islands Council)	Western Isles

BT Changes to Dialling Codes

BT are changing the STD codes for all UK telephone exchanges on 16 April 1995. From August 1994 it will be possible to use the new numbers.

With the exception of Leeds, Sheffield, Nottingham, Leicester and Bristol, all STD codes will have a **1** inserted after the initial **0** For example:

	OLD	*NEW*
Manchester	061	0161
Norwich	0603	01603

The exceptions are:

Leeds	0532	01132
Sheffield	0742	01142
Nottingham	0602	01159
Leicester	0533	01162
Bristol	0272	01179

Also:

International	010	00

The following codes which belong to one of the following groups will not be changed

BT (Callstream)	Kingston Communications
BT (Lo-Call)	MCL
BT (Freephone)	Mercury (Freephone)
Cellnet	Reserved
Hutchinson	Vodata

0201 0321 0331 0336 0338 0345 0370 0374 0385 0390 0447 0500 0585 0589 0632 0640 0645 0660 0696 0701 0774 0800 0802 0831 0836 0839 0850 0860 0881 0891 0894 0897 0898 0910 0921 0941 0956 0958 0973 0976 0987 0990 0999 09797

Please note these changes have been included in this edition of Education Services Year Book.

Guide to Terminology

Academic Board
A board in colleges of further education comprising heads of departments and representatives of teaching staff and students. The board decides on curriculum and monitors effectiveness.

Adult Basic Education
A more accurate term than adult literacy as it embraces a wider context than reading, writing and maths.

Adventure Playground
Play area under supervision with basic equipment such as climbing frames and building materials, to stimulate children's inventive ability.

Advisers
Employed by local education authorities to inspect and monitor school standards and activities. They supervise new staff during the normal probationary period. Advisers serve primary and secondary and some further education establishments, and are often specialists in a particular subject. They are not the same as HMIs.

Aided School
A voluntary school where salaries, equipment and housekeeping costs are funded by the local education authority, whilst the school governors maintain the fabric and appoint the staff.

Ancillary Staff
Non-teaching staff in schools, and unqualified classroom assistants.

Assembly
Collective worship attended by all school pupils every day as required by the 1944 Education Act. Matters of general information are also related at assembly.

Assisted Places Scheme
Financial assistance available from central government for parents, to help with tuition fees of children at private schools. Individual schools select suitable pupils and remit fees according to individual financial circumstances.

Attendance Order
Action taken by a local education authority against parents who are not educating their children, by issuing orders and eventually taking legal action.

Autism
Childhood disorder observed shortly after birth where the child exhibits an inability to relate to both children and adults.

Banding
The allocation of pupils into a series of groups during the school year, on the basis of ability.

Block Release
Employees released for a substantial period to attend college full-time. Periods of release are limited to eighteen weeks in any one academic year.

Bursar
A paid official in a college or school responsible for its financial and domestic administration.

Bursary
Financial assistance notably for post-graduate degree students or in a Scottish university or school.

Campus
Originally a term used to describe the site and buildings of a university, but now extended to any educational establishment.

Capitation Allowance
An allowance granted by local education authorities to schools for the purchase of books, stationery and other materials. It may also include a number of other items such as equipment and educational visits. It is based on the number of children in the school.

Catchment Area
An accurately defined geographical area from which educational establishments draw their pupils.

Certificate of Pre-Vocational Education (CPVE)
A one-year course, for young people of sixteen and over with few examination passes, to prepare them for a future job, or more vocational training.

Child Guidance Clinic
Clinics provided by local education authorities and staffed with social workers and psychologists. Children are referred by schools or family GPs when they have behavioural or educational problems.

Child Minders
Individuals who look after children of all ages in private premises. Child minders must be registered with local authority social service departments, by whom they are inspected.

City Technology College
Secondary School directly funded by the government with some private funding. Follows National Curriculum but specialises in technology or certain other subjects.

Clearing House
Organisation processing applications for admission to a number of different colleges or courses. It eliminates the need to submit a large number of direct individual applications.

Guide to Terminology

Community Home
The replacement for approved schools under the 1969 Act. Administered by local authority social services departments for the treatment of truancy or minor crimes.

Comprehensive School
Secondary school which admits children from a given catchment area regardless of ability.

Crammer
A school or tutor providing intensive preparation for examinations.

Creaming
The selection of more intelligent children for segregated schools, for example sending them to any remaining grammar schools rather than comprehensives.

Creche
A centre where children under school age are looked after while their parents are at work. The creche must be registered and inspected, and may be a commercial enterprise, or provided free by employers.

Credit Transfers
Credits granted by one higher education establishment and recognised by another.

Curriculum
A course of study followed by a pupil or student.

Day Nursery
A centre provided by private organisations or social services departments to care for children, for a fee, where parents need assistance. Private nurseries must be approved and inspected.

Day Release
The release of employees from their jobs for a period each week to attend training courses.

Day School
A school where children do not board.

DFE Circular
Advice issued by the Department for Education to local education authorities. They do not have the status of law.

Dyslexia
A disorder which produces an inability to read or spell accurately.

Emeritus
An honarary title conferred on retiring university professor and readers.

English as a Foreign Language (EFL)
The teaching of English to foreign students, in the UK or abroad.

English as a Second Language (ESL)
The teaching of English to foreigners residing in the UK.

Exhibition
A financial entrance award given by universities, notably Oxford and Cambridge.

First School
Local authority school usually catering for children 5–8 years old.

Further Education
All post school education outside the university sector. Sometimes the term is restricted to apply only to vocational education.

General Certificate of Secondary Education
Examination introduced in 1988 to replace O-level and CSE examinations.

Governor
An appointed member of the governing body of a school or other educational establishment, required by law.

Grant
An amount of money given to an individual or an institution towards the cost of study or research.

Grant Maintained School
Primary or secondary school which has opted out of local authority control and is funded directly from the government.

Grant Related Expenditure (GRE)
Central government's calculation of the finance needed to provide services to a given standard within an overall financial limit.

Greats
Honours degree examination in classics awarded by Oxford University.

Higher Education
Education which is received in a university, or college of higher education and which usually leads to the award of a degree or diploma.

Independent School
A school which receives no state assistance but is financed by fees. All such schools must be registered.

Infants School
A school which caters for children from five to seven years of age. Often associated with a junior school to which the children will progress.

Interim Advisory Committee
Committee set up after the end of the Burnham Committee to recommend on Teachers' Pay and Conditions of Service.

Junior School
A school which caters for seven to eleven year old children.

Language Laboratory
A specially planned room where languages are taught with the aid of tape recordings and sometimes interactive videos.

Learned Journal
An academic Periodical, often produced by a professional association.

Learning Difficulty
Significantly greater difficulty in learning than experienced by the majority of children of the same age. It may be caused by a disability which prevents or hinders a child from using educational facilities generally provided in schools within the area of the local authority concerned.

Liberal Studies
Taught in college of further education to broaden outlook and interests of students. Usually includes social studies, literature and the arts.

Local Education Authorities (LEAs)
There are 104 LEAs, each with its own education committee, in England and Wales–ILEA, 20 outer London boroughs, 36 metropolitan districts, 47 counties. Each authority has a statutory duty to provide an education service.

Local Management of Schools
Delegation to governing body of management of schools' budget share.

Maintenance Grant
A discretionary grant paid by a local education authority to help to meet housekeeping costs of students attending college or school.

Mandatory Grant
Financial assistance which a local education authority has a duty to provide to students attending higher education courses who satisfy national regulations.

Mature Student
An adult of 25 years of age or older receiving higher education and who may not possess normal entry qualifications.

Middle School
Caters for children from 8 to 12 or 9 to 13 years of age. Legally they are either primary or secondary schools depending on the preponderance of age groups in the school population – i.e. under or over 11 years of age.

Moderator
An examiner who monitors marking and examining to ensure that standards are consistent in a number of colleges and schools.

Nursery Class
Local authority and private establishments, providing pre-school education, usually ages 2–5.

Opting Out
The ERA allows LEA schools to apply for Grant Maintained Status and opt out if permission granted.

Outreach Staff
Staff employed by the youth service and in adult education establishments to promote their aims within the community.

Peripatetic Teacher
A teacher who is not attached to any one school, but travels to several.

PICKUP
Professional, industrial and commercial updating. Concerns the work that colleges, polytechnics and universities do for workforces in all sectors of the economy.

Playgroups
Groups of children under five years of age, supervised by adults who are not required to be qualified teachers. Playgroups must be registered with the social services department who inspect premises.

Play Leader
An adult who supervises a playscheme or adventure playground. Many playleaders are qualified youth workers or teachers.

Pre-School Education
General term embracing the different types of education available for the under-fives. Includes nursery schools, nursery classes and pre-school playgroups.

Preparatory School
Independent school for children aged eight to thirteen preparing for the common entrance examination.

Primary School
A school for children from five to eleven. It may also be used as a generic term to cover infant, first, junior and middle schools.

Public School
Independent secondary school usually in membership of the Headmasters' Conference, the Governing Bodies Association or Governing Bodies of Girls' Schools Association. Pupils are aged from thirteen to eighteen.

REPLAN
Government scheme funded by DES to improve and extend educational opportunities for unemployed adults in England and Wales.

Rate Support Grant
A sum of money allocated to local authorities by the government to supplement local rates and income.

Reception Class
A class organised for new entrants to an infant or first school, which helps introduce children to school life.

Salary Scale
Salary scales are set out in the Burnham Reports on teachers salaries. The number of posts on different scales depends on the size of the school, the ages of the pupils and limited discretion used by the LEA.

Sandwich Course
A course which combines full-time higher education college study with periods of full-time work, under supervision, in industry or commerce.

Scholarship
Financial award, usually based on merit, granted to a student.

Secondary Schools
Cater for the 11–18 age group generally, although sixth form and tertiary colleges, where they exist, cater for 16–18 year olds. Most secondary schools are comprehensive schools.

Guide to Terminology

Secondment
A temporary attachment to a different school, or to a special course away from the normal place of employment.

Sixth Form College
16–19 year olds may transfer from a secondary school to a sixth form college. A wide range of GCE courses at Ordinary and Advanced level are offered, together with an increasing number of vocational and pre-vocational courses for students of all abilities.

Special Educational Needs
Term used to describe the requirements of children with difficulties in one or more of the following areas: learning, behaviour, or emotional, social, physical development. Also, additional arrangements to those generally available designed for children with special education needs. If a child is deemed to require such provision, the LEA is obliged to issue a formal statement of the child's needs with proposals to meet them.

Streaming
The separation of pupils into separate groups according to ability in a school. The opposite of mixed-ability grouping.

Supply Teacher
Teachers appointed by local education authorities to fill vacancies in establishments due to absences of staff. The period of attachment to a particular school may vary from half a day to several weeks.

Teachers' Centre
A local education authority building provided for the in-service training of teachers, providing a useful forum for the exchange of ideas and information.

Tertiary College
An educational establishment offering sixth form and further education through a full range of courses for the 16–19 age group.

Voluntary School
School owned by a voluntary body, usually religious, but receiving financial assistance from the local education authority. Classified as 'aided', 'controlled', or 'special agreement'.

Work Experience
An arrangement by which pupils, usually in their last year at school, may gain experience of being at work through employment (without pay) for a short period, often three weeks.

Guide to Abbreviations

AACE Association for Adult and Continuing Education
AAI Association of Art Institutions
AASSH Anglican Association of Secondary School Heads
ABAPSTAS Association of Blind and Partially Sighted Teachers and Students
ABE Adult Basic Education
ABRC Advisory Board for the Research Councils
ACACE Advisory Council for Adult and Continuing Education
ACACHE Association of Career Advisers in Colleges of Higher Education
ACC Association of County Councils
ACCEPT Addictions Community Centres for Education, Prevention, Treatment and Research
ACE Advisory Centre for Education
ACFHE Association of Colleges of Further and Higher Education
ACG Annual Capital Grants
ACOST Advisory Council on Science and Technology
ACS Average Class Size
ACU Association of Commonwealth Universities
ADAR Art and Design Admissions Registry
ADE Association of Directors of Education
ADES Association of Directors of Education in Scotland
AEAS Association of Educational Advisers in Scotland
AEB Associated Examining Board
AEC Association of Education Committees
AEP Association of Educational Psychologists
AFC Association for Colleges
AGCAS Association of Graduate Careers Advisory Services
AGIT Action for Governors Information and Training
AHMPS Association of Head Mistresses of Preparatory Schools
ALA Association of London Authorities
ALBSU Adult Literacy and Basic Skills Unit
ALH Average Lecture Hours in front of classes per week
AMA Association of Metropolitan Authorities
AMG Annual Maintenance Grant
AMTIS Arts Management Training Initiative (Scotland)
APC Association of Principals of Colleges
APER Association of Publishers' Educational Representatives
APFO Association of Playing Fields Officers
APHE Association for Part-Time Higher Education
APL Accreditation of Prior Learning
APLET Association for Programmed Learning and Educational Technology
APR Age Participation Rate
APRE Association for Recruitment and Retention in Education
APS Assisted Places Scheme
APT Association of Polytechnic Teachers
APU Assessment of Performance Unit
APVIC Association of Principals in Sixth Form Colleges
ARE Association for Recurrent Education
ARELS Association of Recognised English Language Schools
ASB Aggregated Schools Budget
ASE Association for Science Education
Association for Special Education
ASH Average Student Hours in class per week
ASHCOG Association for Self-Help and Community Groups
ASLIB Association of Special Libraries and Information Bureaux
ATCODE Association of Teachers in Colleges and Departments of Education
ATD Art Teachers Diploma
ATDS Association of Teachers of Domestic Science
ATL Association of Teachers and Lecturers
ATPU Adult Training Promotions Unit
AUCL Association of University and College Lecturers
AUT Association of University Teachers
AVA Audio-Visual Aid

BA Bachelor of Arts
BAALPE British Association of Advisers and Lecturers in Physical Education
BAAS British Association for the Advancement of Science
BAAT British Association of Art Therapists
BACIE British Association for Commercial and Industrial Education
BAECE British Association for Early Childhood Education
BALT British Association for Language Teaching
BATOD British Association of Teachers of the Deaf
BDA British Dyslexia Association
BEAS British Educational Administration Society
BEd Bachelor of Education
BEMAS British Educational Management and Administration Society
BERA British Education Research Association
BESA British Educational Suppliers Association
BFES British Families Education Service
BIMH British Institute of Mental Handicap
BL British Library
BNF British Nutrition Foundation
BPS British Psychological Society
BR Block Release
BSc Bachelor of Science
BSS Broadcasting Support Services
BTEC Business and Technician Education Council
BYC British Youth Council

CAL Computer Assisted Learning
CASE Campaign for the Advancement of State Education
CASEP Cognitive Acceleration through Science Education Project
CATE Council for Accreditation of Teacher Education
CATS Credit Accumulation and Transfer Service
Christians and Tyneside Schools
CBI Confederation of British Industry
CBT Competency Based Teaching
CCDU Counselling and Career Development Unit
CCETSW Central Council for Education and Training in Social Work
CCPR Central Council of Physical Recreation
CCT Compulsory Competitive Tendering
CCUCB Committee Chairman of University Councils and Boards
CDP Committee of Directors of Polytechnics
CEA Council for Educational Advance
Community Education Association
Conservative Education Association
CEDC Community Education Development Centre
CEDO Centre for Educational Development Overseas
CEE Centre for Environmental Education
CEF Colleges' Employers Forum
CEO Chief Education Officer
CEP Community Enterprise Project
CERI Centre for Educational Research and Innovation
CET Council for Educational Technology
CEWC Council for Education in World Citizenship
CFE College of Further Education
CFG Counties Furniture Group
CGLI City and Guilds of London Institute
CHC Community Health Council
CHE College of Higher Education

Guide to Abbreviations

CI	Chief Inspector
CILT	Centre for Information on Language Teaching and Research
CIPFA	Chartered Institute of Public Finance and Accounting
CLASP	Consortium of Local Authorities Special Program
CLAW	Consortium, Local Authorities Wales
CLEA	Council of Local Education Authorities
CLEA/ST	Council of Local Education Authorities/School Teachers' Joint Committee
CLEAPSS	Consortium of Local Education Authorities for the Provision of School Science
Cmnd	Command paper
COIC	Careers and Occupational Information Centre
COPS	Committee of Polytechnic Secretaries
COSLA	Convention of Scottish Local Authorities
CPD	Continuing Professional Development
CPVE	Certificate of Pre-Vocational Education
CRAC	Careers Research and Advisory Centre
CRE	Commission for Racial Equality
CRYPT	Creative Young People Together
CSE	Certificate of Secondary Education
CSIE	Centre for Studies on Integration in Education
CSTI	Council of Science of Technology Institute
CSV	Community Service Volunteers
CTC	City Technology College
CTC	Central Training College (covering Industrial Training Boards)
CTF	Catholic Teachers Foundation
CVCP	Committee of Vice-Chancellors and Principals
CYSA	Community and Youth Service Association
DE	Department of Employment
Del	Delicate
DFE	Department for Education
DHSS	Department of Health and Social Security
DipHE	Diploma in Higher Education
DMS	Diploma in Management Studies
DoE	Department of the Environment
EBD	Emotional and Behavioural Difficulties
EDU	Educational Disadvantage Unit
EDUCMAT	Education and training in new materials
EdRop	Education Resources for Older People
EFL	English as a Foreign Language
EFVA	Educational Foundation for Visual Aids
EIS	Educational Institute of Scotland
ELAS	Education Law Advisers Service
EmDist	Emotionally Disturbed
EMEU	East Midlands Educational Union
EMIE	Education Management Information Exchange
EnTra	Engineering Training Authority
EOC	Equal Opportunities Commission
EP	Epileptic
EPA	Educational Priority Areas
EPC	Educational Publishers Council
EPIC	Educational Policy Information Service
ERA	Education Reform Act
ESAC	House of Commons Education, Science and Arts Committee
ESG	Education Support Grants
ESHA	European Secondary Heads Association
ESRC	Economic and Social Research Council
ETUCE	European Trade Union Committee on Education
FAS	Funding Agency for Schools
FE	Further Education
FEAST	Fun Eating in Schools Today
FEFCE	Further Education Funding Council for England
FETT	Further Education Teacher Training
FEU	Further Education Unit
FITLOG	Foundation for Information Technology in Local Government
FORCE	Formation Continue en Europe
FSA	Foundation for Sport and the Arts
FT	Full-time
FTE	Full-time Equivalent
GBA	Association of Governing Bodies of Public Schools (Boys)
GBGSA	Association of Governing Bodies of Girls' Public Schools
GCE	General Certificate of Education
GCSE	General Certificate of Secondary Education
GEST	Grants for Education Support and Training
GNVQ	General National Vocational Qualification
GPDST	Girls Public Day School Trust
GRE	Grant Related Expenditure
GSA	Girls' Schools Association
GTC	General Teaching Council
GTTR	Graduate Teachers' Training Registry
HAPA	Handicapped Adventure Playground Association
HAS	Head Teachers of Scotland
HCIMA	Hotel Catering and Institutional Management Association
HE	Higher Education
HECSU	Higher Education Careers Services Unit
HEIST	Higher Education Information Services Trust
HEQC	Higher Education Quality Council
HMC	Head Masters' Conference
HMI	Her Majesty's Inspectorate
HMSO	Her Majesty's Stationery Office
HNC	Higher National Certificate
HND	Higher National Diploma
IAASE	Independent Appeals Authority for School Examinations
IAC	Interim Advisory Committee on School Teachers' Pay and Conditions
IAPS	Incorporated Association of Preparatory Schools
IBA	Independent Broadcasting Authority
IBO	International Baccalaureate Organisation
ICA	Institute for Contemporary Arts
ICCS	International Centre for Child Studies
ICEd	Institute of Craft Education
ICO	Institute of Careers Officers
IFFTU	International Federation of Free Teacher Unions
IGDS	Integrated Graduate Development Scheme
IIP	Investor in People
iLEP	International Institute for Educational Planning
ILEA	Inner London Education Authority
IM	Institute of Management
IMTEC	International Movement Towards Educational Change
INLOGOV	Institute of Local Government (University of Birmingham)
INSET	In-service Training of Teachers
INTO	Irish National Teachers' Organisation
IPPR	Institute for Public Policy Research
IQ	Intelligence Quotient
ISCG	Institute of School and College Governors
ISIS	Independent Schools Information Service
IT	Information Technology
ITB	Industrial Training Board
ITO	Industry Training Organisation
IVS	International Voluntary Service
JCR	Junior Common Room
JNC	Joint Negotiating Committee
KCN	Kids' Clubs Network
LACA	Local Authority Caterers' Association
LACAS	Local Authority Catering Advisory Service
LACSAB	Local Authorities' Conditions of Service Advisory Board (Burnham Secretariat)
LAMSAC	Local Authorities' Management Services and Computer Committee
LAPP	Lower Attaining Pupils Programme
LCCI	London Chamber of Commerce and Industry
LEA	Local Education Authority
LEAP	LEA Project for School Management Training
LEC	Local Enterprise Companies
LETEC	London East Training and Enterprise Council
LETGS	LEA Training Grant Scheme
LGC	Local Government Commission
LINC	Languages in the National Curriculum
LISC	Library and Information Services Council
LMS	Local Management of Schools
MA	Master of Arts
MACE	Metropolitan Architectural Consortium for Education
MANCAT	Manchester College of Arts and Technology
MAST	Monitoring and support time

MCI Management Charter Initiative
MENCAP National Society for Mentally Handicapped Children and Adults
MESU Microelectronics Education Support Unit
METRA Metropolitan Authorities Recruitment Agency
MH Mentally Handicapped
MLA Modern Language Association
MLD Moderate Learning Difficulties
MRO Media Research Officer

NAB National Advisory Board (for public service higher education) now replaced by PCFC
NACAE National Advisory Council on Adult Education
NACE National Association for Able Children in Education
NACESW National Association of Chief Education Social Workers
NACETT National Advisory Council for Education and Training Targets
NACGT National Association of Careers and Guidance Teachers
NACRO National Association for the Care and Resettlement of Offenders
NACYS National Advisory Council for Youth Services
NAFE Non-Advanced Further Education
NAGC National Association for Gifted Children
NAGM National Association of Governors and Managers
NAHT National Association of Head Teachers
NAEIAC National Association of Educational Inspectors, Advisers and Consultants
NAMCW National Association for Maternal and Child Welfare
NAMH National Association for Mental Health
NASEN National Association for Special Educational Needs
NAS/UWT National Association of Schoolmasters/Union of Women Teachers
NASMO *see* LACA
NASWE National Association of Social Workers in Education
NATE National Association of Teachers of English
NATFHE National Association of Teachers in Further and Higher Education (pronounced 'nat-fee')
NAYCEO National Association of Youth and Community Education Officers
NBL National Book League
NCA National Childcare Association
NCE National Commission on Education
NCES National Council for Educational Standards
NCMA National Child Minding Association
NCNE National Campaign for Nursery Education
NCPTA National Confederation of Parent-Teacher Associations
NCSS National Council for Schools' Sports
NCVQ National Advisory Council for Vocational Qualifications
NCVYS National Council for Voluntary Youth Services
NEAB Northern Examinations and Assessment Board
NEC National Extension College
NEEDS New Examinations—Evaluation and Development in Schools
NFAE National Foundation for Arts Education
NFER National Foundation for Educational Research in England and Wales
NFVLS National Federation of Voluntary Literacy Schemes
NIACE National Institute of Adult Continuing Education
NIECE National Institute for Careers Education and Counselling
NJC National Joint Committee
NNEB National Nursery Examination Board
NPFA National Playing Fields Association
NSEAD National Society for Education in Art and Design
NSSA National School Sailing Association
NUS National Union of Students
NUSS National Union of School Students
NUT National Union of Teachers
NVQ National Vocational Qualification
NWRAC North West Regional Advisory Council
NYA National Youth Agency
NYB National Youth Bureau

OAL Office of Arts and Libraries
OCEA Oxford Certificate of Education Archive
OCEA Oxford Consortium for Educational Achievement
OCN Open College Network
OFSTED Office for Standards in Education
OHMCI Department for Her Majesty's Chief Inspector of Schools
OIS Office Information Systems
ONC Ordinary National Certificate
OND Ordinary National Diploma
OU Open University

PA Publishers' Association
PACE Parental Alliance for Choice in Education
PACT Parents against CTC
PAT Professional Association of Teachers
PCFC Polytechnics and Colleges Funding Council
PE Physical Education
PEA Physicial Education Association
PGCE Postgraduate Certificate of Education
PH Physically Handicapped
PHAB Physically Handicapped and Able-bodied
PhD Doctor of Philosophy
PICKUP Professional Industrial and Commercial Updating
PIT Pool of Inactive Teachers
PLEASE Permanent Liaison of Educational Associations and Schools
POO Parents opposed to Opting Out
PPA Pre-school Playgroups Association
PRP Performance Related Pay
PS Partially Sighted
PSI Policy Studies Institute
PtHg Partially Hearing
PT Part-Time
PTA Parent-Teacher Association
PTR Pupil-teacher Ratio

RANSC Records of Achievement National Steering Committee
RC Roman Catholic
R and D Research and Development
RE Religious Education
RISE Research and Information State Education Trust
RMNS Royal Merchant Navy School
ROSLA Raising of the School Leaving Age
RSA Royal Society of Arts
RSG Rate Support Grant
RVQ Review of Vocational Qualifications

SA Special Agreement
SACRES Standing Advisory Council on Religious Education
SALT Scottish Association for Language Teaching
SATIPS Society of Assistants Teaching in Preparatory
SATRO Science and Technology Regional Organisations
SCAA School Curriculum and Assessment Authority
SCALU Scottish Adult Literacy Unit
SCCC Scottish Consultative Council on Curriculum
SCDC School Curriculum Development Council
SCEA Service Children's Education Authority
SCEC Scottish Community Education Council
SCENE Rural Schools Curriculum Enhancement National Evaluation
SCETT Standing Committee for the Education and Training of Teachers in the Public Sector
SCIA Society of Chief Inspectors and Advisors
SCIP School Curriculum Industry Partnership
SCOP Standing Conference of Principals
SCOLA Second Consortium of Local Authorities
SCOTVEC Scottish Vocational Education Council
SCSST Standing Conference on Schools' Science and Technology
SEA Socialist Education Association
SEA Society for Education through Art
SEAC South Eastern Architects' Collaboration
SEB Scottish Examination Board
SEC Secondary Examinations Council
SED Scottish Education Department
SEFT Society for Education in Film and Television
SEMERC Special Education Microelectronic Resource Centres
SEO Society of Education Officers
SERC Science and Engineering Research Council
SHA Secondary Heads Association

Guide to Abbreviations

SHMIS	Society of Headmasters of Independent Schools
SI	Staff Inspector
SLA	School Library Association
	Service level agreement
SLD	Secretarial Language Diploma
	Severe Learning Difficulties
SMH	Severely Mentally Handicapped
SPACE	Satellite Project for Adult and Continuing Education
SPTC	Scottish Parent Teacher Council
SRB	Single regeneration budget
SRC	Science Research Council
SSA	Scottish Schoolteachers' Association
	Standard Spending Assessment
SSR	Staff Student Ratio
STOPP	Society of Teachers Opposed to Physical Punishment
SVEC	Scottish Vocational Education Council
TACADE	The Advisory Council on Alcohol and Drug Education
TASC	Teaching as a Career Unit
TBF	Teachers' Benevolent Fund
TCA	Tertiary College Association
TCR	Teacher Contact Ratio
TEED	Training Education and Enterprise Directorate
TEC	Training and Enterprise Councils
TECBAC	Technological Baccalaureate
TEFL	Teaching English as a Foreign Language
TMEO	Teachers Material Employers Organisation
TPA	Teachers' Pension Agency
TUPE	Transfer of undertakings protective of employment regulations
TVEI	Technical Vocational Educational Initiative
UCAC	(pronounced 'ick-ack') Undeb Canedlaethol Athrawon Cymru (National Association of Teachers of Wales)
UCAS	Universities and Colleges Admissions Service
UCET	Universities Council for the Education of Teachers
UFC	Universities Funding Council (replaces UGC)
UGC	University Grants Committee
ULCI	Union of Lancashire and Cheshire Institutes
ULEAC	University of London Examinations and Assessment Council
UNESCO	United Nations Educational, Scientific and Cultural Organisation
VA	Voluntary Aided
VC	Voluntary Controlled
VCHC	Voluntary Council for Handicapped Children
VSO	Voluntary Service Overseas
WGARCR	Working Group Against Racism in Childrens Resources
WCOTP	(pronounced 'wickertop') World Confederation of Organisations of the Teaching Profession
WEA	Workers Educational Association
WJEC	Welsh Joint Educational Committee
WRFE	Work Related Further Education

Gazetteer

England and Wales

Alphabetical list of Districts showing County Authority

Aberconwy *(Gwynedd)*
Adur *(West Sussex)*
Allerdale *(Cumbria)*
Alnwick *(Northumberland)*
Alyn and Deeside *(Clwyd)*
Amber Valley *(Derbyshire)*
Arfon *(Gwynedd)*
Arun *(West Sussex)*
Ashfield *(Nottinghamshire)*
Ashford *(Kent)*
Aylesbury Vale *(Buckinghamshire)*

Babergh *(Suffolk)*
Barnsley *(South Yorkshire)*
Barrow-in-Furness *(Cumbria)*
Basildon *(Essex)*
Basingstoke and Deane *(Hampshire)*
Bassetlaw *(Nottinghamshire)*
Bath *(Avon)*
Berwick-upon-Tweed *(Northumberland)*
Beverley *(Humberside)*
Birmingham *(West Midlands)*
Blaby *(Leicestershire)*
Blackburn *(Lancashire)*
Blackpool *(Lancashire)*
Blaenau Gwent *(Gwent)*
Blyth Valley *(Northumberland)*
Bolsover *(Derbyshire)*
Bolton *(Greater Manchester)*
Boothferry *(Humberside)*
Boston *(Lincolnshire)*
Bournemouth *(Dorset)*
Bracknell *(Berkshire)*
Bradford *(West Yorkshire)*
Braintree *(Essex)*
Breckland *(Norfolk)*
Brecknock *(Powys)*
Brentwood *(Essex)*
Bridgnorth *(Shropshire)*
Brighton *(East Sussex)*
Bristol *(Avon)*
Broadland *(Norfolk)*
Bromsgrove *(Hereford and Worcester)*
Broxbourne *(Hertfordshire)*
Broxtowe *(Nottinghamshire)*
Burnley *(Lancashire)*
Bury *(Greater Manchester)*

Calderdale *(West Yorkshire)*
Cambridge *(Cambridgeshire)*
Cannock Chase *(Staffordshire)*
Canterbury *(Kent)*
Caradon *(Cornwall)*
Cardiff *(South Glamorgan)*
Carlisle *(Cumbria)*
Carmarthen *(Dyfed)*
Carrick *(Cornwall)*
Castle Morpeth *(Northumberland)*
Castle Point *(Essex)*
Ceredigion *(Dyfed)*
Charnwood *(Leicestershire)*
Chelmsford *(Essex)*
Cheltenham *(Gloucestershire)*
Cherwell *(Oxfordshire)*
Chester *(Cheshire)*
Chester-le-Street *(Durham)*
Chesterfield *(Derbyshire)*
Chichester *(West Sussex)*
Chiltern *(Buckinghamshire)*
Chorley *(Lancashire)*
Christchurch *(Dorset)*
Cleethorpes *(Humberside)*
Colchester *(Essex)*
Colwyn *(Clwyd)*
Congleton *(Cheshire)*
Copeland *(Cumbria)*
Corby *(Northamptonshire)*
Cotswold *(Gloucestershire)*
Coventry *(West Midlands)*
Craven *(North Yorkshire)*
Crawley *(West Sussex)*
Crewe and Nantwich *(Cheshire)*
Cynon Valley *(Mid Glamorgan)*

Dacorum *(Hertfordshire)*
Darlington *(Durham)*
Dartford *(Kent)*
Daventry *(Northamptonshire)*
Delyn *(Clwyd)*
Derby *(Derbyshire)*
Derwentside *(Durham)*
Dinefwr *(Dyfed)*
Doncaster *(South Yorkshire)*
Dover *(Kent)*
Dudley *(West Midlands)*
Durham *(Durham)*
Dwyfor *(Gwynedd)*

Easington *(Durham)*
East Cambridgeshire *(Cambridgeshire)*
East Devon *(Devon)*
East Hampshire *(Hampshire)*
East Hertfordshire *(Hertfordshire)*
East Lindsey *(Lincolnshire)*
East Northamptonshire *(Northamptonshire)*
East Staffordshire *(Staffordshire)*
East Yorkshire *(Humberside)*
Eastbourne *(East Sussex)*
Eastleigh *(Hampshire)*
Eden *(Cumbria)*
Ellesmere Port and Neston *(Cheshire)*
Elmbridge *(Surrey)*
Epping Forest *(Essex)*
Epsom and Ewell *(Surrey)*
Erewash *(Derbyshire)*
Exeter *(Devon)*

Fareham *(Hampshire)*
Fenland *(Cambridgeshire)*
Forest of Dean *(Gloucestershire)*
Forest Heath *(Suffolk)*
Fylde *(Lancashire)*

Gazetteer

Gateshead *(Tyne and Wear)*
Gedling *(Nottinghamshire)*
Gillingham *(Kent)*
Glanford *(Humberside)*
Gloucester *(Gloucestershire)*
Glyndŵr *(Clwyd)*
Gosport *(Hampshire)*
Gravesham *(Kent)*
Great Grimsby *(Humberside)*
Great Yarmouth *(Norfolk)*
Guildford *(Surrey)*

Halton *(Cheshire)*
Hambleton *(North Yorkshire)*
Harborough *(Leicestershire)*
Harlow *(Essex)*
Harrogate *(North Yorkshire)*
Hart *(Hampshire)*
Hartlepool *(Cleveland)*
Hastings *(East Sussex)*
Havant *(Hampshire)*
Hereford *(Hereford and Worcester)*
Hertsmere *(Hertfordshire)*
High Peak *(Derbyshire)*
Hinckley and Bosworth *(Leicestershire)*
Holderness *(Humberside)*
Horsham *(West Sussex)*
Hove *(East Sussex)*
Huntingdon *(Cambridgeshire)*
Hyndburn *(Lancashire)*

Ipswich *(Suffolk)*
Isle of Anglesey *see* Ynys Môn
Islwyn *(Gwent)*

Kennet *(Wiltshire)*
Kerrier *(Cornwall)*
Kettering *(Northamptonshire)*
King's Lynn and West Norfolk *(Norfolk)*
Kingston upon Hull *(Humberside)*
Kingswood *(Avon)*
Kirklees *(West Yorkshire)*
Knowsley *(Merseyside)*

Lancaster *(Lancashire)*
Langbaurgh *(Cleveland)*
Leeds *(West Yorkshire)*
Leicester *(Leicestershire)*
Leominster *(Hereford and Worcester)*
Lewes *(East Sussex)*
Lichfield *(Staffordshire)*
Lincoln *(Lincolnshire)*
Liverpool *(Merseyside)*
Llanelli *(Dyfed)*
Lliw Valley *(West Glamorgan)*
Luton *(Bedfordshire)*

Macclesfield *(Cheshire)*
Maidstone *(Kent)*
Maldon *(Essex)*
Malvern Hills *(Hereford and Worcester)*
Manchester *(Greater Manchester)*
Mansfield *(Nottinghamshire)*
Medina *(Isle of Wight)*
Meirionnydd *(Gwynedd)*
Melton *(Leicestershire)*
Mendip *(Somerset)*
Merthyr Tydfil *(Mid Glamorgan)*
Mid Bedfordshire *(Bedfordshire)*
Mid Devon *(Devon)*
Mid Suffolk *(Suffolk)*
Mid Sussex *(West Sussex)*
Middlesbrough *(Cleveland)*
Milton Keynes *(Buckinghamshire)*
Mole Valley *(Surrey)*
Monmouth *(Gwent)*
Montgomery *(Powys)*

Neath *(West Glamorgan)*
Newark *(Nottinghamshire)*
Newbury *(Berkshire)*
New Forest *(Hampshire)*
Newcastle *(Staffordshire)*
Newcastle-upon-Tyne *(Tyne and Wear)*
Newport *(Gwent)*
North Bedfordshire *(Bedfordshire)*
North Cornwall *(Cornwall)*
North Devon *(Devon)*
North Dorset *(Dorset)*
North East Derbyshire *(Derbyshire)*
North Hertfordshire *(Hertfordshire)*
North Kesteven *(Lincolnshire)*
North Norfolk *(Norfolk)*
North Shropshire *(Shropshire)*
North Tyneside *(Tyne and Wear)*
North Warwickshire *(Warwickshire)*
North West Leicestershire *(Leicestershire)*
North Wiltshire *(Wiltshire)*
Northampton *(Northamptonshire)*
Northavon *(Avon)*
Norwich *(Norfolk)*
Nottingham *(Nottinghamshire)*
Nuneaton and Bedworth *(Warwickshire)*

Oadby and Wigston *(Leicestershire)*
Ogŵr *(Mid Glamorgan)*
Oldham *(Greater Manchester)*
Oswestry *(Shropshire)*
Oxford *(Oxfordshire)*

Pendle *(Lancashire)*
Penwith *(Cornwall)*
Peterborough *(Cambridgeshire)*
Plymouth *(Devon)*
Poole *Dorset)*
Port Talbot *(West Glamorgan)*
Portsmouth *(Hampshire)*
Preseli *(Dyfed)*
Preston *(Lancashire)*
Purbeck *(Dorset)*

Radnor *(Powys)*
Reading *(Berkshire)*
Redditch *(Hereford and Worcester)*
Reigate and Banstead *(Surrey)*
Restormel *(Cornwall)*
Rhondda *(Mid Glamorgan)*
Rhuddlan *(Clwyd)*
Rhymney Valley *(Mid Glamorgan)*
Ribble Valley *(Lancashire)*
Richmondshire *(North Yorkshire)*
Rochdale *(Greater Manchester)*
Rochester upon Medway *(Kent)*
Rochford *(Essex)*
Rossendale *(Lancashire)*
Rother *(East Sussex)*
Rotherham *(South Yorkshire)*
Rugby *(Warwickshire)*
Runnymede *(Surrey)*
Rushcliffe *(Nottinghamshire)*
Rushmoor *(Hampshire)*
Rutland *(Leicestershire)*
Ryedale *(North Yorkshire)*

St Albans *(Hertfordshire)*
St Edmundsbury *(Suffolk)*
St Helens *(Merseyside)*
Salford *(Greater Manchester)*
Salisbury *(Wiltshire)*
Sandwell *(West Midlands)*
Scarborough *(North Yorkshire)*
Scunthorpe *(Humberside)*
Sedgefield *(Durham)*
Sedgemoor *(Somerset)*
Sefton *(Merseyside)*
Selby *(North Yorkshire)*
Sevenoaks *(Kent)*
Sheffield *(South Yorkshire)*
Shepway *(Kent)*
Shrewsbury and Atcham *(Shropshire)*
Slough *(Berkshire)*
Solihull *(West Midlands)*
South Bedfordshire *(Bedfordshire)*
South Bucks *(Buckinghamshire)*
South Cambridgeshire *(Cambridgeshire)*
South Derbyshire *(Derbyshire)*

South Hams *(Devon)*
South Herefordshire *(Hereford and Worcester)*
South Holland *(Lincolnshire)*
South Kesteven *(Lincolnshire)*
South Lakeland *(Cumbria)*
South Norfolk *(Norfolk)*
South Northamptonshire *(Northamptonshire)*
South Oxfordshire *(Oxfordshire)*
South Pembrokeshire *(Dyfed)*
South Ribble *(Lancashire)*
South Shropshire *(Shropshire)*
South Somerset *(Somerset)*
South Staffordshire *(Staffordshire)*
South Tyneside *(Tyne and Wear)*
South Wight *(Isle of Wight)*
Southampton *(Hampshire)*
Southend on Sea *(Essex)*
Spelthorne *(Surrey)*
Stafford *(Staffordshire)*
Staffordshire Moorlands *(Staffordshire)*
Stevenage *(Hertfordshire)*
Stockport *(Greater Manchester)*
Stockton on Tees *(Cleveland)*
Stoke-on-Trent *(Staffordshire)*
Stratford on Avon *(Warwickshire)*
Stroud *(Gloucestershire)*
Suffolk Coastal *(Suffolk)*
Sunderland *(Tyne and Wear)*
Surrey Heath *(Surrey)*
Swale *(Kent)*
Swansea *(West Glamorgan)*

Taff-Ely *(Mid Glamorgan)*
Tameside *(Greater Manchester)*
Tamworth *(Staffordshire)*
Tandridge *(Surrey)*
Taunton Deane *(Somerset)*
Teesdale *(Durham)*
Teignbridge *(Devon)*
Tendring *(Essex)*
Test Valley *(Hampshire)*
Tewkesbury *(Gloucestershire)*
Thamesdown *(Wiltshire)*
Thanet *(Kent)*
Three Rivers *(Hertfordshire)*
Thurrock *(Essex)*
Tonbridge and Malling *(Kent)*
Torbay *(Devon)*
Torfaen *(Gwent)*
Torridge *(Devon)*
Trafford *(Greater Manchester)*
Tunbridge Wells *(Kent)*
Tynedale *(Northumberland)*

Uttlesford *(Essex)*

Vale of Glamorgan *(South Glamorgan)*
Vale Royal *(Cheshire)*
Vale of White Horse *(Oxfordshire)*

Wakefield *(West Yorkshire)*
Walsall *(West Midlands)*
Wansbeck *(Northumberland)*
Wansdyke *(Avon)*
Warrington *(Cheshire)*
Warwick *(Warwickshire)*
Watford *(Hertfordshire)*
Waveney *(Suffolk)*
Waverley *(Surrey)*
Wealden *(East Sussex)*
Wear Valley *(Durham)*
Wellingborough *(Northamptonshire)*
Welwyn Hatfield *(Hertfordshire)*
West Derbyshire *(Derbyshire)*
West Devon *(Devon)*
West Dorset *(Dorset)*
West Lancashire *(Lancashire)*
West Lindsey *(Lincolnshire)*
West Oxfordshire *(Oxfordshire)*
West Somerset *(Somerset)*
West Wiltshire *(Wiltshire)*
Weymouth and Portland *(Dorset)*
Wigan *(Greater Manchester)*
Wimborne *(Dorset)*
Winchester *(Hampshire)*
Windsor and Maidenhead *(Berkshire)*
Wirral *(Merseyside)*
Woking *(Surrey)*
Wokingham *(Berkshire)*
Wolverhampton *(West Midlands)*
Woodspring *(Avon)*
Worcester *(Hereford and Worcester)*
Worthing *(West Sussex)*
Wrekin, The *(Shropshire)*
Wrexham Maelor *(Clwyd)*
Wychavon *(Hereford and Worcester)*
Wycombe *(Buckinghamshire)*
Wyre *(Lancashire)*
Wyre Forest *(Hereford and Worcester)*

Ynys Môn–Isle of Anglesey *(Gwynedd)*
York *(North Yorkshire)*

London

List compiled by the London Research Library
81 Black Prince Road, London SE1 7SZ

Abbey Wood *(Greenwich)*
Acton *(Ealing)*
Acton Green *(Ealing)*
Acton Vale *(Ealing)*
Addington *(Croydon)*
Addiscombe *(Croydon)*
Aldersgate *(City of London)*
Aldgate *(City of London)*
Aldwych *(City of London)*
Alexandra Palace *(Haringey)*
Alexandra Park *(Haringey)*
Alperton *(Brent)*
Anerley *(Bromley)*
Angel *(Islington)*
Archway *(Islington)*
Arnos Grove *(Enfield)*
Aveley *(Havering)*
Avery Hill *(Greenwich)*

Baker Street *(Westminster)*
Balham *(Wandsworth)*
Balls Pond Road *(Islington)*
Bank *(City of London)*
Barbican *(City of London)*
Barking *(Barking & Dagenham)*
Barkingside *(Redbridge)*
Barnehurst *(Bexley)*
Barnes *(Richmond)*
Barnet *(Barnet)*
Barnsbury *(Islington)*
Barons Court *(Hammersmith & Fulham)*
Battersea *(Wandsworth)*
Bayswater *(Westminster)*
Beckenham *(Bromley)*
Becontree *(Barking & Dagenham)*
Becton *(Newham)*
Beddington *(Sutton)*
Bedfont *(Hounslow)*
Bedford Park *(Hammersmith & Fulham)*
Belgravia *(Westminster)*
Bellingham *(Lewisham)*
Belmont *(Sutton)*
Belsize Park *(Camden)*
Belvedere *(Bexley)*
Bermondsey *(Southwark)*
Bethnal Green *(Tower Hamlets)*
Bexley *(Bexley)*
Bexley Heath *(Bexley)*
Bickley *(Bromley)*
Biggin Hill *(Bromley)*
Bishopsgate *(City of London)*
Blackfriars *(City of London)*
Blackheath *(Lewisham)*
Blackwall *(Tower Hamlets)*
Bloomsbury *(Camden)*
Borough *(Southwark)*
Bostall Woods *(Greenwich)*

Gazetteer

Boston Manor *(Hounslow)*
Bounds Green *(Haringey)*
Bow *(Tower Hamlets)*
Bowes Park *(Haringey)*
Brent *(Brent)*
Brent Cross *(Brent)*
Brentford *(Hounslow)*
Brixton *(Lambeth)*
Broad Street *(City of London)*
Brockley *(Brockley)*
Bromley *(Bromley)*
Bromley by Bow *(Tower Hamlets)*
Brompton *(Kensington & Chelsea)*
Brondesbury *(Brent)*
Brook Green *(Hammersmith & Fulham)*
Burnt Oak *(Barnet)*
Bush Hill Park *(Enfield)*
Bushey Mead *(Merton)*

Caledonian Road *(Islington)*
Camberwell *(Southwark)*
Camden Town *(Camden)*
Canary Wharf *(Tower Hamlets)*
Canning Town *(Newham)*
Canonbury *(Lewisham)*
Carshalton *(Sutton)*
Carshalton Beeches *(Sutton)*
Catford *(Lewisham)*
Chadwell Heath *(Barking & Dagenham)*
Chalk Farm *(Camden)*
Charlton *(Greenwich)*
Cheam *(Sutton)*
Cheapside *(City of London)*
Chelsea *(Kensington & Chelsea)*
Chessington *(Kingston Upon Thames)*
Childs Hill *(Barnet)*
Chingford *(Waltham Forest)*
Chislehurst *(Bromley)*
Chiswick *(Hounslow)*
Church End *(Barnet)*
Clapham (Lambeth)
Clapham Common *(Lambeth/Wandsworth)*
Clapham Junction *(Wandsworth)*
Clapham North *(Lambeth)*
Clapham Park *(Lambeth)*
Clapham South *(Wandsworth)*
Clapton *(Hackney)*
Clayhall *(Redbridge)*
Clerkenwell *(Islington)*
Cockfosters *(Enfield)*
Coldharbour Lane *(Lambeth)*
Colindale *(Barnet)*
Collier Row *(Havering)*
Colliers Wood *(Merton)*
Colney Hatch *(Barnet)*
Coombe and Maldon *(Kingston upon Thames)*
Copse Hill *(Merton)*
Copthall *(Brent)*
Cottenham Park *(Merton)*
Coulsdon *(Croydon)*
Covent Garden *(Camden)*
Cowley *(Hillingdon)*
Cranford *(Hounslow)*
Cranham *(Havering)*
Cricklewood *(Brent)*
Cricklewood Broadway *(Barnet)*
Crofton Park *(Lewisham)*
Cromwell Road *(Kensington & Chelsea)*
Crouch End *(Haringey)*
Crouch Hill *(Islington)*
Croydon *(Croydon)*
Crystal Palace *(Bromley)*

Dagenham *(Barking & Dagenham)*
Dalston *(Hackney)*
Dartmouth Park *(Camden)*
Denmark Hill *(Southwark)*
Deptford *(Lewisham)*
Deptford Wharf *(Lewisham)*
Docklands *(Sthwk/Lew/TH/Newham/Grnwch)*
Dollis Hill *(Brent)*
Drayton Green *(Ealing)*
Drayton Park *(Islington)*
Dulwich *(Southwark)*
Dulwich Village *(Southwark)*

Ealing *(Ealing)*
Ealing Common *(Ealing)*
Earlesfield *(Wandsworth)*
Earls Court *(Kensington & Chelsea)*
East Acton *(Ealing/Hammersmith & Fulham)*
East Barnet *(Barnet)*
East Croydon *(Croydon)*
East Dulwich *(Southwark)*
East Finchley *(Barnet)*
East Ham *(Newham)*
East Putney *(Wandsworth)*
East Sheen *(Richmond upon Thames)*
Eastcote *(Hillingdon)*
Edgware *(Barnet)*
Edmonton *(Enfield)*
Elephant & Castle *(Southwark)*
Elm Park *(Havering)*
Eltham *(Greenwich)*
Elthorne Park *(Ealing)*
Emerson Park *(Havering)*
Enfield *(Enfield)*
Erith *(Bexley)*
Euston *(Camden)*

Farnborough *(Bromley)*
Farringdon *(Islington)*
Feltham *(Hounslow)*
Finchley *(Barnet)*
Finsbury/Finsbury Park *(Islington)*
Forest Dale *(Enfield)*
Forest Gate *(Newham)*
Forest Hill *(Lewisham)*
Fortis Green *(Barnet/Haringey)*
Fortune Green *(Camden)*
Friern Barnet *(Barnet)*
Fulham *(Hammersmith & Fulham)*
Furzedown *(Wandsworth)*

Gants Hill *(Redbridge)*
Gidea Park *(Havering)*
Gipsy Hill *(Southwark/Lambeth)*
Gloucester Road *(Kensington & Chelsea)*
Golders Green *(Barnet)*
Goldhawk Road *(Hammersmith & Fulham)*
Goodmayes *(Redbridge)*
Gospel Oak *(Camden)*
Grange Park *(Enfield)*
Greenford *(Ealing)*
Greenwich *(Greenwich)*
Grove Park *(Lewisham)*
Gunnersbury *(Ealing)*

Hackbridge *(Sutton)*
Hackney *(Hackney)*
Hackney Downs *(Hackney)*
Hackney Marshes *(Hackney)*
Hackney Wick *(Hackney)*
Haggerston *(Hackney)*
Hainault *(Redbridge)*
Hale End *(Waltham Forest)*
Ham *(Richmond upon Thames)*
Hammersmith *(Hammersmith & Fulham)*
Hampstead *(Camden)*
Hampstead Garden Suburb *(Barnet)*
Hampton *(Richmond upon Thames)*
Hampton Hill *(Richmond upon Thames)*
Hampton Wick *(Richmond)*
Hanger Lane *(Ealing)*
Hanwell *(Ealing)*
Hanworth *(Hounslow)*
Harefield *(Hillingdon)*
Harlesden *(Brent)*
Harlington *(Hillingdon)*
Harmonsworth *(Hillingdon)*
Harold Hill *(Havering)*
Harold Wood *(Havering)*
Harringay *(Haringey)*
Harrow *(Harrow)*
Harrow Weald *(Harrow)*
Harrow-on-the-Hill *(Harrow)*

Hartington *(Hillingdon)*
Havering *(Havering)*
Havering Atte Bower *(Havering)*
Haydons Road *(Merton)*
Hayes (Kent) *(Bromley)*
Hayes (Middx) *(Hillingdon)*
Hendon *(Barnet)*
Hendon Central *(Barnet)*
Herne Hill *(Southwark)*
Heston *(Hounslow)*
High Wood Hill *(Barnet)*
Higham Hill *(Waltham Forest)*
Highams Park *(Waltham Forest)*
Highbury *(Islington)*
Highgate *(Haringey)*
Hillingdon *(Hillingdon)*
Hither Green *(Lewisham)*
Holborn *(Camden)*
Holland Park *(Kensington & Chelsea)*
Holloway *(Islington)*
Homerton *(Tower Hamlets)*
Honor Oak *(Lewisham/Southwark)*
Hornchurch *(Havering)*
Hornsey *(Haringey)*
Hornsey Rise *(Islington)*
Hounslow *(Hounslow)*
Hounslow Central *(Hounslow)*
Hounslow East *(Hounslow)*
Hounslow West *(Hounslow)*
Hoxton *(Hackney)*
Hyde Park *(Westminster)*
Hyde, The *(Barnet)*

Ickenham *(Hillingdon)*
Ilford *(Redbridge)*
Isle of Dogs *(Tower Hamlets)*
Isleworth *(Hounslow)*
Islington *(Islington)*

Kenley *(Croydon)*
Kennington *(Lambeth/Southwark)*
Kensal Green *(Brent)*
Kensal Rise *(Brent)*
Kensington *(Kensington & Chelsea)*
Kentish Town *(Camden)*
Kenton *(Brent)*
Kew *(Richmond upon Thames)*
Kidbrooke *(Greenwich)*
Kilburn *(Brent)*
Kings Cross *(Camden)*
Kingsbury *(Brent)*
Kingston *(Kingston upon Thames)*
Knightsbridge *(Westminster)*

Ladbroke Grove *(Kensington & Chelsea)*
Ladywell *(Lewisham)*
Lambeth *(Lambeth)*
Lancaster Gate *(Westminster)*
Lavender Hill *(Wandsworth)*
Lee *(Lewisham)*
Lewisham *(Lewisham)*
Leyton *(Waltham Forest)*
Leyton Green *(Waltham Forest)*
Leytonstone *(Waltham Forest)*
Limehouse *(Tower Hamlets)*
Lisson Grove *(Westminster)*
Little Venice *(Westminster)*
London Bridge *(Southwark)*
London Fields *(Hackney)*
Lower Edmonton *(Enfield)*
Lower Holloway *(Islington)*
Lower Sydenham *(Lewisham)*

Maida Vale *(Westminster)*
Malden *(Kingston upon Thames)*
Manor House *(Haringey)*
Manor Park *(Newham)*
Marble Arch *(Westminster)*
Marylebone *(Westminster)*
Mayfair *(Westminster)*
Merton *(Merton)*
Merton Park *(Merton)*
Mile End *(Tower Hamlets)*
Mill Hill *(Barnet)*
Millwall *(Tower Hamlets)*
Mitcham *(Merton)*
Moorgate *(City of London)*
Morden *(Merton)*
Mortlake *(Richmond upon Thames)*
Motspur Park *(Kingston Upon Thames)*
Mottingham *(Lewisham)*
Muswell Hill *(Haringey)*

Neasden *(Brent)*
New Addington *(Bromley)*
New Barnet *(Barnet)*
New Cross *(Lewisham)*
New Cross Gate *(Lewisham)*
New Eltham *(Greenwich)*
New Malden *(Kingston upon Thames)*
New Southgate *(Enfield/Barnet)*
Newbury Park *(Redbridge)*
Newington *(Southwark)*
Newington Green *(Islington)*
Nine Elms *(Wandsworth)*
Norbiton *(Kingston upon Thames)*
Norbury *(Croydon)*
North Acton *(Ealing)*
North Cheam *(Sutton)*
North Chingford *(Waltham Forest)*
North Dulwich *(Southwark)*
North Ealing *(Ealing)*
North End *(Camden)*
North Enfield *(Enfield)*
North Finchley *(Barnet)*
North Harrow *(Harrow)*
North Kensington *(Kensington & Chelsea)*
North Wembley *(Brent)*
North Woolwich *(Newham)*
Northolt *(Ealing)*
Northwood *(Hillingdon)*
Norwood *(Croydon)*
Norwood Junction *(Croydon)*
Notting Hill *(Kensington & Chelsea)*
Notting Hill Gate *(Kensington & Chelsea)*
Nunhead *(Southwark)*

Oakleigh Park *(Barnet)*
Old Ford *(Tower Hamlets)*
Old Kent Road *(Southwark)*
Old Oak Common *(Ealing/Hammersmith)*
Olympia *(Hammersmith & Fulham)*
Orpington *(Bromley)*
Osidge *(Barnet)*
Osterley *(Hounslow)*
Oval *(Lambeth)*

Paddington *(Westminster)*
Palmers Green *(Enfield)*
Park Lane *(Westminster)*
Park Royal *(Brent)*
Parliament Hill *(Camden)*
Parson's Green *(Hammersmith & Fulham)*
Peckham *(Southwark)*
Penge *(Bromley)*
Pentonville *(Islington)*
Perivale *(Ealing)*
Petersham *(Richmond upon Thames)*
Petts Wood *(Bromley)*
Piccadilly *(Westminster)*
Pimlico *(Westminster)*
Pinner *(Harrow)*
Plaistow *(Newham)*
Plumstead *(Greenwich)*
Poplar *(Tower Hamlets)*
Portobello Road *(Kensington & Chelsea)*
Preston Road *(Brent)*
Primrose Hill *(Camden)*
Purley *(Croydon)*
Putney *(Wandsworth)*

Queens Park *(Brent)*
Queensbury *(Barnet/Harrow)*
Queensway *(Westminster)*

Rainham *(Havering)*

Gazetteer

Ravenscourt Park *(Hammersmith & Fulham)*
Rayners Lane *(Harrow)*
Raynes Park *(Merton)*
Redbridge *(Redbridge)*
Regents Park *(Westminster/Camden)*
Richmond *(Richmond upon Thames)*
Roehampton *(Wandsworth)*
Romford *(Havering)*
Rotherhithe *(Southwark)*
Royal Dockyard *(Greenwich)*
Royal Oak *(Westminster)*
Ruislip *(Hillingdon)*
Ruislip Manor *(Hillingdon)*
Rush Green *(Havering)*
Russell Square *(Camden)*

Sanderstead *(Croydon)*
Sands End *(Hammersmith & Fulham)*
Selhurst *(Croydon)*
Selsdon *(Croydon)*
Seven Kings *(Redbridge)*
Seven Sisters *(Haringey)*
Shacklewell *(Hackney)*
Sheen *(Richmond upon Thames)*
Shepherds Bush *(Hammersmith & Fulham)*
Shooters Hill *(Greenwich)*
Shoreditch *(Hackney)*
Shortlands *(Bromley)*
Sidcup *(Bexley)*
Silvertown *(Newham)*
Sipson *(Hillingdon)*
Sloane Square *(Kensington & Chelsea)*
Soho *(Westminster)*
Somers Town *(Camden)*
South Acton *(Ealing)*
South Croydon *(Croydon)*
South Ealing *(Ealing)*
South Hampstead *(Camden)*
South Harrow *(Harrow)*
South Kensington *(Kensington & Chelsea)*
South Lambeth *(Lambeth)*
South Norwood *(Croydon)*
South Ruislip *(Hillingdon)*
South Tottenham *(Haringey)*
South Wimbledon *(Merton)*
South Woodford *(Redbridge)*
Southall *(Ealing)*
Southfields *(Wandsworth)*
Southgate *(Enfield)*
Southwark *(Southwark)*
Spitalfields *(Tower Hamlets)*
St Johns Wood *(Westminster)*
St Katherines Dock *(Tower Hamlets)*
St Mary Cray *(Bromley)*
St Marylebone *(Westminster)*
St Pancras *(Camden)*
St Paul's Cray *(Bromley)*
Stamford Brook *(Hammersmith & Fulham)*
Stamford Hill *(Hackney)*
Stanmore *(Harrow)*
Stepney *(Tower Hamlets)*
Stockwell *(Lambeth)*
Stoke Newington *(Hackney)*
Stone Bridge *(Brent)*
Stratford *(Newham)*
Streatham *(Lambeth)*
Streatham Hill *(Lambeth)*
Streatham Vale *(Lambeth)*
Stroud Green *(Haringey)*
Sudbury *(Brent)*
Summerstown *(Wandsworth)*
Surbiton *(Kingston upon Thames)*
Surrey Docks *(Southwark)*
Sutton *(Sutton)*
Swiss Cottage *(Camden)*
Sydenham *(Lewisham)*

Teddington *(Richmond upon Thames)*
Temple Mills *(Newham)*
Thamesmead *(Bexley/Greenwich)*
The Borough *(Southwark)*
The Hyde *(Barnet)*
Thornton Heath *(Croydon)*
Tolworth *(Kingston upon Thames)*
Tooting *(Wandsworth)*
Tottenham *(Haringey)*
Tottenham Hale *(Haringey)*
Totteridge *(Barnet)*
Tower Bridge *(Southwark/Tower Hamlets)*
Tower Hamlets *(Tower Hamlets)*
Tower Hill *(Tower Hamlets/City of London)*
Tufnell Park *(Islington)*
Tulse Hill *(Lambeth)*
Turnham Green *(Ealing/Hounslow)*
Turnpike Lane *(Haringey)*
Twickenham *(Richmond upon Thames)*
Upminster *(Havering)*
Upney *(Barking & Dagenham)*
Upper Clapton *(Hackney)*
Upper Edmonton *(Enfield)*
Upper Holloway *(Islington)*
Upper Norwood *(Croydon)*
Upper Sydenham *(Lewisham)*
Upper Tooting *(Wandsworth)*
Upton Park *(Newham)*
Uxbridge *(Hillingdon)*

Vauxhall *(Lambeth)*
Victoria *(Westminster)*
Victoria Park (E2/E3) *(Tower Hamlets)*
Victoria Park (E9) *(Hackney)*

Waddon *(Croydon)*
Wallington *(Sutton)*
Walthamstow *(Waltham Forest)*
Walworth *(Southwark)*
Wandsworth *(Wandsworth)*
Wandsworth Common *(Wandsworth)*
Wanstead *(Redbridge)*
Wapping *(Tower Hamlets)*
Warwick Avenue *(Westminster)*
Waterloo *(Lambeth/Southwark)*
Wealdstone *(Harrow)*
Well Hall *(Greenwich)*
Welling *(Bexley)*
Wembley *(Brent)*
Wembley Park *(Brent)*
West Acton *(Acton)*
West Brompton *(Kensington & Chelsea)*
West Croydon *(Croydon)*
West Drayton *(Hillingdon)*
West Dulwich *(Lambeth/Southwark)*
West Ealing *(Ealing)*
West Finchley *(Barnet)*
West Ham *(Newham)*
West Hampstead *(Camden)*
West Heath *(Bexley)*
West Hendon *(Barnet)*
West Kensington *(Hammersmith & Fulham)*
West Norwood *(Lambeth)*
West Penge *(Bromley)*
West Wickham *(Bromley)*
Westbourne Green *(Westminster)*
Westbourne Park *(Westminster)*
Westminster *(Westminster)*
Whetstone *(Barnet)*
White City *(Hammersmith & Fulham)*
White Hart Lane *(Haringey)*
Whitechapel *(Tower Hamlets)*
Whitton *(Richmond upon Thames)*
Willesden *(Brent)*
Willesden Green *(Brent)*
Willesden Junction *(Brent)*
Willis Green *(Brent)*
Wimbledon *(Merton)*
Wimbledon Chase *(Merton)*
Wimbledon Common *(Merton)*
Wimbledon Park *(Merton)*
Wimbledon Village *(Merton)*
Winchmore Hill *(Enfield)*
Wood Green *(Haringey)*
Woodford *(Redbridge)*
Woodford Green *(Redbridge)*
Woodside Park *(Barnet)*
Woolwich *(Greenwich)*
Worcester Park *(Sutton/Kingston upon Thames)*

Yiewsley *(Hillingdon)*

Scotland

Alphabetical list of Districts showing Regional Authority

Aberdeen *(Grampian)*
Angus *(Tayside)*
Annandale and Eskdale *(Dumfries and Galloway)*
Argyll and Bute *(Strathclyde)*

Badenoch and Strathspey *(Highland)*
Banff and Buchan *(Grampian)*
Bearsden and Milngavie *(Strathclyde)*
Berwickshire *(Borders)*

Caithness *(Highland)*
Clackmannan *(Central)*
Clydebank *(Strathclyde)*
Clydesdale *(Strathclyde)*
Cumbernauld and Kilsyth *(Strathclyde)*
Cumnock and Doon Valley *(Strathclyde)*
Cunninghame *(Strathclyde)*

Dumbarton *(Strathclyde)*
Dundee *(Tayside)*
Dunfermline *(Fife)*

East Kilbride *(Strathclyde)*
East Lothian *(Lothian)*
Eastwood *(Strathclyde)*
Edinburgh *(Lothian)*
Ettrick and Lauderdale *(Borders)*

Falkirk *(Central)*

Glasgow *(Strathclyde)*
Gordon *(Grampian)*

Hamilton *(Strathclyde)*

Inverclyde *(Strathclyde)*
Inverness *(Highland)*

Kilmarnock and Loudoun *(Strathclyde)*
Kincardine and Deeside *(Grampian)*
Kirkcaldy *(Fife)*
Kyle and Carrick *(Strathclyde)*

Lochaber *(Highland)*

Midlothian *(Lothian)*
Monklands *(Strathclyde)*
Moray *(Grampian)*
Motherwell *(Strathclyde)*

Nairn *(Highland)*
Nithsdale *(Dumfries and Galloway)*
North East Fife *(Fife)*

Perth and Kinross *(Tayside)*

Renfrew *(Strathclyde)*
Ross and Cromarty *(Highland)*
Roxburgh *(Borders)*

Skye and Lochalsh *(Highland)*
Stewartry *(Dumfries and Galloway)*
Stirling *(Central)*
Strathkelvin *(Strathclyde)*
Sutherland *(Highland)*

Tweeddale *(Borders)*

West Lothian *(Lothian)*
Wigtown *(Dumfries and Galloway)*

Northern Ireland

Alphabetical list of Borough/District Councils showing Education and Library Boards

Antrim *(North Eastern)*
Ards *(South Eastern)*
Armagh *(Southern)*

Ballymena *(North Eastern)*
Ballymoney *(North Eastern)*
Banbridge *(Southern)*
Belfast City *(Belfast)*

Carrickfergus *(North Eastern)*
Castlereagh *(South Eastern)*
Coleraine *(North Eastern)*
Cookstown *(Southern)*
Craigavon *(Southern)*

Derry *(Western)*
Down *(South Eastern)*
Dungannon *(Southern)*

Fermanagh *(Western)*

Larne *(North Eastern)*
Limavady *(Western)*
Lisburn *(South Eastern)*

Magherafelt *(North Eastern)*
Moyle *(North Eastern)*

Newry and Mourne *(Southern)*
Newtownabbey *(North Eastern)*
North Down *(South Eastern)*

Omagh *(Western)*

Strabane *(Western)*

Guide to Reports

The following notes briefly summarise the remits and recommendations of the principal education reports applying to England and Wales since 1926, Northern Ireland from 1979 and to Scotland from 1946. Some of the reports concerned with England and Wales, however, also have implications for Scotland–for example, the Holland Report and the Warnock Report.

England and Wales

1926 Hadow Report
Brief: To report on the education of children up to the age of 15, other than those in secondary schools.
Recommendations: Leaving age to be raised to 15; secondary education for all children in four types of school: 1 grammar, 2 'modern' (where the curriculum during the last two years would be of practical nature); 3 'modern' (similar to 2 but with provision for pupils of differing abilities); 4 'senior classes' within existing elementary schools for pupils not selected for any of the previous type of secondary school.

1931 Hadow Report
Brief: To inquire into and report on courses of study suitable for children (other than infants) up to 11 in elementary schools, with special reference to needs of children in rural areas.
Recommendations: Division between primary and secondary at 11 plus to continue, with transfer from infants of seven plus; close cooperation between primary and secondary schools; pupils to be streamed by the age of 10; curriculum in the primary school to be thought of in terms of activity and experience, rather than of knowledge to be acquired and facts to be stored; primary classes no larger than 40; training of teachers for backward groups; efficiency of schools not to be judged on success in the 'free place' examination.

1938 Spens Report
Brief: To report on secondary schools other than elementary schools with particular regard to the education of pupils who do not remain at school after the age of 16.
Recommendations: Expansion of technical schools secondary education to remain separate in grammar, technical and secondary modern though a 'multi-lateral idea' to be encouraged in the separated schools; introduction of vocational courses and appointment of careers teachers; adoption of a 'tutorial system'; leaving age to be raised to 16; grammar school places for about 15 per cent of the population.

1944 McNair Report
Brief: To consider the supply, recruitment and training of teachers and youth leaders.
Recommendations: Teachers' salaries should be increased, course of training extended to three years. Also three-year full-time course for youth leaders. Salaries comparable with teachers.

1945 Percy Report
Brief: To consider the needs of higher technical education in England and Wales and the roles of universities and technical colleges.
Recommendations: The designation of a selected number of technical colleges as Colleges of Advanced Technology with full-time courses of degree standard.

1954 Gurney-Dixon Report
Brief: To examine why some pupils left secondary schools as early as possible, whether more should be encouraged to stay on until they were 18 and how this could be done.
Recommendations: Better maintenance allowances for needy pupils staying on a school beyond 15; legislation for the payment of family allowances in respect of all children still at school; a higher proportion of grammar school places to be provided in secondary education.

1959 Crowther Report
Brief: The education of boys and girls between the ages of 16 and 18.
Recommendations: School-leaving age should be raised to 16 between 1966 and 1968, even at the cost of larger classes; county colleges (outlined in the 1944 Act) to be introduced in the early 1970s; a target by 1980 of half the girls and the boys in the country staying in full-time education until 18.

1960 Albemarle Report
Brief: To review the Youth Service (i.e. 14 to 20 age group).
Recommendations: Youth clubs should provide opportunity for association, training and challenge; called for 10-year national and local development plans and a Youth Service Development Council. The mix of statutory and voluntary provision of the youth service to be preserved.

1960 Anderson Report
Brief: To examine the administration of grants to students.
Recommendations: The granting of a place on a first-degree course at a university should entitle the student to a grant from public funds; all types of state scholarships to be discontinued; parental contribution to be abolished (though four members of the 16- strong committee dissociated themselves from this); if, however, parental contribution was retained, it should not apply to about 60 per cent of parents and be reduced considerably for the remainder; in assessing the allowance to married students the income of spouses should be ignored.

1963 Newsom Report
Brief: To consider the education of pupils 13 to 16 of less than average ability; education being understood to include extra-curricular activities.
Recommendations: Raising the leaving age to 16; a longer school day, incorporating into the curriculum activities then being undertaken voluntarily; a joint working party on social services in the slum areas; improvement of teacher training with the retention at all costs of 'concurrent' academic and professional training.

1963 Robbins Report
Brief: To review the full-time pattern of higher education in Great Britain.
Recommendations: To raise the percentage of the age group receiving full-time higher education from about eight per cent to about 17 per cent (12 per cent for girls, 22 per cent for men) by 1980; setting-up of a new Ministry of Arts and Sciences; teacher training to be removed from local authorities and integrated, administratively, into the university pattern.

1964 Henniker-Heaton Report
Brief: To report on day release for young people under 18.
Recommendations: Young people on day release to be

doubled between 1964 and 1970, giving a total of 500,000– this to be achieved by voluntary means.

1967 Plowden Report
Brief: To consider primary education in all its aspects and the transition to secondary education.
Recommendations: Areas and schools in which children are most severely handicapped to be classed as educational priority areas; extra teachers to be recruited to reduce all oversize classes in these areas to 40; £120 additional pay for teachers in EPA schools; immediate expansion of part-time nursery education with the addition of full-time for perhaps up to half the children in these areas; middle schools to be established; a single annual starting date in the autumn term for schooling; corporal punishment should be forbidden; recruitment of teachers' aides; in-service training for teachers every five years.

1968 Gittins Report
Brief: To consider in all its aspects primary education in Wales.
Recommendations: Encourage the teaching of Welsh; 60 hours of in-service training for teachers during a five-year period; area schools for 5 to 12 age group to take the place of one to three teacher schools; middle schools for 8 to 12 group; part-time nursery education from three onwards for all, full-time for needy 15 per cent; statutory requirements for religious education should be relaxed.

1968 Newsom Report on Public Schools
Brief: To consider the integration of the public schools with the maintained system of education.
Recommendations: Independent boarding schools suitable and willing to enter an integrated sector should be encouraged as a first step, to admit assisted pupils from maintained schools to at least a half of their places by the end of a build-up period of about seven years; independent schools cater for about 45,000 of the estimated 80,000 children requiring boarding places; there should be an Education Act enabling an integrated sector to develop under the guidance of a Boarding Schools Corporation; Education Secretary to have power in the last resort to compel a school to enter into a scheme of integration if its refusal was prejudicing a successful integration policy.

1969 Haslegrave Report
Brief: To review the courses and examination existing for technicians.
Recommendations: Two new bodies to be set up: a Technician Education Council and a Business Education Council: to be in charge of planning, coordinating and administering technical courses and examinations; school leavers should go on to a Technician Certificate course qualifying the holder to proceed to a Higher Technician Certificate course, followed by the Higher Technician Diploma. HND to stay for the time being. No general change was thought desirable in the existing pattern of certificate and diploma courses in business studies.

1970 Donnison Report
Brief: Identical to that of the Newsom Report, 1968, but with reference to the independent day schools and the direct grant schools.
Recommendations: In principle, integration. Day schools receiving grants from central or local authorities should participate in the movement towards comprehensive reorganisation; legal right of direct grant schools to go independent recognised.

1972 James Report
Brief: To look into present arrangements for the education, training and probation of teachers in England and Wales.
Recommendations: The education and training of teachers should be divided into three consecutive stages or cycles. First, a diploma or degree course (two years leading to DipHE); second, one year of professional studies leading to appointment as 'licensed teacher' followed by a school-based year with at least one day a week at a professional centre leading to 'registered teacher' and BA(Ed); third, a range of in-service training courses with the equivalent of one term full-time training every seven years.

1973 Russell Report
Brief: To review non-vocational adult education in England and Wales.
Recommendations: Establishment of development councils in all LEA areas; also a national development council; regional advisory councils to be set up similar to those for FE; LEAs should also set up area organisations, each with a full-time head and a management committee; DES should continue to give direct grant for certain kinds of adult education work; WEA grant to be paid in one sum to central organisation and not separately to each WEA district; paid educational leave for workers; fees should be charged but should always be modest; all new FE buildings and secondary schools to be designed with the needs of adult education in mind.

1974 Houghton Report
Brief: To examine the pay of non-university teachers in Great Britain. (The committee found that compared with general movements in salaries, teachers' pay had suffered a shortfall of from 15 to 24 per cent).
Recommendations: An increase in pay for all teachers averaging 30 per cent; a common scale for all teachers in FE, including colleges of education; four scales instead of the existing five for school teachers, this to be achieved by merging scales 2 and 3, Graduates to start two increments ahead, good honours graduates four; salary levels for lower headteacher groups to be increased by 32 per cent with similar percentage increase for all headteacher groups.

1975 Bullock Report
Brief: To consider in relation to schools all aspects of teaching the use of English including reading, writing and speech; how present practice might be improved and the role that initial and in-service teacher training might play; how monitoring general level of attainment could be introduced or improved.
Recommendations: These numbered 333 but were summarised to 17 principal recommendations. A system of monitoring should be introduced; language ability should be developed in pre-school, nursery and infant years, this to involve employment of teachers' aides with some training in language; every teacher on the staff to be involved in the school's language policy; one teacher in each school responsible for language and teaching of reading; transmission of records between schools; every LEA to have an English adviser and establish an advisory team; LEAs and schools to introduce early screening procedures; a reading clinic or remedial centre; provision for tuition of adult illiterates; more tuition in English for immigrant children; a standing working party to consider capitation allowances and level of book provision; language education, including the teaching of reading to be part of every primary and secondary school teacher's initial training; a national centre for language in education to be set up.

1976 Court Report
Brief: To study child health services in Britain.
Recommendations: An integrated system should be introduced quickly, with a general practitioner paediatrician (GPP) at the centre, and many more senior house officers, registrars and consultants specialising in child care. There should be a birth to five years surveillance programme involving successively hospitals, baby clinics, GPPs and health visitors, with immediate evaluation of any special care needed, and a statutory medical assessment of every child before school.

1977 Holland Report
Brief: To study measures to help unemployed young people. The working party, which produced the report in May 1977, was first set up under the chairmanship of Mr Geoffrey Holland by the Manpower Services Commission in October 1976. Its main recommendations were accepted by the Government in June 1977.
Recommendations: The working party concluded that youth unemployment was too urgent a problem to allow time to build a new system; nor did it attempt to provide all young unemployed people with an opportunity. Instead, it proposed a programme of nearly 130,000 places providing 234,000 opportunities each year. It recommended that all

those on the programme should be paid a flat-rate allowance of £18 per week. The cost of the programme was estimated at £168m a year. The courses were intended to be of two kinds: work preparation and work experience. All unemployed young people aged 16 to 18 were to be eligible.

1977 Taylor Report
Brief: To review the management and government of maintained primary and secondary schools in England and Wales, the composition and functions of the governing bodies and their relationships with local education authorities, headteachers, staff, parents, pupils and local community.
Report: Report of the committee of enquiry: a new partnership for our schools HMSO 1977.
Recommendations: Entitled A new partnership in our schools, the report proposed reformed governing bodies with equal numbers of representatives from the LEA, the staff including the head, the parents and the community. LEAs would retain formal responsibility for the running of the school, but many powers would be delegated to the governing bodies. Headteachers would be accountable to the governors for the conduct of the school; there should be no area of the school's activities in which the board would have no responsibility. Governors would have powers to set the school's aims, review progress towards these goals and take necessary action to achieve them. They would also have powers to review financial estimates for the school and subject to the approval of the authority to incur expenditure. LEAs would be required to provide training for governors.

1978 Oakes Report
Brief: To consider ways of improving the system of management and control of higher education in the maintained sector of the British Isles.
Recommendations: The report identified four main functions which any HE management system would need to perform: collecting information on demand and supply; planning for change and development; determining provision and allocating resources; and overseeing the system as a whole. To exercise these functions a national body was proposed with its prime role to advise the Secretary of State on the total share to be devoted to capital expenditure and how the agreed provision should be allocated to individual institutions. HE should be financed through a system under which the major part of the cost would be pooled and met from a fixed sum determined annually, and a minor part would be met direct by the maintaining local authority of each institution. The governing bodies of the institutions and the LEAs should not have their responsibilities diminished. The report argued for operational freedom for governing bodies in matters of appointments, and purchasing and contracts. There should be clear demarcation of governing bodies and LEA powers. The report recommended the establishment of nine regional bodies to assist mainly in planning and information, but also in bringing together LEAs with little HE provision, and including the universities and industry.

1978 Warnock Report
Brief: To review educational provision in England, Scotland and Wales for children and young people handicapped by disabilities of body or mind, taking account of the medical aspects of their needs, together with arrangements to prepare them for entry into employment; to consider the most effective use of resources for these purposes; and to make recommendations.
Report: Special educational needs. Report of the committee of enquiry into the education of handicapped children and young people HMSO 1978.
Recommendations: Given its wide remit, the report made as many as 225 recommendations. The discovery and assessment of disabilities formed an important part of the report. The Committee recommended five stages, three of which were school-based and two of which were multi-professional. Warnock concluded that special education needed to start as early as possible. In the earliest stages parents were the main educators, but parents describing local facilities. Once a child showed signs of special needs a 'named person' should be provided as a point of contact. The report attempted to come to terms with the vexed question of integration of special with ordinary schools. It put its own interpretation on Section 10 of the Education Act 1976 which upheld the principle of integration. It concluded that Section 10 should be amended and that every LEA should have a comprehensive and long term plan for special education provisions within which arrangement for individual schools should have their place. Special schools should continue to feature prominently, but their facilities ought to be more widely available. There should be greater efforts made for disabled youngsters on leaving school. Warnock criticised piecemeal development in FE and called for a coordinated approach to the problems of the handicapped on a regional basis.

1978 Waddell Report
Brief: To enquire into a feasibility of a common 16- plus examination which would span both ordinary level GCE and the CSE.
Report: Report of the steering committee to consider proposals for replacing GCE O level and CSE by a common system of examining HMSO 1978.
Recommendations: The steering Committee set up by the Secretary of State in 1976 recommended that a common system should be designed for the same range of ability as O level and CSE together. Examinations should be available through the three modes already established by CSE. Results should be expressed in seven grades on a single scale. The examinations should be teacher controlled and regionally based. Finally, the Schools Council should have a co-ordinating role.

1981 Rampton Report
Brief: To review in relation to schools the education needs the attainments of children from ethnic minority groups taking account, as necessary, of external factors relevant to school performance, including early childhood influences and prospects for school leavers; to consider the potential value of instituting arrangements for keeping under review the educational performance of different ethnic minority groups, and what those arrangements might be; to consider the most effective use of resources for these purposes; and to make recommendations.
Report: West Indian children in schools: interim report of the committee of enquiry into the education of children from minority ethnic groups Cmnd 8723 HMSO 1981.
Recommendations: Cover pre-school provision; reading and language curriculum; books and teaching materials; examinations; pastoral arrangements; school and community links; and special provision, including the ethnic mix of ESN(M) schools. Recommendations also deal with preparation for adult life with reference to the careers service; the need for teacher education and the recruitment and training of West Indian teachers; the need to appoint multi-cultural advisers; and the recording of statistics of ethnic origin of schoolchildren, student teachers and students of universities. Polytechnic and higher education colleges. Finally the Home Office and the DES should review the operation of Section 11 to meet the needs of the ethnic minority communities.

1982 Cockcroft Report
Brief: To consider the teaching of mathematics in primary and secondary schools in England and Wales, with particular regard to the mathematics required in further and higher education, employment and adult life generally, and to make recommendations.
Report: Mathematics counts. Report of the committee of enquiry into the teaching of mathematics in schools HMSO 1982.
Recommendations: Contains a large number of recommendations, many intended to be implemented by teachers, others requiring the initiative of the LEAs. Recommends essential changes including the necessity to improve the quality of mathematics teaching, to establish mathematics co-ordinators, to improve training and increase the provision of teaching facilities and equipment. Examinations at all levels should provide practical targets and reflect suitable curricula. Future needs of students in relationship to employment are a vital factor. Six agencies are identified who must respond fully and actively if the recommendations are to be implemented–teachers, LEAs,

examination boards, central government, training institutions, and agencies who find and initiate educational research.

1982 Swinnerton-Dyer Report
Brief: To consider how far the present scale and nature of provision for postgraduate education, initially in the fields covered by the Science and Engineering Research Council, the Natural Environment Research Council and the Social Science Research Council, meet manpower needs, and to consider the role of the Councils in meeting them.
Recommendations: The SERC and SSRC should maintain statistics of submission rates for the research students they support. These statistics should be published, analysed into individual universities in order to identify any university where the submission rate relevant to that Council was unacceptable; the SERC and SRCC would then be able to exercise sanctions of increasing severity. The DES should further consider the provision of maintenance grants for conversion courses. The DES should consult with other Government Departments to establish a single body for identifying needs and commissioning courses, where the responsibility is at present divided between the Research Councils. UGC, Training Boards and other organisations.

1985 Swann Report
Brief: To review in relation to schools the educational needs and attainments of children from ethnic minority groups taking account of factors outside the formal education system relevant to school performance, including influences in early childhood and prospects for school leavers; consider the potential value of instituting arrangements for keeping under review the educational performance of different ethnic minority groups, and what those arrangements might be; consider the most effective use of resources for these purposes and to make recommendations.
Report: Education for all. The report of the committee of enquiry into the education of children from ethnic minority groups Cmnd 9453 HMSO 1985.
Recommendations: Seven major recommendations are made. Those in 'authority' (the government, LEAs, HMIs, examination boards and others) are asked to study the report and act on its findings. Most importantly they are asked to keep relevant ethnically based statistics. Schools are asked not to withdraw children in need of extra English language tuition from the classroom but to teach them within the main streams of the school. Mother tongue and community languages should be fostered, but not incorporated into the standard school curriculum. The need for the 'daily act of worship' required by the 1944 Education Act, is questioned. The creation of separate schools for minority communities is considered likely to exacerbate the rejection of minorities by the majority (though a number of committee members disagreed on this point). All teacher training courses should prepare students for teaching in a multi-racial society. Action should be taken to recruit more ethnic minority teachers but a 'quota system' is rejected.

1985 Lindop Report
Brief: To identify and examine key issues for the effective and efficient maintenance and improvement of academic standards in the way those responsible for the academic validation of first and higher degree level courses in the public sector in Great Britain discharge their responsibilities, having regard to the validation arrangements of sub-degree higher education courses in the public sector, and distinguishing as necessary between different branches of learning; and to recommend changes as appropriate.
Recommendations: There should be a range of different forms of validation, including external validation of individual degree courses and groups of courses; accreditation of institutions, and perhaps subject areas; and complete self-validation. The Secretary of State to have powers to designate such self-validating institutions with advice from a new advisory committee set up to process applications; the development of a national body to co-ordinate the validation activities of individual universities in the public sector; better scrutiny of student applications without conventional entry qualifications who will not reach degree standard; and the need to examine the legal ties regulating the relationship between local education authorities and the institutes of higher education they maintain. There should be a strengthening of the external examiner system.

1988 Higginson Report
Brief: In the light of the Government's commitment to retain GCE Advanced Level Examinations as an essential means for setting standards of excellence, and with the aim of maintaining or improving the present character and rigorous standards of these examinations:
to recommend the principles that should govern GCE A Level syllabuses and their assessment, so that consistency in the content and the assessment of subjects is secured; to set out a plan of action for subsequent detailed professional work required to give effect to these recommendations.
Report: Advancing A levels: report of a Committee appointed by the Secretary of State for Education and Science and the Secretary of State for Wales, 1988 HMSO 0 11 270652 5.
Recommendations: 'Leaner' and 'tougher' syllabuses with expansion from three to five subjects as a norm for full-time students, together with one Advanced Supplementary (AS) level subject. Courses should offer 'breadth' so that national economic benefits will follow. There should be a compulsory common core for each subject with a review of all A level syllabuses followed by a revision of AS level syllabuses. The number of A level syllabuses should be reduced from the present 400, with important savings in resources. There must be more accurate and uniform marking through explicit assessment criteria. Twenty per cent of the final totals to be based on in-course assessment. There should be a central body to examine appeals, and, together with coordinating the work of the Boards, this should be the school Examinations and Assessment Council (SEAC) the successor to SEC. Finally, for prospective employers, certificates should show the short subject-title together with a brief description of the syllabus and more information of the candidate's achievements at the point of the assessment.

1988 Cleveland Report
Brief: To examine the arrangements for dealing with suspected cases of child abuse in Cleveland since 1st January 1987 including in particular cases of child sexual abuse, and to make recommendations.
Report of the inquiry into abuse in Cleveland 1987.
Chairman Elizabeth Butler-Sloss. 1988 HMSO 0 10 104132 2.
Recommendations: Investigators into child sexual abuse must act in the best interests of the child, ensure good communication with the child, with the minimum of medical examinations and interviews. Parents should be advised of their rights and receive written confirmation of all important decisions. Place of safety orders should be sought for the minimum time necessary to protect the child. Inter-agency co-operation must be developed. Training is a vital element and a major need. The extension of interim care orders should be in the discretion of Magistrates and there is a need for the setting up of a Family Court, with a new Office of Child Protection. Other recommendations related specifically to the work of the various agencies-social services, police, the medical profession-and to the rationalisation and clarity in the work of the Media and Press.

1988 Kingman Report
Brief: to recommend a model of the English language whether spoken or written which would
(i) serve as the basis of how teachers are trained to understand how the English language works
(ii) inform professional discussion of all aspects of English teaching.
To recommend the principles which should guide teachers on how far and in what ways the model should be made explicit to pupils, to make them conscious of how language is used in range of contexts.
To recommend what, in general terms, pupils need to know about how the English language works and in consequence what they should have been taught, and be expected to understand, on this score, at ages 7, 11 and 16.

Guide to Reports

Report of the Committee of inquiry into the teaching of English language 1988 HMSO 0 11 270650 9.
Recommendations: The Committee set out its detailed model and made 16 recommendations. Some of the recommendations arose out of work of the committee and further to the original brief. All subject departments involved in language teaching in secondary schools should develop a co-ordinated policy, whilst primary schools should designate a member of staff 'language consultant' to advise on language work. all prospective primary school teachers to undertake a language course with 50% of the time spent in direct tuition of 'knowledge about language' as outlined in the recommended model in the report, while potential secondary school teachers of English should undertake a special course as recommended in the model.
The Committee also recommend that a first degree in English should be a pre-requisite for English Specialists in the profession.
There should be a National Language Project under the auspices of the SCDC.

1989 Elton Report
Brief: In view of public concern about violence and indiscipline in schools and the problems faced by the teaching profession today, to consider what action can be taken by central government, local authorities, voluntary bodies owning schools, governing bodies of schools, headteachers, teachers and parents to secure the orderly atmosphere necessary in schools for effective teaching and learning to take place.
Report: Discipline in schools: report of the Committee of Enquire chaired by Lord Elton 1989 HMSO 0 11 270665 7.
Recommendations: Over 130 directed towards teachers, parents, pupils, police, governors, LEA and central government, with a strong emphasis on the need for further training. The committee stressed the urgent need for practical training in managing pupil behaviour in the classroom to be required part of initial teacher training; for clear national standards for the amount of time teacher trainers must spend in school and for the management of pupil behaviour as a national priority in the LEA Training Grants scheme for in-service training of teachers in 1990-91. A monitor scheme should be instituted for two years covering procedures for excluding pupils from school. There should be two new Education Support Grants, to tackle truancy and to tackle the problem of difficult pupils, on-site and off. There must be an emphasis within management training programmes for headteachers and other senior staff on the skills required to motivate and lead staff and manage institutional change.

Northern Ireland

1979 Jackson Report
Brief: To enquire into the nature of existing and likely future demand for adult educational guidance; to report on the adequacy of present provision, noting especially the need within socially disadvantaged areas and any relevant experience or research outside Northern Ireland; and to make recommendations on the development of educational guidance services.
Recommendations: A central agency for the co-ordination of adult educational guidance in Northern Ireland should be established. The agency should train counsellors, establish a comprehensive information service, advise the NI DoE, etc.

Scotland

1946 Primary Education
This was a major report of the Advisory Council on Education in Scotland about primary education post war and made recommendations, many of which are still valid. The Advisory Council has not been constituted for some years.

1947 Secondary Education
This was also a major report of the Advisory Council on Education in Scotland about secondary education post war. Many of its recommendations are still valid–see the Munn Report.

1952 Further Education
This was a matching report of the Advisory Council on Education in Scotland to those on primary and secondary education, and reviewed provision in Further Education.

1963 Wheatley Report
The Teaching Profession in Scotland report resulted in the constituting of the General Teaching Council for Scotland in 1966 in terms of the Teaching Council (Scotland) Act 1965. The functions are–to keep under review standards of fitness to teach, to recommend as to the supply of teachers, to be informed of the nature of instruction given in colleges of education, to establish and keep a register of persons who are entitled to be registered, and to determine whether under disciplinary powers registration be withdrawn or refused.

1963 Brunton Report
From School to Further Education 1963 was an enquiry into aims appropriate to the various ability groups and kinds of curricula required in the third and fourth year of secondary education. It proposed that abler pupils follow an academic curriculum, with the Scottish Certificate of Education as the aim, while others follow a curriculum with a vocational impulse. This division has not proved acceptable. Note that the report was made outside the context of the comprehensive system.

1965 Primary Education in Scotland
This was a memorandum to replace *The Primary School in Scotland* which had appeared in 1950. It provides an appraisal of the best practices in primary schools in Scotland and of the principles on which primary education should be based. It was followed in 1971 by a progress report on *Primary Education Organisation and Development*. This was an account of ways in which there had been an attempt to guide teachers in implementation of the suggestions of the *Report on Primary Education in Scotland 1965*; included an evaluation of means by which responsibilities had been discharged.

1971 Before Five
An appraisal of the best practices in nursery schools and classes and of the principles on which pre-school education should be based.

1972 Brunton Report
The Training of Graduates for Secondary Education reviewed arrangements for post graduate teacher training in the secondary sector. The proposals, which involved 'sandwich' arrangements were not accepted by the Secretary of State.

1973 Melville Report
The Training of Staff for Centres for the Mentally Handicapped was an enquiry into staffing of junior occupational centres where children were trained by instructors. It recommended that centres become schools and part of the educational provision with the appointment of teachers in addition to instructors. The Education Mentally Handicapped Children (Scotland) Act 1974 gave education authorities responsibility, and consequent changes have occurred.

1975 Alexander Report
Adult Education: The Challenge of Change was an enquiry to consider aims appropriate to voluntary leisure time courses for adults, which are educational but not specially vocational.

1976 Ruthven Report
Ancillary Staff in Secondary Schools: Administrative and Clerical Staff, Technicians, Auxiliaries was a review of existing services, and recommendations for new ratio of staff to pupils.

1976 Stimpson Report
Non-Teaching Staff in Secondary Schools: Youth and Community Workers, Librarians, Instructors was a review of existing services, and recommendations for new ratio of staff to pupils. There was particular reference to use of instructors.

1977 Munn Report
The Structure of the Curriculum in the Third and Fourth years of the Scottish Secondary School HMSO 1977 011 491501 6 was an enquiry about how the curriculum at S3 and S4 could be structured to ensure that all pupils receive a balanced education suitable to their needs and abilities and to consider implications for earlier and later stages of secondary education.

1977 Dunning Report
Assessment for all: report of the committee to review assessment in the third and fourth years of secondary education in Scotland HMSO 1977 011 491505 9 was an enquiry to identify aims and purposes of assessment and certification in the light of educational and social changes since the introduction of the Ordinary Grade of the Scottish Certificate of Education; to consider forms of examination or assessment likely to meet the needs of fourth year pupils of varying academic ability; to consider the effect of any changes on Higher Grade of the examination and the Certificate of Sixth Year Studies.

1977 Pack Report
Truancy and Indiscipline in Schools in Scotland HMSO 1977 011 491496 6 was an enquiry into truancy and indiscipline among primary and secondary pupils; to consider measures to reduce these problems, circumstances justifying suspension or expulsion of pupils from school, and provision for such pupils and recommend most effective use of available resources.

1978 Sneddon Report
Learning to Teach: a consideration of student teaching practice and the induction of probationer teachers in Scottish schools HMSO 1978 011 491566 0 identified and evaluated experimental work and recent developments in schools and colleges of education designed to improve quality of student teaching practice and arrangements for the induction of probationer teachers.

1978 Learning Difficulties
The Education of Pupils with Learning Difficulties in Primary and Secondary Schools in Scotland HMSO 1978 011 491535 0 was a progress report by H.M. Inspectors which recommended the education of pupils with learning difficulties as part of the normal school provision. It does not refer to those pupils who clearly require special educational treatment. It recommends a different role for remedial specialists as consultants to the class teachers instead of only being teachers who deal with pupils withdrawn from classes for treatment.

1980 Glasgow Report
Scottish School Councils: Policy-making, Participation or Irrelevance? Called for one school council for every school which could virtually be self-financing since they could be clerked by the school or even members of the council. The report wanted the money that would thus be released to be spent on a regional service and information unit and, more especially, a national information and training centre.

1993 Dearing Report
Brief: to examine the scope for slimming down the curriculum. To see how the central administration of the National Curriculum and testing arrangements could be improved; how the testing arrangements might be simplified; and to consider the future of the ten-level scale for recognising children's attainment.
Report: The National Curriculum and its assessment, final report The School Curriculum and Assessment Authority. Chairman Sir Ron Dearing SCAA 1993 1 85838 030 8.
Recommendations: Give more support to teachers by reducing the amount of statutory teaching material. Slim down N.C. at key stages 1,2,3. Time saved will give 20% of teaching time for discretionary use by schools. This discretionary time must have as priority the basics of literacy, oracy and numeracy. Time to be found for sex education as required by law. Primary concern to divide the content of present curriculum orders between statutory core and optional material for each of the ten subjects Key Stages 1–3. The orders to be revised at the same time without change for five years after this review. Mandatory requirement at Key Stage 4 to be limited to English, maths, single science and PE together with short courses in a modern foreign language and technology. R.E. and sex education must be taught by law. The SCAA to encourage stronger links between GNVQS and GCSE. Increased trust placed in schools and teachers to be complemented with proper accountability to parents by information on progress and achievement. National Curriculum to be available to pupils with special educational needs. Work on the revision of the NC should involve teachers of pupils with special educational needs, with liaison with parents over the development of the appropriate curriculum. Ten level scale is acknowledged to be complex and too prescriptive but should be retained, but improved by reducing substantially the number of statements and attainment targets, and by the addition of more steps between the levels. Until revision of the Orders is completed, no statutory teacher assessment beyond the core subjects in primary schools. Future moderated teacher assessment should not create extra work for teachers, or more bureaucracy, whilst underpinning standards.

Guide to Legislation

England and Wales

Education Acts
The Education Acts from 1944 onwards embody the essential law of education. The Education Act 1944 remains the principal act; the acts immediately following were, on the whole, designed to clear up obscurities and extend definitions in the principal act while later legislation introduced major changes in policy. The important provisions of the acts are briefly summarised, by subject, below:

Government of Schools The Education Act 1980 provides for the reconstitution of governing bodies of maintained schools to include governors elected by and from parents and teachers and for a substantial reduction in the practice of grouping of a number of schools under one governing body.

Establishment, maintenance and discontinuance of schools Section 13 of the principal Act, together with numerous amendments, dealt with the procedures for proposals for establishing, maintaining and closing schools and altering the character and size of schools. This section was repealed by the Education Act 1980 and replaced by sections 12–16 of that Act which also state the procedures to be followed by local authorities and governors of voluntary schools when they propose to reduce the number of children to be admitted to a school. Section 14 of the Education Act 1981 brings the procedures to be followed for the discontinuance of a maintained special school into line with those for other schools.

Admission of pupils The Education Act 1980 introduces for the first time central direction of the procedures to be adopted by local education authorities and governors as to the admission of pupils to individual schools. It requires the issuing of information to parents to enable them to express their choice of school; in order to deal with objections made by parents when the places offered for their children are not in a school of their first choice, local authorities and governors must set up appeal committees to consider these objections.

Enlargement of controlled schools Section 1 of the Education Act 1946 (reprinted with amendments in Schedule 3 to the Education Act 1968) deals with the circumstances in which the Secretary of State may direct that an authority shall pay the expenses of enlargement.

Maintenance of voluntary schools The Education Act 1946 contains provisions relating to the duties of local education authorities and of the governors of voluntary schools with respect to the maintenance of such schools.

Assisted places Section 17 of the 1980 Act requires the Secretary of State to establish and operate a scheme for the purpose of enabling pupils who might otherwise not be able to do so to benefit from education at independent schools; participating schools remit fees in respect of pupils selected for assisted places under the scheme and the Secretary of State reimburses the schools for the fees that are remitted. In determining whether to make a participation agreement with any school the Secretary of State is to have regard to the desirability of securing an equitable distribution of assisted places both geographically and between boys and girls. The Secretary of State is to prescribe various details of the scheme by Regulations, and before making such Regulations he is to consult bodies representative of participating schools. Section 18 of the 1980 Education Act authorises the Secretary of State to make regulations providing for grants or the remission of charges for the incidental expenses of assisted pupils.

Nursery education Section 24 of the 1980 Act states that LEAs have a power to establish and maintain nursery schools. This section replaced Section 8(2)(b) of the Education Act 1944.
Section 26 enables local education authorities to make available to a local authority maintained day nursery the services of any teacher employed in one of their nursery schools or nursery classes, provided that the teacher agrees to such an arrangement.

Provision of clothing The Education (Miscellaneous Provisions) Act 1948 as amended by Section 29 of the Education Act 1980, contains the whole of the law relating to the provision of clothing other than distinctive clothing.

Recoupment of the cost of providing education for persons belonging to the providing authority The Education (Miscellaneous Provisions) Act 1948 provided for the replacement by a local education authority of the cost of providing primary and secondary education for children belonging to the area of another authority (or not belonging to any area); the Education (Miscellaneous Provisions) Act 1953 provided similarly for the recoupment of the cost of further education. The Education Act 1980 repeated these provisions, and Section 31 of that Act greatly limits the right of local authorities to refuse to pay these costs.

Contributions and grants for aided and special agreement schools Contributions and grants payable by the Secretary of State towards expenses incurred by governors in the establishment of aided schools and in the maintenance of aided and special agreement schools (see Sections 102 and 103 of the Education Act 1944), were raised to 80 per cent of the total by the Education Act 1967 (Section 1(2)) and to 85 per cent by the Education Act 1975.

School leaving dates The Education Act 1962 reduced from three to two the number of dates on which a pupil could leave school and defined the dates, in relation to a pupil's sixteenth birthday, on which a child ceases to be of compulsory school age. The Education (School Leaving Dates) Act 1976 further defined the date in the Summer term on which a child ceases to be of compulsory school age.

Middle schools The Education Act 1964 permits the establishment of new schools with 'special age limits'—schools now known as middle schools; the Education Act 1968 extends this provision to enable local education authorities to convert an existing school into a middle school. The Education Act 1967 extends to middle schools the power of the Secretary of State to direct a local education authority to defray the expenses of establishing a new controlled school.

Remuneration of Teachers Act 1965. The act deals with the setting up of committees for the purpose of considering the remuneration of teachers and makes provision for arbitration when the committees are unable to agree on their recommendations.

Superannuation of Teachers. The Superannuation Act 1972 covers the superannuation of teachers, and the Teachers Superannuation Regulations 1976 (as amended) made under this Act consolidated the provisions relating to the superannuation of teachers.

Government of colleges of education and other colleges of further education The Education (No.2) Act 1968 requires that, in the case of institutions maintained by local education authorities, every college for the training of teachers and every other institution providing full-time further education pursuant to an approved further education scheme, there shall exist an instrument of government providing for the constitution of a body of governors and articles of government which shall define the respective functions to be exercised by the local education authority, the governors, the principal and the academic board.

Grants to students The Education Act 1962 requires local education authorities to bestow awards on persons with the requisite educational qualifications pursuing first degree university of comparable courses (mandatory awards); it also enables local education authorities to bestow awards on students over compulsory school age attending full-time or part-time courses of further education (discretionary awards). The Education Act 1973 excluded post-graduate courses from this latter provision. The Education Act 1962 also makes provision for the Secretary of State to bestow awards in respect of post-graduate courses and on students above a prescribed age; the Education Act 1975 extends this provision to certain students attending courses at adult education colleges. Under this act local education authorities are required to make mandatory awards to students pursuing full-time courses for the diploma of higher education or a higher national diploma or a higher diploma of BTEC and to students undertaking courses for the initial training of teachers, The Education Act 1973 provides, in special cases, for the supplementation by the Secretary of State of mandatory awards made by local education authorities. The Education Act 1980 empowers the Secretary of State to award industrial scholarships for students pursuing courses in higher education which appear to him relevant to a career in industry. Sections 1 to 4 of the 1962 Act and Schedule 1 thereto are set out (as amended) in Schedule 5 to the 1980 Act.

Handicapped children The Education (Handicapped Children) Act 1970 repealed the provisions of the principal act whereby severely handicapped children could be ascertained as unsuitable for education at school. All children, however seriously handicapped, are now the responsibility of the local education authority for the purposes of education.

The Education Act 1981 completely recast the law relating to special education. It revised the duties of local education authorities in respect of children with special educational needs, and set out more specifically the responsibilities of ordinary schools towards such children. A new system of approval was introduced for independent schools wishing to take pupils with statements of special educational needs placed by local education authorities.

Provision of milk and meals The statutory obligation placed on local education authorities by the principal Act and various amending acts has been removed by the Education Act 1980. Local authorities now have considerable discretion in the provision of milk, in the nature of the mid-day meal and in the payment required. The Act, however, partially limits this discretion by requiring authorities to supply milk and meals free to children whose families are in receipt of supplementary benefits or family income supplement. It also makes it a duty for schools to provide facilities for children to consume meals brought by them to school.

Work experience The Education (Work Experience) Act 1973 enables local education authorities to provide work experience for pupils in their last year of compulsory attendance at school.

Educational trusts The Education Act 1973 provides for the termination and partial replacement of powers possessed by the Secretary of State under the Charities Act 1960 concurrently with the Charity Commissioners or under the Endowed Schools Acts; it also enlarges other powers of the Secretary of State in relation to the modification of educational trusts.

Governing Bodies The Education (No 2) Act 1986, which will be implemented over the next three years, places extra responsibilities on school governing bodies, which must now have an instrument of government, and articles of government, made by order of the local education authority. The Act specifies the composition of the governing body, and the election or co-option of members. Other matters covered by the Act include freedom of speech in universities and polytechnic, sex education, the abolition of corporal punishment and teacher appraisal. Circular 8/86, December 1986 gives commencement dates for the various sections of the Act.

Teacher's Pay and Conditions Act 1987 Ch 1 repeals the Remuneration of Teachers Act 1965 Ch 3 in full and authorises the minister to set up an interim advisory committee on schoolteachers' pay and conditions until 31st March 1990. Provision by order after consulting the Local Education Authority concerned to impose salaries and conditions of service.

Education Reform Act 1988 Ch 40 This legislation is divided into four main areas. For schools there is to be a national curriculum with three corporate bodies–a National Curriculum Council, a Curriculum Council for Wales and a School Examinations and Assessment Council. Special reference is made to religious education with a requirement for all pupils at maintained schools to attend an act of collective worship. Every LEA to constitute a standing advisory council on religious education. LEAs now required to provide the Secretary of State with a scheme for financing county and voluntary schools with provision for the delegation of the management of a school's budget share to the governing body of the school. The Act provides for certain schools to apply for grant-maintained status and opt out of the LEA control. The size and composition of the governing body is detailed, together with the powers and financial arrangements. the procedure for the acquisition of grant-maintained status to include a secret postal ballet of parents, after the publication of the proposals Initial governors to be elected. The second area is that of Higher and Further Education and the removal of the LEAs duty to provide facilities for higher education. The existing institutions (over 50) will become legal entities in their own right. The National Advisory Body for Public Sector Higher Education will be replaced by a Polytechnic and Colleges Funding Council and the University Grants Committee will be replaced by the Universities Funding Council. In further education colleges will still be maintained by LEAs but at least half of their governors must represent 'employment interests' and will be able to influence staff appointments and dismissals, delegated budgets and the provision of a service relevant to the area. The finance and government of further and higher education is detailed in the Act. The third area covered in the Act details the reorganisation of education in inner London consequent upon the abolition of the ILEA on 1.4.1990. The final part of the Act lists miscellaneous matters such as the establishment of the Education Assets Board and the University Commissioners, Grants, unrecognised degrees and the extension of the functions of the Audit Commission are also discussed. For the benefit of your contributor on this section I note

School Teachers' Pay and Conditions Act 1991 Ch 49

"An Act to make provision with respect to the renumeration and other conditions of employment of school teachers; and for connected purposes"

This Act repeals the Teachers' Pay and Conditions Act 1987.

The Act establishes a review body appointed by the Prime Minister to examine and report on the pay and conditions of teachers in England and Wales and such matters as may be referred to the review body of the Secretary of State.

Reports by the review body to be submitted to the Secretary of State and published.

After consultation with local education authorities associations, bodies representing voluntary schools governors, school teachers and governors of grant maintained schools as appropriate, the Secretary of State may make an Order relating to statutory conditions of employment.

Special provisions may apply to grant maintained schools where an application for exemption has been made to Secretary of State and been granted.

Guide to Legislation

The Act contains interpretation, orders and application of provisions of the 1944 Education Act.

Further and Higher Education Act 1992 Ch 13

"An Act to make new provision about further and higher education"

Part One deals with further education and Chapter One outlines the responsibility for this sector. It establishes two Further Education Funding Councils, one for England and one for Wales. The new further education sector is defined as having responsibility for providing further education for full time students aged 16–18 years, part time education for all over 16 and full time education for those over 18. Special arrangments for those aged 16–25 with learning difficulties may be made.

Details are given of the administration of funds by F.E.F.C.s to governing bodies within the further education sector. Finance also available to students for training or carrying out research by means of grant or loan. Reference is made to consultation with governors of a particular institution, and bodies interested in the further education sector, by a F.E.F.C. Each council will provide information to the Secretary of State and will set up a Quality Assessment Committee to advise individual institutions. The committee to consist of a majority of persons with experience in F.E. matters. The majority not to be members of the council. The Act provides for the adjustment of the L.E.A. sector and states their functions in respect of further education, which is defined, and the provision of F.E. in maintained and grant maintained schools.

Chapter Two sets out details for the incorporation of existing educational institutions within the F.E. sector by order including the establishment of a corporate body for new institutions. All corporate bodies to be known as a Further Education Corporation. The powers of the F.E.Cs are given, details of articles of government and arrangements for the transfer of property and staff from L.E.As. Institutions designated as eligible for financial support given as a voluntary aided school, an L.E.A institution other than a school, or a grant aided institution. Special arrangements for voluntary aided sixth form colleges governors and their qualifications.

Chapter Three states the duty to give information to F.E.F.C. as appropriate to their functions by a L.E.A., the governing body of any institution maintained by a L.E.A., G.M. School, City Technology College or City College for the Technology of the Arts. Inspection of L.E.A. institutions (other than schools) the responsibility of the Chief Inspector who will advise the S of S; procedures for the intervention of the S of S in the event of mismanagement are set out.

Part Two establishes two Higher Education Funding Councils, one for England and one for Wales and details the dissolution of the Universities Funding Council and the Polytechnics and Colleges Funding Council with the transfer of property and to the H.E.F.C. for England. Staff of existing Councils (UFC and P.C.F.C.) will not have their contracts terminated but transferred to the new employer i.c.a H.E.F.C. including the Scottish H.E.F.C. The Act states the responsibility for administration of funds and grants and loans by H.E.F.C, and payments to those employed in the provision of higher and further education. Grants to F.E.F.C. by the S of S subject to certain requirements. Establishment of a Quality Assessment Committee as for F.E.F.C.s required.

Other matters in Part Two relate to the constitution and conduct of H.E.C. government and conduct of institutions and transfer from F.E. institutions to H.E. institutions. Also the power to award degrees, to change the name of an educational institution within the H.E. Sector and use the title "University" with the approval of the Privy Council. The Secretary of State may by order provide for the dissolution of the Council for National Academic Awards.

Sections of the Education Act 1944 Education (No 2) Act 1986 the Education Act 1988 are repealed and amendments made to other legislation including Sex Discrimination Act 1975, Race Relations Act 1976 and the Employment Act 1989 among others.

Education Act 1993 Ch 35

"An Act to amend the law about education"

A major piece of legislation, concerned principally with matters relating to funding, to grant maintained schools and standards of education.

Part One chapter one sets out the general duty of the Secretary of State in promoting education in the case of primary, secondary and further education in England and Wales. There is established a Funding Agency for Schools for England and a Schools Funding Council for Wales.

The Act defines "funding authority"; the duties and responsibilities, grants and supervision of the funding authority are specified. Their requirement to provide information is specified. A standing advisory council on religious education to be set up by the L.E.A.

Chapter Two relates to education at school and the responsibility for providing sufficient school places; power to direct admission of a child to school and miscellaneous functions relating to grant-maintained schools.

Part Two deals in great detail with grant maintained schools as set up by the Education Reform Act 1988 ch 40. Chapter Two deals with eligibility and the duty of governors to consider a ballot on G.M. status. The initiation of procedures by parent or governors, the ballot of parents and the approval or rejection of proposals are set out in detail. A G.M. school must be either a secondary school or a primary school.

Chapter Three is concerned with the transfer of staff and property and the control of contracts.

Chapter Four outlines the procedure for establishing new G.M. schools. Chapter Five specifies the government of G.M. schools namely the governing instruments, the categories of governors, their powers, and the selection of the initial first governors. Chapter Six sets out funding arrangements. The alteration or discontinuance of G.M. schools are dealt with in Chapters Seven and Eight, with the arrangements for grouping two or more G.M. schools under a single governing body are given in Chapter Nine. The final chapter tidies up the legal position of G.M. schools in relation to further education, benefits and services provided by the L.E.A. and matters concerned with religious education.

Part Three is concerned with children with special educational needs. "Special educational needs" and "special educational provision" are defined, and the Secretary of State to issue a Code of Practice to L.E.A.s, G.M. schools or G.M. special schools detailing their duties. The arrangements for special educational provision are given, the identification and assessment of children with special needs, the duties of L.E.A., District Health Authority or N.H.S. Trust are stated, the constitution of tribunals and procedures are covered by further sections and arrangements for special schools and independent schools are given.

Part Four deals with school attendance matters, namely school attendance orders, the offence of failing to comply with the order, failure to secure regular attendance at school, and the application of L.E.A. for an education supervision order.

Part Five details arrangments for the identification of schools failing to give an acceptable standard of education and requiring special measures, details special measures to be taken and their monitoring and further inspections. Such measures may include appointment of additional governors, suspension of the right to a delegated budget, or the establishment of educational associations. Such an association to consist of not less than five persons appointed by the Secretary of State, one of whom to be appointed Chairman. One member at least to have had experience in primary or secondary education. Then follows details of the function, supervision and transfer of responsibility for conducting the school to the educational association and its winding up. This section also details the power of the Secretary of State to discontinue schools conducted by educational associations.

Part Six, the final part of the Act contains details of miscellaneous provisions including nursery education in G.M. schools, the National Curriculum, sex education, religious education, and the replacement of the N.C.C.

and S.E.A.C. by the School Curriculum and Assessment Authority.

The Curriculum Council for Wales to be known as the Curriculum and Assessment Authority for Wales.

The Act concludes with details of various financial matters including financing schools maintained by L.E.A., grants for education support and training, assistance for voluntary schools and musical instrument tuition. Details are given for the new compulsory school age. Finally the requirement to establish committees is abolished whilst the Secretary of State has power to direct appointment of members of the committees.

The Act repeals almost the whole of the Education Act 1981, the whole of the Education Act of 1959, and 1975, the whole of the Education (school leaving dates) Act 1976, Sections of the Education Acts of 1944, 1946, 1962, 1967, 1968, 1973, 1980 and the Education Reform Act 1988 are also repealed.

Education (Schools) Act 1992 Ch 38

"An Act to make provision with respect to the inspection of schools and with respect to information about schools and their pupils"

Establishes Her Majesty's Inspectorate of Schools in England to comprise a Chief Inspector of Schools in England, appointed for a period not exceeding five years, and a staff of inspectors. The functions and duties are given, including the power to arrange for inspections.

A similar Inspectorate of Schools in Wales to be established.

The legislation lists the schools to be inspected, at intervals as required, by registered inspectors, in England and Wales namely County Schools, Voluntary Schools, Special Schools, Grant Maintained Schools, Independent Schools, City Technology Colleges, City Colleges for the Technology of the Arts and Maintained Nursery Schools.

All inspectors to be registered with the Chief Inspector for England or the Chief Inspector for Wales. The Act details the method of registration, conditions of appointment and removal from the register and details of appeals regarding registration.

Provision is made for local education authorities to provide a school inspection service for schools in their areas.

The Secretary of State is empowered to require the proprietor of each independent school and the governing body of every school which is maintained by a local education authority, a grant maintained school or a special school not maintained by a local education authority to provide information about the school as prescribed.

The Act details the nature of the information about schools and pupils which may be required, but no pupil may be named. Special arrangements to be made for Scotland. Special arrangements also for denominational education in voluntary and grant maintained schools.

Other Statutes

There are a number of other statutes which contain sections relevant to education. The main ones are listed below.

London Government Act 1963 established the present system of the Inner London Education Authority (ILEA) and the outer London boroughs as education authorities in Greater London.

Local Government Act 1966 transferred from central government to local authorities the cost of school meals and milk; it also provided for a specific grant to local authorities in respect of additional staff employed in connection with the education and welfare of immigrants.

Children and Young Persons Act 1969 places obligations upon local education authorities with regard to the children not receiving efficient full-time education and who appear to be in need of care and control.

Chronically Sick and Disabled Persons Act 1970 makes provision for the design of university and school buildings to include access, parking facilities and sanitary conveniences appropriate for the needs of the disabled.

Immigration Act 1971 and the rules made under it prescribe the conditions for the admission to this country of non-patrial students and teachers for study and work respectively.

Children Act 1972 provides for the minimum age at which children may be employed out of school hours to remain at thirteen.

Local Government Act 1972 established the new education authorities in England and Wales (excluding Greater London) under local government reorganisation. It also specified the local authorities to which teachers employed by a local authority may be elected and it continued the provisions whereby local authorities must establish education committees and appoint a chief education officer; the provision in the Education Act 1944 whereby the Secretary of State must be consulted about the appointment of a chief education officer was repealed by the Act.

National Health Service Reorganisation Act 1973 transferred from local education authorities to the area health authority responsibility for the school health service.

Employment and Training Act 1973 requires local education authorities to provide a careers service for school leavers and for students at educational institutions (other than universities).

Health and Safety at Work etc. Act 1974 defines the measures that must be taken for the health and safety of both teachers and pupils.

Local Government Act 1974 makes provision for the grant to be paid to local authorities in respect of mandatory awards. It also defines the actions of local education authorities which are not subject to investigation by the Commission for Local Adminstration.

Employment Protection (Consolidation) Act 1978 Section 80 defines when, for the purposes of the Act, a teacher in an aided school must be regarded as an employee of the local authority. The provisions of the Act relating to employment protection and redundancy payment apply to teachers as they do to other employees.

Sex Discrimination Act 1975 prohibits discrimination between the sexes in the admission of pupils and students to educational establishments (with provision for exceptions in the case of single sex institutions), in courses within these establishment and in the appointment of staff.

Race Relations Act 1976 requires local education authorities and other bodies responsible for educational establishments to ensure that facilities for education are provided without discrimination on the grounds of race.

Education (Grants and Awards) Act 1984 empowers the Secretary of State to make specific grants to local education authorities, of up to 70% for duly approved projects.

Further Education Act 1985 repeals Section 28(b) of the Education (student loans) Act 1990 Ch 6 Self-governing schools etc (Scotland) Act 1989 Ch 39 Sex Discrimination Act, relating to physical training courses; give polytechnic and local authority colleges the same rights as universities to sell goods and services arising from their educational activities.

Education Act 1994

"An Act to make provision about teacher training and related matters; to make provision with respect to the conduct of students' unions; and for connected purposes."

Sets up Teacher Training Agency and Training as a Career Unit.

Funding of teacher training.

Defines Students' Unions and their management.

Wales

The Education Acts 1944–1981 apply to Wales as they do to England, but, outside universities, ministerial responsibility for Education in Wales rests with the Secretary of State for Wales, apart from certain matters having a national dimension, principally teacher qualifications, salaries, pensions and conduct.

Guide to Legislation

The Education Act 1980 empowers the Secretary of State to make grants to local education authorities and other persons in respect of expenditure incurred in connection with the teaching of the Welsh language or the teaching of other subjects through the medium of Welsh.

Scotland

Education Acts

The Secretary of State for Scotland is responsible to Parliament for education in Scotland and education authorities are responsible for the administration of public education, with limited statutory controls centrally administered by the Scottish Education Department who in turn are answerable to the Secretary of State for Scotland. While Scotland has, in the main, its own legislation some of the Acts which extend to Scotland cover, in general terms, the same provisions as in the equivalent Acts for England and Wales.

The main Scottish legislation is the *Education (Scotland) Act, 1980* which was amended by the *Education (Scotland) Act, 1981* in certain respects. The 1980 Act consolidated, in one Act, a number of Acts passed between 1962 and 1979, and as amended, by the 1981 Act. It covers general requirements in relation to pupils, public schools of all categories, placing in such schools, grant-aided schools and independent schools and makes provision for the Secretary of State for Scotland prescribing regulations to which authorities must conform in carrying out certain functions. Such regulations include (a) the Schools General (Scotland) Regulations 1975, regarding the general conduct of schools; (b) the Education Authority Bursaries (Scotland) Regulations 1969, as amended, relating to school and further education bursaries (students in attendance at central institutions receive awards from the Scottish Education Department). Other provisions in the 1980 Act include:

(i) duties and powers of education authorities to provide facilities for social, cultural and recreative activities for the community;
(ii) matters relating to the rights and duties of parents;
(iii) educational endowments;
(iv) the establishment, maintenance and staffing of denominational schools;
(v) the Scottish Examination Board which conducts examinations for the award of certificates relating to secondary education;
(vi) Committees which formulate settlements regarding teachers' salaries, with provision for arbitration; and
(vii) provisions with regard to children having special educational needs.

Other relevant enactments not repealed by the 1980 Act are:

The Teaching Council (Scotland) Act 1965 which established the General Teaching Council for Scotland and provides for the registration of teachers, for regulating their professional training and for cancelling registration in cases of misconduct.

The Teaching Council (Scotland) Act, 1971, which enables the Secretary of State for Scotland to make regulations for the deduction from the salaries of teachers of fees due to the General Teaching Council for Scotland in respect of renewal of registration with the Council.

The Education (Mentally Handicapped Children) (Scotland) Act, 1974, which brought profoundly mentally handicapped children within the responsibility of the education service from which they had previously been excluded and contained provisions protecting the interests of health and social work staff concerned with such children.

Educational (Amendment) (Scotland) Act 1984 gives the Secretary of State power to require this approval before specified apparatus or materials may be used in educational establishments, where they are or might be a serious risk to health.

Department for Education Publications

The Building Bulletins and Statutory instruments are obtainable from HMSO, PO Box 276, *London SW8 5DT.*
DFE *Publications Centre, PO Box 2193, London E15 2EU.*
The Laboratories Investigation Unit Papers are available free of charge from Laboratories Investigation Unit, Department for Education, Elizabeth Hse, York Rd, London SE1 7PH.

Building Bulletins

7 Fire and the design of schools (6th edition 1988) (ISBN 0-11-270350-X), £3.95
28 Playing fields and hard surface areas (second edition 1982) (ISBN 0-11-270310-0), £4.95
38 School furniture dimensions: standing and reaching (second edition 1974) (ISBN 0-11270347-X), 65p
55 Energy conservation in educational buildings (second edition 1981) (ISBN 0-11-270454-9), £2.50
56 Nursery education in converted space (1978) (ISBN 0-11-270460-3), £2.50
57 The renewal of primary schools: planning for the 80's (1980) (ISBN 0-11-270523-5). £3.50
58 Storage of pupils personal belongings (1980) (ISBN 0-11-270494-8), £3.50
59 The Victoria Centre, Crewe: school and community provision in urban renewal (1981) (ISBN 0-11-270525-1), £4.30
60 Designing a medium-sized public library (1981) (ISBN 0-11-270524-3), £6.75
61 Designing for children with special educational needs: ordinary schools (1984) (ISBN 0-11-270313-5), £3.95
62 Body dimensions of the school population (1985) (ISBN 0-11-270567-7)
63 Craft design and technology accommodation in secondary schools (1985) (ISBN 0-11-270562-6)
64 Adaptable facilities in further education of business and office studies (1986) (ISBN 0-11-270588-X), £3.95
65 Adaptable teaching kitchens in further education (1986) (ISBN 0-11-270589-8), £5.50
66 Adaptable facilities in further education for accommodation studies (1988) (ISBN 0-11-270647-9), £4.95
67 Crime prevention in schools: practical guidance (1987) (ISBN 0-11-270637-1), £4.95
68 Weald College Harrow development project (1989) (ISBN 0-11-270661-4), £7.50
69 Crime prevention in schools: specification, installation and maintenance of intruder alarm systems (1989) (ISBN 0-11-270677-0), £7.50
70 Maintenance of mechanical services: maintenance and renewal of educational buildings (1990) (ISBN 0-11-270717-3), £10.95
71 Outdoor classroom: educational use, landscape design and management of school grounds (1990) (ISBN 0-11-270730-0), £12.95
72 Educational design initiatives in City Technology colleges (1991) (ISBN 0-11-270737-8), £20
73 Guide to energy efficient refurbishment: maintenance and renewal in educational buildings (1991) (ISBN 0-11-270772 6), £8.50
74 School for Armenia (1991) (ISBN 0-11-270773 4), £14.95
75 Closed circuit TV surveillance in educational buildings (1991) (ISN 0-11-2270778 5), £5
76 Maintenance of electrical services: maintenance and renewal in educational buildings (1992) (ISBN 0-11-270799 8) £13.50
77 Designing for pupils with special educational needs: special schools (1992) (ISBN 0-11-270796-3) £14.95
78 Security lighting: crime prevention in schools (1993) (ISBN 0-11 270822-6) £4.25
79 Passive solar schools: a design guide (1994) (ISBN 0-11 270876-5) £19.95

Design Notes

1 Building for nursery eduction (1968) (ISSN 0141-2825)
2 Henry Fanshawe School, Dronfield, Derbyshire (1969)
3 Demonstration rig: component fixing conventions (1969)
6 Sedgefield School, Durham (1970)
7 U.S.A. visit (1970)
8 Polytechnic: planning for development (1972)
10 Designing for the severely handicapped (1972)
11 Chaucer infant and nursery school, Ilkeston (1973)
12 Space Utilization in universities and polytechnics (1974)
14 School and community (2) (1976)
16 Energy conservation in two Oxfordshire schools (1978)
17 Guidelines on environment design and fuel conservation in educational buildings (revised edition) (1981)
18 Access for disabled people to educational buildings
19 Guillemont Junior School: building manual, second edition, 1984 (1979)
20 Polytechnic: planning for change (1979)
21 Sedgefield Secondary School Durham phase 2 (1980)
22 Accommodation for the 16–19 age group, NAFE: designing for change (1980)
23 Accommodation for the 16–19 age group. Four colleges in 1980
24 Compliance with constructional standards (1981)
25 Lighting and acoustic criteria for the visually handicapped and hearing impaired in schools (1981)
26 Opportunities for improvement: Penistone Grammar School (1981)
27 Falling school rolls and premises—related costs (1981)
28 Opportunities for improvement: North-east Wiltshire (1982)
29 Fume cupboards in schools (1982)
30 Educational furniture for the 16–19 age group: specification and design (1982)
31 Educational planning in North America (1982)
32 Designing 8–12 middle schools (1983)
33 Area guidelines for sixth form, tertiary and NAFE colleges (1983)
34 Area guidelines for secondary schools (1983)
35 Accommodation for the new training courses (1983)

Department for Education Publications

36 Secondary school playing fields: North-east Wiltshire (1983)
37 Assessing the capacity of further education building (1984)
38 Meeting the educational needs of children in hospital (1984)
39 Educational furniture for the 16–19 age groups: space standards (1984)
40 Maintenance and renewal in educational buildings: needs and priorities (1985)
41 Accommodation for changes in public sector higher education (1985)
42 The Dukeries complex: a place for the family (1985)
43 CDT accommodation in a secondary school: John Kyrie School, Ross-on-Wye (1985)
44 Area guidelines for advanced further education institutions (1986)
45 Assessing the capacity of public sector higher education buildings (1985)
46 Maintenance and renewal in educational buildings: flat roofs: criteria and methods of assessment, repair and replacement (1985)
47 St. John's School, Sefton: the design of a new Primary school (1989)
48 Graffiti removal and control (1989)
49 Further education and sixth form colleges: development strategies for accommodation (1992)

Laboratories Investigation Unit Papers

1 An approach to laboratory building (1969)
2 Deep or shallow building: a comparison of costs in use (1970)
3 Growth and change in laboratory activity: a paper based on a study of the University of Surrey in Battersea (1971)
4 The economics of adaptability: a comparative study of the initial and life costs of partitions (1971)
5 Conversions of buildings for science and technology (1971)
6 Adaptable furniture and services for education and science (1972)
7 Adaptable laboratories: design and installation (1974)
8 The conversion of buildings for science and technology (1977)
9 Charles Darwin Building, Bristol Polytechnic (1977) (ISBN 0-11-270353-4)
10 Research laboratories: design for flexibility (1977)
11 Better use by sharing (1980)
12 Short life renewal (1982)

Architects and Building Group Papers

1 Abraham Moss Centre, Manchester (1978)
2 Clayton Green District Centre (1978)
3 Delf Hill Middle School: an appraisal (1978)
4 Stockton Sixth Form College space utilisation survey (1979)
5 Briefing process in school design (1979)
6 Accommodation for the 16–19 age group, Hounslow Borough College, space utilization survey (1980)
7 Maintenance and renewal in educational buildings: a paper for discussion (1984)
8 The Victoria Centre, Crewe: an update (1985)
9 Property information systems and the educational building stock: towards a common framework (1986)
10 Property information systems and the educational building stock
11 Guidelines for school building reviews: property management in educational buildings
12 Swindon revisited: an appraisal of a major reorganisation of secondary schools in north-east Wiltshire: property management in educational buildings
13 Northampton property review: property management in educational buildings
14 Primary rationalisation and improvement: the review of a group of schools in South Maidstone, Kent.
15 Lockers and secure storage: and investigation into the provision of secure storage in schools (1991)
16 Bases for primary teacher education in institutions of higher education (1991)
17 Sprinklers in schools: questions and answers (1993)
18 Saving water: managing school facilities Guide 1 (1993)

Statutory Instruments

1990/59 Education (ILEA) (Staff transfer) Order 1990 (ISBN 0-11-003059-1), £2.65
1990/86 Self-governing schools etc. (Scotland) Act 1989 (Commencement) Order 1990 (ISBN 0-11-003086-9), £0.50
1990/124 Education (ILEA) (Property transfer) Order 1990 (ISBN 0-11-003124-5), £3.40
1990/81 Education (School and placing information) (Scotland) Amendment Regulations 1990 (ISBN 0-11-003181-4), £0.50
1990/183 College Councils (Scotland) Regulations 1990 (ISBN 0-11-003183-0), £0.90
1990/221 Education (Training grants) (Amendment) Regulations 1990 (ISBN 0-11-003221-7), £0.90
1990/227 Education (Grants for the training of teachers and community education workers) (Scotland) Regulations 1990 (ISBN 0-11-003277-2), £0.50
1990/725 Schools (Safety and supervision of pupils) (Scotland) Regulations 1990 (ISBN 0-11-003295-0), £0.50
1990/306 Education (Grants) (Travellers and displaced persons) Regulations 1990 (ISBN 0-11-003306-X), £0.90
1990/313 Education (ILEA) (Property transfer) (Amendment) Order 1990 (ISBN 0-11-003313-2), £0.50
1990/353 Education (School financial Statements) (Prescribed particulars etc.) Regulations 1990 (ISBN 0-11-003353-1), £1.35
1990/361 Education (Areas to which pupils and students belong) (Amendment) Regulations (ISBN 0-11-003361-2), £0.50
1990/362 Education (ILEA) (Horniman and Geffrye museums) (Transfer of functions) Order 1990 (ISBN 0-11-003362-0), £0.50
1990/383 Teachers' superannuation (Scotland) Amendment Regulations 1990 (ISBN 0-11-003383-3), £0.90
1990/391 Education Reform Act 1988 (Commencement No. 8 and amendments) Order 1990 (ISBN 0-11-003391-4), £0.90
1990/423 Education (National Curriculum) (Attainment targets and programmes of study in English) (No. 2) Order 1990 (ISBN 0-11-003423-6), £0.90
1990/424 Education (National Curriculum) (Attainment target and programmes of study in technology) Order 1990 (ISBN 0-11-003424-4), £0.90
1990/480 Education (ILEA) (Schools designation) (No. 2) Order 1990 (ISBN 0-11-003480-5), £0.50
1990/481 Education (Gloucestershire College of Arts and Technology) (Higher Education Corporations) (Dissolution) Order 1990 (ISBN 0-11-003481-3), £0.50
1990/482 Education (Harrow College of Higher Education Corporation) (Dissolution) Order 1990 (ISBN 0-11-003482-1), £0.50
1990/513 Education (ILEA) (Staff transfer) (No. 2) Order 1990 (ISBN 0-11-003513-5) (ISBN 0-11-003513-5), £1.95
1990/532 Education (Governing bodies of institutions of higher and further education) (Regulations 1990 (ISBN 0-11-003532-1), £0.90
1990/549 Education (Grant maintained schools) (Finance) Regulations 1990 (ISBN 0-11-003549-6), £2.65
1990/740 Education (London Institute) (Designated staff) Order 1990 (ISBN 0-11-003740-5), £0.50
1990/772 Education (ILEA) (Property transfer) (No. 2) Order 1990 (ISBN 0-11-003772-3), £3.10

1990/773 Education (ILEA) (Transitional and supplementary provisions) Order 1990 (ISBN 0-11-003773-1), £0.55
1990/774 Education (ILEA) (Transitional and supplementary provisions) (No. 2) Order 1990 (ISBN 0-11-003774-X), £0.55
1990/775 Education (ILEA) (Repayments of loans) Order 1990 (ISBN 0-11-003775-8), £0.95
1990/796 Education (Designated institutions) (Amendment) Order 1990 (ISBN 0-11-003976-0), £0.55
1990/800 Self governing schools (Ballots and publication of proposals) (Scotland) Regulations 1990 (ISBN 0-11-003800-2), £0.95
1990/1082 Education (National Curriculum) (Attainment and targets and programmes of study in Welsh) Order 1990 (ISBN 0-11-004082-1), £1.40
1990/1085 Education (Recognised awards) (Amendment) Order 1990 (ISBN 0-11-004108-5), £0.55
1990/1109 Education (School curriculum and related information) (Amendment) Regulations 1990 (ISBN 0-11-004109-7), £1.70
1990/1208 Education (Welsh medium teacher training incentive supplement) Regulations 1990 (ISBN 0-11-004208-5), £0.95
1990/1278 Higher education (Wales) Regulations 1990 (ISBN 0-11-004278-6), £0.55
1990/1281 Education (School teachers' pay and conditions) Order 1990 (ISBN 0-11-004281-6), £0.95
1990/1346 Education (Assisted places) (Scotland) Amendment Regulations 1990 (ISBN 0-11-004346-4), £0.95
1990/1347 Education authority bursaries (Scotland) Amendment Regulations 1990 (ISBN 0-11-004347-2), £0.55
1990/1381 Education (Individual pupil's achievements) (Information) Regulations (ISBN 0-11-004381-2), £0.95
1990/1401 Education (Student loans) Regulations 1990 (ISBN 0-11-004401-0), £2.00
1990/1432 Education (Reorganisation in Inner London) (Redundancy payments) (Amendment) Order 1990 (ISBN 0-11-004432-0), £0.55
1990/1438 Education (Reorganisation in Inner London) (Compensation) (Amendment) Regulations 1990 (ISBN 0-11-004433-9), £0.55
1990/1506 Education (Student loans) (Northern Ireland) Order 1990 (ISBN 0-11-004506-8), £1.70
1990/1524 Education (Special additional needs) (Amendment) Regulations 1990 (ISBN 0-11-004524-6)
1990/1351 Education (National Curriculum) (Attainment targets and programmes of study in technology) (Amendment) Order 1990 (ISBN 0-11-004531-9), £0.55
1990/1534 Education (Access funds) (Scotland) Regulations 1990 (ISBN 0-11-004534-3), £0.55
1990/1543 Education (National Curriculum) (Assessment arrangements for English, mathematics and science) Order 1990 (ISBN 0-11-004543-2), £1.40
1990/1546 Education (Assisted places) (Amendment) Regulations 1990 (ISBN 0-11-004546-7), £0.95
1990/1547 Education (Assisted places) (Incidental expenses) (Amendment) Regulations 1990, £0.95
1990/1548 Education (Grants) (Music and ballet schools) (Amendment) Regulations 1990 (ISBN 0-11-004548-3), £0.95
1990/1551 School pupil records (Scotland) Regulations 1990 (ISBN 0-11-004551-3), £1.70
1990/1555 Education (Further and Higher education institutions access funds) Regulations 1990 (ISBN 0-11-004555-6), £0.55
1990/1560 Further education student records (Scotland) Regulations 1990 (ISBN 0-11-004660-2), £1.70
1990/1561 Education (Teachers) (Amendment) Regulations 1990 (ISBN 0-11-004561-0), £0.55
1990/1599 Education (Bursaries for teacher training (Amendment) Regulations 1990 (ISBN 0-11-004599-8), £0.55
1990/1628 Education (Mandatory awards) Regulations 1990 (ISBN 0-11-004628), £5.15
1990/1637 College councils (Scotland) (No. 2) Regulations 1990 (ISBN 0-11-004637-4), £2.30
1990/1639 Education (National Curriculum) (Assessment amendments in English, Welsh, mathematics and science) (Wales) Order 1990 (ISBN 0-11-004639-0), £1.70
1990/1653 Education (ILEA) (Transitional and supplementary provisions) (No. 3) Order 1990 (ISBN 0-11-004653-6), £0.55
1990 (Training grants) Regulations 1990 (ISBN 0-11-004857-1) (ISBN 0-11-004857-1), £1.40
1990/1989 Education (Grant) Regulations 1990 (ISBN 0-11-004989-6), £1.70
1990/2031 Education (Eligibility of primary schools for grant-maintained status) Order 1990 (ISBN 0-11-005031-2), £0.55
1990/2104 Testing in primary schools (Scotland) Regulations 1990 (ISBN 0-11-005104-1), £0.95
1990/2146 Education (Unrecognised degrees) (Guernsey) Order 1990 (ISBN 0-11-005145-7), £0.55
1990/2279 Education (Grant maintained schools) (Finance) (Amendment) Regulations 1990
1990/2259 Education (Schools and further education) (Amendment) Regulations 1990 (ISBN 0-11-005259-5), £0.55
1990/2351 Education (School premises) (Amendment) Regulations 1990 (ISBN 0-11-005351-6), £0.55
1990/2516 Teachers' pay and conditions Act 1987 (Continuation) Order 1990 (ISBN 0-11-005637-X), £0.55
1990/2518 Education support grants Regulations 1990 (ISBN 0-11-005634-5), £1.40
1990/2551 Special schools (Scotland) Grant Regulations 1990 (ISBN 0-11-005641-8), £0.95
1991/131 Education (Grants) (Travellers and displaced persons) (Amendment) Regulations 1991 (ISBN 0-11-013131-2), £0.60
1991/184 Education (London Residuary Body) (Capital money) Order 1991 (ISBN 0-11-01384-3), £1.45
1991/353 Education (Grant maintained schools) (Finance) Regulations 1991 (ISBN 0-11--13353-6), £2.95
1991/383 Education (Listed bodies) Order 1991 (ISBN 0-11-013383-8), £1.85
1991/384 Education (Recognised bodies) (Amendment) 1991 (ISBN 0-11-013384), £0.60
1991/409 Education Reform Act 1988 (Commencement No. 8) Order 1991 (ISBN 0-11-013409-5), £1.45
1991/410 Education (Variation of standard numbers for primary schools) Order 1991 (ISBN 0-11-013410-9), £1
1991/411 Education (Publication of proposals for reduction in standard number) Regulations 1991 (ISBN 0-11-013411-7), £0.60
1991/449 Education (Special education needs) (Approval of independent schools) Regulations 1991 (ISBN 0-11-013449-4), £1.85
1991/450 Education (Approval of special schools) (Amendment) Regulations 1991 (ISBN 0-11-013450-8), £1
1991/497 Education (London residuary body) (Property transfer) Order 1991 (ISBN 0-11-013497-4), £1.85
1991/550 Education (Thames Valley College of Higher Education higher education corporation) (Dissolution) Order 1991 (ISBN 0-11-013550-4), £0.60
1991/678 Education (National Curriculum) (Attainment targets and programmes of study in geography) (England) Order 1991 (ISBN 0-11-013678-0), £1
1991/681 Education (National Curriculum) (Attainment targets and programmes of study in history) (England) Order 1991 (ISBN 0-11-013681), £1
1991/751 Education (National Curriculum) (Attainment targets and programmes of study in geography) (Wales) Order 1991 (ISBN 0-11-013751-5), £1
1991/752 Education (National Curriculum) (Attainment targets and programmes of study in history) (Wales) Order 1991 (ISBN 0-11-013752-3), £1
1991/829 Education (Student loans) (Amendment) Regulations 1991 (ISBN 0-11-013829-5), £0.60
1991/830 Education (Fees and awards) (Amendment) Regulations 1991 (ISBN 0-11-013830-9), £0.60

Department for Education Publications

1991/834 Education (Fees and awards, allowances and bursaries) (Scotland) (Amendment) Regulations 1991 (ISBN 0-11-013834-1), £1
1991/964 Education (London Residuary Body) (Property transfer) (No. 2) Order 1991 (ISBN 0-11-013964-X), £0.60
1991/1034 Education (Particulars of independent schools) (Amendment) Regulations 1991 (ISBN 0-11-014034-6), £0.60
1991/1134 Education (Teachers) (Amendment) Regulations 1991 (ISBN 0-11-014134-2), £1
1991/1136 Teachers (Entitlement to registration) (Scotland) Regulations 1991 (ISBN 0-11-014136-9), £0.60
1991/1265 Education (Information on school examination results) (England) Regulations 1991 (ISBN 0-11-014265-9), £1.85
1991/1299 Education (Student loans) Regulations 1991 (ISBN 0-11-014299-3), £2.20
1991/1391 Education Reform Act 1988 (Application of Section 122 to institutions in Wales) (ISBN 0-11-014391-4), £0.60
1991/1427 Education (University Commissioners) Order 1991 (ISBN 0-11-014427-9), £0.60
1991/1457 Education (ILEA) (Transfer of functions) Order 1991 (ISBN 0-11-014457-0), £0.60
1991/1459 Education (School teachers' pay and conditions) Order 1991 (ISBN 0-11-014459-7), £1
1991/1495 Education (Assisted places) (Scotland) (Amendment) Regulations 1991 (ISBN 0-11-014495-3), £0.60
1991/1511 Education (School teacher appraisal) Regulations 1991 (ISBN 0-11-0114511-9), £1.45
1991/1522 Students' allowances (Scotland) Regulations 1991 (ISBN 0-11-014522-4), £1.85
1991/1582 Education (Pupils' attendance records) Regulations 1991 (ISBN 0-11-014582-8), £1.45
1991/1657 Education (National Curriculum) (Exceptions) (Wales) Regulations 1991 (ISBN 0-11-0144657-3), £0.60
1991/1658 Education (School curriculum and related information) (Wales) Regulations (1991) (ISBN 0-11-014658-1), £2.60
1991/1668 Education (National Curriculum) (Attainment targets and programmes of study in history) (Wales) (Amendment) Order 1991 (ISBN 0-11-014668-9), £1
1991/1683 Education (National Curriculum) (Attainment targets and programmes of study in Welsh) (Amendment) Order 1991 (ISBN 0-11-014683-2), £3
1991/1767 Education (Assisted places) (Amendment) Regulations 1991 (ISBN 0-11-014767-1), £1.85
1991/1768 Education (Training grants) (Amendment) Regulations 1991 (ISBN 0-11-014768-5), £0.60
1991/1787 Education (London Residual Body) (Property transfer) (No. 3) Order 1991 (ISBN 0-11-014787-1), £1.45
1991/1804 Education (Bursaries for teacher training) (Amendment) Regulations 1991 (ISBN 0-11-014804-5), £1
1991/1813 Education (School curriculum and related information) (Wales) (Amendment) Regulations 1991 (ISBN 0-11-014813-4), £0.60
1991/1830 Education (Assisted places) (Incidental expenses) (Amendment) Regulations 1991 (ISBN 0-11-014830-4), £0.60
1991/1831 Education (Grants) (Music and ballet schools) (Amendment) Regulations 1991 (ISBN 0-11-014831-2), £1.45
1991/1838 Education (Mandatory awards) Regulations 1991 (ISBN 0-11-014838-X), £5.70
1991/1839 Education (Fees and awards) (Amendment) Regulations 1991 (ISBN 0-11-014839-8), £1
1991/1840 Education (Teachers) (Amendment) (No. 2) Regulations 1991 (ISBN 0-11-014840-1), £0.60
1991/1851 Education (National Curriculum) (Assessment arrangements for Welsh second language) (Key Stage 1) Order 1991 (ISBN 0-11-014851-7), £1
1991/1860 Education (National Curriculum) (Assessment arrangements for English, Welsh, maths and science) (Key Stage 1) (Wales) Order 1991 (ISBN 0-11-014860-6), £1.85
1991/1874 School teachers pay and conditions Act 1991 (Commencement No. 1) Order 1991 (ISBN 0-11-014874-6), £0.60
1991/1890 Education (Financial delegation for primary schools) Regulations 1991 (ISBN 0-11-014890-8), £0.60
1991/1975 Education (Grants) (Amendment) Regulations 1991 (ISBN 0-11-014975-0), £0.60
1991/1976 Education (Higher Education Corporations) (Wales) Order 1991 (ISBN 0-11-014976-9), £0.60
1991/2155 Education (South West London College Higher Education Corporation) (Dissolution) Order 1991 (ISBN 0-11-015155-0), £1
1991 Education (National Curriculum) (Assessment arrangements for English, maths and science) (Key Stage 1) Order 1991 (ISBN 0-11-015169-0), £1.45
1991/2170 Education (National Curriculum) (Assessment arrangements for technology) (Key Stage 1) Order 1991 (ISBN 0-11-015170-4), £1
1991/2240 Education (Teachers) (Amendment) (No. 3) Regulations 1991 (ISBN 0-11-015240-9), £0.60
1991/2307 Education (Polytechnic and colleges Funding Council) (Prescribed expenditure) Regulations 1991 (ISBN 0-11-015307-3), £1
1991/2562 Education (National Curriculum) (Attainment targets and programmes of study in geography) (England) (No. 2) Order 1991 (ISBN 0-11-015562-9), £1
1991/2563 Education (National Curriculum) (Attainment targets and programmes of study in modern foreign languages) Order 1991 (ISBN 0-11-015563-7), £1
1991/2567 Education (National Curriculum) (Modern English languages) Order 1991 (ISBN 0-11-015567-X), £1
1991/2589 Education (Bursaries for teacher training) (Amendment) (No. 2) Regulations 1991 (ISBN 0-11-015589-0), £0.60
1991/2608 Education (National Curriculum) (Attainment targets and programmes of study in geography) (Wales) (Amendment) Order 1991 (ISBN 0-11-015966-7), £1
1991/2778 Education (London Residuary Body) (Property transfer) (No. 4) Order 1991 (ISBN 0-11-015889-X), £1.85
1991/2845 Education (School government) (Amendment) Regulations 1991 (ISBN 0-11-015852-0), £1
1991/2896 Education (Attainment targets and programmes of study in maths) Order 1991 (ISBN 0-11-015753-2), £1.05
1991/2897 Education (Attainment targets and programmes of study in science) Order 1991 (ISBN 0-11-015754-0), £1.05
1991/2921 Teachers (Education training and registration) (Scotland) (Amendment) Regulations 1991 (ISBN 0-11-015748-6), £0.65
1991/2943 Education support grants (Amendment) Regulations 1991 (ISBN 0-11-015744-3), £0.65
1991/2944 Teachers pay and conditions Act 1987 (Continuation) Order 1991 (ISBN 0-11-015745-1), £0.65
1992/70 Education (School information) (Amendment) (England) Regulations 1992 (ISBN 0-11-023070-1), £0.65
1992/110 Education (Financial delegation for primary schools) (Amendment) Regulations 1992 (ISBN 0-11-023110-4), £0.55
1992/155 Education (National Curriculum) (Exceptions) Regulations 1992 (ISBN 0-11-023155-4), £1.05
1992/156 Education (National Curriculum) (Exceptions) history and geography at Key Stage 4) Regulations 1992 (ISBN 0-11-023156-2), £1.05
1992/157 Education (National Curriculum) (Exceptions from science at Key Stage 4) Regulations 1992 (ISBN 0-11-023157-0), £0.65
1992/164 Education (Application for financing schemes to special schools) Regulations 1992 (ISBN 0-11-023164-3), £1.05
1992/280 Teachers' superannuation (Scotland) Regulations 1992 (ISBN 0-11-023280-1), £11.85
1992/331 Education (London Residual Body) (Transfer of compensation functions) Order 1992 (ISBN 0-11-023331-X), £1.50

1992/423 Education (Mandatory awards) (Amendment) Regulations 1992 (ISBN 0-11-023423-5), £0.65
1992/427 Education (Universities funding council) (Supplementary functions) Order 1992 (ISBN 0-11-023427-8), £0.65
1992/428 Education (Polytechnic and colleges funding council) Supplementary functions) (ISBN 0-11-023428-6), £0.65
1992/437 Education (London Residual Body) (Transfer of functions and property) Order 1992 (ISBN 0-11-023437-5), £1.50
1992/501 Education (London Residual Body) (Transfer of loans) Order 1992 (ISBN 0-11-023501-0), £1.05
1992/555 Education (Grant maintained schools) (Finance) Regulations 1992 (ISBN 0-11-023555-X), £3.55
1992/586 Education (London Residual Body) (Transitional and supplementary provisions) Order 1992 (ISBN 0-11-023586-X), £0.65
1992/587 Education (London Residual Body) (Property transfer) Order 1992 (ISBN 0-11-023587-8), £2.30
1992/597 Education (National Curriculum) (Attainment targets and programmes of study in music) (England) Order 1992 (ISBN 0-11-023597-5), £0.65
1992/814 Education (School teachers' pay and conditions) Order 1992 (ISBN 0-11-023814-1), £0.65
1992/817 Further and higher education (Scotland) Act 1992 (Commencement No. 1 and saving provisions) Order 1992 (ISBN 0-11-023817-8), £1.90
1992/988 School teachers' pay and conditions Act 1991 (commencement No. 3) Order 1992 (ISBN 0-11-023988-1) £0.65
1992/989 Education (School teachers' pay and conditions) (No2) Order (ISBN 0-11-023989-X), £0.65
1992/1089 Education (individual pupils' achievements, school records and school curriculum) (Amendment) Regulations 1992 (ISBN 0-11-024089-8), £1.50
1992/1095 Education (Grant maintained schools) (Finance) (Amendment) Regulations 1992 (ISBN 0-11-024095-2), £0.60
1992/1157 Education (Schools) Act 1992 (Commencement No 1) Order (ISBN 0-11-024157-6), £0.65
1992/1166 Education (Further and higher education institutions access funds) (Amendment) Regulations 1992 (ISBN 0-11-024166-5) £0.65
1992/1270 Education (Mandatory awards) Regulations 1992 (ISBN 0-11-024270-X), £5.90
1992/1295 Education (Chief inspector of schools in England) Order 1992 (ISBN 0-11-024295-5), £0.65
1992/1296 Transfer of functions (Science) Order 1992 (ISBN 0-11-024296-3), £1.50
1992/1348 Education Assets Board (Transfers under the ERA 1988) Regulations 1992 (ISBN 0-11-024348-X), £1.05
1992/1385 Education (School performance information) (England) Regulations 1992 (ISBN 0-11-024385-4), £1.90
1992/1548 Education (National curriculum) (Foundation subjects at Key Stage 4) Order 1992 (ISBN 0-11-024548-2), £0.65
1992/1626 Local Government Act 1988 (Defined activities) (Exemption) (Small schools) Order 1992 (ISBN 0-11-024626-8), £1.05
1992/1661 Education (Assisted places) (Incidental expenses) (Amendment) Regulations 1992 (ISBN 0-11-024661-6), £0.65
1992/1662 Education (Grants) (Music and ballet schools) (Amendment) Regulations 1992 (ISBN 0-11-024662-4), £1.05
1992/1713 Education (Inspectors of schools in England) Order 1992 (ISBN 0-11-024713-2), £1.05
1992/1798 Education (Assisted places) (Amendment) Regulations 1992 (ISBN 0-11-024798-1), £1.05
1992/1809 Education (Teachers) (Amendment) Regulations 1992 (ISBN 0-11-024809-0), £0.65
1992/1849 Education (Charlotte Mason College of Education Higher Education Corporation) (Dissolution) Order 1992 (ISBN 0-11-024849-X), £0.65
1992/1857 Education (National curriculum) (Assessment arrangements for English, mathematics, science, technology, history and geography) (Key stage 1) Order 1992 (ISBN 0-11-024857-0), £1.50
1992/1858 Education (National curriculum) (Assessment arrangements for English, mathematics, science and technology) (Key stage 3) Order 1992 (ISBN 0-11-024858-9), £1.50
1992/1957 Education (Government of Further Education Corporations) (Former Sixth Form Colleges) Regulations 1992 (ISBN 0-11-024957-7), £3.10
1992/1963 Education (Government of Further Education Corporations) (Former Further Education Colleges) Regulations 1992 (ISBN 0-11-024963-1) £3.10
1992/2025 Education (Registered inspectors) (Fees) Regulations 1992 (ISBN 0-11-025025-7), £0.65
1992/2041 Further and Higher Education Act 1992 (Commencement No. 1 and transitional provisions) Order 1992 (ISBN 0-11-025041-9), £0.65
1992/2097 Education (Further Education Corporations) Order 1992 (ISBN 0-11-025097-4), £2.30
1992/2151 Education (Crewe and Alsager College of Higher Education Corporation) (Dissolution) Order 1992 (ISBN 0-11-025151-2), £0.65
1992/2152 Education (Higher Education Corporations) (No. 8) Order 1992 (ISBN 0-11-025120-0) £0.65
1992/2181 Education (Grants) (Voluntary aided sixth form colleges) Regulations 1992 (ISBN 0-11-025181-4), £0.65
1992/2257 Education (London Residuary Body) (Transfer of functions and property) (No. 2) Order 1992 (ISBN 0-11-025257-8), £3.10
1992/2288 Education Assets Board (transfers under the Further and Higher Education Act 1992) Regulations 1992 (ISBN 0-11-024288-8), £1.05
1992/2315 Education (Further Education Corporations) (No. 2) Order 1992 (ISBN 0-11-025315-9), £0.65
1992/2361 Education Publication of draft proposals and Orders) (Further Education Corporations) Regulations 1992 (ISBN 0-11-025361-2), £1.05
1992/2377 Further and Higher Education Act 1992 (Commencement No. 2) Order 1992 (ISBN 0-11-025377-9), £1.05
1992/2400 Further Education (Sponsoring Bodies) Order 1992 (ISBN 0-11-025400-7), £0.65
1992/2598 Education (Parental ballots for acquisition of grant maintained status) (Prescribed Body) Regulations 1992 (ISBN 0-11-025598-4), £0.65
1992/2649 Teachers' superannuation (Additional voluntary contributions) (Scotland) Regulations 1992 (ISBN 0-11-025984-X, £3.10
1992/3001 Education (Further Education Corporations) (No. 3) 1992 (ISBN 0-11-025802-9), £0.65
1992/3064 Education (University Commissioners) Order 1992 (ISBN 0-11-025756-1), £0.65
1992/3069 School teachers' renumeration, professional duties and working time Order 1992 (ISBN 0-11-025757-X), £0.65
1992/3168 Education (Individual pupils' achievements) (Information) Regulations 1992 (ISBN 0-11-025442-2), £1.30
1992/3237 Education (Grants) Higher Education Corporations) Regulations 1992 (ISBN 0-11-025249-7), £0.65
1992/3275 Education support grants Regulations 1992 (ISBN 0-11-025213-6), £1.50
1993/56 Education (Higher Education Corporations) (Wales) (No. 3) Order 1993 (ISBN 0-11-033056-0), £0.65
1993/72 Education (Training grants) Regulations 1993 (ISBN 0-11-033072-2), £1.55
1993/89 Higher Education (Wales) (Revocation) Regulations 1993 (ISBN 0-11-033089-7), £0.65
1993/97 Education (Further Education Corporations) Order 1993 (ISBN 0-11-033097-8), £0.65 1993/121 Testing in Primary Schools (Scotland) Revocation Regulations 1993 (ISBN 0-11-033121-4), £0.65
1993/113 Education (School Liaison Statements) (Prescribed Particulars). Regulations 1993 (ISBN 0-11-033113-3), £3.70
1993/114 Teachers' Superannuation (Amendments) Regulations 1993 (ISBN 0-11-033114-1), £2.80
1993/215 Education (Designated Institutions in Further

Department for Education Publications

Education) (Wales) Order 1993 (ISBN 0-11-033215-6), £1.10
1993/230 Academic Awards and Distinctions (Queen Margaret College) (Scotland) Order of Council 1993 (ISBN 0-11-033230-X), £0.65
1993/269 Education (Further Education Corporations) Order 1993 (ISBN 0-11-033269-5), £0.65
1993/270 Education (St Austell Sixth Form College and Mid-Cornwall College) (Dissolution) Order 1993 (ISBN 0-11-033270-9), £0.65
1993/271 St Austell College (Government) Regulations 1993 (ISBN 0-11-033271-7), £3.20
1993/404 Education (Designated Institutions) Order 1993 (ISBN 0-11-033404-3), £0.65
1993/424 Designation of Institutes of Higher Education (Scotland) amendment order 1993 (ISBN 0-11-033424-8), £1.10
1993/434 Education (PCFC and UFC Staff) order 1993 (ISBN 0-11-033434-5), £1.10
1993/435 Education (Designated Institutions in Further Education) Order 1993 (ISBN 0-11-033435-3), £1.10
1993/465 Education (Further Education Corporations) (Designated Staff) Order 1993 (ISBN 0-11-033465-5), £0.65
1993/481 Education (Presailed Courses of Higher Education) (Wales) Regulations 1993 (ISBN 0-11-033481-7), £0.65
1993/489 Grant-aided Colleges (Scotland) Grant Amendment Regulations 1993 (ISBN 0-11-033489-2), £1.10
1993/525 Education (Fees and Awards) (Scotland) Amendment Regulations 1993 (ISBN 0-11-033525-2), £0.65
1993/543 Education (Teachers) Regulations 1993 (ISBN 0-11-033543-0), £3.20
1993/555 Academics Awards and Distinctions (Glasgow Caledonian University) (Scotland) Order of Council 1993 (ISBN 0-11-033555-4), £0.65
1993/557 Napier University (Scotland) Order of Council 1993 (ISBN 0-11-033557-0), £2.50
1993/558 University of Paisley (Scotland) Order of Council 1993 (ISBN 0-11-033558-9) £2.40
1993/559 Further and Higher Education Act 1992 (Consequential Amendments) Regulations 1993 (ISBN 0-11-033559-7), £1.10
1993/560 Further and Higher Education Act 1992 (Consequential Amendments) Order 1993 (ISBN 0-11-033560), £0.65
1993/562 Education (Designated Institutions in Further Education) (No 2) Order 1993 (ISBN 0-11-033562-7), £0.65
1993/563 Education (Designated Institutions in Further and Higher Education) (Interpretation) Order 1993 (ISBN 0-11-033870-7), £1.10
1993/568 Education (Grant Maintained Schools) (Finance) Regulations 1993 (ISBN 0-11-033843-X), £3.70
1993/569 Education (Grants) (Travellers and Displaced Persons) Regulations 1993 (ISBN 0-11-033569-4), £1.55
1993/609 Further Education (Attribution of Surpluses and Deficits) Regulations 1993 (ISBN 0-11-033609-7), £1.10
1993/611 Education (Welsh Agricultural College Higher Education Corporation) (Designated Staff) Order 1993 (ISBN 0-11-033611-9), £1.10
1993/612 Education (Further Education Corporations) (Designated Staff) (Wales) Order 1993 (ISBN 0-11-033612-7), £0.65
1993/625 Education (Listed Bodies) Order 1993 (ISBN 0-11-033625-9), £1.95
1993/626 Education (Recognised Bodies) Order 1993 (ISBN 0-11-033626-7), £1.10
1993/628 Education (Queen Elizabeth Atherstone Further Education Corporation) (Dissolution) Order 1993 (ISBN 0-11-033628-3), £0.65
1993/643 Glasgow Polytechnic and The Queens College Glasgow (Closure) (Scotland) Order 1993 (ISBN 0-11-033643-7), £1.55
1993/835 Education (Individual Pupils' Achievements) (Information) (Wales) Regulations 1993 (ISBN 0-11-033835-9), £2.40
1993/901 Further Education (Exclusion of Land From Transfer) Order 1993 (ISBN 0-11-033901-0), £1.95
1993/924 Education (Dissolution of the Council for Academic Awards) Order 1993 (ISBN 0-11-033924-X), £0.65
1993/937 Further Education (Exclusion of Land From Transfer) (No 2) Order 1993 (ISBN 0-11-033937-1), £1.10
1993/962 Education (School Teachers Pay and Conditions) Order 1993 (ISBN 0-11-033962-2), £1.10
1993/974 Education (Grants for Further Training of Teachers and Educational Psychologists etc) (Scotland) Regulations 1993 (ISBN 0-11-033974-6), £1.10
1993/998 Education (School Curriculum and Related Information) (Amendment) (Wales) Regulations 1993 (ISBN 0-11-033998-3), £0.65
1993/1190 Education (Schools) Act 1992 (Commencement No 2 and Transitional Provision) Order 1993 (ISBN 0-11-034190-2), £0.65
1993/1214 Education (Student Loans) Regulations 1993 (ISBN 0-11-034214-3), £2.40
1993/1492 Education (School Inspection) Regulations 1993 (ISBN 0-11-034492-8), £1.55
1993/1502 Education (School Information) (England) Regulations 1993 (ISBN 0-11-034502-9), £3.20
1993/1503 Education (School Performance Information) (England) Regulations 1993 (ISBN 0-11-034503-7), £1.95
1993/1529 Education (School Inspection) (Wales) Regulations 1993 (ISBN 0-11-034529-0), £1.55
1993/1604 Education (School and Placing Information) (Scotland) Amendment etc Regulations 1993 (ISBN 0-11-024604-1), £1.95
1993/1605 Education (Provision of Information as to Schools) (Scotland) Regulations 1993 (ISBN 0-11-034605-X), £1.55
1993/1614 Further Education (Prescriptions of Different Date for Property Agreements) (Scotland) Order 1993 (ISBN 0-11-0346149-9) £0.65
1993/1620 Education (Student Loans) (Amendment) Regulations 1993 (ISBN 0-11-034620-3), £0.65
1993/1659 Education (assisted places) (Scotland) Amendment Regulations 1993 (ISBN 0-11-034659-0), £1.10
1993/1755 Education (School Teachers' Pay and Conditions) (No 2) Order 1993 (ISBN 0-11-034755-2), £0.65
1993/1775 Education (Bursaries for Teacher Training) (Amendment) Regulations 1993 (ISBN 0-11-034775-7), £0.65
1993/1850 Education (Mandatory Awards) Regulations 1993 (ISBN 0-11-034850-8), £6.10
1993/1891 Colleges of Further Education (Changes of Names) (Scotland) Order 1993 (ISBN 0-11-034891-5), £1.10
1993/1892 Education (Access Funds) (Scotland) Amendment Regulations 1993 (ISBN 0-11-034892-3), £0.65
1993/1936 Education (assisted places) (Amendment) Regulations 1993 (ISBN 0-11-034936-9), £1.10
1993/1937 Education (assisted places) (Incidental Expenses) (Amendment) Regulations 1993 (ISBN 0-11-034937-7), £1.10
1993/1938 Education (grants) (Music and Ballet Schools) (Amendment) Regulations 1993 (ISBN 0-11-034938-5) £1.10
1993/1969 Education (Teachers) (Amendment) Regulations 1993 (ISBN 0-11-034969-5), £0.65
1993/1975 Education Act 1993 (Commencement No 1 and Transitional Provisions) Order 1993 (ISBN 0-11-034975-X), £1.95
1993/1976 Education (London Oratory School) (Exemption from Pay and Conditions Orders) Order 1993 (ISBN 0-11-034976-8), £0.65
1993/1977 Further Education (Attribution of Surpluses and Deficits) (Ridge College) Regulations 1993 (ISBN 0-11-034977-6), £0.65
1993/1982 Education (School Inspection) (Wales) (No 2) Regulations 1993 (ISBN 0-11-034982-2), £2.80
1993/1983 Education (National Curriculum) (Assessment Arrangements for the Core Subjects) (Key Stage 1) Order 1993 (ISBN 0-11-034983-0), £1.55

1993/1984 Education (National Curriculum) (Assessment Arrangements for the Core Subjects) (Key Stage 3) Order 1993 (ISBN 0-11-034984-9), £1.10
1993/1986 Education (School Inspection) (No 2) Regulations 1993 (ISBN 0-11-034986-5), £1.95
1993/1987 Education (Further Education in Schools) Regulations 1993 (ISBN 0-11-034987-3), £0.65
1993/1993 Education (Further Education Institutions Information) (England) Regulations 1993 (ISBN 0-11-034993-8), £1.55
1993/2077 Education (School Performance Information) (England) (No 2) Regulations 1993 (ISBN 0-11-035077-4), £1.95
1993/2104 Education (School Performance Information) (Wales) Regulations 1993 (ISBN 0-11-035194-0), £2.80
1993/2169 Education (Further Educational Institutions Information) (Wales) Regulations 1993 (ISBN 0-11-035169-X), £4.15
1993/2190 Education (National Curriculum) (Assessment Arrangements for English, Welsh, Mathematics and Science) (Key Stage 1) (Wales) Order 1993 (ISBN 0-11-035190-8), £1.55
1993/2191 Education (National Curriculum) (Assessment Arrangements for English, Welsh, Mathematics and Science) (Key Stage 3) Order 1993 (ISBN 0-11-035191-6), £1.55
1993/2513 Teachers' (Superannuation and Compensation for Premature Retirement) (Scotland) Amendment Regulations 1993 (ISBN 0-11-035513-X), £2.80
1993/2709 Education (No 2) Act 1986 (Amendment) Order 1993 (ISBN 0-11-035709-4), £0.65
1993/2732 Teachers' (Education, Training and Recommendations for Registration) (Scotland) Regulations 1993 (ISBN 0-11-035732-9), £1.10
1993/2828 Education (Recognised Awards) (Richmond College) Order 1993 (ISBN 0-11-033185-0) £0.65

SI 1994

Statutory Rules of Northern Ireland 1994
12 *Colleges of education (Grant conditions) Regulations (Northern Ireland) 1994* £1.95
13 *Schools (Expulsion of pupils) (Appeal tribunals) Regulations (Northern Ireland) 1994* £1.55
55 *Education and library services etc. grant regulations (Northern Ireland) 1994* £1.10
122 *Education (Individual pupil's achievements) (Information) (Amendment) Regulations (Northern Ireland) 1994*
127 *Education and libraries (1993 Order) (Commencement No. 1) Order (Northern Ireland) 1994*
238 *School and admissions (Appeal tribunals) (Amendment) Regulations (Northern Ireland) 1994* £0.65
230 *Education (Student loans) Regulations (Northern Ireland) 1994* £3.70
295 *Education reform (1989 Order) (Commencement Orders 4 and 5) (Amendment) Order (Northern Ireland) 1994* £1.95
296 *Education reform (1989 Order) (Commencement No. 7) Order (Northern Ireland) 1994* £1.55
298 *Maintenance allowances (Pupils over compulsory school age) Regulations (Northern Ireland) 1994* £1.55
315 *Education (School information and prospectuses) (Amendment) Regulations (Northern Ireland) 1994* £1.10
323 *Education and libraries (Competition in functional work) Regulations (Northern Ireland) 1994* £1.10
324 *Education and libraries (Specified period for functional work) Regulations (Northern Ireland) 1994* £1.10
325 *Education and libraries (Defined activities) (Exemption) Order (Northern Ireland) 1994* £1.55
342 *Secondary schools (Admission criteria) Regulations (Northern Ireland) 1994* £1.10
361 *Education (School information and prospectuses) (Amendment) Regulations 1994* £0.65

Education Act 1944
156 *Education (Grant) (Henrietta Barnett School) Regulations 1994* £0.65
1421 *Education (School information) (England) Regulations 1994* £3.20
2036 *Education (Grants) (Music and ballet Schools) (Amendment) Regulations 1994* £1.10
2102 *Education (Grant) (Amendment) Regulations 1994* £0.65

Education Act 1962
1606 *Education (Mandatory awards) (Amendment) Regulations 1994* £0.65

Education Act 1964
581 *Education (Middle schools) (Amendment) Regulations 1994* £0.65

Superannuation Act 1972
1058 *Teachers' superannuation (Amendment) Regulations 1994* £1.95
1059 *Teachers' (Compensation for redundancy and premature retirement) (Amendment) Regulations 1994* £1.10

Education Act 1980
1048 *Education (Special educational needs) (Information) Regulations 1994* £1.55
2034 *Education (Assisted places) (Amendment) Regulations 1994* £0.65
2035 *Education (Assisted places) (Incidental expenses) (Amendment) Regulations 1994* £0.65
2103 *Education (Pupil referral units) (Application of enactments) Regulations 1994* £1.95

Education (Scotland) Act 1980
351 *Self governing schools (Application and amendment of regulations) (Scotland) Regulations 1994* £1.55
1827 *Education (Assisted places) (Scotland) amendment regulations 1994* £1.10

Education (Grants and Awards) Act 1984
612 *Education (Grants for educational support and training) Regulations 1994* £1.95
2446 *Education (Grants for education support and training) (Amendment) Regulations 1994* £0.65

Education No. 2 Act 1986
692 *Education (No. 2) Act 1986 (Amendment) Order 1994* £0.65
2016 *Education (Bursaries for teacher training) Regulations 1994* £1.55
2092 *Education (No. 2) Act 1986 (Amendment) Order 1994* £1.10

Education Reform Act 1988
222 *Education (Teachers) (Amendment) Regulations 1994* £1.10
277 *Education (Financial delegations to schools) (Mandatory exceptions) Regulations 1994* £1.10
646 *Education (National curriculum) (Assessment arrangements for English, Welsh, maths and science) (Key Stage 1) (Wales) (Amendment) Order 1994* £0.65
647 *Education (National curriculum) (Assessment arrangements for English, Welsh, maths and science) (Key Stage 3) (Wales) (Amendment) Order 1994* £0.65
959 *Education (Individual pupil's achievements) (Information) (Wales) Regulations 1994* £2.40
1255 *Education (Inner London Education Authority) (Property transfer) Order 1994* £0.65
1270 *Education (National curriculum) (Exceptions in Welsh at Key Stage 4) Regulations 1994* £0.65
1420 *Education (School performance information) (English) Regulations 1994* £2.80
1743 *Education (National curriculum) (Attainment targets and programmes of study in history) (Wales) (Amendment) Order 1994* £0.65
1744 *Education (National curriculum) (Attainment targets and programmes of study in geography) (Wales) (Amendment) Order 1994* £0.65
1814 *Education (National curriculum) (Foundation subjects at Key Stage 4) Order 1994* £0.65
1815 *Education (National curriculum) (Attainment targets and programmes of study in modern foreign languages and technology at Key Stage 4) (England) (Amendment) Order 1994* £0.65

Department for Education Publications

1816 *Education (National curriculum) (Attainment targets and programmes of study in history) (England) (Amendment) Order 1994* £0.65
1817 *Education (National curriculum) (Attainment targets and programmes of study in geography) Order 1994* £0.65
1818 *Education (National curriculum) (Modern foreign languages) (Amendment) Order 1994* £0.65
2017 *Education (Norwich School of Art and Design further education corporation) (Transfer to higher education sector) Order 1994* £0.65
2018 *Education (Northern School of Contemporary Dance Leeds further education corporation) (Transfer to higher education sector) Order 1994* £0.65
2019 *Education (Writtle Agriculture further education corporation) (Transfer to higher education sector) Order 1994* £0.65
2099 *Education (National curriculum) (Assessment arrangements for the core subjects) (Key Stage 1) (Amendment) Order 1994* £1.10
2100 *Education (National curriculum) (Assessment arrangements for the core subjects) (Key Stage 2) (England) Order 1994* £1.10
2101 *Education (National curriculum) (Assessment arrangements for the core subjects) (Key Stage 3) (England) Order 1994* £1.10
2112 *Education (National curriculum exceptions) Regulations 1994* £1.10
2163 *Education (Inner London Education Authority) (Property transfer) (Amendment) (No. 2) Order 1994* £0.65
2206 *Education (National curriculum) (Exceptions) (Wales) Regulations 1994* £1.10
2226 *Education (National curriculum) (Assessment arrangements for English, Welsh, mathematics and science) (Key Stage 1) (Wales) (Amendment) Order 1994* £1.10
2227 *Education (National curriculum) (Assessment arrangements for English, Welsh, mathematics and science) (Key Stage 2) (Wales) Order 1994* £1.10
2228 *Education (National curriculum) (Assessment arrangements for English, Welsh, mathematics and science) (Key Stage 3) (Wales) Order 1994* £1.10
2254 *Education (School performance information) (Wales) (No. 2) Regulations 1994* £2.40
2330 *Education (School information) (Wales) Regulations 1994* £3.20

Self Governing Schools etc. (Scotland) Act 1989
431 *Self governing schools grant and recovery (Scotland) Regulations 1994* £3.70
478 *Self governing schools (Change in characteristics) (Scotland) Regulations 1994* £1.10

Education (Schools) Act 1992
717 *Education (Registered inspectors of schools appeal tribunal) (Procedure) Regulations 1994* £2.80
1186 *Education (School performance information) (Wales) Regulations 1994* £1.10
1633 *Education (Chief inspector of schools in England) Order 1994* £0.65
1912 *Education (School performance information) (Wales) (Amendment) Regulations 1994* £0.65

School Teachers' Pay and Conditions Act 1991
910 *Education (School teachers' pay and conditions) Order 1994* £1.10
1673 *Education (School teachers' pay and conditions) (No. 2) Order 1994* £0.65

Further and Higher Education Act 1992
94 *Education (Further education corporations) Order 1994* £0.65
1478 *Education (Gwynedd Technical College and Coleg Pencraig) (Dissolution) Order 1994* £0.65
1741 *Portsmouth College of Art and Design and Further Education (Dissolution) Order 1994* £0.65
1754 *Epsom School of Art and Design (Dissolution) Order 1994* £0.65

Education Act 1993
436 *Education Act 1993 (Commencement No. 2 and transitional provisions) (Amendment) Order 1994* £0.65
610 *Education (Grant-maintained schools) (Finance) (Wales) Regulations 1994* £3.70
507 *Education Act 1993 (Commencement No. 3 and transitional provisions) Order 1994* £2.80
645 *Education (School curriculum and assessment authority) (Transfer of functions) Order 1994* £0.65
650 *Education (Payment for special educational needs supplies) Regulations 1994* £1.10
651 *Education (Special educational needs) (Approval of independent schools) Regulations 1994* £2.40
652 *Education (Special schools) Regulations 1994* £2.40
653 *Education (Grant maintained schools) Regulations 1994* £3.70
654 *Education (Governors of new grant maintained schools) Regulations 1994* £1.10
1041 *Education (Groups of grant maintained schools) Regulations 1994* £4.70
1083 *Education (Schools conducted by educational associations) (Amendment) Regulations 1994* £1.55
1084 *Education (Special schools conducted by educational associations) Regulations 1994* £3.20
1085 *Education (Schools conducted by educational associations) (Initial articles of government) (Amendment) Regulations 1994* £1.10
1195 *Education (Groups of grant maintained schools) (Finance) Regulations 1994* £0.65
1231 *Education (Grant maintained special schools) (Amendment) Regulations 1994* £1.55
1232 *Education (Maintained special schools becoming grant maintained schools) (Ballot information) Regulations 1994* £0.65
1251 *Education (Special educational needs) (Amendment) Regulations 1994* £4.15
1256 *Education (Information as to provision of Education) (England) Regulations 1994* £2.80
1303 *Education (Lay members of appeal committee) Regulations 1994* £0.65
1304 *Religious education (Meetings of local conferences and councils) 1994* £1.10
1321 *Education (Distribution by schools of information about further education institutions) (Wales) Regulations 1994 £1.10*
1520 *Education (National curriculum) (Attainment targets and programmes of study in science) (Amendment order) 1994* £0.65
1558 *Education Act 1993 (Commencement No. 4) Order 1994* £1.95
1697 *Education (Amount to follow permanently excluded pupil) Regulations 1994* £0.65
1861 *Education (Annual consideration of ballot on grant maintained status) (Wales) Order 1994* £0.65
1910 *Special educational needs tribunal Regulations 1994* £3.20
2003 *Education (Initial government of grant-maintained special schools) Regulations 1994* £1.95
2093 *Education (Exclusion from schools) (Prescribed periods) Regulations 1994* £1.10
2094 *Education (Grant-maintained schools) (Initial governing instruments) (Amendment) Regulations 1994* £1.95
2104 *Education (Grant-maintained special schools) (Initial governing instruments) Regulations 1994* £6.10
2111 *Education (Grant-maintained special schools) (Finance) Regulations 1994* £3.20
2156 *Education (Payment for special educational needs supplies) (Amendment) Regulations 1994* £0.65
2167 *Education (Publication of notices) (Special schools) Regulations 1994* £0.65
2248 *Education Act 1993 (Commencement No. 5 and transitional provisions) (Amendment) Order 1994* £0.65

Education Act 1994
2204 *Education Act 1994 (Commencement) Order 1994* £0.65
2463 *Teaching as a career unit (Transfer of property rights and liabilities) Order 1994* £0.65

Broadsheets

1 Nursery education: low cost adaptation of spare space in primary schools (1980)
2 Roscommon: 3 into 1 will go (1980)

3 Remodelling of Jackfield School: an exercise in primary renewal in an urban context (1980)
4 Redundant school buildings used by further education: South Shields Marine and Technical College (1981)
5 Redundant school buildings used by further education: Berkshire College of Art and Design (1982)
6 Alternative use of surplus school buildings: a drama centre (1981)
7 Alternative use of surplus school buildings: magistrates court accommodation (1981)
8 Changing accommodation for junior and middle school age groups (1981)
9 School sites: recreation play and outdoor education (1982)
10 Drama accommodation: remodelling in a tertiary college (1982)
11 Fire precautions: an alternative approach in the design of a primary school (1982)
12 Vandalism in schools and colleges (1983)
13 Blackthorn: the design of a middle school (1983)
14 Accommodation for the 16–19 age group. NAFE: designing for change at Halesowen (1983)
15 Community use of primary schools (1983)
16 Alternative use of surplus school buildings: a day centre (1983)
17 Playing fields-marginal areas (1983)
18 Alternative use of surplus school buildings: special sheltered housing (1984)
19 Opportunities for improvement: staff resource areas (1984)
20 Energy performance in three schools: a comparison of design values with measured consumption (1984)
21 Opportunities for improvement: Wheatley Park School: a rationalisation project serving school and community (1984)
22 Use of heat pumps in rural schools (1986)
23 Introducing art to the community: how the Drumcoon Education Arts Centre in Wigan was set up.
24 Saving energy in schools: 3 case studies in Nottinghamshire (1987)
25 Energy consumption in educational buildings (1988)
26 Childcare provision in existing school buildings (1989)
27 Energy efficient school refurbishment: 3 case studies (1991)
28 School glazing and vandalism (1991)
29 Energy in educational buildings (1991)
30 Engineering services in school (1992)

Administrative Memoranda

8/77 Educational building: minor works
2/79 Constructional standards for maintained and direct
2/81 The education (school premises) regulations 1981
3/84 Further education for unemployed people under the '21 hours rule'
4/84 Proposals made under Sections 12-16 of the Education Act 1980
1/85 Teacher training awards in craft, design and technology 1985-86
1/86 Modification of approval procedures for ILEA school and further education building projects
2/86 Children at school and problems related to AIDS
3/86 The use of asbestos in educational establishments
1/88 Amendment of pupils' registration regulations: Keeping of school records
1/89 Animals and plants in schools: legal aspects
1/90 Treatment and assessment of probationary teachers
2/90 Misconduct of teachers and workers with children and young people
3/90 Animals and plants in schools: legal aspects
1/92 Use of ionising radiations in education establishments in England and Wales

Circulars

1/87 Follow up to HMI Reports
2/87 Education (Publication of proposals to change status of a controlled school) Regulations 1987
3/87 Providing for quality: the pattern of organisation to Age 19
4/87 Arrangements for the approval of advanced further education in England 1987–1988 and 1988–1989
5/87 School teachers' pay and conditions of employment
6/87 Education (No. 2) Act 1986: Regulations made under Sections 51, 61 and 62 and 3rd Commencement Order
7/87 Education (No. 2) Act 1986: Further education
8/87 School teachers' pay and conditions of employment
9/87 Local education authority training grants scheme: financial year 1988–1989
10/87 Approval for courses of further training for school and further education teachers in England 1988–1989
11/87 Sex eduction at school
1/88 Physical and mental fitness to teach of teachers and entrants to teacher training
3/88 School teachers' pay and conditions of employment
4/88 Working together for the protection of children from abuse
5/88 LEA training grants scheme: financial year 1989-90
7/88 Education Reform Act 1988: local management of school
8/88 Education Reform Act 1988: governance of maintained further and higher education colleges
9/88 Education Reform Act 1988: local management of further and higher education colleges: planning and delegation schemes and articles of government
10/88 Education Reform Act 1988: Grant maintained schools
11/88 Admission of pupils to County and Voluntary schools
12/88 Protection of children: disclosure of criminal background of those with access to children
1/89 Education Reform Act 1988: local arrangements for the consideration of complaints
2/89 Education Reform Act 1988: charges for school activities
3/89 Education Reform Act 1988: religious education and collective worship
4/89 Alcohol misuse
5/89 Education Reform Act 1988: the school curriculum and assessment
6/89 Education Reform Act 1988: National Curriculum mathematics and science orders under Section 4
7/89 Teachers (compensation for redundancy and premature retirement)
8/89 Ethnically based statistics on school teachers
9/89 Education Reform Act 1988: modern foreign languages in the National Curriculum
10/89 Education Reform Act 1988: National Curriculum key stage one: order under Section 4
11/89 Education Reform Act 1988: State approval of qualifications under Section 5
12/89 School teachers' pay and conditions of employment
13/89 Local management of schools and further and higher education colleges. Order under Section 222 Education Reform Act 1988
14/89 Education (School curriculum and related information) Regulations 1989
15/89 Education Reform Act 1988: temporary exceptions from the National Curriculum
16/89 Ethnically based statistics on school pupils
17/89 Education (school records) Regulations
18/89 Education (teachers) Regulations 1989
19/89 Adult continuing education and the Education Reform Act 1988: planning and delegation schemes
20/89 Local Education Authority training grants scheme: financial year 1990–1991
21/89 Grant maintained schools: financial arrangements
22/89 Assessment and statements of special educational needs: procedures within the education, health and social services
23/89 Special schools for pupils with emotional and behavioural difficulties

Department for Education Publications

24/89 Initial teacher training: approval of courses
1/90 Education Reform Act 1988: statutory approval of qualifications under Section 5
2/90 Education Reform Act 1988: National Curriculum: English key stages 2-4 Order under Section 4
3/90 Education Reform Act 1988: National Curriculum: Section 4 Order technology: design and technology and information technology
4/90 Arrangements for the establishment of education committees
5/90 Crime prevention: the success of the partnership approach
6/90 School teachers' pay and conditions of appointment
7/90 Management of the school day
8/90 Records of Achievement
9/90 Education Reform Act 1988: the Education (National Curriculum) (Assessment arrangements for English, Mathematics and Science) Order 1990
10/90 Education Reform Act 1988: specific grant for the education of travellers and of displaced persons
11/90 Staffing for pupils with special educational needs
1/91 Education Reform Act 1988: statutory approval of qualifications under Section 5
2/91 Education (Special educational needs) (Approval of independent schools) Regulations 1991
3/91 Approval of special schools
4/91 Education Reform Act 1988: National Curriculum: Section 4 Order history
5/91 Education Reform Act 1988: National Curriculum: Section 4 Order geography
6/91 Implementation of more open enrolment in primary schools
7/91 Local management of schools: further education
8/91 S.I. 1989/2488: Local Government Act 1988 (Competition in sports and leisure facilities) Order 1989
9/91 Education Reform Act 1988: Section 22: The Education (Information on school examination results) (England) Regulations
10/91 School teachers' pay and conditions of employment
11/91 Education (Pupil's attendance records) Regulations 1991
12/91 School teacher appraisal
13/91 Education (Teachers) (Amendment) Regulations 1991
14/91 Education Reform Act 1988: the Education (National Curriculum) (Assessment arrangements for English, maths and science) (Key stage 1) Order 1991 technology (Key Stage 1) Order 1991
15/91 Education Reform Act 1988: modern foreign languages in the National Curriculum
16/91 Education Reform Act 1988: National Curriculum: Section 4 Order geography
17/91 Education Reform Act 1988: National Curriculum: maths and science orders under Section 4
1/92 National Curriculum: flexibility at Key Stage 4
2/92 ERA 1988: National Curriculum: Section 4 Order Art
3/92 ERA 1988: National Curriculum: Section 4 Order Music
4/92 ERA 1988: National Curriculum: Section 4 Order Physical Education
5/92 Reporting Pupils' achievements to parents
6/92 ERA 1988 Statutory approval of qualifications under Section 5
7/92 The Parents Charter: publication of information about school performance in 1992
8/92 School teachers pay and conditions of employment
9/92 Initial teacher training (secondary phase)
10/92 Grants for education support and training 1993-94
11/92 ERA 1988: specific grant for the education of travellers and of displaced persons
12/92 Education (National Curriculum) (Assessment arrangements for English mathematics, science, technology history and geography) (Key Stage 1) order 1992
13/92 Education (National Curriculum) (Assessment arrangements for English mathematics, science and technology) (Key Stage 3) order 1992
14/92 Reports on individual pupils achievements (Replaces Circular 5/92)
1/93 Further and Higher Education Act 1992
3/93 Parents' Charter. Publication of information about the performance of colleges in the Further Education Sector in 1993
4/93 Parents' Charter. Publication of information about secondary schools performance in 1993
5/93 Parents' Charter. Publication of information about primary schools performance in 1993
6/93 Admission to maintained schools
7/93 Inspecting schools: a guide to the inspection provisions of the Education (Schools) Act 1992 in England
8/93 School Teachers' pay and conditions of employment
9/93 Protection of children: disclosure of criminal background of those with access to children
10/93 Grants for educational support and training 1994/5
11/93 Education Reform Act 1988 Education (National Curriculum) (Assessment arrangements for the core subjects) (Key Stage 1) Order 1993
12/93 Education Reform Act 1988 Education (National Curriculum) (Assessment arrangements for the core subjects) (Key Stage 3) Order 1993
13/93 Physical and mental fitness to teach of teachers and of entrants to initial teacher training
14/93 Initial training of primary school teachers: new criteria for courses
15/93 Use of school premises: incorporation of governing bodies in L.E.A. maintained schools
16/93 Reports on pupils achievements
17/93 Schools requiring special measures
18/93 Education Act 1993. Grant-maintained schools: acquisition, transfer and governance
1/94 Religious education and collective worship
2/94 Local management of schools
3/94 Development of special schools
4/94 Statutory approval of qualifications under 1988 Act
5/94 Sex education in schools
6/94 Organisation of special educational provision
7/94 School teachers' pay and conditions of appointment 1994
8/94 Pupil behaviour and discipline
9/94 Education of children with emotional and behavioural difficulties
10/94 Exclusions from school
11/94 Education by LEAs of children otherwise than at school
12/94 Education of sick children
13/94 Education of children being looked after by local authorities
14/94 Parents' Charter: publication of information about secondary school performance in 1994
15/94 Parents' Charter: publication of information about primary schools in 1994
16/94 Parents Charter: publication of information about the performance of colleges in the further education sector in 1994
17/94 Arrangements for money to follow pupils who have been permanently excluded from school
18/94 Grants for education support and training 1995/96
19/94 Arrangements for education committees
20/94 Assessing 14 year olds in 1995
21/94 Assessing 7 and 11 year olds in 1995
22/94 Safety in outdoor activity centres

Parliamentary Committees

The departmental select committee system was introduced after the 1979 general election: Reports are published as House of Commons papers Committee Office, House of Commons, London SW1A 0AA: Tel 071-291-6432

Education w.e.f 1992–1993 session

Session 1982–83

Chairman Christopher Price
First report 1982/83
Prison education
HC 45 April 1983
Second report 1982/83
Further and higher education in Northern Ireland
HC 180 June 1983
Two further enquiries were commenced but not completed in the 1982/83 Session:
HC 81 1982/83 Public Records
HC 133 1983/83 Education and training 14–19 year olds: the new technical and vocational education initiative

Session 1983–84

Chairman Sir William Van Straubenzee
First report
The effects of the abolition of the GLC and Metropolitan Counties upon support for the Arts
HC 264 April 1984
Second report
Prison education
HC 453 June 1984

Session 1984–85

Chairman Sir William Van Straubenzee
First report
The future of the science budget
HC 46 July 1985

Session 1985–86

Chairman Sir William Van Straubenzee
First report
Revised financial arrangements for the national museums and galleries
HC 417 May 1986
Second report
DES Expenditure plans 1986–1987 to 1988–1989
HC 351 July 1986
Third report
Achievement in primary schools
HC 40 September 1986

Session 1986–87

Chairman Sir William Van Straubenzee
First report
Student awards
HC 28 January 1987
Second report
Prison education
HC 138 June 1987
Third report
Special educational needs: implementation of the 1981 Education Act
HC 201 June 1987
Fourth report
Expenditure Plans 1987–1988 to 1989–1990

Session 1987–88

Chairman Timothy Raison
First report
DES and OAL Expenditure plans 1988–1989 to 1990–1991
HC 265 May 1988
First special report
Special educational needs: observations by the Government on the 3rd report of the Committee 198601987 Session
HC 214 January 1988
Second special report
Achievement in primary schools: observations by the government on the 3rd report of the Committee 1987–1988 Session
HC 246 February 1988

Session 1990–91

Chairman Malcolm Thornton
First report
Science Policy and the European Dimension
HC 127 January 1991
First Special Report
Government Response to the Committee's Fourth Report 1989–90
HC 50 December 1990
Second Report
Prison education
HC 311 May 1991
Third report
Standards of reading in primary schools
HC 268 May 1991
Fourth report
Sports in schools
HC 155 June 1991
Fifth report
DES and OAL expenditure plans 1991–92 to 1993–94
HC 507 July 1991
Sixth report
Education and training for the 21st century
HC 529 August 1991
Second special report
Government response to the fifth report of the committee 1990–1991

Session 1991–92

Chairman Malcolm Thornton
First special report
Government response to the third report of the committee 1990–91: Standard of reading in primary schools
HC 22 November 1991
Second special report
Government response to the fourth report to the committee 1990–1991: Sport in schools
HC 166 January 1992
Third special report
Inquiries into information technology in schools and music in schools
HC 314 March 1992
Fourth special report
The role of the science and technology sub-committee
HC 315 March 1992

Session 1992–93

Chairman Malcolm Thornton
First report
Department for education expenditure plans 1992–93 to 1994–95
HC 305 February 1993

Second report
Some aspects of the funding of schools
HC 419 March 1993
Third report
Meeting special educational needs:
Statements of needs and provisions
HC 287 July 1993
First special report
Government response to the first report of the committee 1992–93 (Expenditure plans 1992–1993 to 1994–1995)
HC 695 June 1993
Second special report
Government response to the third report from the committee 1992–93 (Meeting special educational needs)
HC 941 November 1993

Employment Departmental Select Committee

Session 1982–83

Chairman John Golding
Chairman Jim Craigen
First special report 1982–83
The working of the Health and Safety Commission on the sixth report of the committee in session 1981–82
HC 36 November 1982
Second special report 1982–83
Commission for Radical Equality draft code of practice: observations by the Government on the fifth report of the committee in session 1981–82
HC 319 April 1983

Session 1983–84

Chairman Ron Leighton
First report
Trade union legislation: unions in the Government Communications Headquarters
HC 238 March 1984
Second report
Manpower Services Commission's corporate plan 1984–88
HC 340 June 1984
First special report
MSC corporate plan 1984–88; Observations by the Government
HC 441 May 1984

Session 1984–85

Chairman Ron Leighton
First report
The Equal Opportunities Commussion's draft code of practice
HC 59 November 1984
Second report
Proposals for changes in skill centres
HC 125 April 1985
Third report
The implications for industrial relations and employment of the introduction of the polygraph
HC 125 April 1985
Fourth report
MSC corporate plan 1985–89
HC 244 May 1985
Fifth report
Wages councils
HC 254 May 1985
Sixth report
Dismissal of NCB employees
HC 416 July 1985
First special report
Observations by the Government on the 1st report of the Committee 1984–85
(HC 125) EOC draft code of practice
HC 304 April 1985
Second special report
Observations by the Government on the third report of the Committee 1984–85
(HC 98); The implications for industrial relations and employment of the introduction of the polygraph
HC 305 April 1985

Session 1985–86

Chairman Ron Leighton
First report
Special employment measures and the long-term unemployed
HC 199 February 1986
Second report
MSC Corporate plan 1986–1990
HC 265 June 1986
Third report
Government reply to the report on special employment measures and the long-term unemployed
HC 435 June 1986
First special report
MSC Corporate plan 1985–1989; Response from Government
HC 48 November 1985

Session 1987–88

Chairman Ron Leighton
First special report
Discrimination in employment observations by the Government on the first report of the Committee in session 1986–87
HC 221 January 1988
First report
Department of Employment's estimates 1988–89
HC 526 June 1988
Second report
Legionnaire's disease in the working environment
HC 524 July 1988
Third report
The employment effects of urban development corporations
HC 321 Aug 1988

Session 1989–90

Chairman Ron Leighton
First report
Disability and Employment
HC 35 February 1991 (typescript December 1990)
Second report
Recruitment practices
HC 176 February 1991
Third report
Future prospects for levels of employment and unemployment
HC 176 February 1991
Fourth report
European Community social charter
HC 509 August 1991
Fifth report
Training and Enterprise councils and vocational training
HC 285 August 1991
First special report
Recruitment practices: government reply to the second report of the committee 1990–1991
HC 406 May 1991
Second special report
Future prospects for levels of employment and unemployment: government reply to the third report of the committee 1990–1991
HC 675 October 1991
Third special report
European Community social charter: government reply is the fourth report of the committee 1990–1991
HC 676 October 1991
Fourth special report
Training and Enterprise councils and vocational training: government reply to the fifth report of the committee 1990–1991
HC 677 October 1991

Session 1991–92

Chairman Ron Leighton
First report
Employment in prisons and for ex-offenders
HC 30 November 1991

First report
Industrial change: rertaining and redeployment
HC 71 May 1992

Session 1992–93

Chairman Greville Janner
First report
Employment in the horse racing industry and the new VAT regime after 1st January 1993
HC 308 December 1992
Second report
Employment consequences of British Coal's proposed pit closures
HC 263 January 1993
First special report
Industrial change: retraining and redeployment
Government's response to the Second report of the Committee Session 1991–92
HC 219 November 1992
Second special report
Employment in the horseracing industry and the new VAT regime after 1st January 1993.
Government response to first report of the committee session 1992–1993
HC 521 March 1993
Third special report
Employment consequences of British Coals proposed pit closures. Government response to the second report of the committee session 1992–1993
HC 597 April 1993
Third report
Future of maritime skills and employment in the UK
HC 924 November 1993

Session 1993–94

Chairman Greville Janner
First report
Import and export of jobs: the future of manufacturing
HC 160 February 1994
Second report
Management of redundancies
HC 206 March 1994
First special report
Import and export of jobs: government reply to the first report of the committee session 1993–94
HC 325 April 1994
Second special report
Management of redundancies: government reply to the second report of the committee third session 1993–94
HC 400 May 1994
Third special report
The future of maritime skills and employment in the UK
HC 412 June 1994

Session 1993–94

Chairman Malcolm Thornton
First report
Common funding formula for grant maintained schools
HC 255 April 1994
Second report
Disparity in funding between primary and secondary schools
HC 45 July 1994
First special report
Government response to the fourth report of the committee session 1992–93
HC 268 March 1994
Second special report
Government response to the first report of the committee 1993–94: a common funding policy for grant maintained schools
HC 597 July 1994

fur
fair
furniture

1 Central Government

Government Departments England

Ministers of Education Secretaries of State for Education and Science and Secretary of State for Education since 1944

Ministers

Rt Hon R.A. (later Lord) Butler (President of the Board and subsequently Minister until 27.5.45)
Rt Hon Richard Law
28.5.45 to 2.8.45
Rt Hon Ellen Wilkinson
3.8.45 to 6.2.47 (died)
Rt Hon George Tomlinson
10.2.47 to 2.11.51
Rt Hon Florence Horsbrugh
3.11.51 to 17.10.54
Rt Hon Sir David (later Viscount) Eccles
18.10.54 to 12.1.57
Rt Hon Viscount Hailsham
13.1.57 to 16.9.57
Rt Hon Sir Geoffrey Lloyd
17.9.57 to 13.10.59
Rt Hon Sir David (later Viscount) Eccles
14.10.59 to 16.7.62
Rt Hon Sir Edward (later Lord) Boyle
17.7.62 to 31.3.64

Secretaries of State for Education and Science

Rt Hon Quintin Hogg (formerly Viscount Hailsham)
1.4.64 to 17.10.64
Rt Hon Michael (later Lord) Stewart
18.10.64 to 21.1.65
Rt Hon Anthony Crosland
22.1.65 to 28.8.67
Rt Hon Patrick (later Lord) Gordon-Walker
29.8.67 to 5.4.68
Rt Hon Edward Short (later Lord Glenamara)
6.4.68 to 21.6.70
Rt Hon Margaret Thatcher
22.6.70 to 4.3.74
Rt Hon Reginald Prentice
5.3.74 to 10.6.75
Rt Hon Frederick W. Mulley
11.6.75 to 10.9.76
Rt Hon Mrs Shirley Williams
11.9.76 to 4.5.79
Rt Hon Mark Carlisle
5.5.79 to 13.9.81
Rt Hon Sir Keith Joseph
14.9.81 to 20.5.86
Rt Hon Kenneth Baker
21.5.86 to 25.7.89
Rt Hon John MacGregor
26.7.89 to 1.11.90
Rt Hon Kenneth Clarke, QC
2.11.90 to 11.4.92
Rt Hon John Patten
11.4.92

1 Central Government

Secretary of State for Education

Rt Hon John Patten
6.7.92 to 19.7.94
Rt Hon Gillian Shephard
20.7.94

Department for Education

Sanctuary Bldgs, Great Smith St, London SW1P 3BT; Tel 0171-925 5000; Fax 0171-925 6000
Public Enquiry Unit 0171-925 5555
Secretary of State for Education The Rt Hon Gillian Shephard, MP
Private Secretary P. Laidlaw
Parliamentary Private Secretary George Kynoch, MP
Minister of State Eric Forth, MP
Private Secretary Carol Maye
Parliamentary Under Secretary of State Robin Squire, MP
Private Secretary D. McGrath
Parliamentary Under Secretary of State Tim Boswell, MP
Private Secretary David Walsh
Permanent Secretary of State Sir Tim Lankester, KCB
Private Secretary C. Wormald
Chief Inspector S. Sutherland Elizabeth Hse, York Rd, London SE1
Deputy Secretary J.C. Hedger
Deputy Secretary R.J. Dawe
Deputy Secretary P. Owen

Finance Branch

Finance and Accountant-General (Grade 3) R.D. Horne

Division 1

Deputy Accountant General (Grade 5) R.J. Green
Public expenditure planning and parliamentary estimates; Central government expenditure and local authority capital expenditure

Division 2

Assistant Secretary (Grade 5) J.S. Street
Local authorities expenditure; Forecasting; Education standards spending assessments and grants for education; Support and training

Division 3

Assistant Accountant General (Grade 6) T.A.H. Tyler
Government accounting

Division 4

Senior Principal (Grade 5) N.J. Thirtle
Internal audit

Division 5

Accountancy Adviser (Grade 5) P.F. Slade
(Grade 7) P. Askham
(Grade 7) P.G. Dalgleish
(Grade 7) B.M. Smart
(Grade 7) J. Stockwell
(Grade 7) S.D. James
(Grade 7) N. Blackmore
(Grade 7) L.J. McAvoy
(Grade 7) J.J. Watson
(Grade 7) R.J. Gardner
(Grade 7) S.M. Philpotts

Legal Branch

Legal Adviser (Grade 3) R.N. Ricks
Assistant Legal Adviser (Grade 5) S.T. Harker
Assistant Legal Adviser (Grade 5) F.D.W. Clarke
Assistant Legal Adviser (Grade 5) A.D. Preston
(Grade 6) A.K. Fraser
(Grade 6) N.P. Beach
(Grade 7) C.J. Hales
(Grade 7) Ms C.J. Reay
(Grade 7) A.E. Heilpern
(Grade 7) C. Manuel
(Grade 7) A.M. Goodfellow

Information Branch

Director of Information J. Coe
Head of News M. Paterson
Deputy Director of Information K.B. Kerslake

Personnel and Organisation Branch

Director of Services: Head of Personnel and Organisation (Grade 3) P.A. Shaw
Head of Personnel (Grade 4) H. Douglas
(Grade 5) I. Wilye
(Grade 5) L.B. Webb
(Grade 6) H.H. Barrick
(Grade 6) G.H.N. Evans
(Grade 7) K. Fitzgerald
(Grade 7) A.W. Wilshaw
(Grade 7) M. Lyons
SEO S.E. Cook

Analytical Services

(Grade 3) D.E. Allnutt

Information Bureau

Chief Librarian (Senior Librarian) M.H. Wilson
Deputy Librarian (Public Enquiry Section) J.L. Birch
Technical Services R.J. Walters
Information Services J. Kennedy

Statistics

Division A

Chief Statistician (Grade 5) P. Annesley
Statistician (Grade 7) M.R. Boothroyd
Statistician (Grade 7) K.N. Kew
Economic Adviser (Grade 7) J.A. Tarsh
Statistical advice concerning further and higher education: access, participation and qualifications. First employment; student income and expenditure surveys. Liaison with the HEFC and FEFC on statistical matters. Management and performance measures and co-ordination of Branch effort on non-financial modelling and projections

Division B

Chief Statistician (Grade 5) J.W. Gardner
Statistician (Grade 7) A. Barnett
Statistician (Grade 7) P.J.E. Everett
Statistician (Grade 7) R.K. Jain
Statistician (Grade 7) C. Shaw
Statistical advice concerning teachers, curriculum, examinations (including Statistical information requirements resulting from the Education Reform Act and the Parents Charter) and libraries in schools and further education; Co-ordination responsibilities in respect of evaluation of information needs and use of technology for data collection and analysis

Division C

(Grade 6) S.J. Walton
Statistician (Grade 7) S.K. Cook
Statistician (Grade 7) M.J. Davidson
Statistician (Grade 7) A. Kennedy
(Grade 7) D. Daniels

Statistical advice concerning schools, pupils, students in further and higher education, UK education statistics and International comparisons; Branch administration and Branch publications policy. Survey management and system support; Management of Branch computing system

Economics Division

Senior Economic Adviser (Grade 5) D.J. Thompson
Statistician (Grade 7) A.C. Brown
Statistician (Grade 7) A. Ball
Economic Adviser (Grade 7) M. Thompson
Statistician (Grade 7) T.C. Knight
Economics advice to the Department: on investment appraisal, cost-benefit analysis and various financial questions; Labour market indicators and performance aspects. Co-ordination of the Branch's work on performance indicators and investment

Operational Research Unit

(Grade 5) R.B. Ladley
(Grade 7) A.P. O'Connor
(Grade 7) D.L. Dyke
Operational research and financial modelling for the Department: including Rate support Grant forecasting model, Standard Spending Assessment calculations, GM Schools and CTC funding models, teacher and Departmental manpower modelling, teachers pay models and a Local Education Authority briefing system. Co-ordination of the Branch's work on expenditure monitoring, financial modelling and resource allocation modelling

Further and Higher Education; Science

Deputy Secretary (Grade 2) R.J. Dawe

Higher Education Branch

Under-Secretary (Grade 3) C.A. Clark

Funding Division

Assistant Secretary (Grade 5) S. Trundle
(Grade 7) K. Fleay
(Grade 7) S. Gane
(Grade 7) A. Smyth
SEO H. Briant
General higher education policy. University matters. Funding Policy for English HE Funding Council (HEFCE). HEFCE matters. Student numbers. Education for Architecture, Environment, Medicine, Dentistry, Social Work and Professions allied to Medicine. Oxford and Cambridge College Fees. European University Institute and other EC matters relating to HE. General research Policy in HE Institutions. British Academy. Mission drift. Engineering bursaries

Quality Division

Assistant Secretary (Grade 5) A.G. Woollard
(Grade 7) A. Callaghan
(Grade 7) S. Garner
(Grade 7) M. Spearing
SEO J. Nichol
HE Charter. Quality assurance. COMETT. Access Funds. HE/Industry links. Education for Engineering, Law, Business and Management, Mathematics and Science. Credit accumulation and transfer. Access courses. Continuing education in HE. Student welfare and accommodation. Student Unions. ERASMUS, UKCOSA

Student Support Division

Assistant Secretary (Grade 5) J. Moore
(Grade 6) C.E. Treen
(Grade 7) J.L. Spatcher
(Grade 7) D.D. Cook
SEO D.J. Capel
SEO M. Lucking
SEO N. Curley
Existing arrangements and future police on mandatory and discretionary awards in England and Wales, student loans, DFE postgraduate state studentship and bursary schemes; benefits and council tax; other general student support matters not assigned elsewhere. Students Support policy development group. Awards and Loans Group

Further Education Branch

Under-Secretary (Grade 3) D.M. Forrester

Further Education Support Unit

(Grade 4) B.D. Short
(Grade 6) E.F.H. Brittain
(Grade 6) B.J. Smeaton

Organisation and Funding Division

Assistant Secretary (Grade 5) A.M.J. Benham
(Grade 7) Vacancy
(Grade 7) P.S.J. Humfryes
(Grade 7) E. Slater
FE institutional policy and funding; FEFC matters; Relations with DE on TECs, training credits, WRFE, etc

Qualifications Division

Assistant Secretary (Grade 5) S.T. Crowne
(Grade 7) P. Bailey
(Grade 7) P. Long
(Grade 7) C. Trudgett
(Grade 7) J. Bushnell
Post-16 curriculum and qualifications in schools and FE; FE Staff development

Choice and Performance Division

(Grade 5) S.E. Kershaw
(Grade 7) P.M. Tansley
(Grade 7) C. Trudgett

Schools Command

Deputy Secretary (Grade 2) John Hedger
The Schools Command is responsible for policy in relation to the organisation of schools, including grant-maintained schools and the supply of school places; for policy on independent schools, CTCs and technology colleges; school government, funding and financial management; special education; school effectiveness; educational buildings; admissions to schools; pupil welfare; school attendance and discipline; the Parent's Charter; and school performance tables

Schools Organisation Branch

(Grade 3) M.J. Richardson
Policy on school organisation issues and the supply of school places. Grant-maintained schools policy. Outreach casework with LEAs, GM schools and their networks, religious bodies and the Government's Regional Offices. Advice and support for prospective grant-maintained schools. Relations with the Churches over voluntary schools. Capital resources for LA, VA and GM schools (distributed in the case of GM schools by the FAS). Policy on education interest in the Single Regeneration Budget (SRB). New GM and VA schools. GM clusters. Schools assets and premises issues. Policy on under 5s. Liaison with Local Authority Associations, CLEA, SEO etc. Local Government issues. Advice on school buildings issues

1 Central Government

Grant-Maintained Schools Policy Division

(Grade 5) P.J. Thorpe
Information to prospective GM schools. GM ballots. Grants to governors for costs of acquiring GM status. Grant-Maintained Schools Foundation (GMSF) Grant-Maintained Schools Advisory Committee (GMSAC)

Schools North Division

(Grade 5) A.J. Shaw
Policy on supply of school places including on statutory proposals; rationalisation of surplus place capacity. Liaison with North West, Merseyside, North East Government Offices. Schools organisation issues in these areas. Equal opportunities in school organisation issues

Schools Yorks and Midlands Division

Government Officer (Grade 5) B. Glickman
Co-ordination of liaison function: Whitehall liaison over SRB. GM disposals, transfer of assets, contracts and liabilities, sponsorship of EAB. Local Government issues. School Premises issues. Liaison with Yorks and Humberside, and East Midlands, West Midlands Government Offices. Schools organisation issues in these areas

Schools South Division

(Grade 5) J. Whitaker
Policy on and co-ordination of schools capital issues: allocation of LA and VA school capital: liaison with FAS on GM capital allocations. Co-ordination of DFE relations with the Churches. Liaison with South West and South East, Government Offices and schools organisation issues in these areas

Schools East and London Division

(Grade 5) M. Hipkins
Policy on under 5s. New GM schools and voluntary schools for religious minorities. GM clusters. Residual London issues. Liaison with Local Authority Associations. Liaison with Eastern and London. Government Office and school organisation issues in these areas

Architects and Buildings Division

(Grade 5) G.J. Parker, DipArch
Head of Section 1 (Grade 6) J.J. Wilson, DipArch
Voluntary Aided schools; ordinary school accommodation; special school accommodation; statutory requirements and accommodation standards for schools; capital expenditure advice; furniture advice
Head of Section 2 (Grade 6) M.J. Patel, BSc, CEng, FCIBSE, MIMechE
Government-funded schools; CTCs; GM; Building cost advice and data collection; engineering services and environment condition; energy efficiency; security in schools; advice to FAS
Advice on building and property aspects of Departmental policy. School Premises Regulations and constructional standards for educational buildings. Accommodation standards for educational buildings. International liaison on educational building matters (OECD/PEB)

School Curriculum Branch

(Grade 3) C.H. Saville

Primary Division

(Grade 5) S.R. Williams
(Grade 7) J. Baker
(Grade 7) R.D. Pearce
(Grade 7) J.A. Lawrence
National Curriculum: Policy and Legal framework; Primary Curriculum; English; Music; Science; Religious Education and Collective Worship; Cross-curriculur themes; School Curriculum and Assessment Authority (SCAA)

Secondary Division

(Grade 5) C.A. Bienkowska
(Grade 7) B.A. Tovey
(Grade 7) A.J. Pokorny
(Grade 7) S.A. Mellor
Secondary Curriculum; GCSE Health and Safety Education; HIV and AIDS; Personal and Social Education; Careers Education; Vocational Qualifications at 16

Assessment Division

(Grade 5) M.F. Neale
(Grade 7) I.C. Loveless
(Grade 7) R.J. Wood
(Grade 7) T. Linden
(Grade 7) G.G. Beauchamp
National Curriculum Assessment at 7, 11 and 14. History; Art; Mathematics; Geography; Modern Foreign Languages; Physical Education; Classics Heritage Education; Political Education; Human Rights; Citizenship; European awareness; Departmental Interest in Environmental Education; School books; Museums and Libraries; Curriculum complaints and exceptions. National Curriculum Publications

Technology Division

(Grade 5) R. Ritzemd
(Grade 7) D.J. Noble
(Grade 7) A.A. Partridge
(Grade 7) T.C. Tarrant
(Grade 7) S. Jetha
Technology; Information Technology in Schools; Economics; Home Economics; Business Studies; Economic and Industrial Understanding; Sex discrimination; School/industry links; Work Experience; Departmental Interest in Education/business partnerships

Pupils and Parents Branch

(Grade 3) R.L. Smith

Division A

(Grade 5) A.J. Sargent
(Grade 7) A. Short
(Grade 7) L. Chapman
(Grade 7) P. Ginger
School admissions; school performance tables; Parent's Charter; school prospectuses and annual reports; reports to parents and national records of achievement; parental involvement in schools; complaints

Division B

(Grade 5) P.A. Masters
(Grade 7) C. Barnham
(Grade 7) S.V. Dance
(Grade 7) A. Thompson
School attendance; Education Welfare Services; pupil behaviour and discipline; exclusions; crime prevention' school transport; employment of school children

Division C

(Grade 5) T.B. Jeffery
(Grade 7) P.W.L. Clough
(Grade 7) M. Sharpe
(Grade 7) C. Dowe
Grant maintained special schools; SEN code of Practice and Regulations; Independent schools; SEN aspects of the Children Act; emotional and behavioural problems

Division C2

(Grade 6) G.A. Holley
SEO J. Loosley
SEO L. Cunningham
SEO M. Pooley
SEO Mr Reynold
Health and safety of pupils; appeals under the Education Act 1981

Division D

(Grade 5) M.D. Phipps
(Grade 7) R. Mace
(Grade 7) S.A. Clarke
SEO D. Woolley
(Grade 7) Mr Ford
Education of children of Travellers, refugees, racial disadvantage and ethnic minorities, child protection; Independent schools and assisted places scheme; boarding education; education of servicemen's children; charging; school meals, milk and uniforms

Teachers, Schools Curriculum and Assessment

Deputy Secretary (Grade 2) Peter Owen
The Grade 2 post (Peter Owen) has two branches reporting to it; Schools Curriculum (Clive Saville – Grade 3); Teachers Branch (Nick Sanders – Grade 3)

Teachers Branch

Offices Sanctuary Bldgs, Great Smith St, London SW1P 3BT
(Grade 3) N.J. Sanders

Division A

(Grade 5) A.J. Wye
(Grade 7) J.C. Sheridan
SEO J.M.P. Anstey
(Grade 7) M. Barker
Policy on school, HE and FE teachers' pay and conditions of service; Salary arrangements under School Teachers' Pay and Conditions Act 1991; Teachers' misconduct regulations. Support on Teachers' Superannuation Policy

Division B

(Grade 5) S. Scales
(Grade 7) P. Swift
SEO T. Dracup
Initial Teacher Training and policy on Teacher Qualifications; the further professional development of teachers including in-service training (INSET)

Division C

(Grade 5) R. Chattaway
(Grade 7) P. Curran
SEO (Grade 7) J. Robinson
(Grade 7) N.J. Cornwell
Policy on school teacher numbers and deployment including provision for shortage subjects

International Relations, and Youth Branch

Sanctuary Bldgs, Great Smith St, London SW1P 3BT
(Grade 3) E.R. Morgan

International Relations Division

(Grade 5) C.E. Hodkinson
(Grade 7) V.A. Berkeley
(Grade 7) T. Goldman
(Grade 7) L. Hamner
(Grade 7) A.L. Bidewell
Educational aspects of EC, OECD, Council of Europe and Commonwealth activity

Youth Service Unit

(Grade 5) M. d'Armenia
(Grade 7) D. Barwick
(Grade 7) R.E. Troedson

Executive Agencies

Teachers' Pensions Agency

Mowden Hall, Staindrop Rd, Darlington DL3 9BG; Tel (01325) 460155
Chief Executive D. Metcalfe
Director of Policy and Personnel P.M. Bleasdale
Director of Finance and Business Planning D.G. Sanders
Director of Teacher Operations K.M. Miles
Director of Systems and Employer Operations A. Allison
Teachers' Superannuation Scheme policy, legislation and administration

Non-Departmental Public Bodies

Higher Education Funding Council for England (HEFCE)

Northavon Hse, Coldharbour La, Bristol BS16 1QD; Tel (0117) 931 7363; Fax (0117) 931 7463
Chairman Brandon Gough
Chief Executive Prof Graeme Davies
See Chapter 11

Further Education Funding Council (FEFC)

Cheylesmore House, Quinton Rd, Coventry CV1 2WT; Tel (01203) 863000; Fax (01203) 863100
Chairman B. Gunn
Chief Executive W. Stubbs
The FEFC was set up by the Further and Higher Education Act (1992). Its main duties are to fund colleges, to ensure that further education and training facilities in England are adequate and to assess the quality of provision. The council has nine regional committees and nine further education regional offices. The chairmen of the regional committees are: *Greater London* T. Thomas; *Northern* H. Biddle; *North West* P. Blount; *Yorkshire and Humberside* T. Bramall; *East Midlands* Dr E. Cliffe; *West Midlands* C. Darby *Eastern* P. White; *South East* H. Morris; *South West* Vacancy

Regional Committee Chairmen

Greater London Trevor Thomas, CBE
formerly Director, Unilever UK; member of the National Curriculum Council 1990-92; member of the CBI Task Force "Towards a Skills Revolution" 1989; currently a member of the CBI's Education and Training Affairs Committee and an adviser to London First
Northern Haydn Biddle
Former Managing Director, The Newcastle Breweries Limited; Chairman, Tyneside Training and Enterprise Council (TEC)
North West Peter Blount
Head of Personnel, British Aerospace Defence Limited, Dynamics Division, Lostock, Bolton; Chairman, Engineering and Manufacturing Industry Sector Group for the local Engineering Employers' Federation
Yorkshire and Humberside Terry Bramall

Chairman of Keepmoat Holdings plc, Wadworth, Doncaster; Vice-Chairman, Dearne Valley Partnership
East Midlands Dr Eric Cliffe
Chairman of Nottingham Development Enterprise; formerly Executive Director, The Boots Company plc; member of the Board of Governors, The Nottingham Trent University
Eastern Cllr Paul White
Deputy Lieutenant of the County of Essex, Member of Essex County Council for Stock (Chairman, 1989-92); farmer and Company Director
South East Harry Morris, CBE
formerly Director and Chief Executive, Sheerness Steel Company plc
South West Vacancy
West Midlands Charles Darby
Chairman of Bass Taverns and Director of Bass Plc, Chairman of Birmingham TEC

Funding Agency for Schools

Albion Wharf, Skeldergate, York YO1 2XL; Tel (01904) 661661; Fax (01904) 661684
Chief Executive Mike Collier
Planning Director Sandy Adamson
Finance Director John Codling
Director of Personnel and Services Judith Craggs
Grants Director David Halladay
Financial Controller Derek McMahon
Board Secretary Jane Thornhill
Head of Communications Roger Witts
The Funding Agency for Schools is a Non-Departmental Public Body which is responsible for the calculation and payment of recurrent and capital grants to grant-maintained schools, the financial monitoring of grant-maintained schools carrying out value-for-money studies into grant-maintained schools and the planning and provision of school places in certain local education areas. It is accountable to the Secretary of State for Education and, through her, to Parliament. It is run by a Board of up to 15 members appointed by the Secretary of State and operates through a structure of committees, each of which has a clearly defined role and responsibilities

Office for Standards in Education (OFSTED)

Elizabeth Hse, York Rd, London SE1 7PH; Tel 0171-925 6800; Fax 0171-927 6707
Her Majesty's Chief Inspector of Schools (England) C.A. Woodhead
Director of Administration T. Flesher
Finance, tenders, contracts, registration, information, information technology, personnel, management, competition and compliance
Director of Inspection A.C. Millett
Responsible for the development of the policy framwork within which OFSTED will carry out tasks remitted to HMCI by the Secretary of State; the provision of advice on the quality of education, standards achieved, the efficient use of resources, and the spiritual, moral, social and cultural development of pupils; the implementation of legislation related to registered inspectors; the interrogation and evaluation of inspection evidence from HMI and registered inspectors; the direction of the use of HMI manpower through the inspection programme in line with HMCI's responsibilities; the introduction of new professional working arrangements as required; international comparisons and research; external relations
Deputy Director of Inspection M.J. Tomlinson
Responsible for policy matters: post-16 curriculum and assessment including 'A', AS' levels and GNVQs; links with FEFC and NCVQ; monitoring Registered Inspectors; independent schools, CTCs, SCEA, COBISEC, and European Schools; links with HEFCE; teachers' pay and conditions, appraisal of teachers
Deputy Director of Inspection A.J. Rose
Responsible for policy matters including the curriculum 3-16 and its assessment; links with SCAA; training and assessment of Independent Inspectors; territorial teams; primary phase matters including early years and nursery education; special educational needs; equal opportunities for inner cities; educational disadvantage; urban funding; multi-cultural education, including section 11 grant
Competition and Compliance Team C. Bramley
Competition issues; OFSTED point of contact with other Government Departments, judicial review and appeals procedures; Citizen's Charter; complaints
Curriculum and Assessment Team T. Wylie
Curriculum and assessment 3–16, reporting systems and public examinations up to 16; SCAA and examination bodies
Equal Opportunities and Access Team B.E. Fawcett
Education of pupils from ethnic minority groups, use of Section II and Section 210 funding; educational disadvantage including: school attendance and truancy; exclusions and 'education otherwise'; education in secure training units and juvenile justice and gifted pupils;
External Relations Team P. Singh
Developing OFSTED's relationships with external bodies such as heads, teachers, Independent Inspectors, LEAs, the DFE, SCAA, governors etc. International work
Finance Team B.G. Townsend
Finance, tendering and contracts
Independent, International and Island Schools Team B.J. Lewis
Independent schools (including CTCs), SCEA, COBISEC, European and Island schools
Information Systems Team M.L. Childs
Provision of IS systems and services to OFSTED
Information Team J. Lawson
Media relations, publicity and most external communications issues. Liaison with Heads of Information of other government departments
Management Team C.J. Payne
Staff pay, travel and subsistence, superannuation and terms and conditions of service, Training and Development; Welfare; Industrial Relations
Monitoring Team D.I. Shelton
Monitoring standards of the work of Registered Inspectors; re-registration
Personnel Team J.M. Phillips
Personnel matters of OfSTED staff
Post-Compulsory Education Team D.L. West
Quality, efficiency and standards of 16–19 education in schools, adult education and youth work; assessment and curriculum post 16; careers education and guidance, education in prisons; liaison with FEFC, NCVQ, SCCA, GCE boards, vocational awarding bodies, the National Youth Bureau and other appropriate bodies
Quality Assurance and Development Team A.P. Matthews
Schools Framework for Inspection and the Handbook for Inspection; PIs for education including value for money indicators; QA issues
Registration Team J. Grewe
Registrar
Research and Analysis Team D.E. Soulsby
Managing and using the database generated by inspections carried out by HMI and Registered Inspectors
Resource Planning Team D.W. Taylor
Assessing and advising on the efficiency, economy and effectiveness of OFSTED's operational work
Schools at Risk E.L. Passmore
Advice HMCI and DFE on schools deemed by RgIs to be failing; monitor action plans and performance of schools failing; liaise and advise educational associations/LEAs/ Appropriate Authorities charged with improving schools deemed as failing
Special Education Needs Team D.H. Chorley
Standards and quality of SEN provision in special schools in maintained, non-maintained, and independent sectors; advising DFE on approvals and appeals; reorganisation and responses from LEAs and the 1993 Act, especially the Code of Practice
Teacher Education Team V. Green

Reporting on initial teacher training in order to advise DFE, SoS, CATE and HEFCE; teacher supply; induction and INSET of teachers
Territorial Team R.J. Brake
Provision in regions including the work of LEAs, the Funding Agency for Schools (FAS); GEST funded projects; school reorganisations and applications for self-governing (GM) status; school governors and involvement of parents
Training and Assessment of Independent Inspectors Team E.I. Pagliacci
The organisation of provision of training for and assessment of independent inspectors

Inspectors

J.C. Andreae; P. Armitage; W.G. Bakehouse; C.A. Baker; E.M. Baker; M. Banbury; C. Banks; J.M. Barnes; J. Bennetts; N. Blackett; S.B. Blatton; C.M. Bond; M.T. Boyd-Clarke; M.H. Bradley; T.E. Brand; M.E. Brooks; M.A. Buckingham; M.J. Buckley; P.N. Bufton; K. Bull; D.R. Butler; P. Candlish; M.S. Christie; C.R. Clark; G. Clay; R.S.W. Clements; D.A. Coe; J.E.M. Cohn; B. Colbeck; M. Coleman; M.J. Collier; M.A. Cooke; J. Cooper; P. Cradock; G.K. Crawford; M. Cribb; O. Cupid; B.J. Cusdin; C.M. Davies; P.A. Davies; R.V. Davis; P.W. Dougill; R.G. Dyke; K.H. Dyson; M.E. Eade; C. Elliott; L.J. Ellis; P.S. Friend; C.C. Frost; D. Gardiner; K. Gilbert; J.M. Giles; G.A. Gill; C. Goodhead; C. Goulding; D.I. Grant; N.M.J. Green; N. Grenyer; P. Griffiths; S. Grounds; F. Hadley; D.J. Halligan; N.J. Hallmark; J.A. Hamer; P.G. Hancock; S.C. Hands; J.S. Hardwick; S.M. Harrison; R. Hartley; J.M. Hibbs; E.M. Hill; I.A.E. Hill; D. Hinchliffe; D.G. Holford; T. Holland; M.H. Hollingsworth; J.R. Holmes; M.J. Horn; J.E. Hosegood; B.A.F. Hubbard; V.C. Hughes; P.F.J. Irvine; A.R. Ivatts; M.J. Ive; R.K. James; P.W.R. Johnson; H.B. Joicey; B. Jones; M.E. Jones; P.R. Jones; G.N. Kanji; R. Kapadia; A.C. Keelan-Towner; M. Kerrigan; T.J. Key; M.A. Khan; B.L. King; D. Knighton; J.B. Knox; E.J.M. Layson; A.W. Littlewood; W.K.G. Lloyd; R. Long; P.A. Lowe; T.L. Lusty; S. Lyons; M.E. Madden; J.P. Maddick; M.M. Martin; W.P. Massam; J.E. Mattick; E.M. McAndrew; B. McCafferty; D.C. McIntosh; J.D. McKenley; M. McLaughlin; T. McLaughlin; G.W. McLeman; H.P. McVeigh; J.I. Mills; J.A. Mokades; D. Moon; D.L. Moore; K.J. Morgan; S.H. Morris; A.M. Mukhopadhyay; A.A.H. Murrell; P. Muschamp; G.I. Oldham; S. O'Sullivan; R.L. Page-Jones; J.M. Parsons; E.A. Pollard; R.D. Ponchaud; M.R. Potter; C.P. Power; M.P. Pryce; C.J. Redman; J. Reeves; A.W. Reid; J.D. Reid; J.C. Richardson; B. Roberts; A.S. Robertson; I.A. Rodger; S.J.A. Rogers; M.C. Rosen; C. Rowe; J. Sartain; D.J. Scott; S.M. Scott; G.W. Searle; R.V.L. Shannon; R. Shippam; K.A. Shooter; D.E. Simmonds; D. Singleton; P.R. Smith; J.D. Stannard; O. Stannard; M.M. Stone; R. Storrs; N. Straker; M.E. Stride; D.P. Swain; A. Sykes; A.M. Tapsfield; J.A. Taylor; M.D. Thirkell; M.E. Thomas; D.L. Thorburn; J. Tierney; D.S. Tobin; P.N. Toft; E. Tombs; B.D. Tomkins; J.E. Trickey; G.C. Turner; T. Turner; N.G. Warwick; J.M. Watson; M.R. Webb; R.R. Weir; K.J. Wheeldon; R. Whitburn; F. Whiteman; A. Whitlam; S.M. Wiles; J.R. Williams; M.H. Williamson; R.D. Woods; J.I. Wragg; D. Wynne; A.P. Yeomans

Specialist Advisers

Art P.R. Jones
Educational Technology G. Goldstein
Education Years R-6 C.M. Richards
Education Years 7–11 R.C. Frost
English M.J. Convey
Geography and Environmental Education P.R. Smith
History and Political Education J.A. Hamer
Mathematics K. Cross
Modern Languages A. Dobson
Music Vacancy
Physical and Outdoor Education G. Clay
Religious Education J.I. Wragg
Science C. Gould
Spiritual, Moral, Social and Cultural Education, Including PSE D.R. Trainor
Technology M.J. Ive

School Curriculum and Assessment Authority

The work of the School Curriculum and Assessment Authority is governed by sections 244 and 245 of, and Schedule 14 to, the Education Act 1993, and section 20 of the Education Reform Act 1988 (as amended by the 1993 Act). The Authority's long-term responsibilities, in the main, cover England only. It liaises closely with the Curriculum and Assessment Authority for Wales/Awdurdod Cwricwlwm ac Asesu Cymru (ACAC), established in April 1994, on issues of mutual interest
Newcombe Hse, 45 Notting Hill Gate, London W11 3JB; Tel 0171-229 1234; Fax 0171-229 8526
Chairman Sir Ron Dearing, CB
Chief Executive Dr Nicholas Tate
Assistant Chief Executive for Key Stage 1 Judith Morris
Assistant Chief Executive for Key Stage 2 Chris Jones
Assistant Chief Executive for Key Stage 3 John Hamer
Assistant Chief Executive for Key Stage 4 Keith Weller
Assistant Chief Executive for 16–19 Education Geoff Lucas
Assistant Chief Executive for Communications Tony Millns
Assistant Chief Executive for Finance and Personnel Bill Scott
The School Curriculum and Assessment Authority exists: to help to raise the level of educational achievement, particularly through work on the development of the National Curriculum and the associated assessment arrangements; to involve teachers in SCAA's work on the development of the National Curriculum and the arrangements for its assessment, to try to ensure the acceptability of the Authority's proposals in the classroom; and to manage efficiently the flow of information to schools about the curriculum and assessment, and to ensure that it is clear and on time
SCAA's Statutory Functions
The general functions of the School Curriculum and Assessment Authority as set out in section 254(1) of the Education Act 1993 are: a. to keep under review all aspects of the curriculum for maintained schools in England and all aspects of school examinations and assessment;
b. to advise the Secretary of State on such matters concerned with the curriculum for maintained schools in England or with school examinations and assessment as she may refer to the Authority or as the Authority may see fit;
c. to advise the Secretary of State on, and, if so requested by her, assist her to carry out, programmes of research and development for purposes connected with the curriculum for maintained schools in England or with school examinations and assessment;
d. to publish and disseminate, and assist in the publication and dissemination of, information relating to the curriculum for maintained schools in England or to school examinations and assessment;
e. to make arrangements with appropriate bodies for ensuring the quality of assessments made in pursuance of assessment arrangements;
f. to advise the Secretary of State on the exercise of her powers under section 5(1) of the Education Reform Act 1988 (approval of external qualifications)
g. to advise the Secretary of State on such other matters connected with the provision of education in maintained schools in England, or in non-maintained special schools there, as the Secretary of State may specify by order;
h. to carry out such ancillary activities as the Secretary of State may direct

Further Education Unit

From 1st April 1995 the FEU will combine with the staff college to become FEDA (Further Education Development Association)
Citadel Pl, Tinworth St, London SE11 5EH; Tel 0171-962 1280; Fax 0171-962 1266
Chairman Allan Ainsworth
Chief Officer Geoff Stanton
Deputy Chief Officer Mike Granger

1 Central Government

The Further Education Unit (FEU) is an advisory, intelligence and development body for the further education sector. Its general purpose is to promote quality in further education by encouraging the development of more effective, relevent and flexible learning opportunities for individual learners. FEU undertakes a wide range of activities through its central and regional officers, and works closely with other national training and education agencies

FEU manages research and development projects that draw on the experience of the FE system, as well as contributing to the national debate on post-16 education by its membership of national and regional steering groups, advisory committees and working parties

Guidance, advice and information is offered to the field through publications, newletters and shorter bulletins. Funded by the FEFC

Teacher Training Agency

(Due to move to new premises)
Sanctuary Bldgs, Great Smith St, London SW1P 3BT; Tel 0171-925 5992
Chief Executive Vacancy

Special Educational Needs Tribunal

71 Victoria St, London SW1H OHW; Tel 0171-925 6925; Fax 0171-925 6926

The Special Educational Needs Tribunal was set up by the Education Act 1993. It considers parents' appeals against the decisions of Local Education Authorities (LEAs) about a child's special educational needs, where the parents cannot reach agreement with the LEA

Department of Employment

Caxton Hse, Tothill St, London SW1H 9NF; Tel 0171-273 3000; Telex 915564 DEPEMP; GTN 273 3000
Secretary of State for Employment Rt Hon Michael Portillo, MBE, MP
Parliamentary Private Secretary Nigel Evans
Parliamentary Private Secretary Julian Brazier, MP
Special Adviser Alison Broom
Private Secretary Peter Wanless
Private Secretary Jenny Curtis
Minister of State Ann Widdecombe
Private Secretary Simon Wood
Parliamentary Private Secretary Angela Browning
Parliamentary Under-Secretary James Paice, MP
Private Secretary Ann McNicholl
Parliamentary Under-Secretary Philip Oppenheim
Private Secretary Carolyn Pride
Permanent Secretary Sir Nick Monck, KCB
Private Secretary Katie Driver
Parliamentary Clerk Marilyn East
Chief Librarian Duncan Aitchison
East La, Runcorn WA7 2DN; Tel (01928) 715151; Telex GTN 4197 5151
Moorfoot, Sheffield S1 4PQ; Tel (0114) 275 3275

Press Office

Tel 0171-273 4977

Public Enquiry Point

Tel 0171-273 6969

Department of Health

Richmond Hse, 79 Whitehall, London SW1A 2NS; Tel 0171-210 3000
Secretary of State for Health and Chairman of the NHS Policy Board The Rt Hon Virginia Bottomley, JP, MP
Minister of State (Minister for Health) Gerald Malone, MP
Parliamentary Under-Secretary of State The Hon Thomas Sackville, MP
Parliamentary Under-Secretary of State John Bowis, OBE, MP
Parliamentary Under-Secretary of State Baroness Cumberlege, CBE
Permanent Secretary Graham Hart, CB

Department of Social Security

Richmond Hse, 79 Whitehall, London SW1A 2NS; Tel 0171-210 3000; Telex 883669
Secretary of State for Social Security The Rt Hon Peter Lilley, MP
Minister of State for Social Security and Disabled People The Rt Hon William Hague, MP
Parliamentary Under-Secretary of State James Arbuthnot, MP
Parliamentary Under-Secretary of State Alistair Burt, MP
Parliamentary Under-Secretary of State Roger Evans, MP
Permanent Secretary (Social Security) Sir Michael Partridge, KCB

Department of Trade and Industry

Education and Training Branch

Enterprise Initiative Division 2, Bay 547, Kingsgate Hse, 68–74 Victoria St, London SW1E 6SW; Tel 0171-215 2859
Head Mrs E. Ryle

The Patent Office (An Executive Agency of the Department of Trade and Industry)

Cardiff Rd, Newport, Gwent NP9 1RH; Tel (01633) 814000
Comptroller General P.R.S. Hartnack

Home Office

50 Queen Anne's Gate, London SW1H 9AT; Tel 0171-273 3000; Fax 0171-273 2190
Secretary of State for the Home Office Department The Rt Hon Michael Howard, QC, MP
Minister of State Rt Hon Baroness Blatch, CBE
Minister of State Michael Forsyth, MP
Minister of State David Maclean, MP
Parliamentary Under-Secretary of State Nicholas Baker, MP
Permanent Under-Secretary of State R.T.J Wilson, CB

The Home Office is particularly concerned with the administration of justice; criminal law; the treatment of offenders by the police, prison and probation service; immigration and nationality; passport policy matters; community relations; fire and emergency planning. Other subjects dealt with include electoral arrangements, ceremonial and formal business connected with honours; requests for extradition of criminals; grant of licences for animals (scientific procedures); cremations, burials and exhumations; firearms; dangerous drugs and poisons; general policy on laws relating to shops; liquor licensing; gaming and lotteries; theatre and cinema licensing; co-ordination of government action in relation to voluntary social services, race relations and sex discrimination policy. The following Divisions are of educational interest within the Prison Service.
Located at Cleland Hse, Page St, London SW1P 4LN; Tel 0171-217 3000; Fax 0171-217 6635

Chief Education Officer's Branch

Chief Education Officer I.G. Benson
Principal Education Officer D. Marston
Principal Education Officer A. Brown
Principal Education Officer P. Blunt
Principal Education Officer D. Edwards
Principal Education Officer A. Harris
Principal Education Officer J. Temple

NVQ Development Team

NVQ Development Co-ordinator P.J. Rudgard
NVQ Development Officer D. Chinnock
NVQ Development Officer B. Case
NVQ Development Officer C. Gosden
NVQ Development Officer N. Tattersall
NVQ Development Officer A. Town

Physical Education Branch

Chief Physical Education Officer M.W. Denton

Ministry of Agriculture, Fisheries and Food

Postgraduate Agricultural and Food Studentship Scheme
Room 105, Nobel Hse, Smith Sq, London SW1P 3JR; Tel 0171-238 5598
Head of Branch P.R. Apsey
Secretary C. Barker

Foreign and Commonwealth Office

3*Office* King Charles St, London SW1A 2AH; Tel 0171-270 1500
Permanent Under-Secretary of State and Head of the Diplomatic Service Sir John Coles, KCMG

Cultural Relations Department, Foreign and Commonwealth Office

Old Admiralty Bldg, Whitehall, London SW1A 2AF; Tel 0171-210 6281
Superintending Under-Secretary C.R. Battiscombe, CMG
Head of Department A.D. Sprake
Assistant A. Lewis

Ministry of Defence

Whitehall, London SW1 2HB; Tel 0171-218 9000

Educational and Training Services (ARMY)

Worthy Down, Winchester, Hants SO21 2RG; Tel (01962) 880880 Ext 2661
Officers Education, Soldiers Education and Language Training; Tel: (01962) 880880 Ext 2680
Service Childrens Education Authority; Tel: (01962) 880880 Ext 2966

Flag Officer Training and Recruiting Commander Education and Resettlement

Victory Bldg, HM Naval Base, Portsmouth, Hants PO1 3LS; Tel (01705) 727641

Air Officer Commanding and Air Officer Commanding Training Group

Bldg 255, RAF Innsworth, Glos GL3 1EZ; Tel (01452) 712612

Civilian Management (Training) Division

Ministry of Defence, Empress State Bldg, Lillie Rd, London SW6 1TR; Tel 0171-824 4444 Ext 3072

Department of National Heritage

2–4 Cockspur St, London SW1Y 5DH; Tel 0171-211; Fax 0171-211
Secretary of State for National Heritage The Rt Hon Stephen Dorrell, MP
Private Secretary J. Kingman
Parliamentary Private Secretary Giles Brandreth, MP
Parliamentary Under-Secretary of State Iain Sproat, MP
Private Secretary N. Mackenzie
Parliamentary Under-Secretary of State Viscount Astor
Private Secretary L. Sweet
Lady-in-Waiting Baroness Trumpington
Private Secretary C. Sheridan
Parliamentary Clerk C. Hutson
Permanent Secretary (Grade 1) Hayden Phillips
Private Secretary C. Pillmen

Libraries, Galleries and Museums Group

Head of Group (Grade 3) M. O'Mara
Head of Libraries and Information Services Division (Grade 5) P. Bolt
Director, British Library St Pancras Project (Grade 5) R. Pardey
Head of Museums and Galleries Division (Grade 5) P. Gregory
Director, Government Art Collection (Grade 6) Dr Wendy Baron
Head of Cultural Property Unit (Grade 7) C. Morrison

1 Central Government

Arts, Sports and Lottery Group

Head of Group (Grade 3) A. Ramsay
Head of Arts (Grade 5) N. Kroll
Head of National Lottery Division (Grade 5) S. MacDonald
Head of Sports and Recreation Division (Grade 5) A. Stewart

Broadcasting and Media Group

Head of Group (Grade 3) P. Wright
Head of Broadcasting Policy Division (Grade 5) S. Booth
Head of Media Division (Grade 5) P. Edwards

Heritage and Tourism Group

Head of Group (Grade 3) D. Chesterton
Head of Heritage Division (Grade 5) A. Comer
Head of Royal Estate Division (Grade 5) P. Douglas
Head of Tourism Division (Grade 5) J. Evans

Information

Head of Information (Grade 5) A. MacLean

Other Government and Public Offices England

Commission for Racial Equality

Elliot Hse, 10–12 Allington St, London SW1E 5EH; Tel 0171-828 7022; Fax 0171-630 7605
Principal Officer (Education) Philip Barnett

Equal Opportunities Commission

Overseas Hse, Quay St, Manchester M3 3HN; Tel 0161-833 9244; Fax 0161-835 1657
Chair Kamlesh Bahl
Chief Executive Peter Naish
Director of Development: Education and Training Brenda Hancock

Press Office

Swan Hse, 53 Poland St, London W1V 3DF; Tel 0171-287 3953

Forestry Commission

Office 231 Corstorphine Rd, Edinburgh EH12 7AT; Tel 0131-334 0303; Fax 0131-334 4473
Chief Education, Safety and Training Officer W. MacLachlan

National Council for Vocational Qualifications (NCVQ)

222 Euston Rd, London NW1 2BZ; Tel 0171-387 9898
Chairman Michael Heron
Chief Executive J. Hillier
The National Council for Vocational Qualifications provides the framework of National Vocational Qualifications (NVQs) through which everyone at work can be assessed against national agreed standards. NCVQ also offers vocational education through General National Vocational Qualifications (GNVQs) – preparing students for work or higher education. Through its accreditation and monitoring procedures, NCVQ sets the seal on the standards established for occupations. As a result, NVQs are recognised as hallmarks of achievement within each sector, ensuring that employees at every level can gain the recognition they need for a successful and fulfilling career – and can transfer skills to new jobs. Britain urgently needs a more skilled an qualified workforce. The NVQ framework is helping to meet that need

Office of Population Censuses and Surveys

St Catherine's Hse, 10 Kingsway, London WC2B 6JP; Tel 0171-242 0262
Training Manager Miss J.A. Higgins
Press and Publicity Officer Miss S. Wallace
Divisions: Registration; Census; Health Statistics; Population Statistics division; Social Survey; Information Technology; National Health Service Central Register; Finance, Personnel and Administration; Data Services Division; Marketing

Ombudsmen

Commission for Local Administration in England (The Local Government Ombudsmen)

21 Queen Anne's Gate, London SW1H 9BU; Tel 0171-915 3210; Fax 0171-233 0396; DX2376 Victoria 1
Chairman of the Commission and Local Government Ombudsman for Greater London, Surrey, Kent, East Sussex and West Sussex Edward Osmotherly, CB
Local Government Ombudsman for East Anglia; the South West, the West, the South and most of Central England Vacancy The Oaks, Westwood Way, Westwood Business Pk, Coventry CV4 8JB; Tel (01203) 695999; Fax (01203) 695902; DX 702110 Coventry 6
Vice Chairman of the Commission and Local Government Ombudsman for the East Midlands and the North of England Patricia Thomas Beverley Hse, 17 Shipton Rd, York YO3 6FZ; Tel (01904) 630151; Fax (01904) 624058; DX65201 York 5
The Commission, established under the Local Government Act 1974, investigates complaints from citizens alleging injustice caused by maladministration by local authorities. There are three Local Commissioners (Local Government Ombudsmen) each of whom investigates complaints arising in a particular area of the country. A free booklet about the service is called 'Complaint About the Council? How to complain to the Local Government Ombudsman', available from council offices, citizens advice bureaux or direct from the Commission's offices. The Local Government Ombudsmen can investigate complaints about certain education matters. Education matters form about 6% of the total number of complaints received and about 11% of reports issued by the Ombudsmen. Reports of investigations of education complaints are available from the Commission's offices in London

Health Service Commissioners for England, Scotland and Wales

Church Hse, Great Smith St, London SW1P 3BW; Tel 0171-276 2035
Commissioner W.K. Reid, CB

Office of Public Service and Science

Part of the Cabinet Office, and incorporating the Recruitment and Assessment Services Agency and the Office of the Civil Service Commissioners. Alencon Link, Basingstoke Hants, Tel (0256) 29222
Horse Guards Rd, London SW1P 3AL; Tel 0171-270 6000
Permanent Secretary Sir Robin Butler, KCB, CVO
First Commissioner J. Holroyd

Overseas Development Administration

94 Victoria St, London SW1E 5JL; Tel 0171-917 7000
Abercrombie Hse, Eaglesham Rd, East Kilbride, Glasgow G75 8EA; Tel (0135 52) 411
Overseas Development Natural Resources Institute, Chatham Maritime, Chatham, Kent ME4 4TB; Tel (01634) 880088
Permanent Secretary J.M.M. Vereker, CB
Deputy Secretary R.M. Ainscow
Under-Secretary (Africa) B.R. Ireton
Under-Secretary (Asia, and Pacific) J.V. Kerby
Under-Secretary (International) N.B. Hudson
Under-Secretary (Establishment) P.O.M. Freeman
Under-Secretary (Finance) R.G.M. Manning
Under-Secretary (Joint Assistance Unit, Latin America, Carribean, Atlantic, Centraland Eastern Europe) J.A.L. Faint
Chief Natural Resources Adviser A.J. Bennett
Chief Economist J.B. Wilmshurst
Chief Engineering Adviser J.W. Hodges
Chief Health and Population Adviser Dr D.N. Nabarro
Chief Education Adviser M.A. Harrison
Head of Section – Education J. Butler
Senior Education Adviser Dr D. Pennycuick
Senior Education Adviser D.G. Swift
Senior Education Adviser M.A. Seath
Senior Technical Education Adviser Dr C. Lewis
Senior Technical Education Adviser Dr G.R.H. Jones
Senior Education Adviser (Bangkok) M.D. Francis

The Post Office Education Service

4m Fl, White Rose Hse, 28a York Pl, Leeds LS1 2EZ; Tel (01532) 444128
Staff 193,000
Turnover £5345 million

Post Office Education Resources (Film and Video Library)

PO Box 145, Sittingbourne, Kent ME10 1NH; Tel (01795) 426465; Fax (01795) 474871
National Education Manager M. Foley
Contact B. Wiles

Sea Fish Industry Authority

18 Logie Mill, Logie Green Rd, Edinburgh EH7 4HG; Tel 0131-558 3331; Fax 0131-558 1442; Telex 727225

Service Children's Education Authority (SCEA)

UK Headquarters Organisation

Service Children's Education Authority (SCEA), HQ Director General Adjutant General's Corps, Worthy Down, Winchester, Hampshire SO21 2RG; Tel (01962) 887965; Fax (01962) 887963
Controller GP Capt C. Cho-Young
Deputy Controller 1 Wg Cdr P. Reynolds
SCEA 1A Advice to parents on UK and SCEA schools, advice and support to parents on boarding school matters, Extra Command area schools, School/community relations, SCEA Bulletin
Deputy Controller 2 Ms S. Coward, BA
SCEA 2A/B National Curriculum and resources, HMI Inspections, Advisory service, INSET, Careers Service, Public exams, UK/LEA and other agencies liaison, Early Years
Deputy Controller 3 M.H. Smith
SCEA 3A Primary teacher recruitment; SCEA 3B Secondary teacher recruitment; SCEA 3C Recruitment and Personnel management of teachers; SCEA 3D Finance and resources/Admin and Registry. General enquiries

Schools Controlled by Service Children's Schools (NWE)

Commander Education Brigadier P.A. Tuffnell, BSc, MSc(Econ) HQ British Army of the Rhine, (BAOR) BFPO 140
Chief Executive, Service Children's Schools NW Europe I.S. Mitchelson, MA
Deputy Chief Executive I. Forest
Service Children's Schools (North West Europe) now forms part of a Defence Support Agency locally administered to SCEA policy and caters for children of Service personnel stationed in the Federal Republic of Germany, Berlin, Belgium, The Netherlands, Sardinia, and is responsible for 74 primary schools (16,594 pupils); 7 middle schools (2,268 pupils); 7 secondary comprehensive schools (3 day and 3 day/boarding) (5,018 pupils)

Secondary, Day and Boarding Schools

Edinburgh (486) Münster
Prince Rupert (751) Rinteln
Windsor School (1,545) Rheindahlen

Secondary Day Schools

Gloucester (582) Hohne
The Havel (502) Berlin
King's (1,066) Gutersloh

Schools Administered by the Service Children's Education Authority

Belize and Falkland Islands

SCEA caters for children of Service personnel stationed in Belize and Falkland Islands in 2 small primary schools (30 pupils)

Cyprus

Commander Education Lieutenant Colonel C. Martindill, AGC(ETS) HQ British Forces, Cyprus, BFPO 53
SCEA caters for children of Service personnel stationed in Cyprus and is responsible for 7 primary schools, (1,170 pupils) and 2 secondary comprehensive day schools (485 pupils)

Secondary Day Schools

St John's (312) Episkopi
King Richard (173) Dhekelia

Gibraltar

Officer in Charge of Service Children's Schools Commander B.R. Davies, BSc, RN Queensway, Gibraltar, BFPO 52
SCEA caters for children of Service personnel stationed in Gibraltar and is responsible for 1 first/middle school (679 pupils)

Hong Kong

Commander Education Lieutenant Colonel K.O. Winfield, MA, AGC(ETS) HQ British Forces, Hong Kong, BFPO 1
SCEA caters for children of Service personnel stationed in Hong Kong, Brunei and Nepal and is responsible for 8 primary schools (1,172 pupils) and 1 secondary comprehensive day school (438 pupils)

Secondary Comprehensive Day School

St George's (438) Hong Kong

Naples and Denmark

Command Education Officer Wing Commander WG. Cdr D. Skinner, TSE2 HQPTC RAF Innsworth, Glos GL3 1EZ

SCEA caters for children of Service personnel stationed in Naples, Oslo and Denmark and is responsible for 3 primary schools (163 pupils)

Other Government and Public Offices Wales

Equal Opportunities Commission

Caerwys Hse, Windsor La, Cardiff CF1 1LB; Tel (01222) 343552; Fax (01222) 641079

Ombudsmen

Commission for Local Administration in Wales

Local Ombudsman E.R. Moseley

Other Government and Public Offices Scotland

Equal Opportunities Commission

Stock Exchange Hse, 7 Mandela Pl, Glasgow G2 1QW; Tel 0141-248 5833; Fax 0141-248 5834

Ombudsmen

Commissioner for Local Administration in Scotland

23 Walker St, Edinburgh EH3 7HX; Tel 0131-225 5300; Fax 0131-225 9495

Commissioner Frederick C. Marks, OBE

Other Government and Public Offices Northern Ireland

Department of Agriculture for Northern Ireland

Dundonald Hse, Upper Newtownards Rd, Belfast BT4 3SB; Tel (01232) 524618; Fax (01232) 659856

Education, Training and Technology Services

Senior Deputy Chief Agricultural Officer T. McCluggage, BAgr, NDP

Inspector (Grade 1) C.I. Titterington, BAgr, DipAgrComm

Staff Officer Mrs M. Savage

Ombudsmen

Office of the Northern Ireland Commissioner for Complaints

33 Wellington Pl, Belfast BT1 6HN; Tel (01232) 233821

Commissioner for Complaints J. McIvor, CBE, QSM, LLB(Hons)

The Commissioner investigates complaints made by persons who claim to have sustained injustice in consequence of maladministration in connection with the administrative actions of local authorities and certain public bodies specified in the Commissioner for Complaints Act (NI) 1969

Government Departments Wales

The Welsh Office

New Crown Bldg, Cathays Pk, Cardiff CF1 3NQ; Tel (01222) 825111

Secretary of State for Wales The Rt Hon John Redwood, MP

Private Secretary (Grade 5) K. Jennings

Parliamentary Under-Secretary of State Rod Richards, MP

Health, Education, Social Services, Welsh Language

Private Secretary M. Parkinson

Parliamentary Under-Secretary of State Gwilym Jones, MP

Agriculture, transport, forrestry, conservation, youth

Private Secretary V.R. Watkin

Personal Secretary R. Meechan

Head of Education Department (Grade 3) S.H. Martin

Parliamentary Clerk (London office) A. Green

Press Officer (Senior Information Officer) (London Office) A. Thompson, MBE

Responsibility in Wales for ministerial functions relating to health and personal social services; education except for terms and conditions of service of teachers, and for student awards; the Welsh language, arts and culture; local government; housing; water and sewerage; environmental protection; sport; agriculture and fisheries; forestry; land use, including town and country planning; countryside and nature conservation; new towns; ancient monuments and historic buildings; roads; tourism; training and the careers service; financial assistance to industry; urban programme in Wales; operations of the European Regional Development Fund in Wales and other European Community matters; non-departmental public bodies; civil emergencies and all financial aspects of these matters including Welsh support grant; Oversight of economic affairs and regional planning in Wales

London: Gwydyr Hse, Whitehall, London SW1A 2ER; Tel 0171-270 3000; Fax 0171-270 0561

Education Department

Government Bldgs, Ty-Glas Rd, Llanishen, Cardiff CF4 SWE; Tel (01222) 761456; Fax (01222) 761256

Head of Education Department (Grade 3) S.H. Martin Cathays Pk, Cardiff CF1 3NQ; Tel (01222) 825111

Schools Curriculum Division

(Grade 5) R.J. Davies
(Grade 7) E.K. Davies
(Grade 7) C. Peat
(Grade 7) M. Richards
All matters relating to the National Curriculum in Wales, including its assessment arrangements and GCSE/A levels; and arrangements for in-service teacher training

Schools Administration Division

(Grade 5) W.G. Davies
(Grade 7) D.A. Bullen
(Grade 7) J. Booker
(Grade 7) B. Dare
SEO A.M. Jones
All matters relating to maintained (including grant maintained) and independent schools in Wales, except National Curriculum Examinations and qualification matters; School closure and reorganisation; Information for parents; School transport; Admissions; Local management of schools; School Government; Grant maintained schools; Special education needs; Independent schools; Assisted places scheme; School inspection; Voluntary aided schools; School building matters

Further and Higher Education

(Grade 5) H. Evans
Further and higher education policy; Sponsorship of the Further and Higher Education funding Councils for Wales; Student Access funds; Tuition fees and other student matters; Supply and initial training of teachers

Culture and Recreation Division

(Grade 5) Dr H.F. Rawlings
(Grade 7) G.R. Jones
(Grade 7) D.M. Rolph
(Grade 7) Dr E. Roberts
Welsh language; Libraries; Museums; Broadcasting; Arts; Youth matters; Sport and active recreation; Co-ordination of Education Department PES; Co-ordination of Welsh Office interests in National Lottery Bill

Office of Her Majesty's Chief Inspector (Wales) (OHMCI)

Phase 1, Government Bldgs, Ty Glas, Llanishen, Cardiff CF4 5FQ; Tel (01222) 761456 Ext 5310
HM Chief Inspector of Schools R.L. James
Staff Inspector (Primary Education) C. Abbott
Staff Inspector (Secondary Education) P. Thomas
Staff Inspector (Further Education; Education-Industry Links) G. Thomas
Staff Inspector (Independent Schools; Special Education Needs; Educational Disadvantage) Vacancy
Staff Inspector (Language Development and Bilingualism) T.E. Parry
Staff Inspector (Implementation, Monitoring and Evaluation of inspections conducted by registered inspectors) J.R.N. Evans
Staff Inspector (Education and Training of Teachers; Publications; Research and Development) S.J. Adams
Staff Inspector (Independent Schools, Special Educational Needs; GMS Schools; 16–19 Education (Schools) I. Thomas
Professional advice to the Secretary of State on all educational matters; assessing the educational process in Schools and FE Colleges, through inspection and reporting; specialist and general advice to teachers, institutions and local education authorities, through visits, courses and publications; liaison with local authorities and other statutory and voluntary bodies concerned with education

Non Departmental Public Bodies

Further Education Funding Council for Wales (FEFCW)

Lambourne Hse, Cardiff Business Pk, Llanishen, Cardiff CF4 5GL; Tel (01222) 761861
Chairman Malcom Wallace, OBE
Chief Executive Prof John Andrews
Head of Further Education Funding Council Division Linda Gainsbury
Director of Finance and Common Services Division Richard Hirst
Head of Quality Assessment Division Dr Rowland Wynne
The Further Education Funding Council for Wales is responsible for securing the provision of further education and the administration of funds made available by the Secretary of State for Wales, and others, in support of the provision of further education in further education colleges, designated institutions and higher education institutions and by sponsored bodies in Wales, and the performance of such supplementary functions as are required of it by the Further and Higher Education Act 1992

Government Departments Scotland

The Scottish Office

New St Andrew's Hse, St James Centres, Edinburgh EH1 1TG; Tel 0131-556 8400; Fax 0131-244 5151
Secretary of State for Scotland The Rt Hon Ian Lang, MP
Private Secretary M.B. Foulis
Minister of State for Health and Home Affairs The Rt Hon The Lord Fraser of Carmyllie, QC
With responsibility for: European Affairs; Health Policy and Public Health; NHS Management Executive, Health Boards and Common Services Agency; Hospital Services, General Practioner Services (Doctors, Dentists, Chemists and Opticians), Community Health Services, Ambulance Service and Health Education; Superannuation; General Register Office (Scotland); Social Work Services; Policy and Fire Services; Civil Law and Criminal Justice; Civil Defence and Civil Emergencies; Prisons; Scottish Courts Administration Scottish Record Office; Registers of Scotland; Women's Issues; Constitutional Matters; Spokesman – House of Lords, on all Scottish Affairs
Private Secretary S.J. Morrell
Minister for Industry and Local Government J. Allan Stewart, MP
Private Secretary J. Serafini
Minister of State for Agriculture and Environment Sir Hector Monro, MP

1 Central Government

With responsibility for: Agriculture, Fisheries, Scottish Fisheries Protection Agency; Scottish Agricultural Science Agency; Forestry; The Arts; Museums and Libraries; Sport and Recreation; Water, Sewerage and Pollution; Historic Scotland; Natural Heritage; Co-ordination of Rural Affairs
Private Secretary D.T. Robb
Minister for Education and Housing Lord James Douglas-Hamilton, MP
With responsibility for: Education – including Primary, Secondary, Further and Higher Education; Youth and Community Services; Housing; Building Control; Construction Industry; Roads and Transport; Urban Policy; Highlands and Islands Enterprise; Scottish Tourist Board; Co-ordination of Government action in relation to the Highlands and Islands; Spokesman – House of Commons, on Home Affairs
Private Secretary J. Macbeth
Parliamentary Under-Secretary Lord James Douglas-Hamilton, MP
Parliamentary Under-Secretary of State J. Allan Stewart, MP
Parliamentary Under-Secretary of State Sir Hector Monro, JP, DL, MP
Private Secretary S.C. Gartside
London Office Dover Hse, Whitehall, London SW1A 2AU; Tel 0171-270 3000; Fax 0171-270 6730

The Scottish Office Education Department

New St Andrew's Hse, St James Centre, Edinburgh EH1 3TG; Tel 0131-556 8400
Minister for Education and Housing Lord James Douglas-Hamilton
Private Secretary to Lord James Douglas-Hamilton Jane Macbeth
Private Secretary to G.R. Wilson CB F.E. Locke; Tel 0131-244 4409
HM Senior Chief Inspector of Schools T.N. Gallacher
Permanent Under-Secretary of State Sir R.R. Hillhouse, KCB
Private Secretary to Sir R.R. Hillhouse KCB Sally Gartside; Tel 0131-244 4026
Secretary G.R. Wilson, CB
Under Secretary (School Education) J.S.B. Martin; Tel 0131-244 4413
Under Secretary (Further and Higher Education and Arts) W.A.P. Weatherston, CB; Tel 0131-244 5322
Assistant Secretary (Division 1 Schools Special and Early Education) D.S. Henderson
New St Andrew's Hse
Assistant Secretary (Division 2A School Curriculum 5–14 and Careers) N.S. Munro (p/t)
New St Andrew's Hse
Assistant Secretary (Division 2B Upper Secondary Education) V.M. MacNiven (p/t)
Assistant Secretary (Division 3 Teachers and Community Education and Sports Policy) G.A. McHugh
at New St Andrew's Hse
Assistant Secretary (Division 4 Further and Vocational Education) R.D. Jackson 43 Jeffrey St
Assistant Secretary (Division 5 Higher Education) T.J. Kelly 43 Jeffrey St
Chief Executive (Student Awards Agency for Scotland) K. Macrae Gyleview Hse
Chief Statistician (Division 7 Education Statistics) G.C. Jones Jeffrey St
Assistant Secretary (Division 8 Arts) M. Maclean 43 Jeffrey St
The Scottish Education Department is responsible for the administration of public education in Scotland (except in universities), youth and community services, social work services, the arts, libraries, museums, galleries and sport, broadcasting and Gaelic
Dover Hse, Whitehall, London SW1A 2AU; Tel 071-270 3000

43 Jeffrey St, Edinburgh EH1 3DN; Tel 031-556 8400
Gyleview Hse, 3 Redheughs Rigg, Edinburgh EH12 9HH; Tel 031-556 8400

Schools

Under-Secretary J.S.B. Martin, CB
Assistant Secretary D.S. Henderson; Tel 0131-244 5101
Principal T.R. MacDonald
Principal A. McPherson
Principal A. Lindsey
Organisation of schools systems, independent schools and schools services, school boards and parental involvement; resources and coordination; parental involvement; resources and coordination; self-governing schools and Technology Academies; early education and special educational needs

School Curriculum 5–14 and Careers Service

Assistant Secretary N.S. Munro (p/t)
Principal J. Symington

Teachers, Community Education and Sport and Leisure

Assistant Secretary G. McHugh; Tel 0131-244 5126
Principal L.C. Brownlee
Principal J.R. Brown
Principal I. Howie
Salaries and conditions; teacher training and teacher supply; staff development; community education; Sport Leisure and Recreation

Further and Vocational Education

Assistant Secretary R.D. Jackson 43 Jeffrey St, Edinburgh; Tel 0131-244 5382
Principal A.G. Aitken
Senior Principal J.G. Henderson
Principal A. MacLeod
Principal N. Bradford
Further education, college management legislation, vocational qualifications and SCOTVEC

Higher Education

43 Jeffrey St, Edinburgh EH1 1DN; Tel 0131-244 5534
Assistant Secretary T.J. Kelly
Principal J. Lugton
Principal I.N. Walford
Principal A.W. McNaughton
Universities; Central Institutions and Colleges of Education (funding and capital project control)
Higher Education Policy (including wider access and relations with universities), funding and oversight of grant aided colleges of higher education

Student Awards Agency for Scotland

Gyleview Hse, 3 Redheughs Rigg, South Gyle, Edinburgh EH12 9HH; Tel 0131-244 5868
Chief Executive K. MacRae Gyleview Hse, 3 Redheughs Rigg, Edinburgh EH12 9HH; Tel 0131-244 5868
Principal J. Donnelly
Student support policy and student awards

Education Statistics

43 Jeffrey St, Edinburgh EH1 1DN; Tel 0131-244 5532
Chief Statistician G. Jones; Tel 0131-244 5532
Principal (Statistician) A.C.C. Taylor
Principal (Statistician) Mrs F. Roberts
Principal (Statistician) K.M. Barratt
Principal (Statistician) Miss C. McKay

Statistical returns, analysis research and planning, publications

Formal post-School Education

43 Jeffrey St, Edinburgh EH1 1DN; Tel 0131-244 5533
Under Secretary W.A.P. Weatherston, CB

Higher Education – Division B

43 Jeffrey St, Edinburgh EH1 1DN; Tel 0131-244 5587
Principal A.W. McNaughton
Implementation of the Higher Education White Paper and the establishment of a Scottish Higher Education Funding Council; higher education policy including wider access and relations with universities; funding and oversight of grant-aided colleges of higher education

Arts

43 Jeffrey St, Edinburgh EH1 1DN; Tel 0131-244 5100
Assistant Secretary M. Maclean; Tel 0131-244 4494
Principal J.O. Wastle
Principal J. Black
Arts, national institutions, museums, galleries and libraries; broadcasting; Gaelic

HM Inspectors of Schools

New St Andrew's Hse, St James' Centre, Edinburgh EH1 3TG; Tel 0131-244 5138
Senior Chief Inspector T.N. Gallacher
Depute Senior Chief Inspector W.T. Beveridge
Depute Senior Chief Inspector D. Osler
Chief Inspector (Eastern Division) H. Stalker
Chief Inspector (Western Division) G.P.D. Gordon
Chief Inspector (Northern Division) G.H.C. Donaldson
Chief Inspector (Audit Unit) A.S. McGlynn
Chief Inspector (Teacher Education and Supply) K.M. Fairweather
Chief Inspector (Post School Policy; Advice) D.E. Kelso
Chief Inspector (Post School Inspectorate) J.J. McDonald
Chief Inspector (Pre-School and Education 5–14) J. Boyes
Chief Inspector (Education 14–18) R. Tuck
Chief Inspector (Research and Intelligence Unit) M. Roebuck
District Inspector (Lothian) J. Picken
District Inspector (Borders) I.D.S. Robertson
District Inspector (Fife, Central) K.M. Fairweather
District Inspector (Strathclyde) A. Hawke
District Inspector (Strathclyde) J.C. Dignan
District Inspector (Strathclyde) P. Banks
District Inspector (Strathclyde) D.W. Duncan
District Inspector (Dumfries and Galloway) T.A. Rankin
District Inspector (Grampian, Shetland) C.R. Maclean
District Inspector (Tayside) R.F. Dick
District Inspector (Highland, Orkney, Western Isles) Dr G.D. Gray
Staff Inspector (English, Drama, Communication Studies) J.N. Alison
Staff Inspector (Special Education Needs) Mrs M.M. Browning
Staff Inspector (Guidance, Religious and Social Education) J.W. Burdin
Staff Inspector (Social Subjects) L. McCallum
Staff Inspector (Creative and Aesthetic Studies) B. Fryer
Staff Inspector (Languages) J. Boyes
Staff Inspector (Pre-school and Primary Education) T.O. Grieg
Staff Inspector (Science, Biology) Dr J. Jackson
Staff Inspector (Mathematics) G. Mathison
Staff Inspector (Technological Subjects) Mrs M.A. Macfarlane
Staff Inspector (Computing) Vacancy
Staff Inspector (Organisation Management Staff Development, International Relations) J. Mitchell
Staff Inspectors (Teacher Education) M. Cramb
Staff Inspector (Audit Unit) Ms I.S. McGregor
HM Inspector (Media Studies) M.T.J. Axford
HM Inspector (Technological Studies, Health and Safety) A.D. Blair
HM Inspector (Early Education) N. Pegin
HM Inspector (Physics) T.N. Carr
HM Inspector (Art and Design) A.L. Robson
HM Inspector (Craft and Design) W. Geddes
HM Inspector (Religious Studies) S. Ritchie
HM Inspector (Geography) L.A. Hunter
HM Inspector (History) L. MacCallum
HM Inspector (Gaelic) D. McQuarrie
HM Inspector (School Libraries) A. Maltby
HM Inspector (Home Economics) Mrs M. Robertson
HM Inspector (Environmental Education) I.P. Pascoe
HM Inspector (Classics) J. Picken
HM Inspector (Business Studies and Economics) T.A. Rankin
HM Inspector (Assessment) E.P. Spencer
HM Inspector (Drama) A.M. Steele
HM Inspector (Chemistry) Dr. T. Straiton
HM Inspector (Music) R.S. Weir
Staff Inspector – (Mechanical Engineering, Off-shore Engineering, Further Education in Western Division) K.A. Hope
Staff Inspector (Informal Further Education) D.G. Kirkpatrick
Staff Inspector (Technology, Further Education in Northern Division) W.P. Stewart
Staff Inspector (General Studies, Communication Studies, Vocational Education and Training) R. Mauser
Staff Inspector (Civil Engineering, Planning, Architecture, Mining, Further Education in Eastern Division) Dr. R.W.J. Young
HM Inspector – National Responsibilities in Further and Higher Education (Construction, Surveying, Housing Administration) M.J. Brown
HM Inspector – National Responsibilities in Further and Higher Education (Science, Physics) T.N. Carr
HM Inspector – National Responsibilities in Further and Higher Education (Librarianship, Information Science) A. Maltby
HM Inspector – National Responsibilities in Further and Higher Education (Hotel and Catering Studies, Modern Languages) R.H. Manser
HM Inspector – National Responsibilities in Further and Higher Education (Mathematics, Computing) W.M. Patterson
HM Inspector – National Responsibilities in Further and Higher Education (Caring Services) Mrs P.A. Robertson
HM Inspector – National Responsibilities in Further and Higher Education (Art and Design) A.L. Robson
HM Inspector – National Responsibilities in Further and Higher Education (Electrical and Electronic Engineering; Nautical Engineering) D.M. Russell
HM Inspector – National Responsibilities in Further and Higher Education (Technology, Education in Penal Establishments) J.W. Thomson
Inspection of schools, colleges and other educational institutions and organisations; identification of cost-effective ways of meeting educational needs; national development; contribution to policy formulation; educational research and technology, management of education and resources, copyright and international relations

Non-Departmental Public Bodies

Scottish Higher Education Funding Council

Donaldson Hse, 97 Haymarket Terr, Edinburgh EH12 5HD; Tel 0131-313 6500; Fax 0131-313 6501
Chairman Prof John C. Shaw, CBE
Chief Exeucutive Prof John Sizer, CBE

1 Central Government

Secretary to the Council and Director of Administration Dugald M. Mackie
Director of Funding David Wann
Director of Teaching and Learning James T. Donaldson
Director Financial Appraisal and Monitoring Peter Henriksen

The Scottish Higher Education Funding Council (SHEFC) was established in 1992 to provide financial support for teaching, research and associated activities in Scottish universities and higher education colleges. It also has a legal duty to assess the quality of teaching in these institutions. By 1997 the Council's quality assessment programme will result in published reports on the main subject areas offered by the sector. These reports provide useful information on the quality of course provision to prospective students, employers and interested organisations In addition, the council funds special initiatives, eg improving access for students from non-traditional backgrounds, enhancing facilities for students with disabilities, and encouraging the implementation of flexible teaching using new technology

Scottish Office Superannuation Division

St Margaret's Hse, 151 London Rd, Edinburgh EH8 7TQ; Tel 0131-556 8400
Chief Executive N. MacLeod
Principal A. Small
Senior Executive Officer T.N.C. Darling
Principal G. Mowat
Principal J. Edgar
Senior Executive Officer P. Boyd

Social Work Services Group

Assistant Secretary L.J. Clare

Government Departments Northern Ireland

The Northern Ireland Office

Stomont Castle, Belfast BT4 3ST; Tel (01232) 520700
Secretary of State for Northern Ireland Rt Hon Sir Patrick Mayhew, QC, MP
Minister of State Michael Ancram, MP
Minister of State Rt Hon Sir John Wheeler, JP, DL, MP
Parliamentary Under-Secretary of State Baroness Denton
Parliamentary Under-Secretary of State Tim Smith, MP

Department of Education for Northern Ireland

Rathgael Hse, Balloo Rd, Bangor, County Down BT19 7PR; Tel (01247) 279279; Fax (01247) 279100; Telex Telegraphic Address, Education Bangor
Under-Secretary of State Michael Ancram
Permanent Secretary P. Carvill
Under-Secretary (Educational Services) R.D. Hill
Area Boards Co-ordination and Common Services A. McVeigh
Education Administration I D. Woods
Education Administration II J.S. Smith
Curriculum, Assessment and Special Education C. Jendoubi
Policy S.J. Peover
Under-Secretary (Principal Establishment and Finance Officer) P.S. Holmes
Finance and Strategic Planning Dr A.G. McCormick
Higher Education J.A. Mills
Community Relations Recreation, Arts and Youth R.J. Jordan
Education Administration III Dr Davison
Chief Inspector I. Wallace

AB Co-ord and Common Services

Divisional Responsibilities
Area Boards Admin and Personnel; School Transport, Milk and Meals; Area Boards Resource Allocation and Monitoring; Compulsory Competitive Tendering Assessment of Relative needs exercies and Income Generation; Building and Equipment Capital (including Schools and all other Board Capital excluding Youth Services); Energy Efficiency and Emergency Planning; Primary and Secondary Schools Development; Estates Management

Education Administration I Division

Divisional Responsibilities
Nursery and Primary Schools Administration; Council for Catholic Maintained Schools; Integrated Schools; Teachers pay and administration; Teachers' Superannuation; Teachers' Negotiating Machinery;

Education Administration II Division

Divisional Responsibilities
Education Reform Finance; In service training for Teachers; Board Curriculum Support Service; Grammar and Secondary Schools Administration; Voluntary Grammar Schools Finance; Local Management of Schools

Curriculum, Assessment and Special Education Division

Divisional Responsibilities
Special Education; Transfer Procedure; Education/Industry Links; Assessment of Pupils and Reporting; Records of Achievement; Curriculum; Environmental Education, Health Education; Finance and Administration of NICCEA; Examinations, Qualifications and Syllabuses

Policy Division

Divisional Responsibility
Policy Development and Analysis, Economic Appraisal, Co-ordination, Legislation, Private Office, Information Services

Personnel Division

Divisional Responsibilities
Personnel; Department Running Costs, Pay, Travel and Subsistence, Superannuation, Accomodation, Security; Management Services; Information Systems (IT); Staff Training and Development, Success through People, Equal Opportunities; Typing and Support Services

Finance and Strategic Planning Division

Divisional Responsibilities
Accounts; Financial Planning; Strategic Planning; Co-ordination of EC Matters; European Studies Project; Internal Audit; Statistics; Management Information Systems; Output and Performance measurement; Market Testing; Next Steps; Forms Design; Library

Community Relations, Recreation, Arts and Youth Division

Divisional Responsibilities
Community Relations; Community Services; Youth Services; Sport; Arts/Museums; Libraries

Education Administration III Division

Divisional Responsibilities
HE Policy, HE Funding and HE European Issues; Universities; NI Higher Education Council; Armagh Observatory and Planetarium; Student Loans; Access Funds; Postgraduate Awards including Distinction and CAST Awards; Talented Children Awards and Teacher Training Shortage Subject Bursaries; Initial Teacher Training; Colleges of Education; Further Education Policy and Funding, including Adult Education; Workers' Education Association; Educational Guidance Service for Adults; ESF (Vocational Training)

Inspectorate

Divisional Responsibilities
Education and Training Inspectorate; Inspectorate Support

2 Local Authority Associations

Representative Bodies

Association of County Councils

Eaton Hse, 66A Eaton Sq, Westminster, London SW1W 9BH; Tel 0171-235 1200; Fax 0171-235 8458
President of the Association Sir Frank Layfield, QC
Chairman of Executive Council (Lancashire) Josie Farnington
Vice-Chairman of Executive Council (Devon) S.J. Day
Vice-Chairman of Executive Council (Dyfed) J.A.J. Harries, CBE
Vice-Chairman of Executive Council (Northumberland) I. Swithinbank
Vice-Chairman of Executive Council (Somerset) D. Heath
Education Officer J.I. Langtry Eaton Hse, 66a Eaton Sq, Westminster, London SW1V 9BH; Tel 0171-235 1200; Fax 0171-235 8458
Under-Secretary (Education) D.A.L. Whitbread
Policy Officer J.R. Owen
Policy Officer A.R. Duncan

Ex-officio Members

President of the Association, Sir Frank Layfield QC Chairman of the Executive Council J. Farrington (Lancashire); Vice-Chairmen of the Executive Council I.C.E. Swithenbank (Northumberland), D. Heath CBE (Somerset), S. Day (Devon), J.A.J. Harries CBE (Dyfed)

Education Committee

Chair (Devon) Saxon Spence
Vice-Chair (Humberside) L.M. Bird
Spokesperson (Shropshire) Dr Barbara Marsh
Spokesperson (Isle of Wight) Maureen Stolworthy
Spokesperson (Cornwall) F.J.W. Whiting, OBE

Executive Council Members

Warwickshire J. Airey
Humberside L.M. Bird
Avon V. Davey
Avon M. Wheadon
North Yorkshire D.J. Dennis
Hertfordshire R.I.N. Gordon
Powys J.W. Griffiths
Somerset C. Clarke
West Sussex M.E. Collins
Oxfordshire Mrs W.I. Humphries
Clwyd W.A. Jones
Cleveland K. Legg
Wiltshire K.D. Small
Shropshire Dr B.E. Marsh
Berkshire E.J. Singer
Kent T. Dean
Northamptonshire M.A. Young
South Glamorgan P.G. Perkins
Mid Glamorgan R.W.M. Jenkins
Cheshire A. Richardson, OBE, DL
Cumbria Mrs J.E. Robinson
Dorset R. Legg
Lincolnshire P.V. Metcalfe
Isle of Wight Mrs M.O. Stolworthy
Warwickshire Mrs R.M. Styles
Northumberland T.E.C. Weekes
Essex W. Archibald
Essex J.J. Gordon
Durham J. Alderson
Gwynedd G.A. Williams
Buckinghamshire D.C.T. Graves
Staffordshire T.R. Wright
Hereford and Worcester R. Clayton
Cornwall P.B. Cocks, CBE
West Glamorgan D.T.V. Davies
Kent R.G. Ward
Devon M.H. Knight
Devon S.M. Spence

Nottinghamshire F.J. Riddell
Derbyshire D.J. Wilcox

Added Members

Gloucestershire J. Naish
Lancashire Mrs M.P. Case
East Sussex D. Norcross
Suffolk E.R. Echolls
Cheshire P. Nurse
Bedfordshire Mrs A.M. Roberts
Leicestershire Dr A. Duncan
Devon K.J. Watson
Hampshire A.D. Barron
Norfolk C.B. Cogman
Buckinghamshire J.R.W. Huddart
Cambridgeshire I.C. Kidman
Surrey M. King-Hele
Cleveland K. Legg
Gwent A. Lloyd
Bedfordshire J. Thakoordin

Advisers

Chief Executive (Wiltshire) I.A. Browning
Chief Executive (Devon) R.D. Clark
County Treasurer (Somerset) C.N. Bilsland
County Treasurer (East Sussex) J.M. Davies
County Treasurer (Kent) P.A. Martin
County Treasurer (Lincolnshire) M.J. Spink
County Education Officer (Gloucestershire) K.D. Anderson
County Education Officer (Lancashire) A.J. Collier
County Education Officer (Humberside) Dr M.W. Garnett
County Education Officer (East Sussex) D. Mallen
County Education Officer (Buckinghamshire) E.S. Sharp
County Education Officer (Northamptonshire) J.R. Atkinson
County Education Officer (Northumberland) C.C. Tipple
County Education Officer (Devon) S.W.G. Jenkin
County Education Officer (WJEC) Clayton Heycock
Director of Social Services (Surrey) G.G. Gatehouse
County Secretary (Avon) J.E. Orton
County Secretary (Durham) R.J. Humphries
County Personnel Officer (Devon) C.H. Schofield

Association of Directors of Education in Scotland

General Secretary A.B. Watson Director of Education, Tayside Regional Council, Tayside Hse, 28 Crichton St, Dundee DD1 3RJ; Tel (01382) 23281
President J. Dobie Depute Director of Education, Lothian Regional Council, 40 Torphichen St, Edinburgh
Vice-President G. Harcus Depute Director of Education, Strathclyde Regional Council, Strathclyde Hse, 20 India St, Glasgow
Treasurer I.M. Dutton Director of Education, Borders Regional Council, Regional Headquarters, Newton St Boswells, Melrose, Roxburghshire TD6 0SA; Tel (01835) 823301
Assistant Secretary Anne Wilson Senior Assistant Director of Education, Tayside Regional Council, Tayside Hse, 28 Crichton St, Dundee; Tel (01382) 23281

Association of Local Authorities of Northern Ireland

President Cllr A.G. Kane
Secretary R. McKay, BSc(Econ), LLB, FHSM 123 York St, Belfast BT15 1AB; Tel (01232) 249286; Fax (01232) 326645

Association of London Authorities (ALA)

36 Old Queen St, London SW1H 9JF; Tel 0171-222 7799; Fax 0171-799 2339
Chair Cllr Toby Harris
Secretary John McDonnell
Chair Cllr Toby Harris
Head of Publicity and Public Relations Madeleine Williams
Education Officer Julia Bennett

Education Committee

Lewisham (Chair) Cllr Jim Mallory Town Hall, Catford SE6 4RU
Haringey Cllr Mohammed Mehmet Town Hall, Civic Centre, High Rd, London N22 4LE
Hounslow Cllr John Connelly Civic Centre, Lampton Rd, Hounslow, London TW3 3DN
Newham Cllr Linda Jordan Town Hall, East Ham, London E6 2RP
Waltham Forest Cllr Paul Redcliffe Town Hall, Forest Rd, Walthamstow, London E17 4JF
Camden Cllr Julian Fulbrook Town Hall, Euston Rd, London NW1 2RU
Hackney Cllr Patrick Corrigan Town Hall, Mare St, London E8 1EA
Islington Cllr Phil Kelly Town Hall, Upper St, London N1 2UD
Southwark Cllr John McTernan Town Hall, Peckham Rd, London SE5 8UB
Lambeth Cllr Stewart Hunter Town Hall, Brixton Hill, London SW2 1RW
Greenwich Cllr Dave Picton Town Hall, Wellington St, London SE18 6PW
Hammersmith and Fulham Cllr David Williams Town Hall, King St, London W6 9JU
Merton Cllr Sheila Knight Crown Hse, London Rd, Morden SM4 5DX
Barking and Dagenham Cllr Charlie Fairbrass Civic Centre, Dagenham, Essex RM10 7BN

Association of Metropolitan Authorities (AMA)

35 Great Smith St, Westminster, London SW1P 3BJ; Tel 0171-222 8100; Fax 0171-222 0878
President Lord Clinton-Davis
Chairman Cllr J. Beecham
Secretary Rodney Brooke 35 Great Smith St, Westminster, London SW1P 3BJ; Tel 0171-222 8100; Fax 0171-222 0878
Education Officer Alan Parker
Assistant Secretary (Education) John Fowler

Education Committee

Elections for membership of the AMA Education Committee take place in May and June each year. The following held office in the session 1993/194

Greater Manchester

Bolton Cllr D. Eastwood
Bury Cllr R. Walker
Manchester Cllr K. Fry
Oldham Cllr D.R. Jones
Rochdale Cllr R. Colley
Salford Cllr J.D. Merry
Stockport Cllr J. Roberts

Merseyside

Liverpool Cllr G. Ben-Tovim
St Helens M. Newman
Sefton Cllr B. Reynolds

South Yorkshire

Doncaster Cllr P.J. Mullany
Sheffield Cllr Mrs V. Nicholson

Tyne & Wear

Gateshead Cllr A.C. Brazendale
North Tyneside Cllr W.M. Middleton
Sunderland Cllr J. Jordan

West Midlands

Birmingham Cllr A. Howell
Coventry Cllr J.B. Fletcher
Dudley Cllr J.T. Wilson
Solihull Cllr G. Wright

West Yorkshire

Bradford Cllr M.L. Walters
Kirkless Cllr C. Pearce
Leeds Cllr N. Sloane

London Boroughs

Camden Cllr J. Fulbrook
Croydon Cllr D.E. Perry
Enfield Cllr P.G. Elvidge
Hackney Cllr P. Corrigan
Hammersmith and Fulham Cllr D. Williams
Harrow Cllr B. Turner
Hillingdon Cllr P. Ryerson
Hounslow Cllr J. Connelly
Islington Cllr P. Kelly
Kensington and Chelsea Cllr M. Cockell
Kingston upon Thames Cllr P. Clokie
Merton Cllr S. Knight
Newham Cllr G. Lane
Redbridge Cllr Mrs W.J. Roberts
Richmond upon Thames Cllr D. Razzall
Sutton Cllr V. Sharma

Ex-officio

Chair and Vice-Chair of AMA Policy Committee

Advisers

Chief Executive (Liverpool) K.P. Bounds
Chief Executive (Sutton) Mrs Patricia Hughes
Treasurer (Sheffield) M. Newman
Director of Department of Law and Administration (Southwark) Dr C.L. Grace
CEO (Coventry) C. Farmer
Director of Education (Liverpool) F. Cogley
CEO (Manchester) R. Jobson
CEO (Sheffield) Ann Muller
CEO (Sunderland) D.A. Bowers
CEO (Wakefield) A. Lenney
Director of Education (Enfield) G. Hutchinson
Director of Education (Hounslow) J.D. Trickett
Director of Education (Kensington and Chelsea) M. Stoten
Director of Education (Lewisham) Leisha Fullick

Council of Local Education Authorities

Eaton Hse, 66A Eaton Sq, Westminster, London SW1W 9BH; Tel 0171-235 1200/071-235 9554
Joint Secretary Robin Wendt
Joint Secretary Rodney Brooke
Joint Education Officer Ian Langtry
Joint Education Officer Alan Parker
The Administrator Ivor Widdison

Members

ACC

Cllr L.M. Bird Labour Group Office, County Hall, Beverley HU17 9BA
Cllr E.R. Echolls 68 St Philips Rd, Newmarket CB8 0EN
Cllr Dr Barbara Marsh, DL Middle Farm, Chetwynd Aston, Newport TF10 9LE
Cllr D. Pettitt Nottinghamshire County Council, County Hall, West Bridgford, Nottingham NG2 7QP
Cllr E.J. Singer 1 Claremont Rd, Windsor SL4 3AX
Cllr M.O. Stolworthy 2 Brocks Copse Rd, Wootton Bridge PO33 4ND
Cllr V. Davey 29 Norton Rd, Knowle, Bristol BS4 2EZ
F.J. Riddell 200 Cinderhill Rd, Bulwell, Nottingham NG5 8RL
Cllr J.W. Griffiths Bodaioch Hall, Trefeglwys Trimdon Station, Caersws SY17 5PN
Cllr R.S. Norman St Clere, Kemsing, Sevenoaks TN15 6NL
Cllr S.M. Spence 5 Regents Pk, Exeter EX1 2NT
Cllr D. Wilcox Derbyshire County Council, County Offices, Matlock DE4 3AG

AMA

Cllr J. Merry
Cllr V. Nicholson
Cllr Deirdre Razzall
Cllr G. Wright
Cllr A.C. Brazendale 8 The Orchard, Whickham, Newcastle upon Tyne NE16 4HD
Cllr P. Clokie 9 Endsleigh Gdns, Surbiton, Surrey KT6 5JL
Cllr P. Elvidge
Cllr G. Lane
Cllr P. Mullany, 4 Derwent Dr, Kirk Sandall, Doncaster, DN3 1LE
Cllr Kath Fry
Cllr A. Howell

Advisers

Chief Education Officer A.J. Collier Lancashire County Council, PO Box 61, County Hall, Preston PR1 8RY
Chief Education Officer K.D. Anderson Gloucestershire County Council, Shire Hall, Gloucester GL1 2TP
Director of Education Services R. Pryke Kent County Council, Springfield, Maidstone ME14 2LJ
Director of Education Mrs A. Muller Sheffield City Council, PO Box 67, Leopold St, Sheffield S1 1RJ
LGMB C.C. Nolda 41 Belgrave Sq, London SW1X 8NZ
Chief Education Officer C. Farmer Coventry City Council, Earl St, Coventry CV1 5RR
Director of Education M. Stoten Kensington and Chelsea, The Town Hall, Hornton St, London W8 7NX
Treasurer R. Wolstenholme Surrey County Council, County Hall, Penrhyn Rd, Kingston upon Thames KT1 2DN

Observer

Secretary, Welsh Joint Education Committee C. Heycock

Federated Union of Managerial and Professional Officers (MPO)

National Headquarters, Terminus Hse, The High, Harlow, Essex CM20 1TZ; Tel (01279) 434444/3; Fax (01279) 451176
General Secretary Graham Corless
MPO is open to all full-time officers who hold managerial and professional posts graded at NJC Senior Officer level (or equivalent), or above. In addition, membership is open to certain persons who have appropriate professional qualifications but do not meet the 'grading' criterion. Further details of these qualifications are available from the Membership Department at Headquarters.

Society of Education Officers

3-6 Alfred Pl, London WC1E 7EB; Tel 0171-580 5705; Fax 0171-323 0029
President Tony Webster Education Offices, Council Offices, Wellington Rd, Ashton-under-Lyne, Tameside OL6 6DL
Immediate Past President Christopher Tipple Education Dept, County Hall, Morpeth, Northumberland NE61 2EF

Vice-President Vacancy
Hon Treasurer Dr Philip J. Hunter Education Offices, Tipping St, Stafford ST16 2DH
General Secretary Jim Hendy, SEO 3–6 Alfred Pl, London WC1E 7EB
Administrator Jane Haythorne, SEO 3–6 Alfred Pl, London WC1E 7EB
Membership of the council is for 4 years with officers retiring in rotation. Results of annual elections are confirmed at the Society's AGM in January. From January the Vice-President automatically becomes President and the President automatically becomes Immediate Past President.

Council Members

Nationally Elected

Diana Cavanagh Education Offices, PO Box 70, Municipal Offices, Smith St, Rochdale OL16 1YD
Alan Butterworth Education Department, Civic Centre, Sunderland SRZ 7DN
Heather DuQuesnay Education Offices, County Hall, Hertford SG13 8DF
Eric Hardy Education Offices, PO Box 47, Threadneedle Hse, Market Rd, Chelmsford CM1 1LD
John Harrold Education Dept, 5 Portland Sq, Carlisle, Cumbria CA1 1PU
Graham Platts Education Offices, Grimwade St, Ipswich, Suffolk IP4 1LJ
Linda Steynor County Education Office, County Hall, Norwich, Norfolk NR1 2DL
Alf Taylor Education Dept, PO Box 266, Council Hse, Doncaster DN1 3AD
Avril Walton Education Dept, 14 Sir Thomas St, Liverpool L1 6BJ
Hazel Watt Education Offices, Earl St, Coventry CV1 5RS
John Williams Education Dept, County Hall, Newport, IOW PO30 1UD

Regionally Appointed

North Malcolm Shorney Education Offices, Woodlands Rd, Middlesborough, Cleveland TS1 3BN
Yorkshire and Humberside Gail Naylor Education Dept, County Hall, Wakefield WF1 2QL
Northern Ireland Ernie Brown Board Offices, 18 Windsor Ave, Belfast BT9 6EF
Society of Education Officers, Wales Edgar Lewis Education Dept, Shire Hall, Mold, Clwyd CH7 6ND
South East Patrick Finucane Education Dept, Civic Centre, Stockwell Cl, Bromley BR1 3UH
East Anglia Geoffrey Williams Education Offices, County Hall, Hertford SG13 8DF
South West Bryan Slater Education Offices, County Hall, Exeter EX2 4QG
North West Celia Newton Education Dept, Stopford Hse, Town Hall, Stockport SK1 3XE
Midlands Paul Dean Education Dept, St Peter's Sq, Wolverhampton WV1 1RR
Ex Officio David Cracknell Education Dept, County Hall, Chester CH1 1SQ
Ex Officio David Smith Education Dept, City of London Corporation, PO Box 270, Guildhall, London EC2P 2EJ

Regional Secretaries

East Anglia Regional Society Alan Barclay Education Offices, PO Box 47, Threadneedle Hse, Market Rd, Chelmsford CM1 1LD
Midlands Regional Society Anna Lawson Education Offices, Council Hse, Margaret St, Birmingham B3 3BU
North Regional Society Andrew Roberts Education Dept, Woodlands Rd, Middlesbrough, Cleveland TS1 3BN
North West Regional Society Liz Dobie Education Dept, PO Box 70, Municipal Offices, Smith St, Rochdale OL16 1YD
South East Regional Society Michael Nix Education Dept, PO Box 4, County Hall, St Annes Cres, Lewes, E. Sussex BN7 1SG
South West Regional Society G. Heller Education Offices, Crossland Dr, Havant, Hampshire PO9 ZEL
Yorkshire & Humberside Region Regional Society Scott Hollingsworth Area Education Office, 60 Piccadilly, York YO1 1PW
Society of Education Officers, Wales Wynford Thomas Area Education Office, Erlas Hse, Bryn Estyn Rd, Wrexham, Clwyd
Society of Education Offices, Northern Ireland David Cargo Board Offices, 18 Windsor Ave, Belfast BT9 6EF

Welsh Joint Education Committee

245 Western Ave, Cardiff CF5 2YX; Tel (01222) 561231
Chairman Cllr G. Jenkins, JP
Vice-Chairman Cllr R.W.M. Jenkins
Vice-Chairman Cllr J.E. Angell
Secretary C.R. Heycock, MA, MSc

Deputy Secretaries

Finance L.J. Bence, IPFA
Curriculum J.H. Clifford, BSc
Examinations W.R. Lambert, BA, PhD, FRHist
Welsh I.M. Ll Walters, BA

Senior Assistant Secretaries

Principal Assistant Secretary (Examinations) B.F. Evans, BA
Curriculum Education Secretary P. Davies, BA, MEd
Assessment W.G. Roberts, BA
Management D. Jones, BA

Assistant Secretaries

Events & Appeals C.W. Jones, BA
Research R. Adams, BSc, MA
Information Technology R.G. Rees, HNC
Vocational Boards T.A. Garrett, MSc
GNVQs H.B. Mathews, BSc, MEd
Welsh Medium Examinations D. Stockley
MEU (Cymru) M. Williams, MSc, ARCS, MEd, CEng, MIEE
Finance & Common Services C. Weaver, MAAT
Staff Development L. James, MHCIMA
A/AS Levels R. Carter, BA
NVQs R. Alcock, BA
Certificate of Education B. Rogers, BA
GCSE A. Parker, BA, MPhil
Welsh – Humanities A. Treharne, BA
Welsh – Science H. Roberts, BSc
Welsh Resources P. Wyn Jones, BA
National Language Unit H.G. Hughes, BA

Chairpersons of Standing Sub-Committees

Local Authorities Committee Cllr G. Williams
Finance, Establishment and General Purposes Cllr G. Jenkins, JP
Welsh Language and Culture Cllr D. Orwig
Examinations M. Phillips
Strategy & Support Cllr L.J. Rees, CEng, MIEE
Curriculum Cllr C. Moriarty

Convention of Scottish Local Authorities

President (Cumbernauld and Kilsyth) Cllr R. McKenna
Senior Vice-President (Lothian) Cllr K. Geddes
Vice-President (Highland) Cllr P. Peacock

Local Authority Associations

Secretary-General R. MacIver Rosebery Hse, 9 Haymarket Terr, Edinburgh EH12 5XZ; Tel 0131-346 1222; Fax 0131-346 0055
Assistant Secretary (Education) D. Ferguson

Education Committee

Convenor (Lothian) Cllr E. Maginnis
Vice-Convenor (Strathclyde) Cllr T. Farrell
President (Cumbernauld and Kilsyth) Cllr R. McKenna
Senior Vice-President (Lothian) Cllr K. Geddes
Vice-President (Highland) Cllr P. Peacock
Borders Cllr A. Watt
Central Cllr R. Ball
Central Cllr R. Stead
Dumfries & Galloway Cllr R. Greenhow
Fife Cllr J. Farmer
Fife Cllr A.J. Smith
Grampian Cllr J. Towers
Grampian Cllr J.P. Orskov
Highland Cllr V. MacIver
Lothian Cllr A. Aylett
Lothian Cllr P. Boyes
Lothian Cllr J. Hoey
Orkney Cllr I.M. MacDonald
Shetland Islands Cllr W. Smith
Strathclyde Vacancy
Strathclyde Cllr T. Colyer
Strathclyde Cllr R. Campbell
Strathclyde Cllr J. McDowell
Strathclyde Cllr J. Malloy
Strathclyde Cllr H. Revie
Strathclyde Cllr J. Robertson
Tayside Cllr J. Kemp
Tayside Cllr J. Wilson
Western Isles Cllr R. MacDonald

Advisers

Chief Executive (Central) D. Sinclair
Director of Education (Borders) I. Dutton
Director of Education (Fife) B. Welsh
Director of Education (W. Isles) N. Galbraith
Director of Education (Lothian) E. Reid
Director of Education (Strathclyde) F. Pignatelli
Director of Education (Tayside) A. Watson
Director of Finance (Grampian) A.L. McLean
Assistant Chief Executive (Borders) R. Marr
Director of Leisure and Recreation (Stirling) S. Mackenzie
Director of Social Work (Highland) J. Dick

Association of Northern Ireland Education and Library Boards

Education Offices, County Hall, Galgorm Rd, Ballymena, Co Antrim BT1 2NQ; Tel (01266) 3333
Hon Secretary G. Topping, BA(Hons), MSc, MBA, DipED

Executive Council 1992/93

President Cllr F.R.H. Marks 13 Avon Ct, Moylena Rd, Antrim BH41 4PJ
First Vice-President Cllr W.G. Watson, BEd, DipEd, DASE, FInstD Rosguil, 169 Ballynahinch Rd, Lisburn, Co. Antrim BT27 5LP
Second Vice-President Cllr A.M. Odling-Smee, JP, BA 10 Deramore Park South, Belfast BT9 5JY
Past President Cllr N.R.D. Mulligan, OBE 21 Aughintain Rd, Cavanakirk, Clogher, Co. Tyronne
Past President Rev R.W.W. Clarke, MA 8 Grandsden Pk, Eglinton, Co Londonderry BT47 3XL
Past President Alderman S. Semple, MBE, JP, FRSA, MFTCOM, MESP "Cedar Croft", 16 Belsize Rd, Lisburn BT27 4AW
Past President Rev J. McAllister, MA(Hons) Black Bush Cottage, 34 Dickeystown Rd, Glenarm BT44 0BA
Past President Very Rev J.A. Fair, MA, Dean of Connor The Rectory, Lower Cairncastle Rd, Larne, Co Antrim BT40 1PQ
Past President Cllr V.M. McGahie 139 Drumaney Rd, Ardboe, Stewartstown, Dungannon BT71 5NQ
Past President Cllr J.R. Beggs, MP, MPA, MPAC 9 Carnduff Rd, Ballyvernstown, Larne, Co Antrim BT40 3NJ

Belfast

Alderman J.A. Coggle C/o Members' Room, City Hall, Belfast BT1 5GS
Cllr P. Lewsley C/o Members' Room, City Hall, Belfast BT1 5GS
C. Murphy 7 Cheltenham Gdns, Belfast BT6 0NS
Rev P.F. Patterson, BSc, BD 69 Church Rd, Newtownbreda, Belfast BT8 4AN

North-Eastern

D. White Carthall Cottage, 29 Carthall Rd, Coleraine BT51 3LP
Cllr A.P. McConaghy 230 Whitepark Rd, Lisnagunagh, Bushmills, Co Antrim BT57 8SP
Rev J.R. Wilson The Vicarage, 1A Glenkeen, Randalstown, Co Antrim, BT41 3JX
Cllr E.T. Black 186 Coleraine Rd, Portstewart BT55 7PL

South-Eastern

Alderman T.P. Benson 88 Bowtown Rd, Newtownards, Co Down BT23 3SL
Cllr H.E. Bradford, MA Ardkeen, Killaire Rd, Carnalea, Bangor, Co Down BT19 1EY
Rev Canon S.M.J. Dickson 50 St Patrick's Ave, Downpatrick BT40 6DW
H.R. Small 17 Monument Rd, Hillsborough BT26 6HT

Southern

Cllr F.E. Crowe 9 Highfield Pk, Craigavon, Co Armagh BT64 3AF
Rev G.A. Green, BD, MA Cathedral Presbytery, Hill St, Newry, Co Down BT34 1AR
Cllr J.V. McCart 6 Ardkeen Crt, Warrenpoint, Co Down BT34 3LU
Cllr A. McKelvey 19 Edenvale Ave, Banbridge, Co Down BT32 3RQ

Western

Cllr P. Devine 10 Rathlin Gdns, Creggan, Londonderry BT48 9UE
Cllr J. Gallagher 13 Brownhill Pk, Glenmornan, Strabane BT82 0JF
Cllr J.J. Kerr, BSc, MEd, MIEE 27 Clarendon St, Londonderry BT48 7EP
Cllr E. Turner 69 Deerpark Rd, Newtownstewart, Co Tyrone BT78 4LB

Chief Executives

G. Topping, BA(Hons), MSc, MBA, DipEd North-Eastern Education and Library Board, County Hall, 183 Galgorm Rd, Ballymena, Co Antrim BT42 1HN
J.G. Kelly, MA Southern Education and Library Board, 3 Charlemont Pl, The Mall, Armagh BT61 9AZ
T.G.J. Moag, BSc, DIC, CEng, MIMechE Belfast Education and Library Board, 40 Academy St, Belfast BT1 2NQ
M.H.F. Murphy, OBE, BA, HDipEd, FRSA Western Education and Library Board, 1 Hospital Rd, Omagh, Co Tyrone BT79 0AW
T. Nolan, OBE, BA, MSSc, DipEd, FRSA South-Eastern Education and Library Board, 18 Windsor Ave, Belfast BT9 6EF

Chief Librarians

Chief Librarian R.T.A. Farrow, BA, ALA Western Education and Library Board, Dublin Rd, Omagh BT78 1HG

Chief Librarian J.N. Montgomery, ALA Belfast Education and Library Board, Central Library, Royal Ave, Belfast BT1

Association of Chief Executives of Area Boards for Education and Libraries

Honorary Secretary G. Topping, BA(Hons), MSc, MBA, DipEd Chief Executive, North Eastern Education and Library Board, County Hall, 182 Galgorm Rd, Ballymena, Co Antrim BT42 1HN; Tel (01266) 653333; Fax (01266) 46071

Local Education Authorities Research Group (LEARG)

Education Department, PO Box 149, County Hall, Guildhall Rd, Northampton NN1 1AU; Tel (01604) 236280; Fax (01604) 236188
General Secretary Brian Carr
Chairman Dr Brian Roberts
A self-help group which brings together Education Officers, Advisers and others involved in research, planning and statistical work in LEAs. LEARG does not conduct or manage research projects but aims to provide a forum for discussion of current issues in educational research and its management in LEAs and to exchange factual information and to test ideas. Links are maintained with a variety of organisations including DFE, EMIE, NCET, NFER, SEO and FE Staff College

London Boroughs Association (LBA)

College Hse, Great Peter St, London SW1P 3LN; Tel 0171-799 2477; Fax 0171-233 1151
Chairman Cllr Mary Walker, CBE, DL
Secretary John Hall; Tel 0171-233 1665

Education and Training Committee

Chair Cllr Sidney Kallar
Vice-Chair Cllr David Cornwell
Barking and Dagenham Sidney Kallar
Barnet Anne Jarvis
Bexley S. Hall
Brent John Warren
Bromley J. Hatcher
Croydon Valerie Shawcross
Ealing Margaret Majumdar
Enfield Achilleas Georgiou
Harrow A. Groves
Havering Bill Harrison
Kensington and Chelsea Merrick Cockell
Kingston John Heaman
Lambeth John Whelan
Redbridge John Fairley-Churchill
Richmond David Cornwell
Sutton John Dodwell
Tower Hamlets Julia Mainwaring
Wandsworth E. Howlett
Westminster Carolyn Keen
Corporation of London Judith Mayhew

3 Local Government England and Wales

Grant Maintained Schools

For ease of reference, Grant Maintained Schools (also known as Self-Governing State Schools) are listed under the local authority area where they are situated

Grant Maintained Schools are not controlled by local authorities so queries relating to them should either be referred to the school itself, to the Grant Maintained Schools Centre (Chapter 14 under Research and Advisory Bodies) or to the DFE (Chapter 1)

In April 1994 a non–departmental public body, the Funding Agency for Schools (FAS) took over the funding of Grant Maintained Schools. For further details see the FAS entry in Chapter 1.

Avon County Council

Population 953,000
PO Box 11, Avon Hse, The Haymarket, Bristol BS99 7DE; Tel (0117) 929 0777
Chief Executive and Clerk Basil D. Smith
County Solicitor and Deputy Clerk John Orton, MA PO Box 11, Avon Hse, The Haymarket, Bristol BS99 7DE; Tel (0117) 929 0777
County Treasurer D.G. Morgan, MA, IPFA
Director of Social Services Richard Evans
Acting Director of Property Services David Wilcox Middlegate, Whitefriars, Lewins Mead, Bristol BS1 2NW; Tel (0117) 929 0777
Director of Personnel Services Rodney Jarrett, MIPM, ACIS, DMA
Director of Community Leisure David W. Liddle, DMS, ALA, MILAM, MBIM Southey Hse, 33 Wine St, Bristol BS1 2BQ; Tel (0117) 929 0777
County Press and Public Relations Graham H. Terry PO Box 41, Avon Hse North, St James Barton, Bristol BS99 7NF; Tel (0117) 929 0777

Number of Schools and Further Education Establishments
16 nursery (1,321.5) (FTE); 369 primary (74,645) (FT); 59 secondary (52,541); 3 further education establishments; 3 teachers' centres; 3 outdoor pursuits centres; 12 adult education area offices

Special Schools
26 day (1,865 (FTE), includes mixed day and boarding); 4 residential (163)

Population
953,000

Product of 1p Rate
£1,261,650

Other Authorities with whom Joint Purchasing Arrangements are made
Wiltshire, Gloucestershire, Somerset, Dorset, Cornwall, Dyfed

Education Department

PO Box 57, Avon Hse North, St James Barton, Bristol BS99 7EB; Tel (01179) 874000
Director of Education Graham Badman, MA
Deputy Director of Education E.T.R. Watson

Assistant Director (Administrative & Financial Support Services) T. Gillespie
Assistant Director (Executive and Operational Services) R.R. Riddell, MA, MPhil
Principal Adviser E. Williams
Principal Educational Psychologist K. Thompson
Principal Education Welfare Officer W. Horton
Principal Education Officer J. Winter
Education Officer (Secondary) P. Vedmore
Education Officer (External Services) F.M. Courtney
Education Officer (Equal Opportunities) J. Veira (Acting)
Education Officer (Primary) R. Williams
Education Officer (Primary) G. Cleak
Education Officer (Special) F. Newport
Senior Personnel Officer (Education) R. Bull
Senior Personnel Officer (Education) K. Robertson
Senior Personnel Officer (Education) D.C. Williams
Principal Property and Contracts Officer P. Simpson
Education Officer (Sites and Buildings) R. Baynton
Education Officer (Client Group) M. James
Address for Advisers Education Advisory Service, Sheridan Rd, Horfield, Bristol BS7 0PU; Tel (0117) 931 1111
Adviser (Research and Information) F. Ward
Adviser T. Williamson
Adviser D. Roberts
Adviser R. Grist
Adviser Dr D. Clark
Adviser Dr D. DeSouza
Adviser M. Ryan
Adviser M. Kerly
Adviser K. Sadler
Adviser E. Davies
Adviser R. Brock
Adviser D. Towl
Adviser K. Jane
Modern Languages Adviser J. Budd
Adviser J. Plumb
Adviser M. Rose
Physical Education Adviser M. Harlow
Adviser J. Bevan
Adviser G. Baxter

Number of Schools
16 nursery (1,234) (FTE); 366 primary (72,440); 58 secondary (54,234)

Special Schools
26 day (1,851, includes mixed day and boarding); 4 Residential (171)

Day of Committee Meeting
5 weekly cycle

Other Authorities with whom Joint Purchasing Arrangements are made
Wiltshire, Gloucestershire, Somerset, Dorset, Cornwall, Dyfed

Education Committee

Con 10, Lab 14, LD 8

Members of the Committee
Con: P. Cobbold, J. Forrest, J. Gillard MBE, JP, E. Miles, B. Nicholls, B. Pascoe, H. Roberts, T. Smith, P. Taylor, M. Wheadon
Lab: J. Ashton, A. Becker, B. Chalmers, M. Chivers, C. Dando, P. Dunmore, Dr S. Grant, D. Herod, S. Hodkinson, A. Hughes, W. Martin, R. Stone, B. Perry, V. Davey
LD: G. Crump, J. Dagnall, M. Drew, P. Heath, A. Hockridge, P. Hockey, J. Larkins, M. Smith

Special Schools (Day)

Baytree, Baytree Rd, Weston-super-Mare BS22 8HG; Tel (01934) 625567; *Head* C. Penney. SLD
Briarwood, Briar Way, Fishponds, Bristol BS16 4EA; Tel (0117) 965 7536; J. Buxton, BSc. SLD
Claremont, Henleaze Pk, Westbury-on-Trym, Bristol BS9 4LR; Tel (0117) 924 7527; R.G. Coburn. P.H.
Elmfield, Greystoke Ave, Westbury-on-Trym, Bristol BS10 6AY; Tel (0117) 950 1962; M. Lockett, BEd, FCollP. Deaf
Florence Brown, Leinster Ave, Knowle, Bristol BS4 1NN; Tel (0117) 966 8152; H.J. Till, BEd. MLD
Fosse Way, Longfellow Rd, Midsomer Norton, Bath BA3 4BL; Tel (01761) 412198; R. Hanks. MLD
Fulford, Fulford Rd, Hartcliffe, Bristol BS13 9PD; Tel (0117) 964 9806; B. Yates. EBD
Glevum, Kelston Cl, Yate, Bristol BS17 4SZ; Tel (01454) 318219; K.W. Boys. MLD
Grimsbury Pk, Tower Rd North, Warmley, Bristol BS15 2XL; Tel (0117) 967 3422; S. Morris. SLD
Henbury Manor, Rectory Gdns, Henbury, Bristol BS10 7AH; Tel (0117) 950 2868. SLD
Kingsweston, Napier Miles Rd, Kingsweston, Bristol BS11 0UT; Tel (0117) 982 3382; D.J. Capel, BA, MEd. MLD
Lime Gr, Pulteney Rd, Bath BA2 4HE; Tel (01225) 424732; Mrs J.D. Pulham. SLD
New Fosseway, New Fosseway Rd, Hengrove, Bristol BS14 9LN; Tel (01275) 839411; J. Hiscox. SLD
New Siblands, Easton Hill Rd, Thornbury, Bristol BS12 1AU; Tel (01454) 414188; Miss N.S. Tansley, BAM(Ed). SLD
Ravenswood, Pound La, Nailsea, Bristol BS19 1EY; Tel (01275) 854134; G.A. Sawyer (Acting). MLD; SLD
Royal United Hospital, Cynthia Mossman Hse, Combe Pk, Bath BA1 3NJ; Tel (01225) 824223; J. Giles Wessex Hse
Filton Pk, Charborough Rd, Filton, Bristol BS12 7RB; Tel (0117) 969 4224; S. Evans. EBD
Summerfield, Weston Pk East, Bath BA1 2UY; Tel (01225) 423607; T.G. Williams. MLD
Wansdyke, Frome Rd, Odd Down, Bath BA2 5RF; Tel (01225) 832212; J. Ward. EBD
Warmley Tower, Tower Rd North, Warmley, Bristol BS15 2XL; Tel (0117) 967 6572; M. Bell. MLD
Westhaven, Uphill, Weston-super-Mare BS23 4UT; Tel (01934) 632171; K.G. Henton. MLD
Woodstock, Courtney Rd, Kingswood, Bristol BS15 2RF; Tel (0117) 967 1832; G. Parsons. EBD

Special Schools (Residential)

Croydon Hall, Fetlon's Oak, Minehead, Somerset TA24 6QT; Tel (01984) 40249; *Head* P. Thompson (Acting). BP
Kingsdon Manor, Kingsdon, Somerton, Somerset TA11 7JZ; Tel (01935) 840323; J. Lowe. MLD; Senior Boys'
Notton Hse, Notton, Lacock, nr Chippenham, Wilts SM15 2NF; Tel (0124 973) 407; G.M. Gamble, MEd. BP; Boys
Periton Mead, Periton Rd, Minehead, Somerset TA24 8DS; Tel (01643) 702013; D.A. Singleton (Acting). BP

Comprehensive Schools (County 11–18 except where otherwise stated)

Ashton Pk, Blackmoors La, Bower Ashton, Bristol BS3 2IL; Tel (0117) 966 2241; I. Repper. Mixed (703)
Backwell, Station Rd, Backwell, Bristol BS19 3PB; Tel (01275) 463371; R.J. Nosowski, DipEd. Mixed (1354)
Bedminster Down, Donald Rd, Bedminster Down, Bristol BS13 7DQ; Tel (0117) 964 3530; J.H. Black, MEd. Mixed (917)
Brimsham Green, Broad La, Yate, Bristol BS17 5LB; Tel (01454) 310977; *Head* R.E. Warrillow. Mixed (826)
Brislington, Hungerford Rd, Brislington, Bristol BS4 5EY; Tel (0117) 977 3661; G.J. Clements. Mixed (1637)
Broadlands, St Francis Rd, Keynsham, Bristol BS18 2DY; Tel (0117) 986 4791; D. McGregor, BA. Mixed (709)
Broadoak, Broadoak Rd, Weston-super-Mare BS23 4NP; Tel (01934) 629106/7/8; J. Nickerson. Mixed (1237)
The Castle, Park Rd, Thornbury, Bristol BS12 1HT; Tel (01454) 416363; A. Verwoert. Mixed (1125)
Chew Valley, Chew Magna, Bristol BS18 8QB; Tel (01275) 332272/332527; K.J. Biggs. Mixed (922)
Churchill, Churchill Grn, Churchill, Bristol BS19 5QN; Tel (01934) 852771/2; B. Kirkup. Mixed (1353)
Clevedon, Walton Rd, Clevedon, Bristol BS21 6AH; Tel (0117) 987 6744/5/6; E. Dolling. Mixed (1250)
Culverhay, Rush Hill, Bath BA2 2QL; Tel (01225) 426268; A. Wright. Boys (808)
Downend, Westerleigh Rd, Downend, Bristol BS16 6XA; Tel (0117) 956 0244; Mrs J.E. Penge. Mixed (894)

Filton High, New Rd, Filton, Bristol BS12 6QT; Tel (0117) 969 5325; J. Simes. Mixed (1259)
Gordano, St Mary's Rd, Portishead, Bristol BS20 9QR; Tel (0117) 984 2606; *Head* R. Sommers. Mixed (1117)
Grange, Tower Rd North, Warmley, Bristol BS15 2XL; Tel (0117) 967 4481; J.O. Lench, MA. Mixed (1003)
Hanham High, Memorial Rd, Hanham, Bristol BS15 3LA; Tel (0117) 961 5121; F.E. Appleton, MA, DEM. Mixed (992)
Hartcliffe, Teyfant Rd, Hartcliffe, Bristol BS13 0RL; Tel (0117) 964 5155; A.R. Turner, MEd. Mixed (590)
Hayesfield, Upper Oldfield Pk, Bath BA2 3LA; Tel (01225) 426151; J. Bartholomew. Girls (1090)
Henbury, Marissal Rd, Henbury, Bristol BS10 7NJ; Tel (0117) 950 6624; Dr Langton, BA, DPhil, DipEd. Mixed (1333)
Hengrove, Petherton Gdns, Hengrove, Bristol BS14 9BU; Tel (01275) 836077; K.M. Davis, BA. Mixed (1068)
King Edmund, Sundridge Pk, Yate, Bristol BS17 4DX; Tel (01454) 312265/314406; R. Royds, BSc, MEd. Mixed (791)
Kingsfield, Brook Rd, Kingswood, Bristol BS15 4JT; Tel (0117) 967 3277/603665/677007; D. Lewis. Mixed (936)
Lawrence Weston, Stile Acres, Lawrence Weston, Bristol BS11 0QA; Tel (0117) 982 6801; C. Lindup. Mixed (346)
Lockleaze, Romney Ave, Lockleaze, Bristol BS7 9XT; Tel (0117) 969 4355; R.A. Lockey, BA. Mixed (680)
Mangotsfield, Rodway Hill, Mangotsfield, Bristol BS17 3LH; Tel (0117) 956 0525; B.A. Tranter, BSc. Mixed (1138)
Merrywood, Daventry Rd, Knowle, Bristol BS4 1DQ; Tel (0117) 966 8561; T. French. Boys (621)
Merrywood, Downton Rd, Knowle, Bristol BS4 1QB; Tel (0117) 966 1084; Mrs M.C. Lavington. Girls (541)
Monks Pk, Filton Rd, Horfield, Bristol BS7 0XZ; Tel (0117) 969 0811; R. Phillips. Mixed (971)
Nailsea, Mizzymead Rd, Nailsea, Bristol BS19 2HN; Tel (0117) 985 2251/2/3; Dr T.M. White, BSc, FRIC. Mixed (1281)
Norton Hill, Charlton Rd, Midsomer Norton, Bath BA3 4AD; Tel (01761) 412557/8/9; P. Bevan. Mixed (1002)
Patchway High, Hempton La, Almondsbury, Bristol BS12 4AJ; Tel (01454) 612287/613147; B. Spencley. Mixed (781)
Pen Pk, Pen Park Rd, Southmead, Bristol BS10 6BP; Tel (0117) 950 3666; D. Cooling. Girls (270)
Portway, Penpole, Shirehampton, Bristol BS11 0EB; Tel (0117) 982 8442; W. Astley. Mixed (659)
Priory, Queen's Way, St Georges, Weston-super-Mare BS22 0BP; Tel (01934) 511411; J. Saunders. Mixed (944)
Ralph Allen, Claverton Down Rd, Combe Down, Bath BA2 7AD; Tel (01225) 832936; F. Thomas. Mixed (571)
The Ridings High, High St, Winterbourne, Bristol BS17 1JL; Tel (01454) 772347/773679; Fax (01454) 250404; Miss M.V. Sedgwick, JP, MA, LLB, MBIM. Mixed (1561)
St George, Russell Town Ave, St George, Bristol BS5 9JG; Tel (0117) 955 3141; R. Priest. Mixed (1045)
St Katherines, Pill Rd, Ham Grn, Pill, Bristol BS20 0HU; Tel (01275) 373737; R. Gildersleeve. Mixed (846)
Sir Bernard Lovell, North St, Oldland, Bristol BS15 6TS; Tel (0117) 932 2898; G.D Stewart, DFC, BA. Mixed (857)
Somervale, St Chads Ave, Midsomer Norton, Bath BA3 2HG; Tel (01761) 414276; A.J. Sedgley. Mixed (776)
Speedwell, Speedwell Rd, Kingswood, Bristol BS15 1NU; Tel (0117) 961 3123; P. Kent, MA, MPhil. Mixed (982)
Wellsway, Chandag Rd, Keynsham, Bristol BS18 1PH; Tel (0117) 986 4751; D. Whittle. Mixed (1064)
Whitefield Fishponds, Snowdon Rd, Fishponds, Bristol BS16 2HD; Tel (0117) 965 9421; Mrs M.G. Anderson. Mixed (732)
Withywood, Molesworth Dr, Withywood, Bristol BS13 9BL; Tel (0117) 964 4774; B.C. Eales. Mixed (713)
Worle, Redwing Dr, Mead Vale, Worle, Weston-super-Mare BS22 8XX; Tel (01934) 510777; D.M. Roberts, BA. 11–16; Mixed (929)
Writhlington, Knotsbury La, Radstock, Bath BA3 3NQ; Tel (01761) 433581; C.J. English. Mixed (936)
Wyvern, Sandringham Rd, Weston-super-Mare BS23 3QP; Tel (01934) 629307; B.E. Button, BA. 11–16; Mixed (703)

Comprehensive Schools (Voluntary)

Chipping Sodbury, Bowling Rd, Chipping Sodbury, Bristol BS17 6EW; Tel (01454) 316194; Miss K.R. Phillips, BA. VC; 11–18; Mixed (1098)
Marlwood, Vattingstone La, Alveston, Bristol BS12 2LA; Tel (01454) 416844; K. Williams. VC; 11–18; Mixed (1055)
St Bede's R.C., Long Cross, Lawrence Weston, Bristol BS11 0SU; Tel (0117) 982 2393; Dr P.L. Skeets. VA; 11–16; Mixed (645)
St Bernadette R.C., Fossedale Ave, Whitchurch, Bristol BS14 9LS; Tel (0117) 983 2756; R.P. Thornton, MA. SA; 11–16; Mixed (517)
St Gregory's R.C., Combe Hay La, Bath BA2 8PA; Tel (01225) 832873; D. Byrne, MSc. VA; 11–16; Mixed (546)
St Mark's C.E., Baytree Rd, Bath BA1 6ND; Tel (01225) 312661; Rev J. Coates. VA; 11–18; Mixed (479)
St Mary Redcliffe & Temple C.E., Somerset Sq, Redcliffe, Bedminster, Bristol BS1 6RT; Tel (0117) 929 3931; J.R. Eachus, BA. VA; 11–18; Mixed (1007)
St Thomas More R.C., Stottbury Rd, Eastville, Bristol BS7 9NH; Tel (0117) 951 6011; Mrs J. Mead, BA. SA; 11–16; Mixed (630)

Secondary Grammar (County 11–18)

Cotham, Cotham Lawn Rd, Cotham, Bristol BS6 6DT; Tel (0117) 973 5691; M.J. McKay, BA. Mixed (966)
Fairfield, Fairlawn Rd, Montpelier, Bristol BS6 5JW; Tel (0117) 955 7407; W.C. Cox. Mixed (511)

Community Education Offices

Bath and Wansdyke, City of Bath College, Avon St, Bath BA1 1UP; Tel (01225) 312191; *Senior Community Education Co-ordinator* Gwenda Potter
Bristol North & West Area Office, Stoke Lodge, Shirehampton Rd, Bristol BS9 1BN; Tel (0117) 968 3112; *Senior Community Education Co-ordinator* Dr C. Claxton
Bristol, South Merrywood Boys School, Daventry Rd, Knowle, Bristol BS4 1DQ; Tel (0117 9) 530219; *Senior Community Education Co-ordinator* Jane Taylor
Central & East Bristol Area Office, Alexandra Pk, Fishponds, Bristol BS16 2BG; Tel (0117) 965 6957; *Senior Community Education Co-ordinator* B. Woodward
Northavon and Kingswood, Ridgewood, 244 Station Rd, Yate, Bristol, Avon BS17 4AF; Tel (01454) 315603; *Senior Community Education Co-ordinator* Suzanne Bridgewater
Woodspring, Mizzymead Rd, Nailsea, Bristol BS19 2HL; Tel (0117) 981 0659; *Senior Community Education Co-ordinator* Maggy Crook

Outdoor Pursuits Centres

Dean Field Studies Centre, Parkend, Lydney, Glos GL15 4JA; Tel (01594) 562444; *Head of Centre* M. Arnold

Education Resources Service

Bristol Conference Centre, Bishop Rd, Bishopston, Bristol BS7 8LS; Tel (0117) 923 2276; Fax (0117) 924 8072

Grant Maintained Schools

Beechen Cliff School, Alexandra Pk, Bath, Avon BA2 4RE; Tel (01225) 420366; Fax (01225) 314025; *Headmaster* Roy A. Ludlow; *Chairman of Governors* Richard Hall. (Boys) (11–18) Girls in Sixth Form (983)

Oldfield School, Kelston Rd, Bath BA1 9AB; Tel (01225) 423582; Fax (01225) 464986; *Headteacher* Rev A.A.J. Claridge; *Chair of Governors* Lufkin Skeet. (Girls) (11–18) (796)

Barnsley Metropolitan Borough Council

Population 224,700
Town Hall, Church St, Barnsley, S Yorks S70 2TA; Tel (01226) 770770

Education Department

Berneslai Cl, Barnsley, S Yorks S70 2HS; Tel (01226) 770770
Chief Executive Officer J. A. Edwards
Borough Treasurer D. Hoyland
Director of Architecture P. Buckingham
Director of Social Services R. D. Wardell
Librarian C. E. Vickers
Director of Leisure and Amenities J. A. Reid
Chairman Councillor H. Lavender
Vice-Chairman Councillor D. Foster
Director of Education (Acting) M.F. Warrington, BA
Senior Assistant Director Resources W. Webster, BA(Hons), CIPFA
Assistant Director Property Resources T. Storey
Assistant Director Services H Beaumont, BTech
Principal Officer Schools Services P. Rowbotham
Principal Officer Continuing Education Services G. Howarth, BEd(Hons), CertED, DipEd
Governor Management and Training Coordinator Vacancy
Principal Officer Special Services R. Hayward, BA(Hons), MSc, PGCE
Principal Officer Information Services K. Nield
Principal Careers Officer Mrs Howarth, BA(Hons), DipCareersGuidance
Principal Officer; Staffing Services R. Cheetham, CIPFA
Principal Officer; Property Resources G. Sleight, DMA
General Adviser (Early Years) C.A. Davies
General Adviser (Visual and Performing Arts) W. Goodall
General Adviser (Historty, RE, IT) P. Cole
General Adviser (Modern Foreign Languages) M. Thompson
General Assistant (Science and Technology) R. Holmes
General Adviser (Assessment (Primary) Individual Needs) E. Parry
General Adviser (14-19, Business and Careers Education) D. Agnew
Project Trident Director G. Wilkinson
General Adviser (Management Development) M. Eastwood
General Adviser (Management Development) Mr Owen
Basis Service Manager S. Burgin
Appraisal Manager H. Morris
Professional Assistant S. Brailsford
Principal Officer Welfare Services A. Dunkley
Principal Educational Psychologist M. Andrews, BA(Hons)
Number of Schools
2 nursery (which include Primary Classes); 93 Primary
Special Schools
3 Special (175)

Education Committee

Lab 25, Con 1
Members of the Committee
Lab: P.A. Beardshall, D. Bostwick, G. Cooper, J. Ennis, D. Foster, A. Gardiner, B.G. Goddard, G. Hadfield, M. Hall, A.L. Hall, H. Lavender, G. Murphy, W.R. Norbury, R. Robinson, J. Ryan, H.D. Salt, A. Schofield, G.D. Slasor, L.M. Smith, J.H. Thomson, J.D. Wake, R.I. Walker, R.B.E.M. Warden, J. Watts, H. Wilson
Con: B. Hinchliffe

Education Welfare Offices

Berneslai Cl, Barnsley, South Yorks S70 2HS; Tel (01226) 773500

Careers Office

See Chapter 17

Special Day Schools

Crevesford, St Helen's Boulevard, Carlton Rd, Barnsley S71 2AY; Tel (01226) 283068; Mrs V.A. Brewer
The Gables, Bondfield Cres, Wombwell, Barnsley S73 8TL; Tel (01226) 752466; E.A. Brookes
Rockley Mount, Keresforth Hill Rd, Barnsley S70 6RG; Tel (01226) 287165; G.R. Sharples

Comprehensive School (Special Agreement) (11–16)

St Michael's R.C. Carlton Rd, Barnsley S71 2BD; Tel (01226) 282845; J.C. O'Callaghar, BA. (5A) (587)

Comprehensive Schools (County 11–16)

The Kingstone School, Broadway, Barnsley S70 6RA; Tel (01226) 205510; D. Richards, BSc. (1167)
The Foulstone, Nanny Marr Rd, Darfield, Barnsley S73 9AB; Tel (01226) 753223; *Headteacher* A.J. Robertshaw, BA, MPhil. (852)
Darton High, Churchfield La, Kexborough, Barnsley S75 5EW; Tel (01226) 382568; F.W. Myers, BA. (913)
The Dearne High, Clayton La, Thurnscoe, Rotherham S63 OBE; Tel (01709) 892565; Mrs J.E. Rodgers, BA. (1208)
Edward Sheerien, Carlton Rd Site, Barnsley S71 2BB; Tel (01226) 282371/205571; J. Bramley, BSc. (667)
Kirk Balk, Hoyland, Barnsley S74 9HX; Tel (01226) 742286; R. Hilton, BA. (948)
Priory, Lundwood, Barnsley S71 5RG; Tel (01226) 203110; D.J. Gawthorpe, MA. (850)
Royston, Station Rd, Royston, Barnsley S71 4EQ; Tel (01226) 722515; B. Hilditch, BSc. (613)
Willowgarth High, Brierley Rd, Grimethorpe, Barnsley S72 7AJ; Tel (01226) 711542; Dr A.J. Dorney, BSc, BA. (1010)
Wombwell High, Roebuck St, Wombwell, Barnsley, S. Yorks; Tel (01226) 752551; Mrs I. Dalton, MA. (795)
Worsbrough High, Ardsley Rd, Worsbrough Dale, Barnsley S70 4RL; Tel (01226) 284606; D.G. Angus, BA. (656)

Comprehensive School (County 11–18)

Penistone Grammar, Penistone, Sheffield S30 6BU; Tel (01226) 762114; M.A. Bould, BA. (1380)

Comprehensive School (Voluntary 11–16)

Holgate, Shaw La, Barnsley S70 6EP; Tel (01226) 203720; A.V. Kent, BA. (804)

Professional Development Centre

Basis Longcar Professional Development Centre, Longcar La, Barnsley, S. Yorks; Tel (01226) 281961

Bedfordshire County Council

Population 532,400 (Final Mid-1991 OPCS Estimate)
County Hall, Cauldwell St, Bedford MK42 9AP; Tel (01234) 363222
Chief Executive D. Cleggett

Education Department

County Hall, Cauldwell St, Bedford MK42 9AP; Tel (01234) 363222; Fax (01234) 228249
Chief Education Officer D.G. Wadsworth, MA, MPhil
Deputy Chief Education Officer and Head of Policy and Planning Branch P. Brett, BEd
Policy and Planning Branch
Education Manager (Monitoring and Commissioning) K. Fossey
Education Officer (Finance) P. Buckley
Education Officer (Personnel) C. Hooper
Education Officer (Community Education) M. Airs
Education Officer (Equal Opportunities) Dr N. Khanum
Education Officer (Policy) J. Goldsmith
Education Officer (Planning) Dr K. Modi
Education Officer (Capital Programme) S. Bird
Education Officer (Health, Safety and Sites) C. Wooding
Education Officer (Contract Services) J. Miller
Education Officer (Transport and IT) M. Thomson
Principal School Support Officer D. Fraser
Education Co-ordinator, Under 8's G. Wilkinson
Schools and Colleges Branch
Head of Schools and Colleges Branch D. Doran
Education Manager (Inspection and Advice) P. Allen
Education Manager (Management Services) M. Johnson
Service Manager (Advisory Services) T. Collings
Service Manager (Resource Services) P. Dunne
Service Manager (Music Service) I. Smith
Service Manager (Inspection Services) P. Allen
Service Manager (Financial Services) R. Freeman
Service Manager (Personnel Services) M. Johnson
Head of Staff Development and Management Training R. Bollington
Student, Family and Community Branch
Head of Student, Family and Community Branch R. Vandevelde
Education Manager (Learning Support) L. Brown
Education Manager (Assessment and Family Support) P. Butler
Education Officer (Community Education) M. Haynes
Education Manager (Student Support) M. Eastwood
Team Leader (Learning Support) J. Harrop
Team Leader (Sensory Impairment and Communication Difficulties) L. Truscott
Team Leader (Section 11 Projects) H. Abji
Team Leader (Travellers Education) L. Brown
Team Leader (Formal Assessment Team) P. Butler
Team Leader (Education Psychological Service) P. Penrose
Team Leader (Welfare and Home School Liaison) B. Meatyard
Team Leader (Special Needs Monitoring Team) M. Debney
Team Leader (Guidance Services) M. Eastwood
County Senior Inspector (Middle Years) B. Morton
County Senior Inspector (Secondary) D. Young
County Inspector (Special Needs) D. Baldry
County Inspector (Primary) J. Carter
County Inspector (Music) R. Crozier
County Inspector (Religious Education) R. Gregory
County Inspector (English) R. Hancock
County Inspector (Humanities) D. Hawley
County Inspector (Science) A. Jarvis
County Inspector (Technology) M. Patterson
County Inspector (Art/Design) B. Payne
County Inspector (Primary) E. Clark
County Inspector (Mathematics) E. Wakeling
County Inspector (Primary) R. Thompson
County Inspector (Primary) J. Woolhouse
County Adviser (Mathematics) A. Brough
County Adviser (Assessment, Recording and Reporting) K. Harris
County Adviser (Foreign and Community Languages) B. Keenan
County Adviser (Physical Education) G. Keevill
County Adviser (Science) J. O'Sullivan
County Adviser (Design Technology) S. Dakin
County Adviser (Personal and Social Education) C. Weston
County Adviser (Humanities) D. Jones
County Adviser (Special Needs) N. Lomasney
County Adviser (English) S. Wrigley
County Adviser (Early Years) S. Kirk
Office of Corporate Strategy (Chief Executive) D. Cleggett
Office of Corporate Strategy (Director of Finance) B. Phelps
Office of Corporate Strategy (Director of Property Services) P. Buckley
Office of Corporate Strategy (Director of Human Resource Strategy) C. Burgess
Number of Establishments
12 nursery schools (1,488); 49 nursery units (3,679); 67 4+ units; 31 infant schools (6,663); 32 junior schools (9,155); 6 primary schools (1,651); 147 lower schools (22,831); 37 middle schools (16,323); 14 upper schools (11,226); 8 high schools (6,945); 15 special schools (1,207); 23 schools with special provision (180); 3 residential centres; 70 youth clubs/centres; 31 adult continuing education centres
Special Schools
6 for children with moderate learning difficulties; 5 for children with severe learning difficulties; 2 for children with physical disabilities; 2 for children with emotional and behavioural difficulties

Education Committee

Con 10, Lab 11, LD 4
Members of the Committee
Con: R.G. Baker, A.G. Burnage, J.M. Devenish, P.S. Dunington, P. Gershon, R. Gwynne Jones, P. Hollick, E.M. Joy, A.M. Roberts JP, J.E. Scott,
Lab: A.R. Ali, G.K. Burley, B.E. Ellis, M.D. Hand, S. Hinds, J.E. Jefferson, J. Kinchella, N. Mallett, Cllr Mitchell, D.A. Patten, J. Thakoordin
LD: R.F. Hall, N.L. Hills, E. Ledster, J. Skeppelhom

Governor Support Network

Maryland College, Leighton Rd, Woburn, Milton Keynes MK17 9JD; Tel (01525) 290849; Fax (01525) 290058
Senior Admin Officer Mel Blackshaw

AREA YOUTH OFFICES

Luton

Bedfordshire Hse, Stuart St, Luton LU1 5NP; Tel (01582) 402500 Ext 3319

South Bedfordshire

Youth Service Office, Vernon Pl, Dunstable LU5 4EZ; Tel (01582) 665861 Ext 223

Mid Bedfordshire

Shefford Youth Centre, Samuel Whitbread, Upper School and Community College, Shefford Rd, Clifton, Beds; Tel (01462) 811890

North Bedfordshire

Bedford Youth Hse, St Marys St, Bedford MK42 0AP; Tel (01234) 363222

Hospital Teaching Service

Victoria Ward, South Wing Bedford Hospital, Bedford; Tel (01234) 355122; P.A. Sheard
Luton and Dunstable Hospital, c/o Five Springs School, Northwell Dr, Luton LU3 3SP; Tel (01582) 596800; A. McBrayne

Schools for Children with Moderate Learning Difficulties

Five Springs, Northwell Dr, Luton LU3 3SP; Tel (01582) 572880; H.A. Hardie
Grange, Halsey Rd, Kempston, Bedford MK42 8AU; Tel (01234) 852545; C. Woodroffe
Hitchmead, Hitchmead Rd, Biggleswade SG16 0NL; Tel (01767) 601010; P. Latter
Richmond Hill, Sunridge Ave, Luton LU2 7JL; Tel (01582) 21019; M. Love
Weatherfield, Brewers Hill Rd, Dunstable LU6 1AF; Tel (01582) 605632; C. Peters

Schools for Children with Severe Learning Difficulties

Glenwood, Beech Rd, Dunstable LU5 3LY; Tel (01582) 667106; J.S. Wadlow
Hillcrest, Ridgeway Ave, Dunstable LU5 4QL; Tel (01582) 661983; P. Skingley
Rainbow School, Chestnut Ave, Bromham, Bedford MK43 8HP; Tel (01234) 822596; J. Mason
St Johns, Austin Canons, Kempston, Bedford MK42 8AB; Tel (01234) 345565; R. Babbage
Sunnyside, The Baulk, Biggleswade SG18 0PT; Tel (01767) 313662; P.A. Moore

Schools for Children with Physical Difficulties

Ridgeway, Hill Rise, Kempston, Bedford MK42 7EB; Tel (01234) 853602; W. Spurgeon
Lady Zia Wernher, Ashcroft Rd, Luton LU2 9AY; Tel (01582) 28705; J. Jackson

Schools for Children with Emotional and Behavioural Difficulties

Greys Hse, Manor Dr, Kempston, Bedford MK42 7AB; Tel (01234) 852268; P. Caldwell (Acting)
Oak Bank, Sandy La, Leighton Buzzard LU7 8BE; Tel (01525) 374559; D. McIntosh
St Margarets (Residential) School La, Carlton, Bedford MK43 7LQ; Tel (01234) 720213; R.D. Jones

Middle Schools (9–13)

Abbey, Mowbray Rd, Bedford MK42 9XA; Tel (01234) 359519; A. Alsop. (284)
Alameda, Station Rd, Ampthill MK45 2QR; Tel (01525) 404305; M. Meakin. (376)
Arnold, Hexton Rd, Barton-le-Clay MK45 4HZ; Tel (01582) 881392; G. Varney, BA. (295)
Beauchamp Middle School, Hawk Dr, Bedford MK41 7JE; Tel (01234) 359259; R. Stock, BA. (470)
Brewers Hill, Aldbanks, Dunstable LU6 1AJ; Tel (01582) 666668; C.T. Hale-Brown. (470)
Brooklands, Brooklands Dr, Leighton Buzzard LU7 8PE; Tel (01525) 372018; P. Harris. (562)
Burgoyne, Mill La, Potton SG19 2PG; Tel (01767) 260034; D. Birch, MA. (263)
Daubeney, Orchard St, Kempston MK42 7PS; Tel (01234) 852214; D.L. Jones, BEd. (580)
Etonbury, Stotfold Rd, Arlesey SG15 6XS; Tel (01462) 730391; P. Youell. (420)
Five Oaks, Five Oaks, Caddington LU1 4JD; Tel (01582) 26058; Vacancy. (207)
Fulbrook, Weathercock La, Woburn Sands MK17 8NP; Tel (01908) 582022; G. Bent. (390)
Gilbert Inglefield, Vandyke Rd, Leighton Buzzard LU7 8HS; Tel (01525) 372266; K. Jones. (503)
Goldington, Haylands Way, Bedford MK41 9BX; Tel (01234) 261516; P.W. Heighway, BA. (626)
Harrold Priory, The Green, Harrold MK43 7DE; Tel (01234) 720346; K. Atkins. (315)
Harrowden, Acacia Rd, Bedford MK42 0HU; Tel (01234) 353401; A. Ormsby. (198)
Holmemead, Mead End, Biggleswade SG18 8JU; Tel (01767) 318123; W.M. Morgan (Acting). (331)
Kings Houghton Middle, Parkside Dr, Houghton Regis LU5 5PX; Tel (01582) 866133 or 863294; J.P. Iles. (631)
Leighton, Church Sq, Leighton Buzzard LU7 7AE; Tel (01525) 374907; M. Sayward. (478)
Linslade, Mentmore Rd, Linslade, Leighton Buzzard LU7 7PA; Tel (01525) 372640; J. Hooper. (560)
Margaret Beaufort, High St, Riseley MK44 1DR; Tel (01234) 708213; P. Harpin. (312)
Mill Vale, Wilbury Dr, Dunstable LU5 4QP; Tel (01582) 662629; F. Read. (406)
Newnham, Polhill Ave, Bedford MK41 9DT; Tel (01234) 352559; T.W. Hall. (440)
Parkfields, Park Rd, Toddington LU5 6AB; Tel (0152 55) 872555; D. Calcott. (456)
Priory, Britain St, Dunstable LU5 5AB; Tel (01582) 661158; R. Pepworth. (482)
Robert Bloomfield, Bloomfield Dr, Shefford SG17 5BU; Tel (01462) 813366; R. Willis. (550)
Robert Bruce, Hillgrounds, Bedford Rd, Kempston MK42 8PN; Tel (01234) 843888; F. McMahon. (719)
Sandye Place, Park Rd, Sandy SG19 1JD; Tel (01767) 680420; P. Teague. (467)
Stewartby, The Crescent, Stewartby MK43 9NH; Tel (01234) 768224; D.C. Thurgeson. (211)
Streetfield, Dunstable Rd, Caddington LU1 4BB; Tel (01582) 661342; P.R. Lowe. (465)
Westfield, Chester Rd, Bedford MK40 4HW; Tel (01234) 267353; S. Surtees. (315)
Woodland, Malham Cls, Flitwick MK45 1NP; Tel (01525) 713700; C. Henderson, BEd. (654)
Woodside, Church La, Bedford MK41 0DH; Tel (01234) 350584; A. Phillips. (255)

Middle Schools (Voluntary 9–13)

Alban, Silver St, Great Barford MK44 3JN; Tel (01234) 870735; G. Osborne. VA (306)
Edward Peake, Potton Rd, Biggleswade SG18 0EJ; Tel (01767) 314562; P.L. Haines. VC (445)
Henlow, Church Rd, Henlow SG16 6AN; Tel (01462) 813733; G. Redley. VC (465)
St Bede's R.C., 112 Bromham Rd, Bedford MK40 2QJ; Tel (01234) 353858; G. Chapman. VA (300)
St Gregory's R.C., Biddenham Turn, Bedford MK40 9AT; Tel (01234) 268649; D. O'Dwyer (Acting). VA (420)

High School (Voluntary 11–18)

Cardinal Newman R.C., Warden Hill Rd, Luton LU2 7AE; Tel (01582) 597125; R.A. Smith, BA, BD. VA (1168)

High Schools (11–16)

Challney Boys, Stoneygate Rd, Luton LU4 9TJ; Tel (01582) 599921; V. Galyer. Boys (723)
Challney Girls, Stoneygate Rd, Luton LU4 9TJ; Tel (01582) 571427; M. Arthur (Acting). Girls (884)
Denbigh, Alexandra Ave, Luton LU3 1HF; Tel (01582) 36611; Y. Bevan. Mixed (1071)
Halyard, Emerald Rd, Luton LU4 0NE; Tel (01582) 601221; D. Snape. (792)
Lealands, Sundon Park Rd, Luton LU3 2AL; Tel (01582) 576236/7/8; R.F. Tebbutt. (789)
Putteridge, Putteridge Rd, Luton LU2 8HJ; Tel (01582) 415791; J. Arkell. (1130)
South Luton, Cutenhoe Rd, Luton LU1 3NH; Tel (01582) 22333; G. Briggs. (890)

Upper Schools (Voluntary 13–18)

St Thomas More R.C., Tyne Cres, Bedford MK41 7UL; Tel (01234) 341201; J. McManus, BA. VA (797)

Upper Schools (13–18)

Biddenham, Biddenham Turn, Bedford MK40 4AZ; Tel (01234) 342521/2/3; G.J. Fitzhugh. (850)

The Cedars, Mentmore Rd, Linslade LU7 7PA; Tel (01525) 375636; J.G. Mitchell. (1330)
Harlington, Goswell End Rd, Harlington LU5 6NX; Tel (015255) 873836; D. Motion, BSc, MSc. (1000)
Hastingsbury, Hill Rise, Kempston MK42 7EB; Tel (01234) 841500; M. Mathews. (900)
Kingsland Community College, Parkside Dr, Houghton Regis, Dunstable LU5 5PY; Tel (01582) 866166; D.E. Summers, MSc. (276)
John Bunyan, Mile Rd, Bedford MK42 9TR; Tel (01234) 364351; G. Bryan. (702)
Mark Rutherford, Wentworth Dr, Bedford MK41 8PX; Tel (01234) 364541; J.S. Brandon, BA, BSc. (1050)
Northfields, Houghton Rd, Dunstable LU5 5AB; Tel (01582) 608011; K. Horner. (1027)
Redborne Upper, Flitwick Rd, Ampthill, Bedford MK45 2NU; Tel (01525) 404462; N. Croft. (954)
Samuel Whitbread, Shefford Rd, Clifton, Shefford SG17 5RF; Tel (01462) 812798; R.D. Owen, MA. (980)
Sandy, Engayne Ave, Sandy, Beds; Tel (01767) 680598; A. Hill. (1054)
Stratton, Eagle Farm Rd, Biggleswade SG18 8JB; Tel (01767) 312745/314250; B.J. Farman, BA. (877)
Vandyke, Vandyke Rd, Leighton Buzzard LU7 8HS; Tel (01525) 376838; J.B. Oliver. (1155)

Independent Schools (Harpur Trust Schools)

Bedford School, Burnaby Rd, Bedford MK40 2TU; Tel (01234) 353436; Dr I.P. Evans
Bedford High School, Bromham Rd, Bedford MK40 2BS; Tel (01234) 360221; M. Churm
Bedford Modern School, Manton La, Bedford MK41 7NT; Tel (01234) 364331; P.J. Squire, MA
Dame Alice Harpur School, Cardington Rd, Bedford MK42 0BX; Tel (01234) 340871; R. Randle

Adult Continuing Education Centres

Beech Hill Community Schools, Community Wing, Dunstable Road, Luton LU4 8BW; Tel (01582) 429448; J. Hathaway; R. Clunie
Biddenham Community College, Biddenham Upper School, Biddenham Turn, Bedford MK40 4AZ; Tel (01234) 272920; L. Randle
Biggleswade Community College School, Stratton Upper School, Eagle Farm Rd, Biggleswade SG18 8JB; Tel (01767) 312745; T. Creed
Challney Community College, Challney High School (Boys), Stoneygate Rd, Luton LU4 9TJ; Tel (01582) 576400; J. Pinney
Elstow Craft Centre, Silver Jubile Annexe, Acacia Rd, Bedford MK42 0AU; Tel (01234) 271738; S. Freer
Hastingsbury Community College, Hastingsbury Upper School, Hill Rise, Kempston, Bedford MK42 7EB; Tel (01234) 852756; A. Heywood
Kingsland Community College, Houghton Regis Upper School, Parkside Dr, Houghton Regis, Dunstable, Beds LU5 5PY; Tel (01582) 868285; S. Oliver
John Bunyan Community College, John Bunyan Upper School, Mile Rd, Bedford MK42 9TR; Tel (01234) 365313; S. Freer
Lea Manor Community College, Lea Manor High School, Northwell Dr, Luton LU3 3TL; Tel (01582) 595124; J. Andel
Leighton Linslade Community College, Vandyke Upper School, Vandyke Rd, Linslade, Leighton Buzzard LU7 8HS; Tel (01525) 375769; C. Carey
Mark Rutherford Community College, Mark Rutherford Upper School, Wentworth Dr, Bedford MK41 8PX; Tel (01234) 358299; M.E. Knight
Maryland College, Leighton St, Woburn MK17 9JD; Tel (01525) 290688; B. Cairns, DipFA, MA. (Short term residential)
Putteridge Community College, Putteridge High School, Putteridge Rd, Luton LU2 8HJ; Tel (01582) 415591; P. Todd
Redborne Community College, Redborne Upper School, Flitwick Rd, Ampthill, Bedford MK45 2NU; Tel (01525) 404412; N. Reynolds
Samuel Whitbread Community College, Samuel Whitbread Upper School, Shefford Rd, Clifton SG17 5RF; Tel (01462) 811997; J. Robinson
Sandy Community College, Sandy Upper School, Engayne Ave, Sandy SG19 1BL; Tel (01767) 680574; T. Creed
Sharnbrook Community College, Sharnbrook Upper School, Odell Rd, Sharnbrook, Bedford MK44 1JX; Tel (01234) 782581; A. Samain
South Luton Community College, South Luton High School, Cutenhoe Rd, Luton LU1 3NH; Tel (01582) 480886; D. Beaven
Stopsley Community College, Stopsley High School, St Thomas Rd, Luton LU2 7UX; Tel (01582) 417733; G. Davies

Residential Centres

Blue Peris Mountain Centre, Dinorwic, Caernarvon LL55 3ET; Tel (01286) 870853; C.N. Jones
Dell Farm, Whipsnade, Dunstable LU6 2LG; Tel (01582) 872666; H.G. Fletcher
Nether Swell Manor, Stow-on-the-Wold, Cheltenham, Glos GL54 IJZ; Tel (01451) 830113; R. Davis

Service for Sensory Impairment and Communication Difficulties

The Child Development Centre, Hill Rise, Kempston, Bedford MK42 7EB; Tel (01234) 857575; L. Truscott

Support Teams

Bedford Schools Section II Project and Peripatetic Services 66 Cedar Rd, Bedford MK41 7PZ; Tel (01234) 358164; A. Singhal
Home School Liaison and Interpretation Translation Services – Luton Bedfordshire Hse, 111 Stuart St, Luton LU1 5NP; Tel (01582) 409488; S. Ahmed
Home School Liaison and Interpretation Translation Services – Bedford County Hall, Cauldwell St, Bedford MK42 9AP; Tel (01234) 363222; S. Ahmed (based in Luton)
Inner/Outer Luton Schools Section II Projects and Peripatetic Services Leagrave Junior School, Strangers Way, Luton LU4 9ND; Tel (01582) 597318; G.M. McFarlane
Multicultural Education Resource Services 66 Cedar Rd, Bedford MK42 0JE; Tel (01234) 364475; D. Lee

Traveller Education Service

King's Houghton Middle School, Parkside Dr, Houghton Regis LU5 5PX; Tel (01582) 861063; L. Brown

Youth Centres/Clubs (LEA Provided)

Afro-Caribbean Outreach Project, Starlight Youth Club, Inkerman St, Luton, Beds; Tel (01582) 420203; B.R. Baker
Ampthill Youth Club, Redborne Upper School, Ampthill MK45 2NU; Tel (01525) 402619; N. Sackwild
Annapurna, Old Secondary School, Leighton Rd, Toddington, Beds; Tel (01525) 872071
Arlesey Youth Club, High St, Arlesey, Bedford, Beds; Tel (01462) 731451; A. Otway
Asian Girls Outreach Worker, Bedfordshire Hse, Stuart St, Luton, Beds; Tel (01582) 402500 Ext 3396; Mrs N. Mahmood
Bedford Youth Hse, St Marys St, Bedford, Beds; Tel (01234) 228275; R. Lehal; B. Cooper
Biddenham Upper School and Community College, Biddenham Turn, Bedford MK40 4AZ; Tel (01234) 216329; Mrs W. Manning
Biggleswade Youth Club, Holmemead School, Biggleswade SG18 8JU; Tel (01767) 313984; Mrs L. Argent
Caddington Youth Club, Five Oaks Middle School, Caddington LU1 4JD; Tel (01582) 26525; J. Walker
Chapel St Youth Club, Russell St, Luton, Beds; Tel (01582) 23818; S. McKinley
Dunstable Outreach Worker Grove Hse, 76 High St North, Dunstable, Beds; Tel (01582) 607895
Halyard Youth Club, Halyard High School, High St, Leagrave, Luton LU4 0NE; Tel (01582) 607688; G. Deaves

Hastingsbury Upper School and Community College, Hill Rise, Kempston, Bedford MK42 7EB; Tel (01234) 845100; R. Bedford
Houghton Regis Youth Club, Angels La, Houghton Regis, Dunstable, Beds; Tel (01582) 865469; T. Flatman
John Bunyan Youth Club, John Bunyan Upper School, Mile Rd, Bedford MK42 9TR; Tel (01234) 364351; M. Bell
Kempston Youth Club, Kempston Youth Centre, Hillgrounds Rd, Kempston, Bedford, Beds; Tel (01234) 851046; R. Bedford
Lea Manor Youth Club, Lea Manor High School, Northwell Dr, Luton LU3 3TL; Tel (01582) 579714; R. Jackson
Leighton Linslade Youth Clubs, Vandyke Upper School, Vandyke Rd, Leighton Buzzard, Beds LU7 8HS; Tel (015250) 373375; K. Foulkes
Luton Youth Hse, Saint Marys Rd, Luton LU1 3JA; Tel (01582) 29087; Z. Moran; J. Thatcher
Mark Rutherford Upper School and Community College, Wentworth Dr, Bedford MK41 8PX; Tel (01234) 211524; D. Crawford
Ouse Valley Youth Worker, Sharnbrook Upper School, Odell Rd, Sharnbrook MK44 1JX; Tel (01234) 781360; Mrs J. Williams
Outreach Workers (Pakistani, Bangladeshi, Kashmiri and African Caribbean Communities) Outreach Project, Luton Youth Hse, St Marys Rd, Luton, Beds; Tel (01582) 484239; L. Palmer; T. Khan; T. Hassan
Putteridge Youth Club, Putteridge High School, Putteridge Rd, Luton LU2 8HJ; Tel (01582) 27270; Vacancy
Sandy Youth Club, Sandy Place Middle School, Park Rd, Sandy SG19 1JD; Tel (01767) 680583; D. Ploszay
Shefford Youth Club, Shefford Rd, Clifton, Shefford, Beds; Tel (01462) 811890; D. Stott
Starlight Youth Club, Christchurch Youth Club, Inkerman St, Luton, Beds; Tel (01582) 425668; B. Abbey
Stevington Youth Club, Village Hall, Stevington, Bedford, Beds; Tel (012302) 6109; J. Williams
Stratton Upper School and Community College, Eagle Farm Rd, Biggleswade SG18 8JB; Tel (01767) 316901; Miss S. Large
Stotfold Youth Club, Roecroft, Community Centre, Stotfold, Beds; K. Guest
Sundon Pk Youth Club, Youth Wing, Lealands High School, Sundon Pk Rd, Luton LU3 2AL; Tel (01582) 572279; Ms J. Moore
Westfield Youth Club, Chester Rd, Bedford MK40 4HW; Tel (01234) 210406; A. Boulton

Grant Maintained Schools

Ashcroft High, Leagrave Junior School, Strangers Way, Luton LU4 9ND; Tel (01582) 565486; M. Clarke
Ashton, High St North, Dunstable LU6 1NH; Tel (01582) 663511; C. Locke. VA (595)
Gamlingay Village College, Station Rd, Gamlingay, Nr Sandy, Bedfordshire; Tel (01676) 50360; D.J. Longman; *Chair of Governors* D.S. Spink, MBE. (Middle) (9–13) (180)
Holywell, Red Lion Cl, Cranfield MK43 0JA; Tel (01234) 750381; T.F. James. VC (490)
Icknield, Riddy La, Luton LU3 2AH; Tel (01582) 576561; K. Ford. (1260)
Lea Manor High School, Northwell Drive, Luton, Bedfordshire LU3 3TL; Tel (01582) 595121; *Head Teacher* Rachel Jaye, MEd
Lincroft Middle (GM), Station Rd, Oakley MK43 7RE; Tel (01234) 882147; Fax (01234) 825923; C. Evans, BA. (420)
Manshead School, Dunstable Rd, Caddington LU1 4BB; Tel (01582) 608641; Fax (01582) 472732; G. Kellett, BA. VC (689)
Queensbury School, Langdale Rd, Dunstable, Beds LU6 3BU; Tel (01582) 601241; *Headteacher* Dr Keith Barker; *Chairman of Governors* Cllr P.J. Roberts. (Mixed) (13–19) (1020)
Sharnbrook, Odell Rd, Sharnbrook MK44 1JX; Tel (01234) 782211; D.S. Jackson, MA. (1157)
Stopsley, St Thomas Rd, Luton LU2 7UX; Tel (01582) 412233; Fax (01582) 416686; P.T. Haydock. (631)
Wootton Upper, Hall End Rd, Wootton, Bedford MK43 9HT; Tel (01234) 767123; C.J Mackenzie, MA

Berkshire County Council

Population 744,400

Education Department

Shire Hall, Shinfield Pk, Reading RG2 9XE; Tel (01734) 233652; Fax (01734) 750360
Chief Education Officer S.R. Goodchild, CBE, BA, FBIM, FRSA
Assistant Chief Education Officer R.G. Bingham, BA, MA
Assistant Chief Education Officer A.J. Daykin, MA
Assistant Chief Education Officer Keith Evans, BCom, MSocSc
Head of Service (Strategic Planning and Information Systems) M.E. Evans, BA
Head of Service (School Support Service) L. Lewis, BA
Head of Service (Education Property Management) M.G. Melton, BEd
Head of Service (Finance and Resource Allocation) F. Perry, MA, IPFA
Head of Service (Customer Services) M.S. Cox, BA(Hons)
Head of Service (Berkshire Careers Service) J. Watts
Head of Service (Pupils Support Services) R.W. Howles, MA
Head of Service (Admissions, Transport and Awards) M. Gocke, BA
Head of Service (Special Needs) C. Beacham, MA
Head of Service (Youth and Community Services) J.H. Ashdown
Head of Service (Education Corporate Support) M. Holt
Head of Service (Personnel) G.D. Hawkins, DMS
Head of Service (Multicultural Services) M. Anjali
Head of Service (Quality Assurance Services) Rod King
Senior Adviser (Professional Development) Romy Markham
Senior Adviser (Curriculum & Assessment) Paul Sadler
Principal Inspector (Schools) Vacancy
Senior Inspector (Contracts and Consultancy) Chris Emerson
Senior Inspector/Adviser Allison Fletcher
Senior Inspector/Adviser Helen McMullen
Senior Inspector (Primary) Philip Schofield
Senior Inspector (Primary) Dave Futcher
Primary Adviser/Inspector John Burt
Primary Adviser/Inspector Ann Reilly
Primary Inspector/Adviser John Woodcock
Primary Inspector/Adviser Ann Harris
Art Adviser Ged Gast
Design Technology Adviser Andy Tubbs
English Adviser Ms Karen Butler
Geography and Outdoor Education Inspector/Adviser Stuart Armstrong
History Inspector/Adviser Dan Archer
Information Technology Inspector/Adviser Mrs Chris Robson
Music Adviser Philip Litchfield
Modern Languages and Classics Adviser Roslyn Fox
Mathematics Adviser Colin Jarvis
Physical Education Adviser Judy Evans
Science Adviser Pat O'Brien
Special Needs Inspector/Adviser Jean Nicholson
Staff Development Adviser Keith Ridyard
Primary Inspector/Adviser Brian Page
Primary Inspector/Adviser Audrey Cook
Primary Inspector/Adviser Vacancy

Art & Design Inspector Tim Royle
Post-16 Education Inspector/Adviser Leslie Stephen
Drama Inspector/Adviser Marigold Ashwell
English Inspector Mike Harrison
Mathematics Inspector Jean Head
Music Inspector D. Congden
Physical Education Games/Dance Inspector Jenny Murray
RE and Collective Worship Inspector/Adviser Lisa Baveystock
Science Inspector Peter Jackson
Technology Inspector Bob Welch
Technology Consultant Ron Lewin
Principal Education Welfare Officer F. Walter
Principal Educational Psychologist D. Brownhill
Number of Schools
18 nursery, (1,835 FTE); 79 nursery classes in primary schools (2,333 FTE); 261 primary (53,287); 42 secondary (36,775); 8 middle (deemed primary), 4 middle (deemed secondary) (1,671); 1 college of adult education; grant maintained schools (21); 13 special schools; 5 education centres; 3 residential centres
Number of Special Schools
13 (1,663)
Day of Committee Meeting
Wednesday

Education Committee

Con 3, Lab 5, LD 7, Lib 1
Chair A.M. Risman, (LD) Little Spinney, 11 Ravenswood Ave, Crowthorne RG11 6AX; Tel (01344) 772452
Vice-Chair A.C. Snelgrove, (Lab) 51 Firlands, Bracknell RG12 3SB; Tel (01344) 59160
Members of the Committee
Con: D. Cunliffe, P.J. Edwards, J.H. Maisey
Lab: P.M. Jones, R.J. Webb, T. Wheaton
LD: M.T. Bonney, C.S. Bushill, E.A. Clarke, R.J. Day, R. Mowatt, E.J. Singer, J.A. Williams
Lib: A.J. Bradshaw

AREA OFFICES

Bracknell

Divisional Careers Office

See chapter 17

Education Welfare Service

Bracknell and Wokingham Area, Fitzwilliam Hse, Skimped Hill, Bracknell RG12 1JY; Tel (01344) 426421; *Team Leader* Mrs M. Webb

Psychological Service

Adastron Hse,; Educational Psychologist M.J Beswetherick; *Educational Psychologist* Miss A. Colgan

Special Classes and Resources

Adastron Hse Adjustment Centre, Adastron Hse, Crowthorne Rd, Bracknell RG12 4DG; Tel (01344) 54526; *Teacher-in-Charge* Mrs J. Barrett
Broadmoor Language and Literacy Centre, Broadmoor Primary School, Lower Broadmoor Rd, Crowthorne RG11 7HD; Tel (01344) 773188; S. How
Holly Spring Assessment Resource, Holly Spring Infant School, Lily Hill Rd, Bracknell RG12 2SW; Tel (01344) 483920; J.R. Arwas
Holly Spring Language and Literacy Centre, Holly Spring Junior School, Lily Hill Rd, Bracknell RG12 2SW; Tel (01344) 424203; M. Purdy
Meadow Vale Special Resource, Meadow Vale Primary School, Moordale Ave, Bracknell RG12 1SY; Tel (01344) 421046; S. Thornton
Ranelagh School Special Resource, Ranelagh School, Ranelagh Dr, Bracknell RG12 3DA; Tel (01344) 421233; K.M. Winrow

Special Schools

Kennel Lane School, Kennel La, Bracknell RG12 2EX; Tel (01344) 483872; J. Calcroft

Comprehensive Schools

The Brakenhale, Rectory La, Bracknell RG12 4BA; Tel (01344) 423041; Fax (01344) 300397; C.J. Croft, MA. (839)
Easthampstead Pk, Easthampstead Pk, Ringmead, Bracknell RG12 8FS; Tel (01344) 304567; Fax (01344) 867862; J.E. Traies, MA. (1499)
Edgbarrow, Sandhurst Rd, Crowthorne RG11 7HZ; Tel (01344) 772658; J.D. Pitt, BA. (935)
Garth Hill, Sandy La, Bracknell RG12 2JH; Tel (01344) 421122; Fax (01344) 55223; K.H. Brooke. (1200)
Sandhurst, Owlsmoor Rd, Owlsmoor, Camberley GU15 4SD; Tel (01344) 775678; Fax (01344) 771575; T.M. Enright, BA. (1018)

Comprehensive School (Voluntary)

Ranelagh, Ranelagh Dr, Bracknell RG12 3DA; Tel (01344) 421233; K. Winrow. VA (775)

Youth and Community Centres

Bracknell Boys Youth Club, Calfidus Way, Bracknell RG12 3ET; Tel (01344) 483596; J. Knight
Coopers Hill, Bagshot Rd, Bracknell RG12 3QS; Tel (01344) 423583; G. Plant; J. Galvin
Edgbarrow, Edgbarrow School, Sandhurst Rd, Crowthorne RG11 7HZ; Tel (01344) 773998; Mrs W.M. Peddle
Priestwood Y & C Centre, Court Rd, off Windmill Rd, Bracknell RG12 1TU; Tel (01344) 425531; K. Cornford
Sandhurst, Sandhurst School, Owlsmoor Rd, Owlsmoor, Camberley GU15 4SD; Tel (01344) 761414; Fax (01344) 750417; I. Richards

Teachers' Centre

Teaching and Support Service (Bracknell), Fox Hill Primary, Pond Moor Rd, Bracknell RG12 4AY; Tel (01344) 59122; *Co-ordinator* J. Treen

Newbury

Divisional Careers Offices

See chapter 17

Education Welfare Office

Newbury Area, Brook Hse, 60 Northbrook St, Newbury RG13 1AH; Tel (01635) 41535; Ansaphone (01635) 47110; *Team Leader* M. Hayter

Psychological Service

Newbury (East), Orwell Hse, 23 Craven Rd, Reading RG1 5LE; Tel (01734) 313644
Newbury (West), 88 Newtown Rd, Newbury RG14 7ET; Tel (01635) 45888

Special Classes and Resources

The Keevil Special Resource, Speenhamland Primary, Pelican La, Newbury RG13 1NU; Tel (01635) 41077; P. Shaw
Kennet Special Resource, Kennet County Secondary School, Stoney La, Thatcham RG13 4LL; Tel (01635) 862121; P. Dick
Lambourn Special Resource, Lambourn CE Controlled Primary School, Greenways, Lambourn, Newbury RG16 7LJ; Tel (01488) 71479; G.M. Stephens
Newbury Adjustment Centre, 88 Newtown Rd, Newbury RG14 7BT; Tel (01635) 43794; S. Heames
Park Hse Special Resource, Park Hse School, Andover Rd, Newbury RG14 6NQ; Tel (01635) 40165; D. Greenup

Robert Sandilands Assessment Resource, Robert Sandilands Primary School, Digby Rd, Newbury RG13 1TS; Tel (01635) 40318; R. Blofeld
Theale Language and Literacy Centre, Theale CE Controlled Primary School, Church St, Theale, Reading RG7 5BZ; Tel (01734) 303470; J.P. Buckley
Westwood Farm Infant Special Resource, Westwood Farm Infant School, Fulbrook Cres, Tilehurst RG3 6RY; Tel (01734) 426113; V. Davies
Westwood Farm Junior Special Resource, Fulbrook Cres, Tilehurst, Reading RG3 6RY; Tel (01734) 425182; P.M. Booth
Winchcombe Speech and Language Resource, Winchcombe Infant School, Maple Cres, Shaw Estate, Newbury RG13 1LN; Tel (01635) 40923; L.P. Harvey
Winchcombe Language and Literacy Centre, Winchcombe Junior School, Maple Cres, Shaw Estate, Newbury RG13 1LN; Tel (01635) 41767; M.G. Fowler

Special Schools

Brookfields, Sage Rd, Tilehurst, Reading RG3 6SW; Tel (01734) 421382; J.C. Byrne
The Castle (Prince Rupert Hse), Love La, Donnington, Newbury RG13 2JG; Tel (01635) 42976; H.K. Fernie

Comprehensive Schools

John O'Gaunt, Priory Rd, Hungerford RG17 0AN; Tel (01488) 682400; Fax (01488) 681283; M.A. Twelftree. (534)
Kennet, Stoney La, Thatcham RG13 4LL; Tel (01635) 862121; P.G. Dick, BA. (1327)
Little Heath, Littleheath Rd, Tilehurst, Reading RG3 5TY; Tel (01734) 427337; Fax (01734) 421933; C.W. Rowles. (1378)
Park Hse, Andover Rd, Newbury RG14 6NQ; Tel (01635) 40165; Fax (01635) 528884; D.W. Greenup. (875)
Shaw Hse, Church Rd, Shaw, Newbury RG13 2DU; Tel (01635) 41373; Fax (01635) 41373; M.J. Macleod, MA. (518)
Theale Green, Theale, Reading RG7 5DA; Tel (01734) 302741; Fax (01734) 305715; C. Gittens, BSc. (1364)
The Willink, School La, Burghfield Common, Reading RG7 3XJ; Tel (01734) 832030; Fax (01734) 832030; B. Wynn. (719)

Youth and Community Centres

John O'Gaunt, Priory Rd, Hungerford RG17 0AN; Tel (01488) 683692; Fax (01488) 681638; J.H. Gray
Kennet, Kennet School, Stoney La, Thatcham RG13 4LL; Tel (01635) 871558; Fax (01635) 871814; S. Green
Theale Green School, Theale, Reading RG7 5DA; Tel (01734) 302980; Fax (01734) 30274; D.M. Seward
Turnpike, Gaywood Dr, Shaw, Newbury RG13 2PS; Tel (01635) 46484; Fax (01635) 30642; M. Beams
Waterside, Northbrook St, Newbury RG13 1DS; Tel (01635) 41269; G. Schwarz
14–21 Time to Talk Youth Counselling Service, Newbury Youth Service, 1st Fl, 8 Pound St, Newbury RG14 6AA; Tel (01635) 581421; M. Gillies

Education Centres

Newbury Centre, Fir Tree La, Newbury RG13 2QX; Tel (01635) 43351; Fax (01635) 4331; *Head of Centres* R.M. Strapp Shire Hall; Tel (01734) 233424; Lindsey Sandy
Teaching and Support Service, Newbury Teachers' Centre, Fir Tree La, Newbury RG11 2QX; Tel (01635) 30572; *Co-ordinator* R. Riley

Reading

Divisional Careers Office

See chapter 17

Education Welfare Service

Reading, Top Fl, Reading Central Library, Abbey Sq, Reading RG1 3BE; Tel (01734) 580509; *Team Leader* D. Blake

Hospital and Home Service

Hospital and Home Teaching Service (West Berkshire), E.P. Collier, Ross Rd, Reading RG1 8DZ; Tel (01734) 574076; *Head of Service* A.R.M. Phillips

Psychological Service

Orwell Hse, 23 Craven Rd, Reading RG1 5LE; Tel (01734) 313644; *Educational Psychologist* J. Everett; *Educational Psychologist* C. Roberts; *Educational Psychologist* N. Firmin; *Educational Psychologist* L. Foden; *Educational Psychologist* S. Grimstone; *Educational Psychologist* R. Crofts; *Educational Psychologist* J. Roscoe; *Educational Psychologist* H. Mason; *Educational Psychologist* T. Williams; *Educational Psychologist* S. Baldwin; *Principal Psychiatric Social Worker* Y. Gayford; *Psychiatric Social Worker* E. Treadgold; *Psychiatric Social Worker* W. Bennell; *Psychiatric Social Worker* J. Holt; *Psychiatric Social Worker* J. Hopkins

Special Classes and Units

Geoffrey Field Language and Literacy Centre, Geoffrey Field Junior School, Exbourne Rd, Reading RG2 8RH; Tel (01734) 757344; C. Clare
E.P. Collier Assessment Resource, E.P. Collier School, Ross Rd, Reading RG1 8DZ; Tel (01734) 572352; A.E. Patterson
E.P. Collier Speech and Language Class, E.P. Collier Primary School, Ross Rd, Reading RG1 8DZ; Tel (01734) 572352; A.E. Patterson
New Bridge Nursery Class, Montague St, Caversham, Reading RG4 0AU; Tel (01734) 472838; C. Malley
New Town Primary Unit, New Town School, School Terr, Reading RG1 3LS; Tel (01734) 262206; S. Boott
Holy Brook School, 110 Ashampstead Rd, Reading RG3 3LJ; Tel (01734) 413316; J. Male
St Michael's Resource, St Michael's School, Dee Rd, Tilehurst, Reading RG3 4AS; Tel (01734) 428091; M. Aherne
Thameside Language and Literacy Centre, Thameside Junior School, Wolsey Rd, Caversham, Reading RG4 8BY; Tel (01734) 483978; V.A. Cussell

Special Schools

The Avenue, Basingstoke Rd, Reading RG2 0EN; Tel (01734) 871032; Fax (01734) 860179
Reading Alternative, 40 Christchurch Rd, Reading RG2 7AY; Tel (01734) 752095; J.E. Kightley, BA

Grammar Schools

Kendrick Girls, London Rd, Reading RG1 5BN; Tel (01734) 585959; Fax (01734) 505539; M. Elms. Girls (676)

Comprehensive Schools

Ashmead Boys, Northumberland Ave, Reading RG2 8DJ; Tel (01734) 861177; M. Hockley. (648)
Highdown, Surley Row, Emmer Grn, Reading RG4 8LR; Tel (01734) 475022; Fax (01734) 473761; A.P. Clarke, BA. (977)
Meadway, The Meadway, Tilehurst, Reading RG3 4NN; Tel (01734) 429444; R.J.T. Daybell, BA. (769)

Education Centres

Reading Centre, Cranbury Rd, Reading RG3 2TS; Tel (01734) 52634; Fax (01734) 575576; D. Smith
Teaching & Support Service, Reading Teachers' Centre, Cranbury Rd, Reading RG3 2TS; Tel (01734) 509373; R.C. Lynn

3 Local Government England and Wales

Youth and Community Centres

Central Reading Youth Provision, 36/42 London St, Reading RG1 4SQ; Tel (01734) 574421; Fax (01734) 510196; C. Webb; G. Taylor
Dee Park Centre, Tay Rd, Tilehurst, Reading RG3 4DR; Tel (01734) 419955; Vacancy
Emmer Green, Grove Rd, Emmer Green, Reading RG4 8LN; Tel (01734) 476794; P. Jennings
Fairview, Victoria Pk, George St, Reading RG1 7RR; Tel (01734) 576598; D. Garrett
Milestone Centre, Milestone Youth Wing, Northbrook Rd, Caversham Pk Village, Reading RG4 0PW; Tel (01734) 461329; Vacancy
No 5 Youth Counselling Service, 2–4 Sackville St, Reading RG1 1NT; Tel (01734) 585304; P. Francis
Reading Activities Centre, 69 Bulmershe Rd, Reading RG1 5RP; Tel (01734) 261506; Fax (01734) 263070; J. Hills
South Reading, Northumberland Ave, Reading RG2 7AQ; Tel (01734) 871780; Fax (01734) 756789; L. Chandler
Southcote, Coronation Sq, Southcote, Reading RG3 9QP; Tel (01734) 571410; Fax (01734) 594268; D. Fox
Sun St, off Cumberland Rd, Reading RG1 3JX; Tel (01734) 664576; Fax (01734) 664819; S. Ahmed-Khan
Tilehurst, 23 The Triangle, Tilehurst, Reading RG3 4RN; Tel (01734) 421741; K. Terry
Youth Connections (Detached Work Unit), Watlington Hse, Watlington St, Reading RG1 4RJ; Tel (01734) 595141; A. Cadogan; M. Hajnal

Slough

Divisional Careers Office

See chapter 17

Education Welfare Office

Slough Area Revelstoke Hse, 3–5 Chalvey Pk, Slough SL1 2HG; Tel (01753) 576119; *Team Leader* Mrs M. deJode

Psychological Service

Health Centre, Burlington Rd, Slough SL1 2JX; Tel (01753) 535822

Special Classes and Resources

Beechwood Special Resource, Beechwood Secondary School, Long Readings La, Slough SL2 1QE; Tel (01753) 520473; L.D. Wallace
Chalvey Nursery Assessment Resource, Chalvey Nursery, The Green, Chalvey, Slough SL1 2SP; Tel (01753) 572622; S. Backer
Foxborough Combined Hearing Impaired Resource, Foxborough Combined, Common Rd, Slough SL3 8TX; Tel (01753) 546376; D.H. Richards
Langleywood Secondary Resource, Langleywood Secondary School, Langley Rd, Slough SL3 7EF; Tel (01753) 541549; A. McPhee
Ryvers Combined Resource, Ryvers Combined School, Trelawney Ave, Slough SL3 7TS; Tel (01753) 544474; S. Dowling
St Ethelberts Language and Literacy Centre, St Ethelberts RC Aided, Wexham Rd, Slough SL2 5QR; Tel (01753) 522048; J. Boland-Lee

Special Schools

Arbour Vale, Arbor Vale School, Stoke Rd, Slough, Berks SL2 5AY; Tel (01753) 525291; J. Mansfield
Littledown School, Queens Rd, Slough SL1 3QW; Tel (01753) 521734; V.M. Goodwin
The Jonathan Miller School, 112 Burnham La, Slough, Berks SL1 6LR; Tel (01628) 667965; P.R. Barry

Secondary Modern Schools

Baylis Ct, Gloucester Ave, Slough SL1 3AH; Tel (01753) 531760; C.E.P. Pittaway, BA. Girls (434)
Beechwood, Long Readings La, Slough SL2 1QE; Tel (01753) 520473; L.D. Wallace. (522)
Langleywood, Langley Rd, Slough SL3 7EF; Tel (01753) 541549; Fax (01753) 593145; A. McPhee. (511)
Wexham SM School, Norway Dr, Slough SL2 5QP; Tel (01753) 526797; Fax (01753) 512029; J. Richardson. (531)

Secondary Modern Schools (Voluntary)

St Joseph's Catholic High, Shaggy Calf La, Slough SL2 5HW; Tel (01753) 524713; Fax (01753) 579128; J.B. Carvill. SA (451)
Slough and Eton CE, Ragstone Rd, Slough SL1 2PU; Tel (01753) 520824; R. Hadfield. Controlled (409)

Grammar School (Voluntary)

St Bernard's Convent, Langley Rd, Slough SL3 7AF; Tel (01753) 527020; Fax (01753) 693471; Sister Mary Stephen, BA. Girls; VA (764)

Education Centres

Slough Centre, Thomas Gray Centre, Queens Rd, Slough SL1 3QW; Tel (01753) 820268; Fax (01753) 511464; *Administration Officer* C. Franklin
Teaching and Support Service, Slough Tass Centre, Queen's Rd, Slough SL1 3QW; Tel (01753) 578631; *Teacher-in-Charge* P. Treadwell

Youth and Community Centres

Britwell Project, Wentworth Ave, Britwell Est, Slough SL2 2DH; Tel (01753) 526802; G. Harkin
Haymill, 112 Burnham La, Slough SL1 6LZ; Tel (01628) 604760; Fax (01628) 604798; S. Fairweather, K. Brophy
Horsemoor Grn, Common Rd, Langley, Slough SL3 8JU; Tel (01753) 542289; Fax (01753) 593707; G. Carpenter
Orchard, 73a Stoke Poges La, Slough SL1 3PD; Tel (01753) 518544; L. Jack
Project Contact, The Old Morgue, Burlington Ave, Slough SL1 2JT; Tel (01753) 694225; A. Mitchell, T. Statters
Rochford, Uxbridge Rd, Slough SL2 5NU; Tel (01753) 529582; J. Rowlands
Rotunda, Northampton Ave, Slough SL1 3BP; Tel (01753) 532980; Fax (01753) 550585; M. Solanki
S.P.A.C.E. Counselling Service, 81/83 Windsor Rd, Slough SL1 2JL; Tel (01753) 822895; P. Bains
Spirals Centre, c/o Chalvey Youth and Community Centre, Darvills La, Chalvey, Slough SL1 2PH; Tel (01753) 577007; Fax (01753) 552977; Vacancy

Windsor and Maidenhead

Divisional Careers Offices

See chapter 17

Education Welfare Service

Windsor/Maidenhead Area Windsor Magistrates Court, 65B Alma Rd, Windsor SL4 3HH; Tel (01753) 863486; Ansaphone (01753) 865349; *Team Leader* M. Payne

Psychological Service,

Brocket, 15 Boyn Hill Ave, Maidenhead SL6 4EY; Tel (01628) 24408; *Educational Psychologist* T. Lister; *Educational Psychologist* G. Bradley; *Educational Psychologist* H. Green; *Psychiatric Social Worker* S. McNab; *Psychiatric Social Worker* E. Stott

Special School,

Holyport Manor, Holyport, Maidenhead SL6 3LE; Tel (01628) 23196; P. Donkersloot

Special Classes and Resources

Brocket Adjustment Centre, Brocket, Boyn Hill Ave, Maidenhead SL6 4EY; Tel (01628) 31624; *Teacher-in-charge* J. Rushbrooke
Charters Special Resource, Charters School, Sunningdale, Ascot SL5 9QY; Tel (01344) 24826; J.B. Mitchell
Dedworth Special Resource, Dedworth Middle School, Smiths La, Windsor SL4 5PE; Tel (01753) 860561; B.F. Griffin
Ellington Language and Literacy Centre, Ellington Primary School, Cookham Rd, Maidenhead SL6 7JA; Tel (01628) 21741; H. Wood
Ellington Speech and Language Resource, Ellington Primary School, Cookham Rd, Maidenhead SL6 7JA; Tel (01628) 74096; H. Wood
Trevelyan Language and Literacy Centre, Trevelyan Middle School, Clarence Rd, Windsor SL4 5AJ; Tel (01753) 840262; A.W. Fone
Wessex Nursery Hearing Impaired Resource, Wessex Infants School, St Adrian's Cl, Cox Grn, Maidenhead SL6 3AT; Tel (01628) 29607; S. Robinson

Middle Schools

Dedworth County, Smith's La, Windsor SL4 5PE; Tel (01753) 860561; B.F. Griffin. (514)
Trevelyan, Green La, Windsor SL4 3QG; Tel (01753) 864371; A.W. Fone, MA. (554)

Middle Schools (Voluntary)

St Edward's Royal Free Aided, Parsonage La, Windsor SL4 5EN; Tel (01753) 867809; W.F. Merwood. (364)
St Peter's CE Aided Crimp Hill Rd, Old Windsor SL4 2QY; Tel (01753) 866253; D.J. Benson. VA (239)

Comprehensive Schools

Altwood CE Controlled, Altwood Rd, Maidenhead SL6 4PU; Tel (01628) 22236; Fax (01628) 75140; E.M. Allen. (639)
Charters, Charters Rd, Sunningdale, Ascot SL5 9QY; Tel (01344) 24826; Fax (01344) 875182; J.B. Mitchell, BA. (1292)
Cox Green, Highfield La, Maidenhead SL6 3AX; Tel (01628) 29415; M.C. Hearl. (692)
Furze Platt, Furze Platt Rd, Maidenhead SL6 7NQ; Tel (01628) 25308; A.C. Hill, MA. (1076)
Newlands, Farm Rd, Maidenhead SL6 5JB; Tel (01628) 25068; S.M. Benton. Girls (1094)
The Princess Margaret Royal Free CE Aided School, Bourne Ave, Windsor SL4 3JP; Tel (01753) 850109; P.R. Hutchinson. (312)
Windsor Boys, Maidenhead Rd, Windsor SL4 5EH; Tel (01753) 863882; Fax (01753) 833186; P.A. Blake, BA. Boys (876)
Windsor Girls, Imperial Rd, Windsor SL4 3RT; Tel (01753) 861410; G. Hume, BA. Girls (554)

Secondary Modern School

Churchmead, Priory Way, Datchet, Slough SL3 9JQ; Tel (01753) 542707; J. Smart. (440)

Education Centres

Maidenhead Centre, St Edmund's Hse, Ray Mill Rd West, Maidenhead SL6 8SB; Tel (01628) 27467; *Administration Officer* Fran Fletcher
Teaching and Support Service, Maidenhead Teachers' Centre, St Edmunds Hse, Ray Mill Rd West, Maidenhead SL6 8SB; Tel (01628) 70816; S.H. Rehman

Youth and Community Centres

Castle Hill, High Town Rd, Maidenhead SL6 1PB; Tel (01628) 31963; Fax (01628) 788954; P. Brown, C. Hair, D. Harrison
Charters Youth and Community Centre, Charters School, Charters Rd, Sunningdale, Ascot SL5 9QY; Tel (01344) 27982; J. Madgwick
Cox Green, Cox Green School, Highfield La, Maidenhead SL6 3AX; Tel (01628) 36715; B. Harris
No 22 Youth Counselling Service, 22 Cookham Rd, Maidenhead SL6 8AJ; Tel (01628) 36661; M. Luxon
Pinkneys Green, Courthouse Junior School, Blenheim Rd, Maidenhead SL6 5HE; Tel (01628) 28785; C. Davis
Windsor, Alma Rd, Windsor SL4 1HD; Tel (01753) 851508; Fax (01753) 851194; J. Harris, C. Scott

Wokingham

Divisional Careers Office

See chapter 17

Psychological Service

Dromore, 11 Park Ave, Wokingham RG11 2AJ; Tel (01734) 792280
Psychiatric Social Worker P. Ford

Special Classes and Resources

Beechwood Language and Literacy Centre, Beechwood Primary School, Ambleside Cl, Woodley, Reading RG5 4JJ; Tel (01734) 695976; S. Pyall
The Bulmershe Resource, Bulmershe School, Chequers Way, Woodley, Reading RG5 3EL; Tel (01734) 353353; R. Lennox
Dromore Adjustment Centre, 11 Park Ave, Wokingham RG11 2AQ; Tel (01734) 790417; J. Wheatley
Emmbrook Hearing Impaired Resource, Emmbrook School, Emmbrook Rd, Wokingham RG11 1JR; Tel (01734) 894282; E.H.W. Burton
Lambs La Special Resource, Lambs La Primary School, Back La, Spencers Wood, Reading RG7 1JB; Tel (01734) 883820; M. Stevenson
Palmer Special Resource, The Palmer CE Controlled Junior School, Norreys Ave, Wokingham RG11 1UX; Tel (01734) 784671; R. Palmer
Ryeish Green Special Resource, Ryeish Green School, Ryeish Grn, Spencer's Wood, Reading RG7 1ER; Tel (01734) 883133; I. Marshall

Special Schools

Addington, Loddon Bridge Rd, Woodley, Reading RG5 4BS; Tel (01734) 694244; S.G. Armstrong
Sindlesham, Mole Rd, Sindlesham, Wokingham RG11 5DJ; Tel (01734) 786900; Fax (01734) 776185; J.R. Urwin
Southfield School, Gypsy La, Wokingham RG11 2HR; Tel (01734) 771293; B. Allen

Comprehensive Schools

The Bulmershe, Chequers Way, Woodley, Reading RG5 3EL; Tel (01734) 353353; Fax (01734) 352929; R. Lennox. (1253)
The Emmbrook, Emmbrook Rd, Wokingham RG11 1JP; Tel (01734) 784406; Fax (01734) 892059; E.H.W. Burton, BA. (1157)
The Forest, Robin Hood La, Winnersh, Wokingham RG11 5NE; Tel (01734) 781626; Fax (01734) 776018; S.F. Grue, MA. Boys (1103)
The Holt, Holt La, Wokingham RG11 1EE; Tel (01734) 780165; Fax (01734) 890831; L.A.K. Roberts, BA. Girls (1153)
Maiden Erlegh, Off Silverdale Rd, Earley, Reading RG6 2HS; Tel (01734) 262467; W.D. Wills, MA. (1538)
Ryeish Green, Ryeish Green, Spencers Wood, Reading RG7 1ER; Tel (01734) 883133; I. Marshall. (1017)
St Crispin's, London Rd, Wokingham RG11 1SS; Tel (01734) 781144; Fax (01734) 795224; A. Biddle. (704)
Waingels Copse, Denmark Ave, Woodley, Reading RG5 4RF; Tel (01734) 690336; I. Marks, MEd, LCP. (1363)

Comprehensive School (Voluntary)

Piggott CE Controlled, Wargrave Rd, Wargrave, Reading RG10 8DS; Tel (01734) 402357; Dr K.J. Atton, BA. VC (774)

Education Centres

Wokingham Centre, Wokingham Centre, Reading Rd, Wokingham RG11 1RF; Tel (01734) 794046; Fax (01734) 794046; *Administration Officer* V. James

Wokingham Tass Centre, Wokingham Teachers' Centre, Reading Rd, Wokingham RG11 1RF; Tel (01734) 784512; N. Gaunt

Youth and Community Centres

ARC 6a Crescent Rd, Wokingham RG11 2DB; Tel (01734) 776710; M. Mallan

Bulmershe Centre, Woodlands Ave, Woodley, Reading RG5 3EU; Tel (01734) 268799; Fax (01734) 263153; K. Dynan

Earley Centrepoint, Chalfont Cl, Chalfont Way, Lower Earley, Reading RG6 2HZ; Tel (01734) 312951; M. Lush

The Silverdale Centre, Maiden Erlegh Campus, Silverdale Rd, Earley, Reading RG6 2HS; Tel (01734) 669529; Fax (01734) 352479; D. Regan

Twyford, Loddon Hall Rd, Twyford RG10 9JA; Tel (01734) 340891; T. Collis

Wokingham, 31a Broad St, Wokingham RG11 1AU; Tel (01734) 783610; T. Elwood

Woodley Airfield, Hurricane Way, Woodley, Reading, Berks RG5 4UX; Tel (01734) 440449; Fax (01734) 448762; T. Loveys

Berkshire Young Musicians' Trust

County/Finance, Mockbeggar Hse, 25 Whiteknights Rd, Reading RG6 2BT; Tel (01734) 665015; *Principal* R. Hickman

East Berkshire Music Centre, C/o Oakfield First School, Imperial Rd, Windsor SL4 3RJ; Tel (01753) 854598; *Area Head* G. Sanders

South Berkshire Music Centre, Foxhill Primary School, Pond Moor Rd, Bracknell, Berks RG12 4AY; Tel (01344) 360036; *Area Head* R.G. Priestley

West Berkshire, c/o Shaw Hse School, Church Rd, Shaw, Newbury RG13 2DU; Tel (01635) 48814; *Area Head* N. Beach

Grant Maintained Schools

Cippenham Middle School, Elmshott La, Cippenham, Berkshire SL1 5RB; Tel (01628) 604665

Denefield School, Long La, Tilehurst, Reading RG3 6XY; Tel (01734) 413458; Fax (01734) 452847; *Headmaster* J.M. Scott; *Chair of Governors* Mrs J. Baxter. (Mixed 11–18) (1116)

Desborough School, Shoppenhangers Rd, Maidenhead SL6 2QB; Tel (01628) 34505; Fax (01628) 39263; *Headteacher* M.J. Oddie, BA; *Chair of Governors* C.A.R. Cutler. Boys 11–18 (900)

The Downs, Compton, Newbury RG16 0NU; Tel (01635) 578213; Fax (01635) 578913; G.F. Taylor, BSc. (622)

Herschel, Northampton Ave, Slough SL1 3BW; Tel (01753) 520950; I.J. Pejn, MA. (502)

Langley Grammar School Reddington Dr, Langley SL3 7QS; Tel (01753) 810858; Fax (01753) 810850; *Headteacher* Dr A.G. Robinson; *Chair of Governors* A. West. Mixed 12–18 (630)

Reading School, Erleigh Rd, Reading RG1 5LW; Tel (01734) 261406; Fax (01734) 352755; *Headteacher* Dr Peter R. Mason. Boys 11–18 (717)

St Bartholomew's School Andover Rd, Newbury RG14 6JP; Tel (01635) 521255; Fax (01635) 550865; *Headteacher* Stuart Robinson; *Chair of Governors* Ian Campbell. Mixed 11–18 (650) (6th form)

Slough Grammar School, Lascelles Rd, Slough SL3 7PR; Tel (01753) 522892; Fax (01753) 538618; M. Lenton, BA. (600)

Southlands School, Northumberland Ave, Reading, Berks RG2 7PY; Tel (01734) 861336; Fax (01734) 866938; *Headmistress* Genefer Espejo; *Chairman of Governors* Tony Markham; *Financial Administrator* David Rooke. (Female) (with sixth form) (500)

The Westgate School, Cippenham La, Slough SL1 5AH; Tel (01753) 521320; Fax (01753) 521200; W.J. Armstrong. (446)

Birmingham City Council

Population 988,000

Council Hse, Victoria Sq, Birmingham B1 1BB; Tel 0121-235 9944; Fax 0121-235 4906

Education Department

Council Hse Extension, Margaret St, Birmingham B3 3BU; Tel 0121-235 2872/2590; Fax 0121-235 1318

Chairman Councillor A. Howell
Vice-Chairman Councillor P. Rose
Chief Education Officer Professor Timothy Brighouse
Assistant Director of Management John Fox
Office Service Manager John Perkin
Director of Policy and Finance Dr John Blythe
Assistant Director (Planning and Resources) Anna Lawson
Assistant Director (Quality and Development Review) Vacancy
External Funding and Promotions Manager Peter Harding
Chief Research and Statistics Manager John Hill
Information Technology Manager Chris Price
Director of Education Services Nick Hunnisett
Assistant Director Phil Haynes
Assistant Director (Personnel and Staffing) Manny Lewis
Assistant Director (Schools Management Support) Vacancy
Direct Services Organisation Manager Mike Yarnold
Finance Management Office Lynda Summerfield
Director of Individual and Community Support Vacancy
Assistant Director (Parent and Pupil Support) Gulam Mayet
Assistant Director (Community Education Development) Susan Waddington
Head of Careers Service Joe Donovan
Head of Individual Client Services Joyce Nicholls
Head of Ethnic Minorities Support Zahoor Chaudhary
Chief Psychologist L. Pearson
Social Worker/Behaviour Support Officer Tom Tierney

Number of Schools

26 nursery (1,590 & 5 PTE); 335 primary (96,502); 81 secondary (61,407); 30 special (2,833); 3 hospital; 2 hostels

Governor Training Unit

Portland Centre, 304 Portland Rd, Edgbaston B17 8LR; Tel 0121-235 4580/2322; Fax 0121-235 5305

Co-ordinator Governor Training and Support Nargis Rashid, MBE, CertEd, Batchelor of Philosophy

Services Offered

Training courses, conferences; Individual governing body training; Resources library, central and local helpline; Subscription to National Organisations and magazines; Birmingham Governor newsletter termly; Recruitment of governors from business and industry

Careers Offices

See chapter 17

Courts/Child Employment

4th Fl, 35–50 Orphanage Rd, Erdington B24 9HW; Tel 0121-235 5124; Ann Searle

Special Schools

Accident Hospital Teaching Unit, Ward 1, Bath Row, Birmingham B15 1NA; Tel 0121-627 1627 Ext 54687; P. Grady
Beaufort, 16 Coleshill Rd, Birmingham B36 8AA; Tel 0121-783 3886; P. Radford
Baskerville (Residential), Fellows La, Birmingham B17 9TS; Tel 0121-427 3191; Mrs R. Siddles
Braidwood, Perry Common Rd, Birmingham B23 7AT; Tel 0121-373 5558; W.J. Chippendale
Brays, Brays Rd, Birmingham B26 1NS; Tel 0121-743 5730; M.J. Chinner
Bridge, 290 Reservoir Rd, Birmingham B23 6DE; Tel 0121-373 8265; S. White, BPhil(Ed), MEd
Calthorpe, Darwin St, Birmingham B12 0TJ; Tel 0121-773 4637; G.J. Hardy, BEd, DipEd
Charles Burns Hospital School, Queensbridge Rd, Birmingham B13 8QB; Tel 0121-449 3322; S. Boyle, BEd
Cherry Oak, 60 Frederick Rd, Birmingham B29 6PB; Tel 0121-472 1263; Miss J. Furzey
Children's Hospital, Ladywood Middleway, Birmingham B16 8ET; Tel 0121-445 6685; S. Cowley
Dame Ellen Pinsent, Ardencote Rd, Birmingham B13 0RW; Tel 0121-444 2487; S.N. Heap, BEd
Dudley Rd Hospital 'C' Block 5, Dudley Rd, Birmingham B18 7QH; Tel 0121-554 3801, Ext 4617; J. Alkins
East Birmingham Hospital, Yardley Green Rd, Little Bromwich B9 5PX; Tel 0121-766 6611 Ext 2440; C. Coleman, BEd
Fox Hollies, 419 Fox Hollies Rd, Birmingham B27 7QA; Tel 0121-777 6566; S. Parker
George Auden, Bell Hill, Northfield, Birmingham B31 1LD; Tel 0121-475 3826; B.C. Jackson
Good Hope Hospital Teaching Unit, Harvey Ward, Rectory Rd B75 7RR; Tel 0121-378 2211 Ext 2606; C. Homer
Hallmoor, Hallmoor Rd, Birmingham B33 9QY; Tel 0121-783 3972; B.E. Robbins
Hamilton, Hamilton Rd, Birmingham B21 8AH; Tel 0121-554 1676; W.J. Rowthorn
Hunter's Hill Residential, Blackwell, nr Bromsgrove, Birmingham, West Midlands; Tel 0121-445 1320; K. Lewis. (incorporating Cropwood)
Kingstanding, Old Oscott Hill, Birmingham B44 9SP; Tel 0121-360 8222; R. Wallin
Langley, Lindridge Rd, Sutton Coldfield, Birmingham B75 7HU; Tel 0121-329 2929; A.L. Reid
Lindsworth Residential, Monyhull Hall Rd, Birmingham B30 3QA; Tel 0121-444 5211; M.A. Clarke
Longmoor, Coppice View Rd, Sutton Coldfield, Birmingham B73 6UE; Tel 0121-353 7833; Miss M. Castle
Longwill, Bell Hill, Northfield, Birmingham B31 1LD; Tel 0121-475 3923; P. Plant
Mayfield, Finch Rd, Birmingham B19 1HJ; Tel 0121-554 3354; S. Arbrol, MA, MEd
The Pines, Dreghorn Rd, Birmingham B36 8LL; Tel 0121-747 6136; S. Tuft
Priestley Smith, Perry Common Rd, Birmingham B23 7AT; Tel 0121-373 5493; C.G. Lewis, BEd
Queensbury, Wood End Rd, Birmingham B24 8BL; Tel 0121-373 5731; W. Warner
Selly Oak, Oak Tree La, Birmingham B29 6MZ; Tel 0121-472 0876; R. Dowling
Skilts Residential, Gorcott Hill, nr Redditch, Birmingham, West Midlands; Tel 0152-785 3851; Miss M.K. Probert
Springfield House Residential, Kenilworth Rd, Knowle, Solihull, West Midlands; Tel (01564) 775696; B. Evershed
Uffculme, Queensbridge Rd, Birmingham B13 8QB; Tel 0121-449 1081; R. Williams, BEd
Underwood, Rowden Dr, Birmingham B23 5UL; Tel 0121-373 5742; Dr D.T. Haigh. Malad
Victoria, Bell Hill, Northfield, Birmingham B31 1LD; Tel 0121-476 9478; I. Glen
Wilson Stuart, Perry Common Rd, Birmingham B23 7AT; Tel 0121-373 4475; J.C. Grantham
Woodlands Hospital, Bristol Rd South, Northfield, Birmingham B31 2AP; Tel 0121-627 1627 Ext 55346; A. Brown

Secondary Schools (County)

Arthur Terry, Kittoe Rd, Sutton Coldfield, Birmingham B74 4RZ; Tel 0121-308 3300; I.P. Lancaster
Aston Manor, Philips St, Birmingham B6 4PZ; Tel 0121-359 8108; Mrs L. Morris
Bartley Green, Adams Hill, Birmingham B32 3QJ; Tel 0121-476 9246; M. Gannon
Bordesley Green Girls, Bordesley Green Rd, Birmingham B9 4TR; Tel 0121-772 1391; Miss J. Sandland
Bournville, Griffins Brook La, Birmingham B30 1QJ; Tel 0121-475 3881; D. Lavery, BA
Broadway, The Broadway, Birmingham B20 3DP; Tel 0121-356 9444; M. Worsley, BA, FEd, FSE
Byng Kenrick, Central, Gressel La, Tile Cross, Birmingham B33 9UF; Tel 0121-779 6737; J.M. Vickers, BA
Castle Vale, Farnborough Rd, Birmingham B35 7NL; Tel 0121-747 6101; D.J. Walters, BSc
Cockshut Hill, Yardley, Birmingham B26 2HX; Tel 0121-722 2122; D.R. Mayes
Colmers Farm, Bristol Rd South, Rednal, Birmingham B45 9NY; Tel 0121-453 1778; M.R. Gardener
Dame Elizabeth Cadbury, Woodbrooke Rd, Birmingham B30 1UL; Tel 0121-458 4040; L.E. Bourne
Duddeston Manor, Gt Francis St, Birmingham B7 4QR; Tel 0121-359 3931; J. Donnelly
Four Dwellings, Dwellings La, Quinton, Birmingham B32 1RJ; Tel 0121-422 0131; R. Smoldon
Golden Hillock, Golden Hillock Rd, Birmingham B11 2QG; Tel 0121-773 8156/9; T. Probert
Hamstead Hall, Craythorne Ave, Birmingham B20 1HL; Tel 0121-358 5991; R.D. Wright
Handsworth Wood, Church La, Handsworth, Birmingham B20 2HH; Tel 0121-554 7883; G.L. Davies, BSc, MPhil. (Boys)
Handsworth Wood, Church La, Handsworth, Birmingham B20 2HL; Tel 0121-554 8122; E. Foster, BEd. (Girls)
Harborne Hill, Harborne Rd, Edgbaston, Birmingham B15 3JL; Tel 0121-454 2737; C.J. James, BA, MEd, ACp, FRGS
Hillcrest, Stonehouse La, Birmingham B32 3AE; Tel 0121-427 3172; Mrs J.S. Trotman, BA
Hodge Hill, Bromford Rd, Birmingham B36 8EY; Tel 0121-783 3094; Mrs A. Ede, BA. (Girls)
Hodge Hill, Bromford Rd, Birmingham B36 8HB; Tel 0121-783 8381; D.R. Gentle, BA
Holte, Wheeler St, Birmingham B19 2EP; Tel 0121-523 7321; G.C. Gray, BA, MEd
Holyhead, Florence Rd, Birmingham B21 0HN; Tel 0121-523 4207; C.R. Guidici
Jaffray, Fentham Rd, Erdington, Birmingham B23 6AB; Tel 0121-373 1425; A.R. Haynes
John Willmott, Reddicapp Heath Rd, Sutton Coldfield, Birmingham B75 7DY; Tel 0121-378 1946; M.C. Watson, BA
Kingsbury, Kingsbury Rd, Birmingham B24 8RE; Tel 0121-373 1080; Miss P.A. Exley
Kings Heath, Hollybank Rd, Birmingham B13 0RJ; Tel 0121-444 4454; I. Horne, BA, MA(Ed). (Boys)
King's Norton, Northfield Rd, Birmingham B30 1DY; Tel 0121-628 0010; I. Sonley. (Boys)
King's Norton, Selly Oak Rd, Birmingham B30 1HW; Tel 0121-458 1305; Mrs J. Carter. (Girls)
Lordswood, Hagley Rd, Birmingham B17 8BJ; Tel 0121-429 2837; R.J. Gardener. (Boys)
Lordswood, Knightlow Rd, Birmingham B17 8QB; Tel 0121-429 2838; J.R. Hattatt, BSc. (Girls)
Moseley, College Rd, Birmingham B13 9LR; Tel 0121-778 1141; M.J. Miles, MEd
Park View, Naseby Rd, Birmingham B8 3HG; Tel 0121-327 4209; J. Drury
Perry Beeches, Beeches Rd, Great Barr, Birmingham B42 2PY; Tel 0121-360 4242; H. Ridley, BEd
Perry Common, 395 College Rd, Birmingham B44 0HF; Tel 0121-373 1647; G. Rousell

Plantsbrook, Upper Holland Rd, Sutton Coldfield, West Midlands B72 1RB; Tel 0121-355 5626; J. Overend, BA
Primrose Hill, Shannon Rd, King's Norton, Birmingham B38 9DE; Tel 0121-459 4451; W.G. Green, BA
Queensbridge, Queensbridge Rd, Moseley, Birmingham B13 8QB; Tel 0121-449 3383; T. Edinburgh, BEd, MPhil
Saltley, Belchers La, Birmingham B9 5RX; Tel 0121-772 1801; R. Coxon
Selly Park, Pershore Rd, Birmingham B29 7PL; Tel 0121-472 1238; Mrs W.P. Davies
Sheldon Heath, Sheldon Heath Rd, Birmingham B26 2RZ; Tel 0121-743 4428; E.J. Buttery, BSc
Shenley Court, Shenley La, Birmingham B29 4HE; Tel 0121-475 5191; K. Dennis, BPhil
Sir Wilfrid Matineau, Gressel La, Birmingham B33 9UE; Tel 0121-779 2011; S. Parker, BA
Stockland Green, Slade Rd, Erdington, Birmingham B23 7JH; Tel 0121-373 4807; M. Johnson, BA, DipEd
Sutton Coldfield, Jockey Rd, Sutton Coldfield, Birmingham B73 5PT; Tel 0121-354 1479; Mrs J. Jones, BA. (Girls)
Swanshurst, Brook La, Birmingham B13 0TW; Tel 0121-443 3541; M.W. Threadgold, MEd
Turves Green Boys, Northfield, Birmingham B31 4BS; Tel 0121-475 4129, 2281; B. Stokes, BA. (Boys)
Turves Green, Northfield, Birmingham B31 4BP; Tel 0121-476 8346; S.K. Brehony. (Girls)
Washwood Heath, Burney La, Birmingham B8 2AS; Tel 0121-784 7272; J.S. Bailey, MEd
Waverley, Hobmoor Rd, Birmingham B10 9BT; Tel 0121-772 1780; Mrs J. Collett, BEd
Wheelers La, Kings Heath, Birmingham B13 0SF; Tel 0121-444 2864; E.D. Griffiths, BSc
Yardleys, Warwick Rd, Tyseley, Birmingham B11 2LT; Tel 0121-708 2771; Mrs H. Jones, BSc

Secondary Schools (Voluntary)

Archbishop Ilsley R.C., Victoria Rd, Acocks Grn B27 7XY; Tel 0121-706 4200; M. Emm, BA, MEd
The Bishop Challoner R.C., Institute Rd B14 7EG; Tel 0121-444 4161; P. Jenkins, BEd
Bishop Vesey's Grammar, Lichfield Rd, Sutton Coldfield B74 2NH; Tel 0121-354 2552; Mrs H.E. Clarke
Bishop Walsh R.C., Wylde Grn Rd, Sutton Coldfield B76 8QT; Tel 0121-351 3215; A.J. Upton, BA
Cardinal Newman R.C., Poplar Ave, Edgbaston B17 8ES; Tel 0121-429 4356; B. Hickey
Cardinal Wiseman R.C., Old Oscott Hill, Kingstanding B44 9SR; Tel 0121-360 6383; S. O'Donnell
Holy Trinity R.C., Oakley Rd B10 0AX; Tel 0121-772 0184; T. Temple
Lea Mason C of E, Bell Barn Rd, Edgbaston B15 2AF; Tel 0121-622 4832; D. Hess
St Alban's C of E, Angelina St B12 0UU; Tel 0121-440 4034; Miss S. Lyman
St Edmund Campion R.C., Sutton Rd, Erdington B23 5XA; Tel 0121-382 6144; K.P. Ash
St George's C of E, Gt Hampton Rd, Newtown B19 3JG; Tel 0121-236 9177; P.A. Cook, BEd (Acting)
St John Wall R.C., Oxhill Rd B21 8HH; Tel 0121-554 1825; B.J. Toft, BA, MEd
St Paul's R.C., Vernon Rd, Edgbaston B16 9SL; Tel 0121-454 0895; Sister Theresa Brown. (Girls)
St Thomas Aquinas R.C., Wychall La, King's Norton B38 8AP; Tel 0121-458 4643; J.F.T. Bartlett, BA

Grant Maintained Schools

Baverstock School, 501 Bells La, Birmingham B14 5TL; Tel 0121-430 7924; Fax 0121-474 5313; *Chairman of Governors* W. Evans; *Headteacher* C.R. Perks. (Mixed) (11–16 (1100)
Fairfax School, Fairfax Rd, Sutton Coldfield, West Midlands B75 7JT; Tel 0121-378 1288
George Dixon School, City Rd, Edgbaston, Birmingham B17 8LF; Tel 0121-434 4488
Great Barr School, Aldridge Rd, Great Barr, Birmingham B44 9NU; Tel 0121-366 6611; Fax 0121-366 6007; *Headteacher* Brian W. Sherratt; *Chair of Governors* Mrs J. Watts-James. (Mixed) (11–18) (2011)
Hall Green Secondary School, Southam Rd, Birmingham B28 0AA; Tel 0121-628 8782; Fax 0121-702 2182; P. Whittaker
Handsworth Grammar School for Boys, Grove La, Birmingham B21 9ET; Tel 0121-554 2794/3506; Fax 0121-554 5405; *Headteacher* M.H. Cavendish; *Chairman of Governors* E.H. Lear, OBE. (Male) (11–18) (780)
King Edward VI Camp Hill School for Boys, Vicarage Rd, Kings Heath, Birmingham B14 7QJ; Tel 0121-444 3188; R.M. Dancey. (Boys)
King Edward Camp Hill School for Girls, Vicarage Rd B14 7QJ; Tel 0121-444 2150; E.A. Percival, BSc. (Girls)
King Edward VI Aston School, Frederick Rd, Aston B6 6DJ; Tel 0121-327 1130; P.A. Christopher, MA, FRSA. (Boys)
King Edward VI Five Ways School, Scotland La, Bartley Grn B32 4BT; Tel 0121-475 3535; J. Knowles. (Boys + Girls in VI form)
King Edward VI Handsworth School, Rose Hill Rd, Handsworth B21 9AR; Tel 0121-554 2342; E.V. Insch, BSc, DipEd, MPhil, FRGS. (Girls)
Kings Norton Girls School, Selly Oak Rd, Kings Norton, Birmingham B30 1HW; Tel 0121-458 1305
Ninestiles School, Hartfield Cres, Acocks Grn, Birmingham B27 7QG; Tel 0121-628 1311
Small Heath School, Muntz St, Small Heath, Birmingham B10 9RX; Tel 0121-766 7997; Fax 0121-766 8120; *Headteacher* C.G. Knight, OBE; *Chairman of Governors* Dr B. Marson; *Bursar* Miss S. Page. (Mixed) (11–18) (1000)
The Streetly School, Queslett Rd East, Streetly, Sutton Coldfield B74 2EX; Tel 0121-353 2709; Fax 0121-353 0212

Bolton Metropolitan Borough Council

Population 267,400
Civic Centre, Bolton, Lancs BL1 1RU; Tel (01204) 22311; Fax (01204) 392808

Education Department

PO Box 53, Paderborn Hse, Civic Centre, Bolton BL1 1JW; Tel (01204) 522311; Fax (01204) 365492
Chairman Councillor D. Eastwood, JP
Director of Education and Arts B. Hughes, BSc
Deputy Director J.M. Willis, BA
Assistant Director (Services for Schools Division) B.E. Atkinson, BA
Assistant Director (Personal Services Division) B.C. Scanlon, BA, IPFA
Chief Librarian F.N. Parker, FLA, AMBIM; Fax (01204) 363224
Chief Museums Officer Dr J.R.A. Gray, BSc, PhD, AMA, FRES; Fax (01204) 391352
Finance Unit Manager I. Glaister, BA(Hons), DMS
Personnel Unit Manager D. Sutton, DMS
Information Technology Unit Manager G.D. Smith, MMS, DMS
Special Needs Service Manager C.F. Chisholm, BA
Pupil and Student Services Manager J.S. Jackson, DipEd
Policy Development Officer C.H. Swift, BA, MEd, CertEd
Programmes Officer J. Fletcher
Principal Careers Officer R. Abrahamsen
Manager (Curriculum and Management) D.C. Llewellyn, BEd
Manager (Inspection) B. Burke, BA

Senior Youth Services Officer W.D. Alders, MSc, CertEd, DipCommDev New Overdale Youth Training and Conference Centre, 11 Overdale Dr, Bolton BL1 5BT; Tel (01204) 840636; Fax (01204) 492087
Principal Educational Psychologist P. Nicklin, MA
Principal Education Social Worker M.A. Price, MA, MSc
Number of Schools
5 nursery (351 F.T.); nursery classes (1,243 F.T.); 104 primary (25,127); 13 secondary (16,974)
Special Schools
7 day (494)
Day of Committee Meeting
Wednesday, six-week cycle (two weeks prior to council meeting)
Requisition Periods for Schools Supplies
No set period
Other Authorities with whom Joint Purchasing Arrangements are made
Local authorities in area of Greater Manchester County

Governor Training Unit

Training Unit, Bolton MBC, Department of Education and Arts, Paderbourn Hse, Bolton BL1 1JW; Tel (01204) 522311 Ext 2024; Fax (01204) 365492
Teachers Centre, Ryoley St, Bolton BL2 1HW; Tel (01204) 522935; Fax (01204) 371874
Training Unit Manager David Lee, BA, DMA, MITD
Services Offered
School-based and centre-based training for governors, senior staff and teaching and non-teaching staff of schools; Skills training; Management; Education and Law; Finance; Personnel issues; Curriculum issues etc

Careers Office

See chapter 17

Education Welfare Office

Paderborn Hse, Civic Centre, Bolton BL1 1JW

Special Schools

Woodside Senior 425 Chorley New Rd, Bolton, Greater Manchester; Tel (01204) 843637; A.J.T. Johns. Moderate learning difficulties (128)
Woodside Junior 425 Chorley new Rd, Bolton, Greater Manchester; Tel (01204) 840709; J.C. Whittaker. Moderate learning difficulties (96)
Thomasson Memorial Devonshire Rd, Bolton, Greater Manchester; Tel (01204) 843063; Mrs P. Ormerod. Hearing Impaired (45)
Lostock Park School Tempest Rd, Lostock, Greater Manchester; Tel (01204) 840321; G. Wilson, BEd(Hons). (E/B) (46)
Firwood Crompton Way, Bolton, Greater Manchester; Tel (01204) 303499; R.T. Peace, BA. Severe learning difficulties (74)
Green Fold Highfield Rd, Farnworth, Greater Manchester; Tel (01204) 72524; Mrs C.E. Chapman. Severe learning difficulties (71)
Stocks Park Stocks Park Dr, Horwich, Greater Manchester; Tel (01204) 691608; M.R. Waring. (E/B) (34)

County Secondary Schools

The Deane New York, Bolton, Greater Manchester; Tel (01204) 64521; H.E. Speller. (965)
Harper Green Harper Green Rd, Farnworth, Greater Manchester; Tel (01204) 72941/74991; Fax (01204) 793031; A. Atherton, BA, MEd. (1003)
Hayward Lever Edge La, Bolton, Greater Manchester; Tel (01204) 62605/62353/1654608; Fax (01204) 653154; J. Heaton. (982)
Little Lever Church St, Little Lever, Bolton, Greater Manchester; Tel (01204) 709500; Fax (01204) 708029; A. Behan, MA, ADVDiploma Education BA(Hons). (893)
Rivington and Blackrod High (Voluntary Controlled) Rivington La, Horwich, Greater Manchester; Tel (01204) 692511; Fax (01204) 693692; J. Mills, BSc(Hons). (1638)
Sharples Hill Cot Rd, Bolton, Greater Manchester; Tel (01204) 308421; C.R. Atkinson, MA. (828)
Smithills Smithills Dean Rd, Bolton, Greater Manchester; Tel (01204) 842382/842375/846890; Fax (01204) 847473; M.P. Kehoe, BSc. (1442)
Turton High Bromley Cross Rd, Bromley Cross, Bolton, Greater Manchester; Tel (01204) 595888; Fax (01204) 306712; F.E.S. Vigon. (1489)
Westhoughton High Bolton Rd, Westhoughton, Greater Manchester; Tel (01942) 814122; Fax (01942) 817792; K.R. Vann, BA. (966)
Withins Newby Rd, Bolton, Greater Manchester; Tel (01204) 526519; Fax (01204) 361428; Mrs J. Richardson. (1089)

Roman Catholic Comprehensive Schools

Mount St Joseph Greenland Rd, Bolton, Greater Manchester; Tel (01204) 391800; Fax (01204) 389575; Sister Barbara Sexton, MA. (795)
St Joseph's Chorley New Rd, Horwich, Greater Manchester; Tel (01204) 697456; G.F. Boyle. (695)
Thornleigh Salesian College Sharples Park, Bolton, Greater Manchester; Tel (01204) 301351; Fax (01204) 595351; Rev J.M. Williams, BSc, BD. (1540)

Grant Maintained Schools

Canon Slade School Bradshaw Brow, Bolton, Greater Manchester BL2 3BP; Tel (01204) 591441; Fax (01204) 595658; Rev P.W. Shepherd, BA, BD, MA, MPhil. (1504)
George Tomlinson Springfield Rd, Kearsley, Greater Manchester; Tel (01204) 71854/709758; Fax (01204) 794091; *Headteacher* A.T. Buckley. (484)
St James CE School Lucas Rd, Farnworth, Bolton BL4 9RU; Tel (01204) 700008

City of Bradford Metropolitan Council

Population 477,500
City Hall, Bradford BD1 1HY; Tel (01274) 752111; Fax (01274) 752065

Education Directorate

Flockton Hse, Flockton Rd, Bradford BD4 7RY; Tel (01274) 752111; Fax (01274) 390081
Director of Education (Acting) Ken Sutcliffe; Tel (01274) 751700
Acting Assistant Director (Client and Corporate Support) Phil Green; Tel (01274) 751702
Assistant Director (Education and Community Services) Dennis Williams; Tel (01274) 751807
Assistant Director (Education and Business Services) Mike Peters; Tel (01274) 751926
Principal Inspector (Acting) Clive Halliwell
Senior Inspector Carlton Midgley
Senior Inspector (Acting) Linda Chapman
Inspector (Primary) Kay Charlton
Inspector (Language and Drama) Sandra Tweddell
Inspector (Primary) Barbara Davy
Inspector (Further Education) R. White
Senior Inspector (Acting) David Jobbings
Inspector (Early Years) Ann Hedley
Inspector (Information Technology) Brian Parkes
Inspector (Mathematics) Steve Guild

Inspector Science Dr John Skevington
Inspector (Primary) Kathryn Butterfield
Inspector (Physical Education) David Bate
Inspector (Geography and Environmental Education) William Varley
Inspector (Middle Years) Mike Warman
Inspector (Middle Years) Pat Copperthwaite
Inspector (Technology) Ray Watson
Head of Curriculum Training and Support Service T. Cooper
Manager (Music Service) Phillip Skelton
Unit Manager (Technical Support Service) David Watson
Unit Manager (Financial Support Service) Alan Jarvis
Unit Manager (Buildings Service) Frank Gorman
Unit Manager (Personnel Support Service) Lynne Barker
Unit Manager (Policy and Information Team) Francis Marslen-Wilson
Unit Manager (Special Educational Needs Support Service) Judith Moore (Acting)
Unit Manager (Education Welfare Service) Beryl Radford
Unit Manager (Psychological Service) Olwyn Billcliff
Unit Manager (Community and Continuing Education Service) Jane Gledhill
Unit Manager (School Management Support Service) Jennie Sadowskyj
Unit Manager (Staff Development Unit) John Hesketh
Unit Manager (Education Social Work Service) Gabrielle Hall
Unit Manager (Education Library Service) Bob Wilkes
Unit Manager (Outdoor Centres) Ric Halsall
Unit Manager (Training Group) Paul Langham
Unit Manager (Careers Service) Cliff Spraclen
Number of Schools
6 nursery; 164 primary; 61 middle; 19 upper; 4 grant maintained upper; 1 grant maintained first; 2 grant maintained middle
Special Schools
14
Special Centres
4
Assessment Centre
1
Requisition Period for School Supplies
1st April to 31st December

Education Committee

Con 6, Lab 10
Chair Malcolm Walters, (Lab) C/o City Hall, Bradford
Vice-Chair Ralph Berry, (Lab) C/o City Hall, Bradford
Members of the Committee
Con: R. Cope, J. Evans, F. Lee, C. Hobson, P. Pettit, D. Smith
Lab: S. Ahmed, J. Ellison, D. Fairfax, P. Foord, J. Ryan, E. Hey, F, Sunderland, J. Tough

Governor Training Unit

Salts Mill, Victoria Rd, Saltaire BD18 3LB; Tel (01274) 757100; Fax (01274) 530253
Service Co-ordinator Jackie Walters
School Governor Officer Colin Richardson
Services Offered
Provides and commissions full range of governor training and clerk to governors training. Also provides support, advice and information (incl governor library and resources). Also services governor forums, provides termly briefing notes for governors and termly briefing sessions for Clerks; supports School Governors Advisory Group, provides guidance about recruitment appointment and election procedures, processes G.B. resolutions to Committees and provide full-day curriculum experience courses etc

Special Schools

Ashfield, Ellar Carr Rd, Thackley, Bradford BD10 OTD; Tel (01274) 612176; C. Hargreaves (Acting)
Bolling, Anerley St, Bradford BD4 7SY; Tel (01274) 721962; A. Moore (Acting). (L.D.) (110)
Braithwaite, Braithwaite Rd, Keighley BD22 6PR; Tel (01535) 603041; Fax (01535) 691227; D. Foster. (L.D.) (115)
Branshaw, Oxford St, Keighley BD21 1RA; Tel (01535) 662739; J. Graveson. (L.D.) (68)
Chapel Grange, Rhodesway, Bradford BD8 0DQ; Tel (01274) 545425; Fax (01274) 484175; H. Morrison. (L.D.) (95)
Greenfield, Boothroyd Dr, Idle, Bradford BD10 8LU; Tel (01274) 614092; J. Taylor. (L.D.) (152)
Haycliffe, Haycliffe La, Bradford BD5 9ET; Tel (01274) 576123; B. Chatwin. (L.D.) (150)
Heaton Royds, Redburn Dr, Shipley, Bradford BD18 3AZ; Tel (01274) 583759; Fax (01274) 589397; M. Fowler. (L.D.) (48)
Lister La, Lister La, Bradford BD2 4LL; Tel (01274) 637473; W.G. Freeth. (P.H.) (110)
Netherlands Ave, Odsal, Bradford BD6 1EA; Tel (01274) 677711; Fax (01274) 677711; W. Paley. (L.D.) (120)
Temple Bank, Daisy Hill La, Bradford BD9 6BN; Tel (01274) 541714; Fax (01274) 490279. (School and Service for Children with Visual Impairment) (75)
Thorn Pk, Thorn La, off Bingley Rd, Bradford BD9 6RJ; Tel (01274) 497866; Fax (01274) 493279. (School and Service for Children with Hearing Impairment) (85)
Wedgwood, Landscove Ave, Holmewood, Bradford BD4 0NQ; Tel (01274) 686735; Mrs Godward. (L.D.) (80)

Special Service Centres

Tong Park Assessment Centre, Tong Pk, Shipley, Bradford BD17 7QL; Tel (01274) 595339; Fax (01274) 531448; E. Godfrey (Acting)
Whinburn Support Centre, Hollins La, Keighley BD20 6LU; Tel (01535) 602025; K. Pinder. (Residential)

Mainstream School Resourced for Special Educational Needs

Carlton Bolling, Butler St, Bradford BD3 0QS; Tel (01274) 726998; M. Flecknoe

County Middle Schools

Addingham Bolton Rd, Addingham LS29 0MR; Tel (01943) 830944; B.D. Hall. (332)
Allerton Middle, Garforth St, Allerton, Bradford BD15 7HB; Tel (01274) 541515; A.B. Markham. (211)
Belmont Middle School, West La, Baildon BD17 5DH; Tel (01274) 598115; C. Hall. (263)
Bronte Middle, Bogthorn, Oakworth, Keighley BD22 7LU; Tel (01535) 605991; J.L. Rosser. (433)
Broomwood Middle School, Dawson La, Bierley, Bradford BD4 6JF; Tel (01274) 689847; J. Kemp. (286)
Burley Middle School, Langford La, Burley-in-Wharfedale, Ilkley LS29 7EJ; Tel (01943) 862642; J. Rowe. (235)
Buttershaw Middle, Farfield Ave, Buttershaw, Bradford BD6 2JD; Tel (01274) 678544; Fax (01274) 690261; J. Thornton. (493)
Calversyke Middle, School Rd, Guard Hse, Keighley BD22 6JG; Tel (01535) 604285; W.J. Haykin. (255)
Clayton Middle, John St, Clayton, Bradford BD14 6AD; Tel (01274) 882263; V.G. Clarke. (372)
Daisy Hill Middle, Hazelhurst Brow, Bradford BD9 6AB; Tel (01274) 546059; J. Jackson. (360)
Delf Hill Middle, Common Rd, Low Moor, Bradford BD12 0TN; Tel (01274) 670686; J. Cawkwell. (320)
Drummond Middle, Drummond Rd, Manningham, Bradford BD8 8DA; Tel (01274) 543260; Fax (01274) 543119; M. Hearn. (559)
Eccleshill North Middle, Rillington Mead, Bradford BD10 0EF; Tel (01274) 611327; Fax (01274) 620579; M. Milone. (262)
Fairweather Green Middle, Thornton Rd, Bradford BD8 0HJ; Tel (01274) 543061; D.N. Park. (377)
Frizinghall Middle, Salisbury Rd, Frizinghall, Bradford BD9 4HW; Tel (01274) 543061; E. Mirza. (193)
Gt Horton Middle, Cross La, Gt Horton, Bradford BD7 3JT; Tel (01274) 573288; C. Feather. (382)
Gilstead Middle School, Barnaby Rd, Warren La, Bingley, Bradford BD16 3LE; Tel (01274) 568361; P. Sumpter. (367)
Grange Middle, Grange Rd, Riddlesden, Keighley BD20 5AB; Tel (01535) 607528; S. Mitchell. (280)

Gregory Middle, C/o St Blaise RC Middle School, Newhall Rd, Bradford BD4 6AF; Tel (01274) 680510; J.M. Powell. (308)
Hainsworth Moor Middle, Hainsworth Moor Gr, Queensbury, Bradford BD13 2ND; Tel (01274) 882883; Fax (01274) 817136; M. O'Brien. (409)
Hartington Middle, Rawdon Rd, Haworth BD22 3DW; Tel (01535) 642359; J. Smith. (393)
Heaton Middle, Haworth Rd, Bradford BD9 6LL; Tel (01274) 548173; A. Parker. (371)
Highfield Middle, Spencer St, Keighley BD21 2QQ; Tel (01535) 604101; T. Peterson. (457)
Holme Middle, Knowles La, Bradford BD4 9AE; Tel (01274) 681502; Fax (01274) 685798; D.L.N. Chapman. (332)
Hutton Middle, Victoria Rd, Bradford BD2 2DW; Tel (01274) 639382; K. McRae. (206)
Ilkley Middle, Valley Dr, Ben Rhydding, Ilkley LS29 8PA; Tel (01943) 608765; D. Tee. (262)
Ladderbanks Middle School, Coverdale Way, Baildon, Bradford BD17 6TE; Tel (01274) 594686; C. Thirkill. (94)
Lapage Middle, Barkerend Rd, Bradford BD3 8QX; Tel (01274) 664483; Fax (01274) 663832; L. Connolly. (493)
Leaventhorpe Middle Chelwood Dr, Bradford BD15 7YD; Tel (01274) 881955; T.P. McAllister. (147)
Lidget Green Middle, Cemetery Rd, Bradford BD7 2PY; Tel (01274) 573293; Fax (01274) 573293; J. Edwards. (365)
Lower Fields Middle, Fenby Ave, Bradford BD4 8RG; Tel (01274) 393444; Fax (01274) 735217; K. McIlroy. (450)
Mandale Middle, Cooper La, Bradford BD6 3WW; Tel (01274) 672184; M.J. Joyce. (306)
Manningham Middle, Manningham La, Bradford BD8 7HS; Tel (01274) 723648; K. McGee. (596)
Nab Wood Middle School, New Close Rd, Shipley, Bradford BD18 4AB; Tel (01274) 592815; J.E. Wood. (531)
Parkland Middle, Old Park Rd, Bradford BD10 9BG; Tel (01274) 611458; J. Flockton. (163)
Parkside Middle School, Parkside Terr, Cullingworth BD13 5AD; Tel (01535) 272752; R. Quartermain. (432)
Pollard Pk Middle, Byron St, Bradford BD3 0AB; Tel (01274) 726158; C. Crowther. (589)
Priestman Middle, Hutton Rd, Bradford BD5 9DS; Tel (01274) 572088; Fax (01274) 572088; D. Robinson. (579)
Royd Mount, Thornton Rd, Bradford BD13 3NN; Tel (01274) 833839; M. Dean. (225)
Ryan Middle, New Cross St, West Bowling, Bradford BD5 8BT; Tel (01274) 723617; Fax (01274) 723617; G. Ensor. (362)
Ryshworth Middle School, Morton La, Crossflatts, Bingley, Bradford BD16 2EP; Tel (01274) 568855; G.R. Jackson. (228)
Scotchman Middle, Scotchman Rd, Bradford BD9 5GF; Tel (01274) 548178; Fax (01274) 487105; H. Figgess. (135)
Stoney Lee Middle School, Cottingley Moor Rd, Cottingley, Bingley BD16 1SY; Tel (01274) 567545; A. Moffat. (495)
Swain House Middle, Swain House Rd, Bradford BD2 1JN; Tel (01274) 638027; D. Curtin. (456)
Swire Smith Middle, Cherry Tree Rise, Keighley BD21 4RU; Tel (01535) 604182; Fax (01535) 604182; D. Adam. (399)
Thornbury Middle, Leeds Old Rd, Bradford BD3 8JG; Tel (01274) 665812; J. Clarke. (356)
Thorpe Middle, Albion Rd, Bradford BD10 9PY; Tel (01274) 611428; B. Grant. (335)
Undercliffe Middle, Undercliffe Old Rd, Bradford BD2 4RQ; Tel (01274) 639380; Fax (01274) 626544; R. Kunicki. (362)
Waverley Middle, Spencer Rd, Bradford BD7 3HU; Tel (01274) 573297; Fax (01274) 521745; I. McRae. (683)
Wellington Middle, Leeds Rd, Bradford BD2 3AY; Tel (01274) 639938; P. Chaplin. (397)
Whetley Middle, Whetley La, Bradford BD8 9HZ; Tel (01274) 543755; P. Mellor. (378)
Woodend Middle School, Wrose Brow Rd, Shipley, Bradford BD18 2NT; Tel (01274) 583555; R.E. Buckee. (431)
Woodroyd Middle, Woodroyd Rd, Bradford BD5 8EL; Tel (01274) 727524; T. Empson. (208)
Woodside Middle, Fenwick Dr, Bradford BD6 2PG; Tel (01274) 676898; Fax (01274) 676898; G. Astley. (150)
Worth Valley Middle, Bracken Bank Cres, Keighley BD22 7AX; Tel (01535) 604240; M.G. Pickles. (274)
Wycliffe C.E. Middle, Saltaire Rd, Shipley BD18 3HZ; D.J. Hartley
Wyke Middle, Huddersfield Rd, Bradford BD12 8AA; Tel (01274) 678383; Fax (01274) 678383; D. Mitchell. (411)

Voluntary Aided Middle Schools

Cottingley Manor R.C. Middle School, Cottingley New Rd, Bingley, Bradford BD16 1TZ; Tel (01274) 562876; O. Wortley. (236)
St Blaise R.C. Middle, Newhall Rd, Bradford BD4 6AF; Tel (01274) 685313; M. Reynolds. (410)
St Edmund Campion R.C. Middle, Rhodesway, Bradford BD8 0DH; Tel (01274) 542992; J. Kenefick. (320)
St George R.C. Middle, Cliffe Rd, Bradford BD3 0LX; Tel (01274) 638754; M. Frost (Acting). (338)

Upper Schools

Beckfoot Upper, Wagon La, Bingley, Bradford BD16 1EE; Tel (01274) 563803; Fax (01274) 510200; R. Wager. (953)
Belle Vue, Thorn La, Haworth Rd, Bradford BD9 6ND; Tel (01274) 493533; Fax (01274) 483671; B. Berry. (Boys) (575)
Belle Vue, Thorn La, Bingley Rd, Bradford BD9 6NA; Tel (01274) 492341; Fax (01274) 490559; A. Hall (Acting). (Girls) (623)
Buttershaw, Reevy Rd West, Buttershaw, Bradford BD6 3PX; Tel (01274) 676285; Fax (01274) 679228; J. Hull. (1319)
Carlton Bolling College, Undercliffe La, Bradford BD3 0DU; Tel (01274) 633111; Fax (01274) 630635; S.C. Willis. (1129)
Eccleshill, Harrogate Rd, Bradford BD10 0JE; Tel (01274) 614928; Fax (01274) 615234; K. Lickley. (515)
Fairfax Community School, Lister Ave, Bradford BD4 7QT; Tel (01274) 392311; Fax (01274) 390887; A. Hobbs (Acting). (540)
Grange, Haycliffe La, Bradford BD5 9ET; Tel (01274) 573953; Fax (01274) 502693; W.R. Thompson. (988)
Greenhead, Greenhead Rd, Utley, Keighley BD20 6EB; Tel (01535) 662828; Fax (01535) 605327; M. Mizon. (926)
Nab Wood Grammar, Cottingley New Rd, Bingley, Bradford BD16 1TZ; Tel (01274) 567281; Fax (01274) 510688; H. Lynch. (906)
Queensbury, Deanstone's La, Queensbury, Bradford BD13 2AS; Tel (01274) 882214; Fax (01274) 884853; K. Biggs. (614)
Rhodesway, Oaks La, Allerton, Bradford BD15 7RU; Tel (01274) 498015; Fax (01274) 544880; I.A. Bowmaker. (1316)
Salt Grammar, Higher Coach Rd, Baildon, Bradford BD17 5RH; Tel (01274) 584681; Fax (01274) 590604; T. Hagerty. (851)
Tong, Westgate Hill St, Bradford BD4 6NR; Tel (01274) 681455; Fax (01274) 689547; R. Shaw. (1150)
Wyke Manor, Wilson Rd, Wyke, Bradford BD12 9PX; Tel (01274) 674186; Fax (01274) 675835; L. Boon. (595)

Voluntary Aided Upper Schools

The Holy Family School, Spring Gardens La, Keighley BD20 6LH; Tel (01535) 607790; Fax (01535) 606596; C.M. Davis. (692)
St Bede's Grammar, Highgate, Heaton, Bradford BD9 4BQ; Tel (01274) 541221; Fax (01274) 498290; Dr J.M. Hegarty. (Boys) (546)
St Josephs College, Cunliffe Rd, Bradford BD8 7AL; Tel (01274) 542050; Fax (01274) 541060; F. McCarron. (Girls) (780)

Yorkshire Martyrs Collegiate School, Westgate Hill St, Bradford BD4 6NR; Tel (01274) 681262; Fax (01274) 689744; J.A. Clarke. (791)

Voluntary Controlled Upper School

Ilkley Grammar, Cowpasture Rd, Ilkley LS29 8TR; Tel (01943) 608424; Fax (01943) 601285; P.N. Wood. (924)

Teachers' Centres

T.F. Davies Professional Development Centre, Rosemount, Clifton Villas, Manningham La, Bradford BD8 7BY; Tel (01274) 493535; Fax (01274) 481614
Interfaith Education Centre, Listerhills Rd, Bradford BD7 1HD; Tel (01274) 731674; Fax (01274) 731621
Keighley Professional Development Centre, Parson St, Keighley BD21 3HD; Tel (01535) 662653
Manningham Environmental Centre, Manningham La, Bradford BD8 7RZ; Tel (01274) 737839

Grant Maintained Schools

Bingley Grammar School Keighley Rd, Bingley BD16 2RS; Tel (01274) 562557/567688; Fax (01274) 566740; *Headteacher* Ian Plimmer; *Chair of Governors* James Britton
Hanson, Sutton Ave, Swain Hse Rd, Bradford BD2 1JP; Tel (01274) 636278; Fax (01274) 636122; I. Chaplin. (1350)
Laisterdyke G.M. Middle School, Thornbury Rd, Bradford BD3 8HE; Tel (01274) 656139; Fax (01274) 661627; J. Law. (99)
Oakbank, Oakworth Rd, Keighley BD22 7DU; Tel (01535) 662787; J.G. Roberts. (1068)
Thornton Grammar, Leaventhorpe La, Thornton, Bradford BD13 3BH; Tel (01274) 881082; G.J.F. Twistleton. (887)
Wibsey Middle, North Rd, Bradford BD6 1RL; Tel (01274) 678016; D.S. Robinson. (523)

Buckinghamshire County Council

Population 645,700
County Hall, Aylesbury, Bucks HP20 1UA; Tel (01296) 395000
Chief Executive C.M. Garrett, BA
Director of Finance J. Beckerleg, MA County Offices, Aylesbury HP20 1UD; Tel (01296) 395000
County Architect E. Lee, MSc, DipArch, RIBA, MRTPI, FRSA
County Librarian R.J Collis, DMA, ALA, ACIS, AMISM
Director of Social Services J. Jeffery

Education Department

County Hall, Walton St, Aylesbury HP20 1UZ; Tel (01296) 395000; Fax (01296) 383367
Chief Education Officer E.S. Sharp
Deputy Chief Education Officer P.J. Mooney
Assistant Chief Education Officer P. Glover
Senior Education Officer (Personnel) G.A. Jones
Senior Education Officer (Finance) A. Mander
Senior Education Officer (Policy Planning and Information) N.S. Fane
Senior Education Officer (Development) J.M.H Parke
Senior Education Officer (Client Services Special Education) M.A. Williams
Senior Education Officer (Schools and Colleges) A. Eccleston
Senior Education Officer (Arts, Sport and Recreation) P. Thomas
Principal Educational Psychologist N. Lygo-Baker
Senior Educational Psychologist Fieldwork Tutor Dr N. Frederickson 25 Buckingham Rd, Aylesbury HP19 3PT (and University College, London); Tel (01296) 82632
Chief Adviser P.D. Green
Senior Adviser (Schools – Aylesbury Vale) D. Bolton
Senior Adviser (Schools – Chilter/South Bucks) C. Wright
Senior Adviser (Schools – Milton Keynes) Dr D. Gamble
Senior Adviser (Schools – Wycombe) S. Wadsworth
Senior Education Adviser (Special Education) S. Wadsworth
County Adviser (Art and Design) C. Wright
County Adviser (Cross-Curricular Issues) G. Vincent
County Adviser (English) S. Gibson
County Adviser (Humanities) J. Maynard
County Adviser (Information Technology) D. Hodgkinson
County Adviser (Mathematics) G. Morris
County Adviser (Modern Languages) D. Bolton
County Adviser (Multicultural Education) D. Shepherd
County Adviser (Music) H. Blakeman
County Adviser (Physical Education) I. Park
County Adviser (Primary Education – Early Years) P. Martin
County Adviser (Primary Education – Middle Years) G. Marshall
County Adviser (Pupil Assessment) I. Lenham
County Adviser (Religious Education) J. Reynolds
County Adviser (Science) Dr D. Gamble
County Adviser (Science) K. Reed
County Adviser (Special Education) G. Kern
County Adviser (Appraisal and Equal Opportunities) C. Marsh
County Adviser (INSET–Secondary) E. Treacher
County Adviser (INSET–Primary, Aylesbury Vale Area and Management INSET) M. Tennant
County Adviser (INSET–Primary, Chiltern/South Bucks Area and Profiling and ROA) J. Senior
County Adviser (INSET–Primary, Milton Keynes Area) C. Povey
County Librarian R. Collis
County Museum Officer C.V. Dawes
Number of Schools
6 nursery (569); 281 primary (55,982); 35 secondary (27,717); 41 adult education centres (41,000)
Special Schools
10 day; 10 boarding

Education Committee

Con 18, Lab 7, LD 7, Ind 1
Chairman D.C.T. Graves, (Con)
Vice-Chairman J.A. Barnes CBE, (Con)
Members of the Committee
Con: J.A. Barnes, CBE, Mrs P.M.A. Dewar, M.S. Dobbins, A.P. Dransfield, D.C.T. Graves, M.J. Greenburgh, Mrs B.H. Jennings, L.H. Jole, MC, P.M. Lawrence, Mrs E.M. Lay, A.E.N. Marsden, A.S. Moore, P.F.R. Mullins, J.E. Oakes, B.C. Peatey, C.F. Robinson, OBE, D.A.C. Shakespeare, O.G. Taylor
Lab: K.L. Beeley, D.W. Driver, Mrs S.J. Holdridge, J.R.W. Huddart, Mrs H.M. Saunders, Dr B.R. Stenner, A.E. Woodcock
LD: Dr E.S. Henderson, C. Jones, J.B. Monk, A.J. Plumridge, Mrs F.D. Roberts MBE, JP, Mrs P.M. Seymour, Mrs C.S. Willetts
Ind: Mrs S.J. Lee

Governor Training Unit

Buckinghamshire County Council, County Hall, Aylesbury HP20 1UZ; Tel (01296) 383395; Fax (01296) 382877
Governor Training Officer S.R.B. Brackley
Services Offered
Full Training Programme across the County; Teacher-Governor Conferences; Parent-Governor Conferences; Annual Conference; Resource Centres in each Area of County

AREA EDUCATION OFFICES

Aylesbury Vale Area

Sweda House, 24–30 New Street, Aylesbury HP20 2NH; Tel (01296) 383500; Fax (01296) 383532
Area Education Manager D. Ayres
Assistant Area Education Manager (Personnel and Governing Bodies) M. Knight
Assistant Area Education Manager (Finance) A. Tusting
Assistant Area Education Manager (Pupil, Student and Parent Services) W. Yeo
Learning Support Manager G. Scourfield
Area E.W.O M. Horbury

Educational Psychologists

Aylesbury Vale Area, 25 Buckingham Rd, Aylesbury HP19 3PT; Tel (01296) 82632; Fax (01296) 394489; *Senior Area Educational Psychologist* A. Gregor (Acting); *Educational Psychologist* J. Dale; *Educational Psychologist* K. Laws; *Educational Psychologist* Dr P. Whitaker; *Educational Psychologist* M. Stickney

Hospital Class

Stoke Mandeville Hospital, Aylesbury HP21 8BB; Tel (01296) 315067
Teacher-in-Charge Miss L.A. Ward

Special Day Schools

Furze Down School, Verney Rd, Winslow MK18 3EN; Tel (01296) 713385; Fax (01296) 714420; *Head* N.A. Ward. (86)
Kynaston School, Claydon Path, Kynaston Ave, Aylesbury HP21 9EF; Tel (01296) 27221; R.C. Lees. (48)
Park School, Bierton Rd, Aylesbury HP20 1EE; Tel (01296) 23507; Fax (01296) 433353; R.M. Cutler. (73)
Stoke Leys School, Claydon Path, Kynaston Ave, Aylesbury HP21 9EF; Tel (01296) 27441; H.E. Chapman. (86)

Residential Special Schools

Pebble Brook School, Churchill Ave, Aylesbury HP21 8LZ; Tel (01296) 415761/2; Fax (01296) 434442; J.C. Lloyd. (63)
Wendover Hse School, Church La, Wendover HP22 6NL; Tel (01296) 622157/623691; B.T. Exell. (65)

Other Special Needs Provision

Aylesbury Vale Primary Support Centre, Unit 1, Abbey Centre, Weedon Rd, Aylesbury HP19 3NS; Tel (01296) 88447; *Teacher-in-Charge* J.D. Smith
Aylesbury Vale Reading Unit and Learning Support Service, Broughton County Middle School, Broughton Ave, Aylesbury HP20 1NQ; Tel (01296) 431716; *Teacher-in-Charge* J.A. Bennett
Aylesbury Vale Secondary Support Centre, Unit 8, Abbey Centre, Weedon Rd, Aylesbury HP19 3NS; Tel (01296) 431989; *Teacher-in-Charge* Mrs P. Lane

Selective Secondary Schools

Aylesbury Grammar, Walton Rd, Aylesbury HP21 7RP; Tel (01296) 84545; Fax Ask for Ext 265; I.P. Roe. Boys (1049)
Aylesbury High, Walton Rd, Aylesbury HP21 7ST; Tel (01296) 415237; E.J. Wainwright. (Girls) (1086)
The Royal Latin, Brookfields, Buckingham MK18 1AX; Tel (01280) 813065; Fax (01280) 813064; C.A. Galloway. (793)
Sir Henry Floyd Grammar, Oxford Rd, Aylesbury HP21 8PE; Tel (01296) 24781; Fax (01296) 24783; D. May. (732)

Other Secondary Schools

Buckingham, London Rd, Buckingham MK18 1AT; Tel (01280) 814006; K. Panes. (774)
The Grange, Wendover Way, Aylesbury HP21 7NH; Tel (01296) 23905; Fax (01296) 399036; A.R. Silver. (1066)
John Colet, Wharf Rd, Wendover HP22 6HF; Tel (01296) 623834/623348; P.J. Mitchell. (691)
The Mandeville, Ellen Rd, Aylesbury HP21 8ES; Tel (01296) 24472; M.J. Newton. (580)
Quarrendon Upper, Weedon Rd, Aylesbury HP19 3PG; Tel (01296) 28551/3; Fax (01296) 86651; R. Canwell. (581)

Chiltern/South Bucks Area

Council Offices, King George V Rd, Amersham HP6 5AW; Tel (01494) 729000; Fax (01494) 729332
Area Education Officer S. Waterman
Assistant Area Education Manager (Personnel and Governing Bodies) R. Aylott
Assistant Area Education Manager (Finance) J. Capell
Assistant Area Education Manager (Pupil, Student and Parent Services) S. Sheen
Senior Support Teacher M. Armstrong
Area E.W.O G. Parker

Educational Psychologists

Chiltern/South Bucks Area, Council Offices, King George V Rd, Amersham HP6 5AW; Tel (01494) 729000; Fax (01494) 729332; *Senior Area Educational Psychologist* P. Norman; *Educational Psychologist* L. Bennett; *Educational Psychologist* J. Kingswood; *Educational Psychologist* J. Wilson; *Educational Psychologist* C. Sullivan

Special Day School

Heritage Hse School, Cameron Rd, Chesham HP5 3DF; Tel (01494) 771445; Fax (01494) 775892; M. Barrie. (68)

Residential Special Schools

Alfriston School, Penn Rd, Beaconsfield HP9 2TS; Tel (01494) 673740; Fax (01494) 670177; V.J. Gordon. (Girls) (88)
Prestwood Lodge School, Nairdwood La, Prestwood, Great Missenden HP16 0QQ; Tel (01494) 863514/5; M.G. Rosner. (Boys) (43)
Stony Dean School, Orchard End Ave, Off Pineapple Rd, Amersham HP7 9JW; Tel (01494) 762007/762538; Fax (01494) 765631; P.G. Newsholme. (112)

Other Special Needs Provision

Bell La Tutorial Unit, Bell La County Combined School, Bell La, Little Chalfont HP6 6PF; Tel (01494) 764969; *Teacher-in-Charge* C. Neil
Chilbec Centre for Secondary Pupils with Emotional and Behavioural Difficulties Slade Hse, Five Acres, Off Pheasant Rise, Chesham, Bucks; Tel (01494) 772024; *Teacher-in-Charge* G. Stokes; *Teacher-in-Charge* S. Davies
Educational Therapy Unit (Primary), Elangeni County Middle School, Woodside Ave, Amersham HP6 6BG; Tel (01494) 721925; *Teacher-in-Charge* O. Harrison; *Teacher-in-Charge* J. Bower
Learning Support Department (Primary), Lent Rise County Combined School, Coulson Way, Burnham SL1 7NP; Tel (01628) 662913; *Teacher-in-Charge* O. Harrison; *Teacher-in-Charge* S. Burkitt
Special Educational Needs Support Service and Home Tuition Service, Area Education Office, Council Offices, King George V Rd, Amersham HP6 5BY; Tel (01494) 729000; Mrs M. Armstrong
Travellers' Education Service, C/o Robertswood County Combined School, Denham La, Chalfont St Peter SL9 0EW; Tel (01753) 886937; *Teacher-in-Charge and County Co-ordinator* Mrs J. Batchelor

Selective Secondary Schools

Burnham Grammar, Hogfair La, Burnham SL1 7HG; Tel (01628) 604812; Fax (01628) 663559; C.E. Long. (594)
Chesham High, Whitehill, Chesham HP5 1BA; Tel (01494) 782854; Fax (01494) 775414; T.J. Andrew. (849)
Dr Challoner's Grammar, Chesham Rd, Amersham HP6 5HA; Tel (01494) 721685; Fax (01494) 721862; G.C. Hill. (Boys) (1062)
Dr Challoner's High, Cokes La, Little Chalfont, Amersham HP7 9QB; Tel (01494) 763296; S. Lawson. (Girls) (856)

Other Secondary Schools

The Amersham School, Stanley Hill, Amersham HP7 9HH; Tel (01494) 726562; Fax (01494) 434181; S.H. Edgar. (586)
The Beaconsfied School, Wattleton Rd, Beaconsfield HP9 1SJ; Tel (01494) 673450; Fax (01494) 676404; R.A. Harknett. (517)
Burnham Upper, Opendale Rd, Burnham SL1 7LZ; Tel (01628) 662107; Fax (01628) 668057; V.J. Hills. (473)
Chesham Pk Community College, Chartridge La, Chesham HP5 2RG; Tel (01494) 782066; Fax (01494) 783185; N.J. Berry. (558)
Holmer Grn, Parish Piece, Holmer Grn, High Wycombe HP15 6SP; Tel (01494) 712219; Fax (01494) 711103; H.J. Thomas. (613)
The Misbourne, Great Missenden HP16 0BN; Tel (01494) 862869; Fax (01494) 890491; D.F. Selman. (765)

Milton Keynes Area

Witan Ct, 275 Upper Fourth St, Central Milton Keynes MK9 1NT; Tel (01908) 835555; Fax (01908) 835500
Area Education Manager A. Flack
Assistant Area Education Manager (Personnel and Governing Bodies) L. Rougale
Assistant Area Education Manager (Finance) S. English
Assistant Area Education Manager (Pupil, Student and Parent Services) M. Barby
Head of Support Services B. Brown

Educational Psychologists

Milton Keynes Area, Maddison Hse, 123 Queensway, Bletchley, Milton Keynes MK2 2EU; Tel (01908) 367333; Fax (01908) 373337; *Senior Area Educational Psychologist* J. Spicer; *Educational Psychologist* M. Matthews; *Educational Psychologist* A. Facherty; *Educational Psychologist* N. Williamson; *Educational Psychologist* J. Andrew-Barrett; *Educational Psychologist* A.M. Gardner

Special Day Schools

The Redway School, Whalley Dr, Bletchley, Milton Keynes MK3 6EN; Tel (01908) 370000; Fax (01908) 374452; *Head* R. Fraser. (101)
Slated Row School, Old Wolverton Rd, Wolverton, Milton Keynes MK12 5NJ; Tel (01908) 316017; Fax (01908) 315082; *Head* J. Turland. (162)

Residential Special Schools

Gatehouse, Crosslands, Marlborough St, Stantonbury, Milton Keynes MK14 6AX; Tel (01908) 313903; N. Chilton. (40)
Romans Field School, Shenley Rd, Bletchley, Milton Keynes MK3 7AW; Tel (01908) 376011; Fax (01908) 645320; J.H.R. Thomas. (60)
The Walnuts School, Simpson, Milton Keynes MK6 3AF; Tel (01908) 670032; P. Ofield. (31)
White Spire School, Rickley La, Bletchley, Milton Keynes MK3 6EW; Tel (01908) 373266; J.S. Moore. (147)

Other Special Needs Provision

Fenny Hse Stage 2 Secondary Tutorial Unit, Knowles Site, Queensway, Bletchley, Milton Keynes MK2 2HB; Tel (01908) 368268; *Teacher-in-Charge* Mrs P. Clark
Primary Support Service, Queensway Centre, Queensway, Bletchley, Milton Keynes MK2 2HB; Tel (01908) 375072; *Teacher-in-Charge* Mrs M. Harrison-Jones
Romans Field Resource Centre, C/o Manor Rd Centre, Bletchley, Milton Keynes MK2 2HP; Tel (01908) 373676; *Teacher-in-Charge* P. Sadler

Comprehensive Secondary Schools

Denbigh, Burchard Cres, Shenley Church End, Milton Keynes MK5 6EX; Tel (01908) 505030; Fax (01908) 505279; R. Conibear. (1119)
Leon, Fern Gr, Bletchley, Milton Keynes MK2 3HQ; Tel (01908) 270164; Fax (01908) 366703; B.H. Abbott. (944)
Ousedale, The Grove, Newport Pagnell MK16 0BJ; Tel (01908) 210203; Fax (01908) 216574; A. Brown. (1713)
St Paul's Roman Catholic, Woughton Campus, Leadenhall, Milton Keynes MK6 5EN; Tel (01908) 669735; Fax (01908) 676206; M. Manley. (1040)
Sir Frank Markham, Rainbow Dr, Leadenhall, Milton Keynes MK6 5EH; Tel (01908) 607416; Fax (01908) 231759; D.C. McClusky. (1451)

Wycombe Area

Wycombe Education Office, Easton St, High Wycombe HP11 1NH; Tel (01494) 475000; Fax (01494) 475001
Area Education Officer B. Edwards
Assistant Area Education Manager (Personnel and Governing Bodies) C. Neill
Assistant Area Education Manager (Pupil, Student and Parent Services) M. Mill
Learning Team Support Manager K. Hart
Area E.W.O L. Galloway

Educational Psychologists

Wycombe Area, Spring Gdns Centre, Pinions La, High Wycombe, Bucks HP13 7AG; Tel (01494) 473636; Fax (01494) 472992; *Senior Area Educational Psychologist* K. Rider; *Educational Psychologist* M. Foot; *Educational Psychologist* V. Legg; *Educational Psychologist* A. Waterfall; *Educational Psychologist* E. Munro; *Educational Psychologist* S. Geiger

Hospital Class

Wycombe General Hospital, Children's Ward 7, High Wycombe, Bucks; Tel (01494) 526161
Teacher-in-Charge Mrs R. Mitchell

Special Day Schools

Park Crescent School, Cressex Rd, High Wycombe HP12 4PR; Tel (01494) 438018; *Head* H.J. Willdridge. (22)
Verney Ave School, Verney Ave, High Wycombe HP12 3NE; Tel (01494) 530289/436982; Fax (01494) 465967; *Head* S.V. Day. (78)
Vinio Hse School, Cressex Rd, High Wycombe HP12 4PR; Tel (01494) 525728/ 465609 (16 plus); *Head* J. Appleyard. (83)

Residential Special School

Chiltern Gate School, Verney Ave, High Wycombe HP12 3NE; Tel (01494) 532621/532622; *Head* W.M. Marshall. (121)

Other Special Needs Provision (Behaviour Support)

The Grange Centre (Secondary Education), 56 Amersham Hill, High Wycombe, Bucks; Tel (01494) 445815; Fax (01494) 465860; *Head of Centre* Mrs B.M. Flack

Woodland First School Centre, Woodland Primary Centre, 300 Micklefield Rd, High Wycombe HP13 7HT; Tel (01494) 523874; *Teacher-in-Charge* G. Allen; *Teacher-in-Charge* P.M. Coogan
The Wycombe Grange (PRU) 56 Amersham Hill, High Wycombe, Bucks HP13 6PQ; Tel (01494) 445815; Fax (01494) 465860; *Head of Service* B.M. Flack; From Sept 1994 The Wycombe Grange is designated as a Pupil Referral Unit (PRU). It provides education and support for pupils with emotional and behavioural difficulties who are unable to cope at school without additional help. As well as catering for permanently excluded pupils, able pupils and pregnant school girls, the organisation also supports some pupils who have statements of special educational needs

Other Special Needs Provision (Learning Support),

Intensive Literacy Centre, C/o Terriers County Middle School, Highworth Cl, High Wycombe HP13 7PH; Tel (01494) 536681; *Teacher-in-Charge* Mrs R. Greenhill
Learning Support Service, C/o The Special Needs Resource Centre, The Hatters La School, Hatters La, High Wycombe HP13 7NQ; Tel (01494) 463266; *Service Co-ordinator* A. Jeffries

Selective Secondary Schools

John Hampden Grammar, Marlow Hill, High Wycombe HP11 1SZ; Tel (01494) 529589; Fax (01494) 447714; A.J. MacTavish. (Boys) (705)
Sir William Borlase's Grammar, West St, Marlow SL7 2BR; Tel (01628) 482256; Fax (01628) 477886; L.A. Smy. (814)
Wycombe High, Marlow Hill, High Wycombe HP11 1TB; Tel (01494) 523961; Fax (01494) 510354; M.N. Pilkington. (Girls) (1346)

Other Secondary Schools

Cressex, Holmers La, High Wycombe HP12 4QA; Tel (01494) 437729; Fax (01494) 461502; T.M.H. Chakera. (677)
Hatters La, High Wycombe HP13 7NQ; Tel (01494) 529740; Fax (01494) 472850; I. Blood. (492)
Princes Risborough, Merton Rd, Princes Risborough, Aylesbury HP27 0DT; Tel (01844) 345496; Fax (01844) 346147; G. Hartle. (453)
St Bernard's R.C., Daws Hill La, High Wycombe HP11 1PW; Tel (01494) 535196; A.M. Moson. (475)
Sir William Ramsay, Rose Ave, Hazlemere, High Wycombe HP15 7UB; Tel (01494) 815211/2; Fax (01494) 816734; W.D. Richards. (670)
Wycombe West School and Collegiate Centre, Faulkner Way, Downley, High Wycombe HP13 5UA; Tel (01494) 523924; Fax (01494) 462064; G.E. Giles. (389)
Wye Valley, New Rd, Bourne End SL8 5BW; Tel (01628) 819022; Fax (01628) 810689; L.J. Melton. (377)

Adult Continuing Education Service

Education Department, County Hall, Aylesbury, Bucks HP20 1UZ; Tel (01296) 382633; Fax (01296) 383367
Education Officer (Adult Continuing Education and Awards) P. Scott
North Field Office, The Old School Hse, 3A The Almhouses, Parklands, Great Linford, Milton Keynes MK14 5DZ; Tel (01908) 231875; Fax (01908) 231876; *Assistant Education Officer, Adult Continuing Education* A. Noble
South Field Office, Bourne End Centre, Wye Valley School, New Rd, Bourne SL8 5BW; Tel (01628) 522844; Fax (01628) 522842; *Assistant Education Officer, Adult Continuing Education* C. Baker

Consortium 1

Cottingham Centre, Lord Grey School, Rickley La, Bletchley, Milton Keynes MK3 6EW; Tel (01908) 647582; Claire Griffin
Milton Keynes Special Provision Centre, The Old School Hse, 3A The Almhouses, Parklands, Great Linford, Milton Keynes MK14 5DZ; Tel (01908) 231879; Audrey Robinson; Olga Sucharyna. Special Provision
Ouesdale Centre, Ouesdale School, The Grove, Newport Pagnell MK16 0BJ; Tel (01908) 210230; L. Northover
Queensway Centre (ESOL), Bletchley, Milton Keynes MK2 2HB; Tel (01908) 644036; Audrey Robinson; Olga Sucharyna. Special Provision
Radcliffe Centre, The Radcliffe School, Aylesbury St West, Wolverton MK12 5BT; Tel (01908) 316853; *Head* Jill Blackwood
Shenley Centre, C/o Denbigh School, Burchard Cres, Shenley Church End, Milton Keynes MK5 6EX; Tel (01908) 503311; Jill Blackwood
Stantonbury Centre, Stantonbury Campus, Milton Keynes, Bucks; Tel (01908) 220066; *Head* Les Northover
Woughton Centre, Sixth Form Bldg, Woughton Campus, Chaffron Way, Leadenhall, Milton Keynes MK6 5HJ; Tel (01908) 671664; Jill Blackwood

Consortium 2

Aylesbury Vale Special Provision Centre, Holman St, Aylesbury HP19 3LJ; Tel (01296) 398957; Maggie Garai. Special Provision
Buckingham Centre, Buckingham School, London Rd, Buckingham MK18 1AT; Tel (01280) 812852; S. Lipscombe
Grange Centre, The Grange School, Wendover Way, Aylesbury HP21 7HN; Tel (01296) 84672; John Gausden
Haddenham Centre, Woodways, Haddenham, Aylesbury HP17 8DS; Tel (01844) 290241; Jenny Dury
Mandeville Centre, The Mandeville School, Ellen Rd, Aylesbury HP21 8ES; Tel (01296) 82416; Jenny Dury
Quarrendon Centre, Quarrendon School, Weedon Rd, Aylesbury HP19 3PG; Tel (01296) 399572; Jenny Dury
Wendover Centre, John Colet School, Wharf Rd, Wendover, Aylesbury HP22 6HF; Tel (01296) 625019; John Gausden
Wing Centre, Wing School, Wing, Leighton Buzzard, Beds LU7 0NY; Tel (01296) 688632; Alan Owen
Winslow Centre, Park Rd, Winslow MK18 3DN; Tel (01296) 714902; Alan Owen

Consortium 3

Bourne End/Flackwell Health Centre, Wye Valley School, New Rd, Bourne End, High Wycombe SL8 5BW; Tel (01628) 523279; Sue Mayer
English for Speakers of Other Languages Green St First School, Green St, High Wycombe HP11 2RA; Tel (01494) 522021; Christina Maratos. (Special Provision)
Marlow Centre, Great Marlow School, Bobmore La, Marlow SL7 1JE; Tel (01628) 484985; Enid Light
Mill End Centre, Sands County Middle School, Mill End Rd, High Wycombe HP12 4BA; Tel (01494) 521586; Glenda Collins
Special Provision Centre, Sands Middle School, Mill End Rd, High Wycombe HP12 4BA; Tel (01494) 445948; Katie Newell-Jones; Sheran Hill
Stokenchurch Centre, Bartholomew Tipping Way, Stokenchurch, High Wycombe HP14 3RF; Glenda Collins

Consortium 4

English for Speakers of Other Languages, Green St First School, Green St, High Wycombe HP11 2RA; Tel (01494) 522021; Christina Maratos. Special Provision
Holmer Green Centre, Holmer Green Upper School, Parish Piece, Holmer Green, High Wycombe HP15 6SP; Tel (01494) 713245; Judy Mace
Princes Risborough Centre, Princes Risborough Upper School, Merton Rd, Princes Risborough HP27 0DT; Tel (01844) 344977/342994; Fax (01844) 346147; Hilary Cozens
Ramsay Centre, Rose Ave, Hazlemere, High Wycombe, Bucks; Tel (01494) 813313; Ann Simmonds

Special Provision Centre, Sands Middle School, Mill End Rd, High Wycombe HP12 4BA; Tel (01494) 445948; Katy Newell-Jones; Sheran Hill. (Special Provision)
Wellesbourne Centre, Kingshill Rd, Terriers, High Wycombe HP13 5BB; Tel (01494) 532870; Iris Brooksbank

Consortium 5

Amersham Centre, The Amersham School, Stanley Hill, Amersham HP7 9HH; Tel (01494) 726224; Harold Reynolds
Amersham Community Centre, Chiltern Ave, Amersham, Bucks; Tel (01494) 433436; Harold Reynolds
Chesham Centre, Chesham Pk School, Chartridge La, Chesham HP5 2RG; Tel (01494) 778203; Harold Reynolds
Misbourne Centre, The Misbourne School, Great Missenden HP16 0BN; Tel (01494) 862904; Nick Corder

Consortium 6

Beaconsfield Centre, The Centre Bungalow, Wattleton Rd, Aylesbury End, Beaconsfield HP9 1RN; Tel (01494) 674694; Liza Wormell
Burnham Centre, Burnham Upper School, Opendale Rd, Burnham SL1 7LZ; Tel (01628) 665513; Rita Bridgen
Chalfonts Centre, Chalfonts School, Narcot La, Chalfont St Peter SL9 8TP; Tel (01753) 890154 (Evenings); Lesley Alexander, G. Collins
Evreham Centre, Swallow St, Iver SL0 0HS; Tel (01753) 652036; Fax (01753) 529841; Lesley Alexander
The Memorial Centre, Gerrards Cross SL9 7AD; Tel (01753) 880408; Lesley Alexander
Princess Marina Centre, Chalfont Rd, Seer Green, Beaconsfield HP9 2QR; Tel (01494) 874231; Debbie Duce. (Special Provision)
Special Provision for Adults, Waterside County Combined School, Black Horse Ave, Chesham HP5 1QU; Tel (01494) 786812/792451; Fax (01494) 786608; Katherine Woods; Rathi Barrell

Provision for Impaired Sight and Hearing

Educational Audiologist, Wycombe General Hospital, High Wycombe, Bucks; Tel (01494) 526161; Mrs W. Smith
County Support Teacher for the Visually Impaired and Physically Handicapped, Room 27, Quarrendon Upper School, Weedon Rd, Aylesbury HP19 3PQ; Tel (01296) 397698; E.K. Barrett

Support Teachers for the Hearing Impaired

Service for Sensory Impaired, Room 27, Quarrendon Upper School, Aylesbury HP19 3PQ; Tel (01296) 397501; *Primary* M. Hawkins; *Secondary* Ms J. Gannon
Cheena Hse, Denham La, Chalfont St Peter SL9 0EW; Tel (01753) 880484 (9am–1pm only); V. Johnson
The Queensway Centre, Queensway, Bletchley, Milton Keynes, Bucks; Tel (01908) 375072 Ext 226; Vacancy
The Resource Centre, C/o The Hatters La School, Hatters La, High Wycombe HP13 7NQ; Tel (01494) 463266; D. Carter

Support Teachers for the Visually Impaired

The Queensway Centre, Queensway, Bletchley, Milton Keynes MK2 2HB; Tel (01908) 375072; H. Endersby; A. Jones

Computer Centres

Abbey Computer Centre, Weedon Rd, Aylesbury HP19 3NS; Tel (01296) 392304; *Centre Head* Terry Galvin
BEMIST, Great Hampden Centre, Hampden Row, Great Missenden HP16 9RS; Tel (01494) 488750; Fax (01494) 488745; *Centre Head* Derek Ayshford
Holne Chase Computer Centre, Buckingham Rd, Bletchley, Milton Keynes MK3 5HP; Tel (01908) 642100; *Centre Head* Pat Trowbridge
William Harding Technology Centre, C/o Quarrendon School, Weedon Rd, Aylesbury, Bucks HP19 3PG; Tel (01296) 435378; *Centre Head* David Guy

Environmental Education Centres

Amersham Field Study Centre, Amersham Main Sub-Station, National Grid, Mop End, Amersham HP7 0QR; Tel (01494) 721054; Deborah Garland
Ivinghoe, High St, Ivinghoe, Leighton Buzzard, Beds LU7 9EX; Tel (01296) 668820; Ian Duckworth; Sue Lyon
Shortenills, Nightingales La, Chalfont St Giles, Bucks; Tel (01494) 872288; Roy Adams
Urban Environmental Education Centre, Gordon Rd, High Wycombe, Bucks; Tel (01494) 447641; David Dyson

Education/Business Activities

Education Department County Hall, Aylesbury HP20 1UZ; Tel (01296) 383730; *County Co-ordinator* Rusty Ansell
Aylesbury Vale Education Office Sweda Hse, 24–30 New St, Aylesbury HP20 2NH; Tel (01296) 383575/383588/383566; *Education Business Officer* Suzanne Millard; *Work Experience Organiser* Derek Jones
Chilten/South Bucks Education Office Council Offices, King George V Rd, Amersham HP6 5BY; Tel (01494) 722389/729000; *Education Business Manager* Geoff Stubbs; *Work Experience Organiser* Anne Cloke
Milton Keynes Education/Business Partnership Countec Education Business Partnership and the Trident Trust, Chesterton Hse, 352 Avebury Boulevard, Central Milton Keynes MK9 2JH; Tel (01908) 660550; *Chief Executive* Stephen Martin; *EBP Manager* Dianne Taylor; *EBP Co-ordinator* Bill Priest; *EBP Co-ordinator* Sue Mason; *Vocational Education and Training Co-ordinator* Peter Devereux; *Media Relations Manager* Ros Agar; *Project Manager for Youth Credits* Anne Robinson; *Director, Trident Trust* Ray Jupp
Wycombe Area Education Office Easton St, High Wycombe HP11 1NH; Tel (01494) 475240/475341/475240; *Education Business Manager* Penny Askew; *Work Experience Officer* Ann Rimmington

Music Service

Milton Keynes Music Centre, Stantonbury Campus, Milton Keynes MK14 6BN; Tel (01908) 224251; Fax (01908) 224201; *Head* David Greig
Bletchley Office, Tel (01908) 373786; *Co-ordinator* Malcolm Crane
Aylesbury Music Centre, Music Centre Office, Elmhurst County Middle School, Dunsham La, Aylesbury HP20 2DB; Tel (01296) 28941; Fax (01296) 28941; *Head* Hugh Molloy

South Buckinghamshire Music Service

High Wycombe Music Centre, C/o Sands County Middle School, Mill End Rd, High Wycombe HP12 4BA; Tel (01494) 445947; Fax (01494) 442773; *Head* Clem Virgo
Amersham Music Centre, Woodside School Site, Mitchell Walk, Amersham HP6 6NW; Tel (01494) 722291; Fax (01494) 722291; *Co-ordinator* David Crook

Other Centres

Abbey Centre, Weedon Rd, Aylesbury HP19 3NS; Tel (01296) 82452
Holne Chase Centre, Buckingham Rd, Bletchley, Milton Keynes MK3 5HP; Tel (01908) 275098
PVE Resource Base, C/o Stony Dean School, Orchard End Ave, off Pineapple Rd, Amersham HP7 9AW; Tel (01494) 762538/(01494) 762007

Multicultural Resource Centres

Teacher/County Projects Manager (Section 11), Multicultural Resource Centre, C/o Hatters La School, Hatters La, High Wycombe HP13 7NQ; Tel (01494) 471527; F. Mirza

Teacher/Area Projects Leader (Section 11), Multicultural Education Centre (Aylesbury), C/o Elmhurst County Middle School, Dunsham La, Aylesbury HP20 2DB; Tel (01296) 21038; Mrs R. Kazi

Teacher/Area Projects Leader (Section 11), Multicultural Education Centre (High Wycombe), Multicultural Resource Centre, C/o Hatters La School, Hatters La, High Wycombe HP13 7NQ; Tel (01494) 471527; P. Jolly

Teacher/Area Projects Leader (Section 11), Multicultural Resource Centre (Milton Keynes), Alex Campbell Middle School, Buckingham Rd, Bletchley, Milton Keynes MK3 5EN; Tel (01908) 270409; Vacancy

Teacher with Section 11 Responsibility, C/o Chesham Park School, Chartridge La, Chesham HP5 2RG; Tel (01494) 782066; K. Rai

Youth & Community Training Centre

Green Pk Centre, Stable Bridge Rd, Aston Clinton, Aylesbury HP22 5NE; Tel (01296) 630239; Fax (01296) 631894; C. Harris

Grant Maintained Schools

Beaconsfield High School, Wattleton Rd, Beaconsfield HP9 1RR; Tel (01494) 673043; Fax (01494) 670715. (Girls 12–18) (785)

The Chalfonts Community College, Narcot La, Chalfont St Peter SL9 8TP; Tel (01753) 882032; Fax (01753) 890716; *Principal* M.J. Preston, BA, MEd, FRSA. (1213)

Co Hesloe Aylesbury Rd, Wing, Leighton Buzzard, Beds LU7 0NY; Tel (0129) 688264/688215; A.T. Hulse, BEd. (430)

Great Marlow, Bobmore La, Marlow SL7 1JE; Tel (01628) 483752; Fax (01628) 475852; N.P. Howson. (728)

The Lord Grey School Rickley La, Bletchley, Milton Keynes, Bucks MK3 6EW; Tel (01908) 379131

The Radcliffe, Aylesbury St West, Wolverton, Milton Keynes MK12 5BT; Tel (01908) 312579; Fax (01908) 322718; D.J. Gilling, MA. (1652)

The Royal Grammar, Amersham Rd, High Wycombe HP13 6QT; Tel (01494) 524955; R.P. Brown, MA. Boys (1130)

Stantonbury Campus, Milton Keynes, Bucks MK14 6BN; Tel (01908) 220066; Fax (01908) 224201

Waddesdon CE, School La, Waddesdon, Aylesbury HP18 0LQ; Tel (01296) 651382/3; Fax (01296) 658453 (Admin)/(01296) 658832 (Library); A.M. Armstrong, MA, MEd. (660)

Bury Metropolitan Borough Council

Population 180,600

Town Hall, Knowsley St, Bury, Lancs BL9 0SW; Tel 0161-705 5000; Fax 0161-705 5105

Education Offices

Athenaeum Hse, Market St, Bury BL9 0BN; Tel 0161-705 5000; Fax 0161-705 5653

Chairman Cllr P.W. Ainscough
Deputy Chairman Cllr C. Platt
Chief Education Officer J. Beech, BA
Deputy Chief Education Officer G. Talbot, BEd
Head of Research and Information P. Baylis, BA, DMA
Head of Resources B. Westwood, ACIS
Head of Client and Building Services J.S. Riley, DMA
Head of Personnel Services G. Nelson, DMA, DMS
Head of Pupil/Student Services J.M. Roach, BA(Hons), DMA
Principal Careers Officer F.J. Bazeley, BA(Hons)
Head of Central Learning Support P. Dawson, BA(Hons)
Head of English Language Teaching Service M. Waterson, BA
Head of School Based Support B. Charlson, BA(Hons)
Head of Advisory Service H. Williams, BEd, MA
Modern Languages Adviser A. Finbow, BA
Humanities Adviser B. Hardman, BSc
10–13 Adviser Primary/Secondary W. Isles
Mathematics Adviser A. Koskie, BEd
Information Technology Adviser M. Lloyd, BA, MSc
Senior Adviser D. Pritchard
Senior Adviser J. Rowe, MEd
English Adviser J. Saunders, BA
Teacher Adviser Physical Education (Part-time) K. Boden
Teacher Adviser Religious Education (Part-time) A. Entwistle, BA, MEd
Principal Educational Psychologist D.W. Grindey, BA(Hons), DEP
Head of Community Education Service J. Barton

Number of Schools
2 nursery (148); 70 primary (15,826); including 24 voluntary aided and 13 voluntary controlled; 14 high schools (10,421); including 1 voluntary aided; 4 special

Number of Community Education Centres
16

Teachers Centres
Professional Development Centre, Seedfield Centre, Parkinson St, Bury; Tel: 061-763 1441

Day of Committee Meeting
Wednesday 6–8 weekly cycle

Careers Office
see chapter 17

Education Committee

Lab 10, Con 9, LD 1

Chair P.W.E. Ainscough, (Lab) 7A Parliament St, Bury BL9 0TE; Tel 7644887

Deputy Chair C. Platt, (Lab) 24 Heaton St, Prestwich, Manchester M25 1HS; Tel 0161-773 7989

Spokeperson A. Barlow, (Con) 13 Park View Crt, St Ann's Rd, Prestwich, Manchester M25 8QD; Tel 0161-798 9875

Members of the Committee

Lab: J.P. Costello, D.O. Davies, W. Flood, I. Lewis, M. Longworth, W. Ramsey, G. Sharkey, D.P. Willis (Non-voting unless Substitute)

Con: D.B. Bigg, D.L. Gunther, V.G. Guthrie, W. Johnson, P.J. Nesbit, C. Ormrod, H. Taylor, R.E. Walker

LD: V.D. D'Albert

Governor Training Unit

Education Dept, Athenaeum Hse, Market St, Bury, Lancs BL9 0BN; Tel 0161-705 5638; Fax 0161-705 5653

Governor Training Co-ordinator C.J. Gill, GIPM

Services Offered
Full support service for school Governors including central and on-site training as well as advice and consultancy

Special Day Schools

Millwood, Fletcher Fold Rd, Bury BL9 9RX; Tel 0161-761 4149; B.J. Emblem, MEd, DipSpEd. (Learning Difficulty) (Primary)

Elms Bank, Ripon Ave, Whitefield M25 6PJ; Tel 0161-766 1597; L. Lines, BA. (Learning Difficulty) (Secondary)

Summerseat Residential, Burrswood Ave, Bury BL0 9UD; Tel 0161-764 1916; H. Partington, DipEd. Emotional and Behavioural Difficulty) (Res/Day)

High Schools (County)

Broadoak, Hazel Ave, Bury, Greater Manchester; Tel 0161-797 6543; P.J. Jefferies, BA. (Mixed) (470)
Castlebrook, Parr La, Bury, Greater Manchester; Tel 0161-796 9820; J. Gannon, BSc, MSc. (Mixed) (810)
Coney Green, Spring La, Radcliffe, Greater Manchester; Tel 0161-724 8704; T.H. Cowan, MA. (Mixed) (469)
Derby, Radcliffe Rd, Bury, Greater Manchester; Tel 0161-764 1819; G.J. Wilson, BA. (Mixed) (915)
Elton, Walshaw Rd, Bury, Greater Manchester; Tel 0161-764 3199; N. Scruton, BEd. (Mixed) (729)
Parrenthorn, Heywood Rd, Prestwich, Greater Manchester; Tel 0161-773 8634; A.F. Francis, BA. Mixed (562)
Philips, Higher La, Whitefield, Greater Manchester; Tel 0161-766 2720; J. Lövgreen, BA. (Mixed) (781)
Prestwich, Heys Rd, Prestwich, Greater Manchester; Tel 0161-773 2052; J. Challands, BEd. (Mixed) (798)
Radcliffe, Abden St, Radcliffe, Greater Manchester; Tel 0161-723 3110; G. Parker, BEd(Hons). (Mixed) (574)
Tottington, Laurel St, Tottington; Tel (0120 488) 2327; A.F. Scott, BEd. (Mixed) (852)
Woodhey, Bolton Rd West, Holcombe Brook, Ramsbottom, Greater Manchester; Tel (0170 682) 5215; F. Bennett, MSc. (Mixed) (923)

High Schools (Voluntary)

Bury Church, Haslam Brow, Bury, Greater Manchester; Tel 0161-797 6236; R. Haigh, BSc. (Mixed) (620)
St Gabriel's R.C., Bridge Rd, Bury, Greater Manchester; Tel 0161-764 3186; P.E. Hopkins, BA, MEd. (S.A.) (Mixed) (935)
St Monica's R.C., Bury Old Rd, Prestwich, Greater Manchester; Tel 0161-773 6436; W.A. Campbell, MEd, DLCP. (Mixed) (983)

Schools with Resources for Hearing Impaired Children

Elton Primary School, Alston St, Bury; Tel 0161-764 4170
Elton High School, Walshaw Rd, Bury; Tel 0161-763 1434

Schools with Resources for MLD Children

Brandlesholme Primary School, Brandlesholme Rd, Bury; Tel 0161-764 5360
Castlebrook High School, Parr La, Bury; Tel 0161-796 9820
Gorsefield Primary School, Robertson St, Radcliffe; Tel 0161-723 5361
Mersey Drive Primary School, Mersey Dr, Whitefield; Tel 0161-766 6298
Radcliffe High School, Abden St, Radcliffe; Tel 0161-723 3110
St Marie's RC Primary School, The Mosses, Bury; Tel 0161-764 3204
St Paul's C of E Primary School, Porrit St, Bury; Tel 0161-764 3788
Tottington High School, Laurel St, Tottington, Bury; Tel (01284) 882327

Schools with Resources for Children with Speech and Language Disorders

Unsworth Primary School, Blackley Cl, Bury; Tel 0161-766 4876

Learning Support Service

Central Learning Support Service, Geoffrey Kershaw Centre, Maxwell St, Bury; Tel 0161-763 1452. (Hospital Tuition, Home Tuition, Specific Learning Difficulties)
English Language Teaching Service, Geoffrey Kershaw Centre, Maxwell St, Bury; Tel 0161-763 1453
Portage Service, C/o Mersey Drive School, Mersey Dr, Whitefield; Tel 0161-796 8042
School Based Support Service, Geoffrey Kershaw Centre, Maxwell St, Bury; Tel 0171-763 1454. (Literacy Support Behaviour Support)
Sensory Support Service, C/o Radcliffe High School, Abden St, Radcliffe; Tel 0171-724 8337

Calderdale Metropolitan Borough Council

Population 193,700
The Town Hall, Halifax HX1 1UJ; Tel (01422) 357257; Fax (01422) 393102

Education Department

Northgate Hse, Northgate, Halifax HX1 1UN; Tel (01422) 357257; Fax (01422) 392515
Director of Education Jacky Tonge
Principal Support Officer (Policy and Planning) D.I. Jennings, BA
Principal Support Officer (Central Support) C.G. Rushworth, IPFA
Principal Support Officer (Pupil Support) Dr J.J. Deakin
Principal Support Officer (Continuing Education) P. Flower, MA
Director of Finance P.A. Walker, IPFA PO Box 51, Princess St, Halifax HX1 1TP
Chief Librarian D.E. Wood, ALA Central Library, Halifax HX1 1UN; Tel (01422) 357257
Principal Psychologist J.A. Griffiths, BSc
Principal Education Welfare Officer J. Taylor
Principal Careers Officer J.K. Heraty
Number of Schools
87 primary (18,966); 9 comprehensive (11,194); 3 special (200); 2 grant maintained grammar; 4 grant maintained primary; 5 grant maintained secondary
Day of Committee Meeting
Monday in 6 weekly cycle
Requisition Periods for School Supplies
No fixed dates

Education Committee

Con 9, Lab 8, LD 2, Ind 1
Chair T. Fall, (Con) 3 Bracewell Dr, Wheatley, Halifax HX3 5HY
Vice-Chair J.F.B. Ford, (Con) Aysgarth, Greenroyd Ave, Halifax HX3 0LP
Members of the Committee
Con: A. Mellor, A. Sugden, G. Reason, L. Mackrill, B. Wildsmith, W. Carpenter, W. Sharp
Lab: M. Higgins, H. Rivron, A. Metcalfe, J. Tolan, M. Najib, E. Hions, P. Judge, S. Tucker
LD: S. Pearson, E.G. Seward, P. Coles, B. Benster
Ind: R. Thrower

Governor Training Unit

Curriculum Support Team, Governor Training, Health Training and Development Centre, Free School La, Halifax, West Yorks HX1 2PT; Tel (01422) 357832; Fax (01422) 348783
Governor Training Co-ordinator and WEA Tutor Organiser Julian Harber
Governor Training Co-ordinator and Headteacher Peter Rhind
Principal Support Officer (Curriculum Support) Peter Bartle

Services Offered

Comprehensive range of courses addressing issues relative to school government. These courses are available to governors generally or to individual governing bodies. Some of our current courses including those on Personnel Issues and Drawing the Line are marketed nationally

Careers Office

See chapter 17

Special Schools

Highbury, Lower Edge Rd, Rastrick, Brighouse HD6 3LD; Tel (01484) 716319. (E.S.N.(S) (35)
Ravenscliffe High, Skircoat Grn, Halifax HX3 0RZ; Tel (01422) 358621; M. Hirst. (S) (99)
Woodbank, Luddendenfoot, Halifax HX2 6PB; Tel (01422) 884170; I. Fielden. (E.S.N.(S) (31)

Comprehensive Schools (County)

Calder High, Brier Hey La, Mytholmroyd, Hebden Bridge, Halifax HX7 5QN; Tel (01422) 883213; D. Scott. (Mixed) (1216)
The Halifax High, Oxford Rd, Halifax HX1 2QU; Tel (01422) 352106; R. Ridley. (Mixed) (771)
The Ridings School, Nursery La, Ovenden, Halifax HX3 5SX; Tel (01422) 352836; K. Stansfield. (Mixed) (750)
South Halifax High, Park La, Exley, Halifax HX3 9LG; Tel (01422) 362215; A. MacIntosh. (Mixed) (405)
Ryburn Valley High, St Peter's Ave, Sowerby Bridge, Halifax HX6 1DF; Tel (01422) 832070; A.R. Thorne. (Mixed) (1132)
Sowerby Bridge High, Albert Rd, Sowerby Bridge HX6 2NW; Tel (01422) 831011; S. Hull. (Mixed) (815)
Todmorden High, Ewood La, Todmorden, Lancs OL14 7DG; Tel (01706) 813558; N.G. Jepson. (Mixed) (935)

Comprehensive Schools (Voluntary)

Halifax Catholic High, Holdsworth Rd, Holmfield, Halifax HX2 9TH; Tel (01422) 245411; M.J. Savage. (V.A.) (Mixed) (824)

Adult Education Service

Headquarters, PO Box 33, Education Department, Northgate Hse, Northgate, Halifax HX1 1UN; Tel (01422) 357257; Vacancy
Ashlar Area, Brighouse Centre, Church La, Brighouse HD6 1AT; Tel (01484) 714019; *Centre Manager* K. Large Northgate Hse
Calder and Ryburn Area, Sowerby Bridge AE Centre, Wharf St, Sowerby Bridge, Halifax HX6 2EG; Tel (01422) 831973; *Centre Manager* S. Lunn Northgate Hse
Halifax Area AE Centre, Horton Hse, Horton St, Halifax HX1 1PU; Tel (01422) 365344; *Centre Manager* R. Fogg Northgate Hse
Todmorden Area, Calder College of Adult Education, Burnley Rd, Todmorden, Lancs OL14 7BX; Tel (01706) 812743; *Centre Manager* M. Vernon

Teachers' Centres

Health Training and Development Centre, Free School La, Halifax HX1 2PS; Tel (01422) 347015; *Principal Support Officer (Curriculum Support)* P. Bartle, BA; *Senior Adviser (Inset)* P.H. Lloyd, BEd; *Senior Adviser (Curriculum)* A. Collins, BA; *Senior Adviser (Management and Appraisal)* J. Jagger, MEd; *General Adviser (Humanities/RE)* Vacancy; *General Adviser (Science)* C.R. DuQueno, BSc, MEd; *General Adviser (Early Years)* M.M. Carroll, DPSE, ALAM; *General Adviser (Assessment, Recording and Reporting)* Sue Coe; *General Adviser (IT)* C. Parker; *General Adviser (Technology)* M. Walker

Grant Maintained Schools

The Crossley Heath School, Savile Pk, Halifax, West Yorkshire HX3 OHG; Tel (01422) 360272; Fax (01422) 349099; *Headteacher* J.T. Bunch; *Chairman of Governors* Joan Tidswell. (Mixed) (11–18) (700)
Holy Trinity C. of E., Holdsworth Rd, Holmfield, Halifax HX2 9TL; Tel (01422) 244890; Fax (01422) 240033; M.J. Felton. (GM) (Senior) (Mixed) (882)
The North Halifax Grammar School Moorbottom Rd, Illingworth, Halifax HX2 9SU; Tel (01422) 244625; Fax (01422) 245237; *Headteacher* G. Crawley; *Chairman of Governors* Tom Enderby. (Mixed) (11–18) (825)
Rastrick High, Field Top Rd, Rastrick, Brighouse HD6 3XB; Tel (01484) 710235; Fax (01484) 720043; P.D. Clark. (G.M.) (Mixed) (1130)

Cambridgeshire County Council

Population 677,000 (1992 estimate)
Shire Hall, Castle Hill, Cambridge CB3 0AP; Tel (01223) 317111; Fax (01223) 317201
Chief Executive A.G. Lister
Director of Finance and Administration D.T. Earle
Director of Property R. Goodall
Director of Transportation M. Sharpe
Director of Personnel M. Smart
Director of Corporate Planning B.P. Smith
Director of Social Services T.D. Kubisa
Director of Libraries and Heritage B.P. Smith

Education Department

Castle Ct, Shire Hall, Castle Hill, Cambridge CB3 OAP; Tel (01223) 317111
Director of Education J. Ferguson
Assistant Director (Policy Planning & Review) W. Goodwin
Assistant Director (Community and Contracts Management) M. Forbes
Manager Learning Support Services B. Gale
Chief Executive (Careers) D. Yates
County Manager (Information Technology) I. Nelson
Assistant Director (Education Property) B. Harris
Assistant Director Finance & Administration (Education) J.A. Neilson
Director (Education Personnel Management Ltd) B.J.F. Curtis
County Catering Officer H. Witt
Head of Inspectorate and Science Inspector M.D. Edey
Art, Design and Technology Inspector O.M. Nicholson
Community Education Inspector M.N. Groves
English Inspector C.A Oswald
Humanities/History/Social Sciences Inspector J.M. Holling
Microtechnology and Learning Resources Inspector E.M. Cole
Modern Languages Inspector H.J. Whiter
Music Inspector F.C. Williams
Nursery and Primary Education Inspector M. Creasey
Nursery and Primary Education Inspector L.C. Jones
Nursery and Primary Education Inspector P. Overton
Nursery and Primary Education Inspector B.A. Froggatt
Personal and Social Education and Health Education Inspector C. Gilder
Religious Education Inspector Mrs J.A. Ardavan
Special Needs Inspector G. Foster

Number of Schools
7 nursery; 258 primary; 29 secondary; 16 special

School population
102,236 (January 1993)

Requisition periods for school supplies
None

Education Committee

Con 8, Lab 5, LD 5
Chair C.J. Bennett, (Lab)
Members of the Committee
Con: P.C. Booth, S.J. Bradshaw, F.J.W. Brown, J.R. Horrell, S.F. Johnstone, S.B. Normington, A.G. Orgee, P.W. Silby
Lab: C.J. Bennett, A.M. Engel, I.C. Kidman, H. Lakhanpaul, J. Owens
LD: S.V. Brinton, J. Conston, S. Giles, S. Littlewood, R. Martlew

Governor Training Unit

Governor Training and Development Unit, Cambridge Professional Development Centre, Foster Rd, Trumpington, Cambridge CB2 2NL; Tel (01223) 842214; Fax (01223) 842216
County Manager Michael Booker, BEd(Hons), DipEd
Development Officer Karen Harper, GradIPM
Services Offered
Termly programme of training activities; In-house training for governing bodies; Foundation courses for newly appointed governors; Information and training materials loan service; Termly newsletter; Briefing papers and booklets

Careers Office

See chapter 17

Special Schools

Clayton, Orton Goldhay, Peterborough, Cambs PE2 0SD; Tel (01733) 232346; R.C. Telfer. (2–19) (Mixed) (SLD) (Day and Board)
Ellindon, North Bretton, Peterborough, Cambs PE3 8RQ; Tel (01733) 265121; P.D. McGurk. (9–16) (Mixed) (EBD) (Day and Board)
Green Hedges Bar La, Stapleford, Cambs CB2 5BJ; Tel (01223) 843872; R. Hubbard. (2–19) (Mixed) (Day) (SLD)
Heltwate, North Bretton, Peterborough, Cambs PE3 8RL; Tel (01733) 262878; D.R. Smith. (2–16) (Mixed) (Day) (MLD and SLD)
Highfield, Tower Rd, Ely, Cambs CB7 4HW; Tel (01353) 662085; V.M. Ashton. (2–19) (Mixed Day SLD)
The Lady Adrian, Courtney Way, Cambridge CB4 2EE; Tel (01223) 357038; E. Bacon
Littleton Hse, Girton, Cambridge, Cambs CB3 0QL; Tel (01223) 277191; E. Nash. (11–16) (Mixed) (EBD) (Day and Board)
The Manor, Station Rd, Wilburton, Nr Ely, Cambs CB6 3RR; Tel (01353) 740229; T. Moran. (6–13) (Mixed) (EBD) (Day and Board)
Marshfields, Eastern Cl, Eastern Ave, Peterborough, Cambs PE1 4PP; Tel (01733) 68058; B.S. Berryman. (7–16) (Mixed) (MLD) (Day)
Meadowgate, Meadowgate La, Wisbech, Cambs PE13 2JH; Tel (01945) 61836; R.M. Blunt. (2–19) (Mixed) (MLD and SLD) (Day)
Pepys Rd, St Neots, Huntingdon, Cambs PE19 2EW; Tel (01480) 215582; M. Whitehead. (3–16) (Mixed) (MLD and SLD) (Day)
Rees Thomas, Downhams La, Cambridge, Cambs CB4 1YB; Tel (01223) 351928; J.A. Gawlinski. (2–19) (Mixed) (SLD) (Day)
St George's, Lawn Ave, Peterborough, Cambs PE1 3RB; Tel (01733) 62058; B.A. Rudgley. (2–19) (Mixed) (SLD) (Day)
Spring Common, American La, Huntingdon, Cambs PE18 7TY; Tel (01480) 454396; Dr B., Thomas. (2–19) (Mixed) (MLD and SLD) (Day)
Springfields, Thames Rd, Huntingdon, Cambs PE18 7QW; Tel (01480) 453588; S. Keen. (2–10) (Mixed) (MLD and SLD) (Day)
Windmill School, Fulbourn, Cambridge CB1 5EE; Tel (01223) 880980; P.A. Scott. (2–19) (Mixed) (SLD) (Day)

Secondary Schools

Arthur Mellows Village College, Helpston Rd, Glinton, Peterborough, Cambs PE6 7JX; Tel (01733) 252235; F. Mann. (11–18)
Bottisham Village College, Lode Rd, Bottisham, Cambs CB5 9EN; Tel (01223) 811250; K.P. O'Shea. (11–16)
Bretton Woods Community School, Flaxland, Bretton, Peterborough, Cambs PE3 8DF; Tel (01733) 266975; J.L. Gribble. (11–18)
Bushfield Community School, Orton Goldhay, Peterborough, Cambs PE2 5RQ; Tel (01733) 233014; T. O'Grady. (11–16)
Chesterton Community College, Gilbert Rd, Cambridge, Cambs CB4 3NY; Tel (01223) 359269; H. Gilbert. (11–16)
Coleridge Community College, Radegund Rd, Cambridge, Cambs CB1 3RJ; Tel (01223) 247720; L.C., Cooper. (11–16)
Cottenham Village College, High St, Cottenham, Cambridge, Cambs CB4 4UA; Tel (01954) 50444; A.J. Cooper. (11–16)
City of Ely Community College, Downham Rd, Ely, Cambs CB6 2SH; Tel (01353) 667763; R. Daw. (11–18)
Cromwell Community College, Wenny Rd, Chatteris, Cambs PE16 6UU; Tel (0135 43) 2193; A.C. Atkins. (11–16)
Eastholm, Reeves Way, Peterborough PE1 5LQ; Tel (01733) 53241; J.S. Forster. (11–18)
Ernulf Community School, Barford Rd, Eynesbury, St Neots, Huntingdon, Cambs PE19 2SH; Tel (01480) 474748; M. Cragg. (11–18)
Hinchingbrooke, Brampton Rd, Huntingdon, Cambs PE18 6BN; Tel (01480) 451121; P.J. Downes. (11–18)
Impington Village College, New Rd, Impington, Cambridge, Cambs CB4 4NP; Tel (01223) 232835; S. West. (11–18)
John Mansfield, Western Ave, Dogsthorpe, Peterborough, Cambs PE1 4HX; Tel (01733) 66010; C. Walford. (11–18)
Ken Stimpson Community School, Staniland Way, Werrington, Peterborough, Cambs PE4 6JT; Tel (01733) 576595; H. Mullen. (11–16)
Linton Village College, Cambridge Rd, Linton, Cambridge, Cambs CB1 6JB; Tel (01223) 891233; C. Bush. (11–16)
The Manor Community College, Arbury Rd, Cambridge, Cambs CB4 2JF; Tel (01223) 354937 and 354929; S.G. Mummery. (11–16)
Melbourn Village College, The Moor, Melbourn, Royston, Herts SG8 6EF; Tel (01763) 60403; J. Mullen. (11–16)
Neale–Wade Community College Wimblington Rd, March, Cambs PE15 9PX; Tel (01354) 53430; Dr R.J. Ward. (11–18)
The Netherhall, Queen Ediths Way, Cambridge, Cambs CB1 4NN; Tel (01223) 242931; Dr K. Hunter. (11–18)
Parkside Community College, Parkside, Cambridge, Cambs CB1 1EH; Tel (01223) 352828; T.T. Eatough. (11–16)
Ramsey Abbey, Ramsey, Huntingdon, Cambs PE17 1BD; Tel (01487) 813285; Dr D. Langridge. (11–18)
St Bedes' Church, Birdwood Rd, Cambridge, Cambs CB1 3TB; Tel (01223) 248660; R.H. Boon. (11–16)
St Ivo, High Leys, Houghton Rd, St Ives, Huntingdon, Cambs PE17 4RR; Tel (01480) 462881; M. Mahoney. (11–18)
Sir Harry Smith Community College, Eastrea Rd, Whittlesey, Peterborough PE7 1XB; Tel (01733) 203991/2; J. James. (11–16)
Swavesey Village College, 1 Gibraltar La, Swavesey, Cambridge, Cambs CB4 5RS; Tel (01954) 30366; P.J. Talbott. (11–16)
Walton, Mountsteven Ave, Peterborough, Cambs PE4 6HX; Tel (01733) 572501; A. Bilton. (11–18)
Witchford Village College, Manor Rd, Witchford, Ely, Cambs CB6 2JA; Tel (01353) 662053; C.M. Duffy. (11–16)

Adult Education Centre

Peterborough College of Adult Education, Brook St, Peterborough PE1 1TU; Tel (01733) 61361; B.A. Rainey

Field Studies Centre

Upware, Ely; Tel (01353) 720264; G. Revill

Music and Drama Centre

Brookside; Tel (01480) 53420

Outdoor Pursuits Centre

Stibbington Environmental Education Centre, Gt North Rd, Stibbington, Peterborough PE8 6LP; Tel (01780) 782386; R. Edwards

Residential Youth Work Establishments

Burwell Hse, Burwell, Cambridge CB5 OBA; Tel (01638) 741256; *Warden* Graham Whitehead
Grafham Water Residential Centre, West Perry, Huntingdon PE18 OBY; Tel (01480) 810521; J. Leaworthy

Residential Centres

Burwell House Burwell, Cambridge, Cambs; Tel 01638-741256; *Warden* G. Whitehead
Grafham Water Residential Centre West Perry, Huntingdon, Cambs; Tel 01480-810521; *Warden* J. Leaworthy

Teachers' Centres

Cambridge Professional Development Centre, Fawcett Site, Foster Rd, Cambridge CB2 2NL; Tel (01223) 844880; Vacancy
Huntingdon Professional Development Centre Lawrence Ct, Huntingdon, Cambs PE18 6PA; Tel (01480) 52181; Vacancy
March Teachers' Centre, Community Education Centre, Station Rd, March PE15 8LE; Tel (01354) 57735; Miss T. York
Mathematics Centre, Lawrence Ct, Huntingdon, Cambs; Tel (01480) 52181; L. Baker
Peterborough Professional Development Centre, Cottesmore Cl, Westwood, Peterborough PE3 6TP; Tel (01733) 334114; Vacancy
Resource and Technology Centre, Back Hill, Ely, Cambs; Tel (01353) 3486; B. Everitt
Wisbech Teachers' Centre, The Castle, Museum Sq, Wisbech PE13 1EH; Tel (01945) 585096; Miss T. York

Youth Centres

City Centre, 439 Lincoln Rd, Peterborough PE1 2PE; Tel (01733) 65337; D. Gibb
The Howard Mallett Club, Sturton St, Cambridge CB1 2QF; Tel (01223) 357496; *Community Education Tutor* C. Thompson
Huntingdon Youth Centre, Sallowbush Rd, Huntingdon, Cambridge PE18 7AF; Tel (01480) 453543; *Community Education Tutor* S. White
St Ives Youth Centre, Off Broad Leys, St Ives, Huntingdon, Cambs PE17 4QB; Tel (01480) 62069; *Community Education Tutor* S. Blyton
St Neots Youth Centre, Priory Rd, St Neots, Huntingdon, Cambs PE17 4BB; Tel (01480) 472343; *Community Education Tutor* P. Taylor
Stanground Youth Centre, Peterborough Rd, Farcet, Peterborough PE7 3BW; Tel (01733) 68797; R. Lee
Wisbech Community Education Centre, Queen's Rd, Wisbech, Cambs; Tel (01945) 581444; *Community Education Tutor* G. Buckler

Grant Maintained Schools

Ailwyn Community School, Hollow La, Ramsey, Huntingdon, Cambs OE17 1DG; Tel (01487) 812352; D. Wallwork
Comberton Village College, Comberton, Cambridge, Cambs; Tel (01223) 262503; Mrs R., Clayton. 11–16
Deacon's Schoolsponsored by Perkins Group, Database, Apricot Computers, Greater Peterborough TEC, Pearl Assurance and Thomas Cook Queen's Gardens, Peterborough, Cambridgeshire PE1 2UW; Tel (01733) 62451
Gamlingay Village College, Gamlingay, Nr Sandy, Beds SG19 3HA; Tel (01767) 650360; Fax (01767) 650605; R.E. Martin
Jack Hunt, Ledbury Rd, Peterborough PE3 9PN; Tel (01733) 263526; Fax (01733) 330364; R.D. Coombe, BA, MA
Kings CE, Park Rd, Peterborough PE1 2UE; Tel (01733) 64938; *Headteacher* G.L. Longman. (VA)
The King's School, Park Rd, Peterborough, Cambridgeshire PE1 2UE; Tel (01733) 64938
Longsands Community College, St Neots, Huntingdon PE19 1LQ; Tel (01480) 403200; R.L. Gwynne
Marshland High School, West Walton, Wisbech, Cambridgeshire PE14 7HA; Tel (01945) 584146
Orton Longueville, Oundle Rd, Orton Longueville, Peterborough PE2 7EA; Tel (01733) 231971; E. Hasler
The Queen's School, Wisbech PE13 2SE; Tel (01945) 585237; J.H. Piercy
St John Fisher R.C., Park La, Peterborough PE1 5JN; Tel (01733) 436646
St Peter's School, St Peter's Rd, Huntingdon PE18 7DA; Tel (01480) 459581; P.D. Furniss
Sawston Village College, New Rd, Sawston, Cambridge CB2 4BP; Tel (01223) 832217; Fax (01223) 836680; K. McMullen. (11–16)
Sawtry Village College, Fen La, Sawtry, Huntingdon PE17 5TQ; Tel (01487) 830701; J. Stewart
Soham Village College, Soham, Ely, Cambs CB7 5AA; Tel (01353) 720569; A.W. Bullock. (GM) (11–16)
Stanground College, Peterborough Rd, Peterborough PE7 3BY; Tel (01733) 64071; Fax (01733) 347626; B.C. Barker

Cheshire County Council

Population 966,900
County Hall, Chester CH1 1SF; Tel (01244) 602424; Fax (01244) 603800

Education Department

County Hall, Chester CH1 1SQ; Tel (01244) 602330
Group Director, Education Services D. Cracknell
County Education Officer (Education Support) J. Feenan
Education Officer (Schools Liaison) A.A.B. Metcalfe
Education Officer (Heads and Governors) M. Brophy, BA
Education Officer (Service Policy) J.W. Edwards, MA
Education Officer (Continuing Education) A. Tranter
Education Officer (Planning and Information) I.R. Aspden
Capital Development Manager A. Tunnicliffe
Area Education Services Officer J.D Watson
Chief Adviser J.F.C. Plummer
Policy Coordinator V. Krivinskas
Policy Coordinator M. Halliday
Student Awards Manager J.F. Barrett
Administration and Communications Manager J. Tunley
Lead Personnel Officer A. Penny
Senior Personnel Officer R. Pearson, DMA
Training and Staff Development Officer E.L. Renshaw, DipCG
Client Catering Manager J.A. Hesp
Client Technical Services Manager G. Chesworth
Education Information Systems Officer A. Williamson
Projects Development Officer K. White
Committee Support Manager A. Passmore
Buildings Manager R. Mellor
Research and Statistics Manager D. Plunkett

Education Officer, Special Education Needs M. Gledhill, MA, DipEd, ABPsS, MEdPsych
Principal Adviser (Primary) M. Morrin
Principal Adviser (Secondary) C. Valleley
Principal Adviser (INSET and curriculum) A. Siddall
Primary Adviser D.A. Taylor, MEd
Primary Adviser E. Williams
Primary Adviser R. Prys-Jones
Primary Adviser S. Prest
Primary Adviser N.W. Harding
Primary Adviser R.L. Harris, BA
Primary Science Adviser M.W. Barlow, BA
Primary Science Adviser M. Clegg, BA
Secondary Adviser J. Collins
Secondary Adviser E.N. Wardle, DipPE
Secondary Adviser W. Davice
Secondary Adviser S. Edwards
Continuing Education Adviser A. Tranter, MEd
Special Education Adviser L. Jones
TVEI Manager D. Selzer
Physical Education Adviser E.N. Wardle, DipPE
Music Adviser M. Williams
Mathematics Adviser S. Jackson
Micro Electronics/Computer Education A. Whittaker, BEd
Geography Adviser J. Krause, BSc, MEd
Religious Education, History Adviser F. Earle, MA
English Adviser M.R. Jones, MA, MEd
Craft, Design and Technology M.O. Bailey, MA
Drama Adviser S.W. Taylor
Art Adviser D.J. Firmstone, ATD
Science Adviser S. Webster
Community Education/Post 16 Special Needs/Health Education Adviser A. Bowen, BEd

Education Services Committee

Chairman J.P. Findlow, (Con) Glendale, 28 South Acre, Macclesfield, SK11 7EW; Tel (01625) 432661
Members of the Committee
A. Barnes, K. Bland, S.H. Cussons FCA, G.A. Cousins FCA. H. Grange, M.E. Melrose DL, A. Richardson OBE DL, S.E. Woodyatt, D.T. Bateman, L.M. Clarke, J.H. Collins OBE JP DL BSc, E.P. Coop, M.J. Copple, C.H. Gerrard, P.W. Hayward, P. Lloyd-Jones, A. McKinlay, P. Nurse, D. Rudd, L.M. Toale, P. Tyrrell KSG, J.J. Warburton, A.V. Williams, W.T. Woolfall, K.A. Hemsley, W.J.C. Talbot, W.T.A. Foster, L.G. Cookson, T.G. Holman, S.R. Proctor

Governor Training Unit

Education Services Group, Cheshire County Council, County Hall, Chester CH1 1SQ; Tel (01244) 602376; Fax (01244) 603821
PO, Governor Training C. Leigh
Services Offered
Programme of formal courses; In-house courses; Governors Up-date; Conferences for Governors

AREA OFFICES

Chester, Ellesmere Port and Neston Area

85 Wellington Rd, Ellesmere Port L65 6QL; Tel 0151-357 4500
Area Manager G. Stockley
Number of Schools
2 nursery (75 FT equiv.) and 13 classes (420 FT equiv.); 96 primary (16,587); 13 secondary (12,523); 5 special (231)

Area Careers Office

See chapter 17

Special Schools

Capenhurst Grange, Chester Rd, Great Sutton, South Wirral L66 2NA; Tel 0151-339 5141; Fax 0151-348 0348; L. Willday. (Mixed) (50)
Dee Banks, Dee Banks, Sandy La, Chester CH3 5UX; Tel (01244) 324012; Fax (01244) 346723; J. Pendry. (SLD) (Mixed) (72)
Deeside, Mellock La, Neston, South Wirral L64 9RN; Tel 0151-336 1940; C.H. McArdle. SLD (Mixed) (72)
Dorin Park, Wealstone La, Upton-by-Chester CH2 1HD; Tel (01244) 381951; Fax (01244) 390422; D. Llewellyn-Jones. (PH) (Day) (Mixed) (115)
Hinderton, Capenhurst La, Whitby, Ellesmere Port L65 7AQ; Tel 0151-356 5068; A.C. Lakin. Communication Difficulties (Mixed) (35)

Pupil Referral Units/Hospital Teaching Units

St Andrew's Special Unit, 2 Overleigh Rd, Handbridge, Chester CH4 7HL; Tel (01244) 683215; Fax (01244) 682280; C. Akam. (BD) (Mixed) (110)
Countess of Chester Hospital Education Unit, Children's Medical Ward 30, Maternity Wing, Liverpool Rd, Chester CH2 1BQ; Tel (01244) 365095; J. Lloyd. (Mixed); (5–16) (6)

Secondary Comprehensive Schools (11–18)

Malpas Bishop Heber County High, Chester Rd, Malpas SY14 8JD; Tel (01948) 860571; Fax (01948) 860962; M. Carding. (Mixed) (903)
The Bishops' (Blue Coat) CE (Aided) High, Vaughan's La, Gt Boughton, Chester CH3 5XF; Tel (01244) 313806/7; Fax (01244) 312319; J.K. Jackson, BA, MA. (Aided High); (Mixed) (872)
Blacon County High, Melbourne Rd, Blacon, Chester CH1 5JH; Tel (01244) 371475; Fax (01244) 374279; B. Dykes (Acting). (Mixed) (993)
Kingsway County High, Kingsway, Newton, Chester CH2 2LB; Tel (01244) 311355; Fax (01244) 312005; Dr D.M. Gower. (Mixed) (731)
Queen's Park County High, Queen's Park Road, Handbridge, Chester CH4 7AE; Tel (01244) 675468; A.D. Firman. (Mixed) (765)
Christleton County High, Vilage Road, Christleton, Chester CH3 7AD; Tel (01244) 335843; Fax (01244) 332173; G.I. Lawson, BA, MEd. (Mixed) (1197)
Neston County High, Raby Park Rd, Neston L64 9SL; Tel 0151-336 3902; Fax 0151-353 0408; G.W. Sirett, BA, MEd. (Mixed) (1393)
Stanney County High, Stanney La, Ellesmere Port L65 9DB; Tel 0151-355 5245/6; F.S. Evans. (Mixed) (858)
Sutton County High, Woodchurch La, Ellesmere Port L66 3NG; Tel 0151-339 4807/8; Fax 0151-339 4216; N.J. Beattie. (Mixed) (1100)
Upton-by-Chester County High, St James' Ave, Upton-by-Chester CH2 1NN; Tel (01244) 313061; Fax (01244) 312115; J.L. Jackson, MSc. (Mixed) (1624)
Whitby County High, Sycamore Dr, Whitby, Ellesmere Port L66 2NU; Tel 0151-355 8445/6; Fax 0151-357 2955; W.R. Fletcher. (Mixed) (1900)

Secondary Comprehensive Schools (Voluntary 11–18)

Chester Catholic (Voluntary Aided) High, Old Wrexham Rd, Handbridge, Chester CH4 7HS; Tel (01244) 683473; Fax (01244) 681773; V. Ratchford. (Aided) (970); (High); (Mixed) (970)
Ellesmere Port Catholic (Aided) High, Capenhurst La, Whitby, Ellesmere Port L65 7AQ; Tel 0151-355 2373; Fax 0151-356 9154; R.A. Flewitt, BA, MEd. (Aided) (1020)

Youth Centres

Area Youth Worker, c/o New Scene Youth Centre, 12 Newton La, Newton, Chester CH2 2LB; Tel (01244) 323736; Steve Cardiff
Chester Lache Youth Centre, Hawthorn Rd, Chester CH4 8HX; Tel (01244) 683909; G. Moore
Blacon Community Education Project, Youth Centre, Blacon High School, Melbourne Rd, Blacon, Chester CH1 5JQ; Tel (01244) 378357; Andy Mackay
New Scene Youth Centre, 12 Newton La, Newton, Chester CH2 2LB; Tel (01244) 323736; Jo Bennett, Kathy Hardy

Polygon Centre, Whitby Rd, Ellesmere Port, South Wirrall L65 6RS; Tel 0151-355 1718; Paul Garrett
Square One Centre, Thackeray Dr, Off Green La, Great Boughton, Chester CH3 5LR; Tel (01244) 320345; Steve Cardiff, Judi Yandell

Halton Area

Grosvenor Hse, Shopping City, Runcorn WA7 2ED; Tel (01928) 704300
Area Manager Elaine Beech
Number of Schools
4 nursery (227 FT equiv.) and 8 nursery classes (230 FT equiv.); 58 primary (12,836); 8 secondary (8,076); 4 special (325)

Area Careers Office

See chapter 17

Special Day Schools

Brookfields, Moorfield Rd, Widnes WA8 0JA; Tel 0151-424 4329; Fax 0151-495 3460; A. Chryssafi. SLD (Mixed) (84)
Cavendish, Lincoln Cl, Off Clifton Rd, Runcorn WA7 4YX; Tel (01928) 561706; Fax (01928) 566088; B.E. Fowler. (SLD) (Mixed) (87)
Chesnut Lodge, Green La, Ditton, Widnes WA8 7HF; Tel 0151-424 0679; Fax 0151-495 2141; A. Westhead. (PH) (Mixed) (120)
Greenfield, Cawfield Ave, Widnes WA8 7HG; Tel 0151-424 4892; R.H. Windsor (Acting). (MLD) (Mixed) (120)

Secondary Comprehensive Schools (11–16)

Brookvale County Comprehensive, Barnfield Ave, Murdishaw, Runcorn WA7 6EP; Tel (01928) 711643; Fax (01928) 701860; J. Phillips. (Mixed) (1139)
Fairfield County High, Peel House La, Widnes WA8 6TE; Tel 0151-423 3571; Fax 0151-424 3316; D.H. Blacow. (Mixed) (819)
The Grange County Comprehensive, Latham Ave, Runcorn WA7 5DX; Tel (01928) 578115; Fax (01928) 590075; P. Mulraney. (Mixed) (1017)
The Heath County Comprehensive, Clifton Rd, Runcorn WA7 4SY; Tel (01928) 576664; Fax (01928) 568703; D.H. Davies. (Mixed) (1159)
Norton Priory County High, Castlefields Ave Est, Runcorn WA7 2NT; Tel (01928) 563621; Fax (01928) 569296; J. Andrews, BSc. (Mixed) (1206)
Saints Peter and Paul RC Aided High, High School, Milton Ave, Widnes WA8 7XW; Tel 0151-424 3367; M.A.J. Glover. (Aided); (High); (Mixed) (1773)
St Chad's R.C. (Aided) Comprehensive, Grangeway, Runcorn WA7 5YH; Tel (01928) 64106; Fax (01928) 572902; A. Graley. (Aided); (Mixed) (1024)
Wade Deacon County High, Birchfield Rd, Widnes WA8 7TD; Tel 0151-423 2721; Fax 0151-420 5789; J.E. Jackson. (Mixed) (1033)

Youth Centres

Castlefields County Youth Centre, Kingshead Cl, Castlefields, Runcorn WA7 2JQ; Tel (01928) 564569; K. Tonge
CATCH Project (Counselling, Action and Training Centre, Halton), ATVO Building, Palacefields Ave, Runcorn, Cheshire; Tel (01928) 715979; Yvonne McNamara; Barry Littler; Bob Allen
Catch, 2 Frederick St, Widnes WA8 6PG; Tel 0151-420 7888; Pete Marsh
Chapelfield Community Centre (V), Liverpool Rd, Hough Green, Widnes, Cheshire; Tel 0151-495 1662; Justin Rolph
Crow Wood Youth Club, Dykin Rd, Widnes WA8 0HN; Tel 0151-424 7168; S. Lomax
Grangeway Youth and Community Centre, Grangeway, Runcorn, Cheshire WA7 5HA; Tel (01928) 569474; Jacqui Jones
Widnes Ditton Youth and Community Centre, Dundalk Rd, Widnes, Cheshire WA8 8DF; Tel 0151-423 2452/3121; F. Murphy
Widnes Youth Centre, St Paul's Rd, Widnes WA8 7QX; Tel 0151-424 5908; K. Hopkins

Macclesfield Area

Chapel La, Wilmslow SK9 1PU; Tel (01625) 534700
Area Manager S.A. Bell
Number of Schools
11 nursery classes (393 FT equiv.); 62 primary (11,232); 6 secondary (6,983); 1 special (65)

Area Careers Office

See chapter 17

Special Day School

Park Lane, Park La, Macclesfield SK11 8JR; Tel (01625) 423407/511191; Fax (01625) 511191; H.F. Lobell. (SLD) (Mixed) (84)

Pupil Referral Units/Hospital Teaching Units

Macclesfield Young People's Unit, Victoria Rd, Macclesfield SK10 3JF; Tel (01625) 616530; Fax (01625) 615841; A.P. Evans. (Mixed) (2–16) (15)
Education Unit, Ward 21, Schoolroom, Macclesfield District Hospital, Victoria Rd, Macclesfield SK10 3BL; Tel (01625) 661050; J.M.L. Westbrook. (12)

Secondary Comprehensive Schools (11–18)

Knutsford County High, Bexton Rd, Knutsford WA16 0EA; Tel (01565) 633294; Fax (01565) 633796; M. Valleley, BA, DipEd. (Mixed) (1451)
Poynton County High, Yew Tree La, off Dickens La, Poynton SK12 1PU; Tel (01625) 871811; Fax (01625) 874541; J.A.P. Jones. (Mixed) (1875)
Ryles Park County High, Ryles Park Rd, Macclesfield SK11 8AJ; Tel (01625) 429621; Fax (01625) 501857; C.J. Henstock. (Mixed) (661)
Tytherington County High, Manchester Rd, Tytherington, Macclesfield SK10 2EE; Tel (01625) 610220; Fax (01625) 610925; A.T. McCall. (Mixed) (974)
Wilmslow County High, Holly Rd, Wilmslow SK9 1LJ; Tel (01625) 526191; Fax (01625) 536858; R.A. Brent. (Mixed) (1658)

Secondary Comprehensive School (Voluntary 11–18)

All Hallows (Special Agreement) Catholic High, Brooklands Ave, Macclesfield SK11 8LB; Tel (01625) 426138; Fax (01625) 500315; R.K. Weremczyk, MA. (SA) (909); (Mixed)

Youth Centres

"The Attic" (Knutsford County Youth Centre), The Knutsford Centre, Westfield Dr, Knutsford WA16 OBL; Tel (01565) 53980; M.A. Lomas
The Egerton Club (V), Mereheath La, Knutsford, Cheshire; Tel (01565) 3383; Eric Ball
The Fermain Club (V), Oxford Rd, Macclesfield, Cheshire; Tel (01625) 26459; Charles Woodward
Generations (Macclesfield County Youth Centre), Union Rd, Macclesfield, Cheshire; Tel (01265) 21760; C. Lewis
Handforth County Youth Centre, Old Rd, Off Station Rd, Handforth, Wilmslow SK9 3AB; Tel (01625) 529745; J. Hartshorn
Macclesfield Youth Project, 33 Gt King St, Macclesfield SK11 6PR; Tel (01625) 34902; Liam Kealy

South Cheshire Area

Delamere Hse, Delamere St, Crewe CW1 2LL; Tel (01270) 505100
Area Manager S.A. Bell
Number of Schools
1 nursery (72 FT equiv.) and 11 classes (384 FT equiv.); 81 primary (16,235); 15 secondary (11,572); 1 special (105)

Area Careers Office

See chapter 17

Special Day School

Springfield, The Green, Crewe Rd, Crewe CW1 1HS; Tel (01270) 582446/582124; Fax (01270) 258281; D.A. Lewis. SLD (Mixed) (100)

Pupil Referral Units/Hospital Teaching Units

Crewe Secondary Unit, Adelaide St, Crewe CW1 3DT; Tel (01270) 255661; N.J. Lainas. (BD) (Mixed) (23)
Leighton Hospital School, CIO Ward 16, Leighton Hospital, Crewe CW1 4QJ; Tel (01270) 580444; P.I. Jackson. (5–16) (Mixed)

Secondary Comprehensive Schools (11–16)

Brine Leas County High, Audlem Rd, Nantwich CW5 7DY; Tel (01270) 625663/1623435/624191; M.K. Butler. (898)
Coppenhall County High, Coronation St, Crewe CW1 4EB; Tel (01270) 583431; Fax (01270) 501679; D.A. Penn. (786)
Kings Grove County High, Buchan Grove, Crewe CW2 7NG; Tel (01270) 661223; Fax (01270) 661223; C.W. Garnett. (786)
Middlewich County High, King Edward St, Middlewich CW10 9BU; Tel (01606) 833170; P.J. Andrews, BA. (681)
The Ruskin County High, Ruskin Rd, Crewe CW2 7JT; Tel (01270) 60514; Fax (01270) 650248; J.R. Munks. (600)
Shavington County High, Rope La, Shavington, Crewe CW2 5DH; Tel (01270) 662111; Fax (01270) 661305; P.R. Williams. (733)
Victoria Community County High, Meredith Centre, Crewe CW1 2PZ; Tel (01270) 212064; Fax (01270) 212064; G.R. Brown. (934)

Secondary Comprehensive School (Voluntary 11–16)

St Thomas More R.C. (Aided) High, Dane Bank Ave, Crewe CW2 8AE; Tel (01270) 68014; Fax (01270) 650860; G.R. Pollard. (A.) (High) (514)

Secondary Comprehensive Schools (11–18)

Alsager County Comprehensive, Hassall Rd, Alsager, Stoke-on-Trent ST7 2HR; Tel (01270) 873221; Fax (01270) 884335; D.J. Black. (Mixed) (1374)
Dane Valley County High, Jackson Rd, Congleton CW12 1NT; Tel (01260) 273000; Fax (01260) 297352; M.S. Wasserberg. (Mixed) (676)
Heathfield County High, Box La, Congleton CW12 4NS; Tel (01260) 273013/1273133; Fax (01260) 297382; R.K. Whitby. (Mixed) (880)
Westlands County High, Holmes Chapel Rd, Congleton CW12 4NH; Tel (01260) 273604; Fax (01260) 297557; R.D. Haigh. (Mixed) (806)
Holmes Chapel County Comprehensive, Selkirk Dr, Holmes Chapel CW4 7DX; Tel (01477) 534513; Fax (01477) 534489; E.J.C. Duffy. (Mixed) (851)
Malbank School and Sixth Form Centre, Welsh Row, Nantwich CW5 5HD; Tel (01270) 611009; Fax (01270) 610350; A. Kettleday. (1175)
Sandbach County High for Girls, 8iddlewich Rd, Sandbach CW11 9EB; Tel (01270) 765031; Fax (01270) 768544; J.M. Leigh. (Independent) (973)
Sandbach School, Crewe Rd, Sandbach CW11 0NT; Tel (01270) 767321; Fax (01270) 764787; C. Brown. (Independent) (Boys) (809)

Outdoor Education Centres

Beeston Outdoor Education Centre, Beeston, Tarporley CW6 9TR; Tel (01829) 260535; K. Veitch. (Residential)
Burwardsley Outdoor Education Centre, Tattenhall, Chester CH3 9PA; Tel (01829) 70424; J.R. Jones. (Residential)
Cheshire College of Agriculture, Reaseheath, Nantwich CW5 6DF; Tel (01270) 625131; S. Young
Delamere Forest Outdoor Education Centre, Foxhowl, Ashton Rd, Norley, nr Warrington WA6 6PA; Tel (01928) 740393; R.M., Smith. (Residential)
Langley Centre, Main Rd, Langley, Macclesfield, Cheshire; Tel (0126 015) 2713; L.M.A. Hodges. (Day Centre with camping facilities)
The Leighton Centre, Hailton Ave, Leighton, Crewe CW1 3QH; Tel (01270) 255901/(0270) 255732; Paul Boskett
Victoria Community High School Youth Centre, Ludford St, Crewe, Cheshire; Tel (01270) 211422/212064; Nigel Edwards
Congleton County Youth Centre Jackson Rd, Congleton CW12 1NT; Tel (01260) 271937; Eric J. Davies

Vale Royal Area

Watling St, Northwich, Cheshire; Tel (01606) 814900
Area Manager B. Glassonbury
Number of Schools
14 nursery classes (356 full-time equiv.); 58 primary (10,380); 10 secondary (8,930); 7 special (531)

Area Careers Office

See chapter 17

Special Schools

Brook Farm, Brook Rd, Tarporley CW6 9HH; Tel (01829) 732201; Fax (01829) 732824; N. Haslam. (Residential) (BD) (50)
Cloughwood, Stones Manor La, Hartford, Northwich CW8 1NU; Tel (01606) 76671; Fax (01606) 783486; D.H. Smith. (Residential) (BD) (Boys) (65)
Greenbank, Greenbank La, Hartford, Northwich CW8 1LD; Tel (01606) 76521; Fax (01606) 783736; K.D. Boyle
Hebden Green, Woodford La West, Winsford CW7 4EJ; Tel (01606) 594221/2; Fax (01606) 861549; A.R. Brindley. (Residential/Day) (2–19) (P.H) (Mixed) (90)
Oaklands, Cheviot Sq, Winsford CW7 1NU; Tel (01606) 551048; Fax (01606) 861291; I.G. Hopkins. (Day) (Mixed) (112)
Rosebank, Townfield La, Barnton, Northwich CW8 4PU; Tel (01606) 74975; L.P. Dicken (Acting). (Day/Residential) (Diagnostic/Assessment) (2–9) (Mixed)
The Russett School, Middlehurst Ave, Weaverham, Northwich CW8 3BW; Tel (01606) 853005; Fax (01606) 854669; H.M. Watts. (SLD) (Mixed) (116)

Secondary Comprehensive Schools (11–16)

Hartford County High, Hartford Campus, Chester Rd, Hartford, Northwich CW8 1LH; Tel (01606) 79233; Fax (01606) 783941; Dr. P.J. Llewellyn, BA. (Mixed) (1105)
The County High Leftwich, Granville Rd, Leftwich, Northwich CW9 8EZ; Tel (01606) 41511; Fax (01606) 331483; T.B. Hodgkinson. (Mixed) (651)
Rudheath County High, Shipbrook Rd, Rudheath, Northwich CW9 7DT; Tel (01606) 42515; Fax (01606) 46053; D. Martin, BSc. (Mixed) (774)
Weaverham County High, Lime Ave, Weaverham, Northwich CW8 3HT; Tel (01606) 852120; Fax (01606) 854033; E.G. Studd, BA. (Mixed) (939)

Secondary Comprehensive Schools (11–18)

Frodsham County High, Queen's Way, Frodsham, via Warrington WA6 6RP; Tel (01928) 731665; Fax (01928) 732991; R.P. Browne, BSc. (Mixed) (1120)
Helsby County High, Chester Rd, Helsby, via Warrington WA6 0HY; Tel (01928) 723551; Fax (01928) 723093; E.A. Lord, BA. (Mixed) (1172)
Tarporley County High, Eaton Rd, Tarporley CW6 0BL; Tel (01829) 732558; Fax (01829) 733945; N. Gilchrist (Acting). (Mixed) (721)
Verdin County High, Grange La, Winsford CW7 2BT; Tel (01606) 592300; Fax (01606) 863562; S.E. Fitches. (Mixed) (770)

Winsford Woodford Lodge County High, Woodford La West, Winsford CW7 4EH; Tel (01606) 551118; Fax (01606) 863162; P.M. Rourke. (Mixed) (612)

Secondary Comprehensive Schools (Voluntary 11–18)

St Nicholas R.C. (Aided) High, Greenbank La, Hartford, Northwich CW8 1JW; Tel (01606) 77500; Fax (01606) 784586; M.D. O'Connor. (Aided) (High) (Mixed) (984)
Winsford County Youth Centre, Nixon Dr, Grange Est, Winsford CW7 2HG; Tel (01606) 593724; Bob Barton
Rudheath County Youth Centre, Sadbrook Rd, Rudheath, Northwich CW9 7JL; Tel (01606) 41492; J. Bamling

Warrington Area

Priestley Hse, Sankey St, Warrington WA1 1PW; Tel (01925) 444000
Area Manager M. Adkins
Number of Schools
1 nursery (52 full-time equiv.) and 19 nursery classes (544 full-time equiv.); 77 primary (17,033); 12 secondary (12,164); 3 special (295)

Area Careers Office

See chapter 17

Special Schools

Grappenhall Hall, Church La, Grappenhall, Warrington WA4 3EU; Tel (01925) 263895; Fax (01925) 860487; J.P.B. Glennon. (30 Day, EBD, MLD) (55 Residential and 39 Day)
Green Lane, Green La, Padgate, Warrington WA1 4JL; Tel (01925) 811651; Fax (01925) 823099; G. Hunt. (MLD) (Mixed) (140)
Loushers Lane, Loushers La, Warrington WA4 2RF; Tel (01925) 633029; C.J. Fleming. (Mixed) (SLD) (72)
Children's Education Unit, Warrington NHS Trust Hospital, Education Room, Ward 810, Lovely La, Warrington WA5 1QG; Tel (01925) 635911 Ext 2609; *Teacher-in-Charge* H. Aylin. (5–16) (15)

Secondary Comprehensive Schools (11–16)

The Sir Thomas Boteler County High, Grammar School Rd, Warrington WA4 1JL; Tel (01925) 636414; Fax (01925) 417468; J. Higgins. (Mixed) (606)
William Beamont County High, Long La, Orford, Warrington WA2 8PX; Tel (01925) 635807; Fax (01925) 232329; E. James. (Mixed) (955)
Birchwood Community High, Brock Rd, Off Benson Rd, Birchwood, Warrington WA3 7PT; Tel (01925) 827322; Fax (01925) 812570; S. Yates. (Mixed) (829)

Secondary Comprehensive Schools (Voluntary 11–16)

Newman RC Aided High, Bridgewater Ave, Latchford, Warrington WA4 1RX; Tel (01925) 635556; Fax (01925) 241009; V. Love. (Mixed) (573)
St Gregory's R.C. Aided High, Cromwell Ave, Westbrook, Warrington WA5 1HG; Tel (01925) 574888; Fax (01925) 574888; T.J. Brophy. (Aided) (High) (Mixed) (841)

Secondary Comprehensive Schools (11–18)

Bridgewater County High, Broomfields Rd, Appleton, Warrington WA4 3AE; Tel (01925) 263919; Fax (01925) 861434; C.P. Marks. (Mixed) (1436)
Culcheth County High, Withington Ave, Culcheth, Warrington WA3 4JQ; Tel (01925) 762136; Fax (01925) 766373; H.C. Douglas. (Mixed) (934)
Great Sankey County High, Barrow Hall La, Great Sankey, Warrington WA5 3AA; Tel (01925) 724118/9; Fax (01925) 727396; W.J. Britton, BSc. (Mixed) (1316)
Lymm High (Voluntary Aided) Oughtrington La, Lymm WA13 0RB; Tel (01925) 755458; Fax (01925) 758439; S.M. Slater. (Voluntary Controlled) (Mixed) (1460)
Padgate County High, Insall Rd, Padgate, Warrington WA2 0LN; Tel (01925) 822632; Fax (01925) 851418; M. Chuck, BSc. (Mixed) (970)
Penketh County High, Heath Rd, Penketh, Warrington WA5 2BY; Tel (01925) 722298; Fax (01925) 723812; G.H. Bradbury, BSc. (Mixed) (1089)
Woolston County High, Holes La, Woolston, Warrington WA1 4LS; Tel (01925) 816848; Fax (01925) 852903; R.H. Mallows. (Mixed) (1105)
Burtonwood Youth Centre, Phipps La, Burtonwood, Warrington WA5 0JF; Tel (01925) 227580; Derek Smith
Warrington Culcheth Youth Centre, Church La, Culcheth WA3 5OJ; Tel (01925) 764618; Howard Quinn; Mike Whiteley
Warrington Orford Youth Centre, Capesthorne Rd, Orford, Warrington WA2 0JF; Tel (01925) 812475; E. Dean

Adult Education Centres

Alsager Adult Centre, Alsager County Comprehensive School, Hassall Rd, Alsager, Stoke-on-Trent ST7 2HR; Tel (0193 63) 3221
Birchwood Adult Education Centre, Birchwood Community High School, Brock Rd, Birchwood, Warrington WA3 7PF; Tel (01925) 827322
Blacon Adult Centre, Blacon County High School, Melbourne Rd, Blacon, Chester CH1 5JH; Tel (01244) 371475
Kingsway Adult Centre, Kingsway High School, Kingsway, Chester, Cheshire; Tel (01244) 311167
Christleton Adult Education Centre, Christleton High School, Village Rd, Christleton, Chester, Cheshire; Tel (01244) 335843
Congleton Adult Centre, Heathfield County High School, Box La, Congleton CW12 4NS; Tel (01260) 27300
Culcheth Adult Education Centre, Culcheth County High School, Withington Ave, Culcheth WA3 4JE; Tel (01925) 762136
The Bishops and Caldy Valley Adult Education Centre, Bishops Bluecoat C of E Aided High School, Vaughans La, Great Boughton, Chester, Cheshire; Tel (01244) 672048
Dorin Park, Adult Education Centre, Dorin Park School, Wealstone La, Upton, Chester CH2 1HP; Tel (01244) 381951
Ellesmere Port Stanney Adult Education Centre, Stanney County Comprehensive School, Stanney La, Ellesmere Port L65 9DB; Tel 0151-355 5245
Farndon and Tattenhall Adult Education Centre, Farndon County Primary School, Farndon, Nr Chester, Cheshire; Tel (01948) 860281
Frodsham Adult Education Centre, Frodsham High School, Queensway, Frodsham, Cheshire; Tel (01928) 31665 and (01244) 313061
Holmes Chapel Adult Centre, Holmes Chapel County Comprehensive School, Chester Rd, Holmes Chapel, Crewe, Cheshire; Tel (01477) 34513
Knutsford Adult Education Centre, Knutsford County High School, Bexton Rd, Knutsford WA16 0EA; Tel (01565) 3294
Leighton Community Centre, Railton Ave, Crewe, Cheshire; Tel (01270) 255901
Lymm Adult Education Centre, Lymm County High School, Grammar School Rd, Lymm WA13 0BH; Tel (0192575) 2350
Macclesfield North Adult Education Centre, Macclesfield Ryles Park County High School, Ryles Park Rd, Macclesfield SK11 8AJ; Tel (01625) 427366
Malpas Adult Education Centre, Malpas Heber County High School, Chester Rd, Malpas SY14 8JP; Tel (01948) 860281
Middlewich Adult Education Centre, Middlewich County Comprehensive School, King Edward St, Middlewich CW10 9BU; Tel (0160684) 3170/2013
Nantwich Adult Education Centre, Nantwich Malbank County High School, Welsh Row, Nantwich, Cheshire; Tel (01270) 65264/63434/628227
Neston Adult Education Centre, Neston County Comprehensive School, Raby Park Rd, Neston L64 9SW; Tel 01244 537242

Padgate Adult Education Centre, Padgate County High School, Insall Rd, Padgate, Warrington, Cheshire; Tel 0161-969 5604
Penketh Adult Education Centre, Penketh County High School, Heath Rd, Penketh WA5 2BY; Tel 2298/6523
Poynton Adult Education Centre, Poynton County High School, Yew Tree La, Poynton SK12 1PU; Tel (01625) 871811
Rudheath Adult Education Centre, Rudheath High School, Middlewich Rd, Rudheath, Northwich CW9 7DT; Tel (01603) 42515
Runcorn Adult Education Centres I:. Norton Priory Comprehensive School Grange Comprehensive School; Tel (01928) 563621
Runcorn Adult Education Centres II, Brookvale Comprehensive; Tel (01928) 711643
Runcorn Adult Education Centres III, Waterloo Rd Community Centre; Tel (01928) 582895
Runcorn Adult Education Centres IV, The Heath County Comprehensive; Tel (01928) 576664
Sandbach Adult Centre, Sandbach County High School, Middlewich Rd, Sandbach CW11 9EB; Tel (019367) 5031
Shavington Adult Education Centre, Shavington County High School, Rope La, Shavington, Crewe CW2 5DM; Tel 662111
Tarporley Adult Education Centre, Tarporley County High School, Eaton Rd, Tarporley CW6 0BL; Tel (01829) 732830
Upton Adult Education Centre, Upton County High School, St James' Ave, Upton-by-Chester CH2 1NN; Tel (01244) 313061
Victoria Community Centre, Oakley Centre, West St, Crewe, Cheshire; Tel (01270) 211422; N.T. Beckett
Warrington Bewsey Adult Education Centre, Bewsey County High School, Clap Gates Rd, Bewsey, Warrington WA5 5AD; Tel (01925) 444601; *Centre Head*
Weaverham Adult Education Centre, Weaverham High School, Lime Ave, Weaverham, Northwich CW8 3DJ; Tel (01270) 852120; *Centre Manager*
Wilmslow Adult Education Centre Thorngrove County High School, Thorngrove Rd, Wilmslow SK9 1DG; Tel 526191/524313; *Centre Manager*
Winsford Adult Education Centre, Woodford Lodge Comprehensive School, Woodford La, Winsford CW7 4EH; Tel (016065) 551118; *Centre Head*
Woolston Adult Education Centre, Woolston County High School, Holes La, Woolston, Warrington WA1 4LS; Tel (01925) 816848/813195; *Centre Head*

In-Service Centres

Cheshire Micro Unit, Rockmount, Liverpool Rd, Chester; Tel (01244) 390088; Fax (01244) 377688; Alex Whittaker
Kingsley Design Centre, Middle La, Kingsley, Frodsham WA6 6TL; Tel (01928) 787226/787012; Fax (01928) 787112; J. Duffield
Langley Centre, Main Rd, Langley, nr Macclesfield SK11 0BU; Tel (01260) 252713; Fax (01260) 253371; L. Hodges
Mond Primary Science Centre, Hollow La, Kingsley, Frodsham WA6 6YB; Tel (01928) 788737; Fax (01928) 788746; M. Gallimore
South Cheshire Micro Centre, Crewe Rd, Willaston, Nantwich CW5 6NE; Tel (01270) 661045; Fax (01270) 650351; P. Crookall
Tarvin Meadow Professional Centre, Meadow Cl, Tarvin, Chester CH3 8LY; Tel (01829) 741118; Fax (01829) 741592; D. Selzer
Woodford Lodge Professional Centre, Woodford La West, Winsford CW7 4EH; Tel (01606) 557328; Fax (01606) 862113; L. Thomas

Other Centres

The Conway Centre, Plas Newydd, Llanfair PG, Anglesey LL61 6DJ; Tel (01248) 714501; Fax (01248) 714504; A.M. Finnegan. (Residential)
St Mary's Centre, St Mary's Hill, Chester CH1 2DW; Tel (01244) 603320; Sue Wright
Tattenhall Centre, Tattenhall, Chester CH3 9PX; Tel (01829) 70223; J. Buffrey. (Residential)

Grant Maintained Schools

Bankfield High School, Liverpool Rd, Widnes, Cheshire WA8 7HU; Tel 0151-424 5038/4228; *Headteacher* Ray Rutter; *Chairman of Governors* Mrs Janet Murphy. (Mixed) (11–16) (700)
Fallibroome County High School, Priory La, Upton, Macclesfield SK10 4AF; Tel (01625) 827898; Fax (01625) 820051; M.W. Batson, BSc. Mixed (1012)
Henbury High School, Whirley Rd, Macclesfield SK10 3JP; Tel (01625) 422115; G.J. Ward. (Mixed) (880)

Cleveland County Council

Population 560,000

At the time of going to press, the local government structure in Cleveland was under review and no final announcement had been made.

Municipal Bldgs, PO Box 100A, Middlesbrough, Cleveland TS1 2QH; Tel (01642) 248155

Education Department

Woodlands Rd, Middlesbrough, Cleveland TS1 3BN; Tel (01642) 248155; Fax (01642) 246720
County Education Officer B.J. Worthy, MA
Deputy County Education Officer M D. Shorney, BSc, MEd
Second Deputy Education Officer P.M. Maddison, BA
EO (Finance) S.M. Goodhall, BA, IPFA
EO (Community Education) A. Stubbersfield, BA
EO (Prov. Accommodation and Admissions) N. Flight, BA
ISM (Information Systems Services Management) R. Jefferies
PAO (Client and Schools Support) K. Bell, DMA
PAO (Office Services) K. Flanagan, DMS
AEO (Schools Provision and Accommodation) M. Mason, BSc
Deputy Finance Officer A. Duffus
PAO (Staffing Services Officer) G.P. Dooks, DPA, FIPM, ACIS
PAO (Establishment) P. Russell, DMA
Chief Adviser G. Hodgson, BA
Senior Adviser (Secondary Education) (Design Technology) P. Davison, DipLC, MCCEd
Senior Adviser (Primary Education) M. Stillie, BA, ARCS
Senior Adviser (Professional Development and Appraisal) P.J. Walkley, BA
Senior Adviser (School Development & Inspection) (Science) J.E. Vickers
Adviser (Geography) J.W. Puckrin, MA
Adviser (Primary) (Curr. and Ass. KS.1 + KS.2) H. Smith
Adviser (Primary) (Professional Development) B. Lewis, BEd, MEd
Adviser (Mathematics) M.E. Lewis, BSc(Hons)
Adviser (Mathematics) T.R. Aspin, BA(Hons)
Adviser (Music) J. Forsyth, MA, ARCM, LRAM
Adviser (Religious Education and P.S.E) A.J.H. Leech, BA, MA, MEd
Adviser (English and Drama) (School Development and Inspection) P.R.D. Scott, MA
Adviser (History and Social Studies)(Curriculum and Assessment KS.4) Dr L.B.S. Holley, BA, MEd, PhD
Adviser (Modern and Classical Languages)(Curriculum + Assessment KS.3) R.W. Hullcoop, BA
Adviser (Science) M.J. Driver, MA, MSc

Adviser (IT and Business Education) (Professional Development) Eurng H.J. Curtis, BSc, CChem, MRSC, MBCS, CEng
Education Social Work Service Manager J. Watson
Principal Education Psychologist M.S. Woods, BSc, BA, ABPS
Youth and Community Officer R.G. Pettigrew, DPA
EO (Local Management of Schools) A. Roberts, MA(Cantab), PGCE
EO (Special Needs) J. Lewis, PGCE, MA(Ed)
Adviser (Art and Design)(Arts and Community) M. Lockey, BA(Hons), DipEd
Adviser (English and Library) (Equal Opportunities) T. Whitfield, BA(Hons)
Adviser (P.E. Health Education) J.J.M. Pearson, BEd, Adv.Dip in Educ, MA(Ed), FPEA
Adviser (Primary) J.M. Randall, MA
Adviser (Primary) (Curr. and Asses. KS1 and KS2) J.E. Vickers, MA
Adviser (Special Needs) (SEN Co-ordinator) P.B. Elton, AdvDip. RemEd
Adviser (Primary) K.A. Ford, BEd, MEd
Principal Careers Officer P. Furniss

Number of Schools
2 nursery (78); 201 primary (51,811); 41 secondary comprehensive (11-16) (33,170); 3 (11-18) (3,688)

Schools for pupils with learning difficulties
16

Day of Committee Meeting
Wednesday – 6 weekly cycle

Education Committee

Con 6, Lab 23, LD 5
Chair K. Legg, (Lab) 16 Burnmoor Dr, Eaglescliffe, Stockton TS16 0HZ
Vice-Chair A. Cunningham, (Lab) 10 Lapwing La, Crooksbarn Farm, Norton, Stockton-on-Tees TS20 1LT

Members of the Committee
Con: S.M. Fitzgerald, H. Pearson, P.,C. Price, F. Rogers, B.A. Thompson, E. Wild
Lab: K. Legg, A. Cunningham, L. Barnbrook, B.S. Bellerby, P. Barns, R. Cook, J. Coulthard, W. Ferrier MBE, J. Garvey, C. Godfrey, M.P. Goosey, B. Hanson OBE, P. Harford, P.M. Hayden, P.N. Hewitt, I.C. Jeffrey, J.M. Kay, K. Leonard, H. Shan, C.H. Stephenson, M. Taylor MBE, R. Waller, J. Watson
LD: J.J.W. Atkinson, H. Foster, K. Kirkham, C.J. Medlock, B.J. Stonehouse

Governor Training Unit

Governor Support Services, Education Offices, Woodlands Rd, Middlesbrough, Cleveland TS1 3BN; Tel (01642) 262974; Fax (01642) 264720
Governor Support Officer Ian Short, DMS, MInst, AM(Dip)
Governor Training Co-ordinator Graham Barwick, DMS

Services Offered
Foundation training for new governors together with information packs. A training programme of specialist courses including staff selection, financial management, health and safety and premises issues. A programme of "whole governing body" training, some aspects to include senior staff, on such topics as OFSTED inspections, building partnerships and school development planning. There are also chairs briefing sessions, link governor briefings, resource centres containing distance learning materials, a termly newsletter and a governors' helpline

County Psychological Services

Edmund Harvey Centre, Cromwell Ave, Stockton TS18 2EF; Tel (01642) 672080
159 Southfield Rd, 159 southfield Rd, Middlesbrough TS1 3HF; Tel (01642) 246695 and 246656
Redcar C.P.S. Centre, 5 Turner St, Redcar TS10 1AY; Tel (01642) 485610/35317

Special Schools for Pupils with Physical Handicaps

Thornhill Elwick Rd, Hartlepool TS6 0LQ; Tel (01429) 276906; R.T. Watson. (110)
The Endeavour (Primary), Tothill Ave, Ormesby, Middlesbrough TS3 0RH; Tel (01642) 312698/311036; Mrs R. Creek (Acting). (100 Primary)

Special Schools for Pupils with Learning Difficulties

Abbey Hill, Ketton Rd, Hardwick, Stockton TS19 8BU; Tel (01642) 677113; P. Coates
Ash Trees, Bowes Rd, Billingham TS23 2BU; Tel (01642) 563712; M.Q. Green. (140)
Carisbrooke, College Rd, Middlesbrough TS3 9JB; Tel (01642) 240595; C.J. Morris. (110)
Catcote, Catcote Rd, Hartlepool TS25 4EZ; Tel (01429) 264036; N. Carden. (120)
Holmwood, Saltersgill Ave, Middlesbrough TS4 3JS; Tel (01642) 819157; J. Appleyard (Acting). (140)
Kirkleatham Hall, Kirkleatham, Redcar TS10 4QR; Tel (01642) 483009; B. Cornell. (135)
Springwell, Wiltshire Way, Hartlepool TS26 0TB; Tel (01429) 260493; J. Lane. (70)
Tollesby, Saltersgill Ave, Middlesbrough TS4 3JS; Tel (01642) 815765; J. Whittingham, BPhil. (140)
Westlands, Eltham Cres, Thornaby TS17 9RA; Tel (01642) 762929; J.E. Jefferson, BPhil(Ed), MA(Ed) Special Needs. (50 Residential, 90 Day)

Special Schools for Pupils with Emotional and Behavioural Difficulties

Bishopsmill (Day and Residential), Mill Lane, Norton, Stockton TS20 1LG; Tel (01642) 531255/531256; R.J.G. Rose
Cleveland Unit Nursery Middlesbrough General Hospital, Ayresome Green La, Middlesbrough TS5 5AZ; Fax (01642) 850222 Ext 153; Mrs K Morris (Teacher in Charge)
Saltersgill (Boys' Residential/Day), Kirlevington, Yarm TS15 9QD; Tel (01642) 782081; A Riley
Sunningdale, Saltersgill Ave, Middlesbrough TS4 3PT; Fax (01642) 317744; R.E. McGlashan. (70)

Special School for the Deaf

Beverley, Beverley Rd, Middlesbrough TS4 3LQ; Tel (01642) 815500
E. McBean. (80)

Comprehensive Schools (11–18)

Conyers, Green La, Yarm TS15 9ET; Tel (01642) 783253; L. Metcalfe, BSc. (Mixed) (1148)
Egglescliffe, Urlay Nook Rd, Eaglescliffe TS16 0LA; Tel (01642) 783686; Fax (01642) 785566; A. Darnell. (Mixed) (1182)

Comprehensive School (Voluntary 11–18)

English Martyrs R.C., Catcote Rd, Hartlepool TS25 4HA; Tel (01429) 275204/273790; Fax (01429) 273998; F.D.S. Relton, MEd. (V.A.) (Mixed) (1237)

Comprehensive Schools (11–16)

Acklam Grange, Lodore Gro, Middlesbrough TS5 8PB; Tel (01642) 817667; Fax (01642) 816911; J.A. Bate, BSc. (Mixed) (1208)
Bassleton, Baysdale Rd, Thornaby TS17 9DB; Tel (01642) 763244; Fax (01642) 761318; J. McDonough, BPhil. (Mixed) (670)
Billingham Campus, Marsh House Ave, Billingham TS23 3HB; Tel (01642) 560947; Fax (01642) 370104; A.J. Finel, BA. (Mixed) (812)
Bishopsgarth, Harrogate L, Stockton TS19 8TF; Tel (01642) 586262; Fax (01642) 570038; M.V. Bond, BA, MA. (Mixed) (669)
Blakeston, Junction Rd, Stockton TS19 9LT; Tel (01642) 612381; Fax (01642) 675842; W.F. Tevendale, BSc. (Mixed) (859)

Brackenhoe, Marton Rd, Middlesbrough TS4 3RX; Tel (01642) 316900; Fax (01642) 319624; Mrs D.S. Palmer-Jones, BA. (Mixed) (594)
Brierton, Catcote Rd, Hartlepool TS25 4AB; Tel (01429) 265711; Fax (01429) 860996; S.A. Priestley, BA, AdvDipEd Management. (Mixed) (1385)
Bydales, Marlborough Ave, Marske TS11 6AR; Tel (01642) 482932/482695/477348; Fax (01642) 477348; P.J. Wilson, MA. (Mixed) (723)
Coulby Newham, Manor Farm Way, Coulby Newham, Middlesbrough TS8 0RJ; Tel (01642) 593113; Fax (01642) 598903; J.L. Gaskell. (Mixed) (800)
De Brus, Marske La, Skelton TS12 2HA; Tel (01287) 651795; Fax (01287) 653191; K.I. Tonge. (Mixed) (351)
Dyke House, Mapleton Rd, Hartlepool TS24 8NQ; Tel (01429) 266377/264488; Fax (01429) 866404; B. Jordan. (Mixed) (525)
Eston Park, Burns Rd, Eston TS6 9AW; Tel 466101; Fax 466101; M.K. Anderson, BA, MBIM. (Mixed) (846)
Gillbrook, Normanby Rd, South Bank TS6 9AG; Tel 466201/2/3; Fax 463905; D.F. Smith, BPhil. (Mixed) (1141)
Grangefield, Oxbridge Ave, Stockton TS18 4LE; Tel (01642) 672311; Fax (01642) 612217; R.J.F. Nicholson, MEd. (Mixed) (1274)
Hall Garth, Hall Dr, Acklam, Middlesbrough TS5 6JY; Tel (01642) 813776; Fax (01642) 816857; W.P.A. Smith, MA(Ed)
Henry Smith, King Oswy Dr, Hartlepool TS24 9PB; Tel (01429) 273041; Fax (01429) 232235; P.E. Webb, MA. (Mixed) (859)
High Tunstall, Elwick Rd, Hartlepool TS26 0LQ; Tel (01429) 261446; Fax (01429) 222856; P.D. Cutland, BA, MA(Ed). (Mixed) (1117)
Huntcliff, Marske Mill La, Saltburn TS12 1HJ; Tel (01287) 622178; E.A. Gartside, BA. (Mixed) (478)
Keldholme, Ormesby Rd, Middlesbrough TS3 8RE; Tel (01642) 326262; Fax (01642) 300663; J.E. Stead, BSc(Econ). (Mixed) (702)
King's Manor, Hall Drive, Acklam, Middlesbrough TS5 7JY; Tel (01642) 818200; Fax (01642) 850560; A.P. Francis, BSc, MA, FBIM. (Mixed) (940)
Langbaurgh, Sulby Ave, Middlesbrough TS3 8RD; Tel (01642) 314519; Fax (01642) 300419; R. Newitt, BSc, DipManEd. (Mixed) (499)
Laurence Jackson, Church La, Guisborough TS14 6RD; Tel (01287) 636361; Fax (01287) 610309; C.S. Lord, BA. (Mixed) (1414)
Manor, Owton Manor La, Hartlepool TS25 3PS; Tel (01429) 267018; Fax (01429) 861115; Mrs J. Mann, BA(Hons), MA. (Mixed) (782)
Northfield, Thames Rd, Billingham TS22 5EG; Tel (01642) 557373; Fax (01642) 360392; D.J. Youldon, BEd. (Mixed) (1053)
Norton, Berkshire Rd, Stockton TS20 2RD; Tel (01642) 557361; Fax (01642) 360266; G. Frew, BA. (Mixed) (765)
Nunthorpe, Guisborough Rd, Nunthorpe, Middlesbrough TS7 0LA; Tel (01642) 310561/2; Fax (01642) 325672; J.R. Rowling, MSc. (Mixed) (1228)
Ormesby, Stockwith Cl, Netherfields, Middlesbrough TS3 0RG; Tel (01642) 452191; Fax (01642) 463018; D. Richmond, BPhil. (Mixed) (814)
Rosecroft, Rosecroft La, Loftus, Saltburn TS13 4PZ; Tel (01287) 640563; A.D. Hopely, BA, DipEd. (Mixed) (539)
Rye Hills, Warwick Rd, Redcar TS10 2EP; Tel (01642) 484269, 484961, 482889; Fax (01642) 484269; Miss P.M. Rutherford, BA. (Mixed) (1010)
The Dene, Baysdale Rd, Thornaby TS17 9DF; Tel (01642) 614141; Fax (01642) 615903; I.D. Graves. (Mixed) (526)
Warsett, Linden Rd, Brotton TS12 2SJ; Tel (01287) 76305; Fax (01287) 77814; G. Davey. (Mixed) (491)
West Redcar, Kirkleatham La, Redcar TS10 4AB; Tel (01642) 473211; Fax (01642) 489202; S. Robson, BSc(Hons). (Mixed) (871)

Comprehensive Schools (Voluntary 11–16)

Ian Ramsey C.E., Green La, Stockton TS18 5AJ; Tel (01642) 585205; Fax (01642) 570488; B.A. Winter, MA, FRSA. (V.A.) (Mixed) (1163)
The Newlands F.C.J., R.C. (V.A.) (Mixed) (672) Saltersgill Ave, Middlesbrough TS4 3JW; Tel (01642) 825311/2; Fax (01642) 812709; Mrs J. Pickering. (Mixed) (728)
Our Lady & St Bede's R.C., Bishopton Rd West, Stockton TS19 0QH; Tel (01642) 615401; Fax (01642) 603559; J. Maloy, BA. (V.A.) (Mixed) (654)
St Anthony's R.C., Tranmere Ave, Middlesbrough TS3 8PB; Tel (01642) 243624; Fax (01642) 222656; C.J. Griffiths. (V.A.) (Mixed) (396)
St David's R.C., Cowley Rd, Acklam, Middlesbrough TS5 7EY; Tel (01642) 822124; Fax (01642) 829099; P.N. Tucker, BSc. (V.A.) (Mixed) (626)
St Michael's R.C., Beamish Rd, Billingham TS23 3DX; Tel (01642) 560612; Fax (01642) 370618; V. Shanley, BA. (V.A.) (Mixed) (824)
St Peter's R.C., Normanby Rd, South Bank TS6 6SP; Tel (01642) 453462; Fax (01642) 455010; T.J. Roe, BSc, BA. (V.A.) (Mixed) (408)
St Patrick's R.C., Baysdale Rd, Thornaby TS17 9DE; Tel 613327; P.F. Benfield, BA. (V.A.) (Mixed) (418)
Sacred Heart R.C., Derwent Rd, Redcar TS10 1BT; Tel (01642) 473221; Fax (01642) 473741; M.A. Dillon, BEd. (V.A.) (Mixed) (590)

Educational Computing Centre

Prissick Base, Marton Rd, Middlesbrough, Cleveland; Tel (01642) 325417; *Centre Manager* A.R. Hill, BA

Educational Development Centres

Guisborough, Old Northgate School, Guisborough, Cleveland TS14 6JA; Tel (01287) 632572
Hartlepool, Golden Flatts Primary School Site, Seaton Lane, Hartlepool, Cleveland TS25 1HN; Tel 274372
Middlesbrough, Worcester St, Middlesbrough, Cleveland TS1 4NT; Tel (01642) 242075

Outdoor Pursuits Centres

Carlton Centre, Carlton in Cleveland, Middlesbrough, Cleveland TS9 9ED; Tel (01642) 712229; J.F. Chapman, BA
Dukeshouse Wood Centre, Hexham, Northumberland NE47 9AG; Tel (01434) 602622
Lanehead Outdoor Pursuits Centre, Lanehead, Coniston, Cumbria LA21 8AA; Tel (015394) 41293; R.M. Skinner
Stainsacre Hall Residential Youth Centre, Stainsacre, Whitby, North Yorks YO22 4NT; Tel (01904) 603214; A.W. Ritson, BSc

Youth and Community Centres

Beechwood Youth and Community Centre, Kirkham Row, Middlesbrough TS4 3EE; Tel (01642) 815382
Billingham Youth and Community Centre, The Causeway, Billingham TS23 2DA; Tel (01642) 554988
Bishopsgarth Youth and Community Centre, Harrowgate La, Stockton TS19 8TF; Tel (01642) 580365
The Bridge Centre, Burbank St, Hartlepool TS24 7JQ; Tel (01429) 275121
Brierton Centre, Brierton La, Hartlepool TS25 4AB; Tel (01429) 265409
Brinkburn Centre, Blakelock Rd, Hartlepool TS25 5PF; Tel (01429) 265400
Brotton Youth Centre Warsett School, Linden Rd, Brotton TS12 2SJ; Tel (01287) 77141
California Youth Centre, Guisborough St, Eston TS6 9LA; Tel (01642) 453330
Chapel Road Youth Centre, Chapel Rd, Billingham TS23 1DX; Tel (01642) 555010
Conyers Youth and Community Centre, Green La, Yarm TS15 9ET; Tel (01642) 783252 (School); (01642) 784020 (Centre)
Coulby Newham Youth and Community Centre, c/o Coulby Newham Secondary School, Manor Farm Way, Coulby Newham, Middlesbrough TS8 ORJ; Tel (01642) 597126
Dyke Hse Centre, Mapleton Rd, Hartlepool TS24 8NQ; Tel (01429) 265401
Egglescliffe Community College Association, Egglescliffe Comprehensive School, Urlay Nook Rd, Egglescliffe TS16 OLA; Tel (01642) 783686

Elmwood Youth and Community Centre, 53 Darlington La, Hartburn, Stockton TS18 5EP; Tel (01642) 580120/580019
English Martyrs Centre, Catcote Rd, Hartlepool TS25 4HA; Tel (01429) 223080
Eston Park Youth Centre, Eston Park, C.S. School, Burns Rd, Teesville East, South Bank, Middlesbrough TS6 9AW; Tel (01642) 452196
Friarage Centre, Moor Terr, Hartlepool TS24 OPS; Tel (01429) 265403
Grangefield Youth and Community Centre, Oxbridge Lane, Stockton, Cleveland; Tel (01642) 675031
Grangetown Youth & Community Centre, Broadway, Grangetown, Middlesbrough TS6 7HP; Tel (01642) 455435
Grove Hill Youth and Community Centre, Bishopton Rd, Middlesbrough TS4 2RP; Tel (01642) 816384
Guisborough Youth Centre, Laurence Jackson School, Church La, Guisborough TS14 6DD; Tel (01287) 634332
Hardwick Youth Centre, Ketton Rd, Hardwick, Stockton, Cleveland; Tel (01642) 676558
Henry Smith Centre, King Oswy Dr, Hartlepool TS19 9RP; Tel (01429) 261290
High Tunstall Centre, Elwick Rd, Hartlepool TS26 OLG; Tel (01429) 264920
Joe Walton Youth Centre, Penrith Rd, Berwick Hills, Middlesbrough TS3 7JR; Tel (01642) 242564
Kader Youth and Community Centre, Trimdon Ave, Acklam, Middlesbrough, Cleveland; Tel (01642) 850179
Kiora Hall Youth and Community Centre, Ragpath La, Roseworth, Stockton TS19 9JS; Tel (01642) 675066
Lingdale Youth Centre, High St, Lingdale, Cleveland; Tel (01287) 653529
Loftus Youth and Community Centre, Duncan Place, Loftus TS13 4PR; Tel (01287) 640654
Long Newton and Elton Youth and Community Centre, Long Newton, Stockton, Cleveland; Tel (01642) 580031
Manor Centre, Owton Manor La, Hartlepool TS25 3PU; Tel (01429) 265405
Marske Youth Centre, Bydales School, Marlborough Rd, Marske TS11 6AR; Tel (01642) 485602
Newport Settlement Youth and Community Centre, St. Paul's Rd, Middlesbrough TS1 3NQ; Tel (01642) 244047
North Ormesby Youth and Community Centre, Derwent St, North Ormesby, Middlesbrough, Cleveland; Tel (01642) 243581
Norton School Centre, Berkshire Rd, Stockton TS20 2RD; Tel (01642) 360569
Nunthorpe Youth Centre, Guisborough Rd, Nunthorpe, Middlesbrough TS7 OLA; Tel (01642) 316818
Redcar Youth and Community Centre, Ayton Dr, Redcar TS10 4EW; Tel (01642) 478550
Redcar Youth Centre, Burnhamthorpe, Coatham Rd, Redcar TS10 1RP; Tel (01642) 482174
Robert Atkinson Youth and Community Centre, Thorntree Rd, Thornaby, Cleveland; Tel (01642) 676731
Rossmere Centre, Rossmere Way, Hartlepool, Cleveland; Tel (01429) 273741
St Hilda's Youth and Community Centre, Old Town Hall, Market Square, Middlesbrough; Tel (01642) 217142
St Michael's Youth Centre, Beamish Rd, Billingham TS23 3DX; Tel (01642) 560612
Saltburn Youth Centre, Saltburn School Annexe, Marske Rd, Saltburn TS12 1QA; Tel (01287) 623783
Seaton Carew Centre, Elizabeth Way, Hartlepool TS25 2AY; Tel (01429) 265407
Skelton Youth Centre, De Brus School, Skelton, Saltburn TS12 2HA; Tel (01287) 651276
South Bank Youth and Community Centre, Upper Jackson St, South Bank, Middlesbrough TS6 6PD; Tel (01642) 466748
Stillington Youth and Community Centre, Lawson St, Stillington, Stockton TS21 1JE; Tel (01740) 30041
Thornaby Youth Centre, Dene School, Baysdale Rd, Thornaby TS17 9DF; Tel (01642) 606623
Thorntree Youth and Community Centre, Birkhall Rd, Thorntree, Middlesbrough TS3 9JW; Tel (01642) 246827
Tilery Youth Centre, Tilery Primary School, St Annes Terr, Stockton TS18 2HU; Tel (01642) 670308
West Redcar, Youth Annexe, West Redcar School, Kirkleatham La, Redcar TS10 4AB; Tel (01642) 483949
Whinney Banks Youth and Community Centre, Harehills Rd, Middlesbrough TS5 4LL; Tel (01642) 814628

Clwyd County Council

Population 402,800
Shire Hall, Mold, Clwyd CH7 6NB; Tel (01352) 752121; Fax (01352) 758240

Education Department

Education Department, Shire Hall, Mold, Clwyd CH7 6ND; Tel (01352) 752121; Fax (01352) 754202
Chairman Councillor Mrs J.E. Angell
Vice-Chairman Cllr T. Middlehurst
Director of Education K.J. McDonogh, BA, MA(Ed)
Deputy Director of Education E.O. Lewis, BA
Principal Educational Psychologist Vacancy
Inspector/Adviser Special Educational Needs (Special)/SEN coordinator A.I. Wilson, MEd
Senior Adviser (Primary) M. Lloyd Jones, MEd
SEO (Secondary) G.M. Ramage, MA
Assistant Director (Strategic Services) R.E. Williams, MSc, MEd
Assistant Director (Learning Support Services) T. Garner, MA
Music Inspector Adviser Geraint James, BMus, MEd
Welsh Studies Inspector Adviser D. Hughes, BA, MEd
Science Inspector Adviser D. Williams, BSc, MSc
Design Education Inspector Adviser C. Wood, MEd
English Inspector Adviser L. Bithell
Mathematics Inspector Adviser G. Barber, BSc, BA
Humanities Inspector Adviser T.C. Davies, MA
Physical Education Inspector Adviser A. Caughter
Primary Education Inspector Adviser Gareth Hughes
Inspector Adviser of INSET J. Ramsay
Education Officer (Secondary) T. O'Marah
Education Officer (Secondary) W.A. Thomas, BEd
Education Officer (Secondary Special) A.R. Williams, BA(Hons)
LMS Co-ordinator Paul Oliver
Principal Careers Officer J. M'caw
Youth Officer J. Garaway
Number of Schools
3 nursery; 243 primary; 28 secondary; 11 special
Day of Committee Meeting
Tuesday

Special Schools

Assessment Centre, Wrexham, Clwyd; Tel (01978) 290101; G. Derby. (51)
Bryn Glas, Mold; Tel (01352) 758686; S. Smith-Jones, BA. (23)
St Christopher's, Wrexham, Clwyd; Tel (01978) 265237. (E.S.N.) (127)
Ysgol Belmont, Tel (01244) 543971; D.G. Jones. (E.S.N.) (155)
Ysgol Delyn, Mold; Tel (01352) 755701; S. Richards-Jones. (E.S.N.(S.) (50)
Ysgol Plas Brondyffryn, Denbigh; Tel (01745) 813841; G. Pilling. (55)
Ysgol Powys, Gwersyllt; Tel (01978) 755921; Vacancy. (E.S.N.(S) (74)
Ysgol Talfryn, Brynford; Tel (01352) 710698; A. Findley
Ysgol Tir Morfa, Rhyl; Tel (01745) 350388; S. Murphy. (E.S.N.) (180)

Ysgol-y-Bryn, Shotton; Tel (01244) 830281; Mrs. S.L., Taylor. (43)
Ysgol-y-Graig, Colwyn Bay, Clwyd; Tel (01492) 516838; J. Hewitt, MEd, PhD. (E.S.N.(S) (60)

Secondary Schools 11–16

Argoed High, Mynydd Isa; Tel (01352) 56414; Mrs J. Wright, BA. (Mixed) (539)
Bryn Alyn, Gwersyllt; Tel (01978) 720700; J. Wild, MA, BSc. (Mixed) (863)
Bryn Offa, Wrexham, Clwyd; Tel (01978) 266775; L. Webb, BA, MSc. (Mixed) (1040)
Darland, Rossett; Tel (01244) 570588; D.J. Gwilliam, BSc. (Mixed) (830)
The Groves, Wrexham, Clwyd; Tel (01978) 263945/354209; T. Wales, BA, MEd. (Mixed) (980)
St David's, Wrexham, Clwyd; Tel (01978) 265412; G.E. Rate, BSc. (Mixed) (1224)
St Joseph's R.C.M, Wrexham, Clwyd; Tel (01978) 265209; J.K. Thompson, MA, BSc. (Mixed) (491)
Ysgol y Grango, Rhos; Tel (0143 786) 840082; P. Mayhew, BA, MEd. (Mixed) (760)

Secondary Schools 11–18

Alun, Mold; Tel (01352) 4801; D.J. Williams, BSc, MPhil. (Mixed) (1488)
Brynhyfryd, Ruthin; Tel (018242) 3933; J.E. Ambrose, MEd, BA. (Mixed) (950)
Castell Alun, Hope; Tel (01978) 760238; D.E. Platten, MEd. (Mixed) (1083)
Connah's Quay High Tel Deeside 813491; P.G. Evans, BSc. (Mixed) (641)
John Summers High School, Tel (01244) 817575; R. Waterfield, MA. (Mixed) (615)
Denbigh High, Tel (0174 571) 812813; P.A. Bailey, BSc, BPhil. (Mixed) (881)
Dinas Bran, Llangollen; Tel (01978) 860669; Mrs M. Raine, BSc. (Mixed) (842)
Edward Jones, Rhyl, Clwyd; Tel (01745) 343433; M.J. Parry, MA(Ed). (Mixed) (630)
Elfed Buckley; Tel 542217; K. Grandfield, BA. (Mixed) (924)
Flint High, Tel 2269; A.C. Roberts, BSc. (Mixed) (777)
Hawarden High, Hawarden; Tel (01244) 534412; C.J. Harvey, MA, MEd. (Mixed) (1018)
Holywell High, Holywell; Tel (01352) 710011; J.G. Richards, BSc. (Mixed) (1132)
Prestatyn High, Tel 852312; A.K. Keep, BA. (Mixed) (1460)
Rhyl High, Tel (01745) 343533; J.R. Brocklehurst, BSc. (Mixed) (1210)
St David's, Saltney; Tel (01244) 671583; Mrs B. Chalmers, MA. (Mixed) (681)
St Richard Gwyn, Flint; Tel (013526) 2788; M.J. Philpot, BA, MEd. (Mixed) (1015)
Ysgol Glan Clwyd, St Asaph; Tel (01745) 582611; M.L. Rees, BSc. (Mixed) (879)
Ysgol Maes Garmon, Mold; Tel (01352) 4801; Dr. P. Davies. (Mixed) (804)
Ysgol Morgan Llwyd, Wrexham, Clwyd; Tel (01978) 356410; E. Williams, MEd. (Mixed) (321)
Ysgol Rhiwabon, Ruabon; Tel (01978) 820724/822392; J.M. Mackay, MA. (Mixed) (836)

Cornwall County Council

Population 467,000
County Hall, Truro, Cornwall TR1 3AY; Tel (01872) 322000; Fax (01872) 70340
Engineering and Architectural Design R.A. Wills
Director of Social Services N. Druce
Director of Finance and Administration R. Lester
County Librarian and Arts Officer J.E. Farmer

Education Department

County Hall, Truro TR1 3AY; Tel (01872) 322000; Fax (01872) 70340
Chair Cllr V.A. Cox
Vice-Chair Cllr M. Horrell
Secretary for Education J.S. Harris
Assistant Secretary for Education (Policy, Support and Standards) A.K. Morgan
Assistant Secretary for Education (Resources) D.G. Roberts
Principal Education Officer (Special Education) T.G. Cooper
Principal Education Officer (Continuing Education) J.B. Hall
Principal Education Officer (School and Governor Support) J.G. Pykett
Principal Education Officer (Development and Planning) C. Ramsey
Principal Education Officer (Information Technology) I.L. White
Assistant Education Officer (Development and Planning) G.D.A. Adye
Assistant Education Officer (Advisory Service) D.I. Thomas
Assistant Education Officer (Information and Statistics) C.M. Hall
Head of Advisory Service G.R. Aver
Secondary Inspector I.J. Brown
Secondary Inspector C. Stolz
Adviser (Mathematics) C. Banwell
Adviser (Geography) P. Butts
Advisor (History) R.J. Damerell
Adviser (Primary East) K. Davis
Adviser (Primary East) R. Desborough
Adviser (Physical Education) N.H. Dingle
Adviser (Special Education Needs) R.M. Ferrie
Advisor (Modern Languages) G. Grigg
Advisor (Science) R. Jardine
Advisor (Religious Education) W.J. Keast
Advisor (Primary West) P. Kemble
Advisor (Art) P. Kendall
Advisor (Music) D. Kitt
Advisor (Environmental Education) R. Moseley
Advisor (Outdoor Education) F.M. Perry
Advisor (Design and Technology) D.T. Prest
Advisor (Home Economics) G.C. Reeve-Fowkes
Advisor (Primary Mid) J. Shepherd
Advisor (English) J. Sinker
Advisor (Primary Mid) J. Springham
Advisor (Information Technology) U. Wagemakers
Chief Educational Psychologist S.J. Colwill
County Youth Service Manager J. Ross
Education Business Partnership Manager D. Smith
Head of Audiology Service A. Alderman
Head of Instrumental Music Support Service J. Harries
Head of Professional Development M. Cooper
Head of Visually Impaired Service M. Baillie
Principal Careers Officer P. Barnes

Number of Schools
2 nursery 69 (FTE); 250 primary (38,546); 31 secondary (29,545)

Special Schools
1 residential and day (100); 3 day (208)

Day of Committee Meeting
Thursday (quarterly)

Other Authorities with whom Joint Purchasing Arrangements are made
Member of CLEAPSE and FLAG Furniture Consortium and Consortium for Purchasing and Distribution.

Education Committee

LD 12, Ind 6, Lab 2, Con 2
Chair V.A. Cox, (LD)
Vice-Chair M. Horrell, (LD)

Members of the Committee
LD: M.E.R. Burley, P.B. Cocks, D.B. Harris, G. Hillman, A.R.J. Horn, S.L. Luscombe, J.G. Mellor, Brinley Morris, M.J. Moyle, S.G. Richards
Ind: H. Bonson, M.B. Breckon, P.M. Englefield, K. Hodge, H. Northcott, F.J.W. Whiting
Lab: T.G. Smale, C.C. Hailey
Con: J.J. Daniel, G.F. Evans

Governor Training Unit

Cornwall County Council, Education Dept, County Hall, Truro TR1 3AY; Tel (01872) 74282; Fax (01872) 70340
Professional Educational Development Unit Manager Mary Cooper, BA, PGCE
Senior Administrative Assistant Jo M. Wakeham

Special Schools

Curnow School, Drump Rd, Redruth, Cornwall TR15 1LU; Tel (01209) 215432; C. Simpson, MPhil. (Mixed) (97)
Doubletrees, St Blazey, Par, Cornwall PL24 2DS; Tel (01726) 812757; D. Leeson, BA, DipSpecEd. (Mixed) (73)
Nancealverne, Madron Rd, Penzance, Cornwall TR20 8TP; Tel (01736) 65039; H.E. John, BEd, CertSpecEd, MA. (Mixed) (63)
Pencalenick, St Clement, Truro, Cornwall TR1 1TE; Tel (01872) 520385; G.R. Williams, AdvCertSpecEd. (MLD) (Mixed) (Senior) (102)

Comprehensive Schools

Bodmin Community College, Tel (01208) 721144/74575; J. Evans, BSc. (Mixed) (1131)
Brannel, Tel (01726) 822485; P. Salmon. (Mixed) (460)
Budehaven Community, Tel (01288) 353271; J.S. Ward, BA. (Mixed) (979)
Callington School and Community College, Tel (01579) 83292/82118; P.L. Buet, BSc, MA. (Mixed) (1018)
Camborne Community, Tel (01209) 712280; D.G. Adam, MA. (Mixed) (1189)
Cape Cornwall, Tel (01736) 788501; R.J. Spowart. (Mixed) (554)
Falmouth Community, Tel (01326) 372386; S.A. Hosken, MA. (Mixed) (1130)
Fowey Community, Tel (01726) 832302; Dr W.P. Leach, BA, PhD. (Mixed) (813)
Hayle Community, Tel (01736) 753009; A.S. Oliver. (Mixed) (552)
Helston, Tel (01326) 562721; D.C. Johnson, BA(Hons). (Mixed) (1422)
Humphry Davy, Tel (01736) 63559; E.J. Ferguson. (Mixed) (767)
Launceston College, Tel (01566) 772468; C.D. Cooper, MA. (Mixed) (Boys' Boarding places) (1117)
Liskeard School and Community College, Tel (01579) 342344/343350; A.D. Wood, MA. (Mixed) (1257)
Looe Community, Tel (01503) 262625; J.A. Bond, BSc. (Mixed) (483)
Mounts Bay, Tel (01736) 63240; R.A. Moore, BA. (Mixed) (849)
Mullion, Tel (01326) 240098; I.L. Hamilton, BA. (Mixed) (461)
Newquay: Tretherras, Tel (01637) 872080/873536; D.R.M. Paveling, BSc. (Mixed) (1560)
Newquay: Treviglas, Tel (01637) 872076/876308; D. Ingham, MA. (Mixed) (682)
Penair, Tel (01872) 74737; Dr P.J. McGovern. (Mixed) (1070)
Penrice, Tel (01726) 72163; J. Walfreys, MA. (Mixed) (1117)
Penryn Community, Tel (01326) 372379; I.R. Jones. (Mixed) (681)
Poltair, Tel (01726) 75721; J.L. Deacon, BSc. (Mixed) (1157)
Pool School and Community College, Tel (01209) 712220/715011; P.K. Hazlewood, BA. (Mixed) (761)
Redruth Community, Tel (01209) 215507/216516; J.E.D. Shears, OBE, BA. (Mixed) (1386)
Richard Lander, Tel (01872) 73750; B.T. Coldman. (Mixed) (1603)
The Roseland Community, Tel (01872) 53675/53583; D.J. Fletcher, BA. (Mixed) (531)
St Ives School, Tel (01736) 795608; R.T. Zolkiewicz, BA. (Mixed) (649)
Sir James Smith's Community, Tel (01840) 213274; P.A. Perlmutter. (Mixed) (629)
Saltash, Tel (01752) 843715/842825; J. Morris, BA. (Mixed) (1234)
Torpoint, Tel (01752) 812511; R.W. Bright, BSc. (Mixed) (776)
Wadebridge, Tel (01208) 812881; J.C. Godwin, BSc. (Mixed) (947)

Teachers' Centres

Primary Resources Centre, Basset Rd, Camborne TR14 8SL; Tel (01209) 710158
Primary Resources Centre, Pondhu Hse, Penwinnick Rd, St Austell PL25 5DP; Tel (01726) 75751/65952; J. Kell
Curriculum Development Unit (TVEE), Hut 19, Old County Hall, Station Rd, Truro TR1 3AY; Tel (01872) 74282
Residential Teachers Centre, Fowey Hall, Fowey; Tel (01726) 833577

Coventry City Council

Population 304,100
The Council Hse, Coventry CV1 5RR; Tel (01203) 833333

Education Service

New Council Offices, Earl St, Coventry CV1 5RS; Tel (01203) 831511; Fax (01203) 831620
Chairman Cllr J. Clifford
Vice-Chairman Cllr D. Edwards
Chief Education Officer Cathryn Goodwin
Chief Adviser Graham Hall
Head of Strategic Planning Dr Carole Pullin
Head of Student/Community Services Marrilyn Snowden
Principal Finance Officer Charles Aplin
Personnel Manager Chris Burrows
Head of Careers Service Mary Davies

Community Education Area Offices

North East Area

Eburne Primary School Deedmore Rd, Coventry CV2 2AA; Tel (01203) 619367; Fax (01203) 619367; *Area Manager* Bill Malley; *Deputy Manager* Sue Sampson

South East Area

Stretton Ave Willenhall, Coventry CV3 3HY; Tel (01203) 511228; Fax (01203) 511309; *Area Manager* Ian Wilson; *Deputy Manager* Sue Wyatt

South West Area

Alderman Callow School and Community College Mitchell Ave, Coventry CV4 8DY; Tel (01203) 694837; Fax (01203) 471255; *Area Manager* Alan Newbold; *Deputy Manager* Hilary Snell

North West Area

Sherbourne Fields School Rowington Cl, Off Kingsbury Rd, Coventry CV6 1PS; Tel (01203) 598266; Fax (01203) 590517; *Area Manager* Kevin Crawford; *Deputy Manager* Ann Selby

North Area

Southfields South St, Coventry CV1 5EJ; Tel (01203) 227060; Fax (01203) 525752; *Area Manager* Rosalind Bell; *Deputy Manager* Philip Dunn

Careers Office

See chapter 17

Hospital School

Coventry Hospital School, Ward B5, Walsgrave Hospital NHS Trust, Clifford Bridge Rd, Walsgrave, Coventry CV2 2DX; Tel (01203) 611848; A. Edwards, BEd(Hons). (30)

Special Schools and Units

Alice Stevens, Ashington Gr, Coventry CV3 4DE; Tel (01203) 303776; R.I. McAllister, MEd. (M.L.D.) (195)
Baginton Fields, Sedgemoor Rd, Coventry CV3 4EA; Tel (01203) 303854; R.J. Aird. (S.L.D.) (87)
Corley (Coventry), Corley, Nr Coventry CV7 8AZ; Tel (01676) 540218; R. Nason (Acting). (MLD) (45)
Dartmouth, Tiverton Rd, Wyken, Coventry CV2 3DN; Tel (01203) 444141; P.S. Davies, DipEd, BA. E. and B.D.; Boys (51)
Deedmore, Deedmore Rd, Coventry CV2 1EW; Tel (01203) 612271; C. Sharrock, BSc, MEd. (M.L.D.) (80)
Hawkesbury Fields, Rear of 176–8 Alderman's Green Rd, Coventry CV2 1PL; Tel (01203) 367075; J. Thompson, BEd. (S.L.D.) (56)
The Meadows Residential, Hawthorn La, Coventry CV4 9PB; Tel (01203) 462335; W.K. Robinson. (E. and B.D.); (Boys) (27)
Sherbourne Fields, Rowington Cl, off Kingsbury Rd, Coventry CV6 1PS; Tel (01203) 591501/2; Mrs E. Hancox. (P.H.) (119)
Three Spires, Kingsbury Rd, Coventry CV6 1PJ; Tel (01203) 594952; C. Worrall. (M.L.D.) (77)
Tiverton, Rowington Cl, off Kingsbury Rd, Coventry CV6 1PS; Tel (01203) 594954; A. Chave, BPhil(Ed). (S.L.D.) (39)
Wainbody Wood, Stoneleigh Rd, Coventry CV4 7AB; Tel (01203) 418755; J. McGinty, BA, BPhil. E. an B.D. (55)

Secondary Comprehensive Schools

Alderman Callow School & Community College Mitchell Ave, Coventry CV4 8DY; Tel (01203) 467779; A.J. Slater, BEd. (Mixed) (497)
Barr's Hill School & Community College Radford Rd, Coventry CV1 4BU; Tel (01203) 252291; C. Engmann, BSc(Econ), MA. (Mixed) (756)
Bishop Ullathorne R.C. Leasowes Ave, Coventry CV3 6BH; Tel (01203) 414515; P.W. Pitt, BMus. (Mixed) (841)
Blue Coat C. of E., Terry Rd, Coventry CV1 2BA; Tel (01203) 223542; D. Lewin. (Mixed) (952)
Caludon Castle, Axholme Rd, Coventry CV2 5BD; Tel (01203) 444822; Dr J. Conneely, BSc, PhD. (Mixed) (1369)
Cardinal Newman School & Community College R.C., Sandpits La, Coventry CV6 2FR; Tel (01203) 332382; J.B. Connor, BSc, MA. (Mixed) (1070)
Cardinal Wiseman R.C., Potters Green Rd, Coventry CV2 2AJ; Tel (01203) 617231; A.P. Riley, BA, MEd. (Mixed) (1368)
Coundon Court School & Community College, Northbrook Rd, Coventry CV6 2AJ; Tel (01203) 335121; D.E. Kershaw, MA. (Mixed) (1531)
Ernesford Grange School & Community College Princethorpe Way, Coventry CV3 2QD; Tel (01203) 453121; R.J. Carter, MEd, BA, DipEd. (Mixed) (953)
Finham Park, Green La, Coventry CV3 6EA; Tel (01203) 418135; C.J. Hunt, BA. (Mixed) (1381)
Foxford Grange Rd, Coventry CV6 6DB; Tel (01203) 367444; M Layton, MA. (Mixed) (985)
Lyng Hall, Blackberry La, Coventry CV2 3JS; Tel (01203) 689447; J. McGinn, MA, BEd. (Mixed) (563)
President Kennedy School & Community College, Rookery La, Coventry CV6 4GL; Tel (01203) 661416; P.D.F. Tribe, BA, MEd. (Mixed) (1404)
Sidney Stringer School & Community College Cox St, Coventry CV1 5NL; Tel (01203) 251756; I.S. Kershaw, MA. (Mixed) (797)
Stoke Park School & Community College Dane Rd, Coventry CV2 4JW; Tel (01203) 450215; W.T. Wolger, BA, MEd. (Mixed) (1070)
Tile Hill Wood, Nutbrook Ave, Coventry CV4 9PW; Tel (01203) 466726; R.M. Westbrook, MSc, BEd. (Girls) (898)
Whitley Abbey, Abbey Rd, Coventry CV3 4BD; Tel (01203) 302580; J.R. Watkin, MEd. (Mixed) (914)
The Woodlands Broad La, Coventry CV5 7FF; Tel (01203) 462634/5; W.J. Hogarth, BA. (Boys) (1127)
Woodway Park School & Community College Wigston Rd, Coventry CV2 2RH; Tel (01203) 616155; M.C.M. Nicholls, BA. (Mixed) (826)

Plas Dol-y-Moch (Outdoor Education Centre)

Maentwrog, Blaenau Ffestiniog, Gwynedd LL41 3YT; Tel (01766) 762623; D.F. Mobbs

School of Music and Drama

Coventry Centre for the Performing Arts Leasowes Ave, Coventry CV3 6BH; Tel (01203) 418868; *Chief Adviser* G. Hall

Teachers' Centre

Elm Bank, Mile La, Coventry CV1 2LQ; Tel (01203) 228258; B. Blatherwick

Grant Maintained School

Ash Green School, Ash Green La, Ash Green, Coventry CV7 9AH; Tel (01203) 366772; *Headteacher* Kenneth Perris; *Chair of Governors* Brian Shillcock. (Mixed) (12–16) (450)

Cumbria County Council

Population 491,400
The Courts, Carlisle CA3 8L2; Tel (01228) 23456
Chief Executive J.E. Burnet, BA; Fax (01228) 401265
Principal Assistant County Librarian T.K. Grenwood, BA, ALA; Fax (01228) 515998
County Treasurer R.F. Mather, BSc, IPFA; Fax (01228) 401852
Director of Social Services K.E. Whittle, BA 3–7 Victoria Pl, Carlisle, CA1 1EJ; Fax (01228) 514763

Education Department

5 Portland Sq, Carlisle CA1 1PU; Tel (01228) 23456; Fax (01228) 515189
Chairman of Education Committee J. Oswald
Director of Education P. Black, BSc
Division Manager (Quality Assurance) J. Nellist, BSc
Division Manager (Operations) J.L. Harrold, BA

Division Manager (Policy and Commissioning) D.J. Hudson, BA, PhD
Senior Education Officer (Learning Support) E. Dawson
Senior Education Officer (Governor and Staff Support) W.M.A. Fox, BSc
Senior Education Officer (Scheme of Delegation) H. Slater
Senior Education Officer (Personnel) F.G. Turney, FIPM
Assistant Education Officer (Policy Research) M.E. Tattersall
Assistant Education Officer (Information Technology) J. Irving
Assistant Education Officer (Governor Training) S. Naybour
Assistant Education Officer (Customer Relations) M. Shiels
Senior Inspector Adviser S. Davies
Senior Inspector Adviser C. Tiddy, BEd
General Inspector Adviser D. Williams
General Inspector Adviser E. Lowis
General Inspector Adviser K. Tickell
County Inspector Adviser (Home Economics) M.E. Burdon, BEd
County Inspector Adviser (Design and Technology) J.D. Lewis
County Inspector Adviser (Early Childhood Education) J.M. Botham, BA
County Inspector Adviser (English) D. White
County Inspector Adviser (Music) M.J. McNally
County Inspector Adviser (Post 16 Education and Training) A. Carmichael
County Inspector Adviser (Science) C.G. Savory, BSc, PhD
County Inspector Adviser (Special Educational Needs) R. Cavanagh, BEd, MA
County Inspector Adviser (Modern Languages) P. Simmons
Principal Careers Officer P.J. Birbeck, BA
Principal Education Welfare Officer S. Bradburn
Area Manager (Welfare) T. Whitehead
Senior Education Welfare Officer J. Davies
Principal Educational Psychologist M.D. Watmough, BSc, MSc
Senior Educational Psychologist M.J. Dawson, Bsc
Educational Psychologist P.J. Hatcher, Msc
Educational Psychologist N Harbron
County Youth Officer P.E. Davies, BSc
TVEI Project Director B.A. Wind, BSc, MSc
Educational Psychologist D. Brewer
Senior Educational Psychologist D.B. Thompson, MA, MLitt

Number of Schools
7 Nursery 397, 301 Primary (41,493), 31 Secondary (30,702)

Special Schools
5 Severe Learning Difficulties, 1 Moderate Learning Difficulties

Day of Committee Meeting
Quarterly

Requisition Periods for School Supplies
No fixed period

Other Authorities with whom Joint Purchasing Arrangements are made
None

Education Committee

Lab 18, Con 14, LD 7, Ind 1
Chair J.W. Oswald, (Lab) 9 Birdoswald Dr, Scandfield Pk, Carlisle, Cumbria CA2 7XQ; Tel (01228) 39845; Office (01228) 23411 Ext 267
Vice-Chair A. Horne, (Lab) 22 Conway Gdns, Barrow in Furness, Cumbria CA14 3NZ; Tel (01229) 473734
Vice-Chair J.A.J. Leadley, (Lab) 16 Balmoral Rd, Fairfield, Whitehaven, Cumbria CA28 6UT; Tel (01946) 61786

Members of the Committee
Lab: A. Burns, D.T. Clarke, M. Dinning, I. Ellis, A. Graham, J.A. Heaslip, S.J. Matthews, W. Minto, J. Murphy, T.H. Pearson, R.M. Postlethwaite, G. Sear, R. Watson, R. Woodward
Con: R.F. Gyngell, P.M. Halfpenny, P.C. Jackson, C.T. Liversedge, J. Mallinson, B. Metz, D.F.W. Pantry, S. Parry, J.R. Richardson, G.E. Smith, S.F. Stevens, R. Strike, A. Toole, D. Youngman
LD: A.D. Baxter, R. Blight, D. Hutchinson, A.A. Metcalfe, J.E. Robinson, G. Walker, M. Wane
Ind: W. Johnston

Governor Training Unit

Cumbria Education Service, Governor and Staffing Services, 5 Portland Sq, Carlisle, Cumbria CA1 1PU; Tel (01228) 812481; Fax (01228) 812064
Governor Development Officer Sheila M. Naybour

Services Offered
A termly magazine–Cumbrian Governor; Helpline: Support Unit offering Development and training

Whitehaven Area Education Office

Union Hall, Scotch St, Whitehaven CA28 7BG; Tel (01946) 695561; Fax (01946) 691992
General Inspector Adviser R.C. Whittington
Educational Pyschologist P. Crompton
Area Manager (Welfare) C.T. Devlin
Senior Education Welfare Officer A. Dalton
Area Office Manager H. McNeil

Area Careers Office

See chapter 17

Barrow Area Education Office

John Whinnerah Institute, Abbey Rd, Barrow-in-Furness LA14 1XN; Tel (01229) 826782; Fax (01229) 812895
County Inspector Adviser (Maths) P. McGaw
Senior Educational Psychologist J. Heath, BSc, MEd
Educational Psychologist D. Sinclair, MA
Educational Psychologist D. Waters
Educational Psychologist S. Sanderson
Educational Psychologist J. Pinney
Area Manager (Welfare) B. Pickthall
Senior Education Welfare Officer G. McCrae
Area Office Manager I. Troughton

Area Careers Office

See chapter 17

Special Schools

George Hastwell, Moor Tarn La, Walney, Barrow-in-Furness LA14 3LW; Tel (01229) 475253; Fax (01229) 471418; B.J. Gummett. (E.S.N.(S)) (Day)
James Rennie, Kingstown Rd, Carlisle CA3 0BU; Tel (01228) 20536; S.J. Bowditch. (E.S.N.(S)) (Day)
Mayfield, Moresby Rd, Whitehaven CA28 8TU; Tel (01946) 692395; Fax (01946) 692395; S. Leathers. (E.S.N.(S)) (Day)
Sandgate, Sandylands Rd, Kendal LA9 6JG; Tel (01539) 723307; I. Hunter, BA. (E.S.N.(S)) (Day)
Sandside Lodge, Sandside Rd, Ulverston LA12 9EF; Tel (01229) 582137; Fax (01229) 582137; J. Billingham. (E.S.N.(S)) (Day)

Comprehensive Schools

The Alfred Barrow School, Duke St, Barrow in Furness LA14 2LB; Tel (01229) 827355; A.R. Titcombe NOR 450
Beacon Hill, Market Sq, Aspatria CA5 3EZ; Tel (016973) 20509; P.J. Cosham. (Mixed) (163)
Caldew, Dalston, Carlisle CA5 7NN; Tel (01228) 710044; Fax (01228) 710390; M.A. Atherton, MA. (Mixed) (1036)
Cockermouth, Castlegate Drive, Cockermouth CA13 9HF; Tel (01900) 823300; J.M. McMurtry. (Mixed) (1102)
Dowdales, Dalton-in-Furness LA15 8AH; Tel (01229) 62535; Fax (01229) 66372; E.A. Moffatt. (Mixed) (551)
Ehenside, Towerson St, Cleator CA23 3EL; Tel (01946) 810306; Fax (01946) 813671; E.A. Naylor. (Mixed) (430)

John Ruskin, Lake Rd, Coniston LA21 8EW; Tel (015394) 41306; Fax (015394) 41123; C. Ditchfield. (Mixed) (247)
Keswick, Main St, Keswick CA12 5NF; Tel (017687) 72173; Fax (017687) 74813; H.W. Allen, MA, ACE. (Mixed) (942)
The Lakes School, Troutbeck Bridge, Windermere LA23 1HW; Tel (015394) 42427; Fax (015394) 46369; A. Capstick. (Mixed) (815)
Lochinvar, Longtown CA6 5UG; Tel (01228) 791416; Fax (01228) 791701; M.D. Jackson. (Mixed) (219)
Millom, Salthouse Rd, Millom LA18 5AB; Tel (01229) 772300; Fax (01229) 772883; L. Higgins. (Mixed) (682)
Morton, Wigton Rd, Carlisle CA2 6LB; Tel (01228) 20155; Fax (01228) 515531; T.G. Easton. (Mixed) (1104)
Nelson Thomlinson, High St, Wigton CA7 9PX; Tel (016973) 42160; Fax (016973) 42160 Ext 238; P.M. Ireland. (Mixed) (891)
Netherhall, Netherhall Rd, Maryport CA15 6NT; Tel (01900) 813434; Fax (01900) 814867; J.D. Hudson. (Mixed) (883)
Newman, Lismore Pl, Carlisle CA1 1NA; Tel (01228) 22281; Fax (01228) 515588; R.A. Whitaker. (Mixed) (551)
Queen Elizabeth, Kirkby Lonsdale, Carnforth LA6 2HJ; Tel (015242) 71275; C. Clarke. (Mixed) (671); (Boarding places)
Samuel King's, Church Rd, Alston CA9 3QU; Tel (01434) 381236; J.M. Moore. (Mixed) (106)
Settlebeck High, Long La, Sedbergh LA10 5AL; Tel (015396) 20383; Fax (015396) 21024; E. Fraser. (Mixed) (148)
Solway Community, Liddell St, Silloth, Carlisle CA5 4DR; Tel (016973) 31234; Fax (016973) 32749; C. Bush. (Mixed) (192)
Southfield, Moorclose Rd, Workington CA14 5BH; Tel (01900) 603140; Fax (01900) 604246; D.R. Humphries. (Mixed) (895)
St Benedict's R.C. High, Red Lonning, Hensingham, Whitehaven CA28 8UG; Tel (01946) 694688; Fax (01946) 694688; D.T. Kinsella. (Mixed) (945)
St Bernard's R.C., Rating La, Barrow-in-Furness LA13 9LE; Tel (01229) 827629; P.D. Cooper. (Mixed) (782)
St Joseph's R.C., Harrington Rd, Workington CA14 3EE; Tel (01900) 604688; G.J. Smith. (Mixed) (459)
Stainburn, Stainburn Rd, Workington CA14 4EB; Tel (01900) 68383; Fax (01900) 602172; M.G. Fossey. (Mixed) (970)
Thorncliffe, Thorncliffe Rd, Barrow-in-Furness LA14 5QP; Tel (01229) 821235; D.G.B. Tye. (Mixed) (762)
Ullswater High, Wetheriggs La, Penrith CA11 8NG; Tel (01768) 64377; Fax (01768) 890037; D. Robinson, BA. (1222)
Victoria High, Springfield Rd, Ulverston LA12 OEB; Tel (01229) 53005; Fax (01229) 52922; B.K.R. Dower. (Mixed) (1371)
Walney, Sandygap La, Walney, Barrow-in-Furness LA14 3JL; Tel (01229) 471349; S. Aspinall, BA(Hons). (Mixed) (651)
Whitehaven, Cleator Moor Rd, Whitehaven CA28 8TY; Tel (01946) 694444; Fax (01946) 590721; A. Bardgett. (Mixed) (1389)
William Howard, Longtown Rd, Brampton CA8 1AR; Tel (016977) 2212; Fax (016977) 41096; R.T. Alston, BA. (Mixed) (922)
Wyndham, Egremont CA22 2DQ; Tel (01946) 820356; Fax (01946) 823900; J. Wilson, MA. (Mixed) (1009)

Adult Education Establishments

Furness College, Howard St, Barrow-in-Furness LA14 1NB; Tel (01229) 825017; Fax (01229) 870964; M. Chadwick
Carlisle College, Victoria Pl, Carlisle CA1 1HS; Tel (01228) 24464; Fax (01228) 514677; *Principal* J.S.R. Venables
Newton Rigg College, Penrith CA11 0AH; Tel (01768) 63791; Fax (01768) 67249; K.E. Jackson
Cumbria College of Art and Design, Homeacres, Brampton Rd, Carlisle CA3 9AY; Tel (01228) 25333; Fax (01228) 514491; D. Vaughan
Kendal College, Milnthorpe Rd, Kendal LA9 5AY; Tel (01539) 724313; Fax (01539) 733714; D.J. Bolton
NORTH EAST
Alston Centre, Samuel King's School, Church Rd, Alston CA9 3QU; Tel (014343) 81236; R.V. Turner
Appleby Centre, Appleby Grammar School, Battlebarrow, Appleby-in-Westmorland CA16 6XU; Tel (017683) 51580; E. Fraser
William Howard Centre, William Howard School, Longtown Rd, Brampton CA8 1AR; Tel (0169 77) 2212; P. Diggle
Kirkby Stephen Centre, Kirkby Stephen Grammar School, Christian Head, Kirkby Stephen CA17 4HA; Tel (017683) 71693; N. Thompson
Lochinvar Centre, Lochinvar School, Longtown, Carlisle CA6 5UG; Tel (01229) 791488; S. Layden
Ullswater Centre, Ullswater High School, Wetheriggs La, Penrith CA11 8NG; Tel (01768) 64120; D.G. Lord
Trinity Centre, Trinity School, Strand Rd, Carlisle CA1 1JB; Tel (01228) 33400; M. Khan
WEST
Beacon Hill Centre, Beacon Hill School, Market Square, Aspatria CA5 3EZ; Tel (016973) 22330; E. Yates
Ehenside Centre, Ehenside School, Towerson St, Cleator CA23 3EL; Tel (01946) 810306; S. McGlynn
Cockermouth Centre, Cockermouth School, Castlegate Dr, Cockermouth CA13 9XG; Tel (01900) 823389; L. Thomlinson
Lairthwaite Centre, Keswick School, Vicarage Hill, Keswick CA12 5QE; Tel (017687) 73565; S. Pilling
Millom Centre, Millom School, Salthouse Rd, Millom LA18 5AB; Tel (01229) 772300; J. Owen
Netherhall Centre, Netherhall School, Netherhall Rd, Maryport CA15 6NU; Tel (01900) 815765; J. Lindsay
Whitehaven Centre, Whitehaven School, Cleator Moor Rd, Whitehaven CA28 8TY; Tel (01946) 694446; M. Smith
Wigton Centre, Nelson Thomlinson School, High St, Wigton CA7 9PX; Tel (016973) 44514; H. Graham
Workington Centre, Workington 6th Form Centre, Needham Dr, Workington CA14 3SE; Tel (01900) 602119; S.W. Rose
Wyndham Centre, Wyndham School, Main St, Egremont CA22 2DQ; Tel (01946) 824259; L. Close
SOUTH
Barrow-in-Furness Sixth Form College, Rating La, Barrow-in-Furness LA13 9LE; Tel (01229) 828377; Fax (01229) 836874; E.J. Elvish
Cartmel Grange Centre, Headless Cross, Cartmel, Grange Over Sands LA11 7SA; Tel (015395) 36323; C.J. Perkins
Coniston Centre, John Ruskin School, Lake Rd, Coniston LA21 8EW; Tel (015394) 41306; Ms C. Ditchfield
Dalton Centre, Dowdales School, Dalton-in-Furness LA15 8AH; Tel (01229) 62535; J. Wickens
Kirkby Lonsdale Centre, Queen Elizabeth School, Kirkby Lonsdale, Carnforth, Lancs LA6 2HJ; Tel (015242) 71275; P. Bolton
Lakes Centre, Charlotte Mason College, Rydal Rd, Ambleside LA22 9BB; Tel (015394) 33066; Dr J. Thorley
Sedbergh Centre, Settlebeck High School, Long La, Sedbergh LA10 5AL; Tel (015396) 20383; E. Fraser
Ulverston Centre, Victoria High School, Springfield Rd, Ulverston LA12 0EB; Tel (01229) 55113; C.J. Perkins
West Cumbria College, Park La, Workington CA14 2RW; Tel (01900) 64331 (Workington Branch); (01946) 692261 (Whitehaven Branch); B.J. Taylor

Adult Education Residential Centre

Higham Hall, Bassenthwaite Lake, Cockermouth CA13 9SH; Tel (017687) 76276; Fax (017687) 76013; *Warden* A. Galbraith

College of Education

Charlotte Mason College, Rydal Rd, Ambleside LA22 9BB; Tel (015394) 33066; Dr J. Thorley

Enhanced Learning Support Departments

Ashfield Junior School ELSD, Ashfield Junior School, High St, Workington CA14 4ES; Tel (01900) 603415; Fax (01900) 872786
Hensingham Junior School ELSD, Hensingham Junior School, Main St, Whitehaven CA28 8QZ; Tel (01946) 693623
Thomlinson Junior School ELSD, Thomlinson Junior School, High St, Wigton CA7 9PG; Tel (016973) 42432; Fax (016973) 42432
Wigton Infant School ELSD, Wigton Infant School, Longthwaite Rd, Wigton CA7 9JR; Tel (016973) 42649
Wetheriggs Junior School ELSD, Wetheriggs Junior School, Huntley Ave, Penrith CA11 8NU; Tel (01768) 63571
Ehenside School ELSD, Ehenside School, Towerson St, Cleator CA23 3EL; Tel (01946) 810306; Fax (01946) 813671
Southfield School ELSD, Southfield School, Moor Close Rd, Workington CA14 5BH; Tel (01900) 603140; Fax (01900) 604246
Ullswater School ELSD, Ullswater School, Wetheriggs La, Penrith CA11 8NG; Tel (01768) 64377; Fax (01768) 890037
Whitehaven School ELSD Whitehaven School, Cleator Moor Rd, Whitehaven CA28 8TY; Tel (01946) 694444; Fax (01946) 590721

Hearing Units

Bransty School Hearing Unit, Bransty School, Whitehaven CA28 6EG; Tel (01946) 693348
Newlaithes Infant School Hearing Unit, Newlaithes Infant School, Langrigg Rd, Carlisle CA2 6DX; Tel (01228) 28589
Newlaithes Junior School Hearing Unit, Newlaithes Junior School, Langrigg Rd, Carlisle CA2 6DX; Tel (01228) 25023
Morton School Hearing Unit, Morton School, Wigton Rd, Carlisle CA2 6LB; Tel (01228) 20155; Fax (01228) 515531
Victoria High School Hearing Unit, Victoria High School, Springfield Rd, Ulverston LA12 0EB; Tel (01229) 53005; Fax (01229) 52922
Whitehaven School Hearing Unit, Whitehaven School, Cleator Moor Rd, Whitehaven CA28 8TY; Tel (01946) 694444; Fax (01946) 590721

Outdoor Education Centres

Fellside Outdoor Education Centre Fellside Mansion, Caldbeck, Wigton CA7 8HA; Tel (0169 98) 307; *Director* C. Hutchinson
Hawse End Centre, Portinscale, Keswick CA12 5UE; Tel (017687) 72816; Fax (017687) 75108; *Director* A. Hunter

Physical-Medical Units

The Lakes School Physical-Medical Unit, The Lakes School, Troutbeck Bridge, Windermere LA23 1HW; Tel (015394) 42427; Fax (015394) 46369
Walney School Physical-Medical Unit, Walney School, Sandygap La, Walney, Barrow-in-Furness LA14 3JL; Tel (01229) 471349

Reading Centres

Barrow Literacy Centre, Alfred Barrow School, Duke St, Barrow in Furness LA14 2LB; Tel (01229) 813424; P. Maquire
Carlisle Literacy Centre, Pennine Way Junior School, Pennine Way, Carlisle CA1 3RQ; Tel (01228) 32684; B. Weston
Kendal Literacy Centre, Castle Park School, Sedbergh Dr, Kendal LA9 6BE; Tel (01539) 730476; *Teacher-in-Charge* A.J. Evans
Penrith Literacy Centre, County Infant School, Brunswick Rd, Penrith CA11 7LX; Tel (01768) 890544; J. Rogers

Tutorial Centres

Bridge Hse Tutorial Centre, 144 Abbey Rd, Barrow in Furness LA14 5AB; Tel (01229) 811894; *Teacher-in-Charge* J. Sharpe. (4–16)
Brunswick Tutorial Centre, 9 Brunswick St, Carlisle CA1 1PB; Tel (01228) 511305; *Teacher-in-Charge* R. White. (11–16)
College House Tutorial Centre, Flatt Walks, Whitehaven CA28 7RW; Tel (01946) 695008; *Teacher-in-Charge* Mrs J.M. Bethwaite. (7–16)
Kendal Tutorial Centre, Canal Head North, Kendal LA9 7BY; Tel (01539) 732960; *Teacher-in-Charge* Mrs J. Sharpe. (7–16)
Orchard Hse Tutorial Centre, Edward St, Carlisle CA1 2JB; Tel (01228) 818127; R. White
St Michael's Tutorial Centre, Station Rd, Workington CA14 2UY; Tel (01900) 604967; *Teacher-in-Charge* J.E.M. Bethwaite. (7–16)

Youth and Community Centres

Allerdale Office, Allerdale Youth Team, Mossdale Hse, 149 Harrington Rd, Workington CA14 2UP; Tel (01900) 602433; Fax (01900) 870229
Barrow Office, Barrow Youth Team, John Whinnerah Institute, Abbey Rd, Barrow in Furness LA14 1XN; Tel (01229) 826782; Fax (01229) 812895
Carlisle Office, Carlisle Youth Team, 5 Portland Square, Carlisle CA1 1PU; Tel (01228) 812591; Fax (01228) 515189
Copeland Office, Copeland Youth Team, Union Hall, Scotch St, Whitehaven CA28 7BG; Tel (01946) 61639; Fax (01946) 691992
Eden Office, Eden Youth Team, 19–24 Friargate, Penrith CA11 7XR; Tel (01768) 891130; Fax (01768) 891203; I. Bell
South Lakeland Office, South Lakeland Youth Team, Kendal Education Office, County Offices, Kendal LA9 4RQ; Tel (01539) 721000; Fax (01539) 724959

Grant Maintained Schools

Appleby Grammar School, Battlebarrow, Appleby-in-Westmorland, Cumbria CA16 6XU; Tel (017683) 51580; G.I. Holloway; Fax (017683) 52412. (Mixed) (498)
Cartmel Priory CE School, Cartmel, Grange Over Sands, Cumbria LA11 7SA; Tel (015395) 36202; Fax (015395) 36287; D.F. Ingram. (Mixed) (311)
Dallam School, Haverflatts La, Milnthorpe LA7 7DD; Tel (015395) 63224; A. Bancroft. (Mixed) (646); Boarding Places
Harraby Grant Maintained School, (which intends to become the City of Carlisle Technology College); Sponsored by Cavaghan & Gray, Talk-Tel Communication and others Edgehill Rd, Carlisle, Cumbria CA1 3SL; Tel (01228) 31435; Fax (01228) 810962; W.G. Blakemore. (Mixed) (521)
Kirkbie Kendal Comprehensive School, Lound Rd, Kendal LA9 7EQ; Tel (01539) 727422; Fax (01539) 729243; *Headmaster* John D. Lomax; *Chairman of Governors* Rev John G. Hetherington. (Mixed) (11–18) (835)
Kirkby Stephen Grammar School, Christian Head, Kirkby Stephen, Cumbria CA17 4HA; Tel (017683) 71693; P. Hawksworth. (Mixed) (355)
Parkview School, West Ave, Barrow-in-Furness, Cumbria LA13 9AY; Tel (01229) 827348; Fax (01229) 431274; R.J. Wilson. (Mixed) (782)
Queen Elizabeth Grammar School, Ullswater Rd, Penrith CA11 7EG; Tel (01768) 64621; Fax (01768) 890923; *Headteacher* Colin P. Birnie; *Chair of Governors* Robert Good. (Mixed) (11–18) (736)
The Queen Katherine School, Appleby Rd, Kendal LA9 6PJ; Tel (01539) 720045; W.J. Duxbury. (GMS) (1160)
St Aidan's County High School, Lismore Pl, Carlisle CA1 1LY; Tel (01228) 20277; Fax (01228) 31249; D.E. Kemp. (GMS) (680)
Trinity School, Strand Rd, Carlisle CA1 1JB; Tel (01228) 27596; Fax (01228) 401020; B. Dexter, BSc, ARCS. (GMS) (1718)

Derbyshire County Council

Population 934,000
County Offices, Matlock, Derbys DE4 3AG; Tel (01629) 580000
County Director J.S. Raine
County Treasurer P. Swaby
County Purchasing Officer P.H. Bangs
Head of Architectural Services S.D.D. Anderson

Education Department

County Offices, Matlock, Derbyshire DE4 3AG; Tel (01629) 580000
Chairman Cllr D.J. Wilcox
Vice-Chairman Cllr R. Hosker
Chief Education Officer V. Hannon
Assistant Chief Education Officer (Student and Community Services) K. Chapman
Assistant Chief Education Officer (Strategic and Marketing Services) R.V. Taylor
Assistant Chief Education Officer (School and College Services) Vacancy
Principal Adviser (Curriculum Consultancy and Staff Development) A. Howell
Principal Adviser (Quality Assurance and Inspection) P. Arnold
Education Officer (Development) D. Humphrey
Senior Community Education Officer (Adult) D. Rae
Senior Community Education Officer (Youth) W. Sherwood
Education Officer (Student Services) P. Purnell
Education Officer (Careers) B. Gray
Educational Officer (Libraries & Arts) R. Ball
Education Officer (Finance) P. Godfrey
Educational Officer (Personnel and Office Services) G. Soudah
County Educational Psychologist C.J.T. Rogers
Number of Schools
17 nursery; 449 primary; 61 secondary comprehensive; 26 special
Day of Committee Meeting
Thursday-six times a year
Requisition Periods for School Supplies
No fixed period
Other Authorities with whom Joint Purchasing Arrangements are made
None

High Peak and Derbyshire Dales Area

Kents Bank Rd, Buxton, Derbyshire SK17 9HJ; Tel (01298) 26121; Fax (01298) 72191
Senior Area Education Officer K.C. Horncastle
Senior Area Adviser J. Headley

Area Careers Office

See chapter 17

Comprehensive Schools

Chapel-en-le-Frith High School, Long La, Chapel-en-le-Frith, Stockport, Ches SK12 6TG; Tel (01298) 813118; S. Ash. (610)
Glossopdale Community College, Talbot Rd, Glossop SK13 9DR; Tel (01457) 862336; J.B. Lees. (1725)
Hope Valley College, Castleton Rd, Hope, Sheffield S30 2RD; Tel (01433) 620555; L. Hudson. (435)
Highfields School, Lumsdale Rd, Matlock, Derbyshire DE4 5NA; Tel (01629) 56686; D.W. Marshall. (1450)
New Mills, Church La, New Mills, Stockport, Ches SK12 4NR; Tel (01663) 743284; M. James. (845)

Comprehensive Schools (Voluntary)

Anthony Gell, Wirksworth, Derby DE4 4DX; Tel (01629) 825577; R. Leach. (625)
Buxton Community, College Rd, Buxton SK17 9EA; Tel (01298) 23122; D. Brindley. (1230)
Queen Elizabeth's, The Green Rd, Ashbourne, Derbyshire DE6 1EP; Tel (01335) 43685; Dr A.R. Wilks. (1070)
St Philip Howard R.C., St Mary's Rd, Glossop SK13 8DR; Tel (01457) 853611; W.J. McGrath. (425)
St Thomas More R.C., Palace Fields, Buxton SK17 6AF; Tel (01298) 23167; J.A. McCabe. (280)

North East Derbyshire, Chesterfield and Bolsover Area

St Helena Centre, Sheffield Rd, Chesterfield S41 7LN; Tel (01246) 204851
Senior Area Education Officer D. Shaw
Senior Area Adviser S. James

Area Careers Office

See chapter 17

Comprehensive Schools

Bolsover (New), Mooracre La, Bolsover, Chesterfield S44 6XA; Tel (01246) 822105; A.K. Turner. (Mixed) (860)
Brookfield Community, Chatsworth Rd, Chesterfield S40 3NS; Tel (01246) 568115/568442; S.E. Thomas. (1170)
Deincourt, Chesterfield Rd, North Wingfield, Chesterfield S42 5LE; Tel (01246) 851206; A.K. Truckel. (580)
Eckington, Dronfield Rd, Eckington, Sheffield S31 9BR; Tel (01246) 432849/434401; E. Middlemass. (1620)
Frederick Gent, Mansfield Rd, South Normanton, Alfreton, Derby DE55 2ER; Tel (01773) 811737; I.M. Fraser. (660)
Hasland Hall Community, Broomfield Ave, The Green, Hasland, Chesterfield S41 0LP; Tel (01246) 273985; G.R. O'Hagan. (785)
Heritage Community, Broughton La, Clowne, Chesterfield S43 4QG; Tel (01246) 810259; I.J. Alford. (1005)
Meadows Community, High St, Old Whittington, Chesterfield S41 9LG; Tel (01246) 450825; L. Asquith. (625)
Newbold Community, Highfield La, Newbold, Chesterfield S41 8AT; Tel (01246) 230550; T. Gibson. (1295)
Parkside Community, Boythorpe Ave, Boythorpe, Chesterfield S40 2NS; Tel (01246) 273458/233832; D.J. Duncombe. (550)
Shirebrook Community, Common La, Shirebrook, Mansfield, Notts NG20 8QF; Tel (01623) 742722; J.C. Young. (685)
Springwell Community, Middlecroft Rd, South Staveley, Chesterfield S43 3NQ; Tel (01246) 473873; J.L. Simon. (735)
Tibshelf, High St, Tibshelf, Alfreton, Derby DE5 5PP; Tel (9773) 872391; G.T. Moseby. (550)
Tupton Hall, Old Tupton, Chesterfield S42 6LG; Tel (01246) 863127/862032; T.R. Smith. (1725)

Comprehensive School (Voluntary)

The Dronfield, Chesterfield Rd, Dronfield, Sheffield S18 6XD; Tel (01246) 412372/415095; T. Thomas. (1820)

Amber Valley and Erewash Area Office,

Grosvenor Rd, Ripley, Derbyshire DE5 3JE; Tel (01773) 744741; Fax (01773) 746848
Senior Area Education Officer P. Fox
Senior Area Adviser D. Connor

Area Careers Office

See chapter 17

Comprehensive Schools

Aldercar, Dalton's Cl, Langley Mill, Nottingham NG16 4HL; Tel (01773) 712477; R. Feist. (465)
Bennerley, Bennerley Ave, Ilkeston DE7 8PF; Tel (0115) 932 8739; M.J. Dalton. (480)
Ilkeston, King George Ave, Ilkeston DE7 7HS; Tel (0115) 930 3724; M. Burdon. (1145)
John Flamsteed Community, Derby Rd, Denby, Derby DE5 8NP; Tel (01332) 880260; G. Boss. (515)
Kirk Hallam Community, Godfrey Dr, Kirk Hallam, Ilkeston DE7 4HH; Tel (0115) 930 1522; A.D. Shaw. (770)
Long Eaton Community, Tamworth Rd, Long Eaton, Nottingham NG10 1BE; Tel (0115) 973 2438; R.E. Orriss. (1085)
Mortimer Wilson, Grange St, Alfreton, Derby DE55 7JA; Tel (01773) 832331; J.P. Billing. (1130)
Ripley Mill Hill, Peasehill Rd, Ripley, Derby DE5 3JP; Tel (01773) 746334; A.P. Stephens. (1240)
Swanwick Hall, Derby Rd, Swanwick, Derby DE55 1AE; Tel (01773) 602106; J.R.B Lees. (975)
Wilsthorpe, Derby Rd, Long Eaton, Nottingham NG10 4BJ; Tel (0115) 972 9421/2/3; J.F. Leach. (1095)

Comprehensive School (Voluntary)

St John Houghton R.C., Abbot Rd, Kirk Hallam, Ilkeston DE7 4HX; Tel (0115) 932 2896; T.J. Murphy. (440)

Derby and South Derbyshire Area Office

27 St Mary's Gate, Derby DE1 3NN; Tel (01332) 340251; Fax (01332) 292167
Senior Area Education Officer D.H. Curtis
Senior Area Adviser J. Hickman

Area Careers Office

See chapter 17

Comprehensive Schools

Bemrose Community, Uttoxeter Rd, Derby DE22 3HU; Tel (01332) 366711; R. Kenny. (775)
Derby Moor Community, Moorway La, Littleover, Derby DE3 7FS; Tel (01332) 766280; M.A. York. (1155)
Granville Community, Burton Rd, Woodville, Swadlincote, Derbyshire DE11 7JR; Tel (01283) 216765; R.J.L. Watts. (550)
High View Technology Centre, St Andrew's View, Derby DE21 4ET; Tel (01332) 831515; S.H. Wareing. (595)
Lees Brook Community, Morley Rd, Chaddesden DE21 4QQ; Tel (01332) 671723 and 674739; C. Dibbs. (690)
Littleover Community, Pastures Hill, Littleover, Derby DE23 7BD; Tel (01332) 513219; D. Nichols. (1070)
Sinfin Community School, Farmhouse Rd, Sinfin, Derby DE24 3AR; Tel (01332) 769174; P.G. Collings. (885)
The Village Community, Village Street, Derby DE3 8DF; Tel (01332) 767666; A.L. Jamieson. (625)
William Allitt, Sunnyside, Newhall, Derbys DE11 0TL; Tel (01283) 216404/5; D.J. Roles. (680)
Woodlands Community, Blenheim Dr, Allestree, Derby DE22 2LW; Tel (01332) 551921/2; A.K. Wayment. (885)

Comprehensive Schools (Voluntary)

St Benedict R.C., Duffield Rd, Derby DE22 1JD; Tel (01332) 557032; C.B.A. Reynolds. (1450)

Hostels

Holly House, Church St North, Old Whittington, Chesterfield, Derbyshire; Tel (01246) 450530; G. O'Neil. (Boys 7–11, Girls 7–16) (30 boarding, 10 day)
Stretton House, Highstairs La, Stretton, Derby, Derbyshire DE5 6FD; Tel (01246) 862238; N.P. Smith. (Boys) (50; 40 boarding, 10 day)

Special Day Schools

Ashe Hall, Ash La, Etwall, Derby, Derbyshire DE65 6HT; Tel (01283) 732338; D.C. Jones. (55)
Ashgate Croft, Ashgate Rd, Chesterfield, Derbyshire S40 4BN; Tel (01246) 275111; Mrs B. Campbell. (Multi) (Mixed) (267)
Bennerley Fields, Stratford St, Ilkeston, Derbys DE7 8QZ; Tel (0115) 932 6374; M. Wadsley (Acting). (Multi) (Mixed) (142)
Boothby Meadows, Cokayne Ave, Ashbourne, Derbyshire DE6 1EJ; Tel (01335) 344674; P.M. Sillitoe. (Mixed) (40)
Brackenfield, Bracken Rd, Long Eaton, Nottingham, Derbyshire NG10 4DA; Tel (0115) 973 3710; B.J. Jones. (Multi) (Mixed) (118)
Delves, Hayes La, Swanwick, Derby, Derbyshire; Tel (01773) 602198; I.D. Snodin. (Multi) (Mixed) (132)
Ivy House, Ivy Sq, Osmaston Rd, Derby DE23 8LG; Tel (01332) 344694; Mrs M.A. Phillips. (110)
Parkwood, Alfreton Pk, Alfreton, Derbyshire DE5 7AL; Tel (01773) 832019; V.A. Annis. (Mixed) (105)
St Clare's, Rough Heanor Rd, Mickleover, Derby, Derbyshire DE3 5AZ; Tel (01332) 511757; A. Bradley. (Mixed) (135)
St Giles', Hampshire Rd, Chaddesden, Derby DE2 6BT; Tel (01332) 343039; P.J. Walsh. (Mixed) (100)
St Martin's, Wisgreaves Rd, Alvaston, Derby DE2 8RQ; Tel (01332) 571151; W.J. Jepson. (Mixed) (100)
Stanton Vale, Lower Stanton Rd, Ilkeston, Derbyshire DE7 4LR; Tel (0115) 932 4783; J. Jepson. (Mixed) (73)
Stubbin Wood, Burlington Ave, Langwith Junction, Mansfield, Notts NG20 9AD; Tel (01623) 742795; J.M. Youdan. (Mixed) (180)

Residential Special Schools

Alderbrook, Buxton Rd, Chinley, Stockport, Cheshire SK12 6DR; Tel (01663) 750324; D. Smith (Acting). (57 including 41 day and 16 Boarding) (Mixed)
Brookside, Brookside Rd, Breadsall, Derby DE21 5LF; Tel (01332) 831223; S. Pugh (Acting). (Boys) (Including 15 day boys) (80)
John Duncan, Corbar Rd, Buxton, Derbyshire SK17 6RL; Tel (01298) 23130; R.W. Caswell. (Mixed) (45 boarding and 40 day) (85)
Overseal Manor, Hall Croft Ave, Overseal, Burton-on-Trent, Staffs DE12 6JE; Tel (01283) 760393; J. Antcliffe. (Boys) (30)
St Andrew's, St Andrew's View, Breadsall Hilltop, Derby DE21 4EW; Tel (01332) 832746; M. Dawes (Acting). (20 boarding and 76 day) (Mixed) (96)
Southwood Hse, Portway, Holbrook, Derby DE56 0TE; Tel (01332) 880208; S. Elkins (Acting). (40 boarding, 10 day) (Mixed)
Talbot Hse, Talbot Rd, Glossop, Derby, Derbyshire SK13 9DP; Tel (01457) 852006; D. Sims (Acting). (Mixed) (including 30 day) (40)
Westbrook, Thoresby Rd, Long Eaton, Nottingham NG10 3NP; Tel (0115) 972 9769; D.J. Ingham. (Mixed) (including 52 day pupils) (92)

Residential Training Centres

Lea Green Centre, Lea, Matlock, Derbys DE4 5GJ; Tel (01629) 534561; Ms J.E. Cook
White Hall Centre for Open Country Pursuits, White Hall, Long Hill, Buxton SK17 6SX; Tel (01298) 23260; P.D. Jones

Staff Development Centres

Chesterfield Staff Development Centre, Markham Rd, Chesterfield S40 1SS; Tel (01246) 234070; P. Richards
Derby Staff Development Centre, 184 Kedleston Rd, Derby, Derbyshire DE3 1GT; Tel (01332) 371921; P. Richards

Grant Maintained Schools

Belper School, John O'Gaunt's Way, off Kilbourne Rd, Derbys DE6 1RZ; Tel (01773) 825281; Fax (01773) 820875; R.L. Ingham. (1010)
Chellaston School, Swarkestone Rd, Chellaston, Derby DE73 1UA; Tel (01332) 702502; Fax (01332) 703779; H. Thomas. (900)

Ecclesbourne School, Wirksworth Rd, Duffield, Derbyshire DE56 4ES; Tel (01332) 840645; Fax (01332) 841871; *Headteacher* Dr J.R. Dupey; *Chairman of Governors* P. Latham; *Bursar* L. Allen. Mixed (11–18) (1250)
Heanor Gate School, Smalley Hill, Heanor, Derbyshire DE7 7RA; Tel (01773) 716396; S. Spencer. (970)
John Port School, Etwall, Derby DE65 6LU; Tel (01283) 734111; Fax (01283) 734035; M.A. Crane. (1650)
The Merrill Community School, Upper Moor Rd, Allenton, Derbys DE24 9BY; Tel (01332) 700249
Murray Park Community School, Murray Rd, Mickleover, Derby DE3 5LD; Tel (01332) 515921; E.R. Baker. (930)
Netherthorpe School, Ralph Rd, Staveley, Chesterfield, Derbyshire S43 3PU; Tel (01246) 472220; *Headteacher* Rodney D. Wilson; *Deputy Head* Pat A. Bottomley; *Deputy Head* Martin G. Cooper; *Deputy Head* H. Michael Freeman; *Chairman of Governors* John W. Cutts; *Business Manager* Lucie M. Slight. (Mixed) (11–18) (830)
Noel-Baker Community School, Bracknell Dr, Alvaston, Derby DE24 0BR; Tel (01332) 572026; Fax (01332) 573654; G.E. Wynne. (GM) (1185)
St Marys RC High School, Newbold Rd, Upper Newbold, Chesterfield, Derbyshire S41 8AG; Tel (01246) 201191

Devon County Council

Population 1,049,200 (Mid 1993)
County Hall, Topsham Rd, Exeter EX2 4QD; Tel Exeter (01392); Barnstable (01271); Plymouth (01752); Torquay (01803) 382000; Fax Exeter, Barnstaple, Plymouth, Torquay 382286
Chief Executive R.D. Clark, BA, DipEd, FRSA
County Treasurer J. Glasby
Chief Education Officer S.W.G. Jenkin
Chief of Property Services Officer R. Lee
Director of Social Services A. Williamson
County Environmental Director E. Chorlton, CEng, MICE, FIHT, ACIArb, EurIng
County Librarian A.J Shute, BA, ALA Barley Hse, St Thomas, Exeter; Tel (01392) 74142
Chief Purchasing Officer P. Dummett, IPFA 2 Trusham Rd, Marsh Barton, Exeter; Tel (01392) 384635
County Personnel Officer C.H. Schofield
Dartmoor National Park Officer Dr N. Atkinson
County Trading Standards Officer S. Butterworth
Chief Fire Officer A. Currie
County Solicitor P. Jenkinson
Head of Press and PR R.A. Wood
General Manager, Devon Direct Services R. Grigg

Education Department

County Hall, Topsham Rd, Exeter EX2 4QG; Tel (01392) 382000; Fax (01392) 382203
Chairman M.H. Knight
Vice-Chairman K.J. Turner
Chief Education Officer Simon W.G Jenkin
Deputy Chief Education Officer (Policy, Planning and Review) Dr. Paul Gray
Assistant Chief Education Officer Dr Bryan C. Slater
Senior Education Officer (Policy and Student Services) Dr Tony Smith
Senior Education Officer (Premises) Mel L. Atkinson
Senior Education Officer (Special Education) and Principal Educational Psychologist Louise Nichols
Senior Education Officer (Communications and IT) Brian Sussex
Senior Education Officer (Personnel) John Sanders
Senior Education Officer (Stategic Development) Geoff Thomas
Senior Adviser (Primary Education) Jennie Willcock-Bates
Assistant Education Officer (Special Education) Dr Frances Canning
Assistant Education Officer (Finance) Angela Daveney
Assistant Education Officer (Premises) Steve Daw
Assistant Education Officer (Support Services) Rosemary Fardell
Assistant Education Officer (Community Education) Ingrid Fisher
Assistant Education Officer (Student Awards) Terry Green
Assistant Education Officer (Premises) Graham Jones
Assistant Education Officer (School and College Transport) Mike Passmore
Assistant Education Officer (Management Information Systems) Richard Stevens
Assistant Education Officer (Staff Development) Chris Stokes
Assistant Education Officer (Policy) David Sullivan
Devon Learning Resources S. Allardyce
Number of Schools
3 nursery; 438 primary (81,666); 57 secondary (53,760); 21 Special (1,848); 5 professional centres; 6 residential centres
Day of Committee Meeting
Two-monthly cycle

Governor Services Unit

Education Dept, County Hall, Topsham Rd, Exeter EX2 4QG; Tel (01392) 383611; Fax (01392) 382203
AEO (Governor Services) Vicky Rollason
Services Offered
Administration of appointment of County Council representatives on school governing bodies; Maintenance of records of governing body membership; Provision of training and advice to members of school governing bodies and clerks; Provision of information at local resource centres; Publication of information on policies, procedures and good practice

Devon Curriculum Advice

Education Dept, County Hall, Topsham Rd, Exeter EX2 4QG; Tel (01392) 382345; Fax (01392) 382079
Chief Adviser Peter Edwards
Adviser (English) Janet Brennan (KS 1&2)
Adviser (English) Nick Jones
Adviser (English) Martin Phillips
Adviser (Art and Design) Chris Wrightman
Adviser (Foreign Language) Bernard Lien
Adviser (Foreign Language) Chris Wakely
Adviser (Science) Pauline Allen
Adviser (Science) David Butler
Adviser (Science) Stuart Farmer
Adviser (Religious Education) Mark Brimicombe
Adviser (Religious Education) Valerie Pearson
Adviser (Personal and Social Education) Helena Williams
Adviser (Design and Technology) Veronica Matthews
Adviser (Design and Technology) Annette Hardcastle
Adviser (Drama) Jackie Taylor
Adviser (Physical Education) Chris Rose
Adviser (Mathematics) Peter Griffin
Adviser (Mathematics) Keith Holding
Adviser (Mathematics) David Owen
Adviser (Geography and Environmental Education) Ralph Hare
Adviser (History) Chris Taylor
Adviser (History) Gillian Temple
Adviser (Music) Brian Ley
Adviser (Vocational Education Team) John Willis (Post-16)
Adviser (Vocational Education Team) Trevor Hamilton
Adviser (Vocational Education Team) Trevor Day

The Babbage Centre

Dartington Hall, Totnes, Devon TQ9 6EJ; Tel (01803) 867082; Fax (01803) 867086
Couty Adviser for Computer John Ralston

Devon Youth Music

Countess Weir Combined School, Lower Weir Rd, Exeter EX2 7BR; Tel (01392) 876132
Ken Parr

The Devon Schools International Centre

St James High School, Summer La, Exeter EX4 8NN; Tel (01392) 460194; Fax (01392) 460294
Director Brian Cousins

Devon School Library Service

Barley Hse, Isleworth Rd, Exeter EX4 1RQ; Tel (01392) 384304
Head of Service Lyhne Medlock

Devon Learning Resources

21 Old Mill Rd, Torquay, Devon TQ2 6AU; Tel (01803) 605531; Fax (01803) 607127
Stuart Allardyce

Schools Management Information Services (ScoMIS)

Exeter Hawthorn Hse, Emperor Way, Exeter Business Pk, Exeter EX1 3QS; Tel (01392) 445440; Fax (01392) 44522; *Senior MIS Co-ordinator* Brian Hodge
Plymouth ScoMIS, Annexe 12A, The College of St Mark and St John, Derriford Rd, Plymouth PL6 8BH; Tel (01752) 784433; Fax (01752) 78227; *MIS Co-ordinator* Roger Plant

Devon Inspection Service

5A Cranmere Ct, Lustleigh Cl, Matford Business Pk, Exeter EX2 8RD; Tel (01392) 824210; Fax (01392) 824218
Chief Inspector Tessa Stiles

Devon Business Partnership/Teacher Placement Service

c/o Parkins Ltd, 20 Trusham Rd, Marsh Barton, Exeter EX2 8DF; Tel (01392) 494488; Fax (01392) 412417
Director Ann Forsyth
West Devon c/o College of St Mark and St John, Derriford Rd, Plymouth PL6 8BH; Tel (01752) 768799; Fax (01752) 761120; *Manager* Jenny Rhodes

Education, Arts and Libraries Committee

LD 16, Con 8, Lab 8, Ind 1, Lib 1
Members of the Committee
LD: B.H. Berman, R.A. Cook, I.J. Fenton, K.M. Hawkins, K.M. Hill, R.A. Hobson, M.H. Knight, M.W.G. Lane, D.J. Morrish, G.J. Oakes, J. Palk, C.M. Pannell, A.F. Perret-Green, D.H. Strudwick, D.W.S. Thorning, K.J. Turner, J.D. Walker
Con: M.P. Bealey, C. Channon, D.H. Dicker, T.J. Hart, M. Lawley, M.R. Tomlinson, K.J. Watson, B. Willoughby
Lab: D.M. Connelly, V.S. Ellery, E.R. Evans, B.J. Mills, J. Owen, R.C.J. Scott, S.M. Spence, J.F. Wilton

AREA OFFICES

East Devon

Morwenstow, 7 Barnfield Cres, Exeter EX1 1SU; Tel (01392) 383900; Fax (01395) 383926
Area Education Officer Alan MacKenzie
Area Adviser for Secondary Education John Butt
Adviser for Special Education Geoff Hogg
Area Adviser for Primary Education Manny Lewis
Area Adviser for Secondary Education (East and South) John Stephens
Area Adviser for Primary Education "H" Thompson
Area Adviser for Primary Education Grahan Jones
Area Community Education Officer Peter Brewer

Youth and Community Education Centres

Axe Vale Youth and Community Office, Pippins, Lyme Rd, Axminster EX13 5AZ; Tel (01297) 32820; P. Lacey
Cullompton School, Cullompton EX15 1DX; Tel (01884) 38326; P. Hague
East Devon Outdoor Education Centre (Haven Banks), Sailing and Canoeing Centre, 61 Haven Banks, Exeter EX2 8DP; Tel (01392) 434668; *Director* J. Bradford
Exeter '100 Club', Wear Barton Rd, Exeter EX2 7EH; Tel (01392) 873432; *Community Education Tutor* M. Green
Exeter 'Bridge Club', Exeter St Thomas High School, Cowick La, Exeter EX2 9JL; Tel (01392) 432694; A. Dyer
Exeter 'Knight Club', Beacon La, Exeter EX4 8LZ; Tel (01392) 67236; *Community Education Tutor* N. Stuart
Exeter Community Centre, 17 St David's Hill, Exeter EX4 3RG; Tel (01392) 55188; *Community Education Tutor* T. Price
Exeter, The Fountain Community Education Centre, St James Rd, Exeter EX4 6PU; Tel (01392) 57526; N. Stuart
Exeter, The Loft Club, Tin La, St Thomas, Exeter EX2 9BH; Tel (01392) 432694; A. Dyer
Exeter Phoenix Club, Wonford District Centre, Rifford Rd, Exeter EX2 6NF; Tel (01392) 59130; *Community Education Tutor* M. Green
Honiton Youth Centre, School La, Honiton EX14 8QW; Tel (01404) 42102; Mrs L. Martin
QE Community Centre, Old Hayward School, East St, Crediton EX17 3AX; Tel (01363) 772410; R. Stock
Sidmouth Youth Centre, Manstone La, Sidmouth EX10 9TS; Tel (01395) 514819; L. Lavender
Tiverton Youth Centre, Bolham Rd, Tiverton EX16 6SG; Tel (01884) 252642; *Community Education Tutor* B. Freeman

North Devon

Civic Centre, Barnstaple EX31 1EG; Tel (01271) 388540; Fax (01271) 388469
Area Education Officer Sue Pygott
Area Adviser for Secondary Education Andrew Bennett
Adviser for Special Education Denise Morris
Area Adviser for Primary Education Martin Winter
Area Adviser for Primary Education Jim Cobbett
Area Community Education Officer Lynsay Ewbank-Scott

Youth and Community Centres

Barnstaple Abbey Youth Centre, Chaddiford La, Barnstaple EX32 1RF; Tel (01271) 46710; *Community Education Tutor* R.M. Pettifer; *Community Education Tutor* M. Manuel
The Bideford Centre, The Pill, Bideford EX39 2PF; Tel (012372) 475242; J. Fernandez
Holsworthy Youth Centre, Sanders La, Holsworthy EX22 6HE; Tel (01409) 253283; *Community Education Tutor* L. Gurney
The Lantern Centre, High St, Ilfracombe, Devon EX34 9QB; Tel (01271) 865824; D. Dafferty; J. Bell

South Devon

Oldway, Paignton TQ3 2TE; Tel (01803) 217857; Fax (01803) 217859
Area Education Officer Peter Tregenna
Senior Adviser for Special Educational Needs (County) Maria Landy
Area Adviser for Secondary Education Mike Allen, BPhilEd, MPhil
Adviser for Special Educational Needs Victoria Jones

Area Adviser for Primary Education Margaret Turley, BA, BEd
Area Adviser for Primary Education Janet Watts, BA, DipEd
Area Community Education Officer Dick Dyke The Polsham Centre, Higher Polsham Rd, Paignton TQ3 2SZ; Tel (01803) 663282; Fax (01803) 665735

Youth and Community Centres

Brixham Youth Centre, Brixham Community College, Higher Ranscombe Rd, Brixham TQ5 9HF; Tel (01803) 882723; *Community Education Tutor* N. Ohlson
Dartmouth Youth Centre, Ivy La, Dartmouth, Devon TQ6 9QQ; Tel (01803) 835088; G.C. Anderson
Teignmouth Winterbourne Centre, West Lawn, Teignmouth, Devon; Tel (0162 67) 74707; *Community Education Tutor* K. Breeze
Dyrons Youth Centre, Wain La, Newton Abbot TQ12 2SH; Tel (01626) 69283; *Community Education Tutor* K. Wynn
Totnes Youth Centre The Mansion, Fore St, Totnes, Devon; Tel (01803) 862020; *Community Education Tutor* A.F. Nute

West Devon

Civic Centre, Plymouth PL1 2EW; Tel (01752) 385501; Fax (01752) 385500
Area Education Officer Paul Davies
Area Adviser for Primary Education Jean Humphrys
Area Adviser for Primary Education Mary McNaughton
Area Adviser for Secondary Education Philip Braide
Area Adviser for Secondary Education Patrick Playfair
Adviser for Special Education Colin Evans-Moore
Area Adviser for Primary Education Mike Benson
Area Community Education Officer Mike Matthews Martins Gate, Bretonside, Plymouth PL4 0AT; Tel (01752) 253272

Youth and Community Centres

Efford Youth Centre Blandford Rd, Efford, Plymouth PL3 6HU; Tel (01752) 776853; *Community Education Tutor* S. Tate
Honicknowle Youth Centre Honicknowle Gn, Honicknowle, Plymouth PL5 3PX; Tel (01752) 705297; *Community Education Tutor* C. Smith
Plymouth Devonport Project, 20 Marlborough St, Devonport, Plymouth, Devon; Tel (01752) 560374; Vacancy
Plymouth Youth Enquiry Service, YMCA Triangle, Coburg St, Plymouth; Tel (01752) 250144; Fax (01732) 60411; R. Kramer
Plymouth Frederick St Centre, Frederick St, Stonehouse, Plymouth, Devon; Tel (01752) 228906; A. Kemp
Plymouth Morley Youth Centre, Stentaway Dr, Plymstock, Plymouth PL9 8TE; Tel (01752) 404370; Ms C. McMahon
Plymouth Rees Youth Centre, Mudge Way, Plympton, Plymouth PL7 3PS; Tel (01752) 337267; P. Burling
Plymouth Southway Youth Centre, Hendwell Cl, Southway, Plymouth PL6 6TB; Tel (01752) 775969; V. Parker
Plymouth Trelawny Youth and Community Centre, Ham Drive, Plymouth, Devon PL2 2NL; Tel (01752) 362263; K. Morrish
Plymouth Tothill Community Centre, Knighton Rd, St Judes, Plymouth PL4 9DA; Tel (01752) 665919; B. Dent
Plymouth Whitleigh Youth Centre, Lancaster Gdns, Whitleigh, Plymouth, Devon; Tel (01752) 780589; V. Parker
Plymouth Woodland Fort Community Centre, Crownhill Rd, Plymouth PL5 3SQ; Tel (01752) 703180; Mrs J. Dawkins
Tavistock Alexander Centre, 62 Plymouth Rd, Tavistock; Tel (01822) 613522; J. Collacott

Special Schools

Barnstaple, The Lampard-Vachell, St John's La, Barnstaple EX32 9DD; Tel (01271) 45416; M. Buckland. (MLD) 6–16 (Mixed)
Barnstaple, Pathfield, Abbey Rd, Pilton, Barnstaple EX31 1JU; Tel (01271) 42423; Mrs J.F. Hawkes. (SLD) 3–19 (Mixed)
Dartington, Bidwell Brook, Shinners Bridge, Dartington, Totnes TQ9 6JU; Tel (01803) 864120; Fax (01803) 868025; Mrs S.M. Love. (MLD/SLD) 5–16 (Mixed)
Dawlish, Oaklands Pk, John Nash Dr, Dawlish EX7 9RL; Tel (01626) 862363; Fax (01626) 888566; R.W. Pugh. (S.L.D.) 5–17 (Mixed)
Dawlish, Ratcliffe, John Nash Dr, Oaklands Pk, Dawlish EX7 9RL; Tel (01626) 862939; Fax (01626) 888101; C. Hackett. (E.B.D.) 8–17 (Mixed)
Exeter, Barley La, St Thomas, Exeter EX4 1TA; Tel (01392) 430774; P.A. McLoughlin. (EBD) 11–16 (Mixed)
Exeter, Ellen Tinkham, Hollow La, Exeter EX1 3RW; Tel (01392) 467168; Fax (01392) 464011; Mrs F. Larner. (SLD) 3–19 (Mixed)
Exeter, Southbrook, Bishop Westall Rd, Exeter EX2 6JB; Tel (01392) 58373; N.G. Glover. (MLD) 6–16 (Mixed)
Exmouth, Hill Crest, St John's Rd, Exmouth EX8 4ED; Tel (01395) 263480; Fax (01395) 225357; G. Adler. (EBD) 11–16 (Mixed)
Honiton, Mill Water, Littletown, Honiton EX14 8EG; Tel (01404) 43454; S. Leathlean. (MLD/SLD) 3–19 (Mixed)
Paignton, Mayfield, 170b Torquay Rd, Paignton TQ3 2AL; Tel (01803) 557194; Fax (01803) 552014; G.H.J. Dunkerley. (S.L.D.) 3–19 (Mixed)
Plymouth, Courtlands, Widey La, Crownhill, Plymouth PL6 5JS; Tel (01752) 776848; Fax (01752) 769102; D.L. Hughes, MEd. (MLD) 5–12 (Mixed)
Plymouth, Hillside, Bodmin Rd, Whitleigh, Plymouth PL5 4DZ; Tel (01752) 773875; Fax (01752) 775761; A.E. Fry, DipEd. (MLD) 10–16 (Mixed)
Plymouth Hospitals School, Level 12, Derriford Hospital, Plymouth PL6 8DH; Tel (01752) 792476; Fax (01752) 792476; A.C. Thomas. 2–17 (Mixed)
Plymouth, Longcause, St Maurice, Plympton, Plymouth PL7 3JB; Tel (01752) 336881; Fax (01752) 341151; R.L. Howell. (MLD) 6–16 (Mixed)
Plymouth, Mill Ford, Rochford Cres, Ernesettle, Plymouth PL5 2PY; Tel (01752) 365833; Fax (01752) 360992; J. Hill. (SLD/PMLD) (5–16) (Mixed)
Plymouth, Mount Tamar, Row La, Higher St Budeaux, Plymouth PL5 2EF; Tel (01752) 365128; Fax (01752) 351227; W. Hug, MEd. (EBD) 6–16 (Mixed)
Plymouth, Woodlands, Bodmin Rd, Whitleigh, Plymouth PL5 4DZ; Tel (01752) 778229; Fax (01752) 776080; M.A. Vatcher. (P.H.) 3–16 (Mixed)
Plymstock, Downham, Horn La, Plymstock, Plymouth PL9 9BR; Tel (01752) 403214; M.E. Maleham, MPhil. (SLD) 2–19 (Mixed)
Torquay, Combe Pafford, Steps La, Watcombe, Torquay TQ2 8NL; Tel (01803) 327902; Fax (01803) 327902; M.E. Lock, BEd. (M.L.D.) 5–16 (Mixed)
Torquay, Steps Cross, Steps La, Watcombe, Torquay TQ2 8NN; Tel (01803) 328375; Fax (01803) 311460; E.R.J. Blake. (PhH) 4–16 (Mixed)

Hostel for Children with Emotional and Behavioural Difficulties

The Gables, Willand, Cullompton EX15 2PL; Tel (01884) 33241; *Warden* P. Hurring. (EBD) 7–12 (Boys), 5–18 (Girls)

Secondary Grammar Schools

Churston, Greenway Rd, Churston Ferrers, Brixham TQ5 0LN; Tel (01803) 842289; Fax (01803) 846007; J.R. Parsons, MA. (768)
Plymouth Devonport High for Boys, Paradise Rd, Stoke, Plymouth PL1 5QP; Tel (01752) 564682; Fax (01752) 564647; N.M. Pettit, PhD. (791)

Plymouth Devonport High for Girls, Lyndhurst Rd, Peverell, Plymouth PL2 3DL; Tel (01752) 705024; Fax (01752) 791873; E.B. Dunball, BA, MEd. (666)
Plymouth High School for Girls, St Lawrence Rd, Plymouth PL4 6HT; Tel (01752) 224718; R. Stoggall. (471)
Torquay Girls Grammar, Shiphay La, Torquay TQ2 7DY; Tel (01803) 613215; Fax (01803) 616724; P.M. Cross, BA. (821)

Secondary Comprehensive Schools

Axe Valley School, Chard St, Axminster EX13 5EA; Tel (01297) 32146; Fax (01297) 35851; B. Steane, BA. (362)
Barnstaple, The Park, Park La, Barnstaple EX32 9AX; Tel (01271) 73131; Fax (01271) 73167; A. Hodgetts, BA. (995)
Barnstaple, Pilton, Chaddiford La, Barnstaple EX31 1RF; Tel (01271) 74381; Fax (01271) 24271; T.S. Satinet, BA. (School and Community College) (1154)
Bideford College, Abbotsham Rd, Bideford EX39 3AR; Tel (01237) 477611; Fax (01237) 425371; B. Love. (School and Community College) (1494)
Braunton, Barton La, Braunton EX33 2BP; Tel (01271) 812221; Fax (01271) 817145; J.E. Hunkin, BPhil, FCollP. (School and Community College) (636)
Brixham Community College, Higher Ranscombe Rd, Brixham TQ5 9HF; Tel (01803) 858271/72; Fax (01803) 882726; C.P. Turner, BSc. (School and Community College) (554)
Chulmleigh, Chulmleigh EX18 7AA; Tel (01769) 580215; Fax (01769) 580292; M.J. Fielding. (School and Community College) (470)
Clyst Vale Community College, Station Rd, Broadclyst, Exeter EX5 3AJ; Tel (01392) 461407; Fax (01392) 460594; T.J. Green, MA. (School and Community College) (965)
Crediton, Queen Elizabeth's Community College, Western Rd, Crediton EX17 3LU; Tel (01363) 773401; Fax (01363) 777859; Vivian Brasington. (Boarding places) (1286); School and Community College
Cullompton Community College, Exeter Rd, Cullompton EX15 1DX; Tel (01884) 33364; Fax (01884) 38307; K.L. Turner, BA. (School and Community College) (538)
Dartmouth Community College, Milton La, Dartmouth TQ6 9HW; Tel (01803) 834921; Fax (01803) 835350; A.E. Buckingham. (392); School and Community College
Dawlish Community College, Elm Grove Rd, Dawlish EX7 0BY; Tel (01626) 862318; Fax (01626) 866238; J.P.C. Watson, BSc. (591); School and Community College
Exeter, The Priory High, Earl Richards Rd South, Exeter EX2 6AP; Tel (01392) 59112; Fax (01392) 52258; I.M. Weir, BSc. (531)
Exeter, St James' High, Summer La, Exeter EX4 8NN; Tel (01392) 467369; Fax (01392) 462506; F. Hart, BA. (377)
Exeter, St Thomas High, Hatherleigh Rd, Exeter EX2 9JU; Tel (01392) 54336; Fax (01392) 75134; W. Ridley, MEd. (1179)
Exmouth Community College, Gipsy La, Exmouth EX8 3AF; Tel (01395) 264761; Fax (01395) 225355; J.H. Garnett, MA. (2139); (School and Community College)
Great Torrington, Calvesford Rd, Torrington EX38 7DJ; Tel (01805) 23531; D. Nainby, BA, BSc(Econ). (727)
Holsworthy, Community College, Victoria Hill, Holsworthy EX22 6JD; Tel (01409) 253430; M.I.J. Woodward, MA. (School and Community College) (447)
Honiton Community College, School La, Honiton EX14 8QW; Tel (01404) 42283; Fax (01404) 44491; N.J. Tyson. (School and Community College) (754)
Ilfracombe College, Worth Rd, Ilfracombe EX34 9JB; Tel (01271) 863427; Fax (01271) 863477; A. Bacon, BA. (School and Community College) (1175)
Ivybridge Community College, Harford Rd, Ivybridge PL21 0JA; Tel (01752) 691000; Fax (01752) 691247; G. Rees, MA. (School and Community College) (1548)
Kingsbridge School and Community College, Kingsley Rd, Kingsbridge TQ7 1EY; Tel (01548) 852641; Fax (01548) 854277; R. Wolfson, MA. (School and Community College) (1105)
Newton Abbot, Coombeshead College, Coombeshead Rd, Newton Abbot TQ12 1PT; Tel (01626) 334401; Fax (01626) 334401; B.W. Fletcher, BCom. (994)
Okehampton College, Mill Rd, Okehampton EX20 1PW; Tel (01837) 52001; Fax (01837) 55526; P.A. Herriman. (1130); (School and Community College)
Ottery St Mary, The King's School, Ottery St Mary EX11 1RA; Tel (01404) 812982; Fax (01404) 812982; J.B. Teare, BSc(Econ). (805)
Paignton Community College, Waterleat Rd, Paignton TQ3 3UQ; Tel (01803) 557297; Fax (01803) 666550; T.B. Yates, MSc, BEd. (School and Community College) (1333)
Plymouth Eggbuckland, Community College, Westcott Cl, Plymouth PL6 5YB; Tel (01752) 779061; Fax (01752) 766650; H.E. Green. (School and Community College) (1496)
Plymouth Estover, Community College, Miller Way, Estover, Plymouth PL6 8UN; Tel (01752) 784316; Fax (01752) 795235; F.A. Loosmore, BSc, MEd. (School and Community College) (1372)
Plymouth John Kitto Community College, Honicknowle La, Plymouth PL5 3NE; Tel (01752) 705131; Fax (01752) 705191; K. Barter, BA. (School and Community College) (1395)
Plymouth Lipson, Community College, Bernice Terr, Plymouth PL4 7PG; Tel (01752) 671318; Fax (01752) 252140; B. Geddes, MEd, LCP. (School and Community College) (1156)
Plymouth, Parkside School, Park Ave, Devonport, Plymouth PL1 4RL; Tel (01752) 556764; Fax (01752) 607235; V.M. Jones. (600)
Plymouth Sir John Hunt Community College, Lancaster Gdns, Whitleigh, Plymouth PL5 4AA; Tel (01752) 706386; Fax (01752) 767195; M.J.P. Larner, MSc, MA. (School and Community College) (530)
Plymouth Southway Community College, Rockfield Ave, Southway, Plymouth PL6 6DY; Tel (01752) 705195; Fax (01752) 767203; Barbara Maddox. School and Community College (924)
Plymouth Stoke Damerel Community College, Somerset Pl, Stoke, Plymouth PL3 4BD; Tel (01752) 556065; Fax (01752) 605714; M. Thomas, BPhil(Ed). (School and Community College) (1262)
Plymouth Tamarside Community College, Trevithick Rd, Higher St Budeaux, Plymouth PL5 2AF; Tel (01752) 365320; Fax (01752) 369992; R. Desborough, BA. School and Community College (1242)
Plympton, Hele's School, Seymour Rd, Plympton, Plymouth PL7 4LT; Tel (01752) 337193; Fax (01752) 331460; M.R. Urglow. (1222)
Plympton, The Ridgeway School, Moorland Rd, Plympton, Plymouth PL7 3BH; Tel (01752) 338373; Fax (01752) 331559; J.G. Lawson, MEd. (980)
Plymstock Coombe Dean, Charnhill Way, Plymstock, Plymouth PL9 8ES; Tel (01752) 406961; Fax (01752) 482140; P. Reid, MA. (944)
Plymstock, Church Rd, Plymstock, Plymouth PL9 9AZ; Tel (01752) 402679; Fax (01752) 484018; A.E. Parsons. (1361)
Sidmouth College, Primley Rd, Sidmouth EX10 9LG; Tel (01395) 514823; Fax (01395) 578073; M.G. Owen, BA. (School and Community College) (821)
South Dartmoor, Community College, Balland La, Ashburton TQ13 7EW; Tel (01364) 652230; Fax (01364) 654069; R.B. Tarleton, MA. (School and Community College) (788)
South Molton, Community College, Old Alswear Rd, South Molton EX36 4LA; Tel (01769) 572129; Fax (01769) 573357; J.E. Coley, BA, MEd. (School and Community College) (563)
Tavistock College, Crowndale Rd, Tavistock PL19 8DD; Tel (01822) 614231; Fax (01822) 612030; R.P.J. Upton. (School and Community College) (1781)
Teignmouth Community College, Exeter Rd, Teignmouth TQ14 9HZ; Tel (01626) 774091; Fax (01626) 777920; D.W. Clarke, MA. (School and Community College) (982)

Tiverton High School, Bolham Rd, Tiverton EX16 6SQ; Tel (01884) 256655; Fax (01884) 243364; R. Lambert, MA. (1044)
Torquay Audley Park, Barton Rd, Torquay TQ2 7NU; Tel (01803) 329351; Fax (01803) 316297; M. Thomson. (1146)
Totnes, King Edward VI College, Ashburton Rd, Totnes TQ9 5JX; Tel (01803) 862591; Fax (01803) 866159; J.W.N. Frame, LLB. (School and Community College) (1493)

Secondary Comprehensive Schools (Voluntary)

Exeter, St Peter's C. of E. High School, Southam, Exeter EX2 5AP; Tel (01392) 74383; Fax (01392) 423448; J.M. Dobson, BSc. (Aided) (990)
Exeter, St Luke's High, Ringswell Ave, Exeter EX1 3EG; Tel (01392) 367773; M. Cowton, BEd. (V.C.) (586)
Plymouth Notre Dame R.C., Looseleigh La, Crownhill, Plymouth PL6 5HN; Tel (01752) 775101; Fax (01752) 768120; Sister M. Lomax. (V.A.) (Girls) (720)
Torquay, Cuthebert Mayne, Trumlands Rd, Torquay TQ1 4RN; Tel (01803) 328725; Fax (01803) 322273; K.H.J. Thomas, MSc, BA. (V.A.) (Comp) (781)

Secondary Bilateral School

Torquay Westlands, Warbro Rd, Plainmoor, Torquay TQ1 3PS; Tel (01803) 327257; Fax (01803) 323210; G. Madoc-Jones, BSc. (1067)

Adult Education Centres

Axe Valley Community Education, St Clare's Adult Education Centre, Fore St, Seaton EX12 1AN; Tel (012972) 21904; D. Tinker
Barnstaple Pilton Community College, Chaddiford La, Barnstaple EX31 1RF; Tel (01271) 74381; *Community Tutor* S. Daws
Bideford College, Abbotsham Rd, Bideford EX39 3AR; Tel (01237) 477611; Fax (01271) 425371; J. Fernandez
Braunton Community College, Barton La, Braunton EX33 2BP; Tel (01271) 813267; *Community Tutor* C.R. Mandry
Chulmleigh Community College, Chulmleigh EX18 7AA; Tel (01769) 580215; Fax (01769) 580292; *Community Tutor* D.J. Lang
Clyst Vale Community College, Station Rd, Broadclyst EX5 3AJ; Tel (01392) 66643; Fax (01392) 460594; *Community Tutor* R.T. Edwards
Crediton, Queen Elizabeth's Community College, Queen Elizabeth's School, Crediton EX17 3LU; Tel (01363) 773401; Fax (01363) 777859; *Community Tutor* A.M. Hope
Culm Valley Adult Education Centre, Cullompton Community College, Cullompton EX15 1DX; Tel (01884) 38326; *Community Tutor* P.H. Hague; *Community Tutor* K. With
Dartmouth Community College, Milton La, Dartmouth TQ6 9HW; Tel (01803) 834921; *Community Tutor* G. Anderson
Dawlish Community College, Elm Grove Rd, Dawlish EX7 0BY; Tel (01626) 862318; Fax (01626) 866238; *Community Tutor* C. Wrigley
The Eric Palmer Centre, Barley Grove, Castle St, Torrington, Devon; Tel (01805) 623991; Fax (01805) 623055; P. Troke
Exeter Central Adult Education Centre, Exeter Community Centre, 17 St David's Hill, Exeter EX4 3RG; Tel (01392) 55188; *Organiser* E. Wheeler
Exeter Exwick Adult Education Centre, The Old School, Station Rd, Exeter EX4 2AT; Tel (01392) 436178; *Organiser* A. Collins
Exeter, The Fountain Commmunity Education Centre, St James Rd, Exeter EX4 6PU; Tel (01392) 57526; *Organiser* J. Lock
Exeter Learning Centre, 22 St. Davids Hill, Exeter EX4 4JS; Tel (01392) 383127; Fax (01392) 498086; A. Statham
Exeter St Luke's Adult Education Centre, Exeter St Luke's High School, Ringswell Ave, Exeter EX1 3EG; Tel (01392) 361987; *Organiser* T.B. Ham
Exeter Wonford/Priory Adult Education Centre, 100 Club, Wear Barton Rd, Exeter EX2 7EH; Tel (01392) 873522; C. Enefer
Exmouth Community College, Gipsy La, Exmouth EX8 3AF; Tel (01395) 264761; Fax (01395) 225355; *Adult Tutor* E. Brown
Holsworthy Community College, Victoria Hill, Holsworthy EX22 6JD; Tel (01409) 253430; *Community Tutor* L.R. Gurney
Honiton Community College, School La, Honiton EX14 8QW; Tel (01404) 42283; *Community Tutor* L. Martin
Ilfracombe Community College, Worth Rd, Ilfracombe EX34 9JA; Tel (01271) 863427; *Deputy Principal (Community Education)* J.D. Bell; *Community Tutor* D. Rafferty
Ivybridge Community College, Harford Rd, Ivybridge PL21 0JA; Tel (01752) 691000; *Head of Community Education* L. Dent
Kingsbridge Community College, Kingsley Rd, Kingsbridge TQ7 1EY; Tel (01548) 852648; *Adult Tutor* Ms G. Weaver
Newton Abbot Adult Education Centre, Market St, Newton Abbot, Devon; Tel (01626) 54584; L. Carson
North West Plymouth Community Education Team, Sir John Hunt Community College, Lancaster Gdns, Whitleigh, Plymouth, Devon PL5 4AA; Tel (01752) 780589; *Senior Community Education Tutor* B. Steele
Okehampton Community College, Okehampton School, Mill Rd, Okehampton EX20 1PW; Tel (01837) 53800; *Community Tutor* D. Pritchard
Paignton Community College, Waterleat Rd, Paignton, Devon TQ3 3UQ; Tel (01803) 559372; *Community Tutor* Vacancy
Plym Community Education Team Plymstock School, Church Rd, Plymstock, Plymouth, Devon; Tel (01752) 406847; *Community Education Tutor* L. Aston
Plymouth Community Education
Plymouth Eggbuckland Community College, Westcott Cls, Eggbuckland, Plymouth PL6 5YB; Tel (01752) 767788; *Principal* H.E. Green; *Community Tutor* G.L. Peck
Plymouth Estover Community College, Miller Way, Estover, Plymouth PL6 8UN; Tel (01752) 784316; *Principal* F.A. Loosmore, BSc, MEd; *Community Tutor* Dr P.J. Stevens
Plymouth John Kitto Community College, Honicknowle La, Honicknowle, Plymouth PL5 3NE; Tel (01752) 705131; *Principal* K. Barter; *Community Tutor* A.D. Bloomer
Plymouth Lipson Community College, Bernice Terr, Lipson, Plymouth PL4 7PG; Tel (01752) 671318; *Principal* B. Geddes, MEd, LCP; *Community Tutor* D.A. Weekes
Plymouth Stoke Damerel Community College, Somerset Pl, Stoke Damerel, Plymouth PL3 4BD; Tel (01752) 556065; *Principal* M. Thomas, BPhil(Ed); *Community Tutor* R. Phillips; *Community Tutor* B. Fennessy
Plymouth Swarthmore Adult Education Centre, Mutley Plain, Plymouth PL4 6LF; Tel (01752) 665268; *Community Tutor* R. Allman
Sidmouth College, Sidmouth College, Primley Rd, Sidmouth EX10 9LG; Tel (013955) 514823; *Community Tutor* A. Connah
South Dartmoor Community College, Balland La, Asburton TQ13 7EW; Tel (01364) 652230; *Community Tutor* P. Novak
South Molton Community College, Old Alswear Rd, South Molton EX36 4LA; Tel (01769) 572129; Fax (01769) 573351; *Community Tutor* D. Cannon
Tavistock Community College, Crowndale Rd, Tavistock PL19 8DD; Tel (01822) 614231; Fax (01822) 612030; *Community Tutor* A. Ball
Teignmouth Community College, Exeter Rd, Teignmouth TQ14 9HZ; Tel (01626) 774091; Fax (01626) 777920; *Community Tutor* G. Cox
Tiverton, Tiverton Youth and Community Centre, Bolham Rd, Tiverton EX16 6SG; Tel (01884) 252642; Fax (01884) 259262; B. Freeman
Torquay Adult Education Centre, South Devon College of Arts and Technology, Newton Rd, Torquay, Devon TQ2 5BY; Tel (01803) 386393; J. Elston

Totnes King Edward VI College, Ashburton Rd, Totnes TQ9 5JX; Tel (01803) 862020; *Community Tutor* L. Rudling

Devon Curriculum Development Project

Devon Curriculum Development Project, TVEI Centre, St Hilda's, York Rd, Exeter EX4 6PG; Tel (01392) 219615; Fax (01392) 426731; G. Thomas

Drama Centre

Crediton Drama Centre, Old Hayward School, East St, Crediton EX17 3AX; Tel (0136 32) 3260; P. Hamilton

Residential Centres

Beaford Centre, Beaford, Winkleigh EX19 8LU; Tel (0180 53) 202; P. Creek
Dartmoor Training Centre, Two Bridges, Princetown, Yelverton PL20 6SA; Tel (0182289) 207/565; T. Dawson
Grenville Hse Nautical Venture Centre, Berry Head Rd, Brixham TQ5 9AF; Tel (01803) 852797; M. Bennett
Pixies Holt, Dartmeet, Princetown, Yelverton, Devon PL20 6SG; Tel (0136 43) 248; Fax (01392) 383965; A. Tribe
Start Bay Centre, Slapton, Kingsbridge TQ7 2RA; Tel (01548) 580321/(0392) 382158; A. Wiggett
Wembworthy Centre, Wembworthy, Chulmleigh EX18 7QR; Tel (01769) 580667; F. Sendall

Residential Conference and Training Centre

Devon Centre, Dartmoor, Moorlands, Haytor, South Devon TQ13 9XT; Tel (01364) 661407; Fax (01364) 661573; *Conference Manager* S. Eglington

Professional and Teachers' Centres

Exeter Teachers' Centre St James' High School, Summer La, Exeter EX4 8NN; Tel (01392) 464986; Fax (01392) 460655; B. Marshall, MEd
North Devon Professional Centre, Vicarage St, Barnstaple EX32 7HB; Tel (01271) 72048; Fax (01271) 76650; S. Steer
South Devon Professional Centre, Foxhole at Dartington, Dartington, Totnes TQ9 6EB; Tel (01803) 866644; Fax (01803) 863775; Linda Scofield
Tiverton Teachers' Centre, Barrington St, Tiverton EX16 6QP; Tel (01884) 256648; Fax (01884) 242407; M.J. Gent, BSc
West Devon Professional Centre, College of St Mark and St John, Derriford Rd, Plymouth PL5 8BH; Tel (01752) 774404; Fax (01752) 774818; H. Davies

Grant Maintained Schools

Colyton Grammar School, Gully Shoot, Colyford, Devon EX13 6HN; Tel (01297) 552327; Fax (01297) 553853; *Headteacher* B.J. Sindall; *Chairman of Governors* D. Meikle. Mixed (11–18 (590)
Newton Abbot, Knowles Hill, Exeter Rd, Newton Abbot TQ12 2NF; Tel (01626) 67335; Dr C. Pope. (740)
Plymouth St Boniface's College, Tavistock Rd, Crownhill, Plymouth, Devon; Tel (01752) 779051; Rev Brother J. Kavanagh. (GM) (Boys 11–16; Mixed 16–18) (740)
Teign School, Chudleigh Rd, Kingsteignton, Newton Abbot, Devon TQ12 3JQ; Tel (01626) 66969; D.S. Cottam, BA. (817)
Torquay Boys Grammar School, Shiphay Manor Dr, Torquay TQ2 7EL; Tel (01803) 615501; R.E. Pike, BA, BEd. (940)
Uffculme School, Chapel Hill, Uffculme, Cullompton EX15 3AG; Tel (01884) 840458; Fax (01884) 841570; B Gordon, BA. (731)

Doncaster Metropolitan Borough Council

Population 293,453
2 Priory Pl, Doncaster DN1 1BN; Tel (01302) 734444; Fax (01302) 734040

Directorate of Education

P.O Box 266, The Council House, Doncaster DN1 3AD; Tel (01302) 737222; Fax (01302) 737223
Chief Executive Officer J.D. Hale, IPFA 2 Priory Pl, Doncaster
Borough Solicitor J. Rolston, BA(Hons)
Director of Financial Services J.L. Smith, IMTA, CIPFA Council Hse, Doncaster
Director of Planning And Design Services D. M. Ellis, BA, DipTP, FRTPI
Director of Environmental Services R.A. Sprenger, BSc, DMS, FIEH
Borough Engineer R.S. Eyre, TD, BSc, CEng, FICE, MIHT, DMS
Chief Contracting Officer Vacancy
Director of Social Services I. Cartwright, MA, DMA, CQSW, RMN
Director of Recreational and Cultural Services E.J. Chapman, BA, ALA
Director of Housing Services D. Crofts, AIHM
Director of Education Services A.M. Taylor, MA, MEd
Deputy Director of Education Services M.P. Brunt, BA, MEd, MBIM
Assistant Director: Operations R.J. Chapman, BSc
Assistant Director: Resource/Admin A.R. Earley, BA, BSc
Education Officer: South West Area H.N. Cleeve, BSc, MEd
Education Officer: North West Area D.J. Ingall, BA
Education Officer: East Area M.R. Taylor, BA
Education Officer: Special Needs A. Tipton
Education Officer: Admin. Co-ordination J.G. Coupe
Education Officer: Premises/Development A Martin, BSc
Education Assistant: Staff Development S. Howarth
Education Assistant: Governor Training R.P. McCormick, ACIS, ACMA
Senior Education Officer (Reorganisation) R.M. Spensley, BA
Principal Careers Officer M.E. Brown, BA, DipCG
Principal Inspector A.K. Taylor, MA, MPhil
Senior Inspector (Advice and Guidance) A.J. McGregor, MA
Senior Inspector (Professional Development) N.P. Stewart, BA
Senior Inspector (Inspection and Languages) G.K. Vaughan, BA
Inspector (Primary) K. Baines
Inspector (Primary/Geography) J. Deans, BA
Inspector (Primary/Early Years/Equal Opportunities) M. Morgan, BEd, MA
Inspector (Special Education Needs) G. Pirt, BA, MEd
Inspector (Mathematics) G. Haney, BA
Inspector (Science) K. W. Valentine, BSc
Inspector (Technology) J.G. Hughes, BA
Inspector (Physical Education) L.R. Taylor
Inspector (English and Drama) J. Peacock, BA
Inspector (Art and Design) P.D. Freund, BA
Inspector (Computer Education) H.B. Pryce
Inspector (Humanities and Religious Education) P. Gardner
Catering Client Manager L. Poulston
Chief Education Welfare Officer G. Hemsworth, DipSW

Principal Educational Psychologist H.A. Jones, BSc, DipEdPsych, CPsychol, AFBPsS
Educational Psychologist P.W. Atkinson, BA, MLitt, CPsychol, AFBPsS
Educational Psychologist A. Harwood, BSc, MSc, CPsychol, AFBPsS
Educational Psychologist A.E. Harris, CertEd, BA, MSc, DipAppEdPsych
Educational Psychologist S.A. Lister, BA, MSc
Educational Psychologist K. Scorer, BSc, MSc
Educational Psychologist M. Russell, MA, MAp, Sc
Chartered Educational Psychologist B. Willis, BA, MEd, CPsychol, AFBPsS
Educational Psychologist J.B. Smith, BA, MSc
Educational Psychologist C. Grindle, CertEd, BA(Hons), MSc
Assistant Director, Community Development A. Sockett; Tel (01302) 737317; Fax (01302) 737309
Senior Youth Adviser D. Hammerson; Tel (01302) 737370
Youth and Community Organiser K. Rodgers
Youth and Community Organiser R. Hobson
Youth and Community Organiser P. Hemmingway
Youth and Community Organiser D. Churchill
Youth and Community Organiser D. Bird

Number of Schools
60 nursery units (3,469); 110 primary (25,230); 17 middle (5,011); 17 secondary (18,161); 1 teachers' centre

Number of Special Schools
1 day (del. and P.H.) (88); 1 residential and day (E.S.N.(M.) (29 residential, 94 day, mixed); 2 day (E.S.N.(M.), (152 and 115); 3 day (E.S.N.(S.) (74, 81 and 69)

Day of Commitee Meeting
Tuesday

Other Authorities with whom Joint Purchasing Arrangements are made
Yorkshire Purchasing Organisation

Education Committee

Con 3, Lab 23
Chair P.J. Mullany, (Lab) 4 Derwent Dr, Kirk Sandall, Doncaster DN3 1LE
Vice-Chair C.L. Wedd, (Lab) Warmsworth Hse, Quaker La, Warmsworth, Doncaster DN4 9LD

Members of the Committee
Con: J. Dainty, D. Hoyle, Y.D. Woodcock
Lab: P.J. Birks, M.J. Collins, L. Dyson, J.M. Elwick, M.J. Farrington, G. Gallimore, A. Grimson, C.W. Harrison, J. Hawley, M.J. Hepworth, E.E. Jones, W.T. Kelly, A. Lanaghan, J. Meredith, I.D. Oldroyd, A.A. Pratt, J. Riley, T. Roebuck, A. Sellars, P. Shelvin, P.J. Welsh

Governor Training Unit

Doncaster Metropolitan Council, PO Box 266, The Council Hse, College Rd, Doncaster DN1 3AD; Tel (01302) 737190; Fax (01302) 737223
Education Officer (Premises/Development) A. Martin, BA(Hons)
Education Assistant (Governor Training) R.P. McCormick, ACIS, ACMA

Services Offered
The Governor Training Co-ordinator arranges for induction courses to be provided throughout the year to new Governors. Additionally a directory of courses available is circulated to schools and Governing Bodies. Courses can be arranged to meet the identified needs of individual Boards; Boards are also supported by providing briefing sessions for clerks, a Governors' helpline, Resource Centres in Doncaster Libraries and the publication of a newsletter

Careers Offices

See chapter 17

Special Schools

Anchorage Lower School, Cusworth La, York Rd, Doncaster, South Yorkshire DN5 8JL; Tel (01302) 788484; Fax (01302) 390135; J. Taylor, MA. (ESN(M) (Mixed) (Day) (152)
Anchorage Upper School Barnsley Rd, Scawsby, Doncaster DN5 7UB; Tel (01302) 788484
Athelstane School, Old Rd, Conisbrough, Doncaster, South Yorkshire DN12 3LR; Tel (01709) 864978; Fax (01709) 770172; A. Wilkinson. (Mixed) (ESN(M.) (Day) (115)
Cedar School, Cedar Rd, Balby, Doncaster, South Yorkshire DN4 9HT; Tel (01302) 853361; Fax (01302) 853922; T.M. Kellett, BA. (Mixed) (ESN(S) (Day) (74)
Chase School, Ash Hill, Hatfield, Doncaster DN7 6JH; Tel (01302) 844883; Fax (01302) 841528; W.J. Evans. (Mixed) (ESN(S) (Day) (81)
Fernbank School, Village St, Adwick-le-Street, Doncaster, South Yorkshire DN6 7AA; Tel (01302) 723571; Fax (01302) 724196; A.R. Bickerton. (Mixed) (ESN(S)(Day) (69)
Rossington Hall School, Bawtry Rd, Rossington, Doncaster, South Yorkshire DN11 0HS; Tel (01302) 868365; Fax (01302) 865620; M.A. Lovatt. (Mixed) (ESN(M) (94 Day Pupils) (29 Boarding)
Sandall Wood School, Leger Way, Doncaster, South Yorkshire DN2 6HQ; Tel (01302) 322044; Fax (01302) 739927; B.A.J. Wilson. (Del. & P.H.) (Day) (Mixed) (88)

Middle Schools 8–12

Dunscroft Abbey C.E. Middle, Station Rd, Dunscroft, Doncaster DN7 4EG; Tel (01302) 840839; J.P. Wallhead. (Mixed) (63)
Hatfield Ash Hill Middle, Ash Hill Rd, Hatfield, Doncaster DN7 6JJ; Tel (01302) 840109; W. Carr, BA. (Mixed) (177)
Hatfield Manor Middle, Cuckoo La, Hatfield, Doncaster DN7 6QE; Tel (01302) 842164; G. McGarvie. (Mixed) (217)
Stainforth Middle, Church Rd, Stainforth, Doncaster DN7 5AB; Tel (01302) 841246; D. Elsey, MEd. (Mixed) (327)

Middle Schools 9–13

Balby Middle, Oswin Ave, Doncaster DN4 0NY; Tel (01302) 853137; A.K. Woods. (Mixed) (401)
Carr House Middle, Danum Rd, Doncaster DN4 5HF; Tel (01302) 360192; B. Potts. (Mixed) (251)
Ellers Middle, St Michael's Rd, Doncaster DN4 5LU; Tel (01302) 535559; K.M. Brown. (Mixed) (458)
Hexthorpe Middle, Urban Rd, Doncaster DN4 0HH; Tel (01302) 852245; P. Bray. (Mixed) (208)
Intake Middle, Coniston Rd, Doncaster DN2 6JL; Tel (01302) 361450; N.R. Britton. (Mixed) (376)
South Cantley Middle, Plumpton Park Rd, Doncaster DN4 6SL; Tel (01302) 538108; H. Webster. (Mixed) (226)
Thorne Green Lane Middle, Wike Gate Rd, Thorne, Doncaster DN8 5PQ; Tel (01405) 812200; M. Duffin. (Mixed) (264)
Thorne Marshland Middle, Marshland Rd, Moorends, Doncaster DN8 4SB; Tel (01405) 812201; Fax (01405) 740706; J.G. Allen, BA. (Mixed) (288)
Thorne Northfield Middle, North Eastern Rd, Thorne, Doncaster DN8 4BQ; Tel (01405) 812715; Fax (01405) 740661; P.A. Marchant. (Mixed) (293)
Wheatley Hills Middle, Leger Way, Doncaster DN2 5RW; Tel (01302) 365671; R. Leedale, BA. (Mixed) (404)
Wheatley Middle, Beckett Rd, Doncaster DN2 4AL; Tel (01302) 344746; Fax (01302) 738887; M.G. Pagett. (Mixed) (382)
Wilby Carr Middle, Aldesworth Rd, Cantley, Doncaster DN4 6LD; Tel (01302) 536182; R.G. Iball. (Mixed) (179)
Woodfield Middle, Cedar Rd, Balby, Doncaster DN4 9HU; Tel (01302) 859116; P. Watson (Acting). (Mixed) (495)

Secondary Schools

Adwick School, Windmill Balk La, Woodlands, Doncaster, South Yorkshire DN6 7SF; Tel (01302) 722237; Fax (01302) 337345; J.L. Sheppard, BA(Econ). (Mixed) (1623)
Armthorpe Comprehensive School, Mere La, Armthorpe, Doncaster, South Yorkshire DN3 2DA; Tel (01302) 831582; Fax (01302) 300757; D.A. Pearmain, BA. (Mixed) (903)
Balby Carr School, Weston Rd, Balby, Doncaster, South Yorkshire DN4 8ND; Tel (01302) 852247; Fax (01302) 310774; M. Townsend, BSc. (Mixed) (779)
Campsmount School, Ryecroft Rd, Norton, Doncaster, South Yorkshire DN6 9AS; Tel (01302) 700474; T. Butterworth, BSc, AKC, MEd. (Mixed) (760)
Danum School, Armthorpe Rd, Doncaster, South Yorkshire DN2 5QD; Tel (01302) 831385; Fax (01302) 300109; M.J. Vickers, BA. (Mixed) (1033)
Don Valley High School, Jossey La, Scawthorpe, Doncaster, South Yorkshire DN5 9DD; Tel (01302) 781528; Fax (01302) 786252; R.F. Johnson, BSc, FRSA. (Mixed) (1219)
Edlington School, Tait Ave, Edlington, Doncaster, South Yorkshire DN12 1HH; Tel (01709) 864100; A. White, BSc, MEd. (Mixed) (1106)
Hall Cross Comprehensive School, Thorne Rd, Doncaster, South Yorkshire DN1 2HY; Tel (01302) 320626; Fax (01302) 322190; B.G. Ford, BA(Hons). (Mixed) (1457)
Hatfield High School, Ash Hill, Hatfield, Doncaster, South Yorkshire DN7 6JH; Tel (01302) 840961; Fax (01302) 845906; C.A. Smith, BSc. (Mixed) (1077)
The Hayfield School, Hurst La, Auckley, Doncaster, South Yorkshire DN9 3HG; Tel (01302) 770589; G.A. Storey, OBE, BA. (Mixed) (1151)
Hungerhil School, Hungerhill La, Edenthorpe, Doncaster, South Yorkshire DN3 2JY; Tel (01302) 885811; Fax (01302) 880384; A. Leamy, MA. (Mixed) (1023)
McAuley R.C. School, Cantley La, Doncaster, South Yorkshire DN3 3QF; Tel (01302) 537396; Fax (01302) 537891; F.M. O'Halloran, BA. (Mixed) (1591)
Mexborough School, Maple Rd, Mexborough, South Yorkshire S64 9SB; Tel (01709) 585858; Fax (01709) 578080; R.T. Woollard, MA, BSc, M/Mgt. (Mixed) (1186)
Northcliffe School, Gardens La, Conisbrough, Doncaster, South Yorkshire DN12 3JS; Tel (01709) 864001; Fax (01709) 770185; B.P. Thomson, MA. (Mixed) (722)
Scawsby Ridgewood Comprehensive School, Barnsley Rd, Scawsby, Doncaster, South Yorkshire DN5 7UB; Tel (01302) 783939; Fax (01302) 390448; J.F. Sharpe, BSc. (Mixed) (745)
Rossington High School, Bond St, Rossington, Doncaster, South Yorkshire DN11 0BZ; Tel (01302) 868414; Fax (01302) 866252; R.D.G. Allan, BSc, MSc. (Mixed) (640)
Thorne Grammar School, St Nicholas Rd, Thorne, South Yorkshire DN8 5BQ; Tel (01405) 812179; Fax (01405) 740315; A. Brookes, PhD, BSc. (Mixed) (761)

Field Study Centre

Austerfield Field Study Centre Austerfield, Bawtry, Doncaster DN10 6RG; Tel (01302) 710415; Fax (01302) 710415; A. Jagger

Music Centre

William Appleby Music Centre Danum Rd, Doncaster DN4 5HF; Tel (01302) 323556; Fax (01302) 323605; P.R. Bear

Study Base

Cusworth Hall Museum Study Base Cusworth, Doncaster DN5 7TU; Tel (01302) 786925; Fax (01302) 786925; R.M. Ward, BEd

Teachers' Centre

Beechfield Teachers' Support Centre, Chequer Rd, Doncaster DN1 2AF; Tel (01302) 734267; P. Morley

Teaching Support

Teaching Support Service Aldesworth Rd, Doncaster DN4 6LD; Tel (01302) 533444; Fax (01302) 530355; D.W. Houldsworth

Dorset County Council

Population 664,200
County Hall, Dorchester, Dorset DT1 1XJ; Tel (01305) 251000; Fax (01305) 224839
County Librarian C. Earl, BSc, ALA, FRSA
County Treasurer A.P. Peel, BA, IPFA
Director of Social Services R.G. SeQueira, CQSW

Education Offices

County Hall, Dorchester, Dorset DT1 1XJ; Tel (01305) 251000; Fax (01305) 224499
County Education Officer R.H. Ely, MA, FRSA
Number of Schools
188 Primary (42,074) 27 middle (11,330), 28 secondary (24,088), 5 adult education areas, 32 evening adult education centres, 1 centre for community arts, 6 outdoor centres for education, 2 of which are residential, 1 community centre
Special Schools
12 day (1,040), 12 day units (139), 3 residential (37), 2 hostels (19)

Adult Education Service

Principal T. Challis, BSc

Careers Guidance Service

Chief Executive I.C. Gittins

Central Services

Principal Education Officer A.S. Lawson, BA
Education Officer S.E. Cleverly, MA

County Psychological Service

Principal County Education Psychologist R.E. Born, MA, DipEdPsych, CPsychol, AFBPsS
Senior Educational Psychologist N.V. Auston, BA, MEdPsych, AFBPsS, CPsychol
Senior Educational Psychologist C.T. Flann, BSc, DipEdPsych, CPsychol, AFBPsS
Senior Educational Psychologist S. Richards, BSc, MEd(EdPsych), AFBPsS, CPsychol
Senior Educational Psychologist A.H. Salt, BA, MEdPsych, CPsychol
Educational Psychologist J. Adlam-Hill, BSc, CPsychol
Educational Psychologist M. Allebon, DipAD, BA, MEd, CPsychol
Educational Psychologist N.E. Beard, BEd, MA, MEd
Educational Psychologist G. Chapman, BA, MEd(EdPsych), CPsychol
Educational Psychologist K. Cotton, RMN, BA, PGCE, MSc
Educational Psychologist G.J. Davies, BA, MEd
Educational Psychologist M.E. Francis, MA, MSc(EdPsych)
Educational Psychologist S.J. Goddard, BSc, MEd, CPsychol
Educational Psychologist D. Hills, BSc, MSc, CPsychol
Educational Psychologist G. Law, BSc, MSc
Educational Psychologist J. Mansfield, BA, PGCE, CertEd(Hearing Impaired), MEd(EdPsychol)
Educational Psychologist C. Russell, BA, MEd

Educational Psychologist C.F. Sawyer, DCP, MEd, MEd(EdPsych), CPsychol, AFBPsS
Educational Psychologist B. Ward, BSc, MA, MSc, PLD, CPsychol

Dorset Education Business Partnership

Director M.E. Turner, MPhil, CertEd

Management Advice and Support Services

Head of Operations A.S. Taylor, BSc, MIPD
Area Officer Co-ordinator G. Case, BA, CertEd
Area Officer H.P. Richards, MEd
Area Officer V.J. Sandel, CertEd
Area Officer A. Taylor, BEd(Hons)
Area Officer P.M. Toohey, MEd

Personal Services

Principal Education Officer M.A. Bray, MA
SEO F. Canning, BSc(Hons), MSc, PhD
AEO R.J. Boulton
Principal Education Welfare Officer D.E. Bowen, MPhil, CSW, CertEd
Head of County Service for Sensory Impaired Children J. Dalzell
Head of Behaviour Support Services S. Cottrell
Co-Director, Literacy and Numeracy Support Service R. Fullford
Co-Director, Literacy and Numeracy Support Service M. Tepper
Co-Director, Literacy and Numeracy Support Service S. Willcocks

Planning and Development

Principal Education Officer L.H. Saunders, BA
SEO P.G. Speakman, BA
EO P. Robson, BSc, ARCS, MPhil
AEO K. Armstead, BEd

Professional Development Services

Unit Manager (Principal Inspector) M.J. Young, MA
Senior Inspector (INSET) B. Allsop, MA(Ed), BEd(Hons)
Senior Inspector (Management Development) S.A. Billington, BEd(Hons), CertEd
Senior Inspector (School Inspection Services Manager) P.R. Clapham, CertEd
Senior Inspector (Management Development) D.W. Clegg, MEd, BA(Hons)
Senior Inspector (Quality Monitoring) T. Ferris, BA(Hons)
Senior Inspector (IT) M. Graham, BEd
Senior Inspector (Marketing) J. Hart, BA(Hons), MA
Senior Inspector (Management Development) H.R. Turner, BEd, CertEd
Senior Inspector (Management Development) D. Wheatley, BEd(Hons), CertEd, SDES
General Inspector (Design and Technology) J. Adams, BEd(Hons)
General Inspector (Humanities and Museum Education) P. Barton, MA, BA
General Inspector (Creative and Expressive Arts) S. Bugg, BEd, CertEd
General Inspector (Creative and Expressive Arts) M. Dickinson, BA(Hons)
General Inspector (Design and Technology) P.M. Monk, CertEd
General Inspector (Science and Environmental Education) A.B. Stillman, PhD, MEd, BEd
Appraisal Co-ordinator A. Walden, BSc

Youth Services

Principal Youth Services Officer N.W. Palmer

Governor Training Unit

Governor Services, Education Dept, County Hall, Dorchester, Dorset DT1 1XJ; Tel (01305) 224156; Fax (01305) 224499
Co-ordinator of Governor Services David Rees, BEd

Services Offered
Central training courses; whole governing body training; helpline; quarterly magazine; distance learning materials

Education Committee

LD 14, Con 7, Lab 2, DIG 1
Chair A.R.N. Bussey, LD 52 Lake Rd, Verwood, Wimborne BH21 6BX
Vice-Chair C.A. Allington, LD 87 Leybourne Ave, Northbourne, Bournemouth BH10 6ET
Members of the Committee
LD: C.A. Allington, A.R.N. Bussey, N.P. Evans, A.J. Humphries, L. Legg, R.A.S. Legg, M.A. Mackenzie, Dr J. Millward, J.E. Moore, J.F. Noyes, G.W. Rose, A.B. Rowberry, B.M. Williams
Con: G.I. Burns, D. Halton, H. Henning, D.W. Packwood, R. Smith, J.A. Terrett, E. Webb
Lab: P.J. Brushett, L.H. Dibdin
DIG: J.J. Payne, R. Whittaker

Specialist Mainstream Bases for Moderate Learning Difficulties

Beaminster, Beaminster School, Newtown, Beaminster DT8 3EP; Tel (01308) 862633; F.J. Pugsley
Beaminster, St Mary's CE Primary School, Clay La DT8 3BY; Tel (01308) 862201; C.F. Longridge

Specialist Mainstream Bases for Hearing Impaired Children

Ferndown Upper School Partially Hearing Unit, Cherry Gr, Ferndown BH22 9EY; Tel (01202) 871243; Dr D.A. Howard, MA, PhD. (9)
Branksome Heath Middle School Unit for Hearing Impaired Children Branksome Heath Middle School, Livingstone Rd, Parkstone, Poole BH12 3DX; Tel (01202) 747966; M.J. Stead, BA, MEd. (12)
Sylvan First School Unit for Hearing Impaired Children Livingstone Rd, Parkstone, Poole BH12 3DT; Tel (01202) 743064; C.P.W. Innes, BA. (14)

Day Special Schools

Bournmouth; Bicknell School, Petersfield Rd, Bournemouth BH7 6QP; Tel (01202) 424361; M. Hurst
Bournemouth; Linwood School, Alma Rd, Bournemouth BH9 1AJ; Tel (01202) 525107; S. Brown (Acting). (MLD, SLD) (150)
Bournemouth, Slades Farm School, Ensbury Ave, Ensbury Park, Bournemouth BH10 4HG; Tel (01202) 518189; E. Ross. (EBD) (Mixed) (11–16) (57)
Bridport, Mountjoy School, Flood La, Bridport DT6 3QG; Tel (01308) 22250; S.G. Searly (Acting). (SLD) (Mixed) (3–18) (42)
Dorchester, Penwithen, Winterborne Monkton, Dorchester DT2 9PS; Tel (01305) 266842; M. Sherratt. (EBD) (Mixed) (7–16) (50)
Poole, Longspee, Learoyd Rd, Canford Heath, Poole BH17 7PJ; Tel (01202) 674220; M. Amos. (EBD) (5–11) (Mixed) (61)
Poole, Montacute, 3 Canford Heath Rd, Poole BH17 7NG; Tel (01202) 693239; R.P. Sammons. (SLD) (3–18) (Mixed) (71)
Poole, Winchelsea, Guernsey Rd, Parkstone, Poole BH12 4LL; Tel (01202) 746240; R. Barnsley. (MLD) (Mixed) (3–16+) (140)
Sturminster Newton, Yewstock, Honeymead La, Sturminster Newton DT10 1EW; Tel (01258) 72796; Mrs J. Davis. (MLD, SLD) (Mixed) (3–16+) (110)
Weymouth, Westfield, Littlemoor Rd, Preston, Weymouth DT3 6AA; Tel (01305) 833518; P. Silvester. (MLD) (Mixed) (3–16) (140)
Weymouth, Wyvern 307 Chickerell Rd, Weymouth DT4 0QU; Tel (01305) 783660; Miss M. Robinson. (SLD) (Mixed) (3–18) (55)
Wimborne, Beaucroft, Wimborne Rd, Colehill, Wimborne BH21 2SS; Tel (01202) 886083; A. Mears. (MLD) (Mixed) (3–16+) (99)

Day Special Unit for Physically Disabled

Dorchester, The Prince of Wales Special Unit, Maiden Castle Rd, Dorchester DT1 2HH; Tel (01305) 267224; P. Farrington

Special Schools and Specialist Mainstream Bases Residential Establishments

Bicknell Hostel, Petersfield Rd, Bournemouth BH7 7QP; Tel (01202) 424361; Fax (01202) 430592; G. Lucas. (EBD) (7–16) (50)
Slades Farm Hostel, Ensbury Ave, Ensbury Park, Bournemouth BH10 4HG; Tel (01202) 536329; R.A.C. Humphries. (Emotionally and behaviourally disturbed) (Mixed) (7–16) (30)
Penwithen Hostel, Winterborne Monkton, Dorchester, Dorset DT2 9PS; Tel (01305) 264315; A. Bowerman. (EBD) (Mixed) (7–16) (30)

Children's Hospital Education Units

Dorchester, Allington Ward, West Dorset Hospital, Damers Rd, Dorchester DT1 2JX; Tel (01305) 251150 Ext 4219/4253; D. Hussey
Poole, Poole Hospital, Schoolroom Ward B1, Longfleet Rd, Poole BH15 2JB; Tel (01202) 665511 Ext 2383; J. Rogers
Poole, Poole Hospital, Ward E1, Longfleet Rd, Poole BH15 2JB; Tel (01202) 665511 Ext 2269; M. O'Docherty

Behaviour Support Service Bases

Crossways Home Tuition Base, Crossways Youth Centre, Old Farm Way, Crossways, Dorchester DT2 8PU; Tel (01305) 850306; Vacancy
Fernlea Pupil Referral Unit, Fernside Rd, Poole BH15 2QY; Tel (01202) 730587; D. Hankin
Gloucester Rd Centre, Gloucester Rd, Dorchester DT1 2NJ; Tel (01305) 251362; S. Downes (Acting)

Speech and Language Specialist Mainstream Bases

Christchurch Infant Unit, Christchurch C Infants School, Addiscombe Rd, Christchurch BH23 2AE; Tel (01202) 479021; *Head* W. Pickering; *Teacher-in-Charge* Mrs A. Lilley
Christchurch Junior Unit, Christchurch County Junior School, Clarendon Rd, Christchurch BH23 2AA; Tel (01202) 490249; *Head* C. Taylor; *Teacher-in-Charge* J. Wainwright
Dorchester Speech and Language Base, Damers C First School, Damers Rd, Dorchester DT1 2LB; Tel (01305) 264924; *Head* S. Birch; *Teacher-in-Charge* J. Cook
Gillingham Speech and Language Base (Infant), Gillingham C Primary School, School La, Gillingham SP8 4QR; Tel (01747) 823245; *Head* C. Nye; *Teacher-in-Charge* G. Harvey
Gillingham Speech and Language Base (Junior), Gillingham County Primary School, School La, Gillingham SP8 4QR; Tel (01747) 823245; *Head* C. Nye; *Teacher-in-Charge* G. Harvey

Specific Learning Difficulty Mainstream Bases

All Saint's CE School Base, All Saint's CE VSA School, Sunnyside Rd, Wyke Regis, Weymouth DT4 9BY; Tel (01305) 783391; *Head* J.E. Munslow; *Teacher-in-Charge* H. Dick
Allenbourn Base, Allenbourn Middle School, East Borough, Wimborne, Dorset BH21 1PL; Tel (01202) 886738; *Acting Head* R. Wrigley; *Teacher-in-Charge* M. Halliwell
The Gryphon Base, The Gryphon School, Bristol Rd, Sherborne DT9 4EQ; Tel (01935) 813122; *Head* C. Shepperd; *Teacher-in-Charge* C. Johnson

Comprehensive Schools (11–16)

The Grange, Redvers Rd, Christchurch BH23 3AU; Tel (01202) 486536/7; Fax (01202) 487621; A. Cooke. (870)
Twynham, Soper's La, Christchurch BH23 1JF; Tel (01202) 486237; B. Driver, BPhil. (1040)
Royal Manor, Weston Rd, Portland DT5 2DB; Tel (01305) 820262; Fax (01305) 860417; Mrs L.M. Headon. (620)
Sturminster Newton High, Sturminster Newton DT10 1DT; Tel (01258) 72642; S. Carrington. (590)
All Saints C.E., Sunnyside Rd, Wyke Regis, Weymouth DT4 9BJ; Tel (01305) 783391; Mrs J.E. Munslow, MA. (V.S.A.) (590)
The, Wey Valley Dorchester Rd, Weymouth DT3 5AN; Tel (01305) 812855; Fax (01305) 815851; T.D. Norman, MA. (1040)

Comprehensive Schools (11–18)

Lytchett Minster, Post Green Rd, Lytchett Minster, Poole BH16 6JD; Tel (01202) 622413; Fax (01202) 621230; R.W. Castleton, BA. (730)
The Colfox, Ridgeway Est, Bridport DT6 3DT; Tel (01308) 422291; Fax (01308) 420036; C.C. Mason, MA(Ed). (980)

Comprehensive Schools (Voluntary 11–18)

The Dorchester (Thomas Hardye) VA School Queen's Ave, Dorchester DT1 2ET; Tel (01305) 266064; Fax (01305) 250510; I.E. Melvin, BA, PhD. (Voluntary)
Beaminster, Newtown, Beaminster DT8 3EP; Tel (01308) 862633; Fax (01308) 863909; F.J. Pugsley, MSc. (V.C.) (670)
Gillingham, Hardings Lane, Gillingham SP8 4QP; Tel (01747) 822222/3; M. Lenarduzzi, BA. (V.C.) (940)

Comprehensive Schools (11–18)

Ferndown Upper, Cherry Grove, Ferndown BH22 9EY; Tel (01202) 871243; Dr D.A. Howard. (1310)
Corfe Hills Upper, Higher Blandford Rd, Broadstone, Poole BH18 9BG; Tel (01202) 697541; Fax (01202) 658974; Mr A.H. Williams, MA. (1250)
The Purbeck, Worgret Rd, Wareham BH20 4PF; Tel (01929) 556301; Fax (01929) 554025; A.J. Smetham, BA,MA. (1370)

Comprehensive Schools (Voluntary 13–18)

Blandford School, Milldown Rd, Blandford DT11 7SQ; Tel (01258) 451121; S.F. Prewett, BA. (V.C.) (790)
Queen Elizabeth's, Blandford Rd, Pamphill, Wimborne BH21 4DT; Tel (01202) 885233; Fax (01202) 840703; S.S. Tong, MA. (V.C.) (1310)
Shaftesbury School, Salisbury Rd, Shaftesbury SP7 8ER; Tel (01747) 54498; Fax (01747) 51208; A. Jeavons. (Mixed) (870); (VC); (Boarding Places)

Secondary Schools

Ashdown, Adastral Rd, Canford Heath, Poole BH17 7RE; Tel (01202) 604222; Mr A. Pellegrini, BEd, ACP. (12-16)
Carter Community, Blandford Cl, Hamworthy, Poole BH15 4BQ; Tel (01202) 676789; D. Pratten. (630)
Glenmoor, Beswick Ave, Bournemouth BH10 4EX; Tel (01202) 527818; Mrs P.M. Orchard, BA. (Girls) (740)
Kingsleigh, Hadow Rd, Bournemouth BH10 5HS; Tel (01202) 528554; Fax (01202) 528554; K. Allen. (880)
Oakmead, Duck La, Bournemouth BH11 9JJ; Tel (01202) 573266; P. Lawrenson, BA. (Mixed)
The Martin Kemp-Welch School, Herbert Ave, Parkstone BH12 4HS; Tel (01202) 732500; K.R. Baldock, BSc. (12–17)
Portchester, Harewood Ave, Bournemouth BH7 6NZ; Tel (01202) 309841; J.M. Haigh. (Boys) (860)
Summerbee, Mallard Rd, Bournemouth BH8 9PW; Tel (01202) 512697; A. Whelan. (700)
Winton, Coronation Ave, Bournemouth BH9 1TP; Tel (01202) 529738; I. Johnson, MA. (Boys) (670)

Secondary Schools (Voluntary)

St Edward's RC-CE, Dale Valley Rd, Oakdale, Poole BH15 3HY; Tel (01202) 740950; A.J. Murphy, BA. (V.A.) (440)
The Gryphon CE VC School, Bristol Rd, Sherborne DT9 4EQ; Tel (01935) 813122/3; C. Shepperd, BA. (V.C.) (880)

Grammar Schools

Adult Education Centres

Bournemouth Area, Punshon Building, Exeter Rd, Bournemouth BH2 5AJ; Tel (01202) 557131; V. Grayson
Christchurch Area, Christchurch AEC, Sopers La, Christchurch BH23 1JF; Tel (01202) 482789; T. Lewis
North and East Dorset Area, North East Dorset AEC, Mountbatten Dr, Ferndown BH22 9EW; Tel (01202) 875359; Fax (01202) 875379; A. Thomson
Poole and Purbeck Area, The Martin Kemp Welch School, Herbert Ave, Parkstone, Poole BH12 4HS; Tel (01202) 721600; Fax (01202) 721600; K. Fullman
South and West Dorset Area, South and West Dorset AEC, 45 Dorchester Rd, Weymouth DT4 7JT; Tel (01305) 776727; G. Brace

Professional Educational Centres

East Dorset, 40 Lowther Rd, Bournemouth BH8 8NR; Tel (01202) 296071; *Administration Manager* J. Higgs
West Dorset, 45 Dorchester Rd, Weymouth DT4 7JT; Tel (01305) 774802; Fax (01305) 770310; *Director* J. Tirrell

Outdoor Education Centres

Carey Camp Outdoor Education Centre, Wareham BH20 7PB; Tel (01929) 552265
Cranborne Ancient Technology Centre, Cranborne Middle School, Cranborne BH21 5RP; Tel (017254) 618; J. Keen
Hengistbury Head Outdoor Education and Field Studies Centre, Hengistbury Head, Bournemouth BH6 4EW; Tel (01202) 425173; Mrs T. Zimmerman
Leeson Hse Field Studies Centre, Langton Matravers, Swanage BH19 3EU; Tel (01929) 422126; M. Kershaw
Hamworthy Outdoor Education Centre, Hamworthy Park, Lulworth Ave, Poole BH15 4DQ; Tel (01202) 678336; M. Abel
Weymouth Outdoor Education Centre, Knightsdale Road, Weymouth DT4 OHS; Tel (01305) 784927; M. Jones

Youth and Community Centres

"The Planet", 4 Church St, Wimborne BH21 1LT; Tel (01202) 840628; S. Neale
Beaminster Area Youth Centre, 6 Prout Bridge, Beaminster DT8 3AY; Tel (01308) 862384; M. Singer
Blandford Area Youth Centre, Milldown Rd, Blandford DT11 7SQ; Tel (01258) 455106; P. Williams
Bourne Valley Youth Centre, Northmere Rd, Parkstone, Poole BH12 2EA; Tel (01202) 740113; A. Doolin
Bovington Area Youth Centre, Elles Rd, Bovington, Wareham BH20 6JB; Tel (01929) 463503; S. Smith
Bridport Youth Centre, Gundry La, Bridport DT6 3RL; Tel (01308) 422500; A. Woodgate
Broadstone Youth Centre, Moor Rd, Broadstone, Poole, Dorset; Tel (01202) 697303; A. Hebron
Burton Area Youth Centre, Sandy Plot, Burton, Christchurch BH23 6NH; Tel (01202) 470457; P. Cox
896 Club, 896 Christchurch Rd, Boscombe, Bournemouth BH7 6DL; Tel (01202) 426905; G. Meadows
Creekmoor Area Youth Centre, Northmead Rd, Creekmoor, Poole BH17 7YX; Tel (01202) 605340; D. Boler
Crossways Youth Centre, Old Farm Way, Crossways, Dorchester, Dorset DT2 8TU; Tel (01305) 853567; D. Evans
Detached Youth Worker, Punshon Church, Exeter Rd, Bournemouth BH2 5AJ; Tel (01202) 551823; C. Howard
Dorchester YC, Colliton St, Dorchester DT1 1HX; Tel (01305) 262114; M. Hogan
East Howe YC, Kinson Rd, East Howe, Bournemouth BH10 5HT; Tel (01202) 519184; K. Grant; J. Cobley-Pearson
Embassy YC, Brassey Rd, Winton BH9 1PT; Tel (01202) 515684; M. O'Connor; Mrs E. Reavenall; Mrs J. Tiller
Ferndown Area YC, Church Rd, Ferndown, Wimborne BH22 9ET; Tel (01202) 874448; S. Ross
Gillingham YC, Cemetery Rd, Gillingham SP8 4AZ; Tel (01747) 822267; S. Rustage
Harewood Youth Centre, Avonbourne School, Harewood Ave, Boscombe East, Bournemouth BH7 6NY; Tel (01202) 398471; P. Webber
Henry Brown Youth Centre, Cunningham Cres, Kinson, Bournemouth BH11 8DY; Tel (01202) 573388; J. Roberts; P. Harper
"The Junction" 266 Holdenhurst Rd, Bournemouth BH8 8AY; Tel (01202) 399321; J. Edmonds; F. Davies
Littlemoor YC, Littlemoor School, Littlemoor Rd, Weymouth DT3 6AF; Tel (01305) 833560; Mrs C. Murray
Muscliff Park Area Youth Centre, Shillingstone Dr, Muscliff Pk, Bournemouth BH9 3LR; Tel (01202) 546213; A. Farmer; Vacancy
Oakdale Boys Club, Learoyd Rd, Poole BH17 7PJ; Tel (01202) 672318; C. Dutfield
Oakmead Youth Centre, Duck La, Northbourne, Bournemouth BH11 9JJ; Tel (01202) 572898; M. Tatton-Bennett
Outreach Youth Worker, 'Waves', Weymouth Youth Resource Centre, 52 St Marys St, Weymouth, Dorset DT4 8BJ; R. Pryce
Outreach Youth Worker,; Outreach Youth Worker T. Wall Meechs Forge, South Rd, Poole BH15 1QB; Tel (01202) 666439; *Detached Youth Worker* S. Chattaway Canford Heath Pavilion, Learoyd Rd, Canford Heath, Poole BH17 7PJ; Tel (01202) 681204
Parkstone Boys' and Girls' Club Sports Centre, Recreation Rd, Poole BH12 3EA; Tel (01202) 744143; B. Stunt
Pokesdown Youth Centre, 108 Stourvale Rd, Pokesdown, Bournemouth BH6 5JB; Tel (01202) 424133; S. Witt
Portland Youth Centre, Royal Manor School, Weston Rd, Portland DT5 2DB; Tel (01305) 823663; S. Rose
Shaftesbury Boys' Club, Coppice St, Shaftesbury SP7 8PF; Tel (01747) 53195; P. Weaving
Sherborne Youth Centre, Tinneys Lane, Sherborne DT9 3DY; Tel (01935) 814202; P. Bryer
Sturminster Newton Area Youth Centre, The High School, Bath Rd, Sturminster Newton DT10 1DT; Tel (01258) 472368; A. Baverstock
Swanage Youth Centre, Chapel La, Swanage BH19 2PW; Tel (01929) 423421; S. Lacey
Turlin Moor Area Youth Centre, Turlin Rd, Turlin Moor, Poole BH16 5AH; Tel (01202) 670085; B. Bennett
Verwood Area Youth Centre, Howe La, Verwood BH21 6JF; Tel (01202) 825351; Ms E. Paterson
Wareham Youth Centre, Worgret Rd, Wareham BH20 4PH; Tel (01929) 552934; N. Tuffley
Weymouth Boys' Club, 110 Chickerell Rd, Weymouth DT4 0BT; Tel (01305) 771861; T. Lane
The Beacon Centre, Mitchel Rd, Canford Heath, Poole BH17 7UE; Tel (01202) 686965 (club); S. Harwood

Grant Maintained Schools

Avonbourne School, Harewood Ave, Bournemouth, Dorset BH7 6NY; Tel (01202) 398451
Bournemouth Girls' School, Castle Gate Close, Castle La West, Bournemouth, Dorset BH8 9UJ; Tel (01202) 526289; Fax (01202) 548923
Bournemouth School, East Way, Bournemouth, Dorset BH8 9PY; Tel (01202) 512609/519888; Fax (0120) 516095; *Headmaster* A.F.P. Petrie; *Chairman of Governors* B.V. Newman. (Boys) (11–18) (950)
Budmouth School, Chickerell Rd, Weymouth DT4 9SY; Tel (01305) 783057; Fax (01305) 766389; *Headteacher* D.C. Higham; *Chair of Governors* R. Mauger. (Mixed) (11–16 (926)
Highcliffe School, Parkside, Highcliffe, Christchurch, Dorset BH23 4QD; Tel (01425) 273381; Fax (01452) 271405
Parkstone Grammar School, Sopers La, Poole, Dorset BH17 7EP; Tel (01202) 97456
Poole Grammar, Gravel Hill, Poole BH17 7JU; Tel (01202) 692132; A.A.J. Clarke, BA. (Boys) (750)

Poole High School, Wimborne Rd, Poole BH15 2BW; Tel (01202) 670631; Fax (01202) 660674; J.A. Short, BA, MSc. (12–17) (1410)
St Peter's, St Catherine's Rd, Southbourne, Bournemouth BH6 4AH; Tel (01202) 421141; A. McCaffrey. (V.A.) (1570)
The Woodroffe School, Uplyme Rd, Lyme Regis DT7 3LS; Tel (01297) 442232/442234/442235; Fax (01297) 444762; *Head Teacher* Kerrigan Redman, BA; *Chair of Governors* J.A. Terrett. Mixed 11–18 (Comprehensive/day/boarding (850)

Dudley Metropolitan Borough Council

Population 304,615 (1991 Census)
The Council Hse, Priory Rd, Dudley DY1 1HF; Tel (01384) 456000; Fax (01384) 453226

Education Offices

Westox Hse, 1 Trinity Rd, Dudley DY1 1JB; Tel (01384) 456000; Fax (01384) 452216
Chairman Cllr Mrs M.G. Fenton, JP
Vice-Chairman Cllr H.E. Nottingham, JP, FCollP
Chief Education Officer R.K. Westerby, BA, FRSA
Head of Special Needs P.G. Metcalfe, BA,
Head of Schools R.P. Colligan, BEd, MA
Head of Resources H.R. Holt, MA
Head of Continuing Education G.A. Daniels, BSc, MSocSc
Head of Development and Client Services H.R. Holt, MA
Head of Inspection, Support and Advisory Service I.M. Cleland, MA, MBIM, DMS, DASE
Inspector (Music) M.G. Jones
Inspector (Physical Education) P. Whitlam
Inspector (Research, Development and Evaluation) K.M. Lambert, MSc
Inspector (Design and Technology) R. Farman
Inspector (Modern Languages) P.G. Dahl
Inspector (Humanities) C.R. Burns
Inspector (Mathematics) A.J. Wood
Inspector (Religious Education) Rev G. Hodgson
Inspector (Primary) Mrs P. Kenyon
Inspector (English) R.G. Bibby
Inspector (Multi-Cultural Education) A. Sahota
TVEI Manager, Inspector (Management of Learning) D. Darwood
Inspector (Assessment) Mrs H. Roxborough
Inspector (Management) J. Bethel
Inspector (Work Related Curriculum) Mrs C. Emery
Inspector (Entitlement and Progression) Mrs J. Hodgetts
Head of Information Services G. Baker, MInstPS
Education Buildings Officer A.E. Willetts, MBIM
Education Supplier Officer Mrs T. Wharton
Head of Counselling Service A. Patel, BA(Hons)
AEO (Schools) G. Gray-Smith, BScoSc, MEd
AEO (Colleges) J.C. King
AEO (INSET) R. Wilkins, BA
AEO (Continuing Education) Ms J. Hoare
Principal Educational Psychologist R.A. Blakey, BSc, DipEdPsych
Student Awards Officer (Grants) M. Baker
Adult Education Guidance Co-ordinator J. Hoare
Careers Services Manager C. Morgan
Youth and Community Officer A. Lowe
Senior Education Social Worker D. Maybury
Pre-School SEN Support Service M. Lavery

Number of Schools
1 nursery; 83 primary; 21 secondary; 8 special (day);
Day of Committee Meeting
Tuesday, six-weekily

Careers Office

See chapter 17

Special Schools and Special Educational Provision (Age range as given)

The Brier, Cottage St, Brierley Hill, Dudley DY5 1RE; Tel (01384) 78304; D.K. Postlethwaite. (5–16)
Halesbury, Feldon La, Halesowen, Dudley B62 9DR; Tel 0121-422 5521; W.E. Davison. (E.S.N.) (5–16) (100)
Mere Education Centre, Lawnswood Rd, Wordsley, Stourbridge, Dudley LDY8 5PQ; Tel (01384) 273334; R.O. Gibson. (5–11)
Old Park, Corbyn Rd, Russells Hall Est, Dudley DY1 2JZ; Tel (01384) 258476; W.A. Howkins. (3–19)
Pens Meadow, Ridge Hill, Brierley Hill Rd, Stourbridge, Dudley DY8 5ST; Tel (01384) 288201; Mrs J. Rowthorn. (3–19)
Rosewood, Overfield Rd, Russells Hall Est, Dudley DY1 2NX; Tel (01384) 256120; E.M. Williams. (11–16)
Saltwells Hse, Pedmore Rd, Brierley Hill, Dudley, West Midlands; Tel (01384) 77629; N. Harrison. (12–16+)
The Sutton, Scotts Green Cl, Russells Hall Est, Dudley DY1 2DU; Tel (01384) 254766; S. Freer. (5–16)
The Woodsetton, Tipton Rd, Woodsetton, Dudley DY3 1BY; Tel (01902) 663657; C.L. Downing. (5–16)

Middle School (County 8–12)

Red Hall Middle, Zoar St, Lower Gornal, Dudley DY3 2PA; Tel (01384) 214062; D.L. Eades. (360)

Comprehensive Schools (County 11/12–16)

The Buckpool, Brierley Hill Rd, Wordsley, Stourbridge, Dudley DY8 5SP; Tel (01384) 76766/73444; T.P. Jordan. (544)
The Coseley, Ivyhouse La, Coseley, Bilston, Dudley WV14 9JH; Tel (01902) 880381; D. Scott. (644)
Cradley High School, Homer Hill, Halesowen, Dudley B63 2UP; Tel (01384) 66444/68164; Miss J.A. Fowler. (587)
The Dormston, Mill Bank, Sedgley, Dudley DY3 1SN; Tel (01902) 663161/663162; Mrs B.H. O'Connor. (679)
The Earls High, Furnace La, Halesowen, Dudley B63 3SL; Tel 0121-550 1001; Mrs C. Raphael. (898)
The Grange, Grange La, Stourbridge, Dudley DY9 7HS; Tel (01384) 894711/2; M.S. Hursey. (823)
The Hillcrest School and Community College, Simms La, Netherton, Dudley DY2 0PB; Tel (01384) 212121; J. Bateson. (526)
Leasowes High School and Community College, Kent Rd, Halesowen, Dudley B62 8PJ; Tel 0121-422 0265; J.G. Howells. (935)
The Pensnett School of Technology, Tiled House La, Pensnett, Brierley Hill, Dudley DY5 4LN; Tel (01384) 77832, 79319; B.C. Bainbridge. (408)
The Redhill, Junction Rd, Stourbridge, Dudley DY8 1JX; Tel (01384) 395602/376460; C.T. Lacey. (1060)
The Ridgewood High, Park Rd West, Stourbridge, Dudley DY8 3NQ; Tel (01384) 379532; I. Maddock. (885)
The Ridgewood High, Longlands Site, Brook St, Stourbridge DY8 3XB; Tel (01384) 395057/378220
The Thorns School and Community College, off Stockwell Ave, Quarry Bank, Brierley Hill, Dudley DY5 2NU; Tel (01384) 754123; J.W. Thompson. (987)

Comprehensive Schools (County 12/13–18)

The Crestwood, Bromley La, Kingswinford, Dudley DY6 8QG; Tel (01384) 295935; J.S. Grove. (548)
The Summerhill, Lodge La, Kingswinford, Dudley DY6 9XE; Tel (01384) 401909; M.S. Hewitt. (695)

Comprehensive Schools (Voluntary Aided 11/12–18)

The Bishop Milner R.C., Burton Rd, Dudley DY1 3BY; Tel (01384) 255235; D.A. Fagan. (V.A.) (563)
Castle High, St James's Rd, Dudley DY1 3JE; Tel (01384) 253766; G.M. Cresswell. (VA) (694)
Castle High School Annexe, Priory Rd, Dudley DY1 4AB; Tel (01384) 253830

Adult Literacy Centre

Dudley College of Technology, The Broadway, Dudley DY1 4AS; Tel (01384) 455433; *Organiser* Miss J. Manley

Dudley Music Centre

Lawnswood Rd, Wordsley, Stourbridge DY8 5PQ; Tel (01384) 288582; *Head of Music Services* G.V. Johnson

Education Counselling Service

23-25 St James's Rd, Dudley, West Midlands; Tel (01384) 456000
Head of Counselling Service A. Patel

Home & Hospital Tuition Service

Office: Dudley (Saltwells) Education Development Centre, Bowling Green Rd, Dudley, West Midlands; Tel (01384) 634155; *Head of Service* Mrs S. Jewitt

Learning Support Service

Saltwells Education Development Centre, Bowling Green Rd, Dudley, West Midlands; Tel (01384) 634155; *Head of Service* R. Brooks

Multicultural Support Service

Saltwells Education Development Centre, Bowling Green Rd, Dudley LDY2 9LY; Tel (01384) 410025

School Camp Site – Outdoor Education Service

Astley Burf Camp Astley Burf, Stourport-on-Severn, Worcs; Tel (0129 93) 3909; R. Doidge

Services for Hearing-Impaired Children

Office: Ashwood Park Primary School, Off Bells La, Ashwood Pk Est, Wordsley, Stourbridge DY8 5DJ; Tel (01384) 271762; *Teacher in Charge* Miss P. Harrison
Unit for 1st & Middle School Children, Ashwood Park Primary School, off Bells La, Ashwood Pk Est, Wordsley, Stourbridge DY8 5DJ; Tel (01384) 279873 Ext 23; *Tutor* Mrs F. Phillips
Unit for Secondary School Children, Redhill School, Junction Rd, Stourbridge, West Midlands; Tel (01384) 395602/376460; *Tutor* S.D. Whitlow

Service for Visually Impaired Children

Office: Bromley Hills Primary School, Granville Dr, Kingswinford DY6 8LW; Tel (01384) 277071; *Teacher in Charge* Mrs A. Hope
Unit for Primary School Children, Bromley Hills Primary School, Granville Dr, Kingswinford DY6 8LW; Tel (01384) 277071; *Support Teacher* Mrs J. Richards
Unit for Secondary School Children, The Holly Hall School, Scotts Green Cl, Russells Hall Est, Dudley DY1 2DU; Tel (01384) 240250; Mrs L.P Dukes

Sports Centres

Leasowes Sports Centre, Kent Rd, Halesowen, West Midlands; Tel 0121-421 2470; K. Hughes
Thorns Sports Centre, off Stockwell Ave, Quarry Bank, Brierley Hill, Dudley, West Midlands; Tel (01384) 71668; J. Williams

Educational Development Centres

Dudley Teachers' Education and Development Centre, Laburnum Rd, Kingswinford DY6 8EH; Tel (01384) 273531; R. Hartill
Dudley (Saltwells) Educational Development Centre, Bowling Green Rd, Dudley, West Midlands; Tel (01384) 634155; R. Harthill

Youth Centres

Claughton Youth and Community Centre Claughton Hse, Blower Green Rd, Dudley, West Midlands; Tel (01384) 78349
Coseley Youth Centre, Old Meeting Rd, Coseley, Dudley, West Midlands; Tel 0121-557 5187; D. Williams
Dudley Wood Youth Centre, Dudley Wood Rd, Dudley Wood, Dudley, West Midlands; Tel (01384) 67190; Miss E. McPherson
Halesowen Youth Centre, Highfield La, Halesowen, West Midlands; Tel 0121-550 5273; Vacancy
Kingswinford Youth Centre, High St, Kingswinford, Dudley, West Midlands; Tel (01384) 278366; Vacancy
Lower Gornal Youth Centre, Temple St, Lower Gornal, Dudley, West Midlands; Tel (01384) 211559; C. Jones
Lye Youth Centre, Chapel St, Lye, Stourbridge, West Midlands; Tel (01384) 422260; J. Charles
Russells Hall Youth Centre, Overfield Rd, Russells Hall, Dudley, West Midlands; Tel (01384) 254554; M. Javaid
Sedgley Youth Centre, Vale St, Upper Gornal, Dudley, West Midlands; Tel (01902) 884755; C. Jones
Stourbridge Youth Centre, Brook St, Stourbridge, West Midlands; Tel (01384) 394219; Miss M. Martin
The Source, Barnett La, Wordsley, Stourbridge, West Midlands; Tel (01384) 279380; P. Creed
Meadow Rd Youth Centre, Meadow Rd, Dudley, West Midlands; Tel (01384) 258489; R. Singh

Grant Maintained Schools

The Ellowes Hall GM School, Stickley La, Lower Gornal, Dudley DY3 2JH; Tel (01902) 884581/678364; N.R. Smith. (602)
The High Arcal School, High Arcal Dr, Sedgley, Dudley DY3 1BP; Tel (01902) 883887/673956; J.R. Williams. (880)
The Holly Hall, Scotts Green Cl, Russells Hall Est, Dudley DY1 2DU; Tel (01384) 253722; J.S. Cutts. (432)
The Kingswinford GM School, Water St, Kingswinford, Dudley DY6 7AD; Tel (01384) 296596; Fax (01384) 401098; G.J. Harrison. (531)
Old Swinford Hospital School, Stourbridge, West Midlands DY8 1QX; Tel (01384) 370025; Fax (01384) 441686; *Headmaster* C.F.R. Potter; *Chairman of Governors* D. Higgs. (Male) (11–18) (550)
Windsor High School, Richmond St, Halesowen, Dudley B63 4BB; Tel 0121-550 1452; D. Newton. (893)

Durham County Council

Population 604,300
County Hall, Durham DH1 5UG; Tel 0191-386 4411
Assistant Chief Executive C. Shearsmith, IPFA
Director of Community Services N. Smith, CEng, MICE

Education Department

County Hall, Durham DH1 5UJ; Tel (0191) 3864411
Chairman Councillor J. Walker, JP, FInst

Vice-Chairman Councillor F.G. Taylor, JP
Director of Education K. Mitchell, BA, LLB, PGCE
Deputy Director of Education J.J. Fitt, BA, MA, PGCE
Senior Assistant Director (Resources Division) N. Charlton, BA(Hons), CertEd
Principal Education Officer (Physical Resources/Special Projects) J.K. Banks, BA, MEd, DLC, ACP
Principal Education Officer (Personnel/Administration) J.W. Bowman, CIPFA
Principal Education Officer (Finance/Local Management) P. Barclay, DMA
Principal Education Officer (Compulsory Education) P.A. Astle, BA
Principal Education Officer (Community Education) P.B. Robinson, BA
Princpal Education Officer (Careers) J. Bray, BA, DipYESTB
Principal Education Officer (Special Education) M.E. Clare, BEd
Education Officer (Special Education) H. Sawyer, BA
AEO (Compulsory Education) K.R. Bates, BSc, MSc
AEO (Training) Miss J.A. Doxford, BA
AEO (Computing and Information Technology) G.A. Wood, BSc
AEO (LMS) P. Jackson
AEO (Compulsory Education) Mrs A.J. Johnson, BA
Chief Education Inspector G.L. Clarke, BSc, MAEd
Senior Inspector (Secondary, Area 1) P. Livsey, BA
Senior Inspector (Secondary, Area 2) A.O. Sheard, BA
Senior Inspector (Primary Area 3) E.L. Reed, BEd, BPhil
Senior Inspector (14–18, Area 4) R.A. Edwardson, BSc
Senior Inspector (Junior, Area 5) M. Pinch, ACP, BEd, BSc, MPhil, DipManEd
Staff Inspector (Curriculum and Assessment) Ms V.R. Ashfield, BA, MEd
Staff Inspector (In-Service Training) R.A. Langham, BSc
Inspector (Special Education) Mrs E.R. Adams
Inspector (Special Education) R.H. Rubin, BS(USA)
Inspector (Primary Education) Mrs K.J. Chandler
Inspector (Primary Education) C.A. Lumsden, CertEd
Inspector (Primary Education) Mrs D. Yoxall, BEd
Inspector (Continuing Education) G.W. Stephenson, BA
Inspector (Home Economics/Health Education) Miss E. Allen, BEd
Inspector (Primary) D.G. Ford
Inspector (Primary) P. Cass
Inspector (Physical Education) A. Bell, BEd
Inspector (Creative Movement) J. Carey, CertEd
Inspector (Science) J.H. Crossland, BA, MA(Ed)
Inspector (Art and Design) Vacancy
Inspector (Nursery/Infant Education) Vacancy
Inspector (Geography) T. Hemsley, BEd
Inspector (Humanities) R.B. Higgs, BEd, MEd
Inspector (Modern Languages) D. Neil, BA
Inspector (Religious Education) Mrs M. Potter, BEd MA
Inspector (Design and Technology) P.A. Renton, BEd
Inspector (Mathematics) T. Robshaw, BSc
Inspector (Business Studies/Economic Awareness) Ms M. Sinclair, BSc
Inspector (Rural and Environmental Education) M. Tones, BEd
Co-Ordinator Health Education Vacancy
Inspector (Business Studies and Economic Understanding) Vacancy
TVEI Co-ordinator Ms M. Shirren
Inspector (Pre-Vocational Education) Ms B.A. Comiskey, BA
County Catering Adviser Mrs F. Tee, MHC, IMA
International Exchange Officer A. Sutcliffe, BA, CertEd
County Educational Psychologist D.A. Smith, BTech, MEd, PGCE
Area Senior Educational Psychologist M.L. Smith, MEd(EdPsych)
Area Senior Educational Psychologist I.J. Gale, BA, MSc (EdPsych)
Area Senior Educational Psychologist J.I. Edmunds, BSc, MSc(EdPsych)
Area Senior Educational Psychologist P. Withnall
Area Senior Educational Psychologist J.M. Little, BA, Dip(EdPsych)
Specialist Educational Psychologist Mrs M. Portwood, BA, MSc(EdPsych)
Specialist Educational Psychologist Mrs H. Flack, BSc, MSc(EdPsych)
Specialist Educational Psycholgist L. Gibson, BA, MSc(EdPsych), MEd
Specialist Educational Psychologist S. Miller, BA, MSc(EdPsych)
Specialist Educational Psychologist I.A. Keddie, BSc, MSC(EdPsych)
Educational Psychologist Ms S. Hewitt, BSc, MEd(EdPsych)
Educational Psychologist K. Venables, BSc, MA(EdPsych)
Educational Psychologist Ms D. Boutilier, BA, MSc
Educational Psychologist C.D. Hutchinson, BA, MSc(EdPsych)
Specialist Educational Psychologist L. Gibson, BA, MSc(EdPsych), MEd
Educational Psychologist R. Ford, BA, MSc(Ed Psych)
Educational Psychologist J. Sharpe, BSc, MEd(EdPsych)
Educational Psychologist J. Davies, BSc, MSc (Ed Psych)
Educational Psychologist J. Crawford, BA, MSc(EdPsych)
Educational Psychologist M.T. Taylor, BA, DipEdPsych
Educational Psychologist K.R. Linton, BA, MSc(EdPsych)
Educational Psychologist S. Woodcock, BA, MSc(EdPsych)
Educational Psychologist E.G. Cumming, MA, DipEdPsych
Educational Psychologist C. Shearer, BSc, MSc(EdPsych)
Educational Psychologist C. Fletcher, BA, MSc(EdPsych)

Number of Schools
27 nursery (233 full-time, 2,699 part-time) 297 primary (51,285), 45 secondary (37,021)

Day of Committee Meeting
Second Wednesday in January, April, July, October plus annual meeting

Requisition Periods for School Supplies
Main in April; supplementary (if necessary) following September

Other Authorities with whom Joint Purchasing Arrangements are made
None

East Durham Area
York Rd, Peterlee SR8 2DP; Tel (0191) 5872777

Mid Durham Area
New College, Nevilles Cross Premises, Darlington Rd, Durham DH1 4UH; Tel (0191) 3845054

North Durham Area
Education Centre, Stanley DH9 0ST; Tel (01207) 232565

South Durham Area
Craig Lea, Uplands Rd, Darlington DL3 7SW; Tel (01325) 355311

West Durham
Kingsway, Bishop Auckland DL14 7JN; Tel (01388) 663666

Careers Office
See chapter 17

Child Guidance Centres
Annfield Plain Centre, Priory Ct, Annfield Plain DH9 7TG; Tel (01207) 282888
Bishop Auckland Child Guidance Centre, Murphy Cres, Bishop Auckland DL14 6QH; Tel (01388) 661281

Darlington Child Guidance Centre, Craig Lea, Uplands Rd, Darlington DL3 7SW; Tel (01325) 355311
Durham Educational Psychology Centre, Aykley Heads, Durham DH1 5TS; Tel 0191-3865969
Horden Child Guidance Centre, York Rd, Peterlee; Tel 0191-5182602

Special Schools

Consett Villa Real, Villa Real, Consett DH8 6BH; Tel (01207) 503651; Mrs F. Wood
Durham Trinity (Flambard Premises) Aykley Heads, Durham DH1 5TS; Tel 0191-386 4612; J.M. Wynn
Durham Trinity (Kirkham Premises) Aykley Heads, Durham DH1 5TS; Tel 0191-384 7658
Durham Trinity (Bek Premises) Hartside, Durham DH1 5RH; Tel 0191-384 5288
Easington Glen Hill, Crawlaw Rd, Easington Colliery, Peterlee SR8 3BQ; Tel 0191-527 0304; P.R. Bamberough (Acting)
Elemore Hall Residential, Littletown, Sherburn DH6 1QD; Tel 0191-372 0275; M. Davey. (Residential)
Ferryhill Rosebank, Rutherford Terr, Broom, Ferryhill DL17 8AN; Tel (01740) 651555; Mrs S. Stubbs
Hare Law, Catchgate, Annfield Plain, Stanley DH9 8DT; Tel (01207) 234547; Mrs E.A. Collin
Horden Dene View, Cotsford Pk, Horden, Peterlee SR8 4SZ; Tel 0191-586 4166; D. Johnson
Murphy Cres, Murphy Cres, Bishop Auckland DL14 6QH; Tel (01388) 602349; E.A. Hornsey
Newton Aycliffe Walworth, Bluebell Way, Newton Aycliffe DL5 7LP; Tel (01325) 300194; M. McNally (Acting). (Residential & Day)
Spennymoor Whitworth Hse, Whitworth La, Spennymoor DL16 7QW; Tel (01388) 816061; L.E. Ablett
Villa Real, Villa Real, Consett DH8 6BH; Tel (01207) 503651; Mrs F. Wood
Warwick Rd, Warwick Rd, Bishop Auckland DL14 6LS; Tel (01388) 602683; G. Price
Windlestone Hall, Rushyford, Chilton, Ferryhill DL17 0LX; Tel (01388) 720337; P.M. Jonson. (Residential)

Secondary Schools

Barnard Castle Teesdale, Prospect Pl, Barnard Castle DL12 8HH; Tel (01833) 38166 & 37507; K.R. Dodds. (726)
Belmont Comprehensive, Belmont, Durham DH1 2QP; Tel (0385) 3865715; V.A. Reed. (850)
Bishop Barrington Comprehensive, Woodhouse La, Bishop Auckland DL14 6LA; Tel (01388) 603307; N. Donkin. (588)
Blackfyne Comp, Durham Rd, Blackhill, Consett DH8 5TW; Tel (01207) 503515; J.L. Brierley
Branksome, Eggleston View, Darlington DL3 9SH; Tel (01325) 380776; J.J. Le Roi. (689)
Deerness Valley Comprehensive School, Ushaw Moor, Durham DH7 7NG; Tel 0191-373 0336; D.W. Armstrong. (564)
Dene House Comprehensive, Manor Way, Peterlee SR8 5RL; Tel 0191-586 2140; D.L. Roberts. (838)
Durham Johnston Comprehensive Crossgate Moor, Durham DH1 4SU; Tel 0191-384 3887; J.E. Dunford
Durham Sixth Form Centre, Providence Row, Durham DH1 1SG; Tel 0191-384 2217; M. Todd
Easington Comprehensive, Stockton Rd, Easington Village, Peterlee SR8 3AY; Tel 0191-527 0757; G.O. Smith
Eastbourne, The Fairway, Darlington DL1 8RW; Tel (01325) 464657/464357; R.J. Dingle. (846)
Ferryhill Comprehensive, Merrington Rd, Ferryhill DL17 8RW; Tel (01740) 651554; W.I. Wilks. (753)
Framwellgate Moor Comprehensive School, Newton Dr, Framwellgate Moor, Durham DH1 5BQ; Tel 0191-384 8050; A. McNamara. (1221)
Gilesgate Comprehensive, Bradford Cres, Durham DH1 1HN; Tel 0191-384 7505; M. Todd
Greencroft Comprehensive, Greencroft Road Ends, Annfield Plain, Stanley DH9 8PR; Tel (01207) 234466; J.E. Cotton
Greenfield Comprehensive, Greenfield Way, Newton Aycliffe DL5 7LE; Tel (01325) 300378; J.D. Tate. (556)
Haughton, Rockwell Ave, Darlington DL1 2AX; Tel (01325) 380812/3; S.M. Potter. (750)
Hermitage Comprehensive, Waldridge La, Chester-le-Street DH2 3AD; Tel (0385) 3887161; E. Brady. (748)
Hummersknott, Edinburgh Dr, Darlington DL3 8AR; Tel (01325) 461191/2; D. Henderson. (1003)
Hurworth Comprehensive, Croft Rd, Hurworth, Darlington DL2 2JG; Tel (01325) 720424; K. Charlton. (593)
King James I Comprehensive, South Church Rd, Bishop Auckland DL14 7JZ; Tel (01388) 603388; P. Wager. (1219)
Longfield, Longfield Rd, Darlington DL3 OHT; Tel (01325) 380815/6; Dr W.D. Ions. (883)
Moorside Comprehensive Dunelm Rd, Consett DH8 8EG; Tel (01207) 507001; J.D. Hughes. (482)
Park View Comprehensive, Church Chare, Chester-le-Street DH3 3PZ; Tel (0385) 3882248; A.M. Thompson. (1132)
North Lodge, Chester-le-Street DH3 4BB; Tel 3882416
Roseberry Comprehensive, Pelton, Chester-le-Street DH2 1NN; Tel (0385) 3700300; J. Stafeckis. (782)
Sacriston Fyndoune Comprehensive, Findon Hill, Sacriston, Durham DH7 6LU; Tel (0385) 3710277; A. Rand. (594)
Seaham Comprehensive, Burnhall Dr, Seaham SR7 OEN; Tel Wearside 5813262. (1099)
Sedgefield Community College, Sedgefield, Cleveland TS21 3DD; Tel (01740) 620288; A.F. Williams. (748)
Shotton Hall Comprehensive, Waveney Rd, Peterlee SR8 1NX; Tel (01783) 5862580/5863619; P.J. Clark. (1159)
Staindrop Comprehensive School, Cleatham La, Staindrop, Darlington DL2 3JU; Tel (01833) 660285/660447; I.F. Weare. (596)
Stanley Comprehensive, Tyne Rd, South Stanley, Stanley DH9 6PZ; Tel (01207) 232506; C. Johnson. (737)
Sunnydale Comprehensive, Middridge La, Shildon DL4 2EP; Tel (01388) 772526; R.G. Walton. (571)
Tanfield Comprehensive, Nr Good St, Stanley DH9 8AY; Tel (01207) 232881; A.J. Howatt. (636)
Tudhoe Grange Comprehensive, St Charles Rd, Spennymoor DL16 6JY; Tel (01388) 815000; J.M. Mallin
Durham Rd, Spennymoor DL16 6SQ; Tel (01388) 816050
Wellfield Comprehensive, North Rd, East Wingate TS28 5AX; Tel (01429) 838413; Dr J.A. Jordan
Wellfield Rd, Wingate TS28 5JY; Tel 838214
Willington Parkside Comprehensive, Hall Lane, Willington DL15 8QG; Tel (01388) 746396; D.C. Jewell
Wolsingham Comprehensive, Tunstall Rd, Wolsingham, Bishop Auckland DL13 3DN; Tel Weardale 527302/527623; U. O'Reilly. (945)
Woodham Comprehensive, Washington Cres, Newton Aycliffe DL5 4AX; Tel (01325) 300328; S. Harness. (926)

Secondary Schools (Voluntary)

Darlington Carmel R.C., Comprehensive, The Headlands, Darlington DL3 8RN; Tel (01325) 463009; J.S. O'Neill. (Aided) (620)
Lanchester R.C., Comprehensive, Lanchester, Durham DH7 ORD; Tel (01207) 520424; E.G. Dunn. (Aided) (987)
St Bede's R.C., Comprehensive, West Way, Peterlee SR8 LDE; Tel 0191-586 2291; W. Mulligan. (Aided) (811)
St John's R.C., Comprehensive, Woodhouse La, Bishop Auckland DL14 6JT; Tel (01388) 603246/605492; B.A. Jones. (Aided) (754)
St Leonard's R.C., Comprehensive, North End, Durham DH14 NG; Tel 0191-384 8575; S.O. Keeffe. (Aided) (1072)

College of Education

New College, Durham Framwellgate Moor, Durham DH1 5ES; Tel (0385) 3862421; D.L. Turner, BA, FBIM; Formed by the merger of Nevilles Cross College and Durham Technical College, Darlington Rd, Durham DH1 4SY; Tel 3847325

Field Studies Centres

Earls Orchard, Richmond, Yorks DL10 4RH; Tel (01748) 2155; *Head* R. Robinson
Middleton-in-Teesdale, Middleton-in-Teesdale DL12 0QB; Tel 509; *Warden* A. Steventon

Other Establishments

Annfield Plain Day Teaching Unit, Annfield Centre, Priory Court, Annfield Plain, Stanley, Durham; Tel (01207) 231169; Mrs E. Young
Bishop Auckland Combined Child Guidance Centre and Day Teaching Unit, Murphy Cres, Bishop Auckland DL14 6QH; Tel (01388) 601818; R. Heap
Darlington Child Guidance Centre, Craiglea, Uplands Rd, Darlington DL3 7SW; Tel (01325) 355311
Darlington Day Teaching Unit, Hundens La, Darlington DL3 6JY; Tel (01325) 468395; M.P. Grogan
Drama Centre, Arthur Pease Bldg, Trinity Rd, Darlington DL3 7AZ; Tel (01325) 465935; D. Tungate
Durham Child Guidance Clinic, Aykley Heads, Durham DH1 5TS; Tel 0191-386 5969
Durham Day Teaching Unit, Aykley Heads, Durham DH1 5TS; Tel 0191-386 3113; Mrs J. Bach
Education Advisory Centre, New College, Nevill's Cross Centre, Durham DH1 4UH; Tel 0191-384 7325
Horden Child Guidance Centre, York Rd, Peterlee; Tel 0191-518 2602; P.N. Dunn
Music Centre, Borough Rd, Darlington DL1 1SG; Tel (01325) 380757
Peterlee Day Teaching Unit, York Rd, Peterlee; Tel 0191-518 2601
Westgate School Camp, Westgate, Eastgate, Bishop Auckland DL13 1JJ; Tel (01388) 517270; *Caretaker* Mrs P. Fairless

Teachers' Centres

King Edward VIII Terr Shield Row, Stanley DH9 0HQ; Tel 232565; *Warden* W. Robinson
North Lodge, North Rd, Darlington DL1 1TZ; Tel (01325) 61416; F.W. Firth

Dyfed County Council

Population 352,600
County Hall, Carmarthen, Dyfed SA31 1JP; Tel (01267) 224671; Fax (01267) 221737
Chief Executive Officer W.J. Phillips
County Secretary D.R. Irving
County Treasurer H.C. Morse
Director of Personnel and Management Services D.G. Llewellyn
Planning Officer D.P. Brown 40 Spilman St, Carmarthen
County Architect Roy Howell Lime Grove Hse, Lime Grove Ave, Carmarthen
County Engineer and Surveyor D.H. Davies Highways and Transportation Dept, Johnstown, Carmarthen
Director of Cultural Services D.T. Lewis Public Library, St Peter St, Carmarthen
Director of Social Services D. Evans

Education Department

Education Headquarters, Pibwrlwyd, Carmarthen, Dyfed SA31 2NH; Tel (01267) 233333; Fax (01267) 221692
Chairman Cllr D.J. Thomas
Vice-Chairman Cllr J.A.J Harries
Director of Education J.G. Ellis, BSc, MEd, DipEd
Deputy Director of Education G.W. Davies, MA, LLB, MBA
Assistant Director (Research, Development and Forward Planning) R.E. Jones
Assistant Director Officer (Schools and Schools Services) D.G. Hughes
Assistant Director (Administration and Finance) A. Arnott
Principal Education Psychologist J.G. Williams
Principal Careers Officer I.W. Davies
Senior Administrative Officer B. Miles
Principal Advisers D. Morris, D. Norbury (Acting)
Adviser/Inspector (Maths) P.V. Moody, MA Education Resource Centre, St Clears, Dyfed; Tel (01994) 231223; Fax (01994) 231255
Adviser/Inspector (Science) D. Norbury, PhD Education Resource Centre, St Clears, Dyfed; Tel (01994) 231223; Fax (01994) 231255
Adviser/Inspector (D.T) G. Edwards, BEd Education Resource Centre, St Clears, Dyfed; Tel (01994) 231223; Fax (01994) 231255
Adviser/Inspector (English) P.A. Richardson Education Resource Centre, St Clears, Dyfed; Tel (01994) 231223; Fax (01994) 231255
Adviser/Inspector(Information Technology) B. Stephens Education Resource Centre, St Clears, Dyfed; Tel (01994) 231223; Fax (01994) 231255
Adviser/Inspector (Inset-Ordinator) M. Thomas Education Resource Centre, St Clears, Dyfed; Tel (01994) 231223; Fax (01994) 231255
Adviser/Inspector (Modern Languages) M.R. Fowler Education Resource Centre, St Clears, Dyfed; Tel (01994) 231223; Fax (01994) 231255
TVEI Co-ordinator Dr G. Rogers Education Resource Centre, St Clears, Dyfed; Tel (01994) 231223; Fax (01994) 231255
Primary Adviser/Inspector S. Richards Education Resource Centre, St Clears; Tel (01994) 231223; Fax (01994) 231255
Adviser/Inspector (Humanities) W. Williams Education Resource Centre, St Clears, Dyfed; Tel (01994) 231223; Fax ()994) 231255
Adviser/Inspector (Music) E.W. Jones Education Resource Centre, St Clears, Dyfed; Tel (01994) 231223; Fax (01994) 231255

Number of Schools
318 nursery and primary (32,000); 5 special; 31 secondary (24,000)

Committee Meeting
Four per year

Education Committee

Con 1, Lab 22, LD 8, Ind 31, PC 7, RPA 1
Chair Cllr D.J. Thomas
Vice-Chair J.A.J. Harries

Members of the Committee
*Con:*R.J. Buckland
Lab: D.J. Adams, G.M. Davies, W.J. Davies MBE, P.I. Evans JP, M. Evans, A.C. Francis, R.G. Harries, W.G.H. James, H. Jones, J.R. Lawrence, F.H. Levesley, K.W. Lloyd, R. Maddock, S.J. May, K.B. Maynard, M.P. Morris, G.F. Meyler, H.S. Peregrine, Prof H.G. Rees, A.B.D. Pugh, E.A.B. Thomas BScEcon, JP, K. Williams
LD: J.M. Allen, P.W. Eklund, K.J. Evans, E.J. Griffiths, J.D.R. Jones, W.A. Jones, K.D. Rees, T.H. Sinclair
Ind: T.J. Adams-Lewis, W.G. Bennett, J.G. Cawood, D.G.E. Davies CBE, D.T. Davies OBE, MM, H.E. Davies, T.W. Davies, Dr W.E.V.J. Davies, G.J. Earl, A.W. Edwards, W.L. Evans, M.T. Folland, T.R. George OBE, M. Gravell, P.E. Griffiths, R.O. Griffiths, E.R. Harries, J.A.J. Harries CBE, R.R. Hayes, W.H. Hitchings, D.L. James, J.L. James, J.E.J. Jones, T.H. Lewis, R.W. Lewis, T.R.L. Martin, T.G. Parry, J.W.J. Roberts, T. Theophilus, D.J. Thomas, M. Thomas
PC: H.G. Evans, J.R. Evans, W.G. Hopkins, F.M. Jones, W.P. James, D.J.R. Llewellyn, D. Thomas
RPA: W.J.W. Evans

Governor Training Unit

Governor Support Unit, Dyfed Education HQ, Pibwrlwyd, Carmarthen, Dyfed SA31 1NH; Tel (01267) 224512; Fax (01267) 221692
Assistant Director (Schools) Dewi Hughes
Governor Training Co-Ordinator Dilwen Davies
Services Offered
Support to Governors; Training–conference, workshops, seminars termly governors newsletter, advice, information, guidance–consultancy, information packs, documents, library–books, audio, video tapes; Helpline for Governors; Support in Crisis available bilingually in Welsh and English

Aberystwyth Area

County Offices, Marine Terr, Aberstwyth SY23 2DE; Tel (01970) 617581; Fax (01970) 615817
Area Education Officer R.J. Williams, MA
Professional Assistant J.L. Evans
Primary Adviser T. Davies-Jones, BEd
Physical Education Adviser G.A. Williams
Welsh Language Adviser E.P. Davies, BA
Senior Careers Officer R. Thomas
Senior Education Welfare Officer P. Lee-Jones
Education Welfare Officer E.D. Jones
Senior Educational Psychologist L. Roberts
Educational Psychologist S. Jenkins

Carmarthen Area

Area Education Office, 1 Penlan Rd, Carmarthen SA31 1DN; Tel (01267) 233333; Fax (01267) 222419
Area Education Officer D. Hedydd Davies, BSc, MEd, PhD, CChem, MRSC
Primary Adviser A.S. Parry
Language Adviser J.D. Davies
Special Education Managers E. Schiavone, A. Thomas
Educational Psychologist C.H. Storey
Education Psychologist J. Hedges
Educational Psychologist M. ap Steffan
Educational Psychologist L.A.H. Lawrence
Senior Education Welfare Officer C. Randall
Assistant Education Welfare Officer S.D. Giles
Assistant Education Welfare Officer P.M. Jones
Assistant Education Welfare Officer G. Morgan

Haverfordwest Area

County Offices, St Thomas Green, Haverfordwest SA61 1QZ; Tel (01437) 764591; Fax (01437) 769557
Area Education Officer C.H. Llewelyn, BA, DipEd
Welsh Language Adviser E.P. Davies, BA
Primary Education Adviser E.K. James
Educational Psychologist J. Benbow
Educational Psychologist T.C.H. Thomas
Educational Psychologist S. Lewis
Senior Careers Officer P.A. Allingham
Senior Community Education Officer A.R. Organ
Senior Community Education Officer R.A. Morgan
Senior Special Education Teacher Manager of Services to Schools J.E.B. Wilcox
Senior Education Welfare Officer J. Bearne
Manager of Services to Children C.M. Lawrie

Llanelli Area

17 Goring Rd, Llanelli, Dyfed, SA15 3HF; Tel (01554) 774951; Fax (01554) 753110
Area Education Officer T.R. Fowler, BA, MEd
Primary Adviser A.M. Lloyd
Senior Community Education Officer J. Jenkins
Education Welfare Officer C. Mathias
Education Welfare Officer A.J. Jones
Senior Education Welfare Officer A. Edwards
Area Senior Careers Officer G. Evans
Educational Psychologist T. Stallard
Educational Psychologist A. Davies

Careers Offices

See chapter 17

Special Schools

Heol Goffa, Heol Goffa, LLanelli, Dyfed; Tel (01554) 759465; *Head Teacher* R.A. Davies, BEd. (SLD) (E.S.N.(S) (58)
Area Education Office, 17 Goring Rd, Llanelli; Tel (01554) 774951; Fax (01554) 753110
Highmead Residential, Llanybyther, Dyfed SA40 9UN; Tel (01570) 480344; *Headteacher* D.J. Rees. (MLD) (E.S.N.(M) (83); Residential
Area Education Office, Marine Terr, Aberystwyth; Tel (01970) 617581
Overdale, Off Portfield Ave, Haverfordwest SA61 1BS; Tel (01437) 765161; *Headteacher* R.M. Davies (Acting). (MLD) (E.S.N.(M) (32); (Day)
Area Education Office, ST Thomas Grn, Haverfordwest, Dyfed; Tel (01437) 764591
Portfield, Off Portfield Ave, Haverfordwest SA61 1BS; Tel (01437) 762701; *Headteacher* J.T. Morgan. (SLD) (E.S.N.(S) (36)
Area Education Office, St Thomas Grn, Haverfordwest; Tel (01437) 764591
Rhydygors Residential, Llansteffan Rd, Johnstown, Carmarthen, Dyfed; Tel (01267) 231171; *Headteacher* S.C.L. Saunders. (EBD) (Malad.); (Residential)

Comprehensive Schools

Aberaeron, Dyfed SA46 0DT; Tel (01545) 570217; D.J. Thomas, OBE, BSc. (900)
Amman Valley, Ammanford, Dyfed SA18 2NN; Tel (01269) 592441/593866; R.O.P. Jones, MSc(Oxon). (1243)
Bryngwyn, Llanelli, Dyfed; Tel (01554) 750661/2/3/14; A.W. Jones, BA, MA. (1016)
Cardigan, Dyfed SA43 1AD; Tel (01239) 612670; Dr G.F. Griffiths, BSc, PhD. (Mixed) (719)
Coedcae, Llanelli, Dyfed; Tel (01554) 750574; W.H. Jones, BEcon, MSc. (839)
Fishguard, County Secondary School, Heol Dyfed, Fishguard SA65 9DT; Tel (01348) 872268; E. Parry, BSc. (Mixed) (754)
Glanymor, Burry Port, Dyfed; Tel (0155 46) 2507; A.J.C. Davies, BSc, PhD. (705)
The Graig, Llanelli, Dyfed; Tel (01554) 773664; *(Acting Head)* W. Dash. (707)
Greenhill Comprehensive School, Heywood La, Tenby SA70 8BN; Tel (01834) 2560; *Headteacher* R.D. Winder, BA(Hons), MA (Acting). (Mixed) (1338)
Gwendraeth Valley, Drefach, Llanelli SA14 7AB; Tel (01269) 841322; R.W. Garrero. (590)
Lampeter, Lampeter, Dyfed SA48 7BX; Tel (01570) 422214; T.G. Jones, BA. (Mixed) (565)
Ysgol Gyfun Tregib Ffairfach, Llandeilo, Dyfed; Tel (01558) 823477/823743; S.G. Davies. (719)
Ysgol Gyfun Pant Y Celyn Llandovery, Dyfed SA20 ODY; Tel (01550) 20395; R.J. Griffiths. (356)
Milford Haven Comprehensive School, Steynton Rd, Milford Haven SA73 1AE; Tel (01646) 690021; J.A. Cartmell, BSc, BA. (1208)
Pembroke School, Bush, Pembroke SA71 4RL; Tel (01646) 682461; R.A. Palmer, BA, BSc. (Mixed) (1376)
Penglais, Waunfawr, Aberystwyth SY23 3AW; Tel (01970) 624811; H.J. Davey, BA. (1026)
Penweddig, St David's Rd, Aberystwyth, Dyfed; Tel (01970) 624596; A.G. George, BSc. (Bilingual) (562)
Ysgol Gyfun Ddwyieithog y Preseli Crymych SAL1 3QH; Tel (0123 973) 831 406/7; D.M. Lloyd, BSc(Econ). (Mixed) (559)
Queen Elizabeth Cambria, Johnstown, Carmarthen SA31 3NL; Tel (01267) 236451/232300; W.A. Evans, BSc, PhD. (739)
Queen Elizabeth Maridunum, Johnstown, Carmarthen SA31 3NT; Tel (01267) 237650/232051; W.G. Thomas. (690)
St. John Lloyd R.C, Llanelli, Dyfed; Tel (01554) 772589; L.J. Affley, BMus, MEd. (377)

Sir Thomas Picton, Off Queensway, Haverfordwest SA61 2NX; Tel (01437) 765395; Dr G.T. Davies, BSc(Hons), MSc, PhD, MA. (1098)
Tasker-Milward V.C. Comprehensive, Off Portfield Ave, Haverfordwest SA61 1EQ; Tel (01437) 764147/8; C. Jones, BSc. (1153)
Tregaron, Dyfed SY25 6HG; Tel (01974) 298231; Dorian Williams, BA. (Mixed) (302)
Ysgol Dewi Sant, St David's, Haverfordwest SA62 6QH; Tel (01437) 720272; J.M. Roberts, BA(Hons). (Mixed) (337)
Ysgol Gyfun Maes yr Yrfa, Cefneithin, Llanelli SA14 7DT; Tel (01269) 842558; D.A. Thomas, BA. (593)
Ysgol Gyfun Bro Myrddin, Parcyffynnon, Carmarthen SA31 1DU; Tel (01267) 234829; G.H. Evans, BSc. (586)
Ysgol Gyfun Ddwyieithog Dyffryn Teifi, Llandyssul SA44 4HP; Tel (0155 932) 362310; J.A. Davies, BA, BD. (556)
Ysgol Gyfun Emlyn, Newcastle Emlyn, Dyfed; Tel (01239) 710447; T.E. Davies. (642)
Ysgol Gyfun y Strade, Llanelli; Tel (01554) 772986; D. Jones, BA. (638)
Ysgol Dyffryn Taf, North Rd, Whitland SA34 OBD; Tel (01994) 240355; D.K. Davies, PhD. (761)

Residential Centres

Ferryside Residential Education Centre Ferryside, Dyfed SA17 5TE; Tel (0126 785) 207; *Centre Administrator* W. Mountain
Stepney Education Centre, Pendine (School Camp); Tel (0199 45) 659; G. Thomas

Professional Education Centres

Professional Education Centre, Pontyberem, Dyfed; Tel (01269) 870169; M.D. Owen
Felinfach, Lampeter, Dyfed; Tel (01570) 470526; *Head* V. Evans
Trinity College, College Rd, Carmarthen, Dyfed; Tel (01267) 237971; P.H. Griffiths, BA
Pembrokeshire Professional Education Centre St Clements Rd, Neyland, Milford Haven SA73 1SH; Tel (01437) 890069; J.D.D. Harry

East Sussex County Council

Population 716,500
Pelham Hse, St Andrews La, Lewes, E. Sussex BN7 1UN; Tel (01273) 481000; Fax (01273) 473321

Education Department

Education Dept, PO Box 4, County Hall, St Anne's Cres, Lewes, E. Sussex BN7 1SG; Tel (01273) 481000; Fax (01273) 481261
Chairman Cllr Derek Norcross
Vice-Chairman Cllr Richard Austin
County Education Officer David Mallen
Assistant County Education Officer (Planning) D.C. Nelson, MA
Assistant County Education Officer (Operations) A. Atkinson, BSc(Hons)
Assistant County Education Officer (Quality Assurance) M.E. Hewitt, BA(Hons), MEd
Education Officer (Primary Schools) M. Dunkley, BA(Hons)
Education Officer (Secondary Schools) M.G. Nix, BA(Hons)
Education Officer (Special Needs) P.A. Weston, MSc
Head of Resources Planning L.A. Wardle, BA, MIFM, MMS
Head of Operations E.M. Peters, BA
Education Personnel Officer K. Newman
AEO (Corporate and External Relations) B. Bacon, BSc(Hons), PhD
AEO (Community Education) P.E. Penney, BA(Hons)
AEO (Admissions and Transport) Vacancy
AEO (Planning and Development) J.M. Atkin, BA(Hons)
AEO (Administration) R.A. Faulkner, BA(Hons), MSc
Awards Officer C. Bailey
County Education Welfare Officer Vacancy
Client Contracts Manager P. Buckenham
Finance Officer G. Roberts, CIPFA
Principal Inspector M. Jennings, BEd(Hons), MEd, MA
Principal Adviser (Curriculum) Dr D.A. Sands, BSc(Hons)
Principal Adviser (Management) M. Relouf, BA, DAES
Pupil Support Services Manager A. Dempsey, BA, MSc
AEO (Training) S. Marsh
Head of Careers Services D.R. Cleaton
County Adviser (Art) A.G. Jones, BA(Hons), MEd
County Adviser (Design and Technology) I. Punter, BA
County Adviser (English and Drama) P.R. Walker, BA
County Adviser (Humanities) J.J. Lace, BSc(Hons)
County Adviser (Music) K. Brock, BEd
County Adviser (Physical Education) C. Casbon, MEd
County Adviser (Science) T.E.W. Howell, BA
Number of Schools
2 nursery (81 FTE); 218 primary (49,975 FTE); 35 secondary (34,375); 18 youth & community centres; 4 teachers centres
Special Schools
17 day (1,290); 2 day & residential (82)
Day of Committee Meeting
Friday
Council Tax Base
261,759
Non Domestic Rateable Value
£309.8m

Education Committee

LD 13, Con 9, Lab 8
Chair D. Norcross, (LD) 12 Barnfield Cls, Hastings, East Sussex TN34 1TS; Tel (01424) 425305
Vice-Chair R.E. Austin, (Lab) 14 St Nicholas Rd, Brighton, East Sussex BN1 3LP; Tel (01273) 323297
Members of the Committee
LD: L.E. Beckman, K. Field, J.H. Freeman, P. D.Heasman, S. Holmes, M. McPherson, A.H. Moore, S.J. Murphy, D.K. Scott, S. Stokes, D.O.Tutt, N.H. Wilcock
Con: D.H. Barling, T.R. Bennett, W. Clements, D.C. Cumming, J. Langston, P.G. Lewis, K. Mason, P. Wright, S. Wrigley
Lab: E. Furey, L.E. Hamilton, J.A. Hazelgrove, J. Lepper, T. Randell, D. Turner, J.C. Warmington

Western Area

Comprehensive Schools

Blatchington Mill, Holmes Ave, Hove, E. Sussex; Tel (01273) 736244; Fax (01273) 739615; G. Tuffnell, BSc. (1316)
Cardinal Newman, The Upper Drive, Hove, E. Sussex; Tel (01273) 558551; Fax (01273) 508778; P. Evans. (1686)
Dorothy Stringer, Loder Rd, Brighton, E. Sussex; Tel (01273) 557311; Fax (01273) 562225; T. Allen. (1153)
Falmer, Lewes Rd, Falmer, Brighton, E. Sussex; Tel (01273) 691191; Fax (01273) 620478; J.J. Williams, BSc. (594)
Hove Pk, Nevill Rd, Hove, E. Sussex; Tel (01273) 733576; Fax (01273) 730091; P. Bratton, BSc. (1224)
Longhill, Falmer Rd, Rottingdean, Brighton, E. Sussex; Tel (01273) 304086; Fax (01273) 303547; P. Lonsdale (Acting). (987)
Patcham High School, Ladies Mile Rd, Patcham, Brighton, E. Sussex; Tel (01273) 503908; Fax (01273) 562896; E. Fletcher. (789)

Portslade Community College, Chalky Rd, Portslade, E. Sussex; Tel (01273) 416300; Fax (01273) 422129; M. Tait. (814)
Stanley Deason, Wilson Ave, Brighton, E. Sussex; Tel (01273) 692471; Fax (01273) 604137; E. Coleman. (842)
Varndean, Balfour Rd, Brighton, E. Sussex; Tel (01273) 561281; Fax (01273) 564614; P.A. Bowmaker, BA, MA. (829)

Central Area

Comprehensive Schools

Bishop Bell C. of E, Priory Rd, Eastbourne, E. Sussex; Tel (01323) 765151; Fax (01323) 765126; M.W. Ring, BA. (553)
Cavendish, Eldon Rd, Eastbourne, E. Sussex; Tel (01323) 731340; Fax (01323) 739572; A.C. Cornell, BEd, MEd. (906)
Chailey, Mill La, South Chailey, Lewes, E. Sussex; Tel (01273) 890407; Fax (01273) 890893; V.M. Howell. (461)
Crowborough Beacon Community College, East Beeches Rd, Crowborough, E. Sussex; Tel (01892) 653451; Fax (01892) 663763; A. Banks. (1727)
Filsham Valley, Edinburgh Rd, St Leonards on Sea; Tel (01424) 446247; Fax (01424) 722354; W.J. Voice, BSc, MEd. (148)
Hailsham, Battle Rd, Hailsham, E. Sussex; Tel (01323) 841468; Fax (01323) 848900; J.G. Quinn, BA. (1228)
Hampden Pk, Brodrick Rd, Eastbourne, E. Sussex; Tel (01323) 501036; Fax (01323) 500210; F.V. Wright. (871)
Heathfield Community College, Cade St, Heathfield, E. Sussex; Tel (01435) 866066; Fax (01435) 867155; R.S. Robinson, MA, BSc. (1027)
Lewes Priory, Mountfield Rd, Lewes, E. Sussex; Tel (01273) 476231; Fax (01273) 486922; K. Chaplin, BSc. (1026)
Newhaven Tideway, Southdown Rd, Newhaven, E. Sussex; Tel (01273) 517601; Fax (01273) 611182; K.L. Saxby, MA. (1405)
Ratton, Park Ave, Eastbourne, E. Sussex; Tel (01323) 504011; Fax (01323) 520364; A. Cockerham. (996)
Ringmer Community College, Ringmer, Lewes, E. Sussex; Tel (01273) 812220; Fax (01273) 813961; J.W. Wakely. (777)
Seaford Head, Arundel Rd, Seaford, E. Sussex; Tel (01323) 891623; Fax (01323) 492576; R. Precey. (1097)
Uckfield Community College, Downsview Cres, Uckfield, E. Sussex; Tel (01825) 764844; Fax (01825) 762946; D.H.J. Rebbitt, BA, MEd. (1173)
Uplands Community College, Uplands, Wadhurst, E. Sussex; Tel (01892) 782135; Fax (01892) 782135; D.L. James, MA. (912)
Willingdon, Broad Rd, Lower Willingdon, Eastbourne, E. Sussex; Tel (01323) 485254; Fax (01323) 487779; I.J. Jungius. (783)

Eastern Area

Comprehensive Schools

Bexhill High, Down Rd, Bexhill, E. Sussex; Tel (01424) 730722; Fax (01424) 212613; H.B. Baptist, BA. (1283)
Claverham Community College, North Trade Rd, Battle, E. Sussex; Tel (01424) 772155; Fax (01424) 774106; R. Pitts. (973)
The Grove, Darwell Cl, off Harley Shute Rd, St Leonard's, E. Sussex; Tel (01424) 431691; Fax (01424) 440060; P. Martin. (1340)
Helenswood, Cleeve, The Ridge, Hastings, E. Sussex; Tel (01424) 422470; Fax (01424) 446323; J. Blackburn. (1073)
Hillcrest, Rye Rd, Hastings, E. Sussex; Tel (01424) 423756; Fax (01424) 719842; A.L. Russell. (1250)
Robertsbridge Community College, Knelle Rd, Robertsbridge, E. Sussex; Tel (01580) 880360; Fax (01580) 882120; J. Richardson. (414)
St Richard's R.C., Ashdown Rd, Bexhill, E. Sussex; Tel (01424) 731070; Fax (01424) 215623; A. Campbell. (669)
Thomas Peacocke, The Grove, Rye, E. Sussex; Tel (01797) 222545; Fax (01797) 224343; B.M. Loydell. (928)
William Parker, Parkstone Rd, and Park Ave, Hastings, E. Sussex; Tel (01424) 439888; Fax (01424) 461472; R.J. Mitchell, MA, MEd. (1197)

Special Day Schools

Castledean, Lynchet Cl, Brighton BN1 7FP; Tel (01273) 702121; Fax (01273) 702112; V. Ellis
Cuckmere Hse, Eastbourne Rd, Seaford, E. Sussex; Tel (01323) 893319; F. Stanford
The Downs Beechy Ave, Eastbourne, E. Sussex; Tel (01323) 730302; E. Gidlow (Acting)
Downs Pk, Foredown Rd, Portslade, E. Sussex; Tel (01273) 417448; A.S. Jedras, MA
Downs View, Warren Rd, Brighton, E. Sussex; Tel (01273) 601680; Fax (01273) 699420; J. L. Reed
Glyne Gap, Hastings Rd, Bexhill, E. Sussex; Tel (01424) 217720; J.A. Hassell
Grove Pk, Church Rd, Crowborough, E. Sussex; Tel (01892) 663018; V.A. Alexander
Hazel Ct, Shinewater La, off Milfoil Dr, Eastbourne, E. Sussex; Tel (01323) 761061; P. Gordon
Hillside, Foredown Rd, Portslade, E. Sussex; Tel (01273) 416979; Fax (01273) 417512; *Head* R.J. Wall
Inglesea School, Tile Barn Rd, St Leonards-on-Sea, E. Sussex; Tel (01424) 853232; Fax (01424) 853704; L. Bush, BEd(Hons)
The Lindfield, Lindfield Rd, Eastbourne, E. Sussex; Tel (01323) 502988; Fax (01323) 500433; J.A. Nield, BA, DipSEd
Patcham Hse, Old London Rd, Brighton, E. Sussex; Tel (01273) 551028; R.L. Humphrey, BSc
Queensdown, Queensdown School Rd, Off Lewes Rd, Brighton, E. Sussex; Tel (01273) 604472; C.D. Kennedy
Robert Mitchell, All Saints La, Sidley, Bexhill, E. Sussex; Tel (01424) 222300; P.F. Viner, BSc
St Anne's, Rotten Row, Lewes, E. Sussex; Tel (01273) 473018; J. Arch
Saxon Mount, Edinburgh Rd, St Leonards-on-Sea, E. Sussex; Tel (01424) 426303; A. Wood, BA, MEd
Torfield, Croft Rd, Hastings, E. Sussex; Tel (01424) 428228; C.D. Owen, BEd(Hons), ACP
Uplands, Lynchet Cl, Brighton, E. Sussex; Tel (01273) 558622; R.J. Upward, MA

Special Residential School

St Mary's, Horam, Heathfield, E. Sussex; Tel (01435) 812278; Fax (01435) 813019; D.F. Bashford, DipEd

Residential Centre

County Education Centre, Corsica Hall, Cricketfield Rd, Seaford BN25 1BT; Tel (01323) 893556; *Centre Manager* J. Breeds

Professional Centres

T Block (University of Brighton), Falmer, Brighton BN1 9PH; Tel (01273) 601972; Fax (01273) 679248
High St, Uckfield, E. Sussex; Tel (01825) 762437; Fax (01825) 767278
Priory Rd, Hastings, E. Sussex; Tel (01424) 435971; Fax (01424) 443147
Trevin Towers, Gaudick Rd, Eastbourne, E. Sussex; Tel (01323) 643201; Fax (01323) 417657

East Sussex Music School,

Watergate La, Lewes BN7 1UQ; Tel (01273) 472336; Fax (01273) 486396
Director Dr Roy Wales

Essex County Council

Population 1,543,000
County Hall, Duke St, Chelmsford, Essex CM1 1LX; Tel (01245) 492211; Fax (01245) 352710

Education Department

PO Box 47, County Hall, A-Block, Chelmsford, Essex CM1 1LD; Tel (01245) 492211; Fax (01245) 492759
Chairman Cllr J.J. Gordon
Vice-Chairman Cllr D.M. Hardy
County Education Officer R. Michael Sharp, BA
Deputy County Education Officer P. Lincoln
Public Relations-CEO's Support Team M. Barnett
Principal Education Officer – Quality P. Evans
Head of Finance D. Price
Senior Liaison Officer C.R. Baxter
Senior Liaison Officer Mrs T. Canham
Senior Liaison Officer S. Leverett
Senior Liaison Officer B. Mellor
Senior Liaison Officer A. Porter
Senior Liaison Officer R. Slade
Service Unit Manager (Client Services) C. Bragg
Service Unit Manager (Careers and Business Partnerships) B. Catt
Service Unit Manager (Information Systems and Technology) W. Gooch
Service Unit Manager (Community Education and Post 16) J. Harris
Service Unit Manager (Pupil, Student and Parent Services) N. Hunt
Service Unit Manager (Essex Development and Advisory Services) D. Maclean
Service Unit Manager (Inspection Services) M. Phillips-Davies
Service Unit Manager (Learning Support and Special Needs) I.W. Pollard
Senior Education Officer (Special Projects) Vacancy
Education Officer (Consortia Department) D. Bateson
EO (Financial Services) I. Traynier, IPFA
Senior Manager (Major Projects and LMS) E. Hardy
Service Unit Manager (Personnel Services) S. Shipton
Senior Education Officer (Premises) P. Hodge, MA
Education Officer (Premises) K. Dobson, DipEd
Number of Schools (inc. Areas)
2 nursery; 582 primary; 89 comprehensive; 8 secondary selective; 4 secondary modern; 2 secondary boarding; 2 bilateral; 1 short term residential adult college; 3 residential youth centres; 1 residential field studies and sailing centre; 1 residential outdoor pursuits centre; 2 camp sites; 30 centres for community education; 61 youth centres; 7 centres for adult education
Special Schools
30 day; 6 residential
Day of Committee Meeting
Monday (four times a year)
Other Authorities with whom Joint Purchasing Arrangements are made
Essex Local Authority Supplies Consortium (Including London Boroughs), Eastern District Group Uniform Purchasing)

Education Committee

Con 14, Lab 14, LD 14, Ind 1
Chair J.J. Gordon, (LD) 67 High Rd, Rayleigh, Essex SS6 7SE
Vice-Chair D.M. Hardy, (LD) Meadowside School Rd, Kelvedon Hatch, Brentwood, Essex
Members of the Committee
Con: I.E. Abbey, D.F. Cotgrove, B.J. Jones, S. Kay, B.T. Kelly, G.W. McEwan, E. Mickelborough, D.F. Pallett, I. Pommell, D.F. Rex, E.W. Sullivan, B.L. Trevelyan, D.A. Westcott, P.E.W. White
Lab: S. Anderson, W. Archibald, E. Bishop, P. Bolger, P.A. Bruce, F.E.T. Card, F.J. Davis, G. Fox, M.S. Jones, J.M. Lyn, G.R. Miles, E.I.V. Morris, G. Shearwood, R.G. Smith
LD: G.E.E. Allen, M.H. Caton, E.B. Davis, P.G. Evans, M.D. Fisher, K. Jones, J.N. Lefever, M.R. Lubel, D. Rice, P.A. Smith, T.C. Smith-Hughes, A.F. Smuleian
Ind: R. Knight

Governor Training Unit

Governor Development–EDAS, PO Box 47, County Hall, Victoria Rd South, Chelmsford, Essex CM1 1LD; Tel (01245) 494443; Fax (01245) 344652
Governor Development Consultant Dianne Johnstone
Services Offered
Full range of training sessions open to all Governors; Training sessions arranged for individual Governing Bodies, plus Clusters; Conferences for special school and teacher governors packages for GM schools; Termly newsletter and publication of handbooks

North West Essex Area (Uttlesford and Braintree)

Area Education Office, Crossman Hse, Station Approach, Braintree CM7 6QA; Tel (01376) 550202; Fax (01376) 550077
Area Office Manager Heather Currie

Comprehensive Schools (11–16)

Alec Hunter High, Stubbs La, Braintree CM7 6NR; Tel (01376) 321813; H. Ritchie. (7FE)
Honywood, Westfield Dr, Coggeshall CO6 1PZ; Tel (01376) 561231; K Hotchin. 4FE
Mountfitchet, Forest Hall Rd, Stansted CM24 8TZ; Tel (01279) 813384; D. Williams. (4FE)

Comprehensive Schools (11–18)

Hedingham, Yeldham Rd, Sibble Hedingham, Halstead CO9 3QH; Tel (01787) 60470; S. Anderson. (7FE)
Notley High, Notley Rd, Braintree CM7 8JX; Tel (01376) 323601; A. Davison. (7FE)
The Ramsey, Colne Rd, Halstead CO9 2HR; Tel (01787) 472481; A.G. Davies. (7FE)
Tabor High, Panfield La, Braintree CM7 5XP; Tel (01376) 323701; F.R. Snelling. (7FE)

North East Essex Area (Colchester and Tendring)

Area Education Office, Park Rd, Colchester C03 3UP; Tel (01206) 763611; Fax (01206) 574292
Area Office Manager J. Morley

Comprehensive Schools (11–16)

Alderman Blaxill, Walnut Tree Way, Colchester CO2 9BU; Tel (01206) 579693; V. Cresswell. (5FE)
Manningtree County, Colchester Rd, Lawford, Manningtree CO11 2BW; Tel (01206) 392852; M. Nesbitt. (4FE)
St Benedict's R.C., Norman Way, Colchester CO3 3US; Tel (01206) 549222; A. Whelan. (4FE)
Thomas Lord Audley, Monkwick Ave, Monkwick, Colchester CO2 8NN; Tel (01206) 47911; M. Howard. (8FE)

West Essex Area (Epping Forest and Harlow)

Area Education Office, St John's Rd, Epping CM16 5EB; Tel (01992) 560616; Fax (01992) 578831
Area Office Manager B. Harphann

Secondary Comprehensive Schools (11–16)

Brays Grove, Tracyes Rd, Harlow CM18 6JH; Tel (01279) 439161; Fax (01279) 435339; H. Binns, BA MA. (7FE)
Burnt Mill, First Ave, Harlow CM20 2NR; Tel (01279) 421138; Fax (01279) 422651; A.R. Ward. (7FE)
Mark Hall, First Ave, Harlow CM17 9LR; Tel (01279) 439121; Fax (01279) 635113; R.J. James, BSc. (7FE)
Passmores, Tendring Rd, Harlow CM18 6RW; Tel (01279) 431921; Fax (01279) 445515; P. Jarman, BA. (7FE)
Roding Valley High School, Alderton Hill, Loughton IG10 3JA; Tel 0181-508-1173; C.N. Manning
St John's, Tower Rd, Epping CM16 5EN; Tel (01378) 73028; J. Edwards. (7FE)
Stewards, Parnall Rd, Harlow CM18 7NQ; Tel (01279) 421951; Fax (01279) 435307; Rhonda Murthar, BA MA (Ed). (7FE)

Mid Essex Area (Chelmsford, Maldon and Brentwood)

County Hall, A-Block, Chelmsford CM1 1LB
Area Office Manager Vacancy

Secondary Comprehensive Schools (11–18)

Moulsham High, Brian Cl, Chelmsford CM2 9ES; Tel (01245) 260101/2/3; Dr C. Nicholls, BSc, PhD. (8FE)
St John Payne R.C., Patching Hall La, Chelmsford CM1 4DJ; Tel (01245) 256030; J.A. McDonald, LLB Adv.DipEd. (6FE)
St Peter's, Southminster Rd, Burnham-on-Crouch CM0 8QB; Tel (01621) 782377; G.S.W. Nash, BSc. (8FE)
Sandon, Molrams La, Great Baddow CM2 7AQ; Tel (01245) 473611/4; I.S Nicholson, BA. (8FE)
Shenfield, Alexander La, Chelmsford Rd, Shenfield, Brentwood CM15 8RY; Tel (01277) 219131. (7FE)
Ursuline Convent, Queen's Rd, Brentwood CM14 4EX; Tel (01277) 227156; E. Ranzetta, MA. (4FE)

South West Essex Area (Basildon and Thurrock)

Area Education Office, The Knares, Basildon SS16 5RX; Tel (01268) 544022; Fax (01268) 415122
Area Office Manager M. Denmark

Comprehensive Schools (11–18)

Aveley, Nethan Dr, Aveley RM15 4RU; Tel (01708) 865180; G.A. Coop, MA, MEd. (6FE)
Billericay, School Rd, Billericay CM12 9LH; Tel (01277) 655191; R. Goodler, BSc. (9FE)
Fryerns, Craylands, Basildon SS14 3RN; Tel (01268) 525111; T.R. Slater. (10FE)
Grays Convent, College Ave, Grays RM17 5UX; Tel (01375) 376173; (Sister Paul) M.M. O'Reilly. (4FE)
Laindon, High Rd, Laindon, Basildon SS15 6DD; Tel (01268) 545871/545603; P.C. Newton. (8FE)
Mayflower County High, Stock Rd, Billericay CM12 0RT; Tel (01277) 623171; Dr G.H. Smith, BSc, ALC. (10FE)
Nicholas, St Nicholas La, Basildon SS15 5NX; Tel (01268) 543391; J.K. Cooper. (8FE)
St Anselm's R.C., Ghyllgrove, Basildon SS14 2LA; Tel (01268) 281234; (Brother Mark) A.J. O'Rourke, BA. (6FE)
The Ockendon School, Erriff Drive, South Ockendon RM15 5AY; Tel (01708) 851661; M.F. Batten. (6FE)
St Chad's, St Chad's Rd, Tilbury RM18 8LH; Tel (0137 51) 845381; D.A. Anderson. (7FE)
Woodlands, Takely End, Basildon SS16 5BA; Tel (01268) 282146; A. White. (10FE)

South East Essex Area (Southend-on-Sea, Castle Point and Rochford)

Area Education Office, Civic Centre, Victoria Ave, Southend-on-Sea SS2 6DD; Tel (01702) 355000; Fax (01702) 432273
Area Office Manager M. Denmark

Secondary Schools

The Notley High School Notley Rd, Braintree CM7 8JX; Tel (01376) 323601; A. Davison
The Tabor High School Panfield La, Braintree CM7 5XP; Tel (01376) 323701; F.R. Snelling. Boys
The Helena Romanes School; R.W. Street. Boys
The Ramsey School Colne Rd, Halstead C09 2HR; Tel (01787) 472481; A.G. Davies. Boys
Hedingham School Yeldham Rd, Sible Hedingham, Halstead C09 3QH; Tel (01787) 60470; S. Anderson. Boys

Secondary Modern Schools (11–16)

Prittlewell High, Boston Ave, Southend-on-Sea SS2 6JH; Tel (01702) 343233; M. Barr, MA, DipEd. 6FE
The Park, Rawreth La, Rayleigh SS6 9RN; Tel (01268) 781322; J.C. Jackman. (7FE)
Sweyne, Pearsons Ave, Rayleigh SS6 9BZ; Tel (01268) 784721; K. Wood. (7FE)

Secondary Bilateral (Selective/Modern School 11–18)

St Bernard's Convent High, Milton Rd, Westcliffe-on-Sea SS0 7JS; Tel (01702) 343583; J.M. Ballard, BA. (Girls) (4FE)

Secondary Comprehensive School (11–18)

Shoeburyness High, Caulfield Rd, Shoeburyness SS3 9QW; Tel (01702) 292286; J.K.W. Gardiner. (Mixed) (7FE)

Careers Service

See chapter 17

Special Day Schools

Castledon, Bromfords Dr, Wickford SS12 0PW; Tel (01268) 761252; P.B. Webster. (MLD)
Cedar Hall, Hart Rd, Thundersley SS7 3UQ; Tel (01268) 774723; C. Bent. (MLD)
Commonside School, Commonside Rd, Harlow CM18 7EZ; Tel (01279) 427465; M. Woods. (MLD); (Secondary)
Edith Borthwick, Fennes Rd, Church St, Bocking, Braintree CM7 5LA; Tel (01376) 326436; M. Jelly. (MLD) (SLD); (B)
Elmbrook, Church Rd, Basildon SS14 2EX; Tel (01268) 521808; D. Ainsley. (SLD)
Fairview, Fairview Rd, Basildon SS14 1PW; Tel (01268) 552482; J. Lewis. (Emotional & Behavioural)
Glenwood, Rushbottom La, New Thundersley, Benfleet SS7 4LW; Tel (01268) 792575; T. Baker. (SLD)
Kingsdown, Snakes La, Eastwood, Leigh-on-Sea SS2 6XT; Tel (01702) 527486; J.F. Hagyard. (LD and Emotional & Behavioural) (Physical Handicap)
Kingswode Hoe, Sussex Rd, Colchester CO3 3QJ; Tel (01206) 576408; B. Walsh. (MLD)
Knightsmead Fortin Close, South Ockendon RM15 5NH; Tel (01708) 852956; J.P Misra. (SLD)
Lancaster, Prittlewell Chase, Westcliff SS0 0RT; Tel (01702) 342543; D. Victor. (SLD)
Leas, Leas Rd, Clacton CO15 1DY; Tel (01255) 426288; E.A. Barkley. (MLD)
Lexden Springs, Halstead Rd, Lexden, Colchester CO3 5AB; Tel (01206) 563321; S.H. Goldsmith. (SLD)
Market Field, School Rd, Elmstead Market, Nr Colchester CO7 7ET; Tel (01206) 825195; A.S. Kaye. (MLD)
Mead School, Tendring Rd, Harlow CM18 6RN; Tel (01279) 423488; A.J. Fowler. (MLD) (Primary)
Moat House, Church Rd, Basildon SS14 2NQ; Tel (01268) 522077; D.B. Sims. (MLD)
Peter Kirk, Chapel Hill, Stansted CM24 8AG; Tel (01279) 815359; H.M. Philips. (MLD) (SLD)

Priory, Burr Hill Chase, Southend-on-Sea SS2 6PE; Tel (01702) 347490; J. Holliday. (Emotional & Behavioural)
St Christopher, Mountdale Gardens, Leigh-on-Sea SS9 4AW; Tel (01702) 524193; T.G. Wilson. (MLD)
St Luke's School, Borders La, Loughton IG10 1TE; Tel 0181-508 4293; S.P. Armstrong. (MLD) (SLD)
St Nicholas, Philpott Ave, Southend-on-Sea SS2 4RL; Tel (01702) 462322; G.M. Houghton. (MLD)
South View School Black Notley, nr Braintree CM7 8NF; Tel (01376) 326447; G.W. Currie. (D)
Thriftwood, Slades La, Galleywood CM2 8RW; Tel (01245) 266880; P. Smith. (MLD)
Treetops, Dell Rd, Grays RM17 5LH; Tel (01375) 372723; F.D. Pardoe. (MLD)
Tye Green School, Tendring Rd, Harlow CM18 6RN; Tel (01279) 423670; M.A. Henderson. (SLD)
Windsor, Windsor Ave, Clacton CO15 2AH; Tel (01255) 424412; J.M. Hobley. (SLD)
Woodlands, Patching Hall La, Chelmsford CM1 4BX; Tel (01245) 355854; O. Caviglioli. (SLD)

Special Residential Schools

The Heath, Winstree Rd, Stanway, Colchester CO3 5QE; Tel (01206) 571379; C.F.A. Creasy. (Emotional & Behavioural) (Secondary)
Homestead, School Rd, Langham, nr Colchester CO4 5PA; Tel (01206) 272303; W.D. Mitchell. (Emotional & Behavioural) (Secondary)
Nazeing Park School, Betts La, Nazeing Common, Waltham Abbey EN9 2DN; Tel (01992) 893107; D. Wood. (Emotional & Behavioural) (Primary)
Ramsden Hall, Ramsden Heath, Billericay CM11 1HN; Tel (01277) 624580; S. Grant. (Emotional & Behavioural) (Secondary

Secondary Boarding Schools

Elmbridge, Fyfield, Ongar CM5 0HR; Tel (01277) 899207. (Boys) (2FE)
Hockerill, Dunmow Rd, Bishops Stortford CM23 5HX; Tel (01279) 658451; Vacancy. Mixed) (3FE

Teachers' Centres and Curriculum Development Centres

Mid-Essex Curriculum Development Centre, First Floor, Gordon Hall, Duffield Rd, Gr Baddow, Chelmsford CM2 9SW; Tel (01245) 494291; *Centre Manager* Carol Hodgson
North East Curriculum Development Centre, The Sir Charles Lucas School, Acacia Ave, Colchester CO4 3TQ; Tel (01206) 863869/860936; *Centre Manager* Pauline Doubtfire
North West Curriculum Development Centre, Saffron Walden High School, Audley End Rd, Saffron Walden CB11 4UH; Tel (01799) 22761; *Centre Manager* H. Batchelor
South East Curriculum Development Centre, School Way, Off Blenheim Rd, Leigh-on-Sea SS9 4HX; Tel (01702) 471942; *Centre Manager* Vacancy
South West Curriculum Development Centre, Barn Hall, Alderney Gardens, Wickford SS11 7JZ; Tel (01268) 769646; *Centre Manager* Alan Rivers
West Essex Curriculum Development Centre, Abbotsweld, Partridge Rd, Harlow CM18 6TE; Tel (01279) 451854/411490; *Centre Manager* Janet Mumford

Centres for Adult Education and Centres for Community Education

Basildon Centre for Adult Education, Fryerns School, Craylands, Basildon, Essex; Tel (01268) 520599; M.R.G. French
Benfleet/Hadleigh Centre for Community Education, 114 Benfleet Rd, Hadleigh, Essex; Tel (01702) 556622; R. Martin
Billericay Centre for Community Education, Perry St, Billericay CM12 0NX; Tel (01277) 656563
Brentwood Centre for Adult Education, Bishops Hill, Rayleigh Rd, Hutton, Essex; Tel (9972) 218593; A. Bell
Brightlingsea Centre for Community Education, Church Rd, Brightlingsea, Essex; Tel (0120 630) 3511; P.C. Overton
Burnham Centre for Community Education, St Peter's School, Southminster Rd, Burnham-on-Couch, Essex; Tel (01621) 785149; K. Grantham
Canvey Island Centre for Community Education, Furtherwick Park School, Furtherwick Rd, Canvey Island, Essex; Tel (01268) 682426; S. Pollock
Chelmsford Centre for Adult Education, Patching Hall La, Chelmsford, Essex; Tel (01245) 263013; M. Flude
Clacton Centre for Community Education, Green Lodge, 180 Old Rd, Clacton, Essex; Tel (01255) 424151; J. Bird
Colchester Centre for Adult Education, Greyfriars, High St, Colchester, Essex; Tel (01206) 42242; A. Skinner
Culver Centre for Community Education, Daiglen Dr, South Ockendon RM15 5RR
Dunmow Centre for Adult Education, Helena Romanes School, Parsonage Down, Dunmow, Essex; Tel Great Dunmow 874079
Epping Centre for Community Education, St John's Rd, Epping, Essex; Tel (01378) 75055; M. Taylor
Frinton & Walton Centre for Community Education, Tendring High School (Senior), Rochford Way, Frinton-on-Sea, Essex; Tel (0125 56) 6085; C. Hursey
Grays Centre for Adult Education, Bridge Rd, Grays, Essex; Tel (01375) 372476; D. Hale
Halstead Centre for Community Education, Parsonage St, Halstead, Essex; Tel (01787) 472498; D. Marner
Harlow Centre for Adult Education, Hodings Rd, Harlow CM20 1NW; Tel (01279) 427711/2; P. Boshier
Harwich Centre for Community Education, Main Rd, Dovercourt, Harwich, Essex; Tel (0125 55) 2467; C. Thorpe
Hedingham Centre for Community Education, Hedingham School, Yeldham Rd, Sible Hedingham, Halstead, Essex; Tel (01787) 61140; R. Raymond
Hockley Centre for Community Education, Greensward School, Greensward La, Hockley, Essex; Tel (01702) 207070; G. James
Honywood Community School, Honywood School, Westfield Dr, Coggeshall CO6 1PZ
Maldon Centre for Community Education, The Friary, Chequers La, Maldon, Essex; Tel (01621) 853337; C. Badshaw
Mersea Island Centre for Community Education, West Mersea Primary School, Bardfield Rd, West Mersea, Essex; Tel (01206) 382229 (evenings only); S. Powell
Ongar Centre for Community Education, Ongar School Campus, Fyfield Rd, Ongar, Essex; Tel Ongar 363774; K. Trobridge
The Prettygate Centre for Community Education, Philip Morant School, Rembrandt Way, Colchester, Essex; Tel (01206) 577458; L. Barton
Rayleigh Centre for Community Education, 72 Hockley Rd, Rayleigh, Essex; Tel (01268) 742500; O. Stone
Rocheway Centre for Community Education, Rocheway, Rochford, Essex; Tel (01702) 544900; A. Dykes
Saffron Walden Centre for Community Education, Fairycroft, Audley Rd, Saffron Walden, Essex; Tel (01799) 527109; K. Watson
Southend Centre for Adult Education, Ambleside Dr, Southend, Essex; Tel (01702) 610196/7; Dr M.G. Jones
Stanford Centre for Community Education, Hassenbrook School, Hassenbrook Rd, Stanford-le-Hope, Essex
Stansted Centre for Community Education, Lower St, Stanstead, Essex; Tel (01279) 813319; N. Varnam
Stanway Centre for Community Education, Straight Rd, Lexdon, Colchester CO3 5QA
Thorpe-le-Soken Centre for Community Education, Tendring High School (Junior), Landermere Rd, Thorpe le Soken, Clacton-on-Sea, Essex; Tel (01255) 861504; C. Hussey
Tiptree Centre for Community Education, Thurstable School, Maypole Rd, Tiptree, Essex; Tel (01621) 816527; J. Farnsworth
Waltham Abbey Centre for Community Education, King Harold School, Broomstickhall Rd, Waltham Abbey, Essex; Tel Lea Valley 716380

Wickford Centre for Community Education, Beauchamps School, Beauchamps Dr, Wickford, Essex; Tel (0137 44) 734926/762666; R. Olver
William de Ferrers Centre for Community Education, Trinity Sq, South Woodham Ferrers CM3 5JU
Witham Centre for Community Education, Central Office, Spinks La, Witham, Essex; Tel (01376) 516533; J. Thomas
Wivenhoe Centre for Community Education Phillip Rd, Wivenhoe, Essex; Tel (01206) 823746; P. Overton

Outdoor Pursuits Centres

Bradwell Field Studies and Sailing Centre, Bradwell Waterside, nr Southminster CMO 7QY; Tel (01621) 776256; P.G. Gurnell
Harlow Outdoor Pursuits Centre, Burnt Mill La, Harlow, Essex; Tel (01279) 432031; C. Nielson; (non-residential)
Maes-y-Lade Outdoor Pursuits Centre, Tregoyd, Brecon, Powys; Tel (01497) 847287; G.O.I. Evans

Residential Centres

Clarance Hse, Thaxted; Tel (01994) 830245; H. Gascoigne
Wicken Hse, Wicken Bonhunt, nr Newport, Essex; Tel (01799) 40216; B. Hooper

Youth Camps

Danbury Pk, Chelmsford; Tel (01245) 413320; G. Birch
East Mersea, Colchester; Tel (01206) 383226; D. Powell

Grant Maintained Schools

The Appleton School, Croft Rd, Benfleet, Essex SS4 5RN; Tel (01268) 794215; Fax (01268) 759981; G.A. Naylor, BA. (11FE)
Barstable School Grant Maintained, Timberlog Cl, Basildon SS14 1UX; Tel (01268) 552091; A.C. Little. (9FE)
Chalvedon School, Wickford Ave, Pitsea, Basildon SS13 3HL; Tel (01268) 552536; Fax (01268) 551209
Beauchamps GM School, Beauchamps Dr, Wickford, Essex SS11 8LY; Tel (01268) 735466; J.H. Davies. (9FE)
Belfairs School and Sixth Form Centre, Highlands Blvd, Leigh-on-Sea SS9 3TG; Tel (01702) 74496/75783; M. Younie, BSc(Hons), BA. 5FE
The Boswells School, Burnham Rd, Springfield, Chelmsford, Essex CM1 5LY; Tel (01245) 264451; Fax (01245) 350142; K. Arkell, BSc, MEd, MIMgt. 8FE
Brentwood County High, Shenfield Common CM14 4JE; Tel (01277) 226482; Fax (01277) 200853; M.R.J. Trett, BSc. (8FE)
Bromfords School GM, Grange Ave, Wickford, Essex SS12 0LZ; Tel (01268) 763121; N.E.J. Poad. (6FE)
Castle View School, Mapple Ave, Canvey Island, Essex SS8 9RZ; Tel (01268) 696811; E. Simmons, BA. 6FE
Cecil Jones High School, Eastern Ave, Southend-on-Sea SS2 4BU; Tel (01702) 468000; R.B. Hellen, BSc(Hons), MA. (Mixed) (8FE)
Chelmer Valley High School, Court Rd, Broomfield, Chelmsford CM1 5ER; Tel (01245) 440232; D. Franklin, BSc. 7FE
Chelmsford County High School for Girls, Broomfield Rd, Chelmsford, Essex CM1 1RW; Tel (01245) 352592; Fax (01245) 345746; B. McCabe, BA. Girls) (3FE
Clacton County High School, Walton Rd, Clacton-on-Sea CO15 6DZ; Tel (01255) 424266; J. Clay. (8FE)
Colbayns High School, Pathfields Rd, Clacton-on-Sea CO15 3JL; Tel (01255) 428131; J. Holt. (9FE)
Colchester County High School for Girls, Norman Way, Lexden Rd, Colchester CO3 3US; Tel (01206) 576973; Fax (01206) 769302; Dr A.M. Black. (Girls) (3FE)
Colchester Royal Grammar School, Lexden Rd, Colchester CO3 3ND; Tel (01206) 577971; S.A.C. Francis. Boys) (3FE
The Colne Community School and Colne College, Church Rd, Brightlingsea CO7 0QL; Tel (01206) 303511; Fax (01206) 302258; Terry Creissen, MA. (8FE)
The Cornelius Vermuyden School, Dinant Ave, Canvey Island, Essex SS8 9SU; Tel (01268) 685011; S.M. Blackshaw, BSc. 7FE
Davenant Foundation School, Chester Rd, Loughton, Essex IG10 2LD; Tel (01378) 812608; D. Daniels. (5FE)
The Deanes School (Grant Maintained), Daws Heath Rd, Thundersley, Benfleet, Essex SS7 2TD; Tel (01268) 773545; P. Beashel, BEd, MEd. 7FE
Eastwood County High School, Rayleigh Rd, Leigh-on-Sea SS9 5UT; Tel (01702) 524341; A. Harrison, BA. 4FE
The Fitzwimarc School, 72 Hockley Rd, Rayleigh, Essex SS6 8EB; Tel (01268) 743884; D.W. Cox, BA. 7FE
Furtherwick Park, Furtherwick Rd, Canvey Island SS8 7AZ; Tel (01268) 682157/8; L.I. Tooke. 8FE
Gable Hall School, Southend Rd, Corringham, Stanford-le-Hope, Essex SS17 8JT; Tel (01375) 671526; Fax (01375) 642505; J. King. (9FE)
The Gilberd School, Brinkley La, Highwoods, Colchester, Essex C04 4PU; Tel (01206) 842211; D.J. Rowe. (8FE)
The Grays School (GM), Hathaway Rd, Grays RM17 5LL; Tel (01375) 371361; Fax (01375) 382743; J.J.H. Winstone, BSc, MIMgt. (6FE)
Great Baddow, Duffield Rd, Beehive La, Chelmsford CM2 9RZ; Tel (01245) 265821; R. Hunton, MSc. 8FE
The Greensward School, Greensward La, Hockley SS5 5HG; Tel (01702) 202571/2; Fax (01702) 200083; D.A. Triggs, BEd(Hons), MSc. 8FE
The Harwich School, Hall La, Dovercourt, Harwich CO12 3TG; Tel (01255) 506272; T.J. McAleavy. (8FE)
Hassenbrook Grant Maintained School, Hassenbrook Rd, Stanford-le-Hope SS17 0NS; Tel (01375) 671566; Dr G. Casey. (9FE)
The Hedley Walter School, Sawyers Hall La, Brentwood, Essex CM15 9DA; Tel (01277) 220808; D. Spinney, MA. (7FE)
The Helena Romanes School, Parsonage Downs, Great Dunmow CM6 2AU; Tel (01371) 872560; R.W. Street. (8FE)
Hylands School, Hatfield Gr, Chelmsford CM1 3DF; Tel (01245) 266766; T. Mulholland, MA, MSc. (6FE)
Ingatestone Anglo–European School, Willow Grn, Ingatestone, Essex CM4 0DS; Tel (01277) 354018
The John Bramston School, Spinks La, Witham CM8 1EB; Tel (01376) 512911; Fax (01376) 501076; E.N. Rowley. (8FE)
The King Edmund School, Vaughan Cl, Rochford, Essex SS4 1TL; Tel (01702) 545771; Fax (01702) 549662; G.A. Abel, BA, DASE, DMS, MIM. (9FE)
King Edward VI Grammar School, Broomfield Rd, Chelmsford, Essex CM1 3SX; Tel (01245) 353510; Fax (01245) 344741; A.D. Tuckwell, MA, FRSA. (Boys) (3FE)
King Harold School, Broomstick Hall Rd, Waltham Abbey, Essex EN9 1LF; Tel (01992) 714800; M.G. Ward. (8FE)
The King John School, Shipwrights Dr, Thundersley, Benfleet, Essex SS7 1RQ; Tel (01702) 558284; Fax (01702) 555636; *Headteacher* F. Yeomans; *Chair of Governors* Brian Belcher. (Mixed) (11–18) (1475)
Newport Free Grammar School, Newport, Saffron Walden CB11 3TR; Tel (01799) 540237; Fax (01799) 542189; R. Priestley. (4FE)
The Philip Morant School Rembrandt Way, Gainsborough Rd, Colchester, Essex CO3 4QS; Tel (01206) 45222; D. Jones
The Plume School, Fambridge Rd, Maldon CM9 6AB; Tel (01621) 854681; *Headteacher* Alan J. Bilby; *Chair of Governors* Graham Mott. (Mixed) (11–18) (1750)
Rainsford School, Fox Cres, Chelmsford CM1 2BL; Tel (01245) 265511; T.S. Chadd, BA, MEd. (5FE)
Rickstones School, Conrad Rd, Witham, Essex CM2 2SD; Tel (01376) 515756; N. Turner. (5FE)
St Clere's School, Butts La, Stanford-le-Hope SS17 0NW; Tel (01375) 641001; P. Griffiths. (6FE)
St Helena School, Sheepen Rd, Colchester CO3 3LE; Tel (01206) 572253; Fax (01206) 43049; C. Waddington. (6FE)
St Mark's West Essex Catholic Comprehensive School (GM), Tripton Rd, Harlow CM18 6AA; Tel (01279) 421267; D.J. Brunwin. (5FE)
St Martin's School, Hanging Hill La, Hutton, Brentwood CM13 2HG; Tel (01277) 227650; J.W. Telling. (8FE)

St Thomas More RC High School for Boys Grant Maintained, Kenilworth Gdns, Westcliff-on-Sea SS0 0BW; Tel (01702) 344933; F. Keenan, BA. (Boys) (4FE)
Sir Charles Lucas Grant Maintained School, Hawthorn Ave, Colchester CO4 3JL; Tel (01206) 861217/861218; Fax (01206) 865940; L.E. Bamford. (8FE)
South Woodham, The William De Ferrers, Trinity Sq, South Woodham Ferrers CM3 5JU; Tel (01245) 329555; D.J. Parry, BSc. (6FE)
Southend High School, Prittlewell Chase, Southend-on-Sea SS0 0RG; Tel (01702) 343074; E.G. Morris, MA. (Boys) (4FE)
Southend High School for Girls, Southchurch Blvd, Southend-on-Sea SS2 4UZ; Tel (01702) 588852; W. Tribe, BA. (Girls) (4FE)
The Stanway School, Winstree Rd, Stanway, Colchester CO3 5QA; Tel (01206) 575488; Fax (01206) 564164; *Head* I. Carrington. (8FE)
Tendring High Lower, Landermere Rd, Thorpe-le-Soken CO16 0LQ; Tel (01255) 672116; M. Watson. (8FE)
Tendring High School, Rochford Way, Frinton-on-Sea CO13 0AZ; Tel (01255) 672116; Fax (01255) 850210; *Headteacher* M. Watson. 8FE
The Thorpe Bay School, Southchurch Blvd, Southend-on-Sea SS2 4UY; Tel (01702) 586123; B.G. Sandford, BA. (6FE)
Thurstable School, Maypole Rd, Tiptree, Colchester CO5 0EW; Tel (01621) 816526; Fax (01621) 815409; N.H. Hammond. (7FE)
Torells School, Buxton Rd, Grays, Essex RM16 4XN; Tel (01375) 371351; Fax (01375) 394783
West Hatch High School, High Rd, Chigwell, Essex IG7 5BT; Tel 0181-504 8216; G.N. Phipson. (6FE)
Westcliff High School for Boys Kenilworth Gdns, Westcliff-on-Sea, Southend SSO 0BP; Tel (01702) 75443; *Headmaster* Andrew John Baker; *Chair of Governors* Paul Bateman. (11–18) (857)
Westcliff High School for Girls, Kenilworth Gdns, Westcliff-on-Sea, Essex SS0 0BS; Tel (01702) 76026; P. Elliott, MA. (Girls) (4FE)
William de Ferrers School, Trinity Sq, South Woodham Ferrers, Essex CM3 5JU; Tel (01245) 329555; Fax (01245) 321996; D.J. Parry, BSc. 1O FE
William Edwards School, Stifford Clays Rd, Stifford Clays, Grays RM16 3NJ; Tel (01375) 379571; E.R. Van-Tromp. (8FE)

Technology Colleges

Central Technology CollegeSponsored by the Garfield Weston foundation, Systems Integrated Research, Chartwells, Denford Machine Tools, AT Poeton (Gloucester Plating), Permali (Gloucester), C M Downton and Birds Eye Walls Cotteswold Rd, Gloucester GL4 9RN; Tel (01452) 526131; John H. Smith, BSc. (Boys) (Mixed Sixth Form) (750)
Chalvedon School, Sponsored by the Garfield Weston Foundation, Fairfield Catering, MISE, Roy Millard Associates, the SIMS Centre and PMD Associates Wickford Ave, Pitsea, Basildon SS13 3HL; Tel (01268) 552536; Fax (01268) 551209; *Headmaster* Alan Roach; *Chairman of Governors* L. Pounder. Mixed (11–18) (1500)
Saffron Walden Grant Maintained County High School, Sponsored by the Garfield Weston Foundation, Acorn Computers, Messrs Wilby and Burnett and others Audley End Rd, Saffron Walden, Essex CB11 4UH; Tel (01799) 513030; D.J. Boatman. (8FE)

Gateshead Metropolitan Borough Council

Population 203,072

Civic Centre, Regent St, Gateshead, Tyne & Wear NE8 1HH; Tel 0191-477 1011; Fax 0191-477 5154

Education Department

Civic Centre, Regent St, Gateshead, Tyne and Wear NE8 1HH; Tel 0191-477 1011
Chairman Cllr I. Mearns
Vice-Chairman Councillor Cllr P. Mole
Director of Education J.D. Arbon, BA
Deputy Director of Education and Head of Central Services Division P. Johnson, BSc
Head of Curriculum and Inspection G. Carter
Head of Operational Support Division Vacancy
Principal Officer (Financial Management) M. Curry, MA
Principal Officer (Establishment Support) N. Busby, BSc
Principal Officer (Community Education) P. Stout
Principal Officer (Staffing) G. P. Falkenau, BA
Principal Officer (Property Services) P. McIntosh
Principal Officer (Training) E. Forster
Administrative Officer (General Administration) D. Moore
Senior Administrative Officer (Curriculum Administration) J. G. Watson
Principal Officer (Curriculum Development) I. Hills, BA, MEd
Principal Officer (Inspection and Review) D. Sleighholme
Principal Officer (Learning Support) K. Woods
Principal Officer (Staff Training and Development) R.A. Steele
Inspection and Review Officer K. Self
Staff Development Adviser A. Davies
General Phase Adviser P. Pritchard
Staff Development Adviser M.C. Coburn
Staff Development Adviser P. Zarraga
Curriculum Development Adviser R. Hemstock
Curriculum Development Adviser I. Tairns
Curriculum Development Adviser J. Nichol
Learning Support Adviser G. James
Learning Support Adviser R. Bain
Learning Support Adviser D. McNiven
Learning Support Adviser Vacancy
Education Business Partnership Manager C. Nesbitt
Compact Manager P. Saint
Music Development Leader J. Treherne, MA, LTCL
Principal Careers Officer W.M. Howard
Principal Educational Psychologist R.A. Campion
Educational Psychologist E.A. Elliot
Educational Psychologist R.D. Waterhouse
Educational Psychologist V.C. Besag
Educational Psychologist C.P. Martin
Educational Psychologist Vacancy
Educational Psychologist M. Brown
Educational Psychologist J. Hill
Educational Psychologist T. Broderick
TVEI Project Co-ordinator H. Ridley
Chief Executive Officer L. N. Elton
Number of Schools
1 nursery; 35 nursery classes; 81 primary; 13 secondary;
Special Schools
5 day (405); 1 day/residential EBD
Day of Committee Meeting
1st Monday in Month

Education Committee

Lab 21, LD 3, Con 1
Chair Cllr I. Mearns, (Lab) 192 Rodsley Ave, Gateshead NE8 4LB
Vice-Chair P. Mole, (Lab) 58 Merseyside, Leam La NE10 8UN
Members of the Committee
Lab: W. E. Ainsworth, D. Bollands, A.S. Brown, K.M. Dodds, G. Gill, W. Gordon, J.S. Green, L. Green, M. Henry, McNestry, J.I. Mearns, P.J. Mole, M. Robson, T.M. Rook, P.F. Tinnion, G.K. Wilson
LD: F. Hindle, P. Nunn, N.G. Rippeth
Con: M.J. Callanan

3 Local Government England and Wales

Governor Training Unit

Dryden Professional Development Centre, Evistones Rd, Gateshead NE9 5UR; Tel 0191-482 4133 Ext 143; Fax 0191-491 1394
Governor Training Co-ordinator P. Arnold
(Trained teacher with administrative experience)
Services Offered
Training Programme support for individual Governing Bodies in development of their own training programme and use of GEST funding through provision of newsletter, training materials and equipment

Careers Office

See chapter 17

Education Welfare

Education Dept, Civic Centre, Regent St, Gateshead NE8 1HH
Chief Education Welfare Officer K. Johnson

Behavioural Support

Shipcote Centre, Avenue Rd, Gateshead NE8 4LQ

Special Schools

Bleach Green, Blaydon, Tyne and Wear NE21 5HS; Tel 0191-414 4233; B. Howarth (Temp). (4–19) (E.S.N.(S)
The Cedars, Ivy La, Gateshead, Tyne and Wear NE9 6QD; Tel 0191-487 7591; M. Hutchinson. (3–16) (P.H.)
Furrowfield, Whitehills Dr, Felling, Gateshead, Tyne and Wear NE10 9RZ; Tel 0191-469 9499; S. Roberts. (7–16) (Malad.) (Boys)
Hewburn, Wealcroft, Felling, Gateshead, Tyne and Wear NE10 8LT; Tel 0191-469 2462; A. Garbett (Temp). (4–16) (E.S.N.(M)
High Fell, Millway, Sheriff Hill, Gateshead, Tyne and Wear NE9 5PQ; Tel 0191-487 6682; G. Forster (Temp). (4–19) (E.S.N.(S)
Joicey Road, Joicey Rd, Gateshead, Tyne and Wear NE9 5AT; Tel 0191-487 6186; A. Stott (Temp). (4–19) (E.S.N.(M)

Comprehensive School (11–14)

Breckenbeds Junior High, Saltwell Rd South, Gateshead NE9 6LE; Tel (0632) 4876624; J. Day

Comprehensive Schools (11–18)

Blaydon, Shibdon Rd, Blaydon, Tyne and Wear NE21 5NW; Tel (0632) 443233, 443970, 443244; P.S. Warren
Kingsmeadow, Market La, Dunston, Gateshead NE11 9NX; Tel (0632) 4606004; J. Campbell. (11–16)
Heworth Grange, High Lanes, Heworth, Gateshead NE10 0PT; Tel (0632) 4692898; B.H. Huddart. (11–16)
Thomas Hepburn County Community, Swards Rd, Felling, Gateshead NE10 9UZ; Tel (0632) 4694821; C.B. Buddle. (11–16)
Hookergate, High Spen, Rowlands Gill, Tyne and Wear NE39 2BX; Tel (0120 74) 2862; D.A. Roberts. (11–18)
Lord Lawson, Portobello Rd, Birtley, Chester-le-Street DH3 2LP; Tel (0385) 4103511; M. Maltby. (11–18)
Lyndhurst, Beacon Lough Rd, Gateshead NE9 6TA; Tel (0632) 4878248, 4873451; J. Quinn. (11–18)
Ryton Tyne and Wear NE40 3AH; Tel (0632) 2113; J.W. Pearson, BA
Whickham, Burnthouse La, Whickham, Tyne and Wear NE16 5AR; Tel (0632) 4883893, 4887544; J.W. Lea. (11–18)

Comprehensive Schools (14–18)

Heathfield Senior High, Durham Rd, Gateshead NE9 5AS; Tel (0632) 4773862; N. Fearon

Comprehensive Schools (Voluntary Aided 11–18)

St Edmund Campion R.C., Rugby Gdns, Gateshead NE9 7JX; Tel (0632) 4877638, 4875188; G. Rowell. (11–18)
St Thomas More R.C., Croftdale Rd, Blaydon, Tyne and Wear NE21 4BQ; Tel (0632) 4143978; M.N. Zarraga. (11–18)

Professional Development Centre

Evistones Rd, Low Fell, Gateshead NE9 5JR

Outdoor Pursuits Environmental Studies

Dukeshouse Wood Centre, nr Hexham, Northumberland, Tyne and Wear; Tel (01434) 2622; G. Thompson

Youth and Community Organisations

Allerdene Community Centre Smithy La, Allerdene Est, Gateshead; Tel 0191-491 5322; Alwyne Colley
The Avenues Community Education Project, c/o Gladstone Terrace Community Centre, Gladstone Terr, Gateshead; Tel 0191-490 1429; M. Pegg
Barley Mow Village Hall and Youth Club, Vigo La, Barley Mow, Birtley, Chester-le-Street, Co Durham; Tel 0191-410 5334; C. McLelland
Bede Time Out Club Bede Community Primary School, Old Fold Rd, Gateshead; Tel 0191-477 3893; Joan Moon
Bensham Grove Community Centre, Sidney Gr, Bensham, Gateshead; Tel 0191-477 2263; Helen Glegg
Birtley Community Centre, Ravensworth Rd, Birtley, Chester-le-Street, Durham; Tel 0191-410 2343; Cynthia Richardson; Carol Smith
Birtley Youth Club, Birtley Community Centre; Tel 0191-410 2343; Cynthia Richardson; Carol Smith
Blackhall Mill Community Centre, River View, Blackhall Mill, Chopwell, Tyne and Wear; M. Oliver
Blaydon Youth Club,; B. Thompson
Brandling Hall Community Centre, Church Pl, Felling, Gateshead NE10 OHT; Tel 0191-469 2812; D. Bell
Cedars Youth Club, c/o Cedars Special School, Ivy La, Gateshead, Tyne and Wear; Tel (0632) 4877591; Mr Foster
Chopwell Community Centre and Youth Club,; Kath Schofield
Chowdene Boys Club, Glenbrooke Hse, Chowdene Bank, Low Fell, Gateshead NER OJE; Tel 0191-487 6326; Bob Boustead
Clara Vale Village Hall and Youth Club, Clara Vale, Ryton NE40 OJE; Mrs Bainbridge
Creche Mobile Project, C/o Gladstone Terr Community Centre, Gladstone Terr, Gateshead NE8 4EA; Tel 0191-477 3699; Anne Blackie
Deckham Community Centre, Split Crow Rd, Deckham, Gateshead, Tyne and Wear; Tel 0191-477 9210; Graeme Wilkinson
Duke of Edinburgh Award Scheme, c/o Gladstone Terr Community Centre, Gladstone Terr, Gateshead; Tel 0191-478 2780; R. Hoy
Dunston Community Centre, Railway St, Dunston, Gateshead NE11 9EB; Tel 0191-460 4270; June Dobbie
Eighton Banks Village Hall, Black La, Eighton Banks, Gateshead, Tyne and Wear; Tel 0191-491 0183
Felling Crowhall Towers Community Centre, Crowhall La, Felling, Gateshead NE10 ONF; Tel 0191-469 3502; M. Southern
Fellinghouse Playscheme and Community House 1 Greenwood Gdns, Felling, Gateshead NE10 OHB; E. Allan
Fellside Methodist Youth Club, Ancaster Rd, Whickham, Tyne and Wear; R. Dennis
Gateshead International Youth Action Committee (IYAC) Tel 0191-490 1901
Gateshead Outdoor Activity Centre Whinney Hse, Low Fell, Gateshead NE9 5AR; Tel (0632) 4879356; G. Newcomb

Gateshead Working with Women and Girls Gladstone Terr Community Centre, Gladstone Terr, Gateshead, Tyne and Wear; Tel 0191-478 2780; Marion Simpson
Gateshead Young Womens Outreach Project 12 Gladstone Terr, Gladstone Terr, Gateshead; Tel 0191-477 7759; Jo Vary
Gateshead Youth Council, c/o Citizens Advice Bureau, 6 Regent Terr, Gateshead, Tyne & Wear; Tel 0191-490 1900; Terry Eccles
Gladstone Terrace Community Centre, 12 Gladstone Terr, Gateshead NE8 4EA; Tel 0191-477 1005; A. Bell; M. Burns
Greenside and District Community Centre, Main Rd, Greenside, Ryton, Tyne and Wear NE40 4AA; J. Medine
Heathfield Youth Club, C/o Heathfield Senior High School, Durham Rd, Low Fell, Gateshead NE9 5AS; Tel 0191-477 3862; G. Wilson
High Spen Community Centre Park Pavilion, High Spen, Rowlands Gill; K. Charlton
Hookergate Youth Club, C/o Hookergate Comprehensive, Rowlands Gill, Tyne and Wear; G. Thompson
Interface (Felling House/Branding Hall Neighbourhood Project) The Bungalow, 3 Greenwood Gdns, Felling NE10 OHB; Tel 0191-495 2888; Marcia Holmes
Kibbesworth Youth Club, Grange Terr, Kibblesworth, Gateshead NE11 OXN; Tel 0191-410 4736; Den Clark
Leam Lane Community Centre, Leam La Est, Felling, Gateshead NE10 8PP; Tel 0191-469 2269; Anne Connelly
Lobley Hill Youth & Community Centre, Scafell Gdns, Lobley Hill, Gateshead NE11 9LS; Tel (0632) 4604280; D. Allison
Lord Lawson Youth Wing, C/o Lord Lawson County Comprehensive School, Portobello Rd, Birtley, Chester-le-Street DH3 2LP; Tel 0191-410 6790; Marjorie Southwick
Lyndhurst Youth Club, C/o Lyndhurst Comprehensive School, Beacon Lough Rd, Low Fell, Gateshead NE9 6TA; Tel 0191-487 8248; D. Jones
Malton Green Village Hall and Youth Club, Malton Grn, Low Fell, Gateshead NE9 7EF; C. Thompson
Marley Hill Community Centre, Miners Welfare Hall, Marley Hill, Gateshead, Tyne and Wear; Tel 0191-488 0322; G. Haggie
The Mount Community Centre, Sandy La, Eighton Banks, Gateshead NE9 7YB; Tel 0191-487 9269; Mrs Taylor
Pelaw Centre, Shields Rd, Pelaw, Gateshead, Tyne and Wear; Tel 0191-438 6636; Carol Coss
Pelaw Hertfordshire Community Centre, Hertfordshire Hse, Rothbury Ave, Pelaw, Gateshead NE10 OQY; Tel 0191-469 1860; J. Southwick
Redhough Boys Club, c/o Tyne View Primary School, Rose St, Gateshead; Evan Bryson
Route 26 Broadway Centre, Elgin Rd, Carr Hill, Gateshead NE9 5PA; Tel 0191-420 0343; Dave Gaston
Rowlands Gill Community Centre, Strathmore Rd, Rowlands Gill NE39 1JB; Mrs Goodwin
Ryton Community Centre, Cross Hse, Ryton Village NE40 3QP; N. Rippeth
Ryton and District Youth Centre, Barmoor, Ryton, Tyne and Wear; Tel 0191-413 2053; D. Brown
St Cuthbert's Project and Village Hall with Youth Club, c/o Town Centre Project, Gladstone Terr Community Centre, Gladstone Terr, Gateshead; Tel 0191-477 6630; Bob Lewer
St James Village Hall and Youth Club, Sunderland Rd, Gateshead NE8 3NZ; I. Wilson
St Mark's Youth Project, St Mark's Church Hall, Shipcote Terr, Gateshead NE8 4AA; Tel 0191-490 0095; K. Robson
Saltmeadows Community Centre, Nixon St, Saltmeadows, Gateshead NE8 3BD; Tel 0191-477 2877
Smailes Lane Youth Club, C/o Highfield Primary School, Highfield Rd, Rowlands Gill, Tyne and Wear NE39 2LX
Springwell Activity Centre, Aycliffe Ave, Springwell Est, Wrekenton, Gateshead NE9 7BX; Tel 0191-482 5623; Stuart Dearlove
Springwell Community Centre & Youth Club, C/o Village Hall, Lanchester Ave, Springwell, Wrekenton, Gateshead, Tyne and Wear; Tel 0191-487 0169; Stuart Dearlove
Stoneygate Neighbourhood Projects, C/o 6 Stoneygate Gdns, Stoneygate, Felling, Gateshead NE10 OND; J. Burns
Streets Ahead Youth Project, 1 Lobelia Ave, Old Fold, Gateshead, Tyne and Wear; Tel 0191-477 0900; P. Carswell
Swalwell Clavering Youth Club, C/o Holy Trinity Church Hall, Swalwall, Tyne and Wear; Tel 0191-413 2964; Ken Nisbett
Swalwell Community Centre, Clavering Rd, Swalwell, Tyne and Wear; Tel 0191-488 1407; J. Boyd
Teams After School Care Club, C/o Teams Community Centre, Askew Rd, Teams, Gateshead; Tel 0191-478 1003; A. McNeillie
Teams Centre and Youth Club, Askew Rd, Teams, Gateshead NE8 2PW; Tel 0191-478 1003; Peter Bennetts
Thomas Hepburn Community Comprehensive Swards Rd, Felling, Gateshead; Tel 0191-469 4821; Trevor Walmsley
Transport Unlimited C/o Gladstone Terr Community Centre, Gladstone Terr, Gateshead; Tel 0191-477 5321
Trinity Centre, High St, Gateshead, Tyne and Wear; Tel 0191-478 6181; The Secretary
Trinity Methodist Youth Club, Whitehall Rd, Gateshead, Tyne and Wear; P. Jennings
Trinity Town Centre Project, C/o Gladstone Team Community Centre, Gladstone Terr, Gateshead; Tel 0191-477 6630; Anne Nixon
Victoria Rd Youth Club, Victoria Rd, Gateshead, Tyne and Wear; I. Soulsby
Way-Out in Gateshead, The Courtyard, Durham Rd, Low Fell, Gateshead NE9 5AW; Tel 0191-487 9356; Kevin Pearson
Whickham Community Centre, Front St, Whickham, Tyne and Wear; Tel 0191-488 1291; K. Clark
Whickham Fellside Youth Club, C/o Whickham Comprehensive, Burnthouse La, Whickham NE16 5AR; Tel 0191-496 0026; J. Laverick
Whitehouse La Youth Club, Whitehouse La, Wrekenton, Gateshead, Tyne and Wear; Tel 0191-491 0632; J. Langley
Winlaton Centre Youth Club, North St, Winlaton NE21 6BY; Tel 0191-414 4718; John Bell
Winlaton Mill Community Centre, May Avenue, Winalton Mill, Blaydon NE21 6SF; Tel 0191-414 3774; F. Inness
Wrekenton Community Centre Old School, High St, Wrekenton, Gateshead NE9 7JR; Tel 0191-491 0535; Jim Langley

Gloucestershire County Council

Population 545,600 (1993) Est
Shire Hall, Gloucester GL1 2TP; Tel (01452) 425000
Chief Executive M.J. Honey, MA, MSc
County Librarian L. Hopkins, ALA Quayside Wing, Shire Hall, Gloucester GL1 2HY

Education Offices

County Education Office, Shire Hall, Gloucester GL1 2TP; Tel (01452) 425300
Chairman E. Boait
Chief Education Officer K.D. Anderson, BA, DipED, FRSA
Deputy Chief Education Officer J. Braithwaite, MA
Head of Quality Assurance Consultants D. Potter
Head of Pupil and Student Services J.A. Saunders, MA, BA

Head of Careers and Guidance Service R.I. Stokes, BA
Head of Education Finance S.J. King, BA, IPSA
Head of Youth and Community Service M. Counsell, Bed, AdvDipEd Studies
EO D. Howarth, BSc, MEd
EO M. Rousseau, BSoc.Sc
Support Manager, Gloucestershire Training and Enterprise Council E.A. Cousins, BSc
Head of Gloucestershire Music Service R. Ling
Chief Executive M. Honey
County Librarian L. Hopkins
County Property Services Manager I. King
County Treasurer J.R. Cockcroft, IPFA, DMS
Director of Social Services Deryk Mead
Number of Schools
*257 primary (41,521); *14 secondary (15,400); special schools 14 day (1105); 3 residential (223): * Do not include Grant Maintained Schools
Committee Meetings
6 times a year including Budget meeting
Requisition Periods for Schools Supplies
No fixed periods
Other Authorities with who Joint Purchasing Arrangements are made
Somerset County Council; Wiltshire County Council (for Education Stationery & material & cleaning materials)

Gloucestershire Education Management Service (GEMS)

Head of Business Unit G.R. Cane, MA
EO C. Williams, BA, CertEd
EO S. Ellis, BA

Education Planning Group (EPG)

Head of Education Finance S.J. King, BA, IPSA
Head of Youth and Community Service M. Counsell, BEd, AdvDipEd Studies

Professional Development Centre (PDC)

Associate Head of Business Unit D. Burns
Art and Design Inspector A. Penn, BEd
Science Design and Technology Inspector B.J. Gunnell, PhD, BSc
English Inspector K. Jeffrey, MA
Humanities Inspector A. McAleavy, MA
Information Technology and Science Inspector J. Sweeney, MSc
Mathematics Inspector P. Waite, BEd
Primary Inspector R. Arnold, BA
Primary Inspector J.W. Gill
Primary Inspector J. Weltman
Primary Inspector M. Skeet, MEd
Primary Inspector J. Spouse
Design and Technology Inspector B. Gunnell
Secondary Inspector A. Braithwaite, BEd
Special Education Needs Inspector P. Johnson, BA
Head of Pupil and Student Services J.A. Saunders, MA, BA
Head of Careers and Guidance Service R.I. Stokes, BA
Head of Education Finance S.J. King, BA, IPSA
Head of Youth and Community Service M. Counsell, BEd, AdvDipEd Studies
EO D. Howarth

Education Committee

Chair E. Boait Old School Hse, Tibberton, Glos GL19 3AQ
Members of the Committee
T.M. Bliss, J.C. Holmes, J.R. Howe, B.G. Booth, D.A. Hurcombe, T. Workman, B.R. Izett, T.M. Dee, J.B. Leonard, Lady M. Dunrossil, M.A. Levett, D.A. Fidgeon, A.J. Meredith, A. Hanks, R. Merritt, B.W. Hobman, C.J. Morris, P.R. Hodgkinson, J.M. Naish, V.A. Peniket, J.M. Sewell, A.J. Pennington, C.R. Sheppard, V.D. Phillips, F.M. Skinner, E.J. Phillips, J.C. Standing, M. Rutter, F.R. Thompson, H.J. Withers

Governor Training Unit

The Governor Training Section, The Hucclecote Centre, Churchdown La, Hucclecote, Gloucester GL3 3QN; Tel (01452) 425113; Fax (01452) 623037
Governor Training Co-ordinator P. Aplin
Administrator E. Ramshaw
Services Offered
Gloucestershire Governor Training aims to make the Governing Body more effective by: Promoting partnership between heads, governors, staff, parents; Increasing governors' skills, knowledge and confidence; Facilitating understanding of governors' role and responsibility; Helping governors contribute to the improvement of learning processes in school; Encouraging governors to get to know their school; Gloucestershire Governor Training provides: In-house tailor-made training programmes for individual Governing Bodies; County-wide central courses; Clear and relevant information, termly newsletter and Factsheets distributed to all governors

County Curriculum Centre

The Hucclecote Centre, Churchdown La, Hucclecote, Gloucester GL3 3QN; Tel (01452) 623006; *Head of Professional Development Consultancy* D. Berrisford

Educational Psychology Service

Education Department, Shire Hall, Gloucester GL1 2TP; Tel (01452) 425441; *Principal Educational Psychologist* S. Huggett
East Area: Battledown Centre, Harp Hill, Battledown, Cheltenham, Glos GL52 6PZ; Tel (01242) 525448; *Senior Educational Psychologist* Karlo Miklausic
West Area: Maitland Hse Spa Rd, Gloucester GL1 1UY; Tel (01452) 426962/1; *Senior Educational Psychologist* K. Elliott, BA(Hons), MSc
East Area: Beeches Green Health Centre Stroud, Glos GL5 4BH; Tel (01453) 751090/766331; *Senior Educational Psychologist* K. Miklausic, BSc

Special Day Schools

Alderman Knight, Ashchurch Rd, Tewkesbury, Glos GL20 8JJ; Tel (01684) 295639; I.T. Walsh, BA, CertEd, DipSpEd. (85)
Battledown Assessment and Development Centre, Harp Hill, Battledown, Cheltenham, Glos GL52 6PZ; Tel (01242) 525472; Mrs E.M. Rook. (60)
Bettridge, Warden Hill Rd, Cheltenham, Glos GL51 5AT; Tel (01242) 514934; J.R. George, CertEd, DipAdvEd. (96)
Bownham Pk, Rodborough Common, Stroud, Glos GL5 5DA; Tel (01453) 873361; B.P. Kelly, Dip(Physical Ed), Dip(Special Ed), BEd(Hons), MEd. (113)
Brookfield, Warden Hill Rd, Cheltenham, GLOS GL51 5AT; Tel (01242) 526919; Fax (01242) 227827; M.J. Wright, AdvDipEd. (77)
Chamwell, Longford La, Gloucester GL2 9EY; Tel (01452) 523125; A. Farren, BA. (81)
Dean Hall, Speech Hse Rd, Coleford, Glos GL16 7EJ; Tel (01594) 822175; Fax (01594) 826472; J.N. Haddock, BA, BEd. (96)
The Hawthorns, Longford La, Gloucester GL2 9EU; Tel (01452) 500499; M.T. Musson, DipEd. (93)
Longford, Longford La, Gloucester GL2 9EY; Tel (01452) 522637; D. Thomson, BPhil. (121)
Oakdene, Dockham Rd, Cinderford, Glos GL14 2AN; Tel (01594) 822693; K. Sandall, BA, Cert(Physical Activity for Mentally Handicapped). (28)
Paternoster, Watermoor Rd, Cirencester, Glos GL7 1JS; Tel (01285) 652480; P. Barton, CertEd, Dip(Special Ed). (48)
Sandford, Seven Springs, Nr Cheltenham, Glos GL53 9NG; Tel (01242) 870224; Fax (01242) 870331; D.A. Morris, DipEd. (104)
Westlands, Warden Hill Rd, Cheltenham, Glos GL51 5AT; Tel (01242) 525881; G.C. Bellingham. (65)

Special Day and Residential Schools

Amberley Ridge, Stroud, Glos GL5 5DB; Tel (01453) 872536; R. Atherton, BA, DipEd. (85)
Coln Hse, Fairford, Glos GL7 4DB; Tel (01285) 712308; J.W. Davidson, CertEd, AdvDipSpEd. (74)
Cam Hse, Drake La, Cam, Dursley, Glos GL11 5HD; Tel (01453) 542130; T.E. Pascoe, DipEd. (56)

Secondary Schools (11–16)

Cheltenham Kingsmead, Howell Rd, Cheltenham GL51 0ED; Tel (01242) 516008; Fax (01242) 262495; P. Wadsworth. (Grant Maintained) (Mixed) (575)
Oxstalls, Escourt Cl, Gloucester GL1 3LR; Tel (01452) 524879; Fax (01452) 303644; E.O. Rees, BEd. (Mixed) (539)
Thomas Keble, Eastcombe, Stroud GL6 7DY; Tel (01452) 770301; Fax (01452) 770093; J.D. Lewis, BSc, MSc, MEd. (Mixed) (310)

Secondary Schools (Voluntary 11–16)

Barnwood Pk School for Girls St Lawrence Rd, Gloucester GL4 7QT; Tel (01452) 616848; Fax (01452) 613380; E.M. Edney, BA, MEd. (Girls) (266)
Severn Vale, School La, Quedgeley, Glos GL2 6PR; Tel (01452) 720458; Fax (01452) 724900; *Head* P. Jay (Acting). (Mixed) (776)

Secondary Schools (11–18)

Archway, Paganhill, Stroud GL5 4AX; Tel (01453) 763242 or 766543; Fax (01453) 766093; V.P. Warren, BA. (Mixed) (1149)
Beaufort Community School, Windsor Dr, Gloucester GL4 0RT; Tel (01452) 301381; Fax (01452) 380779; A.J. Tetley, BA. (Mixed) (1111)
Berkeley Vale Community School, Wanswell, Berkeley GL13 9RS; Tel (01453) 811396; Fax (01453) 811330; M. Hardwick, BSc. (Mixed) (285)
Brockworth, Mill La, Brockworth, Glos GL3 4QF; Tel (01452) 863372; Fax (01452) 862638; A.D. Folliard, BSc. (Mixed) (978)
Cleeve, Two Hedges Rd, Bishops Cleeve, Cheltenham GL52 4AE; Tel (01242) 672546; Fax (01242) 678604; B.D. Gardiner, BSc. (Mixed) (1411)
The High School for Girls, Denmark Rd, Gloucester GL1 3JN; Tel (01452) 523335; Fax (01452) 309862; M. Bainbridge. (Girls) (559)
Sir Thomas Rich's, Oakleaze, Gloucester GL2 0LF; Tel (01452) 528467; Fax (01452) 382432; *Head* I. Kellie (Acting). (Boys) (562)
Sir William Romney's, Community Lowerfield Rd, Tetbury GL8 8AE; Tel (01666) 502378; Fax (01666) 505864; P. Nicholson, BA. (Mixed) (749)

Secondary Schools (Voluntary 11–18)

Farmor's, The Park, Fairford GL7 4JQ; Tel (01285) 712302/712228; Fax (01285) 713504; C.J. Arnold, MA. (VC) (Mixed) (675)
St Peters High School Stroud Rd, Gloucester GL4 0DD; Tel (01452) 520594; Fax (01452) 385135; L. Montagu, BA. (V.A.) (Mixed) (1253)

Area Resource Centre

The Resource Centre, Gloucestershire Centre for Education and Development, Cheltenham and Gloucester College of H.E., PO Box 220, The Park Campus, Cheltenham GL50 2QF; Tel (01242) 532862; *Manager* M. Cummings

Field Study Centre

The Wilderness Centre, Mitcheldean, Gloucestershire GL17 0HA; Tel (01594) 542551; Fax (01594) 542551; T. Roach

Grant Maintained Schools

Balcarras School, East End Rd, Charlton Kings, Cheltenham GL53 8QF; Tel (01242) 515881; N.E.G. Cooke, BA. Mixed (730)
Cheltenham Bournside Incorporating Cheltenham Sixth Form Centre Warden Hill Rd, Cheltenham GL51 5EF; Tel (01242) 235555; Fax (01242) 226742; G. Stafford. (Mixed) (1527)
Cheltenham Bournside School and Sixth Form Centre, Warden Hill Rd, Cheltenham, Glos GL51 5EF; Tel (01242) 235555; Fax (01242) 226742; *Head* G. Stafford. (Mixed) (1527)
Chipping Campden School, Chipping Campden, Glos GL55 6HU; Tel (01386) 840216; Fax (01386) 840498; J. Price, BA. (Mixed) (845)
Chosen Hill School, Brookfield Rd, Churchdown GL3 2PL; Tel (01452) 713488; A. Winwood, BA, MEd. Mixed (1163)
Churchdown School, Winston Rd, Churchdown GL3 2RB; Tel (01452) 713340; Fax (01452) 857367; P. Goodliffe, BSc. (Mixed) (1133)
Cirencester Deer Pk School, Stroud Rd, Cirencester GL3 2RB; Tel (01285) 653447/8/9; Fax (01285) 640669; D.A. Crossley, BA. (Mixed) (1042)
Cirencester Kingshill School, Kingshill La, Cirencester GL7 1HS; Tel (01285) 651511; Fax (01285) 885652; M.H. Redman, BA. (Mixed) (683)
Cotswold School, Station Rd, Bourton-on-the-Water, Cheltenham GL54 2BD; Tel (01451) 20554; I.P. Sanders, FRSA. (Mixed) (620)
The Crypt Grammar School, Podsmead, Gloucester GL2 6AE; Tel (01452) 524371; Fax (01452) 425301; *Headteacher* William Armiger; *Chair of Governors* Craig Dunne. (Boys 11–18; Girls 16–18) (455)
Cwmcarn G.M. School, Chapel Farm, Cwmcarn, Crosskeys NP1 7NG; Tel (01495) 270982; Fax (01495) 272831; *Headteacher* R.A.R. Woods; *Chair of Governors* D.A. Price. (Mixed) (11–16) (402)
Dene Magna Community School, Mitcheldean, Glos GL17 0DU; Tel (01594) 542370. (Mixed) (548)
The Heywood, Causeway Rd, Cinderford GL14 2AZ; Tel (01594) 822257; Fax (01594) 826240; Mrs C. McManus. (Mixed) (549)
Katharine Lady Berkeley's School, Wotton-under-Edge GL12 8RB; Tel (01453) 842227; J.E. Law, MA. (Grant Maintained) (1157)
Lakers School, Five Acres, Coleford, Glos GL16 7QW; Tel (01594) 832263; Fax (01594) 832486; A.L. Cleaver, BA, MEd. (Mixed) (810)
Maidenhill, Kings Rd, Stonehouse GL10 2HA; Tel (01453) 822469; Fax (01453) 825615; T. Trippett, BA. (Mixed) (547)
Marling School, Stroud, Glos GL5 4HE; Tel (01453) 762251; *Headteacher* Graham Lowe; *Chair of Governors* D.W.H. Jarvis; *Business Manager* R. Hopwood; *Site Manager* Col. P. Haslam. (Boys) (11–19) (772)
Newent Community School, Watery La, Newent GL18 1QF; Tel (01531) 820550; P.E.D. Landau, BA. (Mixed) (1146)
Pate's Grammar School, Upper School, Princess Elizabeth Way, Cheltenham GL51 0HG; Tel (01242) 523169/516756; Fax (01242) 260373 (Bursary); *Headteacher* D.J. Barnes; *Bursar* Miss S.F. Jarritt. (Mixed) (11–18) (977)
Pittville School, Albert Rd, Cheltenham GL52 3JD; Tel (01242) 524787; Fax (01242) 528750; D.P. Abbott, BA. Mixed (712)
Rednock School, Dursley, Glos GL11 4BY; Tel (01453) 543618/9; J. Pritchard, BA, FRSA. (Mixed) (1250)
Ribston Hall High School, Stroud Rd, Gloucester GL1 5LE; Tel (01452) 528178; Fax (01452) 308833; *Headteacher* A.R. Gourd; *Chairman of Governors* M.B. Lewis; *Bursar* B.H. Wooldridge. (Girls) (11–18) (519)
St Benedict's Catholic High School, Arle Rd, Cheltenham GL51 8LE; Tel (01242) 524530; M.G. Whitty. (G.M.) (Mixed) (564)
Stroud High School, Beard's La, Cainscross Rd, Stroud, Glos GL5 4HF; Tel (01453) 764441; *Headteacher* Jean Lord; *Chair of Governors* J.H. Parker. (Girls) (11–18) (790)
Tewkesbury, Ashchurch Rd, Tewkesbury GL20 8DF; Tel (01684) 292152; Fax (01684) 850742; P.F. Cotter, BA, MEd. (Mixed) (1180)

Whitecross, Church Rd, Lydney GL15 5DZ; Tel (01594) 843202; Fax (01594) 842025; D.G. Throp. (Mixed) (682)
Winchcombe, Greet Rd, Winchcombe, Cheltenham GL54 5LB; Tel (01242) 602233; Fax (01242) 604211; R.L. Burcher. (Mixed) (380)
Wyedean School, Beachley Rd, Sedbury, Chepstow, Gwent NP6 7AA; Tel (01291) 625346; Fax (01291) 624251; W.J. Claydon, BA, MA(Oxon). (Mixed) (645)

Greater Manchester Metropolitan Area

The following Metropolitan Councils comprise the Greater Manchester Metropolitan Area and may be found in alphabetical order within this chapter:
Bolton, Bury, Manchester, Oldham, Rochdale, Salford, Stockport, Tameside, Trafford, Wigan.

Gwent County Council

Population 450,000
County Hall, Cwmbran, Gwent NP44 2XB; Tel (01633) 838838; Fax (01633) 838152
Chief Executive Officer M.J. Perry, MA(Oxon), Solicitor
County Treasurer J.P. Walsh, IPFA
Director of Property Services D. Haswell, BArch(Hons)(Edin), RIBA
Director of Social Services C. Lawrence
County Supplies Officer Vacancy Polo Grounds, New Inn, Pontypool, Gwent; Tel (01495) 762431

Education Offices

County Hall, Cwmbran, Gwent NP44 2XG; Tel (01633) 838838; Fax (01633) 838225
Chairman Cllr Mrs A. Lloyd
Vice-Chairman Cllr B. Maurice
Director of Education J.D. Griffiths
Assistant Director of Education (Community Services) P. Ellis
Assistant Director of Education (Strategic Planning and Research) B. Mawby
Education Officer (B&D) J. Howells (Acting)
Education Officer (Schools) J. Sheen, BEd
Education Officer (Finance) J. Pearce
Education Officer (Special Needs) M. Groucutt
Assistant Director of Education D. Hopkins
Chief Staff Development Officer H. Cowen
Senior Staff Development Officer (Primary) I. Lewis
Senior Staff Development Officer (Secondary) D. Williams, BSc
Senior Staff Development Officer (Further Education) D. Martin
Senior Staff Development Officer (Special Needs) A. Jobbins (Acting)
INSET Co-ordinator Mrs B. Jones
Staff Development Officer (Infant Nursery) E. Byard
Staff Development Officer (Junior) M. Morris
Staff Development Officer (Junior) K. White
Staff Development Officer (English) S. Sherlock
Staff Development Officer (Mathematics) H. Probert
Staff Development Officer (Modern Languages) M. Turford
Staff Development Officer (Humanities) M. Trimnell
Staff Development Officer (Music) A. Williams
Staff Development Officer (Science) M. Holmes
Staff Development Officer (Computer Education) P. Cathcart
Staff Development Officer (Computer Education) Dr P. Hepburn
Staff Development Officer (Home Economics) A.E. Hill
Staff Development Officer (Art) D. Barter
Staff Development Officer (Special Needs) R. Miller (Acting)
Staff Development Officer (Youth and Community) A. Griffiths
Staff Development Officer (Geography) K. Lawson
Catering/Cleaning Client Manager S. Clapham
Principal Careers Officer H. Pritchard
Chief Educational Psychologist R. Solomon, BA
Senior (Area) Education Psychologist J. Whiteman
Senior (Area) Educational Psychologist R. Grubb, MA
Senior (Area) Educational Psychologist J.E. Kinge, BSc
Senior Area Educational Psychologist Tom Dyson
Senior Area Educational Psychologist M. Provis
Chief Education Welfare Officer V. Norris
TVEI Manager P. Davies; Tel (0163 33) 838321
Number of Schools
11 Nursery; 215 Primary; 32 Comprehensive; 1 college of higher education (1,513 FT, 2,196 PT); 5 further educational establishments
Special Schools
1 residential (136); 4 non-residential (296)
Other Authorities with whom Joint Purchasing Arrangements are made
None

Governor Training Unit

Education Department, County Hall, Cwmbran, Gwent; Tel (01633) 832796; Fax (01633) 838225
Governor Development Officer Wendy Flynn
Head of Governor Support Unit Julian Williams
Services Offered
Central programme of training courses; Access to training materials in Governors' library; Termly Governor magazine; Telephone helpline; Training for School Clerks

Special Schools

Crown Bridge, Sebastopol, Gwent; Tel (01495) 58739; Mrs A.G. Stephens
Mounton Hse, Chepstow; Tel (01291) 622014; R.A. Hughes
Pen-y-Cwm, Beaufort; Tel (01495) 304031; R. Dickenson
Westfield Lower, Westfield Way, Newport, Gwent; Tel (01633) 855170; C. Matthews (Acting)
Westfield Upper, Maesglas Rd, Newport, Gwent; Tel (01633) 815480; C.M. Evans, BEd

Comprehensive Schools

Abersychan, Talywain, Gwent; Tel (01495) 773068; Miss D. Saunders, BEd. (779)
Abertillery, Tel (01495) 217121; S. Gullick. (851)
Bassaleg, Newport, Gwent; Tel (01633) 892191; I.A. Garrero, BA, MEd. (1346)
Bettws, Newport, Gwent; Tel (01633) 856331; G. Barker. (1069)
Blackwood, Tel 225288; T.J. Warrender. (775)
Caerleon, Caerleon, Gwent; Tel (01633) 420106; C.W. Lapham, MSc. (1195)
Caldicot Caldicot, Gwent; Tel (01291) 421422; J. Norwood, BA. (1308)
Chepstow, Chepstow, Gwent; Tel (01291) 622070; H.W. Gruffydd. (971)
Croesyceiliog, Cwmbran, Gwent; Tel (0163 33) 482453; Mrs M. Mansfield, BA. (1329)
Duffryn, St Bride's Rd, Newport, Gwent; Tel (01633) 816088; A. Williams. (1010)
Ebbw Vale, Tel (01495) 303409; M. Phillips, MA. (14–18) (750)

Ebbw Vale, Glanyrafon, Gwent; Tel (01495) 304226; L.B. Matthews. (11–14) (359)
Ebbw Vale, Glyncoed, Gwent; Tel 303216; R. Lewis. (11–14) (394)
Fairwater, Cwmbran, Gwent; Tel (0163 33) 866523; J.N. Hart. (1197)
Hartridge, Hartridge Farm Rd, Newport, Gwent; Tel (01633) 412487; A.J. Buckle, OBE. (924)
King Henry VIII School Abergavenny, Gwent; Tel (01873) 852701; D.G. Fisher, MSc, PhD. (1248)
Llantarnam, Cwmbran, Gwent; Tel (0163 33) 866711; I.D. Sheen, BSc. (1067)
Lliswerry, Nash Rd, Newport, Gwent; Tel (01633) 277867; J. Brewer, BSc. (1184)
Monmouth, Tel (01600) 712892; D.A. Every, BA, MEd. (1292)
Nantyglo, Tel (01495) 310776; Mrs P. Waite. (14+) (662)
Newbridge, Tel (01495) 243243; A. Raybold, BA. (663)
Oakdale, Blackwood, Gwent; Tel (01495) 225110; G. Hopkins, BA. (813)
Pontllanfraith, Tel (01496) 224929; M.G. Lewis, BSc. (774)
Risca, Tel (01633) 612425; P. Millichamp, BA. (570)
St Joseph's, Tredegar Pk, Newport, Gwent; Tel (01633) 815388; M.J. Dean. (939)
St Julian's, Heather Rd, Newport, Gwent; Tel (01633) 213226; S. Marshall. (1206)
Tredegar, Tel (01495) 723551; G.B. Davies, BA. (938)
Trevethin Comprehensive, Pontypool, Gwent; Tel (01495) 763551; G. Davies. (479)
West Monmouth Comprehensive, Pontypool, Gwent; Tel (01495) 762080; P.J. Phillips, MSc, BEd. (981)
Ysgol Gyfun Gwynllyw, Newbridge, Gwent; Tel (01495) 750405; Mrs L. Jones. (276)

Teachers' Centres

The Hill Residential College, Abergavenny; Tel (01873) 832551; J. Newcombe, MA(Oxon)
Newport, Brynglas Hse, Newport, Gwent; Tel (01633) 821657

Grant Maintained School

St Albans R.C. Pontypool, Gwent; Tel (01495) 762840; K.J.G. Doran, BA, MA. (590)

Gwynedd County Council

Population 235,452 (1991 Census)
County Offices, Shirehall St, Caernarfon, Gwynedd LL55 1SH; Tel (01286) 672255; Fax (01286) 673993
Chief Executive H.V. Thomas, BA, MSc, FBIM, MIPM
County Treasurer T.D. Heald, BA, IPFA
County Secretary and Solicitor G.R. Jones, BA
County Architect G. Harrison, BA
Director of Education G. Jarvis, MA
Director of Social Services L.M. Hughes, BA(Wales), CertSocSc, Home Office Cert
Director of Culture and Leisure E. Mitcheson, BA, DipLib, ALA

Education Department

County Offices, Shirehall St, Caernarfon, Gwynedd LL5 1SH; Tel (01286) 672255; Fax (01286) 677347
Chairman Cllr H.M. Morgan
Vice-Chairman Cllr Dafydd Orwig
Director of Education Gwynn Jarvis, MA
Assistant Director (Personnel/Governors Training) G.H. Jones, BSc
Assistant Director (School Services) R.L. Parry-Jones, MA
Assistant Director (Pupil Services) R.W. Parri, BSc, MEd
Assistant Director (Finance) D. Edwards, BSc
Principal Administrative Officer J.E. Thomas
Welsh Adviser Zac Davies
Humanities Adviser A. Schavoni
Science Adviser M.E. Robertson
Mathematics Adviser H.A. Roberts
Home Economics Adviser B. Portlock
Physical Education Adviser H. Davies
Senior Primary Adviser W.E. Williams
Senior Secondary Adviser Dr Gwynne Jones
Teacher Adviser Infants Huws-Roberts
English Adviser H.M.L. Butler, BA
Number of Schools and Further Education Establishments
193 infant and primary (19,865); 23 secondary (comprehensive) (15,383); 6 special schools (279); 4 colleges of further education

Governor Training Unit

Education Dept, Gwynedd County Council, Caernarfon, Gwynedd LL55 1SH; Tel (01286) 679171; Fax (01286) 677347
Assistant Director of Education G.H. Jones, BSc
Services Offered
Training courses and materials to Governors of seconday, primary and special schools

Special Schools

Hafod Lon School, Y Ffor, Pwllheli, Gwynedd; Tel (01766) 810626; *Vacancy* . (E.S.N.(S)
Treborth School, Bangor; Tel (01248) 353527; Dafydd Evans (Acting). (E.S.N.(M)
Ysgol Gogarth, Llandudno; Tel (01492) 860077; I.G. Jones, MEd. (P.H.)
Ysgol Pendalar, Caernarfon; Tel (01286) 672141; C.M. Jones. (E.S.N.(S)
Ysgol y Bont, Llangefni; Tel (01248) 750151; D. Hughes, BEd. (E.S.N.(M)

Secondary Comprehensive Schools

Ysgol Aberconwy, Conwy LL32 8ED; Tel (0149 263) 3243; R.C.A. Ward, MA, MEd. (684)
Ysgol Ardudwy, Harlech LL46 2UH; Tel (01766) 780331; T.O. Williams, BA. (511)
Ysgol Botwnnog, Botwnnog, Pwllheli LL53 8PY; Tel (0175 883) 220; W.R. Jones, BA. (418)
Ysgol Brynrefail, Llanrug, Caernarfon LL55 4AD; Tel (01286) 672381; J. Grisdale, BSc. (570)
Ysgol Caergybi, Caergybi LL65 1NL; Tel (01407) 762219; M. Chantrell, MA. (1090)
Ysgol David Hughes, Porthaethwy LL59 5SS; Tel (01248) 712287; D. Whitall, BA. (1289)
Ysgol Dyffryn Conwy, Llanrwst LL26 0SD; Tel (01492) 640516; I.G. Evans, BEd. (727)
Ysgol Dyffryn Nantlle, Penygroes LL54 6AA; Tel (01286) 880345; Dr E. Price Jones, BSc, MEd. (413)
Ysgol Dyffryn Ogwen, Bethesda LL57 3NN; Tel (01248) 600291; I. Hughes, BEd, MSc. (424)
Ysgol Eifionydd, Porthmadog LL49 9HS; Tel (01766) 512114; G. Hughes, BA. (535)
Ysgol Friars, Bangor LL57 2LN; Tel (01248) 364905; D.A. Jones, BA. (918)
Ysgol Glanymor, Pwllheli LL53 5HF; Tel (01758) 701244; Dr N.T. Jones, BSc. (637)
Ysgol John Bright, Llandudno LL30 1DL; Tel (01492) 860044; Irene Scott Perry, BA, MEd. (1014)
Ysgol Llangefni, Llangefni LL77 7NG; Tel (01248) 723441; Huw Roberts, BA. (855)
Ysgol Llwchradd Bodedern, Bodedern, Holyhead, Gwynedd; Tel (01407) 74100; John Wyn Jones, BSc. (705)
Ysgol Syr Hugh Owen, Caernarfon LL55 1HW; Tel (01286) 673076; J. Roberts, MSc. (1155)
Ysgol Syr Thomas Jones, Amlwch LL68 9TH; Tel (01407) 830287; O.G. Davies, BSc. (882)
Ysgol Tryfan, Bangor; Tel (01248) 352633; E. Williams, BA. (413)

Ysgol y Berwyn, Bala LL23 7BN; Tel (01678) 520259; G. Llwyd Owain, BA, MEd. (389)
Ysgol y Creuddyn Penrhyn Bay, Penrhyn Bay, Llandudno, Gwynedd; Tel (01492) 544344; E. Roland Jones, BA. (639)
Ysgol y Gader, Dolgellau LL40 1HY; Tel (01341) 422578; C.T. James, BA. (340)
Ysgol y Moelwyn Blaenau Ffestiniog LL41 3DW; Tel (01766) 830435; Dr I. Rees, BSc. (415)
Ysgol y Tywyn, LL36 9EU; Tel (01654) 710256; H.E. James, BSc. (360)

Resources Centre

Maesincla Caernarfon; Tel (01286) 677686

Hampshire County Council

Population 1,541,547
The Castle, Winchester, Hants SO23 8UJ; Tel (01962) 841841; Fax (01962) 846776; Telex 477729
County Chief Executive A.R. Hodgson
County Treasurer J.E. Scotford, CBE, IPFA
County Architect C. Stansfield Smith, CBE, MA, DipArch(Cantab), ARIBA
County Director of Social Services T. Butler
County Librarian P.H. Turner
County Countryside and Community Officer Dr J.R. Thompson
Director Museums Service S. Locke

Education Offices

Education Dept, The Castle, Winchester, Hants SO23 8UG; Tel (01962) 841841; Fax (01962) 842355
County Education Officer P.J. Coles
Deputy County Education Officer A.J. Seber, MA
Senior Management Team
County Education Officer P.J. Coles, MSc
Deputy County Education Officer A.J. Seber, MA
Chief Inspector J.A.A. Morris, BSc, MEd, FIMA
Head of Resources H. Thompson, PhD
ACEO CE Division J.D. Charles, BA, BSc(Econ)
ACEO NE Division E.F.H. Poppitt, MA
ACEO SE Division G.R. Heller, MA
ACEO SW Division R.G. Jones, BA, FBIM
Schools Officer (CE Division) J. Moore
Schools Officer (CE Division) E. Smith
Schools Officer (NE Division) J. Cawthra
Schools Officer (NE Division) S. Dorney-Smith
Schools Officer (SE Division) A. Begley, BSc(Hons), MA
Schools Officer (SE Division) B. Lloyd-Jones, BEd(Hons)
Schools Officer (SE Division) K. Gill, BA, MEd
Schools Officer (SW Division) C. Holt
Schools Officer (SW Division) O. Greenwood, BA(Hons)
Head of Pupil Services (CE Division) A. Munro
Head of Pupil Services (NE Division) P. Lewis
Head of Pupil Services (SE Division) P. Carpenter, BSc(Hons), PGCE
Head of Pupil Services (SW Division) M. Clarke, BA(Hons)
Senior Education Officer (Schools Policy) S. Goodwin, BSc, PhD
Senior Education Officer (Pre-school and Primary Advisory) J. Wilkinson, MA
Development Officer (Special Educational Needs) A. Delyth, BEd, MA
Development Officer (Parents, Pupils and Students) G. Pearce, BA, MA
Service Quality Manager R. Mead, DMA, ACIS
Resource Allocation Manager T. Whiffen, MA, CIPFA
HIASS Finance and Information Manager T. Rath, BA, MSc
Post 16 Development Officer M. Dunn
OFSTED Manager/General Inspector J. Cottee
Capital Planning Manager M. Lee, BA
County Youth Officer T. Caley, MA
Business Unit Manager (Education Information Technology Support Service) S. Cane, BSc, PhD
Business Unit Manager (Hampshire Music Service) H. Dove
Business Unit Manager (Caretaking and Cleaning Support Service) D. Scott-Angell
Business Unit Manager (Education Training Agency) S. Linssen, IPM, MITD
Business Unit Manager (Hampshire Inspection and Advisory Support Service) J.A.A. Morris, BSc, MEd, FIMA
Business Unit Manager (Hampshire Governor Training Service) J. Sheriton, B, PhD
Business Unit Manager (Education Personnel Services) J.D. Wakeling, MIPM
Business Unit Manager (Education Financial Service) R. Zebedee, ACMA
Chief Inspector J.A.A. Morris, BSc, MEd, FIMA
Divisional Senior Inspector (CE Division) D. Caveen, BSc
Divisional Senior Inspector (NE Division) C. Wilson, BEd, MA
Divisional Senior Inspector (SE Division) A. Bartlett, BSc
Divisional Senior Inspector (SW Division) P. Newlands, MA, A DipEd
Principal Educational Psychologist S. Arney, MSc, PGCE
Director Guidance and Careers Service T. Collins
Number of Education Establishments Statistics
Nursery Schools 4 (152 FTE); Nursery Units 29 (833 FTE); Primary Schools 562 (131,553); Secondary Schools (incl 6th Form) 77 (64,084); Grant Maintained Primary Schools 13 (4,065 NOR); Grant Maintained Secondary 17 (15,114 NOR); Grant Maintained Primary Units 1; Grant Maintained Secondary Units 1; Special Schools 74 (3,479 F/T); Special Units (Primary) 29 (233 P/T); Special Units (Secondary) 8

Education Committee

LD17, Con 10, Lab 8, Ind 1
Chairman A.D. Barron, (LD) The Annexe, The Manor Hse, Church La, Holybourne, Alton GU34 4HD
Vice-Chairman B.D. Dash, (LD) 38 Jones La, Hythe, Southampton SO45 6AX
Deputy-Vice Chairman P. Allan, (Lab) 7 Sandown Rd, Shirley, Southampton SO1 5QN
Members of the Committee
LD: A.E. Bailey, P.A. Baker, Dr C.C. Bamber, A.D. Barron, M.J. Clark, B.D. Dash, J.J. Dawson, M.C. Ferguson, B.T. Gurden, J.L. Mauger, A.E. Perry, P.G. Peskett, N.H. Sizer, A. Thame, J.G.L. Wall, J.V. Watson, P.S. Wright
Con: D.G. Allen, Lt Cmdr W.P. Beer, RN(Retd), D.C. Bentall, W.J. Filer, H.F. Hindson, MBE, Dr H.G. Jerrard, S.W. Juniper, P.R. Lillywhite, A. Varden, M.J. Woodhall
Lab: P. Allan, J. Carnell, H.D.L. Khan, K. Morrell, D.D. Morris, K.C.O. Street, T.P. Blair, W.H. Wheeler
Ind: K.P. Jessavala

Central Division

Clarendon Hse, Romsey Rd, Winchester SO22 5PW; Tel (01962) 869611
Assistant County Education Officer J. Charles
Management Support Officer A. Hughes
Head of Pupil Services A. Munro
Schools Officer (Strategic) Judith Moore
Schools Officer (Special) Eric Smith
EOTAS Head of Service Colin Diaper
Divisional Personnel Officer D. Platt
Divisional Training Officer J. Newton
Divisional Finance Officer C. Watson
Divisional Building Planning Officer M. Shefferd
Divisional Staff Development and Training Officer S. Linssen

Divisional Information Officer M. Gamblin
General Inspector Special Needs C. Lloyd
Principal Special Needs Officer J. Reed
Teacher Advisor for Travellers R. Fuszard
Divisional Education Welfare Officer J. McGilvery
Divisional Educational Psychologist C. Turner
Divisional Youth Officer C. Jumar
Divisional Senior Inspector D. Caveen
General Inspector (Primary) K. Hillyer
General Inspector (Primary) T. Hurlin
General Inspector (Primary) T. Walker
General Inspector (Primary) R. Kilgannon
General Inspector (Secondary) M. Newton
County General Inspector (Assessment and Recording of Achievement) G. Hitchcock
County General Inspector (English) K. Marron
General Inspector (History) G. Sherfield
County General Inspector (Mathematics) G. Price
General Inspector (Modern Languages) Kathy Wickstead
General Inspector (Physical Education) S. Poynton
General Inspector (Science) R. Mitchell
Teacher Adviser (Art) W. Richardson
Teacher Adviser (Assessment) D. Tanner
Teacher Adviser (Drama) G. Davies
Teacher Adviser (English) C. Farrow
Teacher Adviser (Geography) J. Stanfield
Teacher Adviser (IT) T. Cook
Teacher Adviser (IT) J. Woollard
Teacher Adviser (Learning Difficulties) E. McAllister
Teacher Adviser (Learning Difficulties) B. Hillier
Teacher Adviser (Modern Foreign Languages) R. Jennings
Teacher Adviser (Music) H. Robberts
Teacher Adviser (Personal, Social and Health Education) P. Forrest
Teacher Adviser (Religious Education) J. Lowndes
Teacher Adviser (Technology) E. Chadwick
Teacher Adviser (Wardrobe) M. Bunyard Hampshire County Wardrobe, Ashbourne Lodge, Andover Rd, Winchester SO22 6AF; Tel (01962) 841581; Fax (01962) 841581

Special Schools

Greenacres School, Andover Rd, Winchester SO22 6AU; Tel (01962) 862450; *Headteacher* D. Skae. (SLD) (5–19)
Icknield, River Way, Andover SP11 6LT; Tel (01264) 365297; Fax (01264) 334794; *Headteacher* S.A. Steer-Smith. (SLD)(2-19)
Lankhills School, Andover Rd, Winchester SO23 7BU; Tel (01962) 854537; Fax (01962) 849419; *Headteacher* D. Nicholls. (MLD) (11–19)
Mark Way, The, Bachelors Barn Rd, Andover SP10 1HR; Tel (01264) 351835; *Headteacher* J.T.P. Mahoney. (MLD)(11-16)
Medecroft Opportunity Centre, Sparkford Rd, Winchester SO22 4NJ; Tel (01962) 860393; *Headteacher* P. Patton. Nursery 2-5
Norman Gate, Vigo Rd, Andover SP10 1JZ; Tel (01264) 323423; *Headteacher* D. Williams. (MLD) (5–11)
Pitmore Special School, Winchester Rd, Chandlers Ford SO5 2DW; Tel (01703) 266633; Fax (01703) 267147; *Headteacher* R. MacDonald. (EBD)
Shepherds Down Special School, Shepherds La, Compton, Winchester SO21 1AJ; Tel (01962) 713453/1713445; *Headteacher* A. Gazzard. (MLD)
Tankerville School, Romsey Rd, Eastleigh SO5 4AJ; Tel (01703) 612639; *Headteacher* G. Clarke. (SLD) (2–19)
Wolverdene School, 22 Love La, Andover SP10 2AF; Tel (01264) 362350; Vacancy. (EBD)(5–11)

Secondary Schools

Alderman Quilley School, Cherbourg Rd, Eastleigh SO5 5EL; Tel (01703) 612330; Fax (01703) 618100; *Headtecher* K. Button. 11–16 Year Olds
The Clere School, Burghclere, Newbury, Berks RG15 9HP; Tel (01635) 27372; Fax (01635) 278538; *Headteacher* D. Thomson. 11–16 Year Olds
Crestwood Community School, Shakespeare Rd, Boyatt Wood, Eastleigh SO5 4FZ; Tel (01703) 641232; Fax (01703) 629373; V. Morley. 11–16 Year Olds
Hamble Secondary School, Satchell La, Hamble-le-Rice, Southampton SO3 5NE; Tel (01703) 452105; Fax (01703) 457439; *Headteacher* R.W. Wilson. 11–16 Year Olds
Harrow Way Community School, Harrow Way, Andover, Hants SP10 3RH; Tel (01264) 364533; *Headteacher* C.J. Overton. 11–16 Year Olds
Henry Beaufort Secondary School, East Woodhay Rd, Harestock, Winchester SO22 6JJ; Tel (01962) 880073; Fax (01962) 883667; *Headteacher* D.J. Dickinson. 11–16 Year Olds
John Hanson Community School, Croye Cl, Andover SP10 3AB; Tel (01264) 352546; Fax (01264) 339685; *Headteacher* G. Wilson. 11–16 Year Olds
Kings Secondary School, Romsey Rd, Winchester SO22 5NP; Tel (01962) 861161; Fax (01962) 849224; *Headteacher* R.W. Bradbury. 11–16 Year Olds
The Mountbatten School, Whitenap La, Romsey SO51 8SY; Tel (01794) 517830; Fax (01794) 511508; *Headteacher* L.K. Morffew. 11–16 Year Olds
Perins Community School, Pound Hill, New Alresford SO24 9BS; Tel (01962) 734361; Fax (01962) 735930; *Headteacher* Glen Strong. 11–16 Year Olds
The Romsey School, Greatbridge Rd, Romsey SO51 8ZB; Tel (01794) 512334; Fax (01794) 511497; *Headteacher* Dr R.A. Skinner. 11–16 Year Olds
Swanmore Secondary School, New Rd, Swanmore, Southampton SO3 2RB; Tel (01489) 892256; Fax (01489) 891453; *Headteacher* A.M. Hillier. 11–16 Year Olds
Test Valley Secondary School, Roman Rd, Stockbridge SO20 6HA; Tel (01264) 810555; Fax (01264) 810173; *Headteacher* W. Morrish. 11–16 Year Olds
Thornden Secondary School, Winchester Rd, Chandlers Ford SO5 2DW; Tel (01703) 269722; Fax (01703) 268393; *Headteacher* Dr R.A. Sykes. 11–16 Year Olds
Toynbee Secondary School, Bodycoats Rd, Chandlers Ford SO5 2PL; Tel (01703) 269026; Fax (01703) 251086; H.J. O'Reilly. 11–16 Year Olds
Westgate Secondary School, Cheriton Rd, Winchester SO22 5AZ; Tel (01962) 854757; Fax (01962) 840080; P.D. Jenner. 11–16 Year Olds
Wildern Secondary School, Wildern La, Hedge End, Southampton SO3 4EJ; Tel (01489) 783473; Fax (01489) 790927; *Headteacher* K. Rockett. 11–16 Year Olds
Winton School, London Rd, Andover, Hants SP10 2PS; Tel (01264) 351822; Fax (01264) 332793; *Headteacher* L.J. Savins. 11–16 Year Olds
The Wyvern Community School, Botley Rd, Fair Oak, Eastleigh SO5 7AN; Tel (01703) 692679; Fax (01703) 602161; *Headteacher* S.P. Campbell. 11–16 Year Olds

Professional Development Centres

Central Division Professional Centre, Falcon Hse, Romsey Rd, Winchester SO22 5PW; Tel (01962) 869611; *Centre Manager* Mrs Moran
Central Division Professional Centre (Andover), St Johns, Junction Rd, Andover SP10 3EG; Tel (01264) 56448

North East Division

Birch Hse, Barley Way, Fleet GU13 8YB; Tel (01252) 812333; Fax (01252) 812363
Assistant County Education Officer E. Poppitt
Management Support Officer I. Bell
Head of Pupil Services P. Lewis
Schools Officer (Strategic) J. Cawthra
Divisional Personnel Officer M. Taylor
Divisional Building Planning Officer D. Kitson
Divisional Finance Officer M. George
Principal Special Needs Officer P. Cawte (Acting)
Divisional Education Welfare Officer J. Heath
Divisional Educational Psychologist S. Turner
Divisional Youth Officer C. Roe
Divisional Senior Inspector Chris Wilson
General Inspector (Primary) L. Smith
General Inspector (Primary) P. Denny

General Inspector (Primary) J. Tyler
General Inspector (Primary) L. Farrow
General Inspector (Primary) J. Dunn
County General Inspector (Drama and Media Studies) A. Black
General Inspector (English) P. Martin
General Inspector (Geography) B. Jones
County General Inspector (Intercultural Education) I. Massey
County General Inspector (Design and Technology) C. Potter
General Inspector (Mathematics) C. Brown
General Inspector (Physical Education) D. Gott
General Inspector (Science) M. Evans
General Inspector (Special Needs) K. Gray
Teacher Adviser Office, Fort Hill Community School, Kenilworth Rd, Basingstoke RG23 8JQ; Tel (01256) 336935/844473; Fax (01256) 57976
Teacher Adviser (Assessment) V. Wainhouse
Teacher Adviser (Drama) C. West
Teacher Adviser (IT) A. Hunt
Teacher Adviser (IT) R. Clough
Teacher Adviser (IT) S. Rees
Teacher Adviser (Music) S. Inglis
Teacher Adviser (Personal, Social and Health Education) M. Davies
Teacher Adviser (Technology) P. Craven
HIASS, Old School Hse, Anstey Rd, Alton GU34 2RA; Tel (01420) 84216
Teacher Adviser (Learning Difficulty) L. Mansfield
Teacher Adviser (Learning Difficulty) M. Pritchard
Teacher Adviser (Learning Difficulty) M. Howells

Special Schools

Dove House Special School, Sutton Rd, Basingstoke RG21 2SU; Tel (01256) 51555; Fax (01256) 29749; *Headteacher* K. Williams. (MLD)(11-16)
The Grange Special School, Croft Rd, Church La East, Aldershot GU11 3HR; Tel (01252) 23583; Fax (01252) 331072; *Headteacher* R. Thompson. (SLD) (5–16)
Green Croft Special School, Ship La, Farnborough GU14 8BX; Tel (01252) 544577; *Headteacher* A.L. Kent. (MLD) (5–11)
Hawthorns School, Pack La, Basingstoke RG22 5TH; Tel (01256) 336601; Fax (01256) 330010; *Headteacher* M. Henderson
Limington House School, St Andrews Rd, Basingstoke RG22 6PS; Tel (01256) 22148; Fax (01256) 58778; *Headteacher* M.J.C. Balson. (SLD)(2-19)
Maple Ridge Special School, Maple Cres, Basingstoke RG21 2SX; Tel (01256) 23639; *Headteacher* F. Fuller
Meadow Special School, Mill Chase Rd, Bordon GU35 0HA; Tel (01420) 474396; *Headteacher* J.L. Owen. (MLD) (5-16)
Samuel Cody School, Lynchford Rd, Farnborough GU14 6BJ; Tel (01252) 314720; Fax (01252) 341869; *Headteacher* L. Bevan. (MLD)(11-16)
Saxon Wood School, Rooksdown La, Basingstoke RG24 9NH; Tel (01256) 56635/6; Fax (01256) 23713; *Headteacher* P.B. Skinner. (PD) (2–11)
Whitedown Special School, Albert Rd, The Butt, Alton GU34 1LP; Tel (01420) 82201; Fax (01420) 542837; *Headteacher* C. Browne. (SLD)(5-19)

Secondary Schools

Amery Hill Secondary School, Amery Hill, Alton GU34 2BZ; Tel (01420) 84545; Fax (01420) 84137; *Headteacher* A. Parry-Jones. 11–16 Year Olds
Bishop Challoner RC (A) Secondary School, St Michael's Rd, Basingstoke RG22 6SR; Tel (01256) 462661; Fax (01256) 810359; *Headteacher* J.F. Murray-Robertson (Acting). 11–16 Year Olds
Brighton Hill Community School, Brighton Way, Basingstoke RG22 4DH; Tel (01256) 50606; Fax (01256) 840116; *Headteacher* A. Kilpatrick. 11–6 Year Olds
Calthorpe Park School, Hitches La, Fleet GU13 8JA; Tel (01252) 613483; Fax (01252) 626091; *Headteacher* C.J. Heasman. 11–16 Year Olds
The Connaught School, Tongham Rd, Aldershot GU12 4AS; Tel (01252) 343723; Fax (01252) 22530; *Headteacher* J.P. Hanna. 11–16 Year Olds
Court Moor School, Spring Woods, Fleet, Aldershot GU13 9SX; Tel (01252) 615065; Fax (01252) 624490; *Headteacher* K. Shorey. 11–16 Year Olds
Cove School, St Johns Rd, Cove, Farnborough GU14 9RN; Tel (01252) 542397; Fax (01252) 524223; *Headteacher* V.M. Hall. 11–16 Year Olds
Cranbourne School, Wessex Cls, Basingstoke, Hants RG21 3NP; Tel (01256) 56056; Fax (01256) 56227; *Headteacher* T.G. Ayres. 11–16 Year Olds
Eggars School, London Rd, Holybourne, Alton GU34 4EQ; Tel (01420) 541194; Fax (01420) 89815; *Headteacher* T.V.B. Morrison. 11–16 Year Olds
Fernhill School, Neville Duke Rd, Fox Lane Est, Farnborough GU14 9BY; Tel (01276) 31777; Fax (01276) 34366; *Headteacher* C. Gilbert. 11–16 Year Olds
Fort Hill Community School, Kenilworth Rd, Basingstoke RG23 8JQ; Tel (01256) 54311; Fax (01256) 25583; *Headteacher* K. Fry. 11–16 Year Olds
Frogmore Community School, Potley Hill Rd, Yateley, Camberley, Surrey GU17 7AG; Tel (01252) 870563; Fax (01252) 890459; *Headteacher* P. Harwood. 11–18 Year Olds
Harriet Costello Secondary School, Crossborough Hill, London Rd, Basingstoke RG21 2AG; Tel (01256) 21263; Fax (01256) 58629; *Headteacher* H. Smith (Acting). 11–16 Year Olds
The Hurst Community School, Brimpton Rd, Baughurst, Basingstoke RG26 5NL; Tel (01734) 817474; Fax (01734) 817976; *Headteacher* R. Bower
John Hunt of Everest Community School, Popley Way, Basingstoke RG24 9AB; Tel (01256) 465547; Fax (01256) 810448; *Headteacher* D. Jones. 11–16 Year Olds
Mill Chase Community School, Mill Chase Rd, Bordon, Hants GU35 0ER; Tel (01420) 472132; Fax (01420) 479986; *Headteacher* A. Philpott. 11–16 Year Olds
Oak Farm Community School, Chaucer Rd, Cove, Farnborough GU14 8SS; Tel (01252) 513333; Fax (01252) 515826; *Headteacher* M. Christian. 11–16 Year Olds
The Petersfield School, Cranford Rd, Petersfield GU32 3LU; Tel (01730) 263119; Fax (01730) 265869; *Headteacher* K. Bell. 11–18 Year Olds
Richard Aldworth Community School, Western Way, Basingstoke, Hants RG22 6HA; Tel (01256) 22691; Fax (01256) 819756; *Headteacher* M. Ward. 11–16 Year Olds
Robert May's School, West St, Odiham RG25 1NA; Tel (01256) 702700; Fax (01256) 703012; *Headteacher* W.R. Sarell. 11–16 Year Olds
The Vyne Secondary School, Vyne Rd, Basingstoke, Hants RG21 2BP; Tel (01256) 473003; Fax (01256) 816956; *Headteacher* R. Green. 11–16 Year Olds
The Wavell School, Lynchford Rd, Farnborough GU14 6BN; Tel (01252) 341256; Fax (01252) 345613; *Headteacher* J. Foxley. 11–16 Year Olds
Yateley School, School La, Yateley, Camberley, Surrey GU17 7NW; Tel (01252) 879222; Fax (01252) 872517; *Headteacher* Dr R.I. Goodall. 11–18 Year Olds

South East Division

River Way, Havant PO9 2EL; Tel (01705) 498200
Assistant County Education Officer G. Heller
Special Needs Inspector J. Samuel
Management Support Officer C. Bassett
Head of Pupil Services P. Carpenter
Schools Officer (Strategic) A. Begley
Schools Officer (Special) K. Gill
Schools Officer (Strategic) B. Lloyd Jones
Divisional Personnel Officer G. Ault
Divisional Projects Manager H. Bancroft
Divisional Building Planning Officer P. Colenutt
Divisional Training and Staff Development Manager T. O'Mahony
Divisional Training Officer A. Scoffin
Divisional Finance Officer R. Barnes
Divisional Information Officer N. Withington
Principal Special Needs Officer F. Dickinson

Divisional Welfare Officer R. Ward
Assistant Principal Educational Psychologist K. Bowen
Divisional Youth Officer M. Limb
Divisional Senior Inspector A. Bartlett
General Inspector (Primary) G. Crosby
General Inspector (Primary) N. Saunders
General Inspector (Primary) J. Warwick
General Inspector (Primary) P. Lamb
General Inspector (Primary) B. Woods
General Inspector (Primary) R. Rix
Secondary Inspector A. Rawlings
County General Inspector (Art) M. Schley
General Inspector (English) K. Wilby
County General Inspector (History) N. Thompson
County General Inspector (Information Technology) M. Wilson
General Inspector (Mathematics) W. Hoskin
County General Inspector (Modern Languages) B. Thomas
General Inspector (Physical Education) J. Drake
County General Inspector (Religious Education) A. Brine
County General Inspector (Science) D. Evans
General Inspector (Special Educational Needs) D. Hogg
HIASS, Divisional Professional Centre, Sundridge Cl, Cosham, Portsmouth PO6 3JL; Tel (01705) 214335; Fax (01705) 201564
Teacher Adviser (Assessment) H. Francis
Teacher Adviser (Drama) S. Sheach
Teacher Adviser (English) G. Ellinas
Teacher Adviser (IT) S. Holroyd
Teacher Adviser (IT) S. Kenny
Teacher Adviser (Learning Difficulties) D. Mitchell
Teacher Adviser (Learning Difficulties) J. Hicks
Teacher Adviser (Learning Difficulties) J. Begley
Teacher Adviser (Music) K. Parkes
Teacher Adviser (Personal, Social and Health Education) S. Falconer
Teacher Adviser (Science) P. Patterson
Teacher Adviser (Technology) C. Thompson
Hampshire Microtechnology Centre, Connaught La, Paulsgrove, Portsmouth PO6 4SJ; Tel (01705) 378266; Fax (01705) 379443
Technical Support Manager
County Co-ordinator for IT in SEN N. Dalton
Centre Manager P. Heinrich
Teacher Adviser (IT) C. Shaw

Special Schools

Baycroft School, Gosport Rd, Stubbington, Fareham PO14 2AE; Tel (01329) 664151; Fax (01329) 668601; *Headteacher* R.A. Hendry. (MLD) (11–16)
Cliffdale Primary School, Battenburg Ave, North End, Portsmouth PO2 0SN; Tel (01705) 662601; Fax (01705) 660506; *Headteacher* L.C. Handford. (MLD) (4–11)
Cliffdale Secondary Special School, Wembley Gr, Highbury, Portsmouth PO6 2RY; Tel (01705) 377500; Fax (01705) 201104; *Headteacher* J.M. Thomas. (MLD) (11–16)
East Shore Special School, Eastern Rd, Milton, Portsmouth PO3 6EP; Tel (01705) 839331; Fax (01705) 872504; *Headteacher* M.J. Vicary. (SLD) (3–19)
Foxbury Special School, Perth Rd, Bridgemary, Gosport PO13 0XX; Tel (01329) 232998; *Headteacher* T.A. Pearson. (MLD)(3–11)
Furzebrook Special School, Cold East Way, Sarisbury Gr, Southampton SO31 7AT; Tel (01489) 582684; Fax (01489) 579915; *Headteacher* J. Bell. (SLD) (2–19)
The Futcher Special School, Drayton La, Drayton, Portsmouth PO6 1HG; Tel (01705) 375318; *Headteacher* J.C. Meek. (PD)(3–16)
Glenwood School, Silvester Rd, Cowplain, Waterlooville PO8 8TR; Tel (01705) 255657; Fax (01705) 253214; *Headteacher* C.A. Hill. (MLD) (11–16)
Heathfield Special School, Oldbury Way, Peak La, Fareham PO14 3BN; Tel (01329) 845150; *Headteacher* E. Muirhead. (MLD/PD) (3–11)
Rachel Madocks School, Eagle Ave, Cowplain, Waterlooville PO8 9XP; Tel (01705) 241818; Fax (01705) 269521; *Headteacher* P. Clarke. (SLD) (3–19)
Riverside School, Middle Park Way, Leigh Pk, Havant PO9 4BZ; Tel (01705) 483733; Fax (01705) 498482; *Headteacher* D.W. Jones. (MLD) (3–12)
St Francis Special School, Patchway Dr, Oldbury Way, Fareham PO14 3BN; Tel (01329) 845730; Fax (01329) 847217; *Headteacher* S. Chalmers. (SLD) (2–19)
Waterloo Special School, Warfield Ave, Waterlooville PO7 7JJ; Tel (01705) 255956; Fax (01705) 241150; G. Davies. (EBD) (5–16)
Waterside Special School, Tipner La, Tipner, Portsmouth PO2 8RA; Tel (01705) 665664; Fax (01705) 670479; T.S. Stokes. (EBD) (6–16)
The Willows Special School, Battenburg Ave, North End, Portsmouth PO2 0SN; Tel (01705) 666918; Fax (01705) 651138; *Headteacher* A.M. Swann. (Nursery 2–5)

Secondary Schools

Bridgemary Community School, Wych La, Gosport PO13 0JN; Tel (01329) 319966; Fax (01329) 319977; *Headteacher* J.M. Barratt. 11–16 Year Olds
Brookfield Community School, Brook La, Sarisbury Grn, Southampton SO31 7DU; Tel (01489) 576335; Fax (01489) 579914; *Headteacher* M.G. Roe. 11–16 Year Olds
Brune Park Secondary School, Military Rd, Gosport PO12 3BU; Tel (01705) 587031; Fax (01705) 525302; *Headteacher* M. Keeping. 11–16 Year Olds
City of Portsmouth Girls Secondary School, St Mary's Rd, Portsmouth PO1 5PF; Tel (01705) 812822; Fax (01705) 872022; *Headteacher* D.P. Smith. 11–16 Year Olds
Cowplain School, Hart Plain Ave, Cowplain, Waterlooville PO8 8RY; Tel (01705) 612020; Fax (01705) 612030; *Headteacher* I.D. Hammond. 11–16 Year Olds
Crookhorn Community School, Stakes Hill Rd, Purbrook, Waterlooville PO7 5UD; Tel (01705) 251120; Fax (01705) 230310; *Headteacher* J. Adam. 11–16 Year Olds
The Hayling School, Church Rd, Hayling Island PO11 0NU; Tel (01705) 466241; Fax (01705) 461835; *Headteacher* J. Moran. 11–16 Year Olds
Henry Cort Community School, Hillson Dr, Fareham PO15 6PH; Tel (01329) 843127; Fax (01329) 846755; *Headteacher* J.H. Bulled. 11–16 Year Olds
Horndean Community School, Barton Cross, Horndean, Portsmouth PO8 9PQ; Tel (01705) 594325; Fax (01705) 571108; *Headteacher* G. Crane. 11–18 Year Olds
King Richard Secondary School, Allaway Ave, Paulsgrove, Portsmouth PO6 4QP; Tel (01705) 370321; Fax (01705) 384811; *Headteacher* P. Warburton. 11–16 Year Olds
Mayfield Secondary School, Mayfield Rd, Portsmouth PO2 0RH; Tel (01705) 693432; Fax (01705) 665298; *Headteacher* R.D. Chester. 11–16 Year Olds
Neville Lovett Community School, St Anne's Grove, Fareham PO14 1JJ; Tel (01329) 282951; Fax (01329) 284007; *Headteacher* N. Dewhurst. 11–16 Year Olds
Park Community School, Middle Park Way, Leigh Pk, Havant PO9 4BU; Tel (01705) 475254; Fax (01705) 481012; *Headteacher* G.R.J. Morris. 11–16 Year Olds
Portchester Community School, White Hart La, Portchester, Fareham PO16 9BD; Tel (01705) 373151; Fax (01705) 201528; *Headteacher* G.M. West. 11–16 Year Olds
Priory Secondary School, Fawcett Rd, Southsea PO4 0DL; Tel (01705) 819115; Fax (01705) 872143; *Headteacher* B.L. Davies. 11–16 Year Olds
St Luke's C.E. (A) Secondary School, Hyde Park Rd, Southsea, Hants PO5 4HL; Tel (01705) 824204; Fax (01705) 829867; *Headteacher* D.P. Bailey. 11–16 Year Olds
Springfield Secondary School, Central Rd, Drayton, Portsmouth PO6 1QY; Tel (01705) 379119; Fax (01705) 388784; *Headteacher* A.L. Knight. 11–16 Year Olds

Staunton Park Secondary School, Wakefords Way, Havant PO9 5JD; Tel (01705) 473031; Fax (01705) 470384; *Headteacher* A.J. Robertson. 11–16 Year Olds
Warblington Secondary School, Southleigh Rd, Havant PO9 2RR; Tel (01705) 475480; Fax (01705) 486127; *Headteacher* E.A. Greenway. 11–16 Year Olds

Professional Development Centre

Divisional Professional Centre, Sundridge Cls, Cosham, Portsmouth PO6 3JL; Tel (01705) 324657; Fax (01705) 201564; *Centre Manager* P. Pond

South West Division

Arundel Towers North, Portland Terr, Southampton SO14 7LN; Tel (01703) 635100; Fax (01703) 232535
Assistant County Education Officer R. Jones
General Inspector Special Needs G. Tester
Management Support Officer G. McGill
Head of Pupil Services Mike Clarke
Schools Officer (Strategic) C. Holt
Schools Officer (Special) O. Greenwood
Divisional Education Personnel Adviser R. O'Reilly
Divisional Building Planning Officer B. Cleightonhills
Training Manager (South West) E. Gower
Financial Services Manager K. Badnell
Divisional Information Officer A. Pollard
Principal Special Needs Officer V. Wales
Divisional Welfare Officer J. Osburn
Divisional Educational Psychologist P. Sharp
Divisional Youth Officer P. Read
HIASS SW Division, Winsor Rd, Bartley, Southampton SO40 2HR; Fax (01703) 814642
Divisional Senior Inspector P. Newlands; Tel (01703) 814603
General Inspector (Primary) C. Poulter; Tel (01703) 813825
General Inspector (Primary) J. Exley; Tel (01703) 814604
General Inspector (Primary) C. Randerson; Tel (01703) 814601
General Inspector (Primary) I. Sandbrook; Tel (01703) 813825
General Inspector (Secondary) T. Byrne; Tel (01703) 814605
General Inspector (Secondary) R. Tong; Tel (01703) 814601
County General Inspector (Careers Education and Guidance/PSE) A. Walkling; Tel (01703) 814604
County General Inspector (Music) R. Howlett; Tel (01703) 814602
County General Inspector (Physical Education) T. Reynolds; Tel (01703) 813825
General Inspector (Mathematics) R. Taylor; Tel (01703) 814605
General Inspector (Science) J. Moore; Tel (01703) 812832
County General Inspector (Geography) A. Pearce; Tel (01703) 814603
Teacher Adviser (Assessment) M. Tumelty; Tel (01703) 814602
Teacher Adviser (English) S. Buckingham; Tel (01703) 812832
Teacher Adviser (History) J. Rowley; Tel (01703) 814601
Teacher Adviser (IT) A. Rothwell; Tel (01703) 814602
Teacher Adviser (IT) M. Steeds; Tel (01703) 814601
Teacher Adviser (Learning Difficulties) M. Brown; Tel (01703) 813825
Teacher Adviser (Learning Difficulties) O. Colvin; Tel (01703) 814601
Teacher Adviser (Learning Difficulties) H. Guilmont; Tel (01703) 814603
Teacher Adviser (Learning Difficulties) S. Stares; Tel (01703) 814602
Teacher Adviser (Mathematics) S. Bird; Tel (01703) 814604
Teacher Adviser (Music) S. Beckett; Tel (01703) 814605
Teacher Adviser (Personal, Social and Health Education) H. Grabham; Tel (01703) 813825
Teacher Adviser (Religious Education) N. Horrigan; Tel (01703) 812832
Teacher Adviser (Technology) B. Cooper; Tel (01703) 814602
Healthy Schools Award Co-ordinator J. Sidonio; Tel (01703) 814605

Special Schools

Buckland School, Paddock Gdns, Off Southampton Rd, Lymington SO41 9ES; Tel (01590) 677133; Fax (01590) 671250; *Headteacher* S. Crowley. (EBD)(10–16)
The Cedar Special School, Redbridge La, Nursling, Southampton SO1 9XN; Tel (01703) 734205; Fax (01703) 738231; *Headteacher* B.C. Hart. (PD) (3-16)
Forest Edge School, Lydlynch Rd, Totton, Southampton SO40 3DW; Tel (01703) 864949; *Headteacher* P. Hodgson. (MLD) (4–11)
Netley Court Special School, Victoria Rd, Netley Abbey, Southampton SO31 5DR; Tel (01703) 453259; *Headteacher* W.R. Ferry. (MLD) (4–11)
Oak Lodge Special School, Roman Rd, Dibden Purlieu, Southampton SO45 5RQ; Tel (01703) 847213; *Headteacher* B.A. Hawker. (MLD) (11–16)
The Polygon Special School, Handel Terr, The Polygon, Southampton SO1 2FH; Tel (01703) 636776; *Headteacher* L.M. Gent. (EBD) (11–16)
Red Lodge School, Vermont Cl, Off Winchester Rd, Southampton SO1 7LT; Tel (01703) 767660; *Headteacher* D.J. Hughes. (MLD) (11–16)
Ridgeway Hse, Peartree Ave, Bitterne, Southampton SO2 7JL; Tel (01703) 448897; *Headteacher* S.J. Savage. (SLD) (3–19)
Salterns Special School, Commercial Rd, Totton, Southampton SO40 3AF; Tel (01703) 864211; *Headteacher* C. Fletcher. (SLD)(3–19)
Vermont School, Vermont Cl, off Winchester Rd, Southampton SO16 7LT; Tel (01703) 767988; *Headteacher* Vacancy. (EBD) (4–11)

Secondary Schools

Bellemoor Secondary School, Bellemoor Rd, Shirley, Southampton, Hants SO15 7QU; Tel (01703) 325333; Fax (01703) 770318; *Headteacher* R. Patterson. 11–16 Year Olds
Bitterne Park Secondary School, Dimond Rd, Southampton, Hants SO18 1BU; Tel (01703) 325200; Fax (01703) 325222; *Headteacher* D.J. Nightingale. 11–16 Year Olds
Cantell Secondary School, Violet Rd, Southampton SO16 3GJ; Tel (01703) 323111; Fax (01703) 322433; *Headteacher* D. Burge. 11–16 Year Olds
Chamberlayne Pk School, Winchfield Cls, Southampton SO2 9JF; Tel (01703) 447820; *Headteacher* R. Hilary (Acting). 12–16 Year Olds
Hounsdown Secondary School, Jacob's Gutter La, Totton, Southampton SO40 9FT; Tel (01703) 862981; Fax (01703) 663160; *Headteacher* M.C. Gibbons. 11–16 Year Olds
Millbrook Community School, Green La, Maybush, Southampton SO16 9LA; Tel (01703) 771881; Fax (01703) 512195; *Headteacher* M. Ellis. 11–16 Year Olds
Noadswood Secondary School, North Rd, Dibden Purlieu, Southampton SO45 4ZF; Tel (01703) 840025; Fax (01703) 843532; *Headteacher* J. Samuels. 11–16 Year Olds
Oaklands Community School, Fairisle Rd, Lords Hill, Southampton SO16 8BY; Tel (01703) 739595; Fax (01703) 731996; Dr P. Hollis. 11–16 Year Olds
Priestlands Secondary School, North St, Pennington, Lymington SO41 8FZ; Tel (01590) 677033; *Headteacher* R.L. Martin. 11–16 Year Olds
Redbridge Community School, Cuckmere La, Southampton SO16 9RJ; Tel (01703) 771381; Fax (01703) 510004; *Headteacher* M. Harris. 11–16 Year Olds

Regents Park Secondary School, King Edward Ave, Regents Pk, Southampton SO16 4GW; Tel (01703) 325444; Fax (01703) 322411; *Headteacher* J.M. Rattle. (Girls) 11–16 Year Olds
Sholing Secondary (Girls) School, Middle Rd, Southampton, Hants SO19 8PH; Tel (01703) 448861; Fax (01703) 422998; *Headteacher* N.G.M. Etheridge. (Girls) (11–16 Year Olds
Weston Park Boys Secondary School, The Grove, Southampton SO2 9LX; Tel (01703) 328128; Fax (01703) 328228; *Headteacher* P.L. Coote. 11–16 Year Olds
Woodlands Community School, Minstead Ave Harefield, Southampton SO18 5FW; Tel (01703) 463303; Fax (01703) 462342; *Headteacher* P. Burke. 11–16 Year Olds
Woolston Secondary School, Portchester Rd, Southampton SO19 2JD; Tel (01703) 448318; Fax (01703) 685729; J. Masters. 11–16 Year Olds

Grant Maintained Schools

Applemore College, Roman Rd, Dibden Purlieu, Southampton SO45 4RQ; Tel (01703) 848804; *Principal* F.C. Callaghan. (SPLD) (11-16)
The Arnewood School, Gore Rd, New Milton BH25 6RS; Tel (01425) 610186; Fax (01425) 612036; *Headteacher* G.R. Skirton; *Chair of Governors* E. Cook. (Mixed (11–18) (1180)
Arnewood Secondary School, Gore Rd, New Milton BH25 6RS; Tel (01425) 610186; G.R. Skirton
Bay House School, Gomer La, Alverstoke, Gosport PO12 2QP; Tel (01705) 587931; *Headteacher* R.J. Cootes. (11–16 Year Olds)
Bohunt Community School, Longmoor Rd, Liphook GU30 7NY; Tel (01428) 724324; *Headteacher* Dr A. Leech. (11–16 Year Olds)
The Burgate School, Salisbury Rd, Fordingbridge SP6 1EZ; Tel (01425) 652039; *Headteacher* C. Nicholls; *Chair of Governors* Colin Knapman. Mixed (11–18) (566)
Cams Hill School, Rooksway Grove, Fareham PO16 8AH; Tel (01329) 283996; Fax (01329) 283996; *Headteacher* J. Hayward. (11–16 Year Olds)
The City of Portsmouth Boys School, London Rd, Hilsea, Portsmouth PO2 9RJ; Tel (01705) 693521; *Headteacher* M.E.B. Lloyd. 12–16 Year Olds
Crofton School, Marks Rd, Stubbington, Fareham PO14 2AT; Tel (01329) 664251; *Headteacher* S.J. Horner. 11–16 Year Olds
Hardley School, Long La, Fawley, Southampton SO4 1PA; Tel (01703) 891192; Fax (01703) 892463; *Headteacher* R. Underwood; *Chair of Governors* M. Galpin. (Mixed) (11–16) (666)
Oaklands RC Comprehensive School, Stakes Hill Rd, Purbrook, Portsmouth PO7 7BW; Tel (01705) 259214; *Headteacher* C. Whitfield. 11–18 Year Olds
Purbrook School, Park Ave, Purbrook, Portsmouth PO7 5DS; Tel (01705) 370351; *Headteacher* M. Dopson. 11–16 Year Olds
Ringwood School, Parsonage Barn La, Ringwood BH24 1RE; Tel (01425) 475000; *Headteacher* Anthony Maw; *Chair of Governors* Rev John Turpin. (Mixed) (11–16) (designated 11–18 from 1.9.95) (824)
St Anne's RC Secondary School, Rockstone Pl, Southampton SO9 4TE; Tel (01703) 631255; Fax (01703) 331767; *Headteacher* C. Hargaden. A) (Girls) (11–18 Year Olds
St Edmund's RC (A) Secondary School, Arundel St, Portsmouth PO1 1RX; Tel (01705) 823766; Fax (01705) 871874; *Headteacher* B.M. Wright. 11–18 Year Olds
St George Catholic School for Boys, Leaside Way, Swaythling, Southampton S016 3DQ; Tel (01703) 322603; Fax (01703) 322606; *Headteacher* D.J. Caswell. 11–16 Year Olds
Testbourne Community School Grant Maintained, Micheldever Rd, Whitchurch RG28 7JF; Tel (01256) 892061; *Headteacher* T.R.T. Pankhurst. 11–16 Year Olds
Testwood School, Testwood La, Totton, Southampton SO4 3ZW; Tel (01703) 862146; Fax (01703) 666514; *Headteacher* M.A. Capsomidis, MA. (11–16 Year Olds)

Hereford and Worcester County Council

Population 694,835
County Hall, Spetchley Rd, Worcester WR5 2NP; Tel (01905) 763763; Fax (01905) 763000; Dx Mailing Number 29941 Worcester 2

Education Offices

County Education Dept, PO Box 73, Worcester WR5 2YA; Tel (01905) 763763; Fax (01905) 768400
County Education Officer D.A.J. Stanley, BA, DipEd, DipPE
PEO (Information and Budgetary Systems) Dr E. Oram
Principal Development Officer (Buildings and Development) G. Salmon, MA(Cantab), MCD, MSc
PEO (Professional and Learning Services) C.C. Bayne-Jardine, MA, MEd
PA EO (Budget) W.R. Powell, FCA
AEO (Buildings) J.S. Glen
AEO (Personnel) P.R. Greenwood, BSc
AEO (Special Services) M.C. Davies
AEO (Administration) E.C. Parkinson, MBA, MIMgtd
AEO (Accommodation) C.C. March
AEO (LMS & Planning) L. Peel, MPhil, BSc(Hon)
AEO (Governor Services) E.J. Dancey, BPhil.Ed
AEO (Operations) A. Heath, BA
AEO (Operations) D.K.N. Kift, BA, MEd
County Careers Officer R.F. Little, BA(Hons)
Head of Inspection, Advice and Training S. Boulter Pitmaston Hse, Malvern Rd, Worcester; Tel (01905) 420818
Senior County Inspector (Curriculum and Development) R. Bentley
Senior County Inspector (Special Education) G. Davies
Senior County Inspector (Primary and Deputy Head) C. Wilkinson
County Inspector (Science) A. Allchin
County Inspector (Primary) M. Carter
County Inspector (Environmental Education) M. Cash
County Inspector (Physical Education) Mrs M. Hunt
County Inspector (Training Assessment and Appraisal) Dr J. Jones
County Inspector (Primary) P. Morris
County Inspector (Arts) P. Murray
County Inspector (Music) C. Polyblank
County Inspector (Humanities) J. Prangnell
County Inspector (English and Drama) M. Riches
County Inspector (Design and Technology) P. Round
County Inspector (Primary) S. Sage
County Inspector (Primary) T. St George
County Inspector (Modern Languages) V. Ward
County Inspector (Primary) G. Warren
Senior County Inspector (Mathematics and Information Technology) R. Westwood
Principal County Youth Officer M. Price, BA(Hons) Education Department, PO Box 73, Worcester WR5 2YA; Tel (01905) 763763; Fax (01905) 768400
Principal County Educational Psychologist T.J. Jellis, MA, MPhil, ABPsS
Number of Schools
281 primary schools; 10 middle (deemed primary); 29 middle (deemed secondary); 42 secondary; 2 county outdoor education centres

Special Schools
14 special schools; 3 day education centres
Day of Committee Meeting
Friday quarterly
Requisition Periods for School Supplies
None
Other Authorities with whom Joint Purchasing Arrangements are made
Shropshire County Council

Education Committee

Lab 9, Con 9, LD 8, Ind 2
Chairman R. Clayton, (Lab) 3 Cherry Orchard Dr, Bromsgrove, Worcs B61 8RJ; Tel (01527) 36693 (Home)
Vice-Chairman Lady Carolyn Harford, (LD) South Hse, South Littleton, Evesham, Worcs WR11 5TJ; Tel (01386) 830478; Fax (01386) 833165
Members of the Committee
Lab: D. Barlow, M. Harford, W.P.A. Hartnett, D.A. Lewis, J.T. O'Reilly, R.W. Passingham, C. Walker, P.D. Wicksteed
Con: J.T. Arnett, L.O. Barnett, M. Bemand, G.L.J. Bruce-Morgan, A.E. Davies, C.K. Davies, P.E. Harling, J.P. Hart, J. Longmuir
LD: B.M. Ingham, C.F. Knock, R.C. Mason, R.P. Neath, M.M.G. Oborski, J.M. Pickering, C.H. Whitaker
Ind: M.J. Davey, E.M. Saunders

East Division

Kingfisher Hse, Kingfisher Walk, Redditch, Worcs B97 4EP; Tel (01527) 66544
Divisional Administrative Officer A. Salerman

North Division

Kidderminster County Bldgs, Bewdley Rd, Kidderminster, Worcs DY11 6RT; Tel (01562) 820840
Divisional Administrative Officer P.G. Bailey

South Division

County Buildings, St Mary's St, Worcester WR1 1HA; Tel (01905) 763763
Divisional Administrative Officer M.L. Hughes

West Division

Bath St, Hereford HR1 2HQ; Tel (01432) 276401
Divisional Administrative Officer M. Chamberlain

Service for Children with Sensory Impairment

17 Castle St, Worcester WR1 3AG; Tel (01905) 765629; *Head of Service* S. Seymour

Special Schools

Alexander Patterson, Park Gate Rd, Wolverley, Kidderminster, Worcs DY10 3PU; Tel (01562) 851396; V.W. Stroud
Barrs Court, Barrs Court Rd, Hereford HR1 1EQ; Tel (01432) 265035; F.W.S. Dove
Blackmarston, Ross Rd, Hereford HR2 7RL; Tel (01432) 272376; F.W. Price
Blakebrook, Bewdley Rd, Kidderminster, Worcs DY11 6RL; Tel (01562) 753066; M. Russell
Chadsgrove, Meadow Rd, Catshill, Bromsgrove, Worcs B61 0JW; Tel (01527) 71511; R.H. Aust
Cliffey Hse, Rhydd, Hanley Castle, Worcester WR8 0AD; Tel (01684) 310336/310524; A.T. Hallett
Manor Park, Turnpike Cl, Oldbury Rd, Worcs WR2 6AB; Tel (01905) 423403; D.C. Palmer
Pitcheroak, Willow Way, Redditch, Worcs B97 6PQ; Tel (01527) 65576; C. Auger
Rigby Hall, Rigby La, Bromsgrove, Worcs B60 2EP; Tel (01527) 75475; P.A. Griffiths
Rose Hill, Windermere Dr, Warndon, Worcs WR4 9JL; Tel (01905) 454828; F.W. Steel, BPhilEd
Stourminster, Comberton Rd, Kidderminster, Worcs DY10 3DX; Tel (01562) 823156/747183 (Headteacher); J. Drew
Thornton House, Wylds La, Worcester WR5 1DR; Tel (01905) 355525 (Nursery Unit 355191); H.B. Thomas. (plus Nursery Unit)(Various handicaps)+ Unit for Autistic children (Mixed) (27)
The Vale of Evesham, Four Pools La, Evesham, Worcs WR11 6DH; Tel (01386) 443367; *Act HT* E.P. Matthews
Westfield, Westfield Walk, Leominster HR6 8HD; Tel (01568) 613147; Mrs P. Chesters

Special Units

The John Corbett Unit, Shaw La, Stoke Prior, Bromsgrove, Worcs B60 4OL; Tel (01527) 78888; W. Briggs
The John Venn Unit, Coningsby St, Hereford HR1 2DY; Tel (01432) 3265153; D. Harris
Hugh Latimer Unit, Thorneloe Rd, Worcester WR1 3HZ; Tel (01905) 21261; L.M. Isaaks

Day Education Centres

Redditch Day Education Centre, Prophets Cl, Batchley, Redditch, Worcs B97 4SD; Tel (01527) 63577; Mrs V.M. Martin
Severnside Day Education Centre, 51 Coventry St, Kidderminster, Worcs DY10 2BZ; Tel (01562) 824309; Mrs S. Nash
Worcester Day Education Centre, Glebe Cls, St John's, Worcester WR2 5BT; Tel (01905) 426881; Mrs B.L. Scott

Middle Schools

Alvechurch C.E., Tanyard La, Alvechurch, Birmingham B48 7LN; Tel 0121-445 1033; C. Nesbitt. Controlled) (9–13
Areley Kings, The Windmill C.E. Princess Way, Walshes Est, Stourport-on-Severn, Worcs DY13 0EL; Tel (01299) 823454; T.M.S. Holland. (Controlled) (9–13)
Bewdley, St Anne's C.E. Wyre Hill, Bewdley, Worcs DY12 2UQ; Tel (01299) 403180; J. Armstrong. (Controlled) (9–13)
Bewdley, Wribbenhall, Stourport Rd, Bewdley, Worcs DY12 1BL; Tel (01299) 401088; J.P.W. Nightingale. 9–13
Bredon Hill Ashton-under-Hill, Evesham, Worcs WR11 6SW; Tel (01386) 881426; C.G. Bourne. (10–13)
Bromsgrove Aston Fields, Drummond Rd, Bromsgrove, Worcs B60 2ET; Tel (01527) 76026; B.V. Dinsdale. 9-13
Bromsgrove Meadow Rd, Catshill, Bromsgrove, Worcs B61 0JW; Tel (01527) 72431; Fax (01527) 37113; J.S. Gould. (9-13)
Bromsgrove Parkside, Stourbridge Rd, Bromsgrove, Worcs B61 0AD; Tel (01527) 73660; L.F. Carroll. County; (9-13)
Bromsgrove, The Lickey First and Middle, Old Birmingham Rd, Rednal, Birmingham B45 8EU; Tel 0121-445 1992; A.C. Ince. (5-12)
Drakes Broughton St Barnabas C.E. First and Middle, Pershore, Worcs WR10 2AW; Tel (01905) 840366; R.F. Godsall. Controlled; 5-12
Droitwich Westacre, Ombersley Way, Droitwich, Worcs WR9 0AA; Tel (01905) 772795; R.F. Derwas. (9-12)
Droitwich Witton, Old Coach Rd, Droitwich, Worcs WR9 8BD; Tel (01905) 773362; Fax (01905) 795474; D.C. Coll. (9-12)
Evesham Blackminster, Station Rd, South Littleton, Evesham, Worcs WR11 5TG; Tel (01386) 830311; Fax (01386) 832024; T. Hodgkinson. (10-13)
Evesham St Egwin's C.E. Worcester Rd, Evesham, Worcs WR11 4JU; Tel (01386) 446924; Fax (01386) 761016; *Head* T.W. Taylor (Acting). (Controlled); (10-13)
Evesham Simon de Montford, Four Pools La, Evesham, Worcs WR11 6DH; Tel (01386) 442204; Fax (01386) 442204; G.A. Burgess. (10–13)

Frankley Frogmill, Wareham Rd, Rubery, Rednal, Birmingham B45 0JS; Tel 0121-453 8659; A. Wood. (8-12)
Frankley Reaside, Tresco Cl, Frankley, Rubery, Rednal, Birmingham B45 0HY; Tel 0121-453 7235; Mrs S.J. Oakes. 8-12
Hagley Park Rd, Hagley, Stourbridge, West Midlands DY9 0NS; Tel (01562) 884375; A.C. Gilmour. (9–13)
Kidderminster Birchen Coppice, Woodbury Rd, Kidderminster, Worcs DY11 7JJ; Tel (01562) 824024; Fax (01562) 862875; G.L. Wainwright. (9–13)
Kidderminster Comberton, Borrington Rd, Kidderminster, Worcs DY10 3ED; Tel (01562) 745339; Fax (01562) 60257; J.A. Harradine. (9-13)
Kidderminster Franche, Chestnut Gr, Kidderminster, Worcs DY11 5QB; Tel (01562) 823794; P.St.C. Frizzelle. 9-13
Kidderminster, St John's C.E. Blakebrook, Kidderminster, Worcs DY11 6AP; Tel (01562) 752155; G.M. Cape. (Controlled) (9–13)
Kidderminster, Sion Hill, Sion Hill, Kidderminster, Worcs DY10 2XT; Tel (01562) 755760; G.G. Perkin. (9–13)
Kidderminster, The Sladen C.E. Hurcott Rd, Kidderminster, Worcs DY10 2QJ; Tel (01562) 822351; Fax (01562) 861313; N.R. Bowring. (Special Agreement) (9–13)
Pershore Abbey Park, Abbey Rd, Pershore, Worcs WR10 1DF; Tel (01386) 552667; T.N. Williams. 9-12
Pinvin St Nicholas C.E., Pershore, Worcs WR10 2ER; Tel (01386) 554196; P. Spurr. (Controlled); (9–12)
Redditch Birchensale, Bridley Moor Rd, Redditch, Worcs B97 6HT; Tel (01527) 68430; Fax (01527) 584190; *Head* I. Bridgewater (Acting). (9–13)
Redditch Church Hill, Wood Piece La, Church Hill, Redditch, Worcs B98 9LR; Tel (01527) 585580; E.J. Jackson. 9-13
Redditch Dingleside, Woodrow North, Redditch, Worcs B98 7SH; Tel (01527) 27116; J.M. Allbut. (9–13)
Redditch Lodge Farm, Studley Rd, Redditch, Worcs B98 7HH; Tel (01527) 27081; Fax (01527) 516586; A.C. Jolly. (9–13)
Redditch Moatfield, Easenhall La, Redditch, Worcs B98 0BJ; Tel (01527) 24484; D.C. Barnes. 9-13
Redditch The Ridgeway, Evesham Rd, Astwood Bank, Redditch, Worcs B96 6BD; Tel (01527) 892867; Fax (01527) 893909; R.S. Cox. (9–13)
Redditch St Peter's C.E. Lowlands La, Redditch, Worcs B98 0JL; Tel (01527) 25725; Miss V.J. Cole. Controlled; 9-13
Redditch St Stephen's C.E. Mabey Ave, Redditch, Worcs B98 8HW; Tel (01527) 62558; F. Brassington. Controlled; (9–13)
Redditch Walkwood C.E. Feckenham Rd, Headless Cross, Redditch, Worcs B97 5AQ; Tel (01527) 543361; Fax (01527) 550232; M. Gallagher. (Controlled); (9–13)
Rubery, Beaconside First and Middle, Hazel Rd, Rubery, Rednal, Birmingham B45 9DX; Tel 0121-453 3801; R.F. Moore. 5-12
Rubery Gannow, Gunner La, Rubery, Rednal, Birmingham B45 9EY; Tel 0121-453 2250; D.J. Roberts. 8-12
Stourport-on-Severn Burlish, Coniston Cres, Burlish Pk, Stourport-on-Severn, Worcs DY13 8LA; Tel (01299) 825763; M.J.A. Underdown. (9–13)
Stourport-on-Severn Lickhill, Lickhill Rd, Stourport-on-Severn, Worcs DY13 8SF; Tel (01299) 822102; Fax (01299) 827128; A.G. MacDonald. (9–13)

Secondary Schools

The Abbey High Easemore Rd, Redditch, Worcs B98 8HB; Tel (01527) 585859; Fax (01527) 65587; E.B. Halsall. (13–18)
Arrow Vale High Greensward La, Matchborough, Redditch, Worcs B98 0EN; Tel (01527) 26800; J.A.P. Smith. (13–18)
Aylestone School Broadlands Hse, Broadlands La, Hereford HR1 1HY; Tel (01432) 357371; Fax (01432) 263925; A.G. Wray. (11–16)
Bewdley High, Stourport Rd, Wribbenhall, Bewdley, Worcs DY12 1BL; Tel (01299) 403277; Fax (01299) 405480; Miss M.O. Griffiths. (13–18)
Bishop of Hereford's Bluecoat Tupsley, Hereford HR1 1UU; Tel (01432) 357481; A.J. Marson. (Aided) (11–16)
Bishop Perowne High Merriman's Hill Rd, Worcester WR3 8LF; Tel (01905) 23766; J.R. Tringham. (Aided) (11–16)
Bridley Moor High Bridley Moor Rd, Redditch, Worcs B97 6HT; Tel (01527) 63191; Fax (01527) 63508; *Head* M.J. Hale (Acting). (13–18)
The Chantry High, Martley, Worcester WR6 6QA; Tel (01886) 888272; P.A. Clayton. 11–16
The Chase High, Geraldine Rd, Malvern, Worcs WR14 3NZ; Tel (01684) 572096; Fax (01684) 566643; D.J. Fawbert. (11–18)
Christopher Whitehead High Bromwich Rd, Worcester WR2 4AF; Tel (01905) 423906; Fax (01905) 420788; M. Cooper (Acting). (11–16)
Droitwich High Ombersley Rd, Droitwich, Worcs WR9 0AA; Tel (01905) 774421; D.C. Owen. (12–18)
The Dyson Perrins C. of E. High, Yates Hay Rd, Malvern, Worcs WR14 1LJ; Tel (01684) 564751; P. Buchanan. (Special Agreement) (11–18)
The Elgar High Bilford Rd, Worcester WR3 8HN; Tel (01905) 54627; Fax (01905) 756517; K.R. Benton. (11–16)
Evesham High Four Pools Rd, Evesham, Worcs WR11 6DQ; Tel (01386) 442060; Fax (01386) 41734; J.E. Andrews. (13–18)
Fairfield High, Peterchurch, Hereford HR2 0SG; Tel (01981) 550231; Fax (01981) 550171; P.C. Fieldhouse. (11–16)
Hagley R.C. High Brake La, Hagley, Stourbridge, West Midlands DY8 2XL; Tel (01562) 883193; Fax (01562) 886816; P.S. Hill. (Special Agreement) (11–18)
Hanley Castle High, Church End, Hanley Castle, Worcester WR8 0BL; Tel (01684) 593241; A.G. Johnston. (Controlled) (11–18)
The Harry Cheshire High Habberley Rd, Kidderminster, Worcs DY11 5PQ; Tel (01562) 741549/741574/741524; Fax (01562) 827719; A.E. Cledwyn-Davies. (13–18)
Haybridge High Brake La, Hagley, Stourbridge, West Midlands DY8 2XS; Tel (01562) 886213; Fax (01562) 887002; Dr M.J. Kershaw. (13–18)
Haywood High Stanberrow Rd, Hereford HR2 7NG; Tel (01432) 355213; T. Thomas. (11–16)
The John Kyrle High, Ross-on-Wye, Hereford HR9 7ET; Tel (01989) 764358; Fax (01989) 65766; P.B. Barlow. (11–18)
The John Masefield High, Mabel's Furlong, Ledbury HR8 2HF; Tel (01531) 631012; C.M. Healy. (11–18)
King Charles I High Hill Grove Hse, Comberton Rd, Kidderminster DY10 1XA; Tel (01562) 60198; Fax (01562) 827813; A. Brooks. (Controlled) (13–18)
Kingstone High Kingstone, Hereford HR2 9HJ; Tel (01981) 250224; M.E. Cousins (Acting). (11–16)
Lady Hawkin's Kington, Herefordshire HR5 3AG; Tel (01544) 230441; I.C. Mayo. (11–18)
The Leys High Woodrow Dr, Redditch, Worcs B98 7UH; Tel (01527) 23088; L.A. McGuigan. (13–18)
The Minster, Leominster, Herefordshire HR6 8JJ; Tel (01568) 613221; Fax (01568) 611646; M.C. Ruckledge. (11–18)
North Bromsgrove High School Dr, Stratford Rd, Bromsgrove, Worcs B60 1BA; Tel (01527) 72375; K.F. Peck. (13–18)
Nunnery Wood High Spetchley Rd, Worcester WR5 2LT; Tel (01905) 356288; Fax (01905) 763482; A.G. Brodrick. (11–16)
Pershore High, Station Rd, Pershore, Worcs WR10 2BX; Tel (01386) 552471; Fax (01286) 555104; M.J. Krier. (12–18)
Queen Elizabeth High, Bromyard, Herefordshire HR7 4QS; Tel (01885) 482230; Fax (01885) 483935; P.A. Jewkes. (11–16)
St Mary's R.C. High, Lugwardine, Herefordshire HR1 4DR; Tel (01432) 850755; Fax (01432) 850416; W.A. Daron. (Aided) (11–16)
South Bromsgrove High, Charford Rd, Bromsgrove, Worcs B60 3NL; Tel (01527) 31783; Fax (01527) 37162; J.A. Baker. (13–18)

Stourport-on-Severn High, Minster Rd, Stourport-on-Severn, Worcs DY13 8AX; Tel (01299) 827027; Fax (01299) 827972; M.S. King. (13–18)
Tenbury High Tenbury Wells, Worcs WR15 8BS; Tel (01584) 810304; M.S. Hird. (11–16)
Waseley Hills High, School Rd, Rubery; Rednal, Birmingham B45 9EL; Tel 0121-453 5211; Fax 0121-457 8851; D.C. Thurbon. (12–18)
Weobley High, Weobley, Hereford HR4 8ST; Tel (01544) 318159; D.R. Noon. (11–16)
Whitecross, Baggallay St, Hereford HR4 0EA; Tel (01432) 359151; D.F.S. Whitcombe. (11–16)
Wigmore High Leominster, Herefordshire HR6 9UW; Tel (0156 886) 323; G.J. Sharratt. (11–16)
Wolverley High, Blakeshall La, Wolverley, Kidderminster, Worcs DY11 5XQ; Tel (01562) 850243; Fax (01562) 851945; M. Beaver. (13–18)
The Woodrush High, Shawhurst La, Hollywood, Birmingham B47 5JN; Tel (01564) 826533; Fax (01564) 822226; H.J. Toogood. (11–18)

Teachers' Centres

Finstall Centre, Stoke Rd, Ashton Fields, Bromsgrove, Worcs B60 3EN; Tel (01527) 570566; Fax (01527) 570763; *Centre Administrator* P. Rea
Inspection, Advice and Training Centre, Pitmaston Hse, Malvern Rd, Worcester WR2 4LL; Tel (01905) 425000/420818; *Administrative Officer* J. Higgs
Music and Arts Centre The Old School, Abberley Rd, Stourport-on-Severn, Worcs DY13 0LH; Tel (01299) 87992

County Outdoor Education Centres

Llanrug Outdoor Education Centre Llanrug, Caernarvon, Gwynedd; Tel (01286) 672136; W. Taylor
West Malvern Outdoor Education Centre, Old Hollow, West Malvern, Worcs WR14 4NR; Tel (01684) 574546; Fax (01684) 893931; *Head of Centre* K. Falconer, BSc MSc

Grant Maintained Schools

Blessed Edward Oldcorne R.C. High School, Timberdine Ave, Worcester WR5 2BE; Tel (01905) 352615; F.J. Ley. (Aided) (11–16)
Prince Henry's High School, Victoria Ave, Evesham, Worcs WR11 4QH; Tel (01386) 765588; B.S. Roberts. (13–18)
Redditch, St Bede's R.C. Holloway La, Redditch, Worcs B98 7HA; Tel (01527) 25916; Fax (01527) 503352; D.F. Thurlow. (Aided); (9–13)
St Augustine's Catholic Grant Maintained School, Hunt End, Redditch, Worcs B97 5LX; Tel (01527) 550400; J.X. Chisnall, BA, BSc, FRSA. (GM) (13–18)
St Bede's Middle School, Holloway La, Redditch, Worcs B98 7HA; Tel (01527) 25916
St John's C.E. Middle School, Watt Cl, Bromsgrove, Worcs B61 7DH; Tel (01527) 32376; Fax (01527) 570258; D.F. Macey. (Aided) (9–13) (Grant Maintained)

Hertfordshire County Council

Population 995,400
County Hall, Hertford SG13 8DN; Tel (01992) 555555
Chief Executive B. Briscoe, MA, DipTP, MRTPI, ARICS; Tel (01992) 555601; Fax (01992) 555505
Director of Corporate Services Lin Homer
Director of Law and Administration W.J. Church; Tel (01992) 555501
Director of Social Services J. Fletcher
Director of Property D. Bennett
Director of Libraries, Arts and Information S. Reeder (Acting)
County Supplies Officer S. Gilbey County Supplies Dept, Mount Pleasant La, Hatfield; Tel (0170 72) 68181

Education Offices

County Hall, Hertford SG13 8DF; Tel (01992) 555827
Director of Education H. DuQuesnay, BA
Deputy Director of Education M.A. Instone, MA
Assistant Director (Planning) J. Evans, MSc
Assistant Director (Finance) P. Fox
Assistant Director (Parent and Student Services) J.R. Crossley-Holland, MA, BEd
Head of Property J. Procter, BSc
Head of Special Projects B. Taylor
Head of Hertfordshire Education Services R. Wilson
Manager of Minority Ethnic Curriculum Support Services J. Hardy
Manager Learning Support Services D. Hills
Head of Conciliation and Advice Service G.A. Williams, MA
Head of Communications R. Stopard
Head of Personnel and Office Services M. Connah (Acting)
Quality Assurance Officer I. Palmer
Art and Design Adviser P. Dawson, BEd
Careers Guidance PSE and Health Education Adviser J. Campbell
Craft, Design & Technology/Home Economics and Technology R. Seviour
English and Drama Adviser Dr R. Anderson
Geography and Environmental Studies Adviser J. Burden
History Adviser J. Harrison, MA
Mathematics Adviser K. Gould
Modern Languages Adviser M. Short
Music Adviser J. Witchell
Nursery Consultant C. Stevenson
Physical Education Adviser A.F.P. Self
Humanities Advsier S. Lavender, BA
Science Adviser L. Ellis
Head of Education Welfare Service D. Ring
Head of Education Psychology B. Ballard
County Careers Officer A. McGowan
Number of Schools (inc divisions)
17 nursery; 418 primary and Infant; 63 secondary and middle
Special Schools
19 day; 10 residential
Day of Committee Meeting
Wednesday
Population
990,600
Other Authorities with whom Joint Purchasing Arrangements are made
Bedfordshire and Suffolk, London Borough of Enfield, Harrow and Haringey

Education Committee

Con 12, Lab 13, LD 8, I 1
Chairman rotating (hung Council)
Spokesperson H. Burningham, (Con)
Spokesperson R. Mays, (Lab)
Spokesperson P. Goggins, (LD)
Members of the Committee
Con: H.A. Burningham, F. Button, L.C. Doyle, R.J.M. Ellis, C.D. Everall, Lt Col Fielder, JA, MBE, A.K. Gray, B. Harlow, J.N.A. Hudson, A. Kilkerr, B.J. Lamb, J. Rose
Lab: F.W. Clayton, C.J. Cushion, N.A.D. Haslam, M. Hudson, T.G.M. Kent, Dr D.L. Kerr, Lady C. Letanka, Sir N. Lindop, R. Mays, S. Meldrum, D.A. Moss, S. Tendeter, M. Warren
LD: T.I. Ambrose, J.M. Blackman, L. Coates, P.V. Goggins, S.J.B. Knott, D.H. Ecob-Newbury, A.F. Rowlands, T.M. Venner
I: T.P. Brooker

Governor Training Unit

Governor and Local Management Service, County Hall, Hertford SG13 8DF; Tel (01992) 555755; (Answerphone) (01992) 555765; Fax (01992) 555754
Head of Governor and Local Management Service Terry Mahoney, BA, MEd, CertEd
Services Offered
All services relating to Governor support, information and training; Clerk support and training; Clerking service; School support staff training; Co-ordination of Briefings, Forums, Consultations

Careers Office

See chapter 17

Area Education Centre (Central)

The Woodside Centre, The Commons, Welwyn Garden City AL7 4RZ; Tel (01707) 325016

Area Education Centre (East)

Rye Pk Centre, Walton Rd, Hoddesdon EN11 0LN; Tel (01992) 469549

Area Education Centre (North)

Centenary House, Grammar School Walk, Hitchin SG5 1JN; Tel (01462) 438158

Area Education Centre (West)

The Bury, Queensway, Hemel Hempstead HP1 1UQ; Tel (01442) 228603

Hospital School

The Edward Jenner, Hill End Hospital, St Albans AL4 0RB; Tel (01727) 831537 Ext 49; B. Brilliant

Special Schools For Children with Learning Difficulties

Schools marked SLD are Severe Learning Difficulties others under the heading of Learning Difficulties are Moderate Learning Difficulties
Amwell View, St Margarets, Stanstead Abbots SG12 8EH; Tel (01920) 870027; J. Mayes. (Day) (S.L.D.) (Mixed) (under 5–19)
Breakspeare, Gallows Hill La, Abbots Langley, Watford WD5 0BU; Tel (0192 32) 63645; G. Williamson. (Day) (S.L.D.) (Mixed) (under 5–19)
The Collett, Lockers Park La, Hemel Hempstead HP1 1TQ; Tel (01442) 253864; P. McCaffery. (Day) (M.L.D.) (Mixed) (5–16)
Colnbrook, Hayling Rd, South Oxley, Watford WD1 6BN; Tel 0181-428 1281; M.J. Clayton. (Day) (M.L.D.) (Mixed) (under 5–16)
Garston Manor, Horseshoe La, Garston, Watford WD2 7HR; Tel (01923) 673757; G. Dunstan. (Day) (M.L.D.) (Mixed) (5–16)
Great Brookmead, Allerton Rd, Boreham Wood WD6 4AH; Tel 0181-953 1920; E. Gibson. (Day) (M.L.D.) (Mixed) (under 5–11)
Greenside, Shephall Grn, Stevenage SG2 9XS; Tel (01438) 315356; A. Biglands. (Day) (S.L.D.) (Mixed) (under 3–19)
Middleton School, South Rd, Standon, Ware SG11 1PS; Tel (01920) 821043. Day) (M.L.D.
Lakeside, Lemsford La, Welwyn Garden City AL8 6YW; Tel (01707) 327410; P.E. Clark. (Day) (S.L.D.) (Mixed) (under 2–19)
Pinewood, Hoe La, Ware SG12 9PB; Tel (01920) 46414; G.R. Rodbard. (M.L.D.) (Day and boarding) (Mixed) (12–19)
St Luke's, Crouch Hall La, Redbourn AL3 7ET; Tel (01582) 792695; M.J. Pearce. (Day) (M.L.D.) (Mixed) (10–16)
The Hyde, Holwell Hyde, Welwyn Garden City AL7 3DH; Tel (01707) 320874; M.B. Philp. (Day) (M.L.D.) (Mixed) (under 5–11)
Watling View, Watling View, St Albans AL1 2NU; Tel (01727) 50560; S.M. Gardner. (Day) (S.L.D.) (Mixed) (5–19)
Woodfield, Malmes Croft, Leverstock Grn, Hemel Hempstead HP3 8RL; Tel (01442) 253476; J. Johnson. (Day) (S.L.D.) (Mixed) (5–19)
Woolgrove, Pryor Way, Letchworth SG6 2PT; Tel (01462) 676754; H.E. Richards. (Day) Junior (M.L.D.) (Mixed) (5–11)

Schools for Children with Emotional and Behavioural Difficulties

Boxmoor House, Box La, Hemel Hempstead HP3 0DF; Tel (01442) 256915; D. Allen. (Senior Boys) (Malad.) (Day and boarding) (11–16)
Epping House, Epping Grn, Nr Hertford SG13 8NF; Tel (01707) 875911; A.J. Hood. (Boarding) (Mixed) (5–11+)
Falconer, Falconer Rd, Bushey, Watford WD2 3AT; Tel 0181-950 2505; J.S.B. Page. (Day and Boarding) (Boys) (Malad.) (11–16)
Hailey Hall, Hailey La, Hertford SG13 7PB; Tel (01992) 465208; M.J. Priestley. (Day and Boarding Boys) (Malad.) (11–16)
High Wick School, Webb Rise, Stevenage SG1 5QU; Tel (01438) 312644; *Vacancy*
Hilltop, Webb Rise, Stevenage SG1 5QU; Tel (01438) 359566; J.R. Moorhouse. (Day and Boarding) (Malad.) (Mixed) (5–11)
Batchwood, Townsend Dr, St Albans AL3 5RP; Tel (01727) 65076; P. Leaper. (Day and Boarding) (Malad.) (Mixed) (11–16)

Schools for Children with Hearing Impairment

Heathlands, Heathlands Dr, St Albans AL3 5AY; Tel (01727) 68596; M. Davis. (Day and boarding) (Mixed) (5–18)
Tewin Water, Tewin Water, Welwyn AL6 0AA; Tel (0143 871) 4288; D. Cox. (Senior Boys and Girls) (Day and Boarding) (Mixed) (10–18)

Schools for Children with Physical Impairment

Hangers Wood, Gosforth La, South Oxley, Watford WD1 6RF; Tel 0181-428 2247; J. Addison. (Day) (P.H.) (Mixed) (under 5–11)
Lonsdale, Webb Rise, Stevenage SG1 5QU; Tel (01438) 357631; M.J. Hall. (Day and Boarding) (P.H.) (Mixed) (5–18)

Middle Schools

Bridgewater, Bridle Way, Billet La, Berkhamstead, Hertfordshire HP4 1ES; Tel (01442) 871231; C.S. Gillon, BSc. (336)
Edwinstree, Norfolk Rd, Buntingford, Hertfordshire SG9 9AW; Tel (01763) 271446; R.M. Knowles. (365)
Furzehill, Furzehill Rd, Boreham Wood, Hertfordshire WD6 2EF; Tel 0181-953 1189; J.P. Fryer. (312)
Greneway, Garden Walk, Royston, Hertfordshire SG8 7JF; Tel (01763) 243650; K.G. Charles. (498)
Holmshill, Shenley Rd, Boreham Wood, Hertfordshire WD6 1TS; Tel 0181-953 2946; C.D. Willis, BA. (345)
Ralph Sadleir, Station Rd, Puckeridge, Hertfordshire SG11 1TF; Tel (01920) 821042; G.A.H. Anderson. (260)
Roysia, Burns Rd, Royston, Hertfordshire SG8 5EQ; Tel (01763) 241555; D.V. Davies. (285)
The Thomas Coram, Swing Gate La, Berkhamstead, Hertfordshire HP4 2RP; Tel (01442) 866757; C.R. Stevens. (334)

Secondary Schools

Adeyfield, Longlands, Hemel Hempstead, Hertfordshire HP2 4DE; Tel (01442) 251803; S.F. Thompson. (798)
The Astley Cooper, St Agnells La, Hemel Hempstead, Hertfordshire HP2 7HL; Tel (01442) 253501; M.T. Ingman. (634)
Barclay, Walkern Rd, Stevenage, Hertfordshire SG1 3RB; Tel (01438) 354673; R.J. Ball. (847)
Barnwell, Barnwell, Stevenage, Hertfordshire SG2 9SW; Tel (01438) 351696; E.P. Gifford. (712)
Beaumont, Oakwood Dr, St Albans, Hertfordshire AL4 0XB; Tel (01727) 54726; M.M. Rawlinson. (880)
Bedwell, Telford Ave, Stevenage, Hertfordshire SG2 0AN; Tel (01438) 351801; H.B. Davies, BSc. (498)
Birchwood High, Parsonage La, Bishop's Stortford, Hertfordshire CM23 5BD; Tel (01279) 655936; R.D. Till. (388)
Bishops Hatfield Girls', Woods Ave, Hatfield, Hertfordshire AL10 8NL; Tel (01707) 275331/2; C.M. Brooks. Girls (667)
Broxbourne, High Rd, Broxbourne, Hertfordshire EN10 7DD; Tel (01992) 464639; Dr A.H. Baines, BSc. (1143)
The Cavendish, Warners End Rd, Hemel Hempstead, Hertfordshire HP1 3DW; Tel (01442) 254566/7; M.L. Griffin. (1121)
The Chauncy, Park Rd, Ware, Hertfordshire SG12 0DP; Tel (01920) 466661; G.J. Field. (472)
Cheshunt, College Rd, Cheshunt, Hertfordshire EN8 9LY; Tel (01992) 24375/6; C.R. Broomfield, MA. (750)
Collenswood, Collenswood Rd, Stevenage, Hertfordshire SG2 9HQ; Tel (01438) 313011; N.G. Tann. (494)
Fearnhill, Icknield Way West, Letchworth SG6 4BA; Tel (01462) 677111; M.L. Monck. (715)
Francis Combe, Horseshoe La, Watford, Hertfordshire WD2 7HW; Tel (01923) 672964; S. Moore. (761)
Heathcote, Shephall Green, Stevenage, Hertfordshire SG2 9XT; Tel (01438) 355605; L. Devlin. (777)
Hemel Hempstead, Heath La, Hemel Hempstead, Hertfordshire HP1 1TX; Tel (01442) 242329/252012; T.A. Phillips. (977)
Herts and Essex High, Warwick Rd, Bishop's Stortford, Hertfordshire CM23 5NJ; Tel (01279) 654127; Mrs A.P. Ewin. Girls (907)
The Highfield, Highfield, Letchworth SG6 3QA; Tel (01462) 685661; P.M. Jackson. (757)
Hillside, Hillside Ave, Boreham Wood, Hertfordshire WD6 1HN; Tel 0181-953 1852; T.E. Westrip. (464)
Hitchin Boys, Grammar School Walk, Hitchin, Herts SG5 1JB; Tel (01462) 432181; A.D.W. Garvie. (Boys) (903)
Hitchin Girls, Highbury Rd, Hitchin, Hertfordshire SG4 9RS; Tel (01462) 432162; R.C. Edwards. (Girls) (913)
John F. Kennedy R.C., Hollybush La, Hemel Hempstead, Hertfordshire HP1 2PH; Tel (01442) 66150; G.M. Stothard, BA. (864)
The John Warner, Stanstead Rd, Hoddesdon, Hertfordshire EN11 0QF; Tel (01992) 462889; A.R. Withell. (734)
King's Langley, Love La, King's Langley, Hertfordshire WD4 9HN; Tel (01923) 264504/264999; A.W. Burge. (677)
The Knights Templar, Park St, Baldock, Hertfordshire SG7 6DZ; Tel (01462) 893083; P. Chapman, MA, MAEd, FRSA. (910)
Langleybury, Hunton Bridge, nr King's Langley, Hertfordshire WD4 8RW; Tel (01923) 262907; D.G. Risdon. (616)
Longdean, Rumballs Rd, Bennett's End, Hemel Hempstead, Hertfordshire HP3 8JB; Tel (01442) 217277; B.M. Roberts. (1081)
Loreto R.C. Girls' College, Hatfield Rd, St Albans, Hertfordshire AL1 3RQ; Tel (01727) 56206; Sister Kathleen Hewitt. (696)
Meridian, Garden Walk, Royston, Hertfordshire SG8 7JH; Tel (01763) 242236; G.T. Kingsley. (715)
Monks Walk, Knightsfield, Welwyn Garden City, Hertfordshire AL8 7NL; Tel (01707) 322846/7; R.F. Foster, BA. (961)
Nicholas Hawksmoor, Cowley Hill, Boreham Wood, Hertfordshire WD6 5LG; Tel 0181-953 3137; P.G. Tompkins. (403)
Nobel, Mobbsbury Way, Stevenage, Hertfordshire SG2 0HS; Tel (01438) 352467; M.F. Titchmarsh. (638)
Norton, Norton Rd, Letchworth, Hertfordshire SG6 1AF; Tel (01462) 682908; P. Wall. (461)
Onslow St Audrey's, Old Rectory Dr, Hatfield, Hertfordshire AL10 8AB; Tel (01707) 264228; T. Williams. (557)
Presdales, Presdales, Hoe La, Ware, Hertfordshire SG12 9NX; Tel (01920) 462210; J.M. Robinson. (Girls) (822)
The Priory, Bedford Rd, Hitchin, Hertfordshire SG5 2UR; Tel (01462) 432748; J.W. Legg. (700)
Richard Hale, Hale Rd, Hertford, Hertfordshire SG13 8EN; Tel (01992) 583441; R.J. James. (Boys) (811)
Roundwood Park, Roundwood Park, Harpenden, Hertfordshire AL5 3AE; Tel (01582) 765344; H.B. Luke, BA, DipEd. (860)
St Albans Girls', Sandridgebury La, St Albans, Hertfordshire AL3 6DB; Tel (01727) 53134; V.A. Booth. (Girls) (999)
St Clement Danes Chenies Rd, Chorleywood, Hertfordshire WD3 6EW; Tel (01923) 284169; P. Conway, MA. (985)
St George's, Carlton Rd, Harpenden, Hertfordshire AL5 4TD; Tel (01582) 765477; N.F. Hoare. (826)
St Mary's Catholic, Windhill, Bishop's Stortford CM23 2NQ; Tel (01279) 654901; P. Jackson. (640)
St Mary's High, Churchgate, Cheshunt, Hertfordshire EN8 9ED; Tel (01992) 29124/5; A. Rowan-Wicks, BSc. (884)
Sandringham, The Ridgeway, St Albans, Hertfordshire AL4 9NX; Tel (01727) 863271; S.P. Andrews. (686)
The Sele, Welwyn Rd, Hertford, Hertfordshire SG14 2DG; Tel (01992) 581455; M.E. Mussell, BA, DipEd. (444)
Sheredes, Cock La, Hoddesdon, Hertfordshire EN11 8JY; Tel (01992) 466902/3; D.A. Wallace. (800)
Simon Balle, Mangrove Rd, Hertford, Hertfordshire SG13 8AY; Tel (01992) 583856; R.C. Sills. (868)
Sir Frederic Osborn, Herns La, Welwyn Garden City, Hertfordshire AL7 2AF; Tel (01707) 323367/327204; J. Downes. (724)
The Sir John Lawes, Manland Way, Harpenden, Hertfordshire AL5 4QP; Tel (01582) 713726; J. Creasey. (529)
Sir John Newsom, Oaken Grove, Welwyn Garden City AL7 4TP; Tel (01707) 328431; V.J. Lindsey, BA. (430)
Stanborough, Lemsford La, Welwyn Garden City, Hertfordshire AL8 6YR; Tel (01707) 321755; D.J. Hitchin, BA. (808)
The Thomas Alleyne, High St, Stevenage, Hertfordshire SG1 3BE; Tel (01438) 354145; H. Parrish. (729)
Townsend, High Oaks, St Albans, Hertfordshire AL3 6DR; Tel (01727) 53047; S.M. Greenfield. (491)
Tring, Mortimer Hill, Tring, Hertfordshire HP23 5JD; Tel (01442) 212303/1213850; M.J. Beloe. (1084)
Turnford, Mill La, Cheshunt, Hertfordshire EN8 0JU; Tel (01992) 27070; C.J. Noble. (836)
Verulam, Brampton Rd, St Albans, Hertfordshire AL1 4PR; Tel (01727) 54576; R.V. Hawkes. (838)
Ward Freman, Bowling Green La, Buntingford, Hertfordshire SG9 9BT; Tel (01763) 271818; R. Harcourt, BA, MA. (603)
Westfield, Tolpits La, Watford, Hertfordshire WD1 8NS; Tel (01923) 31560; A.C. Cunningham. (379)

Advisory & Training Centres

Advisory Unit for Microtechnology in Education Endymion Rd, Hatfield, Hertfordshire; Tel (0170 72) 265443
Dacorum Centre Gadebridge Rd, Hemel Hempstead, Herts; Tel (01442) 40652
East Herts Centre Rye Pk, Walton Rd, Hoddesdon EN11 0LN; Tel (01992) 469549
Hertfordshire Mathematics Centre Burleigh Centre, Wellfield Rd, Hatfield AL19 0BZ; Tel (0170 72) 60152
Mid Herts Centre Burleigh Centre, Wellfield Rd, Hatfield AL19 0BZ; Tel (0170 72) 63148
North Herts Centre The Old Grammar School, Broadway, Letchworth SG6 3QQ; Tel (01462) 686770
Religious Education C/o Dacorum Centre, Gadebridge Rd, Hemel Hempstead HP1 3DT; Tel (01442) 40654
St Albans Centre Woollam Cres, St Albans AL3 6EJ; Tel (01727) 59974

South West Herts Centre Tolpits La, Watford WD1 8NP; Tel (01923) 225758

Stevenage Centre Education Centre, Bedwell JMI Site, Bedwell Cres, Stevenage SG1 1NJ; Tel (9979) 351845

Grant Maintained Schools

Ashylns School, Chesham Rd, Berkhamstead, Hertfordshire HP4 3AH; Tel (01442) 863605; R.F. Warren, BSc, PGCE. (608)

Bishop's Stortford High School, London Rd, Bishop Stortford, Hertfordshire CM23 3LU; Tel (01279) 757515; I. Shaw, BA, PGCE. (959)

Bushey Hall School, London Rd, Bushey, Hertfordshire WD2 3AB; Tel 0181-950 9502; G. Hunter. (1000)

Bushey Mead School, Coldharbour La, Bushey, Hertfordshire WD2 3PA; Tel 0181-950 3000; D.I. Paterson. (829)

Chancellor's School, Pine Grove, Brookmans Pk, Hatfield, Hertfordshire AL9 7BN; Tel (01707) 650702; P. Wormleighton, MA, MEd. (814)

Dame Alice Owen's School, Dugdale Hill La, Potters Bar, Hertfordshire EN6 2DU; Tel (01707) 43441; D.M.W. Bolton, MA(Oxon), BA(Oxon). (1124)

Francis Bacon School, Drakes Dr, St Albans, Hertfordshire AL1 5AR; Tel (01727) 59382/65162; Fax (01727) 810199; *Headteacher* Robert J. Marshall; *Chair of Governors* Charles Gunner. Mixed) (11–18 (450)

Goffs School, Goffs La, Cheshunt, Hertfordshire EN7 5QW; Tel (01992) 627432; Dr J.M.B. Versey, BA. (948)

The John Henry Newman School, Hitchin Rd, Stevenage, Hertfordshire SG1 4AE; Tel (01438) 314643; B.F. Nash, MEd. (913)

Leventhorpe School, Cambridge Rd, Sawbridgeworth, Hertfordshire CM21 9BY; Tel (01279) 722286; *Head* Vacancy. (945)

Lyndhurst, Gateshead Rd, Boreham Wood, Hertfordshire WD6 4NJ; Tel 0181-953 3953; S.I. Jones. (323)

Marlborough School, Watling St, St Albans, Hertfordshire AL1 2QA; Tel (01727) 856874; Fax (01727) 855285; A. Bartlett, MA. (679)

Mount Grace School, Church Rd, Potters Bar, Hertfordshire EN6 1EZ; Tel (01707) 655512; Fax (01707) 663725; C. Elliott. (740)

Nicholas Breakspear R.C. School, Colney Heath La, St Albans, Herts AL4 0TT; Tel (01727) 860079; Paul Patrick. (901)

Parmiter's School, High Elms La, Garston, Nr Watford WD2 7JU; Tel (01923) 671424; Fax (01923) 894195; *Headteacher* B.T. Coulshed; *Chair of Governors* Rev Gp Capt Donald S. Wallace. (Mixed) (11–18) (1050)

Queen Elizabeth's Boys' School Queen's Rd, Barnet, Herts EN5 4DQ; Tel 0181-441 4646; Fax 0181-440 7500; *Headmaster* E. Harris, MA; *Chair of Governors* L.R. Heard, BScEng, CEng, MIEE(Hon), FBIFM; *Bursar* D.M. Blane. (Male) (11–18) (1140)

Queens' School, Aldenham Rd, Bushey, Hertfordshire WD2 3TY; Tel (01923) 224465/8; M.E. Marsh. (1250)

Rickmansworth School, Scots Hill, Rickmansworth, Herts WD3 3AQ; Tel (01923) 773296; *Headmaster* Hugh M.E. Forsyth; *Chairman of Governors* K. Mendelssohn, MBE; *Bursar* Mrs V. Reeves. (Mixed) (11–18) (1071)

St Joan of Arc RC School, High St, Rickmansworth, Hertfordshire WD3 1HG; Tel (01923) 773881; A.W. Sumner. (933)

St Michael's Catholic School, High Elms La, Watford, Hertfordshire WD2 7JT; Tel (01923) 673760; Fax (01923) 680511; L.R. Smith, BA, MA. (807)

Watford Grammar School for Boys Rickmansworth Rd, Watford WD1 7JF; Tel (01923) 224950; Fax (01923) 256131; *Headmaster* J.S. Holman; *Chair of Governors* R.E. Groves. (Male) (11–18) (1070)

Watford Grammar School for Girls, Lady's Cls, Watford WD1 8AE; Tel (01923) 223403; Fax (01923) 223403; *Headteacher* H. Hyde; *Chair of Governors* R. Grove, CBE. (Girls) (11–18) (1100)

Humberside County Council

Population 881,400

County Hall, Beverley, Humberside HU17 9BA; Tel (01482) 867131; Fax (01482) 884992

Education Offices

County Hall, Beverley HU17 9BA; Tel (01482) 867131

Chairman L.M. Bird
Vice-Chairman N. Dickinson
Director of Education Michael Garnett, BA, DPhil
Deputy Director of Education (Schools) Miss J.E. Taylor, BSc(Econ)
Customer Services Group Manager Dr T.W. Thomas, BSc(Hons), PhD
Chief County Adviser M.D. Noddings
Principal Education Officer (Special Needs) S.K. Gardner
Principal Education Officer (Personnel and Administration) B. Merrells, BA(Hons)
Principal Education Officer (Finance and Information) A. Bedford
Senior Education Officer (Adult) P. Robson
Senior Education Officer (Schools) W.J. Rigby, MA, MSc
Senior Education Officer (Schools) Dr B.E. Roberts
Senior Education Officer (Careers Education) M. Peel, BA(Hons), LGTB
Senior Education Officer (Assessment) G.D. Jones, BA(Hons)
Senior Education Officer (Curriculum and Professional Development) B.S. Chubb, BA
Senior Education Officer (Sites and Buildings) C. Parker, MSc, BEd
Senior Area Education Officer (East Riding) R. Morley, MA(Hons)
Senior Area Education Officer (Grimsby) G.G. Hill, MSc(Ed), BSc
Senior Area Education Officer (Hull) C.J. Herrick, MA
Senior Area Education Officer (Scunthorpe) G.A. Green, BSc(Hons), MEd
AEO (Special Needs) Vacancy
AEO (Special Needs) S. Scott
AEO (Special Needs) R.S. Thompson
AEO (Special Needs) S. Oakes
AEO (Special Needs) H. Sail
AEO (Personnel) J.K. Tattersall
AEO (Personnel) K. Green
AEO (Sites and Buildings) J.F. Irving, DMA
AEO (Sites and Buildings) G.E. Hughes
AEO (Catering) D.M. Lamb
Assistant Head of Careers Service (Operations) D. Knibb
Assistant Head of Careers Service (Policy, Quality and Development) D.M. Smith
AEO (CFS) D. Barker
AEO (SFS) A. Williamson
AEO (Information) A. Woodward, BA(Hons)
Area Education Officer (East Riding) A. Green
Area Education Officer (Grimsby) J.E. Lord
Area Education Officer (Hull) I.R. Spencer, BSc(Hons)
Area Education Officer (Scunthorpe) M.B. Pearson, MSc(Phil)
Principal Adviser (Advice and Support) M.H. Wright
Principal Adviser (Inspection and Evaluation) D. Billups
Senior Adviser (SEN) A. Hayward
Senior Adviser (CET) R.H. Crowther
Senior Area Adviser East Riding P. Presland
East Riding General Adviser (Primary) M.S. Saunders
East Riding General Adviser (Geography) D.J. Kennard
East Riding General Adviser (English) N. Jones
East Riding General Adviser (Art and Design) R.C. Tonks
East Riding General Adviser (Religious Education) A. Scott

East Riding General Adviser (Information Technology) N. Waller
East Riding General Adviser (Professional Development) M.D. Marsh
Senior Area Adviser Hull (Secondary) C.C. White
Hull Senior Area Adviser (Primary) B.J. Walker
Hull Area General Adviser (Primary) S.W. Turnbull
Hull Area General Adviser (History and Social Sciences) A. Chrismas
Hull Area General Adviser (Community Education) P.J.C. Hall
Hull Area General Adviser (Science) Dr R.C. Duerden
Hull Area General Adviser (Modern Languages) Dr A.B. Swallow
Hull Area General Adviser (Primary/SEN) A.C. Gurevitch
Hull Area General Adviser (Mathematics) J. Kelly
Hull Area General Adviser (Professional Development) A. Barson
Scunthorpe Senior Area Adviser (Primary) B. Pollard
Scunthorpe Area General Adviser (Primary) C.D. Lea
Scunthorpe Area General Adviser (Music) J.C. Edmondson
Scunthorpe Area General Adviser (English) J. Marum
Scunthorpe Area General Adviser (Technology/SEN) R.E. Eaton
Scunthorpe Area General Adviser (Mathematics) J. Watson
Scunthorpe Area General Adviser (Professional Development) J. Everitt
Grimsby Senior Area Adviser W. Keast
Grimsby Area General Adviser (Primary) J. Barley
Grimsby Area General Adviser (PE/Dance) M.P. Westthorp
Grimsby Area Adviser (Professional Development/SEN) I. Pickles
Grimsby Area Adviser (Science) D.L. Fortune
Grimsby Area Adviser (Technology) S.J. Disbrey
County Educational Psychologist R. Elwood
Humberside TVEI Project Coordinator P.I. Roberts
Number of Schools
10 nursery; 350 primary; 60 secondary; inc 6th form colleges; 15 special; 36 adult education centres; 114 wholly maintained youth centres/clubs.

Education Committee

Lab 9, LD 9, Con 9, Ind 1
Chair R. Clayton, (Lab) 3 Cherry Orchard Dr, Bromsgrove, Worcs B61 8RJ
Vice-Chair Lady Harford, (LD) South Hse, South Littleton, Evesham, Worcs WR11 5TJ
Members of the Committee
Lab: D. Barlow, M. Harford, W.P.A. Hartnett, D.A. Lewis, J.T. O'Reilly, R.W. Passingham, Chris Walker, P.D Wicksteed
LD: M.D. Gardner, B.M. Ingham, C.F. Knock, R.C. Mason, R.P. Neath, June M. Pickering, P.A. Raven, C.H. Witaker
Con: J.T. Arnett CBE, DL, L.O. Barnett, M. Bemand, G.L.J. Bruce-Morgan, A.E. Davies, C.K. Davies, P.E. Harling, J.P. Hart, June Longmuir
Ind: Dr D.J.M. Muffett OBE

Governor Training Unit

Governors' Development Unit, Humberside Education Centre, Coronation Rd North, Hull HU5 5RL; Tel (01482) 566051; Fax (01482) 571992
Co-ordinator Governors' Development Pamela M. Baker, JP, MA
Seconded Headteacher Anthony E. Bridge, BA
Services Offered
Training courses; Conferences; Consultancy; Resource Banks; Distance Learning Materials; Telephone Helpline; Termly Newsletter

East Riding Area

Phoenix House, Grovehill Rd, Beverley HU17 0JQ; Tel (01482) 861251

Child Guidance Centre

Child Guidance Centre, 14 Railway St, Beverley HU17 0DX; Tel (01482) 862948/862249; *County Educational Psychologist* R. Elwood; *Senior Educational Psychologist* J.K. McDonagh

Special Schools

Bridgeview, Ferriby Rd, Hessle HU13 0HR; Tel (01482) 640115; E. Sykes. (Emot/Beh)
Ganton, Springhead Ave, Willerby Rd, Kingston-upon-Hull HU5 6YJ; Tel (01482) 564646; Mrs P.J. Glover. (SLD)
King's Mill, Victoria Rd, Driffield YO25 7UG; Tel (01377) 253375; P.J. Montgomery. (SLD)
St Anne's, St Helen's Dr, Welton, Brough HU15 1NR; Tel (01482) 667379; M. Stubbins. (SLD)

Secondary Schools

Beverley Grammar, Queensgate, Beverley HU17 8NF; Tel (01482) 881531; Fax (01482) 881564; B.H. Roger. (Boys) (Aided) (561)
Beverley High, Norwood, Beverley HU17 9EX; Tel (01482) 881658; Fax (01482) 870935; R. Vincent. (Girls) (720)
Beverley Longcroft, Burton Rd, Beverley HU17 7EJ; Tel (01482) 862171; Fax (01482) 862872; L.R. Hughes. (1228)
Bridlington, Bessingby Rd, Bridlington YO16 4QU; Tel (01262) 672593 (Upper) (01262) 672106 (Lower); Fax (01262) 672593; L. Wright (Boarding places). (Controlled) (1109)
Bridlington Headlands, Sewerby Rd, Bridlington YO16 5UR; Tel (01262) 676198; Fax (01262) 401657; A.J. Halford. (11046)
Cottingham High, Harland Way, Cottingham HU16 5PX; Tel (01482) 847498; Fax (01482) 841053; P.J. Child. (11086)
Driffield, Manorfield Rd, Driffield YO25 7HR; Tel (01377) 253631; Fax (01377) 256922; D.W. Thacker. (1453)
Hessle High Upper School, Tranby Hse, Heads La, Hessle HU13 0JQ; Tel (01482) 648604/643207; D.J. Rose. (827)
Lower School, Boothferry Rd, Hessle HU13 0JQ; Tel (01482) 648761
Hornsea, Eastgate, Hornsea HU18 1DW; Tel (01964) 532727; Fax (01964) 533403; M.J. Day. (1120)
Howden, Derwent Rd, Howden, Goole DN14 7AL; Tel (01405) 430870/430448; Fax (01405) 432435; J.V. Gee. (706)
Market Weighton School, Spring Rd, Market Weighton, York YO4 3JE; Tel (01904) 873450/873848; Fax (01904) 871015; D.M. Anderson. (630)
Pocklington Woldgate, Kilnwick Rd, Pocklington, York YO4 2LL; Tel (01904) 302395; Fax (01904) 306535; J.R.K. Brown, BSc. (1121)
South Holderness, Station Rd, Preston, Hull HU12 8UZ; Tel (01482) 899315; V. Ellis. (1557)
South Hunsley, East Dale Rd, Melton, North Ferriby HU14 3HS; Tel (01482) 631509 (Lower) (01482) 631208/9 (Upper); Fax (01482) 634186; K. Chisholm. (1155)
Wolfreton, South Ella Way, Kirk Ella, Hull HU10 7LU; Tel (01482) 659356/7/8/9; Fax (01482) 658598; M.R. Flecknoe. (1924)
Withernsea High, Hull Rd, Withernsea HU19 2EQ; Tel (01964) 613133/14; Fax (01964) 614560; P.R. Owen. (1156)

Teachers' Centre

Bridlington Teachers' Centre, Sewerby Hall, Sewerby, Bridlington YO15 1EA; Tel (01262) 673228; *Warden* T. O'Reilly

Grimsby Area

Eleanor St, Grimsby DN32 9DU; Tel (01472) 344122; Fax (01472) 341104

Child Guidance Centre

Child Guidance Centre, 100 Wellington St, Grimsby DN32 7DZ; Tel (01472) 350311; *Senior Educational Psychologist* E.J. Marshall

Special Schools

Cambridge Pk, Cambridge Rd, Grimsby DN34 5EB; Tel (01472) 877931; G. Kendall. (MLD)
Sutcliffe, Second Ave, Grimsby DN33 1NU; Tel (01472) 877844; A.A. Zielinski. SLD

Comprehensive Schools (11–16)

Havelock, Holyoake Rd, Grimsby DN32 8JL; Tel (01472) 693946; Fax (01472) 693375; H.G. Horsley. (555)
The Healing, Low Rd, Healing, nr Grimsby DN37 7QD; Tel (01472) 882882; Fax (01472) 885571; C.E.M. Pritchard. (755)
Hereford, Westward Ho, Grimsby DN34 5AH; Tel (01472) 879241; Fax (01472) 879241; T.W. Hutchinson. (1047)
Humberston, Humberston Ave, Humberston, Grimsby DN36 4TF; Tel (01472) 815022/815047; Fax (01472) 815061; W.A. Cormack. (615)
St Mary's R.C., Wootton Rd, Grimsby DN33 1HE; Tel (01472) 878869; K. Higgins. Aided (195)
Western, Cambridge Rd, Grimsby DN34 5TE; Tel (01472) 872151/2; Fax (01472) 874172; W. Carr. (687)
Whitgift, Crosland Rd, Grimsby DN37 9EH; Tel (01472) 887117; Fax (01472) 887634; S. Ireland. (834)
Wintringham, Weelsby Ave, Grimsby DN32 0AZ; Tel (01472) 871811; K. Bardgett. (957)

Comprehensive Schools (11–18)

Immingham, Carver Rd, Immingham DN40 1JT; Tel (01469) 576455; Fax (01469) 576455; R.G. Whyman. (1064)
Lindsey, Grainsby Ave, Cleethorpes DN35 9NX; Tel (01472) 694835/6 (Upper) 691595 (Lower); Fax (01472) 291734; J.D. Walsh. (1496)
Matthew Humberstone, Chatsworth Pl, Cleethorpes DN35 9NF; Tel (01472) 694888 (Upper) 691323 (Lower); Fax (01472) 603702; V. Tolhurst. (1107)
Waltham Toll Bar, Station Rd, New Waltham, Grimsby DN36 4RZ; Tel (01472) 220770; Fax (01472) 821005; D.J. Hampson. (1589)

Education Centre

Holme Hill, Heneage Rd, Grimsby DN32 9DZ; Tel (01472) 353872; Fax (01472) 267154; *Warden* W.F. Jones

Kingston Upon Hull Area

Prospect Hse, Prospect St, Kingston upon Hull HU2 8PU; Tel (01482) 867131; Fax (01482) 218787

Child Guidance Centre

Thoresby Centre, Thoresby St, Hull, Humberside; Tel (01482) 346437; *Senior Educational Psychologist* B. Levy

Special Schools

Derringham, Priory Rd, Kingston upon Hull HU5 5RU; Tel (01482) 561384; R.J. Coates. (MLD)
Frederick Holmes, Inglemire La, Kingston-upon-Hull HU6 8JJ; Tel (01482) 854538; Fax (01482) 806967; P. Donkersloot. (PH)
Northcott, Dulverton Cl, Bransholme, Kingston-upon-Hull HU7 4EL; Tel (01482) 825311; M. Johnson. (Del.)
Teskey-King, Inglemire La, Kingston-upon-Hull HU6 8JH; Tel (01482) 854588; L.A. Purvis. (MLD)
Tweendykes, Tweendykes Rd, Kingston-upon-Hull HU7 4XJ; Tel (01482) 826508; Fax (01482) 839597; K.J. Ogilvie. SLD

Comprehensive Schools (11–16)

Amy Johnson, Ringrose St, Kingston upon Hull HU3 5QB; Tel (01482) 351177; H.M. Roberts. (659)
Andrew Marvell, Barham Rd, Bilton Grange Estate, Kingston upon Hull HU9 4EE; Tel (01482) 799132/3; Fax (01482) 786804; E.S.E. White. (1149)
Archbishop Thurstan C.E., Hopewell Rd, Bilton Grange Estate, Kingston upon Hull HU9 4HD; Tel (01482) 781912/798136; Fax (01482) 798136; G. Broadbent. (Controlled) (650)
David Lister, Rustenburg St, Kingston upon Hull HU9 2PR; Tel (01482) 76304/76414; Fax (01482) 799882; B. Ray. (1110)
Greatfield, Annandale Rd, Kingston upon Hull HU9 5LB; Tel (01482) 708575; F.A. Salt. (723)
Kelvin Hall, Bricknell Ave, Kingston upon Hull HU5 4QH; Tel (01482) 342229/46817; M. Doolan. (931)
Kingston Upper School, Pickering Rd, Kingston upon Hull HU4 7AE; Tel (01482) 352939 (Upper); Fax (01482) 569982; J.A. Peck. (779)
Kingston Lower School, Anlaby Pk Rd South, Kingston upon Hull HU4 7SB; Tel (01482) 561327; Fax (01482) 352939; J.A. Peck
Malet Lambert, James Reckitt Ave, Kingston upon Hull HU8 0JD; Tel (01482) 374211/798135; J. Andrews, BA. (1112)
Newland School for Girls, Cottingham Rd, Kingston upon Hull HU6 7RU; Tel (01482) 343098/346838; A. Mathews. (Girls) (831)
Perronet Thompson, Wawne Rd, Bransholme, Kingston upon Hull, Humberside; Tel (01482) 879967; Fax (01482) 878934; J.A. Lawson. (998)
Sir Henry Cooper, Thorpepark Rd, Orchard Park Est, Kingston upon Hull HU6 9ES; Tel (01482) 854687/8; Fax (01482) 809690; J.G. Laws. (867)
Sydney Smith, First La, Anlaby HU10 6UU; Tel (01482) 652622; Fax (01482) 651690; R. Cooke. (1246)
William Gee, Bishop Alcock Rd, Kingston upon Hull HU5 4RS; Tel (01482) 848123/1844493; Fax (01482) 847419; S. Cook. (Boys) (764)
Winifred Holtby, Midmere Ave, Leads Rd, Bransholme, Kingston upon Hull HU7 4PW; Tel (01482) 826207; Fax (01482) 839589; J. Cooling. (1569)

Comprehensive School (11–18)

St Mary's College, Cranbrook Ave, Kingston upon Hull HU6 7TN; Tel (01482) 851136; Fax (01482) 804522; J.M. Walsh. (Aided) (1343)

Comprehensive School (13–18)

Hull Trinity Hse, Princes Dock St, Kingston upon Hull HU1 2LJ; Tel (01482) 326421; D.J. Taylor. (Aided) (Boys) (274)

Scunthorpe Area

5 Cliff Gardens, Scunthorpe DN15 7PH; Tel (01724) 856101; Fax (01724) 864121

Child Guidance Centre

Child Guidance Centre, Collum La, Ashby, Scunthorpe DN16 2SZ; Tel (01724) 866187; *Senior Educational Psychologist* A.B. Branwhite

Special Schools

Riverside, Ainsty St, Goole DN14 5JS; Tel (01405) 763925; D. Sykes. (MLD)
St Hugh's, Bushfield Rd, Scunthorpe DN16 1NB; Tel (01724) 842960; J.C. Darlington. MLD
St Luke's, Burghley Rd, Scunthorpe DN16 1JD; Tel (01724) 844560; Dr R.W. Ashdown. SLD

Comprehensive Schools (11–16)

Brumby, Cemetery Rd, Scunthorpe DN16 1NT; Tel (01724) 860237; Fax (01724) 281176; Dr T.G. Clark. (584)

Foxhills Comprehensive, Foxhills Rd, Scunthorpe DN15 8LJ; Tel (01724) 860458/9; Fax (01724) 270685; S. Gallaher. (626)
Frederick Gough Comprehensive, Grange La South, Scunthorpe DN16 3NG; Tel (01724) 860151; (Ashby Annexe) 842378; D. Kemp. (1122)
High Ridge Comprehensive, Doncaster Rd, Scunthorpe DN15 7DF; Tel (01724) 842447; Fax (01724) 289660; C.A. Marsh-Edwards. (604)
Huntcliff Secondary, Redbourne Mere, Kirton Lindsey, Gainsborough DN21 4NN; Tel (01427) 648276; Fax (01427) 640390; Dr D.J. Moulson. (767)
North Axholme Comprehensive, Wharf Rd, Crowle, Scunthorpe DN17 4HU; Tel (01724) 710368; L.F. Smith. (366)
South Leys Comprehensive, Enderby Rd, Scunthorpe DN17 2JL; Tel (01724) 868388; Fax (01724) 280768; E.J. Summerfield. (399)
St Bede's R.C. Comprehensive, Collum Ave, Ashby, Scunthorpe DN16 2TF; Tel (01724) 861371/861411; M.G. Nolan. (Aided) (600)
Snaith School, Pontefract Rd, Snaith DN14 9LB; Tel (01405) 860327; W.J. Marshall. (714)
South Axholme Comprehensive, Burnham Rd, Epworth, Doncaster DN9 1BY; Tel (01302) 872121/2; Fax (01302) 875028; M.D. Toms. (736)
Thomas Sumpter Comprehensive, Chandos Rd, Scunthorpe DN17 1HA; Tel (01724) 868666; Fax (01724) 868666; B.W. Parkington. (1237)
Winterton Comprehensive, Newport Drive, Winterton, Scunthorpe DN15 9QD; Tel (01724) 732777; Fax (01724) 733051; D. Houghton. (707)

Comprehensive Schools (11–18)

Baysgarth School, Barrow Rd, Barton-on-Humber DN18 6AE; Tel (01652) 632576; A.C. Fraser. (968)
Sir John Nelthorpe Grammar School, Grammar School Rd, Brigg DN20 8AA; Tel (01652) 656551; Fax (01652) 658229; E.D. Brittain. (Controlled) (753)
Vale of Ancholme, Westmoor House, Grammar School Rd, Brigg DN20 8BA; Tel (01652) 652908/9; Fax (01652) 650245; E. Terry. (629)
Vermuyden School, Centenary Rd, Goole DN14 6AN; Tel (01405) 768621; Fax (01405) 768277; R.A. Lounds. (1088)

Teachers' Centres

Goole In-Service Centre, Parkside Primary School, Western Rd, Goole DN14 0LZ; Tel (01405) 768443; *Warden* M.G. Sargeanston
Scunthorpe Education Centre, South Leys School, Enderby Rd, Scunthorpe DN17 2JL; Tel (01724) 862309; Fax (01724) 270563; *Centre Administrator* C. Atkinson

Isle of Wight County Council

Population 126,300
County Hall, Newport PO30 1UD; Tel (01983) 821000; Fax (01983) 521817
Director of Administrative and Legal Services and Head of Paid Service F.R. Hetherington
Director of Finance and Treasurer J. Pulsford
Consultant County Architect M.E. Rainey, BSc, DipArch, RIBA Rainey Petrie Design; Tel (01983) 822882
Director of Community Services W. Davison, BA, MA
Director of Cultural and Leisure Services Dr K. Brown

Education Offices

County Hall, Newport, I of Wight PO30 1UD; Tel (01983) 821000
Director of Education J.A. Williams, MA, PhD
Head of Central Education Services S.T. Bradford, BSc, MA(Ed), CBiol, BIBiol, MBIM
Principal Education Officer R. Gorley, BA, MSc, BPhil
Principal Education Officer M.P. Lloyd, BA
Assistant Education Officer A. Seaward, BA, ACIS, LIMA,
Assistant Education Officer K. Lane
Head of Schools Service D.C. Harrison, BA, ACE
Principal Inspector P. Birks, MA
County Youth and Community Officer G. Weech
Principal Educational Psychologist R.W. Denman, BSc, ABPsS
Principal Education Welfare Officer J. Wright, CQSW, DipSW
Principal Careers Officer J. Hirons
Music Inspector D. Potts, FRSM, ARCO, ARMCM
Design & Technology Inspector K.R. Simmonds
Science Inspector D. Hussey, MA
Inspector for Special Education Needs C.J. Hartley, DipEd
English Inspector D. Denaro, MA
Assistant Education Officer J. Gardner, ACIS, MIPD
School Catering Management Officer J. Ewell
County Youth and Community Officer G. Weech
Principal Educational Psychologist R.W. Denman, BSc, ABPsS
Principal Careers Officer J. Hirons

Number of Schools
46 primary (7,072 + 140 (nursery) FTE); 16 middle (5,374); 5 high (4,922)

Special Schools
1 E.S.N Physically Handicapped

Day of Committee Meeting
Monday

Requisition Periods for Schools Supplies
April 1st to March 31st; main requisitions in May; supplementary requisitions at any time, as required

Other Authorities with whom Joint Purchasing Arrangements are made
Associate Member of Counties Furniture Group Member of the Consortium for Purchasing and Distribution, Trowbridge

Education Committee

Chair M.O'N. Stolworthy 2 Brocks Copse Rd, Wootton Bridge, Isle of Wight PO33 4ND
Vice-Chair J. Wareham

Members of the Committee
V.A. Anderson, A.R. Axford, A.C. Bartlett, M.G. Barton, P.H.J. Breach, N.P.J. Butchers, B.C. W. Chapman, R.A.S. Cowley, A.R. Drake, M.W. Fletcher, P.G. Harris, R.G.D. Hipkiss, M.A. Jarman, E.G. Keenor, M. Lanfear, A. Leigh, L.E. Rogerson, M. Ross, M.O'N. Stolworthy, V. Taylor, A.H.M. Turner, N.P.J. Wareham, J. White

Governor Training Unit

Training Development Centre, St Mary Passage, Warwick St, Ryde PO33 2RG; Tel (01983) 811020; Fax (01983) 826099

Child Guidance Clinic

Educational Psychology Service, 14 Pyle St, Newport PO30 1JW; Tel (01983) 823506; *Principal Psychologist* R.W. Denman, BSc, ABPsS

Special Day Schools

Medina Hse, School La, Newport PO30 2HS; Tel (01983) 522917; D.M. Hughes, BEd, MA. E.S.N./P.H. (68)
Watergate, Watergate Rd, Newport PO30 1XW; Tel (01983) 524634; A.E. Munt-Davies, BEd(Hons), MA. (E.S.N.) (192)

Secondary High Schools (County 13–18)

Carisbrooke, Mountbatten Dr, Newport PO30 5QU; Tel (01983) 524651; C. Crellin-Whitty, BEd. (969)
Cowes, Crossfield Ave, Cowes PO31 8HB; Tel (01983) 293491; Vacancy. (808)
Medina, Fairlee Rd, Newport PO30 2DX; Tel (01983) 526523; M. Harbour, BA. (1007)
Ryde, Pell La, Ryde PO33 3LN; Tel (01983) 63773; D.L. Pettit, MA. (897)
Sandown, The Fairway, Sandown PO36 9JH; Tel (01983) 402142; P.D. Johnson, BSc. (1241)

Secondary Middle Schools (County 9–13)

Downside, Furrlongs, Barton, Newport PO30 2AX; Tel (01983) 524340; P. Henley, BEd. (279)
Forelands County, Walls Rd, Bembridge PO35 5RH; Tel (01983) 873155; P. Corney, DipEd. (196)
Kitbridge, Forest Rd, Parkhurst, Newport PO30 5SH; Tel (01983) 522329; M. Cooper, BA. (142)
Lake, Newport Rd, Lake PO36 9PE; Tel (01983) 404153; C.J. Gorski, BA. (478)
Nodehill, Upper St James' St, Newport PO30 1LJ; Tel (01983) 522886; I. Morris, MEd. (455)
Osborne, Beatrice Ave, East Cowes PO32 6PA; Tel (01983) 295741; G.R. Cooil, MA, DipEd. (295)
Sandham, Perowne Way, Sandown PO36 9JU; Tel (01983) 404297; J. Dear, BEd. (478)
Solent, Baring Rd, Cowes PO31 8DS; Tel (01983) 295713; D.J. Stradling, BEd. (332)
Somerton, Love La, Cowes PO31 7ES; Tel (01983) 294696; J.M. Iliffe, BA, MA. (239)
Swanmore, Bettesworth Rd, Ryde PO33 3HA; Tel (01983) 62035; I. Coles. (313)
Ventnor, Newport Rd, Ventnor PO38 1BQ; Tel (01983) 852884; K.R. Morris, BEd. (398)
West Wight, Queen's Rd, Freshwater PO40 9ET; Tel (01983) 753103; L.A. Bryant, BEd(Hons). (284)

Secondary Middle Schools (Voluntary 9–13)

Archbishop King R.C., Wellington Rd, Newport PO30 5QT; Tel (01983) 523275; Sister Dolores, BA. (V.A.) (389)
Bishop Lovett C.E., Appley Rd, Ryde PO33 1NE; Tel (01983) 63732/3; I. Harwood. (V.C.) (354)
C.E. Middle, Wellington Rd, Newport PO30 5QY; Tel (01983) 524360; P.J. Bloomfield, MA(Ed), DipEd. (V.A.) (370)
Mayfield C.E., St Vincent's Rd, Ryde PO33 3PT; Tel (01983) 64750; A.F.J. Temel, BA, MA. (V.C.) (372)

Adult Education Service

Adult Education Organiser S. Burgess
(in co-operation with Isle of Wight College)

Drama Centre

Medina Theatre, Medina High School, Fairlee Rd, Newport, IOW; Tel (01983) 527020; *Manager* M.J. Ash, BA

Field Study Centres

Branstone Farm Studies Centre, Branstone, nr Sandown PO36 0LT; Tel (01983) 865540; Fax (01983) 865540; *Warden* T. Gurney
Newtown Nature Reserve, Field Office, Corfe Camp PO30 4NT; Tel (0198 378) 341; *Vacancy*

Outdoor Pursuits/Sports Centres

Mountbatten Centre, Medina High School, Fairlee Rd, Newport, IOW; Tel (01983) 523767; P. Broome
Ryde Sports Centre, Ryde High School, Pell La, Ryde, IOW; Tel 66641; *Manager* N. Searles
South Wight Sports Centre Sandown High School, The Fairway, Sandown, IOW; Tel (01983) 402144; *Manager* P. Biddlecombe

Tutorial Unit

The Clatterford Centre, 63 Clatterford Rd, Carisbrooke, Newport PO30 1NZ; Tel (01983) 524680; G. Salter
Newport Tutorial Unit, Nodehill Middle School, Upper Saint James' St, Newport PO30 1LJ; Tel (01983) 522886; E. Hedley, BEd
Shanklin Tutorial Unit, Shanklin CE Primary School, Albert Rd, Shanklin, IOW; Tel (01983) 862444; S. Gee

Kent County Council

Population 1,538,500
County Hall, Maidstone ME14 1XQ; Tel (01622) 671411; Fax (01622) 690892
Chief Executive P.R. Sabin, DMS, IPFA, MIMgt, FRSA
Director of Finance P.A. Martin, MA, IPFA
Director of Property Vacancy
Director of Social Services P. Smallridge
Director of Arts and Libraries Y. Ezra, BA(Hons), MILAM
Commercial Services Director N. Wang

Education Department

Springfield, Maidstone ME14 2LJ; Tel (01622) 671411; Fax (01622) 690892/696536
Director of Education Services R. Pryke, BA, FRSA
Head of Policy R. Crouch, BA, MSc
Head of Customer and Community Services D. McGahey, MA
Head of Resources G. Reid, DipVG
Head of Finance G. Ward, BSc(Hons), IPFA
Senior County Adviser (Primary) M. Aylen, BA, MA
Senior County Adviser (Review) C. Carter
Senior County Adviser (Secondary) P. Davies, MA
Senior County Adviser (Special Educational Needs) J. Moore, BEd, MEd
County Youth and Community Officer E. Watts, BA, FFA, MIMgt
Principal of Adult Education P. Gibson, BA(Hons), LSIA, DiPMAN, FIMgt Sittingbourne Adult Studies Centre, College Rd, Sittingbourne ME10 1LF; Tel (01795) 435492
Director of Kent Curriculum Support Agency L. Craggs, BA(Hons), PGCE, MEd Southborough Bldgs, Loose Rd, Maidstone ME15 6TL; Tel (01622) 672202
County Commissioner (Special Educational Needs) V. Harvey-Samuel
County Commissioner (Pupil and Student Services) M. Gregory
Manager (Individual Pupil Services) M. McIntosh, MA, DMS
County Educational Psychologist T.M. Redmayne, BSc, MPhil, DipEd(Psych), ABPS
County Educational Psychologist T.M. Redmayne, BSc, MPhil, DipEd(Psych), ABPS

Number of Schools
1 nursery (43); 30 (as at Spring Term 1994) nursery classes (980); 555 primary school departments (119,592); 70 secondary (52,852); 7 middle (2,667); 54 adult education centres (64,315); 2 training and development centres

Special Schools
22 day (2,436); 10 residential (643); 3 hospital special (54); 1 boarding hostel (24)

Education Committee

Con 18, Lab 13, LD 12
Co-Chair T. Dean, (LD)
Spokesperson R.S. Norman, (Con)

Members of the Committee
Con: C.J. Capon, C.C. Coyne, K.A. Ferrin MBE, T. Gates, F. Gibson OBE, J. Hawkes, D.M. Marshall, C. Mullins, R.S. Norman, J. Palmer, J.H. Perry, F. Shutler, Dr F.F. Simpson, A. Smith, C. Thornton, B.P. Trench, P.A. Watkins, P. Wozencroft
Lab: T. Birkett, L. Bishop, C.V. Button, M. Christopher, B.J. Clarke, D. Esterson, J.W.E. Esterson, C. Hall, S. Johnson, I. Jones, J.F. Ovenden, G. Thomsett, R.G. Ward
LD: A. Baker, Dr R. Bond, L. Cufley, T. Dean, M. Featherstone, J.V. Gorton, A. James, P. Kendrick, E. Lowe, D.A. Sinclair, M.J. Vye, F.L. Winslade

Governor Training

Head of Policy Roger Crouch Education Dept, Springfield, Maidstone ME14 2LJ; Tel (01622) 671411; Fax (01622) 690892
School Services Manager David Judson NW Kent Area Education Office, Joynes Hse, 1–4 New Rd, Gravesend DA11 0AT; Tel (01474) 564701; Fax (01474) 320395
School Services Manager Chris Lack North/Mid Kent Area Education Office, Compass Centre, Chatham Maritime, Chatham ME4 4YN; Tel (01634) 880404; Fax (01634) 890120
School Services Manager Richard Spoerry East Kent Area Education Office, Clover Hse, John Wilson Business Pk, Thanet Way, Whitstable CT5 3QZ; Tel (01227) 772992; Fax (01227) 772290
School Services Manager Rod Mailley-Smith West Kent Area Education Office, 39 Grove Hill Rd, Tunbridge Wells TN1 1SL; Tel (01892) 523342; Fax (01892) 511529
School Services Manager Brian Shaw South Kent Area Education Office, 3 Shorncliffe Rd, Folkestone CT20 2SQ; Tel (01303) 850789; Fax (01303) 245015
Services Offered
Each Area offers full Governor Training on all major areas of responsibility to individual Governors, individual schools and consortia of schools

AREA OFFICES

North West/West Kent Area Education Offices

Area Director I. Craig, BA, DMS(PS), FRSA
North West Kent Area Office Joynes Hse, 1–4 New Rd, Gravesend DA11 OAT; Tel (01474) 564701; Fax (01474) 320395
West Kent Area Office 39 Grove Hill Rd, Tunbridge Wells TN1 1SL; Tel (01892) 523342; Fax (01892) 511529

North/Mid Kent Area Education Offices

Area Director K. Davis, MA, MEd
North/Mid Kent Area Office Compass Centre, Chatham Maritime, Chatham ME4 4YN; Tel (01634) 880404; Fax (01634) 890120

East/South Kent Area Education Offices

Area Director K. Jennings, BPhil, FCCEd, FRSA
East Kent Area Office Clover Hse, John Wilson Business Pk, Thanet Way, Whitstable CT5 3QZ; Tel (01227) 772992; Fax (01227) 772290
South Kent Area Office 3 Shorncliffe Rd, Folkestone CT20 2SQ; Tel (01303) 850789; Fax (01303) 245015

Hospital Special Schools

Dartford Hospital School, Manor Rd, Swanscombe DA10 0ES; Tel (01322) 387838; Fax (01322) 381878; J.M. Cobb. (Mixed) (20)
Royal Sea Bathing Hospital School, Canterbury Rd, Westbrook, Margate CT9 5BQ; Tel (01843) 224799; M. Blackman. (Mixed) (18)

Special Day Schools

Abbey Ct, Rede Court Rd, Strood ME2 3SP; Tel (01634) 718153; B. Sherwood. (SLD) (Mixed) (88)
Bower Grove, Fant La, Maidstone ME16 8NL; Tel (01622) 726773/1729315; T.N. Phipps. (MLD) (Mixed) (156)
Bradfields, Churchill Ave, Chatham ME5 0LB; Tel (01634) 847135; P.J. Harris. (MLD) (Mixed) (145)
Danecourt, Watling St, Gillingham ME18 6AA; Tel (01634) 232589; J. Davies. (MLD) (Mixed) (155)
Five Acre Wood, Boughton La, Loose, Maidstone ME15 9QL; Tel (01622) 743925; J.E. Kratchovil. (SLD) (Mixed) (74)
Grange Park College, Birling Rd, Leybourne, Maidstone ME19 5QA; Tel (01732) 842144; J. Walker
Greystones, Hythe Rd, Ashford TN24 0QF; Tel (01233) 621302; Fax (01233) 630467; H.R. Clark. (MLD) (Mixed) (141)
Harbour, Elms Vale Rd, Dover CT17 9PS; Tel (01304) 201964; Fax (01304) 225000; A. Berresford. (MLD) (Mixed) (144)
Highview, Moat Farm Rd, Folkestone CT19 5DJ; Tel (01303) 258755; C. Hurling. (MLD) (Mixed) (Incl Speech and Language Department) (147)
Ifield, Cedar Ave, Gravesend DA12 5JT; Tel (01474) 365485; Fax (01474) 569744; S.M. Harrison. (MLD) (Mixed) (152)
Milestone, (including Meadowcourt Annexe, Gravesend), Milestone Rd, Dartford DA2 6DW; Tel (01322) 220090; E. Flanagan. (SLD) (Mixed) (108)
Orchard, Cambridge Rd, Canterbury CT1 3QQ; Tel (01227) 769220; B.S. Shelley. (MLD) (Mixed) (125)
Ridgeview, Cage Green Rd, Tonbridge TN10 4PT; Tel (01732) 771384; Fax (01732) 770344; J. Donnelly (Acting). (SLD) (Mixed) (66)
Riverside, Clockhouse, Ashford TN23 4YN; Tel (01233) 621468; R.A. Bishop. (SLD) (Mixed) (53)
Rowhill, Stock La, Wilmington, Dartford DA2 7BZ; Tel (01322) 225490; Fax (01322) 291433; S. McGuiness. (MLD) (Mixed) (130)
St Anthony's, St Anthony's Way, Northdown, Margate CT9 3RA; Tel (01843) 292015; R.A. O'Dell. (MLD) (Mixed) (135)
St Bartholomew's, Attlee Way, North St, Milton Regis, Sittingbourne ME10 2HE; Tel (01795) 477888; M. Meakin. (SLD) (Mixed) (62)
St George's, Pembury Rd, Tunbridge Wells TN2 4NE; Tel (01892) 823096; Fax (01892) 823096; P.J. Carr. (MLD) (Mixed) (153)
St Nicholas, Holme Oak Cl, Nunnery Fields, Canterbury CT1 3JJ; Tel (01227) 464316; A. Wiltshire. (SLD) (Mixed) (62)
St Thomas, Attlee Way, North St, Milton Regis, Sittingbourne ME10 2HE; Tel (01795) 477788; P. Rankin. (MLD) (Mixed) (135)
The Foreland, Lanthorne Rd, Broadstairs CT10 3NX; Tel (01843) 863891; P.S. Hare. (SLD) (Mixed) (92)
Waveney School, Waveney Rd, Tonbridge TN10 3JU; Tel (01732) 351917; W. Vaughan. (Del.) (Mixed) (74)

Special Boarding Schools (some with day places)

Broomhill Bank, Broomhill Rd, Rusthall, Tunbridge Wells TN3 0TB; Tel (01892) 522666; P.A. Barnett (Acting). (MLD) (Girls) (70)
Furness, Rowhill Rd, Hextable, Swanley BR8 7RP; Tel (01322) 662937; R.J. Chapman. (EBD) (Mixed) (59)
Gap Hse, South Cliffe Parade, Broadstairs CT10 1TJ; Tel (01843) 861679; I.P. Cooke. (Speech and Language Handicapped) (Mixed) (36)
Halstead Pl, Church Rd, Halstead, Sevenoaks TN14 7HQ; Tel (01959) 533294; N.I.D. Parkinson. (MLD) (Mixed) (58)
Laleham, Northdown Pk Rd, Margate CT9 2TP; Tel (01843) 221946; M.P. Green. (Educationally Vulnerable) (Mixed) (102)
Parkfield, Parkfield Rd, Folkestone CT19 5BY; Tel (01303) 255974/241570; Fax (01303) 241570; C. Soulsby. (Day places) (SLD) (Mixed) (79)
Portal Hse, Sea St, St Margarets-at-Cliffe, Dover CT15 6AR; Tel (01304) 853033; L. Sage. (EBD) (Mixed) (37)

Stone Bay, Stone Rd, Broadstairs CT10 1EB; Tel (01843) 863421; D. Spencer. (SLD) (Mixed) (39)
Swinford Manor, Gt Chart, Ashford TN23 3BT; Tel (01233) 622958; J.L. Davies. (EBD) (Boys) (63)
Valence, Westerham, Sevenoaks TN16 1QN; Tel (01959) 562156; R. Gooding. (PH) (Mixed) (100)

Training and Development Centres

Colyer Hall Centre, Colyer Rd, Northfleet DA11 8BN; Tel (01474) 362733; Fax (01474) 536094; *Centre Manager* Lyn Daly
South Borough Centre, Loose Rd, Maidstone ME15 6TL; Tel (01622) 687261; Fax (01622) 691412; *Centre Manager* Frances McGill

North West Kent Area

High Schools

Northfleet, Hall Rd, Northfleet DA11 8AQ; Tel (01474) 534793/1534222; Fax (01474) 335058; Dr J.R. Keys. (Girls) (773)
West, Highfield Rd, Dartford DA1 2LZ; Tel (01322) 220836; Fax (01322) 289822; P.J. Stratford. (Boys) (637)
West, Heath La, Dartford DA1 2LY; Tel (01322) 224309; Fax (01322) 222445; V.S. Poad. (Girls) (735)
Wilmington, Common La, Wilmington, Dartford DA2 7DR; Tel (01322) 272111; Fax (01322) 222500; J. Lambern. (Mixed) (521)

Grammar Schools

Gravesend Grammar, Church Walk, Milton, Gravesend DA12 2PR; Tel (01474) 534317/352347; Fax (01474) 331589; P.J. Read. (Boys) (798)
Gravesend Grammar Pelham Rd, Gravesend DA11 OJE; Tel (01474) 352896; Fax (01474) 331195; S. Court. (Girls) (852)

Wide Ability Schools (11–18)

Axton Chase, Main Rd, Longfield DA3 7PH; Tel (01474) 705951; Fax (01474) 708309; M. Griffin. (Mixed) (811)
Hextable, Egerton Ave, Hextable, Swanley BR8 7LU; Tel (01322) 668621; Fax (01322) 668703; D.R. Evans. (Mixed) (783)
Swanley, St Mary's Rd, Swanley BR8 7TE; Tel (01322) 665231; Fax (01322) 661006; D.M. MacIldowie. (Mixed) (651)

North and Mid Kent Area

High Schools

The Astor of Hever, Oakwood Rd, Maidstone ME16 8AE; Tel (01622) 752490; Fax (01622) 693789; R.R.S. Barton. (Mixed) (675)
Chapter, Carnation Rd, Strood, Rochester ME2 25X; Tel (01634) 717121; Fax (01634) 726643; S.P. Dore. (Girls) (889)
Chatham South, Letchworth Ave, Chatham ME4 6NT; Tel (01634) 404277; Fax (01634) 829010; T. Nunn. (Mixed) (630)
Christchurch, Magpie Hall Rd, Chatham ME4 5XL; Tel (01634) 845196; Fax (01634) 845196; W.P. Davies. (Girls) (595)
Fort Luton, Magpie Hall Rd, Chatham ME4 5XL; Tel (01634) 845197; N. Armstrong. (Boys) (315)
Holmesdale Community College, Malling Rd, Snodland ME6 5HS; Tel (01634) 240416; Fax (01634) 244041; D. Covell. (Mixed) (534)
Mid Kent School for Girls, Union St, Maidstone ME14 1EE; Tel (01622) 752384; M.J. Cotton. (Girls) (541)
Rainham School for Girls, Derwent Way, Rainham, Gillingham ME8 0BX; Tel (01634) 362746; Fax (01634) 388334; P.J. Gunner. (Girls) (1436)
Sittingbourne Community College, Swanstree Ave, Sittingbourne ME10 4NL; Tel (01795) 472449; A. Barham. (Mixed) (918)
Swadelands School, Swadelands, Lenham, Maidstone ME17 2QJ; Tel (01622) 858267; Fax (01634) 350668; Miss D. Showan. (Mixed) (674)
Temple, Brompton Farm Rd, Rochester ME2 3NN; Tel (01634) 719983; Fax (01634) 290917; B.J. Middleton. (Boys) (679)
Vinters School for Boys, Huntsman La, Maidstone ME14 5DT; Tel (01622) 755169; Fax (01622) 661671; B.J. Cole. (Boys) (472)
Walderslade School for Boys, Bradfields Ave, Walderslade, Chatham ME5 0LE; Tel (01634) 861593; D. Smith. (Boys) (554)
Walderslade School for Girls, Bradfields Ave, Walderslade, Chatham ME5 0LE; Tel (01634) 861596; P. Conibeer. (Girls) (538)
Woodlands, Woodlands Rd, Gillingham ME7 2DT; Tel (01634) 572256/850100; Fax (01634) 280036; K. Masters. (Mixed) (535)

Grammar Schools (11–18 Years)

Borden Grammar, Avenue of Remembrance, Sittingbourne ME10 4DB; Tel (01795) 424192; B.R. Short, MA. (Boys) (582)
Chatham Grammar School for Boys, Holcombe, Maidstone Rd, Chatham ME4 6JB; Tel (01634) 830083; Fax (01634) 826230; D. Marshall. (Boys) (592)
Fort Pitt Grammar School, Fort Pitt, Chatham ME4 6TJ; Tel (01634) 842359; Fax (01634) 817386; M.C. Atkins. (Girls) (744)
Highsted, Highsted Rd, Sittingbourne ME10 4PT; Tel (01795) 424223; J.E.H. Lambert, BA. (Girls) (602)
Maidstone Grammar School for Girls, Great Buckland, Maidstone ME16 0SF; Tel (01622) 752103; Fax (01622) 681947; K. Judson. (Girls) (986)
Maidstone Grammar, Barton Rd, Maidstone ME15 7BT; Tel (01622) 752101; Fax (01622) 753680; N.A. Turrell. (Boys) (1068)
Maidstone Invicta Grammar School for Girls, Huntsman La, Maidstone ME14 5DR; Tel (01622) 755856/761188; Fax (01622) 678584; S. Glanville. (715)
Sir Joseph Williamson's Mathematical School, Maidstone Rd, Rochester ME1 3EL; Tel (01634) 844008; Fax (01634) 818303; K. Williams. (Boys) (870)

Wide Ability (13–18)

Hundred of Hoo, Main Road, Hoo St, Werburgh, Rochester ME2 3HH; Tel (01634) 251443; Fax (01634) 254323; R. Robinson. (Mixed) (1055)

Middle Schools

Danley Halfway Rd, Sheerness ME12 3AU; Tel (01795) 663163; M. Meredith. (Mixed) (643)
St George's CE Middle School, St George's Ave, Sheerness ME12 1QU; Tel (01795) 662687; P.A. Trigwell. (Mixed) (394)

East Kent Area

High Schools

The Abbey, London Rd, Faversham ME13 8RZ; Tel (01795) 532633; Fax (01795) 539931; P. Walker. (Mixed) (1155)
Conyngham High, Stirling Way, Ramsgate CT12 6NB; Tel (01843) 593326; B. Lippett (Acting). (Mixed) (451)
Ellington High, Ellington Pl, Ramsgate CT11 0QQ; Tel (01843) 593522; Fax (01843) 852696; D. Wardley. (Girls) (443)
Hartsdown Secondary, George V Ave, Margate CT9 5RE; Tel (01843) 227957; Fax (01843) 299642; C. Chapman. (Mixed) (916)
Hereson, Lillian Rd, Ramsgate CT11 7DT; Tel (01843) 592067; I.S. Groom. (Boys) (436)
Holy Cross R.C., Ramsgate Rd, Broadstairs CT10 1PJ; Tel (01843) 862729; Fax (01843) 866491; D. Shaw. (Mixed) (489)

King Ethelbert, Canterbury Rd, Birchington CT7 9BL; Tel (01843) 831999; Fax (01843) 831015; K. Ogg. (Mixed) (749)

The Sir William Nottidge Technology, Bellevue Rd, Whitstable CT5 1PX; Tel (01227) 273615/272362; Fax (01227) 770275; J. Mitchell. (Mixed) (799)

Grammar Schools (11–18 Years)

Clarendon House Grammar, Clarendon Gdns, Ramsgate CT11 9BB; Tel (01843) 591074; Fax (01843) 851824; J.M. Bennett. (Girls) (673)

Simon Langton, Old Dover Rd, Canterbury CT1 3EW; Tel (01227) 463711/452543; Fax (01227) 458363; A. Stanton. (Girls) (921)

West Kent Area

Wide Ability Schools (11–18)

Bennett Memorial Diocesan CE, Culverden Down, Tunbridge Wells TN4 9SH; Tel (01892) 521595; Fax (01892) 514424; *Headteacher* Rev John Caperon, BA, MPhil, MSc. (Mixed) (1042)

Eden Valley, Four Elms Rd, Edenbridge TN8 6AD; Tel (01732) 863152; Fax (01732) 864793; P.M.K. Walker, BSc. (Mixed) (292)

Grammar Schools (11–18)

The Judd, Brook St, Tonbridge TN9 2PN; Tel (01732) 771661; K.A. Starling. Boys (769)

Tunbridge Wells Grammar School for Boys, St John's Rd, Tunbridge Wells TN4 9XB; Tel (01892) 529551; D.E. Barnard. (Boys) (850)

Tunbridge Wells Grammar School for Girls, Southfield Rd, Tunbridge Wells TN4 9UJ; Tel (01892) 520902; Fax (01892) 536497; A.S. Daly. (Girls) Grammar (856)

Weald of Kent Grammar, Tudeley La, Tonbridge TN9 2JP; Tel (01732) 352819; Fax (01732) 770536; S.A. Rowell, MA. (Girls) (614)

South Kent Area

Grammar Schools (11–18)

Dover Grammar School for Girls, Frith Rd, Dover CT16 2PZ; Tel (01304) 206625; Fax (01304) 242400; E. Lewis. (587)

Highworth School for Girls, Quantock Dr, Ashford TN24 8UD; Tel (01233) 624910; Fax (01233) 612028; L. Lee. (776)

The Harvey Grammar School, Cheriton Rd, Folkestone CT19 5JY; Tel (01303) 252131; Fax (01303) 220721; E.J. Edwards. (Boys) (802)

The Norton Knatchbull School, Hythe Rd, Ashford TN24 0QJ; Tel (01233) 620045; Fax (01233) 633668; P.G. Cox. (Boys) (692)

High Schools

Archers Court School, Honeywood Rd, Whitfield, Dover CT16 2EG; Tel (01304) 820126; Fax (01304) 821915; S. Alcock. (Mixed) (821)

Astor School, Astor Ave, Dover CT17 0AS; Tel (01304) 201151/202976; Fax (01304) 225170; C.J. Russell. (Mixed) (1338)

Brockhill Park School, Sandling Rd, Saltwood, Hythe CT21 4HL; Tel (01303) 265521; Fax (01303) 262708; A. Lyng. (Mixed) (1028)

Castle High School, Mill Rd, Deal CT14 9BD; Tel (01304) 373363; Fax (01304) 380769; D. Barnes. (Mixed) (635)

The Channel High School, Park Farm Rd, Folkestone CT19 5DN; Tel (01303) 258061; Fax (01303) 221645; R. Fox. (Mixed) (780)

Christ Church CE High School, Millbank Rd, Kennington, Ashford TN23 2RN; Tel (01233) 623465; Fax (01233) 636861; J. Mulrenan. (Mixed) (728)

The North School, Essella Rd, Ashford TN24 8AJ; Tel (01233) 620518; Fax (01233) 612906; K. Hussey. (Mixed) (1111)

The Towers School, Faversham Rd, Kennington, Ashford TN24 9AL; Tel (01233) 634171; Fax (01233) 628326; A.R. Brown. (Mixed) (880)

Walmer School, Salisbury Rd, Walmer, Deal CT14 7QJ; Tel (01304) 375212; Fax (01304) 380766; R. Cross. (Mixed) (666)

Grant Maintained Schools

Angley, Angley Rd, Cranbrook TN17 2PJ; Tel (01580) 715754; Fax (01580) 715434; Stephanie Bedford, BEd(Hons), MA. (Mixed) (810)

The Archbishop's C.E., St Stephen's Hill, Canterbury CT2 7AP; Tel (01227) 765805; A.J. Hogarth. Mixed (680)

Aylesford School, G.M Teapot La, Aylesford ME20 7JU; Tel (01622) 717341; *Headteacher* W.A. Laidler; *Chair of Governors* D. Smyth. Mixed 11–18 (1030)

The Barton Court Grammar, Barton Ct, Longport, Canterbury CT1 1PH; Tel 464600; Dr S. Manning. (Mixed) (506)

The Bradbourne School, Bradbourne Vale Rd, Sevenoaks TN13 3LE; Tel (01732) 454608; Fax (01732) 742262; E.E. Blackburn. (Girls) (490)

Canterbury High, Knight Ave, Canterbury CT2 8QA; Tel (01227) 463971/464872; K.J. Hargrave. (Mixed) (870)

The Charles Dickens School, Broadstairs Rd, Broadstairs CT10 2RL; Tel (01843) 862988; V.R. West. (Mixed) (800)

Chatham House Grammar, Chatham St, Ramsgate CT11 7PS; Tel (01843) 591075; Fax (01843) 851907; J.D. Matthews. (Boys) (663)

Chaucer Technology School, Spring La, Canterbury CT1 1SU; Tel (01227) 763636; Fax (01227) 762352; J. Wynn. (Mixed) (selects pupils on aptitude for technology) (1330)

The Cheyne Middle School, Jefferson Rd, Sheerness ME12 2PU; Tel (01795) 662474; P. Woollacott. (Mixed) (770)

The Cornwallis School, Hubbard La, Linton, Maidstone ME17 4HX; Tel (01622) 743152; Fax (01622) 741866; *Headteacher* M.J. Wood; *Chair of Governors* J.A.R. Hall. (Mixed 11–18) (960)

Cranbrook School, Cranbrook, Kent TN17 3JD; Tel (01580) 712163

Dane Court Grammar, Broadstairs Rd, Broadstairs CT10 2RT; Tel (01843) 864941; R. Curtis. (Mixed) (1014)

Dartford Grammar School for Girls Shepherds La, Dartford DA1 2NT; Tel (01322) 223123; Fax (01322) 294786; *Headteacher* J.M. Hadman; *Chair of Governors* J.V. Rayner. (Girls) (11–18) (836)

Dartford Grammar School, West Hill, Dartford DA1 2HW; Tel (01322) 223039; Fax (01322) 291426; *Headteacher* A.J. Smith; *Chair of Governors* J. Field. (Boys) (11–18) (897)

Dover Grammar School for Boys, Astor Ave, Dover CT17 0DQ; Tel (01304) 206117; Fax (01304) 206074; N. Slater (Acting). (503)

The Folkestone School for Girls, Coolinge La, Folkestone CT20 3RB; Tel (01303) 251125; Fax (01303) 221422; S. Mullett. (Girls) (820)

Fulston Manor, Brenchley Rd, Sittingbourne ME10 4EG; Tel (01795) 475228; Fax (01795) 428144; W.H. Herbert, MA. (Mixed) (935)

Grammar School for Girls, Wilmington Wilmington Grange, Parsons La, Wilmington, Dartford, Kent DA2 7BB; Tel (01322) 226351/226038; Fax (01322) 222607; *Headteacher* Dr Janette Viggers; *Chairman of Governors* Derek Thorogood; *Administrative Officer* Karen Downes. (Girls) (11–18) (575)

The Hayesbrook School, Brook St, Tonbridge TN9 2PH; Tel (01732) 352673; Fax (01732) 367254; N.J.M. Blackburn. (Boys) (474)

Herne Bay, Bullockstone Rd CT6 7NS; Tel (01227) 361221; R. Withington, MA. (Mixed) (700)

Hillview, Brionne Gdns, Tonbridge TN9 2HE; Tel (01732) 352793; Fax (01732) 368718; R.J. Barnfield. (Girls) (657)

Homewood School, Tenterden TN30 6LT; Tel (0158076) 4222; D. Adam, MA, DEA. (Mixed) (1400)
Howard Grammar/High School, Derwent Way, Rainham, Gillingham ME8 0BX; Tel (01634) 235466; A.G. Jarrett. (1826)
Hugh Christie Technology College, Norwich Ave, Tonbridge TN10 4QL; Tel (01732) 353544/358288; Dr Christopher Gerry, BA(Hons), MA, DPhil. (Mixed) (913)
Kelsey Park School Manor Way, Beckenham BR3 3SJ; Tel 0181-650 8694; *Headteacher* C.M. Botten; *Chair of Governors* Dr Mary Horgan. (Boys 11–18) (Girls in Sixth Form) (893)
The Malling School, Beech Rd, East Malling, Maidstone ME19 6DH; Tel (01732) 840995; Fax (01732) 840486; V. Dagger. (Mixed) (589)
Maplesden Noakes School Great Buckland, Maidstone ME16 0JT; Tel (01622) 759036; *Headteacher* D. Kimber; *Chairman of Governors* E. Marchesi; *Financial Administrator* C. Colverly. Mixed 11–16 (714)
Mascalls School, Gedges Hill, Paddock Wood, Tonbridge TN12 6LT; Tel (0189 283) 5366; F. Gale. (Mixed) (1336)
Meopham, Wrotham Rd, Meopham DA13 0AH; Tel (01474) 814646; Fax (01474) 813083; N. Hunt. (Mixed) (415)
Minster College, Minster Rd, Minster-on-Sea, Sheerness, Kent ME12 3JQ; Tel (01795) 873591; Fax (01795) 870107; R.O. Barson. (Mixed) (1300)
Montgomery, Bredlands La, Sturry, Canterbury CT2 0HD; Tel (01227) 710392; Fax (01227) 712370; R. Freakes, MA(Cantab). (Mixed) (650)
Northfleet, Colyer Rd, Northfleet DA11 8BG; Tel (01474) 533802/568170; J.M.B. Hassett. (Boys) (668)
Oakwood Park Grammar School, Oakwood Park, Maidstone, Kent ME16 8AH; Tel (01622) 726683; Fax (01622) 721210. (Boys) (625)
Oldborough Manor Community College Boughton La, Loose, Maidstone ME15 9QL; Tel (01622) 743286; *Headteacher* Colin Barrett; *Chair of Governors* Donald Wright. Mixed 11–18 (600)
Pent Valley High School, Surrenden Rd, Folkestone CT19 4ED; Tel (01303) 277161; Fax (01303) 279342; G.E. Porteous. (Mixed) (979)
Queen Elizabeth's, Abbey Pl, Faversham ME13 7PQ; Tel (01795) 533132; J.W.E. Blackford. (Mixed) (620)
Rainham Mark Grammar School, Pump La, Gillingham ME8 7AJ; Tel (01634) 364151; Fax (01634) 260209; Dr R. Keen. (Mixed) (1003)
Robert Napier, Third Ave, Gillingham ME7 2LX; Tel (01634) 851157; Fax (01634) 280972; R.C. Moreton. (Mixed) (895)
The Rochester Grammar School for Girls, Maidstone Rd, Rochester ME1 3BY; Tel (01634) 843049; A.J. Price. (Girls) (771)
St Anselm's R.C., Old Dover Rd, Canterbury CT1 3EN; Tel (01227) 766263; B.M. McCormack. (Mixed) (900)
St Edmund of Canterbury R.C. Comprehensive School, Old Charlton Rd, Dover CT16 2QB; Tel (01304) 201551; T.S. Connolly. (Mixed) (674)
St George's C.E. School, Westwood Rd, Broadstairs CT10 2LH; Tel (01843) 861696; Fax (01843) 867760; A.J. Fletcher. (Mixed) (920)
St Gregory's Catholic Comprehensive School, Reynolds La, Tunbridge Wells, Kent TN4 9XL; Tel (01892) 527444; Fax (01892) 546621
St John Fisher R.C. School, Ordnance St, Chatham, Kent ME4 6SG; Tel (01634) 842811; K. Findlay. (Mixed) (580)
St John's RC, Rochester Rd, Gravesend DA12 2JW; Tel (01474) 534718/533799; F.J. Clare. (Mixed) (1003)
St Simon Stock R.C., Queens Rd, Maidstone ME16 0JP; Tel (01622) 754551; E. Mulhearn. (Mixed) (988)
Sandown Court Community College, Blackhurst La, Tunbridge Wells TN2 4PY; Tel (01892) 534377; Fax (01892) 516203; D.H. Muir. (Mixed) (869)
Sandwich, Dover Rd, Sandwich CT13 0DA; Tel (01304) 613071; R.C. Elliott. (Mixed) (772)
Senacre Technology School, Sutton Rd, Maidstone, Kent ME15 9DT; Tel (01622) 677471
Simon Langton Grammar School for Boys Nackington Rd, Canterbury CT4 7AS; Tel (01227) 463567; Fax (01227) 456486; *Headteacher* J. Harris, MA(Cantab); *Chair of Governors* P.F. Addis, OBE. (11–19) (738)
Sir Roger Manwood's School, Sandwich CT13 9JX; Tel (01304) 613286; I. Mellor. (Mixed) (653)
Skinners' Company School, St John's Rd, Tunbridge Wells TN4 9PG; Tel (01892) 520732; P. Braggins. (Boys) (685)
Southfields, Singlewell Rd, Gravesend DA11 7RF; Tel (01474) 365818; R. Cochlin. (Mixed) (588)
Southland's Comprehensive School Station Rd, New Romney TN28 8BB; Tel (01797) 364593; Fax (01797) 367315; *Headteacher* Eamonn Cahill; *Chair of Governors* Michael Shannon. Mixed 11–18 (1100)
Thamesview School, Thong La, Gravesend DA12 4LF; Tel (01474) 566552; Fax (01474) 537405; *Headteacher* John R. Strand, BEd(Hons); *Chair of Governors* C.J. Bodle. (Mixed) (11–17) (968)
The Thomas Aveling School, Arethusa Rd, Rochester ME1 2UW; Tel (01634) 844809; Mrs E.R. Ruston. (Mixed) (1004)
Tonbridge Grammar, Deakin Leas, Pembury Rd, Tonbridge TN9 2LR; Tel (01732) 365125; Mrs W. Carey. (Girls) (856)
Upbury Manor, Marlborough Rd, Gillingham ME7 5HT; Tel (01634) 852341; I.J. Gliddon. (Mixed) (904)
The Westlands School, Westlands Ave, Sittingbourne, Kent ME10 1PF; Tel (01795) 477475/6; Fax (01795) 431946
The Wilderness School, Seal Hollow Rd, Sevenoaks, Kent TN13 3SL; Tel (01732) 454617
Wilmington Grammar School for Boys, Wilmington Hall, Common La, Dartford DA2 7DA; Tel (01322) 223090; Fax (01322) 289920; *Headmaster* B.N. Titterington
Wrotham School Borough Green Rd, Wrotham, Sevenoaks TN15 7RD; Tel (01732) 884207; Fax (01732) 884207; *Headteacher* G. Thompson; *Chair of Governors* T. Cowburn. Mixed 11–16 (491)

Technology Centre

Chatham Grant Maintained Grammar School for Girls, Sponsored by the Garfield Weston Foundation, GEC Marconi Avionics, Clifton Reed Consultants, Research Machines, Klick Technology, Data Collection Systems, Architects Joint Partnership and others. Rainham Rd, Chatham ME5 7EH; Tel (01634) 851262; I. Watson. (Girls) (Mixed Sixth Form) (730)

Kirklees Metropolitan Council

Population 385,800
PO Box B24, Civic Centre, Huddersfield HD1 1WG; Tel (01484) 422133; Fax (01484) 442058

Education Service

Oldgate Hse, 2 Oldgate, Huddersfield HD1 6QW; Tel (01484) 422133; Fax (01484) 446764
Chief Education Officer R.W. Vincent, BEng, MCD, MRTPI
Head of Resources (Education and Leisure Services) D.A. Gerrard (Acting)
Head of Community Development Service R. Davies
Group Finance Manager (Education & Leisure Services) R.W. Askham, BA, IPFA
Group Personnel Manager (Education & Leisure Services) E.J. Squires, BA, MIPM
Catering Resource Manager J. Rayner
Service Manager (Schools Management) J. Waddington, BA
Service Manager (Schools Development) G. Tonkin, MA
Service Manager (Inspection & Monitoring) T. Piggott, BEd

Service Manager (Curriculum Support & Development) Dr M.R. Pattison
Service Manager (Special Services) P.J. Robson, BA, MIPM
Service Manager (Careers Service) G.V. Costello, BA, DipCG
Service Manager (Education Social Work) J. Wilson, BSc(Hons), CQSW, DipFT, CMS (Acting)
Service Manager (Psychological Service) R.G. Hedderly, MSc
Education Development Officer (Schools Support) J. Whelan, BEd
Education Development Officer (Research & Planning) Barbara Challenger
Education Development Officer (Ethnic Minorities) A. Schiff, BA
Education Development Officer (FE) T. Irwin, MSc, PhD
Education Development Officer (LMS Development) C.M. Champkin, BSc
Education Development Officer (Governor Training) V. Greenwood, BA
Education Development Officer (Management Development) Dr S. Whitson
Education Development Officer (Special Needs) Vacancy
Chief Inspector T.R. Piggott, BEd(Hons)
Inspector (Art and Design) Vacancy
Inspector (Assessment & Records of Achievement) J. Brown, BSc, MEd
Inspector (Design & Technology) D. Beaumont, MA, DLC
Inspector (Early Years) R. Baldwin, Dip ASEd, NNEB
Inspector (English) Maggie Iles, BA(Cantab), PGCE
Inspector (Humanities/Geography/Environmental Education) B. Dady, BSc, MEd
Inspector (Information Technology) C. Williams, BSc, Dip CE
Inspector (Mathematics) Vacancy
Inspector (Modern Languages/Classics) A. Nutton, BA, MSc, MA
Inspector (Multi-cultural Education) Vacancy
Inspector (Music) A. Simmons, MA, LRAM
Inspector (Primary Education) P. Dennison, BSc(Econ), MEd
Inspector (Primary Education) P. Rawlinson, CertEd, AdvCertEd
Inspector (Primary Education/Middle) M. Shimell, BA, CertEd
Inspector (Special Needs) Dr A. Freeman, BA, MSc, PhD, PGCE
Inspector (TVEI Co-ordinator/Science) D. Gilleard, BEd(Hons)
Inspector (Primary) S. Mulvany, BA(Hons), PGCE, MSc
Inspector (RE) C. Earle, CertEd, BEd, DipTheo, CertHealthEd, AddipEdManagement
Number of Schools
4 nursery; 158 primary (includes 34 controlled and 25 aided); 7 middle; 23 secondary; 9 special

Education Committee

Lab 10, Con 6, LD 4
Chair C. Pearce, (Lab) Ashfield, 8 Station Rd, Golcar, Huddersfield; Tel (01484) 655970
Deputy Chair M. Walton, (Lab) 52 Crosland Hill Rd, Crosland Hill, Huddersfield; Tel (01484) 659591
Members of the Committee
Lab: D. Beetham, J. Brooke, S.D. Hall, M. Harkin, A. Smith, C. Watson
Con: R.C. Light, D.M. Matthews, G.J. Moore
LD: A.E. Denham, J.T. Green, K.M. Pinnock

Governor Training Unit

Oldgate Hse, Huddersfield HD1 6QW; Tel (01484) 446505/446513; Fax (01484) 446764
Education Development Officer Vera Greenwood, BA(Hons), CITD
Admin Assistant Linda Long
Services Offered
Training, support, development

Special Day Schools (Age range as given)

Fairfield, Dale La, Heckmondwike WF16 9PA; Tel (01924) 406363; N.J. Hughes. (Mixed) (3–19); (3–19)
Hartshead Moor, Halifax Rd, Cleckheaton BD19 6LP; Tel (01274) 872384; C. Taylor, MSC, DipEd. (Mixed) (5–16); 5–16
Highfields, Cemetery Rd, Edgerton, Huddersfield HD1 5NF; Tel (01484) 540954. (Mixed) (3–19); 3–19
Longley, Smithy La, Huddersfield HD5 8JE; Tel (01484) 531870; M. Hogarth, MEd DCLD. (Mixed) (5–16); 5–16
Lydgate, Kirkroyds La, New Mill, Huddersfield HD7 7LS; Tel (01484) 683889; B. Goler. (Mixed) (5–16); 5–16
Ravenshall, Ravensthorpe Rd, Dewsbury WF12 9EE; Tel (01924) 469432; C. Newby. (Mixed) (11–16)
Turnshaws, Turnshaws Ave, Kirkburton, Huddersfield HD8 OTJ; Tel (01484) 603863; L. Staves, MEd. (Mixed) (3–19); 3–19

Special Residential Schools (Age range as given)

Nortonthorpe Hall, Busker La, Scissett, Huddersfield HD8 9JU; Tel (01484) 862080 (school); 862565 (residence); J. Craig. (Mixed) (7–13)
Royd Edge, Holmfirth Rd, Meltham, Huddersfield HD7 3DD; Tel (01484) 850610; D.A. Shields, DipEd, MA. (Mixed) (13–16)

Middle Schools (County 9/10–13)

Birkenshaw Middle, Bradford Rd, Gomersal, Cleckheaton BD19 4BE; Tel (01274) 872092; G.M. Harker
R.M. Grylls Middle, Windy Bank, Hightown, Liversedge WF15 8JP; Tel (01274) 873238; J. Dewhirst, BA
Kirkburton Middle, Turnshaws Ave, Kirkburton, Huddersfield HD8 0TJ; Tel (01484) 604040; R.A. Wade, BEd
Scissett Middle, Wakefield Rd, Scissett, Huddersfield HD8 9JX; Tel (01484) 862971/2; M.D. Cole, BSc
West End Middle, South Parade, Cleckheaton BD19 3AE; Tel (01274) 873882; M.L. Halstead, MEd
Whitechapel Middle, Whitechapel Rd, Cleckheaton BD19 6HR; Tel (01274) 876859; G. Trueman

Middle School (Voluntary Controlled 9–13)

Gomersal C.E. Middle, Oxford Rd, Gomersal, Cleckheaton BD19 4PX; Tel (01274) 876856; R.A. Smith, BSc

Comprehensive Schools (County 11–16)

Almondbury High, Fernside Ave, Almondbury, Huddersfield HD5 8PQ; Tel (01484) 427154; I.W. Rees, BA, BSc
Birkdale High, Wheelwright Drive, Dewsbury WF13 4JB; Tel (01924) 457281; D.J. Hall, BEd(Hons)
Earlsheaton High, Old Bank Rd, Earlsheaton, Dewsbury WF12 7DA; Tel (01924) 462730; A.M. Talboys, MEd, CBiol
Fartown High, Woodhouse Hall Rd, Fartown, Huddersfield HD2 1DJ; Tel (01484) 532324; W.E. Firmin, MA(Oxon), MAEd
Holmfirth High, Heys Rd, Holmfirth, Huddersfield HD7 2SE; Tel (01484) 687061; I.D. MacPherson, MA
King James's, St Helen's Gate, Almondbury, Huddersfield HD4 6SG; Tel (01484) 532148; C.P.S. Watkins, LLB
Moor End High, Dryclough Rd, Crosland Moor, Huddersfield HD4 5JA; Tel (01484) 656817; Dr D.M. Rogerson, MA, PhD, FRSA
Newsome High, Castle Ave, Newsome, Huddersfield HD4 6JN; Tel (01484) 539531; G. Hull, BEd (Hons)
Rawthorpe High, Nether Hall Ave, Rawthorpe, Huddersfield HD5 9PG; Tel (01484) 539545; M. Woodcock, BEd, MA
Royds Hall High, Luck La, Paddock, Huddersfield HD3 4HA; Tel (01484) 653587; S.W. Bradbury, BA, MSc
Salendine Nook High, New Hey Rd, Huddersfield HD3 4GN; Tel (01484) 657541/2/3; J.J. Dakers

Spen Valley High School, Roberttown La, Liversedge, W. Yorks WF15 7LX; Tel (01924) 412294; J. Cotterill
Thornhill High, Valley Dr, Thornhill, Dewsbury WF12 0HE; Tel (01924) 465704/469213; J.H. Fowler
Westborough High, Stockhill St, Dewsbury WF13 2JE; Tel (01924) 463431; F.M. Leake, BA, MEd

Comprehensive Schools (County 11–18)

Batley Boys' High, Field Hill, Batley WF17 0BJ; Tel (01924) 474168, 476498; I.L. Hepworth, BSc
Colne Valley High, Gillroyd La, Linthwaite, Huddersfield HD7 5SP; Tel (01484) 842386; A.W. Newton, BSc
Honley High & Sixth Form Centre, Station Rd, Honley, Huddersfield HD7 2QJ; Tel (01484) 661267; B. Conchie
Howden Clough High (Girls), Windmill La, Batley WF17 0LD; Tel (01924) 478179, 478170; D. Drake, BA, MEd

Comprehensive Schools (Voluntary Aided/SpA 11–18)

All Saints' R.C. (A) High, Bradley Rd, Huddersfield HD2 2JT; Tel (01484) 426466; D. Godlington, BSc
St John Fisher R.C. (SpA) High, Oxford Rd, Dewsbury WF13 4LL; Tel (01924) 462927; A.J. Carroll. (S.A.)

Comprehensive Schools (County 13–18)

Mirfield Free Grammar, Kitson Hill Rd, Mirfield WF14 9EZ; Tel (01924) 492069/492434; M.T. Brewis, BA
Shelley High, Huddersfield Rd, Shelley, Huddersfield HD8 8NL; Tel (01484) 863891; P.R.R. Jones, BA

Comprehensive School (Voluntary Controlled 13–18)

Whitcliffe Mount, Turnsteads Ave, Cleckheaton BD19 3AQ; Tel (01274) 876707/8; A.A. Davis

Outdoor Pursuits/Field Study Centre

Cliffe Hse, 140 Lane Head Rd, Shepley, Huddersfield HD8 8DB; Tel (01484) 602303; R.C. Swinden

Adult Education

South and West Areas Head of the School of Continuing Education, Huddersfield Technical College, New North Rd, Huddersfield, W. Yorks HD1 5NN; Tel (01484) 536521; Fax (01484) 511885; *Principal* Dr E.M. Rossiter; *Area Co-ordinator* J. Plested; *Area Co-ordinator* P. Crosbie
Almondbury Adult Education Centre Fernside Ave, Almondbury, Huddersfield HD5 8PQ; Tel (01484) 536333
Colne Valley Adult Education Centre Town Hall, Carr La, Slaithwaite, Huddersfield HD7 5AG; Tel (01484) 842692 (Evening/Term-time only)
Community Adult Education Centre Deighton Rd, Deighton, Huddersfield HD2 1JP; Tel (01484) 519678
Denby Dale/Kirkburton Adult Education Centre Shelley High School, Huddersfield Rd, Shelley, Huddersfield HD8 8NL; Tel (01484) 863882 (Evenings/Term-time only)
Greenhead College Adult Education Centre Greenhead Rd, Huddersfield HD1 4ES; Tel (01484) 422032
Huddersfield Area Office Adult Education Centre, St James's Rd, Marsh, Huddersfield HD1 4QA; Tel (01484) 538454
Newsome Adult Education Centre Newsome High School, Castle Ave, Newsome, Huddersfield HD4 6JN; Tel (01484) 549259
Salendine Nook Adult Education Centre Salendine Nook High School, New Hey Rd, Huddersfield HD3 4GN; Tel (01484) 657541
Upper Agbrigg Area Office Holmfirth Adult Education Centre, Huddersfield Rd, Holmfirth HD7 1AR; Tel (01484) 682511

Teachers' Centres

Banney Royd, Halifax Rd, Egerton, Huddersfield HD3 3BJ; Tel (01484) 427808; *Head of Centre* M.R. Pattison
Curriculum Development Centre, Temple Rd, Dewsbury WF13 3QD; Tel (01924) 465633

Grant Maintained Schools

Castle Hall School, Richard le Thorpe Ave, off Crowlees Rd, Mirfield WF14 9PH; Tel (01924) 493138; Fax (01924) 499232; *Headteacher* M.R. Bell; *Chairman of Governors* J. Temperton. (11–16) (Mixed) (395)
Heckmondwike Grammar, High St, Heckmondwike WF16 0AH; Tel (01924) 402202; Fax (01924) 411345; *Headteacher* M.C. Tweedle; *Chairman of Governors* Dr K. Swann. (Mixed) (11-18) (700)

Knowsley Metropolitan Borough Council

Population 155,500
Municipal Bldgs, Archway Rd, Huyton, Merseyside L36 9UX; Tel 0151-489 6000

Education Department

Huyton Hey Rd, Huyton, Merseyside L36 5YH; Tel 0151-489 6000
Director of Education P.J. Wylie, BA(Hons)
Senior Assistant Director (Resources) S.A. Fairbank, MSc
Assistant Director (Management) C.S. Hilton, BA
Assistant Director (Resources) H.A.J. Garnett, BEd, DEM, LMRSH, ACP
Assistant Director (Support Services) D. Sanders, BSc, PGCE, MEd, PhD
Senior Development Officer (Continuing Education) D.W. Morgan, BSc(Econ)
Continuing Education Officer (Youth & Community) G. Evans-Hughes
Continuing Education Officer (Youth Training & External Finance) B. Pready, BSc, MA
Senior Assistant Director (Curriculum) B. Lord, BSc, ARCS
Senior Inspector (Arts) D.R. Withey, MA, FCCEd, FRSA
Senior Inspector (Humanities) Vacancy
Senior Inspector (Science) Vacancy
Senior Adviser (Special Needs) P. Horn, BA
Music and Drama Adviser Vacancy
PSE Adviser J. Godley, BEd, MEd
English Adviser A. Tregenza, DASE
Principal Education Welfare Officer J. Price
Head of Continuing Education Unit M.J. Garlick
Number of Schools
64 primary (15,071); 10 secondary (8,956); 9 special (608);
Special Schools
9 (608)

Governor Training Unit

Education Offices, Huyton Hey Rd, Huyton, Knowsley, Merseyside L36 5YH; Tel 0151-443 3263; Fax 0151-449 3852
Co-ordinator for Governor Development Paul Evans

Services Offered
Training courses and procedural advice; Resource library; Newsletter; Clerking of Governors' meetings; Governor recruitment publicity; Knowsley Governors' forum

Schools Psychological Service

Huyton Child Guidance Clinic, Liverpool Rd, Huyton, Merseyside L36 3RD; Tel 0151-489 6136 or 6126/7; D. Le Masurier
Kirkby Child Guidance Clinic, Saint Chad's Dr, Kirkby, Merseyside L32 8RE; Tel 0151-546 2451/2; D. Le Masurier

Comprehensive Schools

N.B. All secondary schools bear the word "Knowsley" in their official title
All Saints R.C., Bewley Dr, Southdene, Kirkby L32 9PJ; Tel 0151-546 6881/2; J. Murphy, MEd, DASE. (Mixed) (1228)
Bowring, Western Ave, Huyton, Merseyside L36 4PR; Tel 0151-489 1566/4798; S.S. White, BSc. (Mixed) (799)
Brookfield, Bracknell Ave, Southdene, Kirkby L32 9PP; Tel 0151-546 6804; P. Jervis. (Mixed) (635)
Halewood Comprehensive, The Avenue, Wood Rd, Halewood, Merseyside L26 1UU; Tel 0151-486 2951; E. O'Neill, BA. (Mixed) (1037)
Hey, Seel Rd, Huyton, Merseyside L36 6DG; Tel 0151-489 0276; Dr G. Bedford. (Mixed) (833)
Higher Side, Cumber La, Whistone, Merseyside L35 2XG; Tel 0151-426 5715/9978; C.J. Wilkinson, MA(Cantab). (Mixed) (509)
Prescot, Knowsley Pk La, Prescot, Merseyside L34 3NB; Tel 0151-426 5571/4496; P.A. Barlow, BA, BMus. (Mixed) (824)
Ruffwood, Roughwood Dr, Kirkby L33 8XF; Tel 0151-546 4394/5; J. Jones, BA, MEd. (Mixed) (1182)
St Edmund of Canterbury R.C. Comp, Lordens Rd, Huyton, Merseyside L14 8UL; Tel 0151-489 3944/5911; C.R. Grainger, BA. (533)
St Edmund Arrowsmith R.C., Scotchbarn La, Whiston, Merseyside L35 7JD; Tel 0151-426 6046/430 0924; R. Melia, BSc. (Mixed) (661)

Teachers' Centre

Curriculum Development Centre, Astley Rd, Huyton, Merseyside L36 8HW; Tel 0151-480 8338; P. Winfield

Special Schools

Knowsley Highfield, Baileys La, Halewood, Merseyside L26 0TY; Tel 0151-486 4787
Southern Primary Support Centre, Arncliffe Rd, Halewood, Merseyside L25 9QE; Tel 0151-486 5514; E. Smith
Central Primary Support Centre, Mossbrow Rd, Huyton, Merseyside L36 7SY; Tel 0151-489 5024; H. Petrie, BEd
Northern Primary Support Centre, Bramcote Wk, Northwood, Kirkby, Merseyside L33 9UR; Tel 0151-546 2156; P.E. Edmondson, BA(Hons), MEd
Knowsley Parkfield, Bracknell Ave, Southdene, Kirkby, Merseyside L32 9PW; Tel 0151-546 6355; J.H. Young, MEd
Knowsley Springfield, Cawthorne Cl, Kirkby, Merseyside L32 3XQ; Tel 0151-549 1425; I. Cordingley
Cartbridge, Cartbridge La, Halewood, Merseyside L26 6LH; Tel 0151-487 0575; B. Lindsay (Acting)
The Elms, Roughsedge Hey, Stockbridge Village, Merseyside L28 1RX; Tel 0151-489 6517; E. Craven, BA(Hons), MEd
Service for Hearing Impaired Children, c/o The Health Centre, Old Colliery Old, Whitson, Merseyside L35 3SX; Tel 0151-430 6040; *Head of Service* H.J. Ward, MSc

Lancashire County Council

Population 1,395 300
PO Box 78, County Hall, Preston PR1 8XJ; Tel (01772) 54868; Fax (01772) 263506
Chief Executive/Clerk G.A. Johnson, BA
County Treasurer B. Aldred, BA(Hons), IPFA
Director of Social Services P.A. Oliver, BSc(Hons) PO Box 162, East Cliff County Offices, Preston PR1 3EA
County Librarian M.J. Dolan, MA, FLA, FRSA

Education Department

PO Box 61, County Hall, Preston PR1 8RJ; Tel (01772) 254868; Fax (01772) 261630
Chief Education Officer A.J. Collier, MA
Number of Schools
38 nursery (104 full-time, 3,278 part-time); 595 primary (122,716 full-time, 3,497 part-time); 98 secondary (77,320); 51 evening institutes centres; 2 adult education residential centres; 4 teachers' centres; 9 tutorial centres.
Special Schools
36 day (3,003); 6 residential (233)

Education Committee

Chairman Cllr S. Wright
Vice-Chairman Cllr H. Harding
Day of Committee Meeting
Tuesday

Governor Training Unit

Governor Services Unit, Education Department, PO Box 61, County Hall, Preston PR1 8RJ; Tel (01772) 261899/261869/261560/261593/1261698/261637; Fax (01772) 261886
County Training and Governor Services Manager Dr J. Lea, MA, PHD, PGCE
County Governor Training Officer Dr J. Hashemi, Bsc(Hons), MSc, MEd, PhD
Services Offered
A comprehensive range of training courses for Governors together with special events and conferences. Publication of a twice per term newsletter. Support and training for Clerks to Governors

Community Services Division

PO Box 61, County Hall, Preston PR1 8RJ; Tel (01772) 254868; Fax (01772) 261630
Head of Division R. Comish
Education Psychological Service Team P. Buckley
Education Welfare Service Team A. Hazell
Special Educational Needs Team D. Staton
Support Services Team K. Wales
Youth and Community Service Team J. Goffee
Careers Service Team D. Barber
Adult Education Team C.J. Brooks

Community Services Division – Area Teams

Blackburn

Area Education Office, Joint Divisional Offices, Jubilee St, Blackburn BB1 1ET; Tel (01254) 583328
Area Team Officer Vacancy
Area Special Educational Needs Officer Brenda Castling

Blackpool

Area Education Office, 278A Whitegate Dr, Blackpool FY3 9BS; Tel (01253) 695911
Area Team Officer Peter Skelly
Area Special Educational Needs Officer Edwina Taylor

Burnley

Area Education Office, 14 Nicholas St, Burnley BB11 2AW; Tel (01282) 831031
Area Team Officer Stuart Lovat
Area Special Educational Needs Officer Trish Rymer

Lancaster

Area Education Office, PO Box 606, White Cross Education Centre, Off Quarry Rd, Lancaster LA1 3SQ; Tel (01524) 63243
Area Team Officer Judith Ellis
Area Special Educational Needs Officer Geoff Hiscox

Preston

Area Education Office, 58 Guildhall St, Preston PR1 3US; Tel (01772) 261821
Area Team Officer Philip Wood
Area Special Educational Needs Officer Tony Tawil

West Lancashire

Area Education Office, Greetby Bldgs, Ormskirk L39 2BT; Tel (01695) 573971
Area Team Officer Lindsay Philipson
Area Special Educational Needs Officer Hazel Dodgson

Planning and Policy Division

Head of Division R.J. Marriott
Budget and Financial Services Team J. England
Buildings and Development Team C. Lockwood
Human Resource Management Team G. Stephen
Information Management Strategy Team J. Cousins
Policy Vacancy
Committee and Office Services Team A. Cooper

Quality Development Division

Inspection Team Dr A.G. Dunn
Curriculum Team (Basic) Vacancy
Curriculum Team (Extended) A. Wheatley
Professional Development Team C. Richardson
Area 5 (Blackburn/Hyndburn/Ribble Valley) S. Osborne

Quality Development Division Area Teams

Blackburn

Blackburn Curriculum & Professional Centre, 103 Preston New Rd, Blackburn BB2 6BJ; Tel (01254) 680863/1680850
Area Team Leader Stan Osborne

Blackpool

Education Office, 275A Whitegate Dr, Blackpool FY3 9BS; Tel (01253) 791529
Area Team Leader Helen Brown

Lancaster

White Cross Education Centre, Off Quarry Rd, Lancaster LA1 3SG; Tel (01524) 67376
Area Team Leader Bill Deller

Ormskirk

Chorley and West Lancashire Area Team, Education Offices, Greetby Bldgs, Derby St, Ormskirk L39 2BT; Tel (01695) 573971
Area Team Leader Nigel Edmondson

Preston

Education Department, County Hall, Preston PR1 8RJ; Tel (01772) 261658
Area Team Leader Steve Harrison

Rossendale

Education Office, 1 Grange St, Rawtenstall, Rossendale BB4 7RT; Tel (01706) 831013
Area Team Leader David Sowter

School and College Services Division

Head of Division J. Bennett
School Personnel Services Group C. Lennox
School Financial Services Group A. Taylor
Health and Safety Group M. Glover
Training and Governor Services Group Dr J.H. Lea
Curriculum Support Group R. Hetherington
Special Education (Schools and Services) Group S. Mercer
Competition and Miscellaneous Services Group H. Palmer

Lancaster District

Area Education Office, PO Box 606, White Cross Education Centre, Off Quarry Rd, Lancaster LA1 3SQ; Tel (01524) 63243
Area Team Leader (Personnel) M. Wood
Area Team Leader (Finance) R. Livesey
Area Team Leader (Governor Services) C. Eaves
Number of Schools
2 nursery (80); 52 primary (10,986); 8 secondary (6,565); 2 special (229)

Secondary Modern

Central Lancaster County High, Crag Rd, Lancaster LA1 3LS; Tel (01524) 32636; Fax (01524) 849856; Mrs P. Askew. (Mixed) (549)
Lancaster Skerton County High, Owen Rd, Lancaster LA1 2BL; Tel (01524) 65143; Fax (01524) 843646; P. Schofield, BA. (Mixed) (536)
Lunesdale County High, Melling Rd, Hornby LA2 8LH; Tel (01524) 221471; I. Blaikie. (Mixed) (131)

Comprehensive School (11–18 Voluntary)

Lancaster Our Lady's R.C. High, Morecambe Rd, Lancaster LA1 2RX; Tel (01524) 66689; Fax (01524) 849441; M. Webster. (V.A.) (Mixed) (1026)
Lancaster Ripley St Thomas's C.E. County High, Ashton Rd, Lancaster LA1 4RS; Tel (01524) 64496; Fax (01524) 847069; J.A.V. Lailey. (Aided) (V.A.) (Mixed) (1374)

Comprehensive School (11––16)

Carnforth County High, Kellet Rd, Carnforth LA5 9LS; Tel (01524) 732424; Fax (01524) 720167; P.A. Legon. (Mixed) (654)

Comprehensive Schools (11––18)

Morecambe and Heysham County High, Limes Ave, Morecambe LA3 1HS; Tel (01524) 416830; Fax (01524) 832622; J.M. Thomas, BA. (Mixed) (1068)
Morecambe and Heysham High, Dallam Ave, Morecambe LA4 5BG; Tel (01524) 410207; N.S. Allott. (Mixed) (1227)

3 Local Government England and Wales

Poulton District

Area Education Office, Lockwood Ave, Poulton-Le-Fylde, Blackpool FY6 7AD; Tel (01253) 893614
Area Team Leader (Personnel) D. Singleton
Area Team Leader (Finance) P. Redmond
Area Team Leader (Governor Services) G. Cole
Number of Schools
46 primary (8,477); 6 secondary (5,272); 3 special (167)

Comprehensive Schools (11–16)

Garstang County High, Garstang Rd, Bowgreave, Preston PR3 1YE; Tel (01995) 603226; Fax (01995) 601655; J.D. Falkingham. (Mixed) (797)
Poulton-Le-Fylde Hodgson County High, Moorland Rd, Poulton-le-Fylde FY6 7EU; Tel (01253) 882815; Fax (01253) 899971; J.H. Bowers, BSc. (Mixed) (990)
Thornton Cleveleys Millfield County High Church Rd, Thornton-Cleveleys; Tel (01253) 865017; Fax (01253) 854586; A.P. Harvey. (Mixed) (831)

Comprehensive School (11–18)

Fleetwood County High, Broadway, Fleetwood FY7 8HE; Tel (01253) 876757; M.A. Howseman, BA. (Mixed) (1143)

Comprehensive Schools (Voluntary 11–16)

Fleetwood Cardinal Allen R.C. High, Melbourne Ave, Fleetwood FY7 8AY; Tel (01253) 872659/77160; J. O'Brien, BSc. V.A.) (Mixed (801)
Over Wyre St Aidans CE High, Cartgate, Preesall, Blackpool FY6 0NP; Tel (01253) 810504; Fax (01253) 810244; Rev B.A. Leeson. S.A.) (Mixed (710)

Blackpool District

Area Education Office, 275A Whitegate Dr, Blackpool FY3 9BS; Tel (01253) 791529
Number of Schools
56 primary (16,391); 11 secondary (9,997); 4 special (339)

Comprehensive Schools (Voluntary 11–18)

Blackpool Greenlands County High, Bispham Rd, Blackpool FY2 0NH; Tel (01253) 353155; Fax (01253) 500397; *Headteacher* A.M. Berry. (Girls) (1036)
Blackpool St Mary's R.C. High, St Walburga's Rd, Blackpool FY3 7EQ; Tel (01253) 396286; Fax (01253) 305475
Lytham St Annes St Bede's R.C. High Talbot Rd, Lytham St Annes FY8 4JL; Tel (01253) 737174; Fax (01253) 731243; D.J. Harrison. (S.A.) (Mixed) (551)
St Mary's R.C. High, Garstang Rd West FY3 7UB; Tel (01253) 396291; P.J. McCarthy. (V.A.) (863)

Comprehensive Schools (11–16)

Blackpool Palatine County High, St. Anne's Rd, Blackpool FY4 2AR; Tel (01253) 45522; Fax (01253) 41803; I.E.W. Pike, BA. (627)
Blackpool Highfield High, Highfield Rd, Southshore, Blackpool FY4 3JZ; Tel (01253) 41460; Fax (01253) 401818; C.D. Digman. (Mixed) (916)
Blackpool Montgomery High, All Hallow's Rd, Bispham FY2 0AZ; Tel (01253) 56271; Fax (01253) 52305; P. Moss, MEd, BA, JP. (Mixed) (1079)
Blackpool Collegiate County High, Blackpool Old Rd, Highfurlong, Blackpool FY3 7LS; Tel (01253) 300460; Fax (01253) 395700; K.S. Clark. (1163)
Blackpool St George's County High, Cherry Tree Rd, Blackpool FY4 4PH; Tel (01253) 764169; Fax (01253) 698624; G. Jones. (Mixed) (499)
Blackpool Warbreck County High, Warbreck Hill Rd, Blackpool FY2 0TS; Tel (01253) 55493; Fax (01253) 57981; A.S.B. Olivine, BA. (Boys) (631)

Comprehensive Schools (11–18)

Kirkham Carr Hill County High, Royal Ave, Kirkham PR4 2ST; Tel (01772) 682008; Fax (01772) 673048; J.F. Davies. (Mixed) (1076)
Lytham St Annes County High, Worsley Rd, Lytham St Annes FY8 4DG; Tel (01253) 733192; Fax (01253) 795109; M.E. Payne. (1556)

Preston District

Area Education Office, 58 Guildhall St, Preston PR1 3US; Tel (01772) 261821
Area Team Officer P. Wood
Area Special Educational Needs Officer T. Tawil
Number of Schools
1 nursery (91); 61 primary (13,452); 11 secondary (7,202); 4 special (309)

Comprehensive Schools (11–16)

Broughton High, Woodplumpton La, Broughton PR3 5JJ; Tel (01772) 863849; Fax (01772) 864710; T.A. Harris, BSc. (Mixed) (874)
Fulwood County High, Black Bull La, Fulwood PR2 4YR; Tel (01772) 719060; Fax (01772) 713573; J.F. Byrom. (Mixed) (955)
Longridge County High, Preston Rd, Longridge, Preston PR3 3AR; Tel (01772) 782316; Fax (01772) 782316; P.A. Lewis. (Mixed) (633)
Preston Ashton-on-Ribble County High, Aldwych Dr, Preston PR2 1SL; Tel (01772) 729331; Fax (01772) 721215; G. Hewitson. (Mixed) (794)
Preston Moor Park County High, Moor Park Ave, Preston PR1 6DT; Tel (01772) 795428; Fax (01772) 653912; K.M. Moss. (429)
Preston Ribbleton Hall High, Ribbleton Hall Dr, Preston, Lancs PR2 6EE; Tel (01772) 651110; Fax (01772) 65251; J.H. Deakin. (Mixed) (693)
Preston Tulketh County High, Tag La, Ingol, Preston PR2 3TX; Tel (01772) 729773; K. Curphey. (Mixed) (411)

Comprehensive Schools (Voluntary 11–16)

Longridge, St Cecilia's R.C. High, Chapel Hill, Longridge, Preston PR3 2XA; Tel (01772) 783074; Fax (01772) 786200; C.A. Mason. (V.A.) (395)
Preston Our Lady's R.C. High, St Anthony's Dr, Fulwood, Preston PR2 3SQ; Tel (01772) 726441; Fax (01772) 760212 (A. Greenall); A. Greenall. (V.A.) (929)
Preston Christ The King R.C. High, Lawrence Ave, Frenchwood PR1 4LX; Tel (01772) 252072; Fax (01772) 885674; A. Van Cauwelaert, BSc. (V.A.) (Mixed) (399)
Preston Corpus Christi R.C. High, St Vincent's Rd, Fulwood, Preston PR2 4QY; Tel (01772) 716912; Fax (01772) 718779; M.J. McDermott. (V.A.) (690)

South Ribble District

Area Education Office, Civic Centre, West Paddock, Leyland PR5 1DH; Tel (01772) 421491
Area Team Leader (Personnel) I. Jeynes
Area Team Leader (Finance) L. Rowett
Area Team Leader (Governor Services) B. Bowcott
Number of Schools
41 primary (9,590), 10 secondary (7,563), 2 special (157)

Comprehensive Schools (11–16)

Leyland Wellfield County High, Yewlands Dr, Leyland, Preston PR5 1TP; Tel (01772) 421303; Fax (01772) 454767; M.S. Ainsworth. (Mixed) (612)
Leyland Worden County High, Westfield Dr, Leyland, Preston PR5 1QX; Tel (01772) 421021; D.R. Tilston. (Mixed) (559)
Penwortham Priory County High, Crow Hills Rd, off Crookings La, Penwortham, Preston PR1 0JE; Tel (01772) 744448; Fax (01772) 752426; P.P. Young. (995)

Walton-le-Dale County High, Brindle Rd, Bamber Bridge, Preston PR5 6RN; Tel (01772) 35726; Fax (01772) 39494; R.G. Ashby. (621)
Walton-le-Dale Lostock Hall County High, Todd La North, Lostock Hall, Preston PR5 5UR; Tel (01772) 36293; Fax (01772) 37083; D.W. Hulse. (696)

Comprehensive Schools (11–18)

Hutton Grammar, Liverpool Rd, Hutton, Preston PR4 5SN; Tel (01772) 613112; Fax (01772) 617645; G. Armstong. (V.A.) (842)
Penwortham Girls' County High, Cop La, Penwortham, Preston PR1 0SR; Tel (01772) 743399; Fax (01772) 757475; Mrs J.J. Westwell. (699)

Comprehensive Schools (Voluntary 11–16)

Leyland Balshaw's High, Church Rd, Leyland PR5 2AH; Tel (01772) 421009; P.J. Ingram, BSc. (V.C.) (Mixed) (947)
Penwortham All Hallows R.C. High, Crabtree Ave, Penwortham PR1 0LM; Tel (01772) 746121/2; Fax (01772) 740141; M. Flynn. (V.A.) (Mixed) (888)
Walton-Le-Dale Brownedge St Mary's R.C. High, Station Rd, Bamber Bridge, Preston PR5 6PB; Tel (01772) 39813; Fax (01772) 629236; Dr J.L. McHugh. (S.A.) (704)

West Lancashire District

Area Education Office, Greetby Bldgs, Ormskirk L39 2BT; Tel (01695) 573971
Area Team Officer L. Philipson
Area Special Educational Needs Officer H. Dodgson
Number of Schools
1 nursery (44), 61 primary (10,153), 9 secondary (6,809), 4 special (247)

Comprehensive Schools (11–16)

Burscough Priory High, Trevor Rd, Burscough L40 7RZ; Tel (01704) 893259; Fax (01704) 893307; R.N. Leighton. (Mixed) (690)
Skelmersdale Glenburn County High, Yewdale, Southway, Skelmersdale WN8 6JB; Tel (01695) 24381; P. Hope. (Mixed) (581)
Skelmersdale Lathom County High, Glenburn Rd, Skelmersdale WN8 6JN; Tel (01695) 25653; G. Burnett. (605)
Tarleton County High, Hesketh La, Tarleton PR4 6AQ; Tel (01772) 812644; Fax (01772) 812168; A. Hardiker. (Mixed) (597)
Up Holland County High, Sandbrook Rd, Orrell, nr Wigan WN5 7AL; Tel (01695) 625191; Fax (01695) 633379; G.H. Gorton, MA. (Mixed) (894)

Comprehensive School (11–18)

Ormskirk Cross Hall County High, Wigan Rd, Ormskirk L39 2AT; Tel (01695) 572625; Fax (01695) 572348; J.F. Shemilt. (Mixed) (884)

Comprehensive Schools (Voluntary 11–16)

Ormskirk St Bede's R.C. High, St Annes Rd, Ormskirk L39 4TA; Tel (01695) 570335; Fax (01695) 571686; P. Entwistle. (S.A.) (Mixed) (540)
Skelmersdale Our Lady Queen of Peace R.C. High, Glenburn Rd, Skelmersdale WN8 6JW; Tel (01695) 25635; Fax (01695) 556046; J.J. Glennon. (V.A.) (782)

Comprehensive School (Voluntary 11–18)

Ormskirk Grammar, Ruff La, Ormskirk L39 4QY; Tel (01695) 572405; Fax (01695) 571910; A.C. Richardson. (V.C.) (Mixed) (1236)

Chorley District

Area Education Office, Union St, Chorley PR7 1EB; Tel (01257) 276321
Area Team Leader (Personnel) C. Allison
Area Team Leader (Finance) N. Smith
Area Team Leader (Governor Services) B. Goulding
Number of Schools
2 nursery (81); 50 primary (8,701); 6 secondary (5,106); 2 special (182)

Comprehensive Schools (11–16)

Chorley Albany County High, Bolton Rd, Chorley PR7 3AY; Tel (01257) 262572; Fax (01257) 233725; M. Quirke. (Mixed) (702)
Chorley Parklands High, Southport Rd PR7 1LL; Tel (01257) 264596; Fax (01257) 261215; G. Wright, MEd. (1049)
Chorley Southlands County High, Clover Rd, Chorley PR7 2NJ; Tel (01257) 262704; Fax (01257) 232577; J. Lawson. (Mixed) (907)

Comprehensive Schools (Voluntary 11–16)

Chorley Holy Cross R.C. High Burgh La, Chorley PR7 3NT; Tel (01257) 262093; Fax (10257) 232878; F.A. Charnock, BA. (V.A.) (Mixed) (707)
Chorley St Michael's C.E. High, Astley Rd, Chorley PR7 1RS; Tel (01257) 264740; Fax (01257) 230177; R.H. Hardwick. (V.A.) (Mixed) (1052)
Croston The Bishop Rawstorne C.E. High Out La, Croston PR5 7HJ; Tel (01772) 600349; Fax (01772) 601320; G.H. Lloyd. (S.A.) (Mixed) (689)

Blackburn District

Area Education Office, Joint Divisional Offices, Jubilee St, Blackburn BB1 1ET; Tel (01254) 583328
Area Team Officer Vacancy
Area Special Educational Needs Officer B. Castling
Number of Schools
8 nursery (322); 63 primary (15,492); 8 secondary (8,205); 6 special (464)

Comprehensive Schools (11–16)

Blackburn Beardwood County High Preston New Rd, Blackburn BB2 7AD; Tel (01254) 53126; Fax (01254) 694080; Dr D.R. Eckton. (921)
Blackburn Pleckgate County High, Pleckgate Rd, Blackburn; Tel (01254) 249134; Fax (01254) 245329; G.L. Scott. (1167)
Blackburn Queens Park County High, Shadsworth Road, Blackburn BB1 2HT; Tel (01254) 580665; Fax (01254) 697072; E.A. Sharples. (970)
Blackburn Witton Park County High, Buncer La, Blackburn BB2 6TD; Tel (01254) 51445; Fax (01254) 693699; J.E. Gosling. (1065)
Darwen Moorland County High, Holden Fold, Darwen BB3 3AU; Tel (01254) 702053; Fax (01254) 760910; R.J. Bridges. (Mixed) (1087)
Darwen Vale County High, Blackburn Rd, Darwen BB3 0AL; Tel (01254) 702749; Fax (01254) 706368; J.S. Strivens. (Mixed) (1109)

Comprehensive Schools (Voluntary 11–16)

Blackburn Our Lady & St John R.C. High, North Rd, Blackburn BB1 1PY; Tel (01254) 59055; Fax (01254) 697308; M.T. Humphreys. (Aided) (911)
Blackburn St Bedes R.C. High, Livesey Branch Rd, Darwen BB2 5BU; Tel (01254) 202519; Fax (01254) 207882; J. Challoner. (Aided) (975)

Hyndburn and Ribble Valley District

Area Education Office, Ewbank Hse, Cannon St, Accrington BB5 1PE; Tel (01254) 393824
Area Team Leader (Personnel) W. Hindle
Area Team Leader (Finance) C. Shepherd
Area Team Leader (Governor Services) J. Thompson

Number of Schools
3 nursery (145); 57 primary (11,128); 9 secondary (7,054); 3 special (232)

Comprehensive Schools (11–16)

Accrington Moorhead County High, Cromwell Ave, Accrington BB5 5AF; Tel (01254) 231579; Fax (01254) 872415; A.G. Grey, B.Phil. (Mixed) (1130)
Accrington The Hollins County High, Hollins La, Accrington BB5 2QY; Tel (01254) 233500; Fax (01254) 236970; F. Howard (Acting). (Mixed) (648)
Oswaldtwistle Rhyddings County High, Haworth St, Oswaldtwistle BB5 3EA; Tel (01254) 231051; Fax (01254) 393242; Miss J. Moore. (Mixed) (1052)
Rishton Norden County High, Stourton St, Rishton BB1 4ED; Tel (01254) 885378; Fax (01254) 884372; Miss J.S. Halpin, BA. (Mixed) (570)

Comprehensive Schools (Voluntary 11–18)

Billington St Augustines R.C. High, Elker La, Billington BB6 9JA; Tel (01254) 823362; Fax (01254) 822147; A. McNamara. (V.A.) (Mixed) (924)
Hyndburn Mount Carmel R.C. High, Wordsworth Rd, Accrington BB5 0LU; Tel (01254) 233458; Fax (01254) 236355; W.P. Boylan, BA. (V.A.) (621)
St Christopher's C.E. High, Queens Rd, West Accrington BB5 4AY; Tel (01254) 232992; Fax (01254) 234775; A.D. Coates. (S.A.) (Mixed) (837)

Secondary Modern Schools

Bowland County High, Riversmead, Grindleton, nr Clitheroe, Lancs BB7 4QS; Tel (01200) 41374; G.H. Crossley, BSc, BEd. (Mixed) (343)
Clitheroe Ribblesdale County High, Queens Rd, Clitheroe BB7 1EJ; Tel (01200) 22563; Fax (01200) 442506; Ms G.M. Ward. (Mixed) (929)

Burnley District

Area Education Office, 14 Nicholas St, Burnley BB11 2AW; Tel (01282) 831031
Area Team Officer S. Lovat
Area Special Educational Needs Officer T. Rymer
Number of Schools
13 nursery (579); 38 primary (9,479); 8 secondary (6,043); 3 special (236)

Comprehensive Schools (11–16)

Burnley Barden County High, Heald Rd, Burnley BB10 1JB; Tel (01282) 36324; Fax (01282) 832434; G. Senior, BSc. (Boys) (375)
Burnley Habergham High, Byron St BB12 6NU; Tel (01282) 775131; Fax (01282) 774214; G.D. Clayton. (Mixed) (1137)
Burnley Ivy Bank County High, Byron St BB12 6NU; Tel (01282) 775111; Fax (01282) 779350; S. Ball. (907)
Burnley St Hilda's R.C. Girls High, Coal Clough La, Burnley BB11 5BT; Tel (01282) 36314; Fax (01282) 832198; Miss B. Bleasdale. (S.A.) (Girls) (618)
Burnley Towneley County High, Towneley Holmes, Burnley BB11 3EN; Tel (01282) 36311; Fax (01282) 30247; C.D. Hinks, BA. (Mixed) (766)
Burnley Walshaw County High, Eastern Ave, Burnley BB10 2AT; Tel (01282) 36321; Fax (01282) 830922; Mrs L.F. Towers. (Girls) (808)
Padiham Gawthorpe County High, Burnley Rd, Padiham BB12 8ST; Tel (01282) 772459; T. Nowell, BSc. (Mixed) (653)

Comprehensive School (11–18)

Burnley St Theodore's R.C. High, Ormerod Rd, Burnley BB10 3AA; Tel (01282) 36317; Fax (01282) 832037; C.D. Meehan. (S.A.) (Boys) (779)

Pendle District

Area Education Office, Market St, Nelson BBG 7LQ; Tel (01282) 614332
Area Team Leader (Personnel) C. Healey
Area Team Leader (Finance) S. Grindrod
Area Team Leader (Governor Services) J. Halshaw
Number of Schools
5 nursery (256); 38 primary (8,842); 7 secondary (5,706); 2 special (187)

Comprehensive Schools (11–16)

Barnoldswick West Craven County High, Kelbrook Rd, Barnoldswick, Lancs BB8 5TB; Tel (01282) 812292; Fax (01282) 850427; W.B. Montgomery. (Mixed) (716)
Brierfield Mansfield County High, Elland Rd, Brierfield, Nelson BB9 5RX; Tel (01282) 614640/616380; Fax (01282) 616330; E. Pickup, BA. (1063)
Colne Park County High, Venables Ave, Colne BB8 7DP; Tel (01282) 865200; Fax (01282) 866089; A. Chambers. (913)
Colne Primet County High, Dent St, Colne BB8 8JF; Tel (01282) 863970/865282; Fax (01282) 871276; P.J. Dixon, BA. (949)
Nelson Edge End County High, Hibson Rd, Nelson BB9 0PZ; Tel (01282) 617636/612872; Fax (01282) 619335; M. Burgess. (683)
Nelson Walton County High, Oxford Rd, Nelson BB9 8JG; Tel (01282) 615065/691602; Fax (01282) 619590; D.M. Farrant. (743)

Comprehensive School (Voluntary 11–16)

Colne St John Fisher and Thomas More R.C. High, Gibfield Rd, Colne; Tel (01282) 865299; Fax (01282) 860419; P. Donnelly. (S.A.) (Mixed) (639)

Rossendale District

Area Education Office, 14 Nicholas St, Burnley BB11 2AW; Tel (01282) 831031
Area Team Officer S. Lovat
Area Special Educational Needs Officer T. Rymer
Number of Schools
3 nursery (173); 32 primary (6,502); 5 secondary (3,760); 1 special (78)

Secondary Modern Schools (11–16)

Bacup Fearns County High, Fearns Moss, Stackstead, Bacup OL13 0TG; Tel (01706) 873896; Fax (01706) 875029; N.E. Thornley. (Mixed) (853)
Rawtenstall Alder Grange County High, Calder Rd off Hollin La, Rawtenstall BB4 8HT; Tel (01706) 223171; Fax (01706) 210448; Mrs J. McGrath. (Mixed) (528)

Comprehensive (11–16)

Whitworth County High, Hall Fold, Whitworth, Rochdale OL12 8TS; Tel (01706) 343218; Fax (01706) 343218; N. Robinson. (Mixed) (484)

Comprehensive (11–18)

Haslingden County High, Broadway, Haslingden, Rossendale BB4 4EY; Tel (01706) 215726; Fax (01706) 219861; Miss J. Durbar. (Mixed) (1387)

Comprehensive (Voluntary 11–16)

Rossendale All Saints R.C. High, Haslingden Rd, Rawtenstall, Rossendale BB4 6SJ; Tel (01706) 213693; Fax (01706) 213693; M.J. Brennan. (V.A.) (508)

Hospital Special Schools/Units

Mary Burbury Child Psychiatric Unit, Burnley General Hospital, Casterton Ave, Burnley BB10 2PQ; Tel (01282) 474800; Y. Roberts. (Disturbed Children) (0–12)
Queen's Park Hospital, Day Child Psychiatric Unit, Queens Park Hospital, Haslingden Rd, Blackburn BB2 3HH; Tel (01254) 263555; Mrs A.B. Chenery (Day Child Psychiatric Unit)

Royal Lancaster Infirmary Childrens' Centre Paediatric Ward, Ashton Rd, Lancaster LA1 4RP; Tel (01524) 583412; D.S. Wood. (E.S.N.(S) (Mixed) (4–19)
Royal Preston Hospital Classroom, Childrens Ward 7, Sharoe Green La, Preston PR2 4HT; Tel (01772) 774263; P. Probin
Wrightington Hospital Unit, Wrightington, Wigan WN6 9EP; Tel (01695) 583401; Y. Winstanley. (Orthopaedic) (Mixed) (all ages)

Child Development Centres

Blackpool Child Development Centre, Whitegate Dr, Blackpool FY3 9BS; Tel (01253) 763232; G.B. Farrell
Lancaster, Westbourne Dr, Lancaster LA1 5EE; Tel (01524) 34331; E. Swannie
Ormskirk, Ormskirk and District General Hospital, Wigan Rd, Ormskirk; Tel (01695) 574313; Mrs D. Hughes
Pendle Child Development Centre, Reedley Hall, Reedley, Burnley BB0 2LW; Tel (01282) 602754; S. Wadsley
Rishton, 6 Blackburn Rd, Rishton, Blackburn; Tel (01254) 888503; Mrs M. Birch

Special Day Schools/Units

Blackburn Blackamoor, Roman Rd, Blackburn BB1 2LA; Tel (01254) 52843; A. Abram (Acting). (P.H.) (5–16) (Mixed)
Blackburn Broadlands, Roman Rd, Blackburn BB1 2LA; Tel (01254) 56044; Fax (01254) 56044; Mrs H. Hebden. (Multiply Handicapped) (2–5) (Mixed)
Blackburn Crosshill, Shadsworth Rd, Blackburn BB1 2HR; Tel (01254) 667713; M.J. Hatch. (E.S.N.(M) (5–16) (Mixed)
Blackburn Dame Evelyn Fox, Roman Rd, Blackburn BB1 2LA; Tel (01254) 56808; J.B. Barrie. (E.S.N.(S) (5–16) (Mixed)
Blackpool Highfurlong, Blackpool Old Rd, Blackpool FY3 7LR; Tel (01253) 392188; E. Jackson. (P.H. and Del.) (5–16) (Mixed)
Blackpool Park, Whitegate Dr, Blackpool FY3 9HF; Tel (01253) 764130; E.N.M. Parry. (E.S.N.(M) (5–16) (Mixed)
Blackpool Woodlands, Whitegate Dr, Blackpool FY3 9HF; Tel (01253) 766392; S.J. Forde. (E.S.N.(S) (2–16) (Mixed)
Burnley Calder View School, March St, Burnley BB12 0BU; Tel (01282) 33946; R.J. Barker. (E.S.N.(M) (5–16) (Mixed)
Burnley Partially Hearing SERF Unit (Primary) Todmorden Rd County Primary School, Todmorden Rd, Burnley BB10 4EA; Tel (01282) 37277; *Head* R.W. Marsden; Tel 26670. (5–6 Infants) (E. Large); (7–11) (Mixed) (Junior) (C.O. Else)
Burnley Primrose Hill, Harrogate Cres, Burnley BB10 2NX; Tel (01282) 424216; Fax (01282) 831419; G. McCabe. (P.H. and Del.) (4–16) (Mixed)
Burnley Westway, March St, Burnley BB12 0BU; Tel (01282) 33044; S. West. (E.S.N.(S) (3–17+) (Mixed)
Burnley Partially Hearing Serf Unit (Sec) Ivy Bank High School, Byron St, Burnley BB12 6NU; Tel (01282) 775111; *Teacher in Charge* P.J. Rowbottom. (Partially Hearing) (11–16) (Mixed)
Chorley Astley Pk, Harrington Rd, Chorley PR7 1JZ; Tel (01257) 262227; A.R. Sillitoe. (E.S.N.(M) (5–16) (Mixed)
Chorley Mayfield, Gloucester Rd, Chorley PR7 3HN; Tel (01257) 263063; J.R. Canner. (E.S.N.(S) (2–19) (Mixed)
Colne Gibfield, Gibfield Rd, Colne BB8 8JT; Tel (01282) 865011; Fax (01282) 865011; C.I. Cohen. (E.S.N.(M) (5–16) (Mixed)
The Coppice Walton-Le-Dale, Ash Grove, Bamber Bridge, Preston PR5 6GY; Tel (01772) 36342; A. Jenkins. (E.S.N.(S) (5–16) (Mixed)
Darwen Tullyallan, Salisbury Rd, Darwen BB3 1HZ; Tel (01254) 702317; G. Holman (Acting). (Malad.) (5–16) (Mixed)
Great Harwood North Cliffe, Blackburn Old Rd, Great Harwood, Blackburn BB6 7UW; Tel (01254) 885245; R.L. Whitaker (Acting). (E.S.N.(M) (5–16) (Mixed)
Kirkham Pear Tree, Station Rd, Kirkham, Preston PR4 2HA; Tel (01772) 683609; G.D. Gwilliam. (E.S.N.(S) (5–16+) (Mixed)
Lancaster Hillside Autistic Centre, Chatsworth Rd, Lancaster LA1 4SL; Tel (01524) 60554; Mrs C.J. Farmer. (5–16) (Mixed)
Lancaster The Loyne, Sefton Dr, Lancaster LA1 2PZ; Tel (01524) 64543; Dr J. Steele. (E.S.N.(S) (5–16) (Mixed)
Morecambe and Heysham Morecambe Rd, Morecambe Rd LA3 3AB; Tel (01524) 414384; *Head Teacher* T.G. Pickles. (E.S.N.(M) (5–16) (Mixed)
Nelson Townhouse, Townhouse Rd, Nelson BB9 8DG; Tel (01282) 614013; Fax (01282) 614013; A.J. Worrall. (E.S.N.(S) (2–16) (Mixed)
Ormskirk Parkside, Aughton St, Ormskirk L39 3BS; Tel (01695) 575894; A.E. Rose. (E.S.N.(S) (2–18+) (Mixed)
Oswaldtwistle Broadfield, Fielding La, Oswaldtwistle, Accrington BB5 3BE; Tel (01254) 381782; Fax (01254) 396805; B. McNulty (Acting). (E.S.N.(M) (5–16) (Mixed)
Oswaldtwistle White Ash, Thwaites Rd, Oswaldtwistle, Accrington BB5 4QG; Tel (01254) 235772; E.Y. Twist (Acting). (E.S.N.(S) (2–16+) (Mixed)
Poulton-le-Fylde Wyredale, Fouldrey Ave, Poulton-le-Fylde, Blackpool FY6 7HE; Tel (01253) 886895; D. Woodhouse. (Day) (Malad.) (5–16) (Mixed)
Preston Elms, Moor Pk, Preston PR1 6AU; Tel (01772) 792681; Fax (01772) 654940; J.M. Bacon. (E.S.N.(S) (3–16+) (Mixed)
Preston Moorbrook, Ainslie Rd, Preston PR2 3DB; Tel (01772) 774752; P. Bardsley. (Malad.) (5–16) (Mixed)
Preston Moorfield, Moor Pk, Preston PR1 6AA; Tel (01772) 795378; Fax (01772) 651472; J.R. Dibble. (P.H. and Del.) (5–16) (Mixed)
Preston Partially Hearing Serf Unit (Primary) Holme Slack County Primary, Manor House La, Preston PR1 6HP; Tel (01772) 795257; *Head Teacher* P. Whiteley; *Teacher in Charge (Infant Class 5-7 Mixed)* Mrs P.M. Bradford. (Partially Hearing) (Junior Class 8–11) (Mixed)
Preston Sherburn, Moor Pk, Preston PR1 6AA; Tel (01772) 795749; Fax (01772) 652096; K. Moss. (E.S.N.M) (5–16) (Mixed)
Preston Speech and Language Difficulties Serf Unit (Primary) Savick County Primary School, Ainsdale Dr, Ashton-on-Ribble, Preston PR2 1TU; Tel (01772) 728052; *Head of School* R.F. Adams; *Teacher in Charge* Mrs J.A. Singleton. (Speech Defects) (2–7) (Mixed)
Rossendale Tor View, Clod La, Bentgate, Haslingden BB4 6LR; Tel (01706) 214640; Fax (01706) 214640; M. Morris. (M.L.D. and S.L.D.) (5–16) (Mixed)
Skelmersdale Ashurst School, School La, Chapel Hse, Skelmersdale WN8 8EH; Tel (01695) 22991; J. Hajnryeh. (E.S.N.) (4–18) (Mixed)
Skelmersdale Beacon, Tanhouse Rd, Skelmersdale WN8 6BA; Tel (01695) 21066; J.H. Taylor. (Malad.) (5–16) (Mixed)
Skelmersdale Black Moss, School La, Chapel Hse, Skelmersdale WN8 8EH; Tel (01695) 21487; J.C. Mumby. (E.S.N.(M) (5–16) (Mixed)
Thornton-Cleveleys Great Arley, Holly Rd, Thornton Cleveleys, Blackpool FY5 4HH; Tel (01253) 821072; J.L. Johns. (E.S.N.(M) (5–16) (Mixed)
Thornton-Cleveleys Red Marsh, Holly Rd, Thornton Cleveleys, Blackpool FY5 4HH; Tel (01253) 868451; P. Monk. (E.S.N.(S)
Walton-Le-Dale Moor Hey, Far Croft, Lostock Hall, Preston PR5 5SU; Tel (01772) 36976; C.W.T. Wilson. (E.S.N.(M) (5–16) (Mixed)
Waterloo, County Junior School, Partially Hearing Unit, Waterloo Rd, Blackpool FY4 3AG; Tel (01253) 341350; *Head Teacher* P. Rawcliffe; *Teacher in Charge* Miss J. Shepherd. (5–11) (Mixed)

Residential Special Schools

Bleasdale Hse, 27 Emesgate La, Silverdale, Carnforth LA5 0RG; Tel (01524) 701217; L. Ormrod. (P.H.) (5–16) (Mixed)

Broughton Tower, Broughton-in-Furness, Cumbria LA20 6AA; Tel (01229) 716242; D.J. Norton, BA. (Malad.) (5–13) (Mixed)
Longridge Woodville, Ribchester Rd, Longridge, Preston PR3 3XB; Tel (01772) 782205; K. Saunders. (E.S.N.(M) (Junior) (Mixed)
Rawtenstall Cribden Hse, Haslingden Rd, Rawtenstall, Rossendale BB4 6RX; Tel (01706) 213048; S. Harris. (Malad.) (7–11) (Mixed)
Thelwall Massey Hall, Half Acre La, Thelwall, Warrington WA4 3JQ; Tel (01925) 752016; C. Gleave. (E.S.N.(M) (12–16) (Mixed)
Wennington Hall, Wennington, Lancaster LA2 8NS; Tel (01524) 21333; I. Geary. (Malad.) (Boys) (11–16)

Hostels and Day Classes

Marles Hill Hostel, 150 Wheatley Lane Rd, Barrowford, Nelson BB9 6QQ; Tel (01282) 615862/616924; P.J. Cooper. (E.B.D.) (11–16) (Boys)
Minster Lodge Hostel, Ruff Lane, Ormskirk L39 4QX; Tel (01695) 575486; G.R. Lucy. (E.B.D.) (11–16) (Boys)
Preston Larches Hse, Larches La, Ashton-on-Ribble, Preston PR2 1QE; Tel (01772) 728567; A.G. Chesworth. (Malad.) (Mixed) (6–16)

Autistic Centre

Lancaster Hillside Autistic Centre, Chadsworth Rd, Lancaster; Tel (01524) 60554; C.J. Farmer. (Autistic) (5–16) (Mixed)

Reading and Language Centres

Blackburn, 103 Preston New Rd, Blackburn BB2 6BJ; Tel (01254) 680854; Mrs V.A. England
Blackpool and Fylde, C/o Knowle High School, St. Annes Rd, Blackpool FY4 2AR; Tel (01253) 408981; D. Jones
Burnley, Swindon St, Burnley BB11 4PF; Tel (01282) 425685; B. Dobney (Acting)
Chorley, School House, Highfield County Primary School, Wright St, Chorley PR6 0SP; Tel (01257) 269807; M. Moggridge
District Education Office, 1 Grange St, Rawtenstall, Rossendale BB4 7PR; Tel (01706) 831020; *Teacher in Charge* S. Walker
Hyndburn & Ribble Valley, c/o Woodnook County School, Hudson St, Accrington BB5 2HS; Tel (01254) 382722; B. Hayhurst (Acting)
Lancaster Reading and Language Service, Whitecross Education Centre, PO Box 601, Lancaster LA1 3SB; Tel (01524) 64207; R.L. Lee-Porter
Pendle, Cuerden St, Colne BB8 8JE; Tel (01282) 864049; S.E. Walker
Preston, c/o Brockhalls Wood School, Orrest Rd, Preston PR1 5TT; Tel (01772) 701305; C. Morris
Rossendale, Education Offices, 1 Grange St, Rawtenstall BB4 7RT; Tel (01706) 831020; S.E. Walker
Skelmersdale, C/o Little Digmoor County School, Abbeysteads, Skelmersdale WN8 9NF; Tel (01695) 21656; A. Nuttall (Acting)
South Ribble, Office 23 Centurion Hse, Centurion Way, Farington Leyland PR5 2GR; Tel (01772) 455715; J.M. Snape
Wyre District, Thornton Cleverleys Ringway Tutorial Centre, Ringway, Cleveleys, Blackpool FY5 2NL; Tel (01253) 821516; S.E. Whitaker

Tutorial Centres

Accrington, St James School, Read St, Clayton-le-Moors, Accrington BB5 5LL; Tel (01254) 231553; C. Davies (Acting). (Malad.) (5–11) (Mixed)
Burnley, Swindon St, Burnley BB11 4PF; Tel (01282) 34253; J. Smith. (Malad.) (5–11) (Mixed)
Chorley, Shaftesbury Hse, Stratford Rd, Chorley PR6 0AF; Tel (01257) 275382; I. Glynn. (Malad.) (5–11) (Mixed)
Lancaster, Bowerham Rd, Regent St, Lancaster; Tel (01524) 67164; D. Ramsbottom. (Malad.) (5–11) (Mixed)
Pendle, C/o Hendon Brook School, Townhouse Rd, Nelson; Tel (01282) 693432; J. Sanderson. (Malad.) (5–11) (Mixed)
Preston, Cromwell Rd, Ribbleton, Preston; Tel (01772) 796603; S.E. Bonney. (Malad.) (Mixed)
Rawtenstall, Burnley Rd, Rossendale BB4 8HM; Tel (01706) 215977; J. Lord (Acting). (Malad.) (7–11) (Mixed)
Rishton, Station Rd, Rishton BB1 4HF; Tel (01254) 887116; B. Whittaker (Acting). (Malad.) (5–11) (Mixed)

Adult Education Institutes

Alston Hall College, Alston La, Longridge, Preston PR3 3BP; Tel (01772) 784461; Fax (01772) 785835; B. Leighton
The Adult College, Lancaster, PO Box 603 White Cross Education Centre, Quarry Rd, White Cross, Lancaster LA1 3SE; Tel (01524) 60141; Fax (01524) 849458
Lancashire College of Adult Education, Southport Rd, Chorley PR7 1LF; Tel (01257) 276719; Fax (01257) 241370; A. Burgen

Curriculum Development Centres

Blackburn Curriculum & Professional Centre, 103 Preston New Rd, Blackburn BB2 6BJ; Tel (01254) 680850; S.R. Osborne
Preston Curriculum Development Centre, C/o Savick School, Ainsdale Dr, Ashton-on-Ribble, Preston PR2 1TU; Tel (01772) 728053; J.D. Cowley

Observation & Assessment Centres

Bamber Bridge Intermediate Day Care Centre, Brindle Rd, Bamber Bridge, Preston PR5 6RP; Tel (01772) 35364; C. Burns
Burnley Easden Clough, Morse St, Burnley BB10 4PB; Tel (01282) 30490; C. Hitchen (Acting). (5–15) (Mixed)
Garth Hse, 25 Sandicroft, Ribbleton, Preston; Tel (01772) 795082; M. Frost. (5–16) (Mixed)
Highfield, Kingsfold Dr, Penwortham, Preston PR1 9DN; Tel (01772) 742971; Mrs A.L. Bowe. (5–16) (Mixed)
Wilkinson Hse, 215 Shadsworth Rd, Blackburn; Tel (01254) 582187; Mrs B. Lea. (Category A) (5–16) (Mixed)

Camp School

Whitehough Outdoor Education Centre, New Rd, Barley, Burnley BB12 9LF; Tel (01282) 615688; S. Baggs. (Mixed)

Grant Maintained Schools

Archbishop Temple School, St Vincent's Rd, Fulwood, Preston PR2 4RA; Tel (01772) 717782/718434; Dr D.F. Dennison. (G.M.) (Mixed) (547)
Bacup and Rawtenstall Grammar School Glen Rd, Waterfoot, Rossendale, Lancashire BB4 7BJ; Tel (01706) 217115; Fax (01706) 210960; *Chairman of Governors* David Heap; *Headteacher* Martyn R. Morris. Mixed) (11–18 (950)
Baines School Highcross Rd, Poulton-le-Fylde, Lancs FY6 8BE; Tel (01253) 883019; Fax (01253) 892179; Mrs M.G. Ryding. (G.M.) (Mixed) (820)
Clitheroe Royal Grammar School, York St, Clitheroe BB7 2DJ; Tel (01200) 233118; Fax (01200) 442177; *Headteacher* Stuart Holt, BSc, MPhil, MA; *Chair of Governors* J.B. Parker, JP. Mixed 11–18 (1100)
Lancaster Girls Grammar School Regent St, Lancaster LA1 1SF; Tel (01524) 32010; *Headteacher* P.G. Barber; *Chairman of Governors* P. Oglethorpe. (Female) (11–18) (680)
Lancaster Royal Grammar School East Rd, Lancaster LA1 3EF; Tel (01524) 32109; Fax (01524) 847947; *Headmaster* P.J. Mawby; *Chairman of Governors* Prof R.W. Bray; *Administrator* Jeremy Ranford. (Male) (11–18) (895)
Long Field High School Leicester Rd, Melton Mowbray, Leics LE13 0BZ; Tel (01664) 61234; *Headteacher* L. Moore; *Chairman of Governors* S. Charles; *Financial Administrator* Margaret Perks. (Mixed) (11–14) (430)
Newton Bluecoat CE GM Primary School, School La, Newton, Preston, Lancs PR4 3RT; Tel (01772) 684415
St James's CE School Lucas Rd, Farnworth, Bolton BL4 9RU; Tel (01204) 700008; Fax (01204) 793743; *Headteacher* Chris Hampson, OBE; *Chairman of Governors* Vacancy; *Administrator* Jenny Lane. Mixed 11–16 (920)

Leyland St Mary's RC Grant Maintained School, Royal Ave, Leyland PR5 1BQ; Tel (01772) 421909; J. Clark. (G.M.) (Mixed) (650)
The St Thomas Becket R.C. School, Longview Drive, Huyton-with-Roby, Nr Liverpool L36 6EG; Tel 0151-489 2389/3514; Fax 0151-489 3589; *Head* J.V Wood; *Chairman of Governors* T. Sutherland. (Mixed) (11–18 yrs) (760)
St Wilfrid's C.E. High, Shakespeare St, Blackburn BB2 2JR; Tel (01254) 52935; L. Robinson. (G.M.) (1419)

Leeds City Council

Population 712,200 (approx.)
Civic Hall, Leeds LS1 1UR; Tel (0113) 234 8080
Director of Education J. Strong

Education Department

Merrion Hse, 110 Merrion Centre, Leeds LS2 8JR; Tel (0113) 247 5590; Fax (0113) 247 5611
Chair Cllr K. Wakefield
Deputy Chair Cllr T. Murray
Director of Education Vacancy
Director (Education Services) J. Rawlinson
Director (Resources) M. Hollos
Assistant Director FE (Community) D. Hobbs
Assistant Director (Personnel) I. Metcalfe
Assistant Director (Policy & Administration) C. Booker
Assistant Director (Advisory) M. Pattison
INSET Co-ordinator Staff and Governor Development H. Gardner
Assistant Director (Special Services) M. Robertshaw
Assistant Director (Finance) D.J. McDermott
Principal Finance Officer D. Howell
General Manager (Buildings) P. McKenna
Primary Adviser J. Grady
Primary Adviser (Senior) S.G. Moore
Primary Adviser (Senior) G. Gruen
Primary Adviser V. Reid
Primary Adviser G. Mitchell
Primary Adviser P. Velvick
Primary Adviser L. Guild
Primary Adviser D. Taylor
Primary Adviser P. Mawson
Primary Adviser N. Beck
Advisory Teacher K. Walsh
Advisory Teacher D. Trickett (Acting)
Advisory Teacher P. Kaiserman
Adviser Early Childhood Education P. Booth
Secondary Adviser (Senior) (Support and Development) D. Klemm
Secondary Adviser (Senior) (Monitoring and Review) W.E. Humphrey
Secondary Adviser B.H. Hogg
Secondary Adviser (Acting) S. Lunn
Secondary Adviser (Acting) B. Tuffin
Secondary Adviser A. Evans
Secondary Adviser Mohsin Zulfiqar
Secondary Adviser G. Cooper
Secondary Adviser M. Learoyd
Secondary Adviser R. Bekker
Secondary Adviser L. Hart
Secondary Adviser D. Morris
Secondary Adviser J. Freeman
Secondary Adviser S. Chaplin
Secondary Adviser D. Masterman
Number of Schools
1 nursery (92); 246 primary (69,359); 45 high (42,510)
Special Schools
14 day (1,099)
Day of Committee Meeting
Monday every 6 weeks

Education Committee

Con 7, Lab 7, LD 3
Shadow Chair R. Hughes-Rowlands, (Con) c/o Civic Hall, Leeds
Members of the Committee
Lab: J.P. Jarosz, E.J. McGee, J. McKenna, R. Mitchell, G.F. Morrison, S.E. Perrigo, A. Vollans
Con: M. Addison, P. Crotty, H.J. Gardiner, S.M. Gill, W.S. Hyde, J.M. Procter
LD: W. Winlow, M. Crompton, C. Townsley

Governor Training Unit

Staff and Governor Development, Leeds City Council, Dept of Education, 9th Fl East, Merrion Hse, 110 Merrion Centre, Leeds LS2 8DT; Tel (0113) 247 5666; Fax (0113) 234 1394
Development Officer Angela Bailey
Services Offered
Termly programme of training courses and briefing sessions on a range of topics of current interest and induction training, meetings skills etc; Customised sessions on request, offered to schools on an individual or cluster basis; General support and advice and resources are available from the Governors unit – same address but 9th Fl West

East Education Welfare Service

Brian Yeatman
East Leeds School Tel (0113) 264 1391
Seacroft Tel (0113) 260 2283/1(0113) 264 1391
Crossgates Tel 642724

South

Morley Tel (0113) 256 0622; Colin Whiteley

West

Hough La Centre Tel (0113) 256 0622; Colin Whiteley

North West

West Park Centre Tel (0113) 274 6711; P. Lister

North East

West Park Centre; Tel (0113) 274 6711
P. Lister
Wetherby Tel (01937) 582706

Education Welfare Office

9th Floor East, Merrion Hse, 110 Merrion Centre, Leeds 2; Tel (0113) 247 5607
Principal A. Giles

Child Protection Team

Blenheim Centre, Crowther Pl LS6 2ST; Tel (0113) 242 9111

Education Psychology Service

Blenheim Centre, Crowther Pl, Leeds LS6 2ST; Tel (0113) 242 9111
Principal Educational Psychologist B. McPherson Jones
Peripatetic Service for Deaf and Hearing-Impaired Children, Blenheim Centre, Crowther Pl, Leeds LS2 2ST; Tel (0113) 242 9111; M. Pickersgill
Peripatetic Service for the Visually Impaired, Blenheim Centre, Crowther Pl, Leeds LS2 2ST; Tel (0113) 242 9111; E. Westwood

Special Schools

Broomfield, Broom Pl LS10 3JP; Tel (0113) 277 1603; D.M.W. Dewhirst, BA

Elmete Wood School, Elmete La LS8 2LJ; Tel (0113) 265 5457; J. Kirby
Fearnville, Oakwood La, Leeds LS8 3LF; Tel (0113) 240 1693; B.J. Parker
Grafton, Craven Rd, Leeds LS6 2SN; Tel (0113) 245 1026; E. Clavert
Green Meadows, Bradford Rd, Guiseley LS20 8PP; Tel (01943) 878536/876362; P. Isherwood
John Jamieson, Hollin Hill Dr, Leeds LS8 2PW; Tel (0113) 240 1933; P. Hutchinson
Milestone, Town St, Stanningley LS28 6HL; Tel (0113) 257 4537; Mrs K. Jaques
New Cliff Hse, Fawcett La, Leeds LS12 4PF; Tel (0113) 263 7273; J. Oakes. (Boarding)
Northways, Willow La, Clifford, Wetherby LS23 6JN; Tel (01937) 843766; J. Boulton
Penny Field School, Tongue La, Leeds LS6 4QE; Tel (0113) 278 3577; Mrs H.M. Barrett
Richard Oastler, Cardigan La, Leeds LS4 2LE; Tel (0113) 278 2261; B. Benson, BSc
Stonegate, Stonegate Rd, Leeds LS6 4QJ; Tel (0113) 278 6464; N.R. Richardson
Victoria Pk, Victoria Pk Gr, Leeds LS13 2RD; Tel (0113) 278 3957; B.M.A. Preston
West Oaks, Westwood Way, Boston Spa LS23 6DX; Tel (01937) 844772; H. McEwan

Disruptive Child Units

Armley Park Centre, Rombald's Ave, Armley LS12 2BB; Tel (0113) 263 6810
Craven Road Centre, Leeds 6; Tel (0113) 245 8715

County Comprehensive Schools (11–18)

Benton Park School, Harrogate Rd, Rawdon LS19 6LX; Tel (0113) 250 2330
Boston Spa Comprehensive School, Clifford Moor Rd, Boston Spa, Wetherby LS23 6RW; Tel 01937-842915
Braim Wood (Boys) High School, Wetherby Rd LS8 2LG; Tel (0113) 265 5418
Brigshaw Comprehensive School, Brigshaw La, Allerton Bywater, Castleford WF10 2HR; Tel (0113) 286 5317
Crawshaw School, Robin La, Pudsey LS28 9HU; Tel (0113) 257 617
Garforth Community College, Lidgett La, Garforth LS25 1LJ; Tel (0113) 286 9091
Guiseley School, Fieldhead Rd, Guiseley LS20 8DT; Tel (01943) 872315
Horsforth School, Lee La East, Horsforth LS18 5RF; Tel (0113) 258 1265
Merlyn Rees High School, Middleton Rd LS10 3JA; Tel (0113) 270 2321
Morley Bruntcliffe High School, Bruntcliffe La, Morley LS27 0LZ; Tel (0113) 253 3803. (Resourced school for Hearing Impaired)
Morley High School, Fountain St, Morley LS27 0PD; Tel (0113) 253 2952
Priesthorpe School, Priesthorpe La, Farsley LS28 5SG; Tel (0113) 257 2618
Pudsey Grangefield School, Richardshaw La, Pudsey LS28 7ND; Tel (0113) 257 0278
Rodillian School, Lofthouse, Wakefield WF3 3PS; Tel (01924) 823135
Royds School, Pennington La, Oulton LS26 8EX; Tel (0113) 282 3075
Wetherby High School, Hallfield La, Wetherby LS22 4JS; Tel (01937) 583353
Woodkirk High School, Rein Rd, Tingley, Wakefield WF3 1JQ; Tel (0113) 253 3930

Voluntary Controlled Comprehensive School (12–18)

Otley Prince Henry's Grammar School, Otley LS21 2BB; Tel (01943) 463524

County Comprehensive Schools (13–18)

Allerton Grange High School, Talbot Ave LS17 6SF; Tel (0113) 266 1052
Allerton High School, King La LS17 7AG; Tel (0113) 268 4216
Benjamin Gott High School, Lenhurst Ave LS12 2RE; Tel (0113) 275 2890
City of Leeds School, Woodhouse Ridge Site, Cliff Mount LS6 2HP; Tel (0113) 278 3611
City of Leeds School, Woodhouse La LS2 8BP; Tel (0113) 245 4825/245 3033/1243 9721
Cockburn High School, Gipsy La, Leeds LS11 5TT; Tel (0113) 270 7451
Cross Green School, Cross Green La LS9 0BB; Tel (0113) 249 1501
Farnley Park High School, Chapel La, Farnley LS12 5EU; Tel (0113) 263 0741. (Boys)
East Leeds High School, Brooklands View LS14 6SA; Tel (0113) 260 2141
Intake High School, Calverley La LS13 1AH; Tel (0113) 256 4881
John Smeaton Community High School, Smeaton Approach LS15 8TA; Tel (0113) 264 4251
Lawnswood School, Lawnswood LS16 5AG; Tel (0113) 278 2321
Matthew Murray High School, Brown La LS11 0DJ; Tel (0113) 271 3031
Middleton Park High School, Acre Rd, Leeds LS10 4DE; Tel (0113) 271 7458
Parklands High School, South Parkway LS14 6HB; Tel (0113) 273 1964/5. (Girls)
Primrose Hill High School, Hill St LS9 7NL; Tel (0113) 245 4818
Ralph Thoresby High School, Farrar La LS16 7NQ; Tel (0113) 267 9911
Roundhay School, Gledhow La LS8 1ND; Tel (0113) 266 7711
Wortley High School, Swallow Cres LS12 4RB; Tel (0113) 263 0745. (Girls)
Carr Manor High School, Carr Manor Rd LS17 5DJ; Tel (0113) 268 8352
Temple Moor High School, Field End Grove, Selby Rd LS15 0PT; Tel (0113) 264 5278
West Leeds High School, Congress Mount LS12 3DT; Tel (0113) 263 3426

Church of England Comprehensive Schools (13–18)

Abbey Grange CE High School, Butcher La, Butcher Hill LS16 5EA; Tel (0113) 275 7877/275 7988. (V.A.)
Agnes Stewart C of E High School, Cromwell St LS9 7SG; Tel (0113) 248 2834. (V.A.)

Roman Catholic Comprehensive Schools (13–18 except one)

Cardinal Heenan High School, Tongue La LS6 4QE; Tel (0113) 274 1166
Corpus Christi High School, Neville Rd LS9 0HA; Tel (0113) 248 2666
Mount St Mary's High School, Church Rd LS9 8LA; Tel (0113) 245 5248
Notre Dame Sixth Form College, St Mark's Ave LS2 9BL; Tel (0113) 243 0753
St Mary's Comprehensive School, Bradford Rd, Menston, Ilkley LS29 6AE; Tel (01943) 872951. (11–18)
St Michael's College, St John's Rd LS3 1EY; Tel (0113) 245 2336

Outdoor Pursuits Centres (Shared)

Buckden House Outdoor Pursuits Centre and Local Studies Base, Buckden, Skipton, N. Yorks BD23 5JA; Tel (01756) 760254; *Manager* Ric Halsall
Humphrey Head Outdoor Pursuits Centre, Allithwaite, Grange-over-Sands, Cumbria LA11 7LY; Tel (01539) 532881; *(Head of Centre)* H. Clague
Ingleborough Hall Outdoor Education Centre, Clapham, via Lancaster LA2 8EF; Tel (01524) 251265; *Manager* Ric Halsall

Teachers' Centres

Bramley Grange, Thorner, Leeds LS14 3DW; Tel (0113) 273 7716; *(Director)* S.H. Menzies

Elmete Professional Development Centre Elmete La, Leeds LS8 1PQ; Tel (0113) 232 3046; *Head of Centre* K. Sims

Leicestershire County Council

Population 897,700
County Hall, Glenfield, Leicester LE3 8RF; Tel (0116) 232 3232; Fax (0116) 265 6265; Telex 341478 LCC WKS

Education Department

County Hall, Glenfield, Leicester LE3 8RF; Tel (0116) 232 3232
Director of Education Vacancy
Head of Resources M. Daubney
Head of Quality Development Sue Harrison
Head of Curriculum and Assessment John Turner
Head of School and College Support Stuart Lindeman
Head of Student and Family Support Clive Hadfield
Education Development Officer Roy Evans
Education Development Officer Bob Garnett
Education Development Officer Sylvia Lindoe
Education Development Officer Val Lynch
Education Development Officer Liz Paxton
Head of Curriculum and Assessment J. Turner
Unit Manager (Curriculum, Professional and Inspection) Richard Cheetham
Unit Manager (Design and Communications) Peter Baker
Unit Manager (Finance) David Newport
Unit Manager (M.I.S.) Helen Hughes
Unit Manager (Personnel) Denise Shaw
Unit Manager (Premises) Bob Dutton
Unit Manager (Administration and Governor Support) Sue Ryde
Unit Manager (Assessment and Review) Sylvia Riches
Unit Manager (Provider) Sue Wilton
Number of Schools and Colleges
1 nursery (primary schools with nursery classes 66); 332 primary; 74 secondary;

Education Committee

Con 14, Lab 16, LD 8
Members of the Committee
Con: H. Barber, A.M. Buxton, C.O. Chapman, J.R. Chapman, L.J. Duckham, E.D.T. Goodman, J.T. Griffiths, J.F. Howard, B.A. Hulse, B.C. Jones, H. Richmond, A.J. Thornton, E.F. White, P.G. Winkless
Lab: S.F. Ball, M. Berridge, M.E. Draycott, A.K. Devani, Dr A.M. Duncan, H. Jobanputra, M.T. Jones, F.J. Knaggs, A.R. Osman, A.W.R. Palmer, G.D. Parmar, G.H. Perkins JP, M. Ryan, H. Sankey BEM, D.H. Winttle, J.M. Setchfield, M.B. Wyatt
LD: D.C. Bill, V.P. Bill, R.B. Blackmore, P. Callis, S.J. Galton, P.J.W. Golden, T.R. Lawther, R.M. Wilson

Governor Training Unit

Administration and Governor Support Unit, Education Department, County Hall, Glenfield, Leicester LE3 8RF; Tel (0116) 265 6495; Fax (0116) 265 6634
Service Manager Governor Support and Training Service David Jones
Services Offered
Regular newsletter to governors; Governors' resource centre; Co-ordination of training courses; Support for link Governors and Chairs of Governors; Advice and information service

Special Schools

Ash Field, Broad Ave, Leicester LE5 4PY; Tel (0116) 273 7151; Fax (0116) 273 9962; A.P. Hinchliffe, BA, LCST
Ashmount, 9 Beacon Rd, Loughborough LE11 2BG; Tel (01509) 268506; Fax (01509) 231605; S. Welton
Birkett Hse, Launceston Rd, Wigston Magna, Leicester LE8 2FZ; Tel (0116) 288 5802; Fax (0116) 257 1932; E.W. Ellis
Craven Lodge, Burton Rd, Melton Mowbray LE13 1DJ; Tel (01664) 62246; Fax (01664) 891197; P.D. Coopey
Dorothy Goodman, Middlefield La, Hinckley LE10 0RB; Tel (01455) 634582; V.M. Bradley, NAMH
Emily Fortey, Glenfield Rd, Leicester LE3 6DG; Tel (0116) 285 7395; Fax (0116) 254 6493; J.M. Arnott, BA
Forest Way, Cropston Dr, Coalville LE67 4HS; Tel (01530) 831899; Fax (01530) 814069; L.J. Slinger
Greenacres, Glenfield Rd, Leicester LE3 6DN; Tel (0116) 285 8618; Fax (0116) 285 7393; F.B. Moir, BA
High Leas, Keyham La, Leicester LE5 1FG; Tel (0116) 241 5921; Fax (0116) 243 3259; P.C. Rowlands, JP, FCollP
Long Cl, Hamelin Rd, Leicester LE3 1JP; Tel (0116) 285 6181; Fax (0116) 480043; Vacancy
Manorbrooke, Carisbrooke Gdns, Leicester LE2 3PB; Tel (0116) 270 0741; Fax (0116) 270 8246; R.W. Hannam, DipEd
Maplewell Hall, Maplewell Rd, Woodhouse Eaves, Loughborough LE12 8QY; Tel (01509) 890237; P.A. Minshull
Millgate, 18 Scott St, Leicester LE2 6DE; Tel (0116) 270 4922; Fax (0116) 270 8753; N.H.J. Shaw
The Mount, Leicester Rd, Melton Mowbray LE13 0DA; Tel (01664) 62418; M. Watkins
Nether Hall, Nether Hall Rd, Leicester LE5 1DT; Tel (0116) 241 7258; D.M. Sommefeldt
The Parks Nursery, Barleythorpe Rd, Oakham LE15 6NR; Tel (01572) 756747; Fax (01572) 722369; B. Marchant. (Special Needs)
Royal Infirmary, Infirmary Sq, Leicester LE1 5WW; Tel (0116) 258 5330; Fax (0116) 247 1060; A.C. Osborne
Western Pk, Leicester LE3 6HX; Tel (0116) 285 8225; R.D. Gordon

High Schools

Belvoir High School and Community Centre, Barkestone La, Bottesford, Notts NG13 0AL; Tel (01949) 842367; G.F. Rawlins, BA. (301)
Brockington College Mill La, Enderby, Leics LE9 5LG; Tel (0116) 286 3722; V. Hood. (589)
Brookvale High School, Ratby Rd, Groby, Leics LE6 0FP; Tel (0116) 287 7551/2; S.H. McDemott. (638)
Castle Donnington Community College, Mount Pleasant, Castle Donnington, Derby DE74 2LN; Tel (01332) 810528; A. Morgan, BA. (453)
Castle Rock High School, Warren Hills Rd, Coalville, Leics LE67 4UU; Tel (01530) 834368/9; Fax (01530) 830485; P. Davies, BSc, DipEd. (504)
Garendon High School, Thorpe Hill, Loughborough, Leics LE11 0SQ; Tel (01509) 214378; M.J. Cahill. (776)
Gartree High School, Ridge Way, Oadby, Leics LE2 5TQ; Tel (0116) 271 7421; J.G. Armitage, MA(Ed). (742)
Hastings High School, St Catherines, Burbage, Hinckley, Leics LE10 2QE; Tel (01455) 239414; Vacancy. (634)
Heathfield High School, Belle Vue Rd, Earl Shilton, Leics LE9 7PA; Tel (01455) 842149; J. Graveson, MA. (779)
Humphrey Perkins High School and Community College, Coates Rd, Barrow-on-Soar, Loughborough, Leics LE12 8JS; Tel (01509) 412385; T.J. Riddiough. (741)
Ibstock Community College, Central Ave, Ibstock, Leics LE67 6NE; Tel (01530) 260705; B. Buswell. (550)
Ivanhoe High School and Community College, 7 North St, Ashby-de-la-Zouch, Leics LE65 1HY; Tel (01530) 412756; D.T. Killick, MA. (803)
John Ferneley High School, Scalford Rd, Melton Mowbray, Leics LE13 1LH; Tel (01664) 65901; C.J. Robinson, BA, MA. (411)
Kibworth High School and Community College, Smeeton Rd, Kibworth, Beauchamp, Leics LE8 0LG; Tel (0116) 279 2238; A. Pyle. (519)
Leysland High School, Winchester Rd, Countesthorpe, Leics LE8 5PR; Tel (0116) 277 1841; A.G. Hutchinson, BA

Limehurst High School, Bridge St, Loughborough, Leics LE11 1NH; Tel (01509) 263444; C. Jackson, MA. (483)
Lutterworth High School, Woodway Rd, Lutterworth, Leics LE17 4QH; Tel (01455) 552710; Fax (01455) 552710; T.J. Kinson, BA. (770)
Manor High School, Copse Cl, Oadby, Leics LE2 4FU; Tel (0116) 271 4941; R.H. Moore, MA. (720)
Market Bosworth High School and Community College, Station Rd, Market Bosworth, Nuneaton, Warks CV13 0JT; Tel (01455) 290251; K.A. Illsley, BA. (591)
Martin High School, Link Rd, Anstey, Leics LE7 7EB; Tel (0116) 236 3291; M.S. Furniss, BA, MA(Ed). (384)
Mount Grace High School, Leicester Rd, Hinckley, Leics LE10 1LP; Tel (01455) 238921/2; B.J. Vann. (437)
Newbridge High School, Forest Rd, Coalville, Leics LE67 3SJ; Tel (01530) 831561; N. Fowler. (453)
Redmoor High School, Wykin Rd, Hinckley, Leics LE10 0GP; Tel (01455) 230731/2; D.R. Williams, MA(Ed). (520)
Roundhill Community College, Thurmaston, Leics LE4 8GQ; Tel (0116) 269 3896; N. Gallyot. (596)
St Martin's R.C. High School, Stoke Golding, Nuneaton, Warks CV13 6HT; Tel (01455) 212386; P.A. Scola, MA. (321)
Sarson High School, Barton Rd, Melton Mowbray, Leics LE13 1EA; Tel (01664) 67721; R. Turner. (426)
Shepshed High School, Forest St, Loughborough, Leics LE12 9DB; Tel (01509) 502112; A. Stephenson. (655)
South Charnwood High School, Broad La, Markfield, Leics LE67 9TB; Tel (01530) 242351; J.M. Etchingham. (425)
Stonehill High School, Stonehill Ave, Birstall, Leics LE4 4JG; Tel (0116) 267 3384; Fax (0116) 267 4224; A. Baker. (527)
Thomas Estley Community College, Station Rd, Broughton Astley, Leics LE9 6PT; Tel (01455) 283263; A.P. Gelsthorpe, BA, FRGS. (485)
Welland Park Community College, Welland Pk Rd, Market Harborough, Leics LE16 9DR; Tel (01858) 464795; J.R. Collins, MA. (544)
Winstanley Community College, Kingsway North, Braunstone, Leics LE3 3BD; Tel (0116) 289 8688; J.M. Shapland, BSc, DipEd. (507)
Woodbrook Vale High School, Grasmere Rd, Loughborough, Leics LE11 2ST; Tel (01509) 236208; R. Harris, BSc. (361)
Wreake Valley Community School, Parkstone Rd, Syston, Leics LE7 1LY; Tel (0116) 260 8088; R.A. Longland

Upper Schools

Ashby-de-la-Zouch Grammar School, Nottingham Rd, Ashby-de-la-Zouch, Leics LE65 1DT; Tel (01530) 413748; Fax (01530) 560665; C.R. Ingleton, JP, BA, MEd. (1261)
Beauchamp College, Ridge Way, Oadby, Leics LE2 5TP; Tel (0116) 271 5809; M.D. Cruickshank, MA, MEd. (1205)
Birstall Longslade College, Wanlip La, Birstall, Leics LE4 4GH; Tel (0116) 267 3389; G.A. Newton. (587)
Burleigh College, Thorpe Hill, Loughborough, Leics LE11 0SQ; Tel (01509) 268996; P.A. Watson. (1123)
Countesthorpe College, Winchester Rd, Leics LE8 3PR; Tel (0116) 277 1555; Fax (0116) 277 7027; P.C. Bagshaw. (758)
Desford Bosworth College, Leicester La, Desford, Leics LE9 9JL; Tel (01455) 822841; Fax (01455) 828194; T. Harper. (812)
Earl Shilton Community College, Heath La, Earl Shilton, Leics LE9 7PD; Tel (01455) 845061; R.E.A. Roberts. (607)
Groby Community College, Ratby Rd, Groby, Leics LE6 0GE; Tel (0116) 287 9921/22; Fax (0116) 287 0189; Vacancy. (771)
Guthlaxton Community College, Station Rd, Wigston Magna, Leics; Tel (0116) 288 1611; G.B. Norris, JP, MEd. (1362)
Hinckley John Cleveland College, Forest View, Butt La, Leics LE10 1LE; Tel (01455) 632183; Fax (01455) 234126; N.J. Middleton, MA. (1650)
Hind Leys Community College, Forest St, Shepshed, Leics LE12 9DA; Tel (01509) 504511/2/3; Dr P.J. Sainsbury. (644)
King Edward VII, Burton Rd, Melton Mowbray; Tel (01664) 63484; K. Walsh, BA, MEd. (1162)
King Edward VII Community College, Warren Hills Rd, Coalville, Leics LE67 4UW; Tel (01530) 834925; Fax (01530) 832268; C.R. Holdsworth, BA. (720)
Lutterworth Grammar and Community College, Bitteswell Rd, Leics LE17 4EN; Tel (01455) 554101; Fax (01455) 553725; C.R. Grimwood, BA. (1516)
Market Harborough Robert Smyth Upper School, Burnmill Rd, Leics LE16 7JG; Tel (01858) 465718; J.A.S. Colquhoun. (934)
Melton Mowbray King Edward VII Upper School, Burton Rd, Melton Mowbray, Leics LE13 1DR; Tel (01664) 63484; Fax (01664) 410275; K. Walsh, BA, MEd. (1181)
Rawlins Community College, Loughborough Rd, Quorn, Leics LE12 8DY; Tel (01509) 412406; M.W. Hewlett, BA, MA, MEd. (1076)
Wreake Valley Community College, Parkstone Rd, Syston, Leics LE7 1LY; Tel (0116) 260 8088; Fax (0116) 260 7745; R.A. Longland, BA. (1005)

Secondary Schools (11–16)

Crown Hills and Community College, Gwendolen Rd, Leicester LE5 5FT; Tel (0116) 273 6893; G.A. Coleby, BA(Hons), PGCE. (905)
Fullhurst Community College, Ellesmere Rd, Leicester LE3 1BE; Tel (0116) 282 4326; A.P. Harris. (687)
Hamilton Community College, Keyham La West, Leicester LE5 1RT; Tel (0116) 241 3371; L. Taylor, BA. (610)
John Ellis Community College, Corporation Rd, Leicester LE4 5PW; Tel (0116) 266 3111; S. Thistlethwaite. (584)
Judgemeadow School and Community College, Marydene Dr, Leicester LE5 6HP; Tel (0116) 241 7580; Fax (0116) 243 2314; E.A.W. Green, BA, MEd. (1207)
Lancaster Boys School, Off Knighton La East, Leicester LE2 6FU; Tel (0116) 270 3176; J.E. Blount, MA. (903)
Mary Linwood School, Trenant Rd, Leicester LE2 6UA; Tel (0116) 278 6384; D.R. Corrall, BA. (423)
Moat Community College, Maidstone Rd, Leicester LE2 0TU; Tel (0116) 262 5705; F. Hussain. (834)
Mundella Community College, Wycombe Rd, Leicester LE5 0PR; Tel (0116) 276 2761; E.M. Warren, BA, JP. (575)
New Parks Community College, Greencoat Rd, Leicester LE3 6RN; Tel (0116) 287 2115; N.R. Thompson, BA, MA. (762)
Rowley Fields School and Community College, Lyncote Rd, Leicester LE3 2EL; Tel (0116) 289 9444; A. Waters, BA. (576)
Rushey Mead School, Melton Rd, Leicester LE4 7PA; Tel (0116) 266 3730; S.J. White, MEd. (1094)
Rushey Mead Initial Language Teaching Unit, Melton Rd, Leics LE4 7PA; Tel (0116) 266 3730
Sir Jonathan North Community College, Knighton La East, Leicester LE2 6FU; Tel (0116) 270 8116; V. Keller. (Girls) (804)
Soar Valley Community College, Gleneagles Ave, Leicester LE4 7GY; Tel (0116) 266 1203; D.F. Waterhouse, BA. (1178)
Wycliffe Community College, Hamelin Rd, Leicester LE3 1JN; Tel (0116) 285 8595; M.J. Chapman. (489)

Secondary Schools (11–18)

Alderman Newton's School, Glenfield Rd, Leicester LE3 6DN; Tel (0116) 287 2553; D.G. Butler, BA, MA(Ed). (965)
Babington Community College, Strasbourg Dr, Leicester LE4 0SZ; Tel (0116) 235 4520; F.J. Catton, BEd, MSc. (874)
Beaumont Leys School, Anstey La, Leicester LE4 0FL; Tel (0116) 262 0257; M.J. Fields, BSc, MEd. (768)
City of Leicester School, Downing Dr, Leicester LE5 6LN; Tel (0116) 241 3984; K.B. Lewis, MA. (1281)

De Lisle R.C. School, Thorpe Hill, Loughborough, Leics LE11 0SQ; Tel (01509) 268739; B.N. Kennedy, BA. (1121)
English Martyrs R.C. School, Anstey La, Leicester LE4 0FE; Tel (0116) 251 7740; D.F. McLean. (916)
St Paul's R.C. School, Spencefield La, Leicester LE5 6HN; Tel (0116) 241 4057; E.J. Hayes. (1022)

Youth and Community Centres and Colleges

Ab. Kettleby Community Centre, Tel (01664) 822302; P.J. Fisher
Asfordby Community Centre, Saxelby Rd, Melton Mowbray; Tel (01664) 812630; G. Dexter
Ashby Community College, North St; Tel Ashby 415110; D.T. Killick, MA
Avalon Youth and Community Centre, Duxbury Rd, Leics, LE5 3LR; Tel (0116) 276 6264; M. Solanki
Babington Community College, Leicester; Tel (0116) 235 4520; F. Catton
Barlestone Community Centre, Tel (01455) 290511; W. Glasper
Barrow on Soar Community Centre, Tel (01509) 412385; T. Riddiough
Battling Brook County Primary School and Community Centre, Frederick Ave, Hinckley, Leics LE10 0EX; Tel (01455) 634701; J.N. Hanratty
Beaumont Leys Young People's Centre, Leicester Leys Leisure Centre, Beaumont Way, Leics LE4 1DS; Tel (0116) 236 6004; O. Brown
Beauchamp College, Ridge Way, Oadby LE5 5TP; Tel (0116) 271 5809; M. Cruickshank, MA, MEd
Birstall Community College, Longslade; Tel (0116) 267 4211; G.A. Newton
Bottesford Community Centre, Tel (01949) 842367; G.F. Rawlins
Braunstone Community Centre, Braunstone Ave, Leics LE3 1LE; Tel (0116) 282 4171
Braunstone Millfield Community Centre, Hat Rd LE3 2WF; Tel (0116) 289 7151; B.R. Wilson
Braunstone Winstanley Community College, Kingsway North LE3 3BD; Tel (0116) 289 8713; J.M. Shapland
Breedon on the Hill Community Centre, Tel (01332) 862572; *Warden* M.J. Arkle
Broughton Astley Thomas Estley Community College, Station Rd LE9 6PT; Tel (01455) 283035; A.P. Gelsthorpe, BA, FRGS
Casterton Community College, Great Casterton, Stamford, Lincs PE9 4AT; Tel (01780) 52303; R.J.P. Bird
Castle Donington Community College, Tel (01332) 810528; A. Morgan, BA
Catherine Junior School and Community Centre, Brandon St, Leics LE4 6AZ; Tel (0116) 251 0167; E.A. James
Coalville King Edward VII Community College Warren Hills Rd, Coalville; Tel (01530) 834925; R. Holdsworth, BA
Countesthorpe Community College, Winchester Rd LE8 3PR; Tel (0116) 277 1833; P.C. Bagshaw
Croft Community Centre Brookes Ave, Croft LE9 6GJ; Tel (01455) 282643; B.J. George
Crown Hills Community College Gwendolen Rd LE5 5FT; Tel (0116) 273 9260; G.A. Coleby, BA(Hons), PGCE
Desford Bosworth Community College Tel (01455) 822910; A.T. Harper
Earl Shilton Community College Tel (01455) 845061; R.E.A. Roberts
Ellistown County Primary and Community Centre, Whitehall Rd, Ellistown, Coalville, Leics LE67 1EN; Tel (01530) 260301; *Head* G. Martin
Enderby Brockington Community College, Mill La LE9 5LG; Tel (0116) 286 3722; R.M. Bennett
Eyres Monsell Community Education Project, Tel (0116) 278 7294; C. Ambrose
Farndon Fields Community Centre, Argyle Pk, Market Harborough LE16 9JH; Tel (01858) 464744; B. Poole
Great Glen Community Centre, The Chase LE8 0EQ; Tel (0116) 259 2764; D. Spencer
Groby Community College Ratby Rd LE6 0GE; Tel (0116) 287 9921; Vacancy
Guthlaxton Community College Station Rd, Wigston Magna LE18 2DS; Tel (0116) 288 1611; G.B. Norris, JP, MEd
Hathern Community Centre, Pasture La, Loughborough LE12 5LJ; Tel (01509) 842569; E.E. Glasper
Heatherbrook Community Centre Astill Lodge Rd LE4 1BE; Tel (0116) 235 7721; L. Jewitt
Higham on the Hill Community Centre, Main St, Nuneaton CV13 6AJ; Tel (01455) 212294; J. Nelson
Highfields Youth and Community Centre 96 Melbourne Rd LE2 0DR; Tel (0116) 253 1053; C.P. Thamotheram
Huncote Community Centre Denman La LE9 6BS; Tel (0116) 286 4105; D.J. Owen
Ibstock Community College Central Ave LE67 6NE; Tel (01530) 260705; Ms B. Buswell
John Cleveland Community College Forest View, Butt La, Hinckley; Tel (01455) 632183; N.J. Middleton, MA
Judgemeadow Community College Marydene Dr LE5 6HP; Tel (0116) 241 7234; E.A.W. Green, BA, MEd
Kegworth Community Centre, The Dragwell, Kegworth, Nr Derby DE7 2EL; Tel (0150 9) 672237; J.F. Anderson
Kibworth Community Centre Smeeton Rd, Kibworth Beauchamp LE8 0LG; Tel (0116) 279 3689; A. Pyle
Kingfisher Youth Centre, Boulder La, Saffron La Est, Leics LE2 6LE; Tel (0116) 283 3647
Knighton Fields Primary School and Community Centre, Knighton Fields Rd West, Leics LE2 7NP; Tel (0116) 283 2011; A.E. Manger
Leicester Forest East Community Centre, Tel (0116) 239 2482; C. Meadows
Leicester Hazel Street Community Centre Tel (0116) 254 8401; P.A. Clarke
Leicester Wycliffe Community College, Hamelin Rd LE3 1UN; Tel (0116) 285 8595; M.J. Chapman
Long Whatton Community Centre, The Green, Loughborough LE12 5DB; Tel (01509) 842239; S. Landon
Loughborough Robert Bakewell Community Centre, Barsby Dr LE11 0UJ; Tel (01509) 231646; T. Mason
Loughborough Burleigh Community College Thorpe Hill, Loughborough LE11 0SQ; Tel (01509) 268996; K. Foreman, OBE
Loughborough Shelthorpe Community Centre Woodthorpe Rd LE11 2NF; Tel (01509) 212227; N.B. Jones
Lutterworth Community College, Bitteswell Rd LE17 4EN; Tel (0145 55) 554101; C.R. Grimwood, BA
Market Bosworth Community College Tel (01455) 290251; K.A. Illsley, BA
Market Harborough Community College Welland Park Rd LE16 9DR; Tel (01858) 463645; Mrs J.R. Collins
Medway Primary School and Community Centre, St Stephen's Rd, Leics LE2 1GH; Tel (0116) 254 9305; A.J. Williams
Mellor Community Centre Clarke St LE4 7QN; Tel (0116) 266 1377; S.F. Ball
Melton Sherard Community Centre Grange Rd LE13 1HA; Tel (01664) 65124; M. Smith
Melton St Mary's Community Centre, Tel (01664) 62500; R. Popham
Melton Swallowdale Community Centre Dalby Rd LE13 0BJ; Tel (01664) 65456; R.H. Hill
Moat Community College, Maidstone Rd LE2 0TU; Tel (0116) 262 5705; F. Hussain
The Moira Community Centre, Moira St, Loughborough, Leics LE11 1AX; Tel (01509) 267378; *Head of Centre* Dee Sheils
Mountfields Lodge Youth Centre, Epinal Way, Loughborough, Leics LE11 0QE; Tel (01509) 236043; *Head of Centre* A.S. Lake
Mundella Community College Wycombe Rd LE5 0PR; Tel (0116) 276 6785; E.M. Warren, BA
New Parks Community Centre, St Oswalds Rd, Leics LE3 6RJ; Tel (0116) 287 2334
New Parks Community College and Project Tel (0116) 287 3841; N.R. Thompson, BA, MA
Newbridge Youth Centre, Forest Rd, Coalville LE67 3SJ; Tel (01530) 831561; N. Fowler
Quorn Rawlins Community College, Loughborough Rd LE12 8DY; Tel (01509) 412406; M.W. Hewlett, BA
Roundhill Community College Thurmaston LE4 8GQ; Tel (0116) 269 5812; N. Gallyot

Rowley Fields Community College Lyncote Rd LE3 2EL; Tel (0116) 289 8120; A. Waters, BA
Saffron Community Education Project, Tel (0116) 283 2728; P. Thomson
Shaftesbury Junior School and Community Centre, Latimer School, Leics LE3 0QE; Tel (0116) 254 9939; N.B.P. Gavin
Shepshed Hind Leys Community College Forest St LE12 9DA; Tel (01509) 504511; Dr P. Sainsbury
Sir Jonathan North Community College, Knighton La East LE4 7GY; Tel (0116) 270 5920; V. Keller
Soar Valley Community College Gleneagles Ave; Tel (0116) 266 6377; D.F. Waterhouse, BA
Sparkenhoe Community Centre Sparkenhoe St LE2 0TD; Tel (0116) 251 2686; R.T. Bagrhole
Spinney Hill Community Centre Ventnor St; Tel (0116) 273 4836; D.S. Rzeznik
St Mark's Youth Centre, Dorset St, Leicester; Tel (0116) 262 4304; *Head of Centre* Ivor Stirling
Stocking Farm Youth and Community Centre Tel (0116) 235 2051; A. Legg
Stoney Stanton Community Centre Station Rd LE9 6LQ; Tel (0145 527) 2787; D.E. Schofield
Thringstone Community Centre, The Green, Coalville LE67 8NR; Tel (01530) 222337; L. Goldbourn
Thurnby Lodge Youth and Community Centre Tel (0116) 241 2616; J. Barker
Vale of Catmose Community College, Cold Overton Rd, Oakham; Tel (01572) 724211; P.W. Green
Westfield Youth Centre Hinckley; Tel (01455) 637516; R. Muscutt
Wigston The Meadow Community Centre, Meadow Way LE18 3QZ; Tel (0116) 288 7227; J.R. Sutcliffe
Wigston Fairfield Community Centre Cheshire Dr LE18 4WA; Tel (0116) 278 2424; B.M. Downs
Wigston Lancaster Bell Community Centre Tel (0116) 288 0013; P.J. Lawley
Woodhouse Eaves Community Centre, Meadow Rd LE12 8SA; Tel (01509) 890483; P. Chilvers
Wreake Valley Community College Parkstone Rd, Syston LE7 1LY; Tel (0116) 260 0071; R.A. Longland
Wymondham Sir John Sedley Community Centre Tel (0157 284) 658; J.P.O. Glover

Institute of Adult Education

Leicester Adult Education College, Wellington St, Leicester; Tel (0116) 254 5250; R. Raven

Teachers' Centres

Beaumanor Hall Conference Centre, Old Woodhouse, Loughborough; Tel (01509) 890119; Alan Jacobs
Centre for Multi-Cultural Education, Harrison Rd, Leicester; Tel (0116) 266 5451; R. Wale
Forest Lodge Education Centre Charnor Rd, New Parks, Leicester; Tel (0116) 231 3399
Early Years Centre, C/o Glebelands Primary School, Leicester; Tel (0116) 234 0010
Lansdowne Hse, 113 Princess Rd East, Leicester; Tel (0116) 255 1310; Fax (0116) 255 0132; *Leicester Resource Centre* R. Bradley, MA; *Picture Houses Centre* A. Smalley; *Religious Education Centre* M. Harris
Leicestershire Centre for Educational Technology, Mathematics Centre, Hillsborough Rd, Leicester; Tel (0116) 277 7207; Mrs C. Hunter
Mathematics Centre, Rolleston Teachers' Centre, Leicester; Tel (0116) 277 7207
Science Centre, Rolleston Teachers' Centre, Leicester; Tel (0116) 277 0351
St Paul's Design and Technology Centre, Spencefield La, Leicester; Tel (0116) 243 2312
Woodstock Centre, Marwood Rd, Leicester; Tel (0116) 235 0355. (for Computer Education)

Grant Maintained Schools

Abington High School, Wigston Magna, Leics LE18 2DU; Tel (0116) 288 1228; R.J. Simper, MA. (594)
Bushloe High School, Station Rd, Wigston, Leicestershire LE8 2DT; Tel (0116) 288 1692; E.L. Cook. (724)
Long Field High School, Leicester Rd, Melton Mowbray, Leics LE13 0BZ; Tel (01664) 61234; Fax (01664) 66065; *Head* Linda Moore
South Wigston, Tel (0116) 278 2388; E.D. Bothamley, BA. (773)
Uppingham Community College, London Rd, Uppingham; Tel (01572) 823631; T.P. Macdonald-Pearce, MA. (620)

Lincolnshire County Council

Population 601,400
County Offices, Newland, Lincoln LN1 1YL; Tel (01522) 552222; Fax (01522) 552288

Education Department

County Offices, Newland, Lincoln LN1 1YQ; Tel (01522) 552222; Fax (01522) 553257
Director of Education Norman Riches
Deputy Director of Education D. Trewartha
Assistant Director (Operations) Vacancy
Assistant Director (Curriculum and Inspection) Susan Milton
Acting Assistant Dirctor (Property & Central Services) John Pastor
Acting Assistant Director (Finance Management Information) Julie Flint
Acting Capital Development Manager Ken Redmore
Direct Services Manager M.R. Gardner
Schools Services Manager P.J. Broster
Special Needs Services Manager P.A. Barrett
SEO (Staffing) N.H. Ellerby
Finance Information Manager Vacancy
Principal Education Welfare Officer J. Lister
Principal Educational Psychologist D. Dickinson
Principal Inspector P.J. Scott
General M.H. Whittaker
General Dr T. Lomas
General L. Bensley
General J.H. Good
General G.S. Stowe
General J.H. Slater
English P.S. Jarrett
Mathematics Dr R.V. Williams
Science M.J.P. Seddon
Geography Environmental Education L. Poole
Religious Education P.T. Emmett
Modern Languages R.D. Mayes
Design and Technology C.J. Fowler
Senior Inspector, Evaluation and Appraisal W.A.I. Green
Senior Inspector, Curriculum Development and INSET A.M. Breckon
Testing and Assessment P.S. Niedzwiedzki
National Curriculum Adviser (Primary) R.S. Richardson
Information Technology Officer W.M. Astill

Number of Schools

5 nursery (469), 264 primary (43,759), 37 secondary (20,607), 17 special (137 boarding places, 978 day places), 2 hospital special schools (59)

Requisition Periods for School Supplies

No fixed dates

Other Authorities with whom Joint Purchasing Arrangements are made

Leicestershire County Council, Cambridgeshire County Council, Norfolk County Council and Warwickshire County Council

Education Committee

Con 13, Lab 10, LD 7, Ind 1, Lab and Co-op 1
Chair P.V. Metcalfe, (Lab) 18 Lindum Rd, Lincoln LN2 1NS
Vice-Chair L.P. Pinchbeck, (LD) 16 Burton Rd, Heckington, Sleaford NG34 9QR
Members of the Committee
Con: M.D. Kennedy, J. Smith, W.J. Speechley CBE, J.A. Taylor, C.C. Turner, H.G. Wheat, L. Wilson, W.R. Wyrill, J.M. Baron, P. Bray, B. Brock, I.M. Croft, J.A. Fisher
Lab: P.A. Keddell, P.V. Metcalfe, S.L. Taylor, M.C. Anderson, G. Burrell, E. Davies, E.N. Davies, C. Evans, L.J. Flint, M.C. Flint
LD: M. French, F.M. Martin, L.P. Pinchbeck, M.E. Belton, S.R. Chapman, J.L. Dodsworth, J.L.J. Dyde
Ind: J.A. Kirkman
Lab: P.R. Kenny

Governor Training Unit

Governor Support Initiative, Education Dept, Lincolnshire County Council, County Offices, Newland, Lincoln LN1 1YQ; Tel (01522) 553214; Fax (01522) 553257
School Services Manager P.J. Broster
Senior Admin Officer H.A. Wells
Services Offered
Training offered to School Governors. Chairmen and Clerks to Governing Bodies offer Helpline, termly newsletter and 15 resource libraries

Special Schools

Physical and Medical Disabilities
St Francis School, Wickenby Cres, Lincoln LN1 3TJ; Tel (01522) 526498; *Head* D.G. Williams. (Mixed) (2–18)
Moderate Learning Difficulties
William Harrison School, Middlefield La, Gainsborough DN21 1PU; Tel (01427) 615498; *Head* J. Barton (Acting). (Mixed) (3–16)
Gosberton House School, Westhorpe Rd, Gosberton, Spalding, Lincs PE11 4EW; Tel (01775) 840250; *Head* M.R. Allen. (Mixed) (3–11)
Ambergate School, Dysart Rd, Grantham, Lincs NG31 7LP; Tel (01476) 64957; *Head* V. Millward. (Mixed) (5–16)
St Lawrence School, Bowl Alley La, Horncastle, Lincs LN0 5EJ; Tel (01507) 522563/1523256; *Head* D. Smith. (Mixed) (5–16)
St Christopher's School, Hykeham Rd, Lincoln LN6 8AR; Tel (01522) 528378; *Head* W. Hobson. (Mixed) (3–16)
Priory School, Neville Ave, Spalding, Lincs PE11 2EH; Tel (01775) 724080; *Head* B.J. Howes. (Mixed) (11–16)
Severe Learning Difficulties
John Fielding School, Ashlawn Dr, Boston, Lincs PE21 9PX; Tel (01205) 363395; *Head* M. Brand. (Mixed) (2–19)
The Willoughby School, South Rd, Bourne, Lincs PE10 9JE; Tel (01778) 425203; *Head* J.M. O'Reilly
The Beckett School, White's Wood La, Gainsborough, Lincs DN21 1TW; Tel (01427) 612139; *Head* S.M. Gummerson. (Mixed) (2–19)
Sandon School, Sandon Cl, Sandon Rd, Grantham, Lincs NG31 9AX; Tel (01476) 64994; *Head* E. Mountford. (Mixed) (2–19)
Queen's Park School, South Park, Lincoln LN5 8EW; Tel (01522) 531879; *Head* I.S. Walker. (Mixed) (2–19)
St Bernard's School, Wood la, Louth, Lincs LN11 8RS; Tel (01507) 602776; *Head* M.A. Warren. (Mixed) (2–19)
Garth School, Pinchbeck Rd, Spalding, Lincs PE11 1QF; Tel (01775) 725566; *Head* K.R. Townsend. (Mixed) (2–19)
The Eresby School, Eresby Ave, Spilsby, Lincs PE23 5HU; Tel (01790) 52441; *Head* D.J. Middlehurst. (Mixed) (2–19)

Hospital Schools
Pilgrim Hospital School and Lincolnshire Hospital Education Service, 4th Fl, Sibsey Rd, Boston, Lincs PE21 9QS; Tel (01205) 364801; *Head* J.B. Sykes. (Mixed) (All Ages)
The Ash Villa School, Willoughby Rd, Rauceby Hospital, Sleaford, Lincs NG34 8PP; Tel (01529) 488251 Ext 239; *Head* C.R. Brace. (Mixed) (8–16)
Moderate Learning Difficulties – Schools with Special Provision
Branston Community College, Station Rd, Branston, Lincoln LN4 1LH; Tel (01522) 791279; *Head* B.W. Douglas. (Mixed) (11–16)
The Middlefield School, Middlefield La, Gainsborough DN21 1PU; Tel (01427) 615199; *Head* M. Cox. (Mixed) (11–16)
The Middlecott School, Edinburgh Dr, Kirton, Boston PE20 1JS; Tel (01205) 722336; *Head* G.I. Walters. (Mixed) (11–16)
Christ's Hospital School, Wragby Rd, Lincoln LN2 4PN; Tel (01522) 533561; *Head* D.J. Cox. (Mixed) (11–16)
Myle Cross County Junior School, Macaulay Dr, Lincoln LN2 4EL; Tel (01522) 528006; *Head* A.H. Hearney. (Mixed) (7–11)
St Giles County Infant School, Addison Dr, Lincoln LN2 4LQ; Tel (01522) 523791; *Head* E.A. Burgess. (Mixed) (5–7)
The Cordeaux High School, High Holme Rd, Louth LN11 0HG; Tel (01507) 606555; *Head* P. White. (Mixed) (11–16)
Rasen De Aston School, Willingham Rd, Market Rasen LN8 3RF; Tel (01673) 843415; *Head* A.H. Neal. (Mixed) (11–18)
Ling Moor CP School, Richard Dr, North Hykeham, Lincoln LN6 8QZ; Tel (015220 682602; *Head* R.R. Kirman. (Mixed) (5–11)
St George's Grant Maintained Technology School, Westholme, Westgate, Sleaford NG34 7PD; Tel (01529) 302487); *Head* J.C. Hodgson. (Mixed) (11–16)
Specific Learning Difficulties – Schools with Special Provision
The Central School, Rushcliffe Rd, Grantham, Lincs NG31 8ED; Tel (01476) 66384; *Head* M. Gaul. (Mixed) (11–16)
George Farmer Secondary School, Penny Hill Rd, Holbeach, Spalding, Lincs PE12 7PU; Tel (01406) 423042; *Head* J.M.P. Glenn. (Mixed) (11–16)
The Cordeaux High School, High Holme Rd, Louth, Lincs LN11 0HG; Tel (01507) 606555; *Head* P. White. (Mixed) (11–16)
De Aston School, Willingham Rd, Market Rasen, Lincs LN8 3RF; Tel (01673) 843415; *Head* A.H. Neal. (Mixed) (11–18)
St George''s Grant Maintained Technology School, Westholme, Westgate, Sleaford, Lincs NG34 7PS; Tel (01529) 302487; *Head* J.C. Hodgson. (Mixed) (11–16)
General Learning Difficulties – Schools with Special Provision
John Spendluffe School, Handy La, Alford LN13 9BL; Tel (01507) 462443; *Head* G. Allan. (Mixed) (11–16)
The Aveland School, Birthorpe Rd, Billingborough, Sleaford NG34 0QT; Tel (01529) 240341; *Head* R.M. Lake. (Mixed) (11–16)
The Lafford High School, Fen Rd, Billinghay LN4 4HU; Tel (01526) 860410; *Head* W.J. Hockin. (Mixed) (11–16)
St Bede's RC Secondary School, Tollfield Rd, Boston PE21 9PN; Tel (01205) 365873; *Head* J.A. McGarel. (Mixed) (11–16)
The Haven High School, Marian Rd, Boston PE21 9HB; Tel (01205) 311979; *Head* M. Fox. (Mixed) (11–16)
The Robert Manning School, Edinburgh Cres, Bourne PE10 9DT; Tel (01778) 422365; *Head* M.S. Kee. (Mixed) (11–18)
Yarborough School, Grimsby Rd, Caistor LN7 6QZ; Tel (01472) 851383; *Head* B.R. Tointon. (Mixed) (11–16)
Cherry Willingham Comprehensive School, Croft La, Cherry Willingham LN3 4JP; Tel (01522) 750747; *Head* D.S. Mills. (Mixed) (11–16)

The Charles Read School, Bourne Rd, Corby Glen, Grantham NG33 4NT; Tel (01476) 550333; *Head* J. Gleeson. (Mixed) (11–16)

St Guthlac Comprehensive School, Postland Rd, Crowland, Peterborough PE6 0JA; Tel (01733) 210413; *Head* K.M. Brierley. (Mixed) (11–16)

The Deepings School, Park Rd, Deeping St James, Peterborough PE6 8NF; Tel (01778) 342159; *Head* Dr D.A. Bryars

The Thomas Cowley School, School La, Donington, Spalding PE11 4TF; Tel (01775) 820254; *Head* J.G. Knight. (Mixed) (11–16)

The Castle Hills Grant Maintained School, The Avenue, Gainsborough DN21 1PY; Tel (01427) 612411; *Head* P.L. Elliott. (Mixed) (11–16)

St Hugh's CE Grant Maintained School, The Avenue, Dysart Rd, Grantham NG31 7PX; Tel (01476) 64815; *Head* J. Robinson. (Mixed) (11–16)

St Wulfram' CE High School, Queensway, Grantham NG31 9RA; Tel (01476) 64756; *Head* M.G. Cartwright. (Mixed) (11–16)

The Ancaster High School, Shannon Ave, Lincoln LN6 7JG; Tel (01522) 686124; *Head* J.A. Hillyer. (Mixed) (11–18)

Monks Abbey CP School, Monks Rd, Lincoln LN2 5PF; Tel (01522) 527705; *Head* D.W. Williams. (Mixed) (3–11)

St Peter and St Paul Catholic High School, Western Ave, Lincoln LN6 7SX; Tel (01522) 681101; *Head* S.C. Pitcher. (Mixed) (11–16)

Yarborough School, Riseholme Rd, Lincoln LN1 3SP; Tel (01522) 529203; *Head* K.J. Shanovich. (Mixed) (11–18)

Mablethorpe CP School, High St, Mablethorpe LN12 1EW; Tel (01507) 472472; *Head* A.S. Rothery. (Mixed) (5–11)

The Tennyson High School, Seaholme Rd, Mablethorpe LN12 2DF; Tel (01507) 473331; *Head* G.M. French. (Mixed) (11–16)

The Earl of Scarborough High School, Burgh Rd, Skegness PE25 2QH; Tel (01754) 610073; *Head* S. Elliott. (Mixed) (11–16)

Seathorne CP School, Count Alan Rd, Skegness PE25 1HB; Tel (01754) 764689; *Head* M. Cook. (Mixed) (5–11)

William Alvey's GM Junio School, Eastgate, Sleaford NG34 7EA; Tel (01529) 302772; *Head* I.R. Douglas. (Mixed) (7–11)

Sir John Gleed Technology School, Halmer Gdns, Spalding PE11 2EF; Tel (01775) 722702; *Head* A.D. MacKown. (Boys) (11–16)

Bluecoat CP School, Green La, Stamford PE9 1HE; Tel (01780) 64202; *Head* P. Nuttall. (Mixed) (5–11)

The Queen Eleanor School, Green La, Stamford PE9 1HE; Tel (01780) 51011; *Head* D. Learmouth. (Mixed) (11–16)

The William Lovell CE Secondary School, Main Rd, Stickney, Boston PE22 8AA; Tel (01205) 480352; *Head* R.D. Dring. (Mixed) (11–16)

Sir William Robertson High School, Main Rd, Welbourn LN5 0PA; Tel (01400) 72422; *Head* I.C. Wright. (Mixed) (11–16)

William Farr CE Comprehensive School, Welton, Lincoln LN2 3JB; Tel (01673) 860225; *Head* P. Strong. (Mixed) (11–16)

The Hearing Impaired – Schools with Special Provision

St Thomas' Primary School, Wyberton Low Rd, Boston, Lincs PE21 7RZ; Tel (01205) 362860; *Head* G. Kent. (Mixed) (2–11)

Cherry Willingham Comprehensive School, Croft La, Cherry Willingham, Lincoln LN3 4JP; Tel (01522) 754747; *Head* S.S. Mills. (Mixed) (11–16)

The Thomas Cowley School, School La, Donington, Spalding, Lincs PE11 4TF; Tel (01775) 820254; *Head* J.G. Knight. (Mixed) (11–16)

Ermine County Infant School, Thoresway Dr, Lincoln LN2 2HD; Tel (01522) 530168; *Head* L. Smith. (Mixed) (2–11)

County Service for the Sensory Impaired/Audiology; The Head of Service for the Sensory Impaired/Audiology can be contacted on Lincoln (01522) 553364

Emotional/Behavioural Difficulties

Deighton Close School, Louth, Lincs LN11 0RS; Tel (01507) 605287; *Head* M. Smith. (Boys) (6–16)

Stubton Hall School, Stubton, Newark, Notts NG23 5DD; Tel (01636) 626607; *Head* A.J. Binnie. (Mixed) (6–16)

Nursery Class for Children with Special Needs

Thoresway Nursery, Thoresway Dr, Lincoln LN2 2HD; Tel (01522) 542972; *Teacher-in-Charge* S.J. Stewart. (Mixed) (2–5)

Speech and Language Difficulties – Schools with Special Provision

Fosseway County Primary School, Ash Gr, North Hykeham, Lincoln; Tel (01522) 682020; *Head* I.R. Hirst. (Mixed) (5–11)

Monkhouse County Primary School, Pennygate, Spalding PE11 1LG; Tel (01775) 722006; *Head* D.W. Gale. (Mixed) (5–11)

Learning Difficulties Support Service; A Learning Difficulties Service is available to offer help to schools for children who have learning difficulties including specific learning difficulty. The Head of the Service can be contacted on Lincoln (01522) 553265

English as an Acquired Language; Enquiries to the Teacher/Co-ordinator on Lincoln (01522) 595574

Traveller Children Service; The Teacher/Co-ordinator may be contacted on Lincoln (01522) 553320

Gifted and Able Children Service; Enquiries to the Teacher/Co-ordinator on Lincoln (01522) 752142

Secondary Schools

The Aveland School, Birthorpe Rd, Billingborough, Sleaford NG34 0QT; Tel (01529) 240331; *Head* R.M. Lake. (County, Mixed Modern) (11–16) (236)

Banovallum School, Boston Rd, Horncastle LN9 6DA; Tel (01507) 522232; *Head* A. Darby. (County, Mixed Modern) (352)

Boston High School for Girls, Spilsby Rd, Boston PE21 9PF; Tel (01205) 310505; *Head* J.M. Webb. (County, Girls Grammar) (11–18) (844)

Bourne Grammar School, South Rd, Bourne PE10 9JE; Tel (01778) 422288; *Head* J.F. Nicholson. (Controlled, Mixed Grammar) (11–18) (666)

Caistor Yarborough School, Grimsby Rd, Caistor LN7 6QZ; Tel (01472) 851383; *Head* B.R. Toniton. (County, Mixed Comprehensive) (11–18) (474)

The Central School, Rushcliffe Rd, Grantham NG31 8ED; Tel (01476) 66384; *Head* M. Gaul. (County, Mixed Comprehensive) (636)

The Charles Read School, Bourne Rd, Corby Glen, Grantham NG33 4NT; Tel (01476) 550333; *Head* J. Gleeson. (County, Mixed Comprehensive) (11–16) (236)

Cherry Willingham Comprehensive School, Croft La, Cherry Willingham LN3 4JP; Tel (01522) 750747; *Head* D.S. Mills. (County, Mixed Comprehensive) (11–16) (533)

The City School, Skellingthorpe Rd, Lincoln LN6 0EP; Tel (01522) 683664; *Head* B.J. Peck. (County, Mixed Comprehensive) (861)

The Cordeaux High School, High Holme Rd, Louth LN11 0HG; Tel (01507) 606555; *Head* P. White. (County, Mixed Comprehensive) (11–16) (650)

Coteland's School, Sleaford Rd, Ruskington NG34 9BY; Tel (01526) 832402; *Head* D.P. Veal. (County, Mixed Modern) (11–16) (174)

The Deeping School, Park Rd, Deeping St James, Peterborough PE6 8NF; Tel (01778) 342159; *Head* Dr D.A. Bryars. (County, Mixed Comprehensive) (11–18) (1193)

Donington The Thomas Cowley School, School La, Donington, Spalding PE11 4TE; Tel (01775) 820524; *Head* M.T. Davison. (Controlled, Mixed Modern) (291)

The Earl of Scarborough High School, Burgh Rd, Skegness PE25 2QH; Tel (01754) 610073. (County, Mixed Modern) (11–18) (967)

The George Farmer County Secondary School, Park Rd, Holbeach, Spalding PE12 7PU; Tel (01406) 423042; *Head* J.P.M. Glenn. (County, Mixed Modern) (11–16) (424)

The Haven High School, Marian Rd, Boston PE21 9HB; Tel (01205) 311979; *Head* M. Fox; Tel (01205) 311979. (County, Mixed Comprehensive) (11–16) (608)
John Spendluffe School, Hanby la, Alford LN13 9BL; Tel (01507) 462443; *Head* G. Allan. (County, Mixed Modern) (11–16) (302)
Kesteven and Grantham Girls' School, Sandon Rd, Grantham NG31 9AU; Tel (01476) 63017; *Head* A. Hopkinson. (County, Girls' Grammar) (11–18) (898)
Kesteven and Sleaford High, Jermyn St, Sleaford NG34 7RS; Tel (01529) 302113/1414044; N.W. McFarlane. (Girls) (442)
The Lafford High St, Fen Rd, Billinghay LN4 4HU; Tel (01526) 860410; *Head* W.J. Hockin. (County, Mixed Modern) (11–16) (231)
The Middlecott School Edinburgh Dr, Kirton, Boston PE20 1JS; Tel (01205) 722336; *Head* G.I. Walters. (County, Mixed Modern) (11–16) (557)
The Middlefield School, Middlefield La, Gainsborough DN21 1PU; Tel (01427) 615199; *Head* M. Cox. (County, Mixed Modern) (11–16) 497 (497)
The Peele County Secondary School, 84 Little London, Long Sutton, Spalding PE12 9LF; Tel (01406) 362120; *Head* N. Barton. (County, Mixed Modern) (11–16) (337)
The Queen Eleanor School, Green La, Stamford PE9 1HE; Tel (01780) 51011. (County, Mixed Comprehensive) (500)
Queen Elizabeth's High School, Morton Terr, Gainsborough DN21 2ST; Tel (01427) 612359; *Head* M.F. Pape. (County, Mixed Grammar) (11–18) (925)
Rasen De Aston School, Willingham Rd, Market Rasen LN8 3RF; Tel (01673) 843415; *Head* A.H. Neal. (Controlled, Mixed Comprehensive) (11–18) (1102)
The Robert Manning School, Edinburgh Cres, Bourne PE10 9DT; Tel (01778) 422365; *Head* M.S. Kee. (County, Mixed Comprehensive) (11–18) (775)
St Bede's RC Secondary School, Tollfield Rd, Boston PE21 9PN; Tel (01205) 365873; *Head* J.A. McGarel. (RC Aided, Mixed Modern) (11–16) (192)
St Guthlac Comprehensive School, Postland Rd, Crowland, Peterborough PE6 0JA; Tel (01733) 210413; *Head* K.M. Brierley. (County, Mixed Comprehensive) (11–16) (232)
Sir John Gleed Technology School, Halmer Gdns, Spalding PE11 2EF; Tel (01775) 722702; *Head* A.D. MacKown. (County, Boys' Modern) (11–16) (554)
Spalding Grammar School, Priory Rd, Spalding PE11 2XH; Tel (01775) 724646; *Head* M.J. Stewart. (Aided, Boys' Grammar) (11–18) (720)
Spalding High School for Girls, Stonegate, Spalding PE11 2PJ; Tel (01775) 722110; *Head* A.J. Williams. (County, Girls' Grammar) (11–18) (843)
Spilsby High School, West End, Spilsby PE23 5EW; Tel (01790) 753260; *Head* M.W. Frost. (County, Mixed Bi-lateral) (11–16) (445)
The Tennyson High School, Seaholme Rd, Mablethorpe LN12 2DF; Tel (01507) 473331; *Head* G.M. French. (County, Mixed Modern) (11–16) (304)
The Walton Girls' High School, Harlaxton Rd, Grantham NG31 7JR; Tel (01476) 63251; *Head* M. Banister. (County, Girls Comprehensive) (11–16) (501)
The William Lovell CE Secondary School, Main Rd, Stickney, Boston PE22 8AA; Tel (01205) 480352; *Head* R.D. Dring. (Controlled, Mixed Modern) (11–16) (359)

Schools with Boarding Facilities

The King's School, Brook St, Grantham; Tel (01476) 63180; *Head* D. Lee. (Boys' GM Grammar) (11–18) (70)
The Cordeaux High School, High Holme Rd, Louth; Tel (01507) 606555; *Head* P. White; N.B. The boarding house caters for 11–18 year olds. (Mixed, Comprehensive) (11–16)(Girls 29) (Boys 40)
King Edward VI School, Westgate, Louth; Tel (01507) 600456; *Head* J. Wheeldon. (Mixed, GM Grammar) (14–19) (Boys 40, Girls 35)
De Aston School, Willingham Rd, Market Rasen; Tel (01673) 843415; *Head* A.H. Neal. (Mixed Comprehensive) (11–18) (70)
Skegness Grammar School, Vernon Rd, Skegness PE25 2QS; Tel (01754) 610000; *Head* W.J. Webster. (Mixed, GM Grammar) (11–18) (100)

Grant Maintained Schools

Ancaster High School, Shannon Ave, Lincoln LN6 7JG; Tel (01522) 686124; J.A. Hillyer. (Mixed) (11–18 (580)
Boston Grammar, South End, Boston PE21 6JY; Tel (01205) 366444; J.E. Neal. (11-18)(Boys) (567)
Branston Community College, Station Rd, Branston LN4 1LH; Tel (01522) 791279; Fax (01522) 794484; B.W. Douglas, BA, MSc, FRSA, FIMgt. (Mixed) (11–18 (1050)
Caistor Grammar School, Church St, Caistor, Lincs LN7 6QJ; Tel (01472) 851250; *Headteacher* T.J. Foulkes; *Chair of Governors* J.R. Orr. (Mixed) (11–18) (455)
Carre's Grammar School, Northgate, Sleaford, Lincs NG34 7DD; Tel (01529) 302181; Fax (01529) 413488; *Headteacher* P.C. Freeman; *Chairman of Governors* J.D.P. Duckett. (Boys) (11–18) (528)
Castle Hills GM Community School, The Avenue, Gainsborough DN21 1PY; Tel (01427) 612411/612970; Fax (01427) 677291; P.L. Elliott. (Mixed) (561)
Christ's Hospital School, Wragby Rd, Lincoln LN2 4PN; Tel (01522) 533561; Fax (01522) 511368; *Headteacher* David J. Cox, MA, MSc(Ed); *Chair of Governors* Nevile J. Camamile, BA, FCA. (Mixed 11–18 Grant Maintained) (1295)
Gartree G.M. School Butts La, Tattershall LN4 4PN; Tel (01526) 342399; Fax (01526) 344418; *Headteacher* Jack Walton; *Chair of Governors* V. Dunford. Mixed 11–16 (400)
The Giles School, Church La, Old Leake, Boston PE22 9LD; Tel (01205) 870693; C. Walls. (Mixed) (581)
Gleed Girl's Grant Maintained School Neville Ave, Spalding PE11 2EJ; Tel (01775) 722484; Fax (01775) 760546; M.E. Moorhouse. (Girls) (530)
King Edward VI School Edward St, Louth, Lincs LN11 9LL; Tel (01507) 600456; Fax (01507) 600316; *Headteacher* A.J. Wheeldon; *Chair of Governors* Harry Burgin. (Mixed) (14–18) (560)
The King's School Brook St, Grantham, Lincs NG31 6RP; Tel (01476) 63180; Fax (01476) 590953; *Head Master* D. Lee; *Chair of Governors* Elizabeth Allison; *Bursar* Roger Cross. (Male) (11–18) (850)
Lincoln School of Science and Technology Cross o' Cliff Hill, Lincoln LN5 8PN; Tel (01522) 569977; *Head* A.F.X. Green
Monk's Dyke, Monk's Dyke Rd, Louth LN11 9AW; Tel (01507) 606349; S.M. Williamson. (Mixed) (705)
The North Kesteven, Moor La, North Hykeham LN6 9AG; Tel (01522) 681010; T. O'Toole. (Mixed) (11–18 (1181)
Queen Elizabeth's Grammar School, West St, Horncastle, Lincs LN9 5AD; Tel (01507) 522465; Fax (01507) 527711; *Head* T.J. Peacock. (Mixed-Selective) (600)
Queen Elizabeth's G.M. Grammar School Station Rd, Alford, Lincs LN13 9HY; Tel (01507) 462403; Fax (01507) 462125; *Headteacher* Richard Pryce; *Chair of Governors* Ken Ralph; *Bursarial Secretary* P. Calthorpe; *Administrative Officer* D.C. Morrison. (Mixed) (11–18) (415)
The Robert Pattinson Moor La, North Hykeham, Lincoln LN6 9AF; Tel (01522) 681811; *Head* D.B. Williams
St Hugh's C. of E., The Avenue, Dysart Rd, Grantham NG31 7PX; Tel (01476) 64815; Boyd Chapman. (Mixed) (11–16) (551)
St Peter and St Paul Catholic High, Western Ave, Lincoln LN6 7SX; Tel (01522) 681101; Mrs S.C. Pitcher. (Mixed) (11–16) (450)
St Wulfram's C. of E. High, Queensway, Grantham NG31 9RA; Tel (01476) 64756; Fax (01476) 70140; M.G. Cartwright, BA, MEd, FCollP, LCP, DipTL, ALBC. (Mixed) (11–16) (430)
Sir William Robertson High School, Main Rd, Welbourn, Lincoln LN5 0PA; Tel (01400) 272422/272648; Fax (01400) 273780; I.C. Wright. (Mixed) (11–16) (393)
Skegness Grammar School, Vernon Rd, Skegness, Lincs PE25 2QS; Tel (01754) 610000; Fax (01754) 763947; *Headteacher* W.J. Webster; *Chair of Governors* J. Atkinson; *Bursar* F. Doran. (Mixed) (11–18) (Day and Boarding) (639)

William Farr CE Comprehensive School, Lincoln Rd, Welton, Lincoln LN2 3JB; Tel (01673) 860225; Fax (01673) 862660; Headteacher (01673) 862832; Adult Tutor (01673) 860890; P. Strong, BSc. (Mixed) (11–18) (925)

Yarborough School, Riseholme Rd, Lincoln LN1 3SP; Tel (01522) 529203/1529224; *Headmaster* Kostek Shanovich; *Chair of Governors* Len Mitchell. (Mixed) (11–18) (1100)

Technology Centre

St George's Grant Maintained College of Technology School,Sponsored by Mr Reg Brealey, Database, Apricot Computers and Tandberg (UK) Westholme, Westgate, Sleaford, Lincs NG34 7PS; Tel (01529) 302487; *Principal* J.C. Hodgson; *Chair of Governors* R. Brealey; *Bursar* J. Crow. Mixed 11–18 (1020)

Liverpool City Council

Population 457,000 (1991)

Housing and Consumer Services Directorate, Foster Hse, Canning Pl, Liverpool L1 8HJ; Tel 0151-225 4404; Fax 0151-225 4482

Education Directorate

14 Sir Thomas St, Liverpool L1 6BJ; Tel 0151-227 3911

Director of Education M.F. Cogley, BA

Head of Education Services (Planning, Development and Equal Opportunities) C. Lawton

Head of Education Services (Client Support) D. Barrie

Head of Education Services (Operational Support) W. Carroll

Assistant Director (Planning) J. Richardson

Assistant Director (Curriculum & Staff Development) E. Simpson

Assistant Director (Management Data & Analysis) P. Morgan

Assistant Director (Individual & Special Educational Needs) K. Roberts

Assistant Director (Race Equality) D. Clay

Co-ordinator – Inspection and Advisory Service R. Jones

AEO (Equal Opportunities) S. Brown

AEO (Planning) J. Maskell

AEO (Primary) H. Lindsay

AEO (Secondary) A. Walton

AEO (Youth & Community) M. Croft

Principal Educational Welfare Officer R. Crossley

Principal Educational Psychologist D.T. Jones, BA(Hons)

Principal Careers Officer G. Hogg

Inspector (INSET) J. Arnold

Inspector (Science) M. Bowers

Inspector (Art and Design) M. Dillon

Inspector (Technology) G. Edwards

Inspector (Mathematics) J. Hackney

Inspector (Primary Early Years) M. Haines

Inspector (Science) M. Hannon

Inspector (Modern Languages) E. Kelly

Inspector (Nursery Early Years) J. Morrison

Inspector (PE) M. Potter

Inspector (Music) A. Pugh

Inspector (Primary) D. Roberts

Inspector (Early Years) J. Thomas

Inspector (Special Needs) P. Thomas

Inspector (16-19 RE) J. Toye

Inspector (Humanities) B. Weston

Number of Schools

6 nursery; 189 primary; 35 secondary (27,000); 21 adult centres

Special Schools

19 day; 2 day and residential; 3 residential; 1 hospital special school

Day of Committee Meeting

Monthly

Requisition Periods for School Supplies

March/April

Other Authorities with whom Joint Purchasing Arrangements are made

None

Education Committee

Chair G. Ben-Tovim, (Lab)

Deputy Chair M. McDaid, (Lab) 2 Olive Vale, Liverpool L15 8JH

Members of the Committee

LD: F. Clucas

Lab: S. Hogan

Governor Training Unit

Governor Training, Liverpool Education Advisory Agency, Dulcie Cottages, Riversdale Rd, Liverpool L19 3QN; Tel 0151-225 8129/8149; Fax 0151-494 1597

Co-ordinator and Adviser for Governor Training and Support Stella Owen, CertEd, Advanced Dip Special Educ, MEd

Adviser for Governor Training and Support Len Carter, MSc, PGCE

Services Offered

Training courses; On site training courses; Personal support; Telephone helpline; Newsletter

Hospital School

Alder Hey, Eaton Rd L12 2AP; Tel 0151-228 4811 Ext 2366/2367; A.C. Brereton

Special Day Schools

Acorn Nursery, Lowerson Rd L11 8LW; Tel 0151-226 0309; B. Tonge (Temporary)

Ashfield School, Thingwall La L14 7NX; Tel 0151-228 9500; P. Morrison. (P.H. & Del.)

Clifford Holroyde, Higher La L9 7AG; Tel 0151-525 6943; M. Rees. (Malad.)

Ernest Cookson, Mill La L12 7JA; Tel 0151-220 1874; L.J. Richardson. (Malad.)

Finchlea, Mill La L13 5TF; Tel 0151-228 2578; D. Newman. (S.L.D.)

Grantside, Mill Rd L6 2AS; Tel 0151-263 6417; M.H. Horne. (Malad.)

Greenways Nursery/Infant, Beechwood Rd L19 0LD; Tel 0151-427 1175; I.M. Williams. (E.S.N.)

Longmoor, Sherwoods La L10 1LW; Tel 0151-525 5733; S. Coates (Acting). (S.L.D.)

Margaret Beavan, Almonds Grn L12 5HP; Tel 0151-226 1306; T.B. Flynn. (M.L.D.)

Meadow Bank, Sherwoods La L10 1LW; Tel 0151-525 3451; R. Williams (Temporary). (M.L.D.)

Mersey View, Minehead Rd L17 6AX; Tel 0151-427 1863; K.L. Evans. (M.L.D.)

Millstead, Old Mill La L15 8LW; Tel 0151-722 0974; D. Clifford

Palmerston, Beaconsfield Rd L25 6EE; Tel 0151-428 2128; J.F. Wright. (S.L.D.)

Princes, Selborne St L8 1TY; Tel 0151-709 2602; E.B. Thomas. (S.L.D.)

Sandfield Pk, Sandfield Walk L12 1LH; Tel 0151-228 0324; M. Coghlan (Acting). (P.H.)

Watergate, Speke Rd L25 8QA; Tel 0151-428 5812; P. Richardson. (M.L.D.)

Wheathill, Naylorsfield Rd L25; Tel 0151-498 4811; M.D. Cording. (Malad.)

White Thorn, Sherwoods La L10 1LW; Tel 0151-525 3794; J. Roberts (Acting). (E.S.N.)

Special Residential Schools

Abbots Lea, Beaconsfield Rd, Woolton L25 6EE; Tel 0151-428 1161; G.H. Quick. (P.H. & Del.)

Lower Lee, Beaconsfield Rd L25 6EF; Tel 0151-428 4071; M. Bowers (Temporary). (Malad.)

Special Day and Residential Schools/Units

Alice Elliott, Childwall Abbey Rd L16 5EQ; Tel 0151-722 6199; *Teacher-in-Charge*

Harold Magnay, Woolton Hill Rd, Liverpool L25 6JA; Tel 0151-428 6305; G. Raines (Temporary). (P.H.)

Liverpool Music Centre

1st Floor, 43 Renshaw St L1 25F; Tel 0151-709 9409

County Mixed Community Comprehensive Schools

ALSOP, Queens Dr, Liverpool L4 5SH; Tel 0151-525 2600; A. Yates
Anfield, Priory Rd, Liverpool L4 2SL; Tel 0151-263 5665; Mrs B. Jackson
Breckfield, Hamilton Rd, Liverpool L5 4RX; Tel 0151-263 5349; Mrs V. Valentine
Broadgreen Queens Dr, Liverpool L13 5UQ; Tel 0151-228 6800; I. Andain
Calderstones Harthill Rd, Liverpool L18 HS; Tel 0151-724 2087; B. Davies
Childwall Queens Dr, Liverpool L15 6XZ; Tel 0151-722 1561; J. Nicholson
Croxteth Stonebridge La, Liverpool L11 9AY; Tel 0151-549 1287; G. McKean
Dovecot Fincham Rd, Liverpool L14 9NJ; Tel 0151-228 2752; R.E. Roberts
Fazakerley, Sherwoods La, Liverpool L10 1LB; Tel 0151-521 3418; A. Richmond
Gateacre Grange La, Liverpool L25 4SD; Tel 0151-428 1569; P. Barnes
Netherley Childwall Valley Rd, Liverpool L27 3YA; Tel 0151-487 8346; P.A. Lodge
New Heys Heath Rd, Liverpool L19 4TN; Tel 0151-427 6482; W. May
Queen Mary, Long La, Liverpool L9 6AF; Tel 0151-525 1920; R.W.F. Mander
Shorefields Dingle Vale, Liverpool L8 9SJ; Tel 0151-727 1387; K. Poyser
Speke Central Ave, Liverpool L24 0TP; Tel 0151-486 2612; Mrs P. Belvisi

County Single Sex Comprehensive Schools

Holly Lodge (Girls), Queens Dr, Liverpool L13 0AE; Tel 0151-228 3772; Mrs A.M. Shave
West Derby (Boys), Quarry Rd, Liverpool L13 7DB; Tel 0151-228 7915; P. Fraser

R.C. Comprehensive Schools

Archbishop Beck Cedar Rd L9 9AF; Tel 0151-525 6326; A. Hardman. (Mixed) (1200)
Broughton Hall Yew Tree La L12 8HJ; Tel 0151-228 3622; Sister M. Columba. (Girls) (1080)
Campion Prince Edwin St L5 3RW; Tel 0151-207 1685; E. Wallace. (Boys) (1080)
Cardinal Heenan Honeysgreen La L12 9HZ; Tel 0151-228 3472; J. Gibbons. (Boys) (1080)
De La Salle Carr Lane East L11 4SG; Tel 0151-546 3134; Rev Brother Peter. (Boys) (1080)
Notre Dame Everton Valley L4 4EZ; Tel 0151-263 3104; Sister Eileen. (Girls) (1080)
Nugent Overbury St L7 3HL; Tel 0151-709 6638; J. Nash (Acting). (Boys) (850)
Pope John Paul Alderwood Ave L24 2UB; Tel 0151-486 1267; Mrs B. Arden. (Mixed) (650)
St John Almond Horrocks Ave L19 4PF; Tel 0151-427 5302; Miss C. Davidson. (Mixed) (1080)
St John Bosco, Stonedale Cres L11 9DQ; Tel 0151-546 6360; Sister Helen. (Girls) (1080)
St Julie's Speke Rd L25 7TN; Tel 0151-428 6421; Sister Anne Marie Gammack. (Girls) (1080)
St Mary's Windermere Terrace L8 35B; Tel 0151-727 2064; Sister Mary Gabriel. (Girls) (850)

Voluntary Aided Bilateral Schools

King David (Hebrew) Childwall Rd L15 6UZ; Tel 0151-722 7496; Miss V. Carter. (Mixed) (521)
The Blue Coat School Church Rd L15 9EE; Tel 0151-733 1407/8; J. Speller. (Boys) (685)

Voluntary Aided High Schools

Archbishop Blanch Sefton Park Rd L8 0TH; Tel 0151-727 6055; Mrs K. Zimak. (Girls) (733)
St Hilda's Croxteth Dr, Liverpool L17 3AL; Tel 0151-733 2709; H. Lavery (Acting). (Girls) (644)

City of Liverpool Community College

Canning Place Centre L1 8BT; Tel 0151-709 0541 *Principal* W. Brown
Bankfield Centre Bankfield Rd L13 0BQ; Tel 0151-259 1124
City of Liverpool Community College, Abercromby Site, Myrtle St, Liverpool L7 7DN; Tel 0151-708 0423; *Principal* W. Brown
Corinthian Site, Inigo Rd, Liverpool L13 6SH; Tel 0151-228 1740
Hanover Site, Colquitt St, Liverpool L1 4DB; Tel 0151-709 0541
Mabel Fletcher Site, Sandown Rd, Liverpool L15 4JB; Tel 0151-733 7211
Muirhead Site, Muirhead Ave East, Liverpool L11 1ES; Tel 0151-226 0111
Octagon Site, Grove St, Liverpool L7 7AD; Tel 0151-709 4773
Old Swan Site, Broadgreen Rd, Liverpool L13 5SQ; Tel 0151-254 1239
Riversdale Site, Riversdale Rd, Liverpool L19 3QR; Tel 0151-427 1227
Clarence Street Centre Clarence St L3 5TP; Tel 0151-708 0423
Colquitt Centre Colquitt St L1 4DB; Tel 0151-709 0541
Greenbank Centre Mossley Ave L18 1JB; Tel 0151-733 5511
Hope Street Centre Hope St L1 9EB; Tel 0151-708 0423
Liverpool Adult Basic Education Unit 73 Canning St L8 7NW; Tel 0151-708 9860
Myrtle Street Centre Myrtle St L7 7DN; Tel 0151-708 0423
Rotunda Centre 109, Great Mersey St L5 2PL; Tel 0151-207 2176
Windsor Street Centre Windsor St L8 8EE; Tel 0151-709 5867

Adult Education Establishments

Burton Manor Residential College of Adult Education Neston, South Wirral, Cheshire L64 5SJ; Tel 0151-336 5173; Mrs J. Dawson
Liverbus Project Former Roscommon School Bldg, Roscommon St L5 3NE; Tel 0151-298 2161; *Manager* Ms A. Phizakerlea (Acting)
Newsham Drive Adult Education Centre 83 Newsham Dr L6 7UH; Tel 0151-263 5153; Mrs J. Navein
Prince Edwin Adult Centre Prince Edwin St L5 3LL; Tel 0151-207 0824; Mrs M. Foster

Educational Centres

Educational Development Centre, Dulcie Cottages, Riversdale Rd L19 3QN; Tel 0151-494 1257
Colomendy Centre for Outdoor Education Loggerheads, Near Mold, Clwyd CH7 5LB; Tel (0135285) 381; R.G. Taylor
Craft Stores and Maintenance Unit Gloucester Pl L6 1DZ; Tel 0151-263 3478; E. Forshaw

Grant Maintained Schools

Our Lady of Fatima Margaret St L6 2HN; Tel 0151-263 5602; D. Hart (Acting). (Mixed) (800)
St Francis Xavier's College, High Lee, Beaconsfield Rd, Woolton, Liverpool L25 6EG; Tel 0151-428 6307; Fax 0151-428 8485; *Headteacher* Brother Francis, FIC, OBE, MSc, FRSA; *Chair of Governors* John McGlashan; *Bursar* Mrs C. Walker. (Male) (11–18) (Girls in VI Form) (1179)

St Margaret's CE High School (GM) Aigburth Rd L17 6AB; Tel 0151-427 1825; R.E. Enoch, OBE. (Boys) (820)

Manchester City Council

Population 440,900
PO Box 532, Town Hall, Albert Sq, Manchester M60 2LA; Tel 0161-234 5000; Fax 0161-236 5909
Chief Executive A. Sandford, LLB, DL

Education Offices

Crown Sq, Manchester M60 3BB; Tel 0161-234 7125; Fax 0161-234 7007
Chief Education Officer R. Jobson
Head of Adult, Curriculum and Youth Division B. Clayton
Head of Children's Services M. Smith
Head of Schools Division A. Cant
Head of Support Services Division A. Longworth
Head of Leisure Division J. Byrne
AEO (Support Services) B. O'Keeffe
Head of Adult Education Services R. Corbridge
Head of Inspectorate W. Rogers
Head of Curriculum Services M. Molley
Principal Youth Officer D. Bradley
Head of Manchester Careers Service S. Millward
Head of Under – Fives M. Parker
Play Areas Co-ordinator J. Horsfall (Acting)
Head of Music and Dance Services A. Jones
AEO (Divisional Support Team) Vacancy
AEO (Schools) – North District J.L. Bedford
AEO (Schools) – South District B. Seaborn
AEO (Schools) – Central District A. Seaborn
AEO (Client Support) B. O'Keeffe
AEO (Resources) B. Myers
AEO (Finance) T. Goodwin
AEO (Information Technology/Personnel) J.L. Bedford
Principal Leisure Officer Vacancy
Principal Officer (Client Services) E. O'Rourke
Governors' Training Officer D. Morgan
Chief Education Welfare Officer N. Barlow (Acting)
Education Inspector (Central/North) A. Warm
Senior Education Adviser J. Coghill; Tel 0161-998 5256
Adviser (English) D. Newell; Tel 0161-998 5256
Adviser (Mathematics) G. Hunter; Tel 0161-998 5256
Adviser (Science) L. Jones; Tel 0161-998 5256
Adviser (Modern, Foreign Languages) G. Graus; Tel 0161-998 5256
Adviser (Technology/Information Technology) P. Hemphill; Tel 0161-998 5256
Adviser (History, Geography, Religious Education) R. Isaac; Tel 0161-998 5256
Adviser (Art and Performing Arts) S. Moulson; Tel 0161-998 5256
Adviser (Equal Opportunities) M. Noble; Tel 0161-998 5256
Adviser (P.E. and Health Related Issues) M. Brown; Tel 0161-998 5256
Adviser (Assessment) G. Carter; Tel 0161-998 5256
PAA (LMSS) K. Worrall
PAA (Schools' Budget) C. Pollard
PAA (Schools' Budget) S. Scott
Number of Schools
7 nursery and 173 nursery classes in primary schools (5,432); 176 primary (41,700); 27 secondary
Special Schools
23 day (2,050); 4 boarding (350); 1 hospital (150); 2 hostels
Day of Committee Meeting
Wednesday of week 2 in a 5 week cycle
Requisition Periods for School Supplies
April-March
Other Authorities with whom Joint Purchasing Arrangements are made
None

Education Committee

Con 1, Lab 24, LD 5, Ind Lab 1
Chair K. Fry, (Lab) Flat 23, Dudley Ct, Carlton Rd, Manchester M16 8DA; Tel 0161-226 0097
Deputy Chair M. Hackett, (Lab) 3 Buckland Ave, Blackley, Manchester M9 8FU; Tel 0161-795 8533
Deputy Chair J.E. Keller, (Lab) 14 Nan Nook Rd, Northern Moor, Manchester M23 9BZ; Tel 0161-998 3535
Members of the Committee
Con: W.H. Aikman
Lab: K. Barner, R. Boyle, A. Burns, J. Byrne, V.J. Edwards, T. Eko, M. Enderby, T. Farrell, M. Humphreys, H. Johnson, M. Kane, Y.S. Mambu, N.K. Mogal, A.G. Harding, T. O'Callaghan, W.T. Risby, B. Selby, B.E. Stone, M. Taylor, N. Tilley, V.P. Young
LD: W. Helsby, J. Pearcey, D.J. Sandiford, A. Firth, S. Ashley
Ind Lab: M. Manning

Hospital Schools and Home Tuition Service

Booth Hall Hospital, Charlestown Rd, Blackley M9 7AA; Tel 0161-741 5252; *Head* H.E. Jones

Special Day Schools

Barlow Hall, Darley Ave, Manchester M21 2JA; Tel 0161-881 1934; *Head* A. Scally. (Assessment Unit)
Barnes Green Nursery, Beech Mount, Manchester M9 5XS; Tel 0161-205 1934; *Head* M. Gilmartin. (Assessment Unit)
Central District Support Service, Peacock School, Peacock Cl, Gorton, Manchester M18 8EG; Tel 0161-223 0458; *Head* C. McGrath. (50); (Social and Emotional Difficulties)
Crosby Meadow 71 Victoria Ave East, Blackley M9 7HA; Tel 0161-740 3395; *Head* P. Derbyshire (Acting). (45)
Gorton Brook First School, Belle Vue St, Gorton M12 5PW; Tel 0161-223 1822; *Head* I. John. (100)
Grange, Pilgrim Dr, Manchester M11 3TD; Tel 0161-223 2744; *Head* M. Lucas. (45)
Lancasterian, Elizabeth Slinger Rd, West Didsbury M20 2XA; Tel 0161-445 0123; *Head* R.D. Billinge. (140)
Leacroft, Correlli St, Miles Platting M40 8HX; Tel 0161-205 1839; *Head* P.A. Vermes. (60)
Longsight Park, Cochrane Ave M12 4FA; Tel 0161-273 4894; *Head* J. Holt. (100)
Melland, Holmcroft Rd, Gorton M18 7NG; Tel 0161-223 9915; *Head* J.D. O'Kane. (100)
Mill Hse, Nathan Rd, Poundswick M22 9GH; Tel 0161-437 2058; *Head* S. McFarlane (Acting). (30)
Newbrook School, Newholme Rd, off Elizabeth Slinger Rd, West Didsbury, Manchester M20 2XZ; Tel 0161-445 5172; *Head* S. Parsons (Acting). (Hearing Impaired)
Newton Heath Upper, Hague St, Newton Heath M40 2AE; Tel 0161-205 4782; *Head* P. Walker. (150)
North District Support Service Mead Hill, Middleton Rd M8 6NB; Tel 0161-795 8445; Fax 0161-795 6241; *Head* A.J. Farrell. (50)
Piper Hill, 200 Yew Tree La, Northenden M23 0FF; Tel 0161-998 4068; *Head* J. Andrews. (80)
Queens Park First, Marston St, Collyhurst M40 7US; Tel 0161-205 3667; *Head* M. Russell (Acting). (100)
Rodney Hse, 388 Slade La, Burnage, Manchester M19 2HT; Tel 0161-224 2774; *Head* P. Gibson. (45)
Roundwood Upper School, Roundwood Rd, Northenden M23 4AB; Tel 0161-998 4138; *Head* W.W. Montgomery
Shawgrove, Cavendish Rd, West Disbury M20 1QB; Tel 0161-445 9435; *Head* H.S. Taylor. (80)

South District Support Service Southern Cross, Barlow Hall Rd, Chorlton-cum-Hardy M21 2JJ; Tel 0161-881 2695; *Head* M. Howard. (50)
Telford, Bank House Rd, Blackley M9 8LE; Tel 0161-740 1897/8; *Head* R.D. Billinge (Acting). (110)
The Birches, 77 Dickenson Rd, Rusholme M14 5AZ; Tel 0161-224 7537; *Head* M. Morgan. (50)
Whitworth Park First, Monton St, Moss Side M14 4GP; Tel 0161-226 2079; *Head* K.C. Scrymgeour. (100)
Woodside First, Crossacres Rd, Wythenshawe M22 5DR; Tel 0161-437 5697; *Head* A.M. Stuart. (100)

Residential Schools

Bollin Cross, Styal, Wilmslow, Ches SK9 4HX; Tel (01625) 529571; *Head* G. Beardsell (Acting). (80)
Buglawton Hall, Buxton Rd, Congleton, Cheshire CW12 3PQ; Tel (01620) 274492; *Head* A.K. Williams. (35)
Ewing, Central Rd, Withington M20 4ZA; Tel 0161-445 0745; *Head* D.F. Williams. (58)

County High Schools (11–16)

Abraham Moss High School, Crescent Rd, Crumpsall, Manchester M8 5UF; Tel 0161-740 5141; Fax 0161-721 4973; *Head* D. Watchorn
Brookway High School, Moor Rd, Wythenshawe, Manchester M23 9BP; Tel 0161-998 3992 and 3981; Fax 0161-998 5144; *Head* A. Williams. (900)
Ducie Central High School for Boys, Daisey Bank Rd, Victoria Pk, Manchester M14 5QL; Tel 0161-224 8280; Fax 0161-256 3419; *Head* D. Peters. (750)
Ellen Wilkinson High School, Upper: Palmerston St, Ancoats, Manchester M12 6PT; Tel 0161-274 4667; *Head* Y. Kneen. (900)
Lower: Hyde Rd, Ardwick, Manchester M12 6BA; Tel 0161-273 2793; Fax 0161-272 8427
Levenshulme High School for Girls, Crossley Rd, Manchester M19 1FS; Tel 0161-224 4625/248 6141; Fax 0161-256 1170; *Head* A.E.D. Farrell. (900)
Moston Brook High School, Northampton Rd, Manchester M40 5BP; Tel 0161-202 2244; Fax 0161-202 1101; *Head* R. Howell (Acting). (1050)
Newall Green High School, Upper: Greenbrow Rd, Manchester M23 8SX; Tel 0161-499 3878; Fax 0161-436 8914; *Head* B. Morrison
Lower: Porlock Rd, Baguley M23 9LZ; Tel 0161-998 3103; Fax 0161-945 8701
North Manchester High School for Boys, Chain Bar Bldg, Chain Bar, Moston La, Manchester M10 9RR; Tel 0161-681 1592; Fax 0161-681 8190; *Head* A. Gregory. (Boys) (1050)
Moss Hse Bldg, Charlestown Rd, Blackley, Manchester M9 7BS; Tel 0161-681 1526/682 1199
North Manchester High School for Girls, Brookside Bldg, Brookside Rd, Moston, Manchester M40 9QJ; Tel 0161-681 4678; Fax 0161-684 8946; *Head* J. Gledhill. (Girls) (900)
Shackliffe Bldg, Crofthill Rd, Moston, Manchester M40 9GL; Tel 0161-681 4678
Clough Top Bldg, Raycroft Ave, Blackley, Manchester M9 7EA; Tel 0161-681 4678
Oakwood High School, Nell La, Manchester M21 7SL; Tel 0161-881 4778; Fax 0161-861 8753; *Head* P.J. McBride. (1050)
Darley Ave, Manchester M21 7JB; Tel 0161-881 5133
Plant Hill High School, Plant Hill Rd, Blackley, Manchester M9 0WQ; Tel 0161-740 1831; Fax 0161-720 7254; *Head* A. Schofield. (900)
Poundswick High School, Upper: Simonsway, Manchester M22 7RH; Tel 0161-499 2726; *Head* J.A. Corcoran. (900)
Lower: Portway, Manchester M22 6QN; Tel 0161-499 2824; Fax 0161-499 1147
South Manchester High School, Woodhouse La, Manchester M22 7TH; Tel 0161-437 3156; Fax 0161-499 0408; *Head* P. Taylor. (900)
Spurley Hey High School, Upper: Mount Rd, Manchester M18 7GH; Tel 0161-248 7009; *Head* M. Powell
Lower: Ryder Brow Rd, Gorton, Manchester M18 7EX; Tel 0161-248 7009; Fax 0161-248 7914
Wright Robinson High School, Abbey Hey La, Gorton, Manchester M18 8RL; Tel 0161-370 5121; Fax 0161-371 8287; N. Beischer. (1200)

County High Schools (11–19)

Burnage High School for Boys, Upper: Burnage La, Manchester M19 1BU; Tel 0161-432 1527; *Head* D. Blackwell. (1500)
Lower: Parrs Wood Rd, Manchester M20 9TP; Tel 0161-434 0422/432 1527; Fax 0161-442 2366/061-448 1462
Parrs Wood High School, Wilmslow Rd, East Didsbury, Manchester M20 0PG; Tel 0161-445 8786; Fax 0161-445 5974; *Head* I.R. Hall. (1350)
Whalley Range High School for Girls, Upper: Wilbraham Rd, Whalley Range, Manchester M16 8GW; Tel 0161-861 9727; Fax 0161-881 0617; *Head* G. Bennett
Lower: Doncaster Ave, Withington, Manchester M20 1DN; Tel 0161-445 5432; Fax 0161-448 1645/881 0617

High Schools (Voluntary)

Our Lady's R.C. High, Alworth Rd, Blackley M9 0RP; Tel 0161-795 0711; Fax 0161-740 8641; A. Dolan. (824)
St Alban's R.C. High, Holmcroft Rd, Gorton M18 7NG; Tel 0161-231 1551; Fax 0161-220 8223; F.W. McFadyen. (821)
St Gregory's R.C. High, Stopford St, Higher Openshaw M11 1FG; Tel 0161-370 3111; Fax 0161-370 8420; C. Quinn
St Matthew's R.C. High, Lower: Beverley St, Blackley M9 4ED; Tel 0161-203 4674; B.D. McNulty. (1135)
Upper: Nuthurst Rd, New Moston M10 0EW; Tel 0161-681 6178
St Paul's R.C. High, Firbank Rd, Newall Grn M23 2YS; Tel 0161-437 5841; Fax 0161-499 0860; J. Wilbraham
St Thomas Aquinas R.C. High, Lower: Brantingham Rd, Whalley Range M16 8LY; Tel 0161-881 6253; D.B. Ganderton
Upper: Nell La, Chorlton-cum-Hardy M21 2SW; Tel 0161-881 9448; Fax 0161-882 0164
St Vincent De Paul R.C. High, Denison Rd, Victoria Pk, Manchester M14 5RX; Tel 0161-224 7748; Fax 0161-248 8318; J. McNerney
The Barlow R.C. High, School La, East Disbury, Manchester M20 0JP; Tel 0161-445 8053; Fax 0161-445 6350; P.V. Foley

Secondary Schools (Voluntary)

King David High, Eaton Rd, Crumpsall M8 5DY; Tel 0161-740 7248; Fax 0161-740 0790; F. McDonnell (Acting). (435)
Trinity C.E. High, Cambridge St, Greenheys M15 6HP; Tel 0161-226 2272; Fax 0161-227 9691; M.A. Evans

Detached Services

Inspection and Advisory Service, Acorn Centre, Royal Oak Rd, Wythenshawe, Manchester M23 8EB; Tel 0161-998 5256; Fax 0161-945 4846

Manchester Adult Education Services

Plymouth Grove Centre, Hathersage Rd, Longsight, Manchester M13 6BY; Tel 0161-273 4740
Head D. Corbridge
Abraham Moss Centre, Crescent Rd, Crumpsall, Manchester M8 6UH; Tel 0161-740 1491; Fax 0161-740 5460
Alexandra Community Workshop 14 Bedwell Cl, Alexandra Park Est, Moss Side, Manchester 16; Tel 0161-226 4624
Birtles Centre, Town Centre, Wythenshawe, Manchester M22 5RF; Tel 0161-499 1455; Fax 0161-436 8983
Cambrian Centre, Keymer St, Beswick, Manchester M11 3FY; Tel 0161-273 8130; Fax 0161-272 6792
Chain Bar Centre, North Manchester High School for Boys, Moston La, Manchester M10 9RR; Tel 0161-795 6010

Chorlton Park Centre, Mauldeth Rd West, Manchester M21 2SL; Tel 0161-881 0002; Fax 0161-862 9890
Collyhurst Centre, Teignmouth Ave, Collyhurst, Manchester M10 7QD; Tel 0161-205 1067
Greenheys Centre, Upper Lloyd St, Moss Side, Manchester M14 4HZ; Tel 0161-226 0428; Fax 0161-226 9673
Hulme Centre, Hulme Walk, Hulme, Manchester M15 5FQ; Tel 0161-226 8411; Fax 0161-226 8854
Ladybarn Evening Centre, Burnage High School for Boys (Lower), Parrswood Rd, Manchester M20 9PT; Tel 0161-445 7049
Levenshulme Evening Centre, Levenshulme High School for Girls, Crossley Rd, Manchester M19 1ES; Tel 0161-224 2676
Mill Street Centre, Bradford, Manchester; Tel 0161-220 8825
Moston Centre, Ashley La, Moston, Manchester M9 1WU; Tel 0161-953 5995
Newall Green Evening Centre, Scout Drive, Greenbrow Rd, Newall Grn, Manchester M23 8SX; Tel 0161-437 8505
Newton Heath Evening Centre Hague St, Newton Heath, Manchester M10; Tel 0161-205 4782
Newton Hse, 203 Droylsden Rd, Newton Heath, Manchester M10 6NY; Tel 0161-683 4203
Parent Education Project, Haveley Hey Primary School, Broadoak Rd, Benchill, Manchester M22 7PL; Tel 0161-437 5939
Parent Education Project, Newall Green Primary School, Fairbank Rd, Manchester M23 8YG; Tel 0161-499 1261
Parrswood Evening Centre, Parrswood High School, Wilmslow Rd, Manchester M20 0PG; Tel 0161-445 0591
Plant Hill Centre, Plant Hill Rd, Higher Blackley, Manchester M9 2WP; Tel 0161-795 6010; Fax 0161-740 1831
Plymouth Gr Centre, Hathersage Rd, Longsight, Manchester M13 0BY; Tel 0161-273 7177; Fax 0161-273 6919. (Lower)
Rackhouse Community Education Centre, Rackhouse Primary School, Yarmouth Drive, Northern Moor, Manchester M23 0BT; Tel 0161-998 4728
Royal Green Centre, Weston Grove, Northenden, Manchester M22 4NR; Tel 0161-998 3704
Spurley Hey Adult Centre, Spurley Hey High School (Upper), Mount Rd, Gorton, Manchester M18 6GR; Tel 0161-257 2518; Fax 0161-257 2518
Terry Dowling Centre, 260 Brownley Rd, Wythenshawe, Manchester M22; Tel 0161-437 8898/498 9996
Training Access Centre, Birtles Adult Education Centre, Wythenshawe Town Centre, Manchester M22 5RF; Tel 0161-498 8886; Fax 0161-436 8983
Training Access Centre, Greenheys Adult Education Centre, Upper Lloyd St, Manchester M14 4HZ; Tel 0161-226 4606; Fax 0161-226 9673
Varna Street Centre, Varna St, Openshaw, Manchester M11 1WP; Tel 0161-223 3627; Fax 0161-231 1248
Whalley Range Evening Centre, Whalley Range High School for Girls (Upper), Wilbraham Rd, Manchester M16 8GW; Tel 0161-861 9727. Upper

Music Centres

Medlock School, Wadeson Rd, Manchester M13 9UR; Tel 0161-273 3630; Fax 0161-274 4569
Head of Music and Dance Service A. Jones
Co-ordinator A. Culpeper; Tel 0161-273 3584
Music Service–North 337 St Mary's Rd, Moston M10 0EW; Tel 0161-681 0991; *Co-ordinator* P. Wainwright
Music Service–South Newall Green Junior School, Wythenshawe, Manchester M23 8YQ; Tel 0161-436 1944; *Co-ordinator* J. Fox

Miscellaneous Establishments

Arnfield Tower Field Study Centre, Manchester Rd, Tintwisle, Hyde SK14 7NE; Tel (01457) 852420; Fax (01457) 863480; P.K. Greenough
Debdale Sailing Centre, 1073 Hyde Rd, Gorton, Manchester M18 7LJ; Tel 0161-223 5182; C. Blundell
Language and Learning Support Service Palmerston St, Ancoats M12 6PE; Tel 0161-273 4232; Fax 0161-274 3427; J. Jolliffe
Manchester Dance Centre, Shena Simon College, Whitworth St, Manchester M1 2HB; Tel 0161-236 3095; L. Jordan
North Manchester Resources Centre, c/o Queens Park School, Marston St M10 7US; Tel 0161-205 6012; J.B. O'Neill
South Manchester Resources Centre, Acorn Centre, Royal Oak Primary School, Royal Oak Rd, Wythenshawe, Manchester M23 8EB; Tel 0161-946 0102; Fax 0161-946 0102; D. Hough
Travellers Education Service Parkside Training Centre, Sheepfoot La, Prestwick M25 8BW; Tel 0161-740 1465; Fax 0161-721 4220; M. Small

SERIS (Special Education Resource Information Service)

Westwood St, Moss Side, Manchester M14 4SW; Tel 0161-226 0843
P. Eckersley

Grant Maintained School

Audenshaw High School Hazel St, Audenshaw, Manchester M34 5NB; Tel 0161-336 2133; Fax 0161-320 3046; *Chair of Governors* T.J. Hall; *Headteacher* Graham Locke. Boys) (11–16 (748)

Merseyside Metropolitan Area

The following Metropolitan Councils comprise the Merseyside Metropolitan Area and may be found in alphabetical order within this chapter:
Knowsley, Liverpool, St Helens, Sefton, Wirral.

Mid Glamorgan County Council

Population 541,800
County Hall, Cathays Pk, Cardiff CF1 3NE; Tel (01222) 820820; Fax (01222) 780027

Education Department

Education Dept, County Hall, Cathays Pk, Cardiff CF1 3NF; Tel (01222) 780200
Director of Education K.P. Davies
Deputy Director K.P. Davies, MSc
Assistant Director (Operations) J.N.O. Harries, BA, MEd, BMIM

Assistant Director (Special Education/Liaison other Agencies) D.J.C. Young, MSc
Assistant Director (Finance/Administration) B. Hopkins, IPFA
County Librarian and Arts Officer J.I. Davies, FLA
Assistant Education Officer (Forward Planning and Property Services) G. Avery
Assistant Education Officer (Special Projects) G.R. Dun, DMA, ACIS
Assistant Education Officer (District and School Support) D. Matthews
Personnel Services Division W.A. Davies, MSc, ACIS, MIPM
Forward Planning and Property Services Division L. Stewart, DMA, ACIS
Awards and Benefits Divison L.L. Howells, BA, DipCg
Financial Services Division N. Skett, BA, ACMA
Operational Support Division P. Hulland
Chief Adviser D.R. John
Senior Adviser (Economics, History) D. Maddox
Senior Adviser (Appraisal) M. Keating
Senior Adviser (Primary) V. Morgan
Senior Adviser (Secondary, Personal and Social) T. Woodward
Adviser (CDT) R. Cater
Adviser (PE, Health Education, Outdoor Education) J. Davis
Adviser (Art) Ivan Davies
Adviser (Sensory Handicaps, EBD) G. Davies
Adviser (Primary, Bilingual Primary) C. Edwards
Adviser (Welsh, Bilingual Developments) J. Albert Evans
Adviser (Music) J. Francis
Adviser (Business Studies, IT – Curriculum) F. Gamble
Adviser (RE) T. Guy
Adviser (Primary) R. Howells
Adviser (Mathematics) M. Jones
Adviser (Primary) W.M. Jones
Adviser (INSET) G. Jones
Adviser (Geography) R. Knowles
Adviser (Primary) P. Kyte
Adviser (English) R. Landy
Adviser (Home Economics, Equal Opportunities) I. Manley
Adviser (Physical Science, Electronics) L. Richards
Adviser (Early Years) L. Webster
Adviser (Modern Languages, Classics) R. Williams
Principal Educational Psychologist F.L.U. Holland, BSc, MEd, ABPsS
Senior Educational Psychologist N. Seaton, BA
Senior Educational Psychologist V.E. Board, BA
Senior Educational Psychologist M. Greening, MA, BEd, BSc
Senior Educational Psychologist R. Brown
Senior Educational Psychologist J.C. Noaks, BSc(Econ), MEd
Senior Educational Psychologist R. Davies, BSc, MEd
Senior Educational Psychologist M.E. Edmunds
Educational Psychologist C. Pugh
Educational Psychologist M. Jennings
Educational Psychologist B. Jenkins
Educational Psychologist A. Lawthom
Educational Psychologist S. Winter-Allsop
Educational Psychologist D. Ellis
Educational Psychologist E. Beddoe
Educational Psychologist Mrs McLees
Educational Psychologist C. Thomas
Educational Psychologist A. Mundy
Educational Psychologist A. Appleby
Educational Psychologist J. Garland
County Community Education Officer D.K. Jones, BA
Assistant County Community Education Officer C.J. Berry, CertEd
Principal Education Officer (Careers) W. Feldon, BA
Principal Assistant (Carrers) S. Phillips, BA, DipCg
County Librarian J.I. Davies, FLA
Assistant Librarian A. Croft
Assistant Librarian P.A. Tobin, ALA, BA
Director of Catering Services C. Campbell

Number of Schools
23 nursery (783); 312 primary (50,621); 42 comprehensive (39,795)

Voluntary
16 primary (2,833); 4 comprehensive (2,543)

Special Schools
4 residential (347); 6 day (408)

Day of Committee Meeting
Tuesday. Bi-monthly

Requisition Periods for School Supplies
Twice Yearly

Other Authorities with whom Joint Purchasing Arrangements are made
South Glamorgan, West Glamorgan, Gwent

Education Committee

Chair R.W.M. Jenkins 12 Maes Glas, Brynhyfryd, Bridgend CF31 3RX; Tel (01656) 652979
Vice-Chair L.J. Rees 3 Caemawr Gdns, Porth CF39 9DB; Tel (01443) 682342

Governor Training Unit

Mid Glamorgan Governor Support Unit, Treforest ITEC, Treforest Industrial Estate, Pontypridd, Mid Glam CF37 5YL; Tel (01443) 842561; Fax (01443) 842565
Development Officer M. Drake, BA, MED, PGCE
Assistant Development Officer J. Bird

Services Offered
Structured training programme; Individual negotiated training courses; Resource loan service; Newsletter; Governors study centre for open learning

DISTRICT OFFICES

Ogwr District

District Education Office, County Council, Sunnyside, Bridgend CF31 4AR; Tel (01656) 766211
District Manager H. Williams

Careers Office

See chapter 17

Aided Secondary

Archbishop McGrath R.C. Heol yr Ysgol, Ynysawdre, Tondu, Bridgend CF32 9EH; Tel (01656) 720677; E.P. Hatton, BA. (11–19) (425)

County Secondary (11–19)

Brynteg Comprehensive School Heolgam, Bridgend CF31 3EU; Tel (01656) 652518; Dr C.H. Davies, BSc. (Lower) (11–14)
Brynteg Comprehensive School Ewenny Rd, Bridgend CF31 3ER; Tel (01656) 652608/766218; Dr C.H. Davies, BSc. (Upper) (14–19) (1850)
Bryntirion Comprehensive School Merlin Cres, Cefn Glas, Bridgend CF31 4QR; Tel (01656) 766941; D. Barry. (11–19) (1015)
Cynffig Comprehensive School East Ave, Kenfig Hill, Bridgend CF33 6NP; Tel (01656) 740294/741047; J. Evans. (11–19) (848)
Maesteg Comprehensive School Bridgend Rd, Maesteg, Bridgend CF34 0AX; Tel (01656) 733253; D.J. Painter, BA, MEd. (Lower) (11–14)
Maesteg Comprehensive School Llangynwyd, Bridgend CF34 9RP; Tel (01656) 732991; D.J. Painter, BA, MEd. (Upper) (14–19) (1273)
Ogmore Comprehensive School Spout Hill, Abergarw, Bryncethin, Bridgend CF32 9NA; Tel (01656) 721515; S.F. Davies, BSc. (Upper) (14–19) (649)
Pencoed Comprehensive School Coychurch Rd, Pencoed, Bridgend CF35 5LY; Tel (01656) 860799; L.A. Morgan, BSc, MEd, JP. (11–19) (1150)
Porthcawl Comprehensive School 52 Park Ave, Porthcawl CF36 3ES; Tel (01656) 782300; A.M. Jones, MA. (11–19) (1022)
Ynysawdre Comprehensive School Heol-yr-ysgol, Tondu, Bridgend CF32 9EL; Tel (01656) 720643; E. Williams, LLB. (Senior) (11–19) (910)

Rhondda District

District Education Office, Crawshay St, Ton Pentre, Rhondda CF41 7ER; Tel (01443) 441888
District Manager S. Whippey

Careers Office

See chapter 17

County Secondary

Ferndale Comprehensive School Darren Pk, Ferndale CF43 4LE; Tel (01443) 730450; A.J.G. Chinn, BSc. (Lower) (11–14)
Ferndale Comprehensive School Rear Excelsior Terr, Maerdy CF43 4AR; Tel (01443) 755337; A.J.G. Chinn, BSc. (Upper) (14–19) (924)
Porth Comprehensive School Cemetery Rd, Porth CF39 0BS; Tel (01443) 682137/682148; H.G.G. Thomas, BA(Hons). (11–19) (1250)
Tonypandy Comprehensive School Llewellyn St, Penygraig, Rhondda CF40 1HQ; Tel (01443) 436171; M.J. Jones, MEd. (11–19) (1062)
Treorchy Comprehensive School Pengelli, Treorchy CF42 6UL; Tel (01443) 773128; J. Owen, BA. (11–19) (1243)
Ysgol Gyfon Y Cymer Graigwen Rd, Cymmer, Porth CF39 9HA; Tel (01443) 685811; E.P. Jones. (580)

Cyon Valley District

District Education Office, Old Boys' Grammar School, Hirwaun Rd, Aberdare CF44 8DY; Tel (01685) 877755
District Manager G. Thomas

Careers Office

See chapter 17

Aided Secondary

St John Baptist C. in W. Comprehensive School Glan Rd, Aberdare CF44 8BW; Tel (01685) 875414; J.G. Jones. (11–19) (800)

County Secondary

Aberdare Boys Comprehensive School Cwmdare Rd, Trecynon, Aberdare CF44 8SS; Tel (01685) 872642; Dr T.G.N. Abbott. (11–19) (738)
Aberdare Girls Comprehensive School Gadlys Rd, Gadlys, Aberdare CF44 8AA; Tel (01685) 871130; S.B. Richardson. (Lower) (11–14)
Aberdare Girls Comprehensive School Cwmbach Rd, Aberdare CF44 0NF; Tel (01685) 872460; S.B. Richardson. (Upper) (13–19) (657)
Blaengwawr Comprehensive School Club St, Aberaman, Aberdare CF44 6TN; Tel (01685) 874341; E.S. George, BSc. (11–19) (595)
Mountain Ash Comprehensive School New Rd, Mountain Ash CF45 4DG; Tel (01443) 479199; M.E. Guilfoyle, BA, MEd. (11–19) (1120)

Merthyr Tydfil District

District Education Office, Gwernllwyn Rd, Dowlais, Merthyr Tydfil CF48 3TA; Tel (01685) 722761
District Manager G. Kiss

Careers Office

See chapter 17

Aided Secondary

Bishop Hedley R.C. High School Penydarren, Merthyr Tydfil CF47 9AN; Tel (01685) 721747/8; T.M. Gay, BSc. (11–19) (656)

Secondary Comprehensive Schools (County 11–19)

Afon Taf High Comprehensive School Yew St, Troedyrhiw, Merthyr Tydfil CF48 4ED; Tel (01443) 690401; P. Atkinson, BA. (11–19) (1260)
Cyfarthfa High Comprehensive School Cyfarthfa Pk, Merthyr Tydfil CF47 8RA; Tel (01685) 721772/721725; T.J. Church, MA. (Lower) (11–14)
Cyfarthfa High Comprehensive School Cae Mari Dwn, Queen's Rd, Merthyr Tydfil CF47 0LS; Tel (01685) 721725; T.J. Church, MA. (Upper) (14–19) (1050)
Pen-y-dre High Comprehensive School Gurnos Est, Merthyr Tydfil CF47 9BY; Tel (01685) 721726; J. Williams. (11–19) (1116)
Vaynor and Penderyn Comprehensive School Old Church St, Cefn Coed, Merthyr Tydfil CF48 2RR; Tel (01685) 722030; C.G. Daniel, BSc. (11–19) (396)

Rhymney Valley District

District Education Office, Mid Glamorgan County Offices, Caerphilly Rd, Ystrad Mynach, Hengoed CF8 7EP; Tel (01443) 816016
District Manager S. Lawrence

Careers Office

See chapter 17

County Secondary

Bedwas Comprehensive School Newport Rd, Bedwas NP1 8BJ; Tel (01222) 852500; Dr A.L. Jones, BSc, PhD. (11–19) (730)
Bedwellty Comprehensive School Pengam Rd, Aberbargoed, Bargoed CF8 9UA; Tel (01443) 875502/05/06; G. Jones, BA, MEd. (11–19) (529)
Heolddu Comprehensive School Mountain Rd, Bargoed CF8 8XL; Tel (01443) 875531/2; D.M. Howarth. (11–19) (868)
Lewis Boys Comprehensive School Pengam, Blackwood NP2 1ZH; Tel (01443) 875301; Dr C.J. Howard. (Upper) (14–19) (875)
Lewis Boys Comprehensive School Twyn Rd, Ystrad Mynach, Hengoed CF8 7EU; Tel (01443) 812240; Dr C.J. Howard. (Lower) (11–14)
Lewis Girls Comprehensive School Oakfield St, Ystrad Mynach, Hengoed CF8 7WW; Tel (01443) 813168/813530; M.E. Hemmings, BA. (Upper) (11–19) (997)
Rhymney Comprehensive School Mill Field, Abertysswg, Gwent NP2 5XB; Tel (01685) 840347/842840; J.B. Hogan, BA. (11–19) (700)
St Cenydd Comprehensive School St Cenydd Rd, Trecenydd, Caerphilly CF8 2RP; Tel (01222) 852504; D.W.C. Eynon. (11–19) (930)
St Ilan Comprehensive School Pontygwyndy Rd, Caerphilly CF8 3HD; Tel (01222) 852533/14; A.W. Cornelius, BSc, MEd. (Upper) (14–19) (840)
St Martin Comprehensive School Hillside, Caerphilly CF8 1UW; Tel (01222) 852501/2; S.A. Jones. (11–19) (747)
Ysgol Gyfun Cwm Rhymni Ty Fry Rd, Aberbargoed, Bargoed CF8 9FN; Tel (01443) 875533; H. Thomas, MA. (Lower) (11–13)
Ysgol Gyfun Cwm Rhymni Park Cres, Bargoed CF8 8PN; Tel (01443) 875227; H. Thomas, MA. (Upper) (14–19) (885)

Taff Ely District

District Education Office, The Grange, Tyfica Rd, Pontypridd CF37 2DD; Tel (01443) 486801
District Manager N. Stead

Careers Office

See chapter 17

Aided Secondary

Newman R.C. Comprehensive School Dynea Rd, Rhydyfelin, Pontypridd CF37 5DP; Tel (01443) 486845/6; P. Norman. (11–19) (720)

County Secondary

Bryn Celynnog Comprehensive School Penycoedcae Rd, Beddau, Pontypridd CF38 2AE; Tel (01443) 203411/204642; G. Lloyd, BA. (11–19) (1370)
Coed-y-Lan Comprehensive School Tyfica Rd, Pontypridd CF37 2DF; Tel (01443) 486809; P.E. Raybould. (Lower) (11–14)
Coed-y-Lan Comprehensive School Albion Site, Cilfynydd, Pontypridd CF37 4SF; Tel (01443) 486133/1486812; P.E. Raybould. (Upper) (14–19) (1144)
Hawthorn High School School La, Hawthorn, Pontypridd CF37 5AL; Tel (01443) 841228/9; M.K. Mullins, BA. (11–19) (998)
Hawthorn School La, Hawthorn, Pontypridd CF37 5AL; Tel (01443) 841228; M.K. Mullins. (Middle) (14–16)
Hawthorn School La, Hawthorn, Pontypridd CF37 5AL; Tel (01443) 841228; M.K. Mullins. (Upper) (16–19) (889)
Tonyrefail Comprehensive School Gilfach Rd, Tonyrefail, Porth CF39 8HG; Tel (01443) 670471/671376/670471/673535; T.J. Parry, BA, MEd. (11–19) (1075)
Y Pant Comprehensive School Cowbridge Rd, Talbot Grn, Pontyclun CF7 8YG; Tel (01443) 237701; J. Davies. (11–19) (730)
Ysgol Gyfun Llanharri Llanharri, Pontyclun CF7 9XE; Tel (01443) 237824; P. Griffiths, BA. (11–19) (1260)
Ysgol Gyfun Rhydfelen Glyndwr Ave, Pontypridd CF37 5NU; Tel (01443) 486816/7; D.B. James. (11–19) (1010)

Educational Psychology Service

Office Mid Glamorgan County Hall Cathays Pk, Cardiff CF1 3NF; Tel (01222) 780242; *Principal Educational Psychologist* F.L.U. Holland
District Psychological Centre Old Boys' Grammar School, Hirwaun Rd, Trecynon, Aberdare CF44 8DY; Tel (01685) 876062; M. Greening; A. Mundy
District Psychological Centre Maesglas, Old Gelligaer Village School, Gelligaer, Hengoed; Tel (01443) 875535/875556; M.E. Edmunds; M. Jennings; E. Jones; C. Pugh; S. Winter
District Psychological Centre Nantgwyn, Penygraig Junior School, Hendrecafn Rd, Pengraig CF40 1LJ; Tel (01443) 432067; J. Noaks; A. Appleby; E. Beddoe; J. McLees
District Psychological Centre Tram Rd La, Alexandra Ave, Penyderren, Merthyr Tydfil; Tel (01685) 721733; R. Brown; J. Garland
District Psychological Centre Ty Gwyn, Seaton St, Pwllgwaun, Pontypridd CF37 1JA; Tel (01443) 486331; V.E. Board; C.P. Thomas; D. Ellis
District Psychological Centre Ty Morfa, Minerva St, Bridgend CF31 1TD; Tel (01656) 766223; R. Davies; B. Ferron; A. Lanthom

Special Units

Oaklands Primary School Clifton Cres, Aberaman, Aberdare CF44 1RT; Tel (01685) 882577; J. Oliver. (P.H.)
Afon Taf High Comprehensive School Yew St, Troedyrhiw, Merthyr Tydfil CF48 4ED; Tel (01443) 690401; P. Atkinson. (Hearing Impaired)
Blaengwawr Comprehensive School Club St, Aberaman, Aberdare CF44 6TN; Tel (01685) 874341; E.S. George. (Hearing Impaired)
Brackla Junior School Brackla Estate, Coychurch Rd, Bridgend CF31 2EZ; Tel (01656) 766244; P.C. Jones. (P.H.)
Bryn Celynnog Comprehensive School (P.H., Hearing Impaired) Pencoedcae Rd, Beddau, Pontypridd CF38 2AE; Tel (01443) 203411; G. Jones, BA. (Upper)
Brynmenyn Primary School Bryn Rd, Brynmenyn, Bridgend CF32 9LA; Tel (01656) 720280; P.I. Thomas. (Hearing Impaired)
Caedraw Primary School Caedraw Rd, Merthyr Tydfil CF47 8HA; Tel (01685) 722620; C. Thomas. (P.H.)
Cap-coch Primary School School St, Abercwmboi, Aberdare; Tel (01443) 472746; D.E. Jones. (Hearing Impaired)
Ferndale Comprehensive; A.J.G. Chinn. (Lower)
Greenhill Primary School Penywrlod, Gelligaer, Hengoed CF8 8EU; Tel (01443) 875521; Mrs A. Broughman. (P.H.)
Hendre Infants School St Cenydd Rd, Trecenydd, Caerphilly CF8 2RP; Tel (01222) 883205; J.I. O'Regan. (Hearing Impaired)
Hendre Junior School St Cenydd Rd, Trecenydd, Caerphilly CF8 2RP; Tel (01222) 852518; H.R. Lewis. (Hearing Impaired)
Llwyn-crwn Primary School Llwyn-crwn Rd, Beddau, Pontypridd CF38 2BE; Tel Newtown Llantwit 203557; W.I. Richards. (Hearing Impaired)
Maes-y-Bryn Primary School Lancaster Dr, Llantwit Fardre, Pontypridd CF38 2NS; Tel (01443) 202928; W. Davies. (P.H.)
Pen-rhys Junior School Penrhys, Tylorstown, Ferndale CF43 3PL; Tel (01443) 730037; C.M. Morse. (P.H.)
*Preswylfa Observation & Assessment Centre 109 Merthyr Mawr Rd, Bridgend CF31 3NS; Tel Bridgend 61023
St Cenydd Comprehensive School St Cenydd Rd, Trecenydd, Caerphilly CF8 2RP; Tel (01222) 852504; D.W.C. Eynon. (Hearing Impaired) (P.H.)
Talbot Green Unit Heol-y-Gyfraith (M.H.) Talbot Green, Pontyclun CF7 8AJ; Tel (01443) 223487; *Teacher in Charge* R. Cooper
Tonypandy Comprehensive Llewellyn St, Penygraig, Rhondda; Tel (01443) 436171; M.J. Jones. (Upper) School (Hearing Impaired) (PH)
Tonypandy Primary Primrose St, Tonypandy CF40 1BQ; Tel (01443) 433006; M. Harrison. (Hearing Impaired)
Ynysawdre Comprehensive Heol-yr-Ysgol, Tondu, Bridgend CF32 9EL; Tel (01656) 720643; E. Williams, LLB. (Senior)
Ynysowen Junior School Aberfan, Merthyr Tydfil CF48 4NT; Tel (01443) 690478; W.D. Griffiths. (Hearing Impaired)
Ynyswen Infants School Ynyswen, Treorchy CF42 6ED; Tel (01443) 772410; M.A. Woolford. (P.H.)
Tylorstown Tutorial Centre Edmund St, Tylorstown LF43 3HH; K. Benyon. (Disruptive Pupils)

Special Day Schools

Cherry Gr, Pengam Rd, Ystrad Mynach, Hengoed CF8 8AA; Tel (01443) 812154; Y. Cousins. (58)
Greenfield, Duffryn Rd, Pentrebach, Merthyr Tydfil CF48 4BJ; Tel (01443) 690468; J. Bright. (184)
Heronsbrook, Heol Persondy, Aberkenfig, Bridgend CF32 9RF; Tel (01656) 720225; C. Major. (72)
Park Lane, Park La, Trecynon, Aberdare CF44 8HN; Tel (01685) 874489; A.C. Brown. (42)
Trealaw, Brithweunydd Rd, Trealaw, Rhondda CF40 2UH; Tel (01443) 433046; A. Lawthom. (55)
Ysgol Maes Gwyn, Cwmdare Rd, Aberdare CF44 8RE; Tel (01685) 873933; G.M. Manning. (71)

Special Residential Schools

Ysgol Castell Newydd, Llangewydd Rd, Cefn Glas, Bridgend CF31 4JP; Tel (01656) 767517; K.A. Maw. (65)
Ysgol Cefn Glas, Llangewydd Rd, Cefn Glas, Bridgend CF31 4JP; Tel (01656) 4826; A.R. Bolton. (120)
Ysgol Penybont, Ewenny Rd, Bridgend CF31 3HS; Tel (01656) 653974; D. Evans (Acting). (67)
Ysgol Ty Coch, Lansdale Dr, Tonteg, Pontypridd CF38 1PG; Tel (01443) 203471; A.M. Protheroe. (85)

Adult Education Centres

Aberbargoed A.E.C. Old Drill Hall, Aberbargoed; Tel (01443) 830043 (evening); T. Hourihan
Abercynon A.E.C. Abercynon Old Secondary School; Tel (01443) 740393 (evening); R. Sheldon

Afon Taf A.E.C. Afon Taf High School; Tel (01443) 690594; G. Newton
Aberdare A.E.C. Aberdare Girls Lower Comprehensive School; Tel (01685) 873405; Mrs M.S. Davies
Beddau A.E.C. Bryncelynnog Comprehensive School; Tel (01443) 204531; S.P. Brown
Bedwas Community Centre Bedwas Comprehensive School; Tel (01222) 883324; R. Lewis
Bridgend A.E.C. Brynteg Lower Comprehensive School; Tel (01656) 2518 (evening); O.P. Owen
Caerphilly A.E.C. St Martin's Comprehensive School; Tel (01222) 866647; D. Lyons
Cwm Ogwr A.E.C. Nantymoel Junior School; Tel (01656) 840417; Miss M. Hughes
Cynfig A.E.C. Cynfig Comprehensive School; Tel (01656) 740896; Mrs R.A. Davies
Ferndale Community Education Centre Ferndale Upper Comprehensive School; Tel (01443) 755220; J.E.C. Price
Garw Valley A.E.C. Ynysawdre Comprehensive School; Tel (01656) 870306; Mrs J.L. Ward
Hawthorn A.E.C. Hawthorn Comprehensive School; Tel (01443) 841251; Mrs J. Farr
Heolddu Leisure Centre Heolddu Comprehensive School; Tel (01443) 832443; J.M. Gourley
Maesteg A.E.C. Maesteg Lower Comprehensive School; Tel (01656) 733253; C.B. Rees
Mountain Ash A.E.C. Mountain Ash Upper Comprehensive School; Tel (01443) 473412; Mrs J.L. Morgan
Pencoed A.E.C. Pencoed Comprehensive School; Tel (01656) 860799; J. Webster
Pontypridd A.E.C. Coedylan Lower Comprehensive School; Tel (01443) 402744; Mrs M. Morgan
Porth Community Education Centre Porth Comprehensive School; Tel (01443) 682701; Mrs E. Davies
Porthcawl A.E.C. Porthcawl Comprehensive School; Tel (0165 671) 2300; Mrs G.H. Carlson
Rhondda A.E.C. Rhondda College of Education; Tel (01443) 437722; E. Howells
Rhymney A.E.C. Rhymney Comprehensive School; Tel (01685) 842840; J.A. Williams
Tonyrefail Community Education Centre Tonyrefail Comprehensive School; Tel (01443) 670647; C.G. Lewis
Treorchy Community Education Centre Treorchy Comprehensive School; Tel (01443) 773763; R. Jones

Teachers' Centres

Cynon Valley Resources Centre Old Aberaman Infants School, Gladstone St, Aberaman, Aberdare CF44 6SA; Tel (01685) 884405; G. Jones
Merthyr Tydfil Teachers' Centre Ynysfach Est, Merthyr Tydfil CF48 1AD; Tel (01685) 723617; K. Davies
Ogwr Teachers' Centre Park St, Bridgend CF31 4AZ; Tel (01656) 652634; Miss E. Godwin
Rhondda Educational Centre Porth Resources Centre, Grawen St, Porth CF39 0AG; Tel (01443) 687666
Rhymney Valley Teachers' Centre Mill Rd, Caerphilly CF8 3FD; Tel 852541
Taff Ely Teachers' Centre The Broadway, Treforest, Pontypridd CF37 1BE; Tel (01443) 486848/9; M. Rees

Outdoor Pursuits Centres

Dolygaer Outdoor Education Centre Pontsticill, Merthyr Tydfil; Tel (01685) 721751; *Warden* C. Roberts
Ogmore Recreation Centre Ogmore-by-Sea, Bridgend CF32 0PW; Tel (01656) 880247; *Warden* J.G. Phillips

Newcastle upon Tyne City Council

Population 282,700

Civic Centre, Barras Bridge, Newcastle upon Tyne NE99 2BN; Tel 0191-232 8520; Fax 0191-232 3992

Education Offices

City Education Dept, Civic Centre, Barras Bridge, Newcastle upon Tyne NE1 8PU; Tel 0191-232 8520
Director of Education Nils Purser, BA(Hons)
Deputy Director of Education J.A. Ginnever, BSc, MEd
Principal Adviser Rosemary Morris, MA, BEd (Acting)
General Adviser (Primary Education) K. Wallace, TCert, BPhil, AdDip(CommEd)
General Adviser (Languages) D. Clegg, BA(Hons), PGCE
General Adviser (Music) L. Young, ATCL, ARCM, GRSM
General Adviser (Science) S. Duncan, BTech(Hons), CFPS
General Adviser (Special Needs) D.W. Bennett, AdvDipEd, MA
General Adviser (Humanities) N.C. Tonge, BA(Hons), MA
General Adviser (Mathematics) C. Noble-Nesbitt, BSc, BA(Hons), DipEd
General Adviser (English) M. Shirren
Head of Adult Education P. Flynn
Principal Careers Officer T. Welsh (Acting) College St; Tel 0191-232 9471
Principal Educational Psychologist K.A. Hibbert, BA, DipEdPsych
Chief Executive Officer G. N. Cook, LIB
Number of Schools
7 nursery; 51 nursery classes; 80 primary; 9 middle; 12 secondary; 10 special
School Population
37,549

Education Committee

Con 1, Lab 16, LD3
Chair A.G. Flynn, (Lab) 12 Dilston Terr, South Gosforth, Newcastle upon Tyne NE3 1XX
Vice-Chair D.J. Murphy, (Lab) 171 Biddleston Rd, Heaton, Newcastle upon Tyne NE6 5SP
Vice-Chair K. Taylor, (Lab) 4 Ingram Ave, Newcastle upon Tyne NE3 ZBR
Members of the Committee
Con: M.A. Summersby
Lab: A.G. Flynn, D.J. Murphy, K. Taylor, J. Angus, M.J. Carr, G.W. Douglas, G.A. Johnson, J.C. Kerrigan, S. Khan, J.M. Lamb, J. Marshall, J. O'Shea, R. Robson, R.W. Robson, C. Stephenson. Dr R.C. Woods
LD: C.E. Durose, G.F. Keating, J.W. Shipley

Governor Training Unit

Governor Information Development and Support, Education Department, Civic Centre, Newcastle upon Tyne NE1 8PU; Tel 0191-232 8520; Fax 0191-261 7934
Governor Training Co-ordinator Dr Carol M. Woodhouse, CertEd, BA(Hons), PHd
Services Offered
Training; Clerking service; Conferences; Newsletters; Governor information points; Telephone helpline; Governor forums

Careers Office

See chapter 17

Special Schools

Brunswick Beech Brunswick Village NE13 7DR; Tel 0191-236 2572; M.M. McKay
Castle Dene Freeman Rd, South Gosforth, NE3 1SZ; Fax 0191-284 2516/7; W. Lennox. (Mixed) (E.B.D.) (40)
Jesmond Dene House Jesmond Dene Rd NE2 2EY; Tel 0191-281 0124; R. Heard. (Residential) (Mixed) (35)
Kenton Lodge Kenton Rd, Kenton NE3 4PD; Tel 0191-285 5392; D. Tait. (Residential) (E.B.D.) (Mixed) (34)
Oakfield College Condercum Rd NE4 8XJ; Tel 0191-273 5558; D. Edmundson. (Mixed) (14–19) (upto 200)

Parkway Hillhead Parkway NE5 1DP; Tel 0191-267 4447; Mrs M. Bell
Pendower Hall Bertram Cres NE15 6PY; Tel 0191-273 4440/273 6965; N.O. Stromsoy. (Mixed) (P.H.) (with Res. Unit) (100)
St Peter's Freeman Rd, South Gosforth, Newcastle upon Tyne NE3 1SZ; Tel 0191-284 3533; D. Slater. (Mixed) (Primary) (90)
Walkerdene Westbourne Ave; Tel 0191-263 0261; J.C. Preston
Westlands Hillhead, Parkway NE5 1DS; Tel 0191-267 5435; P. Gilbert
Hospital Teaching Service Freeman Rd, Newcastle NE7 7DN; Tel 0191-284 3111; C.J. Harris

Middle Schools

Chapel Hse off Hillhead Parkway, West Denton NE5 1EL; Tel 0191-267 8367; J.W. Foster
Chapel Park Granville Dr, Chapel Pk NE5 1SH; Tel 0191-267 2931; T.A. Shell
Chevyside Yetholm Pl, Westerhope NE5 4EB; Tel 0191-286 0077; P. Burns
Denton Park Linhope Rd, Westerhope NE5 2NW; Tel 0191-267 1353; G. Sayer
Gosforth Central Great North Rd, Gosforth NE3 1UN; Tel 0191-285 1793; D.E. Darwin
Gosforth East Harewood Rd, Gosforth NE3 5JT; Tel 0191-285 5445; G.H. Oliver
Gosforth West Jubilee Rd, Gosforth NE3 1DY; Tel 0191-285 3060; P. Hugall
Lemington West Denton Rd, Lemington NE15 7LS; Tel 0191-267 6130; D. Hodson
Throckley Hexham Rd, Throckley NE15 9DY; Tel 0191-267 4467; K.B. Gilbert

High Schools

Gosforth Great North Rd, Gosforth, Newcastle upon Tyne NE3 2JH; Tel 0191-285 1000; K.E. Nancekievill. (1300)
Walbottle Walbottle, Newcastle upon Tyne NE15 9TP; Tel 0191-267 8221; G.K. Gulliver, BA. (1650)
West Denton Off West Denton Way, West Denton, Newcastle NE5 2SZ; Tel 0191-267 7036; J. Slater. (1250)

Comprehensive Schools

Benfield Benfield Rd NE6 4NU; Tel 0191-265 6091; R.A. Cardinal. (Mixed) (1500)
Blakelaw Firfield Rd NE5 3HU; Tel 0191-286 3211; J. Curd, BA(Hons), DipEd. (Mixed) (1005)
Heaton Manor Jesmond Pk West NE7 7DP; Tel 0191-281 8486; P. Illingworth, BA. (Mixed) (1740)
Kenton Drayton Rd NE3 3RU; Tel 0191-286 9001; M. Gibbons. (Mixed) (1620)
Westgate Community College, West Rd NE4 9LU; Tel 0191-273 7965; S.M. Clement/Jones. (Mixed) (1520)
Walker Middle St NE6 4BY; Tel 0191-262 0911/4; A. Broady. (Mixed) (1430)

Voluntary Comprehensive

St. Cuthbert's R.C. Benwell Hill NE15 7PX; Tel (0191) 2744510; E. Lovell, MLitt, MEd. (Boys) (1300)
St. Mary's R.C. Benton Park Rd NE7 7PE; Tel 0191-266 8813; D. O'Neill, MPhil, MRIC, Chem. (Mixed) (1300)
Sacred Heart R.C. Fenham Hall Dr NE4 9YH; Tel 0191-274 7373; J.O. Donnelly-Wood. (Girls) (1190)

Education Development Centre

Pendower Hall West Rd NE15 6PP; Tel 0191-274 3620; J. Brocker

Norfolk County Council

Population 769,400 (mid 1993)
County Hall, Martineau La, Norwich NR1 2DH; Tel (01603) 222222; Fax (01603) 222959

Education Department

County Hall, Martineau La, Norwich NR1 2DL; Tel (01603) 222146
County Education Officer M.H. Edwards, BA
Head of Education Personnel Services R.J. Philpott, BSc(Hons), MIPM
Head of Education Financial Services P.R. Fisher, IPFA
Chief Education Accountant D. Slade, BA, IPFA
Head of Technical and Contract Services J. Rhind
County Catering Manager G. Lloyd
Number of Schools
4 nursery; 402 primary and middle (58,637); 55 secondary (43,654);
Special Schools
12
Requisition Periods for School Supplies
Schools order direct from contractors and ESPO
Other Authorities with whom Joint Purchsing Arrangements are made
Member Authority of Eastern Shires Purchasing Organisation

Governor Training Unit

Norfolk Governor Support Unit, County INSET Centre, Witard Rd, Norwich NR7 9XD; Tel (01603) 702902; Fax (01603) 702106
Development Officer Pennie Walker, BA, PGCE
Services Offered
Full programme of training courses; In school training for individual governing bodies; Termly newsletter; Telephone helpline; Information service; Resource loans, books, videos, training packs

Special Schools

Alderman Jackson, Marsh La, Gaywood, Kings Lynn PE30 3AE; Tel (01553) 672779; S.K. Davies
Chapel Rd, Attleborough NR17 2DS; Tel (01953) 453116; P.A. Thomas, DipSpEd
Clare, South Park Ave, Norwich NR4 7AU; Tel (01603) 54199; C. Hocking, BSc
Eaton Hall, Pettus Rd, Norwich NR4 7BU; Tel (01603) 57480; S.T. Lord. (Boarding and Day) (Boys) (7–16) (43)
Edinburgh Rd, Holt NR25 6SL; Tel (01263) 713358; G. Measures
Ethel Tipple, Winston Churchill Dr, Fairstead Est, Kings Lynn PE30 4RP; Tel (01553) 763679; G.H. Scullard
Fred Nicholson, Westfield Rd, Dereham NR19 1JB; Tel (01362) 693915; E. Harvey, BA, DipTHC. (Boarding) (Mixed) (7–16) (98)
The Hall, St Faiths Rd, Old Calton, Norwich NR6 7AD; Tel (01603) 419428; M.J. Dalston (Acting)
Harford Manor, 43 Ipswich Rd, Norwich NR2 2LN; Tel (01603) 51809; D.M. Curl
John Grant, St George's Dr, Caister-on-Sea, Great Yarmouth NR31 0LJ; Tel (01493) 720158; G. Hampson. (Day) (Mixed) (4–19) (68)
Parkside, College Rd, Norwich NR2 3JA; Tel (01603) 52727; I.R. Naylor
Sidestrand Hall, Sidestrand, Cromer Rd, nr Cromer NR27 0NH; Tel (01263) 579336; J.H. Pearman
Child Study Centre Lowestoft Rd, Gorleston, Great Yarmouth NR31 6LZ; Tel (01493) 662923; J. Roberts
Westwood Tutorial Centre 111 Newmarket Rd, Norwich NR2 2HT; Tel (01603) 55531; K. Pomeroy

Secondary Schools (11/12–16)

Alderman Peel County High Market La, Wells-next-Sea NR23 1RB; Tel (01328) 710476; Fax (01328) 710767; D. Thorneycroft. (386)
Attleborough County High Norwich Rd NR17 2AJ; Tel (01953) 452335; Telex 456817; E. Hickling. (618)
Aylsham County High Sir Williams La NR11 6AN; Tel (01263) 733270; Fax (01263) 732918; A. Regan. (574)
Caister County High Windsor Rd, Caister-on-Sea NR30 5LS; Tel (01493) 720542; R.G. Bond. (630)
Dereham Northgate High Cemetery Rd, Dereham NR19 2EU; Tel (01362) 697033; Fax (01362) 698484; J.R. Spradbery. (974)
Framingham Earl County High Norwich Rd NR14 7QP; Tel (01508) 492547; Fax (01508) 493597; W.M. Down. (567)
Hethersett County High Queens Rd, Hethersett NR9 3DB; Tel (01603) 810924; Fax (01603) 812697; M. Chapman. (518)
Hoveton Broadland County High Tunstead Rd, Hoveton NR12 8QN; Tel (01603) 782715; Fax (01603) 784354; G.R. Scott, BA. (614)
Hunstanton Smithdon County High, Downs Rd PE36 5HY; Tel (01485) 534541; Fax (01485) 535251; D. Little. (900)
Litcham County High Church St PE32 2NS; Tel (01328) 701265; Fax (01328) 701850; C. Shaw. (425)
Loddon Hobart County High Kittens La NR14 6JU; Tel (01508) 520359; Fax (01508) 528024; D.L. Osborne. (477)
Long Stratton County High Manor Rd NR15 2XR; Tel (01508) 31244; Fax (01508) 31708; J.T. Chapman. (493)
Methwold County High Stoke Rd IP26 4PE; Tel (01366) 728333; Fax (01366) 728905; K.J. Earle. (630)
North Walsham County High Spenser Ave NR28 9HZ; Tel (01692) 402581; Fax (01692) 500643; K. Johnson. (871)
Old Buckenham County High Abbey Rd NR17 1RL; Tel (01953) 860766; Fax (01953) 860944; N.T.F. Newbury. (478)
Reepham County High Broomhill La, Reepham NR10 4QY; Tel (01603) 870328; Fax (01603) 870988; Dr D.P. Ainsworth, PhD, BSc. (602)
Stalham County High Brumstead Rd NR12 9DG; Tel (01692) 580281; Fax (01692) 581480; J. Chilvers. (473)
Taverham County High Beech Ave, Taverham NR8 6HP; Tel (01603) 860505; Fax (01603) 261525; G. Porter. (631)
Thetford Rosemary Musker, Croxton Rd, Thetford IP24 ILH; Tel (01842) 754875; Fax (01842) 765036; M.P. Brindle. (572)
Watton The Wayland County High, Merton Rd IP25 6BA; Tel (01953) 881514; Fax (01953) 885677; C. Dix. (691)

Secondary Schools (11/12–18)

Blyth Jex Comprehensive St Clement's Hill, Norwich NR3 4BX; Tel (01603) 411721; Fax (01603) 487575; P. Stiven. (1008)
Dereham Neatherd High Norwich Rd NR20 3AX; Tel (01362) 697981; Fax (01362) 698463; J.C. Horsfield. (649)
Diss County High Walcot Rd IP22 3DH; Tel (01379) 642424; Fax (01379) 642428; S.C. Ballantyne. (1004)
Earlham Comprehensive Earlham Rd, Norwich NR4 7NU; Tel (01603) 52628; Fax (01603) 507215; I.E. Daymond. (990)
Eaton Eaton Rd, Norwich NR4 6PP; Tel (01603) 54015; Fax (01603) 58196; Dr T.E. Elkins. Comprehensive (City of Norwich) (1191)
Fakenham County High Wells Rd, Fakenham NR21 9HP; Tel (01328) 862238; Fax (01328) 855337; F.C.L. Muston. (1406)
Gaywood Park County High Queen Mary Rd, King's Lynn PE30 4QG; Tel (01553) 774671; Fax (01553) 770740; C.J. Pearce. (1022)
Heartsease Comprehensive Marryat Rd, Norwich NR7 9DF; Tel (01603) 35178; Fax (01603) 701639; J. Norman, MA. (462)
Hellesdon County High Middleton's La, Hellesdon, Norwich NR6 5SB; Tel (01603) 424711; Fax (01603) 487602; G. Lloyd. (1023)
Hewett Comprehensive Cecil Rd, Norwich NR1 2PL; Tel (01603) 628181; C.E.H. Wade. (2068)
Oriel High Oriel Ave, Gorleston NR31 7JJ; Tel (01493) 662966; Fax (01493) 440715; J.R. Bennett. (570)
Springwood County High Queensway, King's Lynn PE30 4AP; Tel (01553) 773393; Fax (01553) 771405; M.W. Griffiths. (1117)
Sprowston County High Cannerby La, Sprowston, Norwich NR7 8NE; Tel (01603) 485266; Fax (01603) 426213; G. Best. (1405)
Swaffham Hamond's High Brandon Rd PE37 7DZ; Tel (01760) 721480; Fax (01760) 721269; R.L. Young. (767)
Thetford Charles Burrell High, Staniforth Rd, Thetford IP24 3LH; Tel (01842) 763981; Fax (01842) 766561; C.A.L. Wragg, BSc. (490)
Thorpe St Andrew County Laundry La, Thorpe St Andrew, Norwich NR7 0XS; Tel (01603) 37711; Fax (01603) 702107; Dr D.W. Bullard. (1443)
Wymondham County High Folly Rd NR18 0NT; Tel (01953) 602078; Fax (01953) 605518; D. Walker. (718)

Secondary Schools (Voluntary)

The Archbishop Sancroft C.E. High Wilderness La, Harleston IP20 9DD; Tel (01379) 852561; Fax (01379) 854174; F.C. Paice. (V.A.) (456)
King Edward VII High Gaywood Rd, King's Lynn PE30 2QB; Tel (01553) 773606; Fax (01553) 769386; M.J. Walker. (V.C.) (1211)
Notre Dame R.C. High Surrey St, Norwich NR1 3PB; Tel (01603) 611431; Fax (01603) 763381; Sister Mary Cluderay. (V.A.) (1154)

Middle Schools (8–12)

Angel Road Middle Angel Rd, Norwich NR3 3HS; Tel (01603) 425494; L. Holman. (304)
Avenue Middle Avenue Rd, Norwich NR2 3HP; Tel (01603) 620876; J.A. Zarins. (349)
Aylsham Middle Hungate St, Aylsham NR11 6JZ; Tel (01263) 733393; J.K. Elphick. (268)
Bignold Middle Wessex St, Norwich NR2 2SP; Tel (01603) 625721; D. Watkins. (231)
Blackdale Middle Bluebell Rd, Norwich NR4 7LN; Tel (01603) 52196; M.D. Long. (307)
Bradwell Woodlands Middle, Church Walk, Bradwell, Gt Yarmouth NR31 8QQ; Tel (01493) 665314; D. Batley. (409)
Caister-on-Sea Middle Kingston Ave, Caister-on-Sea NR30 5ET; Tel (01493) 728223; K.J. Forsyth. (369)
Catton Grove Middle Middleton Cl, Norwich NR3 3QE; Tel (01603) 426728; R. Atkins (Acting). (321)
Cliff Park Middle Orde Ave, Gorleston, Gt Yarmouth NR31 6SZ; Tel (01493) 663612; J.G. Poulter. (478)
Colman Middle South Park Ave, Norwich NR4 7AU; Tel (01603) 54201; A. Genge. (220)
Dereham Toftwood Middle Westfield Rd, Dereham NR19 1JB; Tel (01362) 694919; D.F. Appleby. (196)
Edward Worlledge Middle Suffolk Rd, Gt Yarmouth NR31 0ER; Tel (01493) 603462; J.R. Nickerson. (206)
Fairway Middle Purtingay Cl, Norwich NR4 6HU; Tel (01603) 502454; D. Gowans. (160)
George White Middle Silver Rd, Norwich NR3 4RG; Tel (01603) 425515; J.E.A. Payne. (264)
Greenacre First and Middle Dickens Ave, Gt Yarmouth NR30 3DT; Tel (01493) 855304; K.H. Nicholls. (456)
Heartsease Middle Rider Haggard Rd, Norwich NR7 9UE; Tel (01603) 34576; J. Wilkinson. (244)
Hellesdon Firside Middle, Middletons La, Hellesdon, Norwich NR6 5NF; Tel (01606) 426550; C. Holmes. (257)
Hellesdon Kinsale Avenue Middle, Kinsale Ave, Hellesdon, Norwich NR6 5SG; Tel (01606) 425662; M.F. Pond. (244)
Herman Middle Oriel Ave, Gorleston, Gt Yarmouth NR31 7JL; Tel (01493) 661355; S.E. Freeman. (212)

Lakenham Middle City Rd, Norwich NR1 2HL; Tel (01603) 627399; Fax (01603) 762363; L. Taylor. (178)
Larkman Middle Clarkson Rd, Norwich NR5 8ED; Tel (01603) 52817; D.J. Adams. (183)
Mattishall Middle Dereham Rd, Mattishall NR20 3AA; Tel (01362) 858451; F.P. Brown. (179)
Mile Cross Middle Valpy Ave, Norwich NR3 2EY; Tel (01603) 425186; Fax (01603) 787035; P.R. Keen. (333)
Mill View Middle Gentry Pl, Norwich NR5 8XZ; Tel (01603) 742969; C. Spinks. (199)
Mulbarton Middle The Common, Mulbarton NR14 8JG; Tel (01508) 78242; B. Chatten. (268)
North Denes Middle Jellicoe Rd, Gt Yarmouth NR30 4HF; Tel (01493) 842063; P.J. Unsworth. (287)
Ormesby Middle North Rd, Ormesby, Gt Yarmouth NR29 3LA; Tel (01493) 730944; A. George. (252)
Peterhouse Middle Magdalen Sq, Gorleston, Gt Yarmouth NR31 7BY; Tel (01493) 661046; Fax (01493) 656832; D. Freear. (226)
South Harford Middle Locksley Rd, Norwich NR4 6LG; Tel (01603) 51903; A. Parsons. (236)
Spixworth Woodland View Middle Ivy Rd, Spixworth, Norwich NR10 3PY; Tel (01603) 898292; L. Towle. (238)
Sprowston Falcon Middle Falcon Rd West, Sprowston, Norwich NR7 8NT; Tel (01603) 429743; A. Waller. (346)
Sprowston Middle Recreation Ground Rd, Sprowston, Norwich NR7 8EW; Tel (01603) 425150; D. Watkins. (236)
Sprowston White Woman Lane Middle White Woman La, Sprowston, Norwich NR6 7JA; Tel (01603) 419203; D.J. Cossey. (293)
Stalham Middle Yarmouth Rd, Stalham NR12 9PS; Tel (01692) 580053; Fax (01692) 582027; J.P. Scott. (513)
Thetford Abbey Farm Middle, Canterbury Way, Thetford IP24 1EB; Tel (01842) 753327; D. Cragoe. (166)
Thetford Admiral's Middle Admiral's Way, Thetford IP24 2JT; Tel (01842) 753993; Fax (01842) 753993; M.K. Dixon. (334)
Thetford Queensway Middle Hillary Rd, Thetford IP24 3DP; Tel (01842) 752387; Fax (01842) 754032; R. Hedley. (194)
Thorpe Hamlet Middle Wolfe Rd, Norwich NR1 4HT; Tel (0603)33014; F. Press. (278)
Wensum Middle Waterworks Rd, Norwich NR2 4DF; Tel (01603) 620877; S. Fisher. (189)
West Earlham Middle Scarnell Rd, Norwich NR5 8HT; Tel (01603) 54569; L. Peloe. (227)
Wroughton Middle Burgh Rd, Gorleston, Gt Yarmouth NR31 8BD; Tel (01493) 662756; Fax (01493) 442917; D.R. Osborne. (408)

Middle Schools (Voluntary)

Belton Breydon Middle, Moorland Way, Belton, Gt Yarmouth NR31 9PA; Tel (01493) 780007; I. Stone. (V.C.) (310)
Bowthorpe St Michaels Middle Chapel Break, Astley Rd, Norwich NR5 9LA; Tel (01603) 745812; K. Lilley. (V.A.) (318)
Dereham Middle, Littlefields, Dereham NR19 1BG; Tel (01362) 693876; A. Milbourne. (V.A.) (420)
Hethersett Middle Queens Rd, Hethersett NR9 3DB; Tel (01603) 810498; Fax (01603) 812423; T.P. Atkins. (V.C.) (250)
Horsford All Saints Middle Mill La, Horsford NR10 3ES; Tel (01603) 897938; Fax (01603) 891779; S.E.G. Slack. (V.C.) (221)
Long Stratton St Mary's Middle, Swan La, Long Stratton NR15 2XN; Tel (01508) 30459; Fax (01508) 32494; A.H. Blake. (V.C.) (353)
Necton Middle School Rd, Necton, Swaffham PE37 8HT; Tel (01760) 22975; J. Potter (Acting). (V.C.) (118)
Old Catton Middle Church St, Old Catton, Norwich NR6 7DS; Tel (01603) 426973; Fax (01603) 424029; R. Jackson. (V.C.) (189)
St Nicholas Middle Priory Plain, Gt Yarmouth NR30 1NJ; Tel (01493) 843552; J.A. Handford. (V.C.) (282)
St Thomas More R.C. Middle Jessop Rd, Norwich NR2 3QB; Tel (01603) 52430; F. Burns. (V.A.) (348)
Swaffham South Greenhoe Middle, Brandon Rd, Swaffham PE37 7EA; Tel (01760) 721831; D. Rice. (V.C.) (349)
Taverham St Edmunds Middle Taverham Rd, Taverham NR8 6SX; Tel (01603) 867740; N. Beacock. (V.C.) (254)

Field Study Centres

Wells Field Study Centre Polka Rd, Wells, Norfolk NR23 1EF; Tel (01328) 710525; C.A. West
Holt Hall Kelling Rd, Holt NR25 7DU; Tel (01263) 713117; Fax (01263) 712396; G. Carrick

Teachers' Centres

Norwich 13 Ipswich Rd NR2 2LL; Tel (01603) 623262; P. Kirby
West Norfolk Teachers' Centre St Edmunds C Primary School, Kilhams Way, King's Lynn PE30 2HU; Tel (01553) 766872; J. Duffill

Outdoor Pursuits Centre

County Sailing Base Hunter's Yard, Ludham, Gt Yarmouth; Tel (01692) 678263; D. Holden

Grant Maintained Schools

Acle High South Walsham Rd, Gt Yamouth NR13 3ER; Tel (01493) 750431; H. Dillon. (472)
Cliff Park County High Kennedy Ave, Gorleston NR31 6TA; Tel (01493) 661504; Fax (01493) 440558; M. Evans. (707)
Costessey High School Middleton Cres, Norwich NR5 0PX; Tel (01603) 742310; Fax (01603) 741875; J. Mann. (780)
Cromer High Norwich Rd NR27 0EX; Tel (01263) 511433; B. King. (514)
Dersingham Middle Admiral's Dr, Dersingham, King's Lynn PE31 6LR; Tel (01485) 540308; R.A. Potts. (V.C.) (238)
Downham Market County High School Grant Maintained Bexwell Rd, Downham Market PE38 9LL; Tel (01366) 388717; Fax (01366) 382529; J. Ingram, BA, FRSA. (1368)
Flegg High Somerton Rd, Martham NR29 4QD; Tel (01493) 740349; Fax (01493) 740223; R.J. Fuller. (540)
Great Yarmouth High Salisbury Rd, Gt Yarmouth NR30 4LS; Tel (01493) 842061; Fax (01493) 332848; I.J. Pegg. (12–16) (650)
Hunstanton Redgate Middle, Collingwood Rd, Hunstanton PE36 5DY; Tel (01485) 533373; Fax (01485) 533126; Z.M. Kentzer. (165)
Lynn Grove Grant Maintained High School Lynn Gr, Gorleston NR31 8AP; Tel (01493) 661406; Fax (01493) 441368; J.P. Fox. (770)
Martham West Flegg Middle, Black St, Martham NR29 4PR; Tel (01493) 740071; R.B. Masterson. (437)
St Clement's High School, Terrington St Clements, Kings Lynn, Norfolk PE34 4LZ; Tel (01553) 828648; Fax (01553) 829320; R.W. Wealthall. (585)
Sheringham High School, Holt Rd NR26 8ND; Tel (01263) 822363; Fax (01263) 825907; N. Ware. (554)
West Walton Marshland High School, School Rd PE14 7HA; Tel (01945) 584146; Fax (01945) 581275; J.B. Bennett. (631)
Wymondham Robert Kett Middle, Hewitts La, Wymondham NR18 0LS; Tel (01953) 603405; Mrs P. Perkins. (400)
Wymondham College, Golf Links Rd, Wymondham, Norfolk NR18 9SZ; Tel (01953) 605566; Fax (01953) 603313; *Principal* J.D. Haden, MA, BPhil; *Chair of Governors* T.C. Eaton. (Mixed) (11–18) (930); (1134)

North Tyneside Metropolitan Borough Council

Population 191,748
14 Northumberland Sq, North Shields, Tyne and Wear NE30 1PZ; Tel 0191-257 5544
Executive Director Brian Drew
Executive Director John Foster
Executive Director Victor Gallant
Executive Director Chris Roberts
Executive Director David Wright

Education Services

Stephenson House, Stephenson St, North Shields, Tyne and Wear NE30 1QA; Tel 0191-257 5544; Fax 0191-296 2439
Chief Education Officer and Head of Education Services J.C. Benneworth, BSc, MEd
Manager (Operations and Resources) D. Nicholson
Education Officer (Governor and School Support) M.R. Alderson
Education Officer (Pupil Support) H. Eadington, BEd
Education Officer (Information and Strategic Planning) Dr N. Reed, BSc, MA(Ed), PhD
TVEI Project Co-ordinator Peter Parish
Senior Inspector Education Advice and Inspection Unit P. Jefferson, BA
Inspector (History/Geography/Modern Languages/RE and Environmental Education) A.F. Heinzman, BA, MEd
Inspector (Physical Education) A. Hamilton, BA, DPE
Inspector (Technology) P. Reynolds
Inspector (English) B. Jordan, BEd(Hons), MA
Inspector (Home Economics, Health & PSE) D. Greaves, B.Phil
Inspector (Art) J. Wells, BA
Inspector (Mathematics) Joan Bell, T.Cert, MADME Dip
Inspector (Music) R. Eaton, MA, FRCO, LRAM, ARCM
Inspector (Primary Education) Julia Bell, T.Cert, DipEd, MEd
Schools Mean Business (Partnership Director) and TVEI Extension Co-ordinator P.G. Parish, MA, MSc
Number of Schools
3 nursery; 58 primary (34) and first (24); 11 middle; 11 high; 5 special
Day of Committee Meeting
Monday four weeks prior to Council meetings

Education Committee

Con 6, Lab 13, LD 3
Chair J. Hunter 6 The Gr, Benton
Deputy-Chair I.G. Gordon 534 Station Rd North, Wallsend
Convenor C.B. Pickard 45 Deepdale Rd, North Shields
Members of the Committee
A.E. Alderson, M. Bell, K.A. Conroy, D.E. Corkey, T.C. Cruikshanks, B. Durham, A. Ferguson, J.M.A. Green, I. Gordon, G. Halliday, D.B. Hedgcock, M.M. Howe, N.J. Huscroft, B. Kane, R. Lackenby, Rev G.M. Lee, F. Lott, I. Macaulay, D. McGarr, H.L. Perks, R. Pinkney, P. Rountree, M. Spicer, R. Stringfellow

Careers Office

See chapter 17

Pupil Support Service

Minton La, North Shields NE29 6DQ; Tel (0191) 2582917/8
Principal Educational Psychologist M.E. Foulkes

Special Day Schools

Ashleigh, Charlotte St, North Shields NE30 1BP; Tel 0191-257 3646; S. Gibbon, MEd. (E.S.N.(S.)
The Glebe, Woodburn Dr, Whitley Bay NE26 3HW; Tel 0191-251 2230; L. Turner, BA. (E.S.N.)
Parkside, Mullen Rd, High Farm, Wallsend NE28 9HA; Tel 0191-262 3846; H.M. Jones, MA. (E.S.N.(S.)
Southlands, Beach Rd, Tynemouth, North Shields NE30 2QR; Tel 0191-257 0551; M. McCabe, BEd. (E.S.N.)
Woodlawn, Langley Ave, Whitley Bay NE25 9DF; Tel 0191-251 2516; N.V. Buckingham, MEd. (P.H. & Del.)

Middle Schools

Central Middle School St Peter's Rd, Wallsend NE28 7LQ; Tel (0191) 2625635; S.A. Hickson, BA
Hadrian Park Middle School Addington Dr, Wallsend NE28 9RT; Tel (0191) 2630916; J. McCalman, BSc
High Farm Middle School Rising Sun Cottages, Wallsend NE28 9JW; Tel (0191) 2624033; C. Kelly, BEd, ADB(Ed)
Killingworth Middle School West La, Killingworth, Newcastle upon Tyne NE12 0BH; Tel (0191) 2684430; I.S.P. Todd, BA
Marden Bridge Middle School Lovaine Ave, Whitley Bay NE25 8RW; Tel (0191) 2521956; A.J. Driver, BSc
Monkseaton Middle School Vernon Dr, Monkseaton, Whitley Bay NE25 8JN; Tel (0191) 2523148; A.E. Wilson, BEd
Shiremoor Middle School Earsdon Rd, Shiremoor, Newcastle upon Tyne NE27 0HJ; Tel (0191) 2533294; D. Currie
Valley Gardens Middle School Valley Gdns, Whitley Bay NE25 9AQ; Tel (0191) 2520411; A. Spencer, BPhil
Western Middle School Forrest Rd, Wallsend NE28 8PY; Tel (0191) 2624009; D.C. Brown, BEd
Westmoor Middle School West Moor, Newcastle upon Tyne NE12 0PT; Tel (0191) 2682898; A. Golightly
Langdale Community Middle School, Langdale Gdns, Wallsend; *Head Teacher* C. Stephenson, BA

County High Schools (11–16)

John Spence Community Preston North Rd, North Shields NE29 9PU; Tel (0191) 2585855; B. Davidson, BA. (Mixed) (708)
Marden Hartington Rd, North Shields NE30 3RZ; Tel (0191) 2574433; V. Bridges, BA. (Mixed) (813)
Norham Alnwick Ave, North Shields NE29 7BU; Tel (0191) 2576131; *Headteacher* L.H. Walton, BA, MEd. (Mixed) (518)

R.C. High School (11–18)

St Thomas More R.C. Lynn Rd, North Shields NE29 8LF; Tel (0191) 2572869; J.T. Marshall, BA. (Mixed) (833)

County High Schools (13–18)

Burnside Community High School Boyd Rd, Wallsend NE28 7AF; Tel (0191) 2624063; D.R. Loveday, BA, MEd. (Mixed) (789)
George Stephenson Community High School Southgate, Killingworth NE12 0SA; Tel (0191) 2682002; N.S. Palmer, BA. (Mixed) (799)
Monkseaton Seatonville Rd, Whitley Bay NE25 9EQ; Tel (0191) 2531325; Dr P. Kelley, BA. (Mixed) (692)
Seaton Burn Community Dudley La, Seaton Burn, Newcastle Upon Tyne NE13 6HB; Tel (0191) 2170505; S.J. Prandle, BA, MEd. (Mixed) (528)
Whitley Bay Deneholm, Whitley Bay NE25 9AS; Tel (0191) 2522323/14; D.M. Oliver, BA; A. Chedburn. (Mixed) (1047)
Willington Community High School Churchill St, Wallsend NE28 7TN; Tel (0191) 2624880; C. Halverson, BA. (Mixed) (606)

Community College (11–18)

Longbenton Community College Hailsham Ave, Longbenton, Newcastle upon Tyne NE12 8ER; Tel (0191) 2662536; J. Cockburn, JP, BSc, MEd. (Mixed) (758)

Adult Continuing Education Centres

Burnside Community High School, Boyd Rd, Wallsend NE28 7AF; Tel (0191) 262 4063
George Stephenson Community High School, Stephenson Centre, Killingworth, Newcastle upon Tyne NE12 0YB; Tel (0191) 268 1601
John Spence Community High School, Linskill Bldg, Linskill Terr, North Shields NE30 2ED; Tel (0191) 258 5707
Longbenton Community High School, Hailsham Ave, Longbenton, Newcastle upon Tyne NE12 8ER; Tel (0191) 2662536
Marden High School, Hartington Rd, North Shields NE30 3RZ; Tel (0191) 257 4433
Monkseaton Community High School, Seatonville Rd, Monkseaton, Whitley Bay NE25 9EQ; Tel (0191) 253 1325
Norham Community High School, Alnwick Avenue, North Shields NE29 7VU; Tel (0191) 257 6131
Seaton Burn Community High School, Dudley La, Seaton Burn, Newcastle upon Tyne NE13 6HB; Tel (0191) 217 0505
Whitley Bay High School, Deneholm, Whitley Bay NE25 9AS; Tel (0191) 253 2177; A. Coe
Willington Community High School, Churchill St, Wallsend NE28 7TN; Tel (0191) 2623497

Grant Maintained School

South Wellfield Middle School Kielder Rd, South Wellfield, Whitley Bay NE25 9QV; Tel (0191) 2529486; J.A. Redhead, BEd

North Yorkshire County Council

Population 720,900
County Hall, Northallerton DL7 8AD; Tel (01609) 780780; Fax (01609) 777951

Education Offices

County Hall, Northallerton DL7 8AE; Tel (01609) 780780; Fax (01609) 778611
County Education Officer F.F. Evans, MA, FRSA
Senior Assistant Director (Planning and Development) C. Welbourn, MA
Chief Adviser D.M. Settle, BSc
Assistant Director (Operations and Customer Services) K.H. Burton, MA
Assistant Director (Resources) G.C. Bateman, IPFA
AEO (14+) G.E.B. Jenkins, MA
Personnel Manager C.S. Parkin, BA, MIPM
AEO (Advisory Support) N.B.M. Price, BA
Head of Pupil Support Services and Principal Educational Psychologist A. Milburn, BSc
AEO (Building and Development) R.E. Allen, BA
AEO (Review and Development) C.A. Bird, BA, ALA
Budget Support Manager R. Jacobs, IPFA
AEO (Resources) A.W. Packer, MA, ACCA
IT Manager F.J. Gilchrist, BA
Principal Education Development Officer C.J. McGee (Acting), BA
AEO (Special Needs) G.B. Allgood, BSc
Client Services Manager (Catering) R. Nichols
Assistant Chief Adviser C. Edwards, BSc
Assistant Chief Adviser J.R. Manning, MA
Senior Adviser (Physical Education) Vacancy
Senior Adviser (Art) J. Bowden
Senior Adviser (Science) T.C. Wood, BSc, PhD
Senior Adviser (Modern Languages) R.P.N. Geoghegan, MA
Senior Adviser (History) M.C. Holyoak, MA
Senior Adviser (Primary) K. Hopwood, MA
Senior Adviser (Technology) G. Howard, BA
Senior Adviser (Religious Education) R. Lohan, MEd
Senior Adviser (Secondary) J. Brown, MEd
Senior Adviser (Information Technology) J. Owen, BSc
Senior Adviser (Music) D.N. Parkinson, GRSM, ARMCM
Senior Adviser (English and Drama) G.R. Phinn, MEd
Senior Adviser (Special Education) J. Jacques
Senior Adviser (Mathematics) P.T. Robbins
Senior Adviser (Assessment/Recording & Reporting) M.P. Viner, BA, MEd
Senior Adviser (Geography) R.J. Pike, BA
Adviser (Mathematics) Vacancy
Adviser (Primary) G. Lund
Adviser (Primary) A.M. Smith, BE, MEd
Senior Adviser (Primary) E.H. Walton, MA
Adviser (Secondary) M. Christian
Adviser (Primary) M. Britton
Adviser (English) P.S. Ellison, MA
Adviser (Science) P. Dawson
Adviser (Technology) M.W. Holroyde, BEd
Adviser (Primary IT) B.M. Ives, BA
Adviser (Humanities) Vacancy
Adviser (Primary) A. Smithers

Number of Schools
5 nursery; 392 primary; 59 secondary; 17 special

Day of Committee Meeting
Friday

Other Authorities with whom Joint Purchasing Arrangements are made
North Yorkshire is a member of Counties Furniture Group and the Yorkshire Purchasing Organisation

Education Committee

Members of the Committee
S.E. Braund, W. Brewis, K. Cooper DL, D.J. Dennis, J.M. Duggan, T. Fairhurst, J.V. Groves, M.D. Haigh, R. Hall, R.G. Heseltine, J. Hill, B. Hill, L.V. Hughes, T.K. Hull, Lt Col J.H. Jacob, J.M. Kenyon, D. Lloyd-Williams, J.M. Looker, A.K. McKenzie, P. Milner, J.P. Morley, T.A. Mould, M. Nicholson, M.F. Pitts, G.K. Rennie, F. Robson, C.M. Seymour, T.N.M. Stow, C.D. Swinglehurst, G.F. Webber, J.K. Weihell, C. Wilson

Governor Training Unit

Room 609, North Yorkshire County Council, Education Dept, County Hall, Northallerton, North Yorkshire DL7 8AE; Tel (01609) 780780 Ext 2816; Fax (01609) 778611
Part-time Training Officer (Governor Support) Julia Spittle, BA(Hons), Corporate Member Institute of Personnel Management
Clerical Assistant (Governor Support) Helen Bosomworth

Services Offered
A Governor Training Programme to groups and individual governing bodies; Governor resource materials for loan; A bi-monthly Governor Newsletter; Advice and support as required

AREA OFFICES

Harrogate/Craven

Area Education Office, 59 Grove Rd, Harrogate HG1 5ER; Tel (01423) 560511
Area Manager E.A. Jones
Water St, Skipton, N. Yorks BD23 1PD; Tel (01756) 792427

Comprehensive Schools (Mixed)

Boroughbridge High Wetherby Rd, Boroughbridge YO5 9JX; Tel (01423) 323540; G. Mitchell, MA, BSc. (600)
Harrogate Grammar Arthur's Ave HG2 0DZ; Tel (01423) 531127; K.S. McAleese, MA, FRSA. (1627)
Harrogate Granby High Avondale Rd, Harrogate HG1 4AR; Tel (01423) 564421; J. Edwards, BA. (784)
Ingleton Middle Ingleton, Carnforth, Lancashire LA6 3BU; Tel (015242) 41301; S.W. Marshall, BA. (173)
King James's King James's Rd, Knaresborough HG5 8EB; Tel 866061; J.R. Forster, MA, MEd. (1375)
Rossett High Green La, Harrogate HG2 9JP; Tel (01423) 564444; J. Whittle, MEd, BA. (1108)
St Aidan's C.E. High Oatlands Dr, Harrogate HG2 8JR; Tel (01423) 885814; D. Richards, BA. (1415)
St John Fisher R.C. High Hookstone Dr, Harrogate HG2 8PT; Tel (01423) 887254; T.T. Keelan, MEd, BA. (776)
Settle High Settle BD24 0AU; Tel (01729) 822451; Fax (01729) 823830; T.J. Wear, BSc. (459)
Settle Middle Settle BD24 0AU; Tel (01729) 823636; J.W. Mansley, MA, MEd. (262)
South Craven Holme La, Crosshills, Keighley BD20 7RL; Tel (01535) 632861; Fax (01535) 632859; J.M. Vickers. (1674)
Upper Nidderdale High Low Wath Rd, Pateley Bridge, Harrogate HG3 5HL; Tel (01423) 711246; N. Metcalfe, BSc. (321)

Secondary Modern Schools (Mixed)

Aireville Gargrave Rd, Skipton BD23 1UQ; Tel (01756) 792965/798151; D. Croll, BA. (514)
Ripon City Clotherholme Rd, Ripon HG4 2DF; Tel (01765) 604564; C.J.M. Newell, BA. (429)
Upper Wharfedale Wharfeside Ave, Threshfield, Grassington, Skipton BD23 5BS; Tel (01756) 752215; Fax (01756) 752363; R.J. Kennedy, BA. (256)

Secondary Grammar Schools

Ermysted's Grammar Gargrave Rd, Skipton BD23 1PL; Tel (01756) 792186; D.M. Buckroyd, MA. (Boys only) (534)
Ripon Grammar Clotherholme Rd, Ripon HG4 2DG; Tel (01765) 602647; A.M. Jones, BA. (Mixed) (623)
Skipton High Gargrave Rd, Skipton BD23 1QL; Tel (01756) 792115; Fax (01756) 701068; S.D.J. Chambers, BA. (Girls only) (566)

Northallerton Area

Area Education Office

1 Racecourse La Bldg, County Hall, Northallerton, N. Yorks DL7 8AE; Tel (01609) 780780; Fax (01609) 778611
Area Manager A.P. Terry, BA

Comprehensive Schools (Mixed)

Allertonshire, Brompton Rd, Northallerton DL6 1ED; Tel (01609) 772888; Fax (01609) 780517; J. Smith, MSc, BA. (933)
Bedale High, Fitzalan Rd, Bedale DL8 2EQ; Tel (01677) 422419; J.E. Critchlow, PhD, BA. (572)
Easingwold, York Rd, Easingwold YO6 3EF; Tel (01347) 821451; Fax (01347) 823301; P. Fletcher, BA, MEd. (1091)
Northallerton College, Grammar School La, Northallerton DL6 1DD; Tel (01609) 774559/774013; Fax (01609) 770265; J. Bell, MA. (787)
Richmond, Darlington Rd, Richmond DL10 7BQ; Tel (01748) 850111; Fax (01748) 850265; J.E. Jack, MA. (1243)
Risedale, Hipswell, Catterick Garrison, Richmond DL9 4BD; Tel (01748) 833501; C.A. Brown, MA. (552)
St Francis Xavier, Darlington Rd, Richmond DL10 7DA; Tel (01748) 823414; R.W. Sparks, BA. (298)
Stokesley, Station Rd, Stokesley TS9 5AL; Tel (01642) 710050/711310/710923; B.P. Owen. (1109)
Thirsk, Topcliffe Rd, Thirsk YO7 1RZ; Tel (01845) 522024; J.C. Lewis, BA. (908)
Wensleydale, Richmond Rd, Leyburn DL8 5HY; Tel (01969) 22244; J.W. Hopkins, BA. (450)

Scarborough/Ryedale

Valley Bridge Pde, Scarborough YO11 2PL; Tel (01723) 361376; Fax (01723) 501496
Area Manager P.L. Mellor, MA, MEd

Comprehensive Schools (Mixed)

Caedmon Airy Hill, Whitby YO21 1QA; Tel (01947) 602570; C.L. Cowell. (560)
Eskdale Stainsacre La, Whitby YO22 4HS; Tel (01947) 602856; D.W. Bradley, BEd. (433)
Filey Muston Rd, Filey YO14 0HG; Tel (01723) 512354; Fax (01723) 512165; V.K. Rees, BA. (502)
Graham Woodlands Dr, off Scalby Rd, Scarborough YO12 6QW; Tel (01723) 366451; Fax (01723) 364102; M. Bowers, BA. (923)
Lady Lumley's, Swainsea La, Pickering YO18 8NF; Tel (01751) 472846/473103; Fax (01751) 477259; N.D. Corner, BEd, BA, MSc. (797)
Malton, Middlecave Rd, Malton YO17 0NH; Tel (01653) 692828; D. Roberts, BA. (532)
Norton, Langton Rd, Norton, Malton YO17 9PT; Tel (01653) 693296; Fax (01653) 693338; P. Barton, BEd. (591)
Pindar Eastfield, Scarborough YO11 3LX; Tel (01723) 582194; Fax (01723) 583110; P. Acaster. (709)
Raincliffe Lady Edith's Dr, Newby, Scarborough YO12 5RL; Tel (01723) 366527/8; Fax (01723) 501580; M.J. Goode, MSc, BA. (732)
Ryedale Nawton, York YO6 5SL; Tel (01439) 71665/71637; G.R. Jenkinson, Ed. (337)
St Augustine's R.C. Sandybed La, off Stepney Hill, Scarborough YO12 5LH; Tel (01723) 363280; K.P. Bear, MA. (285)
Scalby Fieldstead Cres, Newby, Scarborough YO12 6TH; Tel (01723) 362301; Fax (01723) 369226; D.C. Pynn, MA. (965)
Whitby Community College Prospect Hill, Whitby YO21 1LA; Tel (01947) 602406/602750; Fax (01947) 821169; R.M. Totton, BA, MEd. (731)

York/Selby Area

60 Piccadilly, York YO1 1PW; Tel (01904) 628933
Area Manager J.S. Hollingsworth, LLB, MEd

Comprehensive Schools (Mixed)

All Saints' RC, Mill Mount La, York YO2 2BJ; Tel (01904) 647877; A. Elliott, BA, PhD. (984)
Archbishop Holgate's C.E., Hull Rd, York YO1 5HA; Tel (01904) 411341; J. Harris, BA, MPhil. (467)
Barlby High, York Rd, Barlby, Selby YO8 7JP; Tel (01757) 706161; F. Loftus, BA. (507)
Brayton High, Doncaster Rd, Selby YO8 9QS; Tel (01757) 707731; H. Porter, BA. (1048)
Burnholme Community College, Bad Bargain La, York YO3 OLW; Tel (01904) 415906/415885; P. Leech, BA. (467)
Canon Lee, Rawcliffe La, Clifton Without, York YO3 6NS; Tel (01904) 653227; A.A. Brewerton, PhD, BSc. (465)
Fulford, Fulfordgate, Heslington La, Fulford, York YO1 4LY; Tel (01904) 633300/629751; E.K. Hayton, MA. (961)

Holy Family R.C. High, Longhedge La, Carlton, Snaith, Goole DN14 9NS; Tel (01405) 860276; Fax (01405) 860311; P.A. O'Neill. (372)
Huntington, Huntington Rd, Huntington, York YO3 9PX; Tel (01904) 760167; K. Wragg, MA, DPhil. (1430)
Joseph Rowntree, Haxby Rd, New Earswick, York YO3 8BZ; Tel (01904) 768107; Fax (01904) 750458; G. Mills, BA. (1036)
Lowfield, Dijon Ave, Acomb, York YO2 3DD; Tel (01904) 791674; M. Foster, MA. (644)
Manor C.E., Low Poppleton La, York YO2 6BB; Tel (01904) 798722; R.P. Smith, BSc. (610)
Millthorpe, Nunthorpe Ave, York YO2 1PF; Tel (01904) 622736/652310; P. Whitcomb, BSc. (705)
Oaklands, Cornlands Rd, Acomb YO2 3DX; Tel (01904) 782727; Fax (01904) 788395; M.H. Burns, MA. (770)
Queen Anne, Queen Anne's Rd, York YO3 7AA; Tel (01904) 620959/620950; D. Lane, AdvDipEd. (425)
Selby High, Leeds Rd, Selby YO8 OHT; Tel (01757) 703327; Dr D.R. Squires, MSc. (797)
Sherburn High, Sherburn-in-Elmet, Leeds LS25 6AS; Tel (01977) 682442; Fax (01977) 682752; C. Peace, BSc. (797)
Tadcaster Grammar, Toulston, Tadcaster LS24 9NB; Tel (01937) 833466; D. Impey, BA. (1116)

Special Schools

Baliol, Sedbergh; Tel (01587) 20232/21015; R.F.M. Lindsay
Brompton Hall, Brompton by Sawdon, Scarborough; Tel (01723) 859121; J.D. Thorpe, ACP
Brooklands, Burnside Ave, Skipton; Tel (01756) 794028/791654; K. Shorrock, LCP
The Dales, Morton-on-Swale, Northallerton; Tel (01609) 772932; W.F. Rab
The Forest, Park La, Knaresborough; Tel (01423) 864583; S. Wootton
Fulford Cross School, York; Tel (01904) 653219; J. Lock, BA
Galtres School, Bad Bargain La, York YO3 0LW; Tel (01904) 415924; G. Gilmore, BSc, MA
Lidgett Grove, Wheatlands Grove, Acomb, York YO2 5NH; Tel (01904) 791437; R. Nicholls
Mowbray School, Masham Rd, Bedale; Tel (01677) 422446/422447; B.J. McArthur, BA, MEd
Netherside Hall, Grassington, Skipton; Tel (01756) 752324; D.R. Harrison, BA
Northfield, Beckfield La, York; Tel (01904) 791315/791761; W.J.W. Ford, MA
Springhead, Barry's La, Scarborough; Tel (01723) 367829; R. Buckle (Acting)
Springwater, High St, Starbeck, Harrogate; Tel (01423) 883214; G.M. Cook, MA
Welburn Hall, Kirkbymoorside; Tel (01751) 31218; J.V. Hall
The Woodlands, Woodlands Dr, Scarborough; Tel (01723) 373260; C.J. Webley, BA

Northamptonshire County Council

Population: 580,120
County Hall, Northampton NN1 1DN; Tel (01604) 236236; Fax (01604) 236223

Education and Libraries Department

Please note that the Department operates on a split site. The Director is based at the County Hall address and the Deputy Director is based at the John Dryden House address
PO Box No 149, County Hall, Guildhall Rd, Northampton NN1 1AU; Tel (01604) 236236; Fax (01604) 236188; Telex 312516
Director of Education and Libraries J.R. Atkinson, MA, DipEdPsyc, DMS; Tel (01604) 236252
Deputy Director of Education R.L. Pestell, MA, FRSA, FIMgt PO Box No 216, John Dryden Hse, 8–10 The Lakes, Northampton NN4 7DD; Tel (01604) 236218
Chief Education Inspector and Head of NIAS G. Gyte, BA
Assistant County Education Officer (Client Services Planning and Review) J. Fitzpatrick, MA
Assistant County Education Officer (Client Services Planning and Review) D. Johnstone, BA
SAEO (South and West) A.L. Wilkinson, BSc(Econ)
SAEO (Corby and Kettering) A.G. Wilkinson, BA, PGCE
SAEO (Northampton) P. Fair, MEd
SAEO (Wellingborough and East Northants) C.J. Weeden, MA
SAEO (Citizens Charter, Information and Services to Students) J.K. Roberts, MA, MBA
SAEO (Central Services and Public Relations) B.D. Carr, BA
SAEO (Personnel) N. Clegg, DMA, MIPM
Financial Controller Linda Charker, IPFA
Northamptonshire Inspection and Advisory Service
Senior Inspector (Post 16 Education) A. Broadbent, MA
Senior Inspector (Secondary Education) J. Beard, BA, BEd
Senior Inspector (Head of Monitoring and Evaluation) A. Kent, BSc
Senior Inspector (Head of Curriculum Service and Training) M. Lovett, BSc, ENG, ACGI
Senior Inspector (Marketing and Sales) T. Atkins, CEng, MIMechE
Senior Inspector (Primary and Middle Education) D.A. Hill, MEd, Adv, DipEd
Senior Inspector (Head of Inspection) R. Spencer, MA, CertEd
Senior Inspector (Head of Management Services) C. Green, MEd, BEd(Hons)
Senior Inspector (Head of Personnel Finance and Administration) K. Bartley, BA(Hons), PGCE
Senior Inspector (Special Education) B.N. Burnett, BA, CertEd
General Education Inspector (Primary and Early Years) S. Moxon
General Education Inspector (Primary and Early Years) L. Link, CertEd
General Education Inspector (Primary Education) I. Curtis
General Education Inspector (PE and Secondary Education) B. Billingsby
General Education Inspector (Mathematics and Middle Years) H. Scott
General Education Inspector (Curriculum Services and Training) S. Harrison, BSc
General Education Inspector (Secondary Education, Media Studies, English and Drama) A.B. Drane, CertEd
General Education Inspector (Music) D. Bray, BA(Hons), MA
General Education Inspector (Curriculum Services and Training) F. Turner, CertEd, DipMCE
General Education Inspector (Secondary, Personal and Social Education) D. Hill, Adv, DipEd, MEd
General Education Inspector (Secondary Education, Art and Design and Technology) P. Mason, BA
General Education Inspector (Primary Education and Induction) J. Burnham, MEd
General Education Inspector (Primary Education and Information Technology) (Marketing and Sales) M. Rumble, CertEd
General Inspector (Primary Education and Special Educational Needs) Brian Aldridge
General Education Inspector (Secondary Education, Religious Education and Humanities) C. Richards, BEd, CertEd, DPSE
General Education Inspector (Secondary Education and Humanities) (Personnel, Finance and Administration) N. Jackson, BEd, MPhil

General Education Inspector (Secondary Education and Expressive Arts) L.A. Gill, BMUS, ARCO
General Education Inspector (Secondary Education, GCSE/Assessment and Achievement) (Monitoring and Evaluation) M. Brice, BA, MSc, FCollp
General Education Inspector (Primary Education Management Services) M. Riley, MEd, DipEd
General Education Inspector (Special Educational Needs-Secondary) L. Lewis, MEd
General Education Inspector (Secondary Education and Foreign Languages) M.T. Gele
General Education Inspector (Secondary Education and TVEI) J.P. Featherstone, BA
Principal Continuing Education Officer (Adult Education and Leisure) C.R. Dobbs, MEd, DipFE; Tel (01604) 236319
Deputy Principal Youth Officer R. Beard, MEd, FITD, MBIM; Tel (01604) 236313
Head of Support Teaching and Psychology Services (STEPS) D.J. Lucas, BSc(Econ), DipEdPsych, DipYLO; Tel (01604) 236206
Principal Education Welfare Officer J. Sleet, CQSW; Tel (01604) 236203
Principal Careers Officer and Head of Careers Service N. Morris, DMA, DipVG; Tel (01604) 236318
Assistant Principal Careers Officer C. Eagle, DipEd, DipCG; Tel (01604) 236285
Assistant Principal Careers Officer P. Hook, BSc(Hons), DipCG; Tel (01604) 236286
Assistant Principal Careers Officer D. Larmour, BSc(Hons), DipVG Careers Office, St Mary's Rd, Kettering, Northants NN15 7AH; Tel (01536) 513862

Number of Schools
8 nursery (720); 33 nursery units (2,280); 260 primary (46,462); 51 secondary including middle (36,005); 6 Professional Development Centres; 13 Special Schools (1,090)

Day of Committee Meeting
Quarterly, Wednesday

Other Authorities with whom Joint Purchasing Arrangements are made
None

Education and Libraries Committee

Con 10, Lab 15, LD 1
Chair M.A. Young, (Lab) 70 Colwyn Rd, Northampton NN1 3PX
Deputy Chair C. Kalyan, (Lab) 71 Euston Rd, Far Cotton, Northampton NN4 9DX
Deputy Chair M.E. Sneath, (Lab) 35 Weavers Rd, Wellingborough

Members of the Committee
Con: M.J. Bull, R. Cook, B.A. Graves, K.D. Harrington, T.D.R. James, R.J. Middleton, P.J. Mitford-Barberton, J.E. Saxby, P. Higson Smith, K. Ward
Lab: M.A. Young, M.E. Sneath, C. Kalyon, T.A. Atkins, N. Birch, M.G. Boss, W.J.E. Coventon JP, A. Gordon, S.E. Hagen, W.A. Latta, J.J. McIntyre, J.D. Morgan, J.W. Robinson, M.P. Towl, Dr P. Wix
LD: J.B. Cramp

DIVISIONAL YOUTH OFFICES

Northampton Division

The Cottage Youth Centre, Lodge Farm, Rickyard Rd, The Arbours, Northampton NN3 3QZ; Tel (01604) 787022; Fax (01604) 787045
Divisional Youth Officer R. Tims, MA Grad

Northern Division

Divisional Youth Office, The Wm Knibb Centre, Montagu St, Kettering, Northants NN16 8AE; Tel (01536) 523286; Fax (01536) 524524
Divisional Youth Officer C. Taylor
Deputy Divisional Youth Officer S.V. London

Area Office

The Connaughty Centre, Cottingham Rd, Corby NN17 1SY; Tel (01536) 65169
Rushden, Youth Centre, Moor Rd, Rushden NN10 9TP; Tel (01933) 314077
Desborough Youth Centre, Paddock La, Desborough, Kettering NN14 6LZ; Tel (01536) 761286
Thrapston Youth Club, King John Market Rd, Thrapston, Kettering NN14 4JU

Southern Division

St John's Centre, Tiffield, Towcester, Northants NN12 8AA; Tel (01604) 859380
Division Youth Officer G. Sherwood
Deputy Divisional Youth Officer A. Barrow, BEd

Area Office

Brackley Youth Centre, Manor Rd, Brackley, Northants NN13 6EE; Tel (01280) 703911
Brixworth Youth Centre, Church St, Brixworth, Northampton NN6 9BZ; Tel (01604) 880766
Woodford Halse Youth Club, High St, Woodford Halse, Daventry, Northants NN11 6RE

Hospital Education Service

Northampton District

General Hospital, Billing Rd, Northampton NN1 5BD; Tel (01604) 34700 Ext 4853; R.C. Lambert (at Fairfields School)

Kettering District

Schools with Designated Special Provision

Brackley, Southfields Primary School, Banbury Rd, Brackley NW13 6AU; Tel (01280) 702245; W.B. Stimpson. (Day) (Mixed) (5–11)
Daventry Falconers Hill Junior School, Ashby Rd, Daventry NN11 5QE; Tel (01327) 703132; C. Hughes-Rowlands, MEd. (Day) (Mixed) (7–11)
Falconers Hill CE Junior School Ashby Rd, Daventry NN11 5QE; Tel (01327) 702878; C. Hughes-Rowland, MEd
Headlands Lower School,. (Speech and Language Nursery Provision (3–5) (Provision for Severe Learning Difficulties) (3+) (Mixed Day)
Highfields Primary School, Highfield Rd, Kettering NN15 6HY; Tel (01536) 514622; *Headteacher* J.M. Soffe
Magdalen College School High St, Brackley NN13 5AE; Tel (01280) 703911; E. Wotherspoon
Nicholas Hawksmoor Primary School, Balmoral Cl, Towcester NN12 7JA; Tel (01327) 351466; R.F. Edwards, BEd. (Speech and Language Nursery Provision) (3–5)
Southbrook Infants School and Early Education Unit Hawke Rd, Southbrook Est, Daventry NN11 4LJ; Tel (01327) 703440; Mrs D.M. Ogilvie
Spring Lane Lower School Spring La, Northampton NN1 2JW; Tel (01604) 39114; D.J. McAlpine

Education Establishments for Pupils with Special Needs

Kettering District

Brookfield, Friar's Cl, Wellingborough NN8 2LA; Tel (01933) 222332; P. Norton (Acting Head). (Learning difficulties) (Day/Boarding (Mixed) (7–16) (105)
Eastfield Pk, Finedon Rd, Wellingborough NN8 4TF; Tel (01933) 226290; M.C. Richardson, MEd. (Learning difficulties) (Day) (Mixed) (2–11) (105)
Fairlawn School, Spring Gdns, Wellinborough NN8 2AA; Tel (01933) 225280; S. Cullingford-Agnew, DipEd. (Severe learning difficulties) (Day/Boarding) (Mixed) (2–16) (45)
Isebrook School, Eastleigh Rd, Kettering NN15 6PT; Tel (01536) 81606; K.J. McHenry. (Learning difficulties) (Day) (Mixed) (11–16) (74)

Kingsley School, Churchill Way, Kettering NN15 5DP; Tel (01536) 516946/516948; Fax (01536) 415755; J. Williams. (Physically handicapped) (Day) (Mixed) (3–11) (138)
Orchard School, Beatrice Rd, Kettering NN16 9QR; Tel (01536) 513726; V. Payne, BSc. (Behaviourable/emotional problems) (Day) (Mixed) (11–16) (45)
Wren Spinney School, Westover Rd, off Westhill Dr, Kettering NN16 0AP; Tel (01536) 81939; R. Rose, AdDipEd. (Severe learning difficulties) (Day) (Mixed) (3–19) (51)

Northampton District

Billing Brook School, Penistone Rd, Lumbertubs, Northampton NN3 4EZ; Tel (01604) 406329; D. Scott. (Learning Difficulties) (Day) (Mixed) (3–16) (143)
Fairfields School, Trinity Ave, Northampton NN2 6JN; Tel (01604) 714777; R.C. Lambert. (Physically handicapped) (Day) (Mixed) (3–11) (60)
Greenfields School, Harborough Rd, Northampton NN2 8LR; Tel (01604) 843657; J. Moralee. (Severe learning difficulties) (Day) (Mixed) (11–18) (60)
Highfield School, 273 Welford Rd, Northampton NN2 8PW; Tel (01604) 846018; B. Kettleborough. (Behaviourable/emotional difficulties) (Mixed) (5–11) (40)
Northgate School, Queen's Park Parade, Northampton NN2 6LR; Tel (01604) 714098; T. Clay, BEd. (Learning difficulties) (Day) (Mixed) (7–16) (120)
Raeburn School, Raeburn Rd, Northampton NN2 7EU; Tel (01604) 716505; P.D. Snook, BEd(Hons). (Behavioural/emotional problems) (Day) (Mixed) (11–16) (50)

Support Teaching and Educational Psychology Service

Head of Support Teaching and Psychology Service D.J. Lucas, BSc(Econ), DipEdPsych; Tel (01604) 236206
Daventry/South West Area Team, Spencer Centre, Lewis Rd, Northampton NN5 5BJ; Tel (01604) 587052; *Area Team Leader and Senior Educational Psychologist* J. Forrest, BA, MEd(Ed Psych)
Kettering/Corby Area Team William Knibb Cnt, Montagu St, Kettering, Northants NN16 8AE; *Area Team Leader and Senior Teacher* B. Lindop, MA; Tel (01536) 514244/82487; Fax (01536) 414809
Northampton Area Team Springfield Cliftonville, Northampton NN1 5BE; Tel (01604) 30082/32814; Fax (01604) 30283; *Area Team Leader and Senior Educational Psychologist* S. Thomson, BSc, MSc
Wellingborough and North East Area Team, Fairlawn Centre, Spring Grdns, Wellingborough NN8 2AA; Tel (01933) 440289; Fax (01933) 226744; *Area Team Leader and Senior Educational Psychologist* M. Liepins, MA, MEd(C Psych)

Secondary Schools (11–18)

Brackley Magdalen College High St, Brackley NN13 5AE; Tel (01280) 703911; Fax (01280) 704876; E. Wotherspoon. (1067)
Corby Beanfield Glastonbury Rd, Corby NN18 0NG; Tel (01536) 202982; M.A. Tuffin, DLC, BPhil. (529)
Daventry William Parker School Ashby Rd, Daventry NN11 5QE; Tel (01327) 705816; D.D. Johnson. (949)
Daventry Danetre School Hawke Rd, Southbrook Estate, Daventry NN11 4LJ; Tel (01327) 703345/71775; G.C. Rees, MA. 11–16 (995)
Kettering Latimer Castle Way, Barton Seagrave, Kettering NN15 6SW; Tel (01536) 724219; A.W. Matthias, MA. (839)
Northampton Trinity Upper Trinity Ave, Northampton NN2 6JW; Tel (01604) 713621; M.R. Hart, MA. (13–18) (594)
Northampton Weston Favell Upper Booth La South, Northampton NN3 3EZ; Tel (01604) 402121; Fax (01604) 410879; J.C.J. Howard, BD. (13–18) (1278)
Oundle Prince William Upper Herne Rd, Oundle, Peterborough PE8 4BS; Tel (01832) 272881; Fax (01832) 274942; *Personnel* C. Lowe, CBE, BA. (13–18) (901)
Roade School Stratford Rd, Roade, Northampton NN7 2LP; Tel (01604) 862125/6/7; I.C. Willison, BA. (1264)
Rothwell Montsaye Greening Rd, Rothwell, Kettering NN14 2BB; Tel (01536) 418844; Fax (01536) 418282; L.A. Dale, MA. (1037)
Rushden School The Hayway, Rushden NN10 9AD; Tel (01933) 50391; Fax (01933) 411689; C. Fields. (850)
Towcester Sponne Brackley Rd, Towcester NN12 7DJ; Tel (01327) 50284; I. Brown, BSc, MEd. (1089)
Wellingborough John Lea Doddington Rd, Wellingborough NN8 2NJ; Tel (01933) 223180; A.J. Blow, BEd. (392)
Wollaston Irchester Rd, Wollaston, Wellingborough NN9 7PH; Tel (01933) 663501; J. Houlford, BA. (1095)

Secondary Schools (Voluntary)

Corby Our Lady and Pope John XXIII R.C. School Tower Hill Rd, Corby NN18 0TF; Tel (01536) 741832; Fax (01536) 741013; J.E. Platt, BA. (VA) (594)
Northampton Thomas Becket R.C. Upper Kettering Rd North, Northampton NN3 6JF; Tel (01604) 493211/4; J.C. Shoreland, BA, DipEd. (VA) (882)

Middle Schools (9–13)

Northampton Abington Vale Middle Bridgewater Dr, Northampton NN3 3AG; Tel (01604) 37056; A.D.K. Johnston, BEd. (587)
Northampton Bective Middle Whiston Rd, Northampton NN2 7RR; Tel (01604) 715246; P.J. Letts. (271)
Northampton Blackthorn Middle Great Billing Way, Blackthorn, Northampton NN3 4PT; Tel (01604) 402634; M.R. Pead, MEd, MSc. (351)
Northampton Boothville Middle Esher Ct, Paxton Rd, Northampton NN3 3RG; Tel (01604) 406746; N.F.D. Underwood, DipEd. (490)
Northampton Cherry Orchard Middle Birchfield Rd East, Northampton NN3 2TA; Tel (01604) 401241; A.R. Taylor, BEd. (510)
Northampton Cliftonville Middle Cliftonville Rd, Northampton NN1 5BW; Tel (01604) 34984; R.J. Turner, BEd. (220)
Northampton Delapre Middle Rothersthorpe Rd, Far Cotton, Northampton NN4 9SA; Tel (01604) 761456; R. Buntine, BA(Hons). (493)
Northampton Ecton Brook Middle Ecton Brook Rd, Ecton Brook, Northampton NN3 5DY; Tel (01604) 407171; Fax (01604) 786585; R.M. James, BA. (385)
Northampton Goldings Middle Crestwood Rd, Lings Way, Northampton NN3 4JJ; Tel (01604) 647803; S.M. Pearson, BEd. (436)
Northampton Kingsthorpe Middle Northfield Way, Welford Rd, Northampton NN2 8AP; Tel (01604) 842185; N.M. Bramwell, BEd. (512)
Northampton Mereway Middle Mereway, Northampton NN4 9BU; Tel (01604) 702620; Fax (01604) 701668; A. Andres, DipEd. (395)
Northampton Parklands Middle Devon Way, Spinney Hill, Northampton NN3 1DX; Tel (01604) 647119 and 647110; N.L. Smith. (444)
Northampton Ryelands Middle Prestbury Rd, New Duston, Northampton NN5 6XP; Tel (01604) 755125/6; M. Hooper. (445)
Northampton St George's Middle Barrack Rd, Northampton NN1 3RF; Tel (01604) 38855; B. Briggs. (200)
Northampton Spencer Middle Lewis Rd, Northampton NN5 7BJ; Tel (01604) 587778; P. Gillett, BA. (279)
Oundle and Kings Cliffe Middle School Cotterstock Rd, Oundle, Peterborough PE8 5HA; Tel (01832) 272256/273993; Fax (01832) 274348; G. Bate, MSc, DipEd. (623)

Middle Schools (Voluntary 9–13)

Northampton All Saints C.E. Middle Boughton Green Rd, Northampton NN2 7AJ; Tel (01604) 715658; H. Gompertz. (V.A.) (334)

Northampton Emmanuel Church Middle Billing Brook Rd, Lings, Northampton NN3 4NH; Tel (01604) 408033; Fax (01604) 412190; M.C. Bray, JP, BA. (V.A.) (308)
Northampton St David's R.C. Middle Harborough Rd, Northampton NN2 7BB; Tel (01604) 716875; L. Bell, BPhil(Ed), DipEd. (V.A.) (319)
Northampton St Mary's R.C. Middle Grange Rd, Northampton NN3 2AX; Tel (01604) 403838; M.P. Lavelle. (V.A.) (419)

Maintained Youth Centres

Bective Youth Centre Bective Middle School, Whiston Rd, Northampton NN2 7RR; Tel (01604) 712924
Brackley Youth Centre Manor Rd, Brackley NN13 6EE; Tel (01280) 703911
Brixworth Centre Church St, Brixworth, Northampton NN6 9BZ; Tel (01604) 880766
Corby Youth Centre, Connaughty Centre, Cottingham Rd, Corby, Northants NN17 1SY; Tel (01536) 65159
Desborough Youth Centre Paddock La, Desborough NN14 6LZ; Tel (01536) 761286
Duston Folk Centre Duston Upper School, Berrywood Rd, Northampton NN5 6XA; Tel (01604) 751303
Kingsthorpe Upper School Youth Club, Boughton Green Rd, Northampton NN2 7AF; Tel (01604) 711953
Lings Upper School Youth Office, Billing Brook Rd, Northampton NN3 4NH; Tel (01604) 412743
Mereway Upper School Youth Club, Mereway, Northampton NN4 9BU; Tel (01604) 706244
Northampton College Youth Wing, St Gregory's Rd, Booth La South, Northampton NN3 3RF; Tel (01604) 403322
Rushden Youth Centre Moor Rd, Rushden NN10 9TP; Tel (01933) 314077
The Farm Youth Centre Rickyard Rd, The Arbours, Northampton NN3 3QZ; Tel (01604) 405253
Thrapston Youth Club King John School, Market Rd, Thrapston, Kettering NN14 4JU
Wellingborough Youth Centre Rock St, Wellingborough NN8 4LW; Tel (01933) 222095
Woodford Halse Youth Centre High St, Woodford Halse, Daventry NN11 6RE

Youth Service – Training Research and Development

Youth Service/Duke of Edinburgh's Award Scheme Youth Service Office, Grendon Hall, Grendon NN7 1JW; Tel (01933) 663318; *Youth Service/Duke of Edingburgh's Award Scheme Officer* B.F. Ludford-Thomas

Adult Education Service

Principal Adult Education Officer C.R. Dobbs Education and Libraries Department, Northampton Hse, Northampton NN1 2HX; Tel (01604) 236319
Senior Planning and Development Assistant Dr D.R. Wilson, BA, PhD Russell Hse, Rickyard Rd, Northampton NN3 3QZ; Tel (01604) 410236

Adult Education Provision in Towns Other Than Northampton

Daventry Tertiary College Badby Rd, Daventry NN11 4HT; Tel (01327) 300232; C. Harris
Moulton College West St, Moulton, Northampton NN3 7PR; Tel (01604) 491131
Tresham Institute of Further and Higher Education Church St, Wellingborough NN8 4PD; Tel (01933) 224165/22591; D. Wedlake, BA, MEd
Tresham Institute of Further and Higher Education George St, Corby NN17 1QA; Tel (01536) 402252; R. Elias, MEd, CertEd

Adult Education Establishments

Knuston Hall Irchester, Wellingborough NN9 7EU; Tel (01933) 318779; *East Northamptonshire Area Principal* L. Murphy, MA
Open Campus, Northampton College Military Rd, Northampton NN1 3ET; Tel (01604) 734567; *Northampton Area Principal* R. Starkey
The Old Courthouse Watling St, Towcester NN12 7DE; Tel (01327) 359993; *South Northamptonshire Area Principal* W. Nicholson, MA
Brixworth Centre Church St, Brixworth, Northants NN6 9BZ; Tel (01604) 882337; *Uplands (North West Area) Principal* J. Theairs, MA

County Co-ordinators

Adult Basic Skills Co-ordinator S.L. Henderson, MEd Russell Hse, Rickyard Rd, Northampton NN3 3QZ; Tel (01604) 410236
English for Speakers of Other Languages Co-ordinator Z. Ishmail-Bibby Open Campus, Northampton College, Military Road Centre, Military Rd, Northampton NN1 3ET; Tel (01604) 734172
Knuston Hall and Adult Residential College and Training Centre, Knuston Hall, Wellingborough NN9 7EU; Tel (01933) 312104; *Principal* J. Herrick, MEd, BA

Professional Development Centres

Brackley Professional Development Centre 56 Manor Rd, Brackley NN13 6EE; Tel (01280) 702192; D.B. Turner, BEd(Hons), MA
Corby Professional Development Centre Firdale, Cottingham Rd, Corby NN17 1TD; Tel (01536) 266833; Fax (01536) 203642; Antoinette Tuthill
Daventry Professional Development Centre Daventry Tertiary College, Badby Rd West, Daventry NN11 4HJ; Tel (01327) 705418; Fax (01327) 312382; J. Follett, MSc(Ed), BA
Kettering Professional Development Centre William Knibb Centre, Montagu St, Kettering, Northants N15 8AE; Tel (01536) 410579; Fax (01536) 414530; E. Warren, BA
Northampton Professional Development Centre Barry Rd, Northampton NN1 5JS; Tel (01604) 30815; Fax (01604) 22547; A. Raddan, BEd(Hons)
Wellingborough Professional Development Centre 86 Stanley Rd, Wellingborough NN8 1EA; Tel (01933) 225104; Fax (01933) 223925; E. Carr, BA

Units for Hearing Impaired Children

Kettering
Kettering Avondale Infant School, Laburnum Cres, Kettering NN16 9PH; Tel (01536) 512040; H. Cash, Ad, DipEd
Kettering Avondale Junior School, Laburnum Cres, Kettering NN16 9PH; Tel (01536) 513021; C.H. Jervis, BEd, ACP
Kettering Latimer School, Castle Way, Barton Seagrave, Kettering NN15 6SW; Tel (01536) 724219
Northampton
Cherry Orchard Middle, Birchfield Rd East, Northampton NN3 2TA; Tel (01604) 401241; Fax (01604) 787058; A.R. Taylor, BEd
Headlands Lower School Bushland Road, Northampton NN3 2NS; Tel (01604) 407098; G. Roy
St George's Middle School, Barrack Rd, Northampton NN1 3RF; Tel (01604) 38855; B. Briggs
Trinity School, Trinity Ave, Northampton NN2 6JW; Tel (01604) 713621; M.R. Hart, MA
Vernon Terrace Lower School, Vernon Terr, Northampton NN1 5HE; Tel (01604) 33894; M. Starkey, BEd(Hons)
Weston Favell Upper School, Booth La South, Northampton NN3 3EZ; Tel (01604) 402121; Fax (01604) 410879; J.C.J. Howard, BA

Outdoor Education Centre

The Court Hse Longtown, Hereford HR2 0LP; Tel (0187 387) 225; *Head of Centre* R. Burson

Grant Maintained Schools

Danesholme Junior School, Motala Cls, Corby, Northants NN18 9DT; Tel (01536) 741657

The King John Middle School, Market Rd, Thrapston, Kettering NN14 4JU; Tel (01832) 732266; *Headteacher* William T. Mills; *Chair of Governors* R. Steve Clifton. Mixed) (9–13) (284)
Kingsley Park GM Middle School, St George's Ave, Northampton NN2 6JA; Tel (01604) 792221; Fax (01604) 792221; *Headteacher* Colin Shore; *Chair of Governors* B.L. Dee. (Mixed) (9–13) (332)
The Kingswood School, Gainsborough Rd, Corby, Northants NN18 9NS; Tel (01536) 741857/742115; Fax (01536) 460138; *Headteacher* Brian Tyler; *Chair of Governors* Gordon Reynolds. (Mixed) (11–18) (950)
Lodge Park School, Shetland Way, Corby, Northants NN17 2JH; Tel (01536) 203817; N.J. Rumbolow
Manor School, Mountbatten Way, Raunds, Wellingborough, Northants NN9 6ND; Tel (01933) 623921
Montagu School, Weekley Glebe Rd, Kettering, Northants NN16 9NS; Tel (01536) 515644
Moulton Primary School, Church Hill, Moulton, Northants NN3 7SW; Tel (01604) 643061
Northampton School for Boys Billing Rd, Northampton NN1 5RT; Tel (01604) 230240; Fax (01604) 34636; *Headteacher* B. Liddington; *Chair of Governors* Y. Edwards. (Boys) (13–18) (1005)
Sir Christopher Hatton School, The Pyghtle, Wellingborough, Northants NN8 4RP; Tel (01933) 226077; Fax (01933) 271424
Southfield School for Girls Lewis Rd, Kettering, Northants NN15 6HE; Tel (01536) 513063; Fax (01536) 518487; *Headteacher* Mrs Jennifer Morris; *Chair of Governors* J. Dornan. Girls) (11–18 (700)
Weavers School, Weavers Rd, Wellingborough, Northants NN8 3JQ; Tel (01933) 222830
Wrenn School, London Rd, Wellingborough, Northants NN8 2DQ; Tel (01933) 222039

Northumberland County Council

Population 307,100 (mid 1991)
County Hall, Morpeth, Northumberland NE61 2EF; Tel (01670) 533000; Fax (01670) 533253

Education Department

County Hall, Morpeth NE61 2EF; Tel (01670) 533002; Fax (01670) 533750
Director of Education C.C. Tipple, MA
Divisional Director (Policy Review & Management Support Division) Dr K.L. Davies
Senior Education Officer (Policy Review and Management Support Division) C.W. Hurt
Education Officer (Policy Review and Management Support Division) M.J. Trimming
Divisional Director (Services Division) J.D. Haworth
Senior Education Officer (Services Division) D.M. Jenkins
Education Officer (Services Division) S. Smith
AEO (Services Division) F. Dobson
AEO (Services Division) D. Thunder
AEO (Services Division) S. Richard
Education Officer (PRMS) J.P. Clark
Education Officer (PRMS) D. Staples
Education Officer (PRMS) M.A. Tomkinson
Principal Adviser/Inspector D.F. Hume
Senior Adviser/Inspector (Staff Training and Developments and Wansbeck Area) G.L. Howell
Senior Adviser/Inspector (Western Area and First Schools) E.F. Sutton
Senior Adviser/Inspector (Northern Area and Music) A. Rushby
General Adviser/Inspector (Maths) R.S. Bishop
General Adviser/Inspector (Science) F.H. Sambell
General Adviser/Inspector (Technology and Health Education) H.M. Robson
General Adviser/Inspector (IT) M.R. Hall
General Adviser/Inspector (Vocationally Related Education) E. Armstrong
General Adviser/Inspector (Visual Arts) H.G. Thomas
General Adviser/Inspector (Special Needs) S. Pinner
General Adviser/Inspector (First Schools and Small Schools Project) H. Wood
General Adviser/Inspector (First Schools and Assessment) V. Cassell
General Adviser/Inspector (Youth and Community Education) L.M. Banks
General Adviser/Inspector (Technology) R. Taylor
General Adviser/Inspector (PE) B. Blake
General Adviser/Inspector (Outdoor and Environmental Education) P.W. Keighley
General Adviser/Inspector (English and Drama) C. Reeves
General Adviser/Inspector (Humanities and RE) M. Rockett
General Adviser/Inspector (Modern Foreign Languages) Vacancy
General Adviser/Inspector (First Schools) H. Urwin
AEO (Advisory Division) T.M. Richardson
Principal Educational Psychologist B.V. Daly
Senior Educational Psychologist R.L. Parker
Educational Psychologist J. Connelly
Educational Psychologist J.N. Caswell
Educational Psychologist R.M. Dorans
Educational Psychologist J.A. Kirton
Educational Psychologist A.C. Oliver
Educational Psychologist E. Riley
Educational Psychologist D. Lumsdon
Principal Careers Officer L.S. Weir 7/8 Sextant Hse, Freehold St, Blyth NE24 2BA; Tel (01670) 363239

Number of Schools and Further Educational Establishments
64 nursery; 144 first; 45 middle; 15 high; 2 teachers' centres; 3 field studies centres

Special Schools
9 special schools; 1 centre for hearing impaired children; 5 units for hearing impaired children; 3 units for communication disordered pupils

Day of Committee Meeting
Quarterly, Wednesday

Requisition Periods for School Supplies
None

Other Authorities with whom Joint Purchasing Arrangements are made
None

Education Committee

Lab 18, Con 6, LD 4, Ind 1
Chair J. Morris, (Lab) Wesley Cottage, Mile Rd, Widdrington, Morpeth, Northumberland NE61 5QW; Tel (01670) 790331
Vice-Chair T.E.C. Weekes 30 Chipchase Court, New Hartley, Whitley Bay, Tyne and Wear NE25 0SR; Tel Res: 0191-237 2587; Bus: 0191-222 6000 ext 8351

Members of the Committee
Lab: G.R. Arckless, E. Atkinson, W.C. Brown, Dr G.H. Fisher, I. Haves, R.M. Jacobson, I.A. McMinn, D.L. Nicholson, R. Parker, A.D. Patterson, T.R. Saunders, I.C.F. Swithenbank, J.E. Teasdale, B.M.S. Trobe, J. Whiteman, J. Wright
Con: R.L. Bentham, C.J. Darling, D. Jowett, A.W. Purdue, I.M. Smith, T.N. Thorne
LD: A. Davidson, A.M. Mearins, R.M. Nixon, C.J. Rickerby
Ind: B.A. Douglas

Governor Training Unit

PRMS Division, Education Department, County Hall, Morpeth, Northumberland NE61 2EF; Tel (01670) 533609; Fax (01670) 533750
EO (PRMS) David Staples, MA
Services Offered
Governor training; Team of Support Staff whose role includes giving day to day advice to Governing Bodies; Clerking Governing Body meetings

Careers Offices

See chapter 17

Education Welfare Centres

Services Division, Education Department County Hall, Morpeth, Northumberland NE6 2EF; Tel (01670) 533647; Fax (01670) 533750; *Principal Education Welfare Officer* M. Macdonald
Alnwick Education Welfare Office 34 Green Batt, Alnwick, Northumberland NE66 1TU
Blyth Education Welfare Office Wellington House, Wolsey Rd, Blyth NE24 1OD
Hexham Education Welfare Office The Gatehouse, Hexham County Middle School, Wanless La, Hexham NE46 1BU
Morpeth Education Welfare Office 94 Newgate Hse, Newgate St, Morpeth, Northumberland NE61 1BU

Psychological Services

Tyne House, Hepscott Park, Stannington, Morpeth NE61 6NF; Tel (01670) 534300; Fax (01670) 534327; *Principal Educational Psychologist* B.V. Daly

Special Schools

Barndale Hse School, Barndale Hse, Howling La, Alnwick NE66 1DQ; Tel (01655) 602541; J.P. Chappells, BA
Cleaswell Hill School, Guide Post, Choppington NE62 5DJ; Tel (01670) 823182; John C. Airey, MA
Cramlington Hillcrest School, East View Ave, East Farm, Cramlington NE23 9DY; Tel (01670) 713632; Fax (01670) 735695; Keith R. Sargeant, DAES. (Mixed) (10–16) (85)
East Hartford School, East Hartford, Cramlington NE23 9AR; Tel (01670) 713881; Ronald J. Hope, BEd
Gallowhill Hall Boarding School, Gallowhill Hall, Whalton, Morpeth NE61 3TU; Tel (01661) 881662; Fax (01661) 881857; D. Thompson, DipEd, FTC
The Grove School, Grove Gdns, Tweedmouth, Berwick upon Tweed TD15 2EN; Tel (01289) 306390; E.E. Brown. (Mixed) (5–16) (E.S.N.(S) (30)
Hexham Hackwood Pk, Gallows Bank, Hexham NE46 1AU; Tel (01434) 604039; J. Wells
Hexham Priory School, Dene Pk, Hexham NE46 1HN; Tel (01434) 605021; Vacancy
Morpeth Collingwood School, Stobhillgate, Morpeth NE61 1QF; Tel (01670) 516374; C. Hetherington

Units for Communication Disordered Pupils

Hexham East County First School, Beaufront Ave, Hexham NE46 1JD; Tel (01434) 603467
Morpeth Abbeyfields County First School, Abbots Way, Morpeth NE61 2LZ; Tel (01670) 513582
Morpeth Collingwood School, Stobhillgate, Morpeth NE61 1QF; Tel (01670) 516374

Centres and Units for Hearing Impaired Children

Belford County Middle School, Belford NE70 7NX; Tel (01668) 213361
Blyth Horton Grange First School, Kitty Brewster, Blyth NE24 4RE; Tel (01670) 353653; Vacancy
Cramlington County High School, Highburn, Cramlington NE23 6BN; Tel (01670) 712311
Cramlington Southlands County Middle School, Westloch Rd, Southfield Lea, Cramlington NE23 6LW; Tel (01670) 714475

High Schools (County 13+)

Alnwick, The Duchess's County, Howling La, Alnwick NE66 1DH; Tel (01665) 602166; Fax (01655) 510602; R. Todd, BA, MEd
Ashington County Green La, Ashington NE63 8DH; Tel (01670) 812166; Fax (01670) 855377; M.B. Brett
Bedlingtonshire County Palace Rd, Bedlington NE22 7DS; Tel (01670) 822625; Fax (01670) 829378; D.W. Pallett, MA
Berwick-upon-Tweed County, Adams Dr, Berwick TD15 2JF; Tel (01289) 305083; Fax (01289) 302681; P.W. Robinson
Blyth Ridley County, Sixth Ave, Blyth NE24 2SY; Tel (01670) 352641; S.G. Foley
Blyth Tynedale County Tynedale Dr, Blyth NE24 4LN; Tel (01670) 352350; Fax (01670) 352765; G.J. Pritchard, BSc
Coquet County, Acklington Rd, Amble-by-the-Sea, Morpeth NE65 0NG; Tel (92) 710636; Fax (92) 713470; R. Fisk, MEd
Cramlington County, Highburn, Cramlington NE23 6BN; Tel (01670) 712311; Fax (01670) 730598; D.M. Wise
Haydon Bridge County, Haydon Bridge, Hexham NE47 6LR; Tel (01434) 684422; Fax (01434) 684456; C.D. Thompson, MA
(Boarding wings–Haydon Lodge, Haydon Bridge NE47 6LS; Tel (0434) 684269; Ridley Hall, Bardon Mill, Hexham NE47 7BP; Tel (0434) 344282)
Hexham Queen Elizabeth Whetstone Bridge Rd, Hexham NE46 3JB; Tel (01434) 605211; Fax (01434) 660899 (Lower School); (01434) 601068 (Upper School); P.P. Eavis, MA
Hirst County Lichfield Cl, Ashington NE63 9RX; Tel (01670) 816111; Fax (01670) 522565; R. Houlden, BA
King Edward VI, Cottingwood La, Morpeth NE61 1DN; Tel (01670) 515415; Fax (01670) 504116; M.N. Duffy, MA
Ponteland County, Callerton La, Ponteland, Newcastle upon Tyne NE20 9EY; Tel (01661) 824711; Fax (01661) 820831; J. Foster
Prudhoe County, Moor Rd, Prudhoe NE42 5LJ; Tel (01661) 832486; Fax (01661) 832859; J.D. Baumber

High School (Voluntary)

Bedlington St Benet Biscop's R.C. Ridge Terr, Bedlington NE22 6ED; Tel (01670) 822795; Fax (01670) 829427; S.T. Bryce, MA. (V.A.) (13+)

Middle Schools (County 9+–12+)

Allendale County Middle, Allendale, Hexham NE47 9PS; Tel (01434) 683214; D.R.L. Watson
Amble County Middle, South Av, Amble-by-the-Sea, Morpeth NE65 0ND; Tel (01665) 710217; D.R. Sykes
Alnwick The Duke's County Middle, Hope House La, Alnwick NE66 1UN; Tel (01665) 602037; D.W. Gleadall, BEd
Alnwick Lindisfarne County Middle, Lindisfarne Rd, Alnwick NE66 1AX; Tel (92) 602534; B. Cassley
Ashington Alexandra County Middle Second Ave, Ashington NE63 9HB; Tel (01670) 813074; R.I. Stewart
Ashington Bothal County Middle, High Market, Ashington NE63 8NT; Tel (01670) 812360; Fax (01670) 810311; W.J. Gilbert
Ashington Hirst Park County Middle Third Ave, Ashington NE63 9BE; Tel (01670) 813111; K. Elliott, BA
Ashington Seaton Hirst County Middle Norwich Cl, Ashington NE63 9SA; Tel (01670) 815444; M.P. Gilbert
Bedlington Meadowdale County Middle Hazelmere Ave, Bedlington NE22 6HA; Tel (01670) 823170; F.R. Forster
Belford County Middle, Belford NE70 7NX; Tel (01668) 213361; M. Henry
Bellingham County Middle, Bellingham, Hexham NE48 2EN; Tel (01434) 220235; Fax (01434) 220690; E.D. Henderson

Berwick County Middle Lovaine Terr, Berwick upon Tweed TD15 2LB; Tel (01289) 306140; G.W. Cooper
Boarding wing: St Aidan's Hse, Palace Green, Berwick upon Tweed TD15 1HR; Tel (01289) 306355
Blyth Bebside County Middle Kitty Brewster, Blyth NE24 4RE; Tel (01670) 352556; S. Bainbridge, BA, MEd
Blyth Delaval County Middle Plessey Rd, Blyth NE24 3NL; Tel (01670) 353115; C. Smith, MBE, BA
Blyth Tynedale County Middle Tynedale Dr, Blyth NE24 4LQ; Tel (01670) 352256; D.W. Gray
Blyth Wensleydale County Middle Dent St, Blyth NE24 3ED; Tel (01670) 366817; J.F. Coulthard, BA
Corbridge County Middle Corbridge NE45 5HY; Tel (01434) 632191; Fax (01434) 633735; N. Pont
Cramlington Brockwell County Middle Northumbrian Rd, Parkside Grange, Cramlington NE23 9PZ; Tel (01670) 734006; T. Darwin
Cramlington Parkside County Middle Cramlington NE23 9DN; Tel (01670) 712267; J. Elliott, BSc
Cramlington Southlands County Middle Westloch Rd, Southfield Lea, Cramlington NE23 6LW; Tel (01670) 714475; M.Z. Mavro-Michaelis, MA
Cramlington Stonelaw County Middle Highburn, Cramlington NE23 6BW; Tel (01670) 716353; A. Youngs
Druridge Bay County Middle Hadston Rd, South Broomhill, Morpeth NE65 9SD; Tel (01670) 760271; J.H. Little, BEd
Glendale County Middle 15 Brewery La, Wooler NE71 6QF; Tel (01668) 81470; J.N.W. Spowart, MEd
Guide Post County Middle Stakeford La, Guide Post, Choppington NE62 5ET; Tel (01670) 822369; B.C. Buckley
Haltwhistle South Tynedale County Middle Park Ave, Haltwhistle NE49 9BA; Tel (01434) 320491; P.J. Woodward
Hexham County Middle Wanless La, Hexham NE46 1BL; Tel (01434) 602533; D.R. Boas
Morpeth Chantry County Middle Mitford Rd, Morpeth NE61 1RQ; Tel (01670) 512874; D.J. Mitchell, BPhil
Morpeth Newminster County Middle Mitford Rd, Morpeth NE61 1RH; Tel (01670) 513621; P. Lawrence
Newbiggin-by-the-Sea County Middle Cleveland Ave, Newbiggin-by-the-Sea NE64 6RS; Tel (01670) 815824; Fax (01670) 810733; A. Symmonds
Ovingham County Middle Ovingham, Prudhoe NE42 6DE; Tel (01661) 833215; J.G. Swainston
Ponteland County Middle Callerton La, Ponteland, Newcastle-upon-Tyne NE20 9EY; Tel (01661) 824853; Fax (01661) 860020; W.L. Oliver, MA, BEd
Prudhoe Eastwood County Middle Broomhouse Rd, Prudhoe NE42 5EJ; Tel (01661) 832328; R.A.D. Snowdon, BEd
Prudhoe Highfield County Middle Highfield La, Prudhoe NE42 6EY; Tel (01661) 833922; A. Sample
Seahouses County Middle Seahouses NE68 7YF; Tel (92) 720473; J.M. Harris
Seaton Delaval Whytrig County Middle Western Ave, Seaton Delaval, Whitley Bay, Tyne and Wear NE25 0EB; Tel (0191) 2371402; P. Douglas
Seaton Sluice County Middle Alston Grove, Seaton Sluice, Whitley Bay, Tyne and Wear NE26 4JS; Tel (0191) 2370629; Fax (0191) 2373970; Vacancy
Tweedmouth County Middle Billendean Terr, Berwick upon Tweed TD15 2DJ; Tel (01289) 307480; R.S. Thackray
West Sleekburn County Middle West Sleekburn, Bedlington NE22 7BX; Tel (01670) 823084; M.J. Douglas

Middle Schools (Voluntary 9+–12+)

Alnwick Thomas Percy R.C. Middle, Blakelaw Rd, Alnwick NE66 1AZ; Tel (01665) 602650; P. Thomas. (S.A.)
Ashington St Benedict's R.C. Middle Moor House La, Ashington NE63 9LR; Tel (01670) 813658; F.J. Stokoe. (V.A.)
Blyth St Wilfrid's R.C. Back Claremont Terr, Blyth NE24 2LE; Tel (01670) 352919; P.A. Ibbetson. (S.A.)
Cramlington St Peter's R.C. Northumbrian Rd, Alexandra Pk, Cramlington NE23 6DB; Tel (01670) 716343; A.J. Bell. (V.A.)
Hexham St Joseph's R.C. Highford La, Causey Hill, Hexham NE46 2DP; Tel (01434) 605124; Sister J.E. Gilmartin. (V.A.)
Ponteland Coates Endowed Thornhill Rd, Ponteland, Newcastle-upon-Tyne NE20 9BQ; Tel (01661) 823167; Rev P.G. Wolfenden, MA. (S.A.)
Rothbury Thomlinson's C. of E. Silverton La, Rothbury, Morpeth NE65 7RH; Tel (01669) 20287; D.J. Johnson. (S.A.)
Boarding wing: Coquet Hse, Silverton La, Rothbury, Morpeth NE65 7RY; Tel (01669) 20648

Outdoor Education Centres

Deneholm Outdoor Education Centre, Deneholm, Allendale, Hexham NE47 9PX; Tel (01434) 683101; F. Unsworth, BEd
Ford Castle Residential Centre, Ford, Berwick/Tweed TD15 2PX; Tel (01890) 820257; R. Homyer

Teachers' Centre

Education Development Centre Hepscott Park, Stannington, Morpeth NE61 6NF; Tel (01670) 533000

Youth Centre

Beal Residential Youth Centre Beal, Berwick upon Tweed; Tel (01289) 81238; I. Simpson

Grant Maintained Schools

Astley, Elsdon Ave, Seaton Delaval, Whitley Bay, Tyne and Wear NE25 0BP; Tel (0191) 2371505; R.I. Howarth

Nottinghamshire County Council

Population 984,990 (1991 Census)
County Hall, West Bridgford, Nottingham NG2 7QP; Tel (0115) 982 3823; Fax (0115) 981 7945

Education Offices

County Hall, West Bridgford, Nottingham NG2 7QP; Tel (0115) 977 3615; Fax (0115) 981 2824
Director of Education Vacancy
Deputy Director of Education C.R. Valentine
Principal Inspector D.P. Roberts
Senior Assistant Director (Advisory and Inspections Services) J. Berridge
Senior Assistant Director (Pupil and Community Services) A. Dessent
Senior Assistant Director (Operations) M.G.F. Lusty
Senior Assistant (Development) S.C. Parry
Senior Assistant Director (Resources) D.A. Wilson
Assistant Director (Business Planning) P. Kirby
Assistant Director (Development) R.A. Alderson
Assistant Director (Development) P. Foale
Assistant Director (Development) M. Jones
Assistant Education Officer (Development) A. Pae
Assistant Director (Catering and Building Cleaning) D. Clowes
Assistant Director (Careers and Guidance) J. Pardoe Careers Headquarters, 24–32 Carlton Rd, Hockley, Nottingham NG1 1NN; Tel (0115) 948 4484; Fax (0115) 950 8424
Assistant Director (Operations) M. Westhorpe
Assistant Director (Post–16) R. Holloway
Assistant Director (Post–16) M. Matthews
Principal Educational Psychologist P. Gray
Principal Educational Welfare Officer B. Isham

Assistant Director (Pupil and Community Services) P. Richardson
Assistant Director (Pupil and Community Service) J. Price
Assistant Education Officer (Pupil and Community Services) P. Graham
Assistant Education Officer (Pupil and Community Services) D. Smith
Assistant Education Officer B. Wakefield
Assistant Director (Personnel Co-ordinator) Vacancy
Assistant Director (Personnel) N. Clifton
Assistant Director (Personnel) J. McMillan
Assistant Director (Personnel) (Job Share) M. Steel
Assistant Director (Personnel) (Job Share) G. Kandola
Assistant Director (Finance) P.W. Hustings
Head of Information S. Farnsworth
Number of Schools
6 nursery (307); 424 primary (80,035); 79 secondary (61,931);
Special Schools
20 day (1,331); 2 day/residential (141); 1 residential (35). 4 hospitals (135); 3 hostels (3 behavioural and severe learning difficulties); 7 for the hearing impaired; 5 for children with severe communication difficulties; 3 for the visually impaired; As at Jan 94: Nursery = F.T.E, Primary = Excluding Part-time pupils, Secondary = Includes 6th Forms
Day of Committee Meeting
Tuesday every three weeks
Requisition Periods for School Supplies
None
Other Authorities with whom Joint Purchasing Arrangements are made
None

Education Committee

Con 11, Lab 27, LD 3
Chair F. Riddell, BA, Dip(Econ), (Lab) 200 Cinderhill Rd, Bulwell, Nottingham, NG6 8RL
Vice-Chair J. Barker, JP, (Lab) 7 Coppice Cl, Hucknall, Nottingham NG15 6HA
Members of the Committee
Con: E.W. Cheesewright ACIB, P.J. Curry, J.H. Hayes, G.F. Hill, J. Lonergan, V.C. Pepper, T.A.J. Pettengell, T.E. Roach, M.A. Shepherd, H.R. Stanley, S.P. Stuart
Lab: J.E. Anthony, M. Aslam, I.M. Aziz, J. Barker, B.J. Bowker, T.H. Butler, J. Calter, G.M. Gawith, B. Grocock, J. Hunter, G.P. Jackson, D.J. Kirkham, B.A. Larcombe, M.J. Newton, D. Pettitt, F. Riddell BA, DipEcon, W.A. Shaw, G. Skinner, S.M. Smedley JP, N. Smedley, B.G. Smith, G.M. Storey, R. Strauther, M.I. Tewson, J. Thierry, D. Woodward, G.R. Young
LD: T.P. Miller, D.J. Morton OBE, A. Wood

Governor Training Unit

Nottingham Area Education Office, York Hse, Mansfield Rd, Nottingham NG1 3JA; Tel (0115) 941 8511; Fax (0115) 947 6613
Governor Training Officer Kim Garcia
Services Offered
Training for School Governors including 1 to 1 coaching, small group and committee development. Customised courses for whole governing bodies and families of schools. LEA programme of generic and specialist modular courses. Support for school-centred governor development activities. Resource collections and school governor newsletter

Ashfield District

Council Offices, Station Rd, Sutton-in-Ashfield, Nottingham NG17 5JA; Tel (01623) 516508
Area Education Officer T. Howram

Special Day/Residential School

Fountaindale, Nottingham Rd, Mansfield; Tel (01623) 792671; M.S. Dengel. (64 Day, 12 5-day Boarding) (P.H.) (Mixed) (All ages)

Hostel

Chartwell House attached to Bracken Hill School; Tel (01623) 753068; *Warden* D. Cooper. (Moderate Learning Difficulties) (8)

Comprehensive School (Voluntary)

National C.E, Annesley Rd, Hucknall NG15 7DB; Tel (0115) 963 5667; D. Shannon. (V.A.) (1047)

Comprehensive Schools (County)

Ashfield Sutton Rd, Kirkby-in-Ashfield NG17 8HP; Tel (01623) 553492; R. Gillen, MA, MEd. (1613)
Holgate Hillcrest Dr, Hucknall NG15 6PX; Tel (0115) 963 2104; E.J. Round, MPhil, MIBiol. (1316)
Kirkby-in-Ashfield Kirkby Centre Tennyson St, Kirkby-in-Ashfield NG17 7DH; Tel (01623) 756509; R.W. Taylor. (850)
Matthew Holland Chapel Rd, Selston NG16 6BW; Tel Ripley 810321; J.F. Saul, BA, MBIM. (777)
Quarrydale Stoneyford Rd, Sutton-in-Ashfield NG17 2DU; Tel (01623) 554178; A. Flintham. (935)
Sutton Centre High Pavement, Sutton-in-Ashfield NG17 1EE; Tel (01623) 554554; A.R. Mortimer. (765)

Bassetlaw District

Queens Bldgs, Potter St, Worksop S80 2BZ; Tel (01909) 475531
Area Education Officer S. Rees
County Council Offices, Chancery La, Retford, Notts DN22 6EU; Tel (01777) 702681

Comprehensive Schools

Elizabethan High Queen St, Retford DN22 7BH; Tel (01909) 703293; D.J. Willcox, BA. (933)
Hartland Sparken Hill, Worksop S80 1AN; Tel (01909) 472302; K. Poyser. (777)
King Edward VI London Rd, Retford DN22 6AU; Tel (01777) 703654; R.W. Arrowsmith, MA. (647)
North Border Whitehouse Rd, Bircotes, Doncaster DN11 8EF; Tel (01302) 742535; J.F. Graham, BA. (457)
Ordsall Hall Ordsall Rd, Retford DN22 7PL; Tel (01777) 860833; M.P. James, BA. (847)
Portland Sparken Hill, Worksop S80 1AW; Tel (01909) 473656; E.M. Talmadge. (726)
Tuxford Lanfa Gr, Lincoln Rd, Tuxford, Newark NG22 0JG; Tel (01777) 870001; C.K. Atkinson, BA. (904)
Valley Baulk La, Worksop S81 7DG; Tel (01909) 475121; W.A. Miller, BSc. (1437)

Broxtowe District

College Hse, College Rd, Chilwell, Beeston NG9 4AS; Tel (01773) 250226
Area Education Officer Ms B. Burton
Education Offices, Church St, Eastwood, Nottingham NG16 3HQ; Tel (01773) 713598

County Comprehensive Schools

Alderman White Chilwell La, Bramcote, Beeston, Nottingham NG9 3DU; Tel (0115) 922 5727; W. Daniels. (636)
Bramcote Hills Moor La, Bramcote, Beeston, Nottingham NG9 3GA; Tel (0115) 922 1246; D.M. Maltby, BA, MEd. (1126)
Bramcote The Park, Bramcote, Beeston, Nottingham NG9 3GD; Tel (0115) 922 5816; M.N. Taylor, BSc. (504)
Chilwell Queens Rd West, Chilwell, Beeston, Nottingham; Tel (0115) 925 2698; R. Haylock (Acting). (804)
Eastwood Mansfield Rd, Eastwood, Nottingham NG16 3EA; Tel (01773) 716371; C. Hasty. (1131)
Kimberley Newdigate St, Kimberley NG16 2NJ; Tel 383961; J.C. May. (1076)

Eastbourne Centre

Station Rd, Sutton-in-Ashfield, Notts NG17 5FF; Tel (01623) 556804; Fax (01623) 517529
Staff Inspector Sold Services Pam Tulley
Newark and Bassetlaw Area Team
Senior Area Inspector Roger Hyde
General Inspector (Primary Phase) Clive Drake
General Inspector (Primary Phase) Warwick Ellis
General Inspector (Primary Phase) Sue Pilkington
General Inspector (Science) Phil Bunyan
General INspector (Design and Technology) John Culpin
General Inspector (Art) Roger Mountford
General Inspector (Secondary Phase and PSE) Paul Mein
General Inspector (Secondary Phase and Music) Joan Arnold
General Inspector (Special Educational Needs) Margaret Fowkes
Mansfield and Ashfield Area Team
Senior Area Inspector Robin Aldridge
General Inspector (Assessment) Phil Bishop
General Inspector (Primary Phase) Kris Sharma
General Inspector (Primary Phase) Peter Eardley
General Inspector (Secondary Phase) Rob Liley
General Inspector (English) David Allen
General Inspector (Secondary Phase and Humanities incl RE) John Morris
General Inspector (Special Educational Needs) Carol Tennyson
General Inspector (Secondary Phase and Equal Ops) Jan Smith
General Inspector (Secondary Phase and Maths) John Dryden
General Inspector (Consultancy and Training) Gordon Wallace
Co-ordinator (Records of Achievement) Pat Edwards
Co-ordinator (Consultancy and Training) Yvonne Burbanks
Co-ordinator (Consultancy and Training) John Rowland
Rushcliffe Gedling and Broxtowe Area Team
Senior Area Inspector Duncan Smith
General Inspector (Primary Phase) Simon Reynolds
General Inspector (Primary Phase) Lynn Dorling
General Inspector (Post 16 Phase) David Freestone
General Inspector (Post 16 Phase) Tricia Bailey
General Inspector (Secondary Phase and Humanities incl RE) Phil Jones
General Inspector (Secondary Phase and Physical Education) Brian Maydew
General Inspector (Primary Phase and RE) Viv Axford
General Inspector (TVEI Management) Peter Relf
General Inspector (TVEI Review) Roger Whittaker
Co-ordinator (TVEI) Prakash Ross
Co-ordinator (TVEI) Janet Neely
Co-ordinator (TVEI) Roy Haynes

Sandfield Centre

Sandfield Rd, Lenton, Nottingham NG7 1QH; Tel (0115) 953 5000; Fax (0115) 953 5199
Staff Inspector (LEA: Monitoring and Evaluation) Frank Knowles
City Area Team
Senior Area Inspector Diane Morton
General Inspector (Primary Phase) Vacancy
General Inspector (Primary Phase) Brian Crossman
General Inspector (Primary Phase) Alison Day
General Inspector (Secondary Phase) Nick Sparks
General Inspector (Secondary Phase) Mervyn Griffiths
General Inspector (Mathematics) David Rooke
General Inspector (Foreign Languages) Jenny Knowles
General Inspector (Special Educational Needs) Sue Leyden
General Inspector (Information Technology) Mike Thompson
Co-ordinator (Information Technology) Stan Norman
Rushcliffe, Gedling and Broxtowe Area Team
Senior Area Inspector Duncan Smith
General Inspector (Primary Phase) Simon Reynolds
General Inspector (Primary Phase) Lynn Dorling
General Inspector (Post 16 Phase) David Freestone
General Inspector (Post 16 Phase) Tricia Bailey
General Inspector (Secondary Phase and Humanities incl RE) Phil Jones
General Inspector (Secondary Phase and Physical Education) Brian Maydew
General Inspector (TVEI Management) Peter Relf
General Inspector (Primary Phase and RE) Viv Axford

Gedling District

County Offices, Carlton Sq, Carlton, Nottingham NG4 3BZ; Tel (0115) 961 4009
Area Education Officer Dr J. Cornforth

Comprehensive Schools (County)

Arnold Hill Gedling Rd, Arnold, Nottingham NG5 6NZ; Tel (0115) 920 2131; G.R. Wilkinson. (1637)
Carlton Le Willows Wood La, Gedling, Nottingham NG4 4AA; Tel (0115) 961 8919; M.H.A. Naisbitt, BA, MEd, MSc. (1237)
Colonel Frank Seely Flatts La, Calverton NG14 6JZ; Tel (0115) 965 2495; P. Sykes. (1191)
The Wheldon Coningswath Rd, Carlton NG4 3SH; Tel (0115) 955 0010; R.W. Madden. (988)
Gedling Wollaton Ave, Gedling, Nottingham NG4 4HX; Tel (0115) 952 1171; M.F. Lamb. (652)
Redhill Redhill Rd, Arnold, Nottingham NG5 8GX; Tel (0115) 926 1481; D. Parish. (1060)

Comprehensive School (Voluntary)

Christ the King R.C. Darlton Dr, Arnold, Nottingham NG5 7JZ; Tel (0115) 926 3287; G.D. Doust. (V.A.) (632)

Mansfield District

County Offices, St John St, Mansfield NG18 1RJ; Tel (01623) 22551
Area Education Officer F. Beesley, BA, MPhil

Secondary Middle School (Voluntary)

St John's C.E. Middle Saint John St, Mansfield NG18 1QH; Tel (01623) 21753; M. Tomlinson. (VA) (248)

Secondary Middle Schools (County)

Berry Hill Middle Black Scotch La, Mansfield NG18 4JW; Tel (01623) 21023; R. Woolley. (341)
Bull Farm Middle Bright Sq, Mansfield NG19 7LJ; Tel (01623) 23763; P.D. Lane, LCP, DipEd, MSc, FCollP. (262)
Cumberlands Middle Townroe Dr, Mansfield NG19 6JN; Tel (01623) 25577; D.K. Bednall. (363)
Ethel Wainwright Middle Westfield Cl, Westfield La, Mansfield NG19 6BE; Tel (01623) 23588; G. Empson. (288)
High Oakham Middle Nottingham Rd, Mansfield NG18 4SH; Tel (01623) 21345; M.D. Douglass. (494)
Windmill Ridge Abbey Rd, Mansfield NG18 3AF; Tel (01623) 23863; F.A. Allsop, BEd(Hons). (372)

Upper Schools (County)

Brunts The Park, Off Park Ave, Mansfield NG18 2AT; Tel (01623) 23149; J.R. Dalton. (753)
Sherwood Hall Stuart Ave, Forest Town, Mansfield NG19 0AB; Tel (01623) 633167; R.J. Linden, BSc(Econ). (851)

Upper School (Voluntary)

Queen Elizabeth's 150 Chesterfield Rd South, Mansfield NG19 7AP; Tel (01623) 23559; N.M. Atkin

Comprehensive Schools (County)

Garibaldi Garibaldi Rd, Forest Town, Mansfield NG19 0JX; Tel (01623) 20161; R.W. Salisbury, BA, MA. (764)
Manor Park Hall Rd, Mansfield Woodhouse, Mansfield NG19 8QA; Tel (01623) 23843; D.R. Golder, BA. (1302)

Meden Burns La, Warsop, Mansfield NG20 0QN; Tel (01623) 843517; R. Poppleton, BSc. (1156)

Comprehensive School (Voluntary)

All Saints R.C. Broomhill La, Mansfield NG19 6BW; Tel (01623) 634141; P. Whalley, MEd. (V.A.) (1038)

Newark District

Old Magnus Bldgs, Appletongate, Newark NG24 1LA; Tel (01636) 704281
Area Education Officer J.G. Moss, BSc(Hons), DipEd

Comprehensive Schools (Voluntary)

Lilley and Stone Upper London Rd, Newark NG24 1TT; Tel (01636) 703279; L. Saville. (C) (365)
Newark Magdalene High Barnby Rd, Newark NG24 1RR; Tel (01636) 704724; D.A. Geary, DipEd. (C) (501)
Minster C.E. Nottingham Rd, Southwell NG25 0HG; Tel (01636) 814000; P.J. Blinston. (A) (1452)
Thomas Magnus Upper Earp Ave, Newark NG24 4AB; Tel (01636) 704861; F. Hanford. (C) (469)

Comprehensive Schools (County)

Dukeries Community College Whinney La, New Ollerton, Newark NG22 ,9TD; Tel (01623) 860545; R.W. Sowden, BSc. (767)
The Grove London Rd, New Balderton, Newark NG24 3AL; Tel (01636) 705821; I.W. Stuart, BA. (1020)
Joseph Whitaker Warsop La, Rainworth, Mansfield NG21 0AG; Tel (01623) 792327; J.P. Loughton. (1006)
Rufford Mansfield Rd, Edwinstowe NG21 9NP; Tel (01623) 823490; R.H. Baars. (469)
Sconce Hills High Windsor Rd, Newark NG24 4HS; Tel (01636) 703507; W. Cassell, BEd(Hons), MA. (420)

Nottingham District

York House, Mansfield Rd, Nottingham NG1 3JA; Tel (0115) 941 8511
Area Education Officer M.J. Edwards, BA

Comprehensive Schools (County)

Alderman Derbyshire Hucknall La, Bulwell NG6 8AQ; Tel 278425; D.E. Martin, MSc. (503)
Big Wood Bewcastle Rd, Top Valley NG5 9PJ; Tel (0115) 920 3971; C. Singleton. (435)
Elliott Durham Ransom Drive, Mapperley NG3 5LR; Tel (0115) 962 4112; K. Yates. (454)
Ellis Guilford Bar La, Old Basford NG6 0HT; Tel (0115) 978 5845; P.J. Plummer. (865)
Fairham Community College Farnborough Rd, Clifton Estate NG11 9AE; Tel (0115) 984 4668; D.G. Rich. (612)
Farnborough Farnborough Rd, Clifton Est NG11 8JW; Tel (0115) 921 7531; D.J. Mahoney, BSc. (699)
Fernwood Goodwood Rd, Wollaton NG8 2FT; Tel (0115) 928 6326; J.E.A. Gemmell, BEd(Hons). (811)
Forest Gregory Boulevard, NG7 6PA; Tel (0115) 978 7847; A.E. Lawton. (409)
Glaisdale Glenbrook Cres, Bilborough NG8 3GP; Tel (0115) 929 2428; D.J. Higgins. (588)
Haywood Edwards La, Sherwood NG5 3HZ; Tel (0115) 920 4131; J. Chater, MEd, BSc. (601)
Henry Mellish Highbury Rd, Bulwell NG6 9DS; Tel (0115) 927 8133; P.G.L. Morley, MEd. (650)
Manning Robins Wood Rd, Aspley NG8 3LD; Tel (0115) 929 9401; R.W. Allen. (Girls) (597)
Manvers Pierrepont Carlton Rd NG3 2NR; Tel (0115) 958 2011; H. Clarke. (373)
Margaret Glen-Bott Sutton Passey's Cres, Wollaton Pk NG8 1EA; Tel (0115) 928 1291; D. Powell. (473)
Padstow Padstow Rd, Bestwood Estate NG5 5GH; Tel (0115) 927 7711; E.A. Wydenbach. (372)
Top Valley Top Valley Dr West, Hucknall Rd, Nottingham; Tel (0115) 927 9474; C.J. Archer. (781)
Wilford Meadows Coronation Ave, Wilford NG11 7AD; Tel (0115) 981 5896; M.W. Armstrong. (337)
William Crane East Gate, Minver Cres, Aspley NG8 5PN; Tel (0115) 929 3100; C. Wild. (681)
William Sharp Bramhall Rd, Bilborough NG8 4HY; Tel (0115) 929 1492; P.J. Sherlock. (561)

Comprehensive Schools (Voluntary)

Becket R.C. Ruddington La, Wilford NG11 7DL; Tel (0115) 981 7742; D.W. McGawley, MA. (1008)
Bluecoat C.E. Aspley La NG8 5GY; Tel (0115) 929 7445; M.R. Kay. (866)
Trinity R.C. Beechdale Rd, Aspley NG8 3EZ; Tel (0115) 929 6251; B.V. Bonner, MA, DipEd. (721)

Rushcliffe District

21 Musters Rd, West Bridgford, Nottingham NG2 7PP; Tel (0115) 977 3739
Area Education Officer M.R. Morgan, BA

Comprehensive Schools

Bingham Toot Hill The Banks, Bingham NG13 8BL; Tel (01949) 838641; J.D. Eagles, MA. (1170)
Dayncourt Cropwell Rd, Radcliffe on Trent NG12 2FQ; Tel (0115) 933 4327; P.J. Andrew, BSc. (821)
Harry Carlton Lantern La, East Leake, Loughborough, Leics LE12 6QN; Tel (0150 982) 852424; R. Bailey. (1056)
Rushcliffe Boundary Rd, West Bridgford NG2 7BW; Tel (0115) 923 4011; P.D. Chambers, BSc. (1100)
South Wolds Church Dr, Keyworth NG12 5FF; Tel (0115) 937 3506; S. Roser. (1056)
West Bridgford Comprehensive Loughborough Rd, West Bridgford, Nottingham NG2 7FA; Tel (0115) 982 0750; D.A. Cokeham. (1313)

Educational Psychology Service

Bassetlaw 61 Carlton Rd, Worksop S80 1PP; Tel (01909) 478345
Mansfield and Ashfield 12 St John St, Mansfield, Notts NG18 1QJ; Tel (01623) 634524; *Deputy Principal Educational Psychologist* J.M. Bradley, AFBPS
Mundella Centre, Green St, The Meadows, Nottingham NG2 2LA; Tel (0115) 986 8968; *Deputy Principal Educational Psychologist* B. Bennett
Newark and Gedling County Offices, Carlton Sq, Carlton, Nottingham NG4 3BZ; Tel (0115) 961 4009

Special Schools/Individual Needs Centres

Arnold Derrymount, Churchmoor La, Arnold, Nottingham NG5 8HN; Tel (0115) 926 3355; E. Thompson. (Day) (MLD) (Mixed) (plus unit for hearing impaired) (All age) (72)
Ash Lea School, Owthorpe Rd, Cotgrave, Nottingham NG12 3PA; Tel (0115) 989 2744; L. Skillingdon. (Day) (SLD) (Mixed) (All age) (51)
Aspley Wood, Robins Wood Rd, Aspley, Nottingham NG8 3LD; Tel (0115) 929 4887 and 929 5244; G.J. Jamieson. (Day) (P.H.) (Mixed) (All age) (63)
Bassetlaw, Newgate St, Worksop, Notts S80 2LW; Tel (01909) 485737; R.J. Higginbottom. (Day) (37) (MLD) (Senior Mixed) (All age) (13) (5 day boarding)
Beech Hill, Fairholme Dr, Mansfield, Notts NG19 6DX; Tel (01623) 26008; M. Sutton. (Day) (MLD) (Mixed) (Secondary) (83)
Bracken Hill, Chartwell Rd, Kirkby-in-Ashfield, Notts NG17 7HZ; Tel (01623) 753068; D. Cooper. (Day) (MLD and SLD) (Mixed) (97 including 12-place, 5 day Hostel))(3–16+
Carlton Digby, Digby Ave, Mapperley, Nottingham NG3 6DS; Tel (0115) 960 9787; L.M. Day. (Day) (SLD) (Mixed) (All age) (72)
City Hospital and Sandfield Unit, Hucknall Rd, Nottingham NG5 1PB; Tel (0115) 962 7600; P.A. Jordan. (Hospital and S.L.O.) (34)
Ewing, Mansfield Rd, Sherwood, Nottingham NG5 3FN; Tel (0115) 960 7390; P.J. Abell, BA. (Day) (Deaf and Partially Hearing) (Primary) (27)

Foxwood, Bramcote Hills, off Derby Rd, Bramcote, Beeston, Notts NG9 3GF; Tel (0115) 922 4965; J. Baker. (Day) (MLD) (Mixed) (All age) (66)
Hopwell School, Ockbrook, nr Derby DE72 3RW; Tel (01332) 872231; M. Jacobs. (Weekly Boarding) (Behaviour Difficulties) (35) (Boys) (10–16)
Kinder School, Ward C2, School Office, Bassetlaw Hospital, Kilton Hill, Worksop S81 0BD; Tel (01909) 500990 Ext 2281; Dr G.T. Watts, BA, MEd. (Hospital and SLD) (21)
Linden, London Rd, New Balderton, Newark NG24 3AL; Tel (01636) 76947; R. McGrath. (Day) (MLD) (Mixed) (All age) (56)
Mansfield Yeoman Pk, Park Hall Rd, Mansfield Woodhouse, Mansfield NG19 8PS; Tel (01623) 25382; P. Betts. (Day) (SLD) (Mixed) (All age) (80)
Nethergate, Swansdowne Dr, Clifton Est, Nottingham NG11 8HX; Tel (0115) 921 1698; P. Pearce. (Day) (MLD) (Mixed) (All age) (82)
The New Hardwick Chingford Rd, Bilborough, Nottingham NG8 3BT; Tel (0115) 929 3449; P.A. Fallows. (Day) (MLD) (Primary) (42)
Newark Appletongate, Appletongate, Newark NG24 1JR; Tel (01636) 702106; S.P. Jefferies. (Day) (SLD) (Mixed) (43 including 12-place, 5 day Hostel) (All age)
Parkside School, Chewton St, Eastwood, Notts NG16 3HB; Tel (01773) 715804; J.E. Phillips. (Day) (MLD) (Mixed) (All age) (64)
Redgate, Somersall St, Mansfield NG19 6EL; Tel (01623) 27846; K.G. Fallows, MEd. (Day) (MLD) (Mixed) (Primary) (37)
Retford St Giles, North Rd, Retford DN22 7XN; Tel (01777) 703683; C.M. Kirk. (Day) (SLD) (Mixed) (All age) (38)
Rosehill, St Matthias Rd, Nottingham NG3 2FE; Tel (0115) 950 2038; J. Pearson. (Day) (MLD + Secondary Autistic Unit) (Mixed) (All age) (86)
St Ann's Hospital, Fairmead Close, off The Wells Rd NG3 3AL; Tel (0115) 959 0157; D. Richardson (Acting). (Psychiatric) (18)
Shepherd, Harvey Rd, Bilborough, Nottingham NG8 3BB; Tel (0115) 929 1011; D.S. Stewart. (Day) (SLD) (All age) (158)
University Hospital School, Queens Medical Centre, E Fl, East Block, Derby Rd, Nottingham NG7 2UH; Tel (0115) 942 1421, Ext 41753; T. Elston, DipEd, MA. (Hospital) (62)
Westbury, Lortas Rd, New Basford, Nottingham NG5 1EH; Tel (0115) 978 1203; R.J. Lancaster. (Day) (Behaviour Difficulties) (Mixed) (Secondary) (29)
Woodlands, Beechdale Rd, Aspley, Nottingham NG8 3EZ; Tel (0115) 929 5947; J. Campion. (Day) (MLD) (Secondary) (Mixed) (103)

Hostel

Appletongate, attached to Appletongate School; Tel (01636) 702106; *Warden* K. Duddles. Severe Learning Difficulties

Individual Needs Centres for Hearing Impaired Pupils

Hucknall, Annie Holgate Infants', High Leys Rd, Hucknall NG15 6EZ; Tel (0115) 963 2096; D. Watkins
Hucknall, Annie Holgate Junior, High Leys Rd, Hucknall NG15 6EZ; Tel (0115) 963 3880; C. Bumstead
Portland Comprehensive, Sparken Hill, Worksop S80 1AW; Tel (01909) 473656/475429; M. Thomas
William Sharp School, Bramhall Rd, Bilborough, Nottingham NG8 4HY; Tel (0115) 929 1492; P.J. Sherlock
Worksop St Augustine's Infants', Longfellow Dr, Worksop S81 9DW; Tel (01909) 473473; L. Ward
Worksop St Augustines' Junior, Longfellow Dr, Worksop S81 0AW; Tel (01909) 473955; N. Moore
Arnold Derrymount School, Churchmoor La, Arnold, Nottingham NG5 8HN; Tel (0115) 926 3355; E. Thompson

Individual Needs Centres for Children with Severe Communication Difficulties

Arboretum Nursery, Arboretum St, Nottingham NG1 4JA; Tel (0115) 978 9190; A. Crampton, BEd(Hons)
Bosworth Primary, Ainsworth Dr, The Meadows, Nottingham NG2 1FX; Tel (0115) 955 2050; M. Hall
Moor Lane First, Moor La, Mansfield, Notts NG18 5SF; Tel (01623) 28959; C. Hodgkinson
Dalestorth Primary, Hill Cres, Sutton-in-Ashfield, Notts NG17 4JA; Tel (01623) 554089; G.R. Miller

Individual Needs Centres for Visually Handicapped Children

Bramcote The Park, Bramcote, Beeston, Nottingham NG9 3GD; Tel (0115) 922 5816; M.N. Taylor, BSc
Sycamore Infants, Abbotsford Dr, St Anns, Nottingham NG3 4QP; Tel (0115) 950 7471; C. Castleden
Sycamore Junior Abbotsford Drive, St Anns NG3 4QP; Tel (0115) 950 7654; P. Austin

Grant Maintained Schools

Greenwood Dale Sneinton Boulevard NG2 4GL; Tel (0115) 950 5428; B.S. Day. (566)

Technology Centres

George Spencer Grant Maintained School,One of the first twelve Technology College Schools and sponsored by Harry Djanogly CBE, Database, Apricot Computers and Midland Bank, Sandicliffe Motors Arthur Mee Rd, Stapleford, Nottingham NG9 7EN; Tel (0115) 939 9525; Fax (0115) 939 9625; Tom Clark, BA. (1028)

Oldham Metropolitan Borough Council

Population 220,000
PO Box 160, Civic Centre, West St, Oldham OL1 1UG; Tel 0161-911 3000; Fax 0161-911 4936

Education Offices

Old Town Hall, Middleton Rd, Chadderton, Oldham OL9 6PP; Tel 0161-911 4260; Fax 0161-627 2325
Director of Education Dr W.R. Kneen, MA, DipEd
Senior Assistant Director (Central Services) S. Curran, BSc, MEd
Senior Assistant Director (Quality Development) R. Tweed, BA, MSc
Senior Assistant Director (Establishments) H. Holmes, BA
Assistant Director (Financial and Admin) R.G. Teague, DMA, ACIS
Assistant Director (Development) R. Morgan, MA(Cantab), MBA
Assistant Director (Education Personnel) Dr D.J. Hibberd, BA, DipEd
Assistant Director (Continuing Education) K. Edwards
Special Educational Needs D.A. Tweddle, BSc, MSc
Assistant Director (Pupils) D.E.G. Newbury, MA
Catering Manager K. Jackson
Cleaning Manager I. Hughes, BA
AEO (Youth and Community Education Service) J. Brenchley
AEO (Special Educational Needs) D.E.G. Newbury, MA
AEO (Governor Support and Training) L. Tidy, BPhilEd
AEO (Pupils) D. Austin, DMS

AEO (Development) A. Pennington
Head of Youth and Community Education Service S. Stockwell
Senior Inspector (Primary) C. Pickup, BA, MEd, MA
Senior Adviser (Quality Development Service) S. Munby, BA
Senior Inspector (Secondary) I. Middlebrough, BEd, MEd
General Inspector (Humanities) A.B. Goodwin, BScEcon(Hons), MS
General Inspector (Mathematics) I. Hocking, BA, MSc
General Inspector (Modern Foreign Languages) C. Thorne, MA
General Inspector (Equal Opportunities) I. McPhail, CSTD, LUDDA, BPhil(Ed)
General Inspector (Music) Dr E. Bentley, MEd, GRSM, ARMCM(P)
General Inspector (Physical Education) D. Smallwood
General Inspector (Primary) C. Davies, MA, AdDipEd
General Inspector (Primary) R. Gill, BEd(Hons)
General Inspector (Primary/Early Years) B. Hickling, MEd
General Inspector (IT/Technology) P.T. Hill, BA
General Inspector (Science) D. Page, BSc, MEd
Chief Executive Oldham Careers Service A.J. Temple, DMA, DYESTB

Number of Schools
102 primary (22,322); 15 secondary (16,126); 17 adult education centres, 1 music centre, 1 theatre workshop, 1 professional development centre, 1 curriculum development centre

Special Schools
7 (586)

Education Committee

Lab 9, LD 7, Con 2
Chair D.R. Jones, (Lab) 25 Ashton Cres, Chadderton, Oldham OLA 8HE
Vice-Chair S.G.W. Jacobs, (Lab) 120 Foxdenton La, Chadderton, Oldham OL9 9QR

Members of the Committee
Lab: J. Armitage JP, J.B. Battye, G.R. Currie, D.A. Heyes, D.R. Hibbert, A. Jabber, S.G. Jacobs, D.R. Jones, H.G. Sutcliffe
Con: M. Curran, E. McKinley
LD: V. Clayton, C. Dugdale, K. Knox, A. Griffiths, D.W. Joynes, R.D. Knowles, K. Stocks

Governor Training and Support Unit

Education Dept, Old Town Hall, Middleton Rd, Chadderton, Oldham OL9 6PP; Tel 0161-911 4216; Fax 0161-628 0443
AEO Lesley Tidy, CertEd, BPhil(Ed)
Principal Administration Officer David Challen

Services Offered
To give advice and support to governing bodies in accordance with their needs; To ensure that the training needs of governing bodies/governors are met

Special Schools and Units

Ferney Field, Hunt La, Chadderton, Greater Manchester; Tel 0161-624 9913; L. Richardson, MPhil, DipSpecEd
Foxdenton, Foxdenton La, Chadderton, Greater Manchester; Tel 0161-652 5219; M. Farrar, MSc, MEd, AdvDipEd, MBIM
Gorse Bank, Foxdenton La, Chadderton, Greater Manchester; Tel 0161-652 1316; A. Greaves, BEd
Hardman Fold, Dean St, Failsworth, Manchester M35 0DQ; Tel 0161-688 7114; R. Maycock, AdDipEd
HillTop, Arncliffe Rise, Pennine Meadow, Oldham OL4 2LZ; Tel 0161-620 6070
Marland Fold, Rosary Rd, Oldham OL8 2RP; Tel 0161-624 6027
Park Dean, St Martin's Rd, Oldham OL8 2PY; Tel 0161-620 0231; J. O'Garra, MSc, DipSPED, MEd

Special Needs Support Services

Educational Psychology Service, Old Town Hall, Middleton Rd, Chadderton, Oldham OL9 6PP; Tel 0161-911 3204; *Chartered Educational Psychologist* K. Fingleton, MA, MSc
Hospital Home/Tuition Service, Northgate Hse, Firbank Rd, Royton, Oldham OL2 6TU; Tel 0161-627 1764; K. Williams
Pre-School Home Teaching Service, The Bungalow, Dunkerley St, Oldham OL4 2AX; Tel 0161-620 2628; Claire Ward
Primary Special Needs Service, Limeside Primary School, Fourth Ave, Oldham OL8 3SB; Tel 0161-688 9833
Primary Special Needs Service, Hodge Clough Junior School, Conduit St, Oldham OL1 4JX; Tel 0161-628 0608; I. Blackburn, BA
Secondary Special Needs Service, Breeze Hill School, Roxbury Ave, Oldham OL4 5JE; Tel 0161-620 3318; P. Wilkinson, BA, MSc
Service for the Hearing Impaired, Park Dean School, St Martins Rd, Fitton Hill, Oldham OL8 2PY; Tel 0161-620 0231; S. Trotter
Service for the Visually Impaired, Park Dean School, St Martins Rd, Fitton Hill, Oldham OL8 2PY; Tel 0161-620 0231; J. Sweeting

Comprehensive Schools (All Coeducational)

Blue Coat C.E., Horsedge St, Oldham OL1 3FQ; Tel 0161-624 1484; Fax 0161-628 4997; K.W. Pleasant, BA
Breeze Hill, Roxbury Ave, Oldham OL4 5JE; Tel 0161-624 6928/7610; Fax 0161-628 8570; B. Phillips, BA, MEd
Counthill, Counthill Rd, Oldham OL4 2PZ; Tel 0161-624 6366/4701; Fax 0161-633 5909; A. Cunnington, BA, MEd
Crompton Hse C.E., Rochdale Rd, High Crompton, Oldham OL2 7HS; Tel (01706) 845936; Fax (01706) 2914954; M. Taylor, BA, MEd
Failsworth Lower, Partington St, Oldham; Tel 0161-681 3763; D.O. Johnson, BA
Failsworth Upper, Brierley Ave, Oldham M35 9HA; Tel 0161-681 3763; Fax 0161-683 5173; D.O. Johnson, BA
Grange Rochdale Rd, Oldham OL9 6DY; Tel 0161-652 2428; Fax 0161-652 1324; J.D. Owens, BA
Hathershaw Bellfield Ave, Oldham OL8 3EW; Tel 0161-624 7782/3613; Fax 0161-627 2298; C.W. Edney, BA, MSc
Kaskenmoor, Roman Rd, Oldham; Tel 0161-681 4116; Fax 0161-682 8022; Vacancy
North Chadderton Upper, Chadderton Hall Rd, Oldham OL9 0BN; Tel 0161-624 9939; Fax 0161-628 5995; J. McLaren, BA
Lower: Broadway; Tel 0161-624 5883; Fax 0161-628 5995
Our Lady's R.C. Vaughan St, Royton, Oldham OL2 5DL; Tel 0161-624 9974; Fax 0161-627 1871; J. Hughes, BEd, MSc
Radclyffe Lower Broadway, Oldham; Tel 0161-624 2594; Fax 0161-628 5935; M. Warrington, BSc
Upper: Chadderton, Oldham; Tel 0161-633 2120; Fax 0161-633 2183
Royton and Crompton, Blackshaw La, Royton, Oldham OL2 6NT; Tel (01706) 846474; Fax (01706) 842874; J. Watson, BA
Saddleworth High St, Uppermill, Oldham OL3 6BU; Tel (01457) 872072; Fax (01457) 870190; J.M. Hodgkinson, BSc
South Chadderton, Butterworth La, Oldham IL9 8EA; Tel 0161-681 4851; Fax 0161-683 5183; J. Blair, BEd, MBIM
St Augustine of Canterbury RC, Grange Ave, Oldham OL8 4EJ; Tel 0161-624 7089/8055; Fax 0161-627 2138; J.A. Kennedy, BSc

Environmental Centre

Castleshaw Centre Waterworks Rd, Delph, Oldham OL3 5LZ; Tel (01457) 874276; *Head* M. Green

Outdoor Education Service

Castleshaw Centre, Wateworks Rd, Delph OL3 5LZ; Tel (01457) 820551; *Head* D. Faulconbridge

Centre for Professional Development

Fitton Hill School, Rosary Rd, Oldham OL8 2QE; Tel 0161-627 0565; R. Tweed, BA, MSc

Music Centre

The Lyceum, Union St, Oldham OL1 1QG; Tel 0161-627 2332; Dr E. Bentley, Bed, MEd, GRSM, ARMCM(P)

Theatre Workshop

Harrison St, Oldham OL1 1PX; Tel 0161-624 0170

Oxfordshire County Council

Population 590,900
County Hall, New Rd, Oxford OX1 1ND; Tel (01865) 815366; (01865) 726155; Fax (01865) 815447
Assistant Solicitor (Education) S. Dulek

Education Department

Macclesfield Hse, New Rd, Oxford OX1 1NA; Tel (01865) 815449; Fax (01865) 791637
Chief Education Officer J. Stephens, BSc
Chief Executive J. Harwood, MA
Treasurer C. Gray, BA, IPFA
Director of Planning and Property Services D. Young, BA, MRTPI
Director of Social Services I.A. White, MSc, DMS, FCIS
Librarian T. Forrest
County Purchasing Officer T. Stock
Group Spokespersons Variable By Rotation
Chief Education Officer J. Stephens, BSc(PC)
Assistant Chief Education Officer (Planning and Service Management) J.A. Christie, BA; Tel (01865) 815146
Assistant Chief Education Officer (Resources) R. Smith, IPFA
Assistant Chief Education Officer (Curriculum and Inspection) A Kaye
Senior Assistant Education Officer (Policy Development) R. Harmes
Senior Assistant Education Officer (Resources) A.P. Twigger
Senior Assistant Education Officer (Personnel/Central Admin) S.G. Tanner
Divisional Education Officer (South Oxfordshire) R.H. Capstick
Divisional Education Officer (Cherwell) J.A. Crouch
Divisional Education Officer (West Oxfordshire) I.L. Pearson
Divisional Education Officer (Vale of White Horse) M.A. Bullen
Divisional Education Officer (Oxford City) S. Adams
County Careers Officer R. Collier
Principal Education Psychologist/Head of Family Service G. Tee, MSc; Tel (01865) 815125
Senior Inspector (Oxfordshire Quality Schools Association/City Upper Schools) A. Carter
Senior Inspector (Curriculum and Assessment 14–19 Vale and South Secondary Schools) M. Dennison
Senior Inspector (Curriculum Assessment 0–14/City Middle Schools) R. Howard
Senior Inspector (Pupil and Student Progress/Special Schools) G. Jones
Senior Inspector (Inspection Arrangements/Cherwell and West Secondary Schools) R. Long
Primary Inspector (Vale Division/SEN in Primary Schools) R. Border
Primary Inspector (West Division) P. Dorling
Primary Inspector (City Division) J. Head
Primary Inspector (South Division/Assessment and Recording Achievement) D. Kavanagh
Primary Inspector (Cherwell Division) B. Lofthouse
Primary Inspector (Vale Division) B. McCutcheon
Primary Inspector (South Division) L. Martin
Primary Inspector (City Division/Early Years) J. Fisher
Primary Inspector (Cherwell Division) C. Stone
Primary Inspector (West Division/Management Development) D. Westall
Specialist Inspector (SEN) H. Brayton
Specialist Inspector (IT/Business Education) P. Counsell
Specialist Inspector (English and Drama) G. Dean
Specialist Inspector (Humanities) J. Dyson
Specialist Inspector (Mathematics) T. Easterbrook
Specialist Inspector (Science) J. Evans
Specialist Inspector (Music)/Director of Music R. Hallam
Specialist Inspector (Modern Languages) M. Hope
Specialist Inspector (Physical Education) D. Lamb
Specialist Inspector (Multicultural Education) S. Pearse
Specialist Inspector (Personal, Social and Health Education) B. Perigo
Specialist Inspector (Recording Achievement/Teacher Appraisal) R. Reynolds
Specialist Inspector (Religious Education) I. Vale
Specialist Inspector (Design and Technology) G. West
County Youth Development Officer D.T. Holland
Community Education Development Officer (South Oxfordshire) P. Bussell; Tel (01865) 810545
Community Education Development Officer (Oxford City) M. Hanaway; Tel (01865) 815232
Community Education Development Officer (Cherwell) M. Prichard; Tel (01865) 815153
Community Education Development Officer (West Oxfordshire) M. Robbins; Tel (01865) 815119
Community Education Development Officer (Vale of White Horse) C. Sewell; Tel (01865) 810517
Assistant Director of Commercial Services (Catering and Cleaning) R Heaton

Number of Schools

18 nursery; 239 first and primary; 10 middle (9-13) (6 county, 2 aided 2 controlled); 6 Upper (13-18) (5 county, 1 aided); 29 Secondary (27 county, 1 controlled, 1 aided); 30 adult education/community education centres; 1 teachers' centre

Special Schools

11 Learning; 1 physically handicapped; 2 management; 1 hospital

Day of Commitee Meeting

Tuesday, quarterly

Education Committee

Con 9, Lab 9, LD 7
Group Spokesperson D.L.B. Spencer, (Con) Walhall, Bucknell Rd, Bicester OX6 8DG
Group Spokesperson Cllr B. Hodgson, (Lab) 38 Greenfield Cres, Stonesfield, Witney OX8 8EH
Group Spokesperson Cllr Janet Morgan, (LD) 7 Warwick Cl, Abingdon OX14 2HN

Members of the Committee

Con: H.B. Cundall, C.A. Fulljames, N.A.S. Matthews, K.R. Mitchell, A.J. Robertson, D.M. Smith, J.G. Todd, D.M. Turner
Lab: B.H. Duggan, D.S.T. Enright, D.A. Green, J.B. Hodgson, W.I. Humphries, T. Richardson, M.S. Smith, S.J. Thompkins, Vacancy
LD: J.M. Bostock, B.J. Churchill, A.T. Lambert, J. Mayhew-Archer, R.M.C. Morgan, J. Morgan, D.G. Turner

Governor Training Co-ordinators

Community Education Development Officer (West Division) Michele Robbins; Tel (01865) 815119
Community Education Development Officer (South Division) Peter Bussell; Tel (01865) 810545
Community Education Development Officer (City Division) Monica Hanaway; Tel (01865) 815232
Community Education Development Officer (Vale Division) Chris Sewell; Tel (01865) 810517

Community Education Development Officer (Cherwell Division) Mari Prichard; Tel (01865) 815153

Services Offered

Governor training is co-ordinated by the 5 Community Education Development Officers and includes: Countywide and local programmes for both new and experienced governors; Countywide and Divisional newsletters; Resource bases

Hospital Schools

Oxford City (Nuffield & Radcliffe) Hospital Education Service Nuffield Orthopaedic Centre, Headington, Oxford OX3 7LD; Tel (01865) 227554; *Head Teacher* B. Graham. (Orthopaedic and Paediatric) (51)

Special Schools

Bardwell, Hendon Pl, Bicester OX6 7RZ; Tel (01869) 242182; C. Hughes. (E.S.N.(S) (Day) (48)
Bennett Hse, Radley Rd, Abingdon OX14 3RR; Tel (01235) 523843; A. O'Meara (Acting). (Learning) (59); (Day)
Bishopswood, School Office, Sonning Common Primary School, Grove Rd, Sonning Common, Reading RG4 9RJ; Tel (01734) 724311; V. Northfield. (Learning) (42); (Day)
Fitzwaryn, Denchworth Rd, Wantage OX12 9ET; Tel (01235) 764504; M. Tighe (Acting). (Learning) (Day) (76)
Frank Wise, Hornbeam Cl, Broughton Rd, Banbury OX16 9QJ; Tel (01295) 263520; K.A. Griffiths. (Learning) (56); Day
Iffley Mead, Iffley Turn, Oxford OX4 4DU; Tel (01865) 747606; J. Knox. (Learning) (160); (Day)
John Watson, Holton Pk, Wheatley, Oxford OX33 1QJ; Tel (01865) 872515; D. Wilson. (Learning) (35); (Day)
Mabel Prichard, St Nicholas Rd, Littlemore, Oxford OX4 4PN; Tel (01865) 777878; K. Harris. (Learning) (45)
Northern Hse, South Pde, Oxford OX2 7JN; Tel (01865) 57004; R. Howarth. (Management) (55); (Day)
Northfield School, Knights Rd, Blackbird Leys, Oxford OX4 5DQ; Tel (01865) 771703; Fax (01865) 773873; P. Sheldon. (Management) (61); (Day and Residential)
Ormerod, Waynflete Rd, Oxford OX3 8DD; Tel (01865) 744173; Fax (01865) 62776; Vacancy. (Del. & P.H.) (60); (Day)
Springfield, 9 Moorland Cl, Witney, Oxon OX8 5LN; Tel (01993) 703963; S.C. Niner. (Learning) (28); (Day)
Tesdale, Blacknall Rd, Abingdon OX14 5HE; Tel (01235) 555512; E.M. Sims (Acting). (Learning) (57); (Day)
Woodeaton Manor, Woodeaton, Oxford OX3 9TS; Tel (01865) 58722; Fax (01865) 311561; C. Greenhow. (Learning) (50); (Mixed); (Weekly Residential); (6–16)

Upper Schools

Cheney Cheney La, Headington, Oxford OX3 7QH; Tel (01865) 65726; Fax (01865) 67399; A.J. Lane, MA, MSc. (830)
The Cherwell Marston Ferry Rd, Oxford OX2 7EE; Tel (01865) 58719; Fax (01865) 311165; H.M. Roberts, MA. (688)
Milham Ford C. Girls' Harberton Mead, Oxford OX3 0DF; Tel (01865) 243468; Fax (01865) 251354; E. Higgins. (481)
Oxford C. Boys' Glanville Rd, Oxford OX4 2AU; Tel (01865) 777134; Fax (01865) 715086; M. Langford. (663)
Peers Sandy La West, Littlemore, Oxfordshire OX4 5JY; Tel (01865) 774311; Fax (01865) 715677; B. Clarke. (864)
St Augustine of Canterbury R.C./C.E. Iffley Turn, Oxford OX4 4DX; Tel (01865) 778011; Fax (01865) 775187; J.H. Prangley, BA, BPhil. (646)

Middle Schools

Bayswater Bayswater Rd, Oxford OX3 9NU; Tel (01865) 61656; Fax (01865) 742671; D. Parker. (391)
Cardinal Newman R.C. Cricket Rd, Cowley, Oxford OX4 3DR; Tel (01865) 749933; Fax (01865) 717314; J. Batey. (V.A.) (5–12) (265)
Donnington Cornwallis Rd, Oxford OX4 3NH; Tel (01865) 779334; L. Reeves. (388)
Frideswide C.E. Marston, Ferry Rd, Oxford OX2 7EE; Tel (01865) 511285; Fax (01865) 514907; A. Freeney. (557)
Headington Margaret Rd, Headington, Oxford OX3 8NH; Tel (01865) 62504; P. Baum. (422)
Lawn Upton C.E. Sandford Rd, Littlemore, Oxford OX4 4PU; Tel (01865) 779126; Fax (01865) 749362; H.S.M. Turner. (385)
Marston Oxford Rd, Marston, Oxford OX3 0PG; Tel (01865) 242946; Fax (01865) 201843; D. Gillard. (352)
Temple Cowley Temple Rd, Oxford OX4 2HD; Tel (01865) 774668; Fax (01865) 718251; M. Thomas. (454)
The Isis C.E. Middle Meadow La, Oxford OX4 1JJ; Tel (01865) 723841; P. Renshaw. (455)
Wesley Grn Wesley Close, Oxford OX4 5BG; Tel (01865) 774648; P. Reast

Secondary Schools

Banbury Ruskin Rd, Banbury OX16 9HY; Tel (01295) 251451; A.M.C. Higham, BA. (1460)
Bartholomew Witney Rd, Eynsham, Witney OX8 1PQ; Tel (01865) 881430; W.S. Berry, BA. (658)
Bicester Community College Queen's Ave, Bicester OX6 8NS; Tel (01869) 243331; R. Blatchford, Ba, MA. (892)
Blessed George Napier R.C. Addison Rd, Banbury OX16 9DG; Tel (01295) 264216/7; T. O'Flynn, BA, ADB, ACP. (570)
Burford School and Community College Cheltenham Rd, Burford OX18 4PL; Tel (01993) 823303; Vacancy. (1085)
Carterton Community College Upavon Way, Carterton OX18 3BU; Tel (01993) 841611/2; A.D. Klee, MA. (440)
Chiltern Edge Reade's La, Sonning Common, Reading RG4 9LN; Tel (01734) 722666; Fax (01734) 2724116; Dr V. Morris. (880)
Chipping Norton Burford Rd, Chipping Norton OX7 5DY; Tel (01608) 642007; J.G. Howells, BA. (836)
The Cooper Churchill Rd, Bicester, Oxford OX6 7TS; Tel (01869) 242121; K. McClellan. (780)
Didcot Girls' Sherwood Rd, Didcot OX11 0DA; Tel (01235) 812092; Fax (01235) 511245; J. Hebbert. (683)
Drayton Drayton Rd, Banbury OX16 0UD; Tel (01295) 253181; R. Nichol, BEd, BPhil. (684)
Faringdon Fernham Rd, Faringdon SN7 7LB; Tel (01367) 240375; R. Norman, MA(Oxon). (580)
Fitzharrys Northcourt Rd, Abingdon OX14 1NP; Tel (01235) 520698; P. Bloomfield, BSc PhD. (901)
Gillott's Gillott's La, Henley-on-Thames RG9 1PS; Tel (01491) 574315; Fax (01491) 410509; J. Lockyer, BA. (628)
Gosford Hill Oxford Rd, Kidlington OX5 2NT; Tel (01865) 374971; D.J. Rowley, BSc. (1129)
Henry Box Church Grn, Witney OX8 6AX; Tel (01993) 703955; J.D. Barker. (1005)
Icknield Love La, Watlington OX9 5RB; Tel (01491) 612691/2; Fax (01491) 612951; S. Brown, BA. (557)
John Mason Wootton Rd, Abingdon OX14 1JB; Tel (01235) 524664; J.T. Cunningham, MA, MPhil. (945)
King Alfred's Portway, Wantage OX12 9BY; Tel (01235) 763061; M.R.C. Jones, BSc. (1856)
Langtree Reading Rd, Woodcote, Reading, Berks RG8 0RA; Tel (01491) 680514; Fax (01491) 682411; J. Owens. (405)
Larkmead Faringdon Rd, Abingdon OX14 1RF; Tel (01235) 520141; D.R. Walker, MA. (1056)
Lord Williams's Oxford Rd, Thame OX9 2AQ; Tel (01844) 213681; Fax (01844) 261382; D. Kenningham, MA. (1788)
Marlborough Shipton Rd, Woodstock OX20 1LP; Tel (01993) 811431; E. McConnell, BA, MSc. (653)
Matthew Arnold Arnolds Way, Oxford OX2 9JE; Tel (01865) 862232; E.A. Howarth, BA. (830)

St Birinus Boys' Mereland Rd, Didcot OX11 8AZ; Tel (01235) 814444; Fax (01235) 512258; C. Bryan, BA, MA(Ed). (623)
Wallingford St Georges Rd, Wallingford OX10 8LB; Tel (01491) 837115; Fax (01491) 825278; D.G. Kershaw, MA. (902)
The Warriner Banbury Rd, Bloxham, Banbury OX15 4LJ; Tel (01295) 720777/8; R.M. Spencer, BPhil. (963)
Wheatley Park Holton, Oxford OX33 1QH; Tel (01865) 872441; N. Young, BSc. (1181)
Wood Green Woodstock Rd, Witney OX8 6DX; Tel (01993) 702355; P.J. May. (939)

Youth and Community Centres

Berinsfield Campus Youth Centre Wimblestraw Rd, Berinsfield, Wallingford OX10 8LZ; Tel (01865) 340301; K. Chrisp. (151)
Abingdon Youth and Community Centre Stratton Way, Abingdon OX14 3RG; Tel (01235) 521469; C.T. Greenop
Allandale Youth House Burford Rd, Carterton OX18 3AA; Tel (01993) 842416; S. Humphreys
Anne Brown Youth Centre, Icknield School, Watlington OX9 5RB; Tel (01491) 612516; A. Martin
Banbury Youth Centre, Hilton Road, Banbury OX16 0EJ; Tel (01295) 264665; R.A. Smith
Bicester Youth Centre, Launton Rd, Bicester OX6 7DJ; Tel (01869) 252759; J. Brewis. (The Courtyard)
Blackbird Leys Community Centre Blackbird Leys Rd, Oxford OX4 5HW; Tel (01865) 772886; S. Curran
Carterton Community Education Centre Carterton Community College, Upavon Way, Carterton OX18 3BU; Tel (01993) 841776; R. Jones. (342)
Chiltern Edge Community Education Centre Reade's La, Sonning Common, Reading, Berks RG4 9LN; Tel (01734) 723362; L. Boardley. (506)
Chiltern Edge Youth Wing Reade's La, Sonning Common, Reading, Berks RG4 9LN; Tel (01734) 723362; I. Sharp
Chipping Norton Youth Centre, Chipping Norton School, 60 Burford Rd, Chipping Norton OX7 5DY; Tel (01608) 644645; D. Haigh
Cowley & District Community Education Office Union Street Complex, Union St, Oxford 0X4 1JP; Tel (01865) 727148; Mary Hedderwick. (486)
Didcot Youth and Community Centre Park Rd, Didcot OX11 8QX; Tel (01235) 812332; A. Honeyball
East Oxford Youth Centre Union Street Complex, Union St, Oxford OX4 1JP; Tel (01865) 248521; Melanie Clarke
Eynsham Youth Centre Back La, Eynsham, Witney OX8 1QW; Tel (01865) 880630; N. Luxmoore, BA
Faringdon Centre, Faringdon School, Fernham Rd, Faringdon SN7 7LB; Tel (01367) 240922; G. Clitheroe. (566)
The Forum Youth Centre Exeter Cl, Kidlington OX5 1AB; Tel (018675) 5555; R. Clow
Headington Community Education Office, Northway Centre, Maltfield Rd, Oxford OX3 9RG; Tel (01865) 68359; Alison Soskice (Adult); Bob Medcalf (Youth)
Henley Youth Centre 1 Deanfield Ave, Henley-on-Thames RG9 1UH; Tel (01491) 575687; D. Hall
Icknield Community Education Centre, Icknield School, Love La, Watlington OX9 5RB; Tel (01491) 613004; J. Horsup. (326)
Kidlington Community Education Centre Oxford Rd, Kidlington OX5 2NT; Tel (01865) 372165; M. Russell. (1394)
The Mill, Community Education and Arts Centre, Spiceball Park, Banbury OX16 8QE; Tel (01295) 252050; A.J. Snee
North and West Oxford Community Education Committee, The Ferry Centre, Diamond Pl, Banbury Rd, Summertown, Oxford OX2 7PD; Tel (01865) 52295; *Chair and Management Committee* Margaret Bonfiglioni; *Adult* Marianne Moxon; *Youth* Steve Nyman. (1476)
Thame Youth Centre Lord Williams's Lower School, Towersey Rd, Thame OX9 3NW; Tel (01844) 212973; Paula Davies; Anita Martin
Wantage Youth Centre King Alfred's School, Springfield Rd, Wantage OX12 8ET; Tel (01235) 763863; G. Kingett
Wallingford Youth and Community Centre, Clapcot Way, Wallingford OX10 8HS; Tel (01491) 837053; M. Bradley
Wheatley Youth Centre, Littleworth Rd, Wheatley OX9 1NW; Tel (01865) 873916; Paula Davies. (358)
Witney Youth and Community Centre Witan Way, Witney OX8 6YA; Tel (01993) 772731; N. Burnley

Youth Service

Wantage Youth Service, King Alfred's Centre Site, Portway, Wantage OX12 9BY; Tel (01235) 762356; R. Ashwell

Youth Work

Abingdon Detached Youth Work Project, 27 Bridge St, Abingdon OX14 3HN; J. Ralph
Botley Area Youth Work, Area Youth Office, Matthew Arnold School, Arnold's Way, Cumnor, Oxford OX2 9JE; Tel (01865) 864717; J. Linthwaite
Faringdon Area Youth Work Area Youth Office, Faringdon Youth Centre, Faringdon; Tel (01317) 240155; R. Aldridge

Institutes of Adult Education

Banbury Continuing Education Council The Mill Centre, Spiceball Pk, Banbury OX16 8QE; Tel (01295) 266763; P. Scott
Bicester Adult Education Centre Bicester Community College, Queen's Ave, Bicester OX6 8NS; Tel (01869) 241532; P. Smith. (1039)
Burford School and Community College, Cheltenham Rd, Burford OX18 4PL; Tel (01993) 822314; S. Haynes. (172)
Chalgrove Community Education Centre Chalgrove County Primary School, Chalgrove OX44 7ST; Tel (01865) 400169; J. Horsup. (134)
Charlbury Adult Education Centre The Headmaster's Hse, The Playing Cl, Charlbury, Oxford; Tel (01608) 810961; A.A. Grierson. (335)
Chinnor Adult Education Centre St Andrew's C.E. Primary School, Chinnor, Oxford; Tel (01844) 354243; S. Bruce, BSc. (584)
Chipping Norton Area Community Education Council The Community Education Office, 60 Burford Rd, Chipping Norton; Tel (01608) 641644; M. Bardsley. (624)
Cumnor Adult Education Centre Matthew Arnold School, Cumnor OX2 9JE; Tel (01865) 862009; Jan Rogers (Acting). (523)
Didcot Adult Education Centre Park Rd, Didcot OX11 8QX; Tel (01235) 812002/812332; A. Honeyball. (508)
Eynsham Community Education Centre, Bartholomew School, Eynsham, Witney OX8 1PQ; Tel (01865) 880380; B. McLaren. (479)
Faringdon Area Community Education Centre, Faringdon School, Fernham Rd, Faringdon SN7 7LB; Tel (01367) 240922; *Head* H. Dorling
Grove Centre Millbrook, Grove, Wantage, Oxford OX12 7LB; Tel (01235) 764821; P. Coleman. (435)
Hook Norton Adult Education Centre Hook Norton C.E. Primary School, Hook Norton, Banbury OX15 5JS; Tel (01608) 730052; L. Buchanan. (427)
Langtree & Goring Community Education Centres C/o Woodcote Community Centre, Woodcote, Reading RG8 0QY; Tel (01491) 681359; S. Winter
Littlemore Community Education Centre Sandy La West, Littlemore, Oxford OX4 5JY; Tel (01865) 712094/776696; *Adult* Alan Noble; *Youth* Farook Ahmed
Marlborough Adult Education Centre Marlborough School, Shipton Rd, Woodstock OX20 1LP; Tel (01993) 813134; F. Williams. (335)
New Start Guidance, King Alfred's Centre Site, Portway, Wantage OX12 9BY; Tel (01235) 771551; L. Bottomley; J. Williamson
Mount Farm Community Education Centre, Wimblestraw Rd, Berinsfield, Wallingford OX10 7LZ; Tel (01865) 340688; S. Reader

Thame Community Education Centre Towersey Rd, Thame 0X9 3NW; Tel (01844) 213400; Dr S. Holman. (1067)
Wallingford Adult Education Centre St George's Rd, Wallingford OX10 8HR; Tel (01491) 836710; J. Noble. (1410)
Wantage Community Education Centre King Alfred's School, East Site, Springfield Rd, Wantage OX12 8ET; Tel (01235) 765021; T. Mather. (874)

Adult Basic Skills

Vale Community Education Office King Alfred's Centre Site, Portway, Wantage OX12 9BY; Tel (01235) 762356

Special Services

Service for Sensory Impairment

Service for Sensory Impairment c/o John Watson School, Holton Pk, Wheatley, Oxon OX33 1QJ; Tel (01865) 875165; Fax (01865) 875163; *Headteacher* E. Moore

Resource Bases for Pupils with Hearing Impairment

North Oxfordshire Queensway County Primary School, Queensway, Banbury, Oxon OX16 9NF; Tel (01296) 275926; *Team Leader* F. Watton (Acting)
Mid Oxfordshire New Marston First School, Copse La, Headington, Oxford OX3 0AY; Tel (01865) 61522; *Team Leader* Dr N. Ereaut
South Oxfordshire Rush Common County Primary School, Hendred Way, Abingdon, Oxon OX14 2AW; Tel (01235) 531070; Fax (01235) 535863; *Team Leader* A. Holmans

Resource Base for Pupils with Visual Impairments

West Oxford Primary School, Ferry Hinksey Rd, Oxford OX2 0BY; Tel (01865) 792744; *Team Leader* P. Crane

Resource Bases for Pupils with Speech/Language Disorders

North Oxfordshire Queensway County Primary School, Queensway, Banbury, Oxon OX16 9NF; Tel (01295) 275926; *Team Leader* C. O'Keeffe (Acting)
Mid Oxfordshire; Team Leader P. Hudson Rose Hill First School, The Oval, Rose Hill, Oxford OX4 4SF; Tel (01865) 715132; *Team Leader* K. Siddle Donnington Middle School, Cornwallis Rd, Oxford OX4 3NH; Tel (01865) 718392; *Team Leader* P. Hudson. (Mixed) (5–9); (Mixed) (9–13) and outreach service for pupils aged 13+ operates from Donnington Middle School

Service for Motor Impairment

Ormerod School, Waynflete Rd, Headington, Oxford OX3 8DD; Tel (01865) 744173; *Co-ordinator* T. Southgate; *Deputy Co-ordinator* J.M. Williams

Support Service for Autism

Advisory Headteacher C. Simmonds c/o John Watson School, Holton Pk, Wheatley, Oxford OX33 1QJ; Tel (01865) 875172; Fax (01865) 875163
Chinnor St Andrew's Primary School, Station Rd, Chinnor, Oxon OX9 4PU; Tel (01844) 353123; *Teacher-in-Charge* S. Coates
St Nicholas First School, Raymund Rd, Old Marston, Oxford OX3 0PJ; Tel (01865) 726956
Lord William's Upper School, Uplands, Oxford Rd, Thame, Oxon OX9 2AQ; Tel (01844) 218800
Lord William's Lower School East, Towersey Rd, Thame, Oxon OX9 3NN; Tel (01844) 260339

Powys County Council

Population 120,000 (approx)
Powys County Hall, Llandrindod Wells, Powys LD1 5LG; Tel (01597) 826000; Fax (01597) 826230

Education Department

Powys County Hall, Llandrindod Wells, Powys LD1 5LG; Tel (01597) 826000; Fax (01597) 826230
Chief Executive and County Treasurer A.J. Barnish, BCom, IPFA
Director of Architecture and Property Services P. Wharton, DipArch, RIBA
Director of Social Services T.L. Begg
County Librarian Miss E. Ducker
Chairman Councillor H.G. Jones
Vice-Chairman Councillor G. Morgan
Director of Education R.W. Bevan, MA(Ed), BA, DipEd
Deputy Director of Education T.A.V. Evans, BA
Assistant Director of Education: (Administration) W.J. Traylor
Assistant Director of Education: (Schools) M.R.J. Barker, BSc
Assistant Director of Education: (Further Education) A.J. Bell, BA
Senior Assistant Education Officer Mrs J. Howells, BSc
Assistant Education Officer J. Mitson, MA
Drama Adviser J. Greatorex
T.V.E.I Coordinator Dr M. E. Brookes
Languages Adviser D.G. Evans
Mathematics Adviser Mrs K. Pratt
English Adviser Mrs A.D. Hawkins
Modern Languages Adviser M.J. Clarke
Science Adviser G. Gaskill
Early Years Education Adviser Mrs M.E. Morgan
Senior Educational Psychologist J.G. Tuthill
Special Needs Tutor/Organiser D.J. Meredith
Chief Administrative Assistant S. Roderick
Principal Careers Officer J.H. Morris, DCG
Senior Adviser for INSET (Co-ordinator) J. R. Wilson
County Community Development Officer D.W Hall, BA Ladywell Hse, Park St, Newtown, Powys; Tel (01686) 626521
Number of schools
109 primary; 13 comprehensive; 4 special; 8 teachers' centres
Day of Commitee Meeting
Tuesday
Requisition Periods for School Supplies
All year

Governor Training Unit

Powys County Hall, Llandrindod Wells, Powys LD1 5LG; Tel (01597) 826431; Fax (01597) 826230
EO (Development Services) John Mitson, MA
Services Offered
Training courses; Seminars; Surgery sessions; Advice for Governors; Resources and training materials; Termly newsletter; Support for Governors (clerking, preparation of prospectus and minutes, advice at meetings)

Special Schools

Brynllywarch, Kerry, Newtown, Powys; Tel (0168688) 276; D.C. Williams. (Residential) (Boys)
Cyfronydd, Castle Caereinion; Tel (0193 883) 205; E.H. Jones. (Residential) (Girls)
Ysgol Cedewain, Newtown; Tel (01686) 627454; E.M. Edwards
Ysgol Penmaes, Brecon; Tel (01874) 623508; J.R. Lawicki. Mixed

Comprehensive Schools (11–18)

Brecon High Tel (01874) 622361; A. Whiley, BA. (Mixed) (815)
Builth Wells Tel (01982) 553292; I.D. Brown, BSc, MSc. (Mixed) (460)
Crickhowell High Tel (01873) 811033; D.R. Davies, MEd. (Mixed) (610)
Gwernyfed High Three Clocks, Brecon, Powys; Tel (01497) 847445; Mrs P.G. Palin, BA. (Mixed) (505)
John Beddoes Presteigne, Powys; Tel (01544) 267259; J.S. Walbran, MA. (Mixed) (500)
Llandrindod High Dyffryn Rd, Llandrindod Wells, Powys; Tel (01597) 822992; B.P. Heard, BSc, MSc. (Mixed) (750)
Llanfair Caereinion High Tel (01938) 810888; J.E.J. Lewis, BSc. (Mixed) (420)
Llanfyllin High Tel (01691) 648391; Dr D. Leighton. Mixed (530)
Llanidloes High Tel (0155 12) 2289; Dr J.G. Hughes, PhD, LLB, BSc. (Mixed) (470)
Maesydderwen Tudor St, Ystradgynlais, Powys; Tel (01639) 842115; D.B. Marks, BSc. (Mixed) (660)
Newtown High Tel (01686) 626304; D.W. Walters, BA. (Mixed) (1080)
Welshpool High Tel (01938) 552014; S.A. McConaghie, BSc. (Mixed) (680)
Ysgol Bro Ddyfi Machynlleth, Powys; Tel (01654) 702012; C.G. Davies, BA. (Mixed) (325)

Rochdale Metropolitan Borough Council

Population 202,164
Town Hall, Rochdale, Lancs OL16 1AB; Tel (01706) 47474; Fax (01706) 59475

Education Department

PO Box 70, Municipal Offices, Smith St, Rochdale OL16 1YD; Tel (01706) 47474
Director of Education D.L. Cavanagh, MSc
Assistant Director of Education (Business Units) A. Bebb
Customer Liaison Manager J. Bollington
Customer Support Manager D. Laytham
Assistant Director (Finance) J.L. Cook
Education Officer (Pupil Welfare) S. Dearden
Senior Education Officer (Careers) S. Lord, DipCG
Principal Awards Officer I. Denny
SEO (LMR) W. Ollerenshaw
SEO (Development) J. Edmonds
EO (LMR) G. Crowther
Principal Youth Community Officer (Youth Work) Martin Notley
Principal Community Education Officer (Adult/Continuing Education) Jane Black
Principal Community Education Officer (Schools) Nan Jackson
Principal Childrens Services Officer Richard Williams
Professional Assistant H.M. Bambrough
Professional Assistant J. Booth
Professional Assistant Margaret Stouton
Assistant Director/Chief Adviser Dr S. Hodge
General Adviser R. Bramwell
General Adviser S. Hobson
General Adviser S.J. Brown, BA
Team Leader Adviser A. Quaife
General Adviser G. Wilkinson
General Adviser C. Murchie, BEd
General Adviser M.C. Simpson, BEd
Adviser SACRE Rev Freda Jackson
Principal Educational Psychologist D. Williams

Number of Schools
8 nursery; 71 primary; 12 high

Special Schools
7 day; 1 residential

Day of Committee Meeting
Thursday (six-weekly cycle)

Council Tax Payers 1993/194 85,000

Education Committee

LD 8, Con 5, Lab 8
Chair R.D. Colley, (LD) Dewhirst Hse, Dewhirst Rd, Rochdale OL12 9TX
Vice-Chair R. Sarginson, (LD) 11 Knowl View, Smithybridge, Littleborough OL15 0BU

Members of the Committee
LD: R.D. Colley, R. Sarginson, P.W. Barnes, J. Heyworth, N.F. Smith, A. Coric, T. Flynn
Con: J.T. Gartside, R. Keen, J.K. McIntosh, V.A. Mannion, R. Taylor, B.J. Wright
Lab: N.P. Emmott, D.E. Moffat, R.A. Parker, L. Worsley
Lab and Co-op: A.D. Williams, J.P. Brown, A.H. Chowdry, S. Oja-Bello

Governor Training Unit

Governor Support Unit, Fl 8, Municipal Offices, Smith St, Rochdale OL16 1YD; Tel (01706) 47474 Ext 5143; Fax (01706) 865030
Customer Liaison Manager John Bollington
Senior Admin Officer (Governor Support) Jeanette Evans

Services Offered
Governing Body support; Clerking school governing bodies; Governor training

Psychological Service

Fieldhouse School, Greenbank Rd, Rochdale OL12 0HZ; Tel (01706) 40477; D. Williams

Special Schools

Adlington Unit, High Birch Special School, Bolton Rd, Rochdale OL11 4RA; Tel 31752; C. Broomhead (Acting). (16–19) (E.S.N.(S.)
Alderman Kay, Tintern Rd, Hollin, Middleton M24 6JG; Tel 0161-643 4917; Fax 0161-655 4081; J.M. Clarke. (E.S.N.(M.)
Alf Kaufman, Highwood, Norden, Rochdale OL11 5XP; Tel (01706) 359153; P.D. Geldeart, BA. (P.H.) (primary age)
Birtle View, George St, Heywood OL10 4PW; Tel (01706) 368821; Fax (01706) 620760; L. Howarth, MEd. (E.S.N.(S.)
Brownhill, Heights La, Rochdale OL12 0PZ; Tel (01706) 48990; Fax (01706) 48537; J. Novak, MEd. (Malad.)
High Birch, Bolton Rd, Rochdale OL11 4RA; Tel (01706) 31752; C. Broomhead (Acting). (E.S.N.(M.)
Innes, Ings La, Rochdale OL12 7DW; Tel (01706) 46605; Fax (01706) 48783; F.S. Stanley, BPhil(Ed). (E.S.N.(S.)
Knowl View, Norden Rd, Bamford, Rochdale OL11 5PT; Tel (01706) 50511; Fax (01706) 860554. (Malad.) (Boys)
Language Unit Castleton C.P. School, Hillcrest Rd, Rochdale OL11 2QD; Tel (01706) 31858
Rydings, Great Howarth, Wardle Rd, Rochdale OL12 9HJ; Tel (01706) 57993; Fax (01706) 47112; R.A. Jazwinski. (E.S.N.(M.)

High Schools (11–16)

Balderstone Queen Victoria St, Rochdale OL11 2HJ; Tel (01706) 49049/(0706) 49479/(01706) 31387; Fax (01706) 44945; M.J. Von Emloh, BA. (Mixed) (1200)
Falinge Park High Falinge Rd, Rochdale OL12 6LD; Tel (01706) 31246; Fax (01706) 46538; L. Woolley, BEd, MA

Heywood Community Sutherland Rd, Darnhill, Heywood OL10 3PL; Tel (01706) 360466/366344; Fax (01706) 627280; J. Bleakley, DipEd
Matthew Moss High Matthew Moss La, Rochdale OL11 3LU; Tel (01706) 32910; Fax (01706) 523857; A. Raymer, MA
Oulder Hill, Hudsons Walk, Rochdale OL11 5EF; Tel (01706) 55222; Fax (01706) 48404; D.J. Wilson, MA, MEd. (Mixed) (11–18) (1550)
The Queen Elizabeth High School, Hollin La, Middleton M24 5LE; Tel 0161-643 2643; D. Lack, MEd
Siddal Moor Newhouse Rd, Heywood OL12 2NT; Tel (01706) 369436; Fax (01706) 620830; B. Cunliffe, BA, BPhil. (Mixed) (960)
Springhill High Turf Hill Rd, Rochdale OL16 4XA; Tel (01706) 40931; Fax (01706) 524770; A. Hannan, BA

High Schools (Voluntary Aided 11–16)

St Joseph's R.C. High Pot Hall, Heywood OL10 2AA; Tel (01706) 360607; Fax (01706) 620818; M.J. Connolly, BA MEd. (Mixed) (600)

High Schools (11–18)

Middleton Technology Kenyon La, Middleton M24 2DG; Tel 0161-643 5116; Fax 0161-654 6024; P. Coward, BA. (11–18) (1050)

High Schools (Voluntary Aided 11–18)

Cardinal Langley R.C. High Rochdale Rd, Middleton M24 2GL; Tel 0161-643 4009/5899; Fax 0161-655 4050; J.F. Durcan, MA. (Mixed) (1025)
St Cuthbert's R.C. High Shaw Rd, Rochdale, Greater Manchester OL16 4RX; Tel (01706) 47761; Fax (01706) 42378; F.X. Thompson, MEd. (11–18)

School Support Services

Language for Educational Access Project English Teaching Centre, Fieldhouse School, Greenbank Rd, Rochdale OL12 0HZ; Tel (01706) 47078; Fax (01706) 341519; I. Jones (Acting)
Rochdale Music Service Music Centre, Fieldhouse School, Greenbank Rd, Rochdale OL12 0HZ; Tel (01706) 56389; F. Bowker
Pupil Development Support Service, Hamer CP School, Albert Royds St, Rochdale OL16 2SU; Tel (01706) 33613/131520; *Head of Service* A. Florek

Adult Education Centres

Heywood Adult/Continuing Education Hind Hill Centre, Hind Hill St, Heywood; Tel (01706) 367590; Glenys Bentley
Middleton Adult/Continuing Education Durnford St, Middleton, Manchester, Greater Manchester; Tel 0161-643 3618; Desley Sanders
Littleborough/Adult/Continuing Education Littleborough Community Office, Calderbrook Rd, Littleborough, Greater Manchester; Tel (01706) 374900; Rosie Marcus

Grant Maintained Schools

Hollingworth High Cornfield St, Milnrow OL16 3DR; Tel (01706) 41541; P. Mortimer, BEd, MA, PhD, MEd
Wardle High Birch Rd, Wardle, Rochdale OL12 9RD; Tel (01706) 373911; W. Anderson, BA. (Mixed) (including P.H. secondary age) (1125)

Rotherham Metropolitan Borough Council

Population 253,600

Civic Bldg, Walker Pl, Rotherham S65 1UF; Tel (01709) 382121; Fax (01709) 371597

Education Department

Norfolk Hse, Walker Pl, Rotherham S60 1QT; Tel (01709) 382121; Fax (01709) 372056
Director of Education B.H. Yemm, MA
Chief Executive J. Bell, BA, IPFA
Director of Financial Sevices M. Mullins, IPFA
Executive Manager (Department of Architecture) I.H. Russell, ARICS
Director of Social Services P. Nolan, DMA
Director of Libaries, Museum and Arts C.C. Williams, DMA, ALA
Director of Amenities and Recreation R.V. Linegar, FILAM, FI(Hort), MBIM
Chairman Councillor T.R. Sharman
Vice-Chairman Councillor W. Winder
Deputy Director H.C. Bower, BA
Assistant Director: Services A.S. Hercock, BAS, AILGA
Assistant Director: Resources E.S. Langdon, DMA, MILGA
Principal Officer: Employee and Information Services E. Jarvis
Principal Officer: Local Management Development and Monitoring J.H. Ibbotson, BSc, MEd
Principal Officer: Adminstration and Consumer Services D.R. Hill, BSc, ACIS
Principal Officer: Programme Development G. Sinclair, MA
Principal Officer: European Programmes Vacancy
Principal Assistant: Special Education H. Butler, MEd
Principal Assistant: Resources P. Jackson
Principal Careers Advisory Officer S.E. Finnigan, BA
Deputy Principal Carrers Officer M. McNamara
Chief Adviser T. McCormack
Senior Adviser: Secondary C. Kinsella
Senior Adviser: Primary D. Powell
Senior Adviser: Compensatory and Special Education C. Richards
General Adviser: Nursery S. Walker
General Adviser: Infant P.S. Wood
General Adviser: Junior C.H.M. Place
General Adviser: Language Development M.J. Connell
General Adviser: Physical Education B. Chapple
General Adviser: Mathematics, Computer Studies D.C. Harris
General Adviser: Geography, History, Economics S.J. Womack
General Adviser: Music G.H. Thomas
General Adviser: Social and Personal Development and Multi-Cultural Education K. Robinson
General Adviser: Craft, Design and Technology Art, Audio Visual Resouces T. Slack
General Adviser: Modern Languages G.B. Richeux
General Adviser: Primary E. Buxton
General Adviser: TVEI P.G. Laming
Principal Youth & Community Adviser G. Eagle
Principal Educational Psychologist D. Cheetham, MA, ABPsS
Principal Officer: Salaries, Superannuation & Service P. Cook
Principal Officer: Premises B. Appleton, DMA
Education Catering Client Manager L. Handley
Youth & Community Adviser R. Baldwyn
Youth & Community Adviser L. Bailey
Youth & Community Adviser R.A. Boyle
Principal Officer: LMS L. Hill
Principal Officer: Administration S. Buxton
Senior Careers Advisory Officer B.A. Newick
Senior Careers Advisory Officer Vacancy
Chief Education Welfare Officer W. Bycroft

Number of Schools

3 nursery (383); 115 primary (22,573); 17 secondary (16,988)

Special Schools

5 E.S.N. (496); 1 Physically handicapped (89); 1 Maladjusted (30)

Committee Meeting

Monthly except May and August

Requisition Periods for School Supplies; None; Joint Purchasing Arrangement: Yorkshire Purchasing Organisation

Education Committee

Lab 26, Con 1
Chair T.R. Sharman, (Lab) 20 Manor Hse Rd, Kimberworth, Rotherham S61 1NT; Tel (01709) 557580
Vice-Chair W. Winder, (Lab) 14 Rockland Villas, Doncaster Rd, Thrybergh, Rotherham S65 4AG; Tel (01909) 851335
Members of the Committee
Lab: D.A. Appleyard, K.E. Billington, A. Britton, J. Burchby, M.G. Boyes, J. Carr, F. Cooper, M.T. Edgell, G.S. Etchells, A. Gosling, M.J. Hoggard, N. Hamilton, C.A. Kelly, M.R. Kirk, Sir J. Layden JP, P. McSweeney, G.B. Robinson JP, S.D. Russell, A. Senior, T.R. Sharman, I.G.L. St.John, C. Swindell, M. Wainwright, W. Winder, R. Windle, K.J. Wyatt
Con: D.J. Nuttall

Governor Training Unit

Governors Section, Education Offices, Norfolk Hse, Walker Pl, Rotherham S60 1QT; Tel (01709) 822510; Fax (01709) 372056
Training Co-ordinator, School Governors David Borthwick, BEd
Services Offered
Training for Governors; Training for individual Governing Bodies and cluster groups of Governing Bodies; Newsletter, 3 times a year; Training for clerks to Governing Bodies; Training for Link Governors; Learning pack for School Governors; Booklets on Hints and Guideance for Governors and Clerks; Advice and support through Helpline; Resources for Governors personal use

Day Special Schools & Hospital Special Schools

Abbey, Little Common La, Kimberworth, Rotherham S61 2RA; Tel (01709) 740074; J.S. Swain. (134)
Green Arbour, Locksley Dr, Thurcroft S66 9NT; Tel (01709) 542539; I. Hill. (135)
Hilltop, Larch Rd, Maltby S66 8AZ; Tel (01709) 813386; P. Leach. (82)
Kelford, Oakdale Rd, Kimberworth, Rotherham S61 2NU; Tel (01709) 740791; S.L. Greenhough. (75)
Milton, Storey St, Swinton, Mexborough S64 8QG; Tel (01709) 570246; *Head Teacher* C. Garford (Acting). (100)
Newman, East Bawtry Rd, Rotherham S60 3LX; Tel (01709) 828262; J.C.J. Goode. (P.H.) (89)
Whiston Grange, East Bawtry Rd, Rotherham S60 3LX; Tel (01709) 828838; R.J. Brewer. (Malad) (38)

Secondary Schools

Aston Aughton Rd, Swallownest S31 0TF; Tel (0114) 287 2171; G.C. Lowe, MEd. (1690)
Brinsworth Brinsworth Rd, Brinsworth, Rotherham S60 5EJ; Tel (01709) 828383; M. Gray, BA. (1409)
Clifton Middle La, Rotherham S65 2SN; Tel (01709) 828840; D.G. Light, MEd. (1134)
Dinnington Doe Quarry La, Dinnington S31 7NH; Tel (01909) 550066; G. Forster, BSc. (1384)
Kimberworth Kimberworth Rd, Rotherham S61 1HE; Tel (01709) 740471; M. Whale, BSc. (751)
Maltby Braithwell Rd, Maltby S66 8AB; Tel 812864; D. Musson, BA. (1431)
Oakwood Moorgate Rd, Rotherham S60 2UE; Tel (01709) 373664 & 373665; J. Charters, MSc. (852)
Old Hall Kimberworth, Rotherham S61 2BD; Tel (01709) 740232; W.A. Bainbridge, BSc. (1028)
Rawmarsh Monkwood Rd, Rawmarsh Rotherham S62 7ET; Tel (01709) 710672; A.C. Evans, MA. (864)
St Bernard's R.C. Herringthorpe Valley Rd, Rotherham S65 3BE; Tel (01709) 828183; C.T. Giblin, BA. (638)
Swinton Comprehensive East Ave, Swinton S64 8JW; Tel (01709) 570586; D. Bates, BSc. (1150)
Thrybergh Arran Hill, Park La, Thrybergh S65 4BJ; Tel 850471; S.M. Marshall, MSc. (578)
Wales Storth La, Kiveton Pk, Sheffield S31 8QS; Tel (01909) 771291; L. Morton, MEd. (1249)
Wath Comprehensive Sandygate, Wath-on-Dearne, Rotherham S63 7NW; Tel (01709) 760222; D. Kirby, CertEd. (1701)
Wath Pope Pius R.C. Wath Wood Rd, Wath-on-Dearne, Rotherham S63 7PQ; Tel (01709) 760218; D. Roche, MSc. (695)
Wickersley Bawtry Rd, Wickersley, Rotherham S66 0JL; Tel (01709) 542147/543170; J.T. Deeley, BA. (1744)
Wingfield Wingfield Estate, Rotherham S61 4AU; Tel (01709) 740362; M.S. Harris, BSc. (534)

Teachers' Centre

Parkhurst Doncaster Rd, Rotherham S65 2BL; Tel (01709) 828191
Rockingham Centre Roughwood Rd, Wingfield Estate, Rotherham, S Yorks; Tel (01709) 740226

Outdoor Pursuits Centres

Crowden Hadfield, Hyde, Cheshire SK14 7HZ; Tel (01475) 862821
Habershon House Primrose Valley, Filey YO14 9QX; Tel (01723) 513194
Ulley Water Activities Centre Ulley Reservoir, Aughton, Sheffield, S Yorks; Tel (01709) 828151

St Helens Metropolitan Borough Council

Population 180,000
Town Hall, St Helens, Merseyside WA10 1HP; Tel (01744) 456000

Community Education Department

The Rivington Centre, Rivington Rd, St Helens, Merseyside WA10 4ND; Tel (01744) 24061; Fax (01744) 455350
Chairman M. Newman
Deputy Chairman Cllr A. Whiteside
Director of Community Education B. Mainwaring
Assistant Director of Education (Establishment Support Services) Dr I.R. Gault
Assistant Director of Education (Pupil/Student Support Services) M. Smith
Education Management Accountant S. Gaskell
Building and Contract Services Officer M. Farrell
Personnel Officer P. Cunningham
Management Information Services Officer L. Wright
SEO (Entitlement) J.M. Laute
AEO (Community) J.R. Rosier
AEO (External Resources and Training) G.D. Butler
EO (Forward Planning and Statistics) J. Skinley
EO (Governor Services and Training) G. Greenhalgh
Senior Inspector (Primary) J.F.R. Hagan
Inspector (Primary) J. Hunter
Inspector (Primary) D. Twist
Inspector (Primary) C. McBride
Inspector (Primary) P. Snelling
Inspector (Secondary & Post-Compulsory) M.A. Hill
Inspector (Secondary & Post-Compulsory) P. Mather
Inspector (Secondary & Post-Compulsory) J. Stirrup

Professional Assistant (Awards & Admissions) C.W. Smith
Support Services Co-ordinator Vacancy
Statementing Officer E. Braben
Project Director, T.V.E.I A. Witt
Principal Educational Psychologist G. Bradley, BA
Educational Advisory Unit, Gamble Ave, St Helens, Merseyside WA10 6LR; Tel (01744) 22465
Educational Psychologist A. Borg, BSc
Educational Psychologist P.T. Cook, BA(Hons), MSc
Educational Psychologist C.W. Hamer, BA, BEd
Educational Psychologist P. Gallimore, BA, MEd
Educational Psychologist J.R. Hughes, BA, MSc
Educational Psychologist E. Bell
Educational Psychologist C. McCormack
Educational Psychologist V. Stoddart-Cross
Educational Psychologist J. Grainger
Educational Psychologist S. Blackmore
Number of Schools
1 nursery (40); 66 primary (16,795); 12 secondary (12,393)
Special Schools
5 special schools (469)
Day of Committee Meeting
Eight weekly cycle; Friday
Requisition Periods for School Supplies
As and when required

Governor Training Unit

Governor Services Section, Community Education Dept, The Rivington Centre, Rivington Rd, St Helens WA10 4ND; Tel (01744) 455351/2/3/14; Fax (01744) 455350
Education Officer, Governor Services and Training G. Greenhalgh
Services Offered
Support and training in all areas of school governance; Provision of information, agenda items, Instruments and Articles of Government; Membership records; Clerking service

Special Day Schools and Units

Ashtons Grn, Derbyshire Hill Rd, St Helens WA9 2LH; Tel (01744) 26250; V.J. Garston. (2–11)
Hamblett, Rainford Rd, St Helens WA10 6BX; Tel (01744) 23078; P. Whitby, MA. (2–16)
Hurst, Hard La, St Helens WA10 6PN; Tel (01744) 25643; M.J. Carolan, BEd, MA. (5–16)
Mere Hse Unit, Mere Rd, Newton-le-Willows, Merseyside; Tel (0192 52) 224060; O.E. Thomson. (5–11)
Mill Hse, Mill Rd, Newton-le-Willows, Merseyside; Tel (0192 52) 226213; G.C. Brown. (11–19)
Penkford, Wharf Rd, Newton-le-Willows, Merseyside; Tel (0192 52) 224195; J. Halsall. (5–16)

County Comprehensive School (11–16)

Broadway Community High, Broadway, St Helens WA10 3RY; Tel (01744) 24349; Fax (01744) 56047; M.A. Cox, BA. (Mixed) (537)
Haydock High, Clipsley La, Haydock, St Helens WA11 0JG; Tel (01744) 54221/2; Fax (01744) 22319; G.D. Fletcher, BA. (Mixed) (740)
Parr Community High, Fleet La, St Helens WA9 1ST; Tel (01744) 24348; Fax (01744) 56693; L. Webb, BSc, MSc. (Mixed) (635)

Voluntary Comprehensive Schools (11–16)

De La Salle R.C. High, Mill Brow, St Helens WA10 4QH; Tel (01744) 20511; Fax (01744) 20543; P.F. Byron. (V.A.) (Mixed) (971)
St Augustine of Canterbury R.C. High, Boardmans La, St Helens WA11 9BB; Tel (01744) 26110; Fax (01744) 454195; P. Murphy. (V.A.) (Mixed) (581)
St Cuthbert's R.C. Community High, Berry's La, St Helens WA9 3HE; Tel (01744) 55186/7; Fax (01744) 29847; J.S. Boyes, BA. (S.A.) (Mixed) (634)

County Comprehensive Schools (11–18)

Cowley High, Hard La, St Helens WA10 6LB; Tel (01744) 50607; Fax (01744) 454835; M.J. Ryder, BA. (Mixed) (1371)
Newton-le-Willows High, Ashton Rd, Newton-le-Willows WA12 0AQ; Tel (01925) 227209; Fax (019250 291335; P. Reed, BSc. (Mixed) (793)
Rainford High, Higher La, Rainford WA11 8NY; Tel (01744) 885914; Fax (01744) 884642; M. Greenwood (Acting). (Mixed) (1661)
Rainhill High, Warrington Rd, Rainhill L45 6NY; Tel 0151-430 0070; Fax 0151-431 0221; D.R. Atkin, BSc. (Mixed) (1373)
Sutton Community High, Elton Head Rd, St Helens WA9 3NF; Tel (01744) 810011; Fax (01744) 850629; G.F. Caton, BA, MA. (Mixed) (1308)

Voluntary Comprehensive Schools (11–18)

St Aelred's R.C. High, Birley St, Newton-le-Willows WA12 9UW; Tel (01925) 225974; Fax (01925) 290759; J.C. Murray, BA(Hons), MSc. (V.A.) (Mixed) (974)

Salford City Council

Population 235,600 mid 1989. Registrar General est.
Salford Civic Centre, Chorley Rd, Swinton, Salford M27 2AD; Tel 0161-794 4711; Fax 0161-794 6595

Education Department

Education Offices, Chapel St, Salford M3 5LT; Tel 0161-832 9751
Chairman Cllr J.D. Merry
Vice-Chairman Cllr J.D. Warmisham
Chief Education Officer D.C. Johnston, MEd, DipEdMan, DipASE
Deputy Chief Education Officer (Head of Strategic Services Division) John G. Harris, BEd(Hons)
Principal Adviser (Head of Inspection and Advisory Service) H.C. Pickles
Principal Officer (Strategy Unit) J.V.G. Clements, MSc, FIPD, MIMgt
Head of Faculties (Management Division) H. Aston, BA(Hons)
Head of Pupil Services Division J. Baker, BSc(Hons)
Senior Inspector (Adviser) A.H. Hillerton, DipEd
Senior Inspector – Adviser J.D. Perry, BA
Head of Community Services Division D. Mitchell, BA(Hons), LTCL
Management Accountant M.C. Cook, FCA
Education Officer (Community Services) J.E. Harrison, BA, MSc, DipEd
Education Officer (Careers) S. Piazza, BA, DipCG
Assistant Education Officer (Special Educational Needs) R. Rose
Principal Educational Psychologist D.M. O'Hara, MSc, BSc; Tel 0161-745 7488
Principal Education Welfare Officer J.N. Beswick, CQSW
Principal Youth and Community Officer D. Osbaldestin, JP, MTID, MIPM
Principal Officer (Information Technology and Management Support Team) D. Chadwick
Salford Consortium Co-Ordinator C. Hinckley
General Adviser (P.E. and Health) J. Rigby
General Adviser (Primary) B.M. Powell
General Adviser (English) J.A. Paine, BA, MA
General Adviser (Maths) D. Cain
General Adviser (I.T.) P.A. Fell, Bed, MB

General Adviser (Primary) T. Stringer
General Adviser (Primary) D. Winston
Number of Schools
21 nursery; 89 primary (22,413); 17 secondary (11,209)
Special School
6 day (1421); 1 hospital (104)
Day of Committee Meeting
Monthly, second Tuesday after Council

Education Committee

Chairman J.D. Merry 14 Cleveleys Gr, Salford M7 4DE
Vice-Chairman J.D. Warmisham "The Grange", 5 Cliff Grange, Bury New Rd, Higher Broughton, Salford M7 4EZ

Special Day Schools

Ash Field, Walkden Rd, Worsley M28 7FG; Tel 0161-790 4335; *Headteacher* J. Pardoe. (SLD) (Primary) (59)
Greenwood, Stafford Rd, Eccles M30 9ED; Tel 0161-789 4512; *Headteacher* J.H. Mossley. (MLD) (Primary) (81)
New Croft High, Seedley Rd, Salford M6 5JL; Tel 0161-736 6415; *Headteacher* J.S. Chapman. (SLD) (Secondary) (69)
Northumberland High, Northumberland St, Salford M7 4RP; Tel 0161-792 8504; *Headteacher* A. Kennedy. (Emotional & Behavioural) (Secondary) (29)
Oakwood High, Park La, Salford M6 7RQ; Tel 0161-736 3944; *Headteacher* J. Triska. (MLD) (Secondary) (148)
Parkes Field, Barton Rd, Swinton M27 1LP; Tel 0161-794 1486; *Headteacher* A. Darlington. (PD) (Primary) (47)
Royal Manchester Children's Hospital School, Hospital Rd, Pendlebury, Swinton M27 4EY; Tel 0161-794 1151; B.I. Purdy, BEd. (107)
Support Service, Parkes Field School, Barton Rd, Swinton M27 5LP; Tel 0161-728 3734; *Headteacher* R. Attfield; Support to children of all ages with special educational needs in mainstream schools and in the home

Outdoor Education Centre

Lledr Hall Dolwyddelan, Gwynedd, North Wales LL25 0PJ; Tel (0169 016) 214/279; P.L. Branch

School Psychological Child Guidance Service

Education Centre, London St, Salford M6 6QT; Tel 0161-745 7488; M. O'Hara, MSc, BGc

County Comprehensive High Schools (11–16)

Buile Hill, Eccles Old Rd, Salford M6 8RD; Tel 0161-736 1773; J.A.B. Baird, BSc. (812)
Hope, Eccles Old Rd, Salford M6 8BJ; Tel 0161-736 2637; A. Hewitt. (866)
Little Hulton Community, Longshaw Dr, Little Hulton, Worsley M38 0AZ; Tel 0161-790 4214; D.J. Fisher, BSc. (415)
Irlam and Cadishead Community, MacDonald Rd, Irlam M30 M44; Tel 0161-775 5525; A. Lamb, MEd. (816)
Joseph Eastham, Hilton La, Little Hulton, Worsley M38 0SY; Tel 0161-790 5022; A. Walsh. (720)
Kersal, Mesnefield Rd, Salford M7 3QD; Tel 0161-792 1748; R.C. Lewis. (576)
Lowry, Camp St, Salford M7 1LG; Tel 0161-792 1368; M. Shelton. (661)
Moorside, East Lancashire Rd, Swinton M27 3BB; Tel 0161-794 1045; C. Chapman. (1245)
The Swinton, Sefton Rd, Pendlebury, Swinton M27 0FG; Tel 0161-794 6215; E.G. Wynne, BSc. (737)
Walkden, Birch Rd, Walkden, Worsley M28 5FJ; Tel 0161-799 5525; G. Bent, BA. (944)
Wentworth, Wentworth Rd, Eccles M30 9BP; Tel 0161-789 4565; N.J. Harrop, BA. (831)
Windsor, Churchill Way, Salford M6 5BH; Tel 0161-736 4269; G. McConville, MEd. (450)

Voluntary Comprehensive High Schools (11–16)

Eccles C.E. High, Northfleet Rd, Peel Grn, Eccles M30 7PQ; Tel 0161-789 5359; A.N. Whitehead, BA. (648)
Our Lady of Mount Carmel R.C., Weaste La, Salford M5 2JH; Tel 0161-736 4117; S. Almond. (346)
Pope John Paul II R.C., Brittania St, Salford M6 6FX; Tel 0161-736 4074; R. Steele. (358)
St George's R.C., Parsonage Dr, Little Hulton, Worsley M28 3SH; Tel 0161-790 4420; D.E. Moon, BEd. (461)
St Patrick's R.C., Guilford Rd, Winton, Eccles M30 7JF; Tel 0161-789 4678; M. Deegan, BEd. (657)

Teachers'/Resources Centre

Education Centre London St, Salford M6 6QT; Tel 0161-736 8122; A. Ramsbottom

Music Centre

Education Centre, London St, Salford M6 6QT; Tel 0161-745 8374; C. Green

Sandwell Metropolitan Borough Council

Population 294,200
P.O. Box 2374, Sandwell Council Hse, Oldbury, West Midlands B69 3DE; Tel 0121-569 2200

Education Department

PO Box 41, Shaftesbury Hse, 402 High St, West Bromwich B70 9LT; Tel 0121-525 7366; Fax 0121-553 1528
Director of Education S.R. Gallacher
Assistant Director of Education K. Wilson
Assistant Director of Education J.D. Badger
PEO (Governor and Committee Services) E. Hannington
PEO (Primary) M. Robertson (Acting)
PEO (Secondary) J. Davies
PEO (Schools Support Branch) K.W. Smith
PEO (Resource Management) D. Collins
PEO (Personnel, Development and Property and Contract Support) D.M. Edwards
Principal Educational Psychologist P. Watts
Principal Welfare Officer M.N.H. Davis
Advisory Service Manager R. Ashman
Key Stage 1 Adviser Dr D. Dolley
Key Stage 1 Adviser P. Onions
Key Stage 1 Adviser S.J. Shan-Randhawa
Key Stage 2 Adviser B. Cloke
Key Stage 2 Adviser R. Maden
Key Stage 2 Adviser M. Storrie
Key Stage 3 Adviser S. Bardwell
Key Stage 3 Adviser R. Kent
Key Stage 4 Adviser R. Sharif
Special Educational Needs Adviser D. Callicott
Key Stage 4 Adviser R. Worth
Number of Schools
3 Nursery (122); 112 primary (26,714); 19 secondary (24,080); 1 education development centre; 4 residential centres
Special Schools
10 day (821); 2 special residential (53)

Education Committee

Lab, 12, Con 6, Lib 2
Chair T. King, JP (Lab) 27 Roebuck La, West Bromwich, W. Midlands B70 6QP
Vice-Chair L. Turton, (Lab) 87 Edward St, West Bromwich, W. Midlands B70 8NT
Members of the Committee
Lab: A.J. Carey, A.F. Clay, J.S. Gill, L. Horton, E. Matthews, R. Page, G.S. Sidhu, F.D. Smith, B. Tagger, G.I. Wyton JP. *Con*: F.A. Betteridge JP, D.A. Dixon JP, K.A. Fletcher, J. Geddes, V.D. Jones, D. Murdock. *Lib*: I.A.G. Garrett, J. Underhill

Governor Training Unit

Governor and Committee Services, Education Dept, Sandwell MBC, Shaftesbury Hse, 402 High St, West Bromwich, West Midlands B70 9LT; Tel 0121-525 7366; Fax 0121-553 1528
PEO Eddie Hannington
Governor Training Officer W. Beddall, Diploma in Training Management (ITD), C&G 730 Teaching Certificate in Further and Adult Education, RSA Work Based Assessors Award and Open Learning Certificate
Services Offered
Comprehensive range of training courses; Link governor meetings; Clerk support meetings; Governor training advisory committee; Termly newsletter; Support and guidance manuals for governors and clerks; Helplines

Careers Office

See chapter 17

Child Psychology Services

Child Psychology Service, 12 Grange Rd, West Bromwich B70 8PD; Tel 0121-553 7411
Connor Education Centre, Connor Rd, West Bromwich; Tel 0121-588 8337

Special Schools

Albert Bradford, Holly La, Smethwick, Warley B66 1QN; Tel 0121-558 2560; H.G. Smith. (3–19) (46)
Arden, Arden Rd, Smethwick, Warley B67 6AL; Tel 0121-558 0275; Fax 0121-555 6036; B. Miller. (4–16) (95)
Birchley, Throne Rd, Rowley Regis, Warley B65 9JP; Tel 0121-559 4623; S. Rushton. (5–16) (57)
Blakeley, Dudley Rd East, Oldbury, Warley B69 3BU; Tel 0121-552 2237; A. Lockley. (5–16) (109)
Firs, Coopers La, Smethwick, Warley B67 7DW; Tel 0121-558 1069; A. Sanders. (2–11) (62)
Fitzwarren, Upper Church La, Tipton DY4 9PF; Tel 0121-557 2528; A.J. Smith. (4–16) (89)
Glenvale, Jervoise St, West Bromwich B70 9LZ; Tel 0121-525 2873; H. Atkins. (2–18) (84)
Knowle, Dudley Rd, Rowley Regis, Warley B65 8JY; Tel 0121-559 1868; A. Harrington. (4–16) (90)
Millfield, Westminster Rd, West Bromwich B71 2JN; Tel 0121-588 2421; Fax 0121-588 5451; A. Simm. (4–16) (127)
Regent, Red Lion Cl, Tividale, Warley B69 1TP; Tel (01384) 255343; G.A. Lloyd. (3–19) (50)
Shenstone Lodge, Shenstone, Lichfield WS14 0LB; Tel (01543) 480369; Fax (01543) 481104; S.P. Butt. (Residential); (7–11+) (18)
Whittington Grange, Burton Rd, Whittington, Nr Lichfield WS14 9NU; Tel (01543) 432296. (Residential); (11–16)

Comprehensive Schools (County 11–16)

Bristnall Hall High, Bristnall Hall La, Oldbury, Warley B68 9PA; Tel 0121-552 5425; Fax 0121-511 1325; R. Dyson. (Mixed) (918)
Britannia High, Britannia Rd, Rowley Regis, Warley B65 9NF; Tel 0121-559 6361; Fax 0121-559 0068; R.W. Kindon, BSc, MEd. (Mixed) (639)
George Salter High, Claypit La, West Bromwich B70 9UW; Tel 0121-553 4665; Fax 0121-525 5082; H.A. Sargeant. (Mixed) (848)
Holly Lodge High Holly La, Smethwick, Warley B67 7JG; Tel 0121-558 0691; Fax 0121-558 6136; J. Caine. (Mixed) (1139)
Langley High Moat Rd, Oldbury, Warley B68 8ED; Tel 0121-552 1331; Fax 0121-544 1891; J.J. Harland. (Mixed) (569)
Perryfields High, Oldacre Rd, Oldbury, Warley B68 0RG; Tel 0121-421 7979; Fax 0121-421 5718; J.W. Withnall. (Mixed) (933)
Shireland High, Waterloo Rd, Smethwick, Warley B66 4ND; Tel 0121-558 8086; Fax 0121-558 8377; B.M. Worrall. (Mixed) (752)
Warley High, Pound Rd, Oldbury, Warley B68 8NE; Tel 0121-544 7521; Fax 0121-544 1298; G.H. Butler, BA(Hons). (Mixed) (856)
Willingsworth High, Bilston Rd, Gospel Oak, Tipton DY4 0BZ; Tel 0121-556 1351; Fax 0121-502 0038; P. Bishop (Acting). (Mixed) (753)
Wodensborough High Hydes Rd, Wednesbury WS10 0DR; Tel 0121-556 4951; Fax 0121-556 0134; D. Seddon. (Mixed) (731)

Comprehensive Schools (County 11–18)

Alexandra High, Alexandra Rd, Tipton DY4 7NR; Tel 0121-557 4146; Fax 0121-522 2264; C.E.L. Farmer, BSc, AFIMA. (Mixed) (1323)
Churchfields High, Church Vale, West Bromwich B71 4DR; Tel 0121-588 8452; Fax 0121-588 8436; E.F. Smith. (Mixed) (763)
Dartmouth High, Wilderness La, Great Barr, Birmingham B43 7SD; Tel 0121-358 6186; Fax 0121-358 5967; K.E.J. Marsh, BA. (Mixed) (1709)
Menzies High, Clarkes La, West Bromwich B71 2BX; Tel 0121-588 8384; Fax 0121-567 5284; I.J. Pedder. (Mixed) (1386)
Tividale Comprehensive, Lower City Rd, Tividale, Warley B69 2HF; Tel 0121-552 5501; Fax 0121-511 1326; A.R. Birch. (Mixed) (1217)
Wood Green High, Wood Green Rd, Wednesbury WS10 9QU; Tel 0121-556 4131; Fax 0121-505 3376; J.C. King. (Mixed) (1221)

Comprehensive Schools (Voluntary)

St Michael's C. of E. High, Throne Rd, Rowley Regis, Warley B65 9LD; Tel 0121-559 5224; Fax 0121-559 4203; K.E. Briscoe. (V.C.) (11–16) (Mixed) (765)
Stuart Bathurst R.C. High, Wood Green Rd, Wednesbury WS10 9QS; Tel 0121-556 1488; Fax 0121-556 0149; P.J. Moss. (V.A.) (11–18) (734)

Teachers' Centre

Sandwell Education Development Centre, Popes La, Oldbury, Warley B69 4PJ; Tel 0121-552 3373; L. Binsley

Residential Establishments

Edgmond Hall, Edgmond, Newport, Shropshire TF10 8JY; Tel (01952) 810799; C.B. Matthews
Frank Chapman Centre, Park End, Ribbesford, Bewdley, Worcs DY12 2TY; Tel (01299) 403292; Fax (01299) 402724; F.A. Winnall
Ingestre Hall, Ingestre, Stafford ST18 0RF; Tel (01889) 270225; Fax (01889) 270225; *Principal* J. Blake
Plas Gwynant, Nantgwynant, Caernarfon, Gwynedd LL55 4NR; Tel (01766) 890212; D. Firth (Acting)

Grant Maintained Schools

Heathfield High, Wrights La, Cradley Heath, Warley B64 6QU; Tel (01384) 66598; J.B. Parker. (Mixed) (977)
Manor High Community School (Grant Maintained), Friar Park Rd, Wednesbury, Sandwell WS10 0JS; Tel 0121-556 2858; G. Black. (Mixed) (700)
St Ambrose Barlow RC High School Grant Maintained, Shaftesbury Rd, Swinton M27 5SZ; Tel 0161-794 3521; W.G. Livesey, BEd, MEd. (413)

Sefton Metropolitan Borough Council

Population 294,273 (OPCs Mid 93 estimate)
Town Hall, Lord St, Southport, Merseyside PR8 1DA; Tel (01704) 533133; Fax 0151-934 2293

Education Department

Town Hall, Bootle, Merseyside L20 7AE; Tel 0151-922 4040; Fax 0151-934 3349
Director of Education J.A. Marsden, BA
Assistant Director of Education (Operations) S. Faruqi
Assistant Director of Education (Resources) B.J. Marsh
Education Officer (Special Needs) P.C. Birkett, BA
Senior Education Officer (Schools) D.D. Sherwell
Senior Education Officer (Post 16) P. Lally
Senior Education Officer (Personnel) E. Mills
Senior Education Officer (Information Systems) G. Murphy
Technical Services Officer H. Brocklebank
Education Officer (Planning) D.A. Butlin
Education Officer (Budget Services) V. McKeown
Education Officer (Benefits & Admissions) J. Rankin
Senior Adviser J.E. Sharp
Senior Adviser A.J. Holland
Art Adviser M.R. Moody
Assessment Adviser I. Carr
Business Studies & Economics Adviser S. Squires
Craft, Design & Technology E. McGuigan
Drama & Religious Education J.A. Emery
Early Years Adviser M. Cook
English Adviser M.P. Higgins
Geography Adviser M. Fletcher-Hunt
History Adviser A. Powell
Mathematics & Computers in Education J.C. Hall
Modern Language Adviser R. Bretherton
Music Adviser M. Lormor
Physical Education Adviser D. Roberts
Science Adviser A. Potter
Youth Service Adviser Iain Mackenzie
Principal Careers Officer V. Salisbury
Principal Educational Psychologist S. Bloom
Principal Education Welfare Officer A. Bryan
Health Education Co-ordinator N. Scott
Schools Curriculum Industry Partnership (Co-ordinator) J. Murphy
Teacher Placement Organiser G. Crompton
TVEI Co-ordinator G. Taylor

Education Committee

Con 8, Lab 8, LD 7
Chair Cllr B. Reynolds, (Lab) 12 St James' St, Southport PR8 5AE
Vice-Chair Cllr P. Cummins, (Lab) 41 Handfield Rd, Waterloo, Liverpool L22 0NU
Members of the Committee
Con: Cllr Glover, G.R.B. Jones, E.F. Jones, Cllr Lewis, Cllr Parry, Cllr Platt, Cllr Storey, Cllr Whitby
Lab: L. Cluskey, Cllr Fairclough, Cllr Frier, Cllr McCabe, Cllr Moncur, Cllr Tweed
LD: Cllr Dodd, M. Fearn, Cllr Francis, Cllr Mainey, Cllr Pugh, Cllr Tonkiss, Cllr Williams

Governor Training Unit

Sefton Education Dept, Town Hall, Oriel Rd, Bootle, Merseyside L20 7AE; Tel 0151-934 3339; Fax 0151-934 3343
Senior Admin Officer (Training) J. Kavanagh
Services Offered
Training courses planned; Regular newsletter; Helpline for Governors and their clerks; Library of books, videos, cassettes; Training for individual Governing Bodies

Special Schools

Merefield, Westminster Dr, Southport PR8 2QZ; Tel (01704) 577163; B.M. Bramald. (Children with severe learning difficulties) (2–19) (Day)
Newfield School, Edge La, Crosby L23 4TG; Tel 0151-931 3030; J. Taylor, BA, DipSpecialEd. (learning difficulties associated with behavioural problems) (Mixed) (5–16) (Day)
Presfield, Preston New Rd, Southport PR9 8PA; Tel (01704) 27831; E.T. Powell. (children with moderate learning difficulties) (5–16) (Day)
Ronald Hse, De Villiers Ave, Crosby, Merseyside L23 2TH; Tel 0151-924 3671; D.M. Emsley. (Children with moderate learning difficulties) (Mixed) (5–16) (Day)
Rowan Pk (Lower School), St Luke's Rd, Liverpool L23 5SZ; Tel 0151-924 2742; Mrs A. Oldhams. (severe learning difficulties) (Mixed) (Day)
Rowan Pk (Upper School), Menai Rd, Bootle L20 6DU; Tel 0151-922 5625; A. Oldhams. (severe learning difficulties) (Mixed) (Day)
School of the Good Shepherd, Sterrix La, Bootle L21 0DA; Tel 0151-928 6165; A.M. Sullivan. (Learning difficulties associated with physical disability) (Mixed) (2–16) (Day)

Special Educational Needs Support Service

c/o Formby High Lower School, Halsall La, Formby, Liverpool L37; Tel (0170 48) 79608

Comprehensive Schools (County 11–16)

Ainsdale High Sandringham Rd, Ainsdale, Southport PR8 2PJ; Tel (01704) 578231; A.P. Gordon, MEd. (Mixed) (485)
Birkdale High Windy Harbour Rd, Southport PR8 3DT; Tel (01704) 577253, 576155. (Boys) (555)
Bootle High Browns La, Bootle L30 5RN; Tel 0151-521 1734; C.A. Sweeney, BD, MEd. (Mixed) (665)
Greenbank High Hastings Rd, Southport PR8 2LT; Tel (01704) 567591; P. McQuade. (Girls) (830)
Hillside High Breeze Hill, Bootle L20 9NU; Tel 0151-525 2630; C. MacDonald. (Mixed) (670)
Litherland High Sterrix La, Liverpool L21 0DB; Tel 0151-928 4449, 0151-928 6596; J.F. Donnelly, MEd. (Mixed) (645)
Meols Cop High Meols Cop Rd, Southport PR8 6JS; Tel (01704) 531180. (Mixed) (770)
St George of England High Fernhill Rd, Bootle L20 6AQ; Tel 0151-922 3798; V.J. Schwarz, Bsc. (Mixed) (475)
Stanley High Fleetwood Rd, Southport PR9 9TF; Tel (01704) 28940; I.M. Roberts, BA. (Mixed) (600)

Comprehensive Schools (County 11–18)

Chesterfield High Chesterfield Rd, Liverpool L23 9YB; Tel 0151-924 6454; Dr A.K. Irving. (Mixed) (1048)
Annexe: Haigh Rd, Liverpool L22 3XW; Tel 0151-928 1211
Deyes High Deyes La, Maghull, Liverpool L31 6DE; Tel 0151-526 3814; P.H. Middleton, BD, MEd. (Mixed) (1330)
Formby High Freshfield Rd, Liverpool L37 3HW; Tel (0170 48) 73100, 77383; P. Baldock, MA. (Mixed) (645)
Maghull High Ormonde Dr, Maghull, Liverpool L31 7AW; Tel 0151-526 2711, 0151-525 2607; P.R. Perdue, MA. (Mixed) (1130)
Manor High Manor Rd, Liverpool L23 7UL; Tel 0151-924 6778; A.J. Green, BA, MSc. (Mixed) (785)
Range High Stapleton Rd, Liverpool L37 2YN; Tel (0170 48) 79315/6; M.J. Dixon, MA. (Mixed) (980)

Comprehensive Schools (Voluntary 11–16)

St Ambrose Barlow RC Aided Copy La, Bootle L30 7PQ; Tel 0151-526 7044, 0151-531 9878; V.A. McLellan, BA, MEd. (Mixed) (380)

Comprehensive Schools (Voluntary 11–18)

Christ the King RC High Special Agreement, Stamford Rd, Southport PR8 4EX; Tel (01704) 65121; E. Barlow, BSc. (Mixed) (1120)
Holy Family RC High Aided Virgin's La, Thornton, Liverpool L23 4UD; Tel 0151-924 6451; N.W. Hutchins, BA. (Mixed) (850)
Maricourt RC High Aided Hall La, Liverpool L31 3DZ; Tel 0151-531 0531; Sister Mary Teresa, BSc. (Mixed) (1280)
Sacred Heart RC High Aided Liverpool Rd, Liverpool L23 5TE; Tel 0151-931 2971; T. Harrington, BA, MEd. (Mixed) (845)
Annexe: Myers Rd East, Liverpool L23 0QU
St Wilfrid's RC Special Agreement High Orrell Rd, Liverpool L21 8NU; Tel 0151-928 4543, 4021. (865)
Savio RC Aided High School Netherton Way, Bootle L30 2NA; Tel 0151-521 3088; Rev A.J. Bailey, BSc. (Mixed) (920)

Music Support Service

Central Music Centre, Redgate, Formby L37 4EW; Tel (0170 48) 72773; G. Reed, ARCM

Youth Clubs

Aintree Youth Club Oriel Dr, Aintree, Liverpool 10, Merseyside; Tel 0151-526 1177; A. Maddocks
Birkdale Youth Centre Windy Harbour Rd, Birkdale, Southport, Merseyside PR83DT; Tel (01704) 579836; G. Fleming
Crosby Youth Club Coronation Rd, Crosby, Liverpool L23; Tel 0151-924 8048; M. Delamere
Formby Youth Centre Redgate, Formby, Liverpool, Merseyside; Tel (017048) 78770; K. Lee
Manor High Activities Manor High School, Crosby, Liverpool, Merseyside; Tel 0151-924 6778; J. Cook
Meols Cop Youth Club Meols Cop Rd, Southport PR8 6JS; Tel (01704) 538084; P.A. Wilson
Princess Royal Youth Club Deerbarn Dr, Bootle 10, Merseyside; M. Higham
Stafford Moreton Youth Club Liverpool Rd North, Maghull L31; Tel 0151-526 3294; D. Griffiths
Stanley Youth Centre Marshside Rd, Southport PR9 9TF; Tel (01704) 25319; J. Blanchard
Worcester Youth Club Worcester Rd, Bootle L20; Tel 0151-922 1136; K. Lloyd

Teachers' Centre

Sefton Teachers' Centre 225 Park Rd, Formby, Liverpool L37 6EW; Tel (0170 48) 76220; D. Lamb, BA, MEd

Adult Education Centres

53 Cambridge Rd, Liverpool L21 1EZ; Tel 0151-928 0765; S. Jameson, DipEd

Sheffield Metropolitan City Council

Population 529,300 (mid 1991)
Town Hall, Sheffield S1 2HH; Tel (0114) 272 6444

Education Department

Leopold St, Sheffield S1 1RJ; Tel (0114) 273 5721; Fax (0114) 273 6279
Director of Education A. Muller
Deputy Director of Education Vacancy
Assistant Director Education Budget Strategy and IT Systems H. Griffith
Assistant Director Support Services D. Waxman
Assistant Director Community Services M. Marken
Assistant City Treasurer (Education) K. Matthews
Senior Inspector C. Jessop
Senior Inspector P. Budgell
Assistant Director Planning and Development M. Simpson
Assistant Director Client Services J. Potter
Principal Education Psychologist G. Lindsay
Chief Education Welfare Officer D.R. Pennock
Assistant Director Careers and Business Liaison S. Woolliscroft

Education Committee

Lab 24, Con 3, LD 10
Members of the Committee
Lab: J. Barton, J. Bird, M.D. Bower, M. Chaplin, K. Curran, D. Newton, R.J. Eastall, D. Gow, D.M. Hayes, P. Horton, E.J. Lamb, P.M. Smith, W.J. Jordan, P. Midgley, K.C.J. Mountford, D.M. Lawton, J. Lumley, V. Nicholson, E.A. Sargent, V.C.J. McDonald, F. White, V. Shepherd, E. Smith, C. M. Walayat
Con: H.W.T. Comford, A.E. Fry, A. Pratt
LD: T. Bagshaw, R. Hughes, Cllr Anginotti, Sayris, Cllr Bowden, Chadwick, N.K.D. Kime, A.L. Milton, C.A. Ross, C.M.K. Tosseano

Governor Training Unit

Governor Support Team, Education Dept, Leopold St, Sheffield S1 1RJ; Tel (0114) 273 5792; Fax (0114) 273 6279
Principal Officer Erk Pye
Senior Administrative Officer Rob Johnson
Services Offered
Clerking service to Governing Bodies; Support and Training package; including negotiated elements

Special Schools

Bents Green, Ringinglow Rd S11 7TB; Tel (0114) 236 3545/361737; V. Nicholls. (Learning Difficulties) (Mixed) (75)
Broad Elms, Broad Elms La, Sheffield S11 9RQ; Tel (0114) 236 8277; N. Elliott. (Adjustment Difficulties) (Mixed) (36)
Deerlands, Lindsay Rd S5 7WE; Tel (0114) 240 0271/2; C. Trainor. (Adjustment Difficulties) (Mixed) (36)
Dr John Worrall, Maltby St S9 2QA; Tel (0114) 244 1762; B.M. Burdon. (M.L.D. & Behavioural difficulties) (Mixed) (45)
East Hill Primary, East Bank Rd, Sheffield S2 3PX; Tel (0114) 272 9897; A. Berry. (M.L.D.) (Mixed) (56)
East Hill Secondary, East Bank Rd S2 3PX; Tel (0114) 276 0245; K. Jenkins. (MLD) (Mixed) (100)
Folkwood Secondary, Ringinglow Rd S11 7TB; Tel 351635; P.N. Nelson. (Adjustment difficulties) (Mixed) (54)
Hillsborough Hse, Parkside Rd S6 2AA; Tel (0114) 233 0124; L. John
Hospital and Home Education Service, 16 Northumberland Rd S10 2TT; Tel (0114) 275 6390; L. John
Mossbrook, Bochum Parkway S8 8JR; Tel (0114) 237 2768; S.J. Harrison. (Learning Difficulties) (Mixed) (56)
Norfolk Park Primary, Park Grange Rd S2 3QF; Tel (0114) 272 6165; G.M. Croston. (SLD) (Mixed) (60)
Northern General Adolescent Unit, Herries Rd S5 7AU; Tel (0114) 243 4343 Ext 4414; J. Irwin. (Adjustment Difficulties) (Mixed) (26)
Oakes Park, Matthews La S8 8JS; Tel (0114) 255 6754/554533; C.C. Gold. (PH) (Mixed) (70)
Resource for Pregnant Schoolgirls and Schoolgirl Mothers, Park View Hse, 7 Park Grange Rd, S2 3QF; Tel (0114) 272 5932; L. John
The Rowan Primary, Durvale Ct, Furniss Ave S17 3PT; Tel (0114) 235 0479; D.R.K. Quayle. (Specific Learning Difficulties) (Mixed) (65)

Sheaf Unit, The Stables, Sharrow La S11 8AE; Tel (0114) 258 2810; L. John. (Non-attenders) (Mixed)
Shirle Hill Hospital 6 Cherry Tree Rd S11 9AA; Tel (0114) 271 6877; G.D. Lewis, BEng. (Adjustment difficulties) (Mixed) (20)
Talbot Secondary, Norfolk Park Rd S2 3QE; Tel (0114) 272 4417; J. Taylor. (SLD) (Mixed) (105)
Tapton Mount Primary, Manchester Rd S10 5DG; Tel (0114) 266 7151; K. Doney. (Visually Handicapped) (Mixed) (34)
Whirlow Brook, C/o The Moss Limb La S17 3ES; Tel (0114) 236 8121; J.R. Hillman. (Adjustment difficulties) (Mixed) (42)
Woolley Wood Primary, Oaks Fold Rd S5 0TG; Tel (0114) 245 6885; J. Broom, MEd. (Moderate and Severe Learning Difficulties) (Mixed) (45)

Special Units

Maud Maxfield Service for the Hearing Impaired, C/o Hazlebarrow Primary School, Hazlebarrow Cres, Sheffield S8 8AQ; Tel (0114) 237 7611; G. Woods (Acting)
Traveller Education Service, c/o Lowedges Primary School, Lowedges Rd S8 7JG; Tel (0114) 237 2196; P. Nunn

Integrated Special Resources in Schools

Abbeydale Grange Secondary, Hastings Rd S7 2GU; Tel 557301; J. Woodhead. (MLD) (Mixed); (Special Educational Needs)
All Saints R.C. Secondary (Grant Maintained) Granville Rd S2 2RJ; Tel (0114) 272 4851; J.P. Kelly, BA. (Special Educational Needs)
Arbourthorne J, Eastern Ave, Sheffield S2 2GQ; Tel (0114) 239 7291; D. Hutton. (Primary aged) (Mixed)
Arbourthorne NI Special Educational Needs, Eastern Ave, Sheffield S2 2GQ; Tel (0114) 239 8317; A. Cutts. (Nursery) (Mixed)
Bluestones Primary School, Park Grange Dr S2 3SF; Tel (01142) 725645; *Head* M.W. Scott. (SLD)
Chaucer Secondary School, Wordsworth Ave S5 8NH; Tel (01142) 322330; *Head* D.A. Watson
City, Stradbroke Rd S13 8SS; Tel 392571; E.F. Gabbani, MEd. (MLD) (Mixed) (Secondary)
Dr John Worrall, Maltby St, Sheffield S9 2QA; Tel (0114) 244 1762; B.M. Burdon. (Autistic) (Mixed)
East Hill Secondary, East Bank Rd, Sheffield, West Midlands; Tel (0114) 276 0245; A. Berry; K. Jenkins. (Hearing Impaired)
Firth Park Secondary, Barnsley Rd, Sheffield S5 6SZ; Tel (0114) 243 8437/9; S. Adams (Acting). (Hearing Impaired) (Mixed)
Fox Hill Primary, Keats Rd, Sheffield S6 1AZ; Tel (0114) 231 3469; J. Fryer. (MLD) (Mixed)
Gleadless Valley Secondary Matthews La S8 8JS; Tel 746394; R.D. Dunn. (Physically Handicapped) (Mixed)
Greengate Lane Primary, Greengate La S30 4GT; Tel 848322; M.E. Griffin. (Special Educational Needs) (Primary) (Mixed)
Greystones Primary, Greystones Rd, Sheffield S11 7GL; Tel (0114) 266 3413; S.T.K. Gingele. (Hearing Impaired) (Mixed)
Hartley Brook Primary, Hartley Brook Rd, Sheffield S5 0JF; Tel (0114) 245 6882; J. Booth. (Hearing Impaired) (Mixed); (Special Educational Needs); Nursery Unit (Mixed) (17)
Hazlebarrow Primary, Hazlebarrow Cres, Sheffield S8 8AQ; Tel (0114) 237 5778; Mr Driskell. (Hearing Impaired) (Mixed)
High Green Secondary, Pack Horse La, High Green S30 4HY; Tel (0114) 284 8264; R. Russell. (Physically Handicapped)
High Storrs Secondary, Ringinglow Rd, Sheffield S11 7LH; Tel (0114) 267 0000; C.J. Berry. (Hearing Impaired) (Mixed)
King Egbert Secondary School, Furniss Ave S17 3QN; Tel (01142) 369931; *Head* M.R. Evans. (Communication Difficulties) (Mixed)
Nether Green Junior School, Fulwood Rd S10 3QA; Tel (01142) 302461; *Head* P. Jenkins. (SLD)
Nook Lane J, Stannington S6 6BN; Tel 341097; T. Gadd. (Specific Learning Difficulties) (Mixed)
Notre Dame R.C. Secondary, (Grant Maintained) Fulwood Rd S10 3BT; Tel 302536; J. Conway. (Special Educational Needs)
Park Hill Primary, Duke St, Park Hill North S2 5QR; Tel 722049; R. Butcher. (Adjustment Difficulties) (Mixed)
Pipworth Junior and Nursery Infant Schools, Pipworth Rd S2 1AA; *Head (Junior)* S.W. Adams; Tel (01142) 391078; *Head (Nursery Infant)* M. Davey; Tel (01142) 398432. Adjustment Difficulties
Prince Edward Primary School, City Rd S12 2AA; Tel (01142) 397142; *Head* D.J. Tingle. (Special Educational Needs) (Mixed)
The Rowan Primary, Durvale Ct, Furniss Ave, Sheffield S17 3PT; Tel (0114) 235 0479; D.R.K. Quayle. (Communications) (Mixed)
St Thomas of Canterbury R.C. J & I, Chancet Wood Dr S8 7IR; Tel 745597; C.Q. Donnelly. (Special Educational Needs) (Primary Aged) (Mixed)
Sharrow J, South View Rd, Sheffield S7 1DP; Tel (0114) 255 1704; T.P. Bishop. (MLD) (Mixed)
Silverdale Secondary, Bents Cres, Sheffield S11 9RT; Tel (0114) 236 9991; E. Fitzgeorge-Butler. (Hearing Impaired) (Mixed)
Southey Green J Crowder Ave S5 8DN; Tel (0114) 232 6879; R. Butcher. (Specific Learning Difficulties)
Stradbroke Primary, Richmond Rd, Sheffield S13 8LT; Tel (0114) 239 9320; V.B. Greenwood, BEd. (Moderate Learning Difficulties) (Mixed)
Talbot Secondary, Norfolk Park Rd, Sheffield S2 3QE; Tel (0114) 272 4417; J. Taylor. (Mixed) (Hearing Impaired, Visually Handicapped)
Tapton Secondary, Darwin La, Sheffield S10 5RG; Tel (0114) 230 3937; J.E. Bardsley. (Mixed) (Visually Handicapped)
Wharncliffe Side Primary, Brightholmlee La, Sheffield S30 3DD; Tel (0114) 286 2379; D. Rogers (Acting). (Mixed) (Special Educational Needs); (Nursey)
Woolley Wood Primary, Oaks Fold Rd, Sheffield S5 0TG; Tel (0114) 245 6885; J. Broom, MEd. (Visually Handicapped) (Mixed); (Hearing Impaired)
Yewlands Secondary, Creswick La, Sheffield S30 3NN; Tel (0114) 245 2657; P.A. Whittaker. (MLD)(Mixed)

Secondary Schools (County)

Abbeydale Grange, Hastings Rd S7 2GU; Tel (0114) 255 7301; J. Woodhead. (483)
Birley, Thornbridge Ave S12 3AB; Tel 392531/2; R. Latham, BA. (780)
Bradfield, Kirk Edge Rd, Worral S30 3AE; Tel 863861; M. Booth. (791)
Carter Lodge Beighton Rd S12 4LQ; Tel (0114) 248 5367/484091; L.K. Hill, BA. (397)
Chaucer, Wordsworth Ave S5 8NH; Tel (0114) 232 2338/9/0; D.A. Watson. (892)
City Stradbroke Rd S13 8SS; Tel (0114) 239 2571; E.F. Gabbani, MEd. (1078)
Earl Marshal Earl Marshal Rd S4 8LA; Tel (0114) 243 9391; C.R. Searle. (559)
Ecclesfield Ecclesfield S30 3WD; Tel (0114) 246 1156; R.J. Barnes, BSc. (1245)
Firth Park Barnsley Rd S5 6SZ; Tel (0114) 243 8437/9; S. Adams (Acting). (1118)
Gleadless Valley Matthews La S8 8JS; Tel (0114) 274 6394; D.R. Dunn. (458)
Handsworth Grange, Handsworth Grange Rd S13 9HJ; Tel 694801; K. Foden. (800)
Herries, Penrith Rd S5 8UF; Tel (0114) 231 0221/2; D. Burgan. (620)
High Green Pack Horse La, High Green S30 4HY; Tel (0114) 284 7561; R. Russell. (390)
High Storrs, Ringinglow Rd S11 7LH; Tel (0114) 267 0000; C.J. Berry. (1642)
Hinde House Shiregreen La S5 6AG; Tel (0114) 243 8486; G. Elliott, BSc. (762)
King Egbert Furniss Ave, Dore S17 3QN; Tel (0114) 236 9931; M.R. Evans. (781)

King Edward VII Glossop Rd S10 2PW; Tel (0114) 266 2518/305718; M.H.A. Lewis, BA. (1509)
Meadowhead Dyche La S8 8BR; Tel 372723; K.A. Cook. (1550)
Myers Grove, Wood La S6 5HG; Tel (0114) 234 8805/344296; D.C. Lowe. (913)
Myrtle Springs East Bank Rd S2 2AL; Tel 392631; W.M. Thompson, BA. (986)
Newfield Lees Hall Rd S8 9JP; Tel (0114) 255 7331; I.B. Cockburn, BEd. (623)
Park House Bawtry Rd S9 1WD; Tel (0114) 244 9588; J. Monahan. (302)
Silverdale Bents Cres S11 9RT; Tel (0114) 236 9991; E. Fitzgeorge-Butler. (1030)
Stocksbridge, Shay Hse La, Stocksbridge S30 5FD; Tel (0114) 288 3153, 883410; M.C. Ramsdale. (736)
Tapton, Darwin La S10 5RG; Tel (0114) 230 3937; J.E. Bardsley. (1447)
Waltheof, Beaumont Cl S2 1RY; Tel (0114) 239 2661; A. Gardiner. (851)
Westfield, Mosborough S19 5AQ; Tel (0114) 248 5221; C.B. Pickering. (898)
Wisewood Rural La S6 4BH; Tel (0114) 233 3606; C.G. Sisum, BSc. (675)
Yewlands Creswick La S30 3NN; Tel (0114) 245 2657; P.A. Whittaker. (723)

Teachers' Centres

Nether Edge Curriculum and Professional Development Centre, Union Rd, Sheffield S11 9EH; Tel (0114) 255 0174
Northbank Curriculum and Professional Development Centre, Shiregreen La, Sheffield S5 6AG; Tel (0114) 256 2621
Southfield Curriculum and Professional Development Centre, Gleadless Rd, Sheffield S12 2QB; Tel (0114) 264 4010

Grant Maintained Schools

All Saints R.C. Granville Rd S2 2RJ; Tel (0114) 272 4851; Fax (0114) 276 5371; J.P. Kelly, KSG, BA, MPhil. (886)
Notre Dame Fulwood Rd S10 3BT; Tel (0114) 230 2536; J.M. Conway. (987)

Shropshire County Council

Population 412,800 (1992)
The Shirehall, Abbey Foregate, Shrewsbury SY2 6ND; Tel (01743) 251000; Fax (01743) 360315

Education Department

Shirehall, Abbey Foregate, Shrewsbury SY2 6ND; Tel (01743) 251000
Chief Executive Alan Barnish, BCom, IPFA
County Property and Planning Services Officer Dominic Pagett, FRICS
County Treasurer Nigel Pursey, MusB, IPFA
Director of Social Services Michael Hennessey, BA
Chairman Derek Woodvine
Vice-Chairman Roger Walker
County Education Officer Carol Adams, BA, MA
Deputy County Education Officer Dennis Jones, IPFA
Deputy County Education Officer Mike Raleigh, MA
Area Education Officer (Shrewsbury) John Till, MA
Area Education Officer (North Shropshire) Jeremy Clarke, BA
Area Education Officer (Telford) Ken Pattison, BSc
Area Education Officer (South Shropshire) Jamie Wrench, BA
Education Officer (Personnel Services) David James, BA
Education Officer (Community Services) Paul Taylor, BSc
Education Officer (Pupil Services) Christine Davies, BSc
Education Officer (Buildings/Development) Robin Durham, BA
Senior Adviser (Curriculum/Assessment) Keith Hedger
Senior Primary Adviser Mike Brogden
Senior Secondary Adviser Chris Warn, BSc, MA
Primary Team Adviser Brian Allaway
Primary Team Adviser Oliver Aston
Primary Team Adviser Susan Boughey, BSc
Primary Team Adviser Jean Coward
Primary Team Adviser David Dodds, MA
Primary Team Adviser Meurig Jones, BEd
Primary Team Adviser Maggie Langdale
Primary Team Adviser Andy Watters
Secondary Team Adviser (IT) Tony Berkeley
Secondary Team Adviser (Technology) Janet Boult
Secondary Team Adviser (Special Needs) Norma Cadwallader
Secondary Team Adviser (Geography/Environmental Education) Kate Campion
Secondary Team Adviser (Post 16) Frances White, BA
Secondary Team Adviser (Science) John Clawley
Secondary Team Adviser (History/Learning Resources) David Downey, BEd
Secondary Team Adviser (Modern Languages) Mike McAleavy
Secondary Team Adviser (PE/Outdoor Education) David Penlington
Secondary Team Adviser (PSE) Frances Phelps, MEd
Secondary Team Adviser (The Arts/Drama) Neil Rathwell
Secondary Team Adviser (Art/Design) Stewart Smith, DipAD
Secondary Team Adviser (Mathematics) Linton Waters
Secondary Team Adviser (Music) Nigel Taylor
Secondary Team Adviser (English) Peter Traves, MA
Secondary Team Adviser (Religious Education) John Williams, BEd
County Educational Psychologist Colin Carson, BA
County Careers Officer David Peck, DPA, DVG
Client Officer, Catering/Cleaning/Grounds Maintenance Jo Humphreys
Young Farmers' Club Julia Thomas
County Leisure Services Officer John Hirst, BA, DMS, ALA

Number of Schools
2 nursery (80); 209 primary (33,213); 29 secondary (20,684)
Special Schools
2 day special with hostel (227); 5 day special (299)
Day of Committee Meeting
Variable
Other Authorities with whom Joint Purchasing arrangements are made
Hereford and Worcester

Education Committee

Con 8, Lab 7, LD 4, I 1
Chair Derek Woodvine, (Lab) 1 Avondale Dr, Castlefields, Shrewsbury SY1 2TZ; Tel (01743) 362637
Vice-Chair Roger Walker, (Lab) Grasmere, Christchurch La, Market Drayton, Shropshire TF9 1DZ; Tel (01630) 653652
Liberal Democrat Spokesperson Mary Edbrooke, (LD) 21 Highfields, Shrewsbury, Shropshire SY2 6PH; Tel (01743) 354190
Conservative Spokesperson Paddy Hughes, (Con) 20 Babbinswood, Whittington, Oswestry, Shropshire SY11 4PQ; Tel (01691) 662348
Members of the Committee
Con: Brian Gillow, John Handley, Yvonne Holyoak, Pam Larney, Barbara Marsh, George Richey, Eileen Sandford
Lab: Tony Green, Beryl Mason, George Raxster, Anne Roberts, Robert Storey

LD: Peter Dunham, Shirley Green, Andrew Whyte
I: Ray Turnock

Shropshire Psychological and Child and Family Services

Bourne Hse, Radbrook Centre, Shrewsbury, Shropshire; Tel (01743) 232837

Special Schools

Area Special School, Telford – Day with Hostel (Yet to be named) Grange Ave, Stirchley, Telford, Shropshire; Tel (01952) 591881; F.J. Burns. (SLD) (Mixed) (100)
Charles Darwin, North Rd, Wellington, Telford, Shropshire; Tel (01952) 242229; I.R. Crawshaw. (Emot/Behavioural Problems) (24)
Haughton, Queen St, Madeley, Telford, Shropshire; Tel (01952) 684995; R.K. Prince. (MLD) (Mixed) (121)
Hinkshay, Hinkshay Rd, Dawley, Telford, Shropshire; Tel (01952) 591598; P. Hurd. (Emotional & Behavioural) (14)
Area Special School, Shrewsbury – Day with Hostel (Yet to be named) Hearne Way, Monkmoor, Shrewsbury, Shropshire; Tel (01743) 351091; C. Davies, BEd. (SLD) (Mixed) (127)
Southall, Off Rowan Ave, Dawley, Telford, Shropshire; Tel (01952) 592485; A.J. Day. (MLD) (Mixed) (114)
Trench Hall, Tilley Grn, Wem, Shropshire SY4 5PJ; Tel (01939) 232372; C.A. Hargreaves, BEd. (Emot/ Behavioural Problems) (26)

Modern School

The Burton Borough, Audley Ave, Newport, Shropshire; Tel (01952) 811275; P.J. Boulter. (875)

Grammar School

Newport High, Wellington Rd, Newport, Shropshire; Tel (01952) 811040; K.B. Harrison. (Girls) (234)

Comprehensive Schools

Adams' School, Lowe Hill, Wem, Shropshire; Tel (01939) 232328; P.G. Arnold, BA. (Boarding places) (1019)
Belvidere, Crowmere Rd, Shrewsbury, Shropshire; Tel (01743) 235073; M. Bamford. (568)
Bridgnorth Endowed, Northgate, Bridgnorth, Shropshire; Tel (01746) 762103; G. Butler, BA. (988)
Church Stretton, Shrewsbury Rd, Church Stretton, Shropshire; Tel (01694) 722209; D.V. Oliver, MA. (543)
Community College, Bishop's Castle, Shropshire; Tel (01588) 638257; J.D.M. Preshous, MA. (475)
Grange, Worcester Rd, Shrewsbury, Shropshire; Tel (01743) 445493; J.E. Stokes, BPhil. (508)
The Grove, Newcastle Rd, Market Drayton, Shropshire; Tel (01630) 652121; W.G. Dickinson, BSc. (1086)
Harlescott, Corndon Cres, Shrewsbury, Shropshire; Tel (01743) 233476; S.N.E.G. Newell, BA. (549)
Idsall, Coppice Green La, Shifnal, Shropshire; Tel (01952) 460213; J.D. Carr, MA. (1027)
Lacon Childe, Love La, Cleobury Mortimer, Kidderminster, Worcs; Tel (01299) 270312; J.R. Sullivan. (425)
The Lakelands, Oswestry Rd, Ellesmere, Shropshire; Tel (01691) 622543; N.J. Clarke. (347)
Lord Silkin, District Centre, Stirchley, Telford, Shropshire; Tel (01952) 595511; J.A. Harrop, BEd. (905)
Ludlow CE, Bromfield Rd, Burnway, Ludlow, Shropshire; Tel (01584) 872691; P.W. Suthern. (933)
Madeley Court, Court St, Madeley, Telford, Shropshire; Tel (01952) 680306; A. Phillips, BA, MPhil. (562)
The Marches, Morda Rd, Oswestry, Shropshire; Tel (01691) 652959; A.J. Cooper, BA, MEd. (1149)
The Mary Webb, Pontesbury, Shropshire; Tel (01743) 790333; J. Brown, MA. (525)
Meole Brace, Longden Rd, Shrewsbury, Shropshire; Tel (01743) 235961; I.N. Pringle, BA. (1137)
Oldbury Wells, Bridgnorth, Shropshire; Tel (01746) 765454; J.R. Davies, MA. (780)
Orleton Park, Orleton La, Wellington, Telford, Shropshire; Tel (01952) 244204; P.J. Hampson, MA. (484)
The Phoenix, Manor Rd, Dawley, Telford, Shropshire; Tel (01952) 591531; R.A.O. Jones, BSc, MSc. (614)
Priory, Longden Rd, Shrewsbury, Shropshire; Tel (01743) 343769; S.M. Johnes, BA, MEd. (626)
Rhyn Park, St Martins, Oswestry, Shropshire; Tel (01691) 772273; J.A. Warwick. (487)
The Sir John Talbot's, Heath Rd, Whitchurch, Shropshire; Tel (01948) 662207; D.H. Williams, BA, MEd. (691)
The Sutherland, Gibbons Rd, Trench, Telford, Shropshire; Tel (01952) 605571; N.E. Woods. (709)
Wakeman, Abbey Foregate, Shrewsbury, Shropshire SY2 6AA; Tel (01743) 356246; M.G. Boulter, BEd. (651)
William Brookes, Farley Rd, Much Wenlock, Shropshire; Tel (01952) 727606; P. Cooper, BA. (732)
The Wrockwardine Wood, New Rd, Wrockwardine Wood, Telford, Shropshire; Tel (01952) 612461; Dr R. Nash, BA, BEd, MA, PhD. (987)

Professional Centres

Ludlow Centre, Bishop Mascall Centre, Lower Galdeford, Ludlow, Shropshire; Tel (01584) 872435
Market Drayton Centre, Market Drayton Junior School, Alexandra Rd, Market Drayton, Shropshire; Tel (01630) 658347
Shrewsbury Centre, Racecourse Cres, Shrewsbury, Shropshire; Tel (01743) 232761
Telford Centre, Madeley Crt School, Crt St, Madeley, Telford, Shropshire; Tel (01952) 587057

Grant Maintained Schools

Abraham Darby School, Hill Top, Madeley, Telford, Shropshire TF7 5HX; Tel (01952) 432081; K.A. Pattinson, BA. (1136)
Adams' Grammar School, High St, Newport, Shropshire TF10 7BD; Tel (01952) 810698; Fax (01952) 812696; *Headteacher* James M. Richardson; *Chair of Governors* Dr Alan Snead. (Boys) (11–18) (Girls) 16–18) (616)
Charlton (Grant Maintained) School, Severn Dr, Wellington, Telford, Shropshire TF1 3LE; Tel (01952) 223257; K. Cheshire. (697)
The Corbet School, Baschurch, Shrewsbury, Shropshire; Tel (01939) 260296; R.H. Jackson, BA, ACE. (560)
Ercall Wood School, Golf Links La, Wellington, Telford, Shropshire TF1 2DU; Tel (01952) 223923; P. Rubery, Med. (666)

Solihull Metropolitan Borough Council

Population 200,871
PO Box 18, Council Hse, Solihull, West Midlands B91 3QS; Tel 0121-704 6000

Education Department

PO Box 20, The Council Hse, Solihull B91 3QU; Tel 0121-704 6000; Fax 0121-704 6669
Chairman Education Committee Cllr G. Wright
Vice-Chairman Cllr P.M. Lea
Director of Education C.J. Trinick, MA, BPhil, FRSA
Deputy Director of Education D. Nixon, BA
Head of Support Services A.J. Hawkesford
Head of School Services T. Warren

Head of Business and Finance E.A. Nicholson
EO (Careers) D.E. Taylor
EO (Information and Management Services) P. Mayhew
EO (Personnel and Administration) J.M. Royce
EO (Client Services) M.J. Luntley
EO (Special Services) A.G. Ford-Jones
EO (Special Needs Management) D.R. Pearson
EO (Youth) R.G. Jackson
EO (Schools) I. Morrey
Chief Inspector A.J. Parsons, MA
Deputy Chief Inspector B.J. Salter, BSc
Senior Inspector R.D.W. Curtis, MA
Senior Inspector G. Nunn, MSc, BEd
Senior Inspector J.R. Whittell, BSc
General Inspector (Music) M.D. Goldring, MEd, GRSM, ARCM
General Inspector (Physical Education) G.J. Mason
General Inspector (Mathematics) P. Connah, BPhil(Ed)
General Inspector (Modern Languages) M. Howell, BA
General Inspector (Infant/Nursery) S.L. Brown, BEd
General Inspector (Gifted Children) S. Newton, BA, BPhil(Ed)
General Inspector (Special Needs) J. Bond
General Inspector (Euthenics) D.L. Sheffield, MPhil
General Inspector (Humanities) D. Sharp, BEd
Chief Education Welfare Officer P. Fenton
Principal Educational Psychologist A.G. Russell, BSc, DipEdPsych
Youth and Community Officer K.M. Jones, BEd, DipEd(Man)
Purchasing Officer G. Morris
Inspector (Work Related Curriculum) K. Whitehouse

Number of Schools
70 primary (17,369 F.T.E., 868 nursery); 13 secondary (12,235)

Special Schools
4 (264)

Day and frequency of Committee Meetings
Every 6 weeks

Requisition Period for School Supplies
Throughout the year

Other Authorities with whom Joint Purchasing Arrangements are made
Birmingham

Governor Training Unit

Chapel Fields Centre, Richmond Rd, Solihull, West Midlands B92 7RZ; Tel 0121-707 9488; Fax 0121-706 8304
Governor Training Co-ordinator Ian Plowman, BEd

Services Offered
Centralised training; Governing Body training; Resource Centres; Consultancy; Helpline; Newsletters; Governing Body Audits

Careers Office

See chapter 17

Education Psychology Service

Woodlands Centre, Sanda Croft, Chelmsley Wood, Birmingham B36 0NF; Tel 0121-770 6030

Special Needs Advisory and Support

C/o Woodlands Junior and Infant School, Sanda Croft, Chelmsley Wood, Birmingham B36 0NF; Tel 0121-770 6267; B. Cameron

Emotional and Behavioural Difficulties Unit

Lancaster Centre, Lanchester Way, Castle Bromwich, Birmingham B36 9LF; Tel 0121-776 7465; A. O'Boyle

Specific Learning Difficulties Units

Langley Junior and Infant School, St. Bernard's Rd, Olton, Solihull, West Midlands; Tel 0121-706 3932; J.T. Hemmings. (Primary Unit)
Langley School, Kineton Green Rd, Solihull, West Midlands; Tel 0121-706 9771; S. Orlick. (Secondary Unit)
Widney Junior School, Clifton Cres, Solihull B91 3LQ; Tel 0121-705 8516; *Junior Unit* D.R. Todman

Moderate Learning Difficulty Units

Alderbrook School, Alderbrook School, Blossomfield Rd, Solihull, West Midlands; Tel 0121-704 2146; M. Cross, BA. (Secondary Unit)
Chapel Fields School, Lyndon Rd, Solihull, West Midlands; Tel 0121-706 2644; P. Crathorne. (Junior Unit)
Hatchford Brook Junior and Infant School, Old Lode La, Solihull, West Midlands; Tel 0121-743 4691; J. Benoke. (Infant Unit)
Woodlands Junior and Infant School, Sanda Croft, Chelmsley Wood, Birmingham, West Midlands; Tel 0121-770 5720; D.L. Kimble. (Junior Unit)

Physical Difficulty Units

Primary Support Centre, Ulverley Junior and Infant School, Rodney Rd, Solihull, West Midlands; Tel 0121-742 3251; H. Moore
Secondary Support Centre, Langley School, Kineton Green Rd, Solihull, West Midlands; Tel 0121-706 9771; S. Orlick

Pre-School and Home Tuition Service

Wooden Spoon Centre, Lode La, Solihull, West Midlands; Tel 0121-709 0080; *Head of Service* S. Maden

Service for Hearing Impaired Children and Pre-School Hearing Centre

Helen Keller Hse, Kineton Green Rd, Solihull, West Midlands; Tel 0121-708 0499; *Head of Service* P. McCann (Acting)

Hearing Impaired Units

Peterbrook Junior and Infant School, High St, Solihull Lodge, Solihull, West Midlands; Tel 0121-430 2545; E.R. Carter. (Infant and Junior Unit)
Lyndon School, Baylesford Rd, Solihull, West Midlands; Tel 0121-743 3402; M.K. Johnson. (Secondary Unit)
Windy Arbor Junior and Infant School, Woodlands Way, Chelmsley Wood, Birmingham, West Midlands; Tel 0121-770 4964; B. Bowell. (Infant and Junior Unit)

Service for Visually Impaired Children

Helen Keller Hse, Kineton Green Rd, Solihull, West Midlands; Tel 0121-708 0499; A. Nicholds

Comprehensive Schools (County)

Alderbrook, Blossomfield Rd, Solihull B91 1SN; Tel 0121-704 2146/7/8; M. Cross, BA. (1180)
Arden, Station Rd, Knowle, Solihull B93 0PT; Tel 021-560 3348; D.C. Chamberlin. (940)
Heart of England, Gipsy La, Balsall Common, Coventry CV7 7FW; Tel (01676) 34477; Dr D. Snoswell, BSc, MSc, PhD. (979)
Langley, Kineton Green Rd, Solihull B92 7ER; Tel 0121-706 9771; S. Orlick. (865)
Light Hall, Hathaway Rd, Shirley, Solihull B90 2PZ; Tel 0121-744 3835; D.R. Scard, BA. (1100)
Lode Heath, Lode La, Solihull B91 2HW; Tel 0121-704 1421; G. Robb. (803)
Lyndon, Daylesford Rd, Solihull B92 8EJ; Tel 0121-743 3402 (Upper)/2377 (Lower); M.K. Johnson, BA. (911)
Park Hall, Water Orton Rd, Castle Bromwich, Birmingham B36 9HF; Tel 0121-747 2876/748 2121; N. Craven, BSc, PGCE. (1490)
Smiths Wood, Windward Way, Chelmsley Wood, Birmingham B36 0UE; Tel 0121-770 6811; M.D. Fox, BA. (1180)

Tudor Grange, Dingle La, Solihull B91 3PD; Tel 0121-705 01690 (General), 5100 (Lower), 0121-704 1867 (Upper); J.G. Evans, BA. (600)
Whitesmore, Chapelhouse Rd, Chelmsley Wood, Birmingham B37 5JS; Tel 0121-770 4431; S.C.E. Tillott, MSc, BA. (600)

Comprehensive Schools (Voluntary Aided)

Archbishop Grimshaw R.C., Kew Cl, Cooks La, Chelmsley Wood, Birmingham B37 6NY; Tel 0121-770 5331; M. Corrigan, BEd, MA. (1200)
St Peter's R.C., Whitefields Rd, Solihull B91 3NZ; Tel 0121-705 3988; H.K. Mercer, MA. (856)

Special Schools

Forest Oak, Lanchester Way, Castle Bromwich, Birmingham B37 9LF; Tel 0121-748 3411; I.D. Ould, BA
Hazel Oak, Hazel Oak Rd, Shirley, Solihull B90 2AZ; Tel 0121-744 4162; P.A. Wright, MEd
Merstone, Exeter Dr, Chelmsley Wood, Birmingham, West Midlands; Tel 0121-788 8122; P. Thomas, BA, BPhil(Ed), LTCL
Reynalds Cross, Kineton Green Rd, Solihull B92 7ER; Tel 0121-707 3012; M. Daniels, MEd

Teachers' Centre

Solihull Teachers' Centre, Tanworth La, Shirley, Solihull B90 4DD; Tel 0121-744 1276; S. Youngblood

Somerset County Council

Population 472,500
County Hall, Taunton TA1 4DY; Tel (01823) 333451; Fax (01823) 255258
Chief Executive B.M. Tanner, BA, IPFA

Education Services

County Hall, Taunton TA1 4DY; Tel (01823) 333451; Fax (01823) 338139
Chief Education Officer P.N. Henwood, MEd, BA
Chief County Inspector D. Strong
County Inspector G. Briggs
County Inspector P. Cutts
County Inspector F. Jones
County Inspector T. Murray
County Inspector J. Rose
County Inspector M. Turner
Head of Continuing Education Dr W. Gregg, MA
Head of Finance Information and Resources D. Rawlinson, MA
Head of Customer Support and Marketing J. Wreford, MA(Oxon)
Head of Operations and Services D. Parkinson, BA, MEd, DipEd
Inspection Service Manager R.W. Strong
Music Support Service Manager R. Barrell
Somerset Education Consultant Service Manager M. Knight
Adult and Community Education Arts and Leisure Service Manager P. Edkins
Careers Service Manager P.W. Renshaw
Student Grants Service Manager G.A. Mayor
Youth Service Manager S.J. Bolger
Education Financial Services Manager S.J. Fielden
Information Management Service Manager D.K. Woodward
Internal Support Unit D. Knightly-Baker
Customer Support Service Manager G. Musgrave
Contracts Support Services Manager M. Hughes
Schools and Members Services Manager K.A. Fowler
Special Education Support Services Manager J. Cole
Special Education Services Manager S. Wilkinson
Sites and Buildings Development Service Manager A.J. Reid
Personnel Service Manager T.K. Moore
Early Years Officer J. Brooker
Finance Manager M. Pollard
Head of Information Research G. Smith
Adviser (Art and Design) Derek King
Adviser (English and Drama) Rob Joslin
Adviser (Equal Opportunities) Jon Gray
Adviser (Geography and Environmental Education) Paul Birbeck
Adviser (Health Related and Physical Education) Iain Kerr
Adviser (History) Mike Gorman
Adviser (Mathematics) Trevor West
Adviser (Modern Languages) David Ellis
Adviser (Music) Andrew Maddock
Adviser (Religion, Personal and Social Education) Vacancy
Adviser (Science) David White
Number of Schools
228 primary (35,055) plus 3 grant maintained (298); 9 middle (4,386); 28 secondary (23,029); 2 grant maintained (598); 8 special schools (616)
Day of Committee Meeting
Thursday (quarterly)
Other Authorities with whom Joint Purchasing Arrangements are made
Consortium for Purchasing and Distribution (CPD)

Education Committee

LD 15, Con 6, Lab 1
Chair D.C. Wicks, (LD) 3 Upper Farm Cl, Norton St Philip, Bath BA3 6NA; Tel (01373) 834236
Vice-Chair G.M. Cawood, (LD) The Gardener's Cottage, East Cranmore, Shepton Mallet, Somerset BA4 4SG; Tel 01749) 880404/880623
Vice-Chair D.G. Esp, (LD) The Old Post Office, 84 West St, Hinton St George TA17 8SB; Tel (01460) 72355
Members of the Committee
LD: C.M. Bakewell, V. Byrne, D.C. Campbell, N.A. Cant, T.G.R. Carroll, R.B. Clark, D.G.H. Gordon, D. Heath, P.J. Hunter, Liz Palmer, Hazel Prior-Sankey, J.B.D. Shaw, H.P. Strawbridge, J.L. Taylor, H.P.N. Temperley, Lady Winchilsea
Con: M.J. Challes, Lady Gass, Dr J.C. Malin, A.W.C. Merrick, W.J.D. Roach, B. Roberts
Lab: D.R. Theobald

Somerset Education Consultants

Keats Rd, Holway, Taunton TA1 2JB; Tel (01823) 330574; Fax (01823) 330598

Careers Service

See chapter 17

Child Guidance and Family Therapy Services

Child Guidance and Family Therapy Services, Petrel Hse, Broadway Pk, Barclay St, Bridgwater, Somerset TA6 5YA; Tel (01278) 446909
Child Guidance and Family Therapy Service, Balidon Centre, Summerlands Hospital, Preston Rd, Yeovil, Somerset BA20 2BX; Tel (01935) 76130
Child Guidance and Family Therapy Service, Eastgate, East Reach, Taunton, Somerset; Tel (01823) 255810/255816

Community Education

Burnham-on-Sea CE Centre, Princess St, Burnham-on-Sea TA8 1EH; Tel (01278) 783057; J. Pridham
Minehead CE Centre, Middle St, North Hill, Minehead TA24 5JH; Tel (01643) 702986; M. Silverlock

Wellington and District Community Education Centre, Courtlands Rd, Wellington TA21 8ND; Tel (01823) 663000; S. Duffen

Youth and Community Centre

Taunton Youth and Community Centre, Tangier, Taunton TA1 4AY; Tel (01823) 331700; H. Maul

Area Youth Offices

South Somerset, Eastland Rd, Yeovil BA21 4ET; Tel (01935) 26843/125403; Val Webster
Mendip, Portway, Wells BA5 2BG; Tel (01749) 670067; T. Corban
Sedgemoor, First Fl, Resources 4 Learning, Parkway, Bridgwater TA6 4RL; Tel (01278) 422976; J. Batt
West Somerset/Taunton and Deane, 10 Burton Pl, Taunton TA1 4HD; Tel (01823) 252089; Estelle Margereson

Residential Education Centre

Kilve Court Residential Education Centre, Kilve, Bridgwater TA5 1EA; Tel (01278) 741270; R.J. Hancock

Training and Conference Centre

Dillington Computer Centre, Ilminster TA19 9DT; Tel (01460) 52427/53875; *Director* P. Rowe

Special Schools

Bridgwater Elmwood, Hamp Ave, Bridgwater, Somerset TA6 6AP; Tel (01278) 422866; C.P. Williams. Day (4–16) (85)
Elmwood Learning Support Centre, Tel (01278) 444087; *Coordinator* C. Hawkes
Bridgwater Penrose, Albert St, Bridgwater, Somerset TA6 7ET; Tel (01278) 423660; C. Davies. Day (2–19) (43)
Frome Critchill, Nunney Rd, Frome, Somerset BA11 4LB; Tel (01373) 464148; L. Rowsell. Day (2–16) (54)
Critchill Learning Support Centre, Tel (01373) 461837; *Coordinator* D. Hale
Street Avalon, Brooks Rd, Street, Somerset BA16 0PS; Tel (01458) 43081; S.E. Johnson. Day (2–16) (101)
Avalon SN Support Centre, Tel (01458) 46625; J. Maynard
Taunton Monkton Priors, Pickeridge Cl, Taunton, Somerset TA2 7HW; Tel (01823) 275569; A. Hinchliffe. Day (4–16) (95)
Monkton Priors SN Support Centre Tel (01823) 275569
Taunton Selworthy, Selworthy Rd, Taunton, Somerset TA2 8HD; Tel (01823) 284970; D.J. Machell. Day (2–19) (51)
Yeovil Fairmead, Mudford Rd, Yeovil, Somerset BA21 4NZ; Tel (01935) 21295; A.R. Fox. Day (4–16) (129)
Fairmead Learning Support Centre, Tel (01935) 31834; *Coordinators* S. Thomas-Peter, A. Clarke

Other Special Educational Facilities

Brooklands, Langport, Somerset TA10 9SP; Tel (01458) 250307
Mendip Centre, Beckery St, Glastonbury, Somerset; Tel (01458) 835364; J. Castle
Merrifield, Tone Vale Hospital, Norton Fitzwarren, Taunton TA4 1DB; Tel (01823) 432673; C.J. Taylor
Sedgemoor Centre (EBD) Blake St, Bridgwater TA6 3NB; Tel (01278) 421148; C.R. Perry
Service for Hearing-Impaired Children, The Mount, Taunton TA1 3NR; Tel (01823) 336328; *Senior Advisory Tutor/Educational Audiologist* J. Fossey
Yeovil Centre, Reckleford, Yeovil BA20 1JF; Tel (01935) 410793; N. Cooke

Outdoor Education Centres

Charterhouse Outdoor Education Centre, Blagdon, Bristol BS18 6XR; Tel (01761) 462267; T.C. Mathews
Pinkery Outdoor Education Centre, Simonsbath, Minehead, Somerset TA24 7LL; Tel (01643) 83437; *Head of Centre* A. Bailey

Middle Schools (County 9–13)

Dulverton County Dulverton TA22 9EE; Tel (01398) 23223; R.J. Owen. (156)
Fairlands County, Fairlands Way, Cheddar BS27 3NW; Tel (01934) 743186; B.R.E. Parkin. (458)
Maiden Beech County, Lyme Rd, Crewkerne TA18 8HG; Tel (01460) 72677; J. Broad. (554)
Minehead County, Ponsford Rd, Minehead TA24 5RH; Tel (01643) 704191; R.A.D. West, DEM. (611)
Oakfield County, Oakfield Rd, Frome BA11 4JF; Tel (01373) 462539; R.C. Crossman. (675)
Swanmead County, Ditton St, Ilminster TA19 0BL; Tel (01460) 52431; D. Smith. (267)

Middle Schools (Voluntary Controlled)

Danesfield, North Rd, Williton TA4 4SW; Tel (01984) 32581; R.H. Moore. (V.C.) (420)
Hugh Sexey, Wedmore BS28 4ND; Tel (01934) 712211; L. Reeves. (V.C.) (510)
Selwood, Berkley Rd, Frome BA11 2EF; Tel (01373) 462798; G. Wright. (V.C.) (735)

Secondary Comprehensive Schools (County 11–16)

Ansford County, Castle Cary BA7 7JJ; Tel (01963) 50895/50692; D.M. Bardgett. (534)
Bishop Fox's, Kingston Rd, Taunton TA2 7SS; Tel (01823) 289211; C.J. Harvey, MA. (596)
The Blake County, Hamp Ave, Bridgwater TA6 6AW; Tel (01278) 456243/14; D.S. Jordan. (601)
Buckler's Mead County, St John's Rd, Yeovil BA21 4NH; Tel (01935) 24454; Dr N.B. Darby. (867)
The Castle County, Wellington Rd, Taunton TA1 5AU; Tel (01823) 283551/2; D. Speight, BSc. (968)
Chilton Trinity County, Chilton Rd, Bridgwater TA6 3JA; Tel (01278) 455631/2; T.C. Flitton, BSc. (837)
Court Fields County, Mantle St, Wellington TA21 8SW; Tel (01823) 664201; Dr C.A. Stroud. (578)
Crispin County, Church Rd, Street BA10 0AD; Tel (01458) 42048/42714; D. Hancock, BA. (899)
East Bridgewater County, Parkway, Bridgewater TA6 4QY; Tel (01278) 422841/2/3; M. Hayward, BA. (578)
Haygrove County, Durleigh Rd, Bridgwater TA6 7HW; Tel (01278) 455531/2/3; R.A. Ward. (802)
Heathfield County, Monkton Heathfield, Taunton TA2 8PD; Tel (01823) 412396; S Jones. (1002)
Huish Episcopi County, Langport TA10 9SS; Tel (01458) 250501; J.T. Saunders, BA, DipEd. (1211)
King Arthur's County, West Hill, Wincanton BA9 9BX; Tel (01963) 32368; I. Campbell. (659)
Kingsmead County, Wiveliscombe TA4 2NE; Tel (01984) 623483; B.R. Collingridge, BA. (576)
Ladymead County, Cheddon Rd, Taunton TA2 7QP; Tel (01823) 331243/1228247; J.M. Parker. (767)
Preston County, Monk's Dale, Yeovil BA21 3JD; Tel (01935) 71131; J.W. Hollis. (769)
St Dunstan's County, Wells Rd, Glastonbury BA6 9BY; Tel (01458) 832943; J.A. Beer, MA. (599)
Stanchester County, Stoke-sub-Hamdon TA14 6UG; Tel (01935) 823200/823727; G. Ottery. (691)
Westfield County, Stiby Rd, Yeovil BA21 3EP; Tel (01935) 23747; S.G. Walker. (889)
Whitstone County, Charlton Rd, Shepton Mallet BA4 5PF; Tel (01749) 345555; S.P. Chaudoir. (542)

Secondary Comprehensive Schools (13–18)

Frome College, Bath Rd, Frome BA11 2HQ; Tel (01373) 465353; B.J.C. Bates. (1252)
West Somerset County, Alcombe, Minehead TA24 6AY; Tel (01643) 706061; A.B.H. Fell, BA. (925)

Secondary Comprehensive Schools (11–18)

Holyrood County, Zembard La, Chard TA20 1JL; Tel (01460) 63831; R.S. Chant. (11–18) (1092)

The King Alfred County, Burnham Rd, Highbridge TA9 3EE; Tel (01278) 784881; J.G. Ellener, BSc. (1075)

Secondary Comprehensive Schools (Voluntary Controlled)

The Blue School, Kennion Rd, Wells BA5 2NR; Tel (01749) 678799; P.A. Morris. (1247); (11–18)
Kings of Wessex, Station Rd, Cheddar BS27 3AQ; Tel (01934) 742608; T.K. Herring, BSc. (965)
Wadham, Yeovil Rd, Crewkerne TA18 7NT; Tel (01460) 73481; A. Preston. (606)

Secondary Comprehensive Schools (Voluntary Aided)

St Augustine of Canterbury, Lynford Rd, Taunton TA2 7EF; Tel (01823) 337128; D. Whalley. (585)

Approved Independent (Special)

Childscourt Boarding School, Lattiford Hse, Wincanton BA9 8AH; Tel (01963) 32213; J. Malcolm; M. Wilkins. (9–16)
Marchant-Holliday School, North Cheriton, Templecombe BA8 0AH; Tel (01963) 33234; J.M. Robertson. (6–13)
Princess Margaret School, 53 Middleway, Taunton TA1 3ON; Tel (01823) 157917; D. Walker. (5–19) (Barnado's)
Mark College, Mark, Highbridge TA9 4NP; Tel (01278) 641632; Dr S.J. Chinn. (11–16)

Grant Maintained Schools

East Bridgwater Community, Parkway, Bridgwater TA6 4QY; Tel (01278) 422841/2/3; M. Hayward, BA. (578)
Sexey's School, Bruton BA10 ODF; Tel (01749) 813393; Fax (01749) 812870; *Headteacher* David Charman; *Chair of Governors* M. Oliver. (Boarding/Day) (Mixed 11–18) (400)
St Augustine's R.C. School, Wingfield Rd, Trowbridge BA14 9EN; Tel (01225) 753577; Fax (01225) 777303; *Headteacher* Robert Cook; *Chair of Governors* Michael Thorp. (Mixed) (11–16) (600)

South Glamorgan County Council

Population 410,449 (as at Mid 1992)
County Hall, Atlantic Wharf, Cardiff CF1 5UW; Tel (01222) 872000; Fax (01222) 872597

Education Offices

County Hall, Atlantic Wharf, Cardiff CF1 5UW; Tel (01222) 872700; Fax (01222) 872777
Chief Executive Officer B. Davies
Treasurer K. Bray
Director of Social Services C.J. Perry, MA, CSW, MBASW, MISW
Director of Education T. Davies
Principal Assistant Director of Education (Development and Strategic Services) A.G. Davies, BA, PGCEd, PGCEM
Assistant Director of Education (Services to Institutions) K.A. Gregory, BA
Assistant Director of Education (Quality Assurance) H. Knight, MA, PGCE
Assistant Education Officer (Individual and Community Services) J. Rickard; Tel (01222) 872716
Assistant Education Officer (Individual and Special Services) J.E. Davidson, BA
Assistant Education Officer (Schools Support and LMS) D.A.S. Martin, BA, JP
Assistant Education Officer (Secondary and Special Services) G.M. Rowney, BA
Assistant Education Officer (Schools Support and Governing Bodies) C.D. Mason, BA
Principal Officer (Personnel) J.P. Kippest, BA, DipED
Principal Officer (Finance) R.S. Briggs, IPFA, DMA
Senior Adviser (Primary) E. Griffiths, MEd
Senior Adviser (Secondary) I. Evendon, BA, DipEd
Mathematics Adviser M.R. Haylings
Sciences Adviser Dr D.J. Francis, BSc, PhD
History and Geography Adviser A. Geach
Art and DT Adviser S. Gale
RE/PSE inc Child Abuse, Careers, R.O.A. Welsh Adviser D. Treharne, BA
Modern Languages Adviser R. Hopkins, BA
Computing/Information Technology Adviser Dr M.F. Treadaway, BSc, PhD
Primary Adviser D. Watcyn Jones
English Adviser H. Booley
Community Education Adviser W.J. Morris, DipPhysEd; Tel (01222) 872756; Fax (01222) 872777
Community Education Adviser M. Shaugnessy, BA; Tel (01222) 872757
Community Education Adviser D.R. Allinson, BA, MSc(Econ)
County Catering Officer A. Johns
Senior Educational Psychologist C. Tyre, BSc(Hons), DipEd(Psych)
TVEI Co-ordinator P. Roberts

Number of Schools
10 Nursery (includes part-time); 130 primary (31,538); 25 Secondary (27,432) 13 Special (821); 15 full time adult centres; 1 teachers centre

Education Committee

Lab 21, Con 7, LD, 4, Plaid Cymru 1
Chair P.G. Perkins, (Lab) 77 Pentrebane St, Grangetown, Cardiff CF1 7JF
Deputy-Chair A. A'Herne, (Lab) 41 Colwinstone St, Llandaff North, Cardiff CF4 2LB
Deputy-Chair M.E. Drake, (Lab) 4 Llwyn Drysgol, Radyr, Cardiff CF4 8DN
Deputy-Chair P.C. Gray, (Lab) 3 Little Dock St, Cogan, Penarth CF6 1JT

Members of the Committee
Lab: A. A'Herne, N.C. Butler, B. Doughty, M.E. Drake, A. Fennessy, B.A. Finn, B.J. Foday, P.C. Gray, M. Griffiths, G.J. Hinchley, L.S. Hughes, B. Lane, S.J. Lent, R.A. Pearson, D.F. Reed, D.N. Rees, R.G. Perkins, A. Rees, D. Richards, C.E. Roderick, C.V. Watkins
Con: M.R. Davies, J.P. Donovan, H.E. James, A.R. John, M.J. Prior, R.G. Thomas, D.M. Turner
LD: J.A. Gasson, J. Holiday, T.C. Pickets, R.P.J. Rowland
Plaid Cymru: C.P. Franks

Special Schools

Ashgrove, Sully Rd, Penarth CF6 2TW; Tel (01222) 704212; B.M. Brayford, DipSpEd, CTD. (Deaf) (Residential)
The Court, Station Rd, Llanishen, South Glamorgan; Tel (01222) 752713; W.G. Rees, BEd(Hons), DSE. (E.S.N.) (Junior and Infant)
Greenhill, Heol Brynglas, Rhiwbina, Cardiff CF4 6UJ; Tel (01222) 693786; A.R. Lewis, BA, DipSpecEd
The Lindens, Bradford Pl, Penarth, South Glamorgan; Tel (01222) 707645; M. Bull (Acting). (4–16)
Maes y Coed, Gladstone Rd, Barry CF6 9NH; Tel (01446) 732755; B.A. Milhuisen, BEd, DipTHC
Meadow Bank, Colwill Rd, Gabalfa, Cardiff, South Glamorgan; Tel (01222) 616018/9; S.E. Grover. (Residential)
The Hollies, Pentwyn; Tel (01222) 734411; E.C. Griffiths, BA(Hons), DipSpEd, MEd. (Residential)
Riverbank, Vincent Rd, Ely, South Glamorgan; Tel (01222) 563860; G.A. Evans. (E.S.N.) (Junior)

Ty Gwyn, Ty Gwyn Rd, Penylan, South Glamorgan; Tel (01222) 485570; D.W. Dwyer, BEd
Whitchurch Hospital School (Young People's Unit), Velindre Rd, Whitchurch, Cardiff CF4 7JG; Tel (01222) 693591, Ext 118. (Emotionally Disturbed Adolescents)
Woodlands High, Vincent Rd, Ely, South Glamorgan; Tel (01222) 561279; E.A. Dunn, BEd(Hons). (E.S.N.)
Ysgol Erw'r Delyn, St Cyres Rd, Penarth, Cardiff, South Glamorgan; Tel (01222) 707225; *Head* M. Farrell. (P.H.) (Residential)
Ysgol Maes Dyfan, Gibbonsdown Rise, Barry CF6 2QZ; Tel (01446) 732112; M.J. Righton, BEd(Hons)

Comprehensive High Schools

Barry, Upper School, Port Rd West, Barry CF6 9ZJ; Tel (01446) 732072; D.M. Griffiths, BSc(Econ), MEd, MSc, DipEdMan. (Boys) (1828)
Bishop of Llandaff C.W. High, Rookwood Cl, Llandaff, South Glamorgan; Tel 562485; L.T. Parfitt, BSc. (Mixed) (1059)
Bryn Hafren, Merthyr Dyfan Rd, Barry CF6 7YD; Tel (01446) 739314; P.J. Roberts, BA. (Girls) (1740)
Cantonian High, Fairwater Rd, Cardiff, South Glamorgan; Tel (01222) 564501; A.C. Cowell. (Mixed) (1674)
Cardiff High, Llandennis Rd, Cardiff, South Glamorgan; Tel (01222) 757741; G.O. Roberts, BSc. (Mixed) (1173)
Cathays High, New Zealand Rd, Cardiff, South Glamorgan; Tel (01222) 619444; M.A. Wilson, BSc, MA. (Mixed) (1004)
Corpus Christi High, Cyncoed Rd, Cardiff, South Glamorgan; Tel (01222) 484373; G.E. Silke (Sister Mary Peter), BSc(Hons). (Mixed) (997)
Cowbridge Comprehensive, Tel (0144 63) 913/12333/12311; G. James, BA. (Mixed) (1102)
Fitzalan High, Lawrenny Ave, Cardiff, South Glamorgan; Tel (01222) 396246; A.W. Dumphy, BSc(Econ), DMS, MBIM. (Mixed) (1793)
Glan Ely High, Michaelston Rd, Cardiff, South Glamorgan; Tel (01222) 593414/561901; J.E. Bell, BSc, CertEd. (Mixed) (1279)
Glyn Derw High, Penally Rd, Ely, South Glamorgan; Tel 591216; *Head* A.M. Davies (Acting), BSc, DipEd Man. (Mixed) (914)
Llanedeyrn High, Llanedeyrn Est, Cardiff, South Glamorgan; Tel (01222) 734718; R. Graham, BSc. (Mixed) (1325)
Llanilltud Fawr, Llantwit Major, Llanilltud Fawr, South Glamorgan; Tel (0144 65) 915/3301; E.J. Davies, MA, BEd. (Mixed) (1067)
Llanishen High, Llanishen, South Glamorgan; Tel 753357; A.F. Boxford, BA, DEM. (Mixed) (1476)
Llanrumney High, Ball Rd, Cardiff, South Glamorgan; Tel (01222) 792731/2/3; D. Brooks. (Mixed) (1509)
Mary Immaculate High, Caerau La, Ely, South Glamorgan; Tel 593359; M.D. Howells, BA, DipEd. (Mixed) (917)
Radyr, Radyr, South Glamorgan; Tel (01222) 842059; J.O. David, BSc. (Mixed) (1150)
Rumney High, Quarry Hill, Cardiff, South Glamorgan; Tel (01222) 792751/2; R.J. Gullis, BSc(Hons), MEd. (Mixed) (1448)
Sir Richard Gwyn High, Barry, South Glamorgan; Tel (01446) 733599; P.G. O'Neill, BEd(Hons). (Mixed) (448)
St Cyres, Penarth, South Glamorgan; Tel (01222) 708708; B.R. Rowlands, BA, DipEd. (Mixed) (1468)
St David's R.C., 6th Form College, Ty Gwyn Rd; Tel (01222) 498555; P.D. Bryon, BA, MEd(Principal)
St Illtyd's High, Quarry Hill, Rumney CF3 8XG; Tel 78174; P.A. Gamble, BA(Hons), MPhil. (823)
St Teilo's C.W. High, Llanedeyrn Rd; Tel 490234; A.T. Griffiths, BA. (Mixed) (681)
Stanwell, Penarth, South Glamorgan; Tel (01222) 707633; M.D. Parker, BSc, MEd. (Mixed) (1337)
Whitchurch High, Penlline Rd, Cardiff, South Glamorgan; Tel (01222) 612691; G.B. Matthewson. (Mixed) (2128)
Willows High, Willows Ave, Cardiff, South Glamorgan; Tel (01222) 462916; M.W. Davies, BEd, MEd. (Mixed) (1058)
Ysgol Gyfun Gymraeg Glantaf, Bridge Rd, Llandaff North, Cardiff CF4 2JL; Tel (01222) 562305; J.E.M. Thomas, BA(Hons). (Mixed) (Welsh Medium)

Teachers' Centre

Cardiff Teachers Centre, Cefn Rd, Mynachov, Cardiff, South Glamorgan; Tel (01222) 619043; *INSET Manager* B.T. Griffiths

South Tyneside Metropolitan Borough Council

Population 157,300 (mid 1992)
Town Hall and Civic Offices, Westoe Rd, South Shields, Tyne and Wear NE33 2RL; Tel 0191-427 1717; Fax 0191-455 0208

Education Offices

Town Hall and Civic Offices, Westoe Rd, South Shields, Tyne and Wear NE33 2RL; Tel 0191-427 1717; Fax 0191-427 0584
Director of Education I.L. Reid, BSc
Head of Schools Division Vacancy
Head of Continuing Education Division G.K. Lloyd-Williams, MA
Head of Resources Finance and Personnel Division E. Campbell, MSc
Assistant Director (Finance) W. Green, CIPFA
Assistant Director (Special Needs) G. Snowdon, BA
Senior Assistant Education Officer (Personnel) F.M. Emms, DMA, ACIS, MBIM
Senior Assistant Education Officer (Schools) L.D. Rogers, BA
AEO (Governors Admin and Training) M.R. Grady, BA, MEd, PGCE
AEO (Schools) J. Burrow, HND, BA, LLM
AEO (Resourcing) A. Locklan, CEd
Assistant Education Officer M. Pegram, BEd, MEd
Principal Administrative Assistant (Staffing and Salaries) M. Dixon
Principal Administrative Assistant (Resources and Planning) D. Forbes
Principal Administrative Assistant (Development) B. Brown
Senior Administrative Assistant (Governors Administration) K. Thompson
Principal Administrative Assistant (Pupils Awards, FE) D. Morgan
Chief Adviser (Appraisal/RE) A.K. Haye, BA(Hons)
Adviser (English and Drama) Vacancy
Adviser (Music) R.D. McKone, BA, MA
Adviser (Physical Education and Outdoor Pursuits) A. Brown, BPhil
Adviser (Technology and Art) G.C. Miller, BEd
Adviser (Educational Technology, Mathematics, Science) L. Decyk, BSc, DipEd
Adviser (History and Geography) J.H. Gulson, BA, MEd, DAES, PGCE
Adviser (Early Years, Primary and Assessment) M. Chalmers, BA
Education Business Partnership M.A. Frostick, BPhil
School Meals Contractor (In House) G.W. Hedley
Chief Education Welfare Officer J.A. Soulsby, CQSW
School Meals (Client Services) C. Branch
Senior Educational Psychologist C.D.D. Matthew, BSc
Principal Community Education Officer R. McKay, BA
Community Education Organiser T. Cleveland
Community Education Officer L. Watson
Community Education Organiser L. Power
Principal Careers Officer C.S. Laing, BA

Number of Schools
6 nursery (457); 58 primary (14,345 plus 1,843 in Nursery Units 922 FTE); 11 secondary (9,791); 5 Special (375); 1 teachers centre
Day of Committee Meeting
Mondays or Tuesdays on a 5 or 6 week cycle
Other Authorities with whom Joint Purchasing Arrangements are made
North Eastern Purchasing Organisation (certain items only)

Education Committee

Lab 29, LD 2
Chair P. Waggott, (Lab) 186 Hedworth La, Jarrow NE32 4LG; Tel 0191-536 3957
Vice-Chair J.F. Harper, (Lab) 8 Loudon St, South Shields NE34 0LU; Tel 0191-456 4109
Members of the Committee
Lab: T.A. Bamford, E. Battye, C. Bonnar, M. Chenery, E. Doneghan, J. Eales, R. Edwardson, A.L. Elliot, M. Fairley, F.E. Firth, A. Frost, M.A. Hamilton, T. Hanson, J.F. Harper, S. Hepburn, S.F. Hussain, A. Jackson, J. Jackson, M.E. Lightfoot, I. Malcolm, N. Maxwell, C.E. McHugh, M.C. Pearson, J. Phipps, R.W. Reynolds, B. Scorer, A. Tate, L.A. Waggot, P. Waggott
LD: S. Brown, V. Leary

Governor Training Unit

Education Dept, Town Hall Civic Offices, Westoe Rd, South Shields, Tyne and Wear NE33 2RL; Tel 0191-427 1717; Fax 0191-427 0584
Assistant Education Officer Malcolm Grady, BA(Hons); MA in Education
Services Offered
Comprehensive training package to school Governors; Link Governor network; Resource Base; Termly newsletter; Telephone helpline

Special Needs Support/Resource Centre/Child Guidance Centre

Education Welfare Office

Jarrow Town Hall, Jarrow, Tyne and Wear; Tel 0191-489 1141; Fax 0191-428 0416

Careers Office

See chapter 17

Special Schools

Bamburgh, Norham Ave, South Shields NE34 7TD; Tel 0191-454 0671; J.M. Fawcett. (3–19) (Mixed) (94)
Epinay, Clervaux Terr, Jarrow NE32 5UP; Tel 0191-489 8949; S.D. Allsopp, BPhil. (5–19) (Mixed) (96)
Greenfields, Victoria Rd East, Hebburn NE31 1YQ; Tel 0191-489 7480; M. Conway. (3–19) (Mixed) (40)
Margaret Sutton, Ashley Rd, South Shields NE34 0PF; Tel 0191-455 3309; G. Palmer, MEd. (5–19) (Mixed) (102)
Oakleigh Gardens, Oakleigh Gdns, Cleadon, nr Sunderland SR6 7PT; Tel 0191-536 2590; J. Green. (3–19) (Mixed) (43)

Comprehensive Schools (County 11–16)

Boldon New Rd, Boldon Colliery NE35 9DZ; Tel 0191-536 2176; Fax 0191-537 4073; R.R. Tynemouth, BA. (Mixed) (1007)
Brinkburn, McAnany Ave, South Shields NE34 0PJ; Tel 0191-456 8929; Fax 0191-454 0300; I. Hargreaves, BA, MEd. (Mixed) (779)
Harton, Lisle Rd, South Shields NE34 6DL; Tel 0191-456 4226; Fax 0191-454 4956; P.J.H. Turner, BPhil, MEd. (Mixed) (1172)
Hebburn, Campbell Park Rd, Hebburn NE31 2QU; Tel 0191-483 3199/2518; Fax 0191-483 2160; M. Watson, BEd(Hons), MEd. (Mixed) (865)
Hedworthfield, Hedworth Est, Jarrow NE32 4QD; Tel 0191-536 5411; Fax 0191-519 2422; D. Besford, BSc, MEd. (Mixed) (656)
King George, Nevinson Ave, South Shields NE34 8BT; Tel 0191-456 4811; Fax 0191-427 9268; A.M. Brooks, BSc, DipEd. (Mixed) (693)
Mortimer, Reading Rd, South Shields NE33 4UG; Tel 0191-456 6511; Fax 0191-427 1176; R.A. Snowdon, MA, MEd. (Mixed) (1111)
Springfield, Field Terr, Jarrow NE32 5PP; Tel 0191-489 3225; W.R. Porteous, OBE, TD, MSc, BSc, ARIC. (Mixed) (725)
Whitburn, Nicholas Ave, Whitburn, Sunderland SR6 7EA; Tel 0191-529 3712; Fax 0191-529 4202; A.M. Love, BSc, MEd. (Mixed) (740)

Comprehensive School (Voluntary Aided 11–16)

St Wilfrid's R.C., Harton La, South Shields NE34 0PH; Tel 0191-456 9121; Fax 0191-454 5070; P. Bannon, BA, MEd. (Mixed) (815)

Comprehensive School (Voluntary Aided 11–18)

St Joseph's R.C., Mill La, Hebburn NE31 2ET; Tel 0191-483 2619; Fax 0191-428 2160; J.A. Campbell, PhD, BSc. (Mixed) (1229)

Adult Education, Youth and Community Centres

All Saints Community Centre, Stanley St, South Shields, Tyne and Wear; Tel (0191) 4561185
Boldon C.A., Boldon Comprehensive School, New Rd, Boldon Colliery NE35 9DZ; Tel 0191-536 8085
Boldon Colliery Village Hall, ASDA Complex, North Rd, Boldon Colliery, Tyne and Wear; Tel 0191-536 3841
Boldon Lane Community Centre, Boldon La, South Shields NE34 0LZ; Tel 0191-427 0011
Brinkburn C.A., Brinkburn Comprehensive School, McAnany Ave, South Shields NE34 0PJ; Tel 0191-455 8491
Chuter Ede C.A., Galsworthy Rd, South Shields NE34 9UG; Tel 0191-536 0515
Cleadon Park C.A., Sunderland Rd, South Shields, Tyne and Wear; Tel 0191-454 4403
Clegwell C.A., Hebburn Comprehensive School, Campbell Park Rd, Hebburn, Tyne and Wear; Tel 0191-489 7575
Derby Terrace C.A., Derby Terr, South Shields, Tyne and Wear; Tel 0191-455 7506
Euryalus P.H.A.B. Club, Bede Burn Rd, Jarrow, Tyne and Wear; Tel 0191-489 4336
Hartleyburn C.A., Crawley Ave, Hebburn, Tyne and Wear; Tel 0191-428 0555
Harton Community Centre, Lisle Rd, South Shields NE34 6DL; Tel 0191-456 4226
Hebburn C.A., Argyle St, Hebburn, Tyne and Wear; Tel 0191-483 2784; Fax 0191-483 2376
Hedworthfield C.A., Cornhill, Hedworth, Jarrow, Tyne and Wear NE32 4QD; Tel 0191-536 0367
Hill Park C.A., Hill Pk Est, Jarrow, Tyne and Wear NE32 5XT; Tel 0191-428 1244
Horsley Hill C.A., Horsley Hill Sq, South Shields, Tyne and Wear NE34 7HE; Tel 0191-456 4466
Jarrow C.A., Cambrian St, Jarrow, Tyne and Wear NE32 3QL; Tel 0191-489 4100
Low Simonside C.A., Taunton Ave, Jarrow, Tyne and Wear; Tel 0191-489 8224
Lukes Lane C.A., Marine Parade, Hebburn, Tyne and Wear; Tel 0191-489 2358
Mid Tyne Activities Centre, Grange Rd, Jarrow, Tyne and Wear; Tel 0191-489 7594
Mortimer C.A., Mortimer Comprehensive School, Reading Rd, South Shields NE33 4UG; Tel 0191-456 6680
Ocean Road C.A., Ocean Rd, South Shields, Tyne and Wear; Tel 0191-456 0080
Percy Hudson Y.C., Sheridan Rd, Tyneside, Tyne and Wear; Tel 0191-536 2578
Perth Green C.A., Inverness Rd, Jarrow NE32 4AQ; Tel 0191-489 3743

Primrose C.A., Lambton Terr, Jarrow, Tyne and Wear; Tel 0191-489 2792
Simonside Y.C., Saint Simon St, South Shields, Tyne and Wear; Tel 0191-456 3920
South Shields Activity Centre, Gresford St, South Shields NE33 4SD; Tel 0191-454 0925
Trinity House Social Centre, 134 Laygate La, South Shields, Tyne and Wear NE33 4JG; Tel (0191) 456 4239
Tyne Dock Y.C., Barnes Rd, South Shields, South Tyneside; Tel 0191-456 3917
West Park C.A., Whitehall St, South Shields, South Tyneside; Tel 0191-455 1205

Field Study and Outdoor Pursuits Centres

Akenshawburn Centre, Akenshawburn Cottages, Kielder, Northumberland
Thurston Outdoor Education Centre, Coniston, Cumbria LA21 8AB; Tel (0196) 641218
Water Activities Centre, The Groyne, South Shields, South Tyneside; Tel 0191-455 5414

Service Education Centre

Chuter Ede Education Centre, Galsworthy Rd, South Shields, South Tyneside; Tel 0191-519 1909; Fax 0191-519 0600; J. Kranz, BPhil; Special Needs Support/Resource Centre/Child Guidence Centre

South Yorkshire Metropolitan Area

The following Metropolitan Councils comprise the South Yorkshire Metropolitan Area and may be found in alphabetical order within this chapter:
Barnsley, Doncaster, Rotherham, Sheffield.

Staffordshire County Council

Population 1,051,800
PO Box 11, County Bldgs, Martin St, Stafford ST16 2LH; Tel (01785) 223121; Fax (01785) 215153
Chief Education Officer P.J. Hunter, PhD, BSc
County Clerk and Chief Executive B.A. Price, MA, DMS
County Treasurer R.G. Tettenborn, OBE, MA, IPFA; Tel (01785) 223121
Director of Property Services C.J. Savage, DipArch, RIBA, FRSA, BIFM Green Hall, Lichfield Rd, Stafford
Director of Libraries, Arts and Archives R.J. Smith, BA, ACA, MICAM Friars Terr; Tel (01785) 223121
Director of Social Services C. Walby St Chads Pl; Tel (01785) 223121

Education Department

Education Office, Tipping St, Stafford ST16 2DH; Tel (01785) 223121; Fax (01785) 56727
Chairman Cllr T.R. Wright, MA(Oxon), BSc(Econ)
Vice-Chairman Cllr J.R. Brooks
Deputy Chief Education Officer (Management and Support) J.C. Hawkins, BA
Deputy Chief Education Officer (Policy and Resources) D. D'Hooghe, MSc
Principal Education Officer (Inspection and Review) M.E. Beamond
Principal Education Officer (Financial Services) D. Cheeseman, IPFA
Principal Education Officer (Consultancy and Support) D. Goddard, BA, MSc
Principal Education Officer (Policy and Support Services) M. Halstead, LLB, MA(Ed)
Principal Education Officer (Business Manager and Monitoring) D. Hutt, MA
Principal Education Officer (Development – Sites and Buildings) A. Law, BA
Principal Education Officer (Special Services and Welfare) V. McDonnell, MA
Principal Education Officer (Personnel Services) T. Whincup, BA, MIPM
Director of Physical Education A.A. Bailey, DLC
Director of Music W.S. Johnson, AMusLCM
AEO (Development) M. Aston, CertEd
AEO (Development/Planning) D. Coates, BA, DMS
AEO (Resource Management) I.R. Hill, ACIS
AEO (Resource Policy) Dr T.C. Hine, MSc
AEO (Development) R. Hordern, BSc
AEO (Central Issues) J.M. Inman, BA
AEO (Policy and Support Services) J. Kemp, BA
AEO (Youth and Community Education) S. Lapworth, MA, BSc(Hons), PGCE
Professional Assistant J. Heaton, BEd
AEO (Special Education) F.P. Morgan
AEO (Pupil Support) N. Tushingham, BA, DMA, DMS
District Education Officer H.G. Cartlidge, BA
District Education Officer S.G. Cross, MSc, BA, DMA
District Education Officer K.G. Lancaster, BSc(Soc), DMS
District Education Officer R.J. Lord, MA, PGCE
District Education Officer D. Moore, BEd
Chief Educational Psychologist R.G. Booth, BA(Hons)Psych, DipEd, DipEdPsych
Senior Inspector (Further Education) W.G. Smith
General County Inspector (14–19 Education) J. Alexander
General County Inspector – Design and Technology H. Bagshaw
General County Inspector – Religious Education P. Bellingham
General County Inspector – Language/English J.E. Billington
General County Inspector – Humanities J. Bird
General County Inspector – Mathematics D.J. Birdsall
General County Inspector – Primary Education J. Bristow
General County Inspector – Geography R. Carter
General County Inspector – Early Years M.J. Cheadle
General County Inspector – English Dr P.I. Crumpton
General County Inspector – History W. Dewar
General County Inspector – Information Technology M. Grime
General County Inspector – Modern Languages P. Hall
General County Inspector – Marketing N. Hughes
General County Inspector – Science S. Hurst
General County Inspector – 14–19 Education G. Job
General County Inspector – Middle School I. Jones
General County Inspector – Education at Home R. Lambert
General County Inspector (Records of Achievement and Assessment) T. Legge
General County Inspector – Management R.C. Love
General County Inspector – Small Schools J. Mountford
General County Inspector (Special Educational Needs) J. Murphey
General County Inspector – Environmental Education G. Nabney
General County Inspector – PSHE Development/PDC Network P. Owen
General County Inspector – Mathematics G. Smart
General County Inspector – Contracts Manager R.F. Spinks
General County Inspector – Art and Design J. Thirlwall
General County Inspector – Science R.W. Wonnacott
County Youth and Community Education Officer R. Marsh

County Catering Officer M.H. Hulland
Principal County Careers Officer Eileen Manley, BSc(ScoSci)
County Grounds Officer D.R. Kirk
Number of Schools
25 nursery schools; 406 primary; 82 secondary (including middle deemed secondary)
Special Schools
29 (8,144)
Day of Committee Meeting
Variable, five times a year
Other Authorities with whom Joint Pruchasing Arrangements are made
Shropshire, Hereford and Worcester

Education Committee

Lab 29, Con 11, Others 2, LD 3
Chair T.R. Wright
Vice-Chair J.R. Brookes
Members of the Committee
Lab: E.A. Abel, W.F. Austin, F.J. Ball, D. Bamford, J.T. Betteridge, I.T. Bowen, H.D Brookes, J.R. Brooks, M.J. Davey, D.J. Davis, J.E.A. Dean, T.A. Dix, E.N. Drinkwater, F. Duffy, B.A. Dunn, G. Hackney, A.R. Hanchard, D. Hepstonstall, J. O'Leary, G.D. Mardle, J.T. Meir, J. Merry, D.C. Morris, A.N. Pearce, D. Shotton, T.F. Smith, M. Stringer, R. Wise, T.R Wright
Con: E. Ashley, P.E.B. Atkins, H.J. Carter, M.J. Harris, K. Hoare, A.H.R. Johnson, C.L. Jones, F.W. Lewis, R. Roberts, A.G. Ward, G.F.T. Williams
LD: M.U. Fox, A.L. Thomas, J.A. Russell*O*/N. Imamoglu, R.G. Locker

Careers Office

See chapter 17

Southern Area

Comprehensive/High Schools (County)

Barton-under-Needwood, John Taylor High, Dunstall Rd, Barton-under-Needwood, Burton-on-Trent, Staffordshire; Tel (0128 371) 2476; G.P. Gallie. (Mixed) (11–18) (1183)
Burntwood, Chase Terr High, Bridge Cross Rd, Chase Terr, Walsall, Staffordshire; Tel (0154 36) 82286/2850; B. Mather. (Mixed) (11–18) (1292)
Burton-on-Trent, The Paget High, Burton Rd, Branston, Burton-on-Trent, Staffordshire; Tel (01283) 567429; D.A. Ayling. (Mixed) (11–18) (747)
Burton, de Ferrers High, St Mary's Dr, Horninglow, Burton-on-Trent, Staffordshire; Tel (01283) 543371; B.T. Hughes, BSc, MEd. (Mixed) (11–18) (1694)
Burton, Paulet High, Stanton Rd, Stapenhill, Burton-on-Trent, Staffordshire; Tel (01283) 563697; R. Parker. (Mixed) (11–18) (575)
Cheslyn Hay High, Saredon Rd, Cheslyn Hay, Walsall, Staffordshire; Tel (01922) 416024; J.W. Swinburne. (Mixed) (11–18) (1032)
Codsall High, Elliotts La, Codsall, nr Wolverhampton, Staffordshire; Tel (01902) 844931; E. Liddy. (Mixed) (13–18) (1233)
Great Wyrley High Hall La, Gt Wyrley, Walsall, Staffordshire; Tel (01922) 414480; J.A. Large. (Mixed) (11–18) (1008)
Hednesford, The Blake High, Marston Rd, Hednesford, Cannock, Staffordshire; Tel (01543) 422321/422239; H.L. Bowman. (Mixed) (11–18) (838)
Hednesford, Kingsmead High, Kings Ave, Hednesford, Cannock, Staffordshire; Tel (01543) 422268; A.J. Murray. (Mixed) (11–18) (1204)
Kinver, Edgecliffe High, Enville Rd South, Kinver, nr Stourbridge, Staffordshire; Tel (01384) 872342; J.C. Price. (Mixed) (11–18) (533)
Lichfield, The Friary High, Eastern Ave, Lichfield, Staffordshire; Tel (01543) 254441; J.M. Firth, BSc. (Mixed) (11–18) (962)
Lichfield, King Edward VI, Upper Saint John St, Lichfield, Staffordshire; Tel (01543) 255714; P.J. Youngs, MA. (Mixed) (11–18) (1322)
Lichfield, Netherstowe High, St Chad's Rd, Lichfield, Staffordshire; Tel (01543) 263446/263487; D.L. Binnie. (Mixed) (11–18) (905)
Norton Canes High, Burntwood Rd, Norton Canes, Cannock, Staffordshire; Tel (01543) 279325; D.B. Hunter, BScTech. (Mixed) (11–18) (647)
Penkridge, Wolgarston High, Cannock Rd, Penkridge, Stafford, Staffordshire; Tel (01785) 712466; L.V. Cook. (Mixed) (13–18) (799)
Rugeley, Fair Oak High, Penkridge Bank Rd, Rugeley, Staffordshire; Tel (01889) 583365/586822; D.W. Johnson. (Mixed) (11–18) (958)
Rugeley, Hagley Park High, Burnthill La, Rugeley, Staffordshire; Tel (01889) 582469/585775; J.R. Hall. (Mixed) (11–18) (933)
Stafford, Sir Graham Balfour High, Stone Rd, Stafford, Staffordshire; Tel (01785) 223490/223866; J. Conchie. (Mixed) (11–18) (750)
Stafford, King Edward VI High, West Way, Newport Rd, Stafford, Staffordshire; Tel (01785) 58546; T.R. Brown. (Mixed) (11–18) (1017)
Stafford, Walton High, The Rise, Walton-on-the-Hill, Stafford, Staffordshire; Tel (01785) 661547/663200; D. Hardman. (Mixed) (11–18) (1142)
Stafford, Weston Rd High, Blackheath La, Stafford, Staffordshire; Tel (01785) 48124; G.W.A. Cooper. (Mixed) (11–18) (981)
Stone, Alleynes High, Oulton Rd, Stone, Staffordshire; Tel (01785) 813688; C.A. Spears. (Mixed) (13–18) (861)
Tamworth, Belgrave High, Birds Bush Rd, Belgrave, Tamworth, Staffordshire; Tel (01827) 285596; R. Mountford. (Mixed) (11–18) (923)
Tamworth, TORC High, Silverlink Rd, Tamworth, Staffordshire; Tel (01827) 286305/287378; M.T. Wallis, BA. (Mixed) (11–18) (769)
Tamworth, Queen Elizabeth's Mercian High, Ashby Rd, Tamworth, Staffordshire; Tel (01827) 62241/63198; G.L. Owers. (Mixed) (11–18) (990)
Tamworth, The Rawlett High, Comberford Rd, Tamworth, Staffordshire; Tel (01827) 57178; L.P. Barnett. (Mixed) (11–18) (1056)
Tamworth, Wilnecote High, Tinkers Green Rd, Wilnecote, Tamworth, Staffordshire; Tel (01827) 281491; P.A. Prettyman. (Mixed) (11–18) (1043)
Tamworth, Woodhouse High, Highfields Ave, Amington, Tamworth, Staffordshire; Tel (01827) 68651; P.A. Russell, BA. (Mixed) (11–18) (1116)
Uttoxeter, Thomas Alleynes High, Dove Bank, Uttoxeter, Staffordshire; Tel (01889) 563857; P.K. Mitchell. (Mixed) (13–18) (1154)
Wombourne, Ounsdale High, Ounsdale Rd, Wombourne, nr Wolverhampton, Staffordshire; Tel (01902) 892178; G.J. Hoppington. (Mixed) (11–18) (995)

High Schools (Voluntary 11–18)

Burton-on-Trent, The Abbot Beyne Endowed (C), Linnell Bldg, Osbourne St, Burton-on-Trent, Staffordshire; Tel (01283) 545711; A.L. Heyward, BA, MEd. (Mixed) (11–18) (V.C.) (907)
Burton-on-Trent, Robert Sutton R.C., Bluestone La, Stapenhill, Burton-on-Trent, Staffordshire; Tel (01283) 565015/562145; J. Orton, BA. (Mixed) (11–18) (V.A.) (625)
Stafford, Blessed William Howard R.C. High, Rowley Ave, Stafford, Staffordshire; Tel (01785) 44236; R.J.M. Lister. (Mixed) (11–18) (V.A.) (1047)

Northern Area

Comprehensive Schools

Biddulph High, Conway Rd, Knypersley, Stoke-on-Trent, Staffordshire; Tel (01782) 523977; G. Agar, BSc(Hons). (Mixed) (13–18) (809)
Blythe Bridge High, Cheadle Rd, Blythe Bridge, Stoke-on-Trent, Staffordshire; Tel (01782) 392519; J.M. Wyman. (Mixed) (11–18) (852)

Cheadle High, Station Rd, Cheadle, Stoke-on-Trent, Staffordshire; Tel (01538) 753828; V.M. Bailey. (Mixed) (11–18) (789)
Endon High, Leek Rd, Endon, Stoke-on-Trent, Staffordshire; Tel (01782) 502240; E.P. Baskerville. (Mixed) (11–16) (635)
Kidsgrove, Clough Hall High, First Ave, Kidsgrove, Stoke-on-Trent, Staffordshire; Tel (01782) 783281/2; M.J. Readman. (Mixed) (11–18) (1001)
Kidsgrove, Maryhill High, Gloucester Rd, Kidsgrove, Stoke-on-Trent, Staffordshire; Tel (01782) 783749; C. Lamb, BA(Hons). (Mixed) (11–18) (573)
Leek High, Springfield Rd, Leek, Staffordshire; Tel (01538) 385621; K. Hollins. (Mixed) (13–18) (567)
Leek, Westwood High, Westwood Pk, Leek, Staffordshire; Tel (01538) 385737; G.R. Wiskin, BSc(Econ). (Mixed) (13–18) (716)
Madeley High, Newcastle Rd, Madeley, nr Crewe, Staffordshire; Tel (01782) 750368; B.R. Gilson. (Mixed) (11–16) (567)
Newcastle, Chesterton High, Castle St, Chesterton, Newcastle, Staffordshire; Tel (01782) 561251; M.C. Weeks. (Mixed) (11–16) (626)
Newcastle, Clayton High, Clayton La, Newcastle, Staffordshire; Tel (01782) 614901; D.M. Cole. (Mixed) (11–16) (878)
Newcastle, Wolstanton High, Milehouse La, Newcastle, Staffordshire; Tel (01782) 626431; T.B. Lewis. (Mixed) (11–16) (1196)
Newcastle, Sneyd High, Gallows Tree La, Newcastle, Staffordshire; Tel (01782) 619264; H.I. Marsh. (Mixed) (11–16) (720)
Stoke, Berry Hill High, Arbourfield Dr, Bucknall, Stoke-on-Trent, Staffordshire; Tel (01782) 212163; D.J. Bradbury. (Mixed) (11–16) (1016)
Stoke, Birches Head High, Birches Head Rd, Birches Head, Stoke-on-Trent, Staffordshire; Tel (01782) 262815; M. Wilshaw. (Mixed) (11–16) (816)
Stoke, Blurton High, Beaconsfield Dr, Blurton, Stoke-on-Trent, Staffordshire; Tel (01782) 599541; R.G. Prole, MEd. (Mixed) (11–16) (922)
Stoke, The Mitchell High, Corneville Rd, Bucknall, Stoke-on-Trent, Staffordshire; Tel (01782) 202117; L.H. Wild. (Mixed) (11–16) (539)
Stoke, Brownhills High, Brownhills Rd, Tunstall, Stoke-on-Trent, Staffordshire; Tel (01782) 837508; S.A. Chesterton. (Mixed) (11–16) (686)
Stoke, James Brindley High, St Michael's Rd, Chell, Stoke-on-Trent, Staffordshire; Tel (01782) 837381; J.W. Wood. (Mixed) (11–16) (809)
Stoke, Edensor High, Greendock St, Longton, Stoke-on-Trent, Staffordshire; Tel (01782) 599052; J.W. Edwards. (Mixed) (11–16) (1130)
Stoke, Holden La High, Milton Rd, Sneyd Grn, Stoke-on-Trent, Staffordshire; Tel (01782) 261449; D.P. Gray. (Mixed) (11–16) (1121)
Stoke, Longton High, Box La, Meir, Stoke-on-Trent, Staffordshire; Tel (01782) 599232; R.P. Cooke. (Mixed) (11–16) (1024)
Stoke, Sandon High, Sandon Rd, Meir, Stoke-on-Trent, Staffordshire; Tel (01782) 312782; B.M. Hall. (Mixed) (11–16) (601)
Stoke, Haywood High, High La, Burslem, Stoke-on-Trent, Staffordshire; Tel (01782) 836399; Y.C. Jeffries. (Mixed) (11–16) (832)
Stoke, Trent Valley High, Newcastle La, Penkull, Stoke-on-Trent, Staffordshire; Tel (01782) 744667; A. Thomas. (Mixed) (11–16) (844)
Stoke, Trentham High, Allerton Rd, Trentham, Stoke-on-Trent, Staffordshire; Tel (01782) 658704; R. Burgess. (Mixed) (11–16) (858)
Werrington, Moorside High, Cellarhead Rd, Werrington, Stoke-on-Trent, Staffordshire; Tel (01782) 550265; P.E. Horrobin. (Mixed) (11–18) (794)

High Schools (Voluntary)

Cheadle, The Painsley R.C. High, Station Rd, Cheadle, Stoke-on-Trent, Staffordshire; Tel (01538) 752341/754348; F.R. Tunney. (Mixed) (V.A.) (11–16) (472)
Newcastle, St John Fisher R.C. High, Ashfields New Rd, Newcastle, Staffordshire; Tel (01782) 615636; B.W. Voiels. (Mixed) (V.A.) (11–18) (887)
Stoke, St Margaret Ward R.C. High, Little Chell La, Tunstall, Stoke-on-Trent, Staffordshire; Tel (01782) 575570; M.C. Bannon. (Mixed) (V.A.) (11–18) (822)
Stoke, St Peter's C.E. High, Queens Rd, Penkhull, Stoke-on-Trent, Staffordshire; Tel (01782) 47949; D.E. Titley, BA. (Mixed) (V.A.) (11–16) (666)

School Psychological Service

Psychological Service, 15 Sandford St, Lichfield WS13 6QA; Tel (0154 32) 258838; S. Hopwood
Psychological Service, Lindsay Annexe, Cannon St, Hanley, Stoke-on-Trent, Staffordshire; Tel (01782) 279714; C. Barcham; J. Newton
Psychological Service, 13 Lichfield Rd, Stafford ST17 4JX; Tel (01785) 52318; Vacancy

Special Day Schools

Abbey Hill, Greasley Rd, Bucknall, Stoke-on-Trent ST2 8LG; Tel (01782) 534727; M.H. Coutouvidis, BA(Hons). (M.L.D.) (160); (SLD) (35); (Autistic) (18)
Aynsley, Aynsley Dr, Blythe Bridge, Stoke-on-Trent ST11 9HJ; Tel (01782) 392071; I.T. Jeffrey. (M.L.D.) (120)
The Beecroft Hill, Brunswick Rd, Cannock WS11 2SF; Tel (0154 35) 502291; J. Anderson. (S.L.D.) (77)
Bitham, Bitham La, Stretton, Burton-on-Trent DE13 0HB; Tel (01283) 66988; A.R. Tunstall. (M.L.D.) (110)
Blackfriars, Priory Rd, Newcastle-under-Lyme ST5 2TF; Tel (01782) 619415; C.E. Lilley. (P.H.) (172)
Cherry Trees, Giggetty La, Wombourne, Wolverhampton WV5 0AX; Tel (01902) 894484; A.P. Cresswell. (S.L.D.) (28)
The Coppice, Abbots Way, Newcastle ST5 2EY; Tel (01782) 613918; J.M. Bevan, BA. (M.L.D.) (110)
Crown, Bitham La, Stretton, Burton-on-Trent DE13 0HB; Tel (01283) 41500; J. Harris. (S.L.D.) (63)
Greenhall Nursery, 15 Lichfield Rd, Stafford ST17 4JX; Tel (01785) 46159; S.I. Barlow. (P.H.) (32)
Heathfield, Chell Heath Rd, Chell Heath, Stoke-on-Trent ST6 6PD; Tel (01782) 838938; J. Colesby. (S.L.D.) (42)
Kemball, Duke St, Fenton, Stoke-on-Trent ST4 3NR; Tel (01782) 319154; E. Spooner. (S.L.D.) (77)
Marshlands, Lansdowne Way, Wildwood, Stafford ST17 4RD; Tel (01785) 664475; J. Kirby. (S.L.D.) (49)
The Meadows, Tunstall Rd, Biddulph ST8 7AB; Tel (01283) 513908; C. Fielding. (M.L.D.) (110)
Merryfields, Hoon Ave, May Bank, Newcastle ST5 9NY; Tel (01782) 617432; V.M. Christmas. (S.L.D.) (84)
Middlehurst, Turnhurst Rd, Chell, Stoke-on-Trent ST6 6NQ; Tel (01782) 839883; J.D. Kane. (M.L.D.) (100)
The Park, Solway Cl, Leyfields, Tamworth B79 8EB; Tel (01827) 67922; F. Bartlett. (M.L.D.) (140)
Queen's Croft, Birmingham Rd, Lichfield WS13 6PJ; Tel (0154 32) 254672; A. Hardman. (M.L.D.) (140)
Quince Tree, Quince, off Kerria Rd, Amington Heath, Tamworth B77 4EN; Tel (01827) 56719; V.A. Vernon. (S.L.D.) (70)
Rocklands, Wissage Rd, Lichfield WS13 6SW; Tel (0154 32) 263393; G. Jolley. (S.L.D.) (63)
Springfields, Springfield Rd, Leek ST13 6LQ; Tel (01538) 383558; C.A. Moody. (S.L.D.) (30)
The William Baxter, Stanley Rd, off Belt Rd, Wednesford WS12 4JS; Tel (0154 38) 423714; C.M. Allsop. (M.L.D.) (120)

Special Residential Schools

Ashley, Top Rock Rd, Ashley, nr Market Drayton, Shropshire TF9 4LX; Tel (0163 0187) 2454; J. Parker. (Beh. Diff.) (Boys) (45)
Cicely Haughton, Westwood Manor, Wetley Rocks, Stoke-on-Trent ST9 0BX; Tel (01782) 550202; Vacancy. (Beh. Diff.) (Boys) (35)
Horton Lodge, Horton, Leek ST13 8RB; Tel (0153 833) 214; R.M. Orme. (P.H.) (52)
Loxley Hall, Uttoxeter Rd, Loxley, Uttoxeter ST14 8RS; Tel (0188 93) 562388; A.E. Cattermole, BA, DipEd, DipSMS. (M.L.D./Beh. Diff.) (Boys) (70)

The Mount, The Mount, Penkhull, Stoke-on-Trent ST4 7JU; Tel (01782) 44314; B.J. Richards, BA. (Deaf) (36)
Saxon Hill, Kings Hill Rd, Lichfield WS14 9DE; Tel (0154 32) 263231; D.J. Butcher. (P.H.) (112)
Walton Hall, Stafford Rd, Eccleshall, Stafford ST21 6JR; Tel (01785) 850420; R.B. Goldthorpe. (M.L.D.) (120)
Wightwick Hall Education Centre, Tinacre Hill, Wightwick, nr Compton, Wolverhampton WV6 8DA; Tel (01902) 761889; P.H.W. Archer, AdvDipEd. (MLD) (70)

Institutes of Adult Education

Pendrell Hall College of Residential Adult Education Codsall Wood, Nr Wolverhampton WV8 1QP; Tel (01902) 842398; David Evans
Wedgwood Memorial College, Barlaston, Stoke-on-Trent, Staffordshire; Tel (01782) 392105; D. Tatton, MA, PhD

Music Centres

Address for all correspondence:
County Music Service, Corporation St, Stafford ST16 3LX; Tel (01785) 223121, Ext 8840
Centres:Cannock; Newcastle; Stafford; Burton-on-Trent; Lichfield; Stoke-on-Trent South; Stoke-on-Trent North; Rugeley; Tamworth; Moorlands

Outdoor Education Centres

Alrewas Outdoor Education Centre, Mill End La, Alrewas, Burton-on-Trent DE13 7BX; Tel (01283) 790397; P.D. Orton
Chasewater Outdoor Education Centre, Pools Rd, Chasetown, Walsall WS7 8QW; Tel (01543) 686524; R.K. Griffiths
Coven Outdoor Education Centre, Laches La, Slade Heath, Wolverhampton WV10 7PA; Tel (01902) 790388; R.K. Griffiths
Outdoor Education ESU, Standon, STAFFORD ST21 6RD; Tel (01782) 791422; Fax (01782) 791546; P.L. Jones
Shugborough Outdoor Education Centre, Shugborough Pk, Gt Haywood, Stafford, Staffordshire; Tel (01889) 881357; E. Gardner
Standon Bowers Outdoor Education Centre, Standon, nr Stafford, Staffordshire; Tel (01782) 791422; Fax (01782) 791546; P. Murray (Acting)
Stanley Head Outdoor Education Centre, Tomkin Rd, Stanley, Stoke-on-Trent ST9 9LY; Tel (01782) 503208; J.L. Dodd

Resource and Development Centres

Burton Centre, Grange St, Burton-upon-Trent DE14 2ER; Tel (01283) 63014
Cannock Centre, 119 Walsall Rd, Cannock WS11 3JA; Tel (0154 35) 574647
Kingston Centre, Fairway, Stafford ST16 3TW; Tel (01785) 277900
Willfield Centre, Lauder Pl, North Ubberley, Stoke-on-Trent ST 0QL; Tel (01782) 598230
Tamworth Centre, Moorgate, Tamworth B79 7EL; Tel (01827) 65044

Special Units (Assessment Centres)

Burton Special Educational Needs Support Service, The Education Office, Guild St, Burton-on-Trent DE14 1NF; Tel (01283) 45771, Ext 23; R. Rowley
Burton Teaching Unit, The Education Office, Guild St, Burton-on-Trent DE14 1NF; Tel (01283) 45771, Ext 267; S. Hallmark
Burton-on-Trent, Horninglow County Infants Speech and Language Unit, Horninglow Rd North, Burton-on-Trent DE13 0SW; Tel (01283) 63208; M. Makin
Chancel Special Needs Nursery, Wolesley Rd, Rugeley WS15 2EW; Tel (0188 94) 586260; C. Hobson
Cheadle Teaching Unit, Cheadle Primary School, Cheadle, Stoke-on-Trent ST10 1EN; Tel (01538) 753227; J. Pearce
County Peripatetic Service for Hearing Impaired and Visually Handicapped, Flash Ley Centre, Hawksmoor Rd, Stafford ST17 9DR; Tel (01785) 51391; M.W. Garner
Leek, Wall Lane Teaching Unit, 1 & 2 Wall Lane Terrace, Cheddleton ST13 7ED; Tel (01538) 360917; M. Finney
Lichfield Educational Assessment Centre, Purcell Ave, Lichfield WS13 7PH; Tel (0154 32) 253603/1253217; C. Gough
Lichfield, Stowe Teaching Unit, Stowe St, Lichfield WS13 8AP; Tel (015432) 262806; M. Bailey
Newcastle Educational Assessment Centre, Friarswood Junior School, Abbots Way, Newcastle ST5 2ES; Tel (01782) 610961; N.L. Sanderson
Newcastle Reading Centre, Old Orme Boys' School, Pool Dam, Higherland, Newcastle ST5 2RP; Tel (01782) 711596; C. Rivers
Newcastle Teaching Unit, 2 Woodlands Ave, Wolstanton, Newcastle ST5 8AZ; Tel (01782) 610896; J. Gabriel
Special Educational Needs Support Centre-Stafford Area, Flash Ley School, Hawksmoor Rd, Stafford ST17 9DR; Tel (01785) 54944; D. Mitchell
Stafford Educational Assessment Centre, Flash Ley Resource Centre, Hawkesmoor Rd, Stafford; Tel (01785) 55499; L. James
Stafford Special Educational Needs Support Services HQ, Flash Ley Centre, Hawksmoor Rd, Stafford ST17 9DR; Tel (01785) 54939; Mrs M. Newton
Stafford, Nursery Class for Hearing Impaired Children, Sandyford Nursery, Prospect Rd, Stafford ST16 3NN; Tel (01785) 51512; S. Davies
Stafford, Flash Ley Speech and Language Unit, Hawksmoor Rd, Stafford ST17 9DF; Tel (01785) 51202; D.I. Lewis
Stoke, City General Hospital Child Assessment Unit, City General Hospital, Newcastle Rd, Stoke-on-Trent ST4 6QG; Tel (01782) 621133, Ext 2010; L. Rowley
Stoke, Heron Cross Primary Learning Difficulties Unit and Heron Cross Primary Speech and Language Unit, (E.S.N.M.) Grove Rd, Heron Cross, Stoke-on-Trent ST4 4LJ; Tel (01782) 313408; P. Wallbank
Stoke, Hill Top Hearing Impaired Unit, Greenhead St, Burslem, Stoke-on-Trent ST6 4AF; Tel (01782) 89380; R.J. Websdale
Stoke, Sandford Hill Primary Hearing Impaired Unit, Clayfield Grove, Sandford Hill, Stoke-on-Trent ST3 5AQ; Tel (01782) 316340; C.A. Smith
Stoke, Trent Valley High Unit, (Pt. Hg.) Newcastle La, Penkhull, Stoke-on-Trent ST3 3BQ; Tel (01782) 744667; A. Thomas
Stowe Teaching Unit, Stowe St, Lichfield, Staffordshire; Tel (0154 32) 262806; M.A. Bailey
Tamworth, Stoneydelph Infants Hearing Impaired Unit, (Pt.Hg.) Crowden Rd, Stoneydelph, Tamworth B77 4LS; Tel (01827) 895836; C.R. Chapman
Tamworth, Stoneydelph Junior Hearing Impaired Unit, (Pt.Hg.,) Crowden Rd, Stoneydelph, Tamworth B77 4LS; Tel (01872) 896666; A. Burrows
Tamworth, Torc High, Hearing Impaired Unit, Silverlink Rd, Tamworth B77 2HB; Tel (01827) 286305; M.T. Wallis
Uttoxeter, Oldfields Hall Middle Teaching Unit, Stone Rd, Uttoxeter ST14 7PL; Tel (0188 93) 562770; D. Brown
Willfield Resource Centre, Willfield High School, Lauder Pl, North Ubberlay, Stoke-on-Trent ST2 0QL; Tel (01782) 598226; F. Hobson; P. Croft

Teachers' Centres

Information Technology Centre, Technology Hse, Duke St, Burton-upon-Trent DE14 1EB; Tel (01283) 510313; M. Cotterill
Intercultural Support Service, Victoria Rd, Burton-upon-Trent DE14 2LU; Tel (01283) 564150
Information Technology Centre, Chaseley Hse, New Penkridge Rd, Cannock WS11 1HN; Tel (0154 35) 466600; C. Shotton
Staffordshire Design and Technology Education Programme, Kingston Centre, Stafford ST16 3TU; Tel (01785) 57727; H.C. Bagshaw
Educational Computing Centre, Church La, Hixon, Staffs ST18 0PS; Tel (01889) 271317; D. Pacey

Information Technology Centre, Regent Rd, Hanley, Stoke-on-Trent ST1 3EG; Tel (01782) 279423; G.P. Stones
Intercultural Support Service Willfield – Queensbury Community Education Centre, Lauder Pl, North, Bentilee, Stoke on Trent, Staffs ST2 0QL; Tel (01782) 325085; B. Slade

Youth Centres

Address for all correspondence: Youth and Community Education Section, Education Offices, Tipping St, Stafford ST16 2DH; Tel 223121; *Principal Office Youth and Community Education Service* R. Marsh
Centres: 34 centres throughout County

Grant Maintained Schools

Burntwood, Chasetown High, Pool Rd, Chasetown, Staffordshire WS7 8QW; Tel (01543) 685828; Fax (01543) 677485; M.A Podmore, ADvDipEd, DLC. (Mixed) (11–18) (890)
Cannock Chase High (Grant Maintained), Channock Chase High, Hednesford Rd, Cannock, Staffordshire; Tel (0543) 577528; Fax (0543) 577528; D.J. Knight. (Mixed) (11–18) (1181)
Cannock, Cardinal Griffin R.C. Comprehensive, Stafford Rd, Cannock, Staffordshire; Tel (0154 35) 502215/571722; J.F. Lumb. (Mixed) (11–18) (V.A.) (799)
Stafford, Rising Brook High, Rising Brook, Stafford, Staffordshire; Tel (01785) 58383/157614; D.S. Jeffries. (Mixed) (11–18) (659)
St Thomas More R.C. High, Longton Hall Rd, Longton, Stoke-on-Trent, Staffordshire; Tel (01782) 315188; J.F. Challiner. (Mixed) (V.A.) (11–18) (1004)

Stockport Metropolitan Borough Council

Population 284,395 (1991 census)
Town Hall, Stockport SK1 3XE; Tel 0161-474 3061; Fax 0161-474 3099

Education Division

Stopford Hse, Piccadilly, Stockport, Cheshire SK1 3XE; Tel 0161-480 4949; Fax 0161-953 0012
Assistant Chief Education Officer E.R. Blundell
EO (Research and Information) A. Kelly
Head of Service (Pupil Support) H.M. Hewitt
Head of Service (Resources) A. Thurstan
EO Co-ordinator (Curriculum Development and Teacher Training) C. Newton
EO (Research and Information) A. Kelly
Personnel Manager S.E. Lowe
EO (Personnel) D. Chadderton
EO (Schools Finance) T. Conlon
EO (Pupils) G. Edwards
EO (Special Needs) C. Keeble
EO (School Governance) P. Morgan
EO (Adult) G. Turner
EO (Premises) J. Wadsworth
EO (Youth) P. Whittaker
Head of Service (Resources) A. Thurston
Client Service Manager P. Fearn
Chief Education Welfare Officer B. Field
Chief Education Psychologist G.J. Benson
Adviser (Primary) D.R. Baker
Adviser (English) R.A. Bates
Adviser (Primary) A.W. Cross
Adviser (Primary) P. Gadsby
Adviser (History/Geography/RE) C. Howlett
Adviser (Modern Languages) R. Lofkin
Adviser (Mathematics) M. McLachlan
Adviser (Primary) J. Chapman
Adviser (Primary) J. Draper
Adviser (DT/Art Design) S. Powell
Adviser (Science) R. West
Client Service Manager P. Fearn
Chief Education Welfare Officer B. Field
Principal Educational Psychologist G.J. Benson
Personnel Manager S.E. Lowe
Number of Schools
9 nursery (1007) PTE + 1041 PT in nursery classes; 109 primary (24,552); 14 secondary (11–16) (15,083), 1 Sixth Form College
Special Schools
6 day (406); 1 residential (24)
Day of Committee Meeting
Eight week cycle

Education Committee

LD 9, Con 4, Lab 6, I 1
Conservative Spokesperson E.D. Foulkes 34 Cherry Holt Ave, Heaton Mersey, Stockport SK4 3PS; Tel 0161-432 7111 (Home); 0161-764 1813 (Bus)
Labour Spokesperson T.P. McGee 15 Queen's Dr, Heaton Moor, Stockport SK4 3JN; Tel 0161-432 8792
Liberal Democrat Spokesperson A.N. Walker 20 Albany Rd, Bramhall, Stockport SK7 1ND; Tel 0161-440 8357 (Home), 0161-953 5995 Ext 2323 (Bus)

Governor Training Unit

Governing Body Training Unit, Education Division, Stopford Hse, Town Hall, Stockport, Cheshire SK1 3XE; Tel 0161-474 3845; Fax 0161-953 0012
Education Officer (School Management) Tricia Morgan
Services Offered
Provide/Co-ordinate and deliver a comprehensive training programme for individual Governors and collective Governing Bodies; The Unit provides an advice and support helpline to assist governors in the discharging of their duties/responsibilities

Special Schools

Castle Hill School, Lapwing La, Brinnington, Stockport, Greater Manchester; Tel 0161-494 6439; M.E. Marra, BEd
Heaton School, St James' Rd, Heaton Moor, Stockport SK4 4RE; Tel 0161-432 1931; E. Seers
Lisburne, Half Moon La, Offerton, Stockport SK2 5LB; Tel 0161-483 5045; H. White. (5–11)
Overdale, Powicke Dr, Romiley, Stockport SK6 3DG; Tel 0161-494 8176; C. Newall (Acting). (2–11)
Taxal Lodge Residential, Linglongs Rd, Whaley Bridge, Via Stockport SK12 7DS; Tel (01663) 732613; G. Hurt. (11–16)
Thornfield, Mauldeth Rd, Heaton Mersey, Stockport SK4 3NB; Tel 0161-432 3727; L.K. Harris. (7–16)
Valley, Whitehaven Rd, Bramhall, Stockport SK7 1EN; Tel 0161-439 7343; M. Little, MEd. (2–11)

Secondary Schools (County)

Avondale High, Heathbank Rd, Cheadle Heath, Stockport SK3 0UP; Tel 0161-477 2382; I. Tunnard, BA, MEd. (638)
Bramhall High, Seal Rd, Bramhall SK7 2JT; Tel 0161-439 8045; A.M. Debes, MA, BA. (1359)
Cheadle Hulme High, Woods La, Cheadle Hulme SK8 7JY; Tel 0161-485 7201; R. Dixon, BA. (1310)
Hazel Grove High, Jacksons La, Hazel Grove SK7 5JX; Tel 0161-456 4888; C. Longden, BA. (1063)
Marple Hall High, Hill Top Dr, Marple, Stockport SK6 6LA; Tel 0161-427 7966; M. Cuckson, BA. (1531)
Offerton High School, The Fairway, Offerton, Stockport SK2 5DS; Tel 0161-483 9336; M.J. Hubbard, BA. (1050)

Priestnall, Priestnall Rd, Heaton Mersey, Stockport SK4 3HP; Tel 0161-442 8850; K.M. August, BA. (1218)
Reddish Vale, Reddish Vale Rd, Reddish, Stockport SK5 7HD; Tel 0161-477 3544; P.I. Rowe, BA Hons. (1216)
Stockport, Mile End La, Stockport SK2 6BW; Tel 0161-483 3622; K. Ellis, BSc. (908)
The Kingsway School, Foxland Rd, Gatley, Cheadle, Stockport SK8 4QA; Tel 0161-428 7706; R. Lyon, LLB, MEd. (1464)
Werneth School, Harrytown La, Romiley, Stockport SK6 3BX; Tel 0161-494 1222; G. Nolan, BEd. (1252)

Secondary Schools (Voluntary)

Harrytown R.C. High, Harrytown La, Romiley SK6 3BU; Tel 0161-430 5277; G. Roper, BA. (V.A.) (592)
St Anne's R.C. High, Glenfield Rd, Heaton Chapel, Stockport SK4 2QP; Tel 0161-432 8162; A. Carroll, BEd, MEd. (S.A.) (832)
St James' R.C. High, St James' Way, off Stanley Rd, Cheadle Hulme, Cheshire SK8 6PZ; Tel 0161-486 9211; P.A. Doherty, BA, MEd. (V.A.) (559)

Teachers' Centre

Dialstone Centre, Lisburne La, Stockport SK2 7LL; Tel 0161-474 2220

Suffolk County Council

Population 648,000
St Helen Ct, County Hall, Ipswich, Suffolk IP4 2JS; Tel (01473) 230000; Fax (01473) 214549
Chief Executive P.F. Bye, BA, BPhil
County Treasurer P.B. Atkinson, MA, IPFA St Giles Hse, County Hall, Ipswich IP4 2JP; Tel (01473) 265700; Fax (01473) 230157
Director of Social Services W.P. Bulpin, CQSW, DMS St Paul Hse, County Hall, Ipswich IP4 1LH
Director of Libraries and Heritage A.J. Arrowsmith, MA, MBA St Andrew Hse, County Hall, Ipswich IP4 1LJ

Education Offices

St Andrew Hse, County Hall, Ipswich IP4 1LJ; Tel (01473) 230000; Fax (01473) 230395
County Education Officer D. Peachey
Deputy County Education Officer D.J.E. Thornton, MA, MEd
Principal Education Officer (Inspection & Advice) C.J. Coates, BA
Principal Education Officer (Resources) F. Jiggins, CIPFA
Principal Education Officer (Policy) J.W. Carnall, BSc(Econ)
Senior Education Officer (Personnel) A. Aldred, MA, MIPM
Senior Education Officer (Research & I.T.) D.G. Matthews, BSc(Econ)
Senior Education Officer (Finance) R.F. Smith, IPFA
Senior Education Officer (Community Education) N. Williams
Senior Education Officer (Careers) R.J. Gillam, BA(Hons), MA
Senior Education Officer (Development) S.M. Barber, MA(Oxon)
Senior Education Officer (Pupil/Student Support) M.M. Wilson, BA, MA
Assistant Education Officer (Post 16 Planning) R.D. Dool
Assistant Education Officer (Development) I.C. Brown, BA
Senior Adviser for Professional Development R.E. Fern, BA
Senior Adviser (Curriculum & Assessment) R. Loose, BA(Hons), PGCE
Senior Adviser (Monitoring and Evaluation) J. Clarke, BA, MEd, MA
County Adviser (Science) C.I. Sunley, BSc
County Adviser (English) P. Daw, BA, MA, Phd
County Adviser (Music) P.J. Shaw, LTCL, GNSM
County Adviser (Physical Education) S. Cooke, MA
County Adviser (Mathematics) B.W. Reid, BSc
County Adviser (Art and Design) R. Petty, DipArtEd, MSc
County Adviser (Modern Languages) D.S. Sword, BA
County Adviser (Creative and Performing Arts) P.M. Redsell, LRAM
County Adviser (Information Technology) H.B. Massey, BA
County Adviser (Design and Technology) J.E. Sephton, BA
County Adviser (Humanities) M. Oldfield, BA, MA
County Adviser (Home Economics and Social Education) E.M. Rowe, CertEd
Senior Advisory Officer (Northern Area) Vacancy
Senior Advisory Officer (Southern Area) G.C. Platts, BA, MA, PhD
Senior Advisory Officer (Western Area) T.F. Newton, BA, MA(Ed)
Principal Education Welfare Officer G. Morgan, BA(Hons)
County Educational Psychologist W.F. Herbert, BSc(Hons), MEd
County Advisory Officer (TVEI) C.A. Hutchinson, BEd
County Coordinator (Appraisal) G. Smith, BA
Contract Services Manager H.R. Newsome, BA, MA, FBIM, MIPS
County Caretaking and Cleaning Manager J.H. Crossley, MBICSc
County Catering Manager A. Hope, MHCIMA
County Grounds Manager K. Rowton
Transport Manager T.A. Donovan
Number of Schools
1 nursery (50); 255 primary (40,349); 39 middle (16,043); 38 upper and high comprehensive (31,172)
Special Schools
11 special schools
Day of Committee Meeting
Thursday, 5 times a year
Requisition Periods for School supplies
No specific arrangements
Other Authorities with whom Joint Purchasing Arrangements are made
Department of Education & Science and a number of county, borough and district councils

Education Committee

Lab 11, Con 9, LD 6, Ind 2
Chair D.J. Macpherson, (Lab)
Vice-Chair A.K. Lewis, (Lab)
Vice-Chair C.A. Ward, (LD)
Members of the Committee
Lab: B.H. Coleman, H.H. Leg, A.K. Lewis, D.J. Macpherson, N. Owen, C.W. Packard, M.J.E. Rodgers, D.F. Smith, J.D.B. Taylor, S. Thomas, W.M. Wiles
Con: N.R. Alcock, N.D. Brighouse, J. Burgess, R.M. Coates, H. Hall, E. Milburn, C.W.M. Penn, F. Thomason, R.A. Ward
LD: B.H. Bagnall, S.P. Clarke, J.M. Craven, E.R. Echols, C. MacGregor, C.A. Ward
Ind G.B. Langley, J.A. Mitchell

AREA OFFICES

Northern Area

Adrian Hse, Alexandra Rd, Lowestoft NR32 1PL; Tel (01502) 562262
Area Education Manager D.R. Wright, BA
Senior Education Officer (Institutional Support) D.C. Griffiths, BA
Senior Education Officer (Pupil Services) J.P. Taylor, BA

Senior General Adviser A.G. Andrews, BSc, MA
General Adviser V.D. Cumberbirch, BA, MA
General Adviser T. Dentith, BSc
General Adviser J.V. Drinkwater, BEd
General Adviser K.A. Haddock, BA
General Adviser K.A. Harrison, BA
Senior Educational Psychologist M. Marshall-Watts, BA, MA
Educational Psychologist P. Bartley, BA, MSc
Educational Psychologist F.J. Hagley, BSc, MSc
Educational Psychologist S.G. Phillips, BSc, MSc

High Schools

Beccles, Sir John Leman High, Ringsfield Rd, Beccles NR34 9PG; Tel (01502) 713223; I. Sargen, MA, BA. (13-18) (1105)
Benjamin Britten High, Blyford Rd, Lowestoft NR32 4PZ; Tel (01502) 582312; M.E. Harbour, BA. (13-18) (820)
Bungay High, Queen's Rd, Bungay NR35 1RW; Tel (01986) 892140; W.J. Moore, LLB. (13–18) (795)
The Denes High, Yarmouth Rd, Lowestoft NR32 4AH; Tel (01502) 574474; N. English, BSc. (13–18) (595)
Thomas Mills High, Saxtead Rd, Framlingham IP13 9HE; Tel (01728) 723493; A.J. Leach, BD. (11–18) (910)
Hartismere High, Castleton Way, Eye IP23 7BL; Tel (01379) 870315; R.J. Hewitt, BEd, FRSA. (11–16) (440)
Kirkley High, Kirkley Run, Lowestoft NR33 0UQ; Tel (01502) 566321; J.B. Walmsley, BSc, MEd. (13–18) (1095)
Leiston High, Seaward Ave, Leiston IP16 4BG; Tel (01728) 830570; D. Bywater, BA. (13–18) (555)
Stradbroke High, Wilby Rd, Stradbroke, Eye IP21 5JN; Tel (0137 984) 387/388; D. Shorten, BA. (11–16) (300)

High School (Voluntary)

Debenham C.E. High, Gracechurch St, Debenham IP14 6BL; Tel (01728) 860213; M.J. Crawshaw, BA. (Controlled) (11–16) (295)

Special Schools

Ashley Downs, Ashley Downs, Lowestoft, Suffolk NR32 4EU; Tel (01502) 574847/575439; K. Brownsword
Warren, Clarkes La, Lowestoft, Suffolk NR33 8HT; Tel (01502) 561893; P. Laws

Southern Area

Bond St, Ipswich IP4 2JR; Tel (01473) 230000
Area Education Manager J.H. Crompton, BA, DMA
Senior Education Officer (Institutional Support) J.K. Sculpher, BSc
Senior Education Oficer (Pupil Services) M. Brenner, BSc
Senior General Adviser P.R. North, MEd
General Adviser J.J. Connolly, BEd
General Adviser J. Dunn
General Adviser R.M. Leeke, BA
General Adviser I. Lindsley, BSc, MSc
County Senior Educational Psychologist D.J. Hawthorn, BA, MSc
Educational Psychologist L.M. Boyd, BA, MSc
Educational Psychologist J. Busch-Hansen, BA
Educational Psychologist S. Finlayson, BA, MEd, PhD
Educational Psychologist J.S. Hooper, BA, MLitt

Special Schools

Beacon Hill, Stone Lodge Lane West, Ipswich, Suffolk IP2 9HW; Tel (01473) 601175; I.R. Tatchell, BA, DipSpEd
Belstead, Sprites La, Belstead, Ipswich, Suffolk IP8 3ND; Tel (01473) 686119; D. Margerison
Heathside Heath Rd, Ipswich, Suffolk IP4 5SN; Tel (01473) 725508; K.E. Baker
Thomas Wolsey School, 642 Norwich Rd, Ipswich IP1 6LA; Tel (01473) 241433; N. McArdle, BEd

High Schools (County)

Chantry High, Mallard Way, Ipswich IP2 9LR; Tel (01473) 687181; P.J. Senior, MA, BEd, MBIM. (11–18) (1292)
Claydon High, Church La, Claydon, Ipswich IP6 0EG; Tel (01473) 830319; D. Roberts, BA. (11–16) (493)
Copleston High, Copleston Rd, Ipswich IP4 5HD; Tel (01472) 710951; H.A. Stone, BSc. (11–16) (1265)
Deben High, Garrison La, Felixstowe IP11 7RF; Tel (01394) 282602; M.W. Matthews, BA. (11-18) (917)
East Bergholt High, East Bergholt, Colchester, Essex CO7 6RJ; Tel (01206) 298200; M. Humphreys, BA. (11-16) (828)
Farlingaye High, Ransom Rd, Woodbridge IP12 4JU; Tel (01394) 385720; E. Smith, BA, MA(Ed). (11-18) (1116)
Hadleigh High, Highlands Rd, Hadleigh IP7 5HU; Tel (01473) 823496; R.D.J. Davies, BEd, MEd. (11-16) (659)
Holbrook High Holbrook, Ipswich IP9 2QX; Tel (01473) 328317; A.A. Green, BA, MEd. (11-16) (300)
Kesgrave High, Kesgrave, Ipswich IP5 7PB; Tel (01473) 624855; G.M. Thomas, BA. (11-16) (675)
Holywells High Lindbergh Rd, Ipswich IP3 9PZ; Tel (01473) 729222; D. Floyd, MEd. (11-16) (850)
Northgate High, Sidegate La, Ipswich IP4 3DL; Tel (01473) 210123; N. Watts, BA, MA. (11-18) (1411)
Orwell High, Maidstone Rd, Felixstowe IP11 9EF; Tel (01394) 282628; M.N. Smith, JP, BA. (11-18) (977)
Stoke High, Maidenhall Approach, Ipswich IP2 8PL; Tel (01473) 601252; M.E. Liddle, MA, BSc. (11-16) (749)
Thurleston High, Defoe Rd, Ipswich IP1 6SG; Tel (01473) 464545/6; L. Robinson, BSc. (11-16) (668)
Westbourne High, Marlow Rd, Ipswich IP1 5JN; Tel (01473) 42315; K.R.M. Williams, MEd. (11-18) (1419)

High School (Voluntary)

St Alban's R.C. High, Digby Rd, Ipswich IP4 3NJ; Tel (01473) 726178; J.R. Clinton, BA, MPhil, MA(Ed). (V.A.) (11-16) (491)

Western Area

Shire Hall, Bury St Edmunds IP33 2AN; Tel (01284) 763141
Area Education Manager T.H. Scherb, BA
Senior Education Officer (Institutional Support) K. Manley, BSc
Senior Education Oficer (Pupil Services) R.W. Stiff, BA
Senior General Adviser T.A. Priest, BA
General Adviser R.H. Dyer, LRAM(Drama), Assoc Drama Board
General Adviser M.A. Harvey, BA, MEd
General Adviser M.J. Ingham, BAn
General Adviser A. Weekes, MA
General Adviser J. Wellings, BAc
Senior Educational Psychologist B.R. Perrett, BA
Educational Psychologist M. Hunkin, BA
Educational Psychologist J.P. Clandillon, BA, MSc
Educational Psychologist G. Crane, BSc
Educational Psychologist N. Gardner, MSc
Educational Psychologist P.M. Gavin, BA

Special Schools

Hampden Hse, 3 Cats La, Great Cornard CO10 6SF; Tel (01787) 73583; M.W. Charlton
Hillside, Hitchcock Pl, Sudury, Suffolk CO10 6NN; Tel (01787) 72808; J.E. Freeman
Oakwood, Onehouse Rd, Stowmarket, Suffolk IP14 1SZ; Tel (01449) 613931; E.H. deSmith
Priory, Mount Rd, Bury St Edmunds, Suffolk IP32 7BH; Tel (01284) 761934; M. Esherwood
Riverwalk, South Cl, Bury St Edmunds, Suffolk IP32 3JZ; Tel (01284) 764280; B. Ellis

Upper Schools (County)

County, Beeton's Way, Bury St Edmunds IP32 6RF; Tel (01284) 754857; A. Williams, MA. (900)
Great Cornard, Head La, Gt Cornard, Sudbury CO10 0JU; Tel (01787) 375232; D.E. Pickford, OBE, BSc. (950)
Haverhill Castle Manor, Eastern Ave, Haverhill CB9 9JE; Tel (01440) 705501; M.T. Ryan, MEd. (680)
Haverhill Samuel Ward, Chalkstone Way, Haverhill CB9 0LD; Tel (01449) 61511; P.G. Roberts, MA. (615)
Mildenhall, Bury Rd, Mildenhall IP28 7HT; Tel (01638) 714645/714670; T.C. Lewis, MA. (935)
Newmarket, Exning Rd, Newmarket CB8 0EB; Tel (01638) 664412; S.C. Dart, MA. (615)
Stowmarket High, Onehouse Rd, Stowmarket IP14 1QP; Tel (01449) 613541; S. Hargreaves. (940)
Stowupland High, Crown Hill, Stowupland IP14 1BQ; Tel (01449) 674827/8; P.L. Richards, BSc. (585)
Sudbury, Tudor Rd, Sudbury CO10 6NW; Tel (01787) 75131/2; D. Whittaker, MA. (930)

Upper Schools (Voluntary)

King Edward VI, Grove Rd, Bury St Edmunds IP33 3BH; Tel (012284) 761393/14; M.W. Moran, BA. (VC) (1020)
St Benedict's R.C. V.A., Beeton's Way, Bury St Edmunds IP32 6RF; Tel (01284) 753512; P.D. Rossi, MA. (V.A.) (13–18) (400)

Community Education

Area Community Education Officer P. Lee Western Area Education Office, Shire Hall, Bury St Edmunds; Tel (01284) 763141 Ext 213
Area Community Education Officer A.D. Jones Northern Area Education Office, Adrian Hse, Alexandra Rd, Lowestoft NR32 1PL; Tel (01502) 56226 Ext 37
Area Community Education Officer R. Walmsley Southern Area Education Office, St Andrew Hse, County Hall, Ipswich IP4 1LJ; Tel (01473) 230000 Ext 4668

Careers Office

See chapter 17

Residential Centre of Adult Education

Belstead Hse Adult Education and In-Service Training Residential Centre, Sprites La, Belstead, Ipswich IP8 3NA; Tel (01473) 686321; R. Castles

Performing Arts Centres

West Suffolk Performing Arts Centre, Grove Rd, Bury St Edmunds IP33 3BH; Tel (01284) 767141
Northgate Arts Centre, Sidegate La, Ipswich IP4 3DL; Tel (01473) 281866
North Suffolk Performing Arts Centre (Seagull Theatre), Morton Rd, Lowestoft NR33 0JH; Tel (01502) 562863; *Drama Advisory Teacher* R. Kelsey.

Counselling/Advice Centres

'Insight', Commercial Rd, Lowestoft, Suffolk; Tel (01502) 513547; J. Grant
Youth Advice Counselling Centre, Rendezvous, Out Risby Gate, Bury St Edmunds IP33 3RE; L. Bond
Youth Advice Centre, Curriers La, Ipswich, Suffolk; Tel (01473) 225344

Outdoor Education Centres

Alton Water Sports Centre, C/o Education Dept, St Andrews Hse, County Hall, Ipswich IP4 1JL; Tel (01473) 234622; *Contact* G. Chapman
Beccles Water Sports Centre,; Contact P. Fenn Colman's Dyke, off Bridge Rd, Oulton Broad, Lowestoft; Tel (01502) 587163
Oulton Broad Water Sports Centre
Bury and Forest Heath Water Sports Centre, C/o 9A Beauford Rd, Ingham, Bury St Edmunds, Suffolk; Tel (0128 484) 438; C. Butler
Corpusty Residential Centre, Corpusty, Norwich, Suffolk; *Contact* Area Community Education Office, Adrian Hse, Alexandra Rd, Lowestoft; Tel (01502) 562262 Ext 3706
Deben River Water Sports Centre, C/o 10 Truro Cres, Kesgrave, Ipswich, Suffolk; Tel (01473) 624672; *Contact* M. Watts
Felixstowe Ferry Residential Centre, Ferry Rd, Old Felixstowe, Suffolk; Tel (01473) 744187
Iken Campsite; *Contact* Tel (01473) 744187
Neptune Water Sports Centre, C/o Ridgeway, Main Rd, Wolverstone, Ipswich, Suffolk; W. Smith
Oulton Broad Water Sports Centre, Colman's Dyke, off Bridge Rd, Oulton Broad, Lowestoft, Suffolk; Tel (01502) 587163; *Contact* P. Fenn
Santon Downham Campsite,; M. Pollard Community Education Office, The Upper School, Mildenhall, Bury Rd, Mildenhall IP28 7HT; Tel (01638) 715001
Shotley Lodge Residential Centre, Shotley, Ipswich, Suffolk; Tel (01473) 744187
Southwold Water Sports Centre,; P. Fenn Oulton Broad Water Sports Centre, Colman Dyke, off Bridge Rd, Oulton Broad, Lowestoft; Tel (01502) 587163

Professional Development Centres

North Suffolk Professional Development Centre, Lovewell Rd, Lowestoft NR33 0RQ; Tel (01502) 568577; J.A. Fox, BA,MA
South Suffolk Professional Development Centre, Pauls Rd, Ipswich IP2 0AN; Tel (01473) 251635; R.N. Castle, MA
West Suffolk Professional Development Centre, Brooklands Cl, Hospital Rd, Bury St Edmunds IP33 3JY; Tel (01284) 708721; A. Downing, BA

City of Sunderland

Population 297,100 (mid 1992)
Civic Centre, Sunderland SR2 7DN; Tel 0191-567 6161; Fax 0191-510 9104; Telex 537037

Education Department

PO Box 101, Civic Centre, Sunderland SR2 7DN; Tel 0191-567 6161
City Education Officer D.A. Bowers, MA
Deputy City Education Officer A. Butterworth, BSc
Assistant City Education Officer G. Pennington, MA
Assistant City Education Officer M.J. Craddock, MA, BPhil
Head of Planning and Information Service P. B. Gale, BA
Head of Community Education Service M. Barnes
Head of Careers Service E. Hunt, DipCG, MICO
Head of Pupil and Student Service R.A. Grant
Head of Finance Service J. D. Graham
Head of Personnel Service A.K. Herbert
Head of Educational Psychology Service M.A. Baumber, BSc, MEd (LdPsych)
Head of Learning Support Service E. Richardson, BPhil, DAES
Head of Education Social Work Services B. Thompson
Head of Inspectorate and Advisory Service T. Walsh, BA
Senior Inspector (Primary) W. L. Bower, BA
Senior Inspector (Tertiary) E. Smith, BA, MA
Staff Inspector (Special Needs) C. M. Vening, BEd
Adviser (Music) S. Auster
Adviser (Mathematics) S. Feather, BA
Adviser (English) J. McKeague, MEd
Adviser (Humanities) J. M. Watson, BEd
Adviser (Technology) A. Grant, BA
Adviser (Early Years) S. Hatton

Adviser (Primary Education) A. Cassidy
Adviser (Science) V. Wood-Robinson
Adviser (Modern Languages & Classics) H. C. J. Parr, MA
South West Team Co-ordinator W. McKinnie
Community Education Service (East Team Co-ordinator) J. Beresford
Community Education Service (North Team Co-ordinator) K. Smith
Community Education Service (North West Team Co-ordinator) D. Johnson
Community Education Service (South East Team Co-ordinator) J. McGough
Number of Schools
11 nursery; 100 primary; 17 secondary; 8 special
Day of Committee Meeting
Tuesdays, Monthly
Requisition Period for School Supplies
Schools requisition supplies when required
Other Authorities with whom Joint Purchasing Arrangement are made
None

Education Committee

Lab 23, Con 3, LD 1
Chair R.F. Hunter, (Lab) 17 Maria St, New Silksworth, Sunderland
Vice-Chair J. Jordan, (Lab) 11 Baltimore Crt, Washington
Members of the Committee
Lab: B. Charlton, L. Scott, L.A.F. Bramfitt, D. Allan, C.R. Anderson, F. Anderson, R. Bainsbridge, C.E. Bate, E. Branfilt, A. Campbell, M. Clare, J. Connor, R. Heron, J.K. Murray, N.J. Murray, M. Qualie, J.B. Scott, W. Scott, B. Sidawan, A.G. Tunney, D.G. Wharlen
Con: G.W.E. Hilton, R. Smith, J.E. Wynn
LD: W.E. Landgren

Governor Training

Tel 0191-514 5543; Fax 0191-565 6256
Training Co-ordinator (Personnel Service) Martin Lightfoot, BSc
Services Offered
Co-ordination, publicising of Governor Training Programme

Careers Office

See chapter 17

Educational Psychology Service

Educational Psycology Service, Broadway Centre, Springwell Rd, Sunderland SR4 8NW; Tel 0191-528 4706; M.A. Baumber, BSc, MEd

Special Day Schools

Barbara Priestman, Meadowside, Sunderland SR2 7QN; Tel 0191-528 6919; G.F. Haynes. (3–19)
Davenport, Old Durham Rd, Houghton-le-Spring DH5 8NS; Tel 0191-584 3430; K. Marshall. (3–13)
Felstead, Fordfield Rd, Sunderland SR4 0DA; Tel 0191-567 4258; R.W. Wynn. (13–19)
Maplewood, Redcar Rd, Sunderland SR5 5PA; Tel 0191-549 1240; J. Wilson, MEd, BEd, DAES. (7–13)
Portland, Portland Rd, Sunderland SR3 1SS; Tel 0191-528 5927; J. Lumley. (13–19)
Springwell Dene, Swindon Rd, Sunderland SR3 4EE; Tel 0191-528 4975; J.F. McKnight, BEd. (13–16)
Sunningdale, Shaftoe Rd, Sunderland SR3 4HA; Tel 0191-511 0221; E.A. Winthrop, BA. (3–16)
Wellbank, Wellbank Rd, Washington NE37 1NN; Tel 0191-416 2514; L. Pears, BEd. (3–13)

Secondary Schools (County)

Biddick, Biddick La, Washington, Tyne & Wear NE38 8AL; Tel 0191-417 2013; C. Watson. (Mixed)
Castle View Cartwright Rd, Sunderland SR5 3DX; Tel (01783) 5495239; D.W. Carmicheal, BSc. (Mixed)
Farringdon Allendale Rd, Sunderland SR3 3EL; Tel (01783) 5280627; K.S. Stitt, BA. (Mixed)
Hetton North Rd, Houghton-le-Spring, Tyne & Wear DH5 9JZ; Tel (01783) 5263441; R.J. Horn, BA. (Mixed)
Houghton Kepier Dairy La, Houghton-le-Spring, Tyne & Wear DH5 8NA; Tel (01783) 5843122; R.M. Bloodworth. (Mixed)
Hylton Red House Rutherglen Rd, Sunderland SR5 5LN; Tel (01783) 5481054; M. Boundy. (Mixed)
Monkwearmouth Torver Cres, Sunderland SR6 8LQ; Tel (01783) 5487176; J.R. Farnie, BA. (Mixed)
Oxclose, Dilston Cl, Washington, Tyne & Wear NE38 0LN; Tel 0191-416 6522; M.E. Bowman. (Mixed)
Pennywell, Portsmouth Rd, Sunderland SR4 9BA; Tel (01783) 5342247; D. Wilkinson, MA. (Mixed)
Sandhill View, Telford Rd, Sunderland SR3 4EN; Tel (01783) 5282322; C.A. Short, BA, MEd. (Mixed)
Southmoor, Ryhope Rd, Sunderland SR2 7TF; Tel (01783) 5676822; M.J. Crook, BSc, MA. (Mixed)
Thornhill, Thornholme Rd, Sunderland SR2 7NA; Tel (01783) 5671608; A. Westmorland, MSc. (Mixed)
Usworth, Heworth Rd, Washington, Tyne & Wear NE37 2NF; Tel 0191-416 7500; W. Eddy. (Mixed)
Washington, Spout La, Washington, Tyne & Wear NE37 2AA; Tel 0191-416 0000; D. Jones. (Mixed)

Secondary Schools (Voluntary Aided 11–18)

St Aidan's R.C., Willow Bank Rd, Sunderland SR2 9HJ; Tel (01783) 5282613; P.J. Gordon, BA. (Boys)
St Anthony's R.C., Thornhill Terr, Sunderland SR2 7JN; Tel (01783) 5674726; Sister Aelred J.C. Carlin. (Girls)
St Robert of Newminster R.C., Biddick La, Washington, Tyne & Wear NE38 8AF; Tel 0191-417 1097; J.H. O'Neill, BSc. (Mixed)

Unit Provision

Hearing Impaired

Usworth School Heworth Rd, Washington, Tyne & Wear NE37 2NF; Tel 0191-416 7500
Thorney Close Primary School Torquay Rd, Sunderland, Tyne & Wear SR3 4BB; Tel 0191-528 1747
Usworth Colliery Primary School, Manor Cl, Sulgrave, Washington, Tyne & Wear NE37 3BL; Tel 0191-416 3225

Moderate Learning Difficulties

Usworth School Heworth Rd, Washington, Tyne & Wear NE37 2NF; Tel 0191-416 7500
Usworth Grange Primary School, Marlborough Rd, Sulgrave, Washington, Tyne & Wear NE37 3BG; Tel 0191-416 1729
Washington School, Spout La, Washington NE37 2AA; Tel 0191-416 0000

Language and Communication Difficulties

Pallion Primary School Waverley Terr, Pallion, Sunderland, Tyne & Wear SR4 6TA; Tel 0191-510 0770
Castletown Primary School Grange Rd, Castletown, Sunderland, Tyne & Wear SR5 3EQ; Tel 0191-549 5006
New Penshaw Primary School, Langdale Rd, New Penshaw, Houghton-le-Spring, Tyne & Wear DH4 7HY; Tel 0191-385 3986

Advisers' Centre

Broadway Educational Development Centre Springwell Rd, Sunderland SR4 8NW; Tel (01783) 5110333

Outdoor Pursuits Centre

Outdoor Activities Centre Derwent Hill, Keswick, Tyne and Wear; Tel (01596) 72005; I.A.A. Kellas

Surrey County Council

Population 1,036,700
County Hall, Penrhyn Rd, Kingston-upon-Thames, Surrey KT1 2DN; Tel 0181-541 8800

Education Department

County Hall, Kingston-upon-Thames KT1 2DJ; Tel 0181-541 9501
Director of Education Jill Barrow, BA, CertEd, MA(Ed)
Deputy Director of Education P.J. Levell, BA
Senior Assistant Director of Education (Resources) S.A. Clarke
Senior Assistant Director of Education (Schools and Student Support) A. Hunwicks
Assistant Director of Education (Age of Transfer) D.A. Ager, BSc(Econ)
Assistant Director of Education (Age of Transfer Support) J. Ambrose
Assistant Director of Education (Curriculum and Assessment) D. Stokoe, BA(Hons)
Assistant Director of Education (Planning) H.J.M. Patience, BSc, MA, DipEd, MEd, MBIM
Assistant Director of Education (Post Sixteen) M.C. Thompson, BA
Assistant Director of Education (Special Needs) R.J. Collet, MA
EO (Curriculum and Assessment) I. Skelton
EO (Marketing and Communications) I. Seifert, MEd
EO (Performance Monitoring) D. Hall
EO (Post Sixteen) F. Offer
EO (Research and Information) D. Porter, ALA
Chief Advisor F. Handley, BA, MSc, FRSA
Head of Adult and Continuing Education D. Bardell
Head of Awards M. Hardy
Head of Careers Services C. Thompson
Head of Client Catering Services A. Wallis
Head of Curriculum and Management Support Service John Brenchley, BA(Hons), PGCE, FRSA
Curriculum and Management Support Service Management Team (Services to the LEA) Maggie Roger
Curriculum and Management Support Service Management Team (Services to Surrey Schools and Units) Stephen Dengate
Curriculum and Management Support Service Management Team (External Services) Bob Walding
Curriculum and Management Support Service Management Team (TVEE) Roger Bailess
Curriculum and Management Support Service Management Team (Development) Mike Parkhouse
Curriculum and Management Support Service Management Team (Business) Ros Dore
Curriculum and Management Support Service Management Team (Finance) Aileen Assender
County Consultant (Cross-Curricular/Work Related) Anthony Barnes
County Consultant (TVEE) Adrian Carey
County Consultant (School Management-Primary) Dorothy Clark
County Consultant (Music/Arts) Keith Clark
County Consultant (Training Programme Co-ordinator) John Davies
County Consultant (Science) Stephen Dengate
County Consultant (School Management-Secondary) Brian Evans
County Consultant (School Management-Special) Maria Evans
County Consultant (Modern Languages) Amanda Flint
County Consultant (School Management-Primary) Graham Hall
County Consultant (Information Technology) Bob Higham
County Consultant (School Management-Primary) Carol Jones
County Consultant (School Management-Primary) Coral King
County Consultant (School Management-Special) Viv King
County Consultant (History) Peter Limm
County Consultant (Mathematics) John Ling
County Consultant (School Management-Secondary) Mick Michell
County Consultant (School Management-Secondary) Val Napier
County Consultant (Training Programme Co-ordinator/Physical Education) Tony Pannell
County Consultant (School Management-Primary) Colin Parsons
County Consultant (Geography) Paula Richardson
County Consultant (School Management-Secondary) Maggie Roger
County Consultant (School Management-Primary) Sue Sayers
County Consultant (English) Mike Smith
County Consultant (School Management-Primary) Ann Stoker
County Consultant (School Management-Secondary) Bob Walding
County Consultant (Physical Education) Gill Watkins
County Consultant (Design and Technology) Colin Whitfield
County Consultant (School Management-Primary) Vacancy
Adviser (Careers/TVEE) Briony Backhouse
Adviser (Geography) Val Banks
Adviser (Science/Vocational/TVEE) Ron Bibby
Adviser (Music) Christine Canniff
Adviser (Information Technology) Jill Day
Adviser (Reading Recovery) Christine Dingley
Adviser (Information Technology) Judith Gain
Adviser (History) Linda Goddard
Adviser (Careers/TVEE) Jan Godden
Adviser (English) Sue Hackman
Adviser (Induction/Newly Qualified Teachers) Pat Hansard
Adviser (Information Technology) Peter Hopkins
Adviser (Induction/Newly Qualified Teachers) Nerys James
Adviser (Assessment) Angela Kerswill
Adviser (Careers/TVEE) Gordon Kirk
Adviser (Schools Curriculum Industry Partnership (SCIP) Angela Maloney
Adviser (Information Technology/TVEE) Colin Masters
Adviser (Special/Vocational/TVEE) Vicki Macleod
Adviser (Geography/History) Stuart May
Adviser (Maths/Systems Management) Jim Noonan
Adviser (Information Technology) Lynn O'Neill
Adviser (Humanities/TVEE) Penny Plato
Adviser (Reading Recovery) Jean Prance
Adviser (Information Technology) George Rayner
Adviser (Art) Mary Scurlock
Adviser (Science) Maureen Smith
Adviser (Arts/TVEE) Ann Snelgrove
Adviser (Physical Education) Wendy Todd
Adviser (Equal Opportunities/TVEE) Ann Trengove
Adviser (Special/More Able) Liz Trickett
Adviser (Information Technology) Rowena Vickerstaff
Adviser (Health Education) Carole Watts
Adviser (Modern Languages) Richard White
Adviser (Training Programme Co-ordinator) Ken Wild
Head of Educational Psychology Services A. Wright
Head of Financial Services A. Docksey
Head of Information Systems Services R. Case
Head of Media Resources S. Goode
Head of Music and Performing Arts K. Willis
Head of Personnel Services J. White
Head of School and Student Support S. Cooper
Head of Sites and Accommodation Services S. Cosser
Head of Special Needs and Learning Support P. Foster
Head of Youth and Adult Education Service Diana Bardell

Number of Schools

5 nursery; 59 infant; 97 first; 36 junior; 43 middle; 88 primary; 17 first and middle; 39 secondary; 1 school of art and design; 4 staff development centres; 9 adult education institutes

Special Education
16 day schools; 9 residential and hospital schools; 23 day centres; 34 units attached to mainstream schools; 4 extended education centres
Requisition Periods for School Supplies
None
Other Authorities with whom Joint Purchasing Arrangements are made
None

Education Committee

Con 13, LD 11, Lab 3, IND/RA 2
Chair L. Huggins, (Con) Broome Perrow, Old Rd, Buckland, Betchworth RH3 7DY; Tel (01737) 843116
Members of the Committee
Con: Dr B.J. Coffin, D.M. Davis, J. Etherington, A.M. Fraser, C. Gerrard, S.J. Gladman, G.R. Hurst, P.W. King, M.A. Klat, K.P. Payne, Dr A.F. Povey, W. StCReid, R.G. Scott, W.W. Smith
LD: J.E. Dallison, W.R. Derrett, Y.L. Emmerson-Peirce, E.F. Glynn, D.R. Hall, G. Horsnell, Dr C.J. Inglis, M. King-Hele, J.E. Maines, J.S. Pincham, S. Thomas OBE, H.V. Watson
Lab: F. Awcock, J.I. Bullock, D.A. Morris
Ind/RA: D.A. Gollin, J.M. Haward

Governor Training Unit

The Management Development Centre, Hoefield, Bonsey La, Westfield, Woking GU22 9PR; Tel (01483) 721697; Fax (01483) 776128
Adviser (Training) Ken Wild, TCert, DipEd, BA, MCollP
Services Offered
Arrange and deliver a broad programme of courses for Surrey Governors in booklet form which is distributed twice yearly. Produce and distribute a termly newsletter "The Surrey Governor"; Offer distance learning and training resources; Arrange conferences on topical issues; Offer an individual service to schools for identified training needs for governors, staff and parents; Offer discount on AGIT conferences/courses as well as AGIT produced training material

Local Education Offices

North East (Elmbridge, Epsom and Ewell and Spelthorne)

7 Monument Hill, Weybridge KT13 8RZ; Tel (01932) 852811

North West (Runnymede, Surrey Heath and Woking)

Alexander Hse, 55–61 A Commercial Way, Woking GU21 1HN; Tel (01483) 740788

South West (Guildford and Waverley)

14a/b North St, Guildford GU1 4AF; Tel (01483) 572881

South East (Mole Valley, Reigate and Banstead and Tandridge)

123 Blackborough Rd, Reigate RH2 7DA; Tel (01737) 774166

Careers Services

See chapter 17

Home and Hospital Tuition Service

NE Surrey Home and Hospital Tuition Service Sycamore Centre, Long Grove Hospital, Horton La, Epsom, Surrey KT19 8PU; Tel (0137 27) 722939; P. Knight
NW Surrey Home and Hospital Tuition Service Childrens Ward, St Peters Hospital, Guildford Rd, Chertsey, Surrey KT15 OPZ; Tel (01932) 874761; P. Bye
SE and SW Surrey Home and Hospital Tuition Service SE Area Education Office, 123 Blackborough Rd, Reigate, Surrey RH2 7DA; Tel (01737) 774166; Mrs J. Locke

School Psychological Service

Head of Educational Psychology Services A. Wright County Hall, Kingston Upon Thames; Tel 0181-541 9563
North East Area Senior Educational Psychologist N. Adams, BSc,MSc,D 7 Monument Hill, Weybridge KT13 8RZ; Tel (01932) 852811
North West Area Senior Educational Psychologist C. Shilling North West Area Education Office, Alexander Hse, 55A-61A Commercial Way, Woking GU21 1HN; Tel (0148 62) 740788
South East Area Senior Educational Pyschologist J. Falkner, BA,MSc,Dep(Tav) 123 Blackborough Rd, Reigate RH2 7DA; Tel (01737) 774166
South West Area Senior Educational Psychologist A. Jordan, BSc,CertEd,MSc 14a/b North Street, Guildford GU1 4AF; Tel (01483) 572881

Learning Difficulties

The Abbey , Menin Way, Farnham, Surrey; Tel (01252) 725059; D.A. King. (Mixed) (8-16) (Day) (130)
Brooklands School, Wray Park Rd, Reigate RH2 ODF; Tel (01737) 249941; S. Wakenell. (S) (Mixed) (2-19) (75)
Carwarden House, 118 Upper Chobham Rd, Camberley, Surrey; Tel (01276) 63148; J.G. Cope. (Mixed) (8–16) (140)
Clifton Hill, Chaldon Rd, Caterham, Surrey; Tel (01883) 347740; H. Norris. (Mixed) (2–19) (75)
Gosden House, Bramley, Nr Guildford, Surrey; Tel (01483) 892008; J. David. (M) (Mixed) (5–16) (Day and Boarding) (106)
Manor Mead Laleham Rd, Shepperton, Surrey; Tel (01932) 241834; C.D. Morley. (S) (Mixed) (2–11) (92)
The Park, Park Rd, Woking, Surrey; Tel (01483) 772057; J. Lonsdale. (M) (Mixed) (8–16) (130)
Pond Meadow, Pond Meadow, Park Barn Est, Guildford, Surrey; Tel (01483) 32239; A.E. Brighty. (Mixed) (2–19) (80)
Portesbury, Portesbury Rd, Camberley, Surrey; Tel (01276) 63078; A.E. Davies. (Mixed) (2–19) (92)
Philip Southcote, Woburn Hill, Addlestone, Weybridge, Surrey; Tel (01932) 562326; G.L. Rogers. (Mixed) (8–16) (130)
St Nicholas, Taynton Dr, Merstham, Redhill, Surrey; Tel (0173 764) 4031; J.D. Walker, MA. (M) (Boys) (10–19) (Day and boarding) (73)
The Ridgeway, 14 Frensham Rd, Farnham, Surrey; Tel (01252) 724562; S.A. Cooks. (Mixed) (2–19) (62)
Walton Leigh, Queen's Rd, Walton-on-Thames, Surrey; Tel (01932) 223243; L. Curtis. (Mixed) (11–19) (92)
West Hill, Kingston Rd, Leatherhead, Surrey; Tel (01372) 375270; M. Goldie. (Mixed) (8–16) (160)
Woodfield, Sunstone Grove, Merstham, Surrey; Tel (0173 74) 2623; S.M. Plant. (Mixed) (8–16) (130)
Woodlands, Forty Foot Rd, Leatherhead, Surrey; Tel (01372) 377922; H.F. Barnes. (Mixed) (2–19) (92)

Children with Emotional, Behavioural and Social Needs

Day
Freemantles, Hatton Hill, Windlesham, Surrey; Tel (01276) 71409; R.S. Buchan. (Mixed) (5–11) (25)
John Nightingale, Hurst Rd, West Molesey, Surrey; Tel 0181 979 0266; A.J. Withers. (Mixed) (11–16) (60)
Day Centres
Fordway Centre, Stanwell Rd, Ashford, Kent; Tel (01784) 243365; S.E. Francis. (Mixed) (5–11) (24)
The Grove Centre, Grove Rd, Merrow, Guildford, Surrey; Tel (01483) 60394; C.D. Lodge (Acting). (Mixed) (7–12) (15)
Perrymead Centre, Alpine Rd, Redhill, Surrey; Tel (01737) 767521; H.C. Hunter. (Mixed) (5–11) (24)

Pyrford Centre, Engliff La, Pyrford, Surrey; Tel (093 23) 342451; E.M. Webb. (Mixed) (11–16) (30)
Sidlow Bridge Centre, Irons Bottom La, Sidlow Bridge, Reigate, Surrey; Tel (01737) 249079; D.H. Davies. (Mixed) (11–16) (20)
Linden Bridge and Spring Centre, Grafton Rd, Worcester Pk, Surrey; Tel 0181-330 3009; M.M. Golding. (Mixed) (5–16) (Day and Boarding Places) (50)
Starhurst, Chart La South, Dorking, Surrey; Tel (01306) 883763; H.J. Kiernan. (Boys) (11–16) (53)
Thornchace, Grove Rd, Merrow, Guildford, Surrey; Tel (01483) 573859; *Warden Head of Centre* C.D. Lodge. (Mixed) (Juniors) (11–16) (18)
Wey House, Bramley, nr Guildford, Surrey; Tel (01483) 898130; K. Harrison. (Senior Girls, Junior Boys) (7–11) (50)
Wishmore Cross, Alpha Rd, Chobham, Surrey; Tel (01276) 857555; R.A. Lamb

Children with Specific Learning Difficulties (Day Units)

Echelford County Primary, Park Rd, Ashford TW15 1EX; Tel (01784) 253233; A.F. Wilson. (9–12)
Lakeside County Middle, Alphington Ave, Frimley GU16 5LL; Tel (01276) 24055; M.D. Nolan. (8–12)
Marden Lodge County Primary, Croydon Rd, Caterham CR3 6QH; Tel (01883) 343014; M.L. Kelly. (7–11)
Northmead County Junior, Grange Rd, Guildford GU2 6PZ; Tel (01483) 572017; I.C. Hollingsworth. (7–11)
St Andrew's C.E. Primary, Lockhart Rd, Cobham KT11 2AX; Tel (01932) 63452; D.J. Harrison. (7–11)
St Mary's C.E. Middle, Hart Rd, Byfleet KT14 7NJ; Tel (01932) 344177; C.M. Neef. (8–12)
St Peter's C.E. Middle, Little Grn La, Farnham GU9 8TF; Tel (01252) 714115; P.D. Williams. (8–12)
Salfords County Middle, Copsleigh Ave, Salfords, Redhill RH1 5BQ; Tel (01737) 762940; S.P.I. Wareham. (8–12)

Delicate and Physically Handicapped–Day Units

Badshot Lea Unit, Badshot Lea County First School, Farnham, Surrey GU9 9LE; Tel (01252) 20883; S.L. Norman. (P.H.) (Mixed) (5–8) (20)
Bagshot Unit Bagshot County First School, School La, Bagshot, Surrey GU19 5BP; Tel (01276) 73385; Mrs N. Shone. (P.H.) (Mixed) (5–8) (10)
Cordwalles Unit Cordwalles County Middle School, Berkshire Rd, Old Dean Est, Camberley GU15 4DR; Tel (01276) 23298; D.S. Lewis. (P.H.) (Mixed) (8–12) (10)
De Stafford Unit, De Stafford County Secondary, Burntwood La, Caterham CR3 5YX; Tel (01883) 347818; J. Gribben. (P.H.) (Mixed) (30)
Dovers Green Unit, Dovers Green County First School, Rushetts Rd, Reigate RH2 7RF; Tel (0173 72) 245515; S. Batchelor. (P.H.) (Mixed) (5–8) (10)
Eastwick Unit, Eastwick County Infant School, Eastwick Dr, Great Bookham, Surrey; Tel (01372) 53672; S.M. Evans. (P.H.) (Mixed) (5–7) (10)
Eastwick Unit, Eastwick County Junior School, Eastwick Dr, Great Bookham, Surrey; Tel (01372) 53277; J.S. Stevens. (P.H.) (Mixed) (7–11) (10)
Limpsfield Grange, Blue Hse La, Limpsfield, Oxted, Surrey; Tel (01883) 713928; C. Davies. (Girls) (10–16) (Boarding) (46)
Kings Manor Unit, Kings Manor School, Southway, Guildford GU2 6DU; Tel (01483) 67897; G. Gardner. (P.H.) (Mixed) (11–18) (30)
Pyrcroft Unit, Pyrcroft County Primary School, Pyrcroft Rd, Chertsey KT16 9EW; Tel (01932) 504094; S. Beattie. (P.H.) (Mixed) (5–11) (10)
St Matthew's Unit, St Matthew's CE (Aided) First and Middle School, Linkfield La, Redhill RH1 1JF; Tel (01737) 762080; C.S. Joiner. (PH) (Mixed) (5–12) (10)
Sunnydown, Portley Hse, 152 Whyteleafe Rd, Caterham CR3 5ED; Tel (01883) 342281; M. Armstrong. (Boys) (10–16) (Boarding) (70)
William Cobbett Unit, William Cobbett County Middle School, Weybourne Rd, Farnham GU9 9ER; Tel (01252) 312772; C.L. Peppin, DipEd. (P.H.) (Mixed) (8–12) (10)

Day Units (Hearing Impaired Children)

Auriol County Middle School, Vale Rd, Stoneleigh, Ewell, Surrey; Tel 0181-393 4721; P.J. Skelton. (Mixed) (8–12) (20)
Bishop David Brown Secondary School, Albert Dr, Sheerwater GU21 5RF; Tel (01932) 350191; G.D Ellis. (Mixed) (11–16) (20)
Broadmere County Primary, Devonshire Ave, Sheerwater, Woking, Surrey; Tel (0193 23) 43747; G.E. Holloway. (Mixed) (3–11) (20)
The Mead County First School, Newbury Gdns, Ewell, Surrey; Tel 0181 393 0966; S. Walsh. (Mixed) (3–8) (24)

Day Units (Language)

Burpham County First, Burpham Lane, Burpham, Guildford, Surrey; Tel (01483) 572510; G. Malison. (Mixed) (5–7) (10)
Cranleigh County First, High Stret, Guildford, Surrey; Tel (01483) 272478; S. Attenborough. (Mixed) (5–8) (10)
St Catherines County Primary School, Coneybury, Bletchingley, Redhill, Surrey; Tel (01883) 843337; D.L. Davis
Spelthorne County Infant School, Chertsey Rd, Ashford Common, Surrey; Tel (01233) 253942; P. Reading. (Mixed) (5–7) (10)
Spelthorne County Junior School, Feltham Hill Rd, Ashford Common TW15 1LP; Tel (01233) 253311; J.W. Clarke
Stepgates County Primary School, Free Prae Rd, Chertsey KY16 8HT; Tel (0193 28) 563022; J.W. Denison-Smith. (Mixed) 5–11) (10)
Stepgates County Middle School, Free Prae Rd, Chertsey KY16 8HT; Tel (0193 28) 563226. (Mixed) (10)
Stoughton County Junior School, Grange Rd, Guildford GU2 6PZ; Tel (01483) 573937; J.R.C. Squire. (Mixed) (7–11) (10)
The Grove County School, Chosham Rd, Frimley GU16 5PG; Tel (01276) 23947; Mrs G.P. Borlace. (Mixed) (5–8) (8)
Therfield School, Dilston Rd, Leatherhead KY22 7NZ; Tel (01372) 377661; T.J. Reddin
West Ewell County First, Ruxley Lane, West Ewell KY19 OUZ; Tel 0181-393 2417; S.M. Treskian. (Mixed) (5–8) (10)
Woodville County Junior School, Woodville Rd, Leatherhead KY22 7BP; Tel (01372) 373448; E.S. Truscoe. (Mixed) (7–11) (10)

Comprehensive Secondary Schools (County 12–16)

Abbeylands School, School La, Addlestone KT15 1TE; Tel (01932) 847048; Fax (01932) 851680; T. Russell, BA. (612)
Ash Manor, Manor Rd, Ash, Aldershot GU12 6QH; Tel (01252) 23709; Fax (01252) 23228; R.M. Linnell. (555)
The Ashford High, Stanwell Rd, Ashford TW15 3DU; Tel (01784) 243824; W.A. Brookes, BSc(Hons), DipEd. (778)
Bishop David Brown, Albert Dr, Sheerwater, Woking GU21 5RF; Tel (01932) 349696; G.D. Ellis, BA,(Hons). (535)
Broadwater, Summers Rd, Broadwater, Goldalming GU7 3BW; Tel (01483) 414516/7/8; Fax (01483) 425782; M.T. Hall. (647)
Glebelands, Parsonage Rd, Cranleigh GU6 7AN; Tel (01483) 275248; Fax (01483) 268381; J.W. Baker, BA. (683)
Heath End, Hale Reeds, Farnham GU9 9BN; Tel (01252) 733371; Fax (01252) 712999; M.D. Widdows, MA. (706)
Hinchley Wood, Claygate La, Hinchley Wood KT10 0AQ; Tel 0181-398 7161; Fax 0181-339 0046; G.J. Parker, BEd. (483)

Horsell High School, Morton Rd, Horsell, Woking GU21 4TJ; Tel (01483) 770447; Fax (01483) 766960; S.E.A. Williams. (388)
The Magna Carta School, Thorpe Rd, Staines TW18 3HJ; Tel (01784) 454320; Fax (01784) 441214; P.D. Roe. (545)
The Matthew Arnold School, Kingston Rd, Staines TW18 1PE; Tel (01784) 457275; Fax (01784) 450037; T.W. Allen, BSc,MSc. (492)
Oakwood Balcombe Rd, Horley RH6 9AB; Tel (01293) 785363; Fax (01293) 786465; A.S. Thompson. (800)
Reigate, Pendleton Rd, Reigate RH2 7NT; Tel (0173 72) 243166; J. Cain. (373)
Rodborough, Rake La, Milford GU8 5BZ; Tel (01483) 428182; Fax (01483) 417984; J. Latham. (530)
The Royal Alexandra and Albert, Gatton Pk, Reigate RH2 0TW; Tel (01737) 642565; Fax (01737) 642294; B.H.W. Fox. (371)
Sunbury Manor School, Nursery Rd, Sunbury-on-Thames TW16 6LG; Tel (01932) 784258; Fax (01932) 772197; M.J. Sands. (706)
Trinity C.E. School, More La, Esher KT10 8AP; Tel (01372) 468068; Fax (01372) 471058; M.A. Turnbull. (584)
The Warwick School, Noke Dr, Redhill RH1 4AD; Tel (01737) 764356; Fax (01737) 770007; M.A. Tyrell, BEd(Hons). (642)
Weydon, Weydon La, Farnham GU9 8UG; Tel (01252) 725052; Rev J.D.A. Adams, MA, BD, MEd. (662)
The Winston Churchill School, Hermitage Rd, St John's, Woking GU21 1TL; Tel (01483) 476861; Fax (01483) 476479; P.A. Barnard. (1157)
Woolmer Hill, Woolmer Hill, Haslemere GU27 1QB; Tel (01428) 654055; A. Sheen. (689)

Comprehensive Secondary Schools (County 12–18)

Ashcombe County, Ashcombe Rd, Dorking RH4 1LX; Tel (01306) 886312; Fax (01306) 742537; A. Webster, BA. (1160)
France Hill, Watchetts Dr, Camberley GU15 2PQ; Tel (01276) 21233/128441; E.A. Pain. (934)
Fullbrook, Selsdon Rd, New Haw, Weybridge KT15 3HW; Tel (01932) 349301; Fax (01932) 351224; R.A. Elms, MEd. (1158)
George Abbot, Woodruff Ave, Burpham, Guildford GU1 1XX; Tel (01483) 38433; Fax (01483) 302811; G.M. Wilson, BA. (1488)
Howard of Effingham, Lower Rd, Effingham KT24 5JR; Tel (01372) 453694; M.G. Marchant, MA(Hons) (cantab). (912)
Kings Manor School, Southway, Guildford GU2 6DU; Tel (01483) 67897; G.W. Gardner. (635)
Oxted County, Blue House La, Oxted RH8 0AB; Tel (01883) 712425/712225/6; R.A.V. Coles, MSc. (1391)
Rydens, Hersham Rd, Hersham, Walton-on-Thames KT12 5PY; Tel (01932) 242994/5/6; B.J. Love, BA. (993)
Sondes Place, West Bank, Dorking RH4 3DG; Tel (01306) 887337; Fax (01306) 888715; S. Oviatt-Ham. (587)
Therfield, Dilston Rd, Leatherhead KT22 7NZ; Tel (01372) 377661; Fax (01372) 360679; T.J. Reddin. (1064)
Tomlinscote Tomlinscote Way, Frimley GU16 5LY; Tel (01276) 28768; A.A. Ryles, BEd(Hons). (1163)
Warlingham Tithepit Shaw La, Warlingham CR3 9YB; Tel (01883) 624067; Fax (01883) 624026; D.S. Parr, BEd. (845)

Comprehensive Secondary Schools. (Voluntary)

Bishop Reindorp C. of E. Larch Ave, Guildford GU1 1JY; Tel (01483) 37373; Fax (01483) 452725; J.C. Maton, MA. (V.A.) (12–18) (9150)
Bishop Wand C. of E. Laytons La, Sunbury TW16 6LP; Tel (01932) 787537/788128; N. Dunkley. (V.A.) (11–18) (618)
St Andrew's R.C. Hillfield, Grange Rd, Ashstead, Leatherhead KT22 7JP; Tel (01372) 277881; J. McGrath. (V.A.) (12–18) (583)
St Bede's United C. of E./R.C., Carlton Rd, Redhill RH1 2DD; Tel (01737) 763780; Fax (01737) 770006; J.D. Marcus, MA. (V.A.) (12–18) (1119)
St John the Baptist R.C., Elm Bridge La, Kingfield, Woking GU22 9AL; Tel (0148 62) 729343; B.E. McCarthy, BA,DASE. (V.A.) (12–18) (654)
St Peter's R.C., Horseshoe La, Merrow, Guildford GU1 2TN; Tel (01483) 34654; Fax (01483) 306571; C. Richardson. (V.A.) (12–18) (584)
Salesian School R.C. (Aided), Guildford Rd, Chertsey KT16 9LU; Tel (01932) 560030/563233; Fax (01932) 571526; D. Cleworth. (11–18) (180)

Middle Schools (County 8–12)

Auriol County, Vale Rd, Ewell KT19 0PJ; Tel 0181 393 4721; P.J. Skelton. (392)
Banstead County, The Horseshoe, Banstead SM7 2BQ; Tel (0173 73) 351788; J. Stevens. (225)
Bellfields County, Woking Rd, Guildford GU1 1QJ; Tel (01483) 62088; M. Thurbin. (203)
Binscombe County, Green La, Farncombe, Godalming GU7 3TB; Tel (01483) 6477; J.D. Hilyard. (325)
Blackdown County, Newfoundland Rd, Blackdown, Deepcut, Camberley GU16 6TA; Tel (01252) 835676; L. Sheppard. (5–12) (123)
Boxgrove County, Boxgrove La, Merrow, Guildford, Surrey; Tel (01483) 63701; P. Bridge. (5–12) (273)
Brambletye County, Brambletye Park Rd, Redhill RH1 6JX; Tel (01737) 763488; A. Stainer. (375)
Brockham County, Wheelers La, Brockham Green, Betchworth RH3 7LA; Tel (0173 784) 843384; E. Starkie, BEd. (5–12) (288)
Burstow County, Wheelers La, Smallfield, Horley RH6 9PT; Tel (01342) 842010; C.G Lee. (5–12) (304)
Bushy Hill County, Sheeplands Ave, Bushy Hill, Merrow, Guildford GU1 2SG; Tel (01483) 66546; A. Everleigh. (375)
Connaught County, Manor Way, Bagshot GU19 5JY; Tel (01276) 472489; V.R. Armstrong-Smith. (8–12) (318)
Cordwalles County, Berkshire Rd, Old Dean Est, Camberley GU15 4DR; Tel (01276) 23298; D.S. Lewis. (8–12) (206)
Crawley Ridge County, Crawley Ridge, Camberley GU15 2AJ; Tel (01276) 61144; E.A. Kerr. (8–12) (252)
Cuddington Croft County, West Dr, Cheam SM2 7NA; Tel 0181-642 4325; M.L. Farnham. (5–12) (285)
Danetree County, Danetree Rd, W. Ewell KT19 9SE; Tel 0181-393 6406; E. Butcher. (544)
Eastwick County, Eastwick Dr, Great Bookham KT23 3PP; Tel (01372) 53277; J.S. Stevens. (363)
Epsom County, Pound La, Epsom KT19 8SD; Tel (01372) 720608; H.F. Tompkins. (5–12) (286)
Fetcham County, Bell La, Fetcham, Leatherhead KT22 9ND; Tel (01372) 374781; D.P. Blackman. (158)
Furzefield County, Delabole Rd, Merstham, Redhill RH1 3PA; Tel (01737) 642842; R.J. Cumes. (217)
Godalming County, Hallam Rd, Meadrow, Godalming GU7 3HG; Tel (01483) 421597; D.E. Andrews. (167)
Great Bookham County, Griffin Way, Great Bookham KT23 4JL; Tel (01372) 56774; M.C. Lack. (227)
The Grove County, Chobham Rd, Frimley GU16 5PG; Tel (01276) 22447; G. Brown. (8–12) (241)
Hale County, Upper Hale, Farnham GU9 0LR; Tel (01252) 716729; A.J. Scott. (303)
Hammond Middle School, Badger Dr, Lightwater GU18 5TS; Tel (01276) 473972; B.A. Llyod-Jones. (8–12) (297)
Hoefield County, Bonsey La, Westfield, Woking GU22 9PR; Tel (0148 62) 764187; Vacancy. (248)
Holly Lodge County, Stratford Rd, Ash Vale GU12 5PX; Tel (01689) 548390; A.M. Thorpe. (312)
Kingston Rd County Kingston Rd, Staines TW18 4LN; Tel (01784) 455742; C.R. Jones, BEd. (174)
Lakeside County Alphington Ave, Frimley GU16 5LL; Tel (01276) 24055; M.D. Nolan. (246)
Meath Green County Greenfields Rd, Horley RH6 8HW; Tel (01293) 784298; C.A. Neve, BEd(Hons). (280)

Merland Rise County St Leonards Rd, Tattenham Corner, Epsom KT18 5RJ; Tel (0173 73) 354313; J.A. Shettle (Acting). (128)
Northmead County Grange Rd, Guildford GU2 6PZ; Tel (01483) 572017; I.C. Hollingsworth. (303)
Park Mead County Park Mead Est, Cranleigh GU6 7HB; Tel (01483) 274315; J.R. Quee. (369)
Pirbright County School La, Pirbright, Woking GU24 0JN; Tel (0148 67) 3884; Mrs J.M. Bradley. (5–12) (209)
The Raleigh County Northcote Cres, W. Horsley KT24 6LX; Tel (0148 65) 2988; I.R. Nichols, LLAM. (5–12) (317)
Ravenscote County Old Bisley Rd, Frimley GU16 5RE; Tel (01276) 22270; G.J. Gregg. (557)
The Redlands County Goodwyns Rd, Dorking RH4 2LR; Tel (01306) 884506; M. Newman-Horwell. (152)
Reigate Priory County Bell St, Reigate RH2 7RL; Tel (01737) 245065; G.M. Cox, BEd. (446)
Rivermede County Ray Rd, West Molesey KT8 0LG; Tel 0181-979 2694; K.R.G. Bartlett. (218)
Salfords County, Copsleigh Ave, Salfords, Redhill RH1 5BQ; Tel (01737) 762940; S.P. Wareham. (204)
Sandcross County, Sandcross La, Reigate RH2 8HH; Tel (01737) 245467; C. Topping, BEd(Hons). (270)
Sangers County Middle, Sangers Dr, Horley RH6 8AN; Tel (01293) 782839; D. Wood. (250)
Shawley County, Shawley Way, Tattenham Corner, Epsom KT18 5PD; Tel (01737) 350344; C. Gill (Acting). (5–12) (234)
Shottermill County, Lion La, Shottermill GU27 1JF; Tel (01428) 642096; S.M. Buckingham. (8–12) (298)
South Farnham County, Menin Way, Farnham GU9 8DY; Tel (01252) 716155; A.N. Carter. (8–12) (298)
Southcote, Ash Church Rd, Ash GU12 6LX; Tel (01252) 28589; P.A. Pearce. (236)
Stamford Green County, Christchurch Mount, Epsom KT19 8LU; Tel (01372) 725383; J. Nicholson. (5–12) (404)
Stoneleigh County, Sparrow Farm Rd, Ewell KT17 2LW; Tel 0181-393 4152; G.P.S. Turner. (8–12) (217)
Tadworth County, Tadworth St, Heathcote, Tadworth, KT20 5RR; Tel (01737) 354541; J.A. Williamson. (5–12) (357)
Tillingbourne County, New Rd, Chilworth GU4 8NB; Tel (01483) 504384; P. Wood. (8–12) (236)
Wallace Fields County, Dorling Dr, Ewell KT17 3BH; Tel 0181-393 0350; F.M. Crowley. (8–12) (255)
Warren Mead County, Roundwood Way, Nork, Banstead SM7 1EJ; Tel (0173 73) 353725; L.E. Christie. (247)
Watchetts, Frimley Rd, Camberley GU15 2QB; Tel (01276) 63870; M.G. Keys. (8–12) (347)
William Cobbett County, Weybourne Rd, Farnham GU9 9ER; Tel (01252) 312772; C.L.S. Peppin. (8–12) (311)
Woodmansterne County Carshalton Rd, Woodmansterne, Banstead SM7 3HU; Tel (01737) 353120; C.F. Murphy. (5–12) (271)
Wray Common County, Kendall Cl, Wray Common, Reigate RH2 0LR; Tel (01737) 761254; S.U. Thomas. (269)
Yattenden County, Oakwood Rd, Horley RH6 7BZ; Tel (01293) 785491; E.D. Tope. (329)

Middle Schools (Voluntary 8–12)

Bishopsmead C. of E. Sefton Rd, Epsom KT19 9BQ; Tel (0137 27) 728756; M.C. Muirhead. (V.A.) (8–12) (102)
Busbridge C. of E., Brighton Rd, Busbridge, Godalming GU7 1XA; Tel (01483) 417302; M.G. Wilde, BA, BSc. (V.A.) (210)
The Chandler C. of E., Middlemarch, Roke La, Witley, Godalming GU8 5PB; Tel (0142 879) 683071; J.B. Entwhistle. (V.A.) (284)
Chobham St Lawrence C. of E. Bagshot Rd, Chobham, Woking GU24 8AB; Tel (01276) 858336/858366; D. Linfoot. (V.A.) (5–12) (212)
Frimley C. of E., Frimley Grn, Camberley GU16 6ND; Tel (01252) 835440; M.S. Peace. (V.C.) (8–12) (207)
Holy Trinity C. of E., Benner La, West End, Woking GU24 9JG; Tel (01276) 858297; A.A. Butterick. (V.C.) (5–12) (341)
Holy Trinity C. of E. Addison Rd, Guildford GU1 3QF; Tel (01483) 39033; R.J. Rowe. (V.C.) (266)
Potters Gate C. of E., Potters Gate, Farnham GU9 7BB; Tel (01252) 715619; H.M. Hosker. (V.A.) (5–12) (272)
Powell-Corderoy, Longfield Rd, Dorking RH4 3DF; Tel (01306) 883373; D.A. Seume. (V.C.) (5–12) (165)
St Bartholomew's C. of E., Derby Rd, Haslemere GU27 1BP; Tel (01428) 3634; G.C. Jones. (V.A.) (335)
St Bedes C. of E., Bush La, Send, Woking GU23 7HP; Tel (01483) 222143; Mrs J. Jameson. (V.A.) (195)
St Marks C. of E. Franklyn Rd, Godalming GU7 2LD; Tel (01483) 422924; J.A. Bird. (V.A.) (5–12) (161)
St Martin's C. of E. Ashley Rd, Epsom KT18 7AD; Tel (0137 27) 721996; J.A. Ferretter. (V.C.) (286)
St Martin's C. of E. Ranmore Rd, Dorking RH14 1HW; Tel (01306) 883474; G.A. Robertson, BA Annexe at Pixham La, Dorking RH14 1PQ; Tel (01306) 883548. (V.C.) (5–12) (329)
St Matthews C of E, Linkfield La, Redhill RH1 1JF; Tel (01737) 762080; C.S. Joiner. (VA) (342)
St Nicholas C. of E., Parsonage Rd, Cranleigh GU6 7AN; Tel (01483) 273286; A.L. Keig. (V.A.) (8–12) (336)
St Paul's C. of E., St Paul's Rd, Dorking RH4 2HS; Tel (01306) 883547; C.M. Evans. (V.A.) (5–12) (360)
St Peter's C.E. (Aided) Middle Little Green La, Farnham GU9 8TF; Tel (01252) 714115; P.D. Williams
St Tarcisius R.C., Valroy Cl, Knoll Rd, Camberley GU15 3SY; Tel (01276) 65882; C. Smith. (V.A.) (8–12) (208)
St Thomas The Apostle R.C., Eastworth Rd, Chertsey KT16 8DQ; Tel (0193 28) 562251; A.M. Coleman, BEd. (V.A.) (9–13) (318)
St Thomas More R.C., Beauchamp Rd, East Molesey KT8 0PA; Tel 0181-979 5893; K.M. Barraclough. (V.A.) (9–13) (227)
Waverley Abbey C. of E., Tilford, Farnham GU10 2AE; Tel (01252) 782321; T.J. Melling. (V.A.) (8–12) (283)
The Weald C. of E., Beare Grn, Dorking RH5 4QW; Tel (01306) 711719; I.M.R. Hayler. (V.A.) (173)
Weybridge C. of E., Grotto Rd, Weybridge KT13 8PL; Tel (01932) 851762; I.R. Wilson. (V.C.) (265)
Wrecclesham St Peters C. of E., Little Grn La, Shortheath, Farnham GU9 8TF; Tel (01252) 714115; P.D. Williams. (V.A.) (256)

Adult Education Institutes

Elmbridge Adult Education Institute, Henrietta Parker Centre, Ray Rd, West Molesey KT8 0LG; Tel 0181-979 8334; *Principal* Dr P.G. Buck, MA
Guildford Adult Education Institute, Sydenham Rd, Guilford, Surrey; Tel (01483) 60978; *Principal* J.S. Youngs, MA,DipFE
Mid Surrey Adult Education Institute, The Mansion, Church St, Leatherhead KT22 8DA; Tel (01372) 386851; *Principal* A. Gaywood, DippE
Reigate, Banstead and Horley Adult Education Institute, Longmead Centre, Holland Cl, Redhill RH1 1HT; Tel (01737) 773555; *Principal* M. Kitney, MEd,ATD
Spelthorne Adult Education Institute, 36 Kingston Rd, Staines TW18 4LN; Tel (01784) 457153; *Principal* C. Norris
Surrey Heath Adult Education Institute, France Hill Hse, France Hill Dr, Camberley GU15 3QA; Tel (01276) 20145/681923; *Principal* G. Scandrett, ATD
Tandridge Adult Education Institute, Stychens La, Bletchingley RH1 4LL; Tel (01883) 742115; *Principal* E. Dibba, MA
Waverley Adult Education Institute, Bridge Rd, Godalming GU7 3DU; Tel (01483) 421387; *Principal* Dr J.J. Robinson, MA,PhD,FBIM
Woking and Chertsey Adult Education Institute, Danesfield Centre, Grange Rd, Horsell, Woking GU21 4DA; Tel (0148 62) 721425; *Principal* R. Walsh, DipAdEd

Day Units (Visually Impaired)

George Abbott, Woodruff Ave, Burphay, Guildford GU1 14X; Tel (01483) 384433; E.M. Wilson. (11–16)
Oxted County School, Bluehouse Lane, Oxted, Surrey RH8 OAB; Tel (0188 33) 712425; R.A.V Coles. (Mixed) (11–16) (10)
St Stephens C of E, (Aided Primary School) Hunters Chase, South Godstone RH9 8HR; J.R. Howard. (Mixed) (5–11) (10)

Sythwood County Primary, Sythwood, Horsell, Woking GU21 3AX; Tel (01483) 770063; M.W. Thomas. (5–11)

Remedial Centres

Ardmore Centre, Pendleton Rd, Redhill, Surrey; Tel (0173 72) 248130; H.M. Shand. (Mixed) (38)
Bisley Centre, Bisley, Woking, Surrey; Tel (0148 67) 4893; V.B Rooney. (Mixed) (36)
Byfleet Centre, Byfleet First School, Kings Head La, Byfleet, Surrey; Tel (0193 23) 352987; G. Neal. (Mixed) (24)
Caterham Hill Centre, High St, Caterham, Surrey; Tel (01883) 42343; E.M. McCormack. (Mixed) (48)
Chertsey Centre, Stepgates, Chertsey, Surrey; Tel (093 28) 567442; F.M. Brady. (Mixed) (24)
Clayhill Centre, West Hill, Epsom, Surrey; Tel (0137 27) 23462; E. Waldon. (Mixed) (40)
De Clare Centre, Longfield Rd, Dorking, Surrey; Tel (01306) 882764; V. Gavin. (Mixed) (20)
Farnham Centre, Badshot Lea, Farnham, Surrey; Tel (01252) 310774. (Mixed) (40)
Lingfield Centre, High St, Lingfield, Surrey; Tel (01342) 834185; M. Child. (Mixed)
Merrow Centre, Down Rd, Merrow, Guildford, Surrey; Tel (01483) 69162; I.D. Bell. (Mixed) (30)
Normandy Centre, School La, Normandy, Surrey; Tel (01483) 811154; J. Cooper-Tydeman. (Mixed) (30)
Staines Centre, Knowle Grn, Staines, Middx; Tel (01784) 459411; J.F. Auger. (Mixed) (22)
Walton Centre, Ashley First School, Ashley Rd, Walton-on-Thames, Surrey; Tel (01932) 242949; C. Toasland. (Mixed) (36)

Hospital School

Tadworth Court Teaching Centres Tadworth Court Children's Hospital, Tadworth, Surrey; Tel (073 73) 354006; *(Teacher-in-Charge)* Mrs P. Lane

Extended Education Centres for Adults with severe learning difficulties.

Botleys Park Extended Education Centre, Guildford Rd, Chertsey KT16 0QA; Tel (01932) 872589; P. Hibberd
The Manor Extended Education Centre, Christchurch Rd, Epsom KT19 8NL; Tel (01372) 727967; E. Williams
Royal Earlswood Extended Education Centre, Princes Rd, Redhill RH1 6JL; Tel (01737) 761263; L. Martin
St Ebba's Extended Education Centre, Hook Rd, Epsom KT19 8QJ; Tel (01372) 729148; I. Jackson

Staff Development Centres and Units

Curriculum and Assessment Unit, Frenches Road, Redhill RH1 2HP; Tel (01737) 778383; Fax (01737) 768504; *Director* B. Williams
Glyn House SD Centre, Ewell KT17 2AR; Tel 0181-393 6123; J. Brooker
Governor Training Unit, Woking College, Rydens Way, Woking GU22 9DL; Tel (048 62) 757571; P. Coakley
Horsell Staff Development Unit, Horsell high School, Morton Road, Horsell, Woking GU21 4BD
Local Management of Schools, Training Unit, Woking College, rydens Way, Woking GU22 9DL; Tel (0148 62) 757571; K. Wild
N.E. Surrey SD Centre, Bell Farm Middle School, Hersham Rd, Hersham, Walton-on-Thames KT12 5PY; Tel (01932) 253088; A. Leah
North West Surrey SD Centre, Carwarden Hse, 118 Upper Chobham Rd, Camberley GU15 1EJ; Tel (01276) 26681; M.G. Kimberley
Pirbright Curriculum Development Centre, School Lane, Pirbright, Woking GU24 0JN; Tel (0148 62) 797265; J. Day
Runnymede SD Centre, Chertsey Rd, Addlestone KT15 2EP; Tel (0193 28) 564157; K. Bennett
South East Surrey SD Centre, Allingham Rd, South Park, Reigate RH2 8ED; Tel (0173 72) 242561; S.E. Baxter
South West Surrey SD Centre, Pewley Hill, Guildford GU1 3SG; Tel (01483) 37070; H. Toynbee
Teacher Appraisal Training Unit, Annexe to Hoefield County Middle School, Bonsey Lane, Westfield, Woking GU22 9PR; Tel (0148 62) 721697; W.J. Davies
Teacher Recruitment Unit, Annexe to Hoefield County Middle School, Bonsey Lane, Westfield, Woking GU22 9PR; Tel (0148 62) 726143; C. Eames
TVEE Unit Room 28, Runnymede Staff Development Centre, Addlestone KT15 2EP; Tel (0193 28) 565523; R. Bailess

County Music Centres

Surrey County Music Centre, Hoefield County Middle School, Bonsey La, Westfield, Woking GU22 9PU; Tel (0148 62) 27634; *Head of Country Music Dept* P. Gorman, LTCL
Tandridge County Music Centre, de Stafford County Secondary School, Burntwood La, Caterham CR3 5YX; Tel (01883) 44709; A. Massey, GTCL, LTCL
Elmbridge and Mole Valley County Music Centre, Therfield School, Dilston Rd, Leatherhead KT22 7NZ; Tel (01372) 370294; M. Lovell, ARMC
Reigate County Music Centre, Reigate College, Castlefield Rd, Reigate RH2 0SA; Tel (0173 72) 240607; M.H. Hensor, BMus, GRSM, ARCM
South West Surrey County Music Centre, Adult Education Centre, 6 Gosden Common, Bramley, Guildford, Surrey; Tel (01483) 894379; I. Morrish, BA, FTCL, ARCM, LTCL, LRAM
Staines County Music Centre, Adult Education Centre, 36 Kingston Rd, Staines TW18 4LN; Tel (01784) 463844
Woking County Music Centre Woking College, Rydens Way, Woking GU22 9DL; Tel (0148 62) 761039; D. Hamilton, MIL, ARCM

Grant Maintained Schools

All Hallows Catholic School, Weybourne Rd, Farnham, Surrey GU9 9HF; Tel (01252) 319211; *Headteacher* J.V. Madden, BA, MEd, FRSA, JP. (11–18 Year Olds)
The Beacon Grant Maintained School, Picquets Way, Banstead SM7 1AG; Tel (0173 73) 359103; Fax (0173 73) 359867; J.M. Darker, MA, MEd, FRSA. (849)
Collingwood College, Kingston Rd, Camberley GU15 4AE; Tel (01276) 64048; Fax (01276) 676151; *Principal* P.G. Halls-Dickerson, MA, FRSA, FCollP; Sponsored by the Garfield Weston Foundation, GTI Education System, Orade Corporation (UK) and Motorola. (Mixed) (11–18) (2049)
de Stafford, Burntwood La, Caterham CR3 5YX; Tel (01883) 347818; Fax (01883) 343194; C. Gribben, MA, BEd. (600)
Epsom and Ewell High School, Ruxley La, West Ewell, Surrey KT19 9JW; Tel 0181-397 0671; Fax 0181-397 0724; J. Merrigan. (Mixed) (11–18) (919)
Gordon's School West End, Woking GU24 9PT; Tel (01276) 858084; Fax (01276) 855335; *Headteacher* Edward Firth; *Chair of Governors* Brian Carlisle. Boarding and Day) (Mixed 11–16 (315)
Guildford County School, Farnham Rd, Guildford, Surrey GU2 5LU; Tel (01483) 504089; Fax (01483) 300849; *Headmaster* D.N. Smith; *Chair of Governors* Dr D. Cook; *Administrator* N. Pitt. (Mixed) (11–18) (930)
Heathside School (Grant Maintained), Brooklands La, Weybridge KT13 8UZ; Tel (01932) 846162; G.A. Willoughby; *Chairman of Governors* M. Norman, MBE. (820)
Rosebery White Horse Dr, Epsom KT18 7NQ; Tel (0137 27) 720439/723596; H.K. Saunders. (Girls) (1140)
St John the Baptist School, Elm Bridge La, Woking GU22 9AL; Tel (01483) 729343; Fax (01483) 727578; *Headteacher* B.E. McCarthy; *Chair of Governors* J. Sylvester. (Mixed) (11–18) (820)
St Paul's Catholic School, The Ridings, Green St, Sunbury-on-Thames, Middx TW16 6NX; Tel (01932) 783811; Fax (01932) 786485; E.J. Kaye, BSc, AdvDipEd, CBiol, MIBiol. (11–18) (850)
Thamesmead Manygate La, Shepperton TW17 9EE; Tel (01932) 227078; Fax (01932) 244300. (Grant Maintained) (11–16 Mixed Secondary)

Technology Colleges

Collingwood College,Sponsored by the Garfield Weston Foundation, GTi Education Systems, Oracle Corporation (UK) and Motorola Kingston Rd, Camberley GU15 4AE; Tel (01276) 64048; Fax (01276) 676151; *Principal* P.G. Halls-Dickerson, MA, FRSA, FCollP; *Chair of Governors* D. Tiplady, BA(Hons), FRICS. (Mixed) (11–18) (2049)

ADT Technology School,Sponsored by the ADT Group The Kingsway, Ewell, Epsom KT17 1NB; Tel 0181-394 2955; Fax 0181-786 7668; *Headteacher* Stuart Turner; Audrey Cooper. (Boys) (11–18) (1200)

Tameside Metropolitan Borough Council

Population 218,043
Council Offices, Wellington Rd, Ashton-under-Lyne OL6 6DL; Tel 0161-342 3200; Fax 0161-342 3260

Education Department

Council Offices, Wellington Rd, Ashton-under-Lyne, Tameside OL6 6DL; Tel 0161-330 8355
Chairman Councillor P.J. Joinson
Deputy Chairman Councillor Brodie
Director of Education A.M. Webster, BA
Principal Adviser Secondary and Ofsted K.W. Carnaffan, MA(Hons)
Assistant Director (Resource Services) K.J. Cackett, MEd, BSc(Econ)
Assistant Director (Student and Community Services) M.M. Jolly, BA(Hons)
SEO (Strategic Development) A. Melville, BSc(Hons)
EO (Strategic Development) R. Muller
EO (Strategic Development) H.M. Grace
EO (Governance) N.C. Little, AdvDipEd
EO (Community Education) S. Colman
EO (Careers and Business Education) M.I. Lemecha, BA, DipYestb
EO (Personnel and Office Services) J. White (Job Share)
EO (Special) Dr G. Price
AEO (Personnel) M. Forrest
AEO (Student/Special Services) S. Grimshaw
AEO (Student/Special Services) A. Carriline
AEO (Student/Special Services) A.T. Simpkins
AEO (Strategic Development) R. Higson
Principal Education Welfare Officer C. Platt
Principal Educational Psychologist R.H. Bushell, MSc(EdPsychol)
Client Catering Manager C.J. Swailes
Principal Officer (Finance/Employee Unit) J. Hayes
Principal Officer (Finance and Employee Unit) T. Boyle
PAO Inservice Training C. Tapper
Senior Adviser Primary and Ofsted B. Griffiths
Senior Adviser (Curriculum Assessment) Vacancy
Senior Adviser Management and Vocational Education R.S. Moxon, BA(Econ), MA
Senior Adviser (Professional Development) Vacancy
Headteacher Adviser Vacancy
General Adviser Humanities M. Smith, BA, MA
Physical and Health Education Vacancy
Mathematics Adviser Vacancy
General Adviser Primary and Early Years E. Petrie
General Adviser Primary, Appraisal and PE S. Noble
General Adviser Special Educational Needs Dr G. Price, BSc, PhD
Primary/Early Years Adviser Vacancy
General Adviser Modern Languages and Multicultural Education R. Garside
General Adviser Creative Arts D. Bell
General Adviser Science Design & Technology G. Ashford
General Adviser INSET M. Wall
General Adviser English and Learning Resources C. Threllfall
General Adviser Assessment and PSE J. Saunders
Adviser Information Technology U. Daniels
Adviser Business and Careers Education I. Chambers
TVEI Adviser G. Saunders
Co-ordinator for Language in the National Curriculum A. Goddard
Area Health Authority Community Physician (Child Health) M. Roxby, MB, ChB, MFCM, DPH
Education Development Centre Manager N. Sullivan
Library and Information Officer L. Parkin
Community Languages Co-ordinator M. Mehta
Community Languages Teacher S. Khan
Advisory Teacher (Mathematics) W. Blaszczok
Advisory Teacher (Sex Education Co-ordinator) J. Farrell
Advisory Teacher (Information Technology (Primary) A. McCann
Advisory Teacher (Assessment, Recording and Reporting (Primary) P. Walker
Advisory Teacher (Science Design and Technology (Primary) A. Clayton
Advisory Teacher (P.E.) A. Ayin

Number of Schools
3 nursery; 81 primary; 15 secondary (comprehensive); 8 adult education centres/evening institutes; 1 education development centre

Special Schools
2 moderate learning; 2 severe learning; 2 emotional and behavioural difficulties; 1 hospital and home education

Day of Committee Meeting
Tuesdays every five weeks

Requisition Periods for School Supplies
To end of January

Other Authorities with whom Joint Purchasing Arrangements are made
Greater Manchester Purchasing Consortium

Governor Training Unit

Governor Services (Room 2.40), Education Department, Council Offices, Wellington Rd, Ashton-under-Lyne, Tameside OL6 6DL; Tel 0161-342 3218; Fax 0161-342 3260
EO (Governance and Training) N.C. Little, AdvDipEd

Services Offered
Clerking Service for Governing Body Meetings; Technical and procedural support; Briefing Papers; Co-ordination/Delivery of LEA based Governor Training; Co-ordination of Headteacher/Governor Conferences; Support Networks a. Link Governors; b. Black/Asian Governors; c. Chairs/Headteachers; Distance Learning Materials; Access to National Governor Support Organisations

Child Guidance Clinic

Staveley Clinic Health Centre, Stamford St, Stalybridge, Greater Manchester; Tel 0161-338 2278; Dr Davenport; Dr Bowers

Special Schools

Cromwell, Thornley La South, Reddish, Stockport SK5 6QW; Tel 0161-320 8728; I.J.W. Selkirk. SLD (52)

Dale Grove, Wilshaw La, Ashton-under-Lyne OL7 9RF; Tel 0161-330 7595; J. Cousil (Acting), BSc, MSc. (For children with emotional and behavioural difficulties)(Secondary) (32)

Hawthorns, Corporation Rd, Audenshaw M34 5LZ; Tel 0161-336 3389; J.M. Shore, MEd, MSc. (MLD) (109)

Oakdale, Infant Site, Manchester Rd, Ashton-under-Lyne OL7 0EF; Tel 0161-370 3717; I. Howard, BEd. (SLD) (45)

Junior Site, Grange Rd, Hyde, Cheshire SK14 5NU; Tel 0161-368 1718; I. Howard, BEd. (SLD) (42)

Samuel Laycock, Mereside, Stalybridge SK15 1JF; Tel 0161-303 1321; D.W. Lewis, BA. (for children with moderate learning difficulties) (Secondary) (118)
Tameside Hospital School, General Hospital, Darnton Rd, Ashton-under-Lyne OL6 9RW; Tel 0161-330 8373 Ext 208; M. Knight (Acting)

Tutorial Centre

Bankside, Manchester Rd, Droylsden, Tameside M35 6PW; Tel 0161-370 4210; M. Yearn (Acting). (For children with emotional and behavioural difficulties) (17)

Comprehensive Schools (County 11–16)

Copley County High, Huddersfield Rd, Stalybridge SK15 3RR; Tel 0161-338 6684; J. Joyce, BA. (Mixed) (698)
Droylsden County High, Manor Rd, Droylsden, Tameside M35 6QD; Tel 0161-370 2777; J.B. Wilson, BA, MEd. Girls (812)
Dukinfield Astley High, Yew Tree La, Dukinfield SK16 5BL; Tel 0161-338 2374; J.L. Mayes, BA, MEd. Mixed (626)
Egerton Park County High, Egerton St, Denton, Tameside M34 3PB; Tel 0161-336 2039; J.D. Hart. Mixed (498)
Hartshead County High, Greenhurst Rd, Ashton-under-Lyne OL6 9DX; Tel 0161-330 4965; Mrs A.D.B. Ford, BA, MSc. Mixed
Hattersley County High, Fields Farm Rd, Hattersley, Hyde SK14 3NP; Tel 0161-368 5132; A. Leyland, BEd. Mixed (523)
Hyde County High, Old Rd, Hyde SK14 4SP; Tel 0161-368 1353; B.J. Cooke, BSc, MEd. Mixed (872)
Littlemoss County High, Cryer St, Littlemoss, Droylsden, Tameside M35 7LF; Tel 0161-370 3334; R. Coe, BA, MSc. Boys (518)
Longdendale County High, Spring St, off Market St, Hollingworth SK14 8LW; Tel (014576) 4006; D.R. Matthews, MA. Mixed (813)
Mossley Hollins County High, Huddersfield Rd, Mossley OL5 9DL; Tel (014575) 2491; J. Ainsworth, BEd. Mixed (689)
Stamford County High, Mossley Rd, Ashton-under-Lyne OL6 9SD; Tel 0161-330 7437; P.J. Beetlestone, BSc. (Mixed) (886)
Two Trees County High, Two Trees La, Denton, Tameside M34 1QL; Tel 0161-336 2719; M.H. Boysen. (Mixed) (1088)

Comprehensive Schools (Voluntary Aided 11–18)

All Saints R.C. High, Kenyon Ave, Dukinfield SK16 5AR; Tel 0161-338 2120; T. Atkinson, BA. (Mixed) (538)
St Damian's R.C. High, Lees Rd, Ashton-under-Lyne OL6 8BH; Tel 0161-330 5974; P.E. Jackson, BA, MEd. (Mixed) (587)
St Thomas More R.C. High, Town La, Denton, Tameside M34 1AF; Tel 0161-336 2743; J.B. Riley, BA. (Mixed) (521)

Education Development Centre

Tameside Education Development Centre, Lakes Rd, Dukinfield, Greater Manchester; Tel 0161-330 1375; *Manager* N. Sullivan

Adult Education Department

Warrington Hse Church St, Ashton-under-Lyne, Lancs OL6 7PR; Tel 0161-330 2878; M. Ward

Music Centre

Library E.D.O., Lakes Rd, Dukinfield, Lancashire; Tel 0161-330 1375; G.R. Calcutt

Youth and Community Centres

Longdendale, Cannon St, Hollingworth Hyde, Cheshire SK14 8LR; Tel (014577) 64099; S. Mardy
Mossley, Roughtown Rd, Mossley, Ashton-under-Lyne OL5 0SG; Tel (01457) 2361; P. Ainsworth
Broadoak, Broadoak Rd, Ashton-under-Lyne, Lancs OL6 8RP; Tel 0161-339 2302; D. Entwistle
West End, John St, Ashton-under-Lyne, Lancs OL7 0QY; Tel 0161-339 2728; Arlene Lomax
Newton St Community Centre, Newton St, Ashton-under-Lyne OL6 6EJ; Tel 0161-344 0115; S. Ayoub
Denton (Entitlement Unit), Duke St, Denton, Tameside, Greater Manchester; Tel 0161-337 68316; G. Francis
Haughton Green, Lancaster Rd, Haughton Grn, Denton, Tameside M34 1JP; Tel 0161-320 5658; C. Bates
Fairfield, Grove St, Droylsden, Tameside M35 6AJ; Tel 0161-370 1383; P. Briscoe
Moorside, Lees Park, Cedar Dr, Droylsden, Tameside M35 7DU; Tel 0161-301 1320; P. Briscoe
Beyer Peacock, Kershaw La, Audenshaw, Tameside M34 5WS; Tel 0161-301 3520; Janet Taylor
Youth Adventure Tameside, Vicarage Dr, Dukinfield SK16 5LE; Tel 0161-338 2013; Bev Knowles
Hattersley, Hattersley Rd East, Hattersley, Hyde, Cheshire SK14 3EQ; Tel 0161-368 8513; M. Cuffy
Hyde, Lower Bennett St, Hyde, Cheshire SK14 4PP; Tel 0161-368 6372; P. Jones
Hyde Bangladeshi Youth Group, C/o Training and Resources Centre, Greenfield St School, Jackson St, Hyde SK14 1BX; Tel 0161-344 3666; Sanjay Patel
Youth Action Tameside, 45 Clarendon Pl, Hyde, Greater Manchester; Tel 0161-368 1145
Hyde Shapla, 19 Chapel St, Hyde SK14 1JB; Tel 0161-368 1349; E. Hill
Copley Youth and Community Centre, Demesne Dr, Huddersfield Rd, Stalybridge, Cheshire SK15 2QG; Tel 0161-338 6230; G. Harrison

Grant Maintained Schools

Audenshaw High School, Hazel St, Audenshaw, Tameside M34 5NB; Tel 0161-330 2133
Fairfield High School for Girls (Grant Maintained) Fairfield Ave, Droylsden, Manchester; Tel 0161-370 1488; Fax 0161-371 1620
West Hill County High, Thompson Cross, Stalybridge SK15 1LX; Tel 0161-338 2193; L. Hill. Boys (698)

Trafford Metropolitan Borough Council

Population 217,800
Sale Town Hall, Tatton Rd, Sale, Greater Manchester M33 1YR; Tel 0161-872 2101; Fax 0161-969 8023
Director of Education A. Lee, BA

Education Department

Town Hall, Tatton Rd, Sale, Greater Manchester M33 1YR; Tel 0161-872 2101; Fax 0161-969 8023
Director of Education A. Lee, BSc
ADEO (Client Services) J. Waddington, BA
ADEO (Establishment Services) R.G. Totty
ADEO (Resources) R.D. Else, FCISA, DMA
AEO (Staffing) K. Wilkinson
AEO (Governing Bodies) D. Houghton
AEO (Development) R.G. Sigee
AEO (Monitoring/Evaluation) A. Southworth
AEO (Financial Management) J. Samuels
AEO (Supplies and Services) A.A. Warrington
AEO (Awards and Admissions) R.G. Wise
AEO (Careers) G. Derbyshire

AEO (Youth) M. White
AEO (Special Needs) M. Ellis
AEO (Special Needs) S. Roberts
Senior General Adviser (Primary Education) P. Noden
Senior General Adviser (Secondary Education) E. Ruding, BSc
General Adviser (Primary) A.H. Markham, BSc, MEd
General Adviser (Primary) Vacancy
General Adviser (Special Educational Needs) S. Shoesmith
Specialist Adviser (Mathematics) P.V. Fletcher, BSc
Specialist Adviser (Modern Languages) C.J. Hurren
Specialist Adviser (Science) M. McLeod, BSc, MEd
Specialist Adviser (Arts/Design/Tech Studies) M. Stevenson, MA
Specialist Adviser (Drama/English Literature) G.G. Jones, BA
Specialist Adviser (Music) R.M. Coulthard, BA, FRCO
Specialist Adviser (Physical Education) J.E. Wild
Specialist Adviser (Humanities) L. Heath
Senior Educational Psychologist T. Cooke, BSc, DipEdPsych
Educational Psychologist D.J. Moss, BSc, DipEdPsych, ABPsS, CertEd
Educational Psychologist C.W. Bate, BSc, MEd(EdPsych)
Educational Psychologist A.R Wells
Catering Officer A. Cerisola
Cleaning Services Manager M. Greenwood
Number of Schools
78 primary (16,661); 5 secondary grammar; 10 secondary high; 1 secondary comprehensive (total 11,424); 9 youth centres
Special Schools
3 L.D; 2 S.L.D; 1 P.D; 1 E.B.D.
Committee Meeting
4 weekly cycle

Education Committee

Con 12, Lab 7, LD 1
Chair D.F. Silverman, (Con) 14 Hollywood, Bowdon, Altrincham WA14 2LL
Vice-Chair H. Walker, (Con) 6 Cressingham Rd, Stretford M32 9DW
Members of the Committee
Con: D.R. Baldwin, A. Bowker, K. Bullock, P.A. Dixon, R. Godwin, R. Nicholas, T.R. Seddon, B. Sharp, J. Taylor, OBE, MBIM, MIDPM
Lab: D. Acton, M.E. Atherton, BA, J.E. Beugh, MCSP, SRP, P.W. Mitchell, MA, PhD, DIL, MInstP, CPhys, S. Rogers, BA(Hons), J. Williams, BA(Hons)
LD: B.V. Ackroyd, BA

Governor Training Unit

Trafford M.B.C., PO Box 19, Town Hall, Tatton Rd, Sale, Trafford M33 1YR; Tel 0161-875 0828; Fax 0161-969 0823
Assistant Education Officer (Governing Bodies) D. Houghton, MIPM
Services Offered
Comprehensive governor training programme; Governor Support and Advice service; Termly Newsletter; Helpline; Resource Centres; Distance Learning packages

Special Schools

Brentwood, Brentwood Ave, Timperley, Altrincham, Greater Manchester; Tel 0161-928 8109; B. Hayter
Delamere, Irlam Rd, Flixton, Stretford, Greater Manchester; Tel 0161-747 5893; D.J. Quaife, BEd
Grove, Grove La, Timperley, Altrincham, Greater Manchester; Tel 0161-980 3112; I. Jeffrey
Longford Park, Longford Pk, Stretford, Greater Manchester; Tel 0161-881 2341; M.G. Coxe DipE(Special)
Parklands, Kingsway Pk, Davyhulme, Urmston, Greater Manchester; Tel 0161-748 5318; M.D. McGuirk
Pictor, Harboro Rd, Sale, Greater Manchester; Tel 0161-962 5432; B.R. Kinnloy (Acting)
Priory, Urban Rd, Sale, Greater Manchester; Tel 0161-973 4619; A. Eales, BEd

Secondary High Schools

Flixton, Urmston; Tel 0161-748 3512; P. Swain, MA. (Girls) (884)
Green Lane, Altrincham; Tel 0161-980 7173; M. Lloyd, BA. (Mixed) (551)
Lostock, Stretford; Tel 0161-865 6215; E. Smallridge, BSc. (Mixed) (929)
St Anthony's R.C., Tel 0161-748 4571; J.V. Glennon. (Mixed) (433)
Stretford High, Tel 0161-876 4734; J. Atkinson. (Mixed) (586)
Wellacre, Urmston; Tel 0161-748 5011; D. Swallow. (Boys) (518)

Grammar Schools

Altrincham Tel 0161-928 0827; D.H. Welsh. Girls (859)
Altrincham Tel 0161-928 0858; B. Purvis. (Boys) (715)
Sale, Tel 0161-973 3217; J.E. Connelly. (1230)
Stretford, Stretford; Tel 0161-865 2293; P.E.E. Revill, MA. (Mixed) (546)
Urmston, Tel 0161-748 2875; M. Holland, MSc, BSc. (797)

Comprehensive School

Partington Broadoak Comprehensive, Tel 0161-776 1977; W. Redman, MA. (442)

Grant Maintained Schools

Ashton-on-Mersey, Sale, Greater Manchester; Tel 0161-973 1179; D.A. Horsefield. (Mixed) (900)
Blessed Thomas Holford R.C. Altrincham; Tel 0161-928 6020; L.F. Harris. (639)
The New Wellington, Altrincham; Tel 0161-928 4157; J.A. Knowles. (Mixed) (950)
Sale Moor Tel 0161-973 2713; G. Howarth. (558)

Tyne and Wear Metropolitan Area

The following Metropolitan Councils comprise the Tyne and Wear Metropolitan Area and may be found in alphabetical order within this chapter:
Gateshead, Newcastle upon Tyne, North Tyneside, South Tyneside, Sunderland.

Wakefield Metropolitan District Council

Population 317,533
Town Hall, Wood St, Wakefield WF1 2HQ; Tel (01924) 300900; Fax (01924) 305113

Education Department

County Hall, Wakefield WF1 2QL; Tel (01924) 300900; Fax (01924) 305632
Chair Cllr R. Mitchell
Deputy Chair Cllr O. Rowley
Chief Education Officer J. McLeod, MA
Head of School and Community Services and Deputy Chief Education Officer P.W. May, BSc
Head of Education Finance K. Jones, Bsc, IPFA
Education Officer (School and Governor Support) D. Bowen, MA
EO (Pupil and Student Support) S. Chew, BA, DipEd
EO (LMS Development) N. Diamond, MPhil
EO (Special Needs) E.A. Godman, BSc, MEd
EO (Planning and Development) P. Mosby, LLB, ACIS
EO (Administration) K. Watson, ACIS
EO (Personnel) T.J. Young
Project Officer (Area Reviews and Reorganisations) J. Haigh, BA
Pupil Services Officer G. Naylor, BSc
Special Needs Officer H.V. Constantine, BA
Head of Research and Information Services L.A. Aisthorpe, BEd, MEd, MBA
Chief Adviser L. Goodhand (Acting), BSc, AdvDipEd
Senior Adviser and Head of Inspection Services J. Storey
Advisory and Inspection Service Co-ordinator J. Lindley, BA, MEd
Adviser (Modern Languages, Equal Opportunities) D. Barraclough, BA
Adviser (Primary/Early Years) D. Bluett
Adviser (Primary) A. Farrell
Adviser (Primary) M. Gallagher, DipPrimEd
Adviser (Music) G. Gaunt
Adviser (Special Educational Needs) L. Mitchell, BA, MA, DipSE
Adviser (Religious Education, Collective Worship Assessment) S. Hart, BEd
Adviser (Technology) S. Horridge
Adviser (Primary) R. Hunter, MA
Adviser (Personnel and Social Education Careers Education, Vocational Education, Health Education, Business Education) S. MacLeod
Adviser (Humanities; Economics; Environmental Studies; Geography; History; Sociology) C. Parker, BA
Adviser (Primary) D. Peckett
Adviser (Primary) J. Rutherford
Adviser (Science IT) J. Smith, BSc, CBiol, MIBiol, DPSE
Adviser (Art and Design) E. Snaith, BA
Adviser (Mathematics) A. Wigley, BSc
Adult and Community Education Officer P. Elliott, BA
Principal Youth Officer L. Baynes
Principal Careers Officer M.W. Fox, DipCG
Principal Education Welfare Officer E. Dews, CQSW
Principal Educational Psychologist I.W.M. Filtness, BSc
Educational Psychologist C. Borman, BSc, MEd, PGCE
Educational Psychologist C. Dale, BA, MSc, PGCE
Educational Psychologist V. Goddard
Educational Psychologist K. Howie, BA
Educational Psychologist H. Hughes
Educational Psychologist F. Law, MSc
Educational Psychologist J. Smith, BSc, MEd
Educational Psychologist K. Underwood, BA, MSc, PGCE
DSO Manager (Cleaning/Catering) D. Hail
DSO Manager (Catering) D. Northrop

Number of Schools
5 nursery (239 PT); 104 primary (21,327 FT 3,136 PT); 24 first schools (4,072 FT 1,225 PT); 13 middle (3,287); 19 secondary (17,738)

Special Schools
7 day (532); 1 boarding (44); 2 hospital (73)

Education Committee

Lab 33, Con 3, Ind 1
Chair R. Mitchell, (Lab) 3 Agbrigg Rd, Wakefield WF2 6AA
Deputy-Chair O.M. Rowley, (Lab) 160 Agbrigg Rd, Wakefield WF1 5BY

Members of the Committee
Lab: K. Bollard, P.G.H. Box, T. Brennan, G. Burton, G. Bryne JP, G. Clarke, R.P. Clarkson, V. Cliffe BSc, DipTE, R.J. Cook, C.L. Croxall JP, A. Dean, R. Eggett, L. Harrison, N. Hartshorne, C.A. Heinitz, D. Hitchen, F. Hodgson, N. Kennedy, J. Kershaw, D. Lund, P. McNeill, R. Mitchell (Chair), H. Myers, J.V. Newsome, C. Oldroyd, J. Perry, O.M. Rowley (Deputy Chair), G. Stokes, D.S. Thompson, P. Townend, J. Walkden, E. Wrigglesworth, P. Wroe
Con: K. Blackburn, N.J. Hazell MBE, D. Hopkins
Ind: D. Price

Hospital Special Schools

Pinderfields, Aberford Rd, Wakefield WF1 4DG; Tel (01924) 377458; K. Gaukroger
Stanley Fieldhead, Ouchthorpe La, Wakefield WF1 3SP; Tel (01924) 381780; J.D. Mellor

Special Day Schools

The Castle, Poplar Ave, Townville, Castleford WF10 3QT; Tel (01977) 554254; P. Gawthorpe
Green Leas, Green La, Carleton, Pontefract WF8 3NW; Tel (01977) 797872; S.R. Mulligan
Hill Top, Kershaw Ave, Airedale, Castleford WF10 3ES; Tel (01977) 552940; N. Wainwright
Hollygarth, Wakefield Rd, Hemsworth, Pontefract WF9 4AB; Tel (01977) 611408; M. Sharp
The Park, Lawefield La, Wakefield WF2 8SX; Tel (01924) 370971; A.M. Shorter
Roundwood Hill, St Georges Rd, Lupset, Wakefield WF2 8BB; Tel (01924) 364195; M. Smith
West Hall, Aberford Rd, Stanley, Wakefield WF3 4BA; Tel (01924) 822422; D.W. Brown

Special Boarding School

Moor Top, Barnsley Rd, Ackworth, Pontefract WF7 7DT; Tel (01924) 611869; T.R. Howe

Comprehensive Schools

Airedale High, Crewe Rd, Airedale, Castleford WF10 3JU; Tel (01977) 553766; J.P. Dickens. (881)
Castleford High, Ferrybridge Rd, Castleford WF10 4JQ; Tel (01977) 558701; D.R. Earnshaw. (980)
Crofton High, High St, Crofton, Wakefield WF4 1NF; Tel (01924) 862201; J.M. Myers. (630)
Wakefield City High, Warmfield View, Eastmoor, Wakefield WF1 4SF; Tel (01924) 376519; A. Yellup. (541)
Featherstone High, Pontefract Rd, Purston, Featherstone WF7 5AJ; Tel (01924) 795161; A.R. Warden. (636)
Featherstone St Wilfrid's R.C. High, Cutsyke Rd, North Featherstone, Pontefract WF7 6BD; Tel (01977) 792228; C.P. Cotton. (1404)
Hemsworth High, Station Rd, Hemsworth, Pontefract WF9 4HW; Tel (01977) 610366; R. Dunn. (1067)
Horbury, Wakefield Rd, Horbury, Wakefield WF4 5HE; Tel (01924) 272551; M.A. Walsh. (1120)
Kettlethorpe High, Standbridge La, Sandal, Wakefield WF2 7EL; Tel (01924) 250696; B. Tapson. (1401)
The King's High, Mill Hill La, Pontefract WF8 4JF; Tel (01977) 703631; V.S. Kenningham. (866)
Knottingley High, Middle La, Knottingley WF11 0BZ; Tel (01977) 672859; R. Edwards. (819)
Minsthorpe High, Minsthorpe La, South Elmsall, Pontefract WF9 2UJ; Tel (01977) 644141; G.J. Evans. (897)
Normanton Freeston High, Favell Ave, Normanton WF6 1HZ; Tel (01924) 892234; M. Anderson. (925)
North Ossett High, Gawthorpe La, Gawthorpe, Ossett, WF5 9BS; Tel (01924) 271498; S.J.W. Cox. (273)
Ossett, Storrs Hill Rd, Ossett, Wakefield WF5 0DG; Tel (01924) 273356/7; P. Limbert. (1264)
Outwood Grange, Potovens La, Outwood, Wakefield WF1 2PF; Tel (01924) 823181; G.A. Smith. (1986)
Pontefract Carleton High, Green La, Carleton, Pontefract WF8 3NW; Tel (01977) 703263; Rev M.C. Wright. (873)

St Thomas à Becket R.C., Barnsley Rd, Sandal, Wakefield WF2 6EQ; Tel (01924) 250408; P. Oldroyd (Acting Head). (716)
Wakefield The Cathedral School, C/o Thornes Hse, Thornes Pk, Wakefield WF2 8PW; Tel (01924) 372681; *Head* S. Martin. (794)

Pupil Support Services

Ethnic Minority Support Service, Manygates Education Centre, Manygates La, Sandal, Wakefield WF2 7DQ; Tel (01924) 255024; M. Kaur Jones
Flanshaw Education Unit, 6 Springfield Grange, Off Flanshaw La, Wakefield WF2 9QA; Tel (01924) 200348; M. Hirst
In School Support Service, 6 Springfield Grange, Off Flanshaw La, Flanshaw WF2 9QP; Tel (01924) 365711; R. DeCsernatony
Special Needs Support Service, The Crofton Cente, Pontefract Rd, Crofton, Wakefield WF4 1LL; Tel (01924) 862739; B. Young
Traveller Education Service, C/o Sandal Magna J&I School, Belle Vue Rd, Wakefield WF1 5LT; Tel (01924) 255409; C. Brown

Other Centres

Manygates Education Centre, Manygates La, Sandal, Wakefield WF2 2DQ; Tel (01924) 255361; P. Elliott
Wakefield Information Technology Support for Schools Unit, Crofton Old Hall, High St, Crofton, Wakefield; Tel (01924) 865277; Alan Horner
Westfield Resource and Enterprise Centre, Westfield La, South Elmsall WF9 2PU; Tel (01977) 645141; M. Brown
Woolley Hall College, Woolley, Wakefield WF4 2JR; Tel (01226) 382500; *Director* S. Hughes; Teachers Centres; Residential Colleges; Conference Venues

Joint Services

Buckden Hse Outdoor Education Centre, Buckden, Skipton BD23 5JA; Tel (010756) 760254; *Head of Centre* R. Halsall
Clarke Hall, Aberford Rd, Wakefield WF1 4AL; Tel (01924) 375598; S.F. Martin
Education Resource Service, Resource Village, Painthorpe La, Crigglestone WF4 3LB; Tel (01924) 240999; *Director* E. Jones
Hornsea Centre, Hull Rd, Hornsea HU18 1RU; Tel (010964) 532106; *Warden* R. Hall

Walsall Metropolitan Borough Council

Population 263,000
Civic Centre, Darwall St, Walsall WS1 1RG; Tel (01922) 650000

Education Department

Civic Centre, Darwall St, Walsall WS1 1DQ; Tel (01922) 650000; Fax (01922) 722322
Chairman Cllr C.J.P. Wood
Vice-Chairman Cllr C.R. Beilby
Director of Education M.J. Quinn, BA
Policy Co-ordinator J. Round, BA
PEO (Further Education) J.W. Round
AEO (Schools) K.G. Ilett, BA, MEd
AEO (Administration and Finance) C.L. Harden
Chief Inspector Vacancy
AEO (Staffing) A. Meehan
Chief Inspector N. Barlow
Senior Inspector (Secondary) W.K. Baxendale, BA
Head of Pupil Support Services R.W. Hart, BSc, DipEdPsych
Senior Inspector (Primary) J.M. Dickens
General Inspector Miss J. Brookes
General Inspector K. Allison
General Inspector W.S. Houghton-Hill
General Inspector Mrs M.T. Woodcock
General Inspector Mrs M.P.G. Crawford
General Inspector M.C. Dobson
General Inspector Mrs K. Macfarlane
General Inspector H. Smith
Teacher Adviser (Art and Craft) K.H. Jeavons
Teacher Adviser (Outdoor Education) J.G.L. Miller
Teacher Adviser (Home Economics) Miss R. Robinson
Adult Education Organiser J. Lawton
Catering Contracts Manager T. Morgan
Principal Educational Psychologist C.J. Reeve, BSc
Chief Education Welfare Officer W.R. Carter
TVEI Co-ordinator K.G. Worley

Number of Schools
8 nursery (109 FT, 683 PT); 106 primary (27,811); 19 secondary (16,790)

Special Schools
8 day (530); 1 residential (21)

Day of Committee Meeting
Tuesday (every six weeks)

Requisition Period for School Supplies
April 1st (main); 31st March

Other Authorities with whom Joint Purchasing Arrangements are made
None

Governor Training Unit

Training for Governors, Education Department, Civic Centre, Darwall St, Walsall WS1 1DQ; Tel (01922) 652306; Fax (01922) 722322
Co-ordinator, Training for Governors Nick Dodds

Services Offered
Training support and development for governors and teachers. For details of a range of training, materials and services offered to clients outside Walsall schools contact Nick Dodds as above

Comprehensive Schools

Alumwell, Primley Ave, Walsall, West Midlands; Tel (01922) 720741; Miss S.M. Bradford. (930)
Barr Beacon, Old Hull La, Aldridge, West Midlands; Tel 0121-366 6600; D.M. Lobley. (1210)
Blue Coat C. of E., Birmingham St, Walsall, West Midlands; Tel (01922) 720558; A.D. Grounds. (1000)
Brownhills, Deakin Ave, Brownhills, West Midlands; Tel (01543) 452450; A. Jarrett. Mixed (650)
Darlaston, Herberts Pk Rd, Darlaston, West Midlands; Tel 0121-568 6767; M.A. Gibbons. Mixed (1150)
Frank F. Harrison County, Leamore La, Bloxwich, West Midlands; Tel (01922) 710620; R.W. Taylor. Mixed (550)
Joseph Leckie County, Walstead Rd West, Walsall, West Midlands; Tel (01922) 721071; B. Weston. Mixed (745)
Manor Farm, King George Cres, Rushall, Walsall, West Midlands; Tel (01922) 721271; F.A. Fieldhouse. Mixed (600)
Pelsall, Pelsall La, Rushall, Walsall, West Midlands; Tel (01922) 685884; D.J. Sebborn. Mixed (450)
Pool Hayes, Castle Dr, Willenhall, West Midlands; Tel (01902) 368221; P. Mitchell. Mixed (930)
St Francis of Assisi R.C., Erdington Rd, Aldridge, West Midlands; Tel Aldridge 743696; M.A. Moran. Mixed (570)
The Shelfield, Broad Way, High Heath, Pelsall, West Midlands; Tel (01922) 685777/8; A. Collins. Mixed (600)
Sneyd, Sneyd La, Bloxwich, Walsall, West Midlands; Tel (01922) 710298; L.T. Williams. Mixed (1160)

T.P. Riley County, Lichfield Rd, Bloxwich, West Midlands; Tel (01922) 710064; J. Bowman. Mixed (1200)
Willenhall, Furzebank Way, Willenhall, West Midlands; Tel (01902) 368221. Mixed (1405)

Careers Office
See chapter 17

Grant Maintained Schools
Aldridge Comprehensive School, Tynings La, Aldridge, Walsall, West Midlands WS9 0BG; Tel (01922) 743988; D. Gibbons. Mixed (1225)
Queen Mary's Grammar School, Sutton Rd, Walsall, West Midlands WS1 2PG; Tel (01922) 720696
Queen Mary's High School, Upper Forester St, Walsall, West Midlands WS4 2AE; Tel (01922) 721013
St Thomas More Catholic Comprehensive, Bilston La, Willenhall, West Midlands WV13 2JY; Tel (01902) 368798; J.J. O'Donoghue. Mixed (1252)
Shire Oak Grant Maintained Community School, Lichfield Rd, Walsall Wood, Walsall, West Midlands WS9 9PA; Tel (01543) 452618; C.M. Bryan. Mixed (610)

Warwickshire County Council

Population 484,400
Shire Hall, Warwick CV34 4RR; Tel (01926) 410410

Education Department
PO Box 24, 22 Northgate St, Warwick CV34 4SR; Tel (01926) 410410; Fax (01926) 412746
County Education Officer Eric Wood, MSc
Deputy County Education Officer Vacancy
SEO (Community Division) Jim Fitzgibbon
SEO (Policy and Planning) Brian Barnett, BA
Statutory Compliance Services, Principal Assistant County Treasurer J. Mann
Chief Inspector/Schools Team Manager Elizabeth Wylie, BSc(Econ)
Deputy Chief Inspector (Primary) Stella Blackmore, BA(Hons)
Senior Inspector (Equal Opportunities) Sam Sharma
Senior Inspector (Eastern Area and Mathematics) David Bristow, BA
General Inspector (Home & Family Education) Lyz Mitchell, MA
General Inspector (Physical Education) Sue Orton, BPhil
General Inspector (Music) Gary Jones, MA(Hons), DipEd
General Inspector (Primary) Paul Bennett, BEd, MEd
General Inspector (Primary) David Walker, BEd, MSc(pending)
General Inspector (Art) Malcolm W. Wray, DipArtEd
General Inspector (Design & Technology) Danny Owen, BEd
General Inspector (Early Childhood Education) Margaret Heard, BEd
General Inspector (Primary Phase) Mervyn Price, MA
General Inspector (Science) Christine Thompson, BSc
Senior Inspector (Business Studies 16–19) Dianna Turner, MEd
Senior Inspector (Southern Area and English) Shorn Walton, BA
SEN Inspector Christine Air
Number of Schools
9 nursery; 236 primary; 29 secondary

Special Schools
10 day; 2 residential; 1 day/residential
Day of Committee Meeting
Quarterly

Education Committee
Lab 15, Con 10, LD 5, Ind 1
Chair John Airey, (Lab) 29 Waverley Rd, Kenilworth CV8 1JL; Tel 0121-556 6000
Deputy Chair Alan J. Smith, (Lab) 1 Birch Gr, Birchmoor, Tamworth, Staffs B78 1AP
Members of the Committee
Lab: J.B. Beaumont, I.C. Bottrill, C.K.N. Browne, H.W. De'Ath, DL, L.W.Forsyth, R.J. Grant, F. McCarney, A.P. Marshall, M. Singh, B.W.J. Thomas, S.R. Tooth, D.I. Webster, T.R. White
Con: R.D. Bridgewater, J.F. Coggins, G.D. Collett, A.J. Farnell, M. Heatley, D.T. Jacques, P.L. Joslin, J.Lea, M.A. Sankey, M.M. Weddell
LD: C.C.L. Davis, S.A. Juned, D.F. Kohler, H.A. Thomas
Ind: C.B. Stuart

Central Area School Team
Education Office, Shire Hall, Warwick CV34 4XR; Tel (01926) 410410
Schools Officer Peter Thompson
Number of Schools
4 nursery; 60 primary; 6 secondary; 2 day special

Careers Offices
See chapter 17

Day Special Schools
Ridgeway, Montague Rd, Warwick CV34 5LW; Tel (01926) 491987; P.A. Flynn. (E.S.N.(S)
The Round Oak School and Support Service, Pound La, Lillington, Leamington Spa CV32 7RT; Tel (01926) 335566; Fax (01926) 886163; C. Danks. (E.S.N.)

Comprehensive Schools (County)
Aylesford, Shelley Ave, Warwick CV34 6LA; Tel (01926) 491342; Fax (01926) 494194; L.B. King. (Mixed)
Campion, Sydenham Dr, Leamington CV31 1QH; Tel (01926) 336123/14; Fax (01926) 336123; J.S. Hancock. (Mixed)
Kenilworth, Leyes La, Kenilworth CV8 2DA; Tel (01926) 59421/5; Fax (01926) 59426; Dr A.L. Begbie. (Mixed)
North Leamington, Park Rd, Leamington CV32 6LQ; Tel (01926) 338711/6; D. Hazeldine. (Mixed)
Southam, Welsh Rd West, Southam CV33 0JW; Tel (01926) 812560; Fax (01926) 815807; M.J. Thompson. (Mixed)

Comprehensive School (Voluntary)
Trinity R.C., Guy's Cliffe Ave, Leamington CV32 6NB; Tel (01926) 428416; Fax (01926) 337403; *Acting Head* V. Cutler. (Mixed); (V.A.)

Southern Area School Team
Schools' Officer C. Larvin Education Office, Shire Hall, Warwick CV34 4XR
Number of Schools
52 Primary, 8 Secondary, 2 Day Special

Day Special Schools
Lambert, Blue Cap Rd, Stratford upon Avon CV37 6TQ; Tel (01789) 266845; J. Hudson. (E.S.N.(S)
Marie Corelli, Drayton Ave, Stratford upon Avon CV37 9PT; Tel (01789) 205992; M.H. Cobb. (100)
River Hse, Stratford Rd, Henley-in-Arden, Solihull B95 6AD; Tel (01564) 792514; E. Armsden

Grammar School (County)

Stratford upon Avon, Grammar School for Girls, Shottery Manor, Stratford upon Avon CV37 9HA; Tel (01789) 293759; Fax (01789) 293759; R.A. Standbridge. (Girls)

Grammar School (Voluntary)

King Edward VI, Church St, Stratford upon Avon CV37 6HB; Tel (01789) 293351; Fax (01789) 873814; N.W.R. Mellon, MA. (Boys); (V.A.)

High Schools

Alcester, Gerrard Rd, Alcester B49 6QQ; Tel (01789) 762285; Fax (01789) 400095; A. Fothergill. (Mixed)
Henley-in-Arden, Stratford Rd, Henley-in-Arden B95 6AF; Tel (01564) 792364; Fax (01564) 792411; I.T. Jackson. (Mixed)
Kineton, Banbury Rd, Kineton CV35 0JX; Tel (01926) 640465; Fax (01926) 640872; P.D. Logan. (Mixed)
St Benedict's R.C., Kinwarton Rd, Alcester B49 6PX; Tel (01789) 762888; Fax (01789) 400192; T.P. Sara. (Mixed)
Stour Valley Community School, Darlingscote Rd, Shipston-on-Stour CV36 4DY; Tel (01608) 661833; Fax (01608) 663459; E. Dawson. (Mixed)
Stratford upon Avon, Alcester Rd, Stratford upon Avon CV37 9DH; Tel (01789) 268051; Fax (01789) 261919; S.M.E. Tomkins. (Mixed)

Eastern Area School Team

Education Office, Shire Hall, Warwick CV34 4XR
Schools Officer C. James, BSc
Number of Schools
46 primary; 5 secondary; 1 day special

Careers Offices

See chapter 17

Day Special Schools

Brooke, Merttens Dr, Rugby CV22 7AE; Tel (01788) 576145; Fax (01788) 576145; S. Cowen. (E.S.N.(S)
Tyntesfield, Overslade La, Rugby, Warks CV22 6DY; Tel (01788) 812324; *Head* T. Ashton-Jennings (Acting)

Grammar School (Voluntary)

Lawrence Sheriff, Clifton Rd, Rugby CV21 3AG; Tel (01788) 542074; Fax (01788) 567962; Dr R.H. Pogson, MA, PhD. (Boys) (V.A.)

Bilateral School

Ashlawn, Ashlawn Rd, Rugby CV22 5ET; Tel (01788) 573425/6; Fax (01788) 536159; P.A. Rossborough. (Mixed)

High School (County)

Bilton, Lawford La, Bilton, Rugby CV22 7JT; Tel (01788) 814299; Fax (01788) 521592; B.M. Lockwood. (Mixed)

High Schools (Voluntary)

Bishop Wulstan R.C., Oak St, off Dunchurch Rd, Rugby CV22 5EA; Tel (01788) 542928; I. Gordon
Harris C.E., Harris Dr, Overslade La, Rugby CV22 6EA; Tel (01788) 812549; Fax (01788) 816123; E.A. Stalker. (Mixed) (S.A.)

North School Team

Education Office, Shire Hall, Warwick CV34 4XR
Schools Officer D. Potter
Number of Schools
1 nursery; 30 primary; 3 secondary; 2 day special

Careers Offices

See chapter 17

Day Special Schools

Blythe, Packington La, Coleshill, Birmingham B46 3JE; Tel (01675) 463590; Fax (01675) 463584; J. Fathers. (E.S.N.(S)
Sparrowdale, Spon La, Grendon, Atherstone, Warks CV9 2PD; Tel (01827) 713436; B.R. Fitter. (E.S.N.)

Comprehensive Schools (County)

Coleshill, Coventry Rd, Coleshill, Birmingham B46 3EX; Tel (01675) 462435; J.R.R. Rochelle-Towle. (Mixed)
Kingsbury, Tamworth Rd, Kingsbury, Tamworth, Staffs B78 2LF; Tel (01827) 872316; *Head* E. Morgan (Acting). (Mixed)
Polesworth, Dordon Rd, Dordon, Tamworth, Staffs B78 1QT; Tel (01827) 892204; Fax (01827) 330667; M. Reyner. (Mixed)

Nuneaton and Bedworth Area School Team

Schools Officer D. Craddick
Number of Schools
4 nursery; 56 primary; 7 secondary; 3 day special; 1 residential special

Comprehensive Schools (County)

Alderman Smith, Radnor Dr, Stockingford, Nuneaton CV10 7PD; Tel (01203) 341134/5; Fax (01203) 375459; R. Gittins. (Mixed)
Etone, Leicester Rd, Nuneaton CV11 6AA; Tel (01203) 382008/373972; Fax (01203) 352320; D.O. Prior. (Mixed)
George Eliot, Raveloe Dr, Caldwell, Nuneaton CV11 4QP; Tel (01203) 347926; J.M. Wilson. (Mixed)
Higham La, Shanklin Dr, Higham La, Nuneaton CV10 0BJ; Tel (01203) 388123; Fax (01203) 370550; Dr R.T. Tetlow. (Mixed)
Manor Park, Beaumont Rd, Nuneaton CV11 5HJ; Tel (01203) 374099; *Head* C. Staley (Acting). (Mixed)
Nicholas Chamberlaine, Bulkington Rd, Bedworth, Nuneaton CV12 9EA; Tel (01203) 312308; Fax (01203) 643183; K. Scott. (Mixed)

Comprehensive School (Voluntary)

St Thomas More R.C., Greenmoor Rd, Nuneaton CV10 7EX; Tel (01203) 642400; Fax (01203) 353454; M. Moore. (S.A.) (Mixed)

Educational Development Service

Manor Hall, Sandy La, Leamington Spa CV32 6RD; *Director* C. Rhodes; Tel (01926) 413764; Includes Teacher Advisers (0926) 413702, Inter-cultural Curriculum Support Service (0926) 413734, Museum and Archive Education Service (0926) 412034, INSET Services Manager (0926) 413757, The Learning Company (0926) 413728, Manor Hall reception (0926) 413702, Warwickshire Educational Computing Centre (0926) 413741, Schools Library Service (Advice) (0926) 413758; For information about Teachers' Centre
Marle Hall Residential Centre, Tel (01492) 581218

Special Schools

Exhall Grange Special School, Wheelwright La, Coventry CV7 9HP; Tel (01203) 364200; Fax (01203) 645055; *Head* R.G. Bignall. (PS/PH) (230)
Leyland Special School, Leyland Rd, Nuneaton, Warks CV11 4RP; Tel (01203) 385313; *Head* K.R. Holt. (E.S.N.(S)
Red Deeps Special School, Coventry Rd, Nuneaton, Warks CV10 7AX; Tel (01203) 383315; *Head* R.A. Manchester (Acting). (Special)

St Margaret's Special School, Hurst Rd, Bedworth, Nuneaton, Warks CV12 8AD; Tel (01203) 315734; *Head* R.D. Worrall. (E.S.N.)

Grant Maintained Schools

Alcester Grammar School, Birmingham Rd, Alcester, Warks B49 5ED; Tel (01789) 762494; A.W. Shearn. Mixed

Avon Valley School, Newbold Rd, Rugby, Warks CV21 1EH; Tel (01788) 542355; Fax (01788) 572050; *Headteacher* Mark Braine; *Chair of Governors* Pamela Hill. (Mixed) (11–16) (360)

Hartshill Grant Maintained School, Church Rd, Hartshill, Nuneaton CV10 0NA; Tel (01203) 392237; *Headteacher* Ian Hecks; *Chair of Governors* Terry Redfern. (Mixed) (12–16) (670)

Myton, Myton Rd, Warwick CV34 6PJ; Tel (01926) 493805; Fax (01926) 490380; *Headteacher* J.A. Hewlett

Queen Elizabeth School Atherstone, Long St, Atherstone CV9 1AE; Tel (018277) 712477; T.G. Ledgard, MA. (Mixed)

Queen Elizabeth School, Witherley Rd, Atherstone, Warks CV9 1LZ; Tel (01827) 712477; Fax (01827) 715253

Rugby High for Girls, Longrood Rd, Bilton, Rugby CV22 7RE; Tel (01788) 810518; Fax (01788) 811794; M.D. Thornton. (Girls)

West Glamorgan County Council

Population 361,428 (1991 Census)
County Hall, Swansea SA1 3SN; Tel (01792) 471111; Fax (01792) 471340

Education Department

County Hall, Swansea SA1 3SN; Tel (01792) 471111; Fax (01792) 471642
Chairman Cllr D.T.V. Davies
Vice-Chairman Cllr W.P. Davies, JP
Director of Education H.G. Roberts, BA
Assistant Director (Operations/Support) M.N. De Val, BA, MEd
Assistant Director (Advisory Service/Quality Assurance) H.G. Roberts, BA
SEO (Resources/Budget/LMS) S.G. Evans
SEO (Resources/Evaluation/Collaboration) J.B.H. Davies, BSc
AEO (Further and Continuing Education) D.J. Banbury, BSc
AEO (Development/Funding) D.C. Merrey, DMA, FCIS
AEO (Support Services) Mrs P. Davies, BA
AEO (Client/Personnel Services) R.F. Lewis, BA
County Librarian B. Thomas, ALA
County Careers Officer K.H.J. Cook, DipVG
Adviser (Modern Languages) Mrs N. Griffiths
Adviser (English) C. Williams
Adviser (Welsh) M. Prys Jones
Adviser (Geography) A. Herdman
Adviser (History) A.G.B. Kelly
Adviser (TVEI) Mrs A.E. Thomas
Adviser (PE/Leisure) S. Lloyd
Adviser (Computer Education) P. Craddock
Head of Unit (Customer/Client Services) D.R. Sutherland
Section Leader (Human Resources/Client Services) Mrs E.C. Crawford
Senior Admin Officer (Human Resources/Client Services) P.R. Hopkins
Senior Admin Officer (Human Resources/Client Services) R. Evans
Section Leader (Central Admin/Special Needs) A.V. Jones
Senior Admin Officer (Central Admin/Special Needs) P. Hale
Head of Unit (Strategic Planning & Support) A. O'Brien
Section Leader (School Support & Evaluation) G.R. Young, BA, DMA
Senior Admin Officer (School Support & Evaluation) V. Edwards
Section Leader (Management Information & Resources) R.J. Price
Senior Admin Officer (Management Information & Resources) L. Lammas

Number of Schools
2 nursery; 168 primary; 26 comprehensive
Special Schools
5
Day of Committee Meeting
Thursday every sixth week
Requisition Periods for School Supplies
Mainly twice yearly
Other Authorities with whom Joint Purchasing Arrangements are made
Member of the Welsh Purchasing Consortium

Special Schools

Briton Ferry, Ynysmaerdy Rd, Briton Ferry SA11 2TL; Tel (01639) 813100; Mrs M. Scales

Dyfatty, Croft St, Swansea SA1 1QA; Tel (01792) 652388; J.T. Hall. (P.H.)

Penllergaer, Penllergaer Cross, Penllergaer, Swansea SA4 1AX; Tel (01792) 892221; H.A. Davies

Pen-y-bryn, Glasbury Rd, Morriston, Swansea SA6 7PA; Tel (01792) 799064; A.G. Williams. (E.S.N.)

Ysgol Hendre-Bryncoch, Bryncoch, Neath SA10 7TY; Tel (01639) 642786; C.G. White (Acting). (Boarding)

Comprehensive Secondary Schools

Birchgrove, Birchgrove Rd, Birchgrove, Swansea, W Glamorgan; V. Thomas. (619)

Bishopston, The Glebe, Bishopston, Swansea SA3 3JP; Tel (0144 128) 4121; Mrs B.J. Williams. (975)

Bishop Gore, De-la-Beche Rd, Sketty SA2 9RP; Tel (01792) 202983 and 208533; C. Suff. (1257)

Bishop Vaughan R.C. School, Mynydd Garn Lwyd Rd, Morriston SA6 7QG; Tel (01792) 772006; *Headteacher* J.H. Stone; *Chair of Governors* Father Morrissey. Mixed) (11–18 (920)

Cefn Hengoed, Caldicot Rd, Winch Wen SA1 7HX; Tel (01792) 775034/773464; T.G. Davies, MEd. (1036)

Cefn Saeson, Cimla, Neath SA11 3TA; Tel (01639) 635193/1635193; G.A. Burgess. (857)

Cwmtawe Upper, Pontardawe, Swansea SA8 4LE; Tel (01792) 863200; T.E.L. Jones Lower Gwaun-cae-Gurwen, Ammanford SA18 1UL; Tel (01269) 862213. (1089)

Cwrt-sart, Briton Ferry, Neath SA11 2ET; Tel (01639) 812206; K. Napieralla. (584)

Cymer Afan, Cymmer, Port Talbot SA13 2EL; Tel (01639) 850237; L.W. Williams. (430)

Dillwyn Llewelyn John St, Cockett, Swansea SA2 0FR; Tel (01792) 585570/582979; T.W. Hampson. (612)

Dwr-y-Felin Upper, Dwr-y-Felin Rd, Neath SA10 7RE; Tel (01639) 635161; Dr D.H. Stokes Der-y-Felin Lower, Longford, Neath Abbey SA10 7RF; Tel (01792) 812356. (1211)

Dyffryn Upper, Margam, Port Talbot SA13 2AN; Tel (01639) 884200; I.B. Hawkins Lower Talcennau Rd, Port Talbort SE13 1EP; Tel (01639) 886661. (778)

Dynevor, De-la-Beche St, Swansea SA1 3EU; Tel (01792) 460377; A. Smith. (476)

Glanafan Upper, Station Rd, Port Talbot SA13 1LZ; Tel (01639) 883964; G. Williams Lower Velindre, Port Talbot SA13 1BX; Tel (01639) 883852. (592)

Gowerton Upper, Cecil Rd, Gowerton SA4 3DL; Tel (01792) 873461; P.A. Green. (1091)

Llangatwg Upper, Cadoxton, nr Neath SA10 8DB; Tel (01639) 635195/642770; R.W. Skilton Lower, Seeven Sisters, nr Neath SA10 9AS; Tel (01639) 700388. (959)
Morriston Senior, Cwmrhydyceirw, Morriston SA6 6NH; Tel (01792) 797745; P. Washbrook. 13+ (986)
Mynyddbach, Heol Ddu, Treboeth SA5 7HP; Tel (01792) 771935/775543. Girls (653)
Olchfa, Gower Rd, Sketty SA2 7AB; Tel (01792) 201222; J.W. Booth. (1645)
Penlan, Heol Gwyrosydd, Penlan SA5 7BU; Tel (01792) 584018; J.H. Guy. Boys (631)
Pentrehafod Upper, Pentremawr Rd, Hafod, Swansea SA1 2NN; Tel (01792) 652068/652069; R. Samples, BA Pentnehfod Lower, Odo St, Hafod, Swansea; Tel (01792) 652714. (985)
Penyrheol, Pontarddulais Rd, Gorseinon SA4 2FG; Tel (01792) 894174; J. Evans, BA, DipEd, MEd. (896)
Pontarddulais, Caecerrig Rd, Pontarddulais SA4 1PD; Tel (01792) 884556; P.V. Wilcox. (652)
Sandfields, Southdown View, Port Talbot SA12 7AH; Tel (01639) 883852/884246; D.A. Winfield. (737)
St Joseph's R.C., Newton Ave, Port Talbot SA12 6EY; Tel (01639) 884305; Dr E. Jones, MA, JP. (743)
Ysgol Gyfun Gwyr, Talbot St, Gowerton SA4 3DB; Tel (01792) 872403; T.N. Daniel. (466)
Ysgol Gyfun Ystalyfera, Glan-yr-Afan, Ystalyfera, Swansea SA9 2JJ; Tel (01639) 842129/843632. (773)

West Midlands Metropolitan Area

The following Metropolitan Councils comprise the West Midlands Metropolitan Area and may be found in alphabetical order within this chapter:
Birmingham, Coventry, Dudley, Sandwell, Solihull, Walsall, Wolverhampton.

West Sussex County Council

Population 720,770
County Hall, Chichester, W Sussex PO19 1RQ; Tel (01243) 777100; Fax (01243) 777952

Education Department

County Hall, West St, Chichester PO19 1RF; Tel (01243) 777100; Fax (01243) 777229
Director of Education R.D.C. Bunker, MA
Deputy Director of Education J.H. Bottomley, BA
Assistant Director of Education (Personnel, Finance and Administration) D. Monger
EO (Local Management of Schools/IT) M.N. Smith, MA
PAO K.W. Flower, BA, DMA
PAA (Management Information) J.M. Long
PAA (School Supplies and Transport) M.A. Smith
EO (Personnel) P.E. Stapleton, BA, MA, MEd, MIPD
AEO (Health and Safety) D. Robinson, BA
Personnel Operations Manager J.F. Hutter, DMS, DPM, FIPD, MIMgt
Assistant Director of Education (Buildings and Development) J.M. Taylor, BSc
EO (Buildings and Development) R.D. Dean, MSc
AEO (Development) P.N. Proudley, BSc
PAA (Buildings and Development) E.R. Drake
Assistant Director of Education (Pupil Services) L. Wilkins
EO (Special Services) A. Atkins, MA
AEO (Special Services) P.A. Morton, BEd
AEO (Special Services) P. Barlow, BEd
PAA (Special Education) G.M. Miller
PAA (Schools Management) J.V. Miller, DMA
Assistant Director of Education (Further and Community Education) M. Hancock, BA, MA
EO (Adult and Community Education) C. Holliday, BA, MSc, CertEd(FE)
SAO (Further and Community Education) R.J. West
SAO (Further Education Awards) M.C. Brown
International Links Officer C. John, BA
Chief Adviser R.J. Shostak, BA, MSc
Principal Adviser (Performance Review) K. Pritchard, MEd
Senior Adviser (Curriculum and Professional Development) P. Rabbett, BEd, MA
Senior Adviser (North Team) P. Gaunt, BEd, MA, DipEd North Eastern Area Professional Centre, Furnace Dr, Furnace Grn, Crawley RH10 6JB
General Adviser (Primary Management) M. Walmsley, BPhil
General Adviser (Primary Management) P.F. Sowrey, BA
General Adviser (Secondary Management) Vacancy
General Adviser (Secondary Management) P.A. Latham, BA
General Adviser (English) D. Fry, BA, MEd
General Adviser (Mathematics) B.J. Oldfield, BEd, MPhil
General Adviser (Science) R. Waddingham, BSc
General Adviser (Modern Languages) Dr A. Feltham, BA, DPhil
General Adviser (Drama) A. Fenton
General Adviser (Personal and Social Education) S. Samson
General Adviser (Information Technology) N. Roberts, BA, MA(Ed)
General Adviser (Staff Development) R.H. Little, BA, MA
General Adviser (Humanities) J. Lord, BA, MA
Senior Adviser (South Team) S. Davies, BEd, DipEd Westen Area Professional Centre, Stockbridge Rd, Chichester PO19 2EF
General Adviser (Primary Management) J. Barrett, MA(Ed)
General Adviser (Primary Management) S. Toon, BPhil(Ed)
General Adviser (Primary Management) J. Ikin, BA
General Adviser (Secondary Management) M.J. Freeman, BA
General Adviser (Secondary Management) Dr W. Lind, MA, PhD
GeneralGeneral Adviser (Mathematics) A.P. Foster, BSc
General Adviser (Art/Design and Ceramics) S. Kopecek, BA
General Adviser (Music) D. Williams, ARCM, GRSM, BMus
General Adviser (Physical Education) W.A. Turnbull, BA
General Adviser (Science) Dr J. Hudson, MSc, PhD
General Adviser (Religious Education) N.R. Bloodworth
General Advise (Craft/Design and Technology) J. Price, MA
General Adviser (English) E. Cox, BEd, MA
General Adviser (Assessment) I. Hare, MA
General Adviser (Special Educational Needs) B. Capper, BEd
General Adviser (Special Educational Needs) J.E. Cook, BEd
General Adviser (Staff Development) C. Redknap, MEd
General Adviser (Governor and Management Training) Vacancy
County Careers Officer H.J. Westcott, BSc
County Youth and Community Officer R.G. Ralls
Assistant County Youth and Community Officer M.R. Ryall

County Youth and Community Training Officer D. Chilton
County Education Welfare Officer Vacancy
Principal Educational Psychologist R. Flaxbeard, BA, MA, MSc County Bldgs, East St, Littlehampton, West Sussex BN17 6AP; Tel (01903) 726406; Fax (01903) 713445
Number of Schools
See under Area Offices
Day of Committee Meeting
Tuesday, 6 per year

Education Committee

LD 15, Con 10, Lab 4, Ind 1
Chairman M.E. Collins, (LD) Boddinnick, Lewes Rd, East Grinstead, West Sussex RH19 3UD; Tel (01342) 324296
Vice-Chairman M. Brookes, (LD) 1 Rectory Farm Rd, Sompting, Lancing, West Sussex BN15 0DP; Tel (01903) 763390
Conservative Spokesman M.D. Johnson, The Thatched Hse, Roundwood La, Lindfield, Haywards Heath, West Sussex RH16 1SJ; Tel (01444) 414756
Labour Spokesman D.J. Mayne, 164 Weald Dr, Furnace Grn, Crawley, West Sussex RH10 6NN; Tel (01293) 520107
Members of the Committee
M.L. Beeson, A.V. Biggs, M. Brooks, G.A. Bucknall, J.M. Campbell, DL, Dr A.J. Chapman, A.A. Clare, M.E. Collins, M. Dennis, D.G. Dewdney, B.M. Dick, A.J. Edwards, I.R.W. Elliott, D.H. Farmer, D. Fox, H. Hall, M.J. Hammond, J.D. Herniman, N.R. Hilton, E.D.G. Howell, Rev J. Joyce, M.D. Johnson, G.F.H. Lawes, P.J. Lees, N.B. Matthewson, D.J. Mayne, Capt E.M.S. O'Kelly, The Rev F.H. Parsons, L. Parkin, A.E. Peglar, J.C. Rankin, C. Robinson, N.C. Rodgers, H.J. Ross, J.P. Sheridan, D.J. Smith, B. Wallace, Dr J.M.M. Walsh, S. Watson

Governor Training Unit

Governors' Support Programme, Western Area Professional Centre, Stockbridge Rd, Chichester PO19 2EF; Tel (01243) 789635; Fax (01243) 531080
General Adviser (Governor and Management Training) Vacancy
Services Offered
The Governors' Support Programme provides a wide range of training, support and development opportunities for nearly 4,000 governors of West Sussex Schools. A termly newsletter, GEN, is produced for governors

Mid-Sussex Area

Beckworth Hse, Black Hill, Lindfield, Haywards Heath RH16 2DU; Tel (01444) 484321; Fax (01444) 483380
Education Officer for the Area J.B. Cobbett, BA
Assistant Area Education Officer M. Angus, BA
Principal Administrative Assistant A. Wyncoll
Principal Administrative Assistant C.M.P. Simmonds, DMA
Number of Schools
1 nursery (87); 63 primary (11,522); 9 comprehensive (9,904); 3 adult education centres; 1 professional centre
Special Schools
4 day (271); 1 residential (46)

Special Schools

Colwood and Larchwood Hospitals School, Hurstwood La, Haywards Heath RH17 7SH; Tel (01444) 456427; A.W. Mitchener. (E.B.D.) (23)
Court Meadow, Hanlye La, Cuckfield, Haywards Heath RH17 5HN; Tel (01444) 454535; J. Hedges. (S.L.D.); (Day) (76)
Newick Hse, Birchwood Grove Rd, Burgess Hill RH15 0DP; Tel (01444) 233550; A.M. Roberts. (M.L.D.); (Day) (138)
Queen Elizabeth II Silver Jubilee School, Comptons La, Horsham, W Sussex; Tel (01403) 266215; L.K. Dyer. (S.L.D.) (44)

Special Residential School

Abbotsford, Cuckfield Rd, Burgess Hill RH15 8RE; Tel (01444) 235848; Fax (01444) 241786; P. Moxon. (E.B.D.); (Boarding/Day) (68)

Special Classes

Mid-Sussex Area Pupil Referral Unit, Marle Pl, Leyland Rd, Burgess Hill RH15 8JD; Tel (01444) 232771; S. Vickers (Teacher in Charge)
Horsham Pupil Referral Unit, C/o Shelley C.P. School, Broadbridge Heath, Horsham RH12 3JU; Tel (01403) 252307; D. Searle (Teacher in Charge)
Mid-Sussex SSF for Speech and Language Impaired Children, London Meed C.P. School, Chanctonbury Rd, Burgess Hill RH15 9YQ; Tel (01444) 232336; A. Holgate (Teacher in Charge – Infants); R.M. Rodgers (Teacher in Charge – Juniors)
Mid-Sussex Primary SSF for Children with Severe Specific Learning Difficulties, Blackthorns C.P. School, Blackthorns Cls, Lindfield, Haywards Heath RH16 2AY; Tel (01444) 454866; S. Hodgkinson (Teacher in Charge)
Mid-Sussex Secondary SSF for Children with Severe Specific Learning Difficulties, Warden Pk School, Broad St, Cuckfield, Haywards Heath RH17 5DP; Tel (01444) 457881; A. McQueen (Teacher in Charge)

Comprehensive Schools (County)

Downlands, Dale Ave, Hassocks BN6 8LP; Tel (01273) 845892/3; W. Clarke. (Mixed) (881)
The Forest School, Compton's La, Horsham RH13 5NW; Tel (01403) 261086; Fax (01403) 217150; J.A. Fadden, BSc. (Boys) (747)
Millais, Depot Rd, Horsham RH13 5HR; Tel (01403) 254932; Fax (01403) 211729; M.C. Lillyman. (Girls) (1080)
Oakmeeds Community School, Station Rd, Burgess Hill RH15 9EA; Tel (01444) 241691/3; Fax (01444) 235261; V. Nicholas. (Mixed) (1014)
Oathall Community College, Appledore Gdns, Haywards Heath RH16 2AQ; Tel (01444) 414001/3; Fax (01444) 417027; J.A. Rimmer, MEd. (Mixed) (1084)
Tanbridge Hse, Worthing Rd, Horsham RH12 1SR; Tel (01403) 263628; Fax (01403) 211830; N. Chapman, BA. (Mixed) (1146)
Warden Pk, Broad St, Cuckfield, Haywards Heath RH17 5DP; Tel (01444) 457881; Fax (01444) 417024; B.D. Webb, BA. (Mixed) (1480)
Weald, Station Rd, Billingshurst RH14 9RY; Tel (01403) 783123; Fax (01403) 782305; V. Holly. (Mixed) (1460)

Comprehensive School (Voluntary)

St Paul's R.C., Oathall Ave, Haywards Heath RH16 3ET; Tel (01444) 415418; Fax (01444) 417042; J.F. Flower, ACP. (Mixed); (V.A.) (593)

Professional Centre

Mid-Sussex Area Professional Centre Clarence Rd, Horsham RH13 5SQ; Tel (01403) 241111; Fax (01403) 252325; P. Gaunt

Departments of Adult Education

Haywards Heath/Cuckfield, Oathall Community College, Appledore Gdns, Haywards Heath, W Sussex; Tel (01444) 452163/1459037; Fax (01444) 441927; G. Goater
Horsham, Forest Community School, Horsham RH13 6EH; Tel (01403) 261088; Fax (01403) 217150; J. Robbins
Oakmeeds Community School, Marle Pl, Leylands Rd, Burgess Hill RH15 8JD; Tel (01444) 236355; Fax (01444) 235261; A. Davey

Weald School, Station Rd, Billingshurst RH14 9AB; Tel (01403) 784245; Fax (01403) 782305; M.W.J. Peppiat

Careers Office

See chapter 17

North Eastern Area

Centenary Hse, County Bldgs, Woodfield Rd, Crawley RH10 2GP; Tel (01293) 533661; Fax (01293) 519629
Area Education Officer R.W. Rowe, BSc, MSc
Assistant Area Education Officer C.F. Parsons, BEd, DipEd, DPSE
Principal Administrative Assistant J.M. Petty, BA
Number of Schools
35 primary, including first (7,982); 11 middle deemed primary (3,146); 2 middle deemed secondary (472); 7 comprehensive (8,751); 6 adult education departments; 1 professional centre
Special Schools
2 day (227)

Youth and Community Office

Centenary Hse, County Bldgs, Woodfield Rd, Crawley, W Sussex; Tel (01293) 533661; A. Addison

Special Day Schools

Catherington, Martyrs Ave, Langley Grn, Crawley RH11 7SF; Tel (01293) 526873; Fax (01293) 530642; D.L. Reid. (SLD) (80)
Deerswood, Ifield Grn, Ifield, Crawley RH11 0HG; Tel (01293) 520351; T. Ferber. (M.L.D.) (165)

Special Classes

Crawley Physically Disabled SSF, Southgate C.M. School, Barrington Rd, Southgate, Crawley RH10 6DG; Tel (01293) 525372; J. Tomkinson (Teacher in Charge)
Crawley Primary SSF for Children with Severe Specific Learning Difficulties, Ifield C.M. School, Ifield, Crawley RH11 0EL; Tel (01293) 611971/525320; C. Hiley (Teacher in Charge)
Crawley Secondary SSF for Children with Severe Specific Learning Difficulties, Ifield Community College, Lady Margaret Rd, Ifield, Crawley RH11 0DB; Tel (01293) 526467; Vacancy (Teacher in Charge)
Crawley SSF for Hearing Impaired Pupils, Northgate County First, Green La, Northgate, Crawley RH10 2DX; Tel (01293) 526729/614878; A. Walker (Headteacher); K. Tester (Teacher in Charge)
Crawley SSF for Speech and Language Impaired Children, Three Bridges C.M. School, Gales Dr, Three Bridges, Crawley RH10 1PD; Tel (01293) 526888/615864; J. Harthoorn (Teacher in Charge)
Crawley SSF for Speech and Language Impaired Pupils, Three Bridges First School, Gales Pl, Three Bridges, Crawley RH10 1QG; Tel (01293) 524076/615807; A. Keith (Teacher in Charge)
North Eastern Area Pupil Referral Unit, Worth Annexe, Turners Hill Rd, Crawley RH10 7RN; Tel (01293) 883209; A. Burke (Teacher in Charge)
East Grinstead PRU, C/o Halsford Pk C.P. School, Manor Rd, East Grinstead RH19 1LR; Tel (01342) 325857; J. Kane (Teacher in Charge)
Queen Victoria Hospital Special Class, Holtye Rd, East Grinstead RH19 3DZ; Tel (01342) 410210; H. Davison (Teacher in Charge)
Thomas Bennett SSF for Hearing Impaired Children, Thomas Bennett Community College, Ashdown Dr, Tilgate, Crawley RH10 5AD; Tel (01293) 526255/539310; J. Newton (Teacher in Charge)

Comprehensive Schools (County)

Hazelwick, Hazelwick Mill La, Three Bridges RH10 1SU; Tel (01293) 525616; Fax (01293) 512011; J.K. Wilkinson, BA, MA. (1650)
Ifield Community College, Lady Margaret Rd, Ifield RH11 0DB; Tel (01293) 526467; Fax (01293) 526451; G.P. George, MEd, MSc. (1208)
Imberhorne, Imberhorne La, East Grinstead RH19 1QY; Tel (01342) 323562; Fax (01342) 317366; J.Q. Morrison. (1404)
Sackville, Lewes Rd, East Grinstead RH19 3TY; Tel (01342) 410140; Fax (01342) 315544; D.C. Brooks, BSc. (1460)
The Thomas Bennett Community College, Ashdown Dr, Tilgate RH10 5AD; Tel (01293) 526255; Fax (01293) 527704; M.G. Dunman. (1171)

Comprehensive Schools (Voluntary)

The Holy Trinity C.E., Buckswood Dr, Gossops Grn RH11 8JE; Tel (01293) 526903; Fax (01293) 511968; F.I. Barker, BSc. (V.A.) (924)
St Wilfrid's R.C., Oakwood, Old Horsham Rd RH11 8PG; Tel (01293) 615151; Fax (01293) 512057; B.G. Smith. (V.A.) (587)

Middle Schools (Voluntary)

Holy Cross R.C., Shipley Rd, Ifield RH11 0ED; Tel (01293) 532502; Fax (01293) 512054; D. Foley. (V.A.) (248)
Notre Dame R.C., Turners Hill Rd, Pound Hill RH10 4SN; Tel (01293) 883047; Fax (01293) 886634; C. Belok. (V.A.) (268)

Professional Centre

North Eastern Area Professional Centre, Furnace Dr, Furnace Grn, Crawley RH10 6JB; Tel (01293) 553297; P. Gaunt

Departments of Adult Education

Crawley College, College Rd, Crawley RH10 1NR; Tel (01293) 612686; Fax (01293) 522431; J. Sheridan, ACP, FRGS. (inc. Hazelwick)
East Grinstead Area: Adult Education Office, Windmill La, East Grinstead RH19 2OT; Tel (01342) 321874; Fax (01342) 325553; P. Strong
Ifield, Ifield Community College, North Bldg, Lady Margaret Rd, Ifield, Crawley RH11 0DB; Tel (01293) 561016; Fax (01293) 526451; C. Murray
Thomas Bennett, Thomas Bennett Community College, Ashdown Dr, Tilgate, Crawley RH10 5AD; Tel (01293) 523811; Fax (01293) 527704; A.W. Earl, MA

Careers Office

See chapter 17

Southern Area

Southern Area Education Office, 15 Mill Rd, Worthing BN11 4NH; Tel (01903) 700827; Fax (01903) 507366
Area Education Officer D. Gillard
Assistant Area Education Officer H. Williams
Principal Administrative Assistant D.H. Tansley, DMA
Number of Schools
1 nursery (146); 58 primary, including first (12,686); 12 middle deemed primary (14,815); 1 middle deemed secondary (328); 10 comprehensive (10,896); 4 adult education departments; 1 professional centre
Special Schools
3 day (341)

Youth and Community Office

Southern Youth and Community Office, 15 Mill Rd, Worthing, W Sussex; Tel (01903) 502500; D. McGowan

Special Schools

Cornfield School, Cornfield Cl, Worthing Rd, Littlehampton BN17 6HY; Tel (01903) 731277; C.D. Taylor (Headteacher). (E.B.D.); (Day Pupils) (50)

George Pringle, Palatine Rd, Worthing BN12 6JP; Tel (01903) 242835; J.D. Clough. (M.L.D.); (Day) (151)
Herons Dale, Hawkins Cres, Shoreham BN43 6TN; Tel (01273) 596904/596967; S.A. Pritchard. (M.L.D.); (Day) (100)
Highdown, Durrington La, Worthing BN13 2QQ; Tel (01903) 249611; G. Elliker. (S.L.D.); (Day) (92)

Special Classes

Boundstone Pre-School Class for Children with Speech and Language Problems, Boundstone Nursery School, Boundstone La, Lancing BN15 9QX; K. Keith (Headteacher); Z. Rustom (Teacher-in-Charge)
The Lavinia Norfolk SSF for Physically Disabled and Hearing Impaired Children, The Angmering School, Station Rd, Angmering, Littlehampton BN16 4HH; Tel (01903) 772351/773146; G. Tisdall (Teacher in Charge). (P.D.); (Hearing Impaired)
Littlehampton SSF for Hearing Impaired Pupils, Connaught County Junior School, York Rd, Littlehampton BN17 6EW; Tel (01903) 721677/715575; A. Burgess (Teacher in Charge)
Lyndhurst Assessment Class, Lyndhurst County First School, Lyndhurst Rd, Worthing BN11 2DG; Tel (01903) 235390; C. Mayhew (Teacher in Charge)
Southern Area Primary Phase Pupil Referral Unit, C/o Chesswood C.M. School, Chesswood Rd, Worthing BN11 2AA; Tel (01903) 238854; L. Conway (Teacher in Charge)
Southern Area Secondary Phase Pupil Referral Unit, C/o Northbrook College, Design and Technology, Broadwater Rd, Worthing BN14 8HJ; Tel (01903) 211855; D. Gould (Teacher in Charge)
Southwick PRU, C/o Glebe C.M. School, Church La, Southwick, W Sussex BN42 4GB; Tel (01273) 595026; U. Gates (Teacher in Charge)
Steyning Primary SSF for Children with Severe Specific Learning Difficulties, St Andrew's C.E. School, Shooting Field, Steyning BN44 3RX; Tel (01903) 813420; B. Webber (Headteacher); L. Latham (Teacher-in-Charge)
Steyning Secondary SSF for Children with Severe Specific Learning Difficulties, Steyning Grammar School, Steyning BN44 3RX; Tel (01903) 814555; M. Linehan (Teacher in Charge)
Worthing Language SSF for Speech and Language Impaired Pupils, John Selden C.M. School, Nelson Rd, Worthing BN12 6EN; Tel (01903) 243563; A. Regester (Acting Teacher in Charge)
Worthing Physically Disabled SSF, West Park C.E. Middle School, Marlborough Rd, Worthing BN12 4HD; Tel (01903) 243099/506278; P.M. Dockree (Teacher in Charge)
Worthing Primary SSF for Children with Severe Specific Learning Difficulties, West Pk C.E.M. School, Marlborough Rd, Worthing BN12 4HD; Tel (01903) 243099/506278; B. Frith (Teacher in Charge)
Worthing Secondary SSF for Children with Severe Specific Learning Difficulties, Worthing High School, South Farm Rd, Worthing BN14 7AR; Tel (01903) 237864; M. McGlone (Teacher in Charge)
Worthing SSF for Speech and Language Impaired Pupils, John Selden County First School, Nelson Rd, Worthing BN12 6EN; Tel (01903) 700234/242611; E. Longhurst (Teacher in Charge)

Middle School

Rydon Community, Thakeham Rd, Storrington, Pulborough RH20 3AA; Tel (01903) 744138; Fax (01903) 740300; M.C.B. Parfitt, BPhil. (Mixed) (375)

Comprehensive Schools (County)

Angmering, Station Rd, Angmering, Littlehampton BN16 4HH; Tel (01903) 772351; Fax (01903) 850752; R.T. Evea, MA. (Mixed) (1082)
The Boundstone Community College, Upper Boundstone La, Sompting, Lancing BN15 9QZ; Tel (01903) 755894/5/6; Fax (01903) 755848; G.E. Cooke. (Mixed) (1123)
Durrington High, The Boulevard, Worthing BN13 1JX; Tel (01903) 244957; Fax (01903) 507310; H.H. Smith, MA. (Mixed) (1225)
King's Manor, Kingston La, Shoreham-by-Sea BN4 6YT; Tel (01273) 592647; Fax (01273) 870161; A.D. McLean, MA. (Mixed) (1213)
Littlehampton Community School, Hill Rd, Littlehampton BN17 6DQ; Tel (01903) 714361; Fax (01903) 714361; G. Smith, BA. (Mixed) (1466)
Worthing High School, South Farm Rd, Worthing BN14 7AR; Tel (01903) 237864; Fax (01903) 231709; L. Fryer, BSc. (Mixed) (883)

Comprehensive Schools (Voluntary)

Chatsmore Catholic High, Goring St, Worthing BN12 5AF; Tel (01903) 241368; Fax (01903) 240183; M. Forster, BA, MEd. (Mixed); (V.A.) (566)
Davison C.E. High, Selbourne Rd, Worthing BN11 2JX; Tel (01903) 233835; Fax (01903) 211417; S.A. Wallis. (Girls); (V.C.) (787)
St Andrew's C.E. High, Sackville Rd, Worthing BN14 8BG; Tel (01903) 820676; Fax (01903) 231880; P.G. Stewart, BEd. (Boys); (V.A.) (508)
Steyning Grammar, Steyning BN4 3LB; Tel (01903) 814555; Fax (01903) 879146; A. Tonkin. (Mixed) (1511)

Departments of Adult Education

Boundstone, Boundstone Community College, Upper Boundstone La, Lancing BN15 9QZ; Tel (01903) 755895; Fax (01903) 755848; A.R. Everitt
Chanctonbury, The Grammar School, Steyning BN4 3LP; Tel (01903) 814880/814959; Fax (01903) 879146; R. Whitehead
Littlehampton, The Littlehampton Community School, Hill Rd, Littlehampton BN17 6DQ; Tel (01903) 713614; Fax (01903) 714361; R. Ferrier
Rydon Community School, Rock Rd, Storrington, W Sussex; Tel (0190 66) 744129; Fax (01903) 746065; W. Pickford
Shoreham and Southwick Area Adult Education Centre, The Community Centre, 24 Southwick St, Southwick BN42 4TE; Tel (01273) 592514/594898; Fax (01273) 596933; J. Havenhand; *Admin* V. Bray
Worthing Area Adult Education Centre, Elm Lawn Hse, Union Pl, Worthing, W Sussex BN11 1LG; Tel (01903) 237392; Fax (01903) 237375; J.R. Havenhand

Professional Centre

Southern Area Professional Centre, Glebeside Ave, Worthing BN14 7PR; Tel (01903) 210044; C.J. Redknap

Careers Office

See chapter 17

Western Area

Ambassador Hse, Crane St, Chichester PO19 1TP; Tel (01243) 752070; Fax (01243) 778161
Area Education Officer B.H. Taylor, BA
Assistant Area Education Officer C.M.B. WAlsh, MA
Principal Administrative Assistant D. Gwenlan, DMA
Number of Schools
2 nursery (280); 67 primary (including first) (10,453); 2 middle deemed secondary (587); 10 comprehensive (9,678); 7 adult education departments; 1 professional centre
Special Schools
2 day (217); 2 residential (126)

Youth and Community Office

Fernleigh, 40 North St, Chichester, W Sussex; Tel (01243) 776322; G. Tricker

Special Day Schools

Fordwater, Summersdale Rd, Chichester PO19 4PL; Tel (01243) 782475; R. Rendall. (S.L.D.) (75)
St Anthony's, Woodlands La, off St Paul's Rd, Chichester PO19 3PA; Tel (01243) 785965; M.R. Turney. (M.L.D.) (150)

Special Residential Schools

Littlegreen, Compton, Chichester PO18 9NW; Tel (01705) 631259; A.R.M. Bicknell. (E.B.D.) (37); (Boys) (37)
St Cuthman's, Stedham, Midhurst GU29 0QJ; Tel (01730) 812331; Fax (01730) 812335; H.L. Rooks. (M.L.D.) (Boarding/Day) (98)

Special Classes

Barnham Physically Disabled SSF, Barnham C.P. School, Elm Gr, Barnham, Bognor Regis, W Sussex; Tel (01243) 552197; A.J. Smith (Headteacher); J. Currie (Teacher in Charge)
Chichester SSF for Speech and Language Impaired Pupils, St James C.P. School, St James Rd, Chichester PO19 4HR; Tel (01243) 783939/781256; P.R. Denton (Teacher in Charge-Infants); S. Sheach (Teacher in Charge-Juniors)
Chichester Primary SSF for Children with Severe Specific Learning Difficulties, Parklands C.P. School, Durnford Cl, Chichester PO19 3AG; Tel (01243) 788630; R.P. Martin (Headteacher); J. Calder (Teacher in Charge)
Western Area Pupil Referral Unit, Fletcher Pl Bldg, North Mundham, Chichester PO20 6JR; Tel (01243) 788044; P. Saunders (Teacher in Charge)
Western Area Secondary SSF for Children with Severe Specific Learning Difficulties, Bognor Regis Community College, Westloats La, Bognor Regis PO21 5LH; Tel (01243) 864401/841746

Middle Schools

Herbert Shiner, Petworth GU28 0EE; Tel (01798) 342580; Fax (01798) 343195; M. Mattinson, BA. (Mixed) (219)
Midhurst Intermediate, Wheelbarrow Castle, Easebourne, Midhurst GU29 9AG; Tel (01730) 812371; Fax (01730) 815090; S. Davies, MA. (Mixed) (388)

Comprehensive Schools (County)

The Bognor Regis Community College, Westloats La, Bognor Regis PO21 5LH; Tel (01243) 864401; Fax (01243) 841676; A. Duke, MA, BSc, FBIM; *Bursar* Mrs A. Brown. (1574)
The Bourne Community College, Park Rd, Southbourne, Emsworth, Hants PO10 8PJ; Tel (01243) 375691; Fax (01243) 379286; G.L. Hancock, MA. (494)
Felpham Community College, Felpham Way, Felpham, Bognor Regis PO22 8EL; Tel (01243) 826511; Fax (01243) 841021; R.T. Moggridge, BA; *Bursar* M.H. Woods. (954)
Chichester High School for Boys, Kingsham Rd, Chichester PO19 2AE; Tel (01243) 787691; Fax (01243) 531584; R.L. Austin, BA. (Boys) (1378)
Chichester High School for Girls, Stockbridge Rd, Chichester PO19 2EB; Tel (01243) 787014; Fax (01243) 786543; L. Parkin, BA; *Bursar* M. Youden. (Girls) (1350)
The Manhood Community College, School La, Selsey, Chichester PO20 9EH; Tel (01243) 602558; Fax (01243) 604097; S. Crowther. (616)
The Westergate Community College, Ivy La, Westergate, Chichester PO20 6RE; Tel (01243) 542921/2; Fax (01243) 544075; R.J. Hibberd, MA, BEd. (460)

Comprehensive Schools (Voluntary)

Bishop Luffa C.E., Bishop Luffa Cl, Chichester PO19 3LT; Tel (01243) 787741; Fax (01243) 531807; J.B.E.H. Ashwin, MA; *Bursar* H. Bashford. (V.A.) (1169)
Midhurst Grammar, North St, Midhurst GU29 9DT; Tel (01730) 812451/2; Fax (01730) 813524; E.E. Hickford; *(Bursar)* E. Myall. (Cont.) (748)
Saint Philip Howard High, Elm Gr South, Barnham, Bognor Regis PO22 0EN; Tel (01243) 552055; Fax (01243) 552900; V.P. Kelly, BA; *Bursar* N.A. Hull. (Special Agreement); (Mixed) (659)

Professional Centre

Western Area Professional Centre, Stockbridge Rd, Chichester PO19 2EF; Tel (01243) 789635; *Senior Adviser (South)* S. Davies

Residential Centre

Lodge Hill Residential Centre, Watersfield, Pulborough RH20 1LZ; Tel (01798) 831411; Fax (01798) 831972; M. French

Departments of Adult Education

Bognor Regis, The Bognor Regis Community College, Westloats La, Bognor Regis PO21 5LH; Tel (01243) 827422; Fax (01243) 841676; J. Woodhead
Bourne, Bourne Community College, Park Rd, Southbourne, Emsworth, Hants PO10 8PJ; Tel (01243) 379276; Fax (01243) 379286; J. Nicholson
Chichester, Chichester College of Arts, Science and Technology, Westgate Fields PO19 1SB; Tel (01234) 786321; Fax (01243) 539481; T. Hudson
Felpham, Felpham Community College, Felpham Way, Felpham, Bognor Regis PO22 8EL; Tel (01243) 867845; Fax (01243) 841021; W. Hicks
Herbert Shiner School, Petworth GU28 0EE; Tel (01798) 42580; Fax (01798) 343195; B. Houghton
Manhood Community College, Selsey, Chichester PO20 9EH; Tel (01243) 602767; Fax (01243) 604097; J.G. Craven
Midhurst/Petworth, Midhurst Grammar School, North St, Midhurst GU29 9DJ; Tel (01730) 816683; Fax (01730) 813524; C.E. Hughes
Westergate, The Westergate Community College, Ivy La, Westergate PO20 6RE; Tel (01243) 542921/2; Fax (01243) 544878; B. Sullivan

Careers

see chapter 17

West Yorkshire Metropolitan Area

The following Metropolitan Councils comprise the West Yorkshire Metropolitan Area and may be found in alphabetical order within this chapter:
Bradford, Calderdale, Kirklees, Leeds, Wakefield.

Wigan Metropolitan Borough Council

Population 306,590
New Town Hall, Library St, Wigan WN1 1YN; Tel (01942) 44991; Fax (01942) 82745

Education Department

Gateway Hse, Standishgate, Wigan WN1 1AE; Tel (01942) 44991/828891; Fax (01942) 828811
Chairman Cllr B.M. Wilson
Vice-Chairman Cllr W.S. Shaw
Director of Education R.J. Clark, MA
Deputy Director of Education (Policy/Strategy) M.L. Roxburgh, BSc
Assistant Director (Establishment Services) M.V. Carriline, MA
Assistant Director (Pupil/Student Services) S. Richardson, BSc
Assistant Education Officer (Pupil/Student Services) G. McQueen, MA
Assistant Director (Curriculum Services) D.J. Davies, BA
Assistant Education Officer (Policy/Development) A.D. Fordham, MA
Financial Services Officer J.A. Aspinall
Premises and Client Services Officer J. Cunliffe
Principal Officer (Policy/Strategy) T.M. Warren
Finance Officer J. Taylor
Principal Officer (Human Resources) S.J. Hampson
SAO (Payroll) T. Leyland
SAO (Student Services) J.E. Jolley
Assistant Finance Officer L. Haywood
Chief Adviser M. Salisbury, MSc
Senior Adviser J.P. Sudworth
Senior Adviser S.R. Cooper
Senior Adviser (Primary) Vacancy
General Adviser (Evaluation) Vacancy
General Adviser (Performing Arts) K. Gouge
Curriculum Art Adviser B. Edmundson
General Adviser (Humanities) E.R.C. Steed
General Adviser (English) J.E. Cowen
General Adviser (Primary) T.J. Finn
Principal Officer (Student and Community Services) K. Piggott
Client Catering Officer F. Topping
Metropolitan Catering Services Manager G.S. Long
Principal Careers Officer C. Eagle Library St, Wigan WN1 1NU; Tel (01942) 827566; Fax (01942) 827597
Principal Education Welfare Officer D. Greenhalgh
Senior Educational Psychologist J. Yates, MPhil Education Office, Gateway Hse, Standishgate, Wigan WN1 1AE; Tel (01942) 828815
Educational Psychologist C. Lukey
Educational Psychologist C. Dewhurst
Educational Psychologist A. Maguire
Educational Psychologist W.F. Ainslie
Educational Psychologist Mrs P.M. Jackson
Educational Psychologist E. Silk
Educational Psychologist D.E. Philpot
Educational Psychologist Mrs E. Oakes
Chief Youth and Community Education Officer A.J Taylor, MA
Education Business Partnership and Manager, TVEI Co-ordinator J. Devoy
Number of Schools
124 nursery and primary (28,500); 21 secondary comprehensive (19,000); 2 community education centres; 1 arts centre; 2 teachers' centres
Special Schools
3 E.S.N.(M); 3 E.S.N.(S); 1 physically handicapped; 2 maladjusted

Education Committee

Chair Brian M. Wilson 139 Henfold Rd, Astley, Tyldesley M29 7FX
Vice-Chair William S. Shaw 10 Buchanan Dr, Hindley Grn, Wigan WN2 4HJ
Members of the Committee
K. Anderson, J.W. Ball, J.A. Best, E.S. Cartwright, G. Davies, J.E. Hilton JP, J. Horrocks JP, S.T. Jeffers, S. Kennedy, S. Little, R. McAllister JP, K. Pye, J. Riley JP, G. Roberts, C. Roscoe, G.E.R. Seaward, T. Sherratt, P. Smith, B.J. Strett, J. Sumner JP, S. Turner, R. Winkworth, A. Wright

Governor Training Unit

Education Department, Gateway Hse, Standishgate, Wigan WN1 1AE; Tel (01942) 828990; Fax (01942) 828811
Governor Training Co-ordinator Vacancy
Services Offered
Training courses on various subjects are offered free of charge to Governors of schools buying back the Lea's service; There is a termly newsletter, a helpline. The unit will arrange for speakers to attend individual governing bodies or cluster groups

Special Schools

Borsdane Brook, Princess St, Hindley, Wigan WN2 3HJ; Tel (01942) 55585/526146. (MLD)
Green Hall, Green Hall Cl, off Bolton Rd, Atherton, Nr Manchester M46 9HP; Tel (01942) 883928; I. Triska, BEd. (MLD)
Highfield Residential, St John's Rd, Mosley Common, Worsley, Manchester M28 1AL; Tel 0161-790 2698/8424; J.S. Leamon, BSc, MEd. (EBD)
Hope, Scot La, Newtown, Wigan WN5 0PN; Tel (01942) 222018/824150; J.P.R. Dahlstrom. (SLD)
Mere Oaks, Boars Head, Standish, Wigan WN1 2RF; Tel (01942) 43481/2; W. Turner. (P.H.)
Montrose, Montrose Ave, Pemberton, Wigan WN5 9XN; Tel (01942) 223431; A. Farmer. (MLD)
Rose Hill (split sites), Sougher's La, Bryn, Ashton-in-Makerfield, Wigan WN4 0JS; Tel (01942) 727717/58975; G.R. Hallett. EBD
Tanfield, Borsdane Ave, Hindley, Wigan WN2 3HJ; Tel (01942) 55682; E.M. Edge. (SLD)
Two Porches, Gloucester St, Atherton, Manchester M46 0HX; Tel (01942) 882012. (SLD)

Secondary Comprehensive Schools (County) (11–16)

Ashton-in-Makerfield Cansfield High, Old Rd, Ashton-in-Makerfield, Wigan WN4 9TP; Tel (01942) 720711; Mrs G. Gregory. (800)
Golborne High, Lowton Rd, Golborne, Nr Warrington WA3 3EL; Tel (01942) 726842/728320; Vacancy. (580)
Hindley Mornington High, Mornington Rd, Hindley, Wigan WN2 4LG; Tel (01942) 55927; A. Harris. (1100)
Ince-in-Makerfield Rose Bridge High, Holt St, Ince, Wigan WN1 3HD; Tel (01942) 44151; A.M. Ruscoe. (550)
Leigh Bedford High, Manchester Rd, Leigh WN7 2LY; Tel (01942) 671706; B.W. Mell. (1100)
Leigh Westleigh High Westleigh La, Leigh WN7 5NL; Tel (01942) 883709; M.J. Gray. (650)
Lowton High Newton Rd, Lowton, Nr Warrington WA3 1DU; Tel (01942) 603419; Mrs S. Crosdale. (1050)
Orrell Abraham Guest High, Orrell Mount, Wigan WN5 8HN; Tel (01942) 214960; R. Caslake. (980)
Shevington High Shevington La, Shevington, Wigan WN6 8AB; Tel (01257) 423030; Mrs D. Taylor. (600)
Standish High Kenyon Rd, Standish, Wigan WN6 0NX; Tel (01257) 422265; J.G. Ashton. (850)
Tyldesley Fred Longworth High Printshop La, Tydesley M29 8JN; Tel (01942) 883796; A. Colley. (1000)
Wigan Hawkley Hall High Carr La, Hawkley Hall, Wigan WN3 5NY; Tel (01942) 491729; C. Wilkinson. (800)
Wigan Pemberton High Montrose Ave, Pemberton, Wigan WN5 9XL; Tel (01942) 212507; A. Bradshaw. (600)

Secondary Comprehensive Schools (Voluntary) (11–16) except two)

Ashton-in-Makerfield Byrchall High Warrington Rd, Ashton-in-Makerfield, Wigan WN4 9PQ; Tel (01942) 728221; S. Wall. (V.C.) (1060)
Ashton-in-Makerfield St Edmund Arrowsmith R.C. High Rookery Ave, off Warrington Rd, Ashton-in-Markerfield WN4 9PF; Tel (01942) 728651; P. Phillips. (S.A.) (1100)
Atherton Hesketh Fletcher C. of E. High, Hamilton St, Atherton, Nr Manchester M29 0AY; Tel (01942) 882425; D. Vickers. V.A. (950)

Leigh St Mary's R.C. High Manchester Rd, Astley, Tyldesley, Manchester M29 7EE; Tel (01942) 884144; A.E. Bell. (V.A.) (11–18) (1500)
Orrell St Peter's R.C. High Howard's La, Orrell Post, Wigan WN5 8NU; Tel (01942) 214743; A.T. Edwards. (V.A.) (900)
Wigan Deanery C.E. High Frog La, Wigan WN1 1HQ; Tel (01942) 48932/44355; R.J. Williams. (V.A.) (11–18) (1600)
Wigan St John Fisher R.C. High, Baytree Rd, Springfield, Wigan WN6 7RN; Tel (01942) 47377; D.W. Burnett. V.A. (600)
Wigan St Thomas More R.C. High Wood St, Newton, Wigan WN5 0UQ; Tel (01942) 45517; E.A. Kidd. (S.A.) (600)

Institutes of Community Education

Ashton-in-Makerfield Community High School, Cansfield High School, Old Road, Ashton-in-Makerfield, Wigan WN4 9TP; Tel (01942) 727391; Mrs G. Gregory
Golborne Community Education Centre, Golborne High School, Lowton Rd, Golborne, Nr Warrington WA3 3EL; Tel (01942) 726842; P.J. Allsop
Hindley Mornington High School, Mornington Rd, Hindley, Wigan WN2 4LG; Tel (01942) 55927; A. Harris
Lowton Community High School Newton Rd, Lowton, Nr Warrington WA3 1DU; Tel (01942) 603419/0; Mrs S. Crosdale
Orrell Community Education Centre Abraham Guest High School, Orrell Mount, Wigan, Greater Manchester; Tel (01942) 214960; K. Massey
Shevington Community High School Shevington La, Wigan WN6 8AB; Tel (01257) 423659; Mrs D. Taylor
Standish Community High School Kenyon Rd, Standish, Wigan WN6 0NX; Tel (01257) 422265; J.A. Ashton
Wigan Pemberton Community High School, Montrose Ave, Pemberton, Wigan WN5 9XL; Tel (01942) 212507; A. Bradshaw

Wiltshire County Council

Population 575,000
County Hall, Bythesea Rd, Trowbridge, Wilts BA14 8JN; Tel (01225) 713000; Fax (01225) 713999; Telex 44340

Education Department

County Hall, Bythesea Rd, Trowbridge, Wilts BA14 8JB; Tel (01225) 713000; Fax (01225) 713982
Chief Education Officer K. Robinson, PhD
Deputy Chief Education Officer P. Daly, BA, BSc(Econ)
Education Manager (Wiltshire Education Professional Services) W.E.P.S D.G. Pert, MA
Education Manager (Finance and Information) C.C. Dale, BA, IPFA
Education Manager (Services to Individuals) A.K. Moss, MSc
Education Manager (Policy, Planning and Co-ordination) S.C. Corbett, BD, MEd
Education Manager (Special Education Needs) T.J. Harper, BSc
Education Manager (Wiltshire Inspection Service) J.C. Palmer, BSc
Education Manager (Educational Psychological Service) J.L. Presland, MA
Senior Education Manager (Schools Support) P.F. Jefferson, BA, DipEd
Consultant (Assessment) D.P. Hanson
Consultant (History) D. Starkey
Consultant (RE and SPE) A.C. Barrett
Consultant (English) A.C. Howe
Consultant (Modern Languages) Vacancy
Consultant (Music) M. New
Consultant (Geography and Environmental Studies) Vacancy
Consultant (Physical Education) J. Fear
Consultant (Physical Education) M.D. Cooper
Consultant (Science) T. Robson
Consultant (Special Needs/Special Schools) C.E.M. Brotherton
Consultant (Mathematics) I. Farquhar, BSc
Consultant (Art and Design) J. Hockenhull
Consultant (Information Technology) E. Larkin, BA
Consultant (Drama) Vacancy
Consultant (Technology) V. Marriott, BEd
Inspector (Primary) S.Y. Wright
Inspector (Primary) P. Francis, MA
Consultant Adviser (Primary) A. Jensen
Inspector (Primary) A.S. Folker
Primary Consultant (Team Leader) I. Bennett
Primary Consultant C. Hotham
Inspector (Secondary) F. Mikdadi
Inspector (Secondary) E. Long
Inspector (Secondary) J.B. Kerwood
Primary Consultant K. Oram
Education Manager (Wiltshire Training Services) S.M. Beneicke
Primary Consultant I. Gyllenspetz
Primary Consultant J. Messer
Primary Consultant (Central) M. Chislet
Number of Schools
278 first and primary; 5 middle; 23 secondary; 13 special
Other Authorities with whom Joint Purchasing Arrangements are made
Gloucestershire; Somerset; Avon; Dorset; Cornwall; Dyfed; Gwynedd; Powys

Education Committee

LD 13, Con 7, Lab 7
Members of Committee
LD: B.E. Atfield, A.B. Barker, D.C.B. Coleman, M. Connolly, G. Francis, G. Hill, E.H. Hodges, A.A. Joel, A.V. Lye, C. Pym, J.M. Scott, I.C. West, N.S.E. Westbrook
Con: R.J. Baddeley, J.P. Johnson, D.J. Main, P. Rugg, J.B.P. Savage, C.A. Soden, A.J. Winmill
Lab: H.S. Barnett, B.V. Cockbill, J. Norris, R.T. Rogers, K.D. Small, N.R. Tostevin, L. Vardy

Governor Support Unit

Governor Support Team, Wiltshire Education Professional Services (WEPS), Education Department, Wiltshire County Council, Bythesea Rd, Trowbridge BA14 8JB; Tel (01225) 713819; Fax (01225) 713982
Head of Governor Support R.J. Alderman
Services Offered
An annual programme of seminars for governers, headteachers and clerks to governing bodies; Guidance documents; regular newsletter; helpline; resources library

Special Schools

Calne, Springfields Curzon St, Calne SN11 0DS; Tel (01249) 814125; R.E. Nethercott. (10–16)
Chippenham, Allington, Allington Way, Chippenham SN14 0JS; Tel (01249) 653451; R. Smith. (Boys); (9–16)
Chippenham, The St Nicholas, Malmesbury Rd, Chippenham SN15 1QF; Tel (01249) 650435; E.E. Weston. (2–16+)
Devizes, Downland, Downlands Rd, Devizes SN10 5EF; Tel (01380) 724193; D.G. Walsh. (9–16)
Swindon, St Luke's Cricklade Rd, Swindon SN2 5AH; Tel (01793) 705566; G.J.L. Hiscock. (5–16)
Rowde, Rowdeford Rowde, Devizes SN10 2QQ; Tel (01380) 850309; K.H. Roberts. (7–16)
Salisbury, Exeter Hse, Friary La, Salisbury SP1 2HA; Tel (01722) 334168; G.M. Heather. (2–16)

Swindon, Brimble Hill, Lynhurst Cres, Park North, Swindon SN3 2RW; Tel (01793) 617426; R.K. Walker. (2–16)
Swindon, Crowdys Hill, Jeffries Ave, Cricklade Rd, Swindon SN2 6HJ; Tel (01793) 527232; K. Smith. 12–16
Swindon, Nyland, Nyland Rd, Nythe, Swindon SN3 3RR; Tel (01793) 535023; P. Sunners. (5–11)
Swindon, The Chalet, Queen's Dr, Swindon SN3 1AR; Tel (01793) 534537; M. Topping. (2–7)
Swindon, Uplands, Leigh Rd, Penhill, Swindon SN2 5DE; Tel (01793) 724751; M. Bishop (Acting Head). (11–19)
Trowbridge, Larkrise, Ashton St, Trowbridge BA14 7EB; Tel (01225) 761434; M. Hull. (2–16+)

Middle Schools (County)

Mere, Duchy Manor Middle, Springfield Rd, Mere, Warminster BA12 6EW; Tel (01747) 860305; T.P. Sleigh. (9–13) (194)
Salisbury, Avon Middle, Devizes Rd, Salisbury SP2 9LY; Tel (01722) 333941; B.J. Tilbrook. (9–13) (229)
Salisbury, Fisherton Manor Middle, Highbury Ave, Salisbury SP2 7HJ; Tel (01722) 334113; N.J. Wyatt. (9–13) (262)

Middle Schools (Voluntary)

Tisbury, Nadder C.E. Middle, Weaveland Rd, Tisbury, Salisbury SP3 6HJ; Tel (01747) 870480; J. Cadmore. (9–13) (157)
Wilton C.E. Middle, The Hollows, Wilton, Salisbury SP2 0JE; Tel (01722) 742203; S.N. Denovan. (9–13) (334)

Secondary Modern School (County) (11–16)

Downton, Breamore Rd, Downton, Salisbury SP5 3HN; Tel (01725) 510610; M.V. Sparkes. (320)

Secondary Modern Schools (Voluntary) (11–16)

Salisbury, St Edmund's Girls C.E. Church Rd, Laverstock, Salisbury SP1 1RD; Tel (01722) 328565; T.J. Storer. (655)
Salisbury, St Joseph's R.C., St Joseph's R.C. Aided, Church Rd, Laverstock, Salisbury SP1 1QY; Tel (01722) 335380; F. White. (204)

Comprehensive Schools (County)

Amesbury, The Stonehenge, The Stonehenge, Antrobus Rd, Amesbury, Salisbury SP4 7ND; Tel (01980) 623407; D.R. O'Neill. (11–16) (553)
Corsham School, The Tynings, Corsham SN13 9DF; Tel (01249) 713284; C.A. Constantine. (11–18) (959)
Durrington, Upper Avon, Recreation Rd, Durrington, Salisbury SP4 8HN; Tel (01980) 652467; R.C. Clay. 11–18 (733)
Highworth, The Warneford, Shrivenham Rd, Highworth, Swindon SN6 7BZ; Tel (01793) 762426; R.M. Graydon. (11–16) (803)
Malmesbury School, Corn Gastons, Malmesbury SN16 ODF; Tel (01666) 822296; M. Trobe. (11–18) (888)
Melksham, The George Ward, Shurnhold, Melksham SN12 8DQ; Tel (01225) 702771; A.P. McVernon. (11–18) (1153)
Swindon, Churchfields, Salcombe Grove, Swindon SN3 1ER; Tel (01793) 48786; I.F. Taylor. (11–16) (890)
Swindon, Dorcan, St Paul's Dr, Covingham, Swindon SN3 5DA; Tel (01793) 525231; B. Fenby. (11–16) (998)
Swindon, Greendown Community, Grange Park Way, Grange Pk, Swindon SN5 6HN; Tel (01793) 874224; I.J. Matthews. (11–16) (786)
Swindon, Headlands, Cricklade Rd, Swindon SN2 6BQ; Tel (01793) 723625; R.W. Crow. (11–16) (729)
Swindon, Herod Parkway, Akers Way, Moredon, Swindon SN2 2NJ; Tel (01793) 521335; R.W.B. Cleall. (11–16) (1006)
Swindon, Oakfield, Marlowe Ave, Walcot, Swindon SN3 3HW; Tel (01793) 535043; E. Evans. (11–16) (409)
Tidworth, The Castledown, Ludgershall, Tidworth, Andover, Hants SP11 9RR; Tel (01264) 790778; C.P. McDermott. (11–16) (430)
Trowbridge, The Clarendon, Frome Rd, Trowbridge BA14 0DJ; Tel (01225) 762686; B. Wight. (11–18) (993)
Trowbridge, The John of Gaunt, Wingfield Rd, Trowbridge BA14 9EH; Tel (01225) 762637; S.C. Gee. (11–18) (1253)
Warminster, Kingdown, Woodcock Rd, Warminster BA12 9DR; Tel (01985) 846697; *Head* S. Brown. (11–18) (1270)
Wootton Bassett School, Lime Kiln, Wootton Bassett, Swindon SN4 7HD; Tel (01793) 852121; J.H. Thomas. (11–18) (1312)
Wroughton, The Ridgeway, Inverary Rd, Wroughton, Swindon SN4 9DR; Tel (01793) 812824; T.M. Axon. (11–18) (1302)

Comprehensive Schools (Voluntary)

Bradford-on-Avon, St Laurence, Ashley Rd, Bradford-on-Avon BA15 1DZ; Tel (01225) 867691; J.A. Wetz. (11–18) (1170)
Sarum Westwood St Thomas' C.E. Westwood Rd, Salisbury SP2 9HS; Tel (01722) 323431; J. Jefferson. (13–18) (818)

Institute of Adult Education

Urchfont Manor Residential College, Urchfont, Devizes SN10 4RG; Tel (01380) 840495; *Director* Dr. P. Howell. (Adult Education)

Residential Centres

Braeside Residential Centre, Bath Rd, Devizes SN10 2AX; Tel (01380) 722637; *Head of Centre* J.S. Smith
Oxenwood Outdoor Education Centre, Oxenwood, Marlborough SN8 3NQ; Tel (0126 489) 274; *Head of Centre* D. Hope
Plas Pencelli Outdoor Education Centre, Plas Pencelli, Brecon LS3 7LX; Tel (0187 486) 241; *Head of Centre* Vacancy

Teachers' Centre

Devizes Southbroom Professional Development Centre, C/o Southbroom Junior School, Devizes SN10 3AH; Tel (01380) 729358
Swindon Professional Development Centre, Drove Rd, Swindon SN1 3AH; Tel (01793) 616054; Fax (01793) 617773; *Head of Centre* A. Jensen
Wilton Professional Development Centre, C/o Wilton Middle School, The Hollows, Wilton SP2 0JE; Tel (01722) 744331; *Head of Centre* I. Gyllenspetz

Youth and Community Centres

Amesbury Sports and Community Centre, Antrobus Rd, Amesbury SP4 7ND; Tel (01980) 622173; *Manager* B. Smale
Bradford on Avon Centre Frome Rd, Bradford on Avon BA15 1LE; Tel (0122 16) 863485; *Youth and Community Worker* M. Walker
Calne Youth and Community Centre, Priestley Gr, Calne SN11 8EF; Tel (01249) 812509; *Youth and Community Worker* P. Kallmeier
Chippenham, The Bridge Centre, Bath Rd, Chippenham SN15 2AA; Tel (01249) 655249; *Youth and Community Worker* S. Rowland
Corsham, The Mansion Hse Youth and Community Centre, Pickwick Rd, Corsham SN13 9BJ; Tel (01249) 712250; *Youth and Community Worker* Vacancy
Devizes London Rd Centre, London Rd Centre, Eastcourt St, Devizes, Wiltshire; Tel (01380) 722598; *Youth and Community Worker* C.J. Thomas
Devizes, Southbroom Youth and Community Centre, The Green, Devizes SN10 5AB; Tel (01380) 722598; *Youth and Community Worker* C.J. Thomas
Durrington Youth and Community Centre, The Ham, Durrington, Salisbury SP4 8HW; Tel (01980) 654152; *Youth and Community Worker* R. Saul

Focus Youth and Community Centre, Beckhampton St, Swindon SN1 2JY; Tel (01793) 421644; *Head of Centre* Vacancy
Highworth, Youth and Community Centre, Newburgh Pl, Highworth, Swindon SN6 7DN; Tel (01793) 765279; *Youth and Community Worker* H. Wykes
Malmesbury, The Cartmell Youth and Community Centre, Tetbury Hill, Malmesbury SN16 9JB; Tel (01666) 823747; *Youth and Community Worker* I. Brownlie
Marlborough Youth and Community Centre, St Margaret's Mead, Marlborough SN8 4BA; Tel (01672) 512762; *Youth and Community Worker* S. Richards
Melksham Canberra Youth and Community Centre, 56 Spa Rd, Melksham SN12 7NY; Tel (01225) 702355; *Youth and Community Worker* A. Somerville
Pewsey Swimming and Sports Centre, Wilcot Rd, Pewsey SN9 4EW; Tel (01672) 62469; *Manager* I.H. Cook
Purton Youth and Community Centre, Reid's Piece, Purton, Swindon, Wiltshire; Tel (01793) 772267; *Youth and Community Worker* J. Kirk
Salisbury Grosvenor Hse, 26 Churchfields Rd, Salisbury SP2 7NH; Tel (01722) 337850; *Youth and Community Worker* C. Haines
Salisbury Youth and Comunity Centre, Wilton Rd, New Zealand Ave, Salisbury SP2 7JX; Tel (01722) 329717; *Youth and Community Worker* C. Haines
Salisbury Youth Theatre Hall, 169 Fisherton St, Salisbury, Wiltshire SP2 6SH; Tel (01722) 337850; *DYCSO* C. Haines
Stratton Youth and Community Centre, Hyde Rd, Upper Stratton, Swindon SN2 6SH; Tel (01793) 823354; *Head of Centre* M.B Roche
Swindon, Commonweal Youth and Community Centre, Commonweal School, The Mall, Swindon SN1 4JF; Tel (01793) 612207; *Head of Centre* J.M. Prowse
Swindon Connections (Youth Counselling), 178 Victoria Rd, Swindon SN1 3AY; Tel (01793) 612969; Helpline (01793) 695255; *Youth and Community Worker* E. Aspinall
Swindon, Dorcan Youth and Community Centre, Dorcan School, St Paul's Dr, Swindon SN3 5DA; Tel (01793) 524489; *Head of Centre* J. Davies
Swindon, Ferndale and Moredon Youth, Akers Way, Swindon, Wiltshire SN2 2NQ; Tel (01793) 526098; *Head of Centre* Vacancy
Swindon, Greendown Youth Centre, Grange Pk Way, Swindon SN5 6HN; Tel (01793) 877983; *Youth and Community Worker* R. Williams
Swindon, Lawn Youth and Community Centre, Churchfields School, Salcombe Gr, Swindon SN3 1ER; Tel (01793) 538484; *Head of Centre* L. Davis
Swindon, The Link Centre, The Link Officer, Whitehill Way, Westlea, Swindon SN5 7DL; Tel (01793) 871212; *Youth and Community Worker* J. Marchment
Swindon, Park Youth and Community Centre, Oakfield School, Marlowe Ave, Swindon, Wiltshire; Tel (01793) 521615; *Head of Centre* B. Luffman
Swindon, St Joseph's Youth and Community Centre, St Joseph's School, Queen's Dr, Swindon SN3 1AP; Tel (01793) 536589; *Head of Centre* P. Child
Swindon, Westbourne Youth and Community Centre, Westcott St, off Westcott Pl, Swindon SN1 5HS; Tel (01793) 611634; *Head of Centre* D. Kirby
Tidworth, Castledown Sports and Community Centre, Tidworth Rd, Ludgershall, Tidworth, Andover, Hants SP11 9RR; Tel (01264) 790828; *Manager* P.W. Mellors
Tisbury Youth and Community Centre, Weaveland Rd, Tisbury SP3 6HJ; Tel (01747) 871454; *Youth and Community Worker* G. Rotherham
Trowbridge Court Mills Youth and Community Care, Polebarn Rd, Trowbridge BA14 7EG; Tel (01225) 776772; *Youth and Community Worker* M. Perry
Trowbridge Innox Hall Youth and Community Centre, Innox Rd, Trowbridge BA14 9AT; Tel (01225) 776771; *Youth and Community Worker* M. Perry
Warminster Youth and Community Centre, The Close, Warminster BA12 9AL; Tel (01985) 218561; *Youth and Community Worker* W. Fitzhugh
Westbury Youth and Community Centre, Eden Vale Rd, Westbury BA13 3NY; Tel (01373) 822335; *Youth and Community Worker* P. Nicol
Wootton Bassett Youth and Community Centre, Lime Kiln, Wootton Bassett SN4 7HD; Tel (01793) 853198, Ext 30; *Youth and Community Worker* D. Roberts
Wroughton Youth and Community Centre, Inverary Rd, Wroughton SN4 9DR; Tel (01793) 813289; *Youth Tutor* Vacancy

Grant Maintained Schools

The John Bentley School, Silver St, Calne SN11 8YH; Tel (01249) 814214; Anne Burrell. (11–18) (1100)
Chippenham, Hardenhuish, Hardenhuish La, Chippenham SN14 6HW; Tel (01249) 650693; C.E. Smith. (11–18) (980)
Chippenham, Sheldon, Hardenhuish La, Chippenham SN14 6HJ; Tel (01249) 651216; C. Cox. (11–18) (1030)
Devizes School, The Green, Devizes SN10 3AG; Tel (01380) 724886; C.R. Isted. (11–18) (1010)
Highbury School, Church Rd, Laverstock, Salisbury, Wilts SP1 1RE; Tel (01722) 328536
Lavington School, The Spring, Market Lavington, Devizes SN10 4EB; Tel (01380) 812352; Fax (01380) 818492; D. Bury. (11–16) (520)
Marlborough, St John's Orchard Rd, Marlborough SN8 4AX; Tel (01672) 516156; J.T. Price. (11–18) (1362)
Pewsey Vale, Wilcot Rd, Pewsey, Wilts SN9 5EW; Tel (01672) 62481; J. Plante Cleall. (11–16) (420)
Purton, Bradon Forest, The Peak, Purton, Swindon SN5 9BG; Tel (01793) 770570/771063; I.R. Perkins. (11–16) (960)
St Augustines RC School, Wingfield Rd, Trowbridge, Wilts BA14 9EN; Tel (01225) 753577; Fax (01225) 777303
Salisbury, Bishop Wordsworth's Boys' 11 The Close, Salisbury SP1 2EB; Tel (01722) 333851; C.D. Barnett. (11–18) (670)
Salisbury, Highbury Boys', Highbury, Church Rd, Laverstock, Salisbury SP1 1RE; Tel (01722) 328536; W. Reilly. (11–16 (520)
Salisbury, South Wilts Grammar School for Girls, Stratford Rd, Salisbury SP1 3JJ; Tel (01722) 323326; M. Freeman. (11–18) (780)
South Wilts Grammar School for Girls, Stratford Rd, Salisbury, Wilts SP1 3JJ; Tel (01722) 323326
Stratton St Margaret, Kingsdown, Hyde Rd, Stratton St Margaret, Swindon SN2 6SJ; Tel (01793) 822284/825571; D.B. Williams. (11–16) (960)
Swindon, The Commonweal, The Mall, Swindon SN1 4JE; Tel (01793) 612727; M.R. Salt. (11–16) (840)
Swindon, St Joseph's R.C., Nythe Rd, Stratton St, Margaret, Swindon SN3 4AP; Tel (01793) 825998/9; P.J. Wells. (11–18) (1080)
Trowbridge, St. Augustines R.C., St Augustine's R.C. Wingfield Rd, Trowbridge BA14 9EN; Tel (01225) 753577; R.G. Cook. (11–16) (610)
Westbury, The Matravers, Springfield Rd, Westbury BA13 3QH; Tel (01373) 822666; N. Gilhespy. (11–16) (620)

Metropolitan Borough of Wirral

Population 331,744
Town Hall, Brighton St, Wallasey L44 8ED; Tel 0151-638 7070

Education Offices

Hamilton Bldg, Conway St, Birkenhead, Wirral L41 4FD; Tel 0151-666 2121
Director of Education D. Rigby, MEd
Principal Education Officer (Central Services Branch) S.P. Cassie
Principal Education Officer (Client Services Branch) R.J. Clark

Senior Inspector (Development) C.J. Batman
Senior Inspector (Management Services) A.J. Hewitt
Senior Inspector (Staff Development) S.A. Wood
Senior Inspector (Support Services) D.W. Griffith
Senior Inspector (Primary Education) J.P. Latham
Senior Inspector (Secondary Education) H. Cooper
General Inspector (Development) D. Armstrong
General Inspector (Resources) K. Billington
General Inspector (Pupil Services Secondary) J. Bulmer
General Inspector (Primary Curriculum) F. Cheetham
General Inspector (Information Technology) D. Delasalle
General Inspector (TVEI Curriculum) A. Graley
General Inspector (Science) C. Harrison
General Inspector (Modern Languages) J. Holroyd
General Inspector (Design & Technology) M. McEvoy
General Inspector (Early Years) A. McMullan
General Inspector (Personal/Social Education) A. Mayall
General Inspector (Primary) E. Robinson
General Inspector (Pupil Services Primary) C. Royle
General Inspector (Mathematics) A. Sankey
General Inspector (Human/Bus Ed. Home Economics/RE) D. Smith
General Inspector (Central Services) O. Smith
General Inspector (English) M. Stacey
General Inspector (Music and Creative Arts) D. Straughan
General Inspector (Physical Education) C. Stretch
General Inspector (Management Information) P. Waddington
General Inspector (Primary Curriculum) G. Williams
Principal Youth Officer E. Piecha
Principal Catering Officer P. Rutter
Manager Education Social Welfare Service J. Innes
Principal Educational Psychologist B.A. Bourne, BA, MSc,ABP; Tel 0151-666 2121
Supplies Officer K. Brooks
Principal Careers Officer R. Smith

Education Committee

Con 11, Lab 11, LD 2
Members of the Committee
Con: A.V. Adams, V.P. Borg, B.J. Cummings, A.M. Dishman, J.E. Green, H.M. Lea, I.J. Mackenzie, L.C. Moore, L.A. Rennie, J.G. Stedman, L. Turnbull
Lab: M. Cashman, G. Davies, M. Groves, J. Jackson, A.A. Keyes, C.M. Meaden, W.D. Nock, A.E.S. Rose, H. Smith, W.W. Smith, A.P. Witter
LD: A.H. Dunn, P.M. Williams

Governor Training Unit

Governor Training and Support Service, Wirral Education Dept, Hamilton Bldg, Conway St, Birkenhead, Wirral, Merseyside L41 4FD; Tel 0151-666 4283; Fax 0141-666 4207
Principal Officer F.M. Clarke, BSc(Econ)Hons, MA
Services Offered
Governors are offered an extensive range of cross authority and school based training courses looking at all aspects of their role and responsibilities. Attendance at these averages 2,000 Governors per year. Other resources include a termly newsletter, data bank, Helpline and LEA Consultancy services. Latter include the Governor training and support service plus the presence at every Governor meeting of an LEA Officer/Inspector to advise and guide participants

Special Schools and Units

Arrowe Pk Hospital School, Arrowe Pk Rd, Upton, Birkenhead, Merseyside; Tel 0151-678 5111, Ext 2116; Fax 0151-678 5489; I.D. Price. (2–19) (77)
Clare Mount, Fender La, Moreton L46 9PA; Tel 0151-606 9440; L.C. Clare, MEd. (12–19) (150)
Clatterbridge, Bebington L63 4JY; Tel 0151-334 6120, Ext 4236; D.S. Hamilton. (P.H.); (2–13) (45)
Elleray Pk, Elleray Pk, Wallasey L45 0LH; Tel 0151-639 3594; J. Bevan. (P.H.); 2–13 (58)
Foxfield, 100 Douglas Dr, Moreton, Wirral; Tel 0151-677 8555; Fax 0151-678 5480; I.M. Oram, BEd. (S.L.D.); (11–19) (104)
Gilbrook, Pilgrim St, Birkenhead L41 5EH; Tel 0151-647 8411; K.E. Jackson. (E.H.); (4–12) (41)
Hayfield School, Manor Dr, Upton L49 4PJ; Tel 0151-677 9303/14; J.G. Ashley, BA, BEd, MPhil. (M.L.D.); (6–13) (110)
Kilgarth, Cavendish St, Birkenhead L41 8DU; Tel 0151-652 8071; J.M. Dawson, BEd. (E.H.); (11–16) (46)
Meadowside, Pool La, Woodchurch, Birkenhead L49 5LR; Tel 0151-678 7711; Fax 0151-678 9155; G. Abbott. (P.H.); (13–19) (33)
Orrets Meadow Special School, Chapelhill Rd, Moreton L46 9QQ; Tel 0151-678 8070; S.E. Blythe, BEd, MEd. (S.L.D.); (7–12) (66)
Stanley, Pensby Rd, Thingwall, Wirral L61 7UG; Tel 0151-648 3171; R. Moruzzi, DipEd, DASE. (S.L.D.); (2–11) (87)

County Secondary Schools (11–16) (Birkenhead)

Birkenhead Institute, Tollemache Rd L41 0ES; Tel 0151-652 6771/2; Fax 0151-643 8065; M.D. Sutton, BSc. (Boys) (211)
Park, (Lower School), Park Rd North L41 0DD; Tel 0151-652 3435; M. Hopson, BA
Park, (Upper School), Park Rd South L43 4UY; Tel 0151-652 1574; Fax 0151-653 6760. (1128)
Prenton High School for Girls, Hesketh Ave, Rock Ferry L42 6RR; Tel 0151-645 1377; Fax 0151-643 1650; S. Goodall, BA. (627)
Ridgeway, Noctorum Ave, Birkenhead L43 7EB; Tel 0151-677 0013; Fax 0151-678 6571; P.J. Duffy, BEd(Hons). (697)
Rock Ferry, Ravenswood Ave, Rock Ferry L42 4NY; Tel 0151-645 6917; Fax 0151-643 1236; J. Hassall, BA. (1085)
Woodchurch, Carr Bridge Rd, Woodchurch L49 7NG; Tel 0151-677 5257; Fax 0151-678 1906; J. Byrom, BEd. (985)

County Secondary Schools (11–18) (Wallasey)

Mosslands School, (Upper School) Mosslands Dr, Wallasey L45 8PJ; Tel 0151-638 8131; Fax 0151-639 1317. (1254)
(Lower School) Mosslands Dr, Wallasey L44 2EQ; Tel 0151-638 5987/8131/2; W.V. Mitchell, BSc
Oldershaw, (Upper School) Valkyrie Rd, Wallasey L45 4RJ; Tel 0151-639 1956/051-639 1956; Fax 0151-691 1581. (1262)
(Lower School), Wallasey L45 4LP; Tel 0151-639 3983/1638 8570; G.T. Loach, BA, BSc, MEd
Wallasey School–East Wing, Oxley Ave, Leasowe L46 1QA. (1117)
Wallasey School–West Wing, Birket Ave, Moreton L46 1RA; Tel 0151-677 7825/3222; Fax 0151-605 0238; P.G. Johnson, MA
Weatherhead High, Mount Pleasant Rd, Wallasey L45 5HX; Tel 0151-639 7821; Fax 0151-637 1805; S.M. Davies, GRSM. (1222)

Special and Remedial Units

Sanderling/Ravenswood Unit, Rock Ferry High School, Ravenswood Ave, Birkenhead L42 4NY; Tel 0151-644 6670; S.M. Young
Wimbrick Hey Assessment Unit, 61 Burnley Rd, Moreton, Wirral; Tel 0151-606 0826; R. Taylor

Schools Support Service

C/o Birkenhead Institute High School for Boys, Tollemache Rd, Birkenhead L41 0ES; Tel 0151-670 0560/1/2; P. Weston

Hearing Impaired Service

Wirral Education Department, Conway Bldg, Conway St, Birkenhead L41 6JD; Tel 0151-666 4666; Fax 0151-666 4377; C. Peake

Visually Handicapped Service

Wirral Education Department, Conway Bldg, Conway St, Birkenhead L41 6JD; Tel 0151-666 4509; Fax 0151-666 4377; W. Kearns

Grammar Schools (11–18) (Bebington & Deeside)

West Kirby Grammar School, Graham Rd, West Kirby, Wirral L48 5DP; Tel 0151-632 3449; J. Erskine, BSc. (Girls) (1028)
Wirral Grammar School for Girls, Heath Rd, Bebington, Wirral L63 3AF; Tel 0151-644 8282; Fax 0151-643 1332; C.M. Baines, JP, BSc. (921)

High Schools (11–18) (Bebington & Deeside)

Bebington High School, Higher Bebington Rd, Bebington, Wirral L63 2PS; Tel 0151-645 4154/2132; Fax 0151-643 8065; R.J. Burns, BSc(Hons). (928)
Hilbre High School, Frankby Rd, West Kirby, Wirral L48 6EQ; Tel 0151-625 5996/6132; Fax 0151-625 3697; L. Maxim, BA, BEd. (801)
Pensby High School for Boys, Irby Rd, Heswall, Wirral L61 6XN; Tel 0151-648 2111; Fax 0151-648 3128; M.L. Jones, BA. (738)
Pensby High School for Girls, Irby Rd, Heswall, Wirral L61 6XN; Tel 0151-648 1941/5684; Fax 0151-648 8103; S.J. Hyden, BSc(Hons), PGCE. (1051)
South Wirral High School, Plymyard Ave, Eastham, Wirral L62 8EH; Tel 0151-327 3213; Fax 0151-327 7798; P.W. Francis, BA

High Schools (Voluntary)

Plessington R.C. High School, Old Chester Rd, Bebington L63 7LF; Tel 0151-645 5049/1990; Fax 0151-643 1516; A. Burns, MEd. (1080)
St Benedict's R.C. Aided High School, New Hey Rd, Upton Wirral L49 9BZ; Tel 0151-678 1777; J.M. Scott, BEd, LRSC. (702)
St Mary's R.C. College, Wallasey Village, Wallasey L45 3LN; Tel 0151-639 7531; Fax 0151-691 1452; T.J. Lightbown, BA. (1062)

Professional Development Centre

Acre La, Bromborough; Tel 0151-346 1182

Schools Psychological Service

Wirral Education Department, Beechcroft, Whetstone La, Birkenhead L41 2SA; Tel 0151-650 1970

Grant Maintained Schools

Calday Grange Grammar School, Grammar School La, West Kirby, Wirral L48 8AU; Tel 0151-625 2727; N. Briers, BA. (Boys) (11–16); (Mixed 6th form); (1240)
Wirral Grammar School for Boys, Cross La, Bebington, Wirral L63 3AQ; Tel 0151-644 0908; B.J. Treacy, BA. (853)

Wolverhampton Metropolitan Borough Council

Population 242,190
Civic Centre, St Peter's Sq, Wolverhampton WV1 1SH; Tel (01902) 27811; Fax (01902) 26644

Education Department

St Peter's Sq, Wolverhampton WV1 1RR; Tel (01902) 27811; Fax (01902) 314218
Director of Education R. Lockwood, BA
Assistant Director (Financial and Adminstrative Services) D. Rawlinson, MA
Assistant Director (School and Community Services) Vacancy
Chief Inspector/Head of Inspection Services E.L. Griffiths, MSc, BA, DIC, DiPFE, ACP Jennie Lee Professional Centre, Lichfield Rd, Wednesfield, Wolverhampton WV11 3HT; Tel (01902) 27811; Fax (01902) 315966
Chief Psychologist/Head of Children's Services B.A. Keil, MA, MEd(EdPsych) Neackells La – Children's Services, Neackells La, Wednesfield, Wolverhampton WV11 3PP; Tel (01902) 305580; Fax (01902) 865214
Head of Advisory Service T. Warren Jennie Lee Professional Centre, Lichfield Rd, Wednesfield, Wolverhampton WV11 3HT; Tel (01902) 27811; Fax (01902) 315966
Senior Education Manager (Equal Opportunities) A.K.M.H. Rashid, MA, Phil(Humanities)
Education Programme Manager (Schools) P. Dean, BSc, PGCE, ACP
Education Programme Manager (Post School) Vacancy
Senior Staff Inspector (Programme and Review Development) K.V. Sedgebeer, BA
Senior Inspector (Management Development) J. Johnson, BEd, DipMEd
Senior Inspector (Primary/Self Review) E. Way, DipEd Associateship(Scotland)
Senior Inspector (Assessment) P. Wilson, BA
General Inspector (Physical Education and Outdoor Activities A.R. Bayliss
General Inspector (Science and Technology) K. Martin
General Inspector (Post 14/Community Development) P. Cave, BA, PGCE
General Inspector (Key Stage 2 Curriculum and Special Needs) L. Rhodes, BA, MA
General Inspector (Humanities) J. Hallam, BSc, MSc, PGCE
General Inspector (TVEI) J. West, BSc(Econ)
General Inspector (Mathematics) R. Butcher, BSc
Head of Marketing and Management (Jennie Lee Professional Centre) D. Harris, BEd(Hons)
Director of Leisure Services D. Anderson
Number of Schools
10 nursery (840); 96 primary (23,000); 17 secondary (13,300)
Special Schools
6 day (520)
Day of Committee Meeting
Tuesday (every sixth week)
Other Authorities with whom Joint Purchasing Arrangements are made
None

Education Committee

Lab 9, Con 5, LD 1
Chair R.M. Jones, (Lab) 35 Riches St, Wolverhampton WV6 0DP
Vice-Chair A.G. Garner, (Lab) 37 Wanderers Ave, Wolverhampton WV2 3HL
Members of the Committee
Lab: P.T.A. Bateman, M.M. Benton, F. Docherty, S.S. Dutra, A.G. Garner, D. Hawkins, R.M. Jones, R.S. Reynolds, P. Wesley
Con: B.K. Carpenter, J. Davies, J.L.G. Davie, C.V. Mills, D.M. Seiboth
LD: R.F. Whitehouse

Governor Training Service

The Jennie Lee Professional Centre, Lichfield Rd, Wednesfield, Wolverhampton WV11 3HT; Tel (01902) 315293; Fax (01902) 315966
Governor Training Co-ordinator Pam Timmins, BA(Hons)

Services Offered

A varied annual course programme for Governors, including support for specific categories of Governor; An on-site consultancy service to identify Governing Body training needs leading to tailor-made training sessions; An information service including the production of a termly Governor newsletter; Provision of training materials for local and central resource banks.

Special Schools and Resource Areas

Bushbury Hill Junior Resource Area for EBD, Old Fallings La, Wolverhampton WV10 8BY; Tel (01902) 305974; J.K. Smith

Castlecroft Resource Area for Visual Handicap, Castlecroft (J & I), Windmill Cres, Castlecroft, Wolverhampton WV3 8HS; Tel (01902) 761654; D.J. Michie

Collingwood Infant Resource Area for MLD, Collingwood Rd, Bushbury, Wolverhampton WV10 8DS; Tel (01902) 397602; V. Willis

Collingwood Junior Resource Area for MLD, Collingwood Rd, Bushbury, Wolverhampton WV10 8DS; Tel (01902) 397603; Fax (01902) 398294; Elaine Pearson

Colton Hills Resource Area for Physical Handicap, Jeremy Rd, Goldthorn Pk, Wolverhampton WV4 5DG; Tel (01902) 333281; Fax (01902) 620597; R. Pask

Coppice High Resource Area for Mild Learning Difficulties, Ecclestone Rd, Wednesfield, Wolverhampton WV11 2QE; Tel (01902) 305956; Fax (01902) 307674; M.O. Hardacre

Danesmore Pk Resource Area for Mild Learning Difficulties, Russell Cls, Wednesfield, Wolverhampton WV11 2LA; Tel (01902) 305938; Fax (01902) 722226; C.D. Elliott

Deansfield Resource Area for Hearing Impaired, Deans Rd, Wolverhampton WV1 2BH; Tel (01902) 352362; Fax (01902) 351503; H.W. Howe. (Secondary)

East Pk Resource Area for Hearing Impaired, Hollington Rd, Wolverhampton WV1 2DS; Tel (01902) 451667; S.W. Adey

Farndale Junior Resource Area for EBD, Gatis St, Whitmore Reans, Wolverhampton WV6 0ES; Tel (01902) 312174; J.A. Smith

Green Pk, Green Park Ave, Bilston, West Midlands WV14 6EH; Tel (01902) 353924/353923; Fax (01902) 408076; P.D. English

Hospital/Home Tuition Service, Jennie Lee Professional Centre, Lichfield Rd, Wednesfield, Wolverhampton WV11 3HT; Tel (01902) 315947; S. Humphreyson

The Learning Support Team, Neackells La-Children's Services, Neackells La, Wednesfield, Wolverhampton WV11 3PP; Tel (01902) 305971; I. Carter

The Northicote Resource Area for MLD/EBD, Northwood Pk Rd, Bushbury, Wolverhampton WV10 8EP; Tel (01902) 397610; Fax (01902) 397731; L.G. Hampton

Our Lady and St Chad RC Resource Area for MLD, Old Fallings La, Wolverhampton WV10 8BL; Tel (01902) 305961; Fax (01902) 727861; C.J. Cooper

Palmers Cross Resource Area for Language and Communication, Windermere Rd, Tettenhall, Wolverhampton WV6 9DF; Tel (01902) 752373; C.M. Bates

Parkfield High Resource Area for MLD, Wolverhampton Rd East, Wolverhampton WV4 6AP; Tel (01902) 331212; Fax (01902) 341316; A.I. Thompson

Pendeford High Resource Area for MLD with EBD, Marsh La, Fordhouses, Wolverhampton WV10 6SE; Tel (01902) 397613; Fax (01902) 783748; R.J. Stephenson

Penn Fields, Birches Barn Rd, Penn Fields, Wolverhampton WV3 7BJ; Tel (01902) 339786; I.C. Turner

Penn Hall, Vicarage Rd, Penn, Wolverhampton WV4 5HP; Tel (01902) 332025; Fax (01902) 620335; A.J. Stoll

Pupil Referral Unit (Secondary), Bellamy La, Wednesfield, Wolverhampton WV11 1ND; Tel (01902) 305971

Pupil Referral Unit (Primary), Kingston Hse, Bellamy La, Wednesfield, Wolverhampton WV11 1ND; Tel (01902) 305536

St Andrews CE Infant Resource Area for Mild Learning Difficulty, Coleman St, Whitmore Reans, Wolverhampton WV6 0RH; Tel (01902) 759555; V. Currall

St Andrews CE Junior Resource Area for Mild Learning Difficulty, Coleman St, Whitmore Reans, Wolverhampton WV6 0RH; Tel (01902) 751344; A. Hughes

Smestow Resource Area for Visual Handicap, Windmill Cres, Castlecroft, Wolverhampton WV3 8HU; Tel (01902) 764141; Fax (01902) 380314; P. Hawthorne

Special Needs Early Years Team, Wood End Primary School, Wood End Rd, Wednesfield, Wolverhampton WV11 1YQ; Tel (01902) 305560; J. Wellings

Springdale Infant Resource Area for Language and Communication, Warstones Dr, Penn, Wolverhampton WV4 4NJ; Tel (01902) 335794; L.M. Murphy

Springdale Junior Resource Area for Language and Communication, Warstones Dr, Penn, Wolverhampton, West Midlands WV4 4NJ; Tel (01902) 336771; H.C. Grainger

Stowheath Infant Resource Area for Hearing Impaired and Mild Learning Difficulties, Vaughan Rd, Portobello, Willenhall, West Midlands WV13 3UD; Tel (01902) 366833; S. Bonnick

Stowheath Junior Resource Area for Mild Learning Difficulties, Hill Rd, Portobello, Willenhall, West Midlands WV13 3TT; Tel (01902) 366834; Fax (01902) 631282; B.F. Nuttall

Stowlawn Nursery, Green Park Ave, Bilston, West Midlands WV14 6EH; Tel (01902) 353880; A.R. Coates

Tettenhall Wood, School Rd, Tettenhall Wood, Wolverhampton WV6 8EJ; Tel (01902) 758545/744835; Fax (01902) 744835; M. Partington

Valley Pk Resource Area for Mild Learning Difficulties, Cromer Gdns, Wolverhampton WV6 0UA; Tel (01902) 750451; Fax (01902) 747760; J.M. Denton

Westcroft, Greenacres Ave, Underhill, Wolverhampton WV10 8NZ; Tel (01902) 305970/305969; Fax (01902) 732944; A.M. Chilvers

Secondary Schools

Colton Hills, Jeremy Rd, Wolverhampton, West Midlands WV4 5DG; Tel (01902) 333281; Fax (01902) 620597; R. Pask, BA. (Mixed) (1129)

Coppice High, Ecclestone Rd, Wednesfield, Wolverhampton WV11 2QE; Tel (01902) 305956; Fax (01902) 307674; M.O. Hardarce, BEd(Hons). (Mixed) (777)

Deansfield High, Deans Rd, Wolverhampton, West Midlands WV1 2BH; Tel (01902) 352362; Fax (01902) 351503; H.H. Howe. (Mixed) (700)

The Bilston High School, Prosser St, Bilston, West Midlands WV14 0QD; Tel (01902) 353895; Fax (01902) 492270; J. Warden. (Mixed) (360)

Heath Pk High, Prestwood Rd, Wolverhampton, West Midlands WV11 1RD; Tel (01902) 305958; Fax (01902) 305115; B.J. Cade. (Mixed) (894)

Highfields, Boundary Way, Penn, Wolverhampton, West Midlands WV4 4NT; Tel (01902) 333186; Fax (01902) 620601; A.J. Schofield. (Mixed) (1405)

Moreton Community, Old Fallings La, Wolverhampton, West Midlands WV10 8BY; Tel (01902) 305959; Fax (01902) 307545; R.J. Sheppard, BA. (Mixed) (647)

The Northicote, Northwood Park Rd, Bushbury, Wolverhampton, West Midlands WV10 8EP; Tel (01902) 397610; Fax (01902) 397731; L.G. Hampton. (Mixed) (594)

Our Lady & St Chad's R.C., Oldfallings La, Wolverhampton, West Midlands W10 8BL; Tel (01902) 305961; Fax (01902) 727861; C.J. Cooper, BSc, BA. (Mixed) (781)

Parkfield, Wolverhampton Rd East, Wolverhampton, West Midlands WV4 6AP; Tel (01902) 331212; Fax (01902) 341316; A.I. Thompson. (Mixed) (983)

Pendeford High, Marsh La, Fordhouses, Wolverhampton, West Midlands WV10 6SE; Tel (01902) 397613; Fax (01902) 783748; R.J. Stephenson, BSc. (Mixed) (657)
Regis, Regis Rd, Tettenhall, Wolverhampton WV6 8XG; Tel (01902) 756363; Fax (01902) 754048; *Head* M. Gannon. (Mixed) (988)
St Edmund's R.C., Compton Pk, Compton Rd West, Wolverhampton, West Midlands WV3 9DU; Tel (01902) 756371; Fax (01902) 746596; J.M. Sheppee, BSc. (Mixed) (695)
St Peter's Collegiate School, Compton Pk, Compton Rd West, Wolverhampton, West Midlands WV3 9DU; Tel (01902) 756444; Fax (01902) 751952; *Headteacher* P.M. Crook. (Mixed) (985)
Smestow, Windmill Cres, Castlecroft, Wolverhampton, West Midlands WV3 8HU; Tel (01902) 764141; Fax (01902) 380314; P. Hawthorne. (Mixed) (859)
Valley Pk, Cromer Gdns, Wolverhampton, West Midlands WV6 0UA; Tel (01902) 750451; Fax (01902) 747760; J.M. Denton. (Mixed) (366)
Wednesfield High, Lichfield Rd, Wednesfield, Wolverhampton, West Midlands WV11 3ES; Tel (01902) 305965; Fax (01902) 732182; J.D. Allpress, BSc. (Mixed) (1123)

Professional Centre

Jennie Lee Community and Professional Centre, Lichfield Rd, Wednesfield, Wolverhampton WV11 3HT; Tel (01902) 27811; Fax (01902) 315966

Careers Office

See chapter 17

Grant Maintained Schools

Aldersley High School Grant Maintained, Barnhurst La, Codsall, Wolverhampton, West Midlands WV8 1RT; Tel (01902) 758221; Fax (01902) 747598; M.B. Steventon. (Mixed) (530)
Moseley Pk School, Holland Rd, Bilston, Wolverhampton WV14 6LU; Tel (01902) 353901; Fax (01902) 496103. Mixed) (11–16 (1120)
Wolverhampton Girls'High School, Tettenhall Rd, Wolverhampton WV6 0BY; Tel (01902) 312186; Fax (01902) 715834; *Headteacher* M.M. Ribbins; *Chairman of Governors* Denis Grayson; *Finance Officer* Chris Ankers. (Girls) (11–18) (632)

Technology College

St Peter's Collegiate Church of England Voluntary Aided School a Voluntary Aided School, designated as a Technology College, Sponsored by the Garfield Weston Foundation, Database, Apricot Computers, Lucas Aerospace, Dixons Wallcoverings and Unilab. Affiliated to the Woodard Foundation of Church Schools Compton Pk, Compton Rd West, Wolverhampton, West Midlands WV3 9DU; Tel (01902) 756444; Fax (01902) 751952; P.M. Crook, MSc, BEd, FRSA. (Mixed) (1000)

4 Local Government London

Barking and Dagenham London Borough Council

Population 153,443
Civic Centre, Dagenham, Essex RM10 7BN; Tel 0181-592 4500

Education Department

Town Hall, Barking, Essex IG11 7LU; Tel 0181-592 4500; Fax 0181-594 9837
Chairman Councillor C.J. Fairbrass
Vice-Chairman Councillor F.C. Jones
Chief Education Officer A.P. Larbalestier, MA
Head of Education Operations Management (designated deputy) M.T. Carpenter, MA, BSc
Head of Education Management Support J.R. Scott, BA
EO (Schools) Ms I. Darling, BA
EO (Special Needs) J.J. Watt, BA
EO (Resources) M. Freeman, ACIS
EO (Personnel) C.L. Hardiman, BA(Hons), MIPM
EO (Policy and Planning) A. Benton, BA(Hons), MIPM

Education Committee

Chair C.J. Fairbrass, (Lab) c/o Civic Centre, Dagenham, Essex RM10 7BN
Vice-Chair F.C. Jones, (Lab) c/o Civic Centre, Dagenham, Essex RM10 7BN
Members of the Committee
M.R. Arnold, R.R. Beadle, D.F. Best, T.M. Bird, G.J. Bramley, S.J. Bremner, Cllr Brooker, J.E. Bruce, R.J. Curtis, R.C. Dixon, K.A. Golden, I.S. Jamu, S. Kallar, P.J. Manley, G.P.J. Mayor, R.A.J. Patient, T.P. Power, R. Rogers, G.H. Shaw, Cllr Whitebread, Cllr White, P.A. Twomey

Governor Training Unit

London Borough of Barking and Dagenham, Education Dept, Room 18, Town Hall, Barking, Essex IG11 7LU; Tel 0181-592 4500; Fax 0181-594 9837
LMS Co-ordinator Diane Graham
Services Offered
We offer a comprehensive training and support programme for all our Governors, covering a wide area of topics. We also have a Resource Room where Governors may borrow publications, audio, visual equipment etc. Our programme covers group sessions, whole team approach, residential school based and individual support. Link Governor system in operation

R.C. Secondary Comprehensive School

All Saints R.C., Terling Rd, Wood La, Dagenham RM8 1JT; Tel 0181-592 2464; Fax 0181-595 4024; D.P. Smith, MA, BA, AcDip. (1075)

Secondary Comprehensive Schools

Barking Abbey, Sandringham Rd, Barking IG11 9AG; Tel 0181-594 3541/2/3/14; Fax 0181-594 0052; A.J. Maxwell, BA(Hons), DipEd(Cantab). Mixed (1538)
Dagenham Priory, School Rd, Dagenham RM10 9QH; Tel 0181-595 4067; Fax 0181-595 2493; J.R. Torrie, MEd, AdDip, CertEd. Mixed (743)
Eastbury, Dawson Ave, Barking IG11 9QQ; Tel 0181-594 2094/0827; Fax 0181-507 0117; M.B. Dargon, MA, BEd. Mixed (1028)
Eastbrook, Dagenham Rd, Dagenham RM10 7UR; Tel 0181-592 6313/14193; Fax 0181-593 5050; K.G. Drury, BA, BEd. Mixed (1019)
Robert Clack, Gosfield Rd, Dagenham RM8 1JU; Tel 0181-592 3424; Fax 0181-593 2927; J.R. Fitch, BSc, PGCE, DipED. Mixed (1661)

Sydney Russell, Parsloes Ave, Dagenham RM9 5QT; Tel 0181-592 2914; Fax 0181-592 3459; Mrs G.I. Farnell, BA. Mixed (1497)
Warren, Whalebone La North, Chadwell Heath, Romford RM6 6SB; Tel 0181-590 0435/3497; Fax 0181-503 8462; D.J. Bullock, MA, BA, BSc. Mixed (957)

Special Schools

Bentry, Heathway, Dagenham RM10 7SJ; Tel 0181-592 2396; V.A. Jones
Castle, Goresbrook Rd, Dagenham RM9 6XP; Tel 0181-592 2738; T.M. Kilburn, MA
Faircross, Rosslyn Rd, Barking IG11 9UH; Tel 0181-594 5916; T. Kilburn (Acting), MA

Inspection and Advisory Service

Westbury Centre, Ripple Rd, Barking, Essex IG11 7PT; Tel 0181-591 5656; Fax 0181-594 7002
Principal Inspector R.S. Luxton, MA
Senior Inspector (Staff Development) J. Donovan, MEd, BEd
Senior Inspector (Curriculum Development) G. Last, BEd(Hons)
General Inspector (Art) K.L. Wright, BA(Hons)
General Inspector (English) J.L. Hargreaves, MA, BA(Hons)
General Inspector (Humanities) G.S. Rowe, BSc(Econ)
General Inspector (Information Technology) J.S. Lucock, BSc
General Inspector (Mathematics) Vacancy
General Inspector (Modern Languages) J.G. Lee, BA(Hons)
General Inspector (Music) Vacancy
General Inspector (Physical Education) F. Bevan
General Inspector (Primary) D.E. Rosenthal, BEd(Hons)
General Inspector (Primary) R. Medhurst, BA
General Inspector (Science) J.E. Mackie, BSc
General Inspector (Special Education Needs) V.M.K. Southwell-Sander, PGCE
General Inspector (Technology) N. Sagar, BEd(Hons)
General Inspector (Learning and Assessment) J. Moore
DSO Schools Catering Officer G. Clinton
Client Services Catering Manager Vacancy
TVEI Director K. Terrell
Principal Careers Officer L.P. Duffy, BA(Hons)
Principal Youth Officer F. Barns
Chief Education Social Worker K. Pinfold
Principal Educational Psychologist R. Boxer, BSc, MSc(EdPsych), PGCE
Senior Educational Psychologist B.D. Moorhouse, BSc, MSc DipEd
Senior Educational Psychologist M. Challen, BSc, MSc
Head of Language Support Service L. Hannigan
Head of Behaviour and Curriculum Support Service A. Louden
Chief Executive W.C. Smith, MCIBS, MIEEIE, MDBIM
Director of Finance R. Hillier, IPFA, ACMA, ARVA
Controller of Development and Technical Services D.J. Knowles, CEng, MICE, MIHT
Director of Social Services N. Walker, MA, DipSW, CQSW
Borough Librarian A.J. Hill, ALA
Controller of Contract Services D.P. Allen, MBA, DMS, ARICS
Controller of Housing B.F. Crowley
Borough Health and Consumer Services Officer D.W. Woods, DMS, MRSH

Number of Schools and Further Education Establishments
54 primary (14,145); 8 secondary comprehensive schools (9,518) 1 college of adult education
Special Schools
3 day
Day of Committee Meeting
Tuesdays, every 6-8 weeks
Population
148,600

Adolescent and Court Service

115 Marlborough Rd, Dagenham; Tel 0181-592 9442; K. Bradshaw; *Centre Manager* J. James

Adult Education

The Adult College of Barking and Dagenham, Fanshaw Cres, Dagenham RM9 5QA; Tel 0181-595 3237/3238; Fax 0181-595 1395; *Head of Adult College* P. Cooney
Barking and Dagenham Music Centre, The Adult College, Fanshawe Cres, Dagenham RM9 5QA; Tel 0181-593 8257; *Head of Music Support* S. Sharp
Faircross Branch, Hurstbourne Gdns, Barking; Tel 0181-594 4737

Youth Training

Youth Training, Halbutt St, Dagenham, Essex RM9 5AJ; Tel 0181-592 2916; Fax 0181-592 4979; *Manager* M. Balcombe

The Learning Support Service

Seabrook Hse, 22 Shipton Cl, Bennetts Castle La, Dagenham, Essex; Tel 0181-593 7577; *Head of Service* T. Louden

Education Service for Hearing Impaired

C/o Faircross School, Rosslyn Rd, Barking; Tel 0181-591 9236; M. Chandler

Youth Service

Town Hall, Barking, Essex IG11 7LU; *Principal Youth Officer* F. Barns; Tel 0181-592 4500 (Ext 3028); *Youth Service Development Officer* B. Lindsay; Tel 0181-592 4500 (Ext 3027)

Youth Centres

Beacon Youth Centre, 195-211 Becontree Ave, Dagenham; Tel 0181-590 9904; Vacancy
Chadwell Heath Club, Warren Comprehensive School, Whalebone La North, Chadwell Heath, Romford RM6 6SB; Tel 0181-599 8410; *Club Manager* B. Kettle
Erkenwald Club, Marlborough Rd, Dagenham RM8 2HU; Tel 0181-593 8917; *Club Manager* L. Muscat
Longhouse Centre, Charlecote Rd, Dagenham RM8 3LD; Tel 0181-592 1803; Vacancy
Marley Club, Dagenham Priory Comprehensive School, School Rd, Dagenham RM10 9QH; Tel 0181-592 4143; *Club Manager* D. Telfer
Mayesbrook Lake Outdoor Centre, Centre, Mayesbrook Lake, Lodge Ave, Dagenham, Essex; Tel 0181-593 3539; *Senior Instructor* S. Watson
New Cambell Club, Arden Cres, Dagenham RM9 6TD; Tel 0181-592 7793; F. Barns
Oaks Centre, Collier Row Rd, Romford RM5 2DD; Tel 0181-590 5980; *Bursar P/T* M. Fuller
Outdoor Pursuits Centre, Eastbrook Comprehensive School, Dagenham Rd, Dagenham RM10 7UR; Tel 0181-595 3922; *Outdoor Education Development Officer (Land Activities)* P. Newton
River Outdoor Centre, 176 Abbey Rd, Barking IG11 7BT; Tel 0181-594 4335; *Outdoor Education Development Officer (Water Activities)* J. Elsmore; All correspondence to be sent to: Operations Management Team, c/o Chief Education Officer, Education Department, Town Hall, Barking
Spartans, Faircross Special School, Rosslyn Rd, Barking IG11 9UH; Tel 0181-594 5916; *Warden P/T* A. Birch
Thames View Club, Bastable Ave, Thames View Est, Barking IG11 0LG; Tel 0181-594 4089; *Club Manager* S. Gooding
Westbury Club, Westbury Centre, Ripple Rd, Barking IG11 7PT; Tel 0181-594 4009; *Warden P/T* E. Beresford

College of Adult Education

Adult College of Barking and Dagenham, Fanshawe Crescent, Dagenham RM9 5QA; Tel 0181-595 3237/8; Fax 0181-595 1395
Head of College Miss P. Cooney, BA(Hons)

In-Service Centre

Westbury Centre, Ripple Rd, Barking IG11 7PU; Tel 0181-594 5656; Fax 0181-594 7002; *Professional Development Coordinator/Centre Manager* Ms M. Hanke

Outdoor Pursuits Centre

Trewern Outdoor Education Centre, Cusop, Hay-on-Wye, Herefordshire HR3 5RF; Tel (01497) 820512; Fax (01497) 820056; *Head of Centre* D. Daniels

Barnet London Borough Council

Population 304,700
The Town Hall, The Burroughs, Hendon, London NW4 4BG; Tel 0181-202 8282; Fax 0181-202 4981

Community Services Department

Barnet Hse, 1255 High Rd, Whetstone, London N20 0EJ; Tel 0181-446 8511; Fax 0181-446 6426

Educational Services

Educational Services, formerly Friern Barnet Town Hall, Friern Barnet La, London N11 3DL; Tel 0181-368 1255; Fax 0181-361 3794
Director of Educational Services and Chief Education Officer J. Bailey, MA
Chairman Cllr A. Jarvis
Vice Chairman Cllr A. Dickie, MA(Oxon), LLB
Head of Special Educational Needs T.D. Shine, BA(Hons), MA
Quality Manager R. Rickard, BA, MA
Head of Education Policy S. Taylor-Brooke, BEd (Hons), MA
Controller of Libraries, Arts and Museums M. Kempson, ALA
LMS Resources Manager R. McDonaugh, BA
Education Officer (Service Development) H. Steinhof, MA, BA(Hons), CertEd
Education Liaison Officer G. Bird, BA
Education Liaison Officer Vacancy
Staff Development and Training Co-ordinator M. Elliott, MA(Educ)
Pupil and Student Services Manager V. Patty, MA, BSc
Communications Manager Vacancy
Operational Systems Manager A. Stephens
Service Manager (Careers) P. Stevens, BA(Hons), DipVG
Principal Education Welfare Officer N. Flint, BSc(Hons)
Principal Youth Officer E. Finestone, Dip Y&C Studies
Management Officer Special Educational Needs A. Duncan
Principal Educational Psychologist Mrs D. Earl, DipEd, MA, MSc
General Inspector (English and Drama) Ms J. Joyner
Learning Support S. Flockton, BD(Hons), ADDip(SEN)
Emotional Behavioural Difficulties J. Roucroft, CertEd Dip(Sen)
Sensory and Physical V. Standen, MA
Statementing M. Norman-Smith, BA(Hons), Med
Senior Child Psychotherapist T. Woodcock
Senior Child Psychologist A. McCann
Number of Schools
4 nursery (527); 87 primary (22,496); 11 secondary (16,125)

Special Schools

4 day (306)

Education Committee

Con 10, Lab 8, LD 2
Chair Anne Jarvis, (Lab) Members Room, Hendon Town Hall, The Burroughs, Hendon NW4
Vice-Chair Andrew Dickie, MA(Oxon), LLB, (Lab) Members Room, Hendon Town Hall, The Burroughs, Hendon NW4
Members of the Committee
Con: E. Bunn, J. Czarny, A. Finn, J. Hedge, L. Mammatt, K, Patel, J. Rawles, R. Shutz, J. Tiplady, V. Usher
Lab: R. Carney, K. Lyons, M. Packer, G. Sargeant, A. Slocombe, R. Vis
LD: W. Casey, J. Cohen

Governor Training Unit

Training Section, London Borough of Barnet, Educational Services, Friern Barnet La, London N11 3DL; Tel 0181-368 1255; Fax 0181-361 3794
Governors Support and Development Co-ordinator M. Kuhn, BACertEd
Services Offered
Courses offered at a central venue, designed to develop governor skills and assist governing bodies in all areas of their responsibility; Consultancy for individual governing bodies on subjects of their choice; Newsletter; Helpline; Briefing meetings for Link Governors and Chairmen; Resource Centres in Educational Services and in Libraries; Governors Support and Development Forum (advisory and decision-making body on governor matters)

Special Schools

Mapledown, Claremont Rd NW2 1TR; Tel 0181-455 4111; Fax 0181-455 4895; Miss S.A. Mortimer, DipEd. E.S.N.(S) 12-16+ (52)
Northway, The Fairway, Mill Hill NW7 3HS; Tel 0181-959 4232; Fax 0181-959 6436; E.F. Runham, BA. E.S.N.(M) 5–16 (79)
Oak Lodge, Heathview N2 0QY; Tel 0181-444 6711; Fax 0181-444 6711; P.E.M. Carney, BA(Ed). (E.S.N.(M) 5–16+) (113)
Oakleigh, Oakleigh Rd North, Whetstone N20 0DH; Tel 0181-368 5336; Fax 0181-361 6922; Mrs J.L. Charlesworth, BEd. (E.S.N.(S) 2–11) (52)

Secondary Schools (County)

Christ's College, East End Rd, Finchley N2 0SE; Tel 0181-349 3581; Fax 0181-346 7136; B. Fletcher, BA. Boys (11–18) (924)
Copthall, Page St, Mill Hill NW7 2EP; Tel 0181-203 1074; Fax 0181-203 1074; Mrs S.M. Walden, BSc, MEd. Girls (11–18) (1063)
East Barnet, Chestnut Grove, Cat Hill, East Barnet EN4 8PU; Tel 0181-440 4162; Fax 0181-449 9862; R.D. Hurdman, BSc. Mixed (11–18) (1133)
Edgware, Green La, Edgware, Middx HA8 8BT; Tel 0181-958 5310; Fax 0181-905 4193; M.J. Welch, BA. Mixed (11–18) (910)
Friern Barnet County, Hemington Ave, Friern Barnet N11 3LS; Tel 0181-368 2777; Fax 0181-368 3208; Mrs M.R. Stanier, BSc. Mixed (11–16) (610)
Queen Elizabeth's, High St, Barnet EN5 5RR; Tel 0181-449 2984; Fax 0181-441 2322; Vacancy. Girls (11–18) (930)
Ravenscroft, Barnet La N20 8AZ; Tel 0181-445 9205; Fax 0181-343 7466; J.R. Porter, BSc. Mixed (11–18) (955)
Whitefield, Claremont Rd, Cricklewood NW2 1TR; Tel 0181-455 4114; Fax 0181-455 4382; H. Taylor, BA, MSc. Mixed (11–18) (582)

Secondary Schools (Voluntary)

Christ Church C.E., Warnham Rd, Finchley N12 9NR; Tel 0181-445 3249; Fax 0181-343 9368; B. Fox, BSc. V.A. (Mixed) (11–16) (610)

Henrietta Barnet, Central Sq, Hampstead Garden Suburb NW11 7BN; Tel 0181-458 8999; Mrs E.J. De Swiet. V.A. (Girls) (11–18) (625)

Professional Development Centre

Inspection and Advisory Service 451 High Rd, Finchley N12 0AS; Tel 0181-349 9222; Fax 0181-349 1880; *Senior Adviser/Inspector (Primary)* D. Burns, MA, DipEd; *Senior Adviser/Inspector (Secondary)* P. King, BEd, MSc; *Adviser/Inspector (Modern Languages)* D. Boatman, BA(Hons); *Adviser/Inspector (Assessment and Achievement)* K. Crilley, BA(Hons); *Adviser/Inspector (Primary/Physical Education)* S. Gray, DipPE, BEd; *Adviser/Inspector (Primary)* R. Griffiths, BEd(Hons); *Adviser/Inspector (English and Drama)* J. Joyner, BA(Hons), PGCE; *Adviser/Inspector (Information Technology)* A. Ley, MEd, BEd, DipCompEd; *Adviser/Inspector (Science)* V. Pite, BSc(Hons); *Adviser/Inspector (Special Educational Needs)* L. Stone, MEd, CertEd, AdvDipEd; *Adviser/Inspector (14–18 Education)* I. Wilson, BSc, MA, PhD; *Adviser/Inspector (Mathematics)* D. Tobin, BACertEd, AdDipEd; *Adviser (In-Service Training)/Manager of the Professional Development Centre* P. Marvell, BEd(Hons)

Multicultural Education and Language Support Service, (MELSS) Professional Development Centre, 451 High Rd, Finchley N12 0AS; Tel 0181-349 9222; M. Kenny, BA(Econs), PGCE

Manorside Curriculum Development Centre, Squires La, Finchley N3; Tel 0181-349 2793; *Careers Education, Guidance and Records of Achievement* P. Ayers; *Education Business Partnership* B. Thornton; *Education Business Partnership* M. Steene; *Teacher Placement Organiser* L. Knight; *Teaching and Learning Styles* K. Carrick; *TVEI Extension (Barnet Curriculum Enhancement Project) (Co-ordinator Barnet Vocational Education Consortium)* H. Jones

Youth Centres

South District Childs Hill, Garden Suburb, Golders Green, Hendon and West Hendon Electoral Wards

Hendon Youth Sports Centre, Algernon Rd NW4 3TA; Tel 0181-202 6027; *Team Leader* M. Ling

Welsh Harp Youth Sailing Base, Cool Oak La NW9 7BG; Tel 0181-202 6672; *Centre Organiser* H. Mackie

East District East Finchley, Finchley, St Paul's, Totteridge and Woodhouse Electoral Wards

Compton Centre and Youth Club, Summers La N12 0QG; Tel 0181-368 6316; *Acting Centre Manager* C. Oak

Finches Youth Centre, Woodhouse College, Woodhouse Rd N12 9EY; Tel 0181-445 0249; *Youth Worker* A. Forde

Herbert Wilmot Youth Centre, Market Pl, East Finchley N2 8DD; Tel 0181-444 8422; *Youth Worker* L. Murphy

Finchley Youth Theatre, 142 High Rd, Finchley N2 9ED; Tel 0181-883 9957; *Centre Manager* A. Dean

West District Burnt Oak, Colindale, Edgware, Hale and Mill Hill Electoral Wards

Canada Villa Youth Centre, Sanders La NW7 2BU; Tel 0181-959 2811; *Youth Worker* M. Clarke

Grahame Park Youth Centre, Corner Mead, Grahame Park Way, London NW9 9RA; Tel 0181-205 7112; *Team Leader* D. Allen

Log Cabin Adventure Playground, Lanacre Ave, Grahame Pk NW9; Tel 0181-200 6441; *Play Worker* J. Marshall

Moat Mount Camp Site, Barnet By-Pass, Mill Hill NW7 3AL; Tel 0181-959 1807 (Campsite); 0181-368 1255 Ext 3218 (Bookings); *Centre Warden* P. Smyth

Spur Road Youth Club, Community Centre, Green La, Edgware, Middx; Tel 0181-952 9872; *Youth Worker* Miss S.K. Hackett

North District Arkley, Brunswick Park, East Barnet, Friern Barnet and Hadley Electoral Wards

Ashmole Centre, Burleigh Gdns, Southgate N14 5RJ; Tel 0181-368 4984; *Centre Manager/Team Leader* A. Hatvani

Church Farm Youth Centre and the Whalehouse (Alcohol-Free Bar) Church Hill Rd, East Barnet EN4 8XE; Tel 0181-361 3051; *Youth Worker* Vacancy

Queen Elizabeth's Centre, Meadway, Barnet EN5 5RR; Tel 0181-441 2933; *Centre Manager* D. Bagley

Grant Maintained Schools

Ashmole, Cecil Rd, Southgate N14 5RJ; Tel 0181-368 2608; D.G. Pibworth. (Mixed) (11–18) (1011)

Bishop Douglas R.C. High School, Hamilton Rd, East Finchley, London N2 0SQ; Tel 0181-444 5211; Fax 0181-444 0416; J.R. Meadows. (Mixed) (11–18) (1073)

Finchley Catholic High, Woodside La N12 8TA; Tel 0181-445 0105; S.Z. Szemerenyi. (Boys) (11–18) (929)

Hasmonean, Holders Hill Rd, Hendon NW4 1NA; Tel 0181-203 1411; Rabbi M. Roberg, BA, MPhil, DipEd. V.A. (Boys and Girls) (11–18) (910)

Hendon School, Golders Rise, Hendon NW4 2HP; Tel 0181-202 9004; *Headteacher* R.A. Lloyd; *Chair of Governors* J. Foster; *Finance Manager* Mrs Hansford. (Mixed) (11–18) (950)

Mill Hill County High, Worcester Cres, Mill Hill NW7 4LL; Tel 0181-959 0017; D.J. Culley, MA. Mixed (11–18) (1242)

Queen Elizabeth's School Queen's Rd, Barnet, Herts EN5 4DQ; Tel 0181-441 4646; Fax 0181-440 7500; *Headmaster* E. Harris, MA. (Boys 11-18) (1100)

St James' R.C. High School, Orange Hill Rd, Burnt Oak, Edgware HA8 0ST; Tel 0181-959 3410; F.M. Jordan, BA. V.A. (Mixed) (11–18) (1120)

St Mary's C.E., Downage, Hendon NW4 1AB; Tel 0181-203 2827; J.M. Wood, BA. V.A. (Mixed) (11–18) (957)

St Michael's Convent, Nether St, Finchley N12 7NJ; Tel 0181-446 2256; Miss M.P.K. Daly, BSc. V.A. (Girls) (11–18) (615)

Bexley London Borough Council

Population 219,500

Bexley Civic Offices, Broadway, Bexleyheath, Kent DA6 7LB; Tel 0181-303 7777; Fax 0181-301 2661

Directorate of Education

Hillview, Hill View Dr, Welling, Kent DA16 3RY; Tel 0181-303 7777

Director of Education P. McGee (Acting), MSc

Chief Education Inspector L.E. Pearson (Acting), MA(Ed)

Chief Librarian M. Lister, BA, MSc, ALA

Education Services Secretary P. Makin, IPFA

Assistant Education Services Secretary (General Services) C.H. Lewis, MA, DMS

Assistant Education Services Secretary (Committee Services) M.R. Whybrow, DMA, FCIS

Education Finance Office Brian Cole, IPFA

EO (LMS) J. Saunders, MBIM, BA, ADipEd

EO (Special Education) V. Shenton, BEd

Education Officer (Planning) R. Pinniger, BA, MA, MSc, MPhil

Principal Inspector N. Vivian, BSc, MA

Senior Inspector (Primary) C. Jackson, BA, DipEd

Senior Inspector (Secondary) M. Davidson, MA, MSc, DipPth

E0 (Special Needs) D. Drew, MA

SEO (Client Unit) R. Fee

EO (Admissions) K. Porter

EO (Evaluation) M. Cadmann, BSc

EO (Pupils) H. Morton

Principal Careers Officer J.A. Tuggey, LLB, MICD

Principal Youth and Community Officer (Acting) A. Papademitrie

EO (Pupil Assessment) C. Salter, BSc, PGCE, CertEd, Psych

Number of schools
64 primary (16,432); 17 secondary (17,920); 4 day special schools (377)

Education Committee

Chair C.F. Hargrave 10 Appledore Cres, Sidcup, Kent DA14 6RQ
Members of the Committee
N.P. Bretts, D. Briant, A.H. Charlton, M.J. Davey, H.K. Davis, R.N. French, S. Hall, P. Hollamby, B. Huish, P.W. Hurran, B.W. Oliver, R.J. Passey, T. Perrin, P.G. Scopes, K. Smith, C.L. Tandy, P.G.J. Weston

Education Client Unit

Directorate of Education, Hill View Dr, Welling, Kent DA16 3RY; Tel 0181-303 7777 Ext 4393; Fax 0181-319 4302
Co-ordinator for Governor Support and Training Patrick A. Taylor, MA(Cantab), MIC
Services Offered
Comprehensive support and development programme, including; In-house training; Central briefing and training sessions; 24 hour Helpline; Newsletter "Governing Bexley Schools"; Consultancy Resource bases ending facilities

Special Schools

Marlborough, Marlborough Park Ave, Sidcup DA15 9DP; Tel 0181-300 6896; J. Palmer (Acting), CertEd. (2–16+) (60)
Shenstone, Old Rd, Crayford DA1 4DZ; Tel (01322) 524145; D.E. Hall, CertEd. (2–16+) (72)
Westbrooke, South Gipsy Rd, Welling DA16 1JB; Tel 0181-304 1320; R.B. Lovegrove, CertEd. (5–11) (49)
Woodside, Woodside Rd, Crayford DA7 6LB; Tel (01322) 529240; J.R.G. Martin, BEd. (E.S.N. 5–16+) (196)

Secondary Schools (County 11–18)

Blackfen School for Girls, Blackfen Rd, Sidcup DA15 9NU; Tel 0181-303 1887; R.A.A. Henriksen, MSc. (Girls) (890)
Cleeve Park, Bexley La, Sidcup DA14 4JN; Tel 0181-302 6418; G. Coop, BA, MA. (Mixed) (830)
Hurstmere, Hurst Rd, Sidcup DA15 9AW; Tel 0181-300 5665; I.N. Jones, BSc. (Boys) (930)
Trinity School, Belvedere Erith Rd, Belvedere DA17 6HT; Tel 0132 24-41371; R. Slade, BA, MA. (Mixed) (650)
Welling, Elsa Rd, Welling DA16 1LB; Tel 081-304 8531; B.J.C. Ambrose, MSc, BEd. (Mixed) (1100)
Westwood Technology College, The Green, Welling DA16 2PE; Tel 0181-303 2923; K.W.L. Clements, BSc. (Mixed) (540)

Secondary Schools (11–18)

Bexley Grammar, Danson La, Welling DA16 2BL; Tel 0181-304 9538; C. Jones, BSc, MPhil. (Mixed) (890)
Townley Grammar School for Girls, Townley Rd, Bexleyheath DA6 7AB; Tel 0181-304 8311; L. Hutchinson, BA, MA. (Girls) (950)
Bexleyheath, Graham Rd, Bexleyheath DA6 7DA; Tel 081-303 5696; M. Noble, BEd, MA. (Mixed) (1540)
Chislehurst and Sidcup Grammar, Hurst Rd, Sidcup DA15 9AG; Tel 081-302 6511; J.A. Rouncefield, BSc, MA. (Mixed) (1200)
Erith, Avenue Rd, Erith DA8 3BN; Tel 0132 24 48231; T. Hufford, BEd, MPhil. (Mixed) (1770)
Thamesmead Community College Yarnton Way, Thamesmead, Erith DA18 4DW; Tel 0181-310 0111; J. Sherbourne, MA, BA. (Mixed) (700)

Institutes of Adult Education

Administrative Headquarters, Sidcup Arts and Adult Education Centre, Alma Rd, Sidcup, Kent DA14 4ED;
Principal Adult Education Officer R. Easterbrook; Tel 0181-509 5570
Central Area, Brampton Rd Education Centre, 5 Brampton Rd, Bexleyheath DA7 4EZ; Tel 0181-303 2541
Northern Area, Crayford Manor House Adult Centre, Mayplace Rd East, Crayford DA1 4HB; Tel 521463
Southern Area, Sidcup Arts and Adult Education Centre Alma Rd, Sidcup DA14 4ED; Tel 0181-300 1056

Professional Development Centres

Bexley Education Support and Training, Hill View, Hill View Dr, Welling, Kent DA16 3RY; Tel 0181-303 7777 Ext 4343; Gordon Young

Youth Centres

Belvedere Youth Centre, Mitchell Cl, Belvedere DA17 6AA; Tel 0181-311 5550; B. Shoben
Cray Youth Centre, 150 Rectory La, Sidcup DA14 5BT; Tel 0181-302 3868; *Co-ordinator* N. Marjolin
Crayford and Barnehurst Youth Centre, Woodside Rd, Bexleyheath DA7 6EQ; Tel (01322) 527176; A. Ball
Danson Youth Centre, Brampton Rd, Bexleyheath DA7 4EZ; Tel 0181-303 6052; J. Toghill
Northumberland Heath Youth Centre, Sussex Rd, Erith DA8 1JB; Tel (01322) 439043; D. Weekes
Royal Park Youth Centre, Pembury Cres, Albany Pk, Sidcup DA14 4QD; Tel 0181-300 5097; C. Owen
Sidcup Youth Centre, Burnt Oak La, Sidcup DA15 9EZ; Tel 0181-300 3882; J. Emery
South Reach Youth Centre, Howbury Grange Centre, Slade Green Rd, Erith DA8 2HX; Tel (01322) 337299; K. Hunt
Thamesmead Youth Centre Thamesmead Community College, Yarnton Way, Erith DA18 4DW; Tel 0181-310 0247; F. Creed
Welling Youth Centre, Lovel Ave, Welling DA16 3JQ; Tel 0181-854 1639; J. Ballentyne

Grant Maintained Schools

Bexley/Erith Technical High, Hartford Rd, Bexley DA5 1NE; Tel (01322) 56538; J. Tobin, MA. (Boys) (762)
St Catherine's, Watling St, Bexleyheath DA6 7QJ; Tel (01322) 56333; S.A. Mellish, BA. (V.A.) (Girls) (719)
St Mary and St Joseph's, Chislehurst Rd, Sidcup DA14 6BP; Tel 0181-309 7700; Fax 0181-300 6815; A. Fogell, BA(Hons), MEd. G.M. (Mixed) (700)
St Columba's, Halcot Ave, Bexleyheath DA6 7QB; Tel (01322) 553236; S.J. Grummitt, BSc, MA. (Boys) (728)

Brent London Borough Council

Population 243,025 (1991 Census)
Brent Town Hall, Forty La, Wembley, Middx HA9 9EZ; Tel 0181-904 1244; Fax 0181-908 7065

Education, Arts and Libraries Department

Education Offices, Chesterfield Hse, 9 Park La, Wembley, Middx HA9 7RW; Tel 0181-904 1244; Fax 0181-900 5440
Chairman, Education, Arts and Libraries Committee Councillor J. Warren
Executive Director of Education, Arts and Libraries G.F. Benham, BA, MPhil, DipEd, MA, FBIM, FRSA; Tel 0181-900 5553
Director of Community Education Services B.J. Stead, BSc, MA; Tel 0181-900 5554
Head of Policy and Planning W. Mallard, BA, MA
Director (Schools' Support) D. Sassoon, BA, CertEd, MA

Director of Commissioning F. Quigg, BEd(Hons)
Director of Services to Schools P. Doherty, MEd
Chief Inspector of Schools J. Simpson, BSc, MA
Community Education Services A. Basudev, BSc, MA, DipCD, DipYCS
Primary Education Inspector Madeleine Aherne
English and Drama Inspector R. Ive, BEd (Hons)
Humanities and RE Inspector Ms C. Ross, MA(Hons)
Primary Education Inspector R. Johnson, BEd, MA
Primary Education and SEN Inspector R. Sachse, BA, PGCE, MA
Mathematics Inspector Ms S. Sharkey, BA, MSc
Science Inspector Ms B. Tomlinson, BSc
Director of Education Catering A. Burnett, TEC Dip Hotel Catering Inst Mgt, BIM Cert
Principal Careers Officer W. Clark, BSc, ARCS, CertEd, DipCG Careers Office, Triangle Hse, 328–330 High Rd, Wembley, Middx HA9 6AZ; Tel 0181-900 5430
Principal Education Psychologist T. Bryans, BA, DipEd, MSc; Tel 0181-900 5531
TVEI Extension Inspector C. McKearney, BSc, DMS, MA
Modern Languages Inspector Ms F. Ellks, BA
English and Drama Associate General Inspector T. Furlong, BA(Hons), MA(Ed), LRAM, AKC, FRSA
Chief Executive C. Wood, BSc(Civil Eng), MICE, DipTP

Number of Schools
4 Nursery schools (180); 63 Primary (19,944 full-time, 1,673 part-time); 13 secondary (11,675)

Special Schools
5 day

Day of Committee Meeting
Seven Week Cycle approx

Brent Education Psychology Service

The Education Dept, Chesterfield Hse, 9 Park La, Wembley, Middx HA9 7RW; Tel 0181-900 5531
Principal Officer T. Bryans, BA, DipEd, MSc

Secondary Schools

Wembley High, East La, Wembley HA0 3NT; Tel 0181-904 5066; S. Armstrong, MA, PGCE. (833)
Willesden High, Doyle Gdns NW10 3ST; Tel 0181-965 5976; T.C. Buzzard, BA(Hons), MA. (503)
William Gladstone High, Parkside NW2; Tel 0181-450 2631/2; Ms B. Kelly, BA. Mixed (Closing) (518)

Special Schools

Grove Park, Grove Pk, Kingsbury, London NW9 0JY; Tel 0181-204 3293; *Headteacher* Miss J.F. Edwards, MSc, BA(Hons), DipEd(Adv). P.D.
Hay Lane, Grove Pk, Kingsbury, London NW9 0JY; Tel 0181-204 5396; *Headteacher* P.M. Theuma. SLD
Manor Day School, 5/7 The Avenue, London NW6 7YG; Tel 0181-459 8488; *Headteacher* Mrs Drake, MA, BEd. MLD; MLD
Vernon House,; G.S. Davidson, BA, BPhil(Hons), AdvDipEd(Special). E.B.D.
Woodfield, Glenwood Ave, Kingsbury, London NW9 7LY; Tel 0181-205 1977. M.L.D. (Mixed)

Primary Support Service

Co-ordinator Ms L. Harrowell, BA
Sensory Impairment Peripatetic Service; Co-ordinator M. Eminowicz, MEd, CertEd, Dip Deaf and Partially Hearing, Dip Teach

Secondary Support Service

Co-ordinator Rochelle Haussman, BA, MA

Hospital Teaching Service

Co-ordinator Domenica Hanna, MEd

Music Centres

Brent Music Service, The Music Centre, 2/12 Grange Rd, Willesden, London NW10 2QY; Tel 0181-908 7503; Paul Fensom, CertEd

Environmental Education Centres

Gordon Brown Environmental Education Centre, Rotherwick, Nr Basingstoke, Hampshire; Tel (01256) 762824; M.A. Mould
Welsh Harp Day Field Centre, Birchen Grove NW9; Tel 0181-200 0087

Language Service

Brent Language Service, Centre for Staff Development, Gwenneth Rickus Bldg, Brentfield Rd, London NW10 9UE; Tel 0181-900 5964; Mrs L.C. De Zoysa, BA, MA

Brent Adult and Community Education Service

Headquarters, City Challenge Brent Adult College, 1 Morland Gdns, Stonebridge, London NW10 8NP; Tel 0181-838 4426/838 2882; J. Fitzpatrick
Adult Literacy and Numeracy Scheme, 38 Craven Park Rd, Harlesden, London NW10; Tel 0181-961 1315; S. Tomlins
Brent Adult Educational Guidance, Unit 1, Library Pde, Craven Park Rd, London NW10; Tel 0181-961 3703; Gloria Elliot
Copland Evening Centre, Copland Community School, Cecil Ave, Wembley HA9 7DX; Tel 0181-903 9558; S. Barnard
Neighbourhood English Scheme, Ashley Gdns, Preston Rd, Wembley HA9 8NP; Tel 0181-908 4426; D. Weller
Neighbourhood English Scheme, Winkworth Hall, 215 Chevening Rd, Brondesbury Pk, London NW6; Tel 0181-960 6720; D. Weller
Queens Park Community School, Aylestone Ave, London NW6; Tel 0181-459 3418; *Head* Mary Norton; *Community Tutor* Paul Read
The John Kelly Centre, John Kelly Girls High School, Crest Rd NW2; Fax 0181-208 4654; V. Gibson

Grant Maintained Schools

Alperton High, Stanley Ave, Wembley, Middx HAO 4JE; Tel 081-902 2038; Fax 081-900 1236; *Personnel* P.C. Gulab, BSc, PGCE. (841)
Annexe Ealing Rd, Wembley, Middx HAO 4PW; Tel 081-902 5607 and 2293; Fax 081-900 2720
Cardinal Hinsley R.C. High, Harlesden Rd NW10 3RN; Tel 0181-965 3947; Fax 0181-965 3430; M.P. Metcalfe, BA. Boys (808)
Claremont High School Claremont Ave, Kenton, Harrow HA3 OUH; Tel 0181-204 4442; Fax 0181-204 3548; *Headteacher* L. MacDonald; *Chair of Governors* S. Gurevitz. Mixed) (11–18 (857)
Convent of Jesus and Mary High RC, Crownhill Rd NW10 4EP; Tel 0181-965 2986; Fax 0181-838 0071; Mrs M. Richardson, MA. Girls (790)
Copland Community School (GMS), Cecil Ave, Wembley HA9 7DX; Tel 0181-902 6362; Fax 0181-903 1943; A. Davies, MEd. (915)
John Kelly High, Crest Rd NW2 7SN; Tel 0181-452 8700; Fax 0181-452 8700; A. Young, MA. Boys (364)
John Kelly High, Crest Rd NW2; Tel 0181-452 4842; Ms K. Heaps, BSc. Girls (536)
Kingsbury High, Princes Ave, Kingsbury NW9; Tel 0181-204 9814; Fax 0181-206 0715; P.J. Snell, MA. (1638)
Annexe Bacon La, Kingsbury NW9
Preston Manor High, Carlton Ave East, Wembley HA9 8NA; Tel 0181-904 1669; Fax 0181-908 2607; E. Bates, BEd(Hons), MA. (1173)
Queens Park Community School, Aylestone Ave, NW6 7AD; Tel 0181-451 0088; M.A. Norton, MA. (950)
St Gregory's R.C. High, Donnington Rd, Kenton, Harrow HA3 0NB; Tel 0181-907 8828; M.F. Earley, MA(Oxon), MA(Ed), MSc. (1037)

Bromley London Borough Council

Population 290,609
Civic Centre, Stockwell Cl, Bromley, Kent BR1 3UH; Tel 0181-464 3333; Fax 0181-290 0608

Education Offices

Civic Centre, Rochester Ave, Bromley, Kent BR1 3UH; Tel 0181-464 3333; Fax 0181-313 4049
Chairman Education Committee Cllr B. Humphrys
Chairman Education Review Sub Committee Cllr J. Hatcher
Chairman Operational Management Sub-Committee Councillor C. Priest
Director of Education Andrew J. Baxter, BA, MFA, MBIM
Head of Pupils and Student Services R.C. Wood, BA
Head of Planning Support Unit P.M. Finucane, BA, MA(Ed), MBA, DipM, MCIM
Head of Support Services G. Boyd, BSc
Head of Training and Support G.L. Pearson, MEd
Group Manager (Special Educational Needs) G. Treml, BEd
Chief Inspector D.M. Beniston
General Inspector Bill Dalton, MA
General Inspector M. Ralph, MEd
General Inspector P. Relph, MA
General Inspector P. Duffy, MA
Group Manager (Client Services) K. Stephen, MHCIMA
Principal Education Psychologist M.W. Camp, BEd, MSc
Principal Careers Officer P.G. Brander, BA
Principal of Adult Education College I.F. Fraser, BEd, DipADEd
Number of schools
73 Primary (19,155); 5 Secondary (6,026); 10 Adult Education Centres
Special Schools
5 day (400)
Other Authorities with whom Joint Purchasing Arrangements are made
Kent County Council

Education Committee

Con 13, Lab 2, LD 6
Chair Cllr B. Humphrys 62 Goodhart Way, West Wickham BR4 0ES; Tel 0181-777 7573
Vice-Chair Cllr P. Woods c/o Civic Centre, West Wickham, Kent BR4 0ES; Tel 0181-777 7573
Members of the Committee
Con: J. Andrew, P. Ayres, J. Bryant, I. Buckley, E. Goodman, P. Haslop, J. Hatcher, J. Hillier, S. Humphreys, B. Humphrys, A. Miles, C. Priest, P. Woods
Lab: E. Dyer, P. Fookes
LD: D. Craye, C. Gaster, T. Hawthorne, E. Phythian, H. Rabbatts, W. Shekyls

Governor Training Unit

Education Training and Support Division, Education Development Centre, Church La, Bromley BR2 8LD; Tel 0181-462 8911; Fax 0181-462 7786
Principal Officer Susan Cornish
Services Offered
A full support service for school governors including training courses

Secondary Schools

Cator Park, Lennard Rd, Beckenham BR3 1QR; Tel 0181-778 5917; A. Tigin, BA. (Girls) (1237)
Darrick Wood, Lovibonds Ave, Orpington BR6 8ER; Tel (01689) 850271; A.L. Barker, BSc, CChem, FRSC. (Mixed) (1196)
Langley Park Girls, Hawksbrook La, South Eden Park Rd, Beckenham BR3 3BE; Tel 0181-650 7207; J. Sage, MA. (Girls) (1257)
The Priory School, Tingtagel Rd, Orpington BR5 4LG; Tel (01689) 831075; J. Platt, DMS(Ed). (Mixed) (1076)
The Ravensbourne, Hayes La, Bromley BR2 9EH; Tel 0181-460 0083; R. Wood, MA. (Mixed) (1232)

Youth Centres

Castlecombe Youth Centre, Now run by Bromley Youth Agency Castlecombe Rd, Mottingham SE9 4AT; Tel 0181-857 0047; *Youth Leader* K. Bennett
The Duke Youth Centre, Now run by Youth Work UK Ltd Park Rd, St Mary Cray, Orpington BR5 4AS; Tel (01689) 838797; *Youth Leader* A. Glanville
The Link Youth Centre, Now run by Bromley Youth Agency Midfield Way, St Pauls Cray, Orpington BR5 2QL; Tel 081-300 6749; *Youth Leader* D. Barnett
The Magpie Youth Centre, Now run by Bromley Youth Agency Parkfield Way, Bromley BR2 8AE; Tel 0181-467 5802; *Leader* L. King
Club 2000, Now run by Penge, Anerley and Beckenham Youth Agency Ltd 101a Parish La, Penge SE20 7NR; Tel 0181-778 3566; *Youth Leader* L. Mayfield
The Phoenix Youth Centre, Now run by Penge, Anerley and Beckenham Youth Agency Ltd Hawes La, West Wickham BR4 9AE; Tel 0181-777 7938; *Youth Leader* G. Jones
The Spitfire Youth Centre, Youth Work UK Ltd, Church Rd, Biggin Hill, Westerham TN16 3LB; Tel (01959) 574835; *Youth Leader* Vacancy

Teachers' Centres

Bromley Field Studies Centre, Grovelands Rd, Orpington BR5 3EG; Tel 0181-302 7496
Bromley Urban Studies Centre, C/o Royston Primary, High St, Penge SE20; Tel 0181-778 7178
Education Development Centre, Church La, Bromley BR2 8LD; Tel 0181-462 8911; Fax 0181-462 7786; G.L. Pearson, MEd
Teachers Library Service 7th Fl, Central Library, High St, Bromley BR1 1EX; Tel 0181-313 0976; P. Jones

Adult Education Centres

Bromley Adult Education College, Church La, Bromley BR2 8LD; Tel 0181-462 9184; I.F. Fraser, BEd, DipADEd
Elmers End Arts Centre, Kingsworth Cl, Beckenham BR3 4XN; Tel 0181-650 0628
Kentwood Adult Education Centre, Kingsdale Rd, Penge SE20; Tel 0181-659 7635; W. Thomas
Poverest Adult Education Centre, Poverest Rd, Orpington BR5 2DQ; Tel (01689) 822886
Tuition Support for Adults, Leesons Centre, Chipperfield Rd, Orpington BR5 2LS; Tel (01689) 826269; R. Burke

Grant Maintained Schools

Beaverwood School for Girls Beaverwood Rd, Chislehurst BR7 6HE; Tel 0181-300 3156; Mrs K. Patrick. Girls
Bullers Wood School for Girls St Nicolas La, Logs Hill, Chislehurst, Kent BR7 5LJ; Tel 0181-467 2280
Charles Darwin, Jail La, Biggin Hill, Kent TN16 3AU; Tel (01959) 574043; R.C. Higgins, MA. (Mixed) (1006)
Coopers School, Hawkwood La, Chislehurst BR7 5PS; Tel 0181-467 3263; *Headteacher* Robert Dilley; *Chair of Governors* Jim Close. (Mixed) (11–18) (1101)
Hayes School West Common Rd, Hayes, Bromley BR2 7DB; Tel 0181- 462 2767; *Headteacher* John R. Catmull; *Chair of Governors* Cllr E.D. Barkway, CBE. Mixed 11–18 (1189)
Langley Park School for Boys, South Eden Park Rd, Beckenham BR3 3BP; Tel 0181-650 9253; *Headteacher* R.V.P. Sheffield; *Chair of Governors* W.E. Beck. (Boys) (11–18) (1100)
Newstead Wood, Avebury Rd, Orpington BR6 9SA; Tel (01689) 53626; V. Smith. (Girls) (708)
Raven's Wood School for Boys Oakley Rd, Bromley BR2 8HP; Tel (01689) 856050; Fax (01689) 850452;

Headteacher G.T. Berwick; *Chair of Governors* C. Hillier. (Male 11–18)
St John Rigby R.C., Layhams Rd, West Wickham BR4 9HH; Tel 0181-777 8383; Miss C. McCabe. Aided Mixed (972)
St Olave's GMS, Goddington La, Orpington BR6 9SH; Tel (01689) 20101; F.D. Coulson, MA. Aided Boys (622)

Technology College

Kemnal Technology College (GM),Sponsored by the Philip and Pauline Harris Charitable Trust, Architects Joint Partnership, Ballast Nedam Construction, Denford Machine Tools, Klick Technology and Research Machines Bromley DA14 5AA; Tel 0181-300 7112; J. Atkins, BEd, AdvDipEd, FRSA. (Boys) (814)

Camden London Borough Council

Population 188,600
Town Hall, Euston Rd NW1 2RU; Tel 0171-278 4444

Education Department

Crowndale Centre, 218-220 Eversholt St NW1 1BD; Tel 0171-911 1525; Fax 0171-911 1536
Director of Education R. Litchfield
Deputy Director (Support Services) R. Beeden
Deputy Director (Curriculum Inspection and Direct Services) A. Straker
Senior Inspector (Secondary) (Design) M. Grant
Senior Inspector (Primary) (Early Years) L. McGill
General Inspector (English and Language Development) R. Exton
General Inspector (Performing Arts) D. Hornbrook
General Inspector (Humanities) M. Austin
General Inspector (Foreign and Community Languages) C. Walton
General Inspector (Science) B. Twhigg
General Inspector (IT and Learning Resources) S. Davies
General Inspector (Mathematics) C. Macintyre
General Inspector (PE and Health) C. Lenihan
General Inspector (Special Needs) N. Smith
General Inspector (Primary) M. Gifford
EO (Finance) J. Coates
EO (Personnel) A. Sedley
EO (Client Services) P.J. Wilkinson
EO (Services Planning and Contracts) R. Genn
EO (Special Needs) D. Horsford
EO (Development and Property Services) N. Parshotam
EO (Adult Education/Grants, Policy Support) A. Conway
EO (Early Years) J. Williams
Number of Schools
1 nursery; 41 primary; 9 secondary; 6 special schools; 2 hospital schools

Education Committee

Lab 12, Con 2, LD 1
Chair P. Abraham, (Lab)
Vice-Chair P. Abraham, (Lab)
Vice-Chair D. Krymer, (Lab)
Members of the Committee
Lab: P. Bourne, D. Sacks, T. Walker, J. Roberts, A. Swain, R. Shaw, S. Shine, M. Hasan, J. White
Con: P.Chesters, J. Barnes
LD: M. Little

Hospital Schools

Hospital for Sick Children, Great Ormond St, London WC1N 3JH; Tel 0171-405 9200; Y. Hill
Hospital School, 6th Floor, Royal Free Hospital, Pond St, London NW3; Tel 0171-794 0500; B. Andrews

Special Schools

Chalcot, Harmood St, London NW1; Tel 0171-485 2147; J. Robertson
Frank Barnes Primary, Harley Rd, London NW3; Tel 0171-586 4665; P. Makey
Franklin Delano Roosevelt, Avenue Rd, London NW8; Tel 0171-722 4490; M. Bradbury
Jack Taylor, Ainsworth Way, Off Boundary Rd, London NW8; Tel 0171-328 6731; J. Feltham
John Keats, Adelaide Rd, London NW3; Tel 0171-722 0222; G. Collins

Secondary (County)

Acland Burghley, Burghley Rd, London NW5 1UJ; Tel 0171-485 8515; P. O'Hear
Hampstead, Westbere Rd, London NW2 3RT; Tel 0171-794 8133; T. Imison
Haverstock, Crogsland Rd, London NW1 8AS; Tel 0171-267 0975; J. Wallace
Parliament Hill, Highgate Rd, London NW5 1RL; Tel 0171-485 7077; J. Bax
South Camden Community, Charrington St, London NW1 1RG; Tel 0171-387 0126; H. Salisbury

Secondary (Voluntary Aided)

Camden, Sandall Rd, London NW5 2DB; Tel 0171-485 3414; G. Fallows. Girls
Maria Fidelis, 34 Phoenix Rd, London NW1 1TA; Tel 0171-387 3692; Sister J. Grainger
St Richard of Chichester, Royal College St, London NW1 9LY; Tel 0171-485 4593; J. McDonald
William Ellis, Highgate Rd, London NW5 1RN; Tel 0171-267 9346; M. Wheale

Special Boarding School

Penn, Bucks HP10 8LZ; Tel (01494) 813112; C. Jones

Grant Maintained School

The London Oratory School, Seagrave Rd, Fulham, London SW6 1RX; Tel 0171-385 0102; Fax 0171-381 3836; *Headteacher* John McIntosh; *Chair of Governors* The Very Reverend Michael Napier; *Bursar* Sean McGeeney. (Boys) (11–18) (1100); (Girls VI form only) (11–18) (100)

Corporation of London

Population 5,500 Residential; 250,000 Daytime
PO Box 270, Guildhall, London EC2P 2EJ; Tel 0171-606 3030; Fax 0171-796 2621; Telex 265608 London G

Education Department

City of London Corporation, PO Box 270, Guildhall, London EC2P 2EJ; Tel 0171-332 1750; Fax 0171-332 1621
Chairman J. Mayhew, LLM
Vice-Chairman N.J. Anstee
City Education Officer D. Smith, MA, FRSA
Assistant Education Officer S.J. Denny, MA

Hospital Unit

St Bartholomew's Hospital, Tuition Group, Lucas Ward, West Smithfield, London EC1A 7BE; Tel 0171-601 7931
M. Boydle, MA, CertEd

Careers

London Central Careers Unit, 3–6 Alfred Pl, London WC1E 7EB; Tel 0171-631 0077; Fax 0171-631 1742; Mrs L. Taylor 3-6 Alfred Pl, London WC1E 7EB; Tel 0171-631 0077

Croydon London Borough Council

Population 319,200
Taberner Hse, Park La, Croydon CR9 2BA; Tel 0181-686 4433

Education Department

Taberner Hse, Park La, Croydon CR9 1TP; Tel 0181-686 4433; Fax 0181-760 5603
Director of Education P.B. Benians, BSc(Econ)
EO (Schools) M.D. Peckham, BA(Hons)
EO (Planning Systems and Finance) J. Bamfield, MA, MSc
EO (Buildings, Supplies and Services) T.E.C. Osborn, DMA, MBIM
Personnel Manager E. Anderton (Acting), MA, BA(Hons)
AEO (Administration) J.S. Hill, MSc
AEO (Schools) I. Turner, BA
AEO (Schools) K. Livingston, BSc
AEO (Special Needs) M. McCormack, MA
AEO (Careers and Training) I. Foyle, MA, DCG
AEO (Finance) J. Crippen
AEO (Buildings) Vacancy
AEO (Planning and Resources) J.F. Nuttall, MA
AEO (Schools – Projects) S.L. Lee, BSc(Hons)
Head of Continuing Education and Training Service M. Davey
Chief Education Inspector B. Howes, MA
Inspectors Tel 0181-760 5459
Mathematics Inspector A. Hibbert, MA
Physical Education Inspector E. Floyd
PSD Inspector (Curriculum) D. Carter, BSc, Principal
SEN Principal Inspector (Professional Development) Vacancy
Primary Inspector (Assessment) R.A. Simpson, MA(Ed),Principal
General Inspector J. Miles, MA(Ed)
General Inspector J. Briant, MA
General Inspector C. Jones
Music Inspector M.L. Thomas, MA, MusB, LTCL
Science Inspector S. Foster, MSC, MA
Design and Technology Inspector G. Fisher, MA(Ed), BA, FRSA
English/Drama Inspector Sue Frater
Humanities Inspector M. James, BA, MEd
Visual Arts Inspector J.R. Allison-Smith, NDD
Careers, IT and Environmental Studies J. Johnson, MA
Economic/Industry Liaison IT, BS Post 16 Inspector S. Killman
Modern Languages Inspector Dr A. O'Sullivan
Schools Advisory Service (Davidson Professional Centre) Tel 0181-655 1299; Fax 0181-656 1544
Principal Adviser (In-Service Training) R. Pickup, BA
Director of TVEI H. Shaw
Adviser (KSI&2) J. Minton
Adviser (KS3/14) M. Doherty
Adviser (Equal Opportunities/Access In Education) P. Smith
Catering Manager E. Smith
Director of Public Health Medicine Dr E.S. Williams, MB, BCH, MFGP, AFOM, MFPHM
Dental Services Manager N. Kendall, BDS(Wales), MSC(London), DDPH, RCS(England), CHSM, MBIM
Director of Finance P.J. Leeming, BA(Admin), IPFA
Educational Psychology Service Victoria Hse, Southbridge Pl, Croydon CRO 4HA; Tel 0181-686 0393; Fax 0181-680 0890
Chief Educational Psychologist J.P. Edwards, BSc, ADEP
Senior Educational Psychologist O. Lamond
Senior Educational Psychologist A. Moore
Senior Educational Psychologist R. Tyler, BA, MED
Educational Psychologist C. Alders, BA(Hons)
Educational Psychologist P. Briggs, BA, MSc
Educational Psychologist A. Holley, BA
Educational Psychologist V. Hughes, BSc, MSc
Educational Psychologist J. Daniel
Educational Psychologist M. Munro
Educational Psychologist P. Parkhouse
Director of Public Services & Works K.C. Ollier
Number of Schools
4 nursery (548); 95 primary (26,882); 11 secondary (7,405); 10 continuing education and training centres (26,000 P.T.)
Special Schools
6 day (497)
Requisition Periods for Schools Supplies
No special periods arranged
Other Authorities with whom Joint Purchasing Arrangements are made
Greater London Supplies

Education Committee

Con 12, Lab 4, Lab and Co-op 3
Chair T. Laffin, (Lab) 32 Croham Valley Rd, South Croydon CR2 7NB; Tel 0181-657 2647
Vice-Chair V. Shawcross, (Lab) PO Box 391, Croydon CR9 SBG; Tel 0181-656 6198; Fax 0181-656 6198
Members of the Committee
Con: A. Pelling, M. Wunn, M Mead, D. Adamson, G. Bass, P. Campbell, D. Perry
Lab: J. Bushell, M. Jenitt, S. Khan, M. Allen, G. Bernard, R. Chandarana, R. Grantham
Lab and Co-op: B. Khan, M. Walker, I. Payne

Governor Training Unit

Governor Support Team, London Borough of Croydon, Room 9-01, Education Dept, Taberner Hse, Park La, Croydon CR9 1TP; Tel 0181-760 5612; Fax 0181-760 5603
Governor Training Manager Margaret Collins
Governor Support Manager Richard Inge
Services Offered
The Governor Support Team provides a full range of advisory, training, administrative and information services to schools, Governors and Clerks to Governing Bodies. Advice and information is also provided for Members, Head Teachers and Officers

Special Schools

Beckmead, Monks Orchard Rd, Beckenham BR3 3BZ; Tel 0181-777 9311/2; Fax 0181-777 6550; *Head* W.J. Lyttle (Acting). (E.B.D.) (36)
Bensham Manor, Ecclesbourne Rd, Thornton Heath CR7 7BR; Tel 0181-684 0116; *Head Teacher* E.J. Green. (M.L.D.) (157)
Coldharbour, 489 Purley Way, Croydon CR0 4RG; Tel 0181-688 1761/681 8910; B.A. Fox. (S.L.D.) (58)
Priory, Tennison Rd SE25 5RR; Tel 0181-653 8222/653 7879; Fax 0181-771 6761; M. Simpson. (S.L.D.) (50)
St Giles', Pampisford Rd, Croydon CR2 6DF; Tel 0181-680 2141/1536; Fax 0181-681 6359; T. Coldron. P.H. & Del. (98)
St Nicholas, Old Lodge La, Purley CR8 4DN; Tel 0181-660 4861/2; Fax 0181-660 8119; D.A. Bartram. M.L.D. (77)

Secondary Schools (11–16)

Addington, Fairchildes Ave, New Addington, Croydon CR9 0AA; Tel (01689) 842545/6; Fax (01689) 843504; K.J. Osbourne, BSocSci. (Mixed) (705)
Ashburton, Shirley Rd, Croydon CR9 7AL; Tel 0181-656 0222; Fax 0181-656 1474; C. Hiscock. (Mixed) (1062)
Haling Manor, Kendra Hall Rd, South Croydon CR2 6DT; Tel 0181-681 1141/4; Fax 0181-681 1144; M. Round, JP, BA, MBIM. (Mixed) (478)

Ingram, Springfield Rd, Thornton Heath CR7 8DZ; Tel 0181-653 0901/3; Fax 0181-771 7583; J.C. Blackburn, BSc, MEd. (Boys) (574)
Selsdon, Farnborough Ave, South Croydon CR2 8HD; Tel 0181-657 8935/6; Fax 0181-651 6065; S.A. Newton, BSc, MEd, FBIM, CBiol. (Mixed) (810)
Westwood, Spurgeon Rd, Upper Norwood SE19 3UG; Tel 0181-653 1661; Fax 0181-771 6573; J. Stribbling, MA. (Girls) (631)
Woodcote, Meadow Rise, Coulsdon CR5 2EH; Tel 0181-668 6464; Fax 0181-660 9038; I. Wilson, MA. (Mixed) (908)

Secondary Schools (Aided)

Archbishop Tenison's C.E., Selbourne Rd, Croydon CR0 5JG; Tel 0181-688 4014; Fax 0181-681 6336; R.T. Ford, BA. (Mixed) (11–18) (505)
St Andrew's C.E., Warrington Rd, Croydon CR0 4BJ; Tel 0181-686 8306; Fax 0181-681 6320; J.A. Coatman, MA, BSc(Eng), ACGI. (Mixed) (388)
St Mary's R.C., Woburn Rd, Croydon CR0 2AB; Tel 0181-686 3837/9; Fax 0181-681 6305; W.J. Whitmarsh, MA. (Mixed) (11–16) (686)
Stanley Technical, South Norwood Hill SE25 6AD; Tel 0181-771 9961; Fax 0181-771 7588; P.H. Bean, BSc. (Boys) (11–16) (658)

Teachers' Centre

Davidson Professional Centre, Davidson Rd, Croydon CR0 6DD; Tel 0181-655 1299; Fax 0181-656 1544

Grant Maintained Schools

The Archbishop Lanfranc, Mitcham Rd, Croydon CR9 3AS; Tel 0181-689 1255; Fax 0181-683 3113; R.B. Pope, BSc. (Mixed) (837)
Coloma Convent Girls School Upper Shirley Rd, Croydon CR9 5AS; Tel 0181-654 6228; Fax 0181-656 6485; M.M. Dolan, BA. (Girls) (11–18) (807)
Coulsdon High, Homefield Rd, Old Coulsdon CR5 1ES; Tel (01737) 551161/3; Fax (01737) 557410; P. Mennie, MA. (Mixed) (760)
Edenham, Orchard Way, Croydon CR0 7NJ; Tel 0181-776 0220; Fax 0181-777 3904; P.D. Jones, BA. Mixed (1050)
Norbury Manor, Kensington Ave, Thornton Heath CR7 8BT; Tel 0181-679 0062/4; Fax 0181-679 8007; K.M. Jones, MA. (Girls) (614)
Riddlesdown High School, Honister Heights, Purley CR8 1EX; Tel 0181-668 5136; Fax 0181-660 9025; *Headteacher* Dr D.R. Dibbs; *Chair of Governors* Michael G. Simpson. (Mixed) (11–16) (1050)
St Joseph's R.C. College, Beulah Hill, Upper Norwood SE19 3HL; Tel 0181-761 1426/7; Fax 0181-761 7667; Rev Br. Anthony Porter, MA. (Boys) (11–18) (1072)
Shirley, Shirley Church Rd, Shirley CR0 5EF; Tel 0181-656 9755/8; Fax 0181-654 8507; J.G. Harker, MSc, DMS. (Mixed) (850)
Thomas More R.C., Russell Hill Rd, Purley CR8 2XP; Tel 0181-668 6251/3; Fax 0181-660 9003; A.C. Poole, MA, BEd. (Mixed) (11–16) (650)

Ealing London Borough Council

Population 293,700
Town Hall, New Broadway, Ealing W5 2BY; Tel 0181-579 2424

Education Department

Perceval Hse, 14–16 Uxbridge Rd, London W5 2HL; Tel 0181-579 2424
Chairman Cllr M. Majumdar
Vice-Chairman Cllr F. Dunckley
Director of Education and Leisure M. Herman, MA, MTech, BA
Assistant Director (Client Services) S. Haddon, MA, MSc, MA(Ed)
Assistant Director (Planning and Resources Management) S. Hay, BSc, MA, DipEd, PGCE
Assistant Director (Schools Services) C. Ajit Singh, PGCE, MA(Hist), MA(Ed)
Chief Inspector/Deputy Director of Education K. Shaikh, MSc, MPhil, O.Chem, MRSC
Education Officer (Client Services) G. Durham, BA(Hons), MA
Education Officer (Client Services) V. Jordan, BA, DipCG
Education Officer (Finance and Resources) B. Pollock, ICSA
Education Officer (Planning and Development) G. Redhead, BA(Hons), DipSoc Admin
Education Officer (Special Educational Needs) N. Bowes
Education Officer (Staffing Services) H. Shepherdson, BEd(Hons), Dip Guidance & Counselling, Dip Human Resource Mgmt IPD
Senior Inspector (Primary and Nursery) Vacancy
Senior Inspector (Secondary Education) Vacancy
Senior Inspector (Special Educational Needs) M. Brain
Senior Inspector (Externally Funded Projects) Ms V. Davis
General Inspector (Cross Curricular Elements) N. Anastasiou
General Inspector (English) R. Matthews
General Inspector (Humanities) Vacancy
General Inspector (Recruitment and Retention of Staff/Induction) Mrs E.B Camplin
General Inspector (Early Childhood Education) S.A. Morris
General Inspector (Curricular Access and Achievements) K. Rai
General Inspector (Science) R. Brown
General Inspector (Technology/IT/DT and Art) R.J. Carvell
General Inspector (Religious Education) R.E. Butler
General Inspector (Physical Education) P. Canham
General Inspector (Curriculum Evaluation and Assessment) P.E. Lyseight-Jones
General Inspector (INSET Professional and Management Development) A.L. Rooney
Principal Psychologist I. Choudhury
General Inspector (Mathematics/TVEI) Dr. M. Doran
Number of schools
5 infant; 57 Junior/primary; 7 high
Special Schools
7 day
Date of Committee Meeting
Tuesday (four times a year)

Ealing Education Centre

Westlea Rd, London W7 2AD; Tel 0181-840 4050
Manager Sally Davies

Governor Training Unit

Development and Training Services (Education), Ealing Education Centre, Westlea Rd, London W7 2AD; Tel 0181-567 5501; Fax 0181-566 3362
Manager Brian Cheetham, BA, MA, PGCE
Principal Support Officer Tina Abrahams
Services Offered
A full and varied programme of courses for Governors, including support for headteachers, school teaching and support staff

Special Day Schools

Belvue, Rowdell Rd, Northolt UB5 6AG; Tel 0181-845 5766; D. Whitton. (123)
Castlebar, Hathaway Gdns, Ealing W13 0DH; Tel 0181-998 3135; D.J. Perkins. (106)
Cavendish, Compton Cl, off Cavendish Ave, Ealing W13 0JG; Tel 0181-998 6940; N. Roberts. (6)
John Chilton, Compton Cres, Northolt, Middx UB5 5LD; Tel 0181-842 1329; Mrs B. Cursi. (88)

Mandeville, Eastcote La, Northolt UB5 4HW; Tel 0181-864 4921/0911; S. Blee. (79)
St Ann's, Springfield Rd, Hanwell W7 3JP; Tel 0181-567 6291; M. Hughes. (58)
Springhallow, Compton Cl, Off Cavendish Ave, Ealing, London W13 0JE; Tel 0181-998 2700; J.M. Cook. (27)

High Schools (11+ Secondary Comprehensive School)

Acton, Gunnersbury La, Acton W3 8EY; Tel 0181-752 0005; J.M. Leavold, MA. (1198)
Dormers Wells, Dormers Wells La, Southall UB1 3HZ; Tel 0181-813 8161; C.L. Nicholson. (699)
Featherstone, 11 Montague Way, Southall UB2 5HF; Tel 0181-843 0984; T.C. Cox. (894)
Villiers, Boyd Ave, Southall UB1 3BT; Tel 0181-813 8001; I. Wetherall. (1184)
Walford, Bengarth Rd, Northolt UB5 5LQ; Tel 0181-841 4511; M. Clark, BA. (912)

High Schools (Voluntary)

Cardinal Wiseman R.C., Greenford Rd, Greenford UB6 9AW; Tel 0181-575 8222; A.A. MacMillan, MA, DipEd, AFIMA, FCollP. (S.A.) (1597)
Twyford C.E., Twyford Cres, Acton W3 9PP; Tel 0181-752 0141; Rev. Dr. R.W. Buckley, BSc, PhD, MinstE, CPhys. (V.A.) (1153)

Adult Education and Community Services

Central Office Perceval Hse, 14/16 Uxbridge Rd, London W5 2HL; Tel 0181-579 2424

Senior Tutorial Centres (for pupils with learning difficulties)

Longfield Tutorial Centre, 9 Longfield Rd, Ealing W5 2DH; Tel 0181-758 8841
Lower Boston Road Tutorial Centre, Hanwell W7; Tel 0181-840 4484; *Teacher-in-Charge* Ms T. Knox
Park Tutorial Centre, Recreation Rd, Southall, Middx UB2 5PE; Tel 0181-571 1164; *Teacher-in-charge* C.P. Benyon

Grant Maintained Schools

Brentside, Greenford Ave, Hanwell W7 1JJ; Tel 0181-575 9162; Avril Phillips, BA(Hons), MA(Ed). (1200)
Drayton Manor High School, Drayton Bridge Rd, Hanwell W7 1EU; Tel 0181-840 0866; P. Singh, MA. (1483)
The Ellen Wilkinson School for Girls, Queen's Dr, Acton, London W3 0HW; Tel 0181-752 1525; Fax 0181-993 6632; S.M. Parrott. (1235)
The Greenford High School, Ruislip Rd, Greenford UB6 9XX; Tel 0181-578 9152; K. Griffin. (11–19) (1200)
Northolt, Eastcote La, Northolt UB5 4HW; Tel 0181-864 8544; J. Parry, BA, MEd. (1051)

Enfield London Borough Council

Population 264,300
Civic Centre, PO Box 50, Silver St, Enfield, Middx EN1 3XA; Tel 0181-366 6565

Education Department

PO Box 56, Civic Centre, Silver St, Enfield EN1 3XQ; Tel 0181-366 6565; Fax 0181-982 7375
Director of Education Liz Graham, MA
Deputy Director of Education and Assistant Director (Schools and Community) Judith Black, BA(Hons),MA
Assistant Director (Planning and Resources) A.J. Minchella, BSc
Assistant Director (Community Development) Del Goddard
Senior Manager (Special Education) D. Drury
Senior Manager (Direct Support Services) J. March, MA, PGCE
Senior Advisory Officer (School Development) L. Farraway, BA(Hons), MEd
Senior Advisory Officer (Resources and Planning) K. Hostettler, MBA
Senior Advisory Officer (14–19) R. Marsden
Special Service Manager Vacancy
Special Service Manager B. Kennedy
Information and Review Manager B. Hudgell
Senior Advisory Officer (Schools) R. Arnold, MA
Senior Advisory Officer (Special Education) T.J. Bailey, BA, MEd, MEd(Psych), DCP
Mathematics Adviser C. Christofides, BSc, PGCE
Modern Languages Adviser B. Clinton, BA
Music and Performing Arts R. Bunting, BA(Hons)
Physical Education Adviser N. Rousell, BEd, DipEd, MA
Science Adviser S. Sissling, BSc(Hons), PGCE
CDT Adviser D. Feeley, BSc(Hons)
English, Drama and Media Studies Adviser A. Dobson, MA, PGCE
Information Technology Adviser P. Evans, BSc(Hons), MSc
Art and Design Adviser J. Page, CertEd, DipEd, MA
Humanities Adviser K. Moorse, MA
Staff Development and Induction Adviser J. Minchella, BA
Guidance and Enterprise Manager G. Hilborne
Area Guidance Manager J. Christensen
Area Guidance Manager G. Sharp
Client Support and Business Manager G. Barnes, MHCIMA, MRIM
Youth and Community Manager A.W. Hunter
Education Psychology Service Principal Officer E. Holmes, BA
Number of Schools
66 primary (21,909 full-time; 1,714 part-time (875 full-time equivalent of part-time); 11 secondary (12,074)
Special Schools
5 day (438)
Requisition Periods for School Supplies
Any time
Other Authorities with whom Joint Purchasing Arrangements are made
None

Education Committee

Lab 11, Con 7
Chair A. Georgiou, (Lab) 27 Percy Rd, London N21 2JA
Vice-Chair M. Fenton, (Lab) 4 Bush Hill, London N21
Members of the Committee
Lab: Y. Brett, R.Buckley, B.Chaialambous, A. Constantinides, P. Cunneen, G. Devitt, P. Hyden, G. Loake, R. Smythe, P. Sowter, S. Walker
Con: P. Adams, M. Evans, C. Gooch, J. Shankey, A. Thacker, G. Vince, J. Yates

Governor Training Unit

Professional Development Centre, Kimberley Gdns, Enfield EN1 3ST; Tel 0181-363 4148; Fax 0181-367 8554
Governor Training Co-ordinator Satnam Lotay
Services Offered
The LEA offers a central training programme which includes courses for new governors, courses on the curriculum, and those dealing with governors' responsibilities. In addition, the Training Co-ordinator organises Governing Body based sessions in schools; Additionally, advice is available for governors individually on a broad range of issues. A feature of the training programme is a series of "Open Forums" where governors can raise directly any issue with officers from the Authority

Special Schools

Aylands, Keswick Dr, Enfield EN3 6NY; Tel (01992) 761229; P. Hill. (EBD) (Mixed)
Durants, 4 Pitfield Way, Enfield EN3 5BY; Tel 0181-804 1980; K. Bovair. (MLD)
Oaktree, Chase Side, Southgate N14 4HN; Tel 0181-440 3100; J. Harrison. (MLD) (Mixed)
Waverley, 105 The Ride, Enfield EN3 7DL; Tel 0181-805 1858; L.C. Gibbs. (SLD) (Mixed)
West Lea, Haselbury Rd, Edmonton N9 9TU; Tel 0181-807 2656; A. Fox. (Del.) (5–16)

Secondary Schools

Aylward, Windmill Rd, Edmonton, London N18 1NB; Tel 0181-803 1738; J.R. Salisbury, BA. (Mixed) (1272)
Bishop Stopford's, Brick La, Enfield EN1 3PU; Tel 0181-804 1906; B. Pickard, MA. (Mixed) (1044)
Bullsmoor, Bullsmoor, Enfield EN3 6TW; Tel (01992) 763666; J.B. Dunn, MA (Oxon). (591)
Chace Community, Churchbury La, Enfield EN1 3HQ; Tel 0181-363 7321; D.J. Higgins, BSc. (1114)
Edmonton, Great Cambridge Rd, Enfield EN1 1HQ; Tel 0181-360 3158; J.R. Hulley, BA. (Mixed) (1317)
Enfield County, Holly Walk, Enfield EN2 6QG; Tel 0181-363 3030; I.A. Byard, BA. (Girls) (1079)
Kingsmead, Southbury Rd, Enfield EN1 1YQ; Tel 0181-363 3037; G.R.C. Bird, BA. (Mixed) (957)
St. Anne's Catholic High School for Girls, Oakthorpe Rd, Palmers Green N13 5TY; Tel 0181-886 2165; P. McDermott, MA. (Girls) (11–18) (879)
Salisbury, Nightingale Rd, Edmonton N9 8DR; Tel 0181-804 2376; D.J. Shipley, MA. (Mixed) (980)
Southgate, Sussex Way, Barnet, Herts EN4 0BL; Tel 0181-449 9583; P.G. Hudson, BSc, MEd. (Mixed) (1507)
Winchmore, Laburnum Grove, Winchmore Hill N21 3HS; Tel 081-360 7773; G.E. Aretz, JP, BA, MSc, MA(Ed). (Mixed) (1334)

Professional Development Centre

Craddock Rd, Enfield EN1 4ST; Tel 0181-363 4148/9

Youth Centres

2E Advice and Information Centre, Craig Park Cen, Lawrence Rd, Edmonton N18 2HN; Tel 0181-807 0637; Fax 0181-807 5443
Albany Centre, Bell La, Enfield EN3 5PA; Tel 0181-805 4956; Maureen Anderson
Duke of Edinburgh Award Scheme, Churchbury Rd, Enfield EN1 3HQ; Tel 0181-366 1499
Ponders End Centre, Youth Action Motor Project, 129–139 South St, Ponders End, Enfield EN3 4PX; Tel 0181-804 5908/081-804 7426
Youth Office, Ponders End Centre, 129–139 South St, Enfield EN3 4PX; Tel 0181-805 7261; Fax 0181-805 1748

Grant Maintained Schools

Albany, Bell La, Enfield EN3 5PA; Tel 0181-804 6946; D.J. Houghton, BA, AFIMA. (Mixed) (1017)
Broomfield, Wilmer Way N14 7HY; Tel 0181-368 4710; I. Lucas, BSc. (Mixed Comp) (1200)
Enfield Grammar School, Market Pl, Enfield, Middx EN2 6LN; Tel 0181-363 1095; D.W.E. Thomas, MA. (Boys) (1076)
Latymer, Haselbury Rd, Edmonton N9 9TN; Tel 0181-807 4037; Fax 0181-807 4125; G.T. Mills, MA. (Mixed) (1305)
St Ignatius' College, Turkey St, Enfield EN1 4NP; Tel (01992) 717835; M.J. Blundell, MA. (Boys) (1091)

London Borough of Greenwich

Population 217,800

Town Hall, Wellington St, Woolwich SE18 6PW; Tel 0181-854 8888

Education Department

Riverside Hse, High St, Woolwich SE18 6DF; Tel 0181-854 8888; Fax 0181-855 2427
Director of Education J. Kramer
Assistant Director (Strategic Planning and Resource Division) M. Bright
Assistant Director (Schools and Pupil Support Division) J. Cordwell
Assistant Director (Student, Community and Personnel Services Division) Stephanie Cooper
SAEO (Planning & External Grants) S. Mowles
SAEO (School Support Services) J. Ball
SAEO (Youth and Community Education) M. Hyslop
SAEO (Post 16 and External Relations) A. Evans
SAEO (Special Educational Needs) M. Hart
SAEO (Institutional Support) T. Connolly
SAEO (Equalities and Section 11) R. Sivanandan
Principal Inspector B. Weaver
Head of Finance and Information Technology Vacancy
Phase Inspector (Early Years) L. Pound
Phase Inspector M. Croxford
Phase Inspector (Primary) J. Park
Phase Inspector (Primary) T. Edwards
Phase Inspector (Special) M. McDowell
Subject Inspector (Humanities) M. Howell
Subject Inspector (Modern Languages) Vacancy
Subject Inspector (Mathematics) K. Page
Subject Inspector (Continuing Education) A. Sinha
Subject Inspector (Music) C. Harrison
Subject Inspector (PE) Barrie Wigg
Subject Inspector (RE) Vacancy
Subject Inspector (Visual Arts) C. Salter
Subject Inspector (Science) Sa'ad Khaldi
Subject Inspector (Record Keeping and Assessment) N. Laing
Principal Educational Psychologist R. Booker
Principal Psychiatric Social Worker (Child Guidance Service) V. Kirwan
Principal Education/Social Work Officer B. Cooley

Education Committee

Lab 17, Con 3, SDP 1, LD 1
Chair D.J.G. Picton, (Lab) 12 Wellington Gdns, London SE7 7PH
Vice-Chair C. Slee, (Lab) 63 Riverdale Rd, Plumstead SE18 1PD
Members of the Committee
Lab: P. Challis, S. Coker, M. Devaux JP, L.L. Duval, R. Harris, P. Kotz, P. May, Q. Marsh, V. Morse, K.M. Patel, H. Pike, R. Ramsey, D. Smith, B. Taylor, R. Walker
Con: D.D. Poston, D.M. Richards, P.J.H. King
SDP: D. Lewis
LD: D. Woodhead

Special Schools

Charlton Park Boarding Unit, Charlton Park Rd, London SE7 8HX; Tel 0181-854 1838; *Warden* M. McKenzie
Charlton Park, Charlton Park Rd, London SE7 8HX; Tel 081-854 6259. (P.D.)
Churchfield, Church Manorway, London SE2; Tel 0181-854 3739; P. Goulden. (SNC) (Secondary)
Greenwood, Welton Rd, London SE18 2JD; Tel 0181-854 5904; N.A. McNeil. (SNC) (Secondary)
Griffin Manor, Welton Rd, London SE18 2JD; Tel 0181-854 3905; P. Sullivan. (Autistic) (Complex Needs)
Maze Hill, Woodlands Cres, Maze Hill, London SE10 9UP; Tel 0181-858 0265; Mrs P. Hardaker. (S.L.D.)
Moatbridge, Eltham Palace Rd, (Middle Pk Ave), London SE9 5LX; Tel 0181-850 8081; M.L. Dawson. (E.B.D.)
Nine Acres, Glyndon Est, Robert St, London SE18; Tel 0181-317 7659; Mrs P.J. Mathias. (S.L.D.)

Secondary Schools

Abbey Wood, Eynsham Bridge, Abbey Wood SE2 9AJ; Tel 0181-310 9175; I. Mackie. (Mixed)

Blackheath Bluecoat C.E., 129 Old Dover Rd SE3 8SY; Tel 0181-858 8221/4; J.R. Thurley. (Mixed)
Crown Woods, Riefield Rd, Eltham SE9 2QN; Tel 0181-850 7678; P.D. Wells. (Mixed)
Eaglesfield, Red Lion La SE18 4LD; Tel 0181-856 7156; P.J. McCarthy. (Boys)
Eltham Green, Queenscroft Rd SE9 5EQ; Tel 0181-859 0133; *Headteacher* J.J. Aune. (Mixed)
Eltham Hill, Eltham Hill SE9 5EE; Tel 0181-859 2843; M.R. Wallis. (Girls)
John Roan, Maze Hill SE3 7UD; Tel 0181-858 8981; C. Deane. (Mixed)
Kidbrooke, Corelli Rd, Shooters Hill Rd SE3 8EP; Tel 0181-856 2211; R. Goldberg. (Mixed)
Plumstead Manor, Old Mill Rd SE18 1QF; Tel 0181-855 5011; J. Harding. (Girls)
St Paul's R.C., Wickham La SE2 0XX; Tel 0181-311 3868; J. Flannery. (Mixed)
St Thomas More R.C., Footscray Rd SE9; Tel 0181-850 6700; M. Driscoll. (Mixed)
St Ursula's Convent, 70 Crooms Hill SE10 8HN; Tel 0181-858 4613; S. Fulton. (Girls)
Thomas Tallis, Kidbrooke Park Rd SE3 9PX; Tel 0181-856 0115; C. Yardley. (Mixed)
Waterfield, Waterfield Cl, Thamesmead SE28 8AT; Tel 0181-310 1700; G. Bunce. (Mixed)
Woolwich Polytechnic, Sandy Hill Rd SE18 7BB; Tel 0181-854 1114; P.C. Haigh. (Boys)

Greenwich Professional Development Centre

Craigton Road, Eltham, London SE9 1QG; Tel 0181-850 5043; Fax 0181-850 8937; *Head of Centre* P. Woodward

Hackney London Borough Council

Population 181,248
Hackney Town Hall, Mare St, Hackney E8 1EA; Tel 0181-986 3123; Fax 0181-985 3397

Directorate of Education and Leisure Services

Edith Cavell Bldg, Edith Cavell School, Enfield Rd, London N1 5AZ; Tel 0171-214 8400; Fax 0171-214 8531
Director of Education and Leisure Services Gus John
Deputy Director of Education and Leisure Services D. Silverstone
Assistant Director (Clients and Services) Spencer Roberts
Directorate Finance Officer T. Galea

Education and Leisure Services Committee

Lab 15, Con 2, LD 2
Chair P. Corrigan, (Lab)
Vice-Chair S. Siddiqui, (Lab)
Members of the Committee
Lab: T. Allen, P. Corrigan, M. Ece, C. Gardiner, J. Grosskopf, P. Kenyon, J. Lamb, B. Leadbitter, I. Le Bowitz, J. McCufferty, S. Patrick, P. Pearson, S. Siddiqui, N. Tallentire, P. Watson
Con: J. Lobenstein MBE, E. Ollerenshaw OBE
LD: A. Frost, A. Rothwell

Governor Training Unit

Schools Support and Resourcing Team, Hackney Education, Enfield Rd, London N1 5AZ; Tel 0171-214 8473; Fax 0171-214 8531
Schools Management Officer Mike Rosen

Services Offered

Governor training; Training in LMS for school-based staff

Special Schools

Crusoe Hse, Nile St N1 9EX; Tel 0171-251 3932; Irene Flynn. (EBD)
Downsview, Downs Rd E5 8QP; Tel 0181-985 6833; Valerie Hider. (MLD)
Horizon, Wordsworth Rd N16 8DA; Tel 0171-254 8096; Mrs Uhart. (MLD)
Ickburgh, Ickburgh Rd E5 8AD; Tel 0181-806 4638; Hazel Rowley. (SLD)
Shawcroft, Crockenhill Rd, St Mary's Cray, Kent BR5 4ES; Tel (06898) 31366; Fax (06898) 877797; Alan Whitaker. (EBD)
Stormont House, Downs Park Rd E5 8NP; Tel 0181-985 4245; Angela Murphy. (Del.)

Secondary Schools

Cardinal Pole R.C., Kenworthy Rd E9 5RB; Tel 0181-985 5150; Fax 0181-986 6210; T. Mannion Annexe, Victoria Park Rd E9 7HE; Tel 0181-985 5646. (Mixed) (997)
Clapton, Laura Pl E5 ORB; Tel 0181-985 6641; Fax 0181-986 4686; M. Hillson. (Girls) (809)
Hackney Downs, Downs Park Rd E5 8NP; Tel 0181-985 8886; Fax 0181-985 8489; Betty Hales. (Boys) (413)
Hackney Free and Parochial C.E., Paragon Rd E9 6NR; Tel 0181-985 2430; Fax 0181-533 5441; Mary Collier Annexe, Lansdowne Dr E8 3EF; Tel 0171-254 6974; Fax 0171-923 2618. (Mixed) (679)
Haggerston, Weymouth Terr E2 8LR; Tel 0171-739 7324; Fax 0171-739 8603; Pat Collarbone. (Girls) (863)
Homerton Hse, Homerton Row E9 6EB; Tel 0181-986 8144; Fax 0181-533 1356; Geoffrey Dale. (Boys) (608)
Kingsland, Shacklewell La E8 2EY; Tel 0171-254 8722; Fax 0171-249 0289; Sarah Ayers. (Mixed) (874)
Our Lady's Convent, 6–16 Amhurst Pk N16 5AF; Tel 0181-800 2158; Fax 0181-809 1518; Margaret Dixon. (Girls) (543)
Stoke Newington, Clissold Rd N16 9EU; Tel 0171-254 0548; Fax 0171-923 2451; Steven Belk. (Mixed) (859)
Skinners' Company's SG (Vol) 117 Stamford Hill N16 5RS; Tel 0181-800 7411; Fax 0181-809 1382; Mary Ludlow. (739)
Annexe Mount Pleasant La E5 9JG; Tel 0181-806 3128; Fax 0181-806 0690

Professional Development Centre

Queensbridge Bldg, Albion Rd, Hackney E8; Tel 0171-254 5522; Fax 0171-254 6806; Fred Whipp

Hammersmith and Fulham London Borough Council

Population 145,000 approx
Town Hall, King Street, Hammersmith W6 0LJ; Tel 0181-748 3020

Education Department

Cambridge Hse, Cambridge Gr, c/o Town Hall, King St, Hammersmith W6 9JU; Tel 0181-748 3020; Fax 0181-576 5501
Education Committee Chairperson Councillor David Williams
Deputy Chairperson Cllr Huw Davies
Director of Education C. Whatford
Assistant Director (Planning and Operational Management) Graham Brookbank
Assistant Director (Quality Monitoring and Development) Vacancy
Head of Planning and Development Tracey Coventry

Assistant Director (Management Support Services) D. Cross
Assistant Director (Community Learning and Leisure Service) E. Adlington
Head of Contract Services I. Patterson
Head of Individual Progress Geraldine Breen
Head of Information and External Relations B. Beese
Number of establishments and pupils/students
6 nursery; 37 primary, 8 secondary; 5 special needs; 1 maintained college
Requisition Period for School Supplies
Freedom to requisition throughout the year

Governor Training Unit

School Management Support, Education Dept Hammersmith and Fulham, c/o Hammersmith Town Hall, King St, London W6; Tel 0181-576 5353; Fax 0181-576 5534
Head of SMS M. Daniels
Management Support Officer Frank O'Donoghue
Services Offered
Management consultancy; Governor training

Special Schools

Cambridge School, Cambridge Gr, London W6 0LD; Tel 0181-748 7585; J. Barton
Jack Tizard, Finlay St, London SW6 6HB; Tel 0171-736 7949; M. Loughnan
Heathermount School, Devenish Rd, Sunningdale, Berks SL5 9PG; Tel (01344) 875101; S. Lord
Queensmill Primary, Ciancarty Rd SW6 3AA; Tel 0171-384 2330; C. Notley
Gibbs Grn School, Mund St, London W14 9LY; Tel 0171-385 3908; K. Birchley
Wood Lane, Wood La, London W12 0HP; Tel 0181-743 5668; K. Bedford

Secondary Schools

The Hammersmith, The Curve, London W12 7RQ; Tel 0181-749 1141; M. Brooks. (Mixed)
Burlington Danes, Wood La, London W12 0TY; Tel 0181-743 9428; M. Bedford. (Mixed)
Sacred Heart High RC, 212 Hammersmith Rd, London W6 7DG; Tel 0181-748 7600; C. Carpenter. (Girls)
Fulham Cross, Munster Rd, London SW6 6BP; Tel 0171-381 0861; J. Cartwright. (Girls)
Henry Compton, Kingswood Rd, London SW6 6SN; Tel 0171-381 3606; D. Chant. (Boys)
Hurlingham and Chelsea, Peterborough Rd, London SW6 3ED; Tel 0171-731 2581; B. Simmons
Lady Margaret, Parsons Gn, London SW6 4UN; Tel 0171-736 7138; J. Olivier. (Girls)
St Mark's CE, Bishops Ave, London SW6 6FD; Tel 0171-736 2211; L. Mortimer. (Mixed)

Maintained College

Hammersmith and West London College, Gliddon Rd, London W14 9BL; Tel 0181-741 1688

Professional Support Centre

Beaufort House, Lillie Rd SW6 1UF; Tel 0171-381 4111

Haringey London Borough Council

Population 202,650
Civic Centre, High Rd, Wood Green N22 4LE; Tel 0181-975 9700

Education Department

Development Centre, Downhills Park Rd, London N17 6AR; Tel 0181-889 3910; Fax 0181-365 8068
Chair Cllr Lucy Craig
Vice-Chair Cllr P. Jones
Vice-Chair Cllr S. Brasher
Director of Education Services R.L. Jones
Head of Central Support and Administrative Service B. Greed
Senior Inspector A. Boyle
Phase Inspector T. Boohan
Phase Inspector M. Docherty
Policy and Planning Co-ordinator A. Milsted
Phase Inspector N. Shah
General Inspector (Arts, Design and Technology) D. Williamson
Staff Development Co-ordinator Dr D. Pavey
General Inspector (Music) Ms L. Davies
General Inspector (Mathematics) Vera Foster
General Inspector (English, Language and Communication) J. Broadbent
General Inspector (Humanities inc. RE) G. Fisher
General Inspector (Information Technology) A. Lambert
General Inspector (Design & Technology) D. Williamson
General Inspector (Science) M. Newman
General Inspector (PE, Dance & Drama) Ms F. Jackson
General Inspector (Special Educational Needs) J. Keever
General Inspector (Equal Opportunities) Ms R. Minhas
Principal Educational Psychologist Ms J. Gardiner
TVEI Co-ordinator Ms A. York
Principal Careers Adviser G. Smith
Principal Youth & Community Officer B. Hickey
Policy Officer Jayesh Amin
Policy Officer Barbara Beckles
Policy Officer Deborah Dent
Policy Officer Jennifer Le Gendre Williams
Number of Schools
1 pre-school centre; 3 nursery; 77 primary; 9 secondary
Special Schools
5 day
Requisition Periods for School Supplies
Within the financial year
Other Authorities with whom Joint Purchasing Arrangements are made
Counties Furniture Group, Cleapse, ILEA Supplies

Education Committee

Chair Cllr Lucy Craig, (Lab) 14 Dukes Ave, Alexandra Ward, Muswell Hill N10
Vice-Chair Cllr Philip Jones, (Lab) 14 Uplands Rd, South Hornsey Ward N8 9NL
Members of the Committee
N. Cleeveley, P. Daly, K. Fiakkas, B. Harris, S. Horne, C. Keal, J. Patel, C. Sharp, E. Singleton, C. Tikly, C. Zissimos

Special Schools (2 1/2–19)

Blanche Nevile School, Administrative and Resource Centre, Weir Hall Rd N17 8LB; Tel 081-808 4191; J. Ellwood. Day) (D) (Phg) (3–16
Greenfields, Coppetts Rd, Muswell Hill N10 1JP; Tel 0181-444 5366; D.S. Butterfield, BSc. E.B.D.) (Day) (5–16
Moselle, Adams Rd N17 6HW; Tel 0181-808 8869; A. Redpath. (M.L.D.)(Day)
The Vale, Vale Rd N4 1PG; Tel 0181-800 4772; G. Hill. (PhH) (2 1/2–19) (M)
William C. Harvey, Adams Rd N17 6HW; Tel 0181-808 7120; Ms L. Hall. (Day) (SLD) (3–19) (M)

Comprehensive Schools (11–18)

Fortismere School, Tetherdown N10 1NE; Tel 0181-444 5124; A.M. Nixon. (Mixed)
Gladesmore Community School, Gladesmore Rd N15 6TJ; Tel 0181-800 0884; Mrs H.S. Marmot. (Mixed)
Highgate Wood, Montenotte Rd N8 8RN; Tel 0181-340 1771; J.M. Smith, MA. (Mixed)
Hornsey, Inderwick Rd N8 9JF; Tel 081-348 6191; Ms L.M. Powell. (Girls)
Langham School, Langham Rd N15 3RB; Tel 0181-888 1722; Ms E.L. Green. (Mixed)

Northumberland Park Community School, Trulock Rd N17 0PG; Tel 0181-801 0091; A. Cottrell. (Mixed)
White Hart Lane School, White Hart La N22 5QJ; Tel 0181-889 6761; L.G. Warne. (Mixed)

Comprehensive Schools (Voluntary)

The School of St David & St Katharine, Hillfield Ave N8 7DT; Tel 0181-348 6292; T. Farrell. (V.A.) (Mixed)
St Thomas More R.C., Glendale Ave N22 5HN; Tel 0181-888 7122; P.T. Fox, BA. (V.A.) (Mixed)

Education Psychological Service/Child & Family Consultancy Service

Main Office and Hornsey E.P.S./C.F.C.S., 13 Tetherdown N10 1ND; Tel 0181-883 1094; *Principal Educational Psychologist* Ms J. Gardiner
Downhills E.P.S., Downhills Primary School, Philip La N15 5AB; Tel 0181-801 1134; *Senior Educational Psychologist* Mrs M. Bird
Tottenham C.F.C.S., 28 Philip La N15 4JB; Tel 0181-808 2300; *Senior Educational Psychologist* Mrs M. Bird
Wood Green E.P.S./C.F.C.S., 1 Williams Gr N22 5NR; Tel 081-889 0171; *Senior Educational Psychologist* C. Lewis

Outdoor Education Centre

Pendarren Hse Llangenny, nr Crickhowell, Powys NP8 1HE; Tel Crickhowell 810694; J. Harris

Haringey Education Business Partnership

336 Philip La N15 4AB; Tel 081-808 0771; A. York

Music Resources Centre

Tottenham Green Education Centre Town Hall Approach Rd, N15 4RY; Tel 0181-801 6192; P. Kaniou

Grant Maintained School

La Sainte Union Convent School, Highgate Rd, London NW5 1RP

Harrow London Borough Council

Population 209,100 based on 1993 OPCS Mid Year estimates and including boundary changes
Civic Centre, Station Rd, Harrow, Middx HA1 2UH; Tel 0181-863 5611

Education Department

PO Box 22, Civic Centre, Station Rd, Harrow, Middx HA1 2UW; Tel 0181-863 5611; Fax 0181-427 0810
Director of Education Christine Gilbert
Head of Resources Service Paul Higgins
Head of Direct Education Services Tony Kerr
Head of Strategic and Information Services Paul Osburn
Chief Adviser and Head of the Advisory and Inspection Service Maureen Burns
Admissions Officer Madeleine Hitchens
Awards Officer Lynn Hannon
Careers Service Officer Ann Rosenthal
Community, Arts and Youth Service Officer Tom Cooper
Development and Information Officer Janice Beck
Education Personnel Services Officer Paul Turner
Education Psychology Service Officer Paul Phillips
Education Social Workers Officer Gerry Dermody
Financial Services Officer Graham Try
Governor Services Officer Geraldine Sparrow
Learning Support Services Officer Michael Hart
Learning Support Services Officer Kath Cooke
Learning Support Services Officer Godfrey Pryor
Library Service Officer Bob Mills
Policy Review Officer Geoff Wingrove
Research and Information Officer Liz Defries
Teachers Centre Officer Vera Turner
Arts Adviser John Brigden
Assessment, Continuity and Primary Adviser Ann Simpson
Early Years and Primary Adviser Chris Hammond
English Adviser Anne Seeley
Humanities Adviser Hilary Kemeny
Languages Adviser Janet Halliday
Mathematics Adviser Phil Miley
Music Adviser Ros Asher
Professional Development Adviser Keith Hildrew
Science Adviser Anne Whitehead
Technology Adviser Peter Hemingway
TVEI Director Liz Follett
Number of Schools
54 primary (18,332 inc 8 V.A.); 9 high (7,792 inc 1 V.A.)
Special Schools
3 day; 1 hospital

Education Committee

LD 12, Con 7, Lab 6, Ind 1
Chair John Skipworth, (LD)
Vice-Chair J. Branch, (LD)
Members of the Committee
LD: O. Abrahams MA(Cantab), CertEd, B. Campbell, L. Cox, BSc(Hons), PhD, FRAS, M. de Beer BA, LLB, A. Diamond, M. Graham, J. Knight, B. Murphy, MIL, R. Prowse, J.W. Tuck JP
Con: C. Bath, C.A. Bednell, L. Champagnie, SRN, NDN, J.R. Cowan (The Mayoress), J. Cowan, J. Lammiman, FInstD, FIPD, MIH, MAIE, A.R. Olins, BCon(Hons), FCA, (His Worship the Major), BA(Hons), Law, A. Groves JP, D. Redford, R.W.H. Shannon, K. Thammaiah

Special Schools

Alexandra, Alexandra Ave, South Harrow HA2 9DX; Tel 0181-864 2739; Fax 0181-864 9336; Dennis Goldthorpe. (EBD)
Royal National Orthopaedic Hospital School, Brockley Hill, Stanmore, Middx HA7 4LP; Tel 0181-954 2300; Fax 0181-420 6254; Janet Fitzgerald
Shaftesbury, Headstone La, Harrow HA3 6LE; Tel 0181-428 2482; Fax 0181-420 2361; Paul Williams. (MLD)
Whittlesea, Whittlesea Rd, Harrow Weald HA3 6ND; Tel 0181-428 6968; Anne Carruthers. (SLD)

High Schools (12–16)

Bentley Wood, Bridges Rd, Stanmore HA7 3NA; Tel 0181-954 3623; Fax 0181-954 0427; Annette Ford. (Girls) (740)
Canons, Shaldon Rd, Edgware HA8 6AN; Tel 0181-952 1614; Fax 0181-951 5695; Roger Annan. (Mixed) (717)
Gayton High, Gayton Rd, Harrow HA1 2JG; Tel 0181-427 3266; Fax 0181-861 4024; Martin Buck. (Boys) (620)
Hatch End, Headstone La, Harrow HA3 6NR; Tel 0181-428 2251; Fax 0181-420 1932; *Head* Terry Humphreys (Acting). (Mixed) (1187)
Nower Hill, George V Ave, Pinner HA5 5RP; Tel 0181-863 0877; Fax 0181-424 0762; Simon Hensby. (Mixed) (1071)
Park, Thistlecroft Gdns, Stanmore HA7 1PL; Tel 0181-952 2803; Fax 0181-952 6975; Tony Barnes. (Mixed) (939)
Rooks Heath, Eastcote La, South Harrow HA2 9AG; Tel 0181-422 4675; Fax 0181-422 4407; John Stanley. (Mixed) (888)
Whitmore, Porlock Ave, Harrow HA2 0AD; Tel 0181-864 7688/9; Fax 0181-422 3449; Peter Allan. (Mixed) (1050)

Voluntary Aided High School (12–16)

Sacred Heart RC, High St, Wealdstone, London HA3 7AY; Tel 0181-863 9922; Fax 0181-863 3358; Pat Swindells. (Vol. Aided) (Girls) (580)

Middle Schools

Belmont Middle School, Hibbert Rd, Harrow Weald HA3 7JT; Tel 0181-427 0903; Fax 0181- 427 4738; Les Prince
Cannon Lane Middle School, Cannonbury Ave, Pinner HA5 1TS; Tel 0181-868 7809; Fax 0181-866 8144; David Mewes
Cedars Middle School, Whittlesea Rd, Harrow HA3 6LS; Tel 0181-428 4525; Fax 0181-420 1731; Liz Day
Elmgrove Middle School, Kenmore Ave, Kenton, Harrow HA3 8LU; Tel 0181-907 0162; Fax 0181-909 1477; Adrian Parker
Grange Middle School, Welbeck Rd, South Harrow HA2 0RJ; Tel 0181-422 5070; Fax 0181-423 3557; Jo Harrison
Kenmore Park Middle School, Moorhouse Rd, Kenton, Harrow HA3 9JA; Tel 0181-204 6294; Fax 0181-905 0368; Jacqueline Vaz
Longfield Middle School, Duke's Ave, North Harrow HA2 7NZ; Tel 0181-866 7331; Mike Maxwell
Pinner Park Middle School, Melbourne Ave, Pinner HA5 5JT; Tel 0181-863 1239; Fax 0181-424 8618; Richard Johnson
Pinner Wood Middle School, Latimer Gdns, Pinner HA5 3RA; Tel 0181-866 2125; Fax 0181-429 1629; Stephanie McDonnell
Priestmead Middle School, Hartford Ave, Kenton, Harrow HA3 8SZ; Tel 0181-907 2768; Fax 0181-909 1585; Brian Robertson
Roxbourne Middle School, Torbay Rd, South Harrow HA2 9QF; Tel 0181-422 1059; Ray Crocker
Roxeth Manor Middle School, Eastcote La, South Harrow HA2 9AG; Tel 0181-422 4503; Fax 0181-422 9054; Gabrielle Quinnen
Stag Lane Middle School, Collier Dr, Edgware HA8 5RU; Tel 0181-952 2731; Fax 0181-951 3750; David Mills
Stanburn Middle School, Abercorn Rd, Stanmore HA7 2PJ; Tel 0181-954 3823; Fax 0181-954 3227; Vacancy
Weald Middle School, Robin Hood Dr, Harrow Weald HA3 7DH; Tel 0181-954 2733; Fax 0181-954 8845; Paul Wisken
Welldon Park Middle School, Wyvenhoe Rd, South Harrow HA2 8LS; Tel 0181-422 4304; Sheena Maguire
West Lodge Middle School, West End La, Pinner HA5 1AF; Tel 0181-866 9836; Fax 0181-866 3109; Kris Evans

Grant Maintained School

Salvatorian College, High Rd, Harrow Weald, Harrow, Middx HA3 5DY; Tel 0181-863 2706; Fax 0181-863 3435; Kevin Wehrle. (Vol. Aided) (Boys) (GM) (600)

Havering London Borough Council

Population 229,492
Town Hall, Main Rd, Romford, Essex RM1 3BD; Tel (01708) 772222

Education and Community Services

Noak Hill North Centre, Noak Hill Rd, Romford, Essex RM3 7UE; Tel (01708) 772222; Fax (01708) 772672
Chairman (Chairman Youth Community and Continuing Education Sub Committee) Councillor Bill Harrison
Director of Education and Community Services C. Hardy, MEd, BSc
Head of Planning and Resources N. Rigby, BA
Manager (Premises and Client Services) G.G. Allen
Manager (Personnel) C.L. Hague
AEO (Budget and Resources) N. Porter
Manager (LMS Team) S.P. Ward
Head of Community and Library Services M. Hester
Principal Community Officer M. Calvert
Chief Librarian G. Saddington
Principal Careers Officer R.M. Auvray, BA(Hons), DipCG
AEO (Post-16 Education) J. Hooton
Entertainments and Events Manager M. Brown
Arts Officer C. Cole
Senior Recreation Officer S.E. Waller
Principal P. Boshier Havering College of Adult Education
Head of Pupil and Family Services D.J. Porter
EO (Primary and Special Schools) M. Giles, BSc
AEO (Special Needs) P. Howlett, BA, DipEd, DMS
Principal Educational Psychologist R. Foot, BA, MSc
AEO (Pupil and Welfare Services) T. Oakley
Chief Education Welfare Officer D.A. White
AEO (Governing Body Support Unit) S.M. Clarke, BSc(Hons), CertEd
AEO (Pupil and School Support) N. Keylock
Head of Inspection and Advisory Service B.K. Joy, BA, MA
Phase Inspector for Secondary Education S. Berwitz
Phase Inspector for Primary Education J.B. Thomas
Inspector for Primary Education (Religious Education) M. Edwards
Inspector for Primary Education (Early Years) D. Pilbro
Inspector for Primary Education (Teacher Appraisal) A. Pumfleet
Inspector for Secondary Education (Assessment) C. Hall
Senior Adviser (Information Technology) H. Pitts
Adviser (English and Drama) M. Fowler
Primary Science and Technology M. Langford
Adviser (Secondary Science) G. Pittaway
Adviser (Primary Art and History, Secondary Technology) M. Haynes
Adviser (Business Studies Cross Curriculum and Secondary School Vocational Courses) W. McKenzie
Adviser (Primary Geography and Technology) B.T. Marriott
Adviser (Mathematics) N. Morgan
Adviser (Music) J. Morris
Adviser (Physical Education & Health Education) J. Hickman
Adviser (Dance and Drama) D. Wignall
Adviser (Modern languages) C. Whitham
Advisory Teacher (Information Technology – Primary) J. Pugh
Number of Schools
74 primary (28,240); 14 secondary (10,959)
Special Schools
3 (260)
Day of Committee Meeting
Tuesday (6-week cycle)
Requisition Periods for School Supplies
No special period

Education Committee

Lab 10, Con 4, Residents Assoc 5, LD 1
Chair W. Harrison, (Lab) 126 Gubbins La, Harold Wood, Romford
Vice-Chair D.R. O'Flynn, (Lab) 26 Helmsdale Rd, Rise Pk, Romford
Members of the Committee
Lab: G.M. Carr, D. Cook, T. Gordon, G. Karian, R.S Kilbey, D. Martin, H. Moss, M. Wood
Con: L.S.E. Hutton, R.F. Latchford, E. A. Munday, A.E. Watkinson
Residents Assoc: L. Hawthorn, J.P. Lewis, L. Long, O.H.I. Ware, S. Whittaker
LD: D. Parker-Ross

Governor Training Unit

Governing Body Support Unit, Directorate of Education and Community Services, Noak Hill North Centre, Noak Hill Rd, Romford RM3 7UE; Tel (01708) 772685; Fax (01708) 772672
AEO (Governors) S.M. Clarke, BSc(Hons), CertEd
Services Offered
Support to Governing Body meetings; Dealing with matters raised for action by Governors; Advice helpline; Governor training; Governor newsletter and resource library; Governor recruitment

Special Schools

Corbets Tey, Harwood Hall La, Upminster RM14 2YQ; Tel (01708) 225888; A.J. Eades, BPhil. (E.S.N.)
Dycorts, Settle Rd, Harold Hill, Romford RM3 9YA; Tel (01708) 343649; G.S. Wroe, BA, MSc. (E.S.N.)
Ravensbourne, Neave, Faringdon Ave, Romford RM3 0AB; Tel (01708) 341800; M. Cameron. (E.S.N.(S)

Comprehensive Schools (County)

The Albany School, Broadstone Rd, off Albany Rd, Hornchurch RM12 4AJ; Tel (01708) 441537; M. Johnson, MEd. (Mixed) (746)
Bower Park, Havering Rd North, Romford RM1 4YY; Tel (01708) 730244; P. Davies, BA, MSc. Mixed (867)
Brittons, Ford La, Rainham RM13 7BB; Tel (01708) 554361; R. Sheffield, BA. (Mixed) (603)
Chafford, Lambs La, Rainham RM13 9XD; Tel (01708) 552811; *Head* C. Hassell, BA(Hons) (Acting). (Mixed) (722)
Emerson Park, Wych Elm Rd, Wingletye La, Hornchurch RM11 3AD; Tel (01708) 475285; H.W. Philips, BA(Hons), MA, MSc. (Mixed) (736)
Gaynes, Brackendale Gdns, Upminster RM14 3UX; Tel (01708) 222960; J. Winstone. (Mixed) (930)
Hall Mead, Marlborough Gdns, Cranham, Upminster RM14 1SF; Tel (01708) 225684; A. Wunderly, BSc. (Mixed) (910)
Harold Hill Community School, Settle Rd, Harold Hill, Romford RM3 9XX; Tel (01708) 371334/5; P. Maher. (Mixed) (790)
Marshalls Park, Havering Dr, Romford RM1 4BD; Tel (01708) 724134/5; C.G. Hendricks, BSc. (Mixed) (939)
Redden Court, Cotswold Rd, Harold Wood, Romford RM3 0TS; Tel (01708) 342293; J. Colley, MSc. (Mixed) (609)
Royal Liberty, Upper Brentwood Rd, Gidea Pk, Romford RM2 6HJ; Tel (01708) 740544; L.B. Thomas, BA. (Boys) (587)
Sanders Draper, Suttons La, Hornchurch RM12 6RT; Tel (01708) 443068; B. Rogers, BA, MA. (Mixed) (704)

Comprehensive Schools (Voluntary)

The Campion R.C., Wingletye La, Hornchurch RM11 3BX; Tel 452332; J. Johnson, BA(Hons). (V.A.) (Boys) (791)
St Edward's C.E., London Rd, Romford RM7 9NX; Tel (01708) 730462; *Headteacher* G.C.S. Drew, BA. (V.A.) (Mixed) (1088)

Youth and Community Houses

Albemarle Area Youth Hse, Gooshays Dr, Harold Hill, Romford RM3 9ES; Tel (01708) 340161
Bretons Area Youth Hse, Rainham Rd, Rainham RM13 7LP; Tel (01708) 553857
Century Youth Hse, Albert Rd, Romford, Essex RM1 2PS; Tel (01708) 751656
Robert Beard Area Youth Hse, 233 High St, Hornchurch RM11 3XU; Tel (01708) 450609

Music Centre

Dury Falls Campus, The Walk, Hornchurch RM11 3TL; Tel (01708) 450313; E. Forder

Outdoor Pursuits Centres

Stubbers Outdoor Pursuits Centre, Ockendon Rd, North Ockendon, nr Upminster RM14 2TY; Tel (01708) 224753; *Centre Warden* A. Benson
Youth Camp Tel (01708) 220031 (Call Box)

Havering College of Adult Education

Main Office, Noak Hill Centre, Broxhill Rd, Romford RM3 7TQ; Tel (01708) 378877; P. Boshier

Havering Inspection and Advisory Service

Noak Hill Centre, Noak Hill Rd, Romford RM3 7TQ; Tel (01708) 379560/1/2/3
Inspector (Primary, Religious Education) M. Edwards
Inspector (Primary, Early Years) D. Pilbro
Inspector (Primary, Teacher Appraisal) A. Pumfleet
Inspector (Secondary, Assessment) C. Hall
Adviser (Information Technology) H. Pitts
Adviser (Primary Art and History, Secondary Technology) M. Haynes
Adviser (English and Drama) M. Fowler
Adviser (Mathematics) N. Morgan
Adviser (Physical Education and Health Education) J. Hickman
Adviser (Primary, Science and Technology) M. Langford
Adviser (Primary, Technology and Geography) B. Marriott
Adviser (Modern Languages) C. Whitham
Adviser (Business Studies, Cross-curriculum and Secondary School Vocational Courses) W. McKenzie
Adviser (Music) J. Morris
Adviser (Secondary Science) G. Pittaway
Adviser (Dance and Drama) D. Wignall
Advisory Teacher (Information Technology-Primary) J. Pugh
Professional Assistant (Assessment) P. Brown
Computer Centre, Noak Hill Centre, Noak Hill Rd, Romford RM3 7JW; Tel (01708) 349115; *Adviser (Information Technology)* H. Pitts
Europa Centre, Dury Falls Campus, The Walk, Hornchurch RM11 3TL; Tel (01708) 445694/440087; *Co-ordinator (Modern Languages)* C. Whitham
Special Education Needs Support Centre, Noak Hill Centre, Noak Hill Rd, Romford RM3 7TL; Tel (01708) 370918/343693; *Principal Officer* A. Cushway (Acting); *Adviser (ESOL)* I. Thrilling

Grant Maintained Schools

Abbs Cross School, Abbs Cross La, Hornchurch RM12 4YB; Tel (01708) 440304; D.J. Powney, MA. (Mixed) (729)
The Coopers' Company and Coborn School, St Mary's La, Upminster, Essex RM14 3HS; Tel (01708) 250500; Fax (01708) 226109; *Headmaster* C. Churchett, BA. (Boys)
The Frances Bardesley School for Girls, Brentwood Rd, Romford RM1 2RR; Tel (01708) 762484; P. Joughin, JPBA. (Girls) (GM)
Sacred Heart of Mary R.C. School, St Mary's La, Upminster RM14 2QR; Tel (01708) 22260; B.J. Welch, MSc(Lond), MA(Oxon). (Girls)

Hillingdon London Borough Council

Population 228,476
Civic Centre, High St, Uxbridge, Middx UB8 1UW; Tel (01895) 250111

Education Services Group

Civic Centre, High St, Uxbridge, Middx UBB 1UW; Tel (01895) 250111
Group Director, Education Services G.M. Andrews
Deputy Director, Education Services C.D. Shires
Service Manager (Services to Schools) G. Moss, BSc
Service Manager: Policy and Resources A. Matthews
Senior Inspector (Primary Early Years and Special Needs) J. Dewhurst, MA, LCP, DipEd
Inspector: Mathematics and Careers Dr. E. Blaire, BA, PhD
Inspector: English, Drama and Modern Foreign Languages Rosemary Brougham, BA(Hons), MA
Inspector: Primary, IT and Technology D. Hawthorne, BA(Hons)
Inspector: Primary, RE and Equal Opps P. Hoey, MA

Inspector: Science, Environmental Education and Assessment Dr. P.M. Leckstein, BSc, PhD, FRES
Chief Inspector and Inspector: Creative Arts R. Turner, GRSM, MA
Principal Careers Adviser G. Carnan (Acting)
Educational Support and Psychology Services H.J. Dinham
Service Manager: Pupil and Family Services J.A. Wade
Number of Schools
1 nursery (60); 60 primary; 3 secondary; 11 grant maintained primary, 12 grant maintained secondary
Special Schools
6 day
Requisition Periods for School Supplies
Various
Other Authorities with whom Joint Purchasing Arrangements are made
CLEAPSE, CFG

Education Committee

Lab 8, Con 4
Chair P. Ryerson, (Lab)
Vice-Chair John Morse
Members of the Committee
Lab: L. Bliss, J. Gardner, J.Leonard, K. Livney, N. Nunn-Price, G. Sharma
Con: D. Mills, S. James, M. Knight, K. Morris

Careers Offices

See Chapter 17

Child Guidance Clinic

Uxbridge Child Guidance Centre 26 Bennets Yd, off Lancaster Rd, Uxbridge UB8 1JH; Tel (01895) 256521; *Principal Educational Psychologist* Hilary Dinham

Special Schools

Chantry, Falling La, Yiewsley, West Drayton UB7 8AB; Tel (01895) 446747; R. Warnes. (Day) (11–18) (Mixed) (E.B.D.)
Grangewood, Fore St, Eastcote, Pinner HA5 2JQ; Tel (01895) 676401; J.D. Ayres, MA. (Day) (3–11) (Mixed) (SLD)
Hedgewood, Weymouth Rd, Hayes UB4 8NF; Tel 0181-845 6756; M.J. Goddard, BA(Hons). (Day) (5–11) (Mixed) (MLD) (56)
Meadow, Royal La, Hillingdon, Uxbridge UB8 3QU; Tel (01895) 443310; R. Payne. (Day) (11–18) (Mixed) (MLD)
Moorcroft, Harlington Rd, Hillingdon UB8 3HD; Tel (01895) 236430; M.J. Geddes, BA(Hons). (Day) (11–19) (Mixed) (SLD)
The Willows, Stipularis Dr, off Glencoe Rd, Hayes UB4 9QB; Tel 0181-841 7176; F. King

Secondary Schools (11–18)

Evelyns, Appletree Ave, Yiewsley, West Drayton UB7 8DA; Tel (01895) 430066; J. Reavley, BA. (Mixed)
John Penrose, Northwood Way, Harefield, Uxbridge UB9 6ET; Tel (01895) 822108; A. Way, BA. (Mixed)

Secondary School (Voluntary)

Bishop Ramsey C.E., Warrender Way, Ruislip HA4 8EE; Tel (01895) 639227; M. Udall, BSc. (Mixed) (V.A.)

Institutes of Adult Education

Adult Education Office, 86 Long La, Ickenham, Uxbridge UB10 8SX; Tel (01895) 676690
Frays Centre, 65 Harefield Rd, Uxbridge UB8 1PJ; Tel (01895) 254766
North Hillingdon AEC, 86 Long La, Ickenham, Uxbridge UB10 8SX; Tel (01895) 634616
Harlington AEC, Harlington Community School, Pinkwell La, Hayes UB3 1PE; Tel 0181-569 1613
Pinkwell Open Learning Centre, Harlington Community School, Pinkwell La, Hayes UB3 1PE; Tel 0181-569 1614

Hillington Music Service

Compass Theatre, Glebe Ave, Ickenham, Uxbridge UB10 8PD; Tel (01895) 630155

Teachers' Centre

Deanesfield Centre, Queens Wk, South Ruislip HA4 0LR; Tel 0181-841 5472; P. Terry

Grant Maintained Schools

Abbotsfield, Clifton Gdns, Hillingdon, Uxbridge UB10 0EX; Tel (01895) 237350; M. White, MA, BSc. (Boys)
Bishopshalt School Royal La, Hillingdon, Uxbridge, Middx UB8 3RF; Tel (01895) 233909/253665; Fax (01895) 73102; *Headteacher* Dr Leslie Bather; *Chair of Governors* J.E. Carsons. Mixed (1133)
The Douay Martyrs R.C., Edinburgh Dr, Ickenham, Uxbridge UB10 8QY; Tel (01895) 635371; Mrs M. Stubbs, MA, FRSA. (V.A.) (Mixed)
Greenway School, The Greenway, Uxbridge, Hillingdon, Middx UB8 2PR; Tel (01895) 234060; Fax (01895) 256738; *Headteacher* M.B. Trowell; *Chair of Governors* Cllr P. James. Mixed 11–18
Harlington Community School, Pinkwell La, Hayes, Middx UB3 1PB; Tel 0181-569 1610; Fax 0181-569 1624; P.D. Targett, JP, MA. (Mixed)
Haydon School Wiltshire La, Eastcote, Pinner HA5 2LX; Tel 0181-429 0005; *Headteacher* D. Dobson; *Chair of Governors* B. Kester. (Mixed) (11–18) (1300)
The Hayes Manor School Wood End Green Rd, Hayes UB3 2SE; Tel 0181-573 2097; *Headteacher* J.E. Farr; *Chair of Governors* Cllr Alfred G. Langley. (Mixed) (11–18) (800)
Mellow La School, Hewens Rd, Hayes, Middx UB4 8JP; Tel 0181-573 1039; Fax 0181-813 7058
Northwood School Potter St, Northwood HA6 1QG; Tel (01923) 836363; *Headteacher* Kathy Brisbourne; *Chair of Governors* C. Michael Levy. (Mixed) (1100)
Queensmead School Queen's Walk, South Ruislip HA4 OLS; Tel 0181-845 6266; *Headteacher* R. Duggan; *Chair of Governors* C. Quirk. Mixed) (11–18 (1050)
Swakeleys, Clifton Gdns, Hillingdon, Uxbridge UB10 0EJ; Tel (01895) 251962; Fax (01895) 235027; John Taylor, MA. (Girls)
Uxbridge High School The Greenway, Uxbridge UB9 2PR; Tel (01895) 234060; Fax (01895) 256738; *Headteacher* M.B. Trowell; *Chair of Governors* Cllr P. James. Mixed) (11–18) (700)
Vyners School Warren Rd, Ickenham, Uxbridge UB10 8AB; Tel (01895) 34342; Fax (01895) 237955; *Headteacher* B.P. Houghton; *Chair of Governors* R. Puddifoot. (Mixed) (11–18) (920)

Hounslow London Borough Council

Population 200,000
Civic Centre, Lampton Rd, Hounslow, Middx TW3 4DN; Tel 0181-570 7728; Fax 0181-572 4819

Education Department

The Civic Centre, Lampton Rd, Hounslow, Middx TW3 4DN; Tel 0181-570 7728; Fax 0181-572 4819
Director of Education J.D. Trickett, MA
Chairman Cllr M.J. Sterne
Vice-Chairman Cllr J. Connelly
Vice-Chairman Cllr P. Nathan
Senior Assistant Director of Education R.E. Letch, MA, ADipEd

Principal Adviser (Advice and Support Unit) G.M. McIntosh, BEd
Assistant Director of Education (Strategy) H. Warner
Principal Officer (Special Needs) B. Canvin, BA
EO (Personnel) H. Riddell
EO (Special Needs) S. Brown
EO (Further Education) V. Mitchell
EO (Resources) V. Mitchell
EO (Schools) H. McCafferty
General Adviser (Humanities and Religious Educ) J.M. Williamson, BA, LTH, MEd, MA
General Adviser (TVEI) J.E. Bolt, BA
General Adviser (Primary Early Years/Assessment KS1) L.E. Martin, BA
General Adviser (English, Drama & Media Educ/MFL) D. Meaden, BEd, MA
General Adviser (Primary) M. Burslem, BEd
General Adviser (Multicultural Educ/Maths) J. Tanna, BEd, MA
General Adviser (Science, PSE and H.Ed) V. Davies
General Adviser (Professional Development) A.R. Peter, BA
General Adviser (PE/Secondary Assessment) M.A. Symons
General Adviser (Primary/Assessment KS2) L.D. Ireland, BA, AeDipEd
Technology and IT C. Salt
School Meals Adviser B. Headford
Principal Careers Officer J.D. Allen, MA
Principal Youth and Community Officer R. Devonshire
Principal Educational Psychologist Ms N. D'Aeth, BA, MEd
Deputy Principal Educational Psychologist L. Gardner
Educational Psychologist J. Brandon
Educational Psychologist R. Freedman
Educational Psychologist B. Barnett
Educational Psychologist V. Cornish
Educational Psychologist J. Horne
Educational Psychologist K. Duggan
Educational Psychologist M. Schlesinger
Number of Schools
63 primary (14,916); 14 secondary comprehensive (14,827) 2 GM
Special Schools
5 day (636)
Requisition Periods for School Supplies
As required
Other Authorities with whom Joint Purchasing Arrangements are made
None

Governor Training Unit

Governor Training Programme, Education Dept, Civic Centre, Lampton Rd, Hounslow, Middx TW3 4DN; Tel 0181-862 5241; Fax 0181-862 5249
Governor Training Co-ordinator Hilary Strudwick, BA, BSc
Services Offered
Comprehensive programme of centrally-organised training courses; Helpline, advice given on any issue connected with school governance; Central Resource Loan Library; School based Governors' Libraries; access to regional and national governor services through LEA membership of AGIT, NAGM etc; training for individual governing bodies

Teaching Support Service

Tel 0181-570 8547
Head of Service I. Hempstead
Deputy Head of Service J. Capstick

The Service consists of four specialist teams:- Behaviour, Learning, Physical Disability and Sensory Impairment

Careers Centre

See Chapter 17

Special Schools

John Busch School, Twickenham Rd, Isleworth TW7 6AU; Tel 081-560 4300; P. Hrekow, MA
The Lindon-Bennett, Main St, Hanworth TW13 6ST; Tel 0181-898 0479; S. Line
The Marjory Kinnon, Hatton Rd, Bedfont TW14 9QZ; Tel 0181-890 8890; D.J. Harris, BA, MEd
Oaklands, Woodlands Rd, Isleworth TW7 6HD; Tel 0181-560 3569; Vacancy
The Cedars Primary School, High St, Cranford, London; Tel 0181-759 1805; A. Costello, MA

Comprehensive Schools

Brentford, Clifden Rd, Brentford TW8 0PG; Tel 0181-847 4281; J. Senior, MA(Oxon), MA(Lond). (Girls) (637)
Chiswick, Burlington La, Chiswick W4 3UN; Tel 0181-747 0031; Mrs H. Metcalf, MSc, BA(Hons). (1004)
Cranford Community School, High St, Cranford, London; Tel 0181-897 2001; W.S. Atkinson, MA. (1136)
Feltham, Boundaries Rd, Feltham TW13 5EW; Tel 0181-890 0167/9; P.M. Grant, BSc. (1328)
The Green, Busch Cnr, Isleworth TW7 5BB; Tel 081-568 3137; Mrs J.A. Bartlett, BSc. (Girls) (733)
The Heathland, Wellington Rd South, Hounslow TW4 5HU; Tel 0181-572 4411; G.J. Samuel, JP, MA. (1379)
Heston, Heston Rd, Heston TW5 0QR; Tel 0181-572 1931; *Headteacher* A. Bennett, MA, BEd(Hons), LTCL. (853)
Hounslow Manor, Prince Regent Rd, Hounslow TW3 1NE; Tel 0181-572 4461; R.M. Shortt, MA. (731)
Isleworth and Syon, Ridgeway Rd, Isleworth TW7 5LJ; Tel 0181-568 5791; A.C. Phillips, BSc. (Boys) (878)
Lampton, Lampton Ave, Hounslow TW3 4EP; Tel 0181-572 1936; D.M. Jordan, Bsc(Econ). (803)
Longford, Tachbrook Rd, Feltham TW14 9PE; Tel 0181-890 0245/6; D.W. Tanner, BA. (896)
St Mark's R.C., Bath Rd, Hounslow TW3 3EJ; Tel 0181-577 3600; D.J. Sheath, BSc(Hons). (982)

Higher Education Establishment

West London Institute of Higher Education 300 St Margaret's Rd, Twickenham, London; Tel 0181-891 0121; Dr J.E. Kane, MEd Borough Rd, Osterley, Isleworth, Middx

Education Centre

Hounslow Education Centre, Martindale Rd, Hounslow, London TW4 7HE; Tel 0181-569 5840; *Centre Manager* M. Baker

Grant Maintained Schools

Gumley House Convent, St John's Rd, Isleworth TW7 6DN; Tel 0181-568 8692; Sister Brenda Wallace, FCJ, BA, PhD. (Girls) (1080)
Gunnersbury R.C., The Ride, Boston Manor Rd, Brentford TW8 9LB; Tel 0181-568 7281; J.J. Heffernan. (Boys) (1047)

Islington London Borough Council

Population 175,500 (mid-1993 estimate)
Town Hall, Upper St, London N1 2UD; Tel 0171-226 1234; Fax 0171-477 3063

Education Department

Laycock St, London N1 1TH; Tel 0171-457 5566; Fax 0171-457 5555
Director of Education Dr Hilary Nicolle
Deputy Director of Education Mike Clayden
Assistant Director of Education (Special Education, Client and Community Division) Thanos Morphitis

Assistant Director of Education (Head of Trading Services) Adrian Paterson
Senior Inspector (TVEI and Secondary) M. Linington
Head of Inspection and Advisory Services Alastair Mathews
Senior Inspector (Primary) Y. Conolly
Senior Inspector (Special Needs) C. Bodycombe
Number of Schools
3 nursery (143 full-time, 131 part-time); 57 primary (15,218); 6 secondary county, 3 secondary voluntary (7,223)
Special Schools
6 (338)
Barnsbury Complex Barnsbury Pk, London N1 1QF; Tel 0171-457 5566; Fax 0171-457 5738
Laycock St, London N1 1TH; Tel 0171-457 5874; Fax 0171-457 5555

Education Committee

Lab 14, Con 1, LD 1
Chair P. Kelly, (Lab)
Vice-Chair A. Bogi, (Lab)
Members of the Committee
Lab: C. Jeaper, M. Babulall, M. Boye-Anawomah, D. Burridge, A. Clinton, R. Crossman, D. Kleanthaus, A. Laws, M. Leigh, L. McKinstry, M. Messis, S. Twigg
Con: C. Blackwood
LD: C. Pryce

Governor Training Unit

Professional Development Centre, Islington Education Service, Block 'A', Barnsbury Complex, Offord Rd, London N1 1QF; Tel 0171-457 5676; Fax 0171-457 5738
Governor Information and Training Co-ordinator Jane Wright, BA
Services Offered
Production of Annual Central Training programme on offer to Governing Bodies by subscription; Implementation of training, liaising with Islington and external trainers; Production of Open Learning packs; Support for Link/Training Governors; Maintenance and development of Governor Resource Base (books, videos, etc on loan)

Special Schools

Colebrooke, Colebrooke Row, City Rd N1 8AF; Tel 0171-226 5608; Rosemary Arnott
Harborough, Elthorne Rd, Holloway Rd N19 4AB; Tel 0171-272 5739; A. Furze
Richard Cloudesley, Golden Lane EC1Y 0TJ; Tel 0171-251 1161; H. Came
Rosemary, 75 Prebend St N1 8TW; Tel 0171-226 8223; J. Wolger Upper School, Sans Walk EC1; Tel 0171-253 6893
Samuel Rhodes, Dowrey St, Richmond Ave N1 0LS; Tel 0171-837 9075; S. Cochrane

Secondary Schools (County and Voluntary Aided)

Central Foundation, Cowper St EC2A 4AP; Tel 0171-253 3741; A. Marshall. (Boys)
Elizabeth Garrett Anderson, Off Penton Rise N1 9QJ; Tel 0171-837 0739; B.E. Loveridge. (Girls)
George Orwell, Turle Rd N4 3LS; Tel 0171-263 1465; C. Lodge. (Mixed)
Highbury Fields, Highbury Hill N5 1AR; Tel 0171-226 1525; M. Mann. (Girls)
Annex 34 Aberdeen Pk, London, N5 2BL; Tel 0171-359 4832
Highbury Grove Highbury New Pk N5 2EG; Tel 0171-226 7993; P. Searl. (Boys)
Holloway, Hilldrop Rd, London N7 1JG; Tel 0171-607 5885; P. Smith. (Boys)
Islington Green, Prebend St N1 8PQ; Tel 0171-226 8611; C. Peters. (Mixed)
Mount Carmel, Holland Walk, Scholefield Rd N19 3EU; Tel 0171-281 3536; C. Eisen (Acting). (Girls)
St Aloysius' College, Hornsey La, London N6 5LY; Tel 0171-263 1391; M. Pickersgill. (Boys)

Community Education Service

Principal Co-ordinator (Youth and Play) C. Leach; Tel 0171-457 5822
Principal Under Fives Development Officer A. Wilson; Tel 0171-457 5824

Impairment Units

Hargrave Park Partially Hearing Unit, Hargrave Pk, London N19 2DP; Tel 0171-272 7847; P. Lary
George Orwell Visually Impaired Unit, Turle Rd, Tollington Pk, London N4; Tel 0171-281 7127; D. Arnold
Laycock Partially Hearing Unit, Laycock St, Upper St, London N1 1SW; Tel 0171-359 8005; S. Brownson
Robert Blair Language Impaired Unit, Blundell St, Caledonian Rd, London N7 9BL; Tel 0171-700 5386; A. Herbert
Yerbury Visually Impaired Unit, Foxham Rd, Yerbury Rd, London N19 4RR; Tel 0171-281 7127; T. Lee

Kensington and Chelsea

Population 138,394
The Town Hall, Hornton St, Kensington, London W8 7NX; Tel 0171-937 5464; Fax 0171-937 0038

Education Department

The Town Hall, Hornton St, London W8 7NX; Tel 0171-937 5464; Fax 0171-937 0038
Chairman, Education and Libraries Committee Councillor Merrick R. Cockell
Vice-Chairman, Education and Libraries Committee Councillor Adrian J.A.D. Fitzgerald
Executive Director of Education and Libraries Business Group Michael Stoten, BSc, FRSA, FBIM
District Inspector F. Beresford
District Inspector J. Copeland
District Inspector A. Phillips
Head of Performance Review and Planning C. Richardson
Group Personnel Manager J. Walker
Group Finance Manager A. Barcellos
Finance Manager S. Bettle
Contracts Manager C. Levan
Head of Schools Services L. Purcell
Principal Education Welfare Officer H. Shaw
Head of Training, Enterprise and Guidance A. Webster
Principal Awards Officer Ms T. Prior
Head of Community Education Services R. Kiteley
Principal Youth Officer I. Comfort
Principal Education Psychologist M. Evans
Head of Pupil Support Service G. Crosbie
Number of Schools
4 county nursery (252); 12 county primary (3,417); 13 voluntary primary (2,953); 1 county secondary (1,482); 2 voluntary secondary (1,059); 1 special (boarding)

Education and Libraries Committee

Chair M.R. Cockell, (Con) 30 Kenway Rd, London SW5 0RR; Tel 0171-373 6521
Vice-Chair A.J.A.D. Fitzgerald, (Con) 16 Clareville St, London SW7 5AW; Tel 0171-373 9972
Members of the Committee
Con: C. Buckmaster, D. Campion, E.M. Christmas, A. Dalton, Dr J.E.L. Munday, E.P. Tomlin, J. Wheeler, A. Whitfield
Lab: K. Cunningham, R. Horton, M. Lasharie, R. Weems

Governor Training Unit

Isaac Newton Centre for Professional Development, 108a Lancaster Rd, London W11 1QS; Tel 0171-221 4031; Fax 0171-243 1570
Principal of Professional Development Centre (including support for organisationally led programmes) Judith Clulow
Services Offered
Central programme including induction of new governors. Helpline. Information sheet produced twice termly. Information Centre resource section. Borough's representative for AGIT, NAGAM and other related bodies

Youth Service and Centres

Youth Service Administration Campden Institute, 95 Lancaster Rd W11 1QS; Tel 0171-221 3743; Fax 0171-221 0727
Health Information Project, Grand Union Centre, 336A Ladbroke Gr W10 6BX; Tel 0181-960 5510
Chelsea Youth Centre, Carlyle Bldg, Hortensia Rd SW10 0QR; Tel 0171-352 2905
Golborne Youth Centre, 2a Wornington Rd W10 5QQ; Tel 0181-960 6238
Lancaster Youth Centre, 128A Lancaster Rd W11 1QS; Tel 0171-727 1800
One Step, Campden Institute, 95 Lancaster Rd, W11 1QQ; Tel 0171-221 4425
Portobello Project, Basement, Notting Hill Library, 1 Pembridge Sq W2 4EW; Tel 0171-221 4413

Special School

Parkwood Hall, Beechenlea La, Swanley, Kent BR8 8DS; Tel (01322) 664441; Fax (01322) 613163; R. Lane

Secondary School (County)

Holland Park, Airlie Gdns, Campden Hill Rd W8 9DE; Tel 0171-727 5631; Fax 0171-243 0176. (SM) (1450)

Secondary Schools (Voluntary)

St. Thomas More RC, Cadogan St SW3 2QS; Tel 0171-589 9734; Fax 0171-823 7868; J.M. Burn. (SM) (647)
Sion Manning RC, St. Charles Sq W10 6EL; Tel 0181-969 7111; Fax 0181-969 5119; J. Lebrecht. (SG) (373)

Teachers' Centre

Isaac Newton Centre for Professional Development, 108a Lancaster Rd W11 1QS; Tel 0171-221 4031; Fax 0171-243 1570; *Principal* J. Clulow

Grant Maintained School

Cardinal Vaughan Memorial School 89 Addison Rd, London W14 8BZ; Tel 0171-603 8478; Fax 0171-602 3124; *Headteacher* A.S.J. Pellegrini; *Chair of Governors* Very Rev Canon Adrian Arrowsmith. 160 Sixth Form) (11–18) (Boys) (B (470)

Kingston upon Thames

Population 132,996
Guildhall, Kingston upon Thames, Surrey KT1 1EU; Tel 0181-546 2121; Fax 0181-546 2121

Education Directorate

Guildhall 2, Kingston upon Thames, Surrey KT1 1EU; Tel 0181-546 2121; Fax 0181-547 5296
Director of Education W.E. Dickinson, BA(Hons), ADipEd
Senior Assistant Director B. Heritage, BSc
Assistant Director M.R. Bayliss, MA, MSc, FCollP
Assistant Education Officer M.J. Dale, BA(Hons)
Head of Inspection Advice and Training I. Harries, BA, MEd
Inspector P. Munday, BA, MA (Sen.Primary Insp.)
Inspector J. Allcorn, BEd, MEd
Inspector S. Cook, DipEd, Psych, CD
Inspector Dr J. Gravett, MPhill, ADipE
Inspector M.D. Gibson, BSc(Hons), MRIC, CChem
Inspector P. Hunter, BA
Head of Education Finance J. Ball
Head of Education Personnel D.L. Wilson, MIPM
Head of Pupil, Parents and Students G. Waller, BSc(Econ)
Head of Special Education Needs H. Stirling
Educational Psychology Service H. Firth
Head of Learning Support L. Cowdery
Head of English as a Second Language S. Shaw
Head of Community Education (Adult) R. Kandela, BA, MPhil
Head of Community Education (Youth) S. Roberts
Head of Libraries S. Herbertson, BA, MA, ALA
Head of Information Technology B. Durrant
Head of Malden Centre E. Borthwick, BSc(Hons), MSc, MILAM
Head of Careers A. Moore
Head of Music Service J. Child, MA, DPSA, GRSM, ARCM
Number of Schools
2 nursery (63 full-time, 157 part-time); 35 primary (10,771); 6 secondary (4,886); adult education service (23,210)
Special Schools
3 day (236)
Number of Libraries
6 and 1 mobile library

Education and Leisure Services Committee

LD 9, Con 5, Lab 1
Chair I. Reid, (LD) 126 Clayton Rd, Hode, Chessington KT9 1NJ; Tel 0181-397 1396
Vice-Chair J. Heamon 13 Carlton Rd, New Malden KT3 3AJ; Tel 0181-942 6081
Members of the Committee
LD: S. Goodship, G. Goring, A. McLeay, J Oates, J. Ozanne, S. Scrivens, J. Tilley
Con: P. Clokie, D. Doe, Q. Edington, E. Humphrey, R. Pandya
Lab: T. Flux

Training and Development Centre

The Kingdowne Centre, Ewell Rd, Surbiton KT6 6HL; Tel 0181-390 2431; Fax 0181-390 2431
Manager K.O. Fox
Services Offered
Training for Education Staff and Governors

Special Day Schools

Bedelsford, Grange Rd, Kingston upon Thames KT1 2QZ; Tel 0181-546 9838; H.D. Aitken, DipEd. (P.H.)
Dysart, Dukes Ave, Kingston upon Thames KT2 5QY; Tel 0181-546 0610; P.C. Smillie, BEd(Hons)
St Philip's, Harrow Cl, Leatherhead Rd, Chessington KT9 2HP; Tel 0181-397 2672; J.A. Ainley, MSc, DipChildDev, DipEd, HC. (M.L.D.)

Secondary Schools (11–18)

Coombe, Clarence Ave, New Malden KT3 3TU; Tel 0181-942 1242; Fax 0181-942 6385; A.M. Clarke, MA. (Girls) (1097)
Chessington Community College, Garrison La, Chessington KT9 2JS; Tel 0181-974 1157; Fax 0181-974 2603; J.P. Hayes, BSc, DipEd. (Mixed) (573)
Hollyfield, Surbiton Hill Rd, Surbiton KT6 4TU; Tel 0181-399 2657; Fax 0181-547 6833; S.J. Chamberlain, BEd(Hons). (Mixed) (668)
Southborough, Hook Rd, Surbiton KT6 5AS; Tel 0181-391 4324; Fax 0181-391 0177; J. Oborn, BA. (Boys) (570)

Tolworth, Fullers' Way North, Surbiton KT6 7LQ; Tel 0181-397 3854; Fax 0181-974 2600; C.C. Williams, MA. (Girls) (1118)

Secondary Grammar School

Tiffin Girls, Richmond Rd, Kingston upon Thames KT2 5PL; Tel 0181-546 0773; Fax 0181-547 0191; P.V. Cox, BA(Hons), MA, FRGS. (Girls) (860)

Educational Psychology Service

84 Ewell Rd, Surbiton, Surrey KT6 6EX; Tel 0181-390 8151

Adult Education

Kingston Adult Education Service, North Kingston Centre, Richmond Rd, Kingston upon Thames KT2 5PE; Tel 0181-547 6700/1

The Malden Centre

Cocks Crescent, (Leisure/Learning Facility) Blagdon Rd, New Malden KT3 4TA; Tel 0181-949 3330; Fax 0181-949 5135; E. Borthwick, BSc(Hons), MSc, MILAM

Professional Development Centres

The Kingsdowne Centre, Ewell Rd, Surbiton KT6 6HL; Tel 0181-390 2431
IT and Technology Services Tel 0181-547 6847

Youth and Community Centres

Barnfield Youth & Community Centre, Parkfields Rd, Park Rd, Kingston upon Thames KT2 5LY; Tel 0181-546 6982; *Area Youth and Community Worker (North Kingston)* J. Harvie
Chessington Youth and Community Centre, Church La, Chessington KT9 2DR; Tel 0181-397 2495; *Area Youth and Community Worker (South Kingston)* G. Hall
Doris Venner Youth and Community Centre, The Manor Drive, Worcester Park KT4 7LG; Tel 0181-330 2805; *Youth and Community Worker* J. Trend
Duke of Edinburgh's Awards Adviser, North Kingston Centre, Richmond Rd, London; Tel 0181-547 6719; *Enquiries* Vacancy
Hook Youth & Activities Centre, Devon Way, Hook, Chessington KT9 2RJ; Tel 0181-397 2216; *Youth and Community Worker* G. Marshall
Kingsnympton Youth and Community Centre, Kingsnympton Park Est, Kingston Hill, Kingston upon Thames, Surrey; Tel 0181-549 5705; *Youth & Community Worker* J. Dixon
Searchlight Youth and Community Centre, Kingston Rd, New Malden KT3 3RX; Tel 0181-549 4514; *Youth and Community Worker* M. Dyer

Grant Maintained Schools

Beverley, College Gdns, Blake's La, New Malden KT3 6NU; Tel 0181-949 1537; P.A. O'Shea. (Boys) (671)
Holy Cross Convent R.C., Sandal Rd, New Malden KT3 5AR; Tel 0181-949 4884; Mrs M. Watson, BA, MEd, Dueg(Lille), CRE. (Girls) (673)
Richard Challoner R.C., Manor Dr North, New Malden KT3 5PE; Tel 0181-330 5947; J.M. Gwynn, MA(Oxon), MIL. (Boys) (652)
Tiffin, Queen Elizabeth Rd, Kingston upon Thames KT2 6RL; Tel 0181-546 4638; Dr A.M. Dempsey, BSc(Hons). (Boys) (Grammar) (900)

Lambeth London Borough Council

Town Hall, Brixton Hill, Lambeth SW2 1RW; Tel 0171-926 1000

Education Department

Blue Star Hse, 234–44 Stockwell Rd, London SW9 9SP; Tel 0171-926 1000
Director of Education Bebb Burchell
Assistant Director (Education Client and Community Services) Jill Stansfield
Head of Schools Support Services Maggie Pedersen
Head of Inspection and Advisory Services and Chief Inspector Bruce Gill
Number of Schools
5 nursery; 69 primary; 5 secondary; 15 special schools

Education Committee

Spokesperson A. Bottrall
Spokesperson Shelagh Webb
Spokesperson J. Whelan
Members of the Committee
H. Barker, E. Castle, N. Cattermole, D. Cooper-King, J. Denny, J. Driver, C. Elphicke, K. Fitchett, B. Gentry, A. Hamilton-Mayer, D.Hayes-Mojon, S. Hooberman, D. Hughes, M. Jones, T. Murnaghan, J. Pindar, D. Salisbury-Jones, D. Trott, P. Watson

Governor Training

Institution Management, London Borough of Lambeth Education Dept, 234/244 Stockwell Rd, London SW9 9SB; Tel 0171-926 2163 or 0171-926 2729; Fax 0171-926 2633
Head of Institution Management Hilary Lowe
Local Management Officer Davinder Jhuti
Services Offered
Borough wide training programme covering curriculum, LMS, personnel issues. Finance issues, premises and pupl related issues. Provides individual Governing Body training. Advice to Governors over the phone; The section also provides clerking and support services to Governors on statutory and policy issues

Special Schools

Aspen House, Kennington Park Gdns SE11 4AN; Tel 0171-582 3675; Val Kirk (Acting). (Del)
Clapham Park, 127 Park Hill SW4 9PA; Tel 0181-674 5639; Barbara Raybould. (Impaired vision)
Elm Court, Elmcourt Rd, SE27 9BZ; Tel 0181-670 6577; W.J. Hutcheson. (Del)
Enborne Lodge, Enborne St, Wash Common, Newbury, Berks RG14 6RL; Tel (01635) 45732; M.I. Samuels. (EBD)
George Rainey, 66 London Rd, St Leonards-on-Sea TN37 6AS; Tel (01424) 421252; S. Harkins. (Del)
Grove House Primary, Elmcourt Rd SE27 9DA; Tel 0181-670 9429; P. Odlin. (Impaired hearing)
Hyde Farm, Telferscot Rd, SW12 0HW; Tel 0181-673 4758; P.A. Akhurst. (EBD)
Lansdowne, Argyll Cl, Dalyell Rd SW9 9QL; Tel 0171-737 3713; *Head* Wendy Camm (Acting). (MLD)
Mortimer, Dingley La, Woodfield Ave SW16 1AU; Tel 0181-677 7521; T. Woolgar. (Del)
Shelley, Oakden St SE11 4UG; Tel 0171-735 9081; H.V. Parker. (SLD)
Thurlow Park, Elmcourt Rd SE27 9DA; Tel 0181-670 3975; J. Barrow. (Motor Disability)
Turney, Turney Rd SE21 8LX; Tel 0181-670 7220; J. Davies. (MLD)
Warnham Court, Warnham, Nr Horsham RH12 3RX; Tel (01403) 210423; M. Donovan. (Del)
Willowfield, Heron Rd SE24 OHY; Tel 0171-274 4372; J. Loy. (EBD)
Windmill, Mandrell Rd SW2 5DW; Tel 0171-733 0681; *Head* Peter Steel. (SLD)

Secondary Schools

Charles Edward Brooke, Cormont Rd, London SE5 9RF; Tel 0171-274 1666; Jane Cruse. (Girls) (602)
Dick Sheppard, Tulse Hill SW2 2QA; Tel 0181-674 9421; Doreen Hall. (Mixed) (482)
Lilian Baylis, Lollard St SE11 6PY; Tel 0171-735 3105; Greta Akpeneye. (Mixed) (621)

Norwood, Crown Dale SE19 3PD; Tel 0181-670 9382; Paullette Braithwaite (Acting). (Girls) (500)
Stockwell Pk, Clapham Rd, London SW9 0AL; Tel 0171-733 6156; Tony La Mothe. (Mixed) (446)

Teachers' Centre

Lawn Lane Centre, Lawn La, London SW8 1TU; Tel 0171-926 1000

Grant Maintained Schools

Archbishop Tenison's, 55 Kennington Oval SE11 5SR; Tel 0171-735 3771; Brian Jones. (Boys) (430)
Bishop Thomas Grant R.C., Belltrees Grove SW16 2HY; Tel 0181-769 3294; Michael Gibbons. (Mixed) (877)
Dunraven, Leigham Court Rd SW16 2QD; Tel 0181-677 2431/4; Richard Townsend. (975)
La Retraite R.C. Girls School, Atkins Rd SW12 OAB; Tel 0181-673 5644; Fax 0181-675 8577; *Headteacher* M. Howie; *Chair of Governors* M. Arnold. (Girls) (11–16) (625)
St Martin-in-the-Fields High School for Girls 155 Tulse Hill SW2 3UP; Tel 0181-674 5594; Fax 0181-674 1379; Anne Philpott. (Girls) (431)

Lewisham London Borough Council

Population 235,700
Lewisham Town Hall, Catford, London SE6 4RU; Tel 0181-695 6000; Fax 0181-314 5659

Education Department

Lewisham Education, London Borough of Lewisham, Laurence Hse, 1 Catford Rd SE6 4SW; Tel 0181-695 6000; Fax 0181-690 4392
Director Community Education M. O'Neill Headquarter for Community Education, Mornington Rd Centre, Stanley St, London SE8; Tel 0181-691 5959

Governor Training Unit

Laurence Hse, 1 Catford Rd, London SE6 4SW; Tel 0181-695 6000 Ext 8526; Fax 0181-690 4392
Co-ordinator Rosie Fooks, CertEd, Lewisham Governor/ Governor Trainer

Services Offered

Range of school-based and central training offered on termly basis; Briefing papers produced on termly basis; Occasional borough wide conferences/events. Telephone advice

Special Schools

Anerley, Versailles Rd SE20 8AX; Tel 0181-778 5857. (EBD)
Brent Knoll, Mayow Rd SE23 2XH; Tel 0181-699 1047. (Del)
Grafham Grange, Bramley, Nr Guildford, Surrey GU5 0LH; Tel (01483) 892214. (EBD)
Greenvale, 69 Perry Rise SE23 2QU; Tel 0181-699 6515. (SLD)
Meadowgate, Revelon Rd, Brockley SE4 2PR. (MLD)
Meeting House, 59 Pendragon Rd, Bromley BR1 5LD; Tel 0181-698 9738. (MLD)
New Woodlands, 49 Shroffold Rd, Bromley BR1 5PD; Tel 0181-697 3405. (EBD)
Pupil Support Service, St Stephens School, Albyn Rd SE8 4ED; Tel 081-691 0527
Watergate, 12 Church Grove SE13; Tel 0181-690 6144. (SLD)

Secondary Schools

Addey and Stanhope, 472 New Cross Rd SE14 6TJ; Tel 0181-692 3012; *Headteacher* R.B. Barrett. (Mixed) (560)
Bonus Pastor R.C., Winlaton Rd, Bromley BR1 5PZ; Tel 0181-698 7668; *Headteacher* P. Maloney (Acting). (Mixed) (595)
Catford County, Bellingham Rd SE6 2PS; Tel 081-697 8911; *Headteacher* Mrs J. Fisher. (Girls) (730)
Deptford Green, Amersham Vale, New Cross SE14 6LQ; Tel 0181-691 3236; *Headteacher* K. Ajegbo. (Mixed) (672)
Forest Hill, Dacres Rd SE23 2XN; Tel 0181-699 9343; *Headteacher* G. Agnew. (Boys) (1115)
Hatcham Wood, Walbutton Rd SE4 2NY; Tel 0181-732 2122/4; *Headteacher* Ms J. Wilkins. (Mixed) (552)
Malory, Launcelot Rd, Bromley BR1 5EB; Tel 0181-698 1025; *Headteacher* Ms M. Katalawela. (Mixed) (1000)
Northbrook C.E., Taunton Rd, Lee SE12 8PD; Tel 0181-852 3191; *Headteacher* J. Walters. (Mixed) (410)
Prendergast, Rushey Green SE6 4JQ; Tel 0181-690 3710; *Headteacher* Miss M.E. Perry. (Girls) (559)
St Joseph's Academy, 7 Lee Terr SE3 9TY; Tel 0181-852 7433; *Headteacher* F. O'Regan. (Boys) (637)
Christ The King 6th Form College, Belmont Grove off Belmont Hill, Lewisham SE13 5DZ; Tel 0181-852 9416; *Principal* K. Fagan. (Mixed)
Sedgehill, Sedgehill Rd SE6 3QW; Tel 0181-698 8911; *Headteacher* Mrs I. Phillips. (Mixed) (1551)
Sydenham, Dartmouth Rd SE26 4RD; Tel 0181-699 6731; *Headteacher* Miss D. Such. (Girls) (1107)

Field Study Centres

Horton-Kirby Environmental Studies Centre, Dartford, Kent; *Head of Centre* G. Cox
Tyn-y-Benth Mountain Centre, Caris, Nr Machynlleth, Powys; *Head of Centre* J. Grasse

Teachers' Centre

Professional Development Centre Kilmorie Rd SE23 2SP; Tel 0181-291 5005

Merton London Borough Council

Population 165,000
Merton Civic Centre, London Rd, Morden, Surrey SM4 5DX; Tel 0181-543 2222

Education and Leisure Department

Merton Civic Centre, London Rd, Morden, Surrey SM4 5DX; Tel 081-543 2222
Director of Education and Leisure Lesley Kant, MA(Ed), BA(Hons)
Assistant Director of Education (Family Services) Althea Efunsmile
Assistant Director (Schools Services) Jennifer Cairns
Group Manager (Management Support) William Davies, DipAdEd, DMS
Group Manager (Community Services) Ann Beeching, BA, DMA
Group Manager (Special Educational Needs) Stephen Huggett
Manager (Finance and Resources) Richard Edwards, HNC
Manager (Service Co-ordination and IT) Christine Connolly
Senior Administrative Officer (Building and Supplies) Martin Rose
Senior Administrative Officer (Schools Administration) Debbie West
Principal Inspector Vacancy

Group Manager (Curriculum and Assessment) Emily Allardyce, BEd(Hons)
Group Manager (School Effectiveness) Peter Holsworth (Acting)
Child Policy Co-ordinator Janet Yerbury
Group Manager (Pupil Services) Gerard Noyau, BA(Hons)
Principal of Adult Education William Whitham, DipAdEd
Principal Careers Officer Sue Mairis (Acting)
Principal Youth Officer George Banks
Education Establishments
37 First (9,665); 14 middle (6,247); 9 high (5,786); 1 school of art (450 full-time, 130 part-time); 1 adult education centre (14,000 enrolments)
Special Schools
4 day (247)
Other Authorities with whom Joint Purchasing Arrangements are made
I.L.E.A

Education Committee

Lab 10, Con 5, Ind 1, Res 1
Chair S. Knight, (Lab) 104 Links Rd SW17 9ES; Tel 0181-769 3031
Vice-Chair S. Cowling, (Lab) 135 Graham Rd SW19 3SL; Tel 0181-542 2621

Child Guidance Clinic

Worsfold Hse, Chapel Orchard, Church Rd, Mitcham, Surrey CR4 3BE; Tel 0181-648 4066

Special Schools

Cambridge Hse, 159 Pepys Rd, Wimbledon SW20 8NP; Tel 0181-946 9736; Anne Mitchell. (E.B.D. Primary) (16)
Melrose, Church Rd, Mitcham, Surrey CR4 3BE; Tel 0181-646 2620; Pauline Evans, MEd. (EBD Secondary) (47)
Cricket Green School, Lower Green West, Mitcham CR4 3AF; Tel 0181-640 1177; Hilary Gannaway, BA, BEd(Hons), DipRD. (MLD) (90)
St Ann's, Bordesley Rd, Morden, Surrey SM4 5LT; Tel 0181-648 9737; Tina Harvey. (SLD) (69)

Educational Psychology Service

Canterbury Building, Canterbury Rd, Morden, Surrey; Tel 0181-646 6316; *Principal Educational Psychologist* Stephen Hugget, BA, MSc, PhD; *Head of Learning Support Service* Liz Cowne

Voluntary Aided Schools (13-18)

Ursuline Convent, Crescent Rd, Wimbledon, London SW20 8HA; Tel 0181-944 5693; Sister Armida Veglio, BA, BD. (Girls) (757)
Wimbledon College, Edge Hill SW19 4NS; Tel 0181-946 2533; Rev. Michael Smith, SJ, MA. (Boys) (767)

Voluntary Controlled School (12-18)

Rutlish, Watery La SW20 9AD; Tel 0181-542 1212; Anthony Mooney, MA(ED), M.Phil. (Boys) (880)

High Schools (12–16)

Eastfields, Acacia Rd, Mitcham CR4 1SF; Tel 0181-648 6627; Michael Dunman, BA, M.Coll.P.. (Boys) (430)
Garth, Lilleshall Rd, Morden SM4 6DU; Tel 0181-715 1212; Fax 0181-715 1214; John Walters. (Mixed) (552)
Raynes Park, Bushey Rd SW20 0JL; Tel 0181-946 4112; Fax 0181-947 0224; John Massey, BSc. (Mixed) (736)
Ricards Lodge, Lake Rd SW19 7HB; Tel 0181-946 2208; Fax 0181-947 0113; Deidre Kay, BA, DipEd, MSc, LTCL. (Girls) (649)
Rowan, Rowan Rd SW16 5JF; Tel 0181-764 7179; Fax 0181-679 7179; Ann Ayling. (Girls) (405)
Tamworth Manor, Wide Way, Mitcham CR4 1BP; Tel 0181-764 5112; Jennifer Adey, MA. (Mixed) (610)

Institute of Adult Education

Merton Institute of Adult Education, Whatley Ave, London SW20 9NS; Tel 0181-543 9292; *Principal* William Whitham

Other Centres

Arts Education Centre and Merton Music Foundation, Chaucer Bldg, Canterbury Rd, Morden, Surrey; Tel 0181-640 5446; *Head* John Mander
Environmental Education Centre, Stouthall Environmental Education Centre, Reynoldston, West Glamorgan SA3 1AP; Tel (01792) 391086; *Head of Centre* Andrew J. Turney
Merton Professional Development Centre, Chaucer Bldgs, Canterbury Rd, Morden, Surrey SM4 6PX; Tel 0181-640 6067; Fax 0181-640 6066; *Head of Centre* Barbara Newman

Youth Centres

Duke of Edinburgh Awards Centre, Garth High School, Llanthony Rd, Morden, Surrey; Tel 081-648 1786
Tamworth Manor Youth Centre, Tamworth Manor High School, Wide Way, Mitcham, Surrey; Tel 0181-764 0538
John Innes Youth Centre, 61 Kingston Rd SW19 1JN; Tel 0181-542 3579
Eastfields Youth Centre, Eastfields High School, Acacia Rd, Mitcham, Surrey; Tel 0181-648 6749
Pollards Hill Youth Centre, South Lodge Ave, Mitcham, Surrey; Tel 0181-679 2449
South Wimbledon Youth Centre, Haydons Rd, Wimbledon SW19; Tel 0181-542 7537
Wyvern Youth Centre, Arras Ave, Morden, Surrey; Tel 0181-648 7970

Newham London Borough Council

Population 212,000 (1991 Census)
Town Hall, Barking Rd, East Ham E6 2RP; Tel 0181-472 1430; Fax 0181-472 0293

Education Department

Broadway Hse, 322 High St, Stratford, London E15 1AJ; Tel 0181-555 5552; Fax 0181-503 0014
Director of Education Ian Harrison
Deputy Director (School Management, Advice and Support Services) Andrew Panton
Deputy Director (Strategic and Corporate Services) Parin Bahl
Senior Assistant Director (Monitoring, Evaluation and Curriculum Support) David Lister
Assistant Director (Special Educational Needs Assessment and Support) Simon Trotter
Assistant Director (Community Education) Derek Metters
Senior Assistant Director (Client and Community Services) Chris Kiernan
Assistant Director (Management Support Services) Trevor Matthews
Assistant Director (Learning Support Services) Barbara Burke
Assistant Director (Planning and Property Services) Tony Williams
Assistant Director (Finance and Corporate Services) David Yorath
Senior Assistant Director (Client and Community Services) Chris Kiernan
Assistant Director (Strategic Policy and External Relations) Max Krafchik
Assistant Director (Monitoring, Evaluation and Development) David Haggerstone

Assistant Director (Curriculum Support and Consultancy) Carol Radcliffe
Head of Community Education Steve Cameron
Head of Youth Affairs Sushila Khoot
Principal Educational Psychologist Ian Millward
Principal Officer (Corporate Services) Graham Storey
Number of Schools
8 nursery (1100), 66 primary (21,038) (+ 3,631 in nursery units), 13 comprehensive (14,203)
Special Schools
5 day (292)
Day of Committee Meeting
Tuesday
Requisition Periods for School Supplies
None

Education Committee

Lab 17
Chair Graham Lane, (Lab) 110 Humberstone Rd, Plaistow E13 9NJ; Tel 0181-470 3690
Deputy Chair Ted Sparrowhawk, (Lab) 49 Holland Rd, East Ham, London E6 2EW; Tel 0181-472 1890
Vice-Chair Kevin Jenkins, (Lab) 64 Sandford Rd, East Ham E6 3QS; Tel 0181-552 5908/081-472 6652
Vice-Chair Qaisra Khan, (Lab) 16B Idmiston Rd, Stratford E15 1RG; Tel 0181-519 9564
Vice-Chair David McGladdery, (Lab) 151 Wakefield St, East Ham E6 1LG; Tel 0181-471 7575
Vice-Chair Neil Wilson, (Lab) 41 Upperton Rd West, Plaistow E13 9LT; Tel 0181-471 5916
Members of the Committee
Lab: M. Aslam, J. Isted, M. Knight, A. Kellaway, S. Ahmad, B. Brown, A. Griffiths, M. Inverary, D. Maxwell, C. Seddon, R. Wales

Governor Training Unit

In-service Education Centre, Kirton Rd, Plaistow, London E13 9DR; Tel 0181-470 0931; Fax 0181-471 4605
Governor Education Co-ordinator Myanah Saunders, MA
Services Offered
Training courses for individual Governors and Governing Bodies; Support for Governing Bodies

Special Schools

Beckton, Tollgate Rd E16 3LQ; Tel 0171-474 6326; Margaret Angele. (2–18) (Mixed) (49)
Eleanor Smith, North St E13 9HN; Tel 0181-471 0018/9; Michael Leaman. (5–13) (Mixed) (8)
Elizabeth Fry, Prince of Wales Rd, London E16 3HX; Tel 0171-476 3549; Cliff Early. (2–16) (Mixed) (25); PH
Gurney, Knox Rd, London E7 9HW; Tel 0181-534 1528; *Head* Chris Laing (Acting). (5–16) (Mixed) (33)
John F. Kennedy, Pitchford St E15 4RZ; Tel 0181-534 8544; Doreen Ellmore. (2–18) (Mixed) (58)

Education Welfare Service

Education Welfare Service, Broadway House, 322 High Street, Stratford, London E15 1AJ; Tel 0181-555 5552

Secondary Schools (County 11–16)

Brampton Manor, Roman Rd E6 3SQ; Tel 0171-474 0933; Fax 0171-473 5886; Haydn Powell, BSc. (Mixed) (1429)
Cumberland, Barking Rd E16 4DD; Tel 0171-474 0231; Fax 0171-511 2510; Jane Noble, BA(Hons). (Mixed) (816)
Eastlea, Hilda Rd E16 4NP; Tel 0171-474 5808; Ann Brougham, MA. (Mixed) (755)
Forest Gate, Forest St E7 OHR; Tel 081-534 8666; Fax 081-519 8702; Andrew Richardson, BA, FCollP, FRSA. (Mixed) (918)
Langdon, Sussex Rd E6 2PS; Tel 0181-471 2411/2/3; Vanessa Wiseman, BA, AdvDipEd. (Mixed) (1808)
Lister, St Mary's Rd E13 9AE; Tel 0181-471 3311/2/3; Fax 0181-472 1027; Linda McGowan, BA(Hons). (Mixed) (1023)
Little Ilford, Browning Rd E12 6ET; Tel 0171-478 8024; Fax 0181-478 5954; *Head* Pamela Belmow, BEd(Hons). (Mixed) (1209)
Plashet, Plashet Grove E6 1DG; Tel 0181-471 2418; Fax 0181-471 3029; Bushra Nasir, BSc(Hons). (Girls) (1242)
Rokeby, Pitchford St E15 4RZ; Tel 0181-534 8946; Richard Jarman, BA(Hons). (Boys) (810)
Sarah Bonnell, Deanery Rd E15 4LP; Tel 0181-534 6791/2/3; Fax 0181-555 3793; Carolyn Brown, BA. (Girls) (1154)
Woodside, Woodside Rd E13 8RX; Tel 0171-474 0121/2/3; Kate Keefe, MA. (Mixed) (990)

Secondary Schools (Voluntary 11–18)

St Angela's R.C., St George's Rd E7 8HX; Tel 0181-472 6022; Fax 0181-475 0245; Delia Smith, BA, MSc. (V.A.) (Girls) (1024)
St Bonaventure's R.C., Boleyn Rd E7 9QB; Tel 0181-472 3844/3875/2751; Fax 0181-471 2749; Michael Wilshaw, BA. (V.A.) (Boys) (1025)

Arts Education Centre

Newham Arts Education Centre, Hamilton Rd, London E15 3AF; Tel 0171-511 1757; *Head of Centre* Shea Fiddes

Music Centre

Newham Instrumental Music Service, Newham Academy of Music, Wakefield St, London E6 1NG; Tel 0181-472 9895; *Head of Service* Bill Rumford

Outdoor Education Centres

Fairplay Hse, Wickham Bishops, Maldon, Essex; Tel (01621) 891213; Fax (01621) 892759; *Acting Head of Centre* Chris Speed
The Barge Haybay, Heybridge Basin, Maldon, Essex; Tel (01621) 852096

Residential Centre

Debden House Residential Centre, Debden Green, Loughton, Essex; Tel 081-508 3008; Fax 081-508 0284; *Head of Centre* Lorraine Turner

Teachers' Centre

Newham In Service Education Centre, The Credon Centre, Kirton Rd, London E13 9DR; Tel 0181-470 0931/5; Fax 0181-471 4605; Chris Morgan

Youth Centres

Forest Gate Youth Centre, 1 Woodford Rd, Forest Gate, London E7 0DH; Tel 0181-519 7820
Little Ilford Youth Centre, 1A Rectory Rd, Manor Pk, London E12 6JB; Tel 0181-478 3668; Fax 0181-514 0352
Ravenhill Centre, Ravenhill Centre, Ravenhill Rd, Plaistow, London E13 9BU; Tel 0181-472 4435; Fax 0181-470 7302
Resource Centre, Leywick St, London E15 3DD; Tel 0181-519 6626
Shipman Youth Centre, Prince Regent La, Custom Hse, London E16; Tel 0171-476 1189
Youth Information and Advice Service, 49–51 The Broadway, Stratford, London E15 4BD; Tel 0171-473 6582

Grant Maintained School

Stratford School Upton La, London E7 9PR; Tel 0181-471 2415/7; Fax 0181-471 4684; *Headteacher* I.A.I. Snelling, OBE; *Chair of Governors* M. Prisk. (Mixed) (11–19) (600)

Redbridge London Borough Council

Population 226,218
Town Hall, High Rd, Ilford, Essex IG1 1DD; Tel 0181-478 3020; Fax 0181-478 7709

Education Department

Lynton Hse, 255–259 High Rd, Ilford, Essex IG1 1NN; Tel 0181-478 3020; Fax 0181-553 0895
Director of Education D.E. Capper, BA
Assistant Director (Resources) G.P. Peile
Assistant Director (F.E) D.N. Lindley, MA, BSc(Econ)
Borough Librarian M. Timms (Acting), BA, ALA
SEO (Special Services) J.F.G. Pallett, BA, MA(Ed)
EO (Schools) W.J. Swan, BA, DipEd, DPA
SEO (Buildings and Development) P.K. Randall
SEO (Special Projects) J. Grainger, MA, PhD
AEO (South) M. Osborn, MEd
AEO (FE) S. Bloom, MA, CertEd, DipC
AEO (Special Services) C. Stephens, BA
Chief Inspector S.A. Black (Acting), BA
Principal Inspector F. McNeil, MA
Senior Adviser (Physical Education) C.G. Darkes, BA, DipPE
Principal Education Welfare Officer P. Shoults, LLB(Hons)
Senior Education Welfare Officer C. Corbin
Senior Education Welfare Officer S. Flain, BA(Hons)
Senior Adviser (English) A.I. West
Senior Adviser (Assessment and Inspection) M. Buchanan, MA
CDT Adviser R.L. Knowles, BA
Information Technology/TVEX Adviser M.R. Bostock, BSc
INSET Co-ordinator H. Morrall, BA
Mathematics Adviser P. Wylie, MA
Modern Languages Adviser R.P. Percival, BA
Primary Adviser M.D. Owston, MEd
Primary Adviser J.P. Myer, MA
Science Adviser P.M. Slade, BTech
Religious Education Adviser W.A. Gent, MEd
History and Geography Adviser S. Riches, BA
Head of Drama Centre J. Balcombe
Specialist Careers Adviser (Special Needs) G. Sandy
Principal Educational Psychologist C. Shearer, MA, MSc
Senior Educational Psychologist J. Ludlow, BA, MSc, MA
Senior Educational Psychologist R. Paterson, BSc, MEd, CPsychol
Chartered Educational Psychologist J.A. Heathfield, BA, DipEduc, AFBPS
Educational Psychologist K. Hobson, BSc, MSc
Educational Psychologist S. Morris, MA, MSc, DipEd, CPsychol
Educational Psychologist E. Fenty, BEd, AdvDipEd, DipPsyc, MA, MSc
Educational Psychologist B. Graham, BSc, MSc
Number of Schools
54 primary (19,707); 14 secondary (14,237)
Special Schools
5 day (449)
Requisition Periods for School Supplies
At any time
Other Authorities with whom Joint Purchasing Arrangements are made
Essex County Council; Counties Furniture Group; CLEAPSE

Education Committee

Chair J.W. Fairley-Churchill 44 Green La, Ilford, Essex IG1 1YL
Vice-Chair P.J. Laugharne, BSc(Econ)(Hons), PhD 23 North Rd, Ilford, Essex IG3 8AJ
Members of the Committee
K.E. Axon FFA, FIAB, MIMgt, H.J. Borrott, C.H. Bradd, R.W. Brunnen, T.F. Cobb, FSCA, C.H. Connelley BA(Hons), MBSA, C. Elliman, R.E. Golding, D. Green BEd(Hons), M. Hickey, R.H. Hoskins, JP, A.T. Hughes, C.B. Jackson, M.T. Lambert, P. Lawrence, DLHIST(LDN), F.K. Maravala, D.A. Masters, BSc, W.D. Miskin, JP, BSc(Econ), FCA, E. Norman BSc(Socsci), DIPSW, CQSW, L. Perham, JP, BA, ALA, R.J. Scott, DMS, MCIPS, MIMgt, D.A. Sharma, M.J. Stark, BA, AcDipEd(Ldn), N.S. Tuck, K.M. Turner, BSc(Econ)

Governor Training Unit

Education Offices, Lynton Hse, 255-259 High Rd, Ilford, Essex IG1 1NN; Tel 0181-478 3020 Ext 3128; Fax 0181-553 0895
Head of Governors' Support Section Gail Clark, BA
Services Offered
Range of courses offered as part of Central Programme that includes induction training for new governors, chairmanship skills, personnel issues, Financial Administration, Curriculum Training and training for clerks to governing bodies; Tailored sessions for individual governing bodies and clusters, wide range of courses, subject based and sessions on team building, the effective governing body etc; Production of termly newsletter, out of office hours telephone helpline, reference shelves in libraries and resource bank of training materials

Secondary Grammar Schools (11–18)

Ilford County High, Fremantle Rd, Barkingside, Ilford IG6 2JB; Tel 0181-551 6496; S. Devereux, BA, BEd. (Boys) (710)
Woodford County High, High Rd, Woodford Green IG8 9LA; Tel 0181-504 0611; H.R. Cleland, BA. (Girls) (700)

Secondary Comprehensive Schools (County 11–18)

Beal High, Woodford Bridge Rd, Redbridge, Ilford IG4 5LP; Tel 0181-551 4954; M.J. Manuel, MA. (Mixed) (1135)
Caterham High, Caterham Ave, Clayhall, Ilford IG5 0QW; Tel 0181-551 4321; Dr A.J. Atkins, MEd, BSc. (Mixed) (1120)
Hainault Forest High, Harbourer Rd, Hainault, Ilford IG6 3TN; Tel 0181-500 4266; G.S. Deery, BSc(Econ), FRSA. (Mixed) (1003)
King Solomon High School, Forest Rd, Barkingside, Ilford, Essex IG6 2JB; Tel 0181-501 2083; A. Falk, MA(Cantab). (Mixed VA) (86)
Loxford High, Loxford La, Ilford IG1 2UT; Tel 0181-514 4666; H. Farrow, BSc. (Mixed) (1111)
Mayfield High, Mayfield Rd, Castleton Rd, Goodmayes, Ilford IG3 9JY; Tel 0181-590 5211; R. Woolf, MA. (Mixed) (1157)
Seven Kings High, Ley St, Ilford IG2 7BT; Tel 0181-554 8935; A.W. Steer, BA. (Mixed) (1128)
Valentines High, Cranbrook Rd, Gants Hill, Ilford IG2 6HX; Tel 0181-554 3608; R.G. Baker, BSc. (Mixed) (1051)
Wanstead High, Redbridge La West E11 2JZ; Tel 0181-989 2791; G. Ferris, MSc. (Mixed) (1416)
Woodbridge High, St Barnabas Rd, Woodford Green IG8 7DQ; Tel 0181-504 9618; B. Haigh, BA(Hons), AD, DipEd. (Mixed) (1116)

Secondary Comprehensive Schools (Voluntary)

Canon Palmer R.C. High, Aldborough Rd South, Seven Kings, Ilford IG3 8EU; Tel 0181-590 3808; N. Chichon, BSc, MSc. (V./S.A.) (Mixed) (1113)
Trinity High R.C., Mornington Rd, Woodford Wells IG8 0TP; Tel 0181-504 3419; Dr. P.C.D. Doherty, BA. (V.A.) (Mixed) (1391)

Special Schools

Ethel Davis Barley La, Goodmayes, Ilford IG3 8XS; Tel 0181-599 1768; J.H. Coyne, MA, DipEd. (Day) (P.H.) (2–17)

Hatton, Roding La South, Woodford Green IG8 8EU; Tel 0181-551 4131; L. Richardson, BEd, DipEHC. (Day) (MLD) (5–11)
Hyleford, Loxford La, Ilford IG3 9AR; Tel 0181-590 7272; G.D. Morgan. (Day) (SLD) (3–19)
Little Heath, Hainault Rd, Little Heath, Romford RM7 5RX; Tel 0181-599 4864; R.K. Jones, MEd. (Day) (MLD) (11–16)
New Rush Hall, Fencepiece Rd, Hainault, Ilford IG6 2LJ; Tel 0181-501 3951; J.V. d'Abbro, BEd(Hons). (Day) (Behaviour and emotional problems) (5–16)

Child and Family Consultation Centre

Loxford Hall, Loxford La, Ilford, Essex IG1 2PL; Tel 0181-478 7211/3; *Principal Psychiatric Social Worker* A.J. Manning, BA, DipSocSc

Educational Psychology Service

Ground Fl, Lynton Hse, 255–259 High Rd, Ilford, Essex IGI 1NN; Tel 0181-478 3020 Ext 3155/3154
Principal Educational Psychologist C.M. Shearer

Drama Centre

Churchfields, Junior School, South Woodford E18 2RB; Tel 081-504 5451; J. Balcombe

Music Service

Redbridge Music Centre, John Savage Centre, Fencepiece Rd, Hainault, Ilford IG6 2LJ; Tel 0181-501 3944; A.G. Pegrum, BA, ATCL

Outdoor Pursuits Centres

Fairlop Sailing Centre, Forest Rd, Hainault, Ilford IG6 3HN; Tel 0181-500 1468; P.J. Corti
Glasbury Outdoor Education Centre, Glasbury Hse, Glasbury-on-Wye, Nr Hereford HR3 5NW; Tel (01497) 847231; J. Middleton

Special Educational Needs Support Service

Teacher's Centre, Melbourne Rd, Ilford, Essex IG1 4HT; Tel 0181-514 3186; J. Moore, DipEd(SEN), DMS

Teachers' Centre

The Teachers' Centre, Melbourne Rd, Ilford IG1 4HT; Tel 0181-478 3706; *Warden* H. Morrall. (Dane Centre)

Youth Centres

Daton Youth Club, Ethel Davis School, Barley La, Goodmayes, Ilford IG3 8XQ; *Enquiries* N. Norris; Tel 0181-478 3020 Ext 3112
Hainault Youth Centre, Hainault Forest High School, 116 Huntsman Rd, Hainault IG6 2SY; Tel 0181-500 8071; G. Anastasi, MA
John Barker Youth Service Centre, Cricklefields, 474 High Road, Seven Kings, Ilford IG1 1UE; Fax 0181-478 3020 Ext 3141; K. Brokenshire
Kenneth Stagg Youth Centre, Aldersbrook Primary School, Harpenden Rd, Wanstead E12 5HL; Tel 0181-989 8707; *Team Leader* K. Coleman
Loxford Youth Centre, Loxford High School, Loxford La, Ilford IG1 2UT; Tel 0181-478 4306; O. Bowes, CertEd
Mayfield Youth Centre, Goodmayes Sixth Form Centre, Goodmayes La, Goodmayes, Ilford IG3 9PX; Tel 0181-599 8992; M. Smith
Mildmay House Youth Centre, 69 Albert Rd, Ilford IG1 1HS; Tel 0181-553 3617; R. Reynolds
Wanstead Youth Centre, Elmcroft Ave, Wanstead E11 2DB; Tel 0181-989 1711; *Team Leader* K. Coleman
Woodford Youth Centre, Woodbridge High School, St Barnabas Rd, Woodford Green IG8 7DH; Tel 0181-504 1287; *Team Leader* K. Coleman

Grant Maintained School

Chadwell Heath School, Christie Gdns, Chadwell Heath, Romford RM6 4RS; Tel 0181-252 5151; K.E. Wilkinson, BA. (Mixed) (1109)

Richmond upon Thames London Borough Council

Population 154,013 (1991 Census)
Civic Centre, 44 York St, Twickenham, Middx TW1 3BZ; Tel 0181-891 1411

Education Department

Regal Hse, London Rd, Twickenham, Middx TW1 3QB; Tel 0181-891 1411; Fax 0181-891 7714
Director of Education G.A. Alexander, BA
Education Officer (Forward Planning and Administration) S. Calder, BA
Education Officer (Special Educational Needs and Schools) P. Dickinson
Schools Officer M. Waller, BA
Assistant Education Officer (Awards and Administration) L. Wilson, DMS
Assistant Education Officer (Building Development) P.R. West, BEd, MA
Head of Inspection and Advisory Services P.J. Lomax, BEd, MA
Inspector (Language, Communication) H. Burrows
Inspector (Assessment and Secondary Phase) D.N. Edwards
Inspector (Special Educational Needs) L. Rhead
Inspector (Music and Arts) M. Walsh
Inspector (Primary) N. Empringham
Inspector (Primary) J. Bartholomew
Inspector (TVEI) M. Potter
Inspector (Cross Curricular Themes) L. Gerlach
School Facilities Officer P. Spurr
Head of Schools Support Service A. Proffitt, BSc
Head of Careers Guidance and Industry Links C. Glover
LMS Development Officer W.H. Booth
Information Technology Development Manager Dr M. Barrett, BA, MA(Ed), PhD
Principal Youth Officer H. Day
Head of Community Health Services Dr J.D. Williamson
Head of Libraries and Arts D. Jones, MA, FLA
Chief Executive and Director of Finance R.L. Harbord, MPhil, IPFA, FCCA, FDP, MBIM, FRVA
Number of Schools
1 nursery; 40 primary; 8 secondary schools
Special Schools
3 day Special Units 6
Requisition periods for School Supplies
Daily

Education Committee

LD 21, Con 2, Lab 1
Chair D.C. Cornwell, (LD) 4 Clevedon Mansions, Cambridge Rd, Twickenham TW1 2JA
Senior Vice-Chair (Finance and Operations) R. Morgan, (LD) 59 Elmfield Ave, Teddington TWH 8BX
Vice-Chair (Awards and Training) R. King, (LD) 202 Powdermill La, Twickenham TW2 6EJ
Members of the Committee
LD: B.A. Alexander, D. Carr, N. Carthew, M. Lees, S. Hamwee, R. King, D.C. Cornwell, R. Morgan, D. Orchard, A.S. Lourie, G. MacKinney, J.A. Miller, R. Parslow, M.J.M. Woodriff, M. Quelch, G. Rae, P. Style, M. Weber
Con: H. Champion, JP, T. Arbour
Lab: H. Gold

Governor Training Unit

Governor Support Unit, London Borough of Richmond upon Thames, First Floor, Regal Hse, London Rd, Twickenham TW1 3QB; Tel 0181-891 7515/10; Fax 0181-891 7714
Governor Support Co-ordinator Jo Reeves
Services Offered
Advice, guidance and support to individual governors, governing bodies, school staff and clerks; Organise and make necessary arrangements for a training programme for governors within the authority; Distribute a termly 'Director of Education's Report' and Governors' Information Bulletin, as well as any information received from organisations such as AGIT, NAGM or the DFE etc

Education Welfare Service

58 Hampton Rd, Twickenham, Middx; Tel 0181-893 3923

Special Schools and Units

Clarendon, Hanworth Rd, Hampton TW12 3DH; Tel 0181-979 1165; Mrs A. Coward, BA(Hons). (All-age)
Oldfield Hse, Oldfield Rd, Hampton, Middx TW12 2HP; Tel 0181-979 5102 (Junior); 0181-979 3528 (Infants); A. Glenny (Acting)
Strathmore School, Meadlands Dr, Petersham, Richmond TW10 7ED; Tel 0181-948 0047; S. Rosenberg. (All age)

Psychological Service

58 Hampton Rd, Twickenham, Middx; Tel 0181-894 1288

Secondary Schools (11–16)

Christ's C.E. and R.C., Queens Rd, Richmond TW10 6HF; Tel 0181-940 6982; Fax 0181-332 6085; J.W. Sullivan. (Mixed) (680)
Grey Court, Ham St, Ham TW10 7HN; Tel 081-948 1173; Fax 081-332 2428; Vacancy. (Mixed) (998)
Orleans Park, Richmond Rd, Twickenham TW1 3BB; Tel 0181-891 0187; Fax 0181-744 0312; Mrs E. Selman, BA(Hons). (Mixed) (966)
Rectory, Hanworth Rd, Hampton TW12 3HB; Tel 0181-979 3399; Fax 0181-783 0086; Mrs A. Wilson, BSc. (Mixed) (879)
Shene, Park Ave, East Sheen SW14 8RG; Tel 0181-876 8891; Fax 0181-392 9694; S.A.S. Williams, MA. (Mixed) (1073)
Teddington, Broom Rd, Teddington TW11 9PJ; Tel 0181-943 0033/14; Fax 0181-943 2999; R. Ewen, MA, BSc. (Mixed) (1161)
Waldegrave, Fifth Cross Rd, Twickenham TW2 5LH; Tel 0181-894 3244; Fax 0181-893 3670; Ms H. Flint, MA. (Girls) (927)
Whitton, Percy Rd, Whitton TW2 6JW; Tel 0181-894 4503; Fax 0181-894 0690; R. Hibbitt, BA(Hons), MA(Ed). (Mixed) (940)

Adult Education Centres

Barnes Centre, Castelnau Library, Castelnau SW13 9RT; Tel 0181-741 1827
Christ's School Evening Centre, Christ's School West and East, Queen's Rd, Richmond; Tel 0181-940 6982
Grey Court Centre, Grey Court School, Ham St, Ham TW10 7HN; Tel 0181-948 1173
Hampton, 34 Priory Rd, Hampton TW12 2PD; Tel 0181-979 3377
Orleans Evening Centre, Orleans Park School, Richmond Rd, Twickenham; Tel 0181-891 0187
Parkshot Centre, Parkshot, Richmond, Surrey TW9 2RE; Tel 0181-940 0170
Rectory Evening Centre, Rectory School, Hanworth Rd, Hampton, London; Tel 0181-979 3399
Richmond Adult and Community College, Main Centre, Clifden Rd, Twickenham TW1 4LT; Tel 0181-891 5907; *Principal* Mrs A. Risman, BA, MPhil
Shaftesbury Centre, Kew Rd TW9 2PP; Tel 0181-948 5958
Shene Evening Centre, Hertford Bldg, Shene School, Hertford Ave, East Sheen SW14 8RG; Tel 0181-876 2346
Teddington Evening Centre, Broom Rd, Teddington TW11 9PJ; Tel 0181-943 0033
Waldegrave Centre, Fifth Cross Rd, Twickenham TW2 5LH; Tel 0181-894 3244
Whitton Evening Centre, Whitton School, Percy Rd, Whitton, London; Tel 0181-894 4503

Southwark London Borough Council

Population 227,400
Town Hall, Peckham Rd, London SE5 8UB; Tel 0171-525 5000; Fax 0171-525 7277

Education Department

1 Bradenham Cl, London SE17 2QA; Tel 0171-525 5000; Information: 0171-525 5050; Fax 0171-525 5200
Chair S. Murison C/o Southwark Town Hall, Peckham Rd SE5 8UB
Vice-Chair A. Worsley
Director G. Mott
Group Manager (Education Support) S. Evans
Group Manager (Pupil and Student Services) N. Hadjifotiou
Head Pupil Support and SEN Alan Wood
Head of Educational Psychology Tony Tarrent
Head of Careers Carolyn Heathcote
Head of Early Years Bonnie Ure
Number of Schools
5 nursery; 71 primary; 9 secondary; 8 special schools; 2 hospital schools
Poll tax per person
£189
Requisition Periods for School Supplies
As required
Other Authorities with whom Joint Purchasing Arrangments are made
Greater London supplies

Governor Training Unit

Education Resource Centre, Cator St, London SE15; Tel 0171-701 9577; Fax 0171-703 2528
Governor Training Co-ordinator Tony Stubbs
Services Offered
Cluster training five times per year comprising of 45 min introductory session and 3 or 4 1½hr workshops; whole governing body training, heads, chairs, vice chairs, LEA, parent, teacher, teacher governor training

Hospital Schools

Guy's Evelina Hospital School, Evelina Children's Department, Guy's Hospital Tower, St Thomas St, London SE1 9RT; Tel 0171-955 4841; Fax 0171-955 4197
Maudsley and Bethlehem Royal Hospital School, Monks Orchard Rd, Beckenham, Kent BR3 3BX; Tel 0181-777 1897; Fax 0181-777 1897

Educational Psychology Service

Education Dept, Albany Annexe, Albany Rd SE5 0BN; Tel 0171-525 2723; Fax 0171-525 2725

Special Schools

Beormund, Crosby Row, Long La, London SE1 3PS; Tel 0171-407 9484; Fax 0171-407 9283
Bredinghurst, Stuart Rd, London SE15 3AZ; Tel 0171-639 2541; Fax 0171-732 5502

Cherry Garden, Macks Rd, London SE16 3XU; Tel 0171-237 4050; Fax 0171-237 7513
Haymerle, Haymerle Rd, London SE15 6SY; Tel 0171-639 6080; Fax 0171-277 9906
Highshore, Bellenden Rd SE15 5BB; Tel 0171-639 7211; Fax 0171-252 9024
Spa, Monnow Rd SE1 5RN; Tel 0171-237 3714; Fax 0171-237 6601
Tuke, 4 Woods Rd, London SE15 2PX; Tel 0171-639 5584; Fax 0171-635 8937

Comprehensive Schools

Archbishop Michael Ramsey C.E., Farmers Rd, London SE5 0UB; Tel 0171-701 4166; Fax 0171-701 8461; Mrs W. Parmley
Aylwin, 55 Southwark Park Rd, London SE16 3TZ; Tel 0171-237 9316; Fax 0171-237 9204; Maria P. Williams
Geoffrey Chaucer, Harper Rd, London SE1 6AG; Tel 0171-407 6877; Fax 0171-403 8922; M.F.B. Read
Kingsdale, Alleyn Pk, London SE21 8SQ; Tel 0181-670 7575; Fax 0181-766 7051; S.C. Williams
St Saviour's & St Olave's C.E., New Kent Rd, London SE1 4AN; Tel 0171-407 1843; Fax 0171-407 9163; I. Bishop
Walworth, Shorncliffe Rd, London SE1 5UJ; Tel 0171-703 5431; Fax 0171-703 8785; B. Morgan
Warwick Park, Peckham Rd, London SE15 5DZ; Tel 0171-703 4417; Fax 0171-703 4305; Ms N. Gibbes
Waverley, Homestall Rd, London SE22 0NR; Tel 0171-732 2276; Fax 0181-693 0628; H. Dofman
William Penn, Red Post Hill, London SE24 9JH; Tel 0171-737 2336; Fax 0171-738 6746; L. Marshall

Education Development Units

Education Resource Centre, Cator St, London SE15; Tel 0171-525 2804
South London Science and Technology Centre, Wilson Rd, London SE5 8PD; Tel 0171-701 2224/7200; Fax 0171-701 4607; Patrick McKee
Centre for Language in Primary Education, Webber Row, London SE1 8QW; Tel 0171-633 0840/071-401 3382; Myra Barrs
Southwark Education Library Service, Education Resource Centre, Cator St, London SE15; Tel 0171-525 2830; Elveria Brumant

Nursery Schools

Dulwich Wood, Lyall Ave, London SE21 8QS; Tel 0181-670 0372; Jenny Lovell
The Grove, Newert Cl, off Coleman Rd SE15 6ER; Tel 0171-701 6629; Esther Hothersall
Kintore Way, Grange Rd, London SE1 3BW; Tel 0171-237 1894; Beryl Patterson
Nell Gwynn, Meeting Hse La, London SE15 5TT; Tel 0171-252 8265; Steve Cummings
Sumner, Marne Hse, Sumner Est, London SE15 5RF; Tel 0171-703 6577; Georgie McCall
Thomas Calton Community Education Centre, Thomas Calton, Alpha St SE15; Tel 0171-639 6818; Teri Riley

Grant Maintained Schools

The London Nautical School 61 Stamford St, London SE1 9NA; Tel 0171-928 6801; Fax 0171-261 9408; *Headteacher* John C. Brand; *Chair of Governors* Lieutenant Commander R.M. Frampton; *Bursar* Richard L. Gan. (Male) (11–19) (497)
Notre Dame High R.C., 118 St George's Rd, London SE1 6EX; Tel 0171-261 1121; Sister R. O'Callaghan
St Michael's R.C., John Felton Rd, London SE16 4UN; Tel 071-237 6432; Fax 071-252 2411; Sister A. Hoskison
Sacred Heart R.C., Camberwell New Rd, London SE5 0RP; Tel 071-274 6844; Fax 071-737 1713; C.M. Garvey
St Thomas the Apostle R.C., Hollydale Rd, London SE15 2EB; Tel 0171-639 0106; E. Tope

Sutton London Borough Council

Population 171,947
Civic Offices, St Nicholas Way, Sutton, Surrey SM1 1EA; Tel 0181-770 5000; Fax 0181-770 5665

Education Offices

The Grove, Carshalton, Surrey SM5 3AL; Tel 0181-770 6568
Director of Education Chris Blurton, BA
Assistant Director of Education R. Wilkins, MA, MSc, MBA, DipEd, ACIS; Tel 0181-770 6650; Fax 0181-770 6545
Assistant Director of Education C.D. Woodward, BSc; Tel 0181-770 6503; Fax 0181-770 6545
Chief Inspector/Assistant Director of Education I. Birnbaum, MA(Cantab), PhD, MBCS; Tel 0181-770 6505; Fax 0181-770 6545
Principal Youth and Community Officer J. Hurst; Tel 0181-770 6656; Fax 0181-770 6660
Principal Careers Officer J. Ross; Tel 0181-770 6690; Fax 0181-770 6967
Head of Secondary and Further Education Services D.M. Anderson, BA(Hons), MBA; Tel 0181-770 6574; Fax 0181-770 6660
Head of School Management Support Services A.H. Faulkner, BEd(Hons), MA; Tel 0181-770 6516; Fax 0181-770 6636
Acting Head of Special Educational Needs Services C.D. Woodward, BSc; Tel 0181-770 6503; Fax 0181-770 6545
Head of Management Information Services Ray Collins, BA; Tel 0181-770 6667; Fax 0181-770 6545
General Inspector – Modern Languages, Classical Studies, Adult Education, Public Examinations D. Hewett, BA(Hons); Tel 0181-770 6520
General Inspector – Physical Education T. Mahmoud, BEd(Hons) MA; Tel 0181-770 6573
General Inspector – Mathematics T Maslin, MA(Cantab), MA(Lond); Tel 0181-770 6546
General Inspector – PSE, Equal Opportunities, Careers, Health and Drugs Education, Records of Achievement, Education for Citizenship, Youth and Community Education J. Nash, BA(Hons), MA; Tel 0181-770 6558
General Inspector – Humanities, Environmental Education D. Shannon, BEd(Hons), MEd; Tel 0181-770 6547
General Inspector – English, Drama, Language Development, Bilingual Learners (ESL), Flexible Learning H. Betterton, BA(Hons), MA; Tel 0181-770 6518
General Inspector – Technology (including Business Studies, Home Economics, Craft, Design and Technology), Schools/Industry Links, Economic & Industrial Understanding, Further Education I. Smith, MA, AdvDipEd, FTEng; Tel 0181-770 6519
Head of Customer Services Colin Jones, BA, MA, DMS; Tel 0181-770 6568
Head of Resources and Planning Stephen Ingram; Tel 0181-770 6684
General Inspector – Science F. Thornton, BSc(Hons), MA, DipEd; Tel 0181-770 6572
General Inspector – Early Years, Art M. Topliss, AdvDipEd; Tel 0181- 770 6511
Principal Educational Psychologist Judith Pettersen; Tel 0181-770 6780
Professional Assistant for TVEI Extension P. Scott, BEd(Hons), MA, DipEd; Tel 0181-770 6548
Information Officer Duncan Grant, MA; Tel 0181-770 6553
Sutton Catering – Contract Services T. Mason-Morgan Willow Walk Offices, Willow Walk, Sutton, Surrey SM3 9QQ; Tel 0181-770 6076
Chief Education Welfare Officer E. Arnold; Tel 0181-770 6606

Number of Schools

Nursery 2 schools (120 pupils); primary ex-GM 40

schools (11,818 inc GM schools (12,665) secondary ex-GM 6 schools (4,660) inc-GM 14 Schools (11,359)
Special Schools
3 day; 1 hospital
Requisition Periods for School Supplies
None
Other Authorities with whom Joint Purchasing Arrangements are made
Supplies Southfields (service of ILEA); Supplies Tottenham (service of ILEA)

Education Committee

LD 9, Lab 2, Con 1
Chairman Cllr Terry Woods
Vice-Chairman Cllr Richard Broadbent
Members of the Committee
LD: A. Baughan, R. Broadbent, J. Dodwell, G. Jerome, D. Grozdenoric, J. Leach, J. Lowne, R. Roberts, T. Woods
Lab: P. Kane, A. Theobald
Con: L. Ranson

Governor Training Unit

Education Dept, Stonecourt, 2 North St, Carshalton, Surrey SM5 2HU; Tel 0181-770 6696; Fax 0181-770 6636
Training and Development Officer Sally Simpkin, CertEd
Services Offered
Broad range of training courses for all Governors, currently 40 different courses; Individual governor body sessions; Advice and helpline; Governors library and resource centre; Briefings for Chairs and Link Governors; Primary and Special and High Planning Forum for Governors

Special Schools

Carew Manor, Church Rd, Wallington SM6 7NH; Tel 0181-647 8349; B.E. Wilson, DipEd. (MLD) (ESN(M) (Mixed)
Sherwood Park, Streeters La, Wallington SM6 7NP; Tel 0181-643 7718; R.A. Martin, BEd. (Severe learning difficulties) (Mixed)
Sutton Primary Diagnostic Unit Hexham Rd, Morden, Surrey SM4 6NH; Tel 0181-644 5181; Mrs J. Reid. (Diagnosis of children with suspected learning difficulties) (Mixed)
Unit for Hearing Impaired Children, Green Wrythe Primary School, Green Wrythe La, Carshalton SM5 1JP; Tel 0181-644 5181; Mrs S.M. Wooldridge. (Partially Hearing)
Wandle Valley, Welbeck Rd, Carshalton SM5 1LP; Tel 0181-648 1365; D.L. Bone, BA, Dip Special Ed. (Emotional/Behavioural Disorders)

High Schools (County 11–16)

Highview, The Chase, Wallington SM6 8JT; Tel 0181-688 2958; E. Barthaud, BEd. (Mixed) (248)
Stanley Park, Stanley Park Rd, Carshalton SM5 3HP; Tel 0181-647 5842; D.E. Harding, BSc(Eng). (Mixed) (647)

High Schools (County 11–18)

Carshalton, Winchcombe Rd, Carshalton SM5 1RW; Tel 0181-644 7325; G.G.P. Bevan, MA, DipEd. (Boys) (880)
Carshalton, West St, Carshalton SM5 2QX; Tel 0181-647 8294; E. Coate, BA. (Girls) (896)
Glenthorne, Sutton Common Rd, Sutton SM3 9PS; Tel 081-644 6307; L.E. Neal, MA(Cantab). (Mixed) (868)
Greenshaw, Grennell Rd, Sutton SM1 3DY; Tel 0181-641 2080; J.K. Fuller, BSc. (Mixed) (1121)

Teachers' Centre

The Glastonbury Centre, Glastonbury Rd, Morden SM4 6NZ; Tel 0181-770 6745

Youth Centres

Carshalton Boys Club, Wentworth Hall, Ruskin Rd, Carshalton, Surrey; Tel 0181-647 4229
Century Youth Centre, Fellowes Rd, Carshalton SM5 2SX; Tel 0181-647 3627; *Youth Worker* P. Bradley
Club Constellation, (rear of Sainsbury's), 660 London Rd, Cheam, Sutton SM3 9BZ; Tel 0181-644 3362; *Full Time Youth Worker* M. McKenna
Outdoors Unlimited, c/o St Helier Youth Centre, Bishopsford Rd, Morden SM4 6BL; Tel 0181-646 8688
Roundshaw Youth Centre, Mollison Dr, Roundshaw, Wallington SM6 9HY; Tel 0181-647 7132; *Full Time Youth Worker* M. Hurley
St Helier Youth Centre, Bishopsford Rd, Morden, Surrey SM4 6BL; Tel 0181-648 7220
Sutton Youth Centre, Sutton West Hall, Robin Hood La, Sutton SM1 2SD; Tel 0181-642 0634; *Full Time Youth Worker* A. Wilson (Acting)
Youth Action, c/o St Helier Youth Centre, Bishopsford Rd, Morden SM4 6BL; Tel 0181-648 7220
Youth Centre 21, Alcorn Cl, Sutton Common Rd, Sutton SM3 9PT; Tel 0181-644 1428; *Full Time Youth Worker* M. McKenna

Grant Maintained Schools

Cheam High School, Chatsworth Rd, Cheam SM3 8PW; Tel 0181-644 5790; Fax 0181-641 8611; T.J. Vaughan, BA, MLitt. (Mixed) (1220)
The John Fisher, Peaks Hill, Purley CR2 3YP; Tel 0181-660 4555; *Headteacher* R.P.M. Gregory, MA; *Chair of Governors* W.R. Eaton. Boys 11–18 (804)
Nonsuch High School for Girls Ewell Rd, Cheam, Sutton SM3 8AB; Tel 0181-394 1308; Fax 0181-393 2307; *Headteacher* Veronica Barkey; *Chair of Governors* R. Kerslake. Grammar) (11–18 (877)
St Philomena's Catholic High School for Girls, Pound St, Carshalton SM5 3PS; Tel 0181-642 2025; Fax 0181-643 7925; M. Kilkenny, BA, MEd. (Girls) (900)
Sutton Grammar School for Boys, Manor La, Sutton SM1 4AS; Tel 0181-642 3821; Fax 0181-770 9070; G.D. Ironside, MA, CMath, FIMA. (Boys) (700)
Wallington, Woodcote Rd, Wallington SM6 0PH; Tel 0181-647 2380; Fax 0181-773 9884; M.J. Edwards, BSc. (Girls) (849)
Wallington County Grammar, Croydon Rd, Wallington SM6 7PH; Tel 0181-647 2235; J.H. Haworth, Bd, MA, PhD, Re. (Boys) (687)
Wilson's School Mollison Dr, Wallington, Surrey SM6 9JW; Tel 081-773 2931; Fax 081-773 4972; *Headteacher* C.J. Tarrant; *Chairman of Governors* R.E. McAlister; *Finance Manager* Helen Jennings. (Boys) (11–18) (787)

Tower Hamlets London Borough Council

Population 165,000
At time of going to press, the council was undergoing a period of transition of departments and services. For more information please contact: Tower Hamlets Information Centre, 107a Commercial St, London, E1 6BG; Tel: 0171-512 4200 ext 4970/4971; Fax:0171-375 2539
Principal Offices, Mulberry Pl, 5 Clove Cres, London E14 2BG; Tel 0171-512 4200

Education Strategy Group

Mulberry Pl, 5 Clove Cres, London E14 2BG; Tel 0171-512 4200 Ext 4956; Fax 0171-512 4976
Leader of the Council Cllr J. Biggs
Vice-Chair Cllr P.M. Uddin
Director of Education and Community Services Committee Anne Sofer (Acting)
Assistant Director of Education Sue Barrow
Chief Inspector V. Jenkins

Head of Development Unit B. Glockling
AEO (Special Education Needs/Pupil Services) P. Garretty-Crane
Principal Educational Psychologist J. Hutchings
Head of Student Services Unit S. Allen
Principal Careers Officer J. Beadle
Community and Partnership Strategy Manager R. Hall
Director of Social Services Sandra Walmesley
Number of Schools
7 nursery, 74 primary, 14 secondary, +1 GMS
Special Schools
6 day, 1 residential

Education Committee

Chair Cllr J. Mainwaring, (LD) 53 Strahan Rd, London E3 5DA
Vice-Chair Cllr G. Mortuza, (LD) 10 Regal Cl, London E1 5JB
Members of the Committee
S. Alom, S.Moyneaux, R.G. Gipson, D.R. Johnson, G. Mortuza, B. Alom, B. Harris, A. Linton, L.K. Melvin, P.M. Uddin, R.C. Hunn, D. Jones, J. Mainwaring

Governor Training Unit

Governors Services, London Borough of Tower Hamlets, EBU, Mulberry Pl, London E14 2BG; Tel 0171-512 4397
Head of School Services Linda Blyth
School Support Officer Chris Jones
Services Offered
Clerking service; advisory service; delivery of governor training programme; resource library

Special Schools

Beatrice Tate, St Jude's Rd E2 9RN; Tel 0171-739 6249; C. Sibley. (SLD)
Bowden Hse, Firle Rd, Seaford, E. Sussex RN25 2JB; Tel (01323) 893138; A. Lees
Harpley, Globe Rd, London E1 4DZ; Tel 0171-987 2563; P. Doyle. (PH)
Grenfell, Myrdle St E1 1HL; Tel 0171-247 9475; S. Quilter. (MLD)
Phoenix, 49 Bow Rd E3 2AD; Tel 0171-980 4740; S. Harris. (Del)
Harpley, Globe Rd, London E1 4DZ; Tel 0171-790 5170; A. Finch. (MLD)
Weaver's Field, Mape St E2 6HW; Tel 0171-739 6321; S. Sowerbutts. (EBD)

Secondary Schools

Bishop Challoner, Lukin St, E1; Tel 0171-790 3634; Cathrine Myers. (Girls)
Blessed John Roche, Upper North St, London E14 6DU; Tel 0171-987 7028/9; J. Rogerson. (Boys)
Bow, Fairfield Rd E3 2QD; Tel 0181-980 0118; P.J. Stickings. (Boys)
Central Foundation, 31–33 Bow Rd E3 2AE; Tel 0171-981 1131; P.M. Hull. (Girls)
Daneford, Gossett St, Bethnal Green E2 6NW; Tel 0171-729 3535; A. Wandsworth. (Boys)
George Green's, 100 Manchester Rd E14 9DW; Tel 0171-987 6032; J. Craig. (Mixed)
Langdon Park, Byron St E14 0RY; Tel 0171-987 4811; C. Dunne. (Mixed)
Morpeth, Morpeth St E2 OPX; Tel 0171-981 0921; A. Macdonald. (Mixed)
Mulberry, Richard St, Commercial Rd E1 2JP; Tel 0171-790 6327/8; M. Robottom. (Girls)
Oaklands, Old Bethnal Grn Rd, London E2 6PR; Tel 0171-613 1014; S. Leahy. (Mixed)
Sir John Cass Foundation and Redcoat C.E., Stepney Way E1 ORH; Tel 0171-790 6712; J.M. Hayes. Mixed
St Paul's Way, Shelmerdine Cl E3 4AN; Tel 0171-987 1883/15; M. Coles. (Mixed)
Stepney Green, Ben Jonson Rd E1 4SD; Tel 0171-790 6361; S. Mamon. (Boys)
Swanlea, 31 Brady St, London E1 5DJ; Tel 0171-375 3267; L. Austen. (Mixed)

Adult Education Centres

Bethnal Green Neighbourhood, 229 Bethnal Green Rd E2 6AB; Tel 0171-739 8181
Bow Neighbourhood, Tredegar Centre, Stafford Rd E3 5ES; Tel 0181-980 1812
Globe Town Neighbourhood, Wessex Community Centre, Hadleigh St, London E2 0LB; Tel 0181-980 8067
Isle of Dogs Neighbourhood, 2 Lawn Hse Cls, London E14 9YQ; Tel 0171-987 6966
Poplar Neighbourhood, St Paul's Way School, Shelmerdine Cl, Bow E3 4AN; Tel 0181-980 7111
Stepney Neighbourhood, Whitechapel Centre, London E1; Tel 0171-790 1818
Wapping, The Highway E1 9HT; Tel 0171-987 9200

Professional Development Centre

English St E3 4TA; Tel 0181-981 0183

Grant Maintained School

Raines Foundation School Approach Rd, Tower Hamlets E2 9LY; Tel 0181-981 1231; Fax 0181-983 0153; *Headteacher* Gareth Lewis; *Chair of Governors* Steven Richards. (Mixed) (11–18) (910)

Waltham Forest London Borough Council

Population 217,500
Town Hall, Forest Rd, Walthamstow, London E17 4JF; Tel 0181-527 5544; Fax 0181-527 8313

Education Department

Municipal Offices, High Rd, Leyton E10 5QJ; Tel 0181-527 5544; Fax 0181-527 5544 Ext 5163
Chairman P. Redcliffe
Vice-Chairman N.S. Matharoo
Chief Education Officer Andrew Lockhart
Deputy Chief Education Officer and Senior Education Officer (Schools) W.M.G. Meredith, BA
SEO (Finance, Administration and Development) A.G. Chetham, BA
SEO (Community) Ms E. Carpenter, BA
AEO (Development and Research) (Acting) Val Dalson
AEO (Development and Research) (Acting) Hilary Anthony
AEO (Finance and Resources) L. Howells
AEO (Administration) Vacancy
Chief Adviser Bob Hogg
Senior Adviser Scilla Furey
Senior Adviser Joan McKenna
AEO (Primary and Nursery Education)(Acting) A. Saap
AEO (Secondary Education) Vacancy
AEO (Special Services) C.C. Luck, BA, LLB
AEO (Governing Bodies) (Acting) John Frazer
AEO (Community & F.E.) Vacancy
AEO (Post 16) M. Crowley
AEO (Careers Guidance) Ms C. Smith
Professional Assistant Ms T. Doyle
Professional Assistant (LMS) Colin Ablett
Principal Youth and Community Officer Tom Cooper
Adult Education Organiser Vacancy
Chief Education Welfare Officer Vacancy
Education Catering Manager Ms D. Parker
Principal Educational Psychologist I.S. Gersch, BA, DipEdPsych
Community Education Adviser T. Alexander
Modern Languages Adviser Miss J. Campbell, BA
Science Adviser Dr. T. Borrows
Music Adviser J. Chapman
English Adviser Ms A. Gribbin
Mathematics Adviser R. Clarkson
Business Studies, Economics Education and Schools Industry Liaison Adviser P.L. Waller, BA(Hons)

Religious Education Adviser Mrs P. Belmour
Design & Technology Adviser B. Munden
Educational Tech Adviser S. Lucas
Equal Opportunities Adviser Ms R. Frith
Physical Education Adviser B. Martin
Lead Primary Adviser Vacancy
Primary Adviser Shirley French
Early Years Primary Adviser Vacancy
Race Equality Adviser Ms R. Campbell
Number of Schools
4 nursery (375 part-time, 42 full-time); 61 primary (1,066 full-time); 42 nursery classes in 32 nursery units (1,880 part-time, 102 full-time); 19 secondary (11,644)
Special Schools
6 day (749 full-time, 65 part-time)
Requisition Period for School Supplies (Main)
May

Governor Training Unit

Governing Bodies Unit, Education Department, London Borough of Waltham Forest, Leyton Muncipal Offices, High Rd, Leyton, London E10 5QJ; Tel 0181-527 5544 Ext 5164/5168; Fax 0181-518 7114/081-527 5544 Ext 5163
AEO Governing Bodies/Communications John Frazer
Governors' Trainer Kay Collier
Services Offered
Core Training Programme, Individual Governing Body Sessions, Governors' Newsletter, Briefing for Chairs and Link Governors, Governors Helpline, Training for Clerks, Information and Support for Governors including regular mailings to Governors and Chairs of Governors

Child Guidance Centre

Hurst Road Health Centre, Hurst Rd, London E17 3BL; Tel 0181-520 8513

Careers Service

See chapter 16

Special Schools

Brookfield House, Alders Ave, Woodford Green IG8 9PY; Tel 0181-527 2464; P.G.E. Jeffrey. (P.H.)
Hawkswood, Antlers Hill, Chingford E4 7RT; Tel 0181-529 2561; L.G. Batchelor. (Deaf or Partial Hearing)
The Joseph Clarke, Vincent Rd E4 9PP; Tel 0181-527 8818; F.J. Smith. (Blind and P.S.)
Lea Green, Leyton Green Rd, Leyton E10 6DB; Tel 0181-556 0006/7; Mrs M.A. Gross. (E.B.D.)
William Morris, Folly La E17 5NT; Tel 0181-503 2225/6; Mrs S. Duncan. (M.L.D.)
Whitefield, M.L.D., Autistic, Specific Learning Difficulties), Macdonald Rd, London E17 4AZ; Tel 0181-531 3426; P.R. Turner, MEd

Secondary School (Voluntary)

The Holy Family College, Shernall St E17 9RT; Tel 0181-520 3587; G. Green (Acting). (R.C.) (Mixed) (750)

Secondary Schools (11–18 County)

Aveling Park, Roberts Rd E17 4LS; Tel 0181-527 4566; P. Jose, BSc. (Mixed) (720)
Connaught, Connaught Rd E11 4AB; Tel 0181-539 3029; Mrs P. Fyans. (Girls) (360)
George Mitchell, Farmer Rd E10 5DN; Tel 0181-539 6198; C. Ravden. (Mixed) (360)
Heathcote, Normanton Pk E4 6ES; Tel 0181-529 5953; L. Davis. (Mixed) (600)
Kelmscott, Markhouse Rd E17; Tel 0181-521 2115; R.D. Clarke. (Mixed) (360)
Leytonstone, Colworth Rd E11 1JD; Tel 0181-537 4939; H.L. Freed. (Mixed) (950)
McEntee, Billet Rd E17 5DP; Tel 0181-527 3750; L.A. Banister, MA. (Mixed) (800)
Norlington, Norlington Rd E10 6JZ; Tel 0181-556 4657; Ms J. Beaton. (Boys) (360)
Rush Croft, Rushcroft Rd E4 9SG; Tel 0181-531 9231; Mrs P. Cutler. (Mixed) (360)
Tom Hood, Terling Close E11 3NT; Tel 0181-534 3425; W. Ruston, BA. (Mixed) (905)
Warwick, Barrett Rd E17 3ND; Tel 0181-520 4847; M. Boyers. (Boys) (450)
Walthamstow, Church Hill E17 9RZ; Tel 0181-520 0238; Mrs P. Marino, MA(Ed). (Girls) (1100)
Willowfield, Clifton Ave E17 6HL; Tel 0181-527 4065; A. Steel, BA. (Mixed) (360)

Adult Education Centres

Chingford, Chingford Senior High, Nevin Dr E4; Tel 0181-524 1758; R.M. Dewhurst
Davies, 192 Vicarage Rd E10; Tel 0181-539 7205; R. Markham
Essex Road, Leyton Sixth Form College, Essex Rd E10; Tel 0181-558 0842
Friday Hill Hse, Simmons La E4; Tel 0181-529 3380; R.M. Dewhurst
Harrow Green, Harrow Green Library, Cathall Rd E11; Tel 0181-558 5493; Vacancy
Louisa Oakes, Hall La, Chingford E4; Tel 0181-524 4215; S. Smith
McEntee, McEntee Senior High, Billet Rd E17; Tel 0181-527 4110; R. Tennant
Walthamstow, Greenleaf Rd E17; Tel 0181-520 2867; Ms B. Schultz

Field Studies

Suntrap, Church Rd, High Beach, Loughton, Essex; Tel 0181-508 0611; Cate Hickling-Jackson
Hawkwood Lodge, Yardley La E4; Tel 0181-524 4378; Ray Murdoch

Other Establishments

Adult Basic Education Section, (Adult Education Service) Chestnuts Hse, 398 Hoe St E17 9AA; Tel 0181-521 4311; Ms P. Hulin
Daytime Provision Unit, (Youth Service) c/o Pastures Youth Centre, Davies La E11 3DR; Tel 0181-556 2326; S. Hill
Ethnic Minorities Youth Work Unit, Walthamstow Youth Centre, London; Tel 0181-521 0243; Sabino Miranda
Girls and Young Womens' Unit Daytime Provision Unit, Pastures Youth Centre, London; Tel 0181-539 9486; Ms V. Cotton
Hawkswood Hostel, Hawkswood School, Antlers Hill E4 7RT; Tel 0181-524 5611; Mrs J. Anderson
Language Support Section, c/o Adult Education Service, Chestnuts Hse, 398 Hoe St E17 9AA; Tel 0181-521 4311; Mrs J. Croxton
Multicultural Development Service, Markhouse School, Markhouse Rd E17 8BD; Tel 0181-520 4878; Jennifer James
Music Centre, Leyton Manor Bldg, Capworth St, Leyton E10; Tel 0181-558 9224; R. Cracknell
School Library Service, Queens Rd E17 8QS; Tel 0181-521 3246; P. Vicary
School Media Resource Unit c/o George Mitchell High School, Farmer Rd E10 5DN; Tel 0181-558 3004; H. Meteyard
Summerfield Centre, Remedial Centre, Leyton Green Rd E10 6DB; Tel 0181-556 9951; I. Gersch
Teachers' Centre, Queens Rd E17 8QS; Tel 0181-521 3311/4; Vacancy
Youth Counselling Service, (Youth Service) Chestnuts Hse, 398 Hoe St, Walthamstow E17; Tel 0181-521 4311; Vacancy
Waltham Forest Training Agency, Chestnuts Hse, 398 Hoe St, Walthamstow E17 9AA; Tel 0181-521 4311; B. Goldsworthy

Youth Centres

Chingford Hall Youth Club, Chingford Hall Est, Iris Way E4 8QU; Tel 0181-531 5907; C. Long
Heathcote, Normanton Pk E4 6ES; Tel 0181-529 4620; Ms. S. Hargreaves

Highams Park, Church Ave E4 9QY; Tel 0181-527 3030; D. Wallis
Leyton, Crawley Rd E10 6PY; Tel 0181-539 1924; Fred Tchie
Pastures, Davies La E11 3DR; Tel 0181-539 5469; Terri Hallett
Walthamstow, Markhouse Rd E17 8BD; Tel 0181-520 5761; Vacancy
Warwick, Barrett Rd E17 3ND; Tel 0181-520 2434; Vacancy
Wellington Ave, Wellington Ave E4 6RE; Tel 0181-529 7964; Tony Peters
Whittingham, Higham Hill Rd E17 5QX; Tel 0181-527 4073; D. Martin

Grant Maintained Schools

Chingford, Nevin Dr E4 7LT; Tel 0181-529 1853; Miss F. O'Dowd. (Mixed) (1200)
Higham's Park School Handsworth Ave, Higham's Pk E4 9PJ; Tel 0181-527 4051/6744; Fax 0181-503 3349; *Headteacher* A.D. Browne; *Chair of Governors* T. L'Estrange. Mixed 11–16 (1000)

Wandsworth London Borough Council

Population 261,600 (Projection for 1991 from 1991 census)
Wandsworth Town Hall, Wandsworth High St, London SW18 2PU; Tel 0181-871 7890

Education Department

Wandsworth Town Hall, Wandsworth High St, London SW18 2PU; Tel 0181-871 8013
Acting Director of Education Paul Robinson
Deputy Director and Education Officer (Schools) Vacancy
Chief Education Inspector (Quality and Assessment) John Burchill
EO (Finance and Administration) Adrian Butler
Principal Education Officer (Institutions and Client Services) Urszula Topp
Personnel Services Manager Mary White
Head of Careers Service Sue Gray
Principal Education Welfare Officer David Brown
Student Awards Services Manager Stuart Berwick
Governor Services Manager Ray Bruce
EO (Planning/Special Schools) Gillian Bennell
EO (Planning/Mainstream) David Prothero
Pupil Services Manager Graham Carter
Head of Education Finance Keith Nevitt
Head of Resourcing Unit Frank Weeple
Contracts and Services Manager Glenys Lawrence
Head of Education Premises Steven Daniels
Information Technology Manager Fred Parrett
Administration Services Manager Mike Brooks
Senior Inspector (Head of Curriculum and Professional Development Services) Martin Baker
Senior Inspector (Performance and Standards) Jacky Griffin
Head of Integrated Support Services Sue Clarke
Chief Educational Psychologist Elisabeth Powell
AEO (Special Needs) Sue Norgate

Education Committee

Con 12, Lab 3
Chair Cllr E. Howlett, JP, DRSAM, (Con) 42 Inner Pk Rd, London SW19 6DD
Vice-Chair Cllr N.J. Fernyhough, BSc(Econ) (Con) 165 Trentham St, London SW18 5DH
Deputy Chair Jean Lucas
Members of the Committee
Con: R.E. Bloomfield-Smith, M.E. Calcott-James BA(Hons), C. Dixon MA(Oxon), ACA, A. Graham, V. Graham BSc, DipEd, MSc, A.G. Grant, J.F. Grimshaw, A.C. Jessiman, E.J. Lister, J. Lucas BA(Hons), MBE
Lab: A.J. Belton MA, MBCS, T.D. Hosain BSc, MSc, F.M.W. Ponsonby

Special Schools

Beechcroft, Beechcroft Rd SW17 7DF; Tel 0181-874 9096; R.J. Hughes. (EBD Day and Boarding)
Bradstow School, Dumpton Park Dr, Broadstairs, Kent CT10 1RG; Tel (01843) 862123; Elizabeth Holt. (SLD Boarding)
Burrow Hill School, St Catherine's Rd, Frimley, Camberley GU16 5NL; Tel (01252) 835570; Stuart Jones. (EBD B Boarding)
Chartfield, St Margaret's Cres, Roehampton SW15 6HL; Tel 0181-788 7471; Valerie Hand. (Del.)
Garratt Park School, Waldron Rd, Garratt La SW18 3SY; Tel 0181-946 5769; Roger Legate. (MLD)
Greenmead, St Margaret's Cres SW15 6HL; Tel 0181-789 1466; Pamela Hay. (PH Primary)
Linden Lodge, 61 Princes Way SW19 6JB; Tel 0181-788 0107; Tony Hudson
Oak Lodge, 101 Nightingale La SW12 8WA; Tel 0181-673 3453; Peter Merrifield. (Deaf SM Boarding Hostel)
Paddock, Priory La SW15 5RT; Tel 0181-878 1521; Nora Evans. (SLD)
The Vines, Forthbridge Rd SW11 5NX; Tel 0171-228 0602; Anne Holding. (MLD)

Secondary Schools

Battersea Technology College, Dagnall St SW11 5AP; Tel 0171-622 0026; Michael Clarke. (Mixed)
Chestnut Grove School, 45 Chestnut Grove SW12 8JZ; Tel 081-673 8737; Margaret Peacock. (Mixed)
Ernest Bevin School, Beechcroft Rd SW17 7DF; Tel 0181-672 8582; Naz Bokhari. (Boys)

Grant Maintained Schools

Burntwood School, Burntwood La, Tooting SW17 OAQ; Tel 0181-946 6201; Fax 0181-944 6592; *Principal* B. Beattie; *Chair of Governors* Kathleen Hooper, BA. Girls 11–19 (1229)
Elliott School, Pullman Gdns SW15 3DG; Tel 0181-788 3421; V.T. Burgess, MA. (Mixed)
Ethelburga School, Rosenau Rd, Wandsworth, London SW11 4QP; Tel 0171-228 7658
Graveney School, Welham Rd, Tooting SW17 9BU; Tel 0181-682 7000; *Headteacher* G.E. Stapleton; *Chair of Governors* D. Atkins. (Mixed) (11–19) (1550)
John Paul II School (RC) Princes Way SW19 6QE; Tel 0181-788 8142; J. King. (Mixed)
Salesian College (RC), Surrey La, Battersea SW11 3PB; Tel 0171-228 2857; Rev M.J. Blackburn. (Boys)
Southfields School, 333 Merton Rd SW18 5JU; Tel 0181-870 0171; E.A. Nuttall. (Mixed)

Westminster City Council

Population 187,700
PO Box 240, City Hall, Victoria St, London SW1E 6QP; Tel 0171-828 8070

Education and Leisure Department

PO Box 240, Westminster City Hall, 64 Victoria St SW1E 6QP; Tel 0171-828 8070
Director of Education and Leisure D. Tuck

Education Committee

Con 9, Lab 3
Chairman Cllr Markham, (Con)
Chairman Cllr Keen, (Con)

Vice-Chair Cllr Edmund Lazarus, (Con)
Members of the Committee
Con: D. Avery, T. Hunt, R. Jones, G. Kybeth, C. Longworth, J. Lord, T.Mallinson
Lab: J. Rosenberg, K. Wilkins, B. Grahame

Special Schools

College Pk, Monmouth Rd W2 4UT; Tel 0171-229 1524; *Headteacher* Ms M. Lozano
Queen Elizabeth II Jubilee, Kennet Rd W9 3LG; Tel 0171-960 7457; *Headteacher* Mark Moser. (SLD)
Wanstead Hse, Eastern Esplanade, Cliftonville, Margate, Kent CT9 2HH; Tel (01843) 223599; *Headteacher* Mrs R. Ford. (SLD)

Secondary Schools

Grey Coat Hospital Grey Coat Pl, London SW1P 2DY; Tel 0171-828 0968; Mrs M. Parsons. (Girls) (930)
North Westminster Community, Upper School, North Wharf Rd W2 1LF; M. Marland. (Mixed) (1793)
Pimlico, Lupus St SW1V 3AT; Tel 0171-828 0881; Miss K. Wood. (Mixed) (1168)
Quintin Kynaston, Marlborough Hill NW8 0NL; Tel 0171-722 8141. (Mixed) (894)
St Augustine's C.E., Oxford Rd NW6 5SN; Tel 0171-328 3434; J. Morgan. (Mixed) (665)
St Georges Maida Vale R.C. Lanark Rd W9 1RB; Tel 0171-328 0904; Philip Lawrence. (Mixed) (440)
St Marylebone C.E., 64 Marylebone High St W1M 4BA; Tel 0171-935 4704; Mrs E. Phillips. (Girls) (590)
Westminster City C.E., 55 Palace St SW1E 5HJ; Tel 0171-834 7419; Michael Billingham. (Boys) (753)

5 Local Government Scotland

Borders

Population 104,100
Regional Headquarters, Newtown St Boswells, Melrose, Selkirkshire TD6 0SA; Tel (01835) 823301; Fax (01835) 822145

Education Department

Regional Headquarters, Newtown St Boswells, Melrose TD6 0SA; Tel (01835) 823301; Fax (01835) 822145
Director of Education I.M. Dutton, BSc, MSc
Depute Director of Education D. Gordon, MA, MEd, FCIS
Assistant Director (Continuing Education) G. Donald, DPE, DMS
Assistant Director (Schools) K.N. Paterson, BSc, MEd
Assistant Director (Schools) Vacancy
Senior Adviser D. Mallen, MA, DipEd, MEd
Adviser (Sciences) J. Walsh, BA
Adviser (Social and Environmental Studies) D. Burgess, MA
Adviser (Mathematics) T. Renwick, BSc(Hons) Mathematics
Adviser (Learning Support) L. Walker, MA(Hons)
Primary Education Adviser J. Kerr, MA, MEd
Primary Education Adviser D. Reid, MA
Adviser (Arts) D.A. Salmond, DipMusEd, RSAM, ARCM
Adviser (Language) G. Johnson, BEd, DCE, ALIPE
Adviser (Secondary) R. Robotham, BEd
Adviser (PE, Health, Outdoor Education) D.M. Wallace, DPE, BA, BEd
Religious Education Guidance Adviser E.M. MacIntosh, BA, DipEd
SEO (School Boards) A. Dougall
Principal Careers Officer D.H. Blaszk, BA, DCG
Senior Education Officer (Special Educational Needs) B. Hughes, BEd, MEd
Principal Community Education Officer R. MacLeod, BEd
Senior Education Officer J. Taylor, ACCA

Number of Schools
73 primary; 9 secondary

Special Schools
9 special education centres

Day of Committee Meeting
Six per year; Tuesday

Requisition Period for School Supplies
No fixed period

Other Authorities with whom Joint Purchasing Arrangements are made
Cumbria County Council

Special Classes

Berwickshire High School Special Class, Duns TD11 3QQ; Tel (01361) 83710. (Senior)
Duns Primary School Special Class, Duns TD11 3AG; Tel (01361) 83797. (Junior)
Galashiels Academy Special Class, Elm Row, Galashiels TD1 3HU; Tel (01896) 754788. (Senior)
Hawick High School Special Class, Buccleuch St, Hawick TD9 0EG; Tel (01450) 372429. (Senior)
Kelso High School Special Class, Bowmont St, Kelso TD5 7EG; Tel (01573) 224444. (Senior)
Langlee Primary School Special Class, Longlee Dr, Galashiels TD1 2EB; Tel (01896) 757892
Peebles High School Special Class, Springwood Rd, Peebles EH45 9HB; Tel (01721) 720291. (Senior)
Wilton Primary School Special Unit, Wellfield Rd, Hawick TD9 7EN; Tel (01450) 372075

Secondary Schools

Berwickshire High School, Duns, Berwickshire TD11 3QQ; Tel (01361) 883710; J.M. Smith, BA

High School, Earlston, Berwickshire TD4 6HF; Tel (01896) 849282; N.W.K. Roxburgh, BSc
High School, Eyemouth, Berwickshire TD14 5BY; Tel (018907) 750363; N. Morrison, MA
Galashiels Academy, Elm Row, Galashiels, Selkirkshire TD1 3HU; Tel (01896) 754788; B. Keenan, BA
High School, Buccleuch St, Hawick, Roxburghshire TD9 0EG; Tel (01450) 372429; N.M. Horne, BA, MEd
Grammar School, High St, Jedburgh, Roxburghshire TD8 6DQ; Tel (01835) 863273; G. Adams, MA
High School, Bowmont St, Kelso, Roxburghshire TD5 7EG; Tel (01573) 224444; A. Johnston, BSc
High School, Peebles EH45 9HB; Tel (01721) 720291; Dr R.J. Kerr, MA, PhD
High School, Hillside Terr, Selkirk TD7 4EW; Tel (01750) 720246; G.W. Jack, MA

Central

Population 272,100
Viewforth, Stirling FK8 2ET; Tel (01786) 442000; Fax (01788) 443394

Education Department

Viewforth, Stirling FK8 2ET; Tel (01786) 442641; Fax (01786) 442782
Director of Education M. Allan, BA(Hons)
Head of Community Services Jim Findlay
Head of Pre Fives Services Linda Kinney
Head of Personnel Services Vacancy
Head of Resources Dr J.G.B. Young
Head of School Development S. Rae
Head of Support Services E. Boyce
Adviser (Business Studies) I. Gray
Adviser (Home Economics) M. Graham, DipHome
Area Education Officer (Schools) J. Wright
Adviser (Resources) D.M. Dickie, BSc
Adviser (Mathematics) A. Hunter
Principal Officer (Curriculum Planning) E. Carnachan
Adviser (Physical Education) R. McGowan
Area Education Officer (Schools) D. Mackenzie
Adviser (Science) T. Harrison
Adviser (Social Subjects) Nigel Fletcher
Adviser (Special Educational) Vacancy
Adviser (Computing) G. Connell
Adviser (Outdoor Education) D. Michie
Adviser (Art and Design) D. Matheson
Principal Schools' Librarian E. Dickie
Principal Careers Officer Craig Smith
Principal Educational Psychologist H. Wilson, MA, MEd, ABPS
TVEI Co-ordinator D. Seton
Number of Schools
11 nursery schools (1,448); 36 nursery classes (1,588); 116 primary (23,967); 18 secondary (14,585)
Special Schools
9 special schools (332); Main stream schools with Special Units (21); Day Units (8)
Day of Committee Meeting
Every six weeks
Main Requisition Period for School Supplies
April

Careers Office

See chapter 17

Regional Psychological Service and Units

Alloa R.P.S. Centre, 30 Ludgate, Alloa, Central
Alloa Day Unit, Bedford Pl, Alloa, Central
Bannockburn Day Unit, Hillpark Education Centre, Bannockburn, Central
Regional Psychological Service Springwood Hse, Polmaise Rd, Stirling, Central
Dundas Day Unit, C/o Moray Primary School, Grangemouth, Central
Falkirk R.P.S. Centre, 4 Orchard St, Falkirk, Central
Falkirk Day Unit, Hope St, Falkirk, Central
Grangemouth R.P.S. Centre, C/o Moray Primary School, Grangemouth, Central
Moray Day Unit, Moray Middle School, Grangemouth, Central
Park Day Unit, C/o Park Primary School, Alloa, Central
Riverside Day Unit, C/o Riverside Primary School, Stirling, Central
Stenhousemuir R.P.S. Centre, Main St, Stenhousemuir, Central
Weedingshall Education Unit, Polmont, Falkirk, Central

Special Schools (Day)

Bainsford Primary Special Class Waverley St, Bainsford, Falkirk FK2 7NW. (M.H.)(3–12)
Bannockburn High School, Special Class, Broomridge, Bannockburn Rd, Stirling FK7 OHG; Tel (01786) 813519. (M.H.) (12–16)
Bo'ness Academy, Special Class, Bo'ness Academy, Bo'ness EH15 9QD; Tel (01506) 2260. (M.H.) (12–16
Dawson Park, Bainsford, Falkirk FK2 7QY; Tel (01324) 21072; Fax (01324) 28172; M.J. Bergin. (P.H., M.H., P.S.) (6–16
Fairfield, Pompee Rd, Sauchie, Central; M.K. Stewart. (S.M.H. P.H., E.P.)
Graeme High School Special Class Callendar Rd, Falkirk FK1 1SY. (M.H.) (12–16)
Grangemouth Learning Centre, Moray Primary School, Grangemouth FK3 9EF; Tel (01324) 472333; J. Alexander
Kildean, Stirling FK8 1RW; Tel (01786) 73985; Vacancy. (S.M.H.) (3–16)
Lochies Hse, Clackmannan Primary School, Clackmannan FK10 4JS; Tel (01259) 216928; M.K. Stewart. (M.H.) (5–12)
Lornshill Academy Special Class, Lornshill Academy, Tullibody Rd, Alloa FK10 2ES; Tel (01259) 214331. (M.H.) (12–16)
Riverside Primary School Special Class, Forrest Rd, Stirling FK8 1UJ; Tel (0163 583) 63248
Rossvail, 108 Glasgow Rd, Camelon, Falkirk, Central; M.J. Bergin. (S.M.H.) (4–16)
Special Class, Alloa Academy, Claremont, Alloa FK10 2EQ; Tel (01259) 214979
Special Class, Balfron High School, Balfron G63 OPG; Tel (01360) 40469. (M.H.) (12–16)
Torwood, Larbert FK5 4SR; M.J. Bergin. (S.M.H.) (6–16)
Wallace High School Special Class Dumyat Rd, Stirling FK9 5HW. (M.H.) (12–16)
Weedingshall Education Unit, Tillicoultry, Central; Vacancy
Whins of Milton, Whins of Milton, Stirling FK7 0LL; Tel (01786) 812667; Vacancy. (M.H.) (4–12)
Windsor Park, Bantaskin Rd, Falkirk FK1 5HT; Tel (01324) 28026; P.M. Buttress. (Partially Deaf) (4–16)

Secondary Schools (6-year)

Alloa Academy, Tel (01259) 214979; Fax (01259) 211022; J. Strang. (Mixed) (660)
Alva Academy, Tel (01259) 60342; Fax (01259) 769162; I.A. Lamont. (Mixed) (1224)
Balfron High, Tel (01360) 40469; Fax (01360) 40260; J.A. Fleming. (Mixed) (791)
Bannockburn High, Tel (01786) 813519; Fax (01786) 818040; J. McAlpine. (Mixed) (709)
Bo'ness Academy, Tel (01506) 2260; Fax (01506) 828308; W.M. Brown. (Mixed) (1009)
Dunblane High, Tel (01786) 823823; Fax (01786) 824462; J. Gardner. (Mixed) (703)
Denny High, Tel (01324) 823124; Fax (01324) 826457; F. Ellis, MA, BA. (Mixed) (1336)
Falkirk High, Tel (01324) 29511; Fax (01324) 28249; A.G. Easton. (Mixed) (1390)
Graeme High, Falkirk; Tel (01324) 22576/7; Fax (01324) 22595; J. McHardy. (Mixed) (1456)

Grangemouth High, Tel (01324) 485031; Fax (01324) 666795; W. Paxton. (Mixed) (801)
Larbert High, Tel (01324) 554233; Fax (01324) 570729; R. Holmes. (Mixed) (1475)
Lornshill Academy, Alloa; Tel (01259) 214331; Fax (01259) 720402; A.S. McLachlan. (Mixed) (1067)
McLaren High, Callander; Tel (01877) 30156; Fax (01877) 31601; A. Mathie, MA, MEd. (Mixed) (692)
St Modan's High, Stirling; Tel (01786) 70962; Fax (01786) 447117; J. Oates. (Mixed) (890)
St Mungo's High, Falkirk; Tel (01324) 28416; Fax (01324) 32085; H.J. Lynch. (Mixed) (797)
The High School of Stirling, Tel (01786) 72451; Fax (01786) 447127; J. Anderson. (Mixed) (859)
Wallace High, Stirling; Tel (01786) 62166/7; Fax (01786) 447134; W. Brodie. (Mixed) (1053)
Woodlands High, Falkirk; Tel (01324) 29615; Fax (01324) 31343; A. McGibbon. (Mixed) (478)

Dumfries and Galloway

Population 147,805
Council Offices, English St, Dumfries DG1 2DD; Tel (01387) 61234; Fax (01387) 60034
Chairman (Education Committee) Richard G. Greenhow
Vice-Chairman (Education Committee) Ian A. Pennie
Director of Education W.C. Fordyce
Depute Director of Education K.A. MacLeod
Assistant Director of Education (Pre-School and Primary Education) M McA White
Assistant Director of Education (Educational Audit: Performance Indicators) A.I. Marrs
Assistant Director of Education (Secondary Education, Continuing Education, Careers and Bursaries) C.D. Dignan
Assistant Director of Education (Special Education) F. Sanderson
Professional Assistant A. McElroy
Education Adviser G. Murray
Education Adviser (Audit) J. Shankland
Education Adviser K. Best
Education Adviser J. Tait
Education Adviser I. Scott
Education Adviser J. Macaulay
Education Adviser I. Marriott
Education Adviser (CWLD) J. O'Neill
Area Education Adviser C. Brett
Area Education Adviser Dr W. Flood
Regional Adviser T.L. Gilmour
Area Education Adviser D. Mackie
Client Officer (Catering) H.J. Smith, MBE
Head of Careers J. Henderson
Principal Educational Psychologist S.H. Beck
Principal Community Education Officer W. Hume

Number of Schools and Further Education Establishments
29 nursery classes (1,127); primary pupils (12,666); secondary pupils (9,415); FT F.E. students (1,577)

Learning Centres
24

Number of Pupils
23,658

Product of 1p rate
£526.868

Requisition Periods for School Supplies
As necessary

Other Authorities with whom Joint Purchasing Arrangements are made
Cumbria Supplies

Education Offices

30 Edinburgh Rd, Dumfries DG1 1JQ; Tel (01387) 61234
Chairman T.A. McAughtrie
Vice-Chairman W. Clemie
Director of Education W.C. Fordyce, BSc, MEd
Depute Director of Education K.A. McLeod, MA, BA, DipEd
Assistant Director of Education (Staffing) M. McAwhite, MA(Hons)
Assistant Director of Education (Buildings) Miss A.I. Marrs, BSc
Assistant Director of Education (Continuing Education) G.F. Trickey, BEd, MEd
Assistant Director of Education (School Boards) Mrs C.D. Ferguson, MA
Assistant Director of Education (Idea Unit) F. Sanderson, MA
Assistant Director of Education (Professional Assistant) A. McElroy, (Education H.Q)
Primary Adviser G. Murray, BA
Primary Adviser Miss J. Shankland, BA
Primary Adviser K. Best, MA, BEd
Children with Learning Difficulties Adviser J. O'Neill, MA
General Education Adviser M.J. Prowse, MA
General Education Adviser C. Brett, BSc
General Education Adviser Dr W. Flood, BSc, PhD
General Education Adviser Miss F. Corcoran, BSd, BA(Hons)
General Education Adviser D. Mackay, BA
General Education Adviser T.L. Gilmour
Music Adviser M.L. Davies, LTCL, LRAM
Physical Education Adviser I. Scott, DipPE, BA
Physical Education Adviser F. Coulston, DipPE
Art Adviser J. Macauley, DA
Religious Education Adviser D. Mackie, BD
Outdoor Education Adviser I. Marriott, MA, DipEd
Client Officer (Catering) Vacancy
Principal Careers Officer J. Henderson
Principal Educational Psychologist S.H. Beck, BA(Hons), DEP
Principal Community Education Officer W.A. Chalmers; Tel (01387) 61234
Librarian J. Preston, BA, ALA

Number of Schools
10 nursery classes (646); 116 primary schools and departments (12,721); 16 secondary (8,905)

Special Schools
1

Special Classes
22

Number of Pupils
22,535

Day of Committee Meeting
First Tuesday in month

Requisition Periods for School Supplies
As necessary

Other Authorities with whom Joint Purchasing Arrangements are made
Cumbria and Borders Purchasing Partnership

Careers Office

See chapter 17

Special School

Langlands, Loreburn Pk, Dumfries, Dumfries & Galloway; Tel (01387) 67834; Mrs G. Frame. (M.H.) (Mixed) (28)

Secondary Schools

Annan Academy, Anan; Tel (01461) 202954; C. Moncreiff, BSc, MA. (952)
Castle-Douglas High, Dunmuir Rd, Castle-Douglas, Dumfries & Galloway; Tel (01556) 2821. (433)
Dalbeattie High, Haugh Rd, Dalbeattie, Dumfries & Galloway; Tel (01556) 610445; C. McAteer, MA, BA. (338)
Dalry Secondary, Dalry, Castle-Douglas, Dumfries & Galloway; Tel (016443) 259; W.A.M. Hall, MA. (92)

Douglas Ewart High, Newton Stewart; Tel (01671) 3773; J. Judge, BSc, MIBiol. (691)
Dumfries Academy, Dumfries; Tel (01387) 52846; D. Smith, MA(Hons). (892)
Dumfries High Marchmount, Dumfries, Dumfries & Galloway; Tel (01387) 63061; C. Mitchell, BSc. (898)
Kirkcudbright Academy, Kirkcudbright; Tel (01557) 30440; J.M. Manson, BSc. (517)
Langholm Academy, Langholm; Tel (013873) 80418; D.N. Macdonald, BSc(Hons). (275)
Lockerbie Academy, Lockerbie; Tel (0157 62) 2626; A.M. Blake, BSc. (814)
Maxwelltown High, Lochside Rd, Dumfries, Dumfries & Galloway; Tel (01387) 720458; M.N. Cliff, MA. (313)
Moffat Academy, Moffat; Tel (01683) 20114; S.J. Brown, BA(Hons). (193)
St Joseph's College, Craigs Rd, Dumfries, Dumfries & Galloway; Tel (01387) 52893; M.G.J. Taylor, MA. (627)
Sanquhar Academy, Sanquhar; Tel (01659) 50208; W. McIntyre, MA. (287)
Stranraer Academy, Stranraer; Tel (01776) 6484; D. Eastwood, BSc(Hons). (1166)
Wallace Hall Academy, Thornhill, Dumfriesshire; Tel (01848) 30294; N.L. Anderson, BSc. (375)

Fife

Population 351,200
Fife Hse, North St, Glenrothes KY7 5LT; Tel (01592) 414141; Fax (01592) 414142

Education Department

Regional Headquarters, Fife Hse, North St, Glenrothes KY7 5LT; Tel (01592) 414141; Fax (01592) 610726; Telex 727461
Director of Education B. Welsh, MA, BSc
Senior Depute Director of Education J. Travers, MA, BA
Depute Director of Education A. Auchterlonie, LLB
Assistant Director of Education J. Macgregor, MA, DipEd
Assistant Director of Education D.W. Hill, BSc, DipEd, MSc
Assistant Director of Education A. Kindleysides, BSc
Assistant Director of Education M. Stewart, BSc, MEd
Assistant Director of Education Dr A. Hawkins, BSc, PhD
Assistant Director of Education D. Somerville
Assistant Director of Education J.C. McKeown, MA, MEd
Assistant Director of Education A. McKay
Principal Accountant (Education) G. McDonald
Personnel Services Officer (Education) A. Edwards
Office Manager M. Johnston
Section Head (Schools) E. Doonan
Section Head (Teaching Staff) H. Penman
Section Head (Non-Teaching Staff) I. Ogilvie
Section Head (Grants) A. Vallance
Section Head (Building) H. Martin
Senior Adviser (Nursery to P4) A. Beck
Senior Adviser (Assessment & Research) D. Cameron
Adviser in Art & Design A. Watson
Adviser in Science P. Anderson
Adviser in Business Studies E. Milne
Adviser in Home Economics M. Miller
Adviser in Physical Education Vacancy
Adviser in Guidance M. Liston
Adviser in Special Educational Needs E. Shephard
Adviser in Technological Studies I. Yule
Adviser in Computing B. Taylor
Adviser in English Vacancy
Adviser in Modern Languages I. Hirschfeld
Adviser in Music Vacancy
Head of Auchterderran Staff Development and Resources Centre W. McClean
Adviser in Nursery Education N. Taylor
Adviser in Social Subjects K. Muir
Adviser in Religious Education M. Kincaid
Adviser in Mathematics D. Cursiter
Primary Adviser in Environmental Studies T. Coupar
Adviser in Learning Support Services A. Morton
Primary Adviser in Language Arts B. Rasmusen
Primary Adviser in Mathematics Y. Menzies
Primary Adviser in Early Years E. McMillan
TVEI Extension Co-ordinator G. Cockburn
Assistant Adviser, Music R. Tait
Principal Psychologist B. Kirkaldy
Voluntary Services Officer (Community Education) J. Douglas
School Meals/Regional Client Officer L. Clark
Principal Careers Officer M. Barron

Number of Schools
16 nursery and 81 nursery classes in primary schools (4,595); 145 primary (31,136); 19 secondary (22,457)
Departments of Special Education
Moderate learning difficulties, 232
Special Schools
Severe/profound learning difficulties, 158
Other Units
313
Requisition Periods for Schools Supplies
No specific dates
Other Authorities with whom Joint Purchasing Arrangements are made
None

Careers Offices

See chapter 17

Special Schools (Social/Emotional Difficulties)

Linnwood Hall, Linnwood Dr, Leven, Fife; Tel (01333) 423434; J.H. Tollan, BEd
Ovenstone, Pittenweem KY10 2RR; Tel (01333) 311330; A. Cameron

Special Day Classes for Pupils with Moderate Learning Difficulties

Balwearie High School, Balwearie Gdns, Kirkcaldy KY2 5LY; Tel (01592) 266262; G.D. Mackenzie
Bell-Baxter High School, Westfield, Cupar KY15 5DR; Tel (01334) 652094; D. Campbell
Buckhaven High School, Methilhaven Rd, Buckhaven KY8 1HL; Tel (01592) 713691; G. Grant
Lochgelly High School, Station Rd, Lochgelly KY5 8LZ; Tel (01592) 780199; J. Yuile
Madras College, South St, St Andrews KY16 9EJ; Tel (01334) 475777; D.D. Galloway
Woodmill High School, Shields Rd, Dunfermline KY11 4ER; Tel (01383) 725106; I. Watson

Special Schools for Pupils with Severe/ Profound Learning Difficulties

John Fergus School, Alexander Rd, Glenrothes KY7 4EF; Tel (01592) 755354; J. MacKenzie
Headwell School, Headwell Ave, Dunfermline KY12 0JU; Tel (01383) 721589; G. Franklin
Hyndhead School, Barncraig St, Dunbeath KY8 1JE; Tel (01592) 713338; M. Bendex
Kilmaron School, Balgarvie Rd, Cupar KY15 4PE; Tel (01334) 653125; W. Lawson
Lochgelly North School, McGregory Ave, Lochgelly KY5 9PE; Tel (01592) 780528; M. Lorimer
Robert Hendryson School, Linburn Rd, Dunfermline KY11 4LD; Tel (01383) 728004; C. Haldane
Rosslyn School, Veiwforth Terr, Kirkcaldy KY1 3BP; Tel (01592) 651155; E.A. Morice

Residential Schools

Linnwood Hall, Linnwood Dr, Leven KY8 5RB; Tel (01333) 423434; Dr J. Tollan. (S/Ed.) (12–16) (36)

Melville Hse, Monimail, Letham, Cupar KY7 7RJ; Tel (01337) 810343; J.S. Cocker. (S/Ed.) (12–16) (40)
Ovenstone, Pittenweem, Anstruther KY10 2RR; Tel (01333) 311330; A. Cameron. (S/Ed.) (5–12) (18)
Rimbleton Hse, Rimbleton Ave, Glenrothes KY6 2BY; Tel (01592) 758181; Vacancy. (S/Ed.) (5–16) (25)

High Schools (Comprehensive Mixed)

Auchmuty, Dovecot Rd, Glenrothes KY7 5JL; Tel (01592) 756554; A.J. Kelly, MA. (1315)
Balwearie, Balwearie Gdns, Kirkcaldy KY2 5LY; Tel (01592) 266262; G.D. Mackenzie, BA. (1345)
Beath, Foulford Rd, Cowdenbeath KY4 9BH; Tel (01383) 512114; G.M. Munro. (1042)
Bell-Baxter, Westfield Rd, Cupar KY15 5DR; Tel (01334) 652641; D. Campbell, MA. (1622)
Buckhaven, Methilhaven Rd, Buckhaven KY8 1HL; Tel (01592) 713691; G. Grant, BSc. (1452)
Dunfermline, St Leonards Pl, Dunfermline KY11 3BG; Tel (01383) 726207; D. Brown, MA, LLB. (1594)
Glenrothes, Napier Rd, Glenrothes KY6 1HJ; Tel (01592) 756651; A. Hendrie. (975)
Glenwood, South Parks Rd, Glenrothes KY6 1JX; Tel (01592) 752258; A.M. Hannah, BSc. (960)
Inverkeithing, Hillend Rd, Inverkeithing KY11 1PL; Tel (01383) 414551; L.A. Roy, BSc. (1238)
Kirkcaldy, Dunnikier Way, Kirkcaldy KY1 3LR; Tel (01592) 267111; R.D. Fraser, MA. (1442)
Kirkland, Methil Brae, Methil KY8 3LT; Tel (01333) 424607; G.J. Coyle, BSc. (551)
Lochgelly, Station Rd, Lochgelly, Fife; Tel (01592) 780199; J. Yuile, BSc. (952)
Madras College, South St, St Andrews KY16 9EJ; Tel (01334) 475733; D.D. Galloway, MA, BA. (1513)
Queen Anne, Broomhead, Dunfermline KY12 0PQ; Tel (01383) 728188; M.B. Cook, BSc. (1737)
St Andrew's R.C., Overton Rd, Kirkcaldy KY1 3JL; Tel (01592) 651027; A.O.B. Finn, MA. (748)
St Columba's R.C., Woodmill Rd, Dunfermline KY11 4UN; Tel (01383) 724637; R. Conway, BSc. (714)
Viewforth, Loughborough Rd, Kirkcaldy KY1 3DE; Tel (01592) 652891; D. Jolly, BSc. (491)
Waid Academy, St Andrews Rd, Anstruther KY10 3HD; Tel (01333) 310787; T. Watson, MA. (608)
Woodmill, Shields Rd, Dunfermline KY11 4ER; Tel (01383) 725106; I. Watson, MA. (1132)

Arts in Fife

Auchterderran Staff Development and Resources Centre, Woodend Rd, Cardenden KY5 0NE; Tel (01592) 414600; *Principal Arts Officer* B. McConnell

Educational Library Service

Auchterderran Staff Development and Resources Centre, Woodend Rd, Cardenden, Fife; Tel (01592) 414600; *Chief Librarian* W. Elphinstone, ALA

Educational Television Service

Maitland St, Dunfermline; Tel (01383) 725293

Grampian

Population 500,566
Woodhill Hse, Westburn Rd, Aberdeen AB9 2LU; Tel (01224) 682222; Fax (01224) 697445; Telex 739277

Education Department

Woodhill Hse, Westburn Rd, Aberdeen AB9 2LU; Tel (01224) 682222; Fax (01224) 664615; Telex 739277
Director of Education Douglas M. Paterson, MA, DipED, MEd
Depute Director of Education (Community Education) Ian Craik; Tel (01224) 664641; Fax (01224) 697445
Depute Director (Primary/Nursery) Lizbeth Robertson
Depute Director (Secondary) Nicola Webster (Acting)
SEO (Facilities) Iain Wolstenholme
SEO Ann O. Walker
SEO (8–14) Hamish Vernal
SEO (O–8) Andrew Tait
SEO (Secondary) Bruce Robertson (Acting)
Senior Education Officer (Special Educational Needs) Jonathon Mager
Finance and Administrative Officer Ian C. Stephen
Staffing Services Unit Officer Margaret Simpson
Information and Communication Officer S. Vilma McAdam
Regional Community Education Development Officer Kath Beveridge
Regional Community Education Training Officer Terence Reid
Regional Careers Officer Christina M. Allon
Regional Educational Psychologist James Banks
Regional Organiser of Cleaning and Janitorial Services Charles Topp
Regional Schools Librarian Anslem R. DeSilva
Resources Development Officer Colin R. McKenzie
In Service Training Co-ordinator Lawrence Gray
Schools Industry Liaison Officer Dennis Kidd
TVEI Pilot Co-ordinator Alex Leggat
Eduction Development Co-ordinator Joyce Fogg
Adviser (English) Elisabeth Sharp
Adviser (Modern Languages) Rosalind Cantley
Adviser (Mathematical Studies) David G.G. Houston
Adviser (Scientific Studies) Kenneth M. Duncan
Adviser (Technology Activities and Applications) Peter Edwards
Adviser (Home Economics) Thelma E. Birnie
Adviser (Business Studies) Kathleen Manson
Adviser (Geography and Environmental Studies) Robert M.G. O'Brien
Adviser (History and Modern Studies) Frank Cooney
Creative Activities (Art and Design) Hugh A.W. Roche
Creative Activities (Music) Lloyd Davis
Creative Activities (Drama) Graeme Biggs
Physical Education Peter Giles
Religious and Moral Education David Leng (Acting)
Adviser in Special Education W.F. Murdoch
Guidance J. Terry Ashton

Number of Schools
91 nursery schools and departments (4,266); 265 primary (44,246); 37 secondary (30,341); 1 primary attached to secondary; Special schools and units: 45 (1,138)

Day of Committee Meeting
Tuesday; 8 per year

Requisition Period for Schools Supplies
All year round

Other Authorities with whom Joint Purchasing Arrangements are made
None

Education Committee

Con 3, Lab 5, LD 10, SNP 8, Ind 1
Chair J. Orskol, (Lib) 37 New Pk Rd, Mastrick, Aberdeen AB2 6UT
Vice-Chair J. Towers, (SNP) 8 Cairntrodlie, Peterhead AB42 6AG

Members of the Committee
Con: T. Mason, J. Porter, J. Wisely
Lab: A. Farquharson, J. King, J. Lamond, M. Morrell, J. Thomaneck
LD: W. Anderson, R. Hunter, R. Kemp, G. Kirkbride, G. Leslie, M. Levie, V. Maltin, C. Millar, J. Orskov, A. Tunstall

SNP: N. Allan, G. Barnes, M. Howe, G. McDonald, R. Patterson, D. Scaife, B. Topping, J. Towers

Aberdeen East Area

Education Office, Summerhill Education Centre, Stronsay Dr, Aberdeen AB2 6JA; Tel (01224) 208626; Fax (01224) 708674
Area Education Officer John Stodter
Area Careers Officer Sandra McCabe
Area Community Education Officer Ann Landels
Area Finance and Administrative Officer Kate Derbyshire
Area Primary/Nursery Education Officer John T. Finnie
Area Principal Educational Psychologist Bill Maxwell
Area Secondary Education Officer Charles Muir
Area Primary/Nursery Adviser Isobel Gibson

Special Schools

Aberdeen School for the Deaf, Regent Wk, Aberdeen AB2 1SX; Tel (01224) 480303; Fax (01224) 276675; Mairi Macauley
Beechwood School, Raeden Park Rd, Aberdeen AB2 4PE; Tel (01224) 323405; Fax (01224) 208704; *Head Teacher* Andrew Young, BSc, MEd
Educational Unit, RACH (Wards 2 and 4), Lowit Unit, Ward 7, Department of Child and Family Psychiatry, Cornhill Rd, Aberdeen AB9 2AG; Tel (01224) 681818 ext 52714; Lindsey Mackie, MA, MLitt
Language (ESL) Unit, Linksfield Academy, 520 King St, Aberdeen AB2 1SS; Tel (01224) 481343; Maeve McDowell
Raeden Centre (Nursery School), Mid Stocket Rd, Aberdeen AB2 4PE; Tel (01224) 321381; R.M.M. Murray, MS. Nursery School
Sunnybank Primary School (Language Unit), Sunnybank Rd, Aberdeen AB2 3NJ; Tel (01224) 644540; Andrew May, MA
Sunnybank Primary School (Partially Hearing Unit), Sunnybank Rd, Aberdeen AB2 3NJ; Tel (01224) 633363; Andrew May, MA

Secondary Schools (11–18)

Aberdeen Grammar School, Skene St, Aberdeen AB9 1HT; Tel (01224) 642299; William J. Johnston, BSc, DipEd. (Mixed)
Bridge of Don Academy, Braehead Way, Bridge of Don, Aberdeen AB22 8RR; Tel (01224) 703118; *Headteacher* Alexander Garrow (Acting), BSc(Hons) (2nd Class), DipEd. (Mixed)
Harlaw Academy, 18–20 Albyn Pl, Aberdeen AB9 1RG; Tel (01224) 589251; John Murray. (Mixed)
Linksfield Academy, 520 King St, Aberdeen AB2 1SS; Tel (01224) 481343/14/5; Stewart Philip, BA(Hons). (Mixed)
Oldmachar Academy, Jesmond Dr, Bridge of Don, Aberdeen AB22 8UR; Tel (01224) 820887; Joseph Leiper, MA, DipEd
St Machar Academy, St Machar Dr, Aberdeen AB2 3YZ; Tel (01224) 492855; Douglas Marr, MA, MEd. (Mixed)

Aberdeen West Area

Education Office, Summerhill Education Centre, Stronsay Dr, Aberdeen AB2 6JA; Tel (01224) 208626
Area Education Manager Hugh A. Richardson
Area Careers Officer Sandra McCabe
Area Community Education Officer Alexander Scott
Area Finance and Administrative Officer Frances Uren
Area Primary/Nursery Education Officer Hamish Vernal
Area Principal Educational Psychologist Kenneth Edward
Area Secondary Education Officer Sue Muncer
Area Primary/Nursery Adviser Margaret Carlaw

Special Schools

Carden School, Gordon Terr, Dyce, Aberdeen AB2 OBD; Tel (01224) 770362; R. Brown, MA
Cordyce Residential School, Riverview Dr, Dyce, Aberdeen AB2 ONF; Tel (01224) 724215; Fax (01224) 772738; Neil Brown, BEd(Hon) (2nd Class), MEd(SEN). (Malad)
Kincorth Academy, SEN Base, Kincorth Circle, Aberdeen AB1 5NL; Tel (01224) 872881; Michael Stuart. (Mixed)
Kingslea School, Fernielea Rd, Aberdeen AB2 6JU; Tel (01224) 321363; M.I.D. Colburn
Loirston Primary, SEN Base, Loirston Ave, Cove Bay, Aberdeen AB1 4HE; Tel (01224) 897686; Helen Jamieson, MEd
Marlpool School, Cloverfield Gdns, Bucksburn, Aberdeen AB2 9BE; Tel (01224) 712735; Fax (01224) 712524; Margaret Taylor
Pitfodels School, North Deeside Rd, Cults, Aberdeen AB1 9PN; Tel (01224) 868480/861531; Jennifer McMaster
Redcraigs, Craighill School, Hetherwick Rd, Aberdeen AB1 5ST; Tel (01224) 897641; Eileen Millbank
Woodlands School, Woodlands Hospital, Craighton Rd, Cults, Aberdeen AB1 9PR; Tel (01224) 868814; Malcolm Johnston

Secondary Schools (11–18)

Bankhead Acadamy, Bankhead Ave, Bucksburn, Aberdeen AB2 9ES; Tel (01224) 713861; Brian Wilkins, MSc, BSc, DPhil. (Mixed)
Cults Academy, Hillview Dr, Cults, Aberdeen AB1 9SA; Tel (01224) 868801; Graeme Traill. (Mixed)
Dyce Academy, Riverview Dr, Dyce, Aberdeen AB2 0NF; Tel (01224) 725118; Michael T. Taylor, MA, MEd. (Mixed)
Hazlehead Academy, Groat's Rd, Aberdeen AB9 1FJ; Tel (01224) 310184; Brian Wood, BSc(Hons) (2nd Class). (Mixed)
Kincorth Academy, Kincorth Circle, Aberdeen AB1 5NL; Tel (01224) 872881; Michael Stuart. (Mixed)
Northfield Academy, Granitehill Pl, Aberdeen AB2 7AN; Tel (01224) 699715; David Eastwood. (Mixed)
Torry Academy, Tullos Circle, Aberdeen AB1 3HB; Tel (01224) 876733; Robin M. Dyer, MA, MEd. (Mixed)

Banff/Buchan

Area Education Office, Earlsmount, Regent St, Keith, Banffshire AB55 3EJ; Tel (01542) 882281
Area Education Manager Stephen Shaw
Area Careers Officer Patrica Boyd
Area Community Education Officer Ian R. Kerr
Area Finance and Administrative Officer Alexander Bain
Area Primary/Nursery Education Officer Anne McArthur
Area Principal Educational Psychologist Rhoda Dunbar
Area Secondary Education Officer Gordon Bulloch
Area Primary/Nursery Adviser Rose E. Geddes

Psychological Services

Children's and Teachers' Centre, Victoria St, Fraserburgh AB4 5PJ; Tel (01346) 510187
SEBU Unit, Block A, Banff Primary School, Walker Ave, Banff, Grampian AB45 1AQ; Tel (01261) 832665
Peterhead SEBU Unit, Old Infant School, 16 Prince St, Peterhead, Aberdeenshire AB4 6PL; Tel (01779) 73269/70411/70390
Towie Hse, Banff Rd, Turriff, Aberdeenshire; Tel (01888) 62427

Special Schools

Adolescent Unit, Children's and Teachers' Centre, Victoria St, Fraserburgh AB43 5PJ; Tel (01346) 510187; Jennifer Kinnon
The Anna Ritchie School, Grange Gdns, Peterhead AB42 6AP; Tel (01779) 73293; M. Morgan, BSc
Ramsay School, Block B, Walker Ave, Banff AB45 1AQ; Tel (01261) 812598; *Headteacher* Maureen Forsyth (Acting), (3rd Year Primary Cert)
Westfield School, Argyll Rd, Fraserburgh AB43 5RF; Tel (01346) 518699; F.M.S. Allan, MA

Secondary Schools

Banff Academy, Bellevue Rd, Banff AB45 1BY; Tel (01261) 812591; George Sinclair. (Mixed)
Fraserburgh Academy, Dennyduff Rd, Fraserburgh, Aberdeenshire AB43 5NA; Tel (01346) 515771; John B. Rankin, BSc, FRSGS. (Mixed)
Mintlaw Academy, Station Rd, Mintlaw, Aberdeenshire AB42 8FN; Tel (01771) 22994; William McWhirr, MA(Hons) (2nd Class)
Peterhead Academy, Prince St, Peterhead, Aberdeenshire AB42 6QQ; Tel (01779) 72231; George Milne. (Mixed)
Turriff Academy, Victoria Terr, Turriff, Aberdeenshire AB53 7EE; Tel (01888) 63216/63533/168729; Donald Stewart. (Mixed)

Gordon Area

Education Office, Gordon Hse, Blackhall Rd, Inverurie, Aberdeenshire AB51 3WB; Tel (01467) 21291; Fax (01467) 24277
Area Education Manager Andrew D. Dick
Area Careers Officer Katherine Ross
Area Community Education Officer John G.M. Troup
Area Finance and Administrative Officer Edwin G. Duncan
Area Primary/Nursery Education Officer Malcolm A. Catto
Area Principal Education Psychologist Anne Skinner
Area Secondary Education Officer David MacDonald (Acting)
Area Primary/Nursery Adviser Betty McGill

Psychological Service

Area Education Office, Victoria St, Inverurie, Aberdeenshire AB51 9QS; Tel (01467) 25464

Special Schools

Ellon Academy SEN Base, Schoolhill, Ellon, Aberdeenshire AB41 9AY; Tel (01358) 720715; Fax (01358) 23758; Alan I. Cameron, BSc
Ellon Primary SEN Base, Modley Pl, Ellon, Aberdeenshire AB41 9AZ; Tel (01358) 720692; William S. Irvine, MA
Learning Unit, Market Place School, Inverurie, Aberdeenshire AB51 6XN; Tel (01467) 620451; Alexander B. Malley, MA
The Gordon Schools Special Unit, Huntly, Aberdeenshire AB54 4SE; Tel (01466) 792307; Fax (01466) 792180; John Swan, BSc, DipEd
St Andrew's School, St Andrew's Gdns, Inverurie, Aberdeenshire AB51 3XT; Tel (01467) 621215; Fax (01467) 623428; Dorothy Lindsay

Secondary Schools

Alford Academy, Murray Terr, Alford, Aberdeenshire AB33 8JE; Tel (019755) 62251; Robert H. Graham, BSc. (Mixed)
Ellon Academy, Schoolhill, Ellon, Aberdeenshire AB41 9AX; Tel (01358) 720715; Alan I. Cameron, BSc. (Mixed)
The Gordon Schools, Huntly, Aberdeenshire AB54 4SE; Tel (01466) 792181/2; John Swan, BSc, DipEd. (Mixed)
Inverurie Academy, Jackson St, Inverurie, Aberdeenshire AB51 9PX; Tel (01467) 21655; Alastair G. Hogg, MA, MEd. (Mixed)
Kemnay Academy, Bremner Way, Kemnay, Aberdeenshire AB51 9FT; Tel (01467) 643535; Richard A. Bisset, MA. (Mixed)
Westhill Academy, Hay's Way, Westhill, Skene, Aberdeenshire AB32 6XZ; Tel (01224) 740111; Peter R. Gibson, MA. (Mixed)

Kincardine/Deeside Area

Education Office, Queens Rd, Stonehaven, Kincardineshire AB3 2HQ; Tel (01569) 66960
Area Education Manager Brian J. Walker
Area Careers Officer Patrica Barber
Area Community Education Officer Richard C. Stroud
Area Finance and Administrative Officer Hazel Hall
Area Primary/Nursery Education Officer Frances Davidson
Area Principal Educational Psychologist William O'Hara
Area Secondary Education Officer Dr Patricia M. Maclean
Area Primary/Nursery Adviser Evelyn Massie

Psychological Service

Special Schools

Aboyne Academy SEN Base, Bridgeview Rd, Aboyne, Aberdeenshire AB34 5JN; Tel (013398) 86222; Fax (013398) 86004; Sheena M.M. Cooper, MA
Aboyne Primary SEN Base, Aboyne, Aberdeenshire AB34 5JN; Tel (013398) 86638; George P. Graham, MA
Carronhill, Mill of Forest Rd, Stonehaven, Kincardineshire AB3 2GB; Tel (01569) 763886; Fax (01569) 767286; Lesley Paterson

Secondary Schools

Aboyne Academy, Bridgeview Rd, Aboyne, Aberdeenshire AB34 5JN; Tel (013398) 86222; Sheena M.M. Cooper. (Mixed)
Banchory Academy, Schoolhill, Banchory, Kincardineshire AB31 3TQ; Tel (013302) 3357/8/9; *Head Teacher* Stewart Wilson. (Mixed)
Mackie Academy, Slug Rd, Stonehaven, Kincardineshire AB3 2DF; Tel (01569) 62071; John Fraser, MA. (Mixed)
Mearns Academy, Aberdeen Rd, Laurencekirk, Kincardineshire AB3 1AJ; Tel (01561) 378817; John Fraser, DipPhys. (Mixed)
Porthlethen Academy, Bruntland Rd, Portlethen, Aberdeen AB1 4QL; Tel (01224) 782174; Clement A. Stewart, MA, MEd

Moray Area

Education Office, Academy St, Elgin, Morayshire IV30 1LL; Tel (01343) 541144
Area Education Manager Donald Duncan
Area Careers Officer Mrs Susan Chalmers
Area Community Education Officer David MacDonald
Area Finance and Administrative Officer Mrs Lesley Manson
Area Primary Nursery Education Officer Jim Gibson
Area Principal Educational Psychologist Christopher Toon
Area Secondary Education Officer Andrew Todd
Area Primary/Nursery Adviser Frank Reynolds

Psychological Services

66 Carden Pl, Aberdeen AB1 1UL; Tel (01224) 645945
Area Education Office, Gordon Hse, Blackhall Rd, Inverurie AB51 3WB; Tel (01467) 621291; Fax (01467) 622254
Gordon Terr, Dyce, Aberdeen AB2 OBD; Tel (01224) 722316
11 North Guildry St, Elgin, Morayshire IV30 1JR; Tel (01343) 548884; Fax (01343) 550892
Lady Cathcart Bldg, High St, Buckie, Banffshire AB55 3EJ; Tel (01542) 831790
Sinclair Hse, 619 King St, Aberdeen AB2 1SA; Tel (01224) 481678

Special Schools

Buckie High School Special Unit, West Cathcart St, Buckie, Banffshire AB56 1QB; Tel (01542) 832605; Chris J. Sugden, BA
Cranloch/St Andrews School, Lhanbryde, Morayshire IV30 3LB; Tel (01343) 842428; Donald MacAuley, BEd
Forres Academy SEN Base, Burdsyard Rd, Forres, Morayshire IV36 ODG; Tel (01309) 672271; A.A.D. Maclachlan, BA
Hamilton Drive School, Hamilton Dr, Elgin, Morayshire IV30 2NN; Tel (01343) 543162; David Munro

Ogilvie School, School Rd, Keith, Banffshire AB5 3ES; Tel (015422) 882000; Margaret E. Taylor

Secondary Schools

Buckie High, West Cathcart St, Buckie, Banffshire AB56 1QB; Tel (01542) 832605; Chris J. Sugden, BA. (Mixed)
Elgin Academy, Morriston Rd, Elgin, Morayshire IV30 2ND; Tel (01343) 543485; Norman G. Strachan, MA, DipEd. (Mixed)
Elgin High, High School Dr, New Elgin, Morayshire IV30 3YU; Tel (01343) 545181; William Hope. (Mixed)
Forres Academy, Burdsyard Rd, Forres, Morayshire IV36 0DG; Tel (01309) 672271; Alistair A.D. Maclachlan, BA. (Mixed)
Keith Grammar, School Rd, Keith, Banffshire AB55 3ES; Tel (01542) 882461; Gerald Haines, MA. (Mixed)
Lossiemouth High, Coulardbank Rd, Lossiemouth, Morayshire IV31 6JU; Tel (0134381) 2047; William Barber, MA, MEd. (Mixed)
Milne's High, West St, Fochabers, Morayshire IV32 7DJ; Tel (01343) 820611/2/3/14; Lindsay S.G. Matheson, MA, MLitt. (Mixed)
Speyside High, Mary Ave, Aberlour, Banffshire AB38 9QN; Tel (01340) 871522/3; David A. Tierney, BA. (Mixed)
Tomintoul School, Main St, Ballinadalloch, Banffshire AB37 9HA; Tel (01807) 580271; Brendan McGrath. (4-Year Mixed)

Highland

Population 205,900 (1994)
Regional Bldgs, Glenurquhart Rd, Inverness IV3 5NX; Tel (01463) 702144; Fax (01463) 702111

Education Department

Regional Bldgs, Glenurquhart Rd, Inverness IV3 5NX; Tel (01463) 702000; Fax (01463) 702828
Director of Education A.C. Gilchrist, BSc, DipEd
Depute Director J.G. Findlay, BSc, MEd
Depute Director Vacancy
Assistant Director J.W.C. Stevenson, BA, MEd
Assistant Director M. McArthur, BSc, MSc
Assistant Director T. Waters, ACMA
Principal Administrator J.F. Riddoch, DipComm
Divisional Education Officer (Caithness) J.H. Edgar, MA, MEd Rind Hse, West Bank Ave, Wick; Tel (01955) 602362; Fax (01955) 602408
Divisional Education Officer (Sutherland) J.S. Metcalfe, BA Education Office, Brora; Tel (01408) 621382; Fax (01408) 621126
Divisional Education Officer (Ross & Cromarty) A.G. Forsyth, BSc, MSc The Education Centre, Castle St, Dingwall; Tel (01349) 63441; Fax (01349) 63994
Divisional Education Officer (Inverness) N.W. Murray, BSc, MEd 13 Ardross St, Inverness; Tel (01463) 663800; Fax (01463) 663809
Divisional Education Officer (Lochaber) J. McCabe, BA Montrose Ave, Inverlochy, Fort William; Tel (01397) 702466; Fax (01397) 705627
Assistant Divisional Education Officer (Ross & Cromarty) D.R.J. MacDonald, BSc The Education Centre, Castle St, Dingwall; Tel (01349) 863441; Fax (01349) 863994
Assistant Divisional Education Officer (Inverness) M. Gillies, BSc 13 Ardross St, Inverness; Tel (01463) 663800; Fax (01463) 663809
Assistant Divisional Education Officer (Inverness) H.A. Fraser, MA, MEd 13 Ardross St, Inverness; Tel (01463) 663800; Fax (01463) 663809
Senior Adviser J. Fyfe, MA The Education Centre, Castle St, Dingwall; Tel (01349) 863441; Fax (01349) 865671
Adviser (Gaelic) D.J. Macleod, MA, PhD The Education Centre, Castle St, Dingwall; Tel (01349) 863441; Fax (01349) 865671
Adviser (Physical Education) J. Macdonald The Education Centre, Castle St, Dingwall; Tel (01349) 863441; Fax (01349) 865671
Adviser (Primary) A. Sharland, BA, MEd (Principal) The Education Centre, Castle St, Dingwall; Tel (01349) 863441; Fax (01349) 865671
Adviser (Primary) Y. Orr, MA 13 Ardross St, Inverness; Tel (01463) 663800; Fax (01463) 663809
Adviser (Religious Education) Rev J.M. Wilson, MA, BD The Education Centre, Castle St, Dingwall; Tel (01349) 863441; Fax (01349) 865671
Adviser (Social Subjects) J. Leslie, BSc The Education Centre, Castle St, Dingwall; Tel (01349) 63441; Fax (01349) 65671
Adviser (Education/Industry Liaison Officer) Vacancy The Education Centre, Castle St, Dingwall; Tel (01349) 63441; Fax (01349) 65671
Staff Development Officer E. Gibson, BA The Education Centre, Castle St, Dingwall; Tel (01349) 63441; Fax (01349) 65671
TVEI Co-ordinator J. Ritchie, MA The Education Centre, Castle St, Dingwall; Tel (01349) 63441; Fax (01349) 65671

Number of Schools
199 primary; 2 four-year secondary; 24 six-year secondary; 2 nursery; 5 special

Number of Pupils
35,480

Day of Committee Meeting
Wednesday (6-week cycle)

Education Committee

Chair V. MacIver, (Ind) Newton of Novar, Evanton, Ross-shire IV16 9XH; Tel (01349) 830637; Fax (01349) 830620
Vice-Chair A.J. Russell Cairndearg, Newtonmore PH20 1BL; Tel (01540) 673262

Members of the Committee
B.W. Beattie, J.C. Cole, A. Darlington, B.M.S. Dunlop, M. Foxley, D. Fraser, C.L. Goodman, N.J.O. Graham, D. Grant, D.R. Green, J.N. Home, F.R.M. Keith, D.J. McPherson, I.J. Macdonald, J.T. MacDonald, E. Mackenzie, D.I. Macrane, V. MacIver, A.W. MacKenzie, A. Milne, W.A. Mowat, J.S. Munro, A. Murray, J.W. Oag, P.J. Peacock, D. Philip, A. Rhind, A.B. Robertson, A.J. Russell, J. Scott, W.S. Smith

Advisers

The Education Centre, Castle St, Dingwall, Highland; Tel (01349) 863441; Fax (01349) 865671
Senior Adviser J. Fyfe, MA
Adviser (Computer Studies) I. Graham, MA
Adviser (Gaelic) D.J. Macleod, MA, PhD
Adviser (Physical Education) J. Macdonald
Adviser (Primary) A. Sharland, BA, MA
Adviser (Primary) Y. Orr, MA 13 Ardross St, Inverness; Tel (01463) 663800; Fax (01463) 663809
Adviser (Religious Education) Rev J.M. Wilson, MA
Adviser (Social Subjects) J.C. Leslie, BSc
Adviser (English) D. McCartney, MA
Adviser (Home Economics) J. Brown, DDSc
Mathematics G.A. Gibson, BSc, BA
Adviser (Modern Languages) S. Munro, MA
Adviser (Music) H. Richardson, DMusEd
Adviser (Science) R. English, BSc
Adviser (Technical) A. Urquhart
Adviser (Art) A. Cowie, BA
Adviser (Primary) T. Adair, BA
Divisional Office, Brora, Highland; Tel (01408) 621382
Adviser (Primary) J. Muir

Careers Service

46 Church St, Inverness, Highland; Tel (01463) 238866; Fax (01463) 243231
Principal Careers Officer H. Mennie

Catering Service

Regional Client Office, Dalneigh Primary School, Limetree Ave, Inverness, Highland; Tel (01463) 712919; Fax (01463) 710397
Regional Client Officer S. MacKinnon

Community Education

3 High St, Dingwall, Highland; Tel (01349) 864962; Fax (01349) 863781
Regional Community Education Officer J. Morrison, BA

Psychological Service

Culcabock Ave, Inverness IV2 3RG; Tel (01463) 233494; Fax (01463) 713775; *Regional Principal Psychologist* S. Iliffe, BA, MEd

Special Schools

Banavie School Special Unit Banavie, by Fort William, Lochaber, Highland
Drummond School, Inverness; Tel (01463) 233091
St Clement's School, Dingwall; Tel (01349) 863284
St Duthus School, Tain; Tel (01862) 894407
Special Education Unit, Mount Pleasant School, Thurso, Caithness KW1 8HL
Special Education Unit, Pultneytown Academy, Wick, Highland

Secondary Schools (12–16)

Farr Secondary School, Bettyhill, Sutherland KW14 7SS; Tel (0164 12) 217; J.A. Johnston, MA
Kinlochleven Secondary School, Kinlochleven, Argyll PA40 4QL; Tel (01855) 831273; J.D. Kennedy, MA

Secondary Schools (12–18)

Alness Academy, Alness IV17 0UY; Tel (01349) 883341; G.A. MacKenzie, MA
Charleston Academy, Kinmylies, Inverness IV3 6ET; Tel (01463) 234324; T. McCulloch, BSc, MEd
Culloden Academy, Culloden, Inverness IV1 2JZ; Tel (01463) 790851; D.B. McGinn, BA
Dingwall Academy, Dingwall IV15 9LT; Tel (01349) 863071; A. Glass, MA
Fortrose Academy, Fortrose IV10 8TW; Tel (01381) 620310; J.D. Simpson, BSc
Gairloch High School, Gairloch IV21 2BP; Tel (01445) 712275; N.K. Wilkie, MA
Glenurquhart High School, Drumnadrochit IV3 6UG; Tel (01456) 450243; A.S. Maxwell, BSc
Golspie High School, Golspie KW10 6RF; Tel (01408) 633451; D.J. Whyte, MA
Grantown Grammar School, Grantown-on-Spey PH26 3HU; Tel (01479) 872649; M. Maclennan, BSc
Invergordon Academy, Invergordon IV18 0LD; Tel (01349) 852362; J.B. Macmillan, BSc
Inverness High School, Montague Row, Inverness IV3 5DZ; Tel (01463) 233586; R.R. Cunningham, MA
Inverness Royal Academy, Culduthel Rd, Inverness IV1 2AD; Tel (01463) 222884; J. Considine, MA, MEd
Kilchuimen Academy, Fort Augustus PH32 4DL; Tel (01320) 366296; J. Cameron, BSc, PhD
Kingussie High School, Ruthven Rd, Kingussie PH21 1ES; Tel (01540) 661475; T. Taylor, BSc, PhD
Lochaber High School, Fort William PH33 7ND; Tel (01397) 702512; P.V. Brian, BSc
Mallaig High School, Mallaig PH41 4RN; Tel (01687) 462107; J.F. Jackson
Millburn Academy, Diriebught Rd, Inverness IV2 3QR; Tel (01463) 233573; G.C. Spence, MA
Nairn Academy, Duncan Dr, Nairn IV12 4RD; Tel (01667) 453700; C.S. Dickson, MA
Plockton High School, Plockton IV52 8TU; Tel (01599) 544372; D.J. Ferguson, MA, MEd
Portree High School, Portree, Isle of Skye IV51 9ET; Tel (01478) 612030; D. Meek, MA, MEd
Tain Royal Academy, Scotsburn Rd, Tain IV19 1PS; Tel (01862) 892121; J.F. Kirk, BSc
Thurso High School, Ormlie Rd, Thurso KW14 7DS; Tel (01847) 63822; J. Inkster, BSc, BA
Ullapool High School, Ullapool IV26 2UE; Tel (01854) 612078; J. Nicol, BSc
Wick High School, West Banks Ave, Wick KW1 5LU; Tel (01955) 603333; J.G.M. Manson, BSc

Outdoor Education Centres

Kinlocheil Centre, Kinlocheil, Inverness-shire, Highland
Nethybridge Outdoor Centre, Nethybridge, Inverness-shire, Highland
Rumster Outdoor Centre, Latheron, Caithness, Highland
Torrin Outdoor Centre, Torrin, Isle of Syke

Lothian

Population 750,600
Regional Headquarters, George IV Bridge, Edinburgh EH1 1UQ; Tel 0131-229 9292; Fax 0131-469 3010

Education Department

40 Torphichen St, Edinburgh EH3 8JJ; Tel 0131-229 9166
Chairman Cllr E. Maginnis
Vice-Chairman Cllr D. McGrouther
Chair Education Committee Cllr Elizabeth McGuiness 1 Parliament Sq, Edinburgh EH1 1TT
Director of Education E.M. Reid, MA
Depute Director of Education R.O. Williams, MACantab, PGCE
Depute Director of Education A.K. Mackay, MA, MEd
Depute Director F. Henderson, DipPE
Depute Director of Education J. Dobie, MEd, DipEd
Depute Director of Education J.W. Sellars, BSc, MSc
Regional Careers Officer G.R.D. Dick, MA, FICO
Assistant Director Miss M. Macmillan, BSc
Assistant Director R.S. Ferguson, MA
Assistant Director D.H. Steele, MA(Hons), DipEd
Assistant Director A.P. King, DipEd
Assistant Director E.T. Laing, BSc, MSc
Assistant Director A.D. Mackintosh, MA
Assistant Director A.G. Manning, MA
Assistant Director J. Perry, MA(Hons), MEd
Education Officer H. Dick
Assistant Director A.J. Blackie, BA, DipYouth and Community Service
Assistant Director A. Black
Assistant to the Director of Education C.D. Hepburn, MA, DipEd
School Welfare Catering Client Officer K. Downton
School Libraries Officer Vacancy
TVEI Co-ordinator A.D. McAulay
Number of Schools
45 nursery and 100 nursery classes (9,896); 242 primary (56,097); 50 secondary (36,036); 25 special and 23 special classes (1,492); 6 outdoor education centres
Day of Committee Meeting
Every sixth Wednesday
Regional Community Charge product
£556,657

Regional Psychological Centres

Edinburgh East

Regional Psychological Centre, 7 Merchiston Pk, Edinburgh EH10 4PR; Tel 0131-229 4223/14; J. Wilson, MA, MEd

Edinburgh West

Regional Psychological Centre, Easter Drylaw Dr, Edinburgh EH4 2RY; Tel 0131-343 6181; J. Noble, MA, MEd

East Lothian

Musselburgh Unit St Michael's Ave, Musselburgh EH21 7BD; Tel 0131-665 9255; *Principal Psychologist* Graham Cameron, BA(Hons), MEd, MSc, FColl, P.C.Psychol

East Midlothian

Regional Psychological Centre, 31 School Grn, Lasswade EH18 1NB; Tel 0131-654 1070; G. Cameron, BA(Hons), MEd, MSc, FCollPCPsychol

West Lothian

Cedarbank Centre, Ladywell East, Livingston EH54 6DR; Tel (015064) 37395; C.R. Hughes, MA, DipEd

Advisory Staff

Dean Education Centre, Belford Rd, Edinburgh EH4 3DS; Tel 0131-343 3960
Senior Adviser (Nursery/Primary Education) N.T. Henderson
Senior Adviser (Aesthetic & Linguistic Education) T. McMillan
Senior Adviser (Learning Support & Special Needs) R. Maxwell
Senior Adviser (Secondary/Tertiary Education) M. Roebuck
Senior Adviser (Personal and Social Education) Dr W.M. Stephen
Senior Adviser (Scientific & Technological Education) Mrs I. Vass
Art Adviser W. Thomson
Drama and Media Studies Adviser J.A. Turner
Business Education Adviser Mrs E.J.M. Broughton
Information Technology and Education Computing Adviser J.L. Glen
English Adviser Vacancy
Guidance Health and Social Education Adviser Mrs J. Fancey
Home Economics Adviser Miss M. McMullen
Mathematics Adviser Vacancy
Languages Adviser P. Wheeldon
Music Adviser A.R. Kerr
Nursery Education Adviser Vacancy
Outdoor Education Adviser P. Hitt
Physical Education Adviser E. Still
Primary Education Adviser D.M. Oates
Primary Education Adviser Vacancy
Primary Education Adviser G. Wilson
Primary Education Adviser Mrs W. Dignan
Primary Education Adviser F. Monaghan
Primary Education Adviser Mrs P. Slater
Primary Education Adviser (Acting) D.M. Oates
Religious, Moral and Multicultural Education Adviser B. Wallace
Remedial Education Adviser R. Maxwell
Science Adviser R. Dawson
Education/Industry Links Adviser P. Sweeney
Social Subjects Adviser L.A. Wilsher

Community Education Service Offices and Centres

North Edinburgh
Broughton Community Education Office, Carrington Rd, Edinburgh EH4 1EG; Tel 0131-332 6316; D. Clark
Broughton Youth Wing, Carrington Rd, Edinburgh EH4 1EG; Tel 0131-332 6316; Vacancy
Craigmount, Craigs Rd, Edinburgh EH12 8NH; Tel 0131-339 8278/1884; Mrs J. McIntosh
Craigmount Youth Wing, Craigs Rd, Edinburgh EH12 8NH; Tel 0131-339 8278/1884; Vacancy
Craigroyston, 1a Pennywell Rd, Edinburgh EH4 4PH; Tel 0131-332 7360; Ms D. Watt
Fort Community Wing, Fort Primary School, North Fot St, Edinburgh EH6 4HF; Tel 0131-553 1074
Kirkliston, Queensferry Rd, Kirkliston EH29 9AG; Tel 0131-333 4214; Ms F. Edwards
Leith, New Kirkgate, Edinburgh EH6 6AD; Tel 0131-554 4750; Mrs A. McCulloch
Leith Community Resource Centre, 20 Academy Pk, Edinburgh EH6 8JG; Tel 0131-554 1509; K. McCulloch
Newton, 26 Duddingston Cres, Newton EH52 6QG; Tel 0131-331 3290; Vacancy
Norwood Station Rd, Ratho Station EH28 8PT; Tel 0131-333 1021; Ms F. Edwards
Rannoch, Rannoch Terr, Edinburgh EH4 7ER; Tel 0131-339 5351; Mrs P. Crombie
Ratho, 1 School Wynd, Ratho EH28 8TT; Tel 0131-333 1055; L. Arscott
Pirniehall C.E. Field Office, Pirniehall Primary School, West Pilton Cres, Edinburgh EH4 4HP; Tel 0131-315 2088; Ms M. Gray
Royston/Wardieburn, Pilton Dr North, Edinburgh EH5 1NF; Tel 0131-552 5700; A. Dickson
South Queensferry, Kirkliston Rd, South Queensferry EH30 9NZ; Tel 0131-331 2113; Mrs A. Lambourne
Castlebrae Community Education Office, Greendykes Rd, Edinburgh EH16 4DP; Tel 0131-661 7463
South-East Edinburgh
Bingham, Bingham Ave, Edinburgh EH15 3HD; Tel 0131-669 8778; Ms S. Reeves
Burdiehouse/Southhouse, Burdiehouse St, Edinburgh EH17 8EZ; Tel 0131-664 2210; R. Byfield
Cameron Hse, Cameron Hse Ave, Edinburgh EH16 5LF; Tel 0131-667 3762; Ms D. McCann
Craigentinny, Loaning Rd, Edinburgh EH7 6JE; Tel 0131-661 8188/9; E.C. Ross
Craigentinny Health Project Loaning Rd, Edinburgh EH7 6JE; Tel 0131-661 8188/9; Ms L. Mulvey
Craigmillar Boys' Club, Craigmillar Castle Ave, Edinburgh EH16 4DW; Tel 0131-661 4064; J. Headridge
Gilmerton, 4 Drum St, Edinburgh EH17 8QG; Tel 0131-664 2335; C. Gough
Gracemount Sub-Area Office Lasswade Rd, Edinburgh EH16 6TZ; Tel 0131-664 5101; D. Shannon
Gracemount Youth Centre, 128 Lasswade Rd, Edinburgh EH16 6AU; Tel 0131-664 3275; Ms C. Pattullo
Inch 255 Gilmerton Rd, Edinburgh EH16 5TT; Tel 0131-664 4710; J. Travers
Jack Kane, £08 Niddrie Mains Rd, Edinburgh EH16 4ND; Tel 0131-657 1595; D. Brown
Magdalene Magdalene Dr, Edinburgh EH15 3BE; Tel 0131-669 8760
Moredun, Moredun Park View, Edinburgh EH17 7ND; Tel 0131-664 3612; *Caretaker* Mrs Sutherland
Northfield/Willobrae Northfield Rd, Edinburgh EH8 7PP; Tel 0131-661 5723; J. McDougall
Peffermill, Craigmillar Castle Ave, Edinburgh EH16 4DH; Tel 0131-661 4810; Vacancy
Riddles Court, 322 Lawnmarket, Edinburgh EH1 2PQ; Tel 0131-661 8189; *Caretaker* Mrs M. Flynn
St Anne's, 6 South Gray's Cl, Cowgate, Edinburgh EH1 1TQ; Tel 0131-557 0469; Mrs M. Whitfield
South Bridge Centre, Infirmary St, Edinburgh EH1 1LT; Tel 0131-556 2944; Ms P. Brechin
Tollcross, Tollcross Primary School, Fountainbridge, Edinburgh EH3 9QG; Tel 0131-229 8448; D. Easton
Southside, 117 Nicolson St, Edinburgh EH8 9ER; Tel 0131-667 0484; Ms S. Manning
South-West Edinburgh
Area Office Firrhill Community Education Office, Oxgangs Rd North, Edinburgh EH14 1DP; Tel 0131-441 1031/6671; M. Rosendale
Adult Learning Project (ALP) 184 Dalry Rd, Edinburgh EH11 2EP; Tel 0131-337 5442; S. Reeves; V. Galloway
Balerno Community Wing, 5 Bridge St, Balerno EH14 7AQ; Tel 0131-449 2834; D. Hillson
Carrickvale, Stenhouse St West, Edinburgh EH11 3EP; Tel 0131-443 6971; D. Bishop
Clovenstone, 54 Clovenstone Pk, Edinburgh EH14 3EY; Tel 0131-453 4561; Ms N. Farrell
Colinton Mains, Firrhill Loan, Edinburgh EH13 9EJ; Tel 0131-441 6597; C. Page (at Pentland)
Gorgie War Memorial Hall, Gorgie Rd, Edinburgh EH11 2RQ; Tel 0131-337 9098; *Caretaker* Mrs M. Leckie
Juniper Green, Baberton Ave, Edinburgh EH14 5DU; Tel 0131-453 4427; *Caretaker* I. Watson
Pentland, Oxgangs Brae, Edinburgh EH13 9LS; Tel 0131-445 2871; J. Spence
St Brides, Orwell Terr, Edinburgh EH11 2DY; Tel 0131-346 1405; G. Williamson

Sighthill, Sighthill Wynd, Edinburgh EH11 4BL; Tel 0131-453 6078; K. Mullarkey
Springwell Hse, Ardmillan Terr, Edinburgh EH11 2JN; Tel 0131-337 1971; G. Williamson
Stenhouse/Whitson, 80 Stevenson Dr, Edinburgh EH11 3BQ; Tel 0131-443 9125; D. Bishop (at Carwickvale)

East Lothian/Midlothian

Community Education Office, 8 Academy La, Loanhead EH20 9RP; Tel 0131-440 2366; J.W. Hill
Beeslack, Beeslack High School, Edinburgh Rd, Penicuik EH26 0QF; Tel 71 – 678060; R. Cooper
Bridge Community Education Centre Poldrate Mill, Haddington EH41 4DA; Tel 0161-082 3137; G. Horsburgh; J. Clark
Brown Bldg, Gorebridge Primary School, 80 Hunterfield Rd, Gorebridge EH23 4XA; Tel 49-21808; Ms L. Ferguson
Carnethy, Greenlaw Mains, Penicuik EH26 0QP; Tel 71-673594; Miss S. Brown
Fisherrow, South St, Musselburgh EH21 6AT; Tel 0131-665 7590/5860; Miss A. McConaghy
Greenhall Community Wing, Greenhall High School, Gowkshill, Gorebridge EH23 4PE; Tel 49-20181; I. Lawson
Haddington Community Education Office Carlyle Hse, Lodge St, Haddington EH41 2LA; Tel 0161-082 5104; A. Sneddon
Penicuik YM/YWCA, 50a Kirkhill Rd, Penicuik EH26 8JB; Tel 71-674851; Ms E. Taylor; J. Ainslie
Lasswade High School Centre, Eskdale Dr, Bony Rise EH19 2LA; Tel 0131-663 7171/2/8170; D. Hand; J. McRae
Newbattle, 67 Gardiner Pl, Newtongrange EH22 4RT; Tel 0131-663 6055; J. Fairgrieve; K. McGowan
North Berwick, Law Rd, North Berwick EH39 4PN; Tel (01620) 3056; Ms H. Gardner
Paradykes Community Wing, 5 Mayburn Walk, Loanhead EH20 9HG; Tel 0131-440 3169; Ms L. Kelly
Red School Youth Centre, 50A Kirk St, Prestonpans EH32 9DY; Tel 4-812474; L. Isbrand
Sherwood Community Wing, Cockpen Rd, Bonnyrigg EH19 3HR; Tel 0131-663 7181; C. Paterson
Tranent Community Education Office, Sandersons Wynd, Tranent EH33 1QA; Tel (01875) 612919/612910; Mrs M. Galloway
Wallyford Community Centre, Albert Pl, Wallyford, nr Musselburgh EH21 8LB; Tel 0131-653 2804; M. Rodger
Whitecraig, 44A Whitecraig Cres, Whitecraig, Mussleburgh EH21 8NG; Tel 0131-653 2227; Ms J. McRae

West Lothian

Bathgate Community Education Office, Wellpark, Marjoribanks St, Bathgate EH48 1QL; Tel 51 – 54303; M. Fyvie
Addiewell Community Wing, Church St, Addiewell EH55 8PG; Tel (01501) 62796; J. Allison
Almondbank Resource Centre, Almondbank Primary School, The Mall, Livingston EH54 5EJ; Tel 58- 32314; T. Mitchell
Armadale, North St, Armadale EH48 3QB; Tel (01501) 30708; A. Colquhoun
Bathgate Marjoribanks St, Bathgate EH48 1AH; Tel 51-54487; J. Lockhart
Blackburn, The Centre, Ashgrove, Blackburn EH47 7LJ; Tel 51-53014; A. Philip
Blackridge Community Wing, Blackridge Primary School, Main St, Blackridge EH48 3RJ; Tel (01501) 52352; A. Colquhoun
Bridgend, Auldhill Rd, Bridgend EH49 6NZ; Tel (0150 683) 4626; *Caretaker* Mrs L. McCulloch
Broxburn, 205 West Main St, Broxburn EH52 5LJ; Tel 5-852948; M. Mitchell
Carmondean Community Centre Nether Dechmont Farm, Fells Rigg, Livingston EH54 8AX; Tel (01506) 39568; Mrs A. Coia
Crofthead Farm Community Centre Association Templar Rise, Livingston EH54 8DG; Tel (01506) 419100; Mrs V. Wallace
Dechmont Memorial, 71 Main St, Dechmont EH52 6LJ; Tel 5-890348; Mrs A. Ovens
Dedridge Community Wing, Dedridge Primary School, Dedridge East, Livingston EH54 6JQ; Tel 5-412831; Vacancy
East Calder 143 Main St, East Calder EH53 0EP; Tel 5-881557; I. Johnson
East Whitburn, Hen-Ness Rd, East Whitburn EH47 8EX; Tel (01501) 40938; *Caretaker* T. Carty; *Caretaker* J. Wood
Fauldhouse, Lanrigg Rd, Fauldhouse EH47 9JA; Tel (01501) 70552; R. Gillies
Forestbank, Forestbank, Ladywell, Livingston EH54 6DX; Tel 58-30035; Vacancy
Howden St Andrews Community Wing, Howden St Andrews Primary School, Kingsport Ave, Livingston EH54 6BA; Tel 58-35520; Vacancy
Lanthorn, Kenilworth Rise, Dedridge, Livingston EH54 6JL; Tel 5-413394; D. Cairney
Letham Youth Wing, Letham Primary School, Forth Dr, Livingston EH54 5LZ; Tel 58-32013; I. McIntosh
Livingston Station, 4 Main St, Livingston Station EH54 8BE; Tel 58-414002; *Caretaker* I. Kennedy
Livingston Station Youth Centre 7 Main St, Livingston Station EH54 8BE; Tel 5-411295; Ms L. Cunningham
Livingston Village, 1 Kirk La, Livingston Village EH54 7AY; Tel 5-413252; *Caretaker* Mrs S. Oxley
Livingston Youth Centre, 7 Main St, Livingston Station EH54 8BE; Tel 5-411295; Ms L. Cunningham
Mid Calder, School La, Mid Calder EH53 0JR; Tel 5-881246; I. Johnson
Mosswood, 85 Ferguson Way, Knightsbridge, Livingston EH54 8JF; Tel 5-37761; D. Catto
Philpstoun, Main St, Philpstoun EH49 6RA; Tel (0150 683) 4360; *Caretaker* Vacancy
Riverside, Riverside Primary School, The Mall, Livingston EH54 5EJ; Tel 5-32026; I. Mcintosh
Seafield Main St, Seafield EH47 7AL; Tel 58-52394; *Caretaker* J. McGugan
Springfield, Springfield Primary School, 141 Springfield Rd, Linlithgow EH49 7SN; Tel 5-847455; S. Christie
Stoneyburn, 75 Main St, Stoneyburn EH47 8BY; Tel (01501) 62323; J. Kerr
The Low Port Centre Blackness Rd, Linlithgow EH49 7HZ; Tel 5-844802; *Principal* I. Fox
Toronto, Toronto Primary School, Toronto Ave, Howden East, Livingston EH54 6BN; Tel 58-31465; Vacancy
Torphichen, Bowyett, Torphichen EH48 4LZ; Tel 51-52383; J. Lockhart
West Calder, Young St, West Calder EH55 8EG; Tel 51-871278; J. Close
Whitburn, Manse Rd, Whitburn EH47 8EZ; Tel (01501) 43034; A. Mancini
Winchburgh, Craigton Pl, Winchburgh EH52 6RW; Tel 5-890348; M. Mitchell

Schools for Pupils with Special Educational Needs

Hospital and Home Teaching, Willowpark School, Gorgie Rd, Edinburgh EH11 3UB; Tel 0131-337 1622; D. Strathdee (Acting)
Beatlie, Main St, Winchburgh EH52 6RB; Tel (01506) 890350; K.E. White, DipCE. (36)
Beatlie Kirkhill Annexe, Kirkhill Primary School, Rashierigg Rd, Broxburn EH52 6AW; Tel (01506) 855796; K.E. White, DipCE
Cairnpark, Redhalll Hse Dr, Edinburgh EH14 1JA; Tel 0131-443 0903; H. Heslop, Dip.C.E.. (36)
Canonmills, Rodney St, Edinburgh EH7 4EL; Tel 0131-556 6000; M. Wilson, MA. (56)
Cedarbank, Cedarbank, Ladywell East, Livingston EH54 6DR; Tel (01506) 442172; D. Aitken, DipCE, MEd. (53)
Drylaw School, Easter Drylaw Dr, Edinburgh EH4 2RY; Tel 0131-343 6116; J. Perry, NFF. (54)
Forteviot, 14 Hope Terr, Edinburgh EH9 2AR; Tel 0131-536 0560; D. Leach, BA(Hons), DipCE. (18)
The Young People's Unit Royal Edinburgh Hospital, Tipperlinn Hse, Tipperlinn Rd, Edinburgh EH10 5HF; Tel 0131-447 2011; Mrs Margaret Wilson, BA
Gogarburn Hospital, Corstorphine, Edinburgh EH12 9BJ; Tel 0131-339 7416; D. Barkess (Acting). (36)

Graysmill, 1 Redhall Hse Dr, Edinburgh EH14 1JE; Tel 0131-443 8096; I.H. Elfick, BA, DipEd. (119)
Howdenhall Children's Unit, 39 Howdenhall Rd, Edinburgh EH16 6PG; Tel 0131-664 8488; I.A.J. Thom, MA. (10)
Kaimes, 140 Lasswade Rd, Edinburgh EH16 6RT; Tel 0131-664 8241; J. Ruddick, MA(Hons), BD(Hons), MEd. (81)
Kingsinch, 233 Gilmerton Rd, Edinburgh EH16 5UD; Tel 0131-664 1911; Maureen Price, DipHE. (76)
Lugton, Lugton Brae, Dalkeith EH22 1JX; Tel 0131-663 7146; W.B. Reynolds, DipCE. (128)
Oaklands, Broomhouse Cres, Edinburgh EH11 3UB; Tel 0131-455 7311; S. Harland, BSc(Hons)Soc
Piershill, 70 Willowbrae Rd, Edinburgh EH8 7HA; Tel 0131-661 1488; E. Simpson, DipCE. (24)
Pilrig Park, Balfour Pl, Edinburgh EH6 5DW; Tel 0131-554 7024/5; J.H. Mudie, DipCE. (75)
Pinewood, Elm Grove, Blackburn, Bathgate EH47 7OX; Tel (01506) 656374; R. Bayne, DipCE. (55)
Prospect Bank, 81 Restalrig Rd, Edinburgh EH6 8BQ; Tel 0131-553 2239; E.E.R. Little, DipCE. (53)
St Crispin's, Watertoun Rd, Edinburgh EH9 3HZ; Tel 0131-667 4831; M.B. Gillon, MEd, BA, DipCE. (57)
St Joseph's, Rosewell 32 Carnethie St, Rosewell EH24 9AT; Tel 0131-440 2022; Sister G. Keating, DipCE. (14)
St Nicholas', Gorgie Rd, Edinburgh EH11 2RG; Tel 0131-337 6077; C. McLaren, MA, DPSE. (77)
Westfield, Lugton Brae, Dalkeith EH22 1JX; Tel 0131-663 7145; J. Hunt, DipCE. (47)
Willowgrove Hse, 1–6 Willowgrove, Craigshill, Livingston EH54 5LU; Tel (01506) 434274; D. Aitken, DipCE, MEd
Willowpark, Gorgie Rd, Edinburgh EH11 2BG; Tel 0131-337 1622; D. Strathdee (Acting). (78)

Secondary Schools (12–18+)

Armadale Academy, West End, Armadale EH48 3LY; Tel (01501) 30601; R. Wilson, BSc. (701)
Balerno Community High, 5 Bridge Rd, Balerno EH14 7AQ; Tel 0131-449 5833; I.M. Nicol, MA, DipEd. (775)
Bathgate Academy, Edinburgh Rd, Bathgate EH48 1LF; Tel 51-53725; Dr Norman Reid, BSc, DipEd. (728)
Beeslack High, Edinburgh Rd, Penicuik EH26 0QF; Tel 71-678060; R.J. Staite, MA. (894)
Boroughmuir High, Viewforth, Edinburgh EH10 4LR; Tel 0131-229 9703; T.W. Dalgleish, BA, BSc(Hons), DipEd. (1072)
Broughton High, Carrington Rd, Edinburgh EH4 1EG; Tel 0131-332 7805; J. Scott, MA, DipEd. (892)
Broxburn Academy, Cardross Rd, Broxburn EH52 6AG; Tel 5-852521; Mrs K. Aggett, BA, MA. (666)
Castlebrae High, 2A Greendykes Rd, Edinburgh EH16 4DP; Tel 0131-661 1282; E.G. Smith, BA, BSc(Hons), DipEd. (383)
Craigmount High, Craigs Rd, Edinburgh EH12 8NH; Tel 0131-339 6823; W. Trotter, MA. (1201)
Craigroyston Community High, Pennywell Rd, Edinburgh EH4 4QP; Tel 0131-332 7801; H.D. MacKenzie, MA. (419)
Currie High, 31 Dolphin Ave, Currie EH14 5RD; Tel 0131-449 2165; R. Paul, MA(Hons), DipEd. (955)
Dalkeith High, 23 Newmills Rd, Dalkeith EH22 1ET; Tel 0131-663 4642; W.J. Sleater, MA, DipEd. (908)
Deans Community High, Eastwood Pk, Deans, Livingston EH54 8PS; Tel 58-31972; R. Pietrasik, BSc(Hons), PGCE, DipEd. (765)
Drummond Community High, Cochran Terr, Edinburgh EH7 4BJ; Tel 0131-556 2651; K.R. Thomson, BSc(Hons). (476)
Dunbar Grammar, Summerfield Rd, Dunbar EH42 1NJ; Tel (01368) 63339; W.R. Collin, BSc. (547)
Firrhill High, Firrhill, Edinburgh EH14 1DP; Tel 0131-441 4501; J. Grant-Wood, MA. (760)
Forrester High, Broomhouse Rd, Edinburgh EH12 9AE; Tel 0131-334 9262; A. Clapperton, MA(Hons), DipEd, MEd. (865)
Gracemount High, Lasswade Rd, Edinburgh EH16 6TZ; Tel 0131-664 7440; A.G. Smith, BSc(Hons). (461)
Greenhall High, Gowkshill, Gorebridge EH23 4PE; Tel 49-20156; A.C. Pacey, MA(Hons). (394)
Holy Rood R.C. High, Duddingston Rd West, Edinburgh EH15 1ST; Tel 0131-661 5871; J.P. Beynon, BA. (558)
Inveralmond Community High, Willowbank, Ladywell, Livingston EH54 6HN; Tel 58-38093/14/5/6; R. Stewart, MA(Hons), MA(Educ), DipEd. (915)
James Gillespie's High, Lauderdale St, Edinburgh EH9 1DD; Tel 0131-447 1900; C. Finlayson, MA, DipEd. (1132)
Knox Academy, Pencaitland Rd, Haddington EH41 4DT; Tel (0162 0182) 3387; A.B. Ellis, BA, MEd. (797)
Lasswade High School Centre, Eskdale Dr, Bonnyrigg EH19 2LA; Tel 0131-663 7171; H.S. Flockhart, BSc. (1241)
Leith Academy, 20 Academy Pk, Edinburgh EH6 8JQ; Tel 0131-554 0606; K.A. Hyslop, BSc. (854)
Liberton High, Gilmerton Rd, Edinburgh EH17 7PT; Tel 0131-664 7514; J.W. Vettese, MA(Hons), DipEd. (904)
Linlithgow Academy, Braehead Rd, Linlithgow EH49 6EH; Tel 5-843211; J. Low, BSc(Hons). (1076)
Musselburgh Grammar, 86 Inveresk Rd, Musselburgh EH21 7BA; Tel 0131-665 4278/9; T. Christie, BSc. (971)
Newbattle High, 64 Easthouses Rd, Dalkeith EH22 4EW; Tel 0131-663 4191/6623; S.G. Smith, BSc, DipEd. (617)
North Berwick High, Grange Rd, North Berwick EH39 4QS; Tel (01620) 4661; G.M.R. Smuga, MA(Hons), DipEd. (631)
Our Lady's, (R.C. High) West Main St, Broxburn EH52 5LJ; Tel (01506) 853759; J.G. McGovern, BSc, MRSC. (213)
Penicuik High, 39a Carlops Rd, Penicuik EH26 9EP; Tel 71-674165/672175; A. Waugh, BSc(Hons), DipEd. (823)
Portobello High, Duddingston Rd, Edinburgh EH15 1NF; Tel 0131-669 2324; J.H. Purves, MA. (1383)
Preston Lodge High, Park View, Prestonpans EH32 9QJ; Tel 4-811170; D.S. Allen, BSc, DipEd. (954)
Queensferry High, Ashburnham Rd, South Queensferry EH30 9JN; Tel 0131-331 1944; D.M. Lewis, BSc(Hons). (885)
Ross High, Well Wynd, Tranent EH33 2EQ; Tel 4-610433; Dr C.C. Lamont, MA. (790)
St Augustine's High R.C., Broomhouse Rd, Edinburgh EH12 9AD; Tel 0131-334 6801; Vacancy. (650)
St David's R.C. High, Abbey Rd, Dalkeith EH22 3AD; Tel 0131-663 1961/2; T.J. O'Malley, BSc, ARIC, DipEd. (646)
St Kentigern's R.C. Academy, West Main St, Blackburn EH47 7LX; Tel 51-56404/5/6/7; Dr John Watts, MA, MSc. (736)
St Mary's R.C. Academy, Edinburgh Rd, Bathgate EH48 1EQ; Tel 51-54638; P. McCourt, BSc, HNC. (828)
St Thomas of Aquin's R.C. High, 12 Chalmers St, Edinburgh EH3 9ES; Tel 0131-229 8734/5/6; J.P. Dames, BSc. (660)
The James Young High, Quentin Rise, Dedridge, West Livingston EH54 6NG; Tel 5-414244; N. Henriksen, BSc, MEd. (843)
The Royal High, East Barnton Ave, Edinburgh EH4 6JP; Tel 0131-336 2261; M.M. MacIver, MA, DipEd, MEd. (1122)
Trinity Academy, Craighall Ave, Edinburgh EH6 4RT; Tel 0131-552 8101; P.G. Galloway, BA, DipCom. (771)
Tynecastle High, McLeod St, Edinburgh EH11 2NJ; Tel 0131-337 3488; Michael J. Hay, BSc, DipEd. (894)
West Calder High, Limefield, Polbeth, West Calder EH55 8QN; Tel 5-871510; W.A. Gourlay, MA. (833)
Wester Hailes Education Centre, 5 Murrayburn Dr, Edinburgh EH14 2SU; Tel 0131-442 2201; A. Goodall, MA. (600)
Whitburn Academy, Shanks Rd, Whitburn EH47 0HL; Tel (01501) 40675; W. D. Williamson, MA. (988)

Music Centre

Broughton High School, Carrington Rd, Edinburgh EH4 1EG; Tel 0131-332 7805

Outdoor Centres

Allermuir Outdoor Education Resource Base c/o Firrhill High School, Firrhill, Edinburgh EH14 1DP; Tel 0131-441 1001; P. Leach
Benmore, Sandbank, by Dunoon, Argyll PA23 8QX; Tel (01369) 6337; *Deputy Principal* A. Beveridge
Innerwick, Innerwick Field Study Centre, Innerwick EH42 1SE; Tel (0136 84) 319; *Deputy Principal* P. Leach
Lagganlia, Kincraig, Kingussie, Inverness-shire PH21 1NG; Tel (01544) 651265; R.F.J. Arrowsmith
Low Port Centre, 1 Blackness Rd, Linlithgow EH49 7HZ; Tel 5-844802; I. Fox
Prestonpans Education Centre Gardiner Terr, Prestonpans EH32 9ET; Tel 4-814058; N.T. Henderson

Resource Centres

Castlehill Urban Studies Centre, Cannonball House, Castle Hill, Edinburgh EH1 2ND; Tel 0131-226 7467; Mrs H. Quick
Dean Education Centre, Belford Rd, Edinburgh EH4 3DS; Tel 0131-343 3960; R.O. Williams
Dr Bell's Primary Drama Centre, Junction Pl, Edinburgh EH6 5JA; Tel 0131-554 3073; Miss M. Anderson
Midlothian Teachers' Centre, 62a Polton St, Bonnyrigg EH19 3DG; Tel 0131-663 0770; G.A.S. Wilson
Off-Air Recording, Tel 0131-332 6971
Preston Pans Education Centre, Gardiner Terr, Preston Pans EH32 9ET; Tel (01875) 814058; N.T. Henderson
Primary Education, Tel 0131-332 2710
School Libraries, Tel 0131-332 6971
St Bernard's Centre, Dean Park St, Edinburgh EH4 1JY; Miss I.F. Fraser
Teaching Development Centre, Elm Grove, Blackburn EH47 7QW; Tel (01506) 634040; Miss D.L. Jarvis
Theatre Arts Centre, Davie St, Edinburgh EH8 9EB; Tel 0131-667 2388; Ms P. Smith

Orkney Islands

Population 19,612
Council Offices, School Pl, Kirkwall, Orkney KW15 1NY; Tel (01856) 873535; Fax (01856) 874615

Education and Recreation Services Department

Council Offices, School Pl, Kirkwall, Orkney KW15 1NY; Tel (01856) 873535; Fax (01856) 876327
Director of Education and Recreation Services J.J. Anderson, BA, DipEd
Depute Director M.J.F. Drever, MA
Careers Officer C. Cook, BSc(Hons,), DipCG
Careers Officer A.M. Macleod, BA, DCG, FSA(Scot)
General Adviser E. Holt, FTCL, ARCM
Senior Assistant Director L. Manson, MA
Secondary Curriculum Co-ordinator H. Robertson
Catering Manager H. Ziegert
County Librarian R. Leslie Laing St, Kirkwall; Tel (01856) 873166
Principal Educational Psychologist P.J. Shearer, MA
Primary Curriculum Co-ordinator I. Drever

Number of Schools
20 primary (1,601); 2 comprehensive (1,284); 4 secondary & primary (313); 1 special (22)

Day of Committee Meeting
Every sixth Wednesday

Requisition Periods for School Supplies
April

Other Authorities with whom Joint Purchasing Arrangements are made
Counties Furniture Group

Education Committee

Chair I.M. MacDonald 5 Palace Gdns, Kirkwall
Vice-Chair B.M. Murray 2 Alfred Terr, Stromness

Members of the Committee
M. Bichan, J. Foubister, T.S. Hagan, H. Halcro-Johnston, S.R. Hill, J. Marwick, J.W.R. Moar, J. Sinclair, F.F. Scott, K.A. Sutherland

AREA OFFICES

Community Education Office

Stromness Academy, Stromness, Orkney; Tel (01856) 850660
Area Community Education Officer B. Innes
Area Community Education Officer Vacancy

Kirkwall and St Ola Community Centre,

Broad St, Kirkwall, Orkney; Tel (01856) 873354
Area Community Education Officer D.J. Steele

Careers Office

See chapter 17

Comprehensive Schools (12–18)

Kirkwall Grammar School, Kirkwall, Orkney; Tel (01856) 872102; Fax (01856) 872911; E. Sinclair, MA, DipEd. (824)
Stromness Academy, Stromness, Orkney; Tel (01856) 850660; Fax (01856) 850171; D. Sillar, BSc, MEd. (405)

Secondary Schools (12–16)

North Walls Junior High School, Lyness, Stromness, Orkney; Tel (01856) 791246; K.G. Michie. (23)
Pierowall Junior High School, Westray, Orkney, Orkney; Tel (01857) 677353; A. Sangster, MA. (39)
Sanday Junior High School, Sanday, Orkney; Tel (01857) 600228; R. Thorne, MA. (23)
Stronsay Junior High School, Stronsay, Orkney; Tel (01857) 616246; G. Macdonald. (16)

Outdoor Centres

Birsay Outdoor Centre, Birsay, Orkney; Tel (01856) 873535; *Warden* M. Irvine
Hoy Outdoor Centre, Hoy, Orkney; Tel (01856) 873535; *Warden* C. Clark
Rackwick Outdoor Centre, Hoy, Orkney; Tel (01856) 873535; *Warden* K. Wright

Special Education

Glaitness Aurrida School, Kirkwall, Orkney; Tel (01856) 870330. (M.H. Various) (Mixed) (22)

Shetland Islands

Population 22,522
Town Hall, Lerwick, Shetland ZE1 0HB; Tel (01595) 3535; Fax (01595) 4349

Education Department

Schlumberger Base, Lerwick, Shetland Isles ZE1 0PX; Tel (01595) 3800; Fax (01595) 2810
Director of Education J.G. Halcrow, MA, BMus DipEd
Divisional Education Officer (JHS and Secondary) H. Payton, BSc

Divisional Education Officer (Support Services) J. McLaughlin, MA
Divisional Education Officer (Primary/Nursery) L. Millham, DCE
Administration Manager E. Smaaskjaer, BA
Education Adviser (General Secondary) Vacancy
Education Adviser (Pre School) S. Gray, DCE
Assistant Education Adviser (5–14) C. Brown, DCE
Education Adviser (Science and Technology) J. Pedley, BSc
Education Adviser (Special Needs) L. Roberts, BA, DipEd, CertRemEd
Education Adviser (General Primary) M.E. Robertson, DCE
Education Adviser (Health and Physical Education) R. Williamson, DPE
Education Adviser (Creative and Aesthetic Studies) G.D. Yeaman, DipMusEdRSAM, DRSAM
Principal Psychologist J. Kane, MSc, BSc, DipMan(Open), AFBPsS, CPsychol
Client Officer M. Williamson
Senior Careers Officer A. Carter, MA, DipCG
Director of Design and Technical Services J.A. Inkster, BSc, CEng, MICE, FIWEM, FIHT
Director of Finance A. Matthews, CIPFA
Supplies Officer Administration Manager
Director of Leisure and Recreation J. Nicholson, DipYCW
Chief Librarian J.G. Hunter, ALA
Co-ordinator for Youth Training M. McDonald, MInstAM, MISM, AMITD
Education/Industry Liaison Officer E.K. Smith, DCE
Number of Schools
Primary schools 27; secondary school 1, combined secondary/primary schools 8; further education college 1
Day of Committee Meeting
Monday every six weeks
Requisition Period for School Supplies
February
Other Authorities with whom Joint Purchasing Arrangements are made
None

Education Committee

Chair W.A. Smith, BEM, FEIS, JP, 14 Bruce Cres, Lerwick
Vice-Chair P. Malcolmson Skersund, Upper Sand, Lerwick
Members of the Committee
M.U. Colligan, JP, M.L. Flaws, JP, F.B. Grains, JP, L.G. Groat, J.M. Hannah, BA, L.Hutchinson, Rev B. Knight, W.H. Manson, Rev. G. Munro, J.P. Nicolson, MA, DipEd, T.H. Scott, J.L.B. Smith, L.S. Smith, MA, BD, L.S. Smith, W.N. Stove, Rev R.C. Wilson

Careers Office

See chapter 17

Six-year Comprehensive School (12–18)

Anderson High, Lerwick ZE1 0BA; Tel (01595) 2306; G. Jamieson, C.Chem, MRSC. (915)

Junior High Schools (12–16)

Aith, Bixter; Tel (0159 581) 206; G. Moffat, DCE. (144)
Baltasound, Baltasound, Unst, Shetland, Shetland Isles; Tel (0195 781) 316; A. Spence, BSc. (121)
Brae High School, Brae, Shetland Isles; Tel (0180 622) 370; J.A. Irvine, BSc. (12–18) (6 yr Comp)
Mid Yell, Mid Yell, Shetland, Shetland Isles; Tel (01957) 2252; D. Jamieson, MA. (104)
Sandwick, Sandwick, Shetland Isles; Tel (0185 684) 454; R.A.B. Wishart, MA. (208)
Scalloway, Scalloway, Shetland Isles; Tel (0159 588) 546; A. Green, BSc. (301)
Symbister House, Whalsay, Shetland Isles; Tel (0180 66) 210; A.J. Williamson, BSc, JP. (166)

Strathclyde

Population 2,300,000 (1991)
Strathclyde Hse, 20 India St, Glasgow G2 4PF; Tel 0141-204 2900; Fax 0141-227 2870

Education Department

Strathclyde Hse, 20 India St, Glasgow G2 4PF; Tel 0141-204 2900
Chair Tom Farrell
Vice Chair Yvonne Robertson
Vice Chair T. Colyer
Senior Vice Chairman H. Revie
Director of Education F. Pignatelli, MA, MEd, FBIM, FRSA
Senior Depute Director David Montgomery, MA
Depute Director (Educational Development and Quality Assurance) David Alexander, MA, MLitt
Depute Director (Personnel and Head of Pre-Five Services) Keir Bloomer, MA, BA
Depute Director (Social Strategy) J. G. Urulgrew, BSc
Assistant Director D.W. Thomas, IPFA
Assistant Director B. Gardner, BSc, BA
Assistant Director L. Marsh, BA, MBA, DPE
Chief Adviser Ms J. Bowen, MA
Chief Adviser K. Gavin, MA, DipEd
Chief Adviser J. Goodall, BSc, DipEd
Chief Inspector S. Jardine, BSc, PGCE
Chief Inspector Ms G. White, BA, MEd
Head of Staff College Ms V. Casteel, BA
Regional Inspector W. Coyle, BSc
Regional Adviser (Drama) R. Mackie, DSD, CDS
Regional Adviser (European Studies) S. Wilson, BA, MA
Regional Adviser (Pre-Five) Mrs A. Holman, MA, DipSocSc
Regional Adviser (Health Education) A. Ramsay
Regional Adviser (Resource Service) Mrs M. Sked
Regional Adviser (Religious Education) Ms S. Stevenson
Number of Schools
289 Pre-5 Schools and Centres; 893 primary; 177 secondary
Special Schools
166 (including hospital schools and classes)

Careers Offices

See chapter 17

Community Education Accommodation and Community Education Wings Attached to Primary Schools

Eastwood Area
Busby Primary School, Church Rd, Clarkston, Glasgow G76 8EB
East Inverclyde Area
Kings Glen Primary School, Cardross Cres, Greenock PA15 3HT
St. Lawrence's Primary School, Ingleston St, Greenock PA15 1HN
Linwood Area
Cochrane Castle Primary School, Craigview Ave, Johnstone PA5 0JH; Tel (01505) 35873
Lochwinnoch Primary School, Calder St, Lochwinnoch PA12 4DG
Barsail Primary School, Park Moor, Park Mains, Erskine, Strathclyde; Tel 0141-812 4493
St. James Primary School, Albert Rd, Renfrew, Strathclyde
West Inverclyde Area
Larkfield Primary School, Chester Rd, Greenock PA16 0TT
Springfield Primary School, Berwick Rd, Greenock PA16 0HA
St. Joseph's Primary School, Wren Rd, Greenock PA16 7NH

Community Education Accommodation and Community Wings Attached to Secondary Schools

Barrhead High School, Aurs Rd, Barrhead G78 2SJ
Castlehead High School, Camphill, Paisley PA1 1HL; Tel 0141-884 7329
Linwood High School, Stirling Dr, Linwood PA3 3NB
Mearns Castle High School, Waterford Rd, Newton Mearns, Glasgow G77
Merksworth High School, Gockston Rd, Paisley PA3 2NG; Tel 0141-848 1017
Park Mains High School, Park Mains, Erskine, Strathclyde
Port Glasgow H.S., Marloch Ave, Port Glasgow PA14 6PP
Renfrew High School, Hsining Rd, Renfrew PA4 0AN
Sacred Heart High School, Barrhead Rd, Paisley PA2 7LG
St. Columba's High School, Burnside Rd, Gourock PA19 1XX
St. Cuthbert's H.S., Hallhill Rd, Spateston, Johnstone PA5 0SD
St. Luke's High School, Springfield Rd, Barrhead G78 1AH
Wellington Academy, Dempster St, Greenock, Strathclyde; Tel (01475) 28288
Woodfarm High School, Robslee Rd, Thornliebank, Glasgow G46 7HG

Adult Education Centre

Whitletts Rd, Ayr; Tel (01292) 285285

Argyll & Bute Division

Argyll Hse, Alexandra Pde, Dunoon, Argyll PA23 8AJ; Tel (01369) 4000
Divisional Education Officer J.G. Harcus, MA, MEd
Senior Education Officer G.D. Jeyes, MA, MEd
Education Officer B. McLeary, MA
Education Officer R.I. Malcolm, MA, MEd
Senior Adviser J. Queen, DipPE, DipManStudies
Senior Inspector C. Shirley, MSc, DipProfStudies
Inspector J. McGeer, BA, MEd, DipSecStudies
Educational Psychologist D.C. Devine, BSc, MSc
Educational Psychologist J. Clark, BSc, MSc
Educational Psychologist A. Hall, MA
2 Tom-a-Mhoid Rd, Dunoon PA23 7HN; Tel (01369) 6918

Special Schools (Residential)

Drummore, Oban, Argyll PA34 3SB; Tel (01631) 64811; P. McGovern
Meadows, Campbeltown, Argyll PA28 6LE; Tel (01586) 52397; Mrs A.S. Cousin
White Gates, Lochgilphead, Argyll PA31 8SY; Tel (01546) 2583; G.D. Meredith

Secondary Schools

Campbeltown Grammar, Campbeltown, Argyll PA28 6JS; Tel (01586) 52907; P. Fergusson, DPE
Dunoon Grammar, Ardenslate Rd, Kirn, Argyll PA23 8LU; Tel (01369) 5010; J. Rhodes, MA
Islay High, Bowmore, Isle of Islay PA43 7JY; Tel (0149 681) 239; Mrs J. Hunter, MA
Lochgilphead High, Lochgilphead, Argyll PA31 8JY; Tel (01546) 2598; J.Y. Murray, BSc, MEd
Oban High, Oban, Argyll PA34 4JB; Tel (01631) 64231; B.R. Mitchell, BSc
Rothesay Academy, Isle of Bute PA20 0BQ; Tel (01700) 3367; A.P. Gilmour, BSc
Tarbert Academy, Tarbert, Argyll PA29 6TE; Tel (0880820) 269; G. Bishop, MA
Tiree High, Cornaigmore, Isle of Tiree PA77 6XA; Tel (0187 92) 383; A.C.J. Hunter, BA
Tobermory High, Tobermory, Isle of Mull PA75 6PB; Tel (01688) 2062; G.A. Farquharson, MA

Teachers' Centre

Cowal Teachers' Centre, Sandbank, By Dunoon, Argyll PA23 8PA; Tel (01369) 6548/6761

Community Education, Neighbourhood and Youth Centres

Divisional CES Offices HQ, 2 Tom-a-Mhoid Rd, Dunoon PA23 7HN; Tel (01369) 6476
Dunoon C.E. Centre, Edward St, Dunoon, Argyll PA23 7NY; Tel (01369) 4669
Kintyre C.E. Centre, Stewart Rd, Campeltown, Argyll PA28 6AT; Tel (01586) 52732
Lochgilphead C.E. Centre, Manse Brae, Lochgilphead, Argyll PA31 8SY; Tel (01546) 2177
Lorn C.E. Centre, Albany St, Oban, Argyll PA34 4AR; Tel (01631) 62466
The Moat C.E. Centre, Stuart St, Rothesay PA20 0EP; Tel (01700) 3696

Ayr Division

Regional Offices, Ayr KA7 1DR; Tel (01292) 266922
Divisional Education Officer J. Pearson, BSc, MInstP
Senior Education Officer A.P. Craig, MA, MEd, DipRE
Education Officer Mrs M. Burnell, DCE, ITQ
Education Officer E. Darcy, DipBusAdmin
Education Officer M. Maciver, MA, BA, DipEd
Education Officer Miss C.M. Pryce, DipComm
Senior Adviser H. Johnstone, BSc
Senior Inspector S. McKenzie, BA, BEd, DCE
Inspector W. Clark, BSc
Inspector N. Connaughton, MEd
Inspector G. Short, MA, MEd

Psychological Service

Barrhill Rd, Cumnock KA18 1PG; Tel (01290) 22023; D. Manson
6A Kilwinning Rd, Vineburgh Pk, Irvine, Strathclyde; Tel (01294) 72427; A. Mackie
30 North Hamilton St, Kilmarnock KA1 2QL; Tel (01563) 25795; D. Stewart
Donaldson Ave, Saltcoats KA21 5AG; Tel (01294) 63495; T. William
Wills Rd, Ayr KA8 9NL; Tel (01292) 261738

Special Schools (Day)

Craigpark School, Mainholm Rd, Ayr, Strathclyde; Tel (01292) 289326; Ms M. Burns
Haysholm, Bank St, Irvine KA12 0NE; Tel (01294) 72481; Mrs J.M. McDermott
Invergarven School, Henrietta St, Girvan KA26 9EJ; Tel (01465) 2035; Mrs K. Faulder-Branson
James McFarlane School, Dalry Rd, Androssan, Strathclyde; Tel (01294) 61370; Mrs J. Calvert, BSc, DipSpEd
James Reid, Primrose Pl, Saltcoats KA21 6LH; Tel (01294) 67105; Mrs I. Passway
Kirkmichael Hse, Kirkmichael, Maybole KA19 7PR; Tel (0165 55) 212; D. Ridge
Linfern School, London Rd Centre, London Rd, Kilmarnock, Strathclyde; Tel (01563) 34112; Miss C. Murray
Marnock School, London Rd Centre, London Rd, Kilmarnock KA10 2QJ; Tel (01563) 32597; Mrs Telfer
Marnock Senior Unit, London Rd Centre, London Rd, Kilmarnock KA10 2QJ; Tel (01563) 40657; Mrs M. O'Brien
Meadowbank, Bolestyle Rd, Kirkmichael, Maybole KA19 7PN; Tel (0165 55) 249; Miss J.H.D. McArthur
North Ayrshire District General Hospital School, Crosshouse; Mrs H. Donald
Park, Grassyards Rd, Kilmarnock KA3 7BB; Tel (01563) 25316; Mrs A. Wilson
Rosebank School, Belmont Ave, Ayr KA7 2PS; Tel (01292) 269422; Mrs M. Muir

South Park School, Belmont Ave, Ayr, Strathclyde; Tel (01292) 282259; K. O'Hagan
Stanecastle, Burns Cres, Girdle Toll, Irvine KA11 1AQ; Tel (01294) 211914; Mrs O. Heron
Wallaceton Works School, by Maybole KA19 8LU; Tel (0146 581) 274; D. Rule
West Park, Playingfields Rd, Crosshouse, Kilmarnock KA2 0JJ; Tel (01563) 32300; Miss E.A. Clyne
Witchill, Witch Rd, Kilmarnock, Strathclyde; Tel (01563) 33863; Mrs S. Cunningham
Woodstock, 30 North Hamilton St, Kilmarnock KA1 2QJ; Tel (01563) 33550; Mrs A.T. Black

Secondary Schools

Ardrossan Academy, Sorbie Rd, Ardrossan KA22 8AR; Tel (01294) 61931/2; B. Cunningham, DipPE
Arran High, Lamlash, Isle of Arran KA27 8NG; Tel (0177 016) 341; D.A. Oakes, BA
Auchenharvie Academy, Saltcoats Rd, Stevenston KA20 3JW; Tel (01294) 605156; Mrs M.M. Dick, MA
Auchinleck Academy, Sorn Rd, Auchinleck, Cumnock KA18 2LY; Tel (01290) 20617; J.C. Aitken, BSc
Ayr Academy, Fort St, Ayr KA7 1HX; Tel (01292) 262302; A.C. Moir, MA
Belmont Academy, Belmont Rd, Ayr KA7 2PG; Tel (01292) 281733; W. Stewart, MA, BA
Carrick Academy, Kirkoswald Rd, Maybole KA19 8BP; Tel (01655) 82389; M. Goodwin, BSc
Cumnock Academy, Ayr Rd, Cumnock KA18 1EH; Tel (01290) 21228; R. Smith, MA
Doon Academy, Ayr Rd, Dalmellington, Ayr KA6 7ST; Tel (01292) 550521/2; G. Bone, BSc
Garnock Academy, School Rd, Kilbirnie KA25 7AX; Tel (01505) 682685; Dr D.J. White, BSc
Girvan Academy, The Avenue, Girvan KA26; Tel (01465) 3008; T. Proudfoot, BSc
Grange Academy, Beech Ave, Kilmarnock KA1 2EW; Tel (01563) 21969; H.G. Millar, BSc, ARCST
Greenwood Academy, Dreghorn, Irvine KA11 4HL; Tel (01294) 213124; P. Galbraith, BSc
Irvine Royal Academy, Academy Rd, Irvine KA12 8RN; Tel (01294) 76221; A.A. Crawford, BSc
James Hamilton Academy, Sutherland Dr, Kilmarnock KA3 7DF; Tel (01563) 33221; W. McGregor, MA, MEd
Kilmarnock Academy, Elmbank Dr, Kilmarnock KA1 3BS; Tel (01563) 25509; F. Donnelly, MA
Kilwinning Academy, Dalry Rd, Kilwinning, Strathclyde; Tel (01294) 51316; W. Ballantyne, BSc, MA
Kyle Academy, Overmills Rd, Ayr, Strathclyde; Tel (01292) 262234; J.H. Cooke, BSc, MA, DipEd
Largs Academy, Flatt Rd, Largs KA30 9JX; Tel (01475) 675421; William C. Inglis, MA
Loudoun Academy, Glasgow Rd, Galston KA4 8PD; Tel (01563) 820061; R.J. Findlay, MA
Mainholm Academy, Mainholm Rd, Ayr KA8 0QQ; Tel (01292) 281016; Andrew D.C. Allan, MA
Marr College, Dundonald Rd, Troon KA10 7AB; Tel (01292) 311082; Robert McCarrison, BSc, MIBiol
Prestwick Academy, Newdykes Rd, Prestwick KA9 2LB; Tel (01292) 77121; R.G. Storie, DipEd
Queen Margaret Academy, Dalmellington Rd, Ayr KA7 3TL; Tel (01292) 268379; Daniel Boyle
Ravenspark Academy, Kilwinning Rd, Irvine KA12 8SJ; Tel (01294) 78756; R. Reid, MA
Sacred Heart Academy, Henrietta St, Girvan KA26 9AW; Tel (01465) 3732; Brian Murray, MA
Stewarton Academy, Cairnduff Pl, Stewarton, Kilmarnock KA3 3DL; Tel 01560-82342; Richard Barron, MA, MEd
St Andrew's Academy, Jack's Rd, Saltcoats KA21 5NT; Tel 605221; T.F. Moynihan, MA
St Conval's High, Auchinleck Rd, Cumnock KA18 1AN; Tel 20595; D. Brendan Dorrian, BSc
St Joseph's Academy, Grassyards Rd, Kilmarnock KA3 7SL; Tel (01563) 27197; John McEwan, MA, BA
St Michael's Academy, Winton Pl, Kilwinning KA13 6LJ; Tel (01294) 51564; James McCutcheon, MA

Outdoor Pursuits Centres

Arran Outdoor Centre, North High Corrie, Corrie, Isle of Arran KA27 8JB; Tel (0127 0181) 269
Craigenrae Outdoor Centre, Rowantree, Bargrennan, Newton Stewart, Wigtonshire, Strathclyde; Tel (0167 184) 230
Craigie Outdoor Centre, Main St, Craigie, By Kilmarnock KA1 5LY; Tel (0156 386) 209
Craigmalloch Outdoor Centre, Loch Doon, Dalmellington, Ayr KA6 7PE; Tel (01292) 550829
Glaisnock Hse, Glaisnock Rd, Cumnock KA18 4PJ; Tel (01290) 20432
Lendalfoot Outdoor Centre, Lendalfoot, By Girvan KA26 0JG; Tel (0146 589) 236
Newmilns Dry Ski Slope, 35 High St, Newmilns KA16 9EB; Tel Newmilns 223
Seafield Outdoor Centre, Seafield Towers, Ardrossan, Strathclyde; Tel (01294) 64234

Teachers' Centres

Educational Development Service, Newton Centre, Green Street La, Ayr KA8 8BH; Tel (01292) 260325
Greenwood Teachers' Centre, Dreghorn, Irvine KA11 4HL; Tel (01294) 212716
Microcomputer Resource Centre, Green St, Ayr, Strathclyde; Tel (0117) 928 9898
Technician Centre, London Rd, Kilmarnock, Strathclyde; Tel (01563) 44550; Brian Richmond

Youth Centres

Afton Youth Centre, The Castle, Newcumnock, Strathclyde
Annick Community Centre, East Rd, Irvine, Strathclyde; Tel (01294) 78615
Ardbeg Community Centre, Ardbeg Ave, Kilmarnock, Strathclyde; Tel (01563) 35913
Ardchoille Community Centre, Hayocks Rd, Stevenson, Strathclyde; Tel (01294) 604314
Ardeer Youth and Community Centre, Shore Rd, Stevenston, Strathclyde; Tel (01294) 66861
Ardrossan Social and Recreational Wing, Sorbie Rd, Ardrossan, Strathclyde; Tel (01294) 62911
Argyle Youth and Community Centre, Campbell Ave, Saltcoats, Strathclyde; Tel (01294) 67267
Auchenharvie Social and Recreational Wing, Saltcoats Rd, Stevenson, Strathclyde; Tel (01294) 603791
Auchinleck Community Centre, Well Rd, Auchinleck, Strathclyde; Tel (01290) 20329
Ballantrae Community Centre, Main St, Ballantrae, Girvan, Strathclyde
Barr Community Centre, Greig Rd, Barr, Girvan, Strathclyde
Barr Youth and Community Centre, Station Rd, Galston, Strathclyde; Tel (01563) 820951
Barrhill Centre, Bank Ave, Cumnock, Strathclyde; Tel (01290) 21066
Barrhill Community Centre, Barrhill, By Girvan, Strathclyde
Barrmill Community Centre, Barrmill, Beith, Strathclyde
Barshare Community Wing, St John's Primary School, John Weir Ave, Barshare, Cumnock, Strathclyde
Beith Community Centre, 45–47 Kings Rd, Beith, Strathclyde; Tel (0150 55) 3187
Bellsbank Community Wing, Bellsbank Primary School, Craiglea Cres, Bellsbank, Dalmellington, Strathclyde; Tel (01292) 550493
Belmont Social and Recreational Wing, Belmont Rd, Ayr, Strathclyde; Tel (01292) 263237
Bridgend Centre, Bridgend, Kilbirnie, Strathclyde; Tel (01505) 684512
Brown's Institute, McLeod St, Cumnock, Strathclyde
Caley Centre, Station Rd, Stevenston, Strathclyde; Tel (01294) 602027
Carrick Social and Recreational Wing, Kirkeswald Rd, Maybole, Strathclyde; Tel (01655) 82398
Castlepark Community Centre, Irvine; Tel (01294) 311238
Catrine Community Centre, Institute Ave, Catrine, Strathclyde; Tel 50689
Central School Community Wing, Kirkland Rd, Kilbirnie, Strathclyde

Colmonell Community Centre, 37 Main St, Colmonell, Girvan, Strathclyde
Coylton Community Centre, Hillhead, Coylton, Strathclyde; Tel (01292) 539
Cranberry Moss Community Centre, Cambusdoon Pl, Kilwinning, Strathclyde; Tel (01294) 57146
Crookedholm Community Centre, Grougar Rd, Crookedholm, Kilmarnock, Strathclyde
Crosshill Community Centre, Kirkmichael Rd, Crosshill, Maybole, Strathclyde; Tel (016554) 325
Crosshouse Community Centre, Gatehead Rd, Crosshouse, Kilmarnock, Strathclyde
Cumnock Social/Recreation Centre, Cumnock Academy, Ayr Rd, Cumnock, Strathclyde; Tel (01290) 20850
Dailly Community Centre, Main St, Dailly, Girvan, Strathclyde
Dalmellington Community Centre, Ayr Rd, Dalmellington, Strathclyde; Tel (01292) 550429
Dalry Community Centre, St Margaret's Ave, Dalry, Strathclyde; Tel (0129 483) 3288
Dalrymple Community Centre, 38 Barbieston Rd, Dalrymple, Strathclyde; Tel (0129 256) 469
Dalrymple Youth Centre, Barbieston Rd, Dalrymple, Strathclyde
Drongan Community Centre, Milmannoch Ave, Drongan, Strathclyde; Tel (0129 258) 591355
Drongan Youth Centre, Drongan Primary School, Milmannoch Ave, Drongan, Strathclyde
Fairlie Village Hall, Main Rd, Fairlie, Strathclyde
Fullarton Community Centre, Ayr Rd, Irvine, Strathclyde; Tel 78693
Galston Community Centre, Orchard St, Galston, Strathclyde; Tel (01563) 821329
Garnock Social and Recreational Wing, School Rd, Kirbirnie, Strathclyde; Tel (01505) 682687
Girdle Toll Community Centre, Burns Cres, Girdle Toll, Irvine, Strathclyde; Tel (01294) 211356
Girvan Community Centre, Dalrymple St, Girvan, Strathclyde; Tel (01465) 3480
Glenfield Pavilion, Queen's Dr, Kilmarnock, Strathclyde; Tel (01563) 43617
Grange Social & Recreation Wing, Beech Ave, Kilmarnock; Tel (01563) 31860
Greenwood Social and Recreational Wing, Campbell Pl, Dreghorn, Strathclyde; Tel (01294) 213439
Hurlford Community Centre, Hurlford, Kilmarnock, Strathclyde; Tel (01563) 24841
James Street Community Centre, James St, Dalry, Strathclyde; Tel (0129 483) 5007
Kilmaurs Community Centre, East Park Dr, Kilmaurs, Kilmarnock, Strathclyde; Tel (0156 381) 38662
Lamlash Village Hall, Lamlash, Isle of Arran, Strathclyde; Tel (017706) 256
Lanfine Community Centre, Auchenharvie Pl, Girdle Toll, Irvine, Strathclyde; Tel (01294) 215347
Largs Youth Centre, Flatt Rd, Largs, Strathclyde; Tel (01475) 73767
Lendalfoot Community Centre, Outdoor Centre, Lendalfoot, By Girvan, Strathclyde
Lochside Community Centre, Lochside Rd, Ayr, Strathclyde; Tel (01292) 263333
Logan Community Wing, Logangate Terr, Logan, Strathclyde
Longbar Community Centre, Auchengrae Rd, Longbar, Glengarnock, Strathclyde
Longpark Community Centre, Inellan Dr, Kilmarnock, Strathclyde; Tel (01563) 39873
Maidens Community Centre, Harbour Rd, Maidens, Girvan, Strathclyde
Mauchline Community Centre, Kilmarnock Rd, Mauchline, Strathclyde; Tel (01290) 50662
Maybole Community Centre, Ladylands Rd, Maybole, Strathclyde; Tel (01655) 83596
Mossblown and Drumley Community Centre, Annbank Rd, Mossblown, Strathclyde; Tel (01292) 520758
Muirkirk Community Wing, Burns Ave, Muirkirk, Strathclyde; Tel (0129 016) 324
Muirkirk Youth Centre, Main St, Muirkirk, Strathclyde; Tel (01290) 350
Nether Robertland IFE Wing, Pokelly Pl, Stewarton, Strathclyde
Nethermains Community Centre, Nethermains Rd, Kilwinning, Strathclyde; Tel (01294) 53816
Netherthird Community Centre, Ryderston Pl, Cumnock, Strathclyde; Tel (01290) 20105
New Cumnock Community Centre, The Castle, New Cumnock, Strathclyde; Tel (01290) 582
Newmilns Dry Ski Slope, High St, Newmilns, Strathclyde; Tel (01560) 22320
North Ayr Youth Project, 25 Wellington Sq, Ayr, Strathclyde; Tel (01292) 263721
Oakstaple Centre, Murray Pl, Kilmarnock, Strathclyde
Ochiltree CES Store, Main St, Ochiltree, Strathclyde; Tel (0129 017) 515
Ochiltree Community Centre, Main St, Ochiltree, Strathclyde; Tel (0129 017) 383
Ochiltree Youth Centre, Main St, Ochiltree, Strathclyde; Tel (0129 017) 515
Old Dailly Youth Centre, Old Dailly, By Girvan
Onthank Community Centre, Kirkton Rd, Onthank, Kilmarnock, Strathclyde; Tel (01563) 40310
Patna Community Centre, Doonside Ave, Patna, Strathclyde; Tel (01292) 530
Pinwherry Community Centre, Muck Rd, Pinwherry, Girvan, Strathclyde
Prestwick Community Centre, Caerlaverock Rd, Prestwick, Strathclyde; Tel (01292) 78235
Prestwick Social and Recreational Wing, Newdykes Rd, Prestwick, Strathclyde; Tel (01292) 77700
Queen Margaret Social and Recreational Wing, Dalmellington Rd, Ayr, Strathclyde; Tel (01292) 265056
Rankinston Community Centre, Littlemill Pl, Rankinston, Strathclyde; Tel (01292) 590675
Ravenspark Social and Recreational Wing, Kilwinning Rd, Irvine, Strathclyde; Tel (01294) 72182
Redburn Community Centre, Dickson Dr, Irvine, Strathclyde; Tel (01294) 311279
Redburn IFE Project, Dickson Dr, Irvine, Strathclyde; Tel (01294) 73767
Redburn Youth Cafe, Dickson Dr, Irvine, Strathclyde; Tel (01294) 77049
Shortlees Community Centre, Blacksyke Ave, Kilmarnock, Strathclyde; Tel (01563) 25320
Skelmorlie Community Centre, Castle Rd, Skelimore, Wemyss Bay, Strathclyde; Tel (01475) 521856
Springside Community Centre, Overtoun Rd, Springside, Strathclyde; Tel (01294) 214565
St Joseph's Social & Recreation Wing, Grassyards Roads, Kilmarnock, Strathclyde
St Matthew's IFE Wing, McDonald Dr, Kilmarnock, Strathclyde
Stair Community Centre, Trabboch
Stewarton Annick Youth and Community Centre, Stewarton; Tel (01560) 82934
Symington Community Centre, North Rd, Symington, Strathclyde; Tel (01292) 830700
Tarbolton Community Centre, Montgomerie St, Tarbolton, Strathclyde; Tel (01292) 277
Towerlands Community Centre, Towerlands Farm Centre, Bourtreehill, Irvine, Strathclyde; Tel (01294) 211374
Townend Youth & Community Centre, Townfoot, Main St, Dreghorn, Strathclyde; Tel (01294) 212720
Troon Youth Centre, St Meddans St, Troon, Strathclyde; Tel (01292) 313331
Waterside Community Centre, Hareshaw Centre, Waterside, Kilmarnock, Strathclyde
Wellington Leisure Centre, 24 Wellington Square, Ayr, Strathclyde; Tel (01292) 265815
West Kilbride Community Centre, Corse St, West Kilbride, Strathclyde; Tel (01294) 822144
West Park Community Centre, Irvine Rd, Kilmaurs, Strathclyde; Tel (01563) 38348
Whitlees Community Centre, Carrick Pl, Ardrossan, Strathclyde; Tel (01294) 61700/62930
Whitletts Community Centre, Thorneyflat Rd, Ayr, Strathclyde; Tel (01292) 264578

Dunbarton Division

Regional Council Offices, Dumbarton G82 3PU; Tel (01389) 27000

Psychological Service

Clyde Hse, 170 Kilbowie Rd, Clydebank G81 2UA; Tel 0141-952 0311

Gartconner School, Gartshore Rd, Kirkintilloch G66 3TH; Tel 0141-775 2645
Kyle Rd, Kildrum, Cumbernauld G67 2DN; Tel (01236) 731041
Moss Cottage, Bridgend, Dumbarton G82 4AA; Tel (01389) 63279

Special Schools (Day)

Ardlui House School, East Montrose St, Helensburgh, Strathclyde; Tel (01436) 71798; Mrs C. Anderson
Auchentoshan, Mountblow Rd, Dalmuir G81 4SW; Tel (01389) 72171; Miss P.M. Lawrie
Cunard Unit, Whitecrook School, Cochno St, Clydebank, Strathclyde; Tel 0141-952 6614; E. Quinn
East Bay, 32 East Clyde St, Helensburgh G84 7PG; Tel (01436) 75854; Mrs M. Rue
Elmwood, C/o Braehead Primary School, Meadow Rd, Dumbarton G82 2DB; Tel (01389) 62166; Mrs M. Burger
Glencryan, Greenfaulds Rd, Cumbernauld G67 2XJ; Tel (01236) 724125; Miss A. Irvine, MBE
Hillview School, Mossknowe Building, Kildrum Ring Rd, Cumbernauld G67 2EL; Tel (01236) 736904; Mrs S. Gore
Langbrae School, Boghead Rd, Lenzie G66 4DP; Tel 0141-777 6269; Mrs J. McEwan
Merkland, Langmuir Rd, Kirkintilloch G66 2JD; Tel 0141-776 3454; J. Simmons
Mossknowe School, Kildrum Rd, Cumbernauld, Strathclyde; Tel (01236) 720405; *Vacancy* Mrs M. Brown
Mount Blow, Mountblow Rd, Dalmuir, Clydebank G81 4SW; Tel (01389) 72168; J.K. Clark
Middlemuir School, Cedar Dr, Lenzie, Glasgow G66 4RD; Tel 0141-776 3700; R.G. McDowell, BA
Pentland, Pentland Rd, Chryston, Strathclyde; Tel 0141-779 3351; J. Johnson
Waverley Park Hospital School, Kirkintilloch, Strathclyde; Tel 0141-776 5203; Mrs S. Boulton

Secondary Schools (12–18)

Abronhill High, Larch Rd, Cumbernauld, Strathclyde; Tel (01236) 731715; M. MacSween, MA, BLitt
Bearsden Academy, Morven Rd, Bearsden G61 3SU; Tel 0141-942 2297; N. MacLeod, BSc
Bishopbriggs High School, South Crosshill Rd, Bishopbriggs, Glasgow G64 2NN; Tel 0141-772 1529/7954; R.A. Stewart, BSc, ARIC
Boclair Academy, Inveroran Dr, Bearsden, Glasgow, Strathclyde; Tel 0141-943 0717; J. Aitchison, BSc
Braidfield High, Queen Mary Ave, Clydebank G81 2LR; Tel 0141-952 3265; N.I. MacKinnon, MA
Chryston High, Lindsaybeg Rd, Chryston G69 9DL; Tel 0141-779 2221/4131; R.J.B. Paris, MA, MEd, DipEd
Clydebank High, Shelley Dr, Clydebank G81 3EJ; Tel 0141-952 1011/0001; C. O'Brien, MA
Cumbernauld High, South Carbrain Ring Rd, Kildrum, Cumbernauld G67 2UF; Tel (01236) 725511/2; J.M. Mearns, MA
Douglas Academy, Mains Est, Milngavie G62 7HL; Tel 0141-956 2281; G. Wilson, BSc
Dumbarton Academy, Crosslet Rd, Dumbarton G82 2AJ; Tel (01389) 63373; J. Colraine, MA
Greenfaulds High, Athelstane Dr, Cumbernauld G67 4AQ; Tel (0123 67) 727956; A. Gillespie, BSc
Hermitage Academy, Campbell Dr, Colgrain, Helensburgh G84 7TB; Tel (01436) 72145/6; L.B. Young, BSc, PhD
Kilsyth Academy, Balmalloch, Kilsyth, Glasgow G65 9NF; Tel (01236) 822244/821450; J. Mitchell, BSc
Kirkintilloch High, Briar Rd, Kirkintilloch G66 3SA; Tel 0141-776 5293/14; D.H. Matheson, MA, BA
Lenzie Academy, Myrtle Ave, Lenzie G66 4HR; Tel 0141-776 6118/9; C.M. Brown, BSc, ARIC
Our Lady & St. Patrick's, Hawthornhill Rd, Dumbarton G82 4JN; Tel (01389) 62101; G. McDonald, MA, BA
Our Lady's High, Dowanfield Rd, Cumbernauld G67 1LA; Tel (01236) 721612
St Andrew's High, North Douglas St, Clydebank G81 1NQ; Tel 0141-952 7761; J. McHugh, BSc
St Columba's High, Gilmour St, Clydebank G81 2BW; Tel 0141-952 3163/15; L. Duffy, MA
St Maurice's High School, Westfield, Cumbernauld G68 9AG; Tel (01236) 732701; P. Mulheron, MA, BA
St Ninian's High, Bellfield Rd, Kirkintilloch G66 1DT; Tel 0141-776 1585; J. McNeill, BSc
Thomas Muir High, Wester Cleddans Rd, Bishopbriggs, Strathclyde; Tel 0141-762 3110; T.A. Sillars, MA
Turnbull High School, St Mary's Rd, Bishopbriggs, Glasgow G64 2EF; Tel 0141-772 9101; W. Morell, BSc
Vale of Leven Academy, Main St, Alexandria G83 0TS; Tel (01389) 57231; D. Penny, BSc

Community Education, Neighbourhood and Youth Centres

Abronhill C.E. Centre, Larch Rd, Cumbernauld G67 3AZ; Tel (0123 67) 733249
Adult Basic Education Unit, Dalmuir C.E. Centre, Duntocher Rd, Dalmuir G81 4SF; Tel 0141-941 1903
Alexandria C.E. Centre, Main St, Alexandria G83 0NU; Tel (01389) 59927/8
Auchinairn C.E. Centre, Auchinairn Rd, Bishopbriggs, Strathclyde; Tel 0141-762 0787
Bonhill C.E. Centre, Ladyton, Bonhill, Alexandria G83 9BH; Tel (01389) 53841
Clyde C.E. Centre, East Clyde St, Helensburgh G84 7PG; Tel (01436) 72775
Clydebank East C.E. Centre, Fleming Ave, Whitecrook, Clydebank G81 1AJ; Tel 0141-952 6515
Concord C.E. Centre, Town Centre, Dumbarton G82 1LJ; Tel (01389) 64687
Craighead C.E. Centre, Craighead Rd, Milton of Campsie, Strathclyde; Tel (01360) 311884
Dalmonach C.E. Centre, Second Ave, Bonhill G83 9BH; Tel (01389) 51422
Dalmuir C.E. Centre, Duntocher Rd, Dalmuir G81 4SF; Tel 0141-952 0030
Faifley C.E. Centre, Mildam Rd, Fairfley, Clydebank G81 5LB; Tel (01389) 76442
Garrell Vale C.E. Centre, Duncansfield, Kilsyth G65 9JX; Tel (01236) 823871
Gartocharn C.E. Centre, Gartocharn G83 8NE; Tel (01389) 59927
Gibson C.E. Centre, Garelochhead G84; Tel (01436) 72775
Glenhead C.E. Centre, Duntiglennan Rd, Duntocher G81 6HF; Tel (01389) 74130
Haldane C.E. Centre, Miller Rd, Balloch, Strathclyde; Tel (01389) 54328
Hillhead C.E. Centre, 169 Meiklehill Rd, Kirkintilloch, Strathclyde; Tel 0141-776 1365
Hub C.E. Centre, 405 Kilbowie Rd, Clydebank G81 2TY; Tel 0141-952 5455
Kilcreggan C.E. Centre, Kilcreggan, By Helensburgh, Strathclyde; Tel (01436) 72775
Link C.E. Centre, Bron Way, Town Centre, Cumbernauld G67 1EW; Tel (012367) 728200
Milngavie C.E. Centre, Allander Rd, Milngavie G62 8PN; Tel 0141-956 5700
Milton C.E. Centre, Milton, Dumbarton G82 2TH
Muirfield C.E. Centre, Brown Rd, Cumbernauld G67 1AA; Tel (0123 67) 723966
Neighbourhood Unit, Napier St, Clydebank, Strathclyde; Tel 0141-952 5429
Phoenix C.E. Centre, Quarryknowe Rd, Castlehill, Dumbarton G82 5BH; Tel (01389) 65885
Pivot C.E. Centre, Glenmanor Ave, Moodiesburn, Strathclyde; Tel (01236) 874941
Renton C.E. Centre Annexe, Station Rd, Renton G82; Tel (01389) 56669
Renton C.E. Centre, Main St, Renton G82 4LY; Tel (01389) 56592
Rhu C.E. Centre, Hall Rd, Rhu G84 8RR; Tel (01436) 72775
Rosneath C.E. Centre, Rosneath G84 0RF; Tel (01436) 72775
Whitecrook C.E. Centre, Dean St, Clydebank G81 1RQ; Tel 0141-952 8894

Woodhead C.E. Centre, Woodhead Pk, Kirkintilloch, Strathclyde; Tel 0141-775 2483

Outdoor Pursuits Centres

Arrochar Outdoor Centre, Arrochar; Tel (013012) 355
Garelochhead Outdoor Centre, Old School Rd, Garelochhead, Strathclyde; Tel (01436) 810315

Teachers' Centres

Cumbernauld Education Resource Centre, Darroch Way, Seafar, Cumbernauld GG7 9JG; Tel (0123 67) 721608
Dalmuir Education Resource Centre, Singer Rd, Dalmuir, Clydebank G81 4SF; Tel 0141-952 0301
Pirniehall, Croftamie, By Glasgow G63 0HD; Tel (01360) 60226
Science Centre, St Andrew's High School, North Douglas St, Clydebank G81 1NQ; Tel 0141-952 3229

Glasgow Division

129 Bath St, Glasgow G2 2SY; Tel 0141-204 2900
Divisional Education Officer P.K. Corsar, MA, MEd
Senior Education Officer A. Morton, MA, BA
Education Officer I. McDonald, BSc, MEd
Education Officer D. Harvey, BSc, MEd
Education Officer R. O'Connor, MA(Hons), DipEd
Education Officer Mrs A. Batchelor, BSc, MAPPSci
Education Officer G. Gardner, BSc
Education Officer T. McDougall, MA
Education Officer E. Young, BSc
Education Officer Miss M. McDonald, BA
Senior Adviser J. Duffin, MA
Senior Inspector J. McDonach, MA
Inspector C. Campbell, DCE
Inspector A. Capanni, BSc, DipEd
Inspector A. Clinton, DipEd, DipRE
Inspector K. Cunningham, BEd, MEd
Inspector J. McDonald, BA
Inspector N. McKechnie, MA, CPSW
Inspector E. McNeill, DCE
Inspector D. Morrison, BA, MEd, DipEd

Psychological Service

Administrative Office, 140 West Campbell St, Glasgow G2 6DF; Tel 0141-227 6895/6897; *Principal Educational Psychologist* I.J. McDonald, MA, MEd
Bridgeton Office, 96 Main St, Glasgow G40 1JP; Tel 0141-556 1141
Carnwadric Office c/o Carnwadric Primary, 29 Capelrig St, Glasgow G46 8PH; Tel 0141-638 2349
Central Office, 194 Renfrew St, Glasgow G3 6TX; Tel 0141-332 4137
Drumchapel Office c/o Drumry Primary, 3 Abbotshall Ave, Glasgow G15 8PR; Tel 0141-944 8513
Easterhouse Office, Duntarvie Rd, Glasgow G34; Tel 0141-773 0940
Govan Office, 102 Copland Rd, Glasgow G51 2RR; Tel 0141-445 1628
Knightswood Office, 2028 Great Western Rd, Glasgow G13 2HA; Tel 0141-954 8811
Langside Office, Carmichael Pl, Glasgow G42 9UE; Tel 0141-632 0638
Pollok Office, 75 Househillwood Cres, Glasgow G53 6BG; Tel 0141-881 5502
Springburn Office, 48 Gourlay St, Glasgow G21 1AE; Tel 0141-558 5303

Schools for Pupils with Special Educational Needs (Day)

Abercorn, 195 Garscube Rd G4 9QH; Tel 0141-332 6212; Mrs P. Smith, DipSpecEduc
Ashcraig, Avenue End Rd, Glasgow G33; Tel 0141-774 3428; Mrs E. Dowling, MA, DipSpEd
Broomlea, 168 Broomhill Dr G11 7NH; Tel 0141-339 6494; Mrs A. Cunningham
Carnbooth Residential, 80 Busby Rd, Carmunnock G76; Tel 0141-644 2773; Mrs M. McLarty
Cartvale School, 44 Carmichael Pl G42 9SY; Tel 0141-649 4811; Miss M. Castle
Croftcroighn, 180 Findochty St G33 5EP; Tel 0141-774 7777; Mrs W. Craig
Drummore School, 129 Drummore Rd G15 7NH; Tel 0141-944 1323; M.B. Warren (Acting), MA(Hons)
Eastmuir, 211 Hallhill Rd G33 4QL; Tel 0141-771 3464; Mrs J. Henderson
Gadburn, 70 Rockfield Rd G21 3DZ; Tel 0141-558 5373; G. Hercus, DipSpecEd
Glasgow School for the Deaf, 20 Stornoway St G22 7RJ; Tel 0141-772 6752; Mrs J. Sharp
Glenspean, 29 Mamore St G43 2YX; Tel 0141-632 0541; Mrs M. Dunn
Greenview School, 47 Greenhead St G40 1DG; Tel 0141-554 2818; Mrs V. Cook
Hampden, 80 Ardnahoe Ave G42 0DL; Tel 0141-647 7720; B. Smith
Hollybrook, 135 Hollybrook St G42 7HU; Tel 0141-423 5937; A. Blinma
Howford, 487 Crookston Rd G53 7TX; Tel 0141-882 2605; Mrs M. Barwell
Kelbourne, 109 Hotspur St G20 8LG; Tel 0141-946 1405; Mrs I. Thakur
Kelvin, 69 Nairn St G3 8SE; Tel 0141-339 5835; Mrs P. Potter
Kennyhill, 375 Cumbernauld Rd G31 3LP; Tel 0141-554 2765; Mrs K.J. Stalker
Kirkriggs, 500 Croftfoot Rd G45 0NJ; Tel 0141-634 7158; F.C. Muldoon
Kirkton, 201 Kirkton Ave G13 3AF; Tel 0141-959 2910; Mrs A. Gorman
Ladywell School, 94 Duke St, Glasgow G4 0UW; Tel 0141-552 0641; Mrs C. Kemp
Langlands, 100 Mallaig Rd G51 4PE; Tel 0141-445 1132; Miss M. Cammock
Linburn, 77 Linburn Rd G52 4EX; Tel 0141-883 2082; Mrs J. Telfer
Middlefield Hostel, 26 Partickhill Rd G11 5BP; Tel 0141-344 0159; Ms J. Dorby
Milton, 6 Liddesdale Terr G22 7HL; Tel 0141-762 2102; Mrs E.J. McCallum
Newhills, Newhills Rd G33 4HJ; Tel 0141-773 1296; Mrs K. Kennedy
Northland, 146 Danes Dr G14 9BJ; Tel 0141-959 4147; Mrs M. Pallister, DipSpecEd
Parkhouse, Buckley St, Possilpark G22 6DJ; Tel 0141-336 8391; Mrss A. Crilly
Richmond Park, 30 Logan St G5 0HP; Tel 0141-429 6095; Mrs M.M. Pollard, BEd
Rosevale School, 48 Scalpay St G22 7DD; Tel 0141-772 1756; A. Cunningham, BSc
St Aidan's, 255 Rigby St G32 6DJ; Tel 0141-556 6276; A.J. McDonald
St Joan of Arc, 722 Balmore Rd G22 6QS; Tel 0141-336 6885; Miss McCusker, BA
St Kevin's, 25 Fountainwell Rd G21 1RG; Tel 0141-557 3722; Miss A. Beattie, DipSpecEd
St Mungo's Pr, 45 Parson St G4; Tel 0141-552 3120; Miss R. Gibbon. (Hearing Impaired Unit)
St Oswald's, 83 Brunton St G44 3NF; Tel 0141-637 3952; Mrs P. Cosker
St Raymond's, 384 Drakemire Dr G45 9SR; Tel 0141-634 1551; Mrs E.M. Muchan, BA
St Vincent's (Tollcross) (RC)
St Roch's Sec, 40 Royston Rd G21; Tel 0141-552 6016; F.J. Berry, BA, MEd. (Hearing Imparied Unit)
Shakespeare Unit, Shakespeare Pr, 75 Hotspur St G20; Tel 0141-946 1715; Mrs P. Steele
Woodcroft, 7 Findochty St G33 5EQ; Tel 0141-774 2391; J.D. Boyes, MA

Schools for Pupils with Special Educational Needs (Residential)

Nerston, East Kilbride, Glasgow G74 4PD; Tel 0141-332 009. (Mixed) (5–12) (Malad) (25)
St Vincent's, 30 Fullarton Ave G32 8NJ; Tel 0141-778 2254; Mrs A. Crilly. (Tollcross) (R.C.) (Blind/Deaf) (Mixed) (5–16) (Residential) (See also under Special Schools (Day)) (5)

Secondary Schools

All Saints, 21 Scotsburn Rd G21 3HX; Tel 0141-558 1241; A. Harvey, BSc

Bannerman High, Glasgow Rd, Baillieston G69 7NS; Tel 0141-771 7301; I.M. Duncan, BSc, MSc
Bellahouston Academy, 30 Gower Terr G41 5QF; Tel 0141-427 2251; Dr J. Cassells, BSc, MSc
Bellarmine, 42 Cowglen Rd G53 6EW; Tel 0141-881 9244; R.D. Morgan, MA, DipEd
Castlemilk High, 223 Castlemilk Dr G45 9JY; Tel 0141-634 1159/1150; J. Cathcart, MA
Cathkin High, Whitlawburn, Cambuslang G72 8YS; Tel 0141-641 4331
Cleveden, 42 Cleveden Rd G12 0JW; Tel 0141-334 6118; I. Valentine, BSc
Cranhill, 40 Startpoint St G33 3EF; Tel 0141-774 9711; C.S. Ross (Acting), BA
Crookston Castle, 126 Brockburn Rd G53 5RZ; Tel 0141-882 1792/1109; W. Blakey, MA
Eastbank Academy, 26 Academy St G32 9AA; Tel 0141-778 1720; J. Dalziel, BA
Garthamlock, 43 Craigievar St G33 5HG; Tel 0141-774 2212; N.B. Currie, BSc
Govan High, 12 Ardnish St G51 4NB; Tel 0141-445 4464/5; A. McGinley, MA
Hillhead High, Oakfield Ave G12 8LJ; Tel 0141-339 2177/8200; A. Craig, BSc
Hillpark, 36 Cairngorm Rd G43 2XB; Tel 0141-637 1071; D. Welsh, MA
Holyrood, 100 Dixon Rd G42 8AU; Tel 0141-423 8932; P. Mullen, MA, BA
Hyndland, Lauderdale Gardens G12 9RQ; Tel 0141-334 6129/6120; K. Goodwin, BSc, MIBiol
John Bosco, 50 Wolseley St G5 0HR; Tel 0141-429 2505; M. Graham, BSc
John Paul Academy, Arrochar St G23; Tel 0141-945 2666; E. Rafferty, MA
John Street, 96 Main St G40 1JP; Tel 0141-556 2861; S. McLachlan, MA
King's Park, 14 Fetlar Dr G44 5BL; Tel 0141-637 2304; J. Bell, BSc, DipEd
Kingsridge, 41 Achamore Rd G15 8DR; Tel 0141-944 1292/3156; D. McDiarmid, MA
Knightswood, 60 Knightswood Rd G13 2XD; Tel 0141-954 9124/6335; W. Stewart Ross, MA
Lochend, 80 Lochend Rd G34 0LB; Tel 0141-771 3131/7784; A. Struthers, BSc
Lourdes, 47 Kirriemuir Ave G52 3DF; Tel 0141-883 4711/2; R. Healy, BSc
North Kelvinside, 30–60 Oban Dr G20 6QJ; Tel 0141-946 0121; G. Murray, BSc
Notre Dame High, 160 Observatory Rd G12 9LN; Tel 0141-339 3015/8554; Mrs M. McLaughlin, MA
Penilee, 11 Craigmuir Pl G52 4DL; Tel 0141-883 8878; J.D. Turnbull, MA
Queen's Park, 10 Glenmore Ave G42 0EJ; Tel 0141-647 4341; J. Birchall, BSc
Shawlands Academy, Moss-side Rd G41 3TR; Tel 0141-632 1154; G. Wilson, MA, DipEd
Smithycroft, 282 Smithycroft Rd G33 2QU; Tel 0141-770 5595; J. Milligan, BSc
Springbarn Academy, Mansel St G21 4JL; Tel 0141-558 1561; W. Cowan, BSc
St Andrew's, 47 Torphin Cres G32 6QE; Tel 0141-774 9718; B. Malone
St Augustine's, 190 Liddesdale Rd G22 7QS; Tel 0141-772 5011; C. Milarvie, MA
St Gerard's, 80 Vicarfield St G51 2DF; Tel 0141-445 1581; A. Tarbert, BSc
St Gregory's, 61 Crowlin Cres G33 3QD; Tel 0141-774 5266; J. McGonigal, MA
St Leonard's, 62 Lochend Rd G34 0NY; Tel 0141-771 4986/79; T. Breslin, BSc
St Margaret Mary's, 65 Dougrie Rd G45 9NJ; Tel 0141-634 1169; K. Farrelly, BA
St Mungo's Academy, Crownpoint Rd G40; Tel 0141-556 7221; T.M. Burnett, MA
St Pius', 45 Cally Ave G15 7SQ; Tel 0141-944 2281; J. McKenna, BSc, MEd
St Roch's, 40 Royston Rd G21 2NF; Tel 0141-552 6016; F.J. Berry, BA, MEd
St Thomas Aquinas, 80 Westland Dr G14 9PG; Tel 0141-954 5905; M. Murray, BSc
Stonelaw High, Melrose Ave, Rutherglen G73 3BP; Tel 0141-643 0212; N. Love, MA
Trinity High, Glenside Dr, Eastfield, Rutherglen G73 3LW; Tel 0141-641 7741/7; A. Quigley, BSc
Victoria Drive, Larchfield Ave G14 9BZ; Tel 0141-954 2291; D. Nicholson, MA
Waverley, 120 Summerhill Rd G15 7LD; Tel 0141-944 1171; J.B. McNair, BSc
Whitehill, 280 Onslow Drive G31 2QF; Tel 0141-551 8221; R. Hutchison, MA
Woodside, 147 Berkeley St G3 7HP; Tel 0141-221 9562; P. Morrison, MA, BSc

Outdoor Pursuits Centres

Blairvadach Sailing and Outdoor Centre, Rhu, Helensburgh, Dunbartonshire G84 8NN; Tel (01436) 820491
Faskally Outdoor Centre, Faskally Hse, Nr Pitlochry, Perthshire PH16 5LA; Tel (01769) 2137

Teachers' Centres

Seamill Teachers' Centre, 9 Glenbryde Rd, Seamill, Ayrshire KA23 9NJ; Tel (01294) 822351
Woodlands Teachers' Centre, 315 Woodlands Rd, Glasgow G3 6NG; Tel 0141-339 3108

Youth Centres

Bannerman C.E. Centre, Glasgow Rd, Baillieston, Glasgow G69 7NS; Tel 0141-773 2887
Barlanark C.E. Centre, 33 Burnmouth Rd, Glasgow G33 4RZ; Tel 0141-773 1812
Barmulloch C.E. Centre, 46 Wallacewell Quad, Glasgow G21 3PQ; Tel 0141-558 1772
Barrowfield C.E. Centre, 3 Overtown St, Glasgow G31 4AN; Tel 0141-554 8412
Bellcraig Community Education Centre, 10 Gorston St, Glasgow G20; Tel 0141-945 2710
Bellrock Community Education Centre, 71 Skerryvore Rd, Glasgow G33 5NZ; Tel 0141-774 4994
Cadder C.E. Centre, 20 Fara St, Glasgow G23 5AE; Tel 0141-946 3818
Calton Neighbourhood Centre, Tureen St G40; Tel 0141-551 0825
Carnwadric C.E. Centre, 160 Carnwadric Rd, Glasgow G46 8HR; Tel 0141-638 8751
Castlemilk C.E. Centre, 121 Castlemilk Dr, Glasgow G45 9UG; Tel 0141-634 2233
Castlemilk Youth Centre, 146 Castlemilk Dr, Glasgow G45 9UB; Tel 0141-634 1937
Cathkin C.E. Centre, Withlawburn, Cambuslang G72 8YS; Tel 0141-641 7358
Darnley Community Education Arts Centre, 32A Glenlivet Pl, Glasgow G53 7LA; Tel 0141-620 1120
Dolphin Arts Centre, 7 James St, Glasgow G40 1BZ; Tel 0141-554 7449
Drumchapel C.E. Centre, 320 Kinfauns Dr, Glasgow G15 7HA; Tel 0141-944 1009
Drumchapel Youth Centre, 4 Essenside Ave, Glasgow G15 6DX; Tel 0141-944 1151
Easterhouse C.E. Centre, 1 Shandwick St, Glasgow G34 9DP; Tel 0141-771 9056
Easterhouse Youth Centre, 39 Wellhouse Cres, Glasgow G33 5HG; Tel 0141-771 5529
Eastfield Resource Centre, 285 Cambuslang Rd G72 7DB; Tel 0141-641 5056
Elmvale C.E. Centre, Elmvale St, Glasgow G21 1LR; Tel 0141-558 5223
Gairbraid C.E. Centre, 71 Gairbraid Ave, Glasgow G20 8DE; Tel 0141-946 1591
Garthamlock C.E. Centre, 1 Red Castle Sq, Glasgow G33 5EG; Tel 0141-774 0681
Glasgow Arts Centre, 12 Washington St, Glasgow G3 8AE; Tel 0141-221 4526
Govan Neighbourhood Centre, 121 Langlands Rd, Glasgow G51 3TL; Tel 0141-440 0564
Govanhill Community Education Centre, 6 Daisy St, Glasgow G42; Tel 0141-423 6492
Hamiltonhill and Possil C.E.Centre, 69 Ellesmere St, Glasgow G22 5QT; Tel 0141-332 5632
Househill C.E. Centre, 80 Househillwood Rd, Glasgow G53 6BB; Tel 0141-881 8083

Hydepark C.E. Centre, 60 Mollinsburn St, Glasgow G21; Tel 0141-558-5370
John Mains C.E. Centre, 401 Cumberland St, Glasgow G5 0SE; Tel 0141-429 5640
Kingsridge C.E. Centre, 41 Achamore Rd, Glasgow G15 8DR; Tel 0141-944 8262
Kinning Park Neighbourhood Centre, 40 Lambhill St, Glasgow G41 1AU; Tel 0141-427 4173
Knightswood C.E. Centre, 201 Alderman Rd, Glasgow G13 3DD; Tel 0141-959 9419
Knightswood Youth Centre, Dunterlie Ave, Glasgow G13; Tel 0141-954 2998
Linburn Crafts and Hobbies Centre for Retired People, Linburn Rd, Glasgow G52 4EX; Tel 0141-882 4231
Maryhill C.E. Centre, 87 Kelvinside Ave, Glasgow G20 6PU; Tel 0141-946 8793
Milton C.E. Centre, 424 Liddesdale Rd, Glasgow G22 7BX; Tel 0141-772 9100
Molendinar C.E. Centre, Craighead Rd, Glasgow G33 1LH; Tel 0141-770 7248
Netherton C.E. Centre, 358 Netherton Rd, Glasgow G13 1AX; Tel 0141-954 4250
Oatlands Leisure Centre, 50 Kilbride St, Glasgow G5 0HR; Tel 0141-429 4055
Palace of Art, 1121 Paisley Rd West, Glasgow G52 1EQ; Tel 0141-429 2076
Penilee C.E. Centre, 10 Gleddoch Rd, Glasgow G52 4BD; Tel 0141-882 3309
Pollok C.E. Centre, 134 Langton Rd, Glasgow G53 5DP; Tel 0141-882 5869
Possilpoint C.E. Centre, 130 Denmark St, Glasgow G22 5LQ; Tel 0141-336 4057
Quarry Brae C.E. Centre, 35 Quarrybrae St, Glasgow G31 5AS; Tel 0141-554 3283
Ruchazie C.E. Centre, 441–449 Gartloch Rd, Glasgow G33; Tel 0141-774 0670
Ruchill C.E. Centre, 671 Bilsland Dr, Glasgow G20 9NF; Tel 0141-946 8161
Shettleston and Tollcross C.E. Centre, 54 Amulree St, Glasgow G23 7UT; Tel 0141-778 5783
Sighthill C.E. Centre, Fountainwell Sq, Glasgow G21; Tel 0141-557 0710
South Dennistoun Neighbourhood Centre, 13 Whitevale St, Glasgow G31 1QW; Tel 0141-554 5315
South Nitshill C.E. Centre, 31 Wiltonburn Rd, Glasgow G53 7JF; Tel 0141-880 7285
Summertown C.E. Centre, 71 Broomloan Rd, Glasgow G52; Tel 0141-440 1613
Tollcross Youth Centre, 1120 Tollcross Rd, Glasgow G32; Tel 0141-763 0138
Toryglen Geoff Shaw C.E. Centre, 25 Kerrylamont Ave, Glasgow G42 0DN; Tel 0141-647 0969
Whitehill C.E. Centre, 280 Onslow Dr, Glasgow G31 2QF; Tel 0141-551 0469
Whiteinch Neighbourhood Centre, 1199 Dumbarton Rd, Glasgow G14 9UP; Tel 0141-954 2303
Yoker Neighbourhood Centre, 2418 Dumbarton Rd, Glasgow G14 0GL; Tel 0141-952 1652

Lanark Division

Education Department, Regional Offices, Hamilton ML3 0AE; Tel (01698) 454444
Divisional Education Officer J. Hogan, BSc, ARCST
Senior Education Officer J. Travers, MA
Education Officer Mrs H. Munro, MA
Education Officer H.A. Mulholland, BA
Education Officer Mrs C. Pollock, DipDomSci
Education Officer Ms G. Quinn, MA, MEd
Education Officer Dr J. Tulips, MA, PhD
Senior Adviser D. Menzies, MA, DipEd
Senior Inspector K. Arthur, BSc
Inspector J. Bodys, BSc, PhD, DipEd
Inspector J. Cassidy, BSc
Inspector J. Freeland, MA
Inspector M. Lauder, DipEd, MEd, PhD
Inspector I. Ronald, BA, DipTechEd
Inspector M. Watt, BEd, DipEd

Psychological Service

Principal Educational Psychologist J. Foulds, BSc, DipEd, MEd

East Kilbride District, East Dr, Off West Mains Rd, East Kilbride G74 1PU; Tel (0135 52) 36984
Hamilton District, 23–25 Clydesdale St, Hamilton ML3 0DD; Tel (01698) 285580
Lanark District, 21 Hyndford Rd, Lanark, Strathclyde; Tel (01555) 61673
Monklands District, 109–111 Dunbeth Rd, Coatbridge ML5 3ES; Tel (01236) 33371
Motherwell District, Off West Hamilton St, Motherwell ML1 1YD; Tel (01698) 62840/64797

Special Schools (Day) (5–16)

Avon, Carlisle Rd, Hamilton ML3 7EW; Tel (01698) 285444; Mrs M. Gibson
Bellefield Hospital School, Lanark ML11 7RH; Tel (01555) 4584; Mrs W. McEwan
Bothwellpark School, Sanderson Ave, Viewpark, Uddingston G71 6JZ; Tel (01698) 747721; Mrs B. McFarlane
Clyde View School, The Loaning, Motherwell ML1 3NQ; Tel (01698) 64843; Mrs A.T. Robertson
Craighead, Whistleberry Rd, Hamilton ML3 0EG; Tel (01698) 285678; Mrs L. MacDonald, MA, MEd
Dalton, Flemington Rd, Halfway, Cambuslang G72 8YB; Tel 0141-641 3093; Mrs M.A. Calder
Deanbank, Tay St, Coatbridge ML5 2NA; Tel (01236) 20471; Mrs C. Patrick
Drumpark, Coatbridge Rd, Bargeddie G69 7TW; Tel (01236) 23955; Mrs M. O'Neill
Early Learning Unit c/o Avon School, Carlisle Rd, Hamilton ML3 7EW; Tel (01698) 281228
Earnock High, Earnock High, Wellhall Rd, Hamilton, Strathclyde; Tel (01698) 286643/1286618; Miss W. Gunn. (Deaf Unit)
Firpark, Firpark St, Motherwell ML1 2PR; Tel (01698) 51313; J.G. Connelly
Greenburn School, c/o Maxwellton Primary, Maxwellton Ave, Calderwood, East Kilbride, Glasgow G74 3DU; Tel (0135 52) 37278; Miss E. Hamilton
Mavisbank, Mitchell St, Airdrie ML6 0EB; Tel (01236) 752725; Miss H. Rooney
Springhill School, Livingston Dr, East Kilbride, Glasgow G75 0AB; Tel (0135 52) 29657; Mrs S. Cunningham
Victoria Park School, Market Rd, Carluke ML8 4BE; Tel (01555) 50591; Mrs R. Scott
West Mains School, c/o Halfmerke P.S., Logie Pk, East Kilbride G74 4BU; Tel (0135 52) 49938; Mrs M. Bradley
Willowbank School, 299 Bank St, Coatbridge ML5 1EG; Tel (01236) 21911; Mrs J. Mitchell

Special Schools (Residential)

Kittoch Residential School, East Dr, Lymekilns, West Mains Rd, East Kilbride G74 1PU; Tel (0135 52) 44348/9; J. Hughes
Ridgepark Residential School, Mousebank Rd, Lanark ML11 7RA; Tel (01555) 2151; M. Thomson, BA

Careers Service

See chapter 17

Secondary Schools (12–18)

Airdrie Academy, South Commonhead Ave, Airdrie ML6 6NX; Tel (01236) 769164; C. Smith, MA
Ballerup High, Crosshouse Rd, Greenhills, East Kilbride G75 9DG; Tel (0135 52) 25351
Bellshill Academy, Main St, Bellshill ML4 1AR; Tel (01698) 747585; H.M. Tennant, MA
Biggar High, John's Loan, Biggar ML12 6AG; Tel (01899) 20144; P.V. Brian
Blantyre High, Boswell Dr, Blantyre G72 0BL; Tel (01698) 826431; R. Fawkes
Braidhurst High, Dalriada Cres, Motherwell ML1 3XF; Tel (01698) 64005/52470; J. Gallacher, MA
Brannock High, Loanhead Rd, Newarthill, Motherwell ML1 5AY; Tel (01698) 733905; G. Moncrieff, BSc, ARCST
Calderhead High, Dyfrig St, Shotts ML7 4DH; Tel (01501) 20050; E.T. Barr, BSc

Caldervale High, Towers Rd, Airdrie ML6 8PG; Tel (01236) 766711; A.H. McLeod, MA
Cardinal Newman High, Main St, Bellshill ML4 3DW; Tel (01698) 747668/747593; R.A.R. Equi, BSc
Carluke High, Carnwath Rd, Carluke ML8 4EA; Tel (01555) 72302/72780; R. Rodger, BSc, MEd
Claremont High, High Common Rd, St Leonards, East Kilbride G74 2DA; Tel (0135 52) 33671; J. Harvie, MA
Coatbridge High, Albert St, Coatbridge ML5 3ET; Tel (01236) 27676; J.G. Forsyth, MA
Coltness High, Mossland Dr, Coltness, Wishaw ML2 8NA; Tel (01698) 384307/385727; W. Morton, MA
Columba High, Wallace St, Whifflet, Coatbridge ML5 4DE; Tel (01236) 26185/27462; J.P. Ward
Dalziel High, Crawford St, Motherwell ML1 3AG; Tel (01698) 64255; B. Miller, MA
Duncanrig Secondary, Alberta Ave, East Kilbride G75 8HY; Tel (0135 52) 34254/8; Dr D.L. Cook, MA, BD
Earnock High, Wellhall Rd, Hamilton ML3 9UE; Tel (01698) 285665; R. Murdoch, BSc
Garrion Academy, Castlehill Rd, Wishaw ML2 0LS; Tel (01698) 375011; W.L. Gold, BSc
Hamilton Grammar, Auchincampbell Rd, Hamilton ML3 6PF; Tel (01698) 285777; A.W. Butterfield, MA
Holy Cross High, Muir St, Hamilton ML3 6EY; Tel (01698) 283888; T. Loughran, MA, BA
Hunter High, Crawford Dr, East Kilbride G74 3YD; Tel (0135 52) 24363/148266; Dr R. Wardle
John Ogilvie R.C. High, Farm Rd, Burnbank, Hamilton ML3 9LA; Tel (01698) 820811; A.M. Fagan, BSc
Lanark Grammar, Albany Dr, Lanark ML11 9AQ; Tel (01555) 2471; I. Brown, MA
Larkhall Academy, Cherryhill, Larkhall ML9 1QN; Tel (01698) 881570; R.S. Thomson, BSc
Lesmahagow High, School Rd, Lesmahagow ML11 0DL; Tel (01555) 893456; I. Stirling, MA
Our Lady's High, Dalzell Dr, Motherwell ML1 2DG; Tel (01698) 65191; J.A. Quinn, BSc
Rosehall High, Woodhall Ave, Coatbridge ML5 5DB; Tel (01236) 31166; R. Liddell
Strathaven Academy, Crawford St, Strathaven ML10 6AE; Tel (01357) 20126; D. Cameron-Dick, BA
St Aidan's High, Waverley Dr, Wishaw ML2 7EW; Tel (01698) 381013; Miss R. McDonald
St Ambrose High, Blair Rd, Blairhill, Coatbridge ML5 2EW; Tel (01236) 27671; B. Fagan, BSc
St. Andrew's High, Quarry Rd, Greenhills, East Kilbride G75 9JL; Tel (0135 52) 33691; Mrs A.V. Mulgrew, BSc
St Bride's High, Platthorn Dr, East Kilbride G74 1NL; Tel (0135 52) 34134; S. McPartlin
St Margaret's High, Waverley Dr, Airdrie ML6 6EU; Tel (01236) 766881; D.A. Fowles, BA, BSc
St Patrick's High, Muiryhall St, Coatbridge ML5 3NN; Tel (01236) 26191/31375; E. Mullen, MA, BA
Taylor High School, Carfin St, New Stevenston, Motherwell ML1 4JP; Tel (01698) 832219; R. Lynas, MA, MEd
Uddingston Grammar, Station Rd, Uddingston, Glasgow G71 7BS; Tel (01698) 817321; I. Bainton, MA
Wishaw High, Dryburgh Rd, Wishaw ML2 7JL; Tel (01698) 372372/374737; I. Murray, BSc, MEd

Community Education, Neighbourhood and Youth Centres

Airdrie C.E. Centre, 2 Clark St, Airdrie ML6 6DP; Tel (01236) 751538
Bellshill C.E. Centre, John St, Bellshill ML4 1RJ; Tel (01698) 747725
Blantyre C.E. Centre, 291 Glasgow Rd, Blantyre G72 9HJ; Tel (01698) 823796
Braidwood C.E. Centre, Braidwood, Carluke ML8; Tel (01555) 2178. (Old Braidwood P. School)
Burnbank C.E. Centre, Purdie St, Burnbank, Hamilton ML3 0NF; Tel (01698) 286376
Caldervale C.E. Centre, Caldervale High School, Towers Rd, Airdrie ML6 8PG; Tel (01236) 751538
Cardinal Newman C.E. Centre, Cardinal Newman High School, Main St, Bellshill ML4 3DW; Tel (01698) 844952
Carluke C.E. Centre, Carnwath Rd, Carluke ML8 4DR; Tel (01555) 70308
Carstairs C.E. Centre, School Rd, Carstairs Village ML11 8QF; Tel (01555) 870771
Chapelhall C.E. Centre, Gibb St, Chapelhall, Strathclyde; Tel (0123 64) 51538
Claremont C.E. Centre, Clarmont High School, High Common Rd, East Kilbride G74 2DA; Tel (013552) 71355
Coatbridge C.E. Centre, 2 Corsewall St, Coatbridge ML5 1QH; Tel (01236) 31313
Elizabeth Scott C.E. Centre, Logan St, Blantyre, Strathclyde; Tel (01698) 823076
Fairhill C.E. Centre, Neilsland Rd, Fairhill, Hamilton ML3 8HJ; Tel (01698) 284428
Forth C.E. Centre, Main St, Forth, Strathclyde; Tel (01555) 811596
Garrion C.E. Centre, Garrion Academy, Castlehill Rd, Wishaw M12 0LS; Tel (01698) 357359
Harthill C.E. Centre, Main St, Harthill, Strathclyde; Tel (01698) 2604
Hillhouse C.E. Centre, Hillhouse Rd, Hamilton, Strathclyde; Tel (01698) 822369
Holytown C.E. Centre, Stevenston St, Holytown, Strathclyde; Tel (01698) 732561
Larkhall Academy C.E. Centre, Cherryhill, Larkhall ML9 1QH; Tel (01698) 881570
Larkhall C.E. Centre, Montgomery St, Larkhall, Strathclyde; Tel (01698) 282604
Law C.E. Centre, Law, By Carluke; Tel (01555) 50850
Newarthill C.E. Centre, High St, Newarthill, Strathclyde; Tel (01698) 861170
Shotts C.E. Centre, Kirk Rd, Shotts, Strathclyde; Tel (01698) 218266
Tarbrax C.E. Centre, Tarbrax, West Calder, Strathclyde; Tel (01555) 2178
Uddingston C.E. Centre, Bellshill Rd, Uddingston, Strathclyde; Tel (01698) 813383
Udston C.E. Centre, Fleming Way, Hill Hse, Hamilton, Strathclyde; Tel (01698) 829724
Viewpark C.E. Centre, Old Edinburgh Rd, Viewpark, Strathclyde; Tel (01698) 817500
Wrangholm Hall Residential Centre, Jerviston St, New Stevenston, Strathclyde; Tel (01698) 844952

Outdoor Pursuits Centre

Caldercruix Outdoor Education Centre, Caldercruix, By Airdrie; Tel (012364) 842240

Teachers' Centres

Educational Development Centre, The Orchard, 19 Auchingramont Rd, Hamilton ML3 6JP; Tel (01698) 282020
Educational Resource Service, 4 Auchingramont Rd, Hamilton ML3 6JU; Tel (01698) 284868

Renfrew Division

Regional Offices, Cotton St, Paisley PA1 1LE; Tel 0141-842 5000
Divisional Education Officer J.G. Mulgrew, BSc
Senior Education Officer D. Dunbar, MA, MEd
Education Officer O. Aitken, MA
Education Officer M. Burke, BEd
Education Officer B. Biagini, DA
Education Officer M. McMillan, DCE, DipSpEd
Senior Adviser C. Knox, MA, DipEd
Senior Inspector A. Cumming, BSc
Inspector G. Crosbie, BSc
Inspector I. Fraser, BEd, DipEdTech
Inspector D. Meek, MA, MEd

Psychological Service

Principal Educational Psychologist R.B. Rutherford, MA, DEP
Eastwood Centre, Seres Rd, Clarkston, Strathclyde; Tel 0141-638 6694
Inverclyde Centre, Top Floor, St Mary's Primary, Patrick St, Greenock, Strathclyde; Tel (01475) 28226; R.B. Rutherford, MA, DEP, APBS
Paisley Centre, Carbrook St, Paisley PA1 2NW; Tel 0141-887 7821; R.B. Rutherford, MA, DEP, ABPS

St Catherine's Unit, Brabloch Cresc, Paisley PA3 4RG; Tel 0141-887 8626

Support Services

Behaviour Mrs C. Brownlie Merksworth High School, Gockston Rd, Paisley PA3 2NG; Tel 0141-887 5141
Physical Disabilities Mrs P. McDonald St Mirin's High School, Ferguslie, Paisley PA1 2QY; Tel 0141-840 2851
Moderate Learning Difficulties Miss D. Kindlin St Mirin's High School, Ferguslie, Paisley PA1 2QY; Tel 0141-840 2851

Special Schools (Day)

Clippens, Brediland Rd, Linwood, Paisley PA3 3RX; Tel (01505) 25333; Mrs D. McFarlane
Garvel, Chester Rd, Larkfield, Greenock PA16 OTT; Tel (01475) 35477; Miss M. Keir, MA, DipEd
Gateside, Craigielinn Ave, Paisley PA2 8RH; Tel 0141-884 2090; Mrs E. Quinn
Glenburn, Inverkip Rd, Greenock PA16 OQG; Tel (01475) 34611
Kersland, Ben Nevis Rd, Paisley PA2 7BU; Tel 0141-889 8251; Mrs K. Mulhearn
Lilybank, Birkmyre Ave, Port Glasgow, Strathclyde; Tel (01475) 45121; Mrs M. Lyner
The Isobel Mair, Drumby Cres, Clarkston G78 7HN; Tel 0141-620 0330; Mrs C. McLeod
The Mary Russell, Hawkhead Rd, Paisley PA2 7BE; Tel 0141-889 7628; Mrs A. Crossan, MA, DipEd

Secondary Schools (12–18)

Barrhead High, Aurs Rd, Barrhead G78 2SJ; Tel 0141-881 5751; Dr H.W. Cruickshank, PhD, BSc, MEd
Gleniffer High, Amochrie Rd, Paisley PA2 0AG; Tel (01505) 813116; J.D. Aitchison, MA, MEd
Castlehead High, Camphill, Paisley PA1 2HL; Tel 0141-887 4261; Miss J. Rosie
Eastwood High, Capelrig Rd, Glasgow G77 6NQ; Tel 0141-639 6191; I.G. Macpherson, BSc, DipEd
Gourock High, Fletcher Ave, Gourock PA19 1TP; Tel (01475) 31761; A.A. MacDonald, MA, MEd
Wellington Academy, Dempster St, Greenock, Strathclyde; Tel (01475) 29421; J. McCallum, BSc
Greenock High, Inverkip Rd, Greenock PA16 0QG; Tel (01475) 34613; H. Kerr, BSc
Greenock Academy, Madeira St PA16 7XE; Tel (01475) 29337; A. McDougall
Gryffe High, Bridge of Weir Rd, Houston, Strathclyde; Tel (01505) 690633; G.S. Ross, BSc
Johnstone High, Beith Rd, Johnstone PA5 0JN; Tel (01505) 22173; G.T. Steele, MA
Linwood High, Stirling Dr, Linwood PA3 3NB; Tel (01505) 21244; Mrs F. Farmer
Mearns Castle High, Waterfoot Rd, Newton Mearns, Strathclyde; Tel 0141-639 6231; I.C. Climie, MA
Merksworth High, Gockston Rd, Paisley PA3 2NG; Tel 0141-887 5141; D.B. Carnan, MA
Notre Dame High, Peat Rd, Greenock, Strathclyde; Tel (01475) 29131; J. Irvine, BSc, MEd
Paisley Grammar, Glasgow Rd, Paisley PA1 3RP; Tel 0141-889 3484; H.H. Nisbet, MA
Park Mains High, Park Mains, Erskine PA8 6EY; Tel 0141-812 2801; D.B. Smart, MA
Port Glasgow High, Marloch Ave, Port Glasgow PA14 6PP; Tel (01475) 705921; Dr N. Lawrie, BSc, PhD
Renfrew High, Haining Rd, Renfrew PA4 0AN; Tel 0141-886 7511; A.P. Macpherson, MA
St Andrew's Academy, Barrhead Rd, Paisley PA2 7LG; Tel 0141-887 5201; H. Osborne, BSc
St Brendan's High, Middleton Rd, Linwood PA3 3BE; Tel (01505) 29311; C.D. Quinn, BSc, DipEd
St Columba's High, Burnside Rd PA19 1XX; Tel (01475) 33271/2; H.J. McKenna, BSc, MEd
St Cuthbert's High, Hallhill Rd, Spateston, Johnstone PA5 0SD; Tel (0150 57) 3421; J. McLoone, BSc, CChem, MRIC
St Luke's High, Springfield Rd, Barrhead G78 1AH; Tel 0141-881 9321; N. Roarty
St Mirin's High, Ferguslie, Paisley PA1 2QY; Tel 0141-889 9451; L. Winters
St Ninian's High, Eastwood Pk, Rouken Glen Rd, Giffnock, Glasgow, Strathclyde; Tel 0141-638 4934; J. McVittie
St Stephen's High, Southfield Ave, Bardrainney, Port Glasgow, Strathclyde; Tel (01475) 705111; J.F. O'Hagan, BSc, BA
Trinity High, Glebe St, Renfrew PA4 8TT; Tel 0141-886 6121; J.A. Dourish, MA
Williamwood High, Seres Rd, Clarkston, Glasgow G76 7NJ; Tel 0141-638 2600; I. McGillivray, MA, DipEd
Woodfarm High, Robslee Rd, Thornliebank G46 7HG; Tel 0141-638 6541; J. Anderson, MA, MEd

Outdoor Pursuits Centres

Ardentinny Outdoor Education Centre, Ardentinny, Argyll, Strathclyde; Tel 0136-981 271; D.S. Lilley
Fornethy Residential Centre, Fornethy House, Kilry, Blairgowrie PH11 8HR; Tel (01575) 6209

Teachers' Centres

Highholm Resource Centre, Highholm Bldg, Highholm Ave, Port Glasgow, Strathclyde; Tel (01475) 43926; Mrs J. Mcintosh
Robertson Teachers' Centre, 16 Glasgow Rd, Paisley, Strathclyde; Tel 0141-887 3726; Mrs N. Wilson

Tutorial Centre

Hunterhill, Cartha Cres, Paisley, Strathclyde; Tel 0141-889 6876; Mrs M. McCusker

Community Education, Neighbourhood and Youth Centres

Apex C.E. Centre, 1 Westburn Ave, Paisley, Strathclyde; Tel 0141-889 9864
Bargarran C.E. Centre, Bargarran, Erskine, Strathclyde; Tel 0141-812 2000
Branchton C.E. Centre, 28 Branchton Rd, Greenock, Strathclyde
Gourock C.E. Centre, Binnie St, Gourock, Strathclyde; Tel (01475) 34257
Highholm C.E. Centre, Highholm Ave, Port Glasgow, Strathclyde; Tel (01475) 45227
Kilmacolm C.E. Centre, Lochwinnoch Rd, Kilmacolm, Strathclyde; Tel (0150 587) 3432
Linwood C.E. Centre, Brediland Rd, Linwood, Strathclyde; Tel 22233
Paton St Neighbourhood Centre, Bowfarm, Greenock, Strathclyde; Tel (01475) 83525
Shortroods Resource Centre, Inchinnan Rd, Paisley, Strathclyde; Tel 0141-889 6943
Springfield C.E. Centre, Nairn Rd, Greenock, Strathclyde
Stanely Green C.E. Centre, Foxbar Rd, Paisley, Strathclyde; Tel 0141-227 2829

Tayside

Population 394,000
Tayside Hse, Crichton St, Dundee DD1 3RA; Tel (01382) 23281; Fax (01382) 303393

Education Department

Education Office, Tayside Hse, Dundee DD1 3RJ; Tel (01382) 23281; Fax (01382) 305080
Vice-Chairman Cllr B. Paterson
Director of Education A.B. Watson, MA, MEd, FBIM
Senior Depute Director R. McKay, MA, BA
Depute Director (Staffing Admin and Resource Services) J.N. Erskine, MA, BA

Depute Director (Educational Development Services) J. Christie, MTh, DipEd
Senior Assistant Director (0–14) J.A. Anderson, MA, MEd, DipEd
Senior Assistant Director (14+) J.R. McWhirter, BSc, MEd
Senior Assistant Director (FE/Careers/SEP) R.M. Tindall, MA, DipAG
Senior Assistant Director (Property and Support Services) G. McLafferty, BSc
Assistant Director (0–10) Mrs A. Wilson, DipEd
Assistant Director (10–14) I.T. Mills, BSc, MBIM
Assistant Director (14+) Mrs G. Dugdale, MA
Assistant Director (LS/Special Educational Needs/Library Resource Services) Miss K. Treacy, MA, DipSEN
Assistant Director (Community Education/Educational Support Services) F.R. Patrick, BA
Assistant Director (Resources) J.L. Millar, CEng, MIProdE
Assistant Director (Financial Control) A. Weston, ACIS
Senior Adviser (0–10) L.J. McConnell
Senior Adviser (10–14) C.D.G. Taylor
Senior Adviser (14+) Mrs A.D. McVean
Adviser in Nursery Education Mrs M.R. Cummings
Adviser in Primary Education Mrs B.A.S. Adie
Adviser in Primary Education Mrs L.E. Christie
Adviser in Primary Education D.M. Johnstone
Adviser in Primary Education Miss C. Milne
Adviser in Primary Education J. Nowak
Adviser in Guidance Miss P. Menmuir
Adviser in Learning Support Mrs C., Beattie
Adviser in Special Educational Needs Vacancy
Adviser in Education/Industry Liaison Mrs A. Fell, MA
Adviser in School Management and Admin Vacancy
Adviser in Post-Compulsory Education Mrs E. Johnson
Adviser in Art and Design I.M. Scott
Adviser in Business Studies J.L. Bowie, BA
Adviser in Computer Education T. Smith, BA, DipCompEd
Adviser in English Vacancy
Adviser in Home Economics Mrs C. Watkin
Adviser in Mathematics I. Bryers, BSc
Adviser in Modern Languages Mrs C. Flanigan
Adviser in Music A.M. Perry
Adviser in Physical Education I. Mason
Adviser in Religious and Moral Education J.J. Laidlaw, MA
Adviser in Science P.J. Duguid, BSc, MEd
Adviser in Social Subjects P. McAvoy
Adviser in Technology Education A. Blair, BSc
Principal Educational Psychologist L.C. Meade, MA, MEd
Regional Librarian Mrs Eliz Knowles
Regional Catering Adviser Mrs C. Bushby, BA
Principal Careers Officer S. Benwell, BA, DipCG
Principal Educational Social Worker S.M. Faichney
TVEI Extension Project Co-ordinator Mrs J. Wilson

Careers Service

See chapter 17

Community Education Service

Community Education Officer S. Murdoch
Assistant Community Education Officer A.D. Boffey

Angus Area

Education Department, Ravenswood, New Rd, Forfar, Tayside; Tel (01307) 65441
Assistant Director Mrs M.S. Ray, BA
Education Psychologist J.C. Bright, MA, MEd
Number of Schools
1 full-time nursery (30); 9 nursery classes (533 part-time); 56 primary (8,406); 8 secondary (6,018); 8 special units
Population
95,370

Senior Secondary Schools

Arbroath Academy, Tel 72978; J.D. Lusby, BA, MEd. (685)
Arbroath High, Tel 72033; J.H. Whyte, BSc. (1006)
Brechin High, Tel 2135; A, MacCallum, MA, BA. (625)
Carnoustie High, Tel 52601; G.L. Smith, MA, MEd. (962)
Forfar Academy, Tel 64545; D.J. Carson, MA. (1066)
Montrose Academy, Tel 72626; W.H. Faulkner, BA, DipEd. (995)
Webster's High School, Kirriemuir, Tayside; Tel (01575) 72840; M. Baughan, BEd. (606)

Secondary School

Newtyle, Tel 232; J.B. Buick, BA. (73)

Dundee Area

Level 4, 66 Nethergate Centre, Dundee DD1 4BL
Assistant Director N. Logue, MA
Educational Psychologist I.M. McNeill, BSc, MEd, BA
Chief School Attendance Officer L. Forbes
Number of Schools
14 nursery (330 full-time, 1,000 part-time); 15 nursery classes (109 full-time; 239 part-time); 56 primary (14,076); 13 secondary (9,226)
Special Schools
1 day (157); 13 special units
Population
172,860
Requisition Periods for School Supplies
March each year

Special Schools

Kingspark, Gillburn Rd; Tel (01382) 815207; Mrs M. Reid
Resource Centre for Hearing Impaired, 15A Dudhope Terr; Tel 24793; Mrs K.C. Jordan
Duncarse Resources Centre, 15A Dudhope Terr; Tel 26235; Mrs M.E. Flinn

Senior Secondary

Craigie High, Garnett Terr; Tel 43281; D.J. May, MA. Mixed (567)
Grove Academy, Camperdown St, Broughty Ferry, Tayside; Tel 730284; K.D. Anderson, MA. Mixed (742)
Harris Academy, Perth Rd; Tel 67225; A. Johnstone, MA. Mixed (1285)
Kirkton High, Burn St; Tel 86719; J.R. Ganson, BSc, DipEd. Mixed (593)
Lawside Academy, School Rd; Tel 85801; J.M. Freeman, BSc, MSc. Mixed) (R.C. (735)
Linlathen High, Forfar Rd; Tel 455824; A.J. Hendrie, BEd. Mixed (540)
Menzieshill High, Yarrow Terr; Tel 641111; R.K. Miller, BSc. Mixed (740)
Monifieth High, Panmuirfield Terr, Monifieth, Tayside; H.A. Low, MA. Mixed (842)
Morgan Academy, Forfar Rd; Tel 453805; A.W. Constable, BSc. Mixed (971)
Rockwell, Lawton Rd; Tel 811396; C.E. Robertson, BSc. Mixed (347)
St John's, Harefield Rd; Tel 88269; (Brother Bebe) F.B. McCabe, BA. Mixed) (R.C. (721)
St Saviours High, Drumgeith Rd; Tel 500727; A.J. Gavin, BSc, MEd. Mixed) (R.C. (569)
Whitfield High, Berwick Dr; Tel 456636 or 456611; P.A. Murphy, MA, MEd. Mixed (574)

Teachers' Centres

Lawside Road Workshop, Lawside Rd; Tel 26619
Dryburgh Centre, Napier Dr, Dundee, Tayside; Tel (01382) 612086

Perth & Kinross Area

6–8 South Methven St, Perth, Tayside; Tel (01738) 38101
Assistant Director G.T. Waddell, BSc, DipEdTech
Educational Psychologist Mrs H. Myers, BSc 6-8 South Methven St, Perth; Tel (01738) 38101

Number of Schools
2 nursery (213); 14 nursery classes (517); 78 primary (inclusive of primary departments of secondary schools); (9,969); 11 secondary (6,786)
Special Schools
2 hospital special schools (25); 1 residential school for mentally handicapped children (23); 1 special school (22); 1 special unit
Population
125,770
Requisition Periods for School Supplies
March

Special Schools

Cherrybank, Cherrybank, Perth, Tayside; Tel (01738) 22147; G. Hutchison
The Glebe, Abbey Rd, Scone, by Perth, Tayside; Tel (01738) 51493; Mrs N.R. Guthrie

Senior Secondary Schools

Auchterarder, Tel (0176 46) 2182; C. Kiddie, MA. (230)
Blairgowrie High, Tel 3445; A.S. Dunlop, MA. (933)
Breadalbane Academy, Aberfeldy; Tel (01887) 20428; Miss E. Miskimmin, MA. (372)
Crieff, Tel 3383; J. Nicol, BSc. (421)
Kinross, Tel 62430; D.C. Reid, MA, DipEd. (637)
Perth Academy, Tel (01738) 23491; J.A. Waite, MA. (1356)
Perth Grammar, Tel 20071; D. Bader, MA. (912)
Perth High, Tel 28271; I. Agnew, MA. (1304)
St Columba's R.C., Perth; Tel (01738) 22994; *Vacancy* . (341)

Secondary (four-year courses)

Alyth, Tel 2462; G.W.G. Macgregor, BSc. (91)
Pitlochry High, Tel 2900; I. McEwan, MA. (189)

Western Isles

Population 29,600
Council Offices, Sandwick Rd, Stornoway, Isle of Lewis PA87 2BW; Tel (01851) 703773; Fax (01851) 705349

Education and Leisure Services Department (18)

Council Offices, Sandwick Rd, Stornoway PA87 2BW; Tel (01851) 703773; Fax (01851) 705349
Director of Education and Leisure Services N.R. Galbraith, MA(Hons), MEd
Depute Director L.F. Dick, MA, BA(Hons)
Regional Resources Officer C. Hunter, MA
Divisional Education Officer M. MacLeod, MA
Assistant Director (Primary Community) Vacancy
Assistant Director, Divisional Education Officer R. Woolford, MA Lionacleit Education Centre, Benbeluca; Tel (01870) 602043; Fax (01870) 602053
Music Adviser R.A. Barr, DipMusEd, RSAM, LTCL
Gaelic Development Officer C. Dunn, MA
Computer Development Officer C. Hunter, BSc
Principal Educational Psychologist R. Martin, MA, MEd
Educational Psychologist I. Maciver, MA, MEd
Schools Industry Liaison Officer I. Stewart
TVEI Co-ordinator K. Finlayson
Number of Schools
35 primary, 13 primary and secondary, three secondary (2,811 primary, 2,402 secondary); 1 pre-vocational (150); 1 special unit (11)
Day of Committee Meeting
Tuesday
Requisition Period for School Supplies
March
Other Authorities with whom Joint Purchasing Arrangements are made
None

Careers Office

See chapter 17

Special School

Stornoway Primary Special Unit, Tel (01851) 704700; A. McArthur

Six-year Comprehensive School (12–18)

The Nicolson Institute, Stornoway; Tel (01851) 2275; E. Young, MA. (1160)
Sgoil Lionacleit, Tel 2211; W. MacDonald, MA. (408)
Benbecula

Rural Comprehensive Schools with Primary Departments (5–16)

Back, Isle of Lewis, Western Isles; Tel (01851) 82 230; A. MacDonald, MA. (220)
Bayble, Isle of Lewis, Western Isles; Tel (01851) 870 216; D. Macphail, BSc. (158)
Castlebay, Isle of Barra, Western Isles; Tel (0187 14) 471; J. Campbell, MA. (202)
Daliburgh, South Uist, Western Isles; Tel 0187 84276; T. Rankin, MA. (5–14) (188)
Eriskay, South Uist, Western Isles; Tel (0187 86) 275; N. MacDonald, MA. (33)
Sir E. Scott, Harris; Tel (01859) 2339; D. Murray, MA. (5–16) (173)
Leurbost, Isle of Lewis, Western Isles; Tel (01851) 86 281; M. Morrison, BSc. (69)
Leverhulme Memorial, Harris, Western Isles; Tel (01859) 82208; J. Johnston, BSc. (54)
Lews Castle Day School, Isle of Lewis, Western Isles; Tel (01851) 4067; J. Mackenzie, MA. (No Primary) (Age 14–16) (161)
Lionel, Isle of Lewis, Western Isles; Tel (01851) 81 208; I. Maciver, MA. (122)
Paible, North Uist, Western Isles; Tel 0187 65275; D. Macdonald, MA. (5–14) (84)
Scalpay, Harris, Western Isles; Tel (01859) 84245; D.J. Morrison, MA. (32)
Shawbost, Isle of Lewis, Western Isles; Tel (01851) 71 213; D.R.A. Macleod, MA. (97)
Uig, Lewis, Western Isles; Tel (01851) 95228; E. Hay. (5–14) (39)

Vocational

Lews Castle College, Stornoway, Western Isles; Tel (01851) 3311

Outdoor Pursuits Centre

Valtos Centre, Uig, Isle of Lewis, Western Isles

6 Local Government Channel Islands, Isle of Man, Isles of Scilly

Guernsey

Population 58,867

States of Guernsey Education Department

Grange Rd, St Peter Port, Guernsey, Channel Islands GY1 1RQ; Tel (01481) 710821; Fax (01481) 714475
President Cons N.J.M. Tostevin
Vice-President Deputy P. Mellor
Director of Education J.D. Stephenson, BA
Deputy Director of Education D.T. Neale, BA, MA(Ed)
Assistant Director of Education (Resources) J.C. Diligent
Assistant Director of Education M.S. Pitman, BEd
Youth Services Officer N.C. Hunter
Principal Educational Psychologist S.M. Hayward, BA, MSc, EdPsych, ACP, ABPsS(Principal)
Senior Careers Officer M.Crozier BSc, DipCG
Educational Psychologist S.J. Maunder, MA, MSc
School Librarian M.E.R Harris, ALA
States Architect P.J. Reade, ARIBA Sir Charles Frossard Hse, La Charroterie, St Peter Port GY1 1FH; Tel (01481) 717000
Number of Schools
25 Primary (incl. private sector) (4,696); 9 Secondary (3,509)
Special Schools
3 day (128)
Day of Council Meeting
Alternate Mondays
Requisition Periods for School Supplies
No Specific dates
Other Authorities with whom Joint Purchasing Arrangements are made
None

Special Schools

Longfield Centre, Maurepas Rd, St Peter Port, Guernsey GY1 2DS; Tel (01481) 722339; G. George, CertEd. (34)
Mont Varouf School, Le Neuf Chemin, St Saviour's, Guernsey GY7 9FG; Tel (01481) 63135; R.W. Battye, DipEd. (E.S.N.(S.) (38)
Oakvale School, Collings Rd, St Peter Port GY1 1FW; Tel (01481) 723045; P. Garthwaite, MA. (E.S.N.(M.) (77)

Secondary Schools

Les Beaucamps, La Rue Des Delisles, Castel, Guernsey GY5 7DS; Tel (01481) 56477; P.D. LeCheminant, BEd, MA. (Mixed) (433)
La Mare de Carteret; Rue De Galaad, Castel GY5 7FL; Tel (01481) 56588; J.M. Tasker, BA. (Mixed) (462)
St Peter Port; Les Ozouets, St Peter Port GY1 2UB; Tel (01481) 720236; P.G. Lane, BA. (Mixed) (375)
St Sampson's, Delancey Pk, St Sampson's GY2 4HS; Tel (01481) 44411; G.H. Duport, BSc. (Mixed) (518)

Grammar Schools

Blanchelande Girls' College, Rosaire Ave, St Peter Port GY1 1XX; Tel (01481) 724300; C.P.B. Harkins, MA. (Senior and Junior pupils) (160)
Elizabeth College, Grange, St Peter Port, Guernsey GY1 2PY; Tel (01481) 726544; J.H.F. Doulton, MA. (Boys) (574)
The Grammar School, Les Varendes, St Andrews, Guernsey GY6 8TD; Tel (01481) 56571; A.C. Bisson, BA. (804)

Ladies' College, Les Gravees, St Peter Port, Guernsey GY1 1RW; Tel (01481) 721602; M. Macdonald, MA, DipEd. (340)

Peripatetic Music Service

Education Department, Grange Rd, St Peter Port GY1 1RQ
Instrumental Music Organizer J. Whormersley, LRAM, ALCM, CertEd; Tel (01408) 710821

Education Development Centre

Granville Hse, Mount Durand, St Peter Port, Guernsey GY1 1DZ; Tel (01481) 720654; *Centre Manager* Mrs S. Leach

Jersey

Population 84,082 (1991)
States Greffe, Royal Sq, St Helier, Jersey, Channel Islands; Tel (01534) 502000; Fax (01534) 502098

States of Jersey Education Department

PO Box 142, Jersey; Tel (01534) 509500
President Constable Mrs I.M. Le Feuvre Education Committee, La Bercheuse, Grand Route De St Laurent, St Lawrence, Jersey
Vice-President P.J. Le Masurier La Pointe, La Rue des Pallieres, Vinchelez, St Ouen, Jersey
Director of Education B. Grady, BSc
Assistant Director (Resources) Mrs A.C. Esterson
Assistant Director (Curriculum & Management) T. McKeon
Adviser (Physical & Outdoor Education) A. Cross, MEd
Adviser (Music) M. Davison
Primary D.F. Gibaut, BA; Tel (01534) 509471
Chief Librarian I. Sutherland, ALA Central Library; Tel (01534) 877111
Children's Officer A.J. Skinner PO Box 142, St Saviour; Tel (01534) 509384
Careers Officer Miss S. Longson; Tel (01534) 509350
Medical Officer of Health C. R. Grainger, MB, CHB, MFCM, DPH, DObstRCOG, MRCS, FFCM, DPH, DCH, DIH, FRAI Public Health Dept, Cyril Le Marquand Hse, PO Box 421, The Parade, St Helier; Tel (01534) 879111
Consultant Dental Surgeon/Senior School Dental Officer John Fleet, BDS, MRCS, LRCP, SDS, RCS; Tel (01534) 71000
Educational Psychologist J. Birtwistle, MA (ChildPsych); Tel (01534) 509424
Consultant Psychologist Ian Berry, Dip(Tech), MBC(DipPsych); Tel (01534) 71000
Treasurer of the States G. Baird; Tel (01534) 603000
Number of Scools
22 primary (4,587); 7 secondary (3,675); 1 college of further education (260 F.T., 1,363 Day Release, 197 Link)
Day Of Committee Meeting
Second and fourth Wednesday of each month
Requisition Periods for School Supplies
No fixed period
Other Authorities with whom Joint Purchasing Arrangement are made
None

Secondary Schools

Grainville; Tel (01534) 35541. (Mixed) (533)
d'Hautree; Tel (01534) 36524. (Mixed) (501)
Les Quennevais; Tel (01534) 43171. (Mixed) (452)
Le Rocquier School; Tel (01534) 55876. (Mixed) (533)

Secondary Grammar (11–18 part fee-paying)

Jersey College for Girls; Tel (01534) 32401; Miss I. Stevenson, BSc. (460)
Victoria College, Tel (01534) 37591; J. Hydes, BA, MA, MEd. (Boarding places) (585)

High School (14–18)

Hautlieu School; Tel (01534) 36242; D. Bullock, BSc. (387)

Advisory Service

Education Department, PO Box 142, St Saviour, Jersey; Tel (01534) 509500

Learning Support Unit

Education Dept, PO Box 142, St Saviour, Jersey; Tel (01534) 509500

Isle of Man

Population 69,788
Murray Hse, Mount Havelock, Douglas, Isle of Man; Tel (01624) 685859; Fax (01624) 685943

Education Department

Murray Hse, Mount Havelock, Douglas, Isle of Man IMI 2SG; Tel (01624) 685820; Fax (01624) 685834
Director of Education G.A. Baker, BSc
Minister H. Hannan, MHK
Department Member W.D. Corlett, MHK
Department Member P. Karran, MHK
Deputy Director of Education R.B. Cowin, BSc
Finance Officer D. Goldsmith
Administrator R.M. Gash
School Meals Organiser J. Buckley, MHCIMA
Co-ordinating Adviser (Primary Education) S. Loaring, MA
Music Adviser A.H. Pickard, Hon, TCL, FTCL, GRSM(Manc), LTCL, ARMCM
Co-ordinating Adviser (Secondary Education) J. Cain, BEd, MEd
Co-ordinating Adviser (Further Education) P.A. Creighton, MEd
Information Technology Adviser J.M. Thornley, BSc, MBCS
Careers Officer J. Potts; Tel (01624) 685128
Librarian K. Rose Dept of Education Library, Noble's Hall, Westmoreland Rd, Douglas; Tel (01624) 673123
Assistant Education Officer (Youth and Community) C.M. Clague
AEO (Special Needs) J. Kermode, MSc, ABPsS, PGCE
AEO (Buildings) B.W. Harding, MA, MInstAM(Dip), MBIM
Educational Psychologist S.A. Flynn, BA, PGCE, MEd(Ed.Psych)
Educational Psychologist J.E. Harraghy, BEd, MEd, MSc(Ed Psych)
Inspector of Works W.A. Coleman
Number of Schools
33 primary (5,815); 5 secondary (4,570); 1 college (581 full-time)
Special School
1 day (9)
Day of Department Meeting
Wednesday two monthly

Requisition Periods for School Supplies
February, May (main), November
Other Authorities with whom Joint Purchasing Arrangements are made
None

Board of Education

Members of the Board
Dr P.K. Bregazzi MA, PhD, L.A. Cannell, L.M. Chapman, R. Chatel, A.C. Collister, E.A. Collister, D.P. Corrin BA, B.M. Cottier MBE, A.V. Craine, E.M. Deans, J.P. Gill, J. Hinnigan, G.I. Moore, V.A. Quane

Secondary High Schools

Ballakermeen High School; Douglas; Tel (01624) 673958/9; I. Masterton, BSc. (Mixed) (1228)
Castle Rushen High School, Castletown; Tel (01624) 822588; H. Taverner, BA. (Mixed) (935)
Queen Elizabeth II High School, Peel; Tel (01624) 843181; H.A. Galbraith, BEd. (Mixed) (668)
Ramsey Grammar School, Ramsey; Tel (01624) 813202; D.J. Christal, BA. (Mixed) (693)
St Ninian's High School; Douglas; Tel (01624) 629601; J.G. Quayle (Acting), BA. (Mixed) (1046)

Teachers' Centre

In-service Centre Santon; Tel 685820

Outdoor Pursuits Centres

Ardwhallin, West Baldwin, Isle of Man; Tel (01624) 852208; Fax (01624) 852208; *Development Worker* Vacancy
Eary Cushlin, Dalby, Peel; Tel (01624) 822490; Fax (01624) 822490; *Warden* A. Scarlett

Council of the Isles of Scilly

Population 1,950 (including off islands)
Town Hall, St Mary's, Isles of Scilly TR21 0LW; Tel (01720) 422537; Fax (01720) 422202

Education Department

Town Hall, St Mary's, Isles of Scilly TR21 0LW; Tel (01720) 422537; Fax (01720) 422202
Secretary for Education P.S. Hygate, BA
Number of Schools
4 primary (160), 1 secondary (110)
Day of Committee Meetings
Tuesday-Nine weekly cycle
Population
1,900
Requisition Periods for School Supplies
Vary

Education Committee

Chairman Cllr A.I. Oyler
Vice-Chairman Cllr C.J. Bourdeaux

Comprehensive School

Isle of Scilly, St Mary's, Isles of Scilly; Tel Scillonia 22929. (110)

7 Local Government Northern Ireland

Education and Library Boards

Belfast Education and Library Board

40 Academy St, Belfast BT1 2NQ; Tel (01232) 329211
Chief Executive T.G.J. Moag, BSc, DIC, CEng MIMechE
SEO M.D.M. Rea, BSc, DipEd
Chief Finance Officer D.J. Megaughin, ACMA
Chief Administrative Officer W. Kealey, BSc(Econ), DASE
Chief Librarian J.N. Montgomery, ALA
Purchasing Officer R. Gourley, BA, ACIS
Chief Education Welfare Officer E. Martin
Educational Psychologist F. Fee, MA, MEd, LTCl, ABPS, APSI
Pre-School and Primary Education Adviser L. Simpson
Primary Education Adviser F. Thompson
Secondary Education Adviser N. Todd
Secondary Education Adviser S. Rafferty
Careers Adviser S. Doran
Creative and Expressive Studies S. McElhatton
Religious Education Adviser W. Steele
Information Technology Adviser M. Montgomery
Special Education Adviser E. Cunning
Craft, Design Technology Adviser R.A. Stewart
EO (Nursery and Primary) T. McMillan
EO (Secondary) B. Black
EO (Special) J. McCullough
EO (Further Education) T. Neilands
EO (Youth Service) N. Hearst
Number of Schools
17 controlled nursery; 14 maintained nursery; 46 controlled primary; 47 maintained primary; 9 controlled secondary; 14 maintained secondary; 2 controlled grammar; 14 voluntary grammar; 1 school of music
Special Schools
10 controlled; 2 maintained; 2 remedial centres

Education Committee

Chair M. Muldoon 805 Lisburn Rd, Belfast BT9 7GX; Tel (01232) 612266
Vice-Chair N. McCausland, MA 5 Cooldarragh Pk, Belfast BT14 6TG
Members of the Committee
Rev T.D. Cooper BA, MSc, Rev J. McAllister MA, Rev P.F. Patterson BSc, BD, C. Murphy BA, PGCE, M. McGuiness, J. Cooper, M. Cruickshank BSc, MSc, T.D. Hamilton MA, BSc(Econ), M.F. MacNally MBE, PT, MA, O.J. Magill, J.P.A. Murphy BA, MEd, DASE, A. Odling-Smee JP, BA, D.H. Browne, N.A. Dodds MA, BL, L. Lewsley, S. McBride MA, BL, F. Proctor, J. Walker

Special Schools (Maintained)

St Francis de Sales School for Hearing Impaired Children Beechmount Dr BT12 7LU; Tel 245599; Sister Maeliosa Byrne, BA, BMus, HDipEd. (17)
St Gerard's Resource Centre Upper Springfield Rd BT12 7PQ; Tel (01232) 245593; R. Rooney, BA. (218)

Special Schools (Controlled)

Belfast Hospital, Royal Belfast Hospital for Sick Children, Falls Rd BT12 6BE; Tel (01232) 240503; B. Comfort, BEd, DASE. (91)

Cedar Lodge Grays La, Newtownabbey BT36 7GB; Tel (01232) 777292; M.F.Z Vallely. (137)
Fleming Fulton Upper Malone Rd BT9 6TY; Tel (01232) 613877; D.J Mehaffey, MA, DipAdexs. (173)
Glenveagh, Harberton Pk BT9 6TX; Tel (01232) 669907; K. Murphy, MBE. (93)
Greenwood Assessment Centre Greenwood Ave BT4 3JJ; Tel (01232) 471000/471327; Mrs M.A Adams, DipSpecEd. (50)
Harberton Harberton Park BT9 6TX; Tel (01232) 381525; T.G Rollins. (174)
Oakwood Assessment Centre, 67 Broadway BT12 6HF; Tel (01232) 240482; M.E. Watson. (72)
Jaffe Centre Cliftonville Rd BT14 6JX; Tel (01232) 747551; D. McConnell, MSc,BEd. (35)
Mitchell House Marmont, Holywood Rd BT4 2GU; Tel (01232) 768407/760292; M.H. Gibson. (66)
Park Educational Resource Centre 145 Ravenhill Rd BT6 8GH; Tel (01232) 450513; F.T. Mitchell. (111)

Secondary Schools (Maintained)

Christian Brothers Glen Rd BT11 8BW; Tel (01232) 615999; Brother T.A. Monaghan, BA,HDipEd. (736)
Corpus Christi College Beechmount Parade BT12 7LX; Tel (01232) 245645; G. Hamill, MA. (920)
La Salle Boys Junior Glen Rd BT11 8BQ; Tel (01232) 614868. (Boys) (213)
La Salle Boys' Edenmore Dr BT11 8LT; Tel (01232) 614083/1624268; Brother Francis Manning. (Boys) (1147)
Little Flower Girls' 71A Somerton Rd BT15 4DE; Tel (01232) 370647/370665; Miss A. McGrath, BA. (Girls) (508)
Our Lady of Mercy Girls' Ballysillan Rd BT14 7QR; Tel (01232) 391769; Sister M.Regina Caffrey, BSc. (Girls) (614)
St Gabriel's 685 Crumlin Rd BT14 7CD; Tel (01232) 391518; S. McGartland. (Boys) (313)
St Gemma's 51–59 Ardilea St BT14 7DG; Tel (01232) 740375/6; S. McCloskey. (Girls) (263)
St Genevieve's High Edenmore Dr BT11 8LL; Tel (01232) 614084/627151/2; Sister Luca Henry, BA,DipEd. (Girls) (770)
St Joseph's College, 518–572 Ravenhill Rd BT6 0BY; *Principal* M. Marken, VCertEd, BA(Hons); Tel (01232) 491280/491474
St Louise's Comprehensive College, 468 Falls Road BT12 6EN; Tel (01232) 325631/323719; Sister Rosaleen MacMahon. (2470)
St Patrick's, 619 Antrim Rd BT15 4DZ; Tel (01232) 770011/2; G. Salters, BSc,DMS. (Boys) (466)
St Rose's Beechmount Ave BT12 7NA; Tel (01232) 240937; Sister Helen O'Dwyer. (Girls) (285)

Maintained Integrated School

Hazelwood College, Gray's La, Newtownabbey BT36 7EA; Tel (01232) 774202; T. Rowley, BA,DipEd,MEd,DASE. (215)

Secondary Schools (Controlled)

Ashfield High, Holywood Rd BT4 2LY; Tel (01232) 656812; R. Dunn. (Boys) (379)
Ashfield High, Holywood Rd BT4 2LY; Tel (01232) 471744; Miss E.H. Reid, BA,DipEd. (Girls) (517)
Mount Gibert Community College, 237 Ballygomartin Rd BT13 3NL; Tel (01232) 712600; J. Crossan. (334)
Castle High, Fortwilliam Pk BT15 4AR; Tel (01232) 778602/771168; R. Jones, BSc(Econ). (337)
Deramore High, Carolan Rd BT7 3HE; Tel (01232) 692411; W.A Currie, BSc(Econ). (465)
Larkfield High, Black's Rd BT10 0NB; Tel (01232) 301578; H. Artt, BA, DipEd. (345)
Model, Ballysillan Rd BT14 6RB; Tel (01232) 391156/391077; D.J. Thompson, MA,DipEd. (Boys) (990)
Model, Dunkeld Gdns BT14 6NT; Tel (01232) 391768; P. Wilson (Acting). (Girls) (932)
Orangefield High, Cameronian Dr BT5 6AW; Tel (01232) 701122; A.W.J. Hyndman, BA,DASE. Girls (577)

Grammar Schools (Controlled)

Grosvenor High, Cameronian Dr BT5 6AX; Tel (01232) 702777; K.E. Reid, MA,DipEd. (1063)
Wellington College, Annadale Embankment BT7 3EF; Tel (01232) 642539/643646; D. Woods, BSc,BA,DipEd. (665)

Grammar Schools (Voluntary)

Belfast Royal Academy, Cliftonville Rd BT14 6JL; Tel (01232) 740423; W.M. Sillery, MA. (1298)
Bloomfield Collegiate, Astoria Gdns BT5 6HW; Tel (01232) 471214; Miss R.H. Weir, BA. (543)
Campbell College, Belmont BT4 2ND; Tel (01232) 763076; R.J.I. Pollock, BSc,MEd,PhD. (585)
Dominican College 38 Fortwilliam Pk BT15 4AP; Tel 370298; Sister Jacqueline, OPMA. (790)
Hunterhouse College, Finaghy BT10 0LE; Tel (01232) 612293; Miss D.E.M. Hunter, BA,DipEd. (687)
Methodist College, 1 Malone Rd BT9 6BY; Tel (01232) 669550/8/9; T.W. Mulryne, MA. (1609)
Rathmore, Kingsway, Finaghy BT10 0LF; Tel (01232) 610115/301874; Sister Ursula Canavan, BA. (1063)
Royal Belfast Academical Institution, College Sq East BT1 6DL; Tel (01232) 240461; R.M. Ridley, MA. (900)
St Dominic's 135 Falls Rd BT12 6AE; Tel (01232) 320081; Sister Lucina Montague. (910)
St Malachy's, 36 Antrim Rd BT15 2AE; Tel (01232) 748285; Very Rev F.N. Conway, BSc. (918)
St Mary's Christian Brothers, Glen Rd BT11 8BW; Tel (01232) 615321; Br D. Gleeson, CFC, MCSp. (1122)
Strathearn, 188 Belmont Rd BT4 2AU; Tel (01232) 471858; Miss A. Lamb, BA,DipEd. (606)
Victoria College, Cranmore Pk BT9 6JA; Tel (01232) 661506/7; M. Andrews, BSc(Hons). (661)

Music Service

School of Music 99 Donegall Pass BT7 1DR; Tel (01232) 322435; *Senior Tutor* R.J. Hewitt, GRMS, LRAM, ARCM

North Eastern Education and Library Board

County Hall, 182 Galgorm Rd, Ballymena, Co Antrim BT42 1HN; Tel (01266) 653333; Fax (01266) 46071
Chief Executive G. Topping, BA, MSc, MBA, DipEd
SEO (Administration) Vacancy
SEO (Development) Vacancy
SEO (Services) G.B. Leadley, BA
Chief Librarian J.P.E. Francis, BA, FLA
Chief Finance Officer S.N.S. McCurdy, BA, CIPFA
Chief Architect A. Moody, BSc, RIBA Architects' Dept. 50–62 Ballymoney St, Ballymena BT43 6AN; Tel (01266) 655366; Fax (01266) 655277
Principal Educational Psychologist K. Campbell, BA, DipEd, MSc
Chief Education Welfare Officer G.E. Stevenson
Transport Officer W. Henry
Purchasing Officer Vacancy
Personnel Officer J. Fryers, MSc, BA
Information Officer J.A.D. Kenny, BA, MIPR
Primary Adviser J.P. Flynn, BA, DipEd, DMS
English Adviser A.M. McAuley, MA,(EngEducDipinReading Deve(OpenUniv), BA(Hons)(Eng&Educ)
Environmental Studies Adviser P.G. French, MA, BSc, CertEd
Secondary Adviser G.D. Irwin, MEd, DASE
Science and Technology Adviser J.M. Brown, BSc, PhD, DipEd
Information Technology and Mathematics Adviser J.J.G. Magaud, BA, MSc
Religious Education Adviser P. Hewitt, BSc(Hons), PGCE, CRK, DASE

Management Development J.G.W. Campbell, BA, DipEd
Modern Languages W.A. Brodie, MA
Further Education S.D. McClelland, BSc, DipEd
Creative and Expressive N. McConnell
Careers Education and Guidance Adviser D.R. Beattie, MA, BSc(Econ), DipEd
Educational Technology Adviser W. Smyth, MA, DipEd
Youth Welfare Adviser E.G. Bell
Head of Music E. Boyd
Number of Schools
15 controlled nursery, 2 maintained nursery (1,109); 234 primary (40,023 including 7 nursery units); 17 grammar (13,095); 38 other secondary (19,433); 10 controlled special (752), 1 maintained special (123)
Requisition Periods for School Supplies
Free books (main) 1 Feb-10 April

Education Board

Chair Rev R.F.S. Poots, OBE, BA, PhD 27 Boyland Rd, Ballymoney BT53 7EH
Vice-Chair F.R.H. Marks 13 Avon Crt, Moylena Rd, Antrim BT41 4TJ
Members of the Board
Rev S. Allen BA, J.R. Beggs MP, E.T. Black, R.S. Bolton, J. Christie MBE, Rev D. Clarke LLB, BD, C.C. Corrigan BSSc, DipACC, ACA, E.J. Crilly TD, BA, J. Currie BEd(Hons), SDA, S.C. Dickson, Very Rev J.A. Fair MA, L. Frazer, J.A. Gaston JP, D.A. Gillespie, J. Graham, R.J. Hanna, J.B.H. Hill BSc(Econ), D. Hollis, P.A. Kirpatrick, P.A. Lerwill, T.A. Lyttle BSc, A.P. McConaghy, R.E. McCrea, Rev B. McGoldrick BA, BD, P.G. McShane, K. Regan, G.E. Scott BSc(Hons), J.A. Scott BEd(Hons), DipAS(Ed), R.J. Sloan BEd, MSc, D.M. White BA, Rev J.R. Wilson, Rev T.H. Wilson ACII, BD

Special Schools (Maintained)

Jordanstown, Jordanstown, Newtownabbey, Co Antrim; Tel (01232) 863541; D. Byrne. (Auditory/Visual Handicaps) (119)

Special Schools (Controlled)

Antrim, 29 Oldstone Rd, Muckamore Hse, Muckamore, Co Antrim; Tel (0184 94) 28946; T. Wright. (MH/SMH/PMH) (32)
Ballymena, Loughan School, 22 Old Ballymoney Rd, Co Antrim; Tel (01266) 652944; M.H. Norris. (MH/SMH/PMH) (57)
Beechgrove, 91 Fry's Rd, Ballymena, Co Antrim; Tel (01266) 48264; L. Herbison, BA(Hons), MSc. (PH) (19)
Coleraine, Sandelford School, 8 Rubgy Ave, Co Londonderry; Tel (01265) 43062; P.K. McDermott, BEd(Hons). (MH/SMH/PMH) (78)
Dunfane, 91 Fry's Rd, Ballymena, Co Antrim; Tel (01266) 48263; J. Dixon, BA,BPhil. (ESN) (138)
Larne Roddensvale School, The Roddens, Co Antrim; Tel (01574) 272802; Miss M. Lynas, DipTMH. (MH/SMH/PMH) (39)
Magherafelt, Kilronan School, 46 Ballyronan, Co Londonderry; Tel (01648) 32168; J. Clarke, DipTMH. (MH/SMH/PMH) (67)
Newtownabbey Hillcroft School, Abbots Rd, Co Antrim; Tel (01232) 863262; T. Howard. (MH/SMH/PMH) (66)
Rosstulla 2–6 Jordanstown, Newtownabbey, Co Antrim; Tel (01232) 862743; S. McAvoy, BEd. (117)
Thornfield Hse 8–12 Jordanstown, Newtownabbey, Co Antrim; Tel (01232) 865968; A. Ingram, BSc, MSc.Ed. (69)

Grammar Schools (Controlled)

Antrim Grammar Steeple Rd, Antrim; Tel (0184 94) 64091; J.G. Hunniford, BSc(Hons),DipEd,DASE. (690)
Ballyclare High 31 Rashee Rd; Tel (0196 013) 22244; Mr R.J. Fitzpatrick, BA, DipEd, DASE, MA. (1173)
Cambridge House Boys', Cambridge Ave, Ballymena, Co Antrim; Tel (01266) 43151 & 42807; W.J. Wallace, BA,DipEd,DASE,MAEd. (Boys) (410)
Cambridge House Girl's Cambridge Ave, Ballymena; Tel (01266) 652213 & 42806; Miss A. Graham, BSc,MEd,LGSM. (Girls) (547)
Carrickfergus 120 North Rd; Tel (019603) 63615 & 62024; Mr W.K. Irwin, BEd, BA, P.G.DipGC, Adv.Dip.Em. (604)
Coleraine High Lodge Rd, Coleraine; Tel (01265) 43178; Mrs D. Hutchieson, BA,PGCE. (711)

Grammar Schools (Voluntary)

Ballymena Academy 89 Galgorm Rd, Ballymena; Tel (01266) 652782/3; D.B. Jagoe, BSc,DASE. (1168)
Belfast High 740 Shore Rd, Newtownabbey; Tel (01232) 864431; S.R. Hilditch, BSc,DASE. (757)
Coleraine Academical Institution Castlerock Rd, Coleraine; Tel (01265) 44331; S. Forsythe, BSc,DipEd,DASE. (862)
Dalriada St James' Rd, Ballymoney; Tel (0126 56) 63066; W.S. Calvert, MA, MEd. (796)
Dominican College Strand Rd, Portstewart; Tel (0126 583) 2715 & 2525; J.F. Murphy, BSc,MA,DASE. (398)
Larne Grammar 4–6 Cairncastle Rd, Larne; Tel (01574) 272791; H. Morrow, MOD, BA, DASE. (633)
Loreto College Castlerock Rd, Coleraine; Tel (01265) 43611/57149; L. Diamond, BA, MSc, PGCE, DASE. (758)
Rainey Endowed, 79 Rainey St, Magherafelt; Tel (01648) 32478; C.E.T. Flanagan, MA, DipEd, DASE, MIMgt. (591)
St Louis Grammar Cullybackey Rd, Ballymena; Tel (01266) 49534; J. Stuart, BA,MSc,DipEd,DASE. (947)
St MacNissi's 1 Castledawson Rd, Carnlough; Tel (01574) 885202/885214; Very Rev P.J. Delargy, BA,MEd,STL. (560)
St Mary's Convent Magherafelt; Tel (01648) 32320; Sister I. O'Connor, BA,DipEd. (1026)

Secondary Schools (Controlled)

Antrim 17 Lough Rd, Antrim; Tel (018494) 62233 & 62525; R. Smyth, BEd, MSc. (289)
Ardnaveigh Birch Hill Rd, Antrim; Tel (018494) 64034; G. Acheson, BA, DipEd(Comm). (407)
Ballee Community Ballee Road West, Ballymena; Tel (01266) 49327; Mr W. Clarke, B.Ed. (719)
Ballycastle 33 Rathlin Rd, Ballycastle; Tel (0126 57) 62254; D.J. McKeown, BA,DipEd. (255)
Ballyclare Dough Rd, Ballyclare; Tel (0196 013) 22610; S.A. McCrea, MA,BA,BEd. (906)
Ballymoney 17 Garryduff Rd, Ballymoney; Tel (0126 56) 62361 & 62481; C.W. Ridge, BA,DipEd,DASE. (655)
Carrickfergus College, 110 North Rd, Carrickfergus; Tel (0196 013) 62347 & 63015; J.C. Reid, BSc. (896)
Coleraine Boys' Carthall Rd, Coleraine; Tel (01265) 43467; F.G. Ward, BSc, DipEd. (Boys) (512)
Coleraine Girls' Carthall Rd, Coleraine; Tel (01265) 42671; G.H. McKimm, BEd,MSc. (Girls) (545)
Crumlin High, 10 Glenavy Rd, Crumlin; Tel (0184 94) 52497; F.A. Henderson, BA,MEd. (232)
Cullybackey High, 44 Pottinger St, Cullybackey; Tel (01266) 880771; J.C. Crawford, BA,BEd,MSc. (590)
Downshire Downshire Rd, Carrickfergus; Tel (0196 013) 64334; Mrs M.E. Sinnamon, BEd,M.Sc. (520)
Dunclug Doury Rd, Ballymena; Tel (01266) 653665; R.J. Sloane, BEd,MSc. (513)
Dunluce 16 Dunluce Rd, Bushmills; Tel (0126 57) 31448; M.E. Page, MSc,DASE. (Bushmills) (514)
Garvagh Main St, Garvagh, Coleraine; Tel (0126 65) 58216; M. Branagh, BA,MSc,CertEd,DASE. (210)
Glengormley High, 134 Ballyclare Rd, Newtownabbey; Tel (01232) 837223; R.A. Frost, BA,B.Ed,DipEd. (1238)
Larne High 20 Sallagh Pk, Larne; Tel (01574) 272159; S. Polley, BEd, DASE, MSc. (657)
Maghera High, 30 Tobermore Rd, Maghera; Tel (01648) 42454; J. Steele, BSc(Econ),DASE. (218)
Magherafelt High, 30 Moneymore Rd, Magherafelt; Tel (01648) 32385; N. Haugh, MSc, BA, CertEd. (420)
Monkstown Community, Bridge Rd, Monkstown, Newtownabbey; Tel (01232) 867431/2; R. King, BA.MEd. (664)

Newtownabbey Community High School, Rathcoole Dr, Newtownabbey; Tel (01232) 851558; O. Sayliss, BA, DipEd, MSc
Parkhall High, Steeple Rd, Antrim; Tel (0184 94) 62963; R.J. Dickson, BA,. (402)

Secondary Schools (Voluntary Maintained)

Edmund Rice College, Hightown Rd, Glengormley, Newtownabbey, Co Antrim; Tel (01232) 848434; Brother T.F. Moroney, CFC,BA,CertEd. (585)
Cross and Passion College 10 Moyle Rd, Ballycastle; Tel (0126 57) 62473; Miss C.J.F. Nicholl. (590)
Our Lady of Lourdes Castle St, Ballymoney; Tel (01256 56) 62050; M.J. McHenry, MSc, Mem of Inst Biol, AdvDipEd. (291)
St Aloysius High, 60 Coast Rd, Cushendall; Tel (0126 67) 71314; J. Blaney, BPhil(Hons). (172)
St Colm's High, 2 Magherafelt Rd, Draperstown; Tel (01648) 28377; T. Maguire, MSc,BA,DipEd,DEM. (328)
St Comgalls, Drumalis, Bankheads La, Larne; Tel (01574) 272300 & 274605; J.G. Murphy. (394)
St Joseph's High, Beresford Ave, Coleraine; Tel (01265) 43009; P. McGowan. (431)
St Malachy's High, 4 Birch Hill Rd, Antrim; Tel (018494) 63939; R.P. Fulton, BSc. (529)
St Mary's College, 230 Mayogall Rd, Portglenone; Tel (01266) 821370; M.A. Forde, MA,HDipEd. (247)
St Olcan's High, 5 Craigstown Rd, Randalstown; Tel (01849) 472411; P.J. O'Grady, BSc,MSc,DASE. (330)
St Patrick's High, Broughshane Rd, Ballymena; Tel (01266) 656984; W. Raven, BA, CertEd. (644)
St Patrick's College, 25 Coleraine Rd, Maghera; Tel (01648) 42451; S. McElvee, BEd. (1271)
St Paul's High, 11 Bann Rd, Kilrea; Tel (0126 65) 40536; L. McKee, BA, DASE, AdvDipEd. (216)
St Pius X High, 59 Moneymore Rd, Magherafelt; Tel (01648) 32186; A.J. O'Kane, BA,DASE. (836)

Board Centres

Education Garden Centre, 120 North Rd, Carrickfergus, Co Antrim; Tel (019063) 63401; R. Field, BSc, BEd(Hons)
Educational Computer Unit, 101 Ballymoney Rd, Ballymena, Co Antrim; Tel (01266) 42840
Educational Guidance Centres, 10 Loughanmore Rd, Antrim, Co Antrim; Tel (018494) 32725; J.S. Dunlop, MSc, BA(Hons), CertEd, Educational Psychology
Environmental Resource Centre, Giant's Causeway, Bushmills, Co Antrim; Tel (0126 57) 31777; P.G. French, BSc, MA, CertEd
Science and Technology Centre, 10 Steeple Rd, Antrim, Co Antrim; Tel (01849) 460879; J.M. Brown, BSc, PhD, DipEd

Board Centres

Area Resource Centre, Railway St, Antrim, Co Antrim; Tel (01849) 462254; W. Smyth, MA, DipEd
Ballymena, Ballee Community High School Ballee Rd West, Ballymena, Co Antrim; Tel (01266) 43754
Ballymoney 23 Charles St Ballymoney; Tel (0126 56) 62492
Newtownabbey and District, Whitehouse PS 2 Doagh Rd, Whitehouse, Newtownabbey, Co Antrim; Tel (01232) 868895
Coleraine C/o Coleraine Girls' Secondary School, Carthall Rd, Coleraine, Co.Londonderry BT51 3LR; Tel (01265) 55800

Youth Offices

Antrim/Magherafelt, 2 Castle St, Antrim BT41 4JE; Tel (018494) 65003
Ballymena/Moyle, 22 Ballymoney Rd, Ballymena BT43 5BY; Tel (01266) 43625
Coleraine/Ballymoney, 9A Abbey St, Coleraine BT52 1DS; Tel (01265) 52279
Larne/Carrickfergus, 73 Cheston St, Carrickfergus BT38 7BH; Tel (01960) 364188
Newtownabbey, Mossgrove Primary School, Swanston Rd, Newtownabbey BT36 8DN; Tel (012313) 840971

Residential Youth and Outdoor Pursuits Centres

Ballyhome, 21 Ballyhome Rd, Coleraine, Co Londonderry; Tel (01265) 823212
Bushmills, 7 Priestland Rd, Bushmills, Co Antrim; Tel (0126 57) 31599
Derganagh Hse, Rathlin Rd, Ballycastle, Co Antrim; Tel (012657) 62974
Woodhall, Moneygran Rd, Kilrea, Coleraine, Co Londonderry; Tel (012665) 40762/40331

Youth Centres

Ballycraigy Youth Club, Ballycraigy Primary Youth Wing, Bracken Ave, Antrim BT41 1PU; Tel (0184 94) 66577
Ballykeel Youth Club, Ballykeel Youth Centre, 46 Crebilly Rd, Ballymena BT42 4DR; Tel (01266) 41966
Ballysally, Coleraine; Tel (01265) 55122; J. Seaton
Broughshane, Tel (01266) 861725
Coleraine Information Centre, 50 New Row, Coleraine BT52 1AF; Tel (01265) 53179
Garvagh, Tel 52652
Glengormley Youth Club, Glengormley Youth Centre, Glenvarna Dr, Glengormley BT36 8JQ; Tel (01232) 40942
Millgreen Youth Club, Millgreen Youth Centre, 19A Newton Gdns, Whiteabbey BT36 7BX; Tel (01232) 854440
Monkstown Drop-In, Tel (01232) 868059
New Mossley, Campbell Rd, Newtownabbey, Co Antrim; Tel (01232) 841988
Portrush Youth Club, Portrush Youth Centre, Dunluce Ave, Portrush BT56 8DW; Tel (01265) 823030
Rathcoole Youth Club, Rathcoole Youth Centre, The Diamond, Rathcoole, Newtownabbey BT37 9AH; Tel (01232) 851172
Sunlea Youth Club, Sunlea Youth Centre, 4 Ballyrashane Rd, Coleraine BT52 2NL; Tel (01265) 54823
Sunnylands Youth Club, Sunnylands Youth Centre, Hawthorn Ave, Carrickfergus BT38 8ED; Tel (0196 013) 51866
Waveney Youth Club, Waveney Youth Centre, Doury Rd, Ballymena BT43 6JX; Tel (01266) 45522
Whitehead Youth Club, Whitehead Youth Centre, Castleview Rd, Whitehead BT38 9NA; Tel (0196 013) 53984

South Eastern Education and Library Board

18 Windsor Ave, Belfast BT9 6EF; Tel (01232) 381188; Fax (01232) 383290
Chief Executive T. Nolan, OBE, BA, MSSC, DipEd, FRSA
Deputy Chief Executive C.E. Brown, BA, MSc, DipEd, DMS
Chief Librarian D.H. Welch, FLA
SEO E. Preston, BSc, DipEd
Chief Administrative Officer J.B. Fitzsimons, BSc DipM, MIPD
Chief Architect S.K. Savage, ARIBA
Chief Finance Officer K. Brown, BSc(Econ), FCA
Principal Educational Psychologist S.R. Irvine, BA, MSc
Senior Educational Psychologist H. O'Doherty, BSc, MSc
Senior Educational Psychologist J. Hamilton, BSc, MSc
Senior Educational Psychologist J.P. McKeever, BA, MSc
Senior Educational Psychologist N. Alexander (Acting), MSc, PGCE
ASEO D. Cargo, BA(Hons), PGCE, MA
ASEO M.E. Graham, BA
EO W.J. McCarroll, BA
EO A. Hanratty, BEd, MSc, DMS, CIT

EO S. Skelton, BA(Hons), MSc, MITH, MIPD
EO S. Sloan, BSc, DASE, MA(Ed), MSc, MIBIOL, CBIOL
Principal Architect G. Irvine, DipArch, ARIBA
Environment and Society Adviser E. Woods, BSc, DipEd, MEd
Creative and Expressive Studies Adviser R. Gilbert, BEd, MA, DASE
Religious Education Adviser Rev P Hooper, BA, PGCE
Primary Adviser R.D. Harper, MA, CertEd
English Adviser G.J. Thomson, BA, DipEd
Technology and Design Adviser C. King, BEd
Cross-Curricular Themes Adviser J. McCooe, BA, DipEd
Mathematics Adviser P. McGrattan, BA, MPhil
Science Adviser T. Walsh, BSc, MEd
Language Studies Adviser E.A. McQuiston, BA
Assistant Chief Librarian E.M. Irvine, BA, FLA
Assistant Chief Librarian E. Porter, BA, DipLib.Studies, ALA
Assistant Chief Librarian L. Plummer, BA, DLS, ALA
Chief Education Welfare Officer K. Bridge

Number of Schools
11 controlled nursery (768); 6 maintained nursery (402); 105 controlled primary (includes 3 nursery wings) (24,147); 56 maintained primary (12,030); 1 grant maintained integrated primary (24) 19 controlled secondary intermediate (10,233); 9 maintained secondary (4,658); 2 grant maintained integrated secondary (1000) (811); 3 controlled grammar (3,356); 7 voluntary grammar (7,445); 4 outdoor pursuits centres; 3 resources centres; 6 youth centres; 1 music centre; 1 curriculum & resources centre

Special Schools
10 controlled; 5 units for hearing impaired; 1 diagnostic unit; 9 units for primary E.S.N; 6 secondary E.S.N., 2 Language and Communication Units

Requisition Periods for School Supplies
None specified

Joint Purchasing Arrangements
All other boards for some items

Education Committee

Chair H.R. Small
Vice-Chair H.E. Bradford

Members of the Committee
D.G. Andrews, Rev R.G. Bagnall, Rev W.J. Beattie, H.M. Bell, T.P. Benson, W.J.F. Biggerstaff, S.A. Campbell, R.B. Carabine, Rev T.V. Craig, M.J. Curran, I. Davis, Canon S.M.J. Dickson, L.P. Douglas, R. Gibson, R.A. Jones, S.K. Kilpatrick, W.D. Linton, P.M. McAleenan, M.M.McGoran, Rev J.H. McIntyre, W.R. Magill, W.J. Masterson, F.M. Reid, Dr R.J. Rodgers, S. Semple, Canon K.J. Smyth, D. Tennis, A. Thompson, G. Tigchelaar, S.T. Townsley, W.G. Watson, Rev D.N. Whyte

Special Schools (Controlled)

Ardmore Hse, Saul St, Downpatrick, Co Down; Tel (01396) 614881; E.G. Bunting. (Behavioural Difficulties (Mixed) (12)
Beechlawn, 3 Dromore Rd, Hillsborough, Co Down; Tel (01846) 682302; E.S. Gamble. (E.S.N.) (Boys) (223)
Brookfield, 6 Halfpenny Gate Rd, Moira, Craigavon, Co Armagh; Tel (01846) 611498; A.F. Sturgeon. (Junior) (E.S.N.) (Mixed) (84)
Killard Hse, North Rd, Newtownards, Co Down; Tel (01846) 813613; W.E.J. Haddick. (E.S.N.) (Girls and Junior Boys) (214)
The Lindsay School, Forster Green Hospital, 110 Saintfield Rd, Belfast; Tel (01232) 793681; P. Doherty (Acting)
Longstone, Millar's Lane, Dundonald, Belfast; Tel (01232) 480071; W.J. McLaughlin, BA. (E.S.N.) (Mixed) (202)

Special Schools (Severe Learning Difficulties)

Clifton, 15 Ballyholme Rd, Bangor, Co Down; Tel (01247) 270210; R.S. Cunningham. (Mixed) (82)
Tor Bank, Upper Newtownards Rd, Dundonald, Belfast; Tel (01232) 484147; M. Smith. (Mixed) (132)
Knockevin, 29 Racecourse Hill, Killough Rd, Downpatrick, Co Down; Tel (01396) 612167; I. Wallace (Acting). (Mixed) (75)
Parkview, Wallace Ave, Lisburn, Co Antrim; Tel (01846) 601197; M.F. Loney. (Mixed) (102)

Units For Hearing-Impaired Children

Cregagh P. S. Mount Merrion Ave, Belfast BT6 0FN; Tel (01232) 401246; I.D. Parkinson
Donaghadee High School, Northfield Rd, Donaghadee, Co Down; Tel (01247) 882361; S.J. Rowe
Rathmore Primary School Rathmore Rd, Bangor, Co Down; Tel (01247) 270399; A.S. Kennedy
St Colmcilles High School, Killyleagh Rd, Crossgar, Co Down; Tel (01396) 830311; M. McGreevy
Holy Family Primary School, 1 Drumnaconagher Rd, Downpatrick, Co Down; Tel (01396) 830319; D. Cahill

Diagnostic Unit

Knockmore Primary School, Hertford Cres, Lisburn, Co Antrim; Tel (01846) 662600; J. Cooper

Primary E.S.N. Units

Castlewellan P.S., 2 Church St, Castlewellan BT31 9EG; Tel (013967) 78541; J.H. Gardiner
Downpatrick P.S., 10 Mount Cres, Downpatrick BT30 6AF; Tel (01396) 613934; A.J. Greenwood, BEd, MSc
Knockbreda P.S. Wynchurch Rd, Belfast BT6 0JJ; Tel (01232) 401871; Mrs M. Thompson
St Colmans Primary School, 109 Queensway, Lambeg, Lisburn BT27 4QS; Tel (01846) 601532; G.J. O'Gorman
St Colmcille's P.S. Glebetown Dr, Downpatrick BT30 6PZ; Tel (01396) 614177; J. Cahalane
St Malachy's P.S., 33 Lower Sq, Castlewellan BT31 9DN; Tel (013967) 78537; B.A. King
Seymour Hill P.S. Hazel Ave, Dunmurry, Belfast BT17 9QX; Tel (01232) 301046; N. Meharry
Towerview Primary School, Towerview Cres, Bangor BT19 2AZ; Tel (01247) 270480; T.H. Cowan
West Winds Primary School, Sunderland Pk, Newtownards BT23 4RQ; Tel (01247) 815212; J. McCoubrie

Secondary E.S.N. Units

De La Salle H.S., Struell Rd, Downpatrick BT30 6JR; Tel (01396) 612520; Brother P. Collier
De La Salle, St Marys H.S. 23 Ardglass Rd, Downpatrick, Co Down BT30 6JQ; Tel (01396) 612515; C. Murphy
Down Academy, 12 Old Belfast Rd, Downpatrick BT30 6SG; Tel (01396) 612115; D.G. Hunter
Scrabo H.S., Scrabo Rd, Newtownards BT23 4NP; Tel (01247) 813692; A.W. Rose
St Malachy's H.S. 3 Dublin Rd, Castlewellan BT31 9AG; Tel (013967) 78255; D. Farley
St Patricks H.S., Ballinderry Rd, Lisburn BT28 1TD; Tel (01846) 664877; E. Haughey

Secondary Schools (Maintained)

De La Salle H.S. Struell Rd, Downpatrick BT30 6JR; Tel (01396) 612520; Brother P. Collier. (482)
St Colm's, Summerhill Dr, Twinbrook, Dunmurry, Belfast; Tel (01232) 301118; J. Allen. (450)
St Colman's, 52 Crossgar Rd, Ballynahinch, Co Down; Tel (01238) 562518; F.A. Duffy, BA. (537)
St Colmcilles's, Killyleagh Rd, Crossgar, Co Down; Tel (01396) 830311; M. McGreevy. (416)
St Columba's, Ballyphilip Rd, Portaferry, Newtownards, Co Down; Tel (01247) 28323; B.A. Crawford, BA. (363)
St Columbanus', Ballymaconnell Rd, Bangor, Co Down; Tel (01247) 270927; E. Sweeney. (406)
St Malachy's, 3 Dublin Rd, Castlewellan, Co Down; Tel (013967) 78255; D. Farley. (998)

St Mary's, Ardglass Rd, Downpatrick, Co Down; Tel (01396) 612515; C. Murphy. (Girls) (549)
St Patrick's, Ballinderry Rd, Lisburn, Co Antrim; Tel (01846) 664877; E. Haughey. (457)

Grant Maintained Integrated Secondary Schools

Lagan College, 44 Manse Rd, Castlereagh, Belfast; Tel (01232) 401810; Dr B. Lambkin
Shimna College, Murlough Hse, Keel Point, Dundrum; Tel (013967) 51576; K. Lambe

Secondary Schools (Controlled)

Ballynahinch, Belfast Rd, Ballynahinch, Co Down; Tel (01238) 562424; W.J.A. Finlay, BSc(Econ),DipEd. (366)
Gransha, Gransha Rd, Bangor, Co Down; Tel (01247) 463838; R. Gray. (Boys) (726)
Bangor, Castle St, Bangor, Co Down; Tel (01247) 270535; W.R. Flynn, BSc(Econ),DipEd. (Girls) (1041)
Comber, Darragh Rd, Comber, Co Down; Tel (01247) 872361; G. Drennan, BA. (460)
Donaghadee, Northfield Rd, Donaghadee, Co Down; Tel (01247) 882361; S.J. Rowe, BA. (294)
Dundonald, Upper Newtownards Rd, Dundonald, Belfast; Tel (01232) 484271; S. Reilly. (Mixed) (637)
Dunmurry, River Rd, Dunmurry, Belfast, Belfast; Tel (01232) 622828; D. Thompson. (402)
Fort Hill, Belfast Rd, Lisburn, Co Antrim; Tel (01846) 663670; M.G. Tigchelaar, BA(Hons), MBA. (Girls) (715)
Glastry, 14 Victoria Rd, Ballyhalbert, Newtownards, Co Down; Tel (012477) 71226; J.T. Blundell, MSc,DipEd. (554)
Holywood, My Lady's Mile, Holywood, Co Down; Tel (01232) 423481; I.L.G. Arbuthnot. (303)
Down Academy, 12 Old Belfast Rd, Downpatrick, Co Down; Tel (01396) 612115; D.G. Hunter. (228)
Knockbreda High, Upper Knockbreda Rd, Belfast BT6 0NE; Tel (01232) 649302; W. Gordon, Cert.Ed, BSC,DASE. (622)
Laurelhill, Laurelhill Rd, Lisburn, Co Antrim; Tel (01846) 607351; W.J.H. Harvey. (868)
Lisnagarvey, Warren Gdns, Lisburn, Co Antrim; Tel (01846) 662636; N. McClelland, BSc,PGCE. (Boys) (374)
Lisnasharragh, Stirling Ave, Belfast BT6 9LP; Tel (01232) 401041; H. Hamilton. (496)
Movilla Donaghadee Rd, Newtownards, Co Down; Tel (01247) 812079; B.R. Reilly. (752)
Newtownbreda, Newtownbreda Rd, Belfast BT8 4PY; Tel (01232) 645374; R.S. Dickey. (807)
Saintfield, Comber Rd, Saintfield, Ballynahinch, Co Down; Tel (01238) 510356; R.J. Mills. (299)
Scrabo, Scrabo Rd, Newtownards, Co Down; Tel (01247) 813692; A.W. Rose, BSc(Econ),DipEd,MA. (364)

Grammar Schools (Controlled)

Down High, Mount Cres, Downpatrick, Co Down; Tel (01396) 612103; J.W. Ferris. (718)
Glenlola Collegiate, Castle Pk Rd, Bangor, Co Down; Tel (01247) 271152; R.J. Finlay. (Girls) (1038)
Regent Hse, Circular Rd, Newtownards, Co Down; Tel (01247) 813234; N.C. Orr, BA. (1600)

Grammar Schools (Voluntary)

Assumption High, Belfast Rd, Ballynahinch, Co Down; Tel (01238) 562250; M. Carville. (Girls) (864)
Bangor, College Ave, Bangor, Co Down; Tel (01247) 473734; T.W. Patton, MA. (Boys) (1055)
Friends, Magheralave Rd, Lisburn, Co Antrim; Tel (01846) 663995; J.T. Green, BA,PGCE. (1126)
Our Lady and St Patrick's College, Kingsway Gdns, Belfast; Tel (01232) 401184; Rev P. McKenna. (1118)
St Patrick's Grammar, Saul St, Downpatrick, Co Down; Tel (01396) 613200; Brother F.J. McArdle, BSc,MA,PhD. (Boys) (696)
Sullivan Upper, Belfast Rd, Holywood, Co Down; Tel (01232) 428780; J.F. Young, MA. (1242)
Wallace High, Clonevin Pk, Lisburn, Co Antrim; Tel (01846) 672311; I. McCallan. (1344)

Environmental Education Centres

Ardnabannon Outdoor Pursuits Centre, 3 Ardnabannon Rd, Castlewellan, Co Down; Tel (013967) 78555; T. Quinn
Cabra Towers Residential Centre, 24 Convent Rd, Cabra, Newry, Co Down; Tel (018206) 30315; P. Mullan
Killyleagh Outdoor Education Centre, Shore Rd, Killyleagh, Co Down; Tel (01396) 828511; H.E. Gourley
F. H. Ebbitt Field Study Centre, 56 Bryansford Village, Newcastle, Co Down; Tel (013967) 22207; I. Hood

Resources Centres

Bangor Resources Centre, North Down and Ards Institute of Further and Higher Education, Castle Pk Rd, Bangor; Tel (01247) 271235; B. Hepburn
Downpatrick, Mount Cres, Downpatrick, Co Down; Tel (01396) 613304; A. Vance
Rathvarna, 22 Pond Park Rd, Lisburn, Co Antrim; Tel (01846) 670662; V. McClenaghan
Music Centre, Church Rd, Ballynahinch, Co Down; Tel (01238) 562030; B. Agus

Youth Centres

Ardcarnet Youth Centre, Kinross Ave, Belfast BT5; J. Trimble
Ards Arena, South St, Newtownards, Co Down; C. Martin
Saints, Summerhill Rd, Twinbrook, Dunmurry, Belfast BT5; J. McCloskey
Bridge Youth Club, Railway St, Lisburn, Co Antrim
Poleglass Youth Centre, 14 Good Shepherd Rd, Poleglass, Belfast BT17; Mrs R. Burke
Stevenson Youth Centre, Kingsway, Dunmurry, Co Antrim; E. Henderson

Southern Education and Library Board

3 Charlemont Pl, The Mall, Armagh, Co Armagh; Tel (01861) 523811
Chairman Councillor N.R.D. Mulligan
Vice-Chairman Sr O.A.E. McConville
Chief Executive J.G. Kelly, MA
SEO T.R. Oakes, BA, DipEd
SEO H. McClenaghan, BA, MEd
SEO J.G. Martin, BSc
EO W.B. Weir, BA, DipBusAdmin
EO B.J. McConville, BEd
EO E.M. Keville, BA, MSc
EO S. Anthony, BSc
EO Dr. B. Liddy, PhD
Adviser for Technology R.J. Baker
Adviser for Information Technology W. Burke, MSc
Adviser 11–16 Programme and Science J.H. Logan, BSc, DASE
Adviser for Further Education B.J. Rouse, BPhil
Computer Development Officer K.J. Oates, MSc
Internal Auditor K. Orr
Assistant Finance Officer P.P. Kelly, BA
Officer for Careers Education D.G. Wilson, BA
Senior School Meals Organiser M.K. Livingston, MHCIMA
Chief Librarian A. Morrow, ALA
Principal Educational Psychologist M.D. Gilmour, BA, MEd
Chief Education Welfare Officer H.A. Bennett
Assistant Education Officer (Music) E. Benson
Chief Architect A. McGee, RIBA, BArch
Chief Finance Officer T.M. Heron
Purchasing Officer W.A. Neville
Youth Adviser G.P. Butler
Personnel Officer F.J. Carson, MIPM

Transport Officer D. Flannigan
Information Officer P.H. Jackson, MISM
Number of schools
Controlled 6 special; 12 nursery; 113 primary; 17 secondary; 3 grammar maintained 2 nursery; 146 primary; 19 secondary; voluntary grammar 12; Colleges of Further Education 4
Day of board meeting
3rd Thursday of each month
Requisition Periods for School Supplies
Main-March/April; Subsidiary-October
Other Authorities with whom joint purchasing arrangements are made
Other four Northern Ireland Education and Library Boards

Education Welfare Service

Armagh, Railway St, Armagh; Tel (01861) 525780; *Divisional Education Welfare Officer* A.A. Ryan
Augher, Augher Central Primary School, 17 Knockmany Rd, Augher BT77 0BE; Tel (016625) 48443; *Education Welfare Officer* B.E. Law
Banbridge, St Patricks High School, Scarva Rd, Banbridge BT32 3AS; Tel (018206) 62309; *Divisional Education Welfare* A.E. McNabb
Banbridge, Banbridge High School, Primrose Gdns, Banbridge BT32 3EP; Tel (018206) 22471; *Education Welfare Officer* A. McAlinden
Cookstown, Cookstown High School, Coolnafrankie Est, Cookstown BT80 8PQ; Tel (016487) 63632; *Education Welfare Officer* C.M. Mulholland
Cookstown, Holy Trinity College, Chapel St, Cookstown BT80 8QB; Tel (016487) 62420; *Education Welfare Officer* A. Donnelly
Dungannon, Drumglass High School, Carland Rd, Dungannon BT71 4AA; Tel (018687) 22421; *Divisional Education Welfare Officer* J. McCann
Keady, St Patrick's High School, Middletown Rd, Keady, Armagh BT60 3TH; Tel (01861) 531393; *Education Welfare Officer* G. Black
Lurgan, Sloan Ave, Lurgan BT66 8NY; Tel (01762) 322458; *Divisional Education Welfare Officer* F.W. Johns
Newry, Newry Teachers' Centre, Downshire Rd, Newry BT34 1BE; Tel (01693) 62357; *Divisional Education Welfare Officer* A.M. Mackle
Portadown, Upper Bann Institute of Further and Higher Education, 26 Lurgan Rd, Portadown, Co Armagh BT63 5BL; Tel (01762) 337111; *Education Welfare Officer* C. Maxwell
Portadown, Drumcree High School, Moy Rd, Portadown BT62 1QL; Tel (01762) 334725/8; *Education Welfare Officer* G. Joyce

Colleges of Further Education

Armagh, Lonsdale St, Armagh BT61 7HN; Tel (01861) 522205; H.A. McAleavey; 83 Lisanally La, Armagh, BT61 7HF
East Tyrone (Dungannon and Cookstown), Circular Rd, Dungannon BT71 6BQ; Tel (018687) 722323/1(016487) 62620; A.J. Dardis, BA(Hons), MA(Ed), MLit. (919)
Lurgan, Kitchen Hill, Lurgan, Craigavon BT66 6AZ; Tel (01762) 326135; W.L. Lloyd-Lavery, BA, PhD. (576)
Newry and Kilkeel, Patrick St, Newry BT35 8DN; Tel (01693) 61071; R.J. Mullan, BSc, MSC, MBIM. (1403)
Upper Bann Institute of Further and Higher Education, 26 Lurgan Rd, Portadown, Craigavon BT63 5BL; Tel (01762) 337111; *Director* G.H. Byrne, MA, PhD; Tel (018206) 62289 (Banbridge Campus); Fax (01762) 326135 (Lurgan Campus). (1038)

Special Schools (Controlled)

Ceara, Lough Rd, Lurgan, Craigavon BT66 6JJ; Tel (01762) 323312; A. Blakely, BEd
Donard, Ballygowan Rd, Banbridge BT32 3EH; Tel (018206) 62357; F. Wylie, BEd(Hons)
Fallowfield, Lough Rd, Lurgan, Co Armagh; Tel (017622) 322127; R.C. Peden. (Malad) (18)
Lisanally, Lisanally La, Armagh BT61 7HF; M.T. Williams; Tel (01861) 523563
Rathfriland Hill, Rathfriland Hill, Newry BT34 1HU; Tel (01693) 63068; K.V. McParland
Sperrinview, Carland Ross, Dungannon BT71 4AA; Tel (018687) 722467; Mrs M. Keogh

Hospital and Home Teaching Service

Room 216 Craigavon Area Hospital, 68 Lurgan Rd, Craigavon BT63 5QQ; Tel (01762) 33444; D. Archer

Secondary Schools (Maintained 11–16)

St Ciaran's High, 5 Tullybrynn Rd, Ballygawley, Dungannon BT70 2LY; Tel (0166 25) 68640; E. McSorley, BA. (754)
St Columban's College, 127 Newcastle Rd, Kilkeel, Newry BT34 4NL; Tel (01693 37) 62314; T.J. Curran, BA. (524)
St Joseph's Boys' High, 20 Armagh Rd, Newry BT35 6DH; Tel (01693) 62595; O. Magill. (451)
St Joseph's High, 29 School La, Coalisland, Dungannon BT71 4NW; Tel (0186 87) 740510; M. Whitmore. (675 + 15 SP)
St Mary's Girls' Junior High, Waring St, Lurgan, Craigavon BT66 6DQ; Tel (01762) 322446; Miss M.T. O'Neill, BA; Tel (01762) 322446. (555)
St Patrick's Boys' High, 41 Killymeal Rd, Dungannon BT71 6LT; Tel (0186 87) 722205; J.B. Cullinane. (402)
St Patrick's Girls' High, Donaghmore Rd, Dungannon BT70 1HA; Tel (0186 87) 723052; P.M. Carville. (264)
St Paul's Junior High, Francis St, Lurgan, Craigavon BT66 6DL; Tel (01762) 322694; B. McStravick. (528)

Secondary Schools (Maintained 11–18)

Drumcree High School, Moy Rd, Portadown, Craigavon BT62 1QL; Tel (01762) 334725/8; S.A. O'Neill
Holy Trinity College, Chapel St, Cookstown BT80 8QB; Tel (0164 87) 62420; F.G. Kearney. (499)
Lismore Comprehensive, Drumgask, Craigavon BT65 5DU; Tel (01762) 342165; E. McAGee. (1065 + 5 SP)
St Brigid's Boys High School, Windmill Hill, Armagh BT60 4BR; Tel (01861) 523849; C.F. McGleenon, MA
St Catherine's College, Convent Rd, Armagh BT60 4BG; Tel (01861) 523665/522023; Mrs M. Martin. (843)
St Joseph's High, 77 Dundalk Rd, Crossmaglen, Newry BT35 9HD; Tel (01693) 861240; B. Crilly. (568)
St Mark's High, Upper Dromore Rd, Warrenpoint, Newry BT34 3PN; Tel (0169 37) 53366; J. Cull. (801)
St Mary's High, Upper Chapel St, Newry BT34 2DT; Tel (01693) 62851; A. Vallely. (543 + 7 SP)
St Patrick's High, Scarva Rd, Banbridge BT32 3AS; Tel (0182 016) 62309; E.J. Carr, BA. (509)
St Patrick's High, Middletown Rd, Keady, Armagh BT60 3TH; Tel (01861) 531393; P. McAleavey. (843)
St Paul's High, 108 Camlough Rd, Bessbrook, Newry BT35 7EE; Tel (01693) 830309; M. Warde, BA, BComm, HDipEd. (1245 + 20 S)

Grammar Schools (Controlled 11–18 except where otherwise stated)

Banbridge Academy, Lurgan Rd, Banbridge BT32 4AQ; Tel (0182 016) 23220; C.W. Breen, MA,DipEd. (837)
Lurgan College, College Walk, Lough Rd, Lurgan, Craigavon BT66 6JW; Tel (01762) 322083; W. Johnston, MSc,BSc. (352 + 33P); (14–18)
Portadown College, Killicomaine Rd, Portadown, Craigavon BT63 5BU; Tel (01762) 332439; T.W. Flannagan, BSc. (728 + 62P); (14–18)

Grammar Schools (Voluntary 11–18 except where otherwise stated)

Christian Brothers', Courtney Hill, Newry BT34 2ED; Tel (01693) 63142; Rev Brother J.D. McDonald. (710)
Our Lady's, Chequer Hill, Newry BT35 6DY; Tel (01693) 63552; Sister Mary Perpetua McArdle, BA. (812)

Royal School, College Hill, Armagh BT61 9DH; Tel (01861) 522807; T. Duncan, MA,BSc,DASE. (598 + 45P)
Royal School Northland Row, Dungannon BT71 6AS; Tel (0186 87) 22710; P.D. Hewitt, MA,DipEd. (597 + 46P)
Sacred Heart, 10 Ashgrove Ave, Newry BT34 1HD; Tel (01693) 64632; Sister Patricia Rogers. (807)
St Colman's College, 46 Armagh Rd, Newry BT35 6PP; Tel (01693) 62451; Very Rev L. Stevenson. (770)
St Joseph's Convent 58 Castlecaulfield Rd, Dungannon BT70 3HE; Tel (01868) 761227; Mrs H. McRory, BA,BEd. (343)
St Louis' Grammar School, 151 Newry Rd, Kilkeel, Newry BT34 4EU; Tel (0169 37) 62747; Dr C.J. Devlin. (310)
St Michael's High, 12 Cornakinnegar Rd, Lurgan, Craigavon BT67 9JW; Tel (01762) 323192; Sister Mary St Anne, BA. (450); (14–18)
St Patrick's Academy for Boys, 37 Killymeal Rd, Dungannon BT71 6DF; Tel (0186 87) 722668; Very Rev D. Faul. (757)
St Patrick's Academy for Girls, 35 Killymeal Rd, Dungannon BT71 6DF; Tel (0186 87) 722474; Christina Bradley. (797)
St Patrick's Grammar School, Cathedral Rd, Armagh BT61 7QZ; Tel (01861) 522018; Rev Brother L.S. Kelly. (742)

Secondary Schools (Controlled Age range as given)

The City of Armagh High School, Alexander Rd, Armagh BT61 7JH; Tel (01861) 522278; W.J. Craig, BEd. (579); (11–16)
Aughnacloy High School, 23 Carnteel Rd, Aughnacloy BT69 6DU; Tel (0166 25) 57289; M.J. Duffey, BA. (167); (11–16)
Banbridge High, Primrose Gardens, Banbridge BT32 3EP; Tel (0182 016) 22471; W.J. Wilkinson, BA, MSc, DASE. (602 + 30 SP); (11–16)
Brownlow College (Controlled Integrated) Tullygally Rd, Craigavon BT65 5BS; Tel (01762) 342121; E.J. Lemon. (182); (11–16)
Clounagh Junior High, Brownstown Rd, Portadown, Craigavon BT62 3QA; Tel (01762) 332717; G. Hampton, BA. (565 + 29 SP); (11–14)
Cookstown High, Coolnafrankie Estate, Cookstown BT80 8PQ; Tel (016487) 63632 & 63620; S.J. McGuiness, BSc, DPhil, DASE. (1086 + 34); (11–18)
Dromore High, 31 Banbridge Rd, Dromore BT25 1ND; Tel 692278; R. Russell, MA,DLC,DipEd. (777); (11–16)
Drumglass High, Carland Rd, Dungannon BT71 4AA; Tel (01868) 722421; R.F. Palmer, BA. (483); (11–16)
Fivemiletown High, Corcreevy Demesne, Fivemiletown BT75 0SB; Tel 21279; J.G. Burrell, MA,PhD,DipEd,FRSA. (437); (11–18)
Kilkeel High, Knockchree Ave, Kilkeel, Newry BT34 4BP; Tel (01693) 62365; W.D. Cunningham, BA. (663); (11–18)
Killicomaine Junior High, Upper Church La, Portadown, Craigavon BT63 5JE; Tel (01762) 332021; H.E. McCarthy, BSc, MSc, BA. (637); (11–14)
Lurgan Junior High School, Toberhewny La, Lurgan, Craigavon BT66 8SU; Tel (01762) 323242; Mrs M.E. Ferris. (698); (11–14)
Markethill High, 61 Mowhan Rd, Markethill, Armagh BT60 1RQ; Tel (01861) 551270; S.J. Loughrey, MSc, BEd. (445); (11–16)
Newry High, Ashgrove Pk, Newry BT34 1EB; Tel (01693) 62383; B.G. Robb, BSc,PhD. (570); (11–18)
Newtownhamilton High, 9 Armagh Rd, Newtownhamilton, Newry BT35 0DG; Tel (01693) 878246; J.M. Johnston, BSc. (97); (11–16)
Rathfriland High, 76 Newry St, Rathfriland, Newry BT34 5PZ; Tel (01693) 30374; W.A. Turkington, BA, PGCE. (284); (11–16)
Tandragee Junior High, Armagh Rd, Tandragee, Craigavon BT62 2AY; Tel (01762) 840278; J. Larmour, BA. (295 + 23 SP); (11–14)

Divisional Youth Offices

Armagh/Banbridge, 38 Scotch St, Armagh, Co Armagh BT61 7BY; Tel (01861) 528681; A. Taylor
Craigavon, Bann Hse, Bridge St, Portadown, Co Armagh; Tel (01762) 338556; G. Doran
Dungannon/Cookstown, 20/22 Church St, Dungannon, Co Tyrone BT71 6AB; Tel (018687) 722167; M. Finnerty
Newry/Mourne, Multi-Purpose Centre, Downshire Rd, Newry, Co Down BT34 1BE; Tel (01693) 62357; M. Keenan

Music Centres

Dungannon Music Centre, Thomas St, Dungannon BT70 1HW; Tel (01868) 724379
Portadown Music Centre, Bann Hse, Bridge St, Portadown, Co Armagh; Tel (01762) 332371; E. Benson
Newry Music Centre, Downshire Rd, Newry, Co Down BT34 1BE; Tel (01693) 62357; *Senior Tutor* E. Mills

Residential/Outdoor Education Centres,

Binnian Outdoor Education Base, Head Rd, Annalong, Co Down; Tel (0139 67) 68037; *Warden* P. Mornin
Shannaghmore Residential Centre, Ballagh Rd, Newcastle, Co Down BT33 0LA; Tel (013967) 23841; *Warden* P. Mornin
Killowen Outdoor Education Centre, Killowen Point, Rostrevor, Co Down; Tel (016937) 38297; *Warden* T. Mitten
Yellow Water Cottage, Bryansford Rd, Rostrevor, Co Down; Tel (016937) 38297; *Warden* T. Mitten

Teachers' Centres

Armagh Teachers' Centre, Woodford, 1 Markethill Rd, Armagh BT60 1NR; Tel (01861) 525353; Vacancy
Craigavon Teachers' Centre, C/o Brownlow College, Tullygally Rd, Craigavon, Co Armagh; Tel (01762) 342467; C. Burrows
Dungannon Teachers' Centre, C/o Drumglass Multi-purpose Centre, Dungannon, Co Tyrone; Tel (0186 87) 724379; S. Cousins
Newry Teachers' Centre, Downshire Rd, Newry, Co Down; Tel (01693) 62357; H. McLean

Youth Centres

Armagh Youth Centre, Lisanally La, Armagh, Co Armagh; Tel (01861) 525403; Miss G. McCabe
Aughnacloy Youth Centre, Aughnacloy High School, 23 Carnteel Rd, Aughnacloy, Co Tyrone; Tel (0166 25) 2289; M. Beck
Banbridge Youth Centre, Hill St, Banbridge, Co Down; Tel (0182 016) 62509; E. Parkes
Brownlow Resource (Youth) Centre, Brownlow Rd, Craigavon, Co Armagh; Tel (01762) 343259; M. Young
Cookstown Youth Centre, Cookstown High School, Coolnafrankie Est, Cookstown, Co Tyrone; Tel (0164 87) 63632; G. Gourley
Dromore Youth Centre, Dromore High School, 31 Banbridge Rd, Dromore, Co Down; Tel (01846) 693473; P. Quinn
Drumgor Youth Centre, Drumgor Rd, Craigavon, Co Armagh; Tel (01762) 342977; R. McConville
Fivemiletown Youth Centre, Fivemiletown High School, Corcreevy Demesne, Fivemiletown, Co Tyrone; Tel (0136 55) 21279; K. Graham
Lurgan Youth Annex, Toberhewny La, Lurgan, Craigavon BT66 8JA; Tel (01762) 323119; W. Keegan
Newry Youth Information Point, 81A Hill St, Newry, Co Down BT34 1DJ; Tel (01693) 68132; P. Bradley
Taghnevan Youth Centre, Taghnevan Estate, Lurgan, Co Armagh; Tel (01762) 324989; Mrs A. McCormick
The Hub Youth Club, Church Sq, Rathfriland, Co Down; Tel (0182 016) 30348
Tullygally Youth Centre, Tullygally Rd, Craigavon, Co Armagh; Tel (01762) 341441; R. O'Neill

Western Education and Library Board

1 Hospital Rd, Omagh, Tyrone BT79 OAW; Tel (01662) 240240; Fax (01662) 241443
Chairman Mrs B.B. McIvor
Vice-Chairman S.C. Hogg
Chief Executive P.J. Martin, BA, BD
SEO F.B. Horisk, BSc(Econ), BA
SEO Vacancy
Chief Librarian R.T. Farrow
Chief Finance Officer D. Duffield, ACIS, AMBIM
Chief Transport Officer B. McClean
Purchasing Officer P. McKeever
Personnel Officer Ms. S. Cherry
Senior Adviser (Youth, Community and Cultural Services) J.K. Walls
Senior Adviser (Curriculum) Mrs S. McCaul
Senior Adviser (Management) H. Lindsay
Number of Schools
200 primary (37,000); 37 secondary (16,750); 13 grammar (9,775); special 10; nursery 10

Special Schools

Altnagelvin Hospital, North West Hospital, Altnagelvin, Londonderry, BT47 1SB; Tel (01504) 45171; Mrs V. Smallwoods
Belmont Hse, Racecourse Rd, Londonderry BT48 7RE; Tel (01504) 351266; T. McCully. (Residential & Day (Mixed); (Girls)
Cranny School, 4A Deverney Rd, Omagh, Co Tyrone BT79 0JJ; Tel (01662) 242939; T. McCrossan
Erne, Derrygonnelly Rd, Enniskillen, Co Fermanagh BT74 7EX; Tel (01365) 323942; K. Turnbull
Foyle View, 15 Racecourse Rd, Londonderry BT48 7RB; Tel (01504) 263270; J. Hunter
Glasvey, 15 Loughermore Rd, Ballykelly, Limavady, Co Londonderry BT49 9PB; Tel (0150 47) 62462; J.A. McCallum
Glenside, 45A Derry Rd, Strabane, Co Tyrone BT82 8DY; Tel (01504) 883319; Mrs D.M.H. Kinkaid
Greystone Hall, 2 Ballyquin Rd, Limavady, Co Londonderry BT49 9ET; Tel (0150 47) 62351; W.C. Wilson
Heatherbank School, 17 Deverney Rd, Omagh, Co Tyrone BT79 0ND; Tel (01662) 49182; H. McAteer
Killadeas, Killadeas, Irvinestown, Enniskillen, Co Fermanagh BT7 4AY; Tel (0136 56) 21550; Mrs H. Lendrum

Secondary Schools (Voluntary Maintained)

Dean Brian Maguire, 26 Termon Rd, Carrickmore, Omagh, Co Tyrone BT79 9JR; Tel (0166 27) 61272; P. Curran. (Mixed) (415)
Our Lady of Mercy, Springhill, Strabane, Co Tyrone BT82 8HH; Tel (01504) 382331. (Girls) (537)
St Aidan's, Derrylin, Enniskillen, Co Fermanagh BT92 9LD; Tel (0136 57) 48337; J.V. Cassidy. (Mixed) (301)
St Brecan's, Trench Rd, Londonderry BT47 2DS; Tel (01504) 45364; P. Molloy. (Mixed) (371)
St Brigid's, Kelvin Rd, Omagh, Co Tyrone BT78 1LG; Tel (01662) 42716; Mrs G. McCormick. (Girls) (599)
St Brigid's High, Glengalliagh Rd, Londonderry BT48 8DU; Tel (01504) 351002; F. Dunne. (Mixed) (1002)
St Cecilia's, Bligh's La, Londonderry BT48 9PJ; Tel (01504) 365845; Mrs G. McCafferty. (Girls) (925)
St Colman's, 35 Melmount Rd, Strabane, Co Tyrone BT82 9EF; Tel (01504) 382562; P.J. Grimley. (Boys) (936)
St Comghall's, Lisnaskea, Enniskillen, Co Fermanagh BT92 0LA; Tel (0136 57) 21417; J.J. Tracey. (Mixed) (417)
St Eugene's, 1 Cavan Rd, Castlederg, Co Tyrone BT81 7TP; Tel (0166 26) 71543; C. Gallen. (Mixed) (270)
St Eugene's Roslea, Enniskillen, Co Fermanagh BT92 7PR; Tel (0136 575) 258; J.A. Curolun. (Mixed) (228)
St Fanchea's, Mill St, Enniskillen, Co Fermanagh BT74 6AN; Tel (01365) 322919; Sister Anne Marie McQuade. (Girls) (489)
St John's, 37 Omagh Rd, Dromore, Omagh, Co Tyrone BT78 3AL; Tel (01662) 898284; E. McGrade. (Mixed) (438)
St Joseph's, Drumclay, Enniskillen, Co Fermanagh BT74 6DE; Tel (01365) 322918; B. Gallagher. (Boys) (344)
St Joseph's, Creggan Est, Westway, Londonderry BT48 9NX; Tel (01504) 262923; Dr N. McCafferty. (Boys) (841)
St Joseph's, 397 Lisnarragh Rd, Plumbridge, Omagh, Co Tyrone BT79 8AJ; Tel (0166 26) 48349; L. Kennedy. (Mixed) (307)
St Mary's Brollagh Belleek, Enniskillen, Co Fermanagh BT93 3AA; Tel (0136 56) 58257; G.B. Regan. (Mixed) (195)
St Mary's, Fanad Dr, Creggan Est, Londonderry BT48 9QE; Tel (01504) 362154; G.M. Keegan. (Girls) (915)
St Mary's, Irvinestown, Enniskillen, Co Fermanagh BT94 1EL; Tel (0136 56) 21318; Mrs E. Horisk. (Mixed) (251)
St Mary's, Irish Green St, Limavady, Co Londonderry BT49 9AN; Tel (0150 47) 62360; S. Bradley. (Mixed) (829)
St Patrick's, 9 Curragh Rd, Dungiven, Co Londonderry BT47 4SE; Tel (01504) 41324; G. Devenny. (Mixed) (402)
St Patrick's, Kelvin Rd, Omagh, Co Tyrone BT78 1LG; Tel (01662) 242717; T. Maguire. (Boys) (575)
St Patrick's and St Brigid's, 55 Main St, Claudy, Co Londonderry BT47 4HR; Tel (01504) 338317; Mrs J. McAnena. (Mixed) (483)
St Peter's, Southway, Foyle Hill Est, Londonderry BT48 9SE; Tel (01504) 361981; M. Bowen. (Boys) (416)

Secondary Schools (Controlled)

Castlederg, 16 Castlegore Rd, Castledery, Co Tyrone BT81 7RU; Tel (0166 26) 71272; W. McSparron. (Mixed) (351)
Clondermot High, Irish St, Londonderry BT47 2DD; Tel (01504) 43487; J. Magowan. (Mixed) (558)
Duke of Westminster High School, Ballinamallard, Enniskillen, Co Fermanagh BT94 2GG; Tel (01365) 388227; W.D. McKee, BA. (Mixed) (319)
Dungiven, 6 Chapel Rd, Dungiven, Co Londonderry BT47 4RS; Tel (0150 47) 41298; J. Doherty. (Mixed) (87)
Enniskillen, Derrychara, Enniskillen, Co Fermanagh BT74 6JL; Tel (01365) 322923; V. Outram. (Mixed) (495)
Faughan Valley, 35 Drumahoe Rd, Drumahoe, Londonderry BT47 3SD; Tel (01504) 301284; S.G. Reilly. (Mixed) (558)
Limavady, Irish Green St, Limavady, Co Londonderry BT49 9AN; Tel (0150 47) 62526; J.R. Lapsley. (Mixed) (705)
Lisnaskea, Lisnaskea, Enniskillen, Co Fermanagh BT98 0JS; Tel (0136 57) 21283; R. Forde. (Mixed) (202)
Omagh, 14 Crevenagh Rd, Omagh, Co Tyrone BT79 0ET; Tel (01662) 242656; W. Harper. (Mixed) (481)
Strabane, 61 Derry Rd, Strabane, Co Tyrone BT82 8LD; Tel (01504) 882578; F.A. Browne, BSc. (Mixed) (415)
Templemore, Northland Rd, Londonderry BT48 0AP; Tel (01504) 267834; F.G. Wright. (Mixed) (396)

Grammar Schools (Voluntary)

Christian Brothers, Kelvin Rd, Omagh, Co Tyrone BT78 1LD; Tel (01662) 243567; R.B. Tierney. (Boys) (860)
Enniskillen Convent, Mount Lourdes, Enniskillen, Co Fermanagh BT74 6AB; Tel (01365) 322265; Sister Una Began. (Girls) (850)
Foyle and Londonderry College, Duncreggan, Londonderry BT48 0AW; Tel (01504) 269321; W.J. Magill. (Mixed) (960)
Loreto Convent, James St, Omagh, Co Tyrone BT78 1DL; Tel (01662) 243633; C. O'Neill. (Girls) (955)
Portora Royal, Derrygonnelly Rd, Enniskillen, Co Fermanagh BT74 7HA; Tel (01365) 322658; R.L. Bennett. (Boys) (500)
St Columb's College, Buncrana Rd, Londonderry BT48 8NH; Tel (01504) 266439; Rev J.R. Walsh. (Boys) (1742)

St Michael's, Charterhill Rd, Enniskillen, Co Fermanagh BT74 6DG; Tel (01365) 322935; Rev P. MacEntee. (Boys) (770)
Strabane Convent, Curley Hill, Strabane, Co Tyrone BT82 8LP; Tel (01504) 882339; Mr V. Power. (Girls) (480)
Thornhill College, 123 Culmore Rd, Londonderry BT48 8JF; Tel (01504) 351479; Sister Christopher. (Girls) (1500)

Grammar Schools (Controlled)

Academy, 21–23 Dublin Rd, Omagh, Co Tyrone BT78 1HF; Tel (01662) 242688; J.B. McBain, BA,DipEd,DASE. (Mixed) (648)
Enniskillen Collegiate, 1 Cooper Cres, Enniskillen, Co Fermanagh BT74 6DQ; Tel (01365) 322165; G.A. Young, BA. (Girls) (475)
Limavady, 3 Ballyquin Rd, Limavady, Co Londonderry BT49 9ET; Tel (0150 47) 62374; R.B. Matier. (Mixed) (888)
Strabane Grammar School, Milltown Hse, 4 Liskey Rd, Strabane, Co Tyrone BT82 8NW; Tel (01504) 382319; D.W. Todd. (Mixed) (358)

Field Study Centre

Magilligan Field Centre, 375 Seacoast Rd, Limavady, Co Londonderry; Tel (0150 47) 50234; G. Bond

Outdoor Education Centres

Goles Cottage, Keadycarn, Cranagh, Omagh, Co Tyrone; Tel (01648) 28622; *Caretaker* J. Duffy
Carrowmena Outdoor Education Centre, Seacoast Rd, Limavady, Co Londonderry; Tel (0150 47) 63740; *Caretaker* R. Cooke
Corrick Outdoor Education Centre, 3 Corrickbeg Rd, Newtownstewart, Co Tyrone; Tel (0166 26) 48165/61599; *Caretaker* Mrs. E. Pentland
Gortatole Outdoor Education Centre, Florencecourt, Enniskillen, Co Fermanagh; Tel (0136 5) 348888; *Warden* R. Finlay

Teachers' Centres

North West Teacher's Centre, 24 Temple Rd, Strathfoyle, Londonderry BT47 1UP; Tel (01504) 861116; Ms M. McCallion
Omagh Teachers' Centre, Omagh Library, 1 Spillars Pl, Omagh, Co Tyrone BT78 1HL; Tel (01662) 244821; Vacancy
South West Teachers' Centre, Library Headquarters, Hall's La, Enniskillen, Co Fermanagh BT74 7DR; Tel (01365) 323240; Vacancy
Strabane Teachers' Centre, Khiva House, 55 Urney Rd, Strabane, Co Tyrone; Tel (01504) 382632; Vacancy

Youth Centres

Aileach, St Peter's Secondary School, Foyle Hill, Londonderry, Co Londonderry; Tel (01504) 361981; J. McGilloway
Ballinamallard, Duke of Westminster High School, Ballinamallard, Enniskillen, Co Fermanagh; Tel (01365) 388227; Mrs E. Bradshaw
Brollagh, St Mary's Secondary School, Brollagh Belleek, Enniskillen, Co Fermanagh; G. McGurran
Carrickmore Youth Centre, Termon Rd, Carrickmore, Co Tyrone; Tel (0166 27) 61419; F. Daly. (Cont)
Caw, Seymour Gdns, Londonderry, Co Londonderry; Tel (01504) 310000; V. Rutherford
Claudy, St Patrick's and St Brigid's High School, 55 Main St, Claudy, Co Londonderry; Tel (01504) 338317; G. Burns
Clondermot, Clondermot High School, Irish St, Londonderry, Co Londonderry; Tel (01504) 43096; C. Adjey
Crevenagh, Omagh High School, 14 Crevenagh Rd, Omagh, Co Tyrone; C. McFarland
Derg Valley, Castlederg High School, 16 Castlegore Rd, Castlederg BT81 7RU; Tel (016626) 70195; J. Ireland
Derrychara, Enniskillen High School, Derrychara, Enniskillen, Co Fermanagh; Tel (01365) 323394; G. Milten
Fairview Information Plus Centre, Fairview, Enniskillen, Co Fermanagh; Tel (01365) 326932; J. Rooney
Faughan Valley, Faughan Valley High School, 35 Drumahoe Rd, Drumahoe, Co Londonderry; Tel (01504) 301284; Mr. A. McFarland
Galliagh, Lenamore Rd, Galliagh, Londonderry BT48 8NA; Tel (01504) 352309; D. O'Kane
Glenelly, St Joseph's High School, 397 Lisnarragh Rd, Plumbridge, Co Tyrone; A. McConnell
Holiday Projects West, 18–20 Bishop St, Londonderry, Co Londonderry; Tel (01504) 263262; Mrs C. Delahunt. (Vol)
Irvinestown, Bawnacre Centre, Irvinestown, Enniskillen, Co Fermanagh; Tel (0136 56) 21177; G. Beacon
Kesh, Duke of Westminster High School, Kesh, Enniskillen, Co Fermanagh; Tel (0136 56) 31265/31634; Mrs E. Bradshaw
Limavady Grammar, Limavady Grammar School, 3 Ballyquin Rd, Limavady, Co Londonderry; Tel (0150 47) 62374; Miss J. Miller
Limavady High, Limavady High School, Irish Green St, Limavady, Co Londonderry; Tel (0150 47) 62526; R.J. Robinson
Lisnaskea, Lisnaskea High School, Lisnaskea, Enniskillen, Co Fermanagh; Tel (0136 57) 21283; Dr C. Givan
Londonderry Information Plus Centre, 6 Bayview Terr, Londonderry; Tel (01504) 266339; G. McIntyre
Long Tower Youth Club, Ann St, Londonderry, Co Londonderry; Tel (01504) 260711/264012; F. Campbell. (Vol) (523)
Newtownstewart Model, Newtonstewart Model Primary School, 6 Baronscourt Rd, Newtownstewart, Co Tyrone; D. Loughlin
Omagh Boys & Girls Club, 32A Brookmount Rd, Omagh, Co Tyrone; Tel (01662) 243772; P. McMahon. (Vol)
Omagh Information Plus Centre, Sedan Ave, Omagh, Co Tyrone; Tel (01662) 245954; T. McElholm
Omagh Youth Centre, Old Mountfield Rd, Omagh, Co Tyrone; Tel (01662) 249349; Mrs M. Bradley. (Cont)
Pennyburn Youth Club, 5 Buncrana Rd, Londonderry, Co Londonderry; Tel (01504) 267959; B. Wilkinson. (Vol)
Pilot's Row Youth Club, Rossville St, Londonderry, Co Londonderry; Tel (01504) 269418; Miss S. Gibson. (Cont)
Rosemount Youth Club, Rosemount, Westway, Londonderry, Co Londonderry; Tel (01504) 369264; Miss M. McCourt. (Cont)
Roslea, St Eugene's Secondary School, Roslea, Enniskillen, Co Fermanagh; J. Crudden
St Brecan's, St Brecan's High School, Trench Rd, Londonderry BT47 2DS; Tel (01504) 45364; G. Kelly
St Canice's, St Patrick's High School, 9 Curragh Rd, Dungiven, Co Londonderry; Tel (0150 47) 41324; C. McCartney
St Mary's, St Mary's High School, Irish Green St, Limavady, Co Londonderry; Tel (0150 47) 65443; T. Campbell
St Mary's, Youth Centre, Fanad Dr, Creggan Est, Londonderry; Tel (01504) 265211; C. McCafferty
St Michael's Youth Club, Belmore St, Enniskillen, Co Fermanagh; Tel (01365) 324755; Vacancy. (Vol)
Shantallow Youth Club, Racecourse Rd, Londonderry, Co Londonderry; Tel (01504) 353561; S. Mullin. (Cont)
Sion Mills, Sion Mills Primary School, Sion Mills, Strabane, Co Tyrone; Vacancy
Strabane Youth Association, Melvin Hall, Strabane, Co Tyrone; Tel (01504) 382175; Ms M. McGarrigle. (Cont)
Strathfoyle Youth Centre, Deramore Dr, Strathfoyle, Londonderry, Co Londonderry; Tel (01504) 860334; H. Hastings. (Cont)
Templemore, Templemore Secondary School, Northland Rd, Londonderry, Co Londonderry; Tel (01504) 363407; Miss J. Robinson
Ventures I, Strabane High School, 61 Derry Rd, Strabane, Co Tyrone; Tel (01504) 882578; K. Wilson
Ventures II, St Colman's High School, 35 Melmount Rd, Strabane, Co Tyrone; Tel (01504) 382693; T. McGillicuddy
Waterside Youth Club, 40 Dungiven Rd, Waterside, Londonderry, Co Londonderry; Tel (01504) 261378/49332; J. McLucas. (Vol)

8 Independent Secondary Schools

ABBREVIATIONS
A Participates in Assisted Places Scheme
B Pupils of opposite sex accepted in Sixth Form
C Day pupils of opposite sex accepted
The number in brackets is the approximate number of secondary pupils

England

Avon

Badminton School, Westbury-on-Trym, Bristol BS9 3BA; Tel (0117) 962 3141; Fax (0117) 962 8963 (350) (Girls) (Boarders and Day)
Bath High School GPDST, Hope Hse, Lansdown, Bath BA1 5ES; Tel (01225) 422931; Fax (01225) 484378 (GPDST) (A) (Girls) (418 Senior) (209 Junior)
Bristol Cathedral School, College Square, Bristol BS1 5TS; Tel (0117) 929 1872 (A,B) (Boys)
Bristol Grammar School, Bristol BS8 1SR; Tel (0117) 973 6006; *Headmaster* C.E. Martin (A) (1000) (Mixed)
Bristol Waldorf School, Park Pl, Clifton, Bristol BS8 1JR; Tel (0117) 926 0440; Fax (0117) 929 3561 (250) (Co-ed)
Clifton College, Bristol BS8 3JH; Tel (0117) 973 9187; *Headmaster* A.H. Monro (A) (680) (Mixed) (Boarders) (Day)
Clifton High School, College Rd, Clifton, Bristol BS8 3JD; Tel (0117) 973 0201; Fax (0117) 923 8962; *Headmistress* Mrs J.D. Walters (A) (450) (Boarders)
Colston's Collegiate School, Stapleton, Bristol BS16 1BJ; Tel (0117) 965 5207 (A,B) (600) (mixed) Boys) (Boarders)
Colston's Girls' School, Cheltenham Rd, Bristol BS6 5RD; Tel (0117) 942 4328, 428898 (A) (630)
Downside School, Stratton-on-the-Fosse, Bath BA3 4RJ; Tel (01761) 232206; Fax (01761) 233575 (400) (Boys) (RC) (Boarders)
Highdene Association, The Laurels, Cribbs Causeway, Bristol BS10 7TU; Tel (0117) 950 1857 (16 (Boys) (All-year Boarders for pupils with special educational needs) (Weekly boarders)
King Edward's School, North Rd, Bath BA2 6HU; Tel (01225) 464313; Fax (01225) 481363; *Headmaster* Peter Winter, MA (Oxon) (A,B,C) (690) (Boys 645; 6th Form Girls 45)
Kingswood School, Lansdown, Bath BA1 5RG; Tel (01225) 311627; Fax (01225) 481345 (A,B,C) (253) (Boys) (Girls) (189) (Boarders) (Weekly boarders) (Day)
Monkton Combe, nr Bath BA2 7HG; Tel (01225) 721102; Fax (01225) 721181 (Mixed) (309) (Boarders and some day)
Prior Park College, Bath BA2 5AH; Tel (01225) 835353; *Headmaster* J.W.R. Goulding, MA (463) (Boarders 170) (Day 293) (Boys 271) (Girls 192) (Day pupils 11–18) (Boarders boys 13–18, girls 13–18)
Queen Elizabeth's Hospital, Bristol BS8 1JX; Tel (0117) 929 1856 (A) (500) (Boys) (80) (Boarders)
The Red Maids' School, Westbury-on-Trym, Bristol BS9 3AW; Tel (0117) 962 2641; Fax (0117) 962 1687; *Headmistress* Miss S. Hampton (500) (A) (Girls) (Boarders)
Redland High School for Girls, Redland Ct, Bristol BS6 7EF; Tel (0117) 924 5796 (A) (480) (Girls)
Royal School, Lansdown, Bath BA1 5SZ; Tel (01225) 313877; Fax (01225) 420338 (208) (Boarders) (133) (Day)
St Ursula's High School, Brecon Rd, Westbury-on-Trym, Bristol BS9 4DT; Tel (0117) 962 2616 (Senior) (245) (Girls) (210) (Junior) (Mixed)
Sidcot School, Winscombe BS25 1PD; Tel (0193 484) 3102; *Headmaster* Christopher Greenfield; The Hall School, Sidcot, the pre-prep school for Sidcot – 60 pupils day only (3–9) (Mixed) (390) (Boarders and Day) (Weekly boarders) (9–18)

Silverhill School Winterbourne Hse, Winterbourne, Bristol BS17 1RL; Tel (0117) 977 2156 (Mixed) (3–16) (290) (Day)
Westwing School, Junior/Infant Kyneton Hse, Thonbury, Bristol BS12 2JZ; Tel (0117) 941 2311 (C) (110) (Girls) (Boarders and Day) (Weekly boarders)

Bedfordshire

Bedford High School, Bromham Road, Bedford MK40 2BS; Tel (01234) 360221; Fax (01234) 353552; *Headmistress* M.L. Churm, BA (A) (1000) (Girls) (Boarders) (Weekly boarders) (Day)
Bedford School, Burnaby Road, Bedford MK40 2TU; Tel (01234) 340444 (A) (1130) (Boys) (Boarders/Day)
Bury Lawn School, Steppingley Rd, Flitwick, Beds MK45 1AH; Tel (01525) 718124; Fax (01442) 214346; *Principal* C.G. Symington; *Head* Jon Styler (Mixed 2–18) (Upper School) (200) (Lower School) (200)
The Dame Alice Harpur School, Cardington Rd, Bedford MK42 0BX; Tel (01234) 340871; Fax (01234) 344125; *Headmistress* R. Randle, BA, MA (Ed)
Rushmoor School, 58/60 Shakespeare Rd, Bedford MK40 2DL; Tel (01234) 352031; Fax (01234) 348395 (Boys) (300) (Boarders) (Weekly boarders)
St Andrew's School, Kimbolton Rd, Bedford MK40 2PA; Tel (01234) 267272; Fax (01234) 355105; *Headmistress* J.M. Mark (Girls) (320)

Berkshire

The Abbey School, Kendrick Rd, Reading RG1 5DZ; Tel (01734) 872256; *Headmistress* Miss B.C.L. Sheldon (A) (Girls) (750)
Bearwood College, Wokingham RG11 5BG; Tel (01734) 786915; Fax (01734) 772687; *Headmaster* Dr R.J. Belcher (Co-educational) (204) (Boarders) (Weekly boarders) (Day)
Bradfield College, Bradfield RG7 6AR; Tel (01734) 744203; *Headmaster* P.B. Smith (A,B,C) (Boys) (500) (Girls) (80) (Boarders)
Brigidine School, King's Rd, Windsor SL4 2AX; Tel (01753) 863779 (Girls) (263)
Claires Court School, Ray Mill Rd East, Maidenhead SL6 8TE; Tel (01628) 411470 (Boys) (267)
Douai School, Upper Woolhampton, Reading RG7 5TH; Tel (01734) 715200; Fax (01734) 715241; *Headmaster* Edmund Power, OSB (Co-ed) (225) (Boarders) (Day)
Downe House School, Cold Ash, Newbury RG16 9JJ; Tel (01635) 200286; Fax (01635) 202026; *Headmistress* S.R. Cameron (Girls (524) (Boarders)
Eton College, Windsor; Tel (01752) 866439; *Headmaster* W.E.K. Anderson (Boys) (1250) (Boarders)
Heathfield School, Ascot SL5 8BQ; Tel (01344) 882955; Fax (01344) 890689 (Girls (220) (Boarders
Hemdean Hse, Hemdean Rd, Caversham, Reading RG24 7SD; Tel (01734) 472590; Fax (01734) 464474 (Girls 3-16, Boys 3-11) (156)
Hurst Lodge, Sunningdale SL5 9QG; Tel (01344) 22154; *Principal* Mrs A.M. Smit (Girls) (250) (Boarders) (Weekly boarders and Day)
Leighton Park, Reading RG2 7DH; Tel (01734) 872065; Fax (01734) 866959 (Boys and Girls 360) (Mixed 11-18) (Boarders and Day
Licensed Victuallers' School, London Road, Ascot SL5 8DR; Tel (01344) 882770; *Head* Mrs P.M. Cowley, BA(Hons) (Mixed) (5–18) (700) (Day) (Weekly boarders) (Full Boarders
Luckley-Oakfield School, Wokingham RG11 3EU; Tel (01734) 784175; *Headmaster* R.C. Blake, MA, Mphil (Girls) (272) (Boarders/Weekly Boarders and Day)
Maidenhead College Claires Court Girls, 1 College Ave, Maidenhead SL6 6AW; Tel (01628) 411480; *Headmistress* Dr M. Marwick, BSc, PhD (C) (227) (Girls 3–16) (47) (Boys 3–7)
Marist Convent Senior School, Sunninghill, Ascot SL5 7PS; Tel (01344) 24291; *Headmistress* Sister M. Gaffney (Girls) (400)
Pangbourne College, Pangbourne RG8 8LA; Tel (01734) 842101; Fax (01734) 845443; *Headmaster* A.B.E. Hudson (Boys) (410) (Boarders) (Day)
Presentation College, 63 Bath Rd, Reading RG3 2BB; Tel (01734) 572861; *Headmaster* Rev Simon Sullivan (Boys) (420)
Queen Anne's School, Caversham, Reading RG4 0DX; Tel (01734) 471582 (Girls) (274 Boarders) (118 day girls)
Reading Blue Coat School, Holme Pk, Sonning, nr Reading RG4 0SU; Tel (01734) 441005; Fax (01734) 442690; *Headmaster* A.C.E. Sanders (B) (Boys, Sixth Form Girls) (550) (Boarders) (Weekly boarders) (Day)
St Gabriel's Day School, Sandleford Priory, Newbury RG15 9BB; Tel (01635) 40663; *Headmaster* D.J. Cobb (Girls) (400)
St George's School, Ascot SL5 7DZ; Tel (01344) 20273; Fax (01344) 874213; *Headmistress* A.M. Griggs, BA (Girls) (Boarders and Day) (285)
St Joseph's Convent School, Upper Redland's Rd, Reading RG1 5JT; Tel (01734) 661000 (A) (Girls) (400)
St Mary's School, Ascot SL5 9JF; Tel (01344) 27788; *Headmistress* Sister M.M. Orchard (Girls) (335) (Boarders)
Wellington College, Crowthorne, Berkshire RG11 7PU; Tel (01344) 771588; Fax (01344) 772261 (A,B) (Boys) (750) (Girls) (50) (Boarders)

Buckinghamshire

Akeley Wood School, Buckingham MK18 5AE; Tel (01280) 814110; *Headmaster* J.C. Lovelock (Mixed) (380)
Bury Lawn School, Soskin Drive, Stantonbury Fields, Milton Keynes, Buckinghamshire MK14 6DP; Tel (01908) 220345; Fax (01442) 214346; *Principal* C.G. Symington; *Head* Hilary Kiff (Mixed) (2–18) (200 Lower School) (200 Upper School)
Hampden Manor School, Hampden Manor, Great Missenden HP16 9PS; Tel (01296) 622101 (Mixed) (120)
Holy Cross Convent, Chalfont St Peter, Gerrards Cross SL9 9DW; Tel (01753) 882583; *Headmistress* Sister Kevin Russell (Boarders and Day) (300)
Pipers Corner School, Great Kingshill, High Wycombe HP15 6LP; Tel (01494) 718255; Fax (01494) 715391; *Headmistress* Dr Mary Wilson (Girls (360)
St Mary's Independent Day School for Girls, Gerrards Cross SL9 8JQ; Tel (01753) 883370; *Headmistress* Mrs J.P.G. Smith (Girls) (300)
Stowe, MK18 5EH; Tel (01280) 813164 (A,B) (Boys 13–18) (Girls 16–18) (550) (Boarders, Day)
The Vale School, Peverel Court, Portway Rd, Stone, Aylesbury; Tel (01296) 748786 (Mixed) (155)
Thornton College, Convent of Jesus & Mary, Thornton, Milton Keynes MK17 0HJ; Tel (01280) 812610; Fax (01280) 824042 (Girls) (250) (Boarders) (Day)
Wycombe Abbey School, High Wycombe HP11 1PE; Tel (01494) 520381; Fax (01494) 473836 (Girls) (485) (Limited No. of Day Girls)

Cambridgeshire

Kimbolton School, Kimbolton, Huntingdon PE18 0EA; Tel (01480) 860505; Fax (01480) 860386; *Headmaster* R.V. Peel (A) (Mixed (560) (Day and Boarders)
The King's School, Ely, Cambridgeshire CB7 4DB; Tel (01353) 662824; Fax (01353) 662187; *Head* R.H. Youdale, MA (Mixed) (Boarders) (Weekly boarders) (Age range 4 to 18) (786)
Kirkstone House School, Baston, Peterborough PE6 9NU; Tel (01778) 560350 (Mixed) (151)
The Leys School, Cambridge CB2 2AD; Tel (01223) 355327; *Headmaster* Rev Dr J.C.A. Barrett, MA (A,B) (Mixed) (400) (Boarders and Home Boarders) (Day)
Oundle School, Oundle, Peterborough PE8 4EN; Tel (01832) 273536; Fax (01832) 274967 (Mixed) (Boarder (826)
The Perse School for Boys, Cambridge; Tel (01223) 568300; Fax (01223) 568293; *Headmaster* Nigel Richardson (A) (Boys) (Day) (Co-educational Sixth Form) (473)

The Perse School for Girls, Union Rd, Cambridge CB2 1HF; Tel (01223) 359589; Fax (01223) 467420; *Headmistress* Miss H.S. Smith (A) (550)
Peterborough High School, Westwood House, Thorpe Rd, Peterborough PE3 6JF; Tel (01733) 343357 (C) (310) (Girls) (Boarders) (Weekly Boarders)
St Mary's School, Bateman St, Cambridge CB2 1LY; Tel (01223) 353253; Fax (01223) 357451; *Headmistress* Miss M. Conway (A) (Girls) (600) (Weekly boarders)

Cheshire

Abbey Gate College, Saighton Grange, Saighton, Chester CH3 6EG; Tel (01244) 332077; *Headmaster* E.W. Mitchell (Mixed (350)
Cheadle Hulme School, Claremont Rd, Cheadle Hulme, Cheadle, Cheshire SK8 6EF; Tel 0161-485 4142 (Registrar) 0161-486 9902; Fax 0161-488 4540; *Headmaster* D.J. Wilkinson, BA, MLitt (Warehousemen and Clerks) (A) (920) (Mixed) (Day)
Forest Park School, 27 Oakfield, Sale M33 1NB; Tel (0161) 973 4835; *Headmistress* Rosemarie Smart, TGCE (Mixed (120)
The Grange School, Bradburns La, Hartford, Northwich, Cheshire CW8 1LU; Tel (01606) 74007 (Mixed (4–18) (1080)
Hammond School, Hoole Bank Hse, Mannings La, Hoole, Chester; Tel (01244) 328542; *Headmistress* Mrs P. Dangerfield (Girls (150) (Boarders – dance students) (Day – non-dancers)
Hillcrest Grammar School, Beech Ave, Stockport SK3 8HB; Tel (0161) 480 0329; *Headmaster* D.K. Blackburn (Mixed 4–16) (310)
King's School, Chester CH4 7QL; Tel (01244) 680026; Fax (01244) 678008 (A) (Boys) (673)
The King's School, Macclesfield SK10 1DA; Tel (01625) 618586; *Headmaster* A.G. Silcock, MA (Mixed) (1270) (Mixed 7–11) (195) (Boys 11–16) (590) (Girls 11–16) (200) (Mixed 16–18) (287)
Mount Carmel Convent School, Wilmslow Rd, Alderley Edge SK9 7QE; Tel (01625) 583028; Fax (01625) 590271; *Headmistress* Mrs Marie Moss, BA (Girls (410)
Oriel Bank High School, Devonshire Park Rd, Davenport, Stockport SK2 6JP; Tel (0161) 483 2935; *Headmistress* Mrs Anne P. Perrett (Girls (200)
The Queen's School, City Walls Rd, Chester CH1 2NN; Tel (01244) 312078; Fax (01244) 321507; *Headmistress* Miss D.M. Skilbeck, BA (A) (Girls 4–18, Boys 5–8) (618)
St Hilary's School, Alderly Edge SK9 7AG; Tel (01625) 583532; *Headmistress* Mrs J. Tracey, BSc, AInstP (Girls (245)
Sandbach School, Crewe Rd, Sandbach CW11 0NT; Tel (01270) 767321; *Headmaster* C.R. Brown (A) (900) (Boys) (Independent Comprehensive)
Stockport Grammar School, Buxton Rd, Stockport, Cheshire SK2 7AF; Tel (0161) 456 9000; *Headmaster* D.R.J. Bird, MA (A) (1010) (Mixed)

Cleveland

Ayton School, High Green, Great Ayton, N. Yorks TS9 6BN; Tel (01642) 722141; Fax (01642) 724044; *Headmaster* Christopher J. Scaife (Mixed) (Day) (Boarders) (Weekly Boarders) (5–19) (230)
Mill Hill School, Green La, Middlesbrough, Cleveland TS5 7RY; Tel (01642) 816875 (Mixed (100)
Red House School, 36 The Green, Norton, Stckton on Tees TS20 1DX; Tel (01642) 553370; Fax (01642) 361031 (100) (Mixed)
Teesside High School for Girls, The Avenue, Eaglescliffe, Stockton-on-Tees, Cleveland TS16 9AT; Tel (01642) 782095; Fax (01642) 791207; *Headmistress* Mrs J. Coles (400)
Yarm School, The Friarage, Yarm, Cleveland TS15 9EJ; Tel (01642) 786023; *Headmaster* R. Neville Tate (A,B) (640) (Boys) (Girls 6th form) (Takes Juniors)

Cornwall

Daughters of the Cross, Tremough Convent School, nr Falmouth; Tel (01326) 372226; *Headmistress* Sister Maria (300) (Girls) (Boarders) (Weekly boarders)
The Duchy Grammar School, Tregye, Carnon Downs, Truro TR3 6JH; Tel (01872) 862289; *Headmaster* M.L. Fuller (A,B,C) (180) (Mixed)
St Joseph's School, Launceston PL15 8HN; Tel (01566) 772988; *Headmaster* A.G. Taylor (220) (Girls 11–16) (Mixed Junior School 4–11) (Boarders and Day)
School of St Clare, Polwithen, Penzance TR18 4JR; Tel (01736) 63271; Fax (01736) 330960; *Headmaster* Ian Halford (C) (190) (Girls) (40) (Boys) (Day) (Boarders) (Weekly boarders)
Tremough Convent, Penryn TR10 9EZ; Tel (01326) 372226 (A) (300) (Girls) (Weekly boarders)
Truro High School, Truro; Tel (01872) 72830 (A,B) (497) (Girls) (Boarders) (Weekly boarders) (Takes Juniors)
Truro School, Trennick La, Truro TR1 1TH; Tel (01872) 72763; *Headmaster* G.A.G. Dodd, MA (A,B) (556) (Boys) (258) (Girls) (Boarders) (Weekly boarders)

Cumbria

Austin Friars' School, Carlisle CA3 9PB; Tel (01228) 28042; Fax 01228) 810327 (300) (B,C) (Mainly RC) (Boarding and Day) (Co-Educational)
Casterton School, Kirkby Lonsdale, Cumbria LA6 2SG; Tel (015242) 71202; Fax (015242) 71146; *Headmaster* A.F. Thomas, MA(Cantab) (370) (A) (Girls 8–18) (Boarders and Day)
Lime House School, Holm Hill, Dalston, nr Carlisle CA5 7BX; Tel (01228) 710225; Fax (01228) 710508 (300) (B,C) (Mixed) (Boarders) (Weekly Boarders)
St Anne's School Educational Trust Ltd, Windermere LA23 1NW; Tel (015394) 46164; *Headmaster* C.M.G.R. Jenkins (300) (Girls) (Boarders)
St Bees School, St Bees, Cumbria CA27 0DS; Tel (01946) 8222263; Fax (01946) 823657; *Headmaster* P.A. Chamberlain (155) (Boys) (135) (Girls) (A) (Boarders)
Sedbergh School, Sedbergh; Tel (015396) 20535 (400) (Boys) (A) (Boarders 11–18)

Derbyshire

Derbyshire High School for Girls, Hillsway, Littleover DE3 7DT; Tel (01332) 514267
Michael House School, The Field, Shipley, Heanor DE75 7JH; Tel (01773) 718050; (Mixed (175)
Mount St Mary's College, Spinkhill, Nr Sheffield S31 9YL; Tel (01246) 433388; Fax (01246) 435511; *Headmaster* P.B. Fisher, MA (310) (Mixed) (A,B,C) (Local Boarders, Boarders and Day)
Normanton School, St Johns Rd, Buxton SK17 6SJ; Tel (01298) 22745 (Mixed) (Boarders, Weekly boarders, Day) (80)
Ockbrook School, Moravian Settlement, Ockbrook, Derby DE72 3RJ; Tel (01332) 673532; Fax (01332) 665184; *Headmistress* Dr M. Rennie, BSc, PhD, DipEd (385) (Day) (Boarders) (3–18 Girls) (3–11 Boys) (Weekly Boarders) (Girls 8–18)
Repton School, Repton, Derby DE65 6FH; Tel (01283) 702375; *Headmaster* G.E. Jones (130) (Girls) (470) (Boys) (Boarders)
St Elphin's C. of E. School for Girls, Darley Dale, Matlock DE4 2HA; Tel (01629) 732687; Fax (01629) 733956; *Headmistress* Valerie Fisher, BA, PGCE (260) (Boarders/Day)
Trent College, Long Eaton NG10 4AD; Tel (0115) 946 3114; Fax (0115) 946 3284 (640) (Mixed) (Day/ Boarders)

Devon

Blundell's School, Tiverton EX16 4DN; Tel (01884) 252543; Fax (01884) 243232; *Headmaster* Jonathan Leigh, MA (Boarders) (13–18 Boys and Girls) (240) (Day) (140)
Bramdean School, Homefield Rd, Heavitree, Exeter, Devon EX1 2QR; Tel (01392) 73387; Fax (01392) 439330 (190 Boys and Girls 3–11+) (boys 12–18) (Day and Weekly Boarders)

Croft Lodge Convent, Abbey Rd, Torquay TQ2 5NP; Tel (01803) 292339 (300) (Girls)
Edgehill College, Bideford; Tel (01237) 471701; Fax (01237) 425981; *Headmistress* Mrs E.M. Burton, BSc, AKC (380) (Mixed) (Boarders) (Weekly boarders) (Day) (3–18)
Exeter School, Exeter; Tel (01392) 73679; *Head* N.W. Gamble (740) (Boys) (A,B) (Boarders) (Weekly boarders + 6th form Girls)
Gramercy Hall School, Churston Ferrers, South Devon TQ5 0HR; Tel (01803) 844338; *Contact* G. Nickerson
Grenville College, Bideford EX39 3JR; Tel (01237) 472212; *Headmaster* M.C.V. Cane; Stella Maris (Grenville College Junior School), Bideford EX39 2PN, (01237) 472208, Headmistress L. Maggs-Wellings (Co-educational Day and Boarding) (Senior School 11–18) (400) (Co-educational Day) (2½–11 Junior School) (160)
Kelly College, Tavistock PL19 0HZ; Tel (01822) 613005; *Headmaster* C.H. Hirst, MA (360) (Mixed) (Boarders) (Weekly boarders) (Day)
Kings School, Hartley Rd, Plymouth PL3 5LW; Tel (01752) 771789; Fax (01752) 770826 (Mixed (150)
Maynard School, Exeter EX1 1SJ; Tel (01392) 73417; Fax (01392) 496199 (Girls) (A) (477)
Mount St Mary's Convent School, Wonford Rd, Exeter EX2 4PF; Tel (01392) 436770/433301 (480) (Girls age 3–18) (Boys age 3–7)
Plymouth College, Ford Pk, Plymouth; Tel (01752) 228596; Fax (01752) 221267 (640) (Boys) (A,B) (Boarders)
Rudolf Steiner School, Hood Manor, Dartington, Totes TQ9 6AB; Tel (01803 762) 528; *Chairman of College of Teachers* (Mixed) (250)
St Dunstan's Abbey, North Rd West, Plymouth PL1 5DH; Tel (01752) 663998 (360) (Girls) (Day) (Boarding) (Ages 4–18)
St Margaret's School, Magdalen Rd, Exeter EX2 4TS; Tel (01392) 73197; Fax (01392) 51402; *Headmistress* M. D'Albertanson, MA (440) (Girls)
St Wilfrid's School and Kindergarten, 25-29 St David's Hill, Exeter EX4 4DA; Tel (01392) 76171; *Headmaster* J.G. Bushrod, BSc(Hons), PGCE (Mixed) (120)
Shebbear College, Shebbear, Beaworthy, Devon EX21 5HJ; Tel (01409) 281228; Fax (01409) 281784; *Headmaster* R.J. Buley, MA (Mixed) (Boarders) (275)
Stella Maris School, Bideford EX39 2PW; *Headmistress* Sue Fishleigh; Tel (01237) 472208; Fax (01237) 424136 (205) (Girls) (11–18) (Boarders) (Weekly boarders)
Stoodley Knowle Convent, Anstey's Cove Rd, Torquay TQ1 2JB; Tel (01803) 293160; *Head Teacher* Sister M. Perpetua (Girls) (Day, Weekly boarders) (200)
Stover School, Newton Abbot TQ12 6QG; Tel (01626) 54505; *Head* Mrs W. Lunel (Girls) (Boarders) (Weekly boarders) (Day) (185)
Tower House School, Fisher St, Paignton, Devon TQ4 5EW; Tel (01803) 557077; *Principal* M. Robinson; *Head of Seniors* W.J. Miller (Mixed) (200)
Trinity School, Teignmouth TQ14 8LY; Tel (01626) 778341; Fax (01626) 775491; *Head* C.J. Ashby, BSc(Hons), PGCE (Mixed) (3–18+) (292)
West Buckland School, Barnstaple EX32 0SX; Tel (01598) 760281; Fax (01598) 760546; *Headmaster* M. Downward (550) (Mixed) (A) (Boarders) (Weekly boarders)

Dorset

Allhallows, Rousdon, Lyme Regis DT7 3RA; Tel (01297) 20444; Fax (01297) 24191; *Headmaster* P.S. Larkman, LVO, MA (250) (Mixed) (Boarders) (Weekly boarders) (Day)
Bryanston, Blandford DT11 0PX; Tel (01258) 452411 (660) (Mixed) (Boarders)
Canford School, Wimborne; Tel (01202) 841254 (A,C) (Boarders) (Mixed) (500)
Clayesmore, Iwerne Minster, Blandford DT11 8LL; Tel (01747) 812122; *Headmaster* D.J. Beeby (300) (Mixed) (Boarders and Day)
Croft House, Shillingstone, Blandford, Dorset DT11 0QS; Tel (01258) 860295; Fax (01258) 860552; *Headmaster* M.P. Hawkins (100) (Girls) (Boarders and Day)
Homefield, Salisbury Rd, Winkton, Christchurch BH23 7AR; Tel (01202) 476644; Fax (01202) 477923; *Headmaster* A.C. Partridge (Boys and Girls 3–16+) (Day) (Boarders) (Weekly boarders) (400)
Milton Abbey, nr Blandford Forum, Dorset DT11 0BZ; Tel (01258) 880484; Fax (01258) 881194; R.H. Hardy, MA (230) (Boys) (Boarders) (Day)
St Antony's-Leweston School, Sherborne DT9 6EN; Tel (0196 321) 691; *Headmistress* Mrs P. Cartwright, MA, BSc (348) (Boarders and Day Girls) (400) (Boarders)
St Genevieve's Convent, Les Filles de la Croix, Dorchester; Tel (01305) 64898; *Head Teacher* Mrs B.A. Beakes (Girls (280)
St Mary's School, Shaftesbury, Dorset SP7 9LP; Tel (01747) 54005; Sister M. Campion Livesey, IBVM (300) (Girls) (Boarders/Day)
Sherborne School, Sherborne; Tel (01935) 812249; Fax (01935) 816628; P.H. Lapping, MA (Boys) (Boarders) (650)
Sherborne School for Girls, Sherborne, Dorset DT9 3QN; Tel (01935) 812245; Fax (01935) 814973; *Headmistress* Miss June M. Taylor, BSc (465) (Girls) (Boarders and Day)
Talbot Heath School, Rothesay Rd, Bournemouth, Dorset BH4 9NJ; Tel (01202) 761881; Fax (01202) 768155; *Headmistress* Mrs C. Dipple, BA, M ès L FRSA (Girls) (A) (Day) (Boarders) (Weekly boarders) Pre-Preparatory Dept for boys and girls 3+–7 (547)
Thornlow, Buxton Rd, Weymouth DT4 9PR; Tel (01305) 782977; D.H. Crocker (170) (Mixed) (C) (Boarders) (Weekly boarders)
Uplands School, St Osmund's Rd, Parkstone, Poole BH14 9JY; Tel (01202) 742626; Fax (01202) 731037; *Headteacher* L. Dummett, MED, BEd, CANTAB (Mixed) (350)
Wentworth Milton Mount, College Rd, Boscombe, Bournemouth BH5 2DY; Tel (01202) 423266; Fax (01202) 418030; *Headmistress* Miss S. Coe, BA, FRGS (310) (Girls) (Full and Weekly boarding) (Day)

Durham

Barnard Castle School, Barnard Castle, Co Durham DL12 8UN; Tel (01833) 690222; Fax (01833) 38985; F.S. McNamara (600) (Co-Educational) (Boarders and Day)
Durham High School for Girls Farewell Hall, Durham DH1 3TB; Tel 0191-384 3226; Fax 0191-386 7381; Miss M.L. Walters, BA (Girls) (Senior School) (265) (Junior School) (158)
Durham School, Durham DH1 4SZ; Tel 0191-384 7977; Fax 0191-383 1025; *Headmaster* M.A. Lang, MA (B) (Boys) (Boarders) (Girls in 6th Form) (320)
Polam Hall, Grange Rd, Darlington DL1 5PA; Tel (01325) 463383; Fax (01325) 383539; *Headmistress* Mrs H.C. Hamilton, BSc (A) (338) (Girls) (Day, Weekly Boarders and Boarders)
St Anne's High School, Wolsingham, Bishop Auckland DL13 3AL; Tel (01388) 527298; Sister Mary Micheal (Girls (240)

East Sussex

Battle Abbey School, Battle; Tel (01424) 772385; Fax (01424) 773573; *Headmaster* D.J.A. Teall, BSc (250) (Mixed) (Day) (Boarders)
Brighton College, Eastern Rd, Brighton BN2 2AL; Tel (01273) 605788); J.D. Leach, MA (A) (500) (Mixed) (Boarders and Day) (Weekly and Full boarders)
Brighton and Hove High School, Montpelier Rd, Brighton BN1 3AT; Tel (01273) 734112; Fax (01273) 737120; *Head* Miss R.A. Woodbridge, MA (A) (GPDST) (230) (Girls 4–10) (520) (11–18)
Brighton Steiner School, 363 Ditchling Rd, Brighton BN1 6JU; Tel (01273) 561086; *Chairman of College Teachers* (Mixed) (150)
Buckswood Grange, Uckfield TN22 3PU; Tel (01825) 761666; M B Reiser, BSc,FCA (130) (Mixed)

Charters-Ancaster School, Bexhill-on-Sea TN40 2JQ; Tel (01424) 730499; Fax (01424) 217666; *Headmistress* K Lewis, MA (Cantab) (300) (Girls) (Day 3–18) (Weekly and Full Boarding 11–18) (Boys) (Day 3–8)
Deepdene School, 195 New Church Rd, Hove BN3 4ED; Tel (01273) 418984; Mrs Joyce Shaw, BA,ALAM (180) (Young Boys) (Girls)
Eastbourne College, Eastbourne; Tel (01323) 737655; Fax (01323) 416137; C.M.P. Bush, MA (Boarders) (480)
Frewen College, Brickwall, Northiam Rye, East Sussex TN31 6NL; Tel (01797 25) 2494; *Headmaster* A.B. Fiddian Green, MA (100) (Boys) (Boarders) (Weekly boarders)
Mayfield College, Mayfield, E. Sussex TN20 6PL; Tel (01435) 872041; C.P. Vroege (140) (Co-Ed) (Boys 11-18) (Boarders,Weekly Boarders and Day)
Michael Hall, (B,C) Kidbrooke Park, Forest Row, East Sussex RH18 5JB; Tel (0134 282) 2275 (B,C)(Mixed (Boarders) (Weekly boarders) (600)
Micklefield School, Seaford; Tel (01323) 892457; Fax (01323) 896625; *Headmaster* E Reynolds, BA(Hons),PGCE (220) (Girls) (Boarders and Day)
Moira House School, Upper Carlisle Rd, Eastbourne BN20 7TE; Tel (01323) 644144; Fax (01323) 649720; *Headmaster* A. Underwood, MA, BA, FRSA (380) (Girls) (Boarders and Day)
Newlands Manor School, Sutton Pl, Seaford BN25 3PL; Tel (01323) 890309; Fax (01323) 490100; *Headmaster* Brian F Underwood, MA,DipEd(Oxon) (255) (Mixed) (Boarders) (Weekly Boarders) (Day)
Northease Manor, nr Lewes BN7 3EY; Tel (01273) 472915; Fax (01273) 472202; *Headmaster* R Dennien, MA (96) (Mixed) (Weekly Boarders and Day)
Old Grammar School, High St, Lewes; Tel (01273) 472634; R E Mead (Mixed) (274)
Roedean School, Brighton BN2 5RQ; Tel (01273) 603181; Fax (01273) 676722; Mrs A R Longley, MA (Girls) (Boarders) (450)
St Bede's School, The Dicker, nr Hailsham BN27 3QH; Tel (01323) 843252; *Headmaster* R.A. Perrin (Mixed) (Boarders) (Weekly Boarders) (Day) (400)
St Leonards-Mayfield School, The Old Palace, Mayfield TN20 6PH; Tel (01435) 873652; Fax (01435) 872627; *Headmistress* Sister Jean Sinclair, BSc (525) (Girls) (Boarders)
St Mary's Hall, Eastern Rd, Brighton BN2 5JF; Tel (01273) 606061; Fax (01273) 620782; *Headmistress* P.J. James, BA (400) (Girls 3-18, Boys 3-8, Day & Boarding (8+)
Micklefield Wadhurst, (Inc. the Legat School of Classical Ballet) Mayfield La, Wadhurst, E. Sussex TN5 6JA; Tel (01892) 783193; Miss A.M. Phillips, BEd(Hons) (girls & boys) (Weekly/full boarders and day)
Wilton House School, Catsfield Pl, Battle TN33 9BS; Tel (01424) 830234; Fax (Same as Tel No); *Principal* F. Auer (Mixed) (70) (Senior) (115) (Junior) (Boarders)

Essex

Alleyn Court & Eton House School, Southchurch Lawn, Wakering Rd, Thorpe Bay, Southend-on-Sea SS3 OPY; Tel (01702) 582553; *Head of Senior School* R.N. Slocombe, BA,AdvDipEd,ACP,MBIM (boys) (270)
Bancroft's School, Woodford Green, Essex IG8 ORF; Tel 0181-505 4821; Dr P.C.D. Southern (A) (Mixed) (Day) (750)
Boys' High School, Wellesley Rd, Colchster CO3 3HD; Tel (01206) 573389; A.L. Moore, MA, DipEd (180)
Braeside, 130 High Rd, Buckhurst Hill IG9 5SD; Tel 0181-504-1133; *Headmistress* Mrs C. Naismith (250) (Girls) (4–16)
Brentwood School, Brentwood CM15 8AS; Tel (01277) 212271; Fax (01277) 260218; *Headmaster* J.A.B. Kelsall, MA (725) (A) (Boys 11–18 incl Boarders) (300) (Girls 11–18 incl Boarders)
Chigwell School, High Rd, Chigwell IG7 6QF; Tel 0181-500 1396; Fax 0181-500 6232; A.R.M. Little, MA (Boarders) (A,B) (Weekly Boarders) (Day Pupils)
Colchester Boys' High, Wellesley Rd, Colchester CO3 3HD; Tel (01206) 573389; *Principal* A.L. Moore, MA(Oxon), DipEd,FRGS (174)
Cranbrook College, Mansfield Rd, Ilford, Essex IG1 3BD; Tel 0181-554-1757; *Headmaster* G.T. Reading, MA,CertEd(Oxon) (C) (Boys) (230)
Felsted School, (A,B) Dunmow CM6 3LL; Tel (01371) 820258; Fax (01371) 821179; S.C. Roberts, MA (Mixed) (490)
Friends' School, Saffron Walden CB11 3EB; Tel (01799) 525351; *Head* S.H. Evans, BA,MA (300) (A) (Mixed) (Boarders and Day)
Gosfield School, (C) Halstead CO9 1PF; Tel (01787) 474040; Fax (01787) 478228; *Headmaster* Robert Boyd, BA, DipPhysEd (155) (Mixed) (Boarders and Day)
New Hall School, Boreham, Chelmsford CM3 3HT; Tel (01245) 467588; Sister Margeret Mary, BEd (Girls) (Boarders and Day 9–18) (Boys, Day only 4–11) (490)
St Hilda's, 15 Imperial Ave, Westcliff-on-Sea, Essex SS0 8NE; Tel (01702) 344542; Fax (01702) 435945; *Headmistress* Mrs V.M. Tunnicliffe (Girls) (200)
St John's School, Stock Rd, Billericay CM12 OAR; Tel (01277) 623070; *Head of Senior School* S.E. Hillier (Mixed) (340)
St Mary's School, Lexden Rd, Colchester CO3 3RB; Tel (01206) 572544; *Principal* Mrs G. Mouser, MPhil (Girls) (580)
St Nicholas' School, Hillingdon Hse, Hobbs Cross Rd, Old Harlow; Tel (01279) 429910; G.W. Brant, MA (Mixed)
Thorpe Hall School, Wakering Road, Southend-on-Sea; Tel (01702) 582340; *Headmaster* T. Fawell

Gloucestershire

Bredon School, Pull Ct, Bushley, Tewkesbury GL20 6AH; Tel (01684) 293156; Fax (01684) 298008; *Headmaster* C.E. Wheeler, BEd (310) (Co-ed) (7–18 Boarders, Weekly Boarders) (5–18 Day)
Cheltenham College, Cheltenham, Glos; Tel (01242) 513540; *Headmaster* P.D.V. Wilkes, MA (490) (B) (Boys) (90) (Girls) (Boarders)
The Cheltenham Ladies' College, Cheltenham GL50 3EP; Tel (01242) 520691; Fax (01242) 227882; *Principal* Miss E. Castle, BA (Boarding/Day) (860)
Dean Close School, Cheltenham GL51 6HE; Tel (01242) 522640; C.J. Bacon, MA (Mixed) (440) (Boarders and Day)
Hatherop Castle School, nr Cirencester, Glos GL7 3NB; Tel (01285) 750206; *Headmaster* P. Easterbrook, BEd (217) (Mixed) (Prep) (217) (Nursery) (60) (with Boarding from 7½)
King's School, Gloucester GL1 2BG; Tel (01452) 21251; *Headmaster* P.R. Lacey, MA (500) (Mixed) (Boarders) (Weekly Boarders) (Day)
Rendcomb College, Cirencester GL7 7HA; Tel (01285) 831213; *Headmaster* J.N. Tolputt (B) (270) (Boarding/Day) (Girls and Boys) (11–18)
St Clotilde's School, Lechlade Manor, Lechlade GL7 3BB; Tel (01367) 252259; A.G. Wood, BA(Hons), AdvDipEd (142) (3-18 Girls) (18) (3-8 Boys) (Day and Weekly boarders) (Nursery; Infants; Juniors; Seniors) (weekly boarding from 9 yrs)
St Edward's School, Ashley Rd, Charlton Kings, Cheltenham GL52 6NT; Tel (01242) 526697; Fax (01242) 260986; *Headmaster* A.J. Martin, BA, MA, DipEd, FCollP (720) (Mixed)
Selwyn School, Matson House, Gloucester GL4 9DY; Tel (01452) 305663; Fax (01452) 385907; *Head* L.M. Brown, BA, MA(Ed), PGCE (Girls) (330) (Boarders) (40) (Weekly Boarders) (10) (Day) (235) (Day Boys (3–11) (45) (Girls 3–18)
Westonbirt School, Tetbury GL8 8QG; Tel 0166-688 0333; Fax 0166-688 0364; *Head* Mrs G. Hylson-Smith, BA,DipCEG (250) (Girls) (Boarders and Day)
Wycliffe College, Stonehouse GL10 2JQ; Tel (01453) 822432; D.C.M. Prichard, MA, FRSA, FColP, FBIM (A,B) (Mixed) (Boarders) (Day) (315)
Wynstones (Rudolf Steiner) School, Whaddon Green, nr Gloucester GL4 OUF; Tel (01452) 522475; Fax (01452) 525667 (300) (Mixed) (Boarders)

Hampshire

The Atherley School, Hill La, Southampton SO15 5RG; Tel (01703) 772898; Fax (01703) 779971; *Headteacher* Catherine Madina, BA (Co-ed 3–11, Girls 11–18) (440)
Bedales School, (A) Petersfield GU32 2DG; Tel (01730) 263286; *Headmaster* R.E.I. Newton, MA (472) (Mixed) (Boarders)
Churcher's College, (A) London Rd, Petersfield GU31 4AS; Tel (01730) 263033; Fax (01730) 231437; *Headmaster* G.W. Buttle (Mixed) (586)
Convent of our Lady of Providence, Alton GU34 2NG; Tel (01420) 82070; 83878; *Headmaster* F.A. Martin, BA (Girls) (260)
Ditcham Park School, Ditcham Park, nr Petersfield GU31 5RN; Tel (01730) 825659; *Headmistress* Mrs P.M. Holmes, DipEd (320) (Mixed) (Junior School)
Embley Park, Romsey SO51 6ZE; Tel (01794) 512206; Fax (01794) 518737; D.F. Chapman, BA (220) (Mixed) (Boarders) (Weekly Boarders) (Day) (11–18)
Farnborough Hill, (A) Farnborough GU14 8AT; Tel (01252) 545197; Sister Elizabeth McCormack, RCE (A) (Girls) (500)
Fernhill Manor School, New Milton BH25 5JL; Tel (01425) 611090; Rev Andrew Folks, BA(Hons), DipTh (Boarders) (Weekly Boarders) (Day) (113)
The Gregg School, Townhill Pk Hse, Cutbush La, Southampton SO18 2GF; Tel (01703) 471233; Fax (01703) 471080; R.D. Hart, BEd (Mixed) (215)
Hilsea College, Oakley Hall, Basingstoke RG23 7EJ; Tel (01256) 780222; *Principal* Landon F. Platt (84) (Mixed) (Boarders) (Day)
King Edward VI School, Kellett Rd, Southampton SO15 2UQ; Tel (01703) 704561; Fax (01703) 705937; T.R. Cookson (A,B) (Mixed) (950)
La Sagesse Convent, Abbey Hse, Romsey SO51 8EL; Tel (01794) 522320; Fax (01794) 519829; *Headmistress* Sister Thomas Cox (150) (Girls) (Day)
Lord Wandsworth College, Long Sutton, Basingstoke RG25 1TB; Tel (01256) 862482; Fax (01256) 862563; *Headmaster* G. de W. Waller, MA, MSc (A) (Boys) (Girls in 6th Form) (Boarders and Day) (Weekly boarders) (445)
Mayville High School, Kenilworth Lodge, St Simons Rd, Southsea PO5 2PE; Tel (01705) 734847; Mrs M.I. Russell, ,MA,FRA (Girls) (96)
Meoncross School, Burnt Hse, Burnt House La, Stubbington, Fareham PO14 2EF; Tel (01329) 662182; *Headmaster* C.J. Ford, BEd (Mixed) (410)
North Foreland Lodge, Sherfield-on-Loddon, nr Basingstoke RG27 0HT; Tel (01256) 882431; Fax (01256) 883005; *Headmistress* D.L. Matthews, BA (Girls) (Boarders) (175)
The Portsmouth Grammar School, High St, Portsmouth PO1 2LN; Tel (01705) 819125; Fax (01705) 870184; A.C.V. Evans, MA, MPhil, FIL (Mixed) (820)
Portsmouth High School, 25 Kent Rd, Southsea PO5 3EQ; Tel (01705) 826714; Fax (01705) 814814; *Head* J.M. Dawtrey, BA (G.P.D.S.T.) (A) (Girls) (540)
Ringwood Waldorf School, Ashley, Ringwood BH24 2NN; Tel (01425) 472664 (Co-ed) (140)
Rookwood School, Weyhill Rd, Andover SP10 3AL; Tel (01264) 352855; *Headmistress* Mrs S. Hindle, BA(Hons), FCollP (265) (Girls 7–16) (Boarders) (Weekly boarders) (Day Girls 3–16) (Day Boys 3–11)
Rushmoor Independent School, 40 Reading Rd, Farnborough GU14 6NB; Tel (01252) 544738; Julie Morrish, BEd(Hons) (Mixed) (also Nursey & pre-prep School) (75)
Salesian College, Reading Rd, Farnborough GU14 6PA; Tel (01252) 542919; *Headmaster* Rev M. Delmer, SDB, BEd (A) (Boys) (500)
St Benedict's Convent School, Penton Lodge, Andover SP11 0RD; Tel (01264) 772291; *Headmistress* R.M. Wheelwright (93) (Girls) (Boarders 6–16) (Day 4–16) (Boys 4–9) (Nursery Class 3–4)
St John's College, Grove Rd South, Southsea PO5 3QW; Tel (01705) 815118; Fax (01705) 873603; *Headmaster* Rev Brother Cyril, FSC, BA (A,B) (Boys) (820) (Boarders)
St Mary's College, Bitterne Park, Southampton SO9 4TG; Tel (01703) 671267; Rev Brother Paul, BSc, FIC (Boys) (600)
St Nicholas' School, Branksomewood Rd, Fleet; Tel (01252) 614864; Mrs L.G. Smith, BA(Hons), PGCE (Girls 3–16) (Boys 3–7) (380)
St Swithun's School, Winchester SO21 1HA; Tel (01962) 861316; Dr H.L. Harvey (A) (Girls) (Boarders) (Weekly boarders) (Days) (456)
Stanbridge Earls School, Romsey SO51 0ZS; Tel (01794) 516777; Fax (01794) 511201; H. Moxon, MA (C) (Mixed 11-18) (180) (Boarders) (Weekly boarders)
Winchester College, College St, Winchester SO23 9NA; Tel (01962) 854328; Fax (01962) 842972; J.P. Sabben-Clare, MA (A) (Boys) (Boarders and Day) (669)
Wykeham House School for Girls, East St, Fareham; Tel (01329) 280178; Fax (01329) 823964; Mrs E.M. Moore, BA, FRGS (11–16) (174) (4–16) (318)

Hereford and Worcester

The Alice Ottley School, Worcester WR1 1HW; Tel (01905) 27061; C. Sibbit, MA (A) (Girls) (700)
Belmont Abbey School, Hereford; Tel (01432) 277362; Rev D.C. Jenkins, OSB, MA (C) (Boys) (220) (Boarders) (Day)
Bowbrook House School, Peopleton, nr Pershore WR10 2EE; Tel (01905) 841242; Fax (01905) 840716; *Head Teacher* S.W. Jackson (Mixed) (120)
Bowbrook School, The Village, Hartlebury, Kidderminster DY11 7TE; Tel (01299) 250258; *Headmaster* D.R. Bolam (Mixed) (120)
Bromsgrove School, Bromsgrove B61 7DU; Tel (01527) 579679; T.M. Taylor, MA, DipEd (Mixed) (600) (Boarders and Day)
Dodderhill School, Droitwich WR9 0BE; Tel (01905) 778290; *Headmistress* Mrs M.A. Maybee, BSc (Girls) (120)
Green Hill School, Evesham WR11 4NG; Tel (01386) 442364; *Headmaster* O. Lister (Co-Ed 100) (Boarders and Weekly boarders) (Day)
Heathfield School, Wolverley, nr Kidderminster DY10 3QE; Tel (01562) 850204; *Headmaster* G.L. Sinton, BA, MEd (C) (Co-ed) (260)
Hereford Cathedral School, Hereford HR1 2NN; Tel (01432) 273757; Fax (01432) 344110; Dr H.C. Tomlinson (A) (Mixed) (595) (Boarders) (Weekly boarders)
Hereford Waldorf School, Much Dewchurch, Hereford HR2 8DE; Tel (01981) 540221; (Co-ed) (150)
Holy Trinity School, Birmingham Rd, Kidderminster DY10 2BY; Tel (01562) 822929; S.M. Bell, MEd (Girls) (300)
King's School, Worcester WR1 2LH; Tel (01905) 23016; J.M. Moore, JP, MA, PhD, FRSA (A,C) (800) (Boarders)
Lucton School, Leominster HR6 9PL; Tel (01568) 85686 (Co-Ed) (275) (Boarders) (Day)
Malvern College, Malvern; Tel (01684) 892333; R. de C. Chapman, MA (A) (Co-ed) (675) (Boarders and Day)
Malvern Girls' College, Malvern WR14 3BA; Tel (01684) 892288; Fax (01684) 566204; V. Payne, PhD, MSc, ARCS(London) (Boarders) (430) (Day) (60)
Royal Grammar School, Upper Tything, Worcs WR1 1HP; Tel (01905) 613391; Fax (01905) 726571; W.A. Jones, MA (A) (Boys) (924)
St James's and The Abbey School, West Malvern WR14 4DF; Tel (01684) 560851; Miss E.M. Mullenger, BA, CertEd (Girls) (200) (Boarders and Day)
St Mary's Convent School, Mount Battenhall, Worcester WR5 2HP; Tel (01905) 357786; Mrs M. Kilbride (Girls) (370)

Hertfordshire

Abbot's Hill School, Bunkers La, Hemel Hempstead HP3 8RP; Tel (01442) 240333; Fax (01442) 69981; *Headmistress* Mrs J. Kinsley, MA(Cantab) (Girls) (170) (Boarders) (Weekly boarders) (Day)
Aldenham School, Elstree, Hertfordshire WD6 3AJ; Tel (01923) 858122; Fax (01923) 854410; Michael Higginbottom (A) (B) (Boys) (Boarders and day) (328)
The Arts Educational School, Tring Park, Tring HP23 5LX; Tel (01442) 824255 (Boarders) (155) (Day) (65)

8 Independent Secondary Schools

Berkhamsted School, Berkhamsted HP4 2BB; Tel (01442) 863236; *Headmaster* The Revd K.H. Wilkinson, BA, MA, FRSA (A) (Boys) (Girls in Sixth Form) (Boarders, Weekly boarders and Day) (459)

Berkhamsted School for Girls, Kings Rd, Berkhamsted HP4 3BG; Tel (01442) 862168; *Headmistress* V.E.M. Shepherd, BSc (A) (424) (Boarders) (Weekly boarders)

Bishop's Stortford College, Bishop's Stortford CM23 2QZ; Tel (01279) 657911; S.G.G. Benson, MA (A,B,C) (Boys) (362)

The Haberdashers' Aske's School, Butterfly La, Elstree, Borehamwood, Herts WD6 3AF; Tel 0181-207 4323; Fax 0181-207 4439; *Headmaster* Keith Dawson, MA (A) (Boys) (1300)

Haberdashers' Aske's School for Girls, Aldenham Rd, Elstree WD6 3BT; P.A. Penney, BA, FRSA (A) (1139)

Haileybury, Hertford SG13 7NU; Tel (01992) 462352; Fax (01992) 467603; D.J. Jewell, MA, MSc, FRSA (A,B,C) (Boys) (530) (Girls) (Boarders) (Day) (97)

Northfield Church Rd, Watford WD1 3QB; Tel (01923) 229758; Mrs P. Hargreaves, BSc, MEd (Girls) (150) (Boys) (10) (Age 3–7)

The Princess Helena College, Preston, nr Hitchin SG4 7RT; Tel (01462) 432100; Fax (01462) 431497; H. Davidson-Wall, MA (Girls) (150) (Boarders and Day)

Queenswood School, Brookmans Park, Hatfield, Hertfordshire AL9 6NS; Tel (01707) 652262; Fax (01707) 649267; A.M.B. Butler, MA (Girls) (369) (Boarders) (Day 37)

Rickmansworth Masonic School, Rickmansworth WD3 4HF; Tel (01923) 773168; Fax (01923) 896729; I.M. Andrews, MA(Oxon) (Boarders and Day) (680)

Rudolf Steiner School, Langley Hill, Kings Langley, Herts WD4 9HG; Tel (01923) 262505; Fax (01923) 270958 (Co-ed) (420) (Age 3–4 (KG) to 18)

St Albans High School for Girls, Townsend Ave, St Albans, Herts AL1 3SJ; Tel (01727) 853800; *Headmistress* C.Y. Daly, BSc (A) (690)

St Albans School, Abbey Gateway, St Albans AL3 4HB; Tel (01727) 855521; Fax (01727) 843447; *Headmaster* A.R. Grant, MA (A,B) (Boys and Girls in Sixth Form) (640)

St Christopher School, Letchworth SG6 3JZ; Tel (01462) 679301; C. Reid, MA (Mixed) (350) (Boarders)

St Columba's College, King Harry La, St Albans AL3 4AW; Tel (01727) 855185; Fax (01727) 863997; *Headmaster* J.D. Stuart, MA (Boys) (510)

St Edmund's College, Old Hall Green, Ware SG11 1DS; Tel (01920) 821504; D.J. McEwen, MA (A) (Co-ed) (410) (Girls) (200) (Boarders)

St Francis' College, Letchworth SG6 3PJ; Tel (01462) 670511; M. Hegarty, BA, HDipEd, DMS (Girls) (200) (Boarders and Day) (Weekly boarders)

St Hilda's, High St, Bushey, Herts WD2 3DA; Tel 0181-950 1751; Fax 0181-420 4523; *Head* L. Cavanagh, DipCE (Girls) (200) (3–11)

St Margaret's, Bushey, Herts WD2 1DT; Tel 0181-950-1548; *Headmistress* Miss M. de Villiers (Girls) (430) (Boarders and Day) (Weekly boarders)

Sherrardswood School Welwyn AL6 0BJ; Tel (01438) 714282; Fax (01438) 840616; M.C. Lloyd, MA (Mixed) (125) (Boarders)

Stanborough School, Stanborough Park, Watford WD2 6JT; Tel (01923) 673268; Fax (01923) 893943; A. Luxton, PhD (A,B) (Mixed) (Boarders) (Weekly boarders) (200)

Waterside School, Hassobury, Hazel End, Bishop's Stortford; Tel (01279) 814071; *Principal* Sheila C. Law, MA, LRAM (Mixed 3–11, Girls 11–18) (180)

Humberside

Hull Grammar School, Cottingham Rd, Hull HU5 2DT; Tel (01482) 440144; Fax (01482) 441312; *Contact* R. Haworth

Hull High School, Tranby Croft, Anlaby, North Humberside HU10 7EH; Tel (01482) 657016; Fax (01482) 655389; *Headmistress* M.A. Benson, BA (185) (Weekly boarders) (take Juniors) (Pre-school Kindergarten)

Hymers College, Kingston upon Hull HU3 1LW; Tel (01482) 343555; J.C. Morris, MA (A,B) (Co-ed) (Boys 618) (Girls 306)

St James' School, 22 Bargate, Grimsby, South Humberside DN34 4SY; Tel (01472) 362093; D.J. Berisford (Mixed) (250) (Day) (Boarders) (Weekly boarders)

Isle of Wight

Bembridge School, Bembridge PO35 5PH; Tel (01983) 872101; *Headmaster* J. High (Mixed) (300) (Boarders and Day) (Weekly boarders)

Ryde School, Queen's Rd, Ryde; Tel (01983) 562229; Fax (01983) 564714; *Headmaster* M.D. Featherstone, MA (Mixed) (Borders, Weekly Boarders, Day) (684)

St Therese Presentation Convent School, High St, Ryde; Tel (01983) 67326; Sister M. Paschal McMahon, BA, TTC, DipTh (Girls)

Kent

Ashford School, East Hill, Ashford TN24 8PB; Tel (01233) 625171; Fax (01233) 647185; *Headmistress* Mrs P. Metham, BA(Bristol) (A) (Girls 3–18) (555) (Boarders/Weekly boards 9–18) (91)

Bedgebury School, Bedgebury Park, Goudhurst, Cranbrook, Kent; Tel (01580) 211954; Fax (01580) 212252; *Headmistress* M.E.A. Kaye, MA(Oxon) (Girls 3-18) (360)

Beechwood School Sacred Heart (Sacred Heart School), Beechwood, Pembury Rd, Tunbridge Wells TN2 3QD; Tel (01892) 529193; Fax (01892) 536164; Dr James A. Fallon, MA, PhD, DipEd (Girls) (240) (Boarders) (Weekly boarders) (Day) (Boys 3–7)

Benenden School, Cranbrook, Kent TN17 4AA; Tel (01580) 240592; Mrs G. duCharme, MA(Cantab) (Girls) (424) (Boarders)

Bethany School, Goudhurst TN17 1LB; Tel (01580) 211273; *Headmaster* W.M. Harvey, MA(Oxon) (Co-ed) (Boarders) (Day) (275)

Cannock School, Chelsfield, Orpington BR6 7PH; Tel (01689) 828096; K. Lawrey (Boys and Girls 3–11) (Boys 3–16) (Boarders and Day) (Weekly boarders) (125)

Cobham Hall, Cobham, Nr Gravesend, Kent DA12 3BL; Tel (01474) 824319/823371; Rosalind McCarthy, BA (Girls) (Boarders and Day Girls) (200)

Combe Bank School, Sundridge, Sevenoaks TN14 6AE; Tel (01959) 563720; N. Spurr, BSc (Girls) (230)

Cranbrook School, Cranbrook TN17 3JD; Tel (01580) 712163; Fax (01580) 715365; P.A. Close (Mixed) (Boarders and Day) (720)

Dover College, Dover CT17 9RH; Tel (01304) 205969; *Headmaster* M.P.G. Wright, JP, BA (Mixed) (300) (Boarders and Day)

Duke of York's Royal Military School, Dover CT15 5EQ; Tel (01304) 245024; Col G.H. Wilson, BA, MEd (Boys) (Boarders) (Co-Educational) (480)

Fosse Bank Preparatory School, Quarry Hill, Tonbridge TN9 2NT; Tel (01732) 353820; Mrs J.A. Mills (Boys and Girls 2½ to 11 years) (80)

Gad's Hill School, Higham-by-Rochester ME3 7PA; Tel (01474) 822366; *Headmistress* A. Everitt, BA, AKC (Boys and Girls 3–11) (Girls 11–18) (170)

Kent College Canterbury CT2 9DT; Tel (01227) 763231; Fax (01227) 764777; R.J. Wicks, MA, MSc, ARCM (A) (Mixed) (Boarders) (540)

Kent College Pembury, Pembury, Tunbridge Wells, Kent TN2 4AX; Tel (01892) 822006; Fax (01892) 820221; *Headmistress* Barbara J. Crompton, BSc, CPhys, MInstP (Girls 3–18) (Boarders) (Weekly boarders) (Day) (400)

King's School, Canterbury; Tel (01227) 595501; The Rev Canon A.C.J. Phillips, BD, AKC, PhD (Boys) (Borders and Day) (441) (Girls) (Borders and Day) (272)

King's School, Rochester; Tel (01634) 843913; Fax (01634) 832493; I.R. Walker, BA, PhD, LTh, ABIA, FCollP, FRSA (A,B) (Boys) (280) (Girls) (37) (Boarders) (32) (Weekly boarders) (8)

Perry Court Rudolf Steiner School, Garlinge Green, Chartham CT4 5RU; Tel (01227) 738285; Fax (01227) 731158; (Mixed) (250)

Sackville, Tonbridge Rd, Hildenborough, Tonbridge TN11 9HN; Tel (01732) 838888; J.G. Langdale, BA (Co-Educational 11–16)
St Augustine's College, Canterbury Rd, Westgate-on-Sea CT8 8NL; Tel (01843) 832441; Fax (01843) 833579; *Headmaster* K.C. Doherty, BA (Boys) (Borders) (75) (Day) (50)
St Edmund's School, Canterbury CT2 8HU; Tel (01227) 454575; J.V. Tyson, MA (C) (Boys) (420) (Girls) (Boarders) (160)
St Lawrence College, Ramsgate CT11 7AE; Tel (01843) 592680; J.H. Binfield, MA (B,C) (Mixed) (400) (Boarders)
St Mary's College Senior School, Ravenlea Rd, Folkestone CT20 2JU; Tel (01303) 851363; *Headmistress* Sister B. Milligan (Co-ed) (11–16) (100)
Sevenoaks School, Sevenoaks TN13 1HU; Tel (01732) 455133; Fax (01732) 456143; R.P. Barker, MA (Mixed) (930) (Day and Boarding)
Shernold School, Hill Pl, Queens Ave, Maidstone ME16 0ER; Tel (01622) 52868; Fax (01622) 844093; Mrs E. Drewe, BSc (Girls) (140)
Sutton Valence School, Sutton Valence, Maidstone ME17 3HL; Tel (01622) 842281; *Headmaster* N.A. Sampson, MA (Cantab) (A) (Mixed) (410) (Boarders)
Tonbridge School, Tonbridge TN9 1JP; Tel (01732) 365555; *Headmaster* J.M. Hammond, MA (A) (Boys) (Boarders/Day) (660)
Ursuline Convent School, 225 Canterbury Rd, Westgate-on-Sea, Kent CT8 8LX; Tel (01843) 834431; Fax (01843) 835365; Sister Mary Murphy, OSU (Girls) (300) (Boarders/Day)
Walthamstow Hall, Sevenoaks TN13 3UL; Tel (01732) 451334; Fax (01732) 456156; *Headmistress* Mrs J.S. Lang, MA (A) (Girls) (Boarders) (Weekly boarders) (Day) (520)
West Heath School, Sevenoaks, Kent; Tel (01732) 452541; Ann Williamson, BSc (Girls) (132) (Boarders)

Lancashire

Arnold School, Blackpool FY4 1JG; Tel (01253) 346391; W.T. Gillen, MA (A) (Mixed) (809)
Bentham School, Bentham, Lancaster LA2 7DB; Tel (015242) 61275; Fax (015242) 62944; *Headmaster* N.K.D. Ward, BSc (Mixed) (280) (Boarders)
Bury Grammar School, Tenterden St, Bury, Lancashire BL9 OHN; Tel 0161-797 2700; Fax 0161-763 4655; K. Richards (A) (Boys) (Day) (825) (Senior School) (683) (Junior School) (142)
Elmslie Girls School, Whitegate Dr, Blackpool FY3 9HL; Tel (01253) 763775; *Headmistress* E.M. Smithies, MA (400)
King Edward VII School, Lytham St Annes FY8 1DT; Tel (01253) 736459; P.J. Wilde, MA (A) (Boys) (600)
Kirkham Grammar School, Ribby Rd, Kirkham, nr Preston PR4 2BH; Tel (01772) 671079; Fax (01772) 672747; *Headmaster* B. Stacey (A) (Mixed) (Boarders) (Weekly boarders) (740)
Oakhill College, Wiswell La, Whalley BB7 9AF; Tel (01254) 823546; Fax (01254) 822662; Mrs C.A. Finley, BA (Mixed 3–16) (212)
Queen Elizabeth's Grammar School, Blackburn BB2 6DF; Tel (01254) 59911; Fax (01254) 691423; *Headmaster* E.J. Whittle, JP, BA (A,B) (Boys) (1100) (Girls) (50)
Queen Mary School, Lytham St Annes FY8 1DS; Tel (01253) 723246; Fax (01253) 781766; M.C. Ritchie, JP, BSc (A) (Girls) (650)
Rossall School, Fleetwood FY7 8JW; Tel (01253) 774201; Fax (01253) 774204; *Headmaster* R.D.W. Rhodes, BA(Durham), JP (A,C) (Girls) (38) (Day) (90) (Boarders) (Boys) (45) (Day) (215) (Boarders)
The St Annes College, 293 Clifton Drive South, St Annes FY8 1HN; Tel (01253) 725815; Mrs S.M. Welsby (Co-ed) (2ù–18) (150)
Scarisbrick Hall School, Ormskirk L40 9RQ; Tel (01704) 880200; Fax (01704) 880032; *Headmaster* D.M. Raynor, BA, DipEd (Mixed) (520)
Stonyhurst College, Lancs BB7 9PZ; Tel (01254) 826260; Fax (01254) 826732/826013; R.G.G. Mercer, MA, DPhil (A) (Boys) (6th Form Day Girls) (400) (Boarders and Day Boys)

Westholme School, Meins Rd, Blackburn BB2 6QU; Tel (01254) 53447; Fax (01254) 681459; *Principal* Mrs L. Croston, BSc, ALCM (Girls) (650)

Leicestershire

All Saints' School, 2 St Paul's Rd, Leicester LE3 9DE; Tel (0116) 253 6409; *Director* Fr A.J. Ballard (Mixed) (15)
Leicester Grammar School, 8 Peacock La, Leicester LE1 5PX; Tel (0116) 262 1221; *Headmaster* J.B. Sugden, MA(Cantab), MPhil, FRSA (Mixed) (585)
Leicester High School for Girls, 454 London Rd, Leicester LE2 2PP; Tel (0116) 270 5338; Mrs P.A. Watson, BSc (420)
Loughborough Grammar School, Loughborough LE11 2DU; Tel (01509) 233233; D.N. Ireland, MA (A) (Boys) (Boarders) (940)
Loughborough High School, Burton Walks, Loughborough LE11 2DU; Tel (01509) 212348; Fax (01509) 210486; *Headmistress* J.E.L. Harvatt, BA (A) (Girls) (540)
Oakham School, Chapel Cl, Oakham, Rutland LE15 6DT; Tel (01572) 722487; Fax (01572) 755786; G. Smallbone, MA (Mixed) (1,000) (Boarders and Day)
Our Lady's Convent School, Burton St, Loughborough LE11 2DT; Tel (0116) 226 3901; Sister Mary Mark, BEd (C) (Girls) (575)
Ratcliffe College, Fosse Way, Ratcliffe on the Wreake, Leicester LE7 4SG; Tel (01509) 812522; Fax (01509) 812791; Rev K.A. Tomlinson, STL (B) (Mixed) (Borders) (Day) (473)
Uppingham School, Leicestershire LE15 9QE; Tel (01572) 822216 (Headmaster), 822240 (Bursar), 823584 (Admissions); N.R. Bomford, MA (B) (Boys) (680) (Boarders) (Girls in 6th form)
Woodbank Grammar School, 320 London Rd, Leicester LE2 2PJ; Tel (0116) 270 3287; *Headmistress* A. Dosai (Boys and Girls 5–10) (Girls 11–16) (220)

Lincolnshire

Priory College, St Martin's Without, Stamford PE9 3JW; Tel (01780) 65900; Fax (01780) 56888; *Headmaster* R. Teall, BA(Hons) (Mixed 5–18) (Boarders) (Day) (150)
St Joseph's School, Upper Lindum St, Lincoln LN2 5RW; Tel (01522) 543764; Fax (01522) 537938; *Headmistress* M. Bradley (G.B.G.S.A.G.S.A) (Girls) (Boarders) (Weekly boarders) (220)
Stamford High School, Stamford PE9 2LJ; Tel (01780) 62330; Fax (01780) 481100; *Head* Miss G.K. Bland, BA (A) (Girls) (Boarders) (Weekly boarders) (Day) (712)
Stamford School, Stamford PE9 2BS; Tel (01780) 62171; Fax (01780) 480120; G.J. Timm, MA (A) (Boys) (Boarders) (920)

London

Aldenham School, Elstree WD6 3AJ; Tel (01923) 858122; Fax (01923) 854410; M. Higginbottom, MA, JP (A,B,C) (Boys) (370) (Boarders and Day) (Girls in 6th Form)
Alleyn's School, Dulwich, London SE22 8SU; Tel 0181-693 3422; *Headmaster* Dr C.H.R. Niven, MA, Lès L (A) (Mixed) (920)
The American School in London, 2–8 Loudoun Rd, London NW8 0NP; Tel 0171-722 0101; Fax 0171-586 6885; Judith R. Glickman (Mixed) (1225)
Ashwell Hse Study Centre, Pembridge Hse, London W2 4DS; Tel 0171-229 5874; Fax 0171-229 5874; *Principal* Miss Sheila Clyde, BA
Atholl School, 458 Rayners La, Pinner, Middx HA5 5DT; Tel 0181-866 0271; *Headmaster* C. Dodsworth, BA (Boys 10–16) (160)
Babington House School, Grange Dr, Chislehurst BR7 5ES; Tel 0181-467 5537; *Headmistress* Mrs E.V. Walter, BA (B) (260)
Bancroft's School, Woodford Green IG8 0RF; Tel 0181-505 4821; Fax 0181-559 0032; *Headmaster* Dr P.C.D. Southern (A) (Mixed) (900) (Day) (Also has a Preparatory Dept)

BOARD OF MANAGEMENT FOR METHODIST RESIDENTIAL SCHOOLS

25 Marylebone Road, London NW1 5JP
(Tel: 0171 - 935 3723)
Chairman: The Rev. Dr. R.G. Jones, M.A.
Secretary: Mr. Derek Robson, M.A.

Schools for Boys and Girls

Culford School, Bury St. Edmunds IP28 6TX. Tel: 01284 - 728615
Edgehill College, Bideford, North Devon EX39 3LY. Tel: 012374 - 71701
Kent College, Canterbury CT2 9DT. Tel: 01277 - 763231
Queen's College, Taunton TA1 4QS. Tel: 018232 - 72559
Shebbear College, Shebbear, North Devon EX21 5HJ. Tel: 01409 - 281228
Truro School, Truro, Cornwall TR1 1TH. Tel: 018727 - 2763
Woodhouse Grove School, Apperley Bridge, Yorks BD10 0NR. Tel: 01132 - 502477

Schools for Girls

Farringtons and Stratford House, Chislehurst, Kent BR7 6LR. Tel: 0181 - 467 0256
Kent College, Pembury, Nr. Tunbridge Wells TN2 4AX. Tel: 01892 - 822006

OTHER METHODIST RESIDENTIAL SCHOOLS

Schools for Boys and Girls

Ashville College, Harrogate HG2 9JR. Tel: 01423 - 566358
Kingswood School, Bath, Avon BA1 5RG. Tel: 01225 - 311627
The Leys School, Cambridge CB2 2AD. Tel: 01223 - 355327
Rydal Penrhos School, Colwyn Bay, North Wales LL29 7BT. Tel: 01492 - 532728
Wesley College, Dublin, Tel: Dublin 987066
Methodist College, Belfast 9. Tel: Belfast 669558

Schools for Girls

Queenswood School, Hatfield, Herts AL9 6NS. Tel: 01707 - 52262

A school prospectus, together with the particulars of fees and other information, may be obtained from the Headmaster or Headmistress.
A Central Bursary Fund exists to provide help for Methodist children in boarding need. Details are available from the Board of Management.
Information regarding sources of assistance with fees may be obtained from I.S.I.S., 56 Buckingham Gate, London SW1E 6AG.
Tel: 0171 - 222 7353/0065 and 0171 - 630 8793/4.

Baston School, Baston Rd, Hayes, Bromley BR2 7AB; Tel 0181-462 1010; Fax 0181-462 0438; *Headmaster* C.R.C. Wimble, MA(Cantab) (A) (Girls) (285) (Boarders) (Weekly boarders)
Bishop Challoner School, Bromley Rd, Shortlands, Kent BR2 0BS; Tel 0181-460 3546; *Headmaster* T. Robinson, MSc (B) (Boys) (Mixed 6th Form) (250)
Blackheath High School, GPDST Vanbrugh Pk, London SE3 7AG; Tel 0181-853 2929; Fax 0181-853 3663; Miss R.K. Musgrave, MA (A) (Girls 4–18) (565)
Bromley High School, GPDST, Blackbrook La, Bickley, Bromley BR1 2TW; Tel 0181-468 7981; Fax 0181-295 1062; Mrs E.J. Hancock, BA (A) (Girls) (790)
Channing School, Highgate, London N6 5HF; Tel 0181-340 2328; Fax 0181-341 5698; *Headmistress* Mrs I.R. Raphael, MA(Cantab) (Girls) (460)
Christ's College, 4 St German's Pl, Blackheath SE3 0NJ; Tel 0181-858 0692; Fax 0181-858 7778; *Headmaster* T. Barclay (Boys) (230) (Boarders) (Weekly boarders) (Day)
City of London School, Queen Victoria St, London EC4V 3AL; Tel 0171-489 0291; Fax 0171-329 6887; B.G. Bass (A,B) (Boys) (850)
City of London School for Girls, Barbican, London EC2Y 8BB; Tel 0171-628 0841; Fax 0171-638 3212; *Headmistress* Lady France, MA, FRGS (A) (660)
Colfe's School, Horn Park La, London SE12 8AW; Tel 0181-852 2283/14; *Headmaster* D.J. Richardson, BA PhD (A,B) (Boys) (640) (Girls) (50)
Commonweal Lodge School, Woodcote La, Purley, Surrey CR8 3HB; Tel 0181-660 3179; Fax 0181-660 1385; J.M. Brown, BD (Girls) (250)
Cranbrook College, Mansfield Rd, Ilford IG1 3BD; Tel 0181-554 1757; *Headmaster* G.T. Reading (Boys) (120)
Croham Hurst School, South Croydon CR2 7YN; Tel 0181-680 3064; *Head* S.C. Budgen, BA (Girls) (500)
Croydon High School, GPDST, Old Farleigh Rd, Selsdon, South Croydon, Surrey CR2 8YB; Tel 0181-651 5020; Fax 0181-657 5413; P.E. Davies, BSc, MEd (A) (Girls) (700)
Dulwich College, SE21 7LD; Tel 0181-693 3601; A.C.F. Verity, MA(Cantab) (A) (Boys) (Boarders) (Weekly boarders) (1400)
Ealing College Upper School, 83 The Avenue, Ealing W13 8JS; Tel 0181-997 4346; B. Webb, MA (B) (Boys) (190) (6th form Girls) (10)
Eltham College, Mottingham, London SE9 4QF; Tel 0181-857 1455; *Headmaster* D.M. Green, MA, FRSA (A,B) (Boys) (Boarders) (Weekly boarders) (6th form Girls) (50) (720)
Emanuel School, Battersea Rise, London SW11 1HS; Tel 0181-870 4171; Fax 0181-875 0267; *Headmaster* T. Jones-Parry, MA (A) (Boys) (Girls in 6th Form) (708)
Farringtons and Stratford Hse, Chislehurst BR7 6LR; Tel 0181-467 0256; Mrs B.J. Stock, BA (A) (Girls) (Full Boarders, Weekly Boarders and Day) (410)
Forest School, nr Snaresbrook, London E17 3PY; Tel 0181-520 1744; Fax 0181-520 3656; *Warden* A.G. Boggis, MA (A,C) (Boys) (Girls) (400) (Boy Boarders and Weekly Boarders) (425)
Francis Holland School, Clarence Gate NW1 6XR; Tel 0171-723 0176; Fax 0171-706-1522; *Headmistress* P. Parsonson, MA (Girls) (360)
Francis Holland School, 39 Graham Terr, London SW1W 8JF; Tel 0171-730 2971; Fax 0171-823-4066; *Headmistress* Mrs Jennifer Anderson, MA(Cantab), MA(Lond) (Girls) (180)
Friern Barnet Grammar School, Friern Barnet Rd, London N11 3DR; Tel 0181-368 3777; Fax 0181-368 3220; *Headmaster* J.A. Pearman, BSc, AKC, CertEd (Boys) (150)
Gatehouse School, Sewardstone Rd, London E2 9JG; Tel 0181-980 2978 and 0181-981 5885; Paul Faupel, BEd(Hons) (C) (Mixed) (15)
Godolphin and Latymer School, Iffley Rd, Hammersmith W6 0PG; Tel 0181-741 1936; Fax 0181-746 3352; *Headmistress* Miss Margaret Rudland, BSc (A) (Girls) (700)
Hampton School, Hanworth Rd, Hampton, Middx TW12 3HD; Tel 0181-979 5526; Fax 0181-941 7368; *Headmaster* G.G. Able, MA (A) (Boys) (945)
Harrow School, Harrow-on-the-Hill; Tel 0181-869-1200; *Head Master* N.R. Bomford, MA, FRSA (Boys) (Boarders) (784)
Harvington School Educational Trust Ltd, 20 Castlebar Rd, Ealing, London W5 2DS; Tel 0181-997 1583; Fax 0181-810 4756; Mrs A. Fookes, BA (Girls) (180)
Hasmonean High School, Holders Hill Rd, London NW4; Tel 0181-203 1411 (Boys) and 0181-203 4294 (Girls); Dr D. Coleman (Girls) (400) (Boys) (600)
Hazelhurst School for Girls, 17 The Downs, Wimbledon SW20 8HF; Tel 0181-946 1704; Fax 0181-944 7050; *Principal* Mrs C.W.M. Milner-Williams (Boys and Girls 4.5–7) (Girls 4.5–16) (Girls 140) (Boys 10)
Heathfield School, Beaulieu Dr, Pinner, Middx HA5 1NB; Tel 0181-868 2346; Fax 0181-868 4405; J. Merritt, BA (G.P.D.S.T.) (Girls) (470)
Hellenic College of London, 67 Pont St, London SW1X 0BD; Tel 0171-581 5044/5045; Fax 0171-589 9055; *Headmaster* J.W. Wardrobe (Mixed 2½–18) (215)
Highgate School, London N6 4AY; Tel 0181-340 1524; Fax 0181-340-7674; *Headmaster* R.P. Kennedy (A) (Boys) (Weekly Boarders and Day) (611)
Holy Trinity College, 81 Plaistow La, Bromley BR1 3LL; Tel 0181-313 0399; Fax 0181-466 0151; *Headmistress* Doreen Bradshaw, BA, PGCE, AdvDip, EdMan (Girls) (300)
Ibstock Place, The Froebel School, Clarence La, Roehampton SW15 5PY; Tel 0181-876 9991; Franciska Bayliss (Mixed) (3–16) (450)
International Community School, 4 York Terr East, Regents Pk, London NW1 4PT; Tel 0171-935 1206; Garry Dawson (Mixed) (150)
International School of London, 139 Gunnersbury Ave, London W3 8LG; Tel 0181-992-5823; *Head* Richard Hermon (Mixed 4–18) (235)
Italia Conti Academy of Theatre Arts Ltd, Italia Conti Hse, 23 Goswell Rd, London EC1M 7AJ; Tel 0171-608 0044; Mrs E.M. Sheward (Mixed) (350)
James Allen's Girls' School, East Dulwich Grove SE22 8TE; Tel 0181-693 1181; Fax 0181-693-7842; Marion Gibbs, BA, MLitt (A) (750)
The John Loughborough School, Holcombe Rd, Tottenham, London N17 9AD; Tel 0181-808 7837; Fax 0181-801 6719; Dr Clinton A. Valley, MA, PhD (Mixed) (260)
The John Lyon School, Middle Rd, Harrow HA2 0HN; Tel 0181-422 2046; Fax 0181-422 5008; Rev. T.J. Wright, BD, AKC (A) (Boys) (508)
The King Alfred School, North End Rd, London NW11 7HY; Tel 0181-905-5599; Fax 0181-455-1503; Francis Moran, MA(Cantab), PGCE (Mixed) (470) (4–18)
The King Fahad Academy, Bromyard Ave, Acton W3; Tel 0181-743 0131; Dr Ibtissam Al-Bassam
King's College School, Wimbledon Common, London SW19 4TT; Tel 0181-947 9311; Fax 0181-947 1712; R.M. Reeve, MA (A) (Boys) (700)
Kingston Grammar School, 70 London Rd, Kingston upon Thames, Surrey KT2 6PY; Tel 0181-546 5875; Fax 0181-546 5875; *Headmaster* C.D. Baxter (A) (Boys) (384) (Girls) (214)
Lady Eleanor Holles School, Hanworth Rd, Hampton TW12 3HF; Tel 0181-979 1601; Fax 0181-941 8291; E.M. Candy, BSc (A) (Girls) (680)
Latymer Upper School, Hammersmith, London W6 9LR; Tel 0181-741 1851 (A) (Boys) (1060)
Lubavitch House School, 107–115 Stamford Hill, London N16 5RP; Tel 0181-800 0022; Rabbi Shmuel Lew (Girls) (120)
Lycée Français Charles de Gaulle, 35 Cromwell Rd SW7 2DG; Tel 0171-584 6322; Fax 0171-823 7684; H.L. Brusa (Mixed) (1550) (Jun) (1350)
Marist Convent Independent Day School for Girls, 596 Fulham Rd, Fulham SW6 5NU; Tel 0171-731 3258; *Headmistress* Sister Evelyn Kearns, MA (170)
Marymount International School, George Rd, Kingston upon Thames KT2 7PE; Tel 0181-949-0571; Fax 0181-336-2485; Sister Rosaleen Sheridan, RSHM (Girls) (200) (Boarders and Day)
Merchant Taylors' School, Sandy Lodge, Northwood, Middx HA6 2HT; Tel (01923) 821850; Fax (01923) 835110; *Headmaster* J.R. Gabitass, MA (A) (Boys) (Boarders) (756)

Mill Hill School, Mill Hill Village, London NW7 1QS; Tel 0181-959 1176; A.C. Graham (A,B) (Boys) (540) (Girls) (60) (Boarders)
More House School, 22/24 Pont St SW1; Tel 0171-235 2855; Fax 0171-259 6782; *Head* M. Connell (Lay-Catholic) (Girls) (230)
The Mount School, Milespit Hill, Mill Hill, London NW7 2RX; Tel 0181-959 3403; Fax 0181-959 1503; *Headmistress* M. Pond, BSc (Girls) (440)
Normanhurst School, 68–72 Station Rd, Chingford, E4 7BA; Tel 0181-529 4307; Richard C. Holt (Mixed) (180) (Weekly Boarders Boys only)
North London Collegiate School, Canons, Edgware HA8 7RJ; Tel 0181-952 0912 (Senior School), 0181-952 1276 (Junior School); Fax 0181-951 1391; J.L. Clanchy, MA (A) (Girls) (4+–18) (974)
Northwood College, Maxwell Rd, Northwood HA6 2YE; Tel (01923) 825446; Mrs A. Mayou, MA (Girls (618)
Notting Hill and Ealing High School, 2 Cleveland Rd, Ealing, London W13 8AX; Tel 0181-997 5744; Fax 0181-810 6891; Mrs Susan Whitfield, MA (G.P.D.S.T.) (A) (Girls)
The Old Palace School of John Whitgift, Croydon CR0 1AX; Tel 0181-688 2027; *Headmistress* K.L. Hilton, BA (A) (Girls) (600)
Palmers Green High School, Hoppers Rd, London N21 3LJ; Tel 0181-886 1135; *Headmistress* S. Grant, BMus(Aberystwyth) (Girls) (320)
Park School for Girls (Ilford Ltd), 20/22 Park Ave, Ilford IG1 4RS; Tel 0181-554 2466 (235)
Peterborough and St Margaret's School for Girls, Tanglewood, Common Rd, Stanmore HA7 3JB; Tel 0181-950 3600; *Headmistress* D.M. Tomlinson (101)
Purcell School, Oakhurst, Mount Park Rd, Harrow-on-the-Hill, Middx HA1 3JS; Tel 0181-422 1284; Fax 0181-423-0526; K.J. Bain, MA (A,B,C) (Co-ed Specialist Music School) (Day/Boarders) (165)
Putney High School, GPDST, 35 Putney Hill, London SW15 6BH; Tel 0181-788 4886; Fax 0181-789 8068 (A) (Girls) (575)
Putney Park Upper School, Woodborough Rd, London SW15 6PY; Tel 0181-788 8316 (Girls 11–16) (160) (Lower Mixed) (225)
Queen's College, 43–49 Harley St, London W1N 2BT; Tel 0171-580 1533; Fax 0171-436 7607 (A) (Girls) (370)
Queen's Gate School, 133 Queen's Gate, London SW7 5LE; Tel 0171-589 3587; Fax 0171-584 7691 (Girls (350)
Riverston School, Eltham Rd, Lee Green SE12 8UF; Tel 0181-318 4327; Fax 0181-297 0514; *Principal* D.M. Lewis (Co-ed) (544)
Royal Ballet School, White Lodge, Richmond Park, Richmond, Surrey; Tel 0181-876 5547; Fax 0181-392 2833 (Mixed) (Boarders) (131)
Royal Russell School, Coombe La, Croydon CR9 5BX; Tel 0181-657 4433; *Headmaster* R.D. Balaam (Mixed) (Boarders and Day) (Weekly boarders) (700)
St Augustine's Priory, Hillcrest Rd, Ealing, London W5 2JL; Tel 0181-997 2022; *Headmistress* Mother Mary Gabriel (Girls 4–18) (420)
St Benedict's School, Ealing, London W5 2ES; Tel 0181-997 9828 (A,B) (Boys) (600) (Girls (40)
St Catherine's Convent School, Cross Deep, Twickenham TW1 4QJ; Tel 0181-891 2898; *Head Teacher* Sister Mary Augustine (Girls) (330)
St Christopher's School, 49 Bromley Rd, Beckenham BR3 2PA; Tel 0181-650 2200; *Headmistress* G.M. Scales (Girls and Boys 3–11) (220)
St David's School, Church Rd, Ashford, Middx TW15 3DZ; Tel (01784) 252494; Fax (01784) 248652 (Independent Senior) (Girls) (450) (Boarders) (35) (24) (Day) (210) (Weekley Boarders) (11) (Jun) (Girls) (Day) (164)
St Dunstan's College, Catford SE6 4TY; Tel 0181-690 1274/7 (Co-Ed) (720)
St Helen's School, Eastbury Rd, Northwood, Middx HA6 3AS; Tel (01923) 828511; Direct Line (01923) 826825; Fax (01923) 835824; Dr Yvonne A. Burne, BA, Phd, FRSA; Tel (01923) 828511 (A) (Girls) (Boarders and Day) Christian Based/Inter Denominational (568)
St James' Independent School for Boys, 91 Queen's Gate, London SW7 5AB; Tel 0171-373 5638 (328)
St James' Independent School for Girls, 91 Queen's Gate, London SW7 5AB; Tel 0171-373 5638 (251)
St Margaret's School, 18 Kidderpore Gdns, Hampstead NW3; Tel 0171-435 2439; *Headmistress* S.J. Meaden (Girls) (147)
St Martha's Convent, Senior School, Camlet Way, Hadley, Barnet; Tel 0181-449 6889; *Headmistress* Sister M.Cecile Archer (Girls) (300)
St Paul's Girls' School, Brook Green, Hammersmith W6 7BS; Tel 0171-603 2288; Fax 0171-602 9932 (A) (620)
St Paul's School, Lonsdale Rd, Barnes SW13 9JT; Tel 0181-748 9162; Fax 0181-748 9557 (A) (Boys) (Boarders) (Weekly boarders) (760)
Shaftesbury Independent School, Godstone Rd, Purley, Surrey; Tel 0181-668 8080; *Headmaster* P.A.B. Gowlland (Mixed) (60)
South Hampstead High School, 3 Maresfield Gdns, London NW3 5SS; Tel 0171-435 2899; Fax 0171-431 8022; *Headmistress* J.G. Scott (GPDST) (A) (Girls) (624)
Stowford College, 95 Brighton Rd, Sutton SM2 5SJ; Tel 0181-661 9444; *Principal* A.J. Hennessy (Mixed) (125)
Streatham Hill and Clapham High School, Abbotswood Rd, London SW16 1AW; Tel 0181-677 8400; Fax 0181-677 2001 (G.P.D.S.T.) (A) (Girls) (601)
Surbiton High School, Surbiton Cres, Kingston upon Thames KT1 2JT; Tel 0181-546 5245; Fax 0181-547 0026; Mrs R.A. Thynne, BA, AKC (Girls) (600)
Sutton High School, 55 Cheam Rd, Sutton, Surrey SM1 2AX; Tel 0181-642 0594; Fax 0181-642 2014; *Headmistress* Miss A.E. Cavendish (A) (G.P.D.S.T.) (A) (Girls) (570)
Sydenham High School, GPDST 19 Westwood Hill, London SE26 6BL; Tel 0181-778 8737; Fax 0181-776 8830; *Headmistress* Mrs G. Baker, BSc, FZS (A) (Girls) (712)
Sylvia Young Theatre School, Rossmore Rd, Marylebone, London NW1; Tel 0171-402 0673; Sylvia Young; *Head Teacher* M.T. Melville (Mixed) (139)
Trinity School, Shirley Park, Croydon CR9 7AT; Tel 0181-656 9541; Fax 0181-655 0522; *Headmaster* B.J. Lenon, MA (A) (Boys) (850)
University College School, Frognal, Hampstead NW3 6XH; Tel 0171-435 2215; Fax 0171-431 4385; *Headmaster* G.D. Slaughter, MA (A) (Boys) (700)
Upper Tooting Independent High School, 169 Trinity Rd, Tooting, London SW17 7HL; Tel 0181-672 5676; *Headmistress* Mrs A.M. Abbott (C) (Mixed) (180)
Ursuline High School, Morland Rd, Ilford 1G1 4QS; Tel 0181-554 1995; Miss J. Reddington, MBIM (A) (Girls) (400)
Virgo Fidelis Convent School, Central Hill, Upper Norwood, London SE19 1RS; Tel 0181-670 6917 (Seniors),081-653-2916 (Juniors); Sister Madeleine, BA (Seniors); Sister Renata (Juniors) (Girls) (490) (Seniors and Juniors)
Westminster School, Little Dean's Yard SW1P 3PF; Tel 0171-963 1000; D.M. Summerscale, MA (B) (Boys) (598) (Girls) (70) (Boarders, Weekly Boarders and Day)
Whitgift School, Haling Park, South Croydon CR2 6YT; Tel 0181-688 9222; *Headmaster* C.A. Barnett, MA, DPhil (A) (Boys) (1050)
Wimbledon High School, Mansel Rd, London SW19 4AB; Tel 0181-946 1756; *Head* E.M. Baker, BA(Swansea) (G.P.D.S.T.) (A) (Girls) (804)
Winton School, 205 Addiscombe Rd, Croydon CR0 6SP; Tel 0181-654 1531; *Headmaster* N.G. Murray (Mixed 3–18) (180)

Manchester

Ash Lea School, 1 Half Edge La, Eccles, Manchester M30 9GJ; Tel 0161-789-3892; J.M. Swift, CertEd (Mixed) (155)
Audenshaw High School, Hazel St, Audenshaw, Manchester M34 5NB; Tel 0161-336-2133; Fax 0161-320-3046; *Head* A.A. Crompton (Boys 11-16) (840)
Beech House, 184 Manchester Rd, Rochdale OL11 4JQ; Tel (01706) 46309; *Headmaster* I.R. Barber, BEd (Mixed) (195)

Bolton School, Chorley New Rd, Bolton BL1 4PA; Tel (01204) 840201; Fax (01204) 849477; *Headmaster* A.W. Wright, BSc (A) (Boys) (825)
Bolton School Girls Division, Bolton BL1 4PB; Tel (01204) 840201; E.J. Panton, MA Oxon, FRSA (A) (Girls) (4–18) (Boys) (4–8) (1163)
Bridgewater School, Drywood Hall, Worsley, Manchester M28 4WQ; Tel 0161-794 1463; *Headmaster* Dr B.J. Blundell, BSc, MSc, PhD (Mixed) (470) (Mixed)
Bury Grammar School (Girls), Bury BL9 0HH; Tel 0161-797 2808; Fax 0161-763 4658 (A) (830)
Bury Grammar School, Bury BL9 0HN; Tel 0161-797 2700; K. Richards, MA (A) (Boys) (675)
Cheadle Hulme School, Claremont Rd, Cheadle Hulme, Cheadle, Chesire SK8 6EF; Tel 0161-485 4142; D.J. Wilkinson, BA, MLitt (Warehousemen and Clerks) (A) (Mixed) (920) (Day)
Chetham's School of Music, Long Millgate, Manchester M3 1SB; Tel 0161-834 9644; Fax 0161-839 3609; Rev P.F. Hullah, BD, AKC, FRSA (A) (Mixed) (Boarders) (260)
Culcheth Hall School for Girls, Ashley Rd, Altrincham WA14 2LT; Tel 0161-928 1862; Fax 0161-929 6893; *Headmaster* C.D. Taylor, MA(Cantab), MSc (350)
The Hulme Grammar School, Oldham OL8 4BX; Tel 0161-624 4497; *Headmaster* G.F. Dunkin (A) (Boys) (740)
The Hulme Grammar School for Girls, Chamber Rd, Oldham 0L8 4BX; Tel 0161-624 2523; Fax 0161-620 0234; *Headmistress* M.S. Smolenski, BSc (A) (Day) (630)
Hulme Hall Schools, 75 Hulme Hall Rd, Cheadle Hulme SK8 6LA; Tel 0161-485 4638; *Headmaster* G. Kellock, MEd (C) (Mixed) (450)
Jewish High School for Girls, 10 Radford St, Salford M7 0NT; Tel 0161-792 2118; Rabbi M.I. Young, BA(Hons), DipManEd (A) (107)
Loreto Convent Grammar School, Dunham Rd, Altrincham WA14 4AH; Tel 0161-928 3703; Sister Aileen McEvoy, IBVM, BA (A) (Girls) (810)
The Manchester Grammar School, Manchester M13 0XT; Tel 0161-224 7201/2/3; G.M. Stephen, BA, PhD (A) (Boys) (1453)
Manchester High School for Girls, Grangethorpe Rd, Manchester M14 6HS; Tel 0161-224 0447; Fax 0161-224 6192; E.M. Diggory, BA, FRSA (A) (717)
Manchester Jewish Grammar School, Charlton Ave, Prestwich M25 8PH; Tel 0161-773 1789; P. Pink, BSc(Econ), DipEd (Boys) (170)
North Cestrian Grammar School, Altrincham WA14 4AJ; Tel 0161-928 1856; *Headmaster* P.F. Morton (Boys) (400)
St Ambrose College, Hale Barns, Altrincham WA15 0HF; Tel 0161-980 2711; Fax 0161-980 2323; G.E. Hester, BA (A) (Boys) (700)
St Bede's College, Alexandra Park, Manchester M16 8HX; Tel 0161-226 3323; Fax 0161-226 3813; J. Byrne, BA, MEd (A,B,C) (Boys and Girls) (980)
William Hulme's Grammar School, Spring Bridge Rd, Manchester M16 8PR; Tel 0161-226 2054/2058/2087; Fax 0161-226 8922; *Headmaster* P.D. Briggs, MA (A,C) (Co-ed) (795)
Withington Girls' School, Fallowfield, Manchester M14 6BL; Tel 0161-224 1077; Fax 0161-248 5377; *Headmistress* M. Kenyon (A) (490 Senior School) (100 Junior School)

Merseyside

Beechenhurst, Menlove Ave, Liverpool L18 3EE; Tel 0151-722 3279; Mrs E. Turner (Boys/Girls 3–11)
The Belvedere School, 17 Belvedere Rd, Princes Park, Liverpool L8 3TF; Tel 0151-727 1284; Fax 0151-727 0602; *Headmistress* C.H. Evans (G.P.D.S.T.) (A) (Girls) (655)
Birkenhead High School, Birkenhead L43 1TY; Tel 0151-652 5777; *Headmistress* K. Irving, BSc (G.P.D.S.T.) (A) (Girls) (720)
Birkenhead School, Birkenhead; Tel 0151-652 4014; Fax 0151-653 7412; *Headmaster* S.J. Haggett, MA (A) (Boys) (740)
Elliott-Clarke School, 63 Rodney St, Liverpool L1 9ER; Tel 0151-709 3323; Miss Annette I. Thomson (C) (86)
Highfield School Trust (Birkenhead) Ltd, 96 Bidston Rd, Oxton, Birkenhead L43 6TW; Tel 0151-652 3708; Mrs Sandra Morris (150)
Kingswood Schools, 26 Westcliffe Rd, Birkdale, Southport PR8 2BU; Tel (01704) 563211; Fax (01704) 550399; *Headmaster* E.J. Borowski (B,C) (280)
Liverpool College, Mossley Hill, Liverpool L18 8BE; Tel 0151-724 4000; Fax 0151-729 0105; *Principal* B.R. Martin, MA, MBA, MIMgt, FRSA (A,B) (Boys & Girls) (995)
Merchant Taylors' School, Crosby, Liverpool L23 0QP; Tel 0151-928 3308; Fax 0151-928 0434; *Headmaster* S.J.R. Dawkins, (A) (Boys) (840)
Merchant Taylors' School for Girls, Crosby, Liverpool L23 5SP; Tel 0151-924 3140; *Headmistress* J.I. Mills (A) (658)
Pershore House School, Prenton La, Prenton, Birkenhead L42 8LA; Tel 0151-608 1170; *Headmaster* D.B. Winterford (Mixed) (2–11+) (95)
St Anselm's College, Birkenhead; Tel 0151-652 1408; Fax 0151-652 1957; C.J. Cleugh, MSc (A) (Boys) (650)
St Edward's College, North Dr, Sandfield Park, West Derby, Liverpool L12 1LF; Tel 0151-228 3376; Fax 0151-252 0219; J.E. Waszek, BSc, MA, FRSA (A,B) (Co-Ed) (3–18) (1030)
St Mary's College, Great Crosby, Liverpool L23 3AB; Tel 0151-924 3926; W. Hammond, Esq, MA (A) (Co-ed) (600)
St Wyburn School, 26 Westcliffe Rd, Birkdale, Southport PR8 2BU; Tel (01704) 563211; Fax (01704) 550399; *Headmaster* E.J. Borowski (Part of Kingswood Schools) (Mixed) (B,C) (280)
Streatham House School, 2 Victoria Rd, Crosby, Liverpool L23 8UQ; Tel 0151-924 1514; *Headmistress* Mrs C. Baxter, BA (Girls 2½-16) (180) (Boys 2½-7)
Tower College, Rainhill, Prescot, Merseyside; Tel 0151-426 4333; Fax 0151-426 3338; *Principal* R.J. Oxley (Mixed) (200)
Upton Hall Convent F.C.J., Upton, Wirral L49 6LJ; Tel 0151-677 7696; Fax 0151-677 6868; *Headteacher* Loretta Madigan, BA (A) (Girls) (603)
Wellington School, Bebington, Wirral L63 7NG; Tel 0151-645 2332; *Headmaster* Dr B. Scott, BSc (Mixed) (200)

Norfolk

Bracondale School, Norwich NR1 2AL; Tel 624042; D.M. Gaudoin, BA (Boys) (Weekly boarders) (100)
Bushey Place, Cromer Rd, Aylsham, Norwich NR11 6HF; Tel (01263) 734108; R.G. Horne (Mixed) (60) (Boarders and Day)
Cawston College, Cawston, Norwich NR10 4JD; Tel (01603) 871204; *Headteacher* B. Harrison (C) (Mixed) (125) (Boarders, Weekly Boarders and Day)
Convent of the Sacred Heart, Swaffham PE37 7QW; Tel (01760) 721330/724577; *Headteacher* Sister M. Francis Ridler (Girls) (120) (Weekly boarders) (Day)
Eccles Hall, Quidenham, Norwich NR16 2PA; Tel (0195 387) 217; S.A. Simington, CertEd (Boys) (Boarders) (140)
Gresham's School, Holt; Tel (01263) 713271; J.H. Arkell, MA (Boys) (306) (Girls) (176) (Boarders) (312)
Hethersett Old Hall School, Norwich NR9 3DW; Tel (01603) 810390; Fax (01603) 812094; Mrs V.M. Redington, MA, DipEd(Oxon) (Educational Trust) (Girls) (240) (Boarders and Day)
Langley School, Langley Park, Norwich NR14 6BJ; Tel (01508) 520210; Fax (01508) 528058; *Headmaster* S.J.W. McArthur, (Mixed) (263) (Boarders and Day) (Weekly boarders)
Norwich High School for Girls GPDST, 95 Newmarket Rd, Norwich NR2 2HU; Tel (01603) 53265; Fax (01603) 259891; *Headmistress* Mrs V.C. Bidwell, (A) (Girls) (850)
Norwich School, The Close, Norwich NR1 4DQ; Tel (01603) 623194; *Headmaster* C.D. Brown (A) (Boys 8–18) (Girls (16–18) (600)
Runton and Sutherland School, West Runton, Cromer NR27 9NF; Tel (0126 375) 026375661/2; *Headmistress* D.J. Buckenham (Mixed Junior, Senior Girls only) (170) (Boarders and Day)

8 Independent Secondary Schools

Thetford Grammar School, Bridge St, Thetford IP24 3AF; Tel (01842) 752840; Fax (01842) 750220; *Headmaster* J.R. Weeks, MA, MLit(Oxon) (Mixed) (300)

Thorpe House School, 7 Yarmouth Rd, Thorpe, Norwich NR7 0EA; Tel (01603) 33055; Mrs F.M. Hunt, BA (Girls) (11-15) (225)

North Yorkshire

Ampleforth College, York YO6 4ER; Tel (01439) 788224; Fax (01439) 788330; Rev G.F.L. Chamberlain, OSB, MA (Boarders) (550)

Ashville College, Harrogate HG2 9JP; Tel (01423) 566358; *Headmaster* M.H. Crosby (Mixed) (700) (Boarders) (Weekly boarders)

Belmont-Birklands School Trust Ltd, 68 Kent Rd, Harrogate HG1 2NH; Tel (01423) 502465; V. Arthur, MA (Preparatory) (2–11 years) (Girls) (121) (Boys) (21)

Bootham School, York YO3 7BU; Tel (01904) 623636; Fax (01904) 652106; *Head* I.M. Small, (Co-Ed) (336) (Boarders and Day)

Fyling Hall School, Robin Hood's Bay YO22 4QD; Tel (01947) 880 261/ 880 353; Fax (01947) 880919; *Headmaster* A. Gregg (Acting) (Mixed) (250) (Boarders)

Giggleswick School, Settle BD24 0DE; Tel (01729) 823545; Fax (01729) 824187; *Headmaster* Anthony P. Millard, BSc(Econ), FRSA (A) (Mixed) (8-18) (450) (Boarding and Day)

Harrogate Ladies' College, Clarence Dr, Harrogate HG1 2QG; Tel (01423) 504543; Fax (01423) 568893; *Principal* Jennifer Smith (A) (Girls) (370) (Boarders and Day) (Weekly Boarding) (School Transport from Leeds) (EFL teaching)

The Mount School, Dalton Terr, York YO2 4DD; Tel (01904) 622275; Fax (01904) 627518; *Headmistress* Barbara J. Windle; The Mount School is to merge with York College for Girls in September 1995

Queen Ethelburga's School, Thorpe Underwood Hall, Ouseburn, York YOS 9SZ; Tel (01423) 331480; G.L. Richardson, BA (Girls) (Boarders and Day) (Weekly boarders) (300)

Queen Margaret's School, Escrick Park, York YO4 6EU; Tel (01904) 728261; Fax (01904) 728150 (Girls) (360) (Boarders and Day)

Queen Mary's School, Baldersby Park, Topcliffe, Thirsk, York YO7 3BZ; Tel (01845) 577425; P. Belward (Girls) (230) (Boarders and Day) (Weekly boarders)

Read School, Drax, Selby YO8 8NL; Tel (01757) 618248; A.J. Saddler, MA (Co-ed) (Day 5–8) (Day and Boarding 8–18)

St Hilda's School, Sneaton Castle, Whitby YO21 3QN; Tel (01947) 602079; Fax (01947) 820854; *Headmistress* M. Blain (C) (Mixed) (220) (Boarders and Day)

St Peter's School, York YO3 6AB; Tel (01904) 652079 (Bursar), 623213 (Headmaster); R.N. Pittman, MA (Co-ed) (A) (470) (Boarders)

Scarborough College, Scarborough YO11 3BA; Tel (01723) 360620; Fax (01723) 377265; *Headmaster* D.S. Hempsall, (Mixed) (382) (Boarders) (Weekly boarders)

York College for Girls, 62 Petergate, York YO1 2HZ; Tel (01904) 646421; Fax (01904) 652191; Mrs J.L. Clare, BD (175)

York Steiner School, Fullford Cross, York YO1 4PB; Tel (01904) 654983 (Co-ed) (150)

Northamptonshire

Falcon Manor, Towcester NN12 8BN; Tel (01327) 350544; G.D. Priest (Mixed) (130) (Boarders) (Weekly boarders) (Day)

Laxton School, Oundle PE8 4AR; Tel (01832) 273569; Fax (01832) 273564; *Headmaster* R.I. Briggs, (B) (Co-Ed) (198)

Northampton High School, Newport Pagnell Rd, Hardingstone, Northampton NN4 6UU; Tel (01604) 765765; Fax (01604) 709418 (A) (Girls) (520)

Northamptonshire Grammar School, Pitsford Hall, Pitsford, Northampton NN6 9AX; Tel (01604) 880306; *Headmaster* M.D.W. Tozer, (Boys) (280)

Oundle, The School, Oundle, Peterborough PE8 4EN; Tel (01832) 273536 (Headmaster), 273434 (Bursar); Fax (01832) 274967; *Headmaster* D.B. McMurray (Mixed) (826) (Boarders)

St Peter's School, 52 Headlands, Kettering NN15 6DJ; Tel (01536) 512066; Mrs B. Blakeley, BA(Hons)(London), DipEd(Oxon) (Girls) (63)

Wellingborough School, Wellingborough NN8 2BX; Tel (01933) 222427; Fax (01933) 271986; F.R. Ullmann, MA, ACP, FCollP (A) (Mixed) (780) (Boarders)

Northumberland

Longridge Towers School, Berwick upon Tweed TD15 2XH; Tel (01289) 307584; Fax (01289) 302581; *Headmaster* Dr M.J. Barron (Mixed) (288) (Boarders, Weekly boarders and Day)

Nottinghamshire

Broadgate School, 1 Western Terr, The Park, Nottingham NG7 1AF; Tel (0115) 947 4275; *Principal* T. Osgerby, BA, MEd (Mixed) (120)

Dagfa House School, Broadgate, Beeston, Nottingham NG9 2FU; Tel (0115) 925 4100; *Head* A. Oatway (Co-ed) (2½-16 yrs) (225)

Hollygirt School, Elm Ave, Nottingham NG3 4GF; Tel (0115) 958 0596; Fax (0115) 924 0773; Mrs M.R. Banks, MEd (Girls) (Pay school) (320)

The Lammas School, Lammas Rd, Sutton-in-Ashfield NG17 2AD; Tel (01623) 516879; *Principal* G.H.E. Coleshill (Mixed 4-16) (120)

Nottingham High School, Waverley Mount, Nottingham NG7 4ED; Tel (0115) 978 6056; Fax (0115) 979 2202; C.S. Parker (A) (832) (Boys)

Nottingham High School for Girls, 9 Arboretum St, Nottingham NG1 4JB; Tel (0115) 941 7663; Fax (0115) 924 0757; Mrs C. Bowering, MA (A) (G.P.D.S.T.) (4–18) (1080)

Rodney School, Kirklington, Newark NG22 8NB; Tel (01636) 813281; *Principal* G.R. Howe (Co-ed) (8-18) (Boarders and Day) (250)

Trent College, Long Eaton, Nottingham NG10 4AD; Tel (0115) 973 2737; Fax (0115) 946 3284; J.S. Lee, MA (A) (Fully Co-Ed) (Day and Boarding) (650)

West Bridgford High School, 61–63 Musters Rd, West Bridgford, Nottingham NG2 7PY; Tel (0115) 981 2967; C.W. Redwood, GTCL, LRAM (B) (Boys) (100)

Worksop College, Worksop S80 3AP; Tel (01909) 472391; *Headmaster* R.A. Collard, MA (A) (Mixed) (Boarders and Day) (Weekly boarders) (340)

Oxfordshire

Abingdon School, Oxfordshire, Abingdon OX14 1DE; Tel (01235) 531755; *Headmaster* M. St John Parker, MA (Boys) (Day) (Boarders) (Weekly boarders) (750)

Bloxham School, Bloxham, nr Banbury OX15 4PE; Tel (01295) 720222 Headmaster: (01295) 720206; Fax (01295) 721714 Headmaster: (01295) 721897; *Headmaster* D.K. Exham, MA (Boys) (Boarding and Day) (13–18) (Day) (11–13) (Girls) (16–18) (Boarding and Day)

Carmel College, Mongewell Park, Wallingford, Oxon OX10 8BT; Tel (01491) 837505; *Headmaster* P. Skelker, MA(Oxon) (A) (Mixed) (Boarders) (325)

Cokethorpe School, nr Witney OX8 7PU; Tel (01993) 703921; *Headmaster* D.G. Crawford, BA (B) (Boys) (Day) (Boarders) (Weekly boarders) (175) (Girls) (Day) (30)

Cranford House School, Moulsford, Wallingford, Oxford OX10 9HT; Tel (01491) 651218; *Headmistress* Mrs A.B. Gray, BSc (Girls 3–16) (Boys 3–7) (Girls 172) (Boys 48) (220)

Headington School, Oxford OX3 7TD; Tel (01865) 62711; *Headmistress* Miss E.M. Tucker, MA (Girls) (Boarders and Day) (Weekly boarders) (550)

Kingham Hill School, Kingham, Chipping Norton OX7 6TH; Tel (01608) 658999; Fax (01608) 658658; *Headmaster* M.H. Payne, BSc (Mixed) (Day and Boarders) (Weekly boarders) (200)
Magdalen College School, Oxford OX4 1DZ; Tel (01865) 242191; Fax (01865) 240379; *Master* P.M. Tinniswood, MA, MBA (A) (Boys) (Boarders – Choristers only) (500)
The Oratory School, Woodcote, nr Reading RG8 0PJ; Tel (01491) 680207; Fax (01491) 680020; *Headmaster* S.W. Barrow, BA (Boys) (Day and Boarders) (399)
Our Lady's Convent Senior School, Radley Rd, Abingdon, Oxon OX14 3PS; Tel (01235) 524658; Fax (01235) 535829; *Headmistress* Sister Monica Sheehy, RSM, BEd (Girls) (350)
Oxford High School, Belbroughton Rd, Oxford OX2 6XA; Tel (01865) 59888; Fax (01865) 52343; *Headmistress* Mrs J. Townsend, MA, MSc (G.P.D.S.T.) (A) (Girls) (650)
Radley College, Abingdon OX14 2HR; Tel (01235) 543000; *Headmaster* R.M. Morgan, MA (Boys) (Boarders) (600)
Rye St Antony School, Pullens La, Headington Hill, Oxford OX3 0BY; Tel (01865) 62802; Fax (01865) 63611; *Headmistress* A.M. Jones, BA (Girls) (Boarders) (400)
St Edward's Oxford, Oxford OX2 7NN; Tel (01865) 319204; *Warden* D. Christie, BA, BSc(Econ), FRSA (B) (Boys) (Boarders) (Co-Ed in the V1th Form) (570)
St Mary's School, Wantage Trust Ltd, Newbury St, Wantage OX12 8BZ; Tel (01235) 763571; Fax (01235) 760467; *Headmistress* S. Bodinham, BSc, AKC (Girls) (Boarders) (240)
School of St Helen and St Katharine, Abingdon OX14 1BE; Tel (01235) 520173; *Headmistress* C.L. Hall, MA (Oxon) (A) (Girls) (Day and Weekly Boarding 6th form only) (520)
Shiplake College, Henley-on-Thames RG9 4BW; Tel (01734) 402455; *Headmaster* N.V. Bevan, MA(Oxon) (Boys) (Boarders and Day) (305)
Sibford School, Sibford Ferris, Banbury, Oxon OX15 5QL; Tel (01295) 780441; Fax (01295) 788444; *Headmaster* J. Dunston, MA, AIL, FRSA (Mixed) (Boarders and Day) (320)
Tudor Hall, Wykham Park, Banbury OX16 9UR; Tel (01295) 263434; Fax (01295) 253264; *Headmistress* Miss N. Godfrey, BA (Girls) (Boarders) (260)
Wychwood School, 74 Banbury Rd, Oxford OX2 6JR; Tel (01865) 57976; Fax (01865) 56806; *Headmistress* Mrs M.L. Duffill (Girls) (Boarders) (160)

Shropshire

Acton Reynald School Educational Trust Ltd, Shrewsbury SY4 4DX; Tel (0193928) 365; Mrs D. Matthews (Girls) (110)
Adcote School, Adcote, Little Ness, nr Shrewsbury SY4 2JY; Tel (01939) 260202; Fax (01939) 261300; *Head* Mrs S.B. Cecchet, BSc (Girls) (Full and Weekly Boarders and Day Girls 5–18) (100)
Bedstone College, Bucknell SY7 0BG; Tel (0157) 530303; Fax (0157) 530740; *Headmaster* M.S. Symonds, BSc, PGCE, CPhys, MInstP (B,C) (Mixed) (Boarders and Day, Weekly boarders) (250)
Concord College, Acton Burnell Hall, Shrewsbury SY5 7PF; Tel (0169 44) 631; A.L. Morris, BA (Mixed) (220)
Ellesmere College, Ellesmere SY12 9AB; Tel (01691) 622321; Fax (01691) 623286; *Headmaster* D.R. Du Croz, MA (Coeducational 10–18 Boarding and Day) (10–13 Day only) (350)
Moreton Hall, Weston Rhyn, Oswestry SY11 3EW; Tel (01691) 773671; Fax (01691) 778552; Jonathan Forster Esq, BA (Girls) (Boarders) (Moreton Hall Educational Trust Ltd) (350)
Oswestry School, Oswestry SY11 2TL; Tel (01691) 655711; Fax (01691) 671194; *Headmaster* J.V. Light, MA(Cantab) (Mixed) (Boarders) (Weekly boarders) (300)
Queen's Park School, Oswestry SY11 2HZ; Tel (01691) 652416; Mrs D. Baur (Dyslexic Centre) (Mixed) (Boarders, Weekly boarders) (Day) (50)
Shrewsbury High School, 32 Town Walls, Shrewsbury SY1 1TN; Tel (01743) 362872; *Headmistress* Miss S. Gardner, MA (G.P.D.S.T.) (A) (Girls) (369)
Shrewsbury School, The Schools, Shrewsbury SY3 7BA; Tel (01743) 344537; Fax (01743) 243107; *Headmaster* F.E. Maidment, MA (Boys) (Boarders) (695)
Wrekin College, Wellington, Telford TF1 3BG; Tel (01952) 240131; Fax (01952) 240338; P.M. Johnson, MA (Mixed) (Boarders and Day) (350)

Somerset

Bruton School for Girls, Sunny Hill, Bruton BA10 0NT; Tel (01749) 812277; Fax (01749) 812537; Mrs J.M. Wade, MSc (A) (Day) (Boarders) (Weekly boarders) (560)
Chilton Cantelo School, Yeovil; Tel (01935) 850555; *Headmaster* D.S. von Zeffman, LLB (Mixed) (Boarders and Day) (130)
King's College, Taunton; Tel (01823) 272708; Fax (01823) 334236; *Headmaster* R.S. Funnell, MA (Co-ed) (Boarders) (460)
King's School, Bruton BA10 0ED; Tel (01749) 813326; Fax (01749) 813426; *Headmaster* R.I. Smyth, MA (B) (C) (Boys) (Boarders) (Girls in the Sixth Form) (310)
Millfield, Street BA16 0YD; Tel (01458) 42291; Fax (01458) 47276; C.S. Martin, MA (Mixed) (Boarders and Day) (1250)
The Park School, The Park, Yeovil; Tel (01935) 23514; Fax (01935) 411257; *Headmaster* P.W. Bate, BA, PGCE, DIP MKT (C) (Mixed) (Boarders) (170)
Quantock School, Over Stowey, Bridgwater TA5 1HD; Tel (01278) 732252; *Headmaster* D.T. Peaster; G.R. Warriner, BA (Co-ed) (Boarders) (Weekly boarders) (Boarding places only) (180)
Queen's College, Trull Rd, Taunton, Somerset TA1 4QS; Tel (01823) 272559; Fax (01823) 338430; C.T. Bradnock, MA (A) (Co-ed) (Boarding and Day) (673) (Pre prep 62, Junior 167, Senior 444)
Rossholme School, East Brent, Highbridge TA9 4JA; Tel (01278) 760219; Fax (01278) 760158; S.J.B. Webb (Girls) (Day and Boarders) (100) (Kindergarten boys and girls 3–7)
St Martin's School, 24 Abbey St, Crewkerne TA18 7HY; Tel (01460) 73265; Mrs J.A. Murrell (Mixed) (Ages 4-13) (100)
Shapwick School, Shapwick Manor, Shapwick, nr Bridgwater TA7 9NJ; Tel (01458) 210384; Fax (01458) 210111; D.C. Walker; J.P. Whittock (Dyslexic) (Boys) (90) (Girls) (10) (Boarders and 15 Day)
Taunton School, Taunton TA2 6AD; Tel (01823) 349233; B.B. Sutton, MA (A) (Mixed) (Boarders and Day) (509)
Wellington School, Wellington; Tel (01823) 668800; Fax (01823) 668844; A.J. Rogers, MA (A) (Mixed) (Boarders) (800)
Wells Cathedral School, Wells BA5 2ST; Tel (01749) 72117; *Headmaster* J.S. Baxter, BA (A) (Mixed) (Boarders) (802)

South Yorkshire

Birkdale School, 4 Oakholme Rd, Broomhill, Sheffield S10 3DH; Tel (0114) 266 8409; Rev M.D.A. Hepworth, MA(Cantab) PGCE (Boys) (Co-educational Sixth Form from Sept 1995) (750)
Mount St Mary's College, Spinkhill, Via Sheffield S31 9YL; Tel (01246) 433388; Paul B. Fisher, MA (A) (Mixed) (Day and boarding) (Weekly boarding (320)
Pocklington School, West Green, Pocklington, Yorks YO4 2NJ; Tel (01759) 303125; *Headmaster* J.N.D. Gray, BA (A) (Mixed) (Day and boarder (730)
Sheffield High School, 10 Rutland Pk, Sheffield SI0 2PE; Tel (0114) 266 1435 (Junior Dept); (0114) 266 0324 (Senior School); Mrs M.A. Houston, BA (G.P.D.S.T.) (A,B) (Girls) (693)

Staffordshire

Abbots Bromley School of S Mary and S Anne nr Rugeley WS15 3BW; Tel (01283) 840225/840232; Fax (01283) 840988; *Head* A.J. Grigg, BA, MPhil (A) (Girls) (300)

8 Independent Secondary Schools

Abbotsholme School, Rocester, Uttoxeter, Staffordshire ST14 5BS; Tel (01889) 590217; Fax (01889) 591001; *Headmaster* D.J. Farrant, MA, DipEd, FRSA (Boarder and Day) (Mixed) (240)
Cotton College, Oakamoor, via Stoke-on-Trent ST10 3DP; Tel (01583) 702371; *Headmaster* R.J. Hutchings, BSc, MIBiol (Mixed) (Boarders) (200)
Denstone College, Uttoxeter ST14 5HN; Tel (01889) 590484; Fax (01889) 591295; *Headmaster* H.C.K. Carson, BA (A) (Boys) (207) (Girls) (86) (Boarders, Weekly boarders and Day)
Newcastle under Lyme School, Mount Pleasant, Newcastle under Lyme ST5 1DB; Tel (01782) 633604; Fax (01782) 632765; *Principal* Dr R.M. Reynolds, BSc (A) (Mixed) (1300)
St Dominic's School, 32 Bargate Street, Brewood, Stafford ST19 9BA; Tel (01902) 850248/851201; *Headmistress* K.S. Butwilowska, JP, BA, MEd (Girls 2½–18) (Boys 2½–7) (490)
St Dominic's Priory School, Stone ST15 8EN; Tel (01785) 814181; Fax (01785) 819361; *Headteacher* J.W. Hildreth, BA, MEd (Girls) (352)
St Joseph's Convent, Haunton Hall, Tamworth; Tel (0182 786) 226; *Headmistress* Sister M.S. Armstrong (A) (Girls) (Boarders) (160)
St Joseph's College, Trent Vale, Stoke-on-Trent ST4 5NT; Tel (01782) 48008; Fax (01782) 745487; *Headmaster* John E. Stoer, BA (Co-ed)

Suffolk

All Hallows School, Ditchingham, Bungay NR35 2DU; Tel (01986) 2133; Miss C.A. Harris, BA, DipEd (Boarders) (Weekly boarders) (Day)
Amberfield School, Nacton, Ipswich; Tel (01473) 659265; Fax (01473) 659843; L. Amphlett Lewis, BA (Girls) (275)
Culford School, Bury St Edmunds; Tel (01284) 728615; Fax (01284) 728631; *Headmaster* J.S. Richardson, MA (A) (Mixed) (Boarders and Day) (680)
Felixstowe College, Felixstowe IP11 7NQ; Tel (01394) 284269; Mrs Bridget Patterson, BA (Girls) (Boarders and Day) (Senior Co-ed) (Day) (Junior) (300)
Framlingham College, Framlingham IP13 9EY; Tel (01728) 723789; *Head* G.M. Randall (Boarders) (310) (Day) (134)
Ipswich High School, Woolverstone, Ipswich IP9 1AZ; Tel (01473) 780201; V.C. MacCuish, BA (G.P.D.S.T.) (A) (Girls) (425)
Ipswich School, Henley Rd, Ipswich IP1 3SG; Tel (01473) 255313; Fax (01473) 213831; I.G. Galbraith, MA (A,B) (Boys) (558) (Girls) (44) (Boarders 37) (Weekly boarders)
Royal Hospital School, Holbrook, Ipswich IP9 2RX; Tel (01473) 328342; M.A.B. Kirk MA (Mixed) (Boarders) (650)
St Felix School, Southwold IP18 6SD; Tel (01502) 722175; Mrs S.R. Campion, MA(Cantab) (Girls) (Boarders and Day) (265)
Finborough School, The Hall, Great Finborough, Stowmarket IP14 3EF; Tel (01449) 674479; *Principal* J. Sinclair, BScEcon, FCA (Co-ed) (300)
St Joseph's College, Birkfield, Ipswich IP2 9DR; Tel (01473) 690281; Fax (01473) 602409; *Headmaster* David Hennessy, MA (A,B) (Boys) (Girls in 6th form) (Boarders) (590)
School of Jesus and Mary, Woodbridge Rd, Ipswich IP4 4BB; Tel (01473) 728112/720660; *Headmistress* Mrs E. McKay, BA (Girls) (250)
Stoke College Educational Trust Ltd, Stoke-by-Clare; Tel (01787) 278141; D. Marshall, MA, BA(Hons), AdvDipEd (Mixed) (Day) (Weekly boarders) (132)
Summerhill School, Leiston, Suffolk, IP16 4HY; Tel (01728) 830540; Mrs Z. Readhead (Mixed) (Boarders) (60)
Woodbridge School, Woodbridge, IP12 4JH; Tel (01394) 385547; Fax (01394) 380944; S.H. Cole, MA, CPhys, MInstP (A) (Mixed) (Boarders) (500)

Surrey

Box Hill School, Mickleham, Dorking RH5 6EA; Tel (01372) 373382; Fax (01372) 363942; Dr R.A.S. Atwood, BA, PhD (Mixed) (Boarders) (270)
Caterham School, Harestone Valley, Caterham CR3 6YA; Tel (01883) 343028; Fax (01883) 347795; R.A. Davey, MA (Co-educational 3–18) (Day and Boarding School (Boarding 11–18 only) (Prep School 3–11) (200) (Senior School 11–18) (730)
Charterhouse, Godalming; Tel (01483) 291600 (Headmaster), 291500 (Bursar and Enquiries); Fax (01483) 291647; *Headmaster* P. Hobson, MA (A,B) (Boys) (Boarders) (Girls in Sixth Form) (700)
City of London Freemen's School, co-educational HMC school, Ashtead Park KT21 1ET; Tel (01372) 277933; *Headmaster* D.C. Haywood, MA (Mixed 7–18) (Boarders) (Weekly boarders) (Day) (725)
Claremont Fan Court School, Claremont Dr, Esher KT10 9LY; Tel (01372) 467841; Fax (01372) 471109; *Principal* P.B. Farrar (Mixed) (Boarders) (Weekly boarders) (All boarders Christian Scientists; Day pupils also from other denominations) (385)
Cranleigh School, Cranleigh GU6 8QQ; Tel (01483) 276377; Fax (01483) 267398; Anthony Hart, MA (A,B,C) (Boys) (435) (Boarders) (80) (Day) (includes 76 Sixth Form Girls, 72 Boarders, 4 Day)
Dunottar, High Trees Rd, Reigate, RH2 7EL; Tel (01737) 761945; Fax (01737) 779450; *Headmistress* J. Burnell, CBiol, MIBiol, PGCE (Girls) (460)
Elmhurst Ballet School, Camberley; Tel (01276) 65301; *Principal* J.R. Skitch, BSc (B,C) (Boarders and Day) (300)
Epsom College, Epsom KT17 4JQ; Tel (01372) 723621; Fax (01372) 726277; *Headmaster* A.H. Beadles, MA (A,B,C) (Boys) (Girls 6th form only) (Boarders) (Weekly boarders) (Day) (660)
Ewell Castle School GBA/SHMIS IAPS, Church St, Ewell; Tel 0181-393 7459/081-393 1413; Fax 0181-786 8218; R.A. Fewtrell, MA, JP, FRSA (B) (Mixed) (460)
Frensham Heights, Rowledge, Farnham, Surrey GU10 4EA; Tel (01252) 792134; *Headmaster* P.M. de Voil, MA, DipEd, FRSA (Co-ed) (Boarders and Day) (300)
Gordon's School West End, Woking GU24 9PT; Tel (01276) 858084; Fax (01276) 855335; *Headteacher* Edward Firth; *Chair of Governors* Brian Carlisle (Boarding and Day) (Mixed 11–16 (315)
Greenacre School for Girls Ltd, Sutton La, Banstead, Surrey SM7 3RA; Tel (01737) 352114; Mrs P.M. Wood, BA (Day (380)
The Grove School, Portsmouth Rd, Hindhead GU26 6BW; Tel (01428) 605407; Fax (01428) 607977; *Headmaster* Colin Brooks, BA(Hons) (Girls) (Boarders) (Weekly boarders) (330)
Guildford High School for Girls, London Rd, Guildford GU1 1SJ; Tel (01483) 61440; Fax (01483) 306516; *Head* Mrs S.H. Singer (449)
Halliford School, Russell Rd, Shepperton TW17 9HX; Tel (01932) 223593; Fax (01932) 229781; *Headmaster* J.R. Crook, BA (B) (Boys) (275)
Hawley Place School, Fernhill Rd, Blackwater, Camberley GU17 9HU; Tel (01276) 32028; *Principal* T.G. Pipe (Mixed) (150)
King Edward's School, Witley, Godalming GU8 5SG; Tel (01428) 682572; Fax (01428) 685260; R.J. Fox, MA (A) (Co-ed) (Boarders) (525)
Kingston Grammar School, 70/72 London Rd, Kingston Upon Thames, Surrey KT2 6PY; Tel 0181-546 5875; Fax 0181-974 5177 (A) (Mixed) (Day) (593)
Manor House School, Little Bookham KT23 4EN; Tel (01372) 458538; Mrs L.A. Mendes, BA (Girls) (Day) (Weekly boarders) (260)
More House School, Frensham, Farnham GU10 3AP; Tel (01252) 792303; *Headmaster* B.G. Huggett (Boys) (Boarders and Day) (Weekly boarders) (100)
Notre Dame, Lingfield RH7 6PH; Tel (01342) 832407; *Principal* G.J. Davies, BSc, MEd (Girls) (260)
Notre Dame Senior School, Burwood Hse, Cobham KT11 1HA; Tel (01932) 863560; Fax (01932) 860992; Sister Faith Ede (Girls) (300)
Parsons Mead School, Ottways La, Ashtead KT21 2PE; Tel (01372) 276401; Fax (01372) 278796; *Headmistress* E.B. Plant, BA (Girls) (Weekly boarders) (300)
Pierrepont School, Frensham GU10 3DN; Tel (0125 125) 2110; J.D. Payne, MA (C) (Mixed) (Boy Boarders) (230)

Prior's Field School, Prior's Field, Godalming GU7 2RH; Tel (01483) 810551; Fax (01483) 810180; *Headmistress* J. McCallum, BA (Girls) (Boarders) (Weekly boarders) (Day girls) (250)
Reed's School, Cobham KT11 2ES; Tel (01932) 863076; Fax (01932) 866289 (Bursary); *Headmaster* D.E. Prince, MA; Fax (01932) 869046 (Boys) (365)
Reigate Grammar School, Reigate Rd, Reigate RH2 0QS; Tel (01737) 222231; Fax (01737) 224201; *Headmaster* J.G. Hamlin (Co-ed) (800)
Royal Grammar School, High St, Guildford GU1 3BB; Tel (01483) 502424; Fax (01483) 306127; T.M.S. Young, MA (A) (Boys) (830)
Royal Naval School for Girls, Haslemere, Surrey GU27 1HQ; Tel (01428) 605415; Fax (01428) 607451; *Headmistress* Dr J.L. Clough, BA, PhD (Boarders and Day) (Weekly boarders) (250)
St Catherine's, Bramley, Guildford GU5 0DF; Tel (01483) 893363; *Headmistress* C.M. Oulton, MA(Oxon) (A) (Girls) (Boarders) (465)
St George's College Weybridge, Weybridge KT15 2QS; Tel (01932) 854811; Fax (01932) 851829; *Headmaster* Joseph Peake, BA, MA (A,B) (Boys) (500)
St John's School, Leatherhead; Tel (01372) 372021; Fax (01372) 386606; *Headmaster* D.E. Brown, MA (A,B) (Boys) (Boarders and Day) (450)
St Maur's School, Thames St, Weybridge; Tel (01932) 851411; (01932) 820314 (Headteacher's Office); Maureen Dodds (A) (Girls) (470)
St Michael's, Limpsfield, Oxted RH8 0QR; Tel (01883) 712311; *Headmistress* Dr M.J. Hustler, BSc, PhD (Girls 3–18) (Boys 3–8) (Boarders, Weekly boarders and Day) (250)
St Teresa's School and St Teresa's Preparatory School, Effingham Hill, Dorking RH5 6ST; Tel (01372) 452037; (Prep School: (01372) 453456); *Headmaster* Leslie Allan, BA, MEd (Girls 3–18) (Boarders) (Weekly boarders and Day) (365) (Prep School 220)
Sir William Perkins's School, Guildford Rd, Chertsey, Surrey KT16 9BN; Tel (01932) 562161/560264; Fax (01932) 570841; S. Ross, BSc (A) (Girls) (590)
TASIS England American School, Coldharbour La, Thorpe, Nr Egham TW20 8TE; Tel (01932) 565252; *Headmaster* Lyle D. Rigg (Mixed) (Boarders and Day) (650)
Tormead School, Guildford GU1 2JD; Tel (01483) 575101; Fax (01483) 450592; *Headmistress* Honor E.M. Alleyne, BA, DipEd (Girls) (614)
Wispers School, Haslemere GU27 1AD; Tel (01428) 643646; L.H. Beltran, BA, PGCE, TP (B) (Girls) (Boarding) (Weekly Boarding) (Day Girls) (130)
Woldingham School, Marden Park, Woldingham, Surrey CR3 7YA; Tel (01883) 349431; Fax (01883) 348653; Dr P. Dineen (Girls) (500)
Yehudi Menuhin School, Stoke d'Abernon, Cobham KT11 3QQ; Tel (01932) 864739; Fax (01932) 864633; *Headmaster* P.N. Chisholm, MA(Cantab) (Mixed) (Specialist music school for 8–18 yrs) (Boarders)

Tyne and Wear

Argyle House School, 20 Thornhill Pk, Sunderland SR2 7LA; Tel 0191-510 0726; *Headmaster* J.N. Johnson (Boys) (220)
Central Newcastle High School, GPDST Newcastle upon Tyne NE2 4DS; Tel 0191-281 1768/3811; *Headteacher* Mrs A.M. Chapman, BA (G.P.D.S.T.) (A) (Girls) (876)
Dame Allan's, Newcastle upon Tyne NE4 9YJ; Tel 0191-275 0608; Fax 0191-274 7684; *Principal* T.A. Willcocks, MA (A) (Boys) (450)
Dame Allan's, Newcastle upon Tyne NE4 9YJ; Tel 0191-275 0708; Fax 0191-274 7684; *Principal* T.A. Willcocks, MA (A) (Girls) (445)
Eastcliffe Grammar School, 33 The Grove, Gosforth, Newcastle upon Tyne NE3 1NE; Tel 0191-285 4873; *Headmaster* G.D. Pearson, BA(Hons),PGCE,DipEd (Mixed) (3-18) (250)
The Grainger Grammar School, (Formerly Newcastle Cathedral School) 35 Grainger Park Rd, Newcastle upon Tyne NE4 8SA; Tel 0191-273 3426; Fax 0191-273 3398; *Headteacher* J. Smith (Mixed) (62)
The King's School HMC, Huntington Pl, Tynemouth, North Shields NE30 4RF; Tel 0191-258 5995; Dr D. Younger (B) (Boys) (770) (Girls) (120)
La Sagesse, North Jesmond, Newcastle upon Tyne NE2 3RJ; Tel 0191-281 3474; *Headmistress* D.C. Parker, BA, MII (A) (Girls) (350)
Newcastle upon Tyne Church High School, Tankerville Terr, Jesmond, Newcastle upon Tyne NE2 3BA; Tel 0191-281 4306; *Headmistress* P.E. Davies, MA (Girls) (400)
Newcastle upon Tyne Royal Grammar School, Eskdale Terr, Newcastle upon Tyne NE2 4DX; Tel 0191-281 5711; A.S. Cox, MA (A) (Boys) (Day) (950)
Sunderland High School, Mowbray Rd, Sunderland SR2 8HY; Tel 0191-567 4984; *Head* C.M. Rendle–Short, MEd (B) (Girls) (294) (Boys) (215)
Westfield School, Oakfield Rd, Gosforth, Newcastle upon Tyne NE3 4HS; Tel 0191-285 1948; Fax 0191-213 0734; *Head* M. Farndale, BA (Girls) (350)

Warwickshire

The King's High School, Warwick CV34 4HJ; Tel (01926) 494485; Fax (01926) 403089; *Headmistress* J.M. Anderson, BA(Keele) (A) (Girls) (570)
The Kingsley School, Beauchamp Ave, Leamington Spa CV32 5RD; Tel (01926) 425127; Fax (01926) 831691; Mrs M.A. Webster, BA, MEd (GSA) (Girls) ($2\frac{1}{2}$-18) (Boys $2\frac{1}{2}$–7) (585)
New College, 61 Kenilworth Rd, Leamington Spa CV32 6JU; Tel (01926) 424058; P.S. Fulcher (Co-ed) (Day) (70)
Princethorpe College, Princethorpe, nr Rugby CV23 9PX; Tel (01926) 632147; Fax (01926) 633365; Rev Alan R. Whelan, BA (B) (Boys) (Co-ed 6th form) (Boarders) (Weekly boarders) (Day) (Fully co-educational from Sept 1995) (410)
Rugby School, Rugby; Tel (01788) 565871; Fax (01788) 579745; *Head Master* M.B. Mavor, CVO, MA (Boys) (508) (Girls) (171)
St Joseph's School, Coventry Rd, Kenilworth CV8 2FT; Tel (01926) 55348; L.A. Cox, BSc (Girls) (300)
Warwick School, Myton Rd, Warwick CV34 6PP; Tel (01926) 492484; Fax (01926) 401259; *Headmaster* Dr P.J. Cheshire, BSc, PhD (A) (Boys) (810) (Boarders) (Weekly boarders and Day)
Wroxall Abbey School, Warwick CV35 7NB; Tel (01926) 484220; Fax (01926) 484531; *Headmistress* J.M. Gowen, BSc; *Deputy Head* C.R. Ives, BA (Girls) (100) (Boarders) (Weekly boarders) (Day)

West Midlands

Ardenhurst School, Henley-in-Arden, Solihull, West Midlands B95 6AB; Tel (01564) 792308; *Principal* P.S. Blunt, MA, PGCE (Mixed 3–11)
Bablake School, Coundon Rd, Coventry CV1 4AU; Tel (01203) 228388; Fax (01203) 631947; *Headmaster* Dr S. Nuttall (Mixed) (810)
Edgbaston C. of E. College for Girls, 31 Calthorpe Rd, Birmingham B15 1RX; Tel 0121-625 0398; Fax 0121-625 3340; *Headmistress* A.P.R. Varley-Tipton, MA (350)
Edgbaston College, 249 Bristol Rd, Edgbaston B5 7UH; Tel 0121-472 1034; Fax 0121-414 0064; *Headmaster* A.W.D. Ledwich (Mixed) (227)
Edgbaston High School for Girls, Westbourne Rd, Birmingham B15 3TS; Tel 0121-454 5831; Fax 0121-454 2363; *Headmistress* S. Horsman, MA (900)
Elmfield Rudolf Steiner School, Love La, Stourbridge DY8 2EA; Tel (01384) 394633 (Mixed) (280) (Boarders, Weekly boarders and Day)
Harper Bell School, Camp Hill, Birmingham; Tel 0181-766 7742; *Headteacher* A.J. Kennedy (80)
Highclare School, 241 Birmingham Rd, Wylde Grn, Sutton Coldfield B72 1EA; Tel 0121-354 1882 (B) (Girls) (195)

Holy Child School, Sir Harry's Rd, Edgbaston, Birmingham B15 2UR; Tel 0121-440 4103; Fax 0121-440 3639; *Headmistress* J.M.C. Hill, BA (C) (Girls) (300)
Hydesville Tower School, 25 Broadway North, Walsall WS1 2QG; Tel (01922) 24374; *Headmaster* T.D. Farrell, BA, MEd, FRSA (Mixed 3-16) (337)
King Edward's School, Birmingham B15 2UA; Tel 0121-472 1672; H.R. Wright, MA (A) (Boys) (875)
King Edward VI High School for Girls, Edgbaston Park Rd, Birmingham B15 2UB; Tel 0121-472 1834; Fax 0121-471 3808; *Headmistress* E.W. Evans, BSc (A) (545)
King Henry VIII School, Warwick Rd, Coventry, West Midlands CV3 6AQ; Tel (01203) 673442/675050; Fax (01203) 677102; *Headmaster* G.R. James Esq, BA, MEd (Co-Ed) (Day (834)
Royal Wolverhampton School, Penn Rd, Wolverhampton WV3 0EG; Tel (01902) 341230; Fax (01902) 344496; *Head* B.A. Evans (Mixed) (Boarders) (Full and Weekly boarders and Day) (3½-18) (550)
St Martin's, Malvern Hall, Brueton Ave, Solihull B91 3EN; Tel 0121-705 1265; Fax 0121-711 4529; *Headmistress* Mrs S.J. Williams, MA (Girls) (490)
Solihull School, Solihull B91 3DJ; Tel 0121-705 4273; A. Lee, MA (B) (Boys) (932) (Girls 6th Form) (63)
Tettenhall College, Wolverhampton, West Midlands WV6 8QX; Tel (01902) 751119; Fax (01902) 741940; *Headmaster* W.J. Dale, MA (Mixed) (370) (Boarders and Day)
Wolverhampton Grammar School, Compton Rd, Wolverhampton WV3 9RB; Tel (01902) 21326; *Headmaster* B.St.J. Trafford, MA, MEd (A) (Co-ed) (698)
Wylde Green College, 245 Birmingham Rd, Sutton Coldfield B72 1EA; Tel 0121-354 1505; *Principal* P.J. Burd (Mixed) (160)

West Sussex

Ardingly College, Haywards Heath RH17 6SQ; Tel (01444) 892577; J.W. Flecker, MA (Mixed) (475)
Burgess Hill School, Keymer Rd, Burgess Hill RH15 0EG; Tel (01444) 241050; Fax (01444) 870314; Mrs Rosemary Lewis, BSc (Boarders 60) (Day 510) (Flexible Boarding) (570)
Christ's Hospital, Horsham RH13 7LS; Tel (01403) 252547; R.C. Poulton, MA(Cantab) (Boys) (501) (Girls) (320) (Boarders only)
Farlington School, Strood Pk, Horsham RH12 3PN; Tel (01403) 254967; Fax (01403) 272258; *Headmistress* P.M. Mawer, BA (Girls) (Boarders and Day) (some Weekly boarders) (305)
Hurstpierpoint College, Hurstpierpoint BN6 9JS; Tel (01273) 833636; S.A. Watson, MA (Co-ed 95) (Boarding) (Day) (340)
Lancing College, Sussex BN15 0RW; Tel (01273) 452213; Fax (01273) 464720; C.J. Saunders, MA (B) (Boys) (421) (Boarders) (44) (Day) (Girls) (58) (Boarders) (1) (Day) (Boarders)
Lavant House School, Lavant, Chichester PO18 9AB; Tel (01243) 527211; Fax (01243) 530490; Y.G. Graham, DRS, LITT (Girls) (Boarders and Day 8–18) (Boys and Girls 3–8) (120)
Littlemead Grammar School, Woodfield Hse, Oving, Chichester, W Sussex PO20 6EU; Tel (01243) 787551 (Mixed) (Day & Residential) (140)
Rosemead School, East St, Littlehampton BN17 6AJ; Tel (01903) 716065; Fax (01903) 731247; *Headmistress* H.A. Kingham, BSc (Senior Girls) (250) (Boarders and Day) (Nursery and Preparatory (Co-ed)
St Margaret's Senior School, Convent of Mercy, Midhurst GU29 9JN; Tel (01730) 813899; *Headmistress* Sister Aquinas (Girls) (264)
S Michaels, Burton Park, Petworth GU28 0LS; Tel (01798) 42517; *Lady Warden and Headmistress* L.J. Griffin, BA, BPhil (Girls) (Boarders) (Weekly boarders and Day) (127)
Seaford College, Petworth GU28 0NB; Tel (017986) 392; *Headmaster* R.C. Hannaford, BSc (Boys) (Boarders) (11-18, Day 11-13) (380)
Shoreham College, St Julian's La, Shoreham-by-Sea BN43 6YW; Tel (01273) 592681; Fax (01273) 591673; *Headmaster* D.R. Jarman (C) (Mixed) (165)
Sion School, Gratwicke Rd, Worthing BN11 4BL; Tel (01903) 204063; Fax (01903) 214434; Brian Sexton, MA (Mixed) (500)
Slindon College, nr Arundel; Tel (01243) 814320; A.C. Baldwin, BA, PGCE (Boys) (Weekly, Termly Boarders and Day) (100)
The Towers, Upper Beeding, Steyning BN44 3TF; Tel (01903) 812185; *Headteacher* Sister M. Andrew (Girls) (Boarders) (Weekly boarders) (205) (Boarders) (Weekly boarders)
Worth School, North Abbey, Turners Hill, Crawley RH10 4SD; Tel (01342) 715911; *Headmaster* Rev Father Christopher Jamison, OSB (Boys) (Boarders and Day) (366)

West Yorkshire

Ackworth School Ackworth, Pontefract, West Yorkshire WF7 7LT; Tel (01977) 611401; Diana E. Chadwick, BA (A) (Mixed) (Day and Boarders) (406)
Batley Grammar School, Carlinghow Hill, Batley WF17 0AD; Tel (01924) 474980; Fax (01924) 420513; *Headmaster* C.S. Parker (A,B) (Boys) (580)
Bradford Girls' Grammar School, Squire La, Bradford BD9 6RB; Tel (01274) 545395; *Headmistress* Mrs L.J. Warrington, MEd (A) (690)
Bradford Grammar School, Keighley Rd, Bradford, West Yorkshire BD9 4JP; Tel (01274) 542492; Fax (01274) 548129; D.A.G. Smith, JP,MA (A,B) (Mixed) (1108)
The Fulneck School Foundation (Fulneck Boys' School), Fulneck, Pudsey LS28 8DT; Tel (0113) 257 1864; Fax (0113) 255 7316; *Headmaster* I.D. Cleland, BA, MPhil, FRSA (Boarders) (Weekly boarders) (Day) (330)
Fulneck Girls' School, Fulneck, Pudsey LS28 8DS; Tel (0113) 257 0235; *Headmistress* Mrs B.A. Heppell, BSc (Moravian Foundation) (Boarders) (257)
Gateways School, Harewood, Leeds LS17 9LE; Tel (0113) 288 6345; *Headmistress* J.E. Stephen, BSc (GSA (B) (300)
Kayes' College, New North Rd, Huddersfield HD1 5NE; Tel (01484) 531835; Fax (01484) 456467; *Headteacher* E.J. Jackson (Mixed) (100)
Leeds Girls' High School, Headingley La, Leeds LS6 1BN; Tel (0113) 274 4000; P.A. Randall, BA,MA(Ed) (A) (625)
Leeds Grammar School, Moorland Rd, Leeds LS6 1AN; Tel (0113) 243 3417; B.W. Collins, MSc, MEd (A) (Boys) (1100)
Queen Elizabeth Grammar School, Northgate, Wakefield WF1 3QX; Tel (01924) 373943; Fax (01924) 378871; *Headmaster* R.P. Mardling, MA, FIL, FRSA (A) (Boys) (753)
Rishworth School, Rishworth HX6 4QA; Tel (01422) 822217; Fax (01422) 823231; *Head* M.J. Elford, BSc (Mixed) (Boarders and Day) (Weekly boarders) (630)
Shaw House School, Wilmer Rd, Heaton, Bradford BD9 4AH; Tel (01274) 496299; Mrs J.B. Eccles, BA (80)
Silcoates School, Wrenthorpe, Wakefield WF2 0PD; Tel (01924) 291614; Fax (01924) 368690; *Headmaster* A.P. Spillane (Co-ed) (453) (Boys) (113) (Girls)
Wakefield Girls High School, Wentworth St, Wakefield WF1 2QS; Tel (01924) 372490; Fax (01924) 382080; P.A. Langham, BA,MEd (A) (800)
Woodhouse Grove School, Apperley Bridge, W. Yorks BD10 0NR; Tel (0113) 250 2477; Fax (0113) 250 5290; D.W. Welsh, MA (A) (Mixed) (Boarders) (700)

Wiltshire

Dauntsey's School, West Lavington, nr Devizes SN10 4HE; Tel (01380) 818441; Fax (01380) 813620; C.R. Evans, MA (A) (Mixed) (Boarders) (610)
The Godolphin School, Salisbury SP1 2RA; Tel (01722) 333059; Fax (01722) 411700; *Head* H.A. Fender (Girls) (Boarders and Day) (373)

La Retraite School, Campbell Rd, Salisbury SP1 3BQ; Tel (01722) 333094; R.A. Simmons, BSc (Girls) (250)
Marlborough College, Wiltshire SN8 1PA; Tel (01672) 515511; Fax (01672) 516234; *Master* E.J.H. Gould, MA, FRGS (Mixed) (Boarders) (Day) (852)
St Mary's School Calne, Calne; Tel (01249) 815899; Fax (01249) 822432; Miss D.H. Burns, BA, MSc (Girls) (Boarders and Day) (320)
Stonar School, Cottles Park, Atworth, nr Melksham; Tel (01225) 702309; Mrs S. Hopkinson, BA(Oxon) (Girls) (Boarders and Day) (536)
Warminster School, Warminster BA12 8PJ; Tel (01985) 213038; *Headmaster* T.D. Holgate (Mixed) (Boarders) (Weekly boarders) (Day) (330)

Wales

Clwyd

Howell's School, Denbigh LL16 3EN; Tel (01745) 813631; Fax (01745) 814443; M. Steel, BA (A) (Girls) (Boarders and Day) (300)
Penrhos College, Colwyn Bay LL28 4DA; Tel (01492) 530333; C.M.J. Allen, MA, MSc (A) (Girls) (Boarders) (Weekly boarders) (Day) (300)
Ruthin School, Ruthin, Clywd LL15 1EE; Tel (01824) 702543; Fax (01824) 707141; *Headmaster* J.S. Rowlands, BSc (Mixed) (Boarders and Day) (219)
Rydal, Colwyn Bay, Clywd LL29 7BT; Tel (01492) 530155; Fax (01492) 531872; *Headmaster* N.W. Thorne (A) (Co-ed) (440 from 11+) (130 7–11)
St Brigid's School, Plas yn Green, Denbigh LL16 4BH; Tel (01745) 815228; Fax (01745) 816928; Sister Elizabeth, CSB (Girls) (150)

Dyfed

Llandovery College, Llandovery, Dyfed SA20 0EE; Tel (01550) 20315; Fax (01550) 20168; *Warden* Dr C.E. Evans (A) (Mixed) (Boarders and Day) (242)
Nant-y-Cwm Rudolf Steiner School, Llanycefn, Clynderwen SA66 7QJ; Tel (01437) 563640; (Co-ed) (95)
St Michael's School, Bryn, Llanelli SA14 9TU; Tel (01554) 820325; D.T. Sheehan, BSc(Hons), PGCE (B,C) (304)

Gwent

Haberdashers' Monmouth School for Girls, Monmouth, Gwent NP5 3XT; Tel (01600) 714214; Fax (01600) 772244; *Headmistress* D.L. Newman, BA (A) (Girls) (Boarders) (Weekly boarders) (647)
Monmouth School, Monmouth NP5 3XP; Tel (01600) 713143; Fax (01600) 772701; *Headmaster* R.D. Lane, MA (A) (Boys) (560)
Rougemont School, Stow Hill, Newport NP9 4EA; Tel (01633) 211813; Fax (01633) 855598; *Headmaster* G.R. Sims (Mixed 3–18) (Day)

Gwynedd

Indefatigable School, Plas Llanfair, Llanfairpwll, Anglesey; Tel (01248) 714338; Fax (01248) 715876; *Headmaster* Peter White, BSc(Hons), PGCE (Boys) (Boarders and Day) (160)
St David's College, Llandudno LL30 1RD; Tel (01492) 875974; *Headmaster* W. Seymour (Boys) (Boarders) (234)
St Gerard's School, Ffriddoedd Rd, Bangor, Gwynedd LL57 2EL; Tel (01248) 351656; *Head* Miss A. Parkinson, BA(Hons) (C) (Mixed) (312)
Tower Hse, Harlech Rd, Barmouth LL42 1RF; Tel (01341) 280127; J.M. Pugh, BSc(Hons) (Mixed) (130)

Mid Glamorgan

St Clare's Convent Schools, Newton, Porthcawl CF36 5NR; Tel (01656) 782509 Senior; (01656) 788767 Prep; *Headmistress (Senior)* A. Jarrett; *Headmistress (Prep)* Sr Angela Lyons (RC) (Mixed) (Day Schools 3–18+) (375)

Powys

Brookland Hall School and Golf Academy, Welshpool SY21 9BU; Tel (01938) 552326; Fax (01938) 556578; M.J. Hutchinson (C) (Boarders Boys) (70)
Christ College Brecon, Brecon, Powys LD3 8AG; Tel (01874) 623359; Fax (01874) 611478; S.W. Hockey, MA (A,B) (Boys) (Girls in 6th form) (Boarders and Day) (365)
St David's Ursuline Convent, Brecon LD3 7DN; Tel (01874) 622080; Sister Finbarr Muckley, BA, BA(Mus), HDipEd (C) (Girls 10-18) (50) (Boarders and Weekly boarders) (3-18 and Junior Boys) (130) (Day)

South Glamorgan

Balfour House School, Rectory Dr, St Athan, S. Glam CF6 9PD; Tel (01446) 750236; D.S. Newman (Mixed) (140)
Howell's School, Llandaff GPDST Cardiff CF5 2YD; Tel (01222) 562019; *Headmistress* C.J. Fitz, BSc (A) (Girls 4–18) (690)
Monkton House School, Monkton Hse, The Parade, Cardiff CF2 3UA; Tel (01222) 483130; *Headmaster* P. Cox (Mixed) (200) (11–16 yrs) (6th form) (50)
Reformed Presbyterian Church School, Archer Rd, Ely, Cardiff CF5 4FR; Tel (01222) 596410; Rev D.T.I. Lock, BA; Rev R.H. Holst, BA (Mixed) (64)
Westbourne College, 4 Hickman Rd, Penarth CF6 2AJ; Tel (01222) 705705; Fax (01222) 709988; B.V. Young, PhD (Co-Ed) (51)
Westbourne Schools, 4 Hickman Rd, Penarth, South Glamorgan CF64 2AJ; Tel (01222) 707861; Fax (01222) 709488; *Headmaster* R.H. Harris, MA, MEd (Co-Ed) (144)

West Glamorgan

Ffynone House School, 36 St James' Cres, Swansea SA1 6DR; Tel (01792) 464967; Fax (01792) 455202; *Headmaster* John Rhys Thomas, BSc, DipEd (B.C) (Mixed) (200)
Our Lady's Convent School, The Walk, Cardiff CF2 3AG; Tel (01222) 490907; *Headmistress* Sister M. Imelda (Girls) (204)

Scotland

Central

Dollar Academy, Dollar FK14 7DU; Tel (01259) 42511; J.S. Robertson, MA (Mixed) (Boarders 175) (Day 941) (750)
Queen Victoria School, Dunblane FK15 0JY; Tel (01786) 822288; Fax 0131-310 2519; *Headmaster* B. Raine, BA (Boys) (Boarders) (270)

Fife

St Leonards and St Katharines Schools, St Andrews KY16 9QU; Tel (01334) 472126; May James, BA(York) (A) (Girls) (Boarders and day girls) (335)

Grampian

Aberdeen Waldorf School, 111 Gallowgate, Aberdeen AB1 1BU; Tel (01224) 646111; (Co-Ed) (Steiner Curriculum) (150)
Albyn School for Girls, 17/23 Queen's Rd, Aberdeen AB9 2PA; Tel (01224) 322408; Fax (01224) 209173; *Headmistress* N.H. Smith, BSc, DipEd (A) (Girls) (Boarders) (Weekly boarders) (240)
American School in Aberdeen, Craigton Rd, Cults, Aberdeen AB1 9QD; Tel (01224) 868927; Fax (01224) 869753; John C. Thomas (Mixed) (280)
Gordonstoun, Elgin, Moray; Tel (01343) 830 445; M.C.S.R. Pyper, BA (A) (Mixed) (Boarders) (480)
Robert Gordon's College, Schoolhill, Aberdeen AB9 1FE; Tel (01224) 646346; Fax (01224) 630301; *Headmaster* G.A. Allan, MA (A) (Co-Ed) (Boarders) (930)
St Margaret's School for Girls, 17 Albyn Pl, Aberdeen AB9 1RH; Tel (01224) 584466; Fax (01224) 585600; *Headmistress* L. Ogilvie, BSc(Hons),MSc, FRMetS (A) (Girls) (233) (Senior) (412)

Lothian

Daniel Stewart's and Melville College, Queensferry Rd, Edinburgh EH4 3EZ; Tel 0131-332 7925; Fax 0131-343 2432; *Principal* P.F.J. Tobin, MA (A) (Boys) (Boarders) (763)
The Edinburgh Academy, Henderson Row, Edinburgh EH3 5BL; Tel 0131-556 4603; A.J.D. Rees, MA (921) (A,B) (Boys) (33) (Girls) (71) (Boarders)
The Edinburgh Tutorial College and American School, 29 Chester St, Edinburgh EH3 7EN; Tel 0131-225 9888; A.W. Morris (Mixed) (Boarders) (Weekly boarders) (50)
Fettes College, Carrington Rd, Edinburgh EH4 1QX; Tel 0131-332 2281; Fax 0131-332 3081; M.T. Thyne, MA, FRSE (A) (Mixed) (Boarders) (480)
George Heriot's School, Lauriston Pl, Edinburgh EH3 9EQ; Tel 0131-229 7263; Fax 0131-229 6363; *Headmaster* K.P. Pearson, MA (A) (Mixed) (960)
George Watson's College, Colinton Rd, Edinburgh EH10 5EG; Tel 0131-447 7931; Fax 0131-452 8594; Frank E. Gerstenberg, MA (A) (Mixed) (Boarders) (1240)
Loretto School, Musselburgh EH21 7RE; Tel 0131-665 2567; Fax 0131-653 2773; Rev N.W. Drummond, MA, BD (A,B,C) (Co-educational) (Boarders) (300)
The Mary Erskine School, Ravelston, Edinburgh EH4 3NT; Tel 0131-337 2391; P.F.J. Tobin, MA (A) (29) (Boarders) (628)
Merchiston Castle School, Colinton, Edinburgh EH13 0PU; Tel 0131-441 3797; Fax 0131-441 6060; *Headmaster* D.M. Spawforth, MA (A) (Boys) (Boarders) (Day) (380)
The Rudolf Steiner School of Edinburgh, 60 Spylaw Rd, Edinburgh EH10 5BR; Tel 0131-337 3410; Fax 0131-338 6066; (A) (Mixed) (300)
St Denis and Cranley School for Girls, 3 Ettrick Rd, Edinburgh EH10 5BJ; Tel 0131-229 1500; Fax 0131-229 5753; *Headmistress* Mrs J.M Munro, MA (A) (Boarders) (Weekly boarders) (Day) (Nur) (Jun) (200)
St George's School for Girls, Garscube Terr, Edinburgh EH12 6BG; Tel 0131-332 4575; Dr J. McClure, MA, DPhil(Oxon) (A) (Boarders) (850)
St Margaret's Convent, Edinburgh EH9 1BB; Tel 0131-447 2807; Sister M.B. Carr, MA (Girls) (Boarders) (200)
St Margaret's School, Edinburgh Ltd, East Suffolk Rd, Edinburgh EH16 5PJ; Tel 0131-668 1986; *Principal* Anne C. Mitchell, MA(Hons) (A) (Girls) (Boarders and Weekly boarders) (700)
St Mary's Music School, Old Coates House, Manor Pl, Edinburgh EH3 7EB; Tel 0131-538 7766; *Headmaster* J.P.S. Allison, MA, CertEd (A) (Mixed) (Boarders) (Day) (Scottish Office Aided Places) (31)
St Serf's School, 5 Wester Coates Gdns, Edinburgh EH12 5LT; Tel 0131-337 1015; *Head Teacher* K.D. Hume, BSc (Mixed) (240)

Strathclyde

Belmont House, Sandringham Ave, Newton Mearns, Glasgow G77 5DU; Tel 0141-639 2922; Fax 0141-639 9860; *Headmaster* John Mercer, MA, DipEd (A) (Boys) (259 Secondary) (127 Junior School)
Craigholme School, 72 St Andrews Dr, Glasgow G41 4HS; Tel 0141-427 0375; Fax 0141-427 6396; *Headmistress* Mrs G.R. Burt (A) (Girls) (497)
Fernhill School, Fernbrae Ave, Burnside, Rutherglen, Glasgow G73 4SG; Tel 0141-634 2674; L.M. McLay, MA (Girls) (A) (160)

The Glasgow Academy, Colebrooke St, Glasgow G12 8HE; Tel 0141-334 8558; *Rector* D. Comins (A) (Mixed) (Day) (1010)
The High School of Glasgow, 637 Crow Rd, Glasgow G13 1PL; Tel 0141-954 9628; Fax 0141-959 0191; *Rector* R.G. Easton, MA (A) (Mixed) (600)
Hutchesons' Grammar School, 21 Beaton Rd, Glasgow G41 4NW; Tel 0141-423 2933; Fax 0141-424 0291; *Rector* D.R. Ward, MA (A) (Mixed) (1175)
Keil School, Dumbarton; Tel (01389) 762003; Fax (01389) 764267; *Headmaster* J.A. Cummings, BA, MA (A.B.C) (Mixed) (Boarders) (Weekly boarders) (220)
Kelvinside Academy, 33 Kirklee Rd, Glasgow G12 0SW; Tel 0141-357 3376; Fax 0141-357 5401; *Rector* J.H. Duff, MA(Cantab), MA(Edin) (A) (Boys) (500)
Laurel Bank School, 4 Lilybank Terr, Glasgow G12 8RX; Tel 0141-339 9127; *Head* Miss L.G. Egginton, BSc (A) (Girls) (250)
Lomond School, 10 Stafford St, Helensburgh G84 9JX; Tel (01436) 72476; Fax (01436) 78320; *Headmaster* A.D. Macdonald, MA(Cantab), DipEd (A) (Mixed) (Day/ Some Boarders) (533)
The Park School, 25 Lynedoch St, Glasgow G3 6EX; Tel 0141-332 0426/7; *Headmistress* M.E. Myatt, BSc(Hons) (A) (Girls) (400)
St Aloysius' College, Garnethill, Glasgow G3 6RJ; Tel 0141-332 3190; Fax 0141-353 0426; *Headmaster* Rev Dr James W. Hanvey, SJ, Dphil(Oxon) (RC) (Mixed) (Day) (800)
St Columba's School, Kilmacolm, Renfrewshire PA13 4AU; Tel (01505) 872238; Fax (01505) 873995; A.H. Livingstone, BSc(Hons), DipEd (A) (Mixed) (340)
St Francis Xavier College, Calder Ave, Coatbridge ML5 4JS; Tel (01236) 22166; W. Docherty, BA, BSC, DipAdultEd (Boys) (Boarders) (80)
Wellington School, Ayr KA7 2XH; Tel (01292) 269321; Mrs D.A. Gardner, BA(Hons) (A) Girls) (Boarders) (Weekly boarders) (340)

Tayside

Glenalmond College, Glenalmond, Perth PH1 3RY; Tel 0173-888 442; I.G. Templeton, BA, MA (A) (Boys, 6th form Girls) (Boarders and Day) (300)
High School of Dundee, P.O. Box 16, Euclid Cres, Dundee DD1 9BP; Tel (01382) 202921; Fax (01382) 29822; *Rector* R. Nimmo, OBE, MA, MEd, FRSA, FIM (A) (Mixed) (755)
Kilgraston School, Bridge of Earn, Perthshire PH2 9BQ; Tel 01738 812257/812973; Fax 01738 813410; Mrs J.L. Austin, BA (A) (Girls) (Boarders, Weekly boarders and Day) (A Sacred Heart School) (275)
Morrison's Academy, Crieff PH7 3AN; Tel (01764) 653885; Fax (01764) 655411; H.A. Ashmall, MA, MLitt, FIMgt (A) (Mixed) (Boarders) (600)
Rannoch School, Rannoch PH17 2QQ; Tel (01882) 632332; Fax (01882) 632443; *Headmaster* M. Barratt, MA (A,C) (Boys) (70) (Girls) (Boarders) (250)
Strathallan School, Forgandenny, Perth PH2 9EG; Tel (01738) 812546; Fax (01738) 812549; *Headmaster* A.W. McPhail, MA (350) (A,B) (Boys) (140) (Girls) (Boarders)

Northern Ireland

County Antrim

Friends' School, Magheralave Rd, Lisburn BT28 3BH; Tel (01846) 662156; Fax (01846) 672134; *Headmaster* J.T. Green (A) (Mixed) (Boarders) (Weekly boarders) (1140)

County Armagh

The Royal School, College Hill, Armagh BT61 9DH; Tel (01861) 522807; Fax (01861) 525014; *Headmaster* T. Duncan, MA, BSc, DASE (Mixed) (Boarders) (Weekly boarders) (650)

Belfast

Belfast Royal Academy, Belfast BT14 6JL; Tel (01232) 740423; Fax (01232) 352737; W.M. Sillery (Mixed) (1674)
Campbell College, Belmont Rd, Belfast BT4 2ND, Northern Ireland; Tel (01232) 763076; Fax (01232) 761894; *Headmaster* Dr R.J.I. Pollock, BSc, PhD, CertEd, MEd, CChem, MRIC (Boys) (Boarders 60) (Weekly boarders 40) (Day 630) (690)
Hunterhouse College, Finaghy, Belfast BT10 0LE; Tel (01232) 612293; *Headmistress* Miss D.E.M. Hunter, BA, DipEd (Girls) (785)
Methodist College, 1 Malone Rd, Belfast BT9 6BY; Tel (01232) 669558; *Principal* T.W. Mulryne, MA (Mixed) (Boarders (1825)
The Royal Belfast Academical Institution, College Sq East, Belfast BT1 6DL; Tel (01232) 240461; *Principal* R.M. Ridley, MA (Boys) (1026)
St Mary's Christian Brothers' Grammar School, Glen Rd and Barrack St, Belfast BT11 8NR; Tel (01232) 615321/325867; Fax (01232) 600299; Rev Brother D. Gleeson, CertEd, BD, MCSp, CFC (Boys) (1250)
Victoria College Belfast, Cranmore Park, Belfast BT9 6JA; Tel (01232) 661506; Fax (01232) 666898; M. Andrews (Girls) (Boarders) (980)

County Down

Bangor Grammar School, 13 College Ave, Bangor, Co Down BT20 5HJ; Tel (01247) 473734; T.W. Patton, MA (Boys) (920)
The Holywood Rudolf Steiner School, 34 Croft Rd, Holywood BT18 0PR; Tel (01232) 428029; (Co-Ed) (215)

County Fermanagh

Portora Royal School, 1 Derrygonnelly Rd, Enniskillen BT74 7HA; Tel (01365) 322658; *Headmaster* R.L. Bennett, MA,DipEd (Boys) (430)

County Londonderry

Coleraine Academical Institution, Castlerock Rd, Coleraine BT51 3LA; Tel (01265) 44331; Fax (01265) 52632; *Headmaster* R.S. Forsythe, BSc (Boys) (850) (Boarders) (100)

County Tyrone

Royal School Dungannon, Northland Row, Dungannon BT71 6AP; Tel (018687) 22710; *Headmaster* P.D. Hewitt, MA, DipEd, FRSA, FInstMgt (Mixed) (Boarders and Weekly boarders) (690)

Channel Islands

Guernsey

Blanchelande Girls' College, Rosaire Ave, St Peter Port, Guernsey; Tel (01481) 724300
Elizabeth College, Guernsey GY1 2PY; Tel (01481) 726544; *Principal* J.H.F. Doulton, MA (Boys) (Boarders) (570)
The Ladies' College, Les Graves, St Peter Port, Guernsey GY1 1RW; Tel (01481) 721602; Fax (01481) 724209; *Principal* Miss M.E. Macdonald, MA, DipEd (Girls) (339)

Jersey

Victoria College, Jersey; Tel (01534) 37591; Fax (01534) 27448; *Headmaster* J. Hydes (Boys) (Boarders) (Weekly boarders) (587)

Isle of Man

The Buchan School, Castletown; Tel (01624) 822526; *Headmaster* P.H. Moody, MA (106) (Boys 3-11) (94) (Girls 3-11) (Boarding and Day)

King William's College, Castletown; Tel (01624) 822551; Fax (01624) 824287; *Principal* S.A. Westley, MA (Co-Ed) (Boarders and Day) (320)

City Technology Colleges Trust

9 Whitehall, London SW1A 2DD; Tel 0171-839 9339; Fax 0171-839 5898
Chief Executive Kathleen Lund
Administrative Director Clive Andrews

Establishments in Existence

ADT College, ADT Technology Centre, 100 West Hill, Putney, Wandsworth, London SW15 2UT; Tel 0181-877 0357; David Durban
Bacon's College, Timber Pond Rd, Rotherhithe, London SE16 1AG; Tel 0171-237 1928; Anthony Perry (Acting)
Dixon's Bradford CTC, Ripley St, Bradford BD5 7RR; Tel (01274) 395140; John Lewis
BRIT Performing Arts and Technology School, 60 The Crescent, Croydon CRO 2HN; Tel 0181-665 5242; Anne Rumney
Brooke CTC, Coomb Rd, Great Oakley, Corby, Northants NN18 8LA; Tel (01536) 460108; Gareth Newman
Djanogly CTC, Sherwood Rise, Nottingham Rd, Nottingham NG7 7AL; Tel (0115) 942 4034; Rosemary Potter
Emmanuel College, Lobley Hill, Gateshead, Tyne and Wear NE11 0AN; Tel 0191-460 2099; John Burn
Haberdasher's Aske's Hatcham Schools, PO Box 167, 135 Pepys Rd, New Cross, London SE14 5SF; Tel 0171-277 9333; Roy Baldock
Harris CTC Maberley Rd, Upper Norwood, London SE19 2JH; Tel 0181-771 2261/2030; Lyndon Jones
Kingshurst CTC, PO Box 1017, Cooks La, Kingshurst, Birmingham B37 6NZ; Tel 0121-770 8923; Mrs V. Bragg
Landau Forte College, Fox St, Derby DE1 2LF; Tel (01332) 204040; Peter Shackleton
Leigh CTC, Green St, Green Rd, Dartford DA1 1QE; Tel (01322) 228635/287273; Virginia Waterhouse
Macmillan College, Teeside CTC, PO Box 8, Stockton Rd, Middlesbrough, Cleveland TS5 4YU; Tel (01642) 244144; Robert Howarth
The Thomas Telford School, Ole Park, Telford, Shropshire TF3 4NW; Tel (01952) 200000; Kevin Satchwell

CTC Philosophy and Development

City Technology Colleges are set up by the Secretary of State for Education and are independent of Local Authority control. The main characteristics of CTCs are these: they will normally cater for 11-18 year olds; they will be registered independent schools, subject to inspection by Her Majesty's Inspectorate; they will charge no fees; the industrial and commercial sponsors will own (or lease) and run them, and receive grants on conditions agreed with the Secretary of State; the sponsors will make a substantial contribution towards the costs; they will offer a broad curriculum, with the strong science and technological element which is essential preparation for the changing demands of adult and working life in an advanced industrial society. The CTC Trust runs an Affiliation Scheme which can be joined by secondary schools which comply with stated criteria. Affiliated schools are offered a range of benefits including the opportunity to participate in curriculum development projects.
John Cabot CTC, Potterswood, Britannia Rd, Kingswood, Bristol BS15 2DB; Tel (0117) 947 6142; Fax (0117) 947 8806; from 6th August 1993: Tel (0117) 976 3000; Fax (0117) 976 0631/760632; Keith McCorkindale

9 Independent and Non-Maintained Special Schools & Special FE Establishments

England

Avon

Aspley Hse, 128 Richmond Rd, Bristol BS6 5ER; Tel (0117) 924 3152; *Manager* Mrs S. Browne; Open 52 weeks (S.L.D.) (M) (Mixed) (16–35)

Cintre Community, 54 St John's Rd, Clifton, Bristol BS8 2HG; Tel (0117) 973 8546; *Manager* Robert Hider; *Keyworker* Richard Cull; *Keyworker* Ingrid Ortner (Mixed) (16+)
Training towards independence for young people with learning and/or behavioural difficulties. A second home, Penmaen, has five bed-sits for those who are semi-independent

The Hatch Camphill Community, 23 Castle St, Thornbury, Bristol BS12 1HG; Tel (01454) 413010; Fax (01454) 411860 (Boarding) (Young adults in need of a therapeutic environment) (Mixed) (19–30+) (23)
Member, Assn of Camphill Communities

Ravenscroft School, Farleigh, Hungerford, Nr Bath BA3 6RW; Tel (01225) 753130; *Headteacher* A.M. Gillam (Boarding and Day) (Specific Learning Disability) (Mixed) (10–17) (90)

St Christopher's, 2 Carisbrooke Lodge, Westbury Pk, Bristol BS6 7JE; Tel (0117) 973 3301/736875 (36–52 Week boarding) (All types except Blind and Non-ambulant) (Mixed) (7–19) (50)
No area limit

The Sheiling School, Camphill Community, Thornbury Park, Thornbury, Bristol, Avon BS12 1HP; Tel (01454) 412194; Fax (01454) 411860 (Rudolf Steiner curriculum) (Boarding) (Multiple Handicaps, not severely P.H.) (Mixed) (6–19) (50)
Great Britain and Abroad, Member; Assn of Camphill Communities

Bedfordshire

MacIntyre, East Region Office, 4 & 5 Station Sq, Flitwick, Bedfordshire MK45 1DP; Tel (01525) 713160; *Regional Director (East)* Mike Partner (Residential) (E.S.N.(S) (Mixed) (19+

Berkshire

The Annie Lawson School, Ravenswood Village, Nine Mile Ride, Crowthorne, Berks RG11 6BQ; Tel (01344) 771212; *Headteacher* Anne McNaughton, MA (Residential) (SLD) (Mixed) (5–19 (50)

Bridge House Home School, Padworth, Reading RG7 4JU; Tel (01734) 713176; *Head Teacher* A.R. Olmos (Steiner residential) (E.S.N.) (Mixed) (7–19 (32)
No area limit; also children from overseas
Committee for Steiner Special Education

Bridge House Adult Home, Padworth, Reading; Tel (01734) 713176 (48 week placement for mentally handicapped adults)

Burghclere Grange School, Hart La, Burghclere, Nr Newbury, Berks RG15 9JW; Tel (0163 527) 212; *Principal* G.S. Gibbs; *Headmaster* D.S. Ashworth; *Head of Care* S.L. Gibbs (Boarding) (Educational, Social, Emotional and Behavioural problems) (Boys) (11–17) (41)

High Close, Wiltshire Rd, Wokingham, Berks RG11 1TT; Tel (01734) 785767; *Principal* A. Paterson (Residential) (Educational, emotional/behavioural difficulties) (Mixed) (9–16) (Day unit for 6–9 yr olds) (48)
Barnardo's London Division

The Jonathan Miller School, 112 Burnham La, Burnham, Slough, Berks SL1 6LZ; Tel (01628) 667965; Fax (01628) 660415; *Headteacher* Paul R. Barry, BA, DipEd (Day) (E.B.D.) (Mixed) (11–16) (35 with 15 in Mainstream Support Unit)

Eastwood Grange

Residential School and Children's Centre

For boys aged 11-16+ with Emotional and Behavioural Difficulties

Eastwood Grange is situated in the beautiful Peak District of Derbyshire. Accommodation consists mainly of single bedrooms within three 12-bedded Houses. We offer 38-week and 52-week placements.

We provide a thorough assessment of needs and combine Education, Care and Treatment objectives to formulate individual intervention programmes. All pupils have a Personal Tutor and Personal Counsellor to provide support and monitor progress.

We believe positive approaches will produce positive changes which can compensate for past failure and prepare youngsters for the future.

Within a warm caring environment we offer:

- *Multi-disciplinary Assessment of Needs*
- *Integrated Education and Care Programmes*
- *National Curriculum*
- *Psychological Support*
- *24-hour Curriculum*
- *Post-16 College Links and Independence Training*
- *High Staff: Pupil Ratio*
- *Eclectic Intervention Strategies*
- *Social Skills Training*
- *Reality Therapy*

For further information contact:

The Principal, Eastwood Grange School,
Milken Lane, Ashover, Chesterfield,
Derbyshire S45 0BA.

Telephone: 01246 590255 Fax: 01246 590215

We are registered with the Department for Education and also under the 1989 Children Act as a Children's Home.

Mary Hare Grammar, Arlington Manor, Snelsmore Common, Newbury, Berks RG16 9BQ; Tel (01635) 248303; I.G. Tucker, PhD (Boarding) (Deaf & Partially Hearing) (Mixed) (11–19) (190)
No area limit

Birmingham

Queen Alexandra College, 49 Court Oak Rd, Harborne, Birmingham B17 9TG; Tel 0121-427 4577; Fax 0121-428 2282; *Principal* T.S. Gould, CertEd, DipSpEd, MEd(Psych) (F.E; vocational guidance and training) (Boarding and Day) (Visually Handicapped) (Mixed) (16+) (130)
No area limit; special provision for the Blind and the Blind multi-handicapped; Birmingham Royal Institution for the Blind

Bolton

Birtenshaw Hall School, Darwen Rd, Bromley Cross, Bolton BL7 9AB; Tel (01204) 304230; *Principal* C.D. Jamieson, DipSpEd, MEd (Weekly Residential and Day) (Physical Disabilities esp. Cerebral Palsy) (Mixed) (3–19) (16+ unit) (46)
Must be close enough to return home at weekends; a NAIMS member school

Crowthorn, Broadhead Rd, Turton, Nr Bolton BL7 OJS; Tel (01204) 852143; Fax (01204) 853682; S. Forster, MBA, DAES, SCRCCYP, FCCOMP (Boarding, 38 and 52 week (EBD) (MLD) (SpLD) (Mild Aut) (Mixed) (7–16+) (75)
National Children's Homes, North West Region

Buckinghamshire

Old Manor Hse, Leighton Rd, Wingrave, Bucks HP22 4PD; Tel (01296) 681274; *Principal* Mrs J. Wadhams; Tel (01908) 230100 (Residential) (Mental handicap) (Mixed) (5–19)

Calderdale

The William Henry Smith School, Boothroyd, Brighouse HD6 3JW; Tel (01484) 710123; *Head Teacher* G.R. Darnell (Boarding) (Emotional, social, behavioural and educational problems) (Boys) (10–16) (64)

Cheshire

Bethesda, Schools Hill, Cheadle SK8 1JE; Tel 0161-428 7897; C. Evans (Boarding and Day (PH and Del) (Mixed) (11–19 (80)

Chaigeley School, Thelwall, Nr Warrington WA4 2TE; Tel (0192 575) 2357; A.S. Gray, BA, FRSA (Boarding and Day) (E.B.D.) (Boys) (10–16) (48)
No area limit

The David Lewis School for Epilepsy and Childrens Epilepsy Assessment Unit Mill La, Warford, Nr Alderley Edge, Cheshire SK9 7UD; Tel (0156 587) 2613 (Boarding) (Epilepsy) (Mixed) (5–19) (96)
No area limit

Delamere Forest, Blakemere La, Norley, Warrington WA6 6NP; Tel (01928) 788263; Fax (01928) 788507; S. Lewis (Boarding and Day) (Behavioural, social, educational and specific learning difficulties, language and speech therapy) (Mixed) (5–17) (Jewish) (52)
No area limit: day pupils of any denomination

Royal School for the Deaf, Cheadle Hulme, Cheshire SK8 6RF; Tel 0161-437 5951; Fax 0161-437 7282; B.R. McCracken, BA, DipEd, DEM (Boading and Day) (Deafness, Deafness with multiple handicaps) (Deaf-Blind) (Mixed) (5–mid 20s) (130)
No area limit

The Saint John Vianney Lower School, Didsbury Rd, Heaton Mersey, Stockport, Cheshire SK4 2AA; Tel 0161-432 0510; Fax 0161-442 2095; M. O'Donoghue, BEd(Hons) (Day) (M.L.D.) (Mixed) (5–11) (76)
Manchester, Trafford, Cheshire, Tameside, Oldham, Salford, Stockport, Bolton
Salford Roman Catholic Diocesan Trustees

The Saint John Vianney Upper School, (Day) (MLD) (11–16) (76)

West Kirby Residential School, Meols Dr, West Kirby, Wirral, Merseyside L48 5DH; Tel 0151-632 3201; P.E. Brennan, BSc, BPhil (Boarding) (Mixed) (8–16) (95)

Cornwall

Churchtown Farm Outdoor Education Centre, Lanlivery, Bodmin, Cornwall PL30 5BT; Tel (01208) 872148; Fax (01208) 873377; *Head of Education* David Owens, MPhil, MIBIOL, PGCE (Boarding/Day) (Learning difficulties, mild to severe) (PH) (Blind, Deaf)
Spastics Society

Peredur Farm and Craft Centre, Basill Manor, St Clether, Launceston, Cornwall; Tel (01566) 86575/86245 (Boarding) (Emotionally disturbed) (20+); Sheltered craft workshops and farm training)
Reg Office Peredur Trust, Trebullom, Altarnun, Launceston, Cornwall, PL15 7RF
Registered with Cornwall County Council

Peredur Garden and Craft Centre, Trebullom, Altarnun, Launceston, Cornwall PL15 7RF; Tel (01566) 86575/86245; *Managers* Mr and Mrs S.W. Rudel (Boarding) (Emotionally disturbed) (16–25)
Peredur Trust
Registered with Cornwall County Council under the Registered Homes Act 1984

Cumbria

Eden Grove School, Bolton, Appleby; Tel (01930) 61346; B.E. Cole, MA, MEd (Boarding) (Disturbed boys with mild or moderate learning difficulties) (8–16) (64)
No area limit

Greystone House School, Priestclose La, Gt Strickland, Penrith, Cumbria CA10 3DJ; Tel (01931) 712300; *Co-Principal* B. McCarthy; *Co-Principal* A. McCarthy (Boarding) (EBD) (Boys) (11–16) (19)

Lowgate House School, Witherslack Group of Schools Levens, Kendal LA8 8NJ; Tel (015395) 60124; *Principals* J. & M. Horner; *Head Teacher* S. Brady; *Principal* G.S. McEwan (Boarding) (Specific learning difficulties, emotional/behavioural problems) (Boys) (7–12) (16)

St Anthony's, Plumpton, Penrith, Cumbria CA11 9NP; Tel (01768) 894288; *Registered Owner* S.G. Wilson

Derbyshire

Alderwasley Hall, Alderwasley, Belper, Derbyshire DE56 2SR; Tel (0162 982) 2599; *Director* B.W. Brook; Tel (01629) 822599; *Headmaster* K. Haywood; Tel (01629) 822586 (Boarding/Day) (Speech & Language disorders) (Mixed) (5–19) (Special Annex for 16–19 yr olds) (Boarding) (146) (Day) (30)

Bladon Hse, Newton Solney, Burton-on-Trent DE15 OTA; Tel (01629) 822599; *Director* B.W. Brook Admissions Office, Alderwasley Hall, Belper, Derbys DE56 2SR; Tel (01629) 822599; *Headmaster* R.J. Cubie; Tel (01283) 563787 (Boarding/Day) (Speech and language disorders) (Mixed) (5–16+) (Moderate Learning Difficulties) (Boarding) (116) (Day) (15)

Eastwood Grange, Eastwood Grange School, Milken La, Ashover, Chesterfield, Derbyshire S45 0BA; Tel (01246) 590255 (Boarding) (Mixed) (11–18) (Educational, Social and Emotional Needs)

The Grange Hospital La, Mickleover, Derbyshire DE3 5DR; *Director* Mrs B W Brook Admissions Office, Alderwasley Hall, Belper, Derbyshire DE56 2SR; Tel (01629) 822599 (Day) (Boarding) (Vocational assessment and training centre) (Mixed) (14–19+) (Approved by DSS)

Royal School for the Deaf, Ashbourne Rd, Derby DE3 3BH; Tel (01332) 362512; Fax (01332) 299708; *Principal* T. Silvester; Communication Centre for the Deaf (full range of communication courses); B. Drummond (Centre Administrator) (Boarding and Day) (Deaf and Partially Hearing) (Mixed) (2–21) (including provision for further and continuing education) (180)
No area limit

9 Independent & Non-Maintained Special Schools, Etc

Devon

Bradfield House School, Willand, Cullompton, Devon EX15 2QY; Tel (01884) 33462; Fax (01884) 32008; *Headmaster* R.J. Clarke; *Head of Care* D. Tyler (Boarding) (Emotional/Behavioural) (Disturbed) (Boys) (11–18) (45)

Broomhayes School, 78 Atlantic Way, Westward Ho!, Devon EX39 1JQ; Tel (01237) 473830; *Principal* Mrs W. Brown (Boarding – 52 wks) (Autistic) (Mixed) (10–19 (19)

Chelfham Mill, Chelfham, Barnstaple, Devon; Tel (0127 182) 448; J.R. Burland, MSc, PhD (Boarding and Day) (Malad.) (Boys) (7–13 (46)
Mainly Southern Counties and Midlands

Dame Hannah Rogers, Woodland Rd, Ivybridge, Devon; Tel (01752) 892461 (Day/Boarding, Termly, Weekly) (P.H./Del.) (Communication Problems) (FE Unit) (Intensive Support Unit) (Mixed) (8–19 (50)
No area limit

Grenville College Dyslexia Unit, Grenville College, Bideford, N. Devon EX39 3JR; Tel (01237) 472212; Fax (01237) 477020; *Headmaster* M.C.V. Cane, BSc, PhD; *Director of Dyslexia Unit* A. Lane, BEd (Day) (Boarding) (Large Department with 3 full-time teachers in English skills for dyslexics who are fully integrated into the curriculum, but not a Special School) (Co-educational) (11–18) (400)

Marland School, Peters Marland, Torrington, Devon EX38 8QQ; Tel (01805) 610298; Fax (01805) 601324; W.K. Gerrish (Boarding) (E.B.H.) (Boys) (10–16) (40)
Southern Counties

Netherton Hall School, Farway, Colyton, Devon EX13 6EB; Tel (0140 487) 261/433; *Principal* J.R Hooper, BEd(Hons), ACP (Boarding) (10–18) (Emotional, Behavioural)

Royal West of England Residential School for the Deaf, Exeter EX2 4NF; Tel (01392) 215179 (Further Education Service); Tel (01392) 72692; Fax (01392) 431146; H.P. Jones (Weekly Boarding & Day) (Deaf, Partially Hearing & Deaf/Blind) (Mixed) (3–19) (7 day boarding is available by arrangement) (150)
Priority Western Counties

St Loye's College Foundation, Fairfield Hse, Topsham Rd, Exeter EX2 6EP; Tel (01392) 55428; Fax (01392) 420889; J McCarthy, BSc, FIMgt (Residential) (Assessment, Pre-vocational and Vocational Training) (Employment rehabilitation and Occupational Therapy Training) (Manufacture Leather Workshop)
No area limit

St Luke's School, Exeter Rd, Teignmouth, Devon TQ14 9JG; Tel (01626) 778328; *Principal* J.D. Brandwood (Boarding: 52 week placement) (Male) (11–16) (Behavioural disorders) (Learning difficulties (20)

St Luke's 16 Plus Fairoaks, Dawlish Rd, Teignmouth, Devon TQ14 8TG; Tel (01626) 777171; *Principal* J.D. Brandwood (Boarding: 52 week placement) (Mixed) (16–21) (Behavioural Disorders) (Learning Difficulties) (Independency Training) (16)

St Thomas More's School, East Allington, Totnes TQ9 7QF; Tel (0154 852) 273; *Headteacher* D.R. Eglin (Boarding) (Boys) (E.B.D.) (52 week care and special nurture) (9–16) (70)
No area limit. DES listed

Trengweath School, Hartley Rd, Plymouth PL3 5LW; Tel (01752) 771975; *Head* Mrs J.A. Steward (Boarding) (Physical handicap, C.P., S.L.D.) (Mixed) (2–12 (30)
Spastic Society

Vranch House School, Pinhoe Rd, Exeter, Devon EX4 8AD; Tel (01392) 68333; *Headteacher* M. Boon; An Independent School Approved under the 1981 Education Act (Day) (P.H.) (ESN (S) & (M) (Communication problems) (Mixed) (2–12) (40)
National & Abroad
Devon and Exeter Spastics Society

West of England School for Children with Little or No Sight, Countess Wear, Exeter EX2 6HA; Tel (01392) 436448/413333; *Headmaster* Paul Holland, MEd; Further Education Dept (16–21). Advisory Service for S.W. Region, Regional Assessment Service (V.S) (Boarding & Day) (P.S. & Blind) (Mixed) (5–16) (Day nursery and pre-school assessment unit) (Further Education College) (16–19) (170)
South, South-West Region, Channel Islands and South Wales

Whitstone Head School, Whitstone, Holsworthy EX22 6TJ; Tel (0128 884) 251/207; *Director* E. Gent (Boarding) (Emotional and behavioural problems) (Mixed) (10–17) (36)

Doncaster

Fullerton Hse School, Off Tickhill Sq, Denaby, Doncaster DN12 4AR; Tel (01709) 861633; Fax (01709) 869635; *Head* I. Archer, BA (SLD/Autistic with challenging behaviour) (Mixed) (7–19) (25)
The Hesley Group

Hesley Hall School, Tickhill, Doncaster DN11 9HH; Tel (01302) 868313; Fax (01302) 864059; *Head* M. Gray, CertEd, DipEd (Special Needs) (Boarding) (Boys) (7–13) (Behavioural, social and emotional problems; MLD) (63)
Hesley Group

Wilsic Hall School, Wadworth, Doncaster DN11 9AG; Tel (01302) 856382; Fax (01302) 853608; *Head* A.D. Lemon, MA (Day and Boarding) (Boys) (12–16) (Behavioural, social and emotional problems and moderate learning difficulties) (66)
The Hesley Group

Yorkshire Residential School for the Deaf, Leger Way, Doncaster; Tel (01302) 322122; Plus Doncaster College for the Deaf (Boarding/Day) (Mixed) (250) (16+); R.B. Dickson (Boarding & Day School) (Mixed) (2–16+ (240)
Britain

Dorset

Boveridge Hse, Cranborne, Wimborne BH21 5RV; Tel (01202) 218; Miss P. Harper (Boarding) (E.S.N. with additional handicaps) (Mixed) (7–18 (50)

Edward Hse, 42 Talbot Dr, Parkstone, Poole BH12 5ED; Tel (01202) 536763; *Manager* A.M.N. Allen (Boarding) (People with Special Needs) (Mixed) (Adults) (28)
Dorset Spastics Society

Grangewood Hall, 24 St John's Hill, Wimborne, Dorset; Tel (01202) 883954; M. Jee; P. Edmunds; S.E. Jee (Boarding) (Bd., EBD, MLD) (Mixed) (6–12+) (32)
All areas

Langside School, Langside Ave, Parkstone, Poole BH12 5BN; Tel (01202) 518635; *Headmistress* K.I. Vandervelde; *Sister* D. Bartet, SRN (Day (Children with Special Needs) (Mixed) (2–19) (40)
Dorset Spastics Society

Portfield, 4 Magdalen La, Christchurch, Dorset; Tel (01202) 486626; *Principal* Mrs P. Thomas (Weekly Boarding & Day) (Autism and similar disabilities) (Mixed) (3–18+ (30)
Wessex Autistic Society

The Sheiling Community, Horton Rd, Ashley, Ringwood, Hants BH24 2EB; Tel (01425) 477488; Fax (01425) 479536; Home Life, Education and Training for Children and Young Adults with Special Needs. Comprising: The Sheiling School (Mixed) (50) (6-16); The Sheiling College (Further education and training) (Mixed) (70) (16+) (Multiple Mental Handicaps)(Residential and Day Care)
No area limit
Association of Camphill Communities

Victoria School, 12 Lindsay Rd, Poole BH13 6AS; Tel (01202) 763697; *Principal* Paul A. Warner, BEd, AdvDip (Boarding & Day) (P.H.) (Mixed) (2–19) (70)
No area limit but generally from Southern Counties
The Shaftesbury Society

East Sussex

Chailey Heritage School, North Chailey, Nr Lewes BN8 4EF; Tel (0182 572) 2112; *Headteacher* A.C. Burce, MA; *Deputy Headteacher* S. Wharton; *Bursar* T.H. Mount (Boarding and Day) (P.D.) (Mixed) (2½–19) (100)

Farney Close, Bolney Ct, Bolney; Tel (01444) 82811 (Boarding) (EBD) (Mixed) (8–17 (75)
No area limit. DES approved

Hamilton Lodge School for Deaf Children Walpole Rd, Brighton BN2 2ET; Tel (01273) 682362; *Principal* M.M. Moore, BA (Weekly boarding & Day) (Profoundly deaf) (Mixed) (5–18) (70)
South East area limit
Hazeldene Home School, Highgate Rd, Forest Row; Tel 2797 (Learning difficulties/behavioural problems) (Mixed) (6) (15+)
The Mount Camphill Community, Wadhurst, East Sussex TN5 6PT; Tel (01892) 782025 (Camphill-Steiner) (Boarding) (E.S.N.(M) & (S), (M.H., Malad) (15–25) (42)
Northease Manor School, Lewes BN7 3EY; Tel (01273) 472915; Fax (01273) 472202; *Headmaster* R.J. Dennien, MA (Boarding & Day) (Specific Learning Difficulties) (Co-ed) (10–17) (96)
Ovingdean Hall, Greenways, Brighton BN2 7BJ; Tel (01273) 301929; Fax (01273) 305884; M. Bown, BA (Boarding & Day) (Hearing-impaired) (Mixed) (10–16/FE) (150)
Southern England
Pilgrims School, Firle Rd, Seaford BN25 2HX; Tel (01323) 892697; *Headteacher* V. Steels (Acting) (Boarding) (Mainly asthmatics/eczema) (Mixed) (11–16) (56)
No area limit
Invalid Children's Aid Nationwide
Searchlight Workshops, Claremont Rd, Mount Pleasant, Newhaven; Tel (01273) 514007; Fax (01273) 611289; *Superintendent* T. Reed (Boarding) (P.H./Deaf) (Men) (16+) (50)
St Johns Residential, Walpole Rd, Brighton BN2 2AF; Tel (01273) 570795; Fax (01273) 571509; Michael Hudson (Boarding) (Children with special educational needs; MLD; SLD; (Mixed) (5–19) (76)
No area limit
St Mary's School, Wrestwood Rd, Bexhill-on-Sea TN40 2LU; Tel (01424) 730740; Fax (01424) 733575; *Principal* D. Cassar, MA, CCYW, CEd, MBIM (Boarding) (P.H./Speech and Language) (Mixed) (5–16) (90)
No area limit
St Vincent's School, 80 St Saviour's Rd, St Leonards on Sea TN38 OAT; Tel (01424) 439210; Mrs V. Peters (Boarding & Day) (Emotionally disturbed) (Girls) (10–18) (45)

Essex

Chelmer, Maldon Rd, Chelmsford CM2 7RZ; Tel (01245) 72200; *Principal* C.J. Wright (Residential) (E.B.D.) (Boys) (13–16+) (45)
Doucecroft School, 163 High St, Kelvedon, Colchester; Tel (01376) 570060; *Headteacher* K. Cranmer (Boarding and Day) (Autistic) (Mixed) (3–19) (26 pupils)
Essex Autistic Society
Greenwood, Mill Chase, Halstead, Essex CO9 2DQ; Tel (01787) 472002; C.A. Grandin, BA, BSc, MSc, CertEd (Boarding) (Special Needs – Emotional & Behavioural) (Girls) (7–17) (72)
Royal Eastern Counties Schools, 374 Mill Rd, Colchester CO4 5JF; Tel (01206) 851801
Jacques Hall Foundation, Harwich Rd, Bradfield, Manningtree, Essex CO11 2XW; Tel (01255) 870311; Fax (01255) 870311; *Director* T. Lee (Therapeutic Community) (Mixed) (11–17) (52 weeks) (Emotionally disturbed adolescents)
MacIntyre, Woodacre, 38 D'Arcy Rd, Tolleshunt Knights, Nr Tiptree, Essex CO5 ORT; Fax (01621) 819078; *Project Manager* Jacqueline Huck (Residential and day care for mentally disabled) (Adults (15)
The Oxley Parker School, Mill Rd, Colchester; Tel (01206) 853222; *Headteacher* D.P. King, BEd (Special Needs – EBD) (7–17) (50)
Royal Eastern Counties Schools Ltd, 374 Mill Rd, Colchester CO4 5JF; Tel Colchester 851801
St John's R.C. Special School, Turpins La, Woodford Bridge, Essex IG8 8AX; Tel 0181-504 1818; Fax 0181-559 2409; *Headteacher* Sister M.J. Galvin (MLD/SLD) (Mixed) (5–16+) (100)
Redbridge, W. Essex, Barking, Newham, Havering, Waltham Forest, Haringey, Barnet and Hackney (Sisters of Sacred Hearts of Jesus and Mary)
Woodcroft, Whitakers Way, Loughton, Essex; Tel 0181-508 1369; Fax 0181-502 4855; *Head Teacher* C.D. Renehan (Day) (Special needs), (Disabled, Learning and relationship difficulties) (Mixed) (2–11+ (18)
Essex and neighbouring district authorities

Gloucestershire

Berrow Wood, Pendock, Glos GL19 3PR; Tel (0168481) 225; A. Gorton (Boarding and Day) (EBD) (Boys and Girls) (10–17, 16–19) (63)
Listed by DES
Cotswold Chine Home School, Box, Nr Stroud, Glos GL6 9AG; Tel (01453) 832398; Fax (01453) 834970 (Boarding) (Malad.) (Mixed) (10–16) (42)
No area limit
Committee for Steiner Special Education
New Barns, Church La, Toddington, Cheltenham, Glos GL54 5DH; Tel (01242) 200; R. Alston (Boarding) (Malad.) (Mixed) (7–13+ (32)
Homer Lane Trust
St Rose's, Stroud, Glos GL5 4AB; Tel (01453) 763793; Sister Mary Quentin, OP, BA (Boarding and Day) (P.H.) (Mixed) (5–18) (Nursery 2–5) (Extended Ed. Unit) (16–18)
No area limit
Salesian, Blaisdon Hall, Longhope, Glos GL17 OAQ; Tel Gloucester 830247; Fr P. Kenna, BEd (Boarding) (Malad. and Deprived) (Boys) (10–16) (R.C.) (60)
No area limit

Hampshire

Allington Manor International Special School and Therapeutic Community, Fair Oak, Hants SO50 7DE; Tel Southampton 692621; *Consultant Psychologist* Prof L.F. Lowenstein, MA, DipPsych, PhD, BPs, Chartered Psycho-Diagnostic Assessment Centre; Therapy on premises. Also provides Vocational Assessment and training on the premises and outside through Youth Opportunity Training Programme. Open 52 weeks (From average to below average ability and children of superior intelligence with moderate to fairly severe learning and/or behaviour handicaps) (Mixed) (6 per unit) (10–16)
Coxlease School, Clay Hill, Lyndhurst, Hants SO43 7DE; Tel (01733) 283633; *Head of Care* A.P. Orchard; *Head of Education* D.G. Hendley (Boarding) (E.S.N.(M) Behavioural and social problems, mild medical conditions) (Boys) (9–17) (49)
Grateley Hse School, Andover, Hants SP11 9JR; Tel (01264) 889212; Fax (01264) 889212; *Head* N. Saltrese, CertEd, DipEd (Residential) (Mixed) (Social, emotional and behavioural difficulties) (42)
The Hesley Group
Hill Hse School, Rope Hill, Boldre, Lymington, Hants SO41 8NE; Tel (01590) 672147; Fax (01590) 670535; *Head* A. Sumner, CertEd, AdvDip (Mixed) (8–19) (Autism, SLD with challenging behaviour) (18)
No area limit
The Hesley Group
Hope Lodge School, 41 Belmont Rd, Portswood, Southampton SO2 1GD; Tel (01703) 554729; Fax (01703) 551456; *Principal* Mrs M.E. Rigg (Day and Weekly Boarding) (Autistic and non-communicating) (Mixed) (4–16) (27)
Hampshire Autistic Society
The Loddon School, Wildmoor La, Sherfield on Loddon, Basingstoke, Hants RG27 OJD; Tel (01256) 882394; Fax (01256) 882929; Marion Cornick (Boarding) (Severe learning difficulties, autism and challenging behaviour) (Mixed) (7–19) (22)
Great Britain
The Loddon School Company
Lord Mayor Treloar College, Alton, Hants; Tel (01420) 83508; *Headmaster* H. Heard, MA, MCollP (Boarding and Day) (Wide range of physical disabilities) (Mixed) (8–19) (290)
No area limit
The Treloar Trust
Mordaunt School, Rose Road Centre, Rose Rd, Southampton SO14 6TE; Tel (01703) 229017;

Fax (01703) 336112; *Manager of Education Services* E. Howarth (Day) (PMLD) (Mixed) (2–19) (40)
Rose Rd Association

St Edward's School, Melchet Ct, Sherfield English, nr Romsey, Hants; Tel (01794) 884271/884250; Fax (01794) 884762; *Headmaster* D.J. Doyle, BEd (EBD; SLD; Boys) (10–16) (90)
Independent

Solent View School, Vicars Hill, Boldre, Lymington, Hants SO41 5QB; Tel (01590) 677986; Fax (01590) 677682; *Head* C. Clark, CertEd (Termly boarding) (Mixed) (5–13) (Autism) (18)
The Hesley Group

Southlands School, Vicar's Hill, Boldre, Lymington, Hants SO41 5QB; Tel (01590) 675350; Fax (01590) 671891; *Head* D.L. Jenkins, BA, DipEd (Boarding) (Boys) (11–16) (Behavioural and social problems) (40) (Boys) (Asperger Syndrome) (15)
No area limit
The Hesley Group

Hereford and Worcester

Besford Court R.C. Residential Special School, Ladywood Rd, Besford, Worcester WR8 9AQ; Tel (01386) 552074; *Headmaster* T.P.J. Quigley (Boarding) (Learning, emotional or behavioural problems) (Mixed) (8–16) (80)
No area limit

Kinloss School, Martley, Worcester WR6 6QB; Tel (01886) 888223; Fax (01886) 888095; *Headmaster* D. Tuohy, BA (Learning difficulties caused by dyslexia) (Boys) (11–17) (65)

Royal National College (Further Education and Vocational Training for Blind and Partially Sighted People), College Rd, Hereford HR1 1EB; Tel (01432) 265725; Fax (01432) 353478; *Principal* Colin Housby-Smith, PhD(Cantab), MEd(Wales), DipEE, CEng, MIEE (Boarding) (Mixed) (16+) (200)

RNIB New College Worcester, Whittington Rd, Worcester WR5 2JX; Tel (01905) 763933; Fax (01905) 763277; *Principal* H. Williams, MA (Boarding) (Blind and visually impaired) (Mixed) (11–20) (123)
No area limit
Royal National Institute for the Blind

Hertfordshire

Hengrove School, (The House in the Sun), nr Tring, Herts HP23 6LE; Tel (01296) 622136; A.A. and A.F. Gobell, MA, MEd (Boarding) (Learning and Behavioural Problems) (Girls) (10–16) (24)
No area limit

Meldreth Manor School, nr Royston, Herts SG8 6LG; Tel (01763) 260771; *Head Teacher* Caroline J. Coles (Residential and Day) (PH; SLD and profound learning difficulties) (Mixed) (Difficulties; Specialist in additional visual or hearing impairment) (6–19) (85)
The Spastics Society

Radlett Lodge School (National Autistic Society), Harper La, Radlett, Herts WD7 9HW; Tel (01923) 854922; Fax (01923) 859922; Mrs C.G. Andrews (Day, 5-day Boarding) (Mixed) (3–16) (39)
London Boroughs and Home Counties
National Autistic Society

St Elizabeth's R.C. School, Much Hadham, Herts SG10 6EW; Tel 843451; Sister Veronica Hagen (Boarding) (Epilepsy) (Mixed) (5–19+) (80)
No area limit

South Lodge Residential Special School, High St, Baldock, Herts; Tel (01462) 892715/892815; Fax (01462) 896418; *Principal* W. Bush; Open 52 weeks. Separate training for independence in small groups and in preparation for leaving care (Behavioural problems and Special Education needs) (Girls) (12–18) (26)
No area limit

Humberside

The Small School at Winstead Hall – The Sailors, Winstead, Hull HU12 0NP; Tel (01964) 630396; Steen Thomsen; (See also The Small School at Red House – entry under Norfolk) (Mixed) (11–18) (No area limit)

Isle of Wight

St Catherine's School, Grove Rd, Ventnor, IOW PO38 1TT; Tel (01983) 852722; Provision made for some children to attend local secondary schools (Boarding) (Speech and language disorders) (Mixed) (7–19) (70)
No area limit

Kent

Bourne Place, Nizels La, Hildenborough, Tonbridge, Kent TN11 8NS; Tel (01732) 832666; Fax (01732) 832073; G. Davies (Boarding and Day) (Children with moderate learning difficulties) (Mixed) (8–18
National Children's Home, South East Region

The Caldecott Community, Mersham le Hatch, Ashford, Kent; Tel (01233) 623954; J.F.L. King, OBE; M.R. Jinks (Boarding 52 weeks facility) (Emotionally-disturbed with special educational needs) (Mixed) (5–19) (80)
London and South East Region

Coney Hill and Nash F.E. Centre, Croydon Rd, Hayes, Bromley BR2 7AG; Tel 0181-462 7419/5493; K. Fletcher, MEd (Boarding and Day) (P.H. Speech/ Language disordered) (Mixed) (5–19+ F.E.)
Shaftesbury Society

Dorton House, Seal, Sevenoaks, Kent TN15 0ED; Tel (01732) 61477; Fax (01732) 63363 (Boarding and Day) (Visually Handicapped) (Mixed) (4–19) (Including Nursery and a separate Further Education College – Dorton College (130)
No area limit
The Royal London Society for the Blind

Helen Allison School, Longfield Rd, Meopham, Kent DA13 OEW; Tel (01474) 814878; Fax (01474) 812033; Jacqui Ashton-Smith (Weekly Boarding and Day) (Autism) (Mixed) (5–19) (48)
11, 12, 27 Overcliffe, Gravesend, Kent DA11 0EH (Residential)

Meadows School, London Rd, South Borough, Tunbridge Wells, Kent TN4 0RJ; Tel (01892) 529144; Fax (01892) 527787; *Acting Principal* Mike Price; (Term time only) (Holiday provision can be arranged by APEX Project in certain circumstances) (Day and Boarding) (EBD/ Statement of Special Educational Needs) (Co-educational) (10–16+) (56)
Barnardo's London Division

Ripplevale School, Ripple, Deal, Kent CR14 8JG; Tel (01304) 373866; Fax (01304) 381011; C. Davies and Partners (Boarding) (Learning difficulties/ behavioural problems) (Boys) (9–16)
Ripplevale School Ltd
London, Essex, Kent, Sussex, Herts

Royal School for Deaf Children, Victoria Rd, Margate, Kent; Tel (01843) 227561; Fax (01843) 227637; David E. Bond (Boarding/Day) (Deaf, Deaf with Additional Handicaps and Deaf/Blind) (Mixed) (5–19) (180)
No area limit

Lancashire

Beaumont College, Slyne Rd, Lancaster LA2 6AP; Tel (01524) 64278; Fax (01524) 846896; *Principal* D. Gilbert (2/3 Year Residential Courses for post-school students with physical handicap
Spastics Society

Beech Tree School, Meadow La, Bamber Bridge, Preston PR5 8LN; Tel (01772) 323131; Fax (01772) 322187; *Headteacher* N. Story (Boarding) (Multi-handicapped children with severe challenging behaviour) (Mixed) (52 weeks) (7–16) (14)
SCOPE

Nugent House, Carr Mill Rd, Billinge, nr Wigan, Lancs WN5 7TT; Tel (01744) 892551; C.G. Mills, MA, DipEd; *Director* Miss B. Fann, MA Catholic Social Services, 150 Brownlow Hill, Liverpool (Boarding and Day) (Special educational needs associated with emotional and behavioural disorders) (Boys) (75)
Nationwide
Nugent Care Society

Pontville, Black Moss La, Ormskirk, Lancs L39 4TW; Tel (01695) 578734; Fax (01695) 579224; *Headteachers* Richard Farbon; Attached to school there is a specialised college (Boarding) (MLD(M) with additional emotional problems) (Mixed) (9–19) (70)
British Isles

Royal Cross Primary School, Elswick Rd, Ashton-on-Ribble, Preston PR2 1NT; Tel (01772) 729705 (Day) (Hearing Impaired) (Mixed) (3–11)

Underley Hall School, Kirkby Lonsdale, Carnforth, Lancs LA6 2HE; Tel Kirkby Lonsdale 71206; *Headteacher* T.R. Williams (Emotionally disturbed) (Boys) (9–16+) (52 weeks) (77)

Underley Garden School, Partnership Office, Kirkby Lonsdale, Carnforth, Lancs LA6 2HE; Tel (015242) 72224; Fax (015242) 72581; *Headteacher* J.W. Mager (E.B.D.) (Mixed) (9–16+) (52 weeks) (42)

Witherslack Hall Group of Schools (Cedar House), Kirkby Lonsdale, via Carnforth, Lancs LA6 2HW; Tel Kirkby Lonsdale 71181; *Principal* J. Horner; *Headteacher* J.F. Rimmer (Boarding/Day) (Emotional and Behavioural problems) (Mixed) (9–16) (70)

Leeds

Hawksworth Hall, Guiseley, nr Leeds; Tel (01943) 870058; *Headteacher* Martyn Worrall, MA; Member of the Spastics Society. Boarding provision for 20 children (boys and girls) with profound and multiple learning difficulties, physical disabilities and additional sensory impairment (Residential and Day) (Severe and Complex Learning Difficulties, Physical Handicaps, Long Term Assessment) (Mixed) (5–12+) (20)
The Spastics Society

St John's R.C. School for Hearing Impaired, Boston Spa, Wetherby, W. Yorks LS23 6DF; Tel (01937) 842144; *Headteacher* Thomas Wrynne, BEd, MA; Unit – Deaf and Additional Handicaps; Dept – Deaf and Dyspraxic. 6th form and FE facilities (Boarding and Day) (Deafness) (Mixed) (3–18) (115)
No area limit

Leicestershire

The Grange Therapeutic School Knossington, Oakham, Leics LE15 8LY; Tel (0166 477) 264; Fax (0166 477) 234; *Director and Psychologist* Dr A.J. Smith, MA, MEd, PhD, CPsychol (Boarding) (EBD) (Boys) (7–17) (60)

Lincolnshire

Broughton House College, Brant Broughton, Lincs LN5 OSL; Tel (01400) 72929; Fax (01400) 73438; *Head* R.H. Noble, CertEd, DipEd (Residential) (Mixed) (14–24) (Challenging behaviour, emanating from Autism and SLD) (20)
No area limit
The Hesley Group

Sense, The Manor House, 72 Church St, Market Deeping, Peterborough PE6 8AL; Tel (01778) 344921; Fax (01778) 380078; *Regional Director* D.J. Ford; 2 off-site workshops and 10 group homes) (Long term accommodation available) (Boarding and Day) (Deaf/blind) (Mixed) (17+) (40)
Sense: The National Deaf/Blind and Rubella Association

Liverpool

Royal School for the Blind, Church Rd North, Wavertree, Liverpool L15 6TQ; Tel 0151-733 1012; *Headmaster* J.P. Byrne (Boarding and Day) (Visually impaired with moderate to severe learning difficulties) (3–19) and a range of additional disabilities) (Mixed) (Junior and Senior) (60–75)
No area limit

St Vincent's School for the Blind & Partially Sighted, Yew Tree La, West Derby, Liverpool L12 9HN; Tel 0151-228 9968; Sister Josephine Hawes (Boarding and Day) (Visual Handicap) (Mixed) (4–17) (134)
England and Wales

London

Duncroft School, Moor La, Staines, Middx TW18 4YS; Tel (01784) 450166; *Principal* K. Reece
Barnardo's London Division

MacIntyre Mottingham, Mottingham La, Grove Pk, Lewisham SE12 9AW; Tel 0181-857 2425; Fax 0181-857 9056; *Project Director* R. Barnes (Day) (E.S.N. (M) (Mixed) (19+) (12)

Pield Heath House R.C. School, Pield Heath Rd, Uxbridge, Middx UB8 3NW; Tel (01895) 233092/258507; Fax (01895) 256497; Sister Julie Rose (Boarding and Day) (MLD/SLD) (Mixed) (7–19)
No area limit. Speech and Language Difficulties

RNIB Sunshine House School, Northwood, Middx (Boarding and Day) (Visually Impaired) (Mixed) (2–8) (26)
No area limit
RNIB

Rutherford Day School, 12 Melville Ave, South Croydon, Surrey CR2 7HZ; Tel 0181-688 7560; *Chairman* S. Ellis; *Head of Children's Centre* P.H. Netley (Physical, learning and developmental problems)
Croydon, Sutton and District Spastics Society

The Sybil Elgar School for Autistic Children, 10 Florence Rd, Ealing W5 3TX; Tel 0181-567 9844; *Principal* Andrea Hull, MA(Psych), BEd (Day and Weekly) (Autism) (Mixed) (8–19) (40)
National Autistic Society

Merseyside

Birkdale School for Hearing Impaired Children, 40 Lancaster Rd, Birkdale, Southport PR8 2JY; Tel (01704) 567220; Fax (01704) 568342; *Principal* E. Loxham, BEd, MEd(Aud) (Boarding and Day) (Hearing impairment) (Mixed) (7–18) (114)
North West England

Peterhouse School, Preston New Rd, Church Town, Southport, Merseyside PR9 8PA; Tel (01704) 506682; Fax (01704) 506683; *Principal* Brenda Hatton (Autistic)
Liverpool and Lancashire Autistic Society

RNIB Sunshine House School, 2 Oxford Rd, Birkdale, Southport, Merseyside PR8 2JT; Tel (01704) 567174; Judy Bell (Blind and Partially sighted with Multiple Disabilities) (Mixed) (Under 8) (18)
No area limit

Wargrave House School, 449 Wargrave Rd, Newton-le-Willows, Merseyside WA12 8RS; Tel (01925) 224899; Fax (01925) 291368; *Principal* Pamela Maddock (Day and Boarding) (Autistic) (Mixed) (5–19) (24)
Wargrave House Limited

Newcastle upon Tyne

Northern Counties School for the Deaf, Great North Rd, Newcastle upon Tyne NE2 3BB; Tel 0191-281 5821; Fax 0191-281 5060; K.J.C. Lewis, MA, MSc, DipEd, DipEdDPH (Boarding and Day) (Deaf) (Deaf/Blind) (Multi-handicapped) (Mixed) (2–20) (150)
No area limit

The Percy Hedley School, Station Rd, Forest Hall, Newcastle upon Tyne NE12 8YY; Tel 0191-266 5491; *Headmaster* J. Ferris, BA, MSc; *Secretary* R. Baron (Boarding and Day) (P.H. Speech and Language Disorders) (Mixed) (3–17) (140)

Norfolk

Banham Marshalls College, Mill Rd, Banham, Norwich, Norfolk NR16 2HU; Tel (01953) 888656; *Principal* R. Wilson; *Vice-Principal* B. Taaffe; Education from primary age up to GCSE and beyond, pre- and vocational courses. Pupils with special needs, including emotional, behavioural, learning and speech and language difficulties (Boarding and Day EBD, SLD) (Sp and Lang) (Mixed) (5–17)

The Beaumont College, Rectory Rd, Burston, Diss, Norfolk IP22 3TU; Tel (01379) 741562; *Principal* M.P. Shaw, AdvDipEd, CNAA (52 weeks) (Severe Learning Difficulties) (Mixed) (12–19+) (Life placements accepted) (69)
Beaumont Education Ltd, 1 Lonsdale Gdns, Tunbridge Wells, Kent TN1 1NU

Hilbre, Holway Rd, Sheringham, Norfolk; Tel (01263) 822800; D.C. Younger, CertEd, BEd, MEd (Boarding) (Malad.) (Mixed) (6–12 (24)
No area limit

Reeves Hall, Hepworth, Diss, Norfolk IP22 2PP; Tel (01359) 50217; Mrs J.P. Richards (Boarding and Day) (Learning Difficulties for children of average or above average intelligence) (Mixed) (9–17

Sheridan House School, Child and Family Therapy Unit, Southburgh, Thetford, Norfolk IP25 7TJ; Tel (01953) 850494; Fax (01953) 851498; *Principal* F.R.G.G. Tyler (Residential) (52 week care for children with family difficulties) (10–16) (12)
DFE Approved

The Small School at Red House, Buxton, Norwich NR10 5PF; Tel (01603) 279309; Fax (01603) 279789; Lena Eriksson; (See also The Small School at Winstead Hall – The Sailors entry under Humberside). Fifty-two weeks' care for children with emotional and behavioral problems. Provides a wide range of structured educational, social and leisure activities (Boarding) (Children in care) (Mixed) (10-18)
Registered by the DFE and by Norfolk C.C.

Northamptonshire

Hinwick Hall College of Further Education (Special Needs) Hinwick, nr Wellingborough, Northants; Tel (01933) 312470; Fax (01933) 412470 (Boarding and Day) (P.H.) (Mixed) (F.E.) (16–25) (LD)
No area limit
Shaftesbury Society

Potterspury Lodge, Towcester, Northants; Tel (01908) 542912; G. Lietz (Boarding) (Emotionally Disturbed)(Boys only) (8–16) (45)
No area limit
Committee for Steiner Special Education

RNIB, Rushton Hall, Kettering, Northants NN14 1RR; Tel (01536) 710506; Fax (01536) 418506; *Head Teacher* D. Hussey, BEd, CTB (Boarding) (Blind with additional Handicaps) (Mixed) (5–12+ (42)
No area limit
Royal National Institute for the Blind

Thornby Hall, Thornby, Northants NN6 8SW; Tel (01604) 740001/740353; *Director* A.J. Worthington, BA, DipEd, MPhil (Boarding) (Emotionally Disturbed) (Mixed) (10–16)
No area limit
Member of the Peper Harrow Foundation

North Yorkshire

Breckenbrough, Thirsk, N. Yorks YO7 4EN; Tel (01845) 587238; T.G. Bennett (Boarding) (Malad.) (Intelligent boys) (9–17)
Nationwide
Society of Friends

Henshaw's College, Harrogate, N. Yorks HG1 4ED; Tel (01423) 886451; Fax (01423) 885095; S.C. Jones (Residential Further Education) (Visually handicapped with additional handicaps) (Mixed 16+) (Also Deaf-Blind Unit and Juvenile Battens Disease Unit) (Mixed 14+) (80)
No area limit

Ian Tetley Memorial School, Lund La, Killinghall, Harrogate, N. Yorks HG3 2BQ; Tel (01423) 67258; P.H. Cairns; Extended education unit for students with learning difficulties which may also be physical (16–19) (Boarding). Continued education, 'link' courses, external examinations, work experience and independence training, giving accommodation in independence flats, 30 students. (Boarding and Day) (P.H., M.L.D. Spec. LDs) (Mixed) (4–19+) (50)
West & North Yorkshire and Northern Region
Barnado's Yorkshire Division

Spring Hill, Ripon, N. Yorks HG4 3HN; Tel (01765) 603320; *Principal* D.K. Searle, BA, DipEd (Boarding) (Learning difficulties/behavioural problems) (Mixed) (48)
North of England
Barnardo's Yorkshire Division

Nottingham

Dawn House School, Helmsley Rd, Rainworth, Mansfield, Notts NG21 ODQ; Tel (01623) 795361 (Boarding and Day) (Specific Speech and Language Impairment) (Mixed) (5–16) (90+)
No area limit
Invalid Children's Aid Nationwide

National Autistic Society, Carlton, Notts NG4 IJB; Tel (0115) 940 3773; Fax (0115) 940 1779
Northern Region Office

Rutland House School, 1 Elm Bank, Mapperley Rd, Nottingham NG3 5AJ; Tel (0115) 962 1315; *Headteacher* Mrs Oviatt-Ham; Pre-school nursery facilities for children with cerebral palsy (Boarding and Day) (P.H.) (Learning difficulties, severe) (Mixed) (2–13) (20)
Spastics Society

Sutherland House School, Sutherland Rd, Nottingham NG3 7AP; Tel (0115) 987 3375 (Day) (Autistic) (Mixed) (3–16) (42)
Nottingham Regional Society for Autistic Children and Adults

Whitegates Autistic Community, Sparken Hill, Worksop, Notts; Tel (01909) 475162 (Yearly residential) (Autistic) (Mixed) (16+)
Nottingham Regional Society for Autistic Children and Adults

Oxfordshire

Bessels Leigh School, Besselsleigh, nr Abingdon, Oxon OX13 5QB; Tel (01865) 390436; Fax (01865) 390688; J. Boulton, BEd, MEd (Boarding) (Emotional/Behavioural/Educational Problems) (Boys) (10–17) (36)
No area limit
DFE Approved

Castle Priory, Thames St, Wallingford, Oxon OX10 OHE; Tel (01491) 837551/826350; Fax (01491) 826359; Training and Conference centre for workers involved in the care of people with disabilities

The Mulberry Bush School, Standlake, nr Witney, Oxon OX8 7RW; Tel (01865) 300202; Fax (01865) 300084; R. Rollinson BA, MSc, CQSW (Boarding) (Severe emotional disturbance, average and above average intelligence) (Mixed) (5–12; entry age up to 9 yrs) (36)

Penhurst, Chipping Norton, Oxon OX7 5LN; Tel (01608) 642559; *Head Teacher* D.F. Southeard, BSc, BPhilEd (Boarding and Day) (Physically handicapped plus learning difficulties) (P.H.) (Mixed) (5–19) (Respite Care) (32)
Mainly Midlands and Southern England
National Children's Home, Thames Anglia Region

Swalcliffe Park School Trust, Swalcliffe, nr Banbury, Oxon OX15 5EP; Tel (01295) 780302; Fax (01295) 780302; *Principal/Head Teacher* M. Cooling BSc(Econ), MEd (Boarding) (Special Needs E.B.D.) (Boys) (11–16) (also post 16) (45)
No area limit

Tall Trees, Shipton-under-Wychwood, Oxford OX7 6BD; Tel (01993) 830341; *Project Manager* Clare Campling (Boarding) (Mentally handicapped) (SLD) (PH) (Deaf) (Mixed) (18–50) (9)

Turners Court, Benson, Oxford OX10 6QJ; Tel (01491) 36571; *Principal* M. Cornfield (Boarding) (Adolescents with special needs) (Boys) (14–19) (70)

Shropshire

Condover Hall School for Blind Children, Condover Hall, Condover, Shrewsbury SY5 7AH; Tel (0174 372) 2320; A. Jarvis (Boarding and Day) (Blind with additional Handicaps and Deaf/Blind Unit) (Mixed) (5–19+ (101)
No area limit
Royal National Institute for the Blind

Corvedale Care, Hilltop Community and School with Therapeutic Counselling, Fishmore Rd, Ludlow, Shropshire SY8 3DP; Tel (01584) 875152 or (01588) 672071; *Director* N. Wainwright, CQSW (Boarding, open 52 weeks) (Socially and emotionally disturbed with a range of special educational needs) (Mixed) (11–16) (20)

Cotsbrook Community, Higford, nr Shifnal, Shropshire TF11 9ET; Tel (01952) 87237; *Unit Head* J. Hughes, CertEd, Adv.Dip.SpNeeds; *Head of Education* S. Bale BEd(Hons); All placement enquiries/referrals to Placements Office, Llay Rd, Old Rhosrobin, Wrexham, Clwyd, LL11 4RL; Tel Gresford (0978) 355757 (part of the Bryn Alyn Community – see entry under Wales) (Boarding) (Severely Emotionally/Socially and Educationally Maladjusted) (Mixed) (11–16) (35)

Cruckton Hall, Cruckton, Shrewsbury SY5 8PR; Tel (01743) 860206; *Headteacher* P.D. Mayhew (Residential) (Special educational needs) (Boys) (9–16) (42)
Re-recognised under the 1981 Education Act

Derwen College for the Disabled, Oswestry, Shropshire SY11 3JA; Tel (01691) 661234/5; Fax (01691) 670714; *Director* D.J. Kendall, BEng, FCA, MEd; Further Education, social development and vocational training of young people with disabilities. Courses are residential and usually for a period of 3 years

Loppington House Further Education Unit and Adult Centre, Loppington, Wem, Shropshire SY4 5NF; Tel (01939) 233926; Fax (01939) 235255; *Manager* P. Harris (Boarding) (P.H./M.H.) (E.S.N.(S) (Blind) (Deaf) (Epilepsy, Downs Syndrome) (Mixed) (16+) (Open 52 weeks) (Registered Shropshire Social Services) (40)

Overley Hall School, Wellington, Telford, Shropshire TF6 5HE; Tel Uppington (01952) 740262 (from 0700 hrs) or (01952) 740231 (Boarding) (SLD/PMLD) (Challenging Behaviour) (Mixed) (9–19+); (Open 52 weeks) (34)
No area limit
DFE listed

Somerset

Childscourt, Wincanton, Somerset BA9 8AH; Tel (01963) 32213; Miss J. Malcolm; Mrs M. Wilkins (3-term year), (9–17) (Malad.) (Mixed) (45)

Marchant-Holliday, North Cheriton, Templecombe, Somerset BA8 0AH; Tel (01963) 33234; *Head Teacher* J.M. Robertson, BEd, DipEd (Boarding) (EBD) (Boys) (6–13) (37) (Day Places) (8)
Southern England
DES listed

Princess Margaret, 53 Middleway, Taunton, Somerset TA1 3QN; Tel (01823) 257917; *Principal* D. Walker, BA(Hons), CertEd, CQSW (Boarding and Day) (P.H.) (Mixed) (5–19) (75)
Barnardo's South Wales and SW Division

Sedgemoor College, Lillesdon, Taunton, Somerset TA3 6BY; Tel (01823) 490199; Fax (01823) 491094; *Principal* Peter Forgham, DipEd, MEd; *College Director (Initial Referrals)* Stephen Brunskill, CQSW, MBIM; Tel (01278) 446480; *College Director* Ronnie Gleeson, BEd(Hons), MEd (Residential Care and Education) (Emotionally and behaviourally disturbed) (Female) (11–18), (Main campus: 8 girls max. Off campus resources (7 houses): 3 girls max each. Individual Family Care) (45)

South Yorkshire

Doncaster College for the Deaf (DCD) Leger Way, Doncaster, South Yorkshire DN2 6AY; Tel (01302) 322122; Fax (01302) 344524; *Director* R.B. Dickson; A national and international education and training college for the deaf and hearing impaired people with a total communication policy

Storm House School, 134 Barnsley Rd, Wath-upon-Dearne, Rotherham, South Yorkshire; Tel (01709) 874443; *Principal* Joyce Collins (Day and Weekly Boarding) (Autistic) (Mixed) (3–19) (70)
National Autistic Society

Yorkshire Residential School for the Deaf (YRSD) Leger Way, Doncaster, South Yorkshire DN2 6AY; Tel (01302) 322122; Fax (01302) 344524; A national and international school for deaf and hearing impaired children age 3–16 with a total communication policy

Staffordshire

Longdon Hall, Longdon Grn, nr Rugeley, Staffordshire; *Director* B.W. Brook Admissions Office, Alderwasley Hall, Belper, Derbys DE56 2SR; Tel (01629) 822599; *Headteacher* C. Georgeson; Tel (01543) 490634 (Day) (Boarding) (Autistic) (Mixed) (5–19)
Honormead Group of Special Schools

Westwood (Annex of Longdon Hall School) Blithbury, Rugeley, Staffordshire; Tel (01629) 822599; *Director* B.W. Brook Admissions Office, Alderwasley Hall, Belper, Derbys DE56 2SR; Tel (01629) 822599; *Deputy Head* C. Gee; Tel (0188) 922353 (Residential) (Autistic (Mixed) (5–19) (Motor Therapy) (40)
Honormead Group of Special Schools

Suffolk

Edwardstone Hse, Sherbourne St, Boxford, Suffolk; Tel (01787) 210272; *Principal* C.J. Wright (Residential) (E.B.D.) (Boys) (9–13) (15)

The Ryes School, Little Henny, Sudbury, Suffolk CO10 7EA; Tel (01787) 374998; Fax (01787) 371995; *Principal* Rosemary Stamp; Includes 4 'cluster' houses and a 16+ unit of 6 self-contained flats (Boarding) (Complex emotional, behavioural and learning difficulties) (52 weeks) (Mixed) (7–16) (25)

Sunderland

Thornhill Park School, Sunderland SR2 7LA; Tel 0191-514 0659; *Principal* P. Watson; *Deputy* David Walke (Boarding and Day) (Autistic) (Mixed) (2–19) (76)
Tyne and Wear Autistic Society

Surrey

Banstead Place Rehabilitation and Further Education Centre, Banstead Pl, Park Rd, Banstead, Surrey SM7 3EE; Tel (01737) 356222/351756; *Principal* A.R. Gait (Boarding) (P.H.) (Specialist provision for head injured) (Mixed) (16–30) (30)

Burwood Park School and College, Eriswell Rd, Burwood Pk, Walton-on-Thames, Surrey KT12 5DQ; Tel (01932) 227461; Fax (01932) 229262; *Principal* M.D. Kell, MSc (Boarding) (Day) (Deaf) (Mixed) (11–19) (90)
No area limit

The Grange Centre, Rectory La, Bookham, Surrey KT23 4DZ; Tel (01372) 452608; Fax (01372) 451375; *Principal* Christine Gravestock (Boarding and Day) (P.H.) (16–60) (Training/employment in embroidery, dressmaking, horticulture) (47)
No area limit

Link Primary and Secondary, 138 & 82/84 Croydon Rd, Beddington, Surrey CR0 4PG; Tel 0181-688 5239 (Primary), 7691 (Secondary) (Day) (SLD, specific learning difficulties, emotional problems closely related to learning difficulties) (Mixed) (Primary, 35; Secondary, 35) (5–16+)
No area limit
Link Educational Trust

Meath School, Brox Rd, Ottershaw, Surrey KT16 OLF; Tel (01932) 872302; John Parrott (Boarding) (Speech and Language Disorders) (Special unit 6) (Mixed) (40 + 35 Day) (5–12)
No area limit
Invalid Children's Aid Nationwide

Moor House School, Hurst Green, Oxted, Surrey RH8 9AQ; Tel (01883) 712271; Fax (01883) 716722; *Principal* Alan Robertson; A school for pupils with severe specific speech and language disorders, who are within the range of intelligence found in a mainstream classroom. Provision includes small teaching groups and intensive speech and language therapy. There is additional support from a multi-disciplinary team which includes a nurse and an occupational therapist (Boarding) (Severe Specific Speech and Language Disorders) (Mixed) (7–16) (80) Moor House School Trust Company Limited, Registered Charity No: M18229 Z/18
No area limit

Nanhurst School, Elmridge Rd, Cranleigh, Surrey GU6 8JX; Tel (01483) 275121; Fax (01483) 277187;

ST PIERS LINGFIELD

St. Piers Lingfield enables young people with epilepsy and other neurological disorders to enjoy a full role within society by providing them with the highest standards of integrated education, medical attention and residential care.

The School

Pupils aged 5-16 years are grouped according to age, ability and social maturity. Each class for 6-8 pupils has a teacher and classroom assistant, with extra staff for children with additional special needs. There are good facilities for gardening, woodwork, science, art and craft, home economics and physical education, plus a library and soft play area. The national curriculum is followed.

The Further Education Unit

The FEU prepares students aged 16-19 years for advancement towards nationally recognised qualifications and employment through formal training, work experience and education for leisure in an immensely wide variety of commercial, industrial and social environments.

Social Skills

Our prime objective is to help young people achieve personal goals and autonomy. Self confidence is developed through an integrated programme managed by the teaching and residential staff, which includes a wide range of social and leisure activities.

Medical Facilities

Medical care is provided by the well-equipped hospital, with 24-hour medical and nursing staff, excellent EEG facilities and a small pharmacy. There are also two psychologists, physiotherapy, speech and language and occupational therapy units.

Leisure Facilities

These include the swimming pool, newly built sports hall, large concert hall, youth club, soft play centre, Riding for the Disabled, cricket and football pitches, trampoline and provide every opportunity for community based activities.

Admission

Admissions are accepted from 5-18 years. Parents, children and any interested professionals are welcome to visit St. Piers Lingfield to discuss facilities and programmes and to ensure that our services are indeed suited to the needs of the individual pupil.

Enquiries

Further information and application forms may be obtained from the Admissions Officer, St. Piers Lingfield, St. Piers Lane, Lingfield, Surrey RH7 6PW. Tel: (01342) 833243

School – In the classroom

Sports Hall

Principal Dr A.S. Wisbey; A school for children who are under-achieving for reasons other than a lack of intelligence – usually past or present medical problems. This includes dyslexic children. Provision includes medical facilities and full-time paramedical provision including Physiotherapy, Speech Therapy, Audiology, Orthoptic and Neurophysiology and Allergy Supervision; Teaching programmes prepared to meet individual needs, including those of gifted children (6–18) (6th form) (Mixed) (Full and/or weekly boarding and Day) (48)
No Area Limit
The Audrey Wisbey Foundation Charity No. 326205

Peper Harrow, Godalming, Surrey GU8 6BG; Tel (01483) 415131; *Director* G. Farquharson (Boarding) (Emotionally disturbed of average + above average intelligence) (Mixed) (13+)

Queen Elizabeth's Training College, Leatherhead Ct, Leatherhead, Surrey KT22 OBN; Tel (01372) 842204; *Principal* J.S.B. Peake (Residential and Non-Residential) (All disabilities except total blindness) (19+) (215)
No area limit

RNIB Redhill College, Philanthropic Rd, Redhill, Surrey; Tel (01737) 768935; M. Rowe PhD, MSc, DLC, MIBiol (Boarding) (Registered Blind or Partially Sighted) (Mixed) (16+ – Adult) (115)
U.K.

St Dominic's R.C. School, Hambledon, Godalming, Surrey GU8 4DX; Tel (01428) 684693/1682741; Fax (01428) 685018; *Principal* D. Philipson (Boarding and Day) (Del., Specific learning difficulties, emotional problems, speech and language problems), (Mixed) (6–16) (100)
No area limit; all denominations accepted

St Joseph's, Cranleigh, Surrey GU6 7NQ; Tel (01483) 272449; Fax (01483) 276003; *Principal* A. Lowry (Residential and Day) (Moderate and severe Learning Difficulties) (Mixed) (7–16) (2 yr extended course 16+) (Associated Difficulties) (Speech and Language difficulties) (75)
No area limit
Trustees of the Roman Catholic Diocese of Arundel and Brighton

St Piers Lingfield Lingfield, Surrey RH7 6PW; Tel (01342) 832243; Primary, Secondary and Further Education with Medical nursing and therapy facilities on site; Teaching programmes designed to meet each child's special needs; F.E. Unit (Mixed) (100) (16–19) special educational courses, work experience and social development (Boarding) (Multiple special needs and learning difficulty. Epilepsy is a speciality, other medical needs catered for) (Mixed) (5–19) (225)
No area limit

St Margaret's School, Tadworth Ct, Tadworth, Surrey KT20 5RU; Tel (01737) 357171; Fax (01737) 373848; *Principal* A. O'Connor (Boarding/Day) (48 week education year) (MH) (SLD) (PH) (Blind) (Profoundly multi-handicapped children) (Mixed) (8–19) (34)

White Lodge Children's Centre, Holloway Hill, Chertsey, Surrey KT16 OAE; Tel (01932) 567131; Pauline Baxter; Assessment, out-patient therapy services. Integrated therapy and education (Day) (Cerebral palsy) (Mixed) (0–9)

Warwickshire

Hereward College of Further Education, Bramston Cres, Coventry CV4 9SW; Tel (01203) 461231; Fax (01203) 694305; *Principal* W. Rees-Williams; *Chief Administrative Officer* A.M. Haw (Residential and Day) (Further Education for students with physical and sensory disability) (Mixed) (16+) (120)
Students sponsored by FEFC LEA, Social Services & TECs from all over the UK

West Sussex

Farney Close, Bolney Ct, Bolney, Haywards Heath, W Sussex RH17 5RD; Tel (01444) 881811; Fax (01444)

881957; *Head* J.R. Thompson, BEd(Hons) (Day and Boarding) (EBD) (Mixed) (11–17) (78)
No area limit
DES approved

Ingfield Manor School, Five Oaks, Billingshurst, W Sussex RH14 9AX; Tel (01403) 782294; *Head* C. Donovan; Programmes advised and supported by Peto Institute, Budapest. Working towards Conductive Education (Day and weekly Boarding) (Cerebral Palsied) (3–11) (50)
The Spastics Society
DFE Approved

John Horniman School, 2 Park Rd, Worthing, W Sussex BN11 2AS; Tel (01903) 200317; Janet Dunn (Boarding and Day) (Speech and Language Impairment with Associated Learning Difficulties) (Mixed) (24 + 6 day pupils) (5–10)
No area limit
Invalid Children's Aid Nationwide

Mill Hall Oral School for Deaf Children Whitemans Grn, Cuckfield, Haywards Heath, W Sussex RH17 5HX; Tel (01444) 454000; Fax (01444) 456550; *Principal* P.A. Simpson (Boarding and Day) (Severely and profoundly hearing impaired) (Mixed) (4–12) (50)

Philpots Manor School, West Hoathly, nr East Grinstead, W Sussex RH19 4PR; Tel (01342) 810268; Training Course (16–18) (16); We are a mixed Boarding School for children with emotional and behavioural disturbances and learning difficulties. Numbers 54 from 6–16 yrs, 16 from 16–18 yrs (Boarding) (E.B.D. and MLD) (Mixed) (6–16) (54)
No area limit
Committee for Steiner Special Education

RNIB Sunshine House School, Dunnings Rd, East Grinstead, W Sussex RH19 4ND; *Head Teacher* M.P. Shaw, CertEd (Boarding/Day) (Visually impaired with additional handicaps) (Mixed) (2–10) (15)
No area limit
Royal National Institute for the Blind

West Yorkshire

William Henry Smith School, Boothroyd, Brighouse HD6 3JW; Tel (01484) 710123; *Principal* J.G. Airth, MEd; *Headteacher* R.P. Crampton, BA (Boarding) (Emotional, social, behavioural and educational problems) (Boys) (11–19) (82)

Wiltshire

Burton Hill, Malmesbury, Wilts SN16 OEG; Tel (01666) 822685; Fax (01666) 826022; P. Drake (Boarding and Day) (P.H. with learning difficulties) (Mixed) (8–19) (41)
No area limit
Shaftesbury Society

Sutcliffe, Winsley Hse, Winsley, nr Bradford-on-Avon BA15 2LE; Tel (01225) 722144; P.E. Jones; (Boarding) (E.B.D.) (Boys) (9–16) (43)
No area limit

Wirral

West Kirby Residential, Meols Dr, West Kirby, Wirral L48 5DH; Tel 0151-632 3201; *Headteacher* T.I.F. Price, BEd(Hons), DipSpEd (Boarding and Day) (Health, emotional and social problems) (Mixed) (6–16+ (95)
No area limit

Wales

Aran Hall School, Rhydymain, Dolgellau, Gwynedd LL40 2AR; Tel (01341) 450641; Fax (01341) 450637; *Director* E.V. Jones, MSc; M.B. Jordan, MA; All enquiries to Aran Hall School (Boarding, 52 weeks) (SLD and Challenging Behaviours) (Mixed) (11–19)

Bryn Alyn Community, Bryn Alyn Hall, Gresford, Wrexham, Clwyd LL12 8SA; *Unit Head* John Hughes, CertEd, AdvDip(SPLDS); Also two further residential units in Wrexham Area – Pentre Saeson (20 long-term boys, age on admission 10–13 and Gatewen (20) (Mixed) (Preparation for independence plus Halfway House and Flatlet Schemes). All placement enquiries/referrals to Placements Office, Bryn Alyn Community, Llay Rd, Old Rhosrobin, Wrexham, Clwyd LL11 4RL; Tel (0978) 355757; Fax (0978) 264720 (see also Cotsbrook Community entry under Shropshire) (Boarding) (Severely Emotionally, Socially, and Educationally Maladjusted) (Provides a wide range of educational social and leisure opportunities) (Mixed) (12–16) (40)

Bryn Melyn Community Llandderfel, Bala, Gwynedd LL23 7RA; Tel (01678) 530330; Fax (01678) 530460; *Director* Stephen Elliot

Craig-y-Parc School, Pentyrch, Cardiff CF4 8NB; Tel (01222) 890397; Fax (01222) 891404; M. Fowler, BEd, DipSpecEd, DEM (Boarding) (Cerebral Palsy) (MLD) (Communication Disorders) (Mixed) (3–16) (56)
No area limit
Spastics Society

Furze Mount, Copthorn Rd, Upper Colwyn Bay, Clwyd LL28 5YP; Tel (01244) 881033; All enquiries to Care Concern, Mannanan Hse, Sealand Rd, Sealand, Chester CH1 6BW (Residential, 52 weeks) (16+) (Adults with severe learning difficulties, and physical disabilities with associated behavioural problems)

Headlands, Paget Pl, Penarth, South Glamorgan CF6 1YY; Tel (01222) 709771/2; *Headteacher* P. Carradice, DipEd, MEd (Special school for children with behavioural difficulties) (Mixed) (Plus facilities for 12 Day Pupils) (Fostering/Adoption (40)
National Children's Home (Wales)
DES Reg No 576/6025

MacIntyre Womaston, Womaston Hse, Walton, Presteigne, Powys LD8 2PT; Tel (01544) 230308; *Principal* M. Bertulis (Boarding) (Mental disabilities, moderate to severe learning difficulties and emotional, behavioural problems) (Mixed) (7–19) (18)

St David's (Health Care) Limited Carrog, Corwen, Clwyd; Tel (01490 83) 288; Fax (01490 83) 846; All enquiries to Duncan Pritchard, Manager, St David's (Boarding, 52 weeks) (Mentally handicapped with behavioural and learning difficulties) (Mixed) (16+)

Tregynon Hall School, Tregynon, Newtown, Powys SY16 3PG; Tel (01686) 650330; *Headteacher* Maureen E. Holmes; *Director* P.G. Holmes; *Director* R. Thombs (Boarding, 52 weeks) (Emotionally disturbed) (Mixed) (9–18) (23)

Highfield Park, Llangwyfan, nr Denbigh, Clwyd LL16 4LU; Tel (01824) 790600; All enquiries to The Mental Health Care Group, Highfield Pk, Llangwyfan, Denbigh, Clwyd LL16 4LU; Tel: (01824) 790600 (Residential, 52 weeks) (16+) (Village complex for adults with a mental handicap; social and emotional training, extensive workshops and educational centre)

Scotland

Beannachar, Banchory, Devenick, Aberdeen AB1 5YL; Tel (01224) 868605 and 861825; H. Sargent (Boarding and Day) (Further education and training for a broad range of mentally, emotionally and physically handicapped) (Mixed) (16–25) (27)

Camphill Blair Drummond, Blair Drummond Hse, by Stirling FK9 4UT; Tel (01786) 841573; Fax (01786) 841188 (Residential) (Mixed) (Most handicaps, with training potential) (16+) (F.E. and Training) (50)

Camphill Rudolf Steiner Schools, Central Office, Murtle Hse, Bieldside, Aberdeen AB1 9EP; Tel (01224) 867935; Fax (01224) 868420 (Boarding and Day) (Broad range of mentally and physically handicapped) (Mixed) (5–19) (152)
No area limit

Corseford Residential School Milliken Pk, Howood Rd, Kilbarchan PA10 2NT; Tel (01505) 702141; Fax (01505) 702445; Mrs M. Boyle (Spastic) (Mixed) (5–18) (Early education unit 0–5) (60)

Donaldson's College for Deaf People, West Coates, Edinburgh EH12 5JJ; Tel 0131-337 9911; Fax 0131-337 1654; David R. Scott, MEd, BEd, CTD, MRID (Boarding and Day) (Deafness) (Mixed) (3–18) (+ Adult Provision) (155)
Scotland

East Park Home, 1092 Maryhill Rd, Glasgow G20 9TD; Tel 0141-946 8315; Mrs C.M. Leggate (M.H. and P.H.) (Mixed) (2–18) (50)
Scotland

Easter Anguston Training Farm, Peterculter, Aberdeen AB1 OPJ; Tel (01224) 733627; *Principal Officer* Chris Stewart; Year-round residential farm training and care for young people with mental handicaps. Priority to Grampian Region (Day and boarding) (Mixed) (16 Trainees) (16+)
Administrative Centre: Voluntary Service Aberdeen, 38 Castle St, Aberdeen; Tel (0224) 586395

Garvald Training Centre, West Linton, Dolphinton, West Linton, Peebleshire EH46 7HJ; Tel (01968) 682211; M. Dawson (Boarding) (Brain damage, Downs Syndrome, Autism, Malad.) (Mixed) (16 upwards) (32)
No area limit

Harmeny School, Mansfield Rd, Balerno, Midlothian EH14 7JY; Tel 0131-449 3938; Fax 0131-449 7121; Patrick Webb (Boarding) (Special needs) (Mixed) (6–12) (32)
Scotland
Save the Children Fund

Hillside School, Hillside, Aberdour, Fife KY3 ORH; Tel (01383) 860371; D.A. Harvey, DCE, BA, MEd(Hons) (Day and Boarding) (Malad.) (Boys) (44 residential; 6 day)

Lendrick Muir, Rumbling-Bridge, Kinross; Tel (01577) 840258; R.W. Hayles (Independent) (Learning difficulties, average and above average intelligence) (40 Boarders, 40 Day) (Residential/one day) (Mixed) (10–18)
No area limit

Linn Moor Residential School, Peterculter, Aberdeen AB1 OPJ; Tel (01224) 732246; *Principal* Harry Mulford; Year-round residential care and specialist education for children with mental handicaps, some with social and emotional problems also. Emphasis on individual development. Residential care provided in small family groups (Boarding) (M.H.) (Mixed) (6–18) (32)
Administrative Centre: Voluntary Service, Aberdeen, 38 Castle St, Aberdeen AB1 1AB; Tel (0224) 586395

Ochil Tower (Rudolf Steiner) School, Auchterarder, Perthshire PH3 1AD; Tel (01764) 662416; J.M. Surkamp (Boarding and Day) (Special Care) (Mixed) (6–18) (34)
Scotland

Royal Blind School, Craigmillar Pk, Edinburgh EH16 5NA; Tel 0131-667 1100; Mary L.S. Meek (Visually impaired, V1 + additional handicaps) (3–18) (100)
Scotland
Royal Blind Asylum

Stanmore House Residential and Day School for Spastics, Lanark ML11 7RR; Tel (01555) 665041; *Head Teacher/Manager* J. Bridges (Mixed) (Pre-school-18) (80)

Struan House, 27 and 33 Claremont, Alloa FK10 2DG; Tel (01259) 213435; Fax (01259) 211851; *Principal* J. Taylor (Residential and Day) (Autistic) (5–18) (28)

Tigh-A'-Chomainn Camphill Ltd, 4 Craigton Cres, Peterculter, Aberdeen AB1 OSB; Tel (01224) 732656; Providing a setting for furthering independence within the open community (Community Home for Young Adults with special needs) (Mixed) (16–30) (6)

Westerlea School for Spastic Children, 11 Ellersly Rd, Edinburgh EH12 6HY; Tel 0131-337 1236; *Head Teacher* M. Thompson; Early Education Unit (0–36 months) (Day) (Cerebral Palsy) (Mixed) (3–16+) (70)
Edinburgh and surrounding area
Scottish Council for Spastics

Woodlands School, Corsbie Rd, Newton Stewart, Wigtownshire DG8 6JB; Tel (01671) 2480 and 3740;

Family Support Educational 'Presenting' Centre; Six subjects and FE Modules (List G) (Behavioural problems) (Co-ed) (8–17) (52 and 38 week placements) (Emergency Holiday Provision) (42)

Northern Ireland

Glencraig (Rudolf Steiner) Curative Schools, (Mixed) (5–19) (Camphill School) (70)

Glencraig Camphill Community, Craigavad, Holywood, Co Down BT18 ODB, N. Ireland; Tel (0123 17) 3396 (Residential) (Any forms of Mental Retardation)

Glencraig Young Adult Training Scheme (Rudolf Steiner) (Mixed) (Residential) (18–25) (Camphill) (25)

Jordanstown Schools, 85 Jordanstown Rd, Newtownabbey, Co Antrim BT37 OQE; Tel (01232) 863541; *Principal* Deirdre P. Byrne, MSc, BA, BPhilEd, DipEd (Boarding and Day) (Auditory and Visual) (Mixed) (3–17) (122)

St Gerards Educational Resource Centre, Gort Na Mona, Upper Springfield Rd, Belfast BT12 7QP; Tel (01232) 245593; R.O. Rooney, BA, CertEd, DASE (Day) (M.L.D.) (Mixed) (5–16+) (R.C.) (240)

10 Community Homes/ Schools

The Former Approved Schools are now for the most part known as Community Homes or Community Schools or some variant of these titles. Moreover, the previous classifications into 'Boys Classifying Schools', 'Boys Senior Schools', etc are no longer applicable and they are now classified under local Social Services Authorities. The number of pupils is given in brackets.

England

Counties

Avon

Kingswood Special Unit, Kingswood Schools, Counterpool Rd, Kingswood, Bristol BS15 2DJ; Tel (0117) 960 3846; *Head* W.H. Gregory, MEd, DipSocSt (Boys (20)

Cheshire

Redsands Children's Centre, Crewe Rd, Willaston, Nantwich, Cheshire CW5 6NE; Tel (01270) 664116; *Principal* Roy Grimwood; Status Local authority Community Home with Education (40)

Devon

Heath Barton Centre, William Powlett Hse, Beacon La, Exeter EX4 8LZ; Tel (01392) 51951; *Manager* M. Leitch; Status Controlled Social Service Residential (Mixed) (12)

Durham

Aycliffe Young People's Centre, Newton Aycliffe, Co Durham DL5 6JB; Tel (01325) 300101; *General Manager* Ken Blanch; 11 specialised inter-related facilities for the care of young people within the UK; Status Centre for Children (Mixed) (80)

Gloucestershire

Lismore House, 3 Horton Rd, Glos GL1 3PX; Tel (01452) 309510; *Head of Centre* S. Taylor; Status Pupil Referral Centre (Mixed) (18)

Hampshire

The Brooks School, Andover Site, 86 Andover Rd, Winchester; Tel (01962) 854809; *Head* F. Stanford; Status Community Home with Education (Mixed) (45)

Humberside

St William's Community, Market Weighton, York YO4 3HA; Tel (01430) 722188; Fax (01430) 871294; *Director* Peter Coombes Catholic Child Welfare Society (Middlesbrough Diocese); Status Assisted Community Home with Education (36)

Kent

Barnardo's, Knotley School, Springfield Gdns, West Wickham, Kent BR4 9PX; Tel 0181-777 9232; *Principal* T.J. Hayter; Residential units in Croydon and Bow

Lancashire

The Ashleigh Centre, Heys La, Blackburn, Lancs; Tel (01254) 61655; *Officer in Charge* J. Arnold; Status Intermediate Treatment Centre (Mixed) (40)

The Fylde Community, Poulton-le-Fylde, Blackpool, Lancs FY3 OBE; Tel (01253) 884551; *Principal* S.W. Briggs, MSc, CertEd, MA, DSWA; Status Controlled

Community Home with education on the premises (Boys) (92)
Meadowcroft (Adolescent Girls), Pope La, Whitestake, Preston PR4 4BA; Tel Preston 745231; *Headmaster* P.E. Coughlan; Status Community Home with education on the premises (36)

Northamptonshire

St John's Centre, Tiffield, Towcester, Northants NN12 8AA; Tel Bilsworth 859411; *Principal* L. Pullan; Status Controlled Community Home School (Mixed) (44)

Northumberland

NCH Action for Children (Tynedale Shared Care for Children and Young People with Disabilities), Monksfield, Corbridge Rd, Hexham, Northumberland NE46 1UY; Tel (01434) 601594; Status Voluntary Assisted Community Homes (50)
Netherton Park Observation and Assessment Centre (C.H.E.), Stannington, Morpeth, Northumberland NE61 6DE; Tel (01670) 789351; Fax (01670) 789056; *Principal* A. Mamwell; Status Controlled Community Home

Shropshire

Cotsbrook Community, Higford, Shifnal, Shropshire; Tel (0894) 22237/22371; *Director* J.P. Hughes, CertEd, SP Needs Diploma; *Deputy Head Teacher* S.I. Bale, BEd(Hons); Bryn Alyn Community

Surrey

Chaworth School, Ottershaw, Nr Chertsey, Surrey KT16 OLS; Tel (01932) 874211; *Headmaster* B. Rushworth; Status Community Home School (Girls) (22)
Oaks Centre, Mayford Gr, Woking, Surrey; Tel (01483) 765141; *Head of Centre* D.M. Bowler; Status Community Home with Education

Warwickshire

Warwick C.S.T.(Education Unit), Myton Rd, Warwick CV34 6PX; Tel 492431; *Head of Unit* Louise Giblin; Status Children's Services Team

West Sussex

Shermanbury Grange C.H.(E), Shermanbury, nr Horsham, Sussex RH13 8HB; Tel (01403) 710371; *Centre Manager* Alan P. Dyka; Status Community Home (Education) (Mixed) (24)

Wiltshire

Cotswold Community, Ashton Keynes, nr Swindon, Wilts SN6 6QU; Tel (01285) 861239; *Principal* John Whitwell; Status Therapeutic Community for emotionally disturbed and abused boys (Boys) (9–18) (40)

Metropolitan Districts

Birmingham

St John's Residential Resource Centre, 18 Gravely Hill North, Birmingham B23 6BQ; Tel 0121-373 0562/382 6822; Fax 0121-377 6727; *Principal* Colin Jewitt (Acting); Status Local Authority Community Home School

Kirklees

Hyrstlands School, 28 Track Rd, Batley, W Yorks WF17 7AA; Tel (01924) 465340; *Principal* Capt D. Botting; *Correspondent* Col S. Gauntlett Salvation Army, 280 Mare St, Hackney, London E8; Status Voluntary Community Home (Girls) (16)

Leeds

East Moor School, Tile La, Adel, Leeds; Tel (0113) 261 0031; R.L. Meek; Status Community Home with Education (80)
Shadwell Children's Centre, Shadwell La, Moortown, Leeds LS17 8AG; Tel (0113) 268 4235; *Principal* A. Morris; Status Community School and Assessment Centre (Mixed) (100)

Merseyside

Briars Hey, Mill La, Rainhill L35 6NE; Tel 0151-430 9677; Fax 0151-430 8455; *Principal* R.S. Potter, MEd; Status Community Home School with secure accommodation (Girls) (36)

St Helens

The Orrell School, Blackbrook Rd, St Helens, Merseyside WA11 9RJ; Tel (01744) 22101 and 26531; *Director* Miss B. Fann; *Headteacher* J.M. Yates; Status E.B.D. School – Independent – run by the Nuggent Care Society, 150 Brownlow Hill, Liverpool (Girls) (42)

Sunderland

Wellesley, Links Rd, Blyth, Northumberland NE24 3PF; Tel (01670) 352773; Fax (01670) 366415; *Establishment Manager* Nick Murphy; Status Community Home with Education (42)

London Boroughs

Greenwich

Frant Court, Frant, Tunbridge Wells, Kent TN3 9DE; Tel (0892750) 212; Fax (0892750) 458; *Principal* David Thirlaway; Status Independent Children's Home/Special School (Girls) (11–18) (24)

Hammersmith and Fulham

Finnart Hse, Walsh Manor, Crowborough, E. Sussex; Tel (018926) 652146; *Principal* C.J. Faithfull; Status Community Home with Education (Mixed) (36)

Hounslow

Duncroft Centre, Moor La, Staines, Middx TW18 4YS; Tel (01784) 50166; *Principal* Keith Reece; Status Assisted Community Home School with day pupil provision, Barnardo's, linked with London Borough of Hounslow (Adolescent Girls) (30)

Newham

Ardale School, North Stifford, nr Grays, Essex RM16 1UP; Tel (01375) 382371; *Principal* I.L. Stanger, MA, PQRC; Status Community Home School (Boys) (30)

Wales

Clwyd

Bryn Alyn Community: All placement enquiries to: Placement and Liaison Office; Tel (01978) 355757; *Director* K.J. White
Bryn Alyn Hall, Gresford, Wrexham, Clwyd LL12 8SA; Tel (0197883) 5811; *Principal* Glyn Condiffe, BA, CertEd, ACP(SpNds) (Mixed) (11–18)
Pentre Saeson Hall, Bwlchgwyn, Wrexham, Clwyd; Tel (01978) 757173; *Director* K.M. Taylor, CQSW (Boys) (10–16)

Gwent

Ty Mawr Gilwern, Nr Abergavenny, Gwent NP7 OEB; Tel (01873) 830360; *Principal* C. Phelan; Status Community Home School (Boys) (50)

Scotland: Residential Schools/List 'D' Schools

Central

Ballikinrain School, Balfron, By Glasgow G63 OLL; Tel (01360) 440244/440645; Fax (01360) 440946; *Headmaster* D.H. Denholm; *Correspondent* Director of Social Work Church of Scotland, Charis Hse, 47 Milton Rd, Edinburgh EH15 2SR; Tel 0131-657 2000 (Boys) (8–16) (48)

Snowdon School, Spittal St, Stirling FK8 1DU; Tel (01786) 473449; *Headmaster* A.W. Macintyre, BSc, MSc (Girls) (12–16) (18)

Grampian

Oakbank School, Midstocket Rd, Aberdeen AB9 2XP; Tel 313347; Fax 312017; *Headmaster* C.R. McKail, BA, MSocSc, CertEd, CQSW, MEd (66)

Lothian

St Joseph's Residential School, Tranent, East Lothian EH33 1DT; Tel (01875) 610794; *Headmaster* James Taig, MEd, BA, DPE, DCE, DipSpEd Management through Lothian Reg. Social Work Dept, Shrubhill Hse, Shrub Pl, Edinburgh EH7 4PD; Tel (0131) 554 4301 (Boys and Girls) (38 Residents, 24 Day) (12–16)

Wellington School, Penicuik, Midlothian EH26 8PT; Tel (01968) 72515; *Head* A.D. McCracken (Boys (53)

Strathclyde

Balrossie Residential School, Kilmacolm, Renfrewshire; Tel (01505) 872201/2/3; *Headmaster* D.S.D McCallum; *Correspondent Assistant District Manager* Peter Cairns Social Work Dept, Dalrymple Hse, 195 Dalrymple St, Greenock PA15 1UN; Tel (01475) 892281 (Boys) (48)

Geilsland School, Beith, Ayrs; Tel (01505) 504044; *Head of School* Ranald Mair, BA, MA, CQSW; *Correspondent, Director of Social Work* Church of Scotland Board of Social Responsibility, Charis Hse, 47 Milton Rd East, Edinburgh EH15 2SR; Tel 0131-657 2000 (Boys) (15–18) (35)

Good Shepherd Centre, Bishopton, Renfrewshire PA7 5PF; Tel (01505) 862814; Fax (01505) 864167; *Principal* Sister Andrea Maceachen; *Correspondent* F.P. McCormick Waterloo Chambers, 19 Waterloo St, Glasgow G2 6AH (Girls) (45 Residents and 8 day girls) (Catholic and non-Catholic)

Kerelaw School, Kerelaw Rd, Stevenston, Ayrshire KA20 4JY; Tel (01294) 461536; *Headmaster* R.G. Forrest, MA (Boys and girls—Main School 64) (Boys and girls Secure Unit 24)

Kibbie School, Greenock Rd, Paisley, Renfrews PA3 2LH; Tel 0141-889 0044; Fax 0141-887 6694; *Headmaster* G.M. Bell; *Correspondent* G.N. Walker, CA Craig and Corson, Ashtrees Hse, 9 Orr Sq, Paisley, Renfrews; Tel 0141-887 7811 (Boys) (50 residential pupils, 20 day pupils)

St Mary's Kenmure School, St Mary's Rd, Bishopbriggs, Glasgow G64 2EH; Tel 0141-772 5001; *Headmaster* W. Duffy; *Correspondent* J. McSparran and McCormick SSC, 19 Waterloo St, Glasgow G2 6AH; Tel 0141-248 7962

Springboig St John's R.C. School, 1190 Edinburgh Rd, Glasgow G33; Tel 0141-774 9791/2/3; *Headmaster* W. Fitzgerald, BA; *Correspondents* Mssrs J.McSparran and McCormick SSC, 19 Waterloo St, Glasgow G2 6AH; Tel 0141-248 7962 (Boys)

Tayside

Balnacraig School, Fairmount Terr, Perth; Tel (01738) 36456/7; Fax (01738) 441863; *Headmaster* E.G. Matthew; *Correspondent* D.P. McDonald 10 Blackfriar's St, Perth (0738) 37311 (Co-ed) (24)

Rossie School, Montrose, Angus; Tel (01674) 820204/820271; Fax (01674) 820249; *Chief Executive* A.A. Thompson; *Depute Head* M. Wood (Young People) (Secure Unit) (30)

11 Higher and Vocational Education

Higher and Adult Education Councils and Committees

Advisory Committee on the Supply and Education of Teachers

See Chapter 13

Art and Design Admissions Registry

Penn Hse, 9 Broad St, Hereford HR4 9AP; Tel (01432) 266653
Registrar T.W.M. Gourdie, MA
Information Officer A.E. Charlton, MA (RCA)
The Registry's principal function is to provide an applications service for those wishing to study Art and Design in Higher Education. Courses in the ADAR system are either BA degree in Art and Design or BTEC HND courses in Design and Associated Studies. The Registry also deals with postgraduate courses in Art and Design, including courses leading to secondary school teaching qualifications, and provides a comprehensive advisory and information service on Art and Design education and career opportunities

The Clearing House for Postgraduate Courses in Art and Design Education

Penn Hse, 9 Broad St, Hereford HR4 9AP; Tel (01432) 266653
Registrar T.W.M. Gourdie, MA
The Clearing House provides an application service for thirteen Centres offering one year, full-time, Postgraduate courses in Art and Design teacher training at secondary school level. These centres are located in Birmingham, Cardiff, Leicester, Liverpool, London (Institute, Goldsmiths' and Middlesex), Oxford, Reading, Ulster, and Wakefield. PGCE courses enjoy mandatory grant status. Further information about art and design teacher training and details of how to apply available from the Clearing House secretary at the above address

British Accreditation Council for Independent Further and Higher Education (BAC)

Suite 401, 27 Marylebone Rd, London NW1 5JS; Tel 0171-487 4643; Fax 0171-935 1507
Chief Executive Robin Laidlaw
Acts as the national accreditation authority for independent further and higher education. Institutions listed in the latter half of this chapter with an asterisk are accredited by the BAC

General Teaching Council for Scotland

5 Royal Terr, Edinburgh EH7 5AF; Tel 0131-556 0072; Fax 0131-557 6773

Elected Members (Teachers)
Principals of Teacher Education Institutions
G. Kirk, MA, MEd, FRSA; B.J. McGettrick, KHS, OBE, BSc, MEd; James McCall, BSc, MEd, PhD: G. Wilson, MA, PhD, FRSA
Lecturer in Teacher Education Institutions
G. Livingstone, MA, MEd, FEIS
Further Education
W. Johnson, BSc, CPhys, MInstP
D. Pollock, FTC, LCG, MIMI
Secondary Schools M.T. Allan, MA
Secondary Schools M.R.W. Caden, MA, FEIS
Secondary Schools J. Cairney, DPE
Secondary Schools B. Clark, MA
Secondary Schools P. Dickson, BSc
Secondary Schools A. Finn, MA
Secondary Schools S.M. Forrest, JP, BSc, FEIS
Secondary Schools J. Fraser, MA
Secondary Schools D.T. Hughes, MA
Secondary Schools M.A.M. McCormack, MA
Secondary Schools T. Wallace, BSc
Primary Schools W. Brown, DCE
Primary Schools V. Hanna, DipCE
Primary Schools J. McPherson, MEd, DipCE, DipEdTech
Primary Schools J.M. Hannah, BA, DipCE
Primary Schools C.D. MacLeod, MA, FEIS
Primary Schools J.L. Patton, DipCE
Primary Schools M. Mitchell, AdvDipEd, DipCE, AVPE
Primary Schools A.E. Richardson, DipCE
Primary Schools R. Robertson, MA, MEd
Primary Schools N.A. Watson, DCE, ACE, NFFC
Primary Schools L.S. Young, DipCE, DipEd

Appointed Members
Convention of Scottish Local Authorities
T. Farrell
J. Towers
E. Maginnis
M.J. Rolfe
Association of Directors of Education in Scotland
M. Allan, BA
K. Bloomer, BA
K.A. MacLeod, MA, BA, DipEd
Universities of Scotland S. Brown, BSc
J.R. Ashcroft, BA, MA, PhD
R. Jonathan BS, MA, PhD
C.J. Suckling, BSc, PhD, DSc, CChem, FRSC, FRSA, FRSE
Central Institutions W.J. Emond, BSc, FIMA, FSS
R. Murray, BSc, PhD, CTextATI
Church of Scotland
J.J. Laidlaw, MA
Roman Catholic Church
S. McCormick, MA

Members nominated by Secretary of State for Scotland
J.D. Denny, FIPM; A. Gardner, BSc; A.D. Nicol, CA; B. Steele
Assessors appointed by the Secretary of State
G. McHugh, Assistant Secretary (The Scottish Office Education Dept); K.M. Fairweather, HMCI (The Scottish Office Education Dept)
Registrar D.I.M. Sutherland, MA, MEd, FRSA
Depute Registrar (Administration) H.G. McIntyre, ACIS
Depute Registrar (Education) R.A. Galt, MA, FEIS

National Council for Vocational Qualifications (NCVQ)

222 Euston Rd, London NW1 2BZ; Tel 0171-387 9898
Chairman Sir Bryan Nicholson
Chief Executive J. Hillier
The Council was set up by the government in October 1986 as a registered company limited by guarantee to achieve a coherent national framework for vocational qualifications
Its main task is to design and implement a national framework of vocational qualifications and rationalise and reform the present system. NCVQ accredits awards by certifying bodies where they reflect relevant standards of competence required by industry and commerce. Awarding National Vocational Qualification (NVQ) status will raise standards, encourage more effective training and open up access to qualifications by the removal of unnecessary restrictions on methods and periods of learning, and age barriers

Higher Education Funding Council for England (HEFCE)

Northhavon Hse, Coldharbour La, Bristol BS16 1QD; Tel (0117) 931 7317; Fax (0117) 931 7203
Chairman C. Brandon Gough
Chief Executive Prof Graeme Davies from 1 October 1995 *Prof Brian Fender*

Standing Conference on University Teaching and Research in the Education of Adults (SCUTREA)

Chair M. Zukas Dept of Adult and Continuing Education, University of Leeds, Leeds LS2 9JT; Tel (0113) 233 3242
Hon Secretary Dr Paul Armstrong Mainframe Research and Consultancy Services, Unit 221, The Lee Valley Technopark, Ashley Rd, Tottenham Hale, London N17 9LN; Tel 0181-880 4510
SCUTREA's objective is to further the study of and research into the education of adults. By means of its annual conferences, seminars, study groups and published papers, it provides opportunity for adult educators to share experiences and to discuss research priorities. Membership is open to individuals and institutions who are making a contribution to the study of or research into any aspect of learning, education or training in adulthood

Student Loans Company Ltd

100 Bothwell St, Glasgow G2 7JD; Tel 0141-306 2000
Chief Executive Ronald J. Harrison
Administration of Student Loans Scheme

Universities and Colleges Admissions Service (UCAS)

Fultan Hse, Jessop Ave, Cheltenham, GLOS GL50 3SH; Tel (01242) 222444
UCAS deals with applications for admission to full-time first degree and first diploma courses at all universities and all colleges of HE in the UK. (The Open University does not participate in the UCAS scheme)
Each applicant completes an application form issued by UCAS referring to a UCAS Handbook which is photographed and reduced in size in the UCAS office. Copies of the form are sent simultaneously to all the universities and colleges to which the applicant has decided to apply. The institutions decisions and the replies of the applicant to the offers he or she receives are processed and recorded in the UCAS office
Every applicant applying to a university is required to pay a fee of £12. No application will be accepted unless it is accompanied by this fee

Universities and University Colleges

England

Anglia Polytechnic University

East Rd, Cambridge CB1 1PT; Tel (01223) 663271; Fax (01223) 352973
Victoria Rd South, Chelmsford CM1 1LL; Tel (01245) 493131; Fax (01245) 490835

City College, Norwich

A regional college of Anglia Polytechnic University, Ipswich Rd, Norwich, Norfolk NR2 2LJ; Tel (01603) 660011; Fax (01603) 760326
Contact The Registrar

Colchester Institute

A Partner Institution of Anglia Polytechnic University
Sheepen Rd, Colchester, Essex CO3 3LL; Tel (01206) 778000; Fax (01206) 763041
Contact Student Services

Aston University

Aston Triangle, Birmingham B4 7ET; Tel 0121-359 3611
Chancellor Sir Adrian Cadbury, MA, HonDSc, HonLLD, CIMgt
Vice-Chancellor Prof Sir Frederick Crawford, MSc, PhD, DEng, DSc, FEng, FIEE, FIEEE, FInstP, FIMA, CIMgt
3,873 full-time and sandwich undergraduate students; 379 full-time postgraduates, 475 part-time postgraduates, 235 postgraduates following distance-learning programmes, 35 external research students

University of Bath

Bath BA2 7AY; Tel (01225) 826826; Fax (01225) 462508; Telex 449097
Chancellor Sir Denys Henderson, Kt, MA, LLB, D. Univ, LLD, DSc
Vice-Chancellor Prof V.D. VandeLinde, PhD
No special provision for mature students, but mature students who meet the admission standards are welcomed. Standard fees
4,205 full-time undergraduates; 750 full-time postgraduate students

School of Education

Head Prof J. Calderhead, MA, PhD

University of Birmingham

Edgbaston, Birmingham B15 2TT; Tel 0121-414 3344
Chancellor Sir Alex Jarratt, CB, BCom, HonLLD, HonDSC, HonDUniv
Pro-Chancellor R.S. Burman, CBE, BSc
Vice-Chancellor and Principal Prof Sir Michael Thompson, BSc, DSc, FInstP
Registrar and Secretary D.R. Holmes, MA
11,453 undergraduates; 4,821 postgraduates

School of Education

Head Prof H.R. Thomas, PhD, BA, MEd, PGCE

School of Continuing Studies

Tel 0121-414 5610
Head Prof J. Tann, MA, PhD

Bournemouth University

(formerly Bournemouth Polytechnic)
Poole Hse, Talbot Campus, Fern Barrow, Poole, Dorset BH12 5BB; Tel (01202) 524111; Fax (01202) 513293
Vice-Chancellor Gillian Slater
Pro-Vice-Chancellor (Academic) J. Coyne, BA, MSc, PhD
Pro-Vice-Chancellor (Physical Resources and Finance) D.G. Gibson, BSc, MSc, AFIMA, MBCS
Director of Personnel M. Riordan, BA, BD
Und; M and W
8,000 full-time students
Departments Applied Computing and Electronics; Conservation Sciences; Dorset Business School; Finance and Law; Institute of Health and Community Services; Management Systems; Marketing; Advertising and Public Relations; Media Production; Product Design and Manufacture; Service Industries

University of Bradford

Richmond Rd, Bradford, W Yorks BD7 1DP; Tel (01274) 733466; Fax (01274) 305340; Telex 51309
Chancellor Trevor Holdsworth, Kt, HonDEng, FCA, FRSA
Pro-Chancellors R.W. Suddards, CBE, LMRTPI, FSVA(Hon); Hon DLitt, The Baroness Lockwood of Dewsbury, Hon DLitt, HonLLD
Vice-Chancellor and Principal D.J. Johns PhD, DSc, FEng, FRAeS, FIOA, FCIT
Registrar and Secretary N.J. Andrew, BA
5,505 full-time and 143 part-time undergraduate students; 824 full-time and 526 part-time postgraduate students (1993/194)

Brighton University

(formerly Brighton Polytechnic)
Mithras Hse, Lewes Rd, Brighton, East Sussex BN2 4AT; Tel (01273) 600900
Director Prof D. Watson, MA, PhD
8,268 full-time and sandwich course students; 3,569 part-time students

Faculty of Education, Sport & Leisure

Falmer, Brighton BN1 9PH; Tel (01273) 600900
Dean Ann Markham, MEd

Brunel University

Kingston La, Uxbridge, Middx UB8 3PH; Tel (01895) 270072; Fax (01895) 254760
Chancellor The Rt Hon The Earl of Halsbury, FRS
Pro-Chancellor P.E. Trier, CBE, MA, FEng, FIEE, FInstP, FIMA, HonDTech
Vice-Chancellor and Principal Prof M.J.H. Sterling, PhD, DEng, CEng, FIEE, FInstMC, FRSA
Pro-Vice Chancellor Prof A. Reynolds, BSAc, PhD, DIC, CEng, FiMechE, NASCE, FRSA
Academic Secretary J.B. Alexander
3,726 sandwich undergraduates; 727 full-time and 1,137 part-time postgraduates

University of Bristol

Senate Hse, Tyndall Ave, Bristol BS8 1TH; Tel (0117) 930 3030; Fax (0117) 925 1424
Chancellor Sir Jeremy Morse, KCMG, MA, DLitt, DSc, LLD
Vice-Chancellor Sir John Kingman, FRS, MA, ScD, DSc, LLD, Hon FIS
Registrar J.H.M. Parry, MA
8,682 undergraduates; 1,570 postgraduates

School of Education

Helen Wodehouse Bldg, 35 Berkeley Sq, Bristol BS8 1JA; Tel (0117) 930 3030
Professor of Education, Head of School Prof P.M. Broadfoot, BA, MEd, PhD

Department for Continuing Education

Wills Memorial Bldg, Queen's Rd, Bristol BS8 1HR; Tel (0117) 930 3629
Director C.S.B. Haselgrove, MA, MLitt Senate Hse, Bristol BS8 1TH; Tel (0117) 928 8677; Fax (0117) 928 8675
Head Dr E. Bird, BA, MA, DPhil Wills Memorial Bldg, Queen's Rd, Bristol BS8 1HR; Tel (0117) 930 3629; Fax (0117) 925 4975
Professor of Adult Education Prof E.J. Thomas, MA, MSc, PhD Wills Memorial Bldg, Queen's Rd, Bristol BS8 1HR; Tel (0117) 928 8697; Fax (0117) 925 4975

University of Buckingham

Hunter St, Buckingham MK18 1EG; Tel (01280) 814080; Fax (01280) 822245
Chancellor Baroness Thatcher of Kesteven, OM, FRS
Chairman of the Council Sir Nigel Mobbs, DL, DSc
Vice-Chairman of Council T.B. Collins, MA
Vice-Chancellor The Rt Hon Sir Richard Luce, DL, MA
Executive Pro-Vice-Chancellor Prof P.L. Watson, MSc, FCA
Director of Administration and Resources J. Elder, MAppSci, FIMgt
Finance Officer M.C. Collings, ACIS
1000 students

University of Cambridge

Chancellor HRH The Prince Philip Duke of Edinburgh, HonLLD
Vice-Chancellor Prof Sir David Williams, QC, MA, LLB
Registrary S.G. Fleet, MA, PhD University Registry, The Old Schools, Cambridge; Tel (01223) 332200
Secretary-General of the Faculties D.A. Livesey, MA, PhD
Treasurer J.M. Womack, MA; Tel (01223) 332200
Secretary for Local Examinations M.P. Halstead, MA, PhD Syndicate Bldgs, Hills Rd, Cambridge; Tel (01223) 61111
Secretary to Careers Service A.J. Raban, MA Stuart Hse, Mill La, Cambridge; Tel (01223) 338288
10,500 undergraduates; 3,500 postgraduates

Colleges for Men and Women

With date of foundation

Christ's
Master Prof Sir Hans Kornberg, ScD, FRS; Tel (01223) 334900

Churchill
1960
Master Prof A.N. Broers, BA, PhD, FRS; Tel (01223) 336000

Clare
1326
Master B.A. Hepple, MA, LLB; Tel (01223) 333200

Clare Hall
1966 *Graduates only*
Master Prof G.P.K. Beer, LITTD; Tel (01223) 332360

Corpus Christi
1352
Master Prof E.A. Wrigley, MA, PhD; Tel (01223) 338000

Darwin
1964 *Graduates only*
Master Prof G.E.R. Lloyd, MA, PhD, FBA; Tel (01223) 335660

Downing
1800
Master P. Mathias, LittD, FBA; Tel (01223) 334800

Emmanuel
1584
Master Lord St John of Fawsley, PC, MA, PhD; Tel (01223) 334200

Fitzwilliam
1966
Master A.W. Cuthbert, PhD, FRS; Tel (01223) 332000

Girton
1869
Mistress J.J. d'A. Campbell, CMG, MA; Tel (01223) 338999

Gonville and Caius
1348
Master P. Gray, ScD, FRS; Tel (01223) 332400

Homerton
(Approved Society 1977)
Principal K.B. Pretty, MA, PhD; Tel (01223) 411141

Hughes Hall
1885
President J.T. Dingle, PhD; Tel (01223) 334893

Jesus
1496
Master Prof Lord Renfrew, ScD, FBA; Tel (01223) 339313

King's
1441
Provost Prof P.P.G. Bateson, ScD, FRS; Tel (01223) 331100

Magdalene
1542
Master Prof J.B. Gurdon, FRS; Tel (01223) 332100

Pembroke
1347
Master Sir Roger Tamkys, MA; Tel (01223) 338100

Peterhouse
1284
Master Sir John Meurig Thomas, MA; Tel (01223) 338200

Queen's
1448
President Rev J.C. Polkinghorne, ScD, FRS; Tel (01223) 335511

Robinson
1977
Warden Prof Lord Lewis, ScD, FRS; Tel (01223) 339100

St Catharine's
1473
Master Sir Terence English, MA; Tel (01223) 338300

St Edmund's
1965
Master R.M. Laws, MA, PhD; Tel (01223) 336250

St John's
1511
Master P. Goddard, MA, PhD; Tel (01223) 338600

Selwyn
1882
Master D. Harrison, CBE, ScD; Tel (01223) 335846

Sidney Sussex
1596
Master Prof G. Horn, ScD, FRS; Tel (01223) 338800

Trinity
1546
Master Sir Michael Atiyah, MA, PhD, FRS; Tel (01223) 338400

Trinity Hall
1350
Master Sir John Lyons, LittD, FBA; Tel (01223) 332500

Wolfson
1965 *(Graduates only)*
President G. Johnson, MA, PhD; Tel (01223) 335900

Colleges for Women

Lucy Cavendish
1965
Rt Hon Lady Perry, MA, *President*; Tel (01223) 332190

New Hall
1954
President V.L. Pearl, PhD; Tel (01223) 351721

Newnham
Principal O.S. O'Neill, MA; Tel (01223) 335700

Faculty of Education (Department of Education)

17 Trumpington St, Cambridge; Tel (01223) 332888
Professor of Education Prof D.H. Hargreaves, MA, PhD

Institute of Education
Shaftesbury Rd; Tel (01223) 69631
Director H.W. Bradley, MA

Faculty of Education (Institute of Education)

Shaftesbury Rd, Cambridge CB2 2BX; Tel (01223) 69631; Fax (01223) 324421
Director H.W. Bradley, OBE, MA
Secretary G.M. Morley, MA

Board of Extra-mural Studies

Madingley Hall, Madingley, Cambridge; Tel (01954) 210636
Director M.E. Richardson, MA

University of Central England in Birmingham

Perry Barr, Birmingham B42 2SU; Tel 0121-331 5000
Vice-Chancellor Dr P.C. Knight, BA, FRAS, CPhy, MInstP, DPhil, DUniv
Secretary and Registrar M. Penlington, BA
Pro-Chancellor F.L. Shaw, JP, BCom, FCA, FCMA, FCIS
18,100 full and part-time students

Faculty of Education

Westbourne Rd, Edgbaston, Birmingham; Tel 0121-331 6100
Dean of Faculty Prof S. Buchanan, BA, MSc(Education)
Associate Dean: (Staffing and Resources) Prof D.E. Hellawell, BA, DipEd, MA, MEd, MSc, DMA

University of Central Lancashire

(formerly Lancashire Polytechnic)
Preston PR1 2HE; Tel (01772) 201201; Fax (01772) 892946
Rector Brian G. Booth, JP, BA(Econ), MTech, FSS
University Secretary Pam Ackroyd, BA, MA
9,000 full-time students; 6,000 part-time students

City University

Northampton Sq, London EC1V 0HB; Tel 0171-477 8000
Chancellor The Rt Hon The Lord Mayor of London
Pro-Chancellor Sir John Leahy, KCMG
Deputy Pro-Chancellor M.F. Stonefrost, CBE, DL
Vice-Chancellor and Principal Prof R.N. Franklin, ME, MA, DPhil, DSc, CBIM, FIEE, FEng, FInstP, FIMA
Academic Registrar A.H. Seville, MA, PhD
Schools Liaison Officer C.J. Morris, BA, MA
3,016 undergraduates; 2,727 postgraduates

Coventry University

(formerly Coventry Polytechnic)
Priory St, Coventry CV1 5FB; Tel (01203) 631313; Fax (01203) 838793
Vice-Chancellor Michael Goldstein, BSc, PhD, DSc, CChem, FRSC
Pro-Vice-Chancellor Prof Norman Bellamy, BEng, PhD, CEng, FIEE
Pro-Vice-Chancellor Prof Robert Pryce, BSc, PhD, CChem, FRSC
Pro-Vice-Chancellor Prof Norma Reid, BSc, MSc, DPhil, FSS
Manager, Careers Guidance Jeanne Booth
10,220 undergraduate students (including HND); 1,148 postgraduate students (including full-time, block release, part-time day and evening)

Cranfield University

Cranfield, Beds MK43 0AL; Tel (01234) 750111; Fax (01234) 750972
Chancellor The Lord Kings Norton, DSc, PhD, DIC, FEng
Vice-Chancellor Prof F.R. Hartley, MA, DSc, CChem, FRSC
Secretary/Registrar J.K. Pettifer, MA, CEng, FIEE
Cranfield is a principally post-graduate technological university. There is a total of 2,232 post-graduate students based at Cranfield, and at Silsoe, Bedfordshire MK45 4DT (Tel (01525) 863000 Fax (01525) 861527) and the Royal Military College of Science, Shrivenham, Swindon SN6 8LA (01793) 782551 Fax (01793) 783878). 893 undergraduates also study at Silsoe and Shrivenham

University of Derby

(formerly Derbyshire College of Higher Education)
Kedleston Rd, Derby DE22 1GB; Tel (01332) 47181
Chairman of Governors A. Woods, FCA, Cooper-Parry Prior Palmer, Chartered Accountants
Director R. Waterhouse, BA, MA

Faculty of Education, Humanities and Social Sciences

Dean R. Faithorn, BA, MPhil, PGCE

University of Durham

University Office, Old Shire Hall, Durham DH1 3HP; Tel 0191-374 2000; Fax 0191-374 3740
Chancellor Sir Peter Ustinov, CBE, DLitt, FRSA, FRSL
Vice-Chancellor and Warden E.A.V. Ebsworth, PhD, MA, ScD, FRSC, CChem, FRSE
Pro-Vice-Chancellor and Sub-Warden G.E. Rodmell, BA, PhD
Pro-Vice-Chancellor Prof P.D.B. Collins, BSc, PhD, CPhys, FInstP
Pro-Vice Chancellor M.C. Prestwich, MA, DPhil, FRHistS, FSA
Registrar and Secretary J.C.F. Hayward, MA, FIMgt
Director of Careers Advisory Service V.A. McIntyre, MA University Careers Advisory Service, 49 New Elvet, Durham DH1 3PF; Tel 0191-374 2300

Colleges in Durham

College of St Hild and St Bede
J.V. Armitage, BSc, PhD, FIMA, FRAS, *Principal*, Durham DH1 1SZ; Tel 0191-374 2000; Fax 0191-374 4740

Collingwood College
G.H. Blake, JP, MA, PhD, *Principal* South Rd, Durham DH1 3LT; Tel 0191-374 2000; Fax 0191-374 4595

Grey College
V. Watts, MA, FSA, *Master* South Rd, Durham DH1 3LG; Tel 0191-374 2000

Hatfield College
Professor J.P. Barber, JP, MA, PhD, *Master* North Bailey, Durham DH1 3RQ; Tel 0191-374 2000; Fax 0191-374 7472

St Aidan's College
R.J. Williams, JP, BA, MPhil, *Principal*, Durham DH1 3LJ; Tel 0191-374 2000; Fax 0191-374 4749

St Chad's College
E. Halladay, MA, *Principal* North Bailey, Durham DH1 3RH; Tel 0191-374 2000

St John's College
D.V. Day, BA, MEd, MTheol, *Principal* South Bailey, Durham DH1 3RJ; Tel 0191-374 2000; Fax 0191-374 3573

St Mary's College
Joan M. Kenworthy, BLitt, MA, *Principal* Elvet Hill Rd, Durham DH1 3LR; Tel 0191-374 2000

Trevelyan College
Deborah Lavin, MA, *Principal* Elvet Hill Rd, Durham DH1 3LN; Tel 0191-374 2000; Fax 0191-374 3789

University College
E.C. Salthouse, BSc, PhD, CEng, FIEE, FRSA, *Master* The Castle, Durham DH1 3RW; Tel 0191-374 2000; Fax 0191-374 7470

Ushaw College
The Rt Rev Mgr R. Atherton, OBE, *President*, Durham DH7 9RH; Tel 0191-373 1254

Van Mildert College
Judith Turner, BSc, MA, PhD, *Principal* South Rd, Durham DH1 3LH; Tel 0191-374 2000; Fax 0191-384 7764

St Cuthbert's Society
S.G.C. Stoker, BA, MEd, *Principal* 12 South Bailey, Durham DH1 3EE; Tel 0191-374 2000; Fax 0191-374 4753

The Graduate Society
M. Richardson, BSc, PhD, *Principal* 30 Old Elvet, Durham DH1 3HN; Tel 0191-374 2000

School of Education

Leazes Rd, Durham DH1 1TA; Tel 0191-374 2000
Professors of Education F.J. Coffield, MA, MEd; G.R. Grace, BA, MA, MEd, PhD; D.M. Galloway, MA, MSc, PhD

Department of Adult and Continuing Education

32 Old Elvet, Durham DH1 3JB; Tel 0191-374 2000
Director W. Williamson, BSc(Soc), MA, PhD

University of East Anglia

University Plain, Norwich, Norfolk NR4 7TJ; Tel (01603) 592068/592057
Chancellor The Rev Prof Owen Chadwick, OM, KBE, DD, FBA, HonLittD
Vice-Chancellor Prof D.C. Burke, BSc, PhD, HonLLD
Deputy Vice-Chancellor J.R. Tarrant, BSc, PhD
Pro-Vice-Chancellors R.A.Y. Jones, MA, PhD, MS, FRSA, CChem, FRSC; Prof J.G. Miller, LLM, PhD, LLB
Registrar and Secretary M.C.E. Paulson-Ellis, MA, FCA
4,317 undergraduates; 1,492 postgraduates (both figures include full and part-time students)

School of Education

Professors of Education D. Bridges, BA, PGCE, MA, PhD; G. Brown, MEd, PhD; J. Elliott, DipPhilEd, MPhil; B. Macdonald, MA, MEd, PGCE

University of East London

(formerly Polytechnic of East London)
Longbridge Rd, Dagenham, Essex RM8 2AS; Tel 0181-590 7722; Fax 0181-590 7799
Vice-Chancellor Prof F.W. Gould, MA
Pro Vice-Chancellor Prof J.A. McGinnety, BSc, PhD
11,200 students

Department of Education Studies

Longbridge Rd, Dagenham, Essex RM8 2AS; Tel 0181-590 7722

University of Essex

Wivenhoe Pk, Colchester CO4 3SQ; Tel (01206) 873333; Fax (01206) 873410
Chancellor Rt Hon Sir Patrick Nairne, GCB, MC, MA, LLD, DU
Vice-Chancellor Prof R.J. Johnston, MA, PhD
Registrar and Secretary A.F. Woodburn, BSc, DPA
Director of Continuing Education Dr J.G. Tillett, PhD, DSc, FRSC
4,200 undergraduates; 1,218 postgraduates

University of Exeter

Northcote Hse, The Queen's Dr, Exeter EX4 4QJ; Tel (01392) 263263; Fax (01392) 263108
Chancellor Sir Rex Richards, DSc, FRS, FRSC, HonDSc
Vice-Chancellor Sir Geoffrey Holland, KCB, MA, HonLLD
Registrar and Secretary I.H.C. Powell, MA
Full-time 7,714; Part-time 1,196, mainly postgrad

School of Education

Heavitree Rd, Exeter EX1 2LU; Tel (01392) 263263; Fax (01392) 263108
Professor of Education and Director Charles W. Desforges, BSc, PhD

Professor of Education S.N. Bennett, BEd, PhD
Professor of Education D.N. Burghes, BSc, PhD
Professor of Education Martin Hughes, BA, PhD
Professor of Education M.E. John, BA, PhD
Professor of Education Edward C. Wragg, BA, MEd, PhD, HonDUniv
Professor of Health and Exercise Sciences Neil Armstrong, BEd, MSc, PhD, CBiol, FIBiol

Department of Continuing and Adult Education

Cotley, Streatham Rise, Exeter EX4 4PE; Tel (01392) 74425
Head of Dept and Assistant Director (Cornwall) Richard M. Grady, BA, BMus, PhD
Professor of Adult Education and Director of Continuing Education R.T. Fieldhouse, BA, PhD

University of Greenwich

Wellington St, Woolwich, London SE18 6PF; Tel 0181-331 8000
Vice-Chancellor D.E. Fussey, MA, PhD, CEng, FIMechE, FInstE
Secretary J.M. Charles, MA
Dean of Faculty of Education C.M. Wykes, MA, AcDipEd
Avery Hill Campus
Bexley Rd, Eltham, London SE9 2PQ; Tel 0181-331 8444
Roehampton Campus
Manresa Hse, Holybourne Ave, London SW15 4JD; Tel 0181-331 8000
Dartford Campus
Oakfield La, Dartford, Kent DA1 2SZ; Tel 0181-331 8555
Medway Towns Campus
Grenville Bldg, Central Ave, Chatham, Maritime, Kent ME4 4TB; Tel 0181-331 8000
Woolwich Campus
Wellington St, Woolwich, London SE18 6PF; Tel 0181-331 8000

Faculty of Education

(Avery Hill Campus)

Faculty of Science, Faculty of Technology, Faculty of Business, Faculty of Health and Faculty of Humanities and Social Sciences

(Woolwich Campus)

Faculty of the Built Environment

(Dartford Campus)

University of Hertfordshire

College La, Hatfield, Herts AL10 9AB; Tel (01707) 284458; Fax (01707) 284738; Telex 262413
Director Prof N. Buxton, MA, PhD
Deputy Director T. Wilson, BSc, MA, FBIM
Assistant Director T. Hanahoe, PhD, CBiol, FIBiol
Secretary and Registrar P.G. Jeffreys, BA, MEd
12,589 full-time and sandwich students; 1,700 postgraduate students
Hertford Campus: Business School
Mangrove Rd, Hertford SG13 8QF; Tel (01707) 284000
School of Art & Design
Comet Way, Hatfield, Herts AL10 9TL; Dean C. Hunt ATD, FRSA

Humanities and Education

Watford Campus, Aldenham, Watford, Herts WD2 8AT; Tel (01707) 284000
Dean Prof G. Holderness, BA, BPhil, MA, MPhil, PhD

University of Huddersfield

(formerly Polytechnic of Huddersfield)
Queensgate, Huddersfield HD1 3DH; Tel (01484) 422288; Fax (01484) 516151
Vice-Chancellor and Principal Sir William Taylor, CBE, BScEcon, PhD
Academic Registrar M.E. Bond, MA
8,800 full-time students; 4,100 part-time students

School of Education

Dean of School E. Twigg, BA, MEd
Secretary to the University Council D.J. Lock
2,100 full and part-time students

University of Hull

Hull HU6 7RX; Tel (01482) 346311
Chancellor , PC, CMG, OBE, MA, LLD, DCL
Vice-Chancellor Prof D.N. Dilks, FRHists, FRSL
Registrar P.A. Bolton, BA, MA, PGCE
6,142 undergraduates; 1,109 postgraduates (full-time)

School of Education

University of Hull, Hull HU6 7RX; Tel (01482) 465989
Dean of School Prof V.A. McClelland, MA, PhD, FRSA

Department of Educational Studies

University of Hull, Hull HU6 7RX; Tel (01482) 365989
Professor of Educational Studies Prof V.A. McClelland, MA, PhD, FRSA

Department of Adult and Continuing Education

49 Salmon Gr, Hull HU6 7SZ; Tel (01482) 465415
Head of Department Prof G. Harries-Jenkins, LLB, MA, MPhil, PhD

University of Humberside

Admissions Processing Unit, Registry, Milner Hall, Cottingham Rd, Hull HU6 7RT; Tel (01482) 440550
Contact Admissions Officer

Keele University

Keele, Staffs ST5 5BG; Tel (01782) 621111; Fax (01782) 613847
Chancellor Sir Claus Moser, KCB, CBE
Vice-Chancellor Prof B.E.F. Fender, CMG, MA(Oxon), PhD
Registrar Dr D. Cohen, MA, PhD(Cantab), CChem, FRSC
3,943 undergraduates; 870 full-time postgraduates 1993/194

Department of Education

Head of Department Prof R.F. Kempa, IngChem(Essen), PhD(Lond), CChem, FRSC

Centre for Adult and Continuing Education

Tel (01782) 625116
Co-ordinator Dr J.W. Stanley

University of Kent at Canterbury

Canterbury, Kent CT2 7NZ; Tel (01227) 764000
Visitor The Lord Archbishop of Canterbury
Chancellor R. Horton, BSc, SM(Mass), HonLLD, HonDCL, CBIM, FIChemE
Pro-Chancellor The Rt Hon Lord Brabourne, CBE, DCL(Kent)
Vice-Chancellor Robin J. Sibson, MA, PhD(Cantab), CStat
Deputy Vice-Chancellor J. Craven, MA(Cantab)
Pro-Vice-Chancellor J.A. Connor, MA, PhD, CChem, FRSC
Pro-Vice Chancellor R. de Friend, BA, LLM
Registrar T.J. Mead, BSc, PhD
Director, Careers Advisory Service J.W. Greer, MA, DipPM, DipCG
4,695 undergraduates; 843 graduate students

Colleges of the University

Darwin College
Master R.D. Eager, BSc, MSc, CEng, MBCS

Eliot College
Chris Cherry, BA, MA, BPhil, *Master*

Keynes College
Master Alfred P. Smyth, MA(NV1), DPhil(Oxford), FRHistS, FSA, FRGS

Rutherford College
Master Frank Burnet, BSc, DPhil

School of Continuing Education

Executive Director D.J. Goldman, MA, PhD
School of Continuing Education offers courses for personal advancement or pleasure: literature, history, music, psychology, arts, pre-retirement seminars, Access courses

Kingston University

(formerly Kingston Polytechnic)
Penrhyn Rd, Kingston-upon-Thames, Surrey KT1 2EE; Tel 0181-547 2000
Chairman of Governors Professor R. Coleman, CB, BSc, PhD, FRSChem
Vice-Chancellor Dr R.C. Smith, CBE, BSc, PhD
Pro-Vice-Chancellor Dr R.J. Godfrey, BA, PhD, FRSA
University Secretary E.W. Lang, BSc(Eng), MICE
Academic Registrar Alice Hynes, BA, MA, ACIS
8,943 undergraduate students; 2,828 postgraduate students (heads)

Faculty of Education

Kingston Hill Centre, Kingston Hill, Kingston upon Thames, Surrey KT2 7LB; Tel 0181-547 2000
Dean of the Faculty Dr H.R. Cullis, BSc, MSc, MA, PhD, FRGS, FRSA
1,376 students (heads)

Lancaster University

Lancaster LA1 4YW; Tel (01524) 65201
Chancellor HRH Princess Alexandra The Hon Mrs Angus Ogilvy
Pro-Chancellor Sir Christopher Audland, KCMG
Vice-Chancellor Prof H.J. Hanham, MA, PhD
University Secretary S.A.C. Lamley, MA
7,000 undergraduates; 1,100 full-time graduate students

Lancaster Colleges

With date of foundation

Bowland
1964
Principal Dr I.J. Saunders, MSc, PhD, MInstPCPhys; Tel 65201

Cartmel
1966
Principal Dr C.G. Rogers, BA, PhD, DPhil, FInstP; Tel 65201

Charlotte Mason
Ambleside, Cumbria LA22 9BB; Tel (015394) 33066
Principal Prof J.H. Johnson, BA, MA, PhD, FRGS
Academic Services Officer K. Graves
Und; M and W
1,200 full-time students; resident, day and part-time

The County
1967
E.R.B. Gibson, BA, BPhil, Dr3rdCy, *Principal*; Tel 65201

Furness
1968
Principal J. Clements, MA; Tel 65201

Fylde
1969
Principal Dr A. Thomson, MA, DPhil; Tel 65201

The Graduate
1990
Principal C.C. Park, BSc, PhD; Tel 65201

Grizedale
1975
Principal J.H.E. Wood; Tel 65201

Lonsdale
1964
Principal Vacancy; Tel 65201

Pendle
1974
Dr M.W. Kirby, BA, PhD, *Principal*; Tel 65201

Centre for the Study of Education and Training

Director M. Saunders, BA, MA, PhD

Centre for the Study of Management Learning

Head Dr M. Easterby-Smith

Office for the Associated Institutions

Director of External Affairs S.A.C. Lamley, MA

Department of Educational Research

Head Prof R. Deem, BA, MPhil, PhD

Department of Teaching and Education Studies

Dean of Faculty of Education Prof J.M. MacKenzie, MA, PhD, FRHistS
Head of Department of Teaching and Education Studies C. Skelding, CertEd, BEd, MSc
Head of Centre for Continuing Education, Training and Development K. Joyce, CertEd, MAEd, MBA
Head of In-Service Education and Training Dr M.J. Postle, DipEd, BSc, PhD

University of Leeds

Leeds LS2 9JT; Tel (0113) 243 1751
Chancellor HRH The Duchess of Kent, GCVO, LLD
Pro-Chancellor Col A.C. Roberts, MBE, TD, JP, DL, MPhil, PhD, FIBiol, FCGI
Vice-Chancellor Prof A.G. Wilson, MA
Pro-Vice-Chancellor Prof S.B. Brown, BSc, PhD
Pro-Vice-Chancellor Prof A.J. Chapman, BSc, PhD, CPsychol, FBPsS
Pro-Vice-Chancellor Prof D. Holdcroft, MA
Pro-Vice-Chancellor Prof A.A. Watson, BSc, PhD, FRAS
Registrar E. Newcomb, BA, DipEd, FRSA
Director of Finance John R. Clements, BA, FCA
13,620 full-time undergraduates; 2,631 full-time postgraduates; 294 part-time undergraduates; 1,492 part-time postgraduates

Bretton Hall College

West Bretton, Wakefield, W Yorks WF4 4LG; Tel (01924) 830261; Fax (01924) 830521
Principal Prof G.H. Bell, MA, DipPhilEd, DipPrim Ed, FRSA
Finance Director D. Stone, ACA, MIMC, MIBM
Und; M and W
Faculties Education, Performing Arts; Art, Design and Humanities
1,800 students

Faculty of Education
Head D. Marjoram, NND, ATD, FRSA, FNSEAD

School of Education

Chairman of School and Professor of Primary Education E.W. Jenkins, JP, BSc, MEd, CChem, FRSC, FRSA
Professor of Primary Education R.J. Alexander, MA, PhD, MEd
Professor of Education (Science) Rosalind H. Driver, BSc, PhD
Professor of Computers in Education J.R. Hartley, BA, MA
Professor of Continuing Education J.S. Marriott, MA, MEd, PhD
Professor of Education P. Scott, BA
Professor of Special Needs in Education D.A. Sugden, MSc, PhD

University College, Scarborough: The North Riding College

Filey Rd, Scarborough YO11 3AZ; Tel (01723) 362392; Fax (01723) 370815
Principal Dr R. Withers, BA, PhD
Development Director and Secretary David G. Henderson, BTech, MBIM
Academic Dean George MacDonald Ross, MA
Head of Faculty (Professional Studies Section) Susan Billett, MEd
Faculties: Arts, Business Studies, Humanities, Professional Studies, Sciences
1175 Students

University College of Ripon and York St John

Lord Mayor's Walk, York YO3 7EX; Tel (01904) 656771; Fax (01904) 612512
Principal Prof G. McGregor, AB, MEd, DPhil, DHumLitt, Hon D Litt, Diploma College of Teachers of Blind
Vice Principal Dr J. Axon, BA(Hons), MA, PhD, DipEd
Director of Finance P. Hepburn, BSc(Hons)
Chairman of Governors The Archbishop of York Dr John Habgood
Head of Faculty (Humanities) Dr G. Stoakes, BA(Hons), PhD
Head of Faculty (Creative and Performing Arts) F. Coupar, DA, CertEd, MEd
Head of Faculty (Social Environmental and Life Science) Dr G. Lodge, BA(Hons), MA, DMS, PhD
Head of Faculty (Teaching, Professional and Management Studies) Ken Ridley, CertEd, DipEd, MA
Faculties: Humanites, Creative and Performing Arts, Social Environmental and Life Science, Teaching, Professional and Management Studies
2,628 students

Trinity and All Saints College

Brownberrie La, Horsforth, Leeds LS18 5HD; Tel (01532) 837100; Fax (01532) 837200
Principal Dr G.L. Turnbull, BA, PhD
Assistant Principal (Dean of Academic Affairs) D. Samuel, MA
Assistant Principal (Dean of Planning and Development) Dr M. Coughlan, BA, MPhil, PhD
Assistant Principal (Dean of Resources) J.M. Redding, BA, MBIM
Assistant Principal (Registrar) M.C. Owen, BA
Finance Officer J. Bancroft, IPFA
Head of Faculty (Education) D. Shemilt, BEd
Faculties: Education
2,070 students (full-time equivalent)

Leeds Metropolitan University

(formerly Leeds Polytechnic)
Calverley St, Leeds LS1 3HE; Tel (0113) 283 2600; Fax (0113) 283 3115
Principal and Chief Executive L. Wagner, MA
Deputy Principal (Management Services) G.D. Hitchins, BSc, MSc, PhD
Deputy Principal (Planning) F.J. Griffiths, BSc, MSc
10,330 full-time and sandwich students; 9,000 part-time students

Faculty of Cultural and Education Studies

Beckett Pk, Leeds LS6 3QS; Tel (0113) 283 2600
Dean of Faculty of Cultural and Education Studies B. Duffield, BA
Programme Manager of Teacher Education Wendy Nuttall, BA

The University of Leicester

University Rd, Leicester LE1 7RH; Tel (0116) 252 2522; Fax (0116) 252 2200
Chancellor The Lord Porter, OM, FRS, BSc, MA, PhD, ScD, FRCS
Vice-Chancellor Dr K.J.R. Edwards, BSc, MA, PhD
Registrar and Secretary K.J. Julian, MA
6,016 undergraduates; 1,657 full-time and 862 part-time postgraduates

School of Education

Leicester University, 21 University Rd, Leicester LE1 7RF; Tel (0116) 255 4455
Director Prof M. Mathieson, MA
Secretary C.M. Dunkley, MA

Department of Adult Education,

Leicester University, University Rd, Leicester LE1 7RH; Tel (0116) 252 2468; Fax (0116) 252 2200
Head Prof W. Forster, OBE, MA

University of Liverpool

Senate Hse, Abercomby Sq, PO Box 147, Liverpool L69 3BX; Tel 0151-794 2000; Fax 0151-708 6502
Chancellor The Rt Hon the Viscount Leverhulme, TD, JP, BA, LLD, FRCS, ARCVS
Vice-Chancellor Prof P.N. Love, CBE, MA, LLB
Registrar M.D. Carr, MA
Academic Secretary K.H. Jones, MA
7,584 undergraduates; 1,143 postgraduates

Board of College Studies

19/23 Abercromby Sq, Liverpool L69 3BX; Tel 0151-794 2562

Faculty of Education and Extension Studies

1 Abercromby Sq, Liverpool L69 3BX; Tel 0151-794 2571
Sydney Jones Professor of Education D.F. Hamilton, BSc

Centre for Continuing Education

19 Abercromby Sq, Liverpool L69 3BX; Tel 0151-794 2528
Director of Continuing Education R. Derricott, BA, MEd, DipL, Psychol

Liverpool John Moores University

(formerly Liverpool Polytechnic)
Rodney Hse, 70 Mount Pleasant, Liverpool L3 5UX; Tel 0151-231 3584; Fax 0151-707 0937
Vice-Chancellor Prof Peter Toyne, DL, BA, CBIM, FRSA
Bursar Allan Bickerstaffe
Provost Prof Jennifer Latto, MA, PGCE, DipEdPsy, CPsychol
Development Director Stuart Melhuish, BA
Dean Prof Frank Sanderson, BEd, DCC, MA, PhD
Executive Director Alison M. Wild
9,681 full-time 2,494 sandwich course students; 6,040 part-time; postgraduate 1,167
The Liverpool John Moores University has both a national and international reputation in many areas of research. Last year the University received almost £4 million in research funding

University of London

Senate Hse, Malet St, London WC1E 7HU; Tel 0171-636 8000; Fax 0171-636 5875
Chancellor HRH The Princess Royal

Vice-Chancellor Prof Andrew Rutherford, CBE, BLitt, MA, DLitt
Chairman of the Council The Rt Hon Lord Woolf of Barnes, BS, MA, PhD
Chairman of Convocation Prof Sir William Taylor, CBE, BSc(Econ), PhD
Principal P. Holwell, BSc(Econ), FCA
Director of Administration J. Davidson, BA
Academic Registrar G.F. Roberts, BA
Head of Examinations and External Students J. McConnell, MA
Chief Executive to Examination Assessment Council A. Smith, MA
Secretary to the University Entrance Requirements Committee N. Mohammed, MA

External Programme

University of London degrees and diplomas are available to External Students, who study privately in their own home. There are eight main subject areas: Law; Economics and Management; Humanities; Languages; Divinity; Education; Agriculture; Health and Medicine. Further information from the Director for External Students, University of London, Rm 201, Senate Hse, Malet St, WC1E 7HU; Tel 071-636 8000

Schools, Colleges and Institutes of the University

Birkbeck College
Malet St WC1E 7HX; Tel 0171-580 6622

British Institute in Paris
London
Senate Hse, Malet St WC1E 7HU; Tel 0171-636 8000
Paris
11 rue de Constantine, 75340 Paris Cedex 07, France; Tel (1) 4555 7199

British Postgraduate Medical Federation (BPMF)
Central Office, 33 Millman St WC1N 3EJ; Tel 0171-831 6222
BPMF: Institute of Cancer Research
17A Onslow Gdns SW7 3AL; Tel 0171-352 8133
BPMF: Institute of Child Health
30 Guildford St WC1N 1EH; Tel 0171-242 9789
BPMF: Institute of Dental Surgery
Eastman Dental Hospital, Gray's Inn Rd WC1X 8LD; Tel 0171-837 3646
BPMF: National Heart & Lung Institute
Dovehouse St SW3 6LY; Tel 0171-352 8121
BPMF: Institute of Neurology
The National Hospital, Queen Sq WC1N 3BG; Tel 0171-837 3611
BPMF: Institute of Ophthalmology
11–14 Bath St EC1V 9EL; Tel 0171-608 6800
BPMF: Institute of Psychiatry
De Crespigny Pk, Denmark Hill SE5 8AF; Tel 0171-703 5411

Centre for Defence Studies
King's College London, Strand WC2R 2LS; Tel 0171-836 5454

Centre for Metropolitan History
34 Tavistock Sq WC1H 9EZ; Tel 0171-636 0272

Charing Cross and Westminster Medical School
The Reynolds Bldg, St Dunstan's Rd W6 8RP; Tel 0181-846 7231

Courtauld Institute of Art
North Block, Somerset Hse, Strand WC2R 0RN; Tel 0171-872 0220

Goldsmiths University of London
Lewisham Way, New Cross SE14 6NW; Tel 0181-692 7171

Heythrop College
Kensington Sq W8 5HR; Tel 0171-795 6600

Imperial College of Science, Technology and Medicine
South Kensington SW7 2AZ; Tel 0171-589 5111
St Mary's Hospital Medical School
Norfolk Pl, Paddington W2 1PG; Tel 0171-723 1252

Institute of Advanced Legal Studies
Charles Clore Hse, 17 Russell Sq WC1B 5DR; Tel 0171-637 1731

Institute of Classical Studies
31–34 Gordon Sq WC1H 0PY; Tel 0171-387 7696/7

Institute of Commonwealth Studies
28 Russell Sq WC1B 5DS; Tel 0171-580 5876

Institute of Education
20 Bedford Way WC1H 0AL; Tel 0171-580 1122

Institute of Germanic Studies
29 Russell Sq WC1B 5DP; Tel 0171-580 2711

Institute of Historical Research
Senate Hse, Malet St WC1E 7HU; Tel 0171-636 0272

Institute of United States Studies
Senate Hse, Malet St WC1E 7HU; Tel 0171-580 7372

Institute of Latin American Studies
31 Tavistock Sq WC1H 0HA; Tel 0171-387 5671

Institute of Romance Studies
Senate Hse, Malet St WC1E 7HU; Tel 0171-636 8000

Institute of Zoology
Regent's Pk NW1 4RY; Tel 0171-722 3333

Jews' College
44A Albert Rd NW4 2SJ; Tel 0181-203 6427

King's College London
Strand WC2R 2LS; Tel 0171-836 5454
King's College School of Medicine and Dentistry
Bessemer Rd SE5 9PJ; Tel 0171-274 6222

London Business School
Sussex Pl, Regent's Pk NW1 4SA; Tel 0171-262 5050

The London Hospital Medical College
Turner St E1 2AD; Tel 0171-377 7000

London School of Economics and Political Science
Houghton St WC2A 2AE; Tel 0171-405 7686

London School of Hygiene and Tropical Medicine
Keppel St WC1E 7HT; Tel 0171-636 8636

Queen Mary and Westfield College
Mile End Rd E1 4NS; Tel 0171-975 5555

Royal Academy of Music
Marylebone Rd NW1 5HT; Tel 0171-935 5461

Royal College of Music
Prince Consort Rd SW7 2BS; Tel 0171-589 3643

Royal Free Hospital School of Medicine
Rowland Hill St NW3 2PF; Tel 071-794 0500

Royal Holloway, University of London
Egham Hill, Egham, Surrey TW20 0EX; Tel (01784) 434455

Royal Postgraduate Medical School
Hammersmith Hospital, Du Cane Rd W12 0NN; Tel 0181-743 2030

Royal Veterinary College
Royal College St NW1 0TU; Tel 0171-387 2898

St Bartholomew's Hospital Medical College
West Smithfield EC1A 7BE; Tel 0171-982 6000

St George's Hospital Medical School
Cranmer Terr, Tooting SW17 0RE; Tel 0181-672 9944

School of Oriental and African Studies
Thornhaugh St, Russell Sq WC1H 0XG; Tel 0171-637 2388

School of Pharmacy
29–39 Brunswick Sq WC1N 1AX; Tel 0171-837 7651

School of Slavonic and East European Studies
Senate Hse, Malet St WC1E 7HU; Tel 0171-636 4934

Trinity College of Music
Mandeville Pl W1M 6AQ; Tel 0171-935 5773

United Medical and Dental Schools of Guy's and St Thomas's Hospitals
Lambeth Palace Rd SE1 7EH; Tel 0171-928 9292

University College London
Gower St WC1E 6BT; Tel 0171-387 7050

University College London School of Medicine
Rayne Institute, University St WC1E 6JJ; Tel 0171-387 9300

Warburg Institute
Woburn Sq WC1H 0AB; Tel 0171-580 9663

Wye College
Wye, Ashford, Kent TN25 5AH; Tel (01233) 812401

London Guildhall University

133 Whitechapel High St, London E1 7QA; Tel 0171-320 1000; Fax 0171-320 3424
Chairman of Governors The Earl of Limerick
Provost Prof Roderick Floud, MA, DPhil, FRHistS
Deputy Provost Nigel Brown, MA
Academic Secretary Vacancy
Registrar Vacancy
Chief Librarian Maureen Castens, BSc, MA, DMS, ALA
6,004 full-time and sandwich students; 3,294 undergraduate part-time students (including short courses)

Loughborough University of Technology

Loughborough, Leics LE11 3TU; Tel (01509) 263171; Fax (01509) 219337
Chancellor Sir Denis Rooke, CBE, BSc(Eng), DSc(Hon), DTech(Hon), DEng(Hon), DUniv(Hon), LLD(Hon), FRS, FEng
Vice-Chancellor Prof D.J. Wallace, BSc, PhD, FRS, FRSE, FInstP
Registrar D.E. Fletcher, BA, PhD
Bursar H.M. Pearson, BA(Econ), LLB, ACIS
Careers Officer W.E. Llewellyn, BSc, MEd
7,220 undergraduates; 1,060 postgraduates (full-time)

University of Luton

Park Sq, Luton LU1 3JU; Tel (01582) 34111
Faculties Applied Sciences; Business; Design & Technology; Humanities; Health Care and Social Studies; Management
Putteridge Bury Campus, Hitchin Rd, Luton, Beds LU2 8LE; Tel (01582) 34111

The University of Manchester

Oxford Rd, Manchester M13 9PL; Tel 0161-275 2000
Chancellor Vacancy
Vice-Chancellor Prof M. Harris, MA, PhD
Deputy Vice-Chancellor Prof S.A. Moore, MA(Econ), MBCS
Registrar and Secretary Eddi Newcombe, BA, DipEd
15,124* undergraduates; 4,288* postgraduates
*Full-time, including Faculty of Business Administration

Centre for the Development of Continuing Education

Director J.M. Hostler, MA, PhD, MEd

Hester Adrian Research Centre

(For the study of learning processes in the mentally handicapped)
Director Prof C.C. Kiernan, BA, PhD

Institute of Science and Technology (UMIST)

PO Box 88, Sackville St, Manchester M60 1QD; Tel 0161-236 3311
Principal Prof H.C.A. Hankins, BSc, PhD, CEng, FIEE
Secretary and Registrar P.C.C. Stephenson, MA
Bursar D.G. Keenleside, ICMA
Director of Communications Timothy Yates, MA
3,250 undergraduates; 1,394 postgraduates (full-time)

North Cheshire College

A College of the University of Manchester
Padgate Campus, Fearnhead, Warrington, Cheshire WA2 0DB; Tel (01925) 814343; Fax (01925) 816077
Academic Registrar Wynn Whitehead

Office of Part-time Education

Director K.B. Drake, MA, BSc(Econ)

School of Education

(Incorporating: Centres for Adult and Higher Education, Audiology and education of the deaf; Curriculum policy; Educational guidance and special needs; English language studies in education; Ethnic studies in education; Formative assessment studies; In-service education of teachers; Physical education; Primary education; Science and technology education; Social ethics and policy; Youth studies)
Director and Professor of Special Education P.J. Mittler, MA, MEd, PhD
Professor of Education A.G. Smithers, MSc, PhD
Professor of Education G.K. Varma, BA, MA, DipEd, PhD
Professor of Education J.D. Turner, MA, LLD, PhD, MEd
Professor of Education J.M. Bamford, BA, PhD
Professor of Education P.D. Pumfrey, MEd, MSc

The Manchester Metropolitan University

(formerly Manchester Polytechnic)
All Saints, Manchester M15 6BH; Tel 0161-247 2000; Fax 0161-247 6390
Vice-Chancellor Sir K. Green, MA, DLitt
Deputy Vice-Chancellor Mrs A.V. Burslem, OBE, JP, BA, FRSA
Financial Director G.P. Judge, FCMA
Personnel Director I.W. Hallam, MA
Secretary R.O. Yeo, BA
Pro-Vice-Chancellor (Art and Design) Prof R. Wilson, Dip AD, Dip LFS
Pro-Vice-Chancellor (Community Studies Law and Education) D.W. Pyle, BA, BSc, MSc, DipEd, AFBPsS, CPsychol
Pro-Vice-Chancellor (Hollings) G. Wilson, BEng, PhD, CEng, MIChemE, MMCIMA
Pro-Vice-Chancellor (Humanities and Social Science) S. Kirby, BA, MSc, PhD
Pro-Vice-Chancellor (Management and Business) Prof A.R. Lock, BA, MSc(Econ), PhD, MBLS, FSS, FRSA
Pro-Vice-Chancellor (Science and Engineering) Prof G.L. Slater, MSc, MA, DPhil, CMath, FIMA, FRSA
Pro-Vice-Chancellor (Crewe and Alsager) J.R. Needham, MEd
19,553 (approx) full-time and sandwich students; 9,700 part-time students (including education students)

Faculty of Community Studies Law and Education

799 Wilmslow Rd, Manchester M20 8RR; Tel 0161-247 2020
Assistant Director and Dean of Faculty D. Pyle, BA, MSc, DipEd, ABPsS, CPsychol
Head of School of Education I.S. Kane, BA, CertEd, FRSA

Middlesex University

(formerly Middlesex Polytechnic)
Trent Pk, Bramley Rd, London N14 4XS; Tel 0181-362 5000; Fax 0181-362 6878; Telex 8954762
Vice Chancellor Prof David Melville, BSc, PhD, CPhys, FInstP, FRSA Middlesex University, Trent Pk, Bramley Rd, London N14 4XS; Fax 0181-441 4672
Deputy Vice-Chancellor (Academic) Professor K.H. Goulding, BSc, PhD, FIBiol, CBiol
Deputy Vice-Chancellor (Resources) R. Kirby-Harris, BSc, CPhys, MIP, AFIMA, MBIM
Academic Registrar Gareth Wynford Jones, BA, MA, PGCE
10,516 undergraduates; 1,405 postgraduates
Tottenham, White Hart La, London N17 8HR; Fax 0181-362 6878
Bounds Green Rd, London N11 2NQ; Fax 0181-361 1726
The Burroughs, London NW4 4BT; Fax 0181-202 1539
Cat Hill, Barnet, Herts EN4 8HT; Fax 0181-449 9541
Queensway, Enfield EN3 4SF; Fax 0181-805 0702
Quicksilver Pl, Western Rd, London N22 6XH; Fax 0181-888 6741
Trent Pk, Bramley Rd, London N14 4XS; Fax 0181-441 4672

Education Department

Trent Pk, Bramley Rd, London N14 4XS; Tel 0181-362 5000; Fax 0181-441 4672
Director of Studies, Trent Park Campus Roger Harris

De Montfort University

The Gateway, Leicester LE1 9BH; Tel (0116) 255 1551; Fax (0116) 255 0307
37 Lonsdowne Rd, Bedford MK40 2BZ; Tel (01234) 351966
Kent, Hammerwood Gate, Milton Keynes MK7 4HP; Tel (01908) 695511; Fax (01908) 695581
9 Caythorpe Court, Caythorpe, Grantham NG32 2EP; Tel (01400) 72521; Fax (01400) 72722
Chairman of Governors J.G. White, CBE, BA, PhD, CIMgt, FPRI, FIM
Chief Executive and Vice-Chancellor Prof Kenneth Barker, CBE, MA, BMus, GRSM, FTCL, FLCM, ARCM, FRSA, CIMgt
Pro Vice-Chancellor Prof M.A. Brown, BSc, PhD, MIEE, CEng, MInstP, CPhys, FIMgt
Pro-Vice Chancellor Prof Chiddick, MSc, FRICS, MRTPI, FRSA
Pro Vice-Chancellor Prof B.H. Swanick, BEng, PhD, FIEE, CEng, MInstMC
Pro Vice-Chancellor Prof M. Scott, BA, MA, PGCE, FRSA
Academic Registrar E. Critchlow, BA, MA
Student Facilities Residential; Lodgings assistance; Industrial placement; Counselling; Careers guidance; Health service
14,858 full-time and sandwich course students; 3,639 part-time students; 1,298 postgraduate students

Centre for Postgraduate Teacher Education

Head of Centre Vacancy
55 full-time students; 73 part-time students

University of Newcastle upon Tyne

University of Newcastle, 6 Kensington Terr, Newcastle upon Tyne NE1 7RU; Tel 0191-222 6000
Chancellor The Viscount Ridley, TD
Vice-Chancellor J.R.G. Wright, MA
Pro-Vice-Chancellor Prof B. Farmer, MA, DA, RIBA, FRSA
Pro-Vice-Chancellor A.R. Archibald, BSc, PhD
Pro-Vice-Chancellor Prof A. Hamnett, MA, DPhil, CChem, MRSC
Registrar D.E.T. Nicholson, MA
Bursar H.B. Farnhill, BA, FCA
9,336 undergraduates; 2,534 postgraduates

School of Education

Joseph Cowen Hse, St Thomas' St, Newcastle Upon Tyne NE1 7RU; Tel 0191-222 6000
Head of School of Education Dr M.J. Atkins, BA, PhD
Professor of Education A.D. Edwards, MA, MPhil, PhD
Professor of Education C.T. Fitz-Gibbon, BSc, MA, PhD
Professor of Education D. Reynolds, BA

Centre for Continuing Education

King George VI Bldg, University of Newcastle, Newcastle upon Tyne NE1 7RU; Tel 0191-222 6000
Director I.H. Forster, OBE, BA, DipEd, FIPM, FITD, FBIM
Elderly people are defined as mature students

University of North London

(formerly Polytechnic of North London)
166–220 Holloway Rd, London N7 8DB; Tel 0171-607 2789
Vice-Chancellor Brian Roper
Course Enquiries Office Tel 0171-753 5066/7
7,889 full-time and sandwich students; 3,114 part-time students

University of Northumbria at Newcastle

(formerly Newcastle Polytechnic)
Ellison Bldg, Ellison Pl, Newcastle upon Tyne NE1 8ST; Tel 0191-232 6002
Chairman of the Board of Governors W.R. Atkinson, CB, BA, FBCS
Vice-Chancellor Prof L. Barden, CBE, DSc
Pro-Vice-Chancellor and Deputy Chief Executive Professor J. Rear, MA Barrister at Law
Pro-Vice-Chancellor (Resources) G.C. Campbell, CA, DipMan, DipHSM, FIPM
Pro-Vice-Chancellor (Development) Professor A.R.D. Dickson, BSc(Hon), PhD
Secretary and Registrar R.A. Bott, BSc(Econ), MSc, DMA, FCIS
10,896 undergraduates; 672 postgraduates (full-time); 4,427 undergraduates; 1,723 postgraduate (part-time)

Department of Education Studies

Coach La Campus, Coach La, Newcastle upon Tyne NE7 7XA; Tel 0191-232 6002
Head of Department M. Cornish, BE(Hons), MA, PGCE
Primary; secondary; part day/part residential
620 teacher trainees (full-time) including 35 technology, 35 science, 20 mathematics, 20 CDT, 30 modern languages plus 500 primary age range specialists
Correspondence should be addressed to the Head of the Department of Education Studies

University of Nottingham

University Pk, Nottingham NG7 2RD; Tel (0115) 951 5151
Chancellor Sir Ron Dearing, CB, LLD
Vice-Chancellor Prof Sir Colin M. Campbell, LLB
Registrar D.J. Allen, BA, MEd
Bursar J.H. Cunningham, BA
Head of Careers Advisory Service M.E. Thorne, MA, LRAM
9,354 undergraduates; 1,674 postgraduates (full-time)

Department of Adult Education

14–22 Shakespeare St, Nottingham NG1 4FJ; Tel (0115) 948 3838
Director Dr I.D. Sutton, BSc, PhD

School of Education

Chair Prof C.W. Day, MA, DPhil
Secretary B.A. Rothera, BA

The Nottingham Trent University

Burton St, Nottingham NG1 4BU; Tel (0115) 941 8418; Fax (0115) 948 4266
Vice-Chancellor Prof R. Cowell, BA, PhD
14,689 full-time students; 4,122 part-time students

Faculty of Education

Dean of Faculty J. Lesquereux, BA, DipEd Studies, MEd
1,411 full-time students; 172 part-time students

The Open University

Walton Hall, Milton Keynes MK7 6AA; Tel (01908) 274066
Chancellor The Rt Hon Betty Boothroyd
Pro-Chancellor Sir Kenneth Berrill, GBE, KCB, MA, BSc(Econ), HonLLD, HonDSc, HonDTech, HonDUniv
Vice-Chancellor Sir J.S. Daniel, MA, DesSc, HonDLitt, HonDesSc
Secretary D.J. Clinch, BA, MBA
Pro-Vice-Chancellors:
Presentation and Student Support R. Lewis, BSc, MSc, ACAFC
Programme Development Dr A.R. Floyd, MA, PGCE, PhD
Resources Prof R.J. Housden, MA, PhD, FIMA, FBCS
Strategy G. Peters, BSc, MSc
University Relations and Research Prof J.M. Greene, MA, BA, PhD
Deans and Directors of Studies:
Dean (Arts Faculty) Prof S. Brown, MA, PhD
Dean (School of Education) R.D.T. Glaister, MA, MEd, PhD
Dean (School of Management) D. Asch, MSc(Bradford), FCA
Dean (Mathematics Faculty) P.G. Thomas, BSc, MSc, PhD
Dean (Social Science Faculty) A.D. Cochrane, BA(Oxford), PhD(Oxon)
Dean (Science) A.R. Bassingdale, MSc, DPhil(Sussex)
Dean (Technology Faculty) K. Williams, MA, PhD
Director (Regional Academic Services) D. Sewart, BA, PhD
Director (Institute of Educational Technology) C. Lawless, MA, PhD
Director (Institute of Health, Welfare and Community Education) Prof M. Johnson, BA, DSAS
Admissions information is available in the following guides: 'Studying with the Open University'; 'Guide to the BA and BSc degrees; 'Research Degree Prospectus'. All these guides can be obtained from the Central Enquiry Service (address below)
General enquiries should be addressed to Central Enquiry Service, PO Box 200, Milton Keynes, MK7 6YZ; Tel (0908) 653231 (answering service out of normal office hours)

Regional Directors

London
P.W. Syme, MA Parsifal College, 527 Finchley Rd, Hampstead, London NW3 7BG; Tel 0171-794 0575

South
S. Watts, BSc Foxcombe Hall, Boars Hill, Oxford OX1 5HR; Tel (01865) 327000

South East
G.W.S.V. Rumble, BA, MA(Kent)

South West
S. Clayton, BA, MA 4 Portwall La, Bristol B51 6NB; Tel (0117) 929 9641

West Midlands
Dr G.F. Hancock, BSc, MSc, PhD 66–68 High St, Harborne, Birmingham B17 9NB; Tel 0121-426 1661

East Midlands
G.A. Lammie, MA The Octagon, 143 Derby Rd, Nottingham NG7 1PH; Tel (0115) 947 3072

East Anglia
A.R. Mills, BSc, MSc, DipAdEd, MBiol Cintra Hse, 12 Hills Rd, Cambridge CB2 1PF; Tel (01223) 64721

Yorkshire
P.H.K. Smith, DPhil, DipArch, RegArch 2 Trevelyan Sq, Boars La, Leeds LS1 6ED; Tel (0113) 244 4431

North West
L.A. Goldstone, MA Chorlton Hse, 70 Manchester Rd, Chorlton cum Hardy, Manchester M21 9UN; Tel 0161-861 9823

North
Dr M. Susan Hurley, BSc, PhD Eldon Hse, Regent Centre, Gosforth, Newcastle upon Tyne NE3 3PW; Tel 0191-284 1611

Wales
Dr J.N. McGrath, BSc, MSc, PhD, CEng, FIMerE, FIM 24 Cathedral Rd, Cardiff CF1 9SA; Tel (01222) 397911

Scotland
Dr J. Cowan, MBE, BSc, MSc, PhD, DEng, FIStructE, FEIS 60 Melville St, Edinburgh EH3 7HF; Tel 0131-226 3851

Northern Ireland
Dr R. Hamilton, BSc, PhD 40 University Rd, Belfast BT7 1SU; Tel (01232) 245025

University of Oxford

Chancellor The Rt Hon Lord Jenkins of Hillhead, OM, PC, DCL
Vice-Chancellor Dr Peter North, QC, CBE, DCL, FBA
Registrar A.J. Dorey, MA, DPhil
Secretary of the Chest I.G. Thompson, MA
Secretary of Faculties A.P. Weale, MA
Oxford Delegacy of Local Examinations Secretary Vacancy
Oxford and Cambridge Schools' Examinations Board Elsfield Way, Oxford OX2 8EP
Secretary J.G. Lloyd, MA; Tel (0865) 54421
10,396 undergraduates; 4,172 postgraduates in residence

Oxford Colleges

With date of foundation
All colleges admit both men and women unless otherwise indicated

All Souls
1438
Warden Sir Patrick Neill, QC, BCL, MA, HonDCL; Tel (01865) 279379 (Fellows only)

Balliol
1263–8
Master C.L. Lucas, MA, DPhil, FRHists; Tel (01865) 277777

Brasenose
1509
Principal The Rt Hon Lord Windlesham, PC, CVO, MA; Tel (01865) 277830

Christ Church
1546
Dean The Very Rev J.H. Drury, MA; Tel (01865) 276150

Corpus Christi
1517
President Sir Keith Thomas, MA, FBA; Tel (01865) 276700

Exeter
1314
Rector Prof Marilyn S. Butler, MA, DPHil; Tel (01865) 279600

Hertford
1740
Principal Sir Christopher Zeeman, MA, DPhil, FRS; Tel (01865) 279400

Jesus
1571
Principal P.M. North, CBE, MA, DCL, FBA; Tel (01865) 279700

Keble
1870
Warden Averil M. Cameron, MA, FBA, FSA; Tel (01865) 272727

Lady Margaret Hall
1878
Principal D.M. Stewart, MA; Tel (01865) 274300

Lincoln
1427
Rector E.R. Anderson, MA, MLitt, FRSE; Tel (01865) 279800

Magdalen
1458
President A.D. Smith, CBE, MA; Tel (01865) 276000

Merton
1264
Jessica M. Rawson, FBE, MA, DLitt, CBA; Tel (01865) 276310

New
Warden H. McGregor, QC, MA, DCL; Tel (01865) 279555

Oriel
1326
Provost The Rev E.W. Nicholson, MA, DD, FBA; Tel (01865) 276555

Pembroke
1624
Master R.B. Stevens, MA, DCL; Tel (01865) 276444

Queen's
1340
Provost G. Marshall, MA, FBA; Tel (01865) 279120

St Anne's
1952
Principal R.L. Deech, MA; Tel (01865) 274800

St Catherine's
1963
Master The Lord Plant of Highfield, MA

St Edmund Hall
c. 1278
Principal J.C.B. Gosling, BPhil, MA; Tel (01865) 279000

St Hilda's
1893
Principal E.M. Llewellyn-Smith, CB, MA; Tel (01865) 276884 (W)

St Hugh's
1886
Principal D.A. Wood, QC, BCL, MA; Tel (01865) 274900

St John's
1555
President W. Hayes, MA, DPhil; Tel (01865) 277300

St Peter's
1929
Master J.P. Barron, MA, DPhil, FSA, FRC; Tel (01865) 278900

Somerville
1879
Principal C.E. Hughes, CMG, MA; Tel (01865) 270600

Trinity
1554
President Sir John Burgh, KCMG, CB, MA; Tel (01865) 279900

University
1249
Master Prof W.J. Albery, MA, DPhil, FRS; Tel (01865) 276602

Wadham
1612
Warden Dr J. Flemming, MA, FBA; Tel (01865) 277900

Worcester
1714
Provost R.G. Smethurst, MA; Tel (01865) 278300

Postgraduate Colleges

Green
1979
Warden Sir Crispin Tickell, GCMG, KCVO, MA; Tel (01865) 274770

Kellogg
1994
Director G.P. Thomas, MA

Linacre
1962
Principal Sir Bryan Cartledge, KCMG, MA; Tel (01865) 271650

Nuffield
1937
Warden A.B. Atkinson, MA, FBA; Tel (01865) 278500

St Antony's
1950
Warden Rt Hon Lord Dahrendorf, KBE, MA, FBA,; Tel (01865) 59651

St Cross
1965
Warden R.C. Repp, MA, DPhil; Tel (01865) 278490

Wolfson
1965
President Sir David Smith, MA, DPhil, FRSQA, FRSE; Tel (01865) 274100

Permanent Private Halls

Blackfriars
1921
Regent The Rev P. Parvis, DPhil; Tel (01865) 278400

Campion Hall
1896
Master The Rev A.J. Munitz, MA; Tel (01865) 286100

Greyfriars
1910
Warden The Rev T. Weinandy, MA; Tel (01865) 243694

Manchester
1889
Principal Rev R. Waller, MA; Tel (01865) 271006

Mansfield
1886
Principal D.J. Trevelyan, CB, MA, FIPM; Tel (01865) 270999

Regent's Pk
1810
Principal The Rev P.S. Fiddes, MA, DPhil; Tel (01865) 59887

St Benet's Hall
1897
Master The Rev H. Wansbrough, OSB, MA, STL, LSS; Tel (01865) 515006

Department of Educational Studies

15 Norham Gdns, Oxford; Tel (01865) 274024
Director Prof R.A. Pring, MA, PhD

Oxford Brookes University

(formerly Oxford Polytechnic)
Gipsy La, Headington, Oxford OX3 0BP; Tel (01865) 741111; Fax (01865) 483073
Chairman of Governors Peter Bagnall
Vice-Chancellor C. Booth, MA, PhD
Deputy Vice-Chancellor (Academic Affairs) P. Fidler, MBE, MSc, DiPTP, DipSOC, MRTPI, FRSA
Deputy Vice-Chancellor (Corporate Services) B. Summers, BSc
Deputy Vice-Chancellor (Finance and Marketing) J. Bradshaw, IPFA
Librarian H. Workman, BSc, MA, PhD, ALA, MIInfSc
6,632 full-time students and sandwich students; 1,530 part-time students

School of Education

Head Prof J. Welton, BA, PhD

University of Plymouth

Drake Circus, Plymouth, Devon PL4 8AA; Tel (01752) 233987; Fax (01752) 233984
Vice-Chancellor Professor J. Bull, BSc(Econ), FCCA
Deputy Vice-Chancellor (Secretariat) Dr R.M. Thorpe
10,493 full-time and sandwich course students; 1,045 part-time and short course students

University of Portsmouth

(formerly Portsmouth Polytechnic)
1 Guildhall Wlk, Portsmouth PO1 2RY; Tel (01705) 842726; Fax (01705) 842733
Chancellor Lord Palumbo
Vice-Chancellor N. Merritt
Pro-Vice-Chancellor M. McVicar, MA, PhD
Pro-Vice-Chancellor C.T. Monk, BSc, MBA
Pro-Vice-Chancellor M. Bateman, BA, PhD
Dean of Business School Prof T.M. Podolski, BSc(Econ), MCom, PhD
Dean of Faculty of Engineering (Acting) Prof B. Lee, BSc, PhD
Dean of Faculty of Environmental Studies (Acting) L. Shurmer-Smith, BA
Dean of Faculty of Humanities and Social Sciences (Acting) M. Mitchell, BA, MSc
Dean of Faculty of Science Prof T. Crabb, BSc, PhD, DSc, FRSC
Dean of Fadulty of Technology Prof J. Boardman, PhD
11,100 undergraduate students; 300 postgraduate students and research assistants

University of Reading

Whiteknights, Reading RG6 2AH; Tel (01734) 875123; Fax (01734) 352080
Chancellor The Rt Hon The Lord Carrington, KG, GCMG, CH, MC, PC
Vice-Chancellor Prof R. Williams, MA, MA(Econ)
Registrar D.C.R. Frampton, MA
Bursar R.H.C. Ascott, MA, FBIM
7,416 undergraduates; 3,830 postgraduates

Department of Extended Education

The University of Reading, London Rd, Reading RG1 5AQ; Tel (01734) 318346
Dean Ms M. McCulloch, BSc, MSc, PGCE
Head of Department of Extended Education K.M. Petyt, MA, PhD

University College of Ripon and York St John

Lord Mayor's Walk, York YO3 7EX; Tel (01904) 656771; Fax (01904) 612512
Vol; C of E; M and W
3,200 students; day and mature students accepted
Information The Registrar, The College, Lord Mayor's Walk, York YO3 7EX
College Rd, Ripon HG4 2QX; Tel (01765) 602691; Fax (01765) 600516

University of Salford

Salford M5 4WT; Tel 0161-745 5000; Fax 0161-745 5999/5885; Telex 668680
Chancellor H.R.H. The Duchess of York
Pro-Chancellor Dr J. Goldberg, HonDLitt, MA, BCL, DL
Vice-Chancellor Thomas M. Husband, BSc, MA, PhD(Strathclyde), FEng, FIMechE, Professor of Engineering
Registrar M.D. Winton, BA(Cambridge), MSc, PhD(Manchester)
6,208 undergraduates (full-time/home); 324 undergraduates (full-time/overseas); 280 postgraduates (full-time /home); 419 postgraduates (full-time/overseas); 107 undergraduates (part-time/ home); 657 postgraduates (part-time/home)

University College Salford

(formerly Salford College of Technology)
Frederick Rd, Salford M6 6PU; Tel 0161-736 6541; Fax 0161-745 8386
Principal T.J. Squires, BCom, MSc, MA, FBIM
Deputy-Principal C. Emmott, BSc, PhD, FRICS
Centres: Business; Management and Consumer Studies Design; Manufacture and Technology Media; Performance and Communications; *Departments*: Applied Sciences and Computing Construction and Surveying

University College, Scarborough, The North Riding College

Filey Rd, Scarborough YO11 3AZ; Tel (01723) 362392
Principal Dr R.A. Withers
Undergraduates and postgraduates. Post Graduate Certificate in Education and MEds for serving teachers. Research students accepted for MA and PhD in certain subjects
1175 students

University of Sheffield

Western Bank, Sheffield S10 2TN; Tel (0114) 276 8555; Fax (0114) 273 9826; Telex 547216 UGSHEF G
Chancellor The Rt Hon The Lord Dainton of Hallam Moors, Kt, MA, BSc, PhD, ScD, HonDSc, HonDTech, HonLLD, Hons DCL, HonDLitt, CChem, HonFRCP, HonFRSChem, HonFLA, HonFRCR, FRS
Pro-Chancellors J.E. Eardley, JP; P.W. Lee, DL
Vice-Chancellor Prof G.G. Roberts, BSc, PhD, DSc, MA, HonLLD, CPhys, CEng, FInstP, FIEE, FRS
Registrar and Secretary J.S. Padley, BSc, PhD
undergraduates; postgraduates

Division of Education

Head of Division Professor L.F. Barton, DipEd, BA, MEd
Professor N. Bolton, BA, PhD
Professor J. Rudduck, BA, PGCE, PhD
Professor J.M. Gray, BA, MEd, PGCE, DPhil
Professor G.A. Lindsay, BSc, PhD, FBPsS

Division of Adult Continuing Education

Director of Division G. Mitchell, BA, DipEd
Professor W.A. Hampton, BSc(Econ), PhD

Professor D.G. Hey, BA, MA, PhD, FRHistS
Professor G.E. Chivers, BSc, PhD

Sheffield Hallam University

(formerly Sheffield City Polytechnic)
City Campus, Pond St, Sheffield S1 1WB; Tel (0114) 272 0911; Fax (0114) 253 2096; Telex 54680 SH POLY GT
Principal and Vice-Chancellor J. Stoddart, BA, FRSA, FBIM
Assistant Principal J.M. Hobbs, BSc, PhD, FIMA
Assistant Principal J. Brookes, BSc, PhD, CEng, CPhys, SInstP
Assistant Principal Dianne Willcocks, BSc(Hons), DipMktg
University Secretary Sally Neocosmos, BA
Academic Registrar Jane Tory, BA
Director of Finance R. Lane
15,032 full-time/sandwich students; 2,976 postgraduate students; 5,896 part-time students

South Bank University

(formerly South Bank Polytechnic)
103 Borough Rd, London SE1 0AA; Tel 0171-928 8989
Chairman of Governors Prof W.G. Overend, DSc, FRCS, Master of Birbeck College, University of London
Vice-Chancellor Prof G. Bernbaum
Registrar N.J. Andrew, MA
8,639 full-time and 2,667 sandwich students; 5,936 part-time students

School of Education and Health Studies

Head of School Prof Wendy Couchman, CSS, BAC(Social Sciences), MSc
School Administration Officer David Hunter, BA, AUA
Postgraduate Initial Teacher Education Head of Division S. Wenman, CertEd, BEd, PgDip Language & Literacy, MA
Undergraduate Initial Teacher Education Head of Division D. Orsboyrne, BEd, MA(Ed)

University of Southampton

The University, Highfield, Southampton SO17 1BJ; Tel (01703) 595000; Fax (01703) 593840; Telex 86626 MYNEWS
Chancellor The Rt Hon The Earl Jellicoe, KBE, DSO, MC, HonLLD, FRS, PC
Vice-Chancellor Prof H.J. Newby, PhD, FRSA
Secretary and Registrar John F.D. Lauwerys, BEd, MA
Academic Registrar Rex Kinght, MA
7,515 undergraduates; 1,488 postgraduates

School of Education

Head Prof Helen Simons, BA, DipEd, PhD, PGCE

Department of Adult Continuing Education

Director W.R. Jones, BA, PhD

Staffordshire University

(formerly Staffordshire Polytechnic)
Stoke Site, College Rd, Stoke-on-Trent ST4 2DE; Tel (01782) 294000; Fax (01782) 749109
Chancellor The Rt Hon Lord Ashley of Stoke CH
Vice-Chancellor K.B. Thompson, MA, MEd
University Secretary K.B.G. Sproston, DMA
Academic Registrar F. Francis, BA
Schools and Recruitment Liaison Officer F. Cooke, BA
10,700 full-time and sandwich students; 2,900 part-time students
Stafford Site, Beaconside, Stafford ST18 0AD; Tel (01782) 294000

University College Stockton on Tees

University Boulevard, Thornaby, Stockton on Tees, Cleveland TS17 6BH; Tel (01642) 335300

University of Sunderland

(formerly Sunderland Polytechnic)
Unit 4C, Technology Pk, Chester Rd, Sunderland SR2 7PS; Tel 0191-515 2000; Fax 0191-515 2687
Vice-Chancellor and Chief Executive Dr A. Wright, BA, PhD
University Secretary J.D. Pacey, LLB
Academic Registrar Stuart Porteous, BA, DPP
14,118 undergraduate students; 1,077 postgraduate students; 3,516 part-time students

School of Education

Hammerton Hall, Gray Rd, Sunderland SR2 7EE; Tel 0191-515 2000
Director of School Professor Y.C. Stewart-Smith
1,058 full-time and 639 part-time students

University of Surrey

Guildford, Surrey GU2 5XH; Tel (01483) 300800; Fax (01483) 300803
Chancellor HRH The Duke of Kent, KG, GCMG, GCVO, ADC
Pro-Chancellor Emeritus Sir George Edwards, OM, CBE, FRS
Pro-Chancellors Sir Austin Pearce, CBE, PhD, Sir Diarmuid Downs, CBE, FRS
Vice-Chancellor Prof A. Kelly, CBE, ScD, FEng, FRS
Senior Pro-Vice-Chancellor Prof P.H.W. Butterworth, PhD
Pro-Vice-Chancellors B.H. Archer, PhD, FHCIMA, FTS; J.E. Harding, PhD, CEng, FIStructE, MICE; A.C. Walker, PhD, DSc, CEng, FICE, FIMechE
Treasurer D.A. Main, FCA
Chairman of Council Dr B.F. Street, FEng, FIChemE, CBIM
3,403 undergraduates; 1,883 postgraduates (1992–92); 18,043 Continuing Education

Department of Educational Studies

Tel (01483) 509194
Contact Mrs H. Pawley
Approx 300 courses
Elderly people are defined for Extra-mural courses as those in receipt of a state pension, ie women over 60 years of age, men over 65 years of age

University of Sussex

Arts Bldg, Falmer, Brighton BN1 9QN; Tel (01273) 606755
Chancellor The Earl of March and Kinrara, FCA, DL
Vice-Chancellor Sir Leslie Fielding, KCMG, MA
Senior Pro-Vice-Chancellor Prof F.J. Bayley, MSc, PhD, DSc, FIMechE
Registrar and Secretary G. Lockwood, BSc(Econ), DPhil
Deputy Secretary P.A. Tear, LLB
3,562 undergraduates; 1,590 postgraduates

Institute of Continuing and Professional Education Area

Chairman Prof M.R. Eraut, BA, PhD

University of Teesside

(formerly Teeside Polytechnic)
Middlesbrough, Cleveland TS1 3BA; Tel (01642) 218121; Fax (01642) 342067; Telex 587537
Vice-Chancellor Prof D. Fraser, BA, MA, PhD, FRHistS
Pro-Vice-Chancellor (Resources) Dr J.O. Coulthard, BSc, PhD, CEng, MIM
Pro-Vice-Chancellor (Academic and Staffing) G. Crispin, MPhil
Pro-Vice-Chancellor (External and Research) Ms H.E. Pickering, BA, MSc, MSocSc, FRSA, MIPR
Secretary and Registrar J.M. McClintock, BA, LLB, MA, LLM

Thames Valley University

(formerly Polytechnic of West London)
St Mary's Rd, Ealing, London W5 5RF; Tel 0181-579 5000; Fax 0181-566 1353
Vice-Chancellor Dr Mike Fitzgerald, PhD, MA, FRSA
Schools University Accountancy; Business; Creative, Cultural and Social Studies; English Language Teaching; European and International Studies; Hospitality Studies; Law; Management; Technology and Information Studies; Health and Science
Slough Campus
Wellington St, Slough SL1 1YG; Tel (01753) 534585; Fax (01753) 574264

University of Warwick

Coventry CV4 7AL; Tel (01203) 523523
Chancellor Sir Shridath Ramphal, OE, AC, GCMG, QC, FKC, LLM, HonLLD, HonDUniv, HonDO, HonDHL, HonDCL, HonDLitt, HonDSc
Pro-Chancellor R.J. Williams, BSc
Vice-Chancellor Sir Brian Follett, FRS, BSc, PhD, DSc, HonLLD
Registrar M.L. Shattock, OBE, MA
Deputy Registrar J. Rushton, BA
Academic Registrar J.W. Nicholls, BA, PhD
7,500 undergraduates; 5,200 postgraduates (1993–94)

Dept of Continuing Education

Contact (P/T degrees) J. Blake

Institute of Education

Chairman of Institute of Education Prof J.R.G. Tomlinson, CBE, BA, MA
Chairman of Continuing Education Prof C. Duke, MA, PhD, HonDLitt, PGCE, FACE, FRSA
Chairman of Physical Education M. Ralph, MA, TCert

University of the West of England, Bristol

(formerly Bristol Polytechnic)
Coldharbour La, Frenchay Campus, Bristol BS16 1QY; Tel (0117) 965 6261
Vice-Chancellor A. Morris, MA, FCA, FSS, FRSA
Registrar (Academic) M.J. Carter, BA
Head of Careers Service J.R. Widdows
Careers Adviser D. Bone MA
10,700 full-time students; 5,800 part-time students

Faculty of Education

Redland Hill, Redland, Bristol BS6 6UZ; Tel (0117) 974 1251
Dean R.E. Cuthbert, MA, MSc, MBA, DipEdAdmin

University of Westminster

35 Marylebone Rd, London NW1 5LS; Tel 0171-911 5000; Fax 0171-911 5168
Chairman of the Court of Governors Sir L. Peach
Rector Prof T.E. Burlin, DSc, PhD, FInstP, CEng, FIEE
Deputy Rector Dr G.M. Copland, MA, DPhil, CPhys, MInstP
Academic Registrar Ms J. Hopkinson
5,322 full-time/sandwich students; 20,000 short course/ part-time students
The School of Construction, Housing and Surveying has highly qualified staff professionals who maintain close links with industry and professional institutions. It also houses the internationally renowned Research in Building Group

Centre for Access and Continuing Education

Harrow Campus, Watford Rd, Northwick Pk, Harrow HA1 3TP

University of Wolverhampton

Molineux St, Wolverhampton WV1 1SB; Tel (01902) 321000; Fax (01902) 322680
Vice-Chancellor and Director Prof M.J. Harrison, MA, FBIM
18,352 students; 9,623 full-time; 1.391 full-time sandwich; 7,338 part-time

Faculty of Education and Health Services

Dean Lynn Copcutt, MSc, BEd(CertEd, RGNDN(London), RNT Gorway Rd, Walsall, West Midlands WS1 3BD; Tel (01902) 321050
3,245 full-time students; 2,357 part-time students

University of York

Heslington, York YO1 5DD; Tel (01904) 430000; Fax (01904) 433433; Telex 57933 YORKul
Chancellor Dame Janet Baker, CHDBE (Univ York)
Vice-Chancellor Prof R.U. Cooke, BSc, MSc, PhD, DSc
Registrar D.J. Foster University of York, Heslington, York YO1 5DD; Tel (01904) 430000
3,900 undergraduates; 1,400 postgraduates

Centre for Global Education

Director Vacancy

Department of Educational Studies

Professor of Education I. Lister, MA, CertEd(Cantab)

Wales

University of Wales

Bangor, Gwynedd LL57 2DG; Tel (01248) 351151
Vice Chancellor Prof E. Sunderland, MA, PhD, FIBiol
Registrar Gwyn Thomas, BA, MA
Senior Careers Adviser W.D. Yale, BSocSci
3,616 undergraduate and postgraduate students

Department of Education

Professor of Education I.W. Williams, BSc, PhD, FRSC

Department of Extra-Mural Studies

Director A. Roberts, LLB, MA

University College of Wales

Aberystwyth, Dyfed; Tel (01970) 623111
Principal Prof Kenneth O. Morgan, MA, DPhil, DLitt, FRHists, FBA
Registrar and Secretary D. Gruffydd Jones, BA
Senior Careers Adviser G.R. Jones, BSc
3,801 undergraduate and postgraduate students

Department of Education

Aberystwyth; Tel (01970) 623177
Professor of Education Prof R.A. Daugherty, MA

Department of Extra-Mural Studies

10 Laura Pl, Aberystwyth; Tel (01970) 617616
Director Prof Walford Davies, MA, MLitt

University College of Swansea

Singleton Pk, Swansea SA2 8PP; Tel (01792) 205678 Ext 5318
Principal Prof Robin Williams
Registrar V.J. Carney
Careers Director W.D. Treharne, PhD
5,693 undergraduate and postgraduate students

Department of Education

Professor of Education M.T. Williams, BSc(Econ), MA

Department of Adult and Continuing Education

Berwick Hse, 6 Uplands Terr, Swansea; Tel (01792) 57168
Director D.H. Francis, BA, PhD

University of Glamorgan

Pontypridd, Mid Glam CF37 1DL; Tel (01443) 480480; Fax (01443) 480558; Minicom (01443) 482199
Vice-Chancellor Prof A. Webb, BSocSci, MSc(Econ)
Deputy Vice Chancellor Prof John Flavell
9,139 full-time students; 3,783 part-time students

University of Wales, Lampeter

Lampeter, Dyfed; Tel (01570) 422351
Principal Prof K.G. Robbins, MA, DPhil, FRHistS, FRSE
Registrar and Secretary A.M.S. Kenwright, MA
1,400 undergraduate and postgraduate students

University of Wales

University Registry, Cathays Pk, Cardiff CF1 3NS; Tel (01222) 382656; Fax (01222) 396040
Chancellor HRH The Prince of Wales, KG, KT, GCB, PC
Pro-Chancellor The Rt Hon Lord Williams of Mostyn, QC, LLB, MA
Secretary General J.D. Pritchard, MA
24,186 undergraduate and postgraduate students

University Subject Panel for Education

University Registry, Cathays Pk, Cardiff CF1 3NS; Tel (01222) 382656; Fax (01222) 396040
Acting Registrar J.D. Pritchard, MA
Senior Assistant Registrar D. Gerwyn Lewis, MA, PhD

University of Wales, Cardiff

PO Box 921, Cardiff CF1 3XQ; Tel (01222) 874839
Principal Dr E.B. Smith, MA, DSc, FRSC
Registrar Professor M.J. Bruton, BA, MSc(Eng), DipTP, DIC, FRTPI, FCIT, MIHT
Careers Director D.M.F. Mutlow, BA, DipVG
12,860 undergraduate and postgraduate students

Department of Education

Professor of Education W.B. Davies, BSc(Econ), MA(Ed)

Department of Continuing Education

38 Park Pl, Cardiff CF1 3BB; Tel (01222) 874831
Director J.W. Perkins, BA, FGS, FRGS

The University of Wales College of Medicine

Heath Pk, Cardiff; Tel (01222) 747747
Provost Prof I.R. Cameron, MA, DM, FRCP
Director and Dean of Postgraduate Medical and Dental Education T.M. Hayes, MB, ChB, FRCP
Dean of Clinical Studies D.J.T. Webster, MD, ChB, FRCS
Registrar and Secretary A.W. Roberts, BA, PhD
Deputy Registrar L.F.J. Rees, BA
1889 undergraduate and postgraduate students

Scotland

University of Aberdeen

University Office, Regent Wk, Aberdeen AB9 1FX; Tel (01224) 272000; Fax (01224) 272086
Chancellor Sir Kenneth Alexander, BScEcon, LLD, DUniv, FEIS, FBECScot, FRSE
Vice-Chancellor and Principal Prof J. Maxwell Irvine, MSc, PhD, FIP, FRAS, FRSE, FRSA
7,939 undergraduates; 1,711 postgraduates

Department of Education

Taylor Bldg, King's College, Old Aberdeen AB9 2UB
Head of Department Dr J. Darling

Centre for Continuing Education

Regent Bldg, University of Aberdeen, Aberdeen AB9 1FX; Tel (01224) 272000
Director Dr Melvin T. Dalgarno

University of Dundee

Nethergate, Dundee DD1 4HN; Tel (01382) 23181; Fax (01382) 322638
Chancellor Sir James Black, MB, ChB(St Andrews), FRCP, FRSE, FRS
Principal and Vice-Chancellor Prof M.J. Hamlin, BSc(Bristol), FEng, FICE, FIWEM, FRSE

Centre for Continuing Education

Director Prof M.E. Gerver, BA(Dalhousie), MA(Toronto), PhD(London)
5,720 undergraduates; 778 postgraduates

The University of Edinburgh

Old College, South Bridge, Edinburgh EH8 9YL; Tel 0131-650 1000
Chancellor HRH The Prince Philip Duke of Edinburgh, KG, KT, PC, OM, GBE, LLD, FRS
Principal and Vice-Chancellor Prof Sir David Smith, MA, DPhil, FRS
Secretary M.J.B. Lowe, BSc, PhD
11,844 undergraduates; 2,040 postgraduates (full-time); 405 undergraduates; 1,354 postgraduates (part-time)

University of Glasgow

Glasgow G12 8QQ; Tel 0141-339 8855; Fax 0141-330 5440; Telex 777070
Chancellor Sir Alexander Kirkland Cairncross, KCMG, MA, PhD, LLD, DLitt, DSc(Econ), DUniv, FBA
Principal and Vice-Chancellor Sir William Kerr Fraser, GCB, MA, LLD, FRSE
Secretary of the University Court Robert Ewen, OBE, TD, MA
Registrar J. Michael Black, BA
13,106 undergraduates; 2,736 postgraduates

Department of Education

The University, Glasgow; Tel 0141-339 8855 Ext 7452
Professor of Education N.D.C. Grant, MA, MEd, PhD

Department of Adult and Continuing Education

The University, Glasgow; Tel 0141-339 8855 Ext 394
Director Prof Maria Slowey, BComm, MLitt

Glasgow Caledonian University

City Campus, Cowcaddens Rd, Glasgow G4 0BA; Tel 0141-331 3000; Fax 0141-331 3005
Chairman of University Court C.N.L. Urquhart, MBA
Principal Prof J.S. Mason, BSc, PhD, FIMechE
Vice Principal Prof P.W. Bush, BA(Hons), PhD, FRGS, FRSA
Vice-Principal Prof J.C. Phillips, BSc, FIMA
Senior Assistant Vice-Principal P.B. Finch, BA(Econ), MBIM
Assistant Principal Dr B.M. Fraser, BA(Hons), PhD, DGA, (Now ACIS), FIPM
Assistant Principal (Estates) W.J. Lawrie, BSc, MSc, MInstP, MIOA, CPhys
Head of Academic Administration E.B. Ferguson, BSc, DhS
Dean of Faculty of Business Prof S. McDaid, MBA, CA
Dean of Faculty of Health Prof G. Dickson, MLitt, PhD, FCII, FIRM
Dean of Faculty of Science & Technology Prof C.U. Chisholm, BSc, PhD, CEng, MIM, MIMfgE, MIEE
Approx 10,000 students

Continuing Education
Head W.T. Yule, BSc, Econ(Hons), MPhil, ASCC

Heriot-Watt University

Riccarton, Edinburgh EH14 4AS; Tel 0131-449 5111; Fax 0131-449 5153; Telex 727918 IOEHWU G
Chancellor The Rt Hon The Lord Mackay of Clashfern, PC, QC, MA, LLB, BA, LLD, DUniv, HonFRCSE, HonFICE, FRSE
Principal and Vice-Chancellor Professor A.G.J. MacFarlane, CBE, PhD, DSc, MA, ScD, DEng, FIEE, FRSE, FEng, FRS
Vice Principal Professor R.J. Knops, BSc, PhD, FRSE
Secretary of the University P.L. Wilson, BSc, MA, FBIM, FITD
Registrar D. Sturgeon, BL
4,932 undergraduates; 911 postgraduates (including part-time students)

Moray House College of Education (Institute of Education Heriot-Watt University)

(Incorporating Scottish Centre for Physical Education, Movement and Leisure Studies)
Holyrood Rd, Edinburgh EH8 8AQ; Tel 0131-556 8455
Principal Professor G. Kirk, MA, MEd, FRSA

Napier University Edinburgh

(formerly Napier Polytechnic of Edinburgh)
219 Colinton Rd, Edinburgh EH14 1DJ; Tel 0131-444 2266; Fax 0131-455 7209
Principal Prof J. Mavor, FEng, FRSE
Secretary I.J. Miller, MA, LLB Solicitor
Public Relations Officer M.J. Pate
7,000 full-time students, 2,300 part-time students
Sighthill Ct, Edinburgh EH11 4BN; Tel 0131-444 2266
10 Colinton Rd, Edinburgh EH10 5DT; Tel 0131-444 2266

University of Paisley

(formerly Paisley College of Technology)
High St, Paisley PA1 2BE; Tel 0141-848 3000; Fax 0141-887 0812
Chancellor Sir Robert Easton, CBE Duniv
Chairman of Court Anthony Joyce, GradBritIERE, DipMS
Principal and Vice Chancellor Prof R.W. Shaw, MA
Vice-Principal Prof W.S. Stevely, BSc, DPhil, DipEd, FBiol
Assistant Principal Gordon Wilson, MA, PhD, FRSA
Secretary J.M. Fraser, MA, MEd
6,098 (including part-time)

The Robert Gordon University

(formerly Robert Gordon's Institute of Technology)
Schoolhill, Aberdeen AB9 1FR; Tel (01224) 262000
Chairman of Governors Ian P. Souter, MA, CA
Principal Dr David A. Kennedy, MA, PhD, CChem, FRSC, CBiol, MIBiol
Vice-Principal Gavin T.N. Ross, DA(Edin), DipTP(Edin), MArch(Penn), RIBA, ARIAS, FRSA
Secretary David C. Caldwell, MA, MPhil
6,000 full-time students; 13,00 part-time students

University of St Andrews

The University, St Andrews, Fife KY16 9AJ; Tel (01334) 476161; Fax (01334) 462543
Chancellor Sir Kenneth J. Dover, MA, DLitt, LLD, FRSE, FBA
Principal and Vice-Chancellor Prof Struther Arnott, BSc, PhD, FRS, FRSC, FRSE, SCD, FIBioL
Secretary D.J. Corner, BA, FRHistS
4,121 undergraduates (1992–93)

Centre for Sponsored Programmes

Industrial Liaison Officer Lorna Sillar, BSc

University of Stirling

Stirling FK9 4LA; Tel (01786) 473171
Chancellor Lord Balfour of Burleigh
Principal and Vice-Chancellor Prof Andrew Millar, MA, BSc, PhD, FRSE
University Secretary R.G. Bomont, JP, BSc(Econ), IPFA
3,758 undergraduates; 670 postgraduates (1992)

University of Strathclyde

16 Richmond St, Glasgow G1 1XQ; Tel 0141-552 4400; Fax 0141-552 0775; Telex 77472 (UNSLIB G)
Chancellor The Rt Hon The Lord Tombs of Brailes, BScEcon, LLD, DSc, DUniv, FIMechE, FIEE, FEng
Principal and Vice-Chancellor Prof J.P. Arbuthnott, ScD, FIBiol, MRIA, HonFTCD, FRSE
Secretary P.W.A. West, MA
12,256 full-time students; 2,000 part-time students

Continuing Education Centre

McCance Bldg, 16 Richmond St, Glasgow G1 1XG; Tel 0141-552 4400
Director Archibald M. Fleming, MA, BCom, PhD, FRSA
Director of Senior Studies Institute L.A. Hart, MA

Faculty of Education

Jordanhill Campus, University of Strathclyde, 76 Southbrae Dr, Jordanhill, Glasgow G13 1PP; Tel 0141-950 3000
Dean Prof J. McCall
M and W
2,800 students

Northern Ireland

The Queen's University of Belfast

University Rd, Belfast BT7 1NN; Tel (01232) 245133; Fax (01232) 236618; Telex 682475
Chancellor Sir David Orr, Kt, LLB(Dub), Hon LLD(Dub), Hon LLD(Liverpool), Hon LLD (NUI), Hon DUniv (Surrey), Hon LLD
Vice-Chancellor Sir Gordon Beveridge, BSc, PhD, HonLLD(Dub), HonDSc(UU), ARCST, FEng, FIChemE, FRSE, MRIA, CBIM
Secretary to Academic Council G.A. Baird, BSc, MSc, PhD, FInstP
Bursar J.P.J. O'Kane, BA(CNAA), CIPFA
Administrative Secretary D.H. Wilson, BSc, DipEd
9,442 undergraduates; 3,061 postgraduates

Faculty of Education

Dean A. McEwen, BA, PhD

Institute of Continuing Education

Director J.W. Starr, BSc, DipEd MEd

Physical Education Centre

Director C.A.G. Boreham, BA, MA, CertEd, PhD

University of Ulster at Jordanstown

Newtownabbey, Co Antrim BT37 0GB; Tel (01232) 365731
Chancellor Rabbi Julia Neuberger
Vice-Chancellor Prof T.A. Smith, BSc, LLD, FRHistS CBIM
Deputy to Vice-Chancellor and Pro-Vice Chancellor (Planning and Research) Prof F.C. Monds, BSc, PhD, CEng, MIEE, MIERE, FBIM
Academic Registrar Dr K.I. Millar, BSc, PhD

Faculty of Social and Health Sciences and Education

Dean Prof R.A.F. Ellis, BA, TCert, CPsych, AFBPsS
Heads of School of Education Vacancy

13,862 full and part-time undergraduates; 3,913 postgraduates

Independent Universities

Buckland University College

Ewert Pl, Oxford OX2 7YT; Tel (01865) 53570; Fax (01865) 52961
Academic Registrar A.F. Kerr, MA
Bursar R.M.H. Arnott, MRIN

Lansdowne Independent University College

3–5 Palace Gate, London W8 5LS; Tel 0171-584 8686; Fax 0171-589 9406
President G.R. Rowlands, MA, PhD

Warnborough College, The American College in Oxford

Boar's Hill, Oxford OX1 5ED; Tel (01865) 730901; Fax (01865) 327796
President Dr B.D. Tempest-Mogg
Sciences, Arts and Humanities courses for British and overseas students

Colleges and Institutes of Higher Education

England

Anglia Higher Education College

Chairman of Governors R.W. Dixon-Smith
Director M. Salmon, BA, MEd, FBIM
Vice-Principal K. Swinhoe, MA, PhD
Secretary A.F. Boone, MSc, MCIT
Registrar R. Mepham
6,000 full-time students; 15,000 part-time students
Victoria Rd South, Chelmsford, Essex CM1 1LL; Tel (01245) 493131 Ext 245
Sawyers Hall La, Brentwood, Essex CM15 9BT; Tel (01277) 264504
Danbury Park Management Centre, Danbury; Tel (01245 51) 2141
East Rd, Cambridge CB1 1PT; Tel (01223) 352992

Askham Bryan College

Askham Bryan, York YO2 3PR; Tel (01904) 702121; Fax (01904) 702629

Avon and Gloucestershire College of Health

Glenside, Blackberry Hill, Stapleton, Bristol BS16 1DD; Tel (0117) 958 5655; Contact: Recruitment Office 650485; Fax (0117) 975 8498

Bath College of Higher Education

Newton Pk, Newton St Loe, Bath BA2 9BN; Tel (01225) 873701; Fax (01225) 874123
Director and Chief Executive Prof Brian L. Gomes da Costa, JP, BSc(Soc), MA, FIL
Und; M and W
Faculties Art and Music; Education and Human Sciences; Applied Sciences; Humanities
2,450 FTE; 2,230 full-time students
Sion Hill Pl, Lansdown, Bath BA1 5SF; Tel (01225) 425264; Fax (01225) 445228

Bedford College

Cauldwell St, Bedford, Beds MK41 9AH; Tel (01234) 345151; Fax (01234) 342674
Chief Executive P. Mansell, MA, PhD

Bishop Grosseteste College

Lincoln LN1 3DY; Tel (01522) 527347; Fax (01522) 530243
Principal Prof L.G. Marsh, OBE, MEd, DPhil, FRSA, HONFCP
Clerk to the Governing Body D.C. Peck
Vol; C of E; M and W
850 students (1992–93)
Degree courses: BA/BSc(Hons) 4 year Degree with qualified Teacher Status (QTS) (3–8 Lower Primary and 7–11 Upper Primary); BA(Hons) 3 Year Degree with QTS (4–8 Lower Primary); BA(Hons) Heritage Studies 3 Year Degree; BA(Hons) Arts in the Community (Drama) 3 Year Degree; Post Graduate Certificate in Education (Primary)
In-Service Training Courses: MA 2 year part-time taught course; MEd 2 year part-time Research course; BPhil 2 year part-time taught course; Advanced Diploma and 2 year part-time weekends taught course; Modular Diploma and SEN Diploma Flexible programme covering whole of curriculum and generic issues affecting primary schools

Bolton Institute of Higher Education

School of Education and Health Studies, Chadwick St, Bolton BL2 1JW; Tel (01204) 528851; Fax (01204) 399074
Principal Dr R. Oxtoby, BSc, MEd, PhD, CEng, MInstE, FBIM, FRSA
Vice-Principal H. Horner, BA, MSc
Head of School J. Hughes, BSc(Econ), MSc, MA, ACDipEd
Und; M and W
For FE teachers: Cert Ed, PGCE, BA, MEd; For Nurses: DipHV, DipDN part-time BA, BA (Community Studies)
665 FE Teacher Education students

Bradford and Ilkley Community College

McMillan Bldg, Trinity Rd, Bradford, West Yorkshire BD5 0JD; Tel (01274) 753204; Fax (01274) 307828
Clerk to the Governing Body A.W. Hodgson
LEA; Und; M and W
Schools Adult and General Education; Art, Design and Textiles; Business and Professional Studies; Science and Technology; Teaching and Community Studies

Buckinghamshire College of Higher Education

Queen Alexandra Rd, High Wycombe, Bucks HP11 2JZ; Tel (01494) 22141/9
Director B. Mogford, MA(Cantab)
Deputy Director A.M. d'I Oakeshott, BA, MEd, PhD
Deputy Director M. Hamer, BSc
Chief Administration Officer T. McGowan
Faculties Business Science and Humanities; Design; Health Studies; Technologies; Business School
7,000 students; resident and day

Canterbury Christ Church College

Canterbury CT1 1QU; Tel (01227) 767700
Principal Michael Berry, TD, BA, MEd, FRSA
Director of Admissions Dr T. McCulloch
Vol; C of E; M and W
4,000 students; resident and day

Cheltenham and Gloucester College of Higher Education

PO Box 220, The Park, Cheltenham, GLOS GL50 2QF; Tel (01242) 532700; Fax (01242) 532810
Director Janet Trotter, OBE, BD, MA, MSc
Assistant Director (Academic) Peter Easy, PhD, BA(Hons)

Assistant Director (Finance) David Soulter, MA
Assistant Director (Resources) Prof Chris Turner, MA, BSc, ALA
Clerk to the Governing Body T.R. Morgan
Vol; C of E; M and W
Faculties Arts & Education; Business & Social Studies; Environment and Leisure
7,500 students; 2,000 part-time
Details obtainable from The Admissions Officer, The Park, Cheltenham, Glos GL50 2QF

Chester College of Higher Education

Cheyney Rd, Chester CH1 4BJ; Tel (01244) 375444; Fax (01244) 373379
Principal Rev E.V. Binks, BD, AKC, FRSA
Clerk to the Governing Body R. Downes, MSc, MBIM
Vol; C of E; M and W
2,300 students

The Chichester Institute of Higher Education

Collage La, Chichester, West Sussex PO19 4PE; Tel (01243) 787911
Director J.F. Wyatt, MA, PhD
Ind vol; M and W
BA(QTS)Hons, PGCE, secondary, secondary/junior, junior, infant/early years; BA and BSc honours degrees in Arts, Humanities, Health Studies, Sports Studies; In-service Teacher Training; diplomas, professional qualifications and in-service courses; Social Work; Nursing; Modular courses; part-time BA(Hons); TESOL, ELT, EFL
3,000 students (including part-time, postgraduate and in-service)
also
Upper Bognor Rd, Bognor Regis, W. Sussex; Tel (01243) 865581

Darlington College of Technology

Cleveland Ave, Darlington, Co Durham DL3 7BB; Tel (01325) 503050; Fax (01325) 503000

Edge Hill College of Higher Education

St Helen's Rd, Ormskirk, Lancs L39 4QP; Tel (01695) 575171
Chief Executive Dr John Cater
Clerk to the Governing Body J. McNamara
Und; M and W
Courses Humanities, Environmental and Social Sciences; Management; Initial teacher education; In-service Studies; Nurse Education
3,000 students; resident and day

Gloucestershire College of Arts and Technology

The Pk Campus, 73 The Pk, Cheltenham GL50 2RR; Tel (01242) 532000
Principal Ian Caves, BA(Hons), DMS
3,300 full-time students; 32,000 part-time students

Homerton College

Hills Rd, Cambridge CB2 2PH; Tel (01223) 411141
Principal K. Pretty, MA, PhD
Admissions Secretary G. Eland, BA
Four year upper and lower primary BEd(Hons), and upper and lower primary and secondary PGCE (both of University of Cambridge)
900 students

Humberside College of Higher Education

Cottingham Rd, Hull HU6 7RT; Tel (01482) 440550
Director R. King, BSc, MSocSc
Head of Academic Sciences D. Foster
Und; M and W
Departments Social and Professional Studies; Humberside Business School; Food, Fish and Environmental Studies; Art, Architecture and Design
8,500 students

Kent Institute of Art & Design

Oakwood Pk, Maidstone, Kent ME16 8AG; Tel (01622) 757286
Director Peter Williams, DFA(Lond)
Chief Administrative Officer Ray Moon
Student facilities
Lodgings assistance, counselling, industrial placement, careers guidance
Further Education BTEC: Advanced GNVQ in Art and Design; Foundation Diploma in Art and Design; National Diploma in Design
Higher Education: BTEC Higher National Diplomas: Graphic Design; Fashion Design; Clothing Technology; Design – Precious Metalwork; Design – Modelmaking; Spatial Design; Photography; Design (with English for International Students); BA (Honours) Degrees: Fine Art; Fine Art (part-time); Access course to preceding; Architecture (RIBA Part 1); Communication Media; European Fashion (Product Development); Three Dimensional Design; Design (with English for international students); Graduate Courses: Diploma in Architecture (RIBA Part 2); Interdisciplinary MA in Art and Architecture; MA in Graphic Fine Arts; MA in Art Criticism and Theory; MA in Time-Based Media with Electronic Imaging

King Alfred's College of Higher Education

Winchester SO22 4NR; Tel (01962) 841515
Principal Prof John P. Dickinson, MA, MSc, PhD, FCPA, ACIS
Vol; C of E; M and W
4,300 students; resident and day

Leeds, Trinity and All Saints

Brownberrie La, Horsforth, Leeds LS18 5HD; Tel (0113) 283 7104
Contact Admissions Officer

Liverpool Institute of Higher Education (Christ's and Notre Dame Hall, and S Katharine's Hall)

Stand Pk Rd, Liverpool, Merseyside LI6 9JD; Tel 0151-737 3000
Rector Vacancy
4,000 students; resident and day
Christ's and Notre Dame Hall
Woolton Rd, Liverpool L16 8ND; Tel 0151-737 3000
Vol; RC; M and W
S Katharine's Hall
Stand Park Rd, Liverpool L16 9JD; Tel 0151-737 3000
Vol; C of E; M and W

LSU College of Higher Education

The Avenue, Southampton SO17 1BG; Tel (01703) 228761; Fax (01703) 230944
Principal Dr Anand Chitnis, BA, MA, PhD, FRHistS
Departments Art & Design; English; French; German; Geography; Mathematics; Podiatry; Theology; Historical/Political Studies; Computing; Teaching Studies; Science; Social Studies; European studies; Sport Sciences; Ecology; Life Sciences; Psychology
2,000 students; resident and day; 200 part-time students

Nene College of Higher Education

Park Campus, Boughton Green Rd, Northampton, Northants NN2 7AL; Tel (01604) 735500
Director S. Martin Gaskell, MA, PhD, FRHistS, FRSA
Higher Education Corporation (April '89); Und; W and M
Faculties Applied Sciences; Arts and Social Sciences; Management and Business

10,000 students
St George's Ave, Northampton NN2 6JD; Tel (01604) 735500

Newman and Westhill Colleges

Newman and Westhill Colleges work in academic association with a common academic programme. They form an Academic School of the Faculty of Education and Continuing Studies of the University of Birmingham
Newman College
Bartley Grn, Birmingham B32 3NT; Tel 0121-476 1181;
Principal The Rev G. Benfield, MA, BD, LGSM
Westhill College
Selly Oak, Birmingham B29 6LL; Tel 0121-472 7245;
Principal J. Cuming, PhD, BA, DipEd

Ravensbourne College of Design and Communication

Walden Rd, Chislehurst, Elmstead Woods, Kent BR7 5SN; Tel 0181-468 7071
Chairman of Governors R.A. Brook, BSc, MSc
Principal N.J. Frewing, DesRCA, FCSD
Registrar J.L. Bennett, BA
Librarian J. McKay, MA, ALA

Roehampton Institute, London

(Affiliated to and accredited by the University of Surrey)
Senate Hse, Roehampton La, London SW15 5PU; Tel 0181-392 3000; Fax 0181-392 3131
Rector Dr Stephen C. Holt, MA, PhD
Vol
Faculties Arts and Humanities; Education; Sciences, and Social Sciences
Over 6,000 students, most undergraduates; fifth part-time; over 1,252 residential places
Over 400 undergraduate joint honours and several postgraduate degree programmes leading to BA/BSc or BA degrees of the University of Surrey (with Qualified Teacher Status) plus postgraduate study of Masters and PhD/MPhil level
Teacher Education: wide range of shorter certificate/diploma programmes; postgraduate degrees; professional training for teachers
Colleges
Digby Stuart
(Catholic)
Southlands
(Methodist)
Whitelands
(Anglican)
Froebel Institute

Royal College of Nursing of the United Kingdom

20 Cavendish Sq, London W1M 0AB; Tel 0171-409 3333
Director of Education Miss M.D. Green, OBE, MA(Ed), BA(Hons), SRN, RNT, FRCN

College of St Mark and St John

Derriford Rd, Plymouth, Devon PL6 8BH; Tel (01752) 777188
Principal J. Anderson, BSocSc, MA
Careers Officer I. Hosker
Vol; C of E; M and W
Areas Arts Humanities and Social Sciences; Teacher Education; International Education; Continuing Education and Training
2,230 full-time students

University College of St Martin

Bowerham Rd, Lancaster, Lancs LA1 3JD; Tel (01524) 63446
Principal D. Edynbry, BA, MA, MSc, PhD
C of E; M and W
A range of honours degree courses including Modular Combined Studies Major and Joint Subject Routes (Art and Design, English, Geography, History, Health Promotion, Mathematics, Religious Studies, Social Ethics); Teacher Training (Primary); Christian Ministry, Performing Arts; Community and Youth Studies; Nursing, Diagnostic Radiography, Occupational Therapy, Sports Science and DipHE Imaging Sciences; Postgraduate Teacher Training (Primary and Secondary); Higher Degrees. Also In-Service courses for practising professionals and Short Courses for business and the wider community
2,500 students

St Mary's University College: a college of the University of Surrey

Waldegrave Rd, Twickenham TW1 4SX; Tel 0181-892 0051
Principal Dr A. Naylor, MA, MEd, PhD, MBA
Registrar R. Tank, MA, MPhil
Vol; RC; M and W
1,970 students

University College, Scarborough

Filey Rd, Scarborough, N. Yorks YO11 3AZ; Tel (01723) 362392; Fax (01723) 370815
Head of External Relations and Recruitment Dr E.J. Payne-Ahmadi

South West London College

Tooting Broadway, London SW17 0TQ; Tel 0181-672 2441
Departments Business education; Management studies; Professional accountancy studies; Secretarial and general education; Human resource management; Marketing and short course unit

Southampton Institute

East Park Terr, Southampton SO14 0YN; Tel (01703) 319037
Principal D.G. Leyland, BArch, MCD, MSc, MBA, RIBA, MRTPI
Divisions Accountancy; Built Environment; Systems Engineering; Design; Social Science; Law; Management; Media Arts

Trinity and All Saint's College

Brownberrie La, Horsforth, Leeds LS18 5HD; Tel (0113) 283 7100; Fax (0113) 283 7200
Principal Dr G.L. Turnbull, BA, PhD, PGDE
RC; M and W

Warrington Collegiate Institute

Padgate Campus, Crab La, Fearnhead, Warrington WA2 0DB; Tel (01925) 814343; Fax (01925) 418328
College Principal Steve Broomhead
Academic Registrar (HE) W.M. Whitehead
Information Officer (FE) Audine Hargreaves
Und; M and W
Colleges Technology College (Construction, Engineering, Motor Vehicle, Electrical/Electronics, Hair and Beauty Catering); Community College (Access to Further Education, Community Care, Applied Social and Health, Art and Design, Science and Technology, General Education); Business and Management College (Secretarial Computing and Information Technology, Business Studies, Leisure, Management Studies, Adult Education); Higher Education (Access to Higher Education, Leisure and Recreation, Media, Performing Arts, Sports Science, Environmental Science, Business Management, In-Service Education for Teachers, Counselling Skills/Social Work
1,500 full-time students; 12,000 part-time
Museum St Centre, Museum St, Warrington WA1 1HU; Tel (01925) 32712; Fax (01925) 59241

West London Institute (College of Brunel University)

Gordon Hse, 300 St Margaret's Rd, Twickenham TW1 1PT; Tel 0181-891 0121; Fax 0181-891 0487

Principal J.E. Kane, KCSG, MEd, PhD, FRSA, FCP
Co-ordinator of Academic Registry at Gordon Hse address Caroline Browne
Departments Business and Management Studies; Education; Health and Paramedical Studies; Social Work; Arts and Sciences
3,600 full time equivalent students (3,100 full-time)
Applications: Gordon Hse, 300 St Margaret's Rd, Twickenham, Middx TW1 1PT; Tel 0181-891 0121; Fax 0181-891 0487

West Yorkshire College of Health Studies

Stanley Royd Hospital, Aberford Rd, Wakefield, W. Yorks WF1 4DH; Tel (01924) 814879
The Registrar Gil Stokes

Westminster College

Oxford OX2 9AT; Tel (01865) 247644; Fax (01865) 251847
Principal Rev Dr K.B. Wilson, MA, MLitt, OBE
Clerk to the Governing Body M.C. Sykes, BA, FCA
Vol; Methodist; M and W
1,200 full-time

Worcester College of Higher Education

Henwick Gr, Worcester WR2 6AJ; Tel (01905) 748080; Fax (01905) 748162
Principal D. Urwin, BSc, MA
Vice-Principal Prof R.H. Bryant, BA, PhD
Registrar R. Covency, BA, MA
Undergraduate Modular Scheme subjects:- Art and Design, Biological Science, Business Management, Creative Arts, Drama, Economy and Society, Education Studies, English and Literary Studies, Environmental Science, Geography, Health Studies, History, Home Economics, Information Technology, Mathematics, Music, Primary Education, Psychology, Religious Studies, Renaissance Studies, Sociology, Sports Studies, Theology, Urban Studies and Women's Studies. The College offers a variety of Postgraduate and Post Experience courses and degrees and diplomas in Nursing, Midwifery, Horticulture and Environmental Management
3,500 F/t students, 1,500 P/t students

Wales

Cardiff Institute of Higher Education

Information Office, Central Management, Llandaff Centre, Western Ave, Cardiff CF5 2SG; Tel (01222) 551111 Ext 6045
Director and Chief Executive J. Derek Winslow, BA, MA
LEA; M and W
Faculties Business Information and Management; Education & Sport; Tourism; Hospitality and Food; Community Health Sciences; Art Design & Technology
8,000 students; resident and day

Gwent College of Higher Education

Faculty of Education, Humanities & Science

Caerleon Campus, PO Box 179, Newport, Gwent NP6 1YG; Tel (01633) 432020; Fax (01633) 432006
Principal Dr K.J. Overshott
Registrar J.C. Sexton
M and W
Faculties Newport School of Art and Design, Faculty of Education, Humanities & Science, Newport Business School, Faculty of Technology
6,000 Students

Bangor Normal College

Bangor, Gwynedd LL57 2PX; Tel (01248) 370171; Fax (01248) 370461
Principal H. Gareth, F. Roberts, MA, MEd, PhD
Chief Admin Officer Gwynfor ab Ifor
M and W
1,026 students; resident and day

North East Wales Institute of Higher Education

Newl Plas Coch, Mold Rd, Wrexham, Clwyd LL11 2AW; Tel (01978) 290666; Fax (01978) 290008
Principal/Chief Executive Prof J.O. Williams, PhD, DSc, CChem, FRSC, FInstP
Associate Principal B.R. Williams, BSc, PhD
Faculties Arts and Education; Management Business and Information Technology; Science Health and Medical Studies; Technology; (Built Environment/ Engineering)
3,500 students; 2,137 full-time

Swansea Institute of Higher Education

Townhill Rd, Swansea SA2 0UT; Tel (01792) 203482; Fax (01792) 208683; Telex 48435 WGIHE
Principal and Chief Executive Gerald Stockdale, MEd, MSc, PhD, CEng, MIMinE
Higher Education Corporation; M and W
Faculties Art and Design; Built Environment; Business; Computing; Education; Electronic Engineering; Law; Management and Finance; Tourism, Leisure Management and Health Care, Transport
2,500 full-time students; 2,000 part-time students

Trinity College

Carmarthen SA31 3EP; Tel (01267) 237971/2/3
Principal D. Clive Jones-Davies, OBE, JP, MA, MPhil, FRSA
Clerk to the Governing Body D.A. Davies, BA
Vol; Church in Wales; M and W; Bilingual
Departments Archaeology, Art, Education, English, Geography, History, Information Technology, Mathematics, Music, Physical Education, Religious Studies, Science, Technology, Theatre Studies, Welsh
1,800 students; day and resident

Scotland

St Andrew's College

Duntocher Rd, Bearsden, Glasgow G61 4QA; Tel 0141-943 1424
Principal B.J. McGettrick, BSc, MEd, FRSA
Director of Finance and Administration J.A. McKenna
RC; M and W
1,000 pre-service students; 400 FTE in-service

Northern College of Education

Aberdeen Campus,

Hilton Pl, Aberdeen AB9 1FA; Tel (01224) 283500

Dundee Campus,

Gardyne Rd, Dundee DD5 1NY; Tel (01382) 464000
Principal D.A. Adams, MA
2,000 FTE students; pre-service and in-service

Northern Ireland

St Mary's College of Education

191 Falls Rd, Belfast BT12 6FE; Tel (01232) 327678; Fax (01232) 333719
Principal and Clerk to the Governing Body Rev M. O'Callaghan, BA, BD, LSS
Vol; RCl M and W
Four-year BEd(Hons); one-year postgraduate course (Belfast Queen's University)
690 students

Chairman of Governors B.R. Roberts, MBA
Principal C.E.R. Maddox, BSc, PhD, CBiol, MIBiol, DipManEd
Vice-Principal Dr D.L. Brydon, BSc, PhD, CChem, FRSC
800 full-time students

Stranmillis College

Stranmillis Rd, Belfast BT9 5DY; Tel (01232) 381271
Principal J.R.B. McMinn, BA, PhD
Clerk to the Governing Body Secretary, Stranmillis College
Government College of Education; Und; M and W
700 full-time teacher training students

Central Institutions: Scotland

University of Abertay Dundee

Bell St, Dundee DD1 1HG; Tel (01382) 308000
Chairman of Governors Hugh Smith, MA, DipEd
Principal Prof Bernard King, MSc, PhD, FIWSc, CB
Secretary D.J. Hogarth, MA, LLB
4,000 FTE

Edinburgh College of Art

Lauriston Pl, Edinburgh EH3 9DF; Tel 0131-221 6000
Principal Prof Alistair J. Rowan, DipARCH, PhD, MA, FRIAS, FRSE
Secretary and Treasurer John Nice, DMA
1,366 students (full-time)

Glasgow College

Cowcaddens Rd, Glasgow G4 0BA; Tel 0141-332 7090
Chairman of Governors Prof H.C.S. Wood, BSc, PhD, CChem, FRSC, FRSE
Principal J.S. Mason, BSc, PhD, CEng, FIMechE, FIMarE, MIMinE
Vice-Principal P.W. Bush, BA, PhD, FRGS
Senior Assistant Principal P.B. Finch, BA(Econ), MBIM
College Secretary A. Irons, BA
Registrar I. Struthers
Dean of Faculty of Business and Administration Studies W.J. Elder, MA, MSc, MPhil, MIProdE, MBIM
Dean of Faculty of Life and Social Sciences Prof R.H.C. Bull, BSc, MSc, FBPsS
Dean of Faculty of Science Engineering and Construction W.J. laurie, BSc, MSc, CPhys, MInstP, MIOA

SAC: The National College for Food, Land and Environmental Studies

School of Agriculture, 581 King St, Aberdeen AB9 1UD; Tel (01224) 480291; Fax (01224) 491989
Chairman of Governors W.J. Ferguson
Principal Prof P.C. Thomas
Head of Administration R. Miller
Senior Tutor P.D. Edward
300 full-time students

Queen Margaret College

Clerwood Terr, Edinburgh EH12 8TS; Tel 0131-317 3000
Principal Donald Leach, BSc, CMath, FIMA, CPhys, MInstP, MBCS, CEng, FRSA
2,400 students

Royal Scottish Academy of Music and Drama

100 Renfrew St, Glasgow G2 3DB; Tel 0141-332 4101
Principal Philip Ledger, CBE, MA, MusB, LLD, FRCM, HonRAM, FRNCM, HonGSM, FRSE, FRCO
Secretary and Treasurer Isobel Fowler, BSc
Registrar Thomas W.M. Gourdie, MA
427 students (262 music, 165 drama)

The Scottish College of Textiles

Netherdale, Galashiels TD1 3HF; Tel (01896) 753351; Fax (01896) 758965

Educational Management

The Staff College

Coombe Lodge, Blagdon, Bristol BS18 6RG; Tel (01761) 462503; Fax (01761) 463104
Director T.G. Melling, MA
Deputy Director K.J. Scribbins, BSc(Soc), MA
The College is the management development and training centre for further and higher education in the UK. It is supported by grants from the FE funding councils. The college aims to improve the efficiency and effectiveness of FHE by means of open courses at its own premises and elsewhere, commissioned training, consultancy, research, publication, information and advice services. It brings together senior staff of institutions, officials from central and local government departments, trainers and people from industry and commerce in order to address managerial and organisational issues in FHE and develop solutions to problems. The College has a growing international programme

Business and Technical Education

Business & Technology Education Council (BTEC)

Central Hse, Upper Woburn Pl, London WC1H 0HH; Tel 0171-413 8400; Fax 0171-387 6068
Chairman Sir Michael Lickiss
Chief Executive Dr Christina Townsend
BTEC approves vocational programmes in a wide range of subjects throughout England, Wales and Northern Ireland. It awards qualifications to students who successfully complete these courses. BTEC is working with NCVQ to develop the GNVQ and NVQ Framework of vocational qualifications
Programmes leading to BTEC qualifications are run in schools, colleges, universities, companies and training centres throughout England, Wales and Northern Ireland. They can be studied through different modes including full-time, day release and evening

Scottish Vocational Education Council (SCOTVEC)

Hanover Hse, 24 Douglas St, Glagow G2 7NQ; Tel 0141-248 7900
Chairman David Miller, DUniv (Stirling), MA(Cantab), CBIM, FIPM, FRSA
Chief Executive T. McCool, BSc, HonDEd
SCOTVEC, is the national body with responsibility for accrediting, awarding and developing vocational qualifications in Scotland. Within its qualification's framework, SCOTVEC offers unit-based provision within a range of awards
Modules and Units can be taken individually or in groups and can lead to nationally recognised qualifications such as HNC, HND, General Scottish Vocational Qualifications (GSVQs) or Scottish Vocational Qualifications (SVQs). In addition programmes can be designed which meet the needs of particular organisations and companies
All SCOTVEC awards are designed by SCOTVEC in collaboration with employers, industrial bodies and

professional/technician bodies and are recognised routes to careers and to further study at degree level and beyond

World ORT Union

ORT Hse, London NW3 5HR; Tel 0171-431 1333; Fax 0171-435 4784; Telex 295441 BUSY B. Ref: ORT
Director-General Dr E. Isler
Independent, technological education and training organisation with schools, colleges and teacher training and resource centres worldwide. In Britain supports, sponsors and operates training schemes and co-operates closely with government and local education authorities and industry. For specific needs provides appropriate high technology courses

Management Education

Association of Business Schools

334/345 Gray's Inn Rd, London WC1X 8BP; Tel 0171-837 1899; Fax 0171-837 8189
Represents all of the major providers of business and management education across universities and colleges. ABS aims to advance the education of the public in business and management in particular through the promotion of business and management education, training and development so as to improve the quality and effectiveness of the practice of management in the United Kingdom

Regional Centres of Management Education

East Midlands

East Midlands Regional Management Centre, Clifton Hall, Clifton Village, Nottingham NG11 8NJ
Managing Director G. Gardner
An independent management training and development company whose shareholders are De Montfort University (formerly Leicester Polytechnic), Nottingham Polytechnic and Derbyshire College of Higher Education

Essex

Danbury Pk Conference Centre, Main Rd, Danbury, Chelmsford, Essex CM3 4AT; Tel (01245) 225511; Fax (01245) 226949
General Manager J. Henton

Kingston

Kingston Regional Management Centre, Kingston University, Penrhyn Rd, Kingston-upon-Thames, Surrey KT1 2EE; Tel 0181-549 1141
Director David Miles
Brooklands Technical College, Croydon College, Guildford College of Technology, Kingston College of Further Education, Kingston University, Merton College, North East Surrey College of Technology and West London Institute of Higher Education

London

Duncan Hse, High St, Stratford, London E15 2JB
Head Post Experience Studies C.F Horner, MSc, BSc(Econ), FCCA, FCMA
University of East London, Department of Management

Northern

Northern Regional Management Centre, 3rd Fl, Glendale Hse, Washington Centre, Washington New Town, Tyne and Wear NE38 7SU; Tel 0191-417 1150
Director M. Stephenson
A company set up by the University of Northumbria at Newcastle, University of Sunderland and University of Teesside committed to new approaches to management education and training. Open learning production/delivery. MBA; DBA; CMS; ISM programmes

Sheffield Business School

The Old Hall, Totley Campus, Totley Hall La, Sheffield S17 4AB; Tel (0114) 253 2855; Fax (0114) 253 2870
Director Prof Kevan Scholts, PhD

South West

Bristol Business School, University of the West of England at Bristol, Frenchay, Bristol BS16 1QY; Tel (0117) 965 6261
Prof J.M. Rees, BSc(Eng), MSc, ACGI, CEng, MIEE, FBIM, FRSA (Dean, Bristol Business School)
University of the West of England at Bristol

Staffordshire University Business School

Brindley Building, Leek Rd, Stoke-on-Trent ST4 2DE; Tel (01782) 412515; Fax (01782) 747006
Dean C.J. Brownlees

The following colleges have formal links with the Regional Management Centres Association:

University of Ulster, Faculty of Business and Management

Shore Rd, Newtownabbey, Co Antrim BT37 0QB
Dean of the Faculty of Business and Management Prof W. Ewart
Director of Ulster Business School Prof V. Mageean

Scottish Colleges

Faculty of Management, Dundee Institute of Technology
Bell St, Dundee DD1 1HG; Tel (01382) 308400
Dean G.A. Wright, BA, MPhil

Glasgow Caledonian University
Cowcaddens Rd, Glasgow G4 0BA; Tel 0141-331 3409
Head of Department of Management John F. McKay, BA, MEd

The Robert Gordon University
Business School, Hilton Pl, Aberdeen AB9 1FP; Tel (01224) 482211
Head of School Prof R.T. Hart, BCom, MA, FSS, FBIM, FInstD

Business and Administrative Colleges

England

Ashridge Management College

Berkhamstead, Herts HP4 1NS; Tel (0144 284) 3491
President of Governors Sir John Hedley Greenborough, KBE, LLD, CIMgt
Chief Executive M. Osbaldeston, BSc, MBA, FIPM, FRSA, CIMgt
6,500 students per annum (on 1–4 week courses) plus a 1 and 2 year MBA programme

Aston Business School, Aston University

Nelson Bldg, Aston Triangle, Birmingham B4 7ET; Tel 0121-359 3011
Director of Postgraduate Studies Dr Mark Oakley

University of Bath School of Management

Claverton Down, Bath BA2 7AY; Tel (01225) 826826
Admissions Tutor R.B. Brockington

University of Birmingham, Faculty of Commerce and Social Science
Edgbaston, Birmingham B15 2TT; Tel 0121-414 6622/3
Admissions Officer Undergraduate Admissions Office

Bradford University Management Centre
Emm La, Bradford, W Yorks BD9 4JL
Admissions Officer Postgraduate Secretary

City University Business School
Frobisher Cres, Barbican Centre, London EC2Y 8HB; Tel 0171-477 8000

Cranfield School of Management
Cranfield University, Cranfield, Beds MK43 0AL; Tel (01234) 754025

De Montfort University
The Gateway, Leicester LE1 9BH; Tel (0116) 255 1551; Fax (0116) 255 0307
Vice-Chancellor Prof K. Barker, CBE, MA, BMus, FRSA, CIMgt

University of Derby
(formerly Derbyshire College of Higher Education)
Kedleston Rd, Derby DE3 1GB; Tel (01332) 47181
Vice-Chancellor R. Waterhouse, BA, MA
Dean Prof Russell Syson, MA, FInstFS, MBIM
Registrar J. Fry, BSc
Clerk to the Governors J. Fry
5,500 FTE students
Faculty of Education, Humanities and Social Sciences; *Dean* R. Faithorn, BA, MPhil, PGCE
Institute of Health and Community Studies; *Dean* M. Cullen, BPharm, MCPP, MPS, LHSM, JP

Durham University Business School
Mill Hill La, Durham DH1 3LB; Tel 0191-374 2211
Marketing Officer Kate Bridge
Management Development; Enterprise Training and Development; Research

Henley, Management College
Greenlands, Henley-on-Thames, Oxon RG9 3AU; Tel (01491) 571454; International 44 491 571454; Fax (01491) 571635
Chairman of Governors Sir Denys Henderson
Principal Prof Ray Wild, Phd, MSc, DSC, WhF, CEng, FIMechE, FIMfgE, CBIM, FRSA

University of Humberside
Cottingham Rd, Hull HU6 7RT; Tel (01482) 440550
Dean (School of Management) George Holmes
Dean (School of International Business) Dr Rosina Jones
Dean (School of Computing/Information Systems) Prof Michael Jackson
Dean (School of Economics) Ian Barnes (Acting)
Dean (School of Finance and Law) John Holt (Acting)
Dean (School of Engineering) Roland Stoker (Acting)
5,000 students

Huron University–London Campus
58 Princes Gate, London SW7 2P6; Tel 0171-581 4899; Fax 0171-589 9406
Provost G.W. Bennett, BA, MA, PhD

Lancaster University Management School
Lancaster LA1 4YX
Dean Prof S.R. Watson

University of Leeds
Leeds LS2 9JT; Tel (0113) 233 3993
Senior Administrator (Access Office) C.E. Foote

London Business School
Sussex Pl, Regents Pk, London NW1 4SA; Tel 0171-262 5050
Chairman of Governors D.J. Sainsbury
Principal Prof G.S. Bain, BA, MA, DPhil
Secretary and Treasurer G. Quincey
730 full-time equivalent students

London School of Economics and Political Science
Houghton St, London WC2A 2AE; Tel 0171-405 7686
Admissions Officer (Undergraduates) R. Nixon, Assistant Registrar

University of London, Imperial College: The Management School
53 Prince's Gate, London SW7 2PG; Tel 0181-589 5111
Admissions Tutor R.J. Betts

Manchester Business School
Booth St West, Manchester M15 6PB; Tel 0161-275 6399; Fax 0161-275 6489
Director of Manchester Business School Prof John Arnold, MSc, MA, FCA
Director of Studies (MBA Programme) P.R.N. Barrar, MSc, DipBA, CEng, MIEE, MBPICS
Marketing Manager Anne Keddie, BA(Hons)
Information Officer Janet Cusworth
230 full-time students; 125 part-time students

University of Manchester Institute of Science and Technology, Manchester School of Management
PO Box 88, Sackville St, Manchester M60 1QD; Tel 0161-236 3311; Fax 0161-200 3505
F.T. Professor of Industrial Relations Prof J.F.B. Goodman

The Middlesex University Business School
The Burroughs, London NW4 4BT; Tel 0171-368 1299
Dean Prof M.J. Driscoll, BA, MBIM, FRSA
Administrator L. Morrice, BEd, MA

Missenden Abbey Management Centre
Great Missenden, Bucks HP16 0BD; Tel (01494) 866811; Fax (01494) 866737
Marketing Manager Debbie Edge

North East Worcestershire College
Blackwood Rd, Bromsgrove, Worcs B60 1PQ; Tel (01527) 570020; Fax (01527) 572900
Principal H.B. Sutton, BTech, MTech, PhD, CEng, MIMechE, MInstMC

Open Business School
Customer Service Centre, Open University, PO Box 481, Walton Hall, Milton Keynes MK7 G77; Tel (01908) 653473, 655182
Dean and Director of Studies Prof Andrew Thomson, MBA
Over 15,000 registrations a year

Roffey Pk Management Institute
Forest Rd, Horsham, W Sussex RH12 4TD; Tel (01293) 851644
Chief Executive Valerie Hammond, BA, FRSA, FIMgmt

University of Salford, Department of Business and Management Studies

Salford M5 4WT; Tel 0161-745 500 Ext 7074; Fax 0161-745 5999
Administrative Officer Linda Puttick

Staffordshire University Business School

Brindley Bldg, Leek Rd, Stoke-on-Trent ST4 2DF; Tel (01782) 294060; Fax (01782) 747006
Dean of School C.J. Brownless, BA
School Administrator N. Revell

Sheffield University Management School

9 Mappin St, Sheffield S1 4DT; Tel (01792) 825282; Fax (01792) 725103
Chairman Dr F.A. Fretwell-Downing

University of Southampton

Highfield, Southampton SO17 1BJ; Tel (01703) 595000
Admissions Enquiries Tel (01703) 593712 (undergraduate); (01703) 592837 (postgraduate)

University of Sussex

Management and Professional Development Unit, Institute of Continuing and Professional Education, EDB, Brighton BN1 9RG; Tel (01273) 678348

Sundridge Pk Management Centre

Bromley, Kent BR1 3TP; Tel 0181-313 3131
Chief Executive J.D. Chadwick, BSc(Eng), ACGI, FIMC, CBIM
Marketing Director G. Barrett, MBIM, MIPR
115 students (on 2 day–3 week courses)

University of Greenwich Business School

Riverside Hse, Beresford St, London SE18 6BU; Tel 0181-316 9000; Fax 0181-316 9005
Dean of Faculty Mary Falconer Spence

University of Warwick, Warwick Business School

Coventry CV4 7AL; Tel (01203) 523523 (University); (01203) 524306 (Business School)
Chairman of School Prof Robert D. Galliers, BA, MA, PhD

West of England Management Centre

Engineers' Hse, The Promenade, Clifton Down, Bristol BS8 3NB; Tel (0117) 973 1471
Senior Consultant B. Gardener, CEng, MIMechE, MIProdE, MITD
Enquiries to Administration Centre

Wales

Cardiff Business School, University of Wales

Aberconway Bldg, Colum Dr, Cardiff CF1 3EU; Tel (01222) 874198
Admissions Officer Ms S. Jarratt

University of Wales College of Cardiff

PO Box 494, Cardiff CF1 3YL; Tel (01222) 874404; Fax (01222) 874130
Admissions Officer J. Curran; Tel (01222) 874412

Scotland

Edinburgh University Management School

7 Bristo Sq, Edinburgh EH8 9AL; Tel 0131-650 8066; Fax 0131-650 8077; Telex 727442 UNIVED G
Director J. Moyes

Scottish College of Textiles

Dept of Management Studies, Netherdale, Galashiels TD1 3HF; Tel (01896) 753351; Fax (01896) 758965
Head of Department Jennifer L. Rees, BSc

Strathclyde Graduate Business School, University of Strathclyde

Sir William Duncan Bldg, 130 Rottenrow, Glasgow G4 0GE; Tel 0141-553 6000

University of Stirling, Departments of Economics and of Business and Management, Technological Economics Research Unit

Stirling FK9 4LA; Tel (01786) 73171
University Admissions Officer Vacancy

Agricultural Colleges and Institutes

Agricultural Colleges

For LEA Agricultural and Horticultural Colleges, see appropriate Authority (Chapters 3–7)

Coleg Amaethyddol Cymru/The Welsh Agricultural College

Llanbadarn Fawr, Aberystwyth; Tel (01970) 624471
Chairman of Governors W.C. Philpin, OBE
Dr J.H. Harries, PhD, BSc, CertEd
Registrar C.S. Reynolds
450 full-time students

Enniskillen College of Agriculture

Enniskillen, Co Fermanagh; Tel (01365) 323101
Principal A. Mallon
52 full-time students; 80+ part-time students

Greenmount College of Agriculture and Horticulture

22 Greenmount Rd, Antrim BT41 4PU, N Ireland; Tel (0184 94) 62114/6
Principal R.J. McClenaghan, BAgr, DipAgrComm
Head of Agricultural Education and Training E.F. Boyce, BAgr
Head of Horticulture W.R. Jones, BSc(Hort), MIHort
Head of Agricultural Technology T.A. Stewart, MA, AgrM, CBiol, MIBiol
200 full-time students; 200 part-time students

Harper Adams Agricultural College

Newport, Salop TF10 8NB; Tel (01952) 820280; Fax (01952) 814783
Chairman of Governors The Viscount Boyne, DL, JP
Principal G.R. McConnell, MAgricSc(Hons), Cant, MAIAS
Academic Registrar Dr A. Thomas, BSc, PhD
1,515 full-time and sandwich students

Loughry College of Agriculture and Food Technology

Cookstown, Co Tyrone BT80 9AA; Tel (0164 87) 62491
Principal R.C. Stevenson, BAgr, MS, PhD, CPsychol, AFBPS
Head of Food Technology Education Division W.M.A. Mullan, BSc, MSc, PhD
Head of Food Technology Services Division D. Legge, BSc, MSc, CEng, MIMechE
Head of Agriculture Division J.C. Torney, BAgr, DipAgrComm, CDipAF
360 full-time students

University of Nottingham, Faculty of Agricultural and Food Sciences

Sutton Bonington, Loughborough, Leics LE12 5RD; Tel (0115) 951 6002; Fax (0115) 951 6032
Secretary to the School A.G.S. Whitting

Royal Agricultural College

Cirencester, Glos GL7 6JS; Tel (01285) 652531; 641404 (admissions only); Fax (01285) 650219
Chairman of Governors Sir Michael Angus, BSc, HonDSc, HonDSc(Buck), CIMgt
Principal Prof A.S. Jones, BSc, PhD, CBiol, FIBiol, FBIM, FIAgrM, FRSA
Vice-Principal Prof D.J. Newton, BSc, MSc, PhD
Registrar Mrs S.J. Burton, BSc
760 full-time students

SAC: National College for Food, Land and Environmental Studies

(formerly North of Scotland College of Agriculture, West of Scotland College and East of Scotland College of Agriculture)
Principal Prof P.C. Thomas, BSc, PhD, CBiol, FIBiol SAC Edinburgh, Kings Bldgs, West Mains Rd, Edinburgh EH9 3JG
Chairman of Board of Directors J.A. Inverarity SAC Aberdeen, 581 King St, Aberdeen AB9 1UD
SAC Deputy Principal and Dean W.G.W. Paterson, BSc, MSc SAC Aberdeen
SAC Deputy Principal and Dean of Centre Prof G.D. Barber, BSc, PhD SAC Auchincruive, Ayr KA6 5HW
SAC Deputy Principal and Dean Prof D. Atkinson, BSc, PhD, MIBiol SAC Edinburgh
Academic Registrar SAC Auchincruive, Ayr KA6 5HW; Tel (01292) 520331; Fax (01292) 521119
1,200 full-time students on courses in Agriculture, Aquaculture; Biotechnology; Food Technology; Horticulture; Countryside Conservation; Leisure Management; Rural Resources; Rural Business Management; Poultry Science, Engineering, Rural Recreation, Animal and Plant Science, Pig Production and Environmental Technology

Seale-Hayne Faculty of Agriculture, Food and Land Use: University of Plymouth

Newton Abbot, Devon, TQ12 6NQ; Fax (01626) 325605
Dean Prof F. Harper, BSc, PhD, ARAgS
1,000 full-time and sandwich students

Shuttleworth College (Part of Cranfield University)

Old Warden Pk, Biggleswade, Beds SG18 9DX; Tel (01525) 863100; Fax (01525) 863101
Head of Campus Prof R.W. Radley, BSc, PhD
Director of Studies Dr J. Graham
300 full-time students

Estate Management

College of Estate Management

Whiteknights, Reading, Berks RG6 2AW; Tel (01734) 861101; Fax (01734) 755344
Chairman S.R. Burman, FRICS, FAAV
Hon Treasurer P.D. Hart, FRICS
Principal P.E. Goodacre, RD, MSc, FRICS
Secretary P. Galloway, BA, MSc
Director of Courses E.D. Moir, MA, DipMgmt
Director of Centre for Advanced Land Use Studies J.E. Leonard, BSc, FRICS
Director of Studies K.P. Wiggins, BD, FRICS
Distance learning courses, post-qualification education and training, research and publications

Art and Design

Faculties of Art, and Art Schools

Most of these establishments offer BA(Hons) or MA in Art and Design courses approved by the Council for National Academic Awards in one or more of the following areas: Fine Art (painting or sculpture), Graphic Design, Fashion and Textile Design, Three-Dimensional

Bath Academy of Art

See Bath College of Higher Education under Colleges of Higher Education – England

University of Brighton, Faculty of Art and Design and Humanities

Grand Parade, Brighton BN2 2JY; Tel (01273) 600900
Director Prof D. Watson
Dean of the Faculty Prof Bruce Brown, MA(RCA), FRSA
1,200 students (FTE)

Buckinghamshire College (a College of Brunel University)

Queen Alexandra Rd, High Wycombe, Bucks HP11 2JZ; Tel (01494) 522141; Fax (01494) 538517
Chairman of Governors O.E. Harris
Director P.B. Mogford, MA
Chief Administrative Officer T. McGowan, DMA
4,500 full-time students

Canterbury College of Art

See Kent Institute of Art and Design

Cardiff Institute of Higher Education, Faculty of Art Design and Technology

Howard Gdns, Cardiff CF2 1SP; Tel (01222) 551111
PO Box 377, Western Ave, Cardiff CF5 2SG; Tel (01222) 551111
Principal J. Derek Winslow
Dean of Faculty Robert Brown
1,300 full-time students; 300 part-time students

Birmingham Institute of Art and Design

University of Central England in Birmingham, Corporation St, Gosta Grn, Birmingham B4 7DX; Tel 0121-331 5800
Faculty Registrar F. Johnson
1,900 full-time students; 1,400 part-time students

University of Central Lancashire, Faculty of Design and Technology

Preston PR1 2TQ; Tel (01772) 201201
Dean of Faculty Prof Margaret MacKeith, MA, PhD, DipTP, DipCMS, FRTPI, MIEnvSc, FRSA

Camberwell College of Arts

See London Institute

Central Saint Martin's School of Art

See London Institute

Chelsea College of Art and Design

See London Institute

Coventry University, Coventry School of Art and Design

Gosford St, Coventry CV1 5RZ; Tel (01203) 838547
Head M.J. Tovey, MDes(RCA), MCSD, FRSA
913 full-time students

11 Higher and Vocational Education

Dartington College of Arts

In association with University of Plymouth
Totnes, Devon TQ9 6EJ; Tel (01803) 862224; Fax (01803) 863569
Chairman of Governors Sir Brian Bailey
Principal Prof Kevin Thompson, MA, PhD, GRSM, LRAM, FTCL, FRSA
Vice-Principal (Academic) and Director of Studies John Hall, BA
Vice-Principal (Adminstration) Eric Adams, MIMgt
Library and Resources Officer Dorothy Faulkner, MA, DipLib
Assistant Director of Studies Melinda Drowley, MSc
Director (Music) Trevor Wiggins
Director (Theatre) Roger Sell
Director (Visual Performance) Roger Bourke
Director (Performance Writing) Vacancy
Director (Arts Management) Donna-Lee Iffla
Courses
Modular Degree Courses in the Performance Arts; Music, Performance Writing, Theatre, Visual Performance; Arts Management
400 full time students

University of Derby, Faculty of Art and Design

Kedleston Rd, Derby DE22 1GB; Tel (01332) 47181
Vice-Chancellor R. Waterhouse, BA, MA
Dean Eric Glithero, DipAD, MA
Academic Registrar Jennifer Fry, BSc
Clerk to the Governors Jennifer Fry, BSc
5,500 FTE students

Falmouth School of Art and Design

Woodlane, Falmouth, Cornwall TR11 4RA; Tel (01326) 211077; Fax (01326) 211205
Chairman of Governors M.E. Richards
Principal Prof A. Livingston, BA, FCSD, FRSA
Registrar A.S. Schorah, BA
1,250 full-time students; 100 part-time students

Gloucestershire College of Arts and Technology

The Park Campus, 73 The Park, Cheltenham, Glos; Tel (01242) 532000
Principal I.B.T. Caves, BA(Hons), DMS
3,300 full-time students; 32,000 part-time students
Brunswick Campus, Gloucester; Tel (01452) 426500

Goldsmiths College (Departments of Educational Studies and Design Studies) University of London

Lewisham Way, London SE14 6NW; Tel 0171-919 7171
Chairman of Council Sir Paul Girolami
Warden of the College Prof Kenneth Gregory, PhD, DSc, FRGS
Head of Department of Educational Studies Vacancy
Head of Department of Design Studies Prof Richard Kimbell, BEd, MPhil
Registrar S. Guy, BA
4,000 full-time students (whole college)

Gwent College of Higher Education, Faculty of Art and Design

Clarence Pl, Newport, Gwent NPT 0UW; Tel (01633) 259984
Principal K.J. Overshott, DEng, CEng, FIEE, CPhys
Vice-Principal G.H. Williams, BSc(Econ), DipEd, FBIM
Dean of Faculty N. Trow, MA
Senior Administrative Officer D. Rix, DMA
580 full-time students

University of Hertfordshire

7 Hatfield Rd, St Albans AL1 3RS; Tel (01707) 284000
Dean C. Hunt
School Registrar B. Hart

University of Humberside

Cottingham Rd, Hull HU6 7RT; Tel (01482) 440550
Vice Chancellor Prof R. King

Kent Institute of Art & Design

Oakwood Pk, Maidstone, Kent ME16 8AG; Tel (01622) 757286
Chairman of Governors Dr R.H. Cragg
Director P.I. Williams, DFA(Lond)
Assistant Director/Head of College P. Sanger, BA(Hons), FBIPP, FRPS
Chief Administrative Officer R.H. Moon
Senior Administrative Officer Pat Yarnton
620 full-time students

Constituent Colleges

Kent Institute of Art & Design
New Dover Rd, Canterbury, Kent CT1 3AN; Tel (01227) 769371; Fax (01227) 451320
Assistant Director/Head of College R. Sales, FCCA
Senior Administrative Officer Linda Lough
800 full-time students

Kent Institute of Art and Design at Rochester
Fort Pitt, Rochester, Kent ME1 1DZ; Tel (01634) 830022
Assistant Director/Head of College M. Claridge, BA, ATC, PgD(R)
Senior Administrative Officer Sheila Langley
800 full-time students

Kingston University, Faculty of Design

Knights Pk, Kingston upon Thames KT1 2QJ; Tel 0181-549 6151
Director R.C. Smith, BSc, PhD
Academic Registrar Miss A. Hynes, BA, MA, ACIS
1,040 students

Leeds Metropolitan University, School of Visual and Cultural Studies

Calverley St, Leeds LS1 3HE; Tel (0113) 283 2600
Head of School C.D. Sandle, BA, ABPsS
160 full-time students; 550 part-time students

Liverpool John Moores University

68 Hope St, Liverpool L1 9EB; Tel 0151-231 2133
539 full-time students

London College of Fashion

See London Institute

The London Institute

65 Davies St, London W1Y 2DA; Tel 0171-514 6000; Fax 0171-514 6175
Rector John McKenzie, BSc(Econ), MPhil
Chair of Court of Governors Julian Markham
Secretary Martin Prince

Camberwell College of Arts
43/145 Peckham Rd, London SE5 8UF; Tel 0171-703 0987
Head of College Prof Roger Breakwell
1,150 students (1,020 full-time)

Central Saint Martins College of Art and Design
Southampton Row, London WC1B 4AP; Tel 0171-753 9090; Fax 0171-242 0240
Head of College Prof M. Buck, MA, RCA
2,174 students (2,027 full-time)

Chelsea College of Art and Design
Manresa Rd, Chelsea, London SW3 6LS; Tel 0171-351 3844
Head of College Prof J. Mackenzie
1,300 students (900 full-time)

London College of Fashion
20 John Prince St, London W1M 0BJ; Tel 0171-514 7400
Head of College Prof William Callaway
Specialist College of Higher and Further Education
2,200 students (1,950 full-time)

London College of Printing and Distributive Trades
Elephant and Castle, London SE1 6SB; Tel 0171-735 8484
Head of College Dr J. Clarke, MPhil, PhD
7,200 students (2,400 full-time)

Loughborough College of Art and Design
Radmoor, Loughborough, Leics LE11 3BT; Tel (01509) 261515 Ext 130; Fax (01509) 265515
Chairman of Governors Dr A. Fairbairn, MC, MA, HonDLitt, FRSA
Principal I.M. Pugh
695 full-time (HE) students; 320 full-time (FE) students; 50 part-time students

Maidstone College of Art
See Kent Institute of Art and Design

The Manchester Metropolitan University, Faculty of Art and Design
Grosvenor Bldg, Cavendish St, All Saints, Manchester M15 6BR; Tel 0161-247 1705
Dean of Faculty Prof Roger Wilson
2,300 full-time and sandwich students; 100 part-time students

Medway College of Art and Design and Performing Arts
See Kent Institute of Art and Design

Middlesex University, Faculty of Art, Design and Performing Arts
Cat Hill, Barnet, Herts EN4 8HT; Tel 0181-362 5000
Vice-Chancellor Prof D. Melville, BSc, PhD, CPhys, FInstP
Pro Vice-Chancellor and Dean Prof J. Lansdown, DipArch, RIBA, FBCS, FRSA
1,991 full-time and sandwich students

Norwich School of Art and Design
(incorporating Great Yarmouth College of Art and Design)
St George St, Norwich NR3 1BB; Tel (01603) 610561; Fax (01603) 615728
Chairman of Governors R.J. Fuller
Principal Bruce W. Black, DA(Edin), FRSA
796 full-time students
Trafalgar Rd, Great Yarmouth, Norfolk NR30 2LB; Tel (01493) 843557; Fax (01493) 852216

North East Wales Institute, College of Art and Design Technology (Faculty of Arts and Education)
Cartrefle, Cefn Rd, Wrexham, Clwyd LL13 9NL; Tel (01978) 290666; Fax (01978) 262352
Dean of Faculty R.A. Norris, MA, FCollP, FRSA

University of Northumbria at Newcastle, Faculty of Arts and Design
Squires Bldg, Sandyford Rd, Newcastle upon Tyne NE1 8ST; Tel 0191-227 4413; Fax 0191-227 4559
Dean of Faculty Prof K. McConkey, DipAD, MA(London), FRSA
Faculty Registrar Miss C.M. Covington
1,798 full-time students; 424 sandwich students; 1,044 part-time students

The Nottingham Trent University
Burton St, Nottingham NG1 4BU; Tel (0115) 941 8418
Vice-Chancellor Prof R. Cowell, BA, PhD

Ravensbourne College of Design and Communication
Walden Rd, Elmstead Woods, Chislehurst BR7 5SN; Tel 0181-468 7071; Fax 0181-295 1070
Chairman of Governors Richard Brook, MSc, AFIMA, MIEE, CEng
Director Prof Robin Baker
Registrar James Bennett, BA
A publicly–funded Higher Education Corporation in London which specialises in higher education courses in design and television. It offers degrees in Fashion Design, Graphic Design, Product Design, Interior Design and Furniture and Related Product Design and Higher Diplomas in Television Programme Operations and Television Studio Systems Engineering. Degree courses are validated by the Royal College of Art. Ravensbourne also offers a Foundation course for entry into higher education courses in art and design
630 full-time students

Royal College of Art
Kensington Gore, London SW7 2EU; Tel 0171-584 5020
Provost The Rt Hon The Earl of Gowrie, PC
Pro-Provost Sir Michael Butler, GCMG
Rector and Vice-Provost Professor Anthony Jones, DipAD, MFA
Pro-Rector Professor Christopher Frayling, MA, PhD, FRSA
Director of Administration Dennis Gatland
Registrar Alan Selby, BSc(Econ), DMS
778 students (1994/95)

Sheffield Hallam University, School of Cultural Studies
Psalter La, Sheffield S11 8UZ; Tel (0114) 253 2607
Director of School Mrs M. Ainsworth, BA, MA, CertEd
School Manager J. Hogan, BA
1,800 full-time students

Staffordshire University, School of Design and Ceramics
College Rd, Stoke-on-Trent ST4 2DE; Tel (01782) 294565; Fax (01782) 745637
Dean of School David Weightman, MDes(RCA)
School Administrator C. Rhodes, BSc

Stourbridge College
Hagley Rd, Stourbridge DY8 1QU; Tel (01384) 378531
Chairman of Governors J.E. Simpson
Principal D. Toeman, MSc, BA
Deputy Principal S. Walton, BTech, BA
1,200 full-time students

University of Sunderland, School of Arts, Design and Communications
Ashburne Hse, Backhouse Pk, Ryhope Rd, Sunderland SR2 7EF; Tel 0191-515 2110; Fax 0191-515 2132
Director of School Prof Flavia Swann, BA, FRSA
Chief Administrative Officer J.D. Pacey, LLB
990 full-time students; 240 part-time students

University of Ulster, Faculty of Art and Design
York St, Belfast BT15 1ED; Tel (01232) 328515
Dean Prof Elaine Thomas, DipAD, PGCE
Vice-Chancellor Prof T. Smith, BSc, FRHist
Over 700 full-time students

University of the West of England at Bristol, Faculty of Art, Media and Design
Clanage Rd, Bower Ashton, Bristol BS3 2JU; Tel (0117) 966 0222

Vice-Chancellor Alfred Morris
Registrar (Academic) M. Carter
970 full-time students

Surrey Institute of Art and Design

Farnham Campus, Falkner Rd, Farnham, Surrey GU9 7DS; Tel (01252) 722441; Fax (01252) 733869
Chairman of Governors G.B. Burnett, MA, LLB, CA
Director N.J. Taylor, NDD, ATC, FRSA
Registrar P. Head, BA(Hons)
1,900 full-time students (at Farnham campus)
983 full-time students (at Epsom Campus)
Epsom Campus, Ashley Rd, Epsom, Surrey; Tel (01372) 728811; Fax (01372) 726233

Wimbledon School of Art

Merton Hall Rd, London SW19 3QA; Tel 0181-540 0231; Fax 0181-543 1750
Chairman of Governors D.T. Miller
Principal Colin Painter, NDD, ATD, PhD
Academic Registrar Ms S. Lang, DMS
Administrative Officer P. Close, BA, MISM
650 full and part-time students

Winchester School of Art

Park Ave, Winchester, Hants SO23 8DL; Tel (01962) 842500; Fax (01962) 842496
Chairman of Governors K. Williams
Principal M. Sadler-Forster, BA, FRSA
Director of Academic Affairs K. Crouan, BA
College of Higher Education
667 full-time students; 175 part-time students

Colleges of Art and Crafts

For LEA Colleges, see appropriate Authority (Chapters 3–8)

Byam Shaw School of Art

2 Elthorne Rd, Archway, London N19 4AG; Tel 0171-281 4111; Fax 0171-281 1632
Principal A. Warman

City and Guilds of London Art School

124 Kennington Park Rd, London SE11 4DJ; Tel 0171-735 2306/0171-735 5210; Fax 0171-582 5361
Principal Sir Roger De Grey, KCVO, PPRA

Duncan of Jordanstone College

Perth Rd, Dundee DD1 4HT; Tel (01382) 23261; Fax (01382) 27304
Director Dr Christopher J. Carter, BA(Hons), PhD, MRTPI, FBIH, FRSA
Dean William Barr, BA, MSTD, MCSD, FRSA

Edinburgh College of Art

Lauriston Pl, Edinburgh EH3 9DF; Tel 0131-221 6000
Principal Professor Alistair Rowan, DA, PhD
Secretary and Treasurer John Nice, DMA

Glasgow School of Art

167 Renfrew St, Glasgow G3 6RQ; Tel 0141-353 4500; Fax 0141-353 4746
Director Prof Dugald Cameron, DA, FCSD
Academic Registrar Ewan Hainey, BA, DipHW
Independent, Art School offering a wide range of courses in Architecture, Fine Art and Design. All school's degrees are validated by the University of Glasgow
1,300 FTE students

Inchbald School of Design

7 Eaton Gate, London SW1W 9BA; Tel 0171-730 5508
Principal Jacqueline Duncan
Long and short courses in Interior Design, Design History; Garden Design
Number of students per annum 200
32 Eccleston Sq, London SW1V 1PB; Tel 0171-630 9011

Royal Academy Schools of Painting and Sculpture

Burlington Hse, Piccadilly, London W1V 0DS; Tel 0171-439 7438
Keeper Prof Norman Adams, RA
Secretary Laura Scott

The Scottish College of Textiles

Netherdale, Galashiels, Selkirkshire TD1 3HF; Tel (01896) 753351
Principal Prof C.E.R. Maddox, BSc, PhD, CBiol, MIBiol, DipManEd
790 full-time students

West Dean College

West Dean, Chichester, W Sussex PO18 0QZ; Tel (01243) 811301; Fax (01243) 811343
Principal Dr David Leigh
Short residential courses in Arts, Crafts and Music; 1/2-year courses in Restoration of Antique Furniture, Clocks, Ceramics, Fine Metalwork, Rare Books; 3-year apprenticeships in Musical Instrument Making; 1-year course in Advanced Tapestry Weaving

Music, Dance and Drama Colleges

The Arts Educational London School

14 Bath Rd, Chiswick, London W4 1LY; Tel 0181-994 9366; Fax 0181-994 9274
Principal Peter Fowler, MA, FTCL, LRAM, ARAM, FRSA
Pupils (10–16) Academic education to GCSE and A levels combined with training in the performing arts of the theatre
Students (16+) Course in Dance, Drama, Musical Theatre and Acting Company

The Arts Educational School, Tring Park

Tring Pk, Tring, Herts HP23 5LX; Tel (0144 282) 4255/6; Fax (01442) 891069
Principal Jane Billing, GGSM
Combined academic and vocational training (Dance, Drama, Theatre Studies) to GCSE and A–level. Entry by audition. Girls/Boys Day/Girls Boarding

Barbara Speake Stage School

East Acton La, East Acton, London W3 7EG; Tel 0181-743 1306
Principal Barbara M. Speake, ARAD
200 day pupils full-time academic school

Birmingham Conservatoire

Paradise Pl, Birmingham B3 3HG; Tel 0121-331 5900/1/2/12; Fax 0121-331 5906
Principal Prof G. Caird, BA, FRAM, ARCM
Associate Dean Prof David Brock, MA, BMus, PhD, FTCL, LRAM, ARCM, ARCO

Birmingham School of Speech and Drama

45 Church Rd, Edgbaston, Birmingham B15 3SW; Tel 0121-454 3424
Principal Patricia A. Yardley, LRAM

The Bristol Old Vic Theatre School

2 Downside Rd, Clifton, Bristol BS8 2XF; Tel (0117) 973 3535
Principal Christopher Denys

Britten–Pears School for Advanced Musical Studies

High St, Aldeburgh, Suffolk IP15 5AX; Tel (01728) 452935
Director of Singing Studies Anthony Rolfe Johnson
Director of String Studies Hugh Maguire
Director Katherine Wolfenden
Founded in 1972 by Benjamin Britten and Peter Pears
The Britten–Pears School holds Master Class courses for young singers and string players of outstanding ability and promise who are on the threshold of their professional careers. Each course is taught by distinguished guest teachers, and students from all over the world are selected by audition. Observers are welcome to attend all Master Class courses. The Orchestras of the Britten–Pears School (modern and baroque) meet five or six times a year for courses with world–class conductors, culminating in concerts at Snape Maltings Concert Hall and throughout East Anglia

Central School of Ballet

10 Herbal Hill, Clerkenwell Rd, London EC1R 5EJ; Tel 0171-837 6332; Fax 0171-833 5571
Directors C. Gable; A. Stannard
Training for a professional career in Classical Ballet or Contemporary Dance

Central School of Speech and Drama

Embassy Theatre, 64 Eton Ave, London NW3 3HY; Tel 0171-722 8183
Chairman of Governors G. Laurence Harbottle
Principal Prof Robert S. Fowler, MA(Oxon), LGSM, FRSA
Senior Assistant Principal Debbie Scully, DMS
Student Facilities
Lodgings assistance

Curwen Institute

5 Bigbury Cl, Styvechale, Coventry CV3 5AJ; Tel (01203) 413010
Hon Secretary Barry N. Sampson
President Dr Bernard Rainbow, PhD, MEd
Director John Dowding, LRAM, ARCM

Doreen Bird College of Performing Arts

Birkbeck Centre, Birkbeck Rd, Sidcup, Kent DA14 4DE; Tel 0181-300 3031; Fax 0181-308 1370

Drama Centre London

176 Prince of Wales Rd, Chalk Fm, London NW5 3PT; Tel 0171-267 1177; Fax 0171-485 7129
Principal C. Fettes

East 15 Acting School

South Centre: Hatfields, Rectory La, Loughton, Essex; Tel 0181-508 5983
Director and Founder Margaret Walker
Registrar Pauline Simmons (Sheriff Hutton Park)
3-year acting course; 3-year directors course; 1-year postgraduate acting course; 2-year stage-management courses; 2 Term (24 weeks) FASTSTREAM
North Centre: Sheriff Hutton Pk, Sheriff Hutton, Yorks YO6 1RH; Tel (01347) 878442

Guildford School of Acting

Millmead Terr, Guildford, Surrey GU2 5AT; Tel (01483) 560701
Principal Michael Gaunt
Performance and Stage Management Courses: One Year Acting Course for graduates and mature students accredited by the NCDT
3 year Performance Course (Acting and Musical Theater, 1 year Acting Option for Graduates); 2 year Stage Management Course: 1 year Option for graduates and mature students: 4 week and 2 week Summer Schools in Acting and 6 day Singing School
3 year Performance Course BA(Hons) Theatre Acting and Musical Theatre Pathways validated by the University of Surrey

Guildhall School of Music and Drama

Barbican, London EC2Y 8DT; Tel 0171-628 2571; Fax 0171-256 9438
Principal Ian Horsbrugh, FGSM, FRCM, HonRAM, FRSAMD, FRNCM, FRSA
Director of Music Damian Cranmer, BMus, MA, FGSM
Director of Drama Virginia Snyders, FGSM
Director of Administration David Imrie, MA, BA, HonGSM
Director of Technical Theatre Department S. Thornton

Laban Centre for Movement and Dance

Laurie Grove, New Cross, London SE14 6NH; Tel 0181-692 4070; Fax 0181-694 8749
Director M. North, PhD

London Academy of Music and Dramatic Art (LAMDA)

Tower Hse, 226 Cromwell Rd, London SW5 0SR; Tel 0171-373 9883/14337
Principal Peter James
Vice Principal Colin Cook
Principal of Examinations Shaun McKenna, BA(Hons)
Director of Stage Management Patrick Frazer

Middlesex University School of Dance (incorporating London College of Dance)

Trent Park, Bramley Rd, London N14 4XS
Head of School Prof Christopher Bannerman
The School of Dance incorporating London College of Dance offers the following degree programmes:- BA(Hons) Dance at the London College campus, Bedford – study relates to classical ballet traditions; BA(Hons) Dance Performance, Dance Studies, Performing Arts (Dance), Combined Studies subject options include Spanish, Education and Business Studies and MA in Choreography (subject to validation) at the Trent Park campus London. Study at Trent Park relates to British Contemporary Dance and connected traditions

London Contemporary Dance School

The Place, 17 Dukes Rd, London WC1H 9AB; Tel 0171-387 0152
Principal Richard Ralph, MA, DPhil
Assistant Principal Peter Connell
The major centre for training professional contemporary dancers outside North America, offering 1- and 4-year Diploma and Certificate courses which provide full-time vocational training in contemporary dance, classical ballet, choreography, music and practical stagecraft. There are also a BA(Hons) Degree course and a BA Degree course that emphasise the practical and creative aspects of dance performance supported by required study in related subjects
The LCDS regularly auditions in London and annually in Europe and Australia. Easter and summer courses offer classes in contemporary dance, jazz and classical ballet as recreational and pre-vocational activities, as well as advanced professional and specialised educational courses
LCDS Library includes books on the performing arts, visual arts, music, mythology, literature, etc. The archives of the London Contemporary Dance Theatre and Contemporary Dance Trust are held by the library

and research enquiries should be addressed to the Librarian

London Studio Centre

42–50 York Way, London N1 9AB; Tel 0171-837 7741; Fax 0171-837 3248
Director Nicholas Espinosa
Registrar Sandra Johnson
General Manager Francis Yeoh
3-year full-time professional training in the performing arts
1-year intensive classical graduate class for advanced ballet students intending to join professional companies.
(50–60) Independent

Manchester Metropolitan University, School of Theatre

Capitol Bldg, School La, Didsbury, Manchester M20 0HT; Tel 0161-247 2000 Ext 7123
Head of School Niamh Dowling

Mountview Theatre School Ltd

104 Crouch Hill, London N8 9EA; Tel 0181-340 5885; Fax 0181-348 1727
Principal Peter Coxhead
President Sir John Mills, CBE
Full-time professional courses
The Ralph Richardson Memorial Studios, 1 Kingfisher Pl, Clarendon Rd, Wood Green, London N22 6XF; Tel 0181-881 2201; Fax 0181-365 7635

Queen Margaret College

Clerwood Terr, Edinburgh EH12 8TS; Tel 0131-317 3000
Principal Prof D.F. Leach, BSc, CMath, FIMA, CPhys, MInstP, CEng, MBCS, FRSA

Rose Bruford College

Lamorbey Pk, Sidcup, Kent DA15 9DF; Tel 0181-300 3024; Fax 0181-308 0542
Principal Rob Ely

College of the Royal Academy of Dancing

36 Battersea Sq, London SW11 3RA; Tel 0171-223 0091; Fax 0171-924 3129; Telex 8952105 RADANG G
Principal Ms S. Danby, LRAD, ARAD

Royal Academy of Dramatic Art

62 Gower St, London WC1E 6ED; Tel 0171-636 7076
Principal Nicholas Barter, MA(CANTAB)
Registrar Patricia Myers

Royal Academy of Music

Marylebone Rd, London NW1 5HT; Tel 0171-873 7373
Principal Lynn Harrell, Hon RAM

Royal Ballet School

Upper School: 155 Talgarth Rd, London W14 9DE; Tel 0181-748 6335
Director Dame Merle Park, DBE
Ballet Administrator Rashna Homji-Jefferies
Assistant Director Nigel Grant, BMus(Hons)
Academic and Pastoral Principal Maureen D'Albertanson, MA
Lower School: White Lodge, Richmond Pk, Surrey; Tel 0181-876 5547

Royal College of Music

Prince Consort Rd, London SW7 2BS; Tel 0171-589 3643; Fax 0171-589 7740
Director Janet Ritterman, BMus, MMus, PhD, FICL, DSCM, FRSA
Vice-Director and Director of Studies Nicholas King, MA, MusB, FRCM, FRCO(CHM)
Academic Registrar Kevin Porter, BA
Bursar W. Michael Morgan, FBIM

Royal College of Organists

7 Andrew St, London EC4A 3LQ; Tel 0171-936 3606; Fax 0171-353 8244
Chief Executive Michael Nicholas

Royal Northern College of Music

124 Oxford Rd, Manchester M13 9RD; Tel 0161-273 6283; Fax 0161-273 7611
Principal Sir John Manduell, CBE, CAL, HonDMus, FRAM, FRCM, FRNCM, FRSAMD, FWCMD, HonFTCL, HonGSMD, FBSH, FMP, FRSA

Royal School of Church Music

Addington Palace, Croydon CR9 5AD; Tel 0181-654 7676; Fax 0181-655 2542
Director Harry Bramma, MA, FRCO

Royal Scottish Academy of Music and Drama

100 Renfrew St, Glasgow G2 3DB; Tel 0141-332 4101; Fax 0141-332 8901
Principal Philip Ledger, CBE, MA, MusB, LLD, FRCM, HonRAM, FRNCM, HonGSM, FRCO, FRSE
Director of Finance and Administration Isobel Fowler
523 FTE students (316 music; 207 drama)

Trinity College of Music

Mandeville Pl, London W1M 6AQ; Tel 0171-935 5773; Fax 0171-224 6278
Principal Gavin Henderson

Webber Douglas Academy of Dramatic Art

30 Clareville St, London SW7 5AP; Tel 0171-370 4154
Principal R.B. Jago

Welsh College of Music and Drama

Castle Grounds, Cathays Pk, Cardiff CF1 3ER; Tel (01222) 342854
Principal Edmond Fivet
Director of Music David Nevens
Director of Drama Paul Clements

Adult Education Associations

Adult Residential Colleges Association (ARCA)

Headlands, Church La, Washbrook, Ipswich, Suffolk IP8 3HF; Tel (01473) 730737; Fax (01473) 730737
Chairman Vacancy
Secretary Derek Barbanell
The object of the Association is to promote and disseminate knowledge of the working of the short-term residential colleges to central and local government, other institutions and to the general public

Community Education Development Centre

Lyng Hall, Blackberry La, Coventry CV2 3JS; Tel (01203) 638660; Fax (01203) 681161
Chair Prof Eric Midwinter
Director John Rennie
The Community Education Development Centre provides training, support and consultancy for community educators, by mounting courses and programmes, by publishing and disseminating resources, and by

forming links between community educators nationally and internationally. It provides models for development by carrying out innovative projects, and establishes partnership and collaboration with other services connected with the community

East Midlands Regional Institute of Adult Education (EMRIAE)

c/o 48 Victoria St, Newark, Notts NG24 4UT
Chair Ms S.A. Mills
Secretary Vacancy
To improve the quality of Adult Education in the East Midlands by providing a forum for discussion, by providing seminars, research and publications

National Co-operative Education Association

Stanford Hall, Loughborough, Leics LE12 5QR; Tel (01509) 852333
Chairman of Education Executive A. Thompson
Vice-Chairman of Education Executive E. Hall
Chief Education Officer R. Houlton, MA, PhD
Deputy Chief Education Officer R. Wildgust, BA, ACIS
Officer for Member Education (including Youth Work) M. Wilson, BA

Community Matters (National Federation of Community Organisations)

8/9 Upper St, Islington, London N1 0PQ; Tel 0171-226 0189; Fax 0171-354 9570
National Director Charles Woodd
National Development Officer Olive Bolton Charlton Hse, 36 Hunslet Rd, Leeds LS10 1JN; Tel (0113) 245 6634
President Raymond Clarke
Chairman Michael Clasby
Hon Treasurer D. Watson
Community Matters promotes the activities of local community organisations in the areas of education, recreation and social welfare. The Federation offers support for training, an information and advice service from its Leeds and London offices, and publishes a range of publications. Community Matters also represents the interests of local community organisations nationally

National Institute of Adult Continuing Education

21 De Montfort St, Leicester LE1 7GE; Tel (0116) 255 1451; Fax (0116) 285 4514
President Dick Smethurst
Director Alan Tuckett
NIACE is a national centre for research, advice and information on all forms of adult continuing education. Its governing council has representatives of Local Education Authorities (appointed by the AMA, ACC, and Welsh Joint Education Committee), the Universities, and Colleges, Armed Forces, Home Office, the BBC and IBA, and numerous national voluntary for bodies. The Department for Education appoints assessors. The membership comprises national bodies promoting all forms of adult education, and there are provisions for corporate, and individual membership, Registered Company no. 2603322 and registered charity no. 1002775
NIACE, the national organisation for adult learning also carries out enquiries, publishes *Adults Learning* (monthly), and *Studies in the Education of Adults* (bi-annually), maintains a library and information centre and organises an annual and other conferences. Other regular publications are half-yearly booklets: *Time to Learn* (January and August) and a *Year Book of Adult Continuing Education* (September). NIACE promotes public awareness of study opportunities by organising Adult Learners' week each year
Recent publications include *Wasted Potential (Training and Career Progression for Part-Time and Temporary Workers); Understanding Assessment; Older and Wiser (Participation in Education by Older Black Adults); Women, Education and Training; The Will to Learn; An Adult Higher Education; Flexible Access to Vocational Qualifications; Education and Deaf and Hard of Hearing Adults*

Network Scotland Ltd

Tel 0141-357 1774
Network Scotland Limited provides information services including publishing, telephone counselling and data support services. Network manages the Strathclyde TAP project, which aims to make computerised information on training and education available to the public and business. Services include information audits, information research, data processing, quality control and associated services in the continued updating and maintenance of information

North West Adult International Education Conference

Secretary Jenny Clift 43 Chorley Rd, Hilldale, Parbold, Nr Wigan
Convenor D. Hall
International Secretary David Selby 12 North Houses La, Lytham St Annes, Lancs FY8 4NT; Tel (01253) 723600
Treasurer B. Leighton
This is a voluntary organisation, funded solely by the subscriptions to the annual one-day conference. The prime aim of the committee is to organise the conference for all those in the North West of England who are interested in the development of adult education, whether full-time or part-time staff, from statutory or voluntary organisations, teachers or students and to develop overseas links with adult educators

Northern Ireland Adult Education Association (NIAEA)

c/o 42 Northland Rd, Londonderry BT48 7ND, N Ireland; Tel (01504) 265007
Chair M. Maginn
Vice-Chair P. Patten
Secretary M. Baumann
Treasurer E. Kelly

The Open College

St Pauls, 781 Wilmslow Rd, Didsbury, Manchester M20 2RW; Tel 0161-434 0007; Fax 0161-434 1061
Managing Director Michael Colenso
The Open College specialises in the production of open learning training materials for business and education. Training materials are offered in health and care management and supervisory, business and office skills, technology, and education and training sectors. Most courses lead to recognised national qualifications
In addition to training materials, the College offers support services, especially commissioned and custom-designed training programmes for organisations, accreditation services and consultancy in open and flexible learning. The Open College is dedicated to helping to raise the skills level of the workforce through courses leading to nationally recognised qualifications

Scottish Community Education Council

Rosebery Hse, 9 Haymarket Terr, Edinburgh EH12 5EZ; Tel 0131-313 2488; Fax 0131-313 6800
The Council supports those active in community education to meet the learning needs of people in communities through influencing public policy and awareness, promoting best practice, and providing information, products and services. The Council is active in five main areas: adult education, community work, youth work, international services, and setting training standards

Workers' Educational Association

17 Victoria Park Sq, London E2 9PB; Tel 0181-983 1515; Fax 0181-983 4840
President W. Conboy
General Secretary Robert Lochrie
Deputy General Secretary Mel Doyle

District Secretaries

Thames and Solent
Sarah Grylls 6 Brewer St, Oxford OX1 1QN; Tel (01865) 246270; Fax (01865) 204282

Eastern
Carolyn Daines Botolph Hse, 17 Botolph La, Cambridge CB2 3RE; Tel (01223) 350978; Fax (01223) 300911

East Midlands
Russell Gent 16 Shakespeare St, Nottingham NG1 4GF; Tel (0115) 947 5162; Fax (0115) 924 3513

London
Philippa Langton 44 Crowndale Rd, London NW1 1TR; Tel 0171-388 7261; Fax 0171-383 5668

Northern
Michael Standen 51 Grainger St, Newcastle upon Tyne NE1 5JE; Tel 0191-232 3957; Fax 0191-230 3696

North–Western
Ian Harford 4th Fl, Crawford Hse, University Precinct Centre, Oxford Rd, Manchester M13 9GH; Tel 0161-273 7652; Fax 0161-274 4948

South–Eastern
Vernon Hull 4 Castle Hill, Rochester, Kent ME1 1QQ; Tel (01634) 842140; Fax (01634) 815643

South–Western
E. Weightman Martin's Gate Annexe, Bretonside, Plymouth PL4 0AT; Tel (01752) 664989; Fax (01752) 254195

Western
Dr Joan Smith 40 Morse Rd, Redfield, Bristol BS5 9LB; Tel (0117) 935 1764; Fax (0117) 941 1757

Cheshire, Merseyside & West Lancashire
Dorothea Hall 7/8 Bluecoat Chambers, School La, Liverpool L1 3BX; Tel 0151-709 8023; Fax 0151-708 0046

West Mercia
R.E. Copley 78–80 Sherlock St, Birmingham B5 6LT; Tel 0121-666 6101; Fax 0121-622 2526

Yorks North
Sam Herman 6 Woodhouse Sq, Leeds LS3 1AD; Tel (0113) 245 3304; Fax (0113) 245 0883

Yorks South
Ted Hartley Chantry Bldgs, 6-20 Corporation St, Rotherham S60 1NG; Tel (01709) 837001; Fax (01709) 372121

Scottish Association
Joyce Connon Riddle's Ct, 322 Lawnmarket, Edinburgh EH1 3PG; Tel 0131-226 3456; Fax 0131-220 0306

Residential Colleges

Alston Hall Residential College for Adult Education

Alston La, Longridge, nr Preston, Lancs PR3 3BP; Tel (01772) 784661; Fax (01772) 785835
Principal Brian Leighton, MPhil

Beamish Hall

Stanley, Co Durham DH9 0RG; Tel (01207) 233147; Fax (01207) 281723

Warden T.M. McKeon, MEd
Deputy Warden M.V. Horne

Belstead House Education and Conference Centre

Belstead, Ipswich, Suffolk IP8 3NA; Tel (01473) 686321; Fax (01473) 686664
Manager Ruth Castles
Residential Adult Education Centre In-service Training for Suffolk County Council Residential Conference Centre

Braziers Adult College

Ipsden, Wallingford, Oxon OX10 6AN; Tel (01491) 680221, 680481
Convenor of Studies David Allen, MA

Breanoc Field Study Centre

Goonvrea, St Agnes, Cornwall TR5 0NW; Tel (01872) 2727
Principal Roger Burrows, BA, MIBiol

Burton Manor

Burton-in-Wirral, Cheshire L64 5SJ; Tel 0151-336 5172
Principal Janet Dawson

Burwell Hse Residential Centre

North St, Burwell, Cambridge CB5 0BA; Tel (01638) 741256
Warden G. Parker

Coleg Harlech

Harlech, Gwynedd LL46 2PU; Tel (01766) 780363; Fax (01766) 780169
Warden J.W. England, BA

Co-operative College

Stanford Hall, Loughborough, Leics LE12 5QR; Tel (01509) 852333
Principal R. Houlton, MA, PhD

Debden Hse

Debden Grn, Loughton, Essex IG10 2PA; Tel 0181-508 3008
Head of Centre Claire Tallett, MA, MBA

Denman College (N.F.W.I.)

Marcham, nr Abingdon, Oxon OX13 6NW; Tel (01865) 391991
Principal Graham Jones, BSc

The Devon Centre

Dartington Hall, Totnes, Devon TQ9 6EJ; Tel (01803) 862267
Warden Sylvia Eglington
Deputy Warden Diana Inglesant

Dillington House

Ilminster, Somerset TA19 9DT; Tel (01460) 52427, 53875; Fax (01460) 52433
General Manager Wayne Bennett

Dyffryn Hse

Conference Centre, St Nicholas, nr Cardiff CF5 6SU; Tel (01222) 593328

The Earnley Concourse

Earnley, Chichester, W Sussex PO20 7JL; Tel (01243) 670392; Fax (01243) 670832
The Administrator Owain Roberts
Residential centre for adult education

Easthampstead Park

Easthampstead Pk School, Wokingham, Berks RG11 3DF; Tel (01734) 780986
Principal J.M. Hawe, BA, FRSA

Emerson College

Forest Row, Sussex RH18 5JX; Tel (01342) 822238; Fax (01342) 826055
Education Director G. Locher
(Training in Steiner/Waldorf Education recognised by the Steiner Schools Fellowship in the UK and the Steiner/Waldorf movement worldwide)

Fircroft College

1018 Bristol Rd, Selly Oak, Birmingham B29 6LH; Tel 0121-472 0116
Principal Keith Jackson, MA

Grafham Water Centre

Perry, Huntingdon PE18 0BX; Tel (01480) 810521
Warden John Leaworthy
Deputy Warden Ian Downing

Grantley Hall

Ripon, North Yorkshire HG4 3ET; Tel (01765) 620259; Fax (01765) 620443
Manager K.L. Dart, MHCI, MA

Halsway Manor

Crowcombe, Taunton, Somerset TA4 4BD; Tel (0198 48) 274
Manager Bernard Hucker, MHCIMA

Hawkwood Short Course Residential College and Conference Centre

Stroud, Glos GL6 7QW; Tel (01453) 764607; Fax (01453) 764607
Principal Stephanie Cooper
Principal Tony Cooper

Hawse End Outdoor Education

Portinscale, Keswick, Cumbria CA12 5UE
Administrator Barbara Hunter

Higham Hall Residential Conference and Study Centre

Bassenthwaite Lake, Cockermouth, Cumbria CA13 9SH; Tel (0176 87) 76276; Fax (0176 87) 76013
Director A. Galbraith

The Hill Residential College

Pen-y-pound, Abergavenny, Gwent NP7 7RP; Tel (01873) 855221; Fax (01873) 854817
Principal L.J. Newcombe, MA(Oxon)

Hillcroft Residential College for Adult Education

South Bank, Surbiton, Surrey KT6 6DF; Tel 0181-399 2688
Principal Eileen Aird
A women's college. Mandatory grants, subject to eligibility, for full-time and accelerated entry courses. Many short courses also available

Holly Royde Conference Centre (of Manchester University Continuing Education)

56–62 Palatine Rd, West Didsbury, Manchester M20 3JP; Tel 0161-275 3274; Fax 0161-275 3300
Director Douglas Kaye, BSc

11 Higher and Vocational Education

Horncastle College
Mareham Rd, Horncastle, Lincs LN9 6BW; Tel (01507) 522449; Fax (01507) 524382
Principal Peter Weston, MSc

Knuston Hall Adult Education Residential College
Irchester, Wellingborough, Northants NN9 7EU; Tel (01933) 312104; Fax (01933) 57596
Principal John Herrick, MEd

Lancashire College
Southport Rd, Chorley PR7 1NB; Tel (01257) 276719; Fax (01257) 241370
Principal Andrew Burgen
Vice-Principal Andy Yeomans
Courses Manager Jackie Patry

Little Benslow Hills (Benslow Music Trust)
Benslow La, Hitchin, Herts SG4 9RB; Tel (01462) 459446
Registrar Marie Lucioli, BSc, CPsychol, ALCM
Week–end, mid–week and longer courses for adult musicians of all ages and standards. Summer schools. Private parties accommodated. Details from Registrar

Peak National Park Study Centre
Losehill Hall, Castleton, Derbys S30 2WB; Tel (01433) 620373; Fax (01433) 620346
Director P. Townsend

Maryland Residential College for Adult Education
Woburn, Milton Keynes MK17 9JD; Tel (01525) 290688
Principal Brian Cairns
Vice-Principal Alexander Boyd

Missenden Abbey
Great Missenden, Bucks HP16 0BD; Tel (01494) 890295/6; Fax (01494) 866737
Course Director April Halton

Newbattle Abbey College
Dalkeith, Midlothian EH22 3LL; Tel 0131-663 1921
Principal W.M. Conboy, MA, FRSA

Northern College
Wentworth Castle, Stainborough, Barnsley, S Yorks S75 3ET; Tel (01226) 285426
Principal R.H. Fryer, MA(Cantab)

The Old Rectory
Adult Education College, Upper St, FIttleworth, Pulborough, Sussex RH20 1HU; Tel (01798) 865306
Principal Sue Dawkins
Principal Tony Dawkins

Pendrell Hall College
Codsall Wood, nr Wolverhampton WV8 1QP; Tel (01902) 842398; Fax (01902) 846351
Principal David Evans, MEd, LCP, JP

Plater College
Pullens La, Oxford OX3 0DT; Tel (01865) 741676
Principal M. Blades, MA(Oxon)

Pyke Hse
Battle, Sussex TN33 0AN; Tel (01424) 772495; Fax (01424) 775041
Head of Centre Danny O'Sullivan

Kellogg College
1 Wellington Sq, Oxford OX1 2JA; Tel (01865) 270360
President G.P. Thomas, MA, BSc, PhD, Director of Continuing Education
(36th College of Oxford University, linked to the University's Department for Continuing Education)

Richmond College, The American International University in London
Richmond College Campus (lower division): Queen's Rd, Richmond, Surrey TW10 6JP; Tel 0181-332 9000 (admission enquiries); 0181-332 8200 (all other departments); Fax 0181-332 1596 (admission enquiries); 0181-332 3050 (all other departments)
President Walter McCann
Curriculum based on the American Liberal Arts model. Accredited by Commission on Higher Education of the Middle States Association of Colleges and Schools (USA) as an independent American international university, offering 3 and 4 year degree programmes. Offers BA, BSc degrees in Business Administration Communications, English Literature, Mathematical Sciences, International Business, Political Science, Psychology, Computing, Anthropology/Sociology, Economics, Studio Art, British Studies, History, Theatre Arts. Also offers joint engineering programme with George Washington University (USA). Also offers the degree of Master of Business Administration, all degrees designated by the Department for Education (UK)
Kensington Campus (upper division): 1 St Alban's Gr, London W8 5PN; Tel 0171-368 8400; Fax 0171-937 9724
MBA Program Office, School of Business, 16 Young St, London W8 5EH; Tel 0171-938 1804; Fax 0171-938 3037

Ruskin College
Oxford OX1 2HE; Tel (01865) 54331
Principal Stephen Yeo, MA, DPhil

Urchfont Manor College
nr Devizes, Wilts SN10 4RG; Tel (01380) 840495
Warden Ernest Richards, MA(Cantab), ADB
Deputy Warden Thomas Barklem, BSc, FRGS, FGS

Wansfell College for Residential Adult Education
Theydon Bois, Epping, Essex CM16 7LF; Tel (01992) 813027
Principal Marilyn Taylor, BA, DipACE
(Essex County Council)

Wedgwood Memorial College
Barlaston, Stoke-on-Trent, Staffs; Tel (01782) 372105/373427; Fax (01782) 372393
Principal D. Tatton, MA(Cantab), PhD
(Staffordshire County Council)

Wensum Lodge Residential Centre for Adult and Continuing Education
King St, Norwich, Norfolk NR1 1QW; Tel (01603) 666021; Fax (01603) 765633
Principal Simon J. Pollock

West Dean College (The Edward James Foundation) of Crafts, Arts & Music
West Dean, Chichester, W Sussex PO18 0QZ; Tel (01243) 811301; Fax (01243) 811343
Principal Peter Sarginson

Westham Hse
Barford, Warks CV35 8DP; Tel (01926) 624206
Principal Dr Donn Evans

12 Further, Tertiary and Sixth Form Education

Further Education Colleges

Aberdare College
Cwmdare Rd, Aberdare, Powys CF44 8ST; Tel (01685) 873405; Fax (01685) 876635
Principal G.E. Phillips, BA, MEd, DipEd, FREconS

Aberdeen College of Further Education
College Administration, Gallowgate, Aberdeen, Grampian AB9 1DN; Tel (01224) 640366
Principal J.M. Ferguson, BSc(Econ), MPhil, DipEd, FCIS, FBIM, FRSA, FSA Scot

Aberdeen Technical College
Gallowgate, Aberdeen, Grampian AB9 1DN; Tel (01224) 640366; Fax (01224) 647178
Principal Vacancy

Abingdon College
Northcourt Rd, Abingdon, Oxon OX14 1NN; Tel (01235) 555585; Fax (01235) 553168
Principal R.E. Challis, MA, DipEd

The Adult College–Lancaster
Quarry Rd, White Cross, Lancaster, Lancs LA1 4XQ; Tel (01524) 60141
Principal Peter Garrod

Air Service Training Limited
Perth Aerodrome, Perth, Tayside PH2 6NP; Tel (01738) 52311; Fax (01738) 53006; Telex 76265

Airedale & Wharfedale College
Calverley La, Horsforth, Leeds, W. Yorks LS18 4RQ; Tel (0113) 258 1723; Fax (0113) 259 1138
Principal Vacancy

Alston Hall College
Alston La, Longridge, nr Preston, Lancs PR3 3BP; Tel (01772) 784661; Fax (01772) 785835
Principal Brian Leighton, MPhil

Amersham & Wycombe College
Amersham Campus, Amersham, Bucks HP7 9HN; Tel (01494) 735555; Fax (01494) 735566
Principal D.S. Mason, MSc, FRSA

Angus College
Keptie Rd, Arbroath, Angus DD11 3EA; Tel (01241) 72056
Principal I.S. Ovens, BA(Hons), DMS

Anniesland College
Hatfield Dr, Glasgow, Strathclyde G12 0YE; Tel 0141-357 3969
Principal H.A.D. Walker, BA, DAL

Architectural Association School of Architecture
34–36 Bedford Sq, London WC1B 3ES; Tel 0171-636 0974
Chairman Alan Balfour, DA(Edin), MFA(Princetown), RIBA, AIA

Armagh College of Further Education

Lonsdale Rd, Armagh, Co Armagh BT61 7HN; Tel (01861) 522205
Principal W.K. Lowry, BA, ACP, CertEd

Arnold and Carlton College

Digby Ave, Mapperley, Nottingham, Notts NG3 6DR; Tel (0115) 952 0052; Fax (0115) 953 1210; Student Services (01602) 615886
Principal Ronnie Ogier

Ashridge Management College

Berkhamsted, Herts HP4 1NS; Tel (0144 284) 3491/2311; Fax (0144 284) 3453

Avon & Gloucestershire College of Health

Avon Centre, Glenside, Blackberry Hill, Stapleton, Bristol, Avon BS16 1DD; Tel (0117) 958 5655; Fax (0117) 975 8498 Gloucestershire Centre, Oakes Hse, 55–59 London Rd, Gloucester GL1 3HF

Aylesbury College

Oxford Rd, Aylesbury, Bucks HP21 8PD; Tel (01296) 434111
Principal B. Bennett

Ayr College

Dam Pk, Ayr, Strathclyde KA8 0EU; Tel (01292) 265184; Fax (01292) 263889
Principal F. Burns, BSc(Hons), ASCC(Hons)

Banff and Buchan College of Further Education

Henderson Rd, Fraserburgh, Grampian AB43 5GA; Tel (01346) 25777
Principal Alexander Gordon

Barking College

Principal Ted Parker

Barnet College

Wood St, Barnet, Herts EN5 4AZ; Tel 0181-440 6321
Principal J. Skitt
Russell La, Whetstone, London N20 0AX; Tel 0181-361 5101; Fax 0181-441 5236

Barnfield College

New Bedford Rd, Luton, Beds LU2 7BF; Tel (01582) 507531; Fax (01582) 572264
Principal James Horrocks, BSc, CEng, MIMechE, MBIM, CertEd

Barry College

Colcot Rd, Barry, South Glamorgan CF62 8YJ; Tel (01446) 743519; Fax (01446) 732667
Chief Executive T. Wilmore, BSc, ARCS, CEng, MIEE

Basford Hall College of Further Education

Stockhill La, Nottingham, Notts NG6 0NB; Tel (0115) 970 4541; Fax (0115) 942 2334
Principal John Gray, BSc(Hons), MA, CertEd

Basingstoke College of Technology

Worting Rd, Basingstoke, Hants RG21 1TN; Tel (01256) 54141; Fax (01256) 810007
Principal S.H. Cowser, BSc, MSc(Tech), CEng, MIMechE, MIEE

Beamish Hall

Stanley, Co Durham DH9 0RG; Tel (01207) 233147; Fax (01207) 287723
Warden T.M. McKeon, MEd

The Belfast Institute of Further and Higher Education

Founded 1992 by the merging of The College of Business Studies, Belfast College of Technology and Rupert Stanley College
Park Hse, 87–91 Gt Victoria St, Belfast BT2 7AG; Tel (01232) 325312
Director Prof D. McCloy

Bell College of Technology

Almada St, Hamilton, Strathclyde ML3 0JB; Tel (01698) 283100; Fax (01698) 282131
Principal J. Reid, BSc, CEng, FIMarE, MIMechE

Belstead House Education and Conference Centre

Belstead, Ipswich, Suffolk IP8 3NA; Tel (01473) 686321; Fax (01473) 686664

Beverley College of Further Education

Gallows La, Beverley, Humberside; Tel (01482) 868362
Chairman of Governors P. Downey
Principal J. Carroll, BA(Hons), MA

Bexley College

Tower Rd, Belvedere, Kent DA17 6JA; Tel (01322) 442331; Fax (01322) 448403
Principal J.D. Healy, BSc, PhD, CChem, FRSC

Birmingham College of Food, Tourism and Creative Studies

Summer Row, Birmingham, West Midlands B3 1JB; Tel 0121-604 1000
Principal E.F. McIntyre, BA(Hons), CertEd, MHCIMA

Bishop Auckland College

Woodhouse La, Bishop Auckland, Co Durham DL14 6JZ; Tel (01388) 603052; Fax (01388) 609294
Principal Joanna Tait

Bishop Grosseteste College

Lincoln, Lincs LN1 3DY; Tel (01522) 527347; Fax (01522) 530243
Principal Prof L.G. Marsh, OBE, MEd, DPhil, HonFCP

Blackpool and The Fylde College

Bispham Campus, Ashfield Rd, Bispham, Blackpool, Lancs FY2 0HB; Tel (01253) 352352; Fax (01253) 356127
Principal M.J. McAllister, BSc, FIQA

Bolton College

Manchester Rd, Bolton, Lancs BL2 1ER; Tel (01204) 31411; Fax (01204) 380774
Principal T.J. Hogan

The Borders College of Further Education

Thorniedeam, Melrose Rd, Galashiels, Selkirkshire TD1 2AF; Tel (01896) 57755
Principal R. Campbell Pearson, MSc(Phys), NDA, NDAge

Boston College

Rowley Rd, Boston, Lincs PE21 6JF; Tel (01205) 365701; Fax (01205) 310847
Principal D.J. Pursell, BSc, MSc, FBIM, DipEd

Bournemouth and Poole College of Further Education
Formerly Bournemouth College of Technology and Poole Technical College
Poole Centre (Main Office), North Rd, Parkstone, Poole, Dorset BH14 0LS; Tel (01202) 747600; Fax (01202) 205719
Principal A. Chitty, BSc(Eng), PhD, CEng, FIMechE
Bournemouth Centre Lansdowne, Bournemouth, Dorset BH1 3JJ; Tel (01202) 747600

Bournville College of Further Education
Bristol Rd South, Northfield, Birmingham, West Midlands B31 2AJ; Tel 0121-411 1414; Fax 0121-411 2231
Principal P.M. Twyman, BA, CGLI, CertFE Admin, FRSA

Bracknell College
Church Rd, Bracknell, Berks RG12 1DJ; Tel (01344) 420411
Principal R.R. Lewin, MA, BSc(Econ)

Bradford and Ilkley Community College
Great Horton Rd, Bradford, W. Yorks BD7 1AY; Tel (01274) 753026
Principal Dr P.J. Gallagher

Bramley Grange College
Thorner, Leeds, W. Yorks LS14 3DW; Tel (0113) 273 7716; Fax (0113) 265 0416

Braziers Adult College
Ipsden, Wallingford, Oxon OX10 6AN; Tel (01491) 680221

Bridgend College of Technology
Cowbridge Rd, Bridgend, Mid Glamorgan CF31 3DF; Tel (01656) 766588; Fax (01656) 663912
Principal K. Wylie, MA, CEng, MIProdE, FBIM, FRSA

Brighton College of Technology
Pelham St, Brighton, E. Sussex BN1 4FA; Tel (01273) 667788; Fax (01273) 667703
Principal M.K. Jones, MSc, DipEd

Bromley College of Further and Higher Education
Rookery La, Bromley Common, Bromley, Kent BR2 8HE; Tel 0181-295 7000; Fax 0181-295 7099
Principal R.J. Pritchard, BSc, MSc, PGCE, DipAES, MIBiol

Brooklands Technical College
Heath Rd, Weybridge, Surrey KT13 8TT; Tel (01932) 853300; Fax (01932) 828391
Chairman of Governors M. Klatt
Principal C.B. Staff, BSc, MSc, CPhys, MInstP

Broxtowe College, Nottingham
High Rd, Chilwell, Beeston, Nottingham, Notts NG9 4AH; Tel (0115) 922 8161; Fax (0115) 925 7658
Principal J.N. Lewis, BA

Brunel College of Arts and Technology
Ashley Down Rd, Bristol, Avon BS7 9BU; Tel (0117) 924 1241; Fax (0117) 924 9134
Principal B.D. Styles, BA, MSc

Buckland University College
School of Law, Ewert Pl, Oxford, Oxon OX2 7YT; Tel (01865) 53570; Fax (01865) 52961

Burnley College
Ormerod Rd, Burnley, Lancs BB11 2RX; Tel (01282) 36111; Fax (01282) 415063
Principal John T. Smith, BA, MEd

Burton Manor
Burton, South Wirral, Cheshire L64 5SJ; Tel 0151-336 5172
Principal Janet Dawson

Burton upon Trent Technical College
Lichfield St, Burton upon Trent, Staffs DE14 3RL; Tel (01283) 545401
Principal P. Fearns, MA, BSc(Tech), DBA, ACIS, FBIM, CertEd

Calder College of Adult Education
Burnley Rd, Todmorden, Lancs OL14 7BX; Tel (01706) 812743

Calderdale College
(Previously Percival Whitley College of Further Education)
Francis St, Halifax, W. Yorks HX1 3UZ; Tel (01422) 358221; Fax (01422) 358821
Principal and Chief Executive G. Bate

Camborne School of Mines
Trevenson, Pool, Redruth, Cornwall TR15 3SE; Tel (01209) 714866; Fax (01209) 716977
Principal P. Hackett, BSc, PhD, FEng, FIMM, OBE

Cambridge Regional College
Newmarket Rd, Cambridge, Cambs CB5 8EG; Tel (01223) 357545
Principal Peter Hurrell

Cambuslang College
Hamilton Rd, Cambuslang, Glasgow, Strathclyde G72 7NY; Tel 0141-641 6600
Principal Gordon Robbins, BA(Hons), MIED, MIMgt

Cannock Chase Technical College (A Further Education Corporation)
The Green, Cannock, Staffs WS11 1UE; Tel (01543) 462200; Fax (01543) 574223
Principal and Chief Executive W.A. Tovell, BA, ACP, CertEd, FIMgt, FRSA

Canterbury College
New Dover Rd, Canterbury, Kent CT1 3AJ; Tel (01227) 766081
Principal and Executive Director Susan Pember

Cardonald College
690 Mosspark Dr, Glasgow, Strathclyde G52 3AY; Tel 0141-883 6151/4; Fax 0141-883 1315
Principal R.J. Bailey, CEng, MIERE, MITE

College of Care and Early Education
Broadlands Dr, Lawrence Weston, Bristol, Avon BS11 0NT; Tel (0117) 923 5706; Fax (0117) 982 5904
Principal B.J. Burleton

Carlisle College
Victoria Pl, Carlisle, Cumbria CA1 1HS; Tel (01228) 24464; Fax (01228) 514677
Principal J. Venables, BA, MEd, IPFA, MBIM

Carshalton College

Nightingale Rd, Carshalton, Surrey SM5 2EJ; Tel 0181-770 6800; Fax 0181-770 6899
Principal David Watkins, BA(Hons), PhD, CChem, FRSC, FRSA

Castlereagh College

Montgomery Rd, Belfast BT6 9JD; Tel (01232) 797144
Principal J. McCormick, MA, DipEd

Causeway Institute of Further and Higher Education

Formerly Coleraine Technical College; merged 1 September 1994 with Ballymoney College of Further Education
Union St, Coleraine, Co Londonderry BT52 1QA; Tel (01265) 54717; Fax (01265) 56377
Director I. Williams, BA

Central College of Commerce

300 Cathedral St, Glasgow, Strathclyde G1 2TA; Tel 0141-552 3941; Fax 0141-553 2368
Principal Peter Duncan

Coleg Ceredigion

Llanbadarn Campus, Aberystwyth, Dyfed SY23 3BP; Tel (01970) 624511
Principal M. Lewis, MEng, BSc, CEng, MIMechE, MIPlantE

Charles Keene College of Further Education

Painter St, Leicester, Leics LE1 3WA; Tel (0116) 251 6037; Fax (0116) 253 6553
Principal Bryn Howell, BA(Hons), LLB(Hons), DipEd, FBIM

Chelmsford College

Moulsham St, Chelmsford, Essex CM2 0JQ; Tel (01245) 265611; Fax (01245) 266908
Principal D.F.H. Percival, MA, BPhil, CertEd, CertTEFL

Chesterfield College

Infirmary Rd, Chesterfield, Derbyshire S41 7NG; Tel (01246) 231212; Fax (01246) 558786
Principal D.M. Lyon, JP, BA, MA, PhD

Chichester College of Arts, Science and Technology

Westgate Fields, Chichester, West Sussex PO19 1SB; Tel (01243) 786321; Fax (01243) 530978
Principal J.R. Gorrie, BSc, PhD

Chippenham College

Cocklebury Rd, Chippenham, Wilts SN15 3QD; Tel (01249) 444501; Fax (01249) 653772
Principal G.J. Baskerville, JP, BSc(Hons), MEd, FRSA, FIMgt

City Banking College

7/13 Melior St, London SE1 3QP; Tel 0171-403 3770; Fax 0171-403 8355
Principal K.A. Khan, ACIB, FCCA

City of Bath College

Avon St, Bath, Avon BA1 1UP; Tel (01225) 312191; Fax (01225) 444213
Principal J.C. Togher, MSc, CEng, MIMechE, AMCT

City College of Community Education

All Saints Centre, Cavendish St, All Saints, Manchester, Greater Manchester M15 6BP; Tel 0161-273 5335
Head of Centre N.H. Johnson, BA

City and Islington College – Adult Education Services

Chequer Centre, Chequer St, London EC1Y 8PL; Tel 0171-608 1730
Finsbury Pk Centre, Jack Ashley School, Prah Rd, London N4 2RA; Tel 0171-226 9190
Archway Centre, Holland Walk, off Duncombe Rd, London N19 3EU; Tel 0171-272 4772
Shepperton Centre, Shepperton Rd, London N1 3DQ; Tel 0171-226 6001
Elizabeth Garrett Anderson School, Risinghill St, London N1 9QG; Tel 0171-837 2583
Principal Tom Jupp
Director of Adult Education Erl Lee

City and Islington College – City Campus

Bunhill Row, London EC1Y 8LQ; Tel 0171-638 4171; Fax 0171-588 9024
Pitfield St, London N1 6BX
Willen Hse, 8–26 Bath St, London EC1V 9PL
Rochelle St, Arnold Circus, London E2 7ET
Director Curriculum Planning & Resources Janet Clark, BA

City and Islington College – Islington Campus

444 Camden Rd, London N7 0SP; Tel 0171-609 9981/071-226 1026; Fax 0171-700 1008/071-354 5386
207–255 Essex St, London N1 3PN; Tel 0171-609 9981/071-226 1026; Fax 0171-700 1008/071-354 5386
Principal Tom Jupp

The City Lit

The City Lit, Stukeley St, Drury La, London WC2B 5LJ; Tel 0171-242 9872
Principal W. Tyler, MA(Oxon), MA, MPhil, FRSA

City of Liverpool Community College

Canning Pl Centre, Canning Pl, Liverpool, Merseyside L1 8BT; Tel College Switchboard 0151-252 1515 for all Centres. (There is not a "main" building but the Principalship is based at Canning Place Centre, which is not the largest); Fax 0151-707 0554
Principal Wally Brown

City of Westminster College

(formerly Paddington College)
25 Paddington Grn, London W2 1NB; Tel 0171-723 8826; Fax 0171-258 2700
Principal P. Bellamy

Clackmannan College of Further Education

Branshill Rd, Alloa, Central FK10 3BT; Tel (01259) 215121; Fax (01259) 722879
Principal John M. Taylor, MA, DipEd

Clarendon College Nottingham

Pelham Ave, Mansfield Rd, Nottingham, Notts NG5 1AL; Tel (0115) 960 7201; Fax (0115) 969 3382
Principal Patricia Morgan-Webb

Clydebank College

Kilbowie Rd, Clydebank, Strathclyde G81 2AA; Tel 0141-951 2122
Principal W. Greenock, MA

Coalville Technical College
Bridge Rd, Coalville, Leics LE67 3PW; Tel (01530) 836136; Fax (01530) 814253
Principal G.B. Higginson, BA, MEd, FCIOB

Coatbridge College
Kildonan St, Coatbridge, Strathclyde ML5 3LS; Tel (01236) 422316; Fax (01236) 440266
Principal I. MacIver

Colchester Institute
Sheepen Rd, Colchester, Essex CO3 3LL; Tel (01206) 718600
Marine Parade East, Clacton-on-Sea, Essex CO15 6JQ

Collingham, Brown and Brown Tutorial College
31 St Giles, Oxford, Oxon OX1 3LF; Tel (01865) 728280
Principal Carolyn Llewelyn, MA(Oxon)

Cordwainers College
182 Mare St, Hackney, London E8 3RE; Tel 0181-985 0273; Fax 0181-985 9340
Principal P. Banks, BA(Hons)

Cornwall College
Redruth, Cornwall TR15 3RD; Tel (01209) 712911; Fax (01209) 718802
Principal Dr A. Stanhope

Cornwall College–Falmouth Campus
Killigrew St, Falmouth, Cornwall TR11 3QS; Tel (01326) 313326; Fax (01326) 319461

Coventry Technical College
Butts, Coventry, West Midlands CV1 3GD; Tel (01203) 257221; Fax (01203) 520164
Principal Janey Rees

Craven College
High St, Skipton, N. Yorks; Tel (01756) 791411
Principal S.A. Dey, BA(Hons), CertEd, MIIM

Crawley College
College Rd, Crawley, West Sussex RH10 1NR; Tel (01293) 612686; Fax (01293) 522431
Director J.S. Cox, BSc, MA, CertEd, CEng, MIntMC, AFIMA, MBIM

Croydon College
Fairfield, Croydon, Surrey CR9 1DX; Tel 0181-686 5700
Principal M.J. Field, BA, MSc (Arch), MEd

Cumbernauld College
Tryst Rd, Town Centre, Cumbernauld, Dunbartonshire G67 1HU; Tel (01236) 731811; Fax (01236) 723416
Principal T.J. McGrenary, BSc(Hons)

Darlington College of Technology
Cleveland Ave, Darlington, Co Durham DL3 7BB; Tel (01325) 467651; Fax (01325) 483843
Principal P.R. Shuker, TD, MSc, CertEd, FRSA

Davies, Laing and Dick College
10 Pembridge Sq, London W2 4ED; Tel 0171-727 2797; Fax 0171-792 0730
Principal P.W. Boorman, MA

Debden House Residential Centre for Adult Education
Debden Hse, Debden Grn, Loughton, Essex IG10 2PA; Tel 0181-508 3008
Principal Laraine Turner

Deeside College/Coleg Glannau Dyfrdwy
Kelsterton Rd, Connah's Quay, Deeside, Clwyd CH5 4BR; Tel (01244) 831531; Fax (01244) 814305
Principal A.H. Walker, BA, PhD

Denman College
Marcham, Abingdon, Oxon OX13 6NW; Tel (01865) 391991; Fax (01865) 391966
Principal Graham Jones

Dillington House
Ilminster, Somerset TA19 9DT; Tel (01460) 52427; Fax (01460) 52433

Doncaster College
Waterdale, Doncaster, S. Yorks DN1 3EX; Tel (01302) 553553; Fax (01302) 553559
Principal Dr T.B. Ashurst

Dove Nest Group
The Old Corn Mill, Crosthwaite, Kendal, Cumbria LA8 8BS; Tel (015395) 68824; Fax (015395) 68838

Down College of Further Education
Downpatrick College, Market St, Downpatrick, Co Down BT30 6ND; Tel (01396) 615815; Fax (01396) 615817
Principal J.E. Ellis, BSc
Ballynahinch College Church Rd, Ballynahinch, Co Down BT24 8LP; Tel (01238) 562369
Kircubbin FE Centre Kircubbin, Co Down; Tel (0124 77) 38794

Dudley College of Technology
The Broadway, Dudley, West Midlands DY1 4AS; Tel (01384) 455433; Fax (01384) 455975
Principal G. Hopkins, BSc(Tech)(Hons), MEd, PhD, CChem, FRSC

Dumfries & Galloway College of Technology
Heathhall, Dumfries DG1 3QZ; Tel (01387) 61261; Fax (01387) 50006
Principal J.W.M. Neil

Dundee College
Old Glamis Rd, Dundee, Tayside DD3 8LE; Tel (01382) 834834; Fax (01382) 858117
Principal C.M. Brown, OBE, BSc(Eng)(Hons), MIProdE, FIMgt
30 Constitution Rd, Dundee DD3 6TB; Tel (01382) 29151; Fax (01382) 23299

Dundee Institute of Technology
Bell St, Dundee, Tayside DD1 1HG; Tel (01382) 308000; Fax (01382) 308877
Principal Prof B. King, MSc, PhD, CBiol, FIBiol, FIWSc

Dunford House
Midhurst, West Sussex GU29 0DG; Tel (01730) 812381

Dunstable College
Kingsway, Dunstable, Beds LU5 4HG; Tel (01582) 477776
Principal D.I. Brown, BA, MEd, CertEd, FIMgt

East Berkshire College
Formed 1992 by the merger of Langley College with Windsor and Maidenhead College
Station Rd, Langley, Slough, Berks SL3 8BY; Tel (01753) 793000; Fax (01753) 793316
Principal R.G. Sinclair-Smith, MA, CEng, MIMechE, FinstM

East Birmingham College
Garrets Grn La, Birmingham, West Midlands B33 0TS; Tel 0121-743 4471; Fax 0121-743 9050
Principal A. Henry, BA(Hons), CertEd

East Surrey College
Gatton Point, Redhill, Surrey RH1 2JX; Tel (01737) 772611
Principal R.P. Latham, MSc, BSc(Econ)

East Tyrone College of Further Education
Circular Rd, Dungannon, Co Tyrone BT71 6BQ; Tel (01868) 722323; Fax (01868) 752018
Principal T. Dardis

East Warwickshire College Rugby
Lower Hillmorton Rd, Rugby, Warks CV21 3QS; Tel (01788) 541666; Fax (01926) 413514
Principal D.A. Cotton, BSc(Econ), MEd, CertEd

East Yorkshire College
St Mary's Walk, Bridlington, Humberside YO16 5JW; Tel (01262) 672676; Fax (01262) 671719
Principal P. Watkin, JP, BA(Hons)
Manorfield Rd, Driffield, N. Humberside Y025 7HR

Eastbourne College of Arts and Technology
St Anne's Rd, Eastbourne, E. Sussex BN21 2HS; Tel (01323) 644711; Fax (01323) 412239
Principal John D. Blake, BA(Hons), DPhil

Easthampstead Park
Easthampstead Pk Educational Centre, Wokingham, Berks RG11 3DF; Tel (01734) 780686
Headteacher J.E. Traies, MA, DipEd

Eastleigh College
Chestnut Ave, Eastleigh, Hants SO5 5HT; Tel (01703) 326326; Fax (01703) 322131
Principal Dr A. Roberts, BEng, MBA

Edinburgh's Telford College
Crewe Toll, Edinburgh, Lothian EH4 2NZ; Tel 0131-332 2491; Fax 0131-343 1218
Principal and Chief Executive Michael A. Taylor, BA(Hons), MSc, MEd, PhD

Enfield College
73 Hertford Rd, Enfield, Middx EN3 5HA; Tel 0181-443 3434; Fax 0181-804 7028
Principal A.A. Parker, BA, MA(Ed)

Evesham College of Further Education
Cheltenham Rd, Evesham, Worcs WR11 6LP; Tel (01386) 41091
Principal D. Blades, LLB, CertEd

Falkirk College of Technology
Grangemouth Rd, Falkirk, Central FK2 9AD; Tel (01324) 624981; Fax (01324) 632086
Principal G.M. Clark, BSc, PhD, CChem, FRSC, FIMgt

Farnborough College of Technology
Boundary Rd, Farnborough, Hants GU14 6SB; Tel (01252) 515511
Principal J.F. Potter, BSc, PhD, FGS, CBiol, FIBiol, FIEnvSc

Fermanagh College
Fairview, 1 Dublin Rd, Enniskillen, Co Fermanagh BT74 6AE; Tel (01365) 322431
Principal W.J.A. Millar, BA, DMS, CertEd, MIMgt, FRSA

Field Studies Council
Juniper Hall Field Centre, Dorking, Surrey RH5 6DA; Tel (01306) 883849
Warden J. Bebbington

Fife College of Further and Higher Education
St Brycedale Ave, Kirkcaldy, Fife KY1 1EX; Tel (01592) 268591/262414; Fax (01592) 640225
Principal D.A. Huckle, CA, FIMgt, FCCA

Filton College
Filton Ave, Bristol, Avon BS12 7AT; Tel (0117) 969 4217; Fax (0117) 923 6450
Principal Mrs H. Cowell

Fircroft College of Adult Education
1018 Bristol Rd, Selly Oak, Birmingham B29 6LH; Tel 0121-472 0116/2845; Fax 0121-471 1503
Principal Keith Jackson

Frome College
Bath Rd, Frome, Somerset BA11 2HQ; Tel (01373) 465353; Fax (01373) 452018
Principal B. Bates

Furness College
Howard St, Barrow in Furness, Cumbria LA14 1NB; Tel (01229) 825017; Fax (01229) 870964
Principal Maggie Chadwick

Glasgow College of Building and Printing
60 North Hanover St, Glasgow, Strathclyde G1 2BP; Tel 0141-332 9969; Fax 0141-332 5170
Principal T.B. Wilson, BSc, CEng, MBCS

Glasgow College of Food Technology
230 Cathedral St, Glasgow, Strathclyde G1 2TG; Tel 0141-552 3751
Principal W.R. Bannatyne, BSc, PhD, FIFST, OBE

Glasgow College of Nautical Studies
21 Thistle St, Glasgow, Strathclyde G5 9XB; Tel 0141-429 3201; Fax 0141-420 1690
Principal C.G.W. Hunter, MA

Glenrothes College
Stenton Rd, Glenrothes, Fife KY6 2RA; Tel (01592) 772233; Fax (01592) 772233
Principal T.J. Burness, OBE, MA(Hons), MLitt, DipEd, MIWM, AMBIM

Gloucestershire College of Arts and Technology
Pk Campus, Cheltenham, Glos GL50 2RR; Tel (01242) 532000
Principal I.B.T. Caves, BA(Hons), DMS

Grantham College

Stonebridge Rd, Grantham, Lincs NG31 9AP; Tel (01476) 63141; Fax (01476) 64882
Principal T.K. Jones, MSc, PhD, CChem, FRSC

Grantley Hall

Ripon, N. Yorks HG4 3ET; Tel (0176 620) 259

Great Yarmouth College of Further Education

Southtown, Great Yarmouth, Norfolk NR31 0ED; Tel (01493) 655261
Principal Robin Parkinson, BA, MSc

Grimsby College of Technology and Arts

Nuns Corner, Grimsby, S. Humberside DN34 5BQ; Tel (01472) 279292; Fax (01472) 79924
Principal A. Gothard, BEd(Hons), CEng, FIEE

Guernsey College of Further Education

Route des Coutanchez, St Peter Port, Guernsey GY1 2TT; Tel (01481) 727121; Fax (01481) 714153
Chairman of College Dep B. Torode
Principal R.M. McDonald, BA, MBIM

Guildford College of Further and Higher Education

Stoke Pk, Guildford, Surrey GU1 1EZ; Tel (01483) 31251
Principal Gill Anslow

Hackney Community College

Brooke Hse, Kenninghall Rd, London E5 8BP; Tel 0181-985 8484
Principal C. Farley

Halton College

Kingsway, Widnes, Cheshire WA8 7QQ; Tel 0151-423 1391; Fax 0151-420 2408
Principal M.D. Jenkins

Hammersmith and West London College

Gliddon Rd, Barons Ct, London W14 9BL; Tel 0181-563 0063 Course Information Centre (for all course enquiries); Fax 0181-741 2491
Principal A.M. Illis

Handsworth College

The Council Hse, Soho Rd, Birmingham, West Midlands B21 9DP; Tel 0121-551 6031
Principal C.J. Webb, BA, MEd

Coleg Harlech

Harlech, Gwynedd LL46 2PU; Tel (01766) 780363; Fax (01766) 780169

Harrison Centre and Gymnasium Blackburn College

Lower Hollin Bank St, Blackburn, Lancs BB2 4AF; Tel (01254) 52743

Harrogate College

Hornbeam Pk, Harrogate, N. Yorks HG2 8QT; Tel (01423) 879466; Fax (01423) 879829
Principal P.A. Clarke, MIBiol, FIMgt, ACP

Hartlepool College of Further Education

Stockton St, Hartlepool, Cleveland; Tel (01429) 275453
Principal G.H. Morris

Hastings College of Arts and Technology

Archery Rd, St Leonards-on-Sea, E. Sussex TN38 0HX; Tel (01424) 442222
Principal Judy Vegh

Havering Adult College

Noak Hill North Centre, Noak Hill Rd, Romford, Essex RM3 7TQ; Tel (01708) 378877
Principal Peter Boshier

Havering College of Further and Higher Education

Ardleigh Grn Rd, Hornchurch, Essex RM11 2LL; Tel (01708) 455011; Fax (01708) 477961
Principal K.H. Clarke, BSc(Econ), CertEd, FRSA

Hawkwood Adult College and Conference Centre

Painswick Old Rd, Stroud, Glos GL6 7QW; Tel (01453) 764607
Co-Principals Tony and Stephanie Cooper

Hendon College

Grahame Pk, Corner Mead, Colindale, London NW9 5RA; Tel 0181-200 8300
Principal J.A. Hoyland, BA, CertEd

Henley Management College

Greenlands, Henley-on-Thames, Oxon RG9 3AU; Tel (01491) 571454
Principal Prof Ray Wild, MSc, PhD, MSc, DSc, WhF, CEng, FIMechE, FIEE, CIMgt, FRSA

Herefordshire College of Technology

Folly La, Hereford, Hereford and Worcester HR1 1LS; Tel (01432) 352235; Fax (01432) 353449
Principal G.J. Bateman, MSc, CEng, FIM, AUMIST

Hereward College of Further Education

Bramston Cres, Tile Hill La, Coventry, West Midlands CV4 9SW; Tel (01203) 461231; Fax (01203) 694305
Principal W.R. Williams, BEd

Hertford Regional College

Broxbourne Centre, Turnford, Broxbourne, Herts EN10 6AE; Tel (01992) 466451; Fax (01992) 440645
Principal G.J. Evans, MSc(Man), MSc(Cran), FBIM, CEng, MIMechE
Ware Centre Scotts Rd, Ware, Herts SG12 9JF; Tel (01920) 465441

High Peak College

Harpur Hill, Buxton, Derbys SK17 9JZ; Tel (01298) 71100; Fax (01298) 27261
Principal Mike Taylor, BSc, MBA, CertEd

Highbury College

Dovercourt Rd, Cosham, Portsmouth, Hants PO6 2SA; Tel (01705) 383131; Fax (01705) 325551
Principal G.L. Moss, BSc, MSc, MA, CPhys, MInstP

Highlands College

St Saviour, Jersey; Tel (01534) 608608; Fax (01534) 608600
Principal Dr M. Le Guillou

Hilderstone College

St Peters Rd, Broadstairs, Kent CT10 2AQ; Tel (01843) 869171; Fax (01843) 603877
Principal Peter Worley

The Hill Residential College
Pen-y-Pound, Abergavenny, Gwent NP7 7RP; Tel (01873) 855221; Fax (01873) 854817
Principal L.J. Newcombe, MA(Oxon)

Hillcroft College
South Bank, Surbiton, Surrey KT6 6DF; Tel 0181-399 2688
Principal Eileen M. Aird, BA, MLitt, DipPsych

Hinckley College
London Rd, Hinckley, Leics LE10 1HQ; Tel (01455) 251222; Fax (01455) 633930
Principal Ifor Jones, BA(Hons), MEd, DMS

Hooke Park College
Beaminster, Dorset DT8 3PH; Tel (01308) 863130
General Manager Peter Goulden, NDD, DipRes(Leics), MCSD

Horncastle College
Mareham Rd, Horncastle, Lincs LN9 6BW; Tel (01507) 522449; Fax (01507) 524382
Principal P.J. Weston, MSc, CertEd

Huddersfield Technical College
New North Rd, Huddersfield, W. Yorks HD1 5NN; Tel (01484) 536521; Fax (01484) 511885
Chairman of Corporation E. Thompson
Principal M.E. Rossiter, BSc(Eng), ACGI, MIMechE, CEng, PhD

Hull College of Further Education
Queen's Gdns, Hull, Humberside HU1 3DG; Tel (01482) 329943
Principal P.A. Moseley, BSc, CertEd

Huntingdonshire Regional College
California Rd, Huntingdon, Cambs PE18 7BL; Tel (01480) 52346
Principal R. Summers

Institute of Advanced Nursing Education of the Royal College of Nursing
20 Cavendish Sq, London W1M 0AB; Tel 0171-409 3333
Principal John Wells, BA, MA, RGN, RMN, RNT

International Co-operative College
Stanford Hall, Loughborough, Leics LE12 5QR; Tel (01509) 852333; Fax (01509) 856500
Principal R. Houlton, MA, PhD

Inverness College
3 Longman Rd, Longman South, Inverness, Highland IV1 1SA; Tel (01463) 236681; Fax (01463) 711977
Principal James Hedley, BA(Hons), DipEd, HonMCGLI, FRSA

Irwin College
164 London Rd, Leicester, Leics LE2 1ND; Tel (0116) 255 2648; Fax (0116) 285 4935
Principal A.J. Elliott, BA(Oxon), MPhil(Cantab)

Isle of Man College
Homefield Rd, Douglas, Isle of Man; Tel (01624) 623113; Fax (01624) 661432
Principal B. Hallworth, BSc(Econ), MSc, MEd, FIMgt

Isle of Wight College
Medina Way, Newport, IOW PO30 5TA; Tel (01983) 526631; Fax (01983) 521707
Principal B. Marriott, MEd, DipFE, FAMEME, MIPlantE, MBIM

Islington Federal College
Annette Rd, Islington, London N7 6EX; Tel 0171-609 8401; Fax 0171-609 8401
Director Margaret Chittick

James Watt College of Further and Higher Education
Finnart St, Greenock, Strathclyde PA16 8HF; Tel (01475) 24433; Fax (01475) 888079
Principal T. Davies, BSc, MSc, MInstP, FIPC, MBIM

Jewel and Esk Valley College
Newbattle Rd, Eskbank Centre, Dalkeith, Midlothian EH22 3AE; Tel 0131-663 1951; Fax 0131-663 0271
Principal J. Lisgo, BSc(Econ), DipEd
Milton Rd Centre 24 Milton Rd East, Edinburgh EH15 2PP; Tel 0131-669 8461; Fax 0131-657 2276

John Wheatley College
1346 Shettleston Rd, Glasgow, Strathclyde G32 9AT; Tel 0141-778 2426; Fax 0141-763 2384
Principal Ian Graham

Joseph Priestley College
71 Queen St, Morley, Leeds, W. Yorks LS27 8DZ; Tel (0113) 253 3749/532782; Fax (0113) 252 8654
Principal G. Binks, MA, BA, MBIM

Keighley College
Cavendish St, Keighley, W. Yorks BD21 3DF; Tel (01535) 618555
Principal D.B. Hardaker

Kendal College
Milnthorpe Rd, Kendal, Cumbria LA9 5AY; Tel (01539) 724313
Principal Mike Wright

Kensington and Chelsea College
Hortensia Rd, London SW10 0QS; Tel 0171-351 7127; Fax 0171-351 0956
Principal Michael Baber

Kent Adult Education Service
Sittingbourne College, College Rd, Sittingbourne, Kent ME10 1LF; Tel (01795) 435492
Principal Pam Gibson

Kidderminster College
Hoo Rd, Kidderminster, Worcs DY10 1LX; Tel (01562) 820811
Principal Dr T. Seddon, PhD, MSc, CEng, MIEE, CPhys, MInstP

Kilmarnock College
Holehouse Rd, Kilmarnock, Ayrshire KA3 7AT; Tel (01563) 23501/4; Fax (01563) 38182
Principal James A. Flynn, MA, MEd

Kingston College
Kingston Hall Rd, Kingston upon Thames, Surrey KT1 2AQ; Tel 0181-546 2151; Fax 0181-547 2292
Principal A.B. Cotterell, MA, FRSA, CertEd, DipEdAdmin

Kingsway College
Grays Inn Centre, Sidmouth St, Grays Inn Rd, London WC1H 8JB; Tel 0171-306 5700; Fax 0171-306 5800
Principal P. Haikin

Clerkenwell Centre Sans Walk, London EC1R 0AS; Tel 0171-306 5832; Fax 0171-306 5850
Vernon Sq Centre Penton Rise, London WC1X 9EL; Tel 0171-306 5888; Fax 0171-306 5900
Kentish Town Centre 87 Holmes Rd, London NW5 3AX; Tel 0171-306 5932; Fax 0171-306 5910
Regents Pk Centre London NW1 3HB; Tel 0171-306 5954; Fax 0171-306 5950

Kirby College of Further Education

Roman Rd, Linthorpe, Middlesbrough, Cleveland TS5 5PJ; Tel (01642) 813706; Fax (01642) 816250
Principal F.A. Clifford, MA, BA, CertEd

Kirkwall College of Further Education

Kirkwall, Orkney KW15 1QN; Tel (01856) 872839/872102; Fax (01856) 872911
Principal Eric Sinclair, MA, DipEd

Knuston Hall

Irchester, Wellingborough, Northants NN9 7EU; Tel (01933) 312104; Fax (01933) 57596
Principal J. Herrick, MEd

Lancaster and Morecambe College

Morecambe Rd, Lancaster, Lancs LA1 2TY; Tel (01524) 66215
Principal D.H. Blezard, OBE, BA, DipSpEd

Langside College

50 Prospecthill Rd, Glasgow, Strathclyde G42 9LB; Tel 0141-649 4991
Principal A.M. Tyre, FHCIMA, DipSHS, MBIM

Larne College of Further Education

32–34 Pound St, Larne BT40 1SQ; Tel (01574) 272268
Principal A.J. McKinley, CEng, MIMechE

Lauder College

Halbeath, Dunfermline, Fife KY11 5DY; Tel (01383) 726201; Fax (01383) 621109
Principal Dr Alan C., Brown BSc, PhD, MIBiol, CBiol

Leeds College of Building

North St, Leeds, W. Yorks LS2 7QT; Tel (0113) 243 0765; Fax (0113) 242 2136
Principal R.D. Roberts, BEd(Hons), FCIOB

Leeds College of Technology (formerly Kitson College, Leeds)

Cookridge St, Leeds, W. Yorks LS2 8BL; Tel (0113) 243 0381; Fax (0113) 234 0365
Principal R.J. O'Brien, BSc, CPhys, MInstP

Leek College of Further Education and School of Art

Stockwell St, Leek, Staffs ST13 6DP; Tel (01538) 398866; Fax (01538) 399506
Principal A.P. Price, BTech, PhD, CertEd

Leicester South Fields College

Aylestone Rd, Leicester, Leics LE2 7LW; Tel (0116) 254 1818
Principal A.F. Warren, MA(Cantab), PGCE

Lewisham College

Lewisham Way, London SE4 1UT; Tel 0181-692 0353; Fax 0181-694 9163
Principal Ruth Silver

Lews Castle College

Stornoway, Isle of Lewis, Western Isles PA86 0XR; Tel (01851) 3311
Principal M. Roebuck, BSc, MEd

Limavady College of Further Education

Main St, Limavady, Co Londonderry BT49 0EX; Tel (0150 47) 62334; Fax (0150 47) 22229
Principal R.E. Wright

Lisburn College

39 Castle St, Lisburn, Co Antrim BT27 4SU; Tel (01846) 677225; Fax (01846) 677291
Principal Vacancy

Llandrillo College

Llandudno Rd, Rhos-on-Sea, Colwyn Bay, Clwyd LL28 4HZ; Tel (01492) 546666; Fax (01492) 543052
Principal Huw Evans, BSc, MPhil, FBIM

London City College (LCC)

51–55 Waterloo Rd, London SE1 8TX; Tel 0171-928 0029/0938; Fax 0171-401 2231; Telex 8812438 (Scol G)
Principal W.G. Leader, MIM, DipIM

London College of Printing and Distributive Trades

(A constitutent College of The London Institute)
Elephant and Castle, London SE1 6SB; Tel 0171-514 6500; Fax 0171-514 6535
Head of College Leslie Grindle
Back Hill, Clerkenwell Rd, London EC1R 5EN
65 Davies St, London W1Y 2DA

London Foot Hospital and College of Podiatric Medicine

33 Fitzroy Sq, London W1; Tel 0171-636 0602
Principal A.S.H. Wilson

London School of Business Education

1A Harberson Rd, Balham, London SW12 9QW; Tel 0181-675 0220

Longlands College of Further Education Corporation

Douglas St, Middlesbrough, Cleveland TS4 2JW; Tel (01642) 248351; Fax (01642) 245313
Chairman of Governors John Sefton
Chief Executive A.B. Shaw, BSc, PhD, MInstP, ACP, MIEE, MInstAM, AMBIM, FRSA, MCollP

Loughborough College

Radmoor, Loughborough, Leics LE11 3BT; Tel (01509) 215831; Fax (01509) 232310
Chief Executive and Principal J.E. Mutton, BA

Lowestoft College

St Peter's St, Lowestoft, Suffolk NR32 2NB; Tel (01502) 583521
Principal A. Nicholson

Macclesfield College

Park La, Macclesfield, Cheshire SK11 8LF; Tel (01625) 427744; Fax (01625) 501084
Principal M. Lawson, BSc(Econ), FBIM, FTS, MCIT, AMInstTA

Malvern Hills College for Adult Education

Albert Rd North, Malvern, Worcs WR14 2TW; Tel (01684) 565351/2; Fax (01684) 561767

Manchester College of Arts and Technology

City Centre Campus, Lower Hardman St, Manchester, Greater Manchester M3 3ER; Tel 0161-953 5995; Fax 0161-953 2259
Principal G.A. Rowlands, BA, FRSA, FBIM, DipEd
Openshaw Campus Whitworth St, Openshaw, Manchester M11 2WH; Tel 0161-953 5995; Fax 0161-953 3909
Moston Campus Ashley La, Moston, Manchester M9 1WU; Tel 0161-953 5995; Fax 0161-953 4293

The Marine Society College of the Sea

202 Lambeth Rd, London SE1 7JW; Tel 0171-261 9535; Fax 0171-401 2537; Telex 934089
Principal R.M. Frampton, FNI, FRSA

The Mary Ward Centre

42 Queen Square, London WC1N 3AQ; Tel 0171-831 7711; Fax 0171 831 5431
Principal Patrick Freestone

Maryland College

Woburn, Milton Keynes, Bucks MK17 9JD; Tel (01525) 290688
Director R. Bollington

Matthew Boulton College of Further and Higher Education

Sherlock St, Birmingham, West Midlands B5 7DB; Tel 0121-446 4545; Fax 0121-446 4324
Principal and Chief Executive A.P. Colton, BEd(Hons), BA, MEd, DipEd(Fe), CertEd, MBIM

Coleg Meirion–Dwyfor

Dolgellau Barmouth Rd, Dolgellau, Gwynedd LL40 2SW; Tel (01341) 422827; Fax (01341) 422393
Principal Denis P. McAteer
Pwllheli Penrallt, Pwllheli, Gwynedd LL53 2AB; Tel (01758) 701385
Glynllifon Caernarfon Rd, Caernarfon, Gwynedd LL54 5DU; Tel (01286) 830261

Melton Mowbray College of Further Education

Asfordby Rd, Melton Mowbray, Leics LE13 0HJ; Tel (01664) 67431
Principal K.A.W. Masters, MSc

Coleg Menai

Formed 1 August 1994 by merger of Coleg Pencraig and Gwynedd Technical College
Ffriddoedd Rd, Bangor, Gwynedd LL57 2TP; Tel (01248) 370125; Fax (01248) 370052
Principal H.E. Edwards, BSc, PhD, CChem, FRSC

Merthyr Tydfil College

Ynysfach, Merthyr Tydfil, Mid Glamorgan CF48 1AR; Tel (01685) 723663; Fax (01685) 721782
Principal Frank Marsh

Merton College

Morden Pk, London Rd, Morden, Surrey SM4 5QX; Tel 0181-640 8001; Fax 0181-640 0835
Principal J.J. Duncan, BA, DipEd, MA, MITD, MBIM

Mid Cheshire College

Hartford Campus, Northwich, Cheshire CW8 1LJ; Tel (01606) 74444; Fax (01606) 75101
Principal J.E. Howard, MA, BA, CertEd, MInstMgt, MIPD

Mid–Kent College of Higher and Further Education

Horsted, Maidstone Rd, Chatham, Kent ME5 9UQ; Tel (01634) 830633; 402020 (Central College Helpline for information on all courses); Fax (01634) 830224; (other Centres in Maidstone and Rochester)
Principal D.J. de Mesquita, MSc(Eng), CEng, MIEE

Mid–Warwickshire College, Royal Leamington Spa

Warwick New Rd, Leamington Spa, Warks CV32 5JE; Tel (01926) 311711; Fax (01926) 426910
Principal Mrs H.C. Stockford, BTech, CBiol, MIBiol

Milton Keynes College

Chaffron Way Centre, Woughton Campus West, Leadenhall, Milton Keynes, Bucks MK6 5LP; Tel (01908) 684444

Moray College of Further Education

Moray St, Elgin, Grampian IV30 1NQ; Tel (01343) 554321; Fax (01343) 540830
Principal Doctor R.J. Chalmers

Morley College

61 Westminster Bridge Rd, London SE1 7HT; Tel 0171-928 8501; Fax 0171-928 4074
Principal Bev Walters

Motherwell College

Dalzell Dr, Motherwell, Lanarkshire ML1 2DD; Tel (01698) 259641; Fax (01698) 275430
Principal R. Millham

National Sea Training College

Denton, Gravensend, Kent DA12 2HR; Tel (01474) 363656; Fax (01474) 566364
Chairman F.M. Marchant
Principal Capt M. Bolton

Nene College

Park Campus, Boughton Grn Rd, Northampton, Northants NN2 7AL; Tel (01604) 735500
Director S. Martin Gaskell, MA, PhD, FR, HistS, FRSA

New College Durham

Framwellgate Moor, Durham, Co Durham DH1 5ES; Tel (0385) 386241
Principal D.L. Turner, BA, DipEd, FBIM
Neville's Cross Centre Durham DH1 4SY; Tel (0385) 3847325

Newark and Sherwood College

Friary Rd, Newark, Notts NG24 1PB; Tel (01636) 705921/3; Fax (01636) 701990
Principal G.T. Williams, HCIMA

Newbattle Abbey College

Dalkeith, Midlothian EH22 3LL; Tel 0131-663 1921
Principal W.M. Conboy, MA, FRSA

Newbury College

Oxford Rd, Newbury, Berks RG13 1PQ; Tel (01635) 37000/42824; Fax (01635) 41812
Principal G.A. Bull, MSc, MHCIMA, CertEd

Newcastle College

Ryehill Campus, Scotswood Rd, Newcastle upon Tyne, Tyne and Wear NE4 7SA; Tel 0191-200 4000; Fax 0191-226 1742
Principal G.M. Rowarth, OBE, MA(Oxon), MEd, MIPM

Newcastle College of Further Education
Donard St, Newcastle, Co Down BT33 0AP; Tel (0139 67) 22451; Fax (0139 67) 26203
Principal T.L. Place, MSc, BA, DPM, MIPM

Newham College of Further Education
East Ham Campus, High St South, London E6 4ER; Tel 0181-471 6688; Fax 0181-470 8435
Principal M. Tolhurst
Stratford Campus Welfare Rd, London E15 4HT; Tel 0181-471 6688; Fax 0181-534 3314

Newman College
Gartley Grn, Birmingham, West Midlands B32 3NT; Tel 0121-476 1181
Principal J. Cuming, PhD, BA, DipEd

Newry and Kilkeel Further Education Area
Patrick St, Newry, Co Down; Tel (01693) 61071
Principal R.J. Mullan, MSc, BSc(Econ)(Hons), MIM
Greencastle St, Kilkeel, Co Down; Tel (0169 37) 62582

Newsham Drive Adult Education Centre
83 Newsham Dr, Liverpool, Merseyside L6 7UH; Tel 0151-263 5153
Principal Mrs J.M. Navein, DASE

Newtownabbey College of Further Education
(To merge with Larne College of Further Education in September 1994)
400 Shore Rd, Newtownabbey, Co Antrim BT37 9RS; Tel (01232) 864331; Fax (01232) 862076
Principal J.B.H. Hill, BSc(Econ)

Norfolk College of Arts and Technology
Tennyson Ave, King's Lynn, Norfolk PE30 2QW; Tel (01553) 761144; Fax (01553) 764902
Principal/Chief Executive C.H. Dixon, OBE, BA(Econ), LTCL, CertEd

Normal College, Bangor
George Site, Bangor, Gwynedd LL57 2PX; Tel (01248) 370171
Principal Gareth Roberts

North Antrim College of Further Education
2 Coleraine Rd, Ballymoney, Co Antrim BT53 6BP; Tel (0126 56) 62258/62339; Fax (0126 56) 64529
Principal I. Williams, BA

North Birmingham College (formerly Brooklyn College) Great Barr
Aldridge Rd, Birmingham, West Midlands B44 8NE; Tel 0121-360 3543; Fax 0121-325 0828

North Down and Ards Institute of Further and Higher Education–Bangor Centre
Castle Park Rd, Bangor, Co Down BT20 4TF; Tel (01247) 271254; Fax (01247) 270034
Principal J. Masterson, MSc, BEd, Adv, ResCCCert
Newtownards Centre, Victoria Ave, Newtownards, Co Down BT23 3ED; Tel (01247) 812116; Fax (01247) 812911
Holywood Adult Education Centre, My Lady's Mile, Holywood; Tel (01232) 423454; Fax (01232) 422838

North East Institute of Further and Higher Education
Formed 1994 by merger of Antrim, Ballymena and Magherafelt Colleges
Antrim Campus, Fountain St, Antrim, Co Antrim BT41 4AL; Tel (01849) 463916; Fax (01849) 465132
Director S.M. Owen-Jones, PhD

The College of North East London
Tottenham Centre, High Rd, London N15 4RU; Tel 0181-802 3111; Fax 0181-442 3091
Principal I. Macwhinnie
Bounds Green Centre Park Rd, London N11 2QF; Tel 0181-802 3111
Muswell Hill Centre Rhodes Ave, London N22 4UT; Tel 0181-802 3111
Tottenham Green Centre Town Hall Approach Rd, London N15 4RX
Tetherdown Centre Tetherdown, London N10 1ND; Tel 0181-883 9241
Falkland Centre Falkland Rd, London N8 0NU
Adult Reading Centre Mattison Rd, London N8 1BD

North East Surrey College of Technology
Reigate Rd, Ewell, Epsom, Surrey KT17 3DS; Tel 0181-394 1731; Fax 0181-394 3030
Principal J.A. Strickson, BSc, PhD, CChem, FRSC

The North East Wales Institute
Plas Coch, Mold Rd, Wrexham, Clwyd LL11 2AW; Tel (01978) 290666; Fax (01978) 290008
Executive Principal Prof J.O. Williams, DSc, PhD, CChem, FInstP, FRSC

North East Worcestershire College
Bromsgrove Campus Blackwood Rd, Bromsgrove, Worcs B60 1PQ; Tel (01527) 570020; Fax (01527) 572900
Chairman A.F. George, LIM, MA, BSc
Principal Dr H.B. Sutton, BTech, MTech, PhD, CEng, MIMechE, MInstMC
Redditch Campus Peakman St, Redditch, Worcs B98 8DW; Tel (01527) 570020; Fax (01527) 572901

North Glasgow College
Springburn Campus 110 Flemington St, Glasgow, Strathclyde G21 4BX; Tel 0141-558 9001; Fax 0141-558 9905
Principal I.G.T. Miller, BSc(Hons), CEng, AFIMA, MBCS, FRSA
Barmulloch Campus 186 Rye Rd, Barmulloch, Glasgow G21 3JY; Tel 0141-558 9071; Fax 0141-558 9744

North Hertfordshire College
Stevenage Centre Monkswood Way, Stevenage, Herts SG1 1LA; Tel (01462) 424242 (all Centres)
Principal Roger Gochin
Shephalbury Centre Lodge Way, Stevenage, Herts SG2 8DB
Letchworth Centre Broadway, Letchworth, Herts SG6 3PB
Hitchin Centre Cambridge Rd, Hitchin, Herts SG4 0JD

North Lincolnshire College
Monks Rd, Lincoln, Lincs LN2 5HQ; Tel (01522) 510530
Principal A.E. Crease, PhD, BSc
Morton Terr, Gainsborough, Lincs DN21 2SU; Tel (01427) 617471
Riverhead Rd, Louth LN11 7AH; Tel (01507) 601041

North Lindsey College
Kingsway, Scunthorpe, S. Humberside DN17 1AJ; Tel (01724) 281111; Fax (01724) 294020
Principal R. Snelling, BA(Hons), PGCE

North Nottinghamshire College
Carlton Rd, Worksop, Notts S81 7HP; Tel (01909) 473561; Fax (01909) 485564
Principal Rev W. Wilson, MEd, HND(Mech), MISM, MIIM, MBIM

North Oxfordshire College and School of Art
Broughton Rd, Banbury, Oxon OX16 9QA; Tel (01295) 252221; Fax (01295) 250381
Principal G.J. Wharton, MSc, MWeldI, FRSA

North Trafford College of Further Education
Talbot Rd, Stretford, Manchester, Greater Manchester M32 0XH; Tel 0161-872 3731; Fax 0161-872 7921
Principal D.M. Colenutt, BTech, BA, MPhil, CertEd

North Tyneside College
Embleton Ave, Wallsend, Tyne and Wear NE28 9NJ; Tel 0191-262 5000; Fax 0191-295 0301
Principal L.K. Toye, BA, DipEd

North Warwickshire College of Technology and Art
Hinckley Rd, Nuneaton, Warks CV11 6BH; Tel (01203) 349321
Principal A.B.G. Stokes, BA, MA(Ed), FBIM

North West Institute of Further and Higher Education
Strand Rd, Londonderry, Co Londonderry BT48 7BY; Tel (01504) 266711
Principal P.P. Gallagher, BA, CCCE, MA(Ed), FRSA

North West Kent College of Technology
Miskin Rd, Dartford, Kent; Tel (01322) 225471; Fax (01322) 288139
Principal D.T.L. Jones
Dering Way, Gravesend, Kent; Tel (01474) 352049; Fax (01474) 320523

College of North West London
Dudden Hill La, London NW10 2XD; Tel 0181-208 5000
Principal Michael Shoefield

Northampton College
Booth La, Northampton, Northants NN3 3RF; Tel (01604) 734567; Fax (01604) 784625
Principal R. Barden, BSc(Econ)

Northbrook College of Design and Technology
Littlehampton Rd, Goring-by-Sea, Worthing, West Sussex BN12 6NU; Tel (01903) 830057
Principal M.F.A. Thrower, BSc(Econ)(Hons), FBIM

Northern College
Aberdeen Campus Hilton Pl, Aberdeen, Grampian AB9 1FA; Tel (01224) 283500; Fax (01224) 487046
Principal D. Adams, MA
(All enquiries should be directed to Aberdeen Campus)
Dundee Campus Gardyne Rd, Dundee, Tayside DD5 1NY; Tel (01382) 464000; Fax (01382) 464900

Northern Ireland Hotel & Catering College
Ballywillan Rd, Portrush, Co Antrim BT56 8JL; Tel (01265) 823768; Fax (01265) 824733
Director Ciaran P. O'Cathain

Northumberland College of Arts and Technology
College Rd, Ashington, Northumberland NE63 9RG; Tel (01670) 841200; Fax (01670) 841201
Principal W.S. Mills

Norton Radstock College
South Hill Pk, Radstock, Bath, Avon BA3 3RW; Tel (01761) 433161; Fax (01761) 436173
Director Richard Gorringe

Norwich City College of Further and Higher Education
Ipswich Rd, Norwich, Norfolk NR2 2LJ; Tel (01603) 660011; Fax (01603) 760326
Principal J.S. Lewis, RD, BSc(Eng), MSc, PhD, CEng, FIMechE

Oak Hill College
Chase Side, Southgate, London N14 4PS; Tel 0181-449 0467; Fax 0181-441 5996
Principal Rev Canon Gordon Bridger, MA

Oaklands College
Principal Keith Gardner
St Albans City Campus St Peters Rd, St Albans, Herts AL1 3RX; Tel (01727) 847070; Fax (01727) 847071
Borehamwood Campus Elstree Way, Borehamwood, Herts WD6 1JZ; Tel 0181-953 6024; Fax 0181-207 5721
Oaklands Campus Hatfield Rd, St Albans, Herts AL4 0JA; Tel (01727) 850651; Fax (01727) 847987
Welwyn Garden City Campus Welwyn Garden City, Herts AL8 6AH; Tel (01707) 326318; Fax (01707) 377544
Harpenden Campus Victoria Rd, Harpenden, Herts AL5 4EA; Tel (01582) 762040; Fax (01582) 461383
Hatfield Campus Woods Ave, Hatfield, Herts AL10 8EW; Tel (01707) 273439; Fax (01707) 270104
Lemsford La Campus Lemsford La, Welwyn Garden City, Herts AL8 6YW; Tel (01707) 326318; Fax (01707) 377544
Potters Bar Campus The Walk, Potters Bar, Herts EN6 1QN; Tel (01707) 644311; Fax (01707) 649110

School of Occupational Therapy
Part of Nene College
St Andrew's Hospital, Northampton, Northants NN1 5DG; Tel (01604) 29696; Fax (01604) 259637

Oldham College
Rochdale Rd, Oldham, Greater Manchester OL9 6AA; Tel 0161-624 5214; Fax 0161-627 3635
Principal R. Chapman

Oldham Community Education
Chaucer St, Oldham, Greater Manchester; Tel 0161-652 3085
Principal D.C. Rogers, MA

Omagh College of Further Education
Mountjoy Rd, Omagh, Co Tyrone BT79 7AH; Tel (01662) 245433/14; Fax (01662) 241440
Principal J.J. Devlin, BA, BSc(Econ)

Orpington College
The Walnuts, Orpington, Kent BR6 0TE; Tel (01689) 839336
Principal and Chief Executive John D. Parnham, MA, MSc, MSc(Econ), DipIA, DipM, CDipAF, CertEd

Overbridge Continuing Education Centre
63 St Andrew's Dr, Pollokshields, Glasgow, Strathclyde G41 5EY; Tel 0141-423 2064
Principal Officer Megan Wilson

Oxford College of Further Education
Oxpens Rd, Oxford, Oxon OX1 1SA; Tel (01865) 245871; Fax (01865) 248871
Principal C.R. Wickens, BSc, MSc, CChem, MRSC

Padworth College
Nr Reading, Berks RG7 4NR; Tel (01734) 832644/5; Fax (01734) 834515
Principal Dr S.M. Villazon, MA, PhD(Edin)

Park Lane College
Park La, Leeds, W. Yorks LS3 1AA; Tel (0113) 244 3011; Fax (0113) 244 6372
Principal J.E. Taylor, BSc(Econ)(Hons), CertEd, FRSA

Pembrokeshire College
Haverfordwest, Dyfed SA61 1SZ; Tel (01437) 765247
Principal I.H. Morgan, BSc(Hons), CBiol, MIBiol, CertEd

Pendrell Hall College
Codsall Wood, Nr Wolverhampton, Staffordshire WV8 1QP; Tel (01902) 842398; Fax (01902) 846351
Principal D. Evans

Perth College
Crieff Rd, Perth, Tayside PH1 2NX; Tel (01738) 621171; Fax (01738) 631364
Principal M.A. Webster, BA, DMS, MIMgt

Peterborough Regional College
Park Cres, Peterborough PE1 4DZ; Tel (01733) 67366
Principal K. Stapleford, MSc, PhD

Pitman Business Training
154 Southampton Row, London WC1B 5AX; Tel 0171-837 4481

Plater College
Pullens La, Oxford, Oxon OX3 0DT; Tel (01865) 741676; Fax (01865) 60371
Principal M. Blades, MA

College of Further Education, Plymouth
Kings Rd, Devonport, Plymouth, Devon PL1 5QG; Tel (01752) 385300
Principal G. Rospigliosi, BA

Pontypridd Technical College
Ynys Terr, Rhydyfelin, Pontypridd, Mid Glamorgan CF37 5RN; Tel (01443) 486121; Fax (01443) 409345
Principal J.R. Cocks, BA(Hons), MEd

Portslade Community College
Chalky Rd, Portslade, Brighton, E. Sussex BN41 2WS; Tel (01273) 416300
Principal M. Tait, BA, MEd

Coleg Powys
Penlan, Brecon, Powys LD3 9SR; Tel (01874) 625252; Fax (01874) 622165
Principal J.L. Stephenson, MA, MSc, MInstP
Llanidloes Rd, Newtown, Powys SY16 4HU; Tel (01686) 622722; Fax (01686) 622246
Spa Rd, Llandrindod Wells, Powys LD1 5ES; Tel (01597) 822696; Fax (01597) 825122

Pyke House
Battle, E. Sussex; Tel (01424) 772495; Fax (01424) 775041
Head of Centre Danny O'Sullivan

Reading College of Arts and Technology
Crescent Rd, Reading, Berks RG1 5RQ; Tel (01734) 583501; Fax (01734) 352271
Principal Fred McCrindle

Redbridge College
Little Heath, Romford, Essex RM6 4XT; Tel 0181-599 5231; Fax 0181-599 8224
Principal J.A. McGrath, BA(Hons), CertEd

Reid Kerr College
Renfrew Rd, Paisley, Strathclyde; Tel 0141-889 4225; Fax 0141-889 3958
Principal D. Morrison, BA, DipCom

Rhondda College
Llwynypia, Tonypandy, Mid Glamorgan CF40 2TQ; Tel (01443) 432187
Principal Sandy Grant, BA, PGCE

Rockingham College of Further Education
West St, Wath-upon-Dearne, Rotherham, S. Yorks S63 6PX; Tel (01709) 760310 (24 hours); Fax (01709) 872799 (24 hours)
Principal D.H. Davison, BA(Hons), MCIT, CertEd

Roehampton Institute London
(Affiliated to the University of Surrey)
Senate Hse, Roehampton La, London SW15 5PU; Tel 0181-392 3000
Digby Stuart College Roehampton La, London SW15 5PH; Tel 0181-392 3200
Principal Sister Bernadette Porter, CertEd, BEd, PhD
Southands College Wimbledon Parkside, London SW19 5NN; Tel 0181-392 3400
Principal M.D. Leigh, BA, DipEd
Whitelands College West Hill, London SW15 3SN; Tel 0181-392 3500
Principal Rev D. Peacock, BA, MA, PGCE

Roffey Park Management Institute
Roffey Pk Inst Limited, Forest Rd, Horsham, West Sussex RH12 4TD; Tel (01293) 851644; Fax (01293) 851565

Rother Valley College
Doe Quarry La, Dinnington, S. Yorks S31 7NH; Tel (01909) 550550; Fax (01909) 550504
Principal D. Wilce

Rotherham College of Arts and Technology
Eastwood La, Rotherham, S. Yorks S65 1EG; Tel (01709) 362111
Principal J.K. Molyneux, PhD, MA, DMS, DipEd, FIMgt

Royal National College for the Blind
Royal National College, College Rd, Hereford, Hereford and Worcester HR1 1EB; Tel (01432) 265725; Fax (01432) 353478
Principal Colin Housby-Smith, PhD(Cantab), MEd(Wales), DipEE

Ruskin College
Walton St, Oxford, Oxon OX1 2HE; Tel (01865) 54331
Principal Stephen Yeo, DPhil, MA

St Andrews College
Bearsden, Glasgow, Strathclyde G61 4QA; Tel 0141-943 1424; Fax 0141-943 0106
Principal Bartholomew J. McGettrick, KHS, BSc, MEd, FRSA

St Austell College
Formed April 1993 by merger of St Austell Sixth Form College with Mid-Cornwall CFE
Trevarthian Rd, St Austell, Cornwall PL25 4BU; Tel (01726) 67911; Fax (01726) 68499
Principal W.J. Hill, BA, PGCE

St Helens Community College
St Helens, Merseyside WA10 1PZ; Tel (01744) 33766
Principal J.W. West, BA, MA, MSc, FRSA, FBIM

St Loye's School of Occupational Therapy
Millbrook Hse, Millbrook La, Exeter, Devon; Tel (01392) 219774; Fax (01392) 435357
Principal Barbara Paul, BSc, DipCOT, SROT

Salford College
Worsley Campus, Walkden Rd, Worsley, Manchester, Greater Manchester M28 4QD; Tel 0161-702 8272; Fax 0161-703 8716
Principal M. Humphries, MA, BSc
The Quays Campus Craven Dr, Salford M5 3DJ; Tel 0161-702 8272; Fax 0161-886 5200
The Crescent Campus Windsor Bldg, Withington St, Salford M6 5BG; Tel 0161-702 8272; Fax 0161-886 5400
Wardley Campus Mardale Ave, Swinton M27 3QP; Tel 0161-702 8272; Fax 0161-886 5500

Salisbury College
Southampton Rd, Salisbury, Wilts SP1 2LW; Tel (01722) 323711; Fax (01722) 326006
Principal Gillian Brain

Sandwell College of Further and Higher Education
Woden Rd South, Wednesbury, Sandwell, West Midlands WS10 0PE; Tel 0121-556 6000
Principal D.W.M. Keith, MA(Hons), CertEd

Sandy Community College
Engayne Ave, Sandy, Beds SG19 1BL; Tel (01767) 680574

Shetland College of Further Education
Gremista, Lerwick, Shetland Isles ZE1 0PX; Tel (01595) 5514; Fax (01595) 4830
Principal Gordon Dargie

Shipley College
Exhibition Rd, Shipley, West Yorkshire BD18 3JW; Tel (01274) 757222; Fax (01274) 757201
Principal Jean McAllister

Shrewsbury College of Arts and Technology
London Rd, Shrewsbury, Shropshire SY2 7PR; Tel (01743) 231544
Principal Dr B.D. McIntosh

Solihull College
Blossomfield Rd, Solihull, West Midlands B91 1SB; Tel 0121-711 2111; Fax 0121-711 2316
Principal Colin Flint

Somerset College of Arts and Technology
Wellington Rd, Taunton, Somerset TA1 5AX; Tel (01823) 283403; Fax (01823) 331014
Principal H.E. Rexworthy, BA, ACE(Soc), MITD

Soundwell College
St Stephen's Rd, Soundwell, Bristol, Avon BS16 4RL; Tel (0117) 967 5101; Marketing Unit; Tel (0117) 967 5152; Fax (0117) 935 2753
Principal D. Ekinsmyth, BSc, CertEd, FCII

South Birmingham College
Cole Bank Rd, Birmingham, West Midlands B28 8ES; Tel 0121-694 5000
Principal A.R. Birks, BSc, BA, MBIM, CertEd

South Devon College
Newton Rd, Torquay, Devon TQ2 5BY; Tel (01803) 386404; Fax (01803) 386403
Principal Dr T.R. Keen, PhD, BA(Hons), CertEd, FBIM, ABPsS

South East Essex College of Arts and Technology
Carnarvon Rd, Southend-on-Sea, Essex SS2 6LS; Tel (01702) 220400; Fax (01702) 432320; Minicom (01702) 220642

South Kent College of Technology
Shorncliffe Rd, Folkestone, Kent CT20 2NA; Tel (01303) 850061; Fax (01303) 220354
Maison Dieu Rd, Dover, Kent CT16 1DH; Tel (01304) 204573
Jemmett Rd, Ashford, Kent TN23 2RJ; Tel (01233) 624513
Principal B. Thomason, PhD, MSc, CEng, FIEE, FBIM, FRSA

South London College
Knights Hill, London SE27 0TX; Tel 0181-670 4488
Principal J. Clark

South Nottingham College
Greythorn Dr, West Bridgford, Nottingham, Notts NG2 7GA; Tel (0115) 981 2125
Principal Robert Harrison

South Thames College
Wandsworth High St, London SW18 2PP; Tel 0181-870 2241; Fax 0181-874 6163
Principal W.A. Bridge, BSc(Hons), PhD, MITD

South Trafford College
Manchester Rd, West Timperley, Altrincham, Cheshire WA14 5PQ; Tel 0161-973 7064; Fax 0161-969 6099
Principal Dr R.S. Baker

Southampton Technical College
St Mary St, Southampton, Hants SO9 4WX; Tel (01703) 635222; Fax (01703) 636728
Principal Dr P. Lavery, BA, PhD, MRIPI, FTS

Southern England Nursery Training College
Admissions Office, 81 Lansdowne Rd, Bournemouth, Dorset BH1 1RP; Tel (01202) 780010; Fax (01202) 780009
Director A.M. Barnes, BA, MBIM, CertEd

Southgate College
High St, Southgate, London N14 6BS; Tel 0181-886 6521; Fax 0181-882 9522
Principal M. Blagden, JP, BSc, MSc, CEng, MIMechE

Southport College
Mornington Rd, Southport, Merseyside PR9 0TT; Tel (01704) 500606; Fax 0151-934 2702
Principal B. Mitchell, BSc(Econ)(Hons)

Southwark College
Surrey Docks Centre, Drummond Rd, London SE16 4EE; Tel 0171-815 1500; Fax 0171-815 1525
Principal Stuart Evans, MSc, MIM, FRSA, CertEd
Waterloo Centre The Cut, London SE1 8LE; Tel 0171-815 1500; Fax 0171-261 1301
Bermondsey Centre Tanner St, London SE1 3DP; Tel 0171-815 1500; Fax 0171-237 8640
Blackfriars Centre 209–215 Blackfriars Rd, London SE1 8NL; Tel 0171-815 1500; Fax 0171-261 1301
Camberwell Centre Southampton Way, London SE5 7EW; Tel 0171-815 1500; Fax 0171-815 4751
Peckham Centre Asylum Rd, London SE15 2RJ; Tel 0171-815 1500; Fax 0171-639 1689

The Staff College
Coombe Lodge, Blagdon, Bristol, Avon BS18 6RG; Tel (01761) 462503; Fax (01761) 463104
Director T.G. Melling, MA
Deputy Director K.J. Scribbins, BSc(Soc), MA

Provides training and development activities for managers in further and higher education; updating conferences and seminars for senior staff in post-secondary institutions, authorities, industry and commerce, and central government; customised consultancy and external training. Also undertakes research and development projects and provides an information and publications service

Independent

Stafford College
Earl St, Stafford, Staffs ST16 2QR; Tel (01785) 223800; Fax (01785) 59953
Principal A.J. Haydon, MA, DPhil

Stafford House
Hassocks, Sussex BN6 8QJ; Tel (01273) 845530

Stamford College
Drift Rd, Stamford, Lincs PE9 1XA; Tel (01780) 64141; Fax (01780) 63313
Principal A.P. Middleton, BSc(Econ), MSc, CertEd

Stevenson College, Edinburgh
Bankhead Ave, Sighthill, Edinburgh, Midlothian EH11 4DE; Tel 0131-453 6161; Fax 0131-458 5067
Principal M. Leech, MA(Ed), BA(Hons), DipEd, FRGS

Stockport College of Further and Higher Education
Wellington Rd South, Stockport, Cheshire SK1 3UQ; Tel 0161-958 3110; Fax 0161-480 6636
Principal Dr Richard Evans, BSc, MEd, PGCE, CPhys, FInstP

Stockton and Billingham College of Further Education
The Causeway, Billingham, Cleveland TS23 2DB; Tel (01642) 552101; Fax (01642) 363805
Principal M. Armstrong, BEd, CertEd

Stoke on Trent College
Cauldon Campus, Stoke Rd, Shelton, Stoke on Trent, Staffs ST4 2DG; Tel (01782) 208208; Fax (01782) 203504
Director N.J. Preston, BSc, MHCIMA

Stourbridge College
Hagley Rd, Stourbridge, Dudley, West Midlands DY8 1QU; Tel (01384) 378531/443233
Principal D. Toeman, BA, BSc(Hons), MSc, PGCE

Stow College
43 Shamrock St, Glasgow, Strathclyde G4 9LD; Tel 0141-322 1786
Principal D.W. Snaith, MSc, PhD, CEng, MIM, CChem, FRSC

Stranmillis College
Stranmillis Rd, Belfast BT9 5DY; Tel (01232) 381271; Fax (01232) 664423
Principal J.R.B. McMinn, BA, PhD, DipEd

Stratford-upon-Avon College
The Willows North, Alcester Rd, Stratford-upon-Avon, Warks CV37 9QR; Tel (01789) 266245; Fax (01789) 267524
Principal R.G. Moore, BSc(Econ), MA

Stromness Academy Nautical Department
Stromness, Orkney; Tel (01856) 851021
Principal David Sillar, BSc, MEd

Stroud College of Further Education
Stratford Rd, Stroud, Glos GL5 4AH; Tel (01453) 763424; Fax (01453) 753543
Principal J.M. Hockey, MSc, BSc(Tech), MNI, FBIM, FRSA

Suffolk College
(An Associate College of the University of East Anglia)
Rope Walk, Ipswich, Suffolk IP4 1LT; Tel (01473) 255885; Fax (01473) 230054
Principal Derek Mortimer, OBE, BSc, MEd

Sutton Coldfield College of Further Education
Lichfield Rd, Sutton Coldfield, West Midlands B74 2NW; Tel 0121-355 5671; Fax 0121-355 0799
Principal R.H. Hollyhock, BSc, BA, DipEd
Erdington Centre, Edwards Rd, Birmingham B24; Tel 0121-373 4214; Fax 0121-382 1798

Swindon College
Regent Circus, Swindon, Wilts SN1 1PT; Tel (01793) 491591
Principal C. Brain, OBE, BA(Hons), MSc(Econ), FBIM, FRSA, CertEd
North Star Ave, Swindon SN2 1DY
Euclid St, Swindon SN1 2TQ
Ferndale Rd, Swindon SN2 1HL

TACK Training International
TACK Hse, Longmoore St, London SW1V 1JJ; Tel 0171-834 5001

Tameside College of Technology
Beaufort Rd, Ashton-under-Lyne, Tameside OL6 6NX; Tel 0161-330 6911; Fax 0161-343 2738
Principal J.A. Sanderson, BA(Econ), FCIT, DASTE, FRSA

Tamworth College
Croft St, Upper Gungate, Tamworth, Staffs B79 8AE; Tel (01827) 310202; Fax (01827) 59437
Principal C.A. Herd, BA

Telford College of Arts and Technology
Haybridge Rd, Wellington, Telford, Shropshire TF1 2NP; Tel (01952) 642237; Fax (01952) 243657
Principal D.F. Boynton, BSc, MSC, PGCE, CEng, MIMechE, FRSA
Hartsbridge Rd, Oakengates, Telford TF2 6BA

Thanet College
Ramsgate Rd, Broadstairs, Kent CT10 1PN; Tel (01843) 865111
Principal G.F. Burney, BSc, MPhil, CEng, MIMechE, CertEd

Thomas Danby College
Roundhay Rd, Leeds, W. Yorks LS7 3BG; Tel (0113) 249 4912; Fax (0113) 249 4912
Principal H.W. Jones

Thurrock College
Woodview, Grays, Essex RM16 4YR; Tel (01375) 391199
Principal J.W. Wallace, BEd, MA

Thurso College
Ormlie Rd, Thurso, Caithness, Highland KW14 7EE; Tel (01847) 66161; Fax (01847) 63872
Principal Raymond Murray, BEd

Tile Hill College of Further Education
Tile Hill La, Coventry, West Midlands CV4 9SU; Tel (01203) 694200; Fax (01203) 464903
Principal H.E. Avery, OBE, BSc, PhD

Tower Hamlets College
Poplar Centre, Poplar High St, London E14 0AF; Tel 0171-538 5888
Principal A. Zera

Tresham Institute of Further and Higher Education
Corby Campus, George St, Corby, Northants NN17 1QA; Tel (01536) 402252
Principal C.K. Rowland, BA, FBIM
Kettering Campus St Mary's Rd, Kettering, Northants NN15 7BS; Tel (01536) 410252; Fax (01536) 522500
Wellingborough Campus Church St, Wellingborough, Northants NN8 4PD; Tel (01933) 224165; Fax (01933) 441832

Trinity College
Carmarthen, Dyfed SA31 3EP; Tel (01267) 237971; Fax (01267) 230933
Principal D.C. Jones-Davies, OBE, JP, MA, MPhil, FRSA

Trowbridge College
College Rd, Trowbridge, Wilts BA14 0ES; Tel (01225) 766241; Fax (01225) 777148
Principal G. Bright

Upper Bann Institute of Further and Higher Education
Formed 1995 from the former Portadown College of Further Education, Banbridge College and Lurgan College
Portadown Campus, 26–44 Lurgan Rd, Portadown, Craigavon BT63 5BL; Tel (01762) 337111
Director Dr G. Byrne

Urchfont Manor Residential College of Adult Education
Urchfont Manor College, Urchfont, Devizes, Wilts SN10 4RG; Tel (01380) 840495
Director Patricia Howell, BSc, PhD

Uxbridge College
Park Rd, Uxbridge, Middx UB8 1NQ; Tel (01895) 230411; Fax (01895) 811482
Principal T.J. Hannagan, BSc, MSc, FRSA, FIMgt
Hayes Centre Central Ave, Hayes, Middx UB3 2DD; Tel 0181-756 0414; Fax 0181-569 3063

Walsall College of Arts and Technology
St Paul's St, Walsall, West Midlands WS1 1XN; Tel (01922) 720824
Principal R.A.J. Gray

Waltham Forest College
Forest Rd, London E17 4JB; Tel 0181-527 2311; Fax 0181-523 2376
Principal M.J. Bourke, MA(Ed), BEd(Hons)

Wansfell College
30 Piercing Hill, Theydon Bois, Epping, Essex CM16 7LF; Tel (01992) 813027
Principal Marilyn Taylor, BA, DipACE

Warrington Collegiate Institute
(Formerly North Cheshire College)
Padgate Campus, Crab La, Warrington, Cheshire WA2 0DB; Tel (01925) 814343
Principal and Chief Executive Steven Broomhead
Padgate Campus Crab La, Warrington, Cheshire WA2 0DB; Tel (01925) 814343; Fax (01925) 816077
Museum St Centre Museum St, Warrington, Cheshire; Tel (01925) 32712; Fax (01925) 59241

Wedgwood Memorial College
Barlaston, Stoke on Trent, Staffs ST12 9DG; Tel (01782) 372105/373427; Fax (01782) 372393
Principal D. Tatton, BA(Cantab), PhD

The Wellingborough College
Church St, Wellingborough, Northants NN8 4PD; Tel (01933) 224165; Fax (01933) 441832
Assistant Principals (Resources) J.J. Cutlack, IEng, FIEEIE; (Courses) E.J. Livingstone. BSc(Econ); (Students and Staff) J. Brown, DMS, DipM. FBTS, CertEd

West Cheshire College
Arts Centre, Blacon Ave, Blacon, Chester, Cheshire CH1 5BD; Tel (01244) 377595
Principal C.D. Rees, BA, MEd
Grange Centre Regent St, Ellesmere Port, Cheshire L65 8EJ; Tel 0151-356 2300
Greenbank Centre Eaton Rd, Chester, Cheshire CH4 7ER; Tel (01244) 677677
Handbridge Centre Eaton Rd, Handbridge, Chester, Cheshire CH4 7ER; Tel (01244) 677677

West Cumbria College
Park La, Workington, Cumbria CA14 2RW; Tel (01900) 64331; Fax (01900) 65017
Principal B.J. Taylor, BSc, PhD
Flatt Walks, Whitehaven; Tel (01946) 692261
Lillyhall Main Centre; Tel (01946) 830427
Lillyhall Construction Centre; Tel (0990) 66646

West Dean College
West Dean, Chichester, West Sussex; Tel (01243) 811301; Fax (01243) 811343
Principal P. Sarginson

West of England Management Centre
The Promenade, Clifton Down, Bristol, Avon BS8 3NB; Tel (0117) 9731471; Fax (0117) 9744288
Senior Consultant Bob Gardener

West Herts College
Watford Campus Hempstead Rd, Watford, Herts WD1 3EZ; Tel (01923) 257500
Principal F.H. Baker, BSc, PhD, MIEE, CEng
Cassio Campus Langley Rd, Watford, Herts WD1 3EZ; Tel (01923) 240311
Dacorum Campus Marlowes, Hemel Hempstead, Herts HP1 1HD; Tel (01442) 63771
Leggatts Campus Leggatts Way, Watford, Herts WD2 6BJ; Tel (01923) 684848

West Kent College
Brook St, Tonbridge, Kent TN9 2PW; Tel (01732) 358101; Fax (01732) 771415
Chief Executive Graham S. Hollands

West London College
Avon Hse, 360–366 Oxford St, London W1; Tel 0171-491 1841; Fax 0171-499 5853
Principal Peter Rainey, PostgradDip Marketing, MInstM, MABE

West Lothian College
Marjoribanks St, Bathgate, West Lothian EH48 1QJ; Tel (01506) 634300; Fax (01506) 634860
Principal A.J. Godden, BSc, MRSH, AIHE
Lammermuir Hse Livingston, West Lothian EH54 6PW; Tel (01506) 418484; Fax (01506) 460461

West Nottinghamshire College
Derby Rd, Mansfield, Notts NG18 5BH; Tel (01623) 27191; Fax (01623) 23063
Principal J. Aleander, MA

West Oxfordshire College
Holloway Rd, Witney, Oxon OX8 7EE; Tel (01993) 703464
Principal A.J. Stewart, BSc, CPhys, MInstP

West Suffolk College
Out Risbygate, Bury St Edmunds, Suffolk IP33 3RL; Tel (01284) 701301; Fax (01284) 750561
Principal J.M. Shipston

West Thames College
London Rd, Isleworth, Middx TW7 4HS; Tel 0181-568 0244; Fax 0181-569 7787
Principal Gerard O'Donnell, BA(Hons), FRAI, ACP, FRSA

Westham House Adult College
Barford, Warwick, Warks CV35 8DP; Tel (01926) 624206
Principal Donn Evans, MEd, PhD

Westminster College
Battersea Pk Rd, London SW11 4JR; Tel 0171-720 2121
Principal Mrs P.C. Burgess, BA, DipEd
Vincent Sq, London SW1P 2PD
Castle La, London SW1E 6DR
Peter St, London W1V 4HS

Weston-super-Mare College
Knightstone Rd, Weston-super-Mare, Avon BS23 2AL; Tel (01934) 411411; Fax (01934) 411410
Principal G.T. Williams

Wigan and Leigh College
PO Box 53, Parsons Walk, Wigan, Lancs WN1 1RR; Tel (01942) 501501; Fax (01942) 501551
Principal P. Hoddinott, BSc, MSc, FSS, DipEd

Wigan College of Technology
PO Box 53, Parsons Walk, Wigan, Lancs WN1 1RS; Tel (01942) 494911
P. Hoddinott, BSc, MSc, DipEd, FSS

Wigston College of Further Education
Station Rd, Wigston, Magna, Leicester, Leics LE18 2DW; Tel (0116) 288 5051
Principal D.M. Gurr, BSc, MSc(Soc), DipEdAdmin, MIBiol, MIHE

Wirral Metropolitan College
Borough Rd, Birkenhead, Merseyside L42 9QD; Tel 0151-653 5555
Principal J. Shackleton, BA(Hons)
Carlett Pk, Eastham L62 0AY; Tel 0151-327 4331
Withens La, Wallasey L45 7LT; Tel 0151-639 8371

Wolverhampton College of Adult Education
Old Hall St, Wolverhampton, West Midlands WV1 3AU; Tel (01902) 312059; Fax (01902) 312202
Principal Co-ordinator S.A. Thompson, CertEd

Woolwich College, Plumstead Centre
Villas Rd, Plumstead, London SE18 7PN; Tel 0181-855 1216; Fax 0181-854 2194
Principal Geoff Pine, BSc(Econ), PGCE, DipEdAdmin

Worcester College of Technology
Deansway, Worcester, Hereford and Worcester WR1 2JF; Tel (01905) 723383; Fax (01905) 28906
Principal J. Henderson, BA(Hons), MSc, FIMEMME, FIMgt, CertEd

Workers' Educational Association
Temple Hse, 17 Victoria Pk Sq, London E2 9PB; Tel 0181-983 1515; Fax 0181-983 4040
General Secretary Robert Lochrie, MA

Workers' Educational Association North Wales
33 College Rd, Bangor, Gwynedd LL57 2AP; Tel (01248) 353254; Fax (01248) 371181

Workers' Educational Association South Wales
11 Station Terr, Cowbridge Rd West, Cardiff CF5 4AA; Tel (01222) 552277; Fax (01222) 578829
Director Graham Price, MA

Working Mens College
44 Crowndale Rd, London NW1 1TR; Tel 0171-387 2037; Fax 0171-383 5561

Wulfrun College
Paget Rd, Wolverhampton, West Midlands WV6 0DU; Tel (01902) 317700; Fax (01902) 23070
Principal G.K. Mothersdale, BSc(Hons), PhD, CText, FTI

YMCA National Centre
Lakeside, Ulverston, Cumbria LA12 8BD; Tel (0153 95) 31758

York College of Further and Higher Education
Tadcaster Rd, York, N. Yorks YO2 1UA; Tel (01904) 704141; Fax (01904) 770499
Principal Dr David R. Mason

Yorkshire Coast College
Lady Edith's Dr, Scalby Rd, Scarborough, N. Yorks YO12 5RN; Tel (01723) 372105; Fax (01723) 501918
Principal S.A. Dey, BA(Hons), CertEd, MIIM

Ystrad Mynach College
Ystrad Mynach, Hengoed, Mid Glamorgan CF8 7XR; Tel (01443) 816888; Fax (01443) 816973
Principal D.E. Brooks, MEd, BA

Agriculture and Horticulture Colleges

Askham Bryan College
Askham Bryan, York, N. Yorks YO2 3PR; Tel (01904) 702121; Fax (01904) 702629
Principal/Chief Executive M.D. Pollard, NDA, SDDH

The Barony College
Parkgate, Dumfries & Galloway DG1 3NE; Tel (01387) 86251; Fax (01387) 86395
Principal David Rose, BA, NDA, ARAgS

Berkshire College of Agriculture
Hall Pl, Burchetts Grn, Maidenhead, Berks SL6 6QR; Tel (01628) 824444; Fax (01628) 824695
Principal P. Thorn, BSc(Hons), MCIM

Bicton College of Agriculture
East Budleigh, Budleigh Salterton, Devon EX9 7BY; Tel (01395) 568353; Fax (01395) 567502
Principal M. Florey, MA, NDA, CertEd

Bishop Burton College
York Rd, Bishop Burton, Beverley, Humberside HU17 8QG; Tel (01964) 550481; Fax (01964) 551190
Principal H.W. Petch, NDA(Hons)

Brackenhurst College
Southwell, Notts NG25 0QF; Tel (01636) 812252; Fax (01636) 815404
Principal J.P. Benson, BSc(Hons), FRAgS

Brinsbury College
West Sussex College of Agriculture and Horticulture, North Heath, Pulborough, West Sussex RH20 1DL; Tel (01798) 873832
Principal E.I. Hoyland

Brooksby College
Brooksby, Melton Mowbray, Leics LE14 2LJ; Tel (01664) 434291; Fax (01664) 434572
Principal J. Gusterson

Broomfield College
Derbyshire College of Agriculture and Horticulture, Morley, Ilkeston, Derbys DE7 6DN; Tel (01332) 831345; Fax (01332) 830298
Principal J.C. Field, MA(EdStudies), BSc (Hons), PGCE, DFPS, CIBiol, MIBiol

Cambridgeshire College of Agriculture and Horticulture
Landbeach Rd, Milton, Cambridge CB4 6DB; Tel (01223) 860701; Fax (01223) 860262
Principal J.P.L. Whittington, NDA, CertEd

Cannington College
Somerset College of Agriculture and Horticulture Cannington, Bridgwater, Somerset TA5 2LS; Tel (01278) 652226
Principal B.J. Gimbert

Capel Manor Horticultural and Environmental Centre
Bullsmoor La, Enfield, Middx EN1 4RQ; Tel 0181-366 4442; Fax (01992) 717544
Chief Executive Dr S.R. Dowbiggin, PhD, FIHort

Cranfield (Shuttleworth College)
Old Warden Pk, Biggleswade, Beds SG18 9DX; Tel (01525) 863100

De Montfort University Lincoln School of Agriculture and Horticulture
Caythorpe Ct, Caythorpe, Grantham, Lincs NG32 3EP; Tel (01400) 272521; Fax (01400) 272722
Associate Pro-Vice-Chancellor Prof J. Moverley, MA(Cantab)
Riseholme Campus Riseholme Hall, Riseholme, Lincoln LN2 2LG
Holbeach Campus Park Rd, Holbeach, Lincs PE12 7PT

Durham College of Agriculture and Horticulture
Houghall, Durham, Co Durham DH1 3SG; Tel 0191-386 1351; Fax 0191-386 0419
Principal A. Hetherington, BSc

Easton College
Easton, Norwich, Norfolk NR9 5DX; Tel (01603) 742105; Fax (01603) 741438
Principal D.C. Lawrence, DMS, LCG, CertEd, MIMgt

Elmwood College
Cupar, Fife KY15 4JB; Tel (01334) 652781; Fax (01334) 656795
Principal Norval Black

Enniskillen College of Agriculture
Enniskillen, Co Fermanagh; Tel (01365) 323101
Principal P.A. Mallon, Bsc

Greenmount College of Agriculture and Horticulture
Antrim, Co Antrim BT41 4PU; Tel (0184 94) 62114
Principal R.J. McClenaghan, BAgr, DipAgrComm

Guisborough College of Agriculture and Horticulture (Askham Bryan)
Avenue Pl, Redcar Rd, Guisborough, Cleveland TS14 6AX; Tel (01287) 633870
Principal M.D. Pollard

Hadlow College of Agriculture and Horticulture
Hadlow, Tonbridge, Kent TN11 0AL; Tel (01732) 850551; Fax (01732) 851957
Principal R.A.E. Turner, NDA, CDFM

Harper Adams (A University Sector College)
Salop, Newport, Shropshire TF10 8NB; Tel (01952) 820280; Fax (01952) 814783
Principal Graham McConnell, BSc, MSc

Hartpury College
Hartpury Hse, Gloucester, Glos GL19 3BE; Tel (01452) 700283
Principal M. Wharton, BEd(Hons), NDA, MRAC

Hereford College of Agriculture
Holme Lacy, Hereford and Worcester HR2 6LL; Tel (01432) 870316/870319
Principal J.M.W. Hood

Kingston Maurward College
Dorset College of the Countryside, Dorchester, Dorset DT2 8PY; Tel (01305) 264738; Fax (01305) 250059
Principal R. Bowers, BSc

Kirkley Hall College
Ponteland, Northumberland NE20 0AQ; Tel (01661) 860808; Fax (01661) 860047
Principal P.W. Thompson, NDA, NDD

Lackham College
Lacock, Chippenham, Wilts SN15 2NY; Tel (01249) 443111; Fax (01249) 444474
Principal P.W. Morris, MA, NDA, DipTAd, CIAgrE, FRAgS

Llysfasi College
North Wales College of the Countryside, Ruthin, Clwyd LL15 2LB; Tel (01978) 790263; Fax (01978) 790468
Principal D.F. Cunningham, BSc(Agric), NDD

Loughry College of Agriculture and Food Technology
Cookstown, Co Tyrone BT80 9AA; Tel (0164 87) 62491; Fax (0164 87) 61043
Principal Dr R.C. Stevenson, BAgr, MSc, PhD

Merrist Wood College
Worplesdon, Guildford, Surrey GU3 3PE; Tel (01483) 232424; Fax (01483) 236518
Principal and Chief Executive J.G. Riddle, MHort(RHS), MSc, MBA

Moulton College
Moulton, Northampton, Northants NN3 7RR; Tel (01604) 491131; Fax (01604) 491127
Principal C. Moody, BSc(Hons), MEd, PGCE, MBIM

Myerscough College (Associate College of The University of Central Lancashire)
Myerscough Hall, Bilsborrow, Preston, Lancs PR3 0RY; Tel (01995) 640611; Fax (01995) 640842
Principal A. Fox, BSc, NDA

Newton Rigg College
Penrith, Cumbria CA11 0AH; Tel (01768) 63791; Fax (01768) 67249
Principal K.E. Jackson, BSc(Hons), MSc, Grad, CertEd

Oatridge Agricultural College
Ecclesmachan, Broxburn, Midlothian EH52 6NQ; Tel (01506) 854387
Principal C.W. Nixon, NDA

Otley College of Agriculture and Horticulture
Formerly known as East Suffolk College of Agriculture and Horticulture
Otley, Ipswich, Suffolk IP6 9EY; Tel (01473) 785543; Fax (01473) 785353
Principal A.B. Ferguson, BSc(Hons)

Pencoed College
Tregroes, Pencoed, Bridgend, Mid Glamorgan CF35 5LG; Tel (01656) 860202/860635
Principal J.D.B. Thomas

Pershore College of Horticulture
'Avonbank', Pershore, Worcs WR10 3JP; Tel (01386) 552443; Fax (01386) 556528
Principal David A. Hall, BSc, PhD, Grad. Cert.Ed

Plumpton College
Lewes, E. Sussex BN7 3AE; Tel (01273) 890454; Fax (01273) 890071
Chief Executive Vacancy

Reaseheath College
Reaseheath, Nantwich, Cheshire CW5 6DF; Tel (01270) 625131; Fax (01270) 625665
Principal V.J. Croxson, NDA, CertEd

Rodbaston College
Rodbaston, Penkridge, Staffs; Tel (01785) 712209
Principal R.A. Holtom, BSc, CertEd

Royal Agricultural College
Cirencester, Glos GL7 6JS; Tel (01285) 652531; Fax (01285) 650219
Principal Prof A.S. Jones, BSc, PhD, CBiol, FIBiol, FIAgrM, FBIM, FRSA

Royal Botanic Garden, Edinburgh
Edinburgh, Midlothian EH1 5LR; Tel 0131-552 7171
Regius Keeper Prof D.S. Ingram

Royal Botanic Gardens, Kew School of Horticulture
Richmond, Surrey TW9 3AB; Tel 0181-332 5545; Fax 0181-332 5574
Principal I. Leese

Rycotewood College
Priest End, Thame, Oxon OX9 2AF; Tel (0184 421) 2501
Principal P.L. Shirtcliff, CertEd, FIMIT, CIAgrE

The Scottish Agricultural College
The Registrar SAC Auchincruive, Ayr, Strathclyde KA6 5HW; Tel (01292) 520331; Fax (01292) 520287
Principal Prof P.C. Thomas, BSc, PhD, FIBiol, CBiol
SAC Aberdeen 581 King St, Aberdeen AB9 1UD
SAC Edinburgh Kings Bldgs, West Mains Rd, Edinburgh EH9 3JG

Sparsholt College Hampshire
Sparsholt, Winchester, Hants SO21 2NF; Tel (01962) 776441; Fax (01962) 776587
Principal L. Norman, PhD, BSc(Reading), MSc(Wales), FRAgS

Walford College, Shropshire

Walford, Baschurch, Shrewsbury, Shropshire SY4 2HL; Tel (01939) 260461; Fax (01939) 261112
Principal K.W. Dann, MA, FBIM, CertEd

Warwickshire College for Agriculture, Horticulture, Equine Studies

Moreton Hall, Moreton Morrell, Warwick, Warks CV35 9BL; Tel (01926) 651367/8; Fax (01926) 651190
Principal R.H.G. Suggett, JP, MEd, BSc, NDA, FIBiol, FRAgS, FRSA

Welsh Agricultural College

Llanbadarn Fawr, Aberystwyth, Dyfed SY23 3AL; Tel (01970) 624471; Fax (01970) 611264
Principal J.H. Harries, PhD, BSc, CertEd

Welsh College of Horticulture

Northop, Mold, Clwyd; Tel (01352) 840861
Principal G.A. Limb, JP, BSc, NDA, FIHort

West Sussex College of Agriculture and Horticulture

Brinsbury, North Heath, Pulborough, W Sussex RH20 1DL; Tel (01798) 873832; Fax (01798) 875222
Principal E.J. Hoyland

Worcestershire College of Agriculture

Hindlip, Worcester, Hereford and Worcester WR3 8SS; Tel (01905) 451310
Principal R.B. Brighton, BSc(Hons), NDA, MRAC

Writtle College

Chelmsford, Essex CM1 3RR; Tel (01245) 420705
Principal Prof M.D. Alder, BSc(Hons), MSc, MIBiol, DipTAd

Art & Design and Performing Arts Colleges

Berkshire College of Art and Design

Raymond Rd, Maidenhead, Berks SL6 6DE; Tel (01628) 24302
Principal John Aston, FCSD, FRSA

Bournemouth and Poole College of Art and Design

Wallisdown, Poole, Dorset BH12 5HH; Tel (01202) 533011; Fax (01202) 537729
Principal A.J. Marshall, FSTD, FISTC, FTC

Camberwell College of Arts

Peckham Rd, London SE5 8UF; Tel 0171-703 0987; Fax 0171-703 3689

Central Saint Martins College of Art and Design

(A constituent College of the London Institute)
Southampton Row, London WC1B 4AP; Tel 0171-753 9090; Fax 0171-242 0240
Head Margaret Buck, MA(RCA)
107–109 Charing Cross Rd, London WC2H 0DU
27–29 Long Acre, London WC2E 9LA
Back Hill, Clerkenwell, London EC1R 5EN

Central School of Speech and Drama

Embassy Theatre, 64 Eton Ave, London NW3 3HY; Tel 0171-722 8183
Principal Robert Fowler, MA(Oxon), LGSM, FRSA

Chelsea College of Art and Design

(A constituent College of the London Institute)
Manresa Rd, London SW3 6LS; Tel 0171-351 3844/6
Head of College Bridget Jackson

City and Guilds of London Art School

124 Kennington Pk Rd, London SE11 4DJ; Tel 0171-735 2306/5210; Fax 0171-582 5361
Principal Sir Roger de Grey, KCVO, PPRA

City of Leeds College of Music

Cookridge St, Leeds, W. Yorks LS2 8BH; Tel (0113) 245 2069/432491; Fax (0113) 243 8798

Cleveland College of Art and Design

Green La, Linthorpe, Middlesbrough, Cleveland TS5 7RJ; Tel (01642) 821441; Fax (01642) 823467
Principal R. Jobson, MA, CertRAS, NDD, CertEd

Cumbria College of Art and Design

Brampton Rd, Carlisle, Cumbria CA3 9AY; Tel (01228) 25333
Principal Prof David G. Vaughan, BA(Hons)

Dartington College of Arts

Totnes, Devon TQ9 6EJ; Tel (01803) 862224; Fax (01803) 863569
Principal Prof Kevin Thompson

De Montfort University Lincoln, School of Applied Arts and Design

Lindum Rd, Lincoln, Lincs LN2 1NP; Tel (01522) 512912; Fax (01522) 542167
Head of School Lynne Staley-Brookes (Acting)

Guildhall School of Music and Drama

Barbican, London EC2Y 8DT; Tel 0171-628 2571
Principal Ian Horsbrugh, FGSM, FRCM, FRSA

Herefordshire College of Art and Design

Folly La, Hereford, Hereford and Worcester HR1 1LT; Tel (01432) 273359; Fax (01432) 341099
Principal and Chief Executive Gwynne Williams, DFA(Lond), ATC, FRSA

Ingestre Hall Residential Arts Centre

Ingestre, Stafford, Staffs ST18 0RF; Tel Weston on Trent 270225
Principal Ms J.K. Blake

Kent Institute of Art and Design

Oakwood Pk, Maidstone, Kent ME16 8AG; Tel (01622) 757286; Fax (01622) 692003

Leeds College of Art and Design

Jacob Kramer Bldg, Blenheim Wk, Leeds, W. Yorks LS2 9AQ; Tel (0113) 243 3848
Principal Edmund Wigan

The London Academy of Music and Dramatic Art (LAMDA)
Tower Hse, 226 Cromwell Rd, London SW5 0SR; Tel 0171-373 9883; Fax 0171-370 4739
Principal Peter James

London Contemporary Dance School
The Place, 17 Dukes Rd, London WC1H 9AB; Tel 0171-387 0152; Fax 0171-383 4851
Principal R. Ralph, MA, DPhil

London College of Dance
10 Linden Rd, Bedford, Beds MK40 2DA; Tel (01234) 213331
Principal Patricia Whittock

London College of Fashion
30 John Princes St, London W1M 0BJ; Tel 0171-514 7400; Fax 0171-514 7484
Head of College Prof William Callaway, BA, MSc, DipTP, MRTPI

Loughborough College of Art and Design
Radmoor, Loughborough, Leics LE11 3BT; Tel (01509) 261515; Fax (01509) 265515
Principal Ieuan Pugh

Northern School of Contemporary Dance
98 Chapeltown Rd, Leeds, West Yorkshire LS7 4BH; Tel (0113) 262 5359; Fax (0113) 237 4585
Principal Nadine Senior, MEd, MBE

Norwich School of Art and Design
St George St, Norwich, Norfolk NR3 1BB; Tel (01603) 610561; Fax (01603) 615728
Principal R.J. Fuller
Trafalgar Rd, Great Yarmouth, Norfolk NR30 2LB; Tel (01493) 843557; Fax (01493) 852216

Parnham College
Parnham Hse, Beaminster, Dorset DT8 3NA; Tel (01308) 862204; Fax (01308) 863494/863444
Principal Robert Ingham, DLC, NDD, DipEd

Plymouth College of Art and Design
Tavistock Pl, Plymouth, Devon PL4 8AT; Tel (01752) 385969; Fax (01752) 385972
Principal M.W. Brindley, MCSD, FBID, CGLI (FTC)

Portsmouth College of Art, Design and Further Education
Winston Churchill Ave, Portsmouth, Hants PO1 2DJ; Tel (01705) 826435/7
Principal H.A. Rees, MA

Ravensbourne College of Design and Communication
Walden Rd, Elmstead Woods, Chislehurst, Kent BR7 5SN; Tel 0181-468 7071
Director Prof R. Baker, MAPes, RCA, FCSD

Royal Academy of Music
Marylebone Rd, London NW1 5HT; Tel 0171-873 7373; Fax 0171-873 7374
Principal Lynn Harrell, HonDMus, HonRAM

Royal College of Music
Prince Consort Rd, London SW7 2BS; Tel 0171-589 3643; Fax 0171-589 7740
Director Janet Ritterman, BMus, MMus, PhD, FTCL, DSCM, FRSA

Royal Northern College of Music
124 Oxford Rd, Manchester, Greater Manchester M13 9RD; Tel 0161-273 6283; Fax 0161-273 7611
Principal Sir John Manduell, CBE, Chevalier des Arts et Lettres, HonDMus(Lancaster), HonDMus(Manchester), FRAM, FRCM, FRNCM, FRSAMD, HonFTCL, HonGSM, FBSM, FMP, FWCMD, FRSA

Royal Scottish Academy of Music and Drama
100 Renfrew St, Glasgow, Strathclyde G2 3DB; Tel 0141-332 4101
Principal Philip Ledger, CBE, MA, MusB, LLD, FRCM, HonRAM, FRNCM, HonGSM, FRSE, FRCO

School of Music
99 Donegall Pass, Belfast BT7 1DR; Tel (01232) 322435; Fax (01232) 329201
Senior Tutor R.J. Hewitt, GRSM, LRAM, ARCM

The Surrey Institute of Art and Design
(In 1994 West Surrey College of Art and Design merged with Epsom School of Art and Design to form the Surrey Institute of Art and Design)
Falkner Rd, Farnham, Surrey; Tel (01252) 722441
Director N.J. Taylor, NDD, ATC, FRSA

Sutton College of Liberal Arts
St Nicholas Way, Sutton, Surrey SM1 1EA; Tel 0181-770 6900
Principal G. Russell, MEd

Trinity College of Music
Mandeville Pl, London W1M 6AQ; Tel 0171-935 5773
Principal Gavin Henderson

Welsh College of Music and Drama
Castle Grounds, Cathays Pk, Cardiff, South Glamorgan CF1 3ER; Tel (01222) 342854
Principal Edmond Fivet, MA, FRCM, FRSA

Wimbledon School of Art
Merton Hall Rd, London SW19 3QA; Tel 0181-540 0231; Fax 0181-543 1750
Principal C. Painter

Winchester School of Art
Park Ave, Winchester, Hants SO23 8DL; Tel (01962) 842500
Principal Michael Sadler-Forster, BA, FRSA
C. Barra de Ferro 2, 08003 Barcelona, Spain

Tertiary Colleges

Accrington and Rossendale College
Sandy La, Accrington, Lancs BB5 2AW; Tel (01254) 389933; Fax (01254) 354001
Principal G.M. Austin, MA(Cantab), DipEd(Oxon)

12 Further, Tertiary and Sixth Form Education

Afan College
Margam, Port Talbot, West Glamorgan SA13 2AL; Tel (01639) 882107; Fax (01639) 886163
Principal Tony Halsall

Alton College
Old Odiham Rd, Alton, Hants GU34 2LX; Tel (01420) 88118; Fax (01420) 80012
Principal M.S. Gray, MA

Barnsley College
Old Mill La Site, Church St, Barnsley, S. Yorks S70 2AX; Tel (01226) 730191; Fax (01226) 298514

Basildon College
Nethermayne, Basildon, Essex SS16 5NN; Tel (01268) 532015
Principal S.J. Woodrow

Bilston Community College
Westfield Rd, Bilston, Wolverhampton, West Midlands WV14 6ER; Tel (01902) 353877; Fax (01902) 401897
Principal I.K. Wymer

Blackburn College
Feilden St, Blackburn, Lancs; Tel (01254) 55144
Principal John Bolton, BA

Braintree College
Church La, Bocking, Braintree, Essex; Tel (01376) 321711; Fax (01376) 340799
Principal M.N. Bates

Bridgwater College
Bath Rd, Bridgwater, Somerset TA6 4PZ; Tel (01278) 455464; Fax (01278) 444363
Principal Fiona McMillan

Brockenhurst College
Brockenhurst, Hants SO42 7ZE; Tel (01590) 623565; Fax (01590) 623969
Principal M.J. Snell, BSc(Econ), MA, ACIS, CertEd

Bury College
Market St, Bury, Lancs BL9 0BG; Tel 0161-763 1505
Principal A.A. Robinson, MA

Cardiff Tertiary College/Coleg Glan Hafren
Trowbridge Rd, Rumney, Cardiff, South Glamorgan CF3 8XZ; Tel (01222) 794226; Fax (01222) 797041
Principal Dr C.S. Williams, BSc, PhD, PGCE

Carmarthenshire College of Technology and Art
Alban Rd, Llanelli, Dyfed SA15 1NG; Tel (01554) 759165; Fax (01554) 758189
Principal I. Price, MSc(Eng), CEng, FIMechE, FRSA

Cirencester College
Fosse Way Campus, Stroud Rd, Cirencester, Glos GL7 1XA; Tel (01285) 640944
Principal N.P. Robbins, MA, PGCE, MEd

Cleveland Tertiary College
Corporation Rd, Redcar, Cleveland TS10 3QN; Tel (01642) 473132; Fax (01642) 490856
Principal M.D. Clark, BSc(Eng), CertEd
(Mixed) (310)

Cricklade College, Andover
Charlton Rd, Andover, Hants SP10 1EJ; Tel (01264) 363311; Fax (01264) 332088
Principal R.J. Evans, BA

Daventry Tertiary College
Badby Rd West, Daventry, Northants NN11 4HJ; Tel (01327) 300232; Fax (01327) 300942
Principal Dr D.J. Rogers
Learner Support Manager Ann Forgon

Derby Tertiary College Mackworth
Prince Charles Ave, Mackworth, Derby, Derbys DE22 4LR; Tel (01332) 519951; Fax (01332) 510548
Principal A.B. Harrison, BA, PGCE

Derwentside College
Park Rd, Consett, Co Durham DH8 5EE; Tel (01207) 502906
Principal Mrs J. Round, BA(Hons), MA, CertEd, CDipAFMiMgt

Dewsbury College
Halifax Rd, Dewsbury, W. Yorks WF13 2AS; Tel (01924) 465916; Fax (01924) 457047
Principal and Chief Executive V. Hall, BSc, MBA, PGCE, DMS, MBIM

Ealing Tertiary College
Mill Hill Rd, Acton, London W3 8UX; Tel 0181-231 6000 (All sites); Fax 0181-896 3334
Director Ian Wallis

Formed in 1992 by the amalgamation of three Colleges: Acton College, Norwood Hall Institute of Horticultural Education, Southall College of Technology
Ealing Centre Ealing Grn, London W5 5EW
Acton Centre Mill Hill Rd, Acton W3 8UX
Southall Centre Beaconsfield Rd, Southall, Middx UB1 1DP

East Devon College
Bolham Rd, Tiverton, Devon EX16 6SH; Tel (01884) 254247; Fax (01884) 259262
Principal F.J. Rosamond, MA(Econ), BA(Econ)(Hons), CertEd

Epping Forest College
Borders La, Loughton, Essex IG10 3SA; Tel 0181-508 8311
Principal Gordon Bell, MA, MEng

Exeter College
Hele Rd, Exeter, Devon EX4 4JS; Tel (01392) 382000; Fax (01392) 210282
Principal John Capey, OBE, MA, MSc, PhD

Fareham College
Bishopsfield Rd, Fareham, Hants PO14 1NH; Tel (01329) 220844; Fax (01329) 822483
Principal Richard Parker, PhD, BA(Hons)

Gateshead College
Durham Rd, Gateshead, Tyne and Wear NE9 5BN; Tel 0191-490 0300; Fax 0191 490 2313
Principal C.J. Hughes

Gorseinon College
Belgrave Rd, Gorseinon, Swansea, West Glamorgan SA4 2RF; Tel (01792) 898283; Fax (01792) 898729
Principal Penelope Ryan, BA(Hons), PGCE, MEd, FTCL, FLCM, ARCM, FRSA

Greenhill College, Harrow
Lowlands Rd, Harrow, Middx HA1 3AQ; Tel 0181-422 2388; Fax 0181-423 5183
Principal Fergus Pollard

Gwent Tertiary College (Usk Campus)
The Rhadyr, Usk, Gwent NP5 1XJ; Tel (01291) 672311; Fax (01291) 672256
Principal Dr W. Bleazard
Pontypool Campus Blaendare Rd, Pontypool, Gwent NP4 5YE; Tel (01495) 755141; Fax (01495) 751040

Gwent Tertiary College (Crosskeys College Campus)
Crosskeys, Gwent NP1 7ZA; Tel (01495) 270295
Principal W.R. Williams, BA(Hons), DipEd, MBIM

Gwent Tertiary College (Ebbw Vale College Campus)
College Rd, Ebbw Vale, Gwent NP3 6LE; Tel (01495) 302083; Fax (01495) 350149
Campus Principal G. Neale

Gwent Tertiary College (Newport College Campus)
Nash Rd, Newport, Gwent NP9 0TS; Tel (01633) 274861; Fax (01633) 273045
Campus Principal R.D. Giles

Halesowen College
Whittingham Rd, Halesowen, West Midlands B63 3NA; Tel 0121-550 1451; Fax 0121-585 0369
Acting Principal Dr Stephen Griffiths

Harlow College
West Site College Sq, The High, Harlow, Essex CM20 1LT; Tel (01279) 441288; Fax (01279) 420139
Principal Sue Parker, BSc, MSc
East Site The Hides, Harlow, Essex CM20 3RA; Tel (01279) 441288; Fax (01279) 442538

The Henley College
Deanfield Ave, Henley-on-Thames, Oxon RG9 1UH; Tel (01491) 579988; Fax (01491) 410099
Principal G.D.J. Phillips, BA, MEd, FBIM

Henley College Coventry
Henley Rd, Bell Grn, Coventry, West Midlands CV2 1ED; Tel (01203) 611021; Fax (01203) 611837
Principal Greg Smith, BA, MBA, PGCE

Hopwood Hall College
Rochdale Rd, Middleton, Greater Manchester M24 6XH; Tel 0161-643 7560; Fax 0161-643 2114
Principal Ray Dowd
Rochdale Campus St Mary's Gate, Rochdale, Greater Manchester OL12 6RY; Tel (01706) 345346; Fax (01706) 41426

Hugh Baird College of Technology
Balliol Rd, Bootle, Merseyside L20 7EW; Tel 0151-922 4040
Principal J. McGregor, BSc, MInstP, CertEd

Isle College, Wisbech
Ramnoth Rd, Wisbech, Cambs PE13 0HY; Tel (01945) 582561
Principal Mark Taylor, BA, CertEd

Knowsley Community College
Cherryfield Dr, Kirkby, Merseyside L32 8SF; Tel 0151-443 5400
Principal G. Sweeney, BA, MA
Rupert Rd, Roby, Merseyside L36 9TD; Tel 0151-443 2600

Lambeth College
Founded 1992 by the merging of Brixton College, South London College and Vauxhall College
Principal Adrian Perry
Brixton Centre 56 Brixton Hill, London SW2 1QS; Tel 0171-737 1166
Norwood Centre Knights Hills, London SE27 0TX; Tel 0181-670 4488
Vauxhall Centre Belmore St, Walworth Rd, London SW8 2JY; Tel 0171-498 1234; Fax 0171-498 7569

Lewes Tertiary College
Mountfield Rd, Lewes, E. Sussex; Tel (01273) 483188; Fax (01273) 478561
Principal H. Ball

City College, Manchester
Address for Principal: Wythenshawe Centre, Moor Rd, Wythenshawe, Manchester, Greater Manchester M23 9BQ; Tel 0161-957 1500; Fax 0161-945 8047
Principal D.W. Gibson
Abraham Moss Centre Crescent Rd, Crumpsall M8 5UF
Arden Centre Sale Rd, Northenden M23 0DD
Fielden Centre Barlow Moor Rd, West Didsbury M20 2PQ

Monkwearmouth College of Education
Swan St Centre, Swan St, Sunderland, Tyne and Wear SR5 1EB; Tel 0191-548 7119; Fax 0191-516 2000
Principal G.H. Milton, BA(Econ)(Hons), BPhil, DipEd, MBIM (Swan St Centre)
Redcar Rd Centre Redcar Rd, Sunderland SR5 5DB; Tel 0191-516 2000; Fax 0191-516 2280
Shiney Row Centre Success Rd, Philadelphia, Houghton-le-Spring, Tyne and Wear DH4 4TL; Tel 0191-516 2000; Fax 0191-516 2180

Neath College
Dwr-y-Felin Rd, Neath, West Glamorgan SA10 7RF; Tel (01639) 634271; Fax (01639) 637453
Principal R.J. Trebilcock, MSc, BSc(Hons), MInstP

Nelson and Colne College
Scotland Rd, Nelson, Lancs BB9 7YT; Tel (01282) 603151; Fax (01282) 602588
Principal Helen M. Gilchrist, BA(Hons), PhD

New College, Swindon
Helston Rd, Park North, Swindon, Wilts SN3 2LA; Tel (01793) 611470; Fax (01793) 496355
V. MacLeod

North Derbyshire Tertiary College
Rectory Rd, Clowne, Nr Chesterfield, Derbys S43 4BQ; Tel (01246) 810332; Fax (01246) 810514
Chief Executive David Bunch

North Devon College
Old Sticklepath Hill, Barnstaple, Devon EX31 2BQ; Tel (01271) 45291; Fax (01271) 388121
Principal D. Trueman, BSc, FBIM

North Shropshire College
College Rd Campus, Oswestry, Shropshire SY11 2SA; Tel (01691) 653067; Fax (01691) 670243
Principal R. Pugh, MSc

Penwith College
St Clare St, Penzance, Cornwall TR18 2SA; Tel (01736) 62604 (College), (01736) 64746 (Adult/Continuing Ed Dept); Fax (01736) 51599

Principal J. Sherrington, BA, DipEd(Admin), CertEd
Adult and Continuing Education Department Morrab Rd, Penzance, Cornwall TR18 4EP; Tel (01736) 64746

The People's College of Tertiary Education

Maid Marian Way, Nottingham NG1 6AB; Tel (01602) 417721; Fax (01602) 483749
Principal D.L. Barrell

Peterlee College

Peterlee, Co Durham SR8 1NU; Tel 0191-518 2000; Fax 0191-586 7125
Acting Principal and Chief Executive W.N. Husband, BSc, CertEd

Preston College

St Vincent's Rd, Fulwood, Preston, Lancs PR2 4UR; Tel (01772) 716511; Fax (01772) 712530
Principal M.A. Clegg, BA, FRSA

Richmond upon Thames College

Egerton Rd, Twickenham, Middx TW2 7SJ; Tel 0181-892 6656; Fax 0181-891 5998
Principal E.F. Kirby, BSc, MSc, FRSA

Royal Forest of Dean College

Five Acres Campus, Berry Hill, Coleford, Glos GL16 7JT; Tel (01594) 833416; Fax (01594) 837497
Principal Mrs G. Young, MA

Runshaw College

Langdale Rd, Leyland, Lancs PR5 2DQ; Tel (01772) 622677; Fax (01772) 642009
Chairman John Oliver
Principal and Chief Executive B. O'Connell, MA, MEd, BSc(Econ)

Selby College

Abbot's Rd, Selby, N. Yorks YO8 8AT; Tel (01757) 702606; Fax (01757) 213137
Principal A. Stewart

Sheffield College

Head Office, PO Box 345, Sheffield, S. Yorks S2 2YY; Tel (0114) 260 2600; Fax (0114) 260 2601
Chief Executive/Principal Ken Ruddiman; Tel (0114) 260 2663
Castle Campus Granville Rd, Sheffield S2 2RL; Tel (0114) 260 2100; Fax (0114) 260 2101
Loxley Campus Myers Grove La, Sheffield S6 5JL; Tel (0114) 260 2200; Fax (0114) 260 2201
Norton Campus Dyche La, Sheffield S8 8BR; Tel (0114) 260 2300; Fax (0114) 260 2301
Parkwood Campus Shirecliffe Rd, Sheffield S5 8XZ; Tel (0114) 260 2400; Fax (0114) 260 2401
Parson Cross Campus Remington Rd, Sheffield S5 8PB; Tel (0114) 260 2500; Fax (0114) 260 2501
Stradbroke Campus Spinkhill Dr, Sheffield S13 8FD; Tel (0114) 260 2700; Fax (0114) 260 2701

Skelmersdale College

Northway, Skelmersdale, Lancs WN8 6LU; Tel (01695) 28744; Fax (01695) 51890
Principal Philip Lewis

South Bristol College

Marksbury Rd, Bedminster, Bristol, Avon BS3 5JL; Tel (0117) 963 9033
Principal David Smetherham

South Cheshire College

Dane Bank Ave, Crewe, Cheshire CW2 8AB; Tel (01270) 69133
Principal D.J. Collins, MA(Hons), PhD, MBIM

South East Derbyshire College

Field Rd, Ilkeston, Derbys DE7 5RS; Tel (0115) 932 4212
Principal M.F. Brown, BA(Econ), MA, CertEd
Ilkeston Rd, Heanor DE7 7DW; Tel (0115) 932 4212
Mundy St, Heanor DE7 7DZ; Tel (0115) 932 4212

South Tyneside College

St George's Ave, South Shields, Tyne and Wear NE34 6ET; Tel 0191-456 0403; Fax 0191-427 0267
Principal J.R. Wells, BA(Hons), MA, DipEd, FRSA
Hebburn Premises Mill La, Hebburn, Tyne and Wear NE31 2ER; Tel 0191-483 2741

Strode College

Church Rd, Street, Somerset BA16 0AB; Tel (01458) 42277; Fax (01458) 47944
Principal R.A. Dimbleby, MA, CertEd

Swansea College

Ty Coch Rd, Sketty, Swansea, West Glamorgan SA2 9EB; Tel (01792) 206871; Fax (01792) 208137
Principal Cyril M. Lewis, MSc, CEng, ME, DMS, MBIM

Truro College

College Rd, Truro, Cornwall TR1 3XX; Tel (01872) 264251; Fax (01872) 222360
Principal Jonathan Burnett

Wakefield College

Margaret St, Wakefield, W. Yorks WF1 2DH; Tel (01924) 370501; Fax (01924) 810340
Principal J. Muskett, BSc(Hons), CEng, MIEE, MBIM

Weald College

Brookshill, Harrow Weald, Middx HA3 6RR; Tel 0181-954 0671; Fax 0181-420 7570
Principal J.D. Harland, BA, FRSA

Wearside College

Tunstall Centre, Sea View Rd West, Sunderland, Tyne and Wear SR2 9LH; Tel 0191-567 0794; Fax 0191-564 0620
Principal A. Cass, BSc(Eng)(Hons), CEng, MIMechE, MIEE, Grad CertEd

Weymouth College

Cranford Ave, Weymouth, Dorset DT4 7LQ; Tel (01305) 761100; Fax (01305) 208892
Principal D. Brierley, MA(Cantab), PGCE

Yeovil College

Ilchester Rd, Yeovil, Somerset BA21 3BA; Tel (01935) 23921; Fax (01935) 29962
Principal N.F. Kershaw, MA(Oxon), MPhil

Sixth Form Colleges

Acklam Sixth Form College

Hall Dr, Acklam, Middlesborough, Cleveland TS5 7DY; Tel (01642) 814381; Fax (01642) 821620
Principal John Merrick

Aquinas College
Nangreave Rd, Stockport SK2 6TH; Tel 0161-487 3237; Fax 0161-483 4072
Principal Dr Ambrose J. Smith

Ashton-Under-Lyne Sixth Form College
Darnton Rd, Ashton-Under-Lyne, Lancs OL6 9RL; Tel 0161-330 2330; Fax 0161-339 1772
Principal G.P. Higgins, MA, MPhil, FRSA
(724)

Barrow-in-Furness Sixth Form College
Rating La, Barrow-in-Furness, Cumbria LA13 9LE; Tel (01229) 828377; Fax (01229) 836874
Principal E.J. Elvish
(604)

Barton Peveril Sixth Form College
Cedar Rd, Eastleigh, Hants SO5 5ZA; Tel (01703) 613131; Fax (01703) 650056
Principal Peter Harris, BA

Bede College
(Incorporated Sixth Form College)
Hale Rd, Billingham, Cleveland TS23 3ER; Tel (01642) 561444; Fax (01642) 565497
Principal M. Stanton, MA(Oxon), LLB
Mixed

Bexhill College
Turkey Rd, Bexhill-on-Sea, East Sussex TN39 5HF; Tel (01424) 214545; Fax (01424) 215050
Principal John Beckett

Bilborough Sixth Form College
Bilborough Rd, Nottingham NG8 4DQ; Tel (01602) 299436; Fax (01602) 425561
Principal H.G. Brown

Birkenhead Sixth Form College
Park Rd West, Birkenhead, Merseyside L43 8SQ; Tel 0151-652 5575; Fax 0151-653 4419
Principal Roger Cracknell, MA

Blackpool Sixth Form College
Highfurlong, Blackpool FY3 7LR; Tel (01253) 394911; Fax (01253) 300459
Principal C.P.J. Fulford

Brighton, Hove and Sussex Sixth Form College
205 Dyke Rd, Hove, E. Sussex BN3 6EG; Tel (01273) 552200/502928/541133; Fax (01273) 563139
Principal Vaughan Williams, MA

Cadbury Sixth Form College
Downland Cls, Redditch Rd, Birmingham, West Midlands B38 8QT; Tel 0121-458 3898; Fax 0121-459 4434
Principal F.J. Farrell

Cardinal Newman College
Lake Hill Rd, Preston, Lancs PR1 4HD; Tel (01772) 556847/556793; Fax (01772) 204671
Principal K. Quigley

Carmel College
Prescot Rd, St Helens, Merseyside WA10 3AG; Tel (01744) 22876; Fax (01744) 453843
Principal Peter Rushton

Christ the King Sixth Form College
Belmont Gr, London SE13 5DZ; Tel 0181-297 9433; Fax 0181-297 1460
Principal Kieran Fagan

City and Islington College – Sixth Form Centre
Annette Rd, London N7 6EX; Tel 0171-609 8401; Fax 0171-700 4406
Principal Tom Jupp

The Sixth Form College – Colchester
North Hill, Colchester, Essex CO1 1SN; Tel (01206) 577266; Fax (01206) 573217
Principal John A. Edwards, BSc

Coulsdon College
Placehouse La, Old Coulsdon, Surrey CR5 1YA; Tel (01737) 551176
Principal Peter Sharples, BSc, ARCS, BD
Mixed (1050)

De La Salle College
Weaste La, Salford, Greater Manchester M6 8QS; Tel 0161-736 2302; Fax 0161-737 1918
Principal John R. McDermott

East Norfolk Sixth Form College
Church La, Gorleston, Great Yarmouth NR31 7BQ; Tel (01493) 662234; Fax (01493) 441405
Principal Andrew Thomson

Eastbourne College
King's Dr, Eastbourne, E Sussex BN21 2UN; Tel (01323) 503475; Fax (01323) 508778
Principal Phil Frier, BA, MA

Eccles College
Chatsworth Rd, Eccles M30 9FJ; Tel 0161-789 5876; Fax 0161-789 1123
Principal C. Lee-Jones, MA

Esher College
Weston Grn Rd, Thames Ditton, Surrey KT7 0JB; Tel 0181-398 0291; Fax 0181-339 0207
Principal P.F. Miller, MA

The Sixth Form College – Farnborough
Prospect Ave, Farnborough, Hants GU14 8JX; Tel (01252) 514663; Fax (01252) 540308

Farnham College
Morley Rd, Farnham, Surrey GU9 8LU; Tel (01252) 716988; Fax (01252) 723969
Principal Kathleen Kimber, BA
(508)

Franklin College
Chelmsford Ave, Grimsby, S. Humberside DN34 5BY; Tel (01472) 753175; Fax (01472) 874764
Principal Peter Newcome
(715)

Gateway Sixth Form College
The Newarke, Leicester, Leics LE2 7BY; Tel (0116) 255 3079; Fax (0116) 255 3079
Chairman of Governors Canon M. Wilson
(720)

Godalming College
Tuesley La, Godalming, Surrey GU7 1RS; Tel (01483) 423526
Principal M.E. Hobrough, BA, MEd, MTh FRSA
(981)

Greenhead College
Greenhead Rd, Huddersfield, W. Yorks HD1 4ES; Tel (01484) 422032; Fax (01484) 518025
Principal Dr J.K. Conway

Hartlepool Sixth Form College
Brinkburn, Blakelock Rd, Hartlepool, Cleveland TS25 5PF; Tel (01429) 272389; Fax (01429) 862175
Principal D.J.M. Lownds
Mixed (520)

Havant College
New Rd, Havant, Hants PO9 1QL; Tel (01705) 483856; Fax (01705) 470621
Principal R.Trevor Rowell

Havering Sixth Form College
Wingletye La, Hornchurch, Essex RM11 3TB; Tel (01708) 620962; Fax (01708) 437270
Principal David Blake, MA

Haywards Heath College
Harlands Rd, Haywards Heath, West Sussex RH16 1LT; Tel (01444) 456281; Fax (01444) 417047
Principal B.W. Derbyshire
Mixed (958)

Hereford Sixth Form College
Folly La, Hereford HR1 1LS; Tel (01432) 355166; Fax (01432) 355891
Principal Dr D.W. Hudson

High Pavement Sixth Form College
Gainsford Cres, Nottingham, Notts NG5 5HT; Tel (0115) 927 1235/927 6918; Fax (0115) 975 0052
Principal Trevor Dawson, MA, CertEd, MIMgt

Hills Road Sixth Form College
Hills Rd, Cambridge, Cambs CB2 2PE; Tel (01223) 247251; Fax (01223) 416979
Principal C.A. Greenhalgh, MA
16–19 and Adult

Holy Cross College
Manchester Rd, Bury, Lancs BL9 9BB; Tel 0161-763 1290; Fax 0161-797 5203
Principal M.J. O'Hare, BSc

Huddersfield New College
New Hey Rd, Huddersfield, W. Yorks HD3 4GL; Tel (01484) 652341; Fax (01484) 649923
Principal Mrs S.J. Yeats, BA

Hyde-Clarendon College
Clarendon Rd, Hyde, Cheshire SK14 2JZ; Tel 0161-368 2188/6446; Fax 0161-368 6697
Principal Richard Adams

Itchen College
Middle Rd, Bitterne, Southampton, Hants SO19 7TB; Tel (01703) 435636; Fax (01703) 421911
Chairman David Prowles
Principal Peter Church, BSc

John Leggott College
West Common La, Scunthorpe, S. Humberside DN17 1DS; Tel (01724) 282998; Fax (01724) 281631
Principal D.P. Linnell, BSc, MSc, FInstP
(1070)

John Ruskin College
Selsdon Pk Rd, South Croydon, Surrey CR2 8JJ; Tel 0181-681 1151; Fax 0181-681 4011
Principal A.E. Smith, MA
(Mixed) (810)

Joseph Chamberlain Sixth Form College
Balsall Heath Rd, Highgate, Birmingham, West Midlands B12 9DS; Tel 0121-440 4288; Fax 0121-440 0798
Principal John Nankivell, MA(Oxon)

Josiah Mason College
Slade Rd, Erdington, Birmingham, West Midlands B23 7JH; Tel 0121-382 4757; Fax 0121-377 6076
Principal Sian Macdonald

King Edward VI College
Lower High St, Stourbridge, West Midlands DY8 1TD; Tel (01384) 394223; Fax (01384) 441699
Principal Philip Eyles, MA

King George V College
Scarisbrick New Rd, Southport, Merseyside PR8 6LR; Tel (01704) 530601; Fax (01704) 548656
Principal Mrs H.M. Anslow, BA, MEd
Mixed (605)

Leyton Sixth Form College
Essex Rd, Leyton, London E10 6EQ; Tel 0181-539 3185; Fax 0181-556 9907
Principal Terry A. Keogh, MA

Long Road Sixth Form College
Long Rd, Cambridge, Cambs CB2 2PX; Tel (01223) 247810; Fax (01223) 416118
Principal Madeleine Craft
(16–19)

Loreto College
Chichester Rd, Manchester M15 5PB; Tel 0161-226 5156; Fax 0161-227 9174
Principal Sister Patricia M. Goodstadt

Ludlow College
Mill St, Ludlow, Shropshire SY8 1BE; Tel (01584) 872846; Fax (01584) 876012
Principal David Pafford

Luton Sixth Form College
Bradgers Hill Rd, Luton, Beds LU2 7EW; Tel (01582) 412005; Fax (01582) 486307
Principal B.A. Howseman
(1522)

Margaret Danyers College
North Downs Rd, Cheadle Hulme, Cheadle, Cheshire SK8 5HA; Tel 0161-485 4372; Fax 0161-488 4354

Marton College
Marton Rd, Middlesbrough, Cleveland TS4 3RZ; Tel (01642) 315500; Fax (01642) 313290
Principal E.J.D. Swabey

Merton Sixth Form College
Central Rd, Morden, Surrey SM4 5SE; Tel 0181-648 4993; Fax 0181-640 9564
Principal Joann Jackson, MA

NEW College – Pontefract
Park La, Pontefract, W. Yorks WF8 4QR; Tel (01977) 702139; Fax (01977) 600708
Principal Robert Phillips
(544)

New College – Telford
King St, Wellington, Telford, Shropshire TF1 1NY; Tel (01952) 641892; Fax (01952) 243564
Principal G. Clark
(939)

Newham Sixth Form College
Prince Regent La, Plaistow, London E13 8SG; Tel 0171-473 4110; Fax 0171-511 9463
Principal Sid Hughes

North Area College
Buckingham Rd, Heaton Manor, Stockport, Cheshire SK4 4RA; Tel 0161-442 7494; Fax 0161-442 2166
Principal C.R. Chapman

North Bolton Sixth Form College
Smithills Dean Rd, Bolton BL1 6JT; Tel (01204) 86215; Fax (01204) 848589
Principal M.F. Ingham

Notre Dame Sixth Form College
St Mark's Ave, Leeds, W. Yorks LS2 9BL; Tel (0113) 243 0753; Fax (0113) 242 8487
Principal T. Metcalfe

Oldham Sixth Form College
Union St West, Oldham, Greater Manchester OL8 1XU; Tel 0161-628 8000; Fax 0161-633 7577
Principal N.M. Brown, BA, MPhil

Palmer's College
Chadwell Rd, Little Thurrock, Grays, Essex RM17 5TD; Tel (01375) 370121; Fax (01375) 385479
Principal D.M. Kelly, BA

Parkview Sixth Form Centre
Moor La, Bramcote, Notts NG9 3GA; Tel (0115) 922 1246; Fax (0115) 967 8717
Director D. Sullivan, BA

Paston Sixth Form College
Grammar School Rd, North Walsham, Norfolk NR28 9JL; Tel (01692) 402334; Fax (01692) 500630
Principal Mollie Whitworth, BA

Pendleton College
Dronfield Rd, Salford, Greater Manchester M6 7FR; Tel 0161-736 5074; Fax 0161-737 4103
W.J. Mills
(745)

Peter Symonds' College
Owens Rd, Winchester, Hants SO22 6RX; Tel (01962) 852764; Fax (01962) 849372
Principal N.A. Hopkins, BSc, MEd

Portsmouth College
Tangier Rd, Portsmouth, Hants PO3 6PZ; Tel (01705) 667421; Fax (01705) 693833
Principal T.C.H. Jackson

Priestley College
Loushers La, Warrington, Cheshire WA4 6RD; Tel (01925) 33591; Fax (01925) 413887
Principal David Henderson

Prior Pursglove College – Guisborough
Church Wk, Guisborough, Cleveland TS14 6BU; Tel (01287) 610272; Fax (01287) 610895
Principal E.W. Middleton, MA, MEd, DipTh, FRSC
Mixed (521)

Queen Elizabeth Sixth Form College
Vane Terr, Darlington, Co Durham D3 7AU; Tel (01325) 468520; Fax (01325) 361705
Principal David J. Heaton

Queen Mary's College
Cliddesden Rd, Basingstoke RG21 3HF; Tel (01256) 20861; Fax (01256) 26097
Principal Ivan Peters

Reigate College
Castlefield Rd, Reigate, Surrey RH2 0SD; Tel (01737) 221118; Fax (01737) 222657
Principal G.G. Johnson, BSc(Hons)
(741)

The College of Richard Collyer in Horsham
Hurst Rd, Horsham, West Sussex RH12 2EJ; Tel (01403) 210822; Fax (01403) 211915
Principal D.J. Arnold, MA

The Richard Huish College
South Rd, Taunton, Somerset TA1 3DZ; Tel (01823) 270171; Fax (01823) 324181
Principal P.A. Brennan, MA

The Ridge College
Hibbert La, Marple, Stockport, Cheshire SK6 7PA; Tel 0161-427 7733; Fax 0161-427 8054
Principal A.P.G. MacDonald, BA(Hons)
(1211)

Rowley Regis College
Hawes La, Rowley Regis, Warley, West Midlands B65 9AH; Tel 0121-559 5951; Fax 0121-559 0502
Principal Robert G. Ensum

Rutland College
Barleythorpe Rd, Oakham, Rutland, Leics LE15 6QH; Tel (01572) 722863; Fax (01572) 756707
Principal L.A. Kidd, MEd, BSc, FRSA
(480)

St Brendan's Sixth Form College
Broomhill Rd, Brislington, Bristol, Avon BS4 5RQ; Tel (0117) 977 7766; Fax (0117) 972 3351
Dr M. Davies

St Charles Catholic Sixth Form College
74 St Charles Sq, London W10 6EY; Tel 0181-968 7755; Fax 0181-968 1061
Principal John Rourke, MA

St David's RC Sixth Form College
Ty Gwyn Rd, Penylan, Cardiff, South Glamorgan CF2 5YD; Tel (01222) 498555; Fax (01222) 472594
Principal P.Dominic Bryon, BA, MEd

St Dominic's Sixth Form College
Mount Pk Ave, Harrow-on-the-Hill, Middx HA1 3HX; Tel 0181-422 8084/081-864 4226; Fax 0181-422 3759
Principal John L. Lipscomb, MA, MSc

St Francis Xavier Sixth Form College
Malwood Rd, London SW12 8EN; Tel 0181-673 7122; Fax 0181-673 7480
Principal Bryan Snalune

St John Rigby Sixth Form College
Gathurst Rd, Orrell, Wigan, Lancs WN5 0LJ; Tel (01942) 214797; Fax (01942) 216514
Principal J.R. Haines, BA
Mixed (800)

St Mary's Sixth Form College
Saltersgill Ave, Middlesbrough, Cleveland TS4 3JP; Tel (01642) 814680; Fax (01642) 819624
Principal P.L. Monnelly, BA, LLB

St Philip's RC Sixth Form College
Hagley Rd, Birmingham B16 8UF; Tel 0121-454 3263; Fax 0121-452 1887
Principal Eddie Picardo

St Vincent College
Mill La, Gosport, Hampshire PO12 4QA; Tel (01705) 588111; Fax (01705) 511186
Principal P. Lynn Lee

Scarborough Sixth Form College
Sandybed La, Scarborough, N. Yorks YO12 5LF; Tel (01723) 365032; Fax (01723) 367049
Principal G.E. Mountfield, MA
(640)

Shena Simon College
Whitworth St, Manchester, Greater Manchester M1 3HB; Tel 0161-236 3418; Fax 0161-237 5621
Principal E.G. Young, BA

Shrewsbury Sixth Form College
Priory Rd, Shrewsbury, Shropshire SY1 1RX; Tel (01743) 235491; Fax (01743) 242735
Principal William E. Dowell, BEd

Sir George Monoux College
Chingford Rd, Walthamstow, London E17 3RE; Tel 0181-527 2518; Fax 0181-503 3886
Principal A.J. Harvey, MSc

Sir John Deane's College
Northwich, Cheshire CW9 8AF; Tel (01606) 46011; Fax (01606) 47170
Principal J.R.W. Tasker, MSocSc
Mixed (741)

Solihull Sixth Form College
Widney Manor Rd, Solihull, West Midlands B91 3JG; Tel 0121-704 2581; Fax 0121-711 1598
Principal J.M. Korzeniewski
(1850)

South Bolton Sixth Form College
Lever Edge La, Bolton, Lancs BL3 3HH; Tel (01204) 62524; Fax (01204) 660218
Principal R. Whittle, MA, MPhil, FRSA

South East Essex Sixth Form College
Runnymede Chase, Thundersley, Benfleet, Essex SS7 1TW; Tel (01268) 756111; Fax (01268) 565515
Principal M.B.A. Francis, BA, MEd

South Park Sixth Form College
South Pk Ave, Normanby, Middlesbrough, Cleveland TS6 0NT; Tel (01642) 468338; Fax (01642) 464482
Principal Tony Simpson

Spelthorne College
Church Rd, Ashford, Middx TW15 2XD; Tel (01784) 248666; Fax (01784) 254132
Principal Jane Curry, MEd, BA
(433)

Stanmore College
Elm Pk, Stanmore, Middx HA7 4BQ; Tel 0181-954 9481; Fax 0181-420 6502
Principal Russell V. Woodrow

Stockton Sixth Form College
Bishopton Rd West, Stockton-on-Tees, Cleveland TS19 0QD; Tel (01642) 612611; Fax (01642) 618225
Principal H.R. Clarke, BSc(Econ), MSc(Oxon)
Mixed (800)

City of Stoke-on-Trent Sixth Form College
Victoria Rd, Fenton, Stoke-on-Trent ST4 2RR; Tel (01782) 48736; Fax (01782) 747456
Principal R.J. Stephenson

Strode's College
High St, Egham, Surrey TW20 9DR; Tel (01784) 437506; Fax (01784) 471794
Principal Pamela Maryfield, MA, FRSA
(567)

Taunton's College
Hill La, Southampton, Hants SO15 5RL; Tel (01703) 511811; Fax (01703) 511991
Principal Rodney M. Lyons, BA(Oxon)

Thomas Rotherham College
Moorgate, Rotherham, S. Yorks S60 2BE; Tel (01709) 828606; Fax (01709) 838193
Principal N.F. Briggs, MA

Totton Sixth Form College
Water La, Totton, Sothampton SO40 3ZX; Tel (01703) 872323; Fax (01703) 667922
Principal Kenneth Johnson

Tynemouth College
Queen Alexandra Rd West, North Shields, Tyne and Wear NE29 9BZ; Tel 0191-257 8414; Fax 0191-258 1533
Principal R.C. Bailey, BSc

Varndean College
Surrenden Rd, Brighton, E. Sussex BN1 6WQ; Tel (01273) 508011; Fax (01273) 542950
Principal Alan Jenkins, BA
(804)

Widnes Sixth Form College
Cronton La, Widnes, Cheshire WA8 9AW; Tel 0151-424 1515; Fax 0151-495 1891
Principal M. Hoyle

Wilberforce College
Saltshouse Rd, Hull, Humberside HU8 9HD; Tel (01482) 711688; Fax (01482) 798991
Principal John E. Gwinnell, MA
(690)

Winstanley College
Winstanley Rd, Billinge, Wigan, Lancs WN5 7XF; Tel (01695) 633244; Fax (01695) 633409
Principal Dennis Lavelle
(Mixed)

Woking College

Rydens Way, Old Woking, Surrey GU22 9DL; Tel (01483) 761036; Fax (01483) 728144
Principal Jill Ferguson, BA, FRSA
(505)

Woodhouse College

Woodhouse Rd, North Finchley, London N12 9EY; Tel 0181-445 1210; Fax 0181-445 5210
Principal Dr Colin S. Wharton, MA, PhD
(Mixed) (720)

Worcester Sixth Form College

Spetchley Rd, Worcester, Hereford and Worcester WR5 2LU; Tel (01905) 763999; Fax (01905) 764752
Principal John Tredwell

Worthing Sixth Form College

Bolsover Rd, Worthing, West Sussex BN13 1NS; Tel (01903) 243389; Fax (01903) 243390
(Mixed)

Wyggeston Collegiate Sixth Form College

Regent Rd, Leicester, Leicestershire LE1 7LW; Tel (0116) 255 4629; Fax (0116) 254 5680
Principal O.R.B. Cosham

Wyggeston and Queen Elizabeth I College

University Rd, Leicester, Leics LE1 7RJ; Tel (0116) 255 3206; Fax (0116) 255 3729
Principal Dr Robert E. Wilkinson
(871)

Wyke Sixth Form College

Grammar School Rd, Hull, Humberside HU5 4NX; Tel (01482) 346347; Fax (01482) 473336
Principal Martin Ward, BA, MSc

Xaverian College

Lower Pk Rd, Manchester M14 5RB; Tel 0161-224 1781; Fax 0161-248 9039
Principal Teresa M. Quinn

Yale College

Crispin La, Wrexham, Clwyd LL11 2HT; Tel (01978) 351211; Fax (01978) 364254
Principal Emlyn R. Jones, OBE, BSc, MEd
(784)

York Sixth Form College

Sim Balk La, Tadcaster Rd, York, N. Yorks YO2 1UD; Tel (01904) 701816; Fax (01904) 705712
Principal J.B. Harris, MA

13 Independent Further Education

† Indicates that there are boarders. The number in brackets is the approximate number of students

‡ Includes a course of English for foreign students

Independent Further Education Establishments

British Accreditation Council for Independent Further and Higher Education

Suite 401, 27 Marylebone Rd, London NQ1 5JS; Tel 0171-487 4643; Fax 0171-486 4253
President Sir Wilfred Cockcroft
Chairman Eric Meats, CBE

Profile: Established in 1984 in succession to an earlier scheme run by the Department of Education and Science. Its sponsors include the chief bodies responsible for the maintenance of academic standards in Britain: universities and colleges, national validating bodies, public and professional examining boards, and also those bodies, such as the British Council, with a particular concern for overseas students. The BAC is constituted as a Company Limited by Guarantee and recognised as a Registered Charity. At present 92 institutions are accredited by the BAC enrolling almost 30,000 students from Britain and overseas on an extremely wide range of courses

Aims and Objectives: The BAC exists to define, monitor and improve standards in independent further and higher education institutions in Britain. It does this by inspecting institutions which, if they meet the BAC criteria for accreditation, are recognised as efficient by the BAC

Criteria: Institutions seeking BAC accreditation must satisfy the BAC under *all* the following heads: 1 *Premises and learning resources;* 2 *Administration and staffing;* 3 *Quality control, including the effectiveness of the monitoring of experiences of students in joining and pursuing the programmes provided;* 4 *Welfare arrangements, including career advice and counselling where appropriate;* 5 *Teaching, involving assessment of the professional competence of academic staff*

In addition, the BAC receives legal and financial information from institutions. The criteria used by the BAC are consistent with those required by the Home Office of bona fide institutions enrolling overseas students. The BAC inspectorate which carries out all inspections contains over 100 inspectors and includes: former HM (Her Majesty's) Inspectors of Education: former local education authority advisers and inspectors: current and former heads and senior staff members of Universities, colleges and institutes of higher education and colleges of further education

Procedures: The process of accreditation involves an initial application; the determination of eligibility for accreditation, including a preliminary visit by an inspector; and a full institutional inspection followed by a decision on accreditation by the Accreditation and Recognition Committee of the BAC. Accreditation is conditional upon re-inspection within five years. The BAC reserves the right, however, to review the accreditation of an institution at any time if reasonable grounds exist

Institutions accredited by the BAC are indicated by an asterisk **(*)** next to their entry

England

Avon

Bath Tutors ‡
South Dale, 48 Greenway La, Bath BA2 4LW; Tel (01225) 310162 R.Y. Clarke

(Licensed tutorial agency; all subjects)

Bedfordshire

Bedford Study Centre ‡
94–96 Midland Rd, Bedford MK40 1QE; Tel (01234) 364161; Fax (01234) 270637 Besc G Denis L. Trussler, BA, DipEd, MIMgl, FInstSMM; (Mixed) (100)

Bedford Tutorial College
36 Lansdowne Rd, Bedford; Tel (01234) 46157 C. Spender, BSc; (Mixed) (110)

Berkshire

*** Padworth College †‡**
Padworth, nr Reading RG7 4NR; Tel (01734) 832644/5; Fax (01734) 834515
Principal Dr Sheila Villazon, MA, PhD; (Girls) (130)

Buckinghamshire

*** International Management Centre from Buckingham**
Castle St, Buckingham MK18 1BS; Tel (01280) 817222; Fax (01280) 813297; Telex 51317

Cambridgeshire

*** Cambridge Centre for Sixth Form Studies †**
1 Salisbury Villas, Station Rd, Cambridge CB1 2JF; Tel (01223) 316890; Fax (01223) 358441 Dr A.M. Dawson, MA; (210)

*** Cambridge Seminars**
4 Hawthorn Way, Cambridge CB4 1AX; Tel (01223) 313464; Fax (01223) 355352

Cambridge Tutors ‡
119 Mill Rd, Cambridge CB1 2AZ; Tel + 44 (0) 1223 312944; Fax + 44 (0) 1223 312944; Telex 8954102 BBSLON G S.A. Agar

(Individual tuition–all subjects); (Mixed)

*** St Andrews**
2A Free School La, Cambridge CB2 3QA; Tel (01223) 60040/64652

Devon

Tutorial College ‡
44–46 Magdalen Rd, Exeter EX2 4TE; Tel (01392) 73781 Kenneth Jack; (Mixed) (60–80)

Dorset

Hospitality Career College
43 Norwich Av West, Bournemouth, Dorset BH2 6AJ; Tel (01202) 291877; Fax (01202) 293046

Symondsbury College †‡
Symondsbury, Bridport, Dorset DT6 6HD; Tel (01308) 456288 Tutorial College; Fax (01308) 456525 P.W. Hitchin; Tel (01308) 427339 Art College

East Sussex

*** Bellerbys College, Hove ‡**
44 Cromwell Rd, Hove BN3 3ER; Tel (01273) 723911 A.M. Burton; (Mixed) (200)

*** Eastbourne College of Food and Fashion**
1 Silverdale Rd, Eastbourne BN20 7AA; Tel (01323) 730851; Fax (01323) 416924

*** Ecole de Cuisine Française**
Clapham Hse, Litlington, Sussex BN26 5EQ; Tel (01323) 870047; Fax (01323) 870526

LTC International College of English †‡
Compton Pk, Compton Place Rd, Eastbourne BN21 1EH; Tel (01323) 727755; Fax (01323) 728279 Deborah-Jane Lear, BEd(Hons), MSc, RSA(TEFL), MInstAM(Dip); (Mixed) (120)

*** St Giles College ‡**
13 Silverdale Rd, Eastbourne BN20 7AJ; Tel (01323) 729167, 641502; Fax (01323) 721332 R.M. Elder; (Mixed) (180)

Gloucestershire

*** National Star Centre College of Further Education**
Ullenwood, Cheltenham, Glos GL53 9QU; Tel (01242) 527631; Fax (01242) 222234

Hereford

*** Royal National College for the Blind**
College Rd, Hereford HR1 1EB; Tel (01432) 265725; Fax (01432) 353478

Kent

Kent Institute of Art & Design
Oakwood Pk, Oakwood Rd, Maidstone, Kent ME16 8AG; Tel (01622) 757286 P.I. Williams, DFA(Lond)
Constituent Colleges
New Dover Rd, Canterbury, Kent CT1 3AN; Tel (01227) 769371; Roger Sales, FCCA

Oakwood Pk, Oakwood Rd, Maidstone, Kent ME16 8AG; Tel (01622) 757286; P. Sanger, BA(Hons), FBIPP, FRPS

Fort Pitt, Rochester, Kent ME1 1DZ; Tel (01634) 830022; M. Claridge, BA, ATC, PGDip

*** Rochester Tutors' Independent College**
3 New Rd, Rochester, Kent ME1 1BD; Tel (01634) 828125; Fax (01634) 405667
Principal S. Salkeld, MA, LRAM

*** Stafford House Tutorial College †‡**
68 New Dover Rd, Canterbury CT1 3EQ; Tel (01227) 453237/8/9; Fax (01227) 451685; Telex 965991 J.A. Allsopp A.J. Bennett; (Mixed) (150)

Lancashire

*** Beaumont College of FE**
Slyne Rd, Lancaster LA2 6AP; Tel (01524) 64278; Fax (01524) 846896

Leicestershire

*** Brooke House VIth Form College †‡**
Brooke Hse, Market Harborough LE16 7AU; Tel (01858) 462452; Fax (01858) 462487 F. Colyer, MA(Oxon); (Mixed) (100)

*** Irwin College †**
164 London Rd, Leicester LE2 1ND; Tel (0116) 255 2648 D.J. Williams, BA(Hons), PGCE; (Mixed) (75)

London

Atcfoulks Lynch
28 Farringdon St, London EC4A 4EU; Tel 0171-634 1000; Fax 0171-250 0786

*** Albany College ‡**
23–24 Queens Rd, London NW4 2TL; Tel 0181-202 9748, 5965 Robert J. Arthy; (Mixed) (170)

*** Cambridge Tutors Sixth Form College †‡**
Water Tower Hill, Croydon CR0 5SX; Tel 0181-688 5284 D.N. Wilson, BA, MLitt(Oxon), MIL, FCollP; (Mixed) (220)

13 Independent Further Education

*** Cavendish College**
209–212 Tottenham Court Rd, London W1P 9AF; Tel 0171-580 6043/14074; Fax 0171-255 1591; Telex 296253 STAMCO G

Central London College ‡
213–215 Tottenham Court Rd, London W1; Tel 0171-636 2212; Fax 0171-636 0019 N. Kailides; (Mixed) (500)

*** Central Tutorial College**
8 Herbrand St, Russell Sq, London WC1 1HZ; Tel 0171-278 6622; Fax 0171-837 6077; Telex 265148

*** City College of Higher Education**
67–83 Seven Sisters Rd, Holloway, London N7 6BU; Tel 0171-263 5937/8; Fax 0171-281 9298
Principal A. Andrews

*** Collingham**
23 Collingham Gdns, London SW5 0HL; Tel 0171-244 7414 Gerald Hattee, MA; (Mixed) (300)

*** David Game Tutorial College and Kensington Academy of English †‡**
86 Old Brompton Rd, London SW7 3LQ; Tel 0171-584 7580, 9097; Fax 0171-584 2637; Telex 296 253 STAMCO G David Game; (Mixed) (250)

*** Davies, Laing and Dick Independent Sixth Form College, (DLD)**
10 Pembridge Sq, London W2 4ED; Tel 0171-727 2797; Fax 0171-792 0730 Peter Boorman, MA; (Mixed) (300)

*** Dean College**
97–101 Seven Sisters Rd, Holloway, London N7 7QP; Tel 0171-281 4461/2; Fax 0171-281 7849

*** Duff-Miller Sixth Form College**
59 Queens Gate, London SW7 5JP; Tel 0171-225 0577; Fax 0171-589 5155; Telex 935052

*** E W Fact**
23 Hand Ct, High Holborn, London WC1V 6JF; Tel 0171-404 4545; Fax 0171-405 2953; Telex 262930

Fine Arts College
85 Belsize Park Gdns, London NW3 4NJ; Tel 0171-586 0312; Fax 0171-483 0355

*** Greenwich College**
Meridian Hse, Royal Hill, London SE10 8RT; Tel 0181-853 4484; Fax 0181-305 1782
Principal W.G. Hunt, MA, BEd

Hogarth Tutors ‡
17 Queens Gate Pl, London SW7 5NY; Tel 0181-584 7196 N.N. Browne, BA(Cantab); (Mixed) (10–20)

*** Holborn College**
200 Greyhound Rd, London W14 9RY; Tel 0171-385 3377; Fax 0171-381 3377
Registrar J. Fairhurst

Kensington College of Business
52A Walham Gr, London SW6 1QR; Tel 0171-381 6360; Fax 0171-386 9650 Ian Pirie; (Mixed) (1000)

*** Lansdowne Independent Sixth Form College †‡**
7–9 Palace Gate, London W8 5LS; Tel 0171-581 4866; Fax 0171-823 9978
Principal Paul Murphy, BSc; (Mixed) (300)

*** London City College**
Waterloo Hse, 51–55 Waterloo Rd, London SE1 8TX; Tel 0171-928 0901/0029 0938; Fax 0171-620 1226 W.G. Leader

*** London Electronics College**
20 Penywern Rd, Earls Ct, London SW5 9SU; Tel 0171-373 8721; Fax 0171-244 8733
Principal M.D. Spalding, BSc, CEng, MIEE, PGCE, MCybSoc

*** London Executive College**
"Bank Chambers", 313 Balham High Rd, Tooting Bec, London SW17 7BA; Tel 0181-682 1011; Fax 0181-767 7110
Director M. Arvan, ACIB, CertEd

*** London Montessori Centre**
18 Balderton St, London W1Y 1TG; Tel 0171-493 0165; Fax 0171-629 7808
Principal B. Isaacs

*** The London School of Insurance**
67–83 Seven Sisters Rd, London N7 6BU; Tel 0171-281 9344; Fax 0171-281 5563 Rajendra Sampat, BSc, MBIM; (Mixed) (80)

*** Lucie Clayton Secretarial College**
4 Cornwall Gdns, London SW7 4AJ; Tel 0171-581 0024; Fax 0171-589 9693

*** Mander Portman Woodward**
5 Wetherby Pl, London SW7 4NX; Tel 0171-835 1355; Fax 0171-259 2705

*** Milestone Tutorial College ‡**
85 Cromwell Rd, London SW7; Tel 0171-373 4956 Richard Smart, MA, FBIM, FCollP; (Mixed) (90)

*** Modern Tutorial College †‡**
Kilburn La, London W10 4AA; Tel 0181-960 5899 W.B. Moore, BSc; (Mixed) (150)

Oxford House College †‡
3 Oxford St, London W1R 1RF; Tel 0171-734 3889/580 9785; Fax 0171-287 1623; Telex 261390 OXFORD G C. Polatch

Pitman Central College (Pitman School of English and School of Business and Secretarial Education)
154 Southport Row, London WC1B 5AX; Tel 0171-837 4481; Telex 25569 PITMAN G
Director B. Hilton, BSc, MA, FITD
Principal of the School of English B. Cusack, BA(Hons), DipTEFL
Principal of the School of Business and Secretarial Education E. Summers, CertEd

*** St Godric's Secretarial and Language College †‡**
2 Arkwright Rd, Hamstead, London NW3 6AD; Tel 0171-435 9831 Sir John and Lady Loveridge M.W. Loveridge, MA

Manchester

*** Educare College ‡**
Santaidd, Burnage La, Manchester M19 1DR; Tel 0161-442 0858; Fax 0161-443 2357

Northampton

*** Bosworth Tutorial College † ‡**
9–12 St George's Ave, Northampton NN2 6JA; Tel (01604) 719988; Fax (01604) 791418 Mark A.V. Broadway, BSc, PGCE; (Mixed) (80)

North Yorkshire

*** Harrogate Tutorial College † ‡**
2 The Oval, Harrogate, N. Yorks HG2 9BA; Tel (01423) 501041; Fax (01423) 531110
Principal K.W. Pollard, BSc, DipMaths, DipEd

Oxfordshire

*** Abacus College**
Threeways Hse, George St, Oxford OX1 2BJ; Tel (01865) 240111; Fax (01865) 247259
Principal R. Hazell

*** Cherwell Tutors †‡**
Greyfriars, Paradise St, Oxford OX1 1LD; Tel (01865) 242670 Paul J. Gordon; (Mixed) (100)

*** College of Petroleum Studies**
Sun Alliance Hse, New Inn Hall St, Oxford OX1 2QD; Tel (01865) 250521; Fax (01865) 791474; Telex 838950

*** Collingham, Brown and Brown Tutorial College †‡**
31 St Giles, Oxford OX1 3LF; Tel (01865) 728280; Fax (01865) 240126 C.H. Llewellyn, MA(Oxon); (Mixed) (140)

d'Overbroeck's †
1 Park Town, Oxford OX2 6SN; Tel (01865) 310000 J.D.G. Noel, BA, PGCE R. Knowles, MA, DPhil; (Mixed) (200)

*** Edward Greene's Tutorial Establishment**
45 Pembroke St, Oxford OX1 1BP; Tel (01865) 248308; Fax (01865) 240700; Telex 83147 GREENE

*** Oxford Tutorial College**
16 Gloucester St, Oxford OX1 2BN; Tel (01865) 793333; Fax (01865) 793233
Principal R. Dennison, BA, PGCE

St Aldates College ‡
Rose Pl, St Aldates, Oxford OX1 1SB; Tel (01865) 240963 Pauline Martin; (Mixed) (250)

*** St Clare's †‡**
139 Banbury Rd, Oxford OX2 7AL; Tel (01865) 52031; Fax (01865) 310002; Telex 837379 Margaret Skarland, BA, PGCE; (Mixed) (300)

*** St Joseph's Hall, Independent Sixth Form College ‡**
Junction Rd, Oxford OX4 2UJ; Tel (01865) 711829; Fax (01865) 747791 Simon Fenn, BA, Dip(TEFL), RSA; (Mixed) (50)

Wolsey Hall Tutorial College ‡
66 Banbury Rd, Oxford; Tel (01865) 310310 Ralph Dennison, BA(Hons, PGCE; (Mixed) (100)

Shropshire

*** Concord College†**
Acton Burnell Hall, Shrewsbury, Shropshire SY5 7PF; Tel (016944) 631; Fax (019644) 389; Telex 35457

*** Derwen College for the Disabled**
Oswestry, Shropshire SY11 3JA; Tel (01691) 661234; Fax (01691) 670714
Director D.J. Kendall, BEng, FCA, MEd

Suffolk

Bransons Commonwealth Educational Trust Ltd †‡
Playford, Ipswich IP6 9DW; Tel (01473) 622111 A.M. Llewellyn; (Mixed) (64)

*** International Boatbuilding Training College**
Harbour Rd, Oulton Broad, Lowestoft, Suffolk NR32 3LZ; Tel (01502) 569663/1516097; Fax (01502) 500661

Surrey

*** Banstead Place Rehabilitation and Further Education Centre**
Park Rd, Banstead, Surrey SM7 3EE; Tel (01737) 356222; Fax (01737) 359467
Principal A.R. Gait, BSc, CertEd, DTMHA; (Mixed) (28); (Residential) (PH) (16–30) (Post-medical rehabilitation for young adults with acquired brain damage)

*** Hurtwood House School †‡**
Holmbury St Mary, Nr Dorking RH5 6NU; Tel (01483) 277416 K.R.B. Jackson, MA(Camb); (Mixed) (168)

Richmond College, The American International University in London†
Queens Rd, Richmond, Surrey TW10 6JP;
Tel Admissions Enquiries: 0181-332 9000 All other departments Tel: 0181-332 8200 Walter McCann; (1,046)

*** Surrey College, †‡**
St Michaels Hse, Woodbridge Rd, Guildford, Surrey GU1 4RF; Tel (01483) 65887; Fax (01483) 34777
Principal Dr G.P. Connolly, BA, MA, PhD

*** Tante Marie School of Cookery**
Woodham Hse, Carlton Rd, Woking, Surrey GU21 4HF; Tel (01483) 726957; Fax (01483) 724173
Principal B.A. Childs

West Midlands

Adult Education Management Ltd
5 Squirrels Hollow, Boney Hay, Burntwood, Walsall WS7 8YS; Tel (01922) 693168
Director D.K. Pearce
Director J.B. Pearce

Providing consultancy services to external sector schedule 2 providers – Designers and suppliers of open learning materials for law courses – GCSE Law and GCSE Government by correspondence course

*** The Cable and Wireless College**
IS09001 (BS5750, Part 1)320 Westwood Heath Road, Coventry CV4 8GP; Tel (01203) 868600; Fax (01203) 868650; Telex 310001 Cwcoll G

*** Mander Portman Woodward**
38 Highfield Rd, Edgbaston, Birmingham B15 3ED; Tel 0121-454 9637; Fax 0121-454 6433
Principal K. Munnings, BSc, PGCE

West Sussex

Tobias School of Art
Coombe Hill Rd, East Grinstead, Sussex RH19 4LZ; Tel (01342) 313655/314515

*** West Dean College**
West Dean, Chichester, Sussex PO18 0QZ; Tel (01243) 63301; Fax (01243) 63342

West Yorkshire

North of England College Cavendish Hse
92 Albion St, Leeds LS1 6AG; Tel (0113) 245 3073 Ann Salama, BA(Hons)

Scotland

Lothian

*** The Basil Paterson College ‡**
22 Abercromby Pl, Edinburgh EH3 6QE; Tel 0131-556 7695 R.R. Mackenzie, MA; (Mixed) (75–100)

Wales

Glamorgan

United World College of the Atlantic †‡
St Donat's Castle, Llantwit Major CF61 1WF; Tel (01446) 792530 C.D.O. Jenkins; (Mixed) (340)

*** New College, †**
Bute Terr, Cardiff CF1 2TE; Tel (01222) 463355; Fax (01222) 489616
Principal W. Hoole, BSc, CChem, MRSc, PhC

A Level College, School and English Language School

Independent English Language Schools

British Council English Language Schools Recognition Scheme

Profile: The English Language Schools Recognition Scheme was established in 1982 in succession to an earlier scheme run by the Department of Education and Science. It is administered by the British Council and is open to all independent educational organisations engaged in the teaching of English as a Foreign Language. At present 230 organisations are accredited and entitled to state 'Recognised by the British Council' on publicity. (The British Council also administers a parallel scheme which validates the EFL courses of state sector colleges)

Aims and Obejectives: The Recognition Scheme exists to monitor and improve standards in English Language teaching in the independent sector, in the interest of foreign students, of the proprietors and staff of recognised schools, and in the national interest, so that eligible EFL organisations may be encouraged to aspire to high standards and reflect credit on Britain

Criteria: Organisations undergo a rigorous inspection under six heads as follows: *Management and Administration; Premises: Resources; Professional Qualifications; Teaching; Welfare.* Details of the criteria are set out in the Handbook of the Recognition Scheme available from the British Council on request. The vast majority of organisations go on, after successful inspection, to join ARELS-FELCO, the professional association of recognised schools, which exists to promote and monitor the quality of service offered by its members

Procedures: Organisations are inspected once every three years by inspectors drawn from a panel of fifty, chosen for their experience and pre-eminence in the Teaching of English as a Foreign Language. In addition to the regular inspections, spot-checks may be carried out at any time, without prior warning to the school, to ensure that standards are maintained. A complaints procedure exists, and all reported instances of client dissatisfaction are carefully investigated.

Schools recognised by the Council are indicated by a black square (■) next to their entry .

England

Avon

■ **Abon Language School ‡**
25 St John's Rd, Clifton, Bristol BS8 2HD; Tel (0117) 973 0354; Fax (0117) 973 8696 D. Berrington Davies, BA, CertEd; (Mixed) (60)

■ **Abon Language Centre**
St Peter's Bldg, Dorset Cl, Bath BA2 3RF; Tel (01225) 332211

■ **The Bell Language School**
Henley Lodge, Weston Rd, Bath BA1 2XT; Tel (01225) 426255; Fax (01225) 445716; (Mixed) (150)

■ **Bristol Institute of Language Studies**
1 Lower Pk Row, Bristol BS1 5BJ; Tel (0117) 929 7667

■ **The Canning School**
Bath, 1 Brock St, Bath BA1 2LN; Tel (01225) 335323

■ **English Language Centre Bristol ‡**
44 Pembroke Rd, Bristol BS8 3DT; Tel (0117) 973 7216; Fax (0117) 923 9638; Telex 449752
Principal John Duncan

■ **SERCO-IAL Ltd Bailbrook College †‡**
39 London Rd West, Bath BA1 7JD; Tel (01225) 858941 John Price; (Mixed) (250)

OISE Bristol Institute of Language Studies
1 Lower Prk Row, Bristol BS1 5BJ; Tel (0117) 929 7667 Martin Jenkins; (Mixed) (max 8 students/class)

Berkshire

■ **Heathfield Summer School**
London Rd, Ascot, Royal Berkshire SL5 8BQ; Tel (01344) 885197; Fax (01344) 882235

■ **Padworth College †‡**
Padworth, Nr Reading RG7 4NR; Tel (01734) 832644
Principal Dr Sheila Villazon; (Girls) (135)

■ **Thames Valley Cultural Centres Ltd**
15 Park St, Windsor, Berks SL4 1LU; Tel (01753) 852001

■ **Vacational Studies †‡**
Pepys' Oak, Tydehams, Newbury RG14 6JT; Tel (01635) 523333; Fax (01635) 523999 Ian G. Mucklejohn; (Mixed) (100)

■ **Windsor English Language Centre ‡**
51 Albany Rd, Windsor, Berks SL4 1HL; Tel (01753) 866966; Fax (01733) 866966 Michael Osborn; (Mixed) (max 12 per class)

Buckinghamshire

■ **Merrion House Centre for English Studies ‡**
60 Penn Rd, Beaconsfield HP9 2LS; Tel (01494) 673769 M. Roundell Greene, DipCAM, RSADip, TEFL; (Mixed) (20)

Cambridgeshire

■ **Anglo-World Cambridge**
75 Barton Rd, Cambridge CB3 9LJ; Tel (01223) 357702; Fax (01223) 311939
Principal Kevin Higgins, BA(Hons), RSADipTEFL; (Mixed) (150)

■ **The Bell Language School**
Red Cross La, Cambridge CB2 2QX; Tel (01223) 247242; Fax (01223) 412410; (Mixed) (220)

■ **The Bell Language Schools Head Office and Central Registration Dept**
Hillcross, Red Cross La, Cambridge CB2 2QX; Tel (01223) 212333; Fax (01223) 410282
The Senior Registrar

See The Bell Language Schools listed under Avon, Cambridgeshire, Essex, London and Norfolk

■ **Cambridge Academy of English**
65 High St, Girton, Cambridge CB3 0QD; Tel (01223) 277230; Fax (01223) 277606
Principal A. de Waal, MA, MPhil; (Mixed) (70–90 Winter, 130–160 Summer)

■ **Cambridge Centre for Languages, CCL ‡**
Sawston Hall, Sawston, Cambridge CB2 4JR; Tel (01223) 835099 Dr S. Bayraktaroglu, MA, PhD; (Mixed) (180)

■ **Cambridge School of Languages**
119 Mill Rd, Cambridge CB1 2AZ; Tel (01223) 312333; Fax (01223) 323257; Telex 8954102 BBSLON G
Principal M.E. Davies, MA, DipEd, RSADipTEFLA; (Mixed)

■ **EF International School of English ‡**
221 Hills Rd, Cambridge CB2 2RW; Tel (01223) 240020; Fax (01223) 412474; Telex 817713 Alan Wilson, MA, PGCE, DTEFLA; (Mixed)

■ **Eurocentre, Cambridge**
62 Bateman St, Cambridge CB2 1LX; Tel (01223) 353607; Fax (01223) 68531 A.J. Crosby, BA(Hons), DipLing; (Mixed) (225)

■ **International Language Academy**
12–13 Regent Terr, Cambridge CB2 1AA; Tel (01223) 350519; Fax (01223) 464730
Contact N. Kenny

■ **Language Studies International**
41 Tenison Rd, Cambridge CB1 2DG; Tel (01223) 61783
Principal M. Wicks

■ **New School of English ‡**
52 Bateman St, Cambridge CB2 1LR; Tel (01223) 358089; Fax (01223) 315276 T. Hedger; (Mixed)

■ **Newnham Language Centre**
8 Grange Rd, Cambridge CB3 9DU; Tel (01223) 311344; Fax (01223) 461411; Telex 818231-NLC G M. Short, BA, DipEd; (140)

■ **The Studio School of English**
6 Salisbury Villas, Station Rd, Cambridge CB1 2JF; Tel (01223) 69701; Fax (01223) 314944
Principal Geoff Brock, MA, PGCE, DMS
Managing Director Christopher Roberts; (220)

Cheshire

■ **English in Chester ‡**
9–11 Stanley Pl, Chester CH1 2LU; Tel (01244) 318913; Fax (01244) 320091 Richard J. Day; (Mixed) (100)

Derbyshire

■ **English Language Systems †‡**
The Old Rectory, Church La North, Old Whittington, Chesterfield, Derbys S41 9QY; Tel (01246) 450503; (Mixed) (120 Max)

Devon

■ **The Devon School of English**
The Old Vicarage, 1 Lower Polsham Rd, Paignton, Devon TQ3 2AF; Tel (01803) 559718/521440/666499; Fax (01803) 551407
Principal/Managing Director Brian Hawthorne

■ **Exe College of English**
The Manor Hse, Cowick La, Exeter EX2 9JG; Tel (01392) 433955/6/7; Fax (01392) 422664 D. Russell

■ **Exeter Academy**
64 Sylvan Rd, Exeter, Devon EX4 6HA; Tel (01392) 430303; Fax (01392) 437309

■ **The Globe English Centre (GEC)**
71 Holloway St, Exeter, Devon EX2 4JD; Tel (01392) 71036; Fax (01392) 427559

■ **International Language Academy †**
Castle Circus, Union St, Torquay TQ1 3DE; Tel (01803) 297166; Fax (01803) 298184 Rob Hamilton

■ **The International School**
1 Mount Radford Cres, Exeter EX2 4EW; Tel (01392) 54102, 50096 G. Bryant; (Mixed) (150)

■ **The Isca School of English ‡**
4–5 Mount Radford Cres, Exeter EX2 4JN; Tel (01392) 55342; Fax (01392) 437320 R.F. Tomlinson, BA(Hons), PGCE, PostGradDipEFL, RSADipTEFLA; (Mixed) (40 Winter, 100 Summer)

■ **ISI Language Courses Ltd**
Belgrave Hse, 2 Winner St, Paignton, Devon TQ3 3BJ; Tel (01803) 524169

■ **St Hilary School of English**
284 Midvale Rd, Paignton, Devon TQ4 5BD; Tel (01803) 559223

Sidmouth International School
May Cottage, Sidmouth, Devon EX10 8EN; Tel (01395) 516754/512643; Fax (01395) 579270 M.S. Michelmore

Year-round intensive courses for adults and teenagers (Summer and easter courses for teenagers including juniors) (all main examinations); (Mixed)

■ **Suzanne Sparrow Plymouth Language School Ltd**
'Barncroft', 72–74 North Rd East, Plymouth, Devon PL4 6AL; Tel (01752) 222700; Fax (01752) 222040

■ **Torbay Language Centre**
Conway Rd, Paington, Devon TQ4 5BP; Tel (01803) 558555

■ **Torquay International School**
15–17 Marychurch Rd, Torquay TQ1 3HY; Tel (01803) 295576/298854; Fax (01803) 299062 J.J.K. Hands

■ **Totnes School of English**
51B High St, Totnes, Devon TQ9 5NP; Tel (01803) 865722; Fax (01803) 865722

Dorset

■ **Anglo World Bournemouth**
136 Poole Rd, Westbourne BH4 9EF; Tel (01202) 752200; Telex 41187 G. Witt, MA(Oxon), RSA, CertTEFL; (Mixed) (100)

■ **Anglo-Continental School for Juniors †‡**
33 Wimborne Rd, Bournemouth BH2 6NA; Tel (01202) 557414; Fax (01202) 556156
Director F.E. Herring; (Mixed) (320)

■ **Anglo-Continental School of English ‡**
29–35 Wimborne Rd, Bournemouth BH2 6NA; Tel (01202) 557414; Fax (01202) 556156
Director F.E. Herring; (Mixed) (600)

■ **BEET Language Centre ‡**
Nortoft Rd, Charminster, Bournemouth, Dorset BH8 8PY; Tel (01202) 397721/397609

■ **Bournemouth International School ‡**
711–713A Christchurch Rd, Bournemouth BH7 6AF; Tel (01202) 393112/398824; Fax (01202) 309638 V.S. Currie, MD; (Mixed) (75)

■ **Eagle International School**
7 Springfield Cres, Parkstone, Poole, Dorset BH14 0LL; Tel (01202) 745175

■ **The English Language Centre**
163–169 Old Christchurch Rd, Bournemouth BH1 1JU; Tel (01202) 291919; Fax (01202) 559292; Telex 418416 ELANG D.W. Monks; (Mixed) (150)

■ **Eurocentre UK ‡**
26 Dean Pk Rd, Bournemouth BH1 1HZ; Tel (01202) 554426 I.M.D. Ferris, MA, Dip(TEFL)RSA; (Mixed) (350)

■ **Interlink School of English**
126 Richmond Pk Rd, Bournemouth BH8 8TH; Tel (01202) 290983; Fax (01202) 291141

■ **International Language Academy Bournemouth**
Hinton Chambers, Hinton Rd, Bournemouth BH1 2EN; Tel (01202) 557522; Fax (01202) 297046
Manager L. Di Re
Principal David Brown, MA

■ **Harrow Hse International College**
Harrow Hse, Harrow Dr, Swanage, Dorset BH19 1PE; Tel (01929) 424421

■ **International Teaching and Training Centre**
674 Wimbourne Rd, Winton, Bournemouth BH9 2EG; Tel (01202) 531355

King's College of F.E.
31 Poole Rd, Bournemouth BH4 9DL; Tel (01202) 763615; Fax (01202) 293922 C. Brent, MA, MSC, PGCE

■ **King's School of English ‡**
58 Braidley Rd, Bournemouth BH2 6LD; Tel (01202) 293535; Fax (01202) 293922; Telex 41205 R.Q. Watts; (Mixed) (300)

■ **Kings School of English**
Cranfield Ave, St John's Hill, Wimbourne Minster, Dorset BH21 1BB; Tel (01202) 885119

■ **MLS International College**
8 Verulam Pl, Bournemouth, Dorset BH1 1DW; Tel (01202) 291556/299552; Fax (01202) 293846

■ **Richard Language College ‡**
43–45 Wimborne Rd, Bournemouth BH3 7AB; Tel (01202) 555932; Fax (01202) 555874 D.P. Vann, BA(Hons), CertEd; (Mixed) (100)

■ **Scanbrit School of English**
22 Church Rd, Southbourne, Bournemouth BH6 4AT; Tel (01202) 428252; Fax (01202) 428926 A. Hardy, BA; (Mixed) (100)

■ **Southbourne School of English ‡**
30 Beaufort Rd, Southbourne, Bournemouth BH6 5AL; Tel (01202) 422300; Fax (01202) 417108; Telex 418269 ELSS G Patricia A. Marchiori-White; (Mixed) (300)

■ **The Wessex Academy ‡**
84–86 Bournemouth Rd, Parkstone, Poole BH14 0HA; Tel (01202) 744700/740365; Fax (01202) 716266 M.H. Francis; (Mixed) (150)

East Sussex

■ **Buckswood Grange † ‡**
Uckfield, Sussex TN22 3PU; Tel (01825) 761666; Fax (01825) 765010

■ **The East Sussex School of English**
19 Reynolds Rd, Hove, E. Sussex BN3 5RJ; Tel (01273) 777784

■ **Eastbourne School of English**
8 Trinity Trees, Eastbourne BN21 3LD; Tel (01323) 721759; Fax (01323) 639271 D.S. Rippon, DipTEFL, RSA CertTEFL; (Mixed) (120)

■ **E.F. International School of English ‡**
1–2 Sussex Sq, Kempton, Brighton BN2 1FJ; Tel (01273) 571780 Dermot A. Tobin, BA(Hons), Dip(TEFL)RSA; (Mixed) (900)

■ **E.F. International School of English**
74–80 Warrior Sq, St Leonards-on-Sea, Hastings, E. Sussex TN37 6BP; Tel (01424) 423998

■ **Embassy School of English ‡**
7 Warrior Sq, St Leonards-on-Sea, E. Sussex TN37 6NH; Tel (01424) 720282 Peter Arnold, BA, RSA, DipTEFL; (Mixed) (15 per class maximum)

■ **The English Centre, Eastbourne**
25 St Anne's Rd, Eastbourne BN21 2DJ; Tel (01323) 725887; Fax (01323) 730727 D.A. Ashdown, CertEd M.S. Ockenden MIL, RSA Dip TEFLA; (Mixed) (60)

■ **The English Language and Equestrian Centre**
Friars Gate Farm, Marden Hill, Crowborough, E. Sussex TN6 1XH; Tel (01892) 661195

■ **The English Language Centre**
33 Palmeira Mansions, Hove BN3 2GB; Tel (01273) 721771; Fax (01273) 720898; Telex 87250 C.N. Harrison, FCA; (Mixed) (500)

■ **Eurocentre Brighton formerly Davies's School of English ‡**
Huntingdon Hse, 20 North St, Brighton BN1 1EB; Tel (01273) 324545; Fax (01273) 746013; Telex 877713 K. Chapman, MA; (Mixed)

■ **GEOS English Academy ‡**
55–61 Portland Rd, Hove, Sussex BN3 5DQ; Tel (01273) 735975/721612; Fax (01273) 732884 Wendy Teraoka; (Mixed) (150)

■ **Hastings English Language Centre**
St Helens Pk Rd, Hastings, E. Sussex TN34 2JW; Tel (01424) 437048; Fax (01424) 716442

■ **House of English ‡**
24 Portland Pl, Kemp Town, Brighton BN2 1DG; Tel (01273) 69418/685918
Principal S. Camilleri

ISI Language Courses Ltd ‡
15 Grand Parade, Brighton; Tel (01273) 674765 P.A. Logan; (Mixed)

■ **ITS English School ‡**
43–45 Cambridge Gdns, Hastings TN34 1EN; Tel (01424) 438025; Fax (01424) 438050 John Palim, MA(TEFL), CertEd; (Mixed) (150)

■ **International Language Centres Group Ltd ‡**
International Hse, White Rock, Hastings TN34 1JY; Tel (01424) 720100; Fax (01424) 720323 M.A. Conlin, MA; (200)

■ **LTC International College†**
Compton Pk, Compton Place Rd, Eastbourne BN21 1EH; Tel (01323) 727755; Fax (01323) 728279 D.J. Lear, MSc, BED(Hons), RSA(TEFL), Minst Admin Dip; (Mixed) (120)

■ **Language Studies International Ltd ‡**
13 Ventnor Villas, Hove, E. Sussex BN3 3DD; Tel (01273) 722060/778417; Fax (01273) 746341
Principal Tony Gill

■ **Mayfield House School of English †**
24 Holland Rd, Hove BN3 1JJ; Tel (01273) 779231; Telex 877159 T. Milton, CertEd; Member of ARELS/FELCO; (Mixed)

■ **Meads School of English**
2 Old Orchard Rd, Eastbourne; Tel (01323) 734335/6 Douglas MacRae-Brown; (Mixed) (150)

■ **Regent Language Training Brighton (Business Professional English) ‡**
52 Dykes Rd, Brighton; Tel (01273) 21771; Fax (01273) 723730 Margaret Khidhayir, MA; (Mixed) (42)

■ **Regent Language Training Hove Centre**
18 Cromwell Rd, Hove BN3 3EW; Tel (01273) 731684; Fax (01273) 324542 Paul Johnston; (Mixed) (115)

■ **St Giles College ‡**
3 Marlborough Pl, Brighton BN1 1UB; Tel (01273) 682747; Fax (01273) 689808 B.D. Graver, MA; (Mixed) (180)

69 Marine Pde, Brighton BN2 1AD

■ **St Giles College**
13 Silverdale Rd, Eastbourne, E. Sussex BN20 7AJ; Tel (01323) 729167/641502

■ **YES Educational Centre**
12 Eversfield Rd, Eastbourne, E. Sussex BN21 2AS; Tel (01323) 644830; Fax (01323) 726260

Essex

■ **Alexanders International School † ‡**
Harlowbury Hse, Old Rd, Old Harlow, Essex CM17 0HE; Tel (01279) 422122; Fax (01279) 445584

■ **The Bell Language School ‡**
South Rd, Saffron Walden, Essex CB11 3DP; Tel (01799) 522918; Fax (01799) 526949; (Mixed) (250)

■ **Colchester English Study Centre**
19 Lexden Rd, Colchester CO3 3PW; Tel (01206) 44422; Fax (01206) 761849; Telex 987578 CESC J.A. Seath; (Mixed) (200)

■ **Essex House School of English**
4 Church Rd, Clacton on Sea, Essex CO15 6AG; Tel (01255) 423465 B.J. Segadelli, MA; (Mixed) (90)

Gloucestershire

■ **Cheltenham English Study Centre**
6 Bournside Rd, Cheltenham, Glos; Tel (01242) 523908

■ **Cheltenham School of English ‡**
87 St George's Rd, Cheltenham GL50 3DU; Tel (01242) 570000; Fax (01242) 227350 K.M. Cawsey; (Mixed) (Term 60 approx, summer school 120)

■ **Western Language Centre Ltd**
Forge Hse, Kemble GL7 6AD; Tel (01285) 770447
Principal Michael Lawlor

Greater Manchester

■ **Eaton Hartley College**
32 York Rd, Sale, Manchester M33 1WH; Tel 0161-962 3105/969 6611

■ **Educare College, ‡**
Burnage La, Manchester M19 1DR; Tel 0161-442 0858
Principal Dr E. Stewart

■ **English Country School**
30 Dundonald Rd, Cheadle Hulme, Cheadle SK8 6LQ; Tel 0161-486 1832; Fax 0161-486 1832; Telex 669755 Office (ATTN.ECS)
Principal Christopher Etchells

■ **Inlingua College Courses**
12 Meadowgate, Urmston, Manchester M41 9LB; Tel 0161-748 2621
Principal D.A. Willey

■ **Linguarama Manchester**
28–32 Princess St, Manchester M1 4LB; Tel 0161-228 3983

■ **Nord-Anglia International Ltd**
10 Eden Pl, Cheadle, Cheshire SK8 1AT; Tel 0161-491 4191; Fax 0161-491 4409/4410; Telex 666807

Hampshire

■ **English Immersion Courses ‡**
59 Belmont Rd, Portswood, Southampton SO2 1GD; Tel (01703) 671861; Fax (01703) 671850

■ **The Greylands School of English**
315 Portswood Rd, Southampton SO2 1LD; Tel (01703) 315180

■ **Language Specialists International**
Elizabeth Hse, 13–19 Guildhall Walk, Portsmouth PO1 2RY; Tel (01705) 291811; Fax (01705) 750435

■ **Lewis School of English**
33 Palmerston Rd, Southampton SO14 1LL; Tel (01703) 228203; Fax (01703) 231395

■ **Linguarama**
Riversdown Hse, Warnford, Southampton, Hants SO3 1LH; Tel (01962) 54488

■ **Meridian School of English ‡**
9 Yarborough Rd, Southsea, Hampshire PO5 3DZ; Tel (01705) 816023; Fax (01705) 833438

■ **Summer School in England**
Longlythe, Stairs Hill, Empshott, Liss, Hampshire GU33 6HW; Tel (01420) 7667

Hereford and Worcester

■ **Abbey College †‡**
253 Wells Rd, Malvern Wells, Worcs WR14 4JF; Tel (01684) 892300; Fax (01684) 892757 R. Bellerby D.M. Arrowsmith; (Mixed) (130)

Hertfordshire

■ **English Language and Cultural Organisation**
'Lowlands', Chorleywood Rd, Rickmansworth, Herts WD3 4ES; Tel (01923) 776731/721577; Fax (01923) 774678
Director Tony Thompson, MA(Cantab)

Kent

■ **Anglian School of English ‡**
81–83 Norfolk Rd, Cliftonville, Margate, Kent CT9 2HX; Tel (01843) 293700; Fax (01843) 226014 Neil Radford, MA (TEFL), CertEd; (Mixed) (80) (17+) (Accommodation with local families)

■ **Churchill House School of English ‡**
40–42 Spencer Sq, Ramsgate CT11 9LD; Tel (01843) 586833 Rex A.P. Stickland, BSc; (Mixed) (160)

■ **Cicero Languages International ‡**
42 Upper Grosvenor Rd, Tunbridge Wells, Kent TN1 2ET; Tel (01892) 547077 Paul Mason; (Mixed) (approx 40) (Family accommodation arranged)

■ **Concorde International Study Centre**
22/24 Cheriton Gdns, Folkestone, Kent CT20 2AT; Tel (01303) 256752; Fax (01303) 220538

■ **Concorde International Summer School**
Arnett Hse, Hawk La, Canterbury, Kent CT1 2NU; Tel (01227) 451035

■ **Fitzroy College of English ‡**
Northdown Hse, Margate, Kent CT9 3TP; Tel (01843) 865547; Fax (01843) 869055 Martin Webber, MA; (Mixed) (85)

■ **Kent School of English**
3, 5, 10, 12 Granville Rd, Broadstairs, Kent CT11 1QD; Tel (01843) 868207

■ **King's School of English**
25 Beckenham Rd, Beckenham BR3 4PR; Tel 081-650 5891; Fax 081-663 3224 J. Hudson, FIL; (Mixed, Foreign adults only) (160)

■ **Living Language Centre ‡**
Highcliffe Hse, Clifton Gdns, Folkestone CT20 2EF; Tel (01303) 258536; Fax (01303) 851455; Telex 966229 Livlan G David O'Clee, MA(TCD); (Mixed) (200)

■ **London House School of English**
51 Sea Rd, Westgate-on-Sea, Kent CT8 8QL; Tel (01834) 31216

■ **Passport Language Schools ‡**
37 Park Rd, Bromley, Kent BR1 3HJ; Tel 0181-464 6925
Director G.S. Cook

■ **Pilgrims †‡**
8 Vernon Pl, Canterbury, Kent CT1 3HG; Tel (01227) 762111 James Dixey, BA, DipEd, DipTEO; (Mixed) (approx 1500 annually)

■ **Regency School of English**
Royal Cres, Ramsgate; Tel (01843) 591212; Fax (01843) 850035 Ciaràn Coyle; (Mixed)

St Mildred's School of English
Sussex Gdns, Westgate on Sea; Tel (01843) 32323 P. Harris-Deans; (Mixed)

■ **St Peter's School of English**
4 St Alphege La, Canterbury CT1 2EB; Tel (01227) 462016 P. Harris-Deans; (Mixed)

■ **School of English Studies**
26 Grimston Gdns, Folkestone CT20 2PX; Tel (01303) 850007; Fax (01303) 256544 Freddy Johnson, MA; (Mixed)

■ **Stafford House Tutorial College and School of English †‡**
68 New Dover Rd, Canterbury CT1 3EQ; Tel (01227) 453237/8/9; Fax (01227) 451685; Telex 965991 J.F. Leader; (Mixed) (150)

Leicestershire

■ **Irwin Academy**
164 London Rd, Leicester LE2 1ND; Tel (0116) 255 2648

London, Greater

■ **Academy International**
3 Queen's Gdns, London W2 3BA; Tel 0171-262 6982.1084 J. Hinwood Turner; (Mixed)

■ **ACE School of English**
1105 High Rd, Whetstone, London N20 0PT; Tel 0181-446 0478

■ **Anglo-European Study Tours Ltd**
8 Celbridge Mews, London W2 6EU; Tel 0171-229 4435

■ **Anglo World London**
8 Queen's Rd, London NW4 2TH; Tel 0181-202 4351; Fax 0181-202 0514 C.H. Raynor, BA(Hons), RSA Dip.TEFL; (Mixed) (100)

■ **Angloschool ‡**
146 Church Rd, London SE19 2NT; Tel 0181-653 7285; Fax 0181-653 9667 J.G. Adams, MA; (Mixed) (120)

■ **The Bell Language School**
34 Fitzroy Sq, London W1P 6BP; Tel 0171-637 8338; Fax 0171-637 4811; (Mixed) (130)

■ **Cambridge School of English ‡**
8 Herbrand St, London WC1N 1HZ; Tel 0171-734 4203 and 278 6622 Alan Wheeler; (Mixed) (150)

■ **The Canning School ‡**
4 Abingdon Rd, London W8 6AF; Tel 0171-937 3233 D.J. Lehmann, BA(Hons); (Mixed)

also at 1 Brock St, Bath BA1 2LN

■ **Central School of English ‡**
1 Tottenham Court Rd, London W1P 9DA; Tel 0171-580 2863; Fax 0171-255 1806; Telex 266110 CENSCH G *Marketing Manager* P. O'Shea; (Mixed) (200)

■ **Ebury Executive English ‡**
132 Ebury St, London SW1W 9QQ; Tel 0171-730 3991; Fax 0171-730 1794

■ **ELS Language Centres (UK)**
3 Muirfield Cres, Millharbour, London E14 9SZ; Tel 0171-512 0600; Fax 0171-512 0640

■ **English and Cultural Studies Centres (ESC)**
40 Village Rd, Enfield, Middx EN1 2EN; Tel 0181-360 4118

■ **English Language Communications**
1–3 Manor Parade, Sheepcote Rd, Harrow, London HA1 2JN; Tel 0181-861 5322

■ **English Language Institute**
Royal Waterloo Hse, 51–55 Waterloo Rd, London SE1 8TX; Tel 0171-928 1372

■ **Eurocentre Lee Green**
21 Meadowcourt Rd, Lee Grn, London SE3 9EU; Tel 0181-318 5633 J.F. Andrews, MA; (Mixed) (360)

■ **Eurocentre London Victoria ‡**
56 Eccleston Sq, London SW1V 1PQ; Tel 0171-834 4155; Fax 0171-834 1866 Martyn Ellis, MA; (Mixed) (252)

■ **Frances King School of English**
18 Dunraven St, Park La, London W1Y 3FE; Tel 0171-629 2904

■ **Greenwich International School of English**
2–3 Turnpin La, Greenwich, London SE10 9JA; Tel 0181-305 0370

■ **Hampstead School of English**
553 Finchley Rd, London NW3 7BJ; Tel 0171-794 3533 *Principal* Jill Sieff

■ **International College**
9 Palace Gate, London W8 5LS; Tel 0171-581 9485; Fax 0171-823 9978

■ **International House**
106 Piccadilly, London W1V 9FL; Tel 0171-491 2598; Fax 0171-495 0284 Charles Lowe, BA(Hons), MA, RSA Dip.TEFL; (Mixed) (600)

■ **International Language Academy London**
4 Russell Gdns, Holland Rd W14 8EY; Tel 0171-371 1344; Fax 0171-602 2978 Ann Ayton; (Mixed) (80)

■ **Language-Link Ltd**
21 Harrington Rd, South Kensington, London SW7 3EU; Tel 0171-225 1065

■ **Language Studies Ltd ‡**
Heath Hse, 13 Lyndhurst Terr, London NW3 5QA; Tel 0171-794 8111/2/3 Jane Gray; (Mixed) (class size max 15)

Language Studies International
Woodstock Hse, 10–12 James St, London W1M 5HN; Tel 0171-499 9621, 0171-491 1731 D.H. Immanuel P.J. Bailey

Lansdowne International College Ltd †‡
9 Palace Gate, Kensington W8 5LS; Tel 0171-581 9485 *Principal* Paul W. Templeton, BSc(Econ); (Mixed) (2,000)

■ **Linguarama Ltd ‡**
Queens Hse, 8 Queen St, London EC4N 1AP; Tel 0171-236 1992 Geoff Monaghan; (Mixed)

■ **Linguarama London**
37 Golden Sq, London W1R 3AA; Tel 0171-434 9262

■ **London School of English ‡**
15 Holland Pk Gdns, London W14 8DZ; Tel 0171-603 1656 Timothy Blake; (Mixed) (100)

■ **The London School of Foreign Trade ‡**
(at Morley College) 61 Westminster Bridge Rd, London SE1 7HT; Tel 0171-928 6810 K.W. Aitken; (Mixed) (300)

■ **London Study Centre ‡**
Munster Hse, 676 Fulham Rd, London SW6 5SA; Tel 0171-731 3549, 0171-736 4990, 0171-731 4565; Fax 0171-731 1498; Telex 8954111 G Colin D Gordon, MA(Hons) Oxon; (Mixed) (700)

■ **Marble Arch Intensive English ‡**
21 Star St, London W2 1QB; Tel 0171-402 9273; Fax 0171-724 2219 Peter Brook; (Mixed) (average 130, maximum (July/August) 350)

■ **Mayfair School of English**
45 Oxford St, London W1R 1RD; Tel 0171-437 9941

■ **Oxford House College †‡**
3 Oxford St, London W1R; Tel 0171-580 9785 Dr S. Shaw; (Mixed) (500)

■ **Pitman School of English ‡**
154 Southampton Row, London WC1B 5AX; Tel 0171-278 6877 Simon Williams; (Mixed) (260)

■ **Poly-Contact Education and Training Ltd †‡**
PO Box 53, Isleworth TW7 4EU; Tel 0181-893 3610 M. Webb

■ **Regent Language Training**
4 Percy St, London W1P 9FA; Tel 0171-580 6552; Fax 0171-580 0122
Managing Director Graham White

General, Executive and Examination Courses in London, Hove and Wales (residential); accommodation arranged

■ **Regent Summer Schools †‡**
19–23 Oxford St, London W1R 1RF; Tel 0171-734 1137; Fax 0171-734 4896
Managing Director Jane Merrick; (mixed) (approx 2,000)

■ **St Giles College**
51 Shepherds Hill Highgate N6; Tel 0181-340 0828 David Swabey, BA(Hons), RSA Dip.TEFL; (Mixed)

■ **St Godric's Secretarial and Language College †‡**
6 Arkwright Rd, Hampstead NW3 6AD; Tel 0171-435 9831 Sir John and Lady Loveridge, M.W. Loveridge; (Mixed) (100)

■ **St Patrick's International School ‡**
24 Great Chapel St, London W1V 3AF; Tel 0171-734 2156/439 0116; Fax 0171-287 6282; Telex 295929 Lynda Fase; (Mixed) (50–150)

■ **St John's Wood School of English ‡**
126 Boundary Rd NW8 0RH; Tel 0171-624 1925; Fax 0171-328 6877 P. Bulmer; (Mixed)

■ **SELS English College London**
64–65 Long Acre, Covent Garden, London WC2E 9JH; Tel 0171-240 2581; Fax 0171-379 5793 Dato Y. Raiss, BA, BSc(Econ), MEd, LTCL, DipsTEFL, EdRes, Hisr, Lit, Intl Affairs, Barrister-at-Law; (Mixed) (200)

■ **Shane English School London**
59 South Motton St, London W1Y 1HH; Tel 0171-499 8533; Fax 0171-499 9374

■ **Stanton School of English**
Stanton Hse, 167 Queensway, London W2 4SB; Tel 0171-221 7259; Fax 0171-792 9047; Telex 2262433 Ref 1545 D.A. Garrett, MA; (Mixed)

■ **Victoria School of English ‡**
28 Graham Terr, London SW1; Tel 0171-730 1333; Fax 0171-823 4175 Robert Baldwin, BA, PGCE, RSADipTEFLA; (Mixed) (60 all year/80 in summer)

■ **The Wimbledon School of English**
41 Worple Rd, Wimbledon SW19 4JZ; Tel 0181-947 1921 David Rodgers; (Mixed) (120)

■ **Youth Service Summer School**
16–20 New Broadway, London W5 2XA; Tel 0181-566 2188

Norfolk

■ **The Bell Languages School ‡**
The Old Hse, Church La, Eaton, Norwich NR4 6NW; Tel (01603) 56321; Fax (01603) 506742; Telex 817916 Bellco G; (Mixed) (84)

■ **The Bell Language School ‡**
Bowthorpe Hall, Bowthorpe, Norwich NR5 9AA; Tel (01603) 745615; Fax (01603) 747669; Telex 817916 Bellco G; (Mixed) (110)

North Yorkshire

■ **Anglolang (Scarborough) Ltd ‡**
20 Avenue Rd, Scarborough, N. Yorks YO12 5JX; Tel (01723) 367141/501991; Fax (01723) 378698

■ **Functional English †‡**
International Christian Language School, 5 Chubb Hill Rd, Whitby YO21 1JU; Tel (01947) 603933 Neil McKelvie, MA, PGCE, Dip(TEFL)RSA; (Mixed 17+) (85)

■ **Harrogate Language Academy ‡**
8A Royal Parade, Harrogate, N. Yorks HG1 2SZ; Tel (01423) 531969; Fax (01423) 531064 Heather Mann

■ **Harrogate Tutorial College † ‡**
2 The Oval, Harrogate, North Yorkshire HG2 9BA; Tel (01423) 501041; Fax (01423) 531110; Telex 57784 MCCL G

■ **Melton College ‡**
Holgate Hill, York YO2 4DH; Tel (01904) 622250; Fax (01904) 6296233 E.M. Hiley, MA

■ **Scarborough International School ‡**
Cheswold Hall, 37 Stepney Rd, Scarborough, N. Yorks YO12 5BN; Tel (01723) 362879; Fax (01723) 366458; Telex 527613 TOSCAR G
Principal Director Rosemary Glyde; (Mixed) (approx 100) (accommodation with English host families)

■ **Specialist Language Services (International)**
9 Marsden Business Pk, Clifton, York YO3 4XG; Tel (01904) 691313; Fax (01904) 691102 Barry Stainthorp; (Mixed)

Oxfordshire

■ **Anglo World Oxford**
108 Banbury Rd, Oxford OX2 6JU; Tel (01865) 515808 Simon Barnes, BEd; (Mixed)

■ **The Eckersley School of English †‡**
14 Friars Entry, Oxford OX1 2BZ; Tel (01865) 721268
Principal J.M. Eckersley, MA; (Mixed) (100)

■ **ELT Banbury**
49 Oxford Rd, Banbury, Oxon; Tel (01295) 263480/263502 Dr T.J. Gerighty

■ **Godmer House School of English**
90 Banbury Rd, Oxford OX2 6JT; Tel (01865) 515566; Fax (01865) 512 538; Telex 838986 GHSE Tony Conway, BA(Hons), RSADipTEFL

■ **International Language Academy ‡**
7 Norham Gdns, Oxford OX2 6PS; Tel (01865) 516402; Fax (01865) 311508
Contact J. Hopwood

■ **The Lake School of English (Teachers' Co-operative) ‡**
14 Park End St, Oxford OX1 1HW; Tel (01865) 724312; Fax (01865) 251360
Administrator Jane R. Baker
Administrator Suzette Starmer; (Mixed) (max 14 in each class) (host family accommodation)

■ **MM Oxford Study Services Ltd**
44 Blenheim Dr, Oxford OX2 8DQ; Tel (01865) 513788

■ **The Oxford Academy**
18 Bardwell Rd, Oxford OX2 6SP; Tel (01865) 512174; Fax (01865) 53751 S.M. Mason; (Mixed) (120) (accommodation in school residences, host families or guesthouses)

■ **Oxford House School of English ‡**
67 High St, Wheatley, Oxford OX33 1XT; Tel (01865) 874786; Fax (01865) 873351

13 Independent Further Education

■ **Oxford Intensive School of English**
OISE Hse, Binsey La, Oxford OX2 0EY; Tel (01865) 249218; Fax (01865) 726726 Till Gins; (Mixed) (19 centres, 8 each class, max. 48 each centre) (family and campus accom.)

■ **The Oxford Study Centre †‡**
17 Sunderland Ave, Oxford OX2 8DT; Tel (01235) 554747 C. Philip; (Mixed) (200–250)

■ **St Clare's †‡**
139 Banbury Rd, Oxford OX2 7AL; Tel (01865) 52031; Fax (01865) 310002; Telex 837379 Margaret Skarland, BA, PGCE; (Mixed) (300)

■ **St Joseph's Hall ‡**
Junction Rd, Cowley, Oxford OX4 2UJ; Tel (01865) 711829; Fax (01865) 747791 Simon Fenn, BA, Dip(TEFL), RSA

■ **UTS Oxford Centre**
Wolsey Hall, 66 Banbury Rd, Oxford OX2 6PR; Tel (01865) 576162; Fax (01865) 310910

■ **Swan School of English‡**
111 Banbury Rd, Oxford OX2 6JX; Tel (01865) 53201; Fax (01865) 52923 H.A. Swan; (Mixed) (120)

Powys

■ **English Plus (Park Hse)**
Hyssington, Montgomery, Powys SY15 6DZ; Tel (015885) 611

■ **The Trebinshun Group**
Trebinshun Hse, Nr Brecon, Powys LD3 7PX; Tel (01874) 730653

Shropshire

■ **Concord College †**
Acton Burnall Hall, Shrewsbury SY5 7PF; Tel (01694) 731631 A.L. Morris, BA; (Mixed) (240)

■ **Lydbury English Centre ‡**
The Old Vicarage, Lydbury North, Shropshire SY7 8AU; Tel (01588) 680233; Fax (01588) 680334

■ **Severnvale Central Language Academy**
20 Castle St, Shrewsbury, Shropshire; Tel (01743) 232505; Fax (01743) 272637

Somerset

■ **Millfield School Village of Education**
Millfield School, Street, Somerset BA16 0YD; Tel (01458) 45823/142291

Suffolk

■ **Academic Travel (Lowestoft) Ltd ‡**
8 Gunton Cliff, Lowestoft, Suffolk NR32 4PE; Tel (01502) 573781/564442

Surrey

■ **Campana International College**
Moor Pk Hse, Moor Pk La, Farnham, Surrey GU10 1QP; Tel (01252) 727111; Fax (01252) 712011

■ **The Elizabeth Johnson Organisation Ltd ‡**
West Hse, 19–21 West St, Haslemere, Surrey GU27 2AE; Tel (01428) 652751

■ **Harven School of English ‡**
The Mascot, Coley Ave, Woking GU22 7BT; Tel (01483) 770969/723638; Fax (01483) 740267 V.G. Maddock, LTCL, TEFL, DipEtSup; (Mixed)

■ **Hurtwood House †‡**
Holbury St Mary, Dorking, Surrey RH5 6NU; Tel (01483) 277416 K.R.B. Jackson, MA; (Mixed) (240)

■ **Surrey Language Centre**
Surrey Language Training Ltd, Sandford Hse, 39 West St, Farnham, Surrey GU9 7DR; Tel (01252) 723494

Tyne and Wear

International House, Newcastle ‡
14–18 Stowell St, Newcastle upon Tyne NE1 4XQ; Tel 0191-232 9551; Fax 0191-232 1126 Gill Mitchell; (Mixed) (30–70)

Warwickshire

■ **Coventry International English Studies Centre (incorporating Coventry Business and Management College) ‡**
9 Priory Row, Coventry CV1 5EX; Tel (01203) 223379; Fax (01203) 223229 J.E. Rendle, MA(Oxon), DMS, FBIM, FRSA; (Mixed)

■ **The Harper School of English ‡**
7 Warwick Row, Coventry CV1 1EX; Tel (01203) 222588; Fax (01203) 258196; Telex 311033 CHACOM G for HSE A.J. Harper; (Mixed) (60) (11–17, 18–80) (family accommodation)

■ **Linguarama, Language Training for Business**
1 Elm Court, Arden St, Stratford-upon-Avon, Warks CV37 6PA; Tel (01789) 296535; Fax (01789) 266462

■ **Stratford-upon-Avon School of English Studies**
Tiddington Rd, Stratford-upon-Avon CV37 7AE; Tel (01789) 269497; Fax (01789) 292955 P.D. Lakey, BA, CertEd; (Mixed) (80)

■ **Swan School of English**
11 Guild St, Stratford-upon-Avon CV37 6RE; Tel (01789) 269161 H.A. Swan; (Mixed) (60)

West Midlands

■ **Linguarama, Language Training for Business**
New Oxford Hse, Waterloo St, Birmingham B2 5UG; Tel 0121-632 5925

West Sussex

■ **Bellerbys**
44 Cromwell Rd, Hove, West Sussex BH3 3ER; Tel (01273) 723911

■ **Chichester School of English ‡**
45 East St, Chichester PO19 1HX; Tel (01243) 789893/1781768; Fax (01243) 531378 A.S. Robertson

■ **The International School of English and Commerce ‡**
Seadown Hse, Farncombe Rd, Worthing, West Sussex BN11 2BE; Tel (01903) 209244; (Mixed) (50–100)

International Students Services ‡
58 Chapel Rd, Worthing, West Sussex BN11 1BG; Tel (01903) 211060; Fax (01903) 230129 J. Foord; (Mixed)

■ **Swandean School of English ‡**
12 Stoke Abbott Rd, Worthing BN11 1HE; Tel (01903) 231330 Bruce Noble; (Mixed) (Term 50, Summer 500)

■ **The West Sussex School of English ‡**
7 High St, Steyning, West Sussex BN44 3GG; Tel (01903) 814512; Fax (01903) 812451

Wiltshire

■ **Salisbury School of English**
36 Fowlers Rd, Salisbury, Wilts SP1 2QU; Tel (01722) 331011

■ **Trythall Language Centre**
42–44 Chipper La, Salisbury, Wilts SP1 1BG; Tel (01722) 412711
Principal John Trythall

Scotland

■ AST School of English †
Perth Aerodrome, Perth PH2 6NP; Tel (01738) 52311
J.G. Beech, MA, MBA

■ Basil Paterson School of English ‡
Dugdale–McAdam Hse, 22/23 Abercromby Pl, Edinburgh EH3 6QE; Tel 0131-556 7695; Fax 0131-557 8503; Telex 727815 BAPACO G R.R. Mackenzie, MA; (Mixed) (80 Winter, 250 Summer)

■ Edinburgh Language Foundation
11 Gt Stuart St, Edinburgh EH3 7TS; Tel 0131-225 8785
Dr W.B. Currie, MA, CertEd, Dip App Ling, PhD; (Mixed)

■ Edinburgh School of English
271 Canongate, The Royal Mile, Edinburgh EH8 8BQ; Tel 0131-557 9200; Fax 0131-557 9192 Margot Huggins; (Junior Courses)

■ Edinburgh Tutorial College † ‡
29 Chester St, Edinburgh EH3 7EN; Tel 0131-225 9888

■ Aberdeen Centre for English
68 Polmuir Rd, Aberdeen AB1 2TH; Tel (01224) 580968; Fax (01224) 575655

■ Highland Language Centre † ‡
Marine Terr, Rossmarkie, Ross-shire IV10 8UR; Tel (01381) 620598; Fax (01381) 621247

Secretarial Colleges

Beckenham Secretarial College
31 Beckenham Rd, Beckenham, Kent BR3 4PR; Tel 0181-650 3321
Principal Elizabeth Wakeling

The Cambridge Secretarial College
6 Salisbury Villas, Station Rd, Cambridge CB1 2JF; Tel (01223) 69701; Fax (01223) 314944/324605
Principal Geoff Brock, MA, PGCE, DMS, MIMgt

Camden Secretarial College
Century Hse, 4 Pierrepont St, Bath BA1 1LE; Tel (01225) 463573
Principal Barbara Edwards, DipRSA, FSBT, LIQPS

Cleve College Ltd
96 Newport Rd, Cardiff CF2 1DG; Tel (01222) 497981
Principal D.C. Meek, PCT, FTBE

The Dugdale-McAdam Secretarial College
23 Abercromby Pl, Edinburgh EH3 6QE; Tel 0131-556 7698
Principal J. Hunter

■ Guildford Secretarial College ‡†
16–19 Chapel St, Guildford, Surrey GU1 3UL; Tel (01483) 64885; Fax (01483) 34777
Principal Debra Tomlinson

French Institute (Institut Français)
Bilingual College, 14 Cromwell Pl, London SW7 2JR; Tel 0171-581 2701; Fax 0171-581 2910
Principal Brigitte Freyche
Registrar Vacancy

Leatherhead Secretarial School
28 Bridge St, Leatherhead, Surrey KT22 8BZ; Tel (01372) 372401
Principal N.C. Wolff, MFTCom

Lucie Clayton Secretarial College
* 4 Cornwall Gdns, London SW7 4AJ; Tel 0171-581 0024
Principal Leslie Kark, MA; (144)

Marlborough Secretarial and Business College
110A High St, Oxford OX1 4HU; Tel (01865) 249484
Principal Frances E. Bull

The Marlborough Secretarial College
Bateman St, Cambridge CB2 1LU; Tel (01223) 67016
Principal Janet H. Allom, BA

The North of England College
Cavendish Hse, 92 Albion St, Leeds LS1 6AG; Tel (0113) 245 3073
Principal Ann Salama, BA(Hons)

■ The Oxford and County Business College †‡
34 St Giles, Oxford OX1 3LH; Tel (01865) 310100
Director Joy Thompson, BA, FBIM, MIEx

Pitman Branch Secretarial Colleges
(Wembley, Wimbledon, Oxford, Cambridge, Leeds)154 Southampton Row, London WC1B 5AX; Tel 0171-837 4481
Director, Branch Colleges Rosemary Lloyd, BA, CertEd, DipLaw

Purley Secretarial and Language College
14 Brighton Rd, Purley CR8 3AB; Tel 0181-660 5060; Fax 0181-668 4022
Principal P.W. Kent

The Queen's Secretarial College
24 Queensberry Pl, London SW7 2DS; Tel 0171-589 8583; Fax 0171-823 9915
Principal Marion Feibush, BA(Hons)

St Aldates College
Rose Pl, Oxford OX1 1SB; Tel (01865) 240963
Principal Pauline Martin

The St James's Secretarial College
4 Wetherby Gdns, London SW5 0JN; Tel 0171-373 3852

Underwood Secretarial College
188–190 Old Schristchurch Rd, Bournemouth BH1 1NU; Tel (01202) 552624/292281
Principal Annette M. Jones

Correspondence Education

The Association of British Correspondence Colleges

6 Francis Gr, London SW19 4DT; Tel 0181-544 9559; Fax 0181-540 7657
Chairman R.D. Mercer
Treasurer A. Young
Secretary H. Owen, BA

The aims of the Association are:

To ensure that its members provide a high standard of tuition and efficient service

To safeguard the interests of all students taking correspondence courses

To be a centre of information and advice on matters pertaining to correspondence education

To co-operate with the Council for the Accreditation of Correspondence Colleges, the Department for Education, local education authorities, universities, professional societies and institutions, and other bodies and persons concerned with further education

To maintain and enhance the prestige of correspondence education

13 Independent Further Education

Membership is open only to correspondence colleges that provide a consistently reliable and efficient tutorial service and who comply with the criteria for membership approved by the Council of the Association

Free broadsheet listing member colleges and their courses is available

Council for the Accreditation of Correspondence Colleges

27 Marylebone Rd, London NW1 5JS; Tel 0171-935 5391; Fax 0171-935 2540
Chairman Eric Glover, MA
Secretary E. Ingham, BA, DipEd

Established in 1968 as an independent body with the co-operation of the Secretary of State for Education. The Council which is non-profit making, is constituted as a Company Limited by Guarantee, and recognised as a Registered Charity, and is the only organisation in the United Kingdom recognised as responsible for the award of Accreditation to Correspondence Colleges. At present 43 Correspondence Colleges are accredited by CACC and at least 300,000 students are enrolled for correspondence courses in those colleges

CACC is established for the public benefit to promote education and in particular to raise standards of tuition, education or training carried out wholly or in part by post. It does this by awarding, where appropriate, the status of accreditation in recognition that the activities of a particular college conform to such standards

Institutions seeking CACC Accreditation must satisfy CACC under all the following heads: Overall Organisation, including legal and financial viability; Educational Policy; Publicity and Recruitment including enrolment procedures and fee arrangements; Educational and Training Materials; Educational Staff and Tuition; Accommodation, equipment and general facilities and procedures for establishing and maintaining quality standards

The accreditation process is carried out by panels of independent and well-qualified Assessors appointed by the Council. All are specialists in their own field

The Process of accreditation involves an initial application: a preliminary visit by the Chief Assessor to determine eligibility for accreditation: a full inspection of the Institution by a panel of Assessors, followed by a Report to Council by the Chief Assessor. A decision on accreditation is then taken by Council. Re-accreditation normally takes place every five years but CACC reserves the right to review the accreditation of an Institution at any time if reasonable grounds exist

Colleges accredited by the Council are indicated by a black dot (•) next to their entry

The Agricultural Correspondence College
16 Notton, Lacock, Chippenham, Wilts SN15 2NF
Partner O.N. Menhinick, MSc

The Animal Care College and Canine Studies Institute
Ascot Hse, High St, Ascot, Berks SL5 7JG; Tel (01344) 28269; Fax (01344) 28269

The Association of British Dispensing Opticians
6 Hurlingham Business Pk, Sulivan Rd, London SW6 3DU; Tel 0171-736 0088; Fax 0171-731 5531
Registrar Derek Baker

ATC Foulks Lynch Distance Learning
Accountancy and Finance, Banking, Chartered Secretaries, Taxation, Book Keeping. 28 Farringdon St, London EC4A 4EU; Tel 0171-634 1000; Fax 0171-250 0786
Principal S.C. Maugham

• Business Training Ltd
Sevendale Hse, 7 Dale St, Manchester M1 1JB; Tel 0161-228 6735/6

• Cambridge Tutorial College
College Hse, St Ouen, PO Box 530, Jersey JE4 8XX, Channel Islands; Tel (01534) 485052; Fax (01534) 485071

• The Chartered Institute of Bankers in Scotland
Director of Education, 19–20 Rutland Sq, Edinburgh EH1 2DE, Scotland; Tel 0131-229 9869; Fax 0131-229 1852

• The Chartered Insurance Institute
Headquarters 20 Aldermanbury, London EC2V 7HY; Tel 0171-606 3835; Fax 0171-726 0131
Director General Dr D.E. Bland, BA, MLitt, PhD, ACII, FSCA

• The Chartered Insurance Institute, Distance Learning Division
Churchill Crt, 90 Kippington Rd, Sevenoaks, Kent TN13 2LL; Tel (01732) 450888; Fax (01732) 457062

• Cheltenham Tutorial College
451 High St, Cheltenham GL50 3HX; Tel (01242) 241279; Fax (01242) 234256
Director M.S. Rigby

• Civil Service Correspondence School
Ware, Herts SG12 9AD; Tel (01920) 465927; Fax (01920) 484909

College of Estate Management
Whiteknights, Reading, Berks RG6 2AW; Tel (01734) 861101; Fax (01734) 755344

The College of Law
Braboeuf Manor, St Catherines, Guildford, Surrey GU3 1HA; Tel (01483) 460200; Fax (01483) 460305

• College of Sales and Marketing
31 Upper George St, Luton, Beds LU1 2RD; Tel (01582) 411130; Fax (01582) 453640
Principal D. Waller, CInstSMM

Financial Training Ltd
151 Freston Rd, London W10 6TH; Tel 0171-792 3990; Fax 0171-792 9070

• Henley College Homestudy Unit
Henley College Coventry, Henley Rd, Bell Grn, Coventry CV2 1ED; Tel (01203) 611021

• The Horticultural Correspondence College
Little Notton Farmhouse, 16 Notton, Lacock, Chippenham, Wilts SN15 2NF; Tel (01249) 730326
Partner O.N. Menhinick, MHort(RHS), NDH(Hons), MSc, BA, MIHort

• Ideal Schools
60 St Enoch Sq, Glasgow G1 4AG; Tel 0141-248 5200

• ILEX Tutorial Services
Kempston Manor, Kempston, Bedford MK42 7AB; Tel (01234) 841010

Law and legal practice for the Institute of Legal Executives, Common Professional Examination, Law Society Finals, LLB, Council for Licensed Conveyancers and Crown Prosecution Service

• Institute of Chartered Shipbrokers–Tutorship
3 Grace Church St, London EC3V 0AT; Tel 0171-626 3058

• Institute of Counselling
15 Hope St, Glasgow G2 6AB; Tel 0141-204 2230

The Institute of Grocery Distribution
Grange La, Letchmore Heath, Watford, Herts WD2 8DQ; Tel (01923) 857141
Head of Business Training Marjorie Newton

• International Correspondence Schools
Intertect Hse, 8 Elliott Pl, Clydeway Centre, Glasgow G3 8EF; Tel 0141-221 2926

• International Graphoanalysis Society
Tutorial Section, Stonedge, Dunkerton, Bath BA2 8AS; Tel (01761) 437809; Fax (01761) 432572

• JEB Distance Learning
The Joint Examining Board, 30A Dyer St, Cirencester, Glos GL7 2PF; Tel (01285) 641747; Fax (01285) 650449

• London Montessori Centre
Correspondence Division, 18 Balderton St, London W1Y 1TG; Tel 0171-493 0165

Courses leading to a teaching diploma in Nursery Primary Special Needs Education and Montessori English Language

• London School of Journalism
22 Upbrook Mews, Bayswater, London W2 3HG; Tel 0171-706 3536
Director Heather Hopkins

• Maritime Studies Ltd
24A Bridge St, Carmarthen, Dyfed SA31 3JS; Tel (01267) 221752; Fax (01267) 221752
Principal Chris Corcoran

(Freepost Carmarthen SA31 3ZZ)

• May's Correspondence College
Cleveland Rd, London E18 2AF; Tel 0181-989 9726
Principal P.A. May

• Mercers College
Ware, Herts SG12 9AD; Tel (01920) 465926; Fax (01920) 484909

• Metropolitan School of Machine Knitting
Correspondence Division, The Pinfold, Poole, Nantwich, Cheshire CW5 6AL; Tel (01270) 628414

• Montessori St Nicholas Centre, Correspondence Division
23–24 Princes Gate, London SW7 1PT; Tel 071-225 1277

• National Extension College
18 Brooklands Ave, Cambridge CB2 2HN; Tel (01223) 316644; Fax (01223) 313586
Director Ros Morpeth

Distance learning courses in general education, learning skills, counselling skills, professional and vocational qualifications including Part 1 and Part 2 Examinations for The Engineering Council certificate in marketing and Advanced Certificate in Marketing; open learning resources including materials for NVQs in business administration, accountancy, marketing, caring and childcare; staff development and training resources; consultancy service

• National Marine Correspondence School
28 Hamilton St, Birkenhead, Merseyside L41 1AL; Tel 0151-647 6777; Fax 0151-647 6777
Principal Capt R.G. Morrison, Master Mariner, MRIN, MNI, MIMgt

• The National School of Salesmanship Concessionaires
Sevendale Hse, 7 Dale St, Manchester M1 1JB; Tel 0161-228 6733/14
Chairman E.H. Metcalfe
Director M.A. Metcalfe

• The Northern Institute of Massage/College of Physical Therapies
100 Waterloo Rd, Blackpool FY4 1AW; Tel (01253) 403548
Principal K. Woodward, FLCSP(Phys)

• The Northumbria School of Navigation
78 Stuart Ct, Kenton, Newcastle-upon-Tyne NE3 2SG; Tel 0191-271 4401

Open College of the Arts
Houndhill, Worsbrough, Barnsley S70 6TU; Tel (01226) 730495; Fax (01226) 730838

Open Learning Centre
Methodist Church, Room 501, 25 Marylebone Rd, London NW1 5JR; Tel 0171-486 5502

Over 50 distance learning courses on theological and religious studies subjects for individuals and groups with between 500 and 1,000 students per year.

Pitman Tutorial College
29 Waterloo Pl, Royal Leamington Spa CV32 5LA; Tel (01926) 332071; Fax (01929) 885881
Director M.S. Rigby

The College offers over 150 courses covering professional business, secretarial and leisure studies. It has over 3,500 students from the UK and Commonwealth

• The Rapid Results College
Tuition Hse, London SW19 4DS; Tel 0181-947 7272; Fax 0181-946 7584
Principal Andrew Young, BA, FCA

Courses for a wide variety of recognised examinations in Accountancy, Banking, Bookkeeping, Computing, Law, Safety and Health, Management, Marketing, A Levels and GCSEs

The RRC School for Writers
Tuition Hse, 27-37 St George's Rd, London SW19 4DS

• The School of Phytotherapy (Herbal Medicine)
Bucksteep Manor, Bodle St Grn, Hailsham, E. Sussex BN27 4RJ; Tel (01323) 833812; Fax (01323) 833869

Courses in herbal medicine (FT and correspondence)

Successful Writer School
303–305 Burdett Rd, London E14 7EL; Tel 0171-515 9168
Director of Studies A. Vale

• The Tiller School of Navigation, Sailing and Seamanship
50 Mercury Gdns, Hamble, Southampton SO31 4PA; Tel (01703) 453865

• Transport Tutorial Association
TTA, 80 Portland Pl, London W1N 4DP; Tel 0171-631 3833

• Transworld Education College
8 Elliot Pl, Clydeway Centre, Glasgow G3 8EF; Tel 0141-221 2926
Principal A. McKenzie, FCCA, ACMA

• UNISON Education and Training
1 Mabledon Pl, London WC1H 9AJ; Tel 0171-388 2366; Fax 0171-388 1968
Director of Education and Training Jim Sutherland

• Wheelhouse School of Navigation
Fleet Hse, 173 Haydons Rd, Wimbledon, London SW19 8TB; Tel 0181-545 0750
Principal M. Redway, MRIN, AMNI
Director of Studies Commander D.N.A. Cox

*** Wolsey Hall Oxford Ltd**
66 Banbury Rd, Oxford OX2 6PR; Tel (01865) 310310; Fax (01865) 310969
Marketing Director Jonathan Chalstrey, BA

• The Writers' Bureau
Sevendale Hse, 7 Dale St, Manchester M1 1JB; Tel 0161-228 2362

14 Examining Bodies Research and Advisory Bodies

Examining Bodies

General Certificate of Education

The Associated Examining Board
Secretary General to the Board J.A. Day, BA Stag Hill Hse, Guildford, Surrey GU2 5XJ; Tel (01483) 506506
Head of Bristol Office R.W. Gillingham 23–29 Marsh St, Bristol BS1 4BP; Tel (0117) 927 3434

University of Cambridge Local Examinations Syndicate
Chief Executive and Secretary General Dr M. Halstead, MA, CENg Syndicate Bldgs, 1 Hill Rd, Cambridge CB1 2EU; Tel (01223) 61111; Fax (01223) 460278

Northern Examinations and Assessment Board
Devas St, Manchester M15 6EX; Tel 0161-953 1180; Fax 0161-273 7572; 12 Harter St, Manchester M1 6HL; Tel 0161-953 1170; Fax 0161-953 1177
Chief Executive Kathleen Tattersall, BA, MEd

University of London Examinations and Assessment Council (ULEAC)
Chief Executive A. Smith, BA, DipEd, MA Stewart Hse, 32 Russell Square, London WC1B 5DN; Tel 0171-331 4000; Fax 0171-331 4044/4045

Oxford and Cambridge Schools Examination Board
Secretary-General Vacancy Purbeck Hse, Purbeck Rd, Cambridge CB2 2PU; Tel (01223) 411211
Secretary J.G. Lloyd, MA (Acting) Elsfield Way, Oxford OX2 8EP; Tel (01865) 54421

University of Oxford Delegacy of Local Examinations
Secretary James Pailing Delegacy of Local Examinations, Ewert Hse, Ewert Pl, Summertown, Oxford OX2 7BZ; Tel (01865) 54291

East Midlands Regional Examinations Board
Secretary D.J. Ramsden, OBE, BA, FRSA Robins Wood Hse, Robins Wood Rd, Aspley, Nottingham NG8 3NR

Welsh Joint Education Committee
Secretary Clayton Heycock, MA, MSc 245 Western Ave, Cardiff CF5 2YX; Tel (01222) 561231

General Certificate of Secondary Education

Joint Council for the GCSE

Chairman Dennis J. Hatfield, CBE
Secretary John A. Edmundson, OBE The Joint Council for the GCSE, 6th Fl, Netherton Hse, 23–29 Marsh St, Bristol BS1 4BP; Tel (0117) 921 4379; Fax (0117) 922 6700

The Joint Council for the GCSE was established in 1985. Its constituent members are the examining groups for the GCSE exam: Midland Examining Group (MEG); Northern Examinations and Assessment Board (NEAB); Northern Ireland Council for the Curriculum, Examination and Assessment (NICCEA); Southern Examining Group (SEG); University of London Examinations and Assessment Council (ULEAC) and Welsh Joint Education Committee (WJEC). The Joint Council is a central co-ordinating body which acts as a clearing-house for the exchange of information, as a forum for the discussion of matters of common interest and as the co-ordinator of the groups' activities for those matters on which the groups are expected to adopt uniform policies. The four examining groups in England are represented by six members with a further three nominated by WJEC and two by NISEAC

University of London Examinations and Assessment Council
A. Smith
Mrs J. Fisher
Dr A. Woodthorpe
Prof D. Lawton
M. Morris
Dr W. Roy, CBE

Midland Examining Group
Dr P.H. Andrews, CBE
Dr M.P. Halstead
Dr R.R. McLone
Dr S.G. Raban

Northern Examinations and Assessment Board
D. Battye
D.A. Bowers
K. Tattersall
Dr C.J. Gray

Southern Examining Group
Dr J.S. Rollett
A.S. Worrall, OBE
K.J. Shorey
W.S. Frearson
J.A. Day
J.C. Godwin

Welsh Joint Education Committee
M. Phillips
C. Heycock
Dr W.R. Lambert

Northern Ireland Schools Examination and Assessment Council
W.J. Caves
Prof D. Rea

Midland Examining Group

Chief Executive R.R. McLone, MA, PhD, FIMA Head Office, Syndicate Buildings, 1 Hills Rd, Cambridge CB1 2EU; Tel (01223) 61111; Fax (01223) 327904

The Midland Examining Group was reconstituted on 10 October 1993 as a part of the University of Cambridge Local Examinations Syndicate. The Group has five offices:

Head Office
Syndicate Buildings, 1 Hills Rd, Cambridge CB1 2EU; Tel (01223) 61111

East Midlands Office
Robins Wood Hse, Robins Wood Rd, Aspley, Nottingham NG8 3NR; Tel (0115) 929 6021

West Midlands Office
Mill Wharf, Mill St, Birmingham B6 4BU; Tel 0121-628 2000

Cambridge (OCSEB) Office
Purbeck Hse, Purbeck Rd, Cambridge CB2 2PU; Tel (01223) 411211

Oxford (OCSEB) Office
Elsfield Way, Oxford OX2 8EP; Tel (01865) 54421

Northern Examinations and Assessment Board

Devas St, Manchester M15 6EX; Tel 0161-953 1180; Fax 0161-273 7572; 12 Harter St, Manchester M1 6HL; Tel 0161-953 1170; Fax 0161-953 1177
Chief Executive Kathleen Tattersall, BA, MEd
Assistant Chief Executive Peter Dawson, BA
Assistant Chief Executive John D. Milner, MA, ACP
Assistant Chief Executive Margaret Hutchinson, MA
Assistant Chief Executive Heather James, MSc

Western District Officer Bernard Crooks, BA, MEd Orbit Hse, Albert St, Manchester M30 0WL; Tel 0161-953 1185; Fax 0161-953 1203
Northern District Officer Judith Besford, BA, MEd Wheatfield Rd, Westerhope, Newcastle upon Tyne NE5 5JZ; Tel 0191-201 0180; Fax 0191-271 3314
Eastern District Officer Hazel Adams, BA 31/33 Springfield Ave, Harrogate, N. Yorks HG1 2HW; Tel (01423) 840015; Fax (01423) 523678; Scarsdale Hse, Derbyshire La, Sheffield S8 8SE; Tel (0114) 282 0014; Fax (0114) 255 3750

Southern Examining Group

Central Administration Office, Stag Hill Hse, Guildford, Surrey GU2 5XJ; Tel (01483) 506506
Joint Secretary J.A. Day, BA
Joint Secretary J. Pailing, MA

Southern Examining Group is operated by the Associated Examining Board and Oxford School Examinations Board. The Group has four offices

Guildford Office,
Stag Hill Hse, Guildford, Surrey GU2 5XJ; Tel (01483) 506506

Oxford Office,
Ewert Hse, Ewert Pl, Summertown, Oxford OX2 7BZ; Tel (01865) 54291

Bristol Office,
23–29 Marsh St, Bristol BS1 4BP; Tel (0117) 927 3434

Eastleigh Office,
Unit 23, Monkbrook Ind Pk, Chandler's Ford, Southampton, Hants SO5 3RA; Tel (01703) 644811

University of London Examinations and Assessment Council (ULEAC)

Chief Executive A. Smith, BA, DipEd, MA

Welsh Joint Education Committee

Secretary Clayton Heycock, MA, MSc 245 Western Ave, Cardiff CF5 2YX; Tel (01222) 561231

Northern Ireland Schools Examinations and Assessment Council

See Other Examining Bodies–Northern Ireland

Other Examining Bodies

ARELS Examinations

University of Oxford Delagacy of Local Examinations, Ewert Pl, Summertown, Oxford OX2 7BZ; Tel (01865) 514272; Fax (01865) 510085
Director D.J. Malpass, BSc, FBIM

Associated Board of the Royal Schools of Music

(Royal Academy of Music, Royal College of Music, Royal Northern College of Music and Royal Scottish Academy of Music and Drama)
Chief Executive Richard Morris, MA 14 Bedford Sq, London WC1B 3JG; Tel 0171-636 5400; Fax 0171-436 4520

Business and Technology Education Council (BTEC)

Central Hse, Upper Woburn Pl, London WC1H 0HH; Tel 0171-413 8400; Fax 0171-387 6068
Chairman Sir Michael Lickiss
Chief Executive Dr Christina Townsend

BTEC approves vocational courses in a wide range of subjects throughout England, Wales and Northern Ireland. It awards qualifications to students who successfully complete these courses. BTEC is working with NCVQ to develop the GNVQ and NVQ framework of vocational qualifications

Central Council for Education and Training in Social Work

Derbyshire Hse, St Chad's St, London WC1H 8AD; Tel 0171-278 2455
Chairman Jeffrey Greenwood
Director Tony Hall

City and Guilds of London Institute

76 Portland Pl, London W1N 4AA; Tel 0171-278 2468
Director-General Dr N.A.D. Carey, PhD, MA

An assessment and awarding body operating nationally and internationally under the terms of a Royal Charter conferred in 1900

College of Preceptors

Academic and Membership Office, Coppice Row, Theydon Bois, Epping, Essex CM16 7DN; Tel (01992) 812727; Fax (01992) 814690

Common Entrance Examination to Independent Schools

Common Entrance Board, Jordan Hse, Christchurch Rd, New Milton, Hampshire BH25 6QJ; Tel (01425) 621111; Fax (01425) 620044
Administrator J. Williams

The Common Entrance Board sets examinations for entry to Senior Schools at 11+, 12+ and 13+. Examinations take place in autumn and spring terms for all three age groups and in June for 13+

Examinations take place in autumn and spring terms for all three age groups and in June for 13+

Council for Early Years Awards (CEYA)

8 Chequer St, St Albans, Herts AL1 3XZ; Tel (01727) 47636; Fax (01727) 867609
Director M. O'Hagan

English Speaking Board (International) Ltd

26A Princes St, Southport, Merseyside PR8 1EQ; Tel (01704) 501730
President Christabel Burniston, MBE

Joint Examining Board

Catteshall Manor, Godalming, Surrey GU7 1UU; Tel (01483) 415311; Fax (01483) 418019
Manager Mrs Pat Norman

Vocational Education Unit

46 Britannia St, London WC1X 9RG; Tel 0171-278 3344
Head of Education and Training Sue Fifer

CPVE, Foundation Programmes and Diploma of Vocational Education, all accredited by City and Guilds of London Institute

The London Chamber of Commerce and Industry Examinations Board

Chief Executive Liam Swords Marlowe Hse, Station Rd, Sidcup, Kent DA15 7BJ; Tel 0181-302 0261; Fax 0181-302 4169

National Examining Board for Supervisory Management

76 Portland Pl, London W1N 4AA; Tel 0171-278 2468
Chief Executive Dr Philip Riseborough

Council for Awards in Children's Care and Education (CACHE)

Chief Executive Dr R.C. Dorrance, 8 Chequer St St Albans, Herts, AL1 3XZ, (0727) 847636; Tel (01727) 867609

Pitman Examinations Institute

Catteshall Manor, Godalming, Surrey GU7 1UU; Tel (01483) 415311; Fax (01483) 860435

Regional Advisory Councils for Further Education

see Chapter 12

RSA Examinations Board

Chief Executive Martin F. Cross, MA, FCIS, FIPM, MIMgt
Assistant Company Secretary C. Miles Westwood Way, Coventry CV4 8HS; Tel (01203) 470033; Fax (01203) 468080

Scotland

Scottish Examination Board, Ironmills Rd, Dalkeith, Midlothian EH22 1LE; Tel 0131-663 6601; Fax 0131-654 2664

Northern Ireland

Northern Ireland Schools Examinations and Assessment Council, Beechill Hse, Beechill Rd, Belfast BT8 4RS; Tel (01232) 704666; Fax (01232) 799913
Chief Executive W.J. Caves, BA, MEd
Deputy Chief Executive S.W.W. Mercer, MA

In April 1994, the Northern Ireland Schools Examinations and Assessment Council will amalgamate with the Northern Ireland Curriculum Council (NICC) to form the Northern Ireland Council for the Curriculum, Examinations and Assessment (NICCEA). For further information please contact the Information Officer at NICC Tel: (01232) 381414

Research and Advisory Bodies

Council for the Accreditation of Teacher Education

Elizabeth Hse, York Rd, London SE1 7PH; Tel 0171-934 0946
Chairman Prof Sir William Taylor, CBE
Secretary S.G. Murton, MA, DipEd

The Government's decision to reconstitute CATE was announced on 10 November 1989, in DES Circular 24/89. The Council's terms of reference are: to advise the Secretaries of State for Education and Science, Wales and Northern Ireland on whether individual courses of initial teacher training meet the criteria for course approval; to monitor approved courses to ensure that they continue to meet the criteria; to identify and disseminate good practice in initial teacher training; to keep the criteria for course approval under review and to advise the Secretaries of State on possible changes to them; and to advise the Secretaries of State as requested on other matters relating to initial teacher training

Grant Maintained Schools Centre (GMSC)

Wesley Crt, 4A Priory Rd, High Wycombe, Bucks HP13 6SE; Tel (01494) 474470; Fax (01494) 474480
Managing Director Adrian Pritchard

The centre provides advice and information to and about grant maintained schools, each of which is a separate incorporated body and may be approached individually

Grant Maintained Schools Foundation (GMSF)

36 Great Smith St, London SW1P 3BU
Chairman Sir Robert Balchin
President The Earl of Ilchester
Secretary Adrian Pritchard

To assist grant maintained and charitable schools. Charity Registration No 1000569

Independent Appeals Authority for School Examinations (IAASE)

Newcombe Hse, 45 Notting Hill Gate, London W11 3JB; Tel 0171-243 9245; Fax 0171-221 2141
Chairman Lady Anson, DL, JP
Deputy Chairman J.M. Edwards, CBE, QC
Secretary B.C. Arthur, CBE
Functions The IAASE seeks to ensure that those using the examination system can have confidence that the grades awarded are as fair as possible. It considers whether an examination body's procedures were appropriate and properly applied. It has powers to require an examination body to reconsider a case and to make recommendations

Institute for Schools and College Governors (ISCG)

at Avondale Pk School, Sirdar Rd, London W11 4EE; Tel 0171-229 0200; Fax 0171-229 0651
Director Margaret Jones
Director Margaret Riddell
Director Felicity Taylor

Free advice line. Advice, information, support and training conferences, conventions and services for school and college governors

National Council for Vocational Qualifications

222 Euston Rd, London NW1 2BZ; Tel 0171-387 9898; Fax 0171-387 0978
Chairman Michael Heron
Chief Executive John Hillier

The National Council for Vocational Qualifications provides the framework of National Vocational Qualifications (NVQs) through which everyone at work can be assessed against national agreed standards. NCVQ also offers vocational education through General National Vocational Qualifications (GNVQs). Through its accreditation and monitoring procedures, NCVQ sets the seal on the standards established for occupations. As a result, NVQs and GNVQs are recognised as hallmarks of achievement within each sector, ensuring that employees at every level can gain the recognition they need for a successful and fulfilling career – and can transfer skills to new jobs; The NVQ framework is helping to meet the need for a more skilled and qualified workforce
Members *Senior Lecturer in Political Science, London School of Economics and Political Science* John Barnes
Principal, Exeter College Dr John Capey, OBE
Vice-Chancellor, Nottingham Trent University Professor Raymond Cowell
Chairman, Somerset TEC David Gwyther
Managing Director, Rolls Royce Motor Cars Peter Hill
Chief Executive, NCVQ John Hillier
Managing Director, Prudence Leith Ltd Prudence Leith, OBE
Managing Director, Shotton Paper Company Ltd Kevin Lyden
General Secretary, Banking and Insurance Finance Union Leif Mills
Chairman of Training and Employment Agency (Northern Ireland) and Chairman, Richardsons Fertilisers Ltd Dr John Spence, OBE
Director, Professional Standards and Development Directorate, Law Society John Randall

Principal, Lewisham College Ruth Silver
Managing Director, Mathiesons Family Bakers George Stevenson

School Curriculum and Assessment Authority (SCAA)

The School Curriculum and Assessment Authority (SCAA) was established under the Education Act, 1993 and assumed its responsibilities on 1 October 1993. It replaces the National Curriculum Council (NCC) and the School Examinations and Assessment Council (SEAC). Its main functions are to keep under review all aspects of the curriculum for maintained schools in England and all aspects of school examinations and assessment, and to advise the Secretary of State on these curriculum examinations and assessment matters. SCAA also publishes and disseminates information relating to the curriculum, examinations and assessment, and is responsible for making the necessary arrangements for school-based assessments. Publications include the National Curriculum subject Orders, test materials and non-statutory guidance material. SCAA has a Customer Services Section which deals with orders for publications and enquiries from teachers, governors and parents

Newcombe Hse, 45 Notting Hill Gate, London W11 3JB; Tel 0171-229 1234; Fax 0171-229 8526
Chairman Sir Ron Dearing, CB
Chief Executive Dr Nick Tate
Senior Manager Responsible for Key Stage 1 Judith Morris
Senior Manager Responsible for Key Stage 2 Chris Jones
Senior Manager Responsible for Key Stage 3 John Hamer (Acting)
Senior Manager Responsible for Key Stage 4 Keith Weller
Senior Manager Responsible for 16–19 Education Geoff Lucas
Senior Manager Responsible for Communications Tony Millns
Senior Manager Responsible for Finance and Personnel Bill Scott

Scottish Consultative Council on the Curriculum (Scottish CCC)

Gardyne Rd, Dundee DD5 1NY; Tel (01382) 455053; Fax (01382) 455046

Policy HQ
17 St John St, Edinburgh EH8 8DG; Tel 0131-557 4888; Fax 0131-557 2085
Chief Executive Cameron Harrison
Director, Policy and Administration Donald C. Fraser
Director, Curriculum and Development Ian Barr
Director, Development andf Design Sandy Sloss
Director, Information and Marketing Services Herbert Hayes

The Scottish Consultative Council on the Curriculum is a company limited by guarantee with the following functions: to offer advice to the Secretary of State on matters affecting the school curriculum; to issue curricular guidance to local authorities and schools; to undertake programmes of curricular development. Members of Council, who are non-representative, are invited on the basis of individual merit to serve for three offices, two as above and a third at 74 Southbrae Dr, Glasgow G13 1SU; Tel 041-950 3175; Fax 041-950 3428

Council of SCCC 1991–1994

Chairman Neil Galbraith, Director of Education Western Isles Council
Members *Education Adviser, Lothian Region* May Barclay
Education Adviser, Grampian Region Elizabeth McGill
Headteacher, Our Holy Redeemer's Primary School, Clydebank Anna Smith
Headteacher, St Ninian's High School, Eastwood James McVittie
Headteacher, Forres Academy Alistair MacLachlan
Headteacher, Daniel Stewart's and Melville College, Edinburgh Patrick Tobin
Principal, St Andrew's College of Education, Glasgow Bart McGettrick
Principal, Glenrothes College of Further Education Thom Burness
Department of Sociology, Edinburgh University; Dr Ruth Jonathan
Head of Educational Research, Northern College of Education, Aberdeen Professor Mary Simpson
Personnel Director, John Brown Engineering Ltd Richard Cummings
Chairman, Balerno High School Board Dr Richard Dennis
Parent, Dumfries and Galloway Margaret Gladstone
Depute Director of Education, Grampian Region Hamish Ross
Assessors Scottish Office Education Department; J.W.L. Lornie
HM Depute Senior Chief Inspector of Schools D.W. Mack
Scottish Office Education Department; H. Robertson

Other Research Organisations

British Educational Research Association

Administrative Secretary Anne-Marie Beaucolin BERA Office, c/o SCRE, 15 St John St, Edinburgh EH8 8JR; Tel 0131-557 2944; Fax 0131-556 9454

Centre for Information on Language Teaching and Research

20 Bedfordbury, Covent Gdn, London WC2N 4LB; Tel General enquiries, conferences and publications 0171-379 5101; information and Teacher Resources Library 0171-379 5110; Fax 0171-379 5082
Director Dr L. King
PR Officer Gill Tench

Centre for Institutional Studies

University of East London, Maryland Hse, Manbey Park Rd, Stratford, London E15 1EY; Tel 0181-849 3670; Fax 0181-849 3678
Director Prof John Pratt

CIS undertakes research studies and consultancy into public policy and public institutions, specialising in education in the UK and overseas countries, and in voluntary organisations. It also offers tailor made training programmes

Centre for Research on Learning and Instruction

University of Edinburgh, 12 Buccleuch Pl, Edinburgh EH8 9JT; Tel 0131-650 4323
Director Prof N.J. Entwistle

Research into teaching methods and learning particularly in higher education and professional education. Includes the Godfrey Thomson Unit for Educational Assessment, which develops tests and assessment procedures for use in schools

Centre for the Study of Comprehensive Schools

The Queens Bldg, University of Leicester, Barrack Rd, Northampton NN2 6AF; Tel (01604) 24969/36326

Aims to promote the success of comprehensive schools by publications, research, and sharing of interesting practice with others

Centre for the Study of Education and Training (CSET)

University of Lancaster, Cartmel College, Lancaster LA1 4YL; Tel (01524) 592679; Fax (01524) 844788
Director Dr Murray Saunders

Community Education Development Centre

Lyng Hall, Blackberry La, Coventry CV2 3JS; Tel (01203) 638660; Fax (01203) 681161
Director John Rennie

CEDC is based in Coventry but works nationwide and internationally to promote and develop community education, providing training programmes, consultancy, resources, support and advice, and carrying out innovative projects. CEDC helps to form links between community education workers and encourages the exchange of ideas and good practice through a variety of approaches including its publication *Network* and its National School and Community Network

CEDC's programme areas are: *Family Education* which includes linking home and school, health education issues and responding to child abuse; *Enterprise Development* which includes promoting enterprise development in education, stimulating cross-sector collaboration and supporting enterprise in the community; *Training* which includes management development, whole-school training and award bearing courses

Community and Mental Handicap Educational and Research Association

2 Eastbourne Rd, Trowbridge, Wilts BA14 7HN; Tel (01225) 753984
Director Paul Williams

CMH, the Campaign for People with Mental Handicaps, was set up in 1971 as a pressure group, working for the rights of people with learning disabilities. In 1979 the CMH 'Educational and Research Association' registered as a charity. Its workshops focus on the new ideas about the position of people with learning disabilities in society and the effects these ideas have on service provision. The association works with social services departments, health departments, voluntary organisations, and people with learning disabilities themselves, their parents and friends

Curriculum Council for Wales (CCW)

Castle Bldgs, Womanby St, Cardiff CF1 9SX; Tel (01222) 344946; Fax (01222) 343612
Chairman Rudi Plaut
Vice-Chairman Ieuan Price
Chief Executive Bernard Jones

Independent advisory body appointed by the Secretary of State for Wales to offer professional advice on the curriculum for schools in Wales. Established in August 1988 under the Education Reform Act

Its fourteen members have a wide range of educational experience and knowledge. The Council meetings are conducted bilingually, and there is a bilingual publication policy

The Curriculum Council for Wales is reponsible for keeping all aspects of the curriculum for maintained schools under review; for advising the Secretary of State for Wales on programmes of research and development; for publishing and disseminating information relating to the Curriculum. The Curriculum Council for Wales works very closely with the teaching profession in Wales, and in collaboration with the School Curriculum and Assessment Authority (SCAA)

On 1 April 1994, the Curriculum Council for Wales will become the Curriculum and Assessment Authority for Wales, known by its Welsh acronym ACAC. Its remit will be extended to include some responsibilities for assessment and the Welsh language. The Chairman will continue to be Rudi Plaut. The Deputy Chairman has been named as M.J.F. Wynn, and the new Chief Executive will be John Valentine Williams

Department of Cultural Studies

Faculty of Commerce and Social Science, The University of Birmingham, Edgbaston, Birmingham B15 2TT; Tel 0121-414 6060; Fax 0121-414 6061
Head Michael Green

European Institute of Education and Social Policy

Université de Paris IX-Dauphine, Place du Maréchal de Lattre de Tassigny, F-75116 Paris, France; Tel (33-1) 44 015 40 06; Fax (33-1) 44 015 45 26
Director J.P. Jallade
European Journal of Education (quarterly, Carfax Publishing Co)

Further Education Research Association

City and Guilds, 1 Giltspur St, London EC1A 9HB; Tel 0171-278 2468
Chairmanship floating among members of Management Committee

Further Education Research Network

FERN Centre, Leicester Polytechnic, Scraptoft Campus, Scraptoft, Leicester LE7 9SU; Tel (0116) 243 1011
Co-ordinator David G. Rogers

FERN is an independent, self-financing charity, established and organised by teachers seeking to equip themselves with the knowledge and techniques relevant to contemporary changes in further and higher education. Membership is available to all teachers in further and higher education and the Network is administered by an annually elected executive committee

FERN supports a wide variety of investigations initiated by members, and current research projects include the development of new teaching materials, textbook readability studies and the analysis of classroom interaction. Members receive the *FERN Journal,* published twice a year, and a *FERN Newsletter* three times a year. Libraries and other organisations may subscribe to these publications

The Grubb Institute

Cloudesley St, London N1 0HU; Tel 0171-278 8061; Fax 0171-278 0728
Chairman of the Council M.V. Murphy
Research and Advisory Staff D. Armstrong, J. Bazalgette, J. Hutton, C. Quine

Aims to identify, interpret and work at the organisational pressure points of society. Its staff have particular experience in the field of management and leadership of education in schools, colleges and other human service institutions. They focus on professional and management practice, through advisory work, research and training

Institute of Community Studies

18 Victoria Park Sq, Bethnal Grn, London E2 9PF; Tel 0181-980 6263
Director Michael Young, MA, PhD
Deputy Director Tony Flower, MA, PhD

National Children's Bureau

8 Wakley St, London EC1V 7QE; Tel 0171-836 6000; Fax 0171-278 9512
President The Baroness Faithfull, OBE
Vice-President Joan D. Cooper, CB, BA
Vice-President Lady Callaghan
Vice-Chair Martyn Long, CBE, DL
Chair Barbara Kahan, OBE
Director John Rea Price
Honorary Treasurer Rev Dr Gordon Barritt, OBE
Secretary Anne Weyman, BSc(Soc), FCA

National Foundation for Educational Research in England and Wales

The Mere, Upton Pk, Slough, Berks SL1 2DQ; Tel (01753) 574123; Fax (01753) 691632
President Sir James Hamilton, KCB, MBE
Vice-President Sir Edward Britton, CBE, MA, DEd, FCP, HonFEIS
Vice-President A.W.S. Hutchings, CBE, MA, FEIS, FCP
Vice-President J.E.L. Baird, OBE, MA, FEIS
Chairman of Foundation and of Foundation's Council The Lord Peston
Vice-Chairman of Council N. Harrison, CBE, FCP
Honorary Treasurer R.D.C. Bunker, MA
Director S. Hegarty, BSc, HDipEd, PhD

Education Management Information Exchange (EMIE)

Service Head V. Gee
Senior Information Officer J.L. Griffiths
Senior Information Officer J. Loose
Information Officer S. Woolmer

EMIE is an information service designed primarily for education officers and advisers of Local Education Authorities in England, Wales and Northern Ireland. It was launched as a sponsored research project in 1981. This service is now financed by the local authority associations and NFER and is sponsored by the Society of Education Officers and the National Association of Inspectors, Educational Advisers and Consultants. The Information service is a collaborative enterprise involving LEAs as the main contributors and users

Education Policy Information Centre (EPIC Europe)

National Foundation for Educational Research, The Mere, Upton Park, Slough SL1 2DQ; Tel (01753) 574123; Fax (01753) 691632
Head Dr J.P. Le Métais
Senior Information Officer Dr H. Hayes
Senior Information Officer Ms G. Holt
Information Officer Barbara Dickinson

EPIC Europe is the official link for England, Wales and Northern Ireland to the EURYDICE education policy information network of the European Union. It provides information on education policy issues to LEA education officers and central government staff and to their counterparts in the Member States of the European Union

See Chapter 24

National Primary Centre

National Primary Centre, Westminster College, Oxford OX2 9AT; Tel (01865) 245242
National Director Dr D.R. Winkley

Northern Ireland Council for the Curriculum, Examinations and Assessment (CCEA)

Beechill Hse, 42 Beechill Rd, Belfast BT8 4RS; Tel (01232) 704666; Fax (01232) 799913
Chairman Professor D. Reo
Chief Executive C.M. Coxhead
Deputy Chief Executive W.J. Caves

CCEA was established on 1 April 1994, subsuming the functions previously exercised by the Northern Ireland Curriculum Council (NICC) and the Northern Ireland Schools Examinations and Assessment Council (NISEAC). The role of CCEA is to: keep all aspects of the curriculum, examinations and assessment under review; advise the Department of Education for Northern Ireland (DENI); publish and disseminate curriculum, examinations and assessment materials; conduct and award certificates for examinations; conduct the moderation of relevant examinations and assessments; ensure that standards of the relevant examinations and assessments are recognised and maintained; carry out other activities as directed by the Department of Education for Northern Ireland. The Council works closely with other partners in the education service in Northern Ireland and takes account of the effect of its work on teachers and pupils so that it may ensure that its services are helpful and supportive. For further information please contact the Information Officer at the above number

The Nuffield Foundation

28 Bedford Sq, London WC1B 3EG; Tel 0171-631 0566
Chairman of the Managing Trustees The Rt Hon Lord Flowers, FRS
Director R.J.D. Hazell

Policy Studies Institute

100 Park Village East, London NW1 3SR; Tel 0171-387 2171
Chairman Sir Leonard Peach
Director Pamela Meadows

Public Finance Foundation

CIPFA, 3 Robert St, London WC2N 6BH; Tel 0171-895 8823
Secretary Martin Evans
Administration Manager Judith Sutcliffe
Research Director Chris Trinder

The Public Finance Foundation is the independent research arm of CIPFA – the Chartered Institute of Public Finance and Accountancy. The Foundation provides an impartial forum for debate and the exchange of ideas on public expenditure and related aspects of public finance, and on the management and administration of public services. It aims to promote objective and authoritative analysis and comment on these issues, drawing both on the work of the academic research community and on the practical knowledge and experience of senior financial and general managers from across the public sector

In pursuing this aim, the Foundation: undertakes or commissions original research; disseminates the results of its own or others' research through: a range of publications, and, the Foundation's quarterly journal, *'Public Money and Management'*; and organises conferences, seminars and lectures to promote discussion of topical issues and developments

SISCON Project (Science in a Social Context)

The Combined Studies Centre, Faculty of Science, University of Leeds, Leeds LS2 9JT; Tel (01132) 751618; Fax (01132) 332689; Telex 557939
Project Co-ordinator Dr W.F. Williams

Scottish Council for Research in Education

15 St. John St, Edinburgh EH8 8JR; Tel 0131-557 2944; Fax 0131-556 9454
Chairman Prof Alistair MacFarlane, CBE, FRS, FEng, FRSE
Director Prof Wynne Harlen, OBE, BA, MA, MA(Ed), PhD

Society for Research into Higher Education

President Sir H. Bondi
Chairman Prof John Sizer
Director (SRHE) Cynthia Iliffe, SRHE 344–354 Grays Inn Rd, London WC1X 8BP; Tel 0171-837 7880; Fax 0171-713 0609

Standing Committee for the Education and Training of Teachers (SCETT)

27 Britannia St, London WC1X 9JP; Tel 0171-837 3636; Fax 0171-837 4403
Academic Secretary R. Beardsworth
Chair D. Rivalland
Ex-Chairman Alan John
Honorary Treasurer M. Carney
Office Secretary P.A. Maile

Founded with DES support in 1981 to co-ordinate teacher training organisations and higher educational establishments with responsibility for teacher training

The Committee includes in its membership the representative bodies for teacher education including the major teacher associations, universities and colleges

The Tavistock Institute

30 Tabernacle St, London EC2A 4DE; Tel 0171-417 0407; Fax 0171-417 0566
Secretary Neil Barnes

Universities Council for the Education of Teachers (UCET)

58 Gordon Sq, London WC1H 0NT; Tel 0171-580 8000; Fax 0171-323 0577
Chair Professor A. Edwards
Chair Professor J. Latto
Treasurer H.W. Bradley
Academic Secretary Professor P.H.J.H. Gosden
Secretary M.J. Russell

All universities with courses in education are members of UCET. UCET acts as a national forum for discussion of all matters relating to the education of teachers and the study of education in universities

UCET has 7 Standing Committees, an Executive Committee and a Governing Council; chairs of the Standing Committees are appointed annually; the Chair of UCET is Chair of the Executive Committee

World Association for Educational Research

Secretary General Rijksuniversiteit Gent, Pedagogish Laboratorium, Henri Dunantlaan 1, B-9000 Gent, Belgium; Tel 091/25.41.00
Secretary General Professor Dr M.-L. van Herreweghe
President Professor Dr M. Cipro

Research Councils

Biotechnology and Biological Sciences Research Council

Polaris Hse, North Star Ave, Swindon, Wilts SN2 1UH; Tel (01793) 413200; Fax (01793) 413201
Chairman Sir Alistair Grant
Deputy Chairman and Chief Executive Professor T.L. Blundell, FRS

Aims to promote and support high-quality basic, strategic and applied research, and related postgraduate training in biological systems with the aim of enhancing the management of biological resources and their utilisation and interactions with the environment, placing special emphasis on meeting the needs of users of its research and training output, thereby enhancing the UK's industrial competitiveness and quality of life. The user communities of the Council include: the agricultural, food, biotechnology, pharmaceutical, chemical and health-care industries, together with universities and Government

Economic and Social Research Council (ESRC)

Polaris Hse, North Star Ave, Swindon SN2 1UJ; Tel (01793) 413000; Fax (01793) 413001
Chairman Professor Howard Newby
Secretary William Solesbury

The ESRC is the UK's leading research agency for the social sciences. It is an independent organisation, established by Royal Charter in 1965, and funded mainly by the Government

The ESRC's main aim is to enable Government, business and the public to find out more about social and economic change and the reasons behind it. Subject areas supported by the ESRC include: economics, education, environment and planning, industry, information technology, management, politics, psychology and sociology. The ESRC also makes grants to students for postgraduate instruction in the social sciences

Medical Research Council

20 Park Cres, London W1N 4AL; Tel 0171-636 5422; Fax 0171-436 6179; Telex 24897 MRCHQ G
Chairman Sir David Plastow
Secretary Dr D.A. Rees, FRS

Natural Environment Research Council

Polaris Hse, North Star Ave, Swindon SN2 1EU; Tel (01793) 411500; Fax (01793) 411501
Chairman Robert Malpas
Chief Executive Prof John Krebs

Science and Engineering Research Council (SERC)

Polaris Hse, North Star Ave, Swindon SN2 1ET; Tel (01793) 411000
Chairman Sir Mark Richmond
Director Council Policy and Administration and Secretary to Council J.R. Merchant

The primary purpose of the SERC is to sustain standards of UK postgraduate education and research in such fields as: applied sciences and engineering, astronomy, biological sciences, chemistry, mathematics, physics and nuclear physics. It uses its funds (about £450 million per annum from the national Science Budget, which it receives through the Department of Education and Science) to make grants to university and polytechnic research groups; to award postgraduate studentships and fellowships; to provide national research facilities for academic researchers either at its own establishments or through international collaboration on such projects as satellites, telescopes and particle accelerators; and for the promotion of co-operation between the academic community and industry

SCET (Scottish Council for Educational Technology)

74 Victoria Rd, Glasgow G12 9JN; Tel 0141-337 5000; Fax 0141-337 5050
Chief Executive Nigel Paine

SCET is an advisory, research and development organisation, involved in evaluating the applications of technology in learning. Our role is to enhance the quality of education and training in Scotland—helping people to learn more effectively by making use of today's technology

15 Education Consultants

The Society of Education Consultants

Bartholomew Hse, 178 Beechwood Ave, Earlsdon, Coventry CV5 6PW; Tel (01203) 673765; Fax (01203) 717576

Chairman Molly Hattersley
Secretary Phillipa Cordingley
Assistant Secretary Margaret Spurr
Treasurer Derek Foreman
Committee Angela Brushett
Committee Joan Greenfield
Committee Alan Groves
Committee John Hart
Committee Peter Howlett
Committee Bridget Lawson
Committee John Webb
Observer David Phillips

Bernard Charles Abrams

37 Riverview Way, Cheltenham, Glos GL51 0AF; Tel (01242) 511 689; Fax (01242) 511 689

Undertakes consultancy in the areas of school management systems (school development planning, curriculum information management, project management including new schools, and quality assurance/inspection) and personnel (recruitment procedures, school-centred initial training, induction and appraisal). Recent assignments in these areas cover international consultancy, UK government agency work, conferencing, INSET, and advising governors and senior management

Elizabeth Adams

29 Woodside Hse, Wimbledon, London SW19 7QN; Tel 0181-946 5524

Innovator in records of achievement, in-service education and professional development. Consultancies in USA, Australia, Afghanistan, Mauritius. Former general inspector of education in Surrey. Fellow of University of East London

Geoffrey Adkins

Geoffrey Adkins Education Consultancy, 8 Greig Cl, Hornsey, London N8 8PB; Tel 0181-340 0008

Adult and Continuing Education; community development through education; evaluation of community education programmes; European co-operation in community education. Intended clients are colleges, schools and LEAs, and also professional bodies, companies and charitable organisations wishing to develop educational programmes. Geoffrey Adkins has 25 years experience in managing continuing and community education. Former Principal of a major London Community College

Ivan Andrew

Andrew Consultant Trainer, 55 Patrick Way, Aylesbury, Bucks HP21 9XJ; Tel (01296) 83612

Former Area Education Manager for Bucks County Council and Secondary Headteacher. Wide experience in education management, organisation and administration; introducing educational change; classroom management techniques and governor development. Special interests are governor/staff joint development and training, the self-managing school, appraisal, education industry links and team development. OFSTED accredited inspector. Consultant/clerk to two schools. Experienced presenter on issues relating to governing and managing schools

Wendy Josephine Ashby

24 Noble Corner, Great West Rd, Hounslow, Middx TW5 0PA; Tel 0181-570 6843

Extensive teaching and management experience in independent and LEA schools; advisory work; curriculum; mathematical education. Current involvement includes OFSTED (secondary) inspection and Investment in People initiative. Strong specialisms in small schools, girls' education and development of children of all abilities

Michael Aston

8 Causeway Cl, Potters Bar, Herts EN6 5HW; Tel (01707) 658644; Fax (01707) 273684

Independent advice and consultancy on the use of new technologies in teaching and learning. Experienced in policy development, strategy implementation, specification, teacher training, IT audits, inspection and evaluation. Work already undertaken has included schools in the UK and overseas, Education Ministries in Belgium, Finland, Mauritius and the Middle East and a major evaluation for the Nordic Council of Ministers

John Beardsmore

MSS Associates, 48 Dornden Dr, Langton Grn, Tunbridge Wells, Kent TN3 OAF; Tel (01892) 863532

Formerly Principal Inspector, Bexley and Senior Associate, School Management South; recent involvement with SMTF Training Materials Project. Current involvement includes headteacher appraisal; school focussed management development; appraisal training; school inspection (modern languages and management issues)

Gordon Bell

77 Galleywood Rd, Great Baddow, Chelmsford, Essex CM2 8DN; Tel (01245) 478487

School and college governance; asset management; further education strategic planning; financial management; National Education and training targets

Mervyn Benford

In Education, Cloudshill Cottage, High St, Shutford, Banbury OX15 6HE; Tel (01295) 780308; Fax (01295) 780308

Former teacher, headteacher, advisory headteacher, LEA inspector: primary and secondary expertise; curriculum, organisation, teaching methods; project evaluation; management, school and staff development; long experience of providing INSET at home and abroad; including conferences. Strong specialisms in small schools, education abroad, home and school partnership; freelance broadcaster and writer. All aspects of quality assurance; registered inspector (primary)

David Berrisford

PDC, The Hucclecote Centre, Churchdown La, Gloucester GL3 3QN; Tel (01452) 623068; Fax (01452) 623037

Founded The Professional Development Consultancy in 1991 – interested in training and consultancy in schools and colleges. Client list includes schools throughout the UK and a number of LEAs. Currently advising schools in Russia on Management of Teaching and Learning. The PDC has recently expanded to include Training and Consultancy in other public service areas. OFSTED trained consultants

Jim Bolton

8 Fairfield Cl, Nafferton, Driffield, North Humberside YO25 OJH; Tel (01377) 254404

Former LEA deputy, specialising in employment issues and practice, also appointment processes, governors' training. Policy and implementation aspects of restructuring at institution and LEA levels. Current work includes ATL, Hull University Adult Education Department, Fellow in continuing, vocational education, contributor to post-graduate programmes and International consultancy. Also diocesan body work and District Council adviser

Chris Boothroyd

25 Townsend Cres, Kirkhill, Morpeth, Northumberland NE61 2XP; Tel (01670) 513979

Formerly director Northumberland Supported Self-study Unit (oral evidence to the National Commission on Education); experienced secondary deputy head, English teacher and senior examiner for IB. Particular interest in effective, self-driven learning. Post-16 help and support through consultancy and courses for schools, FE and HE, in the following: learning and teaching methods, preparing student materials, post-16 curriculum issues and course provision, GNVQ management, teaching and assessment, effective organisation of sixth forms, including (with Newcastle University) use of ALIS

Jenny Borsberry

JSB Bursar Services, 21 Brecklands, Mundford, Thetford, Norfolk IP26 5EF; Tel (01842) 878672

JSB Bursar Services provides a range of Bursar and Education services both to GM and LMS schools, including financial management, clerking, personnel services, training for Governors and school administrative staff. Provides advice and practical assistance to schools wishing to become grant-maintained, as well as organising conferences and training sessions for education establishments

Bill Boyle

25 Covertside, Grange, West Kirby, Wirral L48 9UD; Tel 0151-625 8159/0161-275 3418; Fax 0161-275 3552/0151-625 8159

Managing consultant Centre for Formative Assessment Studies (CFAS), School of Education, University of Manchester. Former primary advisory service, Wirral LEA; Multicultural advisory teacher. Production Manager STAIR KS1 SAT development consortium (1988-90). Contributor/editor SEAC guide to Teacher Assessment (1989). National Curriculum geography specialist: Project Manager Geography KS1 and KS3 Assessment Projects (SEAC 1991–93). Author of Sunshine Geography (KS1) and consultant at KS2 for Heinemann Educational. Project Manager KS1 Maths, English Assessment Projects (NISEAC 1993), KS3 Science Assessment Project (NISEAC 1993–94) and KS3 mathematics and science (NICCEA 1994–95). National Curriculum assessment specialist

Geoffrey Boys

East Ashling Hse, Sandy La, East Ashling, Chichester, W Sussex PO18 9AT; Tel (01243) 575786

Former HMI. OFSTED Inspection of schools. Mathematics education, information technology and general secondary matters. Main consultancies: DES school visiting and report writing, Mathematical Association (INSET field officer), Daily Telegraph Good Schools' Guide and publisher advice

David Bradshaw

5 Trippet Ct, Graham Rd, Sheffield S10 3DY; Tel (0114) 230 4340

Main supporting experience lies in management of colleges (principal for nineteen years), analysis of policy (Secretary of ACFHE 1983–88), writing on education and editing. Leading consultancy areas: institutional policy formation and planning, team building, development of core skills through the curriculum process, developing writing skills

Violet Brand

The Stables, Grace's Maltings, Tring, Herts HP23 6DL; Tel (01442) 823243

15 Education Consultants

Specific learning difficulties; adult literacy; underachievement; in-service teacher training. Advisory work – LEAs, colleges, parents and teachers. Member BDA Education and Training Committee and Joint Chairman Music and Dyslexia Committee. Chief Assessor RSA Diploma course

Suzanne Briggs

Lynsted, Clandon Rd, West Clandon, Guildford GU4 7UW; Tel (01483) 222411; Fax (01483) 222411
Specialist knowledge SPLD/Dyslexia, RSA tutor Dip/Cert courses: advisory work LEAs, schools, teachers, parents, all levels of education. Practical workshops, lectures, INSET. Education Consultant to the British Dyslexia Association. Lectured/worked in Pakistan, Italy, Mexico, New Zealand, Australia, S. Africa. Interested in computers in education. Co-editor of the "Hickey Multi-Sensory Language Course" – 2nd edition

William Edgeley Brown

8 Dawn Gdns, Sleepers Hill, Winchester, Hampshire SO22 4NS; Tel (01962) 855527
Education/Management Consultant and Publisher whose interests include: business plans for independent schools, whole school development plans, the management of change, team building, special educational needs including dyslexia, child care in boarding schools, leadership in outdoor education, advice on choosing an independent school. Clients include Which School Limited, Youth Corporation Limited and KGH Computing Solutions. Formerly lecturer in higher education and headmaster of maintained and independent boarding/day schools

Angela Brushett

SchoolSearch NorthWest (Angela Brushett Associates), Ashberry Hse, 41 New Hall La, Bolton BL1 5LW; Tel (01204) 492147; Fax (01204) 840243
(Committee 1993 and 1994/95)
An independent, young and expanding company, specialising in Organisation and Education Management development and training in Secondary schools, for educators and for women in management. Other areas of consultancy: Relocation and School Transfer advice, Education and Outplacement counselling, Public Speaking, Book Reviews. Angela Brushett is an OFSTED Inspector of Schools: School Management, English, Equal Opportunities

Donald G Buckland

6 Dower Hse Cres, Southborough, Tunbridge Wells, Kent TN4 OTS; Tel (01892) 529944; Fax (01892) 514091
Formerly HM Staff Inspector for physical education and dance, with additional national responsibilities for environmental and outdoor education. OFSTED Registered Inspector for primary and secondary schools and Accredited Trainer. Able to inspect PE, DR, DA, PSE, SMSC, EO, SEN, welfare and guidance. Available for appraisal, OFSTED inspections, curriculum review and in-service training assignments

Tyrrell Burgess

Tyrrell Burgess Associates Limited, 34 Sandilands, Croydon CRO 5DB; Tel 0181-656 1770
Specialist in educational and other public institutions, records of achievement and professional development. Consultancies for World Bank and United Nations abroad and LEAs at home, including local financial management in Cambridgeshire

John Cable

Squirrels Oak Tree Corner, Chichester Cl, Witley, Godalming, Surrey GU8 5PA; Tel (01428) 682640
Former member of well integrated LEA inspectorate. Specialism mathematics. Experienced OFSTED inspector for subject and as member of core team

Dennis Carter

4 Belgrave Rd, Wrexham, Clwyd LL13 7ES; Tel (01978) 263037
Former primary headteacher and co-ordinator of Arts in Schools/higher education lecturer. PhD in language, literature and the creative and expressive arts. Director of Clwyd Poetry Project funded by *Gulbenkian*. Author of many reports of innovative arts projects in primary and secondary schools. Main areas of interest: primary management for values and quality; the arts curriculum; creative language development; literature in education at all phases

John Chastney

246 Bishopsgate, London EC2M 4PB; Tel 0171-377 1000; Fax 0171-377 8931
Management consultant and chartered accountant. Former Principal Lecturer in a polytechnic. Partner, Head of Education Sector and in charge of general consultancy at Neville Russell. Specialises in computerised accounting systems, financial, managerial and organisational matters as well as school marketing and publicity. Former External Examiner and sometime Chair of Examining Board. Trainer. Experience at DES and Grade 3 secondment to DTI, 1988-90

Judith Chivers

Touchstone Training, 27 Faversham Hse, Bayham Pl, London NW1 OLA; Tel 0171-387 1563; Fax 0171-388 3964
Touchstone Training is committed to providing quality consultancy and training that meets the needs of clients and gives value for money. Since 1988 Judith has worked with groups of Head and Deputy Headteachers, whole school staff groups, management teams and groups of teachers and governors from across the secondary sector providing consultancy and training to meet specific personal and organisational needs. She has designed and delivered successful tailor-made courses and staff conferences on a variety of professional development topics such as Appraisal, Assertiveness, Career Development, Communication, Managing Change, Developing Middle Managers, Presentation Skills, Quality Improvement, Stress and Time Management

Patricia Clayton

Patricia Clayton Education Consultants, 123 High St, Chard, Somerset TA20 1QT; Tel (014606) 5555; Fax (014606) 5555
Long experience in educational management, in this country and overseas. Specialises in setting up and management of educational projects and new colleges and departments, mostly in the independent sector; international projects, especially USA and Africa. Also Director of the Irlen Institute Southwest, dealing with perceptual learning development. Assessments for Irlen tinted lenses. Teacher Training courses

Ian Clements

ICTC Training and Consultancy, Ash Tree Barn, Coal Pit La, Waterfoot, Rossendale, Lancs BB4 9SA; Tel (01706) 229537; Fax (01706) 229537
Training and consultancy on drugs and drug education, HIV/AIDS, personal and social education, citizenship, cross-curricular planning. Author of two drug education teaching manuals, *Locating Drug Education* and *Taking Drugs Seriously*. Management training and consultancy available in the areas of appraisal, supervision skills, management of change, team building, stress management, time management, counselling, marketing, Look After Your Heart courses and school policies on smoking, drugs, etc. Registered

Health Education and Health Promotion Specialist (No 581). Member of the Institute of Training and Development

Avrille Close

Hillcrest, Kingshill Way, Berkhamsted, Herts HP4 3TP; Tel (01442) 866984; Fax (01442) 870890

Interested in all aspects of management and management development; based on experience in a wide range of schools and colleges. OFSTED trained inspector of secondary schools; Assessor and Consultant for IIP; Consultancy contracts include: TEED; TECS; The Open College; School Management Task Force – as well as LEAs, schools and colleges

Douglas Close

Hillcrest, Kingshill Way, Berkhamsted, Herts HP4 3TP; Tel (01442) 866984; Fax (01442) 870890

Management Consultant in Education. Recently HMI specialising in computing/IT and quality management in further and higher education. Previously consultant and Head of Management Services in industry and commerce; lecturer and head of department in polytechnics. Current consultancy projects include information systems strategy, quality management and quality improvement in a range of colleges and universities. Also TEC consultant under the TECassure initiative; Registered inspector of schools intending to lead teams in 1993/194

Peter Clyne

Peter Clyne Associates, Education and Training Consultancy, 33 Altenburg Gdns, London SW11 1JH; Tel 0171-228 5946; Fax 0171-228 5946

Specialist consultants, advisers, trainers and inspectors covering pre-school to higher education. Experience of curriculum, staff and resource management; Strategic and operational planning; Community education initiatives; Management reviews. Recent clients include schools, colleges, youth service, universities, LEAs, TECs, voluntary organisations, government departments and international organisations. Particular knowledge of education and training for adults, pre and post OFSTED reviews and school/parents/ community links

Ron Cohen

10 Sandhill Dr, Alwoodley, Leeds LS17 8DX; Tel (01532) 680424

Former senior manager in schools and FE colleges. Current governor of schools. Member of British Institute of Management and member of Education Law Association. Areas of interest: Fund-raising and income-generation: the Law and Education: strategic management: human resource development: F/HE links: interface between schools, colleges and business and industry. Consultant to Colleges in Yorkshire for fund-raising and income-generation. Consultant to schools for governor support (training) and fund-raising. Major recent involvement in income generation and sponsorship. Now specialising in this area of work

Eric Colburn

Harvey Whyte Associates, 98 Courtlands Ave, Lee, London SE12 8JB; Tel 0181-318 3249; Fax 0181-318 3249

Senior management experience in three inner city comprehensive schools. OFSTED trained-areas of focus secondary school management and careers education and guidance. Support for senior Management teams and middle managers – pre and post OFSTED – institutional and departmental development plans – monitoring and evaluation. Appraisal, careers education, community education, education/industry links, induction programmes for NQT, marketing, personnel issues, staff development and in-service training, teacher training

Alan Colling

2 Melverley Gdns, Wimborne, Dorset BH21 1HJ; Tel (01202) 885634

Education personnel functions: appointments; conditions of service; teachers' superannuation scheme implications; staff and management support counselling; employment protection; Many years' experience in personnel, management and curriculum matters at senior LEA level

Philippa A Cordingley

178 Beechwood Ave, Coventry CV5 6FW; Tel (01203) 673765; Fax (01203) 717576

Education management researcher, consultant and trainer, specialising in: strategic organisational development; leadership; evaluation and development policy initiatives; equal opportunities. Many years' experience of senior education management at institutional and LEA level. Clients include the Further Education Funding Council, the Association for Colleges, further and higher education colleges, local authorities, LEAs and national institutions including INLOGOV University of Birmingham, CEPP, Brunel University, where she is an associate Fellow

Michael John Creese

9 Church Gdns, Barningham, Bury St Edmonds, Suffolk IP31 1DE; Tel (01359) 221628

Ex-headteacher and LEA governor-trainer who has undertaken PhD research into the work of governing bodies. Has worked with governors and headteachers/ senior staff in a number of LEAs. Particularly interested in governor-teacher relationships, team-building and in helping governing bodies to become more effective. Publisher of resource packs on governor-teacher relationships and effective governing bodies

Leon Crickmore

13 Great Footway, Langton Grn, Tunbridge Wells, Kent TN3 ODT; Tel (01892) 863176; Fax (01892) 863176

Former HMI for further and higher education; more recently HM Staff Inspector for music. Consultant in higher education and training in music. Currently concerned with Quality Assurance in conservatoires

Roy Crowcroft

Scott Crowcroft, 5 Newton Hse, Newton St Cyres, Exeter EX5 5BL; Tel (01392) 851508

Planning, evaluation and quality assurance/control in further and higher education. Background: chartered engineer; wide industrial experience; university teaching/research/consultancy; former HMI(FHE). Recent contracts have included evaluation for DES/ DTI of transbinary initiative, FEU income-generating projects, assessment of management competencies. Main current activities: managing quality assessment exercises for HEFCE, inspection of independent FHE institutions

George Crowther

Little Hill, Colley Manor Dr, Reigate, Surrey RH2 9JS; Tel (01737) 243286

Educational and clinical psychology, special education and education in general. First and second opinion work. Expert witness 1989 Children Act, 1993 Act and Code of Practice on identification and assessment of special educational needs. Inspection – schools, colleges and children's homes. Professional assessment and advice including appraisal, counselling and career progression. Project work with the blind and neurologically impaired in America, France and Israel. Co-production work with Focus in Education on high achieving children. By appointment of the President, member of Independent Appeal Tribunal. South-east convenor for the Society of Education Consultants. Director of the Education Law

Association. Consultant to the Grant Maintained Schools Centre. Expert witness for the Law Society

Kevin Dally

58 Lockesfield Pl, West Ferry Rd, London E14 3AJ; Tel 0171-987 7377; Fax 0171-987 7300

Proprietor of management consultancy specialising in Financial Management, Systems and Operational Processes, Internal Control Reviews, Information Technology and Estate Management. Assignments have included advising and implementing Financial and IT systems, carrying out accommodation strategies, space utilisation surveys and raising finance. We have also provided contract staff to cover deficiencies in clients' resources. Assignments handled in any part of the United Kingdom

Peter Davies

9 Fair Oak, Newport, Shropshire TF10 7LR; Tel (01952) 812658

Taught in comprehensive schools in England and New Zealand; worked as English Adviser and Chief Inspector in LEAs. Advice to governing bodies on staff selection, development and appraisal and on governor-employee relations; assistance to schools with self-appraisal (including classroom observation) and development planning; English, drama and theatre

Trevor Davies

Six Counties Technology, Cooper School, Churchill Rd, Bicester, Oxon OX6 7TS; Tel (01869) 320026

Co-ordinator of this now well developed and respected technology consultancy. Formerly a senior management member of a large secondary school. Support is given to LEAs, schools, colleges and industry concerning any aspect of technology education; teaching and learning, in-service training, management and evaluation including pre and post OFSTED inspection. Leader training development. Curriculum innovation and publication development. Recently engaged in contract work with Australia and Eastern Europe

University of Reading

Dept of Science and Technology Education; Tel (01734) 875123; Fax (01734) 318650

Tim Devlin

Tim Devlin Enterprises, Ramsons, Maidstone Rd, Staplehurst, Kent TN12 ORD; Tel (01580) 893176; Fax (01580) 893431

Marketing and Public Relations Consultant. Help with writing prospectuses. Advice on recruitment of pupils. Runs training courses in marketing and media relations for maintained and independent schools. Public relations audits to see how well schools and colleges are promoting themselves. Author of *Public Relations and Marketing for Schools* (Longman). Former Education Correspondent to *The Times* and National Director of ISIS

Tom Dodd

Cedarwood, Grove La, Chalfont St Peter, Gerrards Cross, Buckinghamshire SL9 9LN; Tel (01753) 885188

Consultant in management training, initial teacher education, curriculum change and the professional development of teachers. Specific areas of interest: design and technology, project monitoring and evaluation, workshop and conference planning, TVEI activities, school inspection

Melody Dougan

56 Sandy Lodge Way, Northwood, Middx HA6 2AS; Tel (01923) 823553

Consultation and training for heads, governors, teachers and parents in the maintained and independent sectors on: heads' and governors' legal responsibilities; recruitment and selection procedures; employment and personnel good practice; all aspects of day to day school management; pupil care – behaviour and discipline policies, attendance, child protection procedures, equal opportunities issues, special educational needs; school/parent relationships; staff structures; school development plans; appraisal; management of change; school review. Extensive experience in teaching and LEA administration (Hertfordshire and Ealing). Former AEO (Special Needs) and Senior Education Officer

Peter Dutton

Peter Dutton Associates Limited, 48 Rochester Rd, Sheffield S10 4JQ; Tel (0114) 230 6174; Fax (0114) 230 6174

Support for uses of information technology in learning, teaching and management. Many years' experience in education-business partnerships at local, regional and national levels. Team member for secondary school inspections organised through OFSTED, specialising in information technology and technology. Recent clients have included National Council for Educational Technology, TVEI Head Office, Sheffield Education Business Partnership, Sanderson CBT Limited, Bromcom Computers Plc, and schools.

Derek Eastham

Scrogg's Cottage, Pamment's La, West Row, Mildenhall, Suffolk IP28 8NN; Tel (01638) 715791; Fax (01638) 715791

Teaching experience in primary, middle and secondary schools in state sector: founding Headteacher of one of Suffolk's successful purpose-built 9–13 middle schools, retiring after 18 years; specialises as expert witness in legal work involving schools and parents; editing schools' work arising from links with industry; marketing schools and school PR; governor training; insurance of pupils, buildings and equipment

Sheila Ebbutt

BEAM, Barnsbury Complex, Offord Rd, London N1 1QH; Tel 0171-457 5535; Fax 0171-457 5906

Director of BEA Mathematician, an established curriculum project for mathematics, publishing a range of materials to help primary schools with the teaching of mathmematics, running training courses, and offering consultancy on any aspect of primary mathematics education. Extensive experience in primary mathematics advisory work, designing and delivering courses, writing materials, providing consultancy to primary schools. HE institutions, and LEAs on policy, management and teaching of mathematics, throughout UK and abroad

Anthony David Edwards

TEAM Education, PO Box 18, Upton, Wirral L49 4WW; Tel 0151-677 0744

Considerable experience as a teacher, teacher trainer and administrator of Technology subjects both here and abroad. Recognised author of books on Design and Technology and an OFSTED trained Primary/Secondary Inspector. Recently worked for British Petroleum as a project leader on an international Technology/Science programme. Offers expertise in design and technology and business/education links including consultancy, project management, training, and resource development to clients regardless of size and location

John Edwards

1 St Margaret's Dr, Twickenham, Middx TW1 1QX; Tel 0181-892 3305

Former Head, Chief Adviser and Deputy Director of Education. Runs the Advisory Service for Salaries in Independent Schools (ASSIS), providing a full personal service for teaching and non-teaching staff, including conditions of service, contracts, pensions, discipline and redundancy. Clerk to the governors of four grant maintained schools. Advice on headship appointments, appraisal and inspection. Hon Secretary Association of Grant Maintained and Aided Schools (AGMAS)

The Education Secretary

Free Church Federal Council, 27 Tavistock Sq, London WC1H 9HH; Tel 0171-387 8413; Fax 0171-383 0150

The Education Committee of the Free Church Federal Council co-ordinates the views, policies and actions of the 21 churches in membership of the FCFC (including the major denominations – Baptist, Methodist, Salvation Army and United Reformed Church) in matters of public education. It relates to the Department for Education, National professional bodies, LEAs, SACREs etc. It is a member of the Churches' Joint Education Policy Committee

Clive Eiles

133 Ruskin Park Hse, Champion Hill, London SE5 8TL; Tel 0171-274 8142

Experience: Local Management of Schools, including: delegation to all schools, and units; development and training of staff and governors, establishing council-wide Performance Review Team. Main areas of interest: Developing effective management at all levels based on the values of learning, growth and development. Consultancy work underaken: London Borough of Hillingdon, and internally for the Kingston Library Service

Janet Elliott

40 Temple Fortune La, London NW11 7UE; Tel 0181-455 2191; Fax 0181-455 1982

Former Chief Executive of international examination board and director of validation bodies. Main areas: Post 16 vocational education and EFL/ESOL in UK, Europe and other overseas, especially qualifications, examinations and assessment but also business and management problem and policy analysis and development, market research and conference and events organising. Recent consultancy for Employment Department, City and Guilds, PEI, AVC International and private training companies

Derek Esp

The Old Post Office, 84 West St, Hinton St George, Somerset TA17 8SB; Tel (01460) 72355; Fax (01460) 72355

Interest in management development and school improvement; policy review in education at national and local education authority levels. Current projects include management development work for independent inspectors and schools; work on school management competences and preparation of flexible learning materials for school management

Alan Evans

22 Talbot St, Cardiff CF1 9BW; Tel (01222) 238074; Fax (01222) 226852

Trains and evaluates in teacher and headteacher appraisal, staff development, management development, mentoring, school improvement, national and transnational education business partnerships and European work experience. He is an appraisal trainer to two LEAs and an appraisal evaluator to two other LEAs. He is the former vice chair of the NSG on teacher appraisal and consultant to the SMTF and Wales Education Management

Roger Evans

11 Avondale Ave, Esher, Surrey KT10 0DB; Tel 0181-224 1985

Former teacher, LEA assistant education officer and present governor in the maintained and independent sectors. Provides advice to school governing bodies as clerk to the governors at grant maintained schools; personnel management and industrial relations in schools; management of school development projects

John Everson

74 Longdown La North, Epsom, Surrey KT17 3JF; Tel (01372) 721556

Formerly HM Chief Inspector for secondary education and teacher training. Expertise in management development; appraisal; assessment; inspection, evaluation and quality assurance; and staff development. Working on setting up an inspection agency, training 'new style' inspectors and with schools, LEAs and higher education institutions on inspection and self evaluation

Andrew N Fairbairn

Vicary Hse, Old Woodhouse, Leicestershire LE12 8UL; Tel (01509) 890309

Former Director of Education, Leicestershire. Special interest in, and experience of, school organisation and staffing; consultancy; curriculum-led local financial management; development or modification of existing and new buildings to meet curriculum/staff needs and direction of architects; arts in the curriculum and out of school; community education development; school links with Europe and its schools. Adviser on fund-raising strategies

Ronald Fell

North West Industry Education Consultants, 15 Tyrers Ave, Lydiate, Merseyside L31 4LD; Tel 0151-531 6170; Fax 0151-531 7695

Former headteacher, TVEI industry education adviser consultancy and advice service on all industry/education matters. Marks and Spencer Fellow for business in the community. National education and training targets; NVQs; investors in people; EBPs, compacts; support to TECs on education matters; EATE; school management; TVEI activities; technology; GNVQs. Developing industry liaison

John Fielden

Poland Hse, Odiham, Hants RG25 1JJ; Tel (01256) 702826; Fax (01256) 704139

Formerly a senior partner in KPMG Peat Marwick, now an independent management consultant specialising in helping universities and institutions of higher education with financial and organisational problems. Has undertaken over 115 studies for institutions, agencies and governments in the UK and overseas. A chartered accountant with 24 years' experience of high level, strategic consultancy

David Figures

Parkside Associates, 2 Weetwood Ave, Leeds LS16 5NF; Tel (0113) 278 6359; Fax (0113) 230 5190

Community Education, from both school and LEA perspective; youth work and adult education review and development; community use of school buildings, costs and charges; staff and governor development in all these areas. Strong support team. Also research and project development, feasibility and evaluation reports

Brian Fletcher

6 Argyll Ave, Curzon Pk, Chester CH4 8AL; Tel (01244) 680036; Fax (01244) 680036

Former headteacher of secondary school, mathematics adviser and school OFSTED inspector. Extensive consulting experience in school management, staff recruitment and appraisal, INSET and marketing

Tony Ford

186A Ashley Gdns, Emery Hill St, London SW1P 1PD; Tel 0171-630 7178

Ex-Chief Inspector, OFSTED accredited Registered Inspector, OFSTED accredited trainer of inspectors and an ex-head teacher. He is able to offer pre and post inspection advice, training and support to head teachers and their teams, governors and staff. He carries out inspection of all kinds and development work in management and training in primary and secondary schools. He is consultant to the London Borough of Islington

Derek Foreman

Cambridge Education Associates, 146 Borstal Rd, Rochester, Kent ME1 3BB; Tel (01634) 408040; Fax (01634) 840528

Director of Operations for CEA, an established management consultancy and staff development company working at all levels within the education service. CEA consultants work as a team in offering an extensive range of support for LEAs and institutions. Derek leads in particular on quality assurance, personnel and resource management

Maurice L Franks, MEd, BSc, MRSC, FRSA

3 Partridge Rd, Stratford-upon-Avon, Warks CV37 9FQ; Tel (01789) 414758

Formerly head of Myton School, Warwick, one of Warwickshire's largest and most successful comprehensive schools. Offer expertise in school organisation, curriculum, administration and management. School marketing and public relations specialist. Also offers consultancy in 'educational relocation' to companies and families moving to the Midlands. Contributor to national newspaper *'Schools Guide'*

Brian Frederick

Education Consultancy, 33 Birch Cl, Broom, Biggleswade, Bedfordshire SG18 9NR; Tel (01767) 313982; Fax (01462) 481102; Office (01462) 424370

Former Divisional Education Officer in Hertfordshire. Special interests include LEA organisational structures, governor training, local management, education/ business partnerships and vocational courses 16–19. Clients include the ODA, LEA, further education colleges and schools; Accredited OFSTED Inspector – Team Member

Nigel Gann

144 Obelisk Rd, Woolston, Southampton SO19 9DP; Tel (01703) 440011

Assisting LEAs, schools and voluntary organisations in: implementation of LMS; costing of premises; developing policies for community education and community use of premises; training school governors, teachers and voluntary workers

Margaret M Gascoigne

110 Wymondley Rd, Hitchin, Herts SG4 9PX; Tel (01462) 434879

Former secondary school PSE co-ordinator, now researcher, teacher trainer, school governor. Interests: planning, materials development, INSET, teaching methodology, involvement of TIE, research in personal, social, health (particularly sex, HIV-AIDS) education. Currently researching provision of HIV-AIDS, sex education for 9–13 year age group

Liz Gerschel

29 Auden Pl, Manley St, London NW1 8NB; Tel 0171-722 6730

Ex-LEA Senior Adviser in Equal Opportunities and Special Educational Needs in Inner London. OFSTED team member. Trainer, consultant, editor and writer. Has worked successfully with universities and colleges, publishers, LEAs, nursery, primary, secondary and special schools (including support staff, parents and governors) on managing equality (race, sex, class, disability and SEN); behaviour and discipline (including exclusions, dealing with bullying and harassment, and setting up school councils); language issues and multi-cultural literature in the curriculum

Marjorie Glynne-Jones

Broome Cottage, Littlebury Gn, Saffron Walden, Essex CB11 4XB; Tel (01763) 838349

Registered Inspector, secondary; inspection team member for music and primary schools. Areas of particular interest: monitoring and evaluation, development and review, equal opportunities, recruitment of senior managers, NQT support and assessment, improving teaching and learning, buildings design for the national curriculum and LMS. National and international consultancy in music education

Rhona Gordon

21 Tudor Cl, Kingsbury, London NW9 8SU; Tel 0181-200 0769

Special educational needs including residential provision: inspection of, and advice to – and on – schools and social services establishments; training for teachers, care workers and auxiliary staff; OFSTED team member for inspections special, secondary and primary; Emotional and Behavioural Difficulties, Severe Learning Difficulties, Hearing Difficulties

Daphne Gould, OBE

Combe Hay Partnership, 193 Lexden Rd, Colchester CO3 4BH; Tel (01206) 563084

Formerly headteacher of a large successful inner city school in Tower Hamlets. A founding Council Member of the National Curriculum Council and a Trustee of the Geffrye Museum, the Citizenship Foundation and the Menerva Trust. As a partner in CHP advises on the wider aspects on management policy relating to inner city schools, Grant Maintained Schools and City Technology Colleges, as well as on the organisational and political implications arising from policy decisions

Duncan Graham, CBE

Gilmour Mews, Battlebarrow, Appleby, Cumbria CA16 6XT; Tel (017683) 52920; Fax (017683) 52920

Former CEO Suffolk and Chairman of the National Curriculum Council. Visiting Professor at Manchester and Exeter Universities. Conference key note addresses and/or chairing – National Curriculum, Quality Assurance, Teacher Appraisal etc. Consultancy in school organisation and curriculum planning

Gavin Graveson

17 Bellevue Rd, Ealing, London W13 8DF; Tel 0181-997 1938; Fax 0181-810 4175

A former senior manager in local, regional and national government organisations. Consultancy and advice on structures and styles for managing change, development planning and project management in LEAs and equivalent organisations. Interests in primary and special education in relation to national curriculum and assessment management; school partnership working; recruitment and employment procedures; governor training. Locum work in LEAs

Harry Gray

Educational Management Services, 5 Oakwood Gdns, Lancaster LA1 4PF; Tel (01524) 69589; Fax (01524) 845136

Further education and higher education sectors. Corporate management, strategic management, management development, Organisation Development (OD), management counselling, consultancy and consultancy training, Investors in People (IIP), MCI, NVA, education-employer partnerships, relationships with employment department and TECs

Joan Greenfield

Yew Tree Cottage, Stanbrook, Thaxted, Essex CM6 2NL; Tel (01371) 830416; Fax (01371) 831247
(Committee 1992 – Present)
Former Chief Inspector and Acting Director of Education. Areas of interest: school inspections (OFSTED) and quality assurance; management development, including team development/building; organisational reviews and the management of change; staff selection, development and appraisal; curriculum and assessment; equal opportunities. Recent and current assignments include SCAA, several District Councils seeking unitary status, various LEAs, companies wishing to tender for OFSTED inspections. Registered Inspector (Primary and Secondary) and OFSTED Accredited Trainer Touche Ross Associate

John Gretton

Quality Teachers, 9a High St, King's Heath, Birmingham B14 7BB; Tel 0121-441 1068; Fax 0121-441 4959
Suppliers of personnel services to schools, including mainstream and special needs cover, and a full range of tailor-made consultancy packages for INSET, inspection, fundraising, marketing, information technology, etc.

Alan Groves

4 Ennerdale Cl, Huntingdon, Cambs PE18 6UU; Tel (01480) 435357
Chairman 1990-92 Committee 1992-94
Former headteacher, CEO of two LEAs and Chairman of Diocesan Education Committee. Conciliation: arbitration: staff appointments: voluntary schools: expert evidence

Lesley Hagon

Thursgill Hse, Cautley, Sedbergh, Cumbria LA10 5LL; Tel (01539) 621579
Lesley offers a wide range of management development training for all phases of education (nursery through to higher education). She also provides consultancy on project management, policy development, implementation and evaluation

Val Hardy

Woldscot Education International, Water La, Walls Quarry, Brimscombe, Stroud, Glos GL5 2ST; Tel (01453) 883734; Fax (01453) 883797
Enrichment through international understanding. Access and bridging courses enhancing ability to communicate effectively in English for business and education. Cultural exchange programmes – active links in Europe, North America and Asia including consultancy work with Japanese Companies. Independent and commissioned TEFL work. Promotional activity for European Business School. Consultancy/training courses preparing international schools students for English education

Peter Harle

9 Fernwood, Marple Bridge, Stockport SK6 5BE; Tel 0161-449 7390
LEA general adviser with specific responsibility for music; in past held responsibility for drama and business studies. For seven years was AMA representative on the National Council for Drama Training, gaining much experience as a panel member on accreditation visits to many drama schools. Extensive OFSTED inspection experience

Patrick Bernard Harrigan

School Croft, Church La, Adel, Leeds LS16 8DE; Tel (01532) 611317; Fax (01532) 611317
Formerly NATFHE National Official. Independent employee relations consultant since 1988. During 1989 temporary assignment as Head of Industrial Relations at Leeds Polytechnic. Interest and experience in employment law, strategic employee relations and HRM. Assignments have included: designing salary structures, assisting in defining employee relations/human resource strategies, development of appraisal schemes and assisting on "people problems"

Michael Harrison

Education Systems Consultant, 20 Robin Hood Chase, Sheffield S6 6FH; Tel (0114) 231 2805
Education and economic performance; technical and vocational education development, post-16 and further and higher education development. Adviser – The Engineering Council and Yorkshire Engineering Council regional organisation; St William's Foundation, York; Sheffield University; FH Partnership; Space-related education. Consultant to: Sheffield University, Department of Employment (further and higher education and higher level NVQs)

John Hart

74 Queen's Rd, Loughton, Essex IG10 1RS; Tel 0181-508 3661
(Committee 1990 Treasurer 1994)
Expertise in education management in LEAs and institutions. Recent consultancies in development planning, financial and resource management, school administrative systems and all aspects of personnel management. Recent research and publications on post-16 issues, school development planning, LEA restructuring and the use of support staff in schools. Locum work in LEAs

Franklin Hartle

Hay Management Consultants, 52 Grosvenor Gdns, London SW1W OAU; Tel (01702) 710305; 0171-730 0833
Director of Performance Management Practice for Hay, following career in teaching and educational administration. Extensive consulting experience with LEAs, individual schools and colleges and professional associations (NAHT, APC, EIS (Scotland).

Molly Hattersley

14 Gayfere St, Smith Sq, London SW1P 3HP; Tel 0171-222 2959; Office 0171-636 6418; Fax 0171-612 6366
Society of Education Consultants (Committee 1990 Chairman 1994)
Specialist in the appraisal of teachers. Consultant on appraisal to a number of local education authorities in inner and outer London, offering advice on the planning and implementation of appraisal schemes, including training of appraisees and appraisers and a monitoring service during process and review. Visiting Fellow, Department of Policy Studies, Institute of Education, London University. Consultant on appraisal at the Management Development Centre there

Geoff Headley

Capital Education Associates, 78 Bartholomew Rd, London NW5 2AL; Tel 0171-267 0757
Capital Education Associates are led by Geoff Headley who is an OFSTED registered inspector, a former teacher, adult educator and LEA inspector. The associates work as a team or individually to provide advice and inspection, consultancy and training to colleges and primary and secondary schools. Expertise is in staff and organisational development and areas of focus include headteacher and teacher appraisal, school governance, strategic planning, curriculum and management development and inspection

Hilary Heffernan

Education Consultant, 243 Yorkland Ave, Welling, Kent DA16 2LH; Tel 0181-301 1024
Specialist in educational/social problems experienced by children of above average intelligence. A teacher for

17 years. Consultant/national organiser: Mensa Foundation for Gifted Children (3 years). Consultant in charge for CHI (Children of High Intelligence)

Barbara Herts

43 Fernside Rd, London SW12 8LN; Tel 0181-675 3912; Fax 1081-675 3912

Extensive career in teaching and education administration (Ealing, Westminster, Newham) Former Assistant Education Officer (Schools) and Assistant Director Head of Early Years Services. Main areas of expertise are: the 1989 Children Act, nursery education and after school provision. Other areas of expertise include school management, services for pupils and students, special educational needs, and TEC/LEA partnership. Experienced trainer of governors, heads and teachers on all aspects of school management, the 1981 Education Act and the 1989 Children Act. Recent clients have included individual establishments, LEAs, Social Services departments, training and enterprise councils and voluntary organisations concerned with children

Ellis Hillman

29 Haslemere Ave, Hendon, London NW4 2PU; Tel 0181-202 7792

Higher and Further Education, management and administration; relationships between universities, colleges of further education, government, local government, professional institutions, communities and unions. Served on LCC, GLC, LEA, currently member of LB Barnet Council. Governor of Imperial College 1969–1991. Currently setting up MSc Management of Cities' Infrastructure Course

Charles Hince

School Administration Management Consultancy, Stretton Hse, Benington, Herts SG2 7LP; Tel (01438) 869311; Fax (01438) 869311

Consultancy specialising in school administration covering: accountancy, banking, catering, cleaning, household and laundry services, employment legislation, fee and debt collection, fund raising, health and safety, grounds and gardens, insurance, office services, professional fees, property management, sports halls and swimming pools, transport and buses, utilities, waste disposal. Supported by other associated specialists available when necessary. Experience: 8 years as a bursar

Kathy Hooper

14 Highlands Heath, Bristol Gdns, London SW15 3TR; Tel 0181-788 3413; Fax 0181-788 3413

Wide experience as a specialist and general senior inspector with a management brief, as a consultant and Chair of Governors of a secondary school. On-going work with primary and secondary schools, including grant maintained, is designed to raise levels of achievement for pupils and teachers through improved educational and personnel management at all levels including the governing bodies. Inspection for OFSTED and LEAs includes technology

Tom C F Hopkins

Sunnyside, 16 Greenhill, Weymouth, Dorset DT4 7SG; Tel (01305) 766 729; Fax (01305) 766 729

Formerly a new university Principal Lecturer; 19 years in FE/HE. Considerable experience of leading and managing developments in Open and Distance Learning, Credit Accumulation and Transfer, Accreditation of Prior Learning and Employment Learning Contracts. Main consultancy areas: HE curriculum and Staff Development; Educational Project Management. Particular interest in working with staff groups on managing the education and training change process. Member of the Association of the Project Managers. Recent work with Open Learning Foundation and Bournemouth University

Miles Howarth

98 The Street, Little Waltham, Chelmsford, Essex CM3 3NT; Tel (01245) 360457; Fax (01245) 360457

Senior Education Officer in Essex for 19 years. Extensive experience of managing capital expenditure, school re-organisation and planning for school premises to meet changing needs. Also National Secretary of the Society of Education Officers International Committee: Involved in practical research, and preparing LEAs and individual establishments to meet the challenge of the new Europe

Peter Howlett

White Barn Cottage, Gedges Hill, Matfield, Tonbridge, Kent TN12 7EA; Tel (01892) 722342; Fax (01892) 724068

Management of education, school and college government, LEA organisational structures and review, local management and local government reorganisation. Clients have included a number of local authorities, the Audit Commission (performance indicators, LEA management reviews), HEFLE and FEFC (College Government). Adviser to Coopers and Lybrand

Neil Jepson

Timetabling Services UK, 39 South St, Emsworth, Hampshire PO10 7EG; Tel (01243) 379944; Fax (01243) 379944

Specialist in computer software for use in the preparation of timetables and managing cover for absent staff. Advice on all aspects: appropriate packages; hardware needed; installation; costs involved; training available; management benefits; Helpline support and timetable interpretation. Neil Jepson, a school timetabler for 30 years, completed a contract with IBM as an Educational adviser and became the UK expert in that company's timetabling products

Anne Jones

23 Queen St, Henley on Thames RG9 1AR; Tel (01491) 578672; Work (01895) 274000; Fax (01491) 521853

Professor and Head of Continuing Education, Brunel University, West London. Visiting Professor, Sheffield University. Registered Inspector OFSTED. Interests: quality management, flexible learning, education-business partnerships, education-industry links, computer integrated systems, guidance and counselling, change management

David Keith

260 Edmond Rd, Sheffield S2 4EN; Tel (01742) 724787

Organisation Development consultancy and training. Staff development in schools and LEAs, person in role, management of self, time, stress. Management and organisation development for team, faculty, whole school, including closure and amalgamation. The nature and management of life as change; peer support and learning; appraisal training; school and LEA project management; vision in education and quality learning culture; the spiritual curriculum. Currently external examiner to Humberside University

Tony Kerr

54 Kingsdown Pde, Bristol BS6 5UF; Tel (01272) 243023; Fax (01274) 41587

Head of Direct Educational Services, Harrow. Worked in Africa, Scandinavia, Spain. Organisational and educational interests include: management development, leadership, selection, appraisal, bilingualism, policy review, project management, special education

Regina Kibel

7 Barham Hse, Molyneux St, London W1H 5HW; Tel 0171-262 9153

(BScEcon) Formerly NALGO Education Officer. Considerable experience of briefing on education policy issues, training needs analysis, the organisation of training programmes, distance learning methods, and of Industry Lead Bodies, the NCVQ, and professional qualifications. Has been a Polytechnic, University, Further Education, and School, Governor, and is a member of a school examinations board

Brian Kington

Consultant in Education Business Partnerships, 11 Lakewood Rd, Chandlers Ford, Hampshire SO53 1ER; Tel (01703) 265938

Areas of interest: education/business partnerships, industrial relevance in the curriculum, education and training policy, business contribution to the management and content of education, skills shortages, access to further and higher education. Recent and current assignments: IBM, Society of Education Officers; Young IT Technician of the Year

Jim Knight

38 Woodhall Cl, Cuckfield, West Sussex RH17 5HJ; Tel (01444) 454174

Experienced management and organisation development consultancy both for schools/LEAs and for business organisations, in designing and running courses in managing innovation, in total quality management and in all forms of experiential and action learning programmes. Special interest in leadership (including use of the outdoors as a vehicle for learning)

Ruth Knox

Chepping Associates, New House, 32a Mount Cl, High Wycombe, Bucks HP12 3PE; Tel (01494) 461283; Fax (01494) 461283

Chepping Associates is a general consultancy offering support for Professional and Organisational Development to schools, voluntary organisations and business. Via associates it also offers Recruitment Consultancy including psychometric assessment. Through TMO Careers we offer Self Marketing training for sixth formers and support to schools wishing to develop their own self marketing programmes. Also Career Planning and Counselling (for adults facing career change)

Margaret Lally

Early Years Consultant, 4 D'Arcy Heights, D'Arcy Rd, Colchester, Essex CO2 8AD; Tel (01206) 369344

Specialist in the education of young children 3–5 years. Runs training courses for early years staff and parents, speaks at conferences and writes on the subject of early education. Course themes include: Working with other adults (eg team leadership, working with parents); child development; the early years curriculum; planning and record-keeping; the role of play in early learning

Frank Lane

1 Alfreda Rd, Whitchurch, Cardiff CF4 2EH; Tel (01222) 626 632

Head of comprehensive schools for over 25 years. Worked with LEA on institutional appraisal. Secretary of NAHT in Wales, 1987–1992. Member, Welsh Joint Education Committee and sub-committees, 1986–1992. Current Chair, Standing Conference for Education in Wales. Staff selection, training and development. School and departmental appraisal, organisation and management. OFSTED team inspector: whole school issues, PSE, History, SEN. Grant Maintained Status issues

Brian Langton

EMDA, 9 Church St, Broughton, Kettering, Northants NN14 1LU; Tel (01536) 791168; Fax (01536) 791168

Formerly Senior Education Officer and Director of the Management Development Unit, Essex LEA. Experience also includes acting as national co-ordinator of a BP/LEA consultant development programme "Managing Change in Education" and as regional liaison officer for East Anglia with the Government's School Management Task Force. Now a Director of Essex Management Development Associates, an established management development consultancy working with schools, colleges, local education authorities and a range of other organisations outside the education service. Areas of particular interest include facilitating organisational change through staff development; appraisal; action learning programmes; leadership and the learning organisation

Ralph Lavender

8 The Granaries, Station Rd, Maldon, Essex CM9 7LQ; Tel (01621) 840974; Fax (01621) 840974

Over 35 years' experience as a primary teacher, headteacher and senior LEA inspector. Author of books and articles about education, especially language, reading and children's books. Advice on English National Curriculum KS 1 and 2, particularly reading, and general implementation of National Curriculum topic work; primary school management; book policy and school library learning resources

Bridget Lawson

LEADA, Five Flies, 9 Sarlsdown Rd, Exmouth, Devon EX8 2HY; Tel (01395) 270124; Fax (01395) 222737

(Committee 1992)

Education Management Consultant and Trainer. Specialises in management training, organisational development and barriers to change, training of trainers and governors. OFSTED Lay Inspector. Is an accredited assessor for NVQs and Crediting Competence (Management Charter Initiative)

Gillian Lea

Educational Development Consultancy, Calf Hse Farm, Abbott Brow, Mellor, Lancs BB2 7HU; Tel (01254) 813248/3209; Fax (01254) 813209

Former headmistress. Consultant for Quest Educational Developments (consultancy and advice for private clients, children and adults, using psychometric testing where appropriate). Advice on efficient and effective use of recruitment and interview procedures. Use of self-evaluation procedures. Assistance with preparation for statutory inspection. Appraisal of staff. Management of stress

Tony Leach

3 Oshawa Dell, Canal La, Pocklington, Yorks YO4 2NW; Tel (01759) 305576; Fax (01759) 305576

Management consultant and trainer. Extensive work with LEAs, TECs, TEED, TVEI, schools and universities. Specialises in appraisal, education-business links. Quality management and improvement, organisation development, management training and development. Counselling skills

Robin Leleux

RVL Consultancy, 113 Northampton Rd, Wellingborough, Northants NN8 3PL; Tel (01933) 224442

Specialist in all employment matters affecting teaching, support, administrative, domestic and maintenance staff, especially in independent and grant-maintained schools, including contracts of employment, conditions of service, disciplinary/grievance hearings, redundancies and school amalgamations and closures. Last post was Deputy Secretary of the Girls' Public Day School Trust, previously Assistant Secretary at AMMA

15 Education Consultants

Grahame Leon-Smith

Tele-School, The Niven Suite, The Mansion, Ottershaw Pk, Surrey KT16 0QG; Tel (01932) 874067; (01932) 874303; Fax (01932) 874068

Secondary educationalist, Head of Townmead School (1974-92), Modern linguist (French, German, Spanish, Esperanto) and IT specialist (CMIS and Computing across the curriculum), European and international education. Advice on all aspects of school management and development including LMS and GMS, problem solving, arbitration and mediation service for all disputes, grievance procedures, appeals panels etc. Evaluation of educational resources and equipment

Michael D Lightfoot

Belmont Consultancy Services (BCS) Belmont Hse, 15 Ashmere Grove, Ipswich IP4 2RE; Tel (01473) 210740; Fax (01473) 211508; Telex 987160

Advice and consultancy on vocational courses in schools (eg RSA Initial Awards, GNVQs) and Assessor/Verifier training and assessment; facilitates the interchange of students on vocational training programmes in EC, Central European and Scandinavian countries (via eg PETRA, Youth for Europe, Kaleidoscope and Overture); provides Primary and Secondary advice and consultancy within OFSTED inspection framework especially in the areas of Science, Music, Drama, PE and RE and Media Studies

John Lipscomb

St Dominic's, Mount Park Ave, Harrow on the Hill, Middx HA1 3HX; Tel 0181-422 8084

Post 16 Education: Management, Curriculum, and Examinations

James Lodge

75 Walmersley Old Rd, Walmersley, Bury BL9 6RH; Tel 0161-761 4663; Fax 0161-763 3769

The James Lodge Consultancy was formed in 1983 to assist education institutions, professional bodies, examiniation boards, and resource providers in the development of overseas activities, in their broadest sense. It has worked in over 40 countries and has undertaken numerous institutional development projects as well as its original British clientele. The consultancy has three offices in UK and a regional office in Malaysia

Flo Longhorn

"Neihaff", L-9161 Ingeldorf, Luxembourg; Tel (+352) 818 910; e mail compuserve 100020,2636 and Hanghorn.eurokom.ie

Catalyst, 35 Send Rd, Woking GU23 7ET; Tel (01483) 223707; Fax (01483) 223707

An independent consultant working mainly in special education both in UK and abroad. Consultancy areas cover special education with particular expertise in severe and profound learning disabilities, alternative therapies and alternative environments in education, fund-raising, resource identification and EEC funding, audit of special needs provision within educational establishments and publication of books on special education

Karen Lynch

Oxford Associates, 52 Ottways La, Ashtead, Surrey KT21 2PJ; Tel (01734) 274066

Former secondary school teacher and education officer for Royal County of Berkshire. Independent trainer and Governor training associate with the Grant Maintained Schools Centre. Oxford Associates provides In Service and Governor training. Design of workshops – roleplay and simulations for use in management training, recruitment and classroom management. Financial management in Primary and Secondary schools. Advice to schools about Quality Assurance (BS 5750) Certification

Henry G Macintosh

Brook Lawn, Middleton Rd, Camberley, Surrey GU15 3TU; Tel (01276) 23950; Fax (01276) 62332

Interests lie in developing and evaluating strategies and materials to help teachers and students to create, use and manage assessment. Specific activities include recording achievement; action planning; portfolios of evidence; whole school assessment policies; moderation and validation; self assessment and appraisal; Core Skills; GNVQs; assessing modular curriculum. Current and recent assignments: Education Division, Department of Employment; British Council; LEAs; UNESCO

Gordon Mackay

Black Gable, 108 North Rd, Hythe, Kent CT21 5DX; Tel (01303) 266555; Fax (01303) 262463

A former member of HM Inspectorate. A team leader for ISJCs accreditation and review inspections. Currently co-ordinating the authorisation of British/International schools in Spain. Other consultancies in Europe and the Middle East

John Mann

Education Systems, 109 Chatsworth Rd, London NW2 4BH; Tel 0181-459 5419; Fax 0181-459 7705

Vice Chairman 1994

Management at institutional, local, regional and national levels. Mergers, re-organisation, negotiation, conciliation. Clients include LM, GM and Independent schools, Association of Teachers and Lecturers, LB Camden, University of California, British Council

Alan Marshall

Alan Marshall Education Consultants Limited, 98 Wheathampstead Rd, Harpenden, Herts AL5 1JB; Tel (01582) 761413; Fax (01582) 467941

Main activity: policy reviews, audits, surveys and reports. Main interests: teacher education, technology in schools, school industry links, information technology. Major consultancies: government departments, educational foundations and trusts, LEAs, teacher training providers. OFSTED Registered Inspector and accredited trainer

Valerie Mason

21 Locks Ride, Ascot, Berks SL5 8RA; Tel (01344) 885375

Extensive experience of educational management at LEA and school level. Main interests: all aspects of management with particular expertise in financial management of school budgets; personnel issues, including employment legislation; health and safety. Accredited OFSTED Inspector

Anne Matthewman

24 Courtyards, Little Shelford, Cambridge CB2 5ER; Tel (01223) 843220; Fax (01223) 846562

Background: extensive career in educational management, administration and teaching in both the school and higher education sectors. Recent experience: transformation of an LEA maintained college to an independent Higher Education Corporation. Areas of interest include: establishment organisation, management and development of systems eg finance, personnel; staff team building and appraisal; assets, premises and estate management, strategic and operational planning. Development and use of computer systems in educational administration, project management, college governance

Kevin J McNeany

Nord Anglia Education PLC, 10 Eden Pl, Cheadle, Cheshire SK8 1AT; Tel 0161-491 4191; Fax 0161-491 4409/4410

Kevin McNeany is leader of a full-time team of educational inspectors, advisers and consultants. Their collective expertise encompasses virtually the whole field of education but the group is especially strong on OFSTED inspections and consultancy, financial management, human and property resource structuring and a full range of curriculum matters

Meiriol Meredith Jones

The Education Consultancy, Added Value Programmes, The Old Rectory, Bodfari, Clwyd LL16 4DA; Tel (01745) 710360; Fax (01745) 710360

Former LEA adviser on special needs and giftedness. Main areas of interest include: individual and whole school strategies to combat underachievement in pupils of all ability levels from 5–19 years; curriculum enrichment and extension programmes; dyslexia; classroom management; staff counselling; APL and GNVQ Training

John Millington

META, John Millington Education and Training Associates, 14 Dingle Rd, Stourbridge, West Midlands DY9 ORS; Tel (01562) 886865; Fax (01562) 886865

Former HMI and industrial education adviser. Vocational education and training; education and industry at all levels, schools, further education, higher education. Work with National Education and Training Targets. Consultancy work for NCVQ; Partnership Awards; NHS Training Agency; Further Education Unit; Engineering Training Authority; Training and Enterprise Councils; Partnership Trust; Beacon Awards

Christopher John Moore

10 Castleview Terr, Torthorwald, Dumfries & Galloway D91 3PX; Tel 0138-775 519; Fax 0138-775 519

After senior management and national curriculum development roles in Further Education, and as a Staff Development Adviser, John became a freelance consultant in 1990. Recent work includes recommendations on Vocational Education and training for the Namibian Government, and a Development Programme for Probationer Teachers in Scotland. He uses the Myers Briggs Type Indicator to help teachers and trainers match teaching and learning patterns

Cathy Moorhouse

48 Cleveland Ave, Chiswick, London W4 1SW; Tel 0181-995 4625

Special educational needs; discipline and grievance policy and practice including conflict management and dealing with poor performance; time management; child protection. Experienced trainer at all levels; also experienced in writing formal procedures

Geoff Morris

108 Huntingdon Rd, Cambridge CB3 OHL; Tel (01223) 353345

Former CEO Cambridgeshire. Organisation review, management processes and change management. Experienced overseas consultant for British Council. Special knowledge of Eastern Europe. Trained career counsellor with successful experience in career change and job search for redundant managers and teachers

David Murray-Smith

Quantock Education and Training Consultants, 16 High St, Cannington, Bridgwater, Somerset TA5 2HE; Tel (01278) 653157

Formerly school teacher, college lecturer, officer and adviser to Liverpool and Somerset LEAs and TEED South West. Particular expertise in strategic and operational planning for all aspects of further and higher education; income generation and commercial activity, Investors in People (IIP). Support for schools, colleges LEAs and TECs. A trained and licensed assessor and adviser for the Investors in People programme currently working with schools, further education colleges and the private sector

Eric V Needham

Education and Training Consultant, 248 Dunchurch Rd, Rugby CV22 6HX; Tel (01788) 815772; Fax (01788) 570772

OFSTED trained and experienced team member (management, history and PE). Offering preparation for and follow up to inspection. Also appraisal of heads and senior staff; appraisal and management training for governors and teachers. Active in LEA, GM and Independent Schools. Has experience also in Oman and Hong Kong. Former Head and LEA Officer

Ian Nelson

Nelson Training Seminars, The Schoolhouse, 152 Sywell Rd, Overstone, Northampton NN6 OAG; Tel (01604) 644209

Freelance consultant, writer and management trainer specialising in personal, professional and organisational development with clients from business, local government, and the voluntary sector. He designs and delivers training courses, writes materials and is an accredited OFSTED inspector. Experience includes primary headships, freelance work with Nene College, Leicester University, and Humberside Curriculum and Staff Development Centre

Paul Nash

Flexible Learning North East, Linskill Site, Linskill Terr, North Shields NE30 2BD; Tel 0191-296 3302; Fax 0191-296 3304

Professional development, effective learning, monitoring, evaluation, design and development of resources, managing change, training the trainers, desk top design, publication of learning materials

Sir Peter Newsam

Institute of Education, University of London, 20 Bedford Way, London WC1 0AL; Tel 0171-612 6000; Fax 0171-612 6126

Mike Nichol

Hazelwood, 73 Plymyard Ave, Bromborough, Wirral L62 6BL; Tel 0151-327 1527

Brian Oakley-Smith

Cambridge Education Associates Limited, Minerva Hse, 618 Newmarket Rd, Cambridge CB5 8LP; Tel (01223) 413399; Fax (01223) 414949

Managing Director of CEA, an established management consultancy and staff development company working at all levels within the education service. CEA consultants work as a team in offering an extensive range of support to LEAs, schools, colleges and educational suppliers. Brian leads, in particular, on strategic management and market research

Louise O'Connor

18 The Haydens, Tonbridge, Kent TN9 1NS; Tel (01732) 399172; Fax (01732) 361803

Specialises in school governor training on management issues, the curriculum, pastoral care and personal, social and health education. Has designed and delivered training packages for a variety of clients including Surrey LEA, North East Surrey College of Technology, Roehampton Institute, and Banking Information Service (BIS). Currently works part time as a senior lecturer and researcher (Education) in higher education, and part time in freelance consultancy

Philip Oswell Jones

69 Barriedale, New Cross, London SE14 6RP; Tel 0181-692 3751

Many years of practical teaching experience with "statemented" children in schools and colleges and adults in "Sheltered Workshops" both in Britain and abroad. Consultancy offers expert advice on behavioural problems, pupil and parent counselling and home programmes designed to manage, modify and change behaviour. Currently working part time as the Vice-Principal of Mycenae College and as an Individual Support Teacher in schools

Marjorie Ouvry

78 Hervey Rd, Blackheath, London SE3 8BU; Tel 0181-856 6050

Former headteacher of the Rachel McMillan Nursery School and former lecturer in Child Development and Education, now runs in-service courses for teachers, nursery nurses, under-fives workers and parents in all aspects of the nursery curriculum, including outdoor play, music, play and learning, child development, observation, assessment and record-keeping, curriculum planning, classroom organisation, staff team building and working with parents

Bryan Owen

Fernlea, Queen St, Houghton Regis, Beds LU5 5BT; Tel (01582) 867909

Former Primary School Head Teacher in VA, VC, and Grant Maintained Schools. Freelance consultant on all aspects of school management and administration specialising in finance and IT systems. Experienced in developing custom IT solutions to meet specific needs and providing on-going technical support in LEA, Voluntary and GM Schools. National Society trained Section 13 Inspector in Voluntary and GM Church Schools

Ray Page

Ray Page Associates, Aldermary Hse, 21 Rodway Rd, Bromley BR1 3JJ; Tel 0181-460 1960; 0181-313 0152; Fax 0181-313 0152

Formerly Deputy Director of South Bank Polytechnic (now South Bank University) and Principal Assistant Director of Education for the London Borough of Bromley, with teacher training, curriculum development, and teaching experience before that. Presently Senior Consultant and Director (Governor Support Services) to the grant maintained School Centre and senior associate of Ray Page Associates. Specialist interests include governor training, strategic and operational planning, senior salary reviews, setting up and training for appraisal schemes, and management reviews. All associates have senior experience in these fields. Major projects include UK, USA and Caribbean universities, LEAs, individual schools, and two companies

Malcolm Pallant

2 The Moorings, Ings La, North Ferriby, East Yorkshire HU14 3ED; Tel (01482) 632061; Fax (01482) 633289

My educational consultancy has been created and designed to provide a personally devised, practical and informed overview of published material currently available. Following some thirty years in Educational Publishing, this unique freelance service (established April 1991) is offered on a nationwide basis, recognised by most major and some minor publishing houses, to school music teachers, music graduates, music groups, instrumental teachers, regional music support services. Enquiries welcomed for INSET and IN-SERVICE courses, teacher 'twilight' and 'cluster' gatherings, summer music schools. Brochure on request

Martin Pavey

5 Vineyards, Bath, Avon BA1 5NA; Tel (01225) 444269

Until recently, Head of comprehensive, voluntary aided grammar and HMC independent schools; OFSTED inspector of English, drama, RE, PSE and management; Education management consultant (secondary); TEFL trainer and adviser on secondary education systems overseas

Eric Peagam

Cranmere Consultancies, Cranmere Bank Hse, Stableford, Bridgnorth, Shropshire WV15 5LP; Tel (01746) 5669; Fax (01746) 5669

22 years in special education, as teacher, head, adviser and researcher. EBD specialist since 1976. PhD study of emotional and behavioural difficulties among urban primary school children. Contributor to specialist literature, consulted by broadcasters, journalists etc. Author of Birmingham "Care Policy for Residential Schools" and other relevant documents. Specialises in training and advice on responses to EBD in mainstream and special schools. Offers pre-inspection advice, on whole-school issues and behaviour/discipline issues

Bergen Peck

91 Hartington Rd, Liverpool L8 0SE; Tel 0151-707 0002; Fax 0151-707 2667

Specialist in performing arts education and training, especially music; event management, including educational travel. Recent consultancies in school-industry liaison, fund raising, PR management and corporate development at secondary, further and higher education levels. European Commission policy and funding for arts and education/training. European/international networking. Development of NVQs in performing arts. Business plans for educational institutions. Clients include Liverpool Institute for Performing Arts (HE curriculum development, building design and institutional development); EC's Task Force, Human Resources, Education, Training and Youth (Music sector chair for Arts Education and Training Initiative); Individual schools in the secondary sector (management advice and school development); work for BTEC and OFSTED; and similar development work in other parts of the European Union

Isobel Pilkington

8 Park Edge, Hathersage, Via Sheffield S30 1BS; Tel (01433) 650395; Mobile 037 444 3667; Fax (01433) 650395

Chartered Educational Psychologist. Independent OFSTED School Inspector in Organisational Change Management Consulting. Expert witness, Education Acts and Children Act

Maurice Plaskow

9 Lakeside, Weybridge, Surrey KT13 9JB; Tel (01932) 222186: 0181-339 0648

Curriculum issues, especially post-16. Education and the arts. Strategies for INSET. Worked on RSA enquiry on Widening Access to HE which produced report "More Means Different" (Sir Christopher Ball). Several enquiries on the arts and education, and consultancies for LEAs on development plans and curriculum guidelines. Currently involved in producing wide range of video material for professional development of teachers, with *Focus in Education Productions*

David Playfoot

Fieldwork Limited, 2 Lower Brook Mews, Ipswich, Suffolk IP4 1RA; Tel (01473) 250294; Fax (01473) 250301

David Playfoot has extensive teaching experience, including three headships. With his partner, Martin Skelton, he founded Fieldwork Limited in 1987. Fieldwork has a wide network of specialist trainers/consultants and is currently working with Bromley, Suffolk, Wiltshire, Essex, Hounslow and Shell International Schools in addition to a number of individual schools. They are also working extensively in Europe, the Middle East, and farther afield in Brazil and Bermuda. Fieldwork's particular interests are in curriculum and management development, including cross-curriculum teaching, school development planning and appraisal training. In addition to consultancy, Fieldwork also provides INSET and a school review service.

Patricia Plummer

18 Bedford Rd, Twickenham TW2 5EW; Tel 0181-898 4914; Fax 0181-994 7921

Although I have taught and lectured to all ages during my long career in education, for the last eighteen years I have been head of a nursery and infant school. I am willing to share my knowledge on all aspects of learning at this stage, also on the management of a delegated budget. Fourteen years ago I set up one of the first After School Care Schemes and have since given advice and help on this in many areas

Ernest W Potter

Special Education Advice Service, 72 Kirkwood Dr, Oakes, Huddersfield HD3 3WJ; Tel (01484) 644561; Fax (01484) 644561

Support for parents on assessment and provision for special educational needs. Former local education authority adviser offering advice and advocacy to parents of children with special educational needs. Member of the Independent Panel for Special Education Advice and the Society of Education Consultants

Bob Powell

9 Moorland Rise, Haslingden, Rossendale, Lancs BB4 6UA; Tel (01706) 220375

Specialises in policy analysis, strategic planning, monitoring, evaluation and quality assurance in further, adult and community education. Formerly Senior Development Officer with UDACE, he has been contracted by the FEFC (England), FEU, NIACE, the Staff College, CEDC and individual colleges, LEAs and services since going freelance in September 1991. Publications include *Securing Adult Learning: Practical Strategies for Implementing the FHE Act 1992*

Marguerite Presman

33 Derwent Gr, East Dulwich, London SE22 8DZ; Tel 0181-693 8758; Fax 0181-693 8184

Former senior inspector (monitoring and evaluation of institutions), advisory headteacher (assessment and examinations), comprehensive school headteacher. Mathematician. All aspects of inspection and monitoring of schools and further education colleges. In particular team inspections organised to advise and support schools prior to an OFSTED quadrenniel inspection. Advice and in-service training on management and curriculum organisation; staff recruitment and selection including headteacher; marketing and public relations; staff appraisal; internal school evaluation; development planning; governor training; local management; time management. Whole-school policies including assessment, recording and reporting; equal opportunities. Conferences organised; OFSTED accredited for secondary and primary school inspections. Have participated in OFSTED school inspections as deputy team leader inspecting most aspects of the Framework and mathematics. For primary schools mathematics, science, management and IT

John Puncher

J.P. Associates; The Old Vicarage, 43 Station Rd, North Ferriby, North Humberside HU14 3DG; Tel (01482) 633512; Fax (01482) 633401

Independent inspector (OFSTED trained). Former Senior Adviser (primary), Consultant and NFER/BGC National Assessment Consortium. Assignments and main interests: school management, appraisal, moderation, curriculum development. Clients include LEAs, SCEA, individual schools, colleges and professional associations

Allan Randall

Focused Learning, Glebe Hse, Ashby Rd, Ticknall, Derbyshire DE7 1JJ; Tel (01332) 862975

Educational consultancy specialising in TQM training and material development. Educational/Business partnership (registered consultant for the Schools Curriculum Industry Project) project and resource development. Consultant on marketing and PR to equipment and service suppliers to education. Also Archive Educational Consultancy developing, writing and publishing learning materials for historic sites. Contributor to Heinemann Our World series and other educational published material. Particular interests in science, technology, history and Family Learning

Neill Ransom

The Chelstoke Educational Group, 4 Heathcoat Bldg, Highfields Science Pk, Nottingham NG7 2QS; Tel (0115) 922 9214; Fax (0115) 922 9330

Formerly Principal of Wreake Valley College and founder of CSCS. Neill now heads The Chelstoke Educational Group comprising Educational Consultants (International), Educational Building Consultants, Educational Computing Consultants, Educational Recruitment and Educational Courses. Working in all sectors in the UK and internationally, the group covers management support and training, financial management, marketing, curriculum and accommodation planning, Refurbishment and Capital Building Management and Development, computing strategies and training and a wide range of staff development

Linda Redford

85 Rodenhurst Rd, London SW4 8AF; Tel 0181-674 1902

A former local authority inspector for special educational needs, Linda Redford is able to offer professional development support to LEAs, schools, colleges and services across the phases and sectors. As well as covering issues such as whole school policies, differentiation and meeting individual needs, she can offer whole institution support on the range of developmental areas including inspection activities, OFSTED inspector

Bob Richardson

Professional and Educational Advisory Services, 73 Shrubland Rd, London E8 4NL; Tel 0171-275 9172; Fax 0171-275 9172

Former headteacher and advisory headteacher interested in corporate development of schools; whole school policies; school governor training; advising governing bodies on interviewing and selection; teacher guidance on appointments; mediation and conciliation. Wide experience as headteacher and national negotiator

Sheila Rosenberg

19 Muncaster Rd, London SW11 6NY

Extensive secondary school, FE, adult education and extra-mural experience in English, ESL and communication skills. Published, organised and lectured nationally in post-16 ESL. ILEA inspector FHCE. LEA senior inspector post-16 education. Experienced OFSTED team member. Experienced FEFC part-time inspector

Trevor J Rothwell

Dragons, Cotterstock, Peterborough PE8 5HD; Tel (01832) 6436; Fax (01832) 6436

Experience as manager of large professional scientific establishment, and as Chairman of Governors of secondary schools, both GM and under LEA. Can assist with issues of organisational structure and management of change; personnel management; training, including role of governors

Alan Rowe

2 Norman Cls, Waltham Abbey, Essex EN9 1PY; Tel (01992) 715886
Former HMI, education manager and lecturer. Specialising in the built environment (construction) vocational education and training, at all levels. Also able to assist with issues of organisation structure; quality assurance; personnel management

William Rumford

31 Pinewood Cl, St Albans, Herts AL4 0DS; Tel (01727) 868102; Fax (01727) 868102
LEA Adviser and head. Extensive teaching and management experience in schools and colleges. Arts education management and training, especially music, project management. Quality performance. Appraisal/appraiser training, middle management training, management of change. Staff development and strategic management

Rodney Sabine

Village Green Associates, 3 Arle Gdns, Alresford, Hampshire SO24 9BA; Tel (01962) 73373
Specialist in School Management including Financial Management and Local Management, Management Skills including Time Management, Team-building, Quality in Education, Management of Change and Marketing. Clients include schools, governing bodies and colleges of higher education. Prepares schools for OFSTED inspections in terms of financial management

Kate Seager

Littlestone Hse, Wall Hill, Ashurst Wood, nr East Grinstead, Sussex RH19 3TQ; Tel (01342) 823588
Broad teaching and management experience in Britain and France. Modern linguist, trained interpreter. Specialist in assessment (nearly five years School Examinations and Assessment Council). Quality assurance of A and AS examinations in all subjects, ten years chief examiner academic and vocational examinations. SEN. Meeting the assessment needs of pupils with SEN and pupils working in a second language. Establishing links in Europe. Registered OFSTED inspector. Extensive experience of public speaking and providing INSET in Britain and abroad. Recent consultancy assignments for the School Curriculum and Assessment Authority, LEAs particularly in relation to National Curriculum assessment, advice on inspections and modern language provision; Cooper Deloitte, Mercury Communications

David Hugh Sharpe

5 High Rigg, Brigham, Cockermouth, Cumbria CA13 0TA; Tel (01900) 824689
Formerly Assistant Education Officer and LEA Inspector/adviser for Religious Education and History with a support function for a clutch of primary and secondary schools. Vice chair of Assoc of RE Advisers and Inspectors 1992-93. OFSTED accredited as team member. Curriculum support, especially for small schools; management of change; development planning in an OFSTED context; staff recruitment, development and appraisal

Jennifer Short

Penfold and Redstone Ltd, 4 Ramilies Rd, Chiswick, London W4 1JN; Tel 0181-994 4707; Fax 0181-994 0194
Current MBA with experience in education, local government and private sector. Devising business and financial strategies and plans to meet organisational, individual and market needs; as authorised Lotus consultants, specifying and supporting major software packages for PC users; quality audits by trained lead assessors; delivering performance improvements by developing the people within organisations

Victor John Shuttleworth

Phoenix Educational Services, 89 Lazy Hill Rd, Aldridge, Walsall, West Midlands W59 8RS; Tel (01922) 52604
Former Head of English department and deputy head teacher. 25 years secondary school experience. Former Director of education/business compact. Pre OFSTED inspection consultancy; OFSTED inspections in English, Management, careers guidance; post OFSTED action planning; curriculum and timetable construction; work related curriculum and business links; management of change and management by objectives; investors in people; experienced examiner and member of Institute of Management

John Simpson

4 Harts La, South Godstone, Surrey RH19 8LZ; Tel (01342) 893070
Offers twenty years experience as head of independent, aided and (one of the first) grant maintained schools

David Sims

55 Coppice Mead, Stotfold, Hitchin, Herts SG5 4JY; Tel (01462) 834862
FHE teacher training and development; teacher assessment. Activity-based programmes for the development of teaching competence, including preparation for City and Guilds 7306 and TDLB standards. For colleges, adult education, refugee organisations and industrial training

Timothy Alan Sinkinson

380 Longbanks, Harlow, Essex CM18 7PG; Tel (01279) 436889; Fax (01279) 436889
Teacher for 17 years in middle and secondary schools, including three years at senior management level before becoming a consultant in 1990. Expertise in management training skills, which I have taught to local government and in the private sector, as well as working in the area of reading development and dyslexia

Martin Skelton

61 Gray's Inn Rd, London WC1X 8TL; Tel 0171-404 2774; Fax 0171-404 2766
Martin Skelton has extensive teaching experience, including two headships. With his partner, David Playfoot, he founded Fieldwork Limited in 1987. Fieldwork has a wide network of specialist trainers/consultants and is currently working with Bromley, Suffolk, Wiltshire, Essex, Hounslow and Shell International Petroleum Company's International Schools in addition to a number of individual schools. They are also working extensively in Europe, the Middle East, and farther afield in Brazil and Bermuda. Fieldwork's particular interests are in curriculum and management development, including cross-curriculum teaching, school development planning and appraisal training. In addition to consultancy Fieldwork also provides INSET and a school review service

Anthony Smith-Roberts

Anthill, Health and Safety Consultancy and Training, 44 Winslow Rd, Granborough, Winslow, Bucks MK18 3NQ; Tel (01296) 670668; Fax (01296) 670664
Experience HM Forces, industry, commerce and both mainstream and special needs teaching. Diploma Education Management, qualified Health and Safety Consultant and Trainer. Clients include British Aerospace, British Rail, Bucks LEA, Glamorgan University. Offers review of systems, development of policy, training for governors, staff, students, risk

management, guidance and counselling in crisis reduction and stress counselling

Peter Cathcart Smith

3 Rosey Row, Woolsthorpe by Belvoir, near Grantham, Lincs NG32 1LZ; Tel (01476) 870801

As a former senior administrative officer at Buckingham University and head of student recruitment/marketing at a US college, I have broad marketing/PR experience within higher education. Consultancy work also undertaken with FE colleges and UK language schools. Main areas of expertise include: overseas student recruitment, preparation of promotional materials and copywriting, staff development, needs analysis, development of alumni networks/fundraising strategies, operational planning, counselling/careers advising, management of change

Margaret Spurr, OBE

Scholaservices OBE, Croxden, Uttoxeter, Staffordshire ST14 5JQ; Tel (01889) 26424; Fax (01889) 26424

Specialist in all aspects of headship appointments, eg. confidential search, contracts of employment, appraisal. Provides consultation and training in the development of educational management for Governors, Heads and Teachers. Counselling and career advice. President of the Girls' Schools Association 1985-6, Chairman of National ISIS Committee 1987-89. Head of large independent day school 1979–94, experienced governor of several schools and a member of the ESU Selection Committee. Governor of Liverpool John Moores University 1994-Governor of the BBC 1983-and Chairman of BBC English National Forum 1994. Vice-Provost Woodard Schools (Midland Division) 1994

Mark Stedman

32 Cedarway, Bollington, Cheshire SK10 5NS; Tel (01625) 575227

Health and Safety specialist. Senior official at ATL Headquarters with responsibility for advice on Health and Safety, 1978–1993. Author of *Safety in Schools* and *Safety Representatives' Briefing*. Advises on school and college safety policies, safety monitoring and safety audits. Trains both governors and staff on current legal requirements

Professor Anne Stennett

3 Upper Hedgemead Rd, Bath, Avon; Tel (01225) 338120; Fax (01225) 874794

Until December 1993, Deputy Director of Bath College of Higher Education. Twenty years' experience of HE institutional management with particular responsibility for academic development and institutional/course validation. Member of former CNAA's Institutions' Committee and CNAA Panels for Accreditation, Institutional review and Course Validation Visits. Member of HE Quality Council Project Team researching Performance Indicators for Course Quality. Principal interests: effectiveness in institutional operations; quality assurance-systems and processes; HE/FE partnerships; staff development; the HE student learner; comparative HE developments (particularly English-French)

David Stephens

The Stillman Eastwick-Field Partnership, Architects, 4 Offord St, London N1 1DH; Tel 0171-609 4400; Fax 0171-609 4044

The Stillman Eastwick-Field Partnership has wide experience of educational buildings from nursery schools to university departments and colleges in both the maintained and independent sectors. Most recent work includes Rugby School Design Centre; a Sixth Form College in Lewisham; a primary school in Croydon and residential accommodation for 120 students at University College, London

John L Stibbs, MA

School Management Services, 93 Ashurst Rd, Barnet, Herts EN4 9LH; Tel 0181-449 5342

Secondary school senior and middle management; staff care, development and appraisal; staff screening and selection; inspections and review of staff performance; management of change; design and preparation of school timetables

David Streatfield

Information Management Associates, 28 Albion Rd, Twickenham TW2 6QZ; Tel 0181-755 0471; Fax 0181-891 5567

Specialist in all aspects of information management in education and public services including IT management, information service evaluation and information skills development. Conducted major consultancies in UK, Europe, Malaysia, Kenya and the Caribbean. Recent clients have included the Health Education Authority, National Council for Educational Technology, National Extension College and Further Education Funding Council as well as the Dental Practice Board and the States of Jersey Health Authority. Member of the Cura Consortium of Consultants in Information Management

Michael Sweet

Heart of England Education Consultancy, 23 The Ridgeway, Warwick CV34 5SH; Tel (01926) 492069

Former CEO. Management consultancy service to LEAs and schools: reorganisations, investigations, trouble-shooting. Adviser to non-metropolitan district councils seeking unitary status. Senior staff appointments. Whole school inspection/appraisal

Bill Tagg

Tagg Oram Partnership, 59 Carlisle Ave, St Albans AL3 5LX; Fax (01727) 868685

Computer Education Specialist. Previously Director of Advisory Unit for Micro-technology in Education in Hatfield. Twenty-five years of experience at home and abroad. Use of PC Compatibles including Laptops a speciality

Graham F Todd

Education Consultancy Services, 4 Seaford Ct, Esplanade, Rochester, Kent ME1 1QA; Tel (01634) 846474; Fax (01634) 846474

A specialist consultancy offering advice and INSET on all aspects of special educational needs to mainstream and day/residential special schools. Recent consultancies include the Service Children's Education Authority, London Borough of Southwark, City of Westminster, Daily Telegraph, Benchmark Educational Services, NAHT Management Development Services. Areas of expertise include pupils' with moderate learning difficulties and emotional and behavioural difficulties. Graham has headship experience and LEA advisory experience and is an OFSTED trained inspector and has inspected SEN in primary, middle, scondary and grant maintained schools

David J Tomlinson

26 Tudor Rd, New Barnet, Herts EN5 5NP; Tel 0181-449 9425; Fax 0181-441 8926

Principal Consultant of Management Consultancy and Training. Areas of special interest: Management and organisational development, strategies for change and uncertainty; performance management including staff appraisal; Investors in People; leadership and learning organisation. Recent clients include schools, LEAs, Ministry of Defence, Crown Prosecution Service

Ellen Tucker-Court

64 Chatsworth Rd, London NW2 4DD

Wide experience and interests in further and higher education

15 Education Consultants

Mary E Van de Water

13 Kennington Pk Pl, London SE11 4AS; Tel 0171-582 1570

A background of wide school (9–18) experience. Specialisms: SEN, ESL, curriculum support (materials, organisation, staff training); staff development. Teacher training for inner city schools. LEA management (teaching staff, special needs, general). Recruitment; analysis, strategies, policy and practical

Don Venvell

Mile Barn, Knapton, Norfolk NR28 ORY; Tel (01263) 720550

Specialist Consultant since 1990 to schools becoming grant maintained, with governor training, on-going advice and clerking, policy reviews, and strategic planning. Previously: Higher Education College bursar; ten years Assistant Education Officer ILEA, i/c secondary education and school support services; Education Officer, LB Haringey; Chief Adviser, Shropshire LEA; Chief Examiner in English

Margaret Vinson

Sotts Hole Cottage, Crouch La, Borough Gn, Sevenoaks, Kent TN15 8QL; Tel (01732) 882524

Former teacher, adviser, LEA inspector (SEN). Currently: OFSTED accredited schools' inspector. Focus: special educational needs, mainstream schools and special. Clients: schools, colleges, parents, LEAs etc. Specialities: trainer for Reuven Feuerstein's Instrumental Enrichment Programme and Mediated Learning Experience: interactive, working with clients to respond to individual needs

Johanna Wanders Turner

2 Vine Cottage, Rodmell, Lewes, E. Sussex BN7 3HE; Tel (01273) 487599; Fax (01273) 487572

OFSTED accredited registered inspector, secondary OFSTED accredited trainer. Formerly HM Staff Inspector for teacher training (INSET) and University teacher/researcher (Psychology). Associate Fellow British Psychological Society with practising certificate. Expertise in staff development, evaluation, inspection, quality assurance, and special educational needs. Currently engaged in conducting inspections, helping schools prepare for inspection, training inspectors and more general educational consultancy

David Ware

David Ware Associates, 84 Brampton Rd, St Albans, Herts AL1 4PX; Tel (01727) 51554

Formerly Head of Department, Senior Teacher and Advisory work in Secondary Education, 11 to 18. Expertise in Business Education, Economics and Technology, including Information Technology and Flexible Learning. Currently consultant to the Central London Training and Enterprise Council (CENTEC) for Flexible Learning and Tutor-Counsellor with the Open University on MA in Education. Qualified OFSTED inspector. Clients include schools, colleges and LEAs. Interests in curriculum and professional development, specifically in developing effective approaches to teaching and learning. Consultancy, support and training for:(1) the management of learning, classroom management, tutoring and resource management and development; (2) development planning and evaluation, particularly the management of educational change and action research

Chris Waterman

11 Hillside Cl, Chalfont St Giles, Bucks HP8 4JN; Tel (01494) 872179

Wide experience in teaching, training and education management. Experience as a senior consultant in information management and training. Principal interests: governing body and school management issues; information management for schools (internal and external communications); governor training; personnel issues; appeals procedures

Peter R Watkins

7 Crofton Way, Swanmore, Southampton SO32 2RF; Tel (01489) 894789

Experience: teaching history; headship of grammar and comprehensive schools; principal of a sixth form college; Deputy Chief Executive of the National Curriculum Council 1988–91. Areas of interest: national curriculum and assessment; secondary curriculum; secondary school management; governor training; writing (books, articles, reviews); speaking; school presentation and marketing; subjects – history and religious education; contributor to *Daily Telegraph Schools Guide*

John Webb

28 Prince's Court, Rope St, London SE16 1TD; Tel 0171-231 5109

(Committee 1992-4)

Managing Consultant – Price Waterhouse, with national responsibility for work in the management of education with DFE, LEAs, further and higher education, TECs

Peter Webb

22 Evenlode Ave, Penarth, South Glamorgan CF6 2PD; Tel (01222) 701320; Fax (01222) 700210

Formerly HM Inspector. Specialisms: statistics, business education, management. Special interests in institutional planning and managerial staff development in education and training, especially further and higher education; in-college consultancy programmes for strategic planning and income-generating development. Current and recent clients include FEU, the Staff College, S.W. Regional Council for further education, various LEAs

Ken Weir

Japan/UK Study Enterprise, Appleton Cottage, Moss La, Madeley, Nr Crewe, Cheshire CW3 9NQ; Tel (01782) 750221; Fax (01782) 712234

Formerly Polytechnic Principal Lecturer and Visiting Professor, Tokyo International University. OFSTED Trained Inspector. All aspects of language in education. Design and implementation of courses on Japan for General Studies programmes, modules in GCSE and A Level courses. INSET courses for teachers of Japanese children in the UK. Educational/business visits to Japan

Tessa Jean West

Kingshall Bungalow, Kingshall St, Rougham, Bury St Edmunds, Suffolk IP30 9LQ; Tel (01359) 270015; Fax (01359) 270015

Specialist in prison education; planning and implementing programmes for prisoners, training prison teachers and officers, and designing educational services to suit individual establishments. Fifteen years' experience of working in prisons and has studied prison education in eastern and western Europe including Scandinavia. Keen to work with organisations that have an interest in prison education, especially colleges of FE, TECs, government departments and international agencies. Currently working with the UN universities, NGOs and private companies

David Whale

56 Arden Rd, Kenilworth, Warks CV8 2DU; Tel (01926) 511515

Classroom and senior school management posts, then substantial LEA experience as senior general inspector and modern languages advisers. Recent work includes OFSTED inspecting, examining, PGCE tutoring, foreign language assistant training (LEA and Central Bureau).

INSET and support offered to modern languages departments, including pre-inspection review. Special interests: educational visits abroad, chanson. Detailed prospectus available

Richard Wheeler

6 Barnsway, Love La, Kings Langley, Herts WD4 9PW; Tel (01923) 263053

Former Dean of Humanities and Education, University of Hertfordshire. Specialist in higher and further education and teacher education. Research in vocational education and training (Enterprise and NVQ/GNVQ). OFSTED (Secondary) and FEFC inspection

Patrick Whitaker

Educational Management Group, Victoria Lodge, 92 Station Rd, Ibstock, Leicestershire LE67 6JJ; Tel (01530) 263053; Fax (01530) 263053

Training and consultancy in leadership, collaborative management, quality management in schools, appraisal, interpersonal and communication skills

Pat White

Education Consultant, 63 Warwick Way, London SW1V 1QR; Tel 0171-834 2692

Careers Service; TEC/LEA partnerships; education and industry links; management (organisation and structures; quality and performance measurement); post school education and training. Recent consultancies: twenty-two TEC/LEA careers service partnerships; Senior Associate – Price Waterhouse

Tim Whiteley

9 Peplins Cl, Brookmans Park, Herts AL9 7UX; Tel (01707) 644586

Chartered Electrical Engineer, with experience as HE lecturer, BTEC Education Adviser, College Principal, Department of Employment Adviser. Interests include Vocational Qualifications particularly at Higher Levels; Access and Progression Post-16 (TVEI, Compacts, Franchising); Engineering Education and Training, supply and demand, high level and intermediate level skills, curriculum revision, occupational standards, lead bodies, Innovative Teaching/Learning/Assessment. FEFC part-time registered inspector

Christopher Wightwick

Education Consultancy, 19 Nottingham Rd, Wandsworth Common, London SW17 7EA; Tel 0181-767 6161; Fax 0181-767 6161

Formerly HM staff inspector for modern languages and HMI assessor to the National Curriculum Modern Foreign Languages Working Group. General inspection of schools, advice on organisation, management and curriculum. Advice on modern languages, including working with teachers on implementing the National Curriculum in the classroom. Director of in-service training courses. Production of reports from data supplied. General editorial work

Angela Wilkinson Tilbrook

Educational Support Services, Churstwood, 51 Maltese Rd, Chelmsford, Essex CM1 2PB; Tel (01245) 258098

Former head of LEA Support Services. All aspects of Special Educational Needs, child protection pre- and post-inspection support. Consultant to National Council for Educational Technology (NCET)

Tony Williams

Ramoth, Little La, Loosley Row, Aylesbury, Bucks HP17 0NX; Tel 0171-473 3818

Has held senior posts in three LEAs; currently working in a London Borough. Interests include property services and capital projects; local management and governing bodies; LEA management structures; re-organisations and amalgamations; and appraisal

Gaynor Wingham

17 Greenham Rd, Eltham, London SE9 1UQ; Tel 0181-889 4678

Wide experience of working within education, social services and the voluntary sector. Former Head of Social Work Services within education. Consultancy and training offered in Child Care legislation and child protection issues, special educational needs legislation and practice, partnership with parents, school attendance, counselling skills, and boarding school care provision

Peter W G Wright

6 Royal Mews, Taswell Rd, Southsea, Hants PO5 2RQ; Tel (01705) 863524

Higher and Further Education: institutional change; quality and quality audit; links with employers; staff development; European links; links between Further and Higher Education; Access; Credit Accumulation and Transfer; Outcomes in Higher Education; links between Vocational qualifications and HE. The Evaluation of Innovation; Open Learning; Work has included: Adviser to the Employment Department on the Enterprise in Higher Education Programme; Professional adviser with the CVCP, Universities' Staff Development Unit; Associate Tutor, the Staff College, Blagdon. Previous clients include the European Commission and the OECD

Carola Zeegan

Lauenburger Strasse 29, 76139 Karlsruhe, Germany; Tel (01721) 689405

Practising primary teacher at European School (EU), Karlsruhe, Germany, seconded by DFE. Author of NFER LINC Paper 10, 1992, Learning through the Familiar: the Inter-Cultural Fairy Tale as a vehicle for Second language Acquisition. Current membership of E2L/EFL (Key Stages 1 and 2) syllabus working party. Consultant to Education Department, Baden-Württemberg (training video produced). INSET to all (eight) European Schools

Nick Zienau

ZTA Consultants, 2 Priory Lodge, Priory Pk, Blackheath, London SE3 9UY; Tel 0181-852 6451; Fax 0181-297 8902

Main themes of current work: management and organisational development – helping professional organisations including schools, colleges and support structures to offer greater quality to their clients. Seminars to develop skills and strategies of consultants and consulting organisations which advise or influence front-line managers. Collaborative projects with the Netherlands and Russia – innovative teacher training and development

Other Consultants

Cambridge Education Associates Ltd

Minerva House, 618 Newmarket Rd, Cambridge CB5; Tel (01223) 413399; Fax (01223) 414949

An established management consultancy and staff development company working at levels within the education service. CEA Consultants work as a team in offering a wide range of support to LEAs, schools, college and educational suppliers. CEA offers teams for OFSTED inspections, as well as pre and post OFSTED consultancy advice

"Catalyst" – ORCA Services Ltd, Educational Services Ltd

35 Send Rd, Send, Woking, Surrey GV23 7ET; Tel (01483) 223707

Contact (UK) Kate Attridge

15 Education Consultants

This consultancy works in the field of severe learning difficulties with a speciality in profound multiple disabilities. "Catalyst" provides workshops, in-service training and management development to a variety of agencies. Work is also undertaken in continental Europe, where learning programmes of the European Commission are monitored
"Neihaff", L-9161 Ingeldorf, Luxembourg; Tel 00 352 81.86.10 (from UK); Fax 00 352 81.86.10 (from UK); *Contact (Luxembourg)* Flo Longhorn

Cavendish Educational Consultants

Oddfellows Cottage, Setley, Brockenhurst, Hampshire SO42 7UF; Tel (01590) 622195; Fax (01590) 624445
Produces the Gap Year Book, annual publication geared towards students taking a year off before University. The booklet describes organisations, colleges and books to aid the student in researching gap year possibilities

The Combe Hay Partnership

Combe Hay Hse, 193 Lexden Rd, Colchester, Essex CO3 4BH; Tel (01206) 563084
The partnership specialises in advising on, and tackling in a practical way, schools within the State, Grant Maintained and CTC sectors that have either been deemed to be "At Risk", or who may have organisational or administrative problems, it also advises on the political and practical implications of government policy related to education

EFTR Associates

30 Gritstone Rd, Matlock, Derbyshire DE4 3GD; Tel (01629) 57501; Fax (01629) 584972
Director Janet Roberts
EFTR Associates provide a wide range of training and consultancy services for a variety of education establishments and other organisations including TECs, companies and the voluntary sector. It offers the services of education, local authority and legal professionals, as well as specialists in the fields of Education Management and Decision Making, Occupational Psychology, Counselling, Total Quality Management and the Accreditation of Prior Learning
National Education Funding Information Service
Annual subscription service in manual form (updated bi-monthly) giving detailed information on possible sources of funding for many areas in Education. Subscription also includes Telephone/Fax Helpline and backup service

Keith Evans

4 Maes yr Haf, Mold, Clwyd CH7 1TR; Tel (01352) 753743
Former Director of Education, Clwyd. Previous experience includes initial teacher training (PGCE), educational producer ITV. Currently Chairman, North Wales Board Arts Council of Wales. Main areas of interest: education, business partnership, management and professional development, arts in education

Clifford French

CFC Consultancy, 340 Windmill Rd, Ealing, London W5 4UR; Tel 0181-569 8770; Mobile (01956) 30608; Fax 0181-569 8770
Specialist in support for grant-maintained schools, from drafting of proposals through to preparation for implementation and provision of consultancy on a wide range of issues, including change of character. Training and support on development plans, budgeting and information systems. Will work with schools' architects on capital bids. Formerly a headteacher and LEA officer

Tom Hinds

Hinds Education and Review, 40 Grove Rd, Windsor SL4 1JQ; Tel (01753) 858123
Work for D.F.E., Action for Governors' Information and Training, the Audit Commission, Brunel University, NAHT, and the National Consumer Council. Interests in local management, governing bodies, performance indicators, and group relations

Roy McHugh

Roy McHugh Education and Training, 46 Polhill Ave, Bedford MK41 9DU; Tel (01234) 261540
Expertise as a consultant to schools, LEAs, universities and industry and commerce. Providing – Organisational, management, staff and curriculum development programmes as well as the training of school governors. Lecturing, research and development, and the application of educational technology to learning/teaching particularly in the field of open learning. Competency-based training in employment and community programmes. Present major contracts with the Open University

Professor Peter Mortimore, OBE, PhD

Institute of Education, University of London, 20 Bedford Way, London WC1 OAL; Tel 0171-580 1122
Courses offered by the Institute range from initial teacher training for graduates, and advanced courses for experienced teachers, to higher degrees in education and related areas. Further information may be obtained from the Student Programmes Office on 0171-612 6104/6102; Secretary and Head of Academic Services: D.J. Warren, BSc; Head of Finance and Administration: G.S. Philpott, BA

NTS Ltd

Brantholme, Mount Pleasant, Arnside, Cumbria LA5 0EW; Tel (01524) 762336; Fax (01524) 762444
Managing Director Tim O'Connor
Event Manager Geoff Storey
Education Consultant Kate O'Connor
Management consultancy and development supporting the development of managers in education, both of support services and teaching staff, with an approach designed to recognise and accommodate the special circumstances of managers in education. 35 consultants, both full and part time

Storey Associates

Pennyleaze, Stainswick La, Shrivenham, Oxford SN6 8DX; Tel (01793) 782918
Principal Consultant Rod Storey
Bespoke short training courses for management in a range of inter-personal and management skills

David Trethowan

David Trethowan Associates, Gorwydd Farm, Llanddewi Brefi, Tregaron, Dyfed SY25 6NY; Tel (01570) 45516
Specialists in human resource management, including performance appraisal, team building, total quality and individual consultancy and training

John Weeks, CBE, MBA

16 Castle Rd, Clevedon, Avon BS21 7DE; Tel (01275) 875189
Co-ordinator of Consultancy for MAPS (Management and Professional Services), associated with the Secondary Heads' Association, using a wide network of SHA members and other specialists as consultants for schools. Previously head of comprehensive schools for 22 years. Was a member of the National Steering Group on Schoolteacher Appraisal. Salaries and Conditions of service Officer for SHA, 1987–90. Main interests: governor training, salaries and conditions of service, appraisal and inspections

16 Confederation of British Industry (CBI) Trades Union Congress (TUC) Association of British Chambers of Commerce

Confederation of British Industry

Centre Point, 103 New Oxford St, London WC1A 1DU; Tel 0171-379 7400; Fax 0171-240 1578; Telex 21332
President Sir Michael Angus
Director-General Howard Davies
Secretary Maurice Hunt
The Confederation is an independent, non-party-political body, financed by industry and commerce. It exists primarily to ensure that governments of all political complexions understand and respond to the interests, needs and problems of British business and, as its acknowledged representative, is consulted by governments. The Confederation publishes a monthly *CBI News*, and runs a comprehensive conference programme

CBI Education Foundation

Chairman Sir Brian Hayes, GCB
Director J.W. Nisbet
The CBI Education Foundation supports Understanding British Industry (UBI) (see below)

CBI Education and Training Directorate

Director A.J. Webb

CBI Regional Offices

The Confederation has 13 Regional Offices (those in Scotland, Wales, Northern and North West have their own Education and Training Committees)

England

Eastern
14 Union Rd, Cambridge CB2 1HE; Tel (01223) 65636
Director A.G. Wilman

East Midlands
17 St Wilfred Sq, Calverton, Nottingham NG14 6FP; Tel (0115) 965 3311
Director K. Barnes

London
Centre Point, 103 New Oxford St, London WC1A 1DU; Tel 0171-379 7400
Director Jane Calvert-Lee

Northern
15 Grey St, Newcastle upon Tyne NE1 6EE; Tel 0191-232 1644
Director Dr A. Foord

North Western
Emerson Hse, Albert St, Eccles, Manchester M30 0LT; Tel 0161-707 2190
Director C. Clifford

South Eastern and Southern
Tubs Hill Hse, London Rd, Sevenoaks, Kent TN13 1BX; Tel (01732) 454040
Director H. Eatock

South Western
8/10 Whiteladies Rd, Clifton, Bristol BS8 1NZ; Tel (0117) 973 7065
Director C.J. Curtis

West Midlands
18th Flr, Metropolitan Hse, 1 Hagley Rd, Edgbaston, Birmingham B16 8TG; Tel 0121-454 7991
Director J. Gunn

Yorkshire and Humberside
Arndale Hse, Station Rd, Crossgates, Leeds LS15 8EU; Tel (0113) 264 4242
Director B. Bigley

Northern Ireland

Fanum Hse, 108 Great Victoria St, Belfast BT2 7PD; Tel (01232) 326658
Director Nigel Smyth

Scotland

Beresford Hse, 5 Claremont Terr, Glasgow G3 7XT; Tel 0141-332 8661
Director D. Maclehose

Wales

Pearl Assurance Hse, Greyfriars Rd, Cardiff CF1 3JR; Tel (01222) 232536
Director I.M. Kelsall

Understanding British Industry (UBI)

UBI has three aims: to improve understanding of industry, commerce and wealth creation among teachers; to help teachers to influence school curricula; bringing the lessons taught in school more into line with the needs of adult life; to improve understanding of the education system among people in industry and business

Headquarters and Information Centre
Sun Alliance Hse, New Inn Hall St, Oxford OX1 2QE; Tel (01865) 722585; Fax (01865) 790014
Director J.L. Brodie
Director, Teacher Placement Service P. Davies
Director, National Education Programmes Unit Ruth Swinhoe
Senior Information Officer Jan Hussey

Directors
Projects Director D. King UBI Midlands, University of Leicester, School of Education, 21 University Rd, Leicester LE1 7RF; Tel (0116) 254 4080; Fax (0116) 285 4275
Projects Director P. Stagg UBI Northern, c/o School of Education, Hillary Pl, University of Leeds, Rm 2.11, Hillary Pl, Leeds LS2 9JT; Tel (0113) 242 4850; Fax (0113) 233 6017
Director V.M. Pugh UBI Scotland and Northern Ireland, Adelphi Education Centre, 12 Commerical Rd, Glasgow G5 0PQ; Tel 0141-429 4575; Fax 0141-420 1710

UBI/INDTEL
Project Director Jose Chambers, MPhil UBI/INDTEL, King Alfred's College, Winchester, Hants SO22 4NR; Tel (01962) 841332; Fax (01962) 849974

Trades Union Congress

Congress Hse, Great Russell St, London WC1B 3LS; Tel 0171-636 4030; Fax 0171-636 0632; Telex 268328 TUC G
General Secretary John Monks
Acting Secretary to Education and Training Committee C. Sherriff
Education and Training Committee C. Brooke; G. Brumwell; T. Burke; N. De Gruchy; Ms J. Drake; Ms P. Dwyer; D. Evans; J. Geldart; Ms A. Gibson; P. Hagger; W.B. Jordan; D. Mc Avoy; H. MacKenzie; L.A. Mills; R. Pickering; Mrs M. Prosser; B. Reamsbottom; Mrs M. Rooney; D. Scard; J. Sheldon; B. Switzer; M. Twomey; J. Weakley;
Secretary to Trade Union Education Committee A. Grant
Trade Union Education Committee Members D.K. Brookman; G. Brumwell; T. Burke; Ms D. Covey; N. De Gruchy; J. Drake; Ms P. Dwyer; J. Edmonds; D. Evans; J. Geldart; P. Hagger; Ms P. Hawkes; D. Hill; Ms B. Hillon; A. Johnson; J. Knapp; D.A.C. Lambert; I. Love; H.U. Mackenzie; D. McAvoy, L.A. Mills; Mrs M. Rooney; D. Scard; B. Switzer; A.I. Young

Trades Union Congress Educational Trust

Congress Hse, Great Russell St, London WC1B 3LS
Trustees J. Knapp (Chairman); L.A. Mills; J. Monks (Treasurer)
Secretary A.F. Grant

Trades Union Congress Regional Education Officers

England

East and West Midland
10 Pershore St, Birmingham B5 4RU; Tel 0121-666 6179; Fax 0121-666 7426
T. Cook

Northern
Swinburne Hse, Swinburne St, Gateshead NE8 1AX; Tel 0191-490 0048
S. Grinter

North Western
Baird Hse, 41 Merton Rd, Bootle, Merseyside L20 7AP; Tel 0151-933 4403
L. Smith

South East and East Anglia
Education Department TUC, Congress Hse, Great Russell St, London WC1B 3LS; Tel 0171-636 4030
B. Bennett

Yorkshire and Humberside
30 York Pl, Leeds LS1 2ED; Tel (0113) 242 9296
M. Ball

Wales and South West England

1 Cathedral Rd, Cardiff CF1 9SD; Tel (01222) 227449
J. Crew

Scotland

16 Woodlands Terr, Glasgow G3 6ED; Tel 0141-332 2045
L. Cairns

Northern Ireland

Belfast
Northern Ireland Committee, Irish Congress of Trade Unions, 3 Wellington Pk, Belfast BT9 6DJ; Tel (01232) 681726
Training and Education Officer T. Moore

Trade Union Education Officers

Amalgamated Engineering Union
110 Peckham Rd, London SE15 5EL; Tel 0171-703 4231
Education Officer J. Richards

Apex Partnership/GMB
Associated Society of Locomotive Engineers and Firemen
9 Arkwright Rd, London NW3 6AB; Tel 0171-431 0275
Education Officer D. Fullick

Association of University Teachers
United Hse, 1 Pembridge Rd, London W11 3HJ; Tel 0171-221 4370
Education Officer Mrs A. Aziz

Bakers, Food and Allied Workers
Stanborough Hse, Great North Rd, Stanborough, Welwyn Garden City, Herts AL8 7TA; Tel (01707) 260159/0
Education Officer N. Bryson

Banking, Insurance and Finance Union
Sheffield Hse, 1B Amity Gr, Raynes Pk, London SW20 0LG; Tel 0181-946 9151
Education Officer P. Ortiz

Broadcasting, Entertainment, Cinematograph and Theatre Union
111 Wardour St, London W1V 4AY; Tel 0171-437 8506; Fax 0171-437 8268
Education Officer A. Egan

Ceramic and Allied Trades Union
Hillcrest Hse, Garth St, Hanley, Stoke-on-Trent ST1 2AB; Tel (01782) 272755
Education Officer G. Bagnall

Civil and Public Services Association
160 Falcon Rd, London SW11 2LN; Tel 0171-924 2727
Education Officer V. Stansfield

College of Radiographers
14 Upper Wimpole St, London W1M 8BN; Tel 0171-934 5726; Fax 0171-487 3483
Director, Professional & Educational Services Peter M. Smith

The Communication Managers' Association
CMA Hse, Ruscombe Business Pk, Twyford, Reading RG10 9JD; Tel (01734) 342300
Officer Responsible for Education

Confederation of Health Service Employees
Glen Hse, High St, Banstead, Surrey SM7 2LH; Tel (0173 73) 53322
Education Officer T. Chandler

Educational Institute of Scotland
46 Moray Pl, Edinburgh EG3 6BH; Tel 0131-225 6244
Education Officer Mr MacCauley

Engineers' and Managers' Association
Flaxman Hse, Gogmore La, Chertsey, Surrey KT16 9JS; Tel (01932) 564131; Fax (01932) 567707
Education Officer F. Adamson

Fire Brigades Union
Bradley Hse, 68 Coombe Rd, Kingston-upon-Thames, Surrey KT2 7AE; Tel 0181-541 1765
Education Officer A. Totterdell

General, Municipal, Boilermakers and Allied Trades Union
GMB National College, College Rd, Whalley Range, Manchester M16 8BP; Tel 0161-861 8788
Director of Training and Education Frank White

Graphical, Paper and Media Union
Keys Hse, 63–67 Bromham Rd, Bedford MK40 2AG; Tel (01234) 351521; Fax (01234) 270580
Head of Education and Training, International and Political Affairs Geoff Hayward, MA(Oxon), PGCE

Inland Revenue Staff Federation
Douglas Houghton Hse, 231 Vauxhall Bridge Rd, London SW1V 1EH; Tel 0171-834 8254
Education Officer K. Burridge

Institution of Professionals, Managers & Specialists
75–79 York Rd, London SE1 7AQ; Tel 0171-928 9951
Education Officer Ms W. Harrison

Iron and Steel Trades Confederation
Swinton Hse, 324 Gray's Inn Rd, London WC1X 8DD; Tel 0171-837 6691; Fax 0171-278 8378
Education Officer J.B. Clarke

MSF
Whitehall College, Dane O'Coys Rd, Bishops Stortford, Herts; Tel (01279) 755677
Education Officer S. Howard

NAS/UWT Education Centre
Hillscourt, Rose Hill, Rednal, Birmingham B45 8RS; Tel 0121-453 6150
Education Officer L. Roberts

National Association of Licensed House Managers
29 Howard St, North Shields, Tyne and Wear NE30 1AR; Tel 0191-258 6891
Education Officer Graham Eastwood

National Association of Teachers in Further and Higher Education
27 Britannia St, London WC1X 9JP; Tel 0171-837 3636
Head of Policy D. Betts

National Communications Union
Alvescot Lodge, Alvescot, Oxon OX18 2PY; Tel (01993) 843373
Education Officer D. Ward

National Union of Civil & Public Servants
124–130 Southwark St, London SE1 0TU; Tel 0171-928 9671
Education Officer Roger McKenzie

National Union of Knitwear, Footwear and Apparel Trades
14 West Walk, Leicester LE1 7NA; Tel (0116) 255 0645
Education Officer David Richardson

National Union of Journalists
Acorn Hse, 314–320 Gray's Inn Rd, London WC1X 8DP; Tel 0171-278 7916
Assistant Secretary R. Norris

National Union of Mineworkers
Holly St, Sheffield S1 2GT; Tel (0114) 276 6900; Fax (0114) 276 6400
Education Officer Ms H. Cave

National Union of Rail, Maritime & Transport Workers
Unity Hse, Euston Rd, London NW1 2DL; Tel 0171-387 4771

Education Centre, Frant Pl, Frant, Tunbridge Wells, Kent, (089 275) 391
Education Officer R. Spry-Shute

National Union of Teachers
Stoke Rochford Hall, Stoke Rochford, nr Grantham, Lincs NG33 5EJ; Tel (0147 683) 421, 337
Director R. Gifford

Society of Telecom Executives
Arthur Willett Hse, 1 Park Rd, Teddington, Middx TW11 0AR; Tel 0181-943 5181
Education Officer Ben Marshall

Trades Union Congress
Congress Hse, Great Russell St, London WC1B 3LS; Tel 0171-636 4030; Fax 0171-636 0632
Head of Organisation and Services Alan Grant

The United Road Transport Union
76 High La, Chorlton-cum-Hardy, Manchester M21 1FD; Tel 0161-881 6245; Fax 0161-862 9127
Education Officer M. Durant

Transport and General Workers' Union
Transport Hse, Smith Sq, London SW1P 3JB; Tel 0171-828 7788

Education Centre, Grand Parade, Eastbourne, E Sussex BN21 4DN; Tel (01323) 21455
Acting Head of Research and Education J. Irvin

Transport Salaried Staffs' Association
Walkden Hse, 10 Melton St, London NW1 2EJ; Tel 0171-387 2101
Education Officer M. Campbell

Union of Communication Workers
UCW Hse, Crescent La, Clapham Common, London SW4 9RN; Tel 0171-622 9977

UCW Education Centre, Elstead Hotel, Knyveton Rd, Bournemouth B41 3QP; *Education Officer* R. Walsh

Union of Construction, Allied Trades and Technicians
UCATT Hse, 177 Abbeville Rd, London SW4 9RL; Tel 0171-622 2442; Fax 0171-720 4081
Education Officer Jennifer Smith

Union of Shop, Distributive and Allied Workers
Oakley, 188 Wilmslow Rd, Fallowfield, Manchester M14 6LJ; Tel 0161-224 2804
Education Officer J. Rees

UNISON
1 Mabledon Pl, London WC1H 9AJ; Tel 0171-388 2366; Fax 0171-387 6692

The Association of British Chambers of Commerce

9 Tufton St, London SW1P 3QB; Tel 0171-222 1555; Fax 0171-799 2202
Director-General Ron Taylor, CBE
Executive Director Alan Bartlett
The Association is the national representative body for 106 Chambers of Commerce and Industry in the United Kingdom which in turn serve over 90,000 businesses of all sizes. It is primarily an information, policy development and representational body, dealing extensively with Government and other national organisations over a range of issues including education and training. Its member Chambers are base organisations for various education–business links, and nominate business governors to all levels of education institution

Chambers of Commerce

Aberdeen
Chamber of Commerce, 5 Hadden St, Aberdeen AB9 1HF; Tel (01224) 212626; Fax (01224) 231221; Telex 73315 CHAMCOM G
Chief Executive D.G. Marnoch, BSc(Eng), AMCA

Barnsley
Chamber of Commerce & Industry, Commerce Hse, Westgate, Barnsley S70 2DX; Tel (01226) 201166; Fax (01226) 298606
Chief Executive R.J. Nunns

Birmingham
Chamber of Industry & Commerce, PO Box 360, 75 Harborne Rd, Birmingham B15 3DH; Tel 0121-454 6171; Fax 0121-455 8670; Telex 338024 BIRCOM G
Director J.K. Warburton, CBE
Area Office: Redditch & District, Chamber of Industry & Commerce, Systems Hse, Unit 2, Moon Pk, Burnt Meadow Rd, North Moons Moat, Redditch B98 9PA; Tel (01527) 67692; Fax (01527) 67861
Office Manager J. Hall
Area Office: Sandwell, Chamber of Commerce & Industry, Sandwell Business Advice Centre, Victoria St, Sandwell, West Bromwich B70 8ET; Tel 0121-553 2821; Fax 0121-553 3079; Telex 338584 SCIC G
Office Manager A.M. Avian
Area Office: Solihull, Chamber of Industry & Commerce, PO Box 360, 75 Harborne Rd, Birmingham B15 3DH; Tel 0121-454 6171; Fax 0121-455 8670; Telex 338024 BIRCOM G
Office Manager D. Burrows

Bolton
Chamber of Commerce & Industry, Silverwell Hse, Silverwell St, Bolton BL1 1PX; Tel (01204) 33896; Fax (01204) 361780; Telex 635109 CHACOM G
Director B. Smith
Training Division: Sun Alliance Hse (4th Floor), 63 Bradshawgate, Bolton BL1 1QP; Tel (01204) 32157

Boston
Chamber of Commerce & Industry, Unit D2, Bolton Industrial Est, Norfolk St, Boston, Lincs PE21 9HG; Tel (01205) 351144; Fax (01205) 352182
Secretary A.M. McCann

Bradford
Chamber of Commerce, Commerce Hse, Cheapside, Bradford BD1 4JZ; Tel (01274) 728166; Fax (01274) 370866, 737615; Telex 51449 CHAMCOM G
Director D. Woodcock, MBE, JP

Burnley see *East Lancashire*

Burton upon Trent & District
Chamber of Commerce & Industry, 158 Derby St, Burton upon Trent DE14 2NZ; Tel (01283) 63761; Fax (01283) 510753
Chief Executive F.M. Shepherd

Bury & District
Chamber of Commerce, Lloyds Bank Chambers, 4 Bolton St, Bury BL9 0LQ; Tel 0161-764 8640
Secretary J. Ridyard

Calderdale
Chamber of Commerce & Industry, Unit OP54/55, Dean Clough Office Pk, Halifax HX3 5AX; Tel (01422) 352517; Fax (01422) 47256; Telex 517129 and 51468
Secretary P.W. Burton, MBE, MC

Cambridge & District
Chamber of Commerce & Industry, The Business Centre, Station Rd, Histon, Cambridge CB4 4LF; Tel (01223) 273414, 237403; Fax (01223) 237405; Telex 817114 CAMCOM G
Chief Executive P.W. Homer

Cardiff
Chamber of Commerce & Industry, 101–108 The Exchange, Mount Stuart Sq, Cardiff CF1 6RD; Tel (01222) 481648; Fax (01222) 489785; Telex 497492 CHACOM G
Chief Executive Dr D. Phillips

Carlisle
Chamber of Commerce, 4 Brunswick St, Carlisle CA1 1PD; Tel (01228) 26288
Director M. Uppard

Central & West Lancashire
Chamber of Commerce & Industry, 9/10 Eastway Business Village, Oliver's Pl, Fulwood, Preston PR2 4WT; Tel (01772) 653000; Fax (01772) 655544; Telex 677467 CHACOM G
Director J.S. White
Area Office: 113 High St, Skelmersdale, Lancs WN8 8AT; Tel (01695) 21436; Fax (01695) 50225
Manager S. Burns
Area Office: 20 Queens St, Blackpool FY1 1PD; Tel (01253) 22958; Fax (01253) 22963
Manager D. Southworth

Central Scotland
Chamber of Commerce, Suite A, Haypark, Marchmont Ave, Polmont, Stirlingshire FK2 0NZ; Tel (01324) 716868; Telex 778583 CHACOM G
Chief Executive T. Lawson

Chester & North Wales
Chamber of Commerce, Reliance Hse, Waterloo Rd, Chester CH2 2AL; Tel (01244) 378776; Fax (01244) 378701; Telex c/o Merseyside Chamber
Director F.R. Bass
Area Office: Selby Towers, 29 Prince Dr, Colwyn Bay, Clwyd LL29 8PE; Tel (01492) 532106; Fax (01492) 531686
Manager P. Rawlings

Colchester & North Essex
Chamber of Commerce, 1 High St, Colchester, Essex CO1 1DA; Tel (01206) 765277; Fax (01206) 578073; Telex 987562 COCHAC G
Secretary J.A. Wellerd

Coventry
Chamber of Commerce & Industry, 123 St Nicholas St, Coventry CV1 4FD; Tel (01203) 633000; Fax (01203) 552908; Telex 311033 CHACOM G
Chief Executive B.V. Willis, FInstPet, FBIM

Croydon
Chamber of Commerce & Industry, Commerce Hse, 21 Scarbrook Rd, Croydon CR9 6HY; Tel 0181-680 2165; Fax 0181-688 4587
Chief Executive P. Broderick, MCAM

Derby & Derbyshire
Chamber of Commerce & Industry, New Enterprise Hse, 9 St Helens St, Derby DE1 3GY; Tel (01332) 47031; Fax (01332) 382028; Telex 377106 CHACOM G
Chief Executive P.K. Farrow
Area Office: Derbyshire Dales District Office, c/o Brittany Chamber of Commerce, Shaw Croft Centre, Dig St, Ashbourne, Derby DE6 1GF; Tel (01335) 300476; Fax (01335) 300296
Manager M. Platt

Doncaster
Chamber of Commerce (Inc), 50 Christchurch Rd, Doncaster DN1 2QN; Tel (01302) 341000; Fax (01302) 328382
Director and Secretary G. Mangan

Dorset
Chamber of Commerce & Industry, Upton Hse, Upton Country Pk, Poole BH17 7BJ; Tel (01202) 682000; Fax (01202) 680315
Chief Executive B.A. Kite

Dudley
Chamber of Industry & Commerce, First Floor, Falcon Hse, The Minories, Dudley DY2 8PG; Tel (01384) 237653; Fax (01384) 238068; Telex 336718 CHACOM G
Manager J.E. Carter

East Lancashire
Chamber of Industry & Commerce, 14 Richmond Terr, Blackburn BB1 7BH; Tel (01254) 664747; Fax (01254) 55465; Telex 63300 CHACOM G
Director J.A. McKinstry
Area Office: Burnley & District, Chamber of Commerce & Industry, 16 Keirby Wk, Burnley, Lancs BB11 2DE; Tel (01282) 36555; Fax (01282) 35620; Telex 63300 BURCOM G
Director G. Beeley

Edinburgh
Chamber of Commerce & Manufactures, 3 Randolph Cres, Edinburgh EG3 7UD; Tel 0131-225 5851; Fax 0131-220 1508; Telex 72465 CHAMCO G
Chief Executive I. Brown

Exeter & District
Chamber of Commerce & Trade, Concord Hse, South St, Exeter EX1 1EG; Tel (01392) 433641/2; Fax (01392) 50402; Telex 42603 CHAMCO G
Secretary M.J.P. Walsh

Fareham
Chamber of Commerce, 75 High St, Fareham PO16 7BB; Tel (01329) 822250
Chief Executive R. Homer

Fife
Chamber of Commerce & Industry, 17 Tolbooth St, Kirkcaldy KY1 1RW; Tel (01592) 201932; Fax (01592) 641187
Chief Executive J.W. Brodie, JP, CEng

Glasgow
Chamber of Commerce & Manufactures, 30 George Sq, Glasgow G2 1EQ; Tel 0141-204 2121; Fax 0142-221 2336; Telex 777967 CHACOM G
Secretary E. Marwick, MA

Goole & District
Chamber of Commerce and Shipping (Inc), 46 Aire St, Goole, North Humberside DN14 5QE; Tel (01405) 769164; Fax (01405) 764991
Secretary G.E. Wragg

Grantham
Chamber of Commerce, c/o Cole, Dickins & Hills, Chartered Accountants, 39 Westgate, Grantham, Lincs NG31 6LY; Tel (01476) 66661
Secretary J.M.D. Morrissey, FCA

Great Yarmouth see *Norwich and Norfolk*

Greenock
Chamber of Commerce, 12 Chapel St, (off Dellingburn St), Greenock, Renfrewshire PA15 1EX; Tel (01475) 83678
Secretary A. MacKenzie, FCCA

Grimsby & Immingham
Chamber of Commerce and Shipping, 4 Victoria St, Mary's Gate, Grimsby DN31 1DP; Tel (01472) 342981; Fax (01472) 250579
Secretary P. Coulbeck

Guernsey
Chamber of Commerce, The States Arcade, Market St, St Peter Port, Guernsey, Channel Islands; Tel (01481) 727483; Fax (01481) 710755; Telex 4191445 CHACOM G
Chief Executive J. Moore

Guildford
Chamber of Commerce, Friary Mews, 28 Commercial Rd, Guildford, Surrey GU1 4SX; Tel (01483) 37449; (01483) 574322 (Export documents only)
Director B.A. Smith

Halton
Chamber of Commerce, 57/61 Church St, Runcorn, Cheshire WA7 1LG; Tel (0192 85) 60958; Telex c/o Merseyside Chamber
Director and Secretary H.C. Nicholls

Hull
Incorporated Chamber of Commerce and Shipping, Samman Hse, Bowlalley La, Hull HU1 1XT; Tel (01482) 324976; Fax (01482) 213962
Secretary D. Myers, JP

Ipswich & Suffolk
Chamber of Commerce, Industry and Shipping, Agriculture Hse, Foundation St, Ipswich IP4 1BJ; Tel (01473) 210611; Fax (01473) 225488; Telex 987703 CHACOM G
Chief Executive and Secretary R. Feltwell

Isle of Man
Chamber of Commerce (including Trade & Industry), 17 Drinkwater St, Douglas, Isle of Man; Tel (01624) 674941; Fax (01624) 663367
Secretary B. O'Hanlon

Isle of Wight
Chamber of Commerce, 24 The Mall, Carisbrooke Rd, Newport, IOW PO30 1BW; Tel (01983) 524390; Fax (01983) 821811
Office Manager P. Reynolds

Jersey
Chamber of Commerce & Industry Incorporated, 19 Royal Sq, St Helier, Jersey, Channel Islands; Tel (01534) 24536, 71031; Fax (01534) 34942
Chief Executive J.M. Snell

Kendal & District
Incorporated Chamber of Commerce, PO Box 27, Exchange Chambers, 10B Highgate, Kendal, Cumbria LA9 4SX; Tel (01539) 720049; Fax (01539) 726177
Secretary J.M. Hopkinson, TD, MA

Kidderminster & District
Chamber of Commerce, Slingfield Mill, Pitts La, Kidderminster, Worcs DY11 6YR; Tel (01562) 515515, 744937; Fax (01562) 747488
Director and Secretary G.A. Kershaw, FBIM

Kirklees & Wakefield
Chamber of Commerce & Industry, Commerce Hse, Wakefield Rd, Aspley, Huddersfield HD5 9AA; Tel (01484) 426591; Fax (01484) 514199; Telex 51458 COMHUDD G
Director K.P. Welton
Area Office: New Commerce Hse, 168 Westgate, Wakefield WF2 9FR; Tel (01924) 200646; Fax (01924) 200564
Head of Policy & Research S.J. Downs
Training Offices: Caldervale Rd, Wakefield WF1 5PF; Tel (01924) 368854; Fax (01924) 364623
Centre Manager J. Cawdron
Garden St, Wakefield WF1 1DX; Tel (01924) 290525
Centre Manager J. Cawdron
44/46 Bradford Rd, Dewsbury WF13 2DR; Tel (01924) 457681; Fax (01924) 458572
Centre Manager M. Fox
15 Wellington Rd, Dewsbury WF13 1HF; Tel (01924) 457982
Centre Manager D. Fox
St Thomas' Rd, Huddersfield HD1 3LG; Tel (01484) 516533; Fax (01484) 423390
Centre Manager M. Fox
Bondgate Industrial Est, Bondgate, Pontefract WF8 2JJ; Tel (01977) 790574; Fax (01977) 702686
Centre Manager J. Cawdron
Industry Hse, Seymour La, Barnsley S70 2NY; Tel (01226) 733838; Fax (01226) 200513
Centre Manager B. Platt
Lidget La, Thurnscoe, Rotherham S63 0DD; Tel (01709) 881988
Centre Manager B. Platt

Lancaster & District
Chamber of Commerce, Trade & Industry, Marton Hse, Marton St, Lancaster LA1 1YA; Tel (01524) 39467; Fax (01524) 63280
Director E.J. Young

Leeds
Chamber of Commerce & Industry, Commerce Hse, 2 St Albans Pl, Wade La, Leeds LS2 8HZ; Tel (0113) 243 0491; Fax (0113) 243 0504; Telex 55293 CHACOM G
Director P. Coles-Johnson

Leith
Chamber of Commerce, 3 Randolph Cres, Edinburgh EH3 7UD; Tel 0131-225 5851; Telex 72465 CHACOM G
Director I. Brown

Lincoln
Incorporated Chamber of Commerce, Commerce Hse, Outer Circle Rd, Lincoln LN2 4HY; Tel (01522) 523713; 542488 (YTS only); Fax (01522) 546667
Secretary R.M. Charnley

London
Chamber of Commerce & Industry, 69 Cannon St, London EC4N 5AB; Tel 0171-248 4444; Fax 0171-489 0391; Telex 888941 LCCI G
Chief Executive A.W.M. Platt, CBE
Enterprise Training Manager M. Horner
The London Chamber is the only one which conducts examinations, nationally recognised, through the Commercial Education Scheme
London Chamber Southern Area and Gatwick Airport Office (documentation only), 13A The Broadway, Crawley, W Sussex RH10 1WP; Tel (01293) 30017
London Chamber SE Region (documentation only), Ashford Hse, County Sq, Ashford, Kent TN23 1YB; Tel (01233) 639562
London Chamber Barking & Dagenham Office (documentation only), 5 Cambridge Hse, Cambridge Rd, Barking IG11 8NW; Tel 0181-594 3195
London Chamber Cricklewood Office (documentation only), 1 Pond Row, Production Village, 110 Cricklewood La, London NW2 2DS; Tel 0181-450 3575
London Chamber Greenford Office, Unit 21, Derby Rd, Metropolitan Centre, Greenford, Middx UB6 8UJ; Tel 0181-575 3542
London Chamber of Commerce & Industrial Examinations Board, Marlowe Hse, 109 Stations Rd, Sidcup, Kent DA15 7BJ; Tel 0181-302 0261; Fax 0181-302 4169
Director C. Bateson

Lowestoft
Incorporated Chamber of Commerce, The Waveney Business Centre, Gordon Rd, Lowestoft, Suffolk NR32 1NL; Tel (01502) 569383; Fax (01502) 501215
Secretary P.J. Stott

Luton, Bedford & District
Chamber of Commerce & Industry, Commerce Hse, Stuart St, Luton LU1 5AU; Tel (01582) 23456, 416943; Fax (01582) 419422; Telex 825562 CHACOM G
Secretary-General P.A. Hoskins, MBE, ACIS
Area Office: 85/87 High St, Bedford MK10 1NE; Tel (01234) 269555; Fax (01234) 219911
Training Division: Unit 6C, Britannia Hse, Leagrave Rd, Luton LU3 1RJ; Tel (01582) 404200, 404300

Manchester
Chamber of Commerce & Industry, 56 Oxford St, Manchester M60 7HJ; Tel 0161-236 3210; Fax 0161-236 4160; Telex 667822 CHACOM G
Chief Executive S.G. Sperryn, MA, MBA, FBIM

Area Office: Salford Chamber of Commerce & Industry, 56 Oxford St, Manchester M60 7HJ; Tel 0161-236 3210; Fax 0161-236 4160; Telex 667822 CHACOM G
Area Office: Tameside Chamber of Commerce & Industry, 56 Oxford St, Manchester M60 7HJ; Tel 0161-236 3210; Fax 0161-236 4160; Telex 667822 CHACOM G
Export Documentation Office, Rm 109, Bldg No 305/ Cargo Centre, Manchester International Airport, Altrincham, Cheshire WA15 8UX; Tel 0161-489 3170; Fax 0161-489 3171
Manager R. Fitzgerald

Medway & Gillingham
Chamber of Commerce, 149 New Rd, Chatham, Kent ME4 4PT; Tel (01634) 830001; Fax (01634) 830950; Telex 966272 MEDCOM G
Chief Executive/General Secretary John Day

Merseyside
Chamber of Commerce & Industry, 1 Old Hall St, Liverpool L3 9HG; Tel 0151-227 1234; Fax 0151-236 0121; Telex 627110 and 628702 CHACOM G
Director H.M.P. Robinson

Milton Keynes
Chamber of Commerce, Silbury Ct, 384 Silbury Blvd, Central Milton Keynes MK9 2HY; Tel (01908) 662123; Fax (01908) 674958; Telex 826932 MKDCCI G
Chief Executive P.A. Eccles, MA, ACIS

Newark
Chamber of Commerce, 67 London Rd, Newark, Notts NG24 1RZ; Tel (01636) 640555; Fax (01636) 605558
Secretary B.C. Tindale

Newport & Gwent
Chamber of Commerce & Industry, Caradog Hse, Cleppa Pk, Newport, Gwent NP1 9UG; Tel (01633) 816689; Fax (01633) 816816
Secretary J.D. Rigby

North Derbyshire
Chamber of Commerce & Industry, Commerce Centre, Canal Wharf, Chesterfield S41 7NA; Tel (01246) 211277; Fax (01246) 203173; Telex 54596
Chief Executive/Director G. Goucher

Northamptonshire
Chamber of Commerce & Industry, 65 The Avenue, Cliftonville, Northampton NN1 5BG; Tel (01604) 22422; Fax (01604) 29858; Telex 311165 CHACOM G
Chief Executive D. Fairweather

Northern Ireland
Chamber of Commerce & Industry, Chamber of Commerce Hse, 22 Great Victoria St, Belfast BT2 7BJ; Tel (01232) 244113; Fax (01232) 247024; Telex 747538 BELCOM G
Director R.T. Jordan, MBE, CEng

North Staffordshire
Chamber of Commerce & Industry, Commerce Hse, Festival Pk, Stoke-on-Trent ST1 5BE; Tel (01782) 202222; Fax (01782) 202448; Telex 36250 CHACOM G
Director B. Carnes

Norwich & Norfolk
Chamber of Commerce & Industry, 112 Barrack St, Norwich NR3 1UB; Tel (01603) 625977, 625992; Fax (01603) 633032; Telex 974247 CHACOM G
Director A. Millar-Brown, MBE
Area Office: Great Yarmouth Chamber of Commerce & Industry, Norwich Union Bldg, Hall Plain, Great Yarmouth NR30 2QD; Tel (01493) 842184; Fax (01493) 857809
Manager M.A. Forbes
Documentation Office: 46 Queen St, King's Lynn, Norfolk PE30 1HT; Tel (01553) 768505
Secretary B. Webb

Nottinghamshire
Chamber of Commerce & Industry, 395 Mansfield Rd, Nottingham NG5 2DL; Tel (0115) 962 4624; Fax (0115) 960 5981; Telex 37605 COMIND G
Chief Executive G.W. Hulse, OBE
Secretary N.J.C. Hough
County Office, Kirkland Ave, Mansfield, Notts NG18 5QP; Tel (01623) 420366; Fax (01623) 24859; Telex 378191 COMIND G
Business Information Centre, 309 Haydn Rd, Nottingham NG5 1DG; Tel (0115) 962 4624; Fax (0115) 985 6612

Oldham
Chamber of Commerce & Industry, 8 Clydesdale St, Oldham, Lancs OL8 1BT; Tel 0161-624 2482
Secretary D.R. Harrison, FCA

Oxford & District
Chamber of Commerce, 30 Cornmarket St, Oxford OX1 3EY; Tel (01865) 792020; Fax (01865) 724243
Secretary P.H. Barley

Paisley
Chamber of Commerce & Industry Ltd, c/o McFadyen & Temple (Solicitors), 6 Gilmore St, Paisley PA1 1BZ; Tel 0141-889 9291; Fax 0141-848 1565
Secretary J.R. McClymont

Peterborough
Chamber of Commerce & Industry, The Lawns, 33 Thorpe Rd, Peterborough PE3 6AB; Tel (01733) 342658, 897561; Fax (01733) 342747; Telex 32849 CHACOM G
Chief Executive C.C. Street, QPM

Plymouth
Chamber of Commerce & Industry, 29 Looe St, Plymouth PL4 0EE; Tel (01752) 221151; Fax (01752) 222589; Telex 45438 PLYCOM G
Chief Executive Brian R. Fox, OBE

Preston see *Central and West Lancs*

Reading & Central Berkshire
Chamber of Commerce, Trade & Industry, Commerce & Industry Hse, 2A Cranbury Rd, Reading RG3 2XD; Tel (01734) 595049; Fax (01734) 500511; Telex 847423 COCR G
Director F.A. Stroud

Rochdale
Chamber of Commerce, Trade & Industry, Lewis Hse, 12 Smith St, Rochdale, Lancs OL16 1TX; Tel (01706) 343810; Fax (01706) 31777
Secretary M. Plane
Assistant Secretary B. Healey

Rotherham
Chamber of Commerce & Industry, Carnson Hse, 1 Moorgate Rd, Rotherham, S Yorks S60 2ED; Tel (01709) 828425; Fax (01709) 820448
Chief Executive/Secretary V.A. Catterall, DMS, MBIM

Rugby & District
Chamber of Commerce, 9 Railway Terr, Rugby, Warks CV21 3EN; Tel (01788) 544951; Fax (01788) 560901; Telex 311794 CHACOM G
Director C. Grigg

St Helens
Chambers of Commerce, Trade & Industry, Court Block, Prescot Rd, St Helens WA10 3TT; Tel (01744) 613068; Fax (01744) 613316; Telex 629861 CHACOM G
Director N. Taylor

Salford see *Manchester*

Sandwell see *Birmingham*

Scunthorpe, Glanford & Gainsborough
Chamber of Commerce, 58 Oswald Rd, Scunthorpe, South Humberside DN15 7PQ; Tel (01724) 842109; Fax (01724) 857659; Telex 527163 FMS PRODUCTS
Chief Executive I.D. Crowther

Sheffield
Incorporated Chamber of Commerce and Manufactures, Commerce Hse, 33 Earl St, Sheffield S1 3FX; Tel (0114) 276 6667; Fax (0114) 276 6644; Telex 547676 CHAMCO G
Director/Secretary J.S. Hambidge, MInstM, FBIM

Shropshire
Chamber of Commerce & Industry Ltd, Industry Hse, Halesfield 16, Telford, Shropshire TF7 4FA; Tel (01952) 588766; Fax (01952) 582503; Telex 35438 TELECOM G
Chief Executive R. Truslove

Solihull see *Birmingham*

South East Hampshire
Chamber of Commerce and Industry, 27 Guildhall Wk, Portsmouth PO1 2RP; Tel (01705) 294111; Fax (01705) 296829
Chief Executive R. Gumbrill
President M. Price

South Essex
Chamber of Commerce, Trade & Industry (Southend) Ltd, 845 London Rd, Westcliff-on-Sea, Essex SS0 9SZ; Tel (01702) 77090, 78380; Fax (01702) 77161; Telex 99450 CHACOM G
General Secretary G. Burn

South of Scotland
Incorporated Chamber of Commerce, 19 Buccleuch St, Hawick, Roxburghshire TD9 0HL; Tel (01450) 77267
Secretary A.L. Rintoul, CA

Southampton
Chamber of Commerce & Industry, Bugle Hse, Bugle St, Southampton SO9 4WP; Tel (01703) 223541; Fax (01703) 227426; Telex 47388 CHACOM G
Chief Executive P.S.J. Beebe

Stockport
Chamber of Commerce & Industry, Victoria Hse, Wellington St, Stockport SK1 3AD; Tel 0161-480 0321/3; Fax 0161-476 0138; Telex 666413 SAC G COC
Chief Executive R.E. Hughes

Sussex
Federation of Industries and Chamber of Commerce, Seven Dials, Brighton, E Sussex BN1 3JS; Tel (01273) 26282; Fax (01273) 207965; Telex 87323 FSI G
Chief Executive Ann A. Crichton
Gatwick Export Enterprise Centre: Rm 35, Gresham Hse, 12–24 Station Rd, Crawley, W Sussex RH13 1HT; Tel (01293) 560884; Fax (01293) 549615
Centre Manager C.H. Melhuish

Swindon
Chamber of Commerce & Industry, Commercial Hse, 1 Commercial Rd, Swindon, Wilts SN1 5NE; Tel (01793) 616544; Fax (01793) 619938
Executive Director P. Stratford, DMS, FInstSMM

Teesside & District
Chamber of Commerce & Industry, Commerce Hse, Exchange Sq, Middlesbrough, Cleveland TS1 1DW; Tel (01642) 230023; Fax (01642) 230105; Telex 58232 CHAMCO G
Chief Executive P.A. Crowe
Darlington Office: Teesside Chamber of Commerce, Enterprise Hse, Valley St North, Darlington, Co Durham DL1 1QE; Tel (01325) 384045; Fax (01325) 384046

Thames–Chiltern
Chamber of Commerce & Industry, Commerce Hse, 2–6 Bath Rd, Slough SL1 3SB; Tel (01753) 77877; Fax (01753) 24644; Telex 848314 CHACOM G
Chief Executive L.P. Robinson, ACIB
Secretary P. Edwards
Heathrow Area Office: London Airport Heathrow 19–20, Bldg 520, Hounslow, Middx TW6 3QW; Tel 0181-759 9321
High Wycombe Area Office: Tooks Ct, Lincolns Rd, Cressex Industrial Est, High Wycombe, Bucks HP12 3RE; Tel (01494) 445909; Fax (01494) 440156
Aylesbury Area Office: Prebendal Ct, Oxford Rd, Aylesbury, Bucks HP19 3EQ; Tel (01296) 434392; Fax (01296) 436427
Bracknell Area Office: Ascot Hse, Doncastle Rd, Southern Industrial Area, Bracknell, Berks RG12 4PE; Tel (01344) 860343; Fax (01344) 860044
Training Centres: The Training Centre, Malton Ave, Trading Est, Slough, Berks SL1 4QU; Tel (01753) 824541, 824129
Cherry Trees Nursery, 27 Bedford Ave, Trading Est, Slough, Berks SL1 4SB; Tel (01743) 32718
Bracken Bears Nursery, Brackenhale Comp School, Rectory La, Bracknell, Berks RG12 4BA; Tel (01344) 868923

Three Counties
Chamber of Commerce & Industry, Commerce Hse, 10 The Moors, Worcester WR1 3EE; Tel (01905) 611611/2; Fax (01905) 611093; Telex 335294 CHACOM G
Chief Executive L.A. Warrilow
Herefordshire Chamber of Commerce & Industry, Yeomans Office Complex, Commercial Rd, Hereford HR1 2BL; Tel (01432) 268795; Fax (01432) 355139; Telex 335294 CHACOM G
Manager J. Hart
Worcester & District Chamber of Commerce & Industry, Commerce Hse, 10 The Moors, Worcester WR1 3EE; Tel (01905) 611611; Fax (01905) 611093; Telex 335294 CHACOM G
Manager T. Thomas

Tyne and Wear
Chamber of Commerce & Industry, 65 Quayside, Newcastle upon Tyne NE1 3DS; Tel 0191-261 1142; Fax 0191-261 4035
Chief Executive R.G. Tilmouth
Training Centres: Pandongate Hse, 5 City Rd, Newcastle upon Tyne NE1 2AL; Tel 0191-261 9555; Fax 0191-232 0506
Centre Manager N.A. Pattison
Town Centre Hse, Crowntree Rd, Sunderland SR1 3EB; Tel 0191-510 9090; Fax 0191-510 0925
Centre Manager G. Richards
Laygate, South Shields, Tyne and Wear NE33 5BU; Tel 0191-427 0663; Fax 0191-427 1489
Centre Manager A. Gilmour

Tynedale
Chamber of Commerce, 14 Gilesgate, Hexham, Northumberland; Tel (01434) 607354, 603164; Fax (01434) 608616
Secretary D. Clay

Walsall
Chamber of Commerce & Industry, Chamber of Commerce Hse, Ward St, Walsall, West Midlands WS1 2AG; Tel (01922) 721777; Fax (01922) 647359; Telex 338212 CHACOM G
Chief Executive D.S. Frost

Warrington
Chamber of Commerce & Industry, 80 Sankey St, Warrington WA1 1SD; Tel (01925) 35054; Fax (01925) 444471
Director G. Willans, BA

Weald & West Kent
Chamber of Commerce & Industry, 10 Crescent Rd, Tunbridge Wells, Kent TN1 2PD; Tel (01892) 546888; Fax (01892) 549849
Manager M.J. Phillips

West Wales
Incorporated Chamber of Commerce, Rms F4/F5, Burrows Chambers, East Burrows Rd, Swansea SA1 1RF; Tel (01792) 653297/2; Fax (01792) 648345
Secretary H.L. Harries

Westminster
Chamber of Commerce, Mitre Hse, 177 Regent St, London W1R 8DJ; Tel 0171-734 2851; Fax 0171-734 0670; Telex 268312
Chief Executive D.R. Allen
Certification Dept: Tel 0171-734 6392
Manager N. Riggs
Area Office: Westminster Chamber of Commerce (Paddington Office), 80 Amberley Rd, London W9 2JJ; Tel 0171-266 2484

Widnes see *Halton*

Wigan & District
Incorporated Chamber of Commerce, 107 Standishgate, Wigan WN1 1XL; Tel (01942) 496074; Fax (01942) 495469
Secretary I. Thomason

Wolverhampton
Chamber of Commerce & Industry, Berrington Lodge, 93 Tettenhall Rd, Wolverhampton WV3 9PE; Tel (01902) 26726; Fax (01902) 26028; Telex 33890 CHAMCO G
Chief Executive J.H. Rice

York
Chamber of Commerce, Trade & Industry, c/o Joseph Terry & Sons, Bishopthorpe Rd, York YO1 1YE; Tel (01904) 629513; Fax (01940) 630985
Chief Executive M.S. Brown

17 Employment and Careers

Training, Enterprise and Education Directorate

TEED is responsible for national policy on vocational education and training, and shares with the Department of Trade and Industry responsibility for enterprise. The Directorate is based mainly in Sheffield and has a network of 10 Regional Offices. Eighty two Training and Enterprise Councils (TECs), which are private sector companies, manage local training and enterprise activities under a performance based contract with the Secretary of State for Employment. Different local arrangements apply in Scotland and Wales, but the Secretary of State for Employment retains responsibility for the UK policy framework on vocational education and training

Policy responsibilities and activities include: working with TECs and Industry Training Organisations; training for work; learning for work, Workstart pilots; Youth Training; Training Credits; Investors in People; National Training Awards; Standards Programme (for use in NVQs); training quality; training standards; learning systems and access to training; Career Development Loans; Education/Business Partnerships; Work Related Further Education; Enterprise in Higher Education; Technical Vocational Education Initiative; Careers Service; Business Start-ups (formerly Enterprise Allowance); Business and Enterprise Training

Moorfoot, Sheffield S1 4PQ; Tel (0114) 275 3275; Fax (0114) 275 8311

Public Enquiry Point Tel London 0171-273 6969; Sheffield (0114) 259 4545

Director General Dr I.A. Johnston; Tel 0171-273 5964/ (0114) 259 4109

Director of Operations S. Loveman; Tel (0114) 259 4812

Director of Adult and Training Strategy Division B. Heatley; Tel (0114) 259 3978

Director of Quality Assurance Division P. Thomas; Tel (0114) 259 3297

Director of Training, Infrastructure and Employers Division D. Grover; Tel (0114) 259 3948

Director of Youth Education Policy Division Mrs V. Bayliss; Tel (0114) 259 3972

Head of Planning F. Everiss; Tel (0114) 259 3234

Regional Offices and TECS

East Midlands

21–23 Castle Gate, Nottingham NG1 7AQ

Regional Director P. Lauener; Tel (0115) 941 0360

Greater Nottingham TEC

Marina Rd, Castle Marina Pk, Nottingham NG7 1TN

Chief Executive Jim Potts; Tel (0115) 941 3313

Leicestershire TEC

1st Flr, Rutland Centre, Halford St, Leicester LE1 1TQ

Chief Executive David Nelson; Tel (0116) 253 8616

Lincolnshire TEC

5th Flr, Wigford Hse, Brayford Wharf East, Lincoln LN5 7AY

Chief Executive David Rossington; Tel (01522) 532266

North Derbyshire TEC

Block C, St Mary's Court, St Mary's Gate, Chesterfield S41 7TD

Chief Executive Stuart Almond; Tel (01246) 551158

North Nottinghamshire TEC

1st Flr, Block C, Edwinstowe Hse, High St, Edwinstowe, Mansfield, Nottinghamshire NG21 9PR

Chief Executive Pat Richards; Tel (01623) 824624

Northamptonshire TEC
Royal Pavilion, Summerhouse Pavilion, Summerhouse Rd, Moulton Pk, Northampton NN3 1WD
Chief Executive Ms C. Jones; Tel (01604) 671200

Southern Derbyshire TEC
St Helens Crt, St Helens St, Derby DE1 3GY
Chief Executive Joy Street; Tel (01332) 290550

Eastern

Victory Hse, Vision Pk, Histon, Cambridge CB4 4ZR
Regional Director Mrs C. Johnson; Tel (01223) 202000

Bedfordshire TEC
Woburn Crt, 2 Railton Rd, Woburn Rd Industrial Est, Kempston, Beds MK42 7PN
Chief Executive Diana McMahon, MBE; Tel (01234) 843100

CAMBSTEC (Central and South Cambridgeshire)
Units 2–3, Trust Crt, Chivers Way, The Vision Pk, Histon, Cambridge CB4 4PW
Managing Director Alan Maltpress; Tel (01223) 235633/1635

Essex TEC
Redwing Hse, Hedgerows Business Pk, Colchester Rd, Chelmsford, Essex, CM2 5PB
Managing Director Michael Clegg; Tel (01245) 450123

Greater Peterborough TEC
Unit 4, Blenheim Crt, Peppercorn Cls, off The Lincoln Rd, Peterborough PE1 2DU
Chief Executive Michael Styles; Tel (01733) 890808

Hertfordshire TEC
New Barnes Mill, Cotton Mill La, St Albans, Herts AL1 2HA
Managing Director Chris Humphries; Tel (01727) 52313

Norfolk and Waveney TEC
Partnership Hse, Unit 10 Norwich Business Pk, Whiting Rd, Norwich NR4 6DJ
Managing Director John Wooddissee; Tel (01603) 763812

Suffolk TEC
2nd Flr, Crown Hse, Crown St, Ipswich IP1 3HS
Managing Director Mike Bax; Tel (01473) 218951

London

236 Grays Inn Rd, London WC1X 8HL
Regional Director Mrs W. Harris; Tel 0171-211 1000

AZTEC
Manorgate Hse, 2 Manorgate Rd, Kingston Upon Thames KT2 7AL
Chief Executive Judith Rutherford; Tel 0181-547 3934

CENTEC (Central London)
12 Grosvenor Cres, London SW1X 7EE
Chief Executive Mrs G. Flower; Tel 0171-411 3500

City and Inner London North TEC
80 Great Eastern St, London EC2A 3DP
Chief Executive Peter Box; Tel 0171-324 2424

London East TEC
Cityside Hse, 40 Adler St, London E1 1EE
Chief Executive Steve Crow; Tel 0171-377 1866

North London TEC
Dumayne Hse, 1 Fox La, Palmers Grn, London N13 4AB
Chief Executive Mike Nixon; Tel 0181-447 9422

North West London TEC
Kirkfield Hse, 118–120 Station Rd, Harrow, Middx HA1 2RL
Chief Executive Roy Bain; Tel 0181-424 8866

SOLOTEC
Lancaster Hse, 7 Elmfield Rd, Bromley, Kent, BR1 1LT
Chief Executive Chris Hubbard; Tel 0181-313 9232

South Thames TEC
200 Great Dover St, London SE1 4YB
Chief Executive Michael Hanson; Tel 0171-403 1990

West London TEC
Sovereign Crt, 15–21 Staines Rd, Hounslow, Middx, TW3 3HA
Chief Executive Dr Phil Blackburn; Tel 0181-577 1010

North West and Merseyside

Washington Hse, Capital Centre, New Bailey St, Manchester
Regional Director (North West) Paul Keen; Tel 0161-833 0251
Regional Director (Merseyside) Peter Houten

Bolton/Bury TEC
Clive Hse, Clive St, Bolton BL1 1ET
Chief Executive Geoff Critchley; Tel (01204) 397350

CEWTEC (Chester, Ellesmere Port, Wirral)
Block 4, Woodside Business Pk, Birkenhead, Wirral L41 1EH
Chief Executive Alan Moody; Tel 0151-650 0555

Cumbria TEC
Venture Hse, Regents Crt, Guard St, Workington, Cumbria CA14 4EW
Chief Executive Steve Palmer; Tel (01900) 66991

ELTEC (East Lancashire)
Red Rose Crt, Petre Rd, Clayton Business Pk, Clayton-Le-Moor, Lancashire BB5 5JR
Chief Executive Mark Price; Tel (01254) 301333

LAWTEC (Lancashire Area West)
4th Flr, Duchy Hse, 96 Lancaster Rd, Preston PR1 1HE
Chief Executive Tony Bickerstaffe; Tel (01772) 200035

Manchester TEC
Bouton Hse, 17–21 Chorlton St, Manchester M1 3HY
Chief Executive Paul Read; Tel 0161-236 7222

Merseyside TEC
3rd Flr, Tithebarn Hse, Tithebarn St, Liverpool L2 2NZ
Chief Executive Linda Bloomfield; Tel 0151-236 0026

METROTEC (Wigan) Ltd
Buckingham Row, Northway, Wigan WN1 1XX
Chief Executive Bill Badrock; Tel (01942) 36312

NORMIDTEC (North and Mid Cheshire)
Spencer Hse, Dewhurst Rd, Birchwood, Warrington WA3 7PP
Chief Executive Andrew Gurr; Tel (01925) 826515

Oldham TEC
Meridian Centre, King St, Oldham OL8 1EZ
Chief Executive Michael Mealing; Tel 0161-620 0006

QUALITEC (St Helens) Ltd
7 Waterside Crt, Technology Campus, St Helens, Merseyside WA9 1UE
Chief Executive John Gracie; Tel (01744) 24433

Rochdale TEC
St James Pl, 160–162 Yorkshire St, Rochdale, Lancashire OL16 2DL
Chief Executive Anne Martin; Tel (01706) 44909

South and East Cheshire TEC
PO Box 37, Middlewich Industrial and Business Pk, Dalton Way, Middlewich, Cheshire CW10 0HU
Chief Executive Richard Guy; Tel (01606) 737009

Stockport/High Peak TEC
1 St Peters Sq, Stockport SK1 1NN
Chief Executive Trevor Jones; Tel 0161-477 8830

17 Employment and Careers

North East

Eastgate Hse, Kings Manor, Newcastle-Upon-Tyne NE1 6PA
Regional Director K. Heslop; Tel 0191-235 7000

County Durham TEC
Valley St North, Darlington DL1 1TJ
Chief Executive David Hall; Tel (01325) 351166

Northumberland TEC
Suite 2, Craster Crt, Manor Walk Shopping Centre, Cramlington NE23 6XX
Chief Executive Stephen Cowell; Tel (01670) 713303

Teesside TEC
Training and Enterprise Hse, 2 Queens Sq, Middlesbrough, Cleveland TS2 1AA
Chief Executive John Howell; Tel (01642) 231023

Tyneside TEC
Moongate Hse, 5th Ave Business Pk, Team Valley Trading Est, Gateshead NE11 0HF
Chief Executive Olivia Grant; Tel 0191-487 5599

Wearside TEC
Derwent Hse, New Town Centre, Washington, Tyne and Wear NE38 7ST
Chief Executive Jules Preston; Tel 0191-416 6161

South East

Telford Hse, Hamilton Cls, Basingstoke RG21 2UZ
Regional Director D. Main; Tel (01256) 29266

Hampshire TEC
25 Thackeray Mall, Fareham, Hampshire, PO16 0PQ
Managing Director Dr Max Wilson; Tel (01329) 230099

Heart of England TEC (Oxfordshire)
26/27 The Quadrant, Abingdon Science Pk, off Barton La, Abingdon OX14 3YS
Acting Chief Executive Brian McCarthy; Tel (01235) 553249

Wight Training and Enterprise
Mill Crt, Furrlongs, Newport, IOW PO30 2AA
Acting Chief Executive Derek Kozel; Tel (01983) 822818

Kent TEC
5th Flr, Mountbatton Hse, 28 Military Rd, Chatham, Kent ME4 4JE
Chief Executive John Forsdyke; Tel (01634) 844411

Milton Keynes and North Buckinghamshire TEC
Old Market Halls, Creed St, Wolverton, Milton Keynes MK12 5LY
Chief Executive Michael Hind; Tel (01908) 222555

Surrey TEC
Technology Hse, 48–54 Goldsmith Rd, Woking, Surrey, GU21 1LE
Managing Director Richard Wormell; Tel (01483) 728190

Sussex TEC
2nd Flr, Electrowatt Hse, North St, Horsham, W Sussex RH12 1RS
Chief Executive Malcolm Allan; Tel (01403) 271471

Thames Valley Enterprise
6th Flr, Kings Point, 120 Kings Rd, Reading RG1 3BZ
Chief Executive Roy Knott; Tel (01734) 568156

South West

The Pithay, Bristol, Avon BS1 2NQ
Regional Director W. Mauger; Tel (0117) 927 3710

Avon TEC
PO Box 164, St Lawrence Hse, 29–31 Broad St, Bristol BS99 7HR
Chief Executive Pat Hall; Tel (0117) 927 7116

Devon and Cornwall TEC
Foliot Hse, Brooklands, Budshead Rd, Crown Hill, Plymouth PL6 5XR
Chief Executive John Mannell; Tel (01752) 767929

Dorset TEC
25 Oxford Rd, Bournemouth BH8 8EY
Chief Executive John Morrison; Tel (01202) 299284

Gloucestershire TEC
Conway Hse, 33–35 Worcester St, Gloucester GL1 3AJ
Chief Executive Graham Hoyle; Tel (01452) 524488

Somerset TEC
Crescent Hse, 3–7 The Mount, Taunton, Somerset, TA1 3TT
Chief Executive Roger Phillips; Tel (01823) 259121

Wiltshire TEC
The Bora Building, Westlea Campus, Westlea Down, Swindon, Wilts SN5 7EZ
Chief Executive John Selway; Tel (01793) 513644

West Midlands

21st Flr, Alpha Tower, Suffolk St, Queensway, Birmingham
Regional Director H. Tollyfield; Tel 0121-631 3555

Birmingham TEC
Chaplin Court, 80 Hurst St, Birmingham B5 4TG
Chief Executive David Cragg; Tel 0121-622 4419

Central England TEC
The Oaks, Clewes Rd, Redditch B98 7ST
Chief Executive Rodney Skidmore; Tel (01527) 545415

Coventry and Warwickshire TEC
Brandon Crt, Progress Way, Coventry CV3 2TE
Chief Executive Scott Glover; Tel (01203) 635666

Dudley TEC
Dudley Crt South, Waterfront East, Level St, Brierley Hill, West Midlands DY5 1XN
Chief Executive John Woodall; Tel (01384) 485000

HAWTEC (Hereford and Worcester)
Haswell Hse, St Nicholas St, Worcester WR1 1UW
Chief Executive Alan Curless; Tel (01905) 723200

Sandwell TEC
1st Flr, Kingston Hse, 438/450 High St, West Bromwich, West Midlands B70 9LD
Chief Executive John Bedingfield; Tel 0121-525 4242

Shropshire TEC
2nd Flr, Hazledine Hse, Central Sq, Telford TF3 4JJ
Chief Executive Stephen Jury; Tel (01952) 291471

Staffordshire TEC
Festival Way, Festival Pk, Stoke on Trent ST1 5TQ
Chief Executive Richard Ward; Tel (01782) 202733

Walsall TEC
5th Flr, Townend Hse, Townend Sq, Walsall WS1 1NS; Tel (01922) 32332
Chief Executive John Hyde; Tel (01922) 32332

Wolverhampton TEC
Pendeford Business Pk, Wobaston Rd, Wolverhampton WV9 5HA
Chief Executive James Wagstaffe; Tel (01902) 397787

Yorkshire and Humberside

City Hse, New Station St, Leeds LS1 4JA
Regional Director J. Walker; Tel (0113) 234 1044

Barnsley and Doncaster TEC
Conference Centre, Eldon St, Barnsley S70 2LJ
Chief Executive Tony Goulborn; Tel (01226) 248088

Bradford and District TEC
Fountain Hall, Fountain St, Bradford BD1 3RA
Chief Executive Simon Cheema; Tel (01274) 723711

Calderdale and Kirklees TEC
Park View Hse, Woodvale Office Pk, Woodvale Rd, Brighouse HD6 4AB
Chief Executive Alastair Graham; Tel (01484) 400770

Humberside TEC
The Maltings, Silvester Sq, Silvester St, Hull HU1 3HL
Managing Director Peter Fryer; Tel (01482) 226491

Leeds TEC
Belgrave Hall, Belgrave St, Leeds LS2 8DD
Chief Executive Derek Pearce; Tel (0113) 234 7666

North Yorkshire TEC
TEC Hse, 7 Pioneer Business Pk, Amy Johnson Way, Clifton Moorgate, York YO3 8TN
Chief Executive Roger Grasby; Tel (01904) 691939

Rotherham TEC
Moorgate Hse, Moorgate Rd, Rotherham S60 2EN
Chief Executive Christopher Duff; Tel (01709) 830511

Sheffield TEC
St Mary's Crt, 55 St Mary's Rd, Sheffield S2 4AQ
Chief Executive Keith Davie; Tel (0114) 270 1911

Wakefield TEC
Grove Hall, 60 College Rd, Wakefield WF1 3RN
Chief Executive Geoffrey Badcock; Tel (01924) 299907

Northern Ireland

Headquarters, Employment Service, Training and Employment Agency, Clarendon Hse, Adelaide St, Belfast BT2 8NR; Tel (01232) 244300
Director of Employment Service J.D. Noble
Careers Officers form part of the all-age placement and guidance service run by the Employment Service Division of the Training and Employment Agency. Careers Officers visit schools to give talks, show films and interview school leavers, and work closely with careers teachers in schools and with employers

Training and Employment Agency

Antrim
25–27 Church St BT41 4BE; Tel (0184 94) 62834; Fax (0894) 28355

Armagh
Ulster Gazette Shopping Centre, Scotch St BT61 7PU; Tel (01861) 523322; Fax (01861) 527994

Ballymena
35–39 Bridge St, Ballymena, Co Antrim BT43 5EL; Tel (01266) 41135; Fax (01266) 651087

Ballymoney
32 Main St, Ballymoney, Co Antrim BT53 6AL; Tel (012656) 62565; Fax (012656) 66786

Ballynahinch
20 High St, Ballynahinch, Co Down BT24 8AB; Tel (01238) 562986; Fax (01238) 565144

Banbridge
Castlewellen Rd, Banbridge, Co Down BT32 3HA; Tel (01820) 62371; Fax (01820) 26872

Bangor
65 High St, Bangor, Co Down BT20 5BE; Tel (01247) 270077; Fax (01247) 465747

Belfast
Gloucester Hse, Chichester St, Belfast BT1 4RA; Tel (01232) 235211; Fax (01232) 234069

Belfast
43-45 Falls Rd BT12 4PD; Tel (01232) 333495; Fax (01232) 313469

Belfast
Newtownabbey, Swinson Hse; Tel (01232) 365171; Fax (01232) 862912

Belfast
178-180 Shankill Rd, Belfast BT13 2BH; Tel (01232) 330063; Fax (01232) 239330

Carrickfergus
20 West St, Carrickfergus, Co Antrim BT38 7AR; Tel (019603) 51449; Fax (019603) 66215

Coleraine
41 Church St, Coleraine, Co Londonderry BT52 IAW; Tel (01265) 51211; Fax (01265) 54780

Cookstown
17 Oldtown St, Cookstown, Co Tyrone BT80 8EE; Tel (016487) 66950; Fax (016487) 61231

Downpatrick
Rathkeltair Hse, Market St, Downpatrick BT30 6LZ; Tel (01396) 612211; Fax (01396) 612936

Dungannon
5 Thomas St Centre, Dungannon, Co Tyrone BT70 1HN; Tel (018687) 22525; Fax (018687) 52981

Enniskillen
Paget Sq, Enniskillen, Co Fermanagh BT74 7HS; Tel (01365) 323511; Fax (01365) 326122

Kilkeel
Newry St, Kilkeel, Co Down BT34 4DN; Tel (0169 37) 62873/162905

Larne
75 Main St, Larne, Co Antrim BT40 1HH; Tel (01574) 273371; Fax (01574) 270178

Limavady
43 Market St, Limavady, Co Londonderry BT49 0AB; Tel (015047) 65967; Fax (015047) 22245

Lisburn
71 Bow St, Lisburn, Co Antrim BT28 1BJ; Tel (01846) 665260; Fax (01846) 664326

Londonderry
5 Waterloo Pl BT48 6BT; Tel (01504) 264294; Fax (01504) 370133

Lurgan
Alexandra Cres, Lurgan, Co Armagh BT66 8AW; Tel (017622) 341177; Fax (017622) 321538

Magherafelt
28 Queen's St, Magherafelt, Co Londonderry BT45 6AB; Tel (01648) 33804; Fax (01648) 33804

Newcastle
113 Main St, Co Down BT33 0AE; Tel (013967) 25001; Fax (013967) 26302

Newry
5–13 Marcus St, Newry, Co Down BT34 1ET; Tel (01693) 61222; Fax (01693) 62675

Newtownards
9 Conway Sq, Newtownards BT23 4DA; Tel (01247) 818653; Fax (01247) 820792

Omagh
10 High St, Omagh, Co Tyrone BT78 1BQ; Tel (01662) 244921; Fax (01662) 242496

Portadown
27 Magowan Bldgs, West St, Portadown, Co Armagh BT62 3PM; Tel (01762) 334141; Fax (01762) 350758

Strabane
26–28 Market St, Strabane, Co Tyrone BT82 8BH; Tel (01504) 382332; Fax (01504) 382172

Waterside
75 Duke St, Londonderry, Co Londonderry BT47 1FP; Tel (01504) 319000; Fax (01504) 319106

Learning Enterprise Councils (Scotland)

Argyll and The Islands Enterprise The Enterprise Centre, Kilmory, Lochgilphead PA31 8SH; Tel (01546) 602281/602563; Fax (01546) 603964; *Chief Executive* David McIntyre; *Chairman* Norman Walker

Caithness and Sutherland Enterprise Scapa Hse, Castlegreen Rd, Thurso, Caithness KW14 7LS; Tel (01847) 66115; Fax (01847) 63383; *Chief Executive* Andrew Thin; *Chairman* Don Clarkson

Inverness and Nairn Enterprise Castle Wynd, Inverness IV3 3DW; Tel (01463) 713504; Fax (01463) 712002; *Chief Executive* Fiona M. Larg; *Chairman* Norman Cordiner

Lochaber Limited St Mary's Hse, Gordon Sq, Fort William PH33 6DY; Tel (01397) 702160/704326; Fax (01397) 705309; *Chief Executive* Douglas MacDiarmid; *Chairman* Stewart MacLean

Moray, Badenoch and Strathspey Enterprise Company Unit 8, Elgin Business Centre, Maisondieu Rd, Elgin IV30 1RH; Tel (01343) 550567; Fax (01343) 550678; *Chief Executive* Dick Ruane; *Chairman* Oliver Russell

Orkney Enterprise 14 Queen St, Kirkwall KW15 1JE; Tel (01856) 874638; Fax (01856) 872915; *Chief Executive* Kenneth Grant; *Chairman* Hugh Clyde

Ross and Cromarty Enterprise 62 High St, Invergordon IV18 0DH; Tel (01349) 853666; Fax (01349) 853833; *Chief Executive* Sandy Cumming; *Chairman* John Shepherd-Barron

Shetland Enterprise Toll Clock Shopping Centre, 26 North Rd, Lerwick ZE1 0PE; Tel (01595) 3177; Fax (01595) 3208; *Chief Executive* William Fraser; *Chairman* Brian Anderson

Skye and Lochalsh Enterprise Kings Hse, The Green, Portree, Isle of Skye IV51 9BT; Tel (01478) 612841; Fax (01478) 612164; *Chief Executive* Lorne Macleod; *Chairman* Jan Nicolson

Western Isles Enterprise (Iomairt nan Etlean Siar) 3 Harbour View, Cromwell Street Quay, Stornoway, Isle of Lewis PA87 2DF; Tel (01851) 703625/703905; Fax (01851) 704130; *Chief Executive* Donald Macaulay; *Chairman* George MacLeod

Dumfries and Galloway Enterprise Company Cairnsmore Hse, Bankend Rd, Dumfries DG1 4TA; Tel (01387) 54444; Fax (01387) 51650; *Chairman* John V. Jameson; *Chief Executive* Irene Walker; *Company Secretary* Stanley D. Cairnie

Fife Enterprise Ltd Huntsman's Hse, 33 Cadham Centre, Glenrothes, Fife KY7 6RU; Tel (01592) 621000; Fax (01592) 742609; *Chairman* Ray Baker; *Chief Executive* Robert McKenzie; *Company Secretary* James Bishop

Grampian Enterprise Company 27 Albyn Pl, Aberdeen AB1 1YL; Tel (01224) 211500; Fax (01224) 213417; *Chairman* Ian Wood; *Chief Executive* Hance Fullerton; *Company Secretary* Keith Brown

Dunbartonshire Enterprise 2nd Fl, Spectrum Hse, Clydebank Business Pk, Clydebank, Glasgow G81 2DR; Tel 0141-951 2121; Fax 0141-951 1907; *Chairman* Alastair Nicol; *Chief Executive* Donald MacInnes; *Company Secretary* Craig Fyfe

Forth Valley Enterprise Laurel Hse, Laurelhill Business Pk, Stirling FK7 9JQ; Tel (017864) 51919; Fax (017864) 78123; *Chairman* Robbie Taylor; *Chief Executive* Bill Morton; *Company Secretary* Billy MacIntyre

Lanarkshire Development Agency New Lanarkshire Hse, Willow Dr, Strathclyde Business Pk, Bellshill M14 3AD; Tel (01698) 745454; Fax (01698) 842211; *Chairman* Ian Livingstone; *Chief Executive* Archie Bethel; *Company Secretary* Ian Carmichael

Renfrewshire Enterprise 25–29 Causeyside St, Paisley PA1 1UG; Tel 0141-848 0101; Fax 0141-848 6930; *Chairman* John Ashworth; *Chief Executive* Tony Cassidy; *Company Secretary* Linda Ellison

Scottish Enterprise Tayside Enterprise Hse, 45 North Lindsay St, Dundee DD1 HTT; Tel (01382) 23100; Fax (01382) 201319; *Chairman* David Sawyer; *Chief Executive* Graham McKee; *Company Secretary* Douglas Black

Enterprise Ayrshire 17–19 Hill St, Kilmarnock KA3 1HA; Tel (01563) 26623; Fax (01563) 43636; *Chairman* John Hornibrook; *Chief Executive* David MacDonald; *Company Secretary* Andrew Downie

Glasgow Development Agency Altrium Ct, 50 Waterloo St, Glasgow G2 6HQ; Tel 0141-204 1111; Fax 0141-248 1600; *Chairman* Forbes MacPherson; *Chief Executive* Stuart Gulliver; *Company Secretary* Brian Jamieson

Lothian and Edinburgh Enterprise Ltd Apex Hse, 99 Haymarket Terr, Edinburgh EH12 5HD; Tel 0131-313 4000; Fax 0131-313 4231; *Chairman* Robert Maiden; *Chief Executive* Des Bomar; *Company Secretary* Colin Donald

Scottish Borders Enterprise Bridge St, Galashiels TD1 1SW; Tel (01896) 58991; Fax (01896) 58625; *Chairman* Derek Bumpstead; *Chief Executive* David Douglas; *Company Secretary* Alan Skutecki

Oil and Gas 10 Queens Rd, Aberdeen AB1 6YT; Tel (01224) 626310; Fax (01224) 627006

Adult Training

NAITeC

Suffolk Enterprise Centre, Russell Rd, Ipswich, Suffolk IP1 2DE; Tel (01473) 233758; Fax (01473) 252489
Marina Marriott
NAITeC has some 60 members who have established themselves as a leading national provider of IT related training and qualifications, including the delivery and assessment of NVQs (National Vocational Qualifications). NAITeC members adhere to a National Code of Practice, and are undertaking ISO 9000 or equivalent quality standards. Standard or personalised short courses are available in almost all popular computer packages and applications. Current clients include: 37 Training and Enterprise Council (LECs in Scotland), Ministry of Defence, Health Authorities and ICI and BAE. The Centres are also approved by many awarding bodies including:- BTEC, RSA, City and Guilds, Entra and Scotvec. Further information on the ITeC in your area and how it might help you is available from the above office

Skillcentres (Astra Training Services)

Scotland Region

West Granton Rd, Edinburgh EH5 1JB; Tel 0131-551 1461

Bellshill Bellshill Industrial Pk, Bellshill, Lanarkshire ML4 3JE; Tel (01698) 748667

Dundee 4 Staffa Pl, Dundee DD2 3SX; Tel (01382) 816733

Dunfermline Townhill, Dunfermline, Fife KY12 0TB; Tel (01383) 721148

Hillington Hillington Industrial Est, Queen Elizabeth Ave, Glasgow G52 4TL; Tel 0141-810 3111

Irvine Ayr Rd, Irvine, Ayrshire KA12 8ES; Tel (01294) 78688

North East Region

Billingham Industrial Est, Leeholme Rd, Billingham-on-Tees TS23 3TE; Tel (01642) 560811

Durham Littleburn Trading Est, Langley Moor, Co Durham DH7 8HG; Tel Durham 780601

Tyneside Green La, Felling, Gateshead NE10 0LA; Tel 0191-469 4314

North West, Yorkshire and Humberside Region

Bradford Common Rd, Low Moor, Bradford, W Yorks BD12 0SF; Tel (01274) 600911

Cheshire Halton Ct, Runcorn, Cheshire WA7 5XR; Tel (01928) 65921
Cumbria Glasson Industrial Est, Maryport, Cumbria CA15 8NY; Tel (01900) 2771
East Lancs Eagle St, Accrington, Lancs BB5 1NS; Tel (01254) 395521
Hull Chamberlain Rd, Hull HU8 8HL; Tel (01482) 20738
Leeds Parkside La, Leeds LS11 5SZ; Tel (0113) 270 4661
Liverpool 105 Boundary St, Kirkdale, Liverpool L5 9YT; Tel 0151-252 4664; Fax 0151-252 4646
Manchester Guiness Rd, Trafford Pk, Manchester M17 1SD; Tel 0161-872 6042
Preston 180 Longridge Rd, Preston, Lancs PR2 5AP; Tel (01772) 652021
Rochdale Chichester St, Rochdale DL16 2AG; Tel (01706) 341514
St Helens Bedford St, Park Industrial Est, St Helens, Merseyside WA9 1PN; Tel (01744) 34134
Sheffield Richmond Pk Rd, Sheffield S13 8HT; Tel (0114) 244 6471
Wakefield Doncaster Rd, Wakefield WF1 5EA; Tel (01924) 75823
Wigan Swan La, Hindley Grn, Wigan WN2 4HD; Tel (01942) 56123

West Midland Region

Conference Centre, Middlemore Rd, Handsworth, Birmingham B21 0BT; Tel 0121-554 6221
Birmingham Middlemore Rd, Handsworth B21 0BT; Tel 0121-554 5222
Coventry Torrington Ave, Coventry CV4 9GR; Tel (01203) 468141
North Staffs Clough St, Hanley, Stoke-on-Trent, Staffs; Tel (01782) 261521
Wolverhampton Craddock St, Whitmore Reans, Wolverhampton WV6 0QJ; Tel (01902) 27173

South West England Region

Strode Rd, Newnham Industrial Est, Plympton, Plymouth PL7 4BG; Tel (01752) 335921; Fax (01752) 344451
Bristol Gill Ave, Fishponds, Bristol BS16 2QL; Tel (0117) 965 7446
Gloucester 117 Bristol Rd, Gloucester GL1 5SP; Tel (01452) 27721
Redruth Wilson Way, Pool Industrial Est, Redruth, Cornwall TS15 3SD; Tel (01209) 213231
Slough Walepole Rd, off Bath Rd, Chippenham, Slough, Berks SL1 6BN; Tel (01753) 5222
Southampton West Bay Rd, Hants SO9 3SH; Tel (01703) 28281
Swindon Faraday Rd, Dorcan, Swindon SN3 5HB; Tel (01793) 41671
West Sussex Churchill Industrial Est, Chartwell Rd, Lancing, W Sussex BN15 8YB; Tel (01903) 764331

South East England Region

Barking 25 Thames Rd, Barking, Essex IG11 0HR; Tel 0181-591 2662
Basildon Bentalls, Cranes Farm Rd, Basildon, Essex SS14 3BT; Tel (01268) 3225´
Chelmsford Farrow Rd, Rodney Way, Widford Industrial Est, Chelmsford, Essex CM1 3TF; Tel (01245) 65333
Deptford 2 Deptford Church St, London SE8 4SJ; Tel 0181-691 5721
Enfield Bilton Way, Enfield, Middx EN3 7NZ; Tel 0181-805 1365
Ipswich White Hse Rd, Ipswich, Suffolk IP1 5NX; Tel (01473) 47464
Lambeth Units 13–14, 11 Lyham Rd, London SW2 5DZ
Letchworth Pixmore Ave, Letchworth, Herts SG6 1JP; Tel (01462) 3084
Medway Courteney Rd, Gillingham, Kent ME8 0RY; Tel (01634) 360404
Milton Keynes Chesney Wold, Bleak Hall, Milton Keynes, Bucks MK16 1LX; Tel (01908) 670001
Norwich Mile Cross Rd, Norwich NR2 4LR; Tel (01603) 429181
Perivale Walmgate Rd, Perrivale, Greenford, Middx UB6 7NE; Tel 0181-998 1451
Peterborough Saville Rd, Westwood, Peterborough PE3 6TQ; Tel (01733) 267242
Twickenham Industrial Est, Rugby Rd, Twickenham, Middx TW1 1DT; Tel 0181-892 6285

Industrial Training

ATB – Landbase

National Agricultural Centre, Kenilworth, Warks CV8 2LG; Tel (01203) 696996; Fax (01203) 696732
Chairman Andy Stewart
ATB – Landbase is the Industry Training Organisation for agriculture and commercial horticulture. Through a national network of training consultants, training providers and instructors, ATB – Landbase provides and advises on a diverse range of management development and skills training courses and issues

Officials of the Board
Chief Executive Nigel Snook
Head of ITO Services Lyn Sawicki
Training Development Manager Terry Howard

British Polymer Training Association

Coppice Hse, Halesfield 7, Telford TF7 4NA; Tel (01952) 587020; Fax (01952) 582065
Business Development Co-ordinator Amanda Cardall
Scope
The polymer industry.
Services offered
Technical training, human resource consultancy, development courses, computer based training, young people training, technical publications, National Vocational Qualifications.

CAPITB PLC

80 Richardshaw La, Pudsey, Leeds LS28 6BN; Tel (0113) 239 3355; Fax (0113) 239 3155
Scope
CAPITB PLC is a leading industrial consultancy group. Divisions include *Kingscourt Consultancies* (DTI listed for quality and manufacturing projects), *Qualifications for Industry Ltd* (awarding body for NVQ and SVQ qualifications), and others covering PR and publicity; work study and management systems; and recruitment.

Officials of the Board
Chief Executive J.W. Dearden

Construction Industry Training Board

Headquarters, CITB Bircham Newton, Kings Lynn, Norfolk PE31 6RH; Tel (01553) 776677; Fax (01553) 692226
Chairman Sir Clifford Chetwood
Deputy Chairman H.W. Try
Scope
The Board covers building, specialist building, civil engineering and brick manufacture.
Central London Office
CITB, 24–30 West Smithfield, London EC1A 9JA; Tel 0171-489 1662; Fax 0171-236 2875

Officials of the Board
Chief Executive Major General E.G. Willmott, CB, OBE
Director and Secretary to the Board M. Smith, FBIM, FIElecIE
Director of Training D.P. Shaw, BSc, CEng, AMIStructE, MICE
Director of Personnel E. Turnbull
Director of Finance and Administration K.D. Owen

Regional Managers
Scotland 4 Edison St, Hillington, Glasgow G52 4XN; Tel 0141-810 3044; D.M. Fergus

North West Parade Chambers, 103 The Parade, Swinton, Manchester M27 2BJ; Tel 0161-794 8931; M. Gee
North East Milton Hse, Queen St, Morley, Leeds LS27 9EL; Tel (0113) 252 1966; J. Lister
East Belton Rd Industrial Est, Prince William Rd, Loughborough, Leics LE11 0GU; Tel (01509) 610266; L.A.S. Scott
South West Lawrence Hse, Lower Bristol Rd, Bath BA2 9ET; Tel (01225) 447914; D.E. Algate
Greater London & South East Radnor Hse, 1272 London Rd, Norbury, London SW16 4EL; Tel 0181-679 8511; J. Hughes
Wales & West Midlands 1st Floor, Shenstone Hse, Dudley Rd, Halesowen, West Midlands B63 3NT; Tel 0121-585 5252; D. Hall

Engineering Training Authority (EnTra)

Vector Hse, 41 Clarendon Rd, Watford WD1 1HS; Tel (01923) 238441; Fax (01923) 256086
Chairman Lord Trefgarne
Scope
EnTra occupies a key place in the Government's national training framework. As the Industry Training Organisation and Industry Lead Body for engineering manufacture, EnTra has responsibility for the development and implementation of standards of competence at all levels in the industry. EnTra is also an Awarding Body for National Vocational Qualifications in engineering manufacture

Officials of EnTra
Chief Executive K.J. Jones
Secretary P.W. Whiteman

Hotel and Catering Training Company

International Hse, High St, Ealing, London W5 5DB; Tel 0181-579 2400; Fax 0181-840 6217
Chairman R. Ackerman
Scope
Hotel and Catering Training Company was formed in September 1989 as the commercial arm of the Hotel and Catering Training Board, which since 1966, has been the industry lead body for the hotel and catering industry. HCTC employs over 350 professional training staff in over 60 training centres ranging from Inverness to St Austell. They are backed by a central team responsible for manpower intelligence, research and the development of new training methods. HCTC were the first of the industry's managing agents for YTS and remain by far the biggest, training between 6,000 and 7,000 young people every year. HCTC publishes a rapidly expanding range of careers films, research reports, and videos and books covering the full range of skills in all sectors of the industry. Information, advice, courses and publications are available for those thinking of starting up their own business in the hotel and catering industry and for those already in business who want to develop their technical or managerial skills. For copies of brochures covering: Business Management, Operational Management, Trainer Training and Craft Training; course calendars; and a full publications catalogue.

Regional Offices
Scottish HCTC, Capital Hse, 9 Logie Mill, Edinburgh EH7 4HG; Tel 0131-557 4677
Central HCTC, Second Floor, Stonebow Hse, The Stonebow, York YO1 2NP; Tel (01904) 626134
Western HTC, Prudential Bldgs, Wine St, Bristol BS1 2PH; Tel (0117) 926 4074
Southern HCTC, International Hse, High St, Ealing, London W5 5DB; Tel 0181-579 2400

Information Technology Training Accreditation Council

ITTAC, IDPM Hse, Edgington Way, Ruxley Corner, Sidcup, Kent DA14 5HR; Tel 0181-309 5496
Secretary Barbara Morris
ITTAC was set up at the end of 1985 to see that the high standards already established by the British computer and computer service industry are maintained; that the names of the best training establishments are communicated abroad; and that Britain remains the overseas student's first choice for IT Training. The training provided by the establishments to be accredited has been thoroughly examined by the Accreditation Committe of ITTAC; moreover they have all undertaken to adhere to the Council's Code of Practice, which is reprinted in the Register. This Register has been distributed widely in the UK and overseas and has the full support of the British Council. It is expected that it will expand substantially over the coming months.

The Local Government Management Board

Arndale Hse, Arndale Centre, Luton LU1 2TS; Tel (01582) 451166
Chairman Harry Jones
Scope
Local authorities in England and Wales
41 Belgrave Sq, London SW1X 8NZ; Tel 0171-235 6081

Officials of the Board
Chief Executive Judith Hunt
Director R. Waterhouse
Director R. Taylor
Director C. Nolda
Scope
The Local Government Management Board brings together a range of services in support of management and people-related matters. Its fundamental role is to help local authorities be more effective in the delivery of services and the provision of democratic leadership in their communities.

Enquiries on management issues, training, NVQs, recruitment and retention, examinations or information to Luton office.
Enquiries concerning pay and conditions, employment issues, industrial relations or research on labour markets to London office.

Man-Made Fibres Industry Training Organisation

Central Hse, Gate La, Sutton Coldfield, West Midlands B73 5TS; Tel 0121-355 7022; Fax 0121-355 7090
Chairman I.E. Quick
General Manager P.A. Grice, MITD, Imtg

Offshore Petroleum Industry Training Organisation

Inchbraoch Hse, South Quay, Ferryden, Montrose DD10 9SL; Tel (01674) 662500; Fax (01674) 662530
Contact John Batchelor
Development and approval of standards of training and competence for the offshore oil and gas industry, training registrars, accreditors and verifiers (successor to Offshore Petroleum Industry Training Board)

Road Transport Industry Training Board

Capitol Hse, Empire Way, Wembley, Middx HA9 0NG; Tel 0181-902 8880
Chairman John Armstrong, CBE
Scope
The Board was originally set up under the Industrial Training Act 1964 and has responsibility for ensuring the provision of training within the road haulage, retail motor trade, motor vehicle maintenance and repair, petrol retail, furniture removals, vehicle body building and repair, motor factoring and vehicle hire industries.

Officials of the Board
Director of Operational and Marketing Services G. Marshment
Director of Finance I.G. Seyler
Director of Administration D.J. Webber
(All enquiries to Marketing Dept)
Number of firms on the Board's Register
27,000

Training and Employment Agency

Clarendon Hse, 9–21 Adelaide St, Belfast BT2 8DJ; Tel (01232) 239944; Fax (01232) 895675
Contact Georgina Campbell

Careers Service

England and Wales

Under the provisions of the Employment and Training Act 1973 all local education authorities in England and Wales were made responsible for the Careers Service.

Careers Offices

Northern Region

Cleveland Careers Service, Business Support and Development Centre, 78 Borough Rd, Middlesbrough, Cleveland TS1 2JH; Tel (01642) 245542
Durham Durham Careers Service, County Hall, Durham DH1 5UJ; Tel 0191-386 4411; Fax 0191-386 0487
Southern Division
Central Hse, Gladstone St, Darlington, Co Durham DL3 6JX; Tel (01325) 346300
Central Division
3rd Floor, Bridge Hse, North Rd, Durham DH1 4PW; Tel 0191-384 9766
Eastern Division
Ridgemount Hse, Bedeway, Peterlee, Co Durham, SR8 1BU; Fax 0191-586 7551
Northern Division
Front St, Stanley, Co Durham DH9 0ST; Tel (01207) 232033
Western Division
4 Market Pl, Bishop Auckland, Co Durham DL14 7NJ; Tel (01388) 603468/605210
Gateshead Gateshead Careers Service, Civic Centre, Gateshead NE8 1HH; Tel 0191-477 1011; Fax 0191-478 3495
Gateshead Careers Centre, Interchange Centre, Gateshead NE8 1BH, UK; Tel 0191-490 1717; Fax 0191-477 9971
Blaydon Careers Centre, Upper Precinct, Wesley Court, Blaydon NE21 SBT, UK; Tel 0191-414 2418; Fax 0191-414 6757
Newcastle upon Tyne Careers Service, College St, Newcastle upon Tyne NE1 8DX; Tel 0191-232 9471; Fax 0191-221 0393
North Tyneside Careers Centre, 205 Park Rd, Wallsend, Wallsend, Tyne and Wear NE28 7NN; Tel 0191-262 5111/3
Northumberland Northumberland County Careers Service, 7/8 Sextant Hse, Freehold St, Blyth NE24 2BA; Tel (01670) 363239; Fax (01670) 363655
South Tyneside Careers Office, Central Library Bldg, Prince Georg Sq, South Shields, Tyne and Wear NE33 2PE; Tel 0191-427 1717; Fax 0191-454 4822
Sunderland City of Sunderland Careers Service, Careers Office, 15 John St, Sunderland SR1 1HT; Tel 0191-514 2441; Fax 0191-565 8273

Yorkshire and Humberside Region

Barnsley Careers Centre, Civic Hall, Eldon St, Barnsley, South Yorkshire S70 2JL; Tel (01226) 205686
Bradford Careers Service, 37/39 Piccadilly Rd, Bradford BD1 3TA; Tel (01274) 752319
Calderdale Careers Office, Northgate Hse, Northgate, Halifax HX1 1UN; Tel (01422) 392579
Doncaster Careers Centre, 24 Thorne Rd, Doncaster, South Yorkshire DN1 2DH; Tel (01302) 734243; Fax (01302) 734339
Humberside County Careers Office, Union St, Albion St, Hull HU2 8HB; Tel (01482) 223081
Kirklees Careers Service Headquarters, Education Service, 7th Floor, Oldgate Hse, 2 Oldgate, Huddersfield HD1 6QW; Tel (01484) 422133 Ext 6714
Leeds Careers Service, Education Dept, Selectapost 17, Merrion Hse, 110 Merrion Centre, Leeds LS2 8DT; Tel (0113) 247 5485
North Yorkshire Careers Guidance Services Ltd, Head Office, Guidance Hse, York Rd, Thirsk YO7 3BT; Tel (01845) 526699; Fax (01845) 526633
Rotherham Careers Office, Norfolk Hse, Walker Pl, Rotherham; Tel (01709) 822632
Sheffield Careers Office, AEU Hse, Furnival Gate, Sheffield S1 3SL; Tel (0114) 273 5461
Wakefield Careers Service, Wood St Hse, 17–19 Cross St, Wakefield WF1 3BW; Tel (01924) 368888

South East Region

Bedfordshire Luton Guidance Centre, Link Hse, 49 Alma St, Luton, Beds MK42 9AE; Tel (01582) 412831; *Information Officer* Ms P. Humphrey
Berkshire Careers Service Headquarters, Dept of Education, Shire Hall, Shinfield Pk, Reading RG2 9XE; Tel (01734) 233551; Fax (01734) 750360
Buckinghamshire County Careers Office, Icknield Hse, Hampden Hall, Aylesbury HP22 5TB; Tel (01296) 395000 Ext 2532; Fax (01296) 387101
Cambridgeshire Training and Information Unit, Castle Court, Castle Hill, Cambridge CB3 0AP; Tel (01223) 317038; Fax (01223) 317024
East Sussex Careers Services Headquarters, County Hall, PO Box 4, Lewes BN7 1SG; Tel (01273) 481000
Essex Careers and Business Partnership, Room 302, Kensal Hse, Springfield Rd, Chelmsford CM2 6TQ; Tel (01245) 348552; Fax (01245) 283407
Hampshire Guidance & Careers Service Headquarters, Monument Hse, 5 Upper High St, Winchester SO23 8NB; Tel (01962) 846493
Hertfordshire County Careers Office, County Hall, Hertford SG13 8DF; Tel (01992) 555794; Fax (01992) 555768
Isle of Wight Careers Centre, 29 High St, Newport, IOW; Tel (01983) 522869; Fax (01983) 521817
Kent Springfield, Maidstone ME14 2LJ; Tel (01622) 671411; Fax (01622) 690892/696536
Norfolk Norfolk Careers Service, County Hall, Martineau La, Norwich NR1 2DL; Tel (01603) 223040
Oxfordshire Education Dept, County Office, Macclesfield Hse, New Rd, Oxford OX1 1NA; Tel (01865) 815449; Fax (01865) 791637
Suffolk County Careers Office, Education Dept, St Andrew Hse, County Hall, Ipswich IP4 1LJ; Tel (01473) 264705; Fax (01473) 230395
Surrey Surrey Careers Services, Farncombe Pl, 10 Farncombe St, Farncombe, Near Godalming, Surrey GU7 3HE; Tel (01483) 860668; Fax (01483) 414980
West Sussex Careers Information Centre, Basildon Chambers, East St, Shoreham-by-Sea BN43 52D; Tel (01273) 454978; Fax (01273) 453789

London

Barking and Dagenham Careers Office, Unit 7 Monteagle Crt, 32-28 Wakering Rd, Barking, Essex IG11 8TE; Tel 0181-591 9999; Fax 0181-591 5111
Barnet (PCO) Educational Services, Friern Barnet La, Friern Barnet, London N11 3DL; Tel 0181-368 1255
Bexley (PCO) Careers Centre, Civic Office, Broadway, Bexleyheath DA6 7LB; Tel 0181-303 7777
Brent Careers Service, Triangle Hse, 328–30 High Rd, Wembley, Middx HA9 6AZ; Tel 0181-900 5434
Bromley The Careers Centre, 83 Tweedy Rd, Bromley, Kent BR1 1RG; Tel 0181-313 4488; Fax 0181-313 4497
Croydon Croydon Careers Service, Careers Centre, College Rd, Croydon CR9 3SU; Tel 0181-401 0301; Fax 0181-401 0300
Selhurst Careers Centre The Crescent, Croydon CR9 2XJ; Tel 0181-689 9288
Ealing Ealing Careers Service, Perceval Hse, 14-16 Uxbridge Rd, London W5 2HL; Tel 0181-579 2424 Ext 53272; Fax 0181-758 8881
Enfield Enfield Careers Service, Enfield Careers Service, PO Box 56, Civic Centre, Silver St, Enfield EN1; Tel 0181-367 7072

17 Employment and Careers

Edmonton Careers Centre Edmonton Centre, South Mall, Edmonton Grn, London N9 0TN; Tel 0181-807 5561
Haringey (PCA) Careers Service, Education Office, 48 Station Rd, Wood Grn, London N22 4TY; Tel 0181-975 9700 (Switchboard) 0181-862 3885 (Direct line)
Harrow Careers Service, London Borough of Harrow, PO Box 147, Civic Centre, Harrow HA1 1FE; Tel 0181-424 1845; Fax 0181-424 1869
Havering PCO, Havering Careers Service, Head Office Holgate Business Centre, 8 Holgate Crt, Western Rd, Romford RM1 3JS; Tel (01708) 738459; Fax (01708) 742366
Hayes Careers Centre, 18/20 East Ave, Hayes UB3 2HP; Tel 0181-573 0719
Hillingdon Careers Centre, Civic Centre, Uxbridge UB8 1UW; Tel (01895) 250773; Fax (01895) 250272
Hounslow PCA Careers Centre, 4 School Rd, Hounslow TW3 1QZ; Tel 0181-577 0555; Fax 0181-572 2653
Kingston upon Thames Head of Careers Service, Careers Office, Guildhall, High St, Kingston upon Thames, Surrey KT1 1EU; Tel 0181-547 4605; Fax 0181-547 5317
Merton Merton Careers Service, 5th Floor, Civic Centre, London Rd, Morden, Surrey SM4 5DX; Tel 0181-545 3320
Newham (PCO) Careers Service, Broadway Hse, 322 High St, Stratford, London E15 1AJ; Tel 0181-534 1374/0181-534 2836
Redbridge Education Office, Lynton Hse, 255–259 High Rd, Ilford IG1 1NN; Tel 0181-478 3020 Ext 3138
Richmond upon Thames Richmond upon Thames College, Egerton Rd, Twickenham TW2 7SJ; Tel 0181-892 6656; Fax 0181-744 9738
Sutton (PCO) Sutton Careers Centre, Westcroft Rd, Carshalton SM5 2TG; Tel 0181-770 6677
Waltham Forest 398A Hoe St, Walthamstow, London E17 9AA; Tel 0181-521 4311; Fax 0181-521 9020

South West Region

Government Office for the South West
Employment and Training Directorate, 4th Fl, The Pithay, Bristol BS1 2NQ; Tel (0117) 945 6941
Avon Careers Service West, 4 Colston Ave, Bristol BS19 4ST; Tel (0117) 987 3700
Gloucestershire Gloucestershire Careers and Guidance Service, 92–96 Westgate St, Gloucester GL1 2PE; Tel (01452) 426900
Wiltshire County Careers Service, Bythesea Rd, Trowbridge BA14 8EZ; Tel (01225) 777442

Midlands Region

Regional Office
Dept of Employment, Cumberland Hse, 200 Broad St, Birmingham B15 1AY; Tel 0121-631 3300
Birmingham Birmingham City Council, Careers HQ, Continuing Education Division, 1 Duchess Pl, Hagley Rd, Birmingham B16 8ND; Tel 0121-235 2655
Coventry Careers Centre, Greyfriars La, Coventry CV1 2GZ; Tel (01203) 831736
Derbyshire Derbyshire Education Offices, County Education Office, Matlock, Derbys DE4 3AG; Tel (01629) 580000
Dudley Careers Service HQ, Education Offices, Westox Hse, 1 Trinity Rd, Dudley DY1 1JB; Tel (01384) 55433
Hereford & Worcester The County Careers Centre, 2nd Floor, County Bldgs, St Marys St, Worcester WR1 1TW; Tel (01905) 763763
Leicestershire Rm 14, County Hall, Glenfield, Leicester LE3 8RF; Tel (0116) 287 1313
Lincolnshire County Council Education Dept, Aquis Hse, Clasketgate, Lincoln LN2 1JZ; Tel (01522) 552222
Northamptonshire Education Dept, 3rd Floor, Northampton Hse, Northampton NN1 2HX; Tel (01604) 236318
Nottinghamshire Careers Service, 24–32 Carlton St, Nottingham NG1 1NN; Tel (0115) 948 4484
Sandwell Education Office, PO Box 41, Shaftesbury Hse, 402 High St, West Bromwich B70 9LF; Tel 0121-525 7366
Shropshire Education Dept, Walker Hse, Radbrook Centre, Shrewsbury SY3 9BJ; Tel (01743) 248597/8
Solihull Careers Advisory Centre, PO Box 20, Council Hse, Solihull B92 3QU; Tel 0121-705 6789
Staffordshire County Education Office, Tipping St, Stafford ST16 2DH; Tel (01785) 323121
Walsall Principal Careers Office, The Education Dept, The Civic Centre, Walsall Metroplitan Borough Council, Darwell St, Walsall; Tel (01922) 21244
Warwickshire County Education Office, 22 Northgate St, Warwick CV34 4SP; Tel (01926) 410410
Wolverhampton Heantun Hse, School St, Wolverhampton, West Midlands WV3 0SN; Tel (01902) 710606

North Western Region

Regional Office
Careers Service Branch, Dept of Employment, Sunley Tower, Piccadilly Plaza, Manchester M60 7JS; Tel 0161-832 9111
Bolton PO Box 53, Paderborn Hse, Civic Centre, Bolton BL1 1JW; Tel (01204) 22311
Bury The Interchange, Haymarket St, Bury BL9 0SN; Tel 0161-705 5779
Cheshire Education Dept, County Hall, Chester CH7 1SQ; Tel (01244) 602407/8
Cumbria 5 Portland Sq, Carlisle CA1 1PU; Tel (01228) 23456
Knowsley Education Offices, Huyton Hey Rd, Huyton, Liverpool L36 5YH; Tel 0151-480 5111
Lancashire Education Dept, County Hall, Preston PR1 8RJ; Tel (01772) 263615
Liverpool 2nd Floor, Merseyside Hse, South John St, Liverpool L1 8BN; Tel 0151-709 5400
Manchester Education Offices, Crown Sq, Manchester M60 3BB; Tel 0161-234 7106-9
Oldham Careers Office, Wellington Bldgs, Hobson St, Oldham OL1 1XG; Tel 0161-624 01505 or 0161-687 4296
Rochdale PO Box 70, Municipal Office, Smith St, Rochdale OL16 1YD; Tel (01706) 48251
St Helens Careers Service Headquarters, 27 Shaw St, St Helens WA10 1PU; Tel (01744) 39333
Salford Careers Office, Halton Hse, 36 Eccles Old Rd, Salford, Lancs M6 7AJ; Tel 0161-736 8931
Sefton Town Hall, Oriel Rd, Bootle, Merseyside L20 7AE; Tel 0151-933 6003
Stockport County Careers Office, Ponsonby Hse, Edward St, Stockport, Cheshire SK1 3UR; Tel 0161-480 4949
Tameside Education Dept, Council Offices, Wellington Rd, Ashton-under-Lyne OL6 6DC; Tel 0161-344 3234
Trafford PO Box 19, Town Hall, Tatton Rd, Sale, Cheshire M33 1YR; Tel 0161-872 2101
Wigan Morrisons Bldgs, Station Rd, Wigan, Lancs WN1 1YQ; Tel (01942) 827566/7
Wirral Education Office, Cleveland St, Birkenhead, Merseyside L41 6NH; Tel 0151-647 7000

Wales

Welsh Office
Careers Guidance Branch, Welsh Office, 3rd Floor, Cathays Pk, Cardiff; Tel (01222) 825863; Telex 825852
Clwyd Careers Service Headquarters, Victoria Hse, Grosvenor St, Mold, Clwyd CH7 1FZ; Tel (01352) 750456; Fax (01352) 750898
Dyfed County Education Office, Pibwrlwyd, Carmarthen, Dyfed SA31 2NA; Tel (01267) 233333 Ext 4528
Gwent Gwent County Offices, County Hall, Cwmbran NP44 2XG; Tel (01633) 838838 Ext 2455
Gwynedd County Careers Office, 2 Castle St, Caernarfon L55 1SE; Tel (01286) 672255
Mid-Glamorgan County Careers Office, Unit G5, Main Ave, Treforest Est, Mid Glamorgan CF37 5YL; Tel (01443) 842207; Fax (01443) 842208
Powys County Careers Headquarters, 4th Floor, Coleg Powys, Llandrindod Wells LD1 5ES; Tel (01597) 824494
South Glamorgan Careers Service Headquarters, Education Offices, County Hall, Atlantic Wharf, Cardiff CF1 5UW; Tel (01222) 872775

West Glamorgan County Careers Office, Education Dept, West Glamorgan Council Council, County Hall, Swansea SA1 3SN; Tel (01792) 471111 Ext 3203

Scotland

Scottish Office Education Dept, Careers Service Branch, New St Andrews Hse, St James's Centre, Edinburgh EH1 3SY; Tel 0131-244 4442

Careers Offices

Border Region

Regional Headquarters, Newtown St Boswells, Melrose TD6 0SA; Tel (01835) 823301

Central Region

Careers Service HQ, Cape Unicentre, Kerse Rd, Stirling FK7 7RW; Tel (01786) 462821

Dumfries and Galloway Region

Careers Service, Education Dept, 30 Edinburgh Rd, Dumfries DG1 1JQ; Tel (01387) 61234

Fife

Regional Headquarters, Fife Hse, North St, Glenrothes, Fife KY7 5LT; Tel (01592) 754411; Fax (01592) 610726

Grampian

Regional Careers Officer, Woodhill Hse, Westburn Rd, Aberdeen AB9 2LU; Tel (01224) 682222
Aberdeen/Gordon/Kincardine & Deeside Old Aberdeen Hse, Dunbar St, Aberdeen AB2 1VE; Tel (01224) 483314
Banff & Buchan 16 Prince St, Peterhead AB4 6PL; Tel (01779) 79345
Moray 11 North Guildry St, Elgin IV30 1JR; Tel (01343) 548884

Highland Region

The Careers Service HQ, Education Dept, 46 Church St, Inverness IV1 1EH; Tel (01463) 236114; Fax (01463) 243231

Lothian Region

Information Unit, Atholl Hse, 2 Canning St, Edinburgh EH3 8EG; Tel 0131-228 7524

Orkney Opportunities Centre,

The Brig, 2 Albert St, Kirkwall, Orkney KW15 1HP; Tel (01856) 872460; Fax (01856) 875515

Shetland

Toll Clock Shopping Centre, 26 North Rd, Lerwick, Shetland Isles ZE1 0PE; Tel (01595) 5791; Fax (01595) 4011

Strathclyde Region

Principal Careers Officer, Strathclyde Region, Dept of Education (FE), Strathclyde Hse, 20 India St, Glasgow G2 4PF; Tel 0141-249 4167/69; Fax 0141-249 4172
Glasgow Division Careers Service, Head Office, 129 Bath St, Glasgow G2 4HH; Tel 0141-204 2900 Ext 6916; Fax 0141-227 6925
Argyll Division Careers Service Head Office, Careers Office, 2 Tom-a-Mhoid Rd, Dunoon PA23 7HN; Tel (01369) 5816; Fax (01369) 3045
Dunbarton Division Careers Service Head Office, 4 South Crosshill Rd, Bishopbriggs, Glasgow G64 2NN; Tel 0141-762 0072; Fax 0141-772 5684
Ayr Division Careers Service Headquarters, Regional Offices, Ayr KA7 1DR; Tel (01292) 612236/7; Fax (01292) 612143
Lanark Division Careers Service Headquarters, Education Dept, Regional Offices, Almada St, Hamilton ML3 0AE; Tel (01698) 454474; Fax (01698) 454467
Renfrew Division Careers Service Headquarters, 6 Glasgow Rd, Paisley PA1 3QA; Tel 0141-887 2281
Adult Guidance Service Continuing Education Gateway, 199 Nithsdale Rd, Glasgow G41 5EX; Tel 0141-422 1070; Fax 0141-422 2006

Tayside Region

Careers Service Headquarters, 3rd Floor, Royal Insurance Bldg, 5 Whitehall Cres, Dundee DD1 4AR; Tel (01382) 303566/303581; Fax (01382) 200476
Perth and Kinross 6–8 South Methven St, Perth; Tel (01738) 38101; Fax (01738) 30818
Angus Bellevue Hse, Springfield Terr, Arbroath DD11 1EL; Tel (01241) 870441
Dundee 2nd Fl, Argyll Hse, Marketgait, Dundee DD1 1QP; Tel (01382) 304100

Western Isles

Careers Office, Council Offices, Sandwick Rd, Stornoway PA87 2BW; Tel (01851) 703773 Ext 445

Northern Ireland

Training and Employment Agency (Northern Ireland)

Headquarters Employment Service Division, Clarendon Hse, 9–21 Adelaide St, Belfast BT2 8DJ; Tel (01232) 239944
Director of Preparation for Work Group J.D. Noble
The group delivers services concerning youth training, training the unemployed, employment and careers services, services to those with disabilities, and the administration of job creation programmes

Training and Employment Agency Offices – Careers Section
Antrim 25–27 Church St, Antrim BT41 4BE; Tel (0184 94) 62834; Fax (0184 94) 28355
Armagh Scotch St, Armagh BT61 7PU; Tel (01861) 523322; Fax (01861) 527994
Ballymena 35–39 Bridge St, Ballymena, Co Antrim BT43 5EL; Tel (01266) 41135; Fax (01266) 651087
Ballymoney 32 Main St, Ballymoney BT53 6AL; Tel (0126 56) 62565; Fax (0126 56) 66786
Ballynahinch 20 High St, Ballynahinch BT24 8AB; Tel (01238) 562986; Fax (01238) 565144
Banbridge 50 Newry St, Banbridge, Co Down BT32 3HA; Tel (0182 016) 62149; Fax (0182 016) 26872
Bangor 65 High St, Bangor BT20 5BE; Tel (01247) 270077; Fax (01247) 465747
Belfast Gloucester Hse, Chichester St, Belfast BT1 4RA; Tel (01232) 235211; Fax (01232) 234069
45 Falls Rd BT12 4AQ; Tel (01232) 333495; Fax (01232) 313469
178–180 Shankill Rd BT13 2BH; Tel (01232) 330063; Fax (01232) 239330
Carrickfergus Crown Bldgs, 20 West St, Carrickfergus, Co Antrim BT38 7AR; Tel (0196 013) 51449; Fax (0196 013) 66215
Coleraine 41 Church St, Coleraine, Co Londonderry BT52 1AW; Tel (01265) 51211; Fax (01265) 54780
Cookstown 17 Oldtown St, Cookstown, Co Tyrone BT80 8EE; Tel (0164 87) 66950; Fax (0164 87) 61231
Downpatrick Rathkeltair Hse, Market St, Downpatrick BT30 6LZ; Tel (01396) 612211; Fax (01396) 612936
Dungannon 5 Thomas St, Co Tyrone BT70 1HW; Tel (0186 87) 22525; Fax (0186 87) 52981
Enniskillen Paget Sq, Enniskillen, Co Fermanagh BT74 7HS; Tel (01365) 323511; Fax (01365) 326122
Kilkeel Newry St, Kilkeel, Co Down BT34 4DN; Tel (0169 37) 62905; Fax (0169 37) 62838
Larne 75 Main St, Larne, Co Antrim BT40 1HH; Tel (01574) 273371; Fax (01574) 270178
Limavady 43 Market St, Limavady, Co Londonderry BT49 0AB; Tel (0150 47) 65967; Fax (0150 47) 22245

Lisburn 71 Bow St, Lisburn BT28 1BJ; Tel (01846) 672214; Fax (01846) 664326
Londonderry 5 Waterloo Pl, Londonderry BT48 6BT; Tel (01504) 264294; Fax (01504) 370133
Londonderry Waterside Hse, 75 Duke St, Londonderry BT47 1DH; Tel (01504) 319000; Fax (01504) 319106
Lurgan 10A High St, Lurgan BT66 8AW; Tel (01762) 344325; Fax (01762) 321538
Magherafelt 28 Queen St, Magherafelt BT45 6AB; Tel (01648) 33804; Fax (01648) 34218
Newcastle 113 Main St, Newcastle, Co Down BT33 0AE; Tel (0139 67) 25001/3; Fax (0139 67) 26302
Newry 5–13 Marcus St, Newry BT34 1ET; Tel (01693) 61222; Fax (01693) 62675
Newtownabbey Swinson Hse, Church Rd, Newtownabbey BT36 7LH; Tel (01232) 365171; Fax (01232) 862912
Newtownards 9 Conway Sq, Newtownards, Co Down BT23 4DA; Tel (01247) 818653; Fax (01247) 820792
Omagh 10 High St, Omagh, Co Tyrone BT78 1BQ; Tel (01662) 244921; Fax (01662) 242496
Portadown 27A Magowan Bldg, West St, Portadown, Co Armagh BT62 3PN; Tel (01762) 334141; Fax (01762) 350758
Strabane 26/28 Market St, Strabane BT82 8BH; Tel (01504) 382332; Fax (01504) 382172

Channel Islands, Isle of Man

Jersey Director of Education, Education Dept, PO Box 142, Jersey, Channel Islands JE4 8QJ; Tel (01534) 509500; Fax (01534) 509800
Guernsey Director of Education, Education Dept, PO Box 32, The Grange, St Peter Port, Guernsey GY1 3AU, Channel Islands; Tel (01481) 710821; Fax (01481) 714475
Isle of Man Careers Office, Markwell Hse, Market St, Douglas, Isle of Man; Tel (01624) 685128

Careers – Advice and Counselling

Banking Information Service, 10 Lombard St, London EC3V 9AT; Tel 0171-626 9386; Fax 0171-283 9655; *Director* Brian Stevens
Cambridge University Careers Service, *Secretary* A.J. Raban Stuart Hse, Mill La, Cambridge CB2 1XE; Tel (01223) 338288
Career Analysts Ltd, Careers Hse, 90 Gloucester Pl, London W1H 4BL; Tel 0171-935 5452; Fax 0171-486 9922; *Contact* Peter Forsyth, MA, CPsychol; *Contact* Sherridan Hughes, MEd, CPsychol
Career and Educational Consultation, Tavistock Institute of Medical Psychology, Tavistock Centre, 120 Belsize La, London NW3 5BA; Tel 0171-794 1309; *Contact* The Secretary
Career Counselling Services, 46 Ferry Rd, Barnes, London SW13 9PW; Tel 0181-741 0335; *Director/Counseller* Robert Nathan, MSc, DipCouns, CPsychol
Career Guidance, 4 Cadogan Lane, London SW1X 9EB; Tel 0171-631 1209; *Director* J.F. Stevenson, MA, MSc
Careers in Focus, The Grange, Elmbridge, Droitwich, Worcs WR9 0DA; Tel (01527) 861898; Fax (01527) 861878; *Managing Director* Craig Nicholl
Careers Guidance Consultants, Hooton Lawn, Benty Heath La, Hooton, Wirral, Cheshire L66 6AG; Tel 0151-327 3894; *Contact* Dr D.W. Blything
Civil Engineering Careers Service, 1/7 Great George St, London SW1P 3AA; Tel 0171-222 7722
CSU (Publications) Ltd, Armstrong Hse, Oxford Rd, Manchester M1 7ED; Tel 0161-236 9816; Fax 0161-236 8541; *Director* A.P. Raderecht
ECCTIS 2000, UK Course Information Service; *Chief Executive* Christopher West ECCTIS 2000 Ltd, Fulton Hse, Jessop Ave, Cheltenham, Glos GL50 3SH; Tel (01242) 518724; Fax (01242) 225914
Educational Guidance, 20 Bloomsbury Sq, London WC1A 2NS; Tel 0171-631 1209; *Director* J.F. Stevenson, MA, MSc
Educational Guidance Service for Adults, 2nd Fl, Glendinning Hse, 6 Murray St, Belfast BT1 6DN; Tel (01232) 244274; Fax (01232) 240892; *Director* E. Kelly, BA, DCG
Engineering Careers Information Service *see* Engineering Training Authority
Gabbitas Educational Consultants Ltd, Broughton Hse, 6/8 Sackville St, London W1X 2BR; Tel 0171-734 0161; Fax 0171-437 1764
Independent Schools Careers Organisation, *National Director* G.W. Searle, MA 12a Princess Way, Camberley, Surrey GU15 3SP; Tel (01276) 21188; Fax (01276) 691833
National Institute for Careers Education and Counselling, Sheraton Hse, Castle Pk, Cambridge CB3 0AX; Tel (01223) 460277; *Director* A.G. Watts, MA, MPhil Sheraton Hse, Castle Pk, Cambridge CB3 0AX; Tel (01223) 460277
Pauline Hyde & Associates Ltd, 20 Lincoln's Inn Fields, London WC2A 3ED; Tel 0171-242 4875; Fax 0171-404 5077; *Chief Executive* Mrs Pauline P. Hyde, CBIM, FInstD, MIPM
Vocational Guidance Association Ltd, 7 Harley Hse, Upper Harley St, London NW1 4RP; Tel 0171-935 2600
The VGA offer counselling to people at all stages of their career by means of psychometric tests and interviews. Clients include students, job-changes, women returners, managers and those about to retire.
WISE (Women into Science and Engineering), c/o The Engineering Council, 10 Maltravers St, London WC2R 3ER; Tel 0171-240 7891; *Contact* Marie-Noelle Barton, Careers Executive

The Services

Royal Navy Educational Establishments

Base Education Centre, H.M.S. Cochrane, Rosyth; Tel (01383) 412121 Ext 62998, 63754
H.M.S. Collingwood, Fareham, Hants PO14 1AS; Tel (01705) 822351 Ext 85212; *Captain* P.F. Wason, RN
Correspondence to the Captain
H.M.S. Sultan, Gosport, Hants PO12 3BY; *Captain* A.D. Ferguson, BA, MSc, CEng, MIMarE, MIMechE, RN; *Commander* I. Edwards, BSc, PhD, ADP, RN
The Britannia Royal Naval College, Dartmouth, Devon TQ6 0HJ; Tel (01803) 832141; *Captain* R.G. Hastilon, RN; *Director of Studies* A.W. Machin, BSc, PhD
Royal Naval Engineering College, Manadon, Plymouth, Devon PL5 3AQ; Tel (01752) 553740, Ext 81213; *Captain* T.J. England, BSc, FIEE, RN; *Dean* J.N. McGrath, MSc, PhD, CEng, FIMarE, FIM, RN
Royal Marines School of Music, Deal, Kent; Tel (01304) 362121
Initial training and music training for the Royal Marines Band Service

Scholarship Scheme, Naval College Entry, Direct Graduate Entry and University Sponsorship
Correspondence in connection with these schemes should be addressed to the Dept of Naval Recruiting, Officer Enquiry Section, Rm 105, Ministry of Defence, Old Admiralty Bldg, Spring Gdns, London SW1A 2BE; Tel 071-218 4740.

Army Staff College

Staff College, Camberley, Surrey GU15 4NP; Tel (01276) 63344
Commandant Maj-Gen C.B.Q. Wallace, OBE
Royal Military College of Science, Cranfield Institute of Technology, Shrivenham, Swindon, Wilts SN6 8LA;

Tel (01793) 782551; *Commandant* Maj-Gen S.A. Cowan, CBE; *Principal* Prof A.C. Baynham, BSc, PhD, rcds

The Royal Military Academy, Sandhurst, Camberley, Surrey GU15 4PQ; Tel (01276) 63344; *Commandant* Maj-Gen T.P. Toyne Sewell; *Director of Studies* B.T. Jones, RD, MA

Royal Military School of Music, Kneller Hall, Twickenham, Middx TW2 7DU; Tel 0181-898 5533/134/35; *Commandant* Brig C.H. Bond, OBE; *Director of Music* Lt-Col F.A. Renton, ARCM, DSM

Scholarship Schemes and Undergraduate Sponsorship

Enquiries about Army Scholarship Schemes may be sent to the Ministry of Defence (DAR1), Empress State Bldg, Lillie Rd, London SW6 1TR; Tel 071-385 1244, Ext 3272.

Headquarters, Director of Army Education

Court Rd, Eltham, London SE9 5NR; Tel 0181-781 4266

Director of Army Education Maj-Gen C.A. Kinvig, MA

Chief Inspector Col T.W. Payne, BSc, MA

Army School of Training Support, RAEC Centre, Wilton Pk, Beaconsfield, Bucks HP9 2RP; Tel (01494) 676121, Ext 3289

Welbeck College, Worksop, Notts S80 3LN; Tel (01909) 476326; *Principal* J.K. Jones, BA

Queen Victoria School, Dunblane, Perthshire FK15 0JY; Tel (01786) 822288; *Headmaster* J.D. Hankinson, MA

Princess Marina College, Arborfield, Reading RG2 9NJ; Tel (01734) 760421, Ext 2437

Army Apprentices College, Beachley, Chepstow, Gwent NP6 7YG; Tel (01291) 627212; *Commandant* Col A.G.R. Holman, OBE; *Senior Education Officer* Lt-Col J.L. Gilders, BSc, MA, RAEC

Army Apprentices College, Harrogate, North Yorkshire HG3 2SE; Tel (01904) 659811 Ext 4294

R.A.F. Educational Establishments

Air Commodore Training Support

Ministry of Defence, Adastral Hse, Theobalds Rd, London WC1X 8RU; Tel 0171-430 7069

Air Commodore Training Support Air Commodore M.D. Smart, BA, RAF

R.A.F. School of Education and Training Support, R.A.F. Newton, Nottingham NG13 8HL; Tel (01949) 20771; *Officer Commanding* Gp-Capt J. Rennie, MA, BSc, FITD, FBIM, RAF

R.A.F. Hereford, Hereford HR4 7DD; Tel (01432) 761555; *Officer Commanding Training Wing* Wg Cdr S.A. Gracie, MA, BA, RAF

Responsible for training Secretarial and Supply Officers and Airmen and the Airmen's Command School.

No 4 School of Technical Training, R.A.F. St Athan, Barry, South Glamorgan CF6 9WA; Tel (01446) 798798, Ext 2751; *Senior Education Officer* Officer Commanding Training Support Squadron

No 1 Radio School, R.A.F. Locking, Weston-super-Mare, Avon BS24 7AA; Tel (01934) 822131

R.A.F. Careers

Further information may be obtained from local R.A.F. Careers Information Offices (addresses are in the telephone book) or direct from H.Q. Inspectorate of Recruiting (R.A.F.), Government Bldgs, London Rd, Stanmore, Middlesex HA7 4PZ; Tel 081-958 6377.

Merchant Navy

Courses for Officer Cadets

The following colleges undertake residential courses leading to ONC/OND in Nautical Studies approved by the Department of Trade for which remission of qualifying service is given. Students attending these courses are sponsored by shipping companies.

Cardiff Institute of Higher Education, Faculty of Design and Technology, Western Ave, Cardiff CF5 2YB; Tel (01222) 551111, Ext 4316; Fax (01222) 578186; *Associate Dean* J. Ayles, BA, CEng, FIEE, FIMarE, MRIN; *Principal* V.D. Wilmslow

Blackpool and The Fylde College, Ashfield Rd, Bispham, Blackpool FY2 OHB; Tel (01253) 352352; Fax (01253) 356127; *Marketing Manager* Patrick E. Stevens

City of Liverpool Community College, Curriculum Support Unit, Riversdale Site, Riversdale Rd, Liverpool L19 3QR; Tel 0151-252 4784; Fax 0151-495 0571; *Principal* Wally Brown; *Cross College Co-ordinator Community Outreach Education* Ms E.M. Galvin

Maritime Division/Maritime Operations Centre, Southampton Institute of Higher Education, Warsash Campus, New Town Rd, Warsash, Southampton SO3 6ZL; Tel (01489) 576161; Fax (01489) 576908; Telex 477362 WRSASH G; *HOD* W. Findlay

South Tyneside College, St George's Ave, South Shields, Tyne and Wear NE34 6ET; Tel 0191-427 3500; Fax 0191-427 3535; *Principal* J.R. Wells, BA(Hons), MA, DipEd, FRSA

Prehsea Courses for Cadets

Hull Trinity Hse School, Princes Dock St, Hull HU1 2LJ; Tel (01482) 326421; *Headmaster* Capt D Thompson, BSc(Hons), ExC, DMS

Courses for Deck, Catering and Engineroom Ratings and Other Merchant Navy Personnel

National Sea Training College, Gravesend, Kent DA12 2HR; Tel (01474) 363656; Fax (01474) 566364

Radiocommunications

DTI Radiocommunications Agency is responsible for examinations for Radio Officers. Enquiries should be addressed to Ships Radio Officers Examinations, Room 804 Waterloo Bridge Hse, Waterloo Rd, London SE1 8UA; Tel 071-215 2292/2007/2104

J.A. Shaw Room 804, Waterloo Bridge Hse, Waterloo Rd, London SE1 8UA; Tel 0171-215 2292/2007/2104; Fax 0171-928 5746

P. Davies

A. Beebeejaun

Kelvin Hughes Ltd, New North Rd, Hainault, Ilford, Essex IG6 2UR; Tel 0181-500 1020

STC International Marine, Intelco Hse, 302 Commonside East, Mitcham, Surrey CR4 1YT; Tel 0181-640 3400; Fax 0181-685 0321

Civil Aviation Authority

Recruitment NATS, Rm T820, CAA Hse, 45–59 Kingsway, London WC2B 6TE; Tel 0171-832 5924

The Civil Aviation Authority (CAA) runs two training schemes, one to train air traffic controllers (ATCOs) and the other to train air traffic engineers (ATEs). ATCOs are responsible for the control of aircraft flying within UK airspace, and ATEs are responsible for maintaining a network of communications equipment, radars, navigational aids and computer systems. Aircrew and aircraft engineers are generally employed by airline operators. Aircraft manufacturers have their own training schemes.

Pilot Training

Courses of ab-initio training for professional pilot's licences are conducted at the following schools approved by the Civil Aviation Authority: *For Aeroplane Licences* Air Services Training, Perth Aerodrome, Scotland PH2 6NP; British Aerospace Flying College Ltd, Prestwick Airport, Ayrshire KA9 2BW; GB Air Academy Ltd, Goodwood Airfield, Chichester, West Sussex PO18 0PH; Oxford Air Training School, Oxford Airport, Kidlington, Oxford OX5 1RA; Trent Air Services, Cranfield Aerodrome, Bedford MK3 0AL. Course duration is approximately 9 months for the basic Commercial Pilot's Licence and 12 months for the Commercial Pilot's Licence and Instrument Rating. *For Helicopter Licences* Bristow Helicopters Ltd, Redhill Aerodrome, Redhill, Surrey RH1 5JZ; Oxford Air Training School, Oxford Airport, Kidlington, Oxford OX5 1RA; Trent Air Services, Cranfield Aerodrome, Bedford MK3 0AL. Course duration is 9 months.

17 Employment and Careers

Applicants for entry to a course of training for a professional pilot's licence must be assessed as medically fit for professional pilot duties by the Civil Aviation Authority. The educational standard assumed for the CPL(A), CPL/IR and CPL(H) full-time approved courses is that the student will have obtained the equivalent of at least the General Certificate of Education of England and Wales, or the Scottish Certificate of Education, or the Northern Ireland General Certificate of Education, with passes in five subjects at O level, including English Language, Mathematics and a science subject. Persons wishing to undertake an approved course who do not meet this minimum educational standard should seek advice on their acceptability for the course from the Flying Training Organisation at which it is to be conducted. Applicants must be aged not less than 18 years when the licence is issued.

Some Airlines and Companies may sponsor trainees, generally on a partial repayment basis. A few companies are offering sponsorship but applications should be made direct to Airlines or Commercial Aeroplane or Helicopter Operators. Companies offering sponsorship usually require applicants to have gained two or more passes at A level in the General Certificate of Education (or equivalent).

Courses of Instruction

The Flight Directory of British Aviation, which may be seen at most public libraries, includes a complete list of universities, colleges, schools and clubs giving training. Requirements for the issue of licences to those seeking a career in civil aviation are set out in appropriate civil aviation publications, which may be obtained from the Civil Aviation Authority, Printing and Publication Services, Greville Hse, 37 Gratton Rd, Cheltenham, Glos GL50 2BN.

Professional Bodies

Accountants

The Association of Accounting Technicians, 154 Clerkenwell Rd, London EC1R 5AD; Tel 0171-837 8600; Fax 0171-410 0906; *Education Officer* Dorothea De Carvalho

Association of International Accountants, South Bank Bldg, Kingsway, Team Valley, Gateshead NE11 0JS; Tel 0191-482 4409; Fax 0191-482 5578; *Director General* J.R.A. Turnbull, FAIA, FSCA, MBIM

The Chartered Association of Certified Accountants, 29 Lincoln's Inn Fields, London WC2A 3EE; Tel 0171-396 5800; Fax 0171-396 5858; *Head of Recruitment, Education and Training* R.M. Protherough, MA, MBIM; *Chief Executive* Anthea Rose

The Chartered Institute of Management Accountants, 63 Portland Pl, London W1N 4AB; Tel 0171-637 2311; *Secretary* Sir George Vallings, KCB; *Director of Student & Technical Affairs* J. Claret, FCA, FCMA

CIPFA (Chartered Institute of Public Finance and Accountancy), 3 Robert St, London WC2N 6BH; Tel 0171-895 8823; Fax 0171-895 8825; *Director* N.P. Hepworth, OBE, IPFA, DPA

The Institute of Chartered Accountants in England and Wales, Chartered Accountants' Hall, PO Box 433, Moorgate Pl, London EC2P 2BJ; Tel 0171-628 7060; *Secretary* A.J. Colquhoun

Institute of Chartered Accountants in Ireland, 11 Donegall Sq South, Belfast BT1 5JE; Tel (01232) 321600; *Director of Education* Ben Lynch; *Administrator* Mary Armstrong

The Institute of Chartered Accountants of Scotland, 27 Queen St, Edinburgh EH2 1LA; Tel 0131-225 5673; Fax 0131-479 4872; *Director of Education* Prof I.F.Y. Marrian, MA, CA

The Institute of Company Accountants, 80 Portland Pl, London W1N 4DP; *Senior Student Administrator* Mrs J.G. Slade

40 Tyndalls Park Rd, Bristol BS8 1PL; Tel (0117) 973 8261; Fax (0117) 923 8292

Institute of Cost and Executive Accountants, Tower Hse, 141–9 Fonthill Rd, London N4 3HF; Tel 0171-272 3925; Fax 0171-281 5723; *Secretary General* S.K. Das Gupta, BCom, ACIS

International Association of Bookkeepers, Burford Hse, 44 London Rd, Sevenoaks, Kent TN13 1AS; Tel (01732) 458080; Fax (01732) 455848; *Chief Executive* J.M. Dean

Actuaries

The Faculty of Actuaries, 40/44 Thistle St, Edinburgh EH2 1EN; Tel 0131-220 4555; Fax 0131-220 2280; *Secretary* W. Wallace Mair, MA

Institute of Actuaries, Staple Inn Hall, High Holborn, London WC1V 7QJ; Tel 0171-242 0106; Fax 0171-405 2482; *Secretary General* A.G. Tait, MA, FIPM

The Institute of Actuaries Education Service, Napier Hse, 4 Worcester St, Oxford OX1 2AW; Tel (01865) 794144; Fax (01865) 704094; *Director of Education* K.L. Gardner, MA, FIMA, FRSA

Administrators

Institute of Paralegal Training (incorporating the Association of Legal Secretaries) The Mill, Clymping St, Clymping, nr Littlehampton, Sussex BN17 5RN; Tel (01903) 714276; *Secretary General* Mrs A.Y. Ibberson

The Association of Personal Assistants & Secretaries Ltd, 14 Victoria Terr, Royal Leamington Spa, Warks CV31 3AB; Tel (01926) 24794, 24844, 30238, 883359; *Chairman* Isobel Brown McPhail

Faculty of Secretaries and Administrators Ltd, 15 Church St, Godalming, Surrey GU7 1EL; Tel (01483) 425144; *Director* D.C. Knight

The Institute of Agricultural Secretaries & Administrators Ltd, NAC Stoneleigh, Kenilworth, Warks CV8 2LZ; Tel (01203) 696592; *Secretary* Mrs Charlotte O'Kane

The Institute of Chartered Secretaries and Administrators, 16 Park Cres, London W1N 4AH; Tel 0171-580 4741; *Secretary* M.J. Ainsworth, DipEd, FCIS

The Institute of Health Services Management, 39 Charlton St, London NW1 1JD; Tel 0171-388 2626; Fax 0171-388 2386

Institute of Qualified Private Secretaries Ltd, 68 Longmoor Rd, Long Eaton, Nottingham NG10 4FP; Tel (0115) 973 3235; *General Manager* N. Harris, FIQPS

Advertising

See Marketing

Aeronautics

The Royal Aeronautical Society (in which are incorporated the Institution of Aeronautical Engineers, the Helicopter Association of Great Britain and the Society of Licensed Aircraft Engineers and Technologists), 4 Hamilton Pl, London W1V 0BQ; Tel 0171-499 3515; Fax 0171-499 6230; Telex 262826 RAESOC; *Director* R.J. Kennett, FBIM, FRAeS

Agriculture

Royal Agricultural Society of England, National Agricultural Centre, Stoneleigh, Kenilworth, Warks CV8 2LZ; Tel (01203) 696969; Fax (01203) 696900; Telex 31697

Arbitrators

Chartered Institute of Arbitrators, International Arbitration Centre, 24 Angel Gate, City Rd, London EC1V 2RS; Tel 0171-837 4483; Fax 0171-837 4185

Archaeology

Council for British Archaeology Bowes Morrell Hse, 111 Walmgate, York YO1 2UA; Tel (01904) 671417; *Director* R.K. Morris, MA, FSA; *Education Officer* D. Henson, BA, MPhil

Architects

Architects and Surveyors Institute St Mary Hse, 15 St Mary St, Chippenham, Wilts SN15 3WD; Tel (01249) 444505; Fax (01249) 443602; *Chief Executive* B.A. Hunt

British Institute of Architectural Technologists, 397 City Rd, London EC1V 1NE; Tel 0171-278 2206; Fax 0171-837 3194; *Education and Membership Officer* Rachel Carter; *Chief Executive* Peter Yeo

Commonwealth Association of Architects, 66 Portland Pl, London W1N 4AD; Tel 0171-636 8276; Fax 0171-255 1541; *Executive Director* George Wilson

The Association of Building Engineers, Jubilee Hse, Billing Brook Rd, Weston Favell, Northampton NN3 8NW; Tel (01604) 404121; *Education and Membership Officer* L.J. Lewis

The Royal Institute of British Architects, 66 Portland Pl, London W1N 4AD; Tel 0171-580 5533; Fax 0171-255 1541; *Director General* The Rt Hon Lord Rodgers of Quarry Bank; *Director, Education and Professional Development* P. Gibbs-Kennet, MA, DipEd

Association and Institute Management

Society of Association Executives, Courtleigh, Westbury, Leigh, Wilts BA13 3TA; Tel (01380) 830964; Fax (01380) 830574; *Secretary* L. Rocker

Auctioneers

See Valuation

Baking

Institute of British Bakers Ltd, 50 Sandygate Rd, Sheffield S10 5RY; Tel (0114) 266 3383; *General Secretary* Peter Skelton, FCCA

Banking

Association of Banking Teachers, c/o CIOB, Emmanuel Hse, Canterbury, Kent CT1 2XJ

The Chartered Institute of Bankers, 10 Lombard St, London EC3V 9AS; Tel 0171-623 3531; Fax 0171-283 1510; *Chief Executive* Gavin Shreeve
4–9 Burgate Ln, Canterbury, Kent CT1 2XJ; Tel (01227) 762600; Fax (01227) 763788

The Chartered Institute of Bankers in Scotland, 19 Rutland Sq, Edinburgh EH1 2DE; Tel 0131-229 9869; *Chief Executive* Charles W. Munn, BA, PhD, ACIBS(Scot)

Biology

Institute of Biology, 20–22 Queensberry Pl, London SW7 2DZ; Tel 0171-581 8333; *General Secretary* Dr R.H. Priestley; *Education Officer* Vacancy; *Executive Editor Journal Biological Education* Clare Chatham

Brewing

The Institute of Brewing, 33 Clarges St, London W1Y 8EE; Tel 0171-499 8144; Fax 0171-499 1156; *Chief Executive* P.W.E. Istead

Building

The Chartered Institute of Building, Englemere, Kings Ride, Ascot, Berks SL5 8BJ; Tel (01344) 23355; *Chief Executive* Keith Banbury, HonAIC, MCIM, FIMgt; *Director of Education* Michael Brown, BSc, MSc, DMS, FCIOB, MIMgt

Business Executives

See Management

Careers

Association of Graduate Careers Advisory Service, Careers Service, Loughborough University, Leics LE11 3TU; Tel (01509) 22052; *Administration Manager* Richard Hill Careers Advisory Service, Sheffield University, 8-10 Favell Rd, Sheffield S3 7QX; Tel (01772) 892584

Institute of Careers Guidance, 27a Lower High St, Stourbridge, West Midlands DY8 1TA; Tel (01384) 376464

Cartography

The British Cartographic Society, c/o The Hon Secretary, 13 Sheldrake Gdns, Hordle, Lymington, Hampshire SO41 0FJ; Tel (01425) 618679; *President* Roger Anson

Ordnance Survey, Romsey Rd, Maybush, Southampton SO9 4DH; Tel (01703) 792639; *Recruitment Officer* Mrs C. Owen

Caseworkers

See Social Work

Catering

Hotel Catering and Institutional Management Association, 191 Trinity Rd, London SW17 7HN; Tel 0181-672 4251; Fax 0181-682 1707; *Director* Stephen Martin-Scott

British Hospitality Association, 40 Duke St, London W1M 6HR; Tel 0171-499 6641; Fax 0171-355 4596; *Chief Executive* Robin Lees, CB, MBE; *Personnel and Training* Susan Harris

European Catering Association (Great Britain), 1 Victoria Parade, by 331 Sandycombe Rd, Richmond, Surrey TW9 3NB; Tel 0181-940 4464; Fax 0181-332 6124; *General Secretary* Ron Barwood

Local Authority Caterers Association, Bourne Hse, Horsell Pk, Woking, Surrey GU21 4LY; Tel (01483) 766777; *LACA Secretariat* Vic Laws

Ceramics

The Institute of Ceramics, Shelton Hse, Stoke Rd, Shelton, Stoke-on-Trent, Staffs ST4 2DR; Tel (01782) 202116; *President* J.E. Troth
(will merge with Institute of Metals in 1993).

Chemistry

Chemical Industries Association Ltd, Kings Bldgs, Smith Sq, London SW1P 3JJ; Tel 0171-834 3399; *Public Affairs Director* G. Liardet, CBE

The Royal Society of Chemistry, Burlington Hse, London W1V 0BN; Tel 0171-437 8656; *Secretary-General* T.D. Inch, DSc, CChem, FRSC

Chiropodists

The Society of Chiropodists and Podiatrists, 53 Welbeck St, London W1M 7HE; Tel 0171-486 3381; Fax 0171-935 6359; *General Secretary* J.G.C. Trouncer, MA, FCIS

Choreology

The Benesh Institute 12 Lisson Gr, London NW1 6TS; Tel 0171-258 3041; Fax 0171-724 6434; *Director* Andrew Ward

Civil Service

The Office of the Civil Service Commissioners, Graduate & Schools Liaison Branch, Alencon Link, Basingstoke, Hants RG21 1JB; Tel (01256) 846414/6415

Cleaning

British Institute of Cleaning Science Ltd, Whitworth Chambers, George Row, Northampton NN1 1DF; Tel (01604) 230075; *Executive Director* C. Hasson

17 Employment and Careers

Clerks of Works

The Institute of Clerks of Works of Great Britain Incorporated, 41 The Mall, Ealing, London W5 3TJ; Tel 0181-579 2917/8; Fax 0181-579 0554; *Secretary* A.P. Macnamara, HonFICW; *Chairman of Examination Board* F.J. Garside, TD, BSc, FICW, ARICS, MCIOB

Clinical Radiology and Oncology

The Royal College of Radiologists, 38 Portland Pl, London W1N 3DG; Tel 0171-636 4432; *Contact* Education Secretary

Colour Technology

See Dyers and Colourists

Commerce

Institute of Commerce, William Hse, 14 Worple Rd, Wimbledon, London SW19 4DD; Tel 0181-879 1973; Fax 0181-946 7153

Commodities

Federation of Commodity Associations (FCA), Gafta Hse, 6 Chapel Crt, Chapel Pl, Rivington St, London EC2A 3DQ; Tel 0171-814 9666; Fax 0171-814 8383; Telex 886984; *Secretary* Pamela Kirby Johnson

Computer Science

British Computer Society, 1 Sanford St, Swindon SN1 1HJ; Tel (01793) 417417; Fax (01793) 480270

The Association of Business & Administrative Computing, The Shaftesbury Centre, Percy St, Swindon SN2 2AZ; Tel (01793) 770259; *Secretary* Graham Minshaw; *Administrative Officer* Pippa Lewis

Concrete

The Concrete Society, 3 Eatongate, 112 Windsor Rd, Slough, Berks SL1 2JA; Tel (01753) 693313; Fax (01753) 692333; *Secretary and Director* T.W. Kirkbride, BSc, MICE

Credit Management

Institute of Credit Management, The Water Mill, Station Rd, South Luffenham, Oakham, Leics LE15 8NB; Tel (01780) 721888; Fax (01780) 721333; *Education and Membership Manager* Lucy Burgin, BA

Dancing

Imperial Society of Teachers of Dancing, Euston Hall, Birkenhead St, London WC1H 8BE; Tel 0171-837 9967; Fax 0171-833 5981; *Chief Executive* Michael J. Browne, FFA, FFBA, FCES, FIAB, FRSA

International Dance Teachers Association Ltd, International Hse, 76 Bennet Rd, Brighton, Sussex BN2 5JL; Tel (01273) 685652; Fax (01273) 674388; *Company Secretary* Jay Dearling

Dentistry

General Dental Council, 37 Wimpole St, London W1M 8DQ; Tel 0171-486 2171; Fax 0171-224 3294; *Registrar* N.T. Davies, MBE, JP, BA

Dietetics

The British Dietetic Association, 7th Floor, Elizabeth Hse, 22 Suffolk St, Queensway, Birmingham B1 1LS; Tel 0121-643 5483; *Organising Secretary* Ms V. Jones

Display

The British Display Society, 70a Crayford High St, Dartford, Kent DA1 4EF; Tel (01322) 555755; Fax (01322) 552807; *Credo Secretarial Services; Examinations Registrar* Mrs S.P. Simpson; Tel (01322) 550544

Dyers and Colourists

The Society of Dyers and Colourists (Incorporated by Royal Charter), PO Box 244, Perkin Hse, 82 Grattan Rd, Bradford, W Yorks BD1 2JB; Tel (01274) 725138; Fax (01274) 392888; *Education Officer* M. Roberts, MA, CCol, ASDC, LRSC

Energy

The Institute of Energy, 18 Devonshire St, London W1N 2AU; Tel 0171-580 7124; Fax 0171-580 4420; *Secretary* J.E. Leach

Engineers

Association of Supervisory and Executive Engineers, Wix Hill Hse, West Horsley, Surrey KT24 6DZ; Tel (01483) 222383; Fax (01483) 211109; *Secretary* D.J. Dacam, OBE, BSc, FCIS

Biological Engineering Society, Royal College of Surgeons, Lincoln's Inn Fields, London WC2A 3PN; Tel 0171-242 7750; *President* L.J. Grant; *Hon Secretary* Dr R.E. Trotman

The Chartered Institution of Building Services Engineers, Delta Hse, 222 Balham High Rd, London SW12 9BS; Tel 0181-675 5211; *Secretary* A.V. Ramsay, MA, CEng, FCIS

The Engineering Council, 10 Maltravers St, London WC2R 3ER; Tel 0171-240 7891; Fax 0171-240 7517; *Senior Executive – General Education* Dr John Williams; *Careers Executive* Marie-Noelle Barton

Institution of Agricultural Engineers, West End Rd, Silsoe, Bedford MK45 4DU; Tel (01525) 861096; Fax (01525) 861660; *Secretary* Michael Hurst, CEng, MIEE

The Institution of Chemical Engineers, (IChemE) Davis Bldg, 165/189 Railway Terr, Rugby, Warks CV21 3HQ; Tel (01788) 578214; Fax (01788) 560833; *General Secretary* T.J. Evans, BSc, PhD, CEng, FIChemE, FBIM

London Office

12 Gayfere St, London SW1P 3HP; Tel 0171-222 2681/2

Institution of Civil Engineers, Great George St, London SW1P 3AA; Tel 0171-222 7722; Fax 0171-222 7500; *Director General/Secretary* R.S. Dobson, OBE, CEng, FICE

Institution of Domestic Heating and Environmental Engineers, 37a High Rd, Benfleet, Essex; Tel (01268) 754266; *Chairman* E.E. Farrow

Institution of Electronics and Electrical Incorporated Engineers, Savoy Hill Hse, Savoy Hill, London WC2R 0BS; Tel 0171-836 3357; Fax 0171-497 9006; *Secretary* A.C. Gingell

Institution of Engineering Designers, Courtleigh, Westbury Leigh, Westbury, Wilts BA13 3TA; Tel (01373) 822801; Fax (01373) 858085; *Secretary* M.J. Osborne

Institute of Engineers and Technicians, 100 Grove Vale, Dulwich, London SE22 8DR; Tel 0181-693 1255; *Secretary General* Dr A.F.L. Deeson

The Institution of Gas Engineers, 21 Portland Pl, London W1N 3AF; Tel 0171-636 6603; Fax 0171-636 6602; *Secretary* S.M. Raine, BA, ACIS

Institution of Highways and Transportation, 3 Lygon Pl, Ebury St, London SW1W 0JS; Tel 0171-730 5245; Fax 0171-730 1628; *Secretary* Dr M. Cragg

Institution of Incorporated Executive Engineers, Wix Hill Hse, West Horsley, Surrey KT24 6DZ; Tel (01483) 222383; Fax (01483) 211109; *Secretary* D.J. Dacam, OBE, BSc, FCIS

The Institution of Electrical Engineers, Savoy Pl, London WC2R 0BL; Tel 0171-240 1871; *Secretary and Chief Executive* J.C. Williams, PhD; *Head of Schools Education and Liaison Service* A.D. Giles; *Courses Information Officer* J. Crabtree

The Institute of Marine Engineers, The Memorial Bldg, 76 Mark La, London EC3R 7JN; Tel 0171-481 8493; Fax 0171-488 1854; *Secretary* J.E. Sloggett, BSc, CEng, FIMarE, FRINA, FICS, CDipAF

The Institution of Mechanical Engineers, 1 Birdcage Walk, London SW1H 9JJ; Tel 0171-222 7899; *Director General* Dr Richard Pike, MA, CEng, FIMechE, FIChemE, FInstPet; *Director, Qualifications* Maurice Harthill, CEng, FIMechE

The Institution of Mechanical Incorporated Engineers, 3 Birdcage Walk, London SW1H 9JN; Tel 0171-799 1808; Fax 0171-799 2243; *Secretary* I.M. Barnes, IEng

The Institution of Mining Electrical and Mining Mechanical Engineers, Danum Hse, 6A South Parade, Doncaster DN1 2DY; Tel (01302) 360104; Fax (01302) 730399; *General Secretary* B. Rolink

The Institution of Mining Engineers, Danum Hse, South Parade, Doncaster DN1 2DY; Tel (01302) 320486; Fax (01302) 340554; *Secretary* Eur Ing Dr G.J.M., Woodrow CEng, FIMinE

Institution of Nuclear Engineers, Allan Hse, 1 Penerley Rd, London SE6 2LQ; Tel 0181-698 1500; *Secretary* Mrs S.M. Blackburn

Institution of Plant Engineers, 77 Great Peter St, London SW1P 2EZ; Tel 0171-233 2855; Fax 0171-233 2604; *Assistant Secretary* P.F. Tye

The Institution of Structural Engineers, 11 Upper Belgrave St, London SW1X 8BH; Tel 0171-235 4535; Fax 0171-235 4294; *Secretary* D.J. Clark, FCIS

The Institution of Water and Environmental Management, 15 John St, London WC1N 2EB; Tel 0171-831 3110; Fax 0171-405 4967; *Executive Director* Tony Bispham

North East Coast Engineering Trust, Great North Hse, Sandyford Rd, Newcastle upon Tyne NE1 8ND; Tel 0191-230 1515; *Secretary* Oscar M. Clemmetsen, CEng

The Society of Engineers, Guinea Wiggs, Nayland, Colchester, Essex CO6 4NF; Tel (01206) 263332; Fax (01206) 262624; *Secretary* L.C.A. Wright

The Welding Institute, Abington Hall, Abington, Cambridge CB1 6AL; Tel (01223) 891162; Fax (01223) 892588; *Associate Director, Professional Affairs* T.J. Jessop

The Women's Engineering Society, Imperial College of Science, Technology and Medicine, Dept Civil Engineering, Imperial College Rd, London SW7 2BU; Tel 0171-594 6025; *Secretary* C.J. MacGillivray

English Language Teaching

Association of Recognised English Language Services (ARELS), 2 Pontypool Pl, Valentine Pl, London SE1 8QF; Tel 0171-242 3136; Fax 0171-928 9378; *Chief Executive* Richard Walker-Arnott

Publishes annual guide on courses offered by member schools and broad range of leaflets for members, students and host families. Raises further the high standards of its members through conferences, training courses, seminars and publications. Represents interests of members and students to government bodies and promotes English language teaching at home and abroad

Environment and Conservation

The Environment Council, 21 Elizabeth St, London SW1W 9RP; Tel 0171-824 8411; Fax 0171-730 9941; *Chief Executive* Steve Robinson

Estate Agents

National Association of Estate Agents, Arbon Hse, 21 Jury St, Warwick CV34 4EH; Tel (01926) 496800; *General Secretary* A.B. Clark, BL(Hons)

Export

Institute of Export, Export Hse, 64 Clifton St, London EC2A 4HB; Tel 0171-247 9812; *Director-General* Ian J. Campbell, BA, MIEx, MIMgt, FRSA; *Education Manager* Miss C.M. Brown, BA, MIEx

Farriers

Farriery Training Service PO Box 49, East of England Showground, Peterborough PE2 6GU; Tel (01733) 394848; *Registrar* B.A. Kavanagh

Food

Institute of Food Science and Technology (UK), 5 Cambridge Ct, 210 Shepherd's Bush Rd, London W6 7NL; Tel 0171-603 6316; *Executive Secretary* Ms H.G. Wild

Meat Training Council, PO Box 141, Winterhill Hse, Snowdon Dr, Winterhill, Milton Keynes MK6 1YY; Tel (01908) 231062; Fax (01908) 231063; *NVQ Co-ordinator* C. Barford

Forestry

Forestry Commission, 231 Corstorphine Rd, Edinburgh EH12 7AT; Tel 0131-334 0303

Institute of Chartered Foresters, 7A St Colme St, Edinburgh EH3 6AA; Tel 0131-225 2705; *Executive Director* Margaret W. Dick; *Secretary and Treasurer* Ms Margaret W. Dick; *Chairman of Training, Education and Research Committee* Dr G.K. Elliott, BSc, PhD, FICFor, FIWSc

Royal Scottish Forestry Society, 62 Queen St, Edinburgh EH2 4NA; Tel 0131-225 8142; Fax 0131-225 8142; *Director* Michael Osborne; *Convener, Technical and Education Committee* Ian Ross

Geology

The Geological Society, Burlington Hse, Piccadilly, London W1V 0JU; Tel 0171-434 9944; *Hon Secretary* Dr A.C. Higgins

(with responsibility for training and education)

Hairdressing

National Hairdressers' Federation, 11 Goldington Rd, Bedford MK40 3JY; Tel (01234) 360332; Fax (01234) 269337; *General Secretary* Ray J. Seymour, ACIS, MBIM

Health

Association of Medical Secretaries, Practice Administrators and Receptionists AMSPAR, Tavistock Hse North, Tavistock Sq, London WC1H 9LN; Tel 0171-387 6005; Fax 0171-388 2648; *General Secretary* Doris Gilhespy, FAMS; *Examinations Officer* Mrs Beverley Alexander

The Health Visitors' Association, Section of Manufacturing, Science & Finance, 50 Southwark St, London SE1 1UN; Tel 0171-378 7255; Fax 0171-407 3251; *Director* Margaret A. Buttigieg

The Institution of Environmental Health Officers, Chadwich Crt, 15 Hatfields, London SE1 8DJ; *Chief Executive* T.J. Brunt

Royal Institute of Public Health and Hygiene, 28 Portland Pl, London W1N 4DE; Tel 0171-580 2731; *Secretary* Group Captain R. Smith, MA, FIMgt, FITD

The Royal Society of Health, RSH Hse, 38A St George's Dr, London SW1V 4BH; Tel 0171-630 0121; Fax 0171-976 6847; *Chief Executive* Anthony J. Byrne

United Kingdom Central Council for Nursing, Midwifery and Health Visiting, 23 Portland Pl, London W1N 3AF; Tel 0171-637 7181; *Registrar and Chief Executive* Colin Ralph, MPhil, RN, DN(Lond)

Health and Safety Inspectors

Health & Safety Executive, Education Service National Interest Group, Maritime Hse, 1 Linton Rd, Barking, Essex IG11 8HF; Tel 0181-594 5522; Fax 0181-591 5183; *Contact* R.W. Hill

Home Economists

Institute of Home Economics, Hobart Hse, 40 Grosvenor Pl, London SW1X 7AE; Tel 0171-823 1109

Horticulture

The Royal Horticultural Society's Garden, Wisley, Woking, Surrey GU23 6QB; Tel (01483) 224234; *Supervisor of Studies and Training* D. Mulford

17 Employment and Careers

Housing

The Chartered Institute of Housing, Octavia Hse, Westwood Way, Coventry CV4 8JP; Tel (01203) 694433; *Chief Executive* Peter McGurk, FCIH

Hypnotherapy

British Society of Hypnotherapists, 37 Orbain Rd, London SW6 7JZ; Tel 0171-385 1166; *General Secretary* S.C. Young, MBSH

British Society of Medical and Dental Hypnosis, 42 Links Rd, Ashtead, Surrey KT21 2HJ; Tel (01372) 73522; *General Secretary* Mrs M. Samuels

Indexers

Society of Indexers, 38 Rochester Rd, London NW1 9JJ; *Hon Secretary* Mrs H.C. Troughton; Tel 0171-916 7809

Industrial Art and Design

The Chartered Society of Designers, 29 Bedford Sq, London WC1B 3EG; Tel 0171-631 1510; Fax 0171-580 2338; *Director* Brian Lymbery

Information Science

The Institute of Information Scientists, 44 Museum St, London WC1A 1LY; Tel 0171-831 8003; *Executive Secretary* Mrs S.A. Carter; *Hon Secretary* K.G. Webster

Insurance

See also Actuaries

Association of British Insurers, 51 Gresham St, London EC2V 7HQ; Tel 0171-600 3333; Fax 0171-696 8999; *Director General* M. Bolèat

The British Insurance and Investment Brokers' Association, BIIBA Hse, 14 Bevis Marks, London EC3A 7NT; Tel 0171-623 9043; Fax 0171-626 9676

The Chartered Insurance Institute, The Hall, 20 Aldermanbury, London EC2V 7HY; Tel 0171-606 3835; Fax 0171-726 0131; *Director General* Dr D. Bland, FSCA, ACII; *Careers Information Officer* Teresa McVey

Journalists

National Council for the Training of Journalists, Latton Bush Centre, Southern Way, Harlow, Essex CM18 7BL; Tel (01279) 430009; Fax (01279) 438008; *Chief Executive* Rob Selwood

Landscape Architecture, Sciences & Management

The Landscape Institute (The Professional Institute for Landscape Architects, Landscape Managers and Landscape Scientists), 6/7 Barnard Mews, London SW11 1QU; Tel 0171-738 9166; *Registrar* P.R. Broadbent, OBE; *Education Officer* Cathy Collins

Laundry and Drycleaning

TRICE (TextilehCare and Rental Industry Council for Education), Forest Hse Laboratories, Knaresborough Rd, Harrogate, North Yorkshire HG2 7LZ; Tel (01423) 885977; Fax (01423) 880045; *Secretary* E.N. Goldthorp

Law

Council of Legal Education (responsible for the Inns of Court School of Law and the Examination for Call to the Bar of England and Wales), Inns of Court School of Law, 39 Eagle St, London WC1R 4AJ; Tel 0171-404 5787; *Dean* Mrs Mary Phillips MA, LLM; *Registrar* G. Hamer, MA, DPMSA

Faculty of Advocates, Advocates Library, Parliament Hse, Edinburgh EH1 1RF; Tel 0131-226 5071; *Administrator* Martin Allan

Institute of Legal Executives, Kempston Manor, Kempston, Bedford MK42 7AB; Tel (01234) 841000; Fax (01234) 840373; *Secretary-General* L.A. Evans, FInstLex, FRSA

The Law Society, Law Society's Hall, 113 Chancery La, London WC2A 1PL; Tel 0171-242 1222; Fax 0171-831 0344; *Secretary-General* J.W. Hayes, LLB; *Director, Professional Standards and Development* John Randall

The Law Society of Scotland, 26 Drumsheugh Gdns, Edinburgh EH3 7YR; Tel 0131-226 7411; Fax 0131-225 2934; *Secretary* Kenneth W. Pritchard, OBE, BL, WS; *Secretary (Legal Education)* Peter S.B. Niven, LLB

Leather

BLC, The Leather Technology Centre Leather Trade Hse, Kings Park Rd, Moulton Pk, Northampton NN3 6JD; Tel (01604) 494131/4; Fax (01604) 648220; *Chief Executive* K.T.W. Alexander, MSc, PhD

Libraries and Information

The Library Association, 7 Ridgmount St, London WC1E 7AE; Tel 0171-636 7543; Fax 0171-436 7218; *Chief Executive* Ross Shimmon, FLA

Linguists

Institute of Linguists, 24a Highbury Gr, London N5 2EA; Tel 0171-359 7445; Fax 0171-354 0202

Local Government

The Institute of Sport and Recreation Management Giffard Hse, 36/38 Sherrard St, Melton Mowbray, Leicestershire LE13 1XJ; Tel (01664) 65531; Fax (01664) 501155; *Education & Training Officer* S. Hackett

Institute of Maintenance and Building Management, Keets Hse, 30 East St, Farnham, Surrey GU9 7SW; Tel (01252) 710994; Fax (01252) 737741; *Director General* A. Grevatt

Institute of Wastes Management, 9 Saxon Ct, St Peters Gdns, Northampton NN1 1SX; Tel (01604) 20426; Fax (01604) 21339; *Membership, Education and Training Secretary* M.R.K. Gibson, MInstWM; *Training Officer* Jane Lawrence

The Institution of Water and Environmental Management, 15 John St, London WC1N 2EB; Tel 0171-831 3110; Fax 0171-405 4967; *Executive Director and Secretary* H.R. Evans

Management

The Association of Business Executives, William Hse, 14 Worple Rd, Wimbledon, London SW19 4DD; Tel 0181-879 1973; *Secretary* John Sewter

The Institute of Administrative Management, 40 Chatsworth Parade, Petts Wood, Orpington, Kent BR5 1RW; Tel (01689) 875555; *Chief Executive* Professor Graham Robinson, FInstAM

Objectives

To promote and develop, for the public benefit, the science of administrative management in all branches, to encourage the attainment of professional academic qualifications, to provide via conferences, seminars, meetings and publications information to enable members to keep up to date with the latest techniques and developments in the field of administrative management

The Institute of Management, Management Hse, Cottingham Rd, Corby, Northants NN17 1TT; Tel (01536) 204 222; Fax (01536) 201 651; *Head of Publishing* Jeremy Kourdi; *Head of Development* Steve Carter; *Head of Information* Bob Norton

Institute of Management Consultants, 5th Floor, 32–33 Hatton Gdn, London EC1N 8DL; Tel 0171-242 1803, 0171-242 2140; Fax 0171-831 4597; *Executive Director* Ms K.L. Hook

Institute of Management Services, 1 Cecil Ct, London Rd, Enfield, Middx EN2 6DD; Tel 0181-363 7452; *Secretary* Frank O'Connolly

Institute of Personnel Management, IPM Hse, Camp Rd, Wimbledon, London SW19 4UX; Tel 0181-946 9100; Fax 0181-947 2570; Telex 947203; *Director-General* Brian Ward Lilley; *Manager, Professional Education* Ms S.C. Murdoch

Women in Management Association, 64 Marryat Rd, Wimbledon, London SW19 5BN; Tel 0181-944 6332; Fax 0181-944 8406; *Secretary* Elizabeth Harman

Market Research

The Market Research Society, 15 Northburgh St, London EC1V 0AH; Tel 0171-490 4911; Fax 0171-490 0608; *Information Officer* Nicola Potts

Marketing/Advertising/Public Relations

Communication Advertising and Marketing Education Foundation, Abford Hse, 15 Wilton Rd, London SW1V 1NJ; Tel 0171-828 7506; Fax 0171-976 5140

Chartered Institute of Marketing, Moor Hall, Cookham, Maidenhead, Berks SL6 9QH; Tel (01628) 524922; *Secretary* C. Lenton, FCIS; *Head of Education* N.E. Waite, MSc, DMS, DipM, FCIM, CertEd, FRSA

The Institute of Practitioners in Advertising, 44 Belgrave Sq, London SW1X 8QS; Tel 0171-235 7020; *Director of Studies* Charles Channon

The Institute of Public Relations, The Old Trading Hse, 15 Northburgh St, London EC1V 0PR; Tel 0171-253 5151; Fax 0171-490 0588; *Executive Director* J.B. Lavelle; *President* Mike Beard, FIPR

Marketing Education Group, Chairman Prof M.J. Thomas; *Membership Secretary* Sean Ennis Marketing, University of Strathclyde, Stenhouse Bldg, 173 Cathedral St, Glasgow G4 ORG

Mathematics

Institute of Mathematics and its Applications, Catherine Richards Hse, 16 Nelson St, Southend-on-Sea, Essex SS1 1EF; Tel (01702) 354020; *Executive Secretary* Adrian M. Lepper, BSc, PhD

Measurement

Institute of Measurement and Control, 87 Gower St, London WC1E 6AA; Tel 0171-387 4949; Fax 0171-388 8431; *Secretary* M.J. Yates, MA

Medical Laboratory Sciences

Institute of Biomedical Science 12 Coldbath Square, London EC1R 5HL; Tel 0171-636 8192; Fax 0171-436 4946; *Chief Executive* A.R. Potter, MPhil, FIMLS; *Head of Education and Development* A.D. Seth-Smith, BA, MA

Society of Cardiological Technicians, c/o Cardiac Dept, The Royal London Trust, London E1 1BB; Tel 0171-377 7659; *Public Relations Officer* Deirdre Harrington

Mining and Metallurgy

The Institute of Metals, 1 Carlton Hse Terr, London SW1Y 5DB; Tel 0171-839 4071; Telex 8814813; *Education Officer* M.P. Stammers, BSc, MEd, CEng, MIM; *Secretary* Dr J.A. Catterall, BSc, PhD, ARSM, DIC, FIP, CEng, FIM

(will merge with Institute of Ceramics and The Plastics & Rubber Institute in 1993)

The Institution of Mining and Metallurgy, 44 Portland Pl, London W1N 4BR; Tel 0171-580 3802; Fax 0171-436 5388; *Secretary* M.J. Jones

The Institute of Quarrying, 7 Regent St, Nottingham NG1 5BS; Tel (0115) 941 1315; Fax (0115) 948 4035; *Technical Director* M.J. Arthur

Motor Industry

The Institute of The Motor Industry, Fanshaws, Brickendon, Herts SG13 8PQ; Tel (01992) 511521; Fax (01992) 511548

Museums

The Museums Association, 42 Clerkenwell Cl, London EC1R 0PA; Tel 0171-608 2933; Fax 0171-250 1929; *Director* Mark Taylor

Nature Conservation

Joint Nature Conservation Committee, Monkstone Hse, City Rd, Peterborough PE1 1JY; Tel (01733) 62626; Fax (01733) 555948; *Chairman* The Earl of Selborne, KBE, FRS; *Chief Officer* C.R. Walker, CB; *Countryside Council for Wales* Prof D.Q. Bowen; *English Nature* The Earl of Cranbrook, DSc, DL; *Scottish Natural Heritage* Prof G.M. Dunnet, OBE; *Department of Environment (Northern Ireland)* Dr J.S. Faulkner; *Countryside Council for Wales* E.M.W. Griffith, CBE, DL; *Independent* Prof J.L. Harper, CBE, FRS; *Countryside Commission* Sir John Johnson; *Independent* Prof J. Knill, DSc, FICE, CEng, FIGeol; *Scottish Natural Heritage* M. Magnusson, KBE; *Independent* Prof R.M. May, FRS; *Council for Nature Conservation and the Countryside (NI)* Prof P. Newbould, BA, FIBiol; *English Nature* Dr D.F. Shaw

Naval Architects

The Royal Institution of Naval Architects, 10 Upper Belgrave St, London SW1X 8BQ; Tel 0171-235 4622; Fax 0171-245 6959; *Secretary* John Rosewarn

Nursing

English National Board for Nursing, Midwifery and Health Visiting, ENB Careers, PO Box 2EN, London W1A 2EA; Tel 0171-391 6200/6205; Fax 0171-391 6207

Head Office

Victory Hse, 170 Tottenham Court Rd, London W1P 0HA; Tel 0171-388 3131

Institute of Advanced Nursing Education of the Royal College of Nursing, 20 Cavendish Sq, London W1M 0AB; Tel 0171-409 3333; *Principal* John Wells, BA, MA, RGN, RMN, RNT

National Board for Nursing, Midwifery and Health Visiting for Scotland, 22 Queen St, Edinburgh EH2 1NT; Tel 0131-226 7371; Fax 0131-225 9970; *Chief Executive* E.C. Mitchell

The Royal College of Nursing of the United Kingdom, 20 Cavendish Sq, London W1M 0AB; Tel 0171-409 3333; *General Secretary* Christine Hancock, BSc(Econ), RGN, RNT; *Director of Education* T.P. Bolger

Occupational Therapy

College of Occupational Therapists, 6–8 Marshalsea Rd, Southwark, London SE1 1HL; Tel 0171-357 6480; Fax 0171-378 1353; *Secretary* M.D. Hall, OBE, GM, FIM, MCIPS, MSAE

Operational Research

Operational Research Society, Seymour Hse, 12 Edward St, Birmingham B1 2RX; Tel 0121-233 9300; Fax 0121-233 0321; *Secretary and General Manager* Dr J.F. Miles

Optics (Ophthalmic Dispensing)

Association of British Dispensing Opticians, 6 Hurlingham Business Pk, Sulivan Rd, London SW6 3DU; Tel 0171-736 0088; Fax 0171-731 5531; *General Secretary* J.W. Roskill; *Director of Education* A.J. Cripps, FBDO(Hons); *Registrar* D.G. Baker

British College of Optometrists, 10 Knaresborough Pl, London SW5 0TG; Tel 0171-373 7765; *Secretary* Peter D. Leigh, FBIM, ANZIPM, MIAP

General Optical Council, 41 Harley St, London W1N 2DJ; Tel 0171-580 3898; Fax 0171-436 3525; *Registrar* R.D. Wilshin, FIMgt, FRSA, Solicitor

17 Employment and Careers

Osteopathy

The British School of Osteopathy, 1–4 Suffolk St, London SW1Y 4HG; Tel 0171-930 9254; *Principal* Sir Norman Lindop, MSc, CChem, FRSC

The General Council and Register of Osteopaths Ltd, 56 London St, Reading RG1 4SQ; Tel (01734) 576585; Fax (01734) 566246; *Secretary* Lt-Col G.P. Blaker, MA, LLB; *Education Adviser* Dr J.M. Sketchley, PhD, MA, MPhil

Packaging

The Institute of Packaging, Sysonby Lodge, Nottingham Rd, Melton Mowbray, Leics LE13 0NU; Tel (01664) 500055; Fax (01664) 64164; *Head of Training* Jim McDermott

Patent Agents

Chartered Institute of Patent Agents, Staple Inn Bldgs, London WC1V 7PZ; Tel 0171-405 9450; Fax 0171-430 0471; *Secretary* Michael C. Ralph, B.Sc

European Patent Office, Erhardtstrasse 27, D-80298 München; Tel (0189) 23 99-0; Fax (0189) 2399-4465; Telex 523656 epmu d; *Contact* Mr Godehard Nowak (Director Public Relations Directorate)

Petroleum

The Institute of Petroleum, 61 New Cavendish St, London W1M 8AR; Tel 0171-467 7100; Fax 0171-255 1472; *Education Liaison Manager* R. Edmondson

Pharmacists

Royal Pharmaceutical Society of Great Britain, 1 Lambeth High St, London SE1 7JN; Tel 0171-735 9141; Fax 0171-735 7629; *Secretary and Registrar* J. Ferguson, FRPharmS

The Pharmaceutical Society of Northern Ireland, 73 University St, Belfast BT7 1HL; Tel (01232) 326927; Fax (01232) 439919; *Secretary and Registrar* D.J. Lawson, FPS

Photographers and Photographic Technicians

British Institute of Professional Photography, 2 Amwell End, Ware, Herts SG12 9HN; Tel (01920) 464011

Physicians

British Medical Association, BMA Hse, Tavistock Sq, London WC1H 9JP; Tel 0171-387 4499; Fax 0171-383 6400; *Secretary* Dr E.M. Armstrong

Royal College of Physicians of London, 11 St Andrew's Pl, London NW1 4LE; Tel 0171-935 1174; Fax 0171-487 5218

The Royal Society of Medicine, 1 Wimpole St, London W1M 8AE; Tel 0171-408 2119; Fax 0171-355 3196; *Executive Director* John T. Green, PhD

Physics

The Institute of Physics, 47 Belgrave Sq, London SW1X 8QX; Tel 0171-235 6111; *Chief Executive* A.D.W. Jones, MA, DPhil, CPhys, FInstP; *Public Affairs Manager* P. Senior

Physiotherapy

The Chartered Society of Physiotherapy, 14 Bedford Row, London WC1R 4ED; Tel 0171-242 1941; Fax 0171-831 4509; *Secretary* Toby Simon

Plastics and Rubber

The Plastics and Rubber Institute, 11 Hobart Pl, London SW1W 0HL; Tel 0171-245 9555; Fax 0171-823 1379; *Secretary-General* J. Hawkins

(will merge with Institute of Ceramics and Institute of Metals 1993)

Printing

British Printing Industries Federation, 11 Bedford Row, London WC1R 4DX; Tel 0171-242 6904; *Director-General* Colin Stanley; *Director of Education and Training* Andrew Brown; *Press and PR* Maria Kane

Institute of Printing, 8 Lonsdale Gdns, Tunbridge Wells, Kent TN1 1NU; Tel (01892) 538118; *Secretary General* D. Freeland, DMS

Psychology

The British Psychological Society, St Andrew's Hse, 48 Princess Rd East, Leicester LE1 7DR; Tel (0116) 254 9568; Fax (0116) 247 0787; *Hon General Secretary* Dr John Groeger

Publishing

Book Trust, Book Hse, 45 East Hill, London SW18 2QZ; Tel 0181-870 9055; Fax 0181-874 4790

Society of Young Publishers, c/o 12 Dyott St, London WC1A 1DF; *Chairman* Suzanne Collier

The Publishers' Association, 19 Bedford Sq, London WC1B 3HJ; Tel 0171-580 6321; Fax 0171-636 5375; Telex 267160 PUBASS; *President* Nicholas Chapman; *Vice-President/Treasurer* Paul Kahn; *Immediate Past President* Sir Roger Elliott

Women in Publishing, c/o 12 Dyott St, London WC1A 1DF; *Information Officer* Vacancy

Young Book Trust Book Hse, 45 East Hill, London SW18 2QZ; Tel 0181-870 9055; Fax 0181-874 4790

Purchasing

The Chartered Institute of Purchasing and Supply, Easton Hse, Easton on the Hill, Stamford, Lincs PE9 3NZ; Tel (01780) 56777; Fax (01780) 51610; *Head of Education* Mrs I. Grickus

Radiographers

The College of Radiographers, 14 Upper Wimpole St, London W1M 8BN; Tel 0171-935 5726; Fax 0171-487 3483; *Chief Executive* Peter M. Smith (Acting)

Refrigeration

British Refrigeration Association, Sterling Hse, 6 Furlong Rd, Bourne End, Bucks SL8 5DG; Tel (01628) 531186

Institute of Refrigeration, Kelvin Hse, 76 Mill La, Carshalton, Surrey SM5 2JR; Tel 0181-647 7033; Fax 0181-773 0165; *Secretary* M.J. Horlick

Retail Trades

National Association of Colleges in Distributive Education and Training, 39 The Birches, Winchmore Hill, London N21 1NJ; Tel 0181-360 4409; *Secretary* J.B. Turner, OBE, OStJ, JP, DL

Rubber

See Plastics and Rubber

Sales and Marketing Management

Institute of Sales and Marketing Management, 31 Upper George St, Luton, Beds LU1 2RD; Tel (01582) 411130

Enquiries to Director of Studies

Secretaries

See Administrators

Shipping

The Institute of Chartered Shipbrokers, 3 Gracechurch St, London EC3V 0AT; Tel 0171-283 1361; Fax 0171-626 2319; *Secretary* B. Fletcher, FICS; *Director of Education* B. Fletcher, FICS

Social Work

British Association of Social Workers, 16 Kent St, Birmingham B5 6RD; Tel 0121-622 3911; *General Secretary* David N. Jones

Speech Therapists

The College of Speech and Language Therapists, 7 Bath Place, Rivington St, London EC2A 3DR; Tel 0171-613 3855; Fax 0171-613 3854; *Professional Director* P. Evans, MCSLT, CHSM

Statistics

The Royal Statistical Society, 12 Errol St, London EC1Y 8LX; *Executive Secretary* I. Goddard

Supervisory Management

The Institute of Supervisory Management, 22 Bore St, Lichfield, Staffs WS13 6LP; Tel (01543) 251346; *Director* G.L.D. Alderson, BA, BSc(Econ), MEd, FRSA

Surgeons

The Royal College of Surgeons of England, 35/43 Lincoln's Inn Fields, London WC2A 3PN; Tel 0171-405 3474; *Secretary* R.H.E. Duffett; *Secretary, Raven Department of Education* Helen Allgrove

Surveyors

Institution of Civil Engineering Surveyors, 26 Market St, Altrincham, Cheshire WA14 1PF; Tel 0161-928 8074; Fax 0161-941 6134; *Secretary* D.H. Daniels; *Chairman, Education Sub-Committee* R.E. Jones

The Royal Institution of Chartered Surveyors, 12 Great George St, Parliament Sq, London SW1P 3AD; Tel 0171-222 7000; *Chief Executive* Michael Pattison, BA

The Society of Surveying Technicians, Surveyor Ct, Westwood Way, Coventry CV4 8JE; Tel (01203) 694757 or 0171-222 7000; Fax 0171-334 3800; *General Secretary* Graham Jones

Television

Royal Television Society, Tavistock Hse East, Tavistock Sq, London WC1H 9HR; Tel 0171-387 1970; *Executive Director* Michael Bruce

Textiles

The Textile Institute, International Headquarters, 10 Blackfriars St, Manchester M3 5DR; Tel 0161-834 8457; Fax 0161-835 3087; *General Secretary* R.G. Denyer, BSc

Town Planning

The Royal Town Planning Institute, 26 Portland Pl, London W1N 4BE; Tel 0171-636 9107; *Secretary-General* David Fryer, OBE, MA, BCL, LMRTPI; *Director, Professional Standards* M. Catran

Training

Institute of Training and Development, Marlow Hse, Institute Rd, Marlow, Bucks SL7 1BD; Tel (01628) 890123; Fax (01628) 890208; *Resource Centre Manager* Hazel Snell

Transport

The Chartered Institute of Transport, 80 Portland Pl, London W1N 4DP; Tel 0171-636 9952; Fax 0171-637 0511; *President* HRH The Princess Royal; *Chairman* The Rt Hon Christopher Chataway; *Director-General and Secretary* R.P. Botwood

Institute of Highway Incorporated Engineers (formerly Highway and Traffic Technicians Association), 20 Queensberry Pl, London SW7 2DR; Tel 0171-823 9093; Fax 0171-823 9409; *Secretary* Miss J.M. Walker

Travel and Tourism

Institute of Travel and Tourism, 113 Victoria St, St Albans, Herts AL1 3TJ; Tel (01727) 854395; Fax (01727) 847415; *Chief Executive* Linda Gibson

International Association of Tour Managers, 397 Walworth Rd, London SE17 2AW; Tel 0171-703 9154; Fax 0171-703 0358; *Executive Manager* John Rooke

The Tourism Society, 26 Chapter St, London SW1P 4ND; Tel 0171-834 0461; Fax 0171-932 0238; *Chairman* Ken Robinson, FTS; *Administrator* Clair Boobyer

Underwater Technology

Society for Underwater Technology, 76 Mark La, London EC3R 7JN; Tel 0171-481 0750; Fax 0171-481 4001; *Executive Secretary* Cdr D.R. Wardle

Valuation

ISVA 3 Cadogan Gate, London SW1X 0AS; Tel 0171-235 2282; Fax 0171-235 4390; *Chief Executive* Hamlyn Whitty

Veterinary Science

The Institute of Animal Technology, 5 South Parade, Summertown, Oxford OX2 7JL

Professional Body for Career Animal Technologists; Enquiries to the Hon Secretary

Royal College of Veterinary Surgeons, 32 Belgrave Sq, London SW1X 8PQ; Tel 0171-235 4971; Fax 0171-245 6100; *Registrar and Secretary* A.R.W. Porter, CBE, MA, Hon Assoc RCVS

Wood

Institute of Wood Science, Stocking La, Hughenden Valley, High Wycombe, Bucks HP14 4NU; Tel (01494) 565374; Fax (01494) 565395; *Director* M.W. Holloway

Youth and Community Work

National Youth Agency, 17–23 Albion St, Leicester LE1 6GD; Tel (0116) 285 6789; Fax (0116) 247 1043; *Contact* Janet Paraskeva (Director)

Sponsored Training and Apprenticeships

Air Products plc

Hersham Pl, Molesey Rd, Walton-on-Thames, Surrey KT12 4RZ; Tel (01932) 249056; Fax (01932) 249565

Graduate Recruitment and Training Officer Monique Leida

Sponsorship available for students wishing to study for Chemical Engineering, Mechanical Engineering & Computer Science Degrees on specific courses only, by invitation each year.

W.H. Allen (NEI-ALLEN Ltd)

Queens Engineering Works, PO Box 43, Bedford MK40 4JB; Tel (01234) 272000 Ext 2632

Training Manager R.A.C. Woodward

Craft apprenticeships, machinists, fitters, sheetmetal and welding, 4 year technical apprenticeships, mechanical technicians, draughtsmen, production technicians. 5 year student engineering training including sponsorship on thick and thin sandwich degree courses.

Alvis Ltd

Holyhead Rd, Coventry, West Midlands CV5 8JH; Tel (01203) 595501

Training and Safety Officer J.R. Brown

4 year craft and technical apprenticeships including day release.

17 Employment and Careers

APV plc
Manor Dr, Paston Parkway, Peterborough PE4 7AP; Tel (01733) 283000; Fax (01733) 283001; Telex 330045
Training and Development Manager R. Morgan
Student sponsorships, on thick or thin sandwich degree courses, in general/mechanical/manufacturing/electrical/electronic/chemical engineering and also in business studies with engineering. Salary during industrial periods and bursary whilst at university. Pre-university year of training based mainly at Peterborough, sponsoring companies at Peterborough, Crawley, Dartford, Stoke-on-Trent and Newcastle–upon–Tyne

Automotive Products plc
Tachbrook Rd, Leamington Spa, Warks CV31 3ER; Tel (01926) 472351
Training Manager W.L. Clarkson
A full range of engineering apprenticeships is offered mainly for local applicants. Commercial apprenticeships for GCE A level school-leavers are more widely offered for training in accountancy, purchasing, marketing and computer applications. These apprenticeships are usually combined with appropriate sandwich courses in cost and management accountancy or business studies, for which financial assistance is given. Day release may be offered as an alternative part-time study where appropriate.

Avdel Systems Ltd
Mundells, Welwyn Garden City, Herts AL7 1EZ; Tel (01707) 328161; Fax (01707) 338828
Chairman and MD J.C. Marley
Director P.M. Gray (General Manager)
Director C. Jackson
Director K. Denham
Engineering Apprenticeships: Technician, Engineer for school-leavers with GCSE Grade C and involving college BTEC to National or Higher National Certificate level. Craft Apprenticeships in toolroom/maintenance gaining City & Guilds qualifications. Sponsored Student Training Scheme to study mechanical or manufacturing engineering or closely-related subject at university or polytechnic. Bursary whilst at university/polytechnic. Salary during industrial placement in company.

BICC Cables Ltd
Central Personnel Dept, Heronsway, Chester Business Pk, Wrexham Rd, Chester CH4 9PZ; Tel (01244) 688492; Fax (01244) 688401
Senior Personnel Adviser D. Dundon
Located in North West and South East.

The Boots Company plc
Head Office, Nottingham NG2 3AA; Tel (0115) 959 2167
Sponsorship Liaison Officer Vacancy; Tel (0115) 959 1491
Sponsorship generally on thin sandwich courses for students reading engineering degrees as follows: mechanical engineering, electrical engineering.

British Broadcasting Corporation (BBC)
Broadcasting Hse, London W1A 1AA; Tel 0171-927 5442; Fax 0171-631 5491
Engineering and Technical Operations Recruitment (enginering and technical enquiries), Secretarial & Clerical Services (secretarial/clerical enquiries) or Corporate Recruitment Services (all other enquiries).
Principal training schemes: secretarial, data preparation, Studio management, news, local radio reporters, production, film, make-up, engineers, camera operation, recording operation. Send for literature regarding entry qualification.

British Gas plc
Corporate Personnel, Rivermill Hse, 152 Grosvenor Rd, London SW1V 3JL; Tel 0171-821 1444; Fax 0171-611 2344
Graduate and Professional Recruitment Manager Barras Stone
Scholarships are available to forward thinking young people, to read Engineering (electronic, chemical, mechanical), Computing, business related and other degrees. You should have a good spread of GCSEs and expect to gain 3 A levels (including 2 at A or B grade) and have a place on a degree course. Current bursary £1300 per annum plus paid holiday work experience. Further details from the above adress. A level entry, craft apprenticeship and school-leaver entry are also provided by British Gas Regions. Applications should be addressed to the local British Gas Region.

British Railways Board
Rm 520, Euston Hse, PO Box 100, London NW1 2DZ; Tel 0171-928 5151 Ext 26374; Fax 0171-922 4157
Manager, Recruitment and Assessment Julian Drury
Graduate training schemes in general management, retail and marketing, personnel, accountancy, engineering, computing, purchasing and supply, engineering research, operational research. University sponsorship for engineering (electrical/electronic, mechanical and civil). Accountancy training opportunities available for A level holders. Brochures available from above address during Oct/Nov. Technical apprenticeship schemes for 16+ school-leavers: applications should go to British Rail offices.

British Telecom
University Sponsorship, FREEPOST, 30/08 Euston Tower, 286 Euston Rd, London NW1 0YH; Tel (0800) 289442
Sponsorships available at the Universities of Aston, Newcastle and York. 4-year courses in Electronics and Software leading to an MEng. British Telecom provides £1200 per annum bursary plus paid vacation work and training.
To apply you should have a good GCSE in English Language and expect to achieve three good A levels including Maths and either Physics or an Engineering or Physical Science subject, OR equivalent qualifications acceptable to the universities.
Selections for places on this scheme will run from late November 1990.

British Timken
Duston, Northampton NN5 6UL; Tel (01604) 52311
Senior Training Officer A.R. Fisher
Student business professional, student engineer, technician engineer, all complying with EITB requirements. Each scheme is associated with attendance on an appropriate degree or higher diploma course. All openings based on Northampton, preference given to applicants living within 20 miles of the company.

Cable & Wireless plc
Mercury Hse, Theobalds Rd, London WC1X 8RX; Tel 0171-242 4433
Manager Recruitment

Carnauld Metalbox
Napier Ct, Napier Rd, Reading, Berks RG1 8BH; Tel (01734) 502323
Graduate Development Manager Peter Mackenzie-Smith
Degree course sponsorships in: mechanical engineering production engineering, electrical engineering, electronic engineering and polymer science.

Courtaulds Chemicals
PO Box 5, Spondon, Derby DE2 7BP; Tel (01332) 661422
Personnel Manager Steve Dallaghan
Courtaulds Chemicals and Courtaulds Research, divisions of Courtaulds plc offer: engineering craft apprenticeships; laboratory technician training; secretarial and office training; vacation training for engineering and chemistry degree courses; day release for part-time courses; financial assistance for full-time degree courses under the Courtaulds University Scholarship Scheme; industrial training placements; YT training in offices, laboratories and catering.

Crabtree Electrical Industries Ltd
Lincoln Works, Lincoln Rd, Walsall WS1 2DN; Tel (01922) 721202 Ext 274
Training Co-ordinator M. Brown

Craft apprenticeships in mechanical and electrical engineering; technician training in mechanical and electrical engineering; student apprenticeships in mechanical, electrical and production engineering. Day release given for part-time courses.

Crane Ltd
Nacton Rd, Ipswich, Suffolk IP3 0QH; Tel (01473) 270222; Fax (01473) 270221
Management Services Officer S. Williams
Opportunities include Graduate Traineeships (enginering or commerical), Commercial Traineeships (for A level school-leavers interested in marketing, sales, finance etc), Craft and Technician Apprenticeships (for GCSE school-leavers interested in engineering, maintenance, production etc), and Manufacturing and Office Traineeships (GCSE qualifications required). All training programmes include planned practical experience, individually tailored training objectives and day release to gain further qualifications.

Eaton Ltd
Industrial Controls Division, Elstow Rd, Bedford MK42 9LH; Tel (01234) 267433
Human Resource Manager D.W. Newman
Electrical and mechanical technician apprenticeships are available in addition to electrical and mechanical craft apprenticeships. Day release is given for part-time City & Guilds and TEC courses.

Electricity plc
Development and Training, Mucklow Hill, Halesowen, West Midlands B62 8BP; Tel 0121-423 2345 Ext 2837/8
Development and Training Manager K.E. Goddard
Graduate vacancies in Electrical Engineering and Systems Analyst/Programming. Industrial placements and vacation work include: 12 month placements in Systems Analysis/Programming for those following a thick sandwich course in Computer Science or IT; and vacation experience in electrical power distribution for students of an electrical related subject. University sponsorships are offered in Enginering to those 16–21 year olds having or expecting 3 A levels at minimum grade B including Maths and Physics or Enginering Science. A level opportunities exist for applicants having or expecting 2 A levels at minimum grade C. Craft apprenticeships are available to applicants having or expecting at least 4 GCSEs at grade E or above, including Maths, English and Science; a craft subject would be an advantage.

European Gas Turbines Ltd
PO Box 1, Lincoln LN2 5DJ
Training Officer R. Bilton
One Year Industrial Training placements leading to final years sponsorships in mechanical engineering, electrical and/or electronic engineering, manufacturing/production engineering, aeronautical engineering, engineering science, or related subjects. A bursary is paid for each academic year whilst at university; salary is paid during industrial training. Candidates will be expected to take up appointments in the company after graduation. Training programmes accredited by IMechE and IEE.

Ferranti International, Simulation and Training UK
Bird Hall La, Cheadle Heath, Stockport SK3 0XQ; Tel 0161-428 01771 Ext 3349
Training Officer R.J. Ball
Applicants within commuting catchment area only: *Technician Apprenticeships:* BTEC: day release: 6 year; *Sponsored Students:* University entry technical subject: bursary; *Programming/Engineering Trainees:* Day release degree: MCR Poly.

Ford Motor Company Ltd
Rm 1/360, Eagle Way, Brentwood, Essex CM13 3BW; Tel (01277) 252202
Senior Training Officer Tessa Williamson
Engineering sponsorship programme; Computer Systems sponsorship programme; Business Technician (A level entry) scheme.

GEC ALSTHOM Electromechanical Division
Newbold Rd, Rugby, Warks CV21 2NH; Tel (01788) 531375
Employee Development Officer Mark Lendon; Tel (01788) 531375
This Division, which includes GEC Alsthom Turbine Generators Ltd and GEC Alsthom Large Machines Ltd, is a world leader in power generation equipment. Opportunities include craft and technician apprenticeships in mechanical and electrical engineering. Student sponsorships leading to engineerng degrees and accountancy sponsorships leading to ICMA accountancy qualifications. Sponsorships include bursary and salary during industrial periods. Graduate traineeships of up to two years' duration in engineering design, R&D, manufacturing, construction, service, project management and commercial functions. United Kingdom locations in Rugby, Manchester and Stafford.

GEC ALSTHOM Transport (UK)
Contact The Company Training Manager, PO Box 134, Manchester M60 1AH
Training Officer R. Ruddick
GEC Alsthom Traction Ltd design and manufacture electric traction control and propulsion systems, with UK sites at Manchester and Preston. A related company, GEC Alsthom Transportation Projects Ltd, design, build and manage railway and mass transportation electrification projects. The company's Birmingham factory (Metro Cammell) specialises in rail vehicle design and assembly.
Opportunities with both companies include design and development, project engineering, manufacturing, applications engineering, software, project and commercial management.
In the same Division is GEC Alsthom Signalling Ltd, with sites at Borehamwood (Herts), Old Trafford (Manchester) and York. This company designs and manufactures railway signalling and reporting systems. Opportunities include applications engineering, software, electronic circuit design engineering, and sales.

GEC–Marconi Communications Ltd
Marconi Hse, New St, Chelmsford, Essex CM1 1PL; Tel (01245) 353221; Fax (01245) 275988
Training Manager S.P. Newton
2–1–1 and thin sandwich courses in electrical & electronic engineering; computer science; production engineering, accountancy. R&D, manufacture, sales and marketing based on 2 sites around Chelmsford.

GEC–Marconi Ltd
102 Arbour La, Chelmsford, Essex CM1 5RN; Tel (01245) 350011; Telex 99201 MARCON G
Administration Officer Mrs S.A. Eaton
University and polytechnic sandwich degree course sponsorships, thick and thin sandwich mainly in electrical and electronic engineering, but other disciplines considered, eg mechanical engineering, physics, business studies, computer science etc. Bursary payable during college terms, and a salary paid during industrial periods. Technician engineer apprentice schemes with day release to HND, HNC and ONC level. Locations: Milton Keynes, Bucks; Basildon, Chelmsford, Essex; Portsmouth, Hants; Stanmore, Middlesex; Frimley, Surrey; Leicester; Rochester, Kent; Edinburgh, Donibristle, Scotland; Borehamwood, Herts.

Haden Young Limited
PO Box 534, 100 High St, Southgate, London N14 6ES; Tel 0181-882 6121
Company Personnel Manager F.J. Davison
The Company recruits school-leavers for engineering student apprenticeships, commercial apprenticeships and craft apprenticeships in the fields of heating, ventilating, air-conditioning, electrical installation, plumbing, quantity surveying and fire protection. The Company has branches in Edinburgh, Glasgow, Newcastle, Leeds, Warrington, Birmingham, Bingham (Nottingham), Cambridge, Bristol, Watford, London, Southampton and Maidstone.

17 Employment and Careers

Higgs and Hill plc
Crown Hse, Kingston Rd, New Malden, Surrey KT3 3ST; Tel 0181-942 8921
Training Officer Jacqueline Stubbs
Major building contractors, offering day release, sandwich course and post–graduate training in building (BSc and TEC), civil engineering and quantity surveying

Imperial Chemical Industries plc
PO Box 90, Wilton, Middlesbrough, Cleveland TS90 8JE
Scholarship Co-ordinator B.M. Husband
ICI Engineering offer Scholarships to students reading university degree courses in mechanical, control, electrical, manufacturing and chemical engineering. Scholarships may also include pre-university training, vacation work or work experience placement. About 25 scholarships are awarded each year.

Kennedy & Donkin Group Ltd
Westbrook Mills, Godalming, Surrey GU7 2AZ; Tel (01483) 25900
Director of Group Trainig D.G. Pilbeam
Graduate training provided to meet the requirements of the engineering institutions in respect of chartered engineer status. Technician training provided with block or day release up to Incorporated Engineer status. Training located in Godalming and Manchester.

John Laing plc
Page St, Mill Hill, London NW7 2ER; Tel 0181-906 5314; Fax 0181-906 5079
Training Adviser A.J. Beames
Three-year training agreements for estimators, planners, buyers, site engineers and quantity surveyors. Day release for technical and professional study given. Degree sponsorships for building, quantity surveying and civil engineering degree sandwich sources. Craft apprenticeships in bricklaying and carpentry/joinery through one year Youth Training Scheme.

London Regional Transport
Engineering Training Centre, 123 Gunnersbury La, Acton, London W3 8J; Tel 0171-227 6682
Senior Training Assistant Mrs C.P. Burvill
Apprenticeships in mechanical engineering, electrical engineering, electronics, fabrication (welding and sheet metal), vehicle building. Day or block release for college, dependent on trade.

Marconi Instruments Ltd
Six Hill Way, Stevenage, Herts SG1 2AN; Tel (01438) 742200 Ext 373
Senior Technical Training Officer Don Scott
MI employs 950 people at sites in Stevenage, St Albans and Luton manufacturing electronic test and measurement equipment. Sponsored student training in electronic engineering on either thick or thin (integrated) sandwich courses. Technician and technician engineer training leading to BTEC, ONC or HNC by day release at a local college.

Marconi Radar Systems Ltd
Writtle Rd, Chelmsford, Essex CM1 3BN; Tel (01245) 267111 Ext 2075
Training Manager
Student apprenticeships for A level school-leavers. Training schemes offered are principally in electronics engineering and software production and application. Sponsored students following a recognised sandwich course will be given relevant industrial training.

Matthew Hall Ltd
7–14 Great Dover St, London SE1 4YR; Tel 0171-407 7272; Fax 0171-378 0559
Training Department
Craft and technician training: electrical installations; heating and air-conditioning; plumbing and domestic heating; fire engineering. All of four to five years duration and include college attendance. All fees paid and some students sponsored for sandwich/degree courses.

The Mineral Industries' Educational Trust
6 St James's Sq, London SW1Y 4LD; Tel 0171-930 2399
Chairman of Trustees R.D. McVean
Secretary G.C. Lloyd Davis
Scholarships and bursaries are offered for courses leading to an honours degree in mining and quarrying engineering, mineral processing, extractive metallurgy or mining or applied geology. Also some sponsorship for one year taught MSc Degrees in these subjects

John Mowlem Construction plc
Westminster Hse, 21 Rugby Rd, Twickenham, Middx TW1 1DS; Tel 0181-891 6000; Fax 0181-892 4425
Training and Development Manager D.N. Littlefair
Technician training for general building, civil engineering, quantity surveying, estimating, supervision, etc. Industrial training for sandwich students in building, civil engineering and quantity surveying. Paid release given for part-time studies. Located in most regions of England, Scotland and Wales.

Ofrex Group Holdings plc
Acco–Rexel Ltd, Bretton Way, Bretton, Peterborough PE3 8YZ; Tel 01733 264711
Director of Personnel and Training C.G. Winchester
Normal apprenticeships in engineering. Industrial training in business studies sandwich degree courses. Training in finance, marketing, sales, computing and distribution. Day and block release given for part-time and professional courses. Financial assistance for examinations and books.

Otter Controls Limited
Hardwick Sq South, Buxton, Derbys SK17 6LA; Tel (01298) 71177
Personnel Services Manager J.H. Bramwell
Industrial training for university or polytechnic students starting at £155 p.w. (with EPI or equivalent). Preference for people normally resident in areas adjacent to Group Factories locations and for students of mechanical-electrical-electronics and similar subjects.
Apprenticeships – per EnTra (Engineering Training Authority) Standard/Guidelines mainly Toolmaking, Electrical/Electronics Technicians. FE encouraged. Currently recruitment via Local College of Further Education Schemes, polytechnics, etc.

Ove Arup Partnership
13 Fitzroy St, London W1P 6BQ; Tel 0171-636 1531; Fax 0171-580 3924
Personnel Manager Ian Patterson
Between 20 and 25 sponsorships per year are available to students who are permanent UK residents and expecting to read for degrees in civil/structural, mechanical, electrical, building services, environmental or general engineering followed by specialisation in those fields.
Degree applicant requirements:
Civil/Structural, Mechanical, Electrical, General Engineering
Six good GCSE grades, including English, Mathematics and Sciences with an expectation of at least 3 good A levels or 5 good grades at SCE Higher Level.
Environmental, Building Services Engineering
5 good grades in English, Mathematics at at least 1 Science at GCSE or BTEC or SCOTEC National Certificates.
Awards of £1000 p.a. (reviewed annually), discretionary supplement and degree prize. Salary during industrial training/vacation employment dependent on age. Opportunities available for pre-degree course experience.

Quarry Products Training Council
Sterling Hse, 20 Station Rd, Gerrards Cross, Bucks SL9 8HT; Tel (01753) 891808; Fax (01753) 891132
Training Officer J.R. George
Training Officer F.H. Hardman
Youth training based on Stages 1 and 2 of the Extractives Industries Apprenticeship Scheme. Some 30 sponsorships a year for attendance on BEng (Ordinary) Degree in Quarry and Road Surface Engineering at Doncaster College.

Racal/Chubb
Wednesfield Rd, Wolverhampton WV10 0EW; Tel (01902) 55111 Ext 4300
Training Manager M.G. Dunn
Craft, technician, commercial apprenticeships, 3–4 year duration. Clerical Training Scheme, 2-year duration. Own off-the-job training centre and staff. Day release given. Business studies and professional engineer trainees sponsorship throughout, with industrial training. Apprenticeships also available at Chubb Security Installations Ltd, Ronald Cl, Kempston, Bedford MK42 7SH.

Racal Electronics plc
Western Rd, Bracknell, Berkshire RG12 1RG; Tel (01344) 483244; Fax (01344) 869727
Senior Training Officer I. Turner
Student sponsorships on university accredited degree courses. All types of electronic and computer degree courses acceptable. Bursary and full pay whilst in-company on Engineering Council registered training programmes. Locations mostly in the south of England.

Rolls–Royce Motor Cars Ltd
Crewe, Cheshire CW1 3PL; Tel (01270) 535004; Fax (01270) 586548
Personnel Officer C. Thelwall
GCSE level: craft apprenticeships in a variety of different trades, usually restricted to local applicants. After the first year a small number of trainees are transferred to the technician training scheme. Also clerical and commercial apprenticeships for local applicants. A level: undergraduate traineeships in mechanical, production or an allied engineering discipline. A 'thin' or 'thick' pattern may be chosen by the students who also choose university study. Students are recruited nationally, paid a wage whilst undergoing industrial training, and receive a bursary (in addition to their LEA grant) whilst at university.

Royal Ordnance plc
PO Box 40, Chorley, Lancs PR7 6AD; Tel (01257) 65511 Ext 2455
Senior Training and Studies Officer K. Gaskill
Intake of 100 craft apprenticeships, 12 sponsored students taking first degree.

R–B (Lincoln) plc
Excavator Works, Beevor St, Lincoln LN6 7DJ; Tel (01522) 525261
Training & Safety Officer B. Atkinson
Apprenticeships in engineering – fitting – thick plate and maintenance crafts. Day release given for part-time courses. EnTra monitored apprenticeships.

Shell Marine Personnel (IOM) Ltd
Manannan Hse, Market Sq, Castletown, Isle of Man; Tel (01624) 825566
Recruitment Officer Sandra Millar
Opportunities for sponsorship as Dual, Deck or Engineer Cadets to become future officers in worldwide shipping fleet
Training spent partly in Technical/Nautical Colleges ashore and partly at sea. Nationally recognised qualifications and Department of Transport certificates obtained by Cadets during training. Entry qualifications range from a minimum of four GCSE Grade C (or equivalent) for Deck and Engineering Cadets, to include the above subjects. (Modified training schemes also operated for A level Cadet entrants). Dual Certificate Cadets should have a minimum of 4 GCSE Grade C (or equivalent) and 1 A level (or equivalent) in Maths and/or Physics and have studied one other numerate subject to A level (or equivalent) standard. Age on entry is 16–18 for cadets, or up to 22 years for A level entrants.

Shell UK Ltd
Shell–Mex Hse, Strand, London WC2R 0DX; Tel 0171-257 1825
Head of Sponsorship R.M. Smeeton (UKPS/3)
Undergraduate sponsorship is available to those applying for a place on courses in engineering and science disciplines at selected universities.

Shepherd Construction Ltd
Frederick Hse, Fulford Rd, York YO1 4EA; Tel (01904) 634431; Fax (01904) 610256
Training Manager P.A. Blackburn
Building craft apprenticeships, building studentships undergraduate sponsorship and graduate trainees in management, planning, quantity surveying and, occasionally, more specialist studentships, with appropriate release to attend further and higher education courses. Located at Darlington, Leeds, Manchester, Northampton, Nottingham, Treforest, York. Participates in government-sponsored Youth Training Scheme.

STC Components
Edinburgh Way, Harlow, Essex CM20 2DE; Tel (01279) 626626
Personnel Manager, Manufacturing L.A. Deakin
Sponsorships for university undergraduates following sandwich courses in electronic engineering, production engineering, manufacturing studies, engineering with marketing. Locations at Footscray, Great Yarmouth and Harlow.

The Steensen Varming Mulcahy Partnership Ltd
Hempstead Hse, 2 Selden Hill, Hemel Hempstead, Herts HP1 1DP; Tel (01442) 231999
Contact R.A. Rushmer
The Practice (of about 110 persons) sponsors students undertaking environmental engineering/building services engineering honours degree courses, arranges for industrial experience and pays a salary during the industrial/vacation periods. Similar sponsorship exists for students for electrical degree courses, geared towards building services. Maximum intake in each category, 1 per year, local applicants preferred.

Taylor Woodrow Construction Holdings Ltd
Group Training Dept, Taywood Hse, 345 Ruislip Rd, Southall, Middx UB1 2QX; Tel 0181-575 4127
Recruitment and Development Manager (Training) P. Donnelly
The Company sponsors students studying for construction related degrees and sponsorship awards are offered in civil engineering, construction management, building, quantity surveying and building services engineering. Both sandwich and full-time courses are acceptable. Applicants must be permanent UK residents under 21 years of age and should have, or expect to obtain, 3 A level passes at grade C or above including one science subject or BTEC passes with merits/distinctions
An attractive bursary is paid during academic periods and guaranteed summer vacation and industrial experience is offered. To qualify for these highly competitive awards you should be able to demonstrate leadership potential, good communication skills and be highly motivated to progress your career with a leading construction group.

The Textile Institute
International Headquarters, 10 Blackfriars St, Manchester M3 5DR; Tel 0161-834 8457; Fax 0161-835 3087
General Secretary R.G. Denyer, BSc
Scholarships are offered to full/part-time students of textiles. Covering all areas from fibre engineering to fashion retailing including clothing, footwear and design. Conditions and application form from Qualifications Officer.

Thorn EMI Electronics (Sensors)
Manor Royal, Crawley, W Sussex RH10 2PZ; Tel (01293) 644230
Training Officer D. Philo
Sponsorships in Electronic Engineering (MEng) at Surrey University and Brighton University and Information Systems Engineering at Surrey University

Vickers Shipbuilding & Engineering Limited
Barrow-in-Furness, Cumbria LA14 1AF; Tel (01229) 873736
Head of Personnel Development and Training R.D. Clark
Student and graduate apprenticeships.

Vosper Thornycroft (UK) Ltd
Company Training Manager, Victoria Rd, Woolston, Southampton, Hants SO9 5GR; Tel (01703) 445144
Student sponsorship; postgraduate training; maximum period of 2 years. Disciplines: naval architecture, all mechanical/marine engineering, electronic/electrical engineering, computer applications, business/commercial training. Training will be given within the Company's 3 divisions as appropriate.

Westinghouse Brake & Signal Holdings Ltd
Westinghouse Training Services, PO Box 74, Chippenham, Wilts; Tel (01249) 441505; Fax (01249) 652322
Assistant Manager, Training Services D.W. Jones
Westinghouse is a group of engineering companies specialising in the supply of signal, brake and door equipment to the railway industry. Sponsored student training in computer science, mechanical, electrical and electronic engineering. Opportunities for 'thick' sandwich and 'thin' sandwich patterns. Financial assistance given during academic periods. Schemes of training meet the requirements of the relevant professional institution.

George Wimpey plc Group
c/o Wimpey Group Services Ltd, Training Dept, Hammersmith Gr, London W6 7EN; Tel 0181-846 3080
Chief Training Officer Edward Booth
Graduates taken in: civil engineering; building, mechanical engineering; business management. School/college leavers with A levels, Highers, or BTEC National Diplomas taken for sandwich (industry-based) courses; building management; civil engineering; quantity surveying; business management; others (at specified establishments). Youth training schemes/part-time release: construction technicians; business administration; bricklaying; carpentry/joinery; painting/decorating; plastering; plant; mechanics; transport. Principal UK locations: Aberdeen Birmingham, Bristol, Cardiff, Edinburgh, Glasgow, Hull, Leeds, Liverpool, London, Luton, Manchester, Middlesbrough, Nottingham, Southampton, Witham.

18 Teachers' and Other Educational Organisations

Salary Negotiation

England and Wales

Teachers Pay & Conditions Act 1987 Ch. 1

Repeals the Renumeration of Teachers Act 1965 Ch. 3 in full and authorises the Minister to set up an interim advisory committee on schoolteachers' pay and conditions until 31st March, 1990. The Secretary of State is seeking parliamentary authority to extend the interim advisory committee's life to 31st March 1991. Provision by order after consulting the Local Education Authority concerned to impose salaries and conditions of service

History (in publication form) of Teachers' Pay and Conditions post the Act

Teachers' Pay and Conditions Act 1987 (Ch. 14) dated 3rd March 1987
Education (School Teachers' Pay and Conditions of Employment) Order 1987 dated 9th April 1987 (SI 1987/650). Revoked by SI 1987/1433
Circular 5/87 (dated 15th May 1987) School Teachers' Pay and Conditions of Service. Includes salary structure for October 1987
Members announced for Interim Advisory Committee on School Teachers' Pay and Conditions 22nd July 1987: Lord Chilver (Chairman); Dr Peter Andrews, CBE; Geoffrey Armstrong; Ray Carter; Mrs Jean Denton; Ken Graham, CBE; Ms Anne Watts; Mrs Rosemary White. Remit: To advise on: a general pay increase for teachers; modifications to the pay of heads and deputies; looking particularly at local management of schools; modifications to selective payments; amendments to the School Teachers' Pay and Conditions document to reflect governors' role in local management of schools and to cover grant-maintained schools
Circular 8/1987 (dated 11th August 1987) School Teachers' Pay and Conditions of Service
Education (School Teachers' Pay and Conditions of Service) Order 1987 dated 13th August 1987 (SI 1987/1433). Revoked by SI 1988/1055
Teachers' Pay and Conditions: a consultative document (Cmd 238) 27th October 1987. Examines options and proposes creation of a new Teachers' Negotiating Group. Replies to be made by 29th January 1988
Report of the Interim Advisory Committee on School Teachers' Pay and Conditions. Chairman Amos Henry Chilver, Baron Chilver (Cmd 363) 19th April 1988
Circular 3/188 School Teachers' Pay and Conditions of Service, 16th June 1988.
Education (School Teachers' Pay and Conditions of Service) Order 1988 dated 21st June 1988 (SI 1988/1055)
Schoolteachers' pay conditions and pensions from 1st April 1988 TASC published August 1988
Education (Amendment of the Teachers' Pay and Conditions Act 1987) Order 1988 9th December 1988 (SI 1988/2074)
Second Report of the Interim Advisory Committee on School Teachers' Pay and Conditions 10th February 1989 (Cmd 625). Chairman Lord Chilver (membership unchanged for original appointments)

Joint Negotiating Committee for Teachers in Residential Establishments

Secretary: Employers' Side C.C. Nolda 41 Belgrave Sq, London SW1X 8NZ; Tel 0171-235 6081
Secretary: Staff Side M. Freedman, MA Hamilton Hse, Mabledon Pl, London WC1H 9BD; Tel 0171-388 6191

Joint Negotiating Committee for Youth and Community Workers

Secretary: Employers' Side C.C. Nolda 41 Belgrave Sq, London SW1X 8NZ; Tel 0171-235 6081
Secretary: Staff Side M. Freedman, MA Hamilton Hse, Mabledon Pl, London WC1H 9BD; Tel 0171-388 6191

The Local Government Management Board

Chief Executive J. Hunt 41 Belgrave Sq, London SW1X 8NZ; Tel 0171-235 6081

Education Negotiating Bodies with which the Board is Associated

National Employers Organisation for School Teachers,
Committee on Salary Scales & Service Conditions of Inspectors, Organisers and Advisory Officers of LEAs (Soulbury)
Joint Negotiating Committee for Youth and Community Workers
JNC for Teachers in Residential Establishments

One of the functions of the Board is to co-ordinate the activities of the employers' sides of local government wage-negotiating organisations, to provide a joint secretariat for those bodies, to maintain liaison with other employers, and to obtain and disseminate information on service conditions and industrial relations matters

The Board, through its secretariat, is available to give local authorities information and advice in all matters concerning their relations with their employees, and in particular, advice relating to establishment problems, grading of all or of individual posts, and industrial relations generally, including the impact of recent legislation in this area

The work of the Board has led to the development of close liaison with employers in other fields of industry

Reports

The Reports embodying the scales for teachers in Social Service Establishments and youth workers and community centre wardens and for inspectors, organisers and advisory officers employed by local education authorities are published by LACSAB, 41 Belgrave Sq, London SW1X 8NZ

Soulbury Committee (Inspectors, Organisers and Advisory Officers of Local Education Authorities)

Chairman Sir John Wordie, CBE, MA, LLB
Employers' Side Secretary C.C. Nolda 41 Belgrave Sq, London SW1X 8NZ
Officers' Side Secretary D. McAvoy Hamilton Hse, Mabledon Pl, London WC1H 9BD

Colleges Employers' Forum (CEF)

7/8 Rathbone Pl, London W1P 1DE; Tel 0171-637 3919; Fax 0171-637 3864

CEF is the national representative body for 95% of Colleges of Further Education (including Tertiary Colleges but excluding Sixth Form Colleges) in England and Wales. CEF activities include nationally negotiated terms and conditions for all leading and non-leading staffs, human resource management, college governance, constitutional and employment legal advice and liaison with the European Union, the Welsh and English Funding Councils and the relevant government agencies

Scotland

The Employers' Association for the Scottish Further Education Colleges

Chief Executive John W. Sellars Falkirk College, Falkirk FK2 9AD

Scottish Joint Negotiating Committee for Teaching Staff in School Education (SJNC/SE)

Management Side Secretary Roy MacIver Rosebery Hse, 9 Haymarket Terr, Edinburgh EH12 5XZ; Tel 0131-346 1222

Management Side

Convention of Scottish Local Authorities (15)
Secretary of State (2)

Teachers' Side

Educational Institute of Scotland (13)
Scottish Secondary Teachers Association (3)
National Association of Schoolteachers/Union of Women Teachers (1)
Professional Association of Teachers (2)

Teachers' Organisations and Other National Salary Committees

Association of Principals of Colleges

President D.L. Turner, BA, DipEd, FRSA, FBIM New College, Durham Framwellgate Moor, Durham DH1 5ES; Tel (0191) 384 7325
General Secretary D.A. Humphreys, OBE, MA, FRSA, 12 Fir Cl, Poynton, Stockport CHES, SK12 1PD; Tel (01625) 859413; Fax (01625) 859413

Association of Teachers and Lecturers (ATL)

7 Northumberland St, London WC2N 5DA; Tel 0171-930 6441; Fax 0171-930 1359
President Roger Green, BA Queen's Park High School, Queen's Park, Chester CH4 7AE; Tel (01244) 675468; Fax (01244) 679491; *Home*: 24 Hooton Rd, Willaston, South Wirral, L64 1SJ; Tel/Fax 0151-327 8323; Pager (01399) 715030
Senior Vice-President Gillian Pickup, BSc Sandal Endowed Junior Middle School, Barnsley Rd, Wakefield WF2 6AS; Tel (01924) 250516; *Home* 13 Marriott Gr, Sandal, Wakefield, WF2 6RP; Tel (01924) 257098
Junior Vice-President Terry McElligott Abbeydale Grange, Upper School Bldg, Bannerdale Rd, Sheffield S2 2GU; *Home*: 122 Button Hill, Ecclesall, Sheffield S11 9HJ; Tel: (01585) 679806; Message Service: (01399) 747256; Fax: (0114) 2621288
Ex-President Anne Keeble, AcDipEd *Home* Northumberland Ave, Aylesbury, Bucks HP21 7HJ; Fax (01296) 415696
Honorary Secretary Kay Larkin, MA *Home* The Teathes, Kirkland, Frizington, Cumbria CA26 3YB; Tel (01946) 861265; Fax (01946) 862093
Honorary Secretary John Puckrin Forest Hill School, Dacres Rd, London SE23; Tel 0181-699 9343; *Home* 55 Hindmans Rd, London, SE22 9NQ; Tel: 0181-693 3695
Honorary Treasurer Julie Grant, BA The Howard School, Derwent Way, Rainham, Gillingham, Kent ME8 0BX; Tel (01634) 388765; Fax (01634) 388558; *Home* 43 Beresford Ave, Rochester, Kent ME1 2QX; Tel (01634) 846872
Honorary Treasurer Martin Lawes, BEd Paget High School, Burton Rd, Brantson, Burton-upon-Trent DE14 3DR; Tel (01283) 567429; *Home*: Glebe Cl, Rolleston, Burton-upon-Trent, DE13 9BP; Tel: (01283) 815395
General Secretary Peter Smith, MA, FRSA

Deputy General Secretary Gerald Imison, BA, FRSA
Deputy General Secretary Vacancy
Accounts Manager Sheila Harris
Deputy Accounts Manager Elias Dos Remedios
Benevolent Fund Valerie Shield
Commercial Director Ron Mills, MCAM, DipPA
Head of Communications Department Janet Manning
Communications Rosa Drohomirecka, BA
Executive Secretary Anne Powell
Facilities Manager David Brooks, BSc, CEng, MIMechE, MIMgt, MBIFM
Information Technology Manager Graham Carter, BA, FIAP, MBIM
Legal Services Senior Solicitor Philip Lott, MA
Legal Services Sharon Liburd, Solicitor, FInstLEx
Legal Services Gill Sage, Solicitor, BA, FRSA
Legal Services Professional Assistant Sally Davies
Head of Member Services Department Martin Pilkington, Solicitor, BA, LLM
Member Services David Authers, MA
Member Services Steven Crane, MBA, MA, BA
Member Services Janet Martyn, BA
Member Services Penelope Taylor, BEd
Member Services Professional Assistant Doreen Clinch
Head of Membership and Subscriptions Department Vacancy
Deputy Head of Membership and Subscriptions Department Sonja Hines
Personnel Manager Esi Kpeglo, MITM
Head of Policy Unit Meryl Thompson, BA, MA(Ed), FRSA
Policy Unit Sheila Dainton, BEd(Hons), MA
Policy Unit Anthony Meredith
Policy Unit, Professional Assistant Chris Seaman
Press and Public Relations Director Richard Margrave, BSc(Econ), PhD
Press and Public Relations Sarah Loughran
Head of Superannuation Department Susan Johnson
Deputy Head of Superannuation Department Marion Bird
Head of Training Department Roland Wiles, BSc, MIMgt, MIPD
Training Fiona Kennedy

Executive Committee Members

Avon and Gloucestershire
Neil Foster Clevedon School, Valley Rd, Clevedon, Avon BS21 6AH; Tel (01275) 876744; Fax (01275) 340935 Home 33 Roath Rd, Portishead, Avon BS20 9AW; Tel (01275) 842827
Gill Pyatt Barnwood Park School, St Lawrence Rd, Gloucester GL4 7QU; Tel (01452) 616848 Home 77 Cirencester Rd, Cheltenham, Glos GL53 8DB; Tel (01242) 519856

Barking, Enfield, Haringey, Havering, Newham, Redbridge and Waltham Forest
Neil Johnson St Ignatius College, Turkey St, Enfield, Middx EN1 4NP; Tel (01992) 717835; Fax (01992) 652070; Home 27 Park Rd, Hampton Wick, Kingston upon Thames, Surrey KT1 4AS; Tel 0181-977 0452
Keith McGovern St Thomas More RC School, Glendale Ave, Wood Green, London N22 5HN; Tel 0181-888 7122; Fax 0181-889 8496; Home 72 Cambridge Gdns, Muswell Hill, London N10 2LN; Tel 0181-444 2431

Barnet, Brent, Ealing, Harrow, Hillingdon and Hounslow
Yolande Phillips Kingsbury High School, Princes Ave, London NW9 9JR; Tel 0181-204 9814; Fax 0181-206 0715; Home 42 Ickenham Road, Ruislip, Middlesex HA4 7DQ; Tel (01895) 638496
Nigel Purchon Kingsbury High School, Princes Ave, London NW9 9JR; Tel 0181-204 9814; Home 54 Gondar Gdns, London NW6 1HG; Tel 0171-794 8693

Barnsley, Doncaster, Rotherham and Sheffield
Laraine Ansley Wickersley Comprehensive School, Bawtry Rd, Wickersley, Rotherham S66 0JL; Tel (01709) 703465; Home 111 Northfield La, Wickersley, Rotherham S66 0HW; Tel/Fax (01709) 545716
John Parkinson Don Valley High School, Jossey La, Doncaster DN5 9DD; Tel (01302) 781528; Home Cherry Tree Cottage, Back La, Campsall, Doncaster DN6 9AH; (01302) 701620

Bedfordshire and Buckinghamshire
Rupert Butterfield John Hampden Grammar School, Marlow Hill, High Wycombe, Buckinghamshire HP11 1SZ; Tel (01494) 529589; Home 27 Greenside, Bourne End, Buckinghamshire SL8 5TW; Tel (01628) 531409
Geoffrey Venn Sharnbrook Upper School, Odell Rd, Sharnbrook, Bedfordshire MK44 1JX; Tel (01234) 782211; Home 10 The Avenue, Bletsoe, Bedford MK44 1QF; Tel: (01234) 781634

Berkshire and Oxfordshire
Michael Edwards Battle Primary School, Cranbury Rd, Reading, Berkshire RG3 2TD; Tel (01734) 590113; Home 31 Grantham Rd, Reading, Berkshire RG3 3NJ; Tel (01734) 581392
Janice Johnson Tudor Hall School, Wykham Pk, Banbury, Oxfordshire OX16 9UR; Tel (01295) 263434; Home Ashburne, Barford-St-Michael, Banbury, Oxfordshire OX15 0RD; Tel (01869) 338312

Bexley, Bromley, Croydon, Kingston, Merton, Richmond and Sutton
Ruth Arnold Coombe Girls' School, Clarence Ave, New Malden, Surrey KT3 3TU; Tel 0181-942 1242; Fax 0181-942 6385; Home Struan Cottage, Woodham Rd, Woking, Surrey GU21 4DL; (01483) 764944
Ian Page Chislehurst and Sidcup Grammar School, Hurst Rd, Sidcup DA15 9AG; Tel 0181-302 6511; Home 35 Cottage Field Cl, Sidcup, Kent DA14 4PD

Birmingham
Vanessa Holt Bordesley Green Girls' School, Bordesley Grn, Birmingham B9 4TR; Tel 0121-772 1881/1391; Fax 0121-773 0122; Home 9 Elm Tree Rd, Harborne, Birmingham B17 9AP; Tel: 0121-426 4734
Raymond Rowe ATL Office: Harborne Hill School, Harborne Rd, Edgbaston, Birmingham B15 3JL; Tel 0121-454 2754; Home 3 Hazelbank, Kings Norton, Birmingham B38 8BT; Mobile 037 4489861

Bolton, Bury, Oldham, Rochdale and Wigan
Ron Cole Standish Community High School, Kenyon Rd, Standish, Wigan WN6 0NX; Tel (01257) 427755; Fax (01257) 425858; Home 40 The Farthings, Astley Village, Chorley PR7 1TP; Tel: (01257) 268387
Gill Stainthorpe Geoffrey Kershaw Centre, Maxwell St, Bury BL9 7QT; Tel 0161-763 1453; Home 24 Lynmouth Cl, Radcliffe, Manchester M26 2RR; Tel: 0161-723 4257

Bradford, Calderdale, Kirklees and Wakefield
Hilary Pollard Rawthorpe High School, Nether Hall Ave, Rawthorpe, Huddersfield, Yorkshire HD5 9PG; Tel (01484) 517532; Fax (01484) 450822; Home 98 Penistone Rd, Waterloo, Huddersfield, Yorkshire HD5 8QX; Tel (01484) 429106
Mike Waters New College, Park La, Pontefract, West Yorkshire WF8 4QR; Tel (01977) 702139; Home 3 Cliff Villas, Tanshelf Dr, Pontefract, West Yorkshire WF8 4DJ; Tel (01977) 701678

Cambridgeshire and Northamptonshire
Jeremy Cole Latimer School, Castle Way, Barton Seagrave, Kettering, Northamptonshire NN15 6SW; Tel (01536) 724219; Home 1 Hood Walk, Kettering, Northamptonshire NN15 6PZ; Tel (01536) 515689
Peter Wake The Village College, Soham, Ely, Cambridgeshire CB7 5AA; Tel (01353) 720569; Fax (01353) 624379; Home 63 Burwell Rd, Exning, Newmarket, Suffolk CB8 7DU; Tel: (01638) 577431

Cheshire and Staffordshire
Elizabeth Williams Cheslyn Hay Primary School, Saredon Rd, Cheslyn Hay, Walsall WA6 7JQ; Tel (01922) 412527; Home 79 Bugeley Rd, Hazelslade, Cannock, Staffordshire WS12 5PQ; (01543) 876150

Pamela Stanley *The Queens School, City Walls Rd, Chester CH1 2NN; Tel (01244) 312078; Home* 8 The Cobbles, Overleigh Rd, Chester CH4 7HY; (01244) 678701

Cleveland, Durham, South Tyneside and Sunderland
Walter Peacock *Tanfield Comprehensive School, Tanfield Lea Road, Stanley, Co Durham DH9 8AY; Tel (01207) 232881; Fax (01207) 282922; Home* 5 Grange Rd, Stanley, Co Durham DH9 7RQ; Tel (01207) 232862
Malcolm Wilkinson *Houghton Kepier School, Dairy La, Houghton-le-Spring, Tyne and Wear DH4 5BH; Tel (0191) 5841674; Home* 43 Derwent Cl, Seaham, Co Durham SR7 7BS; Tel: (0191) 5812480

Clwyd and Gwynedd
Clive Sweeting *Ysgol Friars, Lon Y Bryn, Bangor, Gwynedd LL57 2LN; Tel (01248) 364905; Fax (01248) 352235; Home* 10 Wexham St, Beaumaris, Gwynedd LL58 8AB; Tel: (01248) 810982
Paul May, Yale College, Crispin La *Wrexham, Clwyd LL11 2HT; Tel (01978) 351211; Home* 42 Parc-Y-Llan, Llanfair DC, Ruthin, Clwyd LL15 2YL; Tel (01824) 703776

Cornwall and Devon
John Beattie *Exmouth Community College, Gypsy La, Exmouth, Devon EX8 3AF; Tel (01395) 264761; Fax (01395) 225355; Home* Ilex, Clyst St Mary, Exeter, Devon EX5 1BB; Tel (01392) 875708
Cynthia Watmore *Camborne Community Centre, South Terr, Camborne, Cornwall TR14 5UU; Tel (01209) 718844; Fax (01209) 712620; Pool School and Community College, Church Rd, Pool, Redruth, Cornwall TR15 3PZ; Tel: (01209) 715011, Fax: (01209) 612070*

Coventry, Solihull and Warwickshire
Alan Oglesby *Princethorpe College, Princethorpe, Nr Rugby CV23 9PX; Tel (01926) 632147; Home* 84 Nod Rise, Broad La, Coventry CV5 7JJ; Tel (01203) 469320

Cumbria and Scotland
Judith Rowley *Morton School, Wigton Rd, Carlisle, Cumbria CA2 6LB; Tel (01228) 20155; Fax (01228) 515531; Home* 8 St Peter's Dr, Lowry Hill, Carlisle, Cumbria CA3 0QB; Tel (01228) 38617
Elizabeth Simpson *Victoria Junior School, Pilgrim St, Workington, Cumbria CA14 2QT; Tel (01900) 602296; Home* "Tirol", Church Cl, Distington, Workington, Cumbria CA14 5ST; Tel (01946) 832323

Derbyshire and Nottinghamshire
Jennifer Bangs *West Park School, West Rd, Spondon, Derby DE21 7BT; Tel (01332) 662337; Fax (01332) 280767; Home* 8 Chatsworth Dr, Little Eaton, Derby DE21 5AP; Tel (01332) 880282
Jack, Billington *High Pavement College, Gainsford Crescent, Bestwood, Nottingham NG5 5HT; Tel (0115) 927 1235; Fax (0115) 975 0052; Home* 11A Abingdon Gdns, Woodthorpe, Nottingham NG5 4NP; Tel (0115) 926 5162

Dudley, Sandwell, Walsall and Wolverhampton
Mike Kelley *Langley High School, Moat Rd, Oldbury, Warley, West Midlands B68 8ED; Tel Home* "Willowbank", 28 Fieldfare Cl, Cradley Heath, Warley, West Midlands B64 5QH
Peter Moore *Bluecoat Church of England Comprehensive School, Birmingham St, Walsall WS1 2ND; Tel (01922) 720558; Home* 57 Grosvenor Rd, Harborne, Birmingham B17 9AL; Tel: 0121-426 6624

Dyfed, Powys, and West Glamorgan
Susan Evans *Olchfa School, Gower Rd, Sketty, Swansea SA2 7AB; Tel (01792) 201222; Home* 16 Pentre Banadl, Killay, Swansea SA2 7DD; Tel (01792) 206949
John Hughes *Home* Poplar, Dewi Rd, Tregaron, Dyfed SY25 6JW; Tel (01974) 298513; Fax (01974) 298513

East Sussex and West Sussex
Yvonne Howe *Torfield School, Croft Rd, Hastings, East Sussex; Home* Hurst Cottage, Broad Oak La, Bexhill-on-Sea, East Sussex TN39 4HE; Tel: (01424) 220731
Michael Rice *Durrington High School, The Boulevard, Worthing BN13 1JX; Tel (01903) 244957; Home* "Normandy Lodge", Wellingham La, High Salvington, Worthing, Sussex BN13 3AU; Tel (01903) 263840

Essex and Germany
Arthur Razzell *The Plume School, Fambridge Rd, Maldon, Essex CM8 6AB; Tel (01621) 854681; Home* 6 Beacon Hill, Maldon, Essex CM9 6HR; Tel (01621) 852077

Gateshead, Newcastle, North Tyneside and Northumberland
Betty Hughes *St Bartholomew's CofE Primary (Aided) School, Nursery Unit, Front St, Longbenton, Newcastle upon Tyne NE12 8AE; Tel 0191-266 2660; Home* 29 Cranham Cl, Ashdown Manor, Old Killingworth, Northumberland NE12 0FV; Tel 0191-268 6166

Hampshire, Dorset and Isle of Wight
David Jones *Alton College, Alton, Hampshire GU34 2LX; Tel (01420) 88118; Fax (01992) 652070; Home* 2 Vectis Cl, Four Marks, Alton, Hampshire GU34 5AB; Tel (01420) 562351
Don Rogers *Home* 88 West Way, Broadstone, Dorset BH18 9LS; Tel (01202) 697058

Hereford and Worcester and Shropshire
John Bosworth *Droitwich High School, Ombersley Rd, Droitwich, Worcestershire WR9 0AA; Tel (01905) 774421; Home* 153 Columbia Dr, Lower Wick, Worcester WR2 4XG; Tel (01905) 422789
Josie Huntingdon *Christopher Whitehead High School, Bromwich Rd, Worcester WR2 4AF; Tel (01905) 423906; Fax (01905) 420788; Home* 36 Silverdale Ave, Worcester WR5 1PX; Tel (01905) 351906

Hertfordshire
David Clout *Home* 9 Watling Knoll, Radlett, Hertfordshire WD7 7HW; Tel (01923) 854403

Humberside
Mary Grady *Hull High School for Girls, Tranby Croft, Anlaby, Hull HU10 7EH; Tel (01482) 657016; Fax (01482) 655389; Home* 83 Swanland Rd, Hessle, North Humberside HU13 0NS; Tel (01482) 648044
Sally Webster *Parkwood Junior School, Plymouth Rd, Scunthorpe DN17 1SS; Tel (01724) 861009; Home* 20 Nursery Cl, Barton upon Humber, South Humberside DN18 5LB; Tel (01652) 633596

Kent
Vacancy

Knowsley, Liverpool, Sefton, St Helens and Wirral
Richard Neale *Thornton Hough Primary School, St Georges Way, Thorton Hough, Bebington, Wirral, Merseyside L63 1JJ; Tel 0151-336 3427; Home* 6 Cambridge Rd, Prenton, Birkenhead, Merseyside L42 8PR; Tel 0151-608 4296
Brian Waggett *Range High School, Stapleton Rd, Formby, Merseyside L37 2YN; Tel (017048) 79315; Home* 20 Melrose Ave, Southport, Merseyside PR9 9UY; Tel: (01704) 29800

Lancashire and Isle of Man
Michael Hodgson *Queen's Drive County Primary School, Black Bull La, Fulwood, Preston, Lancashire PR2 3LA; Tel (01772) 718344; Fax (01772) 787126; Home* 72 Ainslie Rd, Fulwood, Preston, Lancashire PR2 3DE; Tel (0772) 715944
Vic Luscombe *Millfield High School, Belvedere Rd, Thornton-Cleveleys, Nr Blackpool FY5 5DG; Tel (01253) 865929; Home* 28 Rivington Ave, Bispham, Blackpool FY2 9ER; Tel (01253) 355855

Leicestershire and Lincolnshire
Joyce Frost North Lincolnshire College, Park St, Lincoln LN2 5HQ; Tel (01522) 510530; Fax (01522) 510530; Home 3 High St, Heighington, Lincoln LN4 1RG; Tel (01522) 794242

London I: Hammersmith & Fulham, Kensington & Chelsea, Westminster, Camden, Southwark, Lambeth and Wandsworth
Briget Sam-Bailey St Mark's School, Bishop's Ave, London SW6 6ED; Tel 0171-736 2211; Home 41 Blagdon Rd, Lewisham, London SE13 7HH; Tel: 0181-244 6857
Robert Skelly Alleyn's School, Townley Rd, London SE22 8SU; Tel 0181-693 3422; Fax 0181-299 3671; Home 137B Barry Rd, London SE22 0HW; Tel 0181-299 0600

London II: Islington, Hackney, City of London, Tower Hamlets, Greenwich and Lewisham
Elizabeth Coston Lee Manor Primary School, Leahurst Rd, London SE13 5LS; Tel 0181-852 7688; Home: 28 Westholme, Erith, Kent DA8 3NS; Tel: (01322) 338990
Neville Jarrett Home 7 Isabella Rd, Hackney, London E9 6DX; Tel 0181-985 1460

Manchester, Salford, Stockport, Tameside and Trafford
Michael Moore Little Hulton Community High School, Longshaw Dr, Little Hulton, Manchester M38 0AZ; Tel 0161-790 4214/1851; Fax 0161-790 2165; Home 12 Camellia Cl, Heaton, Bolton BL1 4NY; Tel (01204) 846183
Clifford Parry Loreto Grammar School, Dunham Rd, Altrincham, Cheshire WA14 4AS; Tel 0161-928 3703; Fax 0161-928 7659; Home 12 Upton Ave, Cheadle Hulme, Cheadle, Cheshire SK8 7HX; Tel: 0161-486 0118

Mid Glamorgan, South Glamorgan and Gwent
Ken Farrar Cardinal Newman RC Comprehensive School, Dynea Rd, Dynea, Rhydyfelin, Pontypridd CF37 5DP; Tel (01443) 486845/6; Fax (01443) 485342; Home Dan-Y-Bryn, Merthyr Tydfil CF47 0ES; Tel (01685) 722847
Gwyn Moses Llanrumney High School, Ball Rd, Llanrumney, Cardiff, South Glamorgan CF3 9YW; Tel (01222) 792731; Fax (01222) 778412; Home "Maesycoed", 29 Warren Dr, Caerphilly, Mid Glamorgan CF8 1HQ; Tel (01222) 883816

Norfolk and Suffolk
Andrew Garner Chantry High School, Mallard Way, Ipswich IP2 9LR; Tel (01473) 687181; Fax (01473) 602693; Home 31 Hatfield Rd, Ipswich, Suffolk IP3 9AF; Tel (01473) 717570
David Stammers Home 12 Birch Ave, Bacton, Stowmarket, Suffolk IP14 4NT; Tel (01449) 781577

North Yorkshire and Leeds
George Dobson Northallerton College, Grammar School La, Northallerton, North Yorkshire DL6 1DD; Tel (01609) 773340; Home The Millings Lodge, 5 North End, Bedale, North Yorkshire DL8 1AF; Tel: (01677) 423017
Hazel Saxton Agnes Stewart C of E High School, Cromwell St, Leeds LS9 7SG; Tel (0113) 248 2834; Home 19 Victoria Mount, Horsforth, Leeds LS18 4PU; Tel (0113) 258 1848

Northern Ireland
Eddie Ferguson Cross and Passion College, 10 Moyle Rd, Ballycastle, Co Antrim BT54 6LA; Tel (012657) 62473; Home 61 Moyle Rd, Ballycastle, Co Antrim BT54 6LG; Tel (012657) 62949
Pearl Miskelly Millisle Primary School, Abbey Rd, Millisle, Co Down BT22 2DD; Tel (01247) 861471; Home 9 Ballymacormick Cres, Bangor, Co Down BT19 6BS; Tel: (01247) 457823

Somerset and Wiltshire
Elizabeth Cragg Frome Community College, Bath Rd, Frome, Somerset BA11 2HQ; Tel (01373) 465353; Fax (01373) 452583; Home 94 Wyville Rd, Frome, Somerset BA11 2BT; Tel (01373) 463614
Peter Greed New College, Helston Rd, Park North, Swindon, Wiltshire SN3 2LA; Tel (01793) 611470; Home 18 Nursteed Pk, Devizes, Wiltshire SN10 3AN; Tel (01380) 723839

Surrey, Guernsey and Jersey
Shirley Smith The Grammar School, Les Varendes, St Andrews, Guernsey; Tel (01481) 56571; Fax (01481) 51236; Home 2 Tall Pines, Route des Capelles, St Sampson, Guernsey; Tel (01481) 725884
Keith Willingham Spelthorne College, Park Rd, Ashford TW15 2XD; Tel (01784) 248666; Home 75 Hillsborough Pk, Camberley, Surrey GU15 1HG; Tel: (01276) 63913

Branch Secretaries

Avon
J.A. Main Culverhay School, Rush Hill, Bath BA2 2QL; Tel (01225) 444753; Fax (01225) 447036; Home 37 Huntingdon Rise, Bradford on Avon, Wiltshire BA15 1RJ; Tel (01225) 865933

Barking and Dagenham
M.A. Cooper Barking Abbey Comprehensive School, Sandringham Rd, Barking, Essex IG11 9AG; Tel 0181-594 3541; Home 23 Southampton Rd, London NW5 4JU; Tel 0171-482 4343

Barnet
Vacancy

Barnsley
R.J. Bone Willowgarth High School, Brierley Rd, Grimethrope, Barnsley S72 7AJ; Tel (01226) 711542; Home 'Ghyllburn', 12 Shaw La, Staincross, Barnsley S74 6JN; (01226) 383782

Bedfordshire
D. King Challney Girls' High School, Stoneygate Rd, Luton, Beds LU4 9TJ; Tel (01582) 571427; Home 15 Hemingford Dr, Luton, Beds LU2 7BA; Tel (01582) 508345

Berkshire
M. Edwards Battle Primary School, Cranbury Rd, Reading RG3 2TD; Tel (01734) 590113; Home 31 Grantham Rd, Reading, Berkshire RG3 3NJ; Tel (01734) 581392
A.B. Jones Aldryngton Primary School, Silverdale Rd, Earley, Reading RG6 2HB; Tel (01734) 265843; Home 9 Elmley Cl, Wokingham, Berkshire RG11 1HP; Tel (01734) 789847

Bexley
I.A. Page Chislehurst & Sidcup Grammar School, Hurst Rd, Sidcup, Kent DA15 9AG; Tel 0181-302 6511; Home 35 Cottage Field Cl, Sidcup, Kent DA14 4PD

Birmingham
R.A. Rowe ATL Office, Harborne Hill School, Harborne Rd, Edgbaston, Birmingham B15 3JL; Tel 0121-454 2754; Home 3 Hazlebank, Kings Norton, Birmingham B38 8BT; Mobile: 0374 489861

Bolton
P.W.R. Wells Turton High School, Bromley Cross, Bolton BL9 7LT; Tel (01204) 595888; Fax (01204) 306712; Home 7 Swan Rd, Greenmount, Bury BL8 4ES; Tel: (01204) 885164

Bradford
P.M. De Villiers Home 2 Kirklands, Church St, Cleckheaton BD19 3RW; Tel (01274) 872634

18 Teachers' and Other Educational Organisations

Brent
N. Purchon Kingsbury High School, Princes Ave, London NW9 9JR; Tel 0171-204 9814; Home 54 Gondar Gdns, London NW6 1HG; Tel 0171-794 8693

Bromley
B. Humphreys Ravens Wood Boys (GMS), Oakley Rd, Bromley BR2 8HP; Tel (01689) 857160; Home 1 Edgewood Dr, Orpington, Kent BR6 6LG; Tel/ Fax (01689) 862378

Buckinghamshire
G. Bell Dr Challoner's Grammar School, Amersham, Bucks HP6 5HA; Tel (01494) 721685; Home 4 Cherry Way, Hazlemere, High Wycombe, Bucks HP15 7UD; Tel (01494) 712388

Bury
M. Price Home 69 Meadow Way, Tottington, Bury, Lancs BL8 3HU; Tel (01204) 885428

Calderdale
I. Whitehill Moorside Junior School, Keighley Rd, Ovenden, Halifax, W. Yorks HX2 8AP; Tel (01422) 365236; Home The Sidings, 23 Crossley Hill, Salterhebble, Halifax HX3 6PL; Tel: (01422) 355193

Cambridgeshire
D.M. Best St Bede's Comprehensive Church School, Birdwood Rd, Cambridge CB1 3TB; Tel (01223) 248660; Fax (01223) 249196; Home 24 Ainsdale, Cherry Hinton, Cambridge CB1 4JT; Tel: (01223) 243053

Cheshire
T.E.H. Capper (Casework) Bridgewater County High School, Broomfields Rd, Appleton, Warrington WA7 6QH; Tel (01925) 263919; Fax (01925) 861434; Home Flat 'S' 4, Norton Hill, Windmill Hill, Runcorn WA7 6QH; Tel: (01928) 712057
S.A. Barnwell (Admin) Bridgewater County High School, Lower Site, Hall Dr, Appleton, Warrington WA7 6QH; Tel (01565) 734031; Fax (01925) 861449; Home 'Mollis', Pickmere La, Pickmere, Cheshire WA16 0JU; Tel (01565) 733604

Cleveland
K.A. Pratt Billingham Campus School, Marsh House Ave, Billingham, Cleveland TS23 3HB; Tel (01642) 560947; Home 67 Wimpole Rd, Stockton-on-Tees, Cleveland TS19 7LR; Tel (01642) 581172

Clwyd
D.M. Hytch St David's High School, St David's Terr, Saltney, Chester CH4 0AE; Tel (01244) 671583; Fax (01244) 680309; Home Twmpath Top, Rhydymwyn, Mold, Clwyd CH7 5HS; Tel (01352) 741837

Cornwall
V. MacFarlane Home 10 Condurrow Rd, Beacon, Camborne TR14 7SW; Tel (01209) 713222
J. Cloke Home 3 Westheath Rd, Bodmin PL31 1QQ; Tel (01208) 73495

Coventry
E. Langdale President Kennedy School, Rookery La, Coventry CV6 4GL; Tel (01203) 661416; Home 62 Rochester Rd, Earlsdon, Coventry CV5 6AG; (01203) 673895

Croydon
D. Webb Norbury Manor Girls School, Kensington Ave, Thorton Heath CR4 8BT; Tel 0181-679 2412; Home Flat 1, 104 Lansdowne Pl, Hove BN3 1FJ; Tel (01273) 821211

Cumbria
J. McCormick Lochinvar School, Longtown, Carlisle, Cumbria CA6 5UG; Tel (01228) 791416/792350; Fax (01228) 791701; Home Low Flatts, Armathwaite, Carlisle CA4 9PB; Tel: (016974) 72205
K.M. Larkin Home The Teathes, Kirkland, Frizington, Cumbria CA26 3YB; Tel (01946) 861265; Fax (01946) 862093

Derbyshire
J.K. Bishton Home 73 Windsor Dr, Wingerworth, Chesterfield, Derbys S42 6TQ; Tel (01246) 207796
D.J. Gent Queen Elizabeth's Grammar School, Ashbourne, Derbys DE6 1EP; Tel (01335) 43685; Home 1 Gorsey Cl, Belper, Derbyshire DE5 2TT; Tel: (01773) 825035

Devon
J.A. Pering Ellacombe Primary School, Ellacombe Church Rd, Torquay, Devon TQ1 1TG; Tel (01803) 293040; Home 12 Lydwell Pk Rd, Wellswood, Torquay, Devon TQ1 3TQ; Tel: (01803) 21440
K.C. Lewis King Edward VIth College, Ashburton Rd, Totnes, Devon TQ9 5JX; Tel (01803) 862591; 2 Whitehall Cl, Newton Abbot, Devon TQ12 6QY; Tel (01626) 68620

Doncaster
J.S. Parkinson Don Valley High School, Jossey La, Scawthorpe, Doncaster DN5 9DD; Tel (01302) 781528; Home Cherry Tree Cottage, Back La, Campsall, Doncaster DN6 9AH; Tel (01302) 701620

Dorset
D.H. Rogers Home 88 West Way, Broadstone, Dorset BH18 9LS; Tel (01202) 697058
P.D. Jacques Shaftesbury School, Salisbury Rd, Shaftesbury SP7 8ER; Tel (01747) 54498; Home 4 Maple Cl, Wincanton, Somerset BA9 9SQ; Tel (01963) 34853

Dudley
Vacancy

Durham
W. Peacock Tanfield Comprehensive School, Tanfield Lea Rd, Stanley, Co Durham DH9 8AY; Tel (01207) 232881; Fax (01207) 282922; Home 5 Grange Rd, Stanley, Co Durham DH9 7RQ; Tel (01207) 232862
E. Boyd Home 4 Aykley Gn, Whitesmocks, Durham DH1 4LN; Tel 0191-384 9473

Dyfed
J.M. Hughes Home Poplar, Dewi Rd, Tregaron, Dyfed SY25 6JW; Tel (01974) 298513; Fax (01974) 298513

Ealing
C.C. Burke Acton High School, Gunnersbury La, Acton, London W3 8EY; Tel 0181-752 0005; Home 35 Bockhampton Rd, Kingston upon Thames, Surrey KT2 5JU; Tel 0181-549 4982

Enfield
R.N. Johnson St Ignatius College, Turkey St, Enfield, Middx EN1 4NP; Tel (01992) 717835; Fax (01992) 652070; Home 27 Park Rd, Hampton Wick, Kingston upon Thames KT1 4AS; Tel 0181-977 0452

Essex
J. Delves Home Pound Hse, 3 Pound La, Hadleigh, Nr Ipswich IP7 5BQ; Tel (01473) 824239
H.V. Powell Essex Traveller Education Service; Tel (01376) 513901; Home 20 Wolmers Hey, Gt Waltham, Chelmsford CM3 1DA; Tel: (01245) 360400

South-East Sub-Branch
J. Raith, Home 5 Doric Ave Rochford, Essex SS4 3DF; Tel (01702) 545083

Gateshead
V.A. Taylorson Home Rhuadatain, 6 Ashfield Rise, Wickham, Newcastle NE16 4PN; Tel 0191-488 7034

Germany
M. Ramsden Edinburgh School, Munster BFPO 17; Tel 00-4925120061 (Ext 294)

Gloucestershire
M. Rear *Home* 106 Malleson Rd, Gotherington, Cheltenham, Gloucestershire GL52 4EY; Tel (01242) 674470; Fax (01242) 674470

Guernsey
C.W. Ogier Education Development Centre, Granville House, Mount Durand, St Peter Port, Guernsey; Tel (01481) 720654; Home La Fosse, La Rue des Fosses', St Martin, Guernsey GY4 6QR; Tel: (01481) 39243

Gwent
D. Harding Home 12 Caradog Cl, Caerleon, Newport, Gwent NP6 1FN; Tel (01633) 422485

Gwynedd
B. Thomas Ysgol Aberconwy, Morfa Dr, Conwy, Gwynedd LL32 8ED; Tel (01492) 593243; Home 5 Parc Sychnant, Conwy, Gwynedd LL32 8SB; Tel (01492) 593473

Hampshire
D. Hinchliffe Meon Junior School, Meon Rd, Southsea PO4 8NW; Tel Home 31 Hazleton Way, Cowplain, Waterlooville, Hants PO8 9BP

Central Division
T. Hilton Alderman Quilley School, Cherbourg Rd, Eastleigh SO5 5EL; Tel (01703) 612330; Home 36 Oval Gdns, Alverstoke, Gosport PO12 2RB; Tel: (01705) 581696

South East Division
D. Belfield Cowplain School, Hart Plain Ave, Waterlooville, Hampshire PO8 9EJ; Tel (01705) 254222; Home 78 Greenfield Cres, Cowplain, Waterlooville, Hampshire PO8 9EJ; Tel: (01705) 648185

South West Division
R. Holt Springhill R.C. First and Middle School, Milton Rd, Southampton, Hampshire SO1 2HW; Tel (01703) 333954; Home 7 Devonshire Gdns, Butts Ash, Hythe, Hampshire SO4 6QZ; Tel: (01703) 846995

North East Division
P. Hake Robert Mays School, West St, Oldham, Basingstoke RG25 1NA; Tel (01256) 702700; Home 48 Riverdale, Wrecclesham, Farnham, Surrey GU10 4PJ; Tel: (01252) 723160

Haringey
K. McGovern St Thomas More R.C. School, Glendale Ave, Wood Grn, London N22 5HN; Tel 0181-888 7122; Home 72 Cambridge Gdns, Muswell Hill, London N10 2LN; Tel: 0181-444 2431

Harrow
J. Betts Home 171 Mount Pleasant La, Bricket Wood, St Albans AL2 3XW; Tel (01923) 674918

Havering
A. Bolton (Contact person) Albany School, Broadstone Rd, Hornchurch RM12 4AH; Tel (01708) 441537; Home 24 Woodlands Rd, Harold Wood, Romford RM30; Tel (01708) 375739

Hereford and Worcester
J. Huntingdon (Negotiations) Christopher Whitehead High School, Bromwich Rd, Worcester WR2 4AF; Tel (01905) 423906; Home 36 Silverdale Ave, Worcester WR5 1PX; Tel (01905) 351906
H.T. Sandison (Casework) Home Feochan, Hillside, Martley, Nr Worcester WR6 6QN; Tel (01886) 888393

Hertfordshire
D. Clout Home 9 Watling Knoll, Radlett, Hertfordshire WD7 7HW; Tel (01923) 854403

Hillingdon
P.A. Smith Home 9 Evelyn Ave, Ruislip, Middx HA4 8AR; Tel (01895) 672251

Hounslow
P.J. Taylor Longford School, Tachbrook Rd, Hounslow TW14 9PE; Tel 0181-890 0245; Home Langdale, Crown Rd, Virginia Water, Surrey GU25 4HT; Tel (01344) 843701

Humberside
S.A. Webster Home 20 Nursery Cl, Barton-on-Humber DN18 5LB; Tel (01652) 633596

East Riding Sub-Branch
W.E. Blair Home 129 Park Ave, Hull HU5 3ED; Tel (01482) 492809

Hull Sub-Branch
J. Forth Maybury Primary School, Maybury Rd, Hull HU9 5RJ; Tel (01482) 701387; Home 115 Main St, Burstwick, Hull HU12 9EB; Tel (01964) 623382

Grimsby Sub-Branch
B.P.M. Kutty Whitgift School, Crosland Rd, Grimsby DN37 9EH; Tel (01472) 887117; Home 27 Station Ave, New Waltham, Grimsby DN36 4QS; Tel (01472) 814569

Scunthorpe Sub-Branch
S.A. Webster Home 20 Nursery Cl, Barton-upon-Humber DN18 5LB; Tel (01652) 633596

Isle of Man
P.J. Fletcher Ramsey Grammar School, Ramsey, IOM; Tel (01624) 813202; Home "Hillview", East Loughan, Jurby, IOM; Tel (01624) 897970

Isle of Wight
R.A. Lister Medina High School, Fairlee, Newport PO30 2DX; Tel (01983) 526523; Home 55 Albert St, Cowes PO31 7ND; Tel: (01983) 299537

Jersey
R. Dupre (Contact person) Hantlieu School, Wellington Rd, St Saviour, Jersey; Tel (01534) 36242; Home Le Picachon, 4 Clos Royale, Grouville, Jersey JE3 9DF; Tel (01534) 856378

Kent
P. MacMillan Home 19 Prospect Row, Brompton, Gillingham ME7 5AL; Tel (01634) 247242

Kingston
R.F. Arnold Coombe Girls School, Clarence Ave, New Malden, Surrey KT3 3TU; Tel 0181-942 1242; Home Struan Cottage, Woodham Rd, Woking, Surrey GU21 4DL; Tel (01483) 764944

Kirklees
H. Pollard Rawthorpe High School, Nether Hall Ave, Rawthorpe, Huddersfield HD5 9PG; Tel (01484) 517532; Fax (01484) 426141; Home 98 Penistone Rd, Waterloo, Huddersfield HD5 8QX; Tel (01484) 429106

Knowsley
M. Penfold Eastcroft Primary School, Tower Hill, Kirkby L33 1EB; Tel 0151-548 0545; Home 61 Elmers Green, Skelmersdale, Lancashire WN8 6SG; Tel (01695) 31488

Lancashire
M. Hodgson Queen's Drive County Primary School, Black Bull La, Fulwood, Preston PR2 3LA; Tel (01772) 718344; Fax (01772) 787126; Home 72 Ainslie Rd, Fulwood, Preston PR2 3DE; Tel (01772) 715944
F. Martin Our Lady's High School, Morecambe Rd, Lancaster LA2 3RX; Tel (01524) 66689; Fax (01524) 849441; Home 24 South Ave, Morecambe LA4 5RJ; Tel (01524) 426316

Leeds
A.C. Felston Lawnswood School, Ring Rd, Leeds LS16 5AG; Tel (0113) 278 2321; Home 19 Southlands Drive, Leeds LS17 5NZ; Tel (0113) 268 9708

Leicestershire
A. Glithero Heathfield High School, Belle Vue Rd, Earl Shilton, Leicester LE9 7PA; Tel (01455) 842149; Fax (01455) 840535; Home 56 Arbor Rd, Croft, Leicester LE9 3GD; Tel (01455) 284096

Lincolnshire
J. Frost North Lincolnshire College, Park St, Lincoln LN2 5HQ; Tel (01522) 510530; Home 3 High Street, Heighington, Lincoln LN4 1RG; Tel (01522) 794242

Liverpool
G.J. Stewart Eileen Craven CP School, Walton La, Liverpool L4 4HQ; Tel 0151-298 2421; Home 1 College Rd North, Blundellsands, Liverpool L23 8UD; Tel 0151-924 1509

London
M.E. Kay Emanuel School, Battersea Rise, Wandsworth, London SW11 1HS; Tel 0181-870 6799; Home 9 Wilhelmina Ave, Coulsdon, Surrey CR5 1NL; Tel (01737) 554703

Camden Sub-Branch
M.J. Whelehan St Richard of Chichester School, 40 Prince of Wales Rd, Kentish Town, London NW5 2LN; Tel 0171-485 3561; Home 97 Glengall Rd, London NW6 7HG; Tel 0171-328 2271

City of London Sub-Branch
J. Hazel City of London School, Queen Victoria St, London EC4V 3AL; Tel 0171-489 0291; Home 23 Haldon Rd, London SW18 1QD; Tel 0181-874 5108

Greenwich Sub-Branch
G.A. Nice Home 4 Blessington Cl, London SE13 5ED; Tel 0181-852-7072

Hackney Sub-Branch
J.E. Bloom Hackney Teacher's Centre, Queensbridge Bldg, Albion Dr, London E8 4ET; Tel 0171-241 5522; Home 29 Belmont Cls, Cockfosters, Herts EN4 9LS

Hammersmith and Fulham Sub-Branch
B.A. Sam-Bailey St Mark's School, Bishop's Ave, London SW6 6ED; Tel 0171-736 2211; Home 41 Blagdon Rd, London SE13 7HH; Tel 0181-244 6857

Islington Sub-Branch
M. Rinsler St Mary's Primary CE School, Fowler Rd, London N1 2EP; Tel 0171-359 1870; Home 63A Dresden Rd, London N19 3BG; Tel: 0171-272 1739

Kensington and Chelsea Sub-Branch
A. Walter Colville Primary School, Lonsdale Rd, London W11; Tel 0171-229 6540; Home 38 Temple Sheen Rd, East Sheen, London SW14 7QG; Tel: 0181-876 2370

Lambeth Sub-Branch
W.M. Stevens Dick Sheppard School, Tulse Hill, London SW2 2QA; Tel 0181-674 8443; Home 333 Lyham Rd, London SW2 5NS; Tel 0181-674 9387

Lewisham Sub-Branch
E. McInulty Holbeach JMI School, Holbeach Rd, Catford, London SE5 4QB; Tel 0181-690 4713; Home 33 Colfe Rd, Forest Hill, London SE23 2ES; Tel: 0181-291 9252

Southwark Sub-Branch
P. Reeves Waverley School, Homestall Rd, Peckham Rye, London SE22 0NR; Tel 0171-732 2276; Home 24 Glengarry Rd, East Dulwich SE22 8Q; Tel 0181-693 3830

Tower Hamlets Sub-Branch
Vacancy

Wandsworth Sub-Branch
M.E. Kay Emanuel School, Battersea Rise, Wandsworth, SW11 1HS; Tel 0181-870 6799; Home 9 Wilhelmina Ave, Coulsdon, Surrey CR5 1NL; Tel (01737) 554703

Westminster Sub-Branch
J.E. Seymour St Mary's Hospital, School Room, Great Western Ward, 7th Fl, QEQM Wing, Praed St, London W2 1NY; Tel 0171-725 6257; Home 13 Ewhurst Rd, Crofton Pk, London SE4 1AG; Tel 0181-690 4522

Manchester
B. Waters Moston Fields County Primary School, Brookside Rd, Moston, Manchester M10 9GN; Tel 0161-681 1801; Home 10 Pentland Way, Matley La, Hyde, Cheshire SK14 4US; Tel 0161-682 8321

Merton
E.A. Kington Rutlish School, Watery La, Merton Pk, London SW20 9AD; Tel 0181-542 1212; Home 8 Woodland Cl, Ewell, Surrey KT19 0BQ; Tel 0181-224 2946

Mid Glamorgan
K.G. Farrar Newman RC Comp School, Dynea Rd, Dynea, Rhydyfelin, Pontypridd CF37 5DP; Tel (01443) 486845; Fax (01443) 485342; Home Dan-y-bryn, Merthyr Tydfil CF47 0ES; Tel (01685) 722847

Newcastle upon Tyne
A. Gardner-Medwin Home Flocktons, Station Rd, Heddon on the Wall NE15 0EG; Tel (01661) 852318

Newham
P.J. Jolly Langdon School, Sussex Rd, East Ham E6 2PS; Tel 0181-471 2411; Home 25 Braintree Ave, Redbridge, Ilford, Essex IG4 5PY; Tel 0181-550 8097

Norfolk
D. Lancaster Eaton (City of Norwich) School, Eaton Rd, Norwich NR4 6PP; Tel (01603) 54015; Home 12 Romany Walk, Poringland, Norwich, Norfolk NR14 7QZ

North Tyneside
R.C. Butler Willington Community High School, Churchill St, Wallsend NE28 7TN; Tel 0191-262 4880; Home 54 Ringway, Stakeford, Choppington, Northumberland NE62 5YW; Tel (01670) 812968
M.E. Hughes St Bartholomew's CofE Primary (Aided) School, Nursery Unit, Front St, Longbenton, Newcastle-upon-Tyne NE12 8AE; Tel 0191-266 2660; Home 29 Cranham Cl, Ashdown Manor, Old Killingworth NE12 0FJ; Tel 0191-268 6166

North Yorkshire
G. Dobson Northallerton College, Grammar School La, Northallerton DL6 1DD; Tel (01609) 773340; Home The Millings Lodge, S. North End, Bedale, N. Yorkshire DL8 1AF; Tel: (01677) 423017

Northamptonshire
D. Weinberg Cherry Orchard Middle School, Birchfield Rd East, Northants NN3 2TA; Tel (01604) 401241; Home Hillside, Sywell Rd, Holcot, Northants NN65 9SN; Tel: (01604) 781645

Northern Ireland
S. Woods ATL Office 397A Holywood Rd, Belfast BT4 2LY; Tel (01232) 471412; Fax (01232) 471535; Omagh Christian Brothers Grammar School, Kevlin Rd, Omagh, Co Tyrone BT78 1LD; Tel: (01662) 243567; *Home* 14 Aughadulla Rd, Omagh, Co Tyrone BT78 1PQ; Tel: (01662) 898661

Northumberland
R. Woolhouse Ponteland High School, Callerton La, Ponteland, Newcastle NI20 9EY; Tel (01661) 824711; Home 55 The Turn, Morpeth NE61 2DU; Tel (01670) 513234
R. Smith Hirst Pk Middle School, Third Ave, Ashington NE63 9BE; Tel (01670) 813111; Home 34 The Ave, Morpeth NE61 2DF; Tel (01670) 514086

Nottinghamshire
B. Robins Joseph Whitaker School, Warsop La, Rainworth, Mansfield, Notts NG21 0AG; Tel (01623)

792327; Home Manor Lodge, Manor Rd, Caunton, Newark, Notts NG23 6AR; Tel (01636) 636321

J.J. Billington High Pavement College, Gainsford Cres, Bestwood Est, Nottingham NG5 5HT; Tel (0115) 927 1235; Fax (0115) 975 0052; Home 11A Abingdon Gdns, Woodthorpe, Nottingham NG5 4NP; Tel (0115) 926 5162

Oldham

J. Ward Hathershaw Comprehensive School, Bellfield Ave, Oldham OL8 3EP; Tel 0161-624 7782; Home 43 Armit Rd, Greenfield, Oldham OL3 7LN; Tel: (01457) 873383

Oxfordshire

R. Martyn Burford School, Cheltenham Rd, Burford OX8 4PL; Tel (01993) 823303; Home 29 North Hinksey Village, Oxford OX2 0NA; Tel (01865) 246408

Powys

R. Carrotte (Contact Person) Maesydderwen High School, Ystradgynlais, Powys SA9 1RP; Tel (01639) 842115; Home Ty Bont, Talachddu, Brecon, Powys LD3 0UG; Tel (01874) 754515

Redbridge

J.N. Hill Wanstead High School, Redbridge La West, Wanstead, London E11 2JZ; Tel 0181-989 2791; Fax 0181-530 8879; Home 46 Belgrave Rd, Wanstead, London E11 3QW; Tel: 0181-989 9377

Richmond

Vacancy

Rochdale

A. Hague Queensway County Primary School, Hartley La, Rochdale OL11 2LR; Tel (01706) 47743; Home 19 Deepdale Ave, Rochdale OL16 4AN; Tel (01706) 42004

Rotherham

L. Ansley Wickersley Comprehensive School, Bawtry Rd, Wickersley, Rotherham S66 0JL; Tel (01709) 703465; Home 111 Northfield La, Wickersley, Rotherham S66 0HW; Tel and Fax (01709) 545716

St Helens

T. Mulrooney (Contact Person) ATL Office Eileen Craven CP School, Walton La, Liverpool L4 4HQ; Tel 0151-298 2421; *Home* 6 Kingscourt Rd, Liverpool L12 8RD; Tel 0151-228 4297

Salford

M. Moore Little Hulton Community High School, Longshaw Dr, Little Hulton, Manchester M38 0AZ; Tel 0161-790 4214; Fax 0161-790 2165; Home 12 Camellia Cl, Heaton, Bolton BL1 4NY; Tel (01204) 846183

Sandwell

A. Porter Perryfields High School, Oldacre Rd, Oldbury, Warley, West Midlands B68 0RG; Tel 0121-421 7979; Home 7 Newlands Dr, Halesowen, West Midlands B62 9DX; Tel 0121-421 8040

Sefton

B. Waggett (Headquarters) Range High School, Stapleton Rd, Formby, Merseyside L37 2YN; Tel (01708) 79315; Home 20 Melrose Ave, Southport, Merseyside PR9 9UY; Tel (01704) 29800

H. Hollinghurst (Negotiations) Chesterfield High School, Chesterfield Rd, Crosby L23 9YB; Tel 0151-924 6454; Home 37 St Michael's Rd, Blundellsands L23 7UJ; Tel 0151-924 7889

Sheffield

R.D. Pidd (Admin and Headquarters) Tapton School, Darwin La, Sheffield S10 5RG; Tel (0114) 230 3937; Home 39 Westwick Rd, Sheffield S8 7BT; Tel (0114) 274 6383

T. McElligott (Representation) Abbeydale Grange, Upper School Bldg, Bannerdale Rd, Sheffield S2 2GU; Tel Home 122 Button Hill, Sheffield S11 9HJ; Tel: (01585) 679806; Message Service (0399) 747256; Fax (0114) 2621288

Shropshire

Vacancy

Solihull

A.K. Martin Alderbrook School, Blossomfield Rd, Solihull, West Midlands B91 1SN; Tel 0121-704 2146; Home 62 Jersey Cl, Church Hill North, Redditch, Worcs B98 9LT; Tel (01527) 67391

Somerset

A.J. Lock Home 'Bluehills', East Nynehead, Wellington, Somerset TA21 0DA; Tel (01823) 461214

South Glamorgan

R. Baker (Branch) Llanedeyrn High School, Roundwood, Llanedeyrn, Cardiff CF3 7US; Tel (01222) 734718; Home 36 Brynawelon Rd, Cyncoed, Cardiff CF2 6QR; Tel (01222) 753905

South Tyneside

M. Shiels St Josephs Comprehensive School, Mill La, Hebburn NE31 1HT; Tel (0191) 483 2827; Home 12 Westmoreland Gdns, Lowfell NE9 6HP; Tel: (0191) 487 7489

Staffordshire

M.D. Kamm John Taylor High School, Barton under Needwood, Burton on Trent DE13 8AZ; Tel (01283) 712476; Home 71 Rotten Row, Lichfield WS13 6JB; Tel (01543) 253016

Southern

M.S. Lawes Paget High School, Burton Rd, Branston, Burton-upon-Trent DE14 3DR; Home 7 Glebe Cl, Rolleston, Burton-upon-Trent, Staffordshire DE13 9BP; Tel: (01283) 815395

Northern

C. Marriott Aynsley Special School, Aynsley Dr, Blythe Bridge, Stoke-on-Trent ST11 9HJ; Home 130 Stallington Rd, Blythe Bridge, Stoke-on-Trent ST11 9PA; Tel: (01782) 395471

Stockport

A.K. Tootill Bramhall High School, Seal Rd, Bramhall, Stockport SK7 2JT; Tel 0161-439 8045; Home 3 Arkwright Rd, Marple, Stockport SK6 7DB; Tel 0161-427 7978

Suffolk

A. Block Westbourne High School, Marlow Rd, Ipswich IP1 5JN; Tel (1473) 742315; Home Hou Cottage, 2 Hollesley Rd, Alderton, Woodbridge IP12 3BX; Tel: (01394) 411660

Sunderland

M. Wilkinson Houghton Kepier School, Dairy La, Houghton-Le-Spring, Tyne and Wear DH4 5BH; Fax 0191-584 1674; Home 43 Derwent Cl, Seaham, Co Durham SR7 7BS; Tel: 0191-581 2480

Surrey

J.F. Welch Marden Lodge Primary School, Croydon Rd, Caterham CR3 6QE; Tel (01883) 343014; Home 23 Buckhurst Cl, Redhill RH1 2AQ; Tel: (01737) 762812

Sussex East

N.J. Chalkley Blatchington Mill School, Holmes Ave, Hove, East Sussex BN3 7LF; Tel (01273) 736244; Home 10 Glynn Rise, Peacehaven, East Sussex BN10 7SG; Tel (01273) 588291

Sussex West

A.S. Niven Chatsmore Catholic High School, Goring St, Goring-by-Sea BN12 5AF; Tel (01903) 241368; Home 20 Ashurst Dr, Goring-by-Sea, West Sussex BN12 4SW; Tel (01903) 240001

Sutton
A.V. Mitchell Wallington County Grammar School, Croydon Rd, Wallington, Surrey SM6 7PH; Tel 0181-647 2235; Home 38 Foresters Dr, Wallington, Surrey SM6 9DG; Tel 0181-647 8484
E.C. Robinson Wallington High School for Girls, Woodcote Rd, Wallington SM6 0PH; Tel 0181-647 2380; Home 'Far End', 50 Woodcote Ave, Wallington, Surrey SM6 0QY; Tel 0181-647 3270

Tameside
H. Sweeney Two Trees High School, Two Trees La, Denton, Manchester M34 1QL; Tel 0161-336 2719/8678; Home 14 Woodville Dr, Staylebridge SK15 3EA; Tel: 0161-338 6041

Trafford
T. Dewhurst Lostock School, Selby Rd, Stretford, Manchester M32 9BX; Tel 0161-865 6215; Home 66 Sandy La, Stretford, Manchester M32 9BX; Tel 0161-865 2044

Wakefield
J.B. Brookling Lawefield Junior School, Lawefield La, Wakefield WF2 8ST; Tel (01924) 373098;Home 3 Primrose La, Calder Gr, Wakefield WF4 3DD; Tel: (10924) 277969
J. Waters New College, Park La, Pontefract, West Yorkshire WF8 4QR; Tel (01977) 702139; Home 3 Cliff Villas, Tanshelf Dr, Pontefract, West Yorkshire WF8 4DJ; Tel (01977) 701678

Walsall
H. Poulsom ATL Office: Pelsall School Site, Pelsall La, Rushall, Walsall WS4 1NG; Tel (01922) 694099; *Home* 12 Brackenhill Rd, Chase Terr, Walsall WS7 8HY; Tel (01543) 686341

Waltham Forest
C.F. Mackley Home 'Camaroth', Coppice Row, Theydon Bois, Essex CM16 7DW; Tel (01992) 812167

Warwickshire
P. Jones Red Deeps School, Coventry Rd, Nuneaton CV10 7AX; Tel (01203) 383315; Home 15 Park View, Sharnford, Leicester LE10 3PT; Tel: (01455) 273861

West Glamorgan
S. Evans Olchfa School, Gower Rd, Sketty, Swansea SA2 7AB; Tel (01792) 201222; Home 16 Pentre Banadl, Killay, Swansea SA2 7DD Tel: (01792) 206949

Wigan
R.J. Cole Standish Community High School, Kenyon Rd, Standish, Wigan WN6 0NX; Tel (01257) 422755; Fax (01257) 425858; Home 40 The Farthings, Astley Village, Chorley, Lancashire PR7 1TP; Tel: (01257) 268387

Wiltshire
J.M. Clampit Home White's Cottage, High St, Damerham, Fordingbridge SP6 3EU; Tel (01725) 3326

Wirral
J.S. Williamson Wirral Professional Development Centre, Acre La, Bromborough, Wirral L62 7BZ; Tel 0151-346 1182; Home 'Lindores' 35 Wood La, Greasby, Wirral L49 2PT; Tel: 0151-677 6310

Wolverhampton
E.S. Bechler ATL Office: Graisley Centre, Graisley Hill, Wolverhampton WV2 4NE; Tel (01902) 21158; Pendeford High School, Marsh La, Wolverhampton WV10 6SG; Tel: (01902) 397613; Fax: (01902) 783748; Home 10 Greaves Cres, Willenhall, West Midlands WV12 5AJ

National Association of Head Teachers

1 Heath Sq, Boltro Rd, Haywards Heath, W Sussex RH16 1BL; Tel (01444) 458133; Fax (01444) 416326
President John McNicholas, MEd Molescroft CP School, St Leonard's Rd, Beverley, N Humberside HU17 7HF; Tel (01482) 861762 and West Garth, Main St, Sigglesthorne, N Humberside HU11 5QA; Tel/Fax (01964) 535599
Vice-President George Varnawa 21 Hugo Rd, London N19 5EU; Tel 0171-607 5825; Fax 0171-609 8021
Ex-President Pat Partington, BA, FRSA Bramcote Hills Primary School, Moor La, Bramcote Hills, Beeston, Nottingham NG9 3GE; Tel (0115) 925 8644; 48 Balmoral Dr, Bramcote Hills, Beeston, Nottingham NG9 3FU; Tel: (0115) 224949
National Treasurer Esme Corner, MSc, DipEd Heacham Middle School, College Dr, Heacham, Kings Lynn, Norfolk PE31 7JY; Tel (014855) 72699; Fax (014855) 72367; Meadow Cottage, Church La, Heacham, Kings Lynn, Norfolk PE31 7HJ; Tel/Fax (014855) 72179
General Secretary David M. Hart, OBE, FRSA
Deputy General Secretary David A. Burbidge, BA, FRSA

Council Members

District 1A–County of Northumberland; Metropolitan Districts of Gateshead, Newcastle upon Tyne, North Tyneside, South Tyneside, Sunderland
Council Member R. Fisk, MEd, DAES Coquet High School, Acklington Rd, Amble by the Sea, Morpeth, Northumberland NE65 0NG; Tel (01665) 710636; Overdale, Hillside Rd, Rothbury, Morpeth, Northumberland NE65 7YG; Tel/Fax (0669) 20495

District 1B–Counties of Cleveland and Durham
Council Member T.F. Williams, BSc, PGCE, FCollP, MBIM Sedgefield Community College, Sedgefield, Stockton on Tees, Cleveland TS21 3DD; Tel (01740) 620288; Fax (01740) 622988; North View, North St, Ferryhill, Co Durham DL17 8HX; Tel (01740) 651403

District 1C–County of Cumbria
Council Member J.R. Francis Stramongate Primary School, Blackhall Rd, Kendal, Cumbria LA9 4BT; Tel (01539) 722160; Fax (01539) 734020 and The Bield, Princes Way, Heversham, Milnthorpe LA7 7EE; Tel (015395) 63170

District 2A–County of Cheshire; Metropolitan Districts of Stockport, Manchester, Trafford
Council Member T.J. Weston Shavington Primary School, Southbank Ave, Shavington, Crewe CW2 5BP; Tel (01270) 661527; Fax (01270) 650567; 2 Broadleigh Way, Wistaston, Crewe CW2 6TT; Tel: (01270) 662887

District 2B–Metropolitan Districts of Knowsley, Liverpool, St Helens, Sefton, Wirral; Other Authorities: Isle of Man
Council Member Donald Craig Joseph Williams JMI School, Naylorsfield Dr, Liverpool L25 2RH; Tel 0151-487 0811 and 51 Bryanston Rd; Liverpool L17 7AL; Tel 0151-728 7481

District 2C–Metropolitan Districts of Bolton, Bury, Salford, Oldham, Tameside, Wigan
Council Member J. Hatch St Bede's CEP School, Morris Gr La, Bolton, Lancs BL3 3LT; Tel (01204) 61899; Fax (01204) 61344; Netherbarrow Fm, East Lancashire Rd, Glazebury, Warrington, Ches WA3 5QL; Tel/Fax (01942) 262336

District 2D–County of Lancashire; Metropolitan District of Rochdale
Council Member N.E. Thornley, BSc, PGCE, ADvDipEd, MEd Fearns High School, Fearns Moss, Bacup, Lancs; Tel (01706) 873896; Fax (01706) 875029; 28 Heywood Hall Rd, Heywood, Lancs OL10 4UU; Tel/Fax: (01706) 360755

District 3A–County of North Yorkshire (Harrogate and Skipton Education Areas); Metropolitan Districts of Bradford, Calderdale, Kirklees, Leeds
Council Member A.D. Parker Lilycroft First School, Lilycroft Rd, Bradford, W. Yorks BD9 5AD; Tel (01274) 543357; Fax (01274) 543357; 23 Warren Pk, Hove

Hedge, Brighouse, W. Yorks HD6 2RR; Tel/Fax (01484) 716920 (send mail to school address)

District 3B–Metropolitan Districts of Barnsley, Doncaster, Rotherham, Sheffield, Wakefield
Council Member E.C. Paver, ACP Intake First School, Sidney Rd, Intake, Doncaster DN2 6EW; Tel (01302) 344743; Fax (01302) 360811; 113 Warning Tongue La, Bessacarr, Doncaster DN4 6TB; Tel (01302) 530706

District 3C–Counties of North Humberside (East Riding and Hull Education Areas) and North Yorkshire (Northern Dales, Ryedale, Scarborough, Whitby and York Education Areas)
Council Member J. McNicholas, MEd Molescroft CP School, St Leonard's Rd, Beverley, N Humberside HU17 7HF; Tel (01482) 861762; West Garth, Main St, Sigglesthorne, N Humberside HU11 5QA; Tel/Fax: (01964) 535599

District 4A–Counties of Dyfed, Gwent, Mid Glamorgan, South Glamorgan, West Glamorgan
Council Member D. Allan Jones, BEd, MEd Penybont Primary School, Minerva St, Bridgend, Mid Glamorgan CF31 1TD; Tel (01656) 652609; Fax (01656) 648409; 40 Danygraig Ave, Porthcawl, Mid Glamorgan CF36 5AA; Tel (01656) 785817

District 4B–Counties of Clwyd, Gwynedd, Powys
Council Member Mrs M. Morgan, BEd, MEd Cornist Pk CP School, Cornist Dr, Flint, Clwyd CH6 5HJ; Tel (01352) 735657; Fax (01352) 730438; Arthog, Cefn Bychan Rd, Pantymwyn, Mold CH7 5EN; Tel (01352) 740385

District 5A–County of Hereford and Worcester; Metropolitan Districts of Birmingham and Dudley
Council Member D. Shipton Westminster St Peters, College Rd, Saltley, Birmingham B8 3TE; Tel 0121-486 2984; Fax 0121-327 6560

District 5B–Counties of Leicestershire, Northamptonshire, Warwickshire; Metropolitan Districts of Coventry, Solihull
Council Member R.W. Hewins, DipEd Holliers Walk CP School, Holliers Walk, Hinckley, Leicester LE10 1PL; Tel (01455) 610186 (NAHT line); Fax (01455) 250915; 99 Gwendoline Dr, Countesthorpe, Leicester LE8 5SJ; Tel (0116) 2775926

District 5C–Counties of Shropshire, Staffordshire; Metropolitan Districts of Sandwell, Walsall, Wolverhampton
Council Member Paul Henbury Brookhouse Green Primary School, Wellfield Rd, Bucknall, Stoke on Trent, Staffs ST2 0DP; Tel (01782) 281122; Fax (01782) 205013; The Croft, Picadilly La, Upper Mayfield, Ashbourne, Derbys DE6 2HP; Tel: (01335) 346103; Mobile (0585) 708990

District 6A–Counties of South Humberside and Lincolnshire
Council Member M.G. Cartwright, BA, MEd, LCP, FCollP, DipTh, ALBC, FRSA St Wulfram's CE High School, Queensway, Grantham, Lincs NG31 9RA; Tel (01476) 590565 (NAHT line); Fax (01476) 70140; Mijoy, 30 Welby Gdns, Grantham, Lincs NG31 8BN; Tel/Fax (01476) 71063

District 6B–Counties of Derbyshire and Nottinghamshire
Council Member P. Partington, BA, FRSA Bramcote Hills Primary School, Moor La, Bramcote Hills, Beeston, Nottinghamshire NG9 3GE; Tel (0115) 925 8644; 48 Balmoral Dr, Bramcote Hills, Beeston, Nottingham NG9 3FU; Tel/Fax: (0115) 922 4949

District 7A– Counties of Cambridgeshire, Norfolk, Suffolk
Information not available at time of going to press.

District 7B–Counties of Bedfordshire and Hertfordshire; Outer London Boroughs of Barnet, Enfield, Haringey, Waltham Forest
Council Member C.A. Pidgeon Wheatfields Junior School, Downes Rd, St Albans, Herts AL4 9NT; Fax (01727) 810058 (NAHT line); 4 Mafeking Rd, Enfield, Middlesex EN1 3SS; Tel 081-364 6283

District 7C–County of Essex; Outer London Boroughs of Barking and Dagenham, Havering, Newham, Redbridge
Council Member Jenny Crockett, AdvDipEd St Andrew's Infant School, Hickory Ave, Greenstead, Colchester CO4 3QJ; Tel (01206) 864510; Fax (01206) 792995 and 14 Foundry Lane, Copford, Colchester, Essex CO6 1BH; Tel/Fax (01206) 212884

District 8A–Inner London Boroughs (North of Thames); Camden, Hackney, Hammersmith & Fulham, Islington, Kensington & Chelsea, London (City), Tower Hamlets, Westminster
Council Member M. Russell Malmsbury Junior School, Coborn St, Bow, London E3 2AB; Tel 0181-980 1591; 5 Dacre Cl, Chigwell Essex IG7 5HQ; Tel/Fax 081-501 0497

District 8B–Inner London Boroughs (South of Thames); Greenwich, Lambeth, Lewisham, Southwark, Wandsworth
Council Member G. Varnava, LesL, FIL 21 Hugo Rd, London N19; Tel 0171-607 5825; Fax 0171-609 8021

District 9A–Counties of Buckinghamshire and Oxfordshire; Outer London Boroughs of Brent, Ealing, Harrow, Hillingdon, Hounslow, Richmond
Council Member J.C. White, BEd New Bradwell C School, Bounty St, New Bradwell, Milton Keynes MK13 0BQ; Tel (01908) 312244; Fax (01908) 222869; 36 The Craven, Heelands, Milton Keynes, Bucks MK13 7NJ; Tel/Fax (01908) 225867

District 9B–Counties of Berkshire and Surrey; Outer London Boroughs of Croydon, Kingston upon Thames, Merton, Sutton
Council Member Michael Round, JP, BA, CertEd, MBM, FRSA, FRA Haling Manor High School, Kendra Hall Rd, South Croydon CR2 6DT; Tel 0181-681 1141/2/3; Fax 0181-681 1144; Bula Matra, 205 Sanderstead Rd, South Croydon CR2 0PN; Tel 0181-657 5710/2572

District 10A–County of Kent, Outer London Boroughs of Bexley, Bromley, Havering
Council Member C.E. Spear, BEd(Hons), MA Staplehurst CP School, Gybbon Rise, Staplehurst, Tonbridge, Kent TN12 0LZ; Tel (01580) 893747 (NAHT Line); Fax (01580) 891291; Cobwebs, Mill La, Smarden, Ashford, Kent TN27 8NN; Tel/Fax (01233) 770350

District 10B–Counties of East Sussex and West Sussex
Council Member John Kenward Bourne CP School, Melbourne Rd, Eastbourne, E Sussex BN22 8BD; Tel (01323) 724729; Fax (01323) 411638; Brown Cottage, Glynleigh Rd, Hankham, East Sussex BN24 5BJ; Tel/Fax (01323) 764334

District 10C–Counties of Hampshire and Isle of Wight; Other Authorities–Guernsey, Jersey
Council Member G. Wilson, BSc(Econ) John Hanson School, Croye Cl, Andover, Hants SP10 3AB; Tel (01264) 352546; Fax (01264) 339685; Tollgate, 67 High St, Overton, Basingstoke RG25 3HQ; Tel/Fax: (01256) 770648

District 11A–Counties of Avon, Gloucestershire, Somerset
Council Member John Massey, DLC, LCP, DipSMS, AdvDipEd Pill CE VC Junior School, Westward Dr, Pill, Bristol BS20 0JP; Tel (01275) 372508; Fax (01275) 375562; Clandown, 5 Walnut Cl, Easton in Gordane, Bristol BS20 OPW; Tel: (01275) 374663; Fax: (01275) 374519

District 11B–Counties of Dorset and Wiltshire
Council Member Sid Willcocks, BEd(Hons), FCollP The Epiphany School, Shillingstone Dr, Bournemouth BH9 3PE; Tel (01202) 530706 (NAHT line); Fax (01202) 547377; 18 Lone Pine Dr, West Parley, Dorset BH22 8LS; Tel: (01202) 897824; Fax: (01202) 861561

District 11C–Counties of Cornwall and Devon, The Isles of Scilly
Council Member David W. Blackford, BSc, FCollP Schools Liaison Officer, Fal Bldg, New County Hall, Truro TR1 3AY; Tel (01872) 323505; Fax (01872) 323500; 11 Hendras Parc, Carbis Bay, St Ives, Cornwall TR26 2TT; Tel/Fax: (01736) 795090

District 12–Northern Ireland
Council Member D. Mehaffey, MA, DipEDEXS Fleming Fulton Special School, Upper Malone Rd, Belfast BT9 6TY; Tel (01232) 613877; Fax (01232) 627975; 14 Edgcumbe Gdns, Belfast BT4 2EG; Tel/Fax: (01232) 656116

National Association of Schoolmasters Union of Women Teachers (NASUWT)

Registered Offices and Administrative Headquarters, Hillscourt Education Centre, Rose Hill, Rednal, Birmingham B45 8RS; Tel 0121-453 6150
President Roger Kirk, BA
Ex-President John Rowland, BA
Senior Vice-President Olwyn Gunn
Junior Vice-President Peter Cole
Hon Treasurer Mick Carney
General Secretary Nigel de Gruchy, BA
Deputy General Secretary Eamonn O'Kane, MA, DipEd
Assistant General Secretary Bill Herron, BSc(Econ)
Assistant Secretary (Salaries) Brian Clegg, BSc
Assistant Secretary (Education) Henry Iven, BA(Hons)
Assistant Secretary (Recruitment) Barry Gandy

Negotiating and Federation Secretaries

Avon
G.R. Owen 82 Brockley Cres, Bleadon Hill, Weston-Super-Mare BS24 9LG; Tel (01934) 853140

Bedfordshire
T.C. Ramsden 3 Ivester Crt, Leighton Buzzard, Beds LU7 7NN; Tel (01525) 382543

Berkshire
K. Murphy PO Box 514, Windsor, Berks SL4 3HF; Tel (01753) 840400

Buckinghamshire
J.W.M. Hollis 'Beechbrook', 12 Farriers Mead, Wendlebury, Bucks OX6 8PW; Tel (01869) 252581

Cambridgeshire
D.W. Wright 4 Prestland, Market Deeping, Peterborough PE6 8DT; Tel (01778) 342248

Cheshire
A. Forster 79 Whitehouse La, Nantwich, Cheshire CW5 6HG; Tel (01270) 626570

Cleveland
N. Ogden Spout Hse, Moorsholm, Saltburn TS12 3JH; Tel (01287) 660462

Cornwall
D.L. Buttivant Dene Ct, Trenance, Mawgan Porth, Newquay TR8 4BY; Tel (01637) 860627

Cumbria
G.A. Reay 31 Kelvin Gr, Morton, Carlisle CA2 6HE; Tel (01228) 591047

Derbyshire
P. Hunt 15 Park News, Church St, Riddings, Derbyshire DE55 4D8; Tel (01773) 608056

Devon
J. Ramsey Beech Dene, 5 Rundell Rd, Newton Abbot, Devon TQ12 2PJ; Tel (01626) 68144

Dorset
A.J. Middlemas 5 High St, Winfrith, Dorchester, Dorset DT2 8JW; Tel (01305) 853295

Durham
M. Lyons 20 Broomside La, Belmont, Durham DH1 2HR; Tel (0191) 384 8340

East Sussex
R.E. Bellingham 24 Downs View Rd, Seaford, E Sussex BN25 4PT; Tel (01323) 893381

Essex
A. Aldsworth 18 Milton Cres, Gants Hill, Ilford, Essex IG2 6DN; Tel 0181-220 8602

Gloucestershire
R.J. Harris Ferndale, Selsley Rd, North Woodchester, Stroud, Glos GL5 5PH; Tel (0145 38) 72317

Hampshire
M. Stephens 15 Manor Rd, Verwood, Wimborne, Dorset BH21 6DS; Tel (01202) 822992

Hereford & Worcester
P.L. Crosher Rydal Lodge, 38 Somerleyton Ave, Kidderminster, Worcs DY10 3AS; Tel (01562) 515255

Hertfordshire
I.J. Gibson 3 Wimborne Gr, Watford, Herts WD2 3JE; Tel (01923) 224025

Humberside
J. Needham 35 Brumby Wood La, Scunthorpe, Humberside DN17 1AA; Tel (01724) 857275

Isle of Wight
D. Porter Woodbury, Lingwood Hill, nr Yarmouth, Isle of Wight PO41 9XP; Tel (01983) 760636

Kent
A.V. Craig 56 Spratling St, Ramsgate, Kent CT12 5AL; Tel (01843) 587729

Lancashire
M.J. Harrison 4 Vicarage Ave, Padiham, Lancs BB12 8JY; Tel (01282) 76295

Leicester
J. Mark 10 Maidwell Cl, Wigston Magna, Leicester LE8 1WV; Tel (0116) 288 3536

Lincolnshire
J. Maddison 3 Auden Cl, off Lee Rd, Lincoln LN2 4BS; Tel (01522) 525129

Norfolk
M. Keable 22 Ashwood Cl, Caister-on-Sea, Great Yarmouth NR30 5RF; Tel (01493) 728474

North Yorkshire
G.I. Ibbetson Fern Lea, Normanby, Whitby, N Yorks; Tel (01947) 880520

Northampton
I.J. Byrnes 47 Oakleas Rise, Thrapstone, Kettering, Northants NN4 4JZ; Tel (01832) 732002

Northumberland
A. Symonds 2 Simonside Cl, Kirkhill Est, Morpeth NE61 2XY; Tel (01670) 514588

Nottinghamshire
Ms M. Hartford 3 Amot Hill Rd, Arnold, Nottingham NG5 6LJ; Tel (0115) 926 4994

Oxford
C.D. Harris 10 Wittenham Cl, Wallingford, Oxford OX10 8JY; Tel (01491) 39057

Shropshire
B.C. Oakley 10 Severn Way, Cressage, Shrewsbury, Shropshire SY5 6DS; Tel (01952) 510546

Somerset
F.W. Redford The Cottage, Broad St, Charlton Adam, Somerton, Somerset TA11 7AT; Tel (01458) 223710

Staffordshire
W.R. Howell NASUWT Office, Great Bache Ave, Penkhull, Stoke on Trent ST4 7JY; Tel (01782) 746467

Suffolk
K. Machej 30 Fitzroy St, Newmarket, Suffolk CB8 0JW; Tel (01638) 661050

Surrey
A.E. Glennon 2 Merrow Crt, Levylsdene, Merrow, Guildford, Surrey GU1 2SA; Tel (01483) 505712

Warwickshire
A. Arthur Feldon Hill La, Cleeve Prior, Evesham, Worcs WR11 5JZ; Tel (01789) 778469

West Sussex
M.N. Brayshaw, JP 58 Upper Brighton Rd, Worthing, W Sussex BN14 9HT; Tel (01903) 39753

Wiltshire
P.A. Smith Hill Grove Cott, 79 Pickwick Rd, Corsham, Wilts SN13 9BJ; Tel (01249) 713770

London (Inner)

Camden/Westminster
C.B. Clifton-Dey Flat 35 Southside Carleton Rd, London N7 0GH

Greenwich
R.G. Moore 35 Domberg Rd, Blackheath, London SE3 7BZ; Tel 0181-858 9829

Hackney
T.G.N. Jones 54 Southwell Gr, Leytonstone, London E11 4PP; Tel 0181-539 4836

Islington
Refer to London Office NASUWT Nunhead Centre, Peckham Rye School, Whorlton Rd, London SE15 3PD; Tel 0181-858 9829

Lewisham
M. Johnson 44a Amyruth Rd, Crofton Pk, London SE4 1HQ; Tel 0181-690 3266

Lambeth
K. Waterhouse 103 Birch Hanger Rd, South Norwood, London SE25 5RH; Tel 0181-656 7674

Southwark
B.M. Bishop 8 Honor Oak Rd, London SE23 3SF; Tel 0181-699 2070

Tower Hamlets
S. Searson 13 Young Rd, Custom Hse, London E16 3RP; Tel 0171-474 4560

Wandsworth
M. Richardson 96 Sheepcote La, Battersea, London SW11; Tel 0171-223 0775

London (Outer)

Barking/Dagenham
D.E. Moore 55 Egglefield Rd, Shooters Hill, London SE18 3HU; Tel 0181-856 8271

Barnet
A.T.E. Homes 22 Wycherley Cres, Barnet, Hert BN5 1AR; Tel 0181-440 3433

Bexley
J.W. Hughes 49 Brittains La, Sevenoaks, Kent TN13 2JP; Tel (01732) 452974

Brent
R.F. Thyer 18 Dewent Cres, Whetstone, London N20 0QQ; Tel 0181-445 6183

Bromley
N.W. Proudfoot 68 Northlands Ave, Orpington, Kent BR6 9LZ; Tel (01689) 854869

Croydon
G. Cluer 12 Bingham Rd, Addiscombe, Croydon CR0 7EB; Tel 0181-654 3146

Ealing
J.D. Hubberstey 33 Lee Rd, Perivale, Greenford, Middx UB6 7BS; Tel 0181-998 6908

Enfield
H.A. Burt 17 Trapstyle Rd, Ware, Herts SG12 0BA; Tel 0181-364 7955

Haringey
Miss S.R. Beagle 70 Woollard St, Waltham Abbey, Essex EN9 1HB; Tel (01992) 716725

Harrow
C.G. Gear 40 Kingsfield Rd, Oxhey, Herts WD1 4PS; Tel (01923) 245755

Havering
D.A. Argent 3 Mulberry Cl, Romford, Essex RM2 6DX; Tel (01708) 454039

Hillingdon
A. Howarth 13 Skylark Rd, Tatling End, Denham, Bucks UB9 4HR; Tel (01895) 832533

Hounslow
R.H. O'Neill 12 Eswyn Rd, Tooting, London SW17 8TP; Tel 0181-767 6009

Kingston
G.K. Thorogood 208 Worpole Rd, West Wimbledon, London SW20 8RH; Tel 0181-946 2792

Merton
K.J. Hickman 89 Penwortham Rd, Streatham, London SW16 6RH; Tel 0181-677 9557

Newham
M. McShea 208 Portway, Stratford, London E15 3QY; Tel 0181-472 5696

Redbridge
H.F. Banks 12 Forest Approach, Woodford Green, Essex IG8 9EW; Tel 0181-505 2012

Richmond
E. Connolly 12 Seymour Rd, Hampton Wick, Kingston KT1 4HW; Tel 0181-977 2770

Sutton
S.E. Smith 23 Pine Walk, Carshalton, Surrey SM5 4ES; Tel 0181-643 4642

Waltham Forest
A.I. Moyes 80 Orford Rd, Walthamstow, London E17 9QL; Tel 0181-521 6258

Greater Manchester

Bolton
M.B. Doyle 18 Winslow Ave, Sharples, Bolton BL1 7AX; Tel (01204) 304798

Bury
N.E. Fairclough 8 Weycroft Cl, Breightmet, Bolton BL2 6TP; Tel (01204) 383914

Manchester
H.W. Spooner NASUWT, Prince of Wales Bldg, 4 Newton St, Manchester M1 2AW; Tel 0161-228 1300

Oldham
P. Patterson 43 Top St, Greenacres, Oldham, Lancs OL4 2DR; Tel 0161-624 9639

Rochdale
C.P. Clissold 141 Hereford Way, Middleton, Manchester M24 2NL; Tel 0161-643 7560

Salford
J.H. Langley 140 Light Oaks Rd, Salford, Greater Manchester M6 8WL; Tel 0161-737 2953

Stockport
P. McCloughlin 44 Chatsworth Rd, Hazel Grove, Stockport SK7 6BT; Tel 0161-487 4095

Tameside
P.A. Goode 22 Four Lanes, Mottram, Hyde, Cheshire SK14 6PP; Tel (01457) 762056

Trafford
P.J. Davis 57 Victoria Ave, Didsbury, Manchester M20 8QX; Tel 0161-445 6988

Wigan
S.L. Wilson 536 Atherton Rd, Hindley Grn, Wigan WN2 4LY; Tel (01942) 701150

Merseyside
Knowsley
J.M. Reilly 45 Hampton Dr, Cronton, Widnes, Cheshire WA8 9DA; Tel 0151-424 6002

Liverpool
J.J. Snape 136 Stuart Rd, Walton, Liverpool L4 5QY; Tel 0151-724 1724

St Helens
W.D. Bradbury 2 Clifton Rd, Birchley, Billinge, nr Wigan WN5 7TP; Tel (01744) 894213

Sefton
D.A. Griffiths Strathdene, High La, Ormskirk, Lancs L40 7SL; Tel (01695) 576744

Wirral
J.N. Reilly 4 Devizes Dr, Irby, Wirral, Merseyside L61 2XL; Tel 0151-648 2926

South Yorks
Barnsley
S. Davies 11 Bradwell Ave, Dodworth, Barnsley S75 3QU; Tel (01226) 299696

Doncaster
M. Goddard 4 North Moor Dr, Walkeringham, Doncaster DN10 4LN; Tel (01427) 890455

Rotherham
F. Ramsbottom 272 Wickersley Rd, Rotherham, S Yorks S60 4JR; Tel (01709) 362404

Sheffield
D. Battye 136 Langsett Ave, Sheffield, Yorks S6 4AD; Tel (0114) 234 9952

Tyne & Wear
Gateshead
M. Brennan Westview, 129 Spoot La, Washington NE37 2UD; Tel 0191-416 6582

Newcastle
J.K. Hall 59 Stannington Rd, North Shields NE29 7JX; Tel 0191-259 0934

North Tyneside
G.T. Dawson 29 Helde Ave, Blythe, Northumberland NE24 3TP; Tel (01670) 361121

South Tyneside
A. Porter 11 Coventry Way, Fellgate Est, Jarrow NE32 4TQ; Tel 0191-489 5317

Sunderland
M.J. Johnson 15 Calderwood Cres, Low Fell, Gateshead NE9 6PU; Tel 0191-487 5194

West Midlands
Birmingham
C. Keates NASUWT Office, Maypole Business Centre, Maypole La, Birmingham B14 5JT; Tel 0121-430 2878

Coventry
D.A. Sedgwick 8 Axminster Cl, Horestone Grange, Nuneaton CV11 6YP; Tel (01203) 375178

Dudley
E. Todd 15 Ludford Rd, Bartley Grn, Birmingham B32 3PG; Tel (01384) 69834

Sandwell
P.I. Cole 35 Springfield Ave, Wollescote, Stourbridge, West Midlands DY9 3XU; Tel 0121-555 6351

Solihull
J.L. Earl 8 Grange Fm, Bearley, Stratford on Avon CV37 0SE; Tel (01564) 779719

Walsall
I.G. Crossland NASUWT, Pelsall School, Pelsall La, Rushall WS41 1NG; Tel (01922) 694901

Wolverhampton
G.W. Harries NASUWT Office, The Graiseley Centre, Pool St, Graiseley WV1 4JL; Tel (01902) 312185

West Yorks
Bradford
I.M. Davey "Brandelhow", 20 Manscombe Rd, Allerton, Bradford BD15 7AE; Tel (01274) 821356

Calderdale
C. Grunstein 15 Saville Cls, Clifton, Brighthouse, West Yorks HD6 4JW; Tel (01484) 513397

Kirklees
S.A. Brook NASUWT, Deighton High Bldgs, Deighton Rd, Huddersfield HD2 1JP; Tel (01484) 513397

Leeds
J. Jackson 10 Cawley Garth, Heckmondwike, W Yorks WF16 0QA; Tel (01924) 401160

Wakefield
B. Garvey 11 Greenfields, Pollington, Goole, North Humberside DN14 0UG; Tel (0113) 282 7441

Wales
Clwyd
W.D. Smith Bodlondes, Holywell, Clwyd CH8; Tel (01352) 780522

Dyfed
G. Davies 9 Glenafon, Panteg Rd, Aberaeron, Dyfed SA46 0EW; Tel (01545) 570150

Gwent
M. Rees 15 St Andrews Ave, Chepstow, Gwent NP6 5LD; Tel (01291) 624518

Gwynedd
V. Rowlands Fron, Pen-Y-Berth, Llanfairpwll, Gwynedd LL61 5YT; Tel (01248) 714173

Mid Glamorgan
P. O'Donnell 10 Coed yr Esgob, Llantrisant, Mid Glam CF7 8EL; Tel (01443) 224714

Powys
S.M. Dawkins 22 Derwen Fawr, Crickhowell, Powys NP8 1DP; Tel (01873) 810071

South Glamorgan
J.R. Phillips 21 Avonridge, Thornhill, Cardiff CF4 9AU; Tel (01222) 692809

West Glamorgan
A.H. Hughes 5 Padleys Cl, Garth, Maesteg, Mid Glam CF34 0TX; Tel (01656) 734603

Other authorities
Guernsey
W.A. Holland La Pouquelaye, Les Prins Est, Vale, Guernsey, CI; Tel (01481) 55129

Jersey
M. Kielty Flat 4, Appart De Pierre, Trinity Hill, St Helier, Jersey JE2 4NJ; Tel (01534) 66948

Isle of Man
A.J. Miller 5 Peveril Terr, Peel, Isle of Man; Tel (01624) 842995

Isle of Scilly
J.P. Hanley Poltair, Church St, St Marys, Isle of Scilly TR21 0JT; Tel (01720) 422640

National Primary Teacher Education Conference (NaPTEC)

University of Greenwich, School of Primary and Secondary Education, Mansion Site, Avery Hill Campus, Bexley Rd, Eltham SE9 2PQ; Tel 0181-316 9432/9500
Chair Jack Hogbin The Manchester Metropolitan University, School of Education, 799 Wilmslow Rd, Manchester M20 8RR
Deputy Chair Leslie James Dept of Science and Technology Education, University of Reading, Bulmershe Court, Earley, Reading RH6 1HY
Secretary Robert Young University of Greenwich, School of Primary and Secondary Education, Avery Hill Campus, Bexley Rd, London SE9 2PQ; Tel 0181-316 9432/9500
Treasurer and Membership Secretary John Bushell University College of Ripon & York, St John College Rd, Ripon HG4 2QX; Tel (01765) 602691

National Union of Teachers (NUT)

Hamilton Hse, Mabledon Pl, London WC1H 9BD; Tel 0171-388 6191; Fax 0171-387 8458
President J. Bills
Vice-President C. Regan
Ex-President S. Sinnott
Hon Treasurer A. Moran
General Secretary Doug N. McAvoy
Deputy General Secretary Vacancy
Assistant Secretary (Education and Equal Opportunities) J. Bangs
Assistant Secretary (Salaries, Conditions of Service and Superannuation) G.B. Fawcett
Assistant Secretary (Accountant) A.G. Wills
Assistant Secretary (Membership and Communications) A. Jarman
Assistant Secretary (Legal and Professional Services) K. Thompson
Assistant Secretary (Organisation and Administration) D. Macfarlane

Regional Councils & Federations

Northern Regional Council
Chair M. Dann 8 Yukon Gdns, Longlands, Middlesborough TS4 2NL
Secretary T.M. Buckler NUT Regional Office, Auckland Hse, High Claire, Chester-le-Street DH3 3PX
Treasurer W. Muir 180 Doncaster Rd, Sandyford, Newcastle-upon-Tyne NE6 5RE

North West Regional Council
Chair A. Wingate 55 Harden Hills, Shaw, Oldham OL2 8NE
Secretary R. Palframan NUT Regional Office, 25 Chorley New Rd, Bolton BL1 4QR; Tel (0124) 21434
Treasurer E. Ritson 63 Station Rd, Woolton, Liverpool L25 3PY

Yorkshire/Midlands Regional Council
Chair P. Harris 38 Calverly La, Horsforth, Leeds LS18 4EE
Secretary M. Anderson NUT Regional Office, 7/9 Chequer Rd, Doncaster DN1 2AA

Eastern Regional Council
Chair I. Bourne 124 Thorndon Ave, W. Horndon, Brentwood, Essex CB13 3TR
Secretary A. Ward NUT Regional Office, Peel Hse, Falmouth Ave, Newmarket, Suffolk CB8 0NB
Treasurer R.J. Russell 3 Manorside, Dersingham, Kings Lyn, Norfolk PE31 6LE

South East Regional Council
Chair D. Butler 6 Glenleigh Ave, Bexhill-on-Sea, East Sussex
Secretary R. Boland NUT Regional Office, 14–16 Sussex Rd, Haywards Heath RH16 4EA

South-Western Federation
Chair A. Johnson 8 The Maples, Cirencester, Glos GL7 1TQ
Secretary R. Card NUT Regional Office, 1–5 Lover Ave, Heavitree, Exeter, Devon EX1 2PR; Tel (01392) 580028
Treasurer J. Pearce 5 Marshfield Pk, Downend, Bristol BS16 2TA

London West Regional Council
Chair C. Blower 62 Cobbold Rd, London W12 9LW
Secretary S Cankett London West Regional Office, Bemco Hse, Bridge End Rd, London SW19 1TW; Tel 0181-874 0034
Treasurer D. North 7 Telford Ave, London SW2 4XJ

London East Regional Council
Chair B. Ghale Ben Jonson Rd, Stepney Grn, London E1 4SD
Secretary T. Harrison NUT Regional Office, 267 Cranbrook Rd, Ilford, Essex IG1 4TD; Tel 0181-554 5525
Treasurer P. Cronan 73 Devanay Rd, Stratford, London E15 4AZ

Secretaries

Tyne & Wear Metropolitan County

Newcastle-upon-Tyne
Secretary T.A. Denholm 23 King Edward Rd, Heaton, Newcastle-upon-Tyne, Tyne & Wear NE6 5RE; Tel 0191-265 9687; Kenton CS, Drayton Rd, Newcastle-upon-Tyne NE3 3RU

North Tyneside
Secretary S. Best 114 Weardale Ave, Forest Hall, Newcastle-upon-Tyne, Tyne & Wear NE12 OJA; Tel 0191-266 5128

Gateshead Metropolitan Division
Gateshead
Secretary D. Jackson 5 North View Terrace, Birches Nook, Stocksfield, Northumberland NE34 7JN; Tel (01661) 843125; Joicey Rd SpS, Joicey Rd, Gateshead, Tyne & Wear NE9 5AT; Tel: 0191-487 6186

South Tyneside Metropolitan Division
South Tyneside
Joint Secretary D. Johnson 140 King George Rd, South Shields, Tyne & Wear NE34 0ET
Joint Secretary M. Skevington 90 Beckenham Ave, East Boldon, Tyne & Wear NE36 0EQ

Wearside Metropolitan Division
Wearside Teachers' Association
Secretary H.W. Brown 2 South View, Haswell, Co Durham DH6 2ED; Tel (01850) 195506

West Yorkshire Metropolitan County

Bradford Metropolitan Division
Bradford District
Secretary J. Murch 67 Aireville Rd, Frizinghall, Bradford BD9 4HN; Tel (01274) 771090

Calderdale Metropolitan Division
Calderdale
Secretary I. Buckley 23 Mill Bank Cl, Triangle, Sowerby Bdge, West Yorks HX6 3HB; Tel (01422) 822567

Kirklees Metropolitan Division
Kirklees Teachers
Secretary H.E. Roberts 22 Huddersfield Rd, Holmfirth, Huddersfield HD7 1JS; Tel (01484) 682959

Leeds Metropolitan Division
Leeds Area
Secretary T. Hales 14 Trinity Pl, Bingley BD16 2PR; Tel (01274) 562453

Wakefield Metropolitan Division
Wakefield Teachers
Secretary G. Pygott 'Caravelle', 36 Carrs La, Cudworth, Barnsley, S. Yorks S72 8EJ; Tel (01226) 714174; Moorthorpe Firs, Regent St, Moorthorpe, South Elmsall, Pontefract WF9 2BI; Tel: (01977) 642987

South Yorkshire Metropolitan County

Barnsley Metropolitan Division
Barnsley
Secretary P.S. Bevis NUT Office, 15 Manchester Rd, Thurlstone, Sheffield S30 6QR; Tel (01226) 765930; Fax (01226) 765930; St Hilda's JS, Laithes La, Barnsley S71 3AF; Tel: (01266) 288675

Doncaster Metropolitan Division
Doncaster & District
Secretary P. Morley 105 Warning Tongue La, Bessacar, Doncaster DN4 6TB; Tel (01302) 532022

Sheffield Metropolitan Division
Sheffield
Secretary D. Tucker 33 Bowood Rd, Sheffield S11 8YF; Tel (01742) 641251

Rotherham Metropolitan Division
Rotherham
Secretary D. Bates 2 Three Hills Cl, Rotherham, South Yorkshire S65 4PH; Tel (01709) 850103; Swinton CS, East Ave, Swinton, Mesborough S64 8JW; Tel: (01709) 570586/7

Greater Manchester Metropolitan County

Wigan Metropolitan Division
Wigan
Secretary G.C. Kemp 11 Elgin Ave, Garswood, Ashton in Makerfield, Wigan, Lancs WN4 ORH; Tel (01942) 717090; NUT Office (01942) 825147; Lamberhead Green CIS, 121 Kershaw St, Lamberhead Green, Orrell, Wigan, Lancs WN5 OAW; Tel: (01942) 214080

Bolton Metropolitan Division
Bolton
Secretary C. Wright 8 Moorside Ave, Smithills, Bolton, Greater Manchester BL1 6BE; Tel (01204) 840121

Bury Metropolitan Division
Bury Metropolitan Teachers
Secretary H. Andrews 81 Heights Ave, Rochdale, Greater Manchester OL12 6JH; Tel (01706) 30143; Derby Hs, Radcliffe Rd, Bury BL9 9NH; Tel: 0161-764 1819

Rochdale Metropolitan Division
Rochdale
Secretary P. Matthews 10 Wimbourne Ave, Chadderton, Oldham, Greater Manchester OL9 OBR; Tel 0161-652 2284; Hopwood Hall College, Rochdale Rd, Middleton, Manchester M24 3XH; Tel: 0161-643 7560 ext 232

Salford Metropolitan Division
Salford
Secretary J. Dyson 29 Simister La, Prestwich M25 5RY; Tel 0161-798 7606; Eccles HS, Northfleet Rd, Peel Green, Eccles M30 7PO; Tel: 0161-789 5339

Manchester Metropolitan Division
Manchester
Secretary J. Watters 5 Morrell Rd, Northendon, Manchester M22 4WJ; Tel 0161-998 4795

Oldham Metropolitan Division
Oldham
Secretary A. Buckley Moorlands, 5 Range Lane, Denshaw, Oldham, Greater Manchester OL3 5RZ; Tel (01457) 870626; Breeze Hill S, Roxbury Ave, Salem, Oldham OL4 5JE; Tel: 0161-624 6928

Trafford Metropolitan Division
Trafford
Secretary C. McAinsh 65 Kenmore Rd, Sale, Cheshire; Tel 0161-969 4857; Sale Girls CS, Marsland Rd, Sale, Cheshire M33 3NH; Tel: 0161-973 3217

Stockport Metropolitan Division
Stockport
Secretary M. Pollard 28 Malton Rd, Heaton Moor, Stockport, Cheshire SK4 4DE; Tel 0161-432 7232

Tameside Metropolitan Division
Tameside
Secretary M.R. Custance 5, Rothbury Ave, Ashton-under-Lyne, Greater Manchester OL7 9SQ; Tel 0161-339 2179; Corrie PS, Cemetry Rd, Denton, Tameside M34 1FG; Tel: 0161-336 4265

Merseyside Metropolitan County

Sefton Metropolitan Division
Sefton
Joint Secretary E. Ritson 74 Baldwin Ave, Childwall, Liverpool L16 3GD; Tel 0151-722 7358; Bootle HS, Brown's La, Bootle; Tel: 0151 521 1734
Joint Secretary D. Lamb 33a Victoria Rd, Freshfield, Formby L37 7DH; Tel (01704) 878700; Sefton Teachers' Centre, 225 Park Rd, Formby L37 6EW; Tel: (01704) 876220

Liverpool Metropolitan Division
Liverpool
Secretary R. Knox Liverpool NUT Office, c/o AUEU Bldgs, 46–48 Mount Pleasant, Liverpool L3 5SD; Tel 0151-707 0900

St Helens Division
St Helens
Secretary L. Merriman 3 Colburn Cl, Hawkley Hall, Wigan WN3 5RF; Tel (01942) 496755

Knowsley Division
Knowsley
Secretary S. Yates 20 Cumberland Ave, Liverpool L17 2AQ; Tel 0151-734 3529

Wirral Division
Wirral
Secretary P.E. Bishop Vyner S, Hoylake Rd, Bidston, Birkenhead, Wirral, Merseyside L43 7AU; Tel 0151-652 7093; Fax 0151-670 0641

West Midlands Metropolitan County

Wolverhampton Metropolitan Division
Wolverhampton
Secretary D. Cole Wolverhampton NUT Office, The Graiseley Centre, Pool St, Wolverhampton, West Midlands WV2 4NE; Tel (01902) 352341; Eastfield Hse, Marsh La, Fordhouses, Wolverhampton WV10 6SE; Tel: (01902) 785085

Walsall Metropolitan Division
Walsall
Secretary R. Grainger 79a Brook La, Walsall Wood, Walsall WS9 9NA; Alumwell Comms, Primley Ave, Walsall, WS2 9UA; Tel: (01922) 720741

Dudley Metropolitan Division
Dudley
Secretary S. Miller 20 Inkebarrow Rd, The Huntlands, Halesowen, West Midlands B63 4NF; Tel 0121-550 3934

Sandwell Metropolitan Division
Sandwell
Secretary R. Broadbent 31 Barnford Hill Cl, Oldbury, Warley B68 AE5; Tel 0121-544 6866; Bearwood PS, Bearwood Rd, Smethwick, Warley B66 4HB; Tel: 0121-434 4499, Fax: 0121-434 4799

Birmingham Metropolitan Division
Birmingham
Secretary M. Bailey 81 Glascote Cl, Solihull B90 2TA; Tel 0121-744 8606

Solihull Metropolitan Division
Solihull
Joint Secretary H. Greenhalgh 62 Wychwood Ave, Knowle, Solihull B93 9DQ; Tel (01564) 773550
Joint Secretary P. Tough 16 Oxford Rd, Moseley, Birmingham B13 9EH; Tel 0121-442 4382; Lode Heath S, Lode La, Solihull, West Midlands B91 2HW; Tel: 0121-704 1421

Coventry Metropolitan Division
Coventry
Joint Secretary A. Duggan 95 Stanley Rd, Earlsdon, Coventry CV5 6FG; Tel (01203) 677212; Coundon Court S, Northbrook Rd, Coundon, Coventry CV6 6DV; Tel: (01203) 335121
Joint Secretary J. Ivens 4 Gloucester St, Coventry CV1 3BZ; Tel (01203) 222041; Foxford S, Grange Rd, Coventry CV6 6DV; Tel: (01203) 367444

London West

Barnet
Secretary P. Taylor 115 Mayfield Ave, London N12 9HY; Tel 0181-446 1625; (NUT Line 0181-446 4304); Northside JMI, Albert St, North Finchley N12 8BJ; Tel: (0181-445 4730)

Brent
Secretary M. Horne 'Chatterings' Orchard Gr, Chalfont St Peter, Bucks SL9 9ET; Tel (01753) 883739

Camden
Secretary K. Courtney 65 Glenarm Rd, London E5 0LY; Tel 0181-985 8789; NUT Camden Office, 100 Stanhope St, London NW1 3JX; Tel: 0171-916 4524

Ealing
Joint Secretary J. Seacombe Ravenor F&MS, Greenford, Middx UB6 9SB
Joint Secretary 58 Haslemere Ave, Hanwell, London W13 1UL; Tel 0181-840 4914

Enfield
Secretary R.A. Gow 29 Forest Rd, Freezeywater, Enfield, Middx EN3 6ST; Essex & Albany SS, Bell La, Enfield, Middx, EN3 5PA; Tel: 0181-443 2594

Hammersmith & Fulham
Secretary C. Blower 62 Cobbold Rd, London W12 9LW; Tel 0181-749 5169

Harrow
Secretaries The Officers, Harrow Teachers' Assoc, c/o Harrow Teachers' Centre, Tudor Rd, Harrow HA3 5QD; Tel 0181-427 1291/424 3860

Hillingdon
Secretary D. Rogers 5 Bumer Cl, Sipson, W. Drayton, Middx UB7 0JP; Tel 0181-897 8221

Hounslow
Secretary S. Jenkins 58 Oakley Cl, Isleworth, Middx TW7 4HZ; Tel 0181-560 8791

Kensington & Chelsea
Secretary R. Sulatycki 97 Moore Park Rd, London SW6 2DA; Tel 0171-736 7216; Holland Park S, Airlie Grdns, London W8 7AF; Tel: 0171-727 5631

Kingston-upon-Thames
Secretary M. Darke 15 Barnfield, New Maldon, Surrey KT3 5RH; Tel 0181-949 2677

Lambeth
Secretary G. Monks 22 Drewstead Rd, Streatham, London SW16 1AB; Tel 0181-677 2812

Merton
Secretary M. Sharp 21 Moreton Rd, Worcester Park, Surrey KT4 8EY; Tel 0181-337 8707; Garth HS, Lilleshall Rd, Mordon, Surrey SN4 6DU; Tel: 0181-715 1212

Richmond-upon-Thames
Secretary P. Clayton 3 Cloister Cl, Teddington, Middx TW11 0XX; Tel 0181-977 4312; Heathfield JS, Cobbett Rd, Twickenham, Middx TW2 6EN; Tel: 0181-894 3525

Sutton
Secretary L. Warne 14 Arundel Ave, Morden, Surrey SM4 4DP; Tel 0181-395 4641; Tweeddale JS, Tweeddale Rd, Carshalton, Surrey SM5 1SR; Tel: 0181-644 5665

Wandsworth
Secretary J. Alterman 37 Archbishops Pl, London SW2 2AH; Tel 0181-671 8635; Southfields S, 333 Merton Rd, London SW18 5JU; Tel: 0181-870 0171

Westminster
Joint Secretary B. Regan WTA Office, Ebury Bridge Centre, Sutherland St, London SW1V 4LH; Tel 0171-828 0834
Joint Secretary M. Brady Flat 7, 244 Evering Rd, London E5 8AJ; Tel 0181-806 6681; North Westminster Comm S, Penfold St, London NW1 6RY; Tel: 0171-262 8000

London East

Barking & Dagenham
Secretary N. James 7 Stopford Rd, Plaistow, London E13 0LY

Bexley Division
Secretary H. Bucky 2 Broomhill Rd, Dartford, Kent DA1 3HT; Tel (01322) 224974; Welling S, Elsa Rd, Welling, Kent DA16 1LB; Tel: 0181 304 8531

Bromley
Secretary B. Calderbank 17 Falkland Pk Ave, London SE25 6SQ; Tel 0181-653 1496; Pickhurst JS, Pickhurst La, West Wickham BR4 0HL; Tel: 0181-462 5867

Croydon
Secretary D. Harvey 65 Zion Rd, Thornton Heath, Surrey CR4 8RJ; Tel 0181-683 1380; Ecclesbourne JS,

Bert Rd, Thornton Heath, Surrey CR4 7EP; Tel: 0181-684 5704

Greenwich
Secretary G. Graham 179 Herbert Rd, Plumstead, London SE18 3QE; Tel 0181-855 0643; Plumstead Manor S, Old Mill Rd, Plumstead, London SE18 1QF; Tel: 0181-855 5011

Hackney
Joint Secretary R. Rieser 78 Mildmay Gr, London N1 4PI; Tel 0171-254 3197
Joint Secretary M. McCarthy Flat 4, St James Hse, 215-217 Lower Clapton Rd, Clapton, London E5 8EY

Haringey
A. Brockman 14a Thane Villas, London N7 7PA; Tel 0181-700 3207; White Hart La CS, White Hart La, London N22 5QJ; Tel: 0181-365 3207

Havering
Secretary S. Kortlandt 91 Marlborough Gdns, Upminster, Essex RM14 1SQ; Tel (01708) 225617; Sanders Draper S, Suttons La, Hornchurch, Essex RM12 6RT; Tel: (01708) 443068

Islington
Secretary D. Murphy 20 Marlborough Rd, Bowes Parks, London N22; Tel 0181-889 5143; Holloway SS, Hilldrop S, London N7 OJG; Tel: 0171-607 5885

Lewisham
Secretary M. Powell-Davies Catford County Girls' School, Bellingham Rd, Catford SE6 2RS; Tel 0181-697 8911

London (East)
Secretary A. Kenny 31A Argyle Rd, Stepney, London E1 4EQ; Tel 0171-790 6776

Newham
Secretary P. Smith 9 Eversleigh Rd, East Ham, London E6 1HG; Tel 0181-472 7568; c/o INSEC, Credon Centre, Kirton Rd, London E13

Redbridge
Secretary M. Sanders 40 Northumberland Ave, London E12 5HD; Tel 0181-989 0408; Wanstead HS, Redbridge La West, London E11 2JS; Tel: 0181-989 2791/9755

Southwark & District
Secretary R. Tabor 28 Kerfield Cres, London SE5 8SU; Tel 0171-701 2546; Snowfields PS, Kirby Gr, London SE1 3TD; Tel: 0171-407 5194/357 7965

Waltham Forest
Secretary R. Haycock c/o JCC Education Centre, Queens Rd, London E17 8QS; Tel 0181-521 3311

SCS (NWE)

J. Fisher Rheindahlen Teachers' Centre BFPO40; Tel (01049) 2163 4722 954

Central Associations

Central Overseas Service Schools Association
Secretary (Head of Membership Department) A. Jarman NUT, Hamilton Hse, Mabledon Pl, London WCLH 9BD
Cyprus Sub-Group
Secretary J. Male The Primary S, Episkopi BFPO 53
Hong Kong Sub-Group
Secretary Vacancy

National Association of Youth & Community Education Officers
Executive Secretary J.E. Tate Cross Pk, Ringmore, Kingsbridge, South Devon TQ7 4HW; Tel (01548) 810238; Office: (01752) 221312

County Divisions

Avon
M. Plaster 4 Florence Pk, Westbury Pk, Bristol BS6 7LP; Tel (01272) 247325

Bedfordshire
Treasurer/Secretary T. Dunning 47 Harroden Rd, Bedford MK2 ORS; Tel (01234 216312); St Thomas More US, Tyne Crescent, Bedford MK41 7UL; Tel (01234 341201)

Berkshire
Secretary R. Ketley 13 Matlock Rd, Caversham, Reading, Berks RG4 7BP; Tel (01734) 476564; Highdown S, Surley Row, Emmer Grn, Reading, Berks; Tel (01734) 475022

Buckinghamshire
Secretary N.L. Miles Conifer Cottage, 9 Slated Row, Old Wolverton, Milton Keynes, Bucks MK12 5NJ; Tel (01908) 3127542; The Radcliffe S, Aylesbury St West, Wolverton, Milton Keynes, Bucks MK12 5BT; Tek (01908) 312579

Cambridgeshire
Secretary M. Slater 26 St Mary's St, Eynesbury, St Neots, Cambs PE19 2TA; Tel (01480) 476690; Ernulf CS, Eynesbury, St Neots, Cambs PE19 2SH; Tel (01480) 474748

Cheshire
Secretary J. Williams 42 Crewe Rd, Shavington, Crewe CW2 5JB; Tel (01270) 67034

Cleveland
Secretary M. Watters 2 Kestrel Hide, Guisborough, Cleveland TS14 8PF

Clwyd
Secretary G. Donaldson, BSc 18 Lon Isaf, Mold, Clwyd CH7 1XA

Cornwall
Secretary V.J. Burton White Cottage, Rosewarne Downs, Camborne, Cornwall TR14 OBD; Tel (01209) 714935; Camborne S, Cranberry Rd, Camborne, Cornwall TR14 7PJ; Tel (01209) 712280

Cumbria
Secretary J.M. Wilson 7 Parkfield, Swarthmoor, Ulverston, Cumbria LA12 OHY; Tel (01229) 52929; St James' JS, Blake St, Barrow-in-Furness, Cumbria LA14 1NY; Tel (01229) 821354

Derbyshire
Secretary C.M. Tarrant 15 Lambourne Ave, Ashbourne, Derby DE6 1BP

Devon
Secretary P. Layton 26A South Ave, Exeter EX1 2DZ; Tel (01392) 438351; Tiverton S, Bolham Rd, Tiverton, Devon EX16 6SQ; Tel: (01884) 256655

Dorset
Secretary I. Kent 62 North Allington, Bridport, Dorset DT6 5DY; Tel (01308) 24591

Durham
Secretary T. Blacklock 128 Hilda Pk, Chester-le-Street, Co Durham DH2 2JY; Tel 0191-388 3755

Dyfed
Secretary B. Nelson Llys Y Gwynt, Llangynin, St Clears, Dyfed SA33 4JZ; Tel (01994) 230036; Sir Thomas Picton CS, Queensway, Haverfordwest, Dyfed SA61 2NX; Tel: (01437) 765394

Essex
Secretary J. Glazier 85 Chalkwell Lodge, London Rd, Westcliff on Sea, Essex SSO 9HX; Tel (01702) 333444

Glamorgan (Mid)
Secretary R. Davies 'Ty Sion', Cardiff Rd, Creigiau, Cardiff CF4 8NL; Tel (01222) 890766

Glamorgan (South)
Secretary G. Lewis 29 Millbrook Cl, Dinas, Powys, S. Glamorgan C86 4DD; Tel (01222) 512299

Glamorgan (West)
Secretary P. George 39 Cambridge Rd, Langland, Swansea, W. Glamorgan SA3 4PQ; Tel (01792) 290059

Gloucestershire
Secretary A.R. Johnson 8 The Maples, Cirencester, Gloucestershire GL7 1TQ; Tel (01285) 656581; Fax (01285) 641967; Cirencester Kingshill S, Kingshill La, Cirencester, Gloucs GL7 1HS; Tel: (01285) 651511

Gwent
M. Phillips, MA 71 Badminton Gr, Ebbw Vale, Gwent NP3 5NA; Tel (01495) 303018; Ebbw Vale CS, Wainpound Rd, Ebbw Vale, Gwent NP3 6LE; Tel: (01495) 303409

Gwynedd
Secretary N. Foden 'Oakmere' 2 Queen's Gdns, Craigy-Don, Llandudno, Gwynedd LL30 1RU; Tel (01492) 870417; Friars S, Lon-y-Bryn, Eithinog, Bangor, Gwynedd; Tel (01248) 364905

Hampshire
Secretary K. Gardiner 8 Woodpath, Southsea PO5 3DX; Tel (01705) 293332

Herefordshire/Worcestershire
Secretary E.E. Simms 14 Oakland Ct, Ross-on-Wye, Herefordshire HR9 7HE; Tel (01989) 65701; John Kyle HS, Ledbury Rd, Ross on Wye, Herefordshire; Tel: (01989) 764358

Hertfordshire
Secretary J. Berry 61 Cambridge Rd, St Albans, Herts AL1 5LE; Tel (01727) 835554

Humberside
Secretary S. Green 44 Riversdale Rd, Beverley High Rd, Hull HU6 7HA

Kent
Secretary P.H. Vokes 26 Harvest Way, Singleton, Ashford, Kent TN23 5WP; Tel (01233) 645769; Thomas Aveling S, Arethusa Rd, Rochester, Kent ME1 2UW; Tel: (01634) 844809

Lancashire
Secretary F. Shuttleworth 35 Kentmere Dr, Blackburn, Lancs BB2 5HG; Tel (01254) 21931; Shadsworth JS, Arran Ave, Blackburn BB1 2ET; Tel: (01254) 698016, Office: (01254) 694440

Leicestershire
Secretary P. Town 9 Palmerston Rd, Melton Mowbray, Leics LE13 OSS; Tel (01664) 62325; Queniborough PS, Coppice Lane, Queniborough, Leics LE7 8DJ; Tel: (01533) 606700

Lincolnshire
Secretary P.E. Forman Appelgarth, Bardney Rd, Fiskerton, Lincs LN3 4HU; Tel (01526) 398316; North Kesteven S, Moor La, North Hykenham, Lincoln; Tel: (01522) 681010

Norfolk
Secretary R.J. Russell, JP 3 Manorside, Dersingham, Kings Lynn, Norfolk PE31 6LE; Tel (01485) 540522; Fairstead PS, Kings Lynn, Norfolk PE30 4RR; Tel: (01553) 774666

Northamptonshire
Secretary M.T. Johnson 181 St John's Rd, Kettering, Northants NN15 5AW; Tel (01536) 515199; St Brendans JS, Cottingham Rd, Corby, Northants NN18 OAZ; Tel: (01536) 203725

Northumberland
Secretary L. Wilkin 2 Thorp Cl, Blyth, Northumberland NE24 4PW; Tel (01670) 362135; Newsham FS, Warwick St, Blyth, Northumberland NE24 4NX; Tel: (01670) 353124

North Yorkshire
Secretary J.M. Silvester Flat 13, Walkers Fold, Union St, Knaresborough HG5 8DN; Tel (01423) 866065; King James, King James Rd, Knaresborough, North Yorks HG5 8EB; Tel: (01423) 866061

Nottinghamshire
Secretary B. Helliwell 2 Holmecroft Dr, Selston, Nottingham NG16 6EZ; Tel (01773) 810041

Oxfordshire
Secretary R. Leach 28 Pegasus Rd, Blackbird Leys, Oxford OX4 5DW; Tel (01865) 777851; Gosford Hill S, Oxford Rd, Kidlington, Oxon; OX5 2NT; Tel: (0186) 754971

Powys
Secretary G. Haslock Fir Tree Cottage, Penybont, Llandrindod Wells, Powys; Tel (01597) 851556

Shropshire
Secretary C. Hargest 58 Abbey Foregate, Shrewsbury SY2 6BQ; Tel (01742) 358865

Somerset
Secretary G. Morris Cranford, Halse, Taunton, Somerset TA4 3AB

Staffordshire
Secretary M. Davis 377 Cannock Rd, Hednesford, Cannock, Staffs WS11 2TD; Tel (01543) 426363

Suffolk
Secretary M.J. Goold 1 Gainsborough Rd, Bury St Edmunds, Suffolk IP33 3RX; Tel (01284) 763980; Thurston US, Thurston, Bury St Edmunds, Suffolk, IB31 3PB; Tel: (01259) 30885; Telex: (01359) 30880

Surrey
Secretary C. Caswell 63 Carshalton Park Rd, Carshalton, Surrey SM5 3SJ; Tel 0181-647 9200; Curriculum and Management Support Service, Runnymede Centre, Chertsey Rd, Addlestone, Surrey KT15 2EP; Tel: (01932) 569663

Sussex (East)
Secretary Dr T. Lucas 2 Friars Ct, 52–54 South Coast Rd, Peacehaven, E Sussex BN10 8SH; Tel (01273) 586777; Priory S, Mountfield Rd, Lewes, E. Sussex BN7 2XD; Tel: (01275) 576231

Sussex (West)
Secretary J. Esden 32 Wood St, Bognor Regis, W Sussex DO21 2PJ; Tel (01243) 534354; Fax (01243) 534354; Bognor Regis Comm College, Westloats La, Bognor Regis, West Sussex PO21 5LF; Tel: (01243) 864401

Warwickshire
Secretary R. Crowther 10 Clarendon St, Leamington Spa CV32 5ST; Tel (01926) 330712; Milverton Combined S, Greatmeed Rd, Leamington Spa CV32 6ES; Tel: (10926) 424043

Wiltshire
Secretary W. Hollingworth 'Callington' 12 New Zealand Ave, Salisbury, Wilts SP2 7JX; Tel (01722) 332300; Upper Avon S, Recreation Rd, Durrington, Salisbury, Wilts; Tel: (01980) 52467

Professional Association of Teachers (PAT)

2 St James' Ct, Friar Gate, Derby DE1 1BT; Tel (01332) 372337; Fax (01332) 290310/292431
Founder President R.V. Bryant
Founder President C.R. Leicester
Chairman D.T. Jones (8/94–7/95)
Past Chairman B. Wilson (8/94–7/95)
Hon Secretary E. Arnold-Davies
Hon Treasurer D. Walker
General Secetary John R. Andrews, DipSMS, FIMgt, FRSA
Deputy General Secretary Dr David Jones, PhD, BSc, ARCS, DIC
Deputy General Secretary Jackie M. Miller, GGSM, FRSA
Solicitor David J. Brierley, MA(Cantab)
Accountant Richard Willcocks, FCMA
Professional Officer (Education) Geoffrey Carver, BA
Professional Officer (Publications) Elizabeth Gabriel, BA
Professional Services Officer Alan Manasseh, BSc
Professional Officer (Tertiary Education) Antony Thompson, BSc, PGCE
Professional Officer (Legal Services) Sheila Wheatcroft

Council Members in England, Northern Ireland and I.O.M.

Area A–Northumberland, Tyne & Wear, Durham
Council Member G. Sewell; Tel (01833) 28286 (home), (01833) 650491 (school)

Area B–Cumbria, Lancashire
Council Member N. Wilson; Tel (015242) 62272 (home), (01254) 59911 (school)

Area C–Cleveland, North Yorkshire
Council Member N. Henderson; Tel (01287) 634953 (home)

Area D–Merseyside, Greater Manchester, Isle of Man
Council Member Vacancy

Area E–West Yorkshire, South Yorkshire
Council Member P. Jenkins; Tel (0114) 230 5592 (home)

Area F–Humberside, Lincolnshire
Council Member P. Withers; Tel (01482) 833184 (home), 855271 (school)

Area G–Derbyshire, Nottinghamshire, Leicestershire
Council Member Mrs J. Smedley; Tel (01509) 852247 (home), (01509) 852276 (school)

Area H–Cheshire, Staffordshire, Shropshire
Council Member Vacancy

Area J–West Midlands
Council Member J. Hetherington; Tel 0121-382 3233 (home), 0121-373 3457 (school)

Area K–Hereford and Worcester, Warwickshire, Gloucestershire
Council Member H.D.J. Nicklin; Tel (01684) 541082 (answerphone), (01684) 40277 (school)

Area L–Buckinghamshire, Oxfordshire, Berkshire
Council Member B. Matthews; Tel (01494) 437208 (home), 522141 (school)

Area M–Northamptonshire, Bedfordshire, Hertfordshire
Council Member P. Kairis; Tel (01327) 78102 (home), (01604) 716106 (school)

Area N–Cambridgeshire, Norfolk
Council Member S. Firth; Tel (01487) 822958 (home)

Area O–Essex, Suffolk
Council Member Dr R.G. Taylor; Tel (01787) 310874 (home), 375131 (school)

Area P1–Hounslow, Hillingdon, Ealing, Harrow, Brent, Barnet
Council Member Vacancy

Area P2–Enfield, Haringey, Waltham Forest, Redbridge, Newham, Barking, Havering
Council Member Vacancy

Area P3–Bexley, Bromley, Croydon, Sutton, Merton, Kingston, Richmond
Council Member J. Lovey; Tel (01372) 810636 (home)

Area Q1–Hammersmith, Kensington & Chelsea, Camden & Westminster, Islington, Lambeth, Wandsworth
Council Member Vacancy

Area Q2–Hackney, Inner City & Tower Hamlets, Greenwich, Lewisham, Southwark
Council Member Vacancy

Area R–Cornwall, Devon, Scilly Isles
Council Member J. Goffey; Tel (01837) 54389 (home), (01837) 52866 (school)

Area T–Somerset, Dorset, Channel Isles
Council Member Vacancy

Area U–Northern Ireland
Council Member S. Mulholland; Tel (01266) 43672 (home), 49534 (school)

Area V–Avon, Wiltshire
Council Member Vacancy

Area X–Hampshire, Isle of Wight
Council Member R. Griffiths; Tel (01705) 384584 (home), (01705) 829424 (school)

Area Y–Surrey, West Sussex
Council Member K. Barraclough; Tel 0181-668 2918 (home), 0181-979 5893 (school)

Area Z–Kent, East Sussex
Council Member R. Cribb; Tel (01634) 374782 (home), 845197 (school)

Professional Association of Teachers in Wales

Headquarters Staff
Secretary for Wales R. Wynn Cowell, LLB, DPA
Bodnant, Borth, Dyfed SY24 5NL; Tel (01970) 871401; Fax (01970) 871401

Welsh Advisory Group
W. Bowen; Tel (01874) 87492 (home), (01874) 623038 (school)
D.T. Jones; Tel (01978) 364712 (home), 311794 (college)
P. Evans; Tel (01633) 858465 (home), (01495) 755141 (college)

Council Members in Wales
Area W1–Gwynedd, Clwyd
Council Member D.T. Jones; Tel (01978) 364712 (home), (01978) 311794 (college)

Area W2
West Glamorgan, Dyfed, Powys
W. Bowen; Tel (01874) 87492 (home), (01874) 623036 (school)

Area W3–South Glamorgan, Gwent, Mid Glamorgan
Council Member P. Evans; Tel (01633) 858465 (home), (01495) 755141 (college)

Professional Association of Teachers in Tertiary Education

Officers of the Tertiary Education Committee
Chairman M. Lewry
Vice-Chairman V. Parkinson

Tertiary Education Committee
North East A.W. Gray; Tel (01207) 520656 (home), (01207) 502906 (college)
North West M.G. Lewry; Tel 0161-958 3256 (college)
East Midlands V. Parkinson; Tel (01695) 573147 (home), (01472) 279222 (college)
West Midlands P. Wright; Tel (01926) 339895 (home), (01203) 694200 (college)
North Thames M. Hughes; Tel (01895) 230411 (college)
Wales D.T. Jones; Tel (01978) 364712 (home), (01978) 311794 (college)
Scotland Dr J. Forrester; Tel (01241) 874945 (home), (01382) 834834 (college)

Council Members (Elected to Represent Tertiary)
M.G. Lewry; Tel 0161-958 3256 (college)
W. Paxton; Tel (01482) 651701 (home), (01482) 329943 (college)

Council Members (Elected on a Council Area Basis)
B. Matthews; Tel (01494) 437208 (home), (01494) 522141 (college)
D.T. Jones; Tel (01978) 364712 (home), (01978) 311794 (college)
P. Evans; Tel (01633) 858465 (home), (01495) 755141 (college)

Co-opted to Council
M. Corry; Tel (01752) 564402 (home), (01752) 385300 (college)

School Teachers' Review Body (STRB)

Office of Manpower Economics, 76 Oxford St, London W1N 9FD; Tel 0171-636 1742; Fax 0171-467 7248
Secretary P.J.H. Edwards (civil servant)
Chairman J. Gardiner
To examine and report on such matters relating to the statutory conditions of employment of school teachers in England and Wales as may from time to time be referred to the review body by the Secretary of State. Takes formal evidence from bodies representative of LEAs, Governors of Voluntary and GM schools and school teachers. 8 members

Secondary Heads Association (SHA)

(Formed from the amalgamation of the Association of Headmistresses and the Head Masters' Association)
130 Regent Rd, Leicester LE1 7PG; Tel (0116) 247 1797; Fax (0116) 247 1152

Officers

President P.J. Downes Hinchingbroke School, Brampton Rd, Huntingdon, Cambs PE18 6BN; Tel (01480) 458017; Fax (01480) 435799
Immediate Past President M.S. Hewitt Summerhill School, Lodge La, Brierley Hill, Kingswinford, W. Midlands DY6 9XE; Tel (01384) 401909; Fax (01384) 400635
Vice-President Dr J.E. Dunford Durham Johnston Comprehensive School, Crossgate Moor, Durham DH1 4SU; Tel (0191) 384 3887; Fax (0191) 384 5771
Treasurer J. Mullen Melbourn Village College, The Moor, Melbourn, Royston, Herts SG8 6EF; Tel (01763) 260403; Fax (01763) 263425
General Secretary J.S. Sutton SHA Headquarters, 130 Regent Rd, Leicester LE1 7PG; Tel (0116) 247 1797; Fax (0116) 247 1152
Hon Secretary B. Hilditch Royston Comprehensive School, Station Rd, Royston, Barnsley, South Yorkshire S71 4EQ; Tel (01226) 722515; Fax (01226) 728664
Legal Secretary B. Douglas Branston School and Community College, Station Rd, Branston, Lincs LN4 1LH; Tel (01522) 791279; Fax (01522) 794484
Publications Officer P.G. Collings Sinfin Community School, Farmhouse Rd, Sinfin, Derby DE24 3AR; Tel (01332) 769174; Fax (01332) 270455
Salaries and Conditions of Service Officer D. Hancock Crispin School, Church Rd, Street, Somerset BA16 OAD; Tel (01458) 42714; Fax (01458) 47955
Chair, Deputy Head V. Parker Longcroft School, Burton Rd, Beverley, Humberside HU17 7EJ; Tel (01482) 862171; Fax (01482) 862872

National Representatives

K. Brooke Garth Hill School, Sandy La, Bracknell RG12 2JH; Tel (01344) 421122; Fax (01344) 55223
P. Miller Wrenn School, Doddington Rd, Wellinborough NN8 2JJ; Tel (01933) 222793; Fax (01923) 225334
Dr J.E. Dunford Durham Johnston Comprehensive School, Crossgate Moor, Durham DH1 4SU; Tel 0191-384 3887; Fax 0191-384 5771
F. Raval Bruntcliffe High School, Bruntcliffe La, Morley, Leeds LS27 0LZ; Tel (01532) 533803; Fax (01532) 529435
B. Hilditch Royston Comprehensive School, Station Rd, Royston, Barnsley, South Yorks S71 4EQ; Tel (01226) 722515; Fax (01226) 728664
M. Cruickshank Beauchamp College, Ridgeway, Oadby, Leicester LE2 5TP; Tel (0116) 271 5809; Fax (0116) 271 5454

Undeb Cenedlaethol Athrawon Cymru

(National Association of the Teachers of Wales)
Swyddfa UCAC, Pen Roc, Rhodfa'r Môr, Aberystwyth, Dyfed SY23 2AZ
President Edwin Williams
General Secretary G. Wyn James, BSc, DipEd
Vice-President Jenni Jones-Annetts
Administrative Secretary Anne O. James
Treasurer J.D.E. Jones, BA

Ysgrifenyddion Cymdeithasau Sir (County Association Secretaries)

Gwynedd
Selwyn Jones Hafan, 5 Bron Arfon, Rachub, Bethesda, Gwynedd LL57 3LW; Tel (01248) 600984

Clwyd
Trefor Jones 9 Llys y Fron, Ffordd Hendy, Yr Wyddgrug, Clwyd CH7 1QZ; Tel (01352) 757375

Dyfed
Gwylon Phillips Carwyn, Llandudoch, Aberteifi SA43 3DS; Tel (01239) 613646

Powys
Dafydd L. Evans Felin Rhyg, 8 Heulfryn, Llanfair Caereinion SY21 0BH; Tel (01938) 810705

Morgannwg Ganol
S. Ellis Danycastell, Heol yr Eglwys, Coity, Ger Penybont ar Ogwr; Tel (01656) 654975

De Morgannwg
Owen John Thomas 4 Llwyn y Grant Pl, Penylan, Caerdydd CF3 7EX; Tel (01222) 499868

Gwent
Richard Morse 35 Waun Rd, St Dials, Cwmbran NP44 7JN; Tel (01633) 870664

Gorllewin Morgannwg
Edwyn Williams Annedd Wen, 37 Heol Waterloo, Capel Hendre, Rhydaman SA18 3SF; Tel (01269) 845435

The University and College Lecturers' Union (NATFHE)

15–27 Britannia St, London WC1X 9JP; Tel 0171-387 3636; Fax 0171-837 4403
President Doreen Cameron
General Secretary John Akker

Regional Secretaries

Inner London
C. Powell The Garden Fl, 39 Morginton Terr, London NW1 7RS; Tel 0171-387 0908; and Westminster College; Tel: 0171-720 2121

Outer London
Ken King 59 Malvern Rd, Thornton Heath, London CR7 7LW; Tel 0181-689 0879; and College of N.W. London; Tel: 0181-208 5313

South-East
M. Dawson 37 Ridgemount, Guildford GU2 5TH; Tel (01483) 65035; and Brooklands College; Tel: (01932) 853300

Southern
A. Murray 5 Paces Yd, Winchester St, Whitechurch RC28 7AM; Tel (01256) 893409 (home), (2064) 63311 (college)

South-West
T. Jolliffe 28 Raddicombe Dr, Brixham, Devon TQ5 0EZ; Tel (01804) 57178; and South Devon CAT; Tel: (01803) 217597

Western
A.N. Gatehouse Carinya Oldcroft, Lydney GL15 4NR; Tel (01594) 562913; and Royal Forest of Dean College; Tel: (01594) 833416

West Midlands
N. Varney 86 Solihull Rd, Birmingham B11 3AG; Tel 0121-777 8212; and Solihull College of Technology; Tel: 0121-711 2111

East Midlands
J. Atkinson 9 Devonshire Rd, Nottingham NG5 2EW; Tel (0115) 962 0764; and Peoples College of Technology; Tel: (01602) 417721

Anglia
A. Coupe 1 Hanford Manor Cl, Norwich NR2 2LW; Tel (01603) 53955; and Norwich City College of F&HE; Tel: (01603) 660011

Yorkshire & Humberside
Secretary E.H. Lawrence 187 Springvale Rd, Sheffield S6 3NT; Tel 0114-208 3243; and Sheffield Hallam University; Tel: 0114-253 2274
Treasurer Ms M. Cooper 153 Warminster Rd, Sheffield S8 8PP

North-West
Secretary Ms A. McConnell 4 Harlow Cl, Thelwall, Warrington, Cheshire WA4 2HD

Northern
R. Grace Castle Brae, Castle Hill, Haltwhistle, Northumberland NE49 0DX; Tel (01434) 320373; and at Newcastle Poly; Tel: 0191-232 6002 Ext 3416

Wales
Secretary A. Screen 116 Riverview, Handaff North, Cardiff CF4 2QH

Northern Ireland
Secretary Jonathan Smith 12 Cleland Park Central, Bangor BT20 3EP; Tel (01247) 467827; Fax (01247) 271254

Scottish Teachers' Organisations

The Educational Institute of Scotland

46 Moray Pl, Edinburgh EH3 6BH; Tel 0131-225 6244; Fax 0131-220 3151

General Secretary James B. Martin, BA(Econ)
Depute General Secretary Frederick L. Forrester, MA(Hons), DipEd, MBIM, FEIS

NAS/UWT (Scotland)

34 West George St, Glasgow G2 1DA; Tel 0141-332 2688; Fax 0141-332 0608
President A. Richardson St Mary's Rectory, Newport-on-Tay DD6 8DA; Tel (01382) 543311 (home); St Rosebank PS (0382) 21721
Scottish Regional Officer J. O'Neill, BEd, FSA(Scot), MSc
NAS/UWT (Scotland) Office, 34 West George St, Glasgow G2 1DA; Tel 041-332 2688
Scottish Representative NAS/UWT Executive T. Ferri 8 Clydeford Dr, Uddingston G71 7DH; Tel (01698) 813405; St Margarets High School, Airdrie; Tel (0236) 766881

District Officers

Strathclyde
Glasgow
R. Dickson 98 Hillington Rd, Glasgow G52 2AJ; Tel 0141-883 8634; Hillpark Secondary School, Glasgow; Tel 041-637 1071
K. Fee 157 Urrdale Rd, Glasgow G41 5DG; Tel 0141-427 0117; Penilee Secondary School, Glasgow; Tel 041-883 8878

County of Lanark
R. Santangeli 23 Fauldshead Rd, Renfrew PA4 0RY; Tel 0141-886 2318; St Aloysius College; Tel 041-332 3190

Counties of Renfrew and Bute
E. Hotchkin 11 Fletcher Ave, Gourock, Renfrewshire PA19 1TU; Tel (01475) 34430 (home); Slaemuir Primary, (0475) 705470

County of Dunbarton
J. Kelly 9 Woodside Ave, Rutherglen, Glasgow; Tel 0141-647 2966; St Ninian's HS; Tel 041-776 1585

County of Ayr
J. Hunter 3 Duncan Dr, Irvine KA12 0HY; Tel (01294) 79409

Dumfries
County of Dumfries
S. Anderson 195 Church St, Maxwelltown, Dumfries DG2 7AZ; Lockerbie PS (0576) 203361

Wigtownshire
S. Flower Fotheringham, Lewis St, Stranraer DG9 7AQ; Stranraer Academy; Tel (0776) 6484

Central and Fife
Counties of Fife, Stirling and Clackmannan
R. Robertson Flat 14, Dryburgh Ave, Denny, Stirlingshire; Tel (01324) 825374; Alva Primary School, Brook St, Alva; Tel (0259) 60987

Tayside
City of Dundee and Counties of Perth, Kinross and Angus
A. Richardson St Marys Rectory, Newport-on-Tay DD6 8DA; Tel (01382) 543311; Rosebank Primary School; Tel (0382) 21721

Grampian
C.R. McKail Oakbank Lodge, Oakbank School, Midstockit Rd, Aberdeen AB9 2XP; Tel (01224) 313347

Highland and Islands
J. Macleod 64 Blackwell Ave, Culloden, Inverness; Tel (01463) 792900; Kinmylies Primary School, Inverness; Tel (0463) 239720

Lothian
C. Wakeling 13 St Ninian's Terr, Edinburgh EH10 5NL; Tel 0131-447 6959; Firrhill HS; Tel 031-441 4501

College Organisers
NAS/UWT West of Scotland
St Leonard's SECY; Tel 0141-771 4986
J. Duffy 27 Starpoint St, Glasgow G33 3DS; Tel 0141-774 7349

NAS/UWT East of Scotland
H. Armstrong 3 Laird St, Monifieth, Dundee DD5 4ED; Tel (01382) 534295; Grove Academy, Dundee; Tel (0382) 730284

Regional Secretaries

Strathclyde
J. Duffy, MA 27 Startpoint St, Glasgow G33 3DS; Tel 0141-774 7349; St Leonard's Secondary, Glasgow; Tel 041-771 4986

Grampian
J. Crawford 6 Middleton Cres, Bridge of Don, Aberdeen AB6; Tel (01224) 820574; Northfield Academy (0224) 699715

Tayside
W. Matthew, BSc 15 Seymour St, Dundee DD2 1HD; Tel (01382) 60810; Menziehill High School, Dundee; Tel (0382) 641111

Fife and Central
R. Robertson 8a Allanvale Rd, Bridge of Allan FK9 4NU; Tel (01786) 833808; Alva Primary School, Brook St, Alva; Tel (0259) 760987

Highlands and Islands
R. MacCrimmon 51 Balnakyle Rd, Lochardil, Inverness IV2 4DJ; Tel (01463) 235629; Holm PS Inverness; Tel (0463) 232697

Professional Association of Teachers in Scotland

4/6 Oak La, Edinburgh EH12 6XH; Tel 0131-317 8282; Fax 0131-317 8111

Headquarters Staff
Secretary for Scotland Robert J.S. Christie, BSc, FRSA
Professional Services Officer John A. Anderson, GTCL, LLB

Officers of the Scottish Executive Committee
Chairman Sally Alexander
Immediate Past Chairman Merle MacLean
Vice-Chairman Ian Elfick
Hon Secretary Maureen Laing
Hon Treasurer R.S. Smith

Scottish Executive Committee
Borders
B. Kelly; Tel (0183 57) 253 (home), (01896) 4788 (school)

Central
Jane Reid; Tel (01324) 38632 (home), (01324) 21882 (school)

Dumfries and Galloway
Dr D. Hawley; Tel (01848) 30719 (home), (01387) 52846 (school)

Fife
M. Laing; Tel (01592) 741881 (home), (01592) 752258 (school)

Grampian
P. Doyle; Tel (01542) 882691 (home)
S. Alexander; Tel (01224) 314743 (home), 825062 (school)

Highland
K. Paterson; Tel (01463) 220120 (home), (01381) 620369 (school)

Lothian
I. Elfick; Tel 0131-445 5369 (home), 0131-443 8096 (school)
I. Brydon; Tel 0131-339 7244 (home), 0131-0506 418484 (school)

Orkney
R. Russell; Tel (01856) 78206

Shetland
B. Moar; Tel (01595) 3116 (home), (01595) 2973 (school)

Strathclyde
D. Cameron; Tel 0141-954 5114 (home)
Anne-Marie McLaughlan; Tel 0141-881 01349 (home), 0141-810 4792 (school)
M. MacLean; Tel 0141-638 5414 (home), 0141-248 4899 (school)

Tayside
Margaret Bowman; Tel (01738) 51615 (home), (01738) 828283 (school)

Western Isles
A.M. MacLeod; Tel (01859) 2461 (home), (01859) 2224 (school)

Council Members in Scotland
Area S1–Dumfries and Galloway, Lothian, Borders
Council Member Brian Kelly; Tel (0183 57) 253 (home), (01896) 4788 (school)

Area S2–Strathclyde
Council Member R. Smith; Tel (01290) 425598 (home), (01290) 421228 (school)

Area S3–Tayside, Central, Fife
Council Member Jane Reid; Tel (01324) 38632 (home), (01324) 21882 (school)

Area S4–Highland, Grampian, Orkney, Shetland, Western Isles
A. Macleod; Tel (01859) 2461 (home), (01859) 2224 (school)

Scottish Secondary Teachers' Association

15 Dundas St, Edinburgh EH3 6QG; Tel 0131-556 5919/0605; Fax 0131-556 1419
President M.T. Allan, MA Holy Rood High School
Immediate Past President J. Small, BEd
General Secretary A.M. Lamont, MA
General Treasurer J.R. McKelvie, BA, DipCom Arbroath High School

Regional Secretaries

Region 1 G.M.J. Stocks, BSc Lorien, 89 Obsdale Pk, Alness
(Dingwall Academy)
Region 2 J.D. Gray, MA, MSc 72 Beechgrove Terr, Aberdeen
(Oldmachar Academy, Aberdeen)
Region 3 W.A.L. Guthrie, BSc 21 Argyle St, Dundee
(Perth High School)
Region 4 I.M. Martin, BSc 6 Taylor Dr, Glenrothes
Glenrothes High School
Region 5 J. Docherty, BSc 11 Dovecot Pk, Linlithgow
(St Kentigern's Academy, Blackburn)
Region 6 J. McMenemy, DipTech 11 Broomlea, Kelso
(Kelso High School)
D.B. Cousin, BSc 74 Stirling St, Tillicoultry
(Alloa Academy)
Region 8 A.C. Chambers, BA 3 Nithsdale View, Thornhill DG3 5DX
(Wallace Hall Academy, Thornhill)
Region 9 J. Doherty, MA, BA 'Highview', 59 Southwold Rd, Paisley PA1 3AL
(St Columba's High School, Gourock)

Region 10 D.C. Farrow, BA 39 Spey Rd, Troon
(Cumnock Academy)
Region 11 G. Paterson, MA 3R, 320 Dumbarton Rd, Partick, Glasgow
(Douglas Academy, Milngavie)
Region 12 T. Wallace, BSc 40 Rowallan Gdns, Glasgow G11 7LJ
Springburn Academy
Region 13 A.R. Taylor, MA 16 Ochiltree Dr, Earnock Gdns, Hamilton ML3
(Brannock High School, Motherwell)

Headteachers' Association of Scotland

Jordanhill College of Education, 76 Southbrae Dr, Glasgow G13 1PP; Tel 0141-950 3298; Fax 0141-950 3268
Secretary James B.O. McNair, BSc

Association of Head Teachers in Scotland

Room D36, Northern College of Education, Gardyne Rd, Dundee DD5 1NY; Tel (01382) 458802
Secretary Room D36, Northern College of Education, Gardyne Rd, Dundee DD5 1NY; Tel (01382) 458802

Association of Educational Advisers in Scotland

Management Committee 1994/95

President Deidre McVean, Senior Adviser 14+ Tayside Regional Council, Educational Development Service, Floor D, Gardyne Rd, Dundee DD5 1NY; Tel (01382) 462857
Past President John Muir, Adviser in Primary Education Highland Regional Council, Education Offices, Brora, Sutherland KW9 6PG
Secretary Frank Cooney, Adviser in Social Subjects Grampian Regional Council, Summerhill Education Centre, Stronsay Dr, Aberdeen AB9 6JA; Tel (01224) 208205
Treasurer Gordon Johnston Education Department, Borders Regional Council, Newton St, Boswells TD6 0SA; Tel (01835) 23301
Conference Secretary Alistair Horne, Adviser in English Tayside Regional Council, Educational Development Service, Gardyne Rd, Dundee DD5 1NY; Tel (01382) 462857
Publicity Secretary Hugh Roche, Adviser in Art and Design Grampian Regional Council, Advisory Service, Summerhill Education Centre, Stronsay Dr, Aberdeen AB9 6JA; Tel (01224) 208205

Committee Members (Secondary)

Colin Laird, Adviser in Modern Languages Strathclyde Regional Council, Dumbarton Division, Educational Development Service, St Andrew's High School, North Douglas St, Clydebank G81 1NQ; Tel 0141-951 2028
Gordon Johnston, Adviser in Language (Treasurer) Education Department, Borders Regional Council, Newton St Boswells TD6 0SA; Tel (01835) 23301
Hugh Roche, Adviser in Art and Design (Publicity) Grampian Regional Council, Advisory Service, Summerhill Education Centre, Stronsay Dr, Aberdeen AB9 6JA; Tel (01224) 208205

Committee Members (Primary)

Yvonne Orr, Adviser in Primary Education Highland Regional Council, Divisional Education Office, 13 Ardross St, Inverness; Tel (01463) 237411
David Johnstone, Adviser in Primary Education Tayside Regional Council, Educational Development Service, Floor D, Gardyne Rd, Dundee DD5 1NY; Tel (01382) 462857

Irish Teachers' Organisations

Irish National Teachers' Organisation (INTO)

35 Parnell Sq, Dublin 1; Tel Dublin 8722533; Fax Dublin 8722462
General Secretary J. O'Toole
President M. McGarry
General Treasurer M. Moroney
Aims to unite and organise the teachers of Ireland and to provide a means for the expression of their collective opinion on educational matters; to safeguard and improve the conditions of employment of its members; to afford advice and assistance to individual members on professional matters; to promote the interests of education; and to cultivate a spirit of fraternal co-operation with kindred organisations in this and other countries

Regional Office
23 College Gdns, Belfast BT9 6BS; Tel (01232) 381455; Fax (01232) 662803
Northern Secretary F. Bunting

Ulster Teachers' Union (U.T.U.)

94 Malone Rd, Belfast BT9 5HP; Tel (01232) 662216; Fax (01232) 663055
General Secretary D. Allen
Assistant General Secretary R. Calvin
Field Officer A. Chatterley
Founded in 1919, the U.T.U. is now one of the largest and strongest organisations of teachers in Northern Ireland. Recognised teachers of all types, irrespective of status, belong to this comprehensive Union and enjoy its protection, benefits and services

Subject Teaching Associations

Council of Subject Teaching Associations

19 Green La, North Duffield, Selby YO8 7RR; Tel (01757) 706161; Fax (01757) 213699
Hon Secretary F. Loftus, BA, BPhil
COSTA was established in February 1972, with the following aims:
1. To provide an effective means of involving Subject Teaching Associations in decision and policy making at national and regional levels
2. To provide a means of communication between Associations on their activities, methods of organisation and economic planning
3. To provide a forum for discussion of matters of common interest
4. To take common action, where appropriate, on behalf of member associations, without thereby committing member associations as a whole, and protecting the right of any constituent association to act individually or to record a dissenting view
Membership of COSTA is open to all Subject Teaching Associations

Association of Agricultural Education Staffs

NATFE Agricultural & Allied Education Sector
Chair D. Owen Kirkley Hall College, Ponteland, Newcastle upon Tyne NE20 0AQ; Tel (01661) 24141
Sector Official R. Eve NATFE, 27 Britannia St, London WC1X 9JP; Tel 0171-837 3636

18 Teachers' and Other Educational Organisations

Association for Language Learning

16 Regent Pl, Rugby CV21 2PN; Tel (01788) 546443; Fax (01788) 544149
Secretary General Christine Wilding, BA
The Association for Language Learning (ALL) is the major UK subject teaching association for all those involved in the teaching and learning of modern foreign languages in all sectors of education, both state and independent, and at all levels from 5–18 to Further, Higher and Adult Education and Training. ALL provides advice and services for teachers of different languages and in different sectors of education. The Association enables language teachers to speak with a unified voice on matters of national and local policy, and maintains and develops international links. ALL is committed to the teaching, learning and use of languages in education and society as a whole

National Association of Careers and Guidance Teachers

Portland Hse, 4 Bridge St, Usk, Gwent NP5 1BG; Tel (01291) 672985; Fax (01291) 672090
President A. Barnes
General Secretary J. Cook
Treasurer A. Vincent

Council for Education in World Citizenship (CEWC)

Seymour Mews Hse, Seymour Mews, London W1H 9PE; Tel 0171-935 1752; Fax 0171-935 5548
Provides a service to member schools, colleges, organisations and individuals including current affairs broadsheets, speakers, conferences, use of Resource Centre, teaching materials and general guidance on all aspects of education for international understanding

Classical Association

c/o 5 Grove Ave, London N10 2AS; Tel 0181-444 5065
Secretary Ann Hunt

Joint Association of Classical Teachers

31/34 Gordon Sq, London WC1H 0PY
Executive Secretary B. Bell

National Association for the Teaching of Drama

30 Heathdene Rd, Streatham, London SW16 3PD; Tel 0181-679 3361
Hon Secretary Maggie McNeill

Earth Science Teachers Association

(formerly the Association of Teachers of Geology)
Department of Geography, University of Wales Swansea, Singleton Pk, Swansea SA2 8PP; Tel (01792) 295141; Fax (01792) 205556
Secretary G. Owen

The Economics and Business Education Association

1A Keymer Rd, Hassocks, W Sussex BN6 8AD; Tel (01273) 846033; Fax (01273) 844646
Administrative Officer Carole V. Dyer
Development Officer Richard Young 31 Newland Mill, Witney, Oxon OX8 6HH; Tel (01933) 774393; Fax (01933) 706150

National Association for the Teaching of English

NATE Office, 50 Broadfield Rd, Sheffield S8 OXJ; Tel (0114) 255 5419; Fax (0114) 255 5296

Officers

General Secretary Anne Barnes NATE Office
Chair Shona Walton Emberley Leys, Chaple La, Ratley, Banbury, Oxon OX15 6DS; Tel 0129-587 596
Vice-Chair Alastair West 33 Parkway, Shenfield, Brentwood, Essex CM15 8LH; Tel (01277) 214493
Secretary Ann Malcolm 106 Richmond Rd, Wolverhampton WV3 9JJ; Tel (01902) 23852
Treasurer Bob Bibby 32 Buckingham Rd, Penn, Wolverhampton WV4 5TJ; Tel (01902) 341649
Publications Officer Angel Scott 4 The Avenue, Durham City DH1 4ED; Tel 0191-384 0684
Conference Officer Contact NATE Office
Newsletter Editor Andrew Burn 6 Fox's Cl, Milton, Cambridge CB4 4BT

Esperanto Teachers' Association

Esperanto Centre, 140 Holland Pk Ave, London W11 4UF; Tel 0171-727 7821

European Association of Teachers (UK Section)

(Representing teachers of European Studies on Council of Subject Teaching Associations)
20 Brookfield, Highgate West Hill, London N6 6AS; Tel 0181-340 9136 (office available part-time 0171-284 3748)
Chairman John Jeffery University College of Greenwich, Wellington St, London SE18 6DF
Hon Secretary Mary E. Duce
Promotes education about Europe

Geographical Association

343 Fulwood Rd, Sheffield S10 3BP; Tel (0114) 267 0666; Fax (0114) 267 0688
Joint Hon Secretary C. Harris
Joint Hon Secretary G. Ranger

Association of Teachers of German see *Association for Language Learning*

Historical Association

59A Kennington Pk Rd, London SE11 4JH; Tel 0171-735 3901; Fax 0171-582 4989
Secretary Madeline Stiles

National Association of Teachers of Home Economics and Technology

Hamilton Hse, Mabledon Pl, London WC1H 9BJ; Tel 0171-387 1441; Fax 0171-383 7230
Secretary Geoffrey Thompson

Association of Teachers of Italian see *Association for Language Learning*

British Association for Language Teaching see *Association for Language Learning*

Centre for Information on Language Teaching and Research

see Chapter 14

Modern Language Association see *Association for Language Learning*

School Library Association

see Chapter 25

Mathematical Association

259 London Rd, Leicester LE2 3BE; Tel (0116) 270 3877; Fax (0116) 244 8508
Executive Secretary Heather Whitby

Association of Teachers of Mathematics

7 Shaftesbury St, Derby DE23 8YB; Tel (01332) 346599; Fax (01332) 204357
Administrative Officer Marian Keeling
Hon Secretary Marjorie Gorman
Hon Treasurer Alan Bloomfield

National Association for Pastoral Care in Education

c/o Education Department, The University of Warwick, Coventry CV4 7AL; Tel (01203) 523810; Fax (01203) 524110
Officer in the Chair Chris Watkins
Vice-Chair Caroline Lodge
President Prof J.R.G. Tomlinson, Prof of Education The University of Warwick
Treasurer Alan Dodds
Development Officer David Lambourn

National Society for Education in Art and Design (NSEAD)

The Gatehouse, Corsham Court, Corsham, Wilts SN13 0BZ; Tel (01249) 714825; Fax (01249) 716138
General Secretary J. Steers, NDD, ATC, DAE
President M. Yeomans Knockinelder Hse, 4 Kearney Rd, Portaferry, Newtonards, Co Down BT22 1QF
Vice-President P. Hay 6 Ainslies Belvedere, Lansdown Rd, Bath BA1 5HT
2nd Vice-President D. Buss Pump Cottage, Pump St, Newton St Syres, Exeter EX5 5BY
Hon Treasurer J.D. Lloyd 24 Ashwood Dr, Gellinudd, Pontardawe, Swansea SA8 3HL

District Representatives

East Anglia
Simon Smith 38 Queens Rd, Bury St Edmunds, Suffolk IP33 3EP

East Midlands
Rose Walters 1 Waterhouses, Dalbury Lees, Derby DE6 5BR

London and Home Counties
K. Mathieson 49 Goat La, Enfield, Middx EN1 4UA

North
Vacancy

North West
Stewart Griffin Holly Cottage, Barton Rd, Farndon, Chester CH3 6NL

Northern Ireland
Vacancy

South
K. Howard-Harris The Old Cottage, Lidsey, Bognor Regis, W. Sussex PO22 9PQ

South West
Vacancy

Wales
Vacancy

West Midlands
K. Jeavons 6 The Village, Kingswinford, West Midlands DY6 8AY

Yorkshire and Humberside
D. Mason 14 Burton Rd, Hornsea, North Humberside HU18 1QY

Scotland
Vacancy

Representatives of Education Sectors

Higher Education
Vacancy

Further Education
A. Seabourne 45 Hopton La, Upper Hopton, Mirfield, W. Yorks WF14 8ER
Jill Lewin 18 Upper Regents Pk, Bradford On Avon, Wiltshire BA15 1EB

Secondary Education
Amrik Varkalis 227 Thornhill Rd, Rastrick, Brighouse, West Yorkshire HD6 3HL

Primary Education
P. Hay 6 Ainslies Belvedere, Lansdown Rd, Bath BA1 5HT

Journal of Art and Design Education

Journal of Art and Design Education–Principal Editor
Prof John Swift, UCE International Hse, Lancaster St, Birmingham

Journal of Art and Design Education, Editorial Board-Chair
M. Buchanan Robinsfield, Crishall, Nr Royston, Herts SG8 8QJ

Observers

CHEAD Representative
Prof. D. Vaughan Cays Hse, Roweltown, Carlisle, Cumbria CA6 6JH

OFSTED Observer
Peter Jones 101 Leomansley View, Lichfield, Staffs WS13 8AP

AAIAD Observer
Roger Mountford The Eastbourne Centre, Lawn View, Station Rd, Sutton-in-Ashfield, Notts NG17 5FJ

Arts Council Observer
Mary McDonagh 14 Great Peter St, London SW1P 3NQ

ACADTE Observer
John French Brighton Polytechnic, Faculty of Education, Falmer, Brighton BN1 9PH

Politics Association

Studio 16, I–Mex Business Pk, Hamilton Rd, Longsight, Manchester M13 0PD; Tel 0161-256 3906
Chairman C. Thomas 34 Park Rd, Street, Somerset BA16 0JN
General Secretary Y. Botham 9 Mount Cottages, Old Common Rd, Cobham, Surrey KT11 1BS
Vice-Chairman W. Cullen 40 St Margarets Rd, Old Town, Swindon SN3 1RX
Executive Secretary Sylvia Llewellyn 69 Osborne Parc, Helston, Cornwall TR13 8TZ
Hon Treasurer Chris Robinson 24 Chesnut Ave, Queens Rd, Hull HU5 2RH
Membership Secretary Jean Prout 64 Westhill Dr, Dartford, Kent DA1 3EA; Tel (01322) 275145
Editor, 'Grass Roots' Terry Ford 68 Raglan Gdns, Oxley, Watford, Herts WD1 4LL
Editor, 'Teaching Politics' Dr Lynton Robins 46 The Fairway, Oadby, Leics LE2 2HJ
Resource Centre Studio 16, I–Mex Business Pk, Hamilton Rd, Longsight, Manchester M13 0PD; Tel 0161-256 3906

Professional Council for Religious Education

(Incorporating the Association for Religious Education and the Professional Committee of the Christian Education Movement)
Royal Bldgs, Victoria St, Derby DE1 1GW; Tel (01332) 296655; Fax (01332) 343253

Association for Professional Development in Education

Clock Cott, Edington, Bridgwater, Somerset TA7 9JP; Tel (01278) 723063
Chair Pat Murgatroyd Isle of Wight Teachers' Centre
Hon Secretary Keith Martin
Hon Treasurer Jim Hewitson 12 Coronation Dr, Whitehaven, Cumbria

The National Association for Special Educational Needs (NASEN)

Units 4 and 5, Amber Business Village, Amber Cl, Amington, Tamworth, Staffordshire B77 4RP

Association of Teachers of Russian see *Association for Language Learning*

Schools Music Association

Contact Maxwell Pryce SMA, 71 Margaret Rd, New Barnet, Herts EN4 9NT; Tel 0181-440 6919; Fax 0181-440 6919
Founded 1938 to support music in schools

Association for Science Education

College La, Hatfield, Herts AL10 9AA
General Secretary Dr D.S. Moore; Tel (01707) 267411; Fax (01707) 266532

Association for the Teaching of the Social Sciences

PO Box 461, Sheffield S2 2RH
Secretary Tony Breslin 97 Princes Ave, Watford, Hertfordshire WD1 7RR; Tel (01923) 213788

Association of Teachers of Spanish and Portuguese see *Association for Language Learning*

Society of Industrial Tutors

Secretary Jean Cooke Middlesex University, Queensway, Enfield EN3 4SF; Tel 0181-362 5342

Women in TEFL

Contact Joy Pascoe Flat 4, 6 Clifton Cres, Folkestone, Kent CT20 2EW; Tel (01303) 258096

Professional Educational Associations

Heads, Governing Bodies and Administrators (Schools)

Association of College Registrars and Administrators

Hon Secretary J.H. Kenyon ACRA National Office, Kingston College North Kingston Centre, Richmond Rd, Kingston Upon Thames, Surrey KT2 5PE; Tel 0181-541 4940; Fax 0181-546 7151

Association of Educational Psychologists

Association Secretary David Webster, BA, MSc 3 Sunderland Rd, Durham DH1 2LH; Tel 0191-384 9512; Fax 0191-386 5287

Association of Heads of Independent Schools

Chairman B. Blakeley, St Peters School, 52 Headlands Kettering, Northants NN15 6DJ

Association of Heads of Outdoor Education Centres

Secretary T. Winnall Frank Chapman Centre, Park End, Bewdley, Worcestershire DY12 2TY; Tel (01299) 403292; Fax (01299) 402724

Association of Principals of Sixth Form Colleges

Secretary Sandy Macdonald The Ridge College, Hibbert La, Marple, Stockport SK6 7PA; Tel 0161-427 7733; Fax 0161-427 8054
Press Officer Pamela Maryfield Strode's College, Egham, Surrey TW20 9DR; Tel (01784) 437506

Centre for Adviser and Inspector Development: NAEIAC Training

Woolley Hall, Woolley, Wakefield, W Yorks WF4 2JR; Tel (01226) 387582
Director Harold Heller
Provides training and development opportunities for Local Authority Advisers and Inspectors and Independent Consultants

Committee of Scottish Higher Education Principals (COSHEP)

3rd Fl, St Andrew Hse, 141 West Nile St, Glasgow G1 2RN; Tel 0141-353 1880
Chairman Prof J.P. Arbuthnott, Principal University of Strathclyde, Glasgow G1 1XQ
Secretary Dr R.L. Crawford COSHEP Office, 3rd Fl, St Andrew Hse, 141 West Nile St, Glasgow G1 2RN

Governing Bodies' Association

Secretary D.G. Banwell, BA Windleshaw Lodge, Withyham, nr Hartfield, E Sussex TN7 4DB; Tel (01892) 770879

Governing Bodies of Girls' Schools Association

Secretary D.G. Banwell Windleshaw Lodge, Withyham, nr Hartfield, E Sussex TN7 4DB; Tel (01892) 770879

Headmasters' Conference

130 Regent Rd, Leicester LE1 7PG; Tel (0116) 285 4810; Fax (0116) 247 1152
Chairman H.R. Wright King Edward's School, Birmingham B15 2UA
Vice-Chairman R de C Chapman Malvern College, Worcs WR14 3DF
Hon Treasurer T.D. Wheare Bryanston School, Blandford, Dorset DT11 OPX
Secretary V.S. Anthony
Membership Secretary R.N.P. Griffiths

Headteachers' Association of Scotland

Secretary James B.O. McNair, BSc University of Strathclyde, Jordanhill Campus, Southbrae Dr, Glasgow G13 1PP; Tel 0141-950 3298; Fax 0141-950 3268

Independent Schools Bursars' Association

Secretary D.J. Bird Woodlands, Closewood Rd, Denmead, Waterlooville, Hants PO7 6JD; Tel (01705) 264506

London Head Teachers' Association

Hon General Secretary K. Brooker 10 Holroyd Rd, London SW15; Tel 0181-788 4470 (home), 0181-969 0629 (school)

National Association of Governors and Managers

21 Bennetts Hill, Birmingham B2 5QP; Tel 0121-643 5787
Secretary Ian Rule

National Association of Educational Inspectors, Advisers and Consultants

President P. Jefferson N. Tyneside C.C.
Immediate Past President M. Jolley LB Croydon
General Secretary W.H. Wright, BA, MEd 1 Heath Sq, Boltro Rd, Haywards Heath, W Sussex RH16 1BL; Tel (01444) 441279

School Secretaries' Association

Secretary D. Hancox King Edward VI Camp Hill School for Girls, Vicarage Rd, King's Heath, Birmingham B14 7QJ; Tel 0121-444 2150

Society of Headmasters and Headmistresses of Independent Schools

Hon Secretary A.E.R. Dodds, MA Mantons, Park Rd, Winchester SO23 7BE; Tel (01962) 862579; Fax (01962) 878981

Society of Schoolmasters

Secretary M.S. Freeburn Hall Farm Dairy, Wood Norton, Dereham, Norfolk NR20 5AR

Standing Conference of Tertiary and Sixth Form College Principals

Chairman Alan Donson Strode Tertiary College, Church Rd, Street, Somerset BA16 0AB; Tel (01458) 42277
Compendium Secretary Geraldine Evans King George V College, Scarisbrick New Rd, Southport, Merseyside PR8 6LR; Tel (01704) 30601

Welsh Secondary Schools' Association

Hon Secretary Catherine James Ysgol y Gader, Dolgellau, Gwynedd LL40 1HY; Tel (01341) 422578

Higher and Further Education–Staff and Administration

Association for Colleges

344–354 Gray's Inn Rd, London WC1X 8BP; Tel 0171-833 1933; Fax 0171-833 1934
Chief Executive Ruth Gee

Association of Higher Academic Staff in Colleges of Education in Scotland

Chairman David A. Adams, MA, Principal Northern College of Education, Hilton Pl, Aberdeen AB9 1FA; Tel (01224) 283609
Secretary J. Alistair Campbell, MA, DipEd, Vice-Principal Northern College of Education, Hilton Pl, Aberdeen AB9 1FA; Tel (01224) 283611

Association of Higher Education Institutions concerned with Home Economics

Secretary Stella M. Walsh Consumer Services Management, Leeds Metropolitan University, Calverley St, Leeds LS1 3HE; Tel (0113) 283 2600

Association of Principals of Colleges (Northern Ireland Branch)

T.L. Place, MSc, BA, DPM, FIPD, Principal East Down Institute of Further and Higher Education At Newcastle, Donard St, Newcastle, Co Down BT33 0AP; Tel (013967) 22451; Fax (013967) 26203

Association of Vice-Principals of Colleges

President V. Robinson Havering College of Further and Higher Education, Ardleigh Grn Rd, Hornchurch, Essex RM11 2LL; Tel (01708) 455011

National Association for Staff Development in Post-16 Education (NASD)

Hon Secretary Don Scott 30 St Helena Rd, Colchester CO3 3BA; Tel (01206) 571258
Chairman Ian Strachan West Herts College, Langley Rd, Watford

Standing Conference of Principals Ltd

Chairman Dr J. Burke Rector Liverpool Institute of Higher Education, St Katherines College, Stand Pk Rd, Liverpool L16 9JD; Tel 0151-722 2361; Fax 0151-722 7179
Executive Secretary T.J. Cox, MA, MEd PO Box 190, Cheltenham, Glos GL50 3SJ; Tel (01242) 225925; Fax (01242) 221502

Conference for Independent Further Education

Secretary Myles Glover, MA Buckhall Farm, Bull La, Bethersden, Nr Ashford, Kent TN26 3HB; Tel (01233) 820797; Fax (01233) 820797

Independent Schools' Association Incorporated

Boy's British School, East St, Saffron Walden, Essex CB10 1LS; Tel (01799) 523619; Fax (01799) 524892
General Secretary Timothy Ham, MA, DipEd

Librarians

Association of Cheshire School Librarians

Honorary Secretary Linda Riley, BA, ALA Woolston High School, Holes La, Warrington WA1 4LS; Tel (01925) 816848; Fax (01925) 852903

Librarians of Institutes and Schools of Education

Secretary R.F. Smeaton University of Hull Education Library, Brynmor Jones Library, Cottingham Rd, Hull HU6 7RX; Tel (01482) 465556

Society of County Children's and Education Librarians

Hon Secretary Catherine Blanshard, ALA, Assistant Head of Library Service Hertfordshire Libraries Arts and Information, New Barnfield, Travellers La, Hatfield, Herts AL10 8XG

Management

Cambridge Education Associates (CEA) Ltd

Minerva Hse, 618 Newmarket Rd, Cambridge CB5 8LP; Tel (01223) 413399; Fax (01223) 414949
Consultancy and advice to LEAs, schools, and inspection contracts for OFSTED. Located in Cambridge and

London, CEA are committed to the creation of a lasting improvement in the quality of leadership and the management of learning

Centre for Higher Education Management

Danbury Pk Conference Centre, Danbury, Chelmsford, Essex CM3 4AT; Tel (01245) 225511; Fax (01245) 224331
Director Prof Ian McNay
Provision of postgraduate teaching programmes, mid career development programmes and short courses for practising managers in further and higher education institutions and governmental agencies in the field of institutional management, and a range of in-service programmes and consultancy and research in UK and overseas

Education Management: North West

North Cheshire College, Fearnhead, Warrington WA2 0DB; Tel (01925) 816882; Fax (01925) 838675
Director David Ward
Directorate John Apthomas
Directorate Shirley Wright
Educational management consultancy service and INSET training for staff in Primary and Secondary Schools

Educational Building Consultants

Head Office, 2 Heathcoat Bldg, Highfield Science Pk, University Boulevard, Nottingham NG7 2QS; Tel (0115) 922 9214; Fax (0115) 922 9330
Director Neill Ransom
Educational Building Consultants, part of The Chelstoke Educational Group, offer specialist accommodation planning, preparation of building bids for refurbishments, extensions and new builds, and project management of building projects. £60m of educational projects completed

Educational Courses

Waterside Centre, Abbey Meadows, Abbey Park Rd, Leicester LE4 5AE; Tel (0116) 251 6953; Fax (0116) 251 0624
Contact Bookings Secretary
Specialists in management courses for teachers and administrators

National Development Centre for Educational Management and Policy

School of Education, University of Bristol, 35 Berkeley Sq, Bristol BS8 1JA; Tel (0117) 930 3030 Ext B7008
Director Prof Eric Hoyle
Co-ordinator David Oldroyd

Northern Ireland Education and Library Boards Regional Training Unit

Larkfield High School, Blacks Rd, Belfast BT10 0NB; Tel (01232) 618121; Fax (01232) 629745

Scottish Centre for Studies in School Administration

Moray Hse, Heriot Watt University, Institute of Education, Holyrood Rd, Edinburgh EH8 8AQ; Tel 0131-558 6179; Fax 0131-557 3458
Director J.E.A. Havard

Parents–Teachers Associations

Campaign for State Education (CASE)

158 Durham Rd, London SW20 0DG; Tel 0181-944 8206; Fax 0181-944 8206
A pressure group, campaigning for the right of all to experience the highest quality state education regardless of race, gender, home circumstances, ability or disability. It supports a fully comprehensive and locally accountable education system and campaigns for the development of partnership between home, school and the community and a recognition of the achievements of state education. CASE is politically non-aligned
Membership £10 per year, £5 unwaged, groups (minimum 5 members) £15 per year

Officers and Committee

President Joan Sallis 49 Lauderdale Dr, Petersham, Richmond, Surrey; Tel 0181-940 8677
Chair Nichola Gregory 64 Emscote Rd, Warwick CV34 5QG; Tel (01926) 491934
Executive Secretary Margaret Tulloch 158 Durham Rd, London SW20 0DG; Tel 0181-947 5758; 0181-944 8206
Treasurer John Coe 155 High St, Chalgrove, Oxford OX44 7ST; Tel (01865) 890281
Editor, 'Parents & Schools' Nicky Adamson Akeman Hse, High St, Stretham, Ely, Cambs; Tel (01353) 649238; Fax (01353) 648184
Vice-Chair Barbara Collins 54 Broadwalk, London E18 2DW; Tel 0181-989 4356

Greater London Federation of Parent–Teacher Associations

Secretary D. Backhouse 20 Airlie Gdns, Ilford IG1 4LB

Home and School Council

Committee
Chairman HSC 40 Sunningdale Mount, Sheffield S11 9HA
Secretary Barbara Bullivant 40 Sunningdale Mount, (ACE) Ecclesall, Sheffield S11 9HA; Tel (0114) 236 4181; Fax (0114) 236 4181
Treasurer C. Davis, (NAPE) 3 Hartland Dr, Melton Mowbray, Leics LE13 0BX
Editor HSC 40 Sunningdale Mount, Sheffield S11 9HA

Members
M. Mansfield (CASE)
A. Mountfield (CASE)
J. Coe (CASE)
S. Naybour (NCPTA)
D. Wright (NCPTA)
P. Rippon (NCPTA)
Treasurer C. Davis (NAPE)
J. Morgan (NAPE)
J. Middlewood (NAPE)
E. Wallis (ACE)
Secretary B. Bullivant (ACE)

Observers from Teachers' Organisations
G. Harries (NAS/UWT)
J. Mulholland (NAHT)
C. Blower (NUT)

National Confederation of Parent–Teacher Associations

2 Ebbsfleet Industrial Est, Stonebridge Rd, Gravesend, Kent DA11 9DZ; Tel (01474) 560618; Fax (01474) 564418
For further information of Affiliated Federations, contact the Membership Secretary

National Education Association

Secretary M. Smith 1 Hinchley Way, Hinchley Wood, Esher, Surrey KT10 0BD; Tel 0181-398 1253
Voluntary non-political body representing parents throughout the country. It has over twenty branches and is financed entirely by members' subscriptions and donations

Social Work, Disability and Counselling

Association of Chief Education Social Workers

Hon General Secretary J.A. Price Bank Hse, 76 Nutgrove Rd, Nutgrove, St Helens; Tel 0151-430 0112

Association for Student Counselling

Division of BAC, 1 Regent Pl, Rugby CV21 2PJ; Tel (01788) 550899; Fax (01788) 562189

Association of Workers for Children with Emotional and Behavioural Difficulties (EBD)

Administrative Officer A. Rimmer
Hon General Secretary S. Panther 20 Carlton St, Kettering NN16 8EB; Tel (01536) 518455

British Association of Art Therapists

11A Richmond Rd, Brighton BN2 3RL; Tel (01734) 265407; Fax (01734) 685852
Chairperson Val Huett
Hon Secretary G. Hicks

British Association of Teachers of the Deaf

Hon Secretary BATOD Ann Underwood 41 The Orchard, Leven, Beverley, North Humberside HU17 5QA; Tel (01964) 544243 (voice/minicom and fax)
The British Association of Teachers of the Deaf is the only Association representing the interests of Teachers of the Deaf in this country. Regional and National Meetings are organised to promote issues connected with the education of hearing impaired children. BATOD publishes a refereed Journal and an Association Magazine in Jan, March, May, Sept and Nov. Articles and advertising should be submitted to the Association Hon Secretary. An information pack about the Association and matters related to the education of deaf and hearing impaired children and their teachers is obtainable from the Secretary on receipt of an A4 SAE (43p)

Community and Youth Workers' Union

Unit 202A, The Argent Centre, 60 Frederick St, Hockley, Birmingham B1 3HS; Tel 0121-233 2815

British Association for Counselling (BAC)

1 Regent Pl, Rugby CV21 2PJ; Tel (01788) 550899; Information Line Tel (01788) 578328; Fax (01788) 562189

The Dyslexia Institute

133 Gresham Rd, Staines TW18 2AJ; Tel (01784) 463851; Fax (01784) 460747
Executive Director E.J. Brooks

National Association of Advisory Officers for Special Education

Hon Secretary C. Dyer 32A Pleasant Valley, Saffron Walden, Essex CB11 4AP; Tel (01799) 521257; Fax (01799) 521257

National Association of Professionals Concerned with Language Impaired Children (NAPLIC)

c/o Visiting Teacher Service, Birmingham Education Authority, Vauxhall Gdns, Barrack St, Birmingham B7 4HA
President David Crystal
Chair Ann Locke
Membership Secretary Alison Reevey
Treasurer Keith Haywood
Promote professional awareness of the needs of the language impaired child and encourage teaching skills

National Association of Social Workers in Education

Hon General Secretary Grace Cheese 9 Ash Cl, Swaffham, Norfolk PE37 7NH; Tel (01603) 223473

National Association of Youth and Community Education Officers

Executive Secretary John Tate Cross Pk, Ringmore, S Devon TQ7 4HW; Tel (01548) 810891

Professional Association of Nursery Nurses (PANN)

2 St James Ct, Friar Gate, Derby DE1 1BT; Tel (01332) 343029
Chairperson L. Underhill
Vice-Chairperson D. Barnes
Immediate Past Chairperson A. Campbell
Hon Secretary L. Porter
Hon Treasurer P. Bonner
A registered trade union with a Certificate of Independence and a membership of 4,000. Promotes professionalism within nursery nursing and negotiates with local authorities. It is the only trade union run by nursery nurses for nursery nurses and is expanding rapidly

National Council

South East Region
R. Williams 27 Manor Rd, West Ealing, London

North West Region
L. Porter 22 Barrett Crt, Bury, Lancs

East Midlands Region
J. Benniston 113A Melbourne Rd, Ibstock, Leics LE6 1NN

West Midlands Region
S. Smith 128 Clent View Rd, Bartley Grn, Birmingham B32 4LY

North East Region
W. Jackson 8 Brantford Villas, Bradford

Subject Advisers/Societies

Association for Astronomy Education

Secretary Teresa Grafton R.A.S., Burlington Hse, Piccadilly, London W1V ONL

Association of Law Teachers

Nottingham Law School, Burton St, Nottingham NG1 4BU; Tel (0115) 941 8418 Ext 2550; Fax (0115) 948 6489
Secretary John Hodgson

Association for Liberal Education

Secretary Barbara Crosbie Eastleigh College of Further Education, Chestnut Ave, Eastleigh, Hants SO5 5HT; Tel (01703) 644011

Association of Motor Vehicle Teachers

Secretary T. Mellard 23 Hilland Dr, Bishopston, Swansea SA3 3AJ; Tel (0144 128) 2843

Association for the Teaching of Psychology
c/o British Psychology Society, St Andrew's Hse, 48 Princes Rd East, Leicester LE1 7DR; Tel (0116) 245 9568

Christian Education Movement
Royal Bldgs, Victoria St, Derby DE1 1GW; Tel (01332) 296655; Fax (01332) 343253
General Secretary Stephen Orchard, MA, PhD

Centre for Design and Technology Education
Head R.J. Booth University of Wolverhampton, Castle View, Dudley, West Midlands DY1 3HR; Tel (01902) 323532

General Studies Association
6 New Row, Wass, W York YO6 4BG; Tel (0134 76) 388
Chair F.I. Magee

Incorporated Society of Musicians
10 Stratford Pl, London W1N 9AE
Chief Executive Neil Hoyle; Tel 0171-629 4413; Fax 0171-408 1538

Music Advisers National Association
Secretary Keith Willis County Music Centre, Westfield Primary School, Bonsey La, Westfield, Woking, Surrey GU22 9PR; Tel (01483) 728711

Music Masters' and Mistresses' Association
Administrator Mrs Alexandra White 71 Portsmouth Rd, Guildford, Surrey GU2 5BS; Tel (01483) 34481; Fax (01483) 69920

National Association for Design Education
General Secretary F. Zankor, MA(Ed), NDD, DLC, FRSA, 26 Dorchester Cl, Mansfield, Notts, NG18 4QW; Fax (01623) 631551

National Association of Advisers and Inspectors in Design and Technology (NAAIDT)
Secretary R.H. Welch 124 Kidmore Rd, Caversham Heights, Reading, Berks RG4 7NB; Tel (01734) 470615 (home), (01734) 233682 (office)

National Association of Educational Inspectors, Advisers and Consultants
General Secretary W.H. Wright, BA, MEd 1 Heath Square, Boltro Rd, Haywards Heath, West Sussex RH16 1BL; Tel (01444) 441279; Fax (01444) 458178
President P. Jefferson N. Tyneside County Council
Immediate Past-President M. Jolley L.B. Croydon

National Association of Language Advisers
Hon Secretary R.S. Heald Education Services Adviser, Education Dept, Margaret St, Birmingham B3 3BU; Tel 0121-235 2706

National Association of Mathematics Advisers
Secretary Ann Hibbert General Education Inspector, Education Dept, Taberner Hse, Park La, Croydon CR9 1TP; Tel 0181-686 4433 Ext 2147

National Association for Teaching English and Other Community Languages to Adults
NATECLA National Centre, South Birmingham College, 524 Stratford Rd, Birmingham B11 4AJ; Tel 0121-694 5070; Fax 0121-766 6618
Administrator Dilys Garrod

National Drama
Chair Geoff Readman Trent Lodge, Main St, North Muskham, Newark NG23 6HD
Secretary Pam Bowell
Treasurer Roger Hancock

Physical Education Association of Great Britain and Northern Ireland
Ling Hse, 5 Western Ct, Bromley St, Digbeth, Birmingham B9 4AN; Tel 0121-753 0909; Fax 0121-753 0170

Society of Teachers in Business Education
88 Springfield Rd, Millhouses, Sheffield S7 2GF
General/Membership Secretary Margaret Maxfield, FSBT

Society of Teachers of Speech and Drama
Hon General Secretary Ann Jones, LRAM, LGSM 73 Berry Hill Rd, Mansfield, Notts NG18 4RU; Tel (01623) 27636; Fax (01623) 27636

Standing Conference on Schools' Science and Technology (SCSST)
76 Portland Pl, London W1N 4AA; Tel 0171-278 2468; Fax 0171-753 5200
President HRH The Duke of Edinburgh, KG, KT, FRS
Chairman Dr N. Brian Smith, CBE
Chief Executive A. Parkin, BSc
SCSST aims to excite young people about science and technology through innovatory approaches in teaching and joint activities between schools and industry. This is done via the activities of the CREST Award Scheme, Young Engineers clubs, and the 50 Science and Technology Regional Organisations (SATROs) throughout the UK (list available). Other activities include accredited INSET courses for teachers

Teachers

Association of Career Teachers
Headquarters Hillsboro, Castledine St, Loughborough, Leics LE11 2DX
Chairman M. Anderson 23 Befoe Cres, Newton Aycliffe, Co Durham; Tel (01325) 312044
Special Educational Needs Team, Durham County Council
Hon Treasurer R.M. Burley 11 Burton St, Loughborough, Leics, (0509) 268735
Sacred Heart RC Primary School, Gray St, Loughborough
General Secretary P. Yaffe Hillsboro, Castledine St, Loughborough, Leics LE11 2DX; Tel (01509) 214617

Association of Christian Teachers
2 Romeland Hill, St Albans, Herts AL3 4ET; Tel (01727) 840298; Fax (01727) 848966

Association of Secondary Teachers in Ireland

General Secretary Charlie Lennon, BA, HDE ASTI Hse, Winetavern St, Dublin 8; Tel Dublin 6719144; Fax Dublin 6719280

CFBT Education Services

Quality Hse, Gyosei Campus, London Rd, Reading, Berks RG1 5AQ; Tel (01734) 756200; Fax (01734) 756365
Chief Executive Neil McIntosh

National Association for Teachers of Religious Knowledge for Jesus and His Cross

Organiser D.C. Howlett Flat 1, 16 Clarendon Rd, Birmingham B16

Swimming Teachers' Association

Anchor Hse, Birch St, Walsall WS2 8HZ; Tel (01922) 645097; Fax (01922) 720628
Company Secretary A.W. Harvey, BA, FSTA
Encouragement of high professional swimming standards, provision of Educational teaching syllabus and certification of teachers of swimming

Ulster Teachers' Union

94 Malone Rd, Belfast BT9 5HP; Tel (01232) 662216; Fax (01232) 663055
General Secretary David Allen
Assistant General Secretary Ray Calvin
Field Officer Avril Chatterley

World Confederation of Teachers

33 rue de Trèves, 1040 Brussels, Belgium; Tel 230.60.90; Fax 230.87.22; Telex 26966 cmtwcl
Secretary General R. Denis

Tutors

Association of Tutors Incorporated

Hon Secretary Dr D.J. Cornelius Sunnycroft, 63 King Edward Rd, Northampton NN1 5LY; Tel (01604) 24171; Fax (01604) 24718

Universities–Teachers and Administrators

Association of University and College Lecturers (AUCL)

Chairman Dr N.A.A. Macfarlane (Nottingham Trent University)
Deputy Chairman K. Harry (Coventry University)
Vice-Chairman Dr J.A. Simmons (University of Westminster)
Senior Vice-Chairman N.C. Gates (University of Hertfordshire)
Vice-Chairman Dr G. Corney (University of Glamorgan)
Vice-Chairman C.H. Minta (Bolton IHE)
Vice-Chairman V. Harrhy (Edge Hill College of HE)
Vice-Chairman Dr R.A. Scott (University of Greenwich)
Treasurer Dr B. Dury (University of the West of England)
Minutes Secretary Dr R.A. Scott (University of Greenwich)
National Secretary Dr M.G. Roberts (UNL)
Assistant National Secretary Dr H.L. Mason (University of Portsmouth)
Chief Executive C. Cheesman 104 Albert Rd, Southsea, Hants PO5 2SN; Tel (01705) 818625; Fax (01705) 838187

Association of University Teachers

General Secretary David Triesman United Hse, 9 Pembridge Rd, London W11 3JY; Tel 0171-221 4370; Fax 0171-727 6547

Association of University Teachers (Scotland)

Regional Officer D. Bleiman, MA, MBA, MIPM, AUT 6 Castle St, Edinburgh EG2 3AT; Tel 0131-226 6694

Committee of Vice-Chancellors and Principals of the Universities of the UK

29 Tavistock Sq, London WC1H 9EZ; Tel 0171-387 9231; Fax 0171-388 8649
Chairman Dr Kenneth Edwards
Secretary Thomas Burgner

Association of University Administrators

Executive Secretary R.G. Ives AUA Office, University of Manchester, Manchester M13 9PL; Tel 0161-275 2063; Fax 0161-275 2036
AUA aims to advance education by fostering the development of sound methods of administration and management in higher education. It holds an annual conference, organises courses, issues publications from time to time and establishes links with administrators and managers in higher education overseas

Engineering Professors' Conference

Chairman Prof P.B. Morice, FEng Dept of Civil Engineering, Southampton University, Southampton SO9 5NH; Tel (01703) 592860; Fax 47661 SOTONU G; Telex (0703) 593017

International Association of University Professors and Lecturers

7 rue Mirabeau, 75016 Paris, France; Tel (1) 40 50 68 11

Standing Conference of Heads of Modern Languages in Polytechnics and Other Colleges

Hon Secretary J.R. French, MA School of Languages and Area Studies, Portsmouth Polytechnic, Wiltshire Bldg, Hampshire Terr, Portsmouth PO1 2BU; Tel (01705) 843059

19 Physical Education and Sport

National Sports Councils and Committees

Sports Council

16 Upper Woburn Pl, London WC1H 0QP; Tel 0171-388 1277
Chairman Sir Peter G. Yarranton
Vice-Chairman Prof J. Allan Patmore, BLitt, MA
Director-General Vacancy
Member Julia Bracewell
Member Trevor Brooking, MBE
Member Gerald Dennis
Member Tim Marshall, MBE
Member Keith Oates
Member Michael Parker
Member David Simon
Member Graeme Simmers, OBE, CA
Member Dr Sarah Springman
Member Jeoff Thompson
Member Ossie Wheatley, MA

The Sports Council received its Royal Charter on 4th February 1972, formally recognising it as an independent body, with the primary aims of promoting sport and physical recreation in Great Britain and of fostering the provision of facilities. For this purpose the Sports Council receives an annual grant-in-aid from the Department of National Heritage

Sports Council Regional Offices

Eastern Region 19 The Cresc, off Tavistock St, Bedford MK40 2QP; Tel (01234) 345222; *Regional Director* H. Darbon
East Midland Region Grove Hse, Bridgeford Rd, West Bridgford, Nottingham NG2 6AP; Tel (0115) 982 1887, 822586; *Regional Director* T. Garfield
Greater London and South East Regions Crystal Palace National Sports Centre, PO Box 480, Ledrington Rd, London SE19 2BQ; Tel 0181-778 8600; *Regional Director London* A. Sutch; *Regional Director South East* M. Lockhart
Northern Region Aykley Heads, Durham DH1 5UU; Tel 0191-384 9595; *Regional Director* D. Dunlop
North West Region Astley Hse, Quay St, Manchester M3 4AE; Tel 0161-834 0338; *Regional Director* C. Clark
Southern Region 51a Church St, Caversham, Reading RG4 8AX; Tel (01734) 483311; *Regional Director* David Dolman
South Western Region Ashlands Hse, Ashlands, Crewkerne, Somerset TA18 7LQ; Fax (01460) 73491; *Regional Director* P. Barson
West Midlands Region Metropolitan Hse, 1 Hagley Rd, Five Ways, Birmingham B16 8TT; Tel 0121-454 3808; *Regional Director* D. Pryor
Yorkshire and Humberside Region Coronet Hse, Queen St, Leeds LS1 4PW; Tel (0113) 243 6443/14; *Regional Director* C. Villiers

National Sports Centres

Bisham Abbey National Sports Centre, nr Marlow, Buckinghamshire SL7 1RT; Tel (0162 84) 76911; *Director* B. Stephens
Crystal Palace National Sports Centre, Norwood, London SE19 2BB; Tel 0181-778 0131; *Director* Peter Lamb
Holme Pierrepont National Water Sports Centre, Adbolton La, Holme Pierrepont, Nottingham NG12 2LU; Tel (0115) 982 1212; *Director* J. Davis
Lilleshall Hall National Sports Centre, Nr Newport, Shropshire TF10 9AT; Tel (01952) 603003; *Director* Bev Stephens
The National Centre for Mountain Activities, Plas y Brenin, Capel Curig, Gwynedd LL24 0ET; Tel (0169 014) 214, 280; *Director* Dave Alcock

19 Physical Education and Sport

Central Council of Physical Recreation

On 1st June 1972 the staff, assets and undertaking of the CCPR were transferred to the Sports Council. The CCPR remains in being as a non-executive body with two main functions: that of constituting a standing forum of the national governing and representative bodies of sport and physical recreation, and acting as a consultative body to the Sports Council

Francis Hse, Francis St, London SW1P 1DE; Tel 0171-828 3163/14

Sports Council for Wales

Welsh Institute of Sport, Sophia Gdns, Cardiff CF1 9SW; Tel (01222) 397571

Chairman O.S. Wheatley, MA

Chief Executive L. Tatham

Sports Centres

Welsh Institute of Sport, Sophia Gdns, Cardiff CF1 9SW; Tel (01222) 397571

Plas Menai National Watersports Centre, Caernarfon, Gwynedd LL55 1UE; Tel (01248) 670964

Scottish Sports Council

Caledonia Hse, South Gyle, Edinburgh EH12 9DQ; Tel 0131-317 7200

Chairman Graeme Simmers, CA, OBE

Vice-Chairman G. Malcolm Murray, FFA

Chief Executive Allan Alstead, CBE, MPhil

Member Michael C. Barron

Member Alan G. Grossett, MA, LLB, WS, NP

Member E. Raistrick

Member Lesley Grant, MA, MBE

Member John Frame

Member P.Fred Nelson, BSc, CEng, MIEE

Member Alan Blackshaw, OBE, VRD, MA, FRGS

Member John F. Loughray

Member Myra Nimmo, BSc, PhD

The Council was established by Royal Charter in 1972 with the objects of fostering the knowledge and practice of sport and physical recreation among the public at large in Scotland. It receives annual grant-in-aid from the Government from which it provides financial assistance to governing bodies of sport – for coaching, administration and international events and to local authorities and others – for sports projects including national and demonstration facilities. The Council also undertakes research, provides information and advisory services, and operates the following three national sports training centres

The Scottish Sports Council has established a Scottish Sports Association, membership of which is open to all the governing bodies of sport and physical recreation (in Scotland) and other appropriate organisations. Its functions include acting as a consultative body to the Scottish Sports Council

National Sports Training Centres

The Scottish National Sports Centre: Cumbrae Largs, Ayrshire KA30 8RW; Tel (01475) 674666; *Director (Inverclyde and Cumbrae)* M.A. McKenzie

The Scottish National Sports Centre: Glenmore Lodge Aviemore, Inverness-shire PH22 1QU; Tel (01479) 861256; *Director* A. Anderson

The Scottish National Sports Centre: Inverclyde Largs, Ayrshire KA30 8RW; Tel (01475) 674666

General Organisations

British Association of Advisers and Lecturers in Physical Education, Nelson Hse, 6 The Beacon, Exmouth, Devon EX8 2AG; Tel (01395) 263247; Fax (01395) 263247; *Gen Secretary* G.M. Edmondson

British Association of Sport and Medicine, Education Officer Nancy Laurenson c/o National Sports Medicine Institute, Medical School of St Bartholomews Hospital, Charterhouse Sq, London EC1M 6BQ; Tel 0171-253 3244; Fax 0171-251 0774; *Executive Officer* Barry Hill The Association gives information on all aspects of sports medicine to individuals and organisations seeking sport injury and educational advice

British Field Sports Society, 59 Kennington Rd, London SE1 7PZ; Tel 0171-928 4742; *Director* Peter Smith The BFSS is the only umbrella organisation supporting all field sports. Provides educational material on request and trained speakers with videos etc

British Olympic Association, 1 Wandsworth Plain, London SW18 1EH; Tel 0181-871 2677; Fax 0181-871 9104; Telex 932312 BOAG Promotes Olympism in Great Britain and organises and ensures participation of a Great Britain team in the Olympic Games

The British Schools Judo Association (BSJA), 21 Finborough Rd, Tooting, London SW17 9HY; Tel 0181-640 6083; Fax 0181-874 8590; *Hon General Secretary* Simon R.W. Hicks Promotion of schools' and colleges' judo, national/international competitions, star award scheme and publication of judo related curriculums and policies

Association of Sports Historians, 16 Faro, Coates Hill Rd, Bickley, Kent BR1 2RR; Tel 0181-295 0188; Fax 0181-295 0190; *Chairman* Prof Wray Vamplew; *Secretary* Chris Harte Stimulates, promotes, and co-ordinates interest in the historical study of sport, physical education, recreation and leisure, particularly relating to UK

British Universities' Sports Federation, 11 Allcock St, Birmingham B9 4DY; Tel 0121-766 8855; Fax 0121-766 8997; *Secretary* Peter Rhodes Student sports administration for British universities in membership

British Veterans' Athletic Federation (BVAF), 67–71 Goswell Rd, London EC1V 7EN; Tel 0171-250 1881; *Hon Administrative Officer* J.F. Fitzgerald Provides athletic competition at national and international level for men over 40 and women over 35 years of age

Civil Service Sports Council (CSSC), 7/8 Buckingham Pl, Bellfield Rd, High Wycombe, Bucks HP13 5HW; Tel (01494) 461800; *General Secretary* F.P. Krinks Sport, recreation and social activities and facilities for Civil Servants, Post Office, British Telecom staff and related bodies

The Commonwealth Games Federation, Knightsbridge Hse, 197 Knightsbridge, London SW7 1RZ; Tel 0171-225 5555; Fax 0171-225 5197; Telex 919156 ELFLDN G; *President* HRH The Prince Edward CVO; *Chairman* A. de O. Sales, CBE, JP; *Hon Secretary* David Dixon, CVO Promotes at four-yearly intervals the Commonwealth Games, establishes rules/regulations for the conduct of the Games (in conformity with technical rules of International Federations governing sports concerned) and encourages amateur sport throughout the Commonwealth by efficient organisation of the Games' competitions

The Institute of Sport and Recreation Management, Giffard Hse, 36/38 Sherrard St, Melton Mowbray, Leics LE13 1XJ; Tel (01664) 65531; Fax (01664) 501155

The Institute of Sport and Recreation Management (Scottish Branch), Kirktown Depot, Broomhill Rd, Spurryhillock Ind Est, Stonehaven AB3 2NH; Tel (01569) 767202; *Training and Education Officer* T. Parker

Institute of Leisure and Amenity Management, Lower Basildon, Reading RG8 9NE; Tel (01491) 874222; *Director* A. Smith; *Assistant Director (Education)* I.C. Fleming

The Institute of Sports Medicine (ISM), Burlington Hse, Piccadilly, London W1V 0LQ; Tel 0171-287 5269 (Ansaphone); *Hon Secretary* Dr W.T. Orton, MB, BCh, DPH, MFPHM Postgraduate medical education in sports medicine

National Coaching Foundation, 114 Cardigan Rd, Headingley, Leeds LS6 3BJ; Tel (0113) 274 4802; *Chief Executive* Sue Campbell, MBE The NCF provides a range of services for coaches at all levels including courses, publications and videos. Coaching

Focus Gold subscription service. Sporting Update current awareness services The NCF is the one-stop shopping centre for all issues relating to coaching and coach education. Its work programmes are delivered locally through a UK network of 16 National Coaching Centres. Products and resources are sold through its trading subsidiary, Coachwise Ltd

National Playing Fields Association (Scottish Branch), 20 Queen St, Edinburgh EH2 1JX; Tel 0131-225 4307; *Chairman* David Reynolds; *Secretary/Treasurer* John E. Tunnah

Northern Ireland Commonwealth Games Council, 22 Mountcoole Pk, Cave Hill, Belfast BT14 8JR; Tel (01232) 716558; R.J. McColgan, MBE

The Physical Education Association of Great Britain and Northern Ireland, Francis Hse, Francis St, London SW1P 1DE; Tel 0171-828 9229; Fax 0171-828 9575; *General Secretary* Peter Harrison Organisation for the physical education profession

Royal Air Force Sports Board, Ministry of Defence, Adastral Hse, Theobald's Rd, London WC1X 8RU

Scottish Association of Advisers in Physical Education, Newton Advisors' Centre, Green St La, Ayr KA8 8BH; *Secretary* Malcolm Renny; Tel (01292) 260325; Fax (01292) 611115; *President* Ian Scott Area Education Office, Dryfe Rd, Lockerbie DG11 2AP; Tel (01576) 202287

Scottish Industrial Sports Association, 34 Caroline Terr, Edinburgh EH12 8QX; *Secretary* Allan G. Shaw

Scottish Universities Physical Education Association, President June Adamson Dept of Physical Education, Edinburgh University, 46 Pleasance, Edinburgh EH8 9TJ; *Secretary* Fraser McGlynn Aberdeen University, Butchart Recreation Centre, University Rd, Aberdeen AB9 2UW

Sport and Recreation Information Group (SPRIG) *Secretary* Stephen Hewett, Centre for Sports Science and History, Main Library, University of Birmingham, Edgbaston Birmingham, B15 2TT, 021-414 5843; *Chair* Lesley Gunter Sports Library, c/o Central Library, Surrey St, Sheffield S1 1XS; Tel (0113) 274 4802 Encourages bibliographic control of the literature and co-operative exploitation of resources, improving dissemination and awareness of sport and recreation documentation

British Universities Sports Association, 8 Union St, London SE1 1SD; Tel 0171-357 8555

National Sports Organisations

England, Scotland, Wales and Northern Ireland

Services

Headquarters: Directorate of Physical and Adventurous Training (Army), Rm 12 Bldg 370, Headquarters Doctrinex Training, Trenchard Lines, Upavon, Nr Pewsey, Wilts SN9 6BE; Tel (01980) 615160

Army School of Physical Training, Queen's Ave, Aldershot, Hants GU11 2LB; Tel (01252) 24431 Ext 2136 (Direct Dial) (01252) 347136

Army Sport Control Board, Ministry of Defence, Clayton Barracks, Aldershot, Hants GU11 2BG

Royal Air Force, Group Captain (Physical Education), HQPTC, RAF Innsworth, Glos GL3 1EZ

Royal Air Force School of Physical Training, RAF Cosford, nr Wolverhampton, West Midlands WV7 3EX; Tel (01902) 372393 Ext 2271

Royal Air Force Sports Board, Ministry of Defence, Adastral Hse, Theobald's Rd, London WC1X 8RU

Royal Marines School of Music, Canada Rd, Deal, Kent CT14 7EH; Tel (01304) 362121 Ext 272

HMS **Temeraire**, Directorate of Naval Physical Training and Sport and RN School of Physical Training, Burnaby Rd, Portsmouth PO1 4QS

RN and RM Sports Control Board, Ministry of Defence, HMS Temeraire, Burnaby Rd, Portsmouth PO1 2HB

Angling

Anglers' Co-operative Association (ACA), Castlegate, Grantham, Lincs NG31 6SW; Tel (01476) 61008; Fax (01476) 60900; *Director* Allen Edwards Common Law actions to prevent pollution of waterways

Confederation of English Fly Fishers (CEFF), 31 Meadow Rd, Hartshill, Nuneaton CV10 0NL; *Hon Secretary* John Hedges Organises international fly fishing events

National Federation of Anglers, Headquarters, Halliday Hse, Egginton Junction, Nr Hilton, Derby DE65 6GU; Tel (01283) 734735; Fax (01283) 734799 Enquiries to Chief Administration Officer. Governing body of coarse angling

National Federation of Sea Anglers, 51A Queen St, Newton Abbot, Devon TQ12 2QJ; Tel (01626) 331330; Fax (01626) 331330; *Development Officer* David Rowe, to whom all enquiries should be sent. The NFSA is the governing body of the Sport within England, and looks after the interests of individual anglers, Sea Angling Clubs, their members, and the development of the sport

Archery

The British Crossbow Society, 2 Vicarage Rd, Chellaston, Derbys DE7 1SD; Tel (01332) 700180; *President* A. Gunn Represents crossbowmen in all matters appertaining to their sport and promotes competitive amateur competition throughout the UK

The British Long–Bow Society, 65 Chiltern Cl, North Common, Warmley, Bristol BS15 5UL; Tel (0117) 967 7223; *Hon Secretary/Treasurer* H.D. Soar Safeguards and perpetuates the custom and usage of the traditional English recreational long–bow through competitive tournaments

Grand National Archery Society, Seventh St, National Agricultural Centre, Stoneleigh, Kenilworth, Warks CV8 2LG; Tel (01203) 696631

National Field Archery Society, 67 Seaburn Rd, Toton, Beeston, Nottingham NG9 6HN; Tel (0115) 972 4615; *Hon Secretary* R. Bickerstaffe Organisation of archery competitions in wooded terrain in which hunting skills are simulated

Northern Ireland Archery Society, Hon Secretary Stephen Ward 8 Ballynahinch Rd, Hillsborough, Co Down BT26 6AR; Tel (01846) 682432 (Home)

Association Football

Amateur Football Alliance, 55 Islington Park St, London N1 1QB; Tel 0171-359 3493/14; Fax 0171-359 5027; *Hon Secretary* W.P. Goss, MSc, BSc, ARCS, DIC Administration of amateur football for member clubs and referees of the Amateur Football Alliance

English Schools' Football Association, 1/2 Eastgate St, Stafford ST16 2NQ; Tel (01785) 51142; Fax (01785) 55485; *Chief Executive* M.R. Berry

The Football Association, 16 Lancaster Gate, London W2 3LW; Tel 0171-262 4542, 0171-402 7151; *Chief Executive* R.H.G. Kelly The Football Association is the governing body of the sport in England and protects and promotes the game at all levels

Football Association of Wales, Plymouth Chambers, 3 Westgate St, Cardiff CF1 1DD; Tel (01222) 372325

Irish Football Association, 20 Windsor Ave, Belfast BT9 6EE; Tel (01232) 669458

19 Physical Education and Sport

Athletics

Amateur Athletic Association of England, 225A Bristol Rd, Edgbaston, Birmingham B5 7UB; Tel 0121-440 5000; Fax 0121-440 0555

Amateur Athletic Association of England Ltd, Francis Hse, Francis St, London SW1P 1DE; Tel 0171-828 4731; M. Hartman, CBE

British Athletics Federation, 225A Bristol Rd, Edgbaston, Birmingham B5 7UB; Tel 0121-456 4050; Fax 0121-456 4061

British Triathlon Association (BTA), Dover Leisure Centre, Townwall St, Dover, Kent CT16 1LN; Tel (01304) 202565; Fax (01304) 214840; *Chief Executive* Elaine Shaw Controls and promotes the sport of Triathlon (swimming, cycling and running) and Duathlon (any two of previous three) against a continuously running clock

English Cross–Country Association (ECCA), 11 Heslop Dr, Darlington, Co Durham DL1 5TQ; Tel (01325) 464822; *Hon Secretary* M. Frazer Encourages and promotes cross–country running and lays down guidelines for affiliated clubs and associations

English Schools' Athletic Association, 26 Newborough Grn, New Malden, Surrey KT3 5HS; Tel 0181-949 1506; Fax 0181-949 1506; D.R. Littlewood

International Amateur Athletic Federation (IAAF), 17 Rue Princesse Florestine, BP 359, MC-98007, Monaco; Tel 33 93 30 70 70; Fax 33 93 15 95 15; *President* Dr Primo Nebiolo; *General Secretary* Istvan Gyulai World governing body for track and field athletics

Kangaroo Club, (Long and Triple Jump) 'Oakdene', The Old Rectory, Lowe Hill Rd, Wem, Shropshire SY4 5UA; Tel (01939) 233220

Northern Ireland Amateur Athletic Federation, House of Sport, Upper Malone Rd, Belfast BT9 5LA; Tel (01232) 381222; Fax (01232) 682757

Road Runners' Club, 21 Station Rd, Welwyn, Herts AL6 0DU; Tel 0171-247 0371; *Chairman* J.C. Legge

Badminton

Badminton Association of England Ltd, National Badminton Centre, Bradwell Rd, Loughton Lodge, Milton Keynes MK8 9LA; Tel (01908) 568822; Fax (01908) 566922

Badminton Union of Ireland, Ulster Branch, The Hse of Sport, Upper Malone Rd, Belfast BT9 5LA; Tel (01232) 381222

International Badminton Federation (IBF), 4 Manor Pk, Mackenzie Way, Cheltenham, Glos GL51 9TX; Tel (01242) 234094; *Executive Director* David Shaw Promotion and development of international badminton

Welsh Badminton Union, 3rd Floor, 3 Westgate St, Cardiff CF1 1JF; Tel (01222) 222082; L. Williams

Baseball and Softball

Welsh Baseball Union, 63 Shakespeare Cres, Newport, Gwent; Tel (01633) 64311; L.C. Mort

Basketball

Basketball Association of Wales, Connies Hse, Rhymney River Bridge Rd, Cardiff CF3 7YZ; Tel (01222) 454395; Fax (01222) 454637

English Basket Ball Association, 48 Bradford Rd, Stanningley, Leeds LS28 6DF; Tel (0113) 236 1166; Fax (0113) 236 1022; David Ransom, MSc

English Mini Basket Ball Association, PO Box 22, Royston, Herts SG8 7BD; Tel (01763) 243650; Evenings (01223) 207213; Fax (01763) 241499; *General Secretary* Kenneth G. Charles, MBE Promotes the development of mini basketball in schools and youth organisations

Billiards and Snooker

The Billiards and Snooker Control Council, 92 Kirkstall Rd, Leeds LS3 1LT; Tel (0113) 244 0586; Fax (0113) 246 8418; *Secretary/Chief Executive* David Ford Governing body of the sport

International Billiards and Snooker Federation (IBSF), 92 Kirkstall Rd, Leeds LS3 1LT; Tel +44 532 440586; Fax +44 532 468418; *Secretary* David Ford World governing body

Bobsleigh

British Bobsleigh Association (BBA), The Secretary, The Chestnuts, 85 High St, Codford, Wilts BA12 0ND; Tel (01985) 850064; Fax (01985) 850064 Promotes the sport of bobsleigh and maintains a high level of international competition

Bowling

British Crown Green Bowling Association, 14 Leighton Ave, Maghull, Merseyside L31 0AH; Tel 0151-526 8367; *Secretary* R. Holt Promotes the game of crown green bowls and develops it throughout the UK

English Bowling Association, Lyndhurst Rd, Worthing, W Sussex BN11 2AZ; Tel (01903) 820222; Fax (01903) 820444

English Bowling Federation (EBF), 62 Frampton Pl, Boston, Lincs PE21 8EL; Tel (01205) 366201; *Secretary* John Webb Promotes, fosters and safeguards the flat-green game of bowls and formulates rules and laws

English Bowls Council, 15 Datchworth Ct, Village Rd, Enfield EN1 2DS; Tel 0181-367 1269; *Hon Secretary* Eric J. Crosbie, MBE, JP A consultative council for all seven codes in England. (Men and women)

English Indoor Bowling Association, 290A Barking Rd, London E6 3BA; Tel 0181-470 1237; Fax 0181-503 5805; *Acting National Secretary* Peter Neighbour Promotes, fosters and safeguards the level green game of indoor bowls for men in England

English Women's Bowling Association (EWBA), 2 Case Gdns, Seaton, Devon EX12 2AP; Tel (01297) 21317; Fax (01297) 21317; *Hon Secretary* Nancie Colling Brings together all women's county associations in England and encourages the game generally

English Women's Indoor Bowling Association (EWIBA), 9 Pine Rd, Whitenap, Romsey, Hampshire SO51 BSG; Tel (01794) 514922; *Secretary* K. Martin Runs national competitions. Encourages both young and old to play bowls. National competitions include 'under 31s'; national competition for 50+; inter-county competition 'Atherley Trophy' plus National Mixed Competition "Egham Trophy"

Guernsey Bowling Association, Meadow View, Mount Row, St Peter Port, Guernsey, Channel Islands; Tel (01481) 25556; *Hon Secretary* Simon D. Masterton

Guernsey Indoor Bowling Association, Hougue du Pommier, Vale, Guernsey, Channel Islands GY6 8BD; Tel (01481) 57100; Fax (01481) 51251; *President* H. Le Tissier

Welsh Bowling Association, 48 Pochin Cres, Tredegar, Gwent NP2 4JS; Tel (01495) 723836; Alan H. Williams

Boxing

The Amateur Boxing Association of England Ltd, Crystal Palace, National Sports Centre, London SE19 2BB; Tel 0181-778 0251; Fax 0181-778 9324; *Secretary* C. Brown

Welsh Amateur Boxing Association, 8 Erw Wen, Rhiwbina, Cardiff CF4 6JW

Camping

The Camping and Caravanning Club, Greenfields Hse, Westwood Way, Coventry CV4 8JH; Tel (01203) 694995; Fax (01203) 694886

Canoeing

British Canoe Union, Adbolton La, West Bridgford, Nottingham NG2 5AS; Tel (0115) 982 1100; *Director* Paul Owen

Canoe Camping Club, 25 Waverley Rd, South Norwood, London SE25 4HT

Caving

British Cave Research Association (BCRA), 20 Woodland Ave, Westonzoyland, Bridgwater, Somerset TA7 0LQ; Tel (01278) 691539; *Administrator* Bryan Ellis Promotion of speleological research and related activities and the provision of support services

National Caving Association, Momomark Hse, 27 Old Gloucester St, London WC1N 3XX

Cricket

The Cricket Council, Lord's Cricket Ground, London NW8 8QZ; Tel 0171-286 4405

Marylebone Cricket Club (MCC), Lord's Cricket Ground, London NW8 8QN; Tel 0171-289 1611; *Secretary* Lt Col J.R. Stephenson, OBE Members' club staging first class cricket for public attendance. Indoor school, banqueting/conference facilities, cricket museum/art gallery, souvenir bookshop, organised tours

National Cricket Association, Lord's Cricket Ground, London NW8 8QZ; Tel 0171-289 6098, 0171-286 4766 (Competitions); *Director of Administration and Development* Terry N. Bates Encourages the playing of cricket, organises the National Coaching Scheme and represents grass roots cricket on the Cricket Council

Northern Cricket Union of Ireland, Hse of Sport, Upper Malone Rd, Belfast BT9 5LA; Tel (01232) 381222

Women's Cricket Association, Warwickshire County Cricket Ground, Edgbaston Rd, Birmingham B5 7QX; Tel 0121-400 0520; Fax 0121-446 6344; *Executive Director* Maria Grant

Croquet

The Croquet Association, Hurlingham Club, Ranelagh Gdns, London SW6 3PR; Tel 0171-736 3148; *Secretary* Tony Antenen

Curling

Royal Caledonian Curling Club, 2 Coates Cres, Edinburgh EH3 7AN; Tel 0131-225 7083; Fax 0131-220 6191; *Principal Officer* A.C.B. Guild Unites curlers throughout the world and regulates by rules the ancient Scottish game of curling

Cycling

British Cycle Speedway Council (BCSC), Central Office, 57 Rectory La, Poringland, Norwich NR14 7SW; Tel (0150 86) 3880; Rod Witham; *Administrator* Ros Burrows; *Administrator* Karen Wells Unification of cycle speedway organisations, gaining national recognition, obtaining grant aid assistance, co-ordination of leagues and competitions

British Cycling Federation, National Cycling Centre, 1 Stuart St, Manchester M11 4DQ; Tel 0161-223 2244; Fax 0161-231 0592

Cyclists' Touring Club (CTC), National HQ, Cotterell Hse, 69 Meadrow, Godalming, Surrey; Tel (01483) 417217 Britain's largest national cycling association for touring, technical, insurance and Legal Aid information. Bi-monthly magazine. Handbook. List of 200 local groups and 200 affiliated groups. Membership details on request

Northern Ireland Cycling Federation, M.K. Wright 8 Wyncairn Rd, Larne, Co Antrim BT40 2DX

Professional Cycling Association (PCA), 30 Windermere Rd, Wolverhampton, West Midlands WV6 9DL; Tel (01902) 751831; *Administrative Officer* S.W. Kite The furtherance of professional cycle racing in Britain

Road Time Trials Council, 77 Arlington Drive, Pennington, Leigh, Lancs WN7 3QP; Tel (01942) 603976; Fax (01942) 262326; P.A. Heaton

Dancing, Movement and Keep Fit

The Dalcroze Society (Incorporated), 41A Woodmansterne Rd, Coulsdon, Surrey CR5 2DJ; Tel 0181-645 0714; *Treasurer and Secretary* Patricia Piqué Develops the basic principles of Eurythmics in the light of modern educational needs through training courses and recreational classes

Dance Council for Wales/Cyngor Dawns Cymru, Thurgarton Hse, Longdown Bank, St Dogmaels, nr Cardigan, Dyfed SA43 3DU; Tel (01239) 612138

The English Folk Dance and Song Society, Cecil Sharp Hse, 2 Regent's Park Rd, London NW1 7AY; Tel 0171-485 2206/(0252) 722938; *Education Officer* Carolyn Robson

Health and Beauty Exercise, 52 London St, Chertsey, Surrey KT16 8AJ; Tel (01932) 564567; Fax (01932) 567566 Exercise system for women and children, with emphasis on correct body alignment, mobility, strength, stretch and tone, Over 300 classes nationwide. Registered charity. Supported by the sports council

Imperial Society of Teachers of Dancing, Euston Hall, Birkenhead St, London WC1H 8BE; Tel 0171-837 9967; Fax 0171-833 5981

International Association of MMM (Margaret Morris Movement), PO Box 1525, Helensburgh, Dumbartonshire G84 0AF; Tel (01436) 810215; *Administrator/Director of Training* Jim Hastie MMM is a unique form of recreative movement and dance. Classes are held for all ages. Teacher training programmes available plus INSET courses for key stages 1 and 2 of the National Curriculum

International Dance Teachers' Association, International Hse, 76 Bennett Rd, Brighton BN2 5JL; Tel (01273) 685652; Fax (01273) 674388

Keep Fit Exercise Association, Northern Ireland, 8 Barnett's Cres, Belfast BT5 7BQ; Tel (01232) 489141; Rosaleen Henry

National Association of Teachers of Dancing, Suite 2, 56 The Broadway, Thatcham, Berks RG13 4HP; Tel (01635) 868888; Fax (01635) 872301

Northern Ireland Society of Dance Teachers, Clarke School of Dancing, Donegall St, Belfast BT1 2FG

Welsh Folk Dance Society/Cymdeithas Ddawns Werin Cymru, Ffynnonlwyd, Trelech, Caerfyrddin, Dyfed SA33 6QZ; Tel (01994) 484496; Dafydd M. Evans

Diving

The British Sub-Aqua Club, Telford's Quay, Ellesmere Port, Wirral L65 4FY; Tel 0151-357 1951

National Snorkellers' Club, 13 Langham Gdns, Wembley, Middx HA0 3RG; Tel 0181-959 6013; *Director* L.F. Blandford Over 450 branches throughout UK, training children aged 9 to 16 years in safe and efficient snorkel diving

Sub Aqua Association, Bryslan Hse, Upper St, Fleet, Hampshire GU13 9PE; Tel (01252) 622415; Fax (01252) 620729 Represents independent sub aqua diving clubs and promotes safe diving within a club environment

Fencing

Amateur Fencing Association, 1 Barons Gate, 33/135 Rothschild Rd, London W4 5HT

Fives

Eton Fives Association (EFA) 5 St Margaret's Cl, Berkhamsted, Herts HP4 2LH; Tel (01442) 864941; *Hon Secretary* P.K. Dicker The promotion and extension of the game of Eton fives, laws and rules, membership, competitions, sponsorship and facilities

Rugby Fives Association, Sutherland Hse, 3 Lloyds Ave, London EC3N 3DS; Tel 0171-702 3171

Flying

Aircraft Owners' and Pilots' Association (AOPA), 50a Cambridge St, London SW1V 4QQ; Tel 0171-834 5632; Fax 0171-834 8623; *Chairman* R.D. Campbell Promotes and protects the safety, aims and interests of the general aviation sector.
Headquarters of the European activities of the International Council of Aircraft owner and Pilot Associations (IAOPA) and the European General Aviation Safety Foundation (EGASF)

British Microlight Aircraft Association (BMAA), Bullring, Deddington, Banbury, Oxford OX15 0TT; Tel (01869) 338888; *Chief Executive* James Bell The governing body for microlight aviation in the UK

Gliding

British Gliding Association, Kimberley Hse, Vaughan Way, Leicester LE1 4SE; Tel (0116) 253 1051

Golf

Council of National Golf Unions, 19 Birch Grn, Formby, Liverpool L37 1NG; Tel (01704) 831800; Fax (01704) 831800; *Hon Secretary* A. Thirlwell Co-ordinates golf administration between the four National Golf Unions (England, Wales, Scotland and Ireland)

English Golf Union, 1/3 Upper King St, Leicester LE1 6XF; Tel (0116) 255 3042; Fax (0116) 247 1322

English Ladies' Golf Association, Edgbaston Golf Club, Church Rd, Birmingham B15 3TB; Tel 0121-456 2088; *Secretary* M.J. Carr Administers ladies' amateur golf in England and organises the English ladies' and girls' championships

Golf Foundation, Foundation Hse, Hanbury Manor, Ware, Hertfordshire SG12 OUH; Tel (01920) 484044

Ladies' Golf Union, The Scores, St Andrews, Fife KY16 9AT; Tel (01334) 75811; *Administrator* Elaine Mackie Upholds the rules of the game, maintains LGU system of handicapping and organises British and international events

National Golf Clubs' Advisory Association, Suite 2, Portland Sq, Bakewell, Derbys DE45 1HB; Tel (01629) 813844; *Secretary* John Crowther Safeguards the interests of member clubs and provides them with legal advice under Opinion of Counsel where necessary

The Professional Golfers' Association, Apollo Hse, The Belfry, Wishaw, Sutton Coldfield, West Midlands B76 9PT; Tel (01675) 470333; *Executive Director* Sandy Jones Protects and advances the interests of golf professionals, identifies and fulfills the needs and interests of the membership, acting as custodians for the traditions of the game, whilst promoting golf for the benefit of all

Welsh Golfing Union, Powys Hse, South Walk, Cwmbran, Gwent NP44 1PB; Tel (01633) 870261; Fax (01633) 871837

Women Professional Golfers' European Tour (WPG European Tour), The Tytherington Club, Macclesfield, Cheshire SK10 2JP; Tel (01625) 611444; Fax (01625) 610406; *Chairman and Chief Executive* Terry Coates Promotes and administers women's professional golf tournaments throughout Europe

Hockey

All England Women's Hockey Association, 51 High St, Shrewsbury, Shropshire SY1 1ST; Tel (01743) 233572; Fax (01743) 233583

British Ice Hockey Association, (Limited by Guarantee) 2nd Floor, 517 Christchurch Rd, Boscombe, Bournemouth BH1 4AG; Tel (01202) 303946; Fax (01202) 398005; *Secretary* D. Pickles Promotes the rapidly growing sport of ice hockey and encourages wider participation both from playing and spectator levels

British Octopush Association (BOA), 25 Brunswick St, Waltham Forest, London E17 9NB; Tel 0181-520 8823; *Promotions Officer (External)* Cliff Underwood The BOA is the controlling and ruling body for all underwater hockey (octopush) in the UK and is part of the world body for the sport (CMAS)

English Mixed Hockey Association, 4 The Sycamore, Horbury, Wakefield, West Yorkshire WF4 5QG; Tel (01924) 274620; *Hon Secretary* J. White Promotes the game of mixed hockey throughout England and the UK at all levels

Great Britain Olympic Hockey Board (GBOHB), 42 Woolacombe Lodge Rd, Selly Oak, Birmingham B29 6PX; Tel 0121-472 3458; *Administrator* Liz Howard Administers the needs of Great Britain men's and women's committees at international level and liaises with the British Olympic Association

Great Britain Men's Olympic Hockey Committee, 42 Woolacombe Lodge Rd, Selly Oak, Birmingham B29 6PX; Tel 0121-472 3458; *Administrator* Liz Howard Selects, trains and participates in Olympic Games. Liaises with Home Countries officiating bodies, Sports Council and Government

Schools and Youth Committee of Hockey Association, 16 Clover Dr, Hardwicke, Gloucester GL2 6TG; Tel (01452) 721247; *Secretary* J.E. Law

Ulster Women's Hockey Union, 41 The Meadow, Antrim BT41 1EY; Tel (01849) 461913; M. Agnew

Welsh Hockey Association, 1 White Hart La, Caerleon NP6 1AB; Tel (01633) 420326 (home) (01222) 584272

Welsh Women's Hockey Association, Welsh Hockey Office, Deeside Leisure Centre, Chester Rd West, Queensferry, Clwyd CH5 1SA; Tel (01244) 811825; Fax (01244) 822662

Horse Driving

Guernsey Horse Driving Society, Bonne Chance, Marais La, Vale, Guernsey, Channel Islands GY6 8BB; Tel (01481) 57868 Promotes horse driving and encourages preservation of horse drawn vehicles, harnesses and their use

Lacrosse

All England Women's Lacrosse Association, 4 Western Ct, Bromley St, Digbeth, Birmingham B9 4AN; Tel 0121-773 4422

English Lacrosse Union (ELU), Ryecroft Mills, Smith St, Ashton-under-Lyne, Lancashire OL7 0DB; Tel 0161-339 7508; *Chief Executive Officer* David Shuttleworth Promotion and development of lacrosse in England.

Welsh Lacrosse Association, 3 Tyla Teg, Pantmawr, Whitchurch, Cardiff

Lifesaving

The Royal Life Saving Society UK, Mountbatten Hse, Studley, Warks B80 7NN; Tel (01527) 853943; Fax (01527) 854453; *Director* Celia J. Godsall, DipM, MInstM

Martial Arts

British Aikido Association (BAA), 2 Heather Rise, Burley in Wharfedale, Ilkley LS29 7RA; Tel (01943) 863857; *Senior Coach BAA and National Squad Team Manager* R. Jones The promotion and development of Tomiki Aikido within Great Britain

Martial Arts Development Commission, PO Box 381, Erith, Kent DA8 1TF; Tel (01322) 431440; Fax (01322) 431465

Modern Pentathlon

Modern Pentathlon Association of Great Britain, Wessex Hse, Silchester Rd, Tadley, Hants RG26 6PX; Tel (01734) 810111; Fax (01734) 819817

Motor Sport

Amateur Motor Cycle Association (AMCA), Darlaston Rd, Walsall WS2 9XL; Tel (01922) 39517; *Chairman* D.T. Green An organisation with 150 clubs who run 'off road' motor cycle sporting events – motocross, scrambling trials, enduros at amateur level

Auto–Cycle Union (ACU), ACU Headquarters, Wood St, Rugby, Warks CV21 2YX; Tel (01788) 540519; Fax (01788) 573585; Telex 311156 ACU G; *Chief Executive* D.R. Barnfield Governing body of motor cycle sport, controlling and promoting all forms of the sport for all age groups

British Automobile Racing Club (BARC), Thruxton Circuit, Andover, Hants SP11 8PN; Tel (01264) 772696, 772697, 772607; Fax (01264) 773794; *Chief Executive* Dennis Carter Organises motor race, sprint and hillclimb meetings in the UK, social events in the UK and France, and training of motorsport marshals

British Motorcyclists' Federation (BMF), Jack Wiley Hse, 129 Seaforth Ave, New Malden, Surrey KT3 6JU; Tel 0181-942 7914; *General Secretary* Jill Preston Protects and promotes the needs of motorcyclists

Motor Cycle Industry Association Ltd (MCI), Starley Hse, Eaton Rd, Coventry CV1 2FH; Tel (01203) 227427; Fax (01203) 229175; *Marketing Manager* Frank Finch Trade Association – Aims are to promote and protect the interests of the motorcycle industry in the UK

Mountaineering

British Mountaineering Council, Crawford Hse, Precinct Centre, Booth St East, Manchester M13 9RZ; Tel 0161-273 5835; Fax 0161-274 3233; *General Secretary* Derek Walker Representative body of mountaineering in UK providing training courses, insurance schemes and advice and information on all mountaineering topics

Netball

Northern Ireland Netball Association, 26 Cresslough Pk, Belfast BT11 9HH; *Hon Secretary* A. Hamill

Welsh Netball Association, 82 Cathedral Rd, Cardiff CF1 9LN; *Secretary* Vacancy

Orienteering

British Orienteering Federation, 'Riversdale', Dale Rd North, Darley Dale, Matlock, Derbys DE4 2HX; Tel (01629) 734042; Fax (01629) 733769; *Director of Coaching* Derek Allison; *Office Manager* Hilda Gregson

Parachuting

British Hang Gliding and Paragliding Association (BHPA), The Old Schoolroom, Loughborough Rd, Leicester LE4 5PJ; Tel (0116) 261 1322; Fax (0116) 261 1323; *Administrator* Jennie Burdett; *Development Officer* Tom Beardsley Promotion, development and co-ordination of paragliding and hang gliding in the UK. Responsible to the CAA for the sport

British Parachute Association, 5 Wharf Way, Leicester LE2 9TF; Tel (0116) 278 5271; Fax (0116) 247 7662 Governing body for the sport in the UK. Examines all Sport Parachute Instructors

Polo

The Hurlingham Polo Association, Winterlake, Kidlington, Oxford OX5 3HG; Tel (01869) 350044; Fax (01869) 350625; *Secretary* J.W.M. Crisp Publishes a year book at £10 (incl postage) which gives detailed information on clubs, rules, fixtures, results etc. every April

Racing

National Greyhound Racing Club Ltd (NGRC), 24–28 Oval Rd, London NW1 7DA; Tel 0171-267 9256; *Secretary* A.H. Newhouse Judicial and disciplinary body for greyhound racing in England, Scotland and Wales

The Racecourse Association Ltd, Winkfield Rd, Ascot, Berks SL5 7HX; Tel (01344) 25912; *Chairman* Sir Paul Fox, CBE; *Managing Director* Stanley Jackson Considers all questions affecting the welfare of racecourse owners and initiates the promotion of improvements in any laws and regulations affecting racecourse owners

Racketball

British Racketball Association (BRA), 50 Tredegar Rd, Wilmington, Dartford, Kent DA2 7AZ; Tel (01322) 272200; Fax (01322) 289295; *Chairman* Di Carrington; *Secretary* Ian Wright Promotes the playing of racketball in Britain and enforces standard rules

Rambling

Ramblers' Association, 1/5 Wandsworth Rd, London SW8 2XX; Tel 0171-582 6878; Fax 0171-587 3799; *Director* Alan Mattingly

Riding

Association of British Riding Schools, Old Brewery Yard, Penzance, Cornwall TR18 2SL; Tel (01736) 69440; Fax (01736) 51390

British Driving Society (BDS), 27 Dugard Pl, Barford, Warks CV35 8DX; Tel (01926) 624420; Fax (01926) 624633; *Executive Secretary* J.M. Dillon Encourages and assists those interested in the driving of horses and ponies. Examining body for carriage DMVUP, including teaching and carriage grooms

British Horse Society, British Equestrian Centre, Stoneleigh, nr Kenilworth, Warks CV8 2LR; Tel (01203) 696697

The Pony Club of Great Britain, BEC, Stoneleigh, nr Kenilworth, Warks CV8 2LR; Tel (01203) 696697; Fax (01203) 692351; *Director* Lt Col T.W. Kopanski Encouraging youngsters to enjoy sports connected with horses. Providing instruction in riding and care of horses. Promoting good sportsmanship

Rowing

Amateur Rowing Association, The Priory, 6 Lower Mall, Hammersmith, London W6 9DJ; Tel 0181-748 3632; Rosemary E. Napp

Welsh Amateur Rowing Association, 30 Lady Mary Rd, Cardiff CF2 5NT; Tel (01222) 754259; G.R.H. Greaves

Women's Rowing Commission (WRC), 30 Denton Gr, Walton-on-Thames, Surrey KT12 3HE; Tel (01932) 240459; *Chairman* D Graham Promotes increased participation by women in the sport of rowing, both competitively and for recreation

Rugby League Football

British Amateur Rugby League Association (BARLA), West Yorkshire Hse, 4 New North Parade, Huddersfield HD1 5JP; Tel (01484) 544131; Maurice F. Oldroyd Governs and promotes ARLF throughout Great Britain and represents the sport on the International Rugby League Board

Rugby Football League, 180 Chapeltown Rd, Leeds LS7 4HT; Tel (0113) 262 4637; Fax (0113) 262 3386

Rugby Union Football

Rugby Football Union, Twickenham, Middx TW1 1DZ; Tel 0181-892 8161; Fax 0181-892 9816

19 Physical Education and Sport

Irish Rugby Football Union (Ulster Branch), 85 Ravenhill Pk, Belfast BT6 0DG; Tel (01232) 649141

Welsh Rugby Union, National Ground, Cardiff Arms Pk, PO Box 22, Westgate St, Cardiff CF1 1JL; Tel (01222) 390111; Fax (01222) 378472

Sailing

British Federation of Sand & Land Yacht Clubs (BFSLYC), 23 Piper Dr, Long Whatton, Loughborough, Leics LE12 5DJ; Tel (01509) 842292; *General Secretary* M. Hampton Governs and promotes the sport, assisting new participants and clubs; providing training and other support

Glenans International Sailing Centres, Ponton des Glenans, Quai Louis Blériot, 75781 Paris CEDEX 16, France; Tel 00-331 42.20.01.40

National School Sailing Association, c/o Bellers Bush, Dover Rd, Sandwich, Kent CT13 0DG; Tel (01304) 613226; *Vice Chairman* Martyn Styles

Royal Yachting Association, RYA Hse, Romsey Rd, Eastleigh, Hampshire SO50 9YA; Tel (01703) 629962; Fax (01703) 629924

Sail Training Association, 2A The Hard, Portsmouth PO1 3PT; Tel (01705) 832055; Fax (01705) 815769; *Chief Executive* John Songhurst

Shooting

The British Association for Shooting and Conservation (BASC), Marford Mill, Rossett, Wrexham, Clwyd LL12 0HL; Tel (01244) 570881; *Education and Training Officer* Stella Rees The national representative body for sporting shooting seeks to promote the highest standards of safety, sportsmanship and courtesy among the shooting public and fosters a practical interest in the countryside, wildlife management and conservation (See also Youth and Education Countryside Trust in Education and Allied Organisations section)

Clay Pigeon Shooting Association, 107 Epping New Rd, Buckhurst Hill, Essex IG9 5TQ; Tel 0181-505 6221; Fax 0181-506 0739

Great Britain Target Shooting Federation, 1 The Cedars, Great Wakering, Southend, Essex; Tel (01702) 219395; Fax (01702) 219250; *Hon Secretary* K. Murray Co-ordination of action and policy on matters affecting the interests of target shooting associations

The National Pistol Association (NPA), 21 Letchworth Gate Centre, Protea Way, Pixmore Ave, Letchworth, Herts SG6 1JT; Tel (01462) 679887; *General Secretary* I.R. McConchie Promotes skill in marksmanship with pistols, and organises competitions. Provides ancillary supplies. Provides competitive, legal and technical advice and organises insurance

National Rifle Association, Bisley Camp, Brookwood, Woking, Surrey GU24 0PB; Tel (01483) 797777; C.C.C. Cheshire

National Small–Bore Rifle Association, Lord Roberts Hse, Bisley Camp, Brookwood, Woking, Surrey GU24 0NP; Tel (01483) 476969

Skateboarding

English Skateboard Association, 50 Park St, Hereford HR1 2RD; Tel (01432) 279133; *Secretary* J.R. Burnham

Skating

National Roller Hockey Association England Ltd, 82 Greenfield Rd, Farnham, Surrey GU9 8TQ; Tel (01252) 723635; Fax (01252) 723635

National Ice Skating Association UK Ltd, 15/27 Gee St, London EC1V 3RE; Tel 0171-253 3824, 0171-253 0910; Fax 0171-490 2589; *Secretary* Mrs C. Waterhouse

Ski–ing

British Association of Ski Instructors (BASI), Grampian Rd, Aviemore, Inverness-shire PH22 1RL; Tel (01479) 810407; Fax (01479) 811222 Training and grading of all ski teachers in Great Britain and the British representative within the International Ski Instructors' Association

The British Ski Federation, 258 Main St, East Calder, West Lothian EH53 0EE; Tel (01506) 884343; Fax (01506) 882952

English Ski Council, Area Library Bldg, Queensway Mall, The Cornbow, Halesowen, West Midlands B63 4AJ; Tel 0121-501 2314; Fax 0121-585 6448; *Chief Executive* Diana King; *Director of Coaching* J.G.M. Shedden

Ski Club of Great Britain, 118 Eaton Sq, London SW1W 9AF; Tel 0171-245 1033; *Contact* Kate Langmuir Ski holidays, clubhouse, resort ski representatives, equipment advice, social events, ski insurance, room hire, resort information, ski magazine and numerous discounts. Individual or commercial membership available

Squash

International Squash Rackets Federation (ISRF), 93 Cathedral Rd, Cardiff CF1 9PG; Tel (01222) 374771; Fax (01222) 374409; Telex 498339 SQUASH G; *Executive Director* Roger Eady Promoting, administering and legislating the game worldwide. The ISRF is now the recognised World Governing Body of the sport incorporating the leading squash playing nations

Squash Rackets Association, West Point, 33–34 Warple Way, Acton, London W3 0RG; Tel 0181-746 1616; *General Secretary* Vacancy

Surfing

British Surfing Association (BSA), Champions Yard, Penzance TR18 2SS; Tel (01736) 60250; Fax (01736) 331077; *Administrator/Development Officer* Colin Wilson Promotion/development of the sport of surfing in the UK. Coaching and competition organisation. Representation of members' interests

Swimming, Diving, Water Polo and Synchronised Swimming

Amateur Swimming Association, Harold Fern Hse, Derby Sq, Loughborough, Leics LE11 0AL; Tel (01509) 230431

English Schools Swimming Association, 3 Maybank Gr, Liverpool L17 6DW; *Hon General Secretary* Don Redman, MBE; Tel 0151-427 3707 (home)

Institute of Swimming Teachers and Coaches Ltd (ISTC), Dawson Hse, 63 Forest Rd, Loughborough, Leics LE11 3NW; Tel (01509) 264357/218827; Fax (01509) 219349; *Secretary* B.W. Relf, JP The education and in–service training of swimming teachers and coaches

Swimming Teachers' Association, Anchor Hse, Birch St, Walsall, West Midlands WS2 8HZ; Tel (01922) 645097

Ulster Branch Irish Amateur Swimming Association, Hse of Sport, Upper Malone Rd, Belfast BT9 5LA; Tel (01232) 381222; *Hon Secretary* Alice McKibbin

Table Tennis

English Table Tennis Association, Queensbury Hse, Havelock Rd, Hastings, Sussex TN34 1HF; Tel (01424) 722525; Fax (01424) 422103

English Schools' Table Tennis Association, 36 Froom St, Chorley, Lancs PR6 0AN; Tel (01257) 26483; *Hon General Secretary* G.R. Gardiner; Tel (01246) 590164

The International Table Tennis Federation, 53 London Rd, St Leonard's-on-Sea, East Sussex TN37 6AY; Tel +44 424 721414; Fax +44 424 431871; *President* Ichiro Ogimura; *Secretary General* Albert

Shipley Control of the sport of table tennis worldwide and the organisation of the World Championships and four other world title events

Table Tennis Association of Wales, 31 Maes-y-Celyn, Griffithstown, Pontypool, Gwent NP4 5DG; Tel (01495) 756112; Fax (01495) 763025; S. Gibbs

Tennis

The British Women's Tennis Association (BWTA), 17 Burkes Rd, Beaconsfield, Bucks HP9 1PB; Tel (01494) 67144; *President* Suzan Livingston Supports and encourages the playing and development of women's tennis at all levels. Tournaments, newsletter, general advice; Information and advice on the professional game including details of European tournaments etc

Lawn Tennis Association, The Queen's Club, West Kensington, London W14 9EG; Tel 0171-381 7000

Tennis and Rackets Association (T & RA), c/o The Queen's Club, Palliser Rd, London W14 9EQ; Tel 0171-386 3447/8; Fax 0171-385 7424; *Chief Executive and Secretary* Brigadier A.D. Myrtle, CB, CBE Administers and controls the games of tennis and rackets and preserves and strengthens their future in Great Britain

Ulster Council of the Irish Lawn Tennis Association, c/o 17 Tennyson Ave, Bangor, Co Down BT20 3SS

Tenpin Bowling

British Tenpin Bowling Association, 114 Balfour Rd, Ilford, Essex IG1 4JD; Tel 0181-478 1745; Fax 0181-514 3665; *General Secretary* Roger Creamer

Trampolining

The British Trampoline Federation Ltd, 146 College Rd, Harrow, Middx HA1 1BH; Tel 0181-863 7278

Volleyball

English Volleyball Association, 27 South Rd, West Bridgford, Nottingham NG2 7AG; Tel (0115) 981 6324

Water Ski–ing

British Water Ski Federation, 390 City Rd, London EC1V 2QA; Tel 0171-833 2855; Fax 0171-837 5879

Weight Lifting

British Amateur Weight–Lifters' Association, 3 Iffley Turn, Oxford OX4 4DU; Tel (01865) 778319; Fax (01865) 778319; Wally Holland, OBE, FADO

Wrestling

British Amateur Wrestling Association, The Wrestling Academy, 41 Great Clowes St, Salford, Manchester M7 9RQ; Tel 0161-832 9209; Fax 0161-833 1120

English Olympic Wrestling Association (EOWA), The Wrestling Academy, 41 Great Clowes St, Salford, Manchester M7 9RQ; Tel 0161-835 2112; Fax 0161-833 1120; *Administrator* C. Barfoot Promotes Olympic style wrestling

Yoga

The British Wheel of Yoga, 1 Hamilton Pl, Boston Rd, Sleaford, Lincs NG34 7ES; Tel (01529) 306851; Nigel Wissett-Warner

Youth Hostels

Youth Hostels Association of England and Wales, Trevelyan Hse, 8 St Stephen's Hill, St Albans, Herts AL1 2DY; Tel (01727) 855215; Fax (01727) 844126

Youth Hostel Association of Northern Ireland, 22 Donegall Rd, Belfast BT12 5JN; Tel (01232) 324733; Fax (01232) 439699

Scotland

Archery

Scottish Archery Association, 30 Gardner St, Partick, Glasgow G11 5NJ; Tel (0141) 339 9188; R. Darling

Athletics

Scottish Athletics Federation, Caledonia Hse, South Gyle, Edinburgh EH12 9DQ; Tel 0131-317 7320; Fax 0131-317 7321

Scottish Schools' Athletic Association, 11 Muirfield St, Kirkcaldy KY2 6SY; Tel (01592) 640233 (business), (01592) 260168 (Home); Fax (01592) 640233; A. Jack

Badminton

Scottish Badminton Union, Cockburn Centre, 40 Bogmoor Pl, Glasgow G51 4TQ; Tel 0141-445 1218; Fax 0141-425 1218

Basketball

Scottish Basketball Association, Caledonia Hse, South Gyle, Edinburgh EH12 9DQ; Tel 0131-317 7260; Fax 0131-317 7489; K.D.A. Johnston

Scottish Schools' Basketball Association, Caledonia Hse, South Gyle, Edinburgh EH12 9DQ; Tel 0131-317 7260; Fax 0131-317 7489

Bowling

Scottish Bowling Association, 50 Wellington St, Glasgow G2 6EF; Tel 0141-221 8999; W.S. Forbes

Scottish Women's Bowling Association, 24 South St, Greenock PA16 8UE; Tel (01475) 24676

Camping

Camping and Caravanning Club (Scottish Region), 70 Douglas Rd, Longniddry, East Lothian EH32 0LJ; A. Strachan

Canoeing

Scottish Canoe Association, Caledonia Hse, South Gyle, Edinburgh EH12 9DQ; Tel 0131-317 7314; Fax 0131-317 7319

Cricket

Scottish Cricket Union, Caledonia Hse, South Gyle, Edinburgh EH12 9DQ; Tel 0131-317 7247; Fax 0131-317 7103

Curling

Royal Caledonian Curling Club, Cairnie Hse, Avenue K, Ingliston Showground, Newbridge, Midlothian EH28 2NB; Tel 0131-333 3003; Fax 0131-333 3323

Cycling

Scottish Cyclists' Union, The Velodrome, Meadowbank Stadium, London Rd, Edinburgh EH7 6AD; Tel 0131-652 0187; Fax 0131-661 0474; *Executive Officer* Jim Riach Governing body for cycle sport. Promotes the sport of cycling for all ages, also encourages the leisure aspect of cycling

Dancing, Movement and Keep Fit

Royal Scottish Country Dance Society, 12 Coates Cres, Edinburgh EH3 7AF; Tel 0131-225 3854; Fax 0131-225 7783

Scottish Official Board of Highland Dancing, 32 Grange Loan, Edinburgh EH9 2NR; Tel 0131-668 3965; Fax 0131-662 0404

19 Physical Education and Sport

Field Sports

British Field Sports Society Scotland, Green Burns, Coupar Angus, Blairgowrie, Perthshire PH13 9HA

Fishing

The Scottish Federation of Sea Anglers, Caledonia Hse, South Gyle, Edinburgh EH12 9DQ; Tel 0131-317 7192

Football

Scottish Amateur Football Association, 'Beechwood', Gateside Rd, Barrhead, Glasgow G78 1EP; I. McTweed

Scottish Football Association Ltd, 6 Park Gdns, Glasgow G3 7YF; Tel 0141-332 6372; Fax 0141-332 7559; Telex 778904; J. Farry

Scottish Schools' Football Association, 50 Lochearn Cres, Airdrie, Strathclyde ML6 6SQ; *General Secretary* J.C. Watson; Tel (01236) 766929 (Home); (01698) 275555 (School); Fax (01236) 275358

Gliding

Scottish Gliding Union, Portmoak Airfield, Scotlandwell, By Kinross KY13 7JJ; Tel (0159 284) 543; *Chairman* J.F. Goudie Gliding holidays, membership, 20 min air experience, instructional flights

Golf

Ladies' Golf Union, The Scores, St Andrews, Fife KY16 9AT; Tel (01334) 75811; A.M. Robertson

Royal and Ancient Golf Club of St Andrews, St Andrews KY16 9JD; Tel (01334) 472112; Fax (01334) 477580

Scottish Golf Union (SGU), The Cottage, 181a Whitehouse Rd, Barnton, Edinburgh EH4 6BY; Tel 0131-339 7546; *Secretary* J.W. Hume Governing body of amateur golf in Scotland

Scottish Ladies' Golfing Association, Rm 1007, Terminal Bldg, Prestwick Airport, Prestwick, Ayrshire KA9 2PL; Tel (01292) 79582; Fax (01292) 671279; *Secretary* L.H. Park Co-ordinates all aspects of women's and girls' amateur golf in Scotland, including organising the national championships and other competitions

Gymnastics

Scottish Amateur Gymnastics Association (SAGA), 8B Melville St, Falkirk FK1 1HZ; Tel (01324) 612308; *President* Louise Martin Encouragement, promotion and control of gymnastics in Scotland

Hockey

Scottish Hockey Union (SHU), 48 Pleasance, Edinburgh EH8 9TJ; Tel 0131-650 8170; Fax 0131-650 8169; *Executive Administrator* S. McQueen Controls, promotes, develops and encourages the playing of the game of hockey in Scotland

Judo

Scottish Judo Federation, Caledonia Hse, South Gyle, Edinburgh EH12 9DQ; Tel 0131-317 7270; Fax 0131-317 7050; Kirsteen Hogg

Karate

Scottish Karate Board, 48 Ryde Rd, Wishaw ML2 7DX; Tel (01698) 357739; Fax (01698) 357739; *Secretary* A. Murdoch; *Chairman* T. Morris

Lawn Tennis

Scottish Lawn Tennis Association, 12 Melville Cres, Edinburgh EH3 7LU; Tel 0131-225 1284; Fax 0131-220 6340

Mountaineering

Mountaineering Council of Scotland, Flat 1R, 71 King St, Crieff, Perthshire PH7 3HB; *Contact* The National Officer

Orienteering

Scottish Orienteering Association, Riversdale, Slitrig Cres, Hawick, Rox TD9 0EN

Parachuting

Scottish Sport Parachute Association, 1B Rosebery Cres, Edinburgh EH12 5JP; *Secretary* Kevin McPhillips

Riding

British Horse Society, Boreland Farm, Aberfeldy, Perthshire, PH15 2PG; *Development Officer for Scotland* I.M. Menzies

British Show Jumping Association (Scottish Branch), Harelaw Farm, Auldhouse, East Kilbride G75 9DR

Rights of Way in Scotland

Scottish Rights of Way Society, Unit 2, John Cotton Business Centre, 10/2 Sunnyside, Edinburgh EH7 5RA; Tel 0131-652 2937; *Secretary* J. Lewis

Rowing

Scottish Amateur Rowing Association, 134 Newton St, Greenock PA16 8SJ

Rugby Union Football

Scottish Rugby Union PLC, Murrayfield, Edinburgh EH12 5PJ; Tel 0131-346 5000; Fax 0131-346 5001; I.A.L. Hogg, CA

Shinty

Camanachd Association, Algarve, Badabrie, Banavie, Fort William; Tel (01397) 772772

Shooting

Scottish Clay Pigeon Association, 10 Balgibbon, Callander, Perthshire FK17 8EU; Tel (01877) 31323

Scottish Pistol Association, Sandhole, Furnace, Inveraray, Argyll PA32 8XU; *Secretariat* M. & T. McCarthy

Skating

The Scottish Ice Skating Association, c/o The Skating Centre, Riverdale Cres, Edinburgh EH12 5XN; Tel 0131-337 3976; *Chairman* W. Findlay

Scottish Speed Skating Union, Hartley Hse, Racecourse View, Ayr KA7 2TX; Tel (01292) 261081

Ski–ing

British Association of Ski Instructors, Grampian Rd, Aviemore, Inverness-shire PH22 1RL; Tel (01479) 810407; Fax (01479) 811222

Scottish National Ski Council, Caledonia Hse, South Gyle, Edinburgh EH12 9DQ; Tel 0131-317 7280

Squash

Scottish Squash Rackets Association, Caledonia Hse, South Gyle, Edinburgh EG12 0DQ; Tel 0131-317 7343

Swimming

Scottish Amateur Swimming Association (SASA), Holmhills Rd, Greenlees Rd, Cambuslang, Glasgow G72 8DT; Tel 0141-641 8818; Fax 0141-641 4443; *Chairman* I. Mason Promotes and encourages the knowledge of swimming, diving, water–polo, synchronised swimming, long–distance swimming and masters swimming

Under–Water Swimming

British Sub-Aqua Club, Telfords Quay, Ellesmere Port, South Wirral L65 4FY; Tel 0151-357 1951; *Regional Coach for North Scotland (Highlands, Islands, Grampian, Tayside)* A. Farrow Veensgarth, Downies Village, Aberdeen AB1 4QX; Tel (01224) 780757; *Regional Coach for South Scotland (Strathclyde, Central, Fife, Lothian, Dumfries & Galloway, Borders)* Clare Peddie Albacore Hse, Kilduncan Poultry Farm, Kings Barns, St Andrews, Fife KY16 8QF; Tel (01334) 880446; *Regional Coach for Northern Ireland* Ralph McBride 2 Ebrington Gdns, Belfast BT4 3BY; Tel (01232) 652772; *Regional Coach for Wales* Ken Parry 27 Lambert Terr, Gadlys, Aberdare, Mid Glamorgan CF44 8AT; Tel (01685) 870124; *Regional Coach for the North (Northumberland, Tyne & Wear, Durham, Cleveland)* Ken Smith 18 Oxford St, South Shields, Tyne & Wear NE33 4BH; Tel 0191-456 5079; *Regional Coach for Yorkshire and Humberside (North, South and West Yorkshire, Humberside)* Nick Nurdin 21 Dunhill Rise, Leeds LS9 0EB; Tel (0113) 249 6419; *Regional Coach for the North West (Cumbria, Lancashire, Greater Manchester, Merseyside, Cheshire, Isle of Man)* Joe Astre 30 Ladysmith Rd, Didsbury, Manchester M20 0HL; Tel 0161-445 0474; *Regional Coach for East Midlands (Derbyshire, Nottinghamshire, Leicestershire, Lincolnshire, Northamptonshire)* Ged Wilkinson 5 Holmecross Rd, Thorplands, Northampton NN3 8AW; Tel (01604) 495459; *Regional Coach for West Midlands (Shropshire, Staffordshire, West Midlands, Warwickshire, Herefordshire, Worcestershire, Gloucestershire)* Tom Grimmett 82 Elmdon La, Marston Grn, Birmingham B37 7EG; Tel 0121-779 2220; *Regional Coach for Eastern (Norfolk, Suffolk, Cambridgeshire, Bedfordshire, Hertfordshire, Essex)* Alison White 47 Brenthall Towers, Potters Street, Harlow, Essex CM17 9AL; Tel (01279) 425234; *Regional Coach for Greater London* Peter ('Tommy') Burton 36 Kentish Rd, Belvedere, Kent DA17 5BN; Tel (01322) 433803; *Regional Coach for South East (Kent, Surrey, East and West Sussex)* John Pederson 8 Holters Way, Seaford, East Sussex BN25 3HS; Tel (01323) 899369; *Regional Coach for the South (Oxfordshire, Buckinghamshire, Berkshire, Wiltshire, Hampshire, Isle of Wight, Channel Islands)* Lizzie Bird Rickyard Cottage, Dunfield, Kempsford, Glos GL7 4HE; Tel (01285) 810911; *Regional Coach for the South West (Cornwall, Devon, Dorset, Somerset, Avon)* Vicky Moore 1 Pontispool Cottage, Norton Fitzwarren, Taunton, Somerset TA4 1BG; Tel (01823) 461759

Scottish Sub-Aqua Club, The Cockburn Centre, 40 Bogmore Pl, Glasgow G51 4TQ; Tel 0141-425 1021

Volleyball

Scottish Volleyball Association, 48 The Pleasance, Edinburgh EH8 9TJ; Tel 0131-556 4633; Fax 0131-557 4314; *Executive Officer* Tafflyn Bradford-James

Water Ski–ing

Scottish Board Sailing Association, Beinn Bhan, Kilmory Rd, Lochgilphead; Tel (01546) 2024; Forbes Johnston

Scottish Water Ski Association, Scottish Water Ski Centre, Townhill Country Pk, Dunfermline KY12 0HT; Tel (01383) 620123

Wrestling

Scottish Amateur Wrestling Association, Kelvin Hall, International Sports Arena, Argyle St, Glasgow G3 8AW; Tel 0141-334 3843

Yachting

Royal Yachting Association Scotland, Caledonia Hse, South Gyle, Edinburgh EH12 9DQ; Tel 0131-317 7388; Fax 0131-317 8566

Youth Hostels

Scottish Youth Hostels Association, 7 Glebe Cres, Stirling FK8 2JA; Tel (01786) 451181; Fax (01786) 450198; *General Secretary* J. Martin

Services

Royal Navy – Scotland and N. Ireland Area, Base Instructor Officer, HMS Cochrane, Rosyth KY11 2XT; Tel (01383) 412121 Ext 62998

Army in Scotland Sports Board, Army HQ Scotland, Edinburgh EH1 2YX; Tel 0131-310 2085

Playing Fields

National Playing Fields Association

25 Ovington Sq, London SW3 1LQ; Tel 0171-584 6445; Fax 0171-581 2402
Patron H.M. The Queen
President H.R.H. The Duke of Edinburgh, KG, KT
Director Elsa Davies
The NPFA is the only independent organisation specialising in play and sports environments. It offers advice on safety and design matters, arranges seminars on grounds maintenance and site management and provides an independent playground and sport safety inspection service

National Playing Fields Assoc (Scottish Branch)

20 Queen St, Edinburgh EH2 1JX; Tel 0131-225 4307
Secretary/Treasurer John E. Tunnah
A charity dedicated to preserving playing space and creating sporting and recreational opportunities for young people, particularly in areas of greatest social need

Sports Turf Research Institute

Bingley, West Yorkshire BD16 1AU; Tel (01274) 565131; Fax (01274) 568191
Patron H.R.H. The Duke of Edinburgh, KG, KT
President Rt Hon Lord Luke, KCVO
Director P. Hayes, PhD, NDA, CBiol, MIBiol, FIHort
Secretary T.R. Wheeldon, FCA
The Institute is the independent national centre for sport and amenity turf. It is a company limited by guarantee and officially recognised by the Department of Trade & Industry as a scientific research association. The affairs of the Institute are administered by a Board of Management comprising representatives of the major sport controlling bodies, which are in turn assisted by advisory committees

Objects

To raise the standard of turf used for all sports, recreational and amenity purposes through scientific research, practical trials, education and advice

Research

The research programme includes contract work commissioned by Government Departments and other bodies. Additionally the Institute finances its own programme within the limits of available funds

Advisory Service

The Institute advises extensively throughout the British Isles and beyond on the maintenance of sports grounds (rugby, soccer, hockey, etc) and golf courses. The service functions through advisory visits supplemented by postal advice and the examination of samples in the Institute's laboratories

For many years, the Institute has also specialised in sports ground construction and drainage. In this connection it undertakes feasibility studies and acts as consultant-in-charge, or as specialist consultant to an architect or engineer

The Sports Council – which assists the Institute financially – has expressed the wish that education authorities should generally make full use of the Institute as a source of information and technical advice.

Association of Landscape Management

38 Highfield Dr, Birstall, Batley, W. Yorks WF17 9BG; Tel (01924) 470292; Fax (01924) 420867
President Martin Ford
General Secretary M.J. Wilby 38 Highfield Dr, Birstall, Batley, W. Yorks WF17 9BG; Tel (01924) 470292; Fax (01924) 420867
Conference Secretary G. Martin
Hon Treasurer C.A. Attwood (Northumberland)
Public Relations Officer N. Baker (Stockport)
Executive Committee P. Negri (Midlands)
Executive Committee D. Pearson (Durham, N.East)
Executive Committee D. Hammond (Cumbria, N.West)
Members of the Association are specialist officers employed by Local Authorities to organise the technical work and staff involved in the construction, maintenance and subsequent management of playing fields. The Association was formed in 1958 to further the general advancement of knowledge of its members through conferences, the publishing of technical papers and personal contact between people with similar problems. Its acts as a consultative body on recreation areas generally, and continues to play an important part in the organisation of specialist seminars on playing fields construction and maintenance. The association also includes members from commercial companies and students

The London Playing Fields Society

Boston Manor Playing Field, Boston Gdns, Brentford, Middx TW8 9LR; Tel 0181-560 3667 (HQ); Fax 0181-568 3475
Secretary D.C. Northwood
The aim of the London Playing Fields Society is to provide playing fields for the adults and youths of Greater London
Douglas Eyre Sports Centre *Coppermill La, Walthamstow,* London E17 7HE
Fairlop Oak Playing Field *Forest Rd, Hainault,* Ilford, Essex
Prince George's Playing Field *Grand Dr, Raynes Pk,* London SW20
Wadham Lodge Sports Centre *Wadham Rd, Walthamstow,* London E17 4HR
Morden Park Sports Centre *Hillcross Ave, Morden,* Surrey SM4 4AF

Sport for the Disabled

British Amputee Sports Association

Harvey Rd, Aylesbury, Bucks HP21 9PP
For all those who are without all or part of an arm or leg, from any cause (accident, illness or from birth), BASA encourages improved health, fitness and well-being of amputees through sporting activities of all kinds at local, national and international level

British Blind Sport

67 Albert St, Rugby CV21 2SN; Tel (01788) 536142; Fax (01788) 536142
Director Tim Hamper

British Deaf Sports Council

7A Bridge St, Otley LS21 1BQ; Tel (01943) 850214 (voice); (01943) 850081 (minicom); Fax (01943) 850828
Executive Director R. Haythornthwaite
Promotes and controls amateur sports and games for the deaf of Great Britain and Northern Ireland on a national and international plane

British Disabled Water Ski Association (BDWSA)

The Tony Edge National Centre, Heron Lake, Hythe End, Wraysbury, Middx TW19 6HW; Tel (01784) 483664; Fax (01784) 482747
Chairman Robin Nichols
Teaches the disabled to water ski, enabling them to participate in the sport with able-bodied friends

British Wheelchair Sports Foundation

(formerly British Paraplegic Sports Society)
Guttmann Sports Centre, Harvey Rd, Stoke Mandeville, Bucks HP21 9PP; Tel (01296) 84848; Fax (01296) 24171
Encourages men, women and children paralysed by injury to the spinal cord, or who have physical disabilities such as spina bifida, polio and amputation of the lower limbs, to participate in wheelchair sports. Opportunities are provided for all ages and standards to take part at local clubs and at organised events. BWSF organises national and world events at Aylesbury and raises funds to meet the cost of training, equipment, facilities and travel to international events

British Ski Club for the Disabled

Springmount, Berwick St John, Shaftesbury, Dorset SP7 0HQ; Tel (01747) 828515
Chairman Hubert Sturges
Ski-ing on artificial slopes in UK and on snow abroad; able-bodied volunteers always needed

British Sports Association for the Disabled

The Mary Glen Haig Suite, Solecast Hse, 13–27 Brunswick Pl, London N1 6DX; Tel 0171-490 4919; Fax 0171-490 4914

The Calvert Trust

Little Crosthwaite, Underkiddaw, Keswick, Cumbria CA12 4QD; Tel (0176 87) 72254

Warden John Crosbie
Holidays, educational or personal development courses designed to meet the needs of individual clients. Activities can include rock climbing, abseiling, hill walking, sailing, canoeing, kayaking, horse riding, trap driving, swimming, fishing, bird watching, indoor archery and hockey. Standard or specially adapted equipment available. Staff hold National Governing Body awards, where appropriate, and are empathetic to the needs of our clients. Comfortable fully serviced accommodation in a converted farmhouse with wheelchair access throughout. Heated indoor swimming pool, large games room, TV/video lounge, library and quiet room. Special diets catered for

Committee for the Promotion of Angling for the Disabled

The Scottish Sports Association for the Disabled, Fife Sports Institute, Viewfield Rd, Glenrothes, Fife KY6 2RA; Tel (01592) 771700
Chairman M. Tudor
Promotes angling for disabled and handicapped persons in Scotland

English National Association of Visually Handicapped Bowlers

Founded in 1975
Hon Secretary G. Rawlinson 11 Wordsworth Rd, Clevedon, Avon BS21 6PQ; Tel (01275) 875969
Patron Tony Alcock, MBE
Charity for blind bowlers in England with 39 member clubs and 470–500 members. Helps to promote national and international tournaments. Affiliated to IBBA and BBS

Great Britain Wheelchair Basketball Association

The Woodlands, Brookend, Keysoe, Beds MK44 2HR; Tel (01234) 708741
National Development Officer Gordon Perry
Promotes and governs the game of wheelchair basketball in Great Britain

HAPA Ltd

Fulham Palace, Bishops Ave, London SW6 6EA; Tel 0171-736 4443. National Information Service 0171-731 1435
Maintains five adventure playgrounds in London for children and young people with disabilities and special educational needs. The National Information Service offers advice and information to individuals and organisations in the UK and abroad who are interested in play/disability and may wish to set up similar playgrounds

National Association of Swimming Clubs for the Handicapped

The Willows, Mayles La, Wickham, Hants PO17 5ND; Tel (01329) 833689
Administrator Rosemary O'Leary
Recognises the value of swimming for the rehabilitation of the disabled and encourages, promotes and develops swimming amongst the handicapped. Produces a register of swimming clubs and organised swimming sessions for handicapped people

National Federation of GATEWAY Clubs

Mencap National Centre, 117 Golden La, London EC1Y 0RT; Tel 0171-454 0454
Chairman Roger W., Galletley
Promotes leisure, recreation and social educational opportunities for people with learning difficulties

Riding for the Disabled Association

Ave R, National Agricultural Centre, Kenilworth, Warks CV8 2LY; Tel (01203) 696510
Provides the opportunity of riding to disabled people who might benefit in their general health and well-being

Scottish Sports Association for the Disabled

Fife Sports Institute, Viewfield Rd, Glenrothes, Fife KY6 2RA
Administrator Margaret McPhee; Tel (01592) 771700
National governing body for sport for all disability groupings in Scotland and has a nationwide structure of branches

Sports Club for the Blind (London)

3 Westland Terr, Balham, London SW12; Tel 0181-673 4010
Chairman John Stancombe
For a very small membership fee, many sports and activities are made available

United Kingdom Sports Association for People with a Learning Disability

Solecast Hse, 13–27 Brunswick Pl, London N1 6DX; Tel 0171-250 1100; Fax 0171-250 0110
National Development Officer Mark Southam
Co-ordinates and promotes sporting and recreational opportunities for people with a learning disability. Organises training workshops, seminars and national/international conferences

Welsh Paraplegic and Tetraplegic Sports Association

Secretary J. Bridgeman 1 Greenway Ave, Rumney, Cardiff CF3 8HQ; Tel (01222) 778026; Fax (01222) 360483
Welfare and sports for paraplegics and tetraplegics

YOU & ME Yoga Centre,

The Cottage, Burton-in-Kendal, Carnforth, Lancs LA6 1ND; Tel (01524) 782103
Founder Maria Gunstone
Trains teachers, carers and parents together with people who have learning difficulties, in a simple systematic yoga approach combined with teaching materials, designed to meet the needs of people with learning difficulties and the development of their potential
Whole-Body-Movement Teaching Video (sponsored by MENCAP) and You and Me Colour Code Instruction Pack available from above address

School Sports Organisations

ENGLAND AND WALES

Association for Archery in Schools

President Miss Margaret Lewis Whitemill, Marston La, Frome, Somerset BA11 4DG
Vice-President Bro Alan Garman Salesian School, Longhope, Glos GL17 0AQ
Vice-President Dr David Hill 27 Park Rd, Woking, Surrey GU22 7BX
Vice-President John Kember-Smith, Southview, Scotland Hill, Sandhurst Camberley, Surrey, GU17 8JR

Achievement Badge Scheme Secretary Ken Barnes 27 Harty Ave, Wigmore, Gillingham, Kent ME8 0NA; Tel (01634) 234921
Chairman and Indoor Championship Organiser Mark Davis 44 Bramerton Rd, Beckenham, Kent BR3 3PB; Tel 0181-650 4648
Postal Leagues Organiser Nick Forbes 17 Sycamore Rd, New Ollerton, Newark, Notts NG22 9PS; Tel (01623) 863848
'Frostbite' and Clout League Organiser B. Burgoyne 63 Northgate, Oakham, Rutland LE15 6QR; Tel (01572) 722487
Hon Secretary and Treasurer and Championship Organiser Chris Fletcher-Campbell All Saints' School, Bloxham, Banbury, Oxon OX15 4PE; Tel (01295) 720443; Fax (01295) 721714

Committee

Joan Kember-Smith Southview, Scotland Hill, Sandhurst, Camberley, Surrey GU17 8JR; Tel (01252) 876641
John Tether 16 Lerwick Cl, Kingswinford, West Midlands; Tel (01384) 839342
Alan Rose 4 Mill Field, Bagshot, Surrey GU19 5DR; Tel (01276) 474356

Cymdeithas Athletau Ysgolion Cymru (Welsh Schools' Athletic Association)

Hon Secretary David J. Phillips Neuadd Wen, Trefegwys Rd, Llanidloes, Powys; Tel (01686) 412156
Hon Treasurer C.E. Hughes, MBE Coleyne, Roe Pk, St Asaph, Clwyd; Tel (01745) 58 2409 (home)
Hon Championship Secretary Graham Coldwell 21 John St, Neyland, Milford Haven, Dyfed; (0646) 602187 (Home) (0473) 764121 (School)

English Schools' Badminton Association

President T.A. Bowker 10 Reynolds Rd, Hove, Sussex BN3 5RJ; Tel (01273) 736535
Chairman E.W. Brown 25 Bounds Green Ct, London N11 2EX; Tel 0181-888 0554
Vice-Chairman M.J. Smith 66 Slayleigh La, Fulwood, Sheffield S10 3RH; Tel (0114) 230 5618
Secretary PO Box 553, Milton Keynes MK8 9EN; Tel (01908) 568822
Hon Treasurer A.J. Bristow 53 Folly Rd, Mildenhall, Suffolk IP28 7BX; Tel (01638) 713967

Executive Committee

A.J. Bristow 53 Folly Rd, Mildenhall, Suffolk IP28 7BX; Tel (01638) 713967
Mrs F.G. Bristow 53 Folly Rd, Mildenhall, Suffolk IP28 7EX; Tel (01638) 713967
Mrs R. Shipley 18 Riley Ave, St Annes, Lancs FY8 1HZ; Tel (01253) 712715
Mrs A.C. Capon 27 Malcolm Rd, Shirley, Solihull, West Midlands B90 2AH; Tel 0121-744 6702
Mrs J. Smith 66 Slayleigh La, Fulwood, Sheffield S10 3RH; Tel (0114) 230 5618
T. Frend 44 Brampton Rd, Oakdale, Poole, Dorset BH15 3RF; Tel (01202) 674729
Mrs S. Chapman 53 Stanwell Way, Wellingborough, Northants
A.J. Winslow Flat 15, The Birches, Marlborough Rd, Swindon, Wilts SN3 1PT
P. Cox 3 Mullion Gr, Padgate, Warrington WA2 0QW; Tel (0925) 812752
A. Dale 30 Grenville Rd, Buckingham MK18 1LR; Tel (01280) 812526
Players Award Secretary C. Byford Byways, 41 West Rd, Dibden Purlieu, Southampton, Hants SO4 5RH; Tel (01703) 848076
Newsletter Editor P. Capon 27 Malcolm Rd, Shirley, Solihull, West Midlands B90 2AH; Tel 0121-744 6702
P. Parish 148 Branks Combe Ave, Stanford Le Hope, Essex SS17 8BY; Tel (01375) 360660
R. Robbins 138 St Nichols Park Dr, Nuneaton, Warks CV11 6EF; Tel (01203) 383820

Affiliated Regions

Midlands East Derbyshire, Leicestershire, Lincolnshire, Northamptonshire, Nottinghamshire
Midlands West Gloucestershire, Worcester, Shropshire, Staffordshire, Warwickshire
North East Tyne & Wear, Yorkshire
North West Cheshire, Cumbria, Lancashire, Isle of Man, Merseyside
South East Kent, Middlesex, Surrey, Sussex
South Berkshire, Buckinghamshire, Hampshire, Isle of Wight, Oxfordshire
East Bedfordshire, Cambridgeshire, Essex, Hertfordshire, Norfolk, Suffolk
South West Avon, Cornwall, Devon, Dorset, Guernsey, Jersey, Somerset, Wiltshire

British Schools' Canoeing Association/British Canoe Youth

Chairman G. Sanders, MBE 4 Barston La, Solihull, West Midlands B91 2SS; Tel 0121-705 2391
Hon General Secretary D.A. Courtman Fairplay Hse, Wickham Bishops, Essex CM8 3JL

British Canoe Youth

Adbolton La, West Bridgford, Nottingham NG2 5AS; Tel (0115) 982 1100; Fax (0115) 982 1797
The youth wing of the British Canoe Union, incorporating the British Schools' Canoeing Association

National Cricket Association

Lord's Cricket Ground, London NW8 8QZ; Tel 0171-289 6098
President M.J.K. Smith, OBE
Director of Administration and Development Terry N. Bates
Director of Finance C.A. Barker
Director of Coaching M.J. Stewart, OBE
National Coach England J. Abrahams (North)
National Coach England R.G.M. Carter (Midlands)
National Coach England L.J. Lenham (South)
National Coach England G.J. Saville (East)
National Coach England G. Lord (South West)
Constituent Members
County Cricket Association of Bedfordshire, Berkshire, Buckinghamshire, Cambridgeshire, Cheshire, Cornwall, Cumbria, Derbyshire, Devon, Dorset, Durham, Essex, Gloucestershire, Guernsey, Hampshire, Herefordshire, Hertfordshire, Huntingdonshire & Peterborough, Isle of Man, Isle of Wight, Jersey, Kent, Lancashire, Leicestershire, Lincolnshire, Middlesex, Norfolk, Northamptonshire, Northumberland, Nottinghamshire, Oxfordshire, Rutland, Shropshire, Somerset, Staffordshire, Suffolk, Surrey, Sussex, Warwickshire, Wiltshire, Worcestershire, Yorkshire; Munster Cricket Union, Leinster Cricket Union, Northern Cricket Union, North West Cricket Union; North, South, East and West of Scotland; and Association of Cricket Coaches, Association of Cricket Umpires, Club Cricket Conference, Combined Services Cricket Association, Council of Cricket Societies, English Schools' Cricket Association, Headmasters' Conference Schools, Incorporated Association of Preparatory Schools, Institute of Groundmanship, League Cricket Conference, Midlands Club Cricket Conference, Minor Counties Cricket Association, National Association of Young Cricketers, Test and County Cricket Board, Welsh Cricket Association, Scottish Cricket Union, Irish Cricket Union, Women's Cricket Association, Marylebone Cricket Club, Lord's Taverners.

English Schools' Cricket Association

Patron Baron Home of the Hirsel, KT, PC
President G.H.G. Doggart, OBE 19 Westgate, Chichester, West Sussex; Tel (01243) 782481
Assistant Secretary R.M. Cuthell 34 Skeffington Cl, Geddington, Kettering, Northants; Tel (01536) 742394
Assistant Treasurer H. Cherry

Welsh Schools' Cricket Association

President A.R. Lewis
Chairman S. Taylor
General Secretary J. Prickett 'Laurie Knowe', Pencoed Rd, Burry Port, Llanelli; Tel (0155 46) 2539
Treasurer G.H. Jenkins Broomfields, 15 Tyn-yr-Heol Rd, Bryncoch, Neath; Tel (01639) 2536

English Schools' Cycling Association

Officers and Executive Committee

Patron R.F. Butlin
President R. Thorn
Chairman G. Banham
General Secretary P.A.W. Dixon 6 Malmers Well Rd, High Wycombe, Bucks; Tel (01494) 446857
Membership Secretary/Treasurer D. Shrubbs 18 St Blaise Rd, Four Oaks, Sutton Coldfield, West Midlands; Tel 0121-308 0455

English Schools' Football Association

Council Members

Chairman D.M. Willacy 36 Hazelmere Rd, St Albans, Herts AL4 9RN; Tel (01727) 865360 (home), (01727) 855521 (school); Fax (01727) 843447
Vice-Chairman M.R. Duffield 52 St Mark's Rd, Castlebank, Dudley, W. Midlands DY2 7SD; Tel (01384) 242526 (home), (01902) 880381 (school); Fax (01384) 242526 (home)
Chief Executive M.R. Berry 4A Eastgate St, Stafford ST16 2NQ; Tel (01785) 51142 (office); Ansaphone: (01785) 54367; Fax (01785) 55485

Area Representatives

Area 1: A.D. Fulton, (1991) Delight Fm, Matfen, Newcastle-upon-Tyne, NE20 0RX, (06661) 886289 (home), 832486 (school); Tel (01661) 832859; J.R. Robson, (1988) 85 Glebe Cres, Washington, Tyne & Wear NE38 7AF; Tel 0191-416 8695 (home); 0191-386 6628 (school); Fax 0191-383 0917; A. Heads, (1987) 39 Glencoe Ave, Southfield Grn, Cramlington, Northumberland NE23 6EH; Tel (01670) 713789 (home); (01912) 531325 (school); Fax 0191-297 0567
Area 2: A.A. Cryer, (1983) 42 Birchdale, Oakwood Pk, Bingley, West Yorks BD16 4SE; Tel (01274) 568401 (home), 307490 (school); Fax (01274) 307490
Area 3: M.J. Hodkinson, (1992) 20 Park La, Great Harwood, Lancs BB6 7RF; Tel (01254) 886340 (home), (01254) 702749 (school); Fax (01254) 706368; C.G. Owen, (1976) 28 Deysbrook La, Liverpool L12 8RF; Tel 0151-220 9961 (home); 0151-546 3134 (school); Fax 0151-548 4146
Area 4: S.J. Abson, (1993) 20 Barry Rd, Nether Hall, Leics LE5 1FA; Tel (01533) 432280 (home), (01533) 782300 (school); J.E. Tarr, (1991) 22 Alderson Rd, Worksop, Notts S80 1XD; Tel (01909) 475754 (home); (01777) 703352/703989 (school); Fax (01777) 703352; Vacancy
Area 5: M.R. Duffield, (1985) 52 St Mark's Rd, Castlebank, Dudley, West Midlands DY2 7SD; Tel (01384) 242526 (home), (01902) 880381 (school); Fax (01384) 242526 (home); P. Rickard, (1993) 36 Ivor Rd, Southcrest, Redditch, Worcester B97 4PE; Tel (01527) 544960 (home); (01527) 585859 (school); Fax (01527) 65587
Area 6: G.L. Lee, (1990) 50 Maybrook Dr, Saltash, Cornwall PL12 4PX; Tel (01752) 843296 (home), (01579) 83292 (school); Fax (01579) 83562
Area 7: R. Wesson, (1991) 25 Elmfield, Kingswood, Bristol BS15 2SS; Tel (01272) 750833 (home), (01272) 777766 (school); Fax (01272) 723351
Area 8: D.J. Lailey, (1982) 47 Longbridge Rd, Bramley, Nr Basingstoke, Hants RG26 5AN; Tel (01256) 881517 (home), (01734) 572861 (school); Fax (01256) 881517 (home), (01734) 572220 (school); S. Inger, (1994) Osmington, The Green, Horton, Slough SL3 9NU; Tel (01753) 685145 (home), (01753) 522892 (school); Fax (01753) 538618
Area 9: T.R. Moore, (1991) 6 Denton Dr, Lowestoft, Suffolk NR33 9DS; Tel (01502) 564943 (home), (01502) 566321 (school); Fax (01502) 566321
Area 10: J.H. Morton, (1987) 16 Greystoke Ave, Pinner, Middlesex HA5 5SL; Tel 0181-723 5415 (home), 0171-262 8000 (school); Fax 0171-224 8418; D.M. Willacy, (1984) 36 Hazelmere Rd, St. Albans, Herts AL4 9RN; Tel (01727) 865360 (home), (01727) 855521 (school); Fax (01727) 843447; D. Woollaston, (1991) 9 Cheyne Cl, Dunstable, Beds LU6 1BX; Tel (01582) 600725 (home), (01582) 576561 (school); Fax (01582) 561533
Area 11: P.J. Harding, (1993) 6 Chestnut Rd, Elms Vale, Dover, Kent CT17 9PY; Tel (01304) 205007 (home), (01303) 252131 (school); Fax (01304) 205007 (home), (01303) 220721 (school); (01850) 154827 (mobile); Vacancy
F.A. Representative: A.W. Brett 5 Ebnal Rd, Shrewsbury SY2 6PW; Tel (01743) 236145 (home); Fax (01743) 236145 (home)

Welsh Schools' Football Association

Chairman P. Hughes-Griffiths
Hon Secretary D. Painter 49 Lanpark Rd, Pontypridd, Mid Glamorgan; Tel (01443) 404442
Hon Treasurer C.M. Evans Watcombe, 170 Cardiff Rd, Newport, Gwent
Hon Assistant Secretary P. Fowler 77 Somerset St, Abertillery, Gwent BP3 1DH; Tel (01495) 213047
Hon Under 15 Secretary E. Blackmore 48 Trevallen Ave, Neath, West Glamorgan; Tel (01639) 639378
Hon Under 18 Secretary D.E. Flye 66 Aberfan Rd, Aberfan, Merthyr Tydfil, Mid Glamorgan; Tel (01443) 690401

The Schools' Association Football International Board (SAFIB)

Chairman D.J. Painter (Wales)
Hon Secretary and Treasurer C.S. Allatt 208 Stechford Rd, Hodge Hill, Birmingham B32 6BL; Tel 0121-783 7657; Fax 0121-783 7657
Victory Shield competition, under 15, UK; Centenary Shield competition, under 18, UK; Control of national schoolboy football. Organises international matches at schoolboy level within the UK and in Western Europe

Rugby Football Schools' Union

Officers

President Brig D.W. Shuttleworth, OBE 'Nonsuch', Warwick Cl, Sheriff Hutton, York YO6 1QW; Tel (01347) 878542
Vice-President R. Davidson 44 Bemersyde Dr, Jesmond, Newcastle Upon Tyne; Tel 0191-281 7203
Hon Treasurer D.M. Franklin 'Arethusa', Bronygarth, Weston Rhyn, Oswestry, Salop SY10 7LY; Tel (01691) 777668
Secretary R.R. Tennick Rugby Football Union, National Centre for Schools and Youth, Castlecroft Stadium,

Castlecroft Rd, Wolverhampton WV3 8NA; Tel (01902) 380302; Fax (01902) 380311

Assistant Secretary R. Milner Rugby Football Union, National Centre for Schools and Youth, Castlecroft Stadium, Castlecroft Rd, Wolverhampton WV3 8NA; Tel (01902) 380302; Fax (01902) 380311

COMMITTEE

County Schools' Union Representatives

Area 1

Northumberland: D. Peffer Benwell Hill, Newcastle-upon-Tyne NE15 7PX; Tel 0191-274 4510

Durham: N.J. Willings 24 Springwell Rd, Northend, Durham DH1 4SZ; Tel (01913) 866286

Yorkshire: G. Liddington 22 The Grove, Hipperholme, nr Halifax; Tel (01422) 201723

Area 2

Cumbria: A. Evans Nandi Hill, Lonsties, Keswick, Cumbria; Tel (01596) 73057

Lancashire: J. Dewhurst Rossall School, Fleetwood, Lancs; Tel (01253) 777767

Cheshire: J. Young 2 Vanderbyl Ave, Bromborough, Wirral, Merseyside; Tel 0151-334 5834

Area 3

Staffordshire: R. Cooper 12 Rushall Manor Cl, Walsall; Tel (01922) 24328, 24696, 26831

North Midlands: J. Escott 42 Elgar Ave, Hereford HR1 1TY; Tel (01432) 273513, 357481

Warwickshire: T. Watton 13 Pilkington Rd, Beechwood Gdns, Coventry CV5 6BG; Tel (01203) 678599

Area 4

Notts, Lincs and Derby: J. Loughton 20 Woodland View, Southwell, Notts NG25 0AG; Tel (01636) 813248

Leicestershire: E. Thorpe 32 Avon Vale Rd, Loughborough, Leics; Tel (01509) 215850/233233

East Midlands: A. Thorp 6 St George's Rd, Bedford; Tel (01234) 344968/353436

Area 5

Eastern Counties: R. Whittle 8 Maria Terr, Stepney, London E1 4NE; Tel 0171-790 8034

Kent: J.D. Hall Jesmond Cottage, Sutton St, Bearsted, Kent; Tel (01622) 730823

Middlesex: C. Bosley 21 Ellesmere Ave, Mill Hill, London NW7; Tel 0181-906 0799

Surrey: C.R. Charlton 28 Woburn Cl, Wimbledon SW19 1DS; Tel 0181-540 8162

Area 6

Berkshire: G. Griffiths 72 Cookham Rd, Maidenhead, Berks; Tel (01682) 31063

Buckinghamshire: B.J. Roberts 55 Craigwell Ave, Aylesbury, Bucks; Tel (01296) 81017, 84545

Hertfordshire: D. Maughan 15 Causeway Cl, Potters Bar, Herts; Tel (01707) 59576, (01540) 8162

Oxfordshire: L. Morgan 9 The Elms, Highworth, Swindon, Wilts SN6 7DD; Tel (01793) 861751; Fax (01367) 240375

Area 7

Cornwall: S.J. Nicholas 2 Hea Villas, Heamoor, Penzance, Cornwall; Tel (01736) 61726, (01726) 73251

Devon: N.T. Clarke 9 Stanford Rd, Broadfields, Exeter; Tel (01392) 78552

Gloucestershire: E. Blackman 4 Merchants Rd, Clifton, Bristol BS8 4EP; Tel (0117) 973 3510

Somerset: B.J.C. Saunders 22 Cherrywood Rise, Worle, Weston-super-Mare; Tel (01934) 510992, 510777

Area 8

Dorset and Wiltshire: M. Summers Holly Cottage, The High St, Blunsdon, Swindon, Wilts; Tel (01793) 722073, 723625

Hampshire: A.P. Scott Embley Pk School, Romsey, Hants S051 6ZE; Tel (01794) 516537/517349

Sussex: C.J. Adams 45 Newtown Ave, Bognor Regis, West Sussex; Tel (01243) 867295/787691

Divisional Representatives

North: J.W. Collard 27 Cookridge La, Leeds, W. Yorks LS16 7LQ; Tel (01532) 674119 (home); T.D. Stirk 27 Cartmell Rd, St Annes-on-Sea, Lancs FY8 1DE; Tel (01253) 724728 (home), (01253) 46391 (work)

Midlands: C.L. Davies Loughborough GS, Burton Walks, Loughborough, Leics LE11 2DU; Tel (01509) 210418 (home); M. Rhodes 39 Redstone Dr, Highley, Bridgnorth, Salop; Tel (01746) 861377 (home)

London and South East: C.R. Kelly 103 Paines La, Pinner Village, Middx HA5 3BP; Tel 0181-866 4297 (home), 0181-866 0067 (work); M.B. Dargon 30 Hillcrest Rd, Loughton, Essex IG10 4QQ; Tel 0181-508 4900 (home), 0181-594 2094 (work); Fax 0181-507 0117

South West: J. Martin Wellington College, Crowthorne, Berks; Tel (01344) 772785 (home), (01344) 772262 (work); K. Gee 88 Stackpool Rd, Bedminster, Bristol B53 1NW; Tel (01272) 669978 (home), (01272) 777766 (work)

Additional Members nominated by the Committee

J. Phillips 84 South View Dr, Upminster, Essex; Tel (0140 22) 29110

F.K. Harding 48 Goodington Rd, Bourne End, Bucks; Tel (016285) 21980 (h), (01923) 836363 (b)

A.D. Pickering Pocklington School, Pocklington, Yorks; Tel (0175 92) 3125

A.J. Turner 'Extra Cover', Edwards Ave, Tangmere, Chichester, W. Sussex; Tel (01243) 773079 (home)

P.F. Jordan Packwood Haugh Prep School, Ruyton-X1-Towns, Shrewsbury, Salop SY4 1HX; Tel (01939) 260217

J.D. Perkins 855 Filton Ave, Filton, Bristol; Tel (01272) 692545 (h), (01272) 291856 (b)

Representatives of the Rugby Football Union Committee

J.H. Addison High Church St, New Basford, Nottingham; Tel (0115) 978 5446

P.M. Johnson, MA Headmaster's House, Wrekin College, Wellington, Shropshire TF1 3BG; Tel (01952) 415001 (h), (01952) 240131 (b); Fax (01952) 240338

P.E. Hughes 361 Padiham Rd, Burnley, Lancs BB12 6SX

M.J. Christie 'Bridle End', 1C Cherney St, Pinner, Middlesex HA5 2TF; Tel 0181-866 0739, 0181-579 9411

B. Williams "Chez Nous", Main Rd, Westerfield, Ipswich IP6 9AJ; Tel (01473) 213339 (h), (01449) 676551 (b); Fax (01473) 213339

Lt Col M.J. Dickinson Tanhouse Cottage, Crockerton, Warminster, Wilts BA12 8AU; Tel (01980) 33371 Ext 2973

Representatives on R.F.U. Committee

D.M. Franklin "Arethusa", Bronygarth, Weston Rhyn, Oswestry, Salop SY10 7LY; Tel (01691) 777668

E.J. Blackman 4 Merchants Rd, Clifton, Bristol B58 4EP; Tel (0117) 973 3510

OFFICERS AND COMMITTEE (18 GROUP)

Officers

Chairman Vacancy

Vice-Chairman E. Thorpe 32 Avon Vale Rd, Loughborough, Leics; Tel (01509) 215850, 214669

Immediate Past Chairman G.E. Griffiths 72 Cookham Rd, Maidenhead, Berks; Tel (01628) 31063 (home)

Hon Secretary A. Rees 1 Fairfield Ave, Whipton, Exeter; Tel (01392) 467119, (01392) 384919

Hon Treasurer B.J. Nightingale 14 Cochrane Cl, Pedmore, Stourbridge, West Midlands DY9 0ST; Tel (01562) 886333; 0121-472 1147

Hon Team Secretary M.R. Summers Holly Cottage, High St, Blunsdon, Swindon, Wilts; Tel (01793) 722073, 723625

Committee

E.J. Blackman 4 Merchant's Rd, Clifton, Bristol; Tel (0117) 973 3510, 24532
D.M. Franklin "Arethusa", Bronygarth, Weston Rhyn, Oswestry, Salop SY10 7LY; Tel (01691) 777668
D.J. Bowers 3 Porchfield Cl, Gravesend, Kent DA12 5PN; Tel (01474) 355796/534317
B. Roberts 55 Craigwell Ave, Aylesbury, Bucks; Tel (01296) 81071, 84545
J.W. Collard 27 Cookridge La, Leeds L16 7LQ; Tel (0113) 267 4119
A.R. Woollard 7 Peacock Cl, Ruddington, Notts NG11 6JF; Tel (0115) 921 1198

OFFICERS AND COMMITTEE (16 GROUP)

Officers

Chairman G.P. Wilson 7 Mount Pleasant, Upton, Macclesfield, Cheshire; Tel (01625) 612865/22505
Vice-Chairman M. Dargon 30 Hillcrest Rd, Loughton, Essex; Tel 0181-508 4900/081-594 2094
Hon Secretary B.C.J. Saunders 22 Cherrywood Rise, Worle, Weston-Super-Mare; Tel (01934) 510992/(0934) 510777
Hon Treasurer A.L. Thompson Boveneyd, Boyne Mead Rd, Kingsworthy, Winchester SO23 7QZ; Tel (01962) 881399
Hon Team Secretary D.N. Sanderson 21 Sycamore Ave, Richmond, N. Yorks; Tel (01784) 3740, 850111

Committee

T. Simpson 17 Fairfield Rd, Ossett, Wakefield WF5 0DZ; Tel (01924) 271783/1474168
R. Davidson 1 Towers Ave, Jesmond, Newcastle upon Tyne NE2 3QE; Tel (0632) 811117
D. Maughan 15 Causeway Cl, Potters Bar; Tel (01707) 59576, 0181-441 4646
J. Phillips 84 South View Dr, Upminster, Essex; Tel (01402) 229110/0181-590 34917
F.K. Harding 48 Goddington Rd, Bourne End, Bucks; Tel (016285) 21980/(0923) 836363
B. Bod Old Church Rd, Mawnan, Falmouth, Cornwall TR11 5HU; Tel (01326) 250508; Fax (01736) 63204
E. Thorpe 32 Avon Vale Rd, Loughborough, Leics; Tel (01509) 215850/233233
T.E. Watton 16 Broadmead Ct, Broad La, Coventry; Tel (01203) 711704, 251756
A.R. Woollard 7 Peacock Cl, Ruddington, Notts NG11 6JF; Tel (0115) 921 1198

Welsh Schools' Rugby Union

Chairman J.D. Rees Ashleigh, Cardiff Rd, Pontypridd, Mid Glamorgan; Tel (01443) 404658 (school), (0144 385) 3482 (home
Hon Secretary (Junior Group) J. Rees (Pontypridd SRU) 'Ashleigh', Cardiff Rd, Pontypridd, Mid Glamorgan; Tel (01443) 404658 (school), (0144 385) 3482 (home)

British Amateur Gymnastics Association

Administration and HQ; Ford Hall, Lilleshall National Sports Centre, Newport, Shropshire TF10 9NB; Tel (01952) 677137; Fax (01952) 820326
President W. Slater, OBE
Deputy President A.G. Strachan (Admin and Finance)
Deputy President Michael Warren (Tech)
General Secretary D.J. Minnery, AFA
Public Relations Officer Natalie Smalley
Promotions Officer Natalie Smalley
Technical Director J. Atkinson, MBE
The Gymnast Magazine Editor T. Low
Bagazine Editor Sue Pygott
Gymnastic award schemes including Gold Top Milk Awards, Gymnastics Awards for Men and Boys, Midland Bank Sports Acrobatics Awards, Lil-lets Awards for Girls, Kit-e-kat Awards; Tel (0435) 866210 (BAGA Awards and Despatch Dept); Persil funfit awards

British Schools' Gymnastic Association (Comprising the Gymnastics Associations of the ESGA, WSAGA, Scottish Schools AGA and Ulster Schools AGA)

Chairman R. Currier 137 Hazelhurst Rd, King's Heath, Birmingham 4; Tel 0121-444 1278
Vice-Chairman J. Jackman Goldrood, South Rd, Brean, Burnham on Sea, Somerset; Tel (01278) 75702
Secretary M. Macleod Talbot Cottage, Forest Rd, Wokingham, Bucks; Tel (01344) 420215
Treasurer H. Todd 184 Dalston Rd, Carlisle; Tel (01228) 29745
National Schools Organiser U. Jackman The Langlands, Church Rd, West Huntspill, Highbridge, Somerset
Boys' Judging Convenor R. Currier 137 Hazelhurst Rd, Birmingham
Girls' Judging Convenor L. Fairbrother Lynsel, 26 Broom Acres, Sandhurst, Camberley, Surrey GU7 8PW; Tel (01276) 776828
Boys' National Coach J. Pirrie 53 Sandyland Pk, Wistaston, Crewe
Girls' National Coach J. Lewis 2 Hawke Rd, Kewstoke, Weston Super Mare
Handbook Officer J. Jackman The Langlands, Church Rd, West Huntspill, Highbridge, Somerset
Sports Acro Officer D. Harrison 11 Grosvenor Cres, Alyn Pk, Rossett, Clwyd

Committee Members

C. Hamilton Orchard Hse, 15 North Common Rd, Uxbridge, Middlesex
B. Benn 203 Rednal Rd, King's Heath, Birmingham B38 8EA
J. Brown 20 Allerton Cl, Ashingdon, Essex SS4 3AR
R. Jeavons Tyrells County Primary School, Tavistock Rd, Springfield, Chelmsford, Essex
J. Levett 9 St Blaize Rd, Romsey, Hants

English Schoolboys' Hockey Association

Chairman D.A. Billson 28 Thorburn Rd, Weston Favell, Northampton NN3 3DA; Tel (01604) 411685
Hon Secretary J.E. Law 16 Clover Dr, Hardwicke, Gloucester GL2 6TG; Tel (01452) 721247
Hon Match Secretary K. Billson 28 Thorburn Rd, Weston Favell, Northampton NN3 3DA; Tel (01604) 411685
HA Coaching Office 6 St Johns, Worcester WR2 5AH; Tel (01905) 426009
Hon Treasurer A.J. Barton The Pines, 30 Roundwood Ave, Hutton Mount, Brentwood, Essex CM13 2LZ; Tel (01277) 211999
Assistant Secretary (Mini Hockey) R.S. Price 70 Pownall St, Macclesfield, Cheshire SK10 1DG; Tel (01625) 614105

Divisional Representatives

East: T.J. Machin Burnaby Hse, 3 Burnaby Rd, Bedford MK40 2TT; Tel (01234) 60118
Midlands: R. McBlane 77 Sutton Ave, Chelaston, Derby
North East: Vacancy
North West: R.S. Price 70 Pownall St, Maclesfield, Cheshire SK10 1DG; Tel (01625) 614105
South (East): V.B. Bowen-West 19 Newlands Rd, Woodford Grn, Essex IG8 0RS; Tel 0181-504 5344
South (West): M.J. Shaw 88 Stoneleigh Ave, Worcester Pk, Surrey KT4 8XY

West: K.R. Moore Old Home Farm, Fousden, Lyme Regis, Dorset DT7 3XR; Tel (01297) 20848

British Schools' Lawn Tennis Association

Chairman J.R. Cochrane, CBE
Executive Director Gilly Crump
Assistant Director Philip Veasey
The British Schools' Lawn Tennis Association, founded in 1980, is administered by the Lawn Tennis Association. Initiatives including in-service training for teachers, coaching programmes and a competitive structure for all ages are available. County Schools' Tennis Associations have been established in most areas. Any school requiring advice or help should write to the Executive Director at The LTA Trust, Queen's Club, West Kensington, London W14 9EG

English Schools' Netball Association

Honorary Officers and Executive

President M. Mallen 89 Marsden Rd, South Shields, Tyne & Wear NE34 6DG; Tel 0191-456 2915
Vice-President C. Stephen 47 Wedderburn Rd, Harrogate, N. Yorks HG2 7QQ; Tel (01423) 884797
Past-President G. Freakley The Bungalow, Canal Side, Newcastle Rd, Stone, Staffs; Tel (01785) 818411
Chairman J.M. Barter 7 Greyfell Cl, Stanmore, Middx; Tel 0181-954 0255
Chairman Elect P. Johns 18 Orchard Rd, Burgess Hill, West Sussex RH15 9PQ; Tel (01444) 235218
Past Chairman Lady S. Driver Conker Tree Cottage, Southbank, Great Budworth, Cheshire CW9 6HG; Tel (01606) 892209
Match & Trials Secretary P. Telford 25 Broomhill Rd, Woodford Green, Essex IG8 9HA; Tel 0181-505 0420
National Team Coach R. Folley 50 Northcote Cres, West Horsley, Surrey KT24 6LY; Tel (01483) 284119
Hon Secretary J. Bracey 76 Macklands Way, Rainham, Kent ME8 7PF; Tel (01634) 376826
Hon Treasurer P. Devine West Common Youth Sports Hall, West Common La, Scunthorpe, Humberside DN17 1DS; Tel (01724) 865407
Inter-County Tournament Secretary S.A. Ellis Foxglove Cottage, 18 Brocklehurst Pl, Old Rd, Chesterfield, Derbyshire S40 2QY; Tel (01246) 236179
National Schools' Tournament Secretary J. Horton 11 Wentworth Cl, Forest Town, Mansfield, Notts NG19 0QT; Tel (0115) 942 3688
Umpiring Secretary J. Burke 24 Thricknells Cl, Luton, Beds LU3 3RP; Tel (01482) 490817
Coaching C. Maylor Pendle Hse, Burcott La, Bierton, Aylesbury, Bucks HP22 5AS; Tel (01296) 23938
N.C.S.S. Representative J., Bracey (Hon Sec)
A.E.N.A. Representative L. McGurk 24 Tynedale Rd, South Shields, Tyne & Wear NE34 6EX; Tel 0191-456 1916
Co-opted O. Place 5 Oakfield Rd, Wellsway, Keynsham, Bristol BS18 15Q; Tel (0117) 986 3263
Team Manager M. Gartland Homlea, Pepworth Rd, Whitely, Guildford, Surrey; Tel (01428) 683777
Publicity K. Edwards 92 Down's Dr, Timperley, Altrincham, Cheshire; Tel 0161-973 0029

Regional Representatives

East: P. Medhurst Tring School, Mortimer Hill, Tring, Herts; Tel (01442) 69776 (home), 822303 (school)
East Midlands: J. Clements 11 Churchill Dr, Stapleford, Nottingham NG9 8PE; Tel (0115) 939 4021; E. Vasey Ilkeston School, Ilkeston, Derbyshire
North: P. Slater Rosecroft Comp School, Rosecroft La, Loftus Saltburn-on-Sea, Cleveland; Tel (01287) 638126; G. Roddam 15 Merrington Cl, Kirk Merrington, Spennymoor, Co Durham DH6 7HU; Tel (01388) 815219
North West: U. Pennington 3 Saunders Mews, Eaves Grn, Chorley, Lancs PR7 3RF, (0257) 233847; M. Wilson Hathershaw School, Bellfield Ave, Oldham, Greater Manchester OL8 3EP; Tel 0161-624 7782
South: J. Hoar Oaklands RC School, Stakes Hill Rd, Waterlooville, Hants; Tel (01705) 259214; J. Wright 32 Church Rd, Chavey Down, Ascot, Berks; Tel (01344) 885475
South East: M. Beardwood 44 Bridge Ave, Hanwell, London W7 3DJ; Tel 0181-578 1350; R. Folley 50 Northcote Cl, West Horsley, Surrey KT24 6LY; Tel (01483) 284119
West: J. Satchell "Heatherbrae" Heatherbrae La, Upton, Poole, Dorset BH16 5LZ; Tel (01202) 631617
West Midlands: A. Hicken 243 Stroud Ave, Willenhall, West Midlands; Tel (01902) 609617; R. Hill 34 Gorseway, Whoberley, Coventry; Tel (01203) 673506
Yorkshire & Humberside: H. Leaver, 3 The Lawns, Eccleshall Sheffield, South Yorks S11 9FL; Tel (01472) 585361

National School Sailing Association

Vice-President A.B. Allison
Vice-President G. Austin
Vice-President J. Evans
Vice-President D.G. Sykes
Vice-President David Bellamy, PhD
Vice-President D.W. Cobden
Vice-President T. Coleman
Vice-President J. Denton
Vice-President John Dudderidge, OBE
Vice-President B.G.M. Dunn
Vice-President M.J. Henley, MA
Vice-President W. Keeble
Vice-President Ian Hunter Edmond
Vice-President Cdr B.W. Lucke
Vice-President M.O. Palmer, MA
Vice-President R.M. Parker, OBE, MA
Vice-President W.C. Primmer, MA, MEd
Vice-President L. Tipper, MBE
Vice-President I. Watson
Vice-President T.W. White, MBE
Vice-President G. Chapman
Vice-President N.L. Ransome
Vice-President K. Anderson
Vice-President Cdr W.B. Smith
Vice-President G. Walton
Vice-President E. Howells
Chairman Michael Edwards, CEO County Hall, Norwich; Tel (01603) 222301
Treasurer Dave Williamson Tower Wood, OE Centre, Windermere, Cumbria; Tel (015395) 31519
Vice-Chairman M.J. Styles Bellers Bush, Dover Rd, Sandwich, Kent CT13 0DG; Tel (01304) 613226
Co-ordinator Course Conference Carol Blundell; Tel 0161-233 5182
Chairman Sailing Committee Bob Grant 2 Nixons Farm Court, Nixons La, Ulnes Walton, Nr Preston PR5 3LD; Tel (01772) 424051
Chairman General Purposes Committee Anna Blannin; Tel 0181-523 1127
Publicity Officer Steve Ells; Tel 0181-531 8107

Cymdeithas Hwylio Ysgolion Cymru (School Sailing Association of Wales)

President A.K. Corey
Chairman A.F. Bond 22 Bryn Estyn Rd, Wrexham, Clwyd; Tel (01978) 352747
Hon Secretary H. Jones Glan Llyn, Llanuwchllyn, Bala, Gwynedd; Tel (0167 84) 607
Committee
Five elected members and representatives from each County Sailing Association in Wales

English Schools' Swimming Association

President Ernie Godin 12 Barlby Gdns, Kensington, London W10 5LW

Hon Awards Secretary N. Bramwell Brackenridge, Builsborough Hill, Hollowell, Northants NN6 8RN; Tel (01604) 740080 (home), 842185 (school)
Hon General Secretary Don Redman, MBE 3 Maybank Gr, Aigburth, Liverpool L17 6DW; Tel 0151-427 3707 (home), 0151-486 1053 (school)
Hon Treasurer John Beddoe 9 Sandringham Rd, Mansfield, Notts NG19 9HN; Tel (01623) 661573 (home), 882494 (school)
Hon Competitions Secretary T. Hyde 20 Pavillion Way, Eastcote, Ruislip, HA 9JN; Tel 0181-207 4323 Ext 228 (school)
Hon Asst Competitions Secretary E. Hartley 49 The Millbank, Ifield, Crawley, West Sussex RH11 0JQ; Tel (01293) 515519
Hon Press and Publicity Secretary Marie Bracey Beech Hurst, Forest Rd, East Horsley, Surrey KT24 5BL; Tel (0148 65) 5488

E.S.S.A. Representatives

National Council for School Sport E. Hartley
National Council for School Sport T. Hyde
National Council for School Sports D. Redman
National Council for School Sport J. Beddoe
Central Council of Physical Recreation E. Hartley
Central Council of Physical Recreation – Council D. Redman
Sports Council Sub-Committee for Swimming for Disabled M.J. Bracey
British Sports Association for Disabled M.J. Bracey
W.I.S.E. Committee D. Redman
W.I.S.E. Committee M. Uglow
National Water Safety Committee N. Bramwell
A.S.A./E.S.S.A. Liaison Committee J. Beddoe
A.S.A./E.S.S.A. Liaison Committee T. Hyde
A.S.A./E.S.S.A. Liaison Committee D. Redman
A.S.A./E.S.S.A. Liaison Committee C.M. Young
D.A.A.G. (Schools) T. Hyde

Annual Championships

E.S.S.A. National Championships, School Team and Diving Championships, Schools' Water Polo Championships. Synchronised Team Championships

Dolphin Trophy Learn to Swim Award Scheme

Hon Secretary N. Bramwell Brackenridge, Guilsborough Hill, Hollowell, Northants NN6 8RN
The Dolphin Trophy Learn to Swim Scheme is open to all schools in England and Wales, the Channel Isles and the Service Children's Education Authority, with primary-aged pupils on their roll, where swimming is part of the curriculum. Special Schools may ignore the upper age limit. Three schools will be selected as national winners and a number of schools will receive a Certificate of Outstanding Achievement. If over half the children in the primary age group are able to swim 25 metres, the school will be sent a Certificate of Merit. The aim of the scheme is to make every child a safe swimmer before the age of 12

Rainbow, Water Skills and A.S.A./ E.S.S.A. Joint Award Schemes

Awards for swimming (including physically handicapped swimmers), diving and water polo

The Teaching Swimming Bath Scheme

Hon Secretary J.B. Beddoe 9 Sandringham Rd, Mansfield, Notts NG19 9HN; Tel (01623) 661573
The Teaching Swimming Bath scheme of the English Schools Swimming Association was started in 1954 to encourage schools to provide their own teaching swimming baths. The Scheme provides interest-free loans to schools building their own pools. The initial funds for the scheme have been augmented by the profits from the Awards Scheme operated by the E.S.S.A. and the A.S.A. The Swimming Pool and Allied Trades Association links and promotes many aspects of pool provision and provides an information service to schools

English Schools' Table Tennis Association

President J. Arnold, BA, Sandal Endowed C.E. Junior School, Barnsley Rd, Wakefield W Yorks, WF2 6AS; Tel (01924) 250516 (school), 372597 (home)
Life Member G.N. Gurney, MA
Life Member E.J. Mitchell
Vice-President I.R. Crickmer
Vice-President D. Harmer, BA(Hons)
Vice-President A. Hydes
Vice-President C. Jaques
Vice-President J.A. Maxwell, BSc(Econ)
Vice-President J.B. Reed
Vice-President P. Townend, BA
Vice-President J.M. Wright, BSc(Hons)
Vice-President C. Villiers
Chairman John Blackbond 5 Fairfield Mount, Highgate, Walsall, West Midlands WS1 3HZ; Tel (01922) 27081 (home), 0121-556 4131 (school)
Vice-Chairman Rea Balmford 30 Glebe Rd, Wawne, Hull, North Humberside HU7 5XR; Tel (01482) 821279
Hon Treasurer Bob Wood 4 Maurice Gr, Blackpool, Lancs FY2 0QH; Tel (01253) 57163 (home)
Hon General Secretary Geoff Gardiner 36 Froom St, Chorley, Lancs PR6 0AN; Tel (01257) 264873 (home)
Hon Assistant General Secretary Grete Willacy 19 Sandymount Rd, Highgate, Walsall WS1 3AR
Hon Team Competition Secretary Paul Birch 23 Kestrel Rd, Bedford MK41 7HR; Tel (01234) 341988 (home)
Hon Individual Competition Secretary Ed Mitchell 12 Newton Cl, Oakenshaw South, Redditch B98 7YR; Tel (01527) 542106 (home)
Hon Handbook Editor John Wilde 60 Hollinwell Ave, Wollaton, Nottingham NG8 1JZ
Representatives from Affiliated Schools' Associations:
Lincolnshire D. Worrell
East Sussex T. Bennett
West Yorkshire R. Hudson
Surrey G.M. McCulloch
Derbyshire L.C. Henry
West Midlands M. Cherry
Cumbria M. Holland
Avon P. Archdale
Shropshire E. Wilson
ESTTA promotes and encourages the playing of table tennis in schools, encourages the formation of County and Local Schools' Table Tennis Associations, organises courses for teachers and players, arranges schools' competitions at any level and assists in the development of schools' table tennis

National Council for Schools' Sports

Chairman B. Latham 257 Woodlands Rd, Batley, West Yorkshire WF17 0QW
Hon Treasurer J. Gates Grove End, Elm Gr, Berkhamsted, Herts HP4 1AE
Hon Secretary D. Lomas 21 Northampton Rd, Croydon, Surrey CR0 7HB
Executive Officer P. Smith 95 Boxley Dr, West Bridgford, Nottingham NG2 7GN
The NCSS was formed in 1948 as an advisory and co-ordinating body for schools' national sports associations involved in extra curricular activities. The membership has now been widened to include any national sports organisation in England and Wales responsible for the development of their sport in schools. The NCSS has also taken on lobbying and development roles and has introduced an information service on the current situation in school sport. The following sports are in membership: National Schools' Associations: Archery, Association Football, Athletics,

Badminton, Basketball, Boxing, Cricket (England and Wales), Cycling, Golf, Gymnastics, Judo, Lawn Tennis, Netball, Rugby League, Rugby Union, Sailing, Ski-ing, Swimming (England and Wales), Table Tennis; National Governing Bodies: Canoeing, Hockey, Lacrosse, Rounders, Rowing, Softball, Squash, Surfing, Trampoline, Volleyball

Physical Education Association of the United Kingdom

Francis Hse, Francis St, London SW1P 1DE; Tel 0171-828 9229; Fax 0171-828 9575
President Neil Armstrong
Vice-President Chris Laws
Vice-President Carolyn Jones
Chairmen of the Sub-Committees:
Finance and General Purposes Dr E.J. Kane
Past President Dick Fisher
General Secretary Peter Harrison
The Association is a non-Governmental body. Founded as the Ling Physical Education Association in 1899, it exists to encourage and facilitate the scientific study of the physical health of the community through physical and health education and recreation; to educate and instruct specialist teachers in physical and health education and recreation in current theory and practice both in the United Kingdom and overseas and in the best methods of improving the physical health of the community; to facilitate the exchange of information, knowledge and thought on these subjects

SCOTLAND

Scottish Schools' Football Association

President's Committee

President R. Thomson 41 Samson Ave, Kilmarnock; Tel (01563) 29007 (home), (01563) 33221 (school)
Vice-President R.M. Docherty 5 Forth Park Gdns, Kirkcaldy; Tel (01592) 261811 (home), (01592) 267111 (school)
General Secretary J.C. Watson 50 Lochearn Cres, Airdrie; Tel (01236) 766929 (home), (01698) 275555 (school)
Hon Treasurer A.B. McMenemy 1 Toppersfield, Kilbarchan PA10 2AG; Tel (0150 57) 5288 (home), 0141-886 7511 (school)
Hon Assistant Secretary G. Liveston 9 Woodlands St, Milngavie, Glasgow; Tel 0141-956 4892 (home), (01698) 283888 (school)
Hon Assistant Secretary W.L. Donaldson 10 Almond Terr, Whitecross, Linlithgow EH49 6LF; Tel (01506) 843668 (home), (01324) 554233 (school)
Hon Assistant Secretary D.P. Lavin 57 Old Evanton Rd, Dingwall; Tel (01349) 64116 (home), (01349) 852362 (school)
Past President and Minute Secretary C. Duggan 2 Burngrange Gdns, West Calder; Tel (01506) 873822 (home)

Physical Education Teacher Training

England and Wales Universities

The University of Birmingham School of Sport and Exercise Sciences, Edgbaston, Birmingham B15 2TT; *Head of School* Prof D.A. Jones, BSc, PhD; *Senior Lecturer* M.D. Lakie, BSc, PhD; *Lecturer* I.M. Cockerill, MEd, PhD; *Lecturer* P.M. Jakeman, BSc, PhD, MSc; *Lecturer* C. Jenkins, BSc, MSc, PhD; *Lecturer* A.K. McConnell, BSc, MSc, PhD; *Lecturer* M.J.N. McDonagh, BA, MA, MSc, PhD; *Lecturer* I.R. Moir, MA, BA; *Lecturer* A.M. Nevill, BSc, PhD; *Lecturer* M.J. White, BSc, PhD; *Lecturer* P.A. van Zyl, MA; *Lecturer* J.H. Challis, BSc, PhD; *Lecturer* F.F. Eves, BSc, PhD; *Lecturer* S.M. Newell, BSc, PhD; *Lecturer* M.D. Brown, BSc, PhD; *Lecturer* M.J. Parkes, BA, MA Sport and Exercise Sciences may be taken as a single (BSc) or joint honours degree in the Faculty of Science. Sport and Recreation Studies may be taken as a single (BA) or offered as one of two subjects in a combined (BA) honours degree in the Faculty of Arts or as a joint (BSocSci) honours degree in the Faculty of Commerce and Social Science. Postgraduate students may carry out research full- or part-time for a higher degree by thesis
University of Leeds Dept of Physical Education, Leeds LS2 9JT; Tel (0113) 243 1751; *Head of Department* M.R. Lindsay, BSc(Eng)(Oklahoma), MPhil(Leeds), PhD(Strathclyde), DipPhysEd(Carnegie); *Senior Fellow* K.K. Mitchell, OBE, DipPhysEd; *Associate Lecturer* S.J. Parry, BA, MEd, MA; *Associate Lecturer* W.D. Patterson, BSc, PGCE; *Sports Administrator* W. Butterworth, MIBRM; *Sports Administrator* Susan M. Jacklin, BEd(Cambridge), MA(Leeds), PhD(Leeds) MPhil and PhD postgraduate research degrees offered; PGCE second method courses in (a) outdoor activities, (b) games

Colleges and Institutes of Higher Education

See Chapter 11

Physical Education Courses

University of Brighton, Faculty of Education, Sport and Leisure, Falmer, Brighton BN1 9PH; Tel (01273) 600900; *Director* Prof D. Watson, MA, PhD; *Dean of Faculty* A. Markham, OBE, CertEd, DipSpeech and Drama, MEd Specialist BA and PostGraduate Certificate Courses in Primary, Art and Design, Design Technology, Technology (Business: Design) Business Education Mathematics and Science Courses; 900 students. In-service and Professional Development courses for serving teachers; 600 students
Eastbourne BN20 7SP; Tel (01273) 600900
Specialist PE courses (M. & W.); BA Hons with QTS (secondary); Sport and Exercise Science BSc; Leisure Policy and Administration BA, Post Graduate Certificate in PE/Dance; 650 students
Liverpool John Moores University, I.M. Marsh Campus, Barkhill Rd, Liverpool L17 6BD; Tel 0151-231 5240; Fax 0151-729 0136; *Correspondent* Rosamund Bull (1) BEd(Hons) four-year degree course in Secondary Physical Education/Dance (W and M); including one other subject from Art, Science, English or Youth/Sport Coordinator; (2) BEd(Hons) four-year degree in Outdoor and Science Education (W and M); (3) BEd(Hons) four-year degree in Design Technology; (4) PGCE one-year course for students (M and W) wishing to teach PE or Art & Design or Design & Technology; (5) BEd(Hons) four-year Primary degree course in Art, Design and Technology, Physical Education, Science and Environmental Studies, Literature and Communication Studies; (6) BA(Hons) Degrees in Home Economics, Consumer Studies, Applied Community Studies, Community Sport/Dance, Philosophy (with another subject), Product Design (with another subject)
Sheffield Hallam University, School of Education, Collegiate Cres Campus, Sheffield S10 2BP; Tel (0114) 253 2306; *Correspondent* School Manager, School of Education Sheffield Hallam University, Collegiate Cres Campus, Sheffield S10 2BP; Tel (0114) 253 2288; Fax (0114) 253 2330
University of Ulster, Jordanstown, Faculty of Education, Dept of Pre-Service Education, Shore Rd, Newtownabbey, Co Antrim BT37 0QB; Tel (01232) 365131; *Head of Department* Prof E.D. Saunders, MA

Other Sports Courses

Lucas–Tooth Gymnasium 11 Heathcote St, Gray's Inn Rd, London WC1N 2AL; Tel 0171-837 9851 Fitness classes and courses enabling students to qualify as PE instructors. Nominal fees

Middlesex University High Level Tennis Centre Middlesex University, White Hart La, London N17 8HR; Tel 0181-362 5943; Fax 0181-362 6341; *Tennis Centre Co-ordinator/Head of Sport and Recreation* John Watson; Tel 0181-362 5943; Fax 0181-362 6341 High level tennis coaching for male and female players aged 18+ who have reached a minimum of county junior standard or its equivalent. All students enrolled must first be accepted on a full- or part-time course at Middlesex University (within the normal range offered). The University does not offer separate courses in sport

20 Youth Service

The Youth Service is administered by the Local Education Authorities and a variety of voluntary organisations. The local authority officers are listed in the chapters devoted to county, metropolitan district or regional administration. Most of the voluntary bodies are linked with the National Conference for Voluntary Youth Services, whose members are listed below.

National Council for Voluntary Youth Services

Coborn Hse, 3 Coborn Rd, Bow, London E3 2DA; Tel 0181-980 5712; Fax 0181-983 4822
Chair John Broadbent
General Secretary Laurie Williams
Administration Secretary Angela Waite

National Voluntary Youth Organisations

Adventure Service Challenge Scheme
376 Hartington Rd, Hillingdon, Middx UB8 3HG; Tel (01895) 444305
Representative R. Butler, FRGS

Army Cadet Force Association
Oakford, Cheltenham Terr, London SW3 4RR; Tel 0171-790 0407
Secretary B.R. MacGregor

Association for Jewish Youth (AJY)
AJY Hse, 128 East La, Wembley, Middx HAO 3NL; Tel 0181-908 4747
Representative M. Shaw

Baptist Union of Great Britain and Alliance of Baptist Youth
Baptist Hse, 129 Broadway, Didcot, Oxon OX11 8RT; Tel (01235) 512077
Representative Iain Hoskins

The Boys' Brigade
Kings Terr, 1 Galena Rd, London W6 0LJ; Tel 0181-741 4001; Fax 0181-741 1721
Brigade Secretary Sydney Jones

British Red Cross Youth
9 Grosvenor Cresc, London SW1X 7EJ; Tel 0171-235 5454
Representative Helen Watson

British Trust for Conservation Volunteers
36 St Mary's St, Wallingford, Oxon OX1 QEU; Tel (01491) 39766
Rob Morley

The Campaigners
Campaigner Hse, St Mark's Cl, Colney Heath, St Albans, Herts AL4 0NQ; Tel (01727) 24065
Chief Executive Rev Kenneth G. Argent

Catholic Youth Services (CYS)
39 Fitzjohn's Ave, London NW3 5JT; Tel 0171-435 3596
General Secretary R.A. Harrow

The Church Army
27 Deans La, Sandbach, Cheshire CW11 9HF; Tel (01270) 766205
Representative Ron Davis

Church Lads' and Church Girls' Brigade
Claude Hardy Hse, 15 Etchingham Park Rd, London N3 2DU; Tel 0181-349 2616/7
Representative Wing Cdr J.S. Cresswell, MBE

Church of England Board of Education
Church Hse, Dean's Yard, Westminster, London SW1P 3NZ; Tel 0171-222 9011
Representative Rev Paul Battersby

Commission for Racial Equality
Elliot Hse, 10/12 Allington St, London SW1E 5EH; Tel 0171-828 7022
Representative M. Forsythe

Community and Youth Workers Union
2 Moomill, Kibblesworth, Gateshead, Tyne and Wear NE11 OYE; Tel 0191-491 1211
National Organiser Margaret Gale

Council for Environmental Education
School of Education, University of Reading, London Rd, Reading RG1 5AQ; Tel (01734) 756061
Representative Libby Grundy

Council of Churches for Britain and Ireland (CCBI)
Inter-Church Hse, 35-41 Lower Marsh, London SE1 7RL; Tel 0171-620 4444
Representative Carmel Heaney

Covenanters
104 Bloom St, Manchester M1 6HU; Tel 0161-236 2305
Director A. Hewerdine

Crusaders
2 Romeland Hill, St Albans, Herts AL3 4ET; Tel (01727) 55422/3
General Secretary E.W. Addicott

Deaf Accord
BP Chanty Base, The Chandlery, 50 Westminster, Bridge Rd, London SE1 7QY
Youth Development Worker Craig Crawley

Drive for Youth
Suite 24B, British Telecom Bldgs, 10–18 Manor Gdns, London N7; Tel 0171-281 7020
Penny Jones

The Duke of Edinburgh's Award
See main entry

Endeavour Training
17A Glumangate, Chesterfield, Derbys S40 1TX; Tel 237201/2
Representative John Williams

Fairbridge Drake Society
202 Lambeth Rd, London SE1 7JW; Tel 0171-928 1704
David James

First Key
Oxford Pl, Methodist Centre, Oxford Pl, Leeds LS1 3AX; Tel Leeds 443898
Representative Lynne Simpson

First Organisation
The St Thomas Centre, Ardwick Green North, Manchester M12 6FZ
Chief Executive Michael Payne

Friends for the Young Deaf (FYD)
East Court Mansion, College La, East Grinstead, West Sussex RH19 3LT; Tel (01342) 323444
Deputy Director Evelyn Carter

Further Youth Trust
Scripture Union Hse, 130 City Rd, London EC1V 2NJ; Tel 0171-782 0013
Secretary and Development Officer Michael Eastman

The Girl Guides Association (GGA)
Penny Cottage, Llansawell, Llandeilo, Dyfed SA19 7SU; Tel (01558) 685595

Girls' Brigade
Girls' Brigade National Council for England and Wales, Brigade Hse, 62 Foxhall Rd, Didcot, Oxon OX11 7BQ; Tel (01235) 510425
General Secretary Daphne Cosser

Girls' Friendly Society
Northolme Hall, Wainfleet, Skegness, Lincs PE24 4AA
Representative Mrs Joy Epton

Inter-Action Youth Projects
Nr Blackfriars Bridge, Victoria Embankment, London EC4Y 0HJ; Tel 0171-583 2652
Representative Ed Berman, HMS President

International Voluntary Service
162 Upper New Walk, Leicester LE1 7QA; Tel (0116) 254 9430
Representative Paul Ticher

Jewish Lads' and Girls' Brigade (JLGB)
Camperdown, 3 Beechcroft Rd, South Woodford, London E18 1LA; Tel 0181-989 5743/18990
Representative C. Kay

Leaving Home Project
The Basement, 38 Pulteney St, London W1R 3DE; Tel 0171-437 2068
Representative Rachel Burnham

Maccabi Union GB
73a Compayne Gdns, West Hampstead, London NW6 3RS; Tel 0171-328 0382
Representative A. Eisen

Methodist Association of Youth Clubs
2 Chester Hse, Pages Lanes, Muswell Hill, London N10 1PR; Tel 0181-444 9845; Fax 0181-365 2471
Representative Rev Dave Martin

National Association of Boys' Clubs
369 Kennington La, London SE11 5QY; Tel 0171-793 0787
Representative Michael Orbell

National Association of Muslim Youth UK (NAMY)
Markfield Dawah Centre, Ratby La, Markfield, Leicester LE6 0RN; Tel (0116) 224 4950; Fax (0116) 224 4946; Telex 341539 SLAMF G
Representative Javed Bostan

National Association of Young People's Counselling and Advisory Services (NAYPCAS)
Magazine Business Centre, 11 Newarke St, Leicester

National Council of Young Men's Christian Associations
640 Forest Gate, London E17 3DZ; Tel 0181-520 5599
Representative John Naylor

National Federation of 18 Plus Groups (18 Plus)
Nicholson Hse, Old Court Rd, Newent, Glos GL18 1AG; Tel (01531) 821210
Representative Madeleine Woodhouse

National Federation of Gateway Clubs
117 Garden La, London EC1Y ORT; Tel 0171-454 0454
Representative John Oliver

National Federation of Young Farmers' Clubs (NFYFC)
NFYFC, YFC Centre, National Agricultural Centre, Kenilworth, Warks CV8 2LG; Tel (01203) 696544
General Secretary Tanner Shields

National Organisation for Work with Girls and Young Women (NOWGYW)
The Frankhurst Centre, 60–62 Nelson St, Chorlton-on-Medlock, Manchester M13 9WP; Tel 0161-274 3421
Representative Vanessa Worrell

National Trust
PO Box 12, Westbury, Wiltshire BA13 4NA; Tel Westbury 826302
Representative Mrs Jenny Baker

20 Youth Service

National Youth Theatre
443/1445 Holloway Rd, London N7 6LW; Tel 0171-281 3863
Edward Wilson

Nautical Training Corps (NTC)
39 Chesham Rd, Brighton BN2 1NB; Tel (01273) 676836
Representative A.E. Sutherwood

NAYCEO
27 St John Terr, Devoran, Truro, Cornwall TR3 6NE
Representative John Walton

New Treatment Church of God
Main Hse, Overstone Pk, Overstone, Northampton NN6 OAD; Tel (01604) 643111
Eric Brown

Ocean Youth Club (OYC)
The Bus Station, South St, Gosport, Hants PO12 1EP; Tel (01705) 523711
Representative Jonathan Cheshire

Scottish Crusaders
23 Royal Exchange Sq, Glasgow; Tel 0141-248 6380
Representative Alister Beaton

Outward Bound Trust
Chesterfield, Regents Pl, Rugby CV21 2PJ; Tel Rugby 60423
Representative I. Fothergill

Oxfam Education Department
23 New Mount St, Manchester M24 4DE; Tel 0161-953 4008
Representative Ailma Sonne

PHAB
c/o Northampton Phab Centre, Bushlands Rd, Weston Raveil, Northampton NN3 2HP; Tel (01604) 785233
Representative Paul Hope

The Pony Club of Great Britain
BEC, Stoneleigh, Kenilworth, Warks CV8 2LR; Tel (01203) 696697; Fax (01203) 696685
Representative Lt Col T.W. Kopanski

Project Trident
17 Trident Trust, The Brewery, 91 Brick La, London E1 6QN; Tel 0171-375 0245
Representative Bob Newman

Reform Synagogue Youth
The Manor Hse Centre for Judaism, 80 East End Rd, Finchley, London N3 2SY; Tel 0181-349 4731

Religious Society of Friends (Quakers)
Children and Young People's Committee, Friends Hse, Euston Rd, London NW1 2BJ; Tel 0171-388 1978
Representative Mina Temple

Royal British Legion
38 Duxbury Rd, Leicester LE5 3LQ; Tel (0116) 274 3171
Richard Clarke

RSPB Youth Unit
The Lodge, Sandy, Beds SG19 2DL; Tel (01767) 680551
Representative Peter Holden

The Salvation Army (SAY)
101 Queen Victoria St, London EC4P 4EP; Tel 0171-236 5222; Fax 0171-236 6272

Save the Children Fund
Southern Regional Office, Goldhawk Hse, 49 Goldhawk Rd, London W12 8QP; Tel 0181-743 3311
Representative Judy Lister

The Scout Association (Incorporated by Royal Chapter)
Baden–Powell Hse, Queen's Gate, London SW7 5JS; Tel 0171-584 7030; Fax 0171-581 9953
Representative Ted Hayden

Scripture Union
Scripture Union Hse, 130 City Rd, London EC1V 2NJ; Tel 0171-782 0013
Representative M. Eastman

The Sea Cadet Association
202 Lambeth Rd, London SE1 7JF; Tel 0171-928 8978; Fax 0171-401 2537
General Secretary Cdr Graham Shaw

Sea Ranger Association
76 Collingwood Gdns, Clayhall, Ilford, Essex IG5 OAN; Tel 0181-550 1109
Representative Doreen Hewitt

South West Association for FE and Training
Bishops Hull Hse, Bishops Hull, Taunton, Somerset TA1 5RA; Tel (01823) 335459
Representative Dillion Hughes

UK Band of Hope Union (UKBHU)
25 (f) Copperfield St, London SE1 0EN; Tel 0171-928 0848
Representative Martin Perry

United Reformed Church, Youth Committee
The U.R.C. Youth Office, 86 Tavistock Pl, London WC1H 9RT; Tel 0171-837 7661
Youth Secretary Paul Franklin

Woodcraft Folk
13 Ritherdon Rd, London, SW17 8QE; Fax 0181-672 6031
National Secretary Tony Billinghurst

Young Christian Workers
120A West Heath Rd, London NW3 7TY; Tel 0181-458 8416
Representative David Stretton

Young Explorers' Trust
Stretton Cottage, Wellow Rd, Ollerton, Newark, Notts NG22 9AX
Representative N.E. Grey

Young Ornithologists' Club (YOC)
The Lodge, Sandy, Beds SG19 2DL; Tel (01767) 680551 (Junior Section of the RSPB); Fax (01767) 292365
Representative Peter N. Holden

Young Women's Christian Association of Great Britain
Claredon Hse, 52 Corn Market St, Oxford OX1 3EJ; Tel 726110
Representative Miss E. Sharples

Youth Clubs UK
Keswick Hse, 30 Peacock La, Leicester LE1 5NY; Tel (0116) 262 9514; Fax (0116) 253 9465
Representative David Stickles

Youth Hostels Association (YHA)
Trevelyan Hse, 8 St Stephen's Hill, St Albans, Herts AL1 2DY; Tel (01727) 55215; Fax (01727) 44126
Representative Christrose Sumner

Local Councils for Voluntary Youth Services

Avon Council for Voluntary Youth Services
Princess St, St Philips, Bristol BS2 0RJ
County Scout Secretary D. Thomas

Bailiwick of Guernsey Council for Voluntary Youth Services
Youth Service Office, Brock Rd, St Peter Port, Guernsey; Tel (01481) 715363
Chairman Stan Green, MBE

Bedfordshire Council for Voluntary Youth Services (CVYS)
1 Wharf View, Buckingham MK18 1XF
Representative John Carr

Berkshire Council for Voluntary Youth Services
452 Basingstoke Rd, Reading, Berkshire RG2 0QE; Tel (01734) 231267; Fax (01734) 231226
Youth and Community Officer Ray Tapken

Birmingham Council for Voluntary Youth Service
133 Scribers La, Hall Green, Birmingham B28 0PW; Tel 0121-744 3412
Representative Tony Mullins

Buckinghamshire Council for Voluntary Youth Services (BCVYS)
The Coach House, Green Pk, Aston Clinton, Aylesbury, Bucks HP22 5NE; Tel (01296) 631911
Executive Officer Don McLaren

Cambridgeshire Council for Voluntary Youth Services
145 Gwydir St, Cambridge CB1 2LJ; Tel (01223) 356615
Representative Mary Sanders

Cheshire Council for Voluntary Youth Services (CCVYS)
15 Windmill Dr, Audlem, Crewe CW3 0BE; Tel (01270) 812135; Fax (01270) 812227
Chairman Peter Ellis

Coventry Council for Voluntary Youth Services
67 Momus Boulevard, Coventry CV1 5NA; Tel (01203) 455749
Representative Kamla Granger

Croydon's Voluntary Youth Sector (CVYS)
The Bungalow, Sir Philip Game Centre, 38 Morland Ave, Addiscombe, Croydon CR0 6EA; Tel 0181-655 1367
Chairperson Pat Creighton, CVYS
Acting Youth Development Officer Jackie Harford

Cumbria Council for Voluntary Youth Service
2 Linden Wk, Stainburn, Workington, Cumbria CA14 4UW; Tel (01900) 603213
Representative Rev Ian Hay

Derbyshire Council for Voluntary Youth Services
17 Meadowside, Whaley Bridge, Via Stockport SK12 7AZ; Tel (01663) 734423; Fax (01663) 735102

Devon Council for Voluntary Youth Services
2 Fore St, Moretonhampstead, Newton Abbot, Devon TQ13 8LL; Tel (01647) 40974; Fax (01647) 40942
Youthwork Organiser Steve Drowley

Dorset Council for Voluntary Youth Services
Rubery, Fairfield Rd, Blandford, Dorset; Tel (01258) 451215
Paul Niemiec

Durham Standing Conference for Voluntary Organisations
58 Thorndale, Belmont, Durham DH1 2AH; Tel 0191-384 2461
Representative Joan Wood

East Sussex Council for Voluntary Youth Services
c/o Youth Clubs Sussex Ltd, The Brighthelm Church and Community Centre, North Rd, Brighton, East Sussex BN1 3LA; Tel (01273) 821789; Fax (01273) 747313
Chair R. Graham Gordon

Essex Council for Voluntary Youth Services (ECVYS)
120 Waterhouse La, Chelmsford, Essex CM1 2QT; Tel (01245) 262312; Fax (01245) 262312
Representative Abbi Thorpe

Gateshead Borough Youth Organisation Council
6 Regent Terr, Gateshead NE8 1LU; Tel 0191-490 1900
Co-ordinator Terry Eccles

Gloucestershire Council for Voluntary Youth Services (GCVYS)
2 Paragate Rd, Cinderford, Glos; Tel (01594) 822602
Chairperson Beryl Evans
Executive Officer K. Tilling c/o Gloucestershire Youth and Community Service, Chequers Bridge Centre, Painswick Rd, Gloucester GL4 7TZ

Greater Manchester Council for Voluntary Youth Services
The St Thomas Centre, Ardwick Green North, Manchester M12 6FZ; Tel 0161-273 7364
Representative M. Payne

Hampshire Council for Voluntary Youth Services
Church Hse, 9 The Cl, Winchester, Hants SO23 9LS; Tel (01962) 844644; Fax (01962) 841815
Chairman Linda Scorey

Hereford and Worcester Council for Voluntary Youth Services (H&WCVYS)
49 Brookside Cl, Shifnal, Shropshire TF11 8HN; Tel (01952) 460364
Representative Martin Lambourne

Hertfordshire Council for Voluntary Youth Services
County Youth and Community Office, The Valley School, Valley Way, Stevenage, Herts SG2 9AB; Tel (01438) 747422
General Secretary John Howat

Humberside Council for Voluntary Youth Services
15 Park Ave, Hull, North Humberside HU5 3EN; Tel (01482) 446095
Representative Eleanor Griffiths

Isle of Wight CVYS
39 Broadsmith Ave, East Cowes, Isle of Wight; Tel (01983) 294035
Representative Angela Stewart

Kent Council for Voluntary Youth Services
c/o County Scout Office, Upbury Manor Youth House, Marlborough Rd, Gillingham, Kent ME7 5HR; Tel (01634) 281770; Fax (01634) 281775
Hon Secretary P.J. Kemp

Knowsley CVYS
Merseyside Youth Association, 86–88 Sheil Rd, Liverpool L6 3AF; Tel 0151-236 0557
Representative Roy Evans

Leicestershire Council for Voluntary Youth Services
15 New St, Leicester LE1 5NR; Tel (0116) 253 9181 Ext 288
Representative Ken Webb

Lincolnshire Council for Voluntary Youth Services
3 Christopher Cl, Heckington, Sleaford, Lincs NG34 9SA; Tel (01529) 60670
Honorary Secretary Capt N. Thomson

Liverpool Youth Organisations Committee
14 Castle St, Liverpool L2 0NJ; Tel 0151-236 7728
Secretary Nadeem Malik

London Youth Matters
c/o YMCA, 640 Forest Rd, London E17 3DZ; Tel 0181-520 6655; Fax 0181-509 3190
Director Graham McDonald

Manchester Council for Voluntary Youth Services
Federation of Boys' Clubs, Playing Fields Hse, Denvent Ave, Chorlton, Manchester M21 2OS; Tel 0161-445 0228
Representative G. Gallop

Norfolk Council for Voluntary Youth services (NCVYS)
St Peters Methodist Church, Park La, Norwich NR2 3EQ; Tel (01603) 625765
Representative Robert Wells

Northamptonshire Council for Voluntary Youth Service
35 Brickwell Ct, Standens, Barn, Northampton NN3 3TS; Tel (01604) 413162
Representative David Greaves

Northumberland Standing Conference of Voluntary Organisations
12 Eleventh Ave, Blyth, Northumberland NE24 2PX; Tel (01670) 367320
Representative Peter Walker

Nottinghamshire Council for Voluntary Youth Services
22 Elm Tree Ave, West Bridgford, Nottingham NG2 7JU; Tel (0115) 981 1735
Administration/Development Officer Sam Leadbetter

Oldham Council for Voluntary Youth Service
Youth Development Office, 122 Rochdale Rd, Oldham, Lancs OL1 1NT; Tel 0161-626 9948
General Secretary and Youth Officer Dr C.W. Shaw
Co-ordinating and Representative Body for Voluntary Youth Work throughout Oldham Borough
The Community and Youth Work Association (YDA) 122 Rochdale Rd, Oldham OL1 1NT; Tel (01457) 834943 or 0161-626 9948; *General Secretary* Dr C.W. Shaw; National Professional Association for Youth and Community Workers
New Institute of Social Welfare, c/o Youth Development Office, 122 Rochdale Rd, Oldham OL1 1NT; Tel (01457) 834943 or 0161 626 9948; General Social Welfare Professional Interest body formed in 1992 similar in format to the old I&W which closed in 1990
Tameside Voluntary Youth Services Steering Group 20 Stockport Rd, Mossley, Ashton-U-Lyne, Lancs OL5 0QY; D. Shaw, CertCYW, MISW; Tel (01457) 834943

Oxfordshire Council for Voluntary Youth Services
Inverbroom, Manor Rd, Towersey, Thame, Oxon OX9 3QS; Tel (01844) 215287
Hon Secretary G.W. Ross Dike

The Prince's Trust, Buckinghamshire,
The Coach Hse, Green Pk, Aston Clinton, Aylesbury HP22 5NE; Tel (01296) 631779
Applications Secretary Don McLaren

Somerset Council for Voluntary Youth Services
The Millstone, Alhampton, Shepton Mallet, Somerset BA5 6PY; Tel (01749) 86216
Representative John Singleton

Staffordshire Council of Voluntary Youth Services (SCVYS)
SCVYS, Youth and Community Service Annexe, 14 Tipping St, Stafford ST16 2LN; Tel (01785) 223121 Ext 8779
SCVYS Development Worker Jenny Harvey

Suffolk Council for Voluntary Youth Services
6 Mornington Ave, Ipswich IP1 4LA; Tel (01473) 742802
Representative Joan Philpot

Surrey Council for Voluntary Youth Services
Felbury Hse, Holmbury St Mary, Dorking, Surrey RH5 6NL; Tel (01306) 730929; Fax (01306) 730610
Representative Beryl Goulston

West Sussex Council for Voluntary Youth Services
19 Pratton Ave, Lancing, W Sussex BN15 9NU; Tel (01903) 755067
Chairman Sheila Cunningham

Wiltshire Council for Voluntary Youth Services
Wiltshire Youth Service Council, 34 Luxfield Rd, Warminster, Wilts BA12 8HN; Tel (01985) 217992
Representative C. Rowberry

Wirral Council for Voluntary Youth Services
c/o Shaftesbury Boys Club, Mendip Rd, Prenton, Birkenhead, Merseyside LA2 8NU; Tel 0151-608 7165
Representative D. Ray

YMCA
The Orchard, Alverton, Penzance TR18 4ET; Tel (01736) 65016
General Secretary Bob Mayfield

Council for Wales of Voluntary Youth Services (CWVYS)

Leslie Crt, Lôn-y-Llyn, Caerphilly, Mid Glam CF8 1BQ; Tel (01222) 880088
Executive Officer Gareth Ioan

Member Organisations

Army Cadet Force
Wales Headquarters of the T.A.V.R. Association Centre Block, Maindy Barracks, Cardiff CF4 3YE; Tel Cardiff 343020
Cadet Executive Officer Major W.G. Gulley

Welsh Alliance of Baptist Youth
Bethel Baptist Church Centre, Heol Miskin, Pontyclun, Mid Glam CF7 9AJ; Tel (01443) 224834
Stephen Collins

Boys' Brigade in Wales
Brigade Hse, 80 Woodville Rd, Cathays, Cardiff CF2 4ED; Tel (01222) 232052
Development Officer Nigel James

British Red Cross Society (Dyfed Branch)
16 Spillman St, Carmarthen, Dyfed
Head Lt Col J.A.S. Rees

Crusaders in Wales
Regal Hse, Gelligaer La, Cathays, Cardiff CF4 3JS
Dellwyn Jones

Cyswllt Ieuenctid/Youthlink Wales
91a Cardiff Rd, Caerphilly CF8 1FQ
Veronica Wilson

The Duke of Edinburgh's Award in Wales
See main entry

Dyfed Youth Council
St Thomas' Grn, Haverfordwest, Dyfed
DYC Education Officer Tony Organ

Further Education and Youth Service Association for Wales
Oak Hse, 12 The Bulwark, Brecon, Powys LD3 7AD
Honorary Secretary Sandra Skinner

Guides Cymru (Girl Guides Association)
Guides Cymru Office, Broneirion, Llandinam, Powys SY17 5DE; Tel (0168 684) 652
General Secretary Betty Cumming

Gweithgareddau Ieuenctid Cymru/Youth Events Wales
Ely Youth Centre, Bishopston Rd, Ely, Cardiff CF5 5DY
Secretary Brian Taylor

URCI Methodists
Persondy, Trallong, Brecon, Powys LD3 8HP
Youth Officer Colin Capewell

Mencap in Wales
169 City Rd, Cardiff CF2 3JB
Keith Roberts

Mudiad Ieuenctid Yr Annibynwyr
Ty John Penry, 11 Heol St Helens, Swansea SA1 4AL; Tel (01792) 467040
Youth Chaplain Rev Robin Samuel

National Federation of Gateway Clubs in Wales
169 City Rd, Cardiff, South Glamorgan; Tel (01222) 494933
Keith Roberts

YFC Wales
Royal Welsh Showground, Llanelwedd, Builth Wells, Powys LD2 3SY; Tel 553502/3
National Development Officer Lynne Bryer

PHAB Council for Wales
179 Penarth Rd, Cardiff CF1 7JW; Tel (01222) 223677
Director Gwynn R. Liscombe

Presbyterian Church of Wales (Youth Service)
Y Coleg, Y Bala, Gwynedd; Tel (01678) 520565
Youth Officer Brian Huw Jones

Church in Wales
Woodland Pl, Penarth, South Glamorgan CF6 3HY; Tel (01222) 705278
Youth Officer Suzie Coles

St John Ambulance Brigade
Priory Hse, Meridian Court, North Rd, Cardiff
Youth and Schools Officer Wyn Jones

Sea Cadet Corps (South Wales)
19 St Mary's Rd, Cardiff CF4 7AH
D.M. Walton

UNA (Wales) IYS
Temple of Peace, Cathays Pk, Cardiff CF1 3AP
Sheila Smith

URC Methodist Church
(see also Methodist)
Youth Officer Colin Capewell

Urdd Gobaith Cymru
Ffordd Llanbadarn, Aberystwyth, Dyfed SY23 1EN; Tel (01970) 3744/5
Director John Eric Williams

WAFTYCW
9 Bridge St, Port Talbot, W Glamorgan SA13 1AG
Secretary Norman Bifield

Welsh National Council of Young Men's Christian Associations
Lord Aberdare Hse, 27 Church Rd, Whitchurch, Cardiff CF4 2DX; Tel 628745/6
National Secretary D.J. Allen

Welsh Scout Council (The Scout Association)
The Old School, Wind St, Llantwit Major, Mid Glam CF61 1RZ
Chief Commissioner and Chairman of the Welsh Scout Council Prof David D. Loades

WFBGG
Western Business Centre, Ely Bridge, Ely, Cardiff CF5 5AS
David Allen-Oliver

Woodcraft Folk/Gwerin y Coed
Manora, Cwmystwyth, Dyfed SY23 4AF
Development Officer John Gurrin

Young Women's Christian Association of Great Britain
87 Ninian Rd, Cardiff CF2 5EP
General Secretary Pat Durbin

Youth Hostels Association (England and Wales)
Wales Regional Headquarters, 1 Cathedral Rd, Cardiff CF1 9HN; Tel (01222) 396766
Regional Director Michael Afia

Observer Bodies

National Council for Voluntary Youth Services
see main entry

Wales Council for Voluntary Action
Crescent Rd, Caerphilly, Mid Glam; Tel 869224
Director Graham Burfield

Welsh Joint Education Committee
see Chapter 2

Welsh Office (Education Dept)
see Chapter 1
Staff with responsibilities for youth service provision:
Culture and Recreation Division Russell Dobbins
Culture and Recreation Division Emyr Roberts
Her Majesty's Inspectorate Elizabeth Kidd
Her Majesty's Inspectorate L. Gainsbury

The Voluntary Youth Network for Northern Ireland

Lamont Hse, Purdy's La, Saintfield Rd, Belfast BT8 4TA; Tel (01232) 643882
President Pat Killen
General Secretary Walter Rader
The Voluntary Youth Network for Northern Ireland has in membership the major voluntary youth work agencies in the Province. Its role is that of an umbrella pressure group, working to provide a platform for the voluntary sector. Youthnet represents the interests of its member organisations and acts on their behalf on issues of common concern

Members

Army Cadet Force
G(PT) Branch, Headquarters, Northern Ireland BFPO 825

Baptist Youth
117 Lisburn Rd, Belfast BT9 7AF

Belfast Girls' Club Union
24 Sandhill Gdns, Belfast BT5 6FF

Boys' Brigade
Rathmore Hse, 126 Glenarm Rd, Larne BT40 1DZ

Boys' and Girls' Clubs of Northern Ireland
2nd Flr, 38 Dublin Rd, Belfast BT2 7HN

British Red Cross Society
87 University St, Belfast BT7 1HP

CABLE
427 Holywood Rd, Belfast BT4 2LT

CATHOG
68 Berry St, Belfast BT1 1FJ

Catholic Guides of Ireland
325 Antrim Rd, Belfast BT15 5AB

CBSI – Scout Foundation
255 Antrim Rd, Belfast BT15 262

Children's Community Holidays
3 Blackwater Rd, Mallusk, Newtownabbey BT36 8TZ

Church of Ireland Youth Council
217 Holywood Rd, Belfast BT4 2DH

Churches Youth Service Council
King's Bldgs, 152 Albert Bridge Rd, Belfast BT5 4GS

Co-operation North
7 Botanic Ave, Belfast BT7 1JG

Conservation Volunteers (NI)
Cherryvale Playing Fields, Ravenhill Rd, Belfast BT6 OBZ

Contact Youth Counselling Service
2a Ribble St, Belfast BT4 1HW

Corrymeela Community
8 Upper Cres, Belfast BT7 1NT

Department of Youth and Childrens Work – Methodist Church
Aldersgate Hse, University Rd, Belfast BT7 1NA

Duke of Edinburgh's Award
See main entry

The Extern Organisation
5–11 Verner St, Belfast BT7 2AA

Girls' Brigade
16 May St, Belfast BT1 4NL

Girl's Friendly Society
36 Upper Leeson St, Dublin 4

The Guide Association
Harmony Community Trust
Glebe Hse, Downpatrick BT30 7NZ

International Voluntary Service
122 Great Victoria St, Belfast BT2 7BG

National Council of YMCAs
37–41 High St, Belfast BT1 2AB

NI Forces Youth Service
HQ Northern Ireland BFPO 825

Northern Ireland Association for the Care and Resettlement of Offenders (NIACRO)
169 Ormeau Rd, Belfast BT7 1SQ

Northern Ireland Children's Holiday Scheme
547 Antrim Rd, Belfast BT15 3B4

Northern Ireland Deaf Youth Association,
Bryson Hse, Bedford St, Belfast

Northern Ireland Federation of Gateway Clubs
Seagal Hse, 4 Annadale Ave, Belfast BT7 3JH

Northern Ireland Scout Council
38 Dublin Rd, Belfast BT2 7HN

Northern Ireland Youth Forum
Lamont Hse, Purdy's La, Saintfield Rd, Belfast BT8 4TA

Northern Ireland Youth Workers' Association
c/o Charter Youth Club, 40 Linfield Rd, Belfast BT12 5GT

Order of Malta Ambulance Corps
St John's Hse, Sloan St, Dungannon, Co Tyrone

Physically Handicapped and Able-Bodied (PHAB)
25 Alexandra Gdns, Belfast BT15 3LJ

Playboard
Unit 2, Quayside Office Pk, 14 Dargon Cres, Belfast BT3 9JP

Presbyterian Youth Department
Church Hse, Fisherwick Pl, Belfast BT1 6DW

Prince's Youth Business Trust
Young Business Centre, 103–107 York St, Belfast BT15 1AB

St John Ambulance Brigade
ERNE, Purdysburn Hospital, Belfast BT8 8RA

Save The Children (NI)
41 Wellington Pk, Belfast BT9 6DN

Scripture Union
157–159 Albertbridge Rd, Belfast BT5 4PS

Share Centre
Smith's Strand, Lisnaskea, Co Fermanagh

Voluntary Service Belfast (VSB)
70–72 Lisburn Rd, Belfast BT9 6AF

Young Farmers' Club of Ulster
475 Antrim Rd, Belfast BT15 3BD

Youth Action Northern Ireland
Hampton, Glenmachan Pk, Belfast BT4 2PJ

Youth Hostel Association of Northern Ireland
56 Bradbury Pl, Belfast BT7 1RU

Youth Initiatives
100 Malone Ave, Belfast BT9 6ES

Youth Link
143a University St, Belfast BT7 1HP

Affiliate Members

Department of Education; Training and Employment Agency; Department of Health and Social Services; Belfast Education and Library Board; North Eastern Education and Library Board; South Eastern Education and Library Board; Southern Education and Library Board; Western Education and Library Board; Probation Board for Northern Ireland; RUC Community Relations; Prince's Trust Volunteers; NUS/USI

Scottish Standing Conference of Voluntary Youth Organisations

Central Hall, West Tollcross, Edinburgh EH3 9BP; Tel 0131-229 0339
Chairman Donald McCalman
Director G. Johnston

Organisations in Membership

The Air Cadets
Air Cadets Regional Headquarters (Scotland and Northern Ireland), RAF Turnhouse, Edinburgh EH12 0AQ; Tel 0131-339 5393 Ext 2254; Fax 0131-339 5393 Ext 2279
Regional Commandant Group Capt Alan Ferguson

Baptist Union of Scotland
14 Aytoun Rd, Glasgow G41 5RT; Tel 0141-423 6169
General Secretary Rev Peter H. Barber
Secretary Rev Ian Mundie

The Boys' Brigade
Carronvale Hse, Carronvale Rd, Larbert FK5 3LH; Tel (01324) 562008
Secretary for Scotland Rev W. Haisley Moore, MA

Boys' and Girls' Clubs of Scotland
88 Giles St, Edinburgh EH6 6BZ; Tel 0131-555 1729
Chief Adviser Les Beaton

British Red Cross Society
Scottish Branch, Alexandra Hse, 204 Bath St, Glasgow G2 4HL; Tel 0141-332 9591
Youth Co-ordinator Mairi Allan

The Campaigners
Scottish Headquarters, 28 Manor Dr, Airdrie, Lanarkshire ML6 0JH; Tel (01236) 763660
Executive Development Officer Sam Bell

Catholic Youth Council (Edinburgh)
Community Education Office, Gillis College, 113 Whitehouse Loan, Edinburgh EH9 1BB; Tel 0131-452 8247
Full Time Community Education Worker Rhona Hutchison

Catholic Youth Council (Glasgow)
Catholic Youth Office, 196 Clyde St, Glasgow G1 4JY; Tel 0141-226 5898
Chairman Father John Quinn

Church of Scotland (Education Department)
St Colm's Education Centre and College, 20 Inverleith Terr, Edinburgh EH3 5NS; Tel 0131-332 0343
National Youth Advisor Rev Fiona Buchan

Duke of Edinburgh's Award
69 Dublin St, Edinburgh EH3 6NS; Tel 0131-556 9097
Secretary for Scotland Colin Shearer

Dumfries and Galloway Regional Group of Voluntary Youth Organisations,
8 Westfield Rd, Dumfries DG1 4AA; Tel (01387) 54285
Secretary David Taylor

Fast Forward Positive Lifestyles Ltd
24A Annandale St, Edinburgh EH7 4AN; Tel 0131-556 3009; Fax 0131-558 1190
Director Simon Jaquet

Frontier Youth Trust
c/o Anderston, Kelvingrove Church, 759B Argyle St, Glasgow G3 8DS; Tel 0141-204 4800
Co-ordinator Feri Salvesen

Girl Guides Association (Scotland)
16 Coates Cres, Edinburgh EH3 7AH; Tel 0131-226 4511
General Secretary Pauline Ashton

The Girls' Brigade
Boys' Brigade Hse, 168 Bath St, Glasgow G2 4TQ; Tel 0141-332 1765
Brigade Secretary Helen McLeod

The Highland Territorial Auxiliary and Volunteer Reserve Association
Seathwood, 365 Perth Rd, Dundee DD2 1LX; Tel (01382) 68283/14/5
Secretary Col J.R. Hensman

The Ocean Youth Club (Scotland)
Kip Marina, Inverkip PA16 OAS; Tel (01475) 521294
Scottish Area Administrator Bet Phillips

PHAB
Princes Hse, 5 Shandwick Pl, Edinburgh EH2 4RG; Tel 0131-229 3559
Scottish Area Director Carol Downie

The Salvation Army
Houldsworth St, Glasgow G3 8DU; Tel 0141-221 3378/9
National Youth Officer Major J. Bradbury

SCOTQUEST
c/o YMCA, 11 Rutland St, Edinburgh EH1 2AE; Tel 0131-469 5790
Chairperson Peter Hitt

Scottish Association of Young Farmers' Clubs
Young Farmers' Centre, Ingliston, Edinburgh EH28 8NE; Tel 0131-333 2445
Director Fiona Bain

Scottish Centres
(Scottish Environmental and Outdoor Education Centres Association Limited), Loaningdale Hse, Carwood Rd, Biggar ML12 6LX; Tel (01899) 21115
Chief Executive Raymond E.B. Thomson

Scottish Child Law Centre
Lion Chambers, 170 Hope St, Glasgow G2 2TU; Tel 0141-333 9305
Business Development Officer Donald Stewart

The Scottish Conservation Projects Trust
Balallan Hse, 24 Allan Pk, Stirling FK8 2QG; Tel (01786) 79697
Director Nicholas Cooke

Scottish Crusaders
23 Royal Exchange Sq, Glasgow G1 3AJ; Tel 0141-248 6380
Scottish Secretary Kevin Simpson

Scottish Episcopal Church
21 Grosvenor Cres, Edinburgh EH12 5EE; Tel 0131-225 6357
Development Officer Rob Whiteman

Scottish National Council of YMCAs
11 Rutland St, Edinburgh EH1 2AE; Tel 0131-228 1464
National General Secretary Rev John Knox

Scottish Office Education Department
44 Jeffrey St, Edinburgh EH1 1DG
HMI Inspectorate Matthew Jack

Scottish Youth Dance Festival
Assembly Rooms, 54 George St, Edinburgh EH2 2LR; Tel 0131-220 6320
Administrative Director Amanda Chinn

Scottish Youth Hostels' Association
7 Glebe Cres, Stirling FK8 2JA; Tel (01786) 51181
General Secretary James Martin

The Scout Association
Fordell Firs, Hillend, Dunfermline, Fife KY11 5HQ; Tel (01383) 419073
Executive Commissioner David Shelmerdine

Scripture Union Scotland
9 Canal St, Glasgow G4 0AB; Tel 0141-332 1162
General Secretary Rev Colin A.M. Sinclair, BA, BD

Sea Cadets Corps
HMS Cochrane (Caledonia), Rosyth, Fife KY11 2XT; Tel (01383) 416300
Area Officer Cdr Sam Baker

SSC
20 South Frederick St, Glasgow G1 1HJ; Tel 0141-552 3658
National Organiser Richard McGhee

Strathclyde Regional Conference of Voluntary Youth Organisations
YMCA Glasgow, 33 Petershill Dr, Glasgow G21 4QQ; Tel 0141-557 2355
Secretary John McMurray

West Lothian Youth Theatre
The Playshed, Maree Walk, Craigshill, Livingston EH54 5BP; Tel (01506) 31727
Scott Johnston

Woodcraft Folk
Strathclyde Project, 95 Morrison St, Glasgow G5 8LP; Tel 0141-429 0952
Project Fieldworker Jim Barr

The Young Ornithologists' Club, The Royal Society for the Protecion of Birds,
RSPB, Scottish Headquarters, 17 Regent Terr, Edinburgh EH7 5BN; Tel 0131-557 3136
Youth Officer (Scotland) Jonathan Osborne

YWCA of Great Britain
Scottish Council, 7 Randolph Cres, Edinburgh EH3 7TH; Tel 0131-225 7592
General Secretary (Scotland) Isabel Carr

Youth Clubs Scotland
Balfour Hse, 17 Bonnington Gr, Edinburgh EH6 4DP; Tel 0131-554 2561
Chief Executive Jessie Todd

Youth For Understanding
YFU Office, Unit 1D3, Templeton Business Centre, 62 Templeton St, Glasgow G40 1DA; Tel 0141-556 1116
James B. Watson

British Youth Council

57 Chalton St, London NW1 1HU; Tel 0171-387 7559
General Secretary Graham Hitchen
Chairperson Vanessa Potter
The British Youth Council is the representative forum in the UK for the young members of National and Local Youth Organisations. It has in membership most major youth organisations in the UK, non party political and

party political included. The council formulates policy and represents this to Government and decision-makers. It has extensive political education and international programmes.

The Prince's Trust and The Royal Jubilee Trusts

Incorporating The Prince's Trust, King George's Jubilee Trust and The Queen's Silver Jubilee Trust
8 Bedford Row, London WC1R 4BA; Tel 0171-430 0524
President HRH The Prince of Wales, KG, KT, GC
Director Tom Shebbeare
The Prince's Trust enables young people, particularly the most disadvantaged, to develop themselves and serve the community

The Duke of Edinburgh's Award

Gulliver Hse, Madeira Wk, Windsor, Berks SL4 1EU; Tel (01753) 810753; Fax (01753) 810666
Director Michael Hobbs, CBE
Secretary for Scotland J. Shepherd 69 Dublin St, Edinburgh EH3 6NS; Tel 0131-556 9097; Fax 0131-557 8044
Territorial Officer (Wales) Mrs S. Skinner Oak Hse, 12 The Bulwark, Brecon, Powys LD3 7AD; Tel (01874) 623086; Fax (01874) 611967
Territorial Officer (Northern Ireland) W.E. Rainey, MBE Northern Bank Hse, 109 Royal Ave, Belfast BT1 1EW; Tel (01232) 232253; Fax (01232) 232386
Regional Officer (North East England) A. Reade PO Box 2, Hadrian Rd, Wallsend, Tyne and Wear NE28 6QL; Tel 0191-262 5306; Fax 0191-295 1660
Regional Officer (North West England) Ms C. Schlichting Churchgate House, 56 Oxford St, Manchester M1 6EU; Tel 0161-228 3688; Fax 0161-228 3690
Regional Officer (Midlands) J.S. Parkes 89–91 Hatchett St, Newtown, Birmingham BL9 3NY; Tel 0121-359 5900; Fax 0121-359 2833
Regional Officer (East England) P. Redrup 17 Lower Southend Rd, Wickford, Essex SS11 8ES; Tel (01268) 571393; Fax (01268) 562060
Regional Officer (South East England) S. Price PO Box 819, Windsor, Berkshire SL4 1AH; Tel (01753) 621622; Fax (01753) 621066
Regional Officer (South West England) D.C. Hewitt Court Gate Hse, Corsham Ct, Corsham, Wiltshire SN13 0BZ; Tel (01249) 701000; Fax (01249) 701050
Regional Officer (London) W. Wreglesworth Suite 502, The Chambers, Chelsea Harbour, London SW10 0XF; Tel 0171-351 4455; Fax 0171-823 3625
The Duke of Edinburgh's Award provides a programme of leisure–time activities offering a wide range of choice to all young people between the ages of 14 and 25. With the voluntary assistance of adults as Leaders, Instructors and Assessors, they can attain one or all of the three Awards, Bronze, Silver and Gold, for each of which they must successfully attempt four Sections: Service, Expeditions, Skills and Physical Recreation. At Gold there is also the Residential Project. The Duke of Edinburgh's Award is operated in schools, youth organisations, firms and through Award Centres and local Committees, in the UK and in 59 countries overseas. Since its inception in 1956 more than two and a half million young people have taken part including an increasing number who have some physical or mental handicap.

Parliamentary Youth Affairs Lobby

57 Charlton St, London NW1 1HU; Tel 0171-387 7559/5882
Honorary President The Rt Hon Edward Heath, MBE, MP
Chairman John Bowis, MP
Vice-Chairman Matthew Taylor, MP
Vice-Chairman Derek Fatchett, MP
Formed in 1978 to provide a link between politicians, young people and those working with them, the Lobby is open to parliamentarians from both Houses and all political parties. Representatives from the British Youth Council and the National Council for Voluntary Youth Services, the Community and Youth Workers' Union, the National Youth Assembly, the National Association of Youth and Community Education Officers and the National Youth Bureau form a liaison group between parliamentarians and young people

National Youth Agency

17–23 Albion St, Leicester LE1 6GD; Tel (0116) 285 6789; Minicom (0116) 247 1305; Fax (0116) 247 1043
Director Janet Paraskeva
The Agency is the resource centre for youth work policymakers and practioners in England. It provides information, publications, curriculum development and quality standards in training to those involved in the informal education of young people, to those involved in the management and training of youth workers, and to those who make policies affecting young people. It endorses professional training. It publishes *Young People Now*. Established in 1991, the Agency is a Government-funded non-departmental public body and a registered charity

Outward Bound Trust

Chestnut Field, Regent Pl, Rugby CV21 2PJ; Tel (01788) 560423
Director I. Fothergill, BA

Centres
Outward Bound Access Programmes, Roscoe Hse, 62 Roscoe St, Liverpool L1 9DW; Tel 0151-707 0202
Outward Bound Eskdale, Eskdale Gn, Holmrook, Cumbria CA19 1TE; Tel (019467) 23281; *Head of Operations* T. Shepherd
Outward Bound Scotland, Loch Eil Centre, By Fort William, Inverness-shire PH33 7NN; Tel (013977) 72866; *Head of Operations* T. Small
Outward Bound Ullswater, Ullswater, Penrith, Cumbria CA11 0JL; Tel (017684) 86347; *Head of Operations* W. Ripley
Outward Bound Wales, Aberdovey Centre, Aberdovey, Gwynedd LL35 0RA; Tel (01654) 767464; *Head of Operations* S. Waring

Field Studies Council

President Ian D. Mercer, BA
Chairman D.J. Stanbury, BSc
Hon Treasurer P. Brackley, Bsc, CChem, FRSC
Director A.D. Thomas, BA, CertEd, AcDipEd
Secretary and Treasurer C.J. Bayliss, FCA Central Services, Preston Montford, Montford Bridge, Shrewsbury SY4 1HW; Tel (01743) 850674/850997

Residential Centres administered by the Council
Blencathra Centre Threlkeld, Keswick, Cumbria CA12 4SG; Tel (017687) 79601
Dale Fort Field Centre Haverfordwest, Dyfed SA62 3RD; Tel (01646) 636205
Epping Forest Field Centre, High Beach, Loughton, Essex IG10 4AF; Tel 0181-508 7714; This modern purpose-built and well equipped centre caters mainly for primary and secondary schools in this area of London, Essex and Herts although it is used by higher education and adult groups as well
Flatford Mill Field Centre, East Bergholt, nr Colchester, Essex CO7 6UL; Tel Colchester 298283
Juniper Hall Field Centre, Dorking, Surrey RH5 6DA; Tel Dorking 883849
Malham Tarn Field Centre, Nr Settle, North Yorks BD24 9PU; Tel Airton 830331
Nettlecombe Court, The Leonard Wills Field Centre, Williton, Taunton TA4 4HT; Tel Washford 40320

Orielton Field Centre, Pembroke, Dyfed SA7 5EZ; Tel Castlemartin 661225
Preston Montford Field Centre Montford Bridge, Nr Shrewsbury SY4 1DX; Tel Shrewsbury 850380
Rhyd-y-Creuau, The Drapers' Field Centre, Betws-y-Coed, Gwynedd LL24 OHB; Tel Betws-y-Coed 710494
Slapton Ley Field Centre, Slapton, Kingsbridge, Devon TQ7 2QP; Tel Kingsbridge 580466

Scottish Field Studies Association

Chairman Prof Joy Tivy Dept of Geography, University of Glasgow; Tel 0141-339 8855 Ext 224
Executive Secretary I.D. Pearson Young Street Financial Services Ltd, 31 Rutland Sq, Edinburgh; Tel 0131-229 7933

Residential Field Centre
Kindrogan Field Centre, Enochdhu, Blairgowrie, Perthshire PH10 7PG; Tel (0125081) 286
Director Dr Alastair Lavery, BSc, PhD

Bowles Outdoor Centre

Eridge Grn, Tunbridge Wells, Kent TN3 9LW; Tel (01892) 665665
Multi-activity and specialist courses in rock-climbing, canoeing, dry ski-ing, orienteering and camping. Courses open to the public and closed courses for schools and colleges. Also courses in management development and team building

Brathay Hall Trust

Brathay Hall, Ambleside, Cumbria LA22 OHP; Tel (015394) 33041; Fax (015394) 34424
Brathay offers experiential programmes that utilise purpose designed activity in and out of doors. Brathay is noted for the very high calibre of its training staff, the flexibility with which programmes are delivered and the breathtaking situation of its residential centre at the head of Lake Windermere
Brathay Hall Trust programmes are concerned with applying outdoor development to personal and interpersonal growth in three key areas 1. Those in education including development for students and facilitation skills for teachers, 2. Youth and youth groups and 3. Young employees. The work of Brathay Hall Trust is directly subsidised to offer high quality at low cost

Brathay Development Training

Tel (015394) 33041; Fax (015394) 34424
Brathay Development Training programmes are most effectively applied to scenarios where a change in approach or attitude to work is required or where the development of personal and interpersonal skills is sought. Each programme is built from the start point of a client's required output. A process is designed around which purpose designed activities are crafted to illustrate the key issues. The programme environment is at once supportive, positive and sensitive whilst being dynamic, challenging and impactful, in a unique and powerful blend designed to meet and exceed expectations

The Trident Trust

Saffron Court, 14B St Cross St, London EC1N 8XA; Tel 0171-242 1616; Fax 0171-430 2975
Representative Colin Cooke-Priest
Director Colin Cooke-Priest
Trident, through its Skills for Life programme, provides a progression of Personal Challenge, Community Involvement and Work Experience. Core Skills learning is recorded and certificated. Nationally Trident supports 70 projects involving more than 160,000 students as a partnership between education, business and voluntary agencies

Endeavour Training

17A Glumangate, Chesterfield, Derbyshire S40 1TX; Tel (01246) 237201; Fax (01246) 203828
Chair Allan Bridgewater
Chief Executive David Howarth
Patron HRH The Duke of Kent, KG, GCMG, GCVO, ADC
Life President The Lord Hunt of Llanfair Waterdine, KG, CBE, DSO
President Sir James Cleminson, KBE, MC, DL
Founder R.S. Allcock, OBE
Endeavour provides programmes of training for personal development. Often long term, it develops personal awareness, confidence and self-esteem. Personal needs are examined alongside those of others within residential programmes, with opportunities for voluntary follow-up and leadership training. Endeavour generates its own voluntary membership, the Endeavour Association. It works for the benefit of the community and is open to anyone. The Association operates through a regional structure and Voluntary Local Groups. The John Hunt Exploration Group provides specialist support for minor expeditions and regularly organises major expeditions with a service element, generally abroad. The Association offers the opportunity to achieve personal growth through committed, responsible effort

Other Youth Organisations

British Schools Exploring Society
Royal Geographical Society, 1 Kensington Gore, London SW7 2AR; Tel 0171-584 0710; Fax 0171-581 7995
Executive Director Lt Col J.W.A. Fleming (Retd)
Administrative Secretary Susannah Cowell, BA
Expeditions Officer Nick Thompson, BA

Combined Cadet Force Association
E Block, Duke of York's Headquarters, London SW3 4RR; Tel 0171-730 9733/14; Fax 0171-730 8264
Secretary Brig R.B. MacGregor-Oakford, CBE, MC

Lindley Training Hollowford Centre
Lindley Training Hollowford Centre, Castleton, Sheffield S30 2WB; Tel (01433) 620377; Fax (01433) 621717
Centre Manager S.J. Short

London Union of Youth Clubs
64 Camberwell Rd, London SE5 OEN; Tel 0171-701 6366
Chief Executive S. Abbott, MA

Peak National Park Centre
Losehill Hall, Castleton, Derbyshire S30 2WB; Tel (01433) 620373
Director Peter Townsend

Reform Synagogues of Great Britain Youth and Students' Division
Sternberg Centre, 80 East End Rd, London N3 2SY; Tel 0181-349 4731
Director Sara Joy Leviten
Deputy Director, Finance and Administration Nora Amswych
Senior Youth Worker and Training Officer Wendy Sugarman

Royal Society of St George
37 Charles St, London W1X 8AB; Tel 0171-499 5430

Young Enterprise
Ewert Pl, Summertown, Oxford OX2 7BZ; Tel (01865) 311180; Fax (01865) 310979
Chief Executive Peter Westgarth
Practical Education programmes for capability and enterprise through the operation of a real-life company; supported by volunteer advisers, age 15–19

years for those in full or part-time education and training

Young Ornithologists' Club
RSPB Youth Unit, The Lodge, Sandy, Beds SG19 2DL; Tel (01767) 680551
National Organiser Peter Holden
The national club for young people interested in birds and wildlife conservation which produces magazines, competitions, projects, local activities and holidays. Special membership rates for schools available

Youth Hostel Association of Northern Ireland
General Secretary Gwynneth Pritchard 56 Bradbury Pl, Belfast BT7 1RU; Tel (01232) 324733; Fax (01232) 439699

Youthaid
322 St John St, London EC1V 4NT; Tel 0171-833 8499
Director Balbir Chatrik
Provides information about the rights and opportunities of young people in training, education, employment and unemployment. Conducts research into the position of young people in the labour market

21 Denominational Education Organisations

Denominational Organisations

Church of England

General Synod Board of Education

Chairman The Bishop of Ripon
General Secretary G.S. Duncan Church Hse, Great Smith St, Westminster, London SW1P 3NZ; Tel 0171-222 9011
Deputy Secretary and Schools Secretary D. Lankshear
FHE Secretary Rev P. Wright
Youth Secretary P. Ball
Deputy Secretary and Adult Education Adviser Yvonne Craig
Adult Education Adviser Hilary Ineson
Children's Officer Rev Ivor Hughes
FE Officer Rev Clifford Jenkins
RE Officer (Schools) Alan Brown
Research and Professional Assistant/Finance Officer Daphne Griffith

Welsh Provincial for Education

Director Jack Davis 7 Holcombe Dr, Llandrindod Wells, Powys DL1 6DN

Diocesan Directors of Religious Education (Church of England)

If the Diocesan Director is not also the Secretary of the Diocesan Education Committee the Secretary's name is shown in brackets

Canterbury
Vacancy Diocesan Hse, Lady Wooton's Grn, Canterbury CT1 1TL

York
Vacancy 8 Minster Yd, York YO1 2HH

London
Rev Prebendary J. Osborn 30 Causton St, London SW1P 4AU

Durham
Rev Canon A. Nugent Hallgarth Hse, Hallgarth St, Durham DH1 3AY

Winchester
Rev Canon M.J. Benton Church Hse, 9 The Cls, Winchester, Hants SO23 9LS

Bangor
Dr Graham Loveluck Diocesan Centre, Cathedral Cl, Bangor, Gwynedd US7 1RL

Bath and Wells
T. Peryer The Old Deanery, Wells, Somerset, BA5 2UE

Birmingham
Rev R. Lindley Church Hse, Harborne Pk Rd, Birmingham B17 0BH

Blackburn
The Rev Canon Canon John Hall Diocesan Office, Cathedral Cl, Blackburn, Lancs BB1 5AA

Bradford
The Rev Canon D.E. Creaser, MA The Vicarage, Askwith, Otley, West Yorks LS21 2HX

Bristol
The Rev Canon R. Protheroe Church Hse, 23 Gt George St, Bristol BS1 5QZ

Carlisle
The Rev Canon R. Chapman Diocesan Church Centre, West Walls, Carlisle CA3 8UE

Chelmsford
The Rev Peter Hartley Diocesan Education Centre, 53 New St, Chelmsford, Essex CM1 1AT

Chester
Jeffrey Turnbull Diocesan Hse, Raymond St, Chester CH1 4PN

Chichester
The Rev John Joyce Diocesan Church Hse, 9 Brunswick Sq, Hove, Sussex, BN3 1EN

Coventry
Rev Canon J. Eardley Church Hse, Palmerston Rd, Coventry CV5 6FJ

Derby
The Rev John Hamilton Church Hse, Full St, Derby DE1 3DY

Ely
The Rev Canon A. Heawood The Rectory, 30 Church Rd, Teversham, Cambs CB1 5AW

Exeter
M. Behenna Education and Resources Centre, St Mary Arches Church, St Mary Arches St, Exeter EX4 3BA

Gloucester
Vacancy Diocesan Education Office, St Mary's Gate, St Mary's St, Gloucester GL1 2QR

Guildford
The Rev Canon A.R. Chanter Education Centre, The Cathedral, Guildford, Surrey GU2 5UP

Hereford
Tristram Jenkins Diocesan Office, The Palace, Hereford HR4 9BL

Leicester
The Rev Canon D. Goodman 3/5 St Martins East, Leicester LE1 5FX

Lichfield
The Rev Canon Peter Lister 67 Park Hall Rd, Walsall WS5 3HL

Lincoln
Rev D. Atkinson Diocesan Education Centre, The Old Palace, Lincoln LN2 1PU

Liverpool
The Rev Canon D. Woodhouse Church Hse, 1 Hanover St, Liverpool L1 3DW

Llandaff
The Rev David Adlington Diocesan Office, Heol Fair, Llandaff, Cardiff CF5 2EE

Manchester
C. Barker-Bennett Diocesan Church Hse, 90 Deansgate, Manchester M3 2GJ
(Allan Plant)

Monmouth
Rev Canon Dr Keith Denison The Vicarage, Whitson, Newport, Gwent NP6 2PG

Newcastle-upon-Tyne
Vacancy Diocesan Office, Church Hse, Grainger Pk Rd, Newcastle-upon-Tyne NE4 8SX

Norwich
Cynthia Wake Diocesan Hse, Dereham Rd, Easton, Norfolk NR9 5ES

Oxford
The Rev T. Williamson Diocesan Church Hse, North Hinksey, Oxford OX2 0NB

Peterborough
George McNeill Bishops Stopford School, The Headlands, Kettering, Northants NN15 6BJ

Portsmouth
Rev Canon David Isaac Cathedral Hse, St Thomas's St, Portsmouth PO1 2HA

Ripon
Ian W.D. MacKenzie Castie CE School, Stockwell, N. Yorks HG3 0JN

Rochester
The Rev Canon E.R. Turner, MA Rochester Diocesan Board of Education, St Nicholas Church, Diocesan Offices, Boley Hill, Rochester, Kent ME1 1SL

St Albans
The Rev Canon J. Birtwistle All Saints Diocesan Education Centre, Hall Grove, Welwyn Garden City, Herts AL7 4PJ

St Asaph
The Rev R. Bird The Rectory, Rhos Common, Four Crosses, Llanmynach, Powys SY22 6RW

St David's
Rev Alan Meats The Vicarage, Swill Valley, Felinfoel, Llanelli, Dyfed SA14 8BS

St Edmundsbury and Ipswich
Rev Clare Sanders Diocesan Hse, 13 Tower St, Ipswich, Suffolk IP1 3BG

Salisbury
Henry Head Audley Hse, 97 Crane St, Salisbury SP1 2QA

Sheffield
John Hoare Diocesan Education Office, St Matthews Hse, 45 Carver St, Sheffield S1 4FT

Sodor and Man
Rev Malcolm Convery Diocesan Committee for Education, 24 Athol St, Crosby, Isle of Man

Southwark
The Rev Canon G. Greenwood 48 Union St, London SE1 1TD; Tel 0171-407 7911

Southwell
Nigel Ladbury Dunham Hse, Westgate, Southwell, Notts NG25 0JL

Swansea and Brecon
The Rev Anthony Pierce Llwynderw Vicarage, Fairwood Rd, West Cross, Swansea SA3 5JT

Truro
Rev Canon P.D. Goodridge St Keyne Hse, Kenwyn, Truro, Cornwall TR1 3DU

Wakefield
Rev Canon I. Knox Church Hse, 1 South Pde, Wakefield WF1 1LP

Worcester
Rev Eric Johnson The Old Palace, Deansway, Worcester WR1 1JE

Church of Scotland

Department of Education

General Secretary Rev John Stevenson, MA, BD

Roman Catholic Church

Catholic Education Service

41 Cromwell Rd, London SW7 2DJ; Tel 0171-584 7491
Chairman Rt Rev J. Hannigan, Bishop of Wrexham
Trustee Rt Rev Mgr E. Mahoney, OBE
Trustee Very Rev Canon J. D'Arcy
Secretary R.F. Cunningham, KCSG, MA
Deputy Secretary M.J. Power

Members Nominated by the Bishops of England and Wales

Sr Cyprian Connolly The Briery, 38 Victoria Ave, Ilkley, W. Yorks
Sr Maureen Coyne Ursuline Provincialate, 10 Coventry Rd, Ilford, Essex
E.M. Brash 14 Gwydrin Rd, Calderstones, Liverpool L18 3HA

Representatives of Dioceses

Westminster
K. O'Gorman, WDES 48 Gt Peter St, London SW1
J. Cullinane 73 St Charles Sq, London W10 6EJ

Arundel and Brighton
J. Ryan Christian Education Centre, 4 Southgate Dr, Crawley, Sussex

Birmingham
Rt Rev Mgr T. Gavin 89 St Bernard's Rd, Olton, Solihull B92 7DG
P. Crook 89 St Bernards Rd, Olton, Solihull, West Midlands B92 7DG

Brentwood
Rev G. Stokes Cathedral Hse, 28 Ingrave Rd, Brentwood, Essex

Cardiff/Menevia
D. Chidgey Archbishop's Hse, Cathedral Rd, Cardiff
Rev M. St Clair St Dyfrig's, Broadway, Treforest, Pontypridd
Rev J. Morrisey The Presbytery, School Rd, Morriston, Swansea

Clifton
J. Placito St Nicholas Hse, Lawford's Gate, Bristol BS5 0RE

East Anglia
Rev P. Leeming 8 Gainsborough Rd, Felixstowe, Suffolk IP11 7HT
M. Amey 38 Glenfield Rd, Felixstowe

Hallam
Very Rev Mgr S. Sullivan 2 Spencer St, Chesterfield, Derbys
Rev J. Ryan St Marie's, Norfolk Row, Sheffield S1 2JB

Hexham and Newcastle
J. McLoughlin St Vincent's Home, The Roman Way, West Denton, Newcastle-upon-Tyne NE15 7RT
Rev R. Richmond St Vincent's Homes, The Roman Way, West Denton, Newcastle upon Tyne NE15 7RT

Lancaster
Very Rev Canon A. Cochrane St Wulstan's Presbytery, Poulton Rd, Fleetwood, Lancs FY7 7JY
Rt Rev Mgr G. Turner The Rectory, Warwick Sq, Carlisle CA1 1LB

Leeds
Rev M. Conlin 7 St Mark's Ave, Leeds

Liverpool
R.J.P. Newman 152 Brownlow Hill, Liverpool L3 5RQ

Middlesbrough
Very Rev Canon K. Coughlan St Thomas More School, Elgar Rd, Hull

Northampton
Rev P. Bailey Brereton Rd, Bedford MK40
Very Rev Mgr Canon N. Burditt St Albans, Sheep St, Winslow, Bucks

Nottingham
Very Rev Canon J.F., Phelan, St Paul's R.C. Church, Lenton Boulevard, Lenton, Nottingham, NG7 2BY

Plymouth
Rev H. Martin 2 West St, Liskeard, Cornwall
Rev K. Collins 4 Lewens La, Wimbourne, Dorset

Portsmouth
R. Fordham St Edmund Hse, Edinburgh Rd, Portsmouth PO1 3QT
J. Stockley St Edmund Hse, Edinburgh Rd, Portsmouth PO1 3QT

Salford
Rev M. Child 5 Gerald Rd, Salford M6 6DL
J. Lester 5 Gerald Rd, Salford M6 6DL

Southwark
Very Rev Mgr C. McGettrick St Edwards Hse, St Pauls, Wood Hill, Orpington, Kent
C. Storr St Edward's Hse, St Paul's, Wood Hill, Orpington, Kent BR5 2SR

Wrexham
Very Rev Canon M.J. Kelly The Presbytery, 35 Lloyd St, Llandudno, Gwynedd LL30 2YA

Co-opted Members
The Very Rev Mgr J. O'Connor, JCD, STL, MA Holy Infant, Baxendale St, Chorley Bridge, Bolton BL1 6QH
Br L. Gillespie Kitimagh, Southdrive, Sandfield Pk, Liverpool L12 1LK
Sr M. Patricia Loreto College, Chichester Rd, Manchester

Colleges of Education Representative

Very Rev D. Beirne, CM, BA, STL, LSS St Mary's College, Strawberry Hill, Twickenham, Middx

University Catholic Federation Representative

P. Wearing 13 Mildred Ave, Northolt, Middx

Catholic Teachers' Federation Representatives

M. Emm 24 Knowlands Rd, Monks Path, Solihull, W. Midlands
M. Ahearne 29 Cecile Pk, Crouch End, London
J. Burns 57 Lake Rd West, Roath Pk, Cardiff CF2 5PH
M. Howells 51 Gwenfd Dr, Cardiff

Conference of Catholic Secondary Schools Representatives

P. Fursey 75 Hollin La, Middleton, Manchester M24 3FE
T. Walsh 9 Agbregg Rd, Sandal, Wakefield, W. Yorks

Association of Teaching Religious Representatives

Sister Josephine Barron, FCJ The Bungalow, 24 Singleton Rd, Salford M7 0WL
Secretary ARE Sister Hilda Mitchell 53 Cromwell Rd, London SW7

National Council for the Lay Apostulate

Mrs Morris Courtyard Cottage, Calcot Pk, Reading RG3 5RN

DIOCESAN SCHOOLS' COMMISSIONERS

Principal Officers

Chairman Rt Rev J. Hannigan Bishop of Menevia, Bishops Hse, Wrexham

Westminster
K. O'Gorman Westminster Education Commission, Archbishop's Hse, Ambrosden Ave, London SW1P
Patrick Topp, WDES 48 Great Peter St, London SW1P 2HB

Arundel and Brighton
J. Ryan, MA Diocesan Schools Commission, 4 Southgate Dr, Crawley, Sussex RH10 6RP

21 Denominational Education Organisations

Birmingham
Very Rev Mgr T. Gavin, MA   89 St Bernard's Rd, Olton, Solihull B92 7DG
P. Crook   89 St Bernard's Rd, Olton, Solihull B92 7DG

Brentwood
Rev G. Stokes   Cathedral Hse, 28 Ingrave Rd, Brentwood

Cardiff/Menevia
D. Chidgey   Inter-Diocesan Schools Commission, Archbishop's Hse, 41/43 Cathedral Rd, Cardiff CF1 9HD
Rev M. St Clair   St Dyfrig's Presbytery, Broadway, Treforest, Pontypridd, Mid Glamorgan CF37 1DB
Rev J. Morrisey   The Presbytery, School La, Morriston, Swansea, W. Glamorgan SA6 6HZ

Clifton
J. Placito   Secretary Diocesan Schools Commission, St Nicholas Hse, Lawford's Gate, Bristol BS5 0RE

East Anglia
Rev P. Leeming   Catholic Presbytery, 8 Gainsborough Rd, Felixstowe, Suffolk IP11 7HT

Hallam
M. Amey   38 Glenfield Rd, Felixstowe, Suffolk IP4 9JL
Very Rev Mgr S.P. Sullivan   2 Spencer St, Chesterfield, Derbys S40 2SD
Rev J. Ryan   St Maries Cathedral Hse, Norfolk Row, Sheffield S1 2JB

Hexham and Newcastle
J. McLoughlin   St Vincent's Home, The Roman Way, West Denton, Newcastle upon Tyne NE15 7RT
Rev A. Duffy   St Vincent's Home, The Roman Way, West Denton, Newcastle Upon Tyne NE15 7RT
Rev R. Richmond   Our Lady & St Joseph's Presbytery, Brooms, Leadgate, Consett, Co Durham DH8 6RS

Lancaster
Very Rev Canon A.J. Cochrane   St Wulstan's Presbytery, poulton Rd, Fleetwood, Lancs FY7 7JY
Rt Rev Mgr G. Turner   The Rectory, Warwick Sq, Carlisle, Cumbria CA1 1LB
E.J. Fox   11 Ashwood Rd, Fulwood, Preston, Lancs PR2 4UB

Leeds
P. Neafsey   Diocesan Schools' Commission, 7 St Mark's Ave, Leeds LS2 9BN
Rt Rev Mgr B. Doyle   St Brigid's Presbytery, Elland Rd, Churwell, Leeds, LS27 7QR

Liverpool
R.J.P. Newman   Diocesan Education Department, 152 Brownlow Hill, Liverpool L3 5RQ
W. Cullen   Diocesan Education Department, 152 Brownlow Hill, Liverpool L3 5RQ
Rt Rev V. Malone   Auxiliary Bishop of Liverpool, Diocesan Education Department, 152 Brownlow Hill, Liverpool L3 5RQ
(Home 17 West Overhill Pk, Liverpool L13 4BN)

Middlesborough
Very Rev Canon K. Coughlan   Diocesan Schools' Commission, St Thomas More School, Elgar Rd, Hull, N. Humberside HU4 7NP
H. Tompkinson   Diocesan Schools' Commission, St Thomas More School, Elgar Rd, Hull, N. Humberside HU4 7NP
Rev A. O'Neill   St Aelred's, 216 5th Ave, Tang Hall, York YO3 0PN
Rev I. Stewart   St Gabriel's Presbytery, Allendale Rd, Middlesborough, Cleveland TS7 9L

Northampton
Rev P. Bailey   2 Brereton Rd, Bedford MK40 1HU

Nottingham
Very Rev Canon J.F. Phelan   St Paul's Presbytery, Lenton Boulevard, Lenton, Notttingham NG7 2BY
Rev C. Taylor   Cathedral Hse, Derby Rd, Nottingham NG1 5AE

Plymouth
Rev H. Martin   2 West St, Liskeard, Cornwall PL14 6BW
Rev K. Collins   4 Lewens La, Wimborne, Dorset, BH21 1LE
P.M. Blake   Heron Cott, Sitterton, Bere Regis, Dorset BH20 7HU
J.F. Martin, MA(Oxon)   20 Holyrood Pl, The Hoe, Plymouth PL6 2BQ
A. Hodson   Penhill, Doddiscombsleigh, Exeter EX6

Portsmouth
J. Stockley   St Edmund Hse, Edinburgh Rd, Portsmouth PO1 3QA
R. Fordham   St Edmund's Hse, Edinburgh Rd, Portsmouth PO1 3QA

Salford
D. O'Brien   Diocesan Schools Commission, Firset Flr, 5 Gerald Rd, Salford M 6DL
Rev M. Child   5 Gerald Rd, Salford M6 6DL
D. Lester   5 Gerald Rd, Salford M6 6DL

Shrewsbury
Very Rt Rev Canon P. O'Neill, VG   2 Park Rd South, Birkenhead L43 4UX
T. Helvin   Diocesan Schools Commission, 2 Park Rd South, Birkenhead L43 4UX

Southwark
Very Rev Mgr J. McGettrick   St Edward's Hse, St Paul's Wood Hill, Orpington, Kent BR5 2SR
C. Storr, MA   Southwark Diocesan Schools Commission, St Edwards Hse, School, St Paul's Wood Hill, Orpington, Kent BR5 2SR
A.J. Woodward   St Edward's Hse, St Paul's Wood Hill, Orpington, Kent BR5 2SR

Wrexham
Very Rev Canon M.J. Kelly   The Presbytery, 35 Lloyd St, Llandudno, Gwynedd LL30 2YA
Rev A. Morrin   The Presbytery, 35 Lloyd St, Llandudno, Gwynedd LL30 2YA

The Free Churches

The Free Church Federal Council

Free Church Federal Council Education Committee

27 Tavistock Sq, London WC1H 9HH; Tel 0171-387 8413; Fax 0171-383 0150
Chairman   A.J. Jennings, BSc   15 Ashtree Way, Hemel Hempstead, Herts HP1 1QS
Secretary   Rev D. Staple, MA, BD   27 Tavistock Sq, London WC1H 9HH
Education Secretary   Vacancy   27 Tavistock Sq, London WC1H 9HH

Education Committee
Chairman of the Council   27 Tavistock Sq, London WC1H 9HH
Dr Jack Priestley, MA   Principal, Westhill College, Weoley Park Rd, Selly Oak, Birmingham B29 6LL
*Dr Mary Ede, JP, MA, DPhil   12 Springfield Pl, Lansdowne, Bath BA1 5RA
Alan Garnham, BSc   Haw Cottage, Haw St, Coaley, Glos GL11 5AY
M. Green   2 Cuffe Rd, Milehouse, Plymouth, Devon PL3 4HR
Vice-Chairman   *Olive Gibbins, BD, MTh   27 Riverside Cl, Kingston-upon-Thames KT1 2JG
Rev T.D. Fletcher
G. Handscomb   11 Tabors Ave, Great Baddow, Chelmsford CM2 7ES
Chairman   *A.J. Jennings, BSc   15 Ashtree Way, Hemel Hempstead, Herts HP1 1QS
Dr Keith Johnston   26 Cottesmore Gdns, Leigh on Sea, Essex SS9 2TG
Rev Eric Lord, BD   349 Woodstock Rd, Oxford OX2 7MX
Gillian G. Wood   Free Church Federal Council, 27 Tavistock Sq, London WC1H 9HH
G. Robson   147 Duffield Rd, Derby DE22 1AH

Rev Dr S. Orchard, MA, PhD Christian Education Movement, Royal Bldgs, Victoria St, Derby DE1 1GW
Katharine Short North Lawns, 23 Harestock Rd, Harestock, Winchester, Hants SO22 6NS
Rev S. Haward 49A Kent Dr, Oadby, Leicester LE2 4PQ
M. Smith, BA 23 Pinewood Cl, Westbury-on-Trym, Bristol BS9 4AJ
*Rev David Staple, MA, BD Free Church Federal Council, 27 Tavistock Sq, London WC1H 9HH
Rev Dr John M. Sutcliffe, MA 159 Old Hal La, Fallowfield, Manchester M14 6HJ
*D. Robson Methodist Division of Education and Youth, 25 Marylebone Rd, London NW1 5JP
F. Cleaves
*Rev Prof J. Tudno Williams, MA, Phd United Thheological College, Aberstwyth, Dyfed SY23 2LT
Dr J.P. Wise 21 Knoll Cres, The Drive, Northwood, Middx HA6 1HH
T. Copley School of Education, St Luke's, Heavitree Rd, Exeter EX1 2LU
Major S. Dalziel Schools and Colleges Information, The Salvation Army, 101 Queen Victoria St, London EC4P 4EP
Rev R.I. Davies 4 Sherwood Ave, Marshalwick, St Albans AL4 9QL
R. Hazeldine 47 West Ave, Stockton Heath, Warrington WA4 6HX
J. Leitch 64A Maryland Sq, London E15 1HE
Rev C. Hughes Smith M.D.E.Y., 2 Chester Hse, Pages La, Muswell Hill, London N10 1PR
S.A. Mortimer Mapledown School, Claremont Rd, Cricklewood, London NW2 1TR
Rev Dr G.A. Patrick 20A Church Plantation, Keele, Staffs ST5 5AY
Dr D.J. Stephens Garforth Community College, Lidgett La, Garforth, Leeds LS25 1LJ
J. Tyler St Mary's CofE Primary School, Kelvedon, Colchester CO5 9DS
P. Roberts Burnside, Llanldloes, Powys SY18
I. Lloyd 134 Lake Rd East, Roath Pk, Cardiff CF2 5NQ

* Also members of the Churches' Joint Education Policy Committee which brings together members of the Church of England Board of Education, The Catholic Education Council and the Free Church Federal Council

The Baptist Union of Great Britain

Head of Mission Department Appointment Pending

Mission Department

Baptist Hse, PO Box 44, 129 Broadway, Didcot, Oxon OX11 8RT; Tel (01235) 512077; Fax (01235) 811537

The Free Church of England (otherwise called Reformed Episcopal Church)

Rt Rev Arthur Ward, BD, ThB, DD 28 Sedgebrook, Liden, Swindon, Wilts SN3 6EY; Tel (01793) 695838

Independent Methodist Churches

Rev John M. Day Old Police Hse, Croxton, Stafford ST21 6PE; Tel (0163 0182) 671

Methodist Church

Division of Education and Youth

General Secretary and Secretary for Higher and Further Education Rev C. Hughes Smith, MA 2 Chester Hse, Pages La, London N10 1PR; Tel 0181-444 9845; Fax 0181-365 2471
Education Secretary and Secretary for Day Schools Derek Robson, MA 25 Marylebone Rd, London NW1 5JP; Tel 0171-935 3723; Fax 0171-224 0702

Division of Ministries

General Secretary The Rev John B. Taylor 25 Marylebone Rd, London NW1 5JR; Tel 0171-486 5502; Fax 0171-935 1507

Moravian Church

Schools Correspondent Rt Rev G.E. Birtill, BA, BD Moravian Church Hse, 5 Muswell Hill, London N10 3TH; Tel 0181-883 3409

Two boarding and day schools are administered by the Provincial Board assisted and advised by a local board of governors for each school

Presbyterian Church of Wales

General Secretary Rev D.H. Owen, BSc, BD 53 Richmond Rd, Cardiff CF2 3UP; Tel (01222) 494913; Fax (01222) 464293
Administrative Officer Dr H.M. Griffiths 53 Richmond Rd, Cardiff CF2 3UP; Tel (01222) 494913; Fax (01222) 464293

Church and Society Board

Chairman Rheinallt Thomas, MA, MEd, JP
Secretary Rev Dr D. Ben Rees, BA, BD, MA, MSc(Econ), FCollP 32 Garth Dr, Liverpool L18 6HW; Tel 0151-724 1989

Union of Welsh Independents

General Secretary Rev D.M. Jones, BA, BD The Welsh Congregational Union, Ty John Penry, 11 St Helen's Rd, Swansea, W. Glamorgan SA1 4AL; Tel (01792) 652542/467040; Fax (01792) 650647
Mission Secretary Rev I.W. Gruffydd, BA, BD

United Reformed Church

General Secretary Rev A.G. Burnham, BA United Reformed Church, 86 Tavistock Pl, London WC1H 9RT; Tel 0171-916 2020; Fax 0171-916 2021

Friends Schools Joint Council

Friends Hse, Euston Rd, London NW1 2BJ; Tel 0171-387 3601
Secretary Peter Norris

There are eight Quaker boarding schools each separately managed by a representative committee of the Society

Interdenominational

Churches Joint Education Policy Committee

Chairman Rt Rev M.E. Adie
Secretary Rev Prof H.W. Marratt 27 Tavistock Sq, London WC1H 9HH

Anglican Members

Rt Rev David N de Z Young, Bishop of Ripon
Rev Preb M.R. Metcalf
Jack Davis
G.S. Duncan
Rev Canon J. Birtwistle
D.W. Lankshear
Rev Canon R. Chapman

Free Church Federal Council Members

Olive Gibbins, MTh
Dr Mary Ede, JP, MA, DPhil
D. Robson
The General Secretary Rev D. Staple, MA, BD
The Education Secretary Vacancy
Arthur Jennings, BSc
Rev Prof J. Tudno Williams, MA, PhD

Roman Catholic Members

Rt Rev David Konstant, Bishop of Leeds
P. Topp
M. Smart
T. Helvin
Rev A. Faley
P. Boylan
Dr G. Turnbull
M. Power

Other Churches' Members

Rev Father Antonious Thabit Shenouda
Senior Apostle James Ozigi
J. Cowing
Janet Scott

Observers

Rev Canon Martin Reardon, Churches Together in England (CTE)
Illtyd Lloyd (CYTUN)

National Ecumenical Agency in Further Education

C/o Methodist Church, Division of Education and Youth, 2 Chester Hse, Pages La, Muswell Hill, London N10 1PR; Tel 0181-444 9845
Chairman P.G. Rossington, MA, BSc, FRSA 15 Chesnut Wk, Upper Halliford, Middx TW17 8QR; Tel (01932) 787377
Vice-Chairman Dr J.W. Lethbridge Stockport College of Technology, Wellington Rd South, Stockport, Cheshire SK1 3UQ; Tel 0161-480 7331
Hon Treasurer Rev Dr E.M. Eggleton, BA, DMin C/o (Methodist Church Division of Education and Youth), 2 Chester Hse, Pages La, Muswell Hill, London N10 1PR; Tel 0181-744 9845

Members

Vacancy (Baptist Union)
John Greenland (Roman Catholic Church), Richmond upon Thames College, Egerton Rd, Twickenham, Middx TW2 7SJ; Tel 0181-892 6656
Rev C. Jenkins (Methodist Church and Church of England Joint F.E. Officer), C/o Board of Education, Church Hse, Great Smith St, London SW1P 3NZ; Tel 0171-222 9011
Rev Tony Cottam (NATFHE), 2 Hilary Cl, Heaton Norris, Stockport SK1 3UG
W.A.G. Easton (Co-opted), 'Lightfoots' Roydon, Harlow, Essex CM19 5HU
Rev R.I. Davies (APC/ACM) Principal, South Cheshire Colege, Dane Bank Ave, Crewe, Cheshire
Vacancy (Church Together in England), Inter Church Hse, 35–41 Lower Marsh, London SE1 7RL
Dr Stephen Orchard (Christian Education Movement), Lancaster Hse, Borough Rd, Isleworth, Middx TW7 5DU
J.D. Green (Dept of Education and Science), Concord Hse, 454–458 London Rd, Croydon CR0 2SS
D.J. Keohane (Roman Catholic Church), Oxford College of Further Education, Oxpens Rd, Oxford, Oxon OX1 1SA
Rev Michael C. Diffey (URC), Ministries Dept, The United Reformed Church, 86 Tavistock Pl, London WC1H 9RT
F. Olney UCCF (Observer), 38 De Montfort St, Leicester LE1 7GP; Tel (0116) 255 1700
Fred Olney (Universities and Colleges Christian Fellowship (Observer), 38 De Montfort St, Leicester LE1 7GP; Tel (0116) 255 1700
Ivor Widdison (CLEA), Eaton Hse, 66A Eaton Sq, London SW1W 9BH; Tel 0171-235 5173
Kevin Swaine (URC), 333 Essex Rd, Canonbury, London N1 3PX

Religious Education Council of England and Wales

1 Raffin Pk, Datchworth, Herts SG3 6RR; Tel (01438) 812416; Fax (01438) 812416
Chairwoman Gwen Palmer
Treasurer Rheinallt Thomas Welsh National Centre for RE, School of Education, UCNW, Bangor, Gwynedd LL57 2UW; Tel (01248) 382761
Secretary and Registrar Dr S. Orchard Christian Education Movement, Royal Bldgs, Victoria St, Derby DE1 1GW; Tel (01332) 296655; Fax (01332) 343253

Member Organisations

Association of University Depts of Theology and Religious Studies;
AMANA The Association of Christian Teachers;
Association of Jewish Teachers;
The Baptist Union of Great Britain and Ireland;
The Board of Deputies of British Jews;
The British Humanist Association;
The Buddhist Society;
The Catholic Bishops' Conference of England and Wales;
The Catholic Education Service;
The Catholic Teachers' Federation;
The Christian Education Movement, CEM (Wales);
The Church of England Board of Education;
Conference of University Lecturers in RE;
Council of African and Afro Caribbean Churches UK;
Culham College Institute;
The Farmington Institute for Christian Studies;
Federation of National and Regional RE Centres;
The Free Church Federal Council;
The Interfaith Network UK;
The IQRA Trust;
ISKCON Education Services;
Islamic Academy;
The Islamic Cultural Centre;
Maha Bodhi Society (UK);
The Methodist Division of Education and Youth;
The Muslim Educational Trust;
NATFHE – Religious Studies Section;
The Association of RE Inspectors, Advisers and Consultants;
National Council of Hindu Temples;
The National Society (C of E) for Promoting Religious Education;
The National Spiritual Assembly of the Baha'is of the United Kingdom;
The Norham Foundation;
The Professional Council for Religious Education;
The Religious Society of Friends;
Roman Catholic National Board of Religious Inspectors and Advisers;
Russian Orthodox Church;
The SHAP Working Party on World Religions in Education;
The Sikh Cultural Society of Great Britain;
Sikh, Divine Fellowship;
Sikh, Education Council;
The Standing Conference on Inter-Faith Dialogue in Education;
The Union of Muslim Organisations NMEC;
Unitarian Youth and Religious Education Department;
The World Congress of Faiths;
Observers
SCAA; NFER; Ofsted; ACAC

Jewish Education

Centre for Jewish Education

Sternberg Centre for Judaism, 80 East End Rd, London N3 2SY; Tel 0181-343 4303; Fax 0181-349 0694
Director Michael J. Shire, MA
Consultant Rabbi Jonathan Black
Consultant Orly Resnick, MA
Consultant Bebe Jacobs, MA
Librarian Pamela Hartog
Consultant Helena Miller, MA

Consultant Sandra Vigon
Programme Administrator Suzanne Zetuni
Northern Resource Centre, c/o Machester Reform Synagogue, Jackson's Row, Albert Sq, Manchester M2 5WD; Tel 0161-831 7092
Peggy Lang Resource Centre, Montagu Centre, 21 Maple St, London W1P 6DS; Tel 0171-580 0214

Institute of Jewish Education

Teachers' Resource Centre, 44A Albert Rd, London NW4 2SJ; Tel 0181-203 6799
Director Vacancy

The Teachers' Resource Centre provides training and resources in support of more effective and forward looking Jewish education. An ongoing programme of lectures, workshops and other events are organised for all types of educators. Institute personnel also regularly visit schools to enable teachers to benefit in their own professional situation. Opportunities for teachers to meet and learn from each other are provided by conferences, seminars and symposia both in the UK and abroad. Our resource centre has the latest educational publications and technology and is used by teachers to research and produce their own material. The Teachers' Resource Centre publishes a journal, *The Jewish Educator,* a fortnightly newsletter *Connections* and other educational publications and teaching aids for the early childhood and primary sectors

The King David Foundation

Administering the King David High School, King David Primary School and King David Kindergarten
Shifron Hse, 433 Smithdown Rd, Liverpool L15 3JL; Tel 0151-733 2292; Fax 0151-734 0212
President of King David Foundation Prof M.H. Rubinstein
Chairman of Governors (High School) H.B. Globe
Chairman of Governors (Primary School) R.N. Goodman
Administration Jewish Welfare Council, Shifrin Hse, 433 Smithdown Rd, Liverpool L15 3JL; Tel 0151-733 2292/3; Fax 0151-734 0212

Manchester Central Board for Hebrew Education and Talmud Torah

Emanuel Raffles' Hse, 57 Leicester Rd, Salford M7 4DA; Tel 0161-708 9200
Chairman S. Pine, BA(Econ), MSc

United Synagogue Board of Religious Education

5th Flr, Woburn Hse, Tavistock Sq, London WC1H 0EZ; Tel 0171-387 4300; Fax 0171-383 4934
Chairman M. De Vmies
Assistant Director of Education J. Leader, DipRd, CertEd
Secretary D. Lerner, BA, MA, PGCE

Islamic Education

The Islamic Academy

23 Metcalf Rd, Cambridge CB4 2DB; Tel (01223) 350976; Fax (01223) 350976
Director General Prof Syed Ali Ashraf
Deputy Director General Dr Shaikh Abdul Mabud
Secretary to Director General M. Sylvester
A religious charity and research-oriented body, aims at making religious values the basis of education

Islamic Academy of Manchester

19 Chorlton Terr, Off Upper Brook St, Brunswick, Manchester M13 9TD; Tel 0161-273 1145
Director Dr Khalid Mahmud, MA, PhD(Birmingham)

Muslim Education Trust

130 Stroud Green Rd, London N4 3RZ; Tel 0171-272 8502; Fax 0171-281 3457
Director Ghulam Sarwar

Union of Muslim Organisations of UK and Eire

109 Campden Hill Rd, London W8 7TL; Tel 0171-229 0538/071-221 6608
Houses the National Muslim Education Council of UK and UMO Youth Council of UK and Eire

22 Educational Visits and Services

Administrative and Co-ordinating Bodies

Association of Independent Museums

President Sir Neil Cossons Science Museum, Exhibition Rd, London SW7 2DD
Chairman Tony Hirst The Boat Museum, Ellesmere Post, South Wirral L65 4EF; Tel 0151-355 5017
Secretary Andrew Patterson Hotties Science and Art Centre, PO Box 68, Chalon Way, St Helens, Merseyside WA9 1LL; Tel (01744) 27766
Editor Diana Zeuner Park Cottage, West Dean, Chichester, Sussex; Tel (01243 013) 364

Cadw–Welsh Historic Monuments

9th Fl, Brunel Hse, 2 Fitzalan Rd, Cardiff CF2 1UY; Tel (01222) 500200 Ext 2241; Fax (01222) 500300
Carries out the statutory responsibilities of the Secretary of State for Wales for protecting and conserving monuments and historic buildings in Wales. These range from prehistoric tombs to Victorian blast furnaces. Naturally they also include most of the castles and abbeys for which Wales is renowned
These monuments are an important educational resource so in order that teachers and lecturers may make full use of this valuable asset to inform and educate their pupils, arrangements have been made for parties of school children and students in full time education to receive free entry to those properties where an admission charge is levied. To take advantage of these arrangements, an application form, obtainable from the above address, should be completed and returned

Council for National Parks

246 Lavender Hill, London SW11 1LJ; Tel 0171-924 4077; Fax 0171-924 5761
President Chris Bonington
Chairman Angus Lunn
Director Amanda Nobbs, MA, MSc
The Council aims to uphold and promote the twin objectives (conservation and recreation) of National Park designation, by representing these interests nationally and through educational and visitor information. 'Know Your National Parks' packs available. New education resource pack available from April 1994

Country Houses Association

41 Kingsway, London WC2B 6UB; Tel 0171-836 1624; Fax 0171-240 1676
Chief Executive R.D. Bratby
Preserved buildings of historic or architectural importance and provides residential apartments with all services

English Heritage

Education Service, Keysign Hse, 429 Oxford St, London W1R 2HD; Tel 0171-973 3442/3; Fax 0171-973 3430
Head of Education Mike Corbishley
Education Officer South West Peter Stone
Education Officer Midlands and East Anglia Liz Hollinshead
Education Officer North Ross Jellicoe
Education Officer South East Jennie Fordham
The official body in England responsible for conserving the historic features of the made environment. English

Heritage produces a wide range of educational material including publications and videos, and offers a professional service for teachers and those working in the heritage education field

Free admission to the monuments in English Heritage care is granted to educational groups. A 'Free Educational Visits' booklet giving details and conditions is available from the above address

Isle of Wight (Including Hurst Castle) English Heritage, Osborne Hse, State Apartments, East Cowes, IOW PO32 6JY; Tel (01983) 200022

South East English Heritage, Historic Properties South East, 1 High St, Tonbridge, Kent TN9 1SG; Tel (01732) 778000

Hampshire (except Hurst Castle), Kent (except Dover, Deal and Walmer), Surrey, East and West Sussex

South West English Heritage, Historic Properties South West, 7/8 King St, Bristol BS1 4EQ; Tel (0117) 975 0700

Avon, Berkshire, Cornwall, Devon, Dorset, Gloucestershire, Isles of Scilly, Oxfordshire, Somerset, Wiltshire

Group for Education in Museums

Chair K. Siliprandi c/o Castle Museum, Norwich, Norfolk NR1 3JU

Secretary S. Morris 63 Navarino Rd, London E8 1AG

Membership Secretary E. Webb c/o Education Department, Museum of London, London Wall, London EC2Y 5HN

The Group exists to promote and co-ordinate interest in and information about, educational work in museums and art galleries, by pooling and exchanging ideas and information concerning the work already being done in and by museums in this country and abroad, and by extending among educationalists and teachers and appreciation of how museums can help them and their students. Membership is open to all who are interested in furthering the Group's aims. The main membership is museum education staff, but there is also an increasing membership of teachers and lecturers

The Heritage Education Trust

Chief Executive A.M. Dyer Heritage Education Trust, The University College of Ripon and York St John, College Rd, Ripon HG4 2QX; Tel (01969) 650294; Fax (01969) 650294

Director Rev the Rt Hon Lord Sandford DSC, 27 Ahley Gdns, London SW1P 1QD

Director Commander Michael Saunders Watson Chairman of Directors, Heritage Education Trust, Rockingham Castle, Market Harborough, Leics LE16 8TH

Director Roy Atkinson Chief Education Officer, Northamptonshire County Council

Director Kathleen Dalyell The Binns, Linlithgow

Director Sir Angus Stirling Director General, The National Trust

Director Susanna Smart Corporate Relations Executive, Reed Elsevir, 6 Chesterfield Gdns, London W1A 1EJ; Tel 0171-491 8276

Director Gordon Lawrence Accountant, Lawrence and Co, 12 St Mary St, Chippenham, Wilts SN15 3JJ

Director Alice Prochaska Special Collections, The British Library WC1B 3DG

Director David A. Hill Senior Education Inspector, Northampton Hse, Northampton NN1 2HX; Tel (01604) 236245

The objective of the Heritage Education Trust (HET) is defined in the Trust Deed as follows: 'The advancement of the education of the public in general and young people in particular in history and archictecture and other environmental subjects through the study of historic buildings, their contents and surroundings and historic landscapes'

The Sandford Award for Heritage Education is made to any heritage property where, for the reception of school or other educational groups, special educational services and facilities are provided which are deemed to meet the educational criteria laid down by the Trust. The Reed Award is a joint award for schools and properties working together to devise school visits projects for children with special educational needs. Both awards are administered by HET and sponsored by Reed Information Services

The official list of award holders is published in the annual guide, *Historic Houses, Castles and Gardens Open to the Public*. HET publishes a periodical, *NIMROD*, annual subscription £6.50

All enquiries to The Chief Executive

A Sandford Award has been given to properties which are judged to have special merit from an educational point of view and these are indicated by an asterisk*

Historic Houses Association

Secretariat Chester St, London SW1X 7BB; Tel 0171-259 5688; Fax 0171-259 5590

Director General Terry Empson

President The Earl of Shelburne

Association of privately owned historic houses. Many of those open to the public offer educational facilities

The Historic Royal Palaces

Hampton Court Palace, East Moseley, Surrey KT8 9AU; Tel 0181-781 9750

Educational Services Manager Gillian Dawson

The Historic Royal Palaces Agency is an executive agency of The Department of National Heritage. The Educational Services Manager is responsible for educational provision at Hampton Court Palace, Kensington Palace, Kew Palace, the Banqueting House and the Tower of London

A new range of curriculum-related teachers' materials are being developed. The service also runs teachers' courses, study days and on-site tuition (storytelling, Tudor music, looking at paintings and costumed interpretation)

Educational visits are to pre-booked school parties Sept to end March. Special schools rate charge now applies Sept to end April

Contact the above address for further information

Royal Commission on the Historical Monuments of England,

National Monuments Record Centre, Kemble Dr, Swindon SN2 2GZ; Tel (01793) 414700; Fax (01793) 414707

Secretary T.G. Hassall, MA, FSA, MIFA

Information Officer Jon Cannon

Maintains the National Monuments Record, the national archive for photographs, drawings, written records and documents relating to the historic environments, which contains over 6.5 million items on architecture, archaeology, air photography and maritime sites. The Royal Commission gathers material for the record through a national programme to survey and record historic buildings and archaeological sites.

Royal Commission on the Historical Monuments of England

National Trust for Places of Historic Interest or Natural Beauty (Registered Charity No. 205846)

36 Queen Anne's Gate, London SW1H 9AS; Tel 0171-222 9251; Fax 0171-222 5097

Director-General A. Stirling

Education Manager Patricia Lankester

Countryside Education Officer Gareth Binns

Young National Trust Theatre Administrator Sally Woodhead

An independent charity established in 1907 to preserve land and buildings of beauty and historic interest for the 'benefit of the nation'. Properties include over 200 houses and castles, 160 gardens and many villages and nature reserves. The National Trust is developing a range of teaching opportunities at its properties, producing educational material and working with Local Education Authorities. The Young National Trust Theatre involves local schools in productions at properties. There is a special membership scheme for schools
Details from the above address

Educational Visits and Services

The following list should prove helpful to those organising school trips of an educational nature. It includes establishments offering education services as well as places of interest for more relaxed enjoyment. Organisers of visits are advised to make advance enquiries for information on facilities available

England

Avon

The American Museum in Britain, Education Centre, Claverton Manor, Bath BA2 7BD; Tel (01225) 463538; Fax (01225) 480726; *Director of Education* Dr John Huitson

Assembly Rooms and Museum of Costume, Bennett St, Bath BA1 2QH; Tel (01225) 461111; *Curator* P. Ruddock
National Trust and Bath City Council
Open daily

Bath Industrial Heritage Centre, Camden Works, Julian Rd, Bath BA1 2RH; Tel (01225) 318348; *Curator* Stuart Burroughs
Recreation of works of Victorian brass founder, engineer, mineral water manufacturer. Also Bath Stone and Bath Cabinet Making Exhibitions. Guided tours and class social history project packs available on loan
Bath Industrial Heritage Trust Ltd

Bath Postal Museum, 8 Broad St, Bath BA1 5LJ; Tel (01225) 460333; *Curator* A.R. Gosling; *Chairman of the Trustees* E. Jenkins
Illustrating the writing and despatch of letters from earliest times to the present day, full size replica Victorian Post Office, special emphasis on Ralph Allen and John Palmer, film and tea rooms. Activities room. Gift shop with souvenirs and collectors' items.

Beckford's Tower and Museum, Lansdown Rd, Bath BA1 9BH; Tel (01225) 338727; *Treasurer* A.M. Bishop
Bath Preservation Trust, 1 Royal Cres, Bath. BA1 2LR

Bristol Zoo Gardens, Clifton, Bristol BS8 3HA; Tel (0117) 973 8951 Information Line; (0117) 970 6176 Enquiries; *Education Officer* Stephen P. Woollard
Admission Charges
Adults £5.50, Children £2.50 (3–13), OAPs, Unemployed, Students £4.00; Group Rates (20 per group): Adults £4.75, Children (School Groups) £2.25, OAPs £3.50, Unemployed, Students £4.00 (valid until April 1995)

City of Bristol Museum and Art Gallery, Bristol Industrial Museum, Georgian House, Red Lodge, Blaise Castle House Museum and Estate, Kingsweston Roman Villa, Maritime Heritage Centre, Ashton Court Visitor Centre and Estate, Education Service, City Museum, Queens Rd, Bristol BS8 1RL; Tel (0117) 922 3623; *Museum Education Officer* Andrew Mathieson
Teaching, advice, information and resources for school groups, teachers and student teachers. Loans service to local schools. Magnet Club for children and parents at weekends and school holidays. Public events programmes at Blaise and Ashton Court Estates

Herschel House and Museum, 19 New King St, Bath BA1 2BL; Tel (01225) 311342; *William Herschel Society Chairman* Francis Ring, MSc; *Administrator* Mary Brown; Tel (01225) 314274
Educational astronomy, music science. Discovery of the plant Uranus in the garden of 19 New King St in 1781 by William Herschel

Holburne Museum and Crafts Study Centre, Great Pulteney St, Bath BA2 4DB; Tel (01225) 466669; *Curator* Barley Roscoe, BA, AMA, MBE
Exhibitions Study facilities by appointment. Fine and decorative art and 20th Century crafts

John Judkyn Memorial, Freshford Manor, Bath BA3 6EF; Tel (01225) 723312; Fax (01225) 723730; *Director* James E. Ayres
Loan service to schools and exhibitions circulated to museums and galleries on the history of U.S.A. as revealed in objects from 16th–20th centuries

Museums and Historic Buildings, 4 Circus, Bath BA1 2EW; Tel (01225) 461111; Fax (01225) 444793; *Museums Education Officer* Essex Havard
Roman Baths Museum, Museum of Costume, Fashion Research Centre, Victoria Art Gallery and the Circus Georgian Garden
Bath City Council Department of Leisure and Tourist Services

SS Great Britain Trading Ltd, Great Western Dock, Bristol BS1 6TY; Tel (01272) 260680/ (0117) 9260680; Fax (01272) 255788/ (0117) 9255788
For full bookings of guided tours for school parties plus Teachers Pack send an A4 stamped addressed envelope together with a cheque for £2.00 made payable to: SS Great Britain and marked attention 'The Schools Officer'. For direct bookings telephone: Bristol (01272) 260680/ (0117) 926-680. School party prices: pupils £1.20/£1.50 From 1st Feb, Adults £1.20/£1.50 From 1st Feb
The SS Great Britain offers a wide range of opportunities for successful educational visits linked to the National Curriculum. It is possible to opt for specific subject work e.g. the Compulsory History Study Visit on Victorian Britain or cross–curricular topic work e.g. Art, English, Geography, Science, Maths etc

The Royal Photographic Society (RPS), The Octagon, Milsom St, Bath BA1 1DN; Tel (01225) 462841; Fax (01225) 448688; *Curator* Pamela G. Roberts
Makes the RPS collection of 24,000 books and periodicals and 120,000 + 6,000 Cameras, Photographs available to a wider public
By appointment only

Westbury Wildlife Park Foundation, Trym Rd, Westbury-on-Trym, Bristol BS9 3ET; Tel (0117) 950 0439
Independent registered charity providing sanctuary for maintenance, preservation and breeding of wildlife

Bedfordshire

Ascott, Ascott Estate Office, Wing, Leighton Buzzard LU7 0PS; Tel (01296) 688242; Fax (01296) 681904; *Administrator* R.A. Inchley
House and grounds with interesting and important paintings and Chinese porcelain collection. Unusual trees and topiary in garden
The National Trust

Bedford Museum, Castle La, Bedford MK40 3XD; Tel (01234) 353323; *Curator* H.J. Turner, FMA; *Museum Education Officer* R. Castling, BA, DipEd
Talks and handling sessions–please book. Small loan service
Bedford Borough Council

Bushmead Priory Nr Colmworth; Tel 730320
English Heritage

Cecil Higgins Art Gallery, Castle Cl, Bedford MK40 3NY; Tel (01234) 211222; *Curator* H. Graham; *Education Officer* Rosalind Castling CHAG and Bedford Museum; Tel (01234) 217418
Furnished Victorian house showing family life of the period. Handling sessions. Reproduction costume to try on. Activity Sheets for all age-groups. Children's

holiday activities. Guided Tours can be arranged. Free entry. Pre-booking essential. Sandford Award winning property
Bedford Borough Council

Chicksands Priory, RAF Chicksands, Shefford; *Contact* R.W. Ward; Tel (01234) 824195
Gilbertine Priory with later additions. Party tours by arrangement
Friends of Chicksands Priory

Luton Museum Service, John Dony Field Centre, Hancock Dr, Bushmead, Luton, Beds LU2 7SF; Tel (01582) 486983
To be found at the centre of the Bushmead Estate, this is a purpose built field study centre consisting of a display area an education room and an ecological garden. The centre forms a base for environmental studies and natural history science work within the environment. Bradgers Hill, in easy walking distance, provides a variety of habitats for fieldwork
Displays interpretation of the surrounding sites; temporary exhibitions on natural history topics
Facilities Toilets (including special needs). Packed lunches may be eaten in education room
Equipment On-site use only. List available on request
Open Mon–Fri 10am–4.30pm. Admission free

Luton Museum Service (Luton Museum and Art Gallery), Wardown Pk, Luton LU2 7HA; Tel (01582) 36941
This is the Town's main museum presenting the local history of the area from earliest times to the present day along with other important collections. Originally a Victorian mansion, the museum is to be found in Wardown Park. The sports pavilion, nearby provides an excellent area for object handling sessions
Displays Archaeology (prehistoric to medieval), straw plait and the hat industry, applied art, costume, lace, childhood, the Beds and Herts regimental collection, Victorian settings, Luton life
Facilities Toilets available in museum (incl special needs) and pavilion. Wheelchair access to museum. Lift. Steps into pavilion
Open Summer weekdays and Saturdays 10am–5pm, Sundays 1pm–5pm. Admission free

Luton Museum Service (Stockwood Craft Museum and Gardens) (Mossman Carriage Collection), Stockwood Country Pk, Farley Hill, Luton LU1 4BH; Tel (01582) 36941
The museum focuses on rural life, in particular crafts, trades and agriculture. It is housed in the stable block of Stockwood House, built in the 1740s and demolished in 1964. The museum, in the middle of Stockwood Country Park, is part of a larger complex including a series of period gardens, craft workshops, the Hamilton Finlay sculpture garden and the Mossman Carriage Collection
Within the Stockwood complex is the unique personal collection, of over 60 original vehicles and replicas of horse drawn transport from Roman times to World War I. It was donated by George Mossman, local businessman and farmer. Carriage rides can be arranged through the stables, phone Graham Ward on (0582) 30131. The Luton Transport Gallery and the Hackney Horse collection are also to be found in this building
Displays Rural life and farming, seed and grain, timber trades, basketmaking, brickmaking, wheelwrighting, blacksmith's forge, horse accessories, town and country crafts
Facilities Toilets on-site (incl special needs). Wheelchair access throughout
Open Summer: Tues–Sat and Bank Holidays 10am–5pm, Sun 10am–6pm; Winter: Sat–Sun 10am–4pm (Tue–Fri School visits by special arrangement)

Luton Hoo, Luton LU1 3TQ; Tel (01582) 22955; Fax (01582) 34437; *Administrator* Zena M. Dickinson
Home of the Wernher Collection, comprising many treasurers including mementoes of Czarist Russia such as jewelled objects by Carl Fabergé

RSPB, The Lodge, Sandy SG19 2DL; Tel (01767) 680551; Fax (01767) 692365; *Head of Education* D.M. Elcome, MSc

Shuttleworth Collection, Old Warden Aerodrome, Nr Biggleswade, Beds SG18 9ER; Tel (01767) 627288; Fax (01767) 627745
Educational Charity. On an active grass aerodrome in a setting reminiscent of the 1930's, a presentation of flyable historic aeroplanes and roadworthy vehicles with aviation and automobile memorabilia. Adjacent to the Swiss Garden, a public beauty spot. 'Time flies at Old Warden'. Special educational events

Whipsnade Wild Animal Park, Nr Dunstable LU6 2LF; Tel (01582) 872171; *Contact: Education Officer* Whipsnade; Tel (01582) 872171
Open everyday except Christmas Day. Educational activities for all ages. Teachers' packs available

Woburn Abbey, Woburn MK43 0TP; Tel (01525) 290666; *Enquiries* P.A. Gregory, Administrator

Woburn Heritage Centre, 1 Leighton St, Woburn, Milton Keynes MK17 9PJ; Tel (01525) 290631; *Chairman* G.M. Green
Interpretation of local history by means of displays and exhibits. Includes items of general interest and a Tourist Information Centre

Woburn Safari Park, Woburn MK17 9QN; Tel (01525) 290407; *Marketing Manager* Cheryl Williams
Woburn Safari Park the Wild Watch new education centre, with a specially commissioned computer programme on wildlife and the environment, linked to the National Curriculum. Full teacher notes are provided. This in addition to many other attractions including adventure ark, indoor adventure playground, educational films in the sealion house and of course over 30 species of wild animals in our open reserves

Wrest House and Gardens, Silsoe, Bedford MK45 4HS; Tel (01525) 60152; *Head Custodian* Alan Hunter
Extensive park illustrating the history of Country House gardens. Also State rooms of 19th century house. Open weekends and Bank Holidays 10.00 to 18.00 Apr (or Easter if earlier)–Sept

Berkshire

Basildon Park, Lower Basildon, Reading RG8 9NR; Tel (01734) 843040; *Administrator* C.J. Leigh
Eighteenth century house with unusual Octagon Room. House contains plasterwork, pictures, furniture and Shell Room. No packs available
National Trust

Calleva Museum, Rectory Gdns, Bramley Rd, Silchester, Reading, Berks; *Secretary to Trustees* Doreen Atton 11 Romans Gate, Pamber Heath, Basingstoke, Hants RG26 6EH; Tel (01734) 700825
The museum provides a pictorial and graphical display of what life was like in Roman Silchester. In September 1993 Hampshire County Council and English Heritage opened a way-marked path with information boards around the repaired Town Walls and fine Amphitheatre. Please note the Museum is unmanned and has no phone: contact the Secretary for information

Cliveden, Taplow, Maidenhead SL6 0JB; Tel (01628) 605069; *Property Manager* T.R.M. Pulverman
Once home of Nancy, Lady Astor. Now hotel with three rooms open to visitors. 375 acres of garden and woodland
National Trust

Courage Shire Horse Centre, Cherry Garden La, Maidenhead Thicket, Maidenhead SL6 3QD; Tel (01628) 824848; *Contact* E.L. Ross
Shire Horse Centre–a working stable with a display of harness, farrier's workshop, demonstration, guided tours, audio-visual presentation. Schools welcomed

Dorney Court, Dorney, Windsor SL4 6QP; Tel (01628) 604638; *Contact* Peregrine Palmer
One of the finest Tudor manor houses in England. Open to the public at certain times in the summer and parties by arrangement

Museum of English Rural Life, University of Reading, Whiteknights, PO Box 229, Reading RG6 2AG; Tel (01734) 318663; *Keeper of Museum* R. Brigden
University of Reading

Museum of Eton Life, Eton College, Windsor, Berks SL4 6DJ; *Curator* P. Hatfield; *Contact* Visits Manager; Tel (01753) 671177; Fax (01753) 617265
Aims :o tell story of Eton College from its foundation in 1440 to the present day

National Dairy Museum, Wellington Country Pk, Riseley, Reading RG7 1SP; Tel (01734) 326444; *Comptroller* P. Aubrey-Fletcher
Exhibition portraying the development of dairying in the UK over 200 years. Contains displays, exhibits and audio visual. Other attractions include Thames Valley Time Trail, Nature Trails, Deer Park, Animal Farm and Miniature Steam Railway. Open daily March to October and winter weekends 10.00 am to 5.00 pm

Newbury District Museum, The Wharf, Newbury RG14 5AS; Tel (01635) 30511; *Curator* A.R. Higgott; *Party Bookings* K. Taylor
Housed in early 17th century and early 18th century buildings connected with cloth manufacture and water transport. Displays covering ballooning, the Kennet and Avon Canal, traditional crafts, costumes and accessories and civil war battles of Newbury with audio-visual presentation plus other local displays. Information folder free on request

The Old Rectory Garden, Burghfield, Nr Reading; Tel (01734) 832206; R.R. Merton

Reading Museum and Art Gallery, Education Section, Yeomanry Hse, Castle Hill, Reading RG1 7TA; Tel (01734) 390909; *Principal Keeper* Barbara Aldridge
Loan service available to individuals, schools, colleges and other establishments in Reading and Berkshire. Also advisory and in-house teaching services

Stanley Spencer Gallery, Kings Hall, High St, Cookham, Berks SL6 9SJ; Tel (01628) 520890/520043
Open Daily Easter–Oct 10.30 am to 5.30 pm
Weekends Nov–Easter 11.00 am to 5.00 pm

Stratfield Saye House, c/o The Wellington Office, Stratfield Saye, Reading RG7 2BT; Tel (01256) 882882; Fax (01256) 882345
Home of the Dukes of Wellington since 1817 and containing many personal possessions of the Iron Duke. Other features of interest are the Funeral Hearse in the Wellington Exhibition, the Walled Garden, the American Garden and the Pleasure Grounds. Open May to Sept 11.30 am to 4.00 pm last ticket 4.00 pm daily except Fridays

Windsor Castle, Windsor SL4 1NJ; Tel (01753) 831118; *Information Officer* Royal Collection Enterprises Ltd, Saxon Tower, Windsor Castle, Windsor, Berkshire SL4 1NJ
Perhaps the largest fortress of its kind in the world, Windsor Castle has belonged to the sovereigns of England for over 900 years and is, by far, the oldest residence still in regular use. The following areas are open to the public: The Precincts, The State Apartments, Queen Mary's Dolls' House, The Gallery, Exhibition of The Queen's Presents and Royal Carriages and St George's Chapel. For pre-recorded opening times and admission prices telephone (0753) 831118

Windsor Safari Park Ltd, Winkfield Rd, Windsor SL4 4AY; Tel (01753) 830886; *Education Officer* S. Struthers

Buckinghamshire

Chicheley Hall, Newport Pagnell; Tel (01234) 391252; Fax (01234) 391388; *Administrator* J.N. Robertson

Chiltern Open Air Museum, Newland Pk, Gorelands La, Chalfont St Giles HP8 4AD; Tel (01494) 871117; *Education Officer* Janet Ahlberg; Tel (01494) 875542
Museum of buildings rescued from demolition and re-erected on a beautiful parkland and woodland site. Iron Age house, Medieval barn, Victorian farmyard and Toll house, Edwardian toilets, 1940's Prefab. Themed visits for schools designed for National Curriculum and include activities. Sandford Award for Heritage Education

City Discovery Centre, Bradwell Abbey, Milton Keynes MK13 9AP; Tel (01908) 227229; P. Mortimer

Claydon House, Middle Claydon, Buckingham MK18 2EY; Tel (0129673) 0349; *Custodians* Mr and Mrs Sandford
Eighteenth century house contains Rococo Staterooms. Florence Nightingale frequently visited Claydon, visitors can see her bedroom and a museum
National Trust

Cowper and Newton Museum, Orchard Side, Market Pl, Olney, Bucks; Tel (01234) 711516; *Custodian* Elizabeth Knight; *Chairman of Trustees* Patricia Osborn
Independent Literary Museum with lace collection
Guided tours and worksheets available if booked in advance

Hughenden Manor, Hughenden Valley, High Wycombe, Bucks HP14 4LA; Tel (01494) 532580; *House Steward* E. Cowan
Bought in 1847 by Disraeli. House contains Disraeli relics including furniture, pictures and books

Milton's Cottage, Chalfont St Giles HP8 4JH; Tel (01494) 872313; *Curator* E.A. Dawson
Conducted tours

The Milton Keynes Museum of Industry and Rural Life, Southern Way, Wolverton, Milton Keynes, Bucks; Tel (01908) 316222/319148; *Schools Co-ordinator* J. Doy
Special visits arranged for school parties

National Trust Regional Office, Thames and Chilterns, Hughenden Manor, High Wycombe HP14 4LA; Tel (01494) 528051

Nether Winchendon House, Nr Aylesbury HP18 0DY; Tel (01844) 290101; *Administrator* Robert Spencer Bernard
Mediaeval manor house with 18th century additions. Home of the last British Governor of Massachusetts. Good English furniture

Schools Museum Service, Buckinghamshire County Museum, Church St, Aylesbury HP20 2QP; Tel (01296) 696012; *Keeper of Education* George Lamb
Disruption to services due to temporary closure of part of premises for rebuilding work. New Art Gallery and Children's Gallery open October 1995; loan service to all schools within county

Stowe School Educational Services Ltd, Buckingham MK18 5EH; Tel (01280) 813650; S.A. Cross

Waddesdon Manor, Aylesbury; Tel (01296) 651282; *Administrator* Lt Col A. Crawforth
Only grounds, aviary, shop and tearoom open in 1992. House reopens 1993
National Trust

West Wycombe Park, Estate Office, West Wycombe; Tel (01494) 24411/2
Ancestral home of the Dashwood family, grounds, church, mausoleum, cars, nature trail, garden centre. Open all year round

Cambridgeshire

Anglesey Abbey and Gardens, Lode, Nr Cambridge CB5 9EJ; Tel (01223) 811200; *Administrator* Graham Moran

Cambridge and County Folk Museum, 2–3 Castle St, Cambridge CB3 0AQ; Tel (01223) 355159; *Principal Curator* Christine Allison
Work sheets available. Exhibitions throughout the year
Council of Management

Cromwell Museum, Grammar School Wlk, Huntingdon, Cambs; Tel (01480) 425830; *Museum Assistant* Cromwell Museum, County Library, Princes St, Huntingdon PE18 6PH
Cambridgeshire County Council

Denny Abbey, Nr Waterbeach; Tel (01604) 730320
English Heritage

Elton Hall, Estate Office, Elton, Peterborough PE8 6SH; Tel (01832) 280468; *Owner* W.H. Proby
Country house lived in by the same family for 300 years. Paintings, library furniture, gardens, teas. Parties catered for

English Heritage, Midlands Regional Office, Hazelrigg Hse, 33 Marefair, Northampton NN1 1SR; Tel (01604) 730320; *Visitor Services Manager* Don Moore
Responsible for properties and East Anglian events

Fitzwilliam Museum, Trumpington St, Cambridge CB2 1RB; Tel (01223) 332900; *Director* S.S. Jervis
University of Cambridge
For education services contact Frances Sword; Tel (01223) 332993

Imperial War Museum, Duxford Airfield, Cambridge CB2 4QR; Tel (01223) 835000; *Education Officer* Sue Chippington
Talks, special studies, and worksheets on topics such as flight and the First and Second World Wars. Free teachers' information pack

Kettle's Yard, Castle St, Cambridge CB3 0AQ; Tel (01223) 352124; *Director* Michael Harrison; *Education* Nicky Boden
Collection of twentieth century art adjoining temporary exhibitions gallery. Education programme includes workshops, talks, clubs and activities for all ages and abilities. INSET and teaching for schools (all keystages) also available

Kimbolton School, Kimbolton School, Kimbolton, Huntingdon PE18 0EA; Tel (01480) 860505; Fax (01480) 860386; *The Headmaster*

Longthorpe Tower, Peterborough; Tel (01733) 268482
14th century tower of manor house, wall paintings of biblical and domestic scenes
English Heritage

Museum of Classical Archaeology, Sidgwick Ave, Cambridge CB3 9DA; Tel (01223) 335153; Fax (01223) 335409; *Curator* Dr N.J. Spivey
University of Cambridge

Museum of Mineralogy and Petrology, Dept of Earth Science, Downing St, Cambridge; Tel (01223) 333405; *Curator* G.A. Chinner
University of Cambridge

Norris Museum, The Broadway, St Ives, Huntingdon PE17 4BX; Tel (01480) 465101; *Education Officer* R.I. Burn-Murdoch
St Ives Town Council

Peakirk Waterfowl Gardens Trust, Waterfowl Gdns, Peakirk, Peterborough PE6 7NP; Tel (01733) 252271; *Centre Manager* B. Clarke
Introductory talk and guided tour, pre-visit briefing sheet, work sheets

Peckover House, 15 North Brink, Wisbech PE13 1JR; Tel (01945) 474008; Fax (01945) 474009; *Tenant* P. Isaac, Esq
National Trust

Peterborough Arts Centre, Goldhay Way, Orton Goldhay, Peterborough PE2 5JQ; Tel (01733) 237073
Drama, dance, curriculum-based arts activities. Exhibitions of visual arts and crafts, concerts; educational programme studies and workshops available, artist residencies promoted. Regular video and photographic training courses

Peterborough City Museum and Art Gallery, Priestgate, Peterborough PE1 1LF; Tel (01733) 343329; *Education Officer* Sarah Burles

Scott Polar Research Institute Museum, Lensfield Rd, Cambridge CB2 1ER; Tel (01223) 336540; *Curator* R.K. Headland
Open 1430 to 1600 hours Monday to Saturday (except some holidays)
Cambridge University

Sedgwick Museum of Geology, Dept of Earth Sciences, Downing St, Cambridge CB2 3EQ; Tel (01223) 333456; *Education Officer* M.G. Dorling
Guided tours of the museum for school parties by appointment
University of Cambridge

Southwick Hall, Peterborough PE8 5BL; Tel (01832) 274064; *Manager* W.J. Richardson
A lived-in historic house with exhibitions open to the public on a limited basis from Easter to August

The Stained Glass Museum, North Triforium, The Cathedral, Ely; Tel (01223) 327367; *Curator* S. Mathews 10 Ferry La, Chesterton CB4 1NT
National collection of stained glass from medieval to modern times plus history information about the craft

University Botanic Garden, Cory Lodge, Cambridge CB2 1JF; Tel (01223) 336265; *Superintendent* P. Orriss
University of Cambridge

University of Cambridge, Collection of Aerial Photographs, Mond Bldg, Free School La, Cambridge CB2 3RF; Tel (01223) 334578; Fax (01223) 334400; *Curator in Aerial Photography*
Committee for Aerial Photography, University of Cambridge

University Museum of Archaeology and Anthropology, Downing St, Cambridge CB2 3DZ; Tel (01223) 337733; *Curator* David W. Phillipson
University of Cambridge

Whipple Museum of the History of Science, Free School La, Cambridge CB2 3RH; Tel (01223) 334540; *Curator* Vacancy
University of Cambridge

Wicken Fen, Lode La, Wicken, Ely CB7 5XP; *Educational Officer* S. Ballard; Tel (01353) 723095
Educational facilities, base camp accommodation. Teachers pack, worksheets
National Trust

Wisbech and Fenland Museum, Museum Sq, Wisbech, Cambs PE13 1ES; Tel (01945) 583817; *Curator* D.C. Devenish, BA, AMA; *Education Officer* S. Burles
Local studies–geology, zoology, archaeology, history (incl. Thomas Clarkson, the Abolitionist); Art–ceramics and ethnography: Temporary Exhibition Gallery

Zoological Gardens, Hadstock Rd, Linton CB1 6NT; Tel (01223) 891308; Fax (01223) 891077; *Director* K. Simmons; *Director* L.G. and D.J. Simmons
Worksheets, guided tours, and talks

Cheshire

Adlington Hall, Macclesfield SK10 4LF; Tel (01625) 829206; Mrs C.J.C. Barnett Legh

Arley Hall and Gardens, Nr Great Budworth, Northwich CW9 6NA; Tel (01565) 777353; Fax (01565) 777465; *Estate Manager* Eric Ransome
An early Victorian historic house set in 12 acres of gardens at the heart of a privately owned estate. School visits Mondays and Fridays. Tours of hall and gardens. Environmental woodland walks, Flora and Fauna. Education Centre, picnic area, shop

Astley Cheetham Art Gallery, Trinity St, Stalybridge; Tel 0161-338 2708/3831
Monthly changing exhibitions of fine art, craft, photography etc

Beeston Castle, Nr Chester; Tel (01829) 260464
English Heritage

The Boat Museum, Dockyard Rd, Ellesmere Port L65 4EF; Tel 0151-355 5017; Fax 0151-355 4079; *Education Officer* Annette Cavell
Information and worksheets, Education and Conference centre

Bramall Hall, Bramhall Pk, Bramhall, Stockport SK7 3NX; Tel 0161-485 3708

Bridgemere Wildlife Park, Nantwich; Tel (0193 65) 223; *Manager* Paul D. Phillips
Education centre–education package for school groups. Guided tours and encounter sessions available. Special rates for visiting schools. 50 acres, birds and mammals

Capesthorne Hall, Macclesfield SK11 9JY; Tel (01625) 861221; *Administrator* Michael Harmer
Home of the Bromley-Davenports, built 1722, with a variety of treasures, a Georgian chapel, gardens, lakes, caravan park, woodland walks and nature trails

Chester Zoo, North of England Zoological Society, Zoological Gdns, Upton-By-Chester CH2 1LH; Tel (01244) 380280; *Head of Education Division* B.M. Norgain, BSc, MA
'Zoo Education Services for Teachers' packs for Primary or Secondary, available free of charge

Churche's Mansion, Hospital St, Nantwich CW5 5RY; Tel (01270) 625933; Mr and Mrs R.V. Myott

Dorfold Hall, Nantwich; Tel (01270) 625245; R.C. Roundell

Dunham Massey Hall, Altrincham WA14 4SJ; Tel 0161-941 4986; Fax 0161-929 7508; *Assistant Administrator* Clive Alford; *Education Co-ordinator* Pauline Mills

Excellent education facilities Sandford award winner. Teachers' resource book. Christmas activities November. Educational Programme available Tue and Thurs during term time, May to October, with use of school party room, which is also available for hire
The National Trust

Fiddler's Ferry Power Station, Widnes Rd, Cuerdley, Warrington, Cheshire WA5 2UT; *Manager* R. Neish
Tours of plant
Central Electricity Generating Board

Gawsworth Hall, Macclesfield; Tel (01260) 223456; Timothy Richards
Tudor Manor House with ancient tilting ground and medieval pleasure gardens. Open every afternoon Easter to October 3rd. Open Air Theatre with covered grandstand – evenings, June, July and August

Gosvenor Museum, Grosvenor St, Chester CH1 2DD; Tel (01244) 321616
Hands-on workshops for the Romans, Tudors and Victorians. Resource packs and information sheets
Further information from Education Service

Little Moreton Hall, Congleton CW12 4SD; Tel (01260) 272018; *Property Manager* S. Adams
Educational tours, room and pack
National Trust

Lyme Hall and Park, Disley, Stockport SK12 2NX; Tel (01663) 762023; Fax (01663) 765035; *The Education Assistant* K.M. Atkinson
National Curriculum based visits to Hall and Park. Period rooms, Tudor, Stuart, Victorian sessions, archives, Red and Fallow deer, trails, orienteering

Norton Priory Museum, Tudor Rd, Runcorn WA7 1SX; Tel (01928) 569895; *Director* Margaret Warhurst, BA, FMA; *Keeper of Education* Amanda Feather, BA, PGCE
Purpose-built museum housing displays and exhibitions, various educational options remains of medieval priory, linked to project work; National Curriculum related worksheets

Orford Castle, Orford
English Heritage
A royal castle built for coastal defence 1165–72

Peover Hall Farm, Over Peover, Knutsford; Tel (01565) 722135; Randle Brooks

****Quarry Bank Mill,*** Styal, Nr Wilmslow SK9 4LA; Tel (01625) 527468; *Education Officer* Christine Chadwick
Museum of textile revolution
Quarry Bank Mill Trust

The Salt Museum, 162 London Rd, Northwich, Cheshire CW9 5AB; *Curator* Stephen Penney; *Education Officer* Julie Williams
Material and information on every aspect of salt and the salt industry, tape/slide show, workroom for study and handling sessions, laboratory facilities, town trails, visits organised to suit each group's curricular activity, TIE workshops, exhibitions and activities during term time, workshops during school holidays

Stretton Mill, off A534, Nr Farndon, Cheshire; Tel (01606) 41331; *Curator* Stephen Penney (The Salt Museum, Northwich, Cheshire); *Education Officer* Julie Williams
Working corn mill with mill pond and eighteenth century wooden mill machinery. Teacher's pack available. Car park and picnic facilities. Open March–October

****Tatton Park,*** Knutsford WA16 6QN; Tel (01565) 750790; Fax (01565) 650179; *Education Manager* Sarah Clegg; *Director* M. Beaufoy
Complete historic country estate with Georgian mansion, gardens, old hall, 1930's working farm, deer park, Woodlands and Meres. Open to schools all year round. Pre-booking essential
Cheshire C.C. for National Trust

Cleveland

Captain Cook Birthplace Museum, Stewart Pk, Marton, Middlesbrough; Tel (01642) 311211; *Curator* Hilary Wade
Describes the early life of James Cook and his 3 epic voyages of discovery, temporary exhibitions. cafeteria, shop, disabled access, auditorium, picnic area
Middlesbrough Borough Council

Cleveland Crafts Centre, 57 Gilkes St, Middlesbrough TS1 5EL; Tel (01642) 226351; *Crafts Officer* Barry Hepton
Gallery and craft workshops. Studio Pottery and jewellery collections on view and educational programme related to exhibitions. Please book in advance

Cleveland Gallery, Victoria Rd, Middlesbrough TS1 3QS; Tel (01642) 262375 during office hours; Fax (01642) 253661; *Exhibitions Officer* Gary Topp
Open Tues–Sat 10–5pm. The Gallery offers a warm welcome to schools and colleges. It is able to offer assistance with projects. A free activities pack is available

Dorman Museum, Linthorpe Rd, Middlesbrough; Tel (01642) 813781; *Curator* Hilary Wade
'What Happened to the Lion?' exhibition, geology, pottery and temporary exhibitions
Middlesbrough Borough Council

Gisborough Priory, Gisborough TS14 6HL; Tel (01287) 38301; *Custodian* B. Wynn
Augustinan priory founded in the first half of the 12th century. remains include the fine east end of a 14th century church
English Heritage–Historic Buildings and Monuments Commission for England

Gray Art Gallery and Museum, Clarence Rd, Hartlepool TS24 8BT; Tel (01429) 268916 Ext 2609; Fax (01429) 869625; *Curator* Frank Caldwell
Hartlepool Borough Council

Maritime Museum, Northgate, Hartlepool, Cleveland TS24 0LD; Tel (01429) 272814
Displays of Hartlepool's maritime past including reconstructed fisherman's cottage and ship's bridge. School parties welcome by arrangement

Newham Gange Leisure Farm, Coulby, Newham, Middlesbrough; Tel (01642) 300202/300261; Fax (01642) 300276
Describes farming in the Cleveland area with farmers general store, Vets, Saddlers and Museum displays. Guided tours available. Children's play area pond, Tea room, picnic areas and vaiours commercial and rare breed animals. Open Easter to Oct, Tues–Sunday, Oct–Easter Sundays only
Middlesbrough Borough Council

Ormesby Hall, Ormesby, Middlesbrough; Tel (01642) 324188; *House Manager* John Baxter

Schools Resources Service, 117 Grange Rd, Middlesbrough, Cleveland TS1 2BE; Tel (01642) 262377; *Resource Officer* C. Rimmington
The School Resources service offers free professional advice, help and a subscription-only book loan service. A limited number of Natural History items are also available on a pay-as-you-borrow basis

Stockton on Tees Borough Council Museum Service, Museum Administration, PO Box 116, Gloicester Hse, 72 Church Rd, Stockton-on-Tees, Cleveland TS18 1YB; Tel (01642) 781184; Fax (01642) 788907; *Contact* The Curator
Three museums including Preston Hall (social history–reconstructed streets and rooms). Green Dragon museum (local history and personalities). School groups booking, educational advice and research material available

Cornwall

Animal World Trenance Pk, Newquay TR7 2LZ; Tel (01637) 873342; *Education Officer* Jon Blount
Wildlife at Night House, lakes and landscaped gardens. Tropical house, education centre, underground rabbit warren and lion House. Breeding programmes for rare and endangered animal species

Antony House, Torpint, Cornwall; Tel (01752) 812191; *The Administrator* J. Morris
National Trust

Archives of the Barnes Museum of Cinematography, Kino Hse, Victoria Pl, St Ives TR26 1NZ
No longer on public display. can be consulted by bona fide students and researchers by appointment

Barbara Hepworth Museum and Sculpture Garden, Barnoon Hill, St Ives, Cornwall TR26 1TG; Tel (01736) 796226; Fax (01736) 794480; *Curator* Michael Tooby
The late Dame Barbara Hepworth's house and garden where she lived and worked from 1949-75. Approximately 47 sculptures and drawings covering the period 1928-75, photographs, documents and other memorabilia. Plus her workshops, housing a selection of tools and some unfinished carvings; Administered jointly with Tate Gallery St Ives
Opening hours; September –May: Sunday 1–5; Closed Monday; Tuesday–Saturday 11–5: June–August; Sunday 1–7; Monday 11–7; Tuesday and Thursday 11–9; Open Bank Holidays 11–5; Closed 24,25,26 December and 1 January. *For admission details see Tate Gallery St Ives*

Camborne School of Mines Geological Museum and Art Gallery, Camborne School of Mines, Pool, Redruth TR15 3SE; Tel (01209) 714866; *Registrar* R. Hancock
Geology teachers resource centre. School parties and all visitors welcome
Admission free
Camborne School of Mines

Chysanster Ancient Village, Nr Gulval; Tel (01736) 61889
English Heritage

Cornish Engines, Agar Rd, Pool, Redruth; *Custodian* Geoffrey Ball; Tel (01209) 216657/(01637) 860140
National Trust

Cotehele House, St Dominick, Saltash; Tel (01579) 50434; *Administrator* E. Proudfoot
Guided tours for school parties. Mon–Thurs only. School parties must book in advance
National Trust

Falmouth Art Gallery, Municipal Offices, The Moor, Falmouth TR11 2RT; Tel (01326) 313863; *Curator* Catherine Wallace, MLIH
Exhibits the town's permanent collection of paintings, and travelling exhibitions, and organises one-man shows and thematic exhibitions

Flambards Village Theme Park, Helston TR13 0GA; Tel (01326) 574549
Three major exhibitions–Flambards Victorian Village, Britain in the Blitz, Cornwall Aero Park. Open every day Easter to end Oct
Plus Cornwall's Exploratorium–A family science playground. Pupils will be safe and are easily supervised and all teachers needs are catered for. Plus famous chemist shop time capsule. Resource packs available to National Curriculum standards. Open Easter to end of October

Godolphin, Breage, Helston, Cornwall TR13 9RE; Tel (01736) 762409; L.M.P. Schofield
Winner of the Sandford Award

Lanhydrock House, Nr Bodmin; Tel (01208) 73320; *Property Manager* Andrea Marchington
The National Trust
Insight into Victorian and Edwardian life
National Trust

Launceston Castle, Launceston; Tel (01272) 750700
English Heritage

The Monkey Sanctuary, Looe; Tel (01503) 262532; *Education Co-ordinator* Ruby Gray
Workshop topics include: monkeys rainforest, other cultures and local wildlife. During the summer monkeys forage freely in the grounds

The National Trust Regional Office, Lanhydrock Pk, Bodmin PL30 4DE; Tel (01208) 74281

Newlyn Art Gallery, New Rd, Newlyn, Penzance TR18 5PZ; Tel (01736) 63715/331578; *Development Officer* Cairney Down
Newlyn Art Gallery presents a changing exhibitions programme of contemporary art from local, regional, national and international artists. The education programme is an integral part of the gallery's activity; projects combine collaboration and interaction between teachers, lecturers, pupils, practising artists, community groups and gallery staff. Events, lectures, guided talks
Newlyn Orion Galleries Ltd

North Cornwall Museum and Gallery, The Clease, Camelford; Tel (01840) 212954; *Contact* Sally Holden
Museum of rural life in North Cornwall. Changing exhibitions in gallery of arts and crafts. Tourist information centre. Open Apr–30th Sept daily. Closed Sundays

Paradise Park, Hayle; Tel (01736) 753365; *Director* M.W. Reynolds
Wildlife conservation sanctuary specialising in worldwide rare and endangered birds. Now home of the World Parrot Trust, The Cornish Otter Sanctuary and the Eagles of Paradise. Write for details of educational information

Pencarrow House, Washaway, Bodmin PL30 3AG; Tel (0120 884) 369; *Educational Officer* The Administrator
A Victorian Experience with teaching pack
Molesworth-St Aubyn Heritage Trust

Pendennis Castle, Falmouth; Tel (01326) 316594; *Head Custodian* J. Wells
English Heritage

Penzance and District Museum and Art Gallery, Penlee Hse, Penlee Pk, Penzance; Tel (01736) 63625; *Museum Officer* J. Holmes
Local history, environmental display, arts and crafts. Permanent exhibition Newlyn School of Art. Help, advice, lectures for local education establishments. Group visits must be pre-booked

Poldark Mine and Heritage Complex, Wendron, Helston TR13 0ER; Tel (01326) 573173/573531; Fax (01326) 563166; *Schools Liaison* K. Toy
Poldark Mine and Heritage Complex

Restormel Castle, Nr Lostwithiel; Tel (01208) 872687
English Heritage

The Royal Cornwall Museum, River St, Truro TR1 2SJ; Tel (01872) 72205; *Schools Service Co-ordinator* Tim German
Schools Service-Curriculum-based workshops; guided school tours
The Royal Institution of Cornwall

St Mawes Castle, St Mawes, Truro TR2 3AA; Tel (01326) 270526; *Head Custodian* Donald Tosh
A Tudor castle of great historical interest, suitable for historical study or delightful relaxation
English Heritage–Historic Buildings and Monuments Commission of England

St Michael's Mount, National Trust, Manor Office, Marazion, Penzance; Tel (01736) 710507; *Agent* O. Bartle
Open Apr-Oct, Mon-Fri. Bookable guided tours on Tuesdays
National Trust

Tate Gallery St Ives Porthmeor Beach, St Ives, Cornwall TR26 1TG; Tel (01736) 796226; Fax (01736) 794480; *Curator* Michael Tooby
The Gallery, designed by architects Evans and Shaley, shows changing groups of work from the Tate Gallery's pre-eminent collection of St Ives painting and sculpture, dating from about 1925 to 1975.
Administered jointly with the Barbara Hepworth Museum
Talks and tours for individual and group visitors. Extensive education programme. A rich educational resource for all levels in the national curriculum
Bookshop; Restaurant; Education Room; Baby change facilities; Disabled access and facilities
Opening Hours; November–April: Closed Monday; Tuesday–Sunday 11–5: May–October; Sunday 11–5; Monday–Saturday 11–7; Tuesday and Thursday 11–9
Open Bank Holidays 11–5
Closed 24,25,26 December and 1 January
Admission; *All tickets inclusive of admission to Barbara Hepworth Museum* £2.50 Adult (includes 1 child/student under 11); £1.50 OAPs, students (over 11), UB40 holders; £10.00/£5.00 Family tickets (2 adults, 2 children; valid 2 weeks); £2.00 Adults and £1.00 OAPs and children in pre-booked groups (over 10 in number)
NB *Early booking essential for group visits*

Tintagel Castle, Nr Tintagel, Cornwall; Tel (01272) 750700
English Heritage

Trerice, Kestle Mill, Newquay, Cornwall TR8 4PG; Tel (01637) 875404; Fax (01637) 879300; *The Administrator* Brian Kirby
National Trust

Trewithen, Grampound Rd, Nr Truro TR2 4DD; Tel (01726) 882763/882418; *Owner* A.M.J. Galsworthy; *Secretary* I. Norman; *Head Gardener* M. Taylor
Gardens internationally renowned for collection of rare trees, shrubs, etc. Famous for rhododendrons, camellias and magnolias
One of only two attractions in Cornwall to be awarded 3 stars by Michelin Guide to the South West

Wheal Martyn China Clay Museum, Carthew, St Austell, Cornwall PL26 8XG; Tel (01726) 850362; *Education Officer* E. McConnell
Open air museum based upon 19th century china clay works. Nature trail and pit viewing area. Education service offers information packs, object and photograph loans, guided tours of historic trail
St Austell China Clay Museum Ltd

Cumbria

Abbot Hall Art Gallery, Kendal, Cumbria LA9 5AL; Tel (01539) 722464; Fax (01539) 722494; *Director* E.T. King, BSc; *Assistant Keeper of Art* P.J. Dalziel, BA; *Education Officer* C. Trelogan
Georgian house decorated with 18th century paintings/furniture. Lake District landscape paintings in new gallery re-creating Picturesque Tour. 20th century British painting. Extensive programme of temporary exhibitions; guides and information sheets, worksheets

Beatrix Potter Gallery, Main St, Hawkshead, Ambleside LA22 0NS; Tel (015394) 36355; *Custodian* F. Clark
Many Beatrix Potter original water-colours on display
National Trust

The Border Regiment and King's Own Royal Border Regiment Museum, The Castle, Carlisle, Cumbria CA3 8UR; Tel (01228) 32774; Fax (01228) 21275; *Curator*
Worksheets, guides, histories of the regiments

Brantwood, Coniston LA21 8AD; Tel (015394) 41396; *Manager* Bruce Hanson
Displays of Ruskin watercolours. Other art and craft exhibitions. Beautifully situated house. Nature walks, boat trips, bookshop and Egon Ronay-recommended tea rooms

Brockhole National Park Visitor Centre, Brockhole, Windermere LA23 1LJ; Tel (015394) 46601
Audio visual presentations, outdoor trails and resource material all relevant to Georgraphy National Curriculum. 30 acres. Open Apr-Oct. Free admission

Brough Castle, Nr Appleby
English Heritage

Brougham Castle, Nr Penrith; Tel 0191-261 1585
English Heritage

Carlisle Castle, Carlisle CA3 8UR; Tel (01228) 591922; *Education Officer* R. Jellicoe English Heritage, Bessle Suntees Hse, 41–44 Sandhill, Newcastle Upon Tyne NE1 3JF; Tel 0191-261 1585
English Heritage

Dalemain Mansion House, Penrith CA11 0HB; Tel (017684) 86450; S. Blaylock
Mediaeval, Tudor and early Georgian House. Fine portraits and furniture. Pele Tower. Museum and beautiful gardens. Open Easter to mid Oct–Sunday to Thurs

The Dock Museum, Barrow Museum Service, North Rd, Barrow in Furness LA14 2PW; Tel (01229) 870871; *Collections Manager* F. Robertson
Open from April 1994; Major social and industrial history exhibition
Barrow in Furness Borough Council

Furness Abbey, Nr Barrow-in-Furness; Tel (01229) 823420
English Heritage

Helena Thompson Museum, Park End Rd, Workington, Cumbria CA14 4DE; Tel (01900) 62598; *Curator* Janet Baker, BA
School parties by appointment, worksheets available
Allerdale Borough Council

Hill Top, Nr Sawrey, Hawkshead LA22 0LF; Tel (015394) 36269
Beatrix Potter wrote many of her books here
National Trust

****Holker Hall and Gardens,*** Cark-in-Cartmel, Grange-over-Sands, Cumbria LA11 7PL; Tel (015395) 58328; *Administrator* Carolyn Johnson
Environmental study days, guided tours, Exhibitions and Listening, Looking and Discovering nature. Plus much, much more. Covering various aspects of the National Curriculum. New!! Learning about Harris Hawks

Hutton-in-the-Forest, Skelton, Penrith CA11 9TH; Tel (017684) 84449; *Administrator* Edward Thompson
The historic home of Lord Inglewood. Open to the public–especially grounds for children. Woodland walk (Countryside Award), dove cote, small lecture room. Grounds open 11–5pm everyday except Saturdays. House open 1–4pm all Bank Holiday Sunday and Mondays, also Thurs, Fri and Sundays from 30 April–1 Oct, also August Wednesdays. Private groups any day by prior arrangement

Kendal Museum (Natural Histrory and Archaeology), also for Abbot Hall Art Gallery and The Museum of Lakeland Life and Industry Station Rd, Kendal LA9 6BT; Tel (01539) 721374; *Educational Out Reach Officer* Cherrie Trelogan, BA(Hons), AMA; *Director* Edward King, BSc(Hons); *Curator Natural History* Carol S. Davies (P/T), AMA, BSc(Hons), PGCE; *Curator* Lynn Fade (P/T), BA, AMA, MA
Newly displayed to reflect the geology, wildlife and human history of the Lake District with new World Wildlife exhibition
Education service for schools and other organisations
Lake District Art Gallery and Museum Trust, Abbot Hall, Kendal, Cumbria

Keswick Museum and Art Gallery, Fitz Pk, Station Rd, Keswick, Cumbria CA12 4NF; Tel (017687) 73263; *Curator* H.A. Davison, BA(Hons), MA

Lake District National Park Education Service, Blencathra Centre, Threlkeld, Keswick CA12 4SG; Tel (017687) 79601
Operates Blencathra Field Centre for Environmental Courses

Lanercost Priory Church and Exhibition, C/o The Vicarage, Lanercost, Brampton, Cumbria; Tel (016977) 2478
Church of England

Levens Hall, Kendal, Cumbria LA8 0PD; Tel (015395) 60321; P. Milner

Lowther Leisure Park, Hackthorpe, Nr Penrith; Tel (01931) 712523
Over 40 attractions set in 150 acres of beautiful parkland

Manjushri Mahayana Buddhist Centre, Conishead Priory, Ulverston, Cumbria LA12 9QQ; Tel (01229) 584029; *Administrative Director* Roy Tyson
A residential centre for the study and practice of Mahayana Buddhism in the New Kadampa tradition
Courses and retreats are held year-round for visitors

Mirehouse, Keswick CA12 4QE; Tel (017687) 72287; *Contact* Clare Spedding
Family house dating from 1666 connected with three Poets Laureate. Wordsworth Southey Tennyson. Children welcomed; quizzes, secrets, things to do. French, German, Spanish spoken by arrangement. Woodland adventure playgrounds. Free preparatory visits by teachers welcomed. School visits can be tailored to special requirements

Muncaster Castle, Gardens and Owl Centre, Ravenglass, Cumbria CA18 1RQ; Tel (01229) 717614/203; Fax (01229) 717010; *Contact* Peter Frost-Pennington

The Museum of Lakeland Life and Industry, Abbot Hall, Kendal LA9 5AL; Tel (01539) 722464; Fax (01539) 722494; *Director* Edward T. King, BSc(Hons); *Education Officer* C. Trelogan

Social and economic history of Lakeland brought to life and interpreted in reconstructed workshops, shops and farmhouse rooms. Craft shop. Arts and crafts movement in Cumbria display. Arthur Ransome and John Cunliffe rooms
Information sheets and worksheets available

National Trust North-West Regional Office, The Hollens, Grasmere, Ambleside LA22 9QZ; Tel (015394) 35599; Fax (015394) 35353

Penrith Museum, Robinson's School, Middlegate, Penrith CA11 7PT; Tel (01768) 64671 Ext 2228; *Curator* Judith Clarke, AMA; *Curator* Dr Sydney T. Chapman, FSA(Scot)
Local Museum for Penrith and the Eden district, with displays illustrating 4,000 years of Man's history in the Eden Valley

Ruskin Museum, Yewdale Rd, Coniston LA21 8DU; Tel (015394) 41164; *Honorary Curator* J. Dawson
Presents the life and work of John Ruskin and his circle; Ruskin lace; local history, scenery and events

Rydal Mount, Ambleside LA22 9LU; Tel (015394) 33002; *Curator* Peter and Marian Elkington

Sizergh Castle, Kendal LA8 8EA; Tel (015395) 60070; *Administrator* B. Doling
Children's discovery sheet
National Trust

South Tynedale Railway Preservation Society, The Railway Station, Alston, Cumbria CA9 3JB; Tel (01434) 381696; *Chairman* E. Dyke
Narrow-gauge railway. Railway locomotives and equipment restored and operating. Tourist Information Centre

Steam Yacht Gondola, Pier Cottage, Coniston LA21 8AJ; Tel (015394) 41288; *Pursar* Lee Bowen
National Trust

Stott Park Bobbin Mill Working Museum, Newby Bridge, Nr Ulverston LA12 8AX; Tel (0153 95) 31087; *Mill Manager* M.J. Nield
Shows an old lake district industry–making bobbins–and also the uses of Lakeland timber. Working static steam engine–Water turbine. Free admission normally available to organised groups of students
English Heritage–Heritage Buildings and Monuments Commission

Townend, Troutbeck, Windermere LA23 1LB; *Custodian* M. Gregg
17th century farmhouse. Discovery sheet. Talk. No coaches
National Trust

Tytup Hall, Dalton-in-Furness LA15 8JR; Tel (01229) 62929; Dr J.R. Edge
By appointment only. Entrance 50p

Whitehaven Heritage Centre, c/o Copeland Borough Council, P.O. Box 19, Catherine St, Whitehaven RA28 7NY; Tel (01946) 693111; *Heritage Centre Manager* Barbara A. Barnes
Opening summer 1995
Three floors of local maritime and industrial history plus a Met Office Weather Gallery
Contact for complete list of Education Resource material
Programme of events and temporary exhibitions featured
Copeland Borough Council

Windermere Steamboat Museum, Rayrigg Rd, Windermere, Cumbria; Tel (015394) 45565
Houses the finest collection of Steamboats in the world, facilities include illustrated talks, educational packs. Model boat pond, magnificent lakeside picnic area, steamboat rides

Wordsworth House, Main St, Cockermouth CA13 9RX; Tel (01900) 824805; *Custodian* Y. Osborne
Displays, audio visuals, discovery sheet
National Trust

Derbyshire

Arkwright's Cromford Mill, The Arkwright Society Ltd, Cromford Mill, Mill La, Cromford DE4 3RQ; Tel (01629) 824297; *Manager* Darrell Clark
Archaeological and historical interpretation of the world's first successful water-powered cotton spinning mill for educational purposes

Bolsover Castle, Castle St, Bolsover S44 6PR; Tel (01246) 823349; *Head Custodian* Sarah Chapman
Historical castle, open 1st April–31st Sept open 10am–6pm 7 days a week; 31st Sept–31st March open 10am–4pm 5 days a week closed on Monday and Tuesday; Admission adults £2.10 concession £1.55 children £1.05

Buxton Micrarium, The Crescent, Buxton SK17 6BQ; Tel (01298) 78662; *Education Officer* Janet Carter
The first 'Planetarium of the microscope'. Push button microscopes projecting onto TV-size screens. Hundreds of specimens to examine

Buxton Museum and Art Gallery, Terrace Rd, Buxton SK17 6DU; Tel (01298) 24658; *Curator* D. Harding; *Assistant Curator* John Leach
Derbyshire County Council

Calke Abbey and Park, Ticknall, Derby DE73 1LE; Tel (01332) 863822; *The Property Manager* K. Usher
The National Trust

Chatsworth, Bakewell DE45 1PP; Tel (01246) 582204; *Comptroller* Eric Oliver
Historic house and garden. Farmyard and adventure playground. Restaurant and shops

Chesterfield Museum and Art Gallery Stephenson's Memorial Hall, St Mary's Gate, Chesterfield, Derbys SH1 7TY; Tel (01246) 559727; Fax (01246) 206667; *Museum Curator* Anne-Marie Knowles
Chesterfield Borough Council

Derby Museums and Art Gallery, The Strand, Derby DE1 1BS; Tel (01332) 255580; *Museums Education Officer* S. Christian
Intra-mural teaching and activities. Holiday sessions for children

Derbyshire Schools Resources Centre, Kedleston Rd, Derby DE3 1GT; Tel (01332) 371921; *Manager* Malcolm F. Plumb
Audio visual equipment and software, school library services, museum exhibits, micro-computer maintenance

The Donington Collection of Single Seater Racing Cars, Donington Pk, Castle Donington, Derby DE74 2RP; Tel (01332) 812919; *Party Bookings* Yvonne Smalley
Donington Park Racing Ltd

Elvaston Castle Estate Museum, Elvaston Castle Country Park, Borrowash Rd, Elvaston, Derby DE72 3EP; Tel (01332) 573799; Fax (01332) 758751; *Booking Clerk* Jo Pocock
Recreation of workshops and domestic life around 1910. Guided tours available

Haddon Hall, Bakewell DE4 1LA; Tel (01629) 812855; *Comptroller* Nicholas Day
Perfectly preserved medieval manor house; a fascinating insight into life in the medival times

Hardwick Hall, Doe Lea, Chesterfield S44 5QJ; Tel (01246) 850430; *Administrator* I. St. C. Hughes
Elizabethan architecture, furniture, tapestries and needlework
National Traust

The High Peak Garden Centre, Bamford; Tel (01433) 651484; *Information Officer*
Large garden centre and grounds with gift shop, tropical fish, cafe and camping/outdoor equipment centre. Sheds and summerhouses

Ilam Park, Ilam, Ashbourne; Tel (0133529) 503; Fax (0133529) 503; *Education Co-ordinator* Jim Barber
Leaflets. Day visit room, walks/talks, resource equipment
National Trust

Matlock Bath Aquarium and Hologram Gallery, North Parade, Matlock Bath, Matlock DE4 3NS; Tel (01629) 583624; *Information Officer* Brian Newton

Melbourne Hall, Estate Office, Melbourne DE73 1EN; Tel (01332) 862502; *Curator* G.A. Weston
Home of Lord Ralph Kerr. Collection of pictures, antique furniture and works of art. One of the most famous formal gardens containing restored wrought iron pergola by Robert Bakewell

The Midland Railway Centre, Butterley Station, Ripley DE5 3TL; Tel (01773) 747674/570140; *General Manager* J. Hett
Large railway museum and operating railway. Fifty-seven acre museum site and 35 acre country park. New undercover museum building now open
The Midland Railway Trust Ltd

National Tramway Museum, Crich, Matlock DE4 5DP; Tel (01773) 852565; *Manager* David Lardge
This 'Action Stop!' offers mile-long scenic journey through period street to open countryside. Biggest national collection of vintage trams plus exhibition hall, video-theatre, playground, shops, café, picnic areas

Old House Museum, Cunningham Pl, Church La, Bakewell DE45 1DD; *Bookings* Dr J.T. Brighton Heald Bank, The Yeld, Bakewell DE45 1FH; Tel (01629) 813165
Folk museum in 16th century house. Open Apr 1 (Good Friday if earlier) to 31 Oct 31
Bakewell and District Historical Society

Peak District National Park Environmental Education Service, *Education Officer* Peak National Park Centre, Losehill Hall, Castleton S30 2WB; Tel (01433) 620373
Advice and information, publications, reference rooms, talks, farm visits, guided field visits and exciting environmental activity days to meet your needs

Peak National Park Centre, Losehill Hall, Castleton S30 2WB; Tel (01433) 620373; Fax (01433) 620346; *Director* Peter Townsend
Residential enviromental centre designed providing training and interpretation for business, local authorities and all those interested and involved in the countryside

Peveril Castle, Castleton; Tel (01604) 730320
English Heritage

Poole's Cavern, Buxton Country Park, Green La, Buxton SK17 9DH; Tel (01298) 26978; *Warden* D.G. Allsop
Showcave suitable for all ages, beautiful formations and archaeological dig, visitor centre with exhibition and video show. Buxton Country Park is 100 acres of woodland with nature trail and viewing tower Solomons Temple, at 1440 feet ASL
Open daily Easter to November 1, 10am – 5pm. Open all year for booked groups

Riber Castle Wildlife Park, Matlock, Derbys DE4 5JU; Tel (01629) 582073; *The Curator*
Home of rare breeds and endangered species. Open all year from 10am. Liaison with teachers. Party rates

Royal Crown Derby Museum, 194 Osmaston Rd, Derby; Tel (01332) 712800; *Curator* John Twitchett
Shows range of Derby china from 1750 to the present day

Sudbury Hall and National Trust Museum of Childhood, Sudbury, Derbys DE6 5HT; Tel (01283) 518022; *Administrator* Robert Parker; *Education Officer* Laura Hetherington
National Trust

Devon

Allhallows Museum, High St, Honiton EX14 8PE; Tel (01404) 44966; *Honorary Curator* Robin Stanes
Museum of local history with special emphasis on Honiton lace

Aqualand, Beacon Quay, Torquay Harbourside; Tel (01803) 294439; *Information Officer* D. Burrell
Largest aquarium in the West Country

Arlington Court, Barnstaple; Tel (01271) 850296; *The Administrator*
Victorian house, with model ships, shells, etc. Large collection of carriages at stables. Carriage rides. Extensive garden and parkland for walks. Shetland ponies, Jacob sheep
National Trust

****Bickleigh Castle,*** Bickleigh, Nr Tiverton; Tel (01884) 855363; O.N. Boxall
900 years of history and architecture. Guided tours, information and 'spotter' sheets. Civil War arms and armour. Mary Rose Exhibition, Model Ships, Museum, Spy and Escape gadgets. Picturesque moated garden Shop. Refreshments and picnic area. Heritage Education award winner

Bowden House, Totnes TQ9 7PW; Tel (01803) 863664; *House Administrator* B. Petersen
Photographic Museum and Bowden House. Costumed guides take children back in time to Tudor Bowdeen and Queen Anne Periods. Good facilities. Cinema for cartoons, seats 76

The British Photographic Museum, Bowden Hse, Totnes TQ9 2PW; Tel (01803) 863664; *Schools Admin. Officer* Belinda Petersen
The last years of British Equipment. Ephemera. Comprehensive collections of still, moving, motion picture equipment from 1880 to 1960. Lecture theatre. Film shows throughout the day from 12 am. Childrens adventure playground. Licenced cafe. Disabled facilities

Brixham Aquarium, 12 The Quay, Brixham; Tel (01803) 882204; *Information Officer* D.W. Pope

Buckland Abbey, Yelverton PL20 6EY; Tel (01822) 853607; *Contact* The Administrator, Buckland Abbey
History of this 700 year old house with displays on Cistercians and Sir Francis Drake, its former occupant. Open 10.30am to 5.30pm April–October, daily (ex. Thurs); 2–5 pm Nov–March 1995 Sat/Sun, plus Wed for pre-arranged parties only. School base room. Secondary school history pack
National Trust

Burton Art Gallery and Museum, Kingsley Rd, Bideford, Devon; Tel (0123 72) 476711 Ext 315; *Museums Officer* Emma Bond; *Curator* John Butler
Torridge District Council

Cadhay, Ottery St Mary EX11 1QT; Tel (01404) 812432; Lady William-Powlett

Castle Drogo, Drewsteignton EX6 6PB; Tel (01647) 433306; *The Administrator*
National Trust

City Museum and Art Gallery, Drake Circus, Plymouth PL4 8AJ; Tel (01752) 264878
School parties by appointment; *Arts Develeopment Officer* Ext 4382. *Education Officer* Ext 4385. For admission by advance booking to The Elizabethan House Museum, 32 New St Plymouth; The Merchants House Museum, 33 St Andrew's St, Plymouth Tel Ext 4878
Plymouth City Council

Coldharbour Mill, The Working Wool Museum, Uffculme, Cullompton EX15 3EE; Tel (01884) 840960
Late 18th century woollen mill where visitors can see turn of the century spinning machinery, still involved in knitting yarn production. Also Carding Engine, Spinning Mule and Weaving Loom, illustrating the woollen processes. Essential visit for any study on Textiles, the Industrial Revolution, Energy and 'How we used to live'. Special events, school Steam Days in 1995. Special rates for school parties. Open throughout the year–please book. Teachers' pack available, cost £5.50. Also 'New World Tapestry' exhibition for groups studying voyages, explorers, the Tudors and Stewarts

Compton Castle, Marldon, Nr Paignton; Tel (01803) 872112; G.E. Gilbert
Parties by arrangment. Open Mon, Wed, Thurs only Apr 1 to end of Oct
National Trust

Connections Discovery Centre, Rougemont Hse, Castle St, Exeter; Tel (01392) 265360/265858; Fax (01392) 421252; *Assistant Director (Museums and Arts)* Katharine Chant; *Museum Services Manager* Julia Simpson; *Press and Events Officer* Ruth Randall; *Education Officer* Frank Gent
A Hands-on interpretation centre for schools and groups. National Curriculum support and resources in all subject areas. Special displays, interpretive guides, teachers resource packs, handling collections, interactive displays, computer games. Classroom, cloakroom and picnic room. Special training sessions available for teachers
Exeter Museums Service

Cookworthy Museum, The Old Grammar School, 108 Fore St, Kingsbridge; Tel (01548) 853235; *Curator* N. Jarvis, MA

School parties welcome, reduced rates charged; during winter–by appointment only; much used by field study groups as it portrays life in south Devon during the last 100 years
Cookworthy Museum Society

Dartmoor Wildlife Park amd West Falconry Centre, Sparkwell, Nr Plymouth; Tel (0175537) 209; *Information Officer* Rosemarie M.B. Hext
Over 125 species of animals, birds and reptiles–tigers, lions, wolves, seals, deer, birds of prey, waterfowl and many more. All weather facilities. Guided tours, worksheets. In school lectures. Full educational facilities. Pony rides. Seating 250. Open daily 10am–dusk

Dartmouth Castle, Dartmouth TQ6 0JN; Tel (01803) 833588
English Heritage

Dartmouth Museum 6 The Butterwalk, Dartmouth TQ6 9PZ; Tel (01803) 832923; *Hon Curator* Ralph Cawthorne

Devon Learning Resources Service, 21 Old Mill Rd, Chelston, Torquay TQ2 6AU; Tel (01803) 605531; Fax (01803) 607127; *Head of Service* S.W. Allardyce
Learning Resource service to schools and education establishments throughout Devon. Services include: Museum Loan Collection, Art Loan Collection, Video and Film Library, Museum Education Officers, Professional Advice and Training as well as Design and Production of Education Material, Exhibition Production, Photography, Video film making and editing, Publishing and Off Air Recording of Educational Material

Devon Zoology Centre, Paignton Zoological and Botanical Gardens, Penwill Way, Paignton TQ4 5JS; Tel (01803) 559674; *Education Officer* R.J. Lovell
Extensive Zoo Education Service including day and residential visits, also roadshow into schools

Education and Guardian Advisory Services, 11 Seaton Ave, Mutley, Plymouth PL4 6QJ; *Information Officer* B.A.E. Stoyel; Tel (01752) 261229; Fax (01752) 261229

Exeter Guided Tours, Civic Centre, Exeter EX1 1JJ; Tel (01392) 265212
Free guided tours operate throughout the year except Christmas Day and Boxing Day. A wide variety of City Centre and Riverside tours. Tours of the port of Topsham in summer. Booking service also operates for large groups. Free brochures sent on request

Exeter Maritime Museum, The Haven, Exeter EX2 8DT; Tel (01392) 58075; *Education Officer* The Secretary
Collection of oar and sail boats which can be boarded at will. Questionnaire for school parties and activity sheets available in the shop or by post. New adventure playship based on Henry VIII Flagship, 'The Great Harry'. Ships and seafarers' themes

Exeter Museums, Queen St, Exeter EX4 3RX; Tel (01392) 265858; Fax (01392) 421252; *Education Officer* Frank Gent; *Press and Events Officer* Julia Simpson
Varied collection including local and natural history. Assistance offered for visits to the Royal Albert Memorial Museum, St Nicholas Priory, Connections Discovery Centre, the Underground Passages and walks around the city; wide variety of handling collections available; holiday activities organised. Temporary exhibition programme

Fairlynch Arts Centre and Museum, 27 Fore St, Budleigh, Salterton EX9 6NP; Tel (01395) 442666; *Chairman of Trustees* P.M. Hull; *Publicity Officer* G.B. Swinyard
Mainly local material–nature, history, archaeology, geology. Period costume. Lace and lace making. reference library. Special exhibitions summer and Christmas

Farway Countryside Park and Nature Reserve, Nr Colyton EX13 6JL; Tel (0140 487) 224/367; *Information Officer* J.M. Forbes-Wood
New Butterfly House with extensive walks and nature trails set in 100 acres of natural countryside and woodlands. Sponsor a tree scheme. Pitch and Put. Craft and gift shop, licenced resturant, children's playground. Open 10 am to 5.30 pm daily, Easter–Oct. Licenced cafe

Fursdon House, Cadbury, Exeter EX5 5JS; Tel (01392) 860860; *Owner* David Fursdon
Historic house open to the public; owned by Fursdon family for 700 years. Family museum, walks, views, tea room

Hartland Abbey, Hartland, Bideford EX39 6DT; Tel (01237) 441264; *Administrator* Mary Heard
Historic House open to the public

Ilfracombe Museum, Runnymead Gdns, Wilder Rd, Ilfracombe EC34 8AF; Tel (01271) 863541; *Education Officer* J. Slocombe
Brass-rubbing Centre
The Trustees of Ilfracombe Museum

Ilfracombe Tropical Wildlife Gardens, Bicclescombe Pk, Ilfracombe; Tel (01271) 62541; *Information Officer* F.G. Elliot Brannochs Pk, Ilfracombe; Tel (01392) 62541

Killerton, Broadclyst, Nr Exeter; Tel (01392) 881345; *The Administrator*
National Trust

Kirkham House, Kirkham St, off Littlegate Rd, Paignton TQ3 3AX; Tel (01803) 522775; Fax (01803) 521617
English Heritage

Knightshayes Court, Bolham, Tiverton EX16 7RQ; Tel (01884) 254665; *The Property Manager*
National Trust

Lydford Gorge, Lydford, Nr Okehampton EX20 4BH; Tel (01822) 820 320/441; Fax (01822) 820 320/441; *Administrator* B. Hague
3 mile walk. Stout footwear, waterproofs and adequate supervision required. walks–leaflet, map. 90ft Waterfall and swirling Devils Cauldron. Party leaders to visit prior to party walk
National Trust

Morwellham Quay Museum, Morwellham Quay, Tavistock PL19 8JL; Tel (01822) 832766; *Director* G. Emerson
Historic copper port and mine; information brochure for schools on request
Morwellham and Tamar Valley Trust

National Trust Regional Office, Devon, Killerton Hse, Broadclyst, Exeter EX5 3LE; Tel (01392) 881691
Contact the Information Office for details of teachers' packs and other facilities for schools at Trust houses, coast and countryside in Devon

North Devon Maritime Museum, Odun Hse, Odun Rd, Appledore EX39 1PT; Tel (01237) 474852; *Contact* P.M. Wiggett
Video interpretation centre for school parties illustrating Devon's maritime history, Victorian schoolroom with costumes, slates, copybooks, etc. Video 'Early Schools'. Send for Teacher's Pack
The North Devon Museum Trust

Okehampton Castle, Castle Rd, Okehampton; Tel (01837) 52844
English Heritage
1 April – 31 October only. 1 November – 31 March to Area Manager

Otterton Mill Centre and Working Museum, Nr Budleigh, Salterton EX9 7HG; Tel (01395) 68521; *Contact* Desna Greenhow
Working watermill museum. Tours gearded to projects/interests/ages of groups e.g. water, power, bread, wheat, industrial archaeology, country crafts

Overbecks Museum and Garden, Sharpitor, Salcombe TQ8 8LW; Tel (01548) 842893; *Curator* A. Scott-Davies
Preparing pack. Children's guide. 1991 Gulbenkian Award winner for best provision for young children. (Commendation.)
National Trust

Parke Rare Breeds Farm, Haytor Rd, Bovey Tracey TQ13 9JQ; Tel (01626) 833909; *Administrator* T. Ash

Plymouth Aquarium, Marine Biological Association of the U.K., The Laboratory, Citadel Hill, Plymouth PL1 2PB; Tel (01752) 222772; *Curator* G.W. Potts

Powderham Castle, Kenton, Exeter EX6 8JQ; Tel (01626) 890243; Fax (01626) 890729
14th century home of the Earls of Devon. Besieged, restored and adapted it has been lived in by the Courtenay family for over 600 years

Quay House Interpretation Centre, The Quay, Exeter EX2 4AN; Tel (01392) 265213; Fax (01392) 265260
Restored 17th century building. Static and audio-visual displays on local history. Open daily 10 am–5 pm Easter–October

Saltram House, Plympton, Plymouth PL7 3UH; Tel (01752) 336546; Fax (01752) 336474; *The Administrator*
18th century house, paintings, parkland. Open 1 April–31 Nov, 12.30–5.30 pm daily except Friday and Saturday
National Trust

Sand, Sidbury, Sidmouth EX10 0QN; Tel (01395) 597230; *Owner* Lt Col P.V. Huyshe
Historic house–bought Huyshe family 1560, rebuilt 1594. Family documents, heraldry, panelling, unspoilt situation

Shaldon Wildlife Trust, Ness Dr, Shaldon, Teignmouth TQ14 0HP; Tel (01626) 872234; *Co-Director* M. Moore; *Co-Director* S. Muir

South Molton Museum, Town Hall, South Molton; Tel (01769) 572951; *Curator*
South Molton Town Council for North Devon District Council

Tiverton Castle, Tiverton, Devon EX16 6RP; Tel (01884) 253200; A.K. Gordon
Fine collection of Civil Wars arms and armour: New World tapestry; Campbell clock collection. Light meals by prior arrangement. Coach parties by appointment only
Open Easter to last Sunday in Sept. Sundays to Thursdays 2.30–5.30. Open other times by appointment to parties of more than 12

Tiverton Museum, St Andrew St, Tiverton EX16 6PH; Tel (01884) 256295; *Curator* Michael Nix
Special co-operation is accorded to school parties. Talks or guided tours by prior arrangement. Admission free to Staff and children, donations requested
Tiverton and Mid Devon Museum Trust

Torquay Museum, 529 Babbacombe Rd, Torquay TQ1 1HG; Tel (01803) 293975; *Curator* Dr Michael Bishop
Natural history, geology, Victorian and Pictorial Records galleries. Important finds from Kents Cavern including the famous 31,000 year old human jaw bone. Archaeology of South Devon. Special facilities available for schools including schoolroom, education packs and handling collection. National Curriculum catered for
Torquay Natural History Society

Torre Abbey, The King's Dr, Torquay TQ2 5JX; Tel (01803) 293593; *Senior Curator* Leslie Retallick; *Principal Curator* Michael Rhodes
12th century monastery, became private house in the 18th century. Houses civic art gallery and museum. Furnished period rooms, educational visits

Totnes Castle, Castle St, Totnes TQ9 5NU; Tel (01803) 864406; *Chairman* Jocelyn Stevens; *Contact Custodian* ; Tel (01803) 864406
Norman Motte and Bailey castle with shell keep and curtain wall built in the 11th century and reconstructed in the 14th century
English Heritage–Historic Buildings and Monuments Commission for England

Totnes Costume Museum, Bogan Hse, 43 High St, Totnes TQ9 5NP; *Hon Curator* P.A. Morel
31 May-30 Sept daily except Saturday 1-31 May and 1-31 October by appointment only. Opening times: Weekdays 11-5 Sundays 2-5. Guided visits by appointment only
Devonshire Collection of Period Costume Trust

Totnes Museum, 70 Fore St, Totnes TQ9 5RU; Tel (01803) 863821; *Curator* L Irwin, BA(Hons)
Museum of local and national interest housed in Tudor Merchant house. Worksheets available. Teachers may borrow (deposit £2) an educational pack on Totnes which consists of slides, maps and booklet on the history of Totnes, architect's elevations; drawings, list of publications and list of useful addresses
Totnes Museum Trust

The Vintage Toy and Train Museum, First Fl, Field's Department Store, Market Pl, Sidmouth EX10 8LU; Tel (01395) 515124 Ext 208; *Founder* R.D.N. Salisbury
Toys and Trains of yesteryear

Dorset

Athelhampton, Nr Dorchester; Tel (01305) 848363; Patrick Cooke
One of the finest examples of 15th Century domestic architecture. Enjoy the lived in famiy house with its great hall, Tudor great chamber; magnificent gardens, all encircled by the river Piddle

The Bournemouth Bears Expocentre, Old Christhchurch La, Bournemouth BH1 1NE; Tel (01202) 293544 or (01305) 269741 (Admin.); Fax (01305) 268885; *Director* Jackie Ridley; *Manager* Tim Batty
Explore the wonderful world of the teddy and meet famous teddy bear personalities. There are old bears, new bears, big bears, tiny bears, bare bears, costume bears and all kinds of bears including limited editions and special creations. Opens daily all year 9.30-5.30 (phone for winter hours)

Brewers Quay, Hope Sq, Weymouth DT4 8TR; Tel (01305) 777622; *Curator* R.M. Alcock
Brewers Quay is an exciting multi-million pound redevelopment within the former Devenish Brewery. Situated near the Harbour, Brewers Quay's major attraction is the 'Timewalk', an atmospheric and educational journey through episodes in Weymouth's long history. The 'Timewalk' includes scenes from the Black Death, the Spanish Armada, a Georgian ballroom and a smuggler's den. Brewers Quay also offers the Weymouth Museum, a museum of brewing, an exhibition gallery and a school/lecture hall as well as shops and resturants

Bridport Museum, South St, Bridport, Dorset DT6 3NR; Tel (01308) 422116; Fax (01308) 458105; *Contact* The Museums Officer
Worksheets. Local History Centre. Guided tours of Bridport by prior arrangement
West Dorset District Council

Chettle House and Gardens, Chettle Hse, Chettle, Blandford DT11 8DB; Tel (01258) 830209; *Contact* J.P.C. Bourke
Aims to give pleasure to gardeners and promote the distribution of unusual plants

Christchurch Tricycle Museum, Quay Rd, Christchurch BH23 1BY; Tel (01202) 479849; *Director* Roger Street
World's first museum devoted solely to multi-wheeled cycles. Forty machines from Victorian times onward. Costumed models

Deans Court, Wimborne BH21 1EE; Sir Michael Hanham, Bt
Historic garden organically cultivated

The Dinosaur Museum, Icen Way, Dorchester DT1 1EW; Tel (01305) 269880/269741 (Admin); Fax (01305) 268885; *Director* Jacqueline Ridley; *Manager* Tim Batty
The Museum educates and entertains people of all ages through interactive and interpretive displays on the fascinating world of dinosaurs. Open all year, daily 9.30–5.30

Dinosaur Safari, Expocentre, Old Christchurch La, Bournemouth BH1 1NE; Tel (01202) 293544/(01305) 269741; Fax (01305) 268885; *Director* Jackie Ridley; *Manager* Tim Batty
Indoor educational attraction features dinosaurs, interactive displays and fossils. Open daily, 9.30–5.30 pm (phone for winter hours)

Dorset County Museum, High West St, Dorchester DT1 1XA; Tel (01305) 262735; *Curator* R.M. de Peyer, BA, AMA; *Schools Organiser* L. Poulsen, BEd, CertEd, MA
Introductory activities for all age ranges to Dorset's geology, natural history, archaeology, social history and Thomas Hardy, relating to the National Curriculum; prior booking essential
Dorset Natural History and Archaeological Society

Dorset Wildlife Trust The Villa, Brownsea Island, Pocle BH15 1EE; Tel (01202) 709445; *The Warden* K.G. Cook
Nature reserve guided tour

East Dorset Heritage Trust (EDHT), Market Hse, Corn Market, Wimborne Minster, Wimborne BH21 1JL; Tel (01202) 888992; Fax (01202) 888992; *Director* A.C. Wilson
Provides environmental education and enhances tourism with particular reference to local history, archaeology, architecture, wild life and landscape

Edmondsham House and Gardens, Edmondsham, Wimborne BH21 5RE; Tel (01725) 517207; *Owner* J.E. Smith
Tudor/Georgian house, stables and gardens. Owner guided tours. Organic gardening tuition days. Telephone for appointments and opening times. Parties welcomed. Teas arranged

Fiddleford Manor, Nr Sturminster Newton
English Heritage

Harbour Museum, Salt Hse, West Bay, Dorset DT6 4SA; Tel (01308) 420997; Fax (01308) 458105; *Contact* The Museums Officer
Activity sheets; demonstrations by prior arrangement (rope making, net making); guided tours of Bridport Harbour by prior arrangement
West Dorset District Council

Kingston Lacy House and Estate, Wimborne BH21 4EA; Tel (01202) 883402; *Education Officer* Barbara Webber
Historic house, furniture, paintings and grounds, 250 acres. Open to the public
The National Trust

Lyme Regis Philpot Museum, Bridge St, Lyme Regis DT7 3QA; Tel (01297) 443370; *Curator* Liz-Anne Bawden; *Honorary Archivist* John Fowles
Lyme Regis Philpot Museum Trust Ltd

Lyme Regis Marine Aquarium and Cobb History, The Cobb, Lyme Regis; Tel (01297) 443678 (Home); *Owner* K.R. Gollop; *Owner* J.B. Gollop
Aquarium of Lyme Bay marine life and static educational displays of the history of the Cobb, the sea, wrecks and wreckage, fishing, working boats etc. Photodisplays of the filming of the 'French Lieutenant's Woman' and 'Persuasion'. Guided walks and talks on the Cobb by ex-Fisherman and historian Ken Gollop. Leaflet available. School group rates 55p per head. Walks and Talks by arrangement. Open May to December

Merley Bird Gardens, Merley, Wimborne, Dorset; Tel (01202) 883790; *Proprietors* A.E. and S.O. Martin
Ideal for children of all ages

The Military Museum of Devon and Dorset The Keep, Bridport Rd, Dorchester DT1 1RN; Tel (01305) 264066; *Education Officer* Maj J. Carroll
Trustess of the Devonshire and Dorset Regimental Charity

Mummies of the Pharaohs ExpoCentre, Old Christchurch La, Bournemouth BH1 1NE; Tel (01202) 293544/(01305) 269741; Fax (01305) 268885; *Director* Dr Michael Ridley; *Manager* Tim Batty
New techniques let you explore the mysteries and magic of the mummies of ancient Egypt, from the first sand dried bodies to the Royal mummies. It's an awe inspiring new exhibition. Open all year daily, 9.30-5.30 (Phone for winter hours)

The Museum of East Dorset Life – The Priest's House 23–27 High St, Wimborne Minster BH21 1HR; Tel (01202) 882533; *Assistant Curator* Sue Tapliss
School parties by arrangement. Hands-on working Victorian kitchen and 1920's ironmongery shop. Accompanying teachers' packs
Priest's House Museum Trust

The Parnham Trust, Beaminster DT8 3NA; Tel (01308) 862204; *Administrator* M. Brook
Parnham College for craftsmen in wood, two years training in design, cabinet making and business studies in preparation for self-employment. One week residential Summer Schools in July/August in cabinet making and wood-turning

Portland Castle, Portland; Tel (01272) 750700
English Heritage

Portland Museum, 217 Wakeham, Portland DT5 1HS; Tel (01305) 821804; *Contact* H. Bailey; Tel (01305) 772444
Visits (with worksheets). Set in two thatched cottages. Community museum of the island displays of Quarrying. Natural history, Shipwrecks and smuggling. Avice's cottage from Thomas Hardy's 'Well Beloved'; school groups–large and small, new gallery, temp exhibitions, garden, shop
Weymouth and Portland Borough Council

Red House Museum and Gardens, Quay Rd, Christchurch BH23 1BU; Tel (01202) 482860; *Curator* Alison J. Carter, MA, AMA
Displays and interprets the local, social and natural history of Christchurch, and exhibits art of local and national importance. Workshops run in conjunction with some exhibitions. New archaeology gallery with resource room and teachers' packs

Russell-Cotes Art Gallery and Museum, East Cliff, Bournemouth BH1 3AA; Tel (01202) 551009
A range of educational facilities

Sandford Orcas Manor House, Sandford Orcas, Sherborne DT9 4SB; Tel (01963) 220206; *Owner/Administrator* Sir Mervyn Medlycott, Bt
Tudor historic house open to public May to Sept, Sundays 2–6 pm and Mondays 10 am–6 pm. Pre-booked parties at other times

Scaplen's Court Museum, High St, Poole; Tel (01202) 683138; *Curriculum Support Teacher* G. Rogers; *Curriculum Support Teacher* Pippa Weekes
Museum of domestic life, activities, re-enactments, handling collections, story telling for primary school children, computer software
Borough of Poole

Sea Life Park, Lodmoor Country Pk, Weymouth, Dorset DT4 7SX; Tel (01305) 788255; *Education Officer* Penny Corp-Palmer
Teachers packs and worksheets available

Shafetsbury and District Local History Museum, Gold Hill, Shaftesbury SP7 4JW; Tel (01747) 852157; *Contact* Pat Gates
Shaftesbury and District Historical Society

Shaftesbury Abbey and Museum and Preservation Trust (Co Ltd), Park Wk, Shaftesbury SP7 8JR; Tel (01747) 852910
Historic abbey ruins and small on-site museum. Open Easter to October

Sherborne Castle, Sherborne; Tel (01935) 813182; Fax (01935) 816727; *Administrator* Sherborne Castle Estates, Cheap St, Sherborne DT9 3PY
Home of Sir Walter Raleigh. Work sheet available

Sherborne Museum, Abbey Gate Hse, Sherborne DT9 3BP; Tel (01935) 812252; *Honorary Curator*
Sherborne Museum Association

Smedmore, Kimmeridge, Wareham BH20 5PG; Tel (01929) 480 719; Dr Philip Mansel

The Tank Museum, Bovington, Dorset BH20 6JG; Tel (01929) 463953; *Education Officer* Graham Holmes
Replies to queries; worksheets for younger visitors; Cinema/seminar room and video thetre; library access for senior students, by prior arrangement with curatorial staff

The Tutankhamun Exhibition, High West St, Dorchester DT1 1UW; Tel (01305) 269571/269741 (Admin); Fax (01305) 268885; *Director* Michael Ridley; *Manager* Tim Batty
The Exhibition superbly captures and recreates the magnificence and mystery of the world's greatest discovery of ancient treasure–the tomb of Tutankhamun. Open all year, daily 9.30–5.30

Waterfront, 4 High St, Poole BH15 1BW; Tel (01202) 683138/661001; *Advisory Teacher* G. Rogers; *Advisory Teacher* Pippa Hall

Weymouth Museum (see Brewers Quay)

Wolfeton House, Dorchester; Tel (01305) 263500; Capt N.T.L. Thimbleby

Durham

Barnard Castle; Castle Hse, Durham DL12 9AT; Tel (01833) 38212
English Heritage

Beamish, The North of England Open Air Museum, Beamish, Co Durham DH9 0RG; Tel (01207) 231811; Fax (01207) 290933
An open air museum of Northern life around the turn of the century with a wealth of educational opportunities. Visit the Town, the Colliery Village, the Home Farm and the Railway Station. Further information from the Education Dept. Open all year (closed Mondays and Fridays in winter)
Consortium of County and District Councils

The Bowes Museum, Barnard Castle, Co Durham DL12 8NP; Tel (01833) 690606; Fax (01833) 37163; *Curator* Elizabeth Conran, MA, FMA; *Administration Officer* M. Keegan; *Antiquities Officer* J. Picken, BA, AMA; Tel (01833) 690107
Wide-ranging collection of European fine and decorative art. Local antiquities. Excellent teaching potential for several courses

Darlington Museum, Tubwell Row, Darlington DL1 1PD; Tel (01325) 463795; *Curator* A. Suddes
Guided tours and talks to schools by appointment
Borough of Darlington

DLI Museum and Arts Centre, Aykley Heads, Durham DH1 5TU; Tel 0191-384 2214; Fax 0191-386 1770; *Manager* Terry Deary
School visits by appointment, access for disabled groups. Coffee bar, parking
Durham County Council Arts, Libraries and Museums Department

Darlington Railway Centre and Museum, North Rd Station, Darlington DL3 6ST; Tel (01325) 460532; *Curator* S.G. Dyke; *Documentation Officer* A.M. Wilson
Darlington Borough Council

Durham Castle, Durham DH1 3RW; Tel 0191-374 3850; Fax 0191-374 7470; *The Bursar*

Durham Cathedral Treasury, The College, Durham DH1 3EH; Tel 0191-386 2489; *Curator* The Revd Canon R.L. Coppin; *Deputy Chapter Librarian* Roger C. Norris
Display of Treasures associated with Durham Cathedral and St Cuthbert. Separate application for access to the exhibition of monastic life 'Craftsmen for Christ'

Durham Light Infantry Museum and Art Gallery, Aykley Heads, Durham DH1 5TU; Tel 0191-384 2214; Fax 0191-386 1770; *Manager* Terry Deary
History of local regiment from 1758 to 1968, plus monthly art/programme exhibition talks, films, concerts, throught the year. Disabled facilities. Parking, coffee bar, souvenirs

Durham University Oriental Museum, University of Durham, Elvet Hill, Durahm DH1 3TH; Tel 0191-374 2911; *Keeper* John Ruffle, MA, FSA
Special rates for school parties. Collections from the Orient. Ancient Egypt and the history of writing; Also displays on Hinduism and Buddhism
University of Durham

Finchale Priory, Brasside, Newton Hall, Co Durham DH1 5SH; Tel (0385) 63828
English Heritage

Museum Education Service, Northgate Bldg, Gladstone St, Darlington DL3 6JY; Tel (01325) 282721; *Museum Education Officer* M.G.C. Wyatt Wheeler
Loan service available within administrative county

Rokeby Park, Nr Barnard Castle, Co Durham DL12 9RZ; Tel (01833) 637334; *Curator* P.I. Yeats
A unique palladian style 18th century country house

East Sussex

Bateman's (Home of Rudyard Kipling), Burwash, Etchingham TN19 7DS; Tel (01435) 882302; *The Administrator* D. Fox
National Trust

Battle and District Historical Society Museum Trust, Langton Hse, Battle TN33 0AQ; *Curator* J. Ede-Borrett; *Chairman* D. Akers; *Honorary Secretary* J.W. Cresswell

Battle Abbey, Battle; Tel (01424) 773792
English Heritage

Bayham Abbey, Nr Lamberhurst; Tel (01892) 890381/(01732) 778000
English Heritage

Bentley Wildfowl and Motor Museum, Halland, Lewes; Tel (01825) 840573; Fax (01825) 840573; *Manager* Barry Sutherland
Study sheets, fieldwork facilities. Slide packs and talks

Bexhill Museum of Costume and Social History, Manor Gdns, Upper Sea Rd, Old Town, Bexhill TN40 1RL; Tel (01424) 210045; *Chairman* Cllr Pauline Bullock; *Education Officer* Mrs M. Rymer
Guided tours, costumes from 1740, doll and toys, sewing machines, household, effects; parties by appointment
Charity Assoc Reg No 803557

Bexhill Museum, Egerton Rd, Bexhill-on-Sea; Tel (01424) 21176; *Curator* Brenda Mason
Class visits welcome from schools and, subject to prior arrangement, additional material from reserve collections provided (local collections, also geology)

The Bluebell Railway (Vintage steam train rides), Sheffield Pk St, Nr Uckfield TN22 3QL; Tel Talking timetable (01825) 722370. Party bookings (01825) 723777; Fax (01825) 724139

Bodiam Castle, Robertsbridge TN32 5UA; Tel (01580) 830436; Fax (01580) 830436; *Administrator* G.E. Bailey
Video shows and children's activity book of the Castle/Education base
National Trust

Booth Museum of Natural History, 194 Dyke Rd, Brighton BN1 5AA; Tel (01273) 552586/713299; *Keeper of the Booth Museum* John A. Cooper
Birds, butterflies, fossils, including dinosaur bones, skeletons, minerals, environment. Educational facilities–classroom and school loan, school parties, talks to schools. Disabled access; C.C.E; temporary exhibitions; outside lectures. Admission free

Butterfly Garden Centre, Royal Parade, Eastbourne BN22 7AQ; Tel (01323) 645522; *Director* Barbara Goodall
Teachers' information packs, special rates for school parties

Charleston Farmhouse, Firle, Nr Lewes BN8 6LL; Tel (01323) 811626; *Administrator* Christina Jeffrey; *Contact* Christina Jeffrey
Historic house open to the public. House and garden were decorated by Bloomsbury painters Vanessa Bell and Duncan Grant
The Charleston Trust

Ditchling Museum, Church La, Ditchling BN6 8TB; Tel (01273) 844744; *Curator* H. Bourne
Preservation of the local past. Thematic exhibitions, research facilities. Assistance with school projects by arrangement. Children's days. The new gallery shows work by Eric Gill and other famous local artists

Drusillas Zoo Park, Alfriston BN26 5QS; Tel (01323) 870656; *Education Officer* David Holland
Educational materials for primary children in line with National Curriculum requirements. Programmes range from variety of animals found in the zoo and how they live to the running of the park

East Sussex Art and Museum Service, Corsica Hall, Cricketfield Rd, Seaford, Sussex BN25 1BT; Tel (01323) 899043; *Head of Art and Museum Service* Grant Jones (County Art Adviser)
Loan and exhibition service to all the county council's schools and education centres

Firle Place, Lewes BN8 6LP; Tel (01273) 858335; *Showing Secretary* Quentin Gage
Georgian house with Tudor core containing connoisseurs' collection of European and British old master paintings, documents relating to the American War of Independence, English and French furniture and notable Sevres porcelain

Fisherman's Museum, Rock-A-Nore Rd, Hastings; Tel (01424) 461446; *Administrator* John Burton
Displays of models and photographs of old Hastings fishing port and the last of the luggers built in Hastings (1912), fully rigged

Glynde Place, Nr Lewes; Tel (0179 159) 227/248

Great Dixter, Northiam TN31 6PH; Tel (01797) 252878; Fax (01797) 252879; *Administrator* Andrew Trump

Hove Museum and Art Gallery, 19 New Church Rd, Hove BN3 4AB; Tel (01273) 779410
Permanent collection and regular exhibitions of historic and contemporary Fine Arts and Crafts, Toys and Local History inluding Pioneer Film makers of Hove, 1896–1914. Occasional childrens events, practical workshops, etc. School visits welcome by arrangement with Curator, T. Wilcox
Hove Borough Council

Lifeboat Museum, Grand Parade, Eastbourne; Tel (01232) 730717; *Honorary Curator* Captain I.M. Shearer, MNI
Open mid March to end of December. No admission charge. Museum shows history of Eastbourne Lifeboats and various rescues etc, and a selection of Lifeboat models. Well stocked souvenir shop

Michelham Priory, Upper Dicker, Nr Hailsham BN27 3QS; Tel (01323) 844224; *Director* A. Jenkinson
Off A22 and A27. Open daily 25 March–31 Oct and Sundays only in Nov and March

Old Mint House, High St, Pevensey, Nr Eastbourne; Tel (01323) 762337; J.C. Nicholson

Pevensey Castle, Pevensey; Tel (01323) 762604
English Heritage

Preston Manor, Preston Pk, Brighton BN1 1UE; Tel (01273) 603005 Ext 3239; *Education Services Officer* c/o Brighton Art Gallery and Museum, Church St, Brighton; Tel (01273) 603005 Ext 3261/2; *Education Officer*
Tour of public rooms including servants quarters, worksheets and servants' role play

Priest House, West Hoathly, W Sussex; Tel (01342) 810479; *Custodian* A. Smith
Open weekdays 11 am to 5.30 pm. Sundays 2 pm to 5.30 pm 1st March to 31st Oct

Redoubt Fortress, Royal Parade, Eastbourne; Tel (01323) 410300; *Curator* Michael Moss
Housing the Sussex Combined Services Museum, the Royal Sussex Regiment Collection and the Museum of the Queen's Irsh Hussars

Royal Pavillion, Art Gallery and Museums Royal Pavillion, Brighton BN1 1EE; *Education Services Section* ; Tel (01273) 603005 Ext 3262; *Head of Museums, Director Royal Pavillion* Jessica Rutherford
Public lectures, talks for school; handling collections; worksheets; teachers' packs on museum collections; holiday activities, Edwardian roleplay

RSPCA Mallydams Wood, Study Centre and Wildlife Sanctuary, Peter James La, Fairlight, Hastings, E. Sussex TN35 4AH; Tel (01424) 812055; *Manager* Trevor Forward
Animal welfare courses to suit all ages groups and educational levels. Topics include: wildlife studies, farm animals and pet care. Facilities for residential and non-residential groups
RSPCA

Rye Museum, Rye Castle, Gungarden, Rye TN31 7HH; Tel (01797) 226728; *Honorary Curator* Mrs M.H. Bird
Cinque Ports, Local history, Rye and Romney Marsh, Maritime Rye.Housed in mediaeval fortress
Rye Museum Association

School Visits Co-ordinator for Eastbourne, The Redoubt Fortress Education Officer, c/o Eastbourne Borough Council, Tourism and Community Services Dept, College Rd, Eastbourne BN21 4JJ; Tel (01323) 410300

Sussex Archaeological Society, Barbican Hse, Lewes; Tel (01273) 486290; *Education Officer* Susan Potter; *Curator* Helen Poole
Educational services available by arrangement at 3 properties in Sussex. Details on request. Also Young Archaeologist of Sussex Club

Towner Art Gallery and Local Museum, Manor Gdns, High St, Old Town, Eastbourne BN20 8BB; Tel (01323) 417961; Fax (01323) 648182; *Curator* Penny J. Johnson
Exhibition from a large collection of 19th and 20th century British Art. Lively temporary exhibitions programme often with workshops. Museum traces the history of Eastbourne. Houses the South-East Arts Association collection of contemporary art, available for loan to public institutions and schools. Teachers packs available for Art and History KS 1 and 2

Wilmington Priory, Wilmington, Polegate BN26 5SW; Tel (01323) 870537; *Administrator* A.C.A. Gottlieb
Collection of Sussex farming implements arranged in picturesque farm building among the ruins of a Benedictine priory

Essex

Audley End House, Saffron Walden CB11 4JF; Tel (01799) 522842/522399
Jacobean house remodelled in 18th and 19th centuries, original furniture and pictures, Capability Brown landscape park, garden buildings by Adam
English Heritage

Basildon Zoo, London Rd, Vange, Bailson; Tel (01268) 553985; *Director* Y.A. Surcouf
Petting area, birds of prey, bat cave, otters, cafe, picnic areas. We cater for the disabled

Beecroft Art Gallery, Station Rd, Westcliff-on-Sea; Tel (01702) 347418; *Curator, Southend-on-Sea Museums* A.C. Wright, AMA
Borough Council administered art gallery. Changing temporary exhibition programme plus works from large permanent collection including topographical works. Admission free. Open Tue to Sat, 9.30–5.00

Blake Hall Gardens, Bobbingworth, Ongar CM5 0DG; Tel (01277) 362502; *Information Officer* B.A. Wilkinson; *Information Officer* G. Terry

Bourne Hall, Bourne Rd, Colchester; Tel (01206) 572422; *Administrator* Mrs Humphries
Limited number by appointments only
National Trust

Central Museum and Planetarium, Victoria Ave, Southend-on-Sea SS2 6EW; Tel (01702) 330214/355130; *Curator* A.C. Wright; *Contact* K.L. Crowe
Collection, conservation, recording, preserving and display of items of archaeological, historical, natural history and social history of South East Essex. Special exhibitions on range of subjects. Open Monday 1–5pm; Tues–Sat 10–5pm. Houses the only public planetarium in the SE outside London
Southend Museums Service (SOUMS)

Chelmsford Museums Service, Chelmsford and Essex Museum (1835) and the Essex Regiment Museum (1975), Oaklands Pk, Moulsham St, Chelmsford, Essex CM2 9AQ; Tel (01245) 353066/260614; *Keeper of Social History* M.D. Bedenham, BA, PGCE (School Loans Advisor); *Keeper of Essex Regiment Museum* Ian Hook, BA; *Keeper of Archaeology* N.P. Wickenden, MA, FSA, AMA; *Keeper of Art* A. Lutyens-Humfrey, MA, AMA; *Keeper of Natural Sciences* A.T. Walentowicz, BSc, PhD; *Keeper of Science and Industry* G. Bowles, BA, DPhil, AMA; *Head of Museum Service* N.P. Wickenden, MA, FSA, AMA
Education service linked to the National Curriculum. Teachers' resource pack. Mounted bird and mammals, archaeology and local and social history project boxes. Keepers are pleased to give talks. Science and Industry Schools Services at the Engine House, Sandford Mill, Chelmsford includes interactive exhibits
Chelmsford Borough Council Museums Service

Clacton Pier Marineland, Clacton Pier, Clacton-on-Sea; Tel (01255) 421115; *Director* F.G. McGinty
Question sheets and lectures

Coalhouse Fort Project, Coalhouse Fort, East Tilbery RM18 8PB; Tel (01375) 844203; *General Secretary* Stephen W. Jarmyn
Restoration of Victorian coastal defence fortifocation through re-arming, refitting and re-enactment of 1874 to 1946, also artillery and aircraft displays

Colchester Museums, Museum Resource Centre, 14 Ryegate Rd, Colchester, Essex CO1 1YG; Tel (01206) 712931/2; Fax (01206) 712937; *Curator and Head of Museum Services* Oliver Green, BA, AMA; *Education Officer* Liz Awty, BA, PGCE
Five museums–major prehistoric and Roman archaeology collections in Norman Castle, local history, costume and toys, clocks, natural history. Loan boxes available. Junior and Secondary activity sheets available. A range of school services available including

guided tours, object handling, archaeological investigation and drama

Colchester Zoo, Maldon Rd, Stanway, Colchester, Essex; Tel (01206) 330253; Fax (01206) 331392; *Marketing Director* Alex Burr

Colne Valley Railway, Castle Hedingham Station, Yeldham Rd, Castle Hedingham, Halstead CO9 3DZ; Tel (01787) 461174; *Managing Director* Dick Hymas
Educational leisure centre for the study of East Anglian railway history. Talks, tours, videos, comprehensive collection of working vintage railwayana and architecture. Special "Steam Days" for schools during June and October. Open all year except Jan

Epping Forest District Museum, 39–41 Sun St, Waltham Abbey EN9 1EL; Tel (01992) 716882; *Museum Officer* Kate Carver; *Education Officer* Sue Davies
Displays relating to the social history of the district plus programmes of exhibitions and exhibition events, outreach activities loans and living history workshops. For details contact Education Officer. Open Fri, Sat, Sun, Mon, 2–5pm; Tues, 12–5 pm, Weds, Thurs, party bookings only

Harlow Museum, Passmore's Hse, Third Ave, Harlow CM18 6YL; Tel (01279) 454959; *Museum Curator* R.W. Bartlett; *Education Officer* vacancy
Local geology, natural history, archaeology, social history, up to the 1950s. Educational talks, loan service. Documentary and oral history archive

The Harwich Society, 4 Hall La, Harwich CO12 3TE; Tel (01255) 503429; *Secretary* Andy Rutter
Educational tours around Harwich Redoubt (circular Napoleonic fort), Harwich Maritime Museum, Harwich Lifeboat Museum, Harwich Treadwheel Crane and Harwich Electric Palace. (Cinema (1911). Enquiries direct to the Guide Panel Secretary, Mrs Sue Lambert, 52 Church St, Harwich CO12 3DS

Hedingham Castle, Castle Hedingham, Nr Halstead, Essex; Tel (01787) 460261; *Manager* Ian Harrington
Fine Norman keep. Worksheets, colouring posters, books, talks, beautiful grounds. Schools welcome all year by appointment
Location On B1058, 1 m off A604 between Cambridge and Colchester. Easy reach of London via M25, M11, A120 and A12; *Opening times* Easter week to end October, 11am–5pm daily 10am–5pm on Bank Holidays; *Admission prices* Children £1.50, teachers and helpers free; *Light refreshments* available, and large picnic area. Beautiful woodland and lakeside walks good for children to learn about birds, animals and nature study

House on the Hill Toy Museum, Bayley Walls, Stansted, Essex CM24 8SP; Tel (01279) 813237; Fax (01279) 816391
One of the largest toy museums in Europe. Housing a vast collection of toys, games and other childhood memorabilia from late Victorian times right up to the 1970's. Many animated displays incl. puppet theatre, meccano, teddy bears' picnic, Peter Pans' bedroom, train layouts and much more. Open all year for pre-booked school parties. Special party rate for schools and free introductory talk

Layer Marney Tower, Colchester CO5 9US; Tel (01206) 330784; Shelia Charrington

Mark Hall Cycle Museum and Gardens, Muskham Rd, Off First Ave, Harlow CM20 2LF; Tel (01279) 439680; *Museum Officer* K.C. Kilvington; *Education Officer* Chris Moffat
Bicycles and accessories illustrating the history and development of the cycle from 1818 to the present day, plus three walled period gardens

The Minories Art Gallery, 74 High St, Colchester CO1 1UE; Tel (01206) 577067; Fax (01206) 577161
Changing exhibitions of contemporary art with accompanying programme of education, talks and activities. School parties welcome. Cafe and education room for on-site creative work. CADVAT also arranges outreach projects with schools, colleges and community groups
The Minories Gallery is managed by Colchester and District Visual Arts Trust (CADVAT)

Mole Hall Wildlife Park and Butterfly Pavilion, Mole Hall, Widdington, Saffron Walden CB11 3SS; Tel (01799) 540400; *Proprietor* Pamela Johnstone
Talks by arrangement

Paycocke's, West St, Coggeshall, Colchester CO6 1NS; Tel (01376) 561305; *Tenant/Custodian* Petra Ward
The National Trust

Prior's Hall Barn, 23 Savile Row, London W1X 1AB
English Heritage

St Osyths Priory, St Osyths CO16 8MZ; Tel (01255) 820492; *Owner* Somerset de Chair; *Contact* G. Colby; Tel (01255) 820242 (9–10am)
Gardens, ancient monuments and art collection. Open to the public Easter weekend and then May 1st–Sept 30th. Adults £3.50, Children £1.00, OAPs £2.00

Saffron Walden Museum, Museum St, Saffron Walden CB10 1JL; Tel (01799) 510333; *Curator* L.M. Pole, BSc, FMA, DipSocAnthrop
Talks and demonstration classes using museum objects eg. Ancient Egypt; Invaders; North American Indians charges £1 per child for Essex C.C. Schools and £1.25 per child for others (GMSet) 'independent' school visits free including teachers and accompanying adults. Free also for teachers making preliminary visits. Otherwise adults admission £1; Discounts 50p; children 18 years and under free. Annual season tickets £3 and £1.50. Pre-booking necessary for all school talks and visits; Open March–Oct, Mon–Sat 10am–5pm; Sundays 2.30–5.00; Nov–Feb, Mon–Sat 11am–4pm; Sundays 2.30–4.30

Stansted Mountfitchet Castle, Bayley Walls, Stansted CM24 8SP; Tel (01279) 813237
Re-construction of 11th-century Norman motte and bailey castle and village on its original site. Open daily mid-March to mid-Nov. Special party rate for schools

Tilbury Fort, Nr Tilbury; Tel (01732) 778000
English Heritage

Upminster Tithe Barn Agricultural and Folk Museum, Hall La, Upminster RM14 1AU; Tel (01708) 447535; *Contact* P.M. Butler
Collection of local artifacts and agricultural items
Hornchurch and District Historical Society

Gloucestershire

Arlington Mill Museum (The Cotswold Country Museum), Bibury, Cirencester GL7 5NL; Tel (0128 574) 368; *Education Officer* D. Alexander

Cheltenham Art Gallery and Museums Outreach Service, Clarence St, Cheltenham GL50 3JT; Tel (01242) 237431; *Community Outreach and Education Officer* Liz Benington; *Community Outreach and Education Officer* Virginia Adsett
Talks, handling sessions, worksheet at all 3 museums; Holst Birthplace Museum, Regency/Victorian/ Edwardian room settings, Victorian cooking/washing facilities. Pittville Pump Room. Displays of costume and jewellery from late 18th century

Berkeley Castle, Berkeley, Glos GL13 9BQ; Tel (01453) 810332
England's oldest inhabited castle and with the same family in residence since it was completed in 1153 at the command on Henry II. Splendidly preserved Norman Castle. Free guided tours. Also outstanding Butterfly House with live butterflies

Birdland, Riverside, Bourton-on-the-Water; Tel (01451) 20689; *Curator* R.A. Hill
Unique collection of tropical birds and penguins

Chastleton House, Chastleton, Nr Moreton-in-Marsh; Tel (0160 874) 355
Undergoing restoration by the National Trust

Chavenage, Tetbury; Tel (01666) 502329; *Contact* D. Lowsley-Williams

Chedworth Roman Villa (National Trust) Yanworth, Cheltenham GL54 3LJ; Tel (01242) 890256; *Property Manager* Philip Bethell; *Administrative Assistant* Damian Baylis
Assistance in project planning, AV presentation, personal introduction to site. Parties must book in advance

Cheltenham Art Gallery and Museum, Clarence St, Cheltenham GL50 3JT; Tel (01242) 237431; *Museum*

Outreach Officer Liz Benington; *Museum Outreach Officer* Virginia Adsett
Arts and Crafts Movement collection; 17th century Dutch and 17th–20th century British paintings, ceramic, glass and metalwork; social hitory archaeological material relating to Cheltenham and Cotwolds

Corinium Museum, Park St, Cirencester GL7 2BX; Tel (01285) 655611; *Assistant Curator* John Paddock
The archaeology of the Cotswolds with particular reference to Roman Britain and the regional capital of Corinium (Cirencester). Full scale reconstructions of kitchen, dinning room and workshop. Special exhibitions. School parties arranged in advance; quiz sheets; slide shows; loans available to teachers; New Medieval Cotswolds gallery
Cotswold District Council

Cotswold Countryside Collection, Northleach, Glos GL54 3JH; Tel (01451) 860715; *Assistant Curator* Ann-Rachel Harwood
Old farm wagons, implements etc, in a former 18th century prison. Also Victorian kitchen and laundry displays. School parties welcome if arranged in advance, quiz sheets, courtroom plays, craft lessons, picnic and play areas; Special exhibitions programme
Cotswold District Council

Cotswold Farm Park Rare Breed Survival Centre, Bemborough Farm, Guiting Power, Nr Stow on the Wold, Cheltenham, Glos GL54 5UG; Tel (01451) 850307
Lectures, teachers' project packs, quiz sheets, farm trail. Lambing, shearing and other seasonal exhibitions

Dean Forest Railway, New Mills, Lydney GL15 4ET; Tel (01594) 843423
Services run from Norchard to Lydney (Lakeside) at regular intervals. Museum and shop at Norchard. Further details, address above

Dean Heritage Centre, Soudley, Forest of Dean, Glos GL14 7UG; Tel (01594) 822170; *Curator* Ian Standing; *General Manager* David Evans
The Unique Museum of the Ancient Forest of Dean; its plants and animals, people and industries

Gloucester, Blackfriars, Tel (01452) 27688
English Heritage

Gloucester City East Gate, Eastgate St, Gloucester (no correspondence to this address); Tel (01452) 524131; *Contact* Director of Museums, City Museum, Brunswick Rd GL1 1HP; Tel (01452) 524131
Roman and medieval gate-towers and moat in an underground exhibition chamber

Gloucester City Museum and Art Gallery, Brunswick Rd, Gloucester GL1 1HP; Tel (01452) 524131; Fax (01452) 410898; *Director* J.F. Rhodes; *Education Assistant* Mrs K.C.M. Kear
Local archaeology and natural history. Georgian furniture and paintings. Children's activities (Roman workshop or Fossil Workshop) by prior appointment. Loan Service

Hailes Abbey, Nr Winchcombe, Cheltenham GL54 5PB; Tel (01242) 602398; *Custodian* E.N. Greenhalf; *Curator* S.C. Jenkins
Museum; exhibition; school parties free by prior arrangement
National Trust/English Heritage

Holst Birthplace Museum, 4 Clarence Rd, Pittville, Cheltenham; Tel (01242) 524846
Regency house, period furnishings; working Victorian kitchen and scullery

Little Dean Hall, Little Dean GL14 3NR; Tel (01594) 24213; *Custodian* D.M. Macer-Wright
Multi period historical site, manor house 11th–19th century. Roman temple. Continuity through the ages. 2,000 years history. Excavated 1990 for permanent exhibition 1st century Roman military cobbled road

Lydney Park Roman Site and Museum, Lydney; Tel (01594) 842844; *Organiser* B. Butcher
Party bookings only–Easter to July

The National Birds of Prey Centre, Newent; Tel (01531) 820286; *Information Officer* M. Garner
Zoo for Birds of prey, flying demonstrations, free guided tour to parties over 12 in number. Teacher's pack and question sheets available. Open 1 Feb–30 Nov. £1.95 child and adult

National Trust Severn Regional Office, Mythe End Hse, Tewkesbury GL20 6EB; Tel (01684) 850051; Fax (01684) 850090

Pittville Pump Room Museum, Pittville Pk, Cheltenham; Tel (01242) 523852; Fax (01242) 526563; *Museum Outreach Officer* Liz Benington; *Museum Outreach Officer* Virginia Adsett; Tel All enquiries (01242) 237431
Displays of costume and jewellery 1780's to 1960's. The museum is on the top floor of the magnificent Pittville Pump Room, in a large park. Open 29th May–30th September

Prinknash Bird Park, Prinknash Abbey, Cranham, Nr Gloucester; Tel (01452) 812727; *Director* P.G. Meigh
The Bird Park is unique in being situated in the middle of a Monastic Estate, with its impressive new Abbey and Historic House once a Hunting Lodge of Henry VIII and the Abbots of Gloucester. The Park has exotic Pheasants, Waterfowl and swans. There are also numerous Peacocks and many Fallow Deer, some of which are so tame they feed out of your hand. The Park has a fishpond teeming with Trout which visitors enjoy feeding. All this and more, you will see in nine acres of including Parkland with lakes in a Monastic background. Opening times 1st March to 31st October 10am–5pm. 1st November to 28th February 10am–4pm

Regiments of Gloucestershire Museum, The Docks, Gloucester GL1 2HE; Tel (01452) 522682; *Curator* Christine Beresford, BA, MSocSc
Tells the story of soldiers in war and peace during the last three centuries. Resource packs. Hands on collection arranged on request. Open Tues–Sun 10–5pm

Snowshill Manor, Broadway; Tel (01382) 852410; *The Administrator* M. Jessup
National Trust

Stroud District Museum, Lansdown, Stroud GL5 1BB; Tel (01453) 763394; *Curator* Susan P. Hayward

Sudeley Castle and Gardens, Winchcombe, Cheltenham, Glos; Tel (01242) 602308
Royal castle dating to 10th century. Open April–Oct

Westonbirt Arboretum, Forestry Commission, Tetbury GL8 8QS; Tel (01666) 880220; *Education Officer* Kevin Beckett
Forest Enterprise

The Wildfowl and Wetlands Trust, Slimbridge GL2 7BT; Tel (01453) 890333; *Director of Education and Public Affairs* Doug Hulyer
Operates 8 centres in UK. Illustrated talks, plus activities, teacher's pack, pre-visit, topic and follow-up material available plus outreach programmes (eg Pondwatch and Waterlands)

Winchcombe Railway Museum, 23 Gloucester St, Winchcombe GL54 5LX; Tel (01242) 602257 or 626410; *Director* Tim Petchey
A collection of railway equipment from the days of steam. Set in ½ acre of enclosed Cotswold gardens. Signals, a signal box and a booking office can all be operated by the visitor. Qualified teacher on staff to give guidance and a resources centre available to teachers bringing school parties

Woolstaplers Hall Museum, High St, Chipping Campden GL55 6HB; Tel (01386) 840289; Fax (01789) 840332; *Curator* P. Woodley
Large collections of town and country bygones, early domestic machines, cinema and cine equipment, cameras, typewriters, sewing machines, apothecary, scientific instruments, victorian flying balloon and paraphernalia and much much more to enlighten and amuse. Open April 1st to October 30th daily. Also Tourist Information Centre and Gift Shop

Hampshire

Aldershot Military Museum, Evelyn Woods Rd, Queen's Ave, Aldershot GU11 2LG; Tel (01252) 314598; *Administrator* Geoffrey Venning
A look behind the scenes at the solider's social and military life in the home of the Britsih Army

Aspex Gallery, Art Space Portsmouth Ltd, 27 Brougham Rd, Southsea PO5 4PA; Tel (01705) 812121; *Director* Les Buckingham
Presents exhibitions of contemporary art with workshops and conferences on current art practice. maintains 26 artists' studio

Avington park, Winchester; Tel (01962) 779260; Ms Bullen

Beaulieu: National Motor Museum and 'Wheels', Palace House and Gardens, Beaulieu Abbey and Exhibition of Monastic Life, John Montagu Bldg, Beaulieu, Brockenhurst, Hampshire SO42 7ZN; Tel (01590) 612345; *Contact* Education at Beaulieu (Montagu Ventures Ltd)
Educational destination with qualified teachers offering National Curriculum subjects and others. Transport, medieval stduies, Victorians, Edwardians

Breamore Countryside Museum and Carriage Museum, Breamore, Nr Fordingbridge; Tel (01725) 512468; *Curator* J. Forshaw
Morning tours by arrangement

Breamore House and Museums, Nr Fordingbridge; Tel (01725) 512468; J. Forshaw
Tours for schools by arrangement

Broadlands, The Home of Lord Mountbatten, Broadlands, Romsey SO51 9ZD; Tel (01794) 517888; *Contact* Eileen Hall

Curtis Museum and Allen Gallery, High St, Alton, Hants GU34 1BA; Tel (01420) 82802; *Curator* T. Cross
Museum workshops held regularly
Hampshire County Council Museum Service

Eling Tide Mill, The Toll Bridge, Totton SO40 9HF; Tel (01703) 869575
Working tide mill regularly producing wholewheat flour as it was done before modern technology; museum and shop. The Mill specialises in educational visits, providing guided tours and video aids for all levels
Eling Tide Mill Trust Ltd

Fort Brockhurst, Gunners Way, Elson, Gosport, Hampshire PO12 4DS; Tel (01705) 581059; *Head Custodian* David Clodfelter
Victorian fort with keep, moat and drawbridges. Exhibition on defences of Portsmouth. Open daily all year; winter–closed Mondays only
English Heritage

The Gilbert White Field Studies Centre, The Oates Memorial Library and Museum and The Gilbert White Museum, Tha Wakes, Selborne, Alton; Tel (0142 0150) 303; *Warden* J.Y. Streeter
Day courses in a wide range of environmental and museum studies; most fieldwork is carried out within a 3-mile radius of Selborne, which has areas of downland, woodland, meadows and fresh water, also heath;and and acid bog. All age and ability groups

Gilbert White's House and Garden and the Oates Museum, The Wakes, Selborne, Alton GU34 3JH; Tel (01420 511) 275
Historic house and garden. Home of Gilbert White, naturalist. Exhibitions include Lawrence Oates of the Antarctic

Gosport Museum, Walpole Rd, Gosport; Tel (01705) 588035; Fax (01705) 501951; *Curator* Ian Edelman, BA, AMA
Open Tues–Sat 10 am to 5 pm. Sunday 1 pm to 5 pm (May to Sept). Admission free
Hampshire County Council Museum Service

Guildhall Gallery, The Guildhall, The Broadway, Winchester SO23 9LJ; Tel (01962) 848289; *Keeper of Exhibitions* Christopher Wardman Bradbury Office Address: Winchester Museums Service, 75 Hyde St, Winchester, Hants SO23 7DW
Changing monthly exhibition programme including topographical paintings and contemporary sculpture, painting, photography crafts, etc, from local and non local artists' groups and students. Open Tues–Sat, 10 am–5 pm. Sun and Mon 2–5 pm. Closed Mon, Oct–March, Admission free

Hampshire County Council Museums Service, (Museums at Petersfield, Alton, Andover, Basingstoke, Christchurch, Eastleigh, Fareham, Havant, Rockbourne Roman Villa Aldershot Gosport) Chilcomb Hse, Chilcomb La, Winchester SO23 8RD; Tel (01962) 846304; Fax (01962) 869836

The Hawk Conservancy, Weyhill, Nr Andover SP11 8DY; Tel (01264) 773850; *Education Officer* J. Baugh
Specialist centre for Birds of Prey, Lectures, demonstrations, worksheets

Hurst Castle, Nr Keyhaven; Tel (01590) 642344
English Heritage

Jane Austen's House, Chawton, Nr Alton GU34 1SD; Tel (01420) 83262; *Curator* Jean Bowden
Carpenters, Mill Hill, London NW7 3NL
Jane Austen Memorial Trust

Manor Farm, Country Park (Hampshire Farm Museum) Bursledon (Junction 8 off M27); Tel (01489) 787055
A working farm of a bygone age, farm animals and mchinery with a traditional Farmstead. Ancient woodland alongside River Hamble, Postal address only: Brook La, Botley, Southampston SO3 2ER

Maritime Museum, Buckler's Hard; *Contact* Education at Beaulieu John Montagu Bldg, Beaulieu, Hants SO42 7ZN; Tel (01590) 612345 Ext 223
Education guides on site. National Curriculum; ships and seafarers, 18th century social/domestic life

Marwell Zoological Park, Colden Common, Nr Winchester SO21 1JH; Tel (01962) 777407/777835; *Head of Education* S.E. Millar
Education service offers illustrated talks, tours , activity and 'hands-on' sessions and written material for teachers and pupils of all ages. All education programmes are National Curriculum related. Special rates for schools

Mary Rose Ship Hall and Exhibition, College Rd, HM Naval Base, Portsmouth PO1 3LX; Tel (01705) 750521; *Chief Executive* John Vimpany; *Visitor Services Manager* Mark Griffin
Preserves and displays Henry VIII's warship, the Mary Rose, and the Tudor treasures discovered with the wreck. Special hands-on facilities for school groups

Museum of Army Flying, Middle Wallop, Stockbridge SO20 8DY; Tel (01980) 674421; Fax (01264) 781694; *Contact* The Museum Curator
Talks the story of 100 years of Army flying from balloons and kites of the 19th century to the present day. Teachers pack available on request

Museums Education Service, Southampton City Heritage, Civic Centre, Southmapton SO9 4XF; Tel (01703) 635904/632493; Tower Hse Office, Town Quay SO1 1LX; Fax (01703) 339601; *Outreach Officer* Siân Jones, BA, AMA; *Education Officer* Hazel Beuret; *Bookings* Jill Neale; Tel (01703) 635904/632493; Fax (01703) 339601
Tudor House Museum, Museum of Social History, Bugle St, Southampton; Bookings (0703) 635904/632493; Tudor Hall; unique Tudor Garden; social and domestic; local history temporary exhibitions
Wool Hse Maritime Museum, Town Quay, Southampton; Bookings (0703) 635904/632493; Southampton Maritime history, especially the liners, and the men and women employed on the ships and in port-based trades
God's Hse Tower Archaeology Museum, Town Quay, Southampton; Bookings (0703) 635904/632493; The collections contain artefacts from the palaeolithic period through to the post-medieval. The museum has displays on the Roman, Saxon and medieval periods of Southampton's history
Workshops, handling sessions and project based activities at each of the city's three museums. Worksheets and teaching resources for all levels
Admission charges: Adults £1.50; Children (5–17 yrs), Senior citizens, registered disabled Museum Association Members (with card) 75p; Leisure Card holders and Friends of Soton Museums and Galleries free; Family ticket £3.00; Visit 3 museums for the price of two £3.00; pre-booked school visits 50p per child, workshops Southampton schools £1.50, other areas £2.50

National Motor Museum, Beaulieu SO42 7ZN; *Contact* Education at Beaulieu; Tel (01590) 612345
Educational material and audio/visual aids; lectures, guided tours, films, role play, Vistorian and Edwardian days

Netley Abbey, Netley; Tel (01703) 453076
English Heritage
Ornamental Farm and Gardens and Tropical Glass Houses Sir George Staunton Country Pk, Middle Pk Way, Havant; Tel (01705) 453405; *Manager* Russell Cleaver
Paultons Park, Nr Romsey SO51 6AL; Tel (01703) 814442; *Marketing Manager* Anne Ruffell
Family leisure park with educational opportunities including Village Life Museum with recreated workshops from turn of century, Romany Experience with unique collection of wagons, many exotic birds and wildfowl from around the world. Also pets corner, hedge maze, nursery rhymes and dinosaurs.
Educational Pack available
Paultons Park
The Pilgrims' School, 3 The Close, Winchester, Hampshire; Tel (01962) 854189
Dean and Chapter, Winchester
Portchester Castle, Nr Fareham; Tel (01705) 378291
English Heritage
Portsmouth City Museums and Records Services, *City Museum; Southsea Castle; D-Day Museum; Cumberland House Natural Science Museum; Charles Dickens Birthplace and Portsmouth City Records Office; Education Officer* Jan Hancock City Museum, Museum Rd, Old Portsmouth PO1 2LJ; Tel (01705) 827261
Facilities for school parties. Loans service to Portsmouth schools
Royal Marines Museum, Southsea, Hampshire PO4 9PX; Tel (01705) 819385; Fax (01705) 838420; *Director* Colonel K.N., Wilkins OBE; *Curator* A. Lane, BEd; *Archive/Librarian* M.G. Little
Ministry of Defence (Navy)
Royal Naval Museum, HM Naval Base, Portsmouth PO1 3LR; Tel (01705) 733060; *Customer Services Manager* M. McKeown
Trustees
Royal Navy Submarine Museum, (Featuring HMS Alliance and Holland 1) Haslar Jetty Rd, Gosport; Tel (01705) 529217; Fax (01705) 511349; *Information Officer* J.A. Nesbitt
Free educational booklets given to children. Available at cost price is a pack of ideas, related where possible to national curriculum attainment levels for Primary school teachers. Also Science and Submarines introduced 1993
Sea Life Centre, Clarence Esplanade, Southsea PO5 3PB; Tel (01705) 734461
Teachers' resource packs; school bookings and information
SEARCH 50 Clarence Rd, Gosport, Hants PO12 1BU; Tel (01705) 501957; Fax (01705) 501921; *Education Officer* Isabel Hughes; *Natural Science Officer* Ann Nicol
SEARCH is Hampshire County Council Museums Service's hands-on centre for history and natural history. It provides an object based educational cente, initially aimed at schools. Disabled access. Admission fee. Visits by arrangement only
Southampton Archaeology Team, The Mission Hall, Southampton; *Site Visits* Dr Andrew Russell; Tel (01703) 634906
The excavation and analysis of the archaeological remains of Southampton and the publication and presentation of the results
Southampton City Council, City Heritage
Southampton City Art Gallery, North Guild, Commercial Rd, Southampton SO14 7LP; Tel (01703) 832743; *Keeper of Art and Exhibitions* Margot Heller; *Outreach Manager* Christine Rawnsley
Art works and related information particularly in respect of the 20th century and contemporary material
Stansted Park, Rowlands Castle PO9 6DX; Tel (01705) 412265; *Events Manager* Brigitta Andresen
Stansted House and Park is available to the public as a venue for recreation, education and leisure
Stansted Park Foundation
Southampton City Heritage, Tower Hse, Town Quay, Southampton, Hants
Tudor house and garden with contemporary and later displays relating to life in Southampton
Southampton City Heritage, Museums Education Service
Bookings (0703) 635904
Uppark, South Harting, Petersfield; Tel (01730) 825317; *Administrator* P.L. Meredith
Teachers' pack video
National Trust
The Vyne, Sherborne St John, Basingstoke RG26 5DX; *The Administrator*
National Trust
Westgate Museum, Upper High St, Winchester; Tel (01962) 848269; *Education Officer* Robin Iles
Winchester City Council; Medieval City gate with displays of armour, weights and measures and a 16th Century painted ceiling. Also brass rubbing activity area
Winchester City Mill Youth Hostel 1 Water La, Winchester; Tel (01962) 853723
YHA Warden
National Trust
Winchester Museums Service, 75 Hyde St, Winchester; Tel (01962) 848269; *Education Officer* Robin Iles
The City Museum. Displays of Roman, Anglo-Saxon and medieval artefacts from Winchester, and reconstructed Victorian Shops
Winchester City Council
Wolvesey, Old Bishop's Place, Winchester; Tel (01962) 854766
English Heritage

Hereford and Worcester

Avoncroft Museum of Historic Buildings, Stoke Heath, Bromsgrove, Worcs B60 4JR; Tel (01527) 831886/831363; *Curator/Education Officer* Dr Simon Penn
Full education service available including teaching sessions, facilities for practical work and special publications
Berrington Hall, Leominster HR6 0DW; Tel (01568) 615721; *Contact* The Administrator
Neo classical house, finely decorated, set in landscaped parkland. School visits welcomed by prior arrangement
Preliminary visit by member of recommended
National Trust
Bewdley Museum, Load St, Bewdley, Worcester DY12 2AE; Tel (01299) 403573; *Museum and Arts Officer* K. Curry
Wyre Forest District Council
Burton Court, Eardislard, Leominster; Tel (0154 47) 231; Lt-Cdr and Mrs R.M. Simpson
Historic costume exhibition. Natural History
Churchill Gdns Museum, Venns La, Hereford; Tel (01432) 268121 Ext 207/334; *Museum Curator* A.E. Sandford
Fine furniture, costumes and paintings of late 19th century. Late 18th and 19th century rooms. Victorian kitchen display. Hatton Gallery exhibition. School visits welcome by appointment
Cider Museum and King Offa Distillery, 21 Ryelands St, Hereford HR4 0LW; Tel (01432) 354207; *Curator* Karen Bradbury; *Shop Manager* Pauline Dabbs
Formally a cider works. Tells the history of cider making through the use of reconstructed areas, displays, sound and slide presentations showing machinery, small objects and documentation.
Educational facilities related to the National Curriculum include Loan Packs of 2-d material and a new publication, "Teachers Guidelines". Gift shop; free parking
The Commandary Civil War Centre, Sidbury WR1 2HU; Tel (01905) 355071; *Contact* The Publicity Assistant

Audio visual displays including the trial of Charles I and a Scots camp on the eve of the Battle of Worcester 1651. Activities for schools throughout the year
Booking essential

Croft Castle, Nr Leominster HR6 9PW; Tel (0156 885) 246; *Administrator* S. Jelfs
Castle with ancient walls and castellated turrets, interior shown as in 18th century. Surrounded by magnificent parkland. Parties must pre-book
National Trust

Droitwich Spa Heritage Centre, St Richard's Hse, Victoria Sq, Droitwich Spa; Tel (01905) 774312; *Tourism Officer* Serena Joule; *Heritage Centre Assistant* Joy King; *Heritage Centre Assistant* Christine Tapson
The history of Droitwich Spa from prehistoric salt town to present day luxury Spa plus temporary exhibitions, brass rubbing centre and tourist information centre

Dyson Perrins Museum of Worcester Porcelain, Severn St, Worcester; Tel (01905) 23221; Fax (01905) 617807; *Curator* H.E. Frost, MA
Tours of the Royal Worcester Porcelain Factory. Visits to the museum containing the finest collection of Worcester porcelain in the world
Coaches welcomed
Trustees of the Dyson Perrins Museum

Eardisley Village Holidays The Cruck Hse, Eardisley, Hereford HR3 6PQ; Tel (01544) 327529; *Co-ordinator* David Gorvett
Heritage and walking breaks to order, staying in villages and half-timbered farmhouses. All meals and accommodation. Guided walks with a historian and/or naturalist

Eastnor Castle, Ledbury, Herefordshire HR8 1RN; Tel (01531) 633160; Fax (01531) 631776; *Administrator* Simon Foster

Forge Mill Needle Museum and Bordesley Abbey Visitor Centre, Needle Mill La, Riverside, Redditch, Worcester B97 6RR; Tel (01527) 62509; *Curator* Barry Mead
Unique 18th century needle mill with working water-wheel and machinery. New visitor centre uses archaeological evidence to tell history of the nearby 12th century Cisterian abbey ruins. Natural history areas. Education Officer and educational facilities available. Open all year except December and January

Goodrich Castle, Nr Ross on Wye HR9 6HY; Tel (01600) 890538; *Head Custodian* G. Duberley
Ruined castle overlooking the Rover Wye, destroyed by Parliamentarians in the Civil War. Keep dates from mid 12th century, main building late 13th century
Open all year round
English Heritage–Historic Building and Monuments Commission

The Greyfriars, Friar St, Worcester WR1 2LZ
written enquiries to The Greyfriars (Tel. (01905) 23571)
Medieval timber-framed house in the heart of Worcester. walled garden. Open April–Oct Weds, Thurs and Bank Holiday Mondays, 2–5.00 pm
The National Trust

Hanbury Hall, Droitwich Spa, Hereford and Worcester WR9 7EA; Tel (01527) 821214; *Property Manager*
Open from April, Sat, Sun, Mon, until end Oct as well as Tues, Wed during August 2–6pm
National Trust

Harvington Hall, Nr Kidderminster DY10 4LR; Tel (01562) 777267; *Resident Custodian* Rev G. Tucker
Archdiocese of Birmingham

Hereford and Worcester County Museum, Hartlebury Caste, Hartlebury, Nr Kidderminster DY11 7XZ; Tel (01299) 250416; *Education Assistant* A. Lloyd
Social history museum with period room settings, role play experiences in the Edwardian schoolroom; early 20th century kitchen/scullery. Special activity days. Shop and refreshments

Hereford City Museum and Art Gallery, Broad St, Hereford HR4 9AU; Tel (01432) 268121 Ext 207; *Curator* A.E. Sandford, BA, AMA
Natural history, archaeology, local history. Art gallery exhibitions by local artists. Open 10 am–6 pm, Tues, Weds and Fri, 10–5 Thurs and Sat (summer, 10–4 Sat (winter), Open Holiday Mondays
Hereford City Council

Hergest Croft Gardens Kington; Tel (01544) 230160; W.L. Banks

Heritage and Tourism Manager, Pepperpot, Church St, Upton Upon Severn; Tel (01684) 594200; *Recreation and Tourism Manager* Ian Hamilton; *Contact* Margaret White; Tel (01684) 892700 Ext 2411
Display on growth and development of town and civil war involvement

Moccas Court, Moccas, Hereford HR2 9LH; Tel (01981) 500381; *Custodian* I. Saunders
Georgian country house on banks of River Wye, decoration designed by Robert Adam. Open Sunday afternoons
April–September

The Old House, Broad St, Hereford HR4 9AU; Tel (01432) 268121 Ext 225
Jacobean house furnished in 17th century style. Open Mon 10am–1pm, Tues–Sat 10am–1pm, 2–5.30pm, Sat 10–1 only winter. Open Bank Holiday Mondays. Open Sundays May–Sept
Hereford City Council

Snowshill Manor, Nr Broadway WR12 7JU; Tel (01386) 852410; *Administrator* M. Jessup
National Trust

Water Mill–Mortimer's Cross, The Mill Hse, Mortimer's Cross, Leominster HR6 9PE; Tel (01568) 708820; Fax (01568) 708765; *Custodian* D.T. Delaney
Restored water-powered fodder mill and Battle (1461) Information Centre open April–Sept, Thursday, Sunday, Bank Holidays, 14.00–17.30. School parties by arrangement

Hertfordshire

Ashridge Estate, Ringshall, Berkhampsted; Tel (01442) 842488; Fax (01442) 842062; *Countryside Manager* Graeme Cannon; *Monument Centre Custodian* Margaret Cleaver; Tel (0144 285) 227
4,000 acre estate including Ashridge Park, Albury, Berkhampsted and Northchurch Commons and restored Pitstone Windmill. Education pack for Teachers; Tel (0494) 528051
National Trust

Barnet Museum, 31 Wood St, Barnet EN5 4BE; Tel 0181-449 0321 Ext 4 and 0181-440 8066; *Curator*
Curatorial Office comprising several officers
Barnet and District Local History Society

Benington Lordship, Stevenage; Tel (01438) 869668; C.H.A. Bott

Chenies Manor House, Chenies, Rickmansworth; Tel (012404) 2888; *Contact* Macleod Mathews
Early Tudor manor open public April–Oct with facilities for school parties. Physic garden, Victorian kitchen garden. Adults £3.50, children half price

The Clock Tower, Market Pl, St Albans; Tel (01727) 853301; *Chairman of Joint Clock Tower Committee* Dennis Owen
Early 15th century curfew tower. Small exhibitions illustrate aspects of local history. Clock mechanism, Curfew Bell, Market Bell. Open Easter–mid Sept on Saturday, Sunday and Bank Holidays
St Albans District Council

First Garden City Heritage Museum, 296 Norton Way South, Letchworth Garden City SG6 1SU; Tel (01462) 482424/482710 (Saturdays); Fax (01462) 480253; *Curator* Robert Lancaster, BA(Hons)
History of first garden city and garden city movement. Covers architecture, palnning, housing, social history. Displays, talks, guided tours, education

Friends of Welwyn Roman Baths, C/o 23 Mill La, Welwyn AL6 9EU; Tel (0143 871) 5300; *Secretary* Tony Rook, BSc, MPhil, FSA
Education by the promotion support, assistance and improvement of Welwyn Roman Baths

Hatfield House, Herts AL9 5NQ; Tel (01707) 262823; Fax (01707) 275719; *Curator* D.G. McCord

Early Jacobean Hse, Great Par,. Nature trails and delightful gardens. Open 25 Mar–13 Oct. Closed Mons. Open Bank Holiday Mondays
Guided Tours Tues–Sats

Hertford Museum, 18 Bull Plain, Hertford SG14 1DT; Tel (01992) 582686; *Senior Curator* Andrea George, BA, AMA; *Administrative Officer* Sheila Every
Displays/collections relate to Hertford, East Herts and Hertfordshire. Social history, archaeology, natural history and photgraphs. School visits/enquiries welcome. Museum shop. Public lavatories. 17th century garden. Disabled access to ground floor and garden

Knebworth House, Garden and Park, Knebworth; Tel (01438) 812661; *General Manager* John Hoy
500 year old stately home, adventure playground with Fort Knebworth, British Raj exhibition; National Curriculum based worksheets available

Lowewood Museum, High St, Hoddesdon EN11 8BH; Tel (01992) 445596; *Curator* Neil Robbins
Local history displays. Varied temporary exhibitions programme. Children's holiday activities. Special educational visits/talks by arrangement

The Manor House, Chenies, Rickmansworth, Herts WD3 6ER; Tel (01494) 762888; A. MacLeod Matthews

Mill Green Museum and Mill, Mill Grn, Hatfield AL9 5PD; Tel (01707) 271362; Fax (01707) 272511; *Curator* Sue Kirby, BA, AMA
Preservation and interpretation of the local environment and its history through exhibitions, displays, guided tours. Craft displays, milling of flour
Welwyn Hatfield Museum Service

Mosquito Aircraft Museum, P.O. Box 107, Salisbury Hall, Nr London Colney; Tel (01727) 822051
Preservation of De Havilland aircraft, engines and aeronautical memorabilia, with special emphasis on Mosquito. Fifteen aircraft and twelve engines on display

Museum of St Albans, (formerly the City Museum) Hatfield Rd, St Albans AL1 3RR; Tel (01727) 819340; *Director, St Albans Museums* Vacancy; *Keeper–Local History* Anne Roach; *Keeper–Natural Sciences* D. Curry; *Curatorial Assistant* M. Wheeler
Collection and exhibition of the story of St Albans from the departure of the Romans to the present day and regular programme of changing exhibitions on wide variety of topics, 'Tools for the Job', new display of the Salaman Collection of trade tools

Museum Education, Museum Resources Centre, Burymead Rd, Hitchin, Herts SG5 1RT; Tel (01462) 422946; *Museum Education Officer* Miss E. Hunter
Loans service, museum classes, teachers' seminars, holiday activities, local fieldwork
North Hertfordshire District Council Museum Service

Paradise Wildlife Park and Education Centre, White Stubbs La, Broxbourne EN10 7QA; Tel (01992) 468001; Fax (01992) 440525

Roman Theatre of Verulamium, Gorhambury, St Albans AL3 6AH; Tel (01727) 835035 (Roman Theatre Kiosk); (01727) 854051 (Estate office); *Contact* Secretary (mornings only)
Only completed theatre in England. It is a theatre with a stage, not amphitheatre. Open every day

RSPB Rye House Marsh Reserve, Rye Hse, Rye Rd, Hoddesdon EN11 0EJ; Tel (01992) 460031; *Contact* Bookings Secretary

Rhodes Memorial Museum and Commonwealth Centre, South Rd, Bishops Stortford, Herts CM23 3JG; Tel (01279) 651746; *Curator* D.R. Parry; *Manager* G.B. Wilcox
Small parties welcome; quiz on arrangement; entry free for accompanied children; small charge for school parties

St Albans Organ Museum, (St Albans Organ Museum is administered by St Albans Musical Museum Society); W. Walker; Tel (01727) 851557
The museum is open and playing every Sunday from 2.00–4.30pm and at other times by appointment. Regular advertised theatre organ concerts featuring UK and International Artists take place throughout the year. The museum houses the Charles Hart collection of mechanical musical instruments including large dance organs and pianos, and two theatre pipe organs. All is housed in a single ground floor level auditorium and Sunday openings include a descriptive commentary. Cost: Adults £1.50; Children 60p

Shaw's Corner, Ayot St Lawrence, Nr Welwyn AL6 9BX; Tel (01438) 820307; *Custodian* D.S. Uttley
Modest Edwardian villa, home of George Bernard Shaw. Downstairs rooms unchanged since his death, contain personal belongings. Open Weds–Sat, 2–5.30pm last admission; Sun and bank hol Mondays 12am–5.30pm. Upstairs room open weekdays only. Price £2.80 adults, children half price
National Trust

Stevenage Museum Education Service, Stevenage Museum, St Georges Way, Stevenage, Herts SG1 1XX; Tel (01438) 354292; *Museums and Arts Officer* Vacancy; *Education Officer* Emma Steed; *Education Officer* Maureen Finn
Full education and activity programme for all ages, on all aspects of the local area. Loan service, research facilities; educational material; monthly Saturday events; holiday activity programmes. Services available to educational groups within Stevenage and the county of Hertfordshire

Verulamium Museum, St Albans, Herts AL3 4SW; Tel (01727) 819341; *Keeper of Education* B.D. Adams, BA, MPhil, DipEd
Roman Material in museum; wall and hypocaust outside. Special school party rate, free to St Albans district schools; Bookable handling sessions
St Albans DC

Watford Museum, 194 High St, Watford WD1 2HG; Tel (01923) 232297; Fax (01923) 249729; *Manager Culture, Museum and Art* Andrew Lewis; *Assistant Curator* Sonia Goodman
Aspects of life in the area from earlist times to present day, special emphasis on brewing and printing industries, Victorian Britain and wartime. Fine Art Collection: 17th and 18th century North European and 19th Century English Landscapes: Includes Hertfordshire artists

Welwyn Hatfield Museum Service (Mill Green Museum and Watermill and Welwyn Roman Baths), Mill Green Museum, Mill Grn, Hatfield AL9 5PD; Tel (01707) 271362; Fax (01707) 272511; *Curator* Sue Kirby, BA, AMA
Talk, quiz sheets and guided tours, advance booking necessary (1 week for Mill and Museum, 1 week for Baths). Resource pack and worksheets available
Welwyn Hatfield District Council

Welwyn Roman Baths, Welwyn By Pass; *Assistant Curator* Wendy Parry, BA, AMA
Correspondence to: Mill Green Museum, Mill Green, Hatfield AL9 5PD; Tel (0707) 271362
A third century A.D. Bath-house, the one visible feature of a villa complex, preserved in a steel vault under the A1(M). Open Thurs–Sun, 2–5pm; other times by arrangement
Welwyn Hatfield Museum Service

Wimpole Hall, Education Office, Wimpole Hall, Arrington, Nr Royston SG8 0BW; Tel (01223) 207801; *Administrator* Graham Damant; *Contact* Education Officer
Education Officer helps schools plan visits to rare breeds farm and Hall, Living History projects, talks, demonstrations, farm trails. Teachers' resource books KS 1 and 2, KS 3 and guides for Hall and farm
National Trust

Humberside

Burnby Hall Gardens and the Stewart Collection, Pocklington; Tel (01759) 302068; *Warden* D.A. Hughes August Cott, Burnby La, Pocklington YO4 2QE
National collection of water lilies, 2 acres of lakes alive with fish. Picnic area. Free coach park. Cafe. Disabled facilities. Children party rate 50p. Excellent day out
Stewart's Trust

Burton Constable Foundation, Hull; Tel (01964) 562400; *Contact* The Director Burton Constable Foundation, Nr Hull HU11 4LN

Open Sun–Thurs Incl Easter Sun–30th Sept. Schools booked in advance

Carlton Towers, Carlton, Nr Goole DN14 9LZ; Tel (01405) 861662; *The Manager* P. Meanwell
Guided tour of historic house with information given regarding present owner and his family

Elsham Hall Country and Wildlife Park, Elsham, Nr Brigg DN20 0QZ; Tel (01652) 688698; *Administrator* (Schools service)
Nature Trails, guided walks, education room, lecture facilities, wild butterfly garden walkway, childrens farmyard, adventure playground, Granary tearooms and restaurant, Giant carp Feeding Jetty, Falconry and Craft Centres. Garden Centre, and New Barn Theatre

Goole Library, Museum and Art Gallery, Carlisle St, Goole DN14 5DS; Tel (01405) 762187; *Team Leader* M.A. Carr
Public library and tourist information. Museum and art gallery

Goole Museum and Art Gallery, Market Sq, Carlisle St, Goole DN14 5AA; Tel (01405) 762187; *Senior Museum Education Officer* Ian Wolseley
Displays providing information about the history of Goole and the surrounding area

Great Grimsby Museum and Heritage Service, Welholme Rd, Great Grimsby DN32 9LP; Tel (01472) 242000 Ext 1385/1795, 242046; *Curator* J. Tierney; *Education Officer* C.M. Parker
Available for educational use only. Social, maritime, local history, archaeology, extensive photographic collection. School loans, ahndling sessions, visits to schools, publications
Museum Education Service for South Humberside

Hornsea Museum, Burn's Farm, 11 Newbegin, Hornsea; Tel (01964) 533443/533430; *Education Officer* M. Kennedy; *Curator* C.F. Walker, BA
19th century home and village life. Victorian activity sessions, teachers packs, fact sheets. Heritage education Trust Sandford Award 1987
Hornsea Museum Trust

Hull City Museums, Art Galleries and Archives, 83 Alfred Gelder St, Hull HU1 1EP; Tel (01482) 593902; Fax (01482) 3593710

Town Docks Museum, Queen Victoria Sq, Hull; *Keeper of Maritime History* Arthur G. Credland
Maritime Museum in Victorian building with displays of whaling, trawling, shipbuilding and commerce relating to Hull, the Humber and Northern waters

Wilberforce House, High St, Hull; *Keeper of Social History* Jayne Tyler
Birthplace of the emancipator, with displays relating to slavery and abolition, other period rooms, costume, silver, etc

Streetlife, Hull Museum of Transport, High St, Hull; *Keeper of Transport* Stephen Goodhand
First phase exhibits of trams and public services' vehicles. Phase two now open containing period street scene and exhibits of cycles and early motor cars; Phases 3 and 4 due to open late 1995

Hull and East Riding Museum, *Keeper of Archaeology* Dr Andrew Foxon
Closed for two years for major new displays on the archaeology, natural history and the environment of Hull and East Riding. Opens late 1995

Old Grammar School, South Church Side; *Keeper* as Wilberforce House
'Story of Hull and its People', new permanent displays and temporary exhibitions, sport opens early 1995

Spurn Lightship, Hull Marina, originally S.E. of Spurn Point, now open to the public

Schools Education Department, 35 High St, Hull; *Keeper of Schools Service* Dennis Northmore
Loans to North Humberside Schools. Information sheets for teachers, worksheets (8–13 age group); talks and tours; handling material; museum classrooms, one each in Wilberfane House, Old Grammar School and Town Docks Museum

Ferens Art Gallery, Queen Victoria Sq, Hull HU1 3RA; *Education Officer, Art* Tracy Teasdale
Old masters, marines portraits and modern art with new exhibition and live art space, lecture room and facilities, enquiries (0482) 593912

Normanby Hall Country Park, Normanby, Scunthorpe; Tel (01724) 720588; Fax (01724) 721248
Regency mansion with period displays and a Farming Museum, set in 350 acres of parkland. Wild and ornamental birds, 2 deer herds, cafe, playground and gift shop. Schools service geared to National Curriculum work in history, science, maths, English, technology, art and geography

Pleasure Island Theme Park Kings Rd, Cleethorpes, South Humberside DN35 0PL; Tel (01472) 211511; Fax (01472) 211087; *Marketing Manager* Isobel Taylor

Scunthorpe Museum and Art Gallery, Oswald Rd, Scunthorpe DN15 7BD; Tel (01724) 843533; *Principal Keeper* Kevin Leahy; *Education Officer* Sally Bailey
The regional museum for South Humberside. Displays of local history, natural science and archaeology. Programme of contemporary art, craft and photography exhibitions, workshops, activities, residencies and courses
Scunthorpe Museums Service

Scunthorpe Museums Service, (Scunthorpe Museum and Art Gallery; Normanby Hall; Normanby Park Farming Museum; Burmby Common Nature Reserve) Northanby Hall, Country Pk, Northanby, Scunthorpe DN15 9HU; Tel (01724) 843533; *Park Manager* Neil Jacques; *Education Officer* Sally Bailey; *Senior Ranger* Jim Forshaw; Tel (01724) 720588

Sewerby Hall Park and Zoo, Bridlington; Tel (01262) 677874
18th century house, local history displays, conference and schools rooms, award-winning cliff-top gardens. Enquiries to Museums Officer, Sewerby Hall, Bridlington, East Yorkshire YO15 1EA; Tel (0262) 677874
East Yorkshire Borough Council

Skidby Mill and Museum, Skidby, North Humberside; Tel (01482) 883817/882255; *Tourist Officer* R.W. Grange
Guided tours; fully restored 19th century tower mill
East Yorkshire Borough of Beverley

Sledmore House, Nr Driffield, North Yorkshire; Tel (01377) 86208; *The House Secretary* N. Dunning

Thornton Abbey, Ulceby DN39 6TU; Tel (01469) 540357; *Head Custodian* N.A. Aspinall
Historic abbey and grounds. Open to the public
English Heritage–Historic Buildings and Monuments Commssion for England

Isle of Man

Curraghs Wildlife Park, Ballaugh, Isle of Man; Tel (01624 89) 7323; Fax (01624 89) 7327; *Director* N.J. Pinder
Over 100 species of animals in natural setting. Schoolroom and resource materials available

Isle of Man Steam Packet Co Ltd, Douglas, Isle of Man; Tel (01624) 623344; *Sales Administration Manager* C.R. Morgan

Port Erin Marine Laboratory, University of Liverpool, Port Erin, Isle of Man; Tel (01624) 832027; Fax (01624) 835788; *Information Officer* Dr A.R. Brand

Isle of Wight

Appuldurcombe House, Nr Wroxhall; Tel (01983) 852484
English Heritage

Bembridge Windmill, Mill Reach, King's Rd, Bembridge PO35 5NT; Tel (01983) 873945; *Custodian* B. Fay
Education packs, schools' tour sheet
National Trust

Carisbrooke Castle Museum, Newport, IOW PO30 1XY; Tel (01983) 523112; *Museum Schools Officer* Rosemary Cooper
Teaching, loan service, information, publications available to Isle of Wight schools. Others contact English Heritage for details (The State Apartments, Osborne Hse, East Cowes PO32 6JY)

Flamingo Park Waterfowl and Watergardens, Springvale, Seaview, IOW; Tel (01983) 612153; *Proprieter* P. Adams

Hurst Castle, C/o Yarmouth Castle, Yarmouth; Tel (01590) 642344
English Heritage–Historic Buildings amd Monuments Commission

Isle of Wight Wax Museum, High St, Brading, IOW PO36 0DQ; Tel (01983) 407286; *Education Officer* B. Webster
Cameos of Island history from Roman times to present day, and includes the early Tudor timber-framed dwelling, the Ancient Rectory Mansion part dating 1066 AD. Chamber of Horrors. Free entry into second museum – World of Nature, alongside. Free information pack and specimen worksheets available

The Needles Old Battery (Fort), West Highdown, Totland Bay, IOW PO39 0JH; Tel (01983) 754772; *Administrator* Vacancy
National Trust

Osborne House, East Cowes, IOW PO32 6JY; Tel (01983) 200022; *Head Custodian* B. Driver
Free admission to pre-booked school groups. Education room with Victorian objects and slides available if pre-booked. Education pack
English Heritage

Robin Hill Country Park, Downeand, Nr Arreton, IOW PO30 2NY; Tel (01983) 527352; *Enquiries to* The Secretary
Learn and play at Robin Hill's 88 acre down and woodland. Nature Work sheets, assault course, toboggan run, café, picnic area and many new attractions for 1995

Roman Villa, Tel (01983) 406223
For bookings contact the Curator
Roman Villa, Brading, IOW PO36 0EN; Tel (0983) 406223 (summer, 404642 (winter)

Yarmouth Castle, Yarmouth, IOW; Tel (01983) 760678
English Heritage

Kent

Archibishops Palace and Heritage Centre, Palace Gdns, Mill St, Maidstone ME15 6YE; Tel (01622) 663006; *Museums and Heritage Manager* Henry Middleton; *Visitor Services Manager* Louise Bruce; *Education Officer* Rosamunde Bell
Recently refurbished Mediaeval Palace of the Archibishops of Canterbury, with Heritage Centre and audio-visual presentation of the history of the Palace and its influence on the history of Maidstone

Bedgebury National Pinetum, Goudhurst, Cranbrook TN17 2SL; Tel (01580) 211044; *Education Officer* Philip Wilson
Forestry Commission

Black Charles, Underriver, Sevenoaks, Kent; Tel (01732) 833036; Mrs and Mrs Hugh Gamon
A hall house, built about 1400

Boughton Monchelsea Place, Maidstone, Kent ME17 4BU; Tel (01622) 743120; C.W. Gooch

The Canterbury Tales Visitor Attraction and Gift Shop, St Margaret's St, Canterbury, Kent CT1 2TG; Tel (01227) 454888; Fax (01227) 765584
Re-Creates the Chaucerian pilgrimage of medieval England. Uses sights, sounds and smells which bring Chaucer's stories to life. Learning can be fun
Heritage Projects

Canterbury Urban Studies Centre, St Alphege La, Canterbury CT1 2EB; Tel (01227) 457009; *Director* Caroline Simpson, BA
Promotes interest in urban affairs in all sections of the community with special reference to the city of Canterbury. Exhibitions, study base, resources for schools, students and general public

Chartwell, Westerham; Tel (01732) 866368; *The Administrator* Jean Broome
National Trust

Chiddingstone Castle, Nr Edenbridge; Tel (01892) 870347; *Managing Trustee* M.R. Eldridge
'Gothic' castle with fine collection furniture, Japanese swords and lacquer, Egyptian antiques, and Royal Stuart memorabilia for enjoyment/instruction of scholars
Denys Eyre Bower Bequest

Cobham Hall, Cobham, Nr Gravesend, Kent DA12 3BL; Tel (01474) 824319/823371; Fax (01474) 822995; *Development Director* Sue Anderson
Elizabethan and 16th century mansion, conference and letting

Museum of Kent Life-Cobtree Lock La, Sandling, Maidstone ME14 3AU; Tel (01622) 763936; *Director* Nigel Chew
Shows the history of the Kent countryside through displays in farm buildings and outside 'live' exhibits including hop garden

The Outreach Collection, KCC, Arts and Libraries, Kings Hill, West Malling, Kent ME19 6QG; Tel (01622) 605226; *Outreach Manager* P.R. Divall
A rich and varied collection of original objects with some high quality models, specimens and replicas. Loan service to KCC schools, Independent schools, libraries, museums and businesses. Catalogue available. Chargeable service

Darwin Museum, Down Hse, Luxted Rd, Downe, Orpington BR6 7JT; Tel (01689) 859119; *Curator* Solene Morris
Prior booking for parties requested. Closed Mon, Tues, and Feb and Mid-Dec to 2 Jan

Deal Castle, Deal; Tel (01304) 372762
English Heritage

Dickens House Museum, Victoria Parade, Broadstairs; Tel (01843) 862853; *Honorary Curator* J. Smith
General talk on house and its associations. Advance booking necessaru
Thanet District Council

Dover Castle: Hellfire Corner, Dover CT16 1HU; Tel (01304) 201628
Military fortress 'key to England'. Norman Keep, Roman Lighthouse (Pharos), saxon Church, Georgian and Victorian Earth Works. Free admission to pre-booked school parties
English Heritage

Dover Museum, Market Sq, Dover CT16 1PB; Tel (01304) 201066; *Education Officer* K. Norton
Dover Distict Council

Dover Roman Painted House, New St, Dover CT17 9AJ; Tel (01304) 203279; *Manager* B.J. Philp
Guided tours by arrangement
Dover Roman Painted House Trust

Ellen Terry Memorial Museum, Smallhythe Pl, Smallhythe, Tenterden TN30 7NG; Tel (01580) 762334 (National Trust); *Custodian* M. Weare
The National Trust
Dame Ellen's home for the last 28 years of her life. Contains collection of theatrical costumes and memorabilia. Open Apr–Oct every day 2–6, except Thurs and Fri. Theatrical history of the last 150 years. Small parties (15 children with 2 teachers). Pre-booking essential. Barn Theatre open most days

Emmetts Garden, Ide Hill, Nr Westerham, Kent; Tel (0173 275) 367 or 429; *The Head Gardener*

Eurotunnel Exhibition Centre, St Martin's Plain, Folkestone, Kent CT19 4QD; Tel (01303) 270111
The award-winning Eurotunnel Exhibition Centre in Folkestone, Kent, provides education for all the family. Since opening in September 1988, the Centre has become a top tourist attraction. The Centre has many special features including a 32m long N-gauge model railway, 5m floor to ceiling illuminated map illustrating road and rail routes, 21m observation tower overlooking the Folkestone Terminal Site as well as a French-style café and a souvenir gift shop

Finchcocks, Living Museum of Music, Goudhurst TN17 1HH; Tel (01580) 211702; Fax (01580) 211007; *Director* Richard Burnett; *Director* Katrina Burnett
18th century house, collection of historical keyboard instruments majority restored to playing condition. Educational programme Apr–Oct for primary to A-level students, concerts, courses and workshops with opportunity to play the instruments

Fleur de Lis Heritage Centre and Museum, Preston St, Faversham ME13 8NS; Tel (01795) 534542; *Honorary Director* A.J. Percival, MBE, BA, DLitt, FSA
The Faversham Society

Folkestone Museum and Arts Room, 2 Grace Hill, Folkestone CT20 1HD; Tel (01303) 850123; Fax (01303) 242907; *Heritage Officer*
Natural history, paintings, local materials
Kent County Council Arts and Libraries (Heritage)

The Friars, Aylesford, Maidstone ME20 7BX; Tel (01622) 717272; *Day Group Visits* Clare Abbotson
13th Century Priory, home of Community of Carmelite Friars as well as Retreat House, Conference Centre and Guest House. All facilities available for day or residential groups, tours by arrangement. Also on site, working pottery, gift and book shop and tea rooms. Open dawn to dusk. No admission charge. Daily Mass at noon

Godinton Park, Godinton Hse, Godinton Pk, Ashford TN23 3BW; Tel (01233) 620773; A. Wyndham-Green

Great Maytham Hall, Rolvenden TN17 4NE; Tel (01580) 241346; *Administrator* D. Bond
Historic hall and grounds
Country Houses Association

Hever Castle, Hever, Edenbridge TN8 7NG; Tel (01732) 865224; Fax (01732) 866796; *Sales and Publicity Officer* Claire Prout
13th Century moated castle, childhood home of Anne Boleyn. Free Schools info pack available. Free preparatory visits for Teachers Apr–Oct. Private tours for school groups available

The Historic Dockyard, Chatham ME4 4TE; Tel (01634) 812551; *Visitor Manager* V. Bunting; *Education Officer* J. Middleton
Georgian/Early Victorian dockyad, being developed as a living, working museum. Opportunities for cross-curricular work and potential in many subject areas for key stages 1–4 and beyond. For information contact the Education Officer

Howletts Wild Animal Park, Bekesbourne, Nr Canterbury, Kent CT4 5EL; Tel (01227) 721286; Fax (01227) 721853; *Education Officer* Terry Lee Cox
75 acres of parkland cares for world's largest colony of captive lowland gorillas. Education packs on National Curriculum of Science. New 1993: Interactive teaching boxes by some of the animal enclosures. New 1994: Animal Diet Booklet gives detailed information on diets of some of the animals cared for at the parks

Hythe Local History Room, Council Offices, Stade St, Hythe CT21 6BG; Tel (01303) 266152/3; Fax (01303) 262912; *Town Clerk*
Hythe Town Council

Ightham Mote, Ivy Hatch, Sevenoaks TN15 0NT; Tel (01732) 810378; *The Administrator* Carole Kenwright

Knole, Sevenoaks TN15 0RP; Tel (01732) 450608; *The Administrator*
National Trust

Leeds Castle, Maidstone ME17 1PL; Tel (01622) 765400; Fax (01622) 735616; *Managing Director* G. Jackson; *Contact* Sales and Reservations Office
Set on two islands in a lake. Castle dates from 857 AD
Attractions include a duckery, maze, grotto, aviary, dog collar museum, gardens and parkland. Educational packs available, free of charge to teachers. Open daily (except Christmas Day and prior to ticketed special events)
Leeds Castle Enterprises Ltd

Lullingstone Castle, Eynsford; Tel (01322) 862114; *Owner* Guy Hart Dyke
A modest Tudor estate still lived in and hosted by descendants of the original owners
Lullingstone Estates Ltd

Lympme Castle, Nr Hythe CT21 4LQ; Tel (01303) 267571; *Owner* Harry Margary
Gives children an insight into life in a medieval building

Maidstone Museum and Art Gallery, Saint Faith's St, Maidstone ME14 1LH; Tel (01622) 754497; *Museum and Heritage Manager* H.S. Middleton; *Education Officer* Rosamunde Bell
Maidstone Borough Council

Milton Chantry, Gravesend; Tel (01474) 321520; Keykeeper; Tel (01634) 842852
English Heritage

National Trust Regional Office, *Kent and E. Sussex*
Scotney Castle, Lamberhurst, Tunbridge Wells TN3 8JN; Tel (01892) 890651

The New College of Cobham, Cobham, Gavesend DA12 3BX; Tel (01474) 814280; *Clerk* Eric G. Gander
Medieval theological college, later renovated and restored to serve as almshouses and modern flats. Architectural features of interest; original college documents

Old Soar Manor, Old Soar, Nr Plaxtol; Tel 0171-973 3443 For booking form
English Heritage

Ospringe, Maison Dieu, Nr Faversham; Tel (01795) 533751
English Heritage

Penshurst Place and Gardens, Nr Tonbridge, Kent; Tel (01892) 870307; Fax (01892) 870866; *Operations Manager* Stephanie Ward

Port Lympne Wild Animal Park Mansion and Gardens, Lympne, Nr Hythe, Kent; Tel (01303) 264647; Fax (01303) 264944; *Education Officer* Terry Lee Cox; *Marketing/P.R.* Annabel Marriot
Education room with qualified educator for talks and slide presentations in historic mansion. 300 acres of parkland for conservation with 50 rare endangered species of animals, safari trailer. Restaurant, picnic areas. Education packs based on National Curriculum for Science. New 1994: Animal Diet Booklet gives detailed information on diets of some of the animals cared for at the parks

Powell-Cotton Museum, Quex Pk, Birchington CT7 0BH; Tel (01843) 842168; *Curator* Derek R. Howlett
Talks; films; colour slides; demonstrations; worksheets; African and Asian natural history, ethnography; local archaeology and antique firearms, cannon, Oriental Fine Arts. Advance booking essential

Quebec House, Quebec Sq, Westerham TN16 1TD; Tel (01959) 562206; *Custodian* Arthur Pratt
Exhibition about the Battle of Quebec, 1759, and the life of General Wolfe. House also contains Wolfe memorabilia. Open Apr to Oct. 2–6pm daily except Thurs and Sat
The National Trust

Richborough Castle, Nr Sandwich CT13 9JW; Tel (01304) 612013
English Heritage

Rochester Cathedral, Cathedral Education Centre, 70a High St, Rochester, Kent ME1 1JY; Tel (01634) 401301; Fax (01634) 401410; *Education and Visits Officer* Mary Hawes
A varied Education Programme for all ages, tailored to suit individual school needs. Activities include workshops on Monasticism, Pilgrimage and Calligraphy, Audio-visuals and Worksheets. Pre-booking is essential

Romney Hythe and Dymchurch Railway, New Romney TN28 8PL; Tel (01797) 362353; Fax (01797) 363591; *Information Officer* D. Smith
Workshops tours, model exhibition, free video hire, different journey to suit time and money

St Augustine's Abbey, Longport, Canterbury, Kent; Tel (01227) 767345
Opening hours: 1st April 1993 7 days a week 10.00am–6.00pm; 1st October 1993 10.00am–4.00pm, closed lunch 1.00–2.00pm
English Heritage

Saltwood Castle, Hythe CT21 4QU; Tel (01303) 267190; The Hon Jane Clark

Squerryes Court, Westerham; Tel (01959) 562345/563118; Fax (01959) 565949; *Owner* John Warde
All ages welcome

Swanton Water Mill, Lower Mersham, Ashford; Tel (01233) 223 and 0171-937 0931; G. Christiansen
Working mill, 3 acre garden

Temple Manor, Knight Rd, Strood ME2 2AH; *Key Keeper*
13th century manor house of the Knights Templars. Open by appointment only (Tel (0304) 211067)
English Heritage–Historic Buildings and Monuments Commission

Tenterden and District Museum, Station Rd, Tenterden, Kent; Tel (01580) 764310

Local history of Tenterden and the Weald of Kent; agricultural and hops; timber framed buildings construction; the Cinque Ports; Col Stephens Light Railway Museum; special terms for school parties by prior arrangement; worksheets available
For further details of services. Tel (0580) 764310

Time-Ball Tower, Victoria Parade, Deal CT14 7BP; Tel (013045) 360897; *Curator* C. Waterman
Dover District Council

Tunbridge Wells Museum and Art Gallery, Civic Centre, Mount Pleasant, Royal Tunbridge Wells, Kent TN1 1JN; Tel (01892) 547221/526121; *Curator* M.L.J. Rowlands, BSc, MSc, PhD
Tunbridge Wells Borough Council
Admission free; Open Mon–Sat, 9.30am–5.00pm; Closed Sundays, Bank Holidays and Easter Saturday; The Museum has displays of local history, Tunbridge ware, dolls, toys, bygones, archaeology, and natural history. In the Art Gallery there are regularly changing exhibitions including showings of the Ashton Bequest of Victorian oil paintings; Groups are asked to book their visits in advance; Parking nearby

Tyrwhitt Drake Museum of Carriages, Archbishop's Stables, Mill St, Maidstone; Tel (01622) 754497; *Museums and Heritage Manager* Henry Middleton; *Education Officer* Rosamunde Bell
One of the finest collection of horse-drawn carriages in Britain, housed in the medieval stables of the Archbishop's palace

Upnor Castle, Upnor; Tel (01634) 718742
English Heritage

Walmer Castle, Kingsdown Rd, Walmer, Deal, Kent CT14 7LJ; Tel (01304) 364288
Open summer daily from Good Friday to 30th Sept 10am–6pm. Winter from 1 Oct to Maundy Thursday 10am–4pm (closed 1–2pm), but closed throughout Jan, Feb and every Monday and Tuesday in Winter and when Lord Warden of Cinque Ports is in residence; Please phone in advance of visit
English Heritage

Whitbread Hop Farm, Beltring, Paddock Wood, Tonbridge TN12 6PY; Tel (01622) 872068; *General Manager* J. Todd
Educational awardwinner. Victorian oasthouses, Hop Story Exhibition, Shire horses, animals village, play area, resturant, picnics, nature trails, owl flying displays. Open all year round 10–6pm (Summer) 10–4pm (Winter)
Whitbread PLC

Wye College Museum of Agriculture, Wye, Ashford, Kent TN25 5AH; Tel (01233) 812401; *Honorary Curator* R.F. Farrar
(Limited Curator)
Please note Museum is sited at Brook, but has no postal address there

Lancashire

Astley Hall, Astley Pk, Chorley PR7 1NP; Tel (01257) 262166; *Cultural Officer* Dorothy M. Constantine
Guided tours and special projects for educational groups
Chorley Borough Council

Blackburn Museum and Art Gallery, Museum St, Blackburn BB1 7AJ; Tel (01254) 667130
Details of wide educational service on request including GCSE work
Blackburn Borough Council, Comunity and Leisure Service Department

Blackpool Tower, Promenade, Blackpool FY1 4BJ; Tel (01253) 22242; *Educational Co-ordinator* Julie Park
Comprehensive educational package catering for both key stages 1 and 2. Package includes, activity sessions, guided tours and workbooks. Subject area's covered are History, Geography, Science and Technology

Blackpool Zoo Park, East Park Dr, Blackpool FY3 8PP; Tel (01253) 765027; *Education Officer* J. Morson
Topics talks with slides and tactiles for primary, secondary and special schools and college students. Teachers' resource publications. Zoo Education Service geared to requirements of National Curriculum

Bolton Museum and Art Gallery (Educational Services), Le Mans Cres, Bolton; Tel (01204) 22311 Ext 2193; *Senior Keeper* David Edwards
Guided tours, talks and loan scheme

Browsholme Hall, Clitheroe BB7 3DE; Tel (01254) 826719; *Director* Diana Parker
Historic house built 1507, Parker family home. School tours based on Granada TV programme 'History Around You'. Juniors, 8 Plus

Council for the Protection of Rural England, Lancashire Branch The Derby Wing, Worden Hall, Leyland PR5 2DJ; Tel (01772) 456181; *Director* John Nairne
Visitor centre. Educational facilities, Theatre available for hire. Regular evening lectures. nature trail in 160 acres of parkland. Exhibitions

Gawthorpe Hall, Padiham, Nr Burnley; Tel (01282) 778511; Fax (01282) 772176
A National Trust property financed and administered by Lancashire County Council, County Museum Service; 17th century house with mid 19th century additions by Sir Charles Barry. Jacobean and Victorian furnishings. National portrait gallery collection of 17th century portraits. Victorian estate life display. Rachel Kay-Shuttleworth Collections of embroidery, lace, costume, etc. Private study available, reference library, courses, exhibitions
Brochures and information from the Principal Keeper

Grundy Art Gallery, Queen St, Blackpool FY1 1PX; Tel (01253) 751701; *Curator* Lynn Fade
Public Art Gallery with permanent collection, temporary art shows, music recitals in winter. Visits welcomed Mon–Sat. Booking preferred, disabled access. Specialist education sessions by arrangement
Blackpool Borough Council

Harris Museum and Art Gallery, Market Sq, Preston PR1 2PP; Tel (01772) 258248; *Museum and Art Officer* Alexandra Walker; *Education Officer (Social History)* Christopher Wyatt
Fine collections of art, decorative art and local history. New galleries of clothes and fashion and water colours, drawings and prints. Lively programme of contemporary art and social history exhibitions and events. Education service available . Quarterly newsletter. Rotunda cafe, shop, disabled access

Haworth Art Gallery, Haworth Pk, Manchester Rd, Accrington BB5 4JS; Tel (01254) 233782; *Curator* J.A. Rennie
Hyndburn Borough Council

Hoghton Tower, Nr Preston PR5 0SH; Tel (01254) 852986; Fax (01254) 852109; *Administrator* Vacancy
Hoghton Tower Preservation Trust

Judges' Lodgings Museum, Church St, Lancaster; Tel (01524) 32808/846315; *Enquiries* S. Sartin

Lancaster City Museums' Service Outreach/Education Dept, Market Sq, Lancaster LA1 1HT; Tel (01524) 64637; Fax (01524) 841692; *Outreach/Education Officer* Fiona O'Neill
Promoting a variety of cross-curricular services to all educational establishments. Located at the City, Maritime and Cottage Museums, Williamson Park, or outreaching to yourselves. Offering hands-on experience in Roman, Georgian, Maritime and Wildlife studies; amongst others. Providing educational consultation, and FREE previsits for schools

Lancaster City Museums, Market Sq, Lancaster LA1 1HT; Tel (01524) 64637; *Curator* Andrew J. White, MA, PhD, FMA, FSA
Provides a comprehensive museum service for North Lancashire and a source of advice on cultural, artistic and historical matters
Lancaster City Council

****Leighton Hall,*** Slackwood Farmhouse, Silverdale, Nr Carnforth LA5 0UF; *Education Officer* A. Oswald Slackwood Hse, Silverdale, Nr Carnforth LA5 0UF; Tel (01524) 701353
School visit programme May to September. Displays and lectures with trained birds of prey. Lectures at schools throughout the Winter. Guided hall tours

Lewis Textile Museum, Exchange St, Blackburn BB1 7JN; Tel (01254) 667130

Most machines are in working order and can be demonstrated to visiting parties by arrangement
Blackburn Borough Council, Community and Leisure Services Department

Meols Hall, Southport PR9 7LZ; Tel (01704) 28171; *Contact* Mrs Plunkett; Tel (01704) 214408
House open to public 15 July to 15 Aug incl. Contains Rossall collection of paintings, furniture, ornaments etc
Robert Fleetwood Hesketh

Metropolitan Wigan Schools' Centre at Wigan Pier, Wigan Pier WN3 4EU; Tel (01942) 323666 Ext 203; *Teacher-in-Charge* M.L. Sumner, BA
Provides an extensive education service for all ages and abilities. Researches and publishes material to the local area

Museum of the Manchesters, Town Hall, Market Pl, Ashton-under-Lyne; Tel 0161-344 3078; *Museum Officer*
A social and regimental history of the Manchester Regiment

Neville Blakey Museum of Locks, Keys and Safes, Burnley Rd, Brierfield, Nr Nelson BB9 5AD; Tel (01282) 63593/602493; *Chairman* W.N. Blakey; *Director* W.N.C. Blakey
Offers interested people the opportunity to see a collection of locks and safes dating from Roman times to the present day. Visits, strictly by appointment only

Pendle Heritage Centre, Park Hill, Barrowfield, Nelson BB9 6JQ; Tel (01282) 695366; *Director* E.M.J. Miller
Heritage education and interpretation

Portland Basin Industrial Heritage Centre, 1 Portland Pl, Portland St South, Ashton-under-Lyne, Tameside OL6 7SY; Tel 0161-308 3374; *Musuem Officer* Vacancy

Ribchester Roman Museum, Riverside, Ribchester, Preston PR3 3XS; Tel (01254) 878261
Educational services by arrangement
Ribchester Museum Trust

Rochdale Art Gallery, Esplanade Arts and Heritage Centre, Esplanade, Rochdale, Lancs OL16 1AQ; Tel (01706) 342154; *Art Gallery Officer* Penny Thompson
Rochdale has a lively exhibitions policy, showing contemporary and historical work, some from the permanent collection. International, Britsh and local artists. Refreshments available in café-bar. Events, workshops, gallery tours run alongside exhibitions

Rossendale Museum, Whitaker Pk, Rawenstall, Rossendale BB4 6RE; Tel (01706) 217777; *Curator* S. Cruise
School parties by arrangement; admission free
Rossendale Borough Council

Rufford Old Hall, Rufford, Nr Ormskirk L40 1SG; Tel (01704) 821254; *Administrator* M.A. Dodsworth
Resource pack
National Trust

Southport Aquarium, Marine Parade, Southport PR8 1SQ; Tel (01704) 532553; *Information Officer* Paul Molineux

Towneley Hall Art Gallery and Museums, Burnley BR11 3RQ; Tel (01282) 424213; *Curator* Susan Bourne, BA, FMA

Turton Tower, Chapeltown Rd, Bolton BL7 0HG; Tel (01204) 852203
Specialist talks and activities. Medieval tower house, woodland gardens, half-timbered wing and Victorian restoration, permanent collection of Lancashire Oak furniture, Civil War armour, exhibitions, contemporary crafts. Guided tours by appointment
Lancashire County Council Museum Service

Warrington Museum and Art Gallery, Bold St, Warrington, Cheshire WA1 1JG; Tel (01925) 442392; *Museum Education Officer* J.E. Hayes, BA, PGCE, AMA; *Assistant Education Officer* M. Draper, BA
School visits. Loan service. Holiday and extra-mural activities

The Wildfowl and Wetlands Trust, Martin Mere, Burscough, Ormskirk L40 0TA; Tel (01704) 895119; *Education Officer* Jackie Le Fevre
Activity-based learning programmes, discovery room, guided tours, lecture theatre, brass-rubbing, pond dipping, badge-making. Internationally important bird reserve and extensive wildfowl collection

Leicestershire

Ashby-de-la-Zouch Castle, Nr Derby; Tel (01503) 413343
English Heritage

Belgrave Hall, Church Rd, Off Thurcaston Rd, Leicester LE4 5PE; Tel (0116) 266 6590
Small Queen Anne County House 1709-13 with period room settings. Coaches and agricultural implements in stables. Outstanding period and botanic gardens, rock and water features. Educational facilitiies and workshops are offered – contact Jill Bourn: Tel: 0116-247 3201
Open Mon-Sat 10.00-17.30; Sun 14.00-17.30; 2 miles from City Centre off Loughborough Rd (A6). Admission is free

The Bell Foundry Museum, Freehold St, Loughborough LE11 1AR; Tel (01509) 233414; *Curator* Vacancy
Exhibits through exhibitions, foundry tours and permanent galleries all aspects of bellfounding, historically and contemporary. Special school tours. Closed Sunday and Monday (except Bank Holiday Mondays)

Bosworth Battlefield, Visitor Centre and County Park, Sutton Cheney, Nr Market Bosworth CV13 0AD; *The Warden* ; Tel (01455) 290429
Leicestershire CC

East Carlton Countryside Park and Heritage Centre, East Carlton, Nr Market Harborough LE16 8YD; Tel (01536) 770977; (01536) 402551 (Tourist Information); *Warden*
History of ironmaking in Corby area. The parkland contains many fine trees with dense woodland and open areas. The Wardens organise guided walks in the summer for the public and a variety of activities for school groups all year round. Other facilities include a classroom, group camping site, a cafe, craft workshops, blacksmith's shop and a picnic area. There are no changes and car-parking is free. Waymarked circular walks exist from the park. Toilets for handicapped

East Midland International Airport Visitor Centre, East Midlands Airport, Castle Donington, Derby DE7 2SA; Tel (01332) 810621 Ext 3361

Great Central Railway, Loughborough Central Station, Gt Central Rd, Loughborough LE11 1RW; Tel (01509) 230726; *Booking Office Manager* Richard Adcock
Fully operative steam railway through the Leicestershire countryside. Twenty-two locomotives, museum, signal boxes. Schools and parties welcome. Party discounts offered. Special Railway Education week in May, exclusively geared to needs of schools (accompanied tours, no discounts)

Guildhall, Guildhall La, Leicester; Tel (0116) 255 4100

Harborough Museum, Council Offices, Adam and Eve St, Market Harborough LE16 7LT; Tel (01858) 432468
Museum of the town of Market Harborough and the surrounding area. Displays from the Symington Collection of corsetry and of a local bootmakers workshop. Temporary exhibitions programme. Educational Facilities and wrokshops are offered – contact Jill Bourn; Tel 0116-247 3201
Open all year Mon-Sat 10.00-16.30; Sun 14.00-17.00; Centre of town above Council Offices, take A6 to Market Harborough. Admission is free

Jewry Wall Museum and Site, St Nicholas Circle, Leicester LE1 4LB; Tel (0116) 255 4100
The archaeology and history of Leicestershire to 1485 displayed in modern building. Site of Roman Baths and remains of massive 2nd Century Roman Jewry Wall. Educational facilities and workshops offered – contact Jill Bourn; Tel 0116-247 3201
Open all year Mon-Sat 10.00-17.30; Sun 14.00-17.30; on West side of City Centre, adjacent to Holiday inn. Admission is free

Kirby Muxloe Castle, Nr Leicester; Tel (0116) 238 6886
English Heritage

Leicestershire Museums and Art Gallery, New Walk, Leicester LE1 6TD; Tel (0116) 255 4100
Major regional Art Gallery with unique collection of 20th Century German Art especially Expressionism. Decorative arts, ceramics and silver collections natural history, geology and egyptology galleries. Temporary exhibitions programme. Educational facilities and workshops are offered – contact Jill Bourn; Tel 0116-247 3201
Open all year; Mon-Sat 10.00-17.30; Sun 14.00-17.30; Off Regent Rd, 5 minutes walk from British Rail Station. Admission is free

Leicestershire Record Office Long St, Wigston Magna, Leicester LE18 2AH; Tel (0116) 257 1080; Fax (0116) 257 1120

Lyddington Bede House, Nr Corby; Tel (01572) 822438
English Heritage

The Manor House, Donington-le-Heath, Nr Coalville, Leicester; Tel (01530) 831259
Fine Medieval Manor House of early 14th Century with later 16th–17th Century alterations. Restored and furnished as period house. Cafe in adjoining stone barn. Educational facilities and workshops are offered – contact Jill Bourn; Tel 0116-247 3201
Open from Weds prior to Easter to end Sept; Wed-Sun 13.00-18.00; also bank holiays (Mondays and Tuesdays) except May Day; South of Coalville, B505 to Hugglescote, take turn to Donington-le-Heath. Admission is free

Melton Carnegie Museum, Thorpe End, Melton Mowbray LE13 1RB; Tel (01664) 69946; *Keeper of Social History* ; Tel 0116-247 3222
Museum illustrating the historic and social life of the Borough of Melton. Sporting paintings, natural history and local exhibitions. Temporary exhibitions programme. Tourist Information Centre within building Open Easter to end of September: Mon-Fri 10.00-17.00; Sat 10.00-16.00; Sun 14.00-17.00; Centre of town at Thorpe End off Crossroads between A607 and B676. Admission is free

Museum of Royal Leicestershire Regiment, The Magazine, Oxford St, Leicester; Tel (0116) 255 5889
History of Royal Leicestershire Regiment (17th foot) housed in late 14th Century Newarke Gateway: regimental momentos, battle trophies and relics on display
Open all year: Mon-Sat 10.00-17.30; Sun 14.00-17.30; Ten minutes walk from City Centre between South Gates and A50. Admission is free

Museum of Technology, Abbey Pumping Station, Corporation Rd, Leicester LE4 5PX; Tel (0116) 266 1330; *Keeper of Science and Industry* Stuart Warburton
Educational facilities and workshops are offered – contact Dorothy Wood; Tel (01530) 510851
The Museum houses 4 Victorian beam engines, which were used to pump sewage up to the sewage treatment farm. Subject to refurbishment and redisplay on the theme of watre and the social issues surrounding its supply, use and disposal. Narrow gauge railway. Restored Victorian manager's house. Special events are held throughout the year including steam days. Funded by Leicestershire County Council Museum Service
Opening hours: Mon-Sat 10.00-17.30; Sun 14.00-17.30. Free admission except on special event days. 3 miles north of Leicester City Centre off A5131 Abbeys Lane, City Bus 54 from City Centre

Newarke Houses Museum, The Newarke, Leicester LE2 7BY; Tel (0116) 247 3222
Social history and crafts from 1485 to present day. Clocks and mechanical instrument 19th Century street scene and early 20th Century grocers shop. Quiet period garden. Temporary exhibition programme. Educational facilities and workshops are offered-contact Jill Bourn; Tel 0116-247 3201
Open all year: Mon-Sat 10.00-17.30; Sun 14.00-17.30; Ten minutes walk from City Centre and in the Castle Park area, A47 into Leicester. Admission is free

Rockingham Castle, Market Harborough LE16 8TH; Tel (01536) 770240; *Secretary* K. Barton; Cdr L.M.M. Saunders Watson
Represents many periods and facets of English domestic life dating from 11th century to present day, an education pack interprets these for teachers and pupils

Rutland County Museum, Catmos St, Oakham, Rutland LE15 6HW; Tel (01572) 723654; Fax (01572) 757576
School visits welcome by prior arrangement
Oakham Castle, Market Pl, Oakham. Enquiries to Rutland County Museum

Snibston Discovery Park, Ashby Rd, Coalville, Leics; Tel (01530) 510851; Fax (01530) 813301; *Education Officer* Dorothy Wood
100 acre science and industrial heritage development

Stanford Hall, Lutterworth LE17 6DH; Tel (01788) 860250; Fax (01788) 860870; Lt Col E.H.L. Aubrey-Fletcher
Stanford, mentioned in the Domesday Book, has been the home of the Cave family, ancestors of Lady Braye, since 1430. The present Hall was built by the Smiths of Warwick for Sir Roger Cave in the 1690s, when the old Manor House was pulled down, and is still occupied by the family. It contains antique furniture, fine pictures including the Stuart Collection, and family costumes; The beautiful 14th century Church has magnificent stained glass windows (removed for restoration but may return during 1995) from the time of Edward II and Henry VII, and exceptionally interesting family monuments and plaques. Visit the walled Rose Garden, the Souvenir Shop and Craft Centre (most Sundays); walk the Nature Trail; see a replica of Percy Pilcher's 1898 Flying Machine (Pilcher was killed flying at Stanford in 1899). Open Easter until end of September, Saturdays and Sundays; also Bank Holiday Mondays and Tuesdays following, 2.30–6pm (last admission 5.30pm). On Bank Holidays and Event Days open 12 noon (House 2.30pm). Open any day or evening during season for pre-booked parties; Tel: The Administrator, Rugby (01788) 860250. Admissions 1995; House and Grounds etc, Adult £3.20, Child £1.50; Reduced fees for parties; Grounds, Rose Garden, Flying Machine, Old Forge, Craft Centre (most Sundays), Adult £1.80, Child 70p (Admission prices subject to increase on some Event days); Parking free. Camping, Caravan, Motor and other rallies may be booked; Fishing tickets available mid-June to mid-March, Conferences and Company Incentive Days may be arranged; Cafeteria (self-service). Motorcycle Museum, the collection of motorcycles in the Stanford Museum has gained a worthy reputation for its quality. The Museum is a living one with constant changes of exhibits and it is organised so that even regular visitors may see something new; The collection of racing motorcycles is outstanding and attracts visitors from all over the world. The exhibits are lent by private owners, as are the splendid and rare photographs. Most exhibits are in running order and many are frequently used for rallies. Admission; Adult £1.00, Child 30p. School parties of 20 or more; Adult free, Child 20p

Twycross Zoo, Norton-Juxta-Twycross, Atherstone CV9 3PX; Tel (01827) 880250; *Education Officer* Denise Cox, BSc(Hons), PGCE; *Education Officer* Alan Bates, BA(Hons), PGCE
Comprehensive programme for schools

Wygston's House, Museum of Costume, Applegate, Leicester; Tel (0116) 247 3506
Important late medieval building housing costume and accessories from 1750 to present day. Reconstruction of drapers shop of 1920s. Outstanding collection of costumes and textiles. Temporary exhibitions programme. Educational facilities and workshops are offered – contact Jill Bourn; Tel 0116-247 3201
Open all year: Mon-Sat 10.00-17.30; Sun 14.00-17.30; Just off A47 near City Centre. 10 minutes walk from bus and rail stations. Admission is free

Lincolnshire

Ayscoughfee Hall, Museum and Gardens, Churchgate, Spalding PE11 2RA; Tel (01775) 725468;

Museum Curator and Tourist Information Officer Susanna Davis
Providing a museum service for the South Holland district in beautiful old house in gardens with famous yew walks

Belton House, Nr Grantham NG32 2LS; Tel (01476) 66116; *Property Manager* D. Bowen
The National Trust

Belvoir Castle, Estate Office, Belvoir Castle, Grantham, Lincs NG32 1PD; Tel (01476) 870262; *Controller* Richard Fenn
The home of the Duke and Duchess of Rutland. Special school facilities, including guided tours, school packs, nature trail and adventure play area

Burgh-Le-Marsh Windmill, Nr Skegness; Tel (01522) 552222; *Honorary Treasurer* F. Skelton 18 Orby Rd, Burgh-le-Marsh, Skegness, Lincs; Tel (01754) 810609
Guided tours available for school parties with volunteer guides
Lincolnshire County Council, Recreational Services

Burghley House, Stamford, Leics; Tel (01780) 52451; *Manager* J. Culverhouse
Burghley House Preservation Trust Ltd

Church Farm Museum, Church Rd South, Skegness PE25 2HF; Tel (01754) 766658; *Curator* P.R. Cousins
Educational guide available. Programme of educational activities i.e. Food and Farming; Woolly days, Victorian, Tastes and Traditions, Steam Threshing. Large open-air site, refreshments, coach park
Lincolnshire County Council Recreational Services

City and County Museum, Broadgate, Lincoln; Tel (01522) 530401; *Keeper* A.B. Page
Archaeology of Lincolshire. Teachers' Roman pack work sheets and handling session. Visit to underground Roman gateway. Medieval teachers' pack, worksheets with handling session. School parties welcome
Lincolnshire County Council Recreational Services

Doddington Hall, Doddington, Lincoln LN6 4RU; Tel (01522) 694308; *The Secretary* ; Tel (01522) 694308
Sandford Award for Heritage Education 1976 and 1987

****Gainsborough Old Hall,*** Parnell St, Gainsborough DN21 2NB; Tel (01427) 612669; *Curator* H.A. Cummins
Unspoiled medieval manor house open to the public all year. Children's worksheets available, temporary exhibitions, special activities for children
Sandford Award for education work
Lincolnshire County Council Recreational Services

Grantham Museum, St Peter's Hill, Grantham NG31 6PY; Tel (01476) 68783; *Museum Assistant* Linda M. Carlisle
Displays on history, archaeology, industrial and military history of Grantham region. Special feature on Isaac Newton and Margaret Thatcher. Temporary exhibition programme. School loan kits, teacher packs, workshops and museum tours
Lincolnshire County Council, Recreational Services

Grimsthorpe and Drummond Castle, Grimsthorpe Estate Office, Nr Bourne PE10 0NB; Tel (01778) 591205; *House and Park Manager* Michael Tebbutt
Guided visits for schools to historic house, various important natural habitats and annual demonstration of the Estate at work
Grimsthorpe and Drummond Castle Trust Ltd

Lincoln: Bishops Palace English Heritage

Lincoln Castle, Castle Hill, Lincoln LN1 3AA; Tel (01522) 511068; Fax (01522) 526431
Historic site with guided tours, education programme, information and special events during the summer. Open Mon to Sat 9.30am–5.30pm (4pm winter); Sun 11.00am–5.30pm (4pm winter)
Lincolnshire County Council

Lincolnshire Recreational Services Museums, County Offices, Newland, Lincoln LN1 1YL; Tel (01522) 552821; *Director* G.N. Keighley

Mablethorpe Animal Gardens, North End, Mablethorpe LN12 1QG; Tel (01507) 473346; *Curator* Paul King

Museum of Lincolnshire Life, Burton Rd, Lincoln; Tel (01522) 528448; *Keeper* P.R. Cousins
Teachers' and pupil's notes, children's activity sheets and school loan kits available, special demonstration and activity days for schools. Please contact for further details
Lincolnshire County Council Recreational Services

Sibsey Trader Windmill, Nr Boston; Tel (01246) 823349
Only open on special milling days
English Heritage

Skegness Natureland, Seal Sanctuary, North parade, Skegness PE25 1DB; Tel (01754) 764345; *Information Officer* J.K.B. Yeadon

Stamford Museum, Broad St, Stamford PE9 1PJ; Tel (01780) 66317; Fax (01780) 480363; *Curator* J.F. Smith, BA, FSA
School parties welcome. Museum staff can visit schools and lead National Curriculum geared specialist tours round the historic town of Stamford. Fee payable for this. School loans and resource packs also available. Lincolnshire County Council schools admitted free to museum. Others, 25p per chld
Lincolnshire County Council Recreational Services

Stamford Steam Museum, All Saints St, Stamford PE9 2PA; Tel (01780) 52816; *Contact* B.M. Galvin
Victorian brewery museum with sound effects

Tattershall Castle, Tattershall, Lincoln LN4 4LR; Tel (01526) 342543; *Custodian* C. Watson
Young persons' guide book
National Trust

Usher Gallery, Lindum Rd, Lincoln LN2 1NN; Tel (01522) 527980; *Assistant Curator* J. Robinson; *Assistant Curator* R. Thomas
Fine and decorative art collections, costume and textiles, plus c 10 exhibitions per annum. Workshops, demonstrations, storytelling, artist-in-residence schemes. Guided tours and study visits by arrangement. Teacher study days, National Curriculum school sessions with Freelance Education Workers available January 1995. Activity sheets. Provision for special needs. Cafe now open
Lincolnshire County Council Recreational Services

London

Apsley House, The Wellington Museum, 149 Piccadilly, Hyde Park Corner, London W1V 9FA; Tel 0171-499 5676; Fax 0171-493 6576
Open Tues to Sunday 11.00–17.00. Free guided tours and admission for pre-booked school and college parties. Closed for maintenance until early 1995

Baden-Powell House, The Scout Association, Baden-Powell Hse, Queen's Gate SW7 5JS; Tel 0171-584 7031; Fax 0171-589 9951; *Manager* W.J. MacKinnon

The Banqueting House, Whitehall, London SW1; Tel 0171-930 4179
Free admission to school parties. Advance booking necessary; Teacher's pack and a 17th century trail (which includes the Banqueting House) available by mail order also occasional on-site tuition; write to Office Manager, The Banqueting Hse, London SW1 2ER

Battersea Park Children's Zoo, Near Pagoda, Battersea Pk, Battersea, London SW11 4NJ; Tel 0181-871 6540 or 0181-871 7530
Wandsworth Borough Council

The Baylis Programme, English National Opera, London Coliseum, St Martin's La, London WC2N 4ES; Tel 0171-836 01111 Ext 354; Fax 0171-379 5530; *Co-Director* Rebecca Meitlis; *Co-Director* David Sulkin; *Administrator* Natalie Sinnadurai
Through creative work and particpation in workshops, young people are encouraged to directly experience the medium of opera, links with schools encouraged
Two youth opera groups 1) Liveculture for 14–25 years; 2) Livewires for 8–14 years

The Bethnal Green Museum of Childhood, Cambridge Heath Rd, London E2 9PA; Tel 0181- 980 2415 (Recorded message)/081-980 3204/4315 and 0181-981 1711; Fax 0181-980 4759; *Education Officer* Peter Kinsey
Service to schools and colleges

Weekend and holiday activities. Teachers' information pack available
Bexley Museum, Hall Pl, Bourne Rd, Bexley, Kent DA5 1PQ; Tel (01322) 526574; Fax (01322) 522921; *Curator* Jessica Vale, BA, AMA
Opens 10 am to 5 pm (Mon–Sat) (to 4.15 pm in winter), 2 pm to 6 pm Sundays (in British Summer Time)
London Borough of Bexley
British Film Institute Education Department, 21 Stephen St, London W1P 1PL; Tel 0171-255 1444; *Head of Education* Cary Bazalgette
Offers advice and materials for media education; also organises conferences and training sessions
British Library, Gt Russell St WC1B 3DG; Tel 0171-412 7783; Fax 0171-412 7508; *Head of Education* Karen Brookfield
Gallery talks and lectures offered; information sheets and reading lists; audio visual programmes. Exhibitions of Western and Oriental manuscripts and printed books on a wide range of subjects. School parties and educational groups welcomed. Information and advice to teachers
The British Library National Sound Archive, 29 Exhibition Rd, London SW7 2AS; Tel 0171-589 6603; Fax 0171-823 8970; *Director* Dr C.H. Roads
Comprehensive collection of sound recordings in all subject areas
British Museum, Gt Russell St, London WC1B 3DG; Tel 0171-323 8511/8854
Information and advice for teachers (including teacher packs), talks, videos and films, teachers' courses, study days for fifth and sixth formers, holiday events for children
Cabinet War Rooms, Clive Steps, King Charles St, London SW1A 2AQ; Tel 0171-930 6961; Fax 0171-839 5897; *Curator* Phil Reed; *Education Officer* Liz Newton
The underground emergency accommodation used to protect Winston Churchill and the British Government during the Second World War. Free personal sound guides. Education programme offers a choice of illustrated talks and project sheets
Carlyle's House, 24 Cheyne Row, Chelsea, London SW3 5HL; Tel 0171-352 7087; *Curator* G.A. Elwes
National Trust
Chapter House, Pyx Chamber and Abbey Museum, East Cloisters, Westminster Abbey, London SW1; Tel 0171-222 5897
English Heritage
Chiswick House, Burlington La, Chiswick, London W4 2RP; Tel 0181-995 0508
English Heritage
Church Farmhouse Museum, Greyhound Hill, Hendon NW4 4JR; Tel 0181-203 0130; *Curator* Gerrard Roots, MA
17th century farmhouse with period furnished kitchen and dining room, exhibitions on local and social history and the decorative arts
London Borough of Barnet Library Services
Commonwealth Institute, Kensington High St W8 6NQ; Tel 0171-603 4535; *Education Centre Teacher* Peter Johnston
Exhibts from over 40 commonwealth countries. Educational programmes for school groups of all ages on and off the site. Conferences and courses for adults
Courtauld Institute Galleries, Somerset Hse, Strand WC2R 0RN; *Director* John Murdoch; *Curator* William Bradford; *Education Officer* Julia Weiner
Princes Gate and Gambier-Parry collections of old master paintings, Samuel Courtauld collection of Impressionist and post-Impressionist paintings. Alastair Hunter collection of 20th Century Masters, Lee and Fry collections. Workshops and guided visits for school groups
MCC Museum, Lord's Cricket Ground, London NW8 8QN; Tel 0171-289 1611; *Curator* Stephen Green
School parties should contact Nick Stewart, Gestetner Tour of Lords, Tel 071-266 3825. Library, paintings, cricketana. Conducted tours arranged
Marylebone Cricket Club
Crystal Palace Park Zoo, Thicket Rd, London SE20 8DT; Tel 0181-778 4487; *Zoo Supervisor* Josephine Hamilton
Cuming Museum, 155–157 Walworth Rd, London SE17 1RS; Tel 0171-701 1342; *Keeper* Caroline Ellis, BA, AMA
The Museum of Southwark's History
The Dickens House Museum, 48 Doughty St, London WC1N 2LF; Tel 0171-405 2127; *Curator* Dr D. Parker
School parties welcome; lectures
Dulwich Picture Gallery, College Rd SE21 7AD; Tel 0181-693 5254; Fax 0181-693 0923; *Head of Education* Gillian Wolfe Advisory Teacher of Southwark
Aims to establish and maintain good relations with schools, by means of talks, practical artwork sessions, concerts, outreach work etc
Enfield, Forty Hall Museum, Forty Hill, Enfield, Middx EN2 9HA; Tel 0181-363 8196; Fax 0181-367 9098; *Museum Officer* J.W. Griffin, BA, AMA; *Taeching Loan Organiser* Anne Orton; Tel 0181-363 8196/4046; Fax 0181-367 9098
Erith Museum, Erith Library, Walnut Tree Rd, Erith, Kent DA8 1RS; Tel (01322) 336582; *Curator* Jessica Vale, BA, AMA
Open Mon, Wed 2.15–5.15pm; Sat 2.15–5pm
London Borough of Bexley
Fenton House, Windmill Hill, Hampsted NW3 6RT; Tel 0171-435 3471; *Administrator* Joy Ashby
Caters particularly for musicians
National Trust
Geffrye Museum, Kingsland Rd E2 8EA; Tel 0171-739 9893; Fax 0171-729 5647; *Keeper of Museum Education* Victoria Woollard, BEd, AMA
Displays period rooms of the British Middle Classes from 1600–1950s. School parties taught during term time by arrangement with museum; leisure activities during all major holidays and Saturdays
The Geological Museum, *see The Natural History Museum*
Goldsmiths' Company, Foster La EC2V 6BN; Tel 0171-606 7010; Fax 0171-606 1511; *Clerk* R.D. Buchanan-Dunlop
The Worshipful Company of Goldsmiths
The Grange Museum, Neasden La, London NW10 1QB; Tel 0181-9087432; *Curator* Finbarr Whooley; *Education Officer* Joy Price
The Grange is the community history museum and local history library for the London Borough of Brent. Victorian parlour. Edwardian draper's shop, 1930s room and displays of local history
Greenwich Borough Museum, 232 Plumstead High St SE18 1JT; Tel 0181-855 3240; Fax 0181-316 5754; *Curator* Bernadette Gillow; *Assistant Curator, (Education)* Beverley Burford; *Assistant Curator, (Collections)* Christopher Foord
Local History Museum for the London Borough of Greenwich. Displays on archaeology, social history, wildlife. Temporary exhibitions, schools service. Saturday club, sales point
Guinness World of Records Exhibition, Trocadero, Piccadilly Circus W1V 7FD; Tel 0171-439 7331; Fax 0171-494 1266; *Contact* Elena Busuttil; *Contact* Mike Tickner
Thousands of staggering facts, feats to delight and amaze. Bought to life by audio-visual computer technology
Gunnersbury Park Museum, Gunnersbury Pk W3 8LQ; Tel 0181-992 1612; Fax 0181-752 0686; *Curator* S. Levitt
Collections include local history, archaeology, transport, social, domestic and industrial history and new costume gallery. Education programmes available for school groups. Contact Sue McAlpine, The Interpretive Officer, 081-992 2247
London Boroughs of Hounslow and Ealing
HMS Belfast, Morgan's La, Tooley St, London SE1 2JH; Tel 0171-407 6434; *Education Officer* Sarah Hogben
Europe's largest preserved WWII warship with seven decks to explore. Moored opposite the Tower of London. Films, talks and quiz trails available, weekdays

only, when booked in advance. Open 7 days a week from 10.00 am
HMS Belfast

Ham House, Nr Richmond, Surrey TW10 7RS; Tel 0181-940 1950; *Administrator* R. Pritchard
The National Trust

Hampton Court Palace, Historic Royal Palaces Agency, East Molesey, Surrey KT8 9AU; Tel 0181-781 9750
Free admission to pre-booked school parties (except May, June, July and Aug). Write to Group Sales Co-ordinator, Hampton Court Palace, or the Educational Services Manager for advice on planning a visit and resource material. Special lower rate admission charges are available to schools who make advance bookings

The Heritage Motor Centre, Banbury Rd, Gaydon, Warks; Tel (01926) 641188; Fax (01926) 641555; *Academic Services Manager* Trevor Lord
Open all year 7 days a week except Christmas and Boxing Day. Display of exhibits is arranged with particular attention to educational requirements of all age groups. Special facilities include video/film viewing, lecture theatres and classrooms. Free preliminary visits for teachers to meet the Education Staff

Hogarth's House, Hogarth La, Great West Rd, London W4 2QN; Tel 0181-994 6757; *Custodian* L.J. Channer
London Borough of Hounslow

Horniman Museum and Gardens, 100 London Rd, Forest Hill SE23 3PQ; Tel 0181-699 2339/1872; Fax 0181-291 5506; *Keeper (Educational Services)* Dr Elizabeth Goodhew, MBE; *Assistant Keeper (Educational Services)* Vivien Golding; *Education Officer* David Judd; *Art and Craft Teacher* Karen Mears; *Pottery Teacher* Carole Dickens; *Education Services Assistant* Modupe Lawanson; *Education Services Assistant* Risikat Odumboni
Talks for all levels. Adult education courses, holiday activities, children's and family workshops Saturday and school holidays

Imperial War Museum, Lambeth Rd SE1 6HZ; Tel 0171-416 5000; *Education Officer* Anita Ballin
Talks, study sessions, films for NC Key Stages 2 and 3 and for GCSE, worksheets and special 6th form events for school and college groups, age-range 9–18 years

Innovation Service, The Design Council, 28 Haymarket, London SW1Y 4SU; Tel 0171-839 8000; *Manager, Innovation NoticeBoard* Susan Cottam
Includes Innovation NoticeBoard, a scheme to link innovators to companies wishing to licence new product innovations. The associated Product Development Advisory Service advises on intellectual property and raising finance for design projects

International Shakespeare Globe Centre and Shakespeare Globe Museum (ISGC), Bear Gdns, Bankside SE1 9EB; Tel 0171-620 01202 (ISGC); 0171-928 6342 (Museum); *Director, Globe Education* Patrick Spottiswoode
Reconstruction of Shakespeare's Globe Theatre on Bankside as focal point of educational complex. ISGC operates Shakespeare Globe Museum, an exhibition of the Shakespearian stage, and London life in the time of Shakespeare. Selection of workshops and lectures to students of all ages

Iveagh Bequest, Kenwood, Hampstead La NW3 7JR; Tel 0181-348 1286
English Heritage

Jewel Tower, Westmister; Tel 0171-222 2219
English Heritage

The Jewish Museum, Woburn Hse, Tavistock Sq WC1H 0EP; Tel 0171-388 4525
Jewish Festivals and history illustrated by attractive ceremonial objects. Two audio-visual programmes of Jusaism. Worksheets for primary and secondary students. School groups welcome by appointment

Dr Johnson's Memorial House, 17 Gough Sq EC4A 3DE; Tel 0171-353 3745; *Curator* Betty Gathergood
18th century house with Johnson relics, prints, furniture, letters. Open all year, closed Suns and Bank Holidays. Admission Charged

Keats House, Wentworth Pl, Keats' Gr, Hampstead, London NW3 2RR; Tel 0171-435 2062; Fax 0171-431 9293; *Curator* C.M. Gee
Home of John Keats, poet. relics of Keats and his circle. Guided tours by appointment
London Borough of Camden

Kensington Palace, State Appartments and Court Dress Collections, Historic Royal Palaces Eduaction Service, Hampton Court Palace, East Molesey, Surrey KT8 9AU; Tel 0181-977 7222
Free admission to school parties; advance booking necessary; write to The Schools' Booking Office, State Apartments, Kensington Palace, London W8 4PX. Education pack available
Department of National Heritage
Historical Royal Palaces Agency

Kenwood, The Iveagh Bequest, Hampstead La NW3 7JR; Tel 0732 778000
English Heritage

Kew Bridge Steam Museum, Green Dragon La, Brentford upon Thames, Middx TW8 0EN; Tel 0181-452 8567 Education Service and Answerphone; Tel 0181-568 4757 Museum Information Desk; *Museum Education Officer* Derek Gooding

Kew Palace and Queen's Cottage, Kew Gdns, Richmond, Surrey; Tel 0181-940 3321
Reduced rate admission to school parties; advance booking necessary; write to Historic Royal Palaces Education Service, Apartment 44, Hampton Court Palace, East Molesey, Surrey KT8 9AU
Department of the Environment

Kingston upon Thames, Kingston Museum and Heritage Service, North Kingston Centre, Richmond Rd, Kingston upon Thames, Surrey KT2 5PE; Tel 0181-547 6755; Fax 0181-547 6747; *Curator (Education and Outreach)* R. Statham
Kingston Museum will reopen in February 1994. New educational services are planned, and a Teachers' Pack is being prepared

Leighton House Museum, 12 Holland Pk Rd W14 9LZ; Tel 0171-602 3316; *Curator* Julia Findlater
High Victorian art collection including painting, sculpting, drawing by Lord Leighton, Millais, Burne Jones. Also collection of Islamic tiles

Linley Sambourne House, 18 Stafford Terr, London W8; *Administrator* S. Ayres
Late 19th century house with original decoration, furnishing and pictures. Open 1 Mar–31 Oct, Weds, 10–4pm and Suns 2–5pm, groups of 20 or more at other times by prior arrangement (fee for opening). No more than 10 children in each group when house is open to the public
The Victorian Society; Tel 0181-994 1019 and 0181-742 3438 (Ansaphone)

London Borough of Greenwich, 'Woodlands', 90 Mycenae Rd, Blackheath SE3 7SE; Tel 0181-858 4631; *Local History Librarian* Julian Watson
Local History Library (Archives, Photographs, Prints, Maps, Census and Newspapers, Miscrofilm)
Visits to schools by Education Officer, visits to 'Woodlands', consultation with environmental projects

The London Butterfly House, Syon Pk, Brentford, Middx TW8 8JF; Tel 0181-560 0378; *Contact* T. Maynard
Stroll among many hundreds of free-flying butterflies in tropical greenhouse gardens. Additional exhibition of British butterflies May to Sept. Plus all-year round exhibitions of other insects, as well as spiders, scorpions, frogs, snakes and lizards. Educational packs and work-sheets available on request

London Planetarium, Marylebone Rd, London NW1 5LR; Tel 0171-486 1121; *Administration* Undine Concannon
School talks 'Earth's Place in the Universe' at 11am weekdays mornings, and regular starshows throughout the day from 12.20–5.00pm. Open every day except Christmas Day. Closed for major refurbishment Jan-May 1995

London Toy and Model Museum, 21–23 Craven Hill, London W2 3EN; Tel 0171-706 8000; Fax 0171-706 1993
Collection of commercially made toys and models, displayed in recently refurbished themed galleries and

garden with operating ride-on and model trains, antique roundabout. Inter-active displays and hands-on sessions for children. Admission charge

London Transport Museum, Covent Garden WC2E 7BB; Tel 0171-379 6344; Fax 0171-836 4118; *Education Officer* Stephen Allen
Special workshops. Activity sheets and education pack available. Holiday activities, Public lectures. Special rates for school groups

London Zoo, Zoological Society of London, Regent's Pk, London NW1 4RY; Tel 0171-722 3333 Ext 551; *Senior Education Officer* Claire Robinson, BEd(Hons)
We offer a wide ranging education programme linked to the National Curriculum for Reception to A-level

Madame Tussaud's, Marylebone Rd, London NW1 5LR; Tel 0171-935 6861
Group Booking Office; New teachers' pack-with worksheets. Schools' discount. Open every day except Xmas Day

Marble Mill House, Richmond Rd, Twickenham, Middx TW1 2NL; Tel 0732 778000
English Heritage

Maritime Trust, 2 Greenwich Church St SE10 9BG; Tel 0181-858 2698; *Contact* The Master
Preserves traditional vessels around the UK including the ship Cutty Sark lying in dry dock at King William Walk, Greenwich SE10 9HT; Tel 0181-858 3445. Famous as the only British built tea and wool clipper in existance. There is a permanent exhibition of figure heads on board and an audio visual display of the history of the ship
Cutty Sark

Markfield Beam Engine and Museum, Markfield Rd, South Tottenham N15 4RB; Tel 0181-800 7061; *Technical Director* A.J. Spackman, MSc, DIC, CEng; Tel (01763) 287331
1886 beam engine. Steam operated by arrangement. Small exhibition, role of pumping engine in public health engineering. Admission charge. Entrance in Crowland Rd. Open second Sunday in Month April to November incl. Other times by appointment

Museum of Artillery, Rotunda, Repository Rd, Woolwich SE18; Tel 0181-316 5402; *Curator* S.C. Walter
Royal Artillery Institution

Museum of Instruments, Royal College of Music, Prince Consort Rd SW7 2BS; Tel 0171-589 3643 Ext 346; *Curator* E.P. Wells
Musical instruments, wind, stringed and keyboard, from 16th–20th centuries. Open Wed in term-time, 2–4.30 (subject to review); party visits by appointment. Admission charge

Museum of London, London Wall, London EC2Y 5HN; Tel 0171-600 3699; *Head of Interpretation* Jane Bywaters, MSc
Prior booking essential

Museum of Mankind (Ethnography Dept of the British Musem), Burlington Gdns W1X 2EX; *Education Officer* B. Burt
A series of changing exhibitions illustrating the variety of non-Western societies and cultures. Its collections come from the indigenous peoples of Africa, Australia and the Pacific Islands, North and South America and parts of Asia and Europe, and include some ancient as well as recent and contemporart cultures. Enquiries and bookings should be made at the Information Desk 0171-323 8043

Museum of the Moving Image, South Bank Arts Centre, Waterloo SE1; Tel 0171-928 3535 (Admin) or 0171-928 3232 (Box Office); *Museum Curator* Leslie Hardcastle, OBE
The story of the development of the moving images of film and television from both a creative and technical point of view

Museum of the Order of St John, St John's Gate, St John's La, Clerkenwell, London EC1M 4DA; Tel 0171-253 6644; Fax 0171-490 8835; *Curator* Pamela Willis; *Deputy Curator* Francesca Alden; *Assistant Curator* Caroline Townend; *Assistant Curator* Piers De Salis
Collection of items relating to the history of the Order and St John Ambulance. Open Mon–Fri, 10am–5pm; Sat, 10am–4pm. Guided tours of St John's Gate and Priory Church, including 12th century crypt, Tues, Fri, Sat at 11am and 2.30pm. Large groups/school visits by arrangement

Museum of the Royal Pharmaceutical Society of Great Britain, 1 Lambeth High St SE1 7JN; Tel 0171-735 9141 Ext 354
Displays reflect the history of British pharmacy and the pharmacist's profession with emphasis on retail, storage and dispensing equipment.

Musical Museum, 368 High St, Brentford, Middx TW8 0BD; Tel 0181-560 8108
A large working collection of automatic musical instruments from small musical boxes to orchestrations and a mighty Wurlitzer theatre organ. Explained and demonstrated between April and October. Sat–Sun, 2–5pm, with additional days in July and August. Party visits at other times by arrangement
The Musical Museum Charitable Trust

National Army Museum, Royal Hospital Rd, London SW3 4HT; Tel 0171-730 0717; Fax 0171-823 6573; *Education Department*; Tel Ext 2228
Illustrated talks for all levels with accompanying handling sessions of period uniforms, weapons, artefacts and documents. Activity sheets, National Curriculum and GCSE study sessions. Facsimile documents and reading lists. Academic lectures (sixth forms and colleges). Summer holiday activities. gallery trails. All free

National Film and Television Archive, 21 Stephen St W1P 1PL; Tel 0171-255 1444; Fax 0171-580 7503; *Curator* Clyde Jeavons; *Cataloguing and other Enquiries*; Tel 0171-255 1444 Ext 319 or direct line: 0171-957 8971
Aims to select, acquire, preserve, document and make permanently available for research and study a national collection of films and TV programmes

National Gallery, Trafalgar Sq, London WC2N 5DN; Tel 0171-389 3321; Fax 0171-930 1681; *Education Officer* Anthea Peppin; *Education Officer* Ailsa Turner; Tel 0171-389 1744 Education Dept Direct Line
Free talks, tours, quizzes and audio-visual programmes for educational groups. Lunch room facilities available. Booking essential

National Maritime Museum, Greenwich SE10 9NF; Tel 0181-858 4422
Gallery teaching, films, planetarium sessions and resource packs; professional development days, programmes for special needs students. Open throughout the year

National Monuments Record *See also* Royal Commission on the Historical Monuments of England
National Monuments Record Centre, Kemble Dr, Swindon SN2 2GZ; Tel (01793) 414600; Fax (01793) 414606; *Secretary* T.G. Hassall, MA, FSA, MIFA; *Information Officer* Jon Cannon
The National Monuments Record is the national archive of heritage information. The collection, which contains over 6½ million items, is used by everyone from local authorities to architects, from GCSE students to national bodies like the National Trust and English Heritage. It is divided into four sections: Buildings, Archaeology, Air Photographs and Maritime sites. It is open to the public at the National Monuments Record Centre in Swindon and can also be consulted through a London Search Room, Tel 0171-208 8200

National Portrait Gallery, St Martin's Pl WC2H 0HE; Tel 0171-366 0055; *Head of Department* John Cooper; *Art Education Officer* Liz Rideal; *Education Officer* Clare Giltings; *Education Officer* Roger Hargreaves
Guided visits, practicle art lessons, introduction to photography, holiday activities

National Postal Museum, King Edward Bldg, King Edward St, London EC1A 1LP; Tel 0171-239 5420; Fax 0171-600 3021; *Manager* Stan Goron; *Group Visits* Barry Tennant
Display of British and foreign stamps and related material. Special Exhibitions about stamps and post office history. Research and group visits possible by prior arrangement

National Theatre, South Bank, London SE1 9PX; Tel 0171-261 9808; *Head of Education* Jenny Harris;

Interact/Outreach Shanti Brahmachari; *BT National Connections* Suzy Graham-Adriani; *Administration* Rachel Dickinson; *Administration* Joe Smith; *Touring* Venu Dhura

The Natural History Museum, Visitor Resources Section, Cromwell Rd, London SW7 5BD; Tel 0171-938 8744 (Teachers' Centre); or 0171-938 9090 (Bookings); *Education Officer* Martin Lawrence
Earth and Life Sciences combined in one Museum. Activity sheets for Key Stages 1–4 and 6th form study guides. Teachers' exhibition guides and newsletter, *Resource.* Guided tours, Discovery Centre and Travelling Discovery Centre for Key Stag 2 pupils. Teachers' Centre and INSET courses. Public events. Special Needs groups welcome. Book free visits (British full-time educational groups) at least three weeks in advance

Newham Museum Service, The Old Town Hall, 29 The Broadway, Stratford, London E15 4BQ; *Principal Assistant Curator (Extension Services)* Teresa Wild
Loans and handling sessions for schools, holiday activities, nature reserve, history trails. North Woolwich Old Station Museum

North Woolwich Old Station Museum, Pier Rd, North Woolwich E16 2JJ; Tel 0171-474 7244
Exhibits in Victorian station and along old platform telling story of the Great Eastern Railway. Talks to schools, holiday activities

Order of St John, Museum and Library of the Order of St John, St John's Gate, St John's La, Clerkenwell, London EC1M 4DA; Tel 0171-253 6644; Fax 0171-490 8835; *Curator* P. Willis
School visits and guided tours by arrangement

Orleans House Gallery, Riverside, Twickenham TW1 3DJ; Tel 0181-892 0221; *Acting Curator* Stephen Nicholls
James Gibbs' Baroque Octagon built circa 1720, with adjacent temporary exhibition gallery and active education programme, is situated in attractive woodland garden

Osterley Park House, Isleworth, Middx TW7 4RB; Tel 0181-560 3918; *Administrator* Barry Williams
Elizabethan mansion, transformed into a grand neo-classical palace by Robert Adam. The superb interiors conjure up a vivid picture of how the well-to-do lived in the 18th Century. Set in 140 acres of landscaped park with lakes. House open April to October, Wed–Sun. Pre-booked school parties: rates on application to the administrator. National Trust Schools Corporate Membership available

Percival David Foundation of Chinese Art, University of London, 53 Gordon Sq WC1H 0PD; Tel 0171-387 3909; Fax 0171-383 5163; *Percival David Professor of Chinese and East Asian Art* R. Whitfield School of Oriental and African Studies, Thornhaugh St, Russell Sq, London, WC1H 0XG; *Curator* R. Scott
Museum with outstanding collection of Chinese Ceramics and teaching foundation with specialist library for East Asian art. Galleries open to the public, Mon–Fri 10.30–5.00, admission free

The Queen's Gallery, Buckingham Palace SW1A 1AA; Tel 0171-799 231; The Information Office, Royal Collection Enterprises Ltd, St James's Palace, London SW1A 1JR
The Queen's Gallery was opened in 1962 to hold annual exhibitions based on the Royal Collection, one of the finest art collections in the world. This years exhibition entitled Fabergé opens mid-March. Tues–Sat 10.00am–5.00pm and Sundays 2.00pm–5.00pm

****Rangers House,*** Chesterfield Wk, Blackheath SE10 8QX; Tel 0181-853 0035 (house)
School workshops and children's holiday projects on the Jacobean portraits and on the history of the house; includes historical dancing and musical activities
English Heritage

Royal Academy of Arts, Piccadilly W1V 0DS; Tel 0171-494 5732/33; *Director of Education* MaryAnne Stevens
Mailing to schools and colleges, school and group bookings; conferences; introductory classes; workshops for primary and secondary schools; teachers' packs; teachers' previews; slide packs, acoustiguides etc

Royal Air Force Museum, Grahame Pk Way, London NW9 5LL; Tel 0181-205 2266; *Education Officer* John Edwards
Britain's National Museum of Aviation. Illustrated talks, handling sessions, activity sheets for junior and secondary pupils, GCSE sessions, assistance with projects, education centre, free 'Plane and Simple' demonstrations of Principles of Flight, lunch room and picnic facilities, flight simulator, shop, large free coach park

Royal Artillery Regimental Museum, Old Royal Military Academy, Woolwich Common SE18 4DN; Tel 0181-781 5628; *Curator* J. Starr
Royal Artillery Institution

Royal Botanic Gardens, Kew, Richmond, Surrey TW9 3AB; Fax 0181-332 5610 Ext 5612/5613; *Education Manager* Gail Bromley; *Education Officer* Laura Ponsonby; *Education Officer (Outreach)* Sharon Hughes
Guided tours on request. In-service Training available. Topic days. Outreach programme

Royal Hospital Chelsea, Royal Hosiptal Rd SW3 4SR; Tel 0171-730 01161 Ext 203; *Curator* Major R.A.G. Courage, CVO, MBE (Ret'd)
Plans, maps, medal collections, uniforms, pictures, open weekdays 10am–12 noon, 2–4pm. Sun 2–4pm. Apr–Oct. Closed Bank Holidays

The Royal Institution of Gt Britain 21 Albemarle St, London W1X 4BS; Tel 0171-409 2992; *Librarian/ Information Officer* I. McCabe
Scientific learned society: scientific research, public understanding of science. Lectures, exhibitions, library, museum

The Royal Mews, Buckingham Palace SW1W 0QH; Tel 0171-799 2331; The Information Office, Royal Collection Enterprises Ltd, St James's Palace, London SW1A 1JR
The Royal Mews, a working department of the Royal Household, provides a unique opportunity to see how the State Carriages and Coaches, together with their horses and equipage, combine to create the familiar pageantry associated with State Occasions. Open of Wednesday 12.00pm–4.00pm throughout the year and additional days in the summer

Royal Society of Painter-Printmakers, Bankside Gallery, 48 Hopton St SE1 9JH; Tel 0171-928 7521; *Secretary* Judy Dixey; *President* Joseph Winkelman
Annual exhibition held. Demonstrations, talks, courses studio visits and other events. Original prints on sale

Royal Watercolour Society, Bankside Gallery, 48 Hopton St SE1 9JH; Tel 0171-928 7521; *Secretary* Judy Dixey; *President* Leslie Worth
Open watercolour exhibition held annually. Demonstrations, talks and events puts on at gallery. Two annual members' shows held and courses

St Bride's Crypt Museum, St Bride's Church, Fleet St EC4Y 8AU; Tel 0171-353 1301/071-583 0239; Fax 0171-583 4867; *Rector* Rev Canon John Oates

The Salvation Army International Heritage Centre, 117 Judd St, King's Cross WC1H 9NN; Tel 0171-387 1656; Fax 0171-387 3768
Student and teacher information packs, slides, films and videos available from *Schools Information Service* Mrs Major Sylvia Dalziel, 101 Queen Victoria St, London EC4P 4EP; Tel 0171-236 5222

Science Museum, Education Unit, Exhibition Rd, South Kensington SW7 2DD; Tel 0171-938 8222; *Education Unit Manager* Alison Porter
Topics include flight, physics, chemistry, industrial history, computers, transport, food, photography, printing, space exploration. Hands-on Launch pad and Flight Lab exhibitions and science box exhibitions. Exhibitions and activities for all ages from pre-school. Free visit planning guide for teachers

The Serpentine Gallery, Kensington Gdns W2 3XA; Tel 0171-402 6075; *Director* Julia Peyton-Jones; *Education Officer* Vivien Ashley
Promotes the visual arts by exhibiting a wide range of painting, sculture and installation from diverse sources

Shakespeare Globe Museum, Bear Gdns, Bankside, London SE1; Tel 0171-928 6342; *Director, Globe Education* Patrick Spottiswoode
Lecture tours, talks and work-shops available by arrangement

Sigmund Freud Museum, 20 Maresfield Gdns, Hampstead NW3 5SX; Tel 0171-435 2002; Fax 0171-431 5452; *Education Officer* Ivan Ward; Tel 0171-435 2002
Public resource with study materials for history and continuing development of psychoanalysis especially. Sigmund Freud's historic environment. Educational visits welcome from primary and secondary schools

Sir John Soane's Museum, 13 Lincoln Inn Fields WC2A 3BP; Tel 0171-405 2107; *Curator* Peter Thornton; *Assistant Curator* Margaret Richardson
Soane's collection of antiques and works of art are freely available in the original setting designed by the architect. Access to the library and collection of 30,000 architectural drawings (Adam, Dance, Soane etc) is by appointment. Groups must book in advance. Introductory talks available. Late evening opening on the first Tuesday on each month, 6–9pm

South Bank Centre, Royal Festival Hall, London SE1 8XX; Tel 0171-921 0600; *Chief Executive* Nicholas Snowman; *Contact* Music Education; Tel 0171-921 0953
Arts centre comprising three concert halls (Royal Festival Hall, Queen Elizabeth Hall, Purcell Room) and Hayward Gallery. The three education units (Visual Arts, Music and Performing Arts) organise events for many sectors of the community, around the artistic programme at the South Bank Centre

South London Gallery, 65 Peckham Rd, London SE5 8UH; Tel 0171-703 6120; *Manager* David Thorp; *Visual Arts Officer* Valerie M. Chang

Southside House, Wimbledon Common, London SW19 4RJ; Tel 0181-947 2491; *Administrator*
Historic house dating from 1687, open to public. Limited number of free, properly supervised, Special school visits upon written application to the Administrator, for serious study by children aged 10–18 years every visitor season between Oct 1st and following May 31st)
Pennington Mellor Charitable Trust (reg no 283266)

Southwark Livesey Museum, 682 Old Kent Rd SE15 1JF; Tel 0171-639 5604; *Keeper* Jill Slaney
Changing hands-on exhibitions and education activities for schools and family groups

Southwark Local Studies Library, 211 Borough High St, London SE1 1JA; Tel 0171-403 3507; *Local Studies Librarian* Janice Brooker, MA, BLS, ALA

BT Museum, 145 Queen Victoria St, London EC4V 4AT; Tel 0171-248 7444

Syon House, Syon Pk, Brentford, Middx TW8 8JF; Tel 0181-560 0881; Fax 0181-568 0936; *Administrative Officer* Vacancy

Tate Gallery, Tate Gallery, Millbank, London SW1P 4RG; Tel 0171-821 1313; *Head of Department* Richard Humphreys; *P.A./Secretary* Julie Gomez; *Young Visitor Programmes (Co-ordinator)* Colin Grigg; *Young Visitor Programmes (Schools and Teachers)* Polly Penrose; *Finance, Young Visitor Programmes and Records (Administrator)* Gloria Hammond; *Young Visitor Programmes (Secretary – part time)* Anne Prothero; *Young Visitor Programmes (Administrator – temp)* Angie Whitbread; *Adult Programmes (Administrator)* Sylvia Lahav; *Adult Programmes (Co-ordinator)* Vacancy; *Slide Curator* Juliette Nissen; *Audio-Visual Technician (part time)* William Rallison; *Audio-Visual Technician (part time)* Deborah Robinson; *Schools Reception* ; Tel Ext 343
All visits must be booked 4 weeks in advance, workshops and talks available for schools

Thames Barrier Visitors Centre, Unity Way, Woolwich SE18 5NJ; Tel 0181-854 1373; *Promotions Officer* M. Sewell; *Admin Officer* G. Roberts
A unique audio-visual exhibition showing how the barrier was built and how it stops London from being flooded. Special rates to school parties on application

Theatre Museum, 1E Tavistock St, Covent Gdn WC2E 7PA; Tel 0171-836 7891; Fax 0171-836 5148; *Head of Education* Stuart Bennett; *Director* Margaret Benton
Exhibitions and events on themes from the history of theatre in England and contemporary productions. Group rates and tours: contact Marketing. Activities and study groups contact Education Dept

Thomas Coram Foundation for Children (Foundling Hospital Art Treasures), 40 Brunswick Sq WC1N 1AZ; Tel 0171-278 2424
Education Pack available

****Tower of London,*** Royal Armouries, H.M. Tower of London EC3N 4AB; Tel 0171-702 0013; *Head of Education* C.L. Scott
Intramural teaching including 'hands-on'. Material for teachers and pupils. Holiday activities. Public lectures

Vestry House Museum, Vestry Rd, Walthamstow E17 9NH; Tel 0181-509 1917; *Contact* Museum
Talks, slide-shows and handling sessions on site, school loans boxes and small travelling exhibitions for loan; advance booking necessary

Victoria and Albert Museum, South Kensington SW7 2RL; Tel 0171-938 8500; *Education Department* ; Tel Ext 8638
Full programme of public courses and activities

The Wallace Collection, Hertford Hse, Manchester Sq, London W1M 6BN; Tel 0171-935 0687; *Director* R.J. Savill; *Assistant to the Director* P. Hughes; *Assistant to the Director* Vacancy; *Head of Administration* A.W. Houldershaw

Wellcome Museum of the History of Medicine, Education Unit, Science Museum, Exhibition Rd, London SW7 2DD; Tel 0171-938 8222; *Education Unit Manager* Alison Porter
Free folder available to teachers, sample activity sheets, back-up material

Wesley's Chapel, House and Museum of Methodism, 49 City Rd, London EC1Y 1AU; Tel 0171-253 2262; *Curator* Alison Taylor, MA
Historical talks by arrangement
Methodist Church

Westminster Abbey, London; Tel 0171-222 5152; Fax 0171-233 2072; *Press Secretary* Emma St John-Smith
Receiver General, The Chapter Office, Dean's Yard, London SW1P 3PA. Introductory talk, guided tours, educational packs available
Dean and Chapter of Westminster

Whitechapel Art Gallery, 80–82 Whitechapel High St, London E1 7QX; Tel 0171-377 5015 (Admin) or 0171-377 0107 (Info); *Head of Education* Jane Sillis; *Director* Catherine Lampert; *Press Officer (Contact)* Mark Sladen
Major exhibitions of modern art and a distinctive education programme which ties the gallery to the local community

Whitehall, 1 Malden Rd, Cheam, Sutton, Surrey SM3 8QD; Tel 0181-643 1236 or 770 4781; Fax 0181-770 4777; *The Curator* Pat Jackson
Tudor timber-framed house built c1500 with later additions, provides a unique opportunity to study the Tudor period and building methods as well as other periods and topics, including domestic history, Nonsuch Palace and the Victorians
Special school visits and guided tours plus resource room for schools
London Borough of Sutton, Leisure Services, Heritage Service

William Morris Gallery, Lloyd Pk, Forest Rd, Walthamstow, London E17 4PP; Tel 0181-527 3782; *Assistant Keeper* Liz Woods
London Borough of Waltham Forest

Wimbledon Lawn Tennis Museum, Church Rd, Wimbledon SW19 5AE; Tel 0181-946 6131; *Contact* The Curator
The displays tell the story of the history of Lawn Tennis. The rich and fascinating collection of paintings, jewellery, ornaments and costume is an unexpected delight. Tea room and shop. Open Tues–Sat, 10.30am–5pm; Sun 2–5pm

Woodlands Art Gallery, 90 Mycenae Rd, Blackheath SE3 7SE; Tel 0181-858 5847; *Gallery Manager* Pat Bowring
Monthly exhibitions of contemporary art. Chosen by exhibitions selection committee from applications made to gallery and by invitation

Manchester

Bolton Museum and Art Gallery (Educational Services), Le Mans Cres, Bolton BL1 1SA; Tel (01204) 2311 Ext 2193; *Senior Keeper* David Edwards
Guided tours, talks, demonstrations, loan service, holiday activities. Service extended to branch museums Halli'th Wood, Smithhills Hall and Local history museums

Bramall Hall, Bramhall Pk, Bramhall, Stockport SK7 3NX; Tel 0161-485 3708; *Schools and Community Education Officer* Judy Oldroyd
Stockport MBC

Bridgewater Packet Boat Service, 8 Benbecula Way, Davyhulme, Manchester M31 2ES; Tel 0161-748 2680; *Contact* Eamon Gall
Canal trips

Bury Art Gallery and Museum, Moss St, Bury BL9 0DR; Tel 0161-705 5882; *Senior Curator* C. Billingham
Open Tues–Sat, 10am–5pm; closed Mon and Sun
Metropolitan Boroygh of Bury

Cornerhouse, Manchester Arts Centre, 70 Oxford St, Manchester M1 5NH; Tel 0161-228 7621; *Exhibitions Director* Stephen Snoddy; *Education Co-ordinator* Julie Jones
Regularly changing programme of exhibitions, film, workshops, lectures, seminars and day schools. Termly and monthly bulletins available

Gallery of English Costume, Platt Hall, Rusholme, Manchester M14 5LL; Tel 0161-224 5217; *Keeper* Anthea M. Jarvis, BA

Heaton Hall, Heaton Pk, Prestwich M25 5SW; Tel 0161-773 1231 (opening hours only); 0161-236 5244 (out of season); *Curator of Decorative Arts* Ruth Shrigley
Late 18th century historic house, restored period rooms, art gallery, free recitals (summer). Group tours by appointment. Provisional opening dates 1996: Easter–Sept, Thur–Sat 10–1pm, 2–5.45pm; Sun 2–5.45pm. Please telephone for up-to-date information 061-236 5244

Manchester Metropolitan Galleries (Holden Gallery, Righton Gallery and Aytoun Gallery) Grosvenor Bldg, Manchester Metropolitan University, Cavendish St, M15 6BR; Tel 0161-247 1708; *Curator* A. Macleod
The Metropolitan galleries encompass three main exhibition venues within the University, reflecting a broad spectrum of today's art making practise. Holden gallery: installed and site specific projects in particular interactive and multi-media work. Righton Gallery: Design aytoun gallery: Wall based work

Manchester Cathedral Brass Rubbing Centre, The Cathedral, Manchester M3 1SX; Tel 0161-833 2220; *Cathedral Head Verger* Geoffrey S. Robinson
Brass rubbing instruction and guided tours

Manchester City Art Galleries, Mosley St M2 3JL; Tel 0161-236 5244; *Contact Education Officer* Jaswant Souel Athenaeum Education Dept re: school visits; Tel 0161-236 5244
Rich permanent collection in Victorian setting. Pre-Raphaelites, Turner, Gainsborough, Stubbs, ceramics and silver. Busy programme of temporary exhibitions

Manchester Galleries Education Service, The Athenaeum, Mosley St, Manchester M2 3JL; Tel 0161-236 9283; *Head of Service* Annette Hollows, NDD, ATD
For all teachers and pupils, working with the city's permanent collections and temporary exhibitions

Manchester Museum, Manchester University M13 9PL; Tel 0161-275 2634; *Education Dept*; Tel 0161-273 2892

Manchester Museum, The University, Oxford Rd M13 9PL; Tel 0161-275 2634; *Education Liaison Keeper, Keeper of Botany* Vacancy
Teaching service and loan service available to all schools

Museum of Science and Industry in Manchester, Liverpool Rd, Castlefield, Manchester M3 4FP; Tel 0161-833 0027; Fax 0161-832 1511; *Education Services Manager* Jacqueline Roberts, BA
Collections of industrial machinery, locomotives, cars, aircraft and space exhibits housed in the world's oldest railway station and warehouse. National Electricity Gallery, 'Underground Manchester'; the 'Making of Manchester'; Interactive gallery Xperiment!; 'Out of this World'; National Electricity Gallery, Gas Gallery. Special events, schools, college, other groups. Classes for school/college groups, guided tours, teachers courses, leaflets on museum machinery; industrial trails; gallery guides for teachers; suggestions for teachers; single copies of appropriate worksheets available for photo copying. Packed lunch area available on first come, first served basis

Museum of Transport, Greater Manchester, Boyle St, Cheetham, Manchester M8 8UW; Tel 0161-205 2122; *Chairman* Dennis Talbot; *Publicity Officer* Stephen Lord
Two- and Three-dimensional exhibition of the history of road passenger transport. School party bookings and enquiries Tel 061-205 2122

Oldham Art Gallery, Union St, Oldham OL1 1DN; Tel 0161-911 4653; *Senior Art Gallery Officer* Tessa Gudgeon; *Principal Museum and Gallery Officer* Vacancy; Fax 0161-627 1025
Temporary exhibitions of contemporary art, craft and design, including video. Changing displays of historical art from the collections. Education workshop programme for schools and groups, special events and talks

Ordsall Hall Museum, Taylorson St, Salford M5 3EX; Tel 0161-872 0251; *Keeper of Social History*
City of Salford

Rochdale Pioneers' Memorial Museum, Toad La, Rochdale OL12 0NU; Tel 0161-832 4300; *Education Officer* T.R. Garratt
Co-operative Union Ltd, Holyoak Hse, Hanover St, Manchester M60 0AS

Salford Mining Museum, Buile Hill Pk, Eccles Old Rd, Salford M6 8GL; Tel 0161-736 1832; *Museum Officer* Alan Davies, BA
Two full size reproduction coalmines. Mining history gallery, childrens worksheets, commentary posts, gallery of mining art, archives, library, souvenirs, books

Salford Museum and Art Gallery, Peel Pk, Salford M5 4WU; Tel 0161-736 2649; *Principal Museums Officer* Mike Leber
Reconstructed period street c. 1900 L.S. Lowry collection, gallery and victorian art

Stockport Art Gallery, Wellington Rd South, Stockport; Tel 0161-474 4453/54; *Outreach Officer* Mike Bloom
Stockport MBC

Stockport Museum, Vernon Pk, Offerton, Stockport SK1 4AR; Tel 0161-474 4460; *Education Officer* Collette Curry; Tel 0161-474 4449
Stockport MBC

Whitworth Art Gallery, University of Manchester, Oxford Rd, Manchester M15 6ER; Tel 0161-273 4865; *Gallery Services Officer*

Wigan Heritage Service, The History Shop, Rodney St, Wigan, Lancs WN1 1DQ; Tel (01942) 828128
School loan service available to all schools in Wigan Metroploitan District. Schools' centre available

Merseyside

Bluecoat Arts Centre, Bluecoat Chambers, School La, Liverpool L1 3BX; Tel 0151-709 5297/5689; Fax 0151-707 0048; *Director* Bryan Biggs
Exhibitions by leading visual artists. Concerts of contemporary, popular and world musics, theatre, dance and performance art. Educational activities allied to both. Regular evening classes in life drawing, etching

The Boat Museum, Dockyard Rd, Ellemere Port L65 4EF; Tel 0151-355 5017; *Education Officer* Annette Cavell
Free preliminary visits. Guided tours and activity sessions for art, drama, history, maths and science. Information and worksheets

Botanic Gardens Aviary, Southport, c/o Pavilion Bldgs, 99–105 Lord St, Southport PR8 1RJ; Tel (01704)

33133; *Chief Recreation and Amenities Officer* T.J. Maple

Botanic Gardens Museum, Churchtown, Southport PR9 7NB; Tel (01704) 27547; *Assistant Keeper (Museums)*
School parties welcomed
Libraries and Arts Services Department, Sefton MBC

****Croxteth Hall and Country Park, Liverpool City Council,*** Croxteth Hall La, Liverpool L12 0HB; Tel 0151-228 5311; *General Manager* E.E. Jackson
Former home of the Earls of Sefton, a complete survival of a working country estate. Hall with furnished rooms and Edwardian 'upstairs downstairs' character figures. Home Farm with traditional breeds, superb walled garden featured on TV, adventure playground, cafe etc. Special living history visits and theme visits on farm and countryside topics for schools. Teaching staff, resource materials etc

Hesketh Park Aviary, Southport, c/o Pavilion Bldgs, 99–105 Lord St, Southport PR8 1RJ; Tel (01704) 33133; *Chief Recreational and Amenities Officer* T.S. Maple

Knowsley Safari Park, Prescot L34 4AN; Tel 0151-430 9009; *Manager* L.D. Tennant

Liverpool Cathedral, St James Rd, Liverpool L1 7AZ; Tel 0151-709 6271; *Information* Cathedral Secretary or Education Officer

The Metropolitan Cathedral of Christ the King, Mount Pleasant, Liverpool L3 5TQ; Tel 0151-709 9222; *The Administrator* Rt Rev Mgr Peter Cookson
School visits service staffed by experienced teachers; free educational visits; worksheets; NPRA units; cathedral guides; free guided tours

National Museums and Galleries on Merseyside

Lady Lever Art Gallery, Port Sunlight Village, Wirral; Tel 0151-207 0001; *Senior Education Officer* Frank Milner
Collection formed by Lord Leverhulme and dedicated to his wife, 18th and 19th century British paintings, furniture, Chinese porcelain. Open daily Mon–Sat 10–5pm; Sun 12–5pm

Liverpool Museum, William Brown St, Liverpool L3 8EN; Tel 0151-207 0001; *Senior Education Officer* Christine Ryan
Intra-mural teaching advice publications and courses for teachers. Planetarium and Natural History Centre. Holiday activities. Open daily Mon–Sat 10–5pm, Sun 12–5pm

Merseyside Maritime Museum, Albert Dock, Liverpool L3 4AA; Tel 0151-207 0001; Fax 0151-478 4590; *Senior Education Officer* Paul Rees
Advice, demonstrations, publications and special events. Port of Liverpool, its ships and people. Displays include Emigrants to the New World, World of Models, Builders of Great Ships, Battle of the Atlantic Gallery, Transatlantic Slavery Gallery. Open daily Mon–Sun, 10.30–5.30pm (Last ticket sold at 4.30pm)

Sudley, Mossley Hill Rd, Liverpool; Tel 0151-207 0001; *Senior Education Officer* Frank Milner
Collection of late 18th and 19th century paintings. Open daily Mon–Sat 10–5pm, Sun 12–5pm

Walker Art Gallery, William Brown St, Liverpool L3 8EL; Tel 0151-207 01001 Ext 266; *Senior Education Officer* F.J. Milner
Schools and College education service. Collection of paintings and sculptures ranging from 13th century Italian to late 20th century abstract pictures. Open daily Mon–Sat 10–5pm, Sun 12–5pm

Pilkington Glass Museum, Prescot Rd, St Helens WA10 3TT; Tel (01744) 692499 (Curator), (01744) 692014 (Information Visits); *Curator* I.M. Burgoyne
Ideal for school visits because many of our exhibits and displays relate to the National Curriculum. A very rare historical glass collection and the many applications of glass in buildings, transport, lighting, science and technology. Many interactive exhibits to include a working periscope and night vision goggles
Pilkington PLC

Prescot Museum of Clock and Watchmaking, 34 Church St, Precot L34 3LA; Tel 0151-430 7787; *Curator* R. John Griffiths
Advice, publications and courses for teachers

St Helens Museum and Art Gallery, College St, St Helens WA10 1TW; Tel (01744) 456961; *Museum and Art Gallery Officer* Roger Hart
Visits, talks, loan service, special exhibitions
St Helens Metropolitan Borough

Southport Zoo and Conservation Trust, Prince's Pk, Southport; Tel (01704) 538102; *Co-Owner* C.A. Petrie; *Co-Owner* D. Petrie; *Information Officer*
Zoological Gardens and Conservation Trust (Charity no 1002352)
Special programme for schools. Open all year from 10.00am to 1 hour before dusk, except Christmas Day

Speke Hall, The Walk, Liverpool L24 1XD; Tel 0151-427 7231; *Contact* Education Advisor at the above address
Advice and publications, teaching sessions

University of Liverpool Art Gallery, 3 Abercromby Sq, PO Box 147, Liverpool L69 3BX; Tel 0151-794 2347; *Curator, Art Collections* Janice A. Carpenter
Permanent display from the University collections for the public. Lectures and conducted tours arranged

Williamson Art Gallery and Museum, Slatey Rd, Birkenhead L43 4UE; Tel 0151-652 4177; Fax 0151-670 0253; *Curator* Colin Simpson
Worksheets; museum/gallery tours; in-school lectures and exhibitions; biennial schools exhibition
Leisure Services Department, Wirral MBC

Middlesex

Animal Ark Studio 29, Somerset Rd, Brentford, Middx TW8 8BT; Tel 0181-560 3029; Fax 0181-560 5762; David Manning; Jo Gaskarth
Visit schools with professionally handled reptiles/amphibians/invertebrates. Cover such topics as classification of animals/rainforests/mini-beasts

Lee Valley Park Countryside Centre, Waltham Abbey; Tel (01992) 713838
The Lee Valley Park offers 23 miles of countryside, including rivers, lakes, marshland and woodland for you to explore. The Youth and Schools' Service offers a series of half-day and full-day educational programmes for primary and secondary schools, designed to meet National Curriculum GCSE and A' Level criteria. There is a wide range of outdoor activities from watersports to conservation, pond dipping to bird watching

Norfolk

Ancient House Museum, White Hart St, Thetford; Tel (01842) 752599
Norfolk Museum

Banham Zoo Ltd, The Grove, Norwich NR16 2HE; Tel (01953) 887771; *Marketing Manager* Simon Lee
Enjoy a great day out at Banham Zoo, where you can see some of the world's rare and endangered wildlife, including Snow Leopards, Cheetahs, Grevy's Zebra, Jackass Penguins, many Exotic Birds and a large collection of primates. Educational facilities available all year round

Berney Arms Windmill, Reedham; Tel (01493) 700605; *Custodian* S.M. Loughlin
English Heritage; Windmill open Apr–Sept 9.00–17.00, Sun 9.00–17.00. Permanent graphic display. Access by train, boat or 3 mile walk–no access for vehicles; 6 mile walk from Gt Yarmouth

Blickling Hall, Blickling, Norwich NR11 6NF; Tel (01263) 733084; Fax (01263) 734924
National Trust

Castle Acre Priory, Castle Acre; Tel (01760) 755394; *Applications for Visits* Education Bookings Clerk, Hazelrigg Hse, 33 Marefair, Northampton NN1 1SR; Fax (01604) 730332
Extensive remains of Clunic priory including church and Prior's lodging. Remains of Norman Castle nearby. Free educational visits
English Heritage

Castle Museum, Norwich NR1 3JU; Tel (01603) 223624; *Head of Education Department* Katrina Siliprandi; *Museums Education Officer* Richard Wood; *Museums Education Officer* Lyn Gash

Norfolk Museums Service Education Dept (0603) 630214
Castle Museum in the heart of the city; with Norman Castle Keep built 12th century, and museum housing displays of art, archaeology, medieval artefacts, natural history, Lowestoft porcelain, Norwich silver, a large collection of paintings (including Norwich school), and famous collection of British ceramic teapots. Changing programme of temporary exhibitions, guided tours of dungeons and battlements. Wide variety of educational activities, lectures, courses, documentary resources, worksheets handling sessions, etc. Provided for children and adults. Inset

Castle Rising Castle, Castle Rising; Tel (0155 387) 330
Mid 12th century domestic keep set in the centre of massive earthwork
English Heritage

Cromer Museum, East Cottages, Tucker St, Cromer NR27 9HB; Tel (01263) 513543; *Curator* M. Warren, BSc, AMA
Norfolk Museums Service

Dragon Hall, 115–123 King St, Norwich NR1 1QE; Tel (01603) 663922; *Director* Sarah Knights
Magnificent medival timber-framed merchant's hall with superb crown post roof and carved and painted dragon. School room available as base for field work within the building and elsewhere in the city
School bookings by arrangement

Euston Hall, Thetford IP24 2QP; Tel (01842) 766366; *Secretary* Linda Campbell
Collection of paintings by Van Dyck, Lely and others of Charles II's family and court, also Stubbs and Reynolds. Open Thurs afternoons June to end Sept and 2 Sundays: the last in June and the first in Sept, 2.30–5pm

Felbrigg Hall, Roughton, Norwich NR11 8PR; Tel (01263) 837444; Fax (01263) 837032; *Marketing Officer*

Grimes Graves, Thetford; Tel (01842) 810656
Extensive group of Neolithic flint mines
English Heritage

Holkham Hall, Holkham, Wells-next-the-Sea; Tel (01328) 710227/(0328) 711707; *Administrator* T.B. Ronnay
18th century Palladian mansion with art collection

How Hill Trust–The Norfolk Broads Study Centre, How Hill, Ludham, Great Yarmouth NR29 5PG; Tel (01692) 678555; *Director* David Holmes
Nature trails and field study facilities. Residential and day courses. Advance booking essential

East Anglian Falconry Centre, Weybourne Rd, Kelling, Holt; Tel (01263) 712235; Fax (01263) 711650; *Proprieter* D. Hopson

Kilverstone Wildlife Park, The Latin American Zoo, Thetford IP24 2RL; Tel (01842) 763666; *Education Officer*
School projects, talks and tours. Primary, secondary and adult facilities. School Video Unit available

King's Lynn Arts Centre (The Guildhall of St George), 27–29 King St, King's Lynn, Norfolk PE30 1HA; Tel (01553) 774725; Fax (01553) 770591; *Director* Lucy Anderson Jones
The Centre promotes the King's Lynn Festival and runs a full year-round arts centre programme. Galleries

King's Lynn Museums, Market St, King's Lynn PE30 1NL; Tel (01553) 775001; 46 Queen St, King's Lynn PE30 5DQ; Tel (01553) 773450; *Museum Education Officer* Faye Kalloniatis
Visits and handling sessions with museum objects, relating to the history, archaeology, social history and natural history of King's Lynn and West Norfolk; school loans services
Norfolk Museums Service

Mannington Gardens and Countryside, Mannington Hall, Norwich NR11 7BB; Tel (01263) 584175 (answerphone); Fax (01236) 761214; *Countryside Warden* Andy Watson
Conservation/countryside interpretation–all ages

Maritime Museum; Elizabethan House Museum; Tolhouse Museum, Nelson's Monument and Exhibitions Galleries, Education Officer, Elizabethan House Museum, 4 South Quay, Gt Yarmouth NR30 2QH; Tel (01493) 855746; *Education Officer* Sheila Watson
Intra-mural services available to all schools and adult groups if pre-booked

Museum Education Department, Castle Museum, Norwich; Tel (01603) 630214; *Head of Education Department* Katrina Siliprandi; *Museums Education Officer* Richard Wood; *Museums Education Officer* Lyn Gash; Tel (01603) 630214
Free intra-mural handling sessions for Norfolk schools. Holiday activities, clubs, worksheets, pre-vocational case studies, GCSE course work assignments, GNVQ materials, workshops, role play events. Inset. Lectures, courses. National Curriculum linked resource packs
Norwich Castle Museum; Strangers Hall Museum; Bridewell Museum; St Peter Hungate Museum; Norfolk Regimental Museum

National Trust Regional Office, East Anglia, The Dairy Hse, Ickworth Park, Horringer, Nr Bury St Edmunds, Suffolk IP29 5QE; Tel (01284) 735480

Norfolk Rural Life Museum, Beech Hse, Gressenhall, Dereham NR20 4DR; *Education Liaison Officer* John Barnwell; Tel (01362) 860294
Lessons, special events. Tel (0362) 860563 for sample worksheets, independent visits and information

Norfolk Wildlife Park, Great Witchingham, Norwich NR9 5QS; Tel (01603) 872274; *Information Officer* The Secretary

Old Merchant House, Gt Yarmouth; Tel (01493) 857900; *Custodian* B. Futter
House open Apr–Sept, weekdays only. Guided tours. Permanent exhibitions

Oxburgh Hall, Oxborough, Nr King's Lynn; Tel (01366) 328258); *Administrator* B. Carter
Young visitors' guide
National Trust

The Rapter Trust, 6 Dukes Way, Earsham, Bungay, Suffolk; Tel (01986) 895673; *Chairman* G. Page
A Charitable Trust running a Treatment Centre for injured birds of prey. Lectures to schools, colleges and evening societies. Rare Species breeding and release scheme. Newsletters

Royal Norfolk Regimental Museum, Shirehall, Market Ave, Norfolk NR1 3JQ
The story of a county regiment and the men who served in it, from 1685 to the present day. Open Mon–Sat, 10am–5pm; Sun 2–5pm

St Andrews and Blackfriars' Halls, St Andrews Plain, Norwich NR3 1AU; Tel (01603) 628477; Fax (01603) 762182; *General Manager* Timothy Aldous
13th century friary: Most complete surviving friary complex in UK. Now refurbished city centre conference banqueting and concert and exhibition complex
Norwich City Council

Sainsbury Centre for Visual Arts, University of East Anglia, Norwich NR4 7TJ; Tel (01603) 456060/592470; Fax (01603) 259401; *Keeper* D.A. Gillman; *Contact* Gallery Administrator
Major holdings of Moore, Giacometti, Bacon, also Picasso, Modigliani, Degas and important examples of African, Oceanic and indigenous American art. Programme of special exhibitions

Sandringham, Estate Office, Sandringham, King's Lynn PE35 6EN; Tel (01553) 772675; Fax (01485) 541571; *Public Access Manager* G.M. Pattinson
Sandringham House, grounds, museum, church and country park are all open to the public on the following days. From 13 April until 1 Oct incl Daily. Please note HOUSE ONLY will be closed to the public from 18 July to 3 Aug incl and Grounds will be closed from 23 July to 2 Aug incl
House and Museum open 11am–4.45pm, Sandringham Grounds 10.30am–5pm

The Shirehall Museum, Common Pl, Little Walsingham NR22 6BP; Tel (01328) 820510; *Curator* M.R. Warren, BSc, AMA
A Georgian courthouse in a medieval building with local history museum, including a display on pilgrimages to Walsingham
Norfolk Museums Service

Strangers' Hall Museum, Charing Cross, Norwich NR2 4AL; Tel (01603) 667229; *Head of Education Department* Katrina Siliprandi; Tel (01603) 630214
Museum of social history including toys, costumes, Victorian and Tudor rooms. Handling sessions, activity days, lectures, courses, documentary resources, worksheets provided for pupils and adults. Inset

Thetford Priory, Thetford, Norfolk; Tel (01842) 766127
English Heritage

Thrigby Hall Wildlife Gardens, Thrigby Hall, Filby, Great Yarmouth NR29 3DR; Tel (01493) 369477; Fax (01493) 368256; *Information Officer* K. Sims

The Thursford Collection, Thursford, Fakenham NR21 0AS; Tel (01328) 877477; *Museum Secretary* Geraldine Rye
A sight and sound spectacular

Walsingham Abbey Grounds, Estate Office, Walsingham NR22 6BP; Tel (01328) 820259
Walsingham Estate Company

North Yorkshire

Aldborough Roman Town, Nr Boroughbridge; Tel (01423) 322768
English Heritage

The ARC, Archaeological Research Centre, St Saviourgate, York; Tel (01904) 654324
A hands-on exploration of archaeology suitable for visitors aged 2–102. Handle archaeological finds and learn how to identify them, try out ancient crafts and use up-to-date computer technology to trace information through the ages. Teachers' notes £3 + 50p p&p. Education Pack £25 + £2.50 p&p. open Mon–Fri, 10am–4pm all year. Sat 1–4pm, all year. For details of Christmas opening hours and prices please ring. Party bookings can be accommodated outside these hours

Beck Isle Museum of Rural Life, Pickering YO18 8DU; Tel (01751) 473653; *Honorary Publicity Officer* T. Johnstone
Rooms with displays from Victorian era. Advance booking necessary for parties (Tel 73707)
Trustees of the Management Committee

Beningborough Hall, York YO6 1DD; Tel (01904) 470666; Administrator
National Trust

Byland Abbey, Nr Ampleforth; Tel (01347) 868614
English Heritage

Castle Howard, York; Tel (01653) 648333; *Administrator* M.E. Carmichael

Clarke Hall, Aberford Hall, Wakefield WF1 4AL; Tel (01924) 375598; Fax (01924) 375598; *Director* Susan Morton, MEd
Restored 17th century house available to all educational establishments in Yorkshire and Humberside. Cost for a full day for schools outside the consortium of 4 LEAs = £10 per pupil (maximum approx 40). Other special public events advertised from time to time. Available also for pre-booked organisations and groups. Please send for a brochure for more information

The Craven Museum, Town Hall, High St, Skipton BD23 1AH; Tel (01756) 794079; *District Museums Officer* Siobhan Kirrane, MA, AMA
School parties welcome, talks available
Craven District Council

Dales Countryside Museum, Station Yard, Hawes, Wensleydale, N. Yorks DL8 3NT; Tel (01969) 667494; *Curator* Martin Gresswell
School visits with or without appointment. Open Apr–Oct daily 10–5pm; Nov–Mar open most weekends

Easby Abbey, Nr Richmond
English Heritage

Educational Resource Service, The Resource Village, Crigglestone, W. Yorks WF4 3LB; Tel (01924) 240999; Fax (01924) 254425; *Director* Evan Jones
Loan service of models, artefacts, photographs and original works of art available to any educational establishments in the North of England and beyond

Embsay Steam Railway, Yorkshire Dales Railway Museum Trust, Embsay Station, Nr Skipton BD23 6AX; Tel (01756) 794727; Fax (01756) 795189; *President* John Keavey; *Chairman* David Barlow; *Business and Marketing Manager* Stephen Walker
Preserves and operates all aspects of rural/industrial steam railway

Fairfax House, Castlegate, York YO1 1RN; Tel (01904) 655543; *Director* Peter Brown
A restored 18th century historic house with outstanding Chippendale furniture, clocks, silver and porcelain. Changing exhibitions on life in Georgian York

Flamingo Land Family Fun Pack, The Rectory, Kirby Misperton, Malton, North Yorkshire YO17 0UX; Tel (01653) 668287; *Marketing Manager* Isobel Taylor

Fountains Abbey and Studley Royal, Ripon; Tel (01765) 608888; *Education Officer* Jenny Deacon
National Trust

Friargate Museum, Castlegate Exhibitions (York) Ltd, Lower Friargate, York YO1 1SL; Tel (01904) 658775; *Director* Trevor G. Hunt; *Administration* Wendy Skelton
The award winning Friargate Museum is taking a leading role in bringing history alive. Over 70 life size models wearing authentically reproduced costumes, together with sound and special lighting effects, give a realistic atmosphere to the museum. 1995 'Elsie Wagstaff Wins' A Home Front Exhibition to celebrate the Anniversary of Victory in Europe (VE day)

Georgian Theatre Royal and Museum, Victoria Rd, Richmond DL10 4DW; Tel (01748) 823021; *Theatre Manager* Bill Sellars
Guided tours for parties by appointment all year. Museum open Easter–Oct 31
Georgian Theatre Trust

Green Howards' Museum, Trinity Church Sq, Richmond DL10 4QN; Tel (01748) 822133; Fax (01748) 826561; *Curator* Lt-Col N.D. McIntosh, MBE
Museum Trustees

Helmsley Castle, Helmsley; Tel (01439) 70442
English Heritage

Impressions Gallery of Photography, 29 Castlegate, York YO1 1RN; Tel (01904) 654724; *Director* Paul Wombell; *Contact* Stefan Sadofski
Photographic gallery with darkrooms and shop. Exhibitions change every six weeks; extensive programme of talks and workshops. Open Mon–Sat 10.30 to 5.30 and cafe open 7 days a week Mon–Sat 9.35–5.30, Sun 10.00–5.00

Jervaulx Abbey, Ripon; Tel (01677) 60226
Privately owned listed Cistercian Abbey set in 120 acre parkland. Open all year. Pay by Honesty Box. I.S. Burdon, Lane House Farm, Jervaulx, Ripon

Jorvik Viking Centre, Coppergate, York YO1 1NT; Tel (01904) 643211; *Education Officer* K. McMahon
Travel back in time to see, hear and smell life in Viking York. Teachers' Information pack and education resource material available

Kirkham Priory, Whitwell-on-the-Hill, York YO6 7JS; Tel (01653) 618768; *Custodian* Lynda Teale
Open to the public. Education, marketing English Heritage. Grounds
English Heritage

Malton Museum, Market Pl, Malton, N. Yorks YO17 0LT; Tel (01653) 695136 and (01653) 692610; *Museum Assistant* P. Wiggle; Tel (01653) 692610
School visits
Malton Museum Foundation

Marvel's Leisure and Amusement Park, Northstead Manor Gardens, North Bay, Scarborough; Tel (01723) 375091

Middleham Castle, Nr Leyburn; Tel (01969) 23899
English Heritage

Mount Grace Priory, Northallerton DL6 3JG; Tel (01609) 883494; *Regional Education Officer* Dr Ross Jellicoe; *Custodian* Harvey Haines
Ancient priory, open to the public. School parties by arrangement
English Heritage–Historic Buildings and Monuments Commission for England

National Railway Museum, Leeman Rd, York YO2 4XJ; Tel (01904) 621261; *Head* Andrew Scott; *Head of Marketing and Development* Rory Wardroper; *Educational Officer* D.W. Mosley

Experience nearly 200 years of technical and social history on the railways and see the way they shaped the world

National Trust Regional Office, Yorkshire, Goddards, 27 Tadcaster Rd, Dringhouses, York YO2 2QG; Tel (01904) 702021; Fax (01904) 707982

Newby Hall and Gardens, Ripon, N. Yorks HG4 5AE; Tel (01423) 322583
Historic House and Gardens. School parties welcomed. Woodland discovery walk. Miniature railway. Adventure gardens for children. Enquiries to Administrator

Norton Conyers, Wath, Ripon HG4 5EH; Tel (01765) 640333; *Contact* Lady Graham
Heritage late medieval house with Stuart and Georgian additions. The home of the Grahams for 370 years. Family pictures, furniture and costumes. Visited by Charlotte Bronte: a family legend is said to have been the inspiration for the mad Mrs Rochester in Jane Eyre and the house is believed to be an original of Thornfield Hall. Large walled garden with 18th century orangery. House Bank Holiday Sundays and Mondays, Sundays from 22 May to 4 September, daily from 25–30 July 2–5.00pm; Garden Wednesdays to Sundays 3 April–4 September, 2–5pm. Closed Mondays (except Bank Holiday Mondays) and Tuesdays

Nunnington Hall, York YO6 5UY; Tel (01439) 748283; Fax (01439) 748284; *Visitor Services Manager* Duncan Pearcey
17th-century manor house. Carlisle collection of 22 miniature rooms. Parties welcome by arrangement

Pickering Castle, Pickering, N. Yorks YO18 7AX; Tel (01751) 74989
English Heritage

Richmond Castle, Richmond, N. Yorks DL10 4QW; Tel (01748) 822493
English Heritage

Richmondshire Museum, Ryder's Wynd, Richmond DL10 4JA; Tel (01748) 825611
Local history and archaeology. Story of Richmond in pictures, models, memorabilia. BBC Herriot surgery. Costumes. Medieval crucks. Lead mining. Toys. Open Easter to end of autumn half-term

Rievaulx Abbey, Nr Helmsley; Tel (014396) 228
English Heritage

Rievaulx Terrace and Temples, Helmsley, York YO6 5LJ; Tel (0143 96) 340; Graham Toase
National Trust

Ripley Castle, Ripley, Harrogate HG3 3AY; Tel (01423) 770152; Fax (01423) 771745; Sir Thomas Ingilby, Bt; *Marketing Co-ordinator* William Myles
Ripley Castle has been the home of the Insilby family since the 1320s. Educational visitors can experience history, along with other subjects in a unique setting. The Castle's educational resource pack offers teachers numerous pre, during and post visit activities in line with the National Curriculum. Study room available. Parties are welcome at £1.75 per child with two teachers free

Ryedale Folk Museum, Hutton-le-Hole, York YO6 6UA; Tel (017515) 367; *Curator* Martin Watts
Yorkshire's leading open-air museum illustrating the everyday life of ordinary people from prehistory to early 20th century. Special rates for school parties. Open daily from 27 March to 30 Oct. For details of our wide range of educational services contact Anne Boyens
Trustees of the Crosland Foundation

Scarborough Art Gallery, The Crescent, Scarborough YO11 2PW; Tel (01723) 374753; *Curator* J. Montgomery
Early 19th century villa housing permanent collection of British art; also the Laughton collection. Annual programme of temporary exhibitions

Scarborough Castle, Scarborough, N. Yorks; Tel (01723) 372451
English Heritage

Scarborough Museum and Art Gallery, *Enquiries* Director of Tourism and Amenities, Londesborough Lodge, The Crescent, Scarborough YO11 2PW; Tel (01723) 369151
Scarborough Borough Council

Shandy Hall, Coxwold, York YO6 4AD; Tel (01347) 868465; *Chairman of Council of the Trust* Nicolas Barker; *Honorary Curator and Honorary Secretary to Laurence Sterne Trust* Julia Monkman
Open to the public on Wed and Sun pm June–Sept, any other time by appointment. Further interest in the works of Sterne. Houses a large collection of Sterneana. Charitable Trust No 529593
The Laurence Sterne Trust

Skipton Castle, Skipton BD23 1AQ; Tel *Enquiries* (01756) 792442; *Contact* J. Parker
The is one of the best preserved mediaeval castles in England. Over 900 years old and fully roofed. Party visits welcomed – free entry for teachers. Guides available at no extra cost, otherwise illustrated Tour Sheets provided in a choice of 8 Languages. Large coach and car park off nearby High Street. Open all year. Castle gift shop now open

Sutton Park, Sutton-on-the-Forest, York YO6 1DP; Tel (01347) 810249
Stately Home. Enquiries to Secretary

Swaledale Folk Museum, Reeth Grn, Reeth, Nr Richmond DL11 6QT; Tel (01748) 84373; *Curator* Donald J. Law
Reflects life traditions, history of the Dale, lead mining, farming, social history, domestic life, religion, pastimes, crafts

Thorp Perrow Arboretum, Thorp Perrow, Bedale, N. Yorks DL8 2PR; Tel (01677) 425323; *Curator* P.G. Robinson

Treasurer's House, Minster Yard, York YO1 2JD; Tel (01904) 624247; *Property Manager* Norma Sutherland
Originally the home to the Treasurer of York Minster. Period rooms, audio-visual programme. Important collection of furniture, pictures. Restaurant

Merchant Adventurers' Hall, Fossgate, York YO1 2XD; Tel (01904) 654818; *Clerk* Ivison S. Wheatley
The finest surviving medieval guild hall in Europe. Exhibitions illustrate the merchants' wealth when York was England's second city
Merchant Adventurers' Company

Whitby Abbey, Whitby; Tel (01947) 603568
English Heritage

Whitby Museum, Pannett Pk, Whitby YO21 1RE; Tel (01947) 602908; *Honorary Keeper* Dr N.T. Nicol, OBE, TD, FRCR
Whitby Museum

Wood End Museum of Natural History, The Crescent, Scarborough YO11 2PW; Tel (01723) 367326; Fax (01723) 376941; *Senior Museums Officer* C.I. Massey
Local natural history and geology exhibits. Aquarium, conservatory, first editions, paintings connected with Sitwell family

York Castle Museum, York YO1 1RY; Tel (01904) 653611; Fax (01904) 671078; *Advisory Teacher, Museum Education Officer* Marilyn Ingle
Museum Education Service for North Yorkshire County Council's Schools. Other enquiries answered. Teachers notes available. Booking service for school parties Tel (01904) 633932

York City Art Gallery, Exhibition Sq, York YO1 2EW; Tel (01904) 551861; *Art Assistant* Catharine MacLeod; *Exhibitions Officer* Helen Grundy
Talks, guided tours, worksheets, advice for teachers, occasional special projects including workshops. Events leaflets available–Free mailing to teachers
York City Council

York: Clifford's Tower, Clifford St, York, N. Yorks YO1 1SA; Tel (01904) 646940
English Heritage

York Story, Castlegate, York; Tel (01904) 628632; *Director of York Castle Museum* Dr A.F. Hodges
Visitor centre containing a mixture of medieval and modern, showing the history of the city through models, reconstructions and audio-visual

Yorkshire Museum, Museum Gdns, York YO1 2DR; Tel (01904) 629745; Fax (01904) 651221
Educational materials specifically designed to meet the criteria of the National Curriculum. Available for booked school parties. Contact the booking office
North Yorkshire CC

Yorkshire Museum of Carriages and Horse Drawn Vehicles, Yore Mill, Aysgarth Falls, N. Yorks DL8 3SR; Tel 01-969 663399; *Trustee* G.W. Shaw
Ex water powered cotton mill, a 3 storey high, Grade II, listed building originally built in 1784. It burned down in in 1852 and was rebuilt 3 years later. It was purchased by G W Shaw of Richmond in 1969 to house part of his unique collection of horse drawn vehicles including coaches, fire engines, hansom cab, haunted coach, and coaching impediments. The Museum gives a varied picture of horse-drawn transport 100 years ago. Open April 1st, until October 31st. Daily 9-30 am to 8-30pm. Guided tours by prior arrangement.

Murton Park, Murton, York YO1 3UF; Tel (01904) 489966; *Assistant Manager/Education Officer* Angela Peirson
Replica Dark Age Village, Derwent Valley Railway and Yorkshire Museum of Farming set in 8 acres of parkland

Northamptonshire

Althorp House, Althorp, Northampton NN7 4HQ; Tel (01604) 770107; *Contact* Lisa Hanlon
Spencer family home. Picture gallery, collection of porcelain and furniture, private carriage collection, shop, tea room, business and private functions catered for by arrangement

****Boughton House,*** Nr Kettering NN14 1BJ; Tel (01536) 515731; Fax (01536) 417255; *Director* Gareth Fitzpatrick
Administered by The Living Landscape Trust, 11,000 acre site. Free school visits to farm, forestry, gamekeeping etc. Nature trails, classroom, interpretive centre

The Canal Museum, Stoke Bruerne, Towcester, Northants; Tel (01604) 862229
Pre-booked party visits. For project information and teacher's packs enclose SAE. Comprehensive collection of publications
British Waterways

Canons Ashby Hse, Canons Ashby, Daventry NN11 6SD; Tel (01327) 860044; *Administrator* L. Richardson
Pack being prepared
National Trust

Castle Ashby House, Castle Ashby, Northampton NN7 1LQ; Tel (01604) 696696; *General Manager* A. McAinsh

Central Museum and Art Gallery, Guildhall Rd, Northampton NN1 1DP; Tel (01604) 233500 Ext 5116, or for general enquiries 5115. Direct Line (01604) 39415; Fax (01604) 238720; *Curator* Sheila M. Stone
Contains one of the largest collections of footwear in the world; Northampton history; Italian 15th–18th century paintings and British art; temporary exhibitions

Deene Park, Corby NN17 3EW; Tel (01780) 450278/ 450223; *Contact* The House Keeper
Delightful 'lived in' historic house, largely 16th century. Home of the Brundenell family since 1514, including the Earl of Cardigan who led the charge of the Light Brigade. Gardens, lake and parkland

Hinwick House, Nr Wellingborough; Tel (01933) 53624; *Owner* R.M. Orlebar
House open to the public for pre-arranged groups. Old Master paintings, tapestries, china, objects d'art, Queen Anne period house

Kirby Hall, Nr Corby; Tel (01536) 203230
English Heritage

****Lamport Study Centre,*** Lamport Hall, Lamport, Northampton NN6 9HD; Tel (0160128) 508; *Study Centre Officer* M.L. Crecraft
Hall and grounds offer a wide variety of resources for historical and environmental studies. Study centre officer available to plan visits

Northampton Museums Education Service, Central Museum Guildhall Rd, Northampton NN1 1DP; Tel (01604) 233500 Ext 5103/5116; *Contact* Education Officer
Two museums, art gallery. Visits, handling sessions and workshops, children's holiday activities

Rushton Triangular Lodge, Nr Desborough; Tel (01536) 710761
English Heritage

Northumberland

Alnwick Castle, Estates Office, Alnwick NE66 1NQ; Tel (01665) 510777; Fax (01665) 510876; *Head Agent to His Grace The Duke of Northumberland* R. Wilson; *Contact* A. Fricker
Magnificent border fortress dating back to 11th century. Principal apartments including the armoury, guard chamber and library are on view. Second largest inhabited castle in England after Windsor

Aydon Castle, Nr Corbridge; Tel (01434) 632450
English Heritage

Bamburgh Castle, Bamburgh; Tel (01668) 214208; *Custodian* D. Armstrong
Historical tour

Belsay Hall, Castle and Gardens, Nr Newcastle; Tel (01661) 881636
English Heritage

Berwick Ramparts, Berwick upon Tweed
English Heritage

Brinkburn Priory, Nr Rothbury; Tel (01665) 570628
English Heritage

Callaly Castle, Whittingham, Alnwick NE66 4TA; Tel (0166 574) 663; Major A.S.C. Browne, DL

Chesterholm Museum, Bardon Mill, Hexham NE47 7JN; Tel (0149 84) 277; *Education Officer* Linda Thompson
Guided tours, excavations in progress. Booklets, information packs and worksheets
The Vindolanda Trust

Chester's Roman Fort and Clayton Collection Museum, Chollerford, Humshaugh, Hexham-on-Tyne NE46 4EP; Tel (01434) 681379
English Heritage

Corbridge Roman Site, Corbridge, Northumberland NE45 5NT; Tel (01434) 632349
English Heritage

Cragside House and Country Park, Rothbury, Morpeth NE65 7PX; Tel (01669) 620333; Fax (01669) 621050; *Property Manager* Rosemary Gillett
National Trust

Dunstanburgh Castle, Nr Alnwick; Tel (01665) 576231
English Heritage

The Farne Islands, 8 St Aidan's, Seahouses NE68 7SR; Tel (01665) 720651; *The Warden*
Pre-booking with Warden essential
National Trust

Grace Darling Museum, 1 Radcliffe Rd, Bamburgh NE69 7AE; *Honorary Curator* Christine Bell; Tel (01668) 214465
(as from 1.4.95)
Exhibits connected with the rescue of 9 survivors of the S.S. Forfarshire by Grace Darling and her father in 1838. Free admission, Open daily 11am–6pm, Easter–1 Oct
Royal National Lifeboat Institution

Heatherslaw Mill, Cornhill on Tweed TD12 4TJ; Tel (01890) 820338; *Manager* J. Bradley; Tel (01890) 820297 (out of hours)
Illustrates milling processes by use of 19th century water driven corn mill. Education resource. Travelling exhibitions. Work room/picnic room available. Tea rooms and shops. Special group rates. Free parking

Housesteads Roman Fort, Haydon Bridge, Hexham; Tel (01434) 344363
English Heritage

Lindisfarne Castle, Holy Island, Berwick on Tweed; Tel (01289) 89244; *Education Liaison Officer*
National Trust, Scots Gap, Morpeth, Northumberland

Meldon Park, Morpeth, Northumberland NE61 3SW; Tel (0167 0172) 661; *Owner* M.J.B. Cookson
An example of John Dobson architecture, built by him for present family's ancestors. Excellent rhododendron spring garden. Open 2–5pm. Open Sat 21 May to 19 June 1994 and 27, 28, 29 August 1994

National Trust, Northumbria Regional Office, Scot's Gap, Morpeth, Northumberland NE61 4EG; Tel (0167 0174) 691

Norham Castle, Nr Berwick-upon-Tweed
English Heritage

Northumbria Craft Centre, The Chantry, Bridge St, Morpeth NE61 1PJ; Tel (01670) 511217; *Manager* Sue Jordan
Northumbria craftsmen's work on display, housed in the 13th century Chantry Building. Visit also the Morpeth Chantry Bagpipe Museum and busy Tourist Information Centre

Preston Tower, Chathill NE67 5DH; Tel (0166589) 227; *Owner and Curator* Major T.H. Baker-Cresswell
A Border Pele Tower providing a realistic picture of the grim way of life under the constant threat of 'Border Reivers'. Open all year in daylight hours

Prudhoe Castle, Prudhoe; Tel (01661) 833459
English Heritage

Wallington House, Garden and Grounds, Cambo, Morpeth NE61 4AR; Tel (01670) 774283; *The Administrator* C.R.A. Olliver
National Trust

Warkworth Castle and Hermitage, Nr Amble; Tel (01665) 711423
English Heritage

Nottinghamshire

Brewhouse Yard Social History Museum, Castle Boulevard, Nottingham NG7 1FB; Tel (0115) 9483504; Fax (0115) 9483504 Ext 3601; *Education Officer* Jocelyn Dodd Castle Museum; Tel Ext 3691
Museum bookings for all parties through Mrs Hogg or Mrs Bombroffe, Ext 3600/1. Self-guided tours or special topics via Education Officer. The Museum offers period rooms and shops, didactic displays and rock-cut caves showing daily life in Nottingham, Many touchables exhibits. Open daily 10am–5pm except Christmas. Admission free: Mon–Fri £1.00 adults, 50p children (Weekends and Bank Holidays) (joint ticket for Castle Museum). All parties must book
Nottingham City Council

Castle Museum and Art Gallery, The Castle Museum, Nottingham NG1 6EL; Tel (0115) 9483504; Fax (0115) 305988
Services include a lecture programme; in-service training for teachers and consultant programme for school visits. Admission free: Mon–Fri £1.00 adults, 50p children (Weekends and Bank Holidays) (joint ticket with Brewhouse Yard Museum)

Clumber Park, Worksop S80 3AZ; Tel (01909) 476592
Open all year. Historic parkland, woodland, grassland, heathland, gardens and a large ornamental lake. Orienteering, fishing, conservation centre. Educational walks and talk. Events, vineries and tools exhibitions, plant centre
Enquiries Estate Office, Clumber Park
National Trust

Creswell Crags Visitor Centre, Welbeck, Worksop; Tel (01909) 720378; *Manager* A. Sumpter
Caves, exhibitions, prehistory, AV aids, events and activities suitable for all ages
Creswell Heritage Trust

Green's Mill and Centre, Windmill La, Sneinton, Nottingham NG2 4QB; Tel (0115) 950 3635; *Keeper of Green's Mill* Denny Plowman
Restored working windmill. Science exhibits and displays tell the story of George Green, (1793–1841), mathematician physicist and miller in the adjacent centre. Open Wed to Sunday plus Bank Holiday Mondays 10am–5pm

Holme Pierrepont Hall, Nottingham NG12 2LD; Tel (0160 73) 2371; *Owners* Mr and Mrs R. Brackenbury
Full educational programme

Mansfield Museum and Art Gallery, Leeming St, Mansfield NG18 1NG; Tel (01623) 663088; *Curator* Elizabeth Weston
Mansfield past and present. Watercolours of Old Mansfield by A.S. Buxton and porcelain collection. Ever changing temporary exhibitions programme

Museum of Costume and Textiles, 51 Castle Gate, Nottingham; Tel (0115) 948 3504; *Education Officer* Jocelyn Dodd Castle Museum
Nottingham City Council

The National Trust, East Midlands Regional Office, Clumber Park Stableyard, Worksop S80 3BE; Tel (01909) 486411; *Regional Director* James Turner; *Contact* A. Pam
Protects through ownership, places of historic interest or natural beauty for public enjoyment

Natural History Museum, Wollaton Hall, Nottingham NG8 2AE; Tel (0115) 928 1333/281130; *Education Officer* A. Thornhill, BSc, MSc
Intra-mural teaching. Lectures, field studies. Nature trails. Excellent habitat displays and much local environment information
Nottingham City Council

Newark Air Museum Ltd, The Airfield, Winthorpe, Newark NG24 2NY; Tel (01636) 707170; *Chairman* R. Bryan; *Contact* R. Blackmore
Extensive display of aircraft aero engines and aviation memorabilia, guided school visits, work sheets etc. Prior appointment necessary. New aircraft display hanger and Engine hall

Newark Museum, Appletongate, Newark NG24 1JY; Tel (01636) 702358; *Museums and Heritage Manager* J. Milford
Archaeology and local history, photographs and slides

Newstead Abbey, Linby NG15 8GE; Tel (01623) 793557; Fax (01623) 793557; *Education Officer* Jocelyn Dodd Castle Museum, Nottingham; Tel (0115) 948 3504 Ext 3691
Nottingham City Council

Ruddington Framework Knitters' Museum, Chapel St, Ruddington, Nottingham NG11 6HE; Tel (0115) 984 6914; *Curator* Jason Doherty
Working museum based in restored 19th century Framework Knitters' workshops and cottages. Guided tours. Working machines and demonstrations. Video. Booked groups throughout the year. £1.25 Children/ OAPs, £5.25 Family, £1 Education Groups/person

Rufford Country Park, Rufford Saw Mill, Newark NG22 9DG; Tel (01623) 824153, Craft Centre (01623) 822944; *Managing Ranger* Frank Eyre
Historical site, ruin of manor house and Abbey. Mill exhibition area. craft centre, shops, resturants
Nottinghamshire CC

Sherwood Forest Visitor Centre, Edwinstowe, Mansfield NG21 9HN; Tel (01623) 823202; *Manager* Sam Dunlop
Video programme, Robin Hood exhibition, teachers' pack. Ranger guides available. 450 acres ancient oak woodland. SSSI Site
Nottinghamshire CC

Sundown Kiddies Adventureland, Rampton, Retford; Tel (01777) 248274; Fax (01777) 248967; *Information Officer* J. Rhodes; *Information Officer* A.B. Rhodes
Theme park specially designed for under 10 years old

Thrumpton Hall, Nottingham NG11 0AX; Tel (0115) 983 0333; *Administrator* Hon George Seymour
Tudor and Jacobean house. School parties welcome; conducted tours by prior arrangement

Vina Cooke Museum of Dolls and Bygone Childhood, The Old Rectory, Cromwell, Nr Newark NG23 6JE; Tel (01636) 821364; *Owner/Curator* Vina Cooke
Displays and explains all aspects of bygone childhood in fascinating setting of old rectory

Interski 95 Outram St, Sutton in Ashfield, Notts NG17 4BG; Tel (0623) 551024; Fax (0623) 558941; *Marketing Manager* Roger Walker

Oxfordshire

Abingdon Museum, The County Hall, Market Pl, Abingdon; Tel (01235) 523703; *Senior Museum Officer* Emily Leach, BA, AMA
Displays or archaeology and local history in a 17th century building. Contemporary Craft Displays. Educational services: contact Oxon County Museum, Fletcher's Hse, Woodstock
Abingdon Town Council and Oxfordshire County Council

Ashmolean Museum, Beaumont St, Oxford OX1 2PH; Tel (01865) 278015; *Clore Education Officer* Katherine Botth Stevens

Guided tours for school parties by appointment. Teachers' Seminars

Banbury Museum, 8 Horsefair, Banbury OX16 0AA; Tel (01295) 259855; Fax (01295) 270556; *Senior Museums Officer* Simon Townsend
Schoolroom available for use by visiting parties. New information pack for use with displays is now available on request. Teaching services in museum
Oxfordshire CC/Cherwell District Council

Bate Collection of Musical Instruments, Faculty of Music, St Aldate's, Oxford OX1 1DB; Tel (01865) 276139/276125; *Curator* Jeremy Montagu, MA, FSA
The most comprehensive collection in England of historical woodwind, brass and percussion instruments and a complete Javanese Gamelan. Many keyboards, including one of Handel's harpsichords, and a bowmaker's workshop. Regular tutorial weekends on instruments and summer schools. Open to the public Monday to Friday, 2.00–5.00pm except Good Friday and Christmas Day. Admission Free. Visits by parties etc are possible in the mornings but only by appointment

Blenheim Palace, Woodstock; Tel (01993) 811091; Fax (01993) 813527; *Education Officer* J.D. Forster

Broughton Castle, Banbury OX15 5EB; Tel (01295) 262624; Lord Saye and Sele
Open throughout the year for parties by appointment

Chiltern Sculpture Trust, PO Box 452, Oxford OX4 1GU; Tel (01865) 483477; Fax (01865) 721136; *Co-ordinator* Jacqui Mansfield
Education Charity managing the Chiltern Sculpture Trail which comprises two walks lasting from 1–2 hours inviting visitors to experience contemporary art in a forest environment. Commissioned artists produce work in response to the location, exploring the possibilities of art beyond the gallery

Christ Church Picture Gallery, Canterbury Quadrangle, Christ Church, Oxford OX1 1DP; Tel (01865) 276172; Fax (01865) 202429; *Assistant Curator* Lucy Whitaker
Old Master paintings and drawings from 14th to 18th century. Tours and talks for schools by arrangement with the Assistant Curator
Christ Church

Cogges Manor Farm Museum, Church La, Cogges, Witney OX8 6LA; Tel (01993) 772602; *Senior Museums Officer* Catherine Mason
A museum of domestic and agricultural life in the late Victorian period with working farmhouse, dairy, stables, farmyard and period livestock, barns, agricultural displays, walled garden, orchard picnic area, nature trail. A wide range of educational talks and demonstrations for all ages. Open Tues–Fri 10.30am–5.30pm; Sat, Sun 12–5.30pm (4.30pm in Oct), Easter to Nov
Oxfordshire County Council, Department of Leisure and Arts

Cotswold Wild Life Park, Bradwell Gr, Burford, Oxford OX18 4JW; Tel (01993) 823006; *General Manager* Colin Fountain; *Park Secretary* Maureen Clifford
Study sheets, talks and brass rubbing available

Didcot Railway Centre, Great Western Society Didcot OX11 7NJ; Tel (01235) 817200; *Marketing* Jeanette Howse
Didcot Railway Centre recreates the golden age of the Western Railway with steam trains, original engine shed and repair shop and reconstructed station

Farnborough Hall, Banbury OX17 1DU; Tel (01295) 690202; *Contact* Mr and Mrs Holbech
Written enquiries to Farnborough Hall. Historic hall of educational interest

Fawley Court, Marian Fathers Historic House and Museum, Fawley Crt, Henley-on-Thames RG9 3AE; Tel (01491) 574917; *Owner* Marian Fathers
Manuscripts, parchments and incunable mostly connected with Poland. Original Laski's Code of Laws, 16th century bible, Polish armoury, Polish paintings, historical maps. Memorabilia of Polish Army, Nay and Air Force during service with Western Allies (1939–1945). Groups welcome by arrangement
All mail to Rev Fr Superior

Greys Court, The National Trust, Rotherfield Greys, Henley-on-Thames RG9 4PG; Tel (01491) 628529
Jacobean house with Georgian additions, amid remains of 14th century fortified house. Walled gardens, Ice House, Tudor donkey wheel and Archbishop's maze in grounds
National Trust

Kingston Bagpuize House and Garden, Kingston Bagpuize, Nr Abingdon OX13 5AX; Tel (01865) 820259; *Owner and Administrator* Lady Tweedsmuir
Charles II manor house, large garden. Open Sundays and Bank Holiday Monday 2.30–5.30 pm, 1 April to 30 Sept, (Closed on Good Friday). Groups on weekdays only by written appointment. Shop, teas

The Manor House, Stanton Harcourt; Tel (01865) 881928; *Contact* The Honorable Mrs A.E. Gascoigne; *Contact* Sarah Pauling; Tel (01993) 811624
The historic manor houses a fine collection of pictures, silver, furniture, and porcelain. The medieval kitchen and Pope's Tower remain

Mapledurham Water Mill, The Estate Office, Mapledurham Hse, Mapledurham, Reading RG4 7TR; Tel (01734) 723350; Fax (01734) 724016; *Administrator* Lucy Boon
Last working watermill on River Thames, still producing flour, all the original working machinery. Schools pack available, tours arranged

Minster Lovell Hall and Dovecot, Nr Witney; Tel (01993) 775315
English Heritage

Museum of the History of Science, Old Ashmolen Bldg, Broad St, Oxford OX1 3AZ; Tel (01865) 277280; Fax (01865) 277288; *Curator* J.A. Bennett; *Assistant Curator* W.D. Hackmann
Early astronomical, mathematical instruments, chemical apparatus, clocks, pharmaceutical exhibits; reference library. Apply to librarian for research purposes. Open weekdays 12pm–4pm Mon–Fri from 1 Oct 94 12pm–4pm Tues–Sat free of charge. Closed Easter and Christmas weeks

Museum of Modern Art, 30 Pembroke St, Oxford; Tel (01865) 722733; *Education Officer* Ian Cole
Talks in gallery, practical workshops, lectures, seminars, films

Museum of Oxford, St Aldate's, Oxford OX1 1DZ; Tel (01865) 815559; *Senior Museums Officer* Dr Lauren Gilmour
The museum displays tell the story of the City and the University. In addition to objects used in the Saxon, Medieval and later periods, there are maps, plans, models and reconstructed Oxford interiors dating from the 16th century to the 1930s. An Audio Tour can be hired to help set the objects on display in a wider historical context (£1.50 per tour). Museum staff also offer handling collections and guided tours of Oxford Castle Motte including the original underground well chamber. Continuous series of temporary exhibitions, with free talks or demonstrations every Thursday lunchtime. Schools and groups very welcome. Please book for handling sessions, worksheets, audio tours, tours of motte, education and Lecture Room facilities

North Leigh Roman Villa, Nr Oxford; Tel (01305) 860853
English Heritage

University of Oxford Botanic Garden Rose Lane, Oxford OX1 4AX; Tel (01865) 276920; *Superintendent* Timothy Walker; *Deputy Superintendent* Marcus Reynolds; *Education Officer* Louise Allen
Education programme aims to encourage a positive attitude to plants and the environment by illustrating the diversity of the plant kingdom, demonstrating the importance of plants and explaining why we need to conserve the world's flora; Open to schools and the general public; Guided Tours for all age groups

Oxford Gallery of Comparative Art/Chinese Arts Centre CAC, 50 High St, Oxford OX1 4AS; Tel (01865) 242167; *Director* G. Aldrick
Gallery of Comparative and Chinese art–contemporary paintings and reproductions, ceramics, books, museum, cassettes, games. Education guides for schools in preparation

The Oxford Story, 6 Broad St, Oxford OX1 3AJ; Tel (01865) 790055; Fax (01865) 791716

Uses innovative techniques to enable visitors to experience collegiate life through the ages and discover the great people and events from this seat of learning. National Curriculum based teachers' pack available
Heritage Projects

Oxfordshire County Council, Dept of Leisure and Arts, Fletcher's Hse, Woodstock, Oxford OX20 1SN; Tel (01993) 811456; Fax (010865) 813239; *Senior Museum Officer (Education)* Carol Anderson, BA, PGCE, AMA
Visit planning and advisory services available to all educational institutions within the county. Handling collections for use in museum. Inset courses available

Pitt Rivers Museum, South Parks Rd, Oxford OX1 3PP; Tel (01865) 270927; *Director* Dr Schuyler Jones; *Contact Secretary* ; Tel (01865) 270927
World wide collections of cultural anthropology and archaeology including musical instruments (audio visual facilities). Graduate teaching department, schools' education service

Rycote Chapel, Nr Thame; Tel (018447) 346
English Heritage

Stonor Park, Stonor, Henley-on-Thames RG9 6HF; Tel (01491) 638587; *Administrator* D. Boddy
Historic house dating from 12th century occupied throughout by Stonor family. Talks and guided tours on history of house, family

Sulgrave Manor, Sulgrave, Banbury OX17 2SD; Tel (01295) 760205; *The Resident Director* Martin Sirot-Smith
The Tudor home of George Washington's ancestors, built in 1539
Sulgrave Manor Board

Upton House, Nr Banbury OX15 6HT; Tel (01295) 670266; *Administrator* Oliver Lane
A major collection of European and English paintings and porcelain in a fine 17th century house. Includes works by El Greco, Brueghel, Bosch, Memling, Guardi, Hogarth and Stubbs. Brussels tapestries, Silver procelain, Chelsea figures
The National Trust

Vale and Downland Museum Centre, The Old Surgery, Church St, Wantage OX12 8BL; Tel (012357) 66838; *Senior Museum Officer* Emily Leach; *Museum Officer* John Lange; *Administrator* Judy Vaughan Williams; *Administrator* Vivienne Hill
Displays of local art and exhibition of history and archaeology of area of the Vale of the White Horse and Wantage. Shop, refreshments

Well Place Zoo, Ipsden; Tel (01491) 680092; *Manager* H. Holtom

Shropshire

Acton Scott Historic Working Farm, Wenlock Lodge, Acton Scott, Church Stretton SY6 6QN; Tel (01694) 781306/307; *Museum Education Officer* Jayne Speakman, BA, PGCE
Working demonstration of horses, crafts and rural life. Free preliminary visits for teachers. Teachers' notes available. Guided tours available to suit the needs of the group. Artefact handling sessions
Shropshire CC

Attingham Park, Nr Shrewsbury; Tel (01743) 709203; *Regional Public Affairs Manager*; Tel (01743) 709203
National Trust
18th Century House set in landscape designed by Humphry Repton, Regency State rooms, painted boudoir, The Nash picture gallery with collection of French and Italian paintings and a collection of Regency Silver. Three woodland walks through the deer park and alongside the river. Tea room and shop. Disabled access. Schools welcome – education officer available for environmental education. Situated on the B4380 (formerly the A5) in Atcham 4 miles east of Shrewsbury. Open 1 April 1995–27 September 1995. Saturday–Wednesday 1.30pm–5.00pm. Bank Holiday Monday 11.00am–5.00pm. October Sat–Sun only 1.30pm–5.00pm. Park open daily dawn to dusk except Christmas Day

Benthall Hall, Broseley TF12 5RX; Tel (01952) 882159; *Custodian/Administrator* June Mitchell
Sixteenth-century stone house, mullioned windows, moulded brick chimneys, carved oak staircase, decorated plaster ceilings. Plantsman's garden, Restoration church. Open 1 April until end of Sept. Every Sunday, Wednesday 1.30–5pm, also Bank Holiday Monday. Mon, Tues by appointment
National Trust

Buildwas Abbey, Nr Telford; Tel (01952) 433274
English Heritage

Carding Mill Valley, Church Stretton, Walks; *Head Warden* Shropshire Hills Office, The Cahlet, Carding Mill Valley, Church Stretton; Tel (01694) 723068
National Trust

Church of St John the Baptist, Stokesay, Craven Arms; Tel (01588) 672797; Rev Allan Toop The Vicarage, Clun Rd, Craven Arms SY7 9QW; Tel (01588) 672797
Guided visits and historical leaflets available for children and adults. Schools should telephone in advance if a guide is required

Clun Local History Museum, Town Hall, Clun; Tel (01588) 640576
Display of flints, domestic and farming bygones, smocks, fossils, geological specimens, local historical finds, Admission Adults 30p Children free

Dudmaston Hall, Quatt, Bridgnorth WV15 6QN; Tel (01746) 780866; *Administrator* Eddie Earl
Seventeenth-century house and furniture. Dutch flower paintings, modern pictures, water colours, botanical art, lakeside garden, dingle walks; Open March 29th to Oct 1st, 2pm–5.30 Wednesday and Sunday only Pre-booked parties Thursdays, pm, Tea Room open 1–2pm Wed and Sun for light lunches. Estate walks starting from Hampton coade car park 6 miles S.E. Bridgnorth and A442
National Trust

Eastern Orthodox Church, Tyn-y-Rhos Hall, Weston Rhyn, Nr Oswestry; Tel (01691) 777898
Museum of the late Victorian period. Free day Retreat service by appointment

Haughmond Abbey, Nr Shrewsbury; Tel (0174377) 661
English Heritage

Ironbridge Gorge Museum Trust, The Wharfage, Ironbridge, Telford TF8 7AW; Tel (01952) 433522; *Education Officer* D.J. Forber
Six main sites: Field study facilities with free preliminary visits for teachers. Guidelines, information, databases, workshops, residential study facilities

Lilleshall Abbey, Nr Oakengates
English Heritage

Ludlow Museum, Castle St, Ludlow, Shropshire SY8 1AS; Tel (01584) 875384; Ludlow Museum Offices, Old St, Ludlow, Shropshire SY8 1NW; Tel (01584) 873857; *Curator of Natural Sciences* Dr Jane Mee; *Education Officer* Jayne Speakman Dept of Leisure Services, Column Hse, 7 London Rd, Shrewsbury SY2 6NW; Tel (01743) 255015
Open April to September Mon–Sat 10.30–1.00, 2.00–5.00 (open Sundays July and August). Admission charge
The story of Ludlow; from the building of the castle and establishment of the town, through medieval prosperity and political intrigue to fashionable Ludlow of the 18th Century. Also 'Reading the Rocks' a celebration of Ludlow's contribution to international geology
Educational Services: Hands on sessions available for schools. Contact Jayne Speakman (see above)
Shropshire CC

Midland Motor Museum, Stourbridge Rd, Bridgnorth; Tel (01746) 761761; *Education Officer* M.H. Barker
Primary teacher guide lines. Camping Park. Open weekends and Bank Holidays 11.00 am–4.00 pm. Open daily July, August and September 11.30 am–5.00 pm. Special opening for pre arranged parties

Much Wenlock Museum, High St, Much Wenlock TF13 6HR; Tel (01952) 727773; *Museum Education Officer* Jayne Speakman
Handling sessions on fossils at the museum and follow-up fieldwork. Excellent Wenlock Olympic

display. There is an outstanding geological display. Teachers' notes and activity sheets available
Shropshire CC

National Trust Regional Office, Mercia, Attingham Pk, Shrewsbury SY4 4TP; Tel (01743) 709343; Fax (01743) 709352
Admission Charges, House and Grounds: Adult £3.50, Child £1.75, Family £8.70; House party rate 20 or more non-members 20% discount; Park and grounds Adult £1.40, Child £0.70

Shipton Hall, Much Wenlock TF13 6JZ; Tel (01746) 785225; *Owner* J.N.R.N. Bishop
Classical Elizabethan Stone Manor House with Georgian additions and elegant Rococo plasterwork by Thomas F. Pritchard. School and educational parties by arrangement

Stokesay Castle, Craven Arms SY7 9AH; Tel (01588) 672544; *Custodian* K.J. Lewis
Thirteenth-century fortified manor house in attractive see=tting, oldest surviving example in England. Refreshments, souvenirs. Open March–November

Upton Cressett Hall, Nr Bridgnorth; Tel (0174 631) 307; W. Cash
Guided tours

Wenlock Priory, Much Wenlock; Tel (01952) 727466
English Heritage

Weston Park, Weston-under-Lizard, Shifnal, Shropshire TF11 8LE; Tel (01952) 850207; Fax (01952) 850430; *Education Officer*

Wroxeter (Viroconium) Roman City, Wroxeter, Shrewsbury, Salop SY5 6PH; Tel (01743) 761330
English Heritage

Somerset

Ambleside Bird Gardens, Lower Weare, Axbridge BS28 2JQ; Tel (01934) 732362; *Owners* John and Teressa Pickford

Axbridge Museum, King John's Hunting Lodge, The Square, Axbridge BS26 2AP; Tel (01934) 732012; *Museum Administrator* Vacancy

Barford Park, Bridgwater; Tel (0127 867) 269; Col Michael Stancombe
House and garden open 16 May to 20 Sept Weds and Thurs 2–6pm and at holiday weekends

Barrington Court, Nr Ilminster TA19 0NQ; Tel (01460) 241480; *Administrator*
Talks and exhibitions occasionally
Farms now privately owned. House and garden run by National Trust

Brympton d'Evercy, Yeovil BA22 8TD; Tel (01935) 862528; *Owner* C.E.B. Clive-Pononby-Fane
Privately owned historic house with award-winning gardens, vineyard, museum and distillery. Cider making, Roman mosaic, photographic and painting exhibitions. 14th century parish church

Cheddar Showcaves, Cheddar Gorge, Somerset BS27 3QF; Tel (01934) 742343; Fax (01934) 744637; *Education Officer* Bob Smart
Beautiful showcaves in spectacular limestone gorge–prehistoric occupation and modern tourism–in SSSI and AONB. Opportunities for study and project work for all ages in Geology, Geography, History and Biology. FREE video loan, worksheets, coach park, toilets, picnic room and guided tours

Cleeve Abbey, Washford, Watchet, Somerset TA23 0PS; Tel (01984) 40377
English Heritage

Coleridge Cottage, 35 Lime St, Nether Stowery, Bridgwater TA5 1NQ; Tel (01278) 732662; *Curator* Derrick Woolf
Home of Coleridge from 1796–1798, open to public. Further knowledge of Coleridge worldwide
National Trust

Combe Sydenham Country Park, Monksilver, Taunton; Tel (01984) 56284; *Education Department* Vacancy
Elizabethan day for schools. A variety of history, geography and environmental education programmes linked to National Curriculum requirements. Free brochure available

Cricket St Thomas Wildlife Park, Nr Chard, Somerset; Tel (01460) 30755 or (01395) 273724
Wildlife park set in a natural valley and containing a wide variety of animals including endangered species. Heavy Horse Centre, Tropical Aviary, Adventure Trail, Scenic Railway, Craft Centre, Gift Shop, Licenced Restaurants together with a Processing Dairy and Ice Cream Factory. Conducted tours available on application. New education room. Crinkly Bottom Themepark

Diocese of Bath and Wells, Education Department, The Old Deanery, Wells, Somerset BA5 2UE; *Contact: Director of Education* Tom Peryer Bath and Wells Diocesan Education Office, The Old Deanery, Wells BA5 2UE; Tel (01749) 670777; Fax (01749) 674240

Dunster Castle, Dunster, Minehead TA24 6SL; Tel (01643) 821314; *Property Manager* Mike MacCormack
National Trust

Farleigh Castle, Farleigh, Hungerford, Nr Bath BA3 6RS; Tel (01225) 754026; *Custodian* B.J. Biddle
Free school visits, mainly tourist, reliving history. Special exhibits, attractions include 16th century armour, tombs, 15th century wall paintings, lead coffins in crypt
English Heritage

Fleet Air Arm Museum, Fleet Air Arm Museum, Box D6, RNAS Yeovilton, Nr Ilchester, Somerset BA22 8HT; Tel (01935) 840565; *Education Adviser* Sue Morse
Free education pack available

Gaulden Manor, Tolland, Lydeard St Lawrence, Nr Taunton TA4 3PN; Tel (019847) 213; *Owner and Administrator* J.H.N. Leg Starkie
Elizabethan historic house of great charm, lived in and shown by owners. Jacobean plasterwork and fine antique furniture. Fascinating gardens

Glastonbury Tribunal and Lake Village Museum and Tourist Information Centre, 9 High St, Glastonbury BA6 9DP; Tel (01458) 832954; Fax (01458) 832949; *Manager* J. Franks
Ancient building, built 1385. Contents, lake, village, items 250 BC–50 AD in numerous rooms. Garden offers quite and peaceful conditions. Tourist Information Centre
English Heritage–Historic Buildings and Monuments Commission

Hatch Court, Hatch Beauchamp, Taunton TA3 6AA; Tel (01823) 480120; Fax (01823) 480058; Dr and Mrs Robin Odgers

Lytes Cary Manor, Nr Somerton; Tel (0145 822) 3297
National Trust

Maunsel Grange Estate, North Newton, Nr Bridgwater; Tel (01278) 663413; *Contact Owner* Sir Benjamin Slade; *Contact* Desmond and Carol Duddridge; Tel (01278) 663413; Fax (01278) 661074
Stately home, historical interest, grade 2, inner hall dates back to 1420, Geoffrey Chaucer stayed. Ancestral home of Mira-Behn–devotee to Gandhi. Wildlife park, picnic and barbecue area. Adventure play area

Midelney Manor, Drayton, Langport TA10 0LU; Tel (01458) 251229; *Owner* J.M.R. Cely Trevilian
Historic connections particularly with Muchelney Abbey. Furniture and items of historical interest. Summer schools, private tours with lunch, tea or supper
Historic Houses Association

Montacute House, Montacute; Tel (01935) 823289; *Regional Education Officer* Barbara Webber
Teacher seminars by arrangement with National Portrait Gallery
National Trust

Muchelney Abbey, Muchelney, Langport, Somerset TA10 0DQ; Tel (01458) 250664
English Heritage

Museum of South Somerset, Hendford, Yeovil; Tel (01935) 24774
Guided school tours. Handling sessions, outreach visits, worksheets
South Somerset District Council

Shoe Museum, C/o C. and J. Clark Ltd, 40 High St, Street BA16 0YA; Tel (01458) 43131; *Public Relations Manager* John Keery
Guided tours by appointment. Free admission. Open Mon–Fri 10am–4.45pm; Sat 10am–6.00pm Sunday 12.00–6.00pm
C. and J. Clark

Somerset Museum Education Service, Weir Lodge, 83 Staplegrove Rd, Taunton TA1 1DN; Tel (01823) 255510; *Organiser, Museum Education Service*
Loan of museum and art objects to Somerset schools. varied programme of activities, events information and advice for schools and the public

Somerset Rural Life Museum, Abbey Farm, Chilkwell St, Glastonbury BA6 8DB; Tel (01458) 831197; *Education Officer, Somerset Museum Education Service*
Somerset CC

Stembridge Tower Mill, High Ham, Langport TA10 9DJ; Tel (01458) 250818; *Curator* G. Rogers
Leaflet. Open 4 April–29 Sept; Sun, Mon, Wed 2–5pm. Parties by appointment only
National Trust

Rode Tropical Bird Gardens, Rode, Nr Bath BA3 6QW; Tel (01373) 830326; *Information Officer*

Wells Museum, Cathedral Grn, Wells BA5 2UE; Tel (01749) 673477; *Curator of Collection* L.A. Kerr; *Administrator* H.W. Gillian
Trustees, Wells Museum

Wookey Hole Caves and Papermill, Wookey Hole, Wells BA5 1BB; Tel (01749) 672243; *Managing Director* Peter Haylings; *Contact* Sylvie Drake
Spectacular caves and variety of exhibitions in Victorian mill

South Yorkshire

Abbeydale Industrial Hamlet, Abbeydale Rd South, Sheffield S7 2QW; Tel (0114) 236 7731; *Keeper* Janet Peatman
18th century water-powered scythe works with crucible steel furnace and workers' houses
Sheffield City Museums Dept

Bishop's House, Norton Lees La, Sheffield S8 9BE; Tel (0114) 255 7701; *Assistant Keeper* Karen Snowden
Tudor-framed yeoman's house with displays of local and social history
Sheffield City Museums Dept

Cannon Hall Museum, Cawthorne, Barnsley S75 4AT; Tel (01226) 790270; *Curator* Brian Murray
Display of decorative arts material such as furniture, glassware, art nouveau pewter and art pottery. Also museum of 13/18th Royal Hussars

City Museum, Weston Pk, Sheffield S10 2TP; Tel (0114) 276 8588; *Director* David Patmore
Outstanding collections of cutlery, Old Sheffield Plate, local archaeology, geology and wildlife. Sheffield Museums run City Ecology Unit; County Archaeology Service; full educational programmes, activities, data banks, information and identification services
Sheffield City Arts and Museums Dept

Conisbrough Castle, Doncaster DN12 3BU; Tel (01709) 863329; *Custodian* Margaret Turner
Late 12th C Fortification, unique original keep, grounds, memorial park and visitors' centre. Open 10–5pm (summer), 10–4pm (winter) and all Bank Holidays except Christmas/New Year. School parties by arrangement. Toilet and Tea Rooms

Cooper Gallery, Church St, Barnsley S70 2AH; Tel (01226) 242905; *Assistant Keeper* Don Bashforth
Lectures, guided tours, films, workshops offered in conjunction with changing exhibition programme as appropriate
Barnlsey MBC, Dept of Education and Leisure

Doncaster Museum and Art Gallery, Chequer Rd, Doncaster DN1 2AE; Tel (01302) 734288; *Assistant Museums and Promotions Officer, Museums Education Service* A. Rodgers
Learning Sessions to school parties, adult organisations, and cultural activities

Doncaster Museum Loans Service, C/o Doncaster Museum, Chequer Rd, Doncaster DN1 2AE; Tel (01302) 734287; *Museums Education and Promotions Officer* P. Anne Pennington-George, BSc, AMA
Loan service to the Metropolitan Borough of Doncaster

Epworth Old Rectory, 1 Rectory St, Epworth, Doncaster DN9 1HX; Tel (01427) 872268; *Warden* C.J. Barton, BSc
This 1709 Queen Anne period house was the boyhood home of John and Charles Wesley, the founders of Methodism. The house contains some items which once belonged to the Wesleys. Some rooms are set out with period furniture, much as the family would have known. There are also portraits, prints, Methodist pottery and other memorabilia. The reference library is available to approved scholars. Open 1st March–31st October daily Mon–Sat 10.00am–12.00pm, 2.00pm–4.00pm; Sun 2.00pm–4.00pm; Admission adults £2.00, children £1.00. Audio visual presentation, refreshments, accommodation and opening at other times, all by prior arrangement with the warden

Graves Art Gallery, Surrey St, Sheffield S1 1XZ; Tel (0114) 273 4789; *Director of Arts* D.N.C. Patmore; *Art Education Officer* Vivienne Sillar
School groups visiting galleries to do art work. Art education officer. Artist residencies organised
Sheffield Arts Department

Huddersfield Art Gallery, Princess Alexandra Wk, Huddersfield HD1 2SU; Tel (01484) 513808 Ext 216; Fax (01484) 531983; *Senior Officer* Robert Hall; *Galleries Officer* Jane Speller
Gallery spaces for contemporary artists working in all media. Permanent collection of 20th century British art. Exciting temporary exhibitions programme

Kelham Island Museum, Alma St (off Corporation St), Sheffield S3 8RY; Tel (0114) 272 2106; *Marketing Officer*
Displays on the industries and industrial development of Sheffield, including working craftsmen and machines, film/slide shows. Class-room facilities. Special talks available by arrangement. Open Mon–Thurs 10am–4pm, Sun 11am–4.45pm. Closed last three weeks of December (please check)
Sheffield City Museums Dept

Mappin Art Gallery, Weston Pk, Sheffield S10 2TP; Tel (0114) 272 6281; *Director of Arts* David Patmore; *Keeper of Mappin Art Gallery* Michael Tooby
Historical and contemporary art from collection and temporary exhibitions, full range of arts and education activities. Closed Mondays
Sheffield Arts Department

Monk Bretton Priory, C/o 17 Abbey La, Barnsley, S. Yorks S71 5QD; Tel (01226) 204089
English Heritage

Roche Abbey, Maltby, Rotherham, S. Yorks S66 8NW; Tel (01709) 812739
English Heritage

Rotherham Art Gallery, Brian O'Malley Arts Centre, Walker Place, Rotherham; Tel (01709) 382121 Ext 3621; *Keeper of Education and Extension Services* Tel (01709) 823633

Rotherham Museum, Clifton La, Rotherham; Tel (01709) 382121 Ext 3635; *Keeper (Education and Extension Services)* T. Brannen; Tel (01709) 823633
Loan service to schools. In-service training for teachers. Extra-mural visits. Purpose-built classroom for schools, with assistance by museum staff. Educational counselling for teachers by museum education staff
Rotherham MBC

Ruskin Craft Gallery, Address and telephone numbers as above; *Principal Keeper* Janet Barnes
Temporary exhibition programme of contemporary crafts

The Ruskin Gallery, Collection of the Guild of St George, 101 Norfolk St, Sheffield S1 2JE; Tel (0114) 273 5299; Fax (0114) 273 5994
Houses museum collection formed by John Ruskin (1819–1900). Temporary exhibition programme

Sheffield City Art Galleries, Education Services, Graves Art Gallery, Surrey St, Sheffield S1 1XZ;

Tel (0114) 273 4789; *Art Education Officer* Vivienne Sillar
Loans of original works available to all schools, colleges and other educational establishments in Sheffield Metropolitan Area. Project work related to exhibitions, worksheets and materials available

Sheffield Manor, Manor La, Sheffield 2; Tel (0114) 276 8588; *Contact*
City Museum for opening arrangements
Sixteenth century manor house ruins, once prison of Mary Queen of Scots and of Cardinal Wolsey
Sheffield City Museums Dept

Shepherd Wheel, *Keeper* Janet Peatman
(Correspondence and telephone as for Abbeydale Industrial Hamlet). Four hundred year old site. Water powered cutlery grinding workshops. Open Wed–Sun 10.00–12.30 and 1.30–5.00. Closes 4.00pm Dec–Feb
Sheffield City Museums Dept

Worsbrough Mill Museum, Worsbrough, Barnsley S70 5LJ; Tel (01226) 203961
A site museum of the corn-milling industry, comprising a 17th-century water-powered mill and a 19th-century engine-driven mill, both fully restored and stoneground flour is still produced for sale. Guided tours for schools. Shop for publications, flour and souvenirs

Staffordshire

Alton Towers, Alton, Staffs ST10 4DB; Tel (01538) 702200
Alton Towers, the UKs no. 1 Theme Park, offers the most magical experience for school visits, by combining 'Learning' with 'Fun'. New for 1995, Alton Towers has National Curriculum Resource packs available on Science and Technology and Mathematics and other interesting Information packs for schools and colleges. With over 125 rides and attractions, and easy ways for schools to pay a discounted rate, Alton Towers is the ideal venue for your school visit. Phone our Information Office (as above) to request a copy of our Schools Brochure – 'The Learning Curve'

The Ancient High House, Greengate St, Stafford ST16 2JA; Tel (01785) 222181; *Contact, Heritage Manager*
The history of England's largest timber-framed Elizabethan Town House (1595) is related through period room settings, video and displays on local history. Costumed tours and workshops are available to school parties and the public
Stafford Borough Council

Bass Museum, Visitor Centre and Shire Horse Stables, Burton-upon-Trent; Tel (01283) 511000 Ext 3505; Fax (01283) 513509; *Education Officer* C. Turner, BA
Presenting the history of brewing and of the Company on a 6 acre site which includes several buildings housing many exhibitions, the Bass Shire Horse Stables, and historic vehicle collection. Guided tours of the Brewery and packaging available. Well equipped Education Dept with study and teaching rooms. Liaison with staff encouraged before visits. Heritage Education Trust 1990 Sandford Award winners

The Brindley Water Mill, Mill St, Leek; Tel (01538) 381446; *Honorary Secretary* David A. Hallen 10 Derby St, Leek, Staffs ST13 5AW; Tel (01538) 399332
A watered powered corn mill containing a museum of the life and achievement of James Brindley, Engineer 1716–1772
The Brindley Mill Preservation Trust

Chatterley Whitfield Mining Museum, Tunstall, Stoke-on-Trent ST6 8UN; Tel (01782) 813337; *Education Officer* Linda Bridges
Tours led by former miners through Museum's New Pit. Free preliminary visits for teachers and a range of free Education Services. Details on request. Home of the national Mining Collection

Drayton Manor Park and Zoo, Nr Tamworth; Tel (01827) 287979
Family leisure park, 45 rides, attractions and zoo. Nature trail. Peel museum, shops and lakes, catering, garden centre. New major indoor ride 'Pirates Adventure'

Ford Green Hall, Ford Green Rd, Smallthorne, Stoke-on-Trent ST6 1NG; Tel (01782) 534771; *Manager* Judith Franklin
Furnished 17th century farmhouse with 18th century brick additions. Educational events and resources
Stoke-on-Trent City Council

Gladstone Pottery Museum, Uttoxeter Rd, Longton, Stoke-on-Trent ST3 1PQ; Tel (01782) 319232/311378; *Bookings* Joy Williams
A restored Victorian 'Potbank' with colourful galleries and demonstrations of pottery making in the original workshops

Hanch Hall, Lichfield WS13 8HH; Tel (01543) 490308; *Owner* Mrs Milton-Haynes
Open Sunday afternoons April to September also Bank Holiday Mondays, afternoons and evenings for groups. Family home. Guided tour. Twenty rooms. Dungeons, gardens, tearooms

Izaak Walton Cottage, Shallowford, Stafford; Tel (01785) 760278; *Contact* Heritage Manager
17th century cottage, with 17th century domestic interiors. Bequeathed to Stafford by Izaak Walton, author of the 'Compleat Angler', period herb garden and fishing collection
Stafford Borough Council

Lichfield Heritage Exhibition and Treasury, Market Sq, Lichfield WS13 6LG; Tel (01543) 256611; *President* J.E. Rackham; *Contact* The Administrator
A cultural exhibition telling the story of Lichfield through its people. Audio-visual theatre, muniment room, coffee, gift shop, viewing platform high in the Spire

Minton Museum, Minton Hse, London Rd, Stoke-on-Trent ST4 7QD; Tel (01782) 744766; *Curator* J. Jones
Comprehensive permanent display of Minton productions since 1793. Also the Minton Archives, the pottery industry's best collection of records

Royal Doulton Museum, Nile St, Burlsem, Stoke-on-Trent ST6 2AJ; Tel (01782) 292292; *Curator* Valerie Baynton, MA, AMA
Permanent displays of Royal Doulton products from 1815. Archive materials, Factory tours

Samuel Johnson Birthplace Museum, Breadmarket St, Lichfield WS13 6LG; Tel (01543) 264972; *Curator* Dr G. Nicholls
Preserves the birthplace and promotes the life, work, and personality of Doctor Samuel Johnson

Shugborough, Nr Stafford; Tel (01889) 881388; *Bookings Officer* Irene Williamson; *Education Officer* Philip Clayton
Mansion house, servants quarters and museum of Staffordshire Life, working Georgian Farmstead, parkland and gardens, tea rooms and NT shop. Educational tours and demonstrations available
National Trust/Staffordshire CC

Shire Hall Gallery, Market Sq, Stafford ST16 2LD; Tel (01785) 278345; Fax (01785) 278327; *Gallery Manager* Hilary Foxley
Historic listed building with Victorian courtrooms available for meetings etc. Exhibitions of fine art, and photography with workshops, lectures and demonstrations by artists and craftspeople for schools, special interest groups and public

Stafford Castle Visitors Centre, Newport Rd, Stafford; Tel (01785) 57698; *Contact* Heritage Manager
Audio visual presentation on the history of Stafford Castle and a recreated Norman guardroom. School tours and education packs are available

Stoke-on-Trent Museum and Art Gallery, Bethesda St, hanley, Stoke-on-Trent ST1 3DE; Tel (01782) 202173; Fax (01782) 205033; *Education Contact* Jane Fineran
Stoke-on-Trent City Council

Tamworth Castle, The Holloway, Tamworth B79 7LR; Tel (01827) 63563; Fax (01827) 52769; *Curator* Esme Ballard, BA, AMA, FRSA
Norman shell-keep with later additions. Fifteen rooms include Dungeon, Norman Exhibition, Haunted Bedroom, 17th century suite, chapel and Victorian wing. Free teachers' resource pack on booking. Giftshop
Tamworth Borough Council

Trentham Gardens, Trentham Leisure Ltd, Trentham, Stoke-on-Trent ST4 8AX; Tel (01782) 657341; *Director* B. Talbot
Ancestral Home and Leisure Centre/Park. Historical and educational value; 750 acre estate. Formal gardens. Wildfowl reserve. Sports facilities, Heritage, Trail Nature Walks (Booklet Guide), Educational Childrens Farm

Wall Roman Site, Watling St, Nr Lichfield, Staffs WS14 0AW; Tel (01543) 480768
English Heritage

Wedgwood Visitor Centre, Barlaston, Stoke-on-Trent ST12 9ES; Tel (01782) 204141/204218; Fax (01782) 204402; *Visitor Centre Manager* Michael Peddar; *Public Relations Executive* Margaret Michell
Purpose-built cinema, craft manufacturing hall, museum and art gallery catering for over 250,000 visitors each year
Josiah Wedgwood and Sons Ltd

Suffolk

Beccles and District Museum, Leman Hse, Ballygate, Beccles NR34 9ND; Tel (01502) 712308; *Chairman of Trustees* G. Standing
The Museum is being relocated during 1995 and will be closed from Jan–Sept. See brochure for details
Trustees of the Beccles and District Museum

Cavendish Manor Vineyards, Nether Hall, Cavendish, Sudbury CO10 8BX; Tel (01787) 280221; *Proprieter* B.T. Ambrose
Listed period house surrounded by own vineyard. Museum, gallery, picnic area, tastings, nature trails, toilets, free parking, wine sales

Christchurch Mansion, Ipswich; *Education Liaison Officer* J.G. Fairclough The Museum, High St, Ipswich IP1 3QH; Tel (01473) 213761

Easton Farm Park, Easton, Nr Wickham Market; Tel (01278) 746475; *Education Officer* C. Barbour
Wide range of farm animals, victorian dairy, modern Dairycentre, Foodcleaning Exhibition and bygone machinery to be seen. School pack available.

Framlingham Castle, Framlingham, Woodbridge IP13 9BP; Tel (01728) 724189
Massive walls and tower of a castle of about 1200AD
English Heritage

Gainsborough's House, 46 Gainsborough St, Sudbury CO10 6EU; Tel (01787) 372958; *Education Officer* Elizabeth Iken
Permanent and temporary exhibitions, library, print workshop
Gainsborough's House Society

Haughley Park, Nr Stowmarket IP14 3JY; Tel (01359) 40205; *Owner* A.J. Williams
Jacobean manor house, built 1620. Open to public Tuesday afternoons May to Sept. House, period furniture, Dutch 16th and 17th century paintings, gardens, woods, fine trees, shrubs. Signposted A45 ignore Haughley signs

Henham Estate, Wangford, Beccles; Tel (01502) 78424; Fax (01502) 78220; *Director* Lady Heidi Crick
4,000 acres of land let to various organisations for use (steam rally, concerts, etc); school tours, scout camps

Ickworth House, Park and Gardens Horringer, Bury St Edmunds IP29 5QE; Tel (01284) 735270; *Property Manager* Caroline Sier
House, park, gardens and deer enclosure with hide. Adventure playground and picnic area. Range of way marked walks in park. House children's guide
National Trust

Ipswich Museum, High St, Ipswich IP1 3QH; Tel (01473) 213761; *Educational Liaison Officer* J.G. Fairclough
Intra- and extra-mural teaching. Loan service. Holiday activities, Saturday club

Kentwell Hall, Long Melford CO10 9BA; Tel (01787) 310207; *Owner* J.G. Phillips

Lavenham Guildhall of Corpus Christi, Market Pl, Lavenham; Tel (01787) 247646; *Administrator* D.W. Head
Medieval buildings and museum
National Trust

Little Hall, Market Pl, Lavenham, Sudbury CO10 9QZ; Tel (01787) 247179; Fax (01787) 248341; *Administrator* Brian Forgham
Guided tour of medieval house with magnificent crown post roof; connections with Cairo and ancient Egyptian history, and with World War 2
Suffolk Building Preservation Trust

Lowestoft Museum, Nicholas Everitt Pk, Lowestoft NR33 9JR; *Honorary Secretary* B.V. Turner; Tel (01502) 565371
Lowestoft Archaeological and Local History Society

Manor House Museum, Honey Hill, Bury St Edmunds IP33 1HF; Tel (01284) 757072; Fax (01284) 757079; *Museums Services Manager* Trevor Meakin
Museum of watches and clocks from the 17th century to the 20th century, together with fine and decorative arts collections displayed in a fine Georgian Building. Groups visits and talks by appointment. Temporary exhibition change every 3 months. Teachers workpacks available on Art and Horology
St Edmundsbury Borough Council

Mechanical Music Museum Trust, Charity Trust Reg. No. 801863 Blacksmith Rd, Cotton, Stowmarket IP14 4QN; Tel (01449) 613876; *Voluntary Workers Registered Trust* Robert Finbow
Musical treasures from small polyphons and music boxes to street pianos and large fair organs. Numerous unusual items, all played. Open Sundays June to Sept 2.30–5.30 for conducted tours. Adults £2.50, Children 50p

Melford Hall, Long Melford, Suffolk CO10 9AA; Tel (01787) 880286; *Administrator* Sir R. Hyde-Parker
Young vistors' guide
National Trust

Moyse's Hall Museum, Cornhill, Bury St Edmunds; Tel (01284) 757488; *Museums Services Manager* Trevor Meakin
Guided tours, handling sessions and teachers' work packs available
St Edmundsbury Borough Council

Museum of East Anglian Life, Stowmarket IP14 1DL; Tel (01449) 612229; *Curator* L. Colsell; *Secretary (school Bookings)* P. Davis; *County Museums Education Liaison Officer* J.G. Fairclough; Tel (01473) 213761/2
Teacher information packs and worksheets; oral history tapes; workroom with audio/visual facilities

National Horseracing Museum, 99 High St, Newmarket CB8 8JL; Tel (01638) 667333; *Curator* Graham Snelling
Exhibition of the development of horseracing housed in Regency Old Subscription Rooms, video programme of classic races. Computer Information on selected racehorses, trainers, jockeys and history of betting

Orford Castle, Woodbridge, Suffolk IP12 2ND; Tel (01394) 450472
English Heritage

Otley Hall, Otley, Ipswich IP6 9PA; Tel (01473) 890264; *Owner* J.G. Mosesson
Fifteenth-century grade 1 listed moated hall. Rich in history. Open to public. Lectures and tours etc by appointment

The Otter Trust, Earsham, Nr Bungay; Tel (01986) 3470
Talks available from Conservation Officer. Educational leaflets available by post

The Priory, Water St, Lavenham CO10 9RW; Tel (01787) 247003; *Owner* Alan Casey
Superb timber-framed historic house dating from 14th century. Paintings and stained glass by Bossanyi. Herb garden, gift shop, lunches, teas. Open Good Friday–31 Oct

Saxtead Green Windmill, Framlington; Tel (01728) 685789
Four-sailed corn mill, medieval in origin, with a 19th century wooden superstructure mounted on a brick round house. In working order
English Heritage

Somerleyton Hall, Nr Lowestoft NR32 5QQ; Tel (01502) 730224; *Administrator* R.T. Hallan
School visits welcome when hall and gardens closed to the public from Easter to 25 September

Southwold Museum, Bartholomew Grn, Southwold IP18 6HZ; *Honorary Curator* George Bumstead

Open daily 2.30 to 4.30pm Easter to 30 Sept.
Admission free
Southwold Archaeological and Natural History Society

Suffolk Wildlife Park, Kessingland, Lowestoft, Suffolk; Tel (01502) 740291; *Director* Martin Goymour; *Contact (Commercial Manager)* Richard Ross
'Take a Walk on the Wild Side' in 100 acres of Suffolk countryside. During your exploration you will see African Wildlife, animals and birds from around the world. Safari Road Train, Bouncy Castle, Crazy Golf and Children's Play Area. Daily entertainments programme during the summer season

Surrey

Birdworld Bird Park and Gardens, Holt Pound, Nr Farnham; Tel (01420) 22140/22992; Fax (01420) 23715; *Director* P. Harvey; *Educational Officer* Janet Newan; *Director* Kate Price; *Wildlife Bookshop Manager* D. Harvey; *Curator of Birds* Rob Harvey
Educational booklets, topic sheets and videos available. Guided tours can be booked

Chertsey Museum, The Cedars, 33 Windsor St, Chertsey KT16 8AT; Tel (01932) 565764; *Curator* Amanda Devonshire; *Education Officer* Christine Finley; *Assistant Curator, Costume Decorative Arts and Temporary Exhibitions* Philip Sykas
Talks, slide shows, loan boxes and quizzes (tailored to teachers' requirements if possible). Programme of temporary exhibitions. Colouring sheets, postcards and information sheets on sale
Runnymeade Borough Council

Chessington World of Adventures, Chessington, Surrey KT9 2NE; Tel (01372) 729560; *Marketing Manager* Lesley Morisetti

Clandon Park, West Clandon, Guildford GU4 7RQ; Tel (01483) 222482; *The Administrator* Dixon Asquith
Palladian country house with marble hall, show rooms; Gubbay collection of porcelain, furniture, needlework; Onslow family pictures; Queen's Royal Surrey Regiment; museum; garden with Maori House
National Trust

Claremont Fan Court School, Claremont Dr, Esher; Tel (01372) 467841; *Bursar* A.R. Oakley
Claremont Fan Court Foundation Ltd

Don Quixote UK, In-Country Language Courses Ltd
2/4 Stoneleigh Park Rd, Stoneleigh, Epsom, Surrey KT19 OQR; Tel 0181-786 8081; Fax 0181-786 8086
Don Quixote is Europe's largest organisation for Spanish language courses in Spain, operating centres in Barcelona, Granada, Salamanca and Màlaga. Also offers advice on funding, transport, insurance, accommodation, excursions, local language courses, study materials and Spanish events (local and national). Will organise parents' evenings and information days on Spanish in Spain at universities, colleges and other educational institutions

Elmbridge Museum, Church St, Weybridge KT13 8DE; Tel (01932) 843573; *Museum Manager* Neil White
Local history museum dealing with archaeology, social and natural history; education workshops for school classes by appointment
Elmbridge Museum Service

Farnham Castle Keep, Castel Hill, Farnham, Surrey GU6 0AG; Tel (01732) 778000
English Heritage

Gatwick Zoo and Aviaries, Russ Hill, Charlwood; Tel (0192 74) 862312; *Information Officers* Terry and Sheila Thorpe

Godalming Museum, 109A High St, Godalming, Surrey GU7 1AQ; Tel (01483) 426510; *Curator* Adela Goodall; *Museum Assistant* J.A. Benson
Local history collections displayed in medieval building; small 'Jekyll' garden. School visits by prior arrangement. Temporary exhibitions, activities
Godalming Museum Trust/Waverley Borough Council

Goddards, Abinger Common, Dorking RH5 6JH; Tel (01306) 730487
Edwardian country house by Sir Edwin Lutyens with Gertrude Jekyll garden. Open to visitors by appointment – please telephone
The Lutyens Trust

Guildford House Gallery, 155 High St, Guildford GU1 3AJ; Tel (01483) 444740; Fax (01483) 444742; *Curator* Miss I.C. Rhodes, BA, MA, AMA
A wide variety of temporary exhibitions; free leaflet available
Guildford Borough Council

Guildford Museum, Castle Arch, Guildford GU1 3SX; Tel (01483) 444750; *Curator* Matthew Alexander
Talks, visits, school loan service
Guildford Borough Council

Little Holland House, 40 Beeches Ave, Carshalton SM5 3LW; Tel 0181-770 4781 (Sutton Leisure Services); Fax 0181-770 4777; *Museum and Historic Houses Officer* V.H. Murphy
House and contents by Frank Dickinson (1874–1961) follower of the Arts and Crafts movement. Open first Sunday of each month, excluding January (and Bank Holiday Sunday and Mondays) 1.30–5.30pm. Group visits available outside normal opening hours

Administered by Sutton Heritage Service, Central Library, St Nicholas Way, Sutton SM1 1EA; Tel 0181-770 4782; Fax 0181-770 4777

Loseley House, Loseley Pk, Guildford GU3 1HS; Tel (01483) 304440; *Visitor Bookings Manager* Penny Swindells
Historic Elizabethan mansion and famous dairy farm with Jersey cows producing renowned additive-free dairy products. House visits and farm tours available

Museum of Farnham, 38 West St, Farnham GU9 7DX; Tel (01252) 715094; *Museum Education Officer* Ruth Watson
Lively new local history displays in an early Georgian town house; temporary exhibitions; schools affiliation scheme, including object loan service; Saturday club for children; holiday activities. The Museum was completely refurbished in 1992

National Trust Regional Office, Southern, Polesden Lacey, Dorking RH5 6BD; Tel (01372) 453401

Petworth House, Petworth GU28 0AE; Tel (01798) 342207; *Administrator* Dr D. Owen
Historic House
Education Room
National Trust

Rural Life Centre Old Kiln Museum, Reeds Rd, Tilford, Farnham GU10 2DL; Tel (01252) 792300/(0252) 795571; *Education Officer* Henry Jackson (Proprietor)
Forge demonstrations, wheelwright talk, worksheets available

Surrey Heath Museum, Knoll Rd, Camberley GU15 3HD; Tel (01276) 686252 Ext 284; *Education Officer* Sharon Cross
Borough of Surrey Heath

Thorpe Park, Staines Rd, Chertsey KT16 8PN; Tel (01932) 569393; Fax (01932) 566367; *Contact* Group Sales and Marketing Department
Our schools' visits programme is closely linked with the National Curriculum for Mathematics, Science and Technology. Free questionnaires, teachers' notes and preliminary visits

The Watts Gallery, Down La, Crompton, Nr Guildford GU3 1DQ; Tel (01483) 810235; *Curator* Richard Jefferies

The Witley Centre, Witley, Godalming GU8 5QA; Tel (01428) 683207; *Education Officer* G. Sully
Educational visits, audio-visual displays and interpretation
National Trust

Tyne and Wear

Bedes World, Church Bank, Jarrow NE32 3DY; Tel 0191-489 2106; Fax 0191-428 2361; *Curator* S.A. Mills
Display of excavated material from Anglo-Saxon and medieval monasteries of St Paul's, Jarrow. Audio/Visual, craft shop, café, temporary exhibitions, herb garden, special events and teachers in service courses. Full educational facilities for schools, who must book visits in advance; education staff. Winner 1988 Heritage Education Trust Sandford Award. Anglo Saxon landscape being developed. Teaching of this

will begin in 1994, will include timber building reconstructions field systems and animals
Jarrow 700 AD Ltd

Gibside Chapel and Grounds, Gibside, Burnopfield, Newcastle upon Tyne NE16 6BG; Tel (01207) 542255; *Custodian-in-Charge* J. Gardener
National Trust

Grindon Museum, Grindon La, Sunderland SR4 8HW; Tel 0191-528 4042; *Education Officer* Joanne Cunningham (based at Sunderland Museum); Tel 0191-514 1235; *Assistant Education Officer* Emma Willson
Turn of the century house with Victorian and Edwardian period rooms, shop reconstructions, quiz sheets, teachers notes, loans
Tyne and Wear Museums

Hancock Museum (Tyne and Wear Museums), The University, Newcastle upon Tyne NE2 4PT; Tel 0191-222 7418; *Assistant Education Officer* Gillian Mason; Tel Daytime school tel no 0191-222 6753
Activities can be signed (BSL) if booked in advance activities and events for schools and families. Worksheets, National Curriculum guides and Teachers Guide are available Audio-guide for Land of the Pharaohs

Hatton Gallery, The University, Newcastle upon Tyne NE1 7RU; Tel 0191-222 6057; *Director* Gavin Robson; *Temporary Secretary* Dr Anthony Parton
Exhibitions of contemporary art; concerts and literary events; collection of 16th–18th century European paintings and 19th, 20th century British paintings. On display Kurt Schwitters 'Elterwater Merzbarn' and Uhlman collection of African sculpture

Hylton Castle, Nr Sunderland
English Heritage

John George Joicey Museum, City Rd, Newcastle upon Tyne NE1 2AS; Tel 0191-232 4562; *Curator* John Millard
Period room settings, militaria and local history, including audio visual presentation of the Great Fire of 1854 and the Tyne Flood of 1771. Special school events throughout the year
Tyne and Wear Museums

The Keep, Castle Garth, Newcastle upon Tyne; Tel 0191-232 7938; *Administrator* J.M. Boyd
A very fine Norman keep containing a museum. The 'Newcastle'. Open every day except Monday, 9.30–16.30
Society of Antiquaries

Laing Art Gallery, Higham Pl, Newcastle upon Tyne NE1 8AG; Tel 0191-232 7734/6989; *Education Officer* Gwen Carr
Talks; worksheets; educational displays; art activities
Tyne and wear museums

Monkwearmouth Station Museum, North Bridge St, Sunderland SR5 1AP; Tel 0191-567 7075; *Education Officer* Joanne Cunningham (based at Sunderland Museum); Tel 0191-514 1235; *Assistant Education Officer* Emma Willson
Victorian station with booking office, rolling stock in siding. Also bicycles, trams and buses in new transport displays. Quizsheets, teachers' notes, loans
Tyne and Wear Museums

Museum of Antiquities of the University and Society of Antiquaries of Newcastle upon Tyne, The University of Newcastle upon Tyne, Newcastle upon Tyne NE1 7RU; Tel 0191-222 7846; *Keeper* Charles Daniels; *Contact* Lindsay Allason-Jones
Prehistoric, Roman, Anglo-Saxon, medieval archaeology of the north of England, particularly Hadrian's Wall and environs, models, reconstructions, book stall

Newcastle Discovery, Blandford Sq, Newcastle upon Tyne NE1 4JA; Tel 0191-232 6789; *Education Officer* Ian Thilthorpe
Incorporating: The Museum of Science and Engineering, Science Factory, Great City, The Peoples Gallery. New Galleries in 1995 are a Fashion Gallery and 'A Soldiers Life'
Tyne and Wear Museums

Shipley Art Gallery, Prince Consort Rd, Gateshead NE8 4JB; *Contact* Diane Gilder; Tel 0191-477 1495
Collections of British and Foreign paintings and applied art
Large permanent collection of traditional and contemporary British Craft. Workshops, seminars, classes, information service
Tyne and Wear Museums

South Shields Museum and Art Gallery, Ocean Rd, South Shields NE33 2AU; Tel 0191-456 8740; *Education Officer* Caroline Lloyd
Quizsheets, teachers notes, help preparing visits, loans, activities in the museum. Education area, temporary exhibitions and shop
Tyne and Wear Museums Education Service

South Shields Roman Fort 'Arbeia', Baring St, South Shields; Tel 0191-456 8740; *Education Officer* South Shields Museum; Tel 0191-456 8740
Teachers pack, quiz sheets, loan materials, help preparing visits, archaeology experience for older children
Tyne and Wear Museums

Sunderland Museum and Art Gallery, Borough Rd, Sunderland SR1 1PP; Tel 0191-514 1235; *Education Officer* Joanne Cunningham; *Assistant Education Officer* Emma Willson
Displays on local history including the history of shipbuilding on the Wear and archaeology, local wildlife and geology, fine and applied art. School loan material; help with preparing visits; worksheets, activities
Tyne and Wear Museums

Tynemouth Priory and Castle, Tynemouth, North Shields NE30 4BZ; Tel 0191-257 1090; *Head Custodian* Neil Moat
Historic site presented as a cultural; amenity; Monastic castle; 1st World War military
Historic Buildings and Monuments Commission for England

Washington 'F' Pit Mining Museum, Albany Way, Albany Village, District 2, Washington NE37 1BJ; Tel 0191-416 7640; *Education Officer* Joanne Cunningham Sunderland Museum, Borough Rd, Sunderland SR1 1PP; Tel 0191-514 1235; *Assistant Education Officer* Emma Willson
The engine house, headgear and steam winding engine are preserved, plus displays about the history and working of the colliery
Tyne and Wear Museums

Washington Old Hall, The Ave, Washington Village; Tel 0191-416 6879; *Administrator* Phoebe Lowery
National Trust

The Wildfowl and Wetlands Trust, Washington, District 15 NE38 8LE; Tel 0191-416 5454; Fax 0191-416 5801; *Centre Manager* C. Francis, BSc, PGCE; *Education Officer* N. Warner, BA
Open every day 9.30 to 5pm (or dusk) except Christmas. Free information sheets regarding educational facilities available

Warwickshire

Arbury Hall, Nuneaton CV10 7PT; Tel (01203) 382804; Fax (01203) 641147; *Administrator* Major W.D. Morris-Barker
Open to public viewing on certain days between Easter and September. Parties, including schools, welcome most days by prior arrangement

Charlecote Park, Wellesbourne, Warwick CV35 9ER; Tel (01789) 470277; *Administrator* Michael Pickard
Education packs, video
National Trust

Children's Farmyard, Royal Argricultural Society of England, National Agricutural Centre, Stoneleigh, Kenilworth CV8 2LZ; Tel (01203) 696969 Ext 315

Coughton Court, Alcester B49 5JA; Tel (01789) 400777; *School Visits Organiser* P. Longstaff
Guided tours for schools Mon–Fri mornings by appointment. Open April–Oct
National Trust

Kenilworth Castle, Kenilworth, Warks CV8 1NE; Tel (01926) 52078
English Heritage

Leamington Spa Art Gallery and Museum, Avenue Rd, Leamington Spa CV31 3PP; Tel (01926) 426559; *Acting Manager* Alison Plumridge
Paintings, decorative art and local history displays. Programme of temporary exhibitions
Warwick District Council

Museum and Art Gallery, Riversley Pk, Nuneaton CV11 5TU; Tel (01203) 376158; *Museum Liaison Officer for Education and Visits* Virginia Quant
Open: Tues–Sat 10.30–4.30; Sun 2.00–4.30
Nuneaton and Bedworth Borough Council

Ragley Hall, Alcester; Tel (01789) 762090; *Business Manager*
Beautiful 17th century Palladian House, home of the Earl and Countess of Yarmouth. Home of the Seymour family for over 300 years. Finest baroque plasterwork in England in Great Hall. Also 'The Temptation', a mural painted by Graham Rust between 1969–1983./ Capability Brown park contains adventure wood, unique 3D maze, woodland walk, lake and picnic area

Royal Shakespeare Theatre Collection, Stratford upon Avon CV37 6BB; Tel (01789) 296655; *Director* Brian Glover
Mon to Sat 9.15–8.00 pm, Sunday 12.00–4.30 pm, Nov–March 11–3.30 pm. Theatre exhibition and tours
Royal Shakespeare Theatre

The Shakespeare Birthplace Trust, Shakespeare Centre, Henley St, Stratford-upon-Avon CV37 6QW; Tel (01789) 204016; Fax (01789) 296083; *Director* Roger Pringle, MA
The Shakespeare Birthplace Trust maintains and preserves Shakespearian properties: Shakespeare's Birthplace; Anne Hathaway's Cottage; Mary Arden's House; Hall's Croft; New Place. Special rates for educational groups are available. Trust also maintains a Shakespearian research library and records office. Range of educational programmes in Shakespeare studies for school, university and general groups

Stratford upon Avon Butterfly Farm, Tramway Wk, Stratford-upon-Avon CV37 7LS; Tel (01789) 299288; *Manager* Richard Lamb

Warwick Castle, Warwick CV34 4QU; Tel (01926) 408000; *General Manager* R.P. Armond
Warwick Castle Ltd

Warwick Doll Museum, Oken Hse, Castle St, Warwick CV34 4BP; Tel (01926) 412034/495546
Further details as per Warwickshire Museum

Warwickshire Museum, Market Pl, Warwick CV34 4SA; *Keeper of Education Service* P. Clarke, BA, ATD Museum Education Service, St John's Hse, Warwick CV34 4NF; Tel (01926) 412034

West Midlands

The Aerospace Museum, Cosford, Shifnal, Shropshire TF11 8UP; Tel (01902) 374872/374172; Fax (01902) 374813; *Education Officer* Donald Prior
One of the largest collections of aviation exhibits in UK. Aircraft, missiles and models. Education: liaison available to support visits at all stages from planning to follow-up

Aston Hall, Trinity Rd, Birmingham B6 6JD; Tel 0121-327 2333; *Head of Schools Liaison Dept* Jan Anderson
Furnished Jacobean House. Teaching sessions with schools liaison for Birmingham LEA Schools

Avery Historical Museum, Foundry La, Smethwick, Warley B66 2LP; Tel 0121-558 1112 Ext 1951; *Curator* H.J. Green
Avery-Berkel

Baddesley Clinton, Knowle, Solihull B93 0DQ; Tel (01564) 783294; *Administrator* Marian Buchanan
Medieval moated manor house and grounds
National Trust

Bantock House Museum, Bantock Pk, Bradmore Rd, Wolverhampton WV3 9LQ; Tel (01902) 312132; *Education Officer* Pauline Thomas
18th/19th century ceramics, enamels, japanned tin and papier maché; dolls and toys and local history, Talks, visits from schools, holiday activities
Metropolitan Borough of Wolverhampton
Address for correspondence:- Wolverhampton Art Gallery, Lichfield St, Wolverhampton WV1 1DU; Tel (01902) 312032

Birmingham Museum of Science and Industry, Newhall St, Birmingham B3 1RZ; Tel 0121-235 1661; Fax 0121-233 9210
Presents and explains science and technology in an objective way which is enlightening to non-specialist vistors. Attractions include "Light on Science" the interactive gallery. School parties are particularly welcome. Open Mon–Sat 10.00–5.00, Sun 12.30–5.00. Admission free

Birmingham Museum and Art Gallery, Chamberlain Sq, Birmingham B3 3DH; Tel 0121-235 3890; Fax 0121-235 1337; *Head of Schools Liaison Department* J. Anderson
Services available to Birmingham and the Midlands schools. Art, ceramics and costume displays; Near East and Egyptian galleries; Social history and natural history displays

Birmingham Nature Centre, Pershore Rd, Edgbaston, Birmingham B5 7RL; Tel 0121-472 7775. School Bookings 0121-471 4925; *Head of Schools Liaison Dept* Jan Anderson
Wide variety of British and European wildlife. Natural habitats for plants and insects. Study base activities with a Schools Liaison Dept teacher for Birmingham Schools. Free admission. Please book in advance. Teachers' notes and illustrated guide available
Birmingham Museums and Art Gallery

The Black Country Museum, Tipton Rd, Dudley DY1 4SQ; Tel 0121-557 9643; Fax 0121-557 4242; *Director* I.N. Walden; *Visit Services Manager* M. Taylor
Open air museum of social and industrial history; guided visits can be tailored to suit the group, covering canals, road transport, mining, social conditions, and Black Country history. Trips into Dudley Canal Tunnel and the 1850's underground coal mining experience. Practical activities for children arranged out of season
The Black Country Museum Trust Ltd

Broadfield House Glass Museum, Barnett La, Kingswinford, West Midlands DY6 9QA; Tel (01384) 273011; Fax (01384) 273952; *Senior Museum Keeper* Charles R. Hajdamach
Displays of English Stourbridge, European glass from 19th and 20th centuries. Videos on request, museum shop, quiz sheets

Chillington Hall, Codsall Wood, Wolverhampton WV8 1RE; Tel (01902) 850236; P. Giffard

Coventry Cathedral Education Service, Cathedral Office, 7 Priory Row, Coventry CV1 5ES; Tel (01203) 227597; *Education Officer* Tina Mead
Comprehensive education programme on a variety of subjects for all age groups and GCSE using cathedral and campus area as a resource. Brochure on request

Coventry Museums, *Education Officer* (all sites); Tel (01203) 832385
Provision for schools at all site includes teaching, activities and workshops, occasional teachers workshops, and courses, information sheets, loans service for Coventry schools only

Herbert Art Gallery and Museum, Jordan Well, Coventry CV1 5QP; Tel (01203) 832385; Fax (01203) 832410
Admission free. Local history. 'Godiva City' exhibition tells the story of the development of the city over 1,000 years through objects, pictures and 'hands on' materials, interactive displays, moving images etc. Publications and gift shop; coffee shop. Toilets – incl wheelchair accessible. Parking for disabled visitors. Lift to first floor. Natural history and visual arts. Good disabled access

Lunt Roman Fort, Baginton, Nr Coventry; Tel (01203) 832381; Fax (01203) 832410
Reconstructed turf and timber fort of 1st century AD. Interpretive centre in Granary. Open beginning April to end September weekends and Bank Holidays only, 10am to 5pm, and every day mid July to end August. Admission £2.50 adults (1.25 children and concessions. Admission charge includes tape tour guide. Special rates apply to pre-booked parties. Educational visits can be arranged outside normal

opening. Publications and gift sales. Toilets (inc Wheelchair accessible). Picnic area. Free Car park

Dudley Museum and Art Gallery, St James's Rd, Dudley DY1 1HU; Tel (01384) 453575; *Senior Keeper* Charles Hajdamach; *Keeper of Geology* Colin Reid
Museum opening Monday–Saturday 10.00am–5.00pm; Galleries and displays; Broadfield House Glass Museum. Dudley Museum Time trail geological gallery. Programme of temporary exhibitions throughout the year including educational and fine art exhibitions. Educational services available for geology and appropriate other exhibitions

Dudley Zoo and Castle, 2 The Broadway, Dudley DY1 4QB; Tel (01384) 252401/2/3; Fax (01384) 456048; *Education Officer* David C. Beeston, PhD
Worksheets, preparatory pack Teachers' notes and lecture service

****Hagley Hall,*** Stourbridge DY9 9LG; Tel (01562) 882408; *Manager* D.C.L. Condy
Open daily except Saturdays 16 Jan–9 March inclusive. The hall will be closed 9th and 10th Feb. From 2pm–5pm, thereafter only April 14–21 inclusive; May 28–June 1 inclusive; Aug 27–29 inclusive

Lapworth Museum, School of Earth Sciences, University of Birmingham, Edgbaston, Birmingham B15 2TT; Tel 0121-414 4173; *Head of School* Prof D.D. Hawkes; *Curator* Dr M.P. Smith

Light House Media Centre, The Chubb Bldgs, Fryer St, Wolverhampton WV1 1HT; Tel (01902) 716055 (Cinema, exhibitions) (01902) 312033 (administrations); *Training Officer* Kate Child
Cinema, video production, video production training including City and Guilds 770 and animation, photographic exhibitions, conferences, events

The Lock Museum, 54 New Rd, Willenhall WV13 2DA; Tel (01902) 634542; *General Manager* John Whistance
Provides an experience of the living working conditions in a Victorian locksmith's family. Keys and locks. Activty days for school parties

****Moseley Old Hall,*** Fordhouses, Wolverhampton WV10 7HY; Tel (01902) 782808; *Administrator* David Lee
National Trust

Museum of British Road Transport, St Agnes La, Hales St, Coventry CV1 1PN; Tel (01203) 832425; *Manager* B.R. Littlewood
Education room; activity sheets; teaching packs; special talsk; free coach parking; cafeteria etc. Over 400 vehicles on display incud-ing cars, motor cycles and commercial vehicles. Also thrust 2 the current holder of the World Land Speed Record. New for 1992 the Tiatsa model collection

The National Motorcycle Museum, Coventry Rd, Bickenhill, Solihull B92 0EJ; Tel (016755) 3311 (Museum)/021-704 2784 (Head Office); *Founding Trustee* W.R. Richards
Catalogues the country's motorcycle industry from its conception to the present day. Six hundred fully restored machines on display

Oak House, Oak Rd, West Bromwich B70 8HJ; Tel 0121-553 0759; *Curator* M. Senior
Sandwell Metropolitan Borough

Packwood House, Lapworth, Solihull B94 6AT; Tel (01564) 782024; *Contact* F. Lyddon
Tudor house, tapestries, furniture, gardens, topiary. Open April to September Weds–Sun and Bank Holiday Mondays, 2–6 pm. October Wed–Sun 12.30 to 4.30 pm
The National Trust

The Patrick Collection Ltd, 180 Lifford La, King's Norton, Birmingham B30 3NT; Tel 0121-459 9111; Fax 0121-433 3048; *Contact, Museum Manager* Graham Drew
'Autoworld' presents motoring in the context of social history. Exhibits range from 1904–1992 housed in converted Victorian papermill. Terraced gardens. Snack bar and gourmet restaurant. The Fina Hall with 'hands-on' activities for school children. Teachers' resource pack.

Sandwell Valley RSPB Nature Centre, 20 Tanhouse Ave, Great Barr, Birmingham B43 5AG; Tel 0121-358 3013; *Warden* Tony Whitehead

Walsall Museum and Art Gallery, Lichfield St, Walsall WS1 1TR; Tel (01922) 653116; Fax (01922) 32824; *Keeper of Fine Art* Jo Digger; *Museums and Galleries Manager* Peter Jenkinson
Garman-Ryan collection. Local history museum and E.M. Flint Gallery with temporary exhibition programme. Work by Epstein, Picasso, Blake, Van Gogh, Cezanne

****Wightwick Manor,*** Wolverhampton WV6 8EE; Tel (01902) 761108; *Administrator* M. Smith
Special prebooked school tours arranged
National Trust

Wolverhampton Art Gallery, Lichfield St, Wolverhampton WV1 1DU; Tel (01902) 312032; Fax (01902) 715582; *Arts and Museums Officer* Nicholas Dodd; *Contact* Promotions Officer
Fine art, applied art, film, television, performance, local history; presentation and interpretation

West Sussex

Amberley Museum, Houghton Bridge, Amberley, Arundel BN18 9LT; Tel (01798) 831370; *Education Officer* Howard Stenning
The working museum in Sussex featuring demonstrating craftsmen, industrial railway, vintage buses, operational machinery, workshops and displays reflecting working life

Arundel Castle, Arundel BN18 9AB; Tel (01903) 883136; Fax (01903) 884581; *Comptroller* P.J.W. Normand, FRICS
Worksheets available
Arundel Castle Trustees Ltd

Arundel Toy and Military Museum, 23 High St, Arundel BN18 9AD; Tel (01903) 883101 or 882908; *Curator/Owner* Diana Henderson
Intriguing extensive private collection of old toys, dolls, famous teddy bears, toy soldiers, curiosities, games, arks, dollshouse, tin toys and small militaria in Georgian cottage. Open winter weekends. most days April–Sept. School and Bank Holidays, (including half-term weeks) or groups anytime pre-arranged

Bignor Roman Villa, Bignor, Pulborough; Tel (01798) 869478; Fax (01798) 869259; *Curator* G. and B. Compton

Chichester District Museum, 29 Little London, Chichester PO19 1PB; Tel (01243) 784683; *Keeper, Social History (job share)* Rosemary Gilmour, BA, AMA; *Keeper, Social History (job share)* Simon Kitchin, BA; *Keeper, Archaeology* Su Fullwood, BA; *Curatorial Assistant* Elizabeth Payce, BA
Branch: Guildhall Museum, Priory Park, Chichester. Loan service for local schools operates from District Museum; worksheets and museum publications. Group visits booked in advance. Chichester Museum open all year Tues–Sat 10–5.30 pm. Guildhall Museum open June–Sept inclusive Sats 1–5pm, othertimes by appointment. Admission free at both museums
Chichester District Council

Denman's Garden, Denmans, Fontwell, Nr Arundel BN18 0SU; Tel (01243 54) 2808; *Director* John Brookes
Garden, plant centre, country shop, tea shop, Clock House School of Garden Design day courses throughout the season

Fishbourne Roman Palace and Museum, Salthill Rd, Fishbourne, Nr Chichester PO19 3QR; Tel (01243) 785859; *Director* D.J. Rudkin; *Education Officer* W. Austin-Ward
Preserves, presents and interprets the archaeological remains of the palace for the public, with special emphasis on school children. Roman garden, and audio visual theatre. Teacher sessions for schools using artefacts and reconstructed Roman kitchen

Goodwood House and Estate, Chichester PO18 0PX; Tel (01243) 774107; *Education Officer* Geoff King
House, farm, forest, nature trail, aerodrome, accommodation
West Sussex Countryside Studies Trust

Hammerwood Park, East Grinstead RH19 3QE; Tel (01342) 86594; Fax (01342) 850864; *Contact* David or Eileen Pinnegar
Gerogian historic house with Repton parkland providing interesting tours for all age groups. Social history, building restoration, costume collection, musical instruments, the history of photography and copy of the Elgin Marbles. Monthly concerts, disabled facilities

Horsham Museum, 9 The Causeway, Horsham RH12 1HE; Tel (01403) 254959; *Curator* Jeremy Knight
Educational talk/visits on request. School loan boxes available on variety of topics
Horsham District Council

Littlehampton Museum, Manor Hse, Church St, Littlehampton BN17 5EP; Tel (01903) 715149; *Curator* Dr Ian Friel
A small, friendly museum – educational visitors welcome. National Curriculum resources in preparation for local archaeology, history and maritime history

Mechanical Music and Doll Collection, Church Rd, Portfield, Chichester; Tel (01243) 785421/(01243) 372646; *Proprietor* Clive Jones
Mechanical instruments, restored and playing. Polyphons, barrel-organs, barrel-pianos, etc/ Over 100 Victorian dolls, magic-lantern, natural history exhibits. Booking any time. 75p each

Pallant House Gallery, 9 North Pallant, Chichester PO19 1TJ; Tel (01243) 774557; *Curator* David E. Coke, BA
Worksheets, publications, Teachers' resource pack

Parham Elizabethan House and Gardens, Pulborough; Tel (01903) 742021; *Administrator* Pat Kennedy
Guided tours for groups by appointment only. Wed and Thurs mornings. Unguided groups welcome on 'open' afternoons: Weds, Thurs, Suns and Bank Hol. Mons, from Easter Sun to first Sun in Oct. 15 and 16 July 1995: Parham House Garden Weekend

Petworth Hse, Petworth GU28 0AE; Tel (01798) 42207; *Administrator* Dr D. Owen
Education Room
National Trust

Rainbows End Family Adventure Park, Hotham Pk, Bognor Regis; *PR/PA and Secretary* J.M. Bull

Uppark, South Harting, Petersfield GU31 5QR; Tel (01730) 825317; *Custodian-in-Charge* P.L. Meredith
National Trust

Warnham War Museum, Durfold Hill, Warnham, Horsham RH12 3RZ; Tel (01403) 65607; *Administrator* A.J. Lynhurst
Large private display of World War II vehicles, equipment, uniforms, badges, documentation, etc

Weald and Downland Open Air Museum, Singleton, Chichester PO18 0EU; Tel (01243) 811348
Weald and Downland open Air Museum. Museum of rescued historic buildings, set in 40 acres of parkland. Domestic and industrial buildings, crafts and trades, through the ages. Demonstrations, hands-on exhibits, special packages, education publications including teachers' kits and childrens' activities

The Wildfowl and Wetlands Centre, Mill Rd, Arundel BN18 9PB; Tel (01903) 883355; *Education Officer* Jane Lovering
Wide range of educational programmes for primary age children in 64 acre landscaped reserve with hundreds of ducks, geese and swans. Special GCSE environmental courses and A level day courses

Worthing Museum and Art Gallery, Chapel Rd, Worthing BN11 1HP; Tel (01903) 239999 Ext 2528 (204229 Saturdays); *Principal Curator* Dr Sally White
Worthing Borough Council

West Yorkshire

Abbey House Museum, Abbey Rd, Kirkstall, Leeds LS5 3EH; Tel (0113) 275 5821; *Curator* J. Bridgwater; *Assistant Curator* A. Garlick, BA, AMA
Set in park and gardens. Abbey house was gate house to Kirkstall Abbeyy 1152–1539. Abbey House Museum is dedicated to folk life of Leeds and Abbey Ruins– costumes, toys, Victorian Leeds. Now open 9.30–5.00 pm all year on Mon–Sat and 1–5pm on Sundays
Leeds City Council, Dept of Leisure Services

Bagshaw Museum, Wilton Pk, Batley, W. Yorks WF17 0AS; Tel (01924) 472514; Fax (01924) 420017; *Contact Senior Museums Officer* Brian Haigh; *Contact Community Officer (Eduction and Interpretation)* Lorraine Greenaid

****Bolling Hall,*** Bowling Hall Rd, Bradford BD4 7LP; Tel (01274) 723057; *Museums Resources Teacher* ; Tel (01274) 492276
Educational service

Bradford Arts, Museums and Libraries, Interpretative Service, Bradford Metropolitan Council; Tel (01274) 631756; Fax (01274) 636362; *City Arts, Museums and Libraries Officer* Paul W.G. Lawson; *Head of Interpretative Service* Graham Wilkinson

Bolling Hall Museum, Bowling Hall Rd, Bradford BD4 7LP; Tel (01274) 723057; *Museum Resources Teacher* Vacancy
Furnished house, 15th–18th century. Decorative arts, furniture, social history

Bracken Hall Countryside Centre, Glen Rd, Baildon, Bradford; Tel (01274) 584140; *Countryside Interpretative Officer* Catherine Rosenbloom; *Assistant Interpretative Officer* John Dallas
Countryside interpretation, information centre, guided walks

Bradford Industrial Museum and Horses at Work, Moorside Mills, Moorside Rd, Eccleshill; Tel (01274) 631756; *Marketing Education Officer, Horses at Work* Lyn Killick; *Assistant Keeper, Museum Education Service (Social History), Bookings Co-ordinator* Janet Davidson; *Assistant Keeper, Technology/Education* Eugene Nykolyszyn
Wool textiles, motive power, transport gallery, horses at work, back to back houses, furnished Mill Manager's house, board school

Cartwright Hall, Lister Pk, Bradford BD9 4NS; Tel (01274) 493313; *Assistant Keeper, MES (Art)* Vicky Mitchell; *Assitant Keepr, MES (Art)* Suzanne Rennie; *Gallery Teacher* Claire Ackroyd
Art Gallery. Fine and contemporary art, temporary exhibition programme

Cliffe Castle Museum, Spring Gardens La, Keighley BD20 6LH; Tel (01274) 758230/(0535) 618230; *Senior Assistant Keeper, Natural Science/MES* Alison Armstrong
Natural history, geology, minerals gallery, social history, temporary exhibitions

The Manor House, Castle Yard, Ilkley LS29 9DT; Tel (01943) 600066; Fax (01943) 817079; *Assistant Keeper (Education)* Mary Bentham
Archaeology, local history, temporary exhibitions by local artists. Activity Centre features interpretative displays on local history, archaeology and environment

Museums Loans Service, T.F. Davies Centre, Block B, Clifton Villas, Bradford; Tel (01274) 492276; *Loans Service Officer* Joyce Myers; *Loans Service Officer* Michele Nagg; *Assistant Loans Service Officer* David Craven; *Loans Service Technician* Sheila Sumner
Loans of objects in all museum and art disciplines to schools, colleges, hospitals, and community centres in Bradford

Bramham Park, C/o Esate Office, Bramham Pk, Wetherby; Tel (01937) 844265; *House Opening Manger* A. Tindall

Brontë Parsonage Museum, Church St, Haworth, Keighley BD22 8DR; Tel (01535) 642323; Fax (01535) 647131; *Administrative Officer* Pat Goff
Video introduction to the Brontës junior or secondary versions available/ Teachers' packs, discovery sheets, special events for schools. Advance booking necessary
Brontë Society

Calderdale Museum Service

Bankfield Museum, Akroyd Pk, Halifax HX3 6HG; Tel (01422) 354823/352334
Costume collection, the Museum of The Duke of Wellington's Regiment, with toy display and travelling exhibitions of textiles, art, craft and ethnography

Calderdale Industrial Museum, Central Works, Square Rd, Halifax; Tel (01422) 358087

Award winning museum reflecting 150 years of Calderdale's industrial history

Heptonstall Old Grammar School, Heptonstall, Hebden Bridge HX7 7LY; Tel (01422) 843738
17th century stone school building (with old school furniture) set in a preserved handloom weaving village. Displays of local history, agricultural and domestic implements

Piece Hall Art Gallery, Halifax HX1 1RE; Tel (01422) 358087
An active gallery with a lively programme. Art gallery specialising in Art and Craft exhibitions. Regular education workshops and activities

Smith Art Gallery, Halifax Rd, Brighouse HD6 2AF; Tel (01484) 3719222
Classical 19th century house contains two art galleries. Display space is devoted to work drawn from the service's own collections, travelling exhibitions, local artist and societies
Metropolitan Borough of Calderdale

Castle Hill and Jubilee Tower, off Lumb La, Almondbury, Huddersfield; Tel (01484) 513808; *Senior Marketing Officer, Kirklees*; Tel (01484) 513808
Iron age hill fort, crowned with Victorian Jubilee Tower. Exhibition in tower, panoramic views. Open Summer afternoonsl other times by appointment
Kirklees Metropolitan Council

Castleford Museum Room, Castleford Library, Carlton St, Castleford WF10 1BB; Tel (01977) 559552; *Museums and Art Galleries Officer* Gordon Watson; *Keeper of Archaeology* Pamela Judkins; *Education and Outreach Officer* Sarah Scaife; Tel (01924) 375402
Displays changed periodically but always of material relating to the local area
Wakefield Art Galleries and Museums

City Art Gallery, The Headrow, Leeds LS1 3AA; Tel (0113) 247 8248; Fax (0113) 244 9689; *Keeper* A. Robertson; *Senior Assistant Keeper (Education)* A. Phillips

Colne Valley Museum, Cliffe Ash, Golcar, Huddersfield; Tel (01484) 659762; *Schools Organiser* S. Osborn; Tel (01484) 653331 (out of hours)
19th century weavers' cottages with restored workshop, living quarters and clog makers workshop. Demonstrations available, and 'Victorian Days' for school parties

Dewsbury Museum, Crow Nest Pk, Heckmondwike Rd, Dewsbury, W. Yorks WF13 2SA; Tel (01924) 468171; *Museums Officer* Richard Butterfield; *Galleries Officer* Helen Robinson
Childhood exhibits. Recreated 1940's schoolroom available for use by groups. Toy displays. Art Gallery space. Handling collections, workshops

East Riddlesden Hall, Keighley BD20 5EL; Tel (01535) 607075; Fax (01535) 691462; *The Property Manager* Ana Chylak
National Trust

Elizabethan Exhibitions Gallery, Brook St, Wakefield; Tel (01924) 370211 Ext 540; (01924) 370087 at weekends; *Principal Leisure Development Officer, Museums, Galleries and Castles* Gordon Watson; *Exhibitions Officer* William Manwaring; *Education and Outreach Officer* Sarah Scaife; Tel (01924) 375402
Mail to Wakefield Art Gallery, Wentworth Terr, Wakefield WF1 3QW
Changing temporary exhibitions of art, craft, history, photography etc, mounted from either the permanent collections or touring exhibitions
Wakefield Art Galleries and Museums

****Harewood House and Bird Garden,*** Estate Office, Harewood, Leeds LS17 9LQ; Tel (0113) 288 6331 Harewood Education Centre; Fax (0113) 288 6467; *Education Officer* Diane Holloway
Heritage Trust's Sandford Award winner for Education, film, theatre, study base, teaching notes. pupils worksheets, workshops on History, Arts, Science, adventure playground, nature trail

Holmfirth Postcard Museum, Huddersfield Rd, Holmfirth HD7 1DH; Tel (01484) 682231; *Senior Library Assistant/Unit Manager* Joyce Carter
Based on local company of Bamforths who for over 100 years have produced saucy seaside postacrds, lanturn slides and silent movies which can be viewed in the cinema
Kirklees Metropolitan Council

Keighley and Worth Valley Railway, Haworth Station, Keighley BD22 8NJ; Tel (01535) 645214; Fax (01535) 647317; *School parties Organiser*
Special school services on steam trains: 9 May and 17–21 June

Ledston Hall, Ledston, Castleford; *Agent* C.M.P. Granger; *Correspondence to* Carter Jonas 82 Micklegate, York YO1 1LF; Tel (01904) 610811
Historic hall open for viewing from the outside only, May–August. Gardens

Leeds City Museum, Municipal Bldgs, Leeds LS1 3AA; Tel (0113) 247 8275/478279; *Director* P. Brears
Exhibitions of archaeology, ethnography, geology, natural history, numismatics and aquaria

Leeds Education Authority Schools Museum and Art Loans Service, Jacob Kramer College Annexe, Rossington St, Leeds 2; Tel (0113) 246 2864
Available to schools and colleges in the Leeds Metropolitan District

Lotherton Hall, Aberford, Leeds LS25 3EB; Tel (0113) 281 3259; *Keeper* Adam White
Leeds Art Galleries and Museums, Leeds City Council

Manor House Art Gallery and Museum, Castle Yard, Ilkley LS29 9DT; Tel (01943) 600066; Fax (01943) 817079; *Assistant Keeper (Education)* Mary Bentham
City of Bradford Metropolitan Council

Metro Arts, Bradford Community Arts Centre, 17–21 Cahpel St, Little Germany BD1 5DT; Tel (01274) 721372; *Community Arts Officer* Shaun Fagan; *Asian Community Arts Assistant* Amerjeat Kaur; *Community Arts Assistant* Anne Armistead
Outreach work with wchools and the public; Centre-based workshops and activities. Open access to darkrooms, graphics areas performance space, meeting rooms. Assistance with funding and skills for voluntary groups and individuals. Recording studio and rehearsal space. Temporary exhibition programme Handling sessions, workshops, lectures, events for all ages. Some events carry a small charge

Museums and Arts Service, The Piece Hall, Halifax HX1 1RE; Tel (01422) 358087; *Director of Leisure Services* Paul Sheehan, MBA, MILAM, MIMgt; *Education Officer* J. Forrester, BA, ATC; *Education Officer* Debbie Newall, BA, DipMusStudies

National Museum of Photography, Film and Television, Pictureville, Bradford BD1 1NQ; Tel (01274) 725347/727488; Fax (01274) 723155; *Head of Education* Nigel Hamilton; *Education Administrator* Sally Tomlinson
Hands-on displays in techniques of photography, television and programme making. Special exhibitions of photography, film and television. Largest cinema screen in UK (IMAX). Unit will assist with visits, contact in advance. Warder Guide tours and theatre in museum performances
Admission to the museum is free. Handling sessions, lectures, workshops for all ages. Special events as advertised for the general public. Some events carry a small charge. For cinema programme and prices telephone Box Office (0274) 732277
Part of the National Museum of Science and Industry

National Museum of Photography, Film and Television, Pictureville, Bradford, W. Yorks BD1 1NQ; Tel (01274) 727488; *Head* Amanda Nevill
Hands-on displays explaining photographic, film and television techniques, exhibitions of contemporary and historical photographs, the history of British television and world's only public cinerama cinema, IMAX largest cinema screen in Britain. Television Heaven archive. The Kodak museum telling The Story of Popular Photography. Education information pack

Nostell Priory, Nostell, Wakefield; Tel (01924) 863892; Fax (01924) 865282; *Contact* Jill Hodgson
Guided tours on weekdays for pre-booked parties
Nostell Priory Enterprises

****Oakwell Hall and Country Park,*** Nutter La, Birstall, Nr Batley, W. Yorks WF17 9LG; Tel (01924) 474926; *Principal Officer (Museum)* Catherine Hall

Elizabethan Manor House furnished as a family home of the 1690s; period gardens and parkland. Visitor centre, shop, nature trail, extensive education programme, classroom facilities, events
Kirklees Metropolitan Council

Pontefract Museum, Salter Row, Pontefract WF8 1BA; Tel (01977) 797289; *Museums and Art Galleries Officer* Gordon Watson; *Curator* Richard Van Riel
Wakefield Museums, Galleries and Castles, West Yorkshire WF1 3QW
Archaeology and history of Pontefract, seventeenth century painting of castle as it was. Changing temporary exhibitions. Education and Outreach Officer available if pre-booked
Wakefield Museums, Galleries and Castles

Red House, Oxford Rd, Gomersal, Cleckheaton; Tel (01274) 872165; *Heritage Officer* Helga Hughes
Period house and grounds reflecting life and work of a prosperous Yorkshire woollen manufacturer and merchant's family in the 1830s

Ripon Prison and Police Museum, St Marygate, Ripon HG4; Tel (01764) 690799; *Honorary Curator* Dr J.K. Whitehead
Museum depicting history of law and order using local examples

RSPB Fairburn Ings Nature Reserve, 2 Springholme, Caudle Hill, Fairburn, Knottingley WF11 9JQ; Tel (01977) 673257
Structured environmental education programme available, all age ranges catered for. Send SAE to the Teacher/Naturalist at above address for details

Shibden Hall, Lister's Rd, Halifax HX3 6XG; Tel (01422) 352246; Fax (01422) 348440; *Museum Officer* Ros Westwood; *Museum Officer (Education)* Vacancy
Early 15th century half-timbered house with examples of 17th, 18th and 19th century furniture.
Reconstruction of an early 19th century village. Also a collection of horse drawn vehicles

Temple Newsam House, Leeds LS15 0AE; Tel (0113) 264 7321; *Keeper of Education* Vacancy
Leeds City Council

Tunnel End Canal and Countryside Centre, Waters Rd, Marsden, Huddersfield HD7 6NQ; Tel (01484) 846062
Former tunnel keeper's cottage at entrance to Standedge Tunnel of Huddersfield Narrow Canal. Canal and countryside interpretation centre with facilities for schools/groups
Kirklees Metropolitan Council

Victorian Reed Organ Museum, Victoria Hall, Victoria Rd, Saltaire, Shipley; Tel (01274) 585601 (after 5pm); *Curator* Philip Fluke
Displays and demonstrates a private collection of about 70 instruments as a visual and musical record of this important development in our history. Open Sun–Thurs 11–4 pm

Wakefield Art Gallery, Wentworth Terr, Wakefield WF1 3QW; Tel (01924) 375402; *Principal Leisure Development Officer, Museums, Galleries and Castles* Gordon Watson; *Keeper of Art* Nino Vella; *Education and Outreach Officer* Sarah Scaife; Tel (01924) 375402
Headquarters of service. Noted collection of 20th century art. Works by Barbara Hepworth and Henry Moore. Changing temporary exhibition. Education Room
Wakefield Art Galleries and Museums

Wakefield Museum, Wood St, Wakefield WF1 2EW; Tel (01924) 295351; (01924) 295356 at weekends; *Principal Leisure Development Officer, Museums, Galleries and Castles* Gordon Watson; *Senior Keeper* Christine Johnstone; *Education and Outreach Officer* Sarah Scaife; Tel (01924) 375402
Museum of local archaeology, historic and social history. Waterton collection of exotic birds and animals. Changing temporary exhibitions. Education Room
Wakefield Art Galleries and Museums

Wallace Arnold, Travel Department, Wallace Arnold Tours Ltd, Gelderd Rd, Leeds LS12 6DH; Tel (0113) 263 6456

The Yorkshire Car & Exhibition Company plc Grange St, Keighley, W Yorks BD21 3EJ; Tel (0535) 690499; *Director* Thomas S.S. Black; *Director* Gordon L. Black, MA(Cantab); *Director* Adam S. Black; *Director* Timothy Dunn, FCA; *School's Contact* June Tuley; Tel (01535) 690499
The Yorkshire Car Collection at Grange St, Keighley, West Yorkshire features about 100 Veteran, Vintage and Classic Cars, imaginatively presented alongside automotive memorabilia and in settings reflecting the times. Special features for School Groups include free 'I-Spy', Motoring Milestones and 'Wordsearch' Competitions. Entry charges are £1.50 per child; £2.00 per College student. Coach parking is free. The Collection is open from 10 am to 5 pm daily from April to October, although we are happy to accommodate pre-booked School parties outside this season. Schools' contact is June Tuley. Telephone (0535) 690499.

Yorkshire Consortium for Education Joint Services
Clarke Hall, Aberford Rd, Wakefield WF1 4AL; Tel (01924) 375598; Fax (01924) 375598; *Director* Susan Morton, MEd
Restored 17th century house available to all educational establishments in Yorkshire, Lancashire and Humberside. Send S.A.E. for information and brochure. Available to organisations and groups (pre-booking essential). Other special public events advertised from time to time. Please ring or write for more information

Educational Resource Service, 71C Northgate, Wakefield WF1 3BT; Tel (01924) 295678; *Director* Evan Jones
Loan service of models, artefacts, photographs and original works of art availableto all educational establishments in the LEAs of North Yorkshire County Council, Metropolitan Districts of Bradford, Kirklees, Wakefield (Administering Authority)

Yorkshire Mining Museum, Caphouse Colliery, New Rd, Overton, Wakefield WF4 4RH; Tel (01924) 848806; *Director* Dr M.L. Faull
Unique underground tour with trained miner guide, allows pupils to experience mining methods and conditions, past and present, at first hand in authentic workings 450 feet below ground. Indoor and outdoor displays cover the social and economic history of the Yorkshire coalfield

Wiltshire

Alexander Keiller Museum, Avebury, Marlborough; Tel (01672) 539250; *Joint Curator* C. Conybeare; *Joint Curator* R. Cleal; *Head Custodian* David Davidge
Preserves and interprets the results of excavations in and around Avebury Stone Circle, especially those conducted by Alexander Keiller
The National Trust

Avebury Museum, Avebury, Wiltshire SN8 1RF; Tel (016723) 250
English Heritage

Corsham Court, Corsham SN13 0BZ; Tel (01249) 712214
Contains a very fine collection of paintings by Old Masters displayed in the magnificent Georgian State Rooms. The 18th century furnishings by Chippendale complement the many other treasures. Open daily 2–4.30 pm except December, also closed Fridays and Mondays (not Bank Hol Mons). From Good Friday to 30 Sept open to 6 pm
The Lord Methuen

Devizes Museum, 41 Long St, Devizes SN10 1NS; Tel (01380) 727369; *Curator* P.H. Robinson, PhD, FSA, AMA; *Education Officer* J. Harvest, CertEd; *Librarian* P. Colman, DipELH, FRSA
Worksheets, talks and topic boxes of artefacts
Wiltshire Archaeological and Natural History Society

Dyrham Park, Nr Chippenham SN14 8ER; Tel (0127 582) 2501; *Administrator* Roger Ashley
Historic house of the William and Mary period set in 300 acre deer park and gardens. Young persons guidebook
National Trust

The Fox Talbot Museum of Photography, Lacock, Nr Chippenham SN15 2LG; Tel (0124 973) 459; *Curator* Michael Gray; Tel (01249) 73459
Museum celebrating Fox Talbot, who invented the negative positive process of photography. family home, built 1232, medieval village. Open Mar–Nov, daily 11am–5.30pm, last admission 5pm. Closed Good Friday

The Great Barn Museum of Wiltshire Life, The Great Barn, Avebury, Malborough SN8 1RF; Tel (01672) 539555; *Curator* Susan Arnold; *TIC Manager* Wendy Gallop
Wiltshire Life Society

Great Western Railway Museum, Faringdon Rd, Swindon SN1 5BJ; Tel (01793) 493189; Fax (01793) 542478; *Museum Keeper* T.F. Bryan
Portraying the history and development of the Great Western Railway including locomotives, photographs, posters, nameplates and other ephemera. Major new exhibition 'Return to Swindon' documents Swindon's role as a railway centre. The railway works, the village and other associated institutions

Lacock Abbey, Nr Chippenham SN15 2LG; Tel (01249) 730227; *Administrator* Charles Pugh
National Trust

Longleat, The Estate Office, Longleat, Warminster; Tel (01985) 844400; Fax (01985) 844885; *Education Officer*

Longleat House and Safari Park, Warminster; Tel (01985) 844400; Fax (01985) 844885; *General Manager and Land Agent* T. Moore

Lydiard Park, Lydiard Tregoze, Swindon SN5 9PA; Tel (01793) 770401; *Keeper* S.E. Finch-Crisp, BA
18th century house, 15th to 19th century family portraits. Wide ranging topic opportunities, eg fine/applied arts, Civil war, life on country estate, Victorians. Teachers' handbook £3.95. Pre-visit consultation with keeper
Thamesdown Borough Council

Mompesson House, Chorister's Gn, The Close, Salisbury SP1 2EL; Tel (01722) 335659; *Administrator* K.E. Rudd
Perfect example of Queen Anne house. Outstanding 18th century craftsmanship in plasterwork ceilings and drinking glasses. Fine period furniture; walled garden. Exhibition of paintings by Barbara Townsend Apr–Oct 1995
National Trust

Swindon Museum and Art Gallery, Bath Rd, Swindon; Tel (01793) 526161 Ext 4530; *Art Education and Exhibitions Officer* Erik Burnett-Godfree
Collection of twentieth century British Art and Ceramics. Gallery talks, activities and events. Outreach to school and community venues
Borough of Thamesdown

National Trust Regional Office, Wessex, Eastleigh Ct, Bishopstrow, Warminster, Wiltshire BA12 9HW; Tel (01985) 847777

Newhouse, Redlynch, Salisbury SP5 2NX; Tel (01725) 20055; *Contact* G. Jffreys
Jacobean house with two Georgian wings containing a collection of costumes. Nelson relics, and an agricultural museum outside

Old Sarum, Castle Rd, Salisbury, Wilts SP1 3SD; Tel (01722) 335398
English Heritage

Old Windsor Castle, Nr Tisbury; Tel (01747) 870487
English Heritage

Salisbury and South Wiltshire Museum, King's Hse, 65 The Close, Salisbury SP1 2EN; Tel (01722) 332151; *Curator* P.R. Saunders
Stonehenge, Early Man, Salisbury history, Pitt Rivers collection, Wedgwood, ceramics, pictures, costume, lace and embroidery. Worksheets and activity packs on Stonehenge and Old Sarum. Wiltshire schools free. Other £8

****Sheldon Manor,*** Chippenham SN14 0RG; Tel (01249) 653120; Martin Gibbs

Stonehenge, Nr Amesbury SP4 7DE
Free entry to pre-booked educational groups.
Tel (0272) 734472
English Heritage

Stourhead House and Garden, Stourton, Nr Warminster BA12 6QH; Tel (01747) 840348; *Administrator* P. Cornick
National Trust

Wilton House, Wilton, Salisbury SP2 0BJ; Tel (01722) 743115; *Tourism and Marketing Manager* Alun Williams
Home of the Earls of Pembroke for 450 years. Dynamic laser disc film re-enacts major events in the family's history, including the Tudor, Stuart, Victorian and Second World War connections. Tudor Kitchen, Victorian Laundry, Adventure Playground and School Room. Free parking. Full Wheelchair access. Teachers' Resource Handbook. Home to the Wareham Bears – around 200 miniature dressed bears set in a variety of scenes

Wiltshire Library and Museum Service, Bythesea Rd, Trowbridge BA14 8BS; Tel (01225) 713744; Fax (01225) 713993; *Manager, Wiltshire Learning Resources* S. McCulloch, BA, ALA; *Local Studies Officer* M.J. Marshman, ALA
Loan and advisory service to LM, GM and independent schools. Payment by subscription or pay-as-use

Wales

Museum of the Welsh Woollen Industry and Craftsworkshop, Dre-fach Felindre, Llandysul, Dyfed SA44 5UP; Tel (01559) 370929; *Curator* J.S. Jones, Museum Officer
Interprets the social and economic history of the Welsh woollen industry through display and working textile machines, together with a working woollen mill, woolshop, craftworkshop, museum café and bookshop

National Museum of Wales, Cathays Pk, Cardiff CF1 3NP; Tel (01222) 397951/9; Fax (01222) 373219; *Co-ordinator, Education Service* Rhina Jones
Education packs, workshops, handling sessions, gallery sheets. Loans to schools in Wales, advice on projects/topics, and training of teachers on use of museum resources

Welsh Folk Museum (National Museum of Wales) St Fagans, Cardiff, South Glamorgan CF5 6XB; Tel (01222) 569441; Fax (01222) 578413; *Education Officer* Walter Jones
100 acre site with 30+ re-erected buildings including farm houses, craft workshops, a chapel, a manor house, a school, a toll house and celtic village. Demonstrations of craft skills and galleries illustrating aspects of domestic life, history of farming and Welsh costume. Contact education department re entry charges, activities INSETS etc

Welsh Industrial and Maritime Museum, Bute St, Cardiff CF1 6AN; Tel (01222) 481919; Fax (01222) 487252; *Keeper* Dr E.S. Owen-Jones
Industrial, transport and maritime history of Wales, illustrated with a wide range of material, all with extensive educational relevance. Weather Satellite

The Welsh Slate Museum, Y Gilfach Ddu, Llanberis, Caernarfon, Gwynedd LL55 4TY; Tel (01286) 870630; Fax (01286) 871906; *Principal Officer* Dr Dafydd Roberts
The museum is located in the former workshops of the Dinorwig slate quarry and relates quarrying history in Wales

Clwyd

Bersham Ironworks and Heritage Centre, Bersham, Wrexham LL14 4HT; Tel (01978) 261529; *Administrator* Hilary Williams
The foundries and furnaces which produced cannon for the American War of Independence and cylinders for James Watt's steam engines are brought alive again at this fascinating museum which tells the story of John 'Iron Mad' Wilkinson and his 18th century ironworks
Clwyd County Council

Bodnant Garden, Tal-y-Cafn, Colwyn Bay; Tel (01492) 650460; *Administrator* M. Puddle

7 miles south of Llandudno and Colwyn Bay
National Trust

Chirk Castle, Chirk, Clwyd LL14 5AF; Tel (01691) 777701; Fax (01691) 774706; *Adminstration* V. Keen
National Trust

Erddig, Wrexham LL13 0YT; Tel (01978) 355314; Fax (01978) 313333; *Property Manager* Robert Dillon
Team of school party guides, audio visual. Must be pre-booked. Mon, Tues, Wed only at 10.15am, April to End-Oct
National Trust, Erddig, Wrexham, Clwyd

Nerquis Hall, Mold; A.W. Furse

Welsh Mountain Zoo and Botanic Gardens, Colwyn Bay LL28 5UY; Tel (01492) 532938; Fax (01492) 530498; *Education Officer* Kim Taylor
Education centre accommodating 40. Talks and tours by arrangement. Chimpanzee World and children's farm. Zoo trails and other educational resources available

Dyfed

Art Gallery and Museum School of Art, The University of Wales, Buarth Mawr, Abersytwyth SY23 1NE; Tel (01970) 622460; Fax (01970) 622461; *Head of School of Art and Keeper of College Collections* Prof Alistair Crawford
Changing exhibitions and reference facility from the college collections of Drawing and Painting, Printmaking, Photography, Decorative Arts
University of Wales, Aberystwyth

Carmarthen Museum, Abergwili, Carmarthen SA31 2JG; Tel (01267) 231691; *County Museum Officer* C.J. Delaney, BSc; *Senior Museums Officer* Ann Dorset, BA
Examples of archaeology, geology, natural history, crafts, costume and folk life of region. School parties free of charge
Cultural Services Department Dyfed CC

Carreg Cennen Castle and Farm, Trap, Llandeilo SA19 6UA; Tel (01558) 822291; *Director* Bernard Llewellyn
Dramatically situated rural Welsh castle with prehistoric cave dwelling. Restored Longhouse, rare farm animals, refreshments, crafts, play area, guided tours

The Catherine Lewis Gallery and Print Room, Hugh Owen Library, The University Of Wales, Panglais, Aberystwyth SY23 1HB; Tel (01970) 622460/623111; Fax (01970) 622461; *Head of School of Art and Keeper of College Collections* Prof Alistair Crawford
Changing exhibitions and reference facility from the collections of the history of printmaking, contemporary photography, including Italian photgraphy, 19th/20th century drawing
University of Wales, Aberystwyth

The Ceraminc Gallery, The Aberystwyth Arts Centre, The University of Wales, Penglais, Aberystwyth SY23 1HB; Tel (01970) 622460/623232; Fax (01970) 622461; *Head of School of Art and Keeper of College Collections* Professor Alistair Crawford
Changing exhibitions and reference facility from the collection of 20th century studio ceramics
University of Wales, Aberystwyth

Ceredigion Museum, Coliseum, Terrace Rd, Aberystwyth SY23 2AQ; Tel (01970) 634212/3; *Curator* M.D. Freeman
School parties are received for conducted tours and/or talks; visits are made to schools in Ceredigion District to give illustrated talks
Ceredigion District Council

Dolaucothi Gold Mines (Dolauchi), Pumpsaint SA19 8RR; Tel (0155 85) 359; *Administrator* Susan Lloyd-Fern
National Trust

Kidwelly Industrial Museum, Kidwelly SA17 4LW; Tel (01554) 891078; *Secretary to the Museum Trust* Freda Phillips
Preservation and interpretation of the remains of a tinplate works (1737–1941) still on its original site. Coal industry also represented

Llwernog Silver-lead Mine, Ponterwyd, Aberystwyth, Dyfed SY23 3AB; Tel (0197 0185) 620; *Curator* P. Lloyd Harvey
Correspondence to: The Mid-Wales Mining Museum Ltd, 15 Market St, Aberaeron, Dyfed SA46 0AU; Tel (0545) 570823
Mid-Wales Mining Museum Ltd

Maesllyn Mill Museum, Llandysul SA44 5LD; Tel (0123 975) 251; *Director* R.G. Martin
Working Woollen mill and museum, Textiles and household artefacts of last hundred years.
Worksheets, shop, coffee shop and nature trail

Manorbier Castle, Manorbier, Nr Tenby; Tel (0183 482) 394; *Managing Director* Beatrice Plunkett
Medieval castle with waxworks and gardens

National Trust Regional Office, South Wales, The King's Head, Bridge St, Llandeilo SA19 6BB; Tel (01558) 822800; Fax (01558) 822872

Pembroke Area Museums
Scolton House and Museum, Spittal, Haverfordwest, Dyfed SA62 5QL; Tel (01437) 731328
Penrhos Cottage, Llanycefn, Clunderwen, Dyfed SA66 7XT; Tel (01437) 731328 *Headquarters*; *County Museums Officer* C.J. Delaney, BSc; *Senior Museums Officer* P.W. Simmonds, BSc, DipEd, AMA, FRES; *Museums Officer* M. Thomas, BA (Scolton Manor Museum). Museum about Pembrokeshire. Archaeology, social and industrial history, costume, furniture, Haverfordwest, militaria and the arts

Rheidol Hydro Scheme, Rheidol Power Station, Cwm Rheidol, Aberystwyth, Dyfed SY23 3NF; Tel (01970 84) 667
Information centre, field study centre, nature trail. Trout fishing. Tour of power station and fish farm. April 1st – October 31st. Guided tours run from 11.00 until 3.30pm daily and by appointment all year

Tenby Museum and Art Gallery, Castle Hill, Tenby SA70 7BP; Tel (01834) 842809; *Honorary Curator* John Beynon, BA, DipEd; *Assistant Curator* Deborah-Anne Wildgust, BA
Community museum and gallery. Geology, archaeology, wildlife and social history of the area. Art and artists of Pembrokeshire interest

Tudor Merchant's House, Quay Hill, Tenby; Tel (01834) 2279; *Administrator* W. Hardy
National Trust

Gwent

Big Pit (Blaenafon) Trust Ltd, Blaenafon, Gwent NP4 9XP; Tel (01495) 790311; Fax (01495) 792618; *Director* Gareth Gregory
Preserved coal mine offering underground tours of 19th/20th century mineworkings together with preserved workshops, machinery, exhibitions, etc

Caldicot Castle, Caldicot, Newport NP6 4HU; Tel (01291) 420241; *Keeper* Shaun Brewer; *Curator* Anne Rainsbury, BA, AMA
Medieval fortifications, country park. Pre-booked educational visits free, with talks by arrangement; children's work sheets subject to availability
Monmouth Borough Council Museums Service

Chepstow Museum, Bridge St, Chepstow NP6 5EZ; Tel (01291) 625981; Fax (01291) 625983; *Curator* Anne Rainsbury, BA, AMA
Educational visits free of charge by arrangement; children's trail sheets; teachers' packs

Gwent Rural Life Museum, The Malt Barn, New Market St, Usk NP5 1AU; Tel (012913) 3777; *Chairman* A. Davies; *Administrator* A. Bowyer; Tel (01291) 673777
Award-winning private collection of agricultural, domestic and craft items from Gwent's rural pst.
Open Easter to end Oct. parties welcome

Junction Cottage, Lower Mill, Pontymoel, Pontypool NP4 0RF; Tel (014955) 52036; *Contact* Visitor Services
Canal exhibition centre housed in Tollkeeper's cottage built in 1814. Open by appointment only. Guided walks along canal

Museum and Art Gallery, John Frost Sq, Newport NPT 1HZ; Tel (01633) 840064; *Contact* Eduaction Officer
Intra-museum education; loan service; activity workshops

The Nelson Museum and Local History Centre Priory St, Monmouth NP5 3XA; Tel (01600) 713519; *Curator* Andrew Helme
Deals with the life, death and commemoration of the famous Admiral, with displays of letters, personal possessions, silver, ceramics, models, weapons, prints paintings and furniture. Local history collections include material on Charles Rolls, co-founder of Rolls Royce. Exhibitions, events, worksheets. School groups free (advance booking)

Newport Museum and Art Gallery, John Frost Sq, Newport NP9 1PA; Tel (01633) 840064; *Curator* Robert Trett, BA, AMA
Displays relating to archaeology, social history, natural history and art. Educational and research facilities. Shop and information centre

****Penhow Castle,*** Nr Newport, Gwent NP6 3AD; Tel (01633) 400800; Fax (01633) 400990; *Administrator* Kathleen Bull
Wales' oldest lived-in castle; Norman keep tower, medieval great hall, 17th century kitchen and more. Audio tours and full educational programme 3 Sandford Awards for Heritage Education

Roman Legionary Museum, Caerleon, High St, Caerleon, Nr Newprt NP6 1AE; Tel (01633) 423134; *Officer in Charge* vacancy
Museum display of Roman artifacts from Caerleon Educational and crafts events. Research and excavation of Roman fortress
Branch Museum of National Museum of Wales

Segontium Roman Fort Museum, Beddgelert Rd, Caernarfon, Gwynedd; Tel (01286) 675625; *Custodian* D.W. Jones; *Education Officer* D. Evans Beddgelert Rd, Caernarfon, Gwynedd; Tel (01286) 675625
Roman workshop, Worksheets and handling material Education and Interpretation Division, National Museum of Wales, Cardiff CF1 3NP

Torfaen Museum Trust, Park Bldgs, Pontypool NP4 6JH; Tel (01495) 752036; *Director* Martin Buckridge; *Curator* Johanne Brown
Provides museum services for Torfaen district of Gwent, operating four properties illustrating its social and industrial history

Tredegar House and Country Park, Newport NP1 9YW; Tel (01633) 815880; *Bookings Officer* V. O'Brian
This authentically restored country house set in 90 acres of parkland which includes lakes, formal gardens and farm outbuilding. An ideal location to study the Victorian upper classes, woodland, architecture servants and farm workers etc. The special schools "Below Stairs" House tour encourages children to discover how their lives would have been 100 years ago. Teachers pack available. Open Easter to Christmas

Gwynedd

Aberconwy House, Castle St, Conwy; Tel (01492) 592246; *Curator* Linda Thorp
National Trust, Trinity Sq, Lladudno

Bryn Bras Castle, Llanrug, Caernarfon LL55 4RE; Tel (01286) 870210; M. Gray-Parry

Cochwillan, Tal Y Bont, Bangor LL57 3AZ; Tel (01248) 364608; *Occupiers* Mr and Mrs P.A.B. Llewellyn
15th-century hall with splendid roof, provides simple demonstration of basic medieval house since there are no additions. Guided tour

Conwy Visitors' Centre, Rosehill St, Conwy, Gwynedd LL32 8LD; Tel (01492) 596288; *Manager* G. Seimann
Films and exhibitions, brass rubbing centre, craft and bookshop
Interviron Ltd

Ffestiniog Pumped Storage Scheme, Tan-y-Grisiau, Blaenau Ffestiniog LL41 3TP; *Visits Officer* Beti Roberts; Tel (01766) 830310
Electricity generation and transmission. Educational tours by appointment; brochure; wall chart; audio-visual presentation; exhibition; working models

Ffestiniog Railway, Harbour Station, Porthmadog LL49 9NF; Tel (01766) 512340; *Marketing Manager* Eamonn Seddon

Llechwedd Slate Caverns, Blaenau Ffestiniog LL41 3NB; Tel (01766) 830306; Fax (01766) 831260; *Contact* Lawrence Manley
Underground tours into slate mine where Victorian conditions are recreated. Miners interpret amidst dramatic surrounding. Exhibitions and demonstrations on surface. Victorian village. Open all year

Lloyd George Museum and Highgate Victorian Cottage, Llanystumdwy, Gwynedd Archives and Museums Service, Victoria Dock, Caernarfon LL55 1SH; Tel (01286) 679090; *Principal Archivist and Museum Officer* Gareth H. Williams, MA; *Contact* Mary Aris; *Contact* Gwenda Williams
Lloyd George museum with school facilities. 'Highgate', his boyhood cottage home. Nature trail along riverbank to his grave. Picturesque village. New Victorian garden

Museum of Childhood, 1 Castle St, Beaumaris, Anglesey LL58 8AP; Tel (01248) 712498; *Education Officer*
Comprehensive guide book, spotters pack. Open anytime for pre-arranged school visits

Narrow Gauge Railway Museum, Wharf Station, Tywyn LL36 9EY; Tel (01654) 710472
Free admission for school parties; teacher pack and worksheets available, open Easter to end of Oct
Narrow Gauge Railway Museum Trust

The Power of Wales, Llanberis, Caernarfon LL55 4UR; Tel (01286) 870636; Fax (01286) 871331; *Keeper* Dr Dafydd Roberts; *Education Officer* Alun Rowlands
Deals with the natural history and industrial past of North Wales, and provides an introduction to the generation of electricity. Trips to the Dinorwig Power Station, temporary exhibitions and displays

National Trust Regional Office, North Wales, Trinity Sq, Llandudno LL30 2DE; Tel (01492) 860123

Penrhyn Castle, Bangor; Tel (01248) 353084; Fax (01248) 371281
For details of Education programme and audio tour contact the Education Coordinator
National Trust

Plas Mawr, High St, Conwy LL32 8DE; Tel (01492) 593413; *Secretary/Curator* L.H.S. Mercer
Original Tudor mansion
Royal Cambrian Academy of Art

Plas Newydd, Llanfairpwll, Anglesey; Tel (01248) 714795; *The Administrator* J.L. Evans
Teachers' pack available
National Trust

Porthmadog Maritime Museum, Oakley Wharf No 1, The Harbour, Porthmadog; Tel (01766) 513736; *Chairman of Board of Trustees* Dr J.L. Jones-Morris
Exhibit to the public items of interest related primarily to the maritime, commercial and marine history of Portmadog and district

Portmerion, LL48 6ET; Tel (01766) 770228; Fax (01766) 771331; *Contact* Glyn Jones
Audio-visual show, provides a guided tour of fairytale Italian village, narrated by Sir Clough William-Ellis, Gardens, beaches, woodlands
Portmerion Ltd

Talyllyn Railway, Wharf Station, Tywyn LL36 9EY; Tel (01654) 710472; Fax (01654) 711755; *Managing Director* Maurice Wilson
Narrow gauge steam trains, running 7 1/4 miles into Snowdonia National Park. Special schools folder, teachers' information pack and project material, talks by arrangement. Facilities for the disabled. Toilets, car parking and Refreshments

Trawsfynydd Nuclear Power Station, Trawsfynydd, Blaenau Ffestiniog LL41 4DT
Tours of plant by prior appointment, audio-visual presentation. Broadsheets and fact sheet available Applications to Information Officer, Tel (0766) 87622; Fax (0766) 87619

Wylfa Nuclear Power Station, Cemaes Bay, Anglesey LL67 0DH; *Manager*
Tours of plant at 10.30 and 14.00 by appointment, Monday to Friday all year. Tel (0407) 710471 for

details. Broadsheets; wall charts; fact sheets; video. Information centre
National Power

Mid Glamorgan

Cyfarthfa Castle Museum and Art Gallery, Cyfarthfa Pk, Merthyr Tydfil; Tel (01685) 723112; *Curator* Stephen Done, BA(Hons)Fine Art, AMA; *Assistant Curator* Derek Phillips, BA, AMA
Ironmaster's Regency period gothic mansion. Open all year round, school parties free if booked in advance. National Curriculum based teaching packs and information displays
Merthyr Tydfil Borough Council

Ponypridd Historical and Cultural Centre, Bridge St, Pontypridd CF37 4PE; Tel (01443) 402077; *Contact* Brian Davies; *Contact* David Gwyer
Working models, oral history on tape, interactive computer programme and audio visuals. Temporary exhibitions on historical, artistic and scientific subjects. Exhibitions on social and industrial history. Illustrated talks on aspects of the history of South Wales by arrangement

Powys

Brecknock Museum, Captain's Wk, Brecon LD3 7DW; Tel (01874) 624121; *Curator* David Moore
Powys CC

Elan Valley Visitor Centre, Elan Valley, Rhayader; Tel (01597) 810880/810898; *Head Countryside Ranger* Pete Jennings
Centre tells history of mans occupation of area, including building of dams and wildlife, using tableaux and audio-visual presentation
Hamdden (Welsh Water plc)

Radnorshire Museum, Temple St, Llandrindod Wells LD1 5DL; Tel (01597) 824513; *Curator* Chris Wilson
Local history museum.

Powis Castle, Welshpool SY21 8RF; Tel (01938) 554336; *Administrator* Mjr H.N. Williams
Children's questionnaire
National Trust

The Robert Owen Memorial Museum, The Cross, Broad St, Newtown, Powys SY16 2BB; Tel (01686) 626345; *Honorary Curator* John H. Davidson
Tells the remarkable story of Robert Owen (1771–1858), industrialist and social reformer, prophet of English socialism, inspirer of the co-operative movement. Admission free. Mon–Fri 9.45–11.45am and 2–3.30pm; Sat 10–11.30am; Curator will meet groups by prior arrangement

South Glamorgan

Cardiff Castle, Castle St, Cardiff CF1 2RB; Tel (01222) 822083; Fax (01222) 231417
Nearly 2000 years of history–Roman, Norman, Medieval. Victorian restoration. Open almost every day through year. Guided tours, groups welcome

Coity Castle, CADW–Welsh Historic Monuments, 9th Fl, Brunel Hse, 2 Fitzalan Rd, Cardiff CF2 1UY; Tel (01222) 465511 Est 241; *Contact* The Education Dept

Welsh Hawking Centre, Weycock Rd, Barry CF62 3AA; Tel (01446) 734687; N. Griffiths
Lectures, birds of prey flying demonstrations, worksheets

West Glamorgan

Aberdulais Falls, Aberdulais, Nr Neath SA10 8EU; Tel (01639) 636674; *Administrator* R. Pool
Lectures tailored to meet specific needs. All groups catered for
National Trust

Cefn Coed Colliery Museum, Blaenant Colliery Site, Crynant, Neath SA10 8SN; Tel (01639) 750556; Fax (01639) 750556; *Manager* Robert Merrill
Museum of the coal industry based in and around the surface buildings of the now disused Cefn Coed colliery

Glynn Vivian Art Gallery and Museum, Alexandra Rd, Swansea SA1 5DZ; Tel (01792) 655006; Fax (01792) 651713; *Curator* Robin Paisey, BA, FMA; *Deputy Curator/Exhibitions Officer* Alison Lloyd, BA; *Education Officer* John Upton, BA; *Community Arts Officer* Robin Hall, BSc, MSc
Educational programme includes film, lectures, workshops and residencies
Swansea City Council

Maritime and Industrial Museum, Museum Sq, Maritime Quarter, Swansea SA1 1SN; Tel (01792) 650351; *Education Officer* Gerald Gabb, MA, PGCE
Education programme includes worksheets for organised school parties and introductory talks
Swansea City Council

Penscynor Wildlife Park, Cilfrew, Neath; Tel (01639) 642189; Fax (01639) 635152; *Education Co-ordinator* Howie Watkins
Teaching kits, worksheets, classroom facilities, guided tours, lectures and AVA all year round. Free inspection tours for teachers

Swansea Museum, Victoria Rd, Swansea SA1 1SN; Tel (01792) 653763; *Education Officer* Gerald Gabb, MA
Worksheets, slide introductions for parties, factsheets, object sessions

Scotland

Borders

Abbotsford House, Melrose, Roxburghshire TD6 9BQ; Tel (01896) 2043; P. Maxwell-Scott

Ayton Castle, Berwickshire TD14 5RD; Tel (018907) 81212 (24 hrs); Fax (018907) 81550; *Contact* The Curator
Scottish Victorian castle, fully restored. Available for conferences, promotional events. Lived in by the owner. Tourist attraction, country sports available

Bowhill House and Country Park, Selkirk TD7 5ET; Tel (01750) 20732; *Countryside Ranger, Education Officer, House Manager*
Nature trail, indoor projects, adventure playground, audio-visual programmes, arts courses, visitor centre, picnic areas. Ranger led Environmental Education Project

Drumlanrig's Tower 1 Tower Knowe, Hawick; Tel (01450) 373457
Opening April 1995: Ideal for school visits. South of Scotland's newest and most exciting visitor centre on Border History from Roman occupation to present day. Features Audio Visuals, Interactive Vice-disks, period room settings, " Aromas of the Past" and stunningly refurbished 18th Century building. Incorporates shop. Booking essential

Dryburgh Abbey, Br St Boswells, c/o Historic Scotland, Longmaore Hse, Salisbury Pl, Edinburgh EH9 1SH; Tel 0131-668 8732; *Education Officer* M. Fry
Medieval ruined abbey and burial place of Sir Walter Scott

Floors Castle, Roxburghe Estates Office, Kelso, Roxburghshire TD5 7SF; Tel (01573) 223333; *Contact* F. Brown
Floors Castle is Scotland's largest inhabited castle. Open Easter weekend until the end of September: daily 10.30am–5.30pm; Oct open Sun and Wed 10.30am–4.30pm. Gift shop, restaurant and Woodland walks

Halliwell's House Museum, Halliwell's Cl, Market Pl, Selkirk TD7 4BC; Tel (01750) 720096; *District Curator* Ian Brown
Social history museum, telling the story of the local area using text, illustration, video, audio. Houses ironmongery, domest history collection. Temporary exhibition gallery

Hawick Museum, Wilton Park Lodge, Hawick; Tel (01450) 373457; *District Museums Curator* Rosemary Capper
School visits welcome, must book; open all year
Roxburgh District Council

Hirsel Homestead Museum and Craft Centre, The Hirsel, Coldstream, Berwickshire TD12 4LP; Tel (01890) 882834; *Factor* Honorable Caroline Douglas-Home
History and natural history of an Estate in the past and present. Archaeology, craftsworkshops, walks, picnic areas. Refreshments

Jedburgh Abbey, Jedburgh, c/o Historic Scotland, Longmore Hse, Salisbury Pl, Edinburgh EH9 1SH; Tel 0131-668 8732
Ruined Augustinian abbey founded about 1138, Visitor Centre

Kelso Museum, Turret Hse, Abbey Court, Kelso; Tel (01573) 225470; *District Museums Curator* Rosemary Capper
School visits welcome by appointment only; open Easter to end Oct
Roxburgh District Council

Manderston, Berwickshire; Tel (01361) 883450; *Owner* The Lord Palmer
"Upstairs, Downstairs" aspects particularly educational; 56 acres of garden, stable, marble dairy, biscuit tin museum

Mary Queen of Scots' House, Queen St, Jedburgh; Tel (01835) 863331
School visits welcome; must book, open March to Mid-Nov

Mellerstain House, Gordon, Berwickshire; Tel (01573) 410225; *Curator* F. Turnbull

Melrose Abbey, Melrose, Longmaore Hse, Salisbury Pl, Edinburgh EH9 1SH; Tel 0131-668 8732
Ruined Cistercian abbey founded about 1136 by David I

Neidpath Castle, Peebles; *The Custodian* ; Tel (01721) 720333 or Estates Office, Longniddry; Tel (018757) 201

Old Gala House, Scott Cres, Galashield TD1 3JS; Tel (01750) 720096; *District Curator* Ian Brown
Former home of Lairds of Gala dates from 1583. Displays relate to the history of the House, the Lairds, the early development of Galashiels and sculptur Thomas Clapperton. There are also three temporary exhibition galleries

Priorwood Gardens, Melrose, Roxburghshire TD6 3PX; Tel (0189 682) 2493; *Dried Flower Manager* Catherine Ross
Dried flower garden, shop, historic apple orchard, exhibition of drying methods, picnic area
National Trust for Scotland

Scottish Museum of Woollen Taxtiles, Tweedvale Mills, Walkerburn, Peeblesshire EH43 6AH; Tel (0189687) 281/3; *Contact* A. Cameron

Thirlestane Castle, Lauder, Berwickshire TD2 6RU; Tel (01578) 722430; Fax (01578) 722761; *Castle Administrator* P.D. Jarvis
16th century castle and family home. Hugh collection of historic toys and Border Country life exhibitions
Thirlestane Castle Trust

Traquair House, Innerleithen, Peeblesshire; Tel (01896) 830323; *Owner* F. Maxwell Stuart
Quiz and guide sheets provided for school

Central

Brannockburn Monument, Stirlingshire; *Respresentative* Heritage Centre; Tel (01786) 812664
National Trust for Scotland

Blair Drummond Safari and Leisure Park, Blair Drummond, Nr Stirling FK9 4UR; Tel (01786) 841456; *Manager* Angela Rennick
Open 1st April–2nd October 1995; daily 10am–5.30pm. Last admission 4.30pm

Falkirk Museums Administration, Kilns House, Kilns Rd, Falkirk FK1 5SA; Tel (01324) 624911 Ext 2202; *Museum Education Officer* Margaret Bowden; Tel (01324) 612134
Provison of historical/ environmental information (Falkirk district) and maintenance of Grangemouth, Callendar House, Falkirk and Kinniel Museums and Kinniel Roman fortlet. Education service to schools and History Research Centre, Callendar House

Motor Museum, Doune, Perthshire; Tel (01786) 841203; *Manager* J. Asher

Smith Art Gallery and Museum, Dumbarton Rd, Stirling FK8 2RQ; Tel (01786) 471917; *Director* Elspeth King; *Education Officer* vacany
Collections of local social and natural history, art and ethnography. All year exhibition and events programme includes contemporary arts, crafts and photography. Theartre, shop, café, assisted disabled access. Termly educational news-letter available on request. Admission free

Stirling Castle, Stirling, c/o Historic Scotland, Longmore Hse, Salisbury Pl, Edinburgh EH9 1SH; Tel 0131-668 8732
The grandest of all Scottish Castles both in its architecture and situation

Dumfries and Galloway

Burns House, Burns St, Dumfries; Tel (01387) 255297; *Museums Manager* Elaine Kennedy, BA, AMA
Open all year. A place of pilgrimage for Burns enthusiasts from around the world, the house retains much of its eighteenth century character and contains many relics of the poet
Nithsdale District Council

Caerlaverock Castle, Nr Dumfries, c/o Historic Scotland, Longmore Hse, Salisbury Pl, Edinburgh EH9 1SH; Tel 0131-668 8732; *Education Officer* M. Fry
One of the finest castles in Scotland. Children's Park and model siege engine in front of castle

Carlyle's Birthplace, The Arched Hse, Ecclefechan, Lockerbie DG11 3DG; Tel (01576) 300666; *Representative* N.B. Walter
Collection of manuscripts and belongings
National Trust for Scotland

Creetown Gem Rock Museum and Crystal Cave, Creetown, Nr Newton Stwart DG8 7HJ; Tel (01671) 820357; Fax (01671) 820554; *Curator* T. Stephenson, FTC, CertEd, FGA
Workshops, craft shop, worldwide collection. Tearoom. Guided tour, quiz available, mineral charts, mineral samples and lapidary equipment for sale incl. mail order. Open 7 days a week

Drumlanrig Castle and Country Park, Thornhill DG3 4AQ; Tel (01848) 331682 (24hr answering service); Country Park (01848) 331555; *Castle Administrator-Archivist* A. Fisher
Open early May to end Aug. School groups welcome in house and woodlands. Unique collection of art treasures and furniture. Teachers' resource material and classroom and audio-visual room available by arrangement. 1994 Sat 30th April–Mon 29th August (inc); Castle closed Thurs

Dumfries Museum, The Observatory, Dumfries DG2 7SW; Tel (01387) 253374; *Museums Manager* Elaine Kennedy, BA, AMA
Open all year. Permanent exhibitions covering the natural and human history of Dumfries and Galloway. Temporary exhibition programme. Camera obscura opens April–Sept

Logan Botanic Garden, Port Logan, Stranraer, Wigtownshire DG9 9ND; Tel (01776) 860231; *Assistant Curator* Barry Unwin

Maxwelton House, Nr Moniaive, Dumfriesshire; Tel (0184 82) 385; M.R.L. Stenhouse
House dates back to the 14th–15th century. Oringinally stronghold of Earls of Glencairn, later birthplace of Anne Laurie. Also includes museum, 19th century chapel, gardens and Greenhouse, tearoom, shop. Open daily from Easter to 30th September

New Abbey Corn Mill, New Abbey Village, c/o Historic Scotland, Longmore Hse, Salisbury Pl, Edinburgh EH9 1SH; Tel 0131-668 8732; *Education Officer* M. Fry
A carefully renovated oatmeal mill

Robert Burns Centre, Mill Rd, Dumfries DG2 7BE; Tel (01387) 264808; *Museums Manager* Elaine Kennedy, BA, AMA
Open all year. Permanent exhibition, models and audio-visual presentation illustrating the life of Robert Burns. Cafe and book shop. Temporary exhibition programme

Shambellie House Museum of Costume, Shambellie Hse, New Abbey, Dumfries DG2 8HQ; Tel (0138 785) 375; *Director* M.E.P. Jones, MA; *Contact* N. Tarrant; *Contact* J.C. Robertson
Display of a selection of costumes and accessories from the National Museums of Scotland
National Museums of Scotland

Sweetheart Abbey, New Abbey Village, c/o Historic Scotland, Longmore Hse, Salisbury Pl, Edinburgh EH9 1SH; Tel 0131-688 8732
Beautiful, ruined 13/14th century Cistercian abbey

Wigtown District Museums Service, Stranraer Museum, The Old Town Hall, George St, Stranraer DG9 7JP; Tel (01776) 705088; *Curator* J.L. Pickin; *Education Officer* S. Curry
Wigtown District Council

Fife

Andrew Carnegie Birthplace Museum, Moodie St, Dunfermline KY12 7PL; Tel (01383) 724302
Guided tours: classroom/seminar room, leaflets, worksheets available
Correspondence to Carnegie Dunferline Trust, Abbey Park Hse, Dunfermline KY12 7PB

Culross Palace, Renovated home of a 17th century merchant.
National Trust for Scotland

Culross: The Study and the Town House, Culross, Fife KY12 8HT; Tel (01383) 880359
The late 16th century Culross Palace is due to re-open on 1st May, renovated and fully furnished. It is a very good example of an early merchant's town house. There will also be a reproduction period garden. Adjacent to the Palace, a 16th century malt house is being converted to provide a tea room, education room and display space for local artists
National Trust for Scotland

Deep-Sea World Deep-Sea World, North Queensferry, Fife KY11 1JR; Tel (01383) 411411; Fax (01383) 410514; *General Manager* Charles Bickett; *Education Officer* Frances J. Oxley
Largest indoor aquarium in Great Britain. Four and a half million litre tank with 3000 fish including sharks viewed via a 112 metre acrylic tunnel. Curriculum related education programme for all age groups from nursery to university
Private company with some public investors eg Fife Enterprise, Scottish Enterprise, Tourist Board. Open all year

Dunfermline District Museum and Small Gallery, Viewfield Terr, Dunfermline KY12 7HY; Tel (01383) 721814; *Director/Curator* Lin Collis
Local social history museum displays on Dunfermline damask linen and history of Dunfermline town. Small Gallery, monthly art, photographic and craft exhibitions

Earlshall Castle, Earlshall Est, Leuchars, St Andrews, Fife KY16 0DP; Tel (01334) 839205; *Owners* Baron and Baronees of Earshall
16th century castle with famous painted ceiling, collection of Broadswords, museum and gun room. Garden with topiary and dovecote

Hill of Tarvit Mansionhouse Cupar KY15 5PB; Tel (01334) 653127; *Property Manager* A. Henderson
Edwardian House by Robert Lorimer; famous collection of paintings, porcelain and furniture; attractive gardens; hill walk. Tea room with home baking
National Trust for Scotland

Inchcolm Abbey, Firth of Forth, c/o Historic Scotland, Longmore Hse, Salisbury Pl, Edinburgh EH9 1SH; Tel 0131-668 8732; *Education Officer* M. Fry
The best preserved group of monastic buildings in Scotland. Reached by ferry for which there is a charge

Inverkeithing Museum, Queen St, Inverkeithing, Fife KY11 1LS; Tel (01383) 410495/721814; *District Curator* Lin Collis
Social and economic history of Inverkeithing and Rosyth. Information on Samuel Greig, born Inverkiething, Father of the Russian Navy

John McDougall Stuart Museum, Rectory La, Dysart; Tel (01592) 260732
Birthplace of Australian explorer. Small exhibition about his journeys, with some Aborigine material. For opening hours and special visits telephone Kirkcaldy Museum (01592) 260732

Kellie Castle and Gardens, Pittenweem KY10 2RF; Tel (01333) 720271; *Property Manager* Patricia Wigston
Audio visual presentation. Kitchen and Victorian nursery. Victorian walled garden

Kirkcaldy Museum and Art Gallery, Kirkcaldy Museum and Art Gallery, War Memorial Gdns, Kirkcaldy KY1 1YG; Tel (01592) 260732; Fax (01592) 645302
Kirkcaldy District Council
Permanent displays of local history material, fine and decorative art. The art collection includes many fine paintings by William McTaggart, Samuel Peploe and the Scottish Colourists. Opening hours: Mon-Sat 10-30am – 5pm; Sun 2pm – 5pm; Closed Public Holidays

Pittencrieff House Museum, Pittencrieff Pk, Dunfermline KY12 2QH; Tel (01383) 722935/721814; *District Curator* Lin Collis
History of Pittencrieff Park and House, costume gallery with changing exhibitions, art gallery. The Dunfermline Giant

Royal Palace of Falkland and Garden, Falkland, Fife; Tel (01337) 857397; *Property Manager* Veronica Woodman
16th century royal palace, centre of Scottish history, architectural masterpiece. Guided tours for schools and costumes, exhibition
National Trust for Scotland

St Andrew's Castle and Cathedral, C/o Historic Scotland, Longmore Hse, Salisbury Pl, Edinburgh EH9 1SH; Tel 0131-668 8732
14th century castle and remains of Scotland's largest cathedral

Scottish Fisheries Museum, St Ayles, Harbourhead, Anstruther KY10 3AB; Tel (01333) 310628
Explains Scotland's fishing industry and fisherfolk, past and present, with model and actual boats, period interiors, ships' gear, paintings, aquarium, wheelchair friendly
Scottish Fisheries Museum Trust Ltd

Grampian

Aberdeen Maritime Museum, C/o Aberdeen Art Gallery, Schoolhill, Aberdeen AB9 1FQ; Tel (01224) 646333; *City Arts and Recreation Officer* Ian McKenzie Smith; *Contact* John Edwards
An award winning museum presenting the story of Aberdeen's maritime history in all its diversity

Aberdeen City Arts & Recreation Division
Aberdeen Pets Corner, Hazlehead Pk, Aberdeen; Tel (01224) 276276 Ext 2231
Doonie's Rane Breeds Farm Coast Rd, Nigg, Aberdeen; Tel (01224) 875879; *Information Officer* Alllan Gawthorpe

Aden Country Park and NE Scotland Agricultural Heritage Centre, Mintlaw, Nr Peterhead, Aberdeenshire AB42 8FQ; Tel (01771) 622857; *Park Manager/Curator* Andrew F. Hill
The preservation and interpretation of NE Scotland's environmental and agricultural heritage. Ranger service and Farm Heritage Centre. Park open all year; Centre open daily May to Sept 11–5 pm and other times by appointment. School parties must book. Adults (16+) £1; Children – Free; School Parties free
Banff and Buchan District Council

Marischal Museum, Marischal College, University of Aberdeen, Aberdeen AB9 1AS; Tel (01224) 273131; *Curator* Charles Hunt
University of Aberdeen

Art Gallery and Museums, Schoolhill, Aberdeen AB9 1FQ; Tel (01224) 646333; *Principal Officer, Programme and Promotions* Ciaran Monaghan

Braemar Castle, Braemar, Aberdeenshire AB35 5XR; Tel (013397) 41219; Fax (013397) 41252; *Estate*

Factor J.S. Blackett; Tel (013397) 41224 (out of season); Fax (013397) 41252
Guided tours daily Easter–to end Oct, 10am–6pm

Brodie Castle, Forres, Moray IV36 0TE; Tel (01309) 641371; Fax (01309) 641600; *Property Manager* Stephanie Blackden
Castle with long unbroken family history. Young persons' publication
National Trust for Scotland

Castle Fraser, Sauchen, Inverurie, Aberdeenshire AB51 7LD; Tel (01330) 833 463; *Property Manager* E. Wilkinson
Magnificent 16th century castle, special activities area, guided tours by arrangement. Formal walled garden, adventure playground, tearoom, walk
National Trust for Scotland

Crathes Castle, Gardens and Estate, Banchory, Kincardineshire AB31 3QJ; Tel (01330) 844525; *Administrator* W.N. Bowman
Magnificent 16th century castle; 600 acre estate with nature trails, ranger service, exhibition and activities area, bird hide, special publications and information sheets in-service training for teachers. Shop, licensed restaurant, adventure area
National Trust for Scotland

Drum Castle, Drumoak, by Banchory, Kincardineshire AB31 3EY; Tel (01330) 811204; *Property Manager* Krista Chisholm
One of the three oldest square towers in Scotland; family story back to Robert the Bruce. Guided tours and self guiding, ranger services
National Trust for Scotland

Fasque, *Manager* Charles Gladstone
Superb Victorian home of the Gladstone Family. Open May–Sept every afternood except Fri

Fyvie Castle, Aberdeenshire; Tel (0165 16) 266; *Representative* D.S. Little
Five towers enshrining over 600 years of Scottish history. Unique collection of portraits, tapestry and armour. 18th century park and man-made loch. Exhibition and tea room
National Trust for Scotland

The Glenfiddich Distillery, Dufftown, Banffshire AB55 4DH; Tel (01340) 820373; *Scottish Public Relations Manager* Elizabeth Lafferty
Visitors' reception centre for promoting traditional methods of manufacture of malt whisky using audio-visual facilities, tour display areas and guides
William Grant and Sons Ltd

Grampian Tranport Museum, Alford, Aberdeenshire AB33 8AD; Tel (019755) 62292; Fax (019755) 62180; *Curator* Mike Ward
Regional road and rail transport history as reflected through extensive collection of vehicles of all types and ages. Demonstration exhibits include 1895 "Craigievar Express" steam tricyclecar

Haddo House, Aberdeen AB41 0ER; Tel (01651) 851440; *Property Manager* Tony Ashby
Important building by William Adam; long Gordon family history
National Trust for Scotland

James Dun's House, C/o Aberdeen Art Gallery, Schoolhill, Aberdeen AB9 1FQ; Tel (01224) 646333; Fax (01224) 632133; *City Arts and Recreation Officer* Ian McKenzie Smith; *Head of Arts and Museums* Alexander Hidalgo
Converted 18th century town house presenting a changing programme of special exhibitions on a wide range of themes

Leith Hall and Gardens, Kennethmont, By Huntly, Aberdeenshire AB5 4NQ; Tel (0146 43) 216; *Property Manager* Eileen Law
Factsheets available on the Hall and surrounding estate. Ranger service by prior arrangement
National Trust for Scotland

The Monymusk Arts Trust, Monymusk, Inverurie, Aberdeenshire AB51 7HL; Tel (01467) 651220
18th century mill, now an arts centre. Crafts for sale, art exhibitions, music and museum of agricultural reforms. Open May–Sept 10–4pmdaily

Moray District Council Museums Division Moray District Council, Department of Leisure and Libraries, Falconer Museum, Tolbooth St, Forres, Moray IV36 9PH; Tel (01309) 673701; *Museums Development Officer* R.B. Inglis
Peter Anson Gallery, Townhouse West, Cluny Pl, Buckie, Moray; Dufftown Museum, The Tower, The Sq, Dufftown, Moray; Tomintoul Visitor Centre, The Sq, Tomintoul, Moray; Tugnet Ice House, Spey Bay, Fochabers; Oldmills Working Mill, Elgin; Falconer Museum, Tolbooth St, Forres; Nelson Tower, Grant Pk, Forres. Organised visits, loan service
Moray District Council

Palace of Holyroodhouse, Edinburgh EH8 8DX; Tel 0131-556 1096; *Principal Officer* Superintendent; Tel 0131-556 7371
The Queen's official residence in Scotland. 17th century building with guided tours throughout the year, closed 3 weeks late May and again late June

Peterhead Arbuthnot Museum, St Peter St, Peterhead, Aberdeenshire AB42 6QD; Tel (01779) 477778; *Curator* J.E. Chamberlain-Mole
Guided tours round the exhibits for school parties, talks by museum staff; adequate booking notice *must* be given (i.e. at least two weeks); with plenty of notice, items not currently on exhibition may be viewed
N.E. Scotland Library and Museums Service Joint Committee

Pitmedden Garden, Ellon, Aberdeenshire AB4 0PD; Tel (01651) 842352; *Representative* Douglas Westland
Formal garden, museum of farming life, collection relating to Aberdeenshire rural life. Open may–Sept, 10–5.30 pm daily. Last admission 5 pm
National Trust for Scotland

Provost Skene's House, C/o Aberdeen Art Gallery and Museums, Schoolhill, Aberdeen AB9 1FQ; Tel (01224) 646333; *City Arts and Recreation Officer* Ian MacKenzie Smith; *Contact* Ciaran Monaghan
17th century town house with period room settings, chapel contains important religious paintings. The top floor houses changing displays

Highland

Balmacara Estate and Lochalsh Woodland Garden, The National Trust for Scotland Lochalsh Hse, Balmacara, Kyle of Lochalsh, Ross-shire IV40 8DN; Tel (01599) 566325; Fax (01599) 566359; *Administrator* D.J.B. Pierce
Woodlands walks

Cawdor Castle, Nairn IV12 5RD; Tel (01667) 404615
Stately home open to the public every day from 1st May to first Sunday in October; 10 am till 5 pm. Questionnaire for children 7–14 years and gift of colouring poster

The Clan Donald Centre, Armadale Castle, Sleat IV45 8RS; Tel (014714) 305/227; *Visitor Services Manager*
Focal point for West Highland history. Woodland gardens. Trails. Help and information from Contryside Ranger service. Audio-visual exhibitions on Lords of the Isles. Resturant and shop. Schools visits welcomed

Culloden, Culloden Moor, Inverness-shire IV1 2ED; *Property Manager* R. Mackenzie Representative's Cottage, Culloden Moor; Tel (01463) 790607; Fax (01463) 794294; *Head of Education* Margaret Cameron
Audio-visual programme, exhibition, publications, battle site with interpretive facilities, guided tours available for school parties, March early June
National Trust for Scotland

Dunrobin Castle, Golspie, Suthreland; Tel (01408) 633177; *Custodian* R. Riley
Display of furniture, paintings and china. Museum, gardens. Open 1 Jun–15 Oct 7 days a week

Dunvegan Castle, Dunvegan; Tel (01470) 521206; *Estate Director* M.J. Lambert

Eileen Donan Castle, Dornie, Kyle, Ross-shire; Tel (0159 985) 202; *Custodian* E. Kennedy

Fort George, Nr Inverness, c/o Historic Scotland, Longmore Hse, Salisbury Pl, Edinburgh EH9 1SH; Tel 0131-668 8732; *Education Officer* M. Fry
A magnificent 18th century artillery fortress

Gairloch Heritage Museum, Achtercairn, Gairloch; Tel (01445) 712287; *Curator* Janette French
Collects, conserves and interprets information (particularly oral history) in both Gaelic and English, covering all aspects of Gairloch Parish

Glenfinnan Monument, Glenfinnan, Inverness-shire PH37 4LT; Tel (01397) 722250; *Property Manager* L. Grant
National Trust for Scotland
Scene of the raising of the standard for the '45 Jacobite rising; exhibition
National Trust for Scotland

Highland Folk Museum, Duke St, Kingussie PH21 1JG; Tel (01540) 661307; *Curator* R. Ross Noble; *Visitor Sevices Manager* Helen Collie
Interprets social and economic history of Scottish Highlands. Open-air museum. farming museum. Demonstrations and live events in summer season
Highland Regional Council

Highland Wildlife Park, Kincraig, Kingussie PH21 1NL; Tel (01540) 651270; *Contact* Education Officer
Royal Zoological Society of Scotland. Project work

Hugh Miller's Cottage, Cromarty, Ross-shire; Tel (01381) 600245; *Custodian* F.C. Gostwick
Church St, Cromarty
Award winning exhibition related to the 19th century scientist, writer and theologian
National Trust for Scotland

Inverewe Garden, Poolewe, Wester Ross IV22 2LQ; Tel (0144 586) 200; *Administrator* K. Gordon
One of the most famous gardens in the UK
National Trust for Scotland

Inverness Museum and Art Gallery, Castle Wynd IV2 3ED; Tel (01463) 237114; *Curator* Catherine Niven
Museum and art gallery

Torridon, The Mains, Torridon, by Achnasheen, Ross-shire IV22 2EZ; Tel (01445) 791221; *Ranger/ Naturalist* S.A. MacNally Countryside Centre
Scenic splendour, natural history, deer museum. Tame herd of red deer
The National Trust for Scotland

The West Highland Museum, Cameron Sq, Fort William PH33 6AJ; Tel (01397) 702169; *Curator/ Secretary* Fiona C. Marwick

Lothian

Brass Rubbing Centre, Trinity Apse, Chalmers Cl, High St, Edinburgh; Tel 0131-556 4364; *Administrative Assistant – Sales* Lesley Stothers
Introduces people to the technique of brass rubbing and provides information about historic brasses. Housed in important historic building

City Art Centre, 2 Market St, Edinburgh EH1 1DE; Tel 0131-529 3993; *Keeper of Fine Art Collection* Ian O'Riordan
Gallery space on six floors, exhibition programme includes international loans, art and crafts, and selections from the City's collection of Scottish art

Dalmeny House, South Queensferry, West Lothian EH30 9TQ; Tel 0131-331 1888; *Administrator* L. Morison
Fabulous collection of works of art, French furniture, tapestries and porcelain, 18th century British portraits, Napoleon collection, beautiful grounds and sea views. Open May–Sept

Dirleton Castle and Garden, Dirleton, East Lothian, c/o Historic Scotland, Longmore Hse, Salisbury Pl, Edinburgh EH9 1SH; Tel 0131-668 8732
An early 13th century castle with later additions. Beautiful gardens

The Edinburgh Butterfly and Insect World, Dobbies Gardening World, Lasswade EH18 1AZ; Tel 0131-663 4932; Fax 0131-654 2548
Free-flying tropical butterflies in exotic surroundings. Insect displays, tropical fish and birds. Bee garden and live honey-bee display. Free guided tours for pre-booked parties. Interesting gift shop

Edinburgh Castle, c/o Historic Scotland, Longmore Hse, Salisbury Pl, Edinburgh EH9 1SH; Tel 0131-668 8732; *Education Officer* M. Fry
The castle houses the crown jewels of Scotland. Visitor display. School parties charged June, July and August

Edinburgh Zoo, Royal Zoological Society of Scotland, Scottish National Zoological Pk, Murrayfield, Edinburgh EH12 6TS; Tel 0131-334 9171; *Education Officer* Robert Ollason

The Fruitmarket Gallery, 29 Market St, Edinburgh EH1 1DF; Tel 0131-225 2383; *Director* Fiona McLeod; *Education Officer* Pat Fisher
Scotland's international venue for contemporary art and design presenting a continuous programme of exhibitions from Great Britain and abroad. During term time exhibitions are accompanied by a full programme of practical activities and guided tours for both primary and secondary schools groups

****The Georgian House,*** 7 Charlotte Sq, Edinburgh EH2 4DR; Tel 0131-225 2160; *Representative* S. Kennedy
Life as it was in Georgian Edinburgh, school parties specially catered for
National Trust for Scotland

Gladstone's Land, 477B Lawnmarket, Edinburgh EH1 2NT; Tel 0131-226 5856; *Property Representative* A. Butler
17th century merchant's house, guided tours, activities room, costumes to dress in
National Trust for Scotland

Historic Scotland, Longmore Hse, Salisbury Pl, Edinburgh EH9 1SH; Tel 0131-668 8732; *Director* Graeme Munro
Manages 330 historic properties open to the public, including Edinburgh and Stirling Castles. Free educational visits scheme. Information on major sites

****Hopetoun House,*** South Queensferry, Nr Edinburgh; Tel 0131-331 2451
18th century state appartments, 100 acres of magnificent parkland, nature trails, seashore and 3 exhibitions: "Horse and Man", "Wildlife" and "The Building of Hopetoun". Free teachers' information pack on request

House of Binns, Linlithgow, West Lothian; Tel (0150 683) 4255; *Representative* Kathleen Dalyell
Family associations with Scottish history, home of Dalyell family since 1612. Home of Gen Tam Dalyell, Royalist General in Civil War, fine plaster ceilings (1630), hilltop viewpoint, guided tours. Advance booking essential for parties. Opening hours 1st May–30th Sept. Every day 2.00–5.00 except Fridays. Closed for major structural repairs. Opening in 1994 season will be delayed until June. Please ring before visiting to check if House has opened
National Trust for Scotland

Huntly House Museum, 142 Canongate, Edinburgh EH8 8DD; Tel 0131-529 4143; *City Curator* Herbert Coutts; *Contact* Sandra Marwick
The history of Edinburgh and collections of Edinburgh silver, glass, shop signs, Earl Haig material and Scottish pottery
Edinburgh District Council

Lennoxlove House, Lennoxlove, Haddington, East Lothian EH41 4NZ; Tel (0162 0182) 3720; *Chairman* Duke of Hamilton; *Contact* E.A. Bouchard
Guided tours of an historic house
Lennoxlove House Ltd

The Almond Valley Heritage Centre, Millfield, Kirkton North, Livingston, West Lothian EH54 7AR; Tel (01506) 414957; *Curator* Dr Robin Chesters
Heritage centre containing the Scottish Shale Oil Museum, local history displays and other exhibitions, working farmstead, restored 18th century watermill, children's farm on 6 acre site, conservation and nature study areas, narrow-gauge railway station. Educational resource room. Open throughout the year

Museum of Childhood, 42 High St, Edinburgh EH1 1TG; Tel 0131-529 4142; *Keeper* John Heyes
The first museum in the world to be solely devoted to the theme of childhood

Museum of Communication, University of Edinburgh, James Clerk Maxwell Bldg, The King's Bldgs, Mayfield Rd, Edinburgh EH9 3JL; Tel (01506) 824507; *Curator/ Founder* C.H.C. Matthews
History of communication and collection of artefacts and library of information. Open Mon–Fri, 9–7; Sat–

Sun, (–7 accompanied only. parties 15 most. Suitable for the disabled

Museum of Flight, East Fortune Airfield, Northern Berwick, East Lothian EH39 5LF; Tel (0162 0188) 308; *Curator* R.J. Major
The museum seeks to exhibit all aspects of flight. There are 30+ aircraft and 70+ engines, together with airships displays

Myreton Motor Museum, Aberlady, East Lothian; Tel (01875) 870288; *Curator* M.J. Mutch
Cars, Motor cycles, commercials, W.W.2. British military vehicles, cycles, period advertising, enamel signs, etc

National Gallery of Scotland, The Mound, Edinburgh EH2 2EL; Tel 0131-556 8921; *Keeper* Michael Clarke; *Contact* Anne-Marie Wagener
An outstanding collection of paintings, drawings and prints by the greatest artists from the Renaissance to Post-Impressionism, also the National Collection of Scottish art

Niddy Castle, Winchburgh, West Lothian; *Contact* Peter and Janet Wright (Owners)
Major castle restoration now nearing completion. Late 15th century towerhouse built by the Sefton family. Gave refuge to Mary Queen of Scots. Archaeological excavation of site

The People's Story Museum, Canongate Tolbooth, 163 Canongate, Edinburgh EH8 8BN; Tel 0131-529 4057; *Keeper of Social History* Helen Clark; *Contact* Sandra Marwick
The People's Story is the museum about the life and work of Edinburgh's people from the late 18th century to the present

Queensferry Museum, Council Chambers, 53 High St, South Queensferry EH30 9HP; Tel 0131-331 5545; *Site Manager* Denise Brace
History of the former Royal Burgh of South Queensferry and of the crossings over the Forth
Edinburgh District Council Museums and Galleries

Royal Botanic Garden, *Senior Education Officer* Dr I. Edwards; *Education Officer* Heather Paul
Leaflet on educational services available

Royal Museum of Scotland, Chambers St, Edinburgh EH1 1JF; *Head of Education* Mary Bryden
Informal and formal educational activities; resources for teachers; the Discovery room is open in Edinburgh for part of the year, and also travels to other venues in Scotland
Queen St, Edinburgh EH2 1JD; Tel 0131-225 7534

Scottish Agricultural Museum, Ingliston, Edinburgh EH28 8NB; Tel 0131-333 2674; Fax 0131-333 2674; *Curator* Gavin Sprott; Tel 0131-333 2674
Shows Country life and work in Scotland over the last two hundred years

Scottish National Gallery of Modern Art, Belford Rd, Edinburgh EH4 3DR; Tel 0131-556 8921; *Keeper* Richard Calvocoressi; *Publicity Officer* Giselle Dye; *Education Officer* Michael Cassin
Scotland's national collection of 20th century painting, sculpture and graphic art

Scottish National Portrait Gallery, 1 Queen St, Edinburgh EH2 1JD; Tel 0131-556 8921; *Keeper* Dr Duncan Thomson; *Information Officer* Lindsey Callander; *Education Officer* Susan Lamb
Portraits of famous Scots from the 16th century to modern times and the national collection of photography

Scottish United Services Museum, Edinburgh Castle, Edinburgh; Tel 0131-225 7534 Ext 404; Fax 0131-225 3848; *Keeper* S.C. Wood, MA; *Librarian* E. Philip
Research and archival function on the armed forces in Scotland
Trustees of the National Museums of Scotland

Stevenson House, Nr Haddington, East Lothian EH41 4PU; Tel (0162 0182) 3376; *Principal Trustee of Family Trust* Mrs A.B. Dunlop
House of historical/architectural interest 16th and 18th century additions. Furnishings, pictures, etc. Family home open to the public Jul/mid-Aug Thurs, Sat, Sun pm, or by appointment May to Oct. Guided tour of House at 3pm, £2, £1.50 concession. Garden open May to Oct also, 50p
The Brown-Dunlop Country Houses Trust

Tantallon Castle, C/o Historic Scotland, Longmore St, Salisbury Pl, Edinburgh EH9 1SH; Tel 0131-668 8732; *Education Officer* M. Fry
A remarkable fortification with a splendid coastal location

Wemyss and March Estates, Estates Office, Longniddry, East Lothian EH32 0PY; Tel (01875) 870201; *The Factor* Estates Office; *The Custodian* Neidpath Castle, Peebles; Tel (01721) 720333
Estate management also public opening of Neidpath Castle, Peebles and Gosford House, East Lothian, and surrounding grounds, woods, walks, etc

Northern Isles

Fair Isle Bird Observatory, Fair Isle, Shetland Isles; *Warden* Dr Roger Riddington; *Administrator* Wendy Christie
Informal participation in daily bird census work. Opportunity to study island's flora and fauna, archaeology, history and social life usuing observatory as base. Groups welcome early Spring, July and August

Jarlshof, Sumburgh Head, Shetland, c/o Historic Scotland, Longmore Hse, Salisbury Pl, Edinburgh EH9 1SH; Tel 0131-668 8732
A Bronze Age village and entire Viking settlement

Orkney Farm and Folk Museum, Kirbuster, Birsay and Corrigall, Harray, Orkney; Tel (0185 677) 268 and (0185 677) 411; *Museum Officer* B.S. Wilson
Collecting and displaying agricultural artefacts in the setting of traditional farm buildings. Two sites

Shetland Croft House Museum, Voe, Dunrossness, c/o The Shetland Museum, Lower Hillhead, Lerwick, Shetland Isles ZE1 0EL; Tel (01595) 5057; *Curator* Tommy Watt, FSA(Scot)
A typical Shetland croft house, steading and water mill, restored to what it would have been circa 1870. Open May to Sept

Shetland Museum, Lower Hillhead, Lerwick, Shetland Isles ZE1 0EL; Tel (01595) 5057; *Curator* Tommy Watt, FSA(Scot)
All the activities and displays in this museum reflects the theme "Life in Shetland through the Ages". Open daily. Admission free. Disabled access

Skara Brae, NW of Kirkwall, c/o Historic Scotland, Longmore Hse, Salisbury Pl, Edinburgh EH9 1SH; Tel 0131-668 8732
The best preserved Stone Age village in W Europe

Stromness Museum, 52 Alfred St, Stromness; Tel (01856) 850025; *Honorary Curator* B.S. Wilson
Specialist collections in natural history and local maritime history
Orkney Natural History Society

Strathclyde

Art Gallery and Museum, Kelvingrove, Glasgow G3 8AG; Tel 0141-334 1131; Fax 0141-357 4537; *Director* Julian Spalding; *Publicity Officer* Vincent Taggart
Archaeology, ethnography, natural history, decorative and fine art. Museum Education Dept offers services for Strathclyde schools. Free guide service available. Open all year
Open daily: 10–5 Sunday 11–5
Admission Free
Wheelchair access throughout
Please ask staff for assistance while improvements are being carried out
Free guided tours

Auchindrain Township Open Air Museum, Inveraray, Argyll PA32 8XN; Tel (014995) 235; *Contact* The Curator
Original old West Highland Township. Restored, furnished and equipped to give living experience of Highland way of life in past

Bachelors' Club, Sandgate St, Tarbolton, Mauchline, Ayrshire KA5 5RB; Tel (01292) 541424; *Custodian* Yule Lithgow; *Contact* Michael L. Tebbutt
Administrator, Culzean Castle and Country Pk, Maybole, Ayrshire KA19 8LE; Tel (016556) 274

Preservation and presentation of Scotland's heritage
National Trust for Scotland

Biggar Gasworks Museum, Biggar, Lanarkshire; Tel (01899) 21070; *Curator* J. Crompton
June–Sept, Mon–Daily 2–5pm. Admission free. See steam engines, domestic appliances and learn how gas was made
Chambers St, Edinburgh EH1 1JF

Bothwell Castle, Nr Uddingston, c/o Historic Scotland, Longmore Hse, Salisbury Pl, Edinburgh EH9 1SH; Tel 0131-668 8732
Largest 13th century stone castle in Scotland

Brodick Castle Gardens, Country Park and Gaotfell, Brodick, Isle of Arran; Tel (01770) 2202; *Administrator* Olive Raymond
Ranger service with guided walks
National Trust for Scotland

Burns' Cottage, Alloway, Ayr KA7 4PY; Tel (01295) 441215; *Curator* John Manson
Birthplace of Robert Burns, 1759–96, Scotland's National Poet. Museum containing many of Burns'relics, songs, poems and manuscripts

The Burrell Collection, Pollok Country Park, 2060 Pollokshaws Rd, Glasgow G43 1AT; Tel 0141-649 7151; Fax 0141-636 0086; *Resident Curator* Stefan Van Raay; *Publicity Officer* Vincent Taggart
Collection of over 8,000 items donated by Sir William Burrell, including European paintings, decorative art, Chinese ceramics, antiques from Iraq, Egypt, Greece and Italy
Glasgow Museums and Art Galleries Department
Open daily: 10–5 Sunday: 11–5
Admission Free
Wheelchair access throughout
Free guided tours

Bute Museum, Stuart St, Rothesay; Tel (01700) 503868; *Curator* A. Speirs
Guides to museum arranged for visiting school parties. Exhibits of local natural history, geology, history and prehistory
Bute Museum Trustees

Clydebank Museum, Old Town Hall, Dumbarton Rd, Clydebank G81 1XQ; Tel 0141-941 1331 Ext 402; *Museum Curator*
Small developing, community museum; local history, industry, shipbuilding, engineering, sewing machines (specialist collection). Educational groups welcome on appointment

Collins Gallery, University of Strathclyde, 22 Richmond St, Glasgow G1 1XQ; Tel 0141-552 4400 Ext 4145/2682; Fax 0141-552 4053; *Exhibition Organiser* Morag Davidson; *Curator* Laura Hamilton
Provides a programme of temporary exhibitions incorporating fine and applied art–historical and contemporary. Contemporary British art collection. Multi-media workshops regularly

Crarae Garden, Crarae Garden Charitable Trust, Inveraray, Argyll PA32 8YA; Tel (01546) 86614/86388; *Administrator* Fiona Sinclair; *Resident Trustees* Sir Ilay and Lady Campbell

**Culzean Castle and Country Park,* Maybole, Ayrshire KA19 8LE; Tel (016556) 274 (general) (016556) 269 (bookings); *Administrator* Jonathan Cardale; *Secretary Reservations* Wendy Hollingworth
Preservation and presentation of a fine example of an 18th century Lowland Scottish estate. Castle built by Robert Adam: interior restored to his original designs
National Trust for Scotland/Local Authorities

David Livingstone Centre, 165 Station Rd, Blantyre, Glasgow G72 9BT; Tel (01698) 823140; *Director* David O'Neill; *Education and Events Officer* Sheila Watt
Comprising The Livingstone Memorial, the birthplace of David Livingstone preserving the house in which he was born and illustrating by maps, models and relics, his life work and Africa travels. Social History Museum, Art Gallery and African Pavilion with exhibitions on modern Africa. Grounds, riverside walk, garden, shop and cafe and Clyde Valley Pottery

Finlaystone Estate, Langbank, Renfrewshire PA14 6TJ; Tel (01475) 540505/540285; *Countryside Ranger* David Pickett
Doll collection, Victoriana, gardens and woodland walks, 'Eye Opener' visitor centre, play and picnic areas, ranger service

Gladstone Court, Greenhill, Moat Park Centre, Biggar ML12 6DT; Tel (01899) 21050; *Education Officer* Brian Lambie
School visits; worksheet; projects boxes, activity programmes
Biggar Museum Trust

Glasgow Botanic Gardens, Western Rd, Glasgow G12 0UE; Tel 0141-334 2422; *Acting Curator* E.G. Donaldson
Guided tours, material for class work, information leaflets
City of Glasgow council

Glasgow Museum of Transport, Kelvin Hall, Glasgow G3; Tel 0141-334 1131 (Educational visits); *Museum Education Officer* Jemima W. Fraser
Intra/extra mural teaching; in-service/in-training courses; art competition; weekend and holiday activities

Glasgow Zoo, Uddingston, Glasgow G71 7RZ; Tel 0141-771 1185; Fax 0141-771 2615; *Education Officer* Dr Stephen Bostock
Education service for Strathclyde schools

The Glencoe and North Lorn Folk Museum, Glencoe Village, Argyll; *Secretary and Treasurer* Miss Fairweather; *President* Mrs Grant; *Vice-President* Mrs Jones
Aims to collect and preserve exhibits of historic interest and to display them or to have them available

Haggs Castle Children's Museum, 100 St Andrew's Dr, Pollokshields, Glasgow G41 4RB; Tel 0141-427 2725; Fax 0141-427 7075; *Senior Curator in Residence* Nat Edwards; *Publicity Officer* Vincent Taggart
A historical castle museum with period rooms, exhibitions and activity sessions designed especially for children. Also base for the Open Museum, which provides small exhibitions and handling kits for use in the classroom and other non-museum venues
Glasgow District Council, Glasgow Museums
Open daily: 10–5 Sunday: 11–5
Admission Free

Hamilton District Council Heritage and Countryside, Chatelherault, Ferniegair, Hamilton ML3 7UE; Tel (01698) 426413; *Keeper of Interpretation and Education* Joyce J.R. Brown, MA(Hons), FSA(Scot)
The Heritage and Countryside Section is responsible for 3 sites – The District Museum, housed in a 17th Century Grade A Listed building; The Cameronian Regimental Museum; and Chatelherault, The Duke of Hamilton's Hunting Lodge, dating from 1732 plus 500 acres of surrounding country park. Displays include archaeology, social and industrial history, costume, paintings, photographs, ceramics and transport. Regular temporary exhibition programme. Introductory talks and guided tours, factsheets and worksheets. Information for teachers and pupils. All day workshops on selected themes. Also holiday activities, concerts, associated events. Ranger Service

Heatherbank Museum of Social Work, Caledonian University, 1 Park Dr, Glasgow G3 6LP; Tel 0141-331 3000 Ext 4402
Changing exhibitions 1993 Disability and Young Offenders. Spring 1994 Homelessness–Spring 1995 Mental Health in Scotland. Reference and picture library. Open by appointment. Admission free (donation welcome)

Hunterian Museum and Art Gallery, University of Glasgow, Glasgow G12 8QQ; Tel 0141-330 4221
Educational activities arranged for school parties and other organised groups. Topics include: Romans, Egyptian, Ancient Greeks, North American Indians, Captain Cook, Early Man, Dinosaurs and Fossils, Rocks and Minerals, "Earth–Life". Advance booking essential for activities. Hours of opening – Mon–Sat 09.30–17.00 hrs. Admission free

Inveraray Castle, Argyll Estates Office, Cherry Pk, Inveraray, Argyll PA32 8XE; Tel (01499) 302203; Fax (01499) 302421

Since the 15th century Inveraray Castle has been the headquarters of Clan Campbell. The present castle was built in the 18th century

Isle of Arran Heritage Museum, Rosaburn, Brodick, Isle of Arran KA27 8DP; Tel (01770) 2636; *Chairperson, Management Committee* Willma Pirie; Tel (01770) 700 337
Heritage museum including school heritage project. Smiddy, agricultural equipment, displays of archaeology, geology. Shipping. Furnished Victorian cottage

Lillie Art Gallery, Station Rd, Milngavie, Glasgow G62 8BZ; Tel 0141-943 3247; *Curator* Elizabeth M. Dent
Exhibits the work of 20th century Scottish artists and of own collection. Organises a programme of temporary exhibitions and educational activities

McLean Museum and Art Gallery, 15 Kelly St, Greenock PA16 8JX; Tel (01475) 723741; *Curator* Valerie Boa
Introductory and guided talks, 2 weeks advance booking
Inverclyde District Council

The McLellan Galleries, 270 Sauchiehall St, Glasgow G2 3EH; Tel 0141-331 1854; Fax 0141-332 9957; *Director* Julian Spalding; *Publicity Officer* Vincent Taggart
The largest temporary exhibition space outside of London, refurbished in 1990 to house the best of temporary exhibitions from around the world

Museum and Art Galleries, High St, Paisley PA1 2BA; Tel 0141-889 3151; *Museum Education Officer* M. Lochrie
Talks on local and social history, wild life, paintings, holiday time activities. Service for schools and children

The Museum of Islay Life, Port Charlotte, Isle of Islay, Argyll PA48 7UA; Tel (01496) 850358; *Hon Curator* Margot Perrons
The exhibits illustrate life in Islay from pre-history to present day, with extensive library, and archive material and photographs relating to Islay

Museum of Transport, Kelvin Hall, 1 Bunhouse Rd, Glasgow G3 8DP; Tel 0141-357 3929; Fax 0141-357 5849; *Senior Curator* Darryl Mead; *Publicity Officer* Vincent Taggart
Many aspects of transport history–road, rail, Clyde ship-building reconstruction of Merkland St underground station
Open daily: 10–5 Sunday: 11–5
Admission Free
Wheelchair access throughout
Free guided tours

The People's Palace, Glasgow Grn, Glasgow G40 1AT; Tel 0141-334 1131 (Edication Service), 554 0223 (Museum); Fax 041-550 0892; *Senior Curator* Mark O'Neill; *Publicity Officer* Vincent Taggart
Museum of the history and development of Glasgow from its founding to the present day. Changing temporary exhibitions. Open all year
City of Glasgow District Council
Open daily: 10–5 Sunday: 11–5
Admission Free
Wheelchair access throughout

Pollok House, Pollok Estate (via 2060 Pollokshaws Rd, Glasgow), Glasgow G43 1AT; Tel 0141-632 0274; *Resident Curator* Rosemary Watt; *Publicity Officer* Vincent Taggart
Ancestral home with 361 acres of gardens and parkland. Open to the public all year. Special arrangements for parties on request
Glasgow Art Galleries and Museums, Museum Education Service Tel 041-334 1131 for school visits
Open daily: 10–5 Sunday: 11–5
Admission Free
Wheelchair access
Please ask staff for assistance
Free guided tours

Provand's Lordship, Castle St, Glasgow G4 0RB; Tel 0141-552 8819; *Senior Curator* Mark O'Neill; *Publicity Officer* Vincent Taggart
15th century house with collection of 15th–17th century furniture and paintings. Open to the public all year. No admission charge
Glasgow Museums and Art Galleries Department
Open daily: 10–5 Sunday 11–5
Admission Free

RSPB Lochwinnoch Nature Centre, Largs Rd, Lochwinnoch PA12 4JF; Tel (01505) 842663; Fax (01505) 843026; *Nature Centre Manager* Graham Christer

Robertson Museum and Aquarium, University Marine, Bological Station, Millport, Isle of Cumbrae KA28 0EG; Tel (01475) 530581/2; *Director* Professor J. Davenport; *Head Museum and Aquarium* Prof P.G. Moore; *Station Secretary* D.J. Murden
Teaching, research, specimen supply in marine biology mainly at tertiary educational level. Visiting classes accommodated. Museum/Aquarium open to the public

Rutherglen Museum, King St, Rutherglen, Glasgow G73 1DQ; Tel 0141-647 0837; *Keeper* Mark O'Neill; *Publicity Officer* Vincent Taggart
Museum of local history
Glasgow District Council Museum and Art Galleries Dept
Open daily 10–5 Sunday: 11–5
Admission Free
Wheelchair access throughout

The St Mungo Museum of Religious Life and Art, 2 Castle St, Glasgow G4 0RH; Tel 0141-553 2557; Fax 0141-552 4744; *Senior Curator* Mark O'Neill; *Publicity Officer* Vincent Taggart
The first museum in the world to look at all the major religious together, from an artistic, historical and social context. Three gallery spaces focus on art, world religious and religion in Scotland. Also, Britain's only authentic Japanese Zen Garden

Scottish Industrial Railway Centre, Minnivey Colliery, Burnton, Dalmellington; Tel (01294) 531144 (day); (01292) 313579 (evenings); *Chairman* Norman Gee; *Contact* Dick Butler; *Contact* Gordon Thompson
Industrial locomotive and rolling stock in preserved working condition and in operation on open days

Souter Johnnie's Cottage, Kirkoswald; Tel (0165 56) 603; *The Administrator* Culzean Castle, Maybole, Ayrshire KA19 8LE; Tel (0165 56) 274; Fax (0165 56) 615
Displays related to the shoemakers craft and his cottage interior
National Trust for Scotland

Strathkelvin District Museums, The Cross, Kirkintilloch, Glsgow G66 1AB; Tel 0141-775 1185; Fax 0141-777 7649; *Curator* Susan M. Selwyn, MA, AMA
Worksheets and activities relating to the displays are available. Postcards and local publications are also available. Guided visits can be arranged and handling sessions if desired; loan service available
Strathkelvin District Council, Tom Johnston Hse, Kirkintilloch, Glasgow G66 1AB; Tel 041-775 1185

Tenement House, 145 Buccleuch St, Glasgow G3; Tel 0141-333 0183; *Representative* Lorna Hepburn
Encapsulation of tenement living in the early 1900's
Phone for details and booking
National Trust for Scotland

University Marine Biological Station, Millport, Isle of Cumbrae KA28 0EG; Tel (01475) 530581/2; *Station Secretary*
Universities of London and Glasgow Field centre with residential accommodation and laboratories for Universities, Colleges and Schools. Also Robertson Museum and Aquarium, open for school parties. Teaching packages available

Weaver's Cottage, The Cross, Kilbarchan, RENFREWSHIRE; *Manager* Irene MacDiarmid 21 Dunrobin Ave, Elderslie, Johnstone, Renfrewshire PA5 9NW; Tel (01505) 324460
The National Trust
18th century handloom weaver's cottage, video on a weaver's family. Demonstrations
National Trust for Scotland

Welfare History Picture Library, Heatherbank Museum of Social Work, Caledonian University, 1 Park Dr, Glasgow G3 6LP; Tel 0141-331 3000
Covers all aspects of social welfare and social work history. Enquiries welcome

Tayside

Angus District Museum–Arbroath Museum; Arbroath Art Gallery; Brechin Museum; Montrose Museum and Art Gallery; William Lamb Memorial Studio, Meffan Institute, Forfar, Angus DD8 1BB; Tel (01307) 66966/7; *District Curator* Norman K. Atkinson
Museum, art gallery, archaeology, natural history, art, local history, maritime history, Pictish stones, fishing history, flax, whaling, Montose and Arbroath silver, shoe-making history, school visits

Angus Folk Museum, Kirkwynd Cottages, Glamis, Angus DD8 1RT; Tel (01307) 840288; V. MacAlister
Special interest on rural life for primary children, collection of early farm machinery.
National Trust for Scotland

Arbroath Abbey, Arbroath, c/o Historic Scotland, Longmore Hse, Salisbury Pl, Edinburgh EH9 1SH; Tel 0131-668 8732; *Education Officer* M. Fry
Substantial monstery ruins and exhibition

Atholl County Collection, The Old School, Blair Atholl, Perthshire; Tel (01796) 481232; *Curator* John Cameron
Tells the interesting story of how the villagers and glen folk lived their lives in days gone by. Open end of May to Mid-Oct

Barrie's Birthplace, 9 Brechin Rd, Kirriemuir, Angus DD8 4BX; Tel (01575) 572646; *Property Manager* Karen Gilmour
Birthplace of Sir J.M. Barrie, author of Peter Pan. Collection of memorabilia, including MSS, costumes. Wash-house–the original Wendy House
National Trust for Scotland

Ben Lawers, Tel (01567) 820397; *Ranger* Helen Cole Visitor Centre
Guided walks
National Trust for Scotland

Blair Castle, Blair Atholl PH18 5TL; Tel (01796) 481207; Fax (01796) 481487; *The Administrator* Brian H. Nodes
Young people's guidebook available. Open to visitors Apr to late Oct. Castle, parklands, deer park, pony trekking, picnic area. 'Diana's Grove'

Branklyn Garden, Dundee Rd, Perth PH2 7BB; Tel (01738) 625535; *Property Manager* R.J. Mitchell
Small ornamental garden. Specialising in Sino Himalayan plants. A plantsman's garden. Open 1 Mar–31 Oct, daily 9.30 to sunset
National Trust for Scotland

Camperdown Wildlife Centre, Camperdown Country Pk, Dundee DD2 4TS; Tel (01382) 432689; *Conservation Officer* Iain Valentine
Visits to schools, guided tours of Centre, nature trail and forest areas

Castle Menzies, Weem by Aberfeldy PH15 2JD; Tel (01887) 820982; *Administrator* R.A. Adam
Historic building, 16th century, seat of Clan Menzies also Clan Museum. Under restoration and open to the public Apr–mid-Oct. Car park. Tea room

Dunblane Cathedral Museum, Cathedral Sq, Dunblane, Perthshire FK15; Tel (01786) 824254; *Honorary Curator* John G. Lindsay
Presents the history of the cathedral of Dunblane, collection of communion tokens, library mainly church history

Discovery Point Discovery Point, Discovery Quay, Dundee DD1 4XA; Tel (01382) 201245; Fax (01382) 225891; *Education Officer*
On-board tour of Captain Scott's Dundee built Antarctic exploration ship RRS Discovery and on-shore audio-visual exhibition bringing alive Discovery's story from design to the present day. Variety of educational tours arranged with access to multi-purpose schools' room and resource facilities

Dundee Art Galleries and Museums (Museum Services), McManus Galleries, Albert Sq, Dundee DD1 1DA; Tel (01382) 432020 Ext 65133/65134; *Education Officer* Nancy Davey; *Curator* Adam B. Ritchie; *Museum Services Technician* James Mann; *Museum Services Officer* Parveen Rodger
Services available in Dundee district for schools, colleges and adult groups. Activity room, school loan service, information service. Booking essential

Glamis Castle, Glamis, Angus DD8 1RJ; Tel (01307) 840242/393; *Estate Office*
Childhood home of HM The Queen Mother, birthplace of HRH The Princess Margaret and the legendary setting of Shakespeare's play Macbeth. School parties welcome. Lecturer with slides available to visit schools

Pass of Killiecrankie, Perthshire PH16 5LG; Tel (01796) 473233; *Ranger-Naturalist* S. Townsend Visitor Centre
History and natural history exhibitions, guided walks
National Trust for Scotland

Perth Museum and Art Gallery, George St, Perth PH1 5LB; Tel (01738) 32488; *Curator* J.A. Blair; *Keeper of Education Services* Barbara Hamilton
Provides, develops and administers a musuem education service for the district and encourages its use by the community. Loan service also available

RSPB Vane Farm Nature Centre, by Loch Leven, Kinross KY13 7LX; Tel (01577) 862355; *Senior Education Development Officer* J. Yuill
Environmental education centre. Programme for primary and secondary pupils, and tertiary students

Scone Palace, Perth PH2 6BD; Tel (01738) 552300; Fax (01738) 552588; *The Administrator* A.R. Robinson
History of Scottish Kings, environmental studies

Scottish Tartans Museum, Drummond St, Comrie, Perthshire PH6 2DW; Tel (01764) 70779; *Executive President* Dr D.G. Teall of Teallach; *Museum Manager* Stan Collingwood
Rare examples of Highland Dress and Tartan, Spinning, Weaving and Dyeing. Over 400 tartans on display with computer access to over 2000 recorded designs in the Register of All Publicly Known Tartans. School visits welcome. Demonstrations and workshops available

Scottish Tartans Society Research Centre Teallach Estates, Pitlochry; Tel (01796) 474079
Researches into Tartans, Highland Dress, Spinning, Weaving and Dyeing. Maintains an archive including 'The Register of All Publicly Known Tartans'. Academic researchers welcome. Limited accommodation available

Sunnyside Museum, Sunnyside Royal Hospital, Hillside, Montrose DD10 9JP; Tel (01674) 830361; *Curator and Consultant Psychiatrist* Dr K.M.G. Keddie
Presents the history of psychiatry in Scotland. The hospital was the first psychiatric hospital to be founded in Scotland in 1781. Open Wed 2–3.30 pm from after Easter to end of Sept

Northern Ireland

County Antrim

Giants Causeway, Visitor Centre, 44 Causeway Rd, Bushmills, Co Antrim BT57 8SU
Audio-visual show and exhibition; Tel (02657) 31855. Guided Walks; Tel (02657) 31855

County Armagh

Ardress House, Annaghmore, Portadown BT62 1SQ; Tel (01762) 851236; *The Administrator* Shan McAnena
National Trust

Armagh County Museum, The Mall East, Armagh BT61 9BE; Tel (01861) 523070; Fax (01861) 522631; *Curator* Catherine M.L. McCullough, MA, DipMAN
The museum presents the history, natural history and art of County Armagh for recreational and educational purposes

Armagh Planetarium, College Hall, Armagh BT61 9DB; Tel (01861) 523689; *Contact* John Flynn; Tel (01861) 524725
The Planetarium provides information and resources on astronomy and space for all users both educational and recreational

Tayto (NI) Ltd, Tandragee Castle, Tandragee, CO ARMAGH BT62 2AA; Tel (01762) 840249; *Contact* R.W.G. Brown

Conducted tours of the factory (which is situated in a 17th century castle) show how crisps and snacks are manufactured

County Down

Arts Council Gallery, 56–60 Dublin Rd, Belfast BT2 7HD; Tel (01232) 321402; *Visual Arts Officer* Noirin McKinney
Located in central Belfast, the Gallery presents exhibitions of contemporary Irish and international art

Belfast Castle, Antrim Rd, Belfast BT15 5GR; Tel (01232) 776925; *Manager* Peter R. McKay
Catering for all types of functions; weddings, dinner dances, conferences, full restaurant facilities, interprative centre, tours, gardens

**Castle Ward,* Strangford BT30 7LS; Tel (0139 686) 204; *Regional Education Officer* James Galway
National Trust

Malone House, Malone Rd, Belfast BT9 5PB; Tel (01232) 681246; *Manageress* Patricia Anderson
Resturant and conference centre with Art Gallery and "Belfast Parks" exhibition

Mount Stewart House and Garden, Mount Stewart, Newtownards BT22 2AD; Tel (012477) 88387; Fax (012477) 88569; *The Administrator* H.R. Hutchman
National Trust

Mullaghbawn Folk Museum, Tullymacrieve, Mullaghbawn, Co Armagh; *Coordinator* M. McCoy; Tel (01693) 838762; Fax (01693) 830208
Mullaghbawn Folk Museum is an old Irish thatched cottage. It provides facilities to give information on tours and coordinating tourist and leisure activities

National Trust Regional Office, Northern Ireland, Rowallane Hse, Saintfield, Ballynahinch BT24 7LH; Tel (01238) 510721

The Newry Museum, The Arts Centre, 1A Bank Parade, Newry, Co Down BT35 6HP; Tel (01693) 66232; *Museum Officer* Margaret Hoben
History of Newry and Mourne through artefacts, models, photographs, maps. Group visits catered for. Seminars, workshops held regularly

North Down Heritage Centre, Town Hall, Castle Pk, Bangor, Co Down BT20 4BT; Tel (01247) 270371/271200; *Manager* I.A. Wilson
To reflect by displays etc full natural, historical and cultural heritage of North Down. Lectures, slide shows and arts events. Restaurant

EXPLORIS – An Exploration of the Irish Sea, The Ropewalk, Castle St, Portaferry, Co Down BT22 1NZ; Tel (012477) 28062; Fax (012477) 28396; *Education Officer* Helana Challinor
Aquarium that takes you on an extraordinary journey from Strangford Lough into the Irish Sea to find the amazing diversity of species, habitats and communities found in these waters. Interactive displays and touch-tanks, resource room/lab, guided tours and shorewalks, gift shop, tearoom, Norman tower house, park and woodland

Streamvale Open Farm, 38 Ballyhanwood Rd, Belfast BT5 7SN; Tel (01232) 483244; *Contact* J. Morrow
To give schools, parents and children an opportunity to see a real farm and have contact with the animals

Ulster Folk and Transport Museum, Eduaction Department, Cultra, Holywood, Co Down BT18 0EU; Tel (01232) 428428; *Director* R.A. Gailey, BA, PhD; *Education Officer* Deirdre A. Brown; *Education Officer* Andrew S. Anderson, BA, CertEd, AMA
Extensive range of educational and leisure services for all ages. Details on request. Educational material and study packs available

Ulster Museum, Botanic Gdns, Belfast BT9 6AB; Tel (01232) 381251; *Director* J.C. Nolan
Gallery lessons with handling materials, activity sheets, talks and study days for children and students. Pre-and in-services teachers' lectures and courses. Talks and tours for continuing education and community groups. Lists of educational resource materials available on request from Education Service Board of Trustees

County Fermanagh

Ardess Craft Centre, Ardess Hse, Kesh, Co Fermanagh BT93 1NX; Tel (013656) 31267
Dorothy Pendryy teachers spinning and weaving throughout the year. Other tutors take courses in various art, craft, pottery and cookery subjects, which are available to residents and non-residents. Contact Mrs Dorothy Pendry for a programme. Guesthouse facilities also available

Florence Court House, Florencecourt, Nr Enniskillen; Tel (01365) 348249
Eighteenth century house in wild rural setting. Irish Georgian furniture, shop and tea room open same as house, pleasure and walled gardens, river, forest walks, water powered sawmill, Marble Arch caves nearby. 3rd Earl's Fossil exhibition. Ice house and hydraulic ram. Education pack £3.50. Party bookings essential. Gardens open: 10.00 am to 1 hour before dusk all year. House open: April, May, Sept Weekends and Bank Holidays, June July Aug everyday (Ex Tues) 1 pm–6pm
National Trust

Marble Arch Caves, Marlbank, Florencecourt, Co Fermanagh; Tel (01365 34) 8855; *Warden* Richard Watson
Guided tours of extensive cave system includes boat journey on underground lake, stalactites, stalagmites and other fine cave features

County Londonderry

Springhill, Moneymore BT45 7NQ; Tel (0164 87) 48210; *Administrator* A. Law
National Trust

County Tyrone

Sperrin Heritage Centre, 274 Glenelly Rd, Cranagh, Gortin, Omagh, Co Tyrone BT79 8LS; Tel (016626) 48142; *Administrator* Karen McFarland
To promote the heritage and culture of the Sperrins which is an area of outstanding natural beauty

Ulster American Folk Park, Camphill, Omagh, Co Tyrone; Tel (01662) 243292; *Education Officer* Evelyn Cardwell; *Assistant Education Officer* Alice C. O'Rawe
Guided tours for schools; crafts demonstrations and workshops; drama and role-play activities; exhibitions; special events; audio-visual presentations; evening lectures

Channel Islands

Guernsey

Castle Cornet, (Branch of Guernsey Museums and Galleries), St Peter Port, Guernsey; Tel (01481) 721657; *Director* Rona Cole; Tel (01481) 726518; Fax (01481) 715177
13th century castle with Elizabethan and later additions. Contains military and maritime museums and art galleries. Noon-day gun daily

Fort Grey Shipwreck Museum, (Branch of Guernsey Museums and Galleries), Rocquaine Bay, Guernsey; Tel (01481) 726518; *Director* Rona Cole; Tel (01481) 726518; Fax (01481) 715177
Converted Martello tower reached by causeway. Displays on shipwrecks off west coast of Guernsey. Within sight of Hanois lighthouse

German Occupation Museum, Forest, Guernsey; Tel (01481) 38205; *Director* R.L. Heaume
To conserve and display all items relating to the German Occupation of the Channel Islands 1940–1945

Guernsey Museum and Art Gallery, Candie Gdns, Guernsey; Tel (01481) 726518; Fax (01481) 715177; *Director* Rona Cole, MA, FSA, FMA
Purpose-built National Museum of Guernsey. Winner of Museum of the Year 1979. Covers archeaology, natural history, history and art. Education Service (0481) 723688

Guernsey Softball Association (GSA), C/o The Secretary, Les Pignons, Longue Rue, St Sampsons, Guernsey GY2 4AB; Tel (01481) 56456; *Contact* Joan Harwood
To foster and promote softball to all age groups. Men's and women's open tournaments held every season

Hauteville House, 38 Hauteville, St Peter Port, Guernsey; Tel (01481) 721911; *Curator* M.C. Lorang
Victor Hugo's house of exile from 1856 to 1870, open April–September every day except Sunday and Bank Holidays

La Vallette Aquarium, *Curator/Director* D.M. Miller; *Manager* S.R. Carter

Priaulx Library, 8andie Rd, St Peter Port, Guernsey; Tel (01481) 721998; Fax (01481) 713804; *Chief Librarian* H. Tomlinson
Channel Islands local studies and family history research

Sausmarez Manor, St Martin, Guernsey; Tel (01481) 35571; Fax (01481) 35572; *Owner* P. De Sausmarez
House and garden open to visits, seminars, functions exhibitions etc. by appointment throughout the year. Also 4 model Railway layouts including 7 gauge ride-on, and 300sq ft "00" gauge, a dolls house collection dating from 1830 to the present day, a putting green, a childrens scrambly castle, a 9 hole par 3 pitch and putt course and pets corner

Jersey

Parkins Pleasure Parks Fantastic Gardens, St. Peter's Valley, Jersey; Tel (01534) 481585; Fax (01534) 47297
Family day out in a world of difference. Open air theatre. Free donkey rides, tropical birds, restaurants, shops. Open Seven days a week. April to October

German Underground Hospital, Meadowbank St, Lawrence, Jersey JE3 1FU; Tel (01534) 36493
Tunnel complex constructed by forced labour between 1941 and 1944 and now the definitive museum of the German Occupation of Jersey

The Jersey Lavender Farm, Rue du Pont Marquet, St Brelade, Jersey; Tel (01534) 42933; Fax (01534) 45613; *Proprietors* David and Elizabeth Christie
Growers/distillers of lavender. Creaters of a range of lavender products. Farm and distillery open to visitors. Tea room and shop

Jersey Motor Museum, St. Peter's Village, Jersey JE3 7AG; Tel (01534) 482966; *Director* F.M. Wilcock
Veteran and vintage cars, motor cycles, Allied and German millitary vehicles of WW2, Jersey Steam Railway exhibition in 1875 carriage

Jersey Museums Service, The Weighbridge, St Helier, Jersey; Tel (01534) 30511; Fax (01534) 66085; *Director of Museum* Michael Day; *Museum Education Officer* Douglas Ford
Administers the public museums and castles in Jersey can provide guided tours, lectures, information sheets on request. Includes *Jersey Museum,* The Weighbridge, St Helier; *La Hougue Bie Museum,* La Hougue Bie, Grouville; *Elizabeth Castle,* St Aubin's Bay, St Helier; *Mont Orgueil,* St Martin. *Sir Frances Cook Gallery,* Augrès, Trinity; *Hamptonne–Jersey's Country Life Museum* Hamptonne, St Lawrence

Jersey Wildlife Preservation Trust, Les Augres Manor, Trinity, Jersey; Tel (01534) 864666; *Education Officer* Phillip Coffey

La Mare Vineyards Ltd, La Mare Vineyards, St Mary, Jersey JE3 3BA; Tel (01534) 481178; Fax (01534) 485210; *Contact* Robert Blayney; *Contact* Andrew Blayney
Working vineyard and winery surrounding 18th century house with attractive grounds offering visitors an enjoyable interpretation of wine making and appreciation

St Peter's Bunker Museum, St. Peter, Jersey JE3 7AF; Tel (01534) 481048; *Contact* Anita Mayne
Museum of genuine military and civilian exhibits of the German Occupation housed in an actual bunker

23 Voluntary Service and Educational Travel

National Travel Organisations

The Central Bureau

The Central Bureau is the national office responsible for the provision of information and advice on all forms of educational vists and exchanges; the development and administration of a wide range of curriculum related pre-service and in-service exchange programmes; the linking of educational establishments and local education authorities with counterparts abroad; the interchange of substantial numbers of English Language Assistants abroad and Foreign Language Assistants in the UK and the organisation of meetings and conferences related to professional international experience. Established in 1948 by the British Government, the Central Bureau is funded in the UK by the Department for Education, the Scottish Office Education Department and the Department of Education for Northern Ireland

The Central Bureau has extensive information and advisory services, responding to the needs of the educational field, and over 20,000 individual enquiries are received and answered each year. The Bureau's publications provide carefully researched, comprehensive information for people of all ages seeking advice on opportunities available for work, study and travel abroad. Since 1 December 1993 the Central Bureau has formed part of The British Council

Seymour Mews Hse, Seymour Mews, London W1H 9PE; Tel 0171-486 5101; Fax 0171-935 5741

Director CBEVE & Secretary UKCEE Tony Male
Deputy Director Bill Musk
Deputy Director Graham Davey
Deputy Director Elspeth Cardy

Scottish Office
3 Bruntsfield Cres, Edinburgh EH10 4HD; Tel 0131-447 8024; Fax 0131-452 8569
Northern Ireland Office
1 Chlorine Gdns, Belfast BT9 5DJ; Tel (01232) 664418; Fax (01232) 661275

Services to Schools
(The Schools Unit and Centre for European Education)

The Schools Unit acts as a central focus for schools in relation to the work of the Central Bureau, and in general to promote the benefits to pupils of curriculum-related international exchange and experience. The Unit provides information and advice to schools and LEAs wishing to establish or develop links and administers a number of specific programmes offering opportunities for international experience to young people at school, including the Project Europe 16–19 Bursary Scheme; German Pupil Courses; English Language Summer Camps in Poland, Hungary and Turkey and the UK/FSU (former Soviet Union) School Exchange Programme. Through the European Awareness Programme, the Unit supports LEAs in order to encourage the development of a European dimension in the curriculum and an awareness of Europe amongst young people at school. The activities of the department are publicised in the *Schools Unit News*, a termly newsletter issued free of charge to schools via LEAs and also direct to individuals requesting copies. The newsletter promotes a wide variety of exchange and other international activities and provides a regular listing of requests from schools in other countries seeking links with partners in the UK. The department now includes the UK Centre for European Education which is one of 15 national Centres in Western European countries (the 12 from the European Union plus Austria, Sweden and Switzerland). UKCEE was established in 1978 in order to co-ordinate and disseminate information about on-going activities designed to develop the promotion of the European dimension in British schools. More than 100 organisations and institutions from the National Conference of the UKCEE, including the UK Education Departments, LEAs, BBC, teachers' unions, subject associations, university departments of education, colleges of higher education, all involved in the development of activities designed to extend and heighten awareness of Europe in our schools and colleges. The UKCEE produces a free twice-yearly newsletter, *EUROEDNEWS*, distributed to schools and colleges via LEAs and direct to individuals who requests copies. It also produces an occasional journal, EDIT (European Dimension in Teaching), which contains articles written by and for teachers presenting practical teaching ideas for the incorporation of the European Dimension in classroom work. The UKCEE runs annually the European Curriculum Awards, which aim to recognise outstanding curriculum development being made in schools and colleges to promote the European dimension

In-Service Training Opportunities for Teachers and Administrators
(Teacher Exchange, Short Courses and Study Visits Departments)

The Bureau administers the official teacher exchange schemes with Austria, Belgium, Denmark, France, Germany, Italy, Spain, Switzerland and the USA for periods ranging from 2 weeks to an academic year. Opportunities also exist for teacher exchanges with other non-Commonwealth countries. It also administers the Teacher Exchange scheme of the European Union and headteacher workshadowing schemes with Denmark, Ireland, the Netherlands and the USA. The bilateral exchanges are operated on a post-to-post basis and applicants must be teaching in the UK in order to be eligible. The Teacher Exchange scheme enables participants to effect a project with a linked institution during a 3-4 week simultaneous or consecutive exchange visit within the European Union

The Central Bureau organises short in-service training courses for teachers of modern languages in France, Germany, Italy and Spain. These courses are chiefly concerned with maintaining and improving teachers' fluency in the spoken language. In addition, a course abroad on the European dimension in the curriculum is held annually. Participants are drawn from a number of European countries. The Central Bureau also organises courses for teachers of English from other countries and administers the German Hospitality Programme as well as a range of study visit schemes. Through the International Study Visit Programme, a bursary allocation is available to every local education authority in England and Wales to support study visits abroad to promote the development of institutional links and staff exchanges and the study of aspects of overseas provision of interest and relevance to the UK. Separate arrangements apply in Scotland and Northern Ireland. In addition, the Bureau administers in the UK the European Union Programme of Short Study Visits for Education Specialists (ARION)

The Central Bureau is the national liaison office in England, Wales and Northern Ireland for the Council of Europe Teacher Bursaries Scheme. It organises courses associated with the scheme in this country for British and overseas participants. Teachers apply to the Bureau for places on couses offered in other member countries. Those who have expressed an intrest in courses using either French, German or English as the working language receive details of the relevant courses

Support for Further and Higher Education Institutions
(Vocational and Technical Education Department)

The Vocational and Technical Education Department provides transnational links and exchanges in further and higher education. It supports and encourages the development of an international dimension in the curriculum through its advisory services and through the management of a number of work placement programmes

As the UK Secretariat of IAESTE (the International Association for the Exchange of Students for Technical Experience), The Bureau liaises with other IAESTE offices throughout the world to arrange for degree level students to have course-related paid work placements in fields such as engineering, sciences, agriculture and the applied arts. Placements are available in 65 countries around the world with the majority lasting for periods of up to 12 weeks during the summer. Longer term placements may sometimes be secured

A bilateral programme with the US called the Career Development Programme enables young professionals from the UK to undertake practical training in the US or vice versa for periods of up to 18 months

The Central Bureau assists the Department of Employment in the management of the PETRA programme in the UK. The beneficiaries are young people in initial vocational training, young workers, young job-seekers and young people on advanced training courses. Financial support is available for training and work experience placements in another Member State and for the development of a network of organisations delivering initial vocational training

The VTE Department also helps colleges to develop course-related links with comparable establishments overseas and provides advice on the introduction of a European dimension in the curriculum, the management of staff/student exchanges and possible sources of funding and information. Topical items on FE exchanges are covered in a termly newsletter called *Link-up* which is distributed to all colleges

The VTE Department administers funds which are used to enable college senior managers and course tutors to develop joint initiatives with counterparts abroad and to promote the development and management of innovative exchange projects which seek to introduce a European dimension into the vocational curriculum

DFE funds are also used to support a number of bilateral programmes under which UK colleges are matched with partner institutions in order to collaborate on project work in specific subject areas. These bilateral programmes are currently running with Finland, France and Spain; any extension to other countries will be announced in *Link-Up*

Exchange of Language Assistants
(The Language Assistants Department)

The Language Assistant Programme currently operates with 26 countries and involves the appointment of English language assistants abroad as well as foreign language assistants in the UK. Nearly 3,500 assistants will have been placed in the last academic year. Participants assist with the teaching of their native tongue in schools and colleges in the host country. The programme is open to students of modern languages and those from other disciplines who are able to offer an adequate knowledge of the target language. Appointments are for one academic year

A six-month Junior Assistant Programme is open to students aged 18–20 with 'A'-level standard or equivalent in the target language. A limited number of appointments are available in France, Germany and Spain and run from January to June

The UK LINGUA Unit
Offices in Scotland and Northern Ireland, *see* Central Bureau Scotland and Northern Ireland above
The UK Lingua Unit, Central Bureau, Seymour Mews Hse, Seymour Mews, London W1H 9PE; Tel 0171-725 9493/4; Fax 0171-224 1906
Information Officer Rosemary Martin
The Lingua Programme was adopted in July 1989 by the Council of Ministers of the European Communities to promote foreign language competence throughout the EC. Its aims are therefore complementary to many of those of the Central Bureau. Its principal objective is to assist Member States with the qualitative and quantitative improvement of foreign language teaching and training, by providing grants in support of mobility schemes and innovative projects in the initial and in-service training of foreign language teachers, language

learning in vocational and higher education and the setting up of strategies for language training in economic life. The languages covered by Lingua are Danish, Dutch, English, French, German, Greek, Irish, Italian, Luxembourgish, Portuguese and Spanish when taught as foreign languages. An important priority of the Programme is to support the teaching and learning of the least widely used and least taught of these languages. The UK Lingua Unit is a department of the Central Bureau and is funded by grants from the UK Education Departments and the European Union

Publications
The publications and prices quoted below were valid during 1993 and may have altered since

Working Holidays 1994: £8.99 ISBN 0 900087 97 8
A Year Between; £8.99 ISBN 0 900087 88 9
Volunteer Work; £8.99 ISBN 0 900087 92 7
Home from Home; £8.99 ISBN 0 900087 85 4
Study Holidays; £8.99 ISBN 0 900087 90 0
Teach Abroad: £8.99 ISBN 0 900087 95 1
Making the Most of Your Partner School Abroad, £4.50 ISBN 0 900087 89 7
The European Dimension in Education: An In-Service Training Handbook: £9.50; ISBN 0 900087 94 3
The European Dimension in FE: A Guide to Good Practice: £10.50 ISBN 0 900087 93 5
The Foreign Language Assistant in the Classroom (Video) £9.75 including notes
European Awareness in Primary Schools (Video) (Price to be agreed)

All publications and videos are sent free of charge

Council for Education in World Citizenship

Seymour Mews Hse, Seymour Mews, London W1H 9PE; Tel 0171-935 1752; Fax 0171-935 5548
CEWC provides a service to member schools, colleges, organisations and individuals which includes current affairs broadsheets, speakers, conferences, use of a Resource Centre, teaching materials and general guidance on all aspects of education for international understanding

The English-Speaking Union of the Commonwealth

Dartmouth Hse, 37 Charles St, London W1X 8AB; Tel 0171-493 3328
Chairman of Education Committee Andrew Stuart
Director of Education Simon Freeman
The English-Speaking Union of the Commonwealth is an independent, non-political and non-sectarian organisation incorporated by Royal Charter, and a registered charity. Its object is to foster mutual understanding, trust and friendship between the people of the United States, the peoples of the Commonwealth, and English-speaking people everywhere through extensive programmes of education and information. It has more than 80 branches in Britain, Australia, France, Germany, Belgium, Bermuda, Canada, Sri Lanka, India, New Zealand, Nigeria and Pakistan which are closely linked with a similar number of branches in the United States

The English-Speaking Union administers educational awards for students and teachers and its programme enables more than 150 people each year to further their education overseas in the United States or the Commonwealth

The International Student Travel Conference

The International Student Travel Conference is an umbrella organisation representing a worldwide network of travel bureaus and other organisations active in the field of student travel. The Student Air Travel Association (SATA), an organisation in its own right, also functions as a commission of the ISTC through which members and other organisations concerned with air travel co-operate. ISTC members work together for young travellers in arranging transportation facilities, work camps, holiday centres, education visits, study tours, and travel aids, and in providing coverage through the International Student Insurance Service (ISIS)

The ISTC seeks to further international understanding by providing indivual students with inexpensive means for meeting their counterparts in other countries. In line with this, and in co-operation with the International Union of Students (IUS) based in Prague, the ISTC issues the International Student Identity Card (ISIC), which entitles its holder to discounts in travel, services accommodation around the world

The following countries are members of the ISTC. Organisations which are also members of SATA are marked with an asterisk (*)

ISTC Secretariate, Weinbergstrasse 31, CH-8006, Zürich; Tel 011-2622620; Fax Telex 815729 istc ch; Telefax 4112622996
SATA Office
Gotherersgade 30, 1123 Copenhagen K; Tel 33-112155; Fax Telex 19279; Telefax 33-114205

Argentina
AAAJ, Talcahuano 214, 2½A, Buenos Aires 1013
ATESA, Av. Callao 1062 8¼ "B", Buenos Aires 1013

Australia
*SSA, (STA), 224 Faraday St, Melbourne 3053, Victoria

Austria
*BfSt, Schreyvogelgasse 3, A-1010 Vienna
*ÖKISTA, Türkenstrasse 4, A-1090 Vienna

Belgium
ACOTRA, rue de la Madeleine 51, 1000 Bruxelles

Brazil
CONTEJ, Rua do Catelle 311, Sala 408, Rio de Janerio

Bulgaria
ORBITA, 45A Stambouliiski Blvd, Sofia

Canada
AOSC Travel Cuts, 187 College St, Toronto, Ontario M5T 1P7

Costa Rica
*OTEC, Edificio Victoria, 2 dopiso, Av 3 Calles 3y5, San Jose 1002

CSSR
CKM, 12 Zitna Ulice, 12105 Prague 2

Denmark
*DIS, Skindergade 28, 1159 Copenhagen K
*SSTS, 17 Hauchsvej, 1825 Frederiksberg C, Copenhagen

Dominican Republic
ODTE, Ave Bolivar No. 456, Apartamentos Gazcue, 2-B, Santo Domingo, DNPO Box 25135

Finland
*FSTS Trevela, Mannerheimintie 5C, SF-00100 Helsinki

France
*OTU, 39 avenue Georges Bernanos, 75005 Paris

Germany
JT-Jurgen and tourist, Alexanderplatz 5, Postfach 57, 1026 Berlin
*ARTU, Hardenbergstrasse 9, 1000 Berlin 12
*RDS, Rentzelstr 16, 2000 Hamberg 13
Asta-Reisen, Kaplerstrasse 17, KS 7000 Stuttgart 1
STR, Wilhelmstrasse 13, 7400 Tübingen

Hong Kong
HKSTB, Rms 833–835 Star Hse, Tsimsatsui, Kowloon, Hong Kong

Hungary
*EXPRESS, Szabadsag Ter 16, Budapest 1395

Iceland
IST, Félagsstofnon Studenta, v/Hringbraut, 101 Reykjavik

India
STIC Rms 5 and 6, Hotel Imperial, Janpath, New Delhi 110001

Ireland
*USIT, Aston Quay/O'Connell Bridge, Dublin 2

Isreal
ISSTA, 109 Ben Yehuda St, Tel Aviv 63401

Italy
*CTS, Via Nazionale 66, 00184 Rome

Jamaica
JOYST, 9 Eureka Cres, Kingston 5

Japan
NFUCA, Sanshin-Hokusei Bldg, 2nd Fl, 2-4-9 Yoyogi, Shibuya, Tokyo 151

Korea
KIYSES, Rm 505, YMCA Bldg, 9 Changro 2-Ka, Chongno-Ku, Seoul

Malaysia
MLS, 1st Fl, Southeast Asia Hotel, 69 Jalan Haji Hussin 50300, Kuala Lumpur

Malta
*NSTF—STF, 220 St Paul St, Valletta

Mexico
SETEJ, Hamburgo 273, Col Juarez 06600, Mexico 6, DF

Netherlands
*NBBS, Schipholweg 101, 2316 XC Leiden

New Zealand
NZSTB, PO Box 4156, 10 High St, Auckland

Norway
UNIVERS, Box 55, Blindern, 0313, Oslo 3

Peru
*INTEJ, Av San Martin 240, Battanco, Lima 4

Philippines
YSTAPHIL, 4227 Tomas Claudio St/Roxas Blvd, Parangue 1700 Metro, Manila

Poland
ALMATUR, Ordynacka 9, 00364 Warsaw

Portugal
ATEJ, Rua Joaquim Antonio de Aguiar, 255, 4300 Porto

Puerto Rico
*OVEJ, PO Box 21448, UPR Station, Rio Piedras 00931

Rumania
BTTR, Onesti St 4–6, Bucharest 1

South Africa
SAST, PO Box 1381, Cape Town 8000

Spain
*TIVE, José Ortega Y Gassett 71, 28006 Madrid

Sweden
*SFS-Resebyrå, Brunnsgaten 9 Box 7144, S-1138 Stockholm

Switzerland
*SSR, Bäckerstrasse 52, 8026 Zurich

Thailand
ETC, Rm 318, Royal Hotel, 2 Rajdumnoen Ave, Bangkok 10200

Tunisia
SOTUTOR, 2 rue de Sparte, Tunis

Turkey
GENCTUR, Yerebatan Cad. 15/3, 34410 Sultanahmet, Istanbul
7-Tur, Inönü Cad, 37/2, Gümüssuyu, Istanbul

Uruguay
AAU, Pablo de Maria 1583/008, C.P. 11200, Montevideo
AUTE, Andes, 1358, Of. 405, Montevideo

USA
*CIEE, 205E, 42nd St, 16th Fl, New York NY 10017

USSR
SPUTNIK, 15 Kosygin St, 117946, Moscow

Venezuela
ONTEJ, Parque Central, Av. Lecuna, Edf. Catuche, Nivel Boliver, PO Box 17697, Caracas 1015—A

Yugoslavia
Yugotours-Narom, Djure Djakovica 31, 11000 Belgrade

League for the Exchange of Commonwealth Teachers

Commonwealth Hse, 7 Lion Yard, Tremadoc Rd, Clapham, London SW4 TNQ; Tel 0171-498 1101
Chairman D. Birchall
Director P. Swain
Honary Treasurer A.H.S. Rees
A non-political, non-secretarian organisation which promotes educational links between Commonwealth countries chiefley by arranging exchanges of teachers (an average of 350 annually). The principal countries in terms of numbers are Canada, Australia and New Zealand. Exchanges are also arranged with The Bahamas, Barbados, Bermuda, Jamaica, Kenya, Trinidad and Tobago, India, Pakistan and Bangladesh

While overseas, exchange teachers continue to be employed by their home authorities, who grant leave of absence and pay salaries. Security of tenure is guaranteed. Teachers located in countries with higher living costs than the UK, receive government grants. In addition, return air fairs are paid

The initial subscription for both UK and overseas exchange teachers is £20 for the first year, and for each subsequent year £5; £25 paid at the outset procures a five-year membership

The League also arranges short-term exchanges for head teachers, deputy heads, heads of departments and local authority officials. A scheme for the exchange of teachers within the UK has been introduced

There are many exchange teachers' clubs, affiliated to the League, distributed throughout the UK and the overseas Commonwealth. They arrange their own programmes and entertain teachers who are currently on exchange in their area

Youth Exchange Centre

The British Council, 10 Spring Gdns, London SW1A 2BN; Tel 0171-389 4030
The Youth Exchange Centre, a department of the British Council, promotes youth exchange between the United Kingdom and other countries. It has responsibility for the development, implementation and evaluation of policy governing youth exchange, and for advice on this to the Government. The YEC administers grants to youth groups, runs projects and provides information, advice and training services to the British youth services on international exchanges. In addition, the Youth Exchange Centre acts as the National Agency for the Youth for Europe programme, which is sponsored by the Commission of the European Community

Tourist Information and Material

The following Tourist Boards produce special information about travel in England

English Tourist Board
Thames Tower, Black's Rd, London W6 9EL; Tel 0181-846 9000

London Tourist Board and Convention Bureau
26 Grosvenor Gdns, London SW1W 0DU; Tel 0171-730 3450 (Administration), 0171-730 3488 (Tourist Information)
Personal callers
Victoria Stn Forecourt: Tourist Information Centre

The South East England Tourist Board
The Old Brew Hse, Warwick Pk, Tunbridge Wells, Kent TN2 5TU; Tel (01892) 540766; Fax (01892) 511008
Chief Executive F.T. Cubbage

Yorkshire and Humberside Tourist Board
312 Tadcaster Rd, York YO2 2HF; Tel (01904) 707961; Fax (01904) 701414; Telex 57715
Director Brian Handley

Heart of England Tourist Board
Larkhill Rd, Worcester WR5 2EF; Tel (01905) 763436

West County Tourist Board
60 St Davids Hill, Exeter, Devon EX4 4SY; Tel (01392) 76351

North West Tourist Board
Swan Hse, Swan Meadow Rd, Wigan Pier, Wigan WN3 5BB; Tel (01942) 821222; Fax (01942) 820002

Cumbria Tourist Board
Ashleigh, Holly Rd, Windermere, Cumbria LA23 2AQ; Tel (015394) 44444; Fax (015394) 44041

Northumbria Tourist Board
Aykley Heads, Durham DH1 5UX; Tel 0191-384 6905 Ext 50; Fax 0191-386 0899

East Anglia Tourist Board
Toppesfield Hall, Hadleigh, Suffolk IP7 5DN; Tel (01473) 822922

East Midlands Tourist Board
Exchequergate, Lincoln LN2 1PZ; Tel (01522) 531521; Fax (01522) 532501
Public Relations Executive June Rowlands
Head of Commercial Services Malcolm Connor

Southern Tourist Board
40 Chamberlayne Rd, Eastleigh, Hants SO5 5JH; Tel (01703) 620006

Guernsey Tourist Board
PO Box 23, White Rock, Guernsey, CI; Tel (01481) 726611; Fax (01481) 721246

Jersey Tourism
Liberation Sq, St Helier, Jersey JE1 1BB, CI; Tel (01534) 500700; Fax (01534) 500899

Isle of Wight Tourism,
Education Officer, Quay Hse, Town Quay, Newport, IOW PO30 2EF; Tel (01983) 524343; Fax (01983) 521606

Isle of Man Department of Tourism
The Sea Terminal, Douglas, Isle of Man IM1 2RG; Tel (01624) 686801; Tourist Information Centre, Harris Promenade, Douglas, Isle of Man IM1 2HH; Tel (01624) 686766
The Sea Terminal Office is for administration/press enquiries; Tourist Information Centre, for literature, general tourist enquiries

Wales Tourist Board
Production Services Dept, Davis St, Cardiff CF1 2FU; Tel (01222) 475226 (literature, price lists); Fax (01222) 482436

Scottish Tourist Board
23 Ravelston Terr, Edinburgh EH4 3EU, Scotland; Tel 0131-332 2433; Fax 0131-343 1513; Telex 72272

Northern Ireland Tourist Board
St Anne's Ct, 59 North St, Belfast BT1 1NB; Tel (01232) 231221; Fax (01232) 240960

Irish Tourist Board
150 New Bond St, London W1Y 0AQ; Tel 0171-493 3201; Fax 0171-493 9065

Exchange Visits and School Travel

This does not claim to be a complete list of firms and organisations offering Educational Travel facilities. Inclusion of an editorial entry does not imply approval; equally exclusion does not imply disapproval

Academic Year in the USA (AYUSA)
Study Associates International, Gold Peak Hse, Wilmerhatch La, Epsom, Surrey KT18 7EH; Tel (01372) 275005; Fax (01372) 273976
UK Programme Director B. Legge
Live with an American Host Family, whilst attending American High School. Innovative curriculum, active social programme, extensive sports, music and drama opportunities. Five and ten month courses, commencing in August and January. Available to students age 15–19 years and ideally suited to students taking a year out prior to university. Limited places available, early application recommended

Accueil des Jeunes en France (A.J.F.)
(Groups) 16 rue du Pont-Louis-Philippe, 75004 Paris; Tel 42.72.72.09; Fax 40.27.08.71; Telex 240909
Central booking office for youth accommodation in Paris (8,000 beds, groups and individuals) and in the Provinces (20,000 beds; groups). AJF proposes accommodations in youth centres, student halls of residence, and tourist hotels and a wide range of services such as tours, visits, excursions, meals, transfers. AJF also provides information about a wide range of leisure and sporting holidays in France
(Individuals)
Plateau Beaubourg, 119 rue Saint-Martin, 75004 Paris; Tel 42.77.87.80; Fax 42.77.70.48
139 Boulevard Saint-Michel, 75005 Paris; Tel 43.54.95.86; Fax 40.46.97.62
Gare Du Nord, 75010 Paris; Tel 42.85.86.19

Accueil Familial des Jeunes Étrangers
23 rue du Cherche-Midi, 75006 Paris, France; Tel (0033) 1 42 22 50 34; Fax (0033) 1 45 44 60 48
Arranges *au pair* places for students (18–30) for the *whole school year* (beginning of September to the end of June) or for a minimum of 6 months and *summer stays* from 1 to 3 months between the 15th of June and the 15th of September. *Paying guest service*: school year Paris and suburb, minimum 18 years old summer and country and seaside, minimum 14 years old

ACE Study Tours
Babraham, Cambridge CB2 4AP; Tel (01223) 835055; Fax (01223) 837394
Arranges study tours and summer schools in history, art and architectural history, archaeology, drama and literature in the British Isles, Western and Eastern Europe, the United States, Mexico, Peru, India, China and Africa

AFS Intercultural Education Programmes
Arden Hse, Wellington St, Bingley, W. Yorks BD16 2NB; Tel (01274) 560677; Fax (01274) 567675
Programmes for 16–18 year olds wishing to learn about another culture through living with a family and attending the local school for a year. Placement possibilities in 60 countries in all world regions

23 Exchange Visits and School Travel

Almatur
9 Ordynacka St, 00-953 Warsaw
Travel Bureau of The Polish Students Association. Offers groups local guided tours; bus tours through Poland; special programmes on economics, politics, architecture, ecology. Programmes for performing and sports groups. Hobby tours: aquatic sports; horse-back riding; ski-ing. Student and Youth Tourist vouchers for bed and breakfast in student hotels (July–August only). No reservation needed for voucher holders. Air tickets (Warsaw only). Homestays with Polish families (small groups and individuals only). Programme: The Experiement in International Living available on request PO Box 3, Poland; Tel 262356; Fax Tx 813474; Fax 262353

Amitié International des Jeunes
Beaver Hse, 10A Woodborough Rd, London SW15 6QA; Tel 0181-788 6857
Finds exchange partners for young people aged 10–18. Escorted travel from London to Paris. If desired, the exchange can be spread over 2 years. Escorted rail and sea travel from London

Anglo-Austrian Society
46 Queen Anne's Gate, Westminster, London SW1H 9AU; Tel 0171-222 01366 (Vienna 1010: Stubenring 24)
Exchange Holidays with Austria for young people aged 12–18 for two or three weeks at Easter or in summer. Escorted travel arranged by air and rail between main centres in Britain and Austria. Also German Language Courses in London, Birmingham and Austria, Youth travel and budget flights to Austria

ASSE
6 Harcourt St, London W1H 2BD; Tel 0171-724 0280; Telex 25405 SKOLEX G
American High School Exchange Programme. Spend school year in USA, attending High School and staying with an American family. Open to 16–18 year olds. Alternatively host an American teenager for 10 months. Also available in Canada, French speaking Canada, New Zealand, France and Germany

ASSET
6 Harcourt St, London W1H 2BD; Tel 0171-724 0280; Telex 25405 SKOLEX G
Exchange visits between Swedish teenagers and English partners. Swedes come to stay with partners for three weeks in July, both go back to Sweden for a two week stay in August. language vourses in the United Kingdom for Swedes all year round upon request

Atherfield Bay Holiday Camp Ltd
nr Chale, Ventnor, IOW PO38 2JD; Tel (01983) 740307
Accommodation and entertainment for school parties during May and June

Avalon Student Travel
11 Marlborough Pl, Brighton BN1 1UB; Tel (01273) 553417; Fax (01273) 559321
Arranges group travel to Western and Eastern European countries. Arranges study tours, family accommodation, sight-seeing and English language training for foreign students both for individuals and groups. Also home stays in California both for individuals and groups

Bienvenue Mutuelle "Les Copains d'Accord"
'L'Eco-Logis, 17320 St-Just-Marennes, France; Tel 46.85.33.35
A non-profit-making organisation which assists its members with travel arrangements, exchange visits, holiday and weekend excursions in Europe, or between Europe and North America. Meetings of French and English young people in Saint-Just-Luzac (17320), near Rochefort, during the summer. Organises the finest toy trains Museum at St Just, open June, July and August

BREAK
7a Church St, Sheringham, Norfolk NR26 89R; Tel (01263) 822161; Fax (01263) 822181
BREAK provides holidays and respite care in a holiday environment for children and adults with learning disabilities/mental handicap at centres on the Norfolk coast. Group holidays available. Individuals and groups welcome, with or without accompanying staff. Full 24 hour care, special diets catered for, varied holiday programme including outings, indoor heated swimming pools, transport with wheelchair lift. Escorted travel. Residential family assessments are offered at 'Magpie' home' (Registered Charity No. 286650)

British American Schools Exchange Club
38 Shepherds Bush Rd, London W6 7PJ; Tel 0171-602 1390/6587
Chairman and Managing Director Kevin J. Shannon, BA
Tours to many parts of the USA with accommodation provided by American families. Groups may wish to host an American school in return. Holidays from 10–21 days duration

British American Soccer Exchange Club
38 Shepherds Bush Rd, London W6 7PJ; Tel 0171-602 1390/6587
Chairman Kevin J. Shannon, BA
Complete holidays including coaching, matches, a full programme of sightseeing activities and accommodation in host team's homes

British Deaf Association
38 Victoria Pl, Carlisle CA1 1HU; Tel (01228) 48844 (Voice and Minicom); Fax (01228) 41420
Educational travel courses arranged by the Education Service especially for the profoundly deaf. Spring and summer. Age range: 6+

British and International Friendship Tourist Association
36 Meredith Rd, Hellesdon, Norwich NR6 6PF; Tel (01603) 486408
Honary Secretary S. Sadler
Affiliated to Naturfreunde Internationale, Birmensdorfer-Strasse 19, 8004 Zürich, Switzerland, which provides inexpensive accommodation for members through its organisations in Austria, Germany, Switzerland, Belgium, France, Holland, Denmark, Isreal, Italy and California. Ski-ing, mountaineering, sailing wild water canoeing, photography and camping courses. Youth opportunity courses in mountain climbing, ski-ing, language. Study of European culture etc

British Universities Accommodation Consortium Ltd
Box EYB95, University Pk, Nottingham NG7 2RD; Tel (0115) 950 4571; Fax (0115) 942 2505
General Secretary C. Formon
Information on accommodation and facilities provided by over 60 member universities nationwide for bed and breakfast or self-catering holiday accommodation for groups, families and individuals and conference/training facilities plus year round availability and study and activity courses

BUNAC
16 Bowling Green La, London EC1R 0BD; Tel 0171-251 3472
Work and travel programmes arranged in USA and Canada during summer months. BUNACAMP counsellors' programme offers jobs to young adults (aged 19½ to 35) working with children in summer camps teaching sports, arts and crafts etc. There are private sports camps. church camps, inner-city and handicapped children's camps. Return flight, visa and insurance arranged by BUNAC. Board and lodging and salary ($400–$460) provided by camp. Up to six weeks to travel after camp

Bureau des Voyages de la Jeunesse
20 rue J.J. Rousseau, 75001 Paris, France; Tel 42.36.88.18, 42.61.66.43 and 42.33.82.10; Fax 42.33.40.53; Telex 213159
International centres in Paris: Paris/Louvre, 20 rue J.J. Rousseau, 75001 Paris; Tel 42.36.88.18, 200 beds; Paris/Opéra, 11 rue Thésèse, 75001 Paris;

Tel 42.60.77.23, 68 beds; Paris/Les Halles, 5 rue du Pélican, 75001 Paris; Tel 40.26.92.45, 55 beds; Corsotel/ Calvi (Corsica) Av.de la Republique 20260 Calvi Tel.95 65 14 15; Centre International de l'Alpe d'Huez Chemin de l'Alaska 38750 Alpe d'Huez Tel.76 80 37 37 and Quartier Latin, 44 rue des Bernardins 75005 Paris; Tel 43.29.34.80

Büro für Studentenreisen (BfSt)
A-1010 Vienna, Schreyvogelgasse 3, Austria; Tel 01222-5333589; Fax 5333499; Telex 135645
Year-round educational visits throughout Austria on request for groups. Year-round weekly stays for minigroups in self-catering Alpine Studenthouse (7 rooms/13 beds, kitchen, bathroom, 2 showers, 2 toilets) in Groebuing/Styria on an altitude of 3700ft. May to October weekly stays in the sailing centres at Mondsee, Neusiedlersee, and Woerthersee for individuals and groups. Year round accommodation and sightseeing services in Vienna. Age range 16–35. English Publications: *'Hotel Service Austria'*. Confidential tariff for groups

Camp America
Dept EYB, 37A Queens Gate, London SW7 5HR
This programme arranges for young people (18–35) to work on American summer camps for 9 weeks, either as a counsellor (looking after children), or as campower worker (working in kitchen, laundry, office etc). There are also places for applicants who wish to look after children in American families (10 weeks). Camp America offers free return flight, board and lodging, pocket money and up to 2 months for independent travel. Applicants must be available from June–September

Canford School of Summer Music
5 Bushey Cl, Old Barn La, Kenley, Surrey CR8 5AU; Tel 0181-660 4766
Varied couses; tuition; musical and social activities including daily concerts

Canopus School Travel Company
16 Silverdale Hesketh Bank, Preston, Lancs PR4 6RZ; Tel (01772) 813456
Organises school journey and educational holidays including sports tours to France, Belgium, FRG, Holland, Sweden

CEI
CEI International Language Teaching Centre and Residence, 60–69 Chepstow Pl, London W2 4TR; Tel 0171-221 8134; Fax 0171-221 0642
Accommodation for 200 persons in individual and multi-bedded rooms, with facilities on each floor. Travel department offering programmes on London and Great Britain all year round. Recognised by the French Government, the CEI runs courses all over France for groups and individuals from 12 years old to adult education and business courses

Centre De Rencontres Internationales Et De Sejour De Dijon
1 boulevard Champollion, 21000 Dijon, France; Tel 80.71.32.12; Fax 80.70.00.61; Telex 351585 CRIDIJ
Accommodation in Burgundy for groups (up to 320) and individuals. Tennis, sailing, study tours, linguistic programmes and cultural programmes can only be arranged for groups

Children's Community Holidays Ltd
3 Blackwater Rd, Mallusk, Newtownabbey BT36 8UA; Tel (01232) 833753
A registered charity which provides summer holidays in Northern Ireland for children aged 8–15 yrs. A number of physically handicapped children are included in suitable holidays. Residential training courses at the beginning of the summer, programme for youth leaders
3 Blackwater Rd, Mallusk, Newtownabbey BT36 8UA; Tel (01232) 833753; Fax (01232) 838107

CKM, Travel and Hotel Corporation
121 05 Prague 2, Zitná ul. 12, Czech Republic; Tel ++42/2/290 535; Fax ++42/2/242 162 10
School journeys with study visits, excursions, outings, lectures, etc. Two International summer youth camps offering water sports, ball games, hiking, etc. International summer work camps. Eight youth hostels

Club du Vieux Manoir
10 rue de la Cossonnerie, Paris 75001, France; Tel 45.08.80.40

Club Europe Educational Tours
Fairway Hse, 53 Dartmouth Rd, London SE23 3HN; Tel 0181-699 7788; Fax 0181-699 7770
Organises: ski courses in Austria, France and Italy; European experience; music, geography field study; drama; technology language tours to Austria, Germany, France, Switzerland, Holland, Italy and Belgium; Sports tours to Holland and Belgium. Euro Disneyland Theme Pk; Bonded members of ABTA, members of SAGTA

Clubtour
666 rue Sherbrooke ouest, Suite 203, Montreal, Quebec H3A 1E7; Tel 844–2851; Telex 05-561983
Tours for young adults in small groups. Transport arranged. Camping, hostels or hotels. Language courses in Austria, Italy, Spain, Mexico and USA

Coat Boloï–Eurauberge
Pleudaniel, 22740 Lézardrieux, France; Tel 96.20.16.59
Youth hostel style accommodation and rural camping for groups and individuals. help with contacts and fieldwork. English/French lessons. French books and maps for sale by post

Commonwealth Youth Exchange Council
7 Lion Yard, Tremadoc Rd, Clapham, London SW4 7NQ; Tel 0171-498 6151; Fax 0171-720 5403
Promotes contact between groups of young people aged 16–25 of Britain and all other Commonwealth countries by means of two-way youth exchanges. Publishes *'Contact'*, a handbook for commonwealth youth exchange 'HARAMBEE' an active learning resource from a youth conference convened by CYEC, 'Safety Welfare Guidelines' essential reading for youth exchange organisers and a newsletter called *'Exchange'*. *Guidelines for Funding* leaflet available on request (s.a.e. appreciated)

Council Travel Services
28A Poland St, London W1V 3DB; Tel 0171-437 7767
Council Travel Services, a travel division of the Council on International Educational Exchange (CIEE), with over 45 offices worldwide, specialises in student and youth travel. Council Travel offers student, youth, teachers and budget travellers of all ages a full range of travel services. These services include student/youth/budget air fairs worldwide. Eurotrain and InterRail cards, low-cost accommodation, car hire, adventure tours, language programmes, international identity cards, youth hostel cards, travel insurance, guidebooks, gear and a group travel department

Countrywide Holidays Association
Birch Heys, 23 Cromwell Range, Manchester M14 6HU; Tel 0161-225 1000
Arranges travel accommodation and outdoor activities for school and youth parties at 13 Country Houses throughout Britain

Cultural and Educational Services Abroad Ltd
Western Hse, Malpas, Truro TR1 1SQ; Tel (01872) 225300; Fax (01872) 225400
Language courses in Europe, Information and Advice Service on a wide range of centres in Europe, courses for juniors (France and Germany), holiday programmes for adults, short term intensive courses for business executives, courses for students working for language exams; and private tuition; Full range of languages covered includes; Chinese, Dutch, French, German, Italian, Greek, Portuguese, Spanish, Japanese and

Russian, French and German can be offered with ski-ing in the afternoons

Daysaway Travel
118 Cromwell Rd, London SW7 4ET; Tel 0171-370 0655
Specialists in providing school and student group accommodation in good class central London hotels. provides qualified guides for sightseeing tours plus coaches and theatre tickets at reduced prices. Also arranges technical vists to factories and arts visits backstage at theatres

Deutsche Sportjugend
Otto-Fleck-Schneise 12, 6000 Frankfurt/Main 71, Germany; Tel 0169 67000
Arranges contacts for international youth exchange. Member federations have sports facilities. International Olympic youth camps

Dick Phillips
Whitehall Hse, Nenthead, Alston, Cumbria CA9 3PS; Tel (01434) 381440
Iceland only. Operators of long-distance walking and motor-assisted tours in uninhabited areas. Full expeditionary service

don Quijote UK, In-Country Language Courses Ltd
2/4 Stoneleigh Park Rd, Stoneleigh, Epsom, Surrey KT19 OQR; Tel 0181-786 8081; Fax 0181-786 8086
Don Quijote is Europe's largest organisation for Spanish language courses in Spain, operating centres in Barcelona, Granada, Salamanca and Màlaga. Also offers advice on funding, transport, insurance, accommodation, excursions, local language courses, study materials and Spanish events (local and national). Will organise parents' evenings and information days on Spanish in Spain at universities, colleges and other educational institutions

Dove Nest Group – Total Adventure
Fallbarrow Hall, Windermere, Cumbria LA23 3DX; Tel (015394) 45454
Provides a range of outdoor pursuits courses including a variety of activities such as canoeing abseiling, gorge walking, sailing, archery, orienteering, overnight camps, assault course etc, for schools, colleges, YT and industrial groups

Educational Travel Service
South Teuchar Farm, Cuminestown, Turriff, Aberdeenshire AB53 8HX, Scotland; Tel (01888) 544243; Fax (01888) 544679
Study tours on general and technical subjects for schools, colleges, universities and professional bodies (groups only) throughout UK and Europe. Family accommodation service

En Famille Overseas
The Old Stables, 60B Maltravers St, Arundel, West Sussex BN18 9BG; Tel (01903) 883266; Fax (01903) 883582
Offers personal paying-guest arrangements with families throughout Europe, for language students and holiday guests of all ages. Available throughout the year. Small teenage groups also organised to France. Stays with individual family; language course at 'O' and 'A' levels plus excursions. Also intensive French coaching and school groups at reduced rates

ESU in Scotland
23 Atholl Cres, Edinburgh EH3 8HQ; Tel 0131-229 1528; Fax 0131-229 1533
Exchanges are arranged between senior school pupils from Scotland and the United States of America. Pupils should be willing to offer reciprocal hospitality

Euro-Academy
77A George St, Croydon, Surrey CR0 1LD; Tel 0181-686 2363/081-680 4618; Fax 0181-681 8850
Learn the language on location in France, Germany, Italy, Spain, Portugal and Austria. Vacation courses for young people Easter and Summer with sports and activities. All-year intensive courses for adults in Paris, Nice, Munich, Vienna, Berlin, Florence, Madrid and Lisbon. Summer university courses in France. Art in Florence all year. French, German and Spanish home-stays all year. We are a member of ABTA

Euro-Sportring Foundation
Unit 10, 18 The Jamb, Corby, Northants NN17 1AY; Tel (01536) 202304; Fax (01536) 400159
Organisation for international sports contacts. Lodging and transport can be arranged

Europa Youth and Student Travel Centre
Viz Mezzocannone 119, 80134 Naples, Italy; Tel 0181 5520947/5520692; Fax 0181-5511642; Telex 710671
School groups, exchange visits, study tours, archaeology work camps courses, holiday centre. Charter flights. Age range; 15–35

Euroyouth
301 Westborough Rd, Westcliffe, Southend-on-Sea, Essex SS0 9PT; Tel (01702) 341434; Fax (01702) 330104; Telex Chacom G 99450 for EUROY
Holiday Guest and Paying Guest Home stays in Germany, Austria, Italy, Turkey, Hungary, Spain, France, Belgium and England, with or without lanuage/sports courses, individual and groups throughout the year. A totally new way to learn a language! Au pair positions in Great Britain only. We arrange English language courses in Southend

Experiment in International Living
West Malvern Rd, Malvern, Worcs WR14 4EN; Tel (01684) 562577; Fax (01684) 562212
Homestay, adventure and education programmes arranged in about 40 countries, promoting learning through direct personel experience. Special home-stays arranged for language students. Legal au pair programme to the USA for 12 months stay. Individuals and groups. Scholarship opportunities available

Express Travel and Hotel Co Ltd
1054 Budapest Szabadsa'g tér 16, Hungary; Tel 1530-660; Fax 36.1.153.3172; Telex 225384/225139; Cable Tourex, Budapest
Arranges stays for groups and individuals throughout Hungary. Paecape tours for schools groups. Study tours on music, folklore, agriculture; special visits for social workers, trainee teachers, sports clubs, unversity parties

Families in Britain
Martins Cottage, Martins La, Birdham, Chichester, Sussex PO20 7AU; Tel (01243) 512222; Fax (01243) 511377
Paying-guest visits. All ages

Faversham Travel Services Ltd
6 Preston Malthouse, St John's Rd, Faversham, Kent ME13 8EW; Tel (01795) 535718; Fax (01795) 539728
Programme Director Kate Stefanko
Educational Travel Consultants. Organisation of tailor-made educational tours for adult groups. Themed tours include art, architecture, archaeology, gardens, music, history, contempory culture. We have special knowledge of Russia, Indonesia, Zimbabwe, China; also Italy, Malta and other European destinations

Federation Internationale Pour Les Schanges Educatifs d'Enfants et d'Adolescents (FIEEA)
10/14 rue Tolian 75020, Paris; Tel 43.67.82.54; Fax 43.67.28.79; Telex 680086F
International federation for educative youth exchanges. Activities; training of international exchanges youth leaders, production of material about youth exchanges. Organisations–members in Morocco, Tunisia, Germany, Italy, France, Spain, Egypt, Belgium, Finland, Cameroon

Finnish Centre for International Exchange Programmes
PL 343, SF-00531 Helsinki, Finland; Tel 3580 7061
Handles arrangements for foreign trainees coming to Finland and Finnish trainees going abroad. Vocational training arranged in Finland. Age range 18–30. Finnish Family Programme; living in Finnish family and

participating in everyday tasks. Age range 18–23. UK inquiries to the Central Bureau for Educational Visits and Exchanges and applications to the address above

Florentina Bureau/Ann Shaw Agency
9 Tower Rd, Orpington, Kent; Tel (01689) 22875
Holiday groups in England for overseas students. Individual stays *en famille* in England and France. Age range: 12+. Group and individual stays for foreign groups: Orpington, Croydon, Bromley, Canterbury, Kendal, Colwyn Bay, Bath, Catford, Sidcup Centres

Foyer International d'Accueil de Paris
30 rue Cabanis, 75014 Paris; Tel 45.89.89.15
Accommodation for groups visiting Paris for research programmes, conferences, exchange programmes, study visits, etc

French Government Tourist Office
178 Piccadilly, London W1V 0AL; Tel (01891) 244123
Provides headmasters and teachers with a list of British tour operators and travel agents specialised in school and group travel and offering a wide range of tours, day-visits, educational tours, holidays, ski-holidays all over France. For information on exchanges, sporting holidays, stays in French families. French courses in France contact Cultural Department, French Embassy, 23 Cromwell Rd, London SW7; Tel: 0171-838 2055, Fax: 0171-838 2088/89

Group and Conference Travel
New Ct, Central Promenade, Douglas, Isle of Man; Tel (01624) 27711
Two night/three night educational 'packages' from Heysham and Liverpool

HF Holidays Ltd
Imperial Hse, Edgware Rd, London NW9 5AL; Tel 0181-905 9556
School party accommodation in UK, in both term and holiday periods; low-cost travel; free preview visits; 1 free place for every ten; supplementary literature available

Inghams Travel
10–18 Putney Hill, Putney, London SW15; Tel 0181-789 6555 (Administration), 0181-785 7777 (Reservations)
Ski-ing holidays in school and holiday periods to more than 60 resorts in 7 countries

Interchange
Interchange Hse, 27 Stafford Rd, Croydon CR0 4NG; Tel 0181-681 3612
Educational visits to most East Eurpean countries for school pupils, young people at work and adult education students. Specialist visits to the former Soviet Union, China and Japan for teachers, youth leaders and student teachers. Travel concessions available

International Farm Experience Programme
YFC Centre, National Agricultural Centre, Kenilworth, Warks CV8 2LG
Agricultural/horticultrual employment for 3–12 months arranged throughout the year to Europe, USA and China. Applicants must have 2 years relevant experience. Age range 18–26 years. Full driver's licence essential

International Study Programmes–ISP
The Manor, Hazleton, Cheltenham GL54 4EB; Tel (01451) 860379
Programmes abroad: 1–3 week language courses in German grammar schools–open to groups and individuals–Scholarships available. Holiday language courses in France and Spain (groups only). Study visits for school/youth groups, concert tours, sports visits etc
Programmes in Britain: Fun with French holiday activities weeks in over 10 English locations for 5–12 year olds

Interschool–"Deutsch in Innsbruck"
Kohlstattgasse 3, A-6020 Innsbruck, Austria; Tel 0512/588957; Fax 0512/588957
Helmut Lerch
German language courses for foreigners at all levels. Summer, Easter and Christman holidays. Ski-ing lessons at Christmas and Easter

INTERVAC International Home Exchange Service
3 Orchard Crt, North Wraxall, Nr Chippenham, Wiltshire SN14 7AD; Tel (01225) 892208
Helps teachers and other professional people to arrange home and youth exchanges, lets and paying-guest accommodation for various holiday periods. Organisers in 50 countries combine to produce a Directory three times a year. There is also a 'Last-minute' computer service for latecomers

IPFS
10015 Ivrea, Italy; Tel 39125 234433
Arranges pen-friend links between students in UK and most foreign countries. Member of FIOCES-UNESCO. Our services are free of charge for the UK. Age range 10–20

John Galleymore
25 High St, Portsmouth PO1 2LZ; Tel 01705) 824095
Language courses and study tours in Austria, France, Italy, Spain and USSR

Juventur Youth Travel Office
01-633 Warsaw, 29/31 Gdanska Str; Tel 33-11-02/33-10-46; Fax 33-10-30; Telex Uohertel: 3912 0928
Travel arrangements to Poland. Study tours, history, geography, architecture, etc. Sailing, canoeing, horse-riding, ski-ing, etc. International youth centres in Zakopane, Miedzyzdroje and Karpacz

Kestours Ltd
Travel Hse, Elmers End, Beckenham, Kent BR3 3QY; Tel 0181-658 7313 (Grouos and Sports Travel, European City Holidays)
Sports tours for schools, youth groups, amateur and professional teams. Regular organised tournaments in Europe. European City holidays for weekends and weeks–short stay programme. Far away holidays to the Caribbean

Kings Ski Club,
24 Culloden Rd, Enfield, Middx EN2 8QD; Tel 0181-363 8202; Fax 0181-363 4605
Marketing Manager Carla Bauer
Sales Manager Tim Amey
Budget sk holidays to France and Austria for students and youth groups. ABTA and ATOL

La Magnanarie
Villedieu, 84110 Vaison-la-Romaine, France; Tel (33) 90.28.92.58
Board and lodging for groups (up to 60 places) on touring or study holidays

The Le Fosso Centre
Le Fosso, 22230 Gomene, France; Tel (00 33) 96 28 47 97
Director Michael Townsend
President Claudine Gaudaire
Secretary Yann Cousin
Bookings Secretary Hilary Townsend
Holidays/field trips in Brittany, France. Set around the original farmyard, two buildings now provide very comfortable accommodation to groups and families. Twenty beds available all accessible to people with disabilities. Options include self catering; full board; organised activities (cultural, educational, sports etc), accompanied by our staff. A registered charity "Le Fosso UK" can assist groups with special needs wishing to visit Le Fosso from the UK

Les Frances
10/14 rue Tolain, 75020 Paris; Tel 43.67.40.00; Fax 43.67.28.29; Telex 680086F
Laic Federation of Educative Leisure Centres for children and adolescents. *Activities;* training of leisure centre leaders and directors; research into leisure centre equipment; production of a newspaper and magazines for scholars; organisation of international exchanges for

children and adolescents; cooperation with developing countries

London Appreciation Society
17 Manson Mews, South Kensington, London SW7 5AF
Worldwide organisation specialising in lesser known corners of London with ancient traditions and ceremonies. Excursions to centres throughout Britain. Weekend and longer visits to Europe. Annual subscription £5.00. Details free on receipt of foolscap s.a.e

Maison des Clubs Unesco
43 rue de la Glaciére, 75013 Paris; Tel 43.36.00.63; Fax 45.35.05.96; Telex MCU 270 144 F
Group and individual accommodation

Maisons Internationales de la Jeunesse et des Etudiants
11 rue du Fauconnier, 75004 Paris; Tel (1) 42.74.23.45; Fax 42.74.08.93; Telex 680863
Advises on and organises journeys and stays in Paris and all French provinces. MIJE has three hotels in Paris in the area of the 'Marais' and can provide transportation, meals, visits and guides. Programmes may be suggested or organised in advance by group leaders, or can be drawn up by the educational services of the MIJE. Individuals and groups

Mostyn Bureau
Camelot, Waverley Ave, Fleet, Hants GU13 8NN; Tel (01252) 6603
Arranges paying guest visits for children in country families. Age range: 6+

National Association of Youth Orchestras
Ainslie Hse, 11 St Colme St, Edinburgh EH3 6AG; Tel 0131-225 4606; Fax 0131-225 3568
Director Carol Main
Courses include Anglo-German Youth Music Week in conjunction with Arbeitskreis für Musik. Festival of British Youth Orchestras, Edinburgh and Glasgow Aug/Sept. NAYO British Reserve Insurance Conducting Prize. Administrators' day Conference, British Reserve Insurance Youth Orchestra Awards. Novello Youth Orchestra Award

Newbourne Transport
73 Parkway, London NW1 7PP; Tel 0171-6663/58/74
Central London coach company approved by ILEA Inexpensive private hire to schools, colleges etc. Specially priced day and weekend trips abroad. School journey programme to Brittany, Normandy and Central France

NLS Travel
83 Auckland Rd, Potters Bar, Herts EN6 3HE; Tel (01707) 50655 (24 hours)
Specialist in school holiday travel. Exchanges and sporting tours arranged. Choice of fixed plan tours or tours tailormade to groups' requirements. Tours to all West and East European Countries

NST (Ltd)
Chiltern Hse, 181 Bristol Ave, Blackpool, Lancs FY1 0FA; Tel (01253) 52525 (10 lines); Fax (01253) 56955; Telex 67164
Leading educational tour operator. Educational and general interest tours by coach and air. Destinations include Greece, Holland, Russia, UK, Austria, Belgium, France, Germany, Italy, Spain, Switzerland and Yugoslavia. Selection of study material for students of French, German, Spanish, History and Environmental studies. Also activity holidays

OIK–Organisation für Internationale Kontakte
Postfach 201051, 5300 Bonn 2, Germany; Tel 01228 356076; Fax 01228 364368
Non-profit making. Arranges stays in youth centres and boarding schools near Cologne and elsewhere. Study tours, field trips, and homestays with German families. Language courses. Sports programmes and music programmes. Own international youth music festival every July. Groups only

Orbita Chain for Youth Tourism – SA
48Hr. Botev Blvd, 1000 Sofia, Bulgaria; Tel 287.91.28; Fax 280.15.06; Telex 22381
Group travel for foreign tourists in Bulgaria, accommodation for individuals. Sightseeing and educational tours, holidays, international youth centres

Progressive Tours
12 Porchester Pl, Marble Arch, London W2 2BS; Tel 0171-262 1676; Fax 0171-724 6941; Telex 25135 (Progtu G); ATOL 447B; ABTA nad SAGTA member
Specialists in study and vacation travel to the USSR and the socialist countries, including China, Mongolia, Nicaragua and Cuba, for schools and colleges. Also to France, Italy and Algeria, and for sports and skiing Study tours for teachers and all educationists with professional and trades union contacts, school and university visits, particularly at Easter and half-terms Russian language courses at all levels in the USSR up to six months duration. Study tours in art, architecture, geography, history, sociology and area studies–most subjects possible, in most countries, through a world-wide network of cooperating organisations in BITEJ and the International Association for Social Tourism. Lowest cost air travel for school exchanges to Russia, the CIS and all other European countries

Regent Holidays (U.K.) Ltd
15 John St, Bristol BS1 2HR; Tel (0117) 921 1711; Fax (0117) 925 4866
School trips to Albania, China, Cuba, Czech Republic, Greenland, Hungary, Iceland, Turkey, Baltics, CIS, Vietnam, and North Cyprus

Rijksuniversiteit Ghent
Stalhof 6-B 9000, Ghent, Belgium; Tel 091.22.09.11
Accommodation in Ghent available during summer. Overnight stays and meals (Price: 500 Bfr bed and breakfast)

The School and Group Travel Association
Honeycroft Hse, Pangbourne Rd, Upper Basildon, Berks RG8 8LP; Tel (01491) 671731
National Director Dr Christina Hill, MA
National association coordinating aspects of educational travel. Membership includes reputable companies specialising in school and youth travel, local education authorities and attractions

School Year Abroad Programme
6 Harcourt St, London W1H 2BD; Tel 0171-724 0280
16–18 years spend 10 months in a family attending local schools in USA, Canada, French speaking Canada, New Zealand, France, Germany, Australia and Japan

Séjours Internationaux Linguistiques et Culturels (S.I.L.C.)
32 rempart de l'Est, 16022 Angouleme Cedex, France; Tel 45 97 41 00; Fax 45 95 41 10; Telex 791193
SILC organises the following programmes in France: Vacation homestays throughout France, all year round for adolescents and adults studying French with the possibility of a different educational theme: Sport, Classique, Langue Accélérée, One to One, School Language in Nantes or University of Toulouse Summer Language Programme. SILC Paris offers: classic French language programmes, Fine Arts and French, semester or summer courses at the famous Sorbonne, courses for foreign teachers and work experience programmes. Academic Year, Semester or Term at school while staying with a French family. International Prep Class in collaboration with SILC Paris in addition to the above academic programme. Academic Year for University students in the Department of French as a Foreign Language of a French university, with family accommodation. Short stays in France from 2 to 6 nights for groups with a full programme of visits. Cultural Stopovers offer the possibility to round off a homestay programme with visits to all the most interesting places

in Paris. Au Pair placements throughout France from 2 months (summer only) to a full year
50 and 51 Cypress Ave, Whitton TW2 7J2; Tel 0181-894 1151

Sing for Pleasure
25 Fryerning La, Ingatestone, Essex CM4 0DD; Tel (01277) 353691; Fax (01277) 353691
National and regional choral events throughout the year and short courses for singers, teachers and conductors held in UK each summer. For children, singing days, weekends and residential summer courses. Also, residential and one-day teachers' courses. Choral music, published for choirs, singing groups and for use in schools. Choir exchanges and visits to festivals in Europe in cooperation with 'A Coeur Joie'

Ski Bound
Olivier Hse, 18 Marine Pde, Brighton, Sussex BN2 1TL; Tel (01273) 677777; Fax (01273) 676410
Managing Director John Bowden
Independent ski tour operator specialising in group travel. Operates school ski tours to Austria, France, Italy and Bulgaria. Member of ABTA and AITO. Took over part of the Quest Leisure Group in March 1991

Society for Co-operation in Russian and Soviet Studies
320 Brixton Rd, London SW9 6AB; Tel 0171-274 2282
MADI Course (Russian language course, beginners and upwards), three weeks in Moscow in August. 5-month studentships at Pushkin and MADI Institute, Moscow for students of Russian (Sept–Jan and Feb–June) at reduced rates to SCR members. Help and advice for school parties on pre-departure study, contacts in FSU, but no travel arrangements. Intensive Russian Language courses in Russia tailored to individuals

Society for International Arts and Language Exchange (SOCIALE)
49 Fog La, Didsbury, Manchester M20 0AR; Tel 0161-434 7475
Travel and exchange for schools and individuals

Spyromilio and Co
Ravine 7, Athens 115 21, Greece
School groups visiting Athens, the Peloponnes and islands, with tours to archaeological and historic sites. Arrangements can be made for independent groups at Easter and during the summer holidays

STA Travel
117 Euston Rd, London NW1
Specialist in independent travel for young people.
Enquiries and bookings Europe 0171-937 9921; Long Haul 0171-937 9962. Round the World 0171-937 1733.
Low cost worldwide flights with special fares for students and academics. Plus tours, holidays and expert advice for the independent traveller
86 Old Brompton Rd, London SW7
25 Queen's Rd, Bristol BS8
38 Sidney St, Cambridge
75 Deansgate, Manchester M3
14a Oxford Rd, Manchester M1
36 George St, Oxford OX1
88 Vicar La, Leeds

and on University Campuses across the UK

STS, School Travel Service
24 Culloden Rd, Enfield, Middx EN2 8QD; Tel 0181-363 8202; Fax 0181-363 4605
Marketing Manager Ms C.D. Bauer
Inclusive educational and project tours to European and worldwide. Tours to France include Paris and environs, Ile de France, Lom Valley, Alsace, Roman France, Auvergne, Languedoc, Pyrenees and Dordogne Valley plus 24 coastal centres in Picardy, Normandy and Brittany. Project Book for use at any of these centres. Allons-y! Language course based near Bolognge, Day trips to Boulogne, Calais and Dieppe. Coach tours to Austria, Belgium, Germany, Holland, Italy and Switzerland. Air tours to Romania. Israel, CIS, Egypt, China, USA, Greece, Turkey, Spain, Italy. Tours to battlefields of the World Wars 1 and 11. Tours for school choirs, bands and orchestras. Sports tours to Belgium, France, Germany and Holland. Tailor made tours available. 60 years of experience in providing school travel

Studentours
3 Harcourt St, London W1H 1DS; Tel 0171-402 5131; Fax (01403) 891439
Accommodation for group visits to London, Scotland, Wales, etc
Educational, school journeys or own specific visit arranged
Gaveston Hall, Sussex (Tel (0403) 891431); youth and student centre, field study centre, nature trail, accommodation 110 persons, open all year. Ideal for field study, school journey, activity holidays. Language study, computer training and educational courses facilities on centre; farm visits; YT courses arranged. Members of FIYTO

Terra Nova Travel
Dronningenst 26, N.0154 Oslo, Norway; Tel (47-22) 42 14 10; Fax (47-22) 42 44 76
Summer group tours to North Cape and fjords region. Winter sports holidays. Arrangements for groups. Accommodation and travel services in Norway in summer and winter. Resort holidays and educational tours

Transcity Link Ltd
152 Maidstone Rd, Sidcup, Kent DA14 5HS; Tel 0181-302 8800; Telex 897497
African camping safaris by expedition truck in Kenya, Tanzania, Egypt, Malawi and Morocco. Equipment and driver/leader provided

Travel Bound
Olivier Hse, 18 Marine Pde, Brighton, East Sussex BN2 1TL; Tel (01273) 677777; Fax (01273) 600999
Managing Director John Bowden
Summer Tours Director Patricia Couchman
Operates school tours in Europe and worldwide "Project Europe" comprises a series of subject specific project tours and study courses, supplemented by course books and background information for teachers.
"Sportsbreaks" offers coaching, tournaments and individual fixture tours as well as Sailsports and Activity Adventures

UK Connection
Deepdene Lodge, Deepdene Ave, Dorking, Surrey RH5 4AZ; Tel (01306) 744666; Fax (01306) 744667
Specialists in school and college group travel worldwide. From a one-night stay to a complete educational programme, committed to providing the best possible prices and itineraries for groups of all ages. Contracted hotels are centrally located close to all places of entertainment and interest. Also sports tours, theatre visits, weekend packages, special event stop-overs, etc (UK Connection is a division of Kuoni Travel Ltd)

UK/US School Exchange Scheme
See Central Bureau for Educational Visits and Exchanges

Ultima Travel Ltd
424 Chester Rd, Little Sutton, South Wirral, Cheshire L66 3RB; Tel 0151-339 6171
Chairman M.M.V. Tudor
Manageing Director (Joint) W.D. Tudor-Morgan
Managing Director (Joint) M.J. Tudor-Morgan
Continental Director W.G.E. Debrock
Study tours linked with courses

Union des Fédérations Régionales des Maisons des Jeunes et de la Culture
168 bis rue Cardinet, 75017 Paris; Tel 627 7974
Education and sports exchanges

Union Française des Oeuvres Laiques d'Education Physique (UFOLEP)
3 rue Réecamier, 75007 Paris; Tel 45.38.97.60
Sports exchanges

Vacances pour Tous
21 rue St Fargeau, 75989 Paris Cedex 20; Tel 4358.95.96; Telex 670 992
Holidays for children and juveniles: holiday centres, camps, sporting holidays (sailing, canoe kayak, riding, windsurfing, etc); junior classes (seaside, mountain country); language courses; cultural holidays in France and foreign countries; family holidays in family guest houses or holiday villages, etc

Vacances-Jeunes
88 rue de Miromesnil, 75008 Paris; Tel (1) 42 89 39 39; Fax (1) 43 59 08 34; Telex 650 113 F VAC JEU
Group accommodation for schools and adult parties. Excursions and tours. Linguistic stays with French families (paying guests) and colleges (12–18 years). Adult courses in Paris, accommodation in hotel. Student courses in Paris, accommodation in University

Venture Abroad
Richmond Hse, High St, Cranleigh, Surrey GU6 8RR; Tel (01483) 273027
Inclusive holidays for youth and school parties. Various sizes of chalets in the Bernese Oberland region of Switzerland; camping and river-cruising in Germany; also holidays in Denmark, Holland and Austria. For groups of between 10 and 50 participants. Transport by coach

Worldwide Christian Travel and Top Ten Travel
50 Coldharbour Rd, Bristol BS6 7NA; Tel (0117) 973 1840/732120; Fax (0117) 973 2434
Managing Director Revd Cyril Hadler
Manager John Hadler
Group travel to Israel/Turkey/Greece/Rome and Continent. Air ticket all over the world
Number of employees 8

Wyvern Schooltours Ltd
Wyvern Hse, 7 Westbourne Gdns, Trowbridge, Wiltshire BA14 9AW; Tel (01225) 766346
Specialist in school trips to Europe, especially visits with a strong educational content

Yorkshire-Lille and Yorkshire-Westphalia Exchanges
Education Department, County Hall, Wakefield, W. Yorks WF1 2QL; Tel (01924) 295658
Secretary J. Ballance
Arranges home to home exchanges for 14–18 year old pupils from Yorkshire and Humberside with partners in the North of France and the Nordrhein-Westfalen district of Germany. Service includes escorted travel and resident escorts during the duration of the exchanges abroad and in England. Also arranges school links with the above areas and Teachers' Exchange visits to France

Young Travellers Ltd
Travel Hse, 34 Station Rd, London SE20 7BQ; Tel 0181-778 6850; Fax 0181-778 9754
Educational and recreational travel for school and adult groups. Junior Journeys for junior and middle schools. Tours and centres in UK mainland, Guernsey, Isle of Wight and Continent of Europe

Your School on the Continent
World Travel, 10 Terminus St, Harlow, Essex; Tel (01279) 418521/4
By coach to Normandy and Paris. Tailor made tours throughout Europe

Youth Travel Bureau, Israel Youth Hostels Association
3 Dorot Rishonim St, PO Box 1075, Jerusalem 91009, Israel; Tel 252706; Fax 250676; Telex 26580
Arranges educational tours for school and student groups throughout the year. Special programmes for school groups; age range 12–20. Living in working on a kibbutz; age range 18–35. Archaeological excavations; age range 18–35. Professional study tours for student groups

Recreational and Residential Courses

This does not claim to be a complete list of fims and organisations offering Recreational and Residential Courses. Inclusion of an editorial entry does not imply approval; equally exclusion does not imply disapproval. Details of such courses may also be obtained from many of the national sports and youth organisations listed in Chapters 19 and 20 and the educational organisations in Chapter 27

Academia Hispano Americana
Mesones 4, San Miguel de Allende GTO, 37700, Mexico; Tel 2-03-49/2-43-49; Fax 2-23-33
Director Gary De Mirjyn
Year-round instruction in Spanish language, history and literature

Academie D'Ete De Nice (C.I.F.M.)
CIFM, Conservatoire National de Région, 24 Boulevard de Cimiez, 06000 Nice, France; Tel 93.81.01.23; Fax 93.53.33.91
Courses in July and August in Music, instrumental, singing and French. Apply to Nadine Haas, Administrator

ACE Study Tours
Babraham, Cambridge CB2 4AP; Tel (01223) 835055; Fax (01223) 837394
Secretary P.B. Barnes
Residential and educational travel

Activity Island
Venture Hse, 108 Park La, Castle Donington, Derby DE74 2JG; Tel (01332) 811400
Specialise in educational visits on the Isle of Wight for primary, junior and middle schools. All accommodation in hotels. Fully qualified instructors operating from recognised centres. Age range: 7+

Aigas House and Field Centre
Aigas House and Field Centre, Beauly, Inverness-shire IV4 7AD; Tel (01463) 782443
Weekly residential courses in Highland Field Study Centre: unparalleled location for geography, natural history and early history studies. School groups over 10 years. Excellent terms

Alliance Française de Paris
101 boulevard Raspail, Paris 6; Tel (1) 45.44.38.28; Fax (1) 45.44.89.42
Practical French courses at all levels throughout the year, except during Christmas and Easter holidays. Teacher training and refresher courses for teachers of French as a foreign language. Brochure and information on request

Allnatt Centres
Joseph Allnatt Centres Ltd, 35 Ulwell Rd, Swanage, Dorset BH19 1LG; Tel (01929) 422122; Fax (01929) 421075
School journey and field study centres in Isle of Wight and Dorset. Field study courses. Able to accommodate whole year groups or small numbers. Personal planning service. Outdoor pursuits, grass-skiing, archery, trampoline, initiative tests, mind games etc. Excellent locations

Atelier Artistique International de Saguret
Seguret, F 84110 Vaison-la-Romaine, Vaucluse, France
Courses in printing, drawing, sculpture, painting, etc., from April to October. Performances, tours and visits in Provence

23 Voluntary Service and Educational Travel

Auberge de la Jeunesse
rue Trencavel, La Cite, 11000 Carcassonne, France; Tel 68 25 23 16; Fax 68 71 14 84
Excursions. Youth hostel accommodation, 120 beds; groups, meals if required individual cooking facilities

Austrian Alpine Club (UK Branch)
Longcroft Hse, Fretherne Rd, Welwyn Garden City, Herts AL8 6PQ; Tel (01707) 324835
Information centre for walking and mountineering in Austria. Two-week summer holidays for adults and suitably experienced 16–18-years-olds, including mountaineering courses with professional Austrian guides; high-level walking tours with British leaders. Air travel and hut voucher packages for individuals and small groups of independent tourers

Loch Morlich Watersports
Glenmore, By Aviemore, Inverness-shire PH22 1QU; Tel (01479) 861221; Fax (01479) 861221
Canoeing, sailing, hill-walking, windsurfing, dry slope ski-ing, mountain biking May–Sept; Accommodation in the Aviemore area; skating and swimming facilities also available

Berwang Holiday Music Centre
The Secretary, Willowdown, Megg La, Chipperfield, Herts WD4 9JN; Tel (01923) 263715
Holiday and music courses in Tyrolean Alpine Village. Classes, informal concerts, swimming, excursions. August to September

Bowles Outdoor Centre
Eridge Grn, Tunbridge Wells TN3 9LW; Tel (01892) 665665
Multi-activity and specialist courses in rock-climbing, canoeing, dry ski-ing, orienteering and camping. Courses open to the public and closed courses for schools and colleges. BS 5750 approved

Boys Clubs of Wales
Sports, Holidays and Conference Centre, West Aberthaw, Nr Barry, South Glamorgan CF6 9JA; Tel (01446) 750741
Accommodation for 180. Facilities for all sports. Mixed groups. Full conference facilities. Contact the Manager

Bradwell and Ardleigh Environmental and Outdoor Education Centre
Bradwell Waterside, nr Southminster, Essex CM0 7QY; Tel (01621) 776256 (Office)/776324 (Students); Fax (01621) 776378
Sailing, canoeing, offshore cruising and windsurfing courses from April to September. Field study courses (geography/biology/environmental studies) from October to March. Fully residential or daily from £10.00 per day

Brathay Hall Trust
See Chapter 20

British Institute in Paris
11 rue de Constantine, 75340, Paris Cedex 07; Tel 45.55.71.99; Fax 45.50.31.55
Term-time and vacation courses in French and in translation at undergraduate and postgraduate levels

British Mountaineering Council
Crawford Hse, Precinct Centre, Booth St East, Manchester M13 9RZ; Tel 0161-273 5835
General Secretary D. Walker
Representative body of mountaineering, providing information, details of training courses, insurance schemes and advice about access and conservation. Member clubs operate reciprocal agreements for the use of huts

British Schools Exploring Society
at The Royal Geographical Society, 1 Kensington Gore, London SW7 2AR; Tel 0171-584 0710; Fax 0171-581 7995
Executive Director Lt Col Jon W.A. Flemming (Ret'd)
Administrative Secretary Susannah Cowell, BA
Expeditions Officer Nick Thompson, BA
Organises two or more expeditions annually (four to seven weeks) in arctic, sub-arctic of 3–4 months for 'gap year' students. July and September. Project expeditions throughout the year. Expeditions of up to 90 (age 16½–20) from schools, industry etc led by experts in the field from universities, national services and industry

Campamarena Adventure Holidays Ltd
Dept E1, Falcon's Nest Hotel, Station Rd, Port Erin, Isle of Man; Tel (01624) 834077
Activity holidays in the Isle of Man offering hill-walking, sailing, canoeing, archery, riding, swimming and orienteering for schools, clubs and individuals. Three centres available with domitory or tented accommodation. Age range: 7–16

The Camping and Caravanning Club
Greenfield Hse, Westward Way, Coventry; Tel (01203) 694995; Fax (01203) 694886
Advice on mobile camping and caravanning in Britain

Casa Internaçional
Rodriguez Sánchez 15, 14003 Cóordoba, Spain
International Spanish courses, two weeks in spring, three weeks in September

Centre Audio-visuel de Royan pour l'Etude des Langues
C.A.R.E.L., BP 219C, 17205 Royan, France; Tel (33) 46 39 50 00; Fax (33) 46 015 27 68; Telex OTROYAN 790441
Full-time French courses throughout the year; minimum age, 18+. Intensive courses in July and August for secondary school pupils (11–17) and residential facilities for supervised groups of teenagers

Centre d'Echanges Internationaux (C.E.I.)
104 rue de Vaugirard, 75006 Paris; Tel 45.49.26.25; Fax 45.49.01.70; Telex ASSCEI 206472F
International centres in Brittany, Loire Valley, Côte d'Azur, Gorges du Tarn and Beaujolais offering sports, arts worksops, photography, excursions and a new centre situated in the heart of London open throughout the year. New: Paris-Langues French School open all year round from 18 up
C/E/I-CLUB des 4 VENTS1 re Gozlin, 75006 PARIS; Tel 43 29 60 20; Fax 43 29 016 21; Telex 202789 F CQV
French School "Paris Langues" open all year round from 18 yrs. and up. All levels. Classic French or Business French, Accommodation at school or in families in Paris. Linguistic stays in families or in residences; from 12 to 25 yrs, 12 cities in France; French tuition with qualified teachers; Leisure activities and excursions
Accommodation: 5 International Centres in Brittany, Loire Valley, Cte d'Azur, Gorges du Tarn and Beaujolais open throughout the year

Centre International d'Etudes Françaises
Université Catholique de l'Ouest, 3 Pl André Leroy, BP 808, 49008 ANGERS Cedex 01, France; Tel 41.88.30.15; Fax 41.87.71.67
Director Renée Cochin
Offers three holiday courses in July and September in French language for students and teachers of French. 2 semesters: October–January; February–June, all levels. Age range: 16+. Open throughout the year except August

Centre Maurice Herzog
100 rue de Lille, 59200 Tourcoing, France; Tel 20 26.96.66
Activity holidays for 14–18 year olds during school holidays. Ski-ing, camping, sailing, climbing, cycling, tours and field studies

Centre Nautique des Glenans
Quai Louis Blériot, 75781 Paris Cedex 16, France; Tel 1-45 20 011 40
Sail training organisation offering one- to two-week sailing courses in Brittany, on the Mediterranean coast, in Ireland and in Great Britain (cruising course in the Scilly Isles). Girls or boys, 15+. Camping. Basic

knowledge of French (for courses in France) and ability to swim 100 yards essential
Address in Great Britain
54C Berefords Rd, London N5 2NZ; Sarah McAlister

Centre Nautique des Rosbras-Brigneau
BP3, 29350 Moëlan-sur-mer, France; Tel 00 33 98 39 60 78
One- to two-week sailing courses at all levels. Ages 8–12, 13–16, and 17+. Group travel from Paris available. Open to school parties all year. Applications direct to Centre

Universite d' Ete de Mentor
c/o Office du Tourisme BP 239 06506, Menton, France; Tel 93575700; Fax 93283599
Three-week summer school course in French for foreigners in July and August. Minimum age: 16. Classes for beginners, intermediate and advanced students and teachers training

Centro Velico Caprera
Corso Italia 10, 20122 Milan; Tel Italy 01039-286452191; Fax 89010826
Sailing school on the island of Caprera, north-east of Sardinia, offering two-week courses from May to October. Three levels of instruction from elementary sailing to offshore cruising. Age range: 17+

Christian Mountain Centre
Gorffwysfa, Tremadog, Porthmadog, Gwynedd LL49 9PS, N. Wales; Tel (01766) 512616
Residential mountaineering, watersports and environmental studies centre. Open all year. Dormitory accommodation for up to 34. Instruction in outdoor pursuits and educational projects. Equipment provided

Club International de Langues et de Vacances
62 avenue de Beauvais, Lanvalley, BP110, 22103-Dinan Cedex, France; Tel 96 39 012 15
Homestays in Dinan and St Malo with French language courses. Age range: 12–20. Two, three or four weeks: Easter, July or August. Study arrangements at a French lycée. Programmes for groups and individual participants, during the school year and the holidays

Club Vercors
24 rue de l'Hotel de Ville, 92200 Neuilly sur Seine, France; Tel (1) 46.40.03.40
Offers sports holidays at Easter (ski-ing, ice skating) and in summer (riding, swimming, tennis, mountain walking, bicycling, camping, sailing, surfing, cruising etc) for foreigners aged 11–16

Collége Actif International
517000 Dormans, France; Tel 26 58.21.12
Intensive holiday courses in French for foreign pupils, aged 8–18 yrs. July to September, instruction in tennis, riding, water ski-ing, sailing, karate, judo, canoeing, football, volleyball, etc. Escorted travel from Paris

Collège de Rivière du Loup
80 rue Frontenac, Rivière du Loup, Quebec G5R 1S8, Canada; Tel 862 6903 Ext 293
Stays with French-speaking families in Canada. Seminars in literature, culture and outdoor recreation (sailing, nature study, canoe trips) conducted in French

CPCV Organisme Protestant de Formation
47 rue de Clichy, 75009 Paris; Tel (1) 42 80 016 99; Fax (1) 42 82 14 63
The CPCV is a french federation of associations who organise educational courses with a fun element

Concorde International Study Centre
22/24 Cheriton Gdns, Folkestone, Kent CT20 2AT; Tel (01303) 256752; Fax (01303) 220538
Administrator J.H. King
Part of Concorde International Summer Schools Ltd Adult students 17/18 years attended Folkestone 12 week examination courses for Cambridge, Oxford, TOEFL, IELTS, GMATT or Intensive General English courses of 4–12 weeks. Canterbury offers intensive business English 2–4 weeks at 3 levels
Arnett Hse, Hawks La, Canterbury, Kent CT1 2NU; Tel (01227) 451035; Fax (01227) 762760; *Director* C. Stone

Contacts Eurovac
55 rue Nationale, 37000 Tours, France; Tel 47 20 20 57; Fax 47 20 68 92
French language courses for individuals or groups of at least ten children or adults; age range; 8+. School parties, homestays and home exchanges for families. Travel and accommodation arrangements. Paying guest accommodation. Operates throughout the year in 15 towns. Courses in French language in Tours, Biarritz, Hyères (Côte d'Azur) and Paris. Au pair positions for the summer holidays or throughout the year. Stays at Teacher's home; Intensive Individual courses; Academic Studies; Discovery sessions; Excursions in the Loire Valley; Transits in Paris. Non-profit-making organisation run by French teachers

Cookery and Activity Holidays
Bridge Courtyard, Donnington, Chichester, West Sussex PO20 7PP; Tel (01243) 779239; Fax (01243) 784241
Holidays every August to give 11–16 year olds opportunity to become familiar with cookery techniques and visit hotels/restaurants to see chefs at work

Council for British Archaeology
Bowes Morrell Hse, 111 Walmgate, York YO1 2UA; Tel (01904) 671417; Fax (01904) 671384
Education Officer Don Henson
YAC Co-ordinator Juliet Mather
Information Officer Mike Heyworth
The CBA works to promote the study and safeguarding of Britain's historic environment, to provide a forum for archaeological opinion, and to improve public knowledge of Britain's past; The CBA produces a regular magazine, *British Archaeological News* (ten issues a year subscription £17.00) which, together with its information supplement *CBA Briefing*, provides news on current developments in British archaeology and lists excavations and other projects, conferences and dayschools in which people can take part. The magazine is available as part of CBA individual membership (£18 per annum, £10 for those in full-time education); The CBA also runs the Young Archaeologists Club for younger members aged between 9 and 16. Its Members receive a quarterly magazine, *Young Archaeologist* and a range of other benefits. Annual membership costs £5, with family membership at £7.50
Education Officer
CBA Northern Office, The King's Manor, York YO1 2EP; Tel (01904) 433925

Countrywide Holidays Association
Birch Heys, Cromwell Range, Manchester M14 6HU; Tel 0161-225 1000
Britain's most experienced outdoor holiday organisation, established 1893. Rambling, fell walking, birdwatching, field studies, photography, dancing, painting and many other holiday courses at 13 holiday centres throughout Britain ideally situated for group work in the countryside

Cours Universitaire d'Eté-Saint Malo
Université Haute Bretagne, 6 Avenue Gaston Berger, 35043 Rennes Cedex, France; Tel 99 33 52 93
Four week residential course (July/August) for foreign students in French language, civilisation and literature

Courtlands Field Studies and Outdoor Pursuits Centre
Kingsbridge TQ7 4BN; Tel (01548) 550227; Fax (01548) 550675
Director Iain Garland
Administrator Sylvia Blomeley
Activity, field study and adventure courses for individuals and groups. Facilities for self-run courses, laboratory, gym, assault course, games field. Close to coast and Dartmoor. Wide range of activities for any age from 9 years. All year round

Cranedale Field Study Centre
Kirby Grindalythe, nr Malton, North Yorkshire YO17 8DB; Tel (01944) 738687
Field study courses (A level, GCSE and Primary/Prep) in Biology, Geography, Geology and Environmental Studies. Courses tailored to specific requirements and tutored by fully qualified staff. Also courses offer blend of outdoor pursuits and environmental studies. Facilities available for self-tutored groups

Cultural Centre of the International Federation of Jeunesses Musicales Groznjan
Cultural Centre FIJM 51924 Groznjan
Summer music courses (instruments masterclasses, chamber, symphony, choir, early music, jazz, dance) and non-musical programmes (comics, architecture, theatre, psychology)
Cultural Centre FIJM, Muzicka Omladina, Trnjanska bb, 41000 Zagreb, Yugoslavia; Tel Zagreb 38 41 53 92 99, 53 97 99; Groznjan (Jun–Sept) 38 53 76 106

Cyclists' Touring Club
Cotterell Hse, 69 Meadrow, Godalming, Surrey GU7 3HS; Tel (01483) 417217
Provides wide range of membership services (insurance, handbook, magazine, touring and technical literature, lists of 200 local groups) and promotes recreational cycling

Dartmoor Expedition Centre
Rowden, Widecombe-in-the-Moor, Newton Abbot, Devon TQ13 7TX; Tel (0136 42) 249
Barn bunkhouse accommodation (maximum 31). Self catering or meals provided. All year round multi-activity and specialist residential courses for schools, youth groups and individuals. Also MLT and instructor's courses. Details from John Earle at above address

Dartmoor Field Study and Activity Centre
Colehayes Pk, Haytor Rd, Bovey Tracey, South Devon TQ13 9LD; Tel (01626) 833033
Contact Peter or Daphne Driver
Georgian mansion situated in 20 acres of Dartmoor National Park. Full board catering for up to 70 people (single to dormoitory bedrooms). Facilities include 2 lounges, bar, dining room, 3 lecture rooms, 2 games rooms, sports field, formal gardens and nature trail. Courses in management training and development, outdoor adventure pursuits. Field study centre caters for primary school to university level

Det Danske Kulturinstitut
Kultorvet 2, DK-1175 Copenhagen, Denmark; Tel +45 33 13 54 48; Fax +45 33 15 10 91
Institute for information about Denmark and cultural co-operation with other countries. Offers seminars, conducted in English, German and French, all for professional people and advanced students, on different aspects and problems of Danish (and Scandinavian) education from pre-school and child care to education for adults and care for the aged, on Danish social policy, library problems, architecture, arts and crafts and design

Did Deutsch-Institut, (deutsch in deutschland) gmbH
Hauptstrasse 26, D-63811 Stockstadt am Main, Germany; Tel (01) 6027/41 77-0; Fax (01) 6027/41 77 41; Telex 4 188 559 did d
German intensive language courses throughout the year for business people, young professionals and students in Frankfurt, München, Berlin and other German cities. Holiday courses for adults, students and pupils in more than one hundred German cities, accommodation in families or in residences, leisure programme and many other activities. Furthermore, Academic Year Programmes, Work and Study and Educational Tours throughout Germany

Dublin University, Trinity College
Accommodation Office, Trinity College, Dublin 2, Ireland; Tel 00-353 7021177; Fax 00-353 6711267; Telex 93782 TCD EI
Summer schools and language courses, conferences

Dryffryn Hall Outdoor Centre
Dryffeyn, Nr Cymmer SA13 3ET; Tel (01639) 851595
Spacious, well equipped centre in the picturesque Afan Valley, with easy access from M4. Dormitory accommodation for 50 people. Large main hall with indoor games area, full central heating and showers. Self-cater and meals provided service available. Optional activity programmes individually structured from more than 30 sessions encompassing educational visits, environmental studies and introductory outdoor pursuits. Prices start from £27 per head plus VAT for a weekend, £53 plus VAT for Mon–Fri

Early Music Days Sopron
Interart Peslivalcenter H-1366 Budapest, POB 80, Hungary
Maria Liszkay

English Folk Dance and Song Society, The
Cecil Sharp Hse, 2 Regents Pk Rd, London NW1 7AY; Tel 0171-485 2206
Information on festivals, events, courses, workshops, clubs, children's activities. Resource centre containing library and folk shop

English Language Institute
99 St Stephen's Grn, Dublin 2, Ireland; Tel 353 (1) 4752965; Fax 353 (1) 4752967
Chairperson E.P. O'Brien
Year-round English language courses. Academic year and business programmes. Summer study holidays. Preparation for all major exams. Accommodation arranged in Irish family homes. On campus residence facilities for July junior school. Extra-curricular activities. Recognised RELSA teacher-training courses. Evening classes for au-pairs. Recognised by the Irish Department of Education. Member of RELSA (recognised English Language Schools Association), FIYTO, Federation of International Youth Travel Oorganisations, Equals, European Association of Quality Language Services

Estudio Internacional Sampere
Castello,50 Bajo Dcha, Madrid, Spain; Tel 275 40 25 and 276 82 64; Fax 2759509; Telex 46080 EISA E
Intensive all-year-round courses in Madrid. Translators, bilingual secretarial training 3/4/8/12/16 weeks. With/ without accommodation. Advanced classes for A-level students
Puerto de Santa Maria,Cielo 40, 11500 Puerto da Santa Maria, Cádiz, Spain; Tel (34 56) 072021; Fax (56) 87 41 09; Telex 76191 EIPSM
Intensive Spanish courses. Tropical climate. Open from March to end November

Europa Cantat–European Federation of Young Choirs
Adersheimer Str 60, D 3340 Wolfenbüttel, Germany; Tel 015331 465 66
Organises several singing week annually and Europa Cantat, a gathering of 3,000 young choristers, triennially, in various European cities

Expedition Advisory Centre
The Royal Geographical Society, 1 Kensington Gore, London SW7 2AR; Tel 0171-581 2057; Fax 0171-584 4447
Jointly founded by the Royal Geographical Society and Young Explorers Trust to provide information and training to those planning scientific or adventurous expeditions overseas from schools, universities or by private groups

FCS Camping Holidays
27 Peter St, Taunton, Somerset TA2 7BY; Tel (01823) 286517
Camping holidays, May, June, July, August and September in Rutland, Hampshire, Sussex, Kent, Northern England, Oxfordshire, France. Minimum age 18 unless accompanied. From £69.00 per week: includes all food and folk music entertainment, reduction for groups

Fédération Internationale des Jeunesses Musicales (FIJM)
Palais des Beaux-Arts, 10 Rue Royale, 1000 Bruxelles, Belgium; Tel (32-2) 513 9774; Fax (32-2) 514 4755
Organises summer music courses all over the world; Level: Musicians with basic training who have studied for about 3 years; Experienced amateur musicians with more than 3 years of tuition; Music students preparing for professional careers; Students in their final year of professional training, young professional musicians, "master-class" standard. Grants are available for travel expenses and course fees

Fédération Unie des Auberges de Jeunesse
27 Rue Pajol, 75018 Paris; Tel 46 017 010 01
Runs nearly 200 youth hostels throughout France. Winter and Summer activities for individuals and groups. Accommodation for groups and special programmes

Felpham Sailing and Sports School
Sea Rd, Felpham, Bognor Regis, West Sussex PO22 7AN; Tel (01243) 826125
Sports include windsurfing, sailing, canoeing, tennis and horse riding. Full programme of leisure activities arranged. Can be combined with English as a foreign language. Specialise in beginners and unaccompanied children. Adults, families and more advanced pupils also welcome. Good reductions for groups. Wide range of accommodation available. Also golf and cultural holidays for adults

Ferienkurs der Stadt Winterhur
Bacheggliweg 22, CH-8405 Winterhur; Tel Switzerland
Holiday German course, July (3 weeks). Open to students and pupils over 14

Field Studies
Youth Hostels Association, Trevelyan Hse, St Albans, Herts AL1 2DY; Tel (01727) 855215
Have 24 Youth Hostels with field study facilities, with day-time access to workrooms for environmental studies, training courses and seminars. Free copy of Groups Away brochure on request

Field Studies Council
Juniper Hall Field Centre, Dorking, Surrey RH5 6DA; Tel (01306) 883849
School (7 years–A level including GCSE; courses can meet most broad balanced science objectives) specialised and amateur courses in history, biology, geography, geology and environmental subjects, photography, art etc

Fondation pour le Connaissance de Paris et le Rayonnement du Tourisme
21 rue du Repos, 75020 Paris; Tel 43.70.70.87; Fax 43.70.28.16
Historic tours and shows inside Paris and the lie de France: monuments and people

Forest School Camps
110 Burbage Rd, London SE24 9HD
Honorary Secretary Lorna English
Purposeful and educational standing camps under canvas for boys and girls aged 6½–17 years. Easter Whitsun and August. Personal tents/equipment required. Also canoeing, mobile and semi-mobile camps, including some foreign ones, potholing. Leadership courses. Apply secretary. Noting on the envelope the service required

Fort Bovisand Underwater Centre
Plymouth, Devon PL9 0AB; Tel (01752) 408021; Fax (01752) 481952
Weekend and 5-day introductory diving courses. One week BS-AC courses in novice and advanced diver training; minimum age 15. Government approved commercial diver training courses to all HSE standards

Gesellschaft für Ost- und Sudostkunde
A-40 24 Wienerstrasse 131, Austria; Tel 01732 33 34/523
International Russian, Czech and Hungarian language seminars: Jan–Feb at Altmuenster, Upper Austria, with skiing (Russina only); Summer ion Crimean penninsula, GUS (Russian only); August at Unterweissenbach, Upper Austria (Russian); Sept Kefermorkz Weinberg (Castle) (Czech and Hungarian); July Budeejovice, CSFR (Czech only). 2 weeks. All levels

Glencoe Outdoor Centre
Glencoe, Argyll PA39 4HS, Scotland; Tel (01855) 811350; Fax (01855) 811644
Located in Scottish Highlands offering multi-activity holidays and specialist courses for individuals, families and groups including schools. Activities include canoeing, hill walking, ski-ing, orienteering, sailing and wind-surfing, climbing and abseiling. Accommodation; facilities include drying room, lounge and games room. Maximum 35 guest. Friendly supportive team, qualified instruction

Goeth-Institut
Postfach 19 04 19, Helene-Weber-Allee 1, D-80604 München, Germany; Tel 0189-15921-0
German language courses for adults (4 or 8 weeks) German for specific fields. Vacation courses for teenagers (14–18 weeks) aged 14 to 18. German in two weeks: Intensive

Hallow Mill Equestrian Centre
Hallow, nr Worcester WR2 6PR; Tel (01905) 640373
Residential holiday courses in riding for individuals and groups

Hans Brinker Stutel/Hotal
Kerkstraat 136, Amsterdam 1017 GR, The Netherlands; Tel 0120-220687; Telex HBS 12127
Hotel accommodation, budget excursions, coach hire, study tours

Harrow Hse International College
Harrow Hse, Harrow Dr, Swanage, Dorset BH19 1PE; Tel (01929) 424421; Fax (01929) 427175
Residential Centre open all year to groups of all ages and interests. Magnificent setting in 5 acres with views overlooking the sea, and Purbeck Hills. Facilities include tennis and squash courts, swimming pool, gymnasium, theatre, sportsdome, bar, video, TV. Clubhouse, lecture and seminar rooms, computer room, playing fields etc

Luftsportjugend des DAeC
Rudolf-Braas-Str-20, D-63150, Heusenstamm, Germany; Tel (06104) 699672; Fax (06104) 699611
International Airport Youth Meetings in Gliding in Germany from April to September. Courses in: gliding, hot air ballooning, aeromodelling, parachuting, microlight

Humboldt-Institut
Schloss Ratzenried, Argenbuehl D-88260, Germany; Tel 07522/4044; Fax 07522/1305
Director Norbert Guethling
Age 16 and over (in summer age 18 and over): Full-year: Intensive German courses, all levels (30 lessons weekly). Ratzenried Castle, Southern Germany. 10 students per class. Activity programme arranged. Accommodation in 16th century castle, institute's guest house, or with family. Also one-to-one courses (40 lessons weekly). *Age 18 and over*: Full-year: Intensive German courses, all levels (30 lessons weekly) at Konstanz, Lake Constance. 10 students per class. Activity programme. Accommodation in the Institute. *Age 28 and over*: Full-year: Intensive one-to-one or two-to-one courses, all levels at Freudental Castle near Konstanz, Lake Constance. *Age 10–14, 15–18 and over*: Numerous summer courses at various locations in Germany from June to August. Please contact the Institute for further details

Institut Catholique de Paris
Cours Universitaires d'Eté, 21 rue d'Assas, 75270 Paris Cedex 06; Tel (33.1) 44.39.52.66 Ext 374; Fax (33.1) 45.44.27.14
Intensive courses in July, all levels. French language, civilisation, literature, phonetics, translation. Language laboratory for all students. Special courses in methodology, written French, Business French,

Excursions. Accommodation provided on request in students' residences. Apply before 1st June enclosing 3 international reply coupons

Institut International Linguistique du Val de Loire
38 Fanbourg Saint Lubin, F-41100 Vendome; Tel 54731256; Fax 54802164
Director Giséle Fillon
Courses in buisness French, conversational French and French for French teachers based in the Loire Valley

Institute for Spanish Studies
Ave Juan Sebastian Elcano 110, Málaga, Spain; Tel (34) 5-2290551; Fax (34) 5-2290551
Small group language courses for all levels. Accommodation with Spanish families or in small apartments

Instituto Allende
San Miguel de Allende, Guanajuato, CP37700, Mexico; Tel 0111-52-415-20190; Fax 0111-52-415-24538
Credit and non-credit courses at undergraduate and graduate levels, specialising in arts, crafts. Spanish. Special escorted field study trips. Age range 16+. Open throughout the year. BFA, MFA degree programs

International Bartók Seminar and Festival
Organised by Interart Festivalcenter
H-1366, Budapest, PO Box 80, Hungary; Tel and Fax 36 1 1179910
Workshops, public concerts and master classes in piano, chamber music, conducting, violoncello, violin, percussion, musicology, composition. 25 June–15 July 1994. Location: Szombathely, West Hungary

International Center of Information and Documentation on Animation Techniques, Cidotam-Fijm
7 Piotra Skargi St, 85-018 Bydgoszcz, Poland; Tel 52/22 23 68/22 019 13
International Music camps with courses on musical animation and composition, music therapy and interdisciplinary art activity

International Centre for the Study of Mosaic (CISIM)
C/o Azienda di Promozione Turistica (APT), Via S. Vitel, 2-48100 Ravenna, Italy; Tel 01544-35755/35756; Telex 550411
International courses on mosaics at Lio Adriano

International Eötvös Institute Budapest
Secretary of the Foundation Maria Mezei
The Institute's goal is a postgraduate program of theoretical and practical training prior to the individual becoming a professional orchestra leader. The program will be divided into 2–4 working periods, each taking place in different European locations in which the students will become acquainted with institutions and orchestras of different characters

Internationaler Arbeitskreis für Musik e.V.
3500 Kassel-Wilhelmshöhe, Heinrich-Schütz-Allee 29, Germany; Tel (01561) 37927; Fax (01561) 313772
Meetings for young and adult musicians in Germany and other European countries during Easter, summer and Christmas holidays. Singing, orchestral and chamber music, dancing, improvisation, etc. Age range: 15–60

Internationales Musikinstitut Darmstadt (IMD)
D Darmstadt, Nieder-Ramstäedter Strasse 190, Germany; Tel (49) 6151 64285; Fax (49) 6151 132405; Telex 4197127 stdad
Information and documentation centre. International vacation courses for the composition and interpretation of contemporary music (biennial, even numbered years). Also, Music Information Centre (MIC) and Archives of the International Society for Contemporary Music (ISCM)

International Junior Camp
PO Box 329, CH-3780 Gstaad, Switzerland; Tel 056/22.67.78 and 030/440-86 (July–August); Fax 056/22 67 75
Summer courses in French, German and English, July to August: Age range: 7–14; Sports, excursions, hiking, summer skiing

International Teen Camp
PO Box 122, CH-1000, Lausanne 12, Switzerland; Tel 056/22-67-78 and 021/652-11-25; Fax July–August 056/22 6775
Summer courses in French, German and English, July to August. Age range: 15–19. Sports, excursions, hiking, summer skiing

The Japan Exchange and Teaching (JET) Programme
The JET Programme Desk, Council on International Educational Exchange, 33 Seymour Pl, London W1H 6AT; Tel 0171-224 8896
Official Japanese government scheme employing graduates for one year as Assistant English Teachers in Japanese secondary schools, and as Co-ordinators for International Relations in local government. Salary: 3.6m yen per annum. Help given to find accommodation. Return travel to Japan provided

Jeunesses Musicales de Suisse
Maison de la Radio, Case postale 233, 1211 Genève 8, Switzerland; Tel 0122 328 70 64
Courses and musical camps

Jeunesses Musicales Deutschland
Marktplatz 12, D-6992 Weikersheim, Germany; Tel 07934/280; Fax 07934/8526
International summer music courses at Schlosss Weikersheim. Opera, chamber music, orchestra. July to August. Age range: 16–30. Grants available. Accommodation available for music groups of up to 120 people throughout the year

John Hall's Pre-University Course in Venice
12 Gainsborough Rd, Ipswich, Suffolk IP4 2UR; Tel (01473) 251223; Fax (01473) 288009
Founded in 1965. Six weeks in Venice (Feb/March). Extension weeks in Florence and Rome. Lectures on art, architecture, history and music. Classes in life drawing, photography and Italian language

Jegendreisesekretariat Tyrol
A-6021 Innsbruck, Meinhardstrasse 9/IV, POB 459, Austria; Tel 0512/582742, 582744; Fax 0512/57327485
Recreational holidays for youth groups, family and adult groups, May to September. Winter ski courses for school groups begin December. Centres in Tyrol, Salzburg and Vorarlberg

Jyvakyla Arts Festival
Kramsunkatu 1, 40600 Jycaskyla, Finland; Tel 0141-615 624
Two-week master classes for musicians, June to July

Landelijk Centrum Voor Amateurdans (LCA)
Oudegracht 25, 3511 AB Utrecht, The Netherlands; Tel 30-334255
Summer, Christmas and Easter courses in international folk dancing, international amateur dance festivals and tuition in children's dance and amateur dance. The LCA also publishes two magazines: 'Dans' and 'Volksdans'

Little Barton Riding and Field Activity Centre
Little Barton Farm, St Cleer, Liskeard, Cornwall PL14 6EH; Tel (01579) 342444
Riding holidays from Easter to September. Excursions. Age range: 10–18

Llanwrtyd Wells Pony Trekking
Pen y Craig, Llandavery Rd, Llanwrtyd Wells, Powys LD5 4TE; Tel (01591) 610 209
Trekking holidays in spectacular scenery for novice and experienced riders. Party bookings welcomed. Open May to September. Short mid week or weekend. Autumn, Winter and Spring

Longtown Outdoor Education Centre
The Court Hse, Longtown, Herefordshire; Tel (0187 387) 225
Outdoor activities for young people 11–21 yrs. School groups during term time – youth groups and adult courses during weekends and school holidays. Courses can include history, geography, biology and outdoor activities. Individuals during summer holiday period. Sponsored by Northamptonshire County Council Education Dept

Medina Valley Centre
Dodnor La, Newport, IOW PO30 5TE; Tel (01983) 522195; Fax (01983) 825962
RYA Dinghay sailing courses. All levels, beginners to instructors. Field Study Courses in Ecology and Geography at GCSE and 'A' level. Environmental Studies and 'Shipshape', Science in Action for primary and middle schools

Millfield School Village of Education
Street, Somerset BA16 0YD; Tel (01485) 45823; Fax (01458) 45102
Holiday courses for young people, adults and families. Approx. 400 courses available in almost 100 games coaching, creative arts and other activities

Minerva Training
Plas Glansevin, Llangadog, Dyfed SA19 9HY; Tel (01550) 777121; Fax (01550) 777890
Development Training. Residential centre near Brecon Beacons accommodating up to 40. Adventure and Personal Development Courses with outdoor activities. Age range 9–18. Also tailored programmes for young employees and adult groups

National Cave Training Centre
See Whernside–National Park Outdoor Recreation and Study Centre

National Centre of International Music Competitions and Festivals
Interart Festivalcenter, H-1366 Budapest, P.O.B. 80, Hungary; Tel 266-3108; Fax 266-3108
Member of the European Association of Music Festivals and the World Federation of International Music Competitions. Runs wide range of courses and competitions

Neige et Merveilles
Hameau de la Minière de Vallanuria, 06430 St Dalmas-de-Tende; Tel 93.04.62.40
One-week holiday courses in Mercantour national park, in the Alpes Maritimes. Age range: 18+
Nice; Tel 92.09.01.61

Nyribátor International Youth Music Camp and Instrumental Competition
Nyribátor Music School, Nyribátor, Szentvér U., I. H-4300
Chamber music, orchestra and individual master courses with public concerts for music students. 18 days in July, 1993

Ocean Youth Club
South St, Gosport, Hants PO12 1EP; Tel (01705) 528421

Oeuvre Departmentale des Centres de Vacances
8 quai Baluze, BP 157, 19004 Tulle, France; Tel (55) 200104
Sailing hoidays in Summer in the Isle of Oléron; ski-ing at Christmas, Easter and in the first term in Chamonix

Orford Arts Centre
CP 280, Magog, Quebec J1X 3W8, Canada; Tel 819 843 3981
Courses and master class on: cello, double bass, viola, violin, french horn, piano, clarinet, flute, oboe, bassoon, percussions, voice, trumpet, trombone, tuba and chamber music

Orkney Field Centre
Links Hse, Birsay, Orkney; Tel (01856) 72221
Courses in birds, flowers and Orkney's 'Heritage'. Student groups welcome. Accommodation for 20 with basic laboratory facilities

Ornitholidays
1–3 Victoria Dr, Bognor Regis, Sussex PO21 2PW; Tel (01243) 821230; Fax (01243) 829574
Principal Officer Nigel R. Jones
Birdwatching and natural history holidays in France, Austria, Spain, N.E. Greece, Poland, Hungary, Canada, India, N. America, Kenya, Brazil, Trinidad and Tobago, The Seychells, Isreal, Cyprus, Botswana, Andorra, Namibia, Australia, Falkland Islands, The Gambia, Venezuela, Costa Rica, Chile, Turkey, Thailand and Japan. Minimum age 15

Out-In Tourist Services
Via Roma, 61, 38064 Folgaria (TN), Italy; Tel 0464/721877; Fax 0464/72.00.71

Outward Bound
Route 9D, R2 Box 280, Garrison NY 10524-9757, USA; Tel 800-243 8520; Fax 914-424 4000
Courses at 5 schools in USA. Self-discovery in a wilderness setting. No previous experience necessary. Backpacking, mountaineering, canoeing, skiing, snowshoeing, sailing, cycling, rafting and caving

Outward Bound Loch Eil
Archdalieu, Fort William, Inverness-shire PH33 7NN; Tel (01397) 772866
Unique courses in the rugged Scottish Highlands, using a wide range of outdoor activities, exciting, adventurous and highly enjoyable, to provide a stimulating framework for all to extend their horizons and realise their potential. Also courses using one particular activity, from specialised ice-climbing to Outward Bound land journeys and sea voyages. Courses open to individuals and groups. Age range: 16–60

The Painting School and Centre for Holidays Study Tours
Calle Mayor 30, Berdun, Huesca, Spain; Tel 974 37 17 48
Cultural/Field studies centre for architectural study, botany, natural history, photography and ornithology in the foothills of the Spanish Pyrenees. Travel agents: Honeyguide Wildlife Holidays, 36 Thunder La, Thorpe St Andrew, Norwich Tel: (01603) 300552. Also Bird Holidays, 115/117 Otley Road, Guiseley, Leeds Tel: (01943) 872464. Also ACE Study Tours, Babraham, Cambridge Tel: (01223) 835055. Also Naturetrek, Chautara, Bighton, Nr Alresford, Hampshire Tel: (01962) 733368 and Cygnus Wildlife, 57 Fore St, Kingsbridge, Devon Tel: (01548) 856178

Pearse House
Parsonage La, Bishop's Stortford, Herts CM23 5BQ; Tel (01279) 757400
School journey visits, activity programmes and specialist creative writing and music courses in centres based throughout England. Qualified tutorial assistance and pastoral help provided. Expertise particularly in the primary sector

Pécs International Music Camp
Jeunesses Musicales Hungary, H-1366 Budapest, PO Box 80; Tel 3611175291; Fax 3611179910; Telex 202861
Pécs Symphony Orchestra Camp. Next camp July 1996

PGL Adventure
Alton Ct, Penyard La, Ross-on-Wye, HEREFORD HR9 5NR; Tel (01989) 764211; Fax (01989) 765451
Britain's leading School Travel operator with choice of 13 UK outdoor pursuit centres in the Wye Valley, Brecon Beacons, Devon, Surrey, Oxfordshire, Isle of Wight and Scotland. Full board and accommodation in dormitories or tents. WTB, BAHA, BCU and RYA Inspected centres. Also canoeing, rafting, windsurfing and sailing in Southern France and Spain at BCU and RYA approved

centres. Tours to London, France, Belgium, Germany, Holland and Eastern Europe. Ski trips to France, Switzerland, Italy, Austria and Romania

Ponies Association (UK)
Chesham Hse, 56 Green End Rd, Sawtry, Huntingdon PE17 5UY
Advice and information on riding holidays, trekking, riding instruction, trail riding etc. Publishes booklet containing full list of approved centres and star ratings awarded. Send SAE for free booklet

Pony Club
British Equestrian Centre, Stoneleigh, Kenilworth, Warks; Tel (01203) 696697; Fax (01203) 692351
Exchange visits between individuals with an interest in horses and riding. 367 branches throughout the British Isles. Both sexes. In school holidays. Usually travelling expenses only

'Pro Musica'
Jeunesse Musicales Secretariate Budapest, PO Box 239, H-1368; Tel 179-910; Telex 22-4121
Courses for Woodwinds 1, Saxophone and Organ in Baja (South-Hungary). Masterclasses, playing possibility also with chamber orchestra

Ramblers Holidays Ltd
Longcroft Hse, Fretherne Rd, Welwyn Garden City, Herts AL8 6PQ; Tel (01707) 331133; Fax (01707) 333276; Telex 24642 RTOURG
Operations Manager David Beer
Walking, trekking, cross-country skiing, alpine mountaineering holidays in 27 countries. Botany, bird watching, city sightseeing and exploring tours

Red Española De Albergues Juveniles
Instito de la Juventud c/o José Ortega y Gasset, no 71, Madrid 28006, Spain; Tel 401.13.00
Youth hostel accommodation for individuals and groups in Spain

John Ridgway International Summer School
Ardmore, Rhiconich, Sutherland IV27 4RB, Scotland; Tel (01971 521) 229; Fax (01971 521) 463
Atlantic rower/round world sailor/Amazon explorer offers adventure holidays, May-September West Highland coast, boys and girls, 12–15, 15–18; men and women 18–30. Instructor; pupil ratio 1:6. Offshore and dinghy sailing, rock-climbing, expeditions, canoeing, self reliance, survival, environment study. 14 days

Sail Training Association
2A The Hard, Portsmouth PO1 3PT; Tel (01705) 832055; Fax (01705) 815769
Chief Executive John Songhurst

School of Continuing Studies, The University of Birmingham
Edgbaston, Birmingham B15 2TT; Tel 0121-414 5606 (24 hour answering service); Fax 0121-414 5619
Vocational Programme; Courses specifically designed to meet the requirements of particular vocational groups (e.g. Applied Social Science, Management, etc) including in-company award bearing courses and training
Public Programme; Courses for the general public, including day and evening courses, day schools, study tours (UK and abroad), residential courses and award bearing courses, in a wide range of subjects
Part-time Degree Programme; a BA&Sc degree by credit accumulation. CATs recognition. Participants study two foundation modules followed by modules from various named routes and electives in two of three academic areas: humanities, social sciences, natural sciences
BPhil(Ed)–Continuation Studies; a two year part-time 'top-up' qualification for those who possess professional qualifications to Diploma level, but who do not possess a first degree
Credit-bearing Public Programme; courses for the general public. No prior entry qualifications required. Mostly modular and most modules qualify for credit
Vocational Consultancy and Courses; designed for specific client groups, particularly the caring professions (especially social work), churches, the NHS

School Management Services
93 Ashurst Rd, Barnet, Herts EN4 9LH; Tel 0181-449 5342
Director John L. Stibbs, MA
A consultant and training agency which works in individual schools, specialising in management issues, staff development and appraisal, and timetable design and preparation

Scottish Centres
Loaningdale Hse, Carwood Rd, Biggar, Lanarkshire ML12 6LX; Tel (01899) 221115; Fax (01899) 220644
Four residential outdoor education centres at Aberfoyle, Meigle, Biggar and West Linton; Accommodation and facilities for groups of 10 to 250 for courses in environmental studies, outdoor pursuits, TVEI and personal development. Assistance with arranging of programmes/courses including visits to local places of educational interest

Scottish Sports Council
Caledonia Hse, South Gyle, Edinburgh EH12 9DQ; Tel 0131-317 7200; Fax 0131-317 7202
Information leaflets on career and education and training opportunities in sport and physical recreation are available from the Scottish Sports Council. Although not exclusively Scottish, the leaflets are angled towards the Scottish market. Brochures outlining details on a series of training courses in sport and outdoor recreation organised by the Council through its three National Sports Training Centres are also available

Scouts de Wiltz
9516 Château de Wiltz, Grand Duchy of Luxembourg; Tel 958 199
International European Scouting centre, providing camping facilities for Schools, Guides and Scouts at 10 homes and 10 campsites plus special site leaders and their families

Scripture Union
130 City Rd, London EC1V 2NJ; Tel 0171-782 0013; Fax 0171-782 0014
Christian holidays and training courses for children and young people aged 9–18 years

Sealyham Activity Centre
Sealyham Mansion, Wolfscastle, Haverfordwest SA62 5NF; Tel (01348) 840763; Fax (01348) 840763
Outdoor pursuits courses for schools including canoeing, climbing, abseiling, sailing, surfing, pony-trekking. Age range 8–18. Full-board and dormitory accommodation in Georgian Mansion house for 100 plus staff. 90 acres of woodland along the River Anghof. Field Study groups also catered for

Society for the Dissemination of Sciences (Budapest)
Budapest H 1088, Muzeum utca 7, Magyarorszag, Hungary; Tel 1-384 250
University course in economics in August. Lectures on the economic life, economic policy and management system of the Hungarian People's Republic for foreigners

Société Spéléologique de Wallonie
93 Rue Belvaux-4030, Liege, Belgium; Tel 010-32-41-426142; Fax 010-32-41-421156
The association co-ordinates the activities of speleology clubs in French-speaking Belgium and owns two speleo-climbing refuges located in Villers-Sainte-Gertrude (about 50 km from Liège) and Jambes (Namur). Group projects arranged during school holidays for affiliated bodies. Age range: 15–35

Spanish Course in Valencia
50 Clewer Hill Rd, Windsor, Berks SL4 4BW
Director R. Clegg
Language course for 'A' level students and undergraduates. 2 weeks in July. Lectures on set texts,

classes in conversation and grammar. Excursions included in inclusive costs of £350. Accommodation in Hall of Residence or with families. Some LEAs give grants for this course. Sponsored by the Hispanic Council

Sports Council
16 Upper Woburn Pl, London WC1H 0QP; Tel 0171-388 1277
Can supply details of organisations running instructional courses in most sports and outdoor activities for adults and young people throughout the year. Centres include 6 national sports centres

Sprachschule Westendorf
6363 Westendorf, Tyrol, Austria; Tel 015334 2266; Fax 015334 6092
Intensive German courses all year round for students of 16+. 2, 3 or 4 week courses or long-term courses. Accommodation included. Optional subjects, such as literature, history, politics, art and music in the Tyrol, traditional and modern folk songs and others are included as well as weekly excursions and most evening programmes; Free time activities in summer: hiking, mountain-biking, tennis, swimming, rafting, summer ski-ing, concerts, barbecues among others. In winter the school lies in the middle of a fantastic ski-ing area. Alpine ski-ing, cross country ski-ing, snow-boarding, skating and tobogganing, weekly excursions and evening programme, etc included. In winter, ski-ing lessons available in the afternoons. Special courses for students of 40+

Station Ornithologique du Bec d'Allier
36 rue Principale, Marzy, 58000 Nevers, France; Tel (86) 59 51 03
Bird-watching near the river Loire. Knowledge of French required

Sterts Arts and Environmental Centre
Upton Cross, Liskeard, Cornwall PL14 5AZ; Tel (01579) 62382
Residential or day courses. Combined arts and environmental centre. Excellent moorland and coastal sites. Field studies, arts/language courses. Music, video, sound-recording, stage-lighting. On-site, open-air theatre and gallery. Primary, secondary, higher education, adults. Self or centre-tutored. Accommodates 35 in high-standard bedroom and workshop areas. Colour brochure available

Stichting International Orgelconcours
Stadhuis, Postbus 3333, 2001 DH Haarlem, Netherlands; Tel (0123) 160574; Fax (0123) 160576
International Summer Academy for Organists, July 11–29 1994

Studentenhaus Birkbrunn
A-1190 Vienna, Linneplatz 3, Austria; Tel (+431) 317 05 63; Fax (+431) 310 61 71
Students residence offering widespread cultural activities and christian formation. Summer courses in German in July and August. Male students only. Age range 16–24. Full tuition ATS 14.500 including course, meals and entrance fees for the cultural programme

Union Belge de Spéléologie–UBS
93 Rue Belvaux-B4030 Liege, Belgium; Tel 32-41-42 61 42; Fax 32-49 42 11 56
Own accommodation for 60 people and a caving school. Mountaineering and caving tuition (beginners to advanced); equipment available for hire. Permanent organisation of technical and cultural activities. Each summer: initiation stage. Age range: 15+

Universidad Interncional de Málaga
Facultad de Letras, San Agustin 6, Málaga, Spain; Tel 21.40.07
Spanish language courses. Summer and winter. Literature, history, art, music geography and Spanish culture. Diploma in Hispanic studies or Certificate of Proficiency in Spanish

University of Peace
B 5000 Namur, 4 Bld du Nord, Belgium; Tel 0181-22 61 02; Fax 23 18 82
International centre for peace studies. One-week summer session alternatively in Belgium and abroad; age range 18–40+ (50 participants). Training sessions whole year round (20–25 participants). Main fields: non-violent communication, mediation, negotiation, non-violent conflict resolution, peace and co-operation education; European, North-South (courses vary from 2 to 5 days); mediation centre; research on conflict resolution

University of Pisa
Dipartimento di Linguistica, Via S. Maria 36, 56100 Pisa, Italy; Tel 050/24773
Two 3/4 week courses for foreigners in Italian language and culture at Viareggio in July and August. Grammar, literature, history of art, political history, history of Italian music. No academic qualification needed for admission. Age range: 18+

Vacances Pour Tous
21 rue Saint Fargeau, PO Box 313-75989, Paris, France; Tel 1-43589593
Residential language courses at centres throughout France

The Venture Centre
Lewaigue Farm, Maughold, Isle of Man IM7 1AW; Tel (01624) 814240; Fax (01624) 815615
Adventure training courses for boys and girls aged 9–15; forty activities including canoeing, sailing, abseiling, grass skiing, archery; Bunk house accommodation, maximum 60; March–October, full board 3–7 nights. BAHA Member. BCU Approved

Village Camps of Switzerland
Village Camps, 34 Wilton Ave, London W4 2HY; Tel 0181-995 5134; Fax 0181-742 3984
Sports, educational and ski-ing tours at competitive pound prices for schools and clubs in Swiss alpine resorts such as Leysin, Anzére and Saas Fee. Also world-wide special interest tours. Special holidays for adults and teachers. Full supervision from our own staff

Whernside Adventure Training Centre
Dent, Sedbergh, Cumbria LA10 5RE; Tel (Office) (0158 75) 213
Offers a range of services to groups visiting the Yorkshire Dales. Accommodation: full board or self-catering. Facilities for outdoor pursuits. Also caving. Full details from Centre Manager

YMCA National Centre–Fairthorne Manor
Curdridge, Southampton SO30 2GH; Tel (01489) 785228
An outdoor education and training centre for schools, colleges, Youth Service and industry. Operates all year round catering for all ages. Environmental Education a speciality. Facilities and activities ideal for summer camps, with access to the Rivers Hamble and Solent. Fully programmed or project-based programmes available

Youth Hostels Association
Youth Hostels Association of England and Wales, Trevelyan Hse, St Albans, Herts AL1 2DY; Tel (01727) 855215
The three Associations provide 400 youth hostels offering simple accommodation for individuals and groups exploring the countryside (special arrangements for schools, colleges and Youth Service including Field Study facilities at some hostels). YHA Great Escapes Holidays provide a variety of outdoor activity holidays in various parts of the country
Scottish Youth Hostels Association, 7 Glebe Cres, Stirling FK8 2JA; Tel (01786) 51181
Youth Hostels Association of Northern Ireland, 56 Bradbury Pl, Belfast BT7 1RU; Tel (01232) 324733

Youth Studies
2 Fontwell Dr, Bickley, Bromley, Kent BR2 8AB; Tel 0181-467 9618

GCSE and 'A' level French, German and Maths courses in London during Easter holidays

Voluntary Service and Working Holidays (Home and Abroad)

Community Service Volunteers (CSV)

237 Pentonville Rd, London N1 9NJ; Tel 0171-278 6601; Fax 0171-833 0149
Executive Director Elisabeth Hoodless
Over 2,500 full time young volunteers (16–35) work for 4–12 months with people in need throughout the UK with free food, accommodation and £21.50 per week pocket money. CSV Education encourages community involvement through in education through publication, workshops, training and local projects. Free publications list on request. Youth employment schemes involve young unemployed people in training and work of community benefit. Over 40 media projects nationwide provide the back-up to various social action broadcasts and develop the use of local media by voluntary/community groups

Coordinating Committee for International Voluntary Service

UNESCO, 1 Rue Miollos, 75015 Paris, France; Tel 45 68 27 31/32
President Thierry Picquart
Director Nigel Watt
CCIVS was founded by UNESCO in 1948 as an international non-governmental organisation and coordinating committee for voluntary service world wide. Its current 125 member organisations implement programmes in the fields of environment, literacy, heritage, refugees, health, emergencies development etc. The programmes are mainly carried out through work-camps and consist of a national or international group working on a common project. CCIVS activities include; organisation of seminars and conferences; distribution of various publications on the topic of voluntary service; fund-raising and allocation of means indespensible for members projects; research and analysis in the area of voluntary service; participation in various international forums. Please note that no work-camps are organised directly by CCIVS or UNESCO, and that CCIVS can NOT undertake recruitment of volunteers due to internal exchange regulations of the member organisations. For list of organisations involved in workcamps or volunteering, contact the CCIVS.

European Regional Clearing House for Community Work

179 Rue du Débarcadère, 6001 Marcinelle, Belgium; Tel 36 63 73; Cables INEIASOC–Marcinelle
President P. Rozen (Secretary General, Inter-University European Institute on Social Welfare)
Community work training (4 training sessions in Community work per year); study tours on community work in Belgium and other European countries. Publishes computerised bibliography on community work and a 3 times yearly review *Community Work and Communication* (COMM)

International Voluntary Service

Old Hall, East Bergholt, Colchester CO7 6TQ; Tel (01206) 298215; Fax (01206) 299043
Honorary Treasurer John Finn
Secretary Steve Davies
International Voluntary Service is the UK Branch of Service Civil International–an international peace movement. It exists to promote true international understanding by bringing together people of different nationalities, backgrounds, ages and beliefs in effective community service. It organises about 60 international workcamps a year in Britain, and sends British volunteers to workcamps in more than 30 countries (minimum age 18)

Voluntary Service Overseas

317 Putney Bridge Rd, London SW15 2PN; Tel 0181-780 2266
Director David Green
VSO is committed to the alleviation of poverty and the building of self reliance in communities in the developing world. Volunteers make a commitment to work for at least two years on project where their skills and expertise can be passed on. There are at present over 1,800 volunteers working overseas in more than 44 countries. Forty-five per cent in various forms of education (mainly English language, maths and science) generally in secondary school or teacher training colleges. Others work in medical, agricultural, engineering, technical, and social and business development projects

VSO provides fares, certain grants and residential briefing courses; the employer overseas provides accommodation and a salary based on local rates. Applicants must be 20 and 70 and in good health. Although requests are increasingly for mature and more experienced volunteers. VSO welcomes applications from newly trained teachers and graduates with a relevant degree. Contact our Enquiries Unit for more information

Other Organisations concerned with Voluntary Service Abroad

Church Missionary Society
157 Waterloo Rd, London SE1 8UU; Tel 0171-928 8681
Stuart Buchanan (Short Service Adviser)

The Guide Association
17–19 Buckingham Palace Rd, London SW1W 0PT; Tel 0171-834 6242; Fax 0171-828 8317
Chief Executive Hilary Williams, BA, MBA, MIMgt

Medical Missionary Association
244 Camden Rd, London NW1 9HE; Tel 0171-485 2672; Fax 0171-485 2672
Administrator D.A. Clarke
Stimultates interest in Christian healthcare work overseas, and provides advice and information relating to Christian Health Professionals working in the Developing World

Methodist Association of Youth Clubs
2 Chester Hse, Pages La, Muswell Hill, London N10 1PR; Tel 0181-444 9845; Fax 0181-365 2471
National Secretary Rev David P. Martin

Returned Volunteer Action
1 Amwell St, London EC1R 1UL; Tel 0171-278 0804

The Salvation Army Schools and Colleges Information Service
Territorial Headquarters, 101 Queen Victoria St, London EC4P 4EP; Tel 0171-236 5222 Ext 2112

The Save the Children Fund
Mary Datchelor Hse, 17 Grove La, London SE5 8RD; Tel 0171-703 5400
Education Unit provides a range of teaching packs and resources. Details available from above address

The Scout Association
Community Development Department (Community Relations), Baden-Powell Hse, Queen's Gate, London SW7 5JS; Tel 0171-584 7030; Fax 0171-581 9953

Student Community and Action Development Unit
Oxford Hse, Derbyshire St, London E2 6HG; Tel 0171-739 9001
Finance and Administrative Officer Josie Neale
Development Worker Julie Christie

Development Worker Kelly Drake
S.C.A.D.U. involved in support and development of student voluntary work through Student Community Action groups based in colleges, polytechnics and universities in the UK

Toc H
1 Forest Cl, Wendover, Aylesbury, Bucks HP22 6BT; Tel (01296) 623911; Fax (01296) 696137
Director Michael Lyddiard

United Nations Association International Service
Suite 3A, Hunter Hse, 57 Goodramgate, York YO1 2LS; Tel (01904) 647799; Fax (01904) 652353
UNAIS works in partnership with organisations in Latin America, West Africa and the Middle East to promote long-term development by providing skilled and experienced people to collaborate with locally organised initiatives. We work mainly in the fields of health, agriculture and water engineering
Contact The Recruitment Administrator, UNAIS, Suite 3A, Hunter Hse, 57 Goodramgate, York YO1 2LS; Tel (01904) 647799; Fax (01904) 652353

United Society for the Propagation of the Gospel
Partnership Hse, 157 Waterloo Rd, London SE1 8XA; Tel 0171-928 8681
Short Term Experience Programmes' Officer Cathi Brereton

Volunteer Missionary Movement
Comboni Hse, London Rd, Sunningdale, Ascot, Berks SL5 0JY; Tel (01344) 875380
Recruits Christian volunteers with medical, pastoral, technical or educational qualifications and experience to work in development projects linked with local churches in Africa. Also promotes mission and development within Britain

Working Holidays

This does not claim to be a complete list of firms and organisations offering Voluntary Work and Working Holidays. The inclusion of an editorial entry does not imply approval; equally exclusion does not imply disapproval

ATD-Fourth World
UK Secretariat: 48 Addington Sq, London SE5 7LB; Tel 0171-703 3231; Fax 0171-252 4276
An international human rights organisation whose aim is to combat extreme poverty and social exclusion in partnership with the poorest themselves. Two week long summer workcamps, street workshops and family holidays with very disadvantaged children and their parents in UK and many countries of Europe during the summer. Working weekends and 3 month introductory programmes in UK for people interested in a long term full time commitment (2 years in the case of third world countries), towards the most deprived people in UK or abroad

Atlantis Youth Exchange
Rolf Hofmosgt. 18, 0655 OSLO, Norway; Tel +47-22670043; Fax +47-22686808
Runs Working Guest programme in Norway. Participants live with a Norwegian family, for between one and three months, usually on a farm, and take part in the daily work in exchange for board and lodging and pocket money. Age range 18–30, some agricultural experience preferred

British Trust for Conservation Volunteers
36 St Mary's St, Wallingford, Oxford OX10 0EU; Tel (01491) 839766
Over 600 week long conservation working holidays throughout England, Wales and Northern Ireland. Also international conservation working holidays in countries such as North America, Iceland, Spain and Romania. Tree planting, coastal work, hedgelaying, protection of wildlife habitats etc. Age range: 16–70. From £28 per week including food and accommodation. Also: active local groups network; environmental training courses; practical publications; midweek conservation projects; and advice to schools

Chantiers d'Etudes Mediévales
4 rue du Tonnelet Rouge, 67000, Strasbourg, France; Tel 88 37 17 20
International workcamps on sites for study and restoration of areas dating back to the Middle Ages. 300–500 volunteers needed every summer

Chantiers Jeunesse Maroc
BP 1351, Rabat RP, Morocco
Summer workcamps. Agricultral, or social work in town or country

Chirstlicher Friedensdienst e.V.
Rendelerstrasse 9–11, 6000 Frankfurt 60, Germany
Voluntary social work projects in Germany, Switzerland, France, Netherlands, Belgium, Italy, England, USA. Work with old people, for local disarmament initiatives, maintenance of buildings and homes, play-schemes, etc. Age range: 17–30. Three- to four-week projects in Summer and spring

Christian Movement for Peace
CMP, 186 St Pauls Rd, Balsall Heath, Birmingham B12 8LZ; Tel 0121-446 5704
Voluntary work with children and the disadvantaged, or manual work on international workcamps in Europe and North America during July–September, lasting 2–4 weeks. Also runs international seminars on topical themes, for which travel subsidies are sometimes available. Would particularly welcome people with experience of, or working with people with linguistic, social or physical needs

Christian Work Camps–Australia
PO Box C199, Sydney, 2000
Workcamps on building projects for 3 or 4 weeks immediately after Christmas. No previous building experience required but it is helpful. Volunteers pay for food only. Camps held in Central Australia and NSW

Club du Vieux Manoir
10 rue de la Cossonnerie, Paris 750001, France; Tel 45 018 80 40
National Association. Work includes archaeology, restoration; environmental protection. Several bases throughout France

Concordia (Youth Service Volunteers) Ltd
8 Brunswick Pl, Hove BN3 1ET; Tel (01273) 772086
Non profit making charity. International voluntary youth camps in France, Germany, Spain, Poland, Belgium, Turkey, Tunisia, Czech Republic, CIS and the Baltic States

Corrymeela Community
Ballycastle, Co Antrim, N Ireland; Tel (0126 57) 62626
An ecumenical Christian community working for reconciliation with a wide range of youth, school, family and community groups from all backgrounds and who stay for 3–4 day residentials on the 120-bed complex. During the months of July and August, volunteers are invited to apply to help for 1–3 weeks with family weeks, youth projects and as resource people in arts and crafts, recreation, kitchen, canoeing
8 Upper Cres, Belfast 7, N Ireland; Tel (01232) 325008

Direction Réegionale des Antiquités Historiques du Centre
6 rue de la Manufacture, 45000 Orleans, France; Tel 16-38 53 91 38
Accepts volunteers for one month minimum on archaeological excavations in Orleans, and other sites in the region

Etudes et Chantiers
33 rue Campagne Première, Paris 14e, France; Tel 322 15 61
Work-camps throughout France in school holidays (Christmas, easter, Summer). Some permanent camps open all year. Workcamp leader training sessions.

Conservation, pollution control, restorations, etc. Camps in West Africa and the Magreb. Exchanges with European associations organising work-camps in Holland, Denmark, Germany, Czechoslovakia, etc. Age range: 13+ in France, 18+ abroad

Friday Bridge International Farm Camp
March Rd, Wisbech, Cambs PE14 0LR; Tel (01945) 860255
Fruit picking for individuals and groups. Age range: 17+. Entertainment provided

Frontiers Foundation/Operation Beaver
2615 Danforth Ave Ste 203, Toronto, Ontario M4C 1L6, Canada; Tel 416 690 3930; Fax 416 690 3934
Voluntary service for 18+ age range. Work with native and/or low income Canadian on housing construction and/or renovation. Three months minimum

Gap Activity Projects (GAP) Ltd
44 Queen's Rd, Reading, Berks RG1 4BB; Tel (01734) 594914; Fax (01734) 576634
Offers work opportunities overseas in 32 different countries for school leavers aged 18–19 in their 'year out' before going on to further education. Placements usually last for 6–9 months, leaving time to travel independently. Those interested should apply as early as possible during their last year at school, preferably in September or October. For details please send large s.a.e. to the above address

International Farm Camp
Hall Rd, Tiptree, Colchester, Essex CO5 0QS; Tel (01621) 815496
Fruit picking during the summer vacation. Students only, age limit 18–25. S.a.e. with applications

Internationale Begegnung in Gemeinschaftsdiensten e.V. (IBG)
Schlosserstrasse 28, 70180 Stuttgart, Germany; Tel 01711-649 11 28
International workcamps for 18–30 age range in Germany and Switzerland. Three weeks during summer. Projects such as construction of playgrounds, paths for hiking, or forest work. For further information or a programme or workcamps please write to IBG in Stuttgart

Internationale Jugendgemeinschaftsdienste
D-53113 Bonn, Kaiserstr 43, Germany; Tel 0228/22 10 01
About 100 three-week international work-camps and work shops for groups of 15–20 young people; minimum age 16. Social work, forestry, archaeological digs, reconstruction work, environment protection. Courses and seminars for training and further education of group leaders and staff. Workcamps and seminars take place all over Germany

Jeunesse et Reconstruction
10 rue de Trevise, 75009 Paris; Tel (1) 4770 15 88
International workcamps in North America, Far East, Western and Eastern Europe, Africa. Travel facilities. Grape-picking in France. Long term voluntary work in France. Social and educational long term stays in Europe, Japan, USA, Costa Rica and Kenya

Kibbutz Representatives
1A Accommodation Rd, London NW11 8ED; Tel 0181-458 9235
Working visits to kibbutzim for a minimum of eight weeks. Free board and lodging. Age range: 18–32

Landdienst-Zentralstelle
Postfach 728, Mühlegasse 13, CH-8025 Zürich, Switzerland; Tel 01/261 44 88; Fax 01/261 44 32
Voluntary farmers' assistants placed all year round (mainly spring to autumn) in German or French-speaking Switzerland for a minimum period of three weeks. Age range: 17+. Free board and lodging and at least Swiss Fr20 pocket money a day. Knowledge of either German or French necessary. Registration form available

Les Moulins des Appentis
Le Moulin de Piot, Cheniers, 23220 Bonnat, France; Tel (55) 62 13 20
Work-camps for teenagers and adults in France. Crafts: pottery, woodwork, weaving, mechanics, plumbing, photography, etc
Courses: French language and civilisation, Esperanto
Leisure: canoe-kayak, riding, walking, etc

Musée des Sciences Naturelles et d'Archeologie
191 rue Saint-Albin – 59500, Douai, France; Tel 27 96 90 60
Work on archaeological digs during school summer holidays. Minimum stay 2 weeks

Nothelfergemeinschaft der Freunde e.V.
Postfach 10 15 10, 52349 Dùren, Germany; Tel 02421 76569; Fax 02421 76468
International work-camps in spring, summer and autumn for male and female volunteers aged 16–26 in Germany, Israel, several African countries, India, Brasilia and other countries. Free board and lodging. Work with the underprivileged, in social institutions and in catastrophe areas. Can place volunteers with associated organisations elsewhere in Europe. Camps outside Germany for Germans only

Österreichischer Bauorden (IBO-Austria)
A-1-1031 Vienna, Hörnesgasse 3, Austria; Tel 01222 7135254; Fax 01222 7138118
Volunteers for community building projects and international exchange. Minimum age 18 years. Engagement only during July and August for periods of 3–4 weeks

Project 67 Ltd
10 Hatton Gdn, London EC1N 8AH; Tel 0171-831 7626
The Kibbutz/Moshav working holidays specialist, for students and young people between the ages of 18–35

Project Trust
Hebridean Centre, Isle of Coll, Argyll PA78 6TE; Tel (0187 93) 444
Projects in Africa, Southern and Central America, Middle and Far East for young men and women aged between 17 and 19 who are about to leave school. Work as teacher-aides, in social service, in development projects etc., for a period of twelve months. Applications must be made by the 1st December for departure overseas in the following August/September

The Royal Society for the Protection of Birds
Reserves Management Department, RSPB, The Lodge, Sandy, Bedfordshire SG19 2DL; Tel (01767) 680551
Residential voluntary wardening schemes on 30 reserves throughout the UK

The Scottish Conservation Projects Trust
Balallan Hse, 24 Allan Pk, Stirling FK8 2QG; Tel (01786) 479696; Fax (01786) 465359

Scripture Union
Scripture Union Hse, 130 City Rd, London EC1V 2NJ; Tel 0171-782 0013; Fax 0171-782 0014
Working with children, young people and families for 1–2 weeks on Christian holidays and missions, mainly July–September. Minimum age 18

SIW International Volunteers Projects
(SIW Inetrnationale Vrijwilligersprojecten)
Two- or Three-week voluntary projects with international group during July and August. Free board and lodging. Combination of work, discussions and excursions and leisure time. Nature conservation projects; Third World solidarity projects; social projects; reconstruction projects, etc
Age range 18–30. British volunteers should apply to QISP, Friends Hse, Euston Hse, Euston Rd, London NW1 2BY or UNA–Wales, Temple of Peace, Cathays Pk, Cardiff, CF1 3AP, Wales

TEJO (Tutmonda Esperantista Junulara Organizo)
World Organisation of Young Esperantists, Nieuwe Binneweg 176, 3015 BJ, Rotterdam, Netherlands; Tel 01104 361539; Fax 01104 361751
Seminars throughout the year on social, political, cultural and linguistic themes in Esperanto (occasionally using other languages). Promotes international travel and understanding by organising an International Youth Conference every summer and a free international host service for Esperanto-speakers, and coordinating the activities of 36 national branches

Tunstead International Farm Camp
C/o R. and J.M. Place Ltd, Church Farm, Tunstead, Norwich, Norfolk NR12 8RQ; Tel (01692) 536337
International farm camp. May to October. Fruit picking and market gardening. Age range: 17+

Union REMPART
1 rue des Guillemites, 75004 Paris, France; Tel (1)-42 71 96 55; Fax (1)-42 71 73 00
Work-camps in all parts of France at weekends and in Easter and summer holidays. Age range, normally 14+. Restoration and conservation work on historic monuments and archaeology

Zentralstelle für Auslandsabteilung (ZAV)
Feuerbachstrasse 42–46, D-6000 Frankfurt/Main 1, Germany; Tel 69-7111.0
Z.A.V. is the federal government office which deals, among other matters, with applicants for foreigners for both temporary and permanent employment

24 Overseas Education

European Organisations

Commission of the European Communities

200 rue de la Loi, 1049 Bruxelles; Tel 235.1111; Telex 21877 COMEU B
President Jacques Delors
Commissioner responsible for Education, Training and Youth V. Papandreou
Chef de Cabinet A. Trifyllis

Task Force Human Resources Education, Training and Youth

Director Hywel C. Jones
Covers vocational training, higher education, continuing training, education at secondary and post secondary levels; youth policy

European Communities Commission, London Office

8 Storey's Gate, London SW1P 3AT; Tel 0171-973 1992
Head of Office John Drew
Education Matters Dr Peter Dixon
Information Unit Carlo Pau

EC Members: Education Ministries

Belgium

Flemish Ministry of Education

Rijksadministrarief Centrum, Arcadengebouw Blk F, 1010 Bruxelles; Tel 02/210 5511

Ministry of National Education (French Speaking)

Cité administrative de l'Etat, rue Royale 204, 1010 Brixelles; Tel 02/210 5511

Conseil Central de l'Enseignment Catholique, Siège Social et Services Françaises 16 rue Edouard Wachen, 400 Liège; Tel 041/52 36666

Nederlandstalige diensten 1 Guimardstraat, 1040 Brussel; Tel 02/513 6880

Denmark

Undervisningsministeriet

Frederiksholms Kanal 21, DK-1220, Copenhagen K; Tel 33 92 50 00
Minister of Education Ole Vig Jensen

France

Ministry of National Education

110 rue de Granelle, 75357 Paris; Tel (1) 45 50 10 10
Minister of National Education M. René Nouon

Federal Republic of Germany

Staendige Konferenze den Kultursminister der Laender in der Bundesrepublik Deutschland

5300 Bonn 1 Nassetr. 8; Tel Bonn 501-0; Fax Bonn 501-301

Federal Ministry of Education and Science

Heinemannstrasse 2, D-53175 Bonn; Tel Bonn 57-0
Minister of Education and Science Prof Dr Karl-Hans Laermann

Federal Ministry for Economic Co-operation

5300 Bonn, Karl-Marx-Strasse 4–6; Tel 5350
Federal Minister Dr Jürgen Warnke

Ireland

Department of Education

Marlborough St, Dublin 1; Tel (00 353) 734700
Minister for Education Mary O'Rourke, TD
Primary Branch
Fl 1, Block 1, Irish Life Centre, Dublin 1; Tel (00 353) 734700
Post-Primary Branch
Apollo Hse, Dublin 2; Tel (00 353) 734700

Hawkins Hse, Dublin 2; Tel (00 353) 734700

Fl 3, Block 1, Irish Life Centre, Dublin 1; Tel (00 353) 734700
Examinations Section
Cornamaddy, Athlone, Co Westmeath; Tel (01902) 74621

Italy

Ministero Della Pubblica Istuzione

Viale Trastevere 76-A, 00153 Roma; Tel 5859
Secretary of State for Education Franca Falcucci

Luxembourg

Ministère de l'Education Nationale

29 rue Aldringen, L-2926 Luxembourg City; Tel 352-478-1
Minister for Education M. Marc Fischbach

The Netherlands

The Ministry of Education and Science

PO Box 25000, 2700 LZ Zoetermeer; Tel 0179 531911
Minister for Education and Science J.M.M. Ritzen

Directorate of International Relations

As above
Contact S.W. van den Ingh

Council of British Independent Schools in the European Communities (COBISEC)

Secretariat, c/o The British School of Brussels 3080, Leuvensesteenweg 19, 3080 Tervuren, Belgium; Tel 322-767 4700; Fax 322-767 8070
Chairman Sir Dick H. Pantlin, CBE
Treasurer M.W.G. Roberts

Belgium

British Primary School, Stationstraat 6, 3080 Tervuren, Belgium; Tel 32 2 767 3098 *Headmistress* Dorothy Guy, CertEd

British School of Brussels, Leuvensesteenweg 19, 3080, Tervuren, Belgium; Tel 32 2 767 4700; Fax 32 2 767 8070 *Principal* Jennifer M. Bray, BA, MA

Brussels English Primary School, Av Franklin Roosevelt 23, 1050 Brussels, Belgium; Tel 32 2 648 4311; Fax 32 2 687 2968 *Director* C.A. Gellar

Brussels English Primary School 2–Limal 13 Rue Deladrière, 1300 Limal, Belgium; Tel 32 10 417227; Fax 32 2 6872968 *Director* C.A. Gellar

France

Mougins School, Ave Dr Maurice Donat 615, BP 101, 06250 Mougins, Cedex, France; Tel 33 93 9015 47; Fax 33 93 75 3140 *The Principal* Dr J. Jackson, BA, PhD

British School of Paris, 38 Quai de l'Ecluse, 78290 Croissy-sur-Seine, France; Tel 33 1 3976 2900; Fax 33 1 3976 3608 *Principal* M.W. Honour, BA, MSc

Germany

British Embassy Prep. School, Tulpenbaumweg 42, D 5300, 53177 Bonn, Germany; Tel (49 228) 32 31 66; Fax (49 228) 32 39 58 *Headmaster* Peter Ward, (AKC)

British High School, Bonn, Friesdorferstrasse 57, D 5300, 5300 Bonn, Germany; Tel (49 228) 31 12 57; Fax (49 228) 31 92 69 *Headmaster* S.V. Wilkerson, MSc

Greece

St Catherine's British Embassy School, C/o The British Embassy, Plutarchou 1, 106 75, Athens, Greece; Tel 30 1 28 29 750; Fax 30 1 28 26 415 *Headmaster* J. Hawkins

Italy

New School, Via della Camillucia 669, 00135 Rome, Italy; Tel 39 6 329 4269; Fax 39 6 329 7546 *Head Teacher* Josette Fusco

Sir James Henderson British School of Milan, Viale Lombardia 66, 20131 Milan, Italy; Tel 39 2 261 3299; Fax 39 2 261 10500 *Headmaster* C.T. Gill Leech, MA

St George's English School, Via Cassia, Km 16, 00123 Rome, Italy; Tel 39 6 3790 141; Fax 39 6 379 2490 *Principal* B. Gardner, MA

Norway

British International School PO Box 7531, Skillebekk, 0205 Oslo 2, Norway; Tel 47 2 444 916; Fax 47 2 551 135 *Headmistress* M.G. Stark, MBE, MA

Stavanger British School, Gauselbakken 107, 4032, Gausel, Norway; Tel 47 4 57 55 99; Fax 47 4 57 15 16 *Headmistress* Z. Roisli, CertEd

The Netherlands

The British School in The Netherlands, Boerderji Rosenburgh, Rosenburgherlaan 2, 2252 BA Voorschoten, The Netherlands; Tel 31 71 616966; Fax 31 71 611412 *Principal* M.J. Cooper, BA, MIBiol

British School of Amsterdam, Jan van Eijckstraat 21, 1077 LG Amsterdam, The Netherlands; Tel 31 206 797840; Fax 31 20 675 8396 *Headmaster* M.W.G. Roberts

Portugal

Colégio International de Vilamoura Apartado 856, 8125 Vilamoura, Portugal; Tel 351 89 366585; Fax 351 89 360888 *Headmaster* L.A. James

St Julian's School (English Section), Carcavelos, 2777, Parede Codex, Portugal; Tel 351 1 457 0140; Fax 351 1 456 6817 *Headmaster* D. Styan, OBE, BSc(Econ), DipEd, FRSA

Spain

Aloha College El Angel, Nueva Andalucia, Marbella, 29660 Malaga, Spain; Tel 34 5 2814133; Fax 34 5 2812729 *Headmaster* P.I. Burnett, MA, PGCE

Baleares International School, San Agustin, 07015 Palma de Mallorca; Tel 34 71 401 812; Fax 34 71 700 319 *Headmaster* J.B. Wiggins, BSc

Bellver International College c/Jose Costa Femer 5, Marivent-Calamayor, 07015 Palma De Mallorca, Spain; Tel 34 71 40 1679/40 4263; Fax 34 71 40 1762 *Director* M. Muirhead

English Montessori School, Avdo La Salle S/N Aravaca, 28023 Madrid, Spain; Tel 34 1 357 2667/357 2126; Fax 34 1 307 1543 *Headmaster* F.J. Poppleton, BA, MA

King's College, Paseo de los Andes, Soto de Vinuelas, 28760 Madrid, Spain; Tel 34 1 803 4800; Fax 34 1 803 65 57 *Headmaster* Dr G.R. Percy, PhD, BA

Runnymeade College, Canino Anch 87, La Moraleja 28109, Alcobencas, Madrid, Spain; Tel 34 1 650 83 02; Fax 34 1 650 82 36 *Headmaster* A.F. Powell, BA

Sierra Bernia School, La Caneta S/N, San Rafael, 03580 Alfaz del Pi, Alicante, Spain; Tel 34 6 6875149 *Headmaster* D.M. Allan, BA

Sweden

British Primary School of Stockholm, Ostra Valhallavagen 17, S182 62 Djursholm, Sweden; Tel 46 8 755 23 75; Fax 46 8 755 26 35 *Headmistress* G. Elliot, CertEd

Switzerland

Aiglon College, 1885 Chesiéres-Villars, Switzerland; Tel 41 25 35 27 21; Fax 41 25 35 28 11 *Headmaster* R. Mcdonald, MA

St George's School, Switzerland, 1815 Clarens, Montreux, Switzerland; Tel 41 21 964 3411; Fax 41 21 964 4932 *Principal* G. Zund

Council of Europe

F-67075 Strasbourg CEDEX, France; Tel + 33 88 41 20 00; Telex 870943F

Secretariat

Secretary General Daniel Tarschys (SW)
Deputy Secretary General Peter Leuprecht

Directorate of Education, Culture and Sport

Director Raymond Weber

European Youth Centre

Director Franco Marziale; Tel 88 41 23 00 (I)

European Youth Foundation

Executive Director André-Jacques Dodin (UK)

Parliamentary Assembly

President Miguel Angel Martinez (Spain)
Clerk H. Klebes (FRG)

Cultural and Education Committee

Chairman L. Fischer (Germany)
Secretary C. Grayson

Science and Technology Committee

Chairman R. Roseta (Portugal)
Secretary B. Perin

Council for Cultural Co-operation

Directorate of Education, Culture and Sport, Council of Europe, F-67075 Strasbourg-CEDEX, France; Tel (88) 41 20 00; Fax 88412788; Telex 870943
Intergovernmental steering committee responsible for the Council of Europe's work on education, culture and cultural heritage, in which 41 States take part
At present major projects are being carried out on: secondary education; language learning; adult education; access to higher education; legislative reform in higher education; books, reading and translation; cultural policies; heritage conservation policies. Other activities include: a teacher bursaries scheme; a network of national information centres on academic mobility and equivalence; regular meetings of directors of education research institutes; a European Education Thesaurus; training of cultural administrators; co-operation with and assistance for countries in Central and Eastern Europe

European Council of International Schools ECIS

21 Lavant St, Petersfield, Hampshire GU32 3EL; Tel (01730) 268244; Fax (01730) 267914
Executive Secretary T.M. Maybury
Administrative Officer Piers Armstrong
ECIS is an independent, non-profit membership organisation representing the interest of more than 360 international schools, in Europe and throughout the World, which provides education for the children of the local expatriate community. Services include teacher recruitment and professional development, assistance with curriculum development admission to university, and school inspection and accreditation. The Council publishes a Directory, price £22.50, detailing all its members and listing some 900 international schools throughout the World

European Cultural Foundation

Jan van Goyenkade 5, 1075 HN Amsterdam; Tel 31 20-6760222; Fax 31 20-6752231
President HRH Margriet, Princess of the Netherlands
Secretary General R. Stephan
Founded 1954 as a non-governmental organisation, supported by private sources, to promote cross-cultural exchange on a multilateral European level. The Foundation initiates and manages its own programmes and projects, manages and administers projects for third parties; administers a limited grants programme in a narrow field, giving priority to Eastern and Central Europe and the Mediterranean; gives network support to representative committees in 20 European countries and to a number of independent Institutes and Centres, such as the Centre Européen de la Culture Genève, European Institute of Education and Social Policy, Paris, Institute for European Environmental Policy; Arnhem, Bonn, Brussels, London and Paris, European Cooperation Fund, Brussels, European Institute for the Media, Düsseldorf, European Foundation Centre, Brussels, Fund for Central and East European Book Project, Amsterdam, Institute for Human Sciences, Vienna, Foundation East/West Parliamentary Practice Project, Amsterdam, Management and service contracts exist for the following: EURYDICE, Brussels. Publications include *Facts and Figures* (Annual Report), *Newsletter* (2x year)

European Educational Research Trust

76 Alfriston Rd, London SW11 6NW; Tel 0171-228 4157
Secretary Lynda M. Dawson

The promotion of Education and Research by the advancement of schemes for the teaching and study of the history, geography, science, languages, art, literature and cultures of the countries of Europe. Provides grants for approved projects

Institut Français d'Ecosse

13 Randolph Cres, Edinburgh EH3 7TT; Tel 0131-225 5366; Fax 0131-220 0648
Director Stéphane Crouzat
General Secretary Rene Levy
Director of Studies Jocelyne Lemoine
The French Institute represents in Scotland the cultural division of the French Ministry of Foreign Affairs. The vocation of the French Institute is to spread the knowledge of French language and culture in Scotland and to promote cultural co-operation between the two countries
Every year, the French institute organises a series of French classes for all levels. There is a public library, gallery, video club, and access to French satellite TV
A lending service offering books, magazines, slides, cassettes and CD's provides documentation of all kinds on French life, literature and society

Institut Français D'Ecosse A Glasgow

7 Bowmont Gdns, Glasgow G12; Tel 0141-357 3632
Director Mélle Bénédicte Madinier
The Institut Français represents the cutural division of the French Ministry of Foreign Affairs in Scotland. Its aim is to promote cultural cooperation between the two countries. Facilities include a lending library

Other Organisations

University Association for Contemporary European Studies

UACES Secretariat, King's College London, Strand, London WC2R 2LS; Tel 0171-240 0206; Fax 0171-240 0206
Chairman Prof M. Smith

Centre for Educational Research and Innovation

Directorate for Education, Employment, Labour and Social Affairs, OECD, Château de la Muette, 2 rue André Pascal, Paris 16e; Tel 45 24 82 00
Director Thomas Alexander

CESA Languages Abroad

Western Hse, Malpas, Truro TR1 1SQ; Tel (01872) 225300; Fax (01872) 225400
Independent language consultancy providing a comprehensive advisory service on language courses abroad, based on personal experience and first hand knowledge of the centres. Areas covered include intensive language programmes for business, short term/holiday courses, examination courses and courses for students. Languages on offer include: French, German, Spanish, Italian, Dutch, Japanese, Russian, Chinese, Portuguese and Greek

Council on International Educational Exchange (CIEE)

33 Seymour Pl, London W1H 6AT; Tel 0171-706 3008; Fax 0171-724 8468
CIEE, a private, non-profit making organisation, was founded in 1947 to further international education. CIEE develops, facilitates and administers a wide variety of international programmes for individuals and groups involved in education, from school teachers to students and faculty of further and higher education institutions, to educational administrators and officials. UK programmes are both outgoing and incoming, and include work exchanges with the USA and Canada, English teaching opportunities in Japan, Japanese teacher visits to the UK, summer, semester and year-long study at British, American and overseas universities for the general public and students, worldwide faculty development seminars, custom-designed programmes for education officials and administrators

don Quijote UK, In–Country Language Courses Ltd

2/4 Stoneleigh Park Rd, Stoneleigh, Epsom, Surrey KT19 0QR; Tel 0181-786 8081; Fax 0181-786 8086
Don Quijote is Europe's largest organisation for Spanish language courses in Spain, operating centres in Barcelona, Granada, Salamanca and Màlaga. also offers advice on funding, transport, insurance, accommodation, excursions, local language courses, study materials and Spanish events (local and national). Will organise parents' evenings and information days on Spanish in Spain at universities, colleges and other educational institutions

Education Policy Information Centre (EPIC Europe)

NFER, The Mere, Upton Pk, Slough, Berks SL1 2DQ; Tel (01753) 574123; Fax (01753) 691632
Head Dr Joanna Le Métais, PhD, FIL, FRSA
Senior Information Officer Gill Holt, BA, ALA, PGDipLibInfMan
Senior Information Officer Heledd Hayes, PhD, PGDipLib
Information Officer Barbara Dickinson
see also National Foundation for Educational Research in England and Wales, Chapter 14
EPIC Europe is the official link for England, Wales and Northern Ireland to the EURYDICE education policy information network of the European Union. It provides information on education policy issues to LEA education officers and central government staff and to their counterparts in the Member States of the European Union

English Speaking Board (International) Ltd

26A Princes St, Southport, Merseyside PR8 1EQ; Tel (01704) 501730
President Christabel Burniston, MBE

English-Speaking Union of the Commonwealth

Dartmouth Hse, 37 Charles St, London W1X 8AB; Tel 0171-493 3328
Chairman The Baroness Brigstocke
Director of Education Simon Freeman

European Association of Teachers

Honorary Secretary (UK Section) M.E. Duce; Tel 0181-340 9136

European Bureau of Adult Education

EAEA–EBAE Amersfoort Office, PO Box 367, 3800 AJ Amersfoort, The Netherlands; Tel ++ 31 33 654116; Fax ++ 31 33 654116
Director W. Bax

EAEA Organisation and Development Office Hotel d'Entitas, C/ Emporda 33, E 08020 Barcelona, Spain; Tel ++ 34 3 2780294; Fax ++ 34 3 2780174
Contact Carme Vendrell

EAEA Relations with European and International Organisms, Kardinaal Mercierplein 1, B 2800 Mechelen; Tel ++ 32 15 401852; Fax ++ 32 15 411858 *Contact* Lucien Mosselaers

EAEA Information and Documentation Office
Museokatu 18 A 9, 00100 Helsinki 10, Finland; Tel ++358 01 449980/449557; Fax ++ 358 01 441794 *Contact* Eeva Sirralo

European Centre for the Development of Vocational Training

CEDEFOP, Bundesallee 22, D-10717 Berlin, Germany
Director Dr Ernst Piehl
Deputy Director Dott Corrado Politi

European Educational Research Trust

41 The Ridings, East Preston, Littlehampton, West Sussex BN16 2TW; Tel (01903) 772494
Cecil Dawson, OBE

European Movement

Europe Hse, 158 Buckingham Palace Rd, London SW1W 9TR; Tel 0171-824 8388; Fax 0171-824 8124
Director Stephen Woodard

European Trade Union Committee for Education (ETUCE)

155 Boulevard, E. Jacqmain, 1210 Bruxelles, Belgium
President Alain Monchoux

International Secretariate for Centres for European Education

Ministério da Educaçào, Av 5 de Outubro 35-7¼, 1000 Lisbon, Portugal
c/o Dr M. Belard

London Europe Society

47 New Rd, Digswell, Welwyn, Herts AL6 0AQ; Tel (01438) 712999
Chairman Derek Prag, Honorary MEP

North Atlantic Treaty Organisation (NATO)

1110 Brussels, Belgium; Tel (32-2) 7284111; Fax (0132-2) 7284579; Telex 23867 OTAN/NATO
Office of Information and Press

UK Centre for European Education

The Central Bureau, Seymour Mews Hse, Seymour Mews, London W1H 9PE; Tel 0171-486 5101
Secretary A.H. Male, BA
Assistant Secretary K.R. Tillin, BA

Western European Union

4, rue de la Régence, 1000 Bruxelles; Tel (32) 02-500 4411; Fax (32) 02-511 3517
Secretary General J. Cutileiro

European Schools

The nine European schools were set up by agreement among the nine member states of the EEC to provide a multinational education for the children of staff employed in the institutions of the European Communities. They are day schools with a 4–19 age range, organised in separate language sections (German, English, Danish, Spanish, French, Greek, Italian, Dutch and Portuguese, depending on local circumstances. For instance, the UK school only has German, English, French, Italian and Dutch language sections). Pupils follow a common curriculum leading in the secondary school to the European Baccalaureate, the schools' own leaving examination

Belgium

European School, 46 Avenue du Vert Chasseur, 1180 Brussels, Belgium J.G. Marshall
No of pupils 3,385

European School, Europawijk 100, 2400 Mol, Belgium; Tel 0114 588835 A. Rodrigues
No of pupils 722

Holland

European School, Molenweidtje 5, Postbus 99, NL-1860 AB Bergen (NH), Holland; Tel 32-2208 90109 I. Murphy
No of pupils 830

Italy

European School, Via Montello 118, 21100, Varese, Italy; Tel 01332 286132/501 285 062; Fax 01332 283782 Jacques Steiwer
No of pupils 1,250

Luxembourg

European School, 23 Boulevard Konrad Adenauer, L-1115 Luxembourg-Kirchberg, Luxembourg; Tel 43 20 82; Fax 43 67 38 Renée Christmann
No of pupils 3,250

Germany

European School, Albert-Schweitzer-Strasse 1, Karlsruhe D-76139, Germany; Tel 683 001 J. Hoffmann
No of pupils 1,250

European School, Elise-Aulinger-Str 21, D-81739 München; Tel 6 37 26 11 Yv Heumann
No of pupils 1,000

United Kingdom

European School, Culham, Abingdon, Oxford OX14 3DZ; Tel (01235) 522621; Fax (01235) 554609 M. Barco
No of pupils 910

Commonwealth Education

Commonwealth Institute

Kensington High St, London W8 6NQ; Tel 0171-603 4535; Fax 0171-602 7374
Acting Chairman David Thompson
Director-General Stephen Cox
The Commonwealth Institute is the centre for Commonwealth education and culture in Britain. Its purpose is to promote a greater understanding of the Commonwealth countries, through a continual programme of exhibitions, education and cultural activities
Situated in the spectacular tent–shaped building in Holland Park, the Institute houses 3 floors of exhibition galleries, designed to show the history, landscape, wildlife, arts, crafts and cultures of the Commonwealth countries. Special exhibitions, live events and cultural festivals are promoted and a diverse Education Programme offers workshops, conferences, educational resources and services.

24 Overseas Education

The *Commonwealth Resource Centre* offers a wealth of information on the Commonwealth including a loan service with up–to–date materials to support teachers working within the National Curriculum and the educational field. Materials include videos, slides, records, posters, wallcharts and information books. A reference collection is also available

The *Education & Curriculum Development* section comprises a team of curriculum developers who work with teachers and pupils on materials arising from the National Curriculum to produce classroom useable packs and handbooks. Conferences, seminars, workshops and in–service training are regularly organised for teachers

The *Literature Unit* promotes a programme of literary events and houses the *Commonwealth Literature Library* which has one of the best and most accessible collections of novels, poems, plays and critical writings from Commonwealth countries

Commonwealth Secretariat, Education Department, Human Resource Development Division

Marlborough Hse, Pall Mall, London SW1Y 5HX; Tel 0171-747 6280; Fax 0171-747 6287

Director, Education Department (HRDD) Vacancy

The Education Department supports educational development in member states by means of commissioned studies, meetings, consultancies and publications and promotes cooperative activities. These are agreed by regular conferences of Commonwealth Education Ministers; eleventh, Barbados 1990

Commonwealth Scholarship Commission in the United Kingdom

Chairman Sir Michael Caine
Joint Secretary A. Christodoulou, CBE
Executive Secretary T.G. Illsley Association of Commonwealth Universities, 36 Gordon Sq, London WC1H 0PF; Tel 0171-387 8572; Fax 0171-387 2655

Offers full support Scholarships and Fellowships for study/research in Commonwealth Countries to candidates nominated by Commonwealth governments and universities

Council for Education in the Commonwealth

c/o LCCI Examinations Board, Marlowe Hse, Station Rd, Sidcup, Kent DA15 7BJ; Tel 0181-302 0261; Fax 0181-302 4169

Contact The Secretary Council for Education in the Commonwealth, c/o LCCI Examinations Board, Marlowe Hse, Station Rd, Sidcup, Kent DA15 7BJ; Tel 0181-302 0261; Fax 0181-302 4169
Patron Lord Peston
Patron Lord Thomson of Monifieth, KT, PC
Patron Baroness Young, PC
Joint Parliamentary Chairman Win Griffiths, MP
Joint Parliamentary Chairman Simon Hughes, MP
Joint Parliamentary Chairman Mark Robinson, MP
Executive Chairman Prof C.D. Sims, OBE
Deputy Executive Chairman P.R.C. Williams
Deputy Executive Chairman M.S. Dalziel, CBE
Honorary Secretary T. Bottomley (Meetings)
Honorary Secretary I.W. Hannaford (Membership)
Honorary Treasurer B.H. Taylor
Activities Secretary J.B. May
Administrative Secretary R. Moore-Devereux
Newsletter Editor M. Stack

The CEC was set up to stimulate public interest in and to create an informed opinion on the problems of education in the Commonwealth and on the contribution of Britain towards these problems. It originated from a parliamentary discussion group, formed at the time of the first Commonwealth Education Conference in 1959, and came into formal being later that year. Its concerns now cover the contribution of the European Community partners, as well as Britain, to Commonwealth education

Australia

London Offices

Enquiries concerning education in particular States should be address to the repective Agents-General

The Office of the Agent-General for Victoria, Victoria Hse, Melbourne Pl, Strand, London WC2B 4LG; Tel 0171-836 2656

The Office of the Agent-General for South Australia, 115 Strand, London WC2R 0AJ; Tel 0171-240 8585

Government of Western Australia European Office, 115 Strand, London WC2; Tel 0171-240 2881

Australian Offices

Australian Government

Library Department of Employment, Education and Training, GPO 9880, Canberra, A.C.T. 2601, Australia

New South Wales

Department of School Education, 55 Market St, Sydney N.S.W. 2000

Victoria

Directorate of School Education, GPO Box 4367, Melbourne 3001, Victoria, Australia; Tel 628 2211

Queensland

Queensland Education Department, PO Box 33, 50 Albert St, Brisbane, Queensland 4002, Australia; Tel (07) 237 0111; Fax (07) 229 0996, (07) 229 0265

South Australia

Department for Education and Children's Services, Education Centre, 31 Flinders St, Adelaide, South Australia 5000

Tasmania

Department of Education and the Arts, 116 Bathurst St, Hobart, Tasmania 7000

Barbados

London Office: Office of the High Commissioner for Barbados, 1 Great Russell St, London WC1B 3JY; Tel 0171-631 4975

Ministry of Education, Jemmott's La, St Michael, Barbados

Botswana

London Office Botswana High Commission, 6 Stratford Pl, London W1N 9AE; Tel 0171-499 0031

Ministry of Education, Private Bag 005, Gaborone, Botswana

Canada

London Office: Canadian High Commission, Canada Hse Trafalgar Sq, London SW1Y 5BJ; Tel 0171-629 9492

Alberta

c/o Office of the Agent General for Alberta, Alberta Hse 1 Mount St, London W1Y 5AA; Tel 0171-491 3430; Fax 0171-629 2296

British Columbia

London Office Office of the Agent General for British Columbia, 1–3 Regent St SW1Y 4NS; Tel 0171-930 6857; Fax 0171-930 2012

The Deputy Minister of Education, Victoria B.C. Canada V8V 2M4; Tel 01101 604 356 2479; Fax 01101 604 356 9121

Manitoba

The Deputy Minister of Education and Training, Rm 162 Legislative Bldg, Winnipeg R3C 0V8

New Brunswick

The Deputy Minister of Education, PO Box 6000, Fredericton, N.B. E3B 5H1

Northwest Territories

Deputy Minister of Education, Department Responsible for Education, Culture and Employment Programmes, PO Box 1320, Yellowknife, Northwest Territories X1A 2L9; Tel 403 920 6240; Fax 403 873 0155

Nova Scotia

London Office of the Agent General for Nova Scotia 14 Pall Mall SW1Y 5LU

The Deputy Minister and Chief Director of Education, Department of Education, Halifax B3J 2S9

Prince Edward Island

The Deputy Minister of Education, Charlottetown C1A 7N8

Québec

Québec Government Office, 59 Pall Mall, London SW1Y 5JH; Tel 0171-930 8314

Ministry of Education, 1035 Rue De La Cheurotière, Québec G1R 5A5; Tel 418-643 7095

Newfoundland and Labrador

The Deputy Minister of Education, PO Box 8700 St John's, Newfoundland A1B 4J6

Cyprus

London Office: Cyprus High Commission, 93 Park St, London W1Y 4ET; Tel 0171-499 8272/071-493 6200
Cultural Counsellor K. Avgoustinos, BA, AMIEd(Lon)

Cyprus

Ministry of Education, Nicosia

Fiji

London Office: Fiji Embassy, 34 Hyde Park Gate, London SW7 5BN; Tel 0171-584 3661/2

Fiji

Ministry of Education, Selbourne St, Suva

The Gambia

London Office: The Gambia High Commission, 57 Kensington Ct, London W8 5DG; Tel 0171-937 6316/7/8

The Gambia

Ministry of Education, Bedford Pl, Banjul

Ghana

London Office: Office of the High Commissioner for Ghana, 104 Highgate Hill, London N6 5HE; Tel 0181-342 8686
Minister/Counsellor Sam Okine
Education Section:
104 Highgate Hill, London N6 5HE

Ghana

Ministry of Education, PO Box M45, Accra

Gibraltar

Department of Education, 40 Town Range, Gibraltar
Minister for Education The Honourable J.L. Moss; Tel 40410
Director of Education J.J. Alcantara, MA, DipEd; Tel 77486
Assistant Director V. Latin; Tel 78638
Higher Executive Officer G. Catania; Tel 75987
General Education Adviser L. Lester, MEd, BSc(Hons); Tel 71430
Assistant Education Adviser P. Scott; Tel 71430
Educational Psychologist A. Trinidad, MA, BEd(Hons); Tel 75373
Education Welfare Officer J. Zammitt; Tel 75373; Fax 71564

Guyana

London Office: Office of the High Commissioner for Guyana, 3 Palace Ct, Baywater Rd, London W2 4LP; Tel 0171-2292 7684; Fax 0171-727 9809

Guyana

Ministry of Education, Brickdam, Georgetown; Tel 2-58511

India

London Office; Education and Science Department, High Commission of India, India Hse, Aldwych, London WC2B 4NA; Tel 0171-836 8484

Union Government

Ministry of Human Resource, Dept of Education, Shastri Bhavan, New Delhi

State Government Departments

Andra Pradesh
Department of Education, Hyderabad
Arunchal Pradesh
Department of Education, Itanagar
Assam
Department of Education, Dispur
Bihar
Department of Education, Patna
Goa
Department of Education, Panaji
Gujarat
Department of Education, Gandhi Nagar
Haryana
Department of Education, Chandigarh
Himachal Pradesh
Department of Education, Simla
Jammu and Kashmir
Department of Education, Jammu/Srinagar
Kerala
Department of Education, Trinadram
Madhya Pradesh
Department of Education, Bhopal
Maharashtra
Department of Education, Bombay
Manipur
Department of Education, Imphal
Meghalaya
Department of Education, Shillong

Mizoram
Department of Education, Aizawal
Nagaland
Department of Education, Kohima
Orissa
Department of Education, Bhubneswar
Punjab
Department of Education, Chandigarh
Tripura
Department of Education, Agartala
Rajasthan
Department of Education, Jaipur
Uttar Pradesh
Department of Education, Lucknow
West Bengal
Department of Education, Calcutta
Sikkim
Department of Education, Gangtok
Tamilnadu
Department if Education, Madras
Karnataka
Department of Education, Bangalore

Union Territories

Andaman and Nicobar Islands
Department of Education, Port Blair
Chandigarh
Department of Education, Chandigarh
Dadra Nagar and Haveli
Department of Education, Silvassa
Daman and Diu
Department of Education, Panaji
Dehli
Department of Education, Delhi
Lakshaweep
Department of Education, Kavaratti
Pondicherry
Department of Education Pondicherry

Jamaica

London Office; Office of the High Commissioner for Jamaica, 1–2 Prince Consort Rd, South Kensington, London SW7 2BZ; Tel 0171-823 9911

Jamaica

Ministry of Education, 2 National Heroes Circle, Kingston 4, Jamaica

Kenya

London Office; Kenya High Commission, 45 Portland Pl, London W1N 4AS; Tel 0171-636 2371/5
High Commissioner J.K.A. Ruto
Education Attaché P.H, Dido

Kenya

Ministry of Education, PO Box 30040, Nairobi, Kenya; Tel 00 2542 334411
Permanent Secretary S. Lesirma
Director of Education E. Njoka

Kiribati

Secretary for Education, Ministry of Education, Science and Technology, PO Box 263, Bikenibeu, Tarawa, Kiribati

Lesotho

London Office; High Commission of the Kingdom of Lesotho, 10 Collingham Rd, London SW5 0NR; Tel 0171-373 8581/2

Lesotho

Ministry of Education, PO Box MS47, Maseru; Tel 323045

Malawi

London Office; Office of the High Commissioner for Malawi, 33 Grosvenor St, London W1X 0DE; Tel 0171-491 4172/7

Malawi

The Ministry of Education and Culture, Private Bag 328, Capital City, Lilingwe 3, Malawi

Malaysia

London Office; Office of the High Commissioner for Malaysia, 45–46 Belgrave Sq, London SW1X 8QT; Tel 0171-235 8033

Students' Department, 44 Bryanston Sq, London W1H 8AJ; Tel 0171-723 2265

Malaysian Tourist Office, 57 Trafalgar Sq, London WC2N 5DU; Tel 0171-930 7932

Malaysia

The Minister for Education, Ministry of Education, Level 7, Block J, Damansara City Centre, 50604 Kuala Lumpar, Malaysia

Malta

London Office: Malta High Commission, 16 Kensington Sq, London W8 5HH; Tel 0171-938 1712/6; Fax 0171-937 8664

Malta

Ministry of Education and Human Resources, Floriana, Malta

Mauritius

London Office: Mauritius High Commission, 32–33 Elvaston Pl, London SW7 5NW; Tel 0171-581 0294

Mauritius

Ministry of Education and Science, 3rd Fl, New Government Centre, Port Louis

New Zealand

London Office: High Commissioner for New Zealand, New Zealand Hse, 80 Haymarket, London SW1Y 4TQ; Tel 0171-930 8422; Fax 0171-839 4580; Telex 24368

New Zealand

Chief Executive, Ministry of Education, PO Box 1666, Wellington, New Zealand; Tel 014-473 5544; Fax 014-499 1327

Nigeria

High Commissioner for Nigeria in the UK, 9 Northumberland Ave, London WC2N 5BX; Tel 0171-839 1244; Fax 0171-839 8746

Head of Consular and Welfare Affairs, 56–57 Fleet St, London EC4Y 1BT; Tel 0171-353 3776

Papua New Guinea

London Office: Papua New Guinea High Commission, 14 Waterloo Pl, London SW1R 4AR; Tel 0171-930 0922

Papua New Guinea

The Secretary, Department of Education, Private Mail Bal, PO Boroko, Papua New Guinea

Seychelles

London Office: Seychelles High Commission, Box 4PE, 2nd Fl, Eros Hse, 111 Baker St, London W1M 1FE; Tel 0171-224 1660

Seychelles

The Principal Scretary, Seychelles Ministry of Education, Mont Fleuri, PO Box 48, Victora, Mahé, Seychelles

Republic of Sierra Leone

London Office: Sierra Leone High Commission, 33 Portland Pl, London W1; Tel 0171-636 6483/6

Sierra Leone

Ministry of Education, New England, Freetown

Singapore

London Office Students Department, Singapore High Commission, 16 Kinnerton St, London SW1X 8ES; Tel 0171-235 5465
Singapore students in the UK are advised and administered at 16 Kinnerton St, London SW1X 8ES; Tel 071-235 5465

Singapore

The Ministry of Education, Kay Siang Rd, Singapore 1024, Republic of Singapore

Solomon Islands

Correspondence to: Permanent Secretary, Ministry of Foreign Affairs and Trade Relations, PO Box G10, Honiara, Solomon Islands
The Permanent Secretary, Ministry of Education, Training and Cultural Affairs, Solomon Islands Ministry of Education

Sri Lanka

London Office: Office of the High Commissioner for the Republic of Sri Lanka, 13 Hyde Park Gdns, London W2; Tel 0171-262 1841
Second Secretary (Education) M.M. Jaffeer

Sri Lanka

Secretary of Education, Ministry of Education, Isurupaya, Sri Jayawardenepura, Battaramulla, Sri Lanka

Swaziland

London Office; Office of the High Commissioner for Swaziland, 58 Pont St, London SW1; Tel 0171-581 4976

Swaziland

Ministry of Education, PO Box 39, Mbabane; Tel 42491

United Republic of Tanzania

London Office: The High Commission of the United Republic of Tanzania, 43 Hertford St, London W1; Tel 0171-499 8951
Minister Counsellor, Education and Culture Fatma S. Abdullah

Tanzania Mainland

Ministry of Education, Dar es Salaam

Zanzibar

Ministry of Education, Zanzibar

Tonga

London Office: Tonga High Commission, 36 Molyneux St, London W1H 6AB; Tel 0171-724 5828; Fax 0171-723 9074
Counsellor M.L. Takapautolo

Tonga

Ministry of Education, Nuku'alofa

Trinidad and Tobago

London Office: The High Commission for the Republic of Trinidad and Tobago, 42 Belgrave Sq, London SW1X 8NT; Tel 0171-245 9351; Fax 0171-823 1065

Trinidad and Tobago

Ministry of Education, Alexandra St, St Clair, Port-of-Spain

Tuvalu

The Director of Education, Ministry of Health, Sport and Human Resources Development, PO Box 36, Funafuti; Tel 20831; Fax 688 832; Telex Govt TV4803

Uganda

Uganda

Permanent Secretary, Ministry of Education, PO Box 7063, Kampala; Tel 234440/6; Telex 61298 EDUCAE UGA

Windward Islands

Ministry of Education and Sports, Government HQ, Roseau, Commonwealth of Dominica

Ministry of Education, St George's, Grenada

Ministry of Education and Health, Castries, St Lucia

Ministry of Education, Youth and Women's Affairs, Kingstown, St Vincent

Zambia

London Office: Office of the High Commissioner for the Republic of Zambia, Zambia Hse, 2 Palace Gate, Kensington W8; Tel 0171-589 6655
First Secretary Education and Recruitment Attaché B. Chomba

Zambia

Ministry of Education, PO Box 50093, Lusaka

Zimbabwe

London Office: The Zimbabwe High Commission, Zimbabwe Hse, 429 Strand, London WC2R 0SA

British Council

Head Office 10 Spring Gdns, London SW1A 2BN; Tel 0171-830 8486
Chairman Sir Martin Jacomb, KT
Director-General John Hanson, CBE
Assistant Director-General Edmund Marsden
Director Professional Services Roger Bowers, OBE
Director Export Promotion (and Co-ordinator for Africa) Peter Mackenzie-Smith
Secretary to the Board Peter Chenery
Director (Central Bureau for Educational Visits and Exchanges) Tony Male

Professional Services

Head Consultancy Group Helen Meixner
Head Education Promotion Group David Elliott
Head Information Group Mary O'Neill
Lead Consultant (English Language) Ian Seaton
Lead Consultant (Education) David Theobald, OBE
Lead Consultant (Health) Dr Douglas Buchanan
Lead Consultant (Science) Dr June Rollinson

The Central Bureau for Educational Visits and Exchanges

Director (Central Bureau for Educational Visits and Exchanges) and Secretary (UK Centre for European Education) Tony Male
Deputy Director (Central Bureau) Bill Musk
Head (UK Lingua Unit and Teacher Exchange) Judith Hemery
Head (Assistants) Anthony Hawick
Head (Vocational and Technical Education) Judy Powell
Head (Courses and Study Units) Dermot George

Ministries and Departments of Education in British Dependent Territories

Anguilla

Chief Education Office, Ministry of Education, Anguilla

Bermuda

Permanent Secretary, Ministry of Education, PO Box HM 1185, Hamilton HM EX BERMUDA

British Virgin Islands

Chief Education Officer, PO Box 72, Road Town, Tortola; Tel 809 494 3408/9 or 5421

Cayman Islands

Chief Education Officer, Harbour Centre, George Town, Grand Cayman

Falkland Islands

Director of Education, Port Stanley, Falkland Islands

Gibraltar

Director of Education, 40 Town Range, Gibraltar; Tel (350) 77486; Fax (350) 71564

Hong Kong

Director of Education, Lee Gdns, 3rd Fl, 33–37 Hysan Ave, Causeway Bay, Hong Kong

Montserrat

Ministry of Education, Health and Welfare, PO Box 103, Plymouth, Monsterrat

St Helena

Chief Education Officer, Jamestown, Island of St Helena

Embassies and Institutes

Educational and Cultural Attachés

Embassy of the Islamic State of Afghanistan

31 Princes Gate, London SW7 1QQ; Tel 0171-589 8891/2

Albania

There is no diplomatic representation in the UK

Algerian Embassy

Cultural Section, 6 Hyde Park Gate, London SW7; Tel 0171-221 7800

Argentine Embassy

53 Hans Pl, London SW1X 0LA; Tel 0171-584 6494
Consular Office
Tel 0171-589 3104

Austrian Embassy

18 Belgrave Mews West, London SW1X 8HU; Tel 0171-235 3731; Fax 0171-235 8025

Austrian Institute

28 Rutland Gate, London SW7 1PQ; Tel 0171-584 8653
Director Dr P. Marginter

Embassy of the State of Bahrain

98 Gloucester Rd, London SW7 4AU; Tel 0171-370 5978
Cultrual Attaché H. Al-Monfaradi

Belgian Embassy

103 Eaton Sq, London SW1W 9AB; Tel 0171-235 5422 Ext 268 and 254
Officer Press and Education Affairs (Education) K. Dockx
Officer Cultural Affairs (Education) A. Van Goethem

Bolivian Embassy

106 Eaton Sq, London SW1W 9AD; Tel 0171-235 4248 and 0171-235 4255 (Consulate)
Correspondence about education should be addressed respectively to the Cultural Attaché or to the Counsul General

Brazilian Embassy

32 Green St, London W1Y 4AT; Tel 0171-499 0877
Counsellor and Head of the Cultural Department Gonçalo de B.C. e Mello Mourâo

Bulgarian Embassy

186–188 Queen's Gate, London SW7; Tel 0171-584 9400/9433
First Secretary (Cultural Affairs) Aglika Markova

Cambodia (Democratic Kampuchea)

At the time of going to press there was no diplomatic representation in the U.K.

Embassy of the Republic of Cameroon

84 Holland Pk, London W11 3SB; Tel 0171-727 0771
Cultural Consellor S.N. Abangma

Chilean Embassy
12 Devonshire St, London W1N 2DS; Tel 0171-580 6392/3/4
Cultural and Press Attaché Florencia Uaras

Embassy of the People's Republic of China
49–51 Portland Pl, London W1; Tel 0171-636 5726
Ambassador Ma Yuzhen

Colombian Embassy
3 Hans Cres, London SW1X 0LN; Tel 0171-589 9177; Fax 0171-581 1829

Côte d'Ivoire Embassy
2 Upper Belgrave St, London SW1X 8BJ; Tel 0171-235 6991; Fax 0171-259 5439

Cuban Embassy
167 High Holborn, London WC1; Tel 0171-240 2488
Press and Information Secretary I. Kennedy
Cultural Attaché M. Vinas

Embassy of the Slovak Republic
25 Kensington Palace Gdns, London W8 4QY; Tel 0171-243 0803
Cultural and Education Attaché Viera Viskupová

Danish Cultural Institute
Carlsberg Hse, 3 Doune Terr, Edinburgh EH3 6DY; Tel 0131-225 7189; Fax 0131-220 6162
Director in Great Britain Finn Andersen

Danish Embassy
55 Sloane St, London SW1X 9SR; Tel 0171-333 0200
Counsellor for Press and Cultural Affairs Jacob Benthien

Office of the High Commissioner for the Commonwealth of Dominica
1 Collingham Gdns, London SW5 0HW

Ecuadorian Embassy
Flat 3b, 3 Hans Cres, London SW1X 0LS; Tel 0171-584 1367/2648
Ambassador Extraordinary and Plenipotentiary Dr José Antonio Correa

Embassy of the Arab Republic of Egypt
Office of the Cultural Counsellor and Egyptian Education Bureau, 4 Chesterfield Gdns, London W1Y 8BR; Tel 0171-491 7720
Cultural Counsellor and Director Prof Younes Elbatrik

El Salvador Embassy
First Fl, 5 Gt James St, London WC1N 3DA; Tel 0171-430 2141
Ambassador Dr Mauicio Rosales

Ethiopian Embassy
Education Dept, 17 Princes Gate, London SW7; Tel 0171-589 7212

Finnish Embassy
38 Chesham Pl, London SW1X 8HW; Tel 0171-235 9531

Gabonese Embassy
27 Elvaston Pl, London SW7 5NL; Tel 0171-823 9986; Telex 919418

Embassy of the Federal Republic of Germany
23 Belgrave Sq, London SW1X 8PZ; Tel 0171-235 5033; Fax 0171-824 1390
Cultural Counsellor Dr R.W. Ehni

Institut Français/French Institute
Bilingual Secretarial College, 14 Cromwell Pl, London SW7 2JR; Tel 0171-581 2701; Fax 0171-581 2910
Principal Brigitte Freyche

Goethe-Institut London (German Cultural Institute)
50 Princes Gate (Exhibition Rd), London SW7 2PH; Tel 0171-411 3400
Director Dr E. Brandt

Greek Embassy
1A Holland Pk, London W11 3TP; Tel 0171-229 3850
The Cultural Section

Guatemala Embassy
All present affairs are handled through the British Embassy
7A Avenida 5–10, Zona 4, Edif Centro Financiero Torre II, Nivel 7, Guatemala City; Tel (502 2) 321601; Fax (502 2) 341904

High Commission for Pakistan
Education Division, 39–40 Lowndes Sq, London SW1X 9JN; Tel 0171-235 2044/2195
Education Counsellor Dr Mohammed Latif Virk; Tel Ext 2195

Hungarian Embassy
35 Eaton Pl, London SW1 8BY; Tel 0171-235 7191/4048; Fax 0171-823 1348
Cultural Attaché G. Turi

Icelandic Embassy
1 Eaton Terr, London SW1W 8EY; Tel 0171-730 5131/2; Fax 0171-730 1683

Indonesian Embassy
38 Gosvenor Sq, London W1; Tel 0171-499 7661
Minister Counsellor for Information Titiek A. Suyono

Embassy of the Republic of Iraq
Cultural Department, 20 Queen's Gate, London SW7 5JG; Tel 0171-584 7141
Cultural Counsellor (Acting) M.A. Al-Hasson

Irish Embassy
17 Grosvenor Pl, London SW1X 7HR; Tel 0171-235 2171
Letters on educational and cultural matters to the Cultural Attaché

Embassy of the Islamic Republic of Islam
Education Department, 50 Kensington Ct, London W8 5DB; Tel 0171-937 5225

Embassy of Israel
2 Palace Grn, London W8; Tel 0171-957 9500
Letters on educational and cultural matters to the Counsellor for Cultural Affairs. Information available from the Information Department

Italian Embassy
14 Three Kings Yard, London W1Y 2EH; Tel 0171-629 8200
Cultural Attaché 39 Belgrave Sq, London SW1X 8NX; Tel 0171-235 1461
Education Officer Dr E. Relton 39 Belgrave Sq, London SW1X 8NX; Tel 0171-235 1461

Italian Institute
39 Belgrave Sq, London SW1X 8NX; Tel 0171-235 1461
Director Prof F. Villari

Embassy of Japan
101–104 Piccadilly, London W1V 9FN
Japan Information and Cultural Centre (Embassy of Japan), 101–104 Piccadilly, London W1V 9FN; Tel 071-465 6500

Embassy of the Hashemite Kingdom of Jordan
6 Upper Phillimore Gdns, London W8 7HB; Tel 0171-937 3685/6/7
Cultural Attach S. Faris

Embassy of the Republic of Korea
4 Palace Gate, London W8 5NF; Tel 0171-581 0247
Education Consultant In Soo Kang

Embassy of the State of Kuwait
45–46 Queen's Gate, London SW7 5HR; Tel 0171-589 4533
Cultural Counsellor Ahmed Al-Duwaisan

Lebanese Embassy
21 Kensington Palace Gdns, London W8 4QM; Tel 0171-229 7265
Letters about education in Lebanon and about Lebanese students in UK to Lebanese (Cultural Section), 21 Kensington Palace Gdns, London W8 4QM

Liberian Embassy
2 Pembridge Pl, London W2 4XB
Ambassador Willie A. Givens

Libyan People's Bureau
At present affairs are handled through the Libyan Interest Section at the Saudia Arbian Embassy, London

Liechtenstein
Diplomatic and consular matters in the UK are handled by the Swiss Embassy (see below)

Luxembourg Embassy
27 Wilton Cres, London SW1X 8SD; Tel 0171-235 6961; Fax 0171-235 9734
Cultural and Educational Matters

Embassy of the Union of Myanmar
19A Charles St, London W1; Tel 0171-629 4486
Cultural Attaché (Counsellor) V Avng BWA

Mexican Embassy
42 Hertford St, London W1Y 7TF; Tel 0171-499 8586
Ambassador Jose Juan de Olloqui

Mongolian Embassy
7 Kensington Ct, London W8; Tel 0171-937 0150

Embassy of the Kingdom of Morocco
49 Queen's Gate Gdns, London SW7 5NE; Tel 0171-581 5001/4 or 0171-724 0719 (Consulate); Fax 071-225 3862

Royal Nepalese Embassy
12A Kensington Palace Gdns, London W8; Tel 0171-229 1594 and 6231
Ambassador H.E. Bharat K. Simha
Counsellor Madhab P. Khanal
Military Attaché Lt Col L.J. Gurung
Attaché Keshab Thaku
Attaché Rameswor Paudel

Royal Netherlands Embassy
38 Hyde Park Gate, London SW7 5DP; Tel 0171-584 5040
Press and Cultural Department

Embassy of Nicaragua
8 Gloucester Rd, London SW7 4PP; Tel 0171-584 4365
Consular Section
8 Gloucester Rd, London SW7 4PP; Tel 0171-584 3231

Royal Norwegian Embassy
25 Belgrave Sq, London SW1X 8QD; Tel 0171-235 7151; Fax 0171-275 6993
General Information is available from the Press and Information Office, information on educational and cultural matters from the Cultural Office

Embassy of the Sultanate of Oman
Cultural Attachés Office, 64 Ennismore Gdns, London SW7 1NH; Tel 0171-581 0129

Embassy of Panama
48 Park St, London W1Y 3PD

Paraguayan Embassy
Braemar Lodge, Cornwall Gdns, London SW7; Tel 0171-937 1253; Fax 0171-937 5687
First Secretary Igor Paugrazio

Embassy of Peru
52 Sloane St, London SW1X 9SP; Tel 0171-235 1917/2545
Consular Section
Tel 0171-235 6867
Cultural Office
Tel 0171-235 1917

Phillippine Embassy
9A Palace Grn, London W8 4QE; Tel 0171-937 1609/1600
Ambassador Tomas T. Syquia
Attaché Juliet M. Posadao

Consular Section
9A Palace Grn, London W8 4QE; Tel 0171-937 3646/7/8

Polish Cultural Institute

34 Portland Pl, London W1N 4HQ; Tel 0171-636 6032; Fax 0171-637 2190
Director Hanna Mausch
Deputy Director (Culture and Art) Aleksandra Czapiewska
Deputy Director (Education and Science) Ryszard Herczynski

Polish Embassy

47 Portland Pl, London W1N 3AG; Tel 0171-580 4324; Fax 0171-323 4018
Cultural Counsellor Karol Drozd
First Secretary Cultural Affairs Barbara Koscielny

Portuguese Embassy

11 Belgrave Sq, London SW1; Tel 0171-235 5331
Cultural Counsellor E. Lisboa

Embassy of the State of Qatar

115 Queen's Gate, London SW7 5LP; Tel 0171-581 8611
Cultural Attaché S. Al-Mannai

Romanian Embassy

4 Palace Grn, Kensington, London W8 4QD; Tel 0171-937 9666
Cultural and Educational Attaché G. Gafita

Saudi Arabian Cultural Bureau

29 Belgrave Sq, London SW1X 8QB; Tel 0171-245 9944/7; Fax 0171-245 9895
Cultural Attaché A. Al-Naser

Senegal Embassy

11 Phillimore Gdns, London W8 7QG; Tel 0171-937 3139 and 0171-937 0925/6
Minister Cllr A.R. Bemgeloum

South African High Commission

Trafalgar Sq, London WC2N 5DP; Tel 0171-930 4488
First Secretary (Cultural Affairs) Vacancy
Counsellor (Information) Vacancy

Embassy of Spain

24 Belgrave Sq, London SW1X 8QA; Tel 0171-235 5555
Cultural Office
39 Chesham Pl, London SW1X 8SB; Tel 0171-201 5522/0171-201 5524; Fax 0171-259 6487
Education Office
20 Peel St, London W8 7PD; Tel 0171-727 2462; Fax 0171-229 4965
Cervantes Institute
102 Eaton Sq, London SW1 9AN; Tel 0171-235 1484/5; Fax 0171-235 4115

Institute of Spain

102 Eaton Sq, London SW1W 9AN; Tel 0171-235 1484/5
Director Fernando Serrano-Suñer
General Secretary Cristina Spink

Embassy of Sweden

11 Montagu Pl, London W1H 2AL; Tel 0171-724 2101
Cultural Counsellor Anders Clason

Swiss Embassy

16–18 Montagu Pl, London W1H 2BQ; Tel 0171-723 0701

Royal Thai Embassy

30 Queen's Gate, London SW7; Tel 0171-589 0173
Education Counsellor Thai Government Students' Office, 28 Princes Gate, London SW7 1QF; Tel 0171-584 4538; Fax 0171-823 9896

Togo Embassy

30 Sloane St, London SW1; Tel 0171-235 0147/9
Charges d'Affaires a.i. Djibril Akanga
Financial Attaché Kilouziba Lanwi Lakignan

Tunisian Embassy

29 Princes Gate, London SW7 1QG; Tel 0171-584 8117
Cultural Counsellor Mohamed Bakir

Turkish Embassy

43 Belgrave Sq, London SW1; Tel 0171-235 5252
Educational Counsellor Educational Counsellor's Dept, Camelot Hse, 76 Brompton Rd, London SW3; Tel 0171-584 4062/2773

United States Embassy

Grosvenor Sq, London W1A 2LH; Tel 0171-499 9000; Fax 0171-491 2485

Cultural Affairs Office

Uruguayan Embassy

48 Lennox Gdns, London SW1X 9DL; Tel 0171-589 8835
Letters about cultural matters to the Embassy

Venezuelan Embassy

56 Graffon Way, London W1P 5LB
Cultural Attaché Yolanda Reyna

Embassy of the Socialist Republic of Vietnam

12–14 Victoria Rd, London W8; Tel 0171-937 1912

Embassy of the Republic of Yemen

57 Cromwell Rd, London SW7 2ED; Tel 0171-584 6607; Fax 0171-589 3350

Cultural Section

Embassy of the Republic of Zaire

26 Chesham Pl, London SW1; Tel 0171-235 6137/8/9

25 Educational Publishing

Educational Correspondents

National Daily and Sunday Newspapers

Daily Express
245 Blackfriars Rd, London SE1 9UX; Tel 0171-928 8000
Education Correspondent Martin Bentham

Daily Mail
Northcliffe Hse, 2 Derry St, Kensington, London W8 5TT; Tel 0171-938 6000
Education Correspondent Ray Massey

Daily Mirror
Canary Wharf, London E14 5DT
Richard Garner

Daily Star
Ludgate Hse, 245 Blackfriars Rd, London SE1 9UX; Tel 0171-928 8000
David Mertens

Daily Telegraph
Canary Wharf, London E14 5DT; Tel 0171-538 5000
John Clare
Paul Marston

The Evening Standard
Northcliffe Hse, 2 Derry St, London W8 5EE; Tel 0171-938 6000

The Guardian
119 Farringdon Rd, London EC1R 3ER; Tel 0171-278 2332; Fax 0171-713 4154
Education Editor James Meikle
Education Correspondent Donald MacLeod
Northern Education Correspondent David Ward 160 Deansgate, Manchester M60 2RR; Tel 0161-832 7200

Sunday Times
1 Pennington St, London E1 9XW; Tel 0171-782 5677
Charles Hymas

The Independent and Independent on Sunday
Canary Wharf, London E14 5DT
Judith Judd
Fran Abrams
Diana Hinds

Mail on Sunday
Northcliffe Hse, 2 Derry St, London W8 5TT; Tel 0171-938 7032
Alison Brace

The Observer
Chelsea Bridge Hse, Queenstown Rd, London SW8 4NN; Tel 0171-278 2332

The Scotsman
20 North Bridge, Edinburgh EH1 1YT; Tel 0131-225 2468
Douglas Fraser

The Sun
1 Virginia St, London E1 9BD; Tel 0171-782 4000
Education Correspondent David Wooding; Tel 0171-782 4184; Fax 0171-488 3253

Sunday Express
121 Fleet St, London EC4; Tel 0171-353 8000 Ext 3866

Sunday People
9 New Fetter La, London EC4A 1AR; Tel 0171-353 01246-822 3189
Peter Bishop

Sunday Telegraph
South Quay, 181 Marsh Wall, London E14 9SR; Tel 0171-538 5000/071-538 7408 (direct Line)
Education Correspondent Fran Abrams

The Times
1 Pennington St, London E1 9XN; Tel 0171-782 5000
Education Editor John O'Leary
Education Correspondent Ben Preston

Provincial Daily Newspapers

Birmingham Evening Mail
PO Box 18, 28 Colmore Circus, Queensway, Birmingham B4 6AX; Tel 0121-236 3366; Telex 337552
Sally Hilton

Birmingham Post
PO Box 18, 28 Colmore Circus, Queensway, Birmingham B4 6AY; Tel 0121-236 3366
Philip Smith

Cambridge Evening News
51 Newmarket Rd, Cambridge CB5 8EJ; Tel (01223) 358877; Fax (01223) 460846
Education Correspondent Pauline Hunt

Coventry Evening Telegraph
Corporation St, Coventry CV1 1FP; Tel (01203) 633633
Julie Chamberlain

Daily Post
PO Box 48, Old Hall St, Liverpool L69 3EB; Tel 0151-227 2000; Fax 0151-236 4682

Dorset Evening Echo
57 St Thomas St, Weymouth, Dorset; Tel (01305) 784804
Editor Michael Woods

East Anglian Daily Times/Evening Star
30 Lower Brook St, Ipswich, Suffolk IP4 1AN; Tel (01473) 230023

Evening Courier
PO Box 19, King Cross St, Halifax, West Yorkshire; Tel (01422) 365711
Michael Peel

Evening Gazette
Borough Rd, Middlesbrough, Cleveland TS1 3AZ; Tel (01642) 245401 Ext 257
Education Reporter Ron Livingstone

Evening Post
8 Tessa Rd, Reading, Berks; Tel (01734) 575833
Estelle Maxwell

Evening News
Nuneaton and District Newspapers Ltd, 11–15 Newtown Rd, Nuneaton CV11 4HR; Tel (01203) 353534; Fax (01203) 353481
Editor Tony Parratt

Express and Star (Evening)
Queen St, Wolverhampton WV1 3BU; Tel (01902) 313131; Fax (01902) 21467
Deputy News Editor James Windle

Herald
195 Albion St, Glasgow G1 1QP; Tel 0141-553 3587 Ext 3447; Fax 0141-552 2288; Direct line 0141-305 3447
Barclay McBain

Huddersfield Daily Examiner (Evening)
Ramsden St, Huddersfield HD1 2TD; Tel (01484) 537444
Peter Hinchcliffe

Irish Independent
90 Middle Abbey St, Dublin, Ireland; Tel 01001 731666; Fax 01001 720304
Fergus Black

Irish News
113–117 Donegall St, Belfast BT1 2GE; Tel (01232) 322226
Marion Sawey

Irish Press/Evening Press/Sunday Press
Irish Press Newspapers Ltd, Burgh Quay, Dublin 2, Ireland; Tel 01001 6713333
Patrick Holmes

Irish Times
10–16 D'Olier St, Dublin 2, Ireland; Tel 0171-353 8970 (London); Telex 5167
Christina Murphy

Jersey Evening Post
PO Box 582, St Saviour, Jersey JE4 8XQ, CI; Tel (01534) 873333; Fax (01534) 879681
Dena Jeune

The Journal
Thomson Hse, Groat Market, Newcastle upon Tyne NE1 1ED; Tel 0191-232 7500; Fax 0191-261 8869
Editor Bill Bradshaw

Lancashire Evening Post
Olivers Pl, Eastway, Fulwood, Preston, Lancs PR2 4ZA; Tel (01772) 54841
Gerrie Burns

Lancashire Evening Telegraph
Newspaper Hse, High St, Blackburn, Lancs; Tel (01254) 678678
Mark Woodhouse

Leicester Mercury (Evening)
St George St, Leicester LE1 9FQ; Tel (0116) 251 2512; Fax (0116) 262 4687
Annemarie Shillito

Manchester Evening News
164 Deansgate, Manchester M60 2RD; Tel 0161-832 7200
Laurie Bullas

Northern Echo
Priestgate, Darlington, Durham; Tel (01325) 381313
Ginny Williams

North–West Evening Mail
Furness Newspapers Ltd, Abbey Rd, Barrow-in-Furness, Cumbria LA14 5QS; Tel (01229) 821835

Oxford Mail (Evening)
Newspaper Hse, Osney Mead, Oxford OX2 0EJ; Tel (01865) 244988
Anne Horner

Paisley Daily Express
14 New St, Paisley, Strathclyde; Tel 0141-887 7911

Press and Journal Aberdeen
PO Box 43, Lang Stracht, Mastrick, Aberdeen AB9 8AF; Tel (01224) 690222
News Editor Eric Stevenson

Scottish Daily Record & Sunday Mail
24 Borden Rd, Glasgow G13 1QX; Tel 0141-959 1454; Fax 0141-954 1880
Mike Ritchie

Shields Gazette (Evening)
Chapter Row, South Shields NE33 1BL; Tel 455 4661

Shropshire Star (Evening)
Ketley, Telford, Shropshire TF1 4HU; Tel (01952) 242424; Fax (01952) 254605
John Simcock

The Star–Sheffield (Evening)
York St, Sheffield, South Yorkshire S1 1PU; Tel (0114) 276 7676
Michael Russell

Telegraph and Argus (Evening)
Hall Ings, Bradford, West Yorkshire BD1 1JR; Tel (01274) 729511
Kathie Griffiths

Western Daily Press
Temple Way, Bristol BS99 7HD; Tel (0117) 920 080
Education Correspondent Neil Morris

Western Mail
Thomson Hse, Cardiff CF1 1WR; Tel (01222) 583583; Fax (01222) 583652
Ruth Davies

Wigan Observer
Lancashire Publications Ltd, Martland Mill, Wigan WN5 OLX; Tel (01942) 228000
Allan Rimmer

Yorkshire Evening Post
Wellington St, Leeds, West Yorkshire LS1 1RF; Tel (0113) 243 2701; Fax (0113) 238 8536
Mike Hurst

Yorkshire Evening Press
PO Box 29, 76/86 Walmgate, York, North Yorkshire YO1 1YN; Tel (01904) 653051
Assistant Editor (News) Richard Neville

National Newspaper Groups

Northcliffe Newspapers Group
32 John St, London WC1N 2QB; Tel 0171-242 7070 Ext 504
Doreen Brooks

Radio

BBC (Radio)
Broadcasting Hse, Portland Pl, London W1A 1AA; Tel 0171-765 5918
Education Correspondent Wendy Jones

News Agencies

Press Association

85 Fleet St, London EC4P 4BE; Tel 0171-353 7440
Ben Preston

Weekly Journals

The Economist
25 St James's St, London SW1A 1HG; Tel 0171-839 7000
Donald Hirsch

Nature
4 Little Essex St, London WC2R 3LF; Tel 0171-836 6633
John Maddox

New Scientist
King's Reach Tower, Stamford St, London SE1 9LS; Tel 0171-261 5000; Fax 0171-261 6464
Maggie McDonald

Information Education,
Unit 24, Enterprise Centre, Bedford St, Stoke-on-Trent ST1 4PZ; Tel (01782) 281643; Fax (01782) 264200
Information Education publishes a range of educational software programs. In addition to cross-cirricular products, IE provides resources for use in English, Drama, Media Studies, Languages for Business, Geography and Environmental Studies, History, Computer Studies, Sociology/Modern Studies, Economics and Catering/Home Economics

Sound Ideas,
117 Athelstan Rd, Bitterne, Southampton SO19 4DG; Tel (01703) 333405; Fax (01703) 235128
Peter Webb
Produces educational tapes for children, teenagers and adults

National Council for Educational Technology

Milburn Hill Rd, Science Park, Coventry CV4 7JJ
Chairman (Acting) Gordon Law

Educational Publishers

A & C Black (Publishers) Ltd
35 Bedford Row, London WC1R 4JH; Tel 0171-242 0946; Fax 0181-881 8478; Telex 32524
Educational Director Jill Coleman
Educational and children's books (including music) for primary, middle and secondary schools: ISBN prefix 0 7136

Addison-Wesley Publishers Ltd
Finchamstead Rd, Wokingham, Berks RG11 2NZ; Tel (01734) 794000; Fax (01734) 794035; Telex 846136 ADIWES G
Managing Director Derek Hall
Editorial Director Andrew Ware
UK Sales Manager Simon Wilkins
University and professional text and reference books; ISBN prefix 0 201

AU Enterprises Ltd
126 Great North Rd, Hatfield, Herts AL9 5JZ; Tel (01707) 266714; Fax (01707) 273684
Marketing Director Alun Hinder
Information technology, computer education, software, special needs, in-service training materials

B.T. Batsford Ltd
4 Fitzhardinge St, London W1H OAH; Tel 0171-486 8484
Secondary and Middle School library books on contemporary world affairs, history, religious education, craft, costume and drama, sports, careers, science and chess. Sixth Form selection, including books on English, history and sociology. Teachers' books on education and in particular, multicultural education; ISBN prefix 0 7134

Better Books and Software
3 Paganel Dr, Dudley, West Midlands DY1 4AZ; Tel (01384) 253276; Fax (01384) 457979
Primary, secondary and F.E. special needs education

Blackwell Publishers
108 Cowley Rd, Oxford OX4 1JF; Tel (01865) 791100; Fax (01865) 791347
Journals Marketing Manager Amanda Wilson
Primary, secondary and university, ISBN prefix 0 631

Butterworth Scientific Ltd
Westbury Hse, Bury St, Guildford GU2 5BH; Tel (01483) 300966
Tertiary technology, mathematics, science medicine and social studies

Butterworth-Heinemann
Linacre Hse, Jordan Hill, Oxford OX2 8DP; Tel (01865) 310366; Fax (01865) 310898

Cambridge University Press
The Edinburgh Bldg, Shaftesbury Rd, Cambridge CB2 2RU; Tel (01223) 312393; Fax (01223) 315052; Telex 817256; Cable Unipress, Cambridge
Managing Director (Publishing Division) and Deputy Chief Executive of the Press Dr Jeremy Mynott
Educational Publishing Director S.A. Seddon
Director (American Branch) Barbara Colson
Archaeology, art and architecture, educational (primary, secondary, tertiary, F.E., micro software, information books), history, language and literature, law, linguistics, medicine, music, oriental, philosophy, economics,

psychology, politics, sociology, anthropology, science (physical and biological), mathematics and computer science, social sciences, theology and religion, Bibles, reference books and prayer books, English language teaching, learned and scientific journals, examination papers; ISBN prefix 0 521

Cassell plc
Villiers Hse, 41–47 Strand, London WC2N 5JE; Tel 0171-839 4900; Fax 0171-839 1804
Editorial Director: Academic/Education Division Stephen Lustig
Cassell publishes at the Primary, Secondary and Tertiary levels; and in Theology, Liturgy and Religious Education under the imprints Geoffrey Chapman and Mowbray; ISBN prefixes (Cassell) 0 304, (Geoffrey Chapman) 0 225 (Mowbray) 0264, Library reference: Mansell imprint ISBN prefex 07201

Child's Play (International) Ltd
Ashworth Rd, Bridgemead, Swindon SN5 7YD; Tel (01793) 616286; Fax (01793) 512795
Director Michael Twinn

Collins Education (incorporating Hart-Davis Educational, Holmes McDougall, Unwin Hyman Educational)
PO Box, Glasgow G4 ONB; Tel 0141-306 3358
Operations Director Jean Fenton
Primary, secondary, F.E., atlases; ISBN prefix 0 00, 0 01

Collins Educational, Harper Collins
77 Fulham Palace Rd, Hammersmith, London W6 8JB; Tel 0181-741 7070; Fax 0181-307 4064; Telex 25611 Colins G
Primary, secondary and FE publishing in all major subject Areas: English, History, Science, Maths, IT, Geography, Economics, Sociology, Special Needs, Learning Skills, RE, Business Studies, Technology, Life Skills, Languages; ISBN prefixes 0 00 32

Dextral Books
Educational Publishers, PO Box 52, South DO, Manchester M20 2PJ; Tel 0161-445 0159; Fax 0161-445 0159
Proprietor Diane Paul

Drake Educational Associates
St Fagans Rd, Fairwater, Cardiff CF5 3AE; Tel (01222) 560333
Primary reading materials, Language Master System, special needs, teacher training programmes, Wallcharts, filmstrips, slides, audio-cassettes, videostrips

Encyclopaedia Britannica International Ltd
Educational Books Division, Carew Hse, Station Approach, Wallington, Surrey SM6 ODA; Tel 0181-669 4355
Reference material; ISBN prefix 0 85229

English Heritage
Keysign Hse, 429 Oxford St, London W1R 2HD; Tel 0171-973 3442/3

European Schoolbooks Ltd
Ashville Trading Estate, The Runnings, Cheltenham, Glos GL51 9PQ; Tel (01242) 245252; Fax (01242) 224137
Sales and Marketing Director D.B. Young
Books, video and other audio-visual materials for foreign language teaching at all levels; paperback literature and background books in French, German, Spanish and Italian; subscription service for foreign newspapers and magazines; also topic-maps for geography and current affairs; ISBN prefix 0 85048

Evans Brothers Ltd
2A Portman Mansion, Chiltern St, London W1M 1LE; Tel 0171-935 7160
Managing Director Stephen Pawley

Faber and Faber Ltd
3 Queen Sq, London WC1N 3AU; Tel 0171-278 6881
Secondary schools texts in English literature, including poetry, plays and criticism and a wide range of books for the school library, both primary and secondary; ISBN prefix 0 571

Folens Ltd
Albert Hse, Apex Business Centre, Boscombe Rd, Dunstable LU5 4RL; Tel (01582) 472788
Managing Director Malcolm Watson
Publishing Director Patricia Harrison
Distribution Manager Philip Hayward
Senior Publisher Margot O'Keeffe
Primary and Secondary Senior Editor Ian Jenkins
Primary and Secondary Editor Catherine Millar
Primary and Secondary Editor Michael Spilling
Primary and Secondary Editor Alison Millar
Primary and Secondary Editor Alyson Jones
Primary and Secondary Editor Edward Rippeth
Publisher Ray Barker
Publisher Chris Moorcroft
All subjects for primary and secondary education including personal and social education, maths, English, science, geography, history, RE; ISBN prefix 185276

Franklin Watts
The Watts Group, c/o Leonard St, London EC3A 4RH; Tel 0171-739 2929 and Orchard Books
Group Sales Manager George Spicer
Promotion Manager Linda Banner
Children's non-fiction books (Franklin Watts); children's fiction, poetry, picture books, novelty and gift books (Orchard Books); ISBN prefix 0 7496 (FW); 185213 (OB)

George Philip Ltd
59 Grosvenor St, London W1X 9DA; Tel 0171-493 5841
Marketing Manager Vacancy
Primary, middle, secondary and above in geography, history, atlases, globes and wall maps; ISBN prefix 0 540
Sales and Inspection Copy Dept, Trade Orders
George Philip Services Ltd, Arndale Rd, Wick, Littlehampton, West Sussex BN17 7EN; Tel (01903) 717453

Ginn and Co Ltd
Prebendal Hse, Parsons Fee, Aylesbury, Bucks HP20 2QY; Tel (01296) 88411 Customer Services; Fax (01296) 25487 Customer Services
Managing Director N. Hall
UK Sales Manager Valerie Fry
Editorial Director Ann Foster
Infant, primary, middle, secondary, remedial; ISBN prefix 0 602

Hamish Hamilton Children's Books
27 Wrights La, London W8 5TZ; Tel 0171-416 3000
Editorial Director Jane Nissen
Children's Marketing Director Sally Gritten
General hardback fiction, all ages; ISBN prefix 0 241

Harcourt Brace & Co Ltd
24/28 Oval Rd, London NW1; Tel 0171-267 4466
Head of Marketing Jane Lawrence
Remedial, primary, middle, secondary, tertiary and university educational books; ISBN prefixes 0 15, 07466, 07295

Hazelnut
Specialist Educational Software, 197 Blackshots La, Grays, Essex RM16 2LL; Tel (01375) 375514; Mobile: (0850) 227358
Hazel Thompson, BEd(Hons)
Pat Morris Esq, BEd(Hons)

Heineman Publishers (Oxford) Ltd, Reed Educational Publishing Ltd
Halley Ct, Jordan Hill, Oxford OX2 8EJ; Tel (01865) 311366; Fax (01865) 314107; Telex 837292 HEBOXF G
Heinemann Educational, Managing Director Bob Osborne

25 Educational Publishing

Heinemann Educational, UK Sales and Marketing Director Simon Watts
Heinemann English Language Teaching, Managing Director Mike Esplen
Heinemann, International Sales and Marketing Director Richard Kemp
Heinemann Educational, International Sales and Marketing Director John Watson
Full range of Textbooks for National Curriculum in all Secondary subjects and publisher of leading Primary Maths Scheme (SPMG/Heinemann Maths) plus primary language and cross-curricular resources. Also children's reference materials, comprehensive range of ELT courses and readers, African and Caribbean paperback fiction and textbooks for overseas countries. ISBN prefixes 0 431 (HCR only), 0 435

Hodder and Stoughton Educational (previously University of London Press Ltd and The English Universities Press Ltd and incorporating the school and F.E. book lists of Edward Arnold)
PO Box 702, Dunton Grn, Sevenoaks, Kent TN13 2YD; Tel (01732) 450111
Managing Director Brian Steven
Marketing Director Oliver Gadsby
All range from infant and primary to undergraduate; ISBN prefix 0 340

James Nisbet and Co Ltd
78 Tilehouse St, Hitchin, Herts SG5 2DY; Tel (01462) 438331; Fax (01462) 431528
Primary and secondary, particularly reading and business management; ISBN prefix 0 7202

John Murray (Publishers) Ltd
50 Albemarle St, London W1X 4BD; Tel 0171-493 4361; Fax 0171-499 1792; Telex 21312 Murray G
Managing Director Nicholas Perren
Educational Marketing Director Judith Reinhold
Primary and science history; Secondary schools and colleges. Biology, chemistry, physics, electronics, English, special needs, mathematics, technical subjects, art and craft, history, geography, modern languages, business studies, economics, social studies, religious education, library; Success Studybooks; ISBN prefix 0 7195

Jonquil Publishing Ltd (Editorial)
24 Broadgate, 727 Barking Rd, London E13 9ER; Tel 0181-470 4335; (Sales) Unit 1, Parson's Grn Est, Boulton Rd, Stevenage, Herts (01438) 314418
Director Philip Joester
Books for primary and secondary schools and youth training

Ladybird Books Ltd
Beeches Rd, Loughborough, Leics LE11 2NQ; Tel (01509) 268021; Fax (01509) 234672
Managing Director Anthony Forbes Watson
Publishing Director Michael Gabb
International Director Brian Cotton
Finance Director Alan Warren
UK Sales Director Charles Sanderson
Production Director Jeff Satterley
Publishers of colour illustrated children's books; ISBN prefix 0 7214

LDA (Learning Development Aids)
Abbeygate Hse, East Rd, Cambridge CB1 1DB; Tel (01223) 65445; Fax (01945) 587361
Product Development Manager Joanne Wroe
Schools Marketing Manager Amanda Clarke
Publishers of educational books and materials and software for children aged 4–16

Learning Materials Ltd
Dixon St, Wolverhampton WV2 2BX; Tel (01902) 454026
Director A. Mellor
Educational suppliers for special needs

Lion Publishing plc
Peter's Way, Sandy La West, Oxford OX4 5HG; Tel (01865) 747550; Telex 837161 LION G
Educational Sales Manager John M. Sutcliffe
Marketing Manager Phil Henderson
Religious Education books (primary and secondary) for class and library use; ISBN prefix O 85648 and 0 7459

Living Earth Foundation
Warwick Hse, 106 Harrow Rd, London W2 1XD
Environmental education charity. Products and services for teachers and pupils. Leading providers of environmental education, locally, nationally and internationally

Longman Group Ltd
Longman Hse, Burnt Mill, Harlow, Essex CM20 2JE; Tel (01279) 426721
Sales and Marketing Director, Longman Education P. Uttley
Books, tapes and other aids covering all subjects for primary and secondary schools and colleges of education; ISBN prefix 0 582

Macmillan Press Ltd,
Houndmills, Basingstoke, Hants RG21 2XS; Tel (01256) 29242
Managing Director A. Soar
Marketing Director Alastair Gordon
Director (College/University) Steven Kennedy
Textbooks and supplementary material for FE colleges, polytechnics and universities; ISBN prefix 0 333

McGraw-Hill Book Co Europe
Shoppenhangers Rd, Maidenhead, Berks SL6 2QL; Tel (01628) 23431; Fax (01628) 76086
Editorial Director Roger Horton
Textbooks and other educational materials for secretarial and business education at schools and colleges. Textbooks for computer science, engineering, economics and business studies at colleges and universities. Business computing and engineering at professional levels. Reference books, dictionaries and encyclopaedias; ISBN prefix 0 07

National Christian Education Council
Robert Denholm Hse, Nutfield, Redhill, Surrey RH1 4HW; Tel (01737) 822411; Fax (01737) 822116
Sales Manager Doug Fletcher
National Christian Education Council publishes books for use as a resource by teachers in collective worship as well as story books for children which can be used as discussion prompters; ISBN prefix 0-7197

National Christian Education Council and International Bible Reading Association
1020 Bristol Rd, Selly Oak, Birmingham B29 6LB; Tel 0121-472 4242; Fax 0121-472 7575
Sales Manager Eric A. Thorn
A company wholly owned by National Christian Education Council. Publishes full-colour story books for first and middle schools; ISBN prefix 0 7197

Nelson Blackie
Thomas Nelson and Sons Ltd, Bishopbriggs, Glasgow G64 2NZ; Tel 0141-772 2311; Fax 0141-762 0897
Commissioning Editor Alison Payne
Customer Services Sheila Morrison
Textbooks for primary, middle, secondary and further education

NFER-NELSON Publishing Company Ltd
Darville Hse, 2 Oxford Rd East, Windsor, Berks SL4 1DF; Tel (01753) 858961
Managing Director Michael Jackson
Financial Director Fiona Penn
Marketing Director Ian Florance
Publishing Director Keith Nettle
UK's leading provider of assessments and assessment information services. Publishers of educational, clinical, psychological and occupational tests and guidance materials, organisers of training courses for industry, education and healthcare markets; ISBN prefixes 0 85633, 0 7005

Old Vicarage Publications
Reades La, Dane in Shaw, Congleton, Cheshire CW12 3LL; Tel (01260) 279276; Fax (01260) 298913
Primary art and craft, classics; secondary classics and rural and environmental studies; tertiary classics, history and rural and environmental studies

Ordnance Survey
Romsey Rd, Maybush, Southampton SO16 4GU; Tel (01703) 792912
The official Mapping Agency for Britain which publishes a full range of maps and guides of the country in both conventional and digital format; ISBN prefix 0 319

Pan Books
Cavaye Pl, London SW10 9PG; Tel 0171-373 6070; Telex 917466
Sales Director Tom Burns
Editorial Director Ian S. Chapman
Editorial Director (Children's Publishing) Mary Tapissier
Complete range of paperbacks for children and young adults (Piccolo and Piper)—fiction and non-fiction—for primary, middle and early secondary. For secondary English Literature classics; Pan Study Aids; Brodie's notes. ISBN prefix 0 330

Pandora
77–85 Fulham Palace Rd, London W6 8JB; Tel 0181-741 7070
Publicity Lucy Daubeny
ISBN prefix 0 04

Penguin Books Ltd
27 Wrights La, London W8 5TZ

Pergamon Educational Productions (PEP)
Hennock Rd, Exeter EX2 9EJ; Tel (01392) 74121
PEP is an imprint of Wheaton's publishers and a member of the Pergamon/Maxwell Communication group. Promotes, distributes, publishes and produces videos, books, other classroom media

Philip Green Educational Ltd
112A Alcester Rd, Studley, Warks B80 7NR; Tel (01527) 854711; Fax (01527) 854385
Primary and rural and environment studies, science, social studies. Remedial education for primary and secondary levels. Poetry. Slides, Filmstrips, Posters, Videos

Pitman Publishing Ltd
128 Long Acre, London WC2E 9AN; Tel 0171-379 7383
Publishers of textbooks in business subjects at secondary and tertiary levels and education management development and reference materials; ISBN prefix 0 273, 0 7121 (Macdonald and Evans titles)

Routledge
11 New Fetter La, London EC4P 4EE; Tel 0171-583 9855
Promotions Controller Alison Grieves
Secondary, tertiary, university; ISBN prefix 0415

Sangram Books Ltd
36 Molyneux St, London W1H 6DS; Tel 0171-402 1522
General list for all levels; ISBN prefixes 0 86125, 0 86131, 0 86132, 0 86311

Schofield and Sims Ltd
Dogley Mill, Fenay Bridge, Huddersfield HD8 0NQ; Tel (01484) 607080; Fax (01484) 606815
Chairman J.S. Nesbitt
Managing Director J.S. Platts
Sales Director J. Brierley
Text and information books for the complete ability range in infant, junior, middle and secondary schools. Revision aids. Educational software and peripheral hardware. Books for technical colleges and children's books for libraries; ISBN prefix 0 7217

Scholastic Publications Ltd
Villiers Hse, Clarendon Ave, Leamington Spa, Warks CV32 5PR; Tel (01926) 887799; Fax (01926) 883331
Book clubs and book fairs for schools from pre-school to secondary level children's books; teachers' magazines; educational books and resource materials; ISBN prefix 0 590

Science Research Associates Ltd
Newtown Rd, Henley-on-Thames, Oxon RG9 1EW; Tel (01491) 410111
Managing Director John Lewis
Multi-media training materials for the purchasers of IBM software and hardware; ISBN prefix 0 574

Stanley Thornes (Publishers) Ltd, incorporating Mary Glasgow Publications
Ellenborough Hse, Wellington St, Cheltenham, Glos GL50 1YD; Tel (01242) 228888; Fax (01242) 221914
Managing Director David Smith
Finance Director Kevin Waterman
Market Development Director Oliver Gadsby
Market Development Director Brian Carvell
Production Director Paul Vinson

The Lutterworth Press
PO Box 60, Cambridge CB1 2NT; Tel (01223) 350865; Fax (01223) 66951
Main range; religious education for primary, secondary and sixth form levels, extensive school library list. ISBN prefix 0 7188

The Oxford University Press
Educational Division, Walton St, Oxford OX2 6DP; Tel (01865) 56767; Fax (01865) 56646
Educational Sales and Marketing Director Martin Cuss
Wide range of textbooks and reference books for infant, primary and secondary schools, and colleges; children's picture books, poetry, encyclopedias and information books and fiction for young adults; ISBN prefix 0 19

The Psychological Corporation Ltd
24 Oval Rd, London NW1 7DX; Tel 0171-267 4466
Marketing Manager Rachel Wheatly
Editor-in-Chief Peter McKay
Primary, middle, secondary and educational psychology tests and assessment systems; ISBN prefix 015, 0 7491

Thomas Nelson and Sons Ltd
Nelson Hse, Mayfield Rd, Walton on Thames, Surrey KT12 5PL; Tel (01932) 252211; Fax (01932) 246109; Telex 929365
Publishing and Development Director Vacancy
Sales and Marketing Director John Tuttle
Textbooks and multimedia product for the complete ability range in infant, junior middle and secondary schools. Strong Reading, Maths, English, Geography, Science and Modern Languages lists. Major FE and Caribbean lists; ISBN prefix 0 17

Transworld Children's Books
61/63 Uxbridge Rd, London W5 5SA; Tel 0181-579 2652; Fax 0181-231 6666
Publish under the following imprints: Doubleday (hardback fiction for all ages), ISBN prefix 0385; Corgi (Picture Corgi, Young Corgi, Corgi and Corgi Freeway – paperback fiction), ISBN prefix 0552; Bantam (Series fiction and Bantam Young Adult – paperback fiction) ISBN prefix 0553; Yearling (paperback fiction for 8–12+), ISBN prefix 0440

Trotman and Company Ltd
12 Hill Rise, Richmond, Surrey TW10 6UA; Tel 0181-940 5668; Fax 0181-948 9267
Careers and higher education material; ISBN prefix 0 85660

Virago Press
42–43 Gloucester Crescent, London NW1 7PD; Tel 0171-916 6066; Fax 0171-916 6101
Books at secondary levels; ISBN prefixes 086068 and 185381

W & R Chambers Ltd
43/45 Annandale St, Edinburgh EH7 4AZ; Tel 0131-557 4571

Managing Director W.G. Henderson
Primary and secondary school books. Wide subject range including mathematics, social studies, reference and commerce. Also dictionaries from pre-school to tertiary levels; ISBN prefix 0 550

W. Foulsham & Co Ltd (incorporating Foulsham Educational and Foulsham Technical Books)
Yeovil Rd, Slough, Berks SL1 4JH; Tel (01753) 26769
Educational Director G.M. Kitchen
Books for primary, secondary and college of education levels; ISBN prefix 0 572

Ward Lock Educational Co Ltd
1 Christopher Rd, East Grinstead, W Sussex RH19 3BT; Tel (01342) 318980; Fax (01342) 410980
Publisher Andrew Thraves
Finance Director Vincent Winter
Books for teachers and students. Infant, junior and secondary books. Kent mathematics project, and Reading Workshop series. Take Part Starters and Take Part Series. Target Science KS1-4, Target Geography KS1-4

Wayland (Publishers) Ltd
61 Western Rd, Hove, East Sussex BN3 1JD; Tel (01273) 722561; Fax (01273) 29314 and 723526
Children's non-fiction information books for primary and secondary schools, including titles for remedial reading, EFL and multi-cultural subjects; ISBN prefixes 0 85078, 0 85340, 185210, 07502

Other Educational Publishers

Consumers' Association
2 Marylebone Rd, London NW1 4DF; Tel 0171-830 6000
Hilary Khawam
Publishers of *Which?, Which Way to Health, Gardening Which?, Good Food Guide, Holiday Which?*

CRAC Learning Materials
Published under licence by Hobsons Publishing PLC, Bateman St, Cambridge CB2 1LZ; Tel (01223) 354551
Managing Director Martin Morgan
Publishing Director Gillian Moore
Publishers for secondary level and FE in careers guidance, science, business studies and PSE; publishers at tertiary level in careers and education guidance; ISBN prefix 185324, 186017

Dryad Press Limited
A division of B.T. Batsford Ltd, 4 Fizhardinge St, London W1H OAH; Tel 0171-486 8484
Educational, conservation, history, science, crafts

Education Correspondents Group
Chairman (The Times) John O'Leary
Secretary (The Guardian) James Meikle
Treasurer (Education) Nick Tester

Scripture Union
Scripture Union Hse, 130 City Rd, London EC1V 2NJ; Tel 0171-782 0013; Fax 0171-782 0014
Sales Manager Eric Lightfoot
Books, assembly materials and activity ideas on Bible and Christian life for all ages from pre-school to adult. ISBN prefix: 0 86201

Educational Journals

Accounting Technician
Quadrant Hse, The Quadrant, Sutton, Surrey SM2 5AS; Tel 0181-661 4800
Editor Ian Mitchell
Monthly; free to members and students of Association of Accounting Technicians

ACE Bulletin
Advisory Centre for Education, 1B Aberdeen Studios, 22 Highbury Gr, London N5 2DQ; Tel 0171-354 8321; Fax 0171-354 9069
6 times a year; annual subscription £15.00

Adults Learning
The National Institute of Adult Continuing Education, 12 De Montfort St, Leicester LE1 7GE; Tel (0116) 255 1451
Editor Christopher Feeney
Monthly; annual subscription (10 issues), £17.50 (£30 institutions)

Adventure Education
12 St Andrews Churchyard, Pemrith, Cumbria CA11 7YE; Tel (01768) 891065; Fax (01768) 891914
Editor C. Loynes
Experimental education consultants, publishers, book shop, administrative services, design and erection of ropes courses
Quarterly; annual subscription £17.50

All-in Success
Centre for the Study of Comprehensive Schools, University of Leicester, Barrack Rd, Northampton NN2 6AF; Tel (01604) 24969; Fax (01604) 29735
Editor The Director
Current topics in education related to comprehensive schools

Amateur Stage
Platform Publications Ltd, 83 George St, London W1H 5PL; Tel 0171-486 1732 (editorial, advertising and admin); Fax 0171-224 2215
Editor Charles Vance
Monthly, 12 per year £1.80; annual subscription £18.00 UK, £26 Europe, £35 rest of the World, post paid. All aspects of stagecraft, new book and play reviews, amateur stage diary, news and opinion covering the whole spectrum of the amateur and community theatre and training

Annual Review of Environmental Education
Council for Environmental Education, University of Reading, London Rd, Reading RG1 5AQ; Tel (01734) 756061
Annual subscription £10 (plus p&p)

Antiquaries Journal
Oxford Journals, Oxford University Press, Pinkhill Hse, Southfield Rd, Eynsham, Oxford OX8 1JJ; Tel (01865) 882283; Fax (01865) 882890
Editor Elizabeth Nichols
Published annually; price £51; Rest of World US$105. Reports of excavations in Britain and abroad. Descriptions of finds, the history of antiquarian studies and studies in ancient and medieval art, crafts, heraldry, and social and economic life

Antiquity
85 Hills Rd, Cambridge CB2 1PG; Tel (01223) 356271; Fax (01223) 322514
Editor Christopher Chippindale
Production Editor Anne Chippindale
Assistant Editor Cyprian Broadbank Institute of Archaeology, 31–4 Gordon Sq, London WC1H 0PY; Tel 0171-380 7523; Fax 0171-383 2572
4 per year; annual price £47; Rest of World US$94. International journal of Record within archaeology, reporting specialist work to the wider readership and larger issues that concern every archaeologist

Applied Linguistics
Oxford Journals, Oxford University Press, Pinkhill Hse, Southfield Rd, Eynsham, Oxford OX8 1JJ; Tel (01865) 882283; Fax (01865) 882890
Editor Rosamond Mitchell
Editor Craig Chaudron
Editor (Reviews) Dr Kees de Bot
4 times yearly, £15 (institutional), £9 (personal); annual subscription, £58 (inst), £30 (pers)

ARENA (Anti-Racist Education News)
Newsletter of the National Antiracist Movement in Education (NAME), 41 Strawberry La, Carshalton, Surrey SM5 2NG; Tel 0181-377 8077 (Answerphone)
Annual membership subscription, £13 (individual), £20 (institutional), £5 (students, unwaged, community organisations)

Art and Craft
Scholastic Publications Ltd, Villiers Hse, Clarendon Ave, Leamington Spa, Warks CV32 5PR; Tel (01926) 887799; Fax (01926) 883331
Editor Vacancy
Monthly, £1.95, annual subscription, £23.40
Creative ideas in art, craft, design and technology following the requirements of the National Curriculum Attainment Targets for primary school teachers

Aspects of Education
University of Hull, Institute of Education, Cottingham Rd, Hull HU6 7RX; Tel (01482) 465406
General Editor V.A. McClelland
Twice yearly; £6.00 per issue
Each issue concentrates on a particular aspect of education and includes articles by experts in the field and authoritative book reviews

Audio Visual
Emap Maclaren Ltd, Maclaren Hse, 19 Scarbrook Rd, Croydon, Surrey CR9 1QH; Tel 0181-688 7788; Fax 0181-681 1672
Publisher/Editor Peter Lloyd, BA(Hons)
Monthly, £3.25; annual subscription, £40; free to educationalists, training officers and commercial managers meeting qualification requirements

AUT Bulletin
Association of University Teachers, United Hse, 9 Pembridge Rd, London W11 3JY; Tel 0171-221 4370; Fax 0171-727 6547
Editor Martin Flynn
Termly: October, January, and April; free to members

Basic Education
Council for Basic Education, 725 Fifteenth St NW, Washington DC 20005, USA; Tel (202) 347 4171
Monthly (except July and August); US$2.50 per copy; subscription US$25; add 20% for foreign postage
Analysis and commentary concerning state of basic education in elementary and secondary schools

Books for Keeps
6 Brightfield Rd, Lee, London SE12 8QF; Tel 0181-852 4953
Editor Chris Powling
Bi-monthly, £2.50; annual subscription, £15

British Education Index
The Brotherton Library, The University of Leeds, Leeds LS2 9JT; Tel (0113) 233 5524; Fax (0113) 233 6017
Editor Philip W. Sheffield
The British Education Index is also available on the "Internatonal ERIC" CD–ROM produced by Dialog Information Services. The CD–ROM includes the British, Australian and Canadian education indexes and their respective national theseuri
Subject and author index to over 300 journals published in the UK and Europe (over 4,000 article refs p.a.)

The British Journal of Aesthetics
Oxford Journals, Oxford University Press, Walton St, Oxford OX2 6DP; Tel (01865) 56767
Editor Prof Peter Lamarque
4 per year; annual price £52 UK Eur; Rest of World US$104
Discussions of general and philosophical aesthetics and articles on the principles of appraisal which apply in the various arts severally, working towards a better understanding of them all and throwing light on the analogies and differences between them

The British Journal of Criminology
Oxford Journals, Oxford University Press, Walton St, Oxford OX2 6DP; Tel (01865) 56767; Fax (01865) 267773
Editor (University of Sheffield) Prof Joanna Shapland
4 per year; annual price UK and Europe £57; Rest of World US$110
Criminology, including social deviance. Has both a British and international focus

British Journal of Educational Psychology
British Psychological Society
Editor Dr Michael Youngman School of Education, University of Nottingham, Nottingham NG7 2RD
£35 a volume of three parts (Feb, June and Nov) or £12 each number

British Journal of Educational Studies
Basil Blackwell Ltd, 108 Cowley Rd, Oxford; Tel (01865) 791100
Editor R. Pring, BA, PhD
Feb, May, Sept, Dec £25 (individuals), £60 (institutions)

British Journal of Educational Technology
Journal of the Council for Educational Technology for the United Kingdom
Editor G.D. Moss, PhD Centre for Educational Technology, University College Cardiff, 8 North Rd, Cardiff CF1 3DY; Tel (01222) 44211 Ext 2232
Thrice yearly; annual subscription £18 from Council for Educational Technology, 3 Devonshire St, London W1N 2BA, Tel 071-636 4186

British Journal of Guidance and Counselling
Carfax Publishing Co, PO Box 25, Abingdon, Oxford OX14 3UE; Tel (01235) 555335
Editor A.G. Watts
3 times a year; annual subscription £42.00 for individuals and £72.00 for institutions plus 20% post and packing
The major British academic/professional journal in the guidance and counselling field

British Journal of Language Teaching (Formerly Audio-Visual Language Journal)
see Language Learning Journal

The British Journal for the Philosophy of Science
Oxford Journals, Oxford University Press, Pinkhill Hse, Southfield Rd, Eynsham, Oxford OX8 1JJ; Tel (01865) 882283; Fax (01865) 882890
Editor (King's College London) David Papineau
4 per year; annual price UK and Europe £35; REs of World US$72
Study of the logic, the method and the philosophy of science as well as those of the various special sciences, including the social sciences

British Journal of Physical Education
The Physical Education Association, 162 Kings Cross Rd, London WC1X 9DH; Tel 0171-278 9311/2
Editor The General Secretary, PEA
Quarterly (March, June, Sept, Dec); to members only

British Journal of Religious Education
Christian Education Movement, Royal Bldgs, Victoria St, Derby DE1 1GW; Tel (01332) 296655
Editor Prof John M. Hull School of Education, University of Birmingham, Edgbaston, Birmingham B15 2TT; Tel 0121-414 4836
3 times a year, annual subscription £24.00, £27.00 from September 1995
Professional journal dealing with religious education (Founded 1934)

British Journal of Special Education
Journal of the National Association for Special Educational Needs
Registered Office: York Hse, Exhall Grange, Wheelwright La, Coventry CV9 7HP
Editor Margaret Peter

Mar, Jun, Sep and Dec; annual subscription, £22.50 (individuals) £45 (institutions); fee to NCSE members, membership fee £20
Editorial Office: 12 Hollycroft Ave, London NW3 7QL

British Library Journal
Organ of the London Services Division of the British Library
Editor C.J. Wright Dept of Manuscripts, The British Library, London WC1B 3DG; Tel 0171-412 7516; Fax 0171-412 7745
Subscriptions Turpin Distribution Services Ltd, Blackhouse Rd, Letchworth, Hertfordshire SG6 1HN
Biannual, £17.50; annual subscription, £35

Bulletin of the Association for Technological Education in Schools
c/o Greenhead School, Greenhead Rd, Keighley, West Yorkshire; Tel (01535) 662828
Editor G.W. Asquith
Once a year, 40p

Bulletin of Hispanic Studies
Department of Hispanic Studies, The University, PO Box 147, Liverpool L69 3BX; Tel 0151-794 2773/4, 2579
General Editor Dorothy Sherman Severin
General Editor Ann L. Mackenzie

Bulletin of the Institute of Mathematics and its Applications
Catherine Richards Hse, 16 Nelson St, Southend, Essex SS1 1EF; Tel (01702) 354020; Fax (01702) 354111
6 times a year; annual subscription £75 (1994)

Bulletin of Physical Education
(British Association of Advisers and lecturers in Physical Education)
Hon Editor Robert Chappell, WLIHE Borough Rd, Isleworth, Middx; Tel 0181-568 8741
Three times yearly; annual subscription, £9; £12 overseas

Business Education International
Journal of the LCCI Examinations Board and the Institute of Commerce, The London Chamber of Commerce and Industry, Examinations Board, Marlowe Hse, Station Rd, Sidcup, Kent DA15 7BJ; Tel 0181-302 0261
Editor David Smith
Quarterly, free

Business Strategy Review
Oxford Journals, Oxford University Press, Pinkhill Hse, Southfield Rd, Eynsham, Oxford OX8 1JJ; Tel (01865) 882283; Fax (01865) 882890
Editor Dr John Cubin
Editor Dr Paul Geroski
3 per year; annual price UK and Europe £52; Res of World US$99

Cambridge Journal of Education
The Journal of the University of Cambridge Institute of Education
Executive Editor B.E. Shannon University of Cambridge Institute of Education, Shaftesbury Rd, Cambridge CB2 2BX; Tel (01223) 69631
Published 3 times yearly by Carfax Publishing Company, PO Box 25, Abingdon, Oxon OX14 3UE; annual subscription £118, personal subscription plan £35
Lively and often seminal articles on matters of current educational concern

The Cambridge Quarterly
Subscriptions: Oxford Journals, OUP, Walton St, Oxford OX2 5DP; Tel (01865) 56767; Fax (01865) 267773
Editorial Address: Clare College, Cambridge CB2 1TL; Tel (01223) 461009
Editor D.C. Gervais
Editor R.D. Gooder
Editor A.P. Newton
Editor F.M. Rosslyn
Editor G. Ward
Administration J. Parker 73 Selwyn Rd, Cambridge CB39 9EA; Tel (01223) 461009
Quarterly; annual price Institutional: UK and Europe £51; Rest of World US$99; Personal subscription: £15
Principally literary criticism, but also articles on painting, sculpture, music and cinema. Each issue contains reviews of important new books as well as major articles on classic and contemporary work

Child Education
Scholastic Publications Ltd, Villiers Hse, Clarendon Ave, Leamington Spa, Warks CV32 5PR; Tel (01926) 887799
Editor Gill Moore
Monthly, £2.10; annual subscription £26.40 (UK), £35.00 (Overseas), 17–15 (Student)

Child and Man
Journal of Steiner Schools Fellowship, The Sprig, Ashdown Rd, Forest Row, Sussex RH18 5BN; Tel (01342) 822115
Editor Brien Masters
Art Editor Peter Ramm

Child: Care, Health and Development
Blackwell Scientific Publications Ltd, 25 John St, London WC1N 2BL; Tel 0171-404 4101
Editor Dr Stuart Logan
Bi-monthly, £84 UK; £87 Overseas; US$150 USA and Canada

Childhood, British Association for Early Childhood Education (formerly NSA)
111 City View Hse, 463 Bethnal Grn Rd, London E2 9QY; Tel 0171-739 7594; Fax 0171-739 7594
Early Education Editor c/o the above address
3 times yearly; free to members

Christian Action Journal
Editor The Revd Canon Eric James 125 Kennington Rd, London SE11 6SF
Quarterly; annual subscription, £10 (£5 senior citizens and students)

Civil Engineering Surveyor
Journal of the Institution of Civil Engineering Surveyors
Editor S.J. Booth 101 Bancroft, Hitchin, Herts SG5 1NB; Tel (01462) 440506; Fax (01462) 440507
10 times a year, £3; annual subscription, £29 (UK, £34 (Europe), £39 (worldwide)

Classical Quarterly
Oxford Journals, Oxford University Press, Pinkhill Hse, Southfield Rd, Eynsham, Oxford OX8 1JJ; Tel (01865) 882283; Fax (01865) 882890
Editor (University of Cambridge) P.C. Millett
Editor (University of Oxford) J.S. Heyworth
Twice per year; annual price UK and Europe £32; Rest of World US$62.
Graeco-Roman antiquity in the English-speaking world. Includes research papers and short notes in the fields of language, literature, history and philosophy, normally in English but sometimes in other languages

Classical Review
Oxford Journals, Oxford University Press, Journals Division, Walton St, Oxford OX2 6DP; Tel (01865) 882283; Fax (01865) 882890
Editor (Royal Holloway, University of London) C. Carey
Editor (King's College, University of London) Dr R.G. Mayer
Twice per year; annual price UK and Europe £30; Rest of World US$58

Collaborative Action Research Network (CARN) Publications
Centre for Applied Research in Education, University of East Anglia, Norwich NR4 7TJ; Tel (01603) 592633; Fax (01603) 593447
Co-ordinator Bridget Somekh
Editors Members of the CARN Steering Group
Regular publications, also annual directory of members' activities. Subscription £15 p.a. includes Directory

Comprehensive Education
Box 1914, London W11 3QH
Editor Caroline Benn
Yearbook, £3 subscription

Computers in Education and Training
Presshouse Publications Ltd, Queen St, Hook Norton, nr Banbury, Oxon OX15 5PH; Tel (01608) 737056
Published in three sections:
Computers in Education and Training Journal—Secondary and Higher Education edition; three times yearly
Primary Computer Learning Supplement—Junior edition; three times yearly
Primary Computer Learning Supplement—Infant edition; three times yearly
Controlled circulation

Conference and Common Room
Belgrave Educational Publishing, PO Box 140, Ipswich, Suffolk IP6 9PL; Tel (01449) 706550; Fax (01449) 709550
Editor C.J. Driver Wellington College, Crowthorne, Berkshire RG11 7PU; Tel (01344) 772261; Fax (01344) 772261
Feb, May, Oct, £2.50 post paid; annual subscription, £7 post paid

Contemporary Physics
Taylor and Francis Ltd, 4 John St, London WC1N 2ET; Tel 0171-405 2237; Telex 858540
Editor (Imperial College, London) P.L. Knight
Bi-monthly; annual subscription, £189 UK and overseas (surface mail; airfreight to India and ASP to Australasia; US$318 USA, Canada and Mexico (airfreight)

CRE-action
Published by CRE (Association of European Universities 10 rue du Conseil General, CH-1211 Geneva 4, Switzerland; Tel 329 26 44 or 329 22 51; Fax 329 28 21
Editor Andris Barblan
Editor Catherine Fayant
CRE is the association of European universities comprising 500 institutions from 36 countries
Occasional, 20 Swiss francs for thematic issues, 50 Swiss francs for Directories
Problems of higher education in Europe and Directory of CRE members and organisations dealing with higher education

Critical Survey
Oxford Journals, Oxford University Press, Pinkhill Hse, Southfield Rd, Eynsham, Oxford OX8 1JJ; Tel (01865) 882283; Fax (01865) 882890
Editor (Roehampton Institute) Bryan Loughrey
3 per year; annual price UK and Europe £25; Rest of World US$52
Literary and cultural studies. The journal publishes detailed readings on individual texts, wide ranging debates on the nature of critical practice, discussion of current educational issues, original short stories and poetry, book reviews and arts coverage with a particular emphasis on theatre, TV and the cinema

Curriculum
Studies in Education Ltd (Nafferton Books), Nafferton, Driffield, North Humberside YO25 OJL; Tel (01377) 44231 and 46861
Editor Mike Bottery
Editor Patrick Costello
Editor Nigel Wright
Editor Jean Whittaker
Three times a year; annual subscription £18.50 overseas £19.50 incl. post

2D Drama and Dance
Knighton Fields Centre, Herrick Rd, Leicester LE2 6DH; Tel (0116) 270 0850/701525
Editor Ken Byron
Twice a year (autumn and summer); annual subscription, £4.50 (UK), £4.50 (surface overseas), £8 (airmail). All subscriptions commence with autumn issue

Dance Research
Oxford Journals, Oxford University Press, Walton St, Oxford OX2 5DP; Tel (01865) 56767; Fax (01865) 882890
Editor Richard Ralph
Twice yearly; annual price UK and Europe £30; Rest of World US$65

Design and Technology Teaching
Trentham Books Ltd, Westview Hse, 734 London Rd, Oakhill, Stoke-on-Trent, Staffordshire ST4 5NP; Tel (01782) 745567; Fax (01782) 745553
Editor Prof John Eggleston
Three times a year; £8; annual subscription; £20.50
Presents new approaches to design and technology teaching in schools, colleges and teacher training

Dutch Crossing
Published by the Centre for Low Countries Studies. Subscription details from The Secretary, Dept of Dutch, University College London, Gower St, London WC1 6BT

The Dyslexia Institute
133 Gresham Rd, Staines, Middx TW18 2AJ; Tel (01784) 463851
Executive Director E.J. Brooks
The Dyslexia Institute has 23 centres nationwide and provides Educational Assessments, Teaching, Teacher Training, issues a range of literature for teachers, parents and employers and publishes the 'As We See It' news twice yearly

Early Music
3 Park Rd, London NW1 6XN; Tel 0171-724 1707; Fax 0171-723 5033
Editor Tess Knighton
Quarterly; annual price UK and Europe £35 (Personal) £45 (Institutional); Rest of World US$68 (Personal) US$82 (Institutional)
Extensively illustrated journal in the field of medieval, renaissance, baroque and classical music

Economic Affairs
Published by City Publications Ltd
1 Wardrobe Pl, London EC4V 5AH; Tel 0171-248 8265 in association with The Institute of Economic Affairs
Editor Prof Colin Robinson Institute of Economic Affairs, 2 Lord North St, London SW1P 3LB
5 times a year £2.50; annual subscription £15 (corporate); £10 (individual)

5–13 Education
Benn Business Magazines Ltd, Bullen La, East Peckham, Tonbridge, Kent TN12 5LP; Tel (01622) 872036; Fax (01622) 872346
7 times a year in Jan, March, April, June, Sep, Oct and Nov; annual subscription, £17 inland, £22 overseas

Education 3–13
Institute of Education, University of Warwick, Coventry CV4 7AL; Tel (01203) 523850; Fax (01203) 524110
Editor Prof R.J. Campbell
3 times yearly; annual subscription £31 (UK), £36/$66 (overseas); from Longman Group UK Ltd, Subscriptions (Journals) Dept, Fourth Ave, Harlow, Essex CM19 5AA; Tel (0279) 29655

Education Equipment
147–151 Temple Chambers, Temple Ave, London EC4Y 0BP; Tel 0171-583 3030; Fax 0171-583 4068
Editor Garry Parker
Monthly except Aug; incorporates special resource features to reflect National Curriculum; annual subscription, £33; Controlled circulation

Education and Health
Schools Health Education Unit, School of Education, University of Exeter, Heavitree Rd, Exeter EX1 2LU; Tel (01392) 264722; Fax (01392) 264761
Managing Editor John W. Balding
Executive Editor James Muirden
5 times a year; price on application

To pass on the results of recent research into health-related behaviour, and to provide a forum for debate among teachers, health-education specialists, and others concerned with the healthy development of young people

Education in Chemistry
The Royal Society of Chemistry, Burlington Hse, Piccadilly, London W1V 0BN; Tel 0171-437 8656
Editor Kathryn Roberts
Bi-monthly; annual subscription, £97 (non-members), £26 (members), £104 (overseas)
The only journal in the UK devoted to chemistry teaching at all levels from secondary school to university

Education in Science
The Association for Science Education, College La, Hatfield, Herts AL10 9AA; Tel (01707) 267411
Editor Dr D.S. Moore
Jan, Apr, June, Sep and Nov; annual subscription, £24 including postage; £5.00 a single copy
Articles relating to current issues in science education

Education and the Law
Longman Group UK Ltd, Longman Hse, Burnt Mill, Harlow, Essex CM20 2JE; Tel (01279) 426721
4 times a year; annual subscription £37

Education Libraries Journal
University of Leicester, Education Library, 21 University Rd, Leicester LE1 7RF
Editor Roy Kirk
Business Manager A. Newton
3 times per annum; annual subscription £15; single issues £6
Microfilm edition available from Xerox University Microfilms
All aspects of bibliography, librarianship and information science applied to education or to related areas of social science

Education Review
National Union of Teachers, Hamilton Hse, Mabledon Pl, London WC1H 9BD; Tel 0171-388 6191
Editor Janet Theakston
Twice a year, annual subscription £6 to members, £14 to non-members, single copies £3 to members, £7 non-members, including postage

Education Today
Journal of the College of Preceptors, Longman Group UK, 6th Flr, Westgate Hse, The High, Harlow, Essex CM20 1YR
Editor Prof Don Moyle
4 times a year; annual subscription £82.50 (UK), £90.00 (overseas); single copy £22 (UK), £24 (overseas)

Education Today and Tomorrow
6 Cynthia St, London N1 9JF; Tel 0171-278 4443
Business Manager K. Ebbutt
3 issues per year, £1; annual subscription, £10 (institutions), £5 (individuals)

Education and Training
MCB University Press Ltd, 62 Toller La, Bradford, W Yorks BD8 9BY; Tel (01274) 499821
Editor Prof Margaret Reid
Bi-monthly; annual subscription, £139.95 post paid

Educational Change and Development
Trentham Books Ltd, Westview Hse, 734 London Rd, Oakhill, Stoke-on-Trent, Staffs ST4 5NP; Tel (01782) 745567; Fax (01782) 745553
Editor Harry Gray
Twice a year; UK £20.00 (including postage); overseas £25.00 (including surface postage)
Editorial matter should be sent to: The Mews Hse, Court Walk, Betley, Crewe, CW3 4DP

Educational Computing and Technology (ECT)
Jubilee Hse, The Oaks, Ruislip, Middx HA4 7LF; Tel (01895) 622112; Fax (01895) 621582
Editor Mark Sealey
Leading monthly journal for all teachers using IT at all phases, all platforms, all curriculum areas. 10 employees/members, private company

Educational Management and Administration
Journal of the British Educational Management and Administration Society
Editor Dr Peter Robbins Senior Lecturer, Centre for Education Management and Policy Studies, School of Education, University of Birmingham, PO Box 363, Birmingham B15 2TT
4 times a year, Longman Group UK Ltd, Subscriptions (Journals) Dept, Fourth Ave, Harlow, Essex CM19 5AA, Tel (0279) 29655

Educational Psychology in Practice
Journal of the Association of Educational Psychologists
Editor Dr R.J. Cameron Dept of Psychology, University College London, Gower St, London WC1E 6BT; Tel 0171-387 7050
Quarterly (April, July, October, January); annual subscription £32.50; single issues £8.75; from Longman Group UK Ltd, Subscriptions (Journals) Dept, Fourth Ave, Harlow, Essex CM19 5AA; Tel (0279) 429655

Educational Review
School of Education, University of Birmingham, Edgbaston, Birmingham B15 2TT
Executive Editor B. Wade
Editorial Board Member M. Mac an Ghaill
Editorial Board Member H. Thomas
Editorial Board Member C. Chitty
Editorial Board Member M. Lawn
Editorial Board Member S. Walker
Editorial Board Member D. Martin
Orders Carfax Publishing Company, PO Box 25, Abingdon, Oxfordshire, OX14 3UE
Feb, June and Nov; annual index and title page bound in the Nov issue
Publishes general articles and accounts of research of interest to teachers, lecturers and research workers in education and educational psychology

Electronics Education
Journal for secondary school teachers of electronics and computing
The Institution of Electrical Engineers, Michael Faraday Hse, Six Hills Way, Stevenage, Herts SG1 2AY
Executive Editor D. Winfield
3 times a year; direct mailing by subscription; mailed free to all secondary schools in the UK

ELT Journal
(English as a Foreign or Second Language), Oxford University Press, Walton St, Oxford OX2 6DP; Tel (01865) 56767; Telex 837330
Editor Keith Morrow Homerton Hse, Cawston Rd, Reepham, Norwich NR10 4LT
Quarterly (Jan, Apr, July, Oct), £6 per copy (institutions, £10); annual subscription, £20 (institutions, £33)(UK)

English Dance and Song
Cecil Sharp Hse, 2 Regents Park Rd, London NW1 7AY; Tel 0171-485 2206
Editor Dave Arther
6 times a year; £1; free to members of English Folk Dance and Song Society

English Historical Review
Brasenose College, Oxford OX1 4AJ
Editor Dr J.R. Maddicott
Editor Prof. R.J.W. Evans
Five times yearly £19; annual subscription £76 from Longman Group UK Ltd, Subscriptions (Journals) Dept, Fourth Ave, Harlow CM19 5AA

English in Education
National Association for the Teaching of English, 50 Broadfield Rd, Broadfield Business Centre, Sheffield S8 0XJ; Tel (0114) 255 5419; Fax (0114) 255 5296
3 times yearly; annual subscription, £35 (£20 for libraries) for individual or institution membership. Also includes NATE News, 3 times yearly, and The English

Magazine, twice yearly, or Language and Learning, three times yearly

Environmental Education and Information
Environmental Resources Unit, Newton Bldg, University of Salford, Salford M5 4WT; Tel 0161-745 5221; Fax 0161-745 5999
Editor Prof Graham Ashworth
Quarterly; annual subscription, £23 UK, £32 Europe; £37 (airmail), £21 (surface) to the rest of the world
For dissemination of research and experience to all involved in environmental education

Esperanto Teacher
Yew Tree Cottage, Ivington Rd, Leominster, Herefordshire HR6 8QD; Tel (01568) 613061
Editor Arnold Pitt
Thrice yearly; annual subscription, £7.50
Articles on educational methods, book reviews and details of forthcoming Esperanto courses

ETTI (Educational and Training Technology International)
The Official Journal of the Association for Educational and Training Technology, c/o Centre for Continuing Education, City University, Northampton Sq, London EC1V OHB
Editor Chris Bell
Quarterly, £15 per single copy; annual subscription, £50 (incl postage). Free to AETT members

EUROEDNEWS, UK Centre for European Education
The Central Bureau, Seymour Mews Hse, Seymour Mews, London W1H 9PE; Tel 0171-486 5101
Editor K.R. Tillin
Provides current information about European educational events, conferences, publications, developments

European Journal of Physics
Institute of Physics, Publishing Ltd, Techno Hse, Redcliffe Way, Bristol BS1 6NX; Tel (0117) 929 7481
Editor (University of Cambridge) Sir Brian Pippard
6 issues annually £24; annual subscription US$408 (USA), £204 (ROW)
Education and scholarly studies in physics and closely related sciences at university level

Evaluation and Research in Education
Editor Keith Morrison Frankfurt Lodge, Clevedon Hall, Victoria Rd, Clevedon, Avon BS21 7SJ; Tel (01275) 876519; Fax (01275) 343096
Three times yearly library £42 (US$89); individual £16 (US$34); student £11 (US$24) (including Postage and Packing); evaluation and research articles on the subject of education, review articles; reviews

FERN Journal
FERN Centre, Scraptoft Campus, Leicester Polytechnic, Leicester LE7 9SU; Tel (0116) 243 1011
Co-ordinator D.G. Rogers
Twice yearly; annual subscription £12 (libraries); £6 (individuals); *Newsletter*, 3 tmes a year, free to members and Journal subscribers
Journal disseminates research initiated or supported by practising teachers

FIEP Bulletin of Physical Education
(Fédération Internationale d'Education Physique)
Editor John C. Andrews, BA, MEd Fédération Internationale d'Education Physique, 4 Cleevecroft Ave, Bishops Cleeve, Cheltenham, Glos GL52 5JZ
Three per year. Tri-Lingual (English/French/Spanish), members' annual subscription, individual £17.50, collective £35, libraries £15 (£2.50 agency discount)

Film
Magazine of the British Federation of Film Socieities, PO Box 1DR, London W1A 1DR
Editor Tom Brownlie
4 times a year; £2.50 a copy; annual subscription, £15.00 members, £20.00 non-members

Focus on Birds
A termly colour poster and news sheet for teachers published by the Royal Society for the Protection of Birds
Contact Geoffrey Abbot, RSPB Education Dept, The Lodge, Sandy, Bedfordshire SG19 2DL; Tel (01767) 680551
Termly; free to all schools via local education authorities; mailed direct to independent schools. Free mailing to RSPB members to request

Focus on Business Education
Journal of the Society of Teachers in Business Education, Trelawne, Southdown Rd, Shawpond, Winchester, Hants SO21 2BY
Editor A.G.H. Elsegood 'Saffron Hill', Uplands Rd, Totland Bay, Freshwater, Isle of Wight PO39 ODY
Quarterly (end Feb, May, Aug, Nov), free to members; subscription rates available

Folk Music Journal
Cecil Sharp Hse, 2 Regent's Park Rd, London NW1 7AY; Tel 0171-485 2206
Editor Dr Julia C. Bishop
Annually; free to members of the English Folk Dance and Song Society; back issues £7.50 plus postage and packing (non-members)
Learned articles on Folk Music, Song and Dance

Forum
Council of Europe, F-67075 Strasbourg Cedex, France; Tel 33 88 41 2000; Fax 33 88 41 2781
Published quarterly in French, English, German and Italian

Forum for Modern Language Studies
Oxford Journals, Oxford University Press, Walton St, Oxford OX2 6DP; Tel (01865) 56767; Fax (01865) 267773
Editor J.R. Ashcroft
Editor I.R.W. Higgins
Editor D.D.R. Owen

Francophonie
French Journal of the Association for Language Learning, 16 Regent Pl, Rugby CV21 2PN; Tel (01788) 546443; Fax (01788) 544149
Editor Allan Smalley Officer des Palmes Académiques, 10 Holt Park Way, Leeds LS16 7QR; Tel (0113) 267 9258 (Home); (0113) 283 2600 Ext 3755 (Work); Fax (0113) 283 3189
Twice yearly (June and December); annual subscription £20 (UK), £21 (overseas), $40 (USA)

French History
Oxford Journals, Oxford University Press, Walton St, Oxford OX2 6DP; Tel (01865) 56767; Fax (01865) 56646
Editor (Univ of Leicester) Prof Richard Bonney
Quarterly; annual price UK and Europe £58; Rest of World US$108

General Education
(Bulletin of the General Studies Association)
Editor Frank Vigon 122 Windmill St, Macclesfield, Cheshire SK11 7LB
Annual, £5

Geo Magazine
Elizabeth Weaver, 90 Tuckingmill, Tisbury, Wilts SP3 6NS; Tel (01747) 870107
Proprietor Elizabeth Weaver
GCSE geography; project work, map work, topical articles, curriculum based text

Geography
The Official Journal of The Geographical Association, 343 Fulwood Rd, Sheffield S10 3BP; Tel (0114) 267 0666; Fax (0114) 267 0688
Editor Dr Derek Spooner
Quarterly; subscription rates available from the above address

Geology Today
Blackwell Scientitic Publications, Osney Mead, Oxford OX2 OEL; Tel (01865) 240201
Editor Peter Smith
6 times a year; 1992 archival subscription, £90 (UK), US$165 (USA and Canada), £95 (overseas); subscription, £24.50 (UK), US$45 (USA and Canada), £27 (elsewhere); the archival subscription includes a bound volume. Further discounts for members of certain geological societies

German History
Oxford Journals, Oxford University Press, Walton St, Oxford OX2 6DP; Tel (01865) 56767; Fax (01865) 267773
Editor (Univ College London) Dr Mary Fulbrook
Editor (Univ of Edinburgh) Jill Stephenson
3 per year; annual price UK and Europe £38; Rest of World US$82 (Check with OUP)
Principally the history of Germany and other German speaking areas, but also other aspects of German life and culture which have a clear historical relevance

German Teaching
German Journal of the Association for Language Learning, Association for Language Learning, 16 Regent Pl, Rugby CV21 2PN; Tel (01788) 546443; Fax (01788) 544149
Editor Alistair Brien 16 Regent Pl, Rugby CV21 2PN
Twice yearly (June and Dec); annual subscription £20 (UK), £21 (overseas), US$40 (USA)
Articles, reviews and information of special interest to learners and teachers of German

Gifted Education International
AB Academic Publishers, PO Box 42, Bicester, Oxon OX6 7NW; Tel (01869) 320949; Fax (01869) 320949
Editor Belle Wallace
3 issues per volume; subscription £49 per volume post paid
Includes evaluation, curriculum development, psychology, practice, resources, reviews, news

Graduate Opportunities
Newpoint Publishing Company, Windsor Ct, East Grinstead Hse, East Grinstead, W Sussex; Tel (01342) 326972
Editor Joyce Lewis
Annual

Greece and Rome
Oxford University Press, Walton St, Oxford OX2 6DP; Tel (01865) 56767
Editor Prof P. Walcot
Editor Ian McAuslan
Biannual, £15; UK annual subscription, £28

Head Teachers Review
1 Health Sq, Boltro Rd, Haywards Heath, W Sussex RH16 1BL; Tel (01444) 458133; Fax (01444) 416326
Editor David Hart, OBE, FRSA
Assistant Editor Peter Hellyer
3 times yearly, £2; annual subscription, £6. Free to members

Headlines
The Secondary Heads Association, 130 Regent Rd, Leicester LE1 7PG; Tel (0116) 247 1797
Editor Michael Duffy King Edward VI School, Morpeth, Northumberland NE61 1DN; Tel (01670) 515415
Oct, Feb, June, £2; annual subscription, £6

Health Education Journal
Health Education Authority, Hamilton Hse, Mabledon Pl, London WC1H 9TX; Tel 0171-413 1987
Editor Margaret Whitehead
Quarterly (spring, summer, autumn, winter); annual subscription, £22 individuals £30 inst, £8 single issue

Healthlines
Health Education Authority, Hamilton Hse, Mabledon Pl, London WC1H 9TX; Tel 0171-413 2646; Fax 0171-383 2408
Editor Sue Jelley
10 times yearly; free to health education/promotion specialists; £20 for other organisations

Higher Education Quarterly (formerly Universities Quarterly)
Basil Blackwell, 108 Cowley Rd, Oxford OX4 1JF
Editor Michael Shattock
Quarterly (Mar, June, Sep, Dec); annual subscription £15 (individuals), £35 (institutions)

Higher Education Review
Tyrrell Burgess Associates Ltd, 34 Sandilands, Croydon CRO 5DB; Tel 0181-656 1770
Editor Prof John Pratt 46 Mercers Rd, London N19 4DR; Tel 0171-263 1620
Once a term; annual subscription, £40

Historical Journal
Cambridge University Press, The Edinburgh Bldg, Shaftesbury Rd, Cambridge CB2 2RU; Tel (01223) 312393
Editor Dr J. Steinberg Trinity Hall, Cambridge
Editor Dr J.S. Morrill Selwyn College, Cambridge; *Correspondence* Faculty of History, West Rd Cambridge CB3 9EF
The Historial Journal publishes papers on all aspects of British, European and World history since the 15th Century. Mar, June, Sep, Dec; £94 institutions, £51 individuals per volume of 4 parts (1995)

History
Historical Association, 59A Kennington Park Rd, London SE11 4JH; Tel 0171-735 3901
Editor (University of Edinburgh) Prof H.T. Dickinson
Oct, Feb, June
Annual subscription (with corporate membership), £49.50; non-members, £35.00 (U/C)

History and Computing
Edinburgh University Press, 22 George Sq, Edinburgh EH8 9LF; Tel 0131-650 4218; Fax 0131-662 0053
Editor (Univ of Edinburgh) R.J. Morris
Covers prosopography, list processing and quantitative methods, free text analysis, image processing, graphical presentation, project management, funding problems, communication and training

History of Education
Taylor & Francis Ltd, 4 John St, London WC1N 2ET; Tel 0171-405 2237/9; Fax 0171-831 2035; Telex 858540
Editor R. Lowe (Univ of Birmingham)
Quarterly; annual subscription, £145 UK only; US$244 (ROW)
Official Journal of History of Education Society

History Today
History Today Ltd, 20 Old Compton St, London W1V 5PE; Tel 0171-439 8315
Editor Gordon Marsden
Monthly £2.75; annual subscription, £28.50 (UK), US $54.95, £49.95 rest of world, US£73 Canada from 20 Old Compton St, London, W1V 5PE, UK
The only illustrated monthly history magazine. Reviews, articles, feature series, news and views from professional historians and writers on all aspects of British, European and international history

History Workshop Journal
Oxford Journals, Oxford University Press, Walton St, Oxford OX2 6DP; Tel (01865) 56767
Editor Sally Alexander
Editor John Barrell
Editor Barbara Bloomfield
Editor Guy Boanas
Editor Susan Bullock
Editor Bernard Canavan
Editor Jane Caplan
Editor Anna Davin
Editor Alun Howkins
Editor Andrew Lincoln
Editor Laura Mulvey

Editor Janet L. Nelson
Editor Alex Potts
Editor Lyndal Roper
Editor Raphael Samuel
Editor Bill Schwarz
Editor Teodore Shanin
Editor Gareth Stedman Jones
Editor Anne Summers
Editor Barbara Taylor
Editor Jeffrey Weeks
Editor Jerry White
Editor Alan Bray
Editor Felix Driver
Editor Laura Crowing
Editor Daniel Pick
2 per year; annual price UK and Europe £30; Rest of World PS$60
Exploration of the 'everyday' in an historical context provides new perspectives on the past and present

Home and School
National Confederation of Parent Teacher Associations
Editor Margaret Morrissey
Editor Diane Wright
Published by Hobsons Publishing plc, Bateman St, Cambridge CB2 1LZ

Home and School Council Working Papers
Home and School Council, 40 Sunningdale Mount, Ecclesall, Sheffield S11 9HA; Tel (0114) 236 4181
Editor Vacancy
Hon Secretary Barbara Bullivant
Three times yearly; annual subscription, £4 inland, post paid
Publishes examples of good practice in home-school relationships

Hospitality
(Official magazine of the Hotel, Catering and Institutional Management Association)
191 Trinity Rd, London SW17 7HN; Tel 0181-672 4251; Fax 0181-682 1707
Editor Alan Sutton 58 Collingdon St, Luton, Beds LU1 1RX
Hospitality is produced six times a year (end Jan, March, May, July, September, November). It carries management articles relating to the hotel and catering industry and associated disciplines. Subscriptions £24 p.a.(UK); £32 p.a. (overseas)

Hungarian Music Quarterly
Editio Musica Budapest, H1051 Budapest, Vorosmarty ter 1, Hungary (Postal address: 1370 Budapest, POB 322)
Editor Antal Boronkay

Iberian Studies
Centre for Iberian Studies, University of Keele, Newcastle, Staffs ST5 5BG; Tel (01782) 621111
Managing Editor John Naylon
Twice a year in spring and autumn; annual subscription, UK £12, other countries £20
Historial and social science studies of modern Spain and Portugal

Industrial and Commercial Training
MCB University Press Ltd, 62 Toller La, Bradford BD8 9BY; Tel (01274) 499821
Editor Bryan Smith
Bi-monthly; annual subscription, £249.95

Industrial and Corporate Change
Oxford Journals, Oxford University Press, Pinkhill Hse, Southfield Rd, Eynsham, Oxford OX8 1JJ; Tel (01865) 882283; Fax (01865) 882890
Editor Giovanni Dosi
Editor Guilio Sapelli
Editor Nick von Tunzelmann
Editor Nathan Rosenburg
Editor David Teece
3 per year; annual price UK and Europe £85; Rest of World US$160
The presentation and interpretation of evidence on corporate and industrial change drawn from an interdisciplinary set of approaches and theories

Industrial Law Journal
Oxford Journals, Oxford University Press, Pinkhill Hse, Southfield Rd, Eynsham, Oxford OX8 1JJ; Tel (01865) 882283; Fax (01865) 882890
Editor Paul L. Davies
Quarterly; annual price UK and Europe £29; Rest of World US$59
Comment in-depth analysis and information for academics, practising lawyers and lay industrial relations experts on all aspects of UK labour law

Infant and Nursery School Education Journal
Presshouse Publications Ltd, Queen St, Hook Norton, nr Banbury, Oxon OX15 5PH; Tel (01608) 737056
Editor Caroline Bond
Termly (ie 3 x yearly); controlled circulation

Infant Projects
Scholastic Publications Ltd, Villiers Hse, Clarendon Ave, Leamington Spa, Warks CV32 5PR; Tel (01926) 887799
Editor Jane Morgan
Bi-monthly, £2.10; annual subscription £12.60 (UK), £17 (Overseas)
Practical Project ideas for teachers of 4 to 8 years olds, for use in the classroom – includes colour posters

The Institute of Careers Guidance
Title of the journal of the Institute of Careers Guidance, is Careers Guidance Today
Editor Sharon Jandu Institute of Careers Guidance, 27A Lower High St, Stourbridge, W Midlands DY8 1TA
4 times yearly

International Education
PEPAR Publications, The Gate Hse, 112 Park Hill Rd, Birmingham B17 9HD; Tel 0121-428 4474
International Education, published since 1990, carries articles by practitioners who are all involved in some aspect of the recruitment, care or tuition of international students. Annual subscription three times a year; Organisation UK £42.50, O/S £47.50; Personal UK £27.50, O/S £32.50

The International Journal of Community Education
The International Community Education Association (ICEA), Lyng Hall, Blackberry La, Coventry CV2 3JS
Editor Alan Blackhurst
Three times a year; annual subscription £19.50

International Journal of Electrical Engineering Education
Published by the Manchester University Press, Oxford Rd, Manchester M13 9PL; Tel 0161-273 5539
Editor Dr M.G. Hartley
Editor Mrs A. Buckley Dept of Electrical Engineering and Electronics, UMIST, Manchester M60 1QD
Quarterly; annual subscription, £105; personal subscription £40

International Journal of Law and the Family
Pembroke College, Oxford OX1 1DW; Tel (01865) 276429; Fax (01865) 276418
Editor (Univ of Oxford) John Eekelaar
Editor (Univ of Nottingham) Robert Dingwall
3 per year; annual price UK and Europe £51; Rest of World US$105
Theoretical analysis of family law; sociological literature concerning the family which is of special interest to law and legal policy; literature in related disciplines (such as medicine, psychology demography) which is of special relevance to law and the family

International Journal of Lexicography
Oxford Journals, Oxford University Press, Walton St, Oxford OX2 6DP; Tel (01865) 56767; Fax (01865) 26773
Editor Robert Ilson

Quarterly; annual price UK and Europe £53; Rest of World US$97; special rates available
Theoretical, practical, diachronic and synchronic aspects of lexicography. Dictionaries and reference works of all types, phrase books, usage guides, encyclopaedias, etc. Related disciplines such as lexicology, terminology, semantics, pragmatics, are also included

International Journal of Lifelong Education
Taylor and Francis Ltd, 4 John St, London WC1N 2ET; Tel 0171-405 2237/9; Fax 0171-831 2035; Telex 858540
Editor Professor P. Jarvis Dept of Adult Education, University of Surrey, Guildford GU2 5XH; Tel (01483) 71281
Editor Prof J.E. Thomas Dept of Adult Education, University of Nottingham, Education Bldg, University Pk, Nottingham NG7 2RD; Tel (0115) 948 4848
Quarterly; annual subscription £83 UK only, US$145 (personal subscription rate available)
Adult, lifelong and continuing education

International Journal of Mathematical Education in Science and Technology
Taylor and Francis Ltd, 4 John St, London WC1N 2ET; Tel 0171-405 2237; Telex 858540
Editor (Univ of Technology, Loughborough) D. Walker
Bi-monthly; annual subscription, £176; US$302 overseas; personal subscription £88, US$151
New teaching aids and techniques are an important feature

The International Journal of Mechanical Engineering Education
Ellis Horwood Ltd, Market Cross Hse, Cooper St, Chichester, W Sussex PO19 1EB; Tel (01243) 789942
Editor J. Atkinson
Editor (University of Manchester Institute of Science and Technology) T.Y. Reddy
Editor (San Jose State University) O.A. Armas, California 95192, USA
Quarterly; annual subscription, £84 (UK), US$176 (overseas airmail)
Covers civil and mechanical engineering, manufacturing engineering sciences and related topics to aid industry and academic and military institutions

International Journal of Refugee Law
Oxford Journals, Oxford University Press, Walton St, Oxford OX2 6DP; Tel (01865) 56767; Fax (01865) 56646
Editor (Carleton Univ, Ottawa, Canada) Prof G.S. Goodwin-Gill
The journal aims to stimulate research and thinking on refugee law and its development. In addition it provides information across the broad field of refugee law; for example, the conclusion and application of relevant international treaties; state practice, such as actions taken, diplomatic exchanges, statements of policy and position made nationally, in the UN General Assembly and other forums; municipal legislative

International Journal of Science Education
Taylor and Francis Ltd, 4 John St, London WC1N 2ET; Tel 0171-405 2237/9; Fax 0171-831 2035; Telex 858540
Editor John Gilbert University of Reading
6/bimonthly times a year; annual subscription, £140 UK only (surface mail; airfreight to India and ASP to Australasia), US$238 USA, Canada and Mexico (airfreight); Personal subscription rates are available
International perspectives on science and technology education; research in science education

International Review of Applied Linguistics
Oxford Journals, Oxford University Press, Walton St, Oxford OX2 6DP; Tel (01865) 56767; Fax (01865) 267773
Editor Gerhard Nickel
Editor Bernard Pottier
Quarterly; annual price UK and Europe £72; Rest of World US$132
Theoretical linguistic research and its practical application to language teaching. Includes synoptic articles on different aspects of applied linguistics, and reports on completed or continuing research projects

International Schools Journal
European Council of International Schools, 21 Lavant St, Petersfield, Hampshire GU32 3EL; Tel (01730) 268244
Editor Edna Murphy 47 St Augustine's Rd, London NW1 9RL, UK
Editor Charles A. Gellar Brussels' English Primary School, 23 Ave
Editor F. Roosevelt 1050 Brussels, Belgium
Twice annually; annual subscription £13 (US$22)
Articles and reviews of interest to educators in schools abroad

IRAL—International Review of Applied Linguistics in Language Teaching
Journals Department, Oxford University Press, Walton St, Oxford OX2 6DP; Tel (01865) 56767; Fax (01865) 267773; Telex 837330
Editor Prof Dr G. Nickel
Single copy DM45; Subscription (institutions DM176, (individuals) DM110

ISCO Careers Scope
Independent Schools Careers Organisation, 4 Connaught Gdns, London N10 3LB; Tel 0181-883 9275; Fax 0181-883 9275
Editor Anna Alston
3 times a year; annual subscription £10
Contains articles on all aspects of careers in business, the professions and public service and monitors changes in further and higher education

The ISIS Magazine
Independent Schools Information Service, 56 Buckingham Gate, London SW1E 6AG; Tel 0171-630 8795
Editor R.C. Davison
Mid Feb, June, Oct; annual subscription (to Friends of Independent Schools) £9 (UK), £12 (overseas)

JACT Review
Journal of the Joint Association of Classical Teachers (JACT), Available through membership of JACT, Application forms from the Secretary, JACT, 31–34 Gordon Sq, London WC1H OPY
Editor Anthony Bowen
Reviews Editor James Stone
Can be bought separately (£2). Cheques to be sent to address above
Biennially (autumn and summer); annual subscription £25 (members also receive three termly Bulletins, the magazine *Omnibus* twice a year, occasional monographs, reports and surveys, and Proceedings of the Classics in schools or universities, and reviews of books, courses and audio visual aids

JET
Mary Glasgow Magazines, 140 Freston Rd, London W10 6TR; Tel 0171-792 3644
Editor Karen Gray
Oct, Feb and May; subscription, £16(UK)
JET is a magazine for teachers of English as foreign language to children of primary level. Contains articles on teaching ideas plus theme pack and poster in the February issue

Journal of African Economies
Oxford Journals, Oxford University Press, Pinkhill Hse, Southfield Rd, Eynsham, Oxford OX8 1JJ; Tel (01865) 882283; Fax (01865) 882890
3 per year; annual price UK and Europe £50; Rest of World US$95

Journal of Biological Education
Institute of Biology, 20–22 Queensberry Pl, London SW7 2DZ; Tel 0171-581 8333; Fax 0171-823 9409
Editor J.A. Barker
Executive Editor C.P. Chatham

Quarterly; vol. 29 subscription £50 UK; Institute members £29 US$105/£57 overseas (1995)

Journal of the British Association of Teachers of the Deaf
Editor R. Elphick 10 Manor Cl, Wilmslow, Cheshire SK9 5PX
Editor I.G. Tucker 9 Grangeway, Handforth, Cheshire SK9 3HY
Circulation Manager G.F.E. Clark Royal School for the Deaf, 50 Topsham Rd, Exeter EX2 4NF
6 times a year; annual subscription £15.50 plus postage, single issue £2.80 plus postage

Journal of Computer Assisted Learning
Blackwell Science Ltd, Osney Mead, Oxford OX2 OEL; Tel (01865) 240201; Fax (01865) 721205
Editor R. Lewis
Four times a year (March, June, September and December); annual subscription rates (1995); individuals; £28.00 Europe, £31.00 Rest of World, US$48.00 USA and Canada: institutions; £115 Europe, £127 Rest of World, US$197 USA and Canada. Subscribers in Canada must add 7% to allow for GST. Subscribers in Europe must quote their VAT registration number or state that they are not registered. Subscribers in the Netherlands who are not VAT registered must add 6% to the subscription price to allow for VAT

Journal of Curriculum Studies
Taylor and Francis Ltd, 4 John St, London WC1N 2ET; Tel 0171-405 2237/9; Fax 0171-831 2035; Telex 858540
Editor I. Westbury
Editor G. Milburn
Editor N. Gough
Editor A. Woodward
Bi-monthly; annual subscription, £95 UK only (surface mail; airfreight to India and ASP to Australasia), US£163 Rest of World inc USA, Canada and Mexico (airfreight). Personal subscription rates available
All aspects of curriculum studies

Journal of Design History
Oxford Journals, Oxford University Press, Pinkhill Hse, Southfield Rd, Eynsham, Oxford OX8 1JJ; Tel (01865) 882283; Fax (01865) 882890
Editor (V&A) Jeremy Aynsley
Editor (Wolverhampton Polytechnic) Christopher Bailey
Editor (Cambridge) Charlotte Benton
Editor (Birkbeck College, London) Annie Coombes
Editor (The Open Univ) Anthony Coulson
Editor (Leicester Polytechnic) Pat Kirkham
Editor (Birmingham Polytechnic) Pauline Madge
Editor (Middlesex Polytechnic) Tim Putnam
Editor (Brighton Polytechnic) Jonathan Woodham
Quarterly; annual price UK and Europe £51; Rest of World US$102
New research in design development and current issues of interest. Promotion of links with other disciplines and exploration of material culture, such as anthropology, architectural history, business history, cultural studies, design management studies, economic and social history, history of science and technology and sociology

Journal of Education for Teaching
Carfax Publishing Co, PO Box 25, Abingdon, Oxford OX14 3UE
Editor Prof Edgar Stones
Publishes original contributions on the subject of teacher education subscription: Institutional; EC £156/Outside EC £179/US$298, Personal: EC £64/Outside EC £72/ US$128 (special discount for individuals) 5 issues a year

Journal of Educational Administration and History
Journal of Educational Administration and History Museum of the History of Education, Parkinson Court, The University, Leeds LS2 9JT; Tel (0113) 243 1751 Ext 4665
Editor Prof J.S. Marriott
Editor Dr J.R. Dunford
Editor Dr P.R. Sharp
January and July, £7.50/US$12.50 (USA); annual subscription, £15/US$25 (USA)
Each issue contains articles on educational history and administration and detailed book reviews. Worldwide coverage

Journal of Environmental Law
Oxford Journals, Oxford University Press, Walton St, Oxford OX2 6DP; Tel (01865) 56757
Editor Richard Macrory Environmental Change Unit, Oxford University, Oxford
2 per year; annual price UK and Europe £45; Rest of World US$95
This journal provides a source of informed analysis in the field. The range of subjects encompassed within environmental law is broad, extending from the more traditional fields of pollution control, waste management, and habitat protection to challenging newer areas such as biotechnology, regulation of hazardous substances, and international regimes for common natural resources

Journal of European Industrial Training
CB University Press Ltd, 62 Troller La, BRADFORD BD8 9BY; Tel (01274) 499821
Editor Roger Bennett
9 times a year; annual subscription, £349.95
Ideas and developments in training within a management and organisation development context

Journal of Further and Higher Education
National Association of Teachers in Further and Higher Education, 27 Britannia St, London WC1X 9JP; Tel 0171-837 3636
Editor Anne Castling
Annual subscription £9 NATFHE members; £17 UK non-members; £20 overseas (surface mail)

Journal of the History of Collections
Oxford Journals, Oxford University Press, Walton St, Oxford OX2 6DP; Tel (01865) 56767; Fax (01865) 267773
Editor Oliver Impey
Editor Arthur MacGregor Ashmolean Museum, Oxford
2 per year, annual price Institutions: UK and Europe £49; Rest of World US$95; Individuals UK and Europe £24.50; Rest of World US$47
This journal is dedicated to the study of collections, ranging from the contents of places and accumulations in more modest households, to the most systematic collections of academic institutions. The journal is interested in the content of these collections, the processes which initiated and controlled their formation and the circumstances of the collections themselves.

Journal of the Institute of Health Education
35 Victoria Rd, Sheffield S10 2DJ; Tel (0114) 266 0790; Fax (0114) 266 0790
Editor F. St. D. Rowntree, OBE, MSc(Med)
Quarterly; annual subscription corporate members (3 copies) £20, individual members (full) £15, (associate) £12 inc p and p (UK), overseas rates on apllication
A quarterly professional journal containing academic articles, reports, book reviews, etc on the behavioural aspects of health and health education, nutrition, biomedical sciences, management etc of interest to medical, nursing and educational workers in the Health, Education and Social Services

Journal of Islamic Studies
Oxford Journals, Oxford University Press, Walton St, Oxford OX2 6DP; Tel (01865) 56767; Fax (01865) 56646
Editor Dr Farhan Ahmad Nizami St Cross Coll, Oxford
2 per year; annual price UK and Europe £50; Rest of World US$95
Dedicated to the multi-disciplinary study of any aspect of Islam and the Islamic world

Journal of Logic and Computation
Oxford Journals, Oxford University Press, Pinkhill Hse, Southfield, Eynsham, Oxford OX8 1JJ; Tel (01865) 882283; Fax (01865) 882890

Editor D.M. Gabby Imperial College of Science, Technology and Medicine
6 per year; annual price UK and Europe £85; Rest of World US$160
Logic has found applications in virtually all aspects of Information Technology, from software engineering and hardware to programming and artificial intelligence. Indeed, logic artifical intelligence and theoretical computing are influencing each other to the extent that a new interdisciplinary area of *Logic and Computation* is emerging. This journal covers that field

Journal of the National Association for Staff Development (NASD Journal)
Editor Anne Castling Southgate College, High St, London N14 6BS
Twice-yearly; subscription: £9 p.a.

Journal of Refugee Studies
Oxford Journals, Oxford University Press, Walton St, Oxford OX2 6DP; Tel (01865) 56767; Fax (01865) 267773
Editor Dr Roger Zetter Refugee Studies Programme, Queen Elizabeth Hse, 21 St Giles, Oxford OX1 3LA; Tel (01865) 270730; Fax (01865) 270721
Quarterly; annual price UK and Europe £54; Rest of World US$102; Personal £27 or $51; Third World Institutions £27 or $51
Academic exploration of the complex problems of forced migration and national and international responses. Includes anthropology, economics, health and education, international relations, law, politics, psychology and sociology

Journal of Research in Reading
Published by Basil Blackwell Ltd for United Kingdom Reading Association
Editor Denis Vincent Dept of Education and Community Studies, University of East London, Longbridge Rd, Dagenham RM8 2AS
Co-editor C. Harrison
Co-editor A.K. Pugh
Co-editor J.M. Ulijn
Co-editor G. Brooks
Co-editor M. Neville
Subscriptions
Basil Blackwell Ltd, 108 Cowley Rd, Oxford OX4 1JF
Biannual; £11 (individual members of UKRA, Reading Association of Ireland and other reading associations in Europe) £11 (School members of UKRA), £36 (comprehensive institutional members of UKRA – includes UKRA's Newsletter and other journal, *Reading*); other individual subscribers, £19.50 individual (UK), £25 (overseas, including Eire), US$37 (USA and Canada); other institutional subscribers, £32 (UK), £39 (overseas, including Eire), US$57.50 (USA and Canada)
Provides forum for researchers into reading and related fields in Britain and Europe

Journal of the Royal Musical Association
Oxford Journals, Oxford University Press, Pinkhill Hse, Southfield Rd, Eynsham, Oxford OX8 1JJ; Tel (01865) 882283; Fax (01865) 882890
Editor Mark Everist
2 per year; annual price UK and Europe £36; Rest of World US$72
New research into all branches of musical scholarship – historical musicology and ethnomusicology, theory and analysis, textual criticism, archival research, organology and performing practice

Journal of Semantics
Oxford University Press, Journal Subscription Department, Walton St, Oxford OX2 6DP; Tel (01865) 56767; Fax (01865) 56646
Managing Editor Peter Bosch IBM Germany, Scientific Centre, PO Box 103068, D-69020 Heidelberg, Germany; Tel +49 6221 594251; Fax +49 6221 593200
Quarterly; annual price UK and Europe £55; Rest of World US£110
This journal publishes articles, notes, discussions, and book reviews in the area of natural language semantics. Its is explicitly interdisciplinary in that it aims at an integration of philosophical, psychological, and linguistic semantics as well as semantic work done in artificial intelligence and anthropology

Journal of Semitic Studies
Department of Middle Eastern Studies, University of Manchester, Oxford Rd, Manchester M13 9PL; Tel 0161-275 3073; Fax 0161-275 3264
Editor P.S. Alexander Univ of Manchester
Editor G.J. Brooke Univ of Manchester
Editor J.F. Healey Univ of Manchester
Editor P.C. Sadgrove Univ of Manchester
Editor G. Rex Smith Univ of Manchester
2 per year; annual price UK and Europe £57.00; Rest of World US$107
Modern and ancient Near East, with special emphasis on research into the languages and literatures of the area

Journal of Teacher Development
Longman Group UK Ltd, Westgate House, The High, Harlow, Essex CM20 1YR; Tel (01279) 442601; Fax (01279) 444501
Editor Professor Rosemary Deem
Three issues per year, February, May and October. Subscriptions: £37 (UK), £43 (overseas).

Journal of Theological Studies
Journals Dept, Oxford University Press, Walton St, Oxford OX2 6DP; Tel (01865) 56767; Fax (01865) 56646
Editor Revd Prof M. Wiles
Editor Prof M. Hooker
Biannual, subscription: £66 UK/Europe; US$138 rest of the world

The Junior Bookshelf
Marsh Hall, Thurstonland, Huddersfield HD4 6XB; Tel (01484) 661811
Editor Miss D.J. Morrell
Bi-monthly; annual subscription for 1995 vol 59 £10.20 inland; £12.50 overseas
Reviews new children's books with occasional articles on children's authors, illustrators, etc

Junior Education
Scholastic Publications Ltd, Villiers Hse, Clarendon Ave, Leamington Spa, Warks CV32 5PR; Tel (01926) 887799
Editor Mrs T. Saunders
Monthly, £2.10; annual subscription £25.20 (UK), £29.00 (overseas)
News and features on education, colour poster and curriculum ideas for the classroom

Junior Focus
Scholastic Publications Ltd, Villiers Hse, Clarendon Ave, Leamington Spa, Warks CV32 5PR; Tel (01926) 887799
Editor Kate Element
Monthly, £2.10; annual subscription £25.20 (UK), £33.00 (overseas)
Practical Project ideas for teachers of 7–12 years old, for use in the classroom—includes colour posters and photocopiable material

Junior and Middle School Education Journal
Presshouse Publications Ltd, Queen St, Hook Norton, Nr Banbury, Oxon OX15 5PH; Tel (01608) 737056
Editor Caroline Bond
Three times yearly; controlled circulation

La Brita Esperantisto (The British Esperantist)
140 Holland Park Ave, London W11 4UF; Tel 0171-727 7821
Editor W. Auld
Bi-monthly, £2.25 including postage; annual postal subscription, £14 including postage

Language Learning Journal
Association for Language Learning, 16 Regent Pl, Rugby CV21 2PN; Tel (01788) 546443; Fax (01788) 544149

Editor Colin Wringe Dept of Education, University of Keele, Keele, Staffs ST5 5BT
Twice yearly (March and September); annual subscription £30 (UK), £33 (overseas) US$60 (USA)
Articles on teaching and learning of languages, applied linguistics, language policy, current issues, and ideas for practical classroom teaching. Also reviews and information. See entries for *Francophonie, German Teaching, Vida Hispanica, Tuttialia, Rusisika and Dutch Crossing*

Language Teaching
Cambridge University Press, The Edinburgh Building, Shaftesbury Rd, Cambridge CB2 2RU; Tel (01223) 312393
Editor Mrs V. Kinsella
Price 1995 (institutions), £56; individuals £27; single parts £15; airmail £12 per year
Experts select articles from about 400 relevant journals for publication in Language Teaching. In this way, teachers are kept up to date with the latest developments in linguistics and applied linguistics. The journal is also of great practical benefit to its readers. It shares ideas for use in the classroom and discusses methods of effective language learning

LCCI Link
Newsletter of the LCCI Examinations Board, London Chamber of Commerce and Industry Examinations Board, Marlowe Hse, Station Rd, Sidcup, Kent DA15 7BJ; Tel 0181-302 0261; Fax 0181-302 4169
Three times yearly, free
Update on the activities of the Examinations Board and information and comment on vocational qualifications generally including National Vocational Qualifications

Lebende Sprachen
(Zeitschrift für fremde Sprachen in Wissenschaft and Praxis, zugleich Fachblatt des Bundesverbandes der Dolmetscher und Übersetzer e.V. (BDU), Langenscheidt-Verlag, Crellestr 28–30 D.1000 Berlin 62 (Schoeneberg); Tel (0130) 780002-0
Editor Prof Dr Gunther Haensch
Editor L.R. Dir Friedrich Krollmann, 8000 Munich
4 copies a year; annual subscription 86 DM, including postage

The Library
Oxford Journals, Oxford University Press, Pinkhill Hse, Southfield Rd, Eynsham, Oxford OX8 1JJ; Tel (01865) 882283; Fax (01865) 882890
Editor Mervyn Jannetta
Quarterly; annual price UK and Europe £50; Rest of World US$104
Official journal of the Bibliographical Society for the history of books, both manuscript and printed, and the role of books in history

Library Association Record
7 Ridgmount St, London WC1E 7AE; Tel 0171-636 7543; Fax 0171-323 6675
Editor Christina Brockhurst
12 issues per year; annual subscription, £79.50 (UK), £98.00 (overseas), US$180.00 (North America)
Professional concerns in librarianship, education, recreation and information

Links 2
Editor Jean Carlisle, BED(SpEd), DipSLD(RSA) Glenwood, Corntown, Bridgend, Mid Glamorgan CF35 5BB
Termly; annual subscription, £15.00
Articles on topics relating to education and allied disciplines

Literary and Linguistic Computing
Oxford Journals, Oxford University Press, Walton St, Oxford OX2 6DP; Tel (01865) 56767; Fax (01865) 267773; Telex 837730 OXPRESG
Editor-in-Chief Gordon Dixon Institute of Advanced Studies, Manchester Metropolitan University, All Saints Bldg, Oxford Rd, Manchester M15 6BH; Tel 0161-247 1947; Fax 0161-247 6390
Quarterly; annual price UK and Europe £70; Rest of World US$130
All aspects of computing applied to literature and language. Scope includes hardware and software, computer-assisted language learning, word-processing for humanities and applications and the teaching of computer techniques to language and literature students

Literature and Theology
Oxford Journals, Oxford University Press, Pinkhill Hse, Southfield Rd, Eynsham, Oxford OX8 1JJ; Tel (01865) 882283; Fax (01865) 882890
Editor (Director of the Centre for the Study of Literature and Theology Revd Dr David Jasper Dept of English, Univ of Glasgow
Quarterly; annual price UK and Europe £54; Rest of World US$100
Interdisciplinary study of serious interest to both theologians and to students of literature

LOGOS
c/o Janice Staines, Delves Junior School, Bell La, Walsall WS5 4PU
Editor Ken Brown
Annual subscription (including membership) £10

Management Bibliographies & Reviews
(incorporating Business Education)
MCB University Press Ltd, 62 Toller La, Bradford BD8 9BY; Tel (01274) 499821
Editor Andrew Ede
8 times a year, £599.95

Mathematical Gazette
The Mathematical Association, 259 London Rd, Leicester LE2 3BE; Tel (0116) 270 3877
Editor Stephen Abbott
Mar, July, Nov; annual postal subscription, £36.00

Mathematical Pie
Mathematical Pie Ltd, 259 London Rd, Leicester LE2 3BE
Editor G. Fowler
Termly, 50p. Discounts on bulk orders. Details on request

Mathematics in School
Journal of the Mathematical Association
Editor D.M. Neal Faculty of Education, University of Central England, Westbourne Rd, Birmingham B15 3TN
Five times yearly, £6; annual subscription, £34.00 from Longman Group UK Ltd, Subscriptions (Journals) Dept, Fourth Ave, Harlow, Essex CM19 5AA (0279) 29655

Mathematics Round the Country
The Mathematical Association, 259 London Rd, Leicester LE2 3BE; Tel (0116) 270 3877
Editor Sylvia Thistle Mathematics Dept, Worcester College of Higher Education, Worcester
Spring, summer, autumn; annual subscription, £2

Mathematics Teaching
Association of Teachers of Mathematics, 7 Shaftesbury St, Derby DE23 8YB; Tel (01332) 346599
Editor Derek Ball
Editor Barbara Ball
4 issues a year. Annual subscription, £55 (institutions), £38 (individuals), £15.25 (students) (inc. 'Micromath'—termly)

MENCAP News
Magazine of MENCAP–the Royal Society for Mentally Handicapped Children & Adults
123 Golden La, London EC1Y ORT; Tel 0171-454 0454
The largest organisation for parents, families and people with a learning disability in the UK providing housing, employment, holidays and further education
Incorporates *Parents Voice*; published 10 times annually

Micro-Scope
99 Foxcote, Wokingham, Berks RG11 3PG; Tel (01734) 733718; Fax (01734) 733718

Editor Mrs C. Robson
Free to members of MAPE; annual membership £15 UK, £20 Overseas

Micromath
Journal of the Association of Teachers of Mathematics, published by the Association of Teachers of Mathematics
7 Shaftesbury St, Derby DE23 8YB; Tel (01332) 346599
Editor Sue Burns
Editor Peter Wilder
3 times a year; annual subscription to Association: Personal £38.00, Institutional £55.00, free to members of the Association of Teachers of Mathematics (incl Mathematics Teaching, 4 issues)

Mind
Oxford Journals, Oxford University Press, Pinkhill Hse, Southfield Rd, Eynsham, Oxford OX8 1JJ; Tel (01865) 882283; Fax (01865) 882890
Editor Mark Sainsbury Kings College London
Quarterly; annual price UK and Europe £28; Rest of World US$53
Leading philosophical ideas of the times. Expresses and gives direction to currents of thought in epistemology, the philosophy of language, metaphysics and philosophical psychology

Minerva: A Review of Science, Learning and Policy
19 Nottingham Rd, London SW17 7EA; Tel 0181-682 1782
Editor Prof Edward Shils
Quarterly; annual subscription, £75 (UK), US$135 (USA), £78 rest of the world

Modern Language Review
Dept of French, The University, Exeter EX4 4QH
Editor Prof M.C. Cook
Quarterly (Jan, Apr, July, Oct); annual subscription, £56

Modus
(The official journal of the National Association of Teachers of Home Economics and Technology)
Hamilton Hse, Mabledon Pl, London WC1H 9BJ; Tel 0171-387 1441
Eight issues yearly; annual subscription, inc postage £25.00; students £16.00; free to members

Multicultural Teaching
Trentham Books Ltd, Westview Hse, 734 London Rd, Oakhill, Stoke-on-Trent, Staffs ST4 5NP; Tel (01782) 745567; Fax (01782) 745553
Editor Gillian Klein
3 times a year, £8; annual subscription, £20.50

Music and Letters
Oxford Journals, Oxford University Press, Walton St, Oxford OX2 6DP; Tel (01865) 56767; Fax (01865) 56646
Editor Nigel Fortune 44 Philip Victor Rd, Birmingham B20 2QD
Editor Tim Carter Department of Music, Royal Holloway, University of London, Egham, Surrey TW20 0EX
Quarterly; annual price UK and Europe £48; Rest of World US$90
All fields of musical enquiry, from earliest times to present day. Includes wide range of reviews: books; scholarly editions of music of the past

Music Teacher
Rhinegold Publishing, 241 Shaftesbury Ave, London WC2H 8EH; Tel 0171-333 1747; Fax 0171-333 1769
Editor Tim Homfray
Monthly, £2.45; annual subscription £26 (UK); overseas: £29 (surface), £33 (Europe airmail), £39, £42 (Zones 1,2 airmail)

Muslim Education Quarterly
The Islamic Academy, 23 Metcalfe Rd, Cambridge CB4 2BD
Editor Prof Syed Ali Ashraf
Quartlery, single copies, £4.90; annual subscription, £13.50 (individual), £19.50 (institutional)
A review of Muslim Education in the modern world both in Muslim majority and in Muslim minority countries, intended as a means of communication for scholars dedicated to the task of making education Islamic in character; also expected to act as an open forum for exchange of ideas between such scholars and others including non-Muslims who hold contrary views

NAGM News
10 Campion Terrace, Leamington Spa, Warks CV32 4SX; Tel (01926) 338765; Fax (01926) 338765
Editor Ian Rule
Magazine of the National Association of Governors and Managers. Published by Campion Communications

NASD Journal
Journal of the National Association for Staff Development
South West Association Further Education and Training, Bishops Hull Hse, Bishops Hull, Taunton, Somerset; Tel (01823) 335491; Fax (01823) 323388
Editor Liz McGrath
Subscription enquiries J. Polkinghorne, Honorary Treasurer
Twice-yearly (January and June); annual subscription £9

NASUWT Career Teacher Journal
National Association of Schoolmasters and Union of Women Teachers (NASUWT), Hillscourt Education Centre, Rose Hill, Rednal, Birmingham B45 8RS; Tel 0121-453 6150; Fax 0121-453 7224
Editor-in-Chief N.R. A.de Gruchy
Executive Editor W.J. Herron, BSc(Econ)
3 times a year

NATFHE Journal
NATFHE, 27 Britannia St, London WC1X 9JP; Tel 0171-837 3636
General Editor Geoff Woolf
Editor Brenda Kirsch
Termly; annual subscription, £8

National Association of Careers and Guidance Teachers
The Journal of the National Association of Careers and Guidance Teachers
169 Melton Rd, West Bridgford, Nottingham NG2 6JL; Tel (0115) 923 1336
Editor Nikki Sims
Three times yearly; annual subscription £25

National Association of Toy and Leisure Libraries Play Matters
Play Matters, 68 Churchway, London NW1 1LT; Tel 0171-387 9592; Fax 0171-383 2714
Play Matters magazine: Four issues per year, free to members. Information about toy and leisure libraries which loan games and toys for all children, and leisure equipment to adults with special needs

National Institute Economic Review
National Institute of Economic and Social Research, 2 Dean Trench St, Smith Sq, London SW1P 3HE; Tel 0171-222 7665; Fax 0171-222 1435
Quarterly; £18 plus postage; annual subscription, £75 Home , £90 Overseas

NCET
National Council for Education Technology, Milburn Hill Rd, Science Pk, Coventry CV4 7JJ; Tel (01203) 416994
The National Council for Educational Technology is a registered charity funded by the Department of Education to develop and promote the use of information technology in every area of education and training

NCVO News
Regent's Wharf, 8 All Saints St, London N1 9RL; Tel 0171-713 6161; Fax 0171-713 6300
Editor Anne Davies

10 times a year; annual subscription £25 for voluntary organisations and individuals, £50 statutory or commercial organisations, foreign and bulk rates on application
Contains information and articles on the voluntary sector, including reviews, features and conference and course listings

NEC News
The National Extension College, 18 Brooklands Ave, Cambridge CB2 2HN; Tel (01223) 316644; Fax (01223) 313586
January, May, September; free

Network
The National Community Education Magazine, published by the Community Education Development Centre, Lyng Hall, Blackberry La, Coventry CV2 3JS
Editor Dick Jenkinson
6 times a year; distributed free to all secondary schools and available to members of CEDC's Community Education Network Forum, annual subscription £20.00

New Community
(A Journal of Research and Policy on Ethnic Relations)
Centre for Research in Ethnic Relations, University of Warwick, Coventry CV4 7AL; Tel (01503) 30904
Editor Malcolm Cross
Quarterly, single/back issue £6 (individuals, £12 institutions); annual subscription, £20 (individual), £36 (institutions)

New Era in Education
Editor (Correspondence) David Turner
3 times yearly, £6; £17 UK individuals; £23, UK institutions; US$44 individuals; US$57 institutions; £20 overseas individuals; £26 overseas institutions
Journal of World Education Fellowship, innovative education in international context

New Home Economics
Forbes Publications Ltd, 2 Drayson Mews, London W8 4LY; Tel 0171-938 1035; Fax 0171-938 4425
Editor Dilys Wells, BSc
10 issues a year; annual subscription, £22; overseas £26 (US$47.50); special student's rate, £17 (single), £16 (5 or more to one address)
Covers food, nutrition, home economics generally, science and technology, life skills, textiles, consumer and health education

New Humanist
88 Islington High St, London N1 8EL; Tel 0171-226 7251
Editor Jim Herrick
Quarterly, £2.50; annual subscription, £12 post paid

Newscheck
Careers and Occupational Information Centre, Department of Employment
Virginia Hse, Foulsham, Dereham, Norfolk NR20 5RX; Tel (01362) 683346; Fax (01362) 683346
Editor J. Widmer
9 issues per annum, free
Brings together careers and occupation-related information and comment, plus reference section

Notes and Queries
Oxford Journals, Oxford University Press, Walton St, Oxford OX2 6DP; Tel (01865) 56767; Fax (01865) 56646
Editor L.G. Black
Editor D. Hewitt
Editor E.G. Stanley
Quarterly; annual price UK and Europe £53; Rest of World US$100
English language and literature, lexicography, history and scholarly antiquarianism. In addition to notes readers' queries and replies there are book reviews. Each issue gives emphasis to the works of a particular period

Nutrition and Food Science
Forbes Publications Ltd, 2 Drayson Mews, London W8 4LY; Tel 0171-938 1035; Fax 0171-938 4425
Editor Dilys Wells, BSc
Bi-monthly (Jan, Mar, May, July, Sep, Nov); annual subscription, £17.50; students £14.50 (single), £13.50 (bulk); overseas, £21 (US$37.50)
All aspects of nutrition, food science and health education

Omnibus
Sixth form classics magazine published by the Joint Association of Classical Teachers (JACT)
31–34 Gordon Sq, London WC1H OPY
Twice yearly; £2 (incl. postage), reduced price for multiple orders

Open Learning
Published in association with the Open University
Editor Alan Tait c/o Ms Jo Matthews, Regional Academic Services, The Open University, Walton Hall, Milton Keynes MK7 6AA
3 times a year; Annual subscription £32.50 (UK), £37/US$66 (overseas) from Longman Group UK Ltd, Subscriptions (Journals) Dept, Fourth Ave, Harlow, Essex, CM19 5AA (0279) 429655
Provides a platform for the latest developments and ideas in this expanding field

Oxford Art Journal
Oxford University Press, Walton St, Oxford OX2 6DP
Andrew Hemingway Department of History of Art, University College London, Gower St, London WC1E 6BT
Biannual; annual subscription, private and individual, £23.00 (UK and Europe), US$44 (Rest of World); libraries and institutions, £38 (UK and Europe), US$74 (Rest of World)

Oxford Journal of Legal Studies
Oxford Journals, Oxford University Press, Pinkhill Hse, Southfield Rd, Eynsham, Oxford OX8 1JJ; Tel (01865) 882283; Fax (01865) 882890
Editor Dr P.M. North Jesus College, Oxford
Quarterly; annual price UK and Europe £58; Rest of World US$125
Emphasis on matters of theory and on broad issues arising from the relationship of law to other disciplines, drawing on Oxford's particular strength in legal philosophy and socio-legal matters. Articles cover comparative and international law, EEC law, legal history and philosophy and interdisciplinary material from, eg the fields of economics and sociology

Paragraph
Edinburgh University Press, 22 George Sq, Edinburgh EH8 9LF; Tel 0131-650 1000; Fax 0131-662 0053
Editor Michael Holland
Editor Roland-François Lack
3 per year; annual price UK and Europe £34; Rest of World US$66
Articles and reviews in English exploring critical theory in general and its application to literature and the other arts

Parents and Schools
Campaign for State Education (CASE)
158 Durham Rd, London SW20 0DG; Tel 0181-944 8206; Fax 0181-944 8206
Editor Nicky Adamson Akeman Hse, High St, Stretham, Cambridge CB6 3JQ
Editor Margaret Tulloch
News and campaigning information on current issues in education
Publishes six times a year; schools, governing bodies and PTAs; LEAs, libraries £20 per year; free to members of CASE 3 copies of each issue

Parliamentary History
Edinburgh University Press, 22 George Sq, Edinburgh EH8 9LF
Editor Clyve Jones Institute of Historical Research, London
3 per year; annual price UK and Europe £50; Rest of World US$98
Research articles and papers of a more general appeal on all aspects of parliamentary history (including the

Scottish and Irish parliaments) from the Middle Ages to the twentieth century and legislatures in British Colonies before independence, covering parliamentary management, political structure, elections and the electorate, architecture and representative art of the various parliaments

PASS
Accountancy Publishing Group, Quadrant Hse, Sutton, Surrey SM2 5AS; Tel 0181-652 4720 (editorial); 0181-652 4688 (advertising)
Editor Graham Hambly
Monthly; annual subscription £22 (UK) £30 (overseas); free to part qualified accountants of the major UK accountancy bodies
Covers exam and student news, reviews, SSAPs and publishes the widest range of job opportunities for part qualified accountants

Past and Present
Oxford Journals, Oxford University Press, Walton St, Oxford OX2 6DP; Tel (01865) 56767; Fax (01865) 514010
Editor Dr Paul Slack Exeter College, Oxford
Editor Joanna Innes Somerville College, Oxford
Quarterly; annual price UK and Europe £54; Rest of World US$125
Primarily concerned with social, economic and cultural changes, their causes and consequences this highly readable journal publishes a wide variety of scholarly and original historical articles

Pastoral Care in Education
The official journal of the National Association for Pastoral Care in Education
Basil Blackwell, 108 Cowley Rd, Oxford OX4 1JF; Tel (01865) 722146
Editor Ron Best
Editor Peter Lang
Editor Margaret Roberts
Editor John Thacker
Available from NAPCE, Dept of Education, University of Warwick, Westwood, Coventry CV4 7AL; Tel Coventry 523810
Four times a year (March, June, Sept and Dec); annual subscription £25 (individual), £6 (student), £27 (primary/special schools), £45 (secondary schools)

Perspective
10 Campion Terrace, Leamington Spa, Warks CV32 4SX; Tel (01926) 457525; Fax (01926) 338765
Editor Julie Smart
Magazine of the National Association of Educational Inspectors, Advisers and Consultants. Published by Campion Communications

Physics Education
Institute of Physics Publishing Ltd, Techno Hse, Redcliffe Way, Bristol BS1 6NX; Tel (0117) 929 7481
Editor John H. Avison Marton Sixth Form College, Middlesbrough
6 issues annually, £14; annual subscription, £102 (ROW), US$204 (USA)
Physics teaching at 16–18 age level

Plus
The Mathematical Association, 259 London Rd, Leicester LE2 3BE; Tel (0116) 270 3877
Editor W. Arthur Dodd
Spring, summer, autumn; annual subscription, £3; discounts on bulk orders, details on request

Political Studies
Dept of Government, The University, Manchester M13 9PL; Tel 0161-275 4931; Fax 0161-275 4932
Editor Prof Michael Moran
Quarterly; annual subscription, £71.00

Postgraduate Study
Newpoint Publishing Company, Windsor Ct, East Grinstead Hse, East Grinstead, W Sussex; Tel (01342) 318011
Editor Carol Stratton

Postgraduate Study in Britain
Newpoint Publishing Company, Windsor Ct, East Grinstead Hse, East Grinstead, W Sussex; Tel (01342) 318011
Editor Carol Stratton

Prep School
Belgrave Educational Publishing, PO Box 140, Ipswich, Suffolk IP6 9PL; Tel (01449) 760550; Fax (01449) 760550
Proprietor Julie Ranson
Editor Mrs Anne Kiggell Straight Ash, Ashampstead Common, Pangbourne, Berks RG8 8QT; Tel (01635) 201385
Feb, May and Oct, £2.50; annual subscription, £7

Primary Geographer
The Geographical Association, 343 Fulwood Rd, Sheffield S10 3BP; Tel (0114) 267 0666; Fax (0114) 267 0688
Editor Wendy Morgan
Quarterly. Subscription rates available from the above address

Primary and Middle School Equipment
131–135 Temple Chambers, Temple Ave, London EC4Y 0BP; Tel 0171-583 3030; Fax 0171-583 6481
Editor Garry Parker
10 issues per annum (Monthly except July and Aug); annual subscription £17 (UK), £22 (overseas)

Proceedings of the London Mathematical Society
Mathematics and Oceanography Bldg, The University of Liverpool, PO Box 147, Liverpool L69 3BX; Tel 0151-794 4009/4017/4062; Fax 0151-794 4061; Telex 837330
Editor Dr S. Brenner
Editor Prof C.T.C. Wall, FRS
Six times a year; price per copy £69 (UK), annual subscription £330 (UK)

Professional Teacher
Journal of the Professional Association of Teachers, 2 St James Ct, Friar Gate, Derby DE1 1BT; Tel (01332) 372337; Fax (01332) 292431
Editorial Jackie M. Miller
Production/Advertising Elizabeth Gabriel
5 times a year, free to members; £6.75 a year non-members

Public Services Yearbook, formerly Public Domain
Published for The Public Finance Foundation, 3 Robert St, London WC2N 6BH; Tel 0171-895 8823
Editor Michaela Lavender
Editor Peter Jackson
Annual; £30
Authoritative annual survey, backed up with charts and tables, of trends and developments in the economy, public sector finance and public service
Chapman and Hall
2–6 Boundary Row, London SE1

Quarterly Journal of Mathematics
Mathematical Institute, 24–29 Giles, Oxford OX1 3LB
Editor B.F. Steer
Editor W.B. Stewart
Quarterly, £21 (UK and Europe), US$38 (rest of world) annual subscription, £70 (UK and Europe), US$125 (Rest of World)

Quarterly Journal of Mechanics and Applied Mathematics
Oxford University Press, Pinkhill Hse, Southfield Rd, Eynsham, Oxford OX8 1JJ; Tel (01865) 882283
Editor L.M. Hocking
Editor P.A. Martin
Editor A.D. Rawlins
Quarterly £25 (UK and Europe), US$50 (US and rest of world); annual subscription £84 (UK and Europe), £165 (US and rest of world)

RE Today
Christian Education Movement, Royal Bldgs, Victoria St, Derby DE1 1GW; Tel (01332) 296655; Fax (01332) 343253
Editor Stephen Orchard
3 times a year, £7.00 (single issue); annual subscription, £17.00
Magazine for RE teachers, circulation approx 12,000

Reading
Administrative Secretary, United Kingdom Reading Association, C/o Warrington Rd, C.P. School, Naylor Rd, Widnes, Cheshire WA8 0BP
Editor David Wray School of Education, University of Exeter, Exeter EX1 2LU
Three times yearly, free to members of UKRA; annual subscription (members), £20 (individuals), £25 (institutions). Non-members can obtain copies from Basil Blackwell, 108 Cowley Rd, Oxford OX4 1JF
Concerned with study and improvement of reading and related processes

Renaissance Studies
Oxford University Press, Walton St, Oxford OX2 6DP; Tel (01865) 56767; Fax (01865) 267773
Editor Dr Gordon Campbell Univ of Leicester; Tel (0116) 252 2633; Fax (0116) 252 2065
Quarterly; 1994 annual price UK and Europe £58; Rest of World US$108
All aspects of Renaissance history and culture. The journal prints multi-disciplinary papers on the history, art, architecture, religion, literature and language of any European country or any country influenced by Europe during the Renaissance period

Report
Journal of the Association of Teachers and Lecturers (ATL)
Editorial, 7 Northumberland St, London WC2N 5DA; Tel 0171-930 6441; Fax 0171-930 1359
8 times a year; annual subscription, £8

Research in Education
Manchester University Press, Oxford Rd, Manchester M13 9PL; Tel 0161-273 5539
Executive Editor Prof Ivan Reid
Editor Dr Ivan Reid
£55 institutional, £35 individual per annum (two issues)
International Disciplinery research in education

Resource
The Professional Council for Religious Education, Royal Bldgs, Victoria St, Derby DE1 1GW; Tel (01203) 523523 Ext 2304
Editor Robert Jackson
Reviews Editor Judith Everington
3 times a year; subscription details from above address
A journal for teachers of religious education

Review of English Studies
Oxford Journals, Oxford University Press, Walton St, Oxford OX2 6DP; Tel (01865) 56767; Fax (01865) 56646
Editor R.E. Alton, MA St Edmund Hall, Oxford
Quarterly (Feb, May, Aug, Nov), £18 institutional; four consecutive numbers, £36 personal, £60 institutional (UK)
English literature and the English language from the earliest period up to the present day. Articles, notes, reviews of recent books, and a summary of periodical literature are included

RISC User
117 Hatfield Rd, St Albans, Herts AL1 4JS; Tel (01727) 840303
Editor Alan Wrigley
Beebug Ltd
Annual subscription £21.90

Royal Air Force Training Bulletin
Department of Educational and Training Technology Development Training Development Support Unit, RAF Newton, Nottingham NG13 8HL; Tel (01949) 20771 Ext 7288
Editor Sqn Ldr M.G. Evans, MED, BED RAF
Annually
Free distribution on request

Rusistika
Russian Journal of the Association for Language Learning
Association for Language Learning, 16 Recent Pl, Rugby CV21 2PN; Tel (01788) 546443; Fax (01788) 544149
Editor Margaret Tejerizo Dept of Slavonic Languages, University of Glasgow, Hetherington Bldg, Bute Gdns, Glasgow G12 8QQ
Twice yearly (June and December); annual subscription £20 (UK), £21 (overseas), US$40 (USA)
Formerly *The Journal of Russian Studies* published by the Association of Teachers of Russian. Articles, reviews and information of special interest to learners and teachers of Russian

Safety Education
Royal Society for the Prevention of Accidents, Cannon Hse, Priory Queensway, Birmingham B4 6BS; Tel 0121-200 2461
Editor Carole Wale
Safety Education Adviser Martin Gomberg
Termly; annual subscription, £6.00 (members); £12 (non-members)

The School Librarian
School Library Association, Liden Library, Barrington Cl, Liden, Swindon, Wilts SN3 6HF; Tel (01793) 617838
Editor Raymond Astbury
Reviews Editor Keith Barker
4 times yearly, current subscription rates from the Executive Secretary
Articles and extensive review section

School Organisation
Carfax Publishing Company, PO Box 25, Abingdon, Oxon OX14 3UE
Editor D. Smetherham South Bristol College
3 issues a year; Institutional: EC£136.00/Outside EC £136.00/US$254.00; Personal: EC £46.00/Outside EC £48.00/US$84.00
Focuses upon the practical organisational and leadership problems in schools

The School Science Review
The Association for Science Education, College La, Hatfield, Herts AL10 9AA; Tel (01707) 267411
Editor A.A. Bishop, MA
Mar, June, Sep and Dec; annual subscription, £52 including postage

Scottish Educational Journal
46 Moray Pl, Edinburgh EH3 6BH; Tel 0131-225 6244; Fax 0131-220 3151
Managing Editor Simon Macaulay
6 issues a year; annual subscription, £8.10 (UK), £13 (overseas) £9.20 (Europe)

Scottish Journal of Political Economy
Department of Social and Economic Research, University of Glasgow, Glasgow G12 8RT; Tel 0141-339 8855 Ext 5060; Fax 0141-330 4940
Editor Prof L.C. Hunter
Editor Prof A. Muscatelli
Quarterly, £20.00; annual subscription, £56.50 (UK), £56.50 (Europe), £65.00 (Rest of World); US$97 (North America) from Basil Blackwell, 108 Cowley Rd, Oxford OX4 1JF

Screen (incorporating Screen Education)
Subscriptions/Enquiries: Oxford Journals, Oxford University Press, Walton St, Oxford OX2 6DP; Tel (01865) 56767; Fax (01865) 267773; Editorial: Screen, John Logie Baird Centre, Glasgow University, Glasgow G12 8QQ; Tel 0141-330 5035; Fax 0141-307 8010
Editor John Caughie
Editor Simon Frith

Editor Sandra Kemp
Editor Norman King
Editor Annette Kuhn
Editor Karen Lury
Editor Jackie Stacey
Quarterly; £6.95 per issue, subscription £48 (institutions), £26 (individuals), £21 (students and unemployed)
Britain's leading journal of film and television studies. Contributions by leading critics, practising writers and film makers. Covers major developments in film theory from the pop video to film noir

The Seafarer
The Marine Society, 202 Lambeth Rd, London SE1 7JW; Tel 0171-261 9535; Fax 0171-401 2537; Telex 934089
Executive Editor Michael Moore, BA
Quarterly (Jan, Apr, Jul, Oct), £2.00; annual subscription, £8

Secondary and Higher Education Journal
Presshouse Publications Ltd, Queen St, Hook Norton, Nr Banbury, Oxon OX15 5PH; Tel (01608) 737056
Editor Caroline Bond
Three times yearly; controlled circulation

Sesame
The Open University, Walton Hall, Milton Keynes MK7 6AA; Tel (01908) 653761
Editor Margaret Salter
6 times yearly, free to students and staff, annual subscription, £4
News and features about Open University studies

Social History of Medicine
Oxford Journals, Oxford University Press, Walton St, Oxford OX2 6DP; Tel (01865) 56767; Fax (01865) 56767
Editor Dr Paul Weindling Wellcome Unit for the History of Medicine, Oxford
Editor Prof Anne Crowther University of Glasgow
3 per year; annual price UK and Europe £44; Rest of World US$86
All aspects of health, illness and medical treatment, as well as the biological aspects of normal life, with patients within their economic, social and political environments and with systems of health and welfare provision

The Sower
A quarterly magazine for growing Christians
The Sower Ltd, 10–12 High St, Great Wakering, Essex SS3 OEQ
Editor Peter Elvy
Annual subscription, £5

Special Needs Education Journal
Presshouse Publications Ltd, Queen St, Hook Norton, Nr Banbury, Oxon OX15 5PH; Tel (01608) 737056
Editor Caroline Bond
Three times yearly; controlled circulation

Spectrum
The Paternoster Press, PO Box 300, Carlisle, Cumbria CA3 0QS
Editor John Shortt 1 Kiteley's Gn, Leighton Buzzard LU7 8LD; Tel (01525) 379709
2 issues a year; £17.90
A journal concerned with current educational thinking from a Christian standpoint sponsored by the Association of Christian Teachers

Speech and Drama
Published by the Society of Teachers of Speech and Drama
4 Fane Rd, Oxford OX3 0SA; Tel (01865) 728304
Editor Dr Paul Ranger
Apr and Oct, £3.50; annual postal subscription, (sterling drawn on a London bank) £6.50 (p.a)
Theatre, speech and drama at a wide range of educational levels. Audio-visual, book and theatre reviews

Spoken English: ideas and developments in oral education
Journal of the English Speaking Board (International), 26A Princes St, Southport, Merseyside PR8 1EQ; Tel (01704) 501730
Editor Malcolm Dale
Twice a year March and Sept. Annual subscription, £15 individual, £20 corporate, both UK and overseas

Sport and Leisure Magazine
16 Upper Woburn Pl, London WC1H 0QP; Tel 0171-388 1277; Fax 0171-383 5740
Editor Louise Fyfe
6 times a year; annual subscription, £9 including postage
The national colour magazine of the Sports Council, featuring the latest developments in the provision of sport and leisure at school, community and national levels

State Education Leader
Education Commission of the States, 707 17th St, Suite 2700, Denver, Colorado 80202-3427, USA
Editor Sherry Freeland Walker
3 time a year; US$15 a year, US$4 per copy
Each issue examines a major educational topic

Statute Law Review
Office of the Clerk of Tynwald, Legislative Bldgs, Douglas, Isle of Man; Tel (01624) 685500; Fax (01624) 685504
Editor (Clerk of Tynwald, Secretary to the House of Keys and Counsel to the Speaker, and of the Univs of Strathclyde and Lancaster) Prof T.St. J.N. Bates
Deputy Editor Prof Gavin Drewry Royal Holloway and Bedford New College
Annual price UK and Europe £57; Rest of World US$110
The legislative process; use of legislation as an instrument of public policy and the drafting and interpretation of legislation

Streetwise
National Association for Urban Studies, University of Brighton, 68 Grand Parade, Brighton BN2 2JY; Tel (01273) 673416; Fax (01273) 673416
Editor Richard Welsh
Quarterly journal for teachers, educationalists, planners, environmentalists, students and anyone concerned with issues involving the built environment

Studies in the Education of Adults
21 De Montfort St, Leicester LE1 7GE; Tel (0116) 255 1451
Editor John Wallis
Bi-annual; annual subscription £17.50; £20 (institutions)
Essays and research studies in adult continuing education

Studies in Science Education
Studies in Education Ltd (Nafferton Books), Driffield Rd, Driffield YO25 0JL; Tel (01377) 44231 and 46861
Editor E. Jenkins
Annually; £17; Overseas £18

Support for Learning (The British Journal of Learning Support)
A journal of NASEN
15 Hall Brow Cl, Ormskirk, Lancs L39 2YX; Tel (01695) 573921
Editor Charles Gains
Quarterly, £7.50; annual subscription, £26 from Basil Blackwell, 108 Cowley Rd, Oxford OX4 1JF, Tel (0865) 791100

Talking Politics
(incorporating Teaching Politics), Journal of the Politics Association, The Politics Association, Studio 16–1 Mex Business Park, Hamilton Rd, Longsight, Manchester M13 0PD
Editor Dr L. Robins De Montfort University, Leicester
3 times a year; annual subscription, £25 for institutions, £18 for individuals; free to members

The Teacher
The National Union of Teachers, Hamilton Hse, Mabledon Pl, London WC1H 9BD; Tel 0171-380 4708
Editor Mitch Howard
8 times a term; free to NUT members
Circulation Department Membership Dept, NUT, Hamilton Hse, Mabledon Pl, London, WC1H 9BD

Teaching Geography
An Official Journal of the Geographical Association, 343 Fulwood Rd, Sheffield S10 3BP; Tel (0114) 267 0666; Fax (0114) 267 0688
Editor Dr David Boardman
Quarterly; Subscription rates available from above address

Teaching History
The Historical Association, 59A Kennington Park Rd, London SE11 4JH; Tel 0171-735 3901
Editor Richard Brown 17 Sunbower Ave, Dunstable, Beds LU6 1UQ
Jan, April, June, Oct; annual subscription (including membership), £35; non-members, £45

Theatre Research International
Oxford Journals, Oxford University Press (in association with the International Federation for Theatre Research), Walton St, Oxford OX2 6DP; Tel (01865) 882283; Fax (01865) 882890
Editor Claude Schumacher Dept of Theatre Studies, Glasgow Univ, Glasgow G12 8QF; Tel 0141-330 5162; Fax 0141-330 4142
3 times yearly, £13; annual price UK and Europe £49; Rest of World US$98
History of criticism of drama conceived as the art of the theatre, providing both a medium of communication for scholars and a service to students of art, architecture, design, music and dramatic literature

The Times Educational Supplement
Admiral Hse, 66–68 East Smithfield, London E1 9XY; Tel 0171-782 3000; Fax 0171-782 3333 (advertising) 0171-782 3200 (editorial)
Editor Patricia Rowan
Weekly (Fri), 90p; annual subscription, £65

The Times Higher Education Supplement
Admiral Hse, 66–68 East Smithfield, London E1 9XY; Tel 0171-253 3000
Editor Auriol Stevens
Weekly (Fri), 90p; annual subscription, £48

TLK (Teaching London Kids)
20 Durham Rd, London SW20 0TW
Bi-Yearly, £1.50 + 50p postage and packing
2 issues, £4.00; 5 back issues, £5 post free
Magazine exploring issues affecting inner-city education

Together
The National Society, Church Hse, Dean's Yard, London SW1P 3NZ; Tel 0171-222 1672; Fax 0171-233 2592
Editor Dorothy Jamal
9 issues a year, 80p; annual subscription, £10
Christian education work with children

Training Officer
Marylebone Press Ltd, Lloyds Hse, 18 Lloyd St, Manchester M2 5WA; Tel 0161-832 4607; Fax 0161-832 8129
Editor Sylvia Worth
10 times a year; annual subscription, £55 (UK)

Tuttitalia
Italian Journal of Association for Language Learning, 16 Regent Pl, Rugby CV21 2PN; Tel (01788) 546443; Fax (01788) 544149
Editor Andrew Wilkin Dept of Modern Languages, University of Strathclyde, Glasgow G1 1XH
Twice yearly (June and Dec); annual subscription £20 (UK), £21 (overseas), US$40 (USA). Available to members of ALL as part of their membership package. Membership subscription £28 (1993) reduced for students and part-time teachers
Formerly *The Association of Teachers of Italian Journal*
Articles, reviews and information of special interest to learners and teachers of Italian

Twentieth Century British History
Oxford Journals, Oxford University Press, Pinkhill Hse, Southfield Rd, Eynsham, Oxford OX8 1JJ; Tel (01865) 882283; Fax (01865) 882890
Editor Dr Ross McKibbin St John's College, Oxford
Editor Dr John Rowett Brasenose College, Oxford
3 per year; annual price UK and Europe £37; Rest of World US$75
Covers all aspects of British history in the twentieth century, drawing together the different branches of historical scholarship and work in all related disciplines

Under Five Contact
Pre-school Playgroups Association, 61–63 Kings Cross Rd, London WC1X 9LL; Tel 0171-833 0991; Fax 0171-837 4942
Editor Ann Henderson
Monthly except Aug and Dec; annual subscription, £21 for individuals, £42 for playgroups. Magazine only, £25 for non-members; £10 for staff/parent in member groups
Post paid from PPA
Play and learning for under-fives, or home and in pre-school groups

Use of English
The English Association University of Leicester, 128 Regent Rd, Leicester LE1 7PA; Tel (0116) 252 5927; Fax (0116) 252 5928
Editor Roger Knight School of Education, 21 University Rd, Leicester LE1 7RF
3 times a year (spring, summer, autumn), £4.25; annual subscription, £13.50 individuals, £15.50 institutions

Utilitas
Edinburgh University Press, 22 George Sq, Edinburgh EH8 9LF; Tel 0131-650 1000; Fax 0131-662 0053
Editor Prof F. Rosen Betham Project, University College, London WC1E 6BT; Tel 0171-380 7123
2 per year, annual price UK and Europe £42; Rest of World US$85
The journal is interested in all aspects of utilitarian thought, and its contemporary application. Each issue is cross disciplinary, publishing material of interest to students of History, Politics, Economics, Philosophy, Law, Sociology and Literature

UTU News
(Ulster Teachers' Union), 94 Malone Rd, Belfast BT9 5HP; Tel (01232) 662216; Fax (01232) 663055
Editor (General Secretary) David Allen
Termly, free to members

Vida Hispanica
Spanish and Portugues Journal of the Association for Language Learning
16 Regent Pl, Rugby CV21 2PN; Tel (01788) 546443; Fax (01788) 544149
Editor Phil Turk 15 North Leigh, Bradford on Avon, Wilts BA15 2RG
Twice yearly (June and December); annual subscription £20 (UK), £21 (overseas), US$40 (USA). Available to members of the Association as part of their membership package. Membership subscription £24 (1991 rate) reduced for students and part-time teachers
Formerly published by the Association of Teachers of Spanish and Portuguese. Articles, reviews and information of special interest to learners and teachers of Spanish and Portuguese

WEA Reportback
A magazine for members and students of the Workers' Educational Association and others interested in adult education
Temple Hse, 17 Victoria Park Sq, London E2 9PB; Tel 0181-983 1515; Fax 0181-983 4840

Founded in 1903, WEA is the largest voluntary adult education organisation in the UK, with 14 WEA districts and over 800 branches
Twice yearly

Welsh Journal of Education
University of Wales Press, 6 Gwennyth St, Cardiff CF2 4YD; Tel (01222) 231919; Fax (01222) 230908
Joint Editor Prof Gareth Elwyn Jones
Joint Editor Anthony Packer
2 a year; annual subscription £10
The journal contains articles (one in Welsh) on issues of general educational interest

Welsh Secondary Schools Review and Pulse
Publications Officer T. Griffiths
4 of Pulse, 1 of Review p.a. free to Heads/Deputies of schools
Secondary education with emphasis on Wales

Women: A Cultural Review
Department of English, Birkbeck College, Malet St, London WC1E 7HX; Tel 0171-631 6324; Fax 0171-580 4510
Editor Helen Carr
Editor Isobel Armstrong
3 per year; annual price UK and Europe £48; Rest of World US$90 Institutional rate; UK and Europe £21.00; US$39 Personal rate
Explores the past and present role and representation of women in the arts and culture

The World Today
Royal Institute of International Affairs, 10 St James's Sq, London SW1Y 4LE; Tel 0171-957 5700; Fax 0171-957 5710
Editor Chris Civic
Monthly, £2; annual subscription, students £19, individuals £25, £30 institutions
Deals and internal politics and economics of countries worldwide and international issues

Young People Now!
National Youth Agency, 17/23 Albion St, Leicester LE1 6GD; Tel (0116) 285 6789; Fax (0116) 247 1043
Editor Mary Durkin
Monthly; annual subscription
The monthly magazine for everyone working with young people

Youth Club With The Edge
Youth Clubs UK, 30 Peacock La, Leicester LE1 5NY; Tel (0116) 262 9514
Editor Mandy Jarvis
Editor Alan Rogers
5 issues a year, free to members; non members, £10 (including postage)

National Library and Publishing Organisations

Advisory Councils

Community Service Volunteers (CSV)

237 Pentonville Rd, London N1 9NJ; Tel 0171-278 6601; Fax 0171-833 0149
Executive Director Elizabeth Hoodless
CSV Education encourages community involvement and volunteering in education through publications, workshops, training and local projects. Free publications list on request. Full-time volunteers (16–35 years old) work away from home for 4–12 months with people in need throughout the UK with board, lodging, fares and pocket money. CSV Training and Enterprise involves young unemployed people in training and work of community benefit. CSV Media projects provide the back-up to over 60 social action broadcasts nationwide and develops the use of local media by voluntary/community groups

Library and Information Services Council (Wales)

Welsh Office (Ed S2), Phase II, Govt Bldgs, TyGlas Rd, Llanishen, Cardiff CF4 5WE; Tel (01222) 761456 Ext 5373
Chairman W. Gwyn Williams
Member Lynda Garfield
Member Dr J. Lionel Madden
Member Ieuan Edwards
Member Tudfil Adams
Member Hywel Roberts
Member John Lancaster
Member Dr Ian Lovecy
Member A. Nick Talbott
Secretary Olwen Griffith

Research

British Library Research and Development Department

2 Sheraton St, London W1V 4BH; Tel 0171-323 7060 (General Enquiries); Fax 0171-323 7251
Director B.J. Perry
Assistant Director Responsible for Information Skills/School Library Research John Burchell
Promotes and supports research and development related to library and information operations in all subject fields and is directed to the benefit of the national library and information systems as a whole. Current research priorities include the use of information in education, incl. the role of the school library. A booklet *Information Skills in Education*, a publications catalogue, and guides to applicants are available free of charge on request

National Libraries

The British Library

Bibliographic Services Division

2 Sheraton St, London W1V 4BH; Tel 0171-323 7070

Humanities and Social Sciences

Great Russell St, London WC1B 3DG; Tel 0171-323 7676

Document Supply Centre

Boston Spa, Nr Wetherby, West Yorkshire LS23 7BQ; Tel (01937) 843434
Chief Executive Kenneth Cooper

British Library National Bibliographic Service

Boston Spa, Wetherby, West Yorkshire LS23 7BQ; Tel (01937) 546585; Fax (01937) 546586
Supplies bibliographic records and services to both the British Library and the whole network of UK libraries. It publishes indexes and bibliographies, operates the BLAISE online information retrieval services and provides bibliographic record supply services

British Library National Sound Archive

29 Exhibition Rd, London SW7 2AS; Tel 0171-412 7429; Fax 0171-412 7416
Publications and Education Officer B. Bergonzi

National Library for the Blind

Cromwell Rd, Bredbury, Stockport SK6 2SG; Tel 0161-494 0217
Director-General A. Leach
The Library is a registered charity. It provides reading of all kinds, in Braille (including music), Moon and large

print. Braille and Moon are lent post free to individual readers; large print through public libraries

National Library for the Handicapped Child: Reach Resource Centre

Wellington Hse, Wellington Rd, Wokingham, Berks RG11 2AG; Tel (01734) 891101; Fax (01734) 790989

National Library of Wales

Aberystwyth, Dyfed SY23 3BU; Tel (01970) 623816; Fax (01970) 615709; Telex 35165
Librarian J. Lionel Madden, MA, PhD, Dip.Lib, ALA

National Library of Scotland

George IV Bridge, Edinburgh EH1 1EW; Tel 0131-226 4531; Fax 0131-220 6662
Librarian I.D. McGowan, BA

National Listening Library (Talking Books for the Disabled and Hospital Patients)

12 Lant St, London SE1 1QH; Tel 0171-407 9417; Fax 0171-403 1377
Chairman Sir Nigel Althaus
Executive Director G.A. Hepworth

Library and Publishers Associations

ASLIB (Association for Information Management)

Information Hse, 20–24 Old St, London EC1V 9AP
President Lord Lloyd of Kilgerran

Association of Learned and Professional Society Publishers

48 Kelsey La, Beckenham, Kent BR3 3NE
Chairman M. Benjamin

Association of Publishers Educational Representatives

Hon Secretary S.W. Hall 88 Haven Chase, Cookridge, Leeds LS16 6SG; Tel (0113) 267 3956

Book Trust

Book Hse, 45 East Hill, London SW18 2QZ; Tel 0181-870 9055/8; Book Information Service Tel 0181-874 8526
Executive Director Brian Perman
Chairman Martyn Goff, OBE
Deputy Chairman Bing Taylor
Hon Treasurer Eric de Bellaigue
Director Willis Pickard
Director Anthony Land
Director Elizabeth Attenborough
Director Pamela Minett
Director Jane Carr
Director Michael Marland
Observer Dr A. Niven
Observer Dr N. Gilroy-Scott

International Board on Books for Young People (British Section)

Head of Children's Book Foundation Wendy Cooling

Booksellers Association of Great Britain and Ireland

Minster Hse, 272 Vauxhall Bridge Rd, London SW1V 1BA; Tel 0171-834 5477; Fax 0171-834 8812
Chief Executive T.E. Godfray
Executive for Training Alyson Smith

Federation of Children's Book Groups

6 Bryce Pl, Currie, Midlothian EH14 5LR; Tel 0131-449 2713

The Library Association

7 Ridgmount St, London WC1E 7AE; Tel 0171-636 7543; Fax 0171-436 7218
Chief Executive Ross Shimmon, FLA

The Publishers Association

19 Bedford Sq, London WC1B 3HJ; Tel 0171-580 6321; Fax 0171-636 5375
President Nicholas Chapman
Vice-President/Treasurer Paula Kahn
Chief Executive Clive Bradley

Educational Publishers' Council

Chairman Roy Davey
Teasurer Jeff Andrew
Director John Davies
Exhibitions Organiser Ruth Stuart Moore

Council of Academic and Professional Publishers

Chairman Dr Iain Stevenson
Vice-Chair John Jarvis
Treasurer Andrew Stevenson
Director John Davies
The Educational Publishers' Council and the Council of Academic and Professional Publishers are divisions of the Publishers' Association whose function is to control policy and activities concerning school and academic and professional publishing respectively in the United Kingdom

School Bookshop Association

6 Brightfield Rd, London SE12 8QF; Tel 0181-852 4953
Director Richard Hill

School Library Association

Liden Library, Barrington Cl, Liden, Swindon, Wilts SN3 6HF; Tel (01793) 617838
President F.N. Hogg, MA, DPA, FLA, OBE

Society of County Children's and Education Librarians

Library HQ, 91 Hoole Rd, Chester CH2 3NG; Tel (01244) 320055
Hon Secretary Janet Hill

Welsh Books Council/Cyngor Llyfrau Cymraeg

Castell Brychan, Aberystwyth, Dyfed SY23 2JB, Wales; Tel (01970) 624151; Fax (01970) 625385
Director Gwerfyl Pierce Jones
Welsh Books Council
Distribution Centre, Glanyrafon Industrial Estate, Aberystwyth, Dyfed SY23 3AQ, Wales; Tel (01970) 624455; Fax (01970) 625506

26 Broadcasting, Audio-Visual Education, Computers in Education

Educational Broadcasting

British Broadcasting Corporation

BBC White City, 201 Wood La, London W12 7TS; Tel 0181-752 5252

Director of Education Jane Drabble
Director's Secretary Michael McLaren
Special Assistant to Director of Education Veron Strachan

The Education Directorate was launched in 1993. The Directorate comprises: two bi-media departments, School Programmes and Continuing Education and Training, producing programmes for radio and television; Publishing Division, a multi-media department producing books, videos, audio cassettes, CD-ROM and public service publishing; the night time service for specialist audiences, BBC Select; The Open University Production Centre, producing radio and television audio and video cassettes and interactive multimedia for the Open University; and Education Policy and Services, responsible for policy and research, press, promotion, and liaison. The cost of both school and continuing education and training broadcasting is met from the general licence revenue. Open University broadcasts are paid for by student fees and a grant from the Higher Education Funding Council

BBC Networking Club

Room 401, Sulgrave Hse, Woodger Rd, London W12 8QT; Tel 0181-576 7799

The BBC Networking Club offers on-line educational and other BBC resources on the global Internet Computer Network and access to a BBC Information and Conferencing service on the BBC Bulletin Board

BBC Education Policy and Services

BBC White City, 201 Wood La, London W12 7TS; Tel 0181-752 5252

Head of Education Policy and Services Lucia Jones
Chief Education Officer (Schools) Julie Cogill
Education Officer Su Hurrell
Education Officer Chris Hughes
Education Officer Samina Miller
Education Officer Chris Durbin
Education Officer Paul Robinson
Chief Education Officer (Continuing Education) Jane Straw
Education Officer Judith Banbury
Education Officer Europe Singh
Education Officer Fiona Russell
Education Officer Catherine McCarthy
Education Officer Chris Bernthal
Education Officer Jacqui Buffon
Education Officer Gill Hind
Education Officer Rachel Harrison
Education Information Officer Rosemary Morgan
Press and Promotions Manager (Press and Promotion Unit) Robert Seatter
Senior Publicity Officer, Schools (Press and Promotion Unit) David Lloyd
Senior Publicity Officer, Continuing Education and Training (Press and Promotion Unit) Caron Jones
Continuing Education and Training Promotions Officer (Press and Promotion Unit) Jennifer Hayes

Education Policy and Services conducts evaluative research into the effectiveness of school and continuing education broadcasts and, through its Education Officers, provides an educational service to assist production departments to relate programme plans to educational needs. Close links are maintained with Education Officers in the Education Departments of the national regions. The department is the focal point for the production of educational information and promotion.

The department also services the Educational Broadcasting Council for the United Kingdom

BBC School Programmes

BBC White City, 201 Wood La, London W12 7TS; Tel 0181-752 5252
Head of School Programmes Terry Marsh
Chief Assistant, School Programmes Jacqueline Johnston
School Programmes Manager Linda Lee-Wright
Executive Producer Len Brown
Executive Producer Richard Langridge
Executive Producer Geoff Marshall-Taylor
Executive Producer Brian Scott-Hughes
Executive Producer Frank Flynn

School Programmes is a bi-media department producing radio and television programmes to help teachers meet the high demands of the curriculum. School Programmes provides a service for school children of all ages from 4 (in nursery schools) up to 18. Programmes are transmitted on BBC2 weekdays and on Radio 3 during the 30 weeks of the school term. All broadcasts are supported by practical and accessible teachers' notes and a range of student materials giving advice about how to use broadcasts and suggestions for follow-up work activities. In 1994 BBC Education celebrated the landmark of 70 years of school broadcasting

BBC Continuing Education and Training

BBC White City, 201 Wood La, London W12 7TS; Tel 0181-752 5252
Head of Education for Adults Glenwyn Benson
Continuing Education and Training Manager Jane Charlton
Executive Producer Jonathan Drori
Executive Producer Chris Lent
Executive Producer Fiona Pitcher

Continuing Education and Training in multi-media department producing radio and television programmes on a wide range of subjects. The main areas of output are relationships, information technology, business and management, citizenship, health and technology and promoting the understanding of the world and other cultures. A number of books and videos are published to accompany the programmes. Programmes are transmitted on both BBC1 and BBC2, and across all the radio networks

BBC Education Publishing Division

BBC White City, 201 Wood La, London W12 7TS; Tel 0181-752 5252
Head of Publishing Division David Mortimer
Head of Educational Publishing Heather Morris
Head of Editorial (Educational Publishing) Sarah Dann BBC Woodlands, 80 Wood La, London W12 0TT; Tel 0181-743 5588
Director (Language Unit) (White City) Martin Mulloy
Head of Educational Developments Angie Mason
Commissioning Editor (Educational Developments) Steve Pollock
Director, BBC for Business (Woodlands) Geoff Flook
Product Development Manager BBC for Business (Woodlands) Victoria Felton

The Department produces a wide range of materials to support educational broadcasts, including books and materials for language learning for teachers and students, training videos for use by employers, and non-profit making publications

BBC Select

BBC Woodlands, 80 Wood La, London W12 0TT; Tel 0181-576 2543
Managing Editor Paul Gerhardt

BBC Select transmits during night-time hours (2am-6am on BBC2) providing specialist education and training programmes to highly targeted specialist professional audiences. All programme services are supplied by outside organisations but within the BBC's editorial guidelines. No decoder is required and all programmes can be recorded and viewed by anyone. Current regular services include: RCN Nursing Update, a continuing education resource for nurses, midwives and health visitors; Voluntary Sector Television, a regular monthly service for charities and voluntary organisations; Benefits Agency Today, a weekly service for BA staff and other benefits advisers; and Pathways to Care, a major training and education initiative for everyone involved in care, childcare and education. Print support is usually supplied and in some services accreditation is offered by appropriate bodies

Open University Production Centre

BBC Walton Hall, Milton Keynes MK7 6BH; Tel (01908) 274033
Head of Open University Production Centre Colin Robinson
Head of Programmes Clive Holloway
Head of Resources Jeff Baker
Head of Personnel and Administration Felicity Cornish
Head of Finance and Management Information Sue Penny
Senior Producer (Arts) Tony Coe
Senior Producer (Continuing Education) Roger Penfound
Senior Producer (Mathematics) John Jaworski
Senior Producer (Technology) Ian Spratley
Senior Producer (Social Sciences) Vic Lockwood
Senior Producer (Education) Meg Sheffield
Senior Producer (Science) Nicholas Watson
Producer (Presentation and Promotions Unit) Christine Palmer

The BBC Open University Production Centre produces radio, television audio and video cassettes and interactive multimedia as integral components of Open University courses. Costs are met through student fees and a grant from the Higher Education Funding Council. The post-production facilities, which are amongst the BBC's most technically advanced, are self-contained at Milton Keynes. Programmes are transmitted on BBC2 weekdays at night and on weekends in the morning, and on Radio 3 (and Radio 4 LW from the start of the academic year 1994)

BBC Educational Broadcasting Council for the United Kingdom

BBC White City, 201 Wood La, London W12 7TS; Tel 0181-752 5252
Chair Christopher Tipple
Head of Education Policy and Services and Secretary, Educational Broadcasting Council Lucia Jones
Senior Education Officer and Secretary, Educational Broadcasting Council, Belfast Northern Ireland Eric Twaddell
Senior Education Officer and Secretary, Educational Broadcasting Council, Edinburgh Scotland John Russell
Head of Educational Broadcasting and Secretary, Education Broadcasting Council, Cardiff Wales Keith Jones

The Educational Broadcasting Council for the United Kingdom validates the formal education output for schools and colleges and advises the BBC about its continuing education output. It delegates the fine detail of its validatory and advisory roles to three programme committees: Primary, Secondary and Continuing Education, and appropriate subject panels. The Education Broadcasting Councils for Scotland, Wales and Northern Ireland perform the same functions in their respective areas. The membership of the Council is representative of the professional world of education, as well as representative of the major 'user' groups of education

Regions

BBC Scotland

Edinburgh
Head of Education and Religious Broadcasting Andrew Bain

Senior Education Officer John Russell
Education Officer Donald Gunn

Glasgow
Education Officer David Smith

BBC Wales

Cardiff
Head of Educational Broadcasting Keith Jones
School and Community Liaison Officer Eleri Wyn Jones

Northern Ireland

Belfast
Senior Education Officer Eric Twaddell

Broadcasting Support Services

Director Keith Smith

This service is independent of the BBC and offers support for a wide range of broadcasts in the areas of social concern and education

BBC Local Radio

London Address BBC Local Radio HQ, G05, Henry Wood Hse, Langham Pl, London W1A 1AA; Tel 0171-580 4468
Education Adviser Cliff Kitney

In the main the output of the BBC's 34 local radio stations includes a substantial amount of programme material which is broadly 'educative' rather than designed for specific school or college audiences. This is to enable a station to maintain a cohesive style and appeal to, and enlighten the lay listener too.
Where there are collaborative links with educational institutions, which often involve teacher or lecturer attachments to the station, such material is also made available as a teaching resource through various archiving systems.
On all stations there is a producer with special responsibility for education who supervises the generation and use of educative material throughout the output. Most stations also provide discrete programmes which have a distinct educational purpose.
All stations have developed links with Local Education Authorities to ensure that information about education, as well as educative programmes, are broadcast.
The subject areas mostly covered by local stations are wide and varied but most concentrate upon social issues, local literature, multi-cultural concerns, the environment, local history, 'Youth' and the developing world of Information Technology
On Station Contacts:

Midlands and East Region

Broadcasting Centre, Pebble Mill, Birmingham B5 7QQ; Tel 0121-414 8888
Head of Local Radio (Midlands) Owen Bentley

Radio Bedfordshire (FM 96.9 stereo and 476m)
Hastings St, Luton, Beds LU1 5BA; Tel (01582) 459111
Manager Mike Gibbons
Education Producer Ian Pearce

Radio Cambridgeshire (FM 96, 292m and 207m)
Broadcasting Hse, 104 Hills Rd, Cambridge CB2 1LD; Tel (01223) 315970
Manager Margaret Hyde
Education Producer Nick Baraclough

BBC Radio Derby (269m or 1116kHz, 104.5MHz, 94.2MHz, 95.3MHz)
Saint Helen's St, Derby DE1 3HY; Tel (01332) 361111
Manager Bryan Harris
Education Producer Jan Rogers

BBC Essex
198 New London Rd, Chelmsford, Essex CM2 9AB; Tel (01245) 262393
Manager Richard Lucas
Education Poducer Martin Ward

BBC Radio Leicester (358m or 837kHz, 95.1MHz)
Epic Hse, Charles St, Leicester LE1 3SH; Tel (0116) 227 113
Manager Jeremy Robinson
Education Producer Vijay Sharma

BBC Radio Lincolnshire (219m or 1368kHz, 94.9MHz)
Radion Bldgs, Newport, Lincoln LN1 3EU; Tel (01522) 40011
Manager David Wilkinson
Education Producer Alan Stennett

BBC Norfolk (FM 95.1, 351 and 344m)
Norfolk Tower, Surrey St, Norwich NR1 3PA; Tel (01603) 617411
Manager Keith Salmon
Programme Organiser Peter Glanville

Radio Northampton (96.6 FM and 271m)
Abington St, Northampton NN1 2BE; Tel (01604) 239100
Manager Peter Davies
Education Producer David Fanville

BBC Radio Nottingham (197m or 152kHz, 189m or 1548kHz, 103MHz)
York Hse, Mansfield Rd, Nottingham NG1 3JB; Tel (0115) 941 5161
Manager Ken Warburton
Education Producer M. Hapgood

BBC Radio Shropshire (397m or 756kHz, 189m or 1584kHz, 96.0MHz, 95.0MHz)
2/4 Boscobel Dr, Shrewsbury, Shropshire SY1 3TT; Tel (01743) 248484
Manager Lawrie Bloomfield
Programme Organiser Vacancy

BBC Radio Stoke-on-Trent (200m or 1503kHz, 94.6MHz)
Conway Hse, Cheapside, Hanley, Stoke-on-Trent ST1 1JJ; Tel (01782) 208080
Manager John Collard
Education Producer Arthur Wood

BBC Radio WM (206m or 1458kHz and 362m or 828kHz, 95.6MHz)
PO Box 206, Pebble Mill Rd, Birmingham B5 7SD; Tel 0121-472 5141
Manager Tony Inchley
Education Producer Mandy Nawn

North Region

New Broadcasting Hse, Oxford Rd, Manchester M60 1SJ; Tel 0161-200 2020

BBC Radio Cleveland (104m or 1548kHz, 95.0MHz, 95.8MHz)
PO Box 1548, Broadcasting Hse, Newport Rd, Middlesborough, Cleveland TS1 5DG; Tel (01642) 225211
Manager John Watson
Education Producer Peter Hedley

Radio Cumbria (FM 95.6 and 397m)
Hilltop Heights, London Rd, Carlisle CA1 2NA; Tel (01228) 31661
Manager Mike Marsh
Education Producer Nigel Holmes

Furness
BBC Radio Furness, Hartingdon St, Barrow-in-Furness; Tel (01229) 26767

GMR (Greater Manchester Radio)
PO Box 90, New Broadcasting Hse, Oxford Rd, Manchester M60 1SJ; Tel 0161-200 2020

Manager Martin Henfield
Education Producer Vacancy

BBC Radio Humberside (202m or 1458kHz, 95.9MHz)
63 Jameson St, Hull HU1 3NU; Tel (01482) 323232
Manager Geoff Sargieson

Radio Lancashire (FM 96.4 and 351m)
20–26 Darwen St, Blackburn, Lancs BB2 2EA; Tel (01254) 62411
Manager Barbara Taylor
Programme Organiser David Sanders

BBC Radio Leeds (388m or 774kHz, 92.4MHz, 95.3MHz)
Broadcasting Hse, Woodhouse La, Leeds LS2 9PN; Tel (0113) 244 2131
Manager John Jefferson
Programme Organiser Richard Rudin

Radio Merseyside (FM 95.8 and 202m)
55 Paradise St, Liverpool L1 3BP; Tel 0151-708 5500
Manager Richard Duckenfield
Education Producer Evelyn Draper

BBC Radio Newcastle (206m or 1458kHz, 95.4MHz, 96.0MHz, 104.4MHz)
Broadcasting Centre, Barrack Rd, Fenham, Newcastle upon Tyne NE99 1RN; Tel 0191-232 4141
Manager Tony Fish
Education Producer V. Jones

BBC Radio Sheffield (290m or 1035kHz, 104.1MHz and 88.6MHz)
60 Westbourne Rd, Sheffield S10 2QU; Tel (0114) 268 6185
Manager Nigel Kay
Programme Organiser Chris van Schaik

BBC Radio York (450m or 666kHz, 238m or 1260kHz, 103.7kHz, 95.5MHz, 104.3MHz)
20 Bootham Row, York YO3 7BR; Tel (01904) 641351
Manager Barry Stockdale
Programme Organiser Tony Fish

South Region

BBC South, Broadcasting Hse, Whiteladies Rd, Bristol BS8 2LR; Tel (0117) 973 2211
Head of Local Radio (South & East) Arnold Miller

Radio Bristol (FM 95.5 and 194m)
3 Tyndalls Park Rd, Bristol BS8 1PP; Tel (0117) 974 1111
Station Manager Roy Roberts
Education Producer Vicki Klein

Radio Cornwall (FM 96.4 and 97.3, 476m and 457m)
Phoenix Wharf, Truro TR1 1UA; Tel (01872) 75421
Manager Mike Hoskin
Education Producer Tim Hubbard

Radio Devon (FM 97.5, 97.0 and 96.2, 303m, 351m, 375m and 206m)
PO Box 100, St David's Hill, Exeter EX4 4DB; Tel (01392) 215651
Manager Roy Corlett

Radio Gloucestershire
London Rd, Gloucester GL1 1SW; Tel (01452) 308585
Manager Peter Gallimore

GLR (Greater London Radio)
35a Marylebone High St, London W1A 4LG; Tel 0171-224 2424
Manager Vacancy
Programme Organiser Vacancy

Radio Guernsey (269m)
Commerce Hse, Les Banques, St Peter Port, Guernsey, CI; Tel (01481) 728977
Manager Roger Bufton

Radio Jersey (292m)
Broadcasting Hse, Rouge Bouillon, St Helier, Jersey, CI; Tel (01534) 70000
Manager Roger Bufton

BBC Radio Kent (290m or 1035kHz, 388m or 774kHz, 187m or 1602kHz, 96.7MHz, 104.2MHz)
Sun Pier, Chatham ME4 4EZ; Tel (01634) 46284
Manager Jim Latham
Education Producer Lynn Wallis-Eade

BBC Radio Oxford (202m or 1485kHz, 95.2MHz)
242/254 Banbury Rd, Summertown, Oxford OX2 7DW; Tel (01865) 53411
Manager John Bright
Programme Ornaiser Stuart Woodcock

Radio Solent
Broadcasting Hse, Havelock Rd, Southampton SO1 0XR; Tel (01703) 631311
Manager Steve Panton
Education Producer Hugh Ashley

Radio Sussex (202m or 1485kHz, 219m or 1368kHz, 1161kHz, 258m or 104.5MHz, 95.3MHz , 104.0MHz)
Marlborough Pl, Brighton BN1 1TU; Tel (01273) 680231
Manager Anne Jones
Programme Organiser Jim Beaman

BBC Wiltshire Sound
Broadcasting Hse, 56–58 Prospect Pl, Swindon SN1 3RW; Tel (01793) 512715
Manager Tony Talmage

Independent Television Commission

33 Foley St, London W1P 7LB; Tel 0171-255 3000; Fax 0171-306 7800
Head of Educational Broadcasting Dr J.R. Moss
Senior Educational Broadcasting Officer Mrs E. Allen

The ITC is the public body responsible for licensing and regulating commercially funded television services provided in and from the UK. These include Channel 3 (ITV), Channel 4, public teletext and a range of cable, local delivery and satellite services. They do not include services provided by the BBC or S4C

The ITC replaced the Independent Broadcasting Authority (IBA) and the Cable Authority on 1 January 1991

Under its powers derived from the Broadcasting Act 1990, the ITC:
licences commercially funded television services in the UK, whether delivered terrestrially or by cable, local delivery or satellite; and licenses services provided from the UK to viewers in other countries;
regulates these services through its published licences, codes and guidelines and has a range of penalties for failure to comply with them;
seeks to ensure that a *wide range of television services* is available throughout the UK and that, takes as a whole, the services are of high quality and appeal to a variety of tastes and interest;
seeks to ensure *fair and effective competition* in the provision of these services

The ITC's Education Department monitors the education and social action output of the ITC's licensees. A Schools Advisory Committee has been established to offer advice to the ITC on Channel 4's service to schools

Schools Advisory Committee

33 Foley St, London W1P 7LB; Tel 0171-584 7011
Head of Education Dr J.R. Moss
Chairman K. Anderson
Members A. Albion; Dr L. Badham; D. Banks; M.H. Coles; C. Gallagher; Mrs J. Hafenrichter; Dr A. Marshall; R. Robertson; Dr J. Solomon; Miss G. White

Assessors E. Lloyd-Williams; G. Goldstein; T.J. Shaw; A. Stewart

The function of the ITC Schools Advisory Committee is to advise the ITC on the quality and suitability of the arrangements to provide a service of schools programmes, and related matters. The Committee undertakes three main roles: planning, monitoring and assessment

The SAC gives advice on the Channel 4 commissioning editor's programme plans. The Committee thus influences the planning of each annual cycle of programmes by Channel 4. By monitoring programmes, liaison and information arrangements, and by study of research and evaluation reports the Committee aims to advise ITC staff on evaluating the effectiveness of the service. Finally, the Committee prepares an annual report to the Commission, assessing how well Channel 4 (or other licensees) are fulfilling their responsibilities

Education is not a mandatory requirement for Channel 3 (ITV) licensees. All licensees have, however, committed themselves to providing some local education/social action programming and many are also interested in submitting proposals for networked adult education series. By contrast, Channel 4's Licence confirm their mandate to provide 'a suitable proportion of programmes of an educational nature', currently an average of seven hours weekly, all supported by publications or other educational arrangements

Channel 4's Licence also requires them to provide a full service for UK schools and commissions programmes from many services. Channel 4 has appointed the Educational Television Company to organise its information service to schools, and its liaison with schools, through a field force of regionally based education officers (see ETC entry)

Channel 4

60 Charlotte St, London W1P 2AX; Tel 0171-631 4444
Commissioning Editor (Education) Karen Brown
Commissioning Editor (Schools) Paul Ashton
Senior Education Officer John Richmond

Educational Television Company

10A Great Titchfield St, London W1P 7AA; Tel 0171-580 8181; Fax 0171-580 9350
Cheif Executive Davina Lloyd
Senior Education Officer Simon Fuller
Education Officer Christine Alford
Education Officer John Austin
Education Officer Mollie Balfour
Education Officer Yvonne Davies
Education Officer Adrienne Jones
Education Officer Peter Logue
Education Officer Liz Meenan
Education Officer Malcolm Ward
Education Officer Robert Duncan Wilson

Independent Television Companies

Anglia Television Ltd
Anglia Hse, Norwich NR1 3JG; Tel (01603) 615151; Telex 97424
Deputy Managing Director, Broadcasting Division (Responsible for Children's and Educational Programming) Colin Ewing
Community Education Officer Cathy Mason
Secretary to Colin Ewing Anne Insall

Anglia Television broadcasts to the East of England, covering Norfolk, Suffolk, Cambridgeshire, Essex, Bedfordshire, Northamptonshire and parts of Hertfordshire and Buckinghamshire

Programmes for the School Year 1992/93
Animals in Action–Natural history, age range 9–13
Earth–the Home Planet–Earth Sciences 11–14

Border Television plc
The Broadcasting Centre, Durranhill, Carlisle CA1 3NT; Tel (01228) 25101
Managing Director J. Graham
Head of Production N. Robinson
Education Liaison Officer J. Johnston

Transmission to the south of Scotland, Cumbria, the Isle of Man and the north of Northumberland

Carlton Television
101 St Martin's La, London WC2N 4AZ; Tel 0171-249 4000

Central Independent Television
Central Hse, Broad St, Birmingham B1 2JP; Tel 0121-643 9898
Head of Education Yvonne Davies
Education Development Manager Anne Suffolk

Channel Television
The Television Centre, La Pouquelaye, St Helier, Jersey, CI; Tel (01534) 68999; Fax (01534) 59446
Managing Director John Henwood

Grampian Television PLC
Education Officer Sandra Arnold
Queen's Cross, Aberdeen AB9 2XJ; Tel (01224) 646464; Fax (01224) 635127
Albany Hse, 68 Albany Rd, West Ferry, Dundee DD5 1NW; Tel (01382) 739363; Fax (01382) 480230
23–25 Huntly St, Inverness IV3 5PR; Tel (01463) 242624; Fax (01463) 223637

Granada Television Ltd
Television Centre, Manchester M60 9EA; Tel 0161-832 7211
Editor, Schools Programmes Brian Nixon

HTV
(HTV Wales) Television Centre, Culverhouse Cross, Cardiff CF5 6XJ; Tel (01222) 590590
Jobline (HTV West) Television Centre, Bath Rd, Bristol BS4 3HG; Tel (0117) 977 8366
Head of Education Gerald Dawson HTV West
Community Education Officer Ceri Black HTV West
Schools Liaison Officer Eleri Lewis HTV Wales

HTV produces a number of adult education series on a variety of subjects for the ITV network, Channel 4, and S4C.
It also produces programmes of community interest in both Wales and the West of England. Its schools productions are concentrated in Wales and are in Welsh and English

LWT
London Television Centre, London SE1 9LT; Tel 0171-620 1620; Telex 918123
Controller of Features and Current Affairs Simon Shaps

LWT produces political, religious, drama, entertainment, arts and wildlife programmes for the London area on ITV network and Channel 4

Meridian Broadcasting
Television Centre, Southampton SO2 0TA; Tel (01703) 222555; Fax (01703) 335050

Scottish Television plc
Cowcaddens, Glasgow G2 3PR; Tel 0141-332 9999
Educational Advisory Committee Chairman D.I.M. Sutherland, Registrar The General Teaching Council for Scotland
Managing Director G. Macdonald
Chief Executive Scottish Television Enterprises A. Moffat
Community Programmes Co-ordinator M. Magowan
Education Senior Producer E. Rayner

Plus representatives from a variety of educational bodies including EIS; GTC; SCCC and the SOED and COSLA

Tyne Tees Television plc
Television Centre, City Rd, Newcastle upon Tyne NE1 2AL; Tel 0191-261 0181
Head of Community Affairs Sheila Browne

Tyne Tees Television's Community Affairs Department provides printed and telephone back-up to national and regional programmes. The Department liaises with community, voluntary and educational organisations, co-ordinating campaigns and providing feedback from viewers to programme-makers

Ulster Television plc
Havelock Hse, Ormeau Rd, Belfast BT7 1EB; Tel (01232) 328122; Fax (01232) 246695
20 The Diamond, Londonderry BT48 6HP; Tel (01504) 266611; Fax (01504) 269048
Senior Education Officer George Fleeton
Community Education Officer Noel Henry
Education Assistant Diane Sloan
Education Advisory Committee Dr G.S.G. Beveridge; M. Bowen; Professor P.P. Daws; J. Hunter; S McCarron; T.G.J. Moag; K. Murphy; W.M. Sillery

Ulster Television is the programme contractor for Northern Ireland to the ITC. The company's programme-making policy gives priority to reflecting the province's way of life and produces a series of programmes for local schools and colleges, and provides televised learning materials for adults on both ITV and Channel 4, all supported by a variety of free information leaflets and priced booklets

Westcountry Television
Western Wood Way, Language Science Pk, Plymouth PL7 5BG; Tel (01752) 333333

Yorkshire Television Ltd
The Television Centre, Leeds LS3 1JS; Tel (0113) 243 8283; Fax (0113) 255 7232; Telex 557232
Community Education Officer Barbara Siedlecki
Head of Education Chris R. Jelley
Head of Non-Broadcasting World-wide Geoff Foster

Yorkshire Television contributes networked series each term to Channel 4 for Schools and a range of adult education programmes for ITV and Channel 4

Cable and Satellite Programme Services

With a current educational purpose or component

Channel e
European Institute for the Media, The University, Manchester M13 9PL; Tel 0161-273 2754
Co-ordinator Philip Crookes

Discovery Channel (Europe)
United Artist Programming, Twyman Hse, 16 Bonny St, London NW1 9PG; Tel 0171-482 4824
Vice-President; Programming Nick Camer-Calder

The Learning Channel
United Artist Programming, Twyman Hse, 16 Bonny St, London NW1 9PG; Tel 0171-813 5000
Vice-President, Programming Nick Comer-Calder
Executive Producer Liz Barron

The Education Channel
Media Centre, Blackburn College, Fielden St, Blackburn BB2 1LH; Tel (01254) 55144
Media Centre Manager Carol Duerden

Education and Training Channel
University of Sunderland, Langham Tower, Ryhope Rd, Sunderland, Tyne and Wear SR2 7EE; Tel 0191-515 2070
Head of Planning and Market Research Services David William Penn

Independent Local Radio

Beacon Radio (97.2MHz(VHF/FM)
267 Tettenhall Rd, Wolverhampton WV6 0DQ; Tel (01902) 838383
Managing Director Alan Mullett
Programme Director Pete Wagstaff
News Editor Tony Attwater

BRMB–FM (96.4MHz FM stereo)
Aston Rd North, Birmingham B6 4BX; Tel 0121-359 4481; Fax 0121-359 1117
Senior Executive M. Owen
Managing Director Ian Rufus
Education Producer and Special Projects Brian Savin

Broadland FM (102.4 FM/(260m) AM 1152kHz)
St George's Plain, Colegate, Norwich NR3 1DB; Tel (01603) 630621
Managing Director Russell Stuart
Programme Director Mike Stewart
Sales Director Robb Young
News Editor Julian Smith

Capital Radio (95.8FM, 1548AM)
Euston Tower, London NW1 3DR; Tel 0171-388 1288
Programme Director Richard Park

Chiltern Radio (South: Herts, Beds and Bucks–VHF 97.6 and 828AM; North: Bedford and South West Cambridgeshire–VHF 96.9 and 792AM)
Broadcast Centre, Chiltern Rd, Dunstable LU6 1HQ; Tel (01582) 666001
Managing Director C.R. Mason
Broadcast Centre, Goldington Rd, Bedford MK40 3LS; Tel (01234) 272400

Clyde One FM (102.5FM)
Clydebank Business Pk, Clydebank, Glasgow G81 2RX; Tel 0141-941 1111; Fax 0141-952 0080

Clyde Two (1152 KHz)
Managing Director James Gordon
Programme Director Alex Dickson

Downtown Radio (96.4, 96.6, 102.4FM; 1026AM)
Newtownards, Co Down BT23 4ES, NI; Tel (01247) 815555; Fax (01247) 815252
Managing Director David Sloan
Head of Programming John Rosborough
Education Adviser Derek Ray

Essex Radio (96.3 and 102.6VHF), Breeze AM (1359 and 1431) or (210/220 Mtrs) MW and Ten 17 (101.7 FM)
Radio Hse, Clifftown Rd, Southend-on-Sea, Essex SS1 1SX; Tel (01702) 333711; Community Action; Tel (01702) 354411; Fax (01702) 345224
Chief Executive Philip Hinton
Programme Controller Peter Holmes
Creative Director Carolyn Rogers
Head of News Tim Gillett

Great Yorkshire Gold; South Yorkshire 1548, 1305, 990 MW; East Yorkshire 1161 MW; West Yorkshire 1530, 1278 MW
Radio Hse, 900 Herries Rd, Sheffield S6 1RH; Tel (0114) 285 2121; Fax (0114) 285 3159
Programme Controller and Head of News Steve Parkinson

GWR East (258 and 321m/1161 and 936kHz MW. 97.2 and 102.6 FM Stereo)
PO Box 2000, Lime Kiln Studios, Wootton Bassett, Wilts SN4 7EX; Tel (01793) 853222
Managing Director/Programme Controller Ralph Bernard
Head of News Lynda Couch
Sales Director Paul Angus
Chief Engineer Quentin Howard

GWR West plc (238m/1260kHz MW. 96.3MHz FM stereo)
PO Box 2000, Watershed, Canon's Rd, Bristol BS99 7SN; Tel (0117) 927 9900
Managing Director/Programme Controller Ralph Bernard
Sales Director Paul Angus
Chief Engineer Quentine Howard
Head of News Mangus Carter

Hereward FM (102.7 VHF FM)
PO Box 225, Queensgate, Peterborough PE11 1XJ; Tel (01733) 460460; Fax (01733) 281445
Station Director Lynda Couch-Smith
Programme Controller Adrian Crookes
Senior Journalist Simon Potter

London Broadcasting Company Ltd (LBC) (VHF 97.3 and 261m)
PO Box 261, Communications Hse, Gough St, London EC4P 4LP; Tel 0171-353 1010
Editorial Director Peter Thornton
Assistant Editor Robin Malcolm
Assistant Editor Philip Bacon
Editor (IRN) John Perkins

Marcher Sound/Sain-Y-Gororau (VHF 103.4 and 238m)
The Studios, Gwersylt, Wrexham, Clywd LL11 4AF; Tel (01978) 752202
Programme Controller Kevin Howard
Managing Director Godfrey Williams
Head of News Andy Ball

Mercury Extra 1476AM 1521
Managing Director Peter S. Perry
Programme Director Martin Campbell
Head of News Jon Royle

Metro FM (97.1FM)
Swalwell, Newcastle upon Tyne NE99 1BB; Tel 0191-488 3131; Fax 0191-488 8611; Telex 537428
Chairman Neil S. Robinson
Managing Director John Josephs
Group Programme Director Mic Johnson
Programme Director Giles Squire
Head of Music Liz Elliot
News Editor Giles Squire

Moray Firth Radio Ltd
PO Box 271, Inverness IV3 6SF; Tel (01463) 224433
Managing Director Thomas Prag
News Editor Mike Hurry
Religious and Community Producer Len Black
Education and Youth Producer Vacancy

Northants Radio
Broadcast Centre, The Enterprise Pk, Boughton Green Rd, Northampton NN2 7AH; Tel (01604) 792411; Fax (01604) 721934
Chief Executive Stuart Reed
Station Organiser Mark Collins

Northsound Radio (1035AM or 96.9FM)
45 Kings Gate, Aberdeen AB2 6BL; Tel (01224) 632234
Managing Director Paul Stevenson
Head of Speech Programmes Edi Stark

Piccadilly Radio Ltd (Piccadilly Key 103 FM and Piccadilly Gold 1152 AM)
PO Box 261, Manchester M1 4AW; Tel 0161-236 9913; PO Box 103, Manchester; Tel 0162-236 0103
Managing Director Neil Jones
Programme Director Mark Story
General Manager Steve Barnes
Piccadilly Action Producer Chris Buckley

Piccadilly Action is Piccadilly Radio's social action broadcasting unit broadcasting some 30 theme weeks a year on diverse social themes

Plymouth Sound Limited (261m, 1152kHz, 97VHF)
Earl's Acre, Plymouth PL3 4HX; Tel (01752) 227272; Fax (01752) 670730
Station Manager Louise Churchill
Programme Controller Louise Churchill

Q103fm
PO Box 103, Vision Pk, Histon, Cambridge CB4 4WW; Tel (01223) 235255; Fax (01223) 235161
Station Director Alastair Wayne
Programme Controller Trevor James
Senior Journalist Matt Hudson

Radio Aire FM/Magic 828 (96.3MHz, 828kHz)
PO Box 2000, Leeds LS3 1LR; Tel (0113) 245 2299; Fax (0113) 242 1830
Chairman R.M. Walker
Managing Director Peter McPartland
Sales Manager Ann Dyson
Director of Programmes Paul Fairburn
Director of Engineering John Orson
News Editor Clive Settle

Radio City – Liverpool (City FM – 96.7MHz VHF, stereo; Radio City Gold – 1548 KHz MW)
PO Box 967, 8–10 Stanley St, Liverpool L69 1TQ; Tel 0151-227 5100; Fax 0151-471 0333
Managing Director Lynne Wood
Programme Director T. McKenzie

Radio Forth (194m, 1548Hz, 97.3VHF)
Managing Director Richard Findlay
Programme Director Tom Steele

Radio Mercury plc (102.7 and 96.4FM) and Mercury Extra A.M. (1521 and 1476 AM)
Broadfield Hse, Brighton Rd, Crawley, Sussex RH11 9TT; Tel (01293) 519161; Fax (01293) 560927; Telex 87503
Managing Director Peter S. Perry
Programme Director Martin Campbell

Radio WABC (330m/990KHz MW)
PO Box 303, Wolverhampton WV6 0DQ

(A Beacon sister-station)

Red Dragon Radio plc (103.2/97.4 FM)
Radio Hse, West Canal Wharf, Cardiff CF1 5XJ; Tel (01222) 384041

Red Rose Radio plc (VHF 97.3 and 301m) Red Rose Gold (AM 999) Red Rose Rock (FM 97.4)
PO Box 301, St Pauls Sq, Preston PR1 1YE; Tel (01772) 556301
Managing Director A.J. Dewhurst
Joint AM and FM Programme Director Jeff Graham
News Editor Marian Kenny

SGRfm – Bury St Edmunds (96.4 FM and 1251 KHz)
Long Brackland, Bury St Edmunds, Suffolk IP33 1JY; Tel (01284) 701511
Managing Director Russell Stuart
Head of News Daragh Croxson
Station Coordinator Nigel Rennie
Programme Controller Mike Stewart

SGRfm – Ipswich (97.1FM and 1170KHz)
Radio Hse, Alpha Business Pk, Whitehouse Rd, Ipswich IP1 5LT; Tel (01473) 461000; Fax (01473) 741200
Managing Director Russel Stuart
Head of News Daragh Croxson
Programme Director Mike Stewart

Signal Radio (257m or 1170kHzm 102.6VHF)
Stoke Rd, Stoke-on-Trent ST4 2SR; Tel (01782) 747047; Fax (01782) 744110
Managing Director Barry H. Machin
Programme Director John Evington
Sales Director Glyn Owen

Southern FM (102.4FM, 102.0FM, 103.5FM, 96.9FM)
PO Box 2000, Brighton BN41 2SS; Tel (01273) 430111; Fax (01273) 430098
Managing Director Rory McLeod
Programme Director Jeremy Scott
Station Director R. Hoad

Swansea Sound (1170kHz, 96.4VHF)
Victoria Rd, Gowerton, Swansea SA4 3AB; Tel (01792) 893751; Fax (01792) 898841
Managing Director Charles Braham

TFM Radio (96.6FM)
74 Dovecot St, Stockton-on-Tees, Cleveland TS18 1HB; Tel (01642) 615111

Chairman The Lord Elliott of Morpeth
Managing Director N.S. Robinson
Director of Programmes and Resources Brian Lister
Sales Manager Sally Marrison
Chief Engineer David Ramsay
News Editor John Ogden
Accounts Supervisor Pat Hutchinson
Head of Administration Nora Barber

Trent–FM (Nottingham) (96.2 and 96.5MHz FM)
29–31 Castle Gate, Nottingham NG1 7AP; Tel (0115) 958 1731; Fax (0115) 958 8614
Station Director Chris Hughes

2 CR-FM (102.3FM) Classic Gold 828 (828AM)
5–7 Southcote Rd, Bournemouth BH1 3LR; Tel (01202) 294881; Fax (01202) 299314
Station Director Roger Brooks

2-TEN FM 'A Better Music Mix' (102.9 and 97FM); Classic Gold 'Good Times Great Oldies' (1431 AM)
PO Box 210, Reading, Berks RG3 5RZ; Tel (01734) 254400
Station Director Jeff Lee

Viking FM (96.9FM)
Commercial Rd, Hull HU1 2SG; Tel (01482) 325141
Programme Controller of Viking FM 96.9 Phil White
Programme Controller of Great Yorkshire Gold (1161 KHz) Steve Parkinson
Sales Controller Iain Clasper
Head of News – Yorkshire Claire Dalton
News Co-ordinator of Viking FM Stephen Edwards

Viking Radio is part of the Metro Radio Group

West Sound (290m, 96.7 and 97.5VHF Stereo)
Radio Hse, Holmston Rd, Ayr KA7 3BE; Tel (01292) 283662
Chairman W. Mowat
Managing Director Joseph Campbell
Programme Controller Gordon MacArthur

The Worlds Greatest Music Station (1332 kHz MW)
PO Box 225, Queensgate, Peterborough PE11 1XJ; Tel (01733) 346225; Fax (01733) 342714

Audio–Visual Education

National Bodies

Educational Foundation for Visual Aids

National Audio-Visual Library, Normal College, (Top Site), Siliwen Rd, Bangor, Gwynedd LL57 2DZ; Tel (01248) 370144; Fax (01248) 351415
Council of Management
Chairman Lt Col A.E.F. Dowse-Brennan; B.H. Laister; E.R. Powell; Rear Admiral J.A. Bell, CB; G.A.R. McHugh; The Earl of Lisburne; K. Parker (DES Observer)

Finance
The Foundation is non-profit-making company recognised as a charity

Charter
The Foundation was established in 1948 to work, in association with the National Committee for Audio-Visual Aids in Education, as a commercial channel through which all audio-visual equipment and materials suitable for teaching purposes would be made available to local education authorities. In recent years, as the relevance of education and training affecting adults in the context of the national economy's needs has developed, the Foundation has expanded its facilities to respond accordingly. Also, when the funding by local education authorities of the National Committee's activities ceased in March 1981, the Foundation took responsibility to continue those of the National Committee's services for which a demand remains evident and which are commercially viable

Functions
The Foundation provides a comprehensive range of facilities and services available in the field of audio-visual and video support to education and training. These are available to UK and overseas clients and include: equipment sales and hire; 16mm films and video tapes for sale and hire; film preview facilities; software (filmstrips, loops and all ancillary expendables associated with audio-visual equipment) and multi-media packages for sale; technical consultancy services for equipment choice and installation; audio and video studios for hire; conference facilities with multi-media provision; video programme production facilities–also available for on-site productions for clients; projectionist for operating audio-visual and video equipment at conferences; training courses in video and tape-slide production and the utilisation of all other audio-visual media; servicing–either on a contractual or on-demand basis–of audio-visual and video equipment; the provision of a book service covering most aspects of educational technology; and the organising of media exhibitions for trade and other clients

Major Centres

National Audio Visual Library
Normal College, (Top Site), Siliwen Rd, Bangor, Gwynedd LL57 2DZ; Tel (01248) 370144; Fax (01248) 351415
Manager B. Mullett

Avon AVA Centre (EFVA)
Unit 5, Little Ann St, St Jude's, Bristol BS2 9EP; Tel (0117) 954 1911; Fax (0117) 955 6991

Northern AVA Centre
Lark La, Penrith, Cumbria CA11 7NS; Tel (01768) 64829

North London AVA Centre
5 The Sidings, Hainault Rd, Leytonstone, London E11 1HD; Tel 0181-539 5407; Fax 0181-539 2047

Service Centres (EFVA)

Aylesbury, Doncaster, Horsham, Newhaven and Rotherham

British National Film and Video Catalogue

British Film Institute, 21 Stephen St, London W1P 1PL; Tel 0171-255 1444; Fax 0171-580 7503
Co-ordinator BNFVC Database Maureen Brown

A national documentation service providing information on films and videos released for non-theatrical screening in Britain (including educational, scientific, cultural and industrial films). Published as a serial from 1963 to 1991 inclusive. NB: It is hoped to resume publication in 1994

Association for Educational and Training Technology

Higher Millbrook, Beavor La, Axminster, Devon EX13 5EQ; Tel (01297) 32030; Fax (01297) 35281
President Peter Clarke, CBE, BSc, PhD, CChem, FRSC, FInstPetHon, DEd(CNAA), HonLLD(Aberdeen)
Chairman Professor H.I. Ellington
Secretary Professor P. Race
Treasurer Squ Ldr N.E. Allen

Aims to bring together individuals and corporate bodies to promote the advancement and diffusion of a knowledge of the technology of education and training.
Membership Open to all interested in educational technology

Services Yearbook; Annual Conferences; Regional Conferences; Journal *Educational and Training Technology International*

Newsletters Network; Conference Proceedings 'Aspects of Educational Technology'; Occasional Publications
Correspondence to: Higher Millbrook, Beavor La, Axminster, Devon EX13 5EQ; Tel (01297) 32030; *A.E.T.T. Administrator* N.R. Winterburn

British Film Institute

21 Stephen St, London W1P 1PL; Tel 0171-255 1444
Chairman of Board of Governors Jeremy Thomas
Director Wilf Stevenson
Principal Education Officer Cary Bazalgette

BFI Education exists to develop education about film, television and video at all levels of the education system through publishing, research and lobbying. It holds conferences, courses and schools for teachers and for the general public. A free catalogue of study materials and a newsletter are available

Children's Film and Television Foundation Ltd

Elstree Studios, Borehamwood, Herts WD6 1JG; Tel 0181-953 0844; Fax 0181-207 0860
Patron H.R.H. The Duchess of Kent
Chairman The Rt Hon Lord Birkett (nominated jointly by the Film Trade Associations)
Director of Production Monica Sims, OBE
Director D. Morphet (nominated by the Producers' Alliance for Cinema and Television (PACT)
Director J. Wilkinson (nominated by the Cinema tograph Exhibitors' Association)
Director J.R.C. Higgins, MBE (nominated by the Society of Film Distributors Limited)
Director A. Sapper (nominated by Broadcast, Entertainment Cinematograph and Theatre Union (BECTU)
Director P. Plouviez (nominated by Performers' Alliance)
Director E. Barnes (nominated by the Children's Film and Television Foundation Limited)
Director F.P. Turner (nominated by the Children's Film and Television Foundation Limited)
Director S. Relph (nominated by the Children's Film and Television Foundation Limited)
Director A. Mitchell, MBE (nominated by the Children's Film and Television Foundation Limited)
Director I.A.R. Smith (nominated by the Children's Film and Television Foundation Limited)
Director D.K. Elstein (nominated by the Children's Film and Television Foundation Limited)
Secretary/Chief Executive S.T. Taylor, FCIS

The Foundation formed in 1952 is a non-profit making organization which was formerly financed by grants from the Eady Levy and subsequently by means of guaranteed income from a distribution deal which expired in February 1986. Such income is applied to the production, promotion, organization and distribution of cinematograph entertainment films especially suitable for showing to children/family audiences through theatrical or television outlets worldwide. The Foundation also gives consideration to possibilities with future productions on a co-production/finance basis with appropriate partners. Free catalogue. Over 200 hours of films

National Film and Television School

Beaconsfield Studios, Station Rd, Beaconsfield, Bucks HP9 1LG; Tel (01494) 671234; Fax (01494) 674042
Director Henning Camre
Chairman David Puttnam
Governor Andy Allan
Governor Lor Brabourne
Governor Moira Armstrong
Governor Roger Bolton
Governor Linda James
Governor Sue Lawley
Governor Gus Macdonald
Governor Frank McGettigan
Governor Jonathan Powell
Governor David Puttnam
Governor Sarah Radclyffe
Governor Noella Smith
Governor Brian Tesler
Governor Stewart Till
Governor Christine Walker
Governor Charles Wesoky
Governor Michael Williams-Jones
Governor Will Wyatt
Governor Alan Yentob
Secretary Anthony Rose

Other Film, Visual and Aural Education Organisations

ASLIB Audio Visual Group

Information Hse, 20–24 Old St, London EC1V 9AP; Tel 0171-253 4488; Fax 0171-430 0514; Telex E-Mail aslib aslib.demon.co.uk
Chair Olwen Terris British Film/Video Council, 55 Greek St, London W1V 5LR

Association of Professional Business Communicators Ltd

PO Box 25, Godalming, Surrey GU7 1PL; Tel (01483) 423429
Chairman Charles Potter, MBE

Audio Visual Association

Herkomer Hse, 156 High St, Bushey, Herts WD2 3DD; Tel 0181-950 5959
Secretary M.A. Simpson, FBIPP

AVP

School Hill Centre, Chepstow, Gwent NP6 5PH; Tel (01291) 625439; Fax (01291) 629671
Managing Director Robin Drewett

Publishers of computer software, audio-visual and video resources for primary and secondary education. Separate secondary catalogues of computer software and videos for all National Curriculum subjects, plus a complete catalogue of computer software for Primary Schools (c.8000 titles)

ABACUS Teaching Systems Ltd

Education Equipment Division, Glensthorpe, Newton St, Llanberis, Gwynedd LL55 4HN; Tel (01286) 870689
Managing Director J.B. Wakeham

Pneumatic teaching aids. Circuits are built using the ABAUCUS flexible, slotted matrix system of mounting components

Bounty Services Ltd

Diss, Norfolk IP22 3HH; Tel (01379) 651081

VHS Video Tape: 'Growing Up–A Guide to Puberty'

British Federation of Film Societies

21 Stephen St, London W1P 1PL; Tel 0171-255 1444; Fax 0171-255 2315
General Secretary Tom Brownlie

British Federation of Film Societies Scottish Group

15 Charlotte St, Ayr KA7 1DZ
Secretary Ronald Currie

British Kinematograph, Sound and Television Society

M6–14 Victoria Hse, Vernon Pl, London WC1B 4DF; Tel 0171-242 8400
Administration Officer Suzie Brewer
Training Officer Anne Fenton

British Library National Sound Archive

29 Exhibition Rd, London SW7 2AS; Tel 0171-412 7440; Fax 0171-412 7416/41
Director A. Crispin Jewitt

British Universities Film and Video Council

55 Greek St, London W1V 5LR; Tel 0171-734 3687; Fax 0171-287 3914
Director Murray Weston

Broadcasting Support Services
Room AG-34, 252 Western Ave, London W3 6XJ; Tel 0181-992 5522
Director Keith Smith

BSS is a charity that provides follow-up services for viewers and listeners and runs long-term helplines

Camerawork
121 Roman Rd, London E2; Tel 0181-980 6256; Fax 0181-983 4714; Telex E-mail cam@camwork.demon.co.uk

Gallery, darkrooms, touring exhibitions, courses, workshops, talks dealing with issues relating to lens-based media

CFL Vision (formerly Central Film Library)
PO Box 35, Wetherby, West Yorkshire LS23 7EX; Tel (01937) 541010; Fax (01937) 541083

Community Service Volunteers (CSV)
237 Pentonville Rd, London N1 9NJ; Tel 0171-278 6601; Fax 0171-833 0149

CSV creates opportunities for people to participate actively in their community through volunteering training, education and the media. Nationwide CSV works with over 3000 full-time volunteers, 15,000 part-time volunteers and 5,000 employment trainees, and in partnership with over 3,000 schools and 50 TV and radio stations each year

Concord Video and Film Council
An Educational Audio Visual Library
201 Felixstowe Rd, Ipswich, Suffolk IP4 9BJ; Tel (01473) 715754/726012; Fax (01473) 274531

A video and film library specializing in social documentary material and the arts

Concordia Books and Films
28 Huntingdon Rd, Cambridge CB3 0HH; Tel (01223) 65113; Fax (01223) 355265

Council for Education in World Citizenship (CEWC)
see Chapter 18

CTVC
Director Barrie Allcott Hillside Studios, Merry Hill Rd, Bushey, Watford WD2 1DR; Tel 0181-950 4426/7; Fax 0181-950 1437

Dean Associates
9 The South West Centre, Troutbeck Rd, Sheffield S7 2QA; Tel (0114) 258 1171; Fax (0114) 258 1338
Senior Partners Christopher G. Dean, Quentin A. Whitlock

Dean Associates are specialists in open learning and the use of computers in training. They run courses in such areas as training design and computer based training and develop CBT and multimedia courseware for clients

Design Initiative
55 Trajan Walk, Andover, Hampshire SP10 5JW; Tel (01264) 351853; Fax (01264) 350943
General Manager M. Doughty

Manufacture and supply of a full range of audio visual teaching, presentation, and display equipment for schools, colleges, and private training organisations. Products include TV, video, overhead projection, slide projection, rear projection equipment and furniture.

Education and Therapy Unit of the Puppet Centre Trust
The Puppet Centre, Battersea Arts Centre, Lavender Hill, London SW11; Tel 0171-228 5335
Contact Education Officer Anna Ledgard

Workshops, courses, schools visits, co-ordination of schools residencies, publications

Educational Television Association
***Administrator* Josie Key 37 Monkgate, York YO3 7PB; Tel (01904) 639212; Fax (01904) 439212**
***Chairman* M. Paterson 1 Laurelbank Rd, Maybole, Ayrshire KA19 8BE; Tel (01655) 883278**
***Deputy Chair (Manager)* Marian Cumpetey Visual and Educational Services, University of Nottingham Medical School, Nottingham NG7 2UH; Tel (01159) 709357**
***Secretary* R.A. Stares, Head of Learning Support University of Luton, Park Sq, Luton LU1 3JU; Tel (01582) 489340**

Annual award scheme (video competition), conference, also open to non-members. Journal and Newsletter. Membership, apply to Administrator

EFM Flamefast Ltd
(Incorporating Flamefast Technology Ltd)
Labtec St, Swinton, Manchester M27 8SE; Tel 0161-793 9333
Chairman/Managing Director S.A. Swinden
Sales and Marketing Manager M. Serridge
Company Secretary C. Kimber

Manufacturers/Distributors/Installers of complete science laboratories Design Technology Furniture and Gas and Technology Modules for teaching Hot Metals and Technology subjects

English Teaching Theatre
c/o 26 Petley Rd, London W6 9ST; Tel 0171-254 9199; 0171-275 8235
Directors Ken Wilson, Hazel Imbert, Doug Case

A professional theatre group aimed at the ELT market in the UK and abroad. Performs a stage show in the UK for summer course students

Fantasy Factory Video Ltd
175 Goswell Rd, London EC1V 7HJ; Tel 0171-608 2227
Joint Co Secretaries Sue Hall, John Hopkins

Flight Electronics International Limited
Flight Hse, Ascupart St, Southampton, Hampshire SO14 1WP; Tel (01703) 227721; Fax (01703) 330039; Telex E.mail: sales @ flight.demon.co.uk
Managing Director M.D. Soffe
General Sales Manager F.R. Walker
UK Sales A. Padley

Educational Micro Electronics Systems and Instrumentation

Focal Point Audio Visual Ltd
251 Copnor Rd, Portsmouth, Hants PO3 5EE; Tel (01705) 665249/645555; Fax (01705) 695723
General Manager David Ellis

Suppliers of audio visual resources for all levels of education: 35mm slide programmes, audio and video cassettes, CD.ROMS and projection equipment. Agents for BBC Educational and Business videos. Free lists available on request

Gateway Audio Visual/Video
472 Green Lanes, London N13 5XF; Tel 0181-882 0177
Managing Director Graham L. Smart

Producers of video, film and tape/slide programmes for training and education

ICA Video
Institute of Contemporary Arts, 12 Carlton Hse Terr, London SW1Y 5AH; Tel 0171-930 0493; Fax 0171-873 0051

Production and distribution of educational videos featuring some of the best of contemporary writers and artists

Institute of Amateur Cinematographers
24C West St, Epsom, Surrey KT18 7RJ; Tel (01372) 739672

Iris Audio Visual
Unit M, Forest Ind Pk, Forest Rd, Hainault, Essex IG6 3HL; Tel 0181-500 2846; Fax 0181-559 8780
Partners Iris Klarnett, Raymond Klarnett

Suppliers of audiovisual and photographic materials to technical, scientific and educational users

JVC Professional Products (UK) Ltd
Ullswater Hse, Kendal Ave, London W3 0XA; Tel 0181-896 6000; Fax 0181-896 6060
Sales Manager Tony Sheen

JVC Professional provide a range of professional video products including cameras, monitors, VCRs and CCTV. New products include the range of 22 Series Super-VHS equipment and recordable CD.ROM hardware and software

L.D.A. (Learning Development Aids)
Duke St, Wisbech, Cambs PE13 2AE; Tel (01945) 63441
Director Dennis Blackmore
Schools Marketing Amanda Clarke

Publishers of Educational Books and Materials; Specialising in children with special educational needs from infant to secondary

London International Film School Ltd
24 Shelton St, London WC2 9HP; Tel 0171-836 9642
Principal Martin M. Amstell
Administrator Phil Mottram

Magiboards Ltd
Stafford Pk 12, Telford, Shropshire TF3 3BJ; Tel (01952) 292111
Chairman A.A. Stallion

Manufacturers and suppliers of visual aids for teaching and training

Masterclass Video Cassettes
see Chapter 25

Museums Association
42 Clerkenwell Cl, London EC1R 0PA; Tel 0171-608 2933
Director Mark Taylor, BA

NCC Audio Visual Centre
Covington St, Northampton NN1 5JU; Tel (01604) 601012; Fax (01604) 34726
Head of Centre David Burridge
Service Manager Jess Rivas
Enquiries/Accounts Kathy Jones

Advisory/training, sales and service on everything audio-visual. Video post-production facilities

The Other Cinema Film and Video Library
79 Wardour St, London W1V 3TH; Tel 0171-734 8508

Pictorial Charts Educational Trust
27 Kirchen Rd, West Ealing, London W13 0UD; Tel 0181-567 9206
Director R. Quiller Barrett

Publishers of wallcharts on a wide range of subjects to support the National Curriculum

Puppet Centre Trust
The Administrator, BAC, Lavender Hill, London SW11 5TN; Tel 0171-228 5335

The Royal Photographic Society
The Octagon, Milsom St, Bath BA1 1DN; Tel (01225) 462841
Secretary Amanda Nevill

The Royal Society for the Protection of Birds Film and Video Department
The Lodge, Sandy, Bedfordshire SG19 2DL; Tel (01767) 680551

RSPB Film Hire Library
15 Beaconsfield Rd, London NW10 2LE; Tel 0181-451 1127
Manager Susan E. Gresham

Royal Television Society
Holborn Hall, 100 Gray's Inn Rd, London WC1X 8AZ; Tel 0171-430 1000; Fax 0171-430 0924

An educational charity with over 3,500 members. The society produces a careers leaflet entitled "I Want to Work in Television" and organises regional workshops where the arts, science and politics of television can be discussed

SCET Training Resources
Distribution Manager John Dyer Dowanhill, 74 Victoria Crescent Rd, Glasgow G12 9JN; Tel 0141-344 9314

Scripture Union
Scripture Union Hse, 130 City Rd, London EC1V 2NJ; Tel 0171-782 0013; Fax 0171-782 0014
Sales Manager Eric Lightfoot

Publishers and suppliers of videos and cassettes on Bible and Christian life for all ages

Staff and Educational Development Association
Gala Hse, 3 Raglan Rd, Edgbaston, Birmingham B5 7RA
Administrator Jill Brookes
Chair David Baume

Tecmedia Ltd
Unit Four, The Courtyard, Stenson Rd, Whitwick Business Pk, Coalville, Leics LE67 4JP; Tel (01530) 815800
Managing Director J.D. Baxter
Company Secretary Karen Paxton

Specialist in the design, development and production of mixed-media information and training packages

Visual Publications
The Green, Northleach, Cheltenham, Glos GL54 3EX; Tel (01451) 860519; Fax (01451) 860215
Managing Director Peter Loveday

Audio-visual publishers to education. Comprehensive slide title library for Art and History, with tapes and handbooks. New cross-curricula titles in preparation. Preview service

Wilson and Garden Ltd
17–21 Newtown St, Kilsyth, Glasgow G65 0JX; Tel (01236) 823291; Fax (01236) 825683
Managing Director J.M. Cooper
Sales Manager R.A. Cooper

Manufacturers of chalkboards, whiteboards, display boards, notice boards, information boards, flipcharts, projection screens and nursery furniture

Computers in Education

National Bodies

National Council for Educational Technology

Milburn Hill Rd, Science Park, Coventry CV4 7JJ
Chief Executive Margaret Bell

The National Council for Educational Technology is a registered charity funded by the Department of Education to be the national focus of expertise in educational technology. NCET develops and promotes the use of technology in every area of education and training

Some Recent Publications
GCSE: a new teaching approach:, edited by Judith Christian-Carter and Jane Burton; It Helps: information technology for FE students with special needs by Peter Fowler; The Open Learning Pocket Workbook, by Roger Lewis with Lesley MacDonald; Supported Self-Study: an introduction for teachers, by Philip Waterhouse; Information Technology in Initial Training, by David Hawkridge; Annual Report 1988–89 Free; Courses leading to Qualifications in Educational Technology 1988–89
Free

Other National Organisations

The Advisory Unit: Computers in Education
126 Great North Rd, Hatfield AL9 5JZ; Tel (01707) 266714; Fax (01707) 273684
Director Mike Aston

The Unit provides advice, training and consultancy on all aspects of computers and information technology in education both nationally and internationally

Advisory Unit for Microtechnology in Education
Wheathampstead Education Centre, Butterfield Rd, Wheathampstead, Herts AL4 8PY; Tel (01582) 830274; Fax (01582) 830273
Co-ordinator Mary Webb

Association of Business and Administrative Computing
29/30 Stone La, Lydiard Millicent, Swindon SN2 9LD; Tel (01793) 514055/(0793) 770259; Fax (01793) 770265
Secretary John Sewter, MABE
Admin Officer P. Lewis

Professional and Examining Association offering Certificate, Certificates available in Word Processing, IT for Managers, Computer Programming, Computer Based Accounting, Computer Fundamentals, Diploma comprised of:- all of 1) Systems Analysis and Design. 2) Programming Methodology. 3) Personal Computer Systems. 4) Project, and by approved project Advanced Diploma

AVP
School Hill Centre, Chepstow, Gwent NP6 5PH; Tel (01291) 625439; Fax (01291) 629671

British Computer Society
13 Mansfield St, London W1M 0BP; Tel 0171-637 0471
Registrar J. Southall, BA, BSc, CEng, FGS, FINucE, MInstE

British Information Technology for Education
Special interest group of the British Educational Equipment Association
see Chapter 27

CAMPUS 2000–The Education Network from BT and The Times
The Times Network Systems Ltd, Priory Hse, St John's La, London EC1M 4HD; Tel 0171-782 7104

CAMPUS 2000 is a service dedicated to the needs of Education, offering a range of Electronic Mail and Information Databases, relevant to both Curriculum and Administrative uses. In addition, access is provided to a range of external Educational databases. Usage by Primary, Secondary, Further and Higher Education users is subsidised by sponsors selected from commercial companies and trade, professional and industrial associations capable of contributing worthwhile information of relevance to education

Ceefax
Rm 7013, BBC Television Centre, Wood La, London W12 7RJ; Tel 0181-576 1801
Editor Graham Norwood
Subtitling Ruth Griffiths
Systems Manager Martin Cooper

Ceefax, the BBC's teletext service offers over 600 pages of current news and information

Cimtech Ltd
University of Hertfordshire, 45 Grosvenor Rd, St Albans, Herts AL1 3AW

Centre for Information Technology in Education
CITE, College of St Mark and St John, Derriford Rd, Plymouth PL6 8BH; Tel (01752) 761104; Fax (01752) 761123
Director Dr Jon Coupland

CITE pursues a wide range of educational initiatives concerning the role of computers in teaching and learning

Department of Trade and Industry, Education and Training Policy Branch
Kingsgate Hse, 66–74 Victoria St, London SW1E 6SW; Tel 0171-215 2861
Contact E. Zimmer

Aims to encourage education and training at all levels to be more responsive to needs of business. Initiatives in schools largely ended except for work-related elements of National Curriculum. Interest in schemes to tackle advanced-level skill shortages, e.g. Teaching Company Scheme, Intergrated Graduate Development Scheme, Advanced IT Skills Initiative

Educational Journals–Computer Education
Acorn User
Audio Visual
AYCE News
Beebug
British Journal of Educatioanl Technology
CET News
Callboard
Computers in Education
Computers in Schools
Education and Training
Education Media International
Electronic Systems News
Interactive Learning International
Journal of Computer Assisted Learning
LOGOS
MUSE Report
Micromath
Micro-scope
PLET (Programmed Learning and Educational Technology)
Primary and Teaching Micros
School Technology
Times Educational Supplement
Times Higher Education Supplement
See Chapter 23

Hertfordshire IT Services
Education Centre, Butterfield Rd, Wheathampstead, Herts AL4 8PY
Director Rhona Seviour

Herts County Council Education Department

Joint Information Systems Committee
Northavon Hse, Coldharbour La, Bristol BS16 1QD; Tel (0117) 931 7230; Fax (0117) 931 7255
Secretary Malcolm G.C. Read

JIIG-CAL,
Careers Research Centre, University of Edinburgh, 5 Buccleuch Pl, Edinburgh EH8 9LW; Tel 0131-650 4310; Fax 0131-650 6533
Director S.J. Closs
Depute Director P.R. MacLean

Provides a range of Careers Guidance and Information Programmes for all ages and abilities. Incorporates Software Packages and comprehensive supporting Resource Materials. Extensive Jobfile Database covering over 650 occupations

MEU Cymru, WJEC
Unit A16/A17 Gwaelod Y Garth Rd, Treforest, Mid Glamorgan CF37 5US; Tel (01443) 841790/1
Director Meurig Williams

Micros and Primary Education
MAPE Administration, The Old Vicarage, Skegby Rd, Normanton on Trent, Notts NG23 6RR; Tel (01636) 821647
Chairman Les Watson Newman College, Bartley Grn, Birmingham B32 3NT; Tel 0121-476 1181 Ext 272
Secretary Alison Galbraith Newcastle LEA

National Computing Centre Ltd
Oxford Rd, Manchester M1 7ED; Tel 0161-228 6333; Fax 0161-228 2579
Director of Education and Training Services R.J. Firth

Provider of IT Training courses, materials and development services

Oracle Teletext
Craven Hse, 25–32 Marshall St, London W1V 1LL; Tel 0171-434 3121; Fax 0171-437 8974
Managing Director Peter Bailey
Features Editor David Klein
News Editor Peter Hall
Subtitling Editor Anne Lester

Provides up to the minute news, features and advertising for viewers. Supplies children's and youth sections to which these viewers contribute
Regional Offices Channel Oracle: TV Centre, St Helier, Jersey, CI; Tel (01534) 873999; *Editor* Gordon St Croix

DIALnet
Western Hse, 43 Smallbrook Queensway, Birmingham B5 4HQ; Tel 0121-624 5050
Managing Director Mark Duddy
Director, Sales and Marketing Sue Froggatt
Director, Operations and Support Keith Rudge
Director, Development and Systems Craig Peppiatt

We operate the DIALnet electronic messaging network used by the Educational Community; In essence DIALnet is an 'electronic post office' or central clearing house for educational data. Technically it is known as a VAN or an EDI Carrier; it offers both an electronic mail and EDI service to administrators, and is used by schools, LEAs, the DFE, Examination Boards, commercial suppliers and other educational organisations to exchange information and data.
The company mission statement is to: 'provide an electronic clearing house for information exhange, which acts as a catalyst for the integration of applications and communications within the educational sector'

Protocol International Ltd
Eldon Lodge, 196–200 Kings Rd, Reading, Berks RG1 4NJ; Tel (01734) 503966
Managing Director Tun Crawford

Provision of education and training in information technology services

School Technology Forum
See Chapter 27

Science Research Council
See Chapter 14

Scottish Micro Electronics Development Programme
See Scottish Council for Educational Technology
The aim of the SMDP is to create an awareness of the potential and application of microelectronics in schools. A significant part of the development of software, and the SDMP maintains a software library of very high quality

Scottish Regional Computer Education Centres
Northern College of Education Computing Services
Head of Dept Norman M. Smart
Aberdeen Campus Computer Education Department, Northern College of Education, Hilton Pl, Aberdeen AB9 1FA; Tel (01224) 283573
Dundee Campus Computer Education Dept, Northern College of Education, Gardyne Rd, Broughty Ferry, Dundee DD5 1NY; Tel (01382) 453433
Department of Business Technology and Administration Clyde Bank College, Kilbowie Rd, Clydebank G81 2AA; Tel 0141-952 7771
Senior Lecturer in Computing R. Elliott
Edinburgh Centre for Computer Education, Moray Hse, College of Edinburgh, Holyrood Rd, Edinburgh EH8 8AQ; Tel 0131-556 8455
P. Barker
Falkirk Computer Studies and Operations, Falkirk College of Technology, Grangemouth Rd, Falkirk F2 9AD; Tel (01324) 24981
Dr J.M. Sharp, Head of Department Computer Studies and Operations, Falkirk College of Technology
Glasgow Department of Computer Education, Jordanhill, College of Education, Southbrae Dr, Glasgow G13 1PP; Tel 0141-950 3233
J. Hawthorn
Schools' Computer Centre, Dundas Vale Teachers' Centre, 6 New City Rd, Glasgow G4 9JR; Tel 0141-332 6762
K.W. Stapely, BSc, Teacher-in-Charge

Social Science Research Council
See Chapter 14

Universities and Colleges Information Systems Association (UCISA)
Information Services, University of Central England, Perry Barr, Birmingham B42 2SU; Tel 0121-331 6234; Fax 0121-331 6789

University of London Computer Centre
20 Guilford St, London WC1; Tel 0171-405 8400; Fax 0171-242 1845
Director Dr R.W. Baker
Head of Systems K. Ashley
Head of User Support M. Keech
Head of Network Operations J.S. Seymour
Head of Operations J. Ralph

Training

The Advisory Unit: Computers in Education
126 Great North Rd, Hatfield, Herts AL9 5JZ; Tel (01707) 266714; Fax (01707) 273684
Training Director Diana Freeman

Provides school based and in-service training both in schools and at the centre in Hatfield. Bespoke courses in all aspects of Computer Education are available on request

Bournemouth Computer and Technology Centre (BCTC)
63 Cavendish Rd, Bournemouth BH1 1RA; Tel (01202) 290943
Principal Ruth Marsden

Short and long term training courses at all levels. C and G, Univ of Cambridge, Univ of London, RSA. Accredited by ITTAC, Borland and many others

Cannock Computer Training Centre (CCTC)
IT and OR Services, British Coal, Walsall Rd, Cannock, Staffs WS11 3HZ; Tel (01543) 462581
Head of Training and Information Dr I.W. Scanlan

Professional trainers of IT. Specialist in commercial programming/systems technique and business users in IT skills for better organisational performance

City and Guilds of London Institute
76 Portland Pl, London W1N 4AA; Tel 0171-278 2468

Britain's largest technical testing and awarding body providing schemes in both computing and its applications and in Information Technology

Comput-Ed Ltd
Long La, Dawlish, Devon EX7 0QR; Tel (01626) 866247
Managing Director John Cooper
Sales Roberta Young

Production and distribution of inexepensive video programmes and Computer Based Training about computing and management subjects

Computer Education Group
Staffordshire University, School of Computing, Beaconside, Stafford ST18 0AD; Tel (01785) 53511

The Association for people involved with IT in Education. Publishers of a journal written by teachers for teachers

Computers in the Curriculum Project
Kings College London (KQC), Centre for Educational Studies–Educational Computing, 552 King's Rd, London SW10 0UA; Tel 0171-351 2488
Project Director Dr Margaret J. Cox

Dean Associates
9 South West Centre, Troutbeck Rd, Sheffield S7 2QA; Tel (0114) 258 1171; Fax (0114) 258 1338
Senior Partner Christopher G. Dean
Senior Partner Quentin A. Whitlock

Dean Associates are specialists in training technology and the use of computers in training. They run courses in such areas as training design and computer based training and develop CBT and multimedia courseware for clients

Department of Computer Science, University of Edinburgh
James Clerk Maxwell Bldg, The King's Bldgs, Mayfield Rd, Edinburgh EH9 3JZ; Tel 0131-650 5112
Contact L.M. McGill

Undergraduate and Postgraduate degrees in Computer Science, also jointly with Artificial Intelligence, Electronic Engineering, Physics, Statistics, Management Science and Mathematics. MSc in Computer Science. PhD by research

ENTEK Training Services
Southgate Hse, Minchenden Complex, High St, London N14 6BJ; Tel 0181-886 0057; Fax 0181-886 4112
Director Peter Chapman
Training Consultants Kevin Challis, Pam Evans

ENTEK offer an extensive range of training services, including: Training Needs Analysis, Short courses and Consultancy. In addition, ENTEK are one of the largest stockist of Open and Flexible Learning materials in the UK, offering independent advice on the setting up, stocking and running of Open and Flexible Learning Centres

Flight Electronics International Limited
Flight Hse, Ascupart St, Southampton SO1 1LU; Tel (01703) 227721; Fax (01703) 330039; Telex 477389 FLIGHT G
Managing Director M.D. Soffe
UK Sales A. Padley

Educational microelectronic systems and instrumentation

Geographical Association Educational Computing Working Group
Exeter School, Victoria Park Rd, Exeter EX2 4NS
Contact John Davidson

Herts IT Service
Education Centre, Butterfield Rd, Wheathampstead, Herts AL4 8PY; Tel (01582) 830260; Fax (01582) 830273

Provides in-service training for teachers and software packages and other materials for sale. In-service training courses

Hoskyns Training
Hoskyns Group plc, Glen Hse, Stag Pl, London SW1E 5AG; Tel 0171-830 6868
Contact Course Registration Team

A wide range of public and in-house customised training courses for IT professionals and user staff. Training consultancy service

ICL Training
ICL Beaumont, Old Windsor, Berkshire SL4 2JP; Tel (01753) 868181; Customer reservations (01753) 851483

ICL covers the full spectrum of IT training requirements from executive education and personal skills to technical and office systems and packaged computer-based training

Dept of Computing, Imperial College of Science, Technology and Medicine
180 Queen's Gate, London SW7 2BZ; Tel 0171-589 5111
Contact Dr S.M. Cox

Provides training in use of computers, Undergraduate and postgraduate full-time courses in Computing Science, Software Engineering, Information Systems Engineering and Advanced Information Technology

Information Technology Centres
See Manpower Services Commission, Chapter 15

L.J. Technical Systems Ltd
Francis Way, Bowthorpe Ind Est, Norwich, Norfolk NR5 9JA; Tel (01603) 748001
Managing Director L.J. Rowe
Works Director T.D. Whiting
Marketing Director D.T. Breeze
Sales Director S.G. Jones

Computer based training for electronics with classroom management, microelectronic, microprocessor and robotic teaching systems and control and communications training systems

Marjon Television Production
College of St Mark and St John, Plymouth PL6 8BH; Tel (01752) 777188/761119; Fax (01752) 761120
General Director Dr Paul Rolph
Projects Officer Richard Wallis

Formerly Video-based Learning Projects Centre. Produces a wide variety of video-based learning material and broadcasts television programmes

MSc (conversion) in Computer Science
Computing Laboratory, The University, Canterbury, Kent CT2 7NF; Tel (01227) 764000 Ext 7697
Director of Computing Lab Professor J.B. Slater
Course Convenor Dr J. Derrick

National Extension College Trust
18 Brooklands Ave, Cambridge CB2 2HN; Tel (01223) 316644; Fax (01223) 313586
Director Ros Morpeth

Programming courses, books and software

NEMEC National Electronics and Microtechnology Education Centre
Univ of Southampton, Southampton SO17 1BJ; Tel (01703) 558379; Fax (01703) 672714
Director Paul Barnes

Develops and disseminates In-Service training and publications in electronics and microtechnology to trainers and teaching staff from schools and further education

Department of Computing Science, University of Newcastle upon Tyne
Newcastle upon Tyne NE1 7RU; Tel 0191-222 8034; Fax 0191-222 8232
Contact Head of Department Professor T. Anderson

University Academic Department of Computing Science. Postgraduate and undergraduate degrees in Computing Science

Nottinghamshire Computer Education Centre
Eaton Hall, Retford, Notts DN22 0PR; Tel (01777) 704875
Contact Deric Ellerby

Provides training in use of computers. Inset and general support for teachers in Nottinghamshire schools and colleges

The University of Huddersfield
School of Computing and Mathematics, The University of Huddersfield, Queensgate, Huddersfield HD1 3DH; Tel (01484) 422288 Ext 2148
Contact Admissions Coordinator

HND/C, Degree MSc and Professional courses in BusinessComputingandInformation Technology. Research. Consultancy. Short courses

Universities and Colleges Information Systems Association (UCISA)
Secretary, Head of Computing Services I.D. Griffiths The Nottingham Trent University, Burton St, Nottingham NG1 4BU; Tel (0115) 948 6444; Fax (0115) 948 4266

Membership enquiries: UCISA Administrator, University of Central England, Computer Services, Perry Barr, Birmingham B42 2SU

Research Machines
New Mill Hse, 183 Milton Pk, Abingdon, Oxford OX14 4SE

Research Machines supply the RM Nimbus range of microcomputer systems

Salford Information Technology Centre Ltd
University Rd, Salford M5 4WR; Tel 0161-736 7852
General Manager Bryan Carrington

Two year full-time training programme for 16–18 year olds covering electronics, modern office skills and microcomputing. The course is split between practicle work within the centre and industrial placement experience. The programme leads to a certificate awarded by the centre and the opportunity exists to obtain a C and G 726 certificate

Maxim Solutions Ltd
2nd Fl, Cavendish Hse, 39/41 Waterloo St, Birmingham B2 5PP; Tel 0121-608 3800; Fax 0121-608 3900

Maxim Solutions can provide consultancy, training and support solutions covering client/server, groupware, desktop databses, development tools, EIS systems, desktop suites and networking technologies

Staff Development Management Systems Ltd (SDMS)
9 Pearson Rd, Central Pk, Telford, Shropshire TF2 9TX; Tel (01952) 200911; Fax (01952) 201563
Managing Director Daivd Stevens
Marketing Manager Adam Green

SDMS specialises in the design of computer systems for Human Resource Management and Quality Development. It is the major provider of training management software for education and social services in the UK, and has a growing customer base in industry and other areas of public services. Our current software range includes Personnel, Staff Development and Training Management, Training Needs Analysis, Training Evaluation, Staff Review and Appraisal plus other specialist areas. All products are fully supported and are available across all the usual computer platforms

Department of Computer Science, University of York
Heslington, York YO1 5DD; Tel (01904) 432727
Contact Dr K.C. Mander

Education, research and consultancy in computing

Wessex Institute of Technology (WIT)
Ashurst Lodge, Ashurst, Southampton SO40 7AA; Tel (01703) 293223; Fax (01703) 292853
Director Prof. C.A. Brebbia

27 Educational and Allied Organisations

Adult Education

Adult Literacy and Basic Skills Unit (ALBSU)
Director Alan Wells Commonwealth Hse, 1–19 New Oxford St, London WC1A 1NU; Tel 0171-405 4017; Fax 0171-404 5038

Educational Centres Association
Fareham Adult Education Centre, Wickham Rd, Fareham, Hampshire PO16 7DA; Tel (01329) 315753; Fax (01329) 826915
Hon Secretary Susan S. Dickinson

Animals and Agriculture

British Field Sports Society
59 Kennington Rd, London SE1 7PZ; Tel 0171-928 4742; Fax 0171-620 1401
Director Peter Smith

The Institute of Horticulture
14/15 Belgrave Sq, London SW1X 8PS; Tel 0171-245 6943; Fax 0171-245 6943
General Secretary A. Clarke

National Dairy Council
5/7 John Princes St, London W1M 0AP; Tel 0171-499 7822; Fax 0171-408 1353
Education Officer Carol Moore

New Zealand Meat Producers' Board
European Director N.W. Taylor Rue de la Loi 99–101, B-1040, Brussels, Belgium; Tel (32) 2 230 6263; Fax (32) 2 230 5067

The Scottish Society for the Prevention of Cruelty to Animals
19 Melville St, Edinburgh EH3 7PL; Tel 0131-225 6418; Fax 0131-220 4675
Chief Executive James Morris, CBE, BSc

Ulster Society for Prevention of Cruelty to Animals
11 Drumview Rd, Lisburn, Co Antrim BT27 6YF; Tel (01232) 813178; Fax (01232) 812260
Chief Executive R.A. Wilson, LLSM

People's Dispensary for Sick Animals (PDSA)
Whitechapel Way, Priorslee, Telford, Shropshire TF2 9PQ; Tel (01952) 290999; Fax (01952) 291035

Royal Agricultural Society of the Commonwealth
55 Sleaford St, London SW8 5AB
Hon Secretary F.R. Francis, LVO, MBE; Tel 0171-627 2111; Fax 0171-978 1824

Art and Design

Arts Council of Northern Ireland
185 Stranmillis Rd, Belfast BT9 5DU; Tel (01232) 381591
Director Brian Ferran

Breakout Theatre Company
Administrator Jane Minton Berkshire Drama Centre, Beechwood Primary School, Ambleside Cl, Woodley, Reading RG5 4JJ; Tel (01734) 441893

The Camden School of Art
19–21 Kidderpore Ave, London NW3 7PS; Tel 0171-431 1292; Fax 0171-794 1439
Director David Carr, DipFA(Lond)

Chartered Society of Designers
Director B. Lymbery 29 Bedford Sq, London WC1B 3EG; Tel 0171-631 1510

Contemporary Applied Arts
43 Earlham St, London WC2H 9LD; Tel 0171-836 6993
Director Tessa Peters

Crafts Council
44A Pentonville Rd, London N1 9BY; Tel 0171-278 7700
Director Tony Ford
Head of Education Section Stephen Burroughs
Education Officers Sarah Mossop; Susan O'Reilly; Sara Bowler

The Design Council's Education and Training Foundation
Interim Director Wendy Powell Haymarket Hse, 1 Oxendon St, London SW1Y 4EE; Tel 0171-839 8000

Design and Industries Association
Co-ordinator Marci

Drama and Theatre Education Council
see British Theatre Institute

Mid–Pennine Arts
Director Nick Hunt The Gallery Downstairs, Yorke St, Burnley, Lancs BB11 1HD; Tel (01282) 421986, 429513
Project Coordinator Jacky Riddell

North West Arts Board
12 Harter St, Manchester M1 6HY; Tel 0161-228 3062; Fax 0161-236 5361
Chief Executive Vacancy

Northern Arts
9–10 Osborne Terr, Jesmond, Newcastle upon Tyne NE2 1NZ; Tel 0191-281 6334; Fax 0191-281 3276
Chief Executive Peter Hewitt

Pauline Turner Crochet Design
17 Poulton Sq, Morecambe LA4 5PZ
Personal Assistant Rita Williams; Tel (01524) 831752; Fax (01524) 833099

The Society for Italic Handwriting
Secretary Janet Pamment 'Timbertrack', 53 Sea Ave, Rustington, West Sussex BN16 2DN; Tel (01903) 783937
Editor of the Journal Duncan Ellison The School, Wellingborough, Northants NN8 2BX
Editor of the Newsletter Nicholas Caulkin 205 Dyas Ave, Great Barr, Birmingham B42 1HN
Chairman David Nicholls 17 Lennox Gdns, London SW1 0DB

Arts Councils

Arts Council of England
14 Great Peter St, London SW1P 3NQ; Tel 0171-333 0100
Chairman Lord Gowrie
Secretary-General Mary Allen
Head of Education Maggie Sample

Arts Council of Wales
Holst Hse, 9 Museum Pl, Cardiff CF1 3NX; Tel (01222) 394711; Fax (01222) 221447
Chief Executive Emyr Jenkins
Information Manager B. Lawton

Arts Council of Wales (West Wales Office)
Red St, Carmarthen, Dyfed SA31 1QL; Tel (01267) 234248; Fax (01267) 233084
Regional Director D. Carwyn Rogers

Arts Council, The Republic of Ireland
70 Merrion Sq, Dublin 2; Tel Dublin 6611840; Fax 6761302
Director Adrian Munnelly
Education Officer Kieran Walsh

East Midlands Arts Board
Chief Executive John Buston Mountfields Hse, Forest Rd, Loughborough, Leics LE11 3HU; Tel (01509) 218292

Eastern Arts Board
Chief Executive Jeremy Newton Eastern Arts Board, Cherry Hinton Rd, Cambridge CB1 4DW; Tel (01223) 215355; Fax (01223) 248075
Director (Planning and Development) Fred Brookes
Director (Performing Arts) Sandy Bailey
Director (Visual and Media Arts) Rosy Greenlees
Director (Resources) Lesley Thompson
Education Officer Karen Dust
Crafts Officer Alison McFarlane
Dance, Mime and New Circus Officer Nicola Crane
Drama Officer Alan Orme
Cinema and Broadcasting Officer Martin Ayres
Literature Officer Don Watson
Music Officer Heather Laing
Information Technology Officer Kofi Owusu
Marketing and Communications Officer Gerry O'Keeffe
Visual Arts Officer Amanda Ryan
Venue Development Officer Peter Thornton
Photography Officer Alastair Haines
Rural Arts Officer Kevin Moore

Scottish Arts Council
12 Manor Pl, Edinburgh EH3 7DD; Tel 0131-226 6051
Director Seona Reid

South East Arts Board
Chief Executive C. Cooper 10 Mount Ephraim, Tunbridge Wells, Kent TN4 8AS; Tel (01892) 515210; Fax (01892) 549383

South West Arts (Arts Board South West Ltd)
Bradninch Pl, Gandy St, Exeter, Devon EX4 3LS; Tel (01392) 218188; Fax (01392) 413554
Chief Executive Christopher Bates
Assistant Director (with responsibility for education) Nicholas Capaldi

Southern Arts Board
Executive Director Sue Robertson 13 St Clement St, Winchester, Hants SO23 9DQ; Tel (01962) 855099; Fax (01962) 861186

West Midlands Arts
82 Granville St, Birmingham B1 2LH; Tel 0121-631 3121; Fax 0121-643 7239
Chief Executive Michael Elliott

Yorkshire and Humberside Arts
Executive Director Roger Lancaster 21 Bond St, Dewsbury, W Yorks WF13 1AX; Tel (01924) 455555; Fax (01924) 466522
Yorkshire and Humberside Arts is one of ten Regional Arts Boards covering the whole of England

Benevolent Funds

Professional Classes Aid Council
10 St Christopher's Pl, London W1M 6HY; Tel 0171-935 0641
Secretary Mrs G.A. Burgess

Blind and Visually Impaired

Association for the Education and Welfare of the Visually Handicapped
41 Stockdale Pl, Westfield Rd, Edgbaston, Birmingham
Secretary S.A. Clamp

College of the Teachers of the Blind
see Association for the Education and Welfare of the Visually Handicapped

Gyde Charity for Blind, Deaf and Dumb Children
4/7 Rowcroft, Stroud, Glos GL5 3BJ; Tel (01453) 763381
Clerk to Trustees P.J. Gadsden

Research Centre for the Education of the Visually Handicapped
University of Birmingham, School of Education, Edgbaston, Birmingham B15 2TT; Tel 0121-414 6733
Director Dr M.J. Tobin

RNIB Education Support Services
RNIB National Education Centre
Garrow Hse, 190 Kensal Rd, London W10 5BT; Tel 0181-968 8600
RNIB Care Training Service
Exhall Grange School, Wheelwright La, Coventry CV7 9HP; Tel (01203) 366133
RNIB Education Centre London
Garrow Hse, 190 Kensal Rd, London W10 5BT; Tel 0181-968 8600
RNIB Education Centre Midlands
RNIB New College Worcester, Whittington Rd, Worcester WR5 2JX; Tel (01905) 763933
RNIB Education Centre Wales
14 Neville St, Canton, Cardiff CF1 8UX; Tel (01222) 668606
RNIB Education Centre North of England
2nd Flr, Emco Hse, 5/7 New York Rd, Leeds LS2 7PJ; Tel (0113) 245 0508
RNIB Education Centre Scotland
10 Magdale Cres, Edinburgh EH12 5BE; Tel 0131-313 1876
RNIB Education Centre South West
Tel Contact (01647) 24326

RNIB Talking Book Service
Mount Pleasant, Wembley, Middx HA0 1RR; Tel 0181-903 6666; Fax 0181-903 6916

Royal National Institute for the Blind
224 Great Portland St, London W1N 6AA; Tel 0171-388 1266; Fax 0171-388 2034
Director-General Ian W. Bruce
Director of Education and Leisure P. Ennals

Business and Industry

Association for Sandwich Education and Training
3 Westbrook Ct, Sharrow Vale Rd, Sheffield S11 8YZ; Tel (01742) 669999; Fax (01742) 683335
Secretary R.M. Brewer ASET Secretary, Sheffield Hallam University, Pond St, Sheffield S1 1WB

Association of Conference Executives (ACE)
Riverside Hse, High St, Huntingdon, Cambs PE18 6SG; Tel (01480) 457595; Fax (01480) 412863
General Manager Peter Worger

British Association for Commercial and Industrial Education (BACIE)
Director B.V. Murphy 16 Park Cres, London W1N 4AP; Tel 0171-636 5351; Fax 0171-436 2624

British Business Graduates Society
Chairman D.L. Rao
Secretary R.W. Boad, Secretariat City of London Polytechnic, 84 Moorgate, London EC2M 6SQ; Tel (01277) 73385

British Nuclear Fuels plc (BNFL),)
Risley, Warrington, Cheshire WA3 6AS; Tel (01925) 835453, 832826
Manager, Education Unit Dr C.P. Squire

Ceylon Tea Bureau
22 Regent St, London SW1Y 4QD

Department of Management Learning
Head Prof J.G. Burgoyne Management School, University of Lancaster, Lancaster LA1 4YX; Tel (01524) 65201 Ext 4019

National Drinkwatchers Network
ACCEPT Clinic, 200 Seagrave Rd, London SW6 1RQ; Tel 0171-381 3157
Essex–Contact
Essex Alcohol Advisory Service, 11 Centurion Hse, Saint John's St, Colchester CO2 7AH; Tel (01206) 575810

Organisation for Economic Co–operation and Development (OECD)
2 rue Andre Pascal, 75775 Paris Cedex 16, France; Tel 45 24 82 00
Director, Employment and Social Affairs T.J. Alexander

Rural Development Commission
141 Castle St, Salisbury, Wilts SP1 3TP; Tel (01722) 336255
Provides technical training in certain disciplines to employees of rural businesses

The Tavistock Institute
30 Tabernacle St, London EC2A 4DE; Tel 0171-417 8310; Fax 0171-417 0566
Secretary N.H. Barnes 30 Tabernacle St, London EC2A 4DE; Tel 0171-417 8310; Fax 0171-417 0566
Social and psychological research, advice and training

Trade Association for Manufacturers and Wholesalers of Musical Instruments and related products
Sponsors of Music for Youth and The National Programme of Training for Primary School Music. Consultants at the University of Reading

United Kingdom Home Economics Federation
Hon Secretary A. Pauline Cooper, DipEd, FIHEc Chairbarrow Hse, 171 Whitechapel Rd, Cleckheaton, West Yorks BD19 6HW; Tel (01274) 872488
A co-ordinating body of Associations dealing with all aspects of home economics

Careers

Association of Graduate Recruiters
Executive Secretary Roly Cockman Sheraton Hse, Castle Pk, Cambridge CB3 0AX; Tel (01223) 356720; Fax (01223) 356720

CareerPlanners
3 Devonshire Ct, 26A Devonshire St, London W1N 1RJ; Tel 0171-487 4027; Fax 0171-486 4232
Principal Dr Judith Haynes
Senior Consultant Peter Kendall
Assessment and advice is provided by independent chartered psychologists. A wide range of services is offered to individuals and direct to schools and colleges. Telephone or write for details

Careers Research and Advisory Centre (CRAC)
Sheraton Hse, Castle Pk, Cambridge CB3 0AX; Tel (01223) 460277; Fax (01223) 311708
Managing Director P.D. Blandford

National Institute for Careers Education and Counselling
Sheraton Hse, Castle Pk, Cambridge CB3 OAX; Tel (01223) 460277; Fax (01223) 311708

Teaching as Career Unit (TASC)
35 Great Smith St, London SW1P 3BJ; Tel 0171-227 2867
Director Jack Dodds, BSc

Charities

A.S. Neill Trust
Secretary P. Dacre Flat 8, Chestnut Mead, Kingsgate Rd, Winchester, Hants, SO23 9QQ

Albany Trust Counselling
Sunra Centre, 26 Balham Hill, London SW12 9EB; Tel 0181-675 6669
Counselling Co-ordinator Gregory Lurie
Director of Training Courses Jeremy Clarke

All Saints Educational Trust
Secretary A.W. Bush, JP, LLB, FRSA St Katharine Cree Church, 86 Leadenhall St, London EC3A 3DH; Tel 0171-283 4485

Anna Westmacott Charity
Clerk to the Trustees Ms V.E. Shield 7 Northumberland St, London WC2N 5DA; Tel 0171-930 6441

Barnardo's
Tanners La, Barkingside, Ilford, Essex IG6 1QG; Tel 0181-550 8822
Senior Director R. Singleton, MA, MSc
Education Adviser Janice Funnell, MA, MSc, CPsychol, AFBPsS
Director of Child Care R.M. Jarman, MA

Berkshire Federation of the Hard of Hearing
4 Shenstone Pk, London Rd, Sunninghill, Ascot SL5 7RE
Hon Secretary June Lamb

Blissymbolics Communication Resource Centre
Rm Q, 102–104 Queenswood, Cardiff Institute of Higher Education, Cyncoed Centre, Cyncoed Rd, Cardiff CF2 6XD; Tel (01222) 757826
National Co-ordinator Ena Davies, LCST
Administrative Secretary Lynne Conway

British and Foreign School Society
Secretary S.M.A. Banister, MA Richard Mayo Hall, Eden St, Kingston upon Thames, Surrey KT1 1HZ; Tel 0181-546 2379

Calouste Gulbenkian Foundation (Lisbon), United Kingdom Branch
Director Ben Whitaker, 98 Portland Pl London, W1N 4ET, 071-636 5313

Chadwick Trust
Secretary to the Management Committee Ian Orchardson Registrar's Division, University College London, Gower St, London WC1E 6BT; Tel 0171-380 7327

Charity Commission
St Albans Hse, 57–60 Haymarket, London SW1Y 4QX; Tel 0171-210 4477; Fax 0171-930 9173
Executive Director E. Shaw

Child Growth Foundation
2 Mayfield Ave, Chiswick, London W4 1PW; Tel 0181-994 7625; 0181-995 0257; Fax 0181-995 9075
Chairman Tam Fry

The Dartington Hall Trust
Company Secretary A. St John Palmer The Dartington Hall Trust, Totnes, Devon; Tel (01803) 862271

Franco–British Society
Rm 623, Linen Hall, 162–168 Regent St, London W1R 5TB; Tel 0171-734 0815; Fax 0171-734 0815
Executive Secretary Marian Clarke, BA(Hons)

Jewish Education Aid Society
C/o Anglo–Jewish Association, Woburn Hse, Upper Woburn Pl, London WC1H 0EP; Tel 0171-387 5937
Secretary E. Salasnik

The Leverhulme Trust
15–19 New Fetter La, London EC4A 1NR; Tel 0171-822 6938
Director Prof B.E. Supple, FRHist, FBA
Awards grants to institutions and individuals for research mainly

Lord Kitchener National Memorial Fund
Enquiries The Secretary LKNMF Salters Grn Fm, Mayfield, E Sussex TN20 6NP; Tel (01892) 852472

Mitchell City of London Educational Foundation
Clerk to the Trustees J. Keyte, OBE The Lodge, 23 Old Lodge La, Purley, Surrey CR8 4DJ

National Federation of Community Organisations (Community Matters)
8/9 Upper St, Islington, London N1 0PQ; Tel 0171-226 0189
Director Charles Woodd
Information Officer Diana Hopkins

National Institute for Social Work
5/7 Tavistock Pl, London WC1H 9SN; Tel 0171-387 9681; Fax 0171-387 7968

The National Meningitis Trust
Fern Hse, Bath Rd, Stroud, Glos GL5 3TJ; Tel (01453) 751738, 24 Hr Helpline (01453) 755049
President HRH The Princess of Wales

National Society for the Prevention of Cruelty to Children (Incorporated by Royal Charter)
Registered Charity No 216401
42 Curtain Rd, London EC2A 3NH; Tel 0171-825 2500
Director Christopher Brown
Head of Child Protection Training Enid Hendry NSPCC Training Centre, 3 Gilmour Cls, Beaumont Leys, Leicester LE4 1EZ
Librarian Catherine Tite, BA, DipLib, ALA, PCM

Pestalozzi Children's Village Trust
Sedlescombe, Battle, Sussex TN33 0RR; Tel (01424) 870444; Fax (01424) 870655

Places for People (National Association for Urban Studies)
University of Brighton, Lewis Cohen Urban Studies Centre, 68 Grand Parade, Brighton, Sussex BN2 2JY
Editor, Streetwise Richard Welsh Lewis Cohen Urban Studies Centre, University of Brighton, 68 Grand Parade, Brighton, Sussex BN2 2JY

Royal Society for Mentally Handicapped Children and Adults (MENCAP,)
MENCAP National Centre, 123 Golden La, London EC1Y 0RT; Tel 0171-454 0454; Fax 0171-608 3254
Chairman Lord Rix, CBE, DL
Chief Executive Fred Heddell
MENCAP is the largest national parent organisation, exclusively concerned with people with a learning disability, their families and carers. The society provides support and help for parents and carers of people with learning disabilities, through its 7 Divisional Offices, its District Officers and a network of 550 Local Societies MENCAP runs residential services, training and

employment services and leisure facilities through the National Federation of Gateway Clubs and holidays. MENCAP also mounts conferences and campaigns to improve public awareness of learning disability and services for people with learning disabilities

Royal Society for the Prevention of Accidents
Cannon Hse, The Priory Queensway, Birmingham B4 6BS; Tel 0121-200 2461; Fax 0121-200 1254
Chief Press Officer Cathy Ward
Education Adviser Martin Gomberg

Royal Society for the Prevention of Cruelty to Animals
Education Dept, Causeway, Horsham, Sussex RH12 1HG; Tel (01403) 264181

Schoolmistresses and Governesses Benevolent Institution
SGBI Office, Queen Mary Hse, Manor Pk Rd, Chislehurst, Kent BR7 5PY; Tel 0181-468 7997
Director and Secretary L.I. Baggott, FCA

Scottish Pre-School Play Association
14 Elliot Pl, Glasgow G3 8EP; Tel 0141-221 4148
National Executive Officer Moira Ferguson

Shaftesbury Society
16 Kingston Rd, London SW19 1JZ; Tel 0181-542 5550; Fax 0181-545 0605
Communications Director Nicky Slater
Founded as the Ragged School Union in 1844, the Shaftesbury Society is a registered Christian caring charity which encourages people with a learning or physical disability to reach their full potential in life

It works with local authorities to provide education, residential care and holidays for people with disabilities. There are residential schools for children, colleges of further education and student hostels. Shared housing units for people with physical and learning disabilities provide differing degrees of independence. Holiday centre for people with learning disabilities. Shaftesbury also runs hostels for young homeless people

The Sidney Perry Foundation (incorporating The Covenantors Educational Trust)
Secretaries and Trustees Atlas Assurance Co Ltd, Executor and Trustee Dept, Civic Dr, Ipswich, Suffolk IP1 2AN

Sir Ernest Cassel Educational Trust
Secretary R. Le Fanu, OBE 8 Malvern Terr, Islington, London N1 1HR; Tel 0171-607 7879

SOS Childrens Villages UK
32 Bridge St, Cambridge CB2 1UJ; Tel (01223) 65589; Fax (01223) 322613
Fund raising organisation supporting family oriented care giving orphaned and abandoned children worldwide a mother, a family, a home and a future

TACADE (The Advisory Council on Alcohol and Drug Education)
Chief Executive Jeffrey Lee
Deputy Chief Executive Vivienne Evans 1 Hulme Pl, The Cres, Salford M5 4QA; Tel 0161-745 8925; Fax 0161-745 8923
TACADE is the leading non–government organisation working in the field of preventive education. Its work encompasses the fields of health and personal and social education. TACADE works in three key areas: Resource Materials, Project Management and Consultancy, Training and Conference Management. For further information please contact TACADE – Telephone: 061-745 8925 or Fax: 061-745 8923

UNICEF(UK) (United Nations Children's Fund)
55 Lincoln's Inn Fields, London WC2A 3NB; Tel 0171-405 5592
Education Officer Heather Jarvis, BA, MA (Educ)

Women's Royal Voluntary Service
Chairman Elizabeth Toulson WRVS Head Office, 234–244 Stockwell Rd, London SW9 9SP; Tel 0171-416 0146; Fax 0171-416 0148

Children

Action for Sick Children (National Association for the Welfare of Children in Hospital)
29–31 Euston Rd,London NW1 2SD; Tel 0171-833 2041
15 Smith's Pl,Edinburgh EH6 8HT; Tel 0131-553 6553

Association of Nursery Training Colleges
Secretary M. Harrison The Norland College, Den Ford Pk, Hungerford, Newbury, RG17 0PQ; Fax (01488) 682252; Telex (0488) 685212

The Boarding Schools Association
Secretary F. Bickerstaff Westmorland, 43 Raglan Rd, Reigate, Surrey RH2 0DU; Tel (01737) 226450; Fax (01737) 226775

British Children's Theatre Association
see National Association for Drama in Education and Children's Theatre

Council for Disabled Children (CDC)
National Children's Bureau, 8 Wakely St, London EC1V 7QE; Tel 0171-843 6061
Principal Officer Mrs P. Russell, BA

Joint Educational Trust (JET),)
Clove Bldg, 4 Maguire St, Butlers Wharf, London SE1 2NQ; Tel 0171-378 1391; Fax 0171-403 0062
Director/Fundraiser Susan E. Bainer, MIPM, ICFM

Kids' Clubs Network
279–281 Whitechapel Rd, London E1 1BY; Tel 0171-247 3009; Fax 0171-247 4490
Director Anne Longfield

The Maria Montessori Training Organisation
26 Lyndhurst Gdns, London NW3 5NW; Tel 0171-435 3646; Fax 0171-431 8096

Montessori Information Line
PO Box 5, Brecon LD3 8XX; Tel (01874) 638007
Admin Officer N.J. Maughan

The Montessori Society, AMI(UK)
26 Lyndhurst Gdns, London NW3 5NW; Tel 0171-435 7874
Chairman Mrs E.A. Hood

National Association for Gifted Children
Park Campus, Boughton Green Rd, Northampton NN2 7AL; Tel (01604) 792300
Director M. Short

National Association for Primary Education (NAPE)
National Centre for Primary Education Queens Bldg, University of Leicester, Barrack Rd, Northampton NN2 6AF; Tel (01604) 36326

National Association of Toy and Leisure Libraries/ The Play Matters
68 Churchway, London NW1 1LT; Tel 0171-387 9592; Fax 0171-383 2714
Director Glenys Carter
National body for toy libraries in the UK. Toy libraries loan carefully selected, good quality toys appropriate to each stage of development. Operate as a preventive service, filling gaps in the existing provision for all families with babies and young children, including those with special needs. Leisure libraries, loan equipment to young people and adults with learning difficulties. Various publications about play – send s.a.e. for list and details nearest Toy or Leisure Library

National Childcare Campaign/Daycare Trust
4 Wild Ct, London WC2B 4AU; Tel 0171-405 5617/405 5618; Fax 0171-831 6632
Director Carol Sherriff

National Children's Home
85 Highbury Pk, London N5 1UD; Tel 0171-226 2033; Fax 0171-226 2537
Principal & Chief Executive Tom White, CBE
Education Adviser Doug Pattison

Nursery and Pre-School Information Line
PO Box 5, Brecon LD3 8YX; Tel (01874) 638007
Contact N.J. Maughan

Peper Harow Foundation
14 Charterhouse Sq, London EC1M 6AX; Tel 0171-251 0672/6072
Chief Executive Michael Willis
Associate Director Brian Bishop, MA, CQSW, DipSocStudies
Aims to foster understanding and recognition of the treatment needed to rehabilitate seriously disturbed children, including advisory services to professionals in the social work, education and health services

Pre-School Playgroups Association
61–63 Kings Cross Rd, London WC1X 9LL; Tel 0171-833 0991; Fax 0171-837 4942, Childcare Helpline: 0171-837 5513
Chief Executive Margaret Lochrie

Rutherford School
1A Melville Ave, South Croydon, Surrey CR2 7HZ; Tel 0181-688 7560
Chairman, Children's Centre Committee S. Ellis
Head of Children's Centre Mrs P.H. Netley
Prepares children who have physical, learning and development problems to be as independent as possible in daily learning skills and helps them reach their full potential and enrich their lives however handicapped they may be, Run by the Croydon, Sutton and District Spastics Society. 2–12 years, day only

World Organisation for Early Childhood Education, UK National Committee (OMEP)
Chairman T. David Institute of Education, University of Warwick, Coventry

Community Work

British Association of Settlements and Social Action Centres (BASSAC),)
13 Stockwell Rd, London SW9 9AU; Tel 0171-733 7428
Head of Agency John Matthews
Membership Services Assistant James Kimmis
Membership Development Worker Vashti Ledford

Interchange Trust Ltd
Interchange Studios, Dalby St, London NW5 3NQ; Tel 0171-267 9421; Fax 0171-482 5292
Director Dr Alan Tomkins
Community development organisation running projects and providing resources for other community groups to do the same. Resources for community groups, including print, community arts, social services, and management training. Legal Advisory Service for charities and trusts and health promotion projects. Central London Conference and training facilities for hire

National Playbus Association
93 Whitby Rd, Bristol BS4 3QF; Tel (0117) 977 5375
Chairperson Jenny Layley
Chief Executive Georgina Payne

Deaf/Without Speech/ Speech Difficulties

Association for All Speech Impaired Children (AFASIC)
347 Central Markets, Smithfield, London EC1A 9NH; Tel 0171-236 3632/6487
Director Norma Corkish

The Beethoven Fund for Deaf Children
2 Queensmead, St John's Wood Pk, London NW8 6RE; Tel 0171-586 8107; Fax 0171-722 9886
Contact Ann Rachlin, MBE, Chairman

British Deaf Association (BDA),)
38 Victoria Pl,Carlisle CA1 1HU; Tel (01228) 48844; Textphone (01228) 28719; Fax (01228) 41420
Chief Executive Elizabeth Wincott

Commonwealth Society for the Deaf
Dilke Hse, Malet St, London WC1E 7JA; Tel 0171-631 5311; Fax 0171-580 8735
Chairman C. Holborow, OBE, TD, MD, FRCS

Council for the Advancement of Communication with Deaf People (CACDP),)
Pelaw Hse, School of Education, University of Durham, Durham DH1 1TA; Tel 0191-374 3607; Fax 0191-374 3605; Minicom answering machine 0191-374 3614
Chief Executive T.S. Simpson, BA, MSc(Econ)

Cumbria Deaf Association
3 Compton St, Carlisle CA1 1HT; Tel (01228) 22885; Fax (01228) 590501; Minicom (01228) 819137
Director Mrs A. Verney

Dance for Everyone (Dance Company Performances and Workshops) in Education, Special Needs, Deaf
Director Miss N. Benari, MA 6 Milverton Rd, London NW6; Tel 0181-451 2000

'I CAN'
Barbican City Gate, 1–3 Dufferin St, London EC1Y 8NA
Co-ordinator Sharon Charteress

International Audiology Society
Sandiane, 16 Nithsdale Rd, Weston-Super-Mare, Avon BS23 4JR; Tel (01934) 415207
Chairman and Honorary Audiology Consultant Mrs E.A. Crellin

National Association for Tertiary Education for Deaf People (NATED)
c/o Service for H.I; Barry College, Colcot Rd, Barry CF62 8YJ
Secretary Karen Every–Clayton
Promotes the exchange of views and experiences of all those concerned in further education and higher education for the Hearing-Impaired

National Deaf Children's Society
24 Wakefield Rd, Rothwell, Leeds LS26 0SF; Tel (0113) 282 3458; Freephone (0800) 252380 (1-5 pm parents only); Fax (0113) 282 4113
Education Officer A. Joseph

NDCS Technology Information Centre
Head of Centre T. Winstanley 4 Church Rd, Birmingham B15 3TD; Tel 0121-454 5151 (Voice and minicom); Fax 0121-454 5044

Nottingham and Notts Society for the Deaf
Institute for the Deaf, 22 Forest Rd West, Nottingham NG7 4EQ; Tel (0115) 970 0516 (voice and text); Tel (0115) 942 3096 (Fax) Tel (0115) 978 5783 minicom 7

Paget Gorman Society (Paget Gorman Signed Speech)
3 Gipsy La, Headington, Oxford OX3 7PT; Tel (01865) 61908
Development Officer R.G. Newey

The Royal National Institute for Deaf People
105 Gower St, London WC1E 6AH; Tel 0171-387 8033; Fax 0171-388 2346
Head of Information Services Division, RNID Judy Walker

Development Education

Development Education Association
Third Fl, 29–31 Cowper St, London EC2A 4AP; Tel 0171-490 8108; Fax 0171-490 8123
Development Education promotes global awareness and international understanding across all educational sectors. It incorporates multicultural, anti-racist and anti-sexist approaches and seeks to enable people to address issues of global inequality, debt, unfair trade, human rights, peace and sustainable development. A network operates across various national bodies and agencies and at the local level through centres. Most centres work with schools and local communities providing in-service training, resources for reference, sale or loan and offer general advice on international perspectives
The following is a list of the members of the Development Education Association
Action Aid Hamlyn Hse, MacDonald Rd, Archway, London N19 5PG; Tel 0171-281 4101
Steve Brace
AIESEC UK 2nd Fl, 29-31 Cowper St, London EC2A 4AP; Tel 0171-336 7939
Kate Berman
Akina Mama wa Afrika c/o London Women's Centre, Wesley Hse, 4 Wild Ct, London WC2B 5AU; Tel 0171-405 0678
Bisi Adeleye-Fayemi
Alternative for India Development 235 Rookery Rd, Handsworth, Birmingham B21 9PU; Tel 0121-554 5854
Joseph Selvam
Anti-Slavery International The Stableyard, Broomgrove Rd, London SW9 9TL; Tel 0171-924 9555
Adam Robertson
Association for Science Education College La, Hatfield AL10 9AA; Tel (01707) 267411
Dr David Moore
Avon International Education School Hse, Bishop Rd, Bristol BS7 8LS; Tel (01272) 240801
Ray Harris
Aylesbury Development Education Centre Elmhurst County Middle School, Dunsham La, Aylesbury HP20 2DB; Tel (01296) 395185
Pauline Roby
Baby Milk Action 23 St Andrew's St, Cambridge CB2 3AX; Tel (01223) 464420
Sonali Kumarakvia Singhe
Bath Development Education Centre 12a Westgate St, Bath BA1 1EQ; Tel (01225) 313274
Roger Davis
Breakthrough Church 52 Fairlight Rd, Tooting, London SW17 0JD; Tel 0181-767 5013
Guy Bevir
Brighton Co-operative Society Ltd 94-101 London Rd, Brighton BN1 4LB; Tel (01273) 606722
John Mileham
Brighton Peace Centre 28 Trafalgar St, Brighton BN1 4ED; Tel (01273) 692880
Wayne Hubbard
CAFOD 2 Romero Cl, Stockwell, London SW9 9TY; Tel 0171-733 7900
Brian Davies
Cambridge Centre for Environment and Development Education The Harambee Centre, 110 Regent St, Cambridge CB2 1DP; Tel (01223) 358116
Charlie Nurse
Catholic Institute for International Relations Unit 3 Canonbury Yard, 190A New North Rd, Islington, London N1 7BJ; Tel 0171-354 0883
Angela Warren
Central Bureau for Educational Visits & Exchanges Seymour Mews Hse, Seymour Mews, London W1H 9PE; Tel 0171-725 9404/486 5101
Elspeth Cardy
Centre for Global Education University College of Ripon & York St. John, Lord Mayors Walk, York YO3 7EX; Tel (01904) 616839
Margot Brown
CHANGE 5 Central Bldgs, Rye La, London SE15 5DW; Tel 0181-277 6187
Charity Projects Ltd 74 New Oxford St, London WC1A 1EF; Tel 0171-436 1122
Rick Scott
Chelmsford One World Resource Centre c/o UNICEF, 1–3 Broomfield Rd, Chelmsford CM1 1SZ; Tel (01245) 354375
Tony Bender
Cheltenham Area Development Education Centre 13 Priory Terr, Cheltenham GL52 6DS; Tel (01242) 520969
Alex Hawkins
Christian Aid 35 Lower Marsh, London SE1 7RL; Tel 0171-620 4444
Barbara Vellacott
Christian Aid (NW Region) The Rectory, Vale Rd, Ellesmere Port L65 9AY; Tel 0151-355 2516
Susanne Garnett
Christian Aid (Wales) 27 Church Rd, Whitchurch, Cardiff CF4 2DX; Tel (01222) 614435
A. Elenid Jones
Christian Brother Schools Resource Centre St Anselm's College, Manor Hill, Birkenhead L43 1UQ; Tel 0151-653 3044
Francis Hall
Christian Concern for One World The Knowle, Philcote St, Deddington, Banbury OX15 0TB; Tel (01869) 38225
Christopher Hall
Christian Fellowship Trust 19 Denbigh Rd, Ealing, London W13 8QA; Tel 0181-997 1095
Alison Harvey
Christian Relief Education and Development c/o Revelation Church, P.O. Box 58, Chichester PO19 2UD; Tel (01243) 531898
Greg Valerio
Church of England, Board of Education Church Hse, Great Smith St, London SW1P 3NZ; Tel 0171-222 9011 Ext 411
Hilary Ineson
Co-operation for Development 118 Broad St, Chesham HP5 3ED; Tel (01494) 775557
Michelle Scully
Comhlamh 61 Lower Camden St, Dublin 2, Ireland; Tel 010 353 1 4783490
Marc Prochasson
Commonwealth Institute Kensington High St, London W8 6NQ; Tel 0171-603 4535
Fennela White
Commonwealth Linking Trust 7 Lion Yard, Tremadoc Rd, London SW4 7NQ; Tel 0171-498 1101
Jean Thompson
Commonwealth TUC Congress Hse, Great Russel St, London WC1B 3LS; Tel 0171-631 0728
Patrick Quinn
Commonwork Land Trust Bore Place Farm, Chiddingstone, Edenbridge TN8 7AR; Tel (01732) 463255
Angela Holland
Cordillera Links 73 Thrayle Hse, Benedict Rd, Stockwell Pk Est, London SW9 0XU; Tel 0171-403 1906/326 0363
Joji Carino
Council for Education in World Citizenship Seymour Mews Hse, Seymour Mews, London W1H 9PE; Tel 0171-935 1752
Patricia Rogers

27 Educational and Allied Organisations

Council for Environmental Education University of Reading, London Rd, Reading RG1 5AG; Tel (01734) 756061
Christine Midgley
Coventry Council for Voluntary Youth Service Bardsley Hse, 7 Priory Row, Coventry CV1 5ES; Tel (01203) 555277
Georgina Price
Craven Dales Development Education Project Wesley Hse, 4 Penyghent View, Settle BD24 9JJ; Tel (01729) 822554
Rev J. Bennett
Cumbria Development Education Centre c/o Faculty of Teacher Education, Charlotte Mason College, University of Lancaster, Ambleside LA22 9BB; Tel (015394) 30231
Jean Crosbie
Daneford Trust 18 Cheverell Hse, Pritchards Rd, London E2 9BN; Tel 0171-729 1928
Anthony Stevens
Dept. of International and Comparative Education Institute of Education, University of London, Bedford Way, London WC1 0AL; Tel 0171-580 1122
Dr E. Thomas
Derby Rainbow Centre 88 Abbey St, Derby DE22 3SQ; Tel (01332) 298185
Cliff James
Derry Development Education Centre 13A Pump St, Derry BT48 6JG; Tel (01504) 269183
Ruth Moore
Development Alternatives 49 Green Rd, Reading RG6 2BS; Tel (01734) 662291
John Cunnington
Development Education Centre (Birmingham) Gillett Centre, 998 Bristol Rd, Selly Oak, Birmingham B29 6LE; Tel 0121-472 3255
Ina Clason
Development Education Centre (South Yorkshire) Woodthorpe School, Woodthorpe Rd, Sheffield S13 8DD; Tel (01742) 656662
Dee Tossell
Development Education in Dorset East Dorset Professional Education Ctr, Lowther Rd, Bournemouth BH8 8NA; Tel (01202) 396932
Angela Joynson
Development Education Project (Manchester) c/o Manchester Metropolitan University, 801 Wilmslow Rd, Didsbury, Manchester M20 8RG; Tel 0161-445 2495
Anne Strachan
Dudley Metropolitan Borough Council Community Development Unit, 8 Parsons St, Dudley DY1 1JJ; Tel (01384) 453190
B. Fryer
Dudley One World Resource Centre Hillcrest School and Community College, Simms La, Netherton, Dudley DY2 0PB; Tel (01384) 457799
D. Tidbury
Eastbourne Professional Centre Trevin Towers, Gaudick Rd, Eastbourne BN20 7SP; Tel (01323) 417657
Ann Wait
Edgewood Educational Orchard Dell, Breakspear Rd, Ruislip HA4 7SE; Tel (01895) 624355
Lynne Kauffman
Education Partners Overseas 10 Barley Mow Passage, London W4 4PH; Tel 0181-742 3757
Jean Burroughs
Environmental Education Centre, Suffolk County Council c/o Otley College, Otley, Ipswich IP6 9EY; Tel (01473) 785543 Ext 159
Alison Wood
European Development Education Network 41 Derby Rd, Melbourne DE73 1FE; Tel (01332) 864794
Pat Gerrard
Eye to Eye Productions 151-153 Clapham High St, London SW4 7SS; Tel 0171-498 5335
Andrew Guy
Falmouth One World Week Group London Wells Farm, Rame Cross, Penryn TR10 9DU; Tel (01209) 860610
Ron Julian
Farmers Link 38–40 Exchange St, Norwich NR2 1AX; Tel (01603) 765670
Alistair Smith
Farmers World Network National Agricultural Ctr, Stoneleigh Pk CV8 2LZ; Tel (01203) 696969
Susan Rabbich
General Assembly of Unitarian & Free Christian Churches 1–6 Essex St, London WC2R 3HY; Tel 0171-240 2384
Ingrid Tavkar
Geographical Association 343 Fulwood Rd, Sheffield S10 3BP; Tel (01742) 670666
Frances Soar
GLADE Centre c/o 40-42 Hendford, Yeovil BA20 1UW; Tel (01935) 33186
Tony Smith
Global Link Resource Ctr, YMCA, China St, Lancaster LA1 1EX; Tel (01524) 36201
Ruth Self
Ann Thomson
Grassroots Programme Luton Industrial College, Chapel St, Luton LU1 2SE; Tel (01582) 29374
David Cowling
Guide Association 17–19 Buckingham Palace Rd, London SW1W 0PT; Tel 0171-834 6242
Barbara Mathieson
Hampshire Development Education Centre Professional Centre, Romsey Rd, Winchester SO22 5PL; Tel (01962) 856106
Pat Francis
Havering Voluntary Youth Forum 34 Maybank Ave, Hornchurch RM12 5SB; Tel (01708) 452043
R.G. Gibbs
Helston One World Week Group 21 Roselidden Parc, Helston TR13 8UH; Tel (01326) 562116
Mary Charnock
Heritage Motor Centre Banbury Rd, Gaydon, Warwick CV35 0BJ; Tel (01926) 645075
Gillian Bardsley
Highland One World Group Development Education Resource Ctr, Old Central School, Kenneth St, Inverness IV3 5DW; Tel (01463) 225449
Helen Meaney
Hull Development Education Centre c/o David Lister School, Rustenberg St, Hull HU9 2PR; Tel (01482) 786488
Adam Ranson
Humanities Association 98 Howard Rd, Leicester LE2 1XH; Tel (01533) 703366
Dan McEwan
Humanities & Development Education Centre Tower Hamlets PDC, English St, London E3 4TA; Tel 0181-981 0183
Margaret Burr
Institute of Ismaili Studies 30 Portland Pl, London W1N 3DF; Tel 0171-436 1736
Nasser Khoja
Intermediate Technology Development Group Myson Hse, Railway Terr, Rugby CV21 3HT; Tel (01788) 560631
Catherine Budgett-Meakin
International Broadcasting Trust 2 Ferdinand Pl, London NW1 8EE; Tel 0171-482 2847
Lynette Aitken
International Community Education Association Lyng Hall, Blackberry La, Coventry CV2 3JS; Tel (01203) 638670
Alan Blackhurst
International Customer Care 48 Findhorn Pl, Edinburgh EH9 2NS; Tel 0131-667 7759
Veronica Wallace
Jabbock Theatre Company 13 Moorfields, Bramley, Leeds LS13 3JZ; Tel (01532) 552557
Roger Harington
Lancashire Development Education Group Global Education Ctr, 37 St Peter's Sq, Preston PR1 7BX; Tel (01772) 252299
Julie Downs
Language & Achievement Project Lewisham Professional Development Ctr, Kilmorie Rd, Forest Hill, London SE23 2SP; Tel 0181-699 1919
Maggie Gravelle
Leaving Home Project Centrepoint, Bewlay Hse, 2 Swallow Pl, London W1R 7AA; Tel 0171-629 2229
Gillian Gholam

Leeds Development Education Centre 151–153 Cardigan Rd, Leeds LS6 1LJ; Tel (01532) 784030
Nigel West
Leicester World Development Centre 10a Bishop St, Leicester LE1 6AF; Tel (01533) 540957
Adam Battersby
Leicestershire Development Education Youth Project 132 Regent Rd, Leicester LE1 7PA; Tel (01533) 543704/543724
Letterbox Library Unit 2D, Leroy Hse, 436 Essex Rd, London N1 3QP; Tel 0171-226 1633
Gillian Harris
Local Government Management Board Arndale Hse, The Arndale Ctr, Luton LU1 2TS; Tel (01582) 451166
LONDEC Instrument Hse, 205–207 King's Cross Rd, London WC1 9DB; Tel 0171-713 7907
Sarbjit Johal
Malvern Third World Centre 22 Church St, Malvern WR14 2AY; Tel (01684) 565796/574392
Isla Williams
Mandela Youth and Community Centre 179–181 Pear Tree Rd, Normanton, Derby DE3 8NQ; Tel (01332) 3678848
Patricia Berry
Masters Curriculum Project in Environment & Development Area of Legal, Political & Social Sciences, South Bank University, 103 Borough Rd, London SE1 OAA; Tel 0171-277 1091
Aileen McKenzie
Matsuyama International Education Center 2–20–8 Furukawaminami, Matsuyama, EHIME, 790, Japan; Tel (01899) 56 8196
Makoto Fujii
Mbaaku Women's Development Project 21A Groveway, Stockwell, London SW9 OAH; Tel 0171-793 0106
Dianne King
Methodist Church Division of Social Responsibility DSR 1 Central Bldgs, Mathew Parker St, London SW1 9NH; Tel 0171-222 8010
Carolyn Maynard
Mexicolore 28 Warriner Gdns, London SW11 4EB; Tel 0171-622 9577
Ian Mursell
Minority Rights Group 379 Brixton Rd, London SW9 7DE; Tel 0171-978 9498
Rachel Warner
Mobile Unit for Development Issues (MUNDI) School of Education, University of Nottingham, University Pk, Nottingham NG7 2RD; Tel (01602) 514485
Lis Martin
Montgomery Development Education Centre c/o Third World Centre, Kirk of St. Nicholas, Back Wynd, Aberdeen AB1 1JZ; Tel (01224) 639294
Sue Good
Anita Gailey
*National Association of Teachers of Home Economics & Technology*Hamilton Hse, Mabledon Pl, London WC1H 9BJ; Tel 0171-387 1441
Geoffrey Thompson
National Committee for Development Education St. Patrick's College, Drumcondra, Dublin 9, Ireland; Tel 01 8371525
Fionnuala Brennan
National Council for Voluntary Youth Services Coburn Hse, 3 Coburn Pl, London E3 2DA; Tel 0181-980 5712
Suzanne Rauprich
National Liaison Committee of Diocesan Justice & Peace Groups Allington Hse, 136/142 Victoria St, London SW1E 5LP; Tel 0171-834 5138
Barbara Ring
Native American Educational Trust 21 Little Preston St, Brighton BN1 2HQ; Tel (01273) 328357
Richard Cupidi
Norfolk Education & Action for Development Third World Centre, 38 Exchange St, Norwich NR2 1AX; Tel (01603) 610993
Sandy Betlem
North Staffordshire Development Education Centre Newcastle-Under-Lyme College, Liverpool Rd, Newcastle-Under-Lyme ST5 2DF; Tel (01782) 711455
Jane Glen
One World Centre (Dundee) 5 Victoria St, Dundee DD4 6EG; Tel (01382) 454603
Ken Mathers
One World Centre (NI) 4 Lower Cres, Belfast BT7 1NR; Tel (01232) 241879
Christine Pradeep
One World Week Inter Church Hse, P.O. Box 100, London SE1 7RT; Tel 0171-620 4444
Tany Alexander
Oxfam 274 Banbury Rd, Oxford OX2 7DZ; Tel (01865) 311311
Tony Williams
Oxfam Education (Brighton) 134A Western Rd (Rear Entrance), Brighton BN1 2LA; Tel (01273) 207014
Oxfam Education (Bristol) Oxfam Office, 62 Cotham Hill, Bristol BS6 6JX; Tel (01272) 734335
Roger James
Oxfam Education (Cardiff) 46–48 Station Rd, Llanishen, Cardiff CF4 5LU; Tel (01222) 757067
Alison Doogan
Oxfam Education (Glasgow) Oxfam Area Office, 5th Fl, Fleming Hse, 134 Renfrew St, Glasgow G3 6ST; Tel 0141-331 2724
Anne Kane
Mary Patience
Oxfam Education – London (North) Primary Education Unit 46A Stoke Newington Church St, London N16 OLU; Tel 0171-249 2632
Bernie Ashmore
Oxfam Education – London (South) Development Education Unit, Effra School, Effra Parade, London SW2 1PL; Tel 0171-737 7967
Sarah Crowley
Oxfam Education (Southampton) The Oxfam Centre, 16 Oakley Rd, Southampton SO9 5TB; Tel (01703) 512222
Jane Dalton
Oxfam Youth Work Unit 23 New Mount St, Manchester M4 4DE; Tel 0161-953 4008
Marianne Flood
Oxford Development Education Centre East Oxford Community Centre, Princess St, Oxford OX4 1HU; Tel (01865) 790490
Pippa Bobbett
Pamoja Third World & Environment Centre Colchester Sixth Form College, North Hill, Colchester CO1 1SN; Tel (01206) 794078
Janet Plummer
Panos Institute 9 White Lion St, London N1 9PD; Tel 0171-278 1111
Steve Percy
Petadists Community Organisation Room 55, Selby Centre, Selby Rd, London N17 8JN; Tel 0181-880 3994
Peter Amadi
Philippine Resource Centre 84 Long La, London SE1 4AU; Tel 0171-378 0296
Mara Stankovitch
Pioneer Agency for Development in Africa 21 Addington Hse, Stockwell Rd, London SW9 0TZ; Tel 0171-274 5252
Dr Ekei U. Etim
Population Concern 231 Tottenham Ct Rd, London W1P 9AE; Tel 0171-631 1546
Sarah Muscroft
Powys Environment and Development Education Centre 12 Great Oak St, Llanidloes SY18 6BU; Tel (01686) 412731
Jonathan Sleigh
Quaker Peace and Service Religious Society of Friends, Friends Hse, Euston Rd, London NW1 2BJ; Tel 0171-387 3601
Marigold Bentley
Reading International Support Centre 103 London St, Reading RG1 4QA; Tel (01734) 586692/594357
Martin Mikhail
Refugee Council 3 Bondway, London SW9 1SJ; Tel 0171-582 6922
Jill Rutter
Religious Education & World Development Resources Centre Trinity College, Carmarthen SA31 3EP; Tel (01267) 237971
Tom Evans

Educational and Allied Organisations

Returned Volunteer Action 1 Amwell St, London EC1R 1UL; Tel 0171-278 0804
Tammy Walker
Royal Anthropological Institute 50 Fitzroy St, London W1P 5HS; Tel 0171-387 0455
J. Benthall
Saltash One World Week Group 1 Churchtown Vale, St Stephens, Saltash PL12 4AN; Tel (01752) 843704
Helen Burke
Save The Children Fund (UK) 17 Grove La, Camberwell, London SE5 8RD; Tel 0171-703 5400 Ext 2440
Andrew Hutchinson
Scottish Catholic International Aid Fund 5 Oswald St, Glasgow G1 4QR; Tel 0141-221 4447
John Dornan
Scottish Development Education Centre Old Play Hse Cl, Moray Hse, Institute of Education, Holyrood Rd, Edinburgh EH8 8AQ; Tel 0131-557 3810
Linda Cracknell
Scottish Education and Action for Development 23 Castle St, Edinburgh EH2 3DN; Tel 0131-225 6550
Linda Gray
Scout Association Gilwell Pk, Chingford, London E4 7QW; Tel 0181-524 5246
Anne Whiteford
Southern Africa Resource Centre 6 West St, Old Market, Bristol BS2 0BH; Tel (01272) 411442
Nick James
Dave Spurgeon
Support and Training Against Racism for Under 5's Workers 7 Barton Bldgs, Old King St, Bath BA1 2JR; Tel (01225) 334415
Mary Fawcett
Survival International 310 Edgware Rd, London W2 1DY
Teeside One World Centre Ayresome Junior School, Parliament Rd, Middlesborough TS1 4NT; Tel (01642) 250930
Trevor Phillips
Third World First 217 Cowley Rd, Oxford OX4 1XG; Tel (01865) 245678/723832
Luis A. Reveco
Third World Resources 464 19th St, Oakland CA 94612, USA; Tel (415) 536 1876, 835 4692
Tibet Support Group UK 9 Islington Green, London N1 2XH; Tel 0171-359 7573
Timothy Nunn
Tourism Concern Southlands College, Wimbledon Parkside, London SW19 5NN; Tel 0181-944 0464
Tricia Barnett
Trade Union International Research and Education Group Ruskin College, Walton St, Oxford OX1 2HE; Tel (01865) 54599
Julie Stevens
Traidcraft Exchange Kingsway, Gateshead NE11 0NE; Tel 0191-491 0591
Sylvia Lough
Trinity Youth Club Burrage Rd, Plumstead, London SE18 7JW; Tel 0181-854 0049
Louise Winstanley
Truro World Development Education Centre Truro Baptist Church, Chapel Hill, Truro TR1 3BN; Tel (01872) 41984
Rev David Rhymer
TZEDEK 26 Goodwyns Vale, London N10 2HA; Tel 0181-883 7453
Steve Miller
UK One World Linking Association Town Hall, Rose Hill, Chesterfield S40 1LP; Tel (01246) 216320
Mary Stead
UNICEF (UK) 55–56 Lincoln's Inn Fields, London WC2A 3NB; Tel 0171-405 5592
Heather Jarvis
United Nations Association Education Committee 3 Whitehall Ct, London SW1A 2EL; Tel 0171-930 2931
Suzanne Long
United Reformed Church Church and Society, 86 Tavistock Pl, London WC1H 9RT; Tel 0171-837 7661
Rev. Peter Brain
Voluntary Service Overseas 317 Putney Bridge Rd, London WC15 2PN; Tel 0181-780 2266
Jane Talbot
Volunteer Missionary Movement Comboni Hse, London Rd, Sunningdale SL5 0JH; Tel (01344) 875380
Claire Casemore
War on Want 37–39 Gt Guildford St, London SE1 0ES; Tel 0171-620 1111
Giampi Alhadeff
Warwickshire Council for Voluntary Youth Services Honiley Hall, Church Rd, Honiley, Nr Kenilworth CV8 1NP
Hugh Disley
Warwickshire World Studies Centre Manor Hall, Sandy La, Leamington Spa CV32 6RD; Tel (01926) 413719
Richard Wright
WaterAid 1 Queen Anne's Gate, London SW1H 9BT; Tel 0171-233 4800
Judith McNeill
Wiltshire World Studies Centre Marlborough Brandt Grp, St John's School, Chopping Knife La, Marlborough SN8 2AU; Tel (01672) 514078
Sam Woodhouse
Workers' Educational Association The National Association, Temple Hse, 17 Victoria Pk Sq, London E2 9PB; Tel 0181-983 1515
Mel Doyle
World Development Education Centre Block A, Bridgewater Hall, Stantonbury Campus, Stantonbury, Milton Keynes MK14 6BN; Tel (01908) 310951
Debbie Greaves
World Development Movement 25 Beehive Pl, London SW9 7QR; Tel 0171-737 6125
David Coe
World Education Development Group The Canterbury Centre, St Alphege La (off Palace St), Canterbury CT1 2EB; Tel (01227) 766552
Marion Walter
World Education Project Welsh National Centre for Religious Education, School of Education, UCNW, Bangor LL57 2UW; Tel (01248) 351151 Ext 2947
Sheila Bennell
World Studies Project c/o School of Education, Manchester Metropolitan University, 799 Wilmslow Rd, Manchester M20 8RR; Tel 0161-247 2316
Miriam Steiner
Worldaware 1 Catton St, London WC1R 4AB; Tel 0171-831 3844
Derek Walker
Worldwise Brightelm, North Rd, Brighton BN1 3LA; Tel (01273) 821220
Jacky Kulkami
Y Care International 640 Forest Rd, London E17 3DZ; Tel 0181-520 5599
Brian Welters
YMCA (Wimbledon and District) 200 The Broadway, Wimbledon, London SW19 1RY; Tel 0181-542 9055
Mark Harrod
York Peace Centre 15A Clifford St, York YO1 1RG; Tel (01904) 642493
Coordinator
Young Women's Christian Association Clarendon Hse, 52 Cornmarket St, Oxford OX1 3EJ; Tel (01865) 726110
Romi Jones
Carol Saker
Youth Clubs UK 11 St Bride St, London EC4A 4AS; Tel 0171-353 2366
John Bateman

Disabled

Centre for Accessible Environments (Architectural Advice and Information)
60 Gainsford St, London SE1 2NY; Tel 0171-357 8182
Chief Executive Sarah Langton-Lockton, BA(Oxon)

Works to improve the design of the built environment to accommodate the needs of all users, including elderly and disabled people. Offers an information service on technical matters, publishes design guidance and a journal *Access by Design*; administers a register of architects with experience of designing for disabled people; runs an extensive seminar programme.

Country Landowners Association Charitable Trust
CLA Fund for the Handicapped, 16 Belgrave Sq, London SW1X 8PQ; Tel 0171-235 0511
Director Major K.J. Smith Bohune Common Hse, Woodborough, Pewsey, Wilts SN9 6LY; Tel (01672) 851207
Encourage and helps landowners to provide facilities on their land for physically and mentally handicapped people to enjoy sport and recreation

CRYPT Foundation (Creative Young People Together),)
Forum, Stirling Rd, Chichester, W Sussex PO19 2EN; Tel (01243) 786064
Chairman Val Fethney

DIAL UK–The Disability Helpline
Park Lodge, St Catherine's Hospital, Tickhill Rd, Doncaster DN4 8QN; Tel (01302) 310123; Fax (01302) 310404
Director Dorothy McGahan
Chairperson Hugh Lyon

Outset
18 Creekside, Deptford, Lewisham, London SE8 3DZ; Tel 0181-692 7141; Fax 0181-469 2532
Contact Robbie Lloyd
Operates a network of innovative vocational training and employment projects in London, Luton, the West Midlands, Cleveland and Kent. Projects focus on the training and employment of people with disabilities in the area of information technology and computerised office skills. OUTSET's Consultancy and Planning division offers organisations and employers a comprehensive range of information, advice, consultancy, research and development services on all aspects of employing and training people with disabilities

Physically Handicapped and Able-Bodied (PHAB)
12–14 London Rd, Croydon CR0 2TA; Tel 0181-667 9443; Fax 0181-681 1399
Secretary Peter Gooch

SCOPE – formerley the Spastics Society
12 Park Cres, London W1N 4EQ; Tel 0171-636 5020; Fax 0171-436 2601
Director of Operations R. Hancock

Scottish Council for Spastics
22 Corstorphine Rd, Edinburgh EH12 6HP; Tel 0131-337 9876/9; Fax 0131-346 7864
Director Ian G. McBain

Sense, The National Deafblind and Rubella Association
11–13 Clifton Terrace, Finsbury Pk, London N4 3SR; Tel 0171-272 7774; Fax 0171-272 6012
Chief Executive Rodney Clark

Skill: National Bureau for Students with Disabilities
336 Brixton Rd, London SW9 7AA; Tel General 071-274 0565 (Voice/Minicom); Fax 071-274 7840
Director D. Cooper

Education

ACE Advisory Centre for Education
1B Aberdeen Studios, 22 Highbury Gve, London N5 2EA; Tel 071-354 8321
An independent non-profit making body providing information and advice for parents and others about the maintained schools system through publications and free afternoon advice lines
ACE Bulletin, a bi-monthly magazine and many publications; send for list

Association of Education Committees Charitable Trust (AEC Trust),)
Midland Personal Financial Services, 70 Pall Mall, London SW1Y 5EY
Contact Miss M.J. Beisley, Area Manager

Bedgebury School
Headmistress M.E.A. Kaye Bedgebury School, Bedgebury Pk, Goudhurst, Cranbrook, Kent TN17 2SH; Tel (01580) 211221

British Dyslexia Association
98 London Rd, Reading, Berks RG1 5AU; Tel (01734) 668271
Administrator George S. Yelland

The British Horological Institute
Secretary W.M. Geoffrey Evans, JP, FBHI, CEng, FFA Upton Hall, Upton, Newark, Notts NG23 5TE; Tel (01636) 813795/6; Fax (01636) 812258

Centre for Studies on Inclusive Education (CSIE) (CSIE)
1 Redland Cl, Elm La, Redland, Bristol BS6 6UE; Tel 0117-923 8450; Fax 0117-923 8460

Dyslexia Institute
Head Office, 133 Gresham Rd, Staines, Middx TW18 2AJ; Tel (01784) 463851

Hornsby Dyslexia Centre
Glenshee Lodge, 261 Trinity Rd, London SW18 3SM; Tel 0181-874 1844; Fax 0181-877 9737
Principal Dr B. Hornsby

National Literacy Association
5 Airspeed Rd, Priory Ind Pk, Christchurch, Dorset BH23 4HD; Tel (01425) 272232; Fax (01425) 270307
Runs 99 by 99 project which aims to ensure that 99% of children leave school with adequate literacy for work and life by 1999

Scottish Consultative Council on the Curriculum
Chief Executive Cameron Harrison Gardyne Rd, Dundee DD5 1NY; Tel (01382) 455053

United Kingdom i.t.a. Federation
Secretary R.A. Threadgall 181 Fleetwood Ave, Holland-on-Sea, Essex CO15 5RA; Tel (01255) 813768

Elderly / Retirement / Pensions

Age Concern England–Education and Leisure
Information and Policy Officer/Education and Leisure Dianne Norton Astral Hse, 1268 London Rd, London SW16 4EJ; Tel 0181-679 8000; Fax 0181-679 6069
Information network for anyone interested in education and leisure for older people. *Information and Leisure Newsletter* published 3 times per annum. Also briefing papers and fact sheets

University of Third Age
U3A National Office, 1 Stockwell Rd, London SW9 9JF; Tel 0171-737 2541
Chairman Mrs Jean Thompson
Secretary Barbara Adkins

Engineering and Technology

The Engineering Council
10 Maltravers St, London WC2R 3ER; Tel 0171-240 7891; Fax 0171-240 7517
General Education Executive John K. Williams

Institute of Science Technology
22 Bore St, Lichfield, Staffs WS13 6LP; Tel (01543) 251346; Fax (01543) 415804
Honorary Secretary D.C.J. Sayers

National Electronics and Microtechnology Education Centre (NEMEC)
University of Southampton, Southampton SO17 1BJ; Tel (01703) 558379; Fax (01703) 672714
Director Paul Barnes
Develops and disseminates In-Service Training in electronics and microtechnology to INSET trainers and teaching staff from schools and further education

School Technology Forum
Secretary Prof G.B. Harrison Nottingham Polytechnic, Burton St, Nottingham NG1 4BU; Tel (0115) 941 8418 Ext 2155

Environment

British Interplanetary Society
Executive Secretary S.A. Jones 27/29 South Lambeth Rd, London SW8 1SZ; Tel 0171-735 3160; Fax 0171-820 1504

Centre for Alternative Technology
Education Officer Ann MacGarry
Education Officer David Reynolds

Civic Trust
Director M.C. Bradshaw 17 Carlton Hse Terr, London SW1Y 5AW; Tel 0171-930 0914
Scottish Civic Trust,24 George St, Glasgow G2 1EF; Tel 0141-221 1466
Director John Ford
Civic Trust for Wales,4th Floor, Empire Hse, Mount Stuart Sq, Cardiff CF1 6DN; Tel (01222) 484606
Director Matthew Griffiths
North East Civic Trust,Floor 4, MEA Hse, Ellison Pl, Newcastle upon Tyne NE1 8XS; Tel 0191-232 9279
Director N. Whittaker

Council for Environmental Education
Director Tim Osborn Jones University of Reading, London Rd, Reading RG1 5AQ; Tel (01734) 756061; Fax (01734) 756264

Countryside Commission
Director-General Michael Dower John Dower Hse, Crescent Pl, Cheltenham, Glos GL50 3RA; Tel (01242) 521381; Fax (01242) 584270

Countryside Education Trust
New Forest Study Centre, Beaulieu, Hampshire SO42 7YL; Tel (01590) 612340
Director P.G. Carter
Contact The Education Officer
Environmental studies from pre-school to 'A' level at a residential farm centre or a day visit woodland study centre

The Environment Council
21 Elizabeth St, London SW1W 9RP

Geologists' Association South Wales Group
Dept of Geography, University College of Swansea, Singleton Pk, Swansea SA2 8PP; Tel (01792) 295141; Fax (01792) 205556
Secretary Geraint Owen

Institution of Environmental Sciences
Hon Secretary Dr R.A. Fuller (Acting) 14 Princes Gate, Hyde Pk, London SW7 1PU; Tel (01778) 394846

The London Wildlife Trust
80 York Way, London N1 9AG; Tel 0171-278 6612; Fax 0171-837 8060
Chair Peter Guest
Secretary Michael Fry
Treasurer Gill Green
Patron Lord Melchett
President Sir William Wilkinson

National Association for Environmental Education
Wolverhampton University, Walsall Campus, Gorway, Walsall WS1 3BD; Tel (01922) 31200
General Secretary Brian Milton

Professional Test Systems
55 Trajan Walk, Andover, Hampshire SP10 5JW; Tel (01264) 351853; Fax (01264) 350943
General Manager M. Doughty
Manufacture of scientific equipment, for use in school and college laboratories. Products include experiment, test, and demonstration equipment for laboratory use, and portable environmental test equipment for field studies of water and environmental pollution. Also swimming pool water testing equipment for use in educational establishments

Royal Geographical Society
(with the Institue of British Geographers)
Director and Secretary Dr J.H. Hemming, CMG 1 Kensington Gore, London SW7 2AR; Tel 0171-589 5466; Fax 0171-584 4447
Librarian Jayne A. Dunlop, BA, ALA

Royal Scottish Geographical Society
Graham Hills Bldg, 40 George St, Glasgow G1 1QE; Tel 0141-552 3330; Fax 0141-552 3331
Director and Secretary A.B. Cruickshank, MA

Town and Country Planning Association
17 Carlton Hse Terr, London SW1Y 5AS; Tel 0171-930 8903; Fax 0171-930 3280
Director David Hall, MA, MRTPI
Education Officer Wendy Wasels

Worldware
Education Officer V.J. Bunce 1 Catton St, Holborn, London WC1R 4AB; Tel 0171-831 3844; Fax 0171-831 1746

Family Welfare

Association of Chief Education Social Workers
National Secretary Jennifer A. Price Bank Hse, 76 Nutgrove Rd, Nutgrove, St Helens WA9 5JL; Tel 0151-430 0112

Both Parents Forever
39 Cloonmore Ave, Orpington, Kent BR6 9LE; Tel (01689) 854343
Coordinator John Bell
National self help group for parents and grandparents following divorce, separation and care proceedings. Information pack: Parents/Grandparents rights in all family proceedings: Parental reponsibility; Residence orders; Contact orders; Education/medical reports; Social workers; Court welfare officers; Child abduction. Files on help available overseas on child abduction. Help

on housing, and children in special need, such education for disabled etc

British Safety Council
Training Manager National Safety Centre, 70 Chancellors Rd, Hammersmith, London W6; Tel 0181-741 1231
Director-General James Tye

British Standards Institution
Linford Wood, Milton Keynes MK14 6LE; Tel (01908) 220022
Chief Executive Dr M.D. Sanderson
Head of Education Derek Prior
Education Officer Kully Jones
Technical Education Officer Maurice Parker

Child Poverty Action Group
4th Floor, 1–5 Bath St, London EC1V 9PY; Tel 0171-253 3406
Director Sally Witcher
Chairman Lynda Bransbury

Education Welfare Officers' National Association
see National Association of Social Workers in Education

Educational Grants Advisory Service
The Family Welfare Association, 501–505 Kingsland Rd, London E8 4AU; Tel 0171-254 6251

Family Education Trust
322 Woodstock Rd, Oxford OX2 7NS; Tel (01865) 56848; Fax (01865) 52774
Chairman Dr S.E. Ellison

Family Service Units
Registered Charity No. 212114
207 Old Marylebone Rd,London NW1 5QP; Tel 0171-402 5175/6; Fax 0171-724 1829
Director Adah Kay

National Gypsy Education Council (NGEC)
47 Evans Rd, London SE6; Tel 0181-461 1402
Secretary Denise Stanley
Vice-Chairman Dr T.A. Acton 82 Evesham Rd, London E15 4AJ; Tel 0181-555 3648

Further Education

Arvon Foundation
Senior Administration (Totleigh) J. Wheadon Totleigh Barton, Sheepwash, Beaworthy, Devon EX21 5NS; Tel (0140 923) 338
Centre Manager (Lumb) Sally Corcos Lumb Bank, Hebden Bridge, W Yorks HX7 6DF; Tel (01422) 843714
Centre Manager (Lumb) Mark Illis

Association for Colleges
Chief Executive Ruth Gee

Learning Resources Development Group
6 St James Ct, Piper Lane, Thirsk, North Yorkshire Y07 IFN; Tel (01845) 526749; Fax (via bureau) (01845) 524347
Chief Executive P.J. Pack

National Association for Staff Development in Post 16 Education
Hon Secretary Don Scott 30 St Helena Rd, Colchester, Essex CO3 3BA; Tel (01206) 571258; Fax (01206) 571258
Chairman I.M. Strachan West Herts College, Langley Rd, Watford WD1 3RH; Tel (01293) 240311; Fax (01293) 247525

Van den Berghs Home Economics
Home Economist S. Batty Sussex Hse, Civic Way, Burgess Hill, Sussex RH15 9AW; Tel (01444) 246300

World Education Fellowship (Great Britain)
Hon Secretary Reg Richardson, MA, BSc 1 Darrell Cl, Chelmsford, Essex CM1 4EL; Tel (01245) 251855
Promotes progressive education emphasising co-operation, peace, continued education throughout life, independent study

Gypsies

ACERT–Advisory Council for the Education of Romany and other Travellers
Moot Hse, The Stow, Harlow, Essex CM20 3AG; Tel (01279) 418666

Health Care/Hospitals/Nursing

Centre for Medical Education
Ninewells Hospital and Medical School, Dundee DD1 9SY; Tel (01382) 60111 Ext 2286/2287
Secretary Mrs E.A. Jeffrey

Church Schoolmasters' and Schoolmistresses' Benevolent Institution (CSSBI)
Secretary Norman E. Smart Gen Arun, 9 Athelstan Way, Horsham, Sussex; Tel (01403) 253881

The Health Education Authority
Registered Office Hamilton Hse, Mabledon Pl, London WC1H 9TX; Tel 0171-383 3833; Fax 0171-387 0550
Chairman Sir Donald Maitland, GCMG, OBE
Chief Executive Dr Spencer Hagard, MB, ChB, PhD, FFOM
A Special Health Authority whose strategic objective is to ensure that by the year 2000 the people of England are more knowledgeable, better motivated and more able to acquire and maintain good health. The HEA provides information and advice about health directly to members of the public; supports other organisaitons, teachers, health professionals and other people who provide health education; and advises the Secretary of State on matters relating to health education. For these purposes the HEA works in co-operation with Government, Health Authorities, Family Health Service Authorities, Local Authorities, Local Education Authorities, voluntary organisaitons, business and commerce, the mass communications media and others. Health Promotion Information Centre offers audio-visual aids, literature on all aspects of health education, an information service, and source lists. Produces free bi-monthly newspaper, posters and leaflets, and a quarterly journal for subscribers. Advice and assistance on request to individuals and LEAs, with in-service courses. Funds a research programme covering the broad spectrum of health education

Health Education Board for Scotland
Woodburn Hse, Canaan La, Edinburgh EH10 4SG; Tel 0131-447 8044; Fax 0131-452 8140
Chairman Ernie Walker, OBE
General Manager Dr Andrew Tannahill, MB, ChB, MSc, FFPHM, MHSM

Health Promotion Agency for Northern Ireland
18 Ormeau Ave, Belfast BT2 8HS; Tel (01232) 311611; Fax (01232) 311711
Contact Dr Jane Wilde
Replaces the Health Education Council in Northern Ireland

Health Promotion Wales
F Fynnon–las, Ilex Cl, Ty Glas Ave, Llanishen CF4 5DZ; Tel (01222) 752222
Director of Education and Training Peter Farley
Responsible for public health education and health promotion programmes in Wales, and professional training and education

Medical Commission on Accident Prevention
Secretary Mrs P.C. McCausland 35–43 Lincoln's Inn Fields, London WC2A 3PN; Tel 0171-242 3176

Medical Officers of Schools Association
Hon Secretary Dr R. Harrington North End Surgery, High St, Buckingham MK18 1NU; Tel (01280) 816612; Fax (01280) 823449

Mental Health Media Council
380–384 Harrow Rd, London W9 2HU
Director Sylvia Hines

The Peppard Trust
c/o Audiology Dept, Royal Berkshire Hospital, Reading, Berks; Tel (01734) 472067, 875111
Chairman Dr Kevin Murphy
Contact D.F. Hand

Public Health Laboratory Service Board
61 Colindale Ave, London NW9 5DF; Tel 0181-200 1295; Fax 0181-905 9729
Deputy Director/Board Secretary K.M. Saunders, IPFA, MHSM, MIMgt

Society of Apothecaries of London
Registrar A.M. Wallington Smith Apothecaries' Hall, Black Friars La, London EC4V 6EJ; Tel 0171-236 1180; Fax 0171-329 3177

United Kingdom Central Council for Nursing, Midwifery and Health Visiting
23 Portland Pl, London W1N 3AF; Tel 0171-637 7181; Fax 0171-436 2924
Registrar and Chief Executive Colin Ralph, MPhil, RN, DN(Lond)

Heritage

Archaeology in Education
Dept of Prehistory & Archaeology, University of Sheffield, Sheffield S10 2TN; Tel (01942) 768555
Director K. Branigan

British Archaeological Association
Hon Secretary Dr L.M. Grant Conway Library, Courtauld Institute, Somerset Hse, Strand, London WC2R 0RN

British Association for Local History
24 Lower St, Harnsham, Salisbury, Wilts SP2 8EY; Tel (01722) 320115

British Numismatic Society
Secretary J.D. Bateson Hunterian Museum, The University, Glasgow G12 8QQ; Tel 0141-339 8855; Fax 0141-307 8059

The Ironbridge Institute
Ironbridge Gorge Museum Trust, Ironbridge, Telford, Shropshire TF8 7AW; Tel (01952) 432751
Contact Dr Michael Stratton

Royal Commission for the Exhibition of 1851
Secretary M.C. Neale, CB Sherfield Bldg, Imperial College, London SW7 2AZ; Tel 0171-225 6110/6111

Society for the Promotion of Roman Studies
Secretary Dr Helen M. Cockle 31/34 Gordon Sq, London WC1H 0PP; Tel 071-387 8157

Higher Education

Association of Colleges Implementing DipHE Programmes (ACID)
Secretary J.M.C. Davidson Centre for Educational Services, University of the West of England at Bristol, Coldharbour La, Bristol BS16 1QY; Tel (0117) 965 6261 Ext 593

British Association for American Studies (BAAS)
School of English Newcastle University, Newcastle-upon-Tyne, Staffs NE1 7RU; Tel 0191-222 7755; Fax 0191-222 8708
Chairman Richard King
Secretary Dr J. Newman

Gilchrist Educational Trust
Secretary Mrs R.A. Everidge Mary Trevelyan Hall, 10 York Terr East, London NW1 4PT; Tel 0171-631 8300

London Mathematical Society
Hon Secretary Prof R.Y. Sharp Dept of Pure Mathematics, University of Sheffield, Sheffield S3 7RH; Tel (0114) 276 8555 Ext 4369
Hon Secretary Dr D.J. Collins School of Math Sciences, Queen Mary & Westfield College, Mile End Rd, London E1 4NS; Tel 0171-975 5480
Administrator S.M. Oakes London Mathematical Society, Burlington Hse, Piccadilly, London W1V 0NL; Tel 0171-437 5377; Fax 0171-439 4629

Maharishi University of Natural Law
Mentmore Towers, Mentmore, Leighton Buzzard, Beds LU7 0QH; Tel (01296) 662186; Fax (01296) 662049; Telex 9312130390 MT G
Vice-Chancellor Geoffrey Clements, DPhil

Open University Students' Association
PO Box 397, Walton Hall, Milton Keynes MK7 6BE; Tel (01908) 652026; Fax (01908) 654326
Permanent Secretary John Needham

Sir Richard Stapley Educational Trust
Charity Reg No. 313812
PO Box 57, Tonbridge, Kent TN9 1ZT

Society for the Promotion of Hellenic Studies
Secretary Dr L. Rodley 31/34 Gordon Sq, London WC1H 0PP; Tel 0171-387 7495

Staff and Educational Development Association (SEDA)
Secretary Chris Rust Educational Methods Unit, Oxford Brookes University, Headington, Oxford OX3 0BP

Universities Association for Continuing Education
Secretary Prof Chris Duke, MA, PhD, Hon DLitt, CertEd Dept of Continuing Education, University of Warwick, Coventry CV4 7AL; Tel (01203) 523835

University of London External Programme
Senate Hse, Malet St, London WC1E 7HU; Tel 0171-636 8000; Fax 0171-636 5894

Universities Statistical Record
PO Box 130, Cheltenham, Glos GL50 3SE; Tel (01242) 225902 (Publications); (01242) 225906 (Statistics)

Virgil Society
Hon Treasurer M.M. Willcock Dept of Latin, University College, Gower St, London WC1E

The Wyvernian Foundation
18 Friar Lane, Leicester LE1 5RA; Tel (0116) 251 6229
Secretary A.R. York, FCA

Housing and Homelessness

The Housing Corporation
Headquarters 149 Tottenham Court Rd, London W1P 0BN; Tel 0171-393 2000; Fax 0171-393 2111
Chairman Sir Brian Pearse
Press and Public Relations Manager Sian Jones

Human Rights/Civil Liberties

The Campaign for Freedom of Information
Director Maurice Frankel 88 Old St, London EC1V 9AR; Tel 0171-253 2445; Fax 0171-608 3325

The Civil Liberties Trust
Secretary Andrew Puddephatt 21 Tabard St, London SE1 4LA; Tel 0171-403 3888

The Institute of Race Relations
Director A. Sivanandan 2/6 Leeke St, London WC1X 9HS; Tel 0171-837 0041; Fax 0171-278 0623

Liberty (National Council for Civil Liberties)
21 Tabard St, London SE1 4LA; Tel 0171-403 3888
General Secretary A. Puddephatt

National Antiracist Movement in Education (NAME)
PO Box 9, Walsall, West Midlands WS1 3SF; Tel 0161-442 2673 (ansaphone)

Runnymede Trust
11 Princelet St, London E1 6QH; Tel 0171-375 1496

Independent Education

Allied Schools:
Stowe; Wrekin; Canford; Westonbirt; Harrogate; Felixstowe; Riddlesworth Hall
General Manager David Harris, BSc, FCA 42 South Bar St, Banbury, Oxon OX16 9XL; Tel (01295) 256441

Girls' Public Day School Trust
Secretary M.A.R. Oakley 26 Queen Anne's Gate, London SW1H 9AN; Tel 0171-222 9595; Fax 0171-222 8771

Girls' Schools Association
Secretary Sheila Cooper, BSc 130 Regent Rd, Leicester LE1 7PG; Tel (0116) 254 1619; Fax (0116) 255 3792

Incorporated Association of Preparatory Schools
General Secretary J.H. Morris 11 Waterloo Pl, Leamington Spa, Warks CV32 5LA; Tel (01926) 887833

Independent Schools Association Incorporated
General Secretary T.M. Ham, MA, DipEd Boys' British School, East St, Saffron Walden CB10 1LS; Tel (01799) 523619

Independent Schools Information Service (ISIS)
Director D.J. Woodhead 56 Buckingham Gate, London SW1E 6AG; Tel 0171-630 8793/4

Independent Schools Joint Council
General Secretary Dr Arthur Hearnden, OBE Grosvenor Gdns Hse, 35–37 Grosvenor Gdns, London SW1W 0BS; Tel 0171-630 0144; Fax 0171-931 0036

International Bureau of Education (UNESCO)
Director J.C. Tedesco 15 route des Morillons, 1218 Le Grand-Saconnex, Switzerland
Contact PO Box 199, 1211 Geneva 20, Switzerland; Tel (00) 41 22 798 1455; Fax (00) 41 22 798 1486; Telex 415771 BIE

King Alfred School Society
Bursar/Secretary G.P. Cooper, MA, FCA 149 North End Rd, London NW11 7HY; Tel 0181-905 5599; Fax 0181-455 1503

Plymouth Tutorial College, Education & Guardian Advisory Services Ltd (EGAS)
11 Seaton Ave, Mutley, Plymouth, Devon PL4 6QJ; Tel (01752) 261229, 267321; Fax (01752) 261229
Director B.A.E. Stoyel, FCollP, ACP, CertEd
Director M.M. Stoyel, BSc and Plymouth Tutorial College
Principal Brian A.E. Stoyel, FCollP, ACP, CertEd

International/Overseas

Britain–Russia Centre/British East-West Centre
14 Grosvenor Pl, London SW1X 7HW; Tel 0171-235 2116/ 0171-823 1990; Fax 0171-259 6254
Director Dr Iain Elliot

Centre for Global Education
University of York, Heslington, York YO1 5DD; Tel (01904) 433444
Director Dr David E. Selby

Commonwealth Linking Trust
7 Lion Yard, Tremadoc Rd, Clapham, London SW4 7NQ; Tel 0171-498 1101
Chairman Jill Dilks
Treasurer P. Hook
Administration J. Thompson

Commonwealth Trust
Commonwealth Hse, 18 Northumberland Ave, London WC2N 5BJ; Tel 0171-930 6733
Director-General Sir David Thorne

English New Education Fellowship
see World Education Fellowship (Great Britain)

Harkness Fellowships of the Commonwealth Fund of New York
28 Bedford Sq, London WC1B 3EG; Tel 0171-631 0411

Institute of International Education
President Dr Richard M. Krasno 809 United Nations Plaza, New York 10017, USA; Tel (212) 883 8200
Director of Communications Ed Battle

International Baccalaureate Organisation
Head Office 15 route des Morillons, CH-1218 Grand-Saconnex/Geneva, Switzerland; Tel (00) 41 22 791 0274; Fax (00) 41 22 791 0277
Director-General Dr Roger M. Peel
Examinations Office
Pascal Cl, St Mellons, Cardiff, South Glamorgan CF3 0YP; Tel (01222) 770770; Fax (01222) 770333; *Director of Examinations* T.C.M. Carthew

International Community Education Association
Lyng Hall, Blackberry La, Coventry CV2 3JS; Tel (01203) 638670; Fax (01203) 681161
Secretary-General Alan Blackhurst
Administrative Officer Ann Stapley
Programme Director Harry Webster

International Friendship League (British Section)
Head Office Peace Haven, 3 Creswick Rd, Acton, London W3 9HE
Hon National Secretary Babs Macdonald

IFL Pen Friend Service
Saltash, Cornwall
IFL Penfriend Service UK
PO Box 17, Leicester
IFL Hospitality Service
4 Wilton Cl, Taunton, Somerset TA1 4EZ; *Organiser* Miss K.M. Suter; Tel (0823) 84533
IFL London Friendship Centre
Peace Haven, 3 Creswick Rd, Acton, London W3 9HE

International Union of Crystallography
2 Abbey Sq, Chester CH1 2HU; Tel (01244) 345431; Fax (01244) 344843
President Prof P. Coppens, Buffalo, USA
Contact M.H. Dacombe

Interserve (International Service Fellowship)
Development Director Dr K. Wycherley 325 Kennington Rd, London SE11 4QH; Tel 0171-735 8227/8; Fax 0171-587 5362

Manchester Development Education Project
C/o The Manchester Metropolitan University, 801 Wilmslow Rd, Didsbury, Manchester M20 2QR; Tel 0161-445 2495
Resource Centre Organiser Anne Strachan
Large resource centre of all kinds of educational materials (slides, videos, posters, sim. games, books, packs) of relevance to development, environment, anti-racism, anti-sexism, multicultural society, peace, politics. Professional advice available

Overseas Development Institute
Regents College, Inner Circle, Regents Pk, London NW1 4NS; Tel 0171-487 7413; Fax 0171-487 7590
Director Dr John Howell

Oxfam
274 Banbury Rd, Oxford OX2 7DZ; Tel (01865) 311311; Fax (01865) 313133
Head of Young People Team T. Williams
Primary Education Worker Ange Grunsell
Youth Worker Alima Sonne
Youth Worker Marianne Flood
Campaign Executive Vicky Cuming
Campaigns Executive Richard Turner
Campaigns Executive Teresa Garlake
Campaigns Executive Pete Davis
Campaigns Executive Harm-Jan Fricke

Royal Commonwealth Society
Secretary-General Sir David Thorne 18 Northumberland Ave, London WC2N 5BJ; Tel 0171-930 6733

Society for Anglo–Chinese Understanding
109 Promenade, Cheltenham, Glos GL50 INW; Tel (01242) 226625
Administrator Isabel Grindley
Book collection housed in Central London. Information sheets available for teachers

TEAM (The European Atlantic Movement)
6 Rowan Ct, Bradford BD2 3LZ; Tel (02741) 780756
Chairman J.W.R. Kempe
Hon Secretary Alan J. Thornton, BA

UKCOSA: The Council for International Education
Director M. Sherlock 9–17 St Albans Pl, London N1 0NX; Tel 0171-226 3762; Fax 0171-226 3373

United States–United Kingdom Educational Commission (Fulbright Commission)
Executive Director James A.A.H. Moore 62 Doughty St, London WC1N 2LS

Victoria League for Commonwealth Friendship
Secretary Mrs S. Barnett, OBE 18 Northumberland Ave, London WC2; Tel 0171-930 1671

Welsh Centre for International Affairs
Temple of Peace, Cathays Pk, Cardiff CF1 3AP; Tel (01222) 395664
Director W.R. Davies

World Confederation of Organisations of the Teaching Profession
Secretary-General R.T. Harris (WCOTP/CMOPE), 5 avenue du Moulin, 1110 Morges (VD), Switzerland; Tel 801 74 67; Fax 0121-801 74 69
Information Officer Nick Grisewood

World Education Fellowship (International Headquarters)
General Secretary R. Crommelin, BA 33 Kinnaird Ave, London W4 3SH

World University Service (UK)
20–21 Compton Terr, London N1 2UN; Tel 0171-226 6747

World–wide Education Service (Home School)
35 Belgrave Sq, London SW1X 8QB; Tel 0171-235 2880; Fax 0171-259 5234

Languages

An Comunn Gaidhealach
109 Church St, Inverness IV1 1EY; Tel (01463) 231226; Fax (01463) 715557
Chief Executive Donald J. MacSween
Major voluntary body promoting the learning and teaching of Scottish Gaelic, and the organisation of National MOD and Gaelic festivals

Association for the Reform of Latin Teaching
Hon Secretary Dr A. Henshaw 15 Hardacre Cl, Melbourne, Derby DE73 1GY

British Association of State Colleges in English Language Teaching (BASCELT)
Executive Officer M. Peirce

English Association
Secretary Dr Ruth Fairbanks-Joseph The Vicarage, Priory Gdns, London W4 1TT; Tel 0181-995 4236

The English Association
University of Leicester, 128 Regent Rd, Leicester LE1 7PA; Tel (0116 2) 525927; Fax (0116 2) 525928
President Prof Martin Dodsworth
Chairman Prof Gordon Campbell
Secretary Helen Lucas
Treasurer Roger J. Claxton
To further knowledge, understanding and enjoyment of the English language and its literature, by means of conferences (5 annually), lectures and publications (journals and annual publications)

Hispanic and Luso Brazilian Council
Canning Hse, 2 Belgrave Sq, London SW1X 8PJ; Tel 0171-235 2303/7; Fax 0171-235 3587
Director-General Sir Michael Simpson–Orlebar, KCMG
Education Officer Miss P.A. Semple

Uned Iaith Genedlaethol Cymru CBAC/WDEC (National Language Unit of Wales)
Dirprwy Ysgrifennydd (Tgymraeg)/Deputy Secretary (Welsh) Iolo M.LL. Walters 245 Western Ave/ Rhodfa'r Gorllewin, Caerdydd/Cardiff CF5 2YX; Tel (01222) 555446; Fax (01222) 575995

Learning Difficulties

National Autistic Society
276 Willesden La, London NW2 5RB; Tel 0181-451 1114; Fax 0181-451 5865
Chief Executive Geraldine Peacock

Local Government

Association of District Councils
Secretary G. Filkin 26 Chapter St, London SW1P 4ND; Tel 0171-233 6868
Represents the 332 non-metropolitan district councils of England and Wales plus the Council of the Isles of Scilly

Bury Metropolitan Arts Association
Director Alan Oatey Market St, Bury, Lancs BL9 0BW; Tel 0161-761 7107; Fax 0161-763 5056

Federated Union of Managerial and Professional Officers (MPO)
General Secretary Graham Corless MPO HQ, Terminus Hse, The High, Harlow, Essex CM20 1TZ; Tel (01279) 434444; Fax (01279) 451176

Hereford and Worcester Education
Co-ordinating Group, 16 Elgar Ave, Hereford HR1 1TY; Tel (01432) 267433
Hon President Rev John Oliver, MA, MLitt
Secretary Carol Clapham, BSc

Mental Health

The Lantern Trust
72 Honey La, Waltham Abbey, Essex EN9 3BS; Tel (01992) 714900
A national charity providing programmes of education for caregivers in the field of loss and bereavement, palliative care, and sexual health. All course are held at The Lantern Trust Education Centre, 4 Bath St, London EC1

Royal College of Psychiatrists
Dean Prof J.L. Cox 17 Belgrave Sq, London SW1X 8PG; Tel 0171-235 2351; Fax 0171-245 1231

MIND (National Association for Mental Health)
Granta Hse, 15–19 Broadway, Stratford, London E15 4BQ; Tel 0181-519 2122; Fax 0181-522 1725

Music and Performing Arts

British Federation of Festivals for Music, Dance and Speech (incorporating the Music Teachers' Association)
Secretary Ms E. Whitehead Festivals Hse, 198 Park La, Macclesfield, Cheshire SK11 6UD; Tel (01625) 428297; Fax (01625) 503229

British Federation of Young Choirs
Hon Secretary Andrew N. Fairbairn 37 Frederick St, Loughborough, Leics LE11 3BW; Tel (01509) 211664; Fax (01509) 233749
Offers practical help in the classroom to schools wishing to revive choral singing or form young choirs

British Library National Sound Archive
29 Exhibition Rd, London SW7 2AS; Tel 0171-412 7430/071-412 7421; Fax 0171-412 7416
Curator of Artefacts B. Berconzi

Choir Schools Association
Administrator Choir Schools Association, The Minster School, Deangate, York YO1 2JA; Tel (01904) 625217; Fax (01904) 632418

Conference of Drama Schools
Hon Secretary c/o Central School of Speech and Drama, Embassy Theatre, Eton Ave, London NW3 3HY; Tel 0171-722 8183

Music Education Council
Music Dept, Institute of Education, 20 Bedford Way, London WC1H 9AL; Tel 0171-612 7640
Chair Prof K. Swanwick
Vice-Chair Prof R. Reeve

Music Industries Association
Grove Court, Hatfield Rd, Slough, Berks SL1 1QU; Tel (01753) 511550; Fax (01753) 539200
Secretary General Bob Kelley, FCIS, FIMgt

Trade Association for Manufacturers and Distributors of Musical Instruments
Also promoters of the annual British Music Fair
see British Federation of Music Festivals

National Association of Youth Orchestras
Ainslie Hse, 11 St Colme St, Edinburgh EH3 6AG; Tel 0131-225 4606; Fax 0131-225 3568
Director C. Main

National Campaign for the Arts
President Melvyn Bragg
Director Jennifer Edwards Francis Hse, Francis St, London SW1P 1DE; Tel 0171-828 4448

National Music Council of Great Britain
Francis Hse, Francis St, London SW1P 1DE
Administrator Jennifer Goodwin

National Operatic and Dramatic Association
1 Crestfield St, London WC1H 8AU; Tel 0171-837 5655
General Administrator M. Thorburn

National School Band Association
Executive Officer Tony Watkins 16 Lodge Cl, Etwall, Derby DE65 6NA; Tel (01283) 733173

National Youth Choir of Great Britain
Executive Director Carl Browning PO Box 67, Holmfirth, W Yorks HD7 1GQ; Tel (01484) 687203; Fax (01484) 681635

The National Youth Orchestra of Great Britain
Director of Music Jill White Causeway Hse, Lodge Causeway, Fishponds, Bristol BS16 3HD; Tel (0117) 965 0036

National Youth Theatre of Great Britain
Administrator Helen Carew 443–445 Holloway Rd, London N7 6LW; Tel 0171-281 3863

The Performing Right Society (PRS)
29–33 Berners St, London W1P 4AA; Tel 0171-580 5544; Fax 0171-631 4138; Telex 892678 PRSLON G
Chairman Wayne Bickerton
Secretary Brian Wilkinson
Collects and distributes royalites for the public performance and broadcasting of copyright musical works, on behalf of its composer and publisher members

Radius (The Religious Drama Society of Great Britain)
Christ Church and Upton Chapel, Kennington Rd, London SE1 7QP; Tel 0171-401 2422
Secretary Howard Bennett

The Rehearsal Orchestra
The London College of Music, Thames Valley University, St Marys Rd, London W5 5RF; Tel 0181-231 2643
Administrator Jean Shannon

Scottish Community Drama Association
Secretary Maggie Gordon 5 York Pl, Edinburgh EH1 3EB; Tel 0131-557 5552; Fax 0131-557 5552

Society for Theatre Research
C/o Theatre Museum, 1E Tavistock Pl, London WC2E 7PA

Prisons, Offenders and Victims

Institute for the Study and Treatment of Delinquency
Director Julia Braggins, BA, DipACE King's College London, Strand, London WC2R 2LS; Tel 0171-873 2822; Fax 0171-873 2823

National Association for the Care and Resettlement of Offenders (NACRO),)
169 Clapham Rd, London SW9 0PU; Tel 0171-582 6500
Assistant Director B. Thompson
National Education Advisory Officer 567A Barlow Moor Rd, Manchester MZ1 2AE; Tel 0161-861 9737

Psychotherapy

Association for Dance Movement Therapy UK
c/o Arts Therapies Dept, Springfield Hospital, Glenburnie Rd, Tooting Bec, London SW17 7DJ
Chair Penelope Best

Sesame Institute
27 Blackfriars Rd, London SE1 8NY; Tel 0171-633 9690
Researches and promotes the use of movement and drama as therapy and trains therapists in this method

Public Health

Society of Public Health (formerly the Society of Community Medicine)
28 Portland Pl, London W1N 4DE
Hon Secretary Dr P.A. Gardner 31 Battye Ave, Huddersfield HD4 5PW; Tel (01652) 659659

Religion

British Humanist Association
Public Relations Officer 14 Lamb's Conduit Passage, London WC1R 4RH; Tel 0171-430 0908; Fax 0171-430 1271

Catholic Student Council of England and Wales
186 St Paul's Rd, Balsall Heath, Birmingham B12 8LZ; Tel 0121-440 3273; Fax 0121-446 4060

Catholic Teachers Federation (of England and Wales)
General Secretary M.H. Emm, BA, MEd 24 Knowlands Rd, Monkspath, Solihull, W Midlands B90 4UG; Tel 0121-745 4265

Central Jewish Lecture and Information Committee and Education and Youth Committee of the Board of Deputies of British Jews
Chief Executive Neville Nagler, MA
Education Officer of the Board & Executive Director of the Committees Laurie Rosenberg Woburn Hse, Tavistock Sq, London WC1H 0EZ; Tel 0171-387 3952; Fax 0171-383 0629

Christian Science Committees on Publication for Great Britain and Ireland
District Manager Alan Grayson 2 Elysium Gate, 126 New Kings Rd, London SW6 4LZ; Tel 0171-371 0600; Fax 0171-371 9204

Church Army
Chief Secretary Capt Phillip Johanson, CA Independents Rd, Blackheath, London SE3 9LG; Tel 0181-318 1226; Fax 0181-318 5258

Church of England Children's Society (known as The Children's Society)
Director Ian Sparks, MA Edward Rudolf Hse, Margery St, London WC1X 0JL; Tel 0171-837 4299

The Church Schools Foundation Ltd/ The Church Schools Company
Chief Executive Ewan Harper, MA Church Schools Hse, Titchmarsh, Kettering, Northants NN14 3DA; Tel (01832) 735105; Fax (01832) 734760

The Council of Christians and Jews
1 Dennington Pk Rd, West End La, London NW6 1AX; Tel 0171-794 8178/9; Fax 0171-431 3500
Executive Director Paul Mendel
Deputy Director Sr Margaret Shepherd

Inter–Varsity Fellowship of Evangelical Unions
see Universities and Colleges Christian Fellowship of Evangelical Unions

Jewish Education Bureau
8 Westcombe Ave, Leeds LS8 2BS; Tel (0113) 266 3613; Fax (0113) 269 7318
Director Rabbi D.S. Charing

Methodist Residential Schools Board of Management
Secretary D. Robson, MA 25 Marylebone Rd, London NW1 5JP; Tel 0171-935 3723

Minaret Hse for Islamic Education Material
9 Leslie Pk Rd, Croydon, Surrey CR0 6TN; Tel 0181-681 2972/081-654 8801; Fax 0181-667 1280

Multifaith Education Centre
Sacred Trinity Church, Chapel St, Salford, Greater Manchester M3 7AJ; Tel 0161-832 3709
Co-ordinator Trish Hardy

Muslim Teachers' Association (MTA)
146 Park Rd, London NW8 7RG; Tel 0171-724 3363/4
President D.Y. Baig
Vice-President Mr Baloch
Secretary S. Syed

National Christian Education Council (International Bible Reading Association)
Robert Denholm Hse, Nutfield, Redhill, Surrey RH1 4HW; Tel (01737) 822411 Ext 215; Fax (01737) 822116

National Society (C. of E.) for Promoting Religious Education
General Secretary G.S. Duncan, BSc(Econ), MA
Deputy Secretary & Schools Officer D.W. Lankshear, LCPL
Promotions and Publications Secretary The Revd J.M. Yates, MA Church Hse, Great Smith St, London SW1P 3NZ; Tel 0171-222 1672/3; Fax 0171-233 2592
Director of R.E. Centre, Kensington A.S. Brown, BA, MPhil 23 Kensington Sq, London W8 5HN; Tel 0171-937 4241
Director R.E. Centre, York Rev Dr P. Doble, MA The College, Lord Mayor's Walk, York YO3 7EX; Tel (01904) 656771

The Scottish Joint Committee on Religious Education
Joint Secretary (Teachers) F.L. Forrester, MA, DipEd, FEIS, 46 Moray Pl, Edinburgh, EH3 6BH; Tel 0131-225 6244; Fax 0131-220 3151
Joint Secretary (Churches) Rev J. Stevenson, MA, BD Church of Scotland, 121 George St, Edinburgh EH2 4YN; Tel 0131-225 5722

Scripture Union in Schools
130 City Rd, London EC1V 2NJ; Tel 0171-782 0013
Contact Lesley Blight

Society for Promoting Christian Knowledge (SPCK)
Holy Trinity Church, Marylebone Rd, London NW1 4DU; Tel 0171-387 5282; Fax 0171-388 2352
Chairman Lionel Scott
General Secretary Paul Chandler

Universities and Colleges Christian Fellowship of Evangelical Unions (formerly Inter-Varsity Fellowship of Evangelical Unions)
38 De Montfort St, Leicester LE1 7GP
General Secretary R.M. Horn, MA 38 De Montfort St, Leicester LE1 7GP; Tel (0116) 255 1700; Fax (0116) 255 5672

Urban Theology Unit
210 Abbeyfield Rd, Sheffield S4 7AZ; Tel (0114) 243 5342
Director Rev Dr John Vincent
Administrator Peter Colby

Research

Birmingham Settlement Research Unit
c/o The Birmingham Settlement, 318 Summer La, Birmingham B19 3RL; Tel 0121-359 3562
Research Director Chris Kunz

British Association for Applied Linguistics (BAAL)
Chair Rosamond Mitchell School of Education, University of Southampton, Highfield, Southampton SO17 1BY

The British Institute of Traffic Education Research
Kent Hse, Kent St, Birmingham B5 6QF; Tel 0121-622 2402/6551; Fax 0121-622 3450
Executive Director Dr A.B. Clayton

Centre for Educational Sociology (CES)
University of Edinburgh, 7 Buccleuch Pl, Edinburgh EH8 9LW; Tel 0131-650 4192
Contact Joan Hughes, Research Administrator

Federal Trust for Education and Research
Director Andrew Duff Europe Hse, 158 Buckingham Palace Rd, London SW1W 9TR; Tel 0171-259 9990; Fax 0171-259 9505
Educational charity running studies, conferences and issuing publications relating to the European Community and the world. It also runs an educational programme on Europe for Schools and Universities

Good Housekeeping Institute–The Food and Consumer Research Centre of Good Housekeeping Magazine
Contact GHI Consumer Research Editor National Magazine Hse, 72 Broadwick St, London W1V 2BP; Tel 0171-439 5000

Institute for Employment Studies
Director Richard Pearson Mantell Bldg, University of Sussex Campus, Falmer, Brighton BN1 9RF; Tel (01273) 686751; Fax (01273) 690430

Modern Humanities Research Association
Hon Secretary Prof D.A. Wells Birkbeck College, Malet St, London WC1E 7HX; Tel 0171-631 6103

Occupational Research Centre (ORC)
Highlands, Gravel Path, Berkhamsted, Herts HP4 2PQ; Tel (01442) 871200
Director M.J. Kirton

Royal Archaeological Institute
Assistant Secretary W. Phillips c/o Society of Antiquaries, Burlington Hse, Piccadilly, London W1V 0HS

Resource Suppliers

Credit Action
Jubilee Centre, 3 Hooper St, Cambridge CB1 2NZ; Tel (01223) 324034; Fax (01223) 61646
Director Alasdair Barron
Credit Action develops money management teaching materials for use in secondary schools

Curriculum Development and Resource Unit
see John Horniman School

Dextral Books
PO Box 52, South D.O., Manchester M20 2PJ; Tel 0161-445 0159; Fax 0161-445 0159
Proprietor Diane Paul

Education and Skills Analysis Branch
Dept of Employment, Moorfoot, Sheffield S1 4PQ; Tel (0114) 259 4449
Head J. Temple
Economic Adviser S. Creigh

Left-Handed Co
PO Box 52, South DO, Manchester M20 2PJ; Tel 0161-445 0159; Fax 0161-445 0159
Proprieter Diane Paul
Teaching aids; utensils; research/bibliography

National Advice and Information Centre (Outdoor Education)
The Director DMIHE, High Melton Site, Doncaster

Newspapers in Education (NIE)
Manager George Kelly The Newspaper Society, Bloomsbury Hse, Bloomsbury Sq, 74–77 Great Russell St, London WC1B 3DA; Tel 0171-636 7014; Fax 0171-631 5119

Reading and Language Information Centre
University of Reading, Bulmershe Ct, Woodlands Ave, Reading RG6 1HY; Tel (01734) 318820

Society of Archivists
Executive Secretary P.S. Cleary Information Hse, 20–24 Old St, London EC1V 9AP; Tel 0171-253 4488; Fax 0171-253 5087

Sciences

Botanical Society of British Isles
Hon General Secretary M. Briggs, MBE C/o Dept of Botany, The Natural History Museum, Cromwell Rd, London SW7 5BD
(sae with enquiries)

British Association for the Advancement of Science
23 Savile Row, London W1X 2NB; Tel 0171-494 3326; Fax 0171-734 1658
Director of Programmes Brian Gamble
Executive Secretary Dr Peter Briggs

British Astronomical Association
British Social Biology Council
Educational Secretary D.M. Jeynes 69 Eccleston Sq, London SW1 1PJ; Tel 0171-834 2091
Business Secretary J. Nimmo-Smith

Geologists' Association
Executive Secretary Sarah Stafford Burlington Hse, Piccadilly, London W1V 9AG; Tel 0171-434 9298; Fax 0171-287 0280
Hon General Secretary Prof R. Stoneley Burlington Hse, Piccadilly, London W1V 9AG; Tel 0171-434 9298; Fax 0171-287 0280

27 Educational and Allied Organisations

The Institute of Mathematics and Its Applications
Catherine Richards Hse, 16 Nelson St, Southend-on-Sea, Essex SS1 1EF; Tel (01702) 354020; Fax (01702) 354111
President Prof J.C.R. Hunt, FRS
Executive Secretary Dr Adrian Lepper

Royal Astronomical Society
Burlington Hse, Piccadilly, London W1V ONL; Tel 0171-734 4582; Fax 0171-494 0166
Executive Secretary J.E.J. Lane

Royal Meteorological Society
Education Officer M.G. Chaplin 104 Oxford Rd, Reading, Berks RG1 7LJ; Tel (01734) 568500; Fax (01734) 568571

Royal Microscopical Society
37/38 St Clements, Oxford OX4 1AJ; Tel (01865) 248768; Fax (01865) 791237
Administrator P.B. Hirst
The Royal Microscopical Society organises courses and meetings on Microscopy including annual courses on Light Microscopy and Electron Microscopy, Immunocyto Chemistry Flow Cytometry and Computers in Microscopy

School Mathematics Project
The University of Southampton, Southampton SO17 1BJ; Tel (01703) 593686; Fax (01703) 594300

'Understanding Electricity' Educational Service for Schools
The Electricity Association, 30 Millbank, London SW1P 4RD; Tel 071-344 5839

United Nations Educational, Scientific and Cultural Organisation (Unesco)
7 place de Fontenoy, 75352 Paris 07 SP, France; Tel 45 68 10 00; Fax 45 67 16 90

WISE Vehicle Programme
C/o The Nottingham Trent University, Burton St, Nottingham NG1 4BU; Tel (0115) 941 8418 Ext 2101; Fax (0115) 947 2780
Joyce Bullimore

Y Gymdeithas Wyddonol Genedlaethol (The Welsh Scientific Society)
Secretary Dr S.E. Pryse Adran Ffiseg, Prifysgol Cymru Aberystwyth, Penglais, Aberystwyth, Dyfed SY23 3BZ; Tel (01970) 622801

Seafarers

The Marine Society College of the Sea
General Secretary Lt Cdr R.M. Frampton, RN, FNI, FRSA 202 Lambeth Rd, London SE1 7JW; Tel 0171-261 9535; Fax 0171-401 2537

The Marine Society Sea Lines
Head of Education Brian Garfield Thomas, MA(Ed), BA, PGCE 22 Lambeth Rd, London SE1 7JW; Tel 0171-261 9535; Fax 0171-401 2537

Societies and Associations

Access Committee for England
Policy Officer Sabrina Aaronovitch 12 City Forum, 250 City Rd, London EC1V 8AF; Tel 0171-250 0008

Association for Lifelong Learning
Department of Continuing Education, Lancaster University, The Storey Institute, Meeting House La, Lancaster LA1 1TH
President Prof Arthur K. Stock, OBE
Chair Dr Frank Molyneux
Secretary Hans R. Klein
Assistant Secretary (Membership) Rosie Cantley
The Association produces news *Digests* and an *Issues* pamphlet and welcomes contributions. *Contact* Rosie Cantley

Association of MBAs
Administrator Pauline North 15 Duncan Terr, London N1 8BZ; Tel 0171-837 3374

Bicycle Association of Great Britain Ltd
Secretary Mrs J. Foster Starley Hse, Eaton Rd, Coventry CV1 2FH; Tel (01203) 553838

British Exhibition Venues Association
'Mallards', Five Ashes, Mayfield, E Sussex TN20 6NN; Tel (01435) 872244; Fax (01435) 872696
Executive Secretary F. Lloyd McLean

British Voice Association
77B Abbey Rd, London NW8 0AE; Tel 0171-372 5109; Fax 0171-372 5109
Chair Janice Chapman
For professionals in medicine and arts concerned with voice. Promotes conferences and research

The Education Industrial Society
Sector Manager–Education UK & Ireland Roger Opie The Industrial Society, Quadrant Ct, 49 Calthorpe Rd, Edgbaston, Birmingham B15 1TH; Tel 0121-454 6769

Folklore Society
c/o University College, Gower St, London WC1E 6BT; Tel 0171-387 5894 (answerphone); 0171-380 7095
Hon Secretary Juliette Wood

Glasgow and West of Scotland Society for the Prevention of Cruelty to Animals
see The Scottish Society for the Prevention of Cruelty to Animals

Greater London Employers' Association
4th Floor, Victoria Station Hse, 191 Victoria St, London SW1E 5NE; Tel 0171-834 8288
Employers' Secretary Huw Jones-Owen
Deputy Director Development & Training C. Lee

Honourable Society of Cymmrodorion
Hon Secretary D.L. Jones, MA 30 Eastcastle St, London W1N 7PD; Tel 0171-631 0502

Inner London Federation of School Associations
General Secretary Ian Sinclair 9 Conyers Rd, London SW16 6LP; Tel 0181-769 2231

London Natural History Society
c/o British Museum (Natural History), Cromwell Rd, London SW7 5BD; Tel 0171-938 9123 Ext 8905
President Ruth Day
Secretary Tony Barrett
Treasurer Mike West

Moral Education Centre
Director Michael Cross St Martins College, Lancaster LA1 3JD; Tel (01524) 62103 Ext 255

National Association for Outdoor Education
Hon Secretary Dr Barbara Humberstone 251 Woodlands Rd, Woodlands, Southampton SO4 2GJ

National Association of Conservative Graduates
Conservative and Unionist Central Office, 32 Smith Sq, London SW1P 3HH; Tel 0171-222 9000
Permanent Secretary Martin Minns

National Dairymen's Association
Chief Executive and Secretary A.D. Moxon 19 Cornwall Terr, London NW1 4QP; Tel 0171-935 4562

National Educational Trust
Administration Mrs M. Smith 1 Hinchley Way, Esher, Surrey KT10 0BD; Tel 0181-398 1253

Playlink (formerly London Adventure Playground Association)
Director Ms S. Melville 279 Whitechapel Rd, London E1 1BY; Tel 0171-377 0314; Fax 0171-247 4490

Radio Society of Great Britain
General Manager Peter Kirby Lambda Hse, Cranborne Rd, Potters Bar, Herts EN6 3JE; Tel (01707) 659015; Fax (01707) 645105

Royal Anthropological Institute of Great Britain and Ireland
Director J. Benthall 50 Fitzroy St, London W1P 5HS

Royal Numismatic Society
Secretary J.E. Cribb Dept of Coins and Medals, British Museum, London WC1B 3DG; Tel 0171-323 8585

The Royal Society
(Founded 1660, Royal Charter granted 1662)
6 Carlton Hse Terr, London SW1Y 5AG; Tel 0171-839 5561; Fax 0171-930 2170
President Sir Michael Atiyah, OM
Treasurer Professor John Horlock, FEng, FRS
Biological Secretary Sir Brian Follett, FRS
Physical Secretary Sir Francis Graham-Smith, FRS
Foreign Secretary Dr Anne McLaren, DBC, FRS
Executive Secretary Dr P.T. Warren
Education Officer R.A. Rees
Founded 1660, Royal Charter granted 1662

Royal Society of Literature
Secretary Maggie Parham 1 Hyde Pk Gdns, London W2 2LT; Tel 0171-723 5104; Fax 0171-402 0199

School Journey Association
Hon Secretary J.U. Lambert, BSc 48 Cavendish Rd, Clapham, London SW12 0DG; Tel 0181-673 4849, 0181-675 6636/9; Fax 0181-673 8763

Socialist Educational Association
110 Humberstone Rd, Plaistow, London E13 9NJ; Tel 0181-470 3690
General Secretary Graham Lane

Society for the Advancement of Games and Simulations in Education and Training
Secretary Alan Cudworth Department of Surveying, The Nottingham Trent University, Burton St, Nottingham NG1 4BU; Tel (0115) 941 8418

Society for Co–operative Dwellings
209 Clapham Rd, London SW9 0HQ; Tel 0171-737 2077
Co-op Development Co-ordinator T. Wood

Society of Authors Educational Writers Group
Secretary Kate Pool 84 Drayton Gdns, London SW10 9SB; Tel 0171-373 6642

Society of Scribes and Illuminators
Chairman I.K. Wymer, BA(Hons), DipEd Principal, Bilston Community College, Westfield Rd, Bilston, Wolverhampton WV14 6ER; Tel (01902) 353877

United Kingdom Reading Association
Hon General Secretary Mary Cooper Administrative Secretary, C/o Warrington Rd CP School, Naylor Rd, Widnes, Cheshire WA8 0BP; Tel 0151-420 2552
Administrative Secretary Mrs B. Malins c/o Ukra, Warrington Rd CP School, Nalyor Rd, Widnes, Cheshire WA8 0BP; Tel 0151-420 2552

Special Educational Needs

Beauchamp Lodge Adult Literacy Scheme
2 Warwick Cres, London W2 6NE; Tel 0171-286 2183
Tutors Mary Kett; Jane Lawrence; Noreen Nolan

British Institute of Learning Disabilities
Wolverhampton Rd, Kidderminster, Worcs DY10 3PP; Tel (01562) 850251
Director Dr J. Harris
Administrator J. Fear
Information Officer Mrs L. Averill

The Cambridge Specific Learning Disabilities Group
Hon Secretary Dept of Education, University of Cambridge, 5 Bene't Pl, Cambridge

Dyslexia Centre
The Helen Arkell, Dyslexia Centre, Frensham, Farnham, Surrey GU10 3BW; Tel (01252) 792400; Fax (01252) 795669
Director Gail Goedkoop, BA, MEd
A registered charity providing a wide range of services for dyslexics of all ages, their teachers and schools

Helen Arkell Dyslexia Centre
see Dyslexia Centre

Institute of Mental Subnormality
see British Institute of Mental Handicap

National Council for Special Education
General Secretary C. Danks Exhall Grange, Wheelwright La, Coventry CV7 9HP; Tel (01203) 352414

SCOPE (Specialised Course Offering Purposeful Education,)
The Oaks, Lindeth, Bowness-on-Winderemere, Cumbria LA23 3NH; Tel (015394) 46265
Principal Beryl Adams
For people with learning difficulties–mental handicap

SENNAC (Special Educational Needs National Advisory Council)
Hon Secretary Ian Petrie Dept of Education, Liverpool University, PO Box 147, Liverpool L69 3BX; Tel 0151-722 3819; Fax 0151-794 2512

Special Educational Needs National Advisory Council
see SENNAC

Spelling Reform: The Simplified Spelling Society
Hon Secretary Bob Brown 133 John Trundle Ct, Barbican, London EC2Y 8DJ; Tel 0171-628 5876; Fax 0171-628 9147

Steiner Schools Fellowship (Waldorf Education)
Kidbrooke Pk, Forest Row, Sussex RH18 5JB; Tel (01342) 82115

Volunteer Reading Help (VRH)
Room 438 High Holborn Hse, 49/51 Bedford Row, London WC1V 6RL; Tel 0171-404 6204
Director Charles Martineau
Recruits and trains volunteers to each help three children to read on a one to one basis by going regularly into primary schools twice a week for a year. The children are chosen by the teachers. Branches in London, Avon, Berkshire, Bolton, Dorset, Kent, Leeds, Liverpool, Northamptonshire, Nottinghamshire, Oxfordshire and Surrey. Charity funded by DFE, LEAs, schools, charitable trusts, companies and individuals

Waldorf Education
see Steiner Schools Fellowship

West Midlands Advisory Council for Special Education
Director of Education M.J. Quinn, BA Education Dept, Civic Centre, Darwall St, Walsall WS1 1DQ; Tel (01922) 652300

World Federation for Mental Health
1021 Prince St, Alexandria, Virginia 22314, USA

Students

Acadynamics
20 West St, Oxford OX2 0BQ; Tel (01277) 220130; Fax (01277) 231838
Director Peter Gleeson
Registrar Michael Handford
Students plan their own programmes for awards up to Masters level. Locations throughout the country.

Malaysian Students Department
44 Bryanston Sq, London W1H 8AJ; Tel 0171-723 2265

National Union of Students
Nelson Mandella Hse, 461 Holloway Rd, London N7 6LJ; Tel 0171-272 8900
President Jim Murphy

National Union of Students in Wales/Undeb Cenedlaethol Myfyrwyr Cymru
107 Walter Rd, Swansea SA1 5QQ; Tel (01792) 643323, 643590; Fax (01792) 648554
President/ Llywydd J. McGreal

National Union of Students, Scotland
11 Broughton Market, Edinburgh EH3 5NU; Tel 0131-556 6598
President J. Murphy
Research Officer Gerald Madill
Research Officer Lynn Henderson
Manager Graeme Campbell

Sudanese Students' Union in United Kingdom and Ireland
Secretary F.B. Abdel Gadir 31 Rutland Gate, London SW7; Tel 0171-589 7577
President M.A. El Noamen

Teachers

Friends Guild of Teachers
see Guild of Friends in Education

The Industrial Society
Sector Manager Education, UK and Ireland R. Opie 49 Calthorpe Rd, Edgbaston, Birmingham B15 1TH; Tel 0121-454 6769; Fax 0121-456 3846

Irish National Teachers' Organisation
General Secretary Senator J. O'Toole, NT, BA, HDE 35 Parnell Sq, Dublin 1; Tel Dublin 8722533; Fax Dublin 8722462

National College of Teachers of the Deaf
see British Association of Teachers of the Deaf

Standing Committee for the Education and Training of Teachers
27 Britannia St, London WC1X 9JP; Tel 0171-837 3636
Chair D. Rivalland
Academic Secretary R. Beardsworth
Founded with DES support in 1981 to co-ordinate teacher training organisations and higher educational establishments with responsibility for teacher training
The Committee includes in its membership the representatives bodies for teacher education including the major teacher associations, universities and colleges

Teacher–Poets Group
Administrator David Orme 27 Pennington Cl, Coldon Common, Winchester, Hants SO21 1UR; Tel or Fax (01962) 712062

Teachers' Guild Benevolent Fund
Secretary Mrs G.A. Burgess 10 St Christopher's Pl, London W1M 6HY; Tel 0171-935 0641
Administered by the Professional Classes Aid Council

World Studies Teacher Training Centre
see Centre for Global Education

Training

British Hypnotherapy Association (BHA)
67 Upper Berkeley St, London W1H 7DH; Tel 0171-723 4443
Chairman R.K. Brian
Secretary Mrs E. Wookey
Maintains a register of qualified trained practitioners who comply with adequate standards of competence and ethics. Aims to care for the interests of patients and members and to collate and disseminate information on hypnotherapy. A voluntary organisation, funded by donations, legacies, subscriptions

Building Crafts College
Director P.C. Quick 153 Gt Titchfield St, London W1P 7FR; Tel 0171-636 0480

Centre for Human Resource Training
1 Holly Terr, Highgate West Hill, London N6 6LX

Civil Service Council for Further Education
Civil Service College, Sunningdale Pk, Larch Ave, Ascot, Berks SL5 0QE; Tel (01344) 634545; Fax (01344) 634233
Secretary M.J. Pearce

Community Development Foundation
Founded 1968
60 Highbury Gr, London N5 2AG; Tel 0171-226 5375; Fax 0171-704 0313
Head of Communications Elizabeth George
Strengthens communities by ensuring the effective participation of people in determining the conditions which affect their lives

Community Education Development Centre (CEDC)
Lyng Hall, Blackberry La, Coventry CV2 3JS; Tel (01203) 638660; Fax (01203) 681161

Community Industry
Victoria Hse, Croft St, Widnes, Cheshire WA8 0NQ; Tel 0151-495 2114/5/6
Managing Director Anne Weinstock, CBE

Directory of Social Change
Radius Works, Back La, London NW3 1HL; Tel 0171-435 8171
Director Michael Norton
Publishers of *The Educational Grants Directory, State Schools–a suitable case for charity?* and guide books. Also runs training courses
The Charitable Status of Schools: What needs to be done?, Anne Mounfield (A4, 64 pages 1992) £12.95 ISBN 0 907164 870; Fundraising for your school: What you need to know, Anne Mountfield June 93 £7.95 ISBN 1 873860 080; Causes for Courses: A Guide for educational material available from the voluntary sector June 93 £7.95
ISBN 1 873860 196

Educational Field Projects
8 St Margaret's Dr, Oakwood, Leeds LS8 1RU

Family Planning Association
Education and Training Dept 27/35 Mortimer St, London W1N 7RJ; Tel 0171-636 7866
Head of Department Mary Porter
Training and Development Officer John Seex
Training and Development Officer Teresa Leo
Administrator Jackie Taylor

NHS Training and Conference Centre
Eastwood Pk, Falfield, Wotton-under-Edge, Glos GL12 8DA; Tel (01454) 260207; Fax (01454) 261370
Director J. Thatcher

Public Service Training Council (PSTC)
6th Floor, Chamber of Commerce Hse, 22 Great Victoria St, Belfast BT2 7BJ; Tel (01232) 230076
Director Philip Anderson

School Management South (SMS)
Professional Centre, Furnace Dr, Furnace Grn, Crawley, W Sussex RH10 6JB; Tel (01293) 611277; Fax (01293) 611326
Director Dr A.J. Bailey
Chairman Dr J. Williams (Chief Executive Officer, Isle of Wight); Tel (01983) 823400

Social Care Association (Education)
Chief Executive R. Clough, OBE 23A Victoria Rd, Surbiton, Surrey KT6 4JZ

Voluntary Groups

Aerospace Education and Recreation Organisation (AERO)
Chairman A.J. Davis
Hon Secretary I.R. Simpson, TD, BA 38 Trelawne Dr, Cranleigh, Surrey GU6 8DB; Tel (01483) 273971

British Epilepsy Association
Anstey Hse, 40 Hanover Sq, Leeds, West Yorkshire LS3 1BE; Tel (0113) 243 9393; Fax (0113) 242 8804
Contact Public Relations Officer

Council for Educational Advance
Hon Secretary K. Ebbutt 2-B Hillfield Rd, London NW6 1QE; Tel 0171-794 8657; Fax 0171-794 8657

Education Otherwise
PO Box 120, Leamington Spa, Warks CV32 7ER; Tel (01926) 886828

Institute of Health Education
Secretary Prof Leo Båric 14 High Elm Rd, Hale Barns, Cheshire WA15 0HS; Tel 0161-980 8276/8696; Fax 0161-980 7446

London Emergency Volunteers
7 Dawlish Dr, Pinner, Middx HA5 5LJ
Secretary Laurence Cornwell 7 Dawlish Dr, Pinner, Middlesex HA5 5LS

London Voluntary Service Council
356 Holloway Rd, London N7 6PA; Tel 0171-700 8107
Director D. Springer; Tel 0171-700 8107; Fax 0171-700 8108

National Adult School Organisation
General Secretary W.J. Scarle MASU Centre, Gaywood Croft, Cregoe St, Birmingham B15 2ED; Tel 0121-622 3400

National Council of Voluntary Child Care Organisations
Director George Thomas Unit 4, Pride Ct, 80–82 White Lion St, London N1 9PF

Network 81
1–7 Woodfield Terrace, Stansted, Essex CM24 8AJ; Tel (01279) 647415; Fax (01279) 816438
A national network of parents of children with special educational needs; journal *Network News*; Publication: Statements – A step–to–step guide to statementing; Individual annual membership £10.00, life membership (individual) £30.00, Annual Associated GP membership £10.00, Annual affiliated GP membership £20.00

Northern Ireland Council for Voluntary Action (NICVA)
127 Ormeau Rd, Belfast BT7 1SH; Tel (01232) 321224; Fax (01232) 438350
Chair Roisin McDonough
Director Quintin Oliver

Rural Voice
C/o ACRE, Somerford Ct, Somerford Rd, Cirencester, Glos GL7 1TW; Tel (01285) 653477; Fax (01285) 654537
Chairman Rev J. Clarke
Vice-Chairman Valerie Gillespie
Secretary Jeremy Fennell
Ten national member organisations seek to campaign for greater recognition of rural socio-economic needs and promote rural self-help

Scottish Council for Voluntary Organisations
18–19 Claremont Cres, Edinburgh EH7 4QD; Tel 0131-556 3882
Director Martin Sime

The Volunteer Centre, UK
Carriage Row, 183 Eversholt St, London NW1 1BU; Tel 0171-388 9888; Fax 0171-383 0448
National resource agency on volunteering specialising in the provision of training, information and research findings

Women

Feminist Library and Information Centre
5A Westminster Bridge Rd, London SE1 7XW; Tel 0171-928 7789
A contemporary feminist library with information on womens' studies courses and conferences, and a Research Index of work in progress

Gender and Mathematics Association (GAMMA)
C/o Lesley Jones Faculty of Education, Goldsmiths' College, New Cross, London SE14 6NW; Tel 0171-919 7171 Ext 2265

National Council of Women of Great Britain
36 Danbury St, Islington, London N1 8JU; Tel 0171-354 2395; Fax 0171-354 9214

National Federation of Voluntary Educational Schemes (NFVES)
Cambridge Hse, 131 Camberwell Rd, London SE5 0HF; Tel 0171-703 8083
National Co-ordinator Amanda Ranson

Townswomen's Guilds (TG)
Chamber of Commerce Hse, 75 Harborne Rd, Edgbaston, Birmingham B15 3DA; Tel 0121-456 3435
National Chairman Marguerite Mitchell
National Secretary Pauline Wilkes

Women Into Science and Engineering (WISE)
C/o The Engineering Council, 10 Maltravers St, London WC2R 3ER; Tel 0171-240 7891; Fax 0171-240 7517
Manager (WISE Campaign) Marie-Noëlle Barton

Young People

The Brandon Centre
26 Prince of Wales Rd, London NW5 3LG; Tel 0171-267 4792/3
Director Geoffrey Baruch, PhD
Counselling and Psychotherapy for young people (12–25) with emotional problems and medical counselling for contraception, pregnancy and related problems

National Organisation for Women's Management Education (NOWME)
Contact Yvonne Sarch 12A Westbere Rd, London NW2 3RR; Tel 0171-794 8734

Shaftesbury Homes and 'Arethusa'
3 Rectory Gr, Clapham, London SW4 0EG; Tel 0171-720 8709
Director Capt N.C. Baird-Murray, CBE, RN

Trust for the Study of Adolescence,
23 New Rd, Brighton, East Sussex BN1 1WZ; Tel (01273) 693311; Fax (01273) 679907
Director Dr John Coleman
The Trust has produced a series of audio tapes and booklets for parents, teenagers and those working with young people and also has a range of publications, videos and games on adolescence for professionals. As well as being involved in research on different aspects of adolescence, the Trust also runs training workshops and conferences

UNA Youth Council
3 Whitehall Ct, London SW1A 2EL; Tel 0171-930 2931/2

Young Explorers' Trust (YET)
The Young Explorers' Trust at the RGS, 1 Kensington Gore, London SW7 2AR; Tel (01623) 861027; Fax (01623) 861027
Secretary Ted Grey

Youth and Education Countryside Trust (YECT)
Marford Mill, Rossett, Wrexham, Clwyd LL12 0HL; Tel (01224) 570881
Secretary Colin Blanchard
Registered Charity Number 293142. Charitable Trust providing free educational material on countryside management

Youth and Music
28 Charing Cross Rd, London WC2H 0DB; Tel 0171-379 6722; Fax 0171-497 0345
Marketing Officer Karen Barnes
Stage Pass – national discount ticket scheme for young people. Discounted tickets and arts magazine for 14–30 year olds

28 Educational Equipment

Purchasing Organisations

Association of County Supplies Officers

C/o Consortium for Purchasing and Distribution, Hammond Way, Trowbridge, Wiltshire BA14 8RR; Tel (01225) 771201; Fax (01225) 771342

Chairman A.J. Gaskell
Vice Chairman S.L. Gilbey
Honorary Secretary J.R. Gould

Professional Officers Association acting on behalf of its Members on matters of purchasing and supply. Also acts an advisory body of Local Authority Associations

CLEAPSS

Director D.A. Tawney CLEAPSS School Science Service, Brunel University, Uxbridge UB8 3PH; Tel (01895) 251496

Consortium of Local Education Authorities for the provision of Science Services was formed in 1963. It supports and controls the School Science Service, an information and advisory service in the field of school and college science laboratory safety and science resources which is offered to teachers (in both primary and secondary schools and in colleges), technicians and county officers. Through its bulletins and guides the Service encourages the wise purchase, careful maintenance and safe use of resources. Several recent guides have been concerned with safety, eg. on fume cupboards, risk assessments and chemical stores; others with micro-electronics and computer interfacing. Other services are the monitoring of laboratory mercury vapour levels and the organisation of courses for teachers and technicians. (Open to all LEAs in England, Wales and Northern Ireland; 117 have joined; also open to colleges and independent and GM schools)

Members
Over 90% of Education Authorities in England, Wales, Northern Ireland and the off-shore islands. Over 1,000 independent schools, GM schools and colleges

Counties Furniture Group

Secretary J. Bower Director of Education, Humberside County Council

C.F.G. (a consortium of Local Authorities) was set up to develop the design, manufacture and supply of a comprehensive range of school furniture for stimulating teaching. The group draws on the collective experience of practising teachers, advisers and administrators to promote a pervasive evolution of new designs and to give a lead in thge achievement of imaginative teaching situations. The range of furniture covers general and specialist needs in primary, secondary and further education. Current contracts are with five manufacturers, in whose supply and delivery arrangements the group's officers have production line influence

Full Members
Bedfordshire, Central Pegion (Scotland), Cheshire, Clywd, Dorset, Dudley, Haringey, Hereford and Worcester, Highlands Region, Humberside, Leicestershire, Lincolnshire, Newcastle upon Tyne, Northamptonshire, Northumberland, North Yorkshire, Orkney Islands, Redbridge, Richmond-upon-Thames, Shropshire, Shetland Islands, Waltham Forest, Warwickshire, Western Isles, West Sussex

A further 22 local authorities are Associate Members

Further information is available from the Design Co-ordinator's Office; County Architect, Shirehall, Shrewsbury, Shropshire SY2 6ND

Consortium for Purchasing and Distribution

Hammond Way, Trowbridge BA14 8RR; Tel (01225) 777333

Chairman
Changes annually, by Election
Supplies Officer J.R. Gould, MInstPS, FBIM
The aims of the consortium are to improve the purchasing performance of member authorities; to undertake the development of ranges of goods required by its customers; to centralise contracting and purchasing arrangements for goods on behalf of its customers; to undertake the storage and distribution of certain common use items; and to provide an information and advisory service
Members
Avon, Cornwall, Dorset, Dyfed, Gloucestershire, Gwynedd, Isle of Wight, Powys, Somerset, Wiltshire
Associate Members
Bath City, Bristol City, Kingswood, Northavon, Wansdyke, Wood-spring, Caradon, Carrick, Kerrier, North Cornwall, Penwith, Restormel, Bournemouth, Christchurch, East Dorset, North Dorset, Poole, Purbeck, West Dorset, Weymouth and Portland, Cartmarthen, Ceredigion, Dinefwr, Llanelli, Preseli, South Pembrokeshire, Cheltenham, Cotswold, Forest of Dean, Gloucester, Stroud, Tewkesbury, Aberconwy, Dwyfor, Isle of Anglesey, meirionnydd, Brecknock, Montgomery, Mendip, Sedgemoor, South Somerset, Taunton Deane, West Somerset, Kennett, North Wiltshire, Salisbury, Thamesdown, West Wiltshire, City of Hereford, City of Plymouth, City of Southampton, East Devon, East Hampshire, Exeter, Fareham, Mid Devon, Newbury, New Forest, North Devon, Reading, Rushmoor, South Hams, Winchester, Wokingham, Elmbridge, Surrey

Yorkshire Purchasing Organisation

41 Industrial Pk, Wakefield, West Yorkshire WF2 0XE; Tel (01924) 824477
Chairman of Management Committee Councillor T. Dixon
Director Arthur Haigh, MCIPS
The Yorkshire Purchasing Organisation is a consortium of local authorities in the North of England which, on local government reorganisation in 1974, took over the functions of the former West Riding County Council Supplies Department. Its agency facilities are available to other local authorities and public bodies outside the consortium
Operating on a commercial budget, the Organisation is currently meeting the requirements of member and user authorities, either via its central stores complex or through the media of contractual arrangements
Member Authorities
Barnsley, Bolton, Bradford, Calderdale, Doncaster, Kirklees, Knowsley, North Yorkshire, Rotherham, St Helens, Wakefield, Wigan
User Authorities
Most of the authorities throughout the North of England and beyond

Building Consortia

Anglian Standing Conference

Design Manager, Property Dept, County Hall, Bedford
Set up in 1964, ir pursues conventional building methods where they are allied to a high degree of organisation and uses a method of constructionappropriate to the local resources of the building industry
Members
Bedfordshire, Norfolk and Cambridgeshire

CLASP

CLASP Development Group, Adam Hse, Player's Crt, Player St, Nottingham NG7 5LZ; Tel (0115) 942 2044; Fax (0115) 942 4768
The CLASP Building System has been used for over 3,000 Education buildings in the UK and overseas since 1957. It is particularly noted for its high quality low maintenance finishes for windows and internal walls and doors. It is the only Building System of its type to have achieved the independent validation of the British Board of Agrément
The System is the only one in the country which is not tied to a contracting organisation. It therefore offers great flexibility of procurement. The benefits of System construction may be achieved with a school's own architect with conventional tendering or by means of a full Design/Build package

CLAW, Consortium Local Authorities, Wales

CLAW Consortium Office, Park Hse, Greyfriars Rd, Cardiff CF1 3UH; Tel (01222) 664041; Fax (01222) 664056
Principal Officer G.N. Price, FRICS
The Consortium is a unique association primarily of Welsh Public Authorities formed in 1962 to assist its many members with their technical requirements and problems associated with their varied building programmes. Above all it assists them in achieving real value for money through the availability, to all participating members, of a wide range of sponsored high quality building components and services obtained through competitive tendering for their new build, maintenance and refurbishment programmes. Membership offers proven products at preferential prices and service
Specialised activities concentrate upon matters of energy efficiency, antivandal and property security measures, and a programme of computer aided design work
Linking all together is a series of regular forums in which all member authorities are able to participate in wide ranging exchanges of technical topics of mutual interest
Members
County Councils: Clywd, Dyfed, Mid Glamorgan, South Glamorgan, West Glamorgan, Gwent, Gwynedd and Powys. District Councils: Cardiff City, Carmarthen, Ceredigion, Dinefwr, Islwyn, Llanelli, Merthyr Tydfil, Newport, Ogwr, Rhymney Valley, South Pembrokeshire. North Wales Police Authority
Associate Members
Glamorgan Holiday Home, Porthcawl; Mid Glamorgan Health Authority; South Wales Police, Bridgend, University College of Wales, Aberystwyth
Honorary Members
Department of Education and Science, Welsh Office

Pillar Consultancy

Director I.M. Cook, RIBA Pillar and Lucy Hse, Merchants Rd, Gloucester GL1 5RG; Tel (01452) 525241; Fax (01452) 303909
A Voluntary association of Local Authorities, formed in 1961, to share resouces and experience in the design and construction of building projects. Previously the second Consortium of Local Authorities (SCOLA)
The co-ordination activities of the Consortium are undertaken by its Central development Group, based in Gloucester whose expertise constitutes a considerable resouce in terms of records, technical knowledge and experience
Whilst the activities of the Central Development Group are primarily directed to the Authorities who are members of the Consortium, the use of this resource is also available to the non-member public and private sectors of the construction industry. Services include:
Technical assistance to anyone concerned with the maintenance or refurbishment of Consortium buildings
Individual commissions on a fee-paying basis
A Structural Steel Frame
A Quality Assurance service and Resource Management Computer Software
A selected range of components
The organisation of Seminars and Technical presentations
A range of commercial package deals, including finance in association with the Consortium Commercial Associate

Trade Associations

British Educational Suppliers Association (BESA)

20 Beaufort Ct, Admirals Way, London E14 9XL; Tel 0171-537 4997; Fax 0171-537 4846
Director and Secretary Dominic J.S. Savage
Assistant Director Eileen Devonshire
Member Services Manager Michael Levitt
BESA is the association representing the educational supply industry. Membership is open to UK based companies manufactoring and supplying products and services to education in the UK who can prove a successful history of supply to UK education and will abide by the Code of Practice
BESA members subscribe to their Code of Practice which offers schools safeguards of choice, quality, safety and service in pusuit of value for money in their purchases
The Code and the companies who subscribe to it are detailed in the BESA membership directory 'The Catalogue of British Educational Suppliers' which is freely available from the BESA offices
BESA is co-organiser of The Education Show held annually in March at the National Exhibition Centre, Birmingham and is industry sponsor of the BETT educational technology exhibition held each January at the National Hall, Olympia. BESA also organises a series of regional educational exhibitions including events in Northern Ireland, Scotland and Wales
BESA also operates a free enquiry service on the companies listed below

3M UK plc, 3M Hse, PO Box 1, Bracknell, Berks RG12 2JU; Tel (01344) 858000; Fax (01344) 858278; *National Sales Manager* B. Wood
3T Productions Ltd (ESPA), Chapel Studio, 47–49 Waterloo Rd, Stockport SK1 3BJ; Tel 0161-476 5553; Fax 0161-476 2988; *Production Director* G. King
ABCeta Playthings Ltd, 19 Torkington Rd, Stockport, Cheshire SK7 4RG; Tel 0161-483 4500; Fax 0161-456 6896; *Managing Director* T.J. Denton
Access to British Training, The Paddock, Maison Dieu Rd, Dover CT16 1DH; Tel (01304) 204890; Fax (01304) 204898; *Director* R. Helmer
Acorn Computers Ltd, Fulbourn Rd, Cherry Hinton, Cambridge CB1 4JN; Tel (01223) 245200; Fax (01223) 210685; *Schools Market Manager* R. Broadie
Acorn (PERCUSSION) Ltd, Unit 34, Abbey Business Centre, Ingate Pl, London SW8 3NS; Tel 0171-720 2243; Fax 0171-627 3020; *Sales Director* M. Vetter
Armfield Ltd (ETEMA), Bridge Hse, West St, Ringwood, Hants BH24 1DY; Tel (01425) 478781; Fax (01425) 470916; *Sales Director* C.J. Addis
AU Enterprises – The Advisory Unit (ESPA), 126 Great North Rd, Hatfield, Herts AL9 5JZ; Tel (01707) 266714; Fax (01707) 273684; *Director of Services* M. Aston
AVP (ESPA), School Hill Centre, Chepstow, Gwent NP6 5PH; Tel (01291) 625439; Fax (01291) 629671; *Managing Director* R. Drewett
AVS Audio Visual Source, PO Box 12, Crowborough, E. Sussex TN6 1QY; Tel (01825) 813655; Fax (01825) 813656; *Director* S.J. Gaster
Balmforth Engineering Ltd, Finway Dallow Rd, Luton, Beds LU1 1TE; Tel (01582) 31171; Fax (01582) 454103; *Sales and Marketing Manager* B. Pettman
Berol Ltd, Oldmeadow Rd, King's Lynn, Norfolk PE30 4JR; Tel (01553) 761221; Fax (01553) 766534; *Educational Sales Manager* M. Reeve
Binney and Smith (Europe) Ltd, Ampthill Rd, Bedford MK42 9RS; Tel (01234) 360201; Fax (01234) 342110; *Sales Director* D. Barker
Blyde-Barton Furniture Ltd, Reepham Rd, Norwich NR6 5LE; Tel (01603) 789000; Fax (01603) 405476; *Works Director* R.A. Brighten
Boxford Ltd (ETEMA), Wheatley, Halifax, W. Yorks HX3 5AF; Tel (01422) 358311; Fax (01422) 355924; *Sales Director* G. Wakeling
British Gas Education, PO Box 70, Wetherby, W. Yorks LS23 7EA; Tel (01937) 843141; Fax (01937) 845381; *Education Liaison Officer* R. Wolfe
British Thornton Ltd, Greenholme Mills, Burley in Wharfedale, W. Yorks LS29 7DX; Tel (01943) 862504; Fax (01943) 862706; *Managing Director* C. Carrick
BT Education Service, BT Centre, 81 Newgate St, London EC1A 7AJ; Tel 0171-356 5674; Fax 0171-356 5675; *Head BT Ed Service* P. Thompson
Budget Direct Plc, Global Hse, 38–40 High St, West Wickham, Kent BR4 0NE; Tel 0181-777 0099; Fax 0181-777 9355; *Sales and Marketing Manager* M. Stevens
R.K. Burt & Co Ltd, 57 Union St, London SE1; Tel 0171-407 6474; Fax 0171-403 3672; *Director* C. Burt
Bytonic (ETEMA), 276 Coleshill Rd, Sutton Coldfield, West Midlands B75 7AX; Tel 0121-378 0613; Fax 0121-311 1774; *General Manager* C. Haden
Cambridge Education Associates Ltd, Sheraton Hse, Castle Pk, Cambridge CB3 0AX; Tel (01223) 460178; Fax (01223) 460178; *Finance Director* E. Tranham
Cambridgeshire Software House (ESPA), 7 Freechurch Passage, St Ives, Huntingdon, Cambs PE17 4AY; Tel (01480) 67945; Fax (01480) 496442; *Partner* B. Richardson
Casio Electronics Co Ltd, Unit 6, 1000 North Circular Rd, London NW2 7JD; Tel 0181-450 9131; Fax 0181-452 6323; *Calculator Sales Manager* D.A. Plater
Clares (ESPA), 98 Middlewich Rd, Northwich, Cheshire CW9 7DA; Tel (01606) 48511; Fax (01606) 48512; *Proprietor* D. Clare
Cochranes of Oxford Ltd, Leafiled, Witney, Oxon OX8 5NY; Tel (01993) 87641; Fax (01993) 87416; *Managing Director* J. Cochrane
Commercial Union Assurance, 1 Undershaft, London EC3P 3DQ; Tel 0171-283 7500 ex 22637; Fax 0171-283 7500 ex; *National Accounts Manager* D. Gray
Commodore Business Machines (UK) Ltd, Commodore Hse, The Switchback, Gardner Rd, Maidenhead SL6 7XA; Tel (01628) 770088; Fax (01628) 71456; *Ed Marketing Manager* C. Steele
Commotion, Redburn Hse, Stockingswater La, Enfield, Middx EN3 7TD; Tel 0181-804 1378; Fax 0181-804 0556; *Managing Director* T. Coote
Community Playthings, Robertsbridge, E. Sussex TN32 5OR; Tel (01580) 880626; *Sales Manager* R. Boucher
Computer Graphics, Belmont Hse, 131 Black Bull La, Preston, Lancs PR2 3PA; Tel (01772) 774930; *Proprietor* T. John
The Concept Keyboard Company, Moorside Rd, Winnall Ind Est, Winchester, Hants SO23 7RX; Tel (01962) 843322; Fax (01962) 841657; *Marketing Manager* P. Goddard
Continental Sports Products Company, Paddock, Huddersfield HD1 4SD; Tel (01484) 542051; Fax (01484) 539148; *Sales Marketing Manager* K. Ibson
Contour Education, Telford Rd, Bicester, Oxon OX6 0TS; Tel (01869) 243102; Fax (01869) 320040; *Managing Director* P. le Feuvre
Coomber Electronic Equipment Ltd, Croft Wk, Worcester WR1 3NZ; Tel (01905) 25168; Fax (01905) 612701; *Director* E. Coomber
Covloc Display Systems Ltd, Unit 14, Windmill Ind Est, Birmingham Rd, Coventry CV5 9QE; Tel (01203) 407317; Fax (01203) 407311; *Sales Director* B. Johnson
Crossbrook Furniture Ltd, Unit 8, Marshgate Trading Est, Marshgate Dr, Hertford SG13 7AJ; Tel (01992) 584547; Fax (01992) 501666; *Director* M. Mitchell
CTI, 56 Copthorne Rd, Leatherhead, Surrey KT22 7EE; Tel (01372) 372689; Fax (01372) 386701; *Partner* W.M. Herten
G Cussons Ltd (ETEMA), 102 Great Clowes St, Manchester M7 9RH; Tel 0161-833 0036; Fax 0161-834 4688; *Managing Director* R. Cowley
Denford Machine Tools (ETEMA), Birds Royd, Brighouse, W. Yorks HD6 1NB; Tel (01484) 712264; Fax (01484) 722160; *International Sales Manager* D. Shears
Dexion Ltd, Maylands Av, Hemel Hempstead, Herts HP2 7EW; Tel (01442) 242261; Fax (01442) 217145; *Marketing Manager* D. Keel

Donmar Ltd, 54 Cavell St, London E1 2HP; Tel 0171-790 1166; Fax 0171-790 6634; *Director* F. MacLean
Drake Educational Associates, St Fagans Rd, Fairwater, Cardiff CF5 3AE; Tel (01222) 560333; Fax (01222) 554909; *Managing Director* R.G. Drake
DRS Data Research Services Ltd, Sunrise Parkway, Linford Wood, Milton Keynes MK14 6LR; Tel (01908) 666088; Fax (01908) 607668; *Director* D. Grashoff
E and L Instruments, Rackery La, Llay, Wrexham LL12 0PB; Tel (01978) 853920; Fax (01978) 854564; *Sales Director* R. Jones
EFM (Chesterfield) Ltd, Grove Rd, Whittington Moor, Chesterfield, Derbyshire S41 8LN; Tel (01246) 455191; Fax (01246) 260221; *Director* P.G. White
ELE International Ltd (ETEMA), Eastman Way, Hemel Hempstead, Herts HP2 7HB; Tel (01442) 218355; Fax (01442) 52474; *Managing Director* D. Beatty
EME Scotland, Blackaddie Rd, Sanquahr, Dumfriesshire DG4 6DE, Scotland; Tel (01659) 50404; Fax (01659) 50107; *Sales Manager* I. Whitehead
Eagle Scientific Ltd, Regent Hse, Lenton St, Sandicare, Nottingham NG10 5DJ; Tel (0115) 949 1111; Fax (0115) 939 1144; *Managing Director* T.J. Johnsen
Earth Science International, The Meadow, 10 Hartfield Hartmoor Rd, Wilts SN10 5JH; Tel (01380) 726767; Fax (01380) 727969; *Managing Director* P. Merritt
Eastlight Ltd, Ashton Rd, Denton, Manchester M34 3NA; Tel 0161-336 9431; Fax 0161-320 8012; *National Contracts Manager* R. Smith
Economics (Education) Ltd, Epic Hse, Darnall Rd, Attercliffe, Sheffield S9 5AA; Tel (0114) 256 1122; Fax (0114) 243 9306; *Managing Director* A. Gunter
Education, 21–27 Lamb's Conduit St, London WC1N 3NJ; Tel 0171-242 2548; Fax 0171-831 2855; *Editor* G. Low
Education Media Film and Video Ltd, 235 Imperial Dr, Rayners La, Harrow, Middx HA2 7HE; Tel 0181-868 1908; Fax 0181-868 1991; *Managing Director* L. Morrell
Educational and Scientific Products Ltd, A2 Dominion Way, Rustington, West Sussex BN16 3HQ; Tel (01903) 773340; Fax (01903) 771108; *Managing Director* P. Seamer
Educational Company Ltd, 1 Mallusk Pk, Mallusk Rd, Newtownabbey, Co Antrim BT36 8GW; Tel (01232) 844023; Fax (01232) 840705; *Operations Director* R.A. McBride
Elite Optics Ltd, 12 Llantrisant Business Pk, Llantrisant, Mid Glamorgan CG7 8LF; Tel (01443) 238833; Fax (01443) 238008; *Managing Director* D. Godsave
Elliott Medway Ltd, Glebe Ct, Glebe Rd, Peterborough PE2 SEE; Tel (01733) 52151; Fax (01733) 313002; *Sales Manager* M. Adams
Eltic Computers, 57–59 Campus Rd, Listerhills Science Pk, Bradford, W. Yorks BD7 1HR; Tel (01274) 309999; Fax (01274) 731713; *Educational Sales Manager* T. Palmer
Emmerich (Berlon) Ltd, Wotton Rd, Ashfield, Kent TN23 2JY; Tel (01233) 622684; Fax (01233) 645801; *Managing Director* C. Emmerich
Encyclopaedia Britannica International, Carew Hse, Station Approach, Wallington, Surrey SM6 0DA; Tel 0181-669 4355; Fax 0181-773 3631; *National Sales Manager* D. Dare
ESM, Abbeygate Hse, East Rd, Cambridge CB1 1DB; Tel (01223) 357788; Fax (01223) 460557; *Managing Director* S. Lyne
Eurotech Associates Ltd, The Old Coach Hse, 56 High St, Harston, Cambridge CB2 5PZ; Tel (01223) 872750; Fax (01223) 872212; *Managing Director* M. Hellowell
John Farnell Ltd, 24 Townhead Mill, Addingham, Ilkley, West Yorks LS29 0PP; Tel (01943) 831504; Fax (01943) 831504; *Managing Director* J. Farnell
GLS Fairway Ltd, Ferry La, Tottenham Hale, London N17 9NQ; Tel 0181-801 7097; Fax 0181-885 7211; *Marketing Manager* Ms J. Bucknall
Feedback Instruments Ltd (ETEMA), Park Rd, Crowborough, E. Sussex TN6 2QR; Tel (01892) 653322; Fax (01892) 663719; *Director* K.J. Hamilton
Felix Design, Unit 15, Tiverton Business Pk, Tiverton EX16 6SR; Tel (01884) 255420; Fax (01884) 242613; *Proprieter* J. Felix
Festo Ltd, Didactic Department, 7 High St, Teddington, Middx TW11 8EH; Tel 0181-943 0018; Fax 0181-943 5253; *Didactic Manager* K. Matthews
First Class Ltd, Imperial Hse, Willoughby La, London N17 0SP; Tel 0181-885 3311; Fax 0181-808 4723; *Director* P. Berglas
Fisher-Marriott (ESPA), 3 Grove Rd, Ansty, Warks CV7 9JD; Tel (01203) 616325; Fax (01203) 616325; *Partner* R. Marriott
Flexible Director Software Ltd (ESPA), PO Box 100, Abingdon, Oxon OX13 6PQ; Tel (01865) 391148; Fax (01203) 616325; *Managing Director* D. Walton
Flight Electronics Ltd (ETEMA), Flight Hse, Ascupart St, Southampton SO1 1LU; Tel (01703) 227721; Fax (01703) 330039; *Managing Director* M.D. Soffe
Focus in Education, C/o Abbeygate Hse, East Rd, Cambridge CB1 1DB; Tel (01223) 357788; Fax (01223) 460557; *Managing Director* S. Lyne
Galt Educational, Brookfield Rd, Cheadle, Cheshire SK8 2PN; Tel 0161-428 8511; Fax 0161-428 4320; *Director* C.J. Bailey
GBC (United Kingdom) Ltd, Rutherford Rd, Basingstoke, Hants RG24 0PD; Tel (01256) 842828; Fax (01256) 842581; *Director of Sales* M. Bonner
Robert Gibson and Sons Glasgow Ltd, 17 Fitzroy Pl, Glasgow G3 7SF; Tel 0141-248 5674; Fax 0141-221 82198; *Director* R.G.C. Gibson
Gopak Ltd, Range Rd, Hythe, Kent CT21 6HG; Tel (01303) 265751; Fax (01303) 268282; *Sales and Marketing Director* D. Enderby
Granada Business Comm, PO Box 31, Ampthill Rd, Bedford MK42 9QQ; Tel (01234) 270082; Fax (01234) 226090; *National Sales Manager* M. Kitchen
Gratnells Ltd, 258 Church Rd, Leyton, London E10 7JQ; Tel 0181-556 9021; Fax 0181-556 3502; *Managing Director* N.A. Hudson
Philip Green Educational Ltd, 12A Alcester Rd, Studley, Warks B80 7NR; Tel (01527) 754711; Fax (01527) 854385; *Managing Director* P. Green
Don Gresswell Ltd, Bridge Hse, Vera Ave, Grange Pk, London N21 1RB; Tel 0181-360 6622; Fax 0181-360 9231; *Marketing Director* N. Woof
Griffin and George, Bishop Meadow Rd, Loughborough, Leics LE11 0RG; Tel (01509) 233344; Fax (01509) 231893; *General Marketing Manager* J. McAvoy
The Guardian, 77–79 Farringdon Rd, London EC1M 3LX; Tel 0171-278 2332; Fax 0171-837 2114; *Class Sales Manager* J. Thomson
Harbautt's Educational and Technical Services, The Mulberrys, Kembroy Pk, Swindon, Wilts SN2 6US; Tel (01793) 488450; Fax (01793) 421331; *Sales Manager* K. Fox
Philip Harris Education, Lynn La, Shenstone, Lichfield, Staffs WS14 0EE; Tel (01543) 480077; Fax (01543) 480068; *Marketing Director* W.J. Foley
TS Harrison and Sons Ltd (ETEMA), Union St, Heckomdwick, W. Yorks WF16 0HN; Tel (01924) 403751; Fax (01924) 407285; *Managing Director* A. Sweeten
Heckmondwick FB Ltd, PO Box 7, Wellington Mills, Liversedge, W. Yorks WF15 7XA; Tel (01924) 410544; Fax (01924) 409972; *Marketing Manager* S. Gordon
Helix Ltd, PO Box 15, Stourbridge, West Midlands DY9 7AJ; Tel (01384) 424441; Fax (01384) 892617; *National Accounts Manager* K. Nicklin
Esmond Hellerman Ltd, Hellerman Hse, Harris Way, Windmill Rd, Sunbury on Thames TW16 7EW; Tel (01932) 781888; Fax (01932) 789573; *Managing Director* E. Hellerman
Helmsman Lockers WB Bawn and Co Ltd, Northern Way, Bury St Edmunds, Suffolk IP32 6NH; Tel (01284) 752812; Fax (01284) 752844; *Sales Director* R. Frisby
Heron Educational Ltd, Carrwood Hse, Carrwood Rd Chesterfield, Derbyshire S41 9QB; Tel (01246) 453354; Fax (01246) 260876; *Managing Director* J. Pye
Hille International Ltd, Hamlet Grn, Haverhill, Suffolk CB9 8QL; Tel (01440) 702537; Fax (01440) 705417; *Sales Director* M. Barker
PA Hilton Ltd (ETEMA), Horsebridge Mill, King's Somborne, Hants SO20 6PX; Tel (01794) 388382; Fax (01794) 388129; *Sales Engineer* I. Mansfield

HME Technology Ltd, Park La Ind Est, Park La, Kidderminster, Worcs DY11 6TT; Tel (01562) 745321; Fax (01562) 745346; *Managing Director* P. Turner
Hope Education Ltd, Orb Hill, Huddersfield Rd, Oldham OL4 2ST; Tel 0161-633 6611; Fax 0161-633 3431; *Sales Director* D. Dyson
Hostess Furniture Ltd, Vulcan Rd, Bilston, West Midlands WV14 7JR; Tel (01902) 493681; Fax (01902) 353185; *Managing Director* I. Freeman
Hunt and Broadhurst Ltd, Calderbank, River St, Brighouse, W. Yorks HD6 1LU; Tel (01484) 400804; Fax (01484) 400839; *Managing Director* R. French
IBM UK Ltd, Education Marketing Group, PO Box 41, Northern Rd, Portsmouth, Hants PO6 3AU; Tel (01705) 370911; Fax (01705) 382426; *Education Specialist* N. Jepson
IMP Workstations, 4 Glynswood, Buckingham Rd, Bucks MK18 1JF; Tel (01280) 813814; *Sole Proprietor* H. Dymond
In Focus, 5 Runnymeade Ct, Egham TW20 9AA; Tel (01784) 437134; *Director* A. Owen-Davies
Interform Contract Furniture, 9 West Hamstead Mews, London NW6 3BB; Tel 0171-328 2340; Fax 0171-624 1777; *Sales Director* J. Rodgers
Invicta Plastics Ltd, Harborough Rd, Oadby, Leicester LE2 4LB; Tel (0116) 272 0555; Fax (0116) 272 0626; *Sales Director* N. Strangeways
Irwin Desman Ltd, 294 Purley Way, Crpydon CR9 4QL; Tel 0181-686 6441; Fax 0181-681 8429; *Manager of Product Sales* F. Campbell
IT Education Ltd, Rackery La, Llay, Wrexham LL12 0PB; Tel (01978) 856226; Fax (01978) 854564; *Managing Director* G. Bennet
Jonathan Press/Clare Publications, Tey Brook Craft Centre, Colchester, Essex CO6 1JE; Tel (01206) 211020; Fax (01206) 212755; *Senior Partner* N. Graham
Kaymar Industrial Furniture Ltd, Brookhill Rd, Brookhill Ind Est, Nottinghamshire NG16 6NS; Tel (01773) 810107; Fax (01773) 580286; *Group Marketing Manager* I. Stokes
Kendata Ltd, Nutsey La, Totton, Southampton SO4 3NB; Tel (01703) 869902; Fax (01703) 860800; *Marketing Manager* P. Fletcher
Klick Superframe, Claverton Rd, Wythenshawe, Manchester M23 9NE; Tel 0161-998 9726; Fax 0161-946 0419; *Managing Director* L. Whitehurst
Kodak Printing and Publishing Imaging, PO Box 66, Station Rd, Hemel Hempstead, Herts HP1 1JU; Tel (01442) 61122; Fax (01442) 243999; *Marketing Specialist – Printing and Publishing* R. Woodhouse
Kuretake, 10 Moons Pk, Burnt Meadow Rd, Redditch B98 9BA; Tel (01527) 62828; Fax (01527) 60765; *Executive Account Manager* P. Jones
Lector Business Machines, 104 Village Rd, Enfield, Middx EN1 2EX; Tel 0181-360 3915; *Director* K. Brereton
LEGO Dacta LEGO UK Ltd, Ruthin Rd, Wrexham, Clwyd LL13 7TQ; Tel (01978) 290900; Fax (01978) 290138; *Overseas Market Dev Manager* B. Sherratt
LETA Telephone Training Ltd, 15 Kingsway, Gerrards Cross, Bucks SL9 8NS; Tel (01753) 882130; Fax (01753) 887168; *Managing Director* J. Hill
Living and Learning (Cambridge) Ltd, Abbeygate Hse, East Rd, Cambridge CB1 1DB; Tel (01223) 357788; Fax (01223) 460557; *Managing Director* S. Lyne
LJ Tech Systems Ltd (ETEMA), Francis Way, Bowthorpe Ind Est, Norwich NR5 9JA; Tel (01603) 748001; Fax (01603) 746340; *Marketing Director* D. Breeze
Locktronics Beverley Electronics Ltd, Unit 1, Avonside Rd, Avonside Ind Est, Bristol BS2 0UQ; Tel (0117) 972 4102; Fax (0117) 972 3616; *Operations Director* B. Chandler
London Emblem plc, Emblem Hse, Blenheim Rd, Longmead Ind Est, Epsom, Surrey KT19 9AP; Tel (01372) 745433; Fax (01372) 745462; *Sales Manager* S. Morse
Longman Logotron Ltd (ESPA), 124 Cambridge Science Pk, Milton Rd, Cambridge CB4 4ZS; Tel (01223) 425558; Fax (01223) 425349; *Managing Director* C. Kington
Magiboards Ltd, Stafford Pk 12, Telford, Shropshire TF3 3BJ; Tel (01952) 292111; Fax (01952) 292280; *Chairman* A. Stallon
Map Marketing Ltd, 102–104 Carnwth Rd, London SW6 3HW; Tel 0171-736 0297; Fax 0171-371 0473; *Maketing Manager* S. Evans
Mattel UK, Meridian West, Leicester LE3 2WT; Tel (0116) 282 6666; Fax (0116) 282 6640; *Marketing Manager* P. Ratcliffe
Mega Electonics, Mega Hse, Grip Ind Est, Linton, Cambs CB1 6NR; Tel (01223) 893900; Fax (01223) 893894; *Sales and Marketing Manager* A. Hawkins
Merricks Sico Ltd, Henwood Ind Est, Ashford, Kent TN24 8OH; Tel (01233) 643311; Fax (01233) 645143; *Chairman* J. Merricks
Mikrodaisy International Ltd, 60 Hamble La, Hamble, Herts SO3 5JS; Tel (01703) 455004; Fax (01703) 457059; *Managing Director* T. Nice
Minerva Software (ESPA), Minerva Hse, Baring Cres, Exeter, Devon EX1 1TL; Tel (01392) 437756; Fax (01392) 421762; *Sole Proprietor* N.A. Fisher
MJP Geopaks, Michael Jay Publications, PO Box 23, St Just, Cornwall TR19 7JS; Tel (01736) 787808; Fax (01736) 787880; *Proprietor* M. Jay
Montessori St Nicholas, Learning Materials, 23–24 Princes Gate, London SW7 1PT; Tel 0171-225 1277; Fax 0171-823 7557; *Company Secretary* A. Wedgeworth
NES Arnold Ltd, Ludlow Hill Rd, West Bridgford, Nottingham NG2 6HO; Tel (0115) 945 2000; Fax (0115) 945 2212; *Sales Director* P.J. Isherwood
The Newspaper Society, Bloomsbury Hse, 74–77 Great Russell St, London WC1B 3DA; Tel 0171-636 7014; Fax 0171-631 5119; *Manager NIE* G.A. Kelly
Ocarina Workshop, PO Box 56, Kettering, Northants NN15 5LX; Tel (01536) 85963; *Partner* D. Liggins
Omtech Callhaven PLC, Rivington St, London EC2A 3AY; Tel 0171-410 9191; Fax 0171-410 9195; *Omtech Project Manager* D. Kennedy
Papworth Group, Papworth Everard, Cambridge CB3 8RG; Tel (01480) 830345; Fax (01480) 830516; *Executive* A.W. Horwood
Pedigree Petfoods Education Centre, The Gryaling Co, 4 Bedford Sq, London WC1B 3RA; Tel 0171-255 2424; Fax 0171-631 0602; *Education Liaison Officer* K. Whittaker
Philip and Tracy Ltd, North Way, Andover, Hants SP10 5BA; Tel (01264) 332171; Fax (01264) 332226; *Managing Director* J. Tracy
Pisces Paper Co, Westwood Studios, West Ave, Crewe CW1 3AD; Tel (01270) 216211; Fax (01270) 586150; *Director* H. Beech
Plaswood Products Ltd, Griston Rd, Watton, Nr Thetford, Norfolk IP25 6DL; Tel (01953) 881799; Fax (01953) 884774; *Sales Manager* M.D. Clarke
Platignum plc, PO Box 1, 20 Greenfield, Royston, Herts SG8 5XX; Tel (01763) 244133; Fax (01763) 247742; *Education Sales Manager* T. Kewley
Playaway Supplies (Scotland) Ltd, 2 Boundary Rd, Shawfield Ind Est, Rutherglen, Glasgow G73 1DB; Tel 0141-647 0531; Fax 0141-613 1565; *Director* A. Keith
Plint and Partners Oakland Park Ltd (ETEMA), Wokingham, Berks RG11 2FD; Tel (01734) 781898; Fax (01734) 772281; *Education Sales* R. Monk
PMS Communications Ltd, Western Hse, 43 Smallbrook, Queensway, Birmingham B5 4HQ; Tel 0121-643 7688; Fax 0121-643 2448; *Marketing Director* S. Froggatt
Polydron UK Ltd, 11 Scotia Cls, Brackmills, Northampton NN4 0HR; Tel (01604) 769144; Fax (01604) 701674; *Managing Dirctor* R.F. Harvey
Portasilo Ltd, New La, Huntingdon, Yorks YO3 9PR; Tel (01904) 624872; Fax (01904) 611760; *General Sales Manager* N. Williams
Potterycrafts Ltd, Campbell Rd, Stoke on Trent, Staffs ST4 4ET; Tel (01782) 745000; Fax (01782) 746000; *Home Sales Manager* P. Hemmings
Rahmqvist UK Ltd, Crabtree Rd, Thorpe Ind Est, Egham, Surrey TW20 8RN; Tel (01784) 439888; Fax (01784) 471419; *Managing Director* C. Mondahl

Reach Open Ltd, 8 Thorndales, Brentwood, Essex CM14 5DE; Tel (01277) 229093; Fax (01277) 261287; *Managing Director* W. Broderick

Remploy Profile, Lakeside Technology Pk, Pheonix Way, Enterprise Pk, Swansea SA7 9FL; Tel (01792) 774421; Fax (01792) 775611; *Marketing and Sales Manager* D. Parry

SJ Research Ltd, J1 The Paddocks, 347 Cherry Hinton Rd, Cambridge CB1 4DH; Tel (01223) 416715; Fax (01223) 416440; *Managing Director* K. Spence-Jones

Research Machines, Mill St, Oxford OX2 0BW; Tel (01235) 826000; Fax (01235) 826999; *Senior Marketing Executive* S. Wharton

Rexel Ltd, Gatehouse Rd, Aylesbury, Bucks HP19 3DT; Tel (01296) 81421; Fax (01296) 395863; *General Sales Manager* P. Phelan

Royal Sovereign Ltd, 9–10 Guinness Rd Training Est, Trafford Pk, Manchester M17 1SD; Tel 0161-872 5781; Fax 0161-873 7964; *Education Buisness Manager* M. Walbank

The Saville Group Ltd, Schools Vision, Millfield La, Nether Poppleton, York YO2 6PQ; Tel (01904) 782782; Fax (01904) 782700; *Manager Training and Schools* Mrs M. Read

Schofield and Sims Ltd, Dogley Mill, Fenay Bridge, Huddersfield BH8 0NQ; Tel (01484) 607080; Fax (01484) 606815; *Chairman* J.S. Nesbitt

Scholarquip Industries Ltd, Manor La, Holmes Chapel, Cheshire CW4 8AG; Tel (01477) 37473; Fax (01477) 35584; *Managing Director* J. Reynard

SD Systems Ltd, Cressex Ind Est, Lancaster Rd, High Wycombe, Bucks HP12 3PY; Tel (01494) 465212; Fax (01494) 465145; *Design Manager* T. Shoosmith

Selective Software (ESPA), 64 Brooks Rd, Street, Somerset BA16 0PP; Tel (01458) 43079; *Partner* A. Pickford

B. Serota Ltd, Acme Works, Rendelsham Rd, Clapton, London E5 8PS; Tel 0181-985 1736; Fax 0181-985 5109; *Director* M. Serota

Sherston Software Ltd (ESPA), Swan Barton, Sherston, Malmesbury, Wilts SN16 0LH; Tel (01666) 840433; Fax (01666) 840048; *Managing Director* W. Bonham

Simon and Schuster Education, Campus 400, Maylands Ave, Hemel Hempstead, Herts HP2 7EZ; Tel (01442) 231900; Fax (01442) 214467; *Educational Marketing Director* M. Maggs

SIMS Education Services Ltd, The SIMS Centre, Abbot's Rd, Priory Business Pk,Cardington, Bedford; Tel (01234) 838080; Fax (01234) 838091; *Director* A. Rayment

Soft Tech Educational (ESPA), Sturgess Farmhouse, Longbridge Deverill, Warminster, Wilts BA12 7EA; Tel (01985) 40329; *Partner* A. Ramsay

Specialist Crafts, PO Box 247, Leicester LE1 9QS; Tel (0116) 251 0405; Fax (0116) 251 5015; *Joint Managing Director* P. Crick

Speedwell Computing Services, Granby Hse, 109 Stimpson Ave, Northampton NN1 4LR; Tel (01604) 30307; Fax (01604) 35991; *Partner* J. Goodison

Staedtler (UK) Ltd, Cowbridge Rd, Pontyclun, Mid Glam CF7 8YJ; Tel (01443) 237421; Fax (01443) 237440; *Director* J. Springett

Stage Systems, PO Box 50, Stage Hse, Pince William Rd, Loughborough, Leicester LE12 0GN; Tel (01509) 611021; Fax (01509) 233146; *Managing Director* A. Hill

Steltube Ltd, The Causeway, Maldon, Essex CM9 7LW; Tel (01621) 857273; Fax (01621) 857732; *Director* M. Panton

Storm Software (ESPA), Coachman's Quarters, Digby Rd, Sherborne, Dorset DT9 3NN; Tel (01935) 817699; Fax (01963) 817699; *Director* A. Miller

Taskmaster Ltd, Morris Rd, Leicester LE2 6BR; Tel (0116) 270 4286; *Director* D.B. Smith

JR Taylor (Wigan) Ltd, Enfield Cabinet Works, Pemberton, Wigan, Lancs WN5 8ER; Tel (01942) 211000; Fax (01942) 215009; *Managing Director* T.N. Taylor

Teacherboards (1985) ltd, 1–8 Airedale Business Pk, Keighley Rd, Skipton BD23 2TR; Tel (01943) 608668; Fax (01943) 816712; *Managing Director* E. Raczkowski

Technology Teaching Systems Ltd, Unit 4, Holmewood Fields Business Pk, Park Rd, Holmewood, Chesterfield, Derbyshire S42 5UY; Tel (01246) 850085; Fax (01246) 855557; *Director* J. Williams

H Tempest Ltd, The Coloir Laboratory, St Ives, Cornwall TR26 3HU; Tel (01736) 752411; Fax (01736) 754851; *Design and Promotion Manager* N. Moon

Texas Instruments Ltd, European Consumer Division (MS24), Manton La, Bedford MK41 7PA; Tel (01234) 223790; Fax (01234) 223512; *Marketing Manager* H. Reid

The Times Network Systems Ltd (TTNS), Priory Hse, St John's La, London EC1M 4HD; Tel 0171-782 7104; Fax 0171-782 7111; *General Manager* R.M. Cullen

The Times Supplements, Priory Hse, St Jon's La, London EC1M 4HD; Tel 0171-253 3000; Fax 0171-215 4698; *Promotions Director* H. Priday

Timestep Weather Systems Ltd, Wickhambook, Newmarket CB8 8QA; Tel (01440) 820040; Fax (01440) 820281; *Director* D. Cawley

TM Enterprises, PO Box 32, Hyde, Cheshire SK14 5NA; Tel 0161-368 1850; *Director* T. Morgan

Topologika (ESPA), PO Box 39, Stilton, Peterborough PE7 3RL; Tel (01733) 244682; Fax (01733) 244682; *Proprietor* B. Kerslake

TQ International (ETEMA), Bonsall St, Long Eaton, Nottingham NG10 2AN; Tel (0115) 972 2611; Fax (0115) 973 1520; *Chief Executive* R.A. Davies

Transaid Audio Visual Services, Francis Gregory and Son Ltd, Radley Rd, Ind Est, Abingdon, Oxon OX14 3RY; Tel (01235) 555002; Fax (01235) 535940; *Managing Director* R.M. Gregory

Treasurer House of Make-Up, Atlas Hse, Chorley Old Rd, Bolton BL1 4JL; Tel (01204) 47436; Fax (01204) 47436; *Director* O. Holt

Tubular Furniture Ltd, Units F2 and F3, Coedcae Ind Est, Pontyclun, Mid Glam CF7 9HG; Tel (01443) 229326; Fax (01433) 222657; *Managing Director* D. Emanuel

Tyne Professional Television Ltd, Unit 2 The Townsend Centre, Blackburn Rd, Houghton Regis, Dunstable, Beds LU5 5BG; Tel (01582) 606266; Fax (01582) 606266; *Managing Director* D. Tyne

Understanding Electricity/Electricity Association Ltd, 30 Millbank, London SW1P 4RD; Tel 0171-834 2333; Fax 0171-233 6640; *Education Liaison Officer* D. Evans

Unilab Ltd, The Science Pk, Hutton St, Blackburn, Lancs BB1 3BT; Tel (01254) 681222; Fax (01254) 681777; *Managing Director* I.D. Newton

Valiant Technology Ltd, 370 Old York Rd, London SW18 1SP; Tel 0181-874 8747; Fax 0181-877 0362; *Managing Director* D. Catlin

Viewtech Film and Video, 161 Winchester Rd, Brislington, Bristol BS4 3NJ; Tel (0117) 977 3422; Fax (0117) 972 4292; *Managing Director* D. Littlechilc

Visible Improvements Ltd, 30–34 Brixton Est, 1–3 Brixton Rd, London SW9 6DE; Tel 0171-735 4030; Fax 0171-587 0746; *Director* M. Cronly

Wayland (Publishers) Ltd, 61 Western Rd, Hove, E Sussex BN3 1JD; Tel (01273) 722561; Fax (01273) 29314; *UK Sales Director* B. Nevin

P and B Weir Electrical, Leafield Trading Est, Corsham, Wilts SN13 9QZ; Tel (01225) 811449; Fax (01225) 810909; *Managing Director* R.H. Crawcour

Noel Whalley and Associates, Downlands Hill Rd, Sandford, Bristol BS19 5RH; Tel (01934) 820444; Fax (01934) 820444; *Partner* N. Whalley

Widgit Software (ESPA), 102 Radford Rd, Leamington Spa, Warks CV31 1LF; Tel (01926) 885303; Fax (01926) 885293; *Proprietor* M. Detheridge

Wilson and Garden Ltd, Newtown St, Kilsyth, Glasgow G65 0JX; Tel (01236) 823291; Fax (01236) 825683; *Managing Director* J. Cooper

World Book – Childcraft International, World Book Hse, 77 Mount Ephraim, Tunbridge Wells, Kent TN4 8AZ; Tel (01892) 547811; Fax (01892) 524702; *Director of Sales* M. Brown

Worlddidac, Bollwerk 21, Postfach 8866 CH, 3001 Berne, Switzerland; Tel 0131 22 76 82; Fax 0131 21 17 44 1393; *Executive Director* A. Kappeler

Engineering Teaching Equipment Manufacturers Association (ETEMA)

ETEMA/BEEA, 20 Beaufort Crt, Admirals Way, London E14 9XL; Tel 0171-537 4997; Fax 0171-537 4846
Chairman John Wilbur
Secretary A.H. Moody, CEng, MIMechE
The Engineering Training Equipment Manufacturers Association is an Association of UK manufacturers of teaching and training equipment for all forms and levels of engineering and technology from research through to vocational training

GAMBICA Association Ltd

(Association for the Instrumentation, Control and Automation Industry in the UK)
Leicester Hse, 8 Leicester St, London WC2H 7BN; Tel 0171-437 0678
Chief Executive G.C. Young
President A.G. Cooper

Technology with Home Economics Resources in Education (THERE)

PO Box 3083, London SW14 8PW; Tel 0181-876 8286; Fax 0181-876 8289
Co-ordinator Jenifer Davies
Technology with Home Economics Resources in Education (THERE) holds the ultimate link between Industry and Education. The Association exists to liaise between Industry and Home Economics/Technology teachers who are educating today's (and tomorrow's) consumers. 'THERE' is responsible for promoting its members' educational facilities to most teachers of 5–18 year olds. 'THERE' publishes two publications a year (Spring and Autumn) sent out free to Home Economics/Technology teachers. Organises two exhibitions

Other Equipment Suppliers

Dr Hadwen Trust

22 Bancroft, Hitchin, Herts SG5 1JW; Tel (01462) 436819; Fax (01462) 436819
General Secretary Terry Huxtable
As an alternative to animal use in education, the Trust offers wide access to the NORINA database of audiovisuals, containing more than 2,200 entries ranging from computer simulations and videos of experiments, through films and slides, to audio tapes, three-dimensional models and wallcharts. The computer database includes detailed descriptions of products, prices, and names and addresses of suppliers

Midnight Sales Ltd

Unit 1, Chelsea Bridge Business Centre, 326 Queenstown Rd, Battersea, London SW8 4NE; Tel 0171-498 7272; Fax 0171-498 8845
Contact Jenny Williams
Drama/Lighting Equipment Supplier

Standard Forms Ltd

Unit 10, Romsey Industrial Estate, Greatbridge Rd, Romsey, Hampshire SO51 0HR; Tel (01800) 304030; Fax (01800) 414041
Marketing Director Iain Stephen

29 Buyers' Guide

Art Materials

Alec Tiranti Ltd
70 High St, Theale, Reading, Berkshire RG7 5AR; Tel (01734) 302776; Fax (01734) 323487

NES Arnold
Ludlow Hill Rd, West Bridgford, Nottingham NG2 6HD; Tel (O115) 945 2200; Fax (0115) 945 2325

Audio Cassette Copiers

The Force Ten Co Ltd
183 Boundary Rd, Woking, Surrey GU21 5BU; Tel (1483) 762711; Fax (1483) 756303

Classroom Furniture & Accessories

EME
Blackaddie Rd, Sanquhar, Dumfrieshire DG4 6DE; Tel (01659) 50404; Fax (01659) 50107

Computer Software

Royal Society for the Prevention of Accidents
Cannon House, The Priory, Queensway, Birmingham B4 6BS; Tel 0121-200 2461; Fax 0121-200 1254

Speedwell Computing Service
The Court Yard, Orchard Hill, Little Billing, Northampton NN3 9AG; Tel (01604) 410041; Fax (01604) 415551

Computer Workstations

EME
Blackaddie Rd, Sanquhar, Dumfrieshire DG4 6DE; Tel (01659) 50404; Fax (01659) 50107

Courses for Further and Higher Education on CD Rom

ECCTIS 2000 Ltd
Fulton Hse, Jessop Av, Cheltenham, Glos GL50 3SH; Tel (01242) 518724; Fax (01242) 225914

Craft Equipment

Alec Tiranti Ltd
70 High St, Theale, Reading, Berkshire RG7 5AR; Tel (01734) 302776; Fax (01734) 323487

Emmerich (Berlon) Ltd
Wotton Rd, Ashford, Kent; Tel (01233) 622684; Fax (01233) 645801

W.G. Ball Ltd
Longton Mill, Anchor Rd, Stoke-on-Trent, Staffordshire ST3 1JW; Tel (01782) 313956; Fax (01782) 598148

Educational Book Suppliers

Royal Society for the Prevention of Accidents
Cannon House, The Priory, Queensway, Birmingham B4 6BS; Tel 0121-200 2461; Fax 0121-200 1254

Educational Equipment

NES Arnold
Ludlow Hill Rd, West Bridgford, Nottingham NG2 6HD; Tel (O115) 945 2200; Fax (0115) 945 2325

Educational Material Suppliers

Alec Tiranti Ltd
70 High St, Theale, Reading, Berkshire RG7 5AR; Tel (01734) 302776; Fax (01734) 323487

Royal Society for the Prevention of Accidents
Cannon House, The Priory, Queensway, Birmingham B4 6BS; Tel 0121-200 2461; Fax 0121-200 1254

Educational Organisations

ALBSU - The Basic Skills Unit
Commonwealth Hse, 1–19 New Oxford St, London WC1A 1NU; Tel 0171-405 4017; Fax 0171-404 5038

Board of Management for Methodists
25 Marleybone Rd, London NW1 5JP; Tel 0171-953 3723; Fax 0171-224 0702

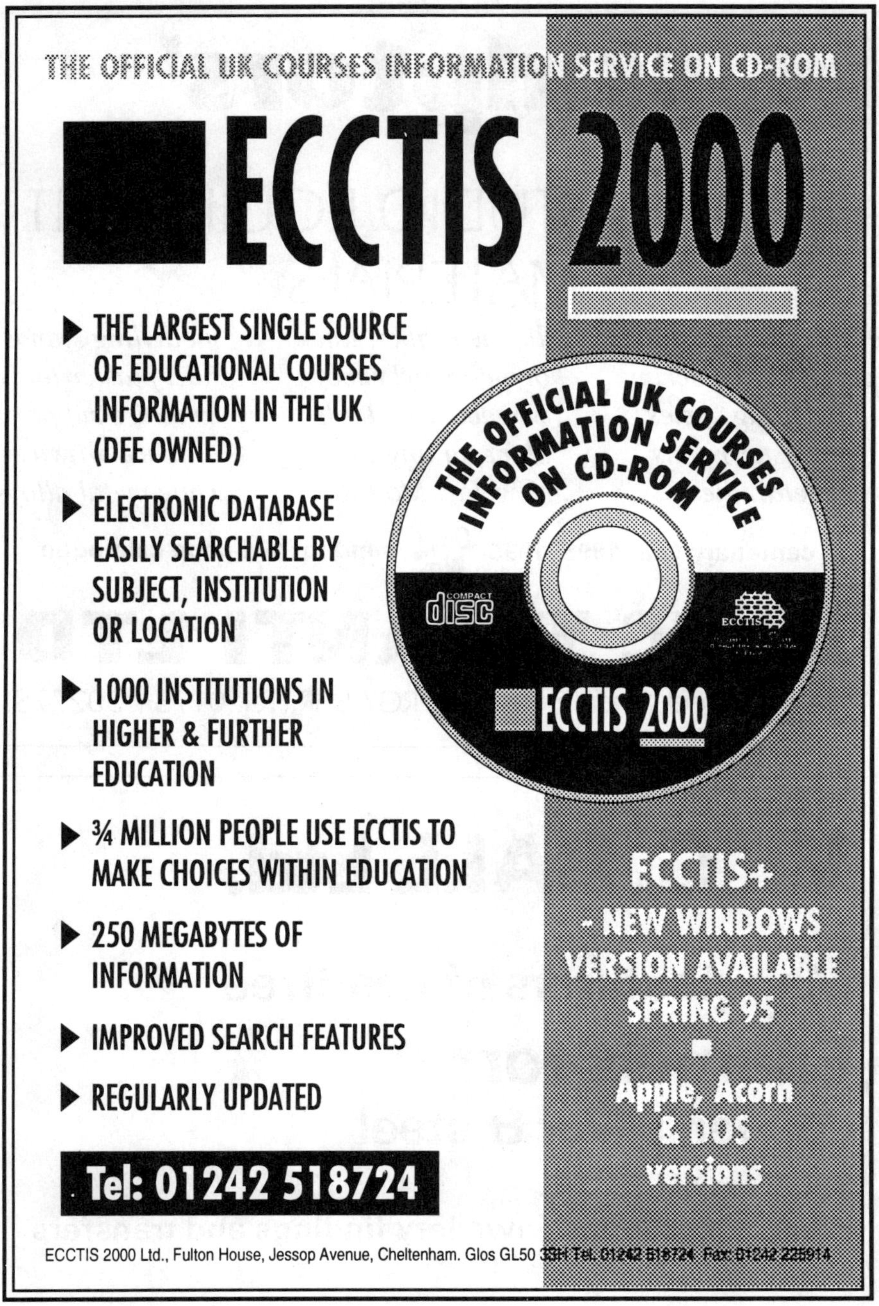

National Confederation of Parent-Teacher Associations
2 Ebbsfleet Estate, Stonebridge Rd, Gravesend, Kent DA11 9DZ, (01474) 560618; Tel (01474) 564418
The Engineering Council
10 Maltravers St, London WC2R 3ER; Tel 0171-240 7891; Fax 0171-240 7517

Educational Psychology

George Crowther MSc AFBPsS (Chartered Education Psychologist)
Little Hill, Colley Manor Dr, Reigate Heath, Surrey RH2 9JS; Tel (01737) 243286
St Piers Lingfield
St Piers La, Lingfield, Surrey RH7 6PW; Tel (01342) 832243; Fax (01342) 834639

Educational Stationery
NES Arnold
Ludlow Hill Rd, West Bridgford, Nottingham NG2 6HD; Tel (0115) 945 2200; Fax (0115) 945 2325

Educational Visits and Services
Skipton Castle
Skipton, N. Yorks BD23 1AQ; Tel (01756) 792200

Engineering
The Engineering Council
10 Maltravers St, London WC2R 3ER; Tel 0171-240 7891; Fax 0171-240 7517

Exhibition Venues
The Normal College
Bangor, Gwynedd LL57 2PX; Tel (01248) 370171; Fax (01248) 370461

Family Literacy
ALBSU - The Basic Skills Unit
Commonwealth Hse, 1–19 New Oxford St, London WC1A 1NU; Tel 0171-405 4017; Fax 0171-404 5038

Gameswear
NOYNA School Aprons
222 Stretford Rd, Urmston, Manchester; Tel 0161-748 2724; Fax 0161-747 8775

Health and Safety
Royal Society for the Prevention of Accidents
Cannon House, The Priory, Queensway, Birmingham B4 6BS; Tel 0121-200 2461; Fax 0121-200 1254

Home Economics Equipment and Craft Aprons
NOYNA School Aprons
222 Stretford Rd, Urmston, Manchester; Tel 0161-748 2724; Fax 0161-747 8775

Independent Boarding Schools
Millfield Schools
Millfield St, Somerset BA16 0YD; Tel (01458) 442291; Fax (01458) 447276

Independent Further Education
St Piers Lingfield
St Piers La, Lingfield, Surrey RH7 6PW; Tel (01342) 832243; Fax (01342) 834639

Independent Schools
Churchers College
Petersfield, Hants GU31 4AS; Tel (01730) 263033; Fax (01730) 231437

Independent Secondary Special Schools
St Lukes School
Exeter Rd, Teignmouth, Devon TQ14 9JG; Tel (01626) 778328

Independent Special Schools
St Joseph's School
Amlets La, Cranleigh, Surrey GU6 7NQ; Tel (01483) 272449; Fax (01483) 276003
St Piers Lingfield
St Piers La, Lingfield, Surrey RH7 6PW; Tel (01342) 832243; Fax (01342) 834639

Information Technology
Speedwell Computing Service
The Court Yard, Orchard Hill, Little Billing, Northampton NN3 9AG; Tel (01604) 410041; Fax (01604) 415551

Journalism Studies
London School of Journalism
22 Upbrook Mews, Bayswater, London W2 3HG; Tel 0171-706 3536; Fax 0171-706 3780

Language Laboratories
The Force Ten Co Ltd
183 Boundary Rd, Woking, Surrey GU21 5BU; Tel (1483) 762711; Fax (1483) 756303

Language Professional Associations
Sels College
64–65 Long Acre, London WCZE 9JH; Tel 0171-240 2581; Fax 0171-379 5793

Low Vision Aid
The Force Ten Co Ltd
183 Boundary Rd, Woking, Surrey GU21 5BU; Tel (1483) 762711; Fax (1483) 756303

Mini Bus New and Late Used Sales
Red Kite Vehicle Consultants
3 Heddons Dr, Three Legged Cross, Wimborne, Dorset BH21 6QU; Tel (01202) 827029; Fax (01202) 827029

Minibus Sales

Red Kite Vehicle Consultants
3 Heddons Dr, Three Legged Cross, Wimborne, Dorset BH21 6QU; Tel (01202) 827029; Fax (01202) 827029

Musical Instruments and Accessories

Chas E. Foote
10 Golden Sq, London W1R 3AF; Tel 0171-437 1811; Fax 0171-734 3095

Non Maintained Special Schools

Royal National Institute for the Blind
224 Great Portland St, London W1N 6AA; Tel 0171-388 1266; Fax 0171-383 4921

Portable Seating

EME
Blackaddie Rd, Sanquhar, Dumfrieshire DG4 6DE; Tel (01659) 50404; Fax (01659) 50107

Professional Associations

Professional Association of Teachers
2 St James Court, Friargate, Derby DE1 1BT; Tel (01332) 372337; Fax (01332) 290310

Professional Educational Associates

Professional Association of Teachers
2 St James Court, Friargate, Derby DE1 1BT; Tel (01332) 372337; Fax (01332) 290310

Publications

Times Educational Supplement
Admiral Hse, 66/68 East Smithfield, London E1 9XY; Tel 0171-782 3000; Fax 0171-782 3398

School Transport

Red Kite Vehicle Consultants
3 Heddons Dr, Three Legged Cross, Wimborne, Dorset BH21 6QU; Tel (01202) 827029; Fax (01202) 827029

Services for Visually Impaired Children

Royal National Institute for the Blind
224 Great Portland St, London W1N 6AA; Tel 0171-388 1266; Fax 0171-383 4921

Special Needs

ALBSU - The Basic Skills Unit
Commonwealth Hse, 1–19 New Oxford St, London WC1A 1NU; Tel 0171-405 4017; Fax 0171-404 5038

Specialising in Examination Assessment and Registration Systems

Speedwell Computing Service
The Court Yard, Orchard Hill, Little Billing, Northampton NN3 9AG; Tel (01604) 410041; Fax (01604) 415551

Sportswear

NOYNA School Aprons
222 Stretford Rd, Urmston, Manchester; Tel 0161-748 2724; Fax 0161-747 8775

Technological Equipment

Emmerich (Berlon) Ltd
Wotton Rd, Ashford, Kent; Tel (01233) 622684; Fax (01233) 645801

Vocational and Careers Guidance

George Crowther MSc AFBPsS (Chartered Education Psychologist)
Little Hill, Colley Manor Dr, Reigate Heath, Surrey RH2 9JS; Tel (01737) 243286

Work Benches and Accessories

Emmerich (Berlon) Ltd
Wotton Rd, Ashford, Kent; Tel (01233) 622684; Fax (01233) 645801

Index

Names of organisations beginning Assoc of/for, British /National Assoc of/for, Institute of/for, Soc of/for, British/ National Soc of/for, have been inverted.

Index

Index

Index

Index

Index

Index

Index

Index

Index

Index

Index

Index

Index

Index

Index

Index

Index

Index

Index

Index

Index

Index

Index to Advertisers

NOTES

NOTES